KF
5640
.A7
G63
2002

OHIO NORTHERN
UNIVERSITY

JUL 1 7 2002

TAGGART LAW LIBRARY

D1289313

UNIVERSITY CASEBOOK SERIES

EDITORIAL BOARD

ROBERT C. CLARK
DIRECTING EDITOR
Dean & Royall Professor of Law
Harvard University

DANIEL A. FARBER
Henry J. Fletcher Professor of Law
University of Minnesota

OWEN M. FISS
Sterling Professor of Law
Yale University

GERALD GUNTHER
William Nelson Cromwell Professor of Law, Emeritus
Stanford University

THOMAS H. JACKSON
President
University of Rochester

HERMA HILL KAY
Dean & Barbara Nachtrieb Armstrong Professor of Law
University of California, Berkeley

HAROLD HONGJU KOH
Gerard C. & Bernice Latrobe Smith Professor of International Law
Yale Law School

DAVID W. LEEBRON
Dean & Lucy G. Moses Professor of Law
Columbia University

SAUL LEVMORE
William B. Graham Professor of Law
University of Chicago

ROBERT L. RABIN
A. Calder Mackay Professor of Law
Stanford University

CAROL M. ROSE
Gordon Bradford Tweedy Professor of Law & Organization
Yale University

DAVID L. SHAPIRO
William Nelson Cromwell Professor of Law
Harvard University

CASES AND MATERIALS

WILDLIFE LAW

by

DALE D. GOBLE
Margaret Wilson Schimke Distinguished Professor of Law
University of Idaho
College of Law

ERIC T. FREYFOGLE
Max L. Rowe Professor of Law
University of Illinois
College of Law

NEW YORK, NEW YORK
FOUNDATION PRESS
2002

Foundation Press, a division of West Group, has created this publication to provide you with accurate and authoritative information concerning the subject matter covered. However, this publication was not necessarily prepared by persons licensed to practice law in a particular jurisdiction. Foundation Press is not engaged in rendering legal or other professional advice, and this publication is not a substitute for the advice of an attorney. If you require legal or other expert advice, you should seek the services of a competent attorney or other professional.

COPYRIGHT © 2002 By FOUNDATION PRESS

     395 Hudson Street
     New York, NY 10014
     Phone Toll Free 1–877–888–1330
     Fax (212) 367–6799
     fdpress.com

All Rights Reserved
Printed in the United States of America

ISBN 1–58778–168–9

 TEXT IS PRINTED ON 10% POST CONSUMER RECYCLED PAPER

For our children — Anna, Camas, and Luke — in the hope that it makes a difference.

*

PREFACE

At first glance, wildlife law would hardly seem to merit a book the size of this one. Why we think otherwise calls for a brief explanation.

In recent decades, natural resources law, environmental law, and land-use planning have all come to address fundamental questions about how people draw sustenance from the larger community of life. Each of these fields is now infused with concerns about ecological interconnection, sustainability, and the dependence of human life and human enterprise on healthy natural systems. Particular resource-use rights, once defined with an eye toward efficiency and fairness, now pay equal attention to the effects of extraction and harvesting on water, soil, and other life forms. Environmental law, once focused on direct threats to human health, now is concerned with assaults on non-human life and disruptions of ecological processes. Land-use planning, once confined to cities and suburbs, has spread across the landscape, focusing on places of critical ecological concern.

At the confluence of these trends is the centuries-old law of wildlife.

Anglo-American jurisprudence has long assigned a prominent role to wildlife. Wild animals held social and symbolic value, as well as economic. Game law reflected and solidified class distinctions; fishing rights decided who could use waterways and how; competing claims to wandering animals highlighted the difficulties of separating sovereign and proprietary powers — and, in time, reconciling landowner rights with the public's ownership of the wild members of the animal kingdom.

Traditional wildlife concerns remain alive today, in disputes over fish, game, and marauding mammals. Linked to those issues, however, are newer, broader concerns about ecosystems, biodiversity, and the quality and sustainability of human life. Wild species are important today, not just because of their direct and indirect value to humans, but because they provide a focal point for a wide array of concerns about how humans live on the land. To manage land to protect biodiversity is to address, along the way, nearly the full range of environmental concerns raised by human land- and resource-use practices. Added to the mix — and demanding increasing attention — are claims that wild animals possess intrinsic value and, as such, deserve respect apart from their contributions to human welfare.

Wildlife law has come of age.

Our book is so bulky largely for four reasons. First, we draw liberally upon the subject's rich history, in law and culture. Without that history, we believe, there can be no firm understanding of the subject. Second, animals are living entities, organized into shifting, complex ecological systems; from the first page, biology plays a critical role in our story. Third, moral sentiments and ethical values have expanded to attend to the plight of particular animals, to species, and to the healthy functioning of communities. Ethical concerns, too, appear here as a key issue.

Finally — and perhaps most importantly — we have, in effect, combined several wildlife law books into one, to give instructors freedom to tailor their courses as they see fit. No one, we trust, will endeavor to use the book in its entirety, nor is there reason to do so. Many of the chapters stand alone and can be used in various combinations.

Foundational issues. At the base of wildlife law are fundamental principles dealing with the private and public interests in animals, including the state ownership doctrine, the rule of capture, the complex links between wildlife and private land, and the rules governing the nature and duration of private rights after capture. These issues occupy Chapters 1-3 and 5. Chapter 1 includes our most extended treatment of animal-welfare issues; we return to them intermittently thereafter.

Biodiversity. Many instructors are likely to focus their courses on the conservation of biodiversity. Chapters 12-14, totaling over 400 pages, cover the subject in some detail, with ample consideration of the science, ethical, and policy implications. When combined with materials from Chapters 1-3 and 5, the casebook provides a rich examination of how biodiversity concerns interact with the common law.

Federal lands/Western issues. Given the particular importance of wildlife on public lands and in the West generally, we offer extensive materials to tailor a wildlife-related course focused on public lands, fisheries, and tribal harvesting rights. Section 3 of Chapter 6 looks at the overall management of federal lands. Chapter 7 explores Indian tribal issues. Chapter 11 examines wildlife refuges, national parks, and wilderness areas; section 2 of Chapter 14 considers federal multiple-use lands. The Endangered Species Act (Chapter 13) is of obvious relevance; less-expansive species-protection laws are taken up in Chapter 10.

State fish and game law administration. As law has come to infuse all aspects of wildlife management, wildlife students are seeing increasing need to study law. (One of us in recent years has had more non-law students take his wildlife law course than law students.) To meet the particular needs of such students, we have included materials on many practical aspects of fish and game management. Chapter 9 looks at state regulatory structures and enforcement issues; sections 1 and 2 of Chapter 10 show how state efforts are supplemented by the federal Lacey Act and various bird-conservation statutes. The constitutional dimensions of federal-state relations are explored in Chapter 6; Chapter 7 adds Indian tribes to the regulatory mix. Instructors interested in private game ranches will likely also want to use Chapter 4 on liability issues. In addition, many of the notes in the opening chapters have been written to explain fundamental legal points to non-law students.

Fisheries. Instructors interested in freshwater and ocean fisheries should find our coverage, we hope, more than adequate. Our foundation chapter on private land — Chapter 3 — spends as much time on waterways (and water rights) as on fast land. For historical reasons, most of the material in Chapter 5 and in section 1 of Chapter 6 deals with aquatic life; fisheries issues also appear conspicuously in Chapter 7 on tribal rights. Our most extended treatment, however, comes in Chapter 8 (international fishery issues), in section 4 of Chapter 10 (marine fisheries), and in section 4 of Chapter 14 (freshwater habitat protection).

Among the chapters that stand alone and that can be used in a variety of mixes are Chapter 4 (liability issues), Chapter 7 (Indian tribes), and Chapter 8 (international wildlife law).

Although wildlife is important and will remain important for many reasons, the central core of the field, we sense, is shifting significantly. Even a generation ago, a course on wildlife law would have focused on wildlife as a distinct natural resource, subject to exploitation and conservation in ways similar to other natural resources. Looking ahead, we see a much different focus: on wildlife as the central, nonhuman element in the ecological communities where humans live and that they help compose. Wildlife is becoming a dominant strand — in many settings, the dominant strand — of large-scale land-use planning. It has become one of the two pillars of modern environmental law. Most disputes over public-lands management now deal with the impacts of human activities on wild species. Indian tribal issues are in few settings more divisive than in the arena of off-reservation fishing and hunting rights, particularly in the salmon regions of the Northwest. Water-rights disputes everywhere — not just in the West — increasingly turn on the effects that diversions, pollution, and blockages have on natural aquatic systems.

To conserve biodiversity is to maintain landscapes where people, too, can thrive.

A final confession: Though the length of this casebook is justified, we hope, by the breadth and important of its subject, a contributing factor, we admit, is that wildlife cares are simply delightful to read. The human drama in them is matched by few other fields. Then there is the wildlife itself, the living creatures that run, slither, fly, crawl, burrow, and creep across our pages. And the cast we have assembled here is large indeed, from spiders to steelheads, mussels to manatees, to beaver, bees, bison, boars, and burros.

In our admittedly biased view, no subject in the curriculum is more enjoyable to teach — and to learn.

*

ACKNOWLEDGMENTS

This project, like so many, gives rise to a mountain of debts that we are happy to acknowledge. To J. Michael Scott, the book's unofficial and (fortunately) unpaid science adviser; Debra Kronenberg, for Latin translations, editorial nudging, and unflagging optimism; Professor Bill Davey, former Legal Advisor of the Word Trade Organization, for his helpful comments on Chapter 8; Dick Hildreth, ocean law guru, for his assistance with ocean fisheries issues; Jane Lear and Carolyn Todd, ILL-wizards who found arcana, some of which is included; Peggy Rasmussen, for a jillion things, large and small; the Rocky Mountain Mineral Law Foundation and Dave Phillips, for a grant to hire a research assistant at a crucial time; Dean Jack Miller, for release time and summer research funding; as well as the numerous colleagues — Michael Bean, Mike Blumm, Fred Cheever, Holly Doremus, Rob Fischman, Doug Grant, Joann Henderson, Jim Huffman, Bob Keiter, Maureen Laflin, Douglas Lind, and Monica Schurtman — who helped us understand; Marc Brown, Dave Jones, Shea Meehan, Liz Merril, Sunil Rammalingam, and Colleen Zahn for their research assistance; and to the several years of students who worked through the iterations of the materials that became this book — we extend our heartfelt thanks.

*

SUMMARY OF CONTENTS

*

TABLE OF CONTENTS

PART 5: BIODIVERSITY

*

TABLE OF CASES

Principal cases are in bold type. Non-principal cases are in roman type. References are to Pages.

CASES AND MATERIALS

WILDLIFE LAW

*

CHAPTER 1

AN INTRODUCTION TO WILDLIFE LAW

SECTION 1. WHAT IS "WILDLIFE"?

This is a casebook on wildlife law. Logically, "wildlife" is all "life" that is "wild." That is, all of the riotously diverse organisms that share the planet with us—animals, plants, fungi, protozoa, bacteria, viruses, and the rest—as long as they have not been domesticated or tamed. But, as Oliver Wendell Holmes noted, logic is not necessarily the best guide to the law.

The common law drew a bright line between plants and animals, a division that retains its hold on the legal imagination: states generally define "wildlife" to include only animals. *See, e.g.,* FLA. STAT. ch. 372.072(3)(a) ("any member of the animal kingdom"); HAW. REV. STAT. § 195D–2 (all members of the animal kingdom); IDAHO CODE § 36–202(g) ("any form of animal life"); IND. CODE § 14–22–6 ("any . . . wild animal"); KAN. STAT. ANN. § 32–958(g) ("any member of the animal kingdom"); MO. REV. STAT. § 252.020(3) ("all . . . wild animals"); N.H. REV. STAT. ANN. § 212–A:2(III) ("any member of any nondomesticated species of the animal kingdom"). Some states are more restrictive and include only a subset of animals. *See, e.g.,* COLO. REV. STAT. § 33–1–102(51) ("vertebrates, mollusks, and crustaceans"); N.M. STAT. ANN. § 17–2–38(G) ("any nondomestic mammal, bird, reptile, amphibian, fish, mollusk, or crustacean"); OR. REV. STAT. § 496.004(17) ("fish, wild birds, amphibians, reptiles, and wild mammals").

Other states have more novel classification schemes. Maryland, for example, defines "wildlife" as "every living creature, not human, wild by nature, endowed with sensation and power of voluntary motion"—except "fish." MD. CODE ANN., NAT. RES. I § 10–101(aa)(1). The separate definition of "fish" reflects jurisdictional needs since management of "wildlife" is vested in one state agency and management of "fish" in another. Furthermore, the statute defines "fish" as "finfish, crustaceans, mollusks, and amphibians and reptiles which spend a majority of their life cycle in water." *Id.* § 4–101(g). In Maryland, frogs are fish and neither are wildlife. Maine has a similar statutory scheme. *See* ME. REV. STAT. ANN. §§ 7001(9), (42). And in Pennsylvania, "fish" includes "[a]ny plant . . . that grows or lives in or upon the water." PA. CONS. STAT. § 34:102.

The statutory definitions raise questions concerning the relationship between law and biology. For example, when a statute defines "wildlife" as "all members of the animal kingdom" what is the effect of changing scientific understanding of the "animal kingdom"?

a. *Life*: Plants, Animals, and Other Life Forms (A Biological Taxonomy)

NOTES

(1) A bit of (scientific) taxonomic history: Diversity is the most apparent fact of life: great blue whales, shrews, swallowtail butterflies, calliope hummingbirds, oak trees, morel mushrooms, lichens, and slime mold are visible examples of the exuberant variety. Our species has faced this diversity (as it has other natural mysteries) guided by a belief that the universe is not chaotic, that there is an underlying structure that can be discovered and studied. In biology, this belief in order is the science of "systematics," the study of the diversity of organisms and the relationships among them.

Systematics seeks to classify organisms according to some relationship. Any number of relationships might be used as a classifying principle: one could, for example, classify animals by their color, number of appendages, or utility to humans. Whatever principle is chosen, it is the "taxonomy"— the general term for the theory guiding a classification.

Systematics and taxonomics are as old as our species: in its simplest form it is nothing more than naming. The history of taxonomy as a formal system, however, begins with Aristotle (384–322 B.C.E.) who classified animals into groups based on observation. On this empirical basis he superimposed a hierarchical, valuing scheme based on four basic properties: hotness, coldness, dryness, and moistness. The relative value of the soul of the animal was determined by its combination of these attributes. Thus, for example, blood—because it was both hot and moist—was particularly important and "blooded" (*i.e.,* vertebrate) animals were "higher" than "bloodless" (*i.e.,* invertebrate) animals.

After Aristotle, the quality of taxonomy declined. With Pliny (ca. 23–79 C.E.), for example, natural history became an uncritical accumulation of fact and fancy in which fabulous creatures mingle with real. During the Christian period, animals became symbols for dogma: to moralize about diligence, one wrote about ants; to explain the resurrection, one pointed to the butterfly emerging from its cocoon. A widely embraced medieval idea was that all life formed a single "great chain of being." God was at the top of the chain, followed by angels, humans (who partake of both the immortal and the material), and all the other forms of life arrayed by their degree of closeness to God. Arthur O. Lovejoy, The Great Chain of Being: A Study of the History of an Idea (1936).

The rediscovery of Aristotle's writings in the fifteenth century contributed to a renewed interest in questions of empirical classification that culminated in the work of Linnaeus. Linnaeus is important for his technical innovation and standardization, which "brought consensus and simplicity back into taxonomy and nomenclature where there had been a threat of total chaos.... [T]his was largely responsible for the unprecedented flowering of taxonomic research on animals and plants during the eighteenth and early nineteenth centuries." Ernst Mayr, The Growth of Biological Thought: Diversity, Evolution, and Inheritance 173 (1982).

Linnaeus, however, was a scholastic, trapped in the dogmatic logic of classifying organisms downward by dichotomous division—a process similar to the parlor game in which one person tries to guess the identity of the object chosen by the other members of the party. The first question—"Is it alive?"—divides the world into living and nonliving; a second—"Is it an animal?"—further divides the world into animal and non-animal. Eventually, however, the method's inability to produce "natural" groupings in the face of increasingly large floras and faunas proved insurmountable and downward, logical-division taxonomies were replaced by upward, compositional systems in which similar species are aggregated into higher, more-encompassing categories. Dogs, wolves, and coyotes, for example, share sufficient similarities to be grouped together in the family *canidae*; canids, in turn, share similarities with other meat eaters and a grouped into the order *carnivora*—an order that includes cats.

The century after the publication of the 10th edition of Linnaeus's *Systema Naturae* in 1758 marked a fundamental transition. The replacement of logical-division taxonomies by compositional taxonomies did not in itself reduce the artificiality of the classification process; some organizing principle remained necessary. The Greeks had been convinced that there was a deeper order underlying the apparently chaotic and diverse surface of nature. In the eighteenth century, natural theology revivified this proposition with grand arguments from design: the order in nature was a reflection of God's plan.

All this was swept away beginning in 1859 with the publication of *On the Origin of Species by Means of Natural Selection or the Preservation of Favored Races in the Struggle for Life* by Charles Darwin. Darwin stated his taxonomic principle as genealogy: "From the first dawn of life, all organic beings are found to resemble each other in descending degrees, so that they can be classed in groups under groups." This Darwinian principle remains the touchstone.

(2) The tree of life: Traditionally, biologists—like common-law lawyers—divided life into two, commonsensical groups: plants and animals. Linnaeus gave this proposition a formal basis in his *Systema Naturae*, but it was present implicitly in Aristotle. Indeed, the roots of this two-kingdom model are ancient, traceable to everyday human experience: animals move and breathe; plants do not.

Conceptual difficulties with the two-kingdom model began as microscopes and other new technologies revealed unexpected and fundamental variations in life-forms. Unicellular organisms presented particular problems because many species exhibited both "plant" and "animal" characteristics. Greater diversity also became apparent among macroscopic life: fungi, for example, differ from plants (with which they were traditionally grouped) on the basis of nutrition since fungi absorb nutrients rather than produce them through photosynthesis.

In 1866, Ernst Haeckel presented a three-kingdom model, arguing that the single-celled organisms—the protists—were neither plants nor animals.

In 1938, H.F. Copeland proposed classifying bacteria—a large group of single-celled organisms—as a separate kingdom, the monera. Robert H. Whitaker proposed a five-kingdom model in 1969 when he argued for the separation of fungi. Whitaker's classification was based primarily upon cellular structure (prokaryotic [lacking organized cellular bodies such as a nucleus] vs. eukaryotic [organized cellular bodies present]) and method of obtaining nutrition (photosynthesis vs. absorption vs. ingestion).[1]

Whitaker's model was the standard model until breakthroughs in biochemistry produced a new type of information. In particular, data derived from the sequencing of the nucleotides of ribonucleic acid (RNA) in ribosomes allows scientists to compare the nucleotides of different species and thus to determine the relationship between species. Based on such sequencing, Carl Woese proposed a three-domain model in 1977: the first two domains (archaea and bacteria) are prokaryotes (species whose cells lack an internal membrane). The third (eukarya) is composed of all eukaryotes with their membrane-enclosed structure containing DNA. Stated differently, the model produced by RNA-sequencing indicates that all the organisms that Linnaeus and his successors up to the twentieth century classified are more closely related to each other than to either bacteria or archaea.

The three-domain model is not without its critics. Ernst Mayr, for example, has argued that the differences between prokaryotes and eukaryotes is of a different "magnitude" than that between bacteria, archaea, and eukarya. In place of the three-domain model, he has proposed a two-domain model:

Domain Prokaryota (Monera)

Subdomain Eubacteria

Subdomain Archaebacteria

Kingdom Crenarchaeota

Kingdom Euryarchaeota

1. The five kingdoms in Whitaker's model are:

1. *monera*, which contains the prokaryotes, species whose cells lack an internal membrane enclosing their deoxyribonucleic acid (DNA). *Monera* are unicellular organisms; examples include several types of bacteria, spirochetes, methanogens, *etc.* Some species of *monera* are autotrophs, species that synthesize their food from simple raw materials such as water and carbon dioxide using an environmental energy source; some *monera* are heterotrophs that feed on tissues or wastes of other organisms. All other organisms are eukaryotes which have at least one membrane-enclosed structure (the nucleus) containing DNA.

2. *protista* are uni-and multicellular organisms such as the diatoms, protozoans, euglenids, and slime molds. Some species of *protista* are photosynthetic autotrophs and some are heterotrophs.

3. *fungi* are mostly multicellular organisms; all species are heterotrophic and rely upon extracellular digestion (they secrete chemicals that break down the food so that it can be absorbed by the fungal cells). Basidiomycetes and ascomycetes—members of the popular category "mushrooms"—are example of *fungi*.

4. *plantae* are mostly multicellular photosynthetic autotrophs.

5. *animalia* are multicellular heterotrophs.

Domain Eukaryota

    Subdomain Protista

    Subdomain Metabionta

        Kingdom Metaphyta (plants)

        Kingdom Fungi

        Kingdom Metazoa (animals)

Ernst Mayr, *A Natural System of Organisms,* 348 NATURE 491 (1990).

More recently, however, the validity of models generated by molecular analysis has been questioned. The problem is that different genes give different relationships because the sharing of bits of genes—"interspecific lateral gene transfer," in the scientific terminology—apparently has been relatively widespread, particularly among unicellular organisms. A recent review disputed the assumption that a universal tree of life could be fashioned out of gene sequences. Because "different genes give different trees, and there is no fair way to suppress this disagreement, then a species (or phylum) can 'belong' to many genera (or kingdoms) at the same time: There really can be no universal phylogenetic tree of organisms based on such a reduction to genes." W. Ford Doolittle, *Phylogenetic Classification and the Universal Tree,* 284 SCI. 2124, 2128 (1999). As the title of a recent *New York Times* article put it, "Life's Origins Get Murkier and Messier." *See* Nicholas Wade, *Life's Origins Get Murkier and Messier*, N.Y. TIMES, June 13, 2000, at D1.

The fundamental point is that our knowledge of the complexity of life and the interrelatedness of its various forms is being dramatically transformed—in ways that may significantly affect our understanding of our place in the universe.

b.   *WILD*: CLASSIFICATIONS OF LIFE (A LEGAL TAXONOMY)

(i)   FOUR DEGREES OF WILDNESS (WILD–FERAL–TAMED–DOMESTICATED)

Koop v. United States

United States Court of Appeals, Eighth Circuit.
296 F.2d 53 (1961).

■ VOGEL, J.:—[Defendants appeal their conviction under the Migratory Bird Treaty Act, 16 U.S.C. §§ 703–711, and its implementing regulations. The regulations prohibit hunting over an area that has been baited with corn or other feed.

[Four of the defendants had paid the fifth defendant, Dr. Herman Koop, to hunt on 1280 acres of land he owned and operated as a dude ranch in Stearns County, Minnesota. In order to attract ducks for hunting, Dr. Koop created several ponds and planted a variety of feed plants. He also fed ducks to keep them in the area. During the 1959 season (when the violations occurred), he fed approximately 250 bushels of corn. Dr. Koop's practice was to discontinue feeding for what he deemed a sufficient length of time before hunting season began so that no corn would remain in the ponds. In 1959, he fed the last corn four days prior to the opening of the hunting season.

[Dr. Koop also raised mallard ducks, using both purchased ducklings and captured wild ducks as brood stock. In 1958, he captured about 70 ducks, maintaining and apparently breeding them over the winter. In the spring of 1959, he bought 50 additional ducks and put them on his ponds together with the captive wild ducks. He contended that his brood stock in 1959, captured in the fall of 1958, was more than two generations removed from the wild. The ducks which were not shot or captured for brood stock, however, migrated in the fall along with the wild ducks attracted to the ponds.

[Dr. Koop testified that] they shot approximately 20% to 25% of the ducks that he raised. The rest disappeared. He did not know where. He stated that he had no way of knowing if the mallards on his ranch were the mallards that were there the year before. This would seem to refute his assertion that his brood stock was more than two generations removed from the wild. He was unable to distinguish between wild mallards and the mallards that he released nor was there any way that he could identify the mallards that he released when they were in the air flying. Until the ducks migrated he claimed that they were his ducks. "The mallard ducks, until the time they migrate from that ranch, leave the ranch, I consider them to be my ducks."

[The five defendants were among approximately 38 people who were present on the Koop Ranch. Dr. Koop had invited the hunters to his premises and charged them $25 per person per day. The hunters were distributed among the ponds on the ranch. The game officers confiscated the six ducks that had been shot by defendants at pond No. 5; one was a pintail and five were mallards. The officers found shelled corn in and near all of the ponds on the Koop Ranch. Oats were also found at pond No. 5. No oats or other grain crops were growing in the vicinity at the time.

[Defendants argued *inter alia* that (1) there was no evidence that they attempted to kill wild ducks; (2) the mallard ducks that they shot were not wild ducks; and (3) the mallard ducks on the premises were more than two generations removed from the wild and did not come under the statute.]

Appellants' next contention ... is that ... the mallards which were shot and shot at were not *wild* ducks within the meaning of the law and the regulations. . . .

It is common knowledge that ducks, and particularly mallard ducks, lend themselves to being tamed or domesticated and that ducks generally found in most farmyards trace their ancestry back to the wild and untamed ducks with whose protection and care the Migratory Bird Treaties and regulations were concerned. Concededly, however, the law was not meant for, nor may it regulate or control the use of, such tamed or domesticated ducks.

It is the contention of Dr. Koop and the other appellants that the mallard ducks which inhabited the ponds at the Koop Ranch which were shot at and shot on October 7, 1959, were more than two generations removed from the wild and that until the ducks migrated in the fall they were "his ducks"; in other words, that they had become domesticated.

... Dr. Koop testified that he could not tell whether the ducks in evidence were "his ducks" or wild ducks, nor could other witnesses so distinguish. The ducks had every appearance of being wild ducks....

But assuming that the mallard ducks were actually raised on the Koop Ranch, our question, then, is whether ducks having been hatched from brood stock which had been captured in the fall of 1958 and confined through the winter by Dr. Koop, and also from ducks purchased by him in the spring of 1959, all of which were nesting upon artificial ponds of his creation, fed by him through the summer in order to keep them there, but which ducks were completely unconfined from flying anywhere they wished and from mingling with other ducks concededly wild, and which ducks did in fact migrate in the fall of the year and which in past years had not been shown to return to Dr. Koop's ponds, can be said not to be wild ducks and thus not included under the Migratory Bird Treaty Act or the regulations.

In determining when a "wild" animal or "wild" birds are no longer considered "wild," courts and writers have made the major consideration one of possession and control. In 2 THOMAS M. COOLEY, TORTS 838 (3d ed., 1906), it is said:

> There is no property in wild animals until they have been subjected to the control of man. If one secures and tames them, they are his property; if he does not tame them, they are still his, so long as they are kept confined and under his control.

In upholding the constitutionality of the Migratory Bird Treaty Act in *Missouri v. Holland,* 252 U.S. 416, 434 (1920), Mr. Justice Holmes said:

> * * * Wild birds are not in the possession of anyone; and possession is the beginning of ownership.

See also Sickman v. United States, 184 F.2d 616, 618 (7th Cir.1950), *cert. denied,* 341 U.S. 939 (1951).

Even if the animals or wild birds have been in the control of a person, thus giving him a property right, once this control is relinquished the property right is destroyed. [ ] In *Graves v. Dunlap,* 152 P. 532, 534 (Wash.1915), the court was dealing with the ownership and right to possession of game animals and birds. The court there stated:

> * * * if the animals return to their wild state, the property right ceases. That the property right is a defeasible one is recognized by Blackstone. In ... Blackstone ... it is said:
>
> > In all these creatures, reclaimed from the wildness of their nature, the property is not absolute, but defeasible; a property that may be destroyed if they resume their ancient wildness and are found at large. For if the pheasants escape from the mew, or the fishes from the trunk, and are seen wandering at large in their proper element, they became *ferae naturae* again, and are free and open to the first occupant that hath ability to seize them. * * *

> Animals *ferae naturae,* if reclaimed and kept in inclosed ground, are property which will pass to the executors and administrators of a deceased person.

Dr. Koop asserts possession and control of the mallards through feeding and leaving them undisturbed throughout the spring and summer up to the hunting season. He claims that the mallards were confined, even though they could obviously fly from one pond to another and, of course, could fly over the four foot fence which surrounded his ranch. The evidence is that neither Dr. Koop nor anyone else could distinguish the mallards he raised from other mallards which might come into the Koop ponds.... There is substantial testimony in the record which indicates that immediately south of the Koop Ranch there were other ponds or areas covered with water and that hundreds of other mallards had been seen flying there shortly before the opening of the hunting season. There was nothing to prevent a commingling of the mallards raised by Dr. Koop with these "strange" mallards. We think it must be held that the mallard ducks here were no more within the possession and control of Dr. Koop than were the pintails, wood ducks and teal that admittedly flew in and out of the ponds on his ranch and which undoubtedly shared in his bounty. They were free to go and come as they would. Admittedly, the mallards hatched and raised on Koop's Ranch and which were not shot or captured in the fall for brood stock migrated yearly. He knew not where, and he did not know if they returned the following spring. Under the circumstances existing on the ranch, therefore, it would seem perfectly clear that even the mallards raised by Dr. Koop, if they could have been identified or distinguished from the other ducks, were wild ducks within the meaning of the law and other regulations. We accordingly hold that the contention of the appellants may not be sustained. A contrary conclusion could defeat the very purpose of the Migratory Bird Treaty Act and handicap beyond measure enforcement of the law and regulations thereunder.

NOTES

(1) The issue in the excerpt from *Koop* came down to the meaning of a single word, "wild," as used in a particular section of the Migratory Bird Treaty Act [MBTA]. The decision illustrates the need to read statutes carefully and, when applying a statute to set of facts, to identify the key words and phrases that generate the uncertainty. In *Koop*, the court turned to the common law to determine the proper meaning of the disputed word, perhaps on the assumption that Congress was aware of the common law of wild animals. Thus, the case also illustrates the continuing importance of the common law of wild animals—even in contemporary disputes centered around statutes and regulations. Of course, Congress could have defined the term "wild" in a much different way. Had it done so, would the court have been obliged to defer?

It is also important to keep in mind that the court in *Koop* decided the meaning of "wild" only for purposes of this particular statutory provision. In other legal settings, the term could have other meanings. Thus, there is not one legal definition of "wild" but many, however similar they might be.

(2) *Koop* suggests that ducks fall into three categories: (i) wild, (ii) tame, and (iii) domesticated. At issue in this case was whether the particular ducks that were shot were wild. Does the court provide enough information about the other two categories to enable us to draw a line between them? Are we given clues about the legal significance, if any, of the distinction between tame and domesticated ducks? Would such a line be drawn on a duck-by-duck basis, or for a species or genetic strain of ducks as a group? We will return to this question in Chapter 2.

(3) Thomas Harelson, a game warden, divided his state's statutes into three groups: (a) *social* statutes such as those prohibiting hunting on Sunday; (b) *traditional* laws such as the rule against hunting waterfowl with a shotgun that has too many shells in the chamber; and (c) *resource protection* statutes such as bag limits. Thomas Harelson, *Streamlining Waterfowl Enforcement,* Proceedings of the International Conference on Improving Hunter Compliance with Wildlife Laws 153 (1992). Based on the *Koop* decision, into which category does the ban on baiting fit? What are the objectives of the ban? Is hunting with bait unsportsmanlike, and thus contrary to good hunting ethics? Does hunting with bait give a hunter an unfair advantage over other hunters, so that the underlying rationale might stem from a concern over fairness among hunters? Might the concerns, instead or in addition, have more to do with the number of ducks that get shot, or with disruptions of the ducks' natural feeding practices, or even with the use of unhealthy food as bait?

If the rationale chiefly has to do with the number of ducks killed during a season, could that rationale be served better simply by reducing bag limits? And if that is the chief rationale, how critical should we be of what Dr. Koop was doing? If he raised and released far more ducks then his guests shot, what harm was he doing to duck populations? Should the court have taken this factor into account in deciding the meaning of "wild"? Should it have considered, too, the fact that Dr. Koop created and maintained several ponds on his property, which apparently supplied good duck habitat? On the other hand, might concerns be raised about breeding game animals in captivity and then releasing them due to possible genetic impacts on wild strains of the same species?

(4) In the last paragraph, the court states that "even the mallards raised by Dr. Koop, if they could have been identified or distinguished from the other ducks, were wild ducks." That comment was not a necessary element of the court's reasoning, given that the court found, on the facts of the case, that Koop's ducks were not capable of being identified or distinguished from other ducks of the same species. Given that the court's statement was *obiter dictum,* why might the court have made it? What if Dr. Koop had successfully bred ducks that contained a visible, peculiar tail feather that allowed them to be identified from a distance. What would the harm be if Dr. Koop's guests simply shot birds raised by Dr. Koop? Would this behavior differ meaningfully from the plainly lawful practice of killing captive-raised ducks? In thinking about these questions, consider the last sentence in the above excerpt, with its claim that a "contrary conclusion could . . . handicap beyond measure enforcement of the law and regulations thereunder." In what way would this be true? For laws and regulations to work, enforcement must be possible, and we shall see other instances in which lawmakers (including courts) consider the practical problems of enforcement when drafting and interpreting wildlife statutes and regulations.

Later chapters take up some of the legal issues presented by game ranches and by various policy proposals that aim to help wildlife by increasing landowner incentives to manage lands in wildlife friendly ways.

(5) *United States v. Conners:* Defendant appealed his conviction under the MBTA for killing mallard ducks. He argued that the ducks were captive-reared and thus not within the scope of the Act. The Tenth Circuit began its analysis by noting that two of the three international treaties—with Great Britain (acting for Canada) and Mexico—that are given effect in the MBTA, specifically include "wild ducks"; the third—with Japan—does not. Thus, the court was faced with an ambiguity: did the MBTA apply to "non-wild" ducks? Since the Fish and Wildlife Service had promulgated regulations that defined the term "migratory game birds" to include "wild ducks," the court reversed the conviction and ordered the magistrate to enter a specific finding on whether the ducks in question were wild or captive-reared.

A dissenter would have affirmed the conviction on the basis of the testimony of federal agents that the birds had been tagged and were wild. The dissenter also thought that the MBTA was broad enough to sustain a conviction for killing the ducks whether captive-reared or wild:

> The majority opinion relies on references ... in the regulations to "migratory game birds" and "wild ducks." In 50 C.F.R., § 20.11, there is a definition of "migratory game birds" for which open seasons are prescribed, and that definition does enumerate "(1) Anatidae (wild ducks, ...)." However this definition is plainly limited to the part of the regulations on "Migratory Bird Hunting." Our case, of course, does not involve such open season hunting. The regulation applicable here, I feel, is the one in 50 C.F.R. § 10.12 with the general definition of "migratory birds." This definition is applicable throughout Subchapter B (see 50 C.F.R. § 10.11) on the "Taking, Possession * * * of Wildlife and Plants." That general definition clearly protects migratory birds "whether or not raised in captivity * * *" We have recently rejected arguments seeking to narrow the protection afforded to migratory birds by the treaties and the regulations. *See United States v. Richards,* 583 F.2d 491 (10th Cir.1978). We stated there that "[t]he Act applies to migratory birds, not wild birds." *Id.* at 494.

United States v. Conners, 606 F.2d 269 (10th Cir.1979).

In *Koop*, the court apparently believed that the MBTA could not apply to non-wild birds ("Concededly ... the law was not meant for, *nor may it regulate or control* the use of ... tamed or domesticated ducks.") Which court is correct? May the federal government regulate the killing of non-wild birds?

(6) Common law classifications: Like early biological taxonomies, common-law taxonomies often proceed through dichotomous distinctions. Thus, the category "animals" was divided into two general classes: animals *domitæ naturæ* (of a domestic nature) or animals *feræ naturæ* (of a wild nature). The dichotomy was legally important in property law: a person might have absolute property in animals *domitæ naturæ* (in the sense that the owner's rights were not lost when the animal wandered away) but a person could only have a qualified property in the second, residual class, animals *feræ naturæ*: ownership rights in wild animals lasted only as long as the animal was physically possessed or had been tamed (*mansueta naturæ*) so that it returned of its own accord (*animus revertendi*). *See generally* 2 WILLIAM BLACKSTONE, COMMENTARIES ON THE LAWS OF ENGLAND *389–97. We will examine the legal effects of these categories in Chapters 2 and 4.

(7) Current categories: The common law's relatively static classification of animals no longer has the power it once did. Although courts continue to employ the traditional categories—stating that animals are wild (*feræ naturæ*), tamed (*mansueta naturæ*), or domesticated (*domitæ naturæ*)—the members of the different classes are no longer a set list of species.

Factually, the lines between the legal categories can also be uncertain. Deer and other game animals, for example, are often fed during the winter; salmon return to hatcheries after growing to maturity in the ocean; mice share our houses; horses roam the western rangelands; people raise wolves as pets. Consider a flyer posted on the announcements boards at the local food co-op in Moscow, Idaho:

Lone Hawk Farm

Domestic Elk for Sale

Prime Three Year Old

Grass Fed

No Hormones or Antibiotics

$1200 Whole or $600 Half

(emphasis added). Even more fundamentally, is an animal "wild" if it exists only at our sufferance? The wolves of Yellowstone, for example, wear radio collars so that biologists can monitor their movements—and can kill them if they step out of line and begin to dine on cattle ("domestic") rather than elk ("wild").

There is no uniform method for deciding this question. Courts often do not analyze the issue, simply assuming the answer, *e.g., Durham v. Barnes,* 124 So.2d 792, 793 (La.App.1960) (horse). Some resort to dictionaries, *e.g., Thurston v. Carter,* 92 A. 295 (Me.1914) (cat), rely on precedent, *e.g., Smith v. State Farm Fire & Casualty Co.,* 381 So.2d 913 (La.App.1980) (cow), or other legal authority, *e.g., Giles v. State,* 431 N.Y.S.2d 781, 784 (N.Y.Ct.Cl. 1980) (*Restatement (Second) of Torts*) (cow); *Smith v. State Farm Fire & Casualty Co.,* 381 So.2d 913 (La.App.1980) (*Am. Jur. 2d*) (cow). Finally, some courts treat the issue as one of fact subject to expert testimony. *E.g., Abrevaya v. Palace Theatre & Realty Co.,* 197 N.Y.S.2d 27 (N.Y.Sup.Ct. 1960) (rhesus monkey); *Sprague–Dawley, Inc. v. Moore,* 155 N.W.2d 579 (Wis.1968) (white rats).

The proffered definitions are equally various:

(a) "wild animals" are "those species of animals that, as a matter of common knowledge, are naturally ferocious, unpredictable, dangerous, mischievous, or . . . 'not by custom devoted to the service of mankind at the time and in the place in which it is kept,' " *Giles v. State,* 431 N.Y.S.2d 781, 784 (N.Y.Ct.Cl.1980) (quoting RESTATEMENT (SECOND) OF TORTS § 506(1)) (milk cow is a domestic animal); *see also Sellers v. Morris,* 64 S.E.2d 662, 663 (N.C.1951) (wild animals are "dangerous, vicious, mischievous, or ferocious, or one termed in law as possessing a vicious propensity"));

(b) "domestic animals," on the other hand, are "tamed, associated with family life, accustomed to live in or near habitations of men," *Commonwealth v. Proctor,* 246 N.E.2d 454, 456 (Mass.1969) (mink not a domestic animal); *Thurston v. Carter,* 92 A. 295 (Me.1914) (cat is a domestic animal).

(c) "domestic animals" are those that are "useful and valuable for one purpose or another," *White v. State,* 249 S.W.2d 877, 878 (Tenn.1952) (coon dogs are domestic animals).

(d) domestic animals are those that are "naturally tame and gentle, or which by long continued association with man, have become thoroughly domesticated and are reduced to a state of subjection to man's will," *Smith v. State Farm Fire & Casualty Co.,* 381 So.2d 913, 914 (La.App.1980).

The definitions have their shortcoming: there are several animals that are "accustomed to live in or near habitations of men" which are not traditionally thought to be domesticated. Rats and house mice, for example, fit this definition—and are, in fact, categorized as "commensals," that is, "eating at the same table." *See generally Sprague–Dawley, Inc. v. Moore,* 155 N.W.2d 579, 582 (Wis.1968). Similarly, although a lion in a circus is "useful and valuable for one purpose or another," it generally is not considered to be domesticated.

Perhaps not surprisingly, however, there is greater uniformity in the outcomes of actual cases than the definitions might suggest. In part this stem from the commingling of two separate questions, one focusing on the *species* and the other on the *individual* animal. For example, are mallards *as a species* "wild" so that *individual* mallards are presumed wild until proven otherwise? Similarly, are horses *as a species* "domesticated" so that *individual* horses are presumed domesticated until proven feral[1]? Note that this approach requires two decisions: (1) whether the species is wild or domesticated; and (2) whether the individual animal is (a) wild or tamed (if the species is wild) or (b) domesticated or feral (if the species is domesticated). In practical effect, the answer to the first issue allocates the burden of proof: a member of a wild species is presumed wild unless tameness is proven; a member of a domesticated species is presumed domesticated unless its feral status is proven.

We will return to this issue in Chapter 4.

PERSPECTIVES

The dance of domestication: Originally, of course, all domestic species were wild. The domestication of plants and animals fundamentally

---

1. That is, having escaped from domestication and become wild.

transformed the relationship of humans to the world: agriculture simplifies ecosystems by reducing the number of plants and animals in a particular place and replacing them with domesticates that redirect larger amounts of solar energy to human use. Monoculture and factory farms are the current manifestation of this simplifying process. DONALD WORSTER, *Transformations of the Earth, in* THE WEALTH OF NATURE 45 (1993).

While the results of domestication are apparent, the defining characteristics remain elusive. Just as there is no completely satisfactory legal definition of "domesticated," so there is also no entirely satisfactory biological definition. Nonetheless, domestication involves capture, taming, and breeding under human control. It is a process of mutual adaptation, an evolutionary strategy for mutual survival. Although our species is wont to think of itself as *the* active agent working its will on a passive nature, domestication was more likely both accidental and interactive, a long, loose association that evolved into the mutual dependence that characterizes "domestication." Seeds gathered for consumption sprout in the camp's midden and thrived on the disrupted edges that humans produce. And in the process both species adapt: humans learn to grow wheat and wheat changes by the selective pressures. Human would naturally favor certain wild plants: those that were less bitter, which had larger seeds, or which had seed heads that did not shatter but had to be threshed. These would be the seeds carried home to eat and which would find there way to the midden to sprout—and evolution would be steered toward mutual compatibility.

The process of animal domestication was probably similar. The wolves that scavenged human kills and human encampments gradually moved into camp, forming a loose association that was advantageous for the hunting of both species. Individual animals that were docile and cooperative likely had a greater chance of surviving and reproducing. Corralling herds of herbivores as walking larders to be killed periodically would have allowed humans to compensate for the periodic absence of migratory species. Animals that were more violent or difficult to manage would be culled from herds and fail to pass on their genes. At some point the process becomes conscious and captive breeding would eventually produce distinctly domesticated varieties.

Another biological element of domestication is revealed by the fact that apparently not all species can be domesticated. The ancient Egyptians, for example, attempted without success to domesticate a number of species such as gazelles, ibexes, antelopes, and hyenas. Many species lack the biological adaptability shared by the major domesticated species: those species that could thrive in the fluctuating environmental conditions at the end of the Ice Age—weedy, highly adaptable, non-specialized, and rapidly reproducing species like ourselves.

There also are ethical and ecological questions raised by domestication. Humans have benefitted enormously from the use of animals for food, travel and transport, as guard animals and pets, and for many other purposes. Domesticated species have also benefitted: cattle, for example, are now found throughout the world. But domestication also has its costs. Perhaps the most significant are the many diseases that humans suffer as germs and viruses harbored by animals mutate and spread to humans, causing over the millennia untold millions of human deaths. HIV–1, the virus that causes AIDs, is one example of such a disease. The disease is believed to have originated in chimpanzees; some 35 million humans are infected with HIV–1. Fen Gao, *et al.*, *Origin of HIV–1 in the Chimpanzee* PAN TROGLODYTES TROGLODYTES, 397 NATURE 436 (1999); Robin A. Weiss & Richard W. Wrangham, *From* PAN *to Pandemic, id.* at 385. The animals have also lost—both freedom and, in many cases, all ability to live in the wild. Certain breeds of dairy cows, for instance, are so dependent on human care that they die within a few days if not regularly milked. Genetic strains of plants and animals that no longer offer economic value are often quick to go extinct. *See* Marian Burros, *Saving Breeds of the Rare and Tasty Sort,* N.Y. TIMES, July 15, 1998, at B11. For a provocative argument that many animals "chose" domestication, *see* STEPHEN BUDIANSKY, THE COVENANT OF THE WILD (1992).

Finally, according to some theorists, the domestication of animals was the key element in the embrace of a new domineering attitude toward nature generally, an attitude that brought, in varied amounts and for varied people, both prosperity and destruction. *See* CALVIN LUTHER MARTIN, IN THE SPIRIT OF THE EARTH: RETHINKING HISTORY AND TIME (1992).

ii.   GAME AND NON–GAME

State ex rel. Hyter v. Teater

Court of Appeals of Ohio.
368 N.E.2d 854 (1977).

■ POTTER, J.:—This case involves the establishment of an open season for the hunting of mourning doves. The issue of whether there should be an open season for mourning doves has evoked a considerable emotional conflict between those who view the mourning dove as a song bird whose plaintive refrains strikes a responsive note in the listener and those who view the dove as an object of sport with the dove having the advantage. However, as the trial court noted, the question of whether there should or should not be a season for hunting mourning doves is not a question before this court. The primary question is whether the legislature delegated to the chief of the division of wildlife, of the Department of Natural Resources of Ohio, authority to establish a season for the hunting of mourning doves in Ohio.[1] When the trial judge denied a temporary restraining order, he found

---

1. By way of comparison, we note that in seventeen states (Alabama, Alaska, California, Colorado, Georgia, Idaho, Massachusetts, Nevada, North Carolina, Pennsylvania, Rhode Island, Tennessee, Texas, Virginia, Washington, West Virginia, Wyoming), the state fish and game commission or its equivalent may, by promulgating rules and regulations, designate and classify wildlife species as game or nongame. In other states, the statutory language is ambiguous, but it appears that in twenty-one states (Arizona, Arkansas, Florida, Hawaii, Kansas, Illinois, Indiana, Iowa, Kentucky, Maine, Michigan, Montana, Nebraska, New Hampshire, New Jersey, New Mexico, North Dakota, Oklahoma, South Carolina, Utah, Wisconsin) the fish and game commission has only enumerated administrative, regulatory, or enforcement powers, which do not include the power to designate game and nongame species. In some of these states, however, there are en-

that the proper procedure was followed to establish such a season. That finding is not challenged on appeal.

Plaintiffs' prayer to permanently enjoin the hunting, shooting and killing of the mourning dove and for such other and further relief to which the plaintiff might be entitled under law and equity was denied....

It is asserted that this is a case of first impression. The wildlife division established the mourning dove season by erroneously extending the effect of the language found in the amendment to R.C. 1531.08, effective January 1, 1974. This section in pertinent part reads as follows:

"The chief [of the division of wildlife] may regulate:

"(A) Taking and possessing wild animals, at any time and place or in any number, quantity, or length, and in any manner, and with such devices as he prescribes * * *."

The above section was a part of an act amending many sections of R.C. Chapter 1531 and Chapter 1533 and was captioned: "An Act to protect endangered species of wildlife." This case involves statutory construction and in construing the statute we must apply the recognized rules of construction. One of the rules for statutory construction is as follows:

"* * * [I]f on the face of a statute there is doubt as to its meaning, and the doubt can be removed and the intent gathered by reference to cognate provisions, it is the duty of the courts to use them in aid of construction to learn and carry out the legislative intent. Thus, a particular statute or section should be construed in the light of, with reference to, or in connection with other statutes and sections, especially where the provisions, though separated in the Code were formerly part of but one section of an act or of the same act. It follows that all such sections and statutes are to be considered and compared with reference to the entire system of which all are parts. A code of statutes relating to one subject is presumed to be governed by one spirit and policy, and intended to be consistent and harmonious, and all of the several sections are to be considered in order to arrive at the meaning of any part, unless a contrary intent is clearly manifest."

See 50 OHIO JURISPRUDENCE 2D 197, *Statutes,* § 221.

dangered species acts which authorize either the commission or a separate environmental agency to designate nongame and/or endangered species, and subsequently to modify the list by addition or deletion. In an additional eleven states (Connecticut, Delaware, Louisiana, Maryland, Minnesota, Mississippi, Missouri, New York, Oregon, South Dakota, Vermont), the commission is given broad general powers, but not specifically the power to designate. For these states it is not possible to determine the scope of the commission's power from the statutory language alone.

Further, doves generally or mourning doves specifically are listed as game birds or migratory game birds in 25 states (Arizona, California, Colorado, Delaware, Florida, Illinois, Indiana, Iowa, Louisiana, Maryland, Mississippi, Nevada, New Hampshire, New Mexico, North Carolina, Oklahoma, Oregon, Pennsylvania, Rhode Island, South Carolina, South Dakota, Tennessee, Texas, Virginia, West Virginia). They are protected by reason of omission from the list of statutory game birds in fourteen states (Arkansas, Connecticut, Hawaii, Kentucky, Maine, Michigan, Montana, Nebraska, New Jersey, New York, North Dakota, Wisconsin, Wyoming). They are specified by name as protected in three states (Idaho, Kansas, Minnesota). Seven states do not list game species by name (Alabama, Alaska, Georgia, Massachusetts, Missouri, Vermont, Washington).

A review of R.C. Chapter 1531, entitled Division of Wildlife, and R.C. Chapter 1533, entitled Hunting and Fishing, reveals too many contradictory and inconsistent sections to permit the holding that the legislature intended to delegate to the chief of the division of wildlife authority to establish a new species for hunting.

R.C. 1531.08 formerly read as follows:

"The council [of the division of wildlife] may regulate: (A) Taking and possessing clams or mussels, crayfish, aquatic insects, fish, frogs, turtles, and game, at any time and place or in any number, quantity, or length, and in any manner, and with such devices as he prescribes
* * *."

It may reasonably be argued that the legislature was substituting the generic words, "wild animals" for the prior listing of specific species.

In comparison with other sections of the chapters, we find that R.C. 1533.02 contains detailed provisions relative to open seasons and bag limits for game birds, fish and fur-bearing animals. R.C. 1531.01(S) defines game birds as follows:

" 'Game birds' includes pheasants, quail, ruffed grouse, sharp-tailed grouse, pinnated grouse, wild turkey, Hungarian partridge, Chukar partridge, woodcocks, black-breasted plover, golden plover, Wilson's snipe or jack-snipe, greater and lesser yellowlegs, rail, coots, gallinules, duck, geese, and brant."

R.C. 1531.01(T), defines nongame birds as follows:

" 'Nongame birds' includes all other wild birds not included and defined as game birds."

Webster's Third New International Dictionary (1971) defines "game bird" as "a bird made legitimate quarry for hunters by state or other law." *See also* 38 C.J.S. *Game* § 1, p. 2. In effect, the order of the chief established the mourning dove as a game bird. This is a usurpation of legislative authority, since game and nongame birds have been clearly defined in R.C. 1531.01.

Further, in construing R.C. 1531.08, it is also necessary to consider a code section that antedates it, R.C. 1533.07, which reads in pertinent part as follows:

"Protection afforded nongame birds.

"No person shall catch, kill, injure, pursue, or have in his possession, either dead or alive, or purchase, expose for sale, transport, or ship to a point within or without the state, or receive or deliver for transportation any bird other than a game bird, or have in his possession any part of the plumage, skin, or body of any bird other than a game bird, except as permitted in Chapters 1531 and 1533 of the Revised Code, or disturb or destroy the eggs, nest, or young of such a bird."

This section is analogous to the former G.C. 1409, which reads as follows:

"No person shall catch, kill, injure, pursue, or have in his possession either dead or alive, or purchase, expose for sale, transport or ship to a point within or without the state a turtle dove or *mourning dove*, sparrow, nut-hatch, warbler, flicker, vireo, wren, American robin, catbird, tanager, bobolink, bluejay, oriole, grosbeak, or redbird, creeper, redstart, waxwing, woodpecker, humming bird, killdeer, swallow, bluebird, blackbird, meadowlark, bunting, starling, redwing, purple martin, brown thresher, American goldfinch, chewink, or ground robin, pewee or phoebe bird, chickadee, fly-catcher, gnat catcher, mousehawk, whippoorwill, snowbird, titmouse, gull, eagle, buzzard, *or any wild bird other than a game bird.* No part of the plumage, skin or body of such birds shall be sold or had in possession for sale."

(Emphasis added.)

To hold that the recent amendment to R.C. 1531.08 modifies R.C. 1533.07, under which mourning doves have until now been protected since they are not game birds, and numerous other sections of the code . . . is to extend the implication of R.C. 1531.08 beyond its scope. If the legislature had intended as a modern concept, to delegate the authority to name species for hunting, in contradiction to its historical practice of doing so by legislative action, it easily could have done so. For example, in 1957, R.C. 1531.01(S) was amended to include the wild turkey as a game bird. As to the early controversy relative to quail, see 1925 OHIO ATTY. GEN. OPS. 775, No. 3032. Further, such a distinct break from the historical precedent established by the legislature would not have occurred in a relatively minor amendment to a single paragraph in an existing section. Such a break from historical precedent would have been in clear and unmistakable language. If the legislature desires such a change it may still so speak. *See* R.C. 1531.02, wherein the legislature has previously declared that the ownership of and the legal title to all wild animals is in the state and the state holds such title in trust for the benefit of all the people.

. . .

For the foregoing reasons, we find that the chief of the division of wildlife did not have authority to declare an open season for the mourning dove and to this extent the appellant's assignment of error is well taken.

The judgment of the Court of Common Pleas of Lucas County is reversed and in rendering the judgment the trial court should have rendered, we order, adjudge and decree that in the state of Ohio all persons are permanently enjoined from the hunting, shooting and killing of the mourning dove.

Judgment reversed.

■ BROWN, P.J., and WILEY, J., concur.

NOTES

(1) For the public, the issue in *Hyter* was whether mourning doves were the sort of animal that should be hunted. The legal issue is different: Did the state agency have the power to add the bird to the list of game birds, or was this a decision that only the legislature could make? The case thus introduces several important points about wildlife law:

(a) Wildlife law often arises within the context of administrative law. The legal issues in wildlife cases often are framed in terms of whether an agency (federal, state, or local) had the power to do what it did. Did the agency properly interpret the statutory guidance that it received from the legislative body? Did it follow the proper procedure in making the decision?

Note the court's statement in the first paragraph of *Hyter* that, according to the trial court, the state agency followed the proper procedure when adding mourning doves to the game list. That ruling, we are told, was not challenged on appeal. If the agency had used an improper procedure, the court likely would have reversed the agency's decision and remanded it to agency.

(b) Wildlife law also concerns the allocation of decisionmaking power. In *Hyter,* the court held that the agency exceeded its substantive powers; it acted *ultra vires.*

Who decides an issue often has considerable impact on the outcome of the decision. This is particularly true in wildlife law since state fish and game departments have long shown a tendency to favor hunting and fishing interests over competing concerns: "He who pays the piper calls the tune." For this reason, a critical issue in wildlife law is the staffing of regulatory agencies because this often affects the agency's responsiveness to the preferences of the public at large. No doubt, pro-hunting advocates in Ohio pushed the state agency to add mourning doves to the game list—rather than asking the legislature to do so—because they believed they would have greater success with a hunter-friendly administrative agency, despite the legal uncertainty about the agency's power to act.

(c) *Hyter* is a relatively uncommon administrative law case because the court held that the procedure was proper but that the agency lacked the substantive authority to act. Most administrative law cases involve the opposite: the agency has the substantive authority but arguably employed improper procedure.

(2) Like *Koop, Hyter* involves a question of statutory construction. In this case the court turned for help, not as *Koop* did to the common law (which, as noted below, did not contain a clear definition of "game" animals), but to other sections of the same statute. In doing so, it assumed that the statute as a whole ought to make sense, and that it should not interpret one provision of a statute in a way either that rendered other sections of the same statute meaningless or that created a direct conflict among statutory sections. The court also noted that the legislature over the years had itself acted to add and delete animals from game lists—evidence that the legislature itself believed that the listing job was one for legislative rather than administrative action. Keep in mind that, if the legislature dislikes an interpretation chosen by an appellate court, it can effectively reverse the decision prospectively by amending the statute to implement its desired meaning.

(3) On what basis might a legislature (or a state agency, if given the authority) decide whether an animal should or should not be a game animal? Historical practice? Public sentiment? Ecological impacts? The importance of particular species for food, hide or fur? Aesthetics? Ethical considerations? The "sport" involved in killing them?

(4) Note, in the statutory sections cited in *Hyter,* the very broad protection granted to nongame birds by the law. It is unlawful, not just to kill them or attempt to kill them, but to disturb them or even possess part of a dead bird. Read literally, the statute prohibits a child from picking up a bluejay feather. Why might the law be so strict? Is a state likely to go after a child with a bird feather collection? Does the answer have something to do with the practical enforcement problems mentioned by the court in *Koop*? If so, how persuasive are such concerns?

(5) Dove hunting at the ballot box: In 1994, the Ohio Legislature narrowly passed a statute amending R.C. 1531.01(S) to provide " 'Game birds' includes mourning doves,...." The legislature thus implicitly reaffirmed the court's decision in *Hyter*, even as it changed the practical result, because it did not give the chief of the division of wildlife power to add birds to the game bird list.

In response to the statute, a group called "Save the Doves" collected more than 100,000 signatures to put the issue of dove hunting on the 1998 ballot. The *Plain Dealer*—Cleveland's newspaper—reported a statement by Jeff Rusnak, a Save The Doves committee member: "There's no need to hunt mourning doves. There are plenty of other animals to be hunted. A mourning dove is a neighborhood bird, a song bird. It's a cruelty issue. A number get shot or wounded or maimed." *The Plain Dealer,* Dec. 10, 1995, at 10B. Wayne Pacelle, vice president of the Washington-based Humane Society of the United States, told one gathering of hunting opponents: "These are entirely inoffensive birds. There is no compelling reason to shoot these birds—either for nuisance or management reasons. It's akin to shooting cardinals or robins." *Id.*, Nov. 9, 1997, at 6B. One reporter commented, "The dove-hunting debate has always been able to stir Ohioans' passions in ways that something like, oh, school funding could never hope to duplicate. There is no middle ground here. Either you're for protecting the sweet, gentle mourning doves, universal symbols of peace since biblical time, or you're for blasting them to smithereens." The issue, he suggested, "has a symbolic resonance beyond the narrow question of whether to add one more species to the 40–some permitted to be hunted in this state" because it "captures the cultural divide that separates citified Ohio from countrified Ohio." Noting that the average dove "yields only about 2 ounces of consumable meat," he concluded, "I'm not rabidly anti-hunting or anything, but I could never see a rationale for dove hunting." Joe Dirck, *One More Shot at Dove Hunting, id.* Dec. 9, 1997, at 1B.

Hunting proponents countered by emphasizing the size of the population of doves and the expertise of the agency's staff. One letter writer stressed that "Division of Wildlife biologists, trained scientific professionals and whose life work is the study of animals, have provided information explaining that mourning doves are one of Ohio's most abundant bird species. Scientific data shows that there are about 500 million doves in the United States, including 3 million to 5 million in Ohio. Doves are hunted in most states, and hunting does not negatively impact their populations." His conclusion: "Vote 'no' on state Issue 1 and keep wildlife management under the direction of professional wildlife biologists and managers." Rick J. Belanger, *Letter to the Editor, id.* Sept. 8, 1998, at 10B. Pro-hunting groups also launched a heavily financed television campaign. The campaign described proponents of a ban on dove hunting as " 'out-of-state extremists' in a series of television ads that barely mentions doves or hunting." Ohioans for Wildlife Conservation, the pro-hunting group, argued that "[i]ssue 1 is a Trojan Horse—innocent on the outside, but loaded with danger inside." The extremists' goal? "not only [to] take doves off the game-bird list, but animals off the farm and meat off our tables . . . animals out of laboratories, pets out of our homes and they would close our zoos. . . . Animal rights is their sole agenda." The ads ended with the punchline: "Tell the extremists it's a bad plan." Paul Souhrada, *Dove-Hunting Ban's Foes Fire off Ads; Campaign Cites Outside "Extremists," id.* Sept. 23, 1998, at 5B.

The proposal to ban dove hunting was defeated 60%–40%.

(6) "Game" and the English common law: The term "game" was not a term of art at the common law; instead, it was applied rather indiscriminately to animals *feræ naturæ* that were hunted. In a House of Lord's decision in 1865, the Lord Chancellor in passing defined the term as "animals *feræ naturæ* which are fit for the food of man." *Blades v. Higgs,* 11 H.L.C. 621, 631, 11 Eng. Rep. 1474, 1478 (H.L. 1865). But this definition—like the previous definitions of "wild" and "domestic"—is problematic since some animals were treated as game that were not eaten, *e.g.,* foxes.

In common speech, the term (of Teutonic origin) has had its present meaning of "amusement, delight, fun, or sport" since at least the 11th century. By the end of the 13th century, the term was used for the fun or sport derived from the chase—and then to the object of the chase, the animal that is hunted. The term is used to refer to wildlife being hunted in *Boke of St. Albans*, a famous text on falconry written at the end of the 15th century. *See generally* 2 The Oxford English Dictionary 36–39 (1933). Thus, as the Lord Chancellor suggested, the term was not a synonym for a particular list of animals but a description of animals put to a specific use.

(7) Feral and "game": What is the legal status of non-native, introduced species that originally were domesticated and whose individual members have become feral?

(a) *Hayward v. Samuel* was a challenge to a decision by the Philadelphia health department to exterminate pigeons that, in the department's opinion, had become a health hazard. The court rejected the challenge, concluding that pigeons are not "game birds" even though they were within the taxonomic order *columbae* which was on the list contained in the statutory definition of "game." The court's decision reflected traditional deference to agency expertise—particularly when public health is involved. *Hayward v. Samuel,* 47 A.2d 251 (Pa.1946).

(b) *State v. Willers*, in contrast, was an appeal from a prosecution for using live pigeons for trap shooting without a hunting license. Defendant argued that the inclusion of the "order *Columbae*" in the statutory definition of game did not include feral pigeons. The court disagreed:

> *Columbae* ... includes all the families, species, and types of pigeons. So that it at once becomes manifest that the pigeons of this region in the feral state fall within the protection of the statute.
>
> The statute does not protect domesticated pigeons, such as are bred and raised in the lofts of farmers, for table consumption, sometimes classified as poultry, but the State in this prosecution having shown the killing by defendant of the type of pigeons which in the feral state the statute protects, made a *prima facie* case....

State v. Willers, 130 S.W.2d 256 (Mo.App.1939).

(c) ***Key v. State*** also involved the relationship between "feral" and "game." Defendants were convicted of hunting out of season. They appealed, arguing that "they were hunting feral hogs and that feral hogs are not protected by the laws of this State and that, therefore, they had a legal right to hunt feral hogs at any time and at any place." The court upheld the conviction since (1) feral hogs were, "[b]y their very definition," wild rather than domesticated animals; (2) that "game" was defined—by *Webster's Dictionary* and *Corpus Juris Secundum*—as wild animals that were hunted; and (3) there was a general closed season on hunting "all game" within the state. *Key v. State,* 384 S.W.2d 22 (Tenn.1964).

Is there a consistent point or do the cases demonstrate only that courts will struggle not to reach what they perceive to be an absurd result?

SECTION 2.   ROLES FOR WILDLIFE LAW

NOTES

(1) Objectives of wildlife law: Like all bodies of law, wildlife law is a human construction. It exists to help people collectively deal with problems that arise among them and to enable people, individually and collectively, to meet their needs and accomplish their goals.

It is useful to give thought to why this body of law was created and what problems it addresses. Why do we need wildlife law? What problems does it help solve? What functions does it perform? What policy concerns influence the ways it has evolved? Such questions are useful because the objectives and underlying, often conflicting, policy considerations that drive an area of law are helpful in understanding that body of law.

Historically, wildlife law has always had a multiplicity of objectives, a schizophrenic nature. The following goals, however, are the most influential:

(a) On the one hand, wildlife law was—and still largely is—a subset of property law. Many of the issues it presents focus on the acquisition of ownership in wild animals and the incidents of that ownership. Often, the acquisition of property is simply the first step in a commercial venture since wildlife was until relatively recently the source of a variety of commodities such as food and furs.

(b) Simultaneously, however, the government—be it the king in Parliament, the state or national governments—has pervasively regulated not only the acquisition of private rights in wildlife, but also the uses to which a landowner might put her land in order to protect wildlife habitat on that land. Traditionally, the regulatory objective was "conservation," that is, regulation that sought to ensure a sustainable harvest of the wildlife species. Hence, governments adopted bag limits, gear restrictions, and closed seasons. Conservation-based regulation can be viewed simply as specifying the steps necessary to acquire property in wildlife; this perspective, however, slights the allocational content. Parliament restricted hunting to reinforce Britain's class structure and states have allocated salmon to sports fishers under the guise of conservation.

(c) Conservation, however, has often also included elements of "preservation," that is, the regulation sought to protect wildlife for purposes that were at least not immediately utilitarian. Kings and queens regulated swans not only to provide food for royal feasts but also because swans were a royal fowl with symbolic importance; Congress similarly enacted legislation to protect the bald eagle for its symbolic rather than economic value.

(d) Most recently, there has been a growing belief that species have an independent moral worth that we, as fellow members of the land community, have an obligation to recognize. The Endangered Species Act, for example, achieves much of its force from its simple statement that *all* species must be protected from extinction.

Although there are obvious tensions along the continuum of these objectives, they are not always in opposition; different legal instruments— be they statutes, regulations, or judicial opinions—frequently spring from a complex mix of these and other objectives.

(2) Wildlife law as natural resources law: As the preceding note suggests, it is essential to recognize that wildlife law is a body of natural resources law and, as such, it necessarily performs many of the same tasks as other bodies of natural resources law:

(a) It allocates private rights in valuable natural resources either directly by granting them to people or indirectly by specifying what people must do to obtain such rights;

(b) It defines the bundle of legal entitlements that a person obtains, *e.g.*, covering such issues as the duration of the rights, possible forfeiture or abandonment, their transferability and divisibility, and how the resource might be used. In doing so, it indirectly facilitates and regulates markets in wildlife-related products;

(c) When a wildlife right is acquired separately from the land where the wildlife lives or might be found, then the law specifies the relative rights of the owner of that wildlife resource vis-a-vis the owner of the land.

One of the most basic functions of all natural resources law is that of allocating private rights and prescribing the steps people can take to acquire such rights. Perhaps the most familiar rule of all wildlife law is one such law: the "rule of capture," under which a person can become the owner of an unowned wild animal by being the first to capture it. This rule sets forth the means by which a person can gain private rights in a wildlife resource; as such, it reflects the method chosen by lawmakers to allocate the resource, out of the many such allocation methods that could be (and are) used. As we shall see in Chapter 2, this familiar rule of capture is subject to severe limits, ones that protect the rights of private landowners and that serve various other aims. As they go about their work, drafters of wildlife laws and regulations rarely mention directly this allocation function, but it is central to all that they do. For instance, a common law rule that vests a landowner with certain rights to control hunting on her land is properly understood (in part) as a rule of resource allocation. The following case, *Madison v. Alaska Department of Fish and Game,* provides a vivid illustration of ongoing disputes about the best means of allocating wildlife, in the context of disputes about the best aims to promote when allocating a scarce resource.

a. CONSUMPTIVE USES

Madison v. Alaska Department of Fish & Game

Alaska Supreme Court.
696 P.2d 168 (1985).

■ MOORE, J.:—This case arises as a consolidated appeal of two cases. It concerns the validity of a Board of Fisheries' (hereafter board) regulation designed to identify eligibility for subsistence fishing in the Cook Inlet region.

Appellants (hereafter Madison and Gjosund) are two groups of Alaskan residents who live along the Kenai coastline and near Homer. For many years, they have fished with set nets for salmon for their personal and family use. Nonetheless, the board denied subsistence permits to Madison and Gjosund because their use of salmon did not meet the board's regulatory definition of subsistence. Both Madison and Gjosund challenged the regulation as exceeding the scope of the state's subsistence law. In both cases, the trial courts upheld the regulation as consistent with the statutory grant of authority. We hold the regulation invalid since it is inconsistent with AS [Alaska Statutes] 16.05.251(b), AS 16.05.940(22) and AS 16.05.940(23) and contrary to the legislature's intent in enacting the 1978 subsistence law.

I. SUMMARY OF FACTS

Records indicate that subsistence fishing in Cook Inlet was minimal through the mid–1970s.[1] However, a core group of residents of each Cook Inlet community has traditionally fished for Cook Inlet salmon for subsistence. Participation in the subsistence salmon fishery is most visible in the

---

1. From 1971 to 1977, the average number of subsistence permits issued annually for the Upper Cook Inlet was 87 and the average catch was 405 salmon. Commercial harvest averaged about two million fish per year. However, this statistical data does not necessarily reveal the total subsistence use since many people did not obtain permits and some commercially caught salmon were used for subsistence.

smaller, more isolated villages, where the subsistence group represents a larger percentage of the population.

In 1977 the board established a comprehensive management policy for Cook Inlet, [ ], which essentially allocated specific salmon stocks to sports fishermen and commercial fishermen on the basis of seasonal fish movements. [ ] Although the policy did not specifically refer to subsistence uses of salmon in Cook Inlet, it had a substantial impact on subsistence fishing. Commercial fishermen, accustomed to taking subsistence salmon from their commercial catch, instead obtained subsistence salmon fishing permits in order to fish for their personal and family use after the commercial season was over.

Before 1978, subsistence fishing was defined in AS 16.05.940(17) as fishing for "personal use and not for sale or barter." In 1978, the Alaska State Legislature enacted ch. 151 SLA 1978 (hereafter the 1978 subsistence law). Subsistence fishing was redefined as fishing for "subsistence uses." Subsistence uses were defined as "customary and traditional uses ... for direct personal or family consumption, and for the customary trade, barter or sharing...." AS 16.05.940(23).[4] Furthermore, the legislation required the board to adopt regulations permitting "subsistence uses" of fish stocks, absent a showing that this use would jeopardize the sustained yield principle. AS 16.05.251(b). Under AS 16.05.251(b), subsistence uses have priority over sport and commercial uses if the board finds it necessary to restrict the taking of fish to assure the maintenance of fish stocks or to assure the continuation of subsistence uses. If further restrictions are necessary after giving priority to all subsistence uses, the legislature established specific criteria to restrict subsistence uses based on the subsistence user's customary and direct dependence on the resource, local residency and availability of alternative resources. *Id.* As a result, the board could no longer allocate for subsistence uses at its discretion [because t]he legislature mandated in AS 16.05.251(b) that the board regulate for the protection of subsistence uses as the priority use of fish and game.

The passage of the 1978 subsistence law, combined with adoption of the board's 1977 management policy, heightened public awareness of the state's subsistence fishing provisions. This public interest resulted in a substantial increase in the demand for subsistence permits and a corre-

---

4. AS 16.05.940(23), (formerly AS 16.05.940(26)), states:

"subsistence uses" means the customary and traditional uses in Alaska of wild, renewable resources for direct personal or family consumption as food, shelter, fuel, clothing, tools, or transportation, for the making and selling of handicraft articles out of nonedible by-products of fish and wildlife resources taken for personal or family consumption, and for the customary trade, barter or sharing for personal or family consumption; for the purposes of this paragraph, "family" means all persons related by blood, marriage, or adoption, and any person living within the household on a permanent basis.

sponding increase in total catch.[7] The board responded to the permit increase by restricting subsistence fishing; it limited areas open to subsistence fishing, length of fishing periods and maximum length of gill nets. Several lawsuits were filed, all of which resulted in decisions unfavorable to the board.

In December 1980, the board held hearings to respond to the 1978 subsistence law and received a considerable amount of testimony on subsistence uses in Cook Inlet. The meeting resulted in the establishment of characteristics for identification of "customary and traditional uses" of Cook Inlet salmon.[8] In addition, the board decided to "adopt a set of criteria drawn from the characteristics . . . and apply [them] to communi-

7. This chart reflects the trend in Upper Cook Inlet:

	Subsistence Use		Commercial Harvest
	Permits Issued	Salmon Caught	
1978	323	3,735	5,118,041
1979	1,161	9,923	1,923,229
1980	1,331	14,775	4,138,648

8. With some modification, these characteristics became the basis of 5 AAC [Alaska Administrative Code] 01.597, which states:

CHARACTERISTICS OF SUBSISTENCE FISHERIES.

(a) The Board of Fisheries finds that certain customary and traditional practices and procedures associated with the utilization of fish in the Cook Inlet Area can be used to identify subsistence uses. Based on testimony to the board, the following characteristics are those that should be evaluated in the identification of subsistence fisheries:

(1) a long-term, stable, reliable pattern of use and dependency, excluding interruption generated by outside circumstances, *e.g.,* regulatory action or fluctuations in resource abundance;

(2) a use pattern established by an identified community, subcommunity or group having preponderant concentrations of persons showing past use;

(3) a use pattern associated with specific stocks and seasons;

(4) a use pattern based on the most efficient and productive gear and economical use of time, energy and money;

(5) a use pattern occurring in reasonable geographic proximity to the primary residence of the community, group or individual;

(6) a use pattern occurring in locations with easiest and most direct access to the resources;

(7) a use pattern which includes a history of traditional modes of handling, preparing and storing the product without precluding recent technological advances;

(8) a use pattern which includes the intergenerational transmission of activities and skills;

(9) a use pattern in which the effort and products are distributed on a community and family basis including trade, bartering, sharing and gift-giving; and

(10) a use pattern which includes reliance on subsistence taking of a range of wild resources in proximity to the community or primary residency.

(b) The board will identify established geographic communities which may be participating in a subsistence system. The board will then apply all of the characteristics in (a) of this section to the communities and to subcommunities, groups and individuals within the communities to determine which uses are customary and traditional and therefore, which communities are eligible for the subsistence priority.

(c) For purposes of this section, a "community" is generally considered to be several households of full-time residents who all reside in a specific geographic area because of common interests.

ties, subcommunities, groups and individuals who wish to continue to participate in an established customary and traditional fishing effort in Cook Inlet."

At its March 1981 meeting, the board received written testimony from the public about subsistence uses of Cook Inlet salmon stock. Subsequently, it decided to apply all of the ten criteria to determine "customary and traditional uses" eligible for the subsistence priority. When the board applied the ten criteria, it determined that no group or community in the Cook Inlet region other than Tyonek, English Bay and Port Graham satisfied all ten of the criteria. The board limited the 1981 subsistence catch to these three communities. As a result, the board eliminated from the protection of the state's subsistence statute the majority of Cook Inlet fishermen who formerly fished under subsistence regulations.

Madison and Gjosund challenged the validity of the board's subsistence criteria ... on several grounds. They claimed that: (1) the criteria were inconsistent with the statutory language and legislative intent of the 1978 subsistence law; .... Both courts issued preliminary injunctions compelling the board to authorize personal use fishing for Madison and Gjosund similar to that allowed in the previous year. The board moved for summary judgment on the plaintiffs' first claim. Both trial courts granted summary judgment to the board, after finding the subsistence criteria consistent with the legislative intent "to provide for and protect personal use ... by persons who reside in rural communities...."

On appeal, Madison and Gjosund seek reversal of the two trial court decisions....

. . .

III. LEGISLATIVE HISTORY OF THE 1978 SUBSISTENCE LAW

Before 1978, subsistence fishing was defined as fishing for "personal use and not for sale or barter." [ ] The 1978 subsistence law redefined subsistence fishing as fishing for "subsistence uses." AS 16.05.940(22). "Subsistence uses" were defined as "the customary and traditional uses in Alaska of wild, renewable resources for direct personal or family consumption ... and for the customary trade, barter or sharing...." AS 16.05.940(23). The board argues that the legislature intended to narrow the scope of subsistence fishing to mean fishing by individuals residing in those rural communities that have historically depended on subsistence hunting and fishing. Under this interpretation, the board asserts that its criteria are consistent with the legislature's intent.

The board's argument reveals a fundamental misconception about the structure of the 1978 subsistence law. There are potentially two tiers of subsistence users under AS 16.05.251(b). The first tier includes all subsistence users. Under the statute, all subsistence uses have priority over sport and commercial uses "whenever it is necessary to restrict the taking of fish to assure the maintenance of fish stocks on a sustained-yield basis, or to assure the continuation of subsistence uses of such resources...." AS 16.05.251(b). If the statutory priority given all subsistence users over commercial and sport users still results in too few fish for all subsistence uses, then the board is authorized to establish a second tier of preferred subsistence users based on the legislative criteria expressed in AS 16.05.251(b), namely, customary and direct dependence on the resource, local residency, and availability of alternative resources.

Criteria like the ten criteria of 5 AAC 01.597(a) could be used to distinguish first-tier general subsistence users from second-tier preferred subsistence users, since most of the criteria relate to either "customary and direct dependence" or "local residency," two of the three criteria set out in AS 16.05.251(b). However, before there is any occasion to restrict subsistence fishing to second-tier preferred subsistence users as distinct from all subsistence users, the board must make two findings. It must find: (1) that it is necessary to restrict the taking of fish for sustained-yield purposes; and (2) that eliminating sport and commercial uses will not assure the maintenance of fish stocks on a sustained-yield basis and, thus, establishing a priority among subsistence users is also necessary. The board erred because it applied the ten criteria without making these findings.

The House Special Committee on Subsistence drafted a letter of intent for House Bill 960 that supports our interpretation. With respect to AS 16.05.251(b) (which was § 6 of House Bill 960), the letter of intent made clear the priority to be given subsistence uses in general over sport and commercial uses and explained the two-tier system among subsistence users.

> *Sections six and seven:* These two sections, which are virtually identical for the Boards of Fisheries and the Board of Game, are intended to statutorily set out the priority given to subsistence use of fish and game resources.... Further, these sections set forth a priority of users if restrictions are needed because of the unavailability of resources. The priority list is an attempt to insure that those with the most dependence upon the fish and game resources are the last to be restricted.

> *If there is a need to restrict the taking of fish or game* in order to avoid damaging the fish stocks or game populations, or in order to assure that subsistence users may continue to take fish or game, *it is the intent of the Committee that sports or commercial use be restricted before subsistence use.* If these restrictions are inadequate, restricting of subsistence use as well is authorized based upon the dependence on the resource, the local residence of the subsistence users, and the availability of alternate resources.

(Emphasis added).

Only in connection with AS 16.05.251(b) does the letter of intent discuss applying residence criteria to subsistence users, and it does so only with respect to second-tier subsistence users. With respect to the definition of subsistence uses in § 17 of House Bill 960 (now AS 16.05.940(23)), the letter of intent does not suggest that the phrase "customary and traditional" was meant to describe users as well as uses. The letter of intent states:

> *Section seventeen:* Subsection (26) defines what uses can be made of subsistence caught fish and game. It allows it to be used for direct personal or family consumption, for barter as defined in subsection (27) and for sharing the subsistence caught fish and game with other

persons. This subsistence caught fish and game which is shared can then only be used for personal or family consumption. This subsection also broadens the definition of family to include the extended family situation.

The letter of intent clearly expressed the legislative resolve to establish a priority for subsistence use of fish and game. The 1978 subsistence law also increased the number of uses qualifying as subsistence fishing by including trade and barter.

The board based its restrictive regulation 5 AAC 01.597, on the words "customary and traditional." The legislature did not define these words in the 1978 subsistence law. In such a case, reference to legislative history may provide an insight into the legislature's intent and a statute's meaning. [ ] In the House floor debate on House Bill 960, Representative Cotton introduced an amendment to delete the words "customary and traditional" from the statute. The floor manager of the bill, Representative Anderson, opposed the amendment in the following speech:

> The two words are used in this context to put some guidelines around the uses of Alaska's freedom of resources. *What we were afraid of,* it was brought to our attention by people who were concerned that this would leave the field of the definition wide open. *That newcomers just coming to the State of Alaska would* automatically be able to establish not only residency in 30 days, but *be able to go out and state that they have a customary and traditional use of Alaska's fish and game resources.* The use of customary and traditional also is in recognition of a *historical use* of fish and game for food, shelter, fuel, clothing, tools, transportation, etc. This is *not only* in conformance with the *aboriginal uses, but also* those that have come in, those people who have come in later.... [T]he *nonnative* people in the State of Alaska have established customary and traditional uses of Alaska's fish and game resources for subsistence purposes. And in order to give the Board of Fish and Game more clarification in the area, we have come up with the [inaudible] of customary and traditional rather than leaving that section wide open. *The design is not to be restrictive but to provide guidelines* and that is basically what I feel and many ... members felt it was necessary in ... adding or retaining those two words "customary and traditional."

(Emphasis added).

. . . Anderson argued for the retention of "customary and traditional" for use as a guideline. His major concern focused on the potential pressure put on resources by newcomers. In his view, the words "customary and traditional" recognized and protected a historical subsistence use by both native and non-native Alaskans. The words were not intended to restrict subsistence use.

Another part of the House debate serves to clarify the statute's meaning. Representative Parr expressed concern that the board might use AS 16.05.251(b) to eliminate Fairbanks residents from subsistence use. Some Fairbanks residents often traveled to the Chitina Dip Net Fishery near the Copper River for their fishing. Representative Anderson responded to these concerns:

> If we get into a condition where the fish stock gets down to the point where there is no way that you can allow any take, the first people that you are going to cut off are the commercial and then the sports, first, and then the last people that you are going to cut off are the subsistence people who have the greatest reliance on the resource.... [I]f it were defined that dip net fishing were for subsistence uses and not for sale or any other purpose, that would be allowed and I would think that people from Fairbanks would fall under these categories. I don't know where else they would go to ... *where people from Fairbanks make it a custom to go down to the Chitina area and if it was determined that that resource was down to the point where only subsistence would be allowed, those people would be taken care of under this section.* I don't see that it is eliminating.

(Emphasis added).

In the House debate, Anderson attempted to assure Parr that residents of urban Fairbanks could be considered priority subsistence users. Contrary to the board's interpretation of the subsistence statutes, there is no indication that legislators understood the 1978 subsistence law to restrict subsistence use to either a rural or a community context. In fact, the House debate indicates that the 1978 subsistence law was necessary to protect subsistence uses as a priority use of Alaska's fish and game resources. This intent is clearly expressed by the preamble to the subsistence law:

> [I]t is in the public interest to clearly *establish subsistence use as a priority use* of Alaska's fish and game resources *and to recognize the needs, customs and traditions of Alaskan residents.* The legislature further finds that beneficial use of those resources by all state residents should be carefully monitored and regulated with as much input as possible from the affected users, so that the viability of fish and game resources is not threatened and so that resources are conserved in a manner consistent with the sustained yield principle.

(Emphasis added).

The legislative history indicates that the legislature intended to protect subsistence use, not limit it. The words "customary and traditional" serve as a guideline to recognize historical subsistence use by individuals, both native and non-native Alaskans. In addition, subsistence use is not strictly limited to rural communities. For these reasons, the board's interpretation of "customary and traditional" as a restrictive term conflicts squarely with the legislative intent.

. . .

The board's regulation, 5 AAC 01.597, is inconsistent with the legislative intent to provide guidelines for the protection of subsistence fishing. The regulation exceeds the authority delegated to the board because it operates too restrictively in its initial differentiation between subsistence and non-subsistence uses. Under a statute designed to protect subsistence uses, the board has devised a regulation to disenfranchise many subsistence users whose interests the statute was designed to protect.

The decision of the two trial courts that 5 AAC 01.597 is consistent with AS 16.05.251(b) and AS 16.05.940(22) and (23) is REVERSED.

NOTES

(1) Like *Hyter, Madison* involved a challenge to action taken by a state administrative agency. The primary claim was that the agency violated the statute that gave it power and defined its responsibilities. The essential question was: Did the agency interpret and apply the statute correctly?

Because the case involved a challenge to an agency interpretation of law—rather than to an agency finding of fact or a policy decision—the appellate court gave little (or no) deference to the agency's decision. It is the job of the appellate court to interpret statutes and to correct misinterpretations by administrative agencies. In the federal court system, courts often defer to "reasonable" agency interpretations of statutes as long as the interpretations do not conflict with the "clear" intent of Congress. *Chevron v. Natural Resources Defense Council*, 467 U.S. 837 (1984). In *Madison*, the Alaska Supreme Court rejected this "reasonable basis" standard of review and independently construed the statute, substituting its interpretation for that of the agency. As in *Hyter*, the *Madison* court looked principally to the language of the statute and to its legislative history to help resolve ambiguities.

(2) Although the Alaska statute proved difficult to interpret, it did set forth a simple scheme for the allocation of salmon. Subsistence uses came first and all others came second. If the fish harvest was insufficient to meet all subsistence uses, then certain substance uses—principally uses by rural communities and by individuals and families economically dependent on the fish—took priority over others. Given the harvest statistics set out in note 7, however, it seems unlikely that any subsistence uses would go unmet; thus, there should be no need to worry about distinguishing among categories of subsistence uses except in isolated instances.

(3) Under the pre–1978 state law, subsistence fishing could only be done for direct personal use. Under the new statute, "subsistence" was broadened in two ways. First, fishing could be done for "family" use as well as personal use, with "family" broadly defined to include "all persons related by blood, marriage, or adoption." Second, subsistence includes not only consumption but also "customary trade" and "barter." These changes expanded the range of subsistence uses. The legal confusion came, of course, when the legislature, in defining "subsistence uses," referred to them as "the customary and traditional uses." How did the court ultimately interpret these words? What would be the most reasonable interpretation of these words, given their location within the definition as a whole and ignoring the legislative history?

Pay careful attention to the comments by Representative Anderson, floor manager for the bill. The words "customary and traditional," Anderson says, were not meant "to be restrictive" but "to provide guidelines." The court interprets this to mean that "[t]he words were not intended to restrict subsistence use." But Anderson also states that the words were "in recognition of historical use." And then there is his worry about "newcomers just coming to the State" and taking up fishing. Are not newcomers being restricted—perhaps completely and forever—from engaging in subsistence uses? If historic use is a key requirement, does the statute restrict only fishing by newcomers to the state or does it also restrict long-time residents who decide to take up fishing for the first time? And what must an applicant show in the way of historical use to gain a permit? A pattern of personal use? A pattern of use by parents or other family members? A pattern of use by neighbors or other nearby community members? And how would this apply to fishing groups from cities such as Fairbanks? In the closing paragraphs, the court states that the new law protects subsistence use and does not limit it, yet it is clear from the opinion that the protection extends only to historically established uses— and perhaps ill-defined new uses that are sufficiently like them—and that subsistence uses by outsiders are not being protected. Can Alaska justify this line-drawing between established natives and outsiders? Is this a distinction that might raise serious questions under the Equal Protection Clause of the federal and state constitutions?

In the end, did the comments by Anderson, and the other evidences of legislative history, provide much help in interpreting the meaning of "subsistence uses"?

(4) What wildlife-related aims or rationales were furthered by the statute at issue in *Madison*? The overall statute had preservation aims, keeping fish populations high enough to permit sustained annual harvests by a wide range of subsistence, sport, and commercial fishing interests. The exact scheme chosen reflected a legislative decision (influenced, as explained below, by the federal government) about how to allocate this valuable resource for consumptive use. As in *Hyter*, note the apparent difference in policy choices by the legislature and the state administrative agency. Why might the Alaska Board of Fisheries have taken such a restrictive interpretation of the definition of subsistence uses? What interests likely dominate the Board?

By enacting the statute, the legislature showed considerable willingness to protect the possibility of subsistence living both by Natives (Indians, Aleuts, and Innupiats) and other state citizens. What is the justification for such an allocational preference? Can it be criticized as an unfair subsidy for a certain class of citizens?

PERSPECTIVES

(1) The role of wildlife in the economy of the United States— biological contributions (pt. 1): It is easy to overlook the economic uses of wildlife in a post-industrial economy such as the United States. The number of subsistence hunter-gatherers who are United States citizens, for example, is minuscule; a trip to the local supermarket reveals few obviously wild products beyond the fish counter. But wild animals are economically significant even in the United States—as a detailed examination of the issue by Christine Prescott–Allen and Robert Prescott–Allen, *The First Resource: Wild Species in the North American Economy* (1986), demonstrated.

The Prescott–Allens begin by categorizing the ways in which our species uses wildlife. Broadly, wildlife species provide both biological and psychological resources. The biological can be broken down into raw materials and services.

(a) **wildlife as a source of raw materials:** The most important use of wild animals in the market economy is fishing. During the period from 1976 to 1980, the United States annually landed some 5.9 billion pounds of fish worth $1.8 billion; an additional 5.5 billion pounds worth $2.3 billion was imported annually. Raw materials for a variety of uses are provided through trapping and collecting wild animals. Ornamental uses of wildlife include skins, ivory, and shells; birds and aquarium fish supply the pet trade; sponges, feathers, and down find their way into kitchens and sleeping bags. The average annual value of such uses was at least $213.8 million between 1976 and 1980; the most economically important commodity was furs ($173.5 million annually). A fourth category of uses are for medicine. Although plants are the primary source of medicine, wild animals supply fish liver oils and some steroids. In addition, some 22,500 non-human primates were used in medical research in 1977. While these animals are increasingly supplied through captive-breeding programs, a significant percentage continue to come from the wild.

(b) **wildlife as a source of services:** In addition to direct economic inputs from harvested resources, wildlife provide a variety of ecological services. Although some of these services have a direct economic value—the value of pollination by wild pollinators, for example, can be determined based on the cost of providing the service with domesticated pollinators—many of the services can be assigned economic value only in the most general of terms. Some view even the attempt to assign dollar values to such things as the services provided by the ecosystem as the clearest example of the old definition of "economist": one who knows the price of everything and the value of nothing.

In one sense, of course, the total value of the "services" is infinite since life is impossible without them. A recent attempt to quantify "the value of the world's ecosystem services and natural capital" concluded that "[t]he services of ecological systems and the natural capital stocks that produce them are critical to the functioning of the Earth's life-support system" and are worth "in the range of US $16–54 trillion ($10^{12}$) per year." Robert Costanza, *et al.*, *The Value of the World's Ecosystem Services and Natural Capital*, 387 NATURE 253 (1997). *See generally* NATURE'S SERVICES (Gretchen C. Daily ed., 1997).

(2) **Subsistence and markets:** The penetration of the market into all regions has impacted even those peoples who still rely to a significant extent upon hunting and gathering. Markets change the nature of subsistence hunting and gathering by converting it into an alternative source for some commodities. The relationship between market and subsistence varies, of course. In some areas, hunting and gathering supplements a primarily market-based life; in others, market commodities add to an essentially

subsistence life. Regardless of the point along this continuum, "the most dramatic kind of environmental change occurs when resource procurement ceases to be aimed at subsistence and is instead market-driven. . . . That is, demand for resources is not based on local nutritional or technological needs, but rather on the opportunities presented by an external market." Raymond Hames, *Wildlife Conservation in Tribal Societies, in* BIODIVERSITY: CULTURE, CONSERVATION, AND ECODEVELOPMENT 172, 178–79 (Margery L. Old-field & Janis B. Alcorn eds., 1991). *See also* RICHARD WHITE, ROOTS OF DEPENDENCE: SUBSISTENCE, ENVIRONMENT, AND SOCIAL CHANGE AMONG THE CHOC-TAWS, PAWNEES, AND NAVAJOS (1983). Much of the change is traceable to the fact that it becomes necessary to produce commodities for trade for the goods purchased. For example, rather than killing enough game for the community larder, hunters need to produce a surplus to trade for market goods. The market and market-based agriculture permit greater population levels than would otherwise be sustainable in an ecosystem and this in turn can increase pressure on local wildlife populations both as a result of habitat destruction and from increased hunting pressures.

(3) Markets for wildlife/market hunting: As the Prescott–Allens note, the primary commercial harvest of wildlife involves fishing. One of the groups that was considered in crafting the regulations attacked in *Madison* were commercial salmon fishers. Why is there a market for commercially harvested wild salmon but not for commercially harvested wild venison or pheasant? The answer is to be found in an intense political battle that climaxed in the early years of the twentieth century.

Beginning in the mid-nineteenth century, writers such as Henry William Herbert (writing as Frank Forester[1]) began to extol the importance of sports hunting as a means for maintaining aristocratic vigor. Herbert's attempts to import an explicitly class-based approach to hunting—empha-sizing the highly stylized language and formal procedures for each type of hunt—did not fare well: the rhetoric of class was simply too unpalatable. Such issues could, however, be presented in the code of The Boone and Crockett Club and the ideal of the "fair chase." As one of the founders of Boone and Crockett subsequently wrote:

> In hunting the finding and killing of the game is after all but a part of the whole. The free, self-reliant, adventurous life, with its rugged and stalwart democracy; the wild surroundings, the grand beauty of the scenery, the chance to study the ways and habitats of the woodland creatures—all these unite to give the career of the wilderness hunter its peculiar charm. The chase is among the best of all national pastimes; it cultivates that vigorous manliness for the lack of which in a nation, as in an individual, the possession of no other qualities can possibly atone.

THEODORE ROOSEVELT, THE WILDERNESS HUNTER, 15 THE WORKS OF THEODORE ROOSEVELT vii (1906). The chase was important, in other words, because of the values that it instilled: it led its participants back to a simpler, more

---

1. *E.g.,* FIELD SPORTS IN THE UNITED   vols. (London: Richard Bentley, 1848).
STATES, AND THE BRITISH PROVINCES OF AMERICA, 2

honest and "natural" life—a hearkening back to the "wilderness" as the defining element of the American character. Coupled with these claims was a political program that sought to restrict access to wildlife to sportsmen. Sportsmen—in conjunction with conservationists—urged states to impose seasons and bag limits on taking wildlife, pass licensing laws, create fish and game commissions, and hire game wardens. By 1920, such limits were nearly universal. What does Roosevelt's paean to hunting suggest about the ban on hunting over bait at issue in *Hyter*?

(4) The psychological contributions of wildlife (pt. 1): Determining the economic value of the psychological uses of wildlife also presents problems. For example, one significant psychological contribution is recreation. Recreation centered on wildlife can be either consumptive—hunting or fishing—or nonconsumptive—birdwatching, for example. In 1996, some 39.7 million hunters and fishers spent $71.9 billion; 69.2 million wildlife-watchers spent a total of $29.2 billion. The primary expenditures by both groups were for equipment and trips (food, lodging, and transportation). *See* United States Department of the Interior & United States Department of Commerce, 1996 National Survey of Fishing, Hunting, and Wildlife-Associated Recreation (1998).

Although economic values can be assigned to the recreational use of wildlife, the values are at best inaccurate proxies because the values that people ascribe to their activities are only partially captured by their expenditures on equipment and trips; participants often view their activities in non-utilitarian terms. For example, Ted Kerasote offers such an explanation: "In my freezer there's the meat of an elk, the being whom I consider the distillate of this country [southeast of Grand Teton National Park]. As I defrost one of his steaks this February morning, the thermometer reading minus twenty-two degrees, a crystalline stratigraphy appears throughout his meat. It's as fine and lovely as the ice flowers on the kitchen windows. When thawed he smells faintly of what he ate last summer: grass and sedge, wildflowers, stream water. He smells of this place, which, when I eat him, becomes an inholding within me. I guess to another I must smell of him, and this place as well. We have joined and it's the hunting that creates the conjunction." Ted Kerasote, Bloodties: Nature, Culture, and the Hunt xv (1993).

b. Animal Welfare/Animal Rights

State v. Cleve

Supreme Court of New Mexico.
980 P.2d 23 (1999).

■ Serna, J.:—Defendant Charles Cleve appeals the Court of Appeals' affirmance of his two convictions of cruelty to animals. A jury found Cleve guilty of two counts of unlawful hunting and two counts of cruelty to animals based on his killing of two deer. Cleve contends that his actions, while within the scope of the prohibition against unlawful hunting, are not contemplated by the prohibition against cruelty to animals. We hold that New Mexico's statute proscribing cruelty to animals applies only to domesticated animals and wild animals previously reduced to captivity.... We therefore reverse Cleve's cruelty-to-animals convictions.

I.   Facts

Cleve owns a one-hundred acre ranch near Elk, New Mexico. At one time, Cleve maintained a herd of approximately three hundred cows on the land. Beginning in the early 1970's, however, Cleve began having difficulty with as many as one hundred deer coming onto his land and destroying his crops and pastures. As a result, Cleve needed to purchase more feed and was forced to reduce the number of cows in his herd.

Around 1977, Cleve began requesting assistance from the New Mexico Department of Game and Fish (Department) in alleviating his deer problems. Over the course of approximately twenty years, the Department, through numerous means, attempted to reduce the number of deer on Cleve's property. The Department eventually leased Cleve's property for two years and used it as a wildlife viewing area. In 1994, the Department, although recognizing the persistence of the deer problem, terminated its lease and, the following year, notified Cleve that it had exhausted its efforts to alleviate his situation.

Three months after receiving the letter from the Department, faced with a continued presence of deer on his land and apparently no further outside assistance, Cleve decided to kill some of the deer. On several occasions, Cleve shot at the deer on his property. Witnesses reported that Cleve shot in the direction of a fishing camp, as well as a highway, and that several bullets had gone into the camp area. Cleve shot at least thirteen deer, five in the abdomen, and snared two others. In one of the snares, a fawn was caught by the neck and died of strangulation, probably within about five minutes of being caught. In the other snare, a spike buck was caught by its antlers and died of either stress-related fatigue, starvation, or dehydration.

The State charged Cleve with three counts of negligent use of a deadly weapon, *see* NMSA 1978, § 30–7–4 (1993), seven counts of cruelty to animals, *see* NMSA 1978, § 30–18–1 (1963), and fifteen counts of unlawful hunting, *see* NMSA 1978, § 17–2–7(A) (1979).... The jury found Cleve guilty of two counts of unlawful hunting, two counts of cruelty to animals, and one count of negligent use of a deadly weapon. The two snared deer formed the basis for the convictions of unlawful hunting and the convictions of cruelty to animals.

Cleve appealed his conviction of two counts of cruelty to animals to the Court of Appeals. Cleve argued that game and fish statutes and regulations preempt application of Section 30–18–1 to game animals. In addition, Cleve contended that Section 30–18–1 is limited to cruelty committed against domesticated animals. The Court of Appeals rejected both of Cleve's arguments and affirmed his convictions. *State v. Cleve*, 949 P.2d 672 (N.M.App. 1997)....

III.   Interpretation of Section 30–18–1

Section 30–18–1 provides:

Cruelty to animals consists of:

    A. torturing, tormenting, depriving of necessary sustenance, cruelly beating, mutilating, cruelly killing or overdriving any animal;

    B. unnecessarily failing to provide any animal with proper food or drink; or

    C. cruelly driving or working any animal when such animal is unfit for labor.

The Court of Appeals concluded that the phrase "any animal" plainly means all animals, including game animals. *See Cleve*, [ ]. The Court of Appeals relied on the lack of definition for "animal" in Section 30–18–1, unlike the cruelty statutes of some other states, [ ], and the lack of alternative protection for many animals if they were excluded from Section 30–18–1. [ ] Additionally, the Court of Appeals reviewed other criminal statutes relating to animals containing specific references to domesticated animals and concluded that the lack of specificity in Section 30–18–1 was a deliberate choice of the Legislature. [ ] We disagree with the Court of Appeals' construction of Section 30–18–1.

In *State v. Buford*, 331 P.2d 1110 (1958), this Court reviewed a statute nearly identical to Section 30–18–1 in defining cruelty to animals. *See id.* at 1110 (quoting in substantial part 1887 NM Laws, ch. 1, § 1 (repealed 1963)). The prosecution in *Buford* charged the defendant with cruelty to animals in relation to a cockfighting incident. [ ] In determining whether New Mexico's cruelty-to-animals statute prohibited cockfighting, we discussed the cruelty-to-animals statutes of a number of other states. [ ] In addition, we reviewed England's Cruelty to Animals Act, which also prohibited the overdriving, abusing, or torturing of any animal and which defined any animal as meaning horses, dogs, cats, and other domestic animals. [ ] We assumed in *Buford* that gamecocks fell within the phrase "any animal" in New Mexico's cruelty-to-animals statute. [ ] In addition, we acknowledged that the terms torture and torment "would seem to embrace fighting cocks equipped with artificial spurs or gaffs capable of cutting deep wounds and sharp gashes in the cocks." [ ] However, we "look[ed] at the statute as a whole," and we noted that "[t]he language of the statute * * * seems to apply only to brute creatures and work animals and the history shows that it was passed in relation to other laws governing livestock." [ ] As a result, because, unlike most states, no New Mexico statute specifically prohibited cockfighting, we applied the rule of lenity and determined that "the type of cruelty to animal statute we are construing was not passed with the intention of prohibiting such sports as cockfighting." [ ]

The Court of Appeals concluded that our discussion of the cruelty-to-animals statute applying only to brute creatures and work animals constituted dicta. We disagree. . . .

In any event, we are persuaded that *Buford* accurately captures the history and scope of cruelty to animals statutes in New Mexico, including the present version contained in Section 30–18–1. First, although under the plain language rule the phrase "any animal" would seem to imply a broad meaning, the language of the statute as a whole negates such an implication. Section 30–18–1 contains three subsections. Section 30–18–1(B) and

Section 30–18–1(C) prohibit behavior that could only apply to domesticated animals or wild animals previously reduced to captivity: unnecessarily failing to provide proper food or drink and cruelly working an animal that is unfit for labor. Despite such a necessarily limited scope, both of these subsections include the phrase "any animal." Clearly, the Legislature did not intend to create a duty on the part of the public to provide sustenance to wild animals. Similarly, while Section 30–18–1(A) prohibits some conduct that could apply to both domesticated and wild animals, such as torturing, tormenting, cruelly beating, mutilating, or cruelly killing any animal, it also proscribes conduct, such as depriving of necessary sustenance and overdriving, that necessarily excludes wild animals. We do not believe the Legislature intended a different meaning for the phrase "any animal" between different subsections of the same statute and within a single subsection. To the contrary, we believe the Legislature intended that the phrase "any animal" denote domesticated animals and wild animals in captivity throughout Section 30–18–1. In fact, the statute at issue in *Buford,* which did not contain discrete subsections like Section 30–18–1, provided:

> If any person torture, torment, deprive of necessary sustenance, cruelly beat, mutilate, cruelly kill or overdrive *any animal,* or unnecessarily fail to provide *the same* with proper food or drink, or cruelly drive or work *the same* when unfit for labor, he shall be punished by a fine....

1887 NM Laws, ch. 1, § 1 (emphasis added). We believe the use of "the same" to describe "any animal," like the repeated use of "any animal" in Section 30–18–1, supports a conclusion that the Legislature intended the same meaning for the phrase throughout the statute. As with Section 30–18–1(B)-(C), it is clear that the Legislature did not intend the latter prohibitions in the prior statute to apply to wild animals. Therefore, from the contextual language of Section 30–18–1, we conclude that the Legislature intended the phrase "any animal" to mean domesticated animals and wild animals previously reduced to captivity.

. . .

... We disagree with the Court of Appeals' assessment that such an intent would be absurd or unjust. While many may regard it presently desirable for New Mexico to protect all animals, including wild animals, from human cruelty, "[a] statute is to be interpreted as the Legislature understood it at the time it was passed." *Pan Am. Petroleum Corp. v. El Paso Natural Gas Co.,* 477 P.2d 827, 830 (N.M.1970). Our role in statutory interpretation is not to sculpt the most just law possible out of the words used by the Legislature or to attribute the meaning to a statute that contemporary ideals would deem preferable. *Cf. Salazar v. St. Vincent Hospital,* 619 P.2d 826, 829 (N.M.Ct.App.1980) ("To construe legislation on the basis of contemporary meanings of words used by the enacting legislature would make a mockery of legislative intent * * *"). Our role is to determine the intent of the Legislature. It has not been uncommon, both at the time the Legislature enacted Section 30–18–1 and at present, for state legislatures to limit cruelty to animals statutes to domesticated animals and wild animals in captivity. *See, e.g.,* Iowa Code § 717B.1(1)(b) (1995) (excluding from the crimes of animal abuse and neglect, among other things, "[a]ny game, fur-bearing animal, fish, reptile, or amphibian" unless owned, confined, or controlled by a person); N.H.Rev.Stat. Ann. § 644:8 (1996 & Supp. 1998) (proscribing cruelty to "any animal" and defining "animal" to mean "a domestic animal, a household pet or a wild animal in captivity"); Okla. Stat. tit. 21, § 1685 (Supp. 1999) (proscribing cruelty to "any animal in subjugation or captivity, whether wild or tame, and whether belonging to [the accused] or to another"); Tex. Penal Code Ann. § 42.09(c)(1) (West Supp. 1999) (defining "animal" in a cruelty to animals statute as "a domesticated living creature and wild living creature previously captured"). A policy decision of this nature should not be second-guessed by the judiciary.... Thus, we conclude that wild game animals, including the deer snared by Cleve in this case, are not covered by Section 30–18–1.

IV. New Mexico's Game and Fish Laws

Even if we had concluded that wild animals are protected by Section 30–18–1, we believe there are additional indications that the Legislature did not intend that Cleve's conduct in this case fall within the meaning of cruelty to animals in Section 30–18–1.... We agree with Cleve that the overall statutory scheme governing hunting and fishing demonstrates a legislative intent to preempt the application of Section 30–18–1 to game and fish with respect to conduct contemplated by game and fish laws....

Cleve contends that the unlawful hunting statute, Section 17–2–7, is a special law that conflicts with the general prohibition against cruelty to animals in Section 30–18–1. In discussing this argument, the Court of Appeals concluded that Section 17–2–7 and Section 30–18–1 serve different purposes, are both necessary to fully protect game animals, and, therefore, do not conflict with one another. *Cleve,* [ ]....

As the Court of Appeals noted, if Section 30–18–1 were to protect wild animals, it would be possible to violate each statute, cruelty to animals and unlawful hunting, independently, without violating the other. *Cleve,* [ ]. For example, many hunters could be convicted of unlawful hunting for killing game without a license, or out of season, and yet fail to satisfy the elements of cruelty to animals. Thus, even if Section 30–18–1 had protected wild animals, the violation of one of these statutes would not commonly result in violation of the other. Further, in assessing "the particular evil sought to be addressed by each offense," and bearing in mind that the description of "social evils can be elusive and subject to diverse interpretation," [ ], we agree with the Court of Appeals that these statutes serve different purposes. [ ] As we have already stated, the cruelty to animals statute serves to define the outer boundaries of acceptable human conduct toward animals. By contrast, the unlawful hunting statute serves to enforce the authority of the Commission in defining the manner and conditions of lawful hunting and fishing in New Mexico and to ensure that hunting and fishing in New Mexico is carried out in a manner consistent with the public policy articulated in NMSA 1978, § 17–1–1 (1931).... Taking into account such statutory factors as language, history, and purpose, we conclude that the Legislature intended to create separately punishable offenses by enacting Section 17–2–7 and Section 30–18–1....

Notwithstanding a lack of conflict between the statutory prohibition against unlawful hunting, by itself, and Section 30–18–1, Cleve also asserts that the overall statutory scheme governing hunting and fishing demonstrates a legislative intent to preempt the application of Section 30–18–1 to game and fish with respect to conduct contemplated by game and fish laws. We agree.... Although the limited proscription against unlawful hunting, standing alone, does not conflict with Section 30–18–1, we conclude that New Mexico's other laws specifically governing hunting and fishing irreconcilably conflict with Section 30–18–1 and that behavior contemplated by the Legislature's authorization of hunting and fishing is excepted from the general proscription against cruelty to animals.

The Legislature has established in New Mexico a system under which game and fish may be "use[d] and develop[ed] for public recreation and food supply." Section 17–1–1. In order to implement this system, the Legislature created the Commission, NMSA 1978, § 17–1–2 (1991), and delegated to it, among other things, the power to "authorize or prohibit the killing or taking of any game animals, game birds or game fish of any kind or sex" and the power to regulate "the manner, methods and devices which may be used in hunting, taking or killing game animals, game birds and game fish," NMSA 1978, § 17–2–1 (1983). The Commission's regulations include provisions governing the hunting of deer, as well as provisions establishing the proper use of traps and snares.

Cleve's cruelty to animals convictions are based on the snaring of two deer. In placing his snares, it is clear that Cleve was engaged in the activity of hunting the deer on his land and that his manner of hunting, trapping by snare, is within the range of hunting activity contemplated by the game and fish statutes. We believe that Cleve's conviction of cruelty to animals for snaring game animals exemplifies the conflict between Section 30–18–1 and the Legislature's provisions governing hunting and fishing in New Mexico. Although the Commission's regulations do not authorize the capturing of deer by snare, see Legal Sporting Arms and Ammunition, Department of Game and Fish, 19 NMAC 31.1.16.4 (April 1, 1995), the Commission has promulgated regulations authorizing the snaring and trapping of furbearing game animals within certain parameters, see Manner and Method of Taking Furbearers, Department of Game and Fish, 19 NMAC 32.1.10 (April 1, 1995). The language of Section 17–2–1 clearly delegates to the Commission the power to determine whether the snaring of particular game animals is consistent with the statutory purposes articulated in Section 17–1–1. It appears from the evidence introduced in the trial court that the manner of death for the two snared deer, strangulation and either starvation, dehydration, or fatigue, is not atypical for a snared game animal. Thus, under the Court of Appeals' interpretation of Section 30–18–1, the lawful snaring of furbearing animals would appear to be equally subject to prosecution for cruelty to animals. Further, a Department official, Assistant Chief of Operations Pat Barncastle, testified that, when the Department traps antelope and deer for purposes such as relocation, it is not uncommon for them to die of stress-related fatigue. This activity would also appear to violate the cruelty to animals statute under the Court of Appeals' construction. Additionally, the State charged Cleve with cruelty to animals for shooting several deer in the abdomen, even though Officer

Barncastle testified that approximately twenty-five to thirty-five percent of deer lawfully taken pursuant to Commission regulations are also shot in the abdomen. Thus, according to the State's interpretation of Section 30–18–1, the lawful hunting of deer would appear to subject a hunter to potential prosecution for cruelty to animals. We believe that these applications of Section 30–18–1 would conflict with the Legislature's authorization of hunting and fishing in New Mexico and would frustrate the Legislature's delegation of power to the Commission to determine the manner in which hunting is to be conducted.

Although Cleve's conduct violated Commission regulations, thereby constituting unlawful hunting, it was not beyond the scope of activity that the Legislature has chosen to place within the regulatory power of the Commission. In fact, the Legislature has recently addressed the specific problems arising in this case, providing that landowners may, in accordance with Commission regulations, take a game animal on private land if the animal "presents an immediate threat to human life or an immediate threat of damage to property, including crops." NMSA 1978, § 17–2–7.2 (1997). Thus, we determine that the Legislature's endorsement of hunting and fishing activity and its delegation of power to the Commission to determine the manner of hunting substantially and irreconcilably conflicts with the cruelty-to-animals statute. Therefore, we conclude that, even if the Legislature had intended to protect wild animals in Section 30–8–1, the Legislature, having dealt with the subject of the hunting of game animals more particularly in the game and fish laws, intended to create an exception from the cruelty-to-animals statute for hunting and fishing activity contemplated by game and fish laws.

[W]e believe the comprehensive nature of the game and fish laws with respect to hunting activity demonstrates a legislative intent to preempt application of Section 30–18–1 to the hunting of game animals. Because Cleve was engaged in the hunting of game animals, specifically deer, and because his manner of hunting was within the range of activity contemplated by game and fish statutes and regulations, we apply the general/specific statute rule and conclude that Section 30–18–1 is inapplicable to the facts of this case.

. . .

IT IS SO ORDERED.

■ Minzner, C.J., Baca and Franchini, JJ., concur.

NOTES

(1) *Cleve* is yet another case about the meaning of a statute, this time a criminal statute enforced by state prosecutors. When construing criminal statutes, courts generally construe them narrowly, resolving ambiguities about their scope in favor of defendants, so that citizens are not surprised by expansive, unexpected applications. The narrow-construction rule, however, is often ignored when the criminal provision is part of a regulatory statute that is chiefly civil in its operation. In resolving the statute's ambiguity, the court employed an interpretive approach different from the tools used in the previous cases: it considered how the particular criminal provision at issue (cruelty to animals) fit with other state laws applicable to the same activity.

(2) Is it possible that the court's interpretation of this statute was swayed by its sympathy for the landowner defendant, who had apparently tried in good faith for years to deal with the deer problem without resorting to killing? What if the defendant had not been a landowner, and was motivated not by defense-of-property concerns but by more plainly malicious ones? Might the court have been swayed by the novelty of the state's attempt to apply the statute in a setting where it had not been applied in the past, thus raising questions about notice to citizens? Note also that Mr. Cleve did not escape punishment; he avoided conviction on the cruelty charges, but did not escape (and apparently did not contest on appeal) conviction on the unlawful hunting charges.

(3) Should the court have felt any sympathy for Mr. Cleve? His land was apparently prime habitat. Why should the owner of such land have any claim to use such land free of wildlife? Why is not the presence of wildlife habitat a condition that limits the uses to which a landowner may put the land?

(4) After *Cleve,* what is the legal status in New Mexico of cockfighting of the type at issue in *State v. Burford* (1958)? Note that the court in *Cleve* relies upon the earlier *Burford* decision, which concluded that cockfighting was not banned by the "nearly identical" 1887 anti-cruelty statute then on the books; that statute, the court decided in *Burford,* applied only to "brute creatures and work animals." Yet, in *Cleve* the court interprets the nearly identical contemporary statute to protect all domesticated animals and captive wild animals. Why the much different interpretation? Might language in a nineteenth-century statute carry different meaning than the same language used in a late-twentieth-century statute?

(5) Following the decision in *Cleve,* the New Mexico legislature rewrote § 30–18–1:

> As used in this section, animal does not include insects or reptiles.

> A.   Cruelty to animals consists of a person:

>> (1) negligently mistreating, injuring, killing without lawful justification or tormenting an animal; or

>> (2) abandoning or failing to provide necessary sustenance to an animal under that person's custody or control.

> B.   As used in Subsection A of this section, "lawful justification" means:

>> (1) humanely destroying a sick or injured animal; or

>> (2) protecting a person or animal from death or injury due to an attack by another animal.

> C.   Whoever commits cruelty to animals is guilty of a misdemeanor. . . .

> D.   Extreme cruelty to animals consists of a person:

(1) intentionally or maliciously torturing, mutilating, injuring or poisoning an animal; or

(2) maliciously killing an animal.

E.   Whoever commits extreme cruelty to animals is guilty of a fourth degree felony....

. . .

H.   The provisions of this section do not apply to:

(1) fishing, hunting, falconry, taking and trapping, as provided in Chapter 17 NMSA 1978;

. . .

J.   The provisions of this section shall not be interpreted to prohibit cockfighting in New Mexico.

Does the new statute apply to free-ranging wildlife as well as to domesticated animals and captured wildlife? Would Cleve be liable for either cruelty or extreme cruelty to animals under the new statute? If Cleve were not liable because he was "hunting"—albeit illegally—is it possible to prosecute anyone killing a game animal? Killing any wild animal?

(6) Hunting and cruelty: Is hunting inherently incompatible with a cruelty prohibition? Note that the New Mexico statute prohibits "cruelly killing" but offers no additional definition of "cruelly." Is "cruelty" sufficient notice on what types of conduct are prohibited? For example, if a hunter wounds an animal, has he engaged in "cruelty"? If he fails to pursue the wounded animal? *See Boushehry v. State,* 648 N.E.2d 1174 (Ind.App.1995) (out-of-season hunter guilty of cruelty for slitting the throat of Canada goose that he had wounded but not for killing another goose with rifle shot); *see also* W.J. Brown, *Cruelty to Wild Animals,* 101 L.J. 425 (1951).

(7) Pigeon shoots: A pigeon shoot uses "pigeons that are trapped in cities are released from cages in a remote area to be shot as part of a contest. An entry fee is paid by the contestants, and prizes are won depending upon how many pigeons a contestant is able to kill. An admission charge is collected from those wishing to view the event." The California Attorney General concluded that pigeon shoots violate the state's animal cruelty statutes because "conducting a pigeon shoot subjects the pigeons to 'needless' suffering, it inflicts 'unnecessary' cruelty upon the birds, it 'abuses' the pigeons, and it takes place after the contest organizers have failed to provide the birds 'with proper food, drink, or shelter.' " The opinion is also careful to note that "nothing contained in this opinion may be said to interfere 'with any of the laws of this state known as the "game laws." ' " CAL. ATT'Y GEN. OP. No. 99–1107 (Mar. 31, 2000). Is the opinion's rationale limited to the special facts of the pigeon shoot—release of previously captured birds—or does the cruelty statute apply to nongame species? *See also Waters v. People,* 46 P. 112 (Colo.1896) (shooting live "doves" released from traps violated state animal cruelty statute).

(8) *State v. Lipsett:* Defendant, owner of Connecticut Pest Elimination Company and a licensed nuisance wildlife control operator, was cited for drowning two trapped raccoons allegedly in violation of Connecticut's statute prohibiting cruelty to animals. Although a nuisance wildlife control officer is encouraged to control nuisance species with nonlethal control practices, including relocation, the Commissioner of Environmental Protection had banned relocation of raccoons by control officers because of the continued threat of rabies. Once defendant trapped the raccoons, he was required to destroy them within 24 hours as a condition of his license. The regulations allowed defendant to shoot the raccoons, but he owned no guns, so he destroyed them by drowning them in the trap. The relevant statute provided: "Any person who overdrives, drives when overloaded, overworks, tortures, deprives of necessary sustenance, mutilates or cruelly beats or kills or unjustifiably injures any animal" was subject to prosecution; "animal" is elsewhere defined to include "all brute creatures and birds."

The Superior Court rejected defendant's argument that the statute was unconstitutionally vague. Relying upon a dictionary definition of "cruelty," the court concluded that the term sufficiently defined the requisite intent. Nonetheless, the court concluded that the state had failed to meet its burden that defendant's conduct was cruel:

> Taking all of the State's evidence as true, all that the State has established is that drowning is not euthanasia and that drowning nuisance wildlife is a practice many people find highly offensive. However, the State has failed to present sufficient evidence from which a jury could conclude defendant's actions were criminal.
>
> Although nuisance wildlife control operators are permitted to destroy nuisance wildlife by shooting, a recognized form of wildlife euthanasia, they are not specifically required by statute or regulation to practice euthanasia or "humane killing" of nuisance wildlife which must be destroyed. If the legislature had intended for nuisance wildlife control operators to use euthanasia or humane killing, it would have said so. [ ] If the Commissioner requires nuisance wildlife control officers to use humane killing when compelled to destroy wildlife, then the regulations, [ ], should be amended or clarified to specify that humane killing or recognized forms of euthanasia must be used. The present regulation which mentions only shooting cannot be read to be mandatory or exclusive, because that would prohibit other forms of animal euthanasia, an undesirable result.

State v. Lipsett, 1997 WL 187133 (Conn.Super.1997).

PERSPECTIVES

Gary L. Francione, Animal Rights and Animal Welfare

48 Rutgers L. Rev. 397, 397–99 (1996).

Over the past century or so, concern about animals' interests was limited to ensuring that they were treated "humanely" and that they were not subjected to "unnecessary" suffering. This position, which is known as the *animal welfare* view, assumes the legitimacy of treating animals instrumentally as means to human ends as long as certain "safeguards" are employed.

The late 1970s marked the emergence of the animal "rights" movement, which "retained the animal welfare tradition's concern for animals as sentient beings that should be protected from unnecessary cruelty," but added "a new language of 'rights' as the basis for demanding" the end of institutionalized animal exploitation. The need to develop a new vocabulary was clear not only in light of certain theoretical inconsistencies between the two positions, but also because the most ardent defenders of institutionalized animal exploitation themselves endorsed animal welfare. Almost *everyone*—including those who use animals in painful experiments or who slaughter them for food—accepts as an abstract proposition that animals ought to be treated "humanely" and not subject to "unnecessary" suffering.

As Bernard Rollin writes, rights are "moral notions that grow out of respect for the individual. They build protective fences around the individual. They establish areas where the individual is entitled to be protected against the state and the majority *even where a price is paid by the general welfare.*"[3] For example, if X's interest in free speech is protected by a right, that generally means that X's interest will be protected *even if* the general welfare would benefit from depriving X of that right simply because people strongly disagree with the content of X's speech.

The theory of animal rights maintains that at least some nonhumans possess rights that function in a manner substantially similar to human rights. Animal rights ensure that relevant animal interests are absolutely protected and may not be sacrificed even if it would benefit humans to do so, or if the animals whose interests are at stake are exploited "humanely" and without "unnecessary" suffering.

Animal rights theory rejects the regulation of animal exploitation and calls unambiguously and unequivocally for its abolition. Rights theory precludes the treatment of animals exclusively as means to human ends, or as the *property* of people. Because animals, like humans, possess certain inherent value, that value must be respected regardless of the consequences to humans of ignoring it in favor of treating animals as instruments. The rights theorist rejects the use of animals in experiments, or for human consumption, because such use violates fundamental obligations of *justice* that humans owe to nonhumans, and not simply because these activities cause animals to suffer.

Citizens to End Animal Suffering & Exploitation, Inc. v. The New England Aquarium

United States District Court, District of Massachusetts.
836 F.Supp. 45 (1993).

■ Wolf, D.J.:—This case is brought by Kama, a dolphin, Citizens to End Animal Suffering and Exploitation ("CEASE"), the Animal Legal Defense

---

3. Bernard E. Rollin, *The Legal and Moral Bases of Animal Rights, in* Ethics and Animals 106, 106 (Harlan B. Miller & William H. Williams, eds., 1983).

Fund, Inc. ("ALDF"), and the Progressive Animal Welfare Society, Inc. ("PAWS"), to protest the transfer of Kama from the New England Aquarium to the Department of the Navy. The parties have named as defendants the New England Aquarium ("the Aquarium"), the Department of the Navy ("the Navy"), the Department of Commerce and two of its subagencies, the National Oceanic and Atmospheric Administration and the National Marine Fisheries Service (collectively referred to as "Commerce").

Defendants have moved to dismiss and for summary judgment on several grounds. They contest the standing of the plaintiffs, the propriety of naming the Aquarium and the Navy as defendants, and the substantive merits of plaintiffs' case.... For the reasons described below, summary judgment should be granted in favor of defendants because plaintiffs lack standing....

I. FACTS

. . .

Kama was born in captivity at Sea World in San Diego in 1981. Kama was transferred to the Aquarium in 1986 for breeding purposes and/or for public display. [ ] Kama, however, did not fit into the social climate at the Aquarium. [ ] As a result, he was not regularly on public display, nor featured in the Aquarium dolphin shows. [ ]

In 1987, the Aquarium wrote to Commerce requesting authorization to transfer Kama and another dolphin to the Naval Oceans Systems Center. [ ] The Navy also wrote to Commerce, requesting authority to purchase and transport the two dolphins, noting, "These two dolphins will be housed in floating bay pens as specified in Marine Mammal Permit Number #195. [ ] Commerce authorized both requests, and sent the Navy a Letter of Agreement (#AN108), to be signed by the Navy, which set forth the obligations of the Navy to ensure the safety and well-being of the dolphins. [ ]

In late 1987, Kama was transferred from the Aquarium to the Navy pursuant to this Letter of Agreement. [ ] Kama is now located in Hawaii, where he is being studied for his sonar capabilities. [ ] The Navy has invested over $700,000 and over 3,500 man hours training Kama. [ ] The Navy contends that Kama is able to associate with wild dolphins on a daily basis, and could swim away if he so desired. [ ]

. . .

III. DISCUSSION

[T]his court's ruling is limited to the issue of plaintiffs' standing. To survive a motion for summary judgment on standing, "[plaintiffs] need show only a 'genuine issue' of material fact as to standing." *Lujan v. Defenders of Wildlife [Lujan v. DOW]*, 504 U.S. 555 (1992) (Blackmun, J., dissenting) (citing F.R. Civ. P. 56(c)). "A 'genuine issue' exists so long as 'the evidence is such that a reasonable jury could return a verdict for the nonmoving party.'" *Id.* [ ] On a motion for summary judgment, the court must view the undisputed facts in the light most favorable to the nonmoving party. [ ]

Defendants assert in their motions to dismiss and/or for summary judgment that plaintiffs lack standing to maintain this suit. The standing requirement is rooted in the constitutional command in Art. III, § 2, that the federal courts' jurisdiction is limited to "Cases" and "Controversies." The standing doctrine serves to preserve the separation of powers, to prevent a flood of lawsuits, to improve judicial decision-making by focussing on actual controversies, and to ensure that "people cannot be intermeddlers trying to protect others who do not want the protection sought." *See E. Chemerinsky, Federal Jurisdiction* § 2.3.1 (1989 ed.). The issue of standing in this case must be addressed on two bases: the standing of Kama, the dolphin, and the standing of the organizational plaintiffs.

A. *Kama Lacks Standing*

There is little case law addressing whether an animal who has allegedly been injured has standing to bring a suit. Plaintiffs assert that Kama has standing, relying on *Palila v. Hawaii Department of Land & Natural Resources*, 852 F.2d 1106, 1107 (9th Cir.1988). In *Palila*, the court stated in its introduction:

> As an endangered species under the Endangered Species Act, * * * the bird (*Loxioides bailleui*), a member of the Hawaiian honey-creeper family, also has legal status and wings its way into federal court as a plaintiff in its own right * * * represented by attorneys for the Sierra Club, the Audubon Society, and other environmental parties.

Id. However, in *Palila*, the defendants did not challenge the propriety of having an animal as a named plaintiff. Similarly, animal species have remained named plaintiffs in other cases in which the defendants did not contest the issue. *See Mt. Graham Red Squirrel v. Yeutter*, 930 F.2d 703 (9th Cir.1991); *Northern Spotted Owl v. Lujan*, 758 F. Supp. 621 (W.D.Wash.1991); *Northern Spotted Owl v. Hodel*, 716 F.Supp. 479 (W.D.Wash.1988).

However, in the only reported case in which the naming of an animal as a party was challenged, the court found that the animal did not have standing to bring suit. In *Hawaiian Crow ('Alala) v. Lujan*, 906 F. Supp. 549 (D.Hawai'i 1991), the court ruled that the 'Alala, an endangered species of birds, did not have standing to maintain a suit challenging the implementation of a program under the Endangered Species Act ("ESA"). The court, while recognizing the authority cited above, denied the 'Alala standing on the bases that: (1) the ESA provided for citizen suits brought by "persons;" (2) the other named parties—various Audubon Societies— could obtain the relief sought; and (3) F.R. Civ. P. 17(c) which provides for suits on behalf of infants or incompetent persons does not apply to animals. *Id.* at 4–6.

The same considerations apply in this case. The MMPA does not authorize suits brought by animals. Rather, the MMPA provides for judicial review of the grant or denial of permits for permit applicants or "any party opposed to such permit" pursuant to 5 U.S.C. § 701 *et seq. See* 16 U.S.C. § 1374(d)(6). Section 702 of Title 5 provides that, "A *person* suffering legal wrong because of agency action, or adversely affected or aggrieved by agency action within the meaning of a relevant statute, is entitled to judicial review thereof." 5 U.S.C. § 702 (emphasis added). Thus, as with regard to the ESA in *'Alala*, the MMPA expressly authorizes suits brought by persons, not animals. This court will not impute to Congress or the President the intention to provide standing to a marine mammal without a clear statement in the statute. If Congress and the President intended to take the extraordinary step of authorizing animals as well as people and legal entities to sue, they could, and should, have said so plainly. Furthermore, as in *'Alala*, citizen groups, if they satisfy the standing requirements, could seek to obtain the relief the amended complaint requests for Kama.

This conclusion is reinforced by consideration of F.R. Civ. P. 17(b), which falls within the section of the Rules entitled "Parties," and discusses the "capacity of an individual ... to sue or be sued." It provides that such capacity "shall be determined by the law of the individual's domicile." While this provision generally addresses the capacity of corporations, partnerships, and other business entities to litigate, there is no indication that it does not apply to other non-human entities or forms of life. While neither Massachusetts nor Hawaii law addresses the precise question of animal standing, cases in each state indicate that animals are treated as the property of their owners, rather than entities with their own legal rights. *See e.g., Massachusetts Society for Prevention of Cruelty to Animals v. Commissioner of Public Health,* 158 N.E.2d 487 (Mass.1959); *State of Hawaii v. Pokini,* 367 P.2d 499 (Haw.1961).

Accordingly, the MMPA and the operation of F.R. Civ. P. 17(b) indicate that Kama the dolphin lacks standing to maintain this action as a matter of law. Defendants have moved, therefore, for the removal of Kama's name from the caption of this case. This motion must be allowed.

B.   Standing of the Organizational Plaintiffs

[The plaintiff organizations asserted standing as representatives for their individual members. They alleged *inter alia* that their members "suffered injury to their aesthetic, conservational, or recreational interests because they can no longer observe Kama at the Aquarium."]

Plaintiffs allege that as a result of Kama's transfer, they have suffered harm by having been deprived of the opportunity to observe and study Kama. In *Lujan v. DOW,* the Court stated:

> Of course, the desire to use or observe an animal species, even for purely aesthetic purposes, is undeniably a cognizable interest for the purpose of standing.* * * But the "injury in fact" requires more than an injury to a cognizable interest. It requires that the party seeking review be himself among the injured. To survive * * * summary judgment * * *, respondents had to submit affidavits or other evidence showing, through specific facts, * * * that one or more of respondents' members would thereby be "directly" affected apart from their " 'special interest' in th[e] subject."

504 U.S. at 562–63 (quoting *Sierra Club v. Morton,* 405 U.S. 727, 734–35 (1972)). In *Lujan v. DOW,* the respondents had sued the Secretary of the Interior for violating the ESA by revising a regulation that required agency review of the environmental consequences of any federal agency action. The

revised regulation required review only of actions taken in the United States or on the High Seas. Members of the organization, Defenders of Wildlife, submitted affidavits which stated that they had visited specific foreign countries to observe wildlife, and noted that specific federal agency actions in those countries would have the effect of destroying the natural habitats of the wildlife. [ ]

The Court held that these allegations of harm were insufficient to create standing. The Court specifically noted that the allegations of unspecified, future visits failed to establish that imminent harm would occur. The Court stated:

> Such "some day" intentions—without any description of concrete plans, or indeed even any specification of when the some day will be—do not support a finding of the "actual or imminent" injury that our cases require.

[ ]

In the present case, plaintiffs also fail to allege actual or imminent harm. . . .

[T]he affiants have not alleged the particular relationship with Kama necessary to cause them to be harmed by his absence even if they plan to return to the Aquarium. In *Lujan v. DOW,* the Court stated that:

> It is clear that the person who observes or works with a particular animal threatened by a federal decision is facing perceptible harm, since the very subject of his interest will no longer exist. It is even plausible—though it goes to the outermost limit of plausibility—to think that a person who observes or works with animals of a particular species in the very area of the world where that species is threatened by a federal decision is facing such harm, since some animals that might have been the subject of his interest will no longer exist.

[ ] The affiants in this case do not, and evidently cannot, state that they ever observed Kama in particular, as opposed to dolphins in general, at the Aquarium.

Plaintiffs seek discovery on whether Kama was ever on public display or included in any dolphin shows at the Aquarium. The Aquarium asserts that Kama was not regularly on display, nor included in any dolphin shows. The fact that neither affiant knows if she actually observed Kama belies any possible assertion that either of them had established a relationship with Kama such that, as a result of his transfer, "the very subject of [the member's] interest will no longer exist." The affiants only allege that they observed *dolphins* during the time that Kama was at the Aquarium. [ ] After Kama's departure, dolphins were still available for observation. [ ] Furthermore, the fact that plaintiffs were, by their own admission, unaware of Kama's transfer until 1990, three years after the transfer took place, indicates that none of plaintiffs' members noted or were harmed by Kama's absence. Rather, the affiants observed dolphins at the Aquarium, and were able to continue to do so after Kama's transfer. As they do not know if they ever observed Kama, did not notice his absence for three years, and because he was not regularly on display, it is unlikely that they ever observed him. In these circumstances, it is evident that the discovery plaintiffs seek would not be helpful. There is simply insufficient evidence for a reasonable factfinder to conclude that they are or will be harmed by Kama's transfer.

. . .

As the Supreme Court has recently reemphasized, in our constitutional democracy courts are empowered to adjudicate only true "Cases" and "Controversies." *Lujan v. DOW*, 504 U.S. at 560. The standing requirements relate directly to this constitutional limitation on the power of the courts.

In this case, viewing the facts in the light most favorable to the plaintiffs, a reasonable factfinder could not find that plaintiffs have suffered, or will suffer, the type harm required to establish standing. In the absence of adequate evidence that any plaintiff has been harmed by Commerce's actions, this court may not address the legality of those actions, for there is no true "Case" or "Controversy."

NOTES

(1) The legal issue in the excerpt is whether Kama and the various animal rights organizations have "standing" to sue. Standing is one of a group of doctrines that have been developed in the federal courts to determine whether a claim is justiciable. It focuses on the plaintiff and the interest that the plaintiff seeks to have redressed. The usual justification for the injury requirement is that unless the plaintiff is a person who will be affected by the court's judgment she cannot be relied upon to present a serious and thorough argument on the issues. *E.g.*, Louis L. Jaffe, *The Citizen as Litigant in Public Actions: The Non–Hofeldian or Ideological Plaintiff*, 116 U. PA. L. REV. 1033, 1037–38 (1968). The difficulty, as Professor Jaffe pointed out, is that an ideological plaintiff is likely to be extremely motivated. Is there any reason to believe that CEASE, ALDF, and PAWS will be less serious or thorough than someone who has suffered a slight economic loss?

The doctrine developed from the common-law idea that a violation of some right was a necessary element of judicial action: thus the emphasis on invasion of a legally protected interest in the various common-law subject areas. Tort actions, for example, are predicated upon the invasion of some legally protected interest—most commonly the interest in being free from physical harm. The central problem raised by the intersection of the justiciability doctrines and the rise of administrative agencies is the difficulty of adapting doctrines intended to govern traditional common-law litigation between private individuals to a public law scheme where the litigants are more likely to represent the interests of groups of individuals: to what extent should a labor union or a trade group be allowed to represent its members? In such contexts, notions of "injury" and "right"—the traditional touchstones of justiciability in a common-law system—take on different connotations and raise problems such as those examined in Kama's case.

Stated from a slightly different perspective, standing is a determination of what interests count. To say that an individual has standing is to say that the interest asserted by that individual is sufficiently important that it is to be accorded protection and, contrariwise, to say that an individual lacks standing is to say that her interest is unworthy of legal protection. Standing thus is a barometer of what interests are deemed worthy of protection.

Why does Kama lack standing? Why doesn't Kama have an "interest" that is sufficient to warrant protection? Does the court's statutory argument exhaust the possibilities?

Why do the organization's members lack standing? Is there any set of allegations that would confer standing on the members? If the members had established an individual relationship with Kama, would they have had standing?

(2) *Kama's case* **(take 2):** Steven Wise, plaintiff's attorney in *Citizens to End Animal Suffering & Exploitation,* offers the following analysis of the court's decision:

> A similar problem [to that of slaves suing for their freedom] is faced when a suit is filed by a nonhuman animal. For example, a suit was filed in 1991 in the name of Kama, a dolphin, that alleged that Kama's transfer to the Navy had been accomplished without benefit of the permits required by the federal Marine Mammal Protection Act. The judge was eventually required to discuss Kama's power-right, or capacity, to sue. Federal Rule of Civil Procedure 17(b) provides that the capacity of any individual to sue or be sued is to be determined "by the individual's domicile." Was Kama an "individual?" He was. "[T]here is no indication that [Rule 17[b]] does not apply to other non-human entities or forms of life." Did Kama have a "domicile"? He did. According to the judge, it was either in Hawaii or Massachusetts. But did Kama have the power-right, or capacity, to sue? No, as neither state permitted dolphins to sue.

Steven M. Wise, *Hardly a Revolution—The Eligibility of Nonhuman Animals for Dignity–Rights in a Liberal Democracy,* 22 VT. L. REV. 793, 821 (1998).

(3) "Theft" vs. "liberation": Are animals *feræ naturæ* property when in the possession of a human or are they like slaves before the Civil War?

Defendant began working at the University of Hawaii marine laboratory as an undergraduate research assistant in January, 1975. During the nearly two years he worked at the lab, Le Vasseur repaired and cleaned the tanks holding two Atlantic Bottlenose dolphins (Kea and Puka); he also fed the dolphins and swam with them. On May 29, 1977, Le Vasseur and four or five other people removed the dolphins from their tanks and transported them by van some fifty miles to Yokohama Bay, on the northwest side of the island of Oahu. The dolphins were taken from the van and released into the ocean. Appellant testified that his intention was to give the dolphins freedom of choice as to whether or not they returned to captivity. Le Vasseur was indicted for theft in the first degree; following a jury trial by jury, he was convicted and sentenced to five years probation with the special condition that he serve six months in jail. He appealed. The Hawai'ian Court of Appeals rejected his argument:

[Le Vasseur] asserted this [choice-of-evils] defense based on the contention that dolphins were included within the meaning of "another" in HRS § 703–302.... Under this theory, appellant contended that he chose the lesser of two possible harms when he released the dolphins. Simply put, he contended that he chose to commit the lesser harm of theft in the first degree in order to avoid greater harm ... to the dolphins.... The trial court's ruling that the choice of evils defense was not available to the appellant is a central issue in this appeal.

In the State of Hawaii, the choice of evils defense is defined by statute as follows:

§ 703–302. *Choice of evils*

(1) Conduct which the actor believes to be necessary to avoid an imminent harm or evil to himself or to another is justifiable provided that:

(a) The harm or evil sought to be avoided by such conduct is greater than that sought to be prevented by the law defining the offense charged; and

(b) Neither the Code nor other law defining the offense provides exceptions or defenses dealing with the specific situation involved; and

(c) A legislative purpose to exclude the justification claimed does not otherwise plainly appear.

(2) When the actor was reckless or negligent in bringing about the situation requiring a choice of harms or evils or in appraising the necessity for his conduct, the justification afforded by this section is unavailable in a prosecution for any offense for which recklessness or negligence, as the case may be suffices to establish culpability.

Appellant contends that because the dolphins were included in a "specific situation" for which "neither the Code nor the law defining the offense [of theft] provides exceptions or defenses," they should be considered within the term "another." This argument must fail because, as the trial court noted, the legislature has provided a specific definition of "another" that does not include dolphins. *HRS* § 701–118(8) defines "another" as "any other person and includes, where relevant, the United States, this State and any of its political subdivisions, and any other state and any of its political subdivisions." Person is defined as a natural person and when relevant a corporation or an unincorporated association. *HRS* § 701–118(7). Thus, the statute makes clear that a dolphin is not "another" under *HRS* § 701–118(8).

State v. LeVasseur, 613 P.2d 1328 (Haw.App.1980)

Note the logic of the court's decision: wild animals (animals *feræ naturæ*) can be property; depriving another person of her property is "theft"; defendant therefore committed theft. Are the categories "property" and "person" mutually inconsistent? Were the categories mutually inconsistent in the antebellum United States?

Why was the choice of evils defense unavailable? If there had been no statutory definition of "another," would the court have been justified in applying the choice-of-evils statute?

At his trial, Le Vasseur sought to argue that dolphins were "persons" within the statutory definition of the choice of evils statute. He was prepared to present expert witnesses who would testify about the size and structure of the dolphin brain, their ability to communicate, and their complex social structure. His argument would have been that, given their large, complex brains, their communication and their social structure, dolphins are more "human" than some humans.

Le Vasseur, of course, sought to raise far broader issues. How ought we treat other animals? Are they the type of beings entitled to moral regard? Are only humans deserving of ethical treatment? He was denied the chance by the court to explain his theory that dolphins ought to have sufficient moral standing to qualify as "another" within the meaning of the state statute. Both the trial and appellate courts had no trouble deciding that dolphins were property as a matter of law so that no factual evidence on the question was needed.

On the decision, *see* Gavan Daws, *"Animal Liberation" as Crime: The Hawaii Dolphin Case, in* ANIMALS AND ETHICS 361–71 (Harlan B. Miller & William H. Williams eds., 1983).

See also State v. Troen, 786 P.2d 751, 753–54 (Or.App.), *review denied,* 801 P.2d 841 (Or.1990), *cert. denied,* 501 U.S. 1232 (1991).

PERSPECTIVES

(1) Ethical rights for animals and nature—the issue: Many people intuitively feel that humans have obligations toward nonhuman animals and nature that are broader than can be explained by purely instrumental arguments. Indeed, public opinion surveys show high levels of support for the moral value of other life forms—particularly for other species as such. A study published in 1995 obtained the following results:

1.   Justice is not just for human beings. We need to be as fair to plants and animals as we are towards people.

Public assent 90%

2.   Our obligation to preserve nature isn't just a responsibility to other people but to the environment itself.

Public assent: 87%

3.   Other species have as much right to be on this earth as we do. Just because we are smarter than other animals doesn't make us better.

Public assent: 83%

4.   All species have a right to evolve without human interference. If extinction is going to happen, it should happen naturally, not through human actions.

Public assent: 87%

Public respondents were less committed to the moral status of individual animals (as opposed to species and biological communities), but moral concern still remained a majority public sentiment.

5. There is nothing wrong with killing individual animals, as in hunting, as long as you don't kill so many that you threaten the population.

Public assent: 43% (meaning 57% opposed hunting)

WILLETT KEMPTON, *ET AL.*, ENVIRONMENTAL VALUES IN AMERICAN CULTURE 106–14 (1995).

Such polls demonstrate that many people believe that we have duties to nonhuman animals and the complex aggregations in which they occur—duties to avoid causing extinctions of species, duties to preserve ecosystems. Duty aside, we could undertake such preservation for purely selfish reasons. We could preserve species and ecosystems because they harbor genetic materials that might cure diseases or improve domestic plants. Similarly, we might justify preservation by pointing to aesthetic values. The difficulty, of course, is that such instrumental arguments fall short of justifying the preservation of all species: if it could be conclusively shown, for example, that a species had *no* instrumental value—no genetic utility or no key role in an ecosystem—then there would be no obligation to preserve the species. This approach, however, strikes many people as fundamentally wrong: to claim that we should preserve pandas or rain forests solely because they are necessary to our lives and goals seems to miss something essential.

On the other hand, trying to specify the source of an obligation to preserve species and ecosystems for noninstrumental reasons seems to require that species and nature possess independent moral status. This claim, however, conflicts with the intuition embraced by many that the existence of intrinsic moral value is dependent upon some degree of consciousness. How can something that is unconscious or inanimate have moral value? *See generally* Donald H. Regan, *Duties of Preservation, in* THE PRESERVATION OF SPECIES 195–96 (Bryan G. Norton ed., 1986).

This challenge—determining the ethics of wildlife—is the focus of the notes in this section. They offer brief examinations of the major justifications put forward for preserving nonhuman animals or species or ecosystems.

We begin with the traditional Western answer: there is no *direct* duty to nonhuman animals as such—apart from duties to other people with respect to wildlife—however wise or virtuous it may be to treat animals kindly.

(2) Ethical rights for animals—the no-rights position: Many people assume that individual humans are intrinsically valuable because they are unique beings. A variety of properties—self-consciousness, the use of language, the capacity for desire—have been offered as the basis for this moral claim. Rene Descartes, for example, used his famous manifesto—"I think, therefore I am"—as a basis for arguing that, since (he believed) animals did not think, they were indistinguishable from automata. RENE DESCARTES, TREATISE ON MAN 2, 4 (1972) (1st ed. Paris 1664) (written 1629–1632).

Descartes's stark view built upon a long-established sense that humans were superior to other species. Aristotle, for example, advocated a hierarchy in which the less rational and hence less perfect served the more rational and thus more perfect:

> Plants exist to give subsistence to animals, and animals to give it to men. Animals, when they are domesticated serve for use as well as for food; wild animals, too, in most cases if not all, serve to furnish man not only with food, but also with other comforts, such as the provision of clothing and similar aids to life.
>
> Accordingly, as nature makes nothing purposeless or in vain, all animals must have been made by nature for the sake of men.

ARISTOTLE, POLITICS 1256b.

The other major font of Western thought—Christianity—had a similar view on the relationship between humans and nonhuman nature. Man is fundamentally different than the rest of nature. While god created man just as he created the beasts, man is different because god created Adam "in his own image," *Genesis* 1:27, and gave man "dominion over the fish of the sea, and over the fowl of the air, . . . and over all the earth and over every creeping thing that creepeth upon the earth." *Id.* 1:26, 28. Thomas Aquinas drove the point home: man, "being made in the image of God, is above other animals, [which] are rightly subject to his government." THOMAS AQUINAS, SUMMA THEOLOGIAE pt. 1, q. 96, art. 1 (Blackfriars ed. 1964) (c. 1267–1273). The concurrence of the biblical and the classical led scholastics such as Aquinas to discern the propriety of man's mastery over the beasts in "the order of nature,"—a refrain shared by John Calvin who concluded that "the Lord himself, by the very order of Creation, has demonstrated that he created all things for the sake of man." JOHN CALVIN, INSTITUTES OF RELIGION bk. 1, ch. 14, § 22 (Beveridge ed. 1983 reprint) (1st ed. Basel 1536).

This traditional Western perspective reached an extreme in the work of the French philosopher Rene Descartes, who argued that animals "are not rational, and that nature makes them behave as they do according to the disposition of their organs; just as a clock, composed only of wheels and weights, can count the hours and measure the time more accurately than we can with all our intelligence." RENE DESCARTES, DISCOURSE ON METHOD pt. 5 (Laurence J. Lafleur trans. 1960) (1637). Animals, in short, were not just beneath humans, they had the same status as machines—which is to say that they had no moral status whatever.

A less extreme perspective on the ethical status of animals is contained in the writings of Immanuel Kant (1724–1804), a professor of philosophy at the University of Konigsberg. Kant argued that the line between rational and nonrational beings was the crucial divide for ethics. Self-conscious, rational beings, he contended, possess the ability to form moral law and to act in conformance with the conception of such laws. This faculty makes rational beings ends-in-themselves rather than means. Nonrational beings, on the other hand, are not ends-in-themselves—and may be treated as means-to-ends:

[S]o far as animals are concerned, we have no direct duties. Animals are not self-conscious and are there merely as a means to an end. That end is man. We can ask, "Why do animals exist?" But to ask, "Why does man exist?" is a meaningless question. *Our duties towards animals are merely indirect duties toward humanity.* Animal nature has analogies to human nature, and by doing our duties to animals in respect of manifestations of human nature, we indirectly do our duty towards humanity. Thus, if a dog has served his master long and faithfully, his service, on analogy of human service, deserves reward, and when the dog has grown too old to serve, his master ought to keep him until he dies. Such action helps to support us in our duties toward human beings, where they are bounden duties. If then any acts of animals are analogous to human acts and spring from the same principles, we have duties towards the animals because thus we cultivate the corresponding duties towards human beings. If a man shoots his dog because the animal is no longer capable of service, he does not fail in his duty to the dog, for the dog cannot judge, but his act is inhuman and damages in himself that humanity which it is his duty to show towards mankind. If he is not to stifle his human feelings, he must practice kindness towards animals, for he who is cruel to animals becomes hard also in his dealing with men.

IMMANUEL KANT, LECTURES ON ETHICS 239–40 (Louis Infield trans. 1930) (ca. 1775–1780).

Does the anti-cruelty statute at issue in *Cleve* reflect a Kantian perspective? Would Kant agree with the court's decision on the construction of the statute? Would he argue that the court was correct as a matter of ethical duty but nonetheless believe that Cleve had behaved in an unethical manner?

Note that animal welfare statutes accept the principle that animals may be used as instruments for attaining human objectives but imposes limits on the methods for such use: animals may be killed for food or furs or sport as long as they are killed humanely; animals may be used for experimental purposes as long as there is no unnecessary suffering.

(3) No rights and the "argument from marginal cases": Both Descartes and Kant claim that humans as a species can be distinguished from non-human species because they are rational—a position in ethics that is often expressed as the ability to understand what it means to act morally and the ability to behave reciprocally in upholding the moral claims of others. One attack on this position is the "argument from marginal cases," which contends that humans—such as infants and the severely mentally disabled—who lack such mental capacities should be accorded the same moral status as animals. Since we do not think that it is right to eat or experiment on infants or the mentally handicapped, it is inconsistent to do such things to non-human animals.

The leading advocates for according animals moral standing disagree that the key criterion for distinguishing morally worthy actors from morally insignificant objects ought to be a high level of mental function. Healthy, adult humans do indeed possess mental capacities that exceed those of other species, but even if this were true for all humans (as it is not), there is the further question as to why this criterion should carry such great weight. After all, humans may excel in this capacity, but they fall far short of other species in nearly all other ways—in their abilities to see, hear, smell, run, fly, swim, etc. Why should mental functioning be the key moral criterion? Animal welfare advocates argue that the primary moral criterion ought to be something else: perhaps consciousness of surroundings and the intentional ability to choose or perhaps merely an ability to experience pain—a criterion that would accord moral significance to a wide range of animal species.

It is important to note—and often ignored by critics—that advocates of animal welfare do not suggest that other species should enjoy the same moral status as humans: only that they ought to have some moral status— that they count for more than nothing, that their interests ought to be given some weight in ethical calculations—even if the weight is insufficient to keep humans from using them when the justification is sufficiently great.

The search for a nonanthropocentric ethic is largely a search for some property or properties that will serve as the basis for acknowledging the intrinsic value of at least some non-human animals or all of non-human nature. In the animal welfare/animal rights context, there are two primary types of challenges to the Kantian position: a utilitarian approach and a deontological or rights-based approach.

The utilitarian position[1] asserts that a morally proper act is one that maximizes utility—pleasure over pain to use a crude measure—with the ultimate objective of producing the best for the most; the deontological argument, on the other hand, claims that certain aspects of actions have intrinsic worth without regard to the consequences—that the killing of innocent individuals is wrong apart from the consequences of the deaths. Both ethical approaches can be used to justify the moral value of at least some non-human animals.

(4) Ethical respect for animals—a utilitarian position: Peter Singer is the primary advocate of a utilitarian justification for the moral value of some non-human animals. Following Jeremy Bentham, Singer argues that the crucial moral property is the capacity for sentience or self-consciousness. The moral considerability of a being depends upon the sentience rather than the rationality of the being because all sentient beings have the capability to suffer:

> Equality is a moral ideal, not a simple assertion of fact. There is no logically compelling reason for assuming that a factual difference in ability between two people justifies any difference in the amount of consideration we give to satisfying their needs and interests. The principle of equality of human beings is not a description of an alleged

1. A utilitarian, of course, need not support recognition of a moral status for the interests of non-human animals in order to justify duties to protect other species and ecosystems since such protection might generate greater utility (however defined) than would be created by destroying the species or ecosystems for economic gain; if so, protection would be morally right independent of any recognition of the intrinsic moral value of other animals.

actual equality among humans; it is a prescription of how we should treat humans.

Jeremy Bentham incorporated the essential basis of moral equality into his utilitarian system of ethics in the formula: "Each to count for one and none for more than one." In other words, the interests of every being affected by an action are to be taken into account and given the same weight as the like interests of any other being. A later utilitarian, Henry Sidgwick, put the point this way: "The good of any one individual is of no more importance, from the point of view (if I may say so) of the Universe, than the good of any other."....

Many philosophers have proposed the principle of equal consideration of interests, in some form or other, as a basic moral principle; but ... not many of them have recognized that this principle applies to members of other species as well as to our own. Bentham was one of the few who did realize this. In a forward-looking passage, written at a time when black slaves in British dominions were still being treated as we now treat nonhuman animals, Bentham wrote:

> The day *may* come when the rest of animal creation may acquire those rights which never could have been witholden from them but by the hand of tyranny. The French have already discovered that the blackness of the skin is no reason why a human being should be abandoned without redress to the caprice of a tormentor. It may one day come to be recognized that the number of legs, the villosity of skin, or the termination of the *os sacrum*, are reasons equally insufficient for abandoning a sensitive being to the same fate. What else is it that should trace the insuperable line? Is it the faculty of reason, or perhaps the faculty of discourse? But a full-grown horse or dog is beyond comparison a more rational, as well as more conversable animal, than an infant of a day, or a week, or even a month, old. But suppose they were otherwise, what would it avail? The question is not, Can they reason? nor Can they *talk*? but, *Can they suffer?*

In this paragraph Bentham points to the capacity for suffering as the vital characteristic that gives a being the *right* to equal consideration. The capacity for suffering—or more strictly, for suffering and/or enjoyment or happiness—is not just another characteristic like the capacity for language, or for higher mathematics.... The capacity for suffering and enjoying things is a pre-requisite for having interests at all, a condition that must be satisfied before we can speak of interests in any meaningful way. It would be nonsense to say that it was not in the interests of a stone to be kicked along the road by a schoolboy. A stone does not have interests because it cannot suffer. Nothing that we can do to it could possibly make any difference to its welfare. A mouse, on the other hand, does have an interest in not being tormented, because it will suffer if it is.

If a being suffers, there can be no moral justification for refusing to take that suffering into consideration.

Peter Singer, *All Animals are Equal, in* ANIMAL RIGHTS AND HUMAN OBLI-GATIONS 148, 152–54 (Tom Regan & Peter Singer eds., 1976).

Singer's central claim is that sentient beings have intrinsic value because what we do to them matters to them. It is in this that they differ from the rock being kicked down the road by the schoolboy. Given sentience, the equality-of-consideration principle becomes operative *as a moral imperative.*

Note that the equality-of-consideration principle does not necessarily preclude all uses of animals nor does it suggest that the interests of all species are the same. The utilitarian position—because it is aggregative—would permit animals to be treated as means to an end when that end produces more utility than non-use would. For example, if a nonhuman species could be used to find a cure for HIV, that use might well be justified by the balance of suffering/utility. *See* Michale Specter, *The Dangerous Philosopher,* NEW YORKER, Sept. 6, 1999, at 46 (a profile of Singer and his views).

(5) Ethical rights for animals—a deontological or rights-based position: In contrast to utilitarian arguments, the deontological position is predicated upon the assertion that it is some quality of the act that justifies ascribing moral status. That is, certain beings possess intrinsic rights and an act is wrong if it violates such a right without regard for the overall utilitarian impacts of the act. Like Singer, Tom Regan contends that certain essential psychological properties are shared by humans and some non-human animals; these include the capacity for belief and desire, the ability to have goals—the crucial elements for Regan's characterization of "self-consciousness." These capacities give rise to equal intrinsic value for those animals that possess them; such animals are "ends in themselves" like people and—like people—therefore possess rights although these rights will differ due to the differences among species.

Regan offers both a critique of Singer's utilitarian view and a defense of his own rights-based position in the following excerpt:

Tom Regan, The Case for Animal Rights *in* IN DEFENSE OF ANIMALS

13–14, 15–16, 18–19, 20–21, 22–23 (Peter Singer ed., 1985).

I regard myself as an advocate of animal rights—as a part of the animal rights movement. That movement, as I conceive it, is committed to a number of goals, including:

* the total abolition of the use of animals in science;

* the total dissolution of commercial animal agriculture;

* the total elimination of commercial and sport hunting and trapping.

There are, I know, people who profess to believe in animal rights but do not avow these goals. Factory farming, they say, is wrong—it violates animals' rights—but traditional animal agriculture is all right. Toxicity tests of cosmetics on animals violates their rights, but important medical research—cancer research, for example—does not. The clubbing of baby seals is abhorrent, but not the harvesting of adult seals. I used to think I understood this reasoning. Not any more. You don't change unjust institutions by tidying them up.

What's wrong—fundamentally wrong—with the way animals are treated isn't the details that vary from case to case. It's the whole system. The forlornness of the veal calf is pathetic, heart wrenching; the pulsing pain of the chimp with electrodes planted deep in her brain is repulsive; the slow, tortuous death of the raccoon caught in the leg-hold trap is agonizing. But what is wrong isn't the pain, isn't the suffering, isn't the deprivation. These compound what's wrong. Sometimes—often—they make it much, much worse. But they are not the fundamental wrong.

The fundamental wrong is the system that allows us to view animals as *our resources*, here for *us*—to be eaten, or surgically manipulated, or exploited for sport or money. Once we accept this view of animals—as our resources—the rest is as predictable as it is regrettable. . . .

We [philosophers] begin by asking how the moral status of animals has been understood by thinkers who deny that animals have rights. Then we test the mettle of their ideas by seeing how well they stand up under the heat of fair criticism. If we start our thinking in this way, we soon find that some people believe that we have no duties directly to animals, that we owe nothing to them, that we can do nothing that wrongs them. Rather, we can do wrong acts that involve animals, and so we have duties regarding them, though none to them. Such views may be called indirect duty views. By way of illustration: suppose your neighbour kicks your dog. Then your neighbour has done something wrong. But not to your dog. The wrong that has been done is a wrong to you. After all, it is wrong to upset people, and your neighbour's kicking your dog upsets you. So you are the one who is wronged, not your dog. Or again: by kicking your dog your neighbour damages your property. And since it is wrong to damage another person's property, your neighbour has done something wrong—to you, of course, not to your dog. . . .

How could someone try to justify such a view? Someone might say that your dog doesn't feel anything and so isn't hurt by your neighbour's kick, doesn't care about the pain since none is felt, is as unaware of anything as is your windshield. Someone might say this, but no rational person will, since, among other considerations, such a view will commit anyone who holds it to the position that no human being feels pain either—that human beings also don't care about what happens to them. A second possibility is that though both humans and your dog are hurt when kicked, it is only human pain that matters. But, again, no rational person can believe this. Pain is pain wherever it occurs. If your neighbour's causing you pain is wrong because of the pain that is caused, we cannot rationally ignore or dismiss the moral relevance of the pain that your dog feels.

. . .

. . . Whatever ethical theory we should accept rationally, . . ., must at least recognize that we have some duties directly to animals, just as we have some duties directly to each other. The next two theories I'll sketch attempt to meet this requirement.

The first I call the cruelty-kindness view. Simply states, this says that we have a direct duty to be kind to animals and a direct duty not to be cruel to them. Despite the familiar, reassuring ring of these ideas, I do not believe that this view offers an adequate theory. To make this clearer, consider kindness. A kind person acts from a certain kind of motive—compassion or concern, for example. And that is a virtue. But there is no guarantee that a kind act is a right act. If I am a generous racist, for example, I will be inclined to act kindly towards members of my own race, favouring their interests above those of others. My kindness would be real and, so far as it goes, good. But I trust it is too obvious to require argument that my kind acts may not be above moral reproach—may, in fact, be positively wrong because rooted in injustice. So kindness, notwithstanding its status as a virtue to be encouraged, simply will not carry the weight of a theory of right action.

Cruelty fares no better. People or their acts if they display either a lack of sympathy for or, worse, the presence of enjoyment in another's suffering. Cruelty in all guises is a bad thing, a tragic human failing. But just as a person's being motivated by kindness does not guarantee that he or she does what is right, so by the absence of cruelty does not ensure that he or she avoids doing what is wrong. Many people who perform abortions, for example, are not cruel, sadistic peoples. But that fact alone does not settle the terribly difficult question of the morality of abortion. The case is no different when we examine the ethics of our treatment of animals. So, yes, let us be for kindness and against cruelty. But let us not suppose that being for the one and against the other answers questions about moral right and wrong.

Some people think that the theory we are looking for is utilitarianism. A utilitarian accepts two moral principles. The first is that of equality: everyone's interests count, and similar interests must be counted as having similar weight or importance. White or black, American or Iranian, human or animal—everyone's pain or frustration matter, and matter just as much as the equivalent pain or frustration of anyone else. The second principle a utilitarian accepts is that of utility: do the act that will bring about the best balance between satisfaction and frustration for everyone affected by the outcome.

As a utilitarian, then, here is how I am to approach the task of deciding what I morally ought to do: I must ask who will be affected if I choose to do one thing rather than another, how much each individual will be affected, and where the best results are most likely to lie—which option, in other words, is most likely to bring about the best results, the best balance between satisfaction and frustration. That option, whatever it may be, is the one I ought to choose. That is where my moral duty lies.

. . .

Serious problems arise for utilitarianism when we remind ourselves that it enjoins us to bring about the best consequences. What does this mean? It doesn't mean the best consequences for me alone, or for my family or friends, or any other person taken individually. No, what we must do is, roughly, as follows: we must add up (somehow!) the separate satisfactions and frustrations of everyone likely to be affected by our choice, the satisfactions on one column, the frustrations in the other. We must total each column for each of the options before us. That is what it means to say the theory is aggregative. And then we must choose that option which is most likely to bring about the best balance of totalled satisfactions over totalled frustrations. Whatever act would lead to this outcome is the one we ought morally to perform—it is where our moral duty lies. And that act quite clearly might not be the same one that would bring about the best results for me personally, or for my family or friends, or for a lab animal. The best aggregated consequences for everyone concerned are not necessarily the best for each individual.

That utilitarianism is an aggregative theory—different individuals' satisfactions or frustrations are added, or summed, or totalled—is the key objection to this theory. My Aunt Bea is old, inactive, a cranky, sour person, though not physically ill. She prefers to go on living. She is also rather rich. I could make a fortune if I could get my hands on her money, money she intends to give me in any event, after she dies, but which she refuses to give me now. In order to avoid a huge tax bite, I plan to donate a handsome sum of my profits to a local children's hospital. Many, many children will benefit from my generosity, and much joy will be brought to their parents, relatives and friends. If I don't get the money rather soon, all these ambitions will come to naught. The once-in-a-lifetime opportunity to make a real killing will be gone. Why, then, not kill my Aunt Bea? . . .

Suppose Aunt Bea is killed and the rest of the story comes out as told. Would I have done anything wrong? Anything immoral? One would have thought that I had. Not according to utilitarianism. Since what I have done has brought about the best balance between totalled satisfaction and frustration for all those affected by the outcome, my action is not wrong. Indeed, in killing Aunt Bea the physician and I did what duty required.

This same kind of argument can be repeated in all sorts of cases, illustrating, time after time, how the utilitarian's position leads to results that impartial people find morally callous. It *is* wrong to kill my Aunt Bea in the name of bringing about the best results for others. A good end does not justify an evil means. Any adequate moral theory will have to explain why this is so. Utilitarianism fails in this respect and so cannot be the theory we seek.

What to do? Where to begin anew? The place to begin, I think, is with the utilitarian's view of the value of the individual—or, rather, lack of value. In its place, suppose we consider that you and I, for example, do have value as individuals—what we call *inherent value*. To say we have such value is to say that we are something more than, something different from, mere receptacles. Moreover, to ensure that we do not pave the way for such injustices as slavery or sexual discrimination, we must believe that all who have inherent value have it equally, regardless of their sex, race, religion, birthplace and so on. Similarly to be discarded as irrelevant are one's talents or skills, intelligence and wealth, personality or pathology, whether one is loved and admired or despised and loathed. The genius and the retarded child, the prince and the pauper, the brain surgeon and the fruit vendor, Mother Teresa and the most unscrupulous used-car salesman—all have inherent value, all possess it equally, and all have an equal right to be treated with respect, to be treated in ways that do not reduce them to the status of things, as if they existed as resources for others. . . .

. . .

The rights view, I believe, is rationally the most satisfactory moral theory. It surpasses all other theories in the degree to which it illuminates and explains the foundation of our duties to one another–the domain of human morality. On this score it has the best reasons, the best arguments, on its side. Of course, if it were possible to show that only human beings are included within its scope, then a person like myself, who believes in animal rights, would be obliged to look elsewhere.

But attempts to limit its scope to humans only can be shown to be rationally defective. Animals, it is true, lack many of the abilities humans possess. They can't read, do higher mathematics, build a bookcase or make *baba ghanoush*. Neither can many human beings, however, and yet we don't (and shouldn't) say that they (these humans) therefore have less inherent value, less of a right to be treated with respect, than do others. It is the *similarities* between those human beings who most clearly, most non-controversially have such value (the people reading this, for example), not our differences, that matter most. And the really crucial, the basic similarity is simply this: we are each of us the experiencing subject of a life, a conscious creature having an individual welfare that has importance to us whatever our usefulness to others. We want and prefer things, believe and feel things, recall and expect things. And all these dimensions of our life, including our pleasure and pain, our enjoyment and suffering, our satisfaction and frustration, our continued existence or our untimely death—all make a difference to the quality of our life as lived, as experienced, by us as individuals. As the same is true of those animals that concern us (the ones that are eaten and trapped, for example), they too must be viewed as the experiencing subjects of a life, with inherent value of their own.

Some there are who resist the idea that animals have inherent value. "Only humans have such value," they profess. How might this narrow view be defended? Shall we say that only humans have the requisite intelligence, or autonomy, or reason? But there are many, many humans who fail to meet these standards and yet are reasonably viewed as having value above and beyond their usefulness to others. Shall we claim that only humans belong to the right species, the species *Homo sapiens*? But this is blatant specieism. Will it be said, then, that all—and only—humans have immortal souls? Then our opponents have their work cut out for them. I am myself not ill-disposed to the proposition that there are immortal souls. Personally, I profoundly hope I have one. But I would not want to rest my position on a controversial ethical issue on the even more controversial question about who or what has an immortal soul. . . .

Well, perhaps some will say that animals have some inherent value, only less that we have. Once again, however, attempts to defend this view can be shown to lack rational justification. What could be the basis of our having more inherent value than animals? Their lack of reason, or autono-my, or intellect? Only if we are willing to make the same judgement in the case of humans who are similarly deficient. But it is not true that such humans—the retarded child, for example, or the mentally deranged—have less inherent value than you or I. Neither, then, can we rationally sustain the view that animals like them in being the experiencing subjects of a life have less inherent value. *All* who have inherent value have it *equally*, whether they be human animals or not.

PERSPECTIVES

(1) The key concept in Regan's theory is inherent value. The concept serves as the basis for the claim that animals have equal moral rights. How does Regan define the concept? What does he offer as the basis for inherent value? Why does inherent value lead to moral rights?

(2) Ethical rights for animals—individuals and aggregations: Like Kant, the animal rights position focuses on individuals—it offers no explicit rationale for the preservation of the complex aggregations of individuals that we call populations, communities, or ecosystems—unless the aggregate is to be protected because of the individuals of which it is composed. Is a rain forest or a desert less independently worthy of protection? At least part of this difficulty is the individualistic bias present in much of western thought; traditional ethics as well as traditional political theory has not focused on groups or aggregations: rights are individual rather than collective. *Cf.* James L. Huffman, *Do Species and Nature Have Rights?*, 13 PUB. LAND L. REV. 51, 55–58 (1992) (a libertarian perspective on rights as the basis of a "community composed of individuals").

(3) Ethical rights/legal rights: Steven M. Wise has recently written a series of law review articles arguing that at least some animals are entitled to "dignity-rights"—a term which, he argues,

> rather than "human rights," better describes fundamental legal rights. This is because the phrase "dignity-rights" emphasizes that fundamental human rights derive not merely from being human, but from the dignity that is associated with qualities alleged or assumed to be universally shared by human beings.

Although Wise's argument is legal in nature—he analyzes rights in the traditional Hohfeldian scheme,[1] cites cases and treaties, and argues that courts should adopt his position—at its core, his argument is the same as that of Regan and Singer: since the universe of human and non-human consciousness overlaps, it is irrational to treat non-human animals differently than humans:

> "[D]ignity" originally referred to one's rank in a social hierarchy, such as the dignity of the king or a noble. Accelerated by the French Revolution, this notion gave way to a natural, inherent, equal, and universal human dignity, heavily influenced by the Kantian ideal of an inherent full rational autonomy incommensurable with what he termed "price."[444] Courts and international treaties often ground hu-

---

1. WESLEY N. HOHFELD, FUNDAMENTAL LE-
GAL CONCEPTIONS (Walter W. Cook ed., 1919).

444. .... "[A] thing has a price if we can put something else in its place as an

man rights upon this sense of dignity which, from a noncomparative perspective, demands treatment as a person and not as a tool, and from a comparative perspective, treats assaults upon universal dignity as denials of equality.

But full Kantian autonomy is a highly problematic standard for dignity, as it is no more empirically verifiable than were Christian and Cartesian incorporeal souls. It is merely presumed to exist in every human being, irrespective of the actual capacities of any particular one.... On the other hand, the actual capacity for full Kantian autonomy can be empirically demonstrated *not to* exist in classes of humans—infants, the persistently vegetative, and many younger children and severely mentally limited who lack the abilities sufficient for rationality, autonomy, self-determination or the capacity to make moral choices. Certainly no human possesses full Kantian autonomy all the time, and normal human adults occupy a sliding psychological and cognitive scale of rationality and autonomy. To adopt full Kantian autonomy as the standard for dignity would require judges who value reasoned judgment and reject invidious discrimination to exclude large numbers of human beings from eligibility for dignity-rights....

It is true that "Anglo American law starts with the premise of thorough-going self determination."[451] But full Kantian autonomy is neither the only nor even the most realistic sense of autonomy and self-determination. Numerous moral and legal philosophers have made Kantian-like arguments that realistically extend autonomy to beings who lack the exceedingly complex cognition required for full Kantian autonomy by emphasizing the simpler ability to act so as to fulfill one's intended purposes or the capacity for mental flexibility and responsiveness. Full Kantian autonomy and realistic autonomy reflect differing capacities for consciousness that range from the most simple awareness of present experience to a much broader and deeper self-awareness, self-reflection, and an awareness of the past, present, and future. The most complex reflexive state of consciousness approximates the high end of full Kantian autonomy, while the more complex of the simple states of consciousness approximate the low end of realistic autonomy.

Full Kantian autonomy is too narrow a condition for dignity for three reasons: It is too idealized. Not all humans possess it to any degree, large numbers of humans possess it only to varying degrees, and no humans possess it all the time, and no one expects them to. Instead, a *realistic* autonomy recognizes that "an agent has a less than perfect ability to choose appropriate actions." A being capable of desires and beliefs, even a nonlinguistic human child, might qualify as autonomous to benefit from fundamental immunity-rights or even to assert claim-rights, if she can have beliefs and desires and is able to make "some, but not necessarily all of the sound inferences from the belief set that are apparently appropriate." Moreover, a far greater number of humans—though still not anencephalic or normal infants,

equivalent. Dignity or worthiness is above all price and has no equivalent or substitute."....

451. Natanson v. Kline, 350 P.2d 1093, 1104 (Kan.1960); [ ].

the most severely retarded adults, or adults in persistent vegetative comas—possess a realistic autonomy than possess full Kantian autonomy. Therefore, it more closely coincides with the way in which human beings are normally understood to be autonomous.

Third, and perhaps most important for our purposes, fundamental common law and constitutional rights were not designed merely to protect those with a full Kantian autonomy. A realistic autonomy thus coincides much more perfectly with the autonomy that judges actually protect.[457] American courts generally hold that incompetent human beings are entitled to the same dignity-rights as are competent human beings. The United States Supreme Court held that a man with an I.Q. below ten and the mental capacity of an eighteen-month-old child had an inextinguishable liberty right to personal security.[458] Every American jurisdiction today recognizes a cause of action in tort, almost always under the common law, for a fetus born alive who suffered prenatal injury after reaching viability. Some jurisdictions permit a common law cause of action for a fetus born alive who suffered even a pre-viability injury. Others allow either a common law or statutory cause of action in favor of the estate of stillborns for prenatal injury that caused their deaths, with courts drawing the line at injuries inflicted both before and after viability.

Once some minimum capacity for autonomy and self-determination is attained, at least with respect to human adults, courts generally respect the choices made within exceedingly wide parameters. This is because a choice emanating from even a flickering autonomy is more highly valued, irrespective of whether the actions are rational or reasonable or often even inimical to one's own best interests, than is any specific choice. Courts are therefore routinely sensitive not only to autonomy's full Kantian sense, but to its realistic sense.

While a realistic autonomy will not produce a diminished dignity, courts may limit the dignity-rights of those who possess the less-than-normal degree of cognition required for full Kantian autonomy to those rights appropriate to the capacity for autonomy and self-determination that they do possess. This would allow normal older children and all but the most seriously retarded human adults a realistic and nonarbitrary measure of dignity-rights. But to avoid the arbitrariness, lack of integrity, and invidious discrimination antithetical to the overarching principles and values of traditional Western law, courts would have to recognize that nonhuman animals who possess capacities for autonomy and self-determination of similar degree, or their equivalents, also possess a dignity sufficient to trigger a realistic and nonarbitrary degree of dignity-rights as well.

. . .

---

457. *See, e.g.,* Schmidt v. Schmidt, 459 A.2d 421, 422–23 (Pa.Super.1983) (holding that a twenty-six year old woman with Down's Syndrome with the mental ability of a child between four and a half and eight years can rationally decide whether to choose to visit a parent).

458. *See* Youngberg v. Romeo, 457 U.S. 307, 309–16 (1982).

.... Recall that in the aftermath of the French Revolution dignity as equality defeated the claim of dignity as hierarchy. The refusal to recognize the dignity of those nonhuman animals otherwise entitled to dignity reinstates the idea of dignity as something reserved for the upper ranks of a hereditary hierarchy, with human beings arbitrarily awarding themselves the upper ranks. This threatens a retreat to the discredited social and political principles that were, in more ignorant ages, modeled on the Great Chain of Being.

Steven M. Wise, *Hardly a Revolution—The Eligibility of Nonhuman Animals for Dignity–Rights in a Liberal Democracy*, 22 Vt. L. Rev. 793, 795, 869–75, 883–84, 887–88 (1998).

Wise believes that "chimpanzees (*Pan troglodytes*) and bonobos (*Pan paniscus*) probably possess a complex cognition that endows them with a reflexive consciousness and a degree of autonomy and self-determination sufficient for the minimal rationality required of an agent.[523] If they do, they should not be deprived of dignity-rights simply because they are not human." *Id.* at 888. On the genetic relationship among humans, chimpanzees, and bonobos, see Jared Diamond, The Third Chimpanzee (1992).

(4) Ethical respect for animals—a gradualist compromise: One problem with both Regan's and Singer's approaches is that, like those who view humans as unique, they end up dividing all life forms into two distinct moral groups. Some species (or individual animals) end up with considerable moral worth; all others end up intrinsically worthless. The following excerpt assesses critically these "two-group" approaches and describes a gradualist approach, purportedly more in keeping with the moral sentiments of many people:

The two-group debate is particularly intense because the proponents of the approach share a vision of a special type of grail. What they seek ... is a single principle that distinguishes between things with and without moral worth. Holders of moral worth enjoy high status; things of no worth are ignored. In the value scheme of these single-line philosophers, the drop-off can be immense.

It is easy to see why arguments among these philosophers are so divisive. Animal rights advocates, mixed up in the middle of this debate, are easy targets for ridicule when they claim to perceive some morally meaningful difference between a chimpanzee and a dog or between a deer and a rabbit. The gradation among species is slight if not arbitrary, and it is disturbing for such grave consequences to rest on so little.

Some scholars—a growing number, it appears—have drifted away from the single-line camp because the whole process seems inevitably unsettling. Their dissent is not so much from any particular line as it is from the idea that we are limited to only one. The alternative approach is some form of gradualism, a philosophic scheme that places organisms in multiple categories and that recognizes gradually declin-

---

523. It is also probable that at least some of the four thousand species of mammals and nine thousand species of birds, and possibly other species as well, possess lesser but still legally significant degrees of autonomy.

ing moral value as we move further and further from the human core. Instead of two groups, we now are offered many, with the rights and entitlements declining in strength as we move down the line to the increasingly less favored....

Ethicists have traditionally favored a single-line system for more than just its economy and elegance. A gradualist system creates multiple moral classes, which means more lines to draw and whole new categories of rules. The more lines and rules there are, the more complex things become and the more prone we are in particular settings to fabricate a new category or rule or to pick and choose among existing options in order to find a justification for what we want to do. The danger is relativity—the lack of rules that really bind—and multitiered schemes commonly must defend against this charge. In the single-line camp there are things that count and things that do not, and the clash between the two produces a clear winner. In gradualism we have harder issues. How do we balance, for example, a moderate need of a higher species against a stronger need of a lower one?.... If a moral scheme becomes too fragmented, the tendency is to develop new rules for each situation—a process not likely to produce rules that are fair and coherent.

To assess the rightness of gradualism, we need to mix our deliberate thoughts about moral value with a few simple intuitions to see where we end up. Although our senses do not organize the world into neat packages, they do send us many messages. On an intuitive level, the gradualist, multi-group approach seems to offer a good deal of accuracy and truth. That intuitive sense supports more logical claims that, as levels of functioning decline among less-developed species, moral value should decline as well.

What we are likely to sense intuitively when we survey the Earth's many life forms is a large element of inequality among species. Bears and elk, it seems, are somehow more precious than mice and beetles, even if we do not know exactly why. The towering oak is more valuable than the patch of common dandelions. A wild stream, we sense, is more valuable for what it is, and its value increases when other wild streams are blocked, diverted, and polluted. An individual condor is more valuable than its bald eagle kin, again because of its relative scarcity.

When we rely on the sense we are likely to come up with many categories, if not a gradual sliding scale. A chimpanzee has value, but we are unlikely to place it exactly on par with a human. The gray squirrel lives in a lower notch still, in part because it is ubiquitous, with most snakes and insects following somewhere below.... By inclination, in short, we approach the world from a gradualist, fragmented perspective. Our categories may be vague and fluid; we may rarely give them thought. But few of us would intuitively develop a hard-and-fast line, even a line that distinguished humans from the rest.

ERIC T. FREYFOGLE, JUSTICE AND THE EARTH: IMAGES FOR OUR PLANETARY SURVIVAL 75–78 (1993).

c. Species Preservation and Land Health

Just v. Marinette County

Wisconsin Supreme Court.
201 N.W.2d 761 (1972).

■ HALLOWS, C.J.:—Marinette county's Shoreland Zoning Ordinance Number 24 ... follows a model ordinance published by the Wisconsin Department of Resource Development in July of 1967. [ ] The ordinance was designed to meet standards and criteria for shoreland regulation which the legislature required to be promulgated by the department of natural resources. . . .

Shorelands for the purpose of ordinances are defined ... as lands within 1,000 feet of the normal high-water elevation of navigable lakes, ponds, or flowages and 300 feet from a navigable river or stream or to the landward side of the flood plain, whichever distance is greater. . . .

There can be no disagreement over the public purpose sought to be obtained by the ordinance. Its basic purpose is to protect navigable waters and the public rights therein from the degradation and deterioration which results from uncontrolled use and developed of shorelands. In the Navigable Waters Protection Act, [ ], the purpose of the state's shoreland regulation program is stated as being to "aid in the fulfillment of the state's role as trustee of its navigable waters and to promote public health, safety, convenience and general welfare." . . .

The shoreland zoning ordinance divides the shorelands of Marinette county into general purpose districts, general recreation districts, and conservancy districts. A "conservancy" district ... is defined ... to include "all shorelands designated as swamps or marshes on the United States Geological Survey maps which have been designated as the Shoreland Zoning Map of Marinette County, Wisconsin or on the detailed Insert Shoreland Zoning Maps." The ordinance provides for permitted uses[3] and conditional uses.[4] One of the conditional uses requiring a permit ... is the

---

3. 3.41 Permitted Uses.

(1) Harvesting of any wild crop such as marsh hay, ferns, moss, wild rice, berries, tree fruits and tree seeds.

(2) Sustained yield forestry subject to the provisions of Section 5.0 relating to removal of shore cover.

(3) Utilities such as, but not restricted to, telephone, telegraph and power transmission lines.

(4) Hunting, fishing, preservation of scenic, historic and scientific areas and wildlife preserves.

(5) Non-resident buildings used solely in conjunction with raising water fowl, minnows, and other similar lowland animals, fowl or fish.

(6) Hiking trails and bridle paths.

(7) Accessory uses.

(8) Signs, subject to the restriction of Section 2.0.

4. 3.42 Conditional Uses. The following uses are permitted upon issuance of a Conditional Use Permit. . . .

(1) General farming provided farm animals shall be kept one hundred feet from any non-farm residence.

(2) Dams, power plants, flowages and ponds.

(3) Relocation of any water course.

(4) Filling, drainage or dredging of wetlands according to the provisions of Section 5.0 of this ordinance.

(5) Removal of top soil or peat.

(6) Cranberry bogs.

filling, drainage or dredging of wetlands.... "Wetlands" are defined ... as "[a]reas where ground water is at or near the surface much of the year or where any segment of plant cover is deemed an aquatic according to N.C. Fassett's *Manual of Aquatic Plants*." Section 5.42(2) of the ordinance requires a conditional-use permit for any filling or grading "Of any area which is within three hundred feet horizontal distance of a navigable water and which has surface drainage toward the water and on which there is: (a) Filling of more than five hundred square feet of any wetland which it contiguous to the water ... (d) Filling or grading of more than 2,000 square feet on slopes of twelve per cent or less."

Several years prior to the passage of this ordinance, the Justs purchased 36.4 acres of land in the town of Lake along the south shore of Lake Noquebay, a navigable lake in Marinette county. This land had a frontage of 1,266.7 feet on the lake and was purchased partially for personal use and partially for resale. During the years 1964, 1966, and 1967, the Justs made five sales of parcels having frontage and extending back from the lake some 600 feet, leaving the property involved in these suits. This property has a frontage of 366.7 feet and the south one half contains a stand of cedar, pine, various hard woods, birch and red maple. The north one half, closer to the lake, is barren of trees except immediately along the shore. The south three fourths of this north one half is populated with various plant grasses and vegetation including some plants which N.C. Fassett in his manual of aquatic plants has classified as "aquatic." There are also non-aquatic plants which grow upon the land. Along the shoreline there is a belt of trees. The shoreline is from one foot to 3.2 feet higher than the lake level and there is a narrow belt of higher land along the shore known as a "pressure ridge" or "ice heave," varying in width from one to three feet. South of this point, the natural level of the land ranges one to two feet above lake level. The land slopes generally toward the lake but has a slope less than twelve per cent. No water flows onto the land from the lake, but there is some surface water which collects on land and stands in pools.

The land owned by the Justs is designated as swamps or marshes on the United States Geological Survey Map and is located within 1,000 feet of the normal high-water elevation of the lake. Thus, the property is included in a conservancy district and ... classified as "wetlands." Consequently, in order to place more than 500 square feet of fill on this property, the Justs were required to obtain a conditional-use permit from the zoning administrator of the county and pay a fee of $20 or incur a forfeiture of $10 to $200 for each day of violation.

[S]ix months after the ordinance became effective, Ronald Just, without securing a conditional-use permit, hauled 1,040 square yards of sand onto this property and filled an area approximately 20–feet wide commencing at the southwest corner and extending almost 600 feet north to the northwest corner near the shoreline, then easterly along the shoreline almost to the lot line. He stayed back from the pressure ridge about 20 feet. More than 500 square feet of this fill was upon wetlands located contiguous to the water and which had surface drainage toward the lake. The fill

(7) Piers, Docks, boathouses.

within 300 feet of the lake also was more than 2,000 square feet on a slope less than 12 percent. It is not seriously contended that the Justs did not violate the ordinance and the trial court correctly found a violation.

The real issue is whether the conservancy district provisions and the wetlands filling restrictions are unconstitutional because they amount to a constructive taking of the Justs' land without compensation. Marinette county and the state of Wisconsin argue the restrictions of the conservancy district and wetlands provisions constitute a proper exercise of the police power of the state and do not so severely limit the use or depreciate the value of the land as to constitute a taking without compensation.

To state the issue more meaningful terms, it is a conflict between the public interest in stopping the despoliation of natural resources, which our citizens until recently have taken as inevitable and for granted, and an owner's asserted right to use his property as he wishes. The protection of public rights may be accomplished by the exercise of the police power unless the damage to the property owner is too great and amounts to a confiscation. The securing or taking of a benefit not presently enjoyed by the public for its use is obtained by the government through its power of eminent domain. The distinction between the exercise of the police power and condemnation has been said to be a matter of degree of damage to the property owner. In the valid exercise of the police power reasonably restricting the use of property, the damage suffered by the owner is said to be incidental. However, where the restriction is so great the landowner ought not to bear such a burden for the public good, the restriction has been held to be a constructive taking even though the actual use or forbidden use has not been transferred to the government so as to be a taking in the traditional sense. [ ] Whether a taking has occurred depends upon whether "the restriction practically or substantially renders the land useless for all reasonable purposes." [ ] The loss caused the individual must be weighed to determine if it is more than he should bear. As this court stated ... "... if the damage is such as to be suffered by many similarly situated and is in the nature of a restriction on the use to which land may be put and ought to be borne by the individual as a member of society for the good of the public safety, health or general welfare, it is said to be a reasonable exercise of the police power, but if the damage is so great to the individual that he ought not to bear it under contemporary standards, then courts are inclined to treat it as a 'taking' of the property or an unreasonable exercise of the police power."

Many years ago, Professor Freund stated in his work on *The Police Power*, § 511, at 546–547, "It may be said that the state takes property by eminent domain because it is useful to the public, and under the police power because it is harmful.... From this results the difference between the power of eminent domain and the police power, that the former recognizes a right to compensation, while the latter on principle does not." Thus the necessity for monetary compensation for loss suffered to an owner by police power restriction arises when restrictions are placed on property in order to create a public benefit rather than to prevent a public harm. [ ]

This case causes us to reexamine the concepts of public benefit in contrast to public harm and the scope of an owner's right to use of his property. In the instant case we have a restriction on the use of a citizens' property, not to secure a benefit for the public, but to prevent a harm from the change in the natural character of the citizens' property. We start with the premise that lakes and rivers in their natural state are unpolluted and the pollution which now exists is man made. The state of Wisconsin under the trust doctrine has a duty to eradicate the present pollution and to prevent further pollution in its navigable waters. This is not, in a legal sense, a gain or a securing of a benefit by the maintaining of the natural *status quo* of the environment. What makes this case different from most condemnation or police power zoning cases is the interrelationship of the wetlands, the swamps and the natural environment of shorelands to the purity of the water and to such natural resources as navigation, fishing, and scenic beauty. Swamps and wetlands were once considered wasteland, undesirable, and not picturesque. But as the people became more sophisticated, an appreciation was acquired that swamps and wetlands serve a vital role in nature, are part of the balance of nature and are essential to the purity of the water in our lakes and streams. Swamps and wetlands, are a necessary part of the ecological creation and now, even to the uninitiated, possess their own beauty in nature.

Is the ownership of a parcel of land so absolute that man can change its nature to suit any of his purposes? The great forests of our state were stripped on the theory man's ownership was unlimited. But in forestry, the land at least was used naturally, only the natural fruit of the land (the trees) were taken. The despoilage was in the failure to look to the future and provide for the reforestation of the land. An owner of land has no absolute and unlimited right to change the essential natural character of his land so as to use it for a purpose for which it was unsuited in its natural state and which injures the rights of others. The exercise of the police power in zoning must be reasonable and we think it is not an unreasonable exercise of that power to prevent harm to public rights by limiting the use of private property to its natural uses.

This is not a case where an owner is prevented from using his land for natural and indigenous uses. The uses consistent with the nature of the land are allowed and other uses recognized and still others permitted by special permit. The shoreland zoning ordinance prevents to some extent the changing of the natural character of the land within 1,000 feet of a navigable lake and 300 feet of a navigable river because of such land's interrelation to the contiguous water. The changing of wetlands and swamps to the damage of the general public by upsetting the natural environment and the natural relationship is not a reasonable use of that land which is protected from police power regulation. Changes and filling to some extent are permitted because the extent of such changes and fillings does not cause harm. We realize no case in Wisconsin has yet dealt with shoreland regulations and there are several cases in other states which seem to hold such regulations unconstitutional; but nothing this court has said or held in prior cases indicate that destroying the natural character of a swamp or a wetland so as to make that location available for human habitation is a reasonable use of that land when the new use, although of a more economical value to the owner, causes a harm to the general public.

Wisconsin has long held that laws and regulations to prevent pollution and to protect the waters of this state from degradation are valid police-power enactments. [ ] The active public trust duty of the state of Wisconsin in respect to navigable waters requires the state not only to promote navigation but also to protect and preserve those waters for fishing, recreation, and scenic beauty. [ ] To further this duty, the legislature may delegate authority to local units of the government, which the state did by requiring counties to pass shoreland zoning ordinances. [ ]

. . .

The Judgment in case number 106, dismissing the Justs' action, is modified to set forth the declaratory adjudication that the shoreland zoning ordinance of respondent Marinette County is constitutional; that the Justs' property constitutes wetlands and that particularly the prohibition in the ordinance against the filling of wetlands is constitutional; and the judgment, as so modified, is affirmed.

NOTES

(1) Although *Just* is only indirectly a wildlife case, it does illustrate the most critical issue surrounding the survival of most species: the preservation of habitat. Most declining species are at risk, not because of overharvesting, but because of habitat loss and degradation, often from the kind of land-development efforts that the Justs wanted to undertake. Laws protecting habitat thus are wildlife laws. Like many other wildlife laws, such laws serve conservation aims—in this case, the conservation not just of wildlife but of entire ecosystems, which perform valuable functions other than providing home and food for wildlife. Wetlands, for instance, provide valuable services in moderating flooding and improving water quality, in addition to their functions as spawning grounds for fish and other aquatic life and feeding and nesting grounds for waterfowl.

(2) The key legal issue in *Just* was a constitutional one: Did the county ordinances lead to an unconstitutional taking of the Justs' private property so as to entitle them to the payment of "just compensation"? This is the "regulatory takings issue" that is common in land-use law generally. To rephrase the issue: Has a regulation so severely interfered with an owner's rights as to be tantamount to physical confiscation, thus triggering the constitutional duty for government to pay for the rights taken?

The regulatory taking doctrine provides a limit on how far lawmakers can go in restricting the use of private land—for wildlife as well as other purposes. We return to this issue in Chapter 6.

(3) In the years since it was decided, *Just* has remained a much-discussed decision, less because of what it said about regulatory takings than for its vision of what it means to own land. The Justs assumed that, as landowners, they had the right to fill in their wetlands for the purposes of development. The law limiting their ability to do so, they claimed, diminished their rights. Note how the court responded to this argument. In the court's view, the inherent rights that the Justs held were shaped and limited by the natural features of the land and the uses to which the land could be put in its natural condition. At least in constitutional terms their rights did not extend to land uses premised on the material alteration of the land.

The test that the court used in resolving the constitutional claim is often referred to as the harm-benefit test. It looks to whether a challenged law halts a landowner from engaging in harmful conduct (which the law can do without compensation) or whether instead it asks a landowner to confer a benefit on the public (which often requires compensation). But which of the two is happening in *Just*? The court grounded its decision in the fact that filling wetlands is a harmful activity because of its impacts on water flows, water quality, and wildlife. As the court saw things, the county ordinance banned a harmful activity. Can the decision also be fairly characterized as forcing the Justs to devote their lands to a public use—as a wildlife sanctuary or a flood control/water purification zone? Did not the law, that is, ask them to confer a benefit on the public? Does the answer depend in part upon how one chooses to define the status quo? That is, are all harms and benefits simply a matter of one's perspective? *Cf.* Ronald Coase, *The Problem of Social Cost*, 3 J.L. & ECON. 1 (1960) (railroads and wheat farmers each impose potential costs on the other party).

To raise this question is to highlight the importance, when applying the harm-benefit test, of having an agreed-upon understanding of which land uses are harmful. When such an understanding exists, the test is relatively easy to apply. Most people would agree, for example, that discharging toxic wastes into a river is harmful; thus, a law that restricts or bans such discharges should not entitle a polluter to compensation. On the other hand, most people would also agree that a zoning ordinance requiring a landowner to devote land to "park purposes" goes too far: it is aimed, not at halting a harm, but at requiring the landowner to devote private land to a public use. How can we apply the test when the existence of a harm is disputed? And what happens when socially accepted ideas of harm are in transition? Many of the environmental problems on which the United States has made the *least* progress are problems that stem from ecologically damaging land uses, including the alteration of wildlife habitat. How do we draw the line when deciding which of these are sufficiently harmful for society to ban them without compensation?

We shall return to this vital issue later, in the specific context of considering laws aimed at protecting wildlife habitat. Before moving on, however, a few key points deserve mention:

(**a**) *Just* is perhaps best understood, not as a constitutional case, but as a case about the shifting meaning of private land ownership. In the United States, property rights are a creation of law, mostly state law, and the laws governing private property have always been subject to change. Ownership norms evolve along with society, however slowly and unobtrusively. *Just*, then, can be seen as simply another step in a continuing process of change.

(**b**) One way to describe the change in *Just* (and in similar cases) is that property law is gradually embracing new definitions of land-use harm. Property law has long banned owners from engaging in harmful land uses—with the meaning of "harm" dependent on the context and evolving social values. With the advent of the environmental age, land uses formerly viewed as innocuous if not beneficial have become viewed as harmful.

(c) Another way to describe *Just* is to say that property law is becoming less abstract: that is, the rights of property ownership are being defined with greater attention to the peculiar features and circumstances of the land that is owned. The rights that an owner has in parcel *A* might well differ from the rights held in parcel *B*, simply because the parcels themselves are physically different—one is sloping and the other flat; one is stable and the other unstable; one is high and dry, the other subject to periodic flooding. In other words, the land itself ought to play a role in the definition of private property rights.

If *Just* is a good indicator of the future of landed property rights, what changes might take place relevant to wildlife law? Might the destruction of important wildlife habitat one day be viewed as a type of land-use harm, akin to dumping toxic wastes? Might current trends lead to a sense that landowners everywhere have a "fair share" duty to leave room for wildlife or to make reasonable accommodations for wildlife?

Aldo Leopold, The Land Ethic *in* A Sand County Almanac
201–26 (1949).

When god-like Odysseus returned from the wars in Troy, he hanged all on one rope a dozen slave-girls of his household whom he suspected of misbehavior during his absence.

This hanging involved no question of propriety. The girls were property. The disposal of property was then, as now, a matter of expediency, not of right and wrong.

Concepts of right and wrong were not lacking from Odysseus' Greece: witness the fidelity of his wife through the long years before at last his black-prowed galleys dove the wine-dark seas for home. The ethical structure of that day covered wives, but had not yet been extended to human chattels. During the three thousand years which have since elapsed, ethical criteria have been extended to many fields of conduct, with corresponding shrinkages in those judged by expediency only.

The Ethical Sequence

This extension of ethics, so far studied only by philosophers, is actually a process in ecological evolution. Its sequences may be described in ecological as well as in philosophical terms. An ethic, ecologically, is a limitation on freedom of action in the struggle for existence. An ethic, philosophically, is a differentiation of social from anti-social conduct. These are two definitions of one thing. The thing has its origin in the tendency of interdependent individuals or groups to evolve modes of co-operation. The ecologist calls these symbioses. Politics and economics are advanced symbioses in which the original free-for-all competition has been replaced, in part, by co-operative mechanisms with an ethical content.

The complexity of co-operative mechanisms has increased with population density, and with the efficiency of tools. It was simpler, for example, to define the anti-social uses of sticks and stones in the days of the mastodons than of bullets and billboards in the age of motors.

The first ethics dealt with the relation between individuals; the Mosaic Decalogue is an example. Later accretions dealt with the relation between the individual and society. The Golden Rule tries to integrate the individual to society; democracy to integrate social organization to the individual.

There is as yet no ethic dealing with man's relation to land and to the animals and plants which grow upon it. Land, like Odysseus' slave-girls, is still property. The land-relation is still strictly economic, entailing privileges but not obligations.

The extension of ethics to this third element in human environment is, if I read the evidence correctly, an evolutionary possibility and an ecological necessity. It is the third step in a sequence. The first two have already been taken. Individual thinkers since the days of Ezekiel and Isaiah have asserted that the despoliation of land is not only inexpedient but wrong. Society, however, has not yet affirmed their belief. I regard the present conservation movement as the embryo of such an affirmation.

An ethic may be regarded as a mode of guidance for meeting ecological situations so new or intricate, or involving such deferred reactions, that the path of social expediency is not discernible to the average individual. Animal instincts are modes of guidance for the individual in meeting such situations. Ethics are possibly a kind of community instinct in-the-making.

The Community Concept

All ethics so far evolved rest upon a single premise: that the individual is a member of a community of interdependent parts. His instincts prompt him to compete for his place in that community, but his ethics prompt him also to co-operate (perhaps in order that there may be a place to compete for).

The land ethic simply enlarges the boundaries of the community to include soils, waters, plants, and animals, or collectively: the land.

This sounds simple: do we not already sing our love for and obligation to the land of the free and the home of the brave? Yes, but just what and whom do we love? Certainly not the soil, which we are sending helter-skelter downriver. Certainly not the waters, which we assume have no function except to turn turbines, float barges, and carry off sewage. Certainly not the plants, of which we exterminate whole communities without batting an eye. Certainly not the animals, of which we have already extirpated many of the largest and most beautiful species. A land ethic of course cannot prevent the alteration, management, and use of these "resources," but it does affirm their right to continued existence, and, at least in spots, their continued existence in a natural state.

In short, a land ethic changes the role of *Homo sapiens* from conqueror of the land-community to plain member and citizen of it. It implies respect for his fellow-members, and also respect for the community as such.

NOTES

(1) The land ethic crafted and articulated by Aldo Leopold[5] is the most visible and celebrated of all holistic visions of humans interacting ethically with the land. Unlike Regan, Singer, and other writers concerned with the treatment of individual organism, Leopold focused his gaze more broadly—on the entire, interdependent community of life, including humans. He encouraged readers to think of nature in just this way—as a community of which they were members. As an ethical matter, we should live, he claimed, in ways that sustained the healthy functioning of this indispensable whole, for the good of ourselves and other life forms. Leopold's masterpiece, *A Sand County Almanac and Sketches Here and There* (1949), is viewed by many as the most important conservation book of twentieth-century America, in part (although only in part) for the ultimate essay in it, from which the above excerpt was taken. A pioneering wildlife ecologist, Leopold was also the author of *Game Management* (1933), the first scientific text on managing lands ecologically for wildlife purposes. He was also the first professor of wildlife management in the United States, and as such was instrumental in shaping the new field.

We shall return to Leopold's thought later, paying particular attention to the idea of "land health" that came to guide his mature thoughts on conservation.

(2) Leopold as a closet utilitarian? Leopold subsequently writes "[a] thing is right when it tends to preserve the integrity, stability, and beauty of the biotic community. It is wrong when it tends otherwise." Aldo Leopold, *The Land Ethic, in* SAND COUNTY ALMANAC 201, 224–25 (1949). Does this differ significantly from the utilitarian position that what is right is what produces the greatest good for the greatest number? Is Peter Singer Leopold's heir?

(3) Holistic vs. individualistic: Holistic visions of the type that Leopold embraced have had far more influence on the modern environmental movement than have ethical visions centered on individual animals, particularly visions such as Regan's that protect only the most biologically advanced organisms. Yet, as an ethical (rather than ecological) matter, moral schemes that focus on abstract components of nature such as species and ecosystems have also drawn criticism. The following excerpt considers that criticism, and distinguishes between individualistic and holistic approaches to our dealings with the rest of nature:

> For many centuries, Western philosophy has assumed that moral worth in the universe lies at the level of the individual organism. This assumption became stronger with the advent of modern science and its claim that all matter was composed of atoms and molecules, the building blocks of life. Modern science promoted a focus that was

5. Aldo Leopold (1886–1948) was an American ecologist who advocated a "land ethic" emphasizing that humans were part of the natural community. While working for the Forest Service in New Mexico, he succeeded in having the Gila Wilderness created; it was the first extensive wilderness area set aside in the United States. He subsequently taught wildlife management at the University of Wisconsin. He is perhaps best known for his posthumously published book of essays, *A Sand County Almanac* (1949).

atomistic and individualistic; both human society and nature as a whole, it seemed, were mere collections of distinct, discrete objects interacting according to the physical laws of motion, however we might categorize them scientifically.

This individualistic focus began to weaken as evolution studies showed the connections among species. But it has been the new science of ecology, born in the twentieth century, that has been the primary stimulus for a new view of life. Ecology is the study of how an organism interacts with its environment. The principal lesson of ecology is that no organism stands alone, no organism can live for long without constant interactions with other organisms and inanimate life, to gain oxygen, water, food, and shelter and in due course to reproduce. Many species live in symbiotic or social relationships and would die in isolation. As more is learned about the complex interactions among life forms, it becomes increasingly clear that the line between the individual and the environment is thin and indistinct. Indeed, for some scientists an individual organism is less a separate piece of life than a focal point or node through which nutrients and energy flow; the individual is fully defined by its interactions.

In important ways, the building blocks of nature are species, communities, and ecosystems. Many philosophers have picked up on this point to assert that moral worth really lies as these higher levels of organization. It is not the individual deer that counts; it is the deer herd or the fir-spruce-aspen ecosystem of which it is a part. Individual animals come and go; value and duty lie in the maintenance of a healthy population in a livable environment.

Philosophers who embrace this view are term "holistic thinkers." Some holistic philosophers believer that all value rests at the species or ecosystem level and that individual organisms get their value only indirectly, by being a part of that larger entity. Others are prone to divide up moral value at the first stage, giving some to entities and some to individual organisms, with some organisms perhaps receiving more than others (as in the multigroup conception) based on higher levels of mental functioning. What distinguishes all of them is a desire to protect healthy wild populations, which translates readily into a concern for protecting nature areas and habitats rather than individual specimens.

Within academic circles this push to attribute moral value to species and ecosystems has not gone unchallenged. The problem, in brief, is that species and ecosystems are intangibles; they are mental constructs or categories that have no physical existence apart from their individual components. A black-footed ferret is a physical object, with a functioning nervous system and an ability to feel pain. The species of black-footed ferrets is nothing more than an idea, an intellectual way to organize all the individual, real-life members. If moral value arises from an ability to think or to feel pain, no species or ecosystem has value.

Holistic philosophers offer varied response to this challenge. Some claim that species and ecosystems do have interests and preferences that are sufficiently strong and distinct to form the locus of moral value. Others attribute moral value in a far different manner, by relying on their deep-seated sentiments about the functioning and interrelatedness of all life on Earth, sentiments that have been distinctly informed and molded by the lessons of ecology. Finally, there are some who claim that species and ecosystems have intrinsic moral value because ecologically informed human observers are around to create and recognize that value. . . .

The importance of holistic thinking, and the extent of its break from our inherited philosophic tradition, can be seen in the distinct strain that exists today between holistic philosophers and animals welfare advocates. The outside observer might assume not just kinship by shared living quarters between these seemingly close compatriots. In fact, their differences are considerable and harsh words have been spoken. Many holistic philosophers, in fact, feel more comfortable with hunters than with animal liberationists.

The claim that holistic thinkers make against animal welfare advocates is that the latter have little sense of ecological balance or are ignoring it if they have it. They don't appreciate that animals must kill one another, and populations must be kept in balance, either naturally or, as needed, by human intervention. If deer populations are too great, they must shrink to avoid habitat destruction, which will harm the deer in the long run. It makes little sense to feed starving deer when the starvation stems from a population too large for its home. If we want to aid deer we should do so naturally, by developing new deer habitat and then leaving them alone.

The responding charge made by those who value the individual organism is, in its starkest form, that of fascism. To the animal welfare advocate, the claim of moral worth at the group level sounds frighteningly like the political claim that the state is all and the individual is nothing. It sounds disturbingly like the idea that individual humans can be freely sacrificed in the name of the nation. If we are to sacrifice individuals for the common good, who is going to make the deadly decisions?

One obvious way around this conflict is to say that holistic reasoning only applies to our dealings with *nonhuman* nature. Among humans we can employ a different moral scheme, one that retains moral value at the individual level. If we follow this approach, as many philosophers have, one set of moral rules will apply to dealings among humans; another set will govern the dealings between humans and the rest of nature. In some manner, these two sets of rules must be knit together with what philosophers call second-order rules—rules that help resolve conflicts when ethical norms among humans point us one way and ethical obligations to nature push us in another.

In many settings, the argument between holistic thinkers and animal welfare advocates is an artificial one, easily set aside. Much of the animal welfare drive has sought to improve the treatment of domesticated animals and wild animals in human captivity. Because these animals are removed from healthy functioning ecosystems, they contribute nothing to ecosystem health. Our dealings with these animals cannot be based on any duty to respect and protect functioning ecosystems; if we have duties, it is to the animals as individuals, not as members of some group. Because these animals are entirely dependent upon humans, they would seem to be in a different moral category from animals in the wild, and different moral rules would seem appropriate. On this issue, it is the reasoning of the animal welfare advocates, not that of holistic thinkers, that is likely to prove most useful.

ERIC T. FREYFOGLE, JUSTICE AND THE EARTH: IMAGES FOR OUR PLANETARY SURVIVAL 80–84 (1993).

(4) Individual worth and species preservation: The disagreement between individualistic and holistic ethical approaches to nature is far more than just an academic debate—it also impacts on-the-ground management decisions:

[In November, 1998,] 58 percent of [California] voters approved a leghold-trap ban called Proposition Four, thereby depriving wildlife managers of their only effective tool for controlling alien red foxes from the East. The foxes, which were brought to California in the 19th century, are in the process of wiping out such endangered birds as the California least tern, the California clapper rail, and the light-footed clapper rail, as well as the threatened western snowy plover. But some animal rights activists would gladly sacrifice whole species to prevent what they perceive as the inhumane treatment of individual animals.

Animal rights groups have told the California Department of Fish and Game that eastern red foxes are "native" because they've been in the state for more than a century and that they should not be killed but caught in humane box traps (even though they won't go into them) and sent to "other states" (even though the other states have said no thanks). Five years ago noted ornithologist and ecologist Lloyd Kiff called alien red foxes the "litmus test that determines whether people are conservationists or animal rights people" and went on to make this prophetic observation: "If not checked soon, [red foxes] will account for more extinctions of bird species than any other single factor in history. These people would rather have red foxes than all these 'weird' birds. If it were put to a vote, I don't know whether we would win this one."

Red foxes nearly wiped out a least tern colony on Anaheim Bay. In 1988 they took eggs from 44 of 69 least tern nests. When the U.S. Fish and Wildlife Service started trapping, in 1986, animal rights groups sued for an injunction, lost, then won an appeal in 1988 that forced the agency to prepare a full-blown environmental impact statement, which cost $500,000. But as a result of the trapping, the tern population has rebounded to about 200 nests. Farther north, in the refuges around San Francisco Bay, foxes and cats had reduced clapper rails from 1,500 in 1980 to 300 in 1991. In the past eight years the Fish and Wildlife Service has removed 458 foxes and 136 feral cats. As a result the rail population has more than doubled.

Despite such successes, the agency ceased trapping everywhere in the state after Proposition Four was voted in. While the federal Endangered Species Act supersedes any state statute, the Fish and Wildlife Service doesn't like to make waves and therefore has a policy of obeying state laws.

Ted Williams, *Management by Majority,* AUDUBON, May–June 1999, at 40, 45–46. *See also National Audubon Society v. Davis*, 144 F.Supp.2d 1160 (N.D.Cal.2000) (suit challenging applicability of state anti-trapping proposition in which animal rights advocates joined as defendants; proposition held preempted by Endangered Species Act).

For animal welfare/animal rights advocates such as Singer and Regan, red foxes and feral cats—because they are cognitively more complex—are likely to be more intrinsically valuable and hence more worthy of moral consideration than endangered clapper rails. As Regan has written, his animal-rights view often works against endangered species: "If, in a prevention[-of-harm] situation, we had to choose between saving the last two members of an endangered species or saving another individual who belonged to a species that was plentiful but whose death would be a greater prima facie harm to that individual than the harm that the death would be to the two, then the rights view requires that we save the individual." TOM REGAN, THE CASE FOR ANIMAL RIGHTS 359 (1983).

Singer has reached the same conclusion: "While individual animals have interests, and no morally defensible line can be drawn between human interests and the interests of nonhuman animals, species as such are not conscious entities and so do not have interests above and beyond the interests of the individual animals that are members of the species. These individual interests ... are no more potent [reasons against killing the individual animal] in the case of rare animals than in the case of common animals." He concludes that there are no intrinsic reasons for preserving endangered species as endangered species: "unless or until better grounds are advanced, the only reasons for being more concerned about interests of animals from endangered species than about other animals are those which relate the preservation of species to benefits for humans and other animals." Peter Singer, *Not for Humans Only: The Place of Non–Humans in Environmental Issues, in* ETHICS AND PROBLEMS OF THE 21ST CENTURY 191, 203, 204 (K.E. Goodpasture & K.M. Sayre, eds., 1979).

Note also that it would arguably be consistent with Singer's and Regan's position to remove all of the clapper rails from the wild, place them in a food rich environment, and prevent them from breeding—thus exterminating the species but not inflicting suffering on any individuals. *See* BRYAN NORTON, WHY PRESERVE NATURAL VARIETY? 168 (1987) (the intrinsic value of species cannot be established with theories that employ the intrinsic value of individuals).

(5) The role of wildlife in the economy of the United States— psychological contributions (pt. 2): In their study of the value of wildlife to humans, the Prescott–Allens divided the types of psychological uses of wildlife into recreational, scientific/educational, aesthetic, and religious/symbolic.

(a) recreational uses were discussed above.

(b) scientific/educational: The human drive to understand the world currently is expressed largely in terms of science—and animals play a large role in the natural sciences. Some of the roles are at least partially quantifiable in economic terms: animals that are used as subjects for experiment, for example, are assigned a value by the market. Similarly, science often blends into engineering, producing products for the market: basic scientific work on DNA, for example, has led to genetic engineering and a large number of potential products. Much of science, however, is unlikely to lead (at least immediately) to marketable commodities—for example, assigning dollar values to research into the genetic relationship between groups of animals or the dietary requirements of voles becomes increasingly unrealistic: the "value" is expressed not in dollars but in an increased understanding of the world of which we are a part.

(c) aesthetic and religious/symbolic: The unreality of proxy values becomes absurdity when applied to the aesthetic and religious or symbolic uses of wildlife. The late Paul Shepard, by training a wildlife biologist and in spirit a philosopher, has argued that animals are what made us human. They were the other that was both different and the same. Our interaction with them, he argued, formed the basis for cognition: they were our first categories, the beginning of abstraction. The residue remains in the metaphors we retain—foxes are cunning, coyote is a trickster—scattered across the night sky as constellations—ursa major and minor, cancer the crab, leo—in the basic positions of yoga—the lion, the cat, the camel. PAUL SHEPARD, THE OTHERS: HOW ANIMALS MADE US HUMAN (1996).

Cleanth Brooks and Robert Penn Warren expressed a similar idea:

language did not develop in a mechanically "pure" form, without the contamination of emotion, but in a form that embodied and expressed the density of experience—the interpenetration of stimulus and response, of object and perception, of idea and emotion, of action and feeling. The word for "bear" not only pointed in a disinterested fashion to a certain kind of creature, but also embodied "bearness"—the terror, awe, power, majesty, and other qualities associated with that creature. Furthermore, language developed in a more specifically metaphorical way by embodying the relation of thing to thing as expressions of human response and feeling. One might be like another in various ways. A man might be like a bear, or a bear like a man, not merely by, let us say, their common ability to stand erect. A certain tribe might be "of the bear," and a member of the tribe would carry a certain "bearness" in him. Or the massive power of the stroke of the bear's paw might equate "bear" with "storm" or "storm" with "bear." The naming process might, in fact, embody such relations. When we find in the Anglo–Saxon poem *Beowulf* the sea being called the "swan's way" or the "whale's bath," we stand at a kind of crossroads: one road leads back to the naming process in the development of language, and the other leads forward toward metaphor as we know it. . . .

CLEANTH BROOKS & ROBERT PENN WARREN, UNDERSTANDING POETRY 4 (4th ed. 1976).

Aldo Leopold, On a Monument to the Pigeon *in* A SAND COUNTY ALMANAC

108–12 (1949).

We have erected a monument to commemorate the funeral of a species. It symbolizes our sorrow. We grieve because no living man will see again the onrushing phalanx of victorious birds, sweeping a path for spring across the March skies, chasing the defeated winter from all the woods and prairies of Wisconsin.

Men still live who, in their youth, remember pigeons. Trees still live who, in their youth, were shaken by a living wind. But a decade hence only the oldest oaks will remember, and at long last only the hills will know.

There will always be pigeons in books and in museum, but these are effigies and images, dead to all hardships and to all delights. Book-pigeons cannot dive out of a cloud to make the deer run for cover, or clap their wings in thunderous applause of mast-laden woods. Book-pigeons cannot breakfast on new-mown wheat in Minnesota, and dine on blueberries in Canada. They know no urge of seasons; they feel no kiss of sun, no lash of wind and weather. They live forever by not living at all.

Our grandfathers were less well-housed, well-fed, well-clothed than we are. The strivings by which they bettered their lot are also those which deprived us of pigeons. Perhaps we now grieve because we are not sure, in our hearts, that we have gained by the exchange. The gadgets of industry bring us much more comforts than the pigeons did, but do they add as much to the glory of the spring?

It is a century now since Darwin gave us the first glimpse of the origin of species. We know now what was unknown to all the preceding caravan of generations: that men are only fellow-voyagers with other creatures in the odyssey of evolution. This new knowledge should have given us, by this time, a sense of kinship with fellow-creatures; a wish to live and let live; a sense of wonder over the magnitude and duration of the biotic enterprise.

Above all we should, in the century since Darwin, have come to know that man, while now captain of the adventuring ship, is hardly the sole object of its quest, and that his prior assumptions to this effect arose from the simple necessity of whistling in the dark.

These things, I say, should have come to us. I fear they have not come to many.

For one species to mourn the death of another is a new thing under the sun. The Cro–Magnon who slew the last mammoth thought only of steaks. The sportsman who shot the last pigeon thought only of his prowess. The sailor who clubbed the last auk thought of nothing at all. But we, who have lost our pigeons would hardly have mourned us. In this fact, rather than in Mr. DuPont's nylons or Mr. Vannevar Bush's bombs, lies objective evidence of our superiority over the beasts.

* * *

This monument, perched like a duckhawk on this cliff, will scan this wide valley, watching through the days and years. For many a March it will watch the geese go by, telling the river about clearer, colder, lonelier waters on the tundra. For many an April it will see the redbuds come and go, and for many a May the flush of oak-blooms on a thousand hills. Questing wood ducks will search these basswoods for hollow limbs; golden prothonotaries will shake golden pollen from the river willows. Egrets will pose on these sloughs in August; plovers will whistle from September skies. Hickory nuts will plop into October leaves, and hail will rattle in November woods. But no pigeons will pass, for there are no pigeons, save only this flightless one, graven in bronze on this rock. Tourists will read this inscription, but their thoughts will not take wing.

We are told by economic moralists that to mourn the pigeon is mere nostalgia; that if the pigeoners had not done away with him, the farmers would ultimately have been obliged, in self-defense, to do so.

This is one of those peculiar truths that are valid, but not for the reasons alleged.

The pigeon was a biological storm. He was the lightning that played between two opposing potentials of intolerable intensity: the fat of the land and the oxygen of the air. Yearly the feathered tempest roared up, down, and across the continent, sucking up the laden fruits of forest and prairie, burning them in a traveling blast of life. Like any other chain reaction, the pigeon could survive no diminution of his own furious intensity. When the pigeoners subtracted from his numbers, and the pioneers chopped gaps in the continuity of his fuel, his flame guttered out with hardly a sputter or even a wisp of smoke.

Today the oaks still flaunt their burden at the sky, but the feathered lightning is no more. Worm and weevil must now perform slowly and silently the biological task that once drew thunder from the firmament.

The wonder is not that the pigeon went out, but that he ever survived through all the millennia of pre-Babbittian time.

* * *

The pigeon loved his land: he lived by the intensity of his desire for clustered grape and bursting beechnut, and by his contempt of miles and seasons. Whatever Wisconsin did not offer him gratis today, he sought and found tomorrow in Michigan, or Labrador, or Tennessee. His love was for present things, and these things were present somewhere; to find them required only the free sky, and the will to ply his wings.

To love what was is a new thing under the sun, unknown to most people and to all pigeons. To see America as history, to conceive of destiny as a becoming, to smell a hickory tree through the still lapse of ages—all these things are possible for us, and to achieve them takes only the free sky, and the will to ply our wings. In these things, and not in Mr. Bush's bombs and Mr. DuPont's nylons, lies objective evidence of our superiority over the beasts.

PERSPECTIVES

Individuals and populations—the parable of the pigeon: In the autumn of 1813, the ornithologist and artist John James Audubon left his home in Henderson, Kentucky to ride to Louisville. A few miles beyond Hardensburgh, he observed a flight of passenger pigeons flying overhead.

> [F]eeling an inclination to count the flocks that might pass within the reach of my eye within one hour, I dismounted, seated myself on an eminence, and began to mark with my pencil, making a dot for every flock that passed. In a short time, finding the task which I had undertaken impracticable, as the birds poured in countless multitudes, I rose, and counting the dots then put down, found that one hundred and sixty-three had been made in twenty-one minutes.... The air was literally filled with pigeons; the light of noonday was obscured as by an eclipse.

JOHN JAMES AUDUBON, ORNITHOLOGICAL BIOGRAPHY *reprinted in* W.B. MERSHON, THE PASSENGER PIGEON 25, 28 (1907). Pigeons continued to pass "in undiminished numbers" for the rest of the fifty-five miles to Louisville "and continued to do so for three days in succession." Audubon estimated that at times more than 300,000,000 pigeons flew by each hour; he also estimated that the flock covered an area of 180 square miles and contained 1,150,-136,000 individuals. The ornithologist Alexander Wilson reported an earlier flight that he estimated contained more than 2 billion birds. ALEXANDER WILSON, WILSON'S AMERICAN ORNITHOLOGY 399 (T.M. Brewer ed., Boston, Otis, Broaders & Co. 1840) (photo. reprint 1970).

The passenger pigeon was endemic to the deciduous forest ecosystem of eastern North America. The species was highly gregarious and nested in colonies containing millions of breeding pairs. One nesting colony in Wisconsin in 1871 covered 850 square miles and contained at least 135,-000,000 adults. The sheer number of birds in a flock was a critical adaptive strategy: "By traveling and nesting in such large groups each pigeon was essentially shielded from predators, a concept known as predator satiation. Wherever the pigeons went there were not enough local predators to seriously detract from their numbers." David E. Blockstein & Harrison B. Tordoff, *A Contemporary Look at the Extinction of the Passenger Pigeon*, 39 AM. BIRDS 845, 846 (1985). This strategy extended to reproduction; nesting was highly synchronous with most eggs laid on a single day. The beech, oak, and chestnut trees that provided the pigeon's dominant food employed a similar strategy: every few years the trees in a particular area would produce a super-abundant crop of nuts that overwhelmed their local seed predators. The pigeons roamed the countryside until they found an area with a heavy mast crop, where they would remain until that crop was exhausted.

The pigeon was probably the most abundant bird on the planet when Audubon recorded his sighting. It existed in such prodigious numbers that it seemed an inexhaustible resource. In 1857, a select committee of the Ohio Senate urged rejection of legislation to restrict hunting since "[t]he passenger pigeon needs no protection. Wonderfully prolific, ... no ordinary destruction can lessen them or be missed from the myriads that are yearly produced." T.S. PALMER, UNITED STATES DEPARTMENT OF AGRICULTURE, BIOLOGICAL SURVEY BULLETIN NO. 41, CHRONOLOGY AND INDEX OF THE MORE IMPORTANT EVENTS IN AMERICAN GAME PROTECTION, 1776–1911 18 (1912).

Pigeons, however, were tasty; they were also used as live predecessors of today's clay "pigeons." Their gregarious habits made them easy to capture or kill: reports of killing a dozen or more with one shot-gun blast are common and they were netted by the thousands. As long as hunting was restricted to subsistence needs, the pigeon population withstood the pressure. It could not, however, withstand market demand. Although commercial marketing of pigeons became a major industry after 1840, it was not until after the Civil War that the nineteenth century's most advanced technology was available in the service of the pigeon netters. The railroad (with its rapid transportation), the refrigerator car (which prevented spoilage), and the telegraph opened markets in eastern cities and allowed netters to determine the locations of nestings.[1] The tonnage of birds shipped to market is as staggering as the reports of their migratory flights: from an 1869 nesting in Michigan more than 7,500,000 pigeons were shipped; in 1874, 40–50 tons of squabs—unfledged nestlings—were shipped from Newaygo County, Michigan and another 1,075,000 pigeons were shipped to market from nearby Shelby. The last large nesting was in Petoskey, Michigan in 1878; the colony covered approximately 100 square miles.

Despite their best efforts, however, the pigeoners did not kill the last pigeons. Market hunting ended when it was no longer profitable—which was before the last pigeon was killed because the profit was in volume: each pigeon was worth comparatively little. During the 1882 season, for example, pigeons costs between $0.35 and $1.00 per dozen. A.W. Schorger, The Passenger Pigeon 217 (1955). Thus the anomaly: "The puzzling aspect of the passenger pigeon's demise lies in the fact that during the last years of its existence the species continued to decline at a rate that seems too great to be accounted for simply by hunting."

Current explanations for the demise of the pigeon focuses on the species' colonial nesting habits. Examination of other colonial nesting species has demonstrated that it has adaptive advantages such as enhancing feeding efficiency and swamping local populations of predators. As one review concludes: "Nest success in these last small colonies and by the lone pairs must have been pitifully low. Without the numerical protection provided by large colonies, the birds were unable to satiate local predators. These last birds were doomed as they attempted solitary nesting, building unconcealed nests, and laying only a single white egg. This very low rate of reproduction was just not enough to save the species, whose whole reproductive strategy depended on mass nesting." David E. Blockstein & Harrison B. Tordoff, *supra*, at 850. It has also been suggested that the species required high population densities to breed. Once the population fell below that threshold, most pigeons ceased to breed. I.L. Brisbin, *The Passenger Pigeon: A Study in the Ecology of Extinction*, Modern Game Breeding, Oct. 1968, at 13, 19–20; T.R. Halliday, *The Extinction of the Passenger Pigeon*,

---

1. The railroads and express companies realized substantial revenue from shipping pigeons. They also had a network of agents with access to telegraph. This network allowed the birds to be tracked on the northward migration. A.W. Schorger, The Passenger Pigeon 146 (1955).

Ectopistes migratorius, *and Its Relevance to Contemporary Conservation*, 17 BIOLOGICAL CONSERVATION 157 (1980).

One parable of the pigeon is that individuals may not be the key to the survival of a species: the pigeon was a social species whose life strategy was based on the presence of thousands if not millions of other individuals. Hence all attempts to breed pigeons in captivity failed. The final disappearance of the pigeon, both in the wild and in captivity, is recounted in engaging detail in CHRISTOPHER COKINOS, HOPE IS THE THING WITH FEATHERS 197–278 (2000).

d. COMMERCE AND CONSERVATION

Cayman Turtle Farm, Ltd. v. Andrus

United States District Court, District of Columbia.
478 F.Supp. 125 (1979).

■ PRATT, D.J.:—Plaintiff Cayman Turtle Farm, Ltd., operates a marine farm, or mariculture operation, on Grand Cayman Island, Cayman Islands, British West Indies, where it breeds green sea turtles in captivity for scientific and commercial purposes. The Company's farmed turtle products, which are exported to the United States and other countries, consist of turtle shell jewelry, steak, soup, meat, leather and turtle oil. In this action, plaintiff specifically seeks to invalidate and enjoin enforcement of the regulations issued by defendant Cecil D. Andrus, Secretary of the Interior, and Juanita M. Kreps, Secretary of Commerce, under the authority of the Endangered Species Act of 1973, [ ] (hereinafter cited as ESA) insofar as these regulations prohibit the importation and trade in the United States of all green sea turtle products produced in mariculture operations.

Plaintiff has filed a motion for summary judgment in which it advances three arguments in support of its position that the Secretaries should be enjoined from prohibiting the importation and trade of farm green sea turtles: (1) the regulations promulgated by the Secretaries are in excess of their authority under the Endangered Species Act of 1973; (2) the regulations are contrary to the Convention on International Trade in Endangered Species of Wild Fauna and Flora, 27 U.S.T. 1087, T.I.A.S. No. 8247 (hereinafter referred to as Convention); and (3) the regulations are without support in the administrative record. The Government of the Cayman Islands has filed an Amicus curiae brief in support of plaintiff's motion for summary judgment. The defendant Secretaries and intervenors Environmental Defense Fund, Inc., have filed cross-motions for summary judgment. We find that there are no genuine issues of material fact which would prevent the grant of a summary judgment. For reasons discussed below, we deny the plaintiff's motion for summary judgment and grant the motions for summary judgment filed by defendants and intervenors.

I. *Procedural History*

The administrative regulations challenged in this action have a lengthy procedural history. [In August 1974, Dr. F. Wayne King, Director of Conservation and Environmental Education of the New York Zoological

Society, petitioned the Departments of Commerce and Interior to list the green sea turtle as endangered. Following a review, the United States Fish and Wildlife Service (USFWS) of the Department of the Interior and the National Marine Fisheries Service (NMFS) of the Department of Commerce published in the Federal Register a proposed regulation listing green, loggerhead, and Pacific ridley sea turtles as threatened species in May, 1975. Among other things, the proposed regulations provided an exception for the importation, exportation, taking, and transporting of sea turtles (and their parts and products) derived from mariculture operations with the provision that after two years the exception would apply only to turtles derived from closed-cycle farming operations which were self-sustaining and independent of wild stocks. Numerous comments on the proposed sea turtle regulations were received by USFWS and NMFS. Many of these comments specifically addressed the proposed mariculture exception.

[In August, 1975, NMFS announced that it would prepare an environmental impact statement on the proposal; the draft environmental impact statement (DEIS) became available for public comment in February, 1976. Public hearings on the proposed listing and on the DEIS were held in Washington, D.C. on February 25–26, 1976. Scientists, conservationists, businessmen, shrimpers and representatives from state and foreign governments participated in the hearings. Plaintiff Cayman Turtle Farm, Ltd. submitted comments on several different occasions in support of the mariculture exception in the proposed regulations; plaintiff also participated in the public hearings. On June 16, 1976, USFWS and NMFS published proposed regulations listing the green, Pacific ridley and loggerhead turtles as threatened. On July 28, 1978, USFWS and NMFS published the final regulations listing the turtles. These regulations prohibited all importation of these turtles with no exception for commercial mariculture operations.

[Plaintiff formally requested USFWS and NMFS to reconsider the sea turtle regulations insofar as they failed to provide an exception for commercial mariculture activities; the stay request was denied. Plaintiff then commenced the present action to challenge the new turtle regulations and to enjoin enforcement of the prohibitions contained therein insofar as they are directed against commercial mariculture activities. Following a hearing on plaintiff's application for a temporary restraining order, USFWS and NMFS agreed to a voluntary stay of enforcement against commercial mariculture activities pending reconsideration by the agencies of the sea turtle regulations pursuant to plaintiff's request, and, if reconsideration was denied, pending the outcome of judicial review of that denial by the United States District Court for the District of Columbia. Plaintiff submitted additional comments to USFWS and NMFS in support of its request for reconsideration. On December 5, 1978, USFWS and NMFS issued a Decision Memorandum denying plaintiff's request to include in the sea turtle regulations an exception for commercial mariculture operations.]

II. *Authority for Mariculture Ban Under the Endangered Species Act*

Plaintiff advances two principal arguments in support of its contention that the withdrawal of an exemption for plaintiff's mariculture activities is an act in excess of the defendant's authority under the Endangered Species

Act of 1973. [ ] First, plaintiff argues that the mariculture ban is contrary to the Act's regulatory mandate to encourage the propagation of protected wildlife. ESA §§ 3(2), 10(a). Second, plaintiff argues that the Endangered Species Act of 1973 does not apply to captive-bred sea turtles which are hatched and raised in a controlled environment.

Defendants and intervenors do not dispute the plaintiff's general contention that a fundamental purpose of the Endangered Species Act of 1973 is to promote measures designed to protect species which are threatened with immediate or foreseeable extinction. Defendants and intervenor, however, do dispute that this general policy requires the establishment of a mariculture exemption in the specific case of threatened or endangered sea turtles. Since plaintiff's argument rests upon the factual assumption that its mariculture operations facilitate the propagation of protected wildlife, we will later treat this argument in the context of plaintiff's challenge to evidentiary basis in the administrative record for the mariculture ban.

Plaintiff's second argument, that the Endangered Species Act of 1973 does not apply to captive-bred sea turtles which are hatched and raised in a controlled environment, is contrary to the clear language of the statute. As defendants and intervenors point out, section 9(b) of the Act, [ ], exempts from the prohibition of the Act only those specimens of a listed species which were "held in captivity or in a controlled environment on December 28, 1973," but not species of fish or wildlife "held in the course of a commercial activity." [ ] While this language clearly evinces a legislative intent to include specimens reared in captivity and in controlled environments within the ambit of the Act, the Act carefully limits the captive specimen exemption to specimens which were (1) in a controlled environment as of December 28, 1973; and (2) not held in the course of a commercial activity. The specimens on the Cayman Turtle Farm cannot qualify for this exemption because they were held in the course of a commercial activity. Moreover, all turtles and the progeny of all turtles acquired after December 28, 1973, would also not qualify for this exemption.

. . .

B.   *Record Support for Elimination of Mariculture Exemption*

. . .

The defendant Secretaries advanced several facts and policy concerns in support of their decision to withdraw the proposed mariculture exemption from the sea turtle regulations. First, the Secretaries found that trade of commercial mariculture products would have a deleterious impact upon sea turtle populations in the wild. Second, the Secretaries found that the likely inadequacy of measures to enforce compliance with a mariculture exemption would also pose a threat to wild populations of sea turtles. Third, the Secretaries found that the benefits of scientific research which would accrue from a mariculture exemption do not outweigh the risks to the survival of wild sea turtle populations. Fourth, the Secretaries found that the Cayman Turtle Farm was not totally independent of wild eggs and wild turtles. [ ] As will be discussed below, each of these findings has a reasonable basis of support in the administrative record.

1. *Deleterious Impact Upon Wild Sea Turtle Population*

The administrative record reveals that there is considerable uncertainty over the precise long-term impact of mariculture activities upon wild sea turtle populations but there is ample evidence to support a finding that such activities would be detrimental to the prospects for the survival of wild sea turtles. Evidence in the administrative record is adequate to support the finding that a mariculture exemption would provide an incentive for the establishment of other turtle farms which, like Cayman Turtle Farm, would at least initially be dependent upon eggs taken from the wild. Even if other turtle farms attempted to acquire wild eggs which would not otherwise have hatched, there is a significant risk that, as in the case of Cayman Turtle Farm, eggs nevertheless may be procured from viable nests thereby depleting the potential stock of wild sea turtles.[4] Moreover, even if other farms procured doomed eggs, there is evidence in the record that the procurement of doomed eggs may reduce the total stock of viable eggs because predators, including man, may then have to resort to viable eggs to satisfy their existing consumptive demands for turtle eggs.

Evidence in the record also supports the Secretaries' contention that the total number of wild sea turtles may be reduced by increased illegal poaching of wild sea turtles. The record contains evidence that plaintiff's marketing of sea turtle products would increase consumer demand for these products.[6] Increased demand would provide a strong economic incentive for the illegal marketing of wild sea turtles. The likelihood of such illegal trade is increased by evidence indicating that the products of wild sea turtles are readily able to be substituted for the products of turtles reared at the Cayman Turtle Farm. The record also contains evidence that such illegal trade has occurred and is increasing. Evidence in the record was therefore more than ample to permit the Secretaries to conclude that the survival of wild sea turtles would be threatened by either the formation of additional turtle farms or by increased illegal poaching. Both of these consequences could reasonably flow from the implementation of a mariculture exemption.

2. *Inadequacy of Enforcement Measures*

The administrative record also adequately demonstrates that the Secretaries had a reasonable factual basis to conclude that the absence of adequate measures to enforce the mariculture exemption increases the likelihood that the products of wild sea turtles will be illegally imported into the United States. As noted previously, evidence in the record is sufficient to demonstrate that many farm sea turtle products, such as oil,

---

4. The very process of establishing a self-sustaining mariculture operation is virtually certain to require the procurement of many wild, potentially viable eggs and wild breeding adults. [ ]

6. Although plaintiff contends that its operation is simply a means to satisfy existing demand for sea turtle products, evidence in the record indicates that plaintiff, a commercial, profit-seeking business, may be seeking to increase its markets and expand the demand for these products. [ ]

soup ingredients, and shell sections, are virtually indistinguishable from wild sea turtle products. The agencies are uniquely situated to determine whether they possess the requisite expertise and resources to enforce mariculture exemption at the points of importation or at other inspection sites. The agencies could reasonably conclude that these inspection and monitoring difficulties would be markedly exacerbated because of limited resources and jurisdictional authority to supervise foreign mariculture operations.

3. *Scientific Research Benefits of Mariculture Facilities*

The administrative record is also adequate to support the Secretaries' finding that the benefits of scientific research performed at the Cayman Turtle Farm do not outweigh the other risks to the species posed by mariculture exemption....

4. *Self Sufficiency of the Operation*

Plaintiff devotes considerable discussion of the evidence in the record which supports their contention that Cayman Turtle Farm is a self-sufficient, closed-cycle operation completely independent of wild stocks of sea turtles. An initial point of contention is whether the Secretaries have properly defined the term "closed-cycle" to include only operations where all farm hatchlings are produced from parents which also were farm hatchlings.[12] According to plaintiff, the term "closed-cycle" should be more loosely interpreted to refer to populations which can be sustained without further acquisition of wild stocks. The interpretation advocated by defendants and intervenor, however, is consistent with the protective policy of the Endangered Species Act of 1973. Moreover, the defendants' and intervenors' more strict definition of "closed-cycle" comports with the terms and underlying policy of the resolution adopted by the parties to the Convention.[13]

The Secretaries had adequate evidence in the record to conclude that plaintiff had not established a closed-cycle operation within the agencies' valid definition of that term. The record contains undisputed evidence that a significant percentage of the breeding herd and of the recent hatchlings were not born of parents which had mated on the farm.[14] In addition, it

---

12. [ ] In an earlier proposed regulation, the Secretaries indicated that a mariculture exemption permit may be issued "if the applicant or permittee can demonstrate to the satisfaction of the Director, that such wildlife is derived from a closed-cycle farming operation consisting of a captive-bred population which is completely self-sustaining and independent of wild stock." [ ]

13. In interpreting the Convention term "bred in captivity," the parties to the Convention stated that "[t]he parental breeding stock must be to the satisfaction of the competent government authorities of the relevant country ... managed in a manner designed to maintain the breeding stock indefi-

nitely." A parental breeding stock shall be considered to be "managed in a manner designed to maintain the breeding stock indefinitely only if it is managed in a manner which has been demonstrated to be capable of reliably producing second-generation offspring in a controlled environment." Resolution of March 27, 1979, adopted at the second meeting of the Conference of the parties to the Convention on International Trade in Endangered Species of Wild Fauna and Flora.

14. Of the nearly 1000 breeding turtles at the Cayman Turtle Farm, approximately 220 were originally taken from the wild. [ ] Until recently, plaintiff has procured substantial numbers of wild turtle eggs. In 1977,

may be premature to determine that the breeding cycle at Cayman Turtle Farm can be completed from farm laid egg to farm laid egg. According to testimony contained in the record, hatchlings from eggs first laid at the farm will not become sexually mature until the early 1980's. Thus, despite evidence of the apparent success of breeding efforts at the Cayman Turtle Farm, the Secretaries had sufficient information before them to conclude that plaintiff had not established the sort of closed-cycle operation which could be entitled to a mariculture exemption if a mariculture exemption was otherwise warranted. However, since the Secretaries also had an adequate basis in the record to conclude that a general mariculture exemption would be contrary to their obligation under and the policies contained in the Endangered Species Act of 1973 and the Convention, the Secretaries' decision to eliminate a mariculture exemption can be sustained without regard to the definitional question of whether Cayman Turtle Farm can be deemed a "closed-cycle" or "self-sufficient" operation.

NOTES

(1) Would the Secretaries have been within their delegated discretion if they had promulgated final regulations that included a mariculture exemption? Note the court's statement: "The administrative record reveals that there is considerable uncertainty over the precise long-term impact of mariculture activities upon wild sea turtle populations but there is ample evidence to support a finding that such activities would be detrimental to the prospects for the survival of wild sea turtles."

Under what circumstances might a mariculture operation contribute to the conservation of species with declining populations? Even if it could be established that Cayman Island was having a positive impact on turtle populations, would the Secretaries be able to permit the import of their products? If not, is this good policy?

(2) A note on terminology: Many of the turtles reared by Cayman Islands were "ranched" rather than "farmed" because the animals were hatched from eggs taken from the wild. At the Third Meeting of the Conference of the Parties to Convention on International Trade in Endangered Species (CITES) in New Delhi, India, in 1981, Conference Resolution 3.15 defined the term "ranching" as "the rearing in a controlled environment of specimens taken from the wild." This definition was maintained in the subsequent Conference Resolution 10.18 adopted at the Tenth Meeting of the Conference of Parties at Harare, Zimbabwe in 1997.

The term "farming" has not been formally defined by the Conference. The term has, however, come to mean "bred in captivity"—a term that was defined in Conference Resolution 10.16 to require the individual to be "born or otherwise produced in a controlled environment" where "the parents mated or gametes were otherwise transferred in a controlled environment" and the breeding stock "is maintained without introduction of specimens from the wild."

for example, plaintiff acquired 20,800 wild   turtle eggs. [ ]

Thus, ranching involves the controlled rearing of wild animals; farming is the controlled rearing of animals bred and born in captivity.

PERSPECTIVES

(1) The role of wildlife in the economy of the United States—biological contributions (pt. 2): A final category of raw materials provided by wildlife is genetic: wild animals that can be domesticated or can serve as a source of genetic material to improve existing domesticates. Several species are currently in the early phases of domestication. These include beaver, sable, Arctic fox, nutria, racoon dog, elk, wapiti, or red deer, musk deer, bison, rainbow trout, channel catfish, and chinook, coho, and Atlantic salmon. In addition, biotechnology now allows technicians to remove genes from one species and insert them into the DNA of another species. As the decoding of genomes increases, the value of raw genetic materials is likely to increase. There are also other, lower technology uses of wild genetic resources: inbreeding of catfish, for example, is a likely cause of increased deformities and slow growth.

(2) Wildlife farming as a wildlife conservation tool: A current buzz-word is "sustainable utilization," which is defined as use of a species so that it maintains its economic value to local human population and thus is preserved. The argument runs thus: the most significant cause of extinction is habitat destruction (due primarily to increasing human numbers) rather than economic exploitation. Thus, prohibiting trade in wildlife does not address the central problem of preserving habitat. Furthermore, bans may in fact be counter-productive by removing all economic incentives for conservation of habitat; faced with an inability to obtain any return, habitat may be converted into agricultural or non-wildlife other uses.

Two potential problems are apparent. First, allowing trade in wildlife can lead to management actions intended to increase the production of the cropped species—actions that often will lead to degraded habitats and a concomitant loss of biological diversity. Since conservation is a largely question of habitat, if the commercial use of a species does not protect habitat it is not conservation. Second, farming operations can become simply a "laundromat for illegally captured wild animals." To the extent that the cropped species is available in local wild populations, there is a potential to include (illegal) wild animals with the (legal) farmed animals.

There is thus far little hard evidence to support the rather grand theoretical arguments of those favoring conservation-through-use. What has been done—although inconclusive—suggests that some skepticism may be appropriate. A review of caiman skins shipped from farming operations in Brazil led the investigators to conclude, "Reality is tragically distant from theory." They concluded that many of the farms were simply fenced wild populations; that wild populations continue to be used to subsidize operations; that many "farmed" animals were in fact wild; etc. Peter Brazaitis, Myrna E. Watanabe, & George Amato, *The Caiman Trade*, SCI. AM., Mar. 1998, at 70–76.

Many of the concerns that FWS and NMFS expressed in prohibiting the importation of Cayman Turtle Farms have on-going analogues. This does not mean that farming—or even ranching—operations cannot play a significant role in wildlife conservation. But it does suggest that "[t]he attempt to derive conservation advantage from using wildlife should not be seen as a bold new conservation initiative for it is not proactive at all; it is a concerned response to an existing, and worsening, situation." Melvin Bolton, *Synthesis and Conclusions, in* Conservation and the Use of Wildlife Resources 266 (Melvin Bolton ed., 1997).

(3) Consumptive uses of wild animals as a conservation tool: Consider the following arguments from a Portland, Oregon chef:

Greg Higgins,

Savor the flavor of wild salmon, and save the species

-o-

*Farm-raised fish may be cheaper, but eating Copper
River salmon helps the environment*

The Sunday Oregonian, July 16, 2000, at G3.

Strawberries in June, tomatoes in July, chanterelles in autumn. I relish the times of year my favorite foods are at their peak.

Some wine lovers make a dash each year when the Beaujolais Noveau is available. But it's hard to imagine any food that garners a more frenzied race for the first taste than the seasonal debut of Alaska's wild Copper River salmon. This is the time of year when lucky supermarkets and restaurants in the Pacific Northwest compete to offer customers their first succulent bite of Copper River salmon just hours after it's caught.

This salmon is one of many wild species that are sustainably-caught, processed and delivered to markets, restaurants and consumers all around the world. Other than Copper River salmon, which are specially marketed, salmon are not labeled or differentiated in any way from their distant cousins, farmed salmon. An unfortunate side effect of this is that wild fish become undervalued, making it difficult for fishermen who catch and distribute wild salmon to afford to stay in business.

At a recent seafood tasting hosted by the Chefs Collaborative in New York City, chefs and food writers unanimously chose four types of wild salmon over farm-raised in a blind tasting. The wild fish were voted superior in aroma, texture and flavor.

Despite the fact that all wild salmon have distinct advantages over farm-raised salmon, a recent national poll by the Mellman Group discovered that environmentally conscious consumers are likely to choose farmed salmon over wild, thinking it's healthier for the environment.

Not so. Farmed salmon is a decent product, but inferior to wild salmon in several important ways. While it is cheaper, it doesn't support traditional family fishing jobs, and it is produced on an industrial scale with considerable ecological impact. Like some agribusiness operations, salmon farming can have negative impacts on water quality, the environment and native species.

Farmed salmon are raised by the thousands in crowded net pens. These conditions encourage the spread of disease that must be countered by antibiotics, vaccines and other chemicals—much of which ends up in the water.

In addition, it takes up to five pounds of anchovies and other feed fish to grow one pound of farmed salmon.

A typical salmon farm generates as much waste as a city of half a million people. This waste pollutes the marine environment, smothering communities of plants and animals beneath salmon cages. Salmon farms are also sitting targets for marine mammals and sea birds looking for a meal. In British Columbia, an estimated 500 harbor seals are shot each year to protect salmon farms. Netting used to exclude marine mammals and birds can entangle and drown hapless animals.

Finally, farmed salmon can directly threaten wild salmon when pens accidentally rip open, releasing non-native species into surrounding water-ways. Besides competing for food and spawning habitat, escaped salmon have been documented interbreeding with wild salmon, polluting their gene pool and further weakening their fitness to survive.

Dozens of species of wild salmon native to the streams and rivers in their southern range are threatened or endangered because of habitat destruction and mismanagement from the past 100 years. However, these runs are off-limits to fishermen. Commercially-available wild salmon come from thriving strongholds, such as northern British Columbia and Alaska, home to the best-regulated, most sustainable wild salmon fisheries in the world. In fact, one of the ways we can help protect wild salmon is to eat it.

When you choose wild salmon, you are eating healthfully too. Wild salmon's oil contains high levels of Omega–3, the unsaturated fat thought to fend off heart disease, psoriasis, rheumatoid arthritis, breast cancer and migraines. FDA studies show that farm-raised salmon have nearly twice the fat, and one-third less protein than wild salmon.

Personal values and ethics are an increasingly important part of our buying choices, as demonstrated by the high demand for sustainably harvested wood products, shade-grown coffee that protects migratory birds, dolphin-safe tuna and the like.

Salmon consumption in the United States hit a record high last year, with farmed salmon capturing the largest share of the market. This trend is shrinking the value and the viability of environmentally friendly wild salmon. Salmon eaters should heed this unconventional wisdom: Eating wild salmon helps save wild salmon.

Strong v. United States

United States Fifth Circuit Court of Appeals.
5 F.3d 905 (1993).

■ PER CURIAM:—Erv and Sonja Strong conduct a commercial tourboat business to transport tourists into the bay by boat for the purpose of feeding dolphins. By this suit the Strongs have challenged the validity of a rule promulgated under the Marine Mammal Protection Act by the Secretary of Commerce which defines the feeding of marine mammals in the wild as prohibited activity. The district court permanently enjoined enforcement of the regulation. 811 F. Supp. 246. We uphold the regulation and vacate the injunction.

By this statute, Title 16 U.S.C. § 1361 *et seq.*, Congress has prohibited the taking of marine mammals without a permit. The term "take" is defined to mean "to harass, hunt, capture, or kill, or to attempt to harass, hunt, capture, or kill any marine mammal." § 1362(12). Congress has directed the Secretary to promulgate regulations with respect to taking and importing of each species of marine mammal. § 1373. Pursuant to that authorization the National Marine Fisheries Service in the Department of Commerce sought the opinions of informed experts on the effect of feeding dolphins, finally concluding that harm was a real possibility and that habitual feeding cruises should be restricted as harassment of the mammal.

The appeal before us does not contest the denial of a permit to conduct feeding cruises. The position of the Strongs is that the Secretary of Commerce has no authority to consider feeding to be a form of harassment or to regulate same. We think the contention asked too much, and that the district court's order infringes upon the authority of the Secretary.

. . .

Here, the precise question addressed by the challenged regulation is whether feeding marine mammals in the wild constitutes a "take." 50 C.F.R. 216.3. The district court rejected the decision of the agency because "to feed" is not among the dictionary definitions of "harass." But "disturb" is synonymous with "harass" and the agency has been given substantial scientific evidence that feeding wild dolphins disturbs their normal behavior and may make them less able to search for food on their own. It is therefore clearly reasonable to restrict or prohibit the feeding of dolphins as a potential hazard to them. The regulation was promulgated by the agency within its authority.

The district court held that the National Marine Fishery Service had improperly established a rule without following rulemaking procedures by issuing a policy statement which required the return without consideration of any application for a public display permit to feed marine mammals in the wild. This holding is not challenged by the United States, and we agree. The judgment only enjoins the enforcement of the regulation, and that is vacated.

NOTES

Is any disruption of the animal's "normal behavior" impermissible? If the mere presence of tourboats altered the dolphin's behavior—for example, if the dolphins either fled or were attracted to the boat—would that be sufficient to prohibit the conduct? Alternatively, is the crucial element of the cases not just that the feeding "disturbs their normal behavior," but that it "may make them less able to search for food on their own," *i.e.*, that the activity impacts a crucial life trait?

Does it make a difference that the conduct was directed at the dolphins? Would it be sufficient if the Strongs operated a ferry between two cities and the boat incidentally altered the dolphins' behavior? If passengers on the ferry fed the dolphins? If the Strongs sold food to feed the dolphins?

PERSPECTIVES

(1) **Eco-tourism** is often promoted as type of use that can be sustainable by providing economic incentives for local people to maintain wildlife habitat. But nonconsumptive wildlife viewing often is in fact highly consumptive: of fossil fuel, water, and often of wildlife habitat itself which is converted to lodging and to agriculture to produce the amenities desired by the eco-tourists. And beyond such matters, there remains the fundamental question of whether ecologically sensitive places can in fact withstand large numbers of visitors. There is a justifiable concern, Timothy Egan has written, "that the world's growing curiosity about, say, blue-footed boobies in the Galapagos or gorillas in the upland mist of Uganda may ultimately put the birds and primates in peril. The ... major cause of worry about the growth of eco-tourism ... is the question of whether the land, people and biological diversity of a given area can be sustained through waves of visitors." Timothy Egan, *Uneasy Being Green: Tourism Runs Wild*, N.Y. Times, May 20, 2001, Travel at 10, 10–12.

(2) **Smooth vs. lumpy—the parable of the pigeon (pt. 2):** Recall the demise of the passenger pigeon, apparently because it could not breed successfully except with throngs of other pigeons and that the commercial harvest of the large nestings was a substantial factor in pushing the species' numbers below this threshold.

In this regard a defense of the pigeon netters—mounted in 1878 by a wholesaler—has a modern ring:

> In conclusion, the pigeons are as much an article of commerce as wheat, corn, hogs, beeves, or sheep. It is no more cruel to kill them for market by the thousand, than it is to countenance the killing at the stock yards in this or any other large commercial centre.... A farmer can market his poultry dead or alive at any time of the year, and the slaughter, the country over, is larger than that of pigeons, yet no one in interest of "justice and humanity" interferes. The pigeon is migratory, it can care for itself. It nests in the impenetrable wilds of Arkansas, the Indian territory, Canada and British America, as often as in the land of civilization where it can be reached for market. It is a source of profit to the poor, or pleasure to the rich. Its benefits to the Emmett county homesteaders as felt through the cold of this Winter alone, are enough to compensate for [any] evils ... , and Emmett county is but a sample of whatever location the birds may settle in. Let the law, in regard to distance, stand as it is; enforce it against all alike. Make no exceptions. Let the rule of supply and demand govern the catching, and you will have something better than all the professors in Michigan can suggest. Let the supply be so large that prices are low and wages can't be made and law or no law the catching will stop. But don't make a law

that will take bread out of the homesteader's mouth, and work from hundreds of poor and honest men; no, not even if the birds should be sacrificed, to a certain extent, for man is above the beasts, and the "beasts of the field and the birds of the air" are given unto him for his benefit and his profit.

Mr. E[dward] T. Martin's Reply to Prof. Roney, CHICAGO FIELD, Jan. 25, 1879.

CHAPTER 2

THE RULE OF CAPTURE

SECTION 1. THE ALLOCATION OF RIGHTS IN WILDLIFE

a. THE ENGLISH COMMON-LAW BACKGROUND

The English common law evolved out of the customs of largely autonomous agricultural communities. Living the seasonal rounds of planting and harvesting during a time when change was nearly nonexistent, people naturally viewed the way things customarily were done as a guide to how they should be done; the past offered solutions even if it did not entirely control the settling of disputes or the allocating of resources.

The imperative to satisfy the material needs of human society produced sophisticated arrangements for distributing and managing natural resources. The rights of different community members often intertwined to create complex patterns of uses on a particular parcel of land: cattle grazed in common on the fields after the crops had been harvested so that their dung fertilized the soil; the grass, herbs, and acorns in a copse of trees provided forage during another part of the seasonal cycle; wood from the trees was used for fuel or building; fish in streams and ponds were netted; wildlife was hunted. Although the patterns were complex, they were spatially limited and focused on subsistence and self-sufficiency.

During the tenth and eleventh centuries, each local community largely settled disputes in line with its own customs and practices; the Anglo–Saxon kingdom had only a limited responsibility for resolving larger-scale disputes and preserving "the King's peace." The Norman Conquest in 1066 overlaid these allocational and managerial patterns with a feudal economic and social system—a hierarchical series of relationships in which lands were held under a lord in return for an obligation of service to that lord. This tenure system mixed Anglo–Saxon and feudal ideas and formed the basis of what evolved into the common law of property.

The imposition of a feudal social and economic structure by the Normans enhanced the centralizing tendencies already at work. At the fore were two institutions: the royal, "common law" courts and the Exchequer.[1] The king's courts—and the common law that those courts created and

---

1. Exchequer is the department of the British government that collects the national revenue. Initially established as the Court of Exchequer by William the Conqueror as part of the *aula regis* (the king's hall), it became one of the four chief courts during the Norman period and was responsible for keeping the king's accounts and collecting royal revenues. In time, it began allowing private litigants to sue one another for money under the theory that the winning party would then be able to pay amounts due the King. The "judicial" functions were gradually separated from the revenue-collection and auditing functions over the next 800 years.

applied—began primarily as a source of revenue and as a means of clarifying the rights and duties in feudal land tenures. In time, however, those courts became a powerful mechanism for asserting authority and increasing royal/national power. These developments were paralleled by the growth of a highly organized auditing function in the Exchequer.

With this transition in perspective, from local to country-wide, came a drive for regularization in the nomenclature and definition of both individual and communal land-use rights. The resource allocation and management patterns in the local manors and villages were abstracted and thereby transformed into "property."[2] The customary rotational grazing system became a "right of common in pasture"; the right to feed pigs on acorns became a "right of pannage"; the custom of taking wood became "estovers"; the customary fishing hole became a "common piscary"; the right to hunt became "chases, parks, or warrens." Custom was transformed into a series of "incorporeal hereditaments"—inheritable intangible property. As Henry de Bracton[3] wrote, "[a] servitude may be constituted in many ways, as that one have the right to pasture in another's property, or the right to cultivate it, to go over it, to draw water from it, to fish in it, to conduct water over it, to hunt on it, and there may be an infinite number of other rights." 4 HENRY DE BRACTON, DE LEGIBUS ET CONSUETUDINIBUS ANGLIAE bk. 4, ch. 37, f. 222a (ca. 1256).

This evolutionary process was as untidy as it was convoluted. A significant complicating force was the confusion of proprietary rights and governmental powers—a confusion that was natural in a system where the lord was chief landholder, leader of the local government, and representative of the distant king. In such a scheme, the powers to hold court and to hang a criminal were forms of property. The king, after all, was only a feudal lord writ large, and the "kingly power . . . a mode of dominium; the ownership of a chattel." 1 FREDERICK POLLOCK & FREDERIC W. MAITLAND, THE HISTORY OF ENGLISH LAW BEFORE THE TIME OF EDWARD I at 513 (2d ed. 1968). One of the great themes of medieval English legal history is the "struggle of ownership and rulership to free themselves from each other." FREDERIC W. MAITLAND, TOWNSHIP AND BOROUGH 31 (Cambridge, 1897).

What we now conceive as "sovereignty"—governmental and regulatory power—generally began as "property" or property-like tenures. In wildlife law, for example, the power to regulate taking or habitat modification has one of its founts in the prerogative of the English kings to declare land to be a "forest"—an area where the King had a property-like right to hunt the "beasts of the forest" such as the king's deer. Stripped of its overly refined technicalities and myriad of finely honed distinctions, the core principle of English wildlife law at the time of the American Revolution was

---

2. "The man of the thirteenth century does not say, 'I agree that you may have so many trees out of my copse every year,' he says, 'I give and grant you so much wood.'" 2 FREDERICK POLLOCK & FREDERIC W. MAITLAND, THE HISTORY OF ENGLISH LAW BEFORE THE TIME OF EDWARD I, at 146 (2d ed. 1968). That is, he creates a property, rather than contractual, relationship.

3. Henry de Bracton (d. 1285) was an English writer on law. *De Legibus et Consuetudinibus Angliae—On the Laws and Customs of England*—is a broad, philosophical treatise often called the most important work on English law before Blackstone.

this: the King in Parliament had broad power to determine, not only who could acquire rights in wildlife and what those rights could be, but also how land could be used when those uses potentially affected wildlife. This power grew out of cases such as:

The Case of Swans

Kings Bench.
7 Co. Rep. 15b, 77 Eng. Rep. 435 (1592).

Between the Queen, and the Lady Joan Young, late the wife of Sir John Young, Knight, deceased, and Thomas Saunger, defendants, the case was such: [In September, 1590, a royal commission visited Dorset County to audit the Crown's interests. The commission reported that there were approximately 500 *unmarked* swans in the county. Upon receipt of the report, Exchequer—the agency responsible for the collection of the Crown's revenue as well as for exercising jurisdiction over cases affecting that revenue—ordered the sheriff to round up all of the unbranded swans on the grounds that they belonged to the queen as sovereign. Joan Young and Thomas Saunger filed a claim to the swans, contending that they owned all of those swimming on the estuary abutting Abbotsbury. Their claim was based on "prescription," a mode of acquiring title to certain types of property based on immemorial or long-continued use rather than on an express grant that could be presented in court. Specifically, Young and Saunger claimed that the previous owners of Abbotsbury "time out of mind ... were accustomed to have and enjoy, the total possession and increase" of the swans and to their use for food. When Queen Elizabeth's father, Henry VIII, renounced the leadership of the Pope, he seized many monastic lands and transferred them to subordinate lords as a means of solidifying power. Abbotsbury was transferred by a deed that included all rights of its prior owners. The right to the swans, Young and Saunger argued, was included within this deed and passed to them by subsequent conveyances. The Queen's attorney denied the claim. In deciding the case, the court handed down a landmark decision on how a person could acquire rights in wildlife and on the duration of those rights.]

1.   It was resolved, that all white [*i.e.*, mature] swans not marked,[1] which having gained their natural liberty, and are swimming in an open and common river, might be seised to the King's use by his prerogative, because ... a swan is a Royal fowl; and all those, the property whereof is not known, do belong to the King by his prerogative:[2] and so whales[3] and sturgeons are Royal fish, and belong to the King by his prerogative. And there hath been an ancient officer of the King's called *magister deductus cignorum*, which continues to this day.

---

1. [Swans were "marked" much as cattle are branded. Marking most commonly involved cutting notches, grooves, or symbols in the bird's upper mandible; lower mandibles, legs, and feet were also marked. NORMAN F. TICEHURST, THE MUTE SWAN IN ENGLAND 80–111 (1957).]

2. ["Prerogative" is an ill-defined concept that is discussed below. At this point, it is sufficient to think of it as a claim that the King has the power to do something simply because he is King.]

3. [Whales, of course, are mammals rather than fish.]

But it was resolved also, that the subject [of the king] might have property in white swans not marked, as some may have swans not marked in his private waters, the property of which belongs to him, and not to the King; and if they escape out of his private waters into an open and common river, he may bring them back and take them again. And therewith agreeth BRACTON, bk. 2., ch. 1, f. 9: ["If wild animals have been tamed, and they have a habit of going out and returning, flying away and flying back, (such as deer, swans, seafowl, and doves and such like) another rule has been approved, that they are so long considered as ours, as long as they have a disposition to return."] But if they have gained their natural liberty, and are swimming in open and common rivers, the King's officer may seise them in the open and common river for the King: for one white swan, without such pursuit as aforesaid, cannot be known from another; and when the property of a swan cannot be known, the same being of its nature a fowl Royal, doth belong to the King; [a prior case was cited o]ut of which case, these points were observed concerning swans:

1. That every one who hath swans within his manor, that is to say, within his private waters, hath a property in them; for the writ of trespass was of wrongful taking his swans....

2. That one may prescribe to have a game of swans[4] within his manor, as well as a warren, or park.

3. That he who hath such a game of swans may prescribe, that his swans may swim within the manor of another.

4. That a swan may be an estray,[5] and so cannot any other fowl, as I have read in any book....

And the law thereof is founded on a reason in nature; for the cock swan is an emblem or representation of an affectionate and true husband to his wife above all other fowls; for the cock swan holdeth himself to one female only, and for this cause nature hath conferred on him a gift beyond all others; that is, to die so joyfully, that he sings sweetly when he dies; upon which the poet[6] saith:

> *Dulcia defecta modulatur carmina lingua, Cantator,*
> *cygnus, funeris ipse sui, & c.*

And therefore this case of the swan doth differ from the case of kine, or other brute beasts. [ ] And it was agreed that none can have a swan mark ... unless it be by the grant of the King, or of his officers authorised

---

4. ["Game" is the term for a group of swans similar to a gaggle of geese, a covey of quail, a murder of crows, and an escheat of lawyers. *See generally* JAMES LIPTON, AN EXALTATION OF LARKS (1968).]

5. [An estray is a wandering animal whose owner is unknown; it has escaped from its owner and strays about.]

6. [The "poet" is Marcus Valerius Martialis, a Roman epigrammatist. Martialis (anglicized as "Martial") was born in what is now Aragon between 38 and 41. He died

there around 104 after spending most of his life in Rome. *See* J.P. Sullivan, *Martial's Life and Works in* EPIGRAMS OF MARTIAL ENGLISHED BY DIVERS HANDS 1 (1987). The epigram quoted by the court is:

> The swan his own death's minstrel's sung
>
> Sweet measured songs with failing tongue.

Id. at 501 (Martial, book 13 verse 77).]

thereto, or by prescription. And if he hath a lawful swan mark, and hath swans swimming in open and common rivers lawfully marked therewith, they belong to him *ratione privilegii*. But none shall have a swan mark, or game of swans, unless he hath lands or tenements of an estate of freehold of the yearly value of five marks, above all charges, on pain of forfeiture of his swans ... and that is by the stat. of 22 Ed. 4 cap. 6 ....

And in [a case decided in the reign of Henry VI] it was resolved, that in some of them which are *feræ naturæ*, a man hath *jus proprietatis*, a right of property; and in some of them a man hath *jus privilegii*, a right of privilege. And there are three manner of rights of property, *scil.* property absolute, property qualified, and property possessory. A man hath not absolute property in any thing which is *feræ naturæ*, but in those which are *domitæ naturæ*. Property qualified and possessory a man may have in those which are *feræ naturæ*; and to such property a man may attain by two ways, by industry [*per industriam*], or *ratione impotentiæ et loci*; by industry as by taking them, or by making them *mansueta, i.e. manui assueta*, or *domesticæ, i.e. domui assueta*: but in those which are *feræ naturæ*, and by industry are made tame, a man hath but a qualified property in them, *scil.* so long as they remain tame, for if they do attain to their natural liberty, and have not *animum revertendi*, the property is lost, *ratione impotentiæ et loci*: as if a man has young shovelers or goshawks, or the like, which are *feræ naturæ*, and they build in my land, I have possessory property in them, for if one takes them when they cannot fly, the owner of the soil shall have an action of trespass, ... [ ] But when a man hath savage beasts *ratione privilegii*, is by reason of a park, warren, & c. he hath not any property in the deer, or conies, or pheasants, or partridges; and therefore in an action, *quare parcum warrennum, & c. fregit et intrav', et 3. damas, lepores, cuniculos, phasianos, perdices, cepit et asportavit,* he shall not say (*suos*) for he hath no property in them, but they do belong to him *ratione privil'* for his game and pleasure, so long as they remain in the privileged place; for if the owner of the park dies, his heir shall have them, and not his executors or administrators, because without them the park, which is an inheritance, is not complete....

And it was resolved, that in the principal case the prescription was insufficient; for the effect of the prescription is to have all wild swans, which are *feræ naturæ*, and not marked ... within the said creek. And such prescription for a warren would be insufficient, *scil.* to have all pheasants and partridges, ... and frequenting within his manor.... But it was resolved, that if the defendants had alleged, that within the said creek there had been time out of mind a game of wild swans not marked, building and breeding; and then had prescribed, that such abbot and all his predecessors, & c. had used at all times to have and take to their use some of the said game of wild swans and their cignets within the said creek, it had been good; for although swans are royal fowls, yet in such a manner a man may prescribe in them; for that may have a lawful beginning by the King's grant: in Rot. Parliam. 30 Ed. 3. part 2. num. 20. the King granted to C.W. all wild swans unmarked between Oxford and London for seven years.... By which it appears that the King may grant wild swans unmarked; and by consequence a man may prescribe in them within a certain place, because it may have a lawful beginning. And a man may prescribe to have royal fish within his manor, as it is held in 39 Ed. 3. 35. for the reason aforesaid. And yet without prescription they do belong to the King by his prerogative.

NOTES

(1) *The Case of the Swans* is a difficult decision but one that is well worth the effort because of its central role in the formulation of English common law on private rights in animals. In making sense of the case, it is useful to separate the court's comments on the various issues it considers: marked versus unmarked swans; swans versus other animals; and methods of acquiring private rights versus the duration of those rights. As noted below, swans were an unusual animal in England because the crown claimed ownership of them as a royal prerogative, just as the crown at the time of the Norman Conquest claimed all land in the realm. As this case explains, private parties—even the loftiest of lords—could claim rights in swans only by proving either a grant from the King or rights acquired by prescription. Presumably the King often made such grants, given that he and his household could not use all of the swans in the realm. Such grants would have been made for the same reasons as other grants: to raise revenue and secure the loyalty of subordinates.

Prescription will crop up again—and take on considerable importance—in later common law cases. Much like its successor, adverse possession, prescription was a means for people to prove their ownership of a thing when they lacked a piece of writing to evidence that ownership. In medieval England, most people could neither read nor write; documents were uncommonly created and easily lost or destroyed. For centuries, even transfers of land could take place by means of a ceremony that included no written instrument of transfer. Thus, many owners whose rights began by express grant, oral or written, had to rely on prescription to prove their rights. The essential element of proof was the unbroken possession and use of a thing so long as anyone could remember (that is, since time immemorial, or for such period as "the memory of man runneth not to the contrary").

(2) Because *The Case of the Swans* dealt only with unmarked swans, the court says little about the rules governing marked ones. What does the court say about how a person can gain the right to mark swans? What level of landholding does a person need to qualify for such interests? What does this landholding requirement tell us about the types of people who were likely to own lawfully marked swans? The social implications of swan ownership are considered below.

(3) In the case of unmarked swans, a person could gain rights to them either by grant from the King or prescription. Here, the defendants either did not have or could not prove an express grant that covered the swans, so they needed to rely on rights gained by prescription. Exactly what was their allegation respecting their claim of prescription? In the end, what does the court require by way of allegation to present a good claim based on prescription? In what ways were the defendants' claims inadequate? Is the court being too picky in terms of the formal rules of pleading?

What does the court say about the rights that a person has in unmarked swans? What happens when a swan swims or flies away from the owner's lands? Is there a uniform rule governing this situation, or does it seem to depend on the habits and dispositions of the particular swan? Finally, how do private rights in swans compare with the private rights that people can acquire in other animal species?

(4) Property in animals: The court presents an elaborate classification of the types of property rights a person could acquire in animals:

(a) It begins with a fundamental dichotomy between animals that are domesticated (*domitæ naturæ*[1]) and those that are wild (*feræ naturæ*). The distinction is reflected in the type of property right that a can be acquired in the animal: a person may have "absolute" property in domesticated animals, but only a "qualified" property in wild animals,[2] *i.e.*, a right that is possessory in the sense that the right ends if the animal escapes from possession.[3] Thus, a person may have absolute property in cattle because they are domesticated but only a possessory property in deer because they are "naturally" wild—even if they have been tamed ("*mansuetæ naturæ*"[4]).

(b) This qualified and possessory property right in wild animals may arise in two ways:

(i) *per industriam,* that is, "by industry as by taking them, or by making them *mansueta*." ¶ 5. The court emphasizes taming as a method of acquiring property *per industriam* and the durational limits imposed on such rights: "in those [animals] which are *feræ naturæ*, and by industry are made tame, a man hath but a qualified property in them ... so long as they remain tame, for if they do attain to their natural liberty, and have not *animum revertendi* [*i.e.*, the spirit of returning], the property is lost." ¶ 5. *See Mallocke v. Eastly,* 3 Lev. 227, 83 Eng. Rep. 663 (K.B. 1685) (tame deer); *Pollexfen v. Crispin,* 1 Vent. 122, 86 Eng. Rep. 84 (K.B. 1671) (fish kept in a pond or tank for the table); *Grymes v. Shack,* Cro. Jac. 262, 79 Eng. Rep. 226 (K.B. 1610) (musk-cats and monkeys held as merchandise); *Ireland v. Higgins,* Cro. Eliz. 125, 78 Eng. Rep. 383 (K.B. 1588) ("a dog is a thing that is tame by industry of man"); *Fines v. Spencer,* 3 Dyer 306b, 73 Eng. Rep. 692 (K.B. 1572) (tamed hawk). At the common law, Dr. Koop would have pled that the mallards were his property *per industriam. See Koop v. United States* in Chapter 1.

Note that, although the court in *The Case of Swans* emphasized taming, its first example of property acquired *per industriam* is "by taking them," *i.e.*, by capture.

(ii) *ratione impotentiæ et loci,* that is, when the animal is powerless to leave "by reason of inability and place," *i.e.*, "as if a man has young shovelers [a species of duck] or goshawks, or the like, which are *feræ naturæ*, and they build in my land, I have possessory property in

---

1. Literally "accustomed to a house," *i.e.*, domesticated.

2. "A man hath not absolute property in any thing which is *feræ naturæ*, [unlike] those which are *domitæ naturæ*." ¶ 5.

3. "Property qualified and possessory a man may have in those [animals] which are *feræ naturæ*." ¶ 5.

4. Literally "accustomed to a hand."

them, for if one takes them when they cannot fly, the owner of the soil shall have an action of trespass.'' ¶ 5. *See also Keble v. Hickringill,* 11 Mod. 73, 88 Eng. Rep. 898 (K.B. 1706) (pleading ownership proper for young hawks). The Latin tag for this category was eventually shortened to *"ratione loci,"* i.e., by reason of location and sometimes restated as *ratione soli, i.e.,* by reason of [ownership] of the soil. This category thus was a recognition that the owner of land had a right to exclude others that implied a possessory interest resulting simply from the animal's presence on her land.

This interest *ratione loci/soli* is to be distinguished from a third category that the court in *The Case of Swans* sets out:

(c) *ratione privilegii.* The owner of a park or warren had a franchise or "privilege" to take game within the confines of the park or warren, *i.e.,* "he hath not any property in the deer, or conies, or pheasants, or partridges ... but they do belong to him *ratione privil[egii]* for his game and pleasure, so long as they remain in the privileged place." ¶ 5. What is important to note at this point is that this type of possessory interest was a result of a grant by the King and differed from the possessory property right that the average landowner held. This type of ownership is considered below in *Sutton v. Moody,* 1 Ld. Raym. 250, 91 Eng. Rep. 1063 (K.B. 1698), and its notes in Chapter 3.

(d) Finally, a person acquired absolute property in animals *feræ naturæ* when they have been killed. *Usher v. Bushnel,* Raym. T. 16, 83 Eng. Rep. 9 (K.B. 1673).

A caveat: As noted in regard to *ratione loci/soli,* terminology was somewhat variable over time. For example, in *Childe v. Greenhill* the court outlined a different group of terms: "a man may have a special or qualified property in things which are *feræ naturæ,* three ways *ratione infirmitatis, ratione loci, & ratione privilegii." Childe v. Greenhill,* March N.R. 48, 82 Eng. Rep. 406 (K.B. 1640), *same case Greenhills Case,* 1 Jones, W. 440, 82 Eng. Rep. 231 (K.B. 1640).

(5) **Writs and property in animals:** The common law of wildlife was substantially shaped by the English system of writs, the "forms of action" at the common law. It was not enough to go into court and allege injury in everyday language: invoking the power of the Crown to settle a dispute required the injured person's attorney to select among a finite number of actions—writs such as an assize of novel disseisin or of entry *sur disseisin* in the *per* and *cui,* actions of replevin, trespass, assumpsit, ejectment, or case. The choice was a choice not only among diverse procedures and facts but also among what we now call substantive law. Although their grip is loosening, it remains true—in Maitland's famous phrase—that "[t]he forms of action we have buried, but they still rule us from their graves.'' F.W. MAITLAND, THE FORMS OF ACTION AT COMMON LAW 2 (1936). That is, disputes about the propriety of the various writs remain important because the legal pigeonholes that the writs created shaped the substance of the common law of wildlife.

Consider the following cases, which concern property rights in wild animals that were not, at the time of alleged wrong, in the actual physical possession of the putative owner. For we moderns, the issue is simply a question of the nature of the rights in the animal; for the common-law courts, on the other hand, this issue was subsumed into the question of whether the appropriate writ had been selected—that is, did the writ protect the type of interest that the plaintiff claimed?

(a) In *Bishop of Canterbury v. Osbert*, plaintiff brought a trespass action, alleging that defendant had trespassed on the plaintiff's warren. A warren was a franchise from the King allowing the franchisee to hunt specified animals on a particular parcel of land. In this case, the warren was located on land owned by defendant. The suit thus involved the relationship between the fanchisee and the landowner who was—in some sense—being sued for interfering with hunting on his land. The court upheld the action, rejecting a claim that a trespass action was appropriate only when the plaintiff owned the property in question (in this case, the wild animals). The court distinguished the case from the similar case of trespass that involved the taking of trees or grass:

> In [a case involving trees or grass] the writ should be . . . *"arbores suas et blada sua,* [my trees and my grass]"* for the writ does not lye for him except that the true property must be stated expressly in the writ, and this by that word (*sua*); but it is not so of hares, or other beasts of warren, for the true property of them does not belong to him to whom the warren belongs; for they belong to him by reason of the warren, *i.e.,* while they are within the warren, and if they go out of the warren, it is lawful for any man to take them.

Bishop of Canterbury v. Osbert, Y.B. 3 Hen. 6, pl. 55 (1425), *reprinted in* 2 JOSEPH CHITTY, A TREATISE ON THE GAME LAWS app. 2 at 730, 730–31 (photo. reprint 1979) (1812). Given the court's statements about animals that leave the warren, what sort of property interest did the warren-owner have in the wild game? How did the ownership differ from that a person might have in the grass or trees? Might it be most apt to say that the property interest was simply in the franchise (the warren) itself rather than in any particular animals?

(b) *Bowlston v. Hardy* was an action on the case brought by a landowner against an adjacent landowner. The defendant had established a coney[5] warren on his land and the number of conies had increased to the point that they were damaging plaintiff's land. The court held that the action would not lie, "for although one hath conies in his land, he hath not any property in them, because they are *feræ naturæ* . . . he who hath damage thereby may well kill them, and they may be said to be his conies when they are upon his land." *Bowlston v. Hardy,* Cro. Eliz. 547, 78 Eng. Rep. 794 (K.B. 1597). *Bowlston* is consistent with *Bishop of Canterbury* since animals escaping a warren are no longer owned by the holder of the warren. But note the facts: in *Bowlston,* the owner of the warren also owned the land and the animals were being raised by the owner as a crop. Should these facts have led to a different outcome in the case? Consider,

---

5. A "coney" or "cony" is a rabbit (*Oryctolagus cuniculus*); "rabbit" was formerly the name for only the young of the species. Coney—which rhymes with honey—dropped from the common tongue in the nineteenth century perhaps because of vulgar associations. 1 OXFORD ENGLISH DICTIONARY 955 (1933).

also: although the warren owner escaped liability for the damage done by the conies, is the court's reasoning likely to be beneficial to him in the long run?

(c) *Fines v. Spencer,* was an action in trover to recover the value of a falcon. Trover[6] was a writ employed to recover the value of personal property that the defendant had either wrongfully destroyed or wrongfully refused to return when asked to do so. Originally it was available only when a plaintiff had lost the item that defendant then found; the allegation of loss and finding, however, soon became a fiction that the defendant could not challenge and the writ became a tool for the recovery of personal property wrongfully held by another. In this case, the defendant "found" the falcon and sold it to a third party. Defendant argued that a trover action was inappropriate unless the plaintiff owned the falcon and that, in the case of an unconfined wild animal, ownership required proof that the animal was "reclaimed." The court agreed. *Fines v. Spencer,* 3 Dyer 306b, 73 Eng. Rep. 692 (K.B. 1572).

(d) *Vincent v. Lesney,* was an action in trespass for killing a hawk. Citing *Fines v. Spencer,* defendant sought judgment on the ground that plaintiff failed to plead that the hawk was "reclaimed." The court rejected the argument and upheld a verdict for plaintiff on the ground that trespass merely required a showing that the plaintiff had possession of the property—unlike trover, which required a showing of ownership. *Vincent v. Lesney,* Cro. Car. 18, 79 Eng. Rep. 621 (K.B. 1625). That is, trover requires a right called "ownership," trespass only possession.

(e) *Holmes v. Morland,* a case that is known only from the reports of a certain Dr. Watson: "Both cases decided, Dr. Watson, and both in my favour. I haven't had such a day since I had Sir John Morland for trespass because he shot in his own warren." SIR ARTHUR CONAN DOYLE, HOUND OF THE BASKERVILLES (1901). Under what facts might Holmes be correct?

(6) The persistence of common-law classifications: Oregon sued to gain possession of "a certain cetacean known as a whale of the classification of *Orca Gladiator,*" which became disoriented and swam inland before dying. The issue was whether the state owned the whale.

> The plaintiff claims that under the law [it] is owner of all "royal fish." Whales within coastal and inland waters have always been a part of the King's own revenue and are denominated "royal fish." 1 BLACKSTONE *290. The rights and prerogatives of the crown under the common law were vested in the state by the Revolution. [ ] The state now has all the prerogatives of sovereignty. Public grants are to be construed strictly. Nothing passes by implication, and all doubts are resolved in favor of the state. [ ]
>
> It is stated in the brief of the plaintiff, and is not challenged by the defendants, that the spectacle of a real whale at play a hundred miles inland from the sea created interest at home and abroad, and was the source of much inquiry from the press and educational institutions in

---

6. Or, "trover and conversion," as it was long called; it is now generally known simply as "conversion."

other parts of the world; that similar events in other countries, as recorded throughout the ages, were cited, and for a time Portland harbor was the object of unusual reference and great publicity; that after the killing, the body of the whale was placed in a tank especially built and donated to the state and preserved by means of donations and placed on exhibit for its educational value. . . .

The distinction between royal fish and other fish and game is clearly set forth in *Parker v. People*, 111 Ill. 581, 611 (1884): "This right, so far as concerned royal fish (whales, porpoises and sturgeon), was held by the sovereign for his own revenues, and so far as concerned all fish not royal, and in tide waters, was said to be in the king, in trust for all his subjects. So royal fish, when taken, were the property of the crown, by whomsoever taken; but fish not royal, taken in tide waters, became the property of the takers."

A different rule prevails in regard to a whale or royal fish from that which pertains to ordinary food fish which are regulated by statute. Defendants seek to apply the latter rule. We find no statutory law enacted in this state governing a whale.

State v. Lessard, 29 P.2d 509 (Or.1934). The supreme court reversed the trial court's dismissal of the state's complaint.

PERSPECTIVES

(1) Bracton and the persistence of Roman law: The court in *The Case of Swans* quoted Bracton for the proposition that animals that had been "tamed" belonged to the person who had tamed them as long as the animal returned. The quote comes from a discussion of the various classes of ownership that individuals might have in animals:

> Things are said to be *res nullius* [property of no one] in several different ways: by nature or the *jus naturale* [natural law],[1] as wild beasts, birds and fish . . . which formerly belonged to the finder by natural law but are now made the property of the prince by the *jus gentium* [human law][2]. . . .
>
> By the *jus gentium* or natural law the dominion of things is acquired in many ways. First by taking possession of things that are owned by no one, and do now belong to the king by the civil law [*i.e.,* the law of a particular state][3], no longer being common as before, as

1. [Bracton offered the following definition of "natural law":

Natural law is defined in many ways. It may first be said to denote a certain instinctive impulse arising out of animate nature by which individual living things are led to act in certain ways. Hence is it thus defined: Natural law is that which nature, that is, God himself, taught all living things. . . .]

HENRY DE BRACTON, DE LEGIBUS ET CONSUETUDINIBUS ANGLIAE bk. 1, chs. 4–5, ff. 3–4 (ca. 1256).

2. [Bracton defined *jus gentium* or "human law" as "the law which men of all nations use, which falls short of natural law since that is common to all animate things born on the earth in the sea or in the air. . . . The *jus gentium* is common to men alone." *Id.*]

3. [Bracton provided the following definition of "civil law":

Civil law, which may be called customary law, has several meanings. It may be taken to mean the statute law of a par-

wild beasts, birds and fish, that is, all the creatures born on the earth, in the sea or in the heavens, that is, in the air, no matter where they may be taken. When they are captured they begin to be mine, because they are forcibly kept in my custody, and by the same token, if they escape from it and recover their natural liberty they cease to be mine and are again made the property of the taker. They recover their natural liberty when they escape from my sight into the free air and are no longer in my keeping, or when, though still within my view, their pursuit is no longer possible.

The taking of possession also includes fishing, hunting and capture. It is not pursuit alone that makes a thing mine, for though I have wounded a wild beast so severely that it may be captured, it nevertheless is not mine unless I capture it; rather it will belong to the one who next takes it, for much may happen to prevent my capture of it....

The taking of possession also includes confinement, as in the case of bees, which are wild by nature. For if they settle in my tree they are no more mine, before I shut them into a hive, than are birds who make their nest there, and therefore if another hives them he will be their owner. A swarm that flies out of my hive is taken to be mine so long as it remains in my sight and its pursuit is not impossible, otherwise it becomes the property of the taker. But if another takes it he does not make the swarm his if he knows it belongs to another; indeed he commits a theft unless he has intention of restoring them. All these rules are true, but sometimes and in some places other rules hold good by custom.

What has been said applies to animals which also remain wild. But if wild animals are tamed and customarily go and come back, or fly away and return, as deer, peafowl and pigeons, another rule is applicable, [namely], that they are taken to be ours so long as they have the intention of returning, for if they cease to have that intention they cease to be ours. They are taken no longer to have the intention of returning when they lose the habit of returning. The same is true of wild hens and wild geese that have become tame. With regard to domestic animals a third rule is applicable, that though they fly out of my view they remain my hens and geese, no matter where they are, and he who takes them with the intention of keeping them commits a theft. This sort of occupation is also applicable to ... things common to all, as the sea and the seashore.

HENRY DE BRACTON, DE LEGIBUS ET CONSUETUDINIBUS ANGLIAE bk. 2, ch. 1, ff. 8b–9 (ca. 1256).

Behind Bracton stands Justinian's *Institutes*,[4] the preeminent "Restatement" of Roman law:

ticular city.... Civil law may also be called all the law used in a state or the like, whether it is natural law, civil law, or the *jus gentium*.]

Id.

4. Justinian I (483–565) was the Byzantine Emperor from 527–565. He was an autocratic emperor who was fortunate to be served by superb generals, who not only kept him in power against popular discontent but also produced a string of military victories

[W]ild animals, birds and fish, *i.e.,* all animals born on land or in the sea or air, as soon as they are caught by anyone, forthwith fall into his ownership by the law of nations: for what previously belonged to no one is, by natural reason, accorded to its captor. Nor does it matter whether the animals and birds be taken on one's own land or on someone else's. Of course, anyone entering another's land to hunt or for fowling can be stopped by the owner, if he be aware of it. But any of these things that you take is considered to be yours so long as it is regulated by your control: but, once it escapes from your custody and resumes its natural state, it ceases to be yours and again becomes open to the next taker. It is regarded as resuming its natural state when either it disappears from your sight or, though you can still see it, pursuit of it is difficult.

The question was raised whether wild animals, which have been so wounded that they could be captured, forthwith become yours. In the opinion of some, it is and is held to be yours at once, so long as you pursue it: but should you give up the chase, it is no longer yours and is again open to the first taker. Others held the view that it becomes yours only if you actually take it. We give our authority to the second view, for many factors may arise by reason of which you do not take it.

. . .

Peacocks and doves are wild by nature nor is it relevant that they are in the habit of flying away and returning: for ... there are deer which are so tame that they go into and out of woods but no one would deny that they are wild by nature. Still, in the case of those animals which normally come and go, the rule has been endorsed that they are treated as yours so long as they have the instinct to return. If they cease to do so, they also cease to be yours and are available to the first taker. And they are regarded as ceasing to have this instinct when they abandon the practice of returning.

THE INSTITUTES OF JUSTINIAN bk. II, tit. 1, §§ 12–13, 15 (1st ed. 533).

The close parallels between Bracton and Justinian and continuing relevance of Roman Law reflected both the Catholicism of medieval England and the fact that English universities taught only Roman and Canon (that is, church) law until Sir William Blackstone[5] became a professor of law at Oxford in 1758 and taught the first courses in English law.

(2) Swans as legal entities: Designation of the swan as a royal fowl had three important legal consequences.

including the reconquest of Africa and Italy. His greatest accomplishment was the codification of Roman law—the *Corpus Juris Civilis*—that was executed under the direction of Tribonian, a Roman jurist.

5. After an unsuccessful legal practice, William Blackstone (1723–1780) became the first Vinerian professor of law at Oxford in 1758. During his tenure, he began the first courses in English law taught at an English university. Between 1765 and 1769, he pub-lished his four volume treatise, the *Commentaries on the Laws of England*. The treatise created order where little had previously existed. The *Commentaries* exerted substantial influence over the legal profession and the teaching of law in the United States. Following its publication, Blackstone resumed his legal practice, served in Parliament, was Solicitor General, and a judge on the Court of Common Pleas.

(a) Swans and property: The designation affected the types of interests that individuals could acquire in swans. The issue in *The Case of Swans*—whether, or under what circumstances, a private individual could acquire ownership of swans—involved questions of grant and prescription.

The Crown could, of course, grant subjects the privilege of keeping swans on public waters. This was Bracton's "special warrant." *The Case of Swans* holds that subjects could also prescribe for (that is, gain by prescription) a privilege to maintain swans on public waters. In Bracton's words, such rights could be acquired

> without a [charter], by long use, with peaceful possession, continuous and uninterrupted, through the knowledge and acquiescence of lords ... which is taken for livery, provided it is not by force, stealth, or at will.

HENRY DE BRACTON, DE LEGIBUS ET CONSUETUDINIBUS ANGLIAE bk. 4, ch. 37, f. 222a (ca. 1256).

(b) Swans and regulation: Designation of the swan as a royal fowl also meant that swans were subject to continuing royal control. This continuing royal interest is also demonstrated in *The Case of Swans*. The modern parallel is the regulatory authority of administrative agencies such as the United States Fish and Wildlife Service and state fish and game commissions.

The case was initiated by the appointment by the Queen of a commission to inquire into the ownership of the swans in Dorset County. Formally termed a "Swanmote," the commission was a body that exercised broad administrative and judicial powers. It was "to enquire into, deal with and award punishments for, transgressions of the swan laws, and to settle disputes between owners and between owners and the Crown"; the commission also "had wide powers to draw up and proclaim additional regulations affecting swan-keeping in their particular area." NORMAN F. TICEHURST, THE MUTE SWAN IN ENGLAND 39 (1957).

In addition to such periodic investigatory and adjudicatory commissions, there was a royal officer—the Master of the King's (or Queen's) Game of Swans (the *magister deductus cignorum*)—who was responsible for the care of the royal swans as well as the general supervision of swan-keeping in England. This involved a large number of tasks including supervising the annual "upping," the round-up of the year's new broods of cygnets and their marking with the parents' swan-marks. This was a process not unlike the annual fall round-up and branding of range cattle: cygnets would be captured with their parents, their parents' swan-marks checked, and the cygnets marked. *Id.* at 54–72.

(c) Swans and revenue: Finally, while the idea of swans as royal fowls (and of whales and sturgeons as royal fish) now has a quaint air, all of these found their way onto the King's table. For example, a twelfth-century description of the Exchequer noted that "if a royal fish, a turbot or a whale, or the like is caught, the necessary materials for salting it and what else are needed are sent by the Sheriff and credited to him without writ." RICHARD, FITZ NIGEL, DIALOGUS DE SCACCARIO bk. II, ch. VIII (Charles Johnson ed. & trans. 1983) (ca. 1176). Swans were the turkeys of the day:

the centerpiece of every self-respecting feast. In 1251, for example, Henry III requisitioned more than 125 swans for Christmas.

The most general point is that the legal procedure has evolved far more radically than have the underlying legal issues. While some translation may be necessary, to see only quaintness is to miss the thread that ties together past and present.

(3) Swans as allegorical entities: The designation of the swan as a royal fowl also offers insights into the early common law's system of categorization. In a related case concerning a possible gold mine, the Queen's attorneys argued that "all mines and ores of gold or silver, which are in the lands of subjects, with power to dig the land, and carry away the ore, and other incidents thereto, belong of right to the King of this realm by prerogative." The first point offered in support of this proposition offers insights into the then-relevant categories:

> [The first reason] why the King shall have mines and ores of gold or silver within the realm, in whatsoever land they are found ... was, in respect of the excellency of the thing, for of all things which the soil within this realm produces or yields gold and silver is the most excellent; and of all persons in the realm the King is in the eye of the law most excellent. And the common law, which is founded upon reason, appropriates every thing to the persons whom it best suits, as common and trivial things to common people, things of more worth to persons in a higher and superior class, and things most excellent to those persons who excel all others; and because gold and silver are the most excellent things which the soil contains, the law has appointed them (as in reason it ought) to the person who is most excellent, and that is the King.

The Case of the Mines, 1 Pl. Com. 310, 315, 75 Eng. Rep. 472, 479 (K.B. 1568). The court in *Case of the Swans* offered a similar analysis, stating that "the law [of swans] is founded on a reason in nature; for the cock swan is an emblem or representation of an affectionate and true husband to his wife above all other fowls." As such, they were "royal" because they were the peak of perfection.

Although much of this allegorical symbolism now seems fanciful[1]—and therefore easily dismissed—in this more rationalist age, to do so unreflectively is to miss an important point on our species' relationship to other species. For much of the medieval period, nature served as a expansive allegory, a symbol-filled landscape leading people to a knowledge of God: as Augustine stated, man "is able to *catch sight of God's invisible nature through his creatures.*" AUGUSTINE, CONFESSIONS bk X, ch. 6, at 212–13 (Penguin ed. 1961) (1st ed. 397–398). The caterpillar, for example, was an emblem of the resurrection, a reminder of the contingency of the world. *See* KEITH THOMAS, MAN AND THE NATURAL WORLD 64 (1983). Swans have occupied a complex and often contradictory role in this mythology. *See* Mary Evans & Andrew Dawnay, *The Swan in Mythology and Art, in* THE SWANS 143–66

---

1. One thing is clear: anyone who writes of the swan's sweet "song" has never heard one squawk.

(Peter Scott ed. 1972); BERYL ROWLAND, BIRDS WITH HUMAN SOULS 169–74 (1978).

(4) Swans as status symbols: Whether because of a worldview that saw the "inherent nature" of swans as an example of royal perfection or simply because of the designation of swans as a royal fowl, swans were symbols of high social status. Ticehurst circumspectly notes that, as a royal fowl, swans "lend a certain air of distinction, well-being and importance to their owner; moreover it is certain also that their possession was, at any rate in early days, regarded as a mark of distinction." NORMAN F. TICEHURST, THE MUTE SWAN IN ENGLAND 11 (1957). To preserve this mark of distinction—by removing swans from "the hands of yeoman and husbandmen, and other persons of little reputation"—Parliament passed the Act for Swans in 1482 which prohibited ownership of swans by anyone who did not meet substantial property requirements; swans held in violation of the Act could be seized by anyone meeting those property requirements. *See* 22 ED. 4, ch. 6 (1482).

Animals have often served as status symbols. This role was particularly well-developed in the hierarchical feudal societies of Christendom and Islam from 500 to 1600. Even more important than swans as status symbols were falcons where, at least for some commentators, each social rank had its particular falcon or hawk. The *Boke of Saint Albans* (1486) provided such a detailed listing: the "Egle" (Golden Eagle) was reserved for the Emperor, the "Gerfalcon & tercett" (Gyrfalcon) for the king, the "Falken gentill" (female Peregrine) for the prince, the "Falken of the rock" (a form of Peregrine) for the duke, the "Falken peregryne" for the earl, the "Bastarde" (bastard or tiercel Peregrine) for the baron, the "Sacre & Sacret" (Saker) for the knight, the "Lanare & Lanrett" (Lanner) for the squire, the "Merlyon" (Merlin) for the lady, the "Hoby" (Hobby) for the page or youngman. The "ignoble hawks" were for the lower classes: the "Goshawke" (female Goshawk) for the yeoman, the "Tercett" (male Goshawk) for the poor man, the "Spare hawke" (female Sparrowhawk) for the priest, and the "Muskyte" (male Sparrowhawk) for the holywater clerk. THE BOKE OF ST. ALBANS f. 27b–28a (1486).

As we shall see, much of the English law on wildlife reflects and reinforces the hierarchical structure of English society—and a good deal of American law is based on a rejections of that social system. Nonetheless, animals retain their power as status symbols in the United States—consider the fur coat.

b. THE COMMON LAW IN A NEW WORLD

Herman Melville, Fast Fish, Loose Fish, in Moby–Dick
ch. 89 (1st ed. London, 1851).

The allusion to the waifs and waif-poles[1] . . . necessitates some account of the laws and regulations, of the whale fishery, of which the waif may be deemed the grand symbol and badge.

---

1. "The waif is a pennoned pole, two or   three of which are carried by every boat; and

It frequently happens that when several ships are cruising in company, a whale may be struck by one vessel, then escape, and be finally killed and captured by another vessel; and herein are indirectly comprised many minor contingencies, all partaking of this one grand feature. For example,—after a weary and perilous chase and capture of a whale, the body may get loose from the ship by reason of a violent storm; and drifting far away to leeward, be retaken by a second whaler, who, in a calm, snugly tows it alongside, without risk of life or line. Thus the most vexatious and violent disputes would often arise between the fishermen, were there not some written or unwritten, universal, undisputed law applicable to all cases.

Perhaps the only formal whaling code authorized by legislative enactment, was that of Holland. It was decreed by the States–General in A.D. 1695. But though no other nation has ever had any written whaling law, yet the American fishermen have been their own legislators and lawyers in this matter. They have provided a system which for terse comprehensiveness surpasses Justinian's Pandects and the By-laws of the Chinese Society for the Suppression of Meddling with other People's Business. Yes; these laws might be engraven on a Queen Anne's farthing, or the barb of a harpoon, and worn round the neck, so small are they.

I.   A Fast–Fish belongs to the party fast to it.

II.   A Loose–Fish is fair game for anybody who can soonest catch it.

But what plays the mischief with this masterly code is the admirable brevity of it, which necessitates a vast volume of commentaries to expound it.

First: What is a Fast–Fish? Alive or dead a fish is technically fast, when it is connected with an occupied ship or boat, by any medium at all controllable by the occupant or occupants,—a mast, an oar, a nine-inch cable, a telegraph wire, or a strand of cobweb, it is all the same. Likewise a fish is technically fast when it bears a waif; or any other recognised symbol of possession; so long as the party waifing it plainly evince their ability at any time to take it alongside, as well as their intention so to do.

These are scientific commentaries; but the commentaries of the whalemen themselves sometimes consist in hard words and harder knocks—the Coke-upon-Littleton of the fist. True, among the more upright and honorable whalemen allowances are always made for peculiar cases, where it would be an outrageous moral injustice for one party to claim possession of a whale previously chased or killed by another party. But others are by no means so scrupulous.

Some fifty years ago there was a curious case of whale-trover litigated in England, wherein the plaintiffs set forth that after a hard chase of a whale in the Northern seas, they (the plaintiffs) had succeeded in harpooning the fish; but at last, through peril of their lives, were obliged to forsake not only their lines, but their boat itself. Ultimately the defendants (the

---

which, when additional game is at hand, are inserted upright into the floating body of a dead whale, both to mark its place on the sea, and also as token of prior possession, should the boats of any other ship draw near." HERMAN MELVILLE, MOBY-DICK ch. 87.

crew of another ship) came up with the whale, struck, killed, seized, and finally appropriated it before the very eyes of the plaintiffs. And when those defendants were remonstrated with, their captain snapped his fingers in the plaintiffs' teeth, and assured them that by way of doxology to the deed he had done, he would now retain their line, harpoons, and boat, which had remained attached to the whale at the time of the seizure. Wherefore the plaintiffs now sued for the recovery of the value of their whale, line, harpoons, and boat.

Mr. Erskine was counsel for the defendants; Lord Ellenborough was the judge. In the course of the defence, the witty Erskine went on to illustrate his position, by alluding to a recent crim. con. case, wherein a gentleman, after in vain trying to bridle his wife's viciousness, had at last abandoned her upon the seas of life; but in the course of years, repenting of that step, he instituted an action to recover possession of her. Erskine was on the other side; and he then supported it by saying, that though the gentleman had originally harpooned the lady, and had once had her fast, and only by reason of the great stress of her plunging viciousness, had at last abandoned her; yet abandon her he did, so that she became a loose-fish; and therefore when a subsequent gentleman re-harpooned her, the lady then became that subsequent gentleman's property, along with whatever harpoon might have been found sticking in her.

Now in the present case Erskine contended that the examples of the whale and the lady were reciprocally illustrative of each other.

These pleadings, and the counter pleadings, being duly heard, the very learned judge in set terms decided, to wit,—That as for the boat, he awarded it to the plaintiffs, because they had merely abandoned it to save their lives; but that with regard to the controverted whale, harpoons, and line, they belonged to the defendants; the whale, because it was a Loose–Fish at the time of the final capture; and the harpoons and line because when the fish made off with them, it (the fish) acquired a property in those articles; and hence anybody who afterwards took the fish had a right to them. Now the defendants afterwards took the fish; ergo, the aforesaid articles were theirs.

A common man looking at this decision of the very learned Judge, might possibly object to it. But ploughed up to the primary rock of the matter, the two great principles laid down in the twin whaling laws previously quoted, and applied and elucidated by Lord Ellenborough in the above cited case; these two laws touching Fast–Fish and Loose–Fish, I say, will, on reflection, be found the fundamentals of all human jurisprudence; for notwithstanding its complicated tracery of sculpture, the Temple of the Law, like the Temple of the Philistines, has but two props to stand on.

Is it not a saying in every one's mouth, Possession is half of the law: that is, regardless of how the thing came into possession? But often possession is the whole of the law. What are the sinews and souls of Russian serfs and Republican slaves but Fast–Fish, whereof possession is the whole of the law? What to the rapacious landlord is the widow's last mite but a Fast–Fish? What is yonder undetected villain's marble mansion with a door-plate for a waif; what is that but a Fast–Fish? What is the ruinous discount which Mordecai, the broker, gets from poor Woebegone, the bankrupt, on a loan to keep Woebegone's family from starvation; what is that ruinous discount but a Fast–Fish? What is the Archbishop of Savesoul's income of 100,000 seized from the scant bread and cheese of hundreds of thousands of broken-backed laborers (all sure of heaven without any of Savesoul's help) what is that globular 100,000 but a Fast–Fish? What are the Duke of Dunder's hereditary towns and hamlets but Fast–Fish? What to that redoubted harpooner, John Bull, is poor Ireland, but a Fast–Fish? What to that apostolic lancer, Brother Jonathan, is Texas but a Fast–Fish? And concerning all these, is not Possession the whole of the law?

But if the doctrine of Fast–Fish be pretty generally applicable, the kindred doctrine of Loose–Fish is still more widely so. That is internationally and universally applicable.

What was America in 1492 but a Loose–Fish, in which Columbus struck the Spanish standard by way of waifing it for his royal master and mistress? What was Poland to the Czar? What Greece to the Turk? What India to England? What at last will Mexico be to the United States? All Loose–Fish.

What are the Rights of Man and the Liberties of the World but Loose–Fish? What all men's minds and opinions but Loose–Fish? What is the principle of religious belief in them but a Loose–Fish? What to the ostentatious smuggling verbalists are the thoughts of thinkers but Loose–Fish? What is the great globe itself but a Loose–Fish? And what are you, reader, but a Loose–Fish and a Fast–Fish, too?

Pierson v. Post

New York Supreme Court.
3 Caines 175 (1805).

[Plaintiff brought a civil action to recover damages, alleging that he (Post) with his hounds did, "upon a certain wild and uninhabited, unpossessed and waste land, called the beach, find and start one of those noxious beasts called a fox." While Post was pursuing the fox with his hounds, Pierson, knowing that Post was hunting the fox, killed the animal. The justice court in Queens County rendered a verdict for plaintiff. The defendant appealed, arguing that the declaration was not sufficient in law to maintain an action.]

■ TOMPKINS, J.:—.... The question submitted by the counsel in this cause for our determination is, whether Lodowick Post, by the pursuit with his hounds in the manner alleged in his declaration, acquired such a right to, or property in, the fox as will sustain an action against Pierson for killing and taking him away?

The cause was argued with much ability by the counsel on both sides, and presents for our decision a novel and nice question. It is admitted that a fox is an animal *feræ naturæ,* and that property in such animals is acquired by occupancy only. These admissions narrow the discussion to the simple question of what acts amount to occupancy, applied to acquiring right to wild animals.

If we have recourse to the ancient writers upon general principles of law, the judgment below is obviously erroneous. Justinian's Institutes, (bk. 2, tit. 1, § 13) and Fleta [ ], adopt the principle, that pursuit alone vests no property or right in the huntsman; and that even pursuit, accompanied with wounding, is equally ineffectual for that purpose, unless the animal be actually taken....

Pufendorf (bk. 4, ch. 6, §§ 2, 10) defines occupancy of beasts *feræ naturæ*, to be the actual corporeal possession of them, and Bynkershoek is cited as coinciding in this definition. It is indeed with hesitation that Pufendorf affirms that a wild beast mortally wounded or greatly maimed, cannot be fairly intercepted by another, whilst the pursuit of the person inflicting the wound continues. The foregoing authorities are decisive to show that mere pursuit gave Post no legal right to the fox, but that he became the property of Pierson, who intercepted and killed him.

It, therefore, only remains to inquire whether there are any contrary principles or authorities, to be found in other books, which ought to induce a different decision. Most of the cases which have occurred in England, relating to property in wild animals, have either been discussed and decided upon the principles of their positive statute regulations, or have arisen between the huntsman and the owner of the land upon which beasts *feræ naturæ* have been apprehended; the former claiming them by title of occupancy, and the latter *ratione soli*. Little satisfactory aid can, therefore, be derived from the English reporters.

Barbeyrac, in his notes on Pufendorf, does not accede to the definition of occupancy by the latter, but, on the contrary, affirms that actual bodily seizure is not, in all cases, necessary to constitute possession of wild animals.... [A]s far as Barbeyrac appears to me to go, his objections to Pufendorf's decision of occupancy are reasonable and correct. That is to say, that actual bodily seizure is not indispensable to acquire right to, or possession of, wild beasts; but that, on the contrary, the mortal wounding of such beasts, by one not abandoning his pursuit, may, with the utmost propriety, be deemed possession of him; since thereby the pursuer manifests an unequivocal intention of appropriating the animal to his individual use, has deprived him of his natural liberty, and brought him within his certain control. So, also, encompassing and securing such animals with nets and toils, or otherwise intercepting them in such a manner as to deprive them of their natural liberty, and render escape impossible, may justly be deemed to give possession of them to those person who, by their industry and labor, have used such means of apprehending them.... The case now under consideration is one of mere pursuit, and presents no circumstances or acts which can bring it within the definition of occupancy by Pufendorf, or Grotius, or the ideas of Barbeyrac upon that subject.

. . . .

We are the more readily inclined to confine possession or occupancy of beasts *feræ naturæ*, within the limits prescribed by the learned authors above cited, for the sake of certainty, and preserving peace and order in society. If the first seeing, starting or pursuing such animals, without having so wounded, circumvented or ensnared them, so as to deprive them of their natural liberty, and subject them to the control of their pursuer, should afford the basis of actions against others for intercepting and killing them, it would prove a fertile source of quarrels and litigation.

However uncourteous or unkind the conduct of Pierson towards Post, in this instance, may have been, yet this act was productive of no injury or damage for which a legal remedy can be applied. We are of opinion the judgment below was erroneous, and ought to be reversed.

■ LIVINGSTON, J.:—My opinion differs from that of the court. Of the six exceptions taken to the proceedings below, all are abandoned except the third, which reduces the controversy to a single question . . .

Whether a person who, with his own hounds, starts and hunts a fox on waste and uninhabited ground, and is on the point of seizing his prey, acquires such an interest in the animal as to have a right of action against another, who in view of the huntsman and his dogs in full pursuit, and with the knowledge of the chase, shall kill and carry him away.

This is a knotty point, and should have been submitted to the arbitration of sportsmen, without poring over Justinian, Fleta, Breakdown, Pufendorf, Locke, Barbeyrac, or Blackstone, all of whom have been cited; they would have had no difficulty in coming to a proper and correct conclusion. In a court thus constituted, the skin and carcass of poor Reynard[1] would have been properly disposed of, and a precedent set, interfering with no usage or custom which the experience of ages has sanctioned, and which must be so well known to every votary of Diana.[2] But the parties have referred the question to our judgment, and we must dispose of it as well as we can, from the partial lights we possess, leaving to a higher tribunal the correction of any mistake which we may be so unfortunate as to make. By the pleadings it is admitted that a fox is a "wild and Noxious beast." Both parties have regarded him, as the law of nations does a pirate. . . . His depredation on farmers and on barnyards, have not been forgotten; and to put him to death wherever found, is allowed to be meritorious, and of public benefit. Hence it follows, that our decision should have in view the greatest possible encouragement to the destruction of an animal, so cunning and ruthless in his career. But who would keep a pack of hounds; or what gentleman, at the sound of the horn, and at peep of day, would mount his steed, and for hours together, "*sub jove frigido*," or a vertical sun, pursue the windings of this wily quadruped, if, just as night came on, and his stratagems and strength were nearly exhausted, a saucy intruder, who had not shared in the honors or labors of the chase, were permitted to come in at the death, and bear away in triumph the object of pursuit? . . . .

It may be expected, however, by the learned counsel, that more particular notice be taken of their authorities. I have examined them all, and feel great difficulty in determining, whether to acquire dominion over a

---

1. [Reynard the Fox was the hero of medieval beast epics, a series of loosely connected tales that usually begin with the summons of Reynard by King Noble (the Lion) to answer the accusations of Isengrim the Wolf and other animals. Most of the stories contain biting satire of the peasants' contempt for the upper classes and the clergy.]

2. [Roman goddess of the hunt; she was identified by ancient Romans with the Greek goddess Artemis.]

thing, before in common, it be sufficient that we barely see it, or know where it is, or wish for it, or make a declaration of our will respecting it; or whether, in the case of wild beasts, setting a trap, or lying in wait, or starting, or pursuing, be enough; or if an actual wounding, or killing, or bodily tact and occupation be necessary. Writers on general law, who have favored us with their speculations on these points, differ on them all; but, great as is the diversity of sentiment among them, some conclusion must be adopted on the question immediately before us. After mature deliberation, I embrace that of Barbeyrac as the most rational and least liable to objection[;] ... that property in animals *feræ naturæ* may be acquired without bodily touch or manucaption, provided the pursuer be within reach, or have a reasonable prospect (which certainly existed here) of taking what he has thus discovered an intention of converting to his own use.

When we reflect also that the interest of our husbandmen, the most useful of men in any community, will be advanced by the destruction of a beast so pernicious and incorrigible, we cannot greatly err in saying that a pursuit like the present, through waste and unoccupied lands, and which must inevitably and speedily have terminated in corporeal possession, or bodily seisin, confers such a right to the object of it, as to make any one a wrong-doer who shall interfere and shoulder the spoil. The justice's judgment ought, therefore, in my opinion, to be affirmed.

Judgment of reversal.

NOTES

(1) The law often embodies its basic propositions in simple, almost-mythic stories. Pierson, Post, and the fox is one such tale—a tale that offers a partial answer to what Carol Rose has noted is "a fundamental puzzle for anyone who thinks about property": "How do things come to be owned?" Carol M. Rose, *Possession as the Origin of Property,* 52 U. CHI. L. REV. 73, 73 (1985).

Pierson came down to the particular issue of how far a person must go in capturing or "occupying" a wild animal before ownership rights arise in that animal. Would the majority allow ownership based on any action short of actual physical capture? In the dissent's view, when in the course of a hunt would such rights arise? What are the factors that a hunter would need to prove to claim ownership, in terms of prospects of capture and intent to conclude the hunt?

(2) Property as allocation: In functional terms, *Pierson* is about the allocation of private rights in wildlife. Note that, from this perspective, the majority and dissent differed only in details. Both assumed that the fox was available for hunters to acquire, and both assumed that the operative legal rule was a rule of capture—that is, a first-in-time allocation scheme. They differed only on the specific application of the rule of capture to the fox-hunting setting: first in time to do what? Neither the majority nor the dissent raised the possibility of alternative allocation methods, nor did they consider the possibility that foxes might be worth protecting because of their role in controlling rodents and other "pests."

Is it surprising that the court finds it necessary in deciding the case to look for precedent in the works of European commentators, dating back to ancient Rome? According to the court, why were English precedents dealing with wild animals irrelevant to the case? Does this irrelevance tell us something about the importance of the rule of capture—standing alone—even in 1809? For an enlightened discussion of the court's use of precedent, see Charles Donahue Jr., *Animalia Ferae Naturae: Rome, Bologna, Leyden, Oxford and Queen's County, N.Y.*, *in* STUDIES IN ROMAN LAW IN MEMORY OF A. ARTHUR SCHILLER 39 (Rogers S. Bagnall & William V. Harris eds. 1986).

(3) Although the justices spend considerable energy exploring old precedents, those precedents were not binding on the court. In fact, one senses that the justices settled upon their respective positions based on policy considerations. What policy factors does the majority cite? In what way would the majority's approach increase certainty in the application of the law? If the majority's approach actually would strike sport hunters as unfair—as Livingston in dissent suggests—would the rule in practice preserve "peace and order in society" and reduce "quarrels and litigation"? Is it important, when considering this issue, to keep in mind that both parties are carrying guns?

On his side, Livingston bases his appeal on fairness, as perceived by sport hunters. Assuming he is factually correct, how relevant is this consideration? If this really is a dispute among sport hunters (as the court-stated facts suggest), should we simply look to see if hunters have informal codes of conduct that govern their affairs? Should hunters alone set the legal rule on this point, or should we consider more widely the views of all citizens? Would the complexity of Livingston's fairness-oriented approach lead to "quarrels and litigation" as the majority suggests? Which is more important in this corner of the law, clarity/ease of application or fairness? Finally, there is Livingston's alternative, farm-focused rationale—that his rule would do a better job encouraging people to kill noxious foxes "in the interest of our husbandmen." Is this likely to be so? And is it clear that farmers of the day would have preferred a fox-less countryside?

(4) The New York Supreme Court viewed *Pierson* as a case dealing with the ownership of a dead fox, no doubt because the lawyers representing the parties presented the case to it in those terms. But is this the only way that it might have thought about the case? Consider Livingston's fairness objection. Why might a hunter in Post's position object to the interference by Pierson? Is it because Pierson ended up with the fox carcass? Or was it because Pierson disrupted the hunt? If the latter, is the key element of the alleged wrong not an invasion of property rights but something else—perhaps an interference with lawful hunting or other lawful enterprise? Might the case have come out differently had it been argued in those terms?

PERSPECTIVES

(1) The missing stories of Pierson, Post, and the fox: Judicial opinions are selective; they tell some stories and leave out others.

(a) Jesse Pierson and Lodowick Post were 25 and 28 at the time the decision was handed down. James Turslow Adams suggests that it was the parties' fathers—Capt. David Pierson and Capt. Nathan Post—who were primarily responsible for turning a dispute over a dead fox into a lawsuit. Another commenter provides the following "facts connected with" the case:

> Jesse Pierson, son of Capt. David, coming from Amagansett, saw a fox run and hide down an unused well near Peters Pond and killed and took the fox. Lodowick Post and a company with him were in pursuit and chasing the fox and saw Jesse with it and claimed it as theirs, while Jesse persisted in his claim. Capt. Pierson said his son Jesse should have the fox and Capt. Post said the same of his son Lodowick and hence the law suit contested and appealed to the highest court in the State which decided that Post had not got the possession of the fox when Pierson killed it and that he had no property in it as against Pierson until he had reduced it into his own possession.... To the public the decision was worth its cost. To the parties who each expended over a thousand pounds, the fox cost very dear.

THE STORY OF A CELEBRATION 60–61 (John E. Heartt ed., 1910). *See also* JAMES T. ADAMS, MEMORIALS OF OLD BRIDGEHAMPTON 166, 319, 334 (1962). On such missing stories, *see generally* JOHN T. NOONAN, PERSONS AND MASKS OF THE LAW (1976).

Note that Heartt writes that "Lodowick Post and a company with him were in pursuit and chasing the fox." Does this suggest that the case grew out of a fox hunt? If so, does this suggest something of the class of the participants? The cost of the fox to the litigants reinforces the inference that this was not a simple case of two individuals seeking to rid the neighborhood of a "wild and Noxious beast."

(b) Another story is teased out of the facts in the following critique:

> The starting point for an analysis of *Pierson* is John Locke, who sought to establish the bona fides of property rights through a narrative of acorns in the wild:

> > He that is nourished by the acorns he picked up under an oak, or the apples he gathered from the trees in the wood, has certainly appropriated them to himself. Nobody can deny but the nourishment is his. I ask, then, When did they begin to be his? when he digested? or when he ate? of when he boiled? or when he brought them home? or when he picked them up? and 'tis plain, if the first gathering made them not his, nothing else could. That *labour* put a distinction between them and common.... And will any one say he had no right to those acorns or apples he thus appropriated, because he had not the consent of all mankind to make them his? Was it a robbery thus to assume to himself what belonged to all in common? If such a consent as that was necessary, man had starved, notwithstanding the plenty God had given him. We see in *commons,* which remain so by compact, that 'tis the taking any part of what is common, the removing it out of the state nature

leaves it in, which *begins the property;* without which the common is of no use.[43]

Pierson authenticates Locke by placing his mythic story in early nineteenth century New York, where it shows the hunter wresting his property from the common by injecting his labor into it.

Locke's nature narrative is a powerful rhetorical tool that establishes two important assumptions about property law. The first is that property rights stem from human biology, specifically from human hunger. The second is that property rights are "naturally" of the on-off (I eat it or you eat it) variety: in other words, that property rights grant exclusive use (and presumably have since men were savages in the wild). This is an important nexus between the strain of Locke that developed into the constitutional rhetoric of absolutism and the somewhat different strain that developed into possessive individualism.

Locke's image of individuals wresting food from a wild terrain also sends messages about the moral status of ownership. *Pierson* intimates that ownership is tied to the sweat of the hunter's brow, thereby implying (without ever being so crass as to state it) that property is open to all and reflects the owner's hard work. *Pierson* intimates that to reconsider the allocation of property rights today would be like tearing the fox from the sweaty hands of the still-panting hunter.

. . .

The . . . wild animal cases also endorse the *Lockean* assumption that ownership is naturally focused on an individual acting alone. The labor of the woman who cooks the hunter's dinner and cares for his children is (for reasons not explained) not of the type that creates property rights. In fact, in [the] wild animal cases, the entire social system is read off the map: the implicit message is that the hunter's dependence on the network of human relationships that created and sustains his life is irrelevant to the design of "his" property rights. In an era supposedly dominated by Hohfeld's analysis of property in terms of social relationships, this is a remarkable achievement.

. . .

Pierson v. Post proves so indispensable not only because it embeds the *Lockean* nature narrative but also the strain of utilitarianism with which the nature narrative ultimately was wedded to create a theory of property Locke himself did not hold. In *Pierson,* both the majority and the dissenting opinions use utilitarian arguments to support their positions, eloquently establishing the point that utilitarian considerations are an inevitable element in cases involving property. When *Pierson* is juxtaposed with Harold Demsetz's modern retelling of the nature narrative,[58] it creates a seamless bond between Locke's nature

---

43. JOHN LOCKE, THE SECOND TREATISE OF GOVERNMENT § 28 (J.W. Gough ed., 1976) (1679–1683).

58. Harold Demsetz, *Toward a Theory of Property Rights,* 57 AM. ECON. REV. 347 (1967).

narrative and the notions that property rights are inevitably *economic* and that their design is tied to wealth creation. Demsetz examines the linkage of property rights with the fur trade and argues that private property replaced common ownership because the latter "naturally" led to waste. Demsetz's modern rewrite of the nature narrative mistakes ideology for history in a way that has been attacked as bad history and bad economics. Yet Demsetz continues to be included, even in casebooks now aware of the need for a long note on the discrediting literature, for the same reason we still teach an 1806 case about wild animals in 1998; it perpetuates and naturalizes a particular vision of property.

Joan Williams, *The Rhetoric of Property,* 83 IOWA L. REV. 277, 285–89 (1988).

As Professor Williams notes, *Pierson* is often understood in the context of John Locke's fictional narrative about how private property rights arose in pre-social times: people mixed their labor with unowned things and thus came to own them. Locke based his argument, however, on the factual assumption that unowned things were so plentiful that they had no value unless and until humans added value to them through work. When that happened, the resulting value was due entirely to the labor supplied by the putative owner, so that it was only fair (Locke assumed) for the laborer to own the thing. How aptly does this narrative apply to a case such as *Pierson*? If the fox was merely a noxious beast, did the labor involving in killing the fox add value to the carcass? And if Pierson and Post really were competing for the same fox, did the living fox (as Locke assumed) have no value?

(c) Finally there is the fox's narrative. This is the most invisible story since "*natural* law" granted the fox no standing. The fox was potential property rather than a legal actor; its interests were of no concern to the lawyers or judges. Recall that for Tom Regan and Steven Wise, the basic problem is that animals are treated as property rather than as individuals worthy of ethical and legal consideration.

(2) *Pierson v. Post,* the fur trade, beaver, and keystone species: *Pierson v. Post* presents property-by-capture with a classic starkness: Post, out with his pack of hounds "upon a certain wild and uninhabited, unpossessed and waste land," found "one of those noxious beasts called a fox" and gave chase; just as he was about to seize his prize, Pierson appeared and killed the beast. In the typical case (well before 1805) this mythic drama on the creation of property was cluttered by questions of land ownership and governmental regulation. But in a number of settings at least, wildlife was there for the taking—and taken it was by a cast of frequently mythic characters, such as the taciturn New England fisherman in his slicker and dory, the hardy mountain man in his fringed buckskins and fur hat, and Buffalo Bill Cody and his Wild West Show. On the unowned (or unpoliced) frontier, *Pierson v. Post* was the basis for the claims of private property in wildlife that so shaped the early history of the European conquest of this continent.

While the fur trade is the stuff of myth, two points are important. First, following the initiation of the fur trade in North America by the

French in the 1580s, imperial rivalry among European nations—and eventually the United States—was repeatedly played out through the discoveries and exploitation of fur traders. It is only a slight exaggeration to say that the early history of Europeans on this continent is a history of fur.

Second, the impact of the fur trade on the environment of North America extended far beyond the death of several million animals. The removal of a species involves more than simply the loss of one biological entity; it changes the selectional environment for all surviving species. The removal of a single species may have unexpected ramifications that ripple through the entire ecosystem, particularly when that species is a "keystone species"—a species that largely determines which alternate, "stable" community is present at a particular time.

The cornerstone of the fur trade was the beaver (*Castor canadensis*), a particularly important keystone species. As is well known, beavers dam streams to create ponds. This not only increases their habitat and food supply and offers protection against predators, dam-building also changes water flows and the physical structure and chemical profile of the stream: run-off is slowed and stored, the channel gradient is altered to a stair-step profile, stream velocity is decreased, sediment and organic matter are retained, the stream's nutrient cycling is modified, and the water table rises, flooding additional soils. Beaver also alter the riparian zone by selectively cropping trees to provide food and dam-building materials. The combination of stream and riparian zone alterations creates a spatial and temporal mosaic that in turn leads to a substantial increase in the total biomass and changes in the other animal species that are present. As beaver were trapped out across the country, their dams fell into disrepair, and stream and riparian zones changed. *See generally* Ronald L. Ives, *The Beaver–Meadow Complex*, 5 J. GEOMORPHOLOGY 191–203 (1942); Robert J. Naiman, *et al., Alteration of North American Streams by Beaver*, 38 BIOSCI. 753–62 (1988); Robert J. Naiman, *et al., Ecosystem Alteration of Boreal Forest Streams by Beaver* (Castor canadensis), 67 ECOLOGY 1254–69 (1986).

(3) The law of the rush: *Pierson v. Post* is the law of the resource rush: the first possessor wins. There were gold rushes and timber rushes, rushes to grow cows and to claim newly opened lands. By converting a bit of nature—grass or trees or animals—into dollars, natural capital could be transformed into personal income. When technology created a market for a previously unvalued piece of nature[1]—as was the case with bison skins and great auk feathers—or allowed marketing of it—as was the case with passenger pigeons—the rush was on.

---

1. The recognition that some piece of nature is a "resource" is a complex act of social definition. For example, suckers are not resources for Euro–Americans in the Pacific Northwest, and agencies nominally acting under "multiple-use resource management" systematically extirpate suckers from trout streams; suckers are, however, highly valued resources for Indians of the region. *See* Eugene S. Hunn, *Mobility as a Factor* *Limiting Resource Use on the Columbia Plateau, in* NORTHWEST LANDS, NORTHWEST PEOPLES 156 (Dale D. Goble & Paul W. Hirt eds. 1999). Bill Cronon's study of New England also demonstrates how the Indians and the English perceived the same habitat in dramatically different ways. WILLIAM CRONON, CHANGES IN THE LAND (1983); *see also* RICHARD WHITE, THE ROOTS OF DEPENDENCE (1983).

The rushes that so characterized United States during its westward irruption reflected common presumptions about the relationship of people to land. Two influential beliefs were that nature was both inexhaustibly fecund and created solely to sustain our species. It was a vast and continuously replenished storehouse. As the Commissioner of Patents Thomas Ewbank triumphantly put it, "The earth was [intended] to be a manufactory and he [the human species] a manufacturer. It was to furnish him with unwrought material, while the sounds of his implements acting upon it were to swell till their reverberations rolled over the whole." THOMAS EWBANK, THE WORLD A WORKSHOP 21 (New York, 1855). Since nature was inexhaustibly bountiful, restrictions on profligacy were unnecessary. Bison could be slaughtered for their tongues and left to rot; passenger pigeons could be left where they fell when picking them up became too onerous.

A pure rule of capture encourages such resource rushes by awarding the first taker the exclusive rights to the resource. When first in time is first in right, speed becomes everything. Because to wait might be to lose, it often makes economic sense to capture in excess of needs. Without cooperation among competitive producers, sustainable use can be impossible. At the same time, the rule embodies a rough sense of justice and equality of opportunity. The right is assigned to the person who takes the initiative, who exhibits the foresight and pluck.

These traits of the rule of capture are intertwined in the prologue of an opinion written by Stephen J. Field, a California mining-camp attorney who went on to sit on the California and United States Supreme Courts:

> The wild bird in the air belongs to no one, but when the fowler brings it to earth and takes it into his possession it is his property. He has reduced it to his control by his own labor, and the law of nature and the law of society recognize his exclusive right to it. . . . So the trapper of the plains and the hunter of the north have a property in the furs they have gathered, though the animals from which they were taken roamed at large and belonged to no one. . . . "So the miners, on the public lands throughout the Pacific States and Territories, by their customs, usages, and regulations everywhere recognized the inherent justice in this principle."

Spring Valley Waterworks v. Schottler, 110 U.S. 347, 374 (1884) (Field, J., dissenting) (*quoting Atchison v. Peterson*, 87 U.S. (20 Wall.) 507, 512 (1874) (Field, J.)).

Legal historian James Willard Hurst has commented that nineteenth-century Americans "[a]ll had in common a deep faith in the social benefits to flow from a rapid increase in productivity; all shared an impatience to get on with the job by whatever means seemed functionally adapted to it, including the law." JAMES WILLARD HURST, LAW AND THE CONDITIONS OF FREEDOM IN THE NINETEENTH-CENTURY UNITED STATES 7 (1956). The profligacy of the extermination of the passenger pigeon and slaughter of millions of buffalo are only the most well-known examples of a recurrent pattern. *See* E. DOUGLAS BRANCH, THE HUNTING OF THE BUFFALO 148–84 (1929); FRANCIS HAINES, THE BUFFALO 190–93 (1970); TOM MCHUGH, THE TIME OF THE BUFFALO 271–90 (1972).

Ghen v. Rich

District Court for the District of Massachusetts.
8 F. 159 (1881).

■ NELSON, D.J.:—This is a libel[1] to recover the value of a fin-back whale. The libellant lives in Provincetown and the respondent in Wellfleet. The facts, as they appeared at the hearing, are as follows:

In the early spring months the easterly part of Massachusetts bay is frequented by the species of whale known as the fin-back whale. Fishermen from Provincetown pursue them in open boats from the shore, and shoot them with bomb-lances fired from guns made expressly for the purpose. When killed they sink at once to the bottom, but in the course of from one to three days they rise and float on the surface. Some of them are picked up by vessels and towed into Provincetown. Some float ashore at high water and are left stranded on the beach as the tide recedes. Others float out to sea and are never recovered. The person who happens to find them on the beach usually sends word to Provincetown, and the owner comes to the spot and removes the blubber. The finder usually receives a small salvage for his services. Try-works[2] are established in Provincetown for trying out the oil. The business is of considerable extent, but, since it requires skill and experience, as well as some outlay of capital, and is attended with great exposure and hardship, few persons engage in it. The average yield of oil is about 20 barrels to a whale. It swims with great swiftness, and for that reason cannot be taken by the harpoon and line. Each boat's crew engaged in the business has its peculiar mark or device on its lances, and in this way it is known by whom a whale is killed.

The usage on Cape Cod, for many years, has been that the person who kills a whale in the manner and under the circumstances described, owns it, and this right has never been disputed until this case. The libellant has been engaged in this business for ten years past. On the morning of April 9, 1880, in Massachusetts bay, near the end of Cape Cod, he shot and instantly killed with a bomb-lance the whale in question. It sunk immediately, and on the morning of the 12th was found stranded on the beach in Brewster, within the ebb and flow of the tide, by one Ellis, 17 Miles from the spot where it was killed. Instead of sending word to Provincetown, as is customary, Ellis advertised the whale for sale at auction, and sold it to the respondent, who shipped off the blubber and tried out the oil. The libellant heard of the finding of the whale on the morning of the 15th, and immediately sent one of his boat's crew to the place and claimed it. Neither the respondent nor Ellis knew the whale had been killed by the libellant, but they knew or might have known, if they had wished, that it had been shot and killed with a bomb-lance, by some person engaged in this species of business.

1. [Libel is the term for the initiatory pleading in an admiralty action; it corresponds to a complaint.]

2. [A now-obsolete meaning of the verb "try" is "To extract (oil) from blubber or fat; to melt down (blubber, etc) to obtain oil; to render." 2 COMPACT EDITION OF THE OXFORD ENGLISH DICTIONARY 3424 (1971).]

The libellant claims title to the whale under this usage. The respondent insists that this usage is invalid. It was decided by Judge Sprague, in *Taber v. Jenny,* 1 Sprague 315 [23 F. Cas. 605 (D.Mass.1856) (No. 13,720)], that when a whale has been killed, and is anchored and left with marks of appropriation, it is the property of the captors; and if it is afterwards found, still anchored, by another ship, there is no usage or principle of law by which the property of the original captors is diverted, even though the whale may have dragged from its anchorage. The learned judge says: "When the whale had been killed and taken possession of by the boat of the Hillman, (the first taker,) it became the property of the owners of that ship, and all was done which was then practicable in order to secure it. They left it anchored, with unequivocal marks of appropriation."

In *Bartlett v. Budd,* 1 Low. 223 [2 F. Cas. 966 (D.Mass.1868) (No. 1,075)], the facts were these: The first officer of the libellant's ship killed a whale in the Okhotsk sea, anchored it, attached a waif to the body, and then left it and went ashore at some distance for the night. The next morning the boats of the respondent's ship found the whale adrift, the anchor not holding, the cable coiled round the body, and no waif or irons attached to it. Judge Lowell held that, as the libellants had killed and taken actual possession of the whale, the ownership vested in them. In his opinion the learned judge says: "A whale, being *feræ naturæ,* does not become property until a firm possession has been established by the taker. But when such possession has become firm and complete, the right of property is clear, and has all the characteristics of property."

He doubted whether a usage set up but not proved by the respondents, that a whale found adrift in the ocean is the property of the finder, unless the first taker should appear and claim it before it is cut in, would be valid, and remarked that "there would be great difficulty in upholding a custom that should take the property of A. and give it to B., under so very short and uncertain a substitute for the statute of limitations, and one so open to fraud and deceit." Both the cases cited were decided without reference to usage, upon the ground that the property had been acquired by the first taker by actual possession and appropriation.

In *Swift v. Gifford,* 1 Low. 110 [23 F. Cas. 558 (D. Mass. 1872) (No. 13,696)], Judge Lowell decided that a custom among whalemen in the Arctic seas, that the iron holds the whale was reasonable and valid. In that case a boat's crew from the respondent's ship pursued and struck a whale in the Arctic ocean, and the harpoon and the line attached to it remained in the whale, but did not remain fast to the boat. A boat's crew from the libellant's ship continued the pursuit and captured the whale, and the master of the respondent's ship claimed it on the spot. It was held by the learned judge that the whale belonged to the respondents. It was said by Judge Sprague, in *Bourne v. Ashley,* an unprinted case referred to by Judge Lowell in *Swift v. Gifford,* that the usage for the first iron, whether attached to the boat or not, to hold the whale was fully established; and he added that, although local usages of a particular port ought not to be allowed to set aside the general maritime law, this objection did not apply to a custom which embraced an entire business, and had been concurred in for a long time by every one engaged in the trade.

In *Swift v. Gifford,* Judge Lowell also said: "The rule of law invoked in this case is one of very limited application. The whale fishery is the only branch of industry of any importance in which it is likely to be much used, and if a usage is found to prevail generally in that business, it will not be open to the objection that it is likely to disturb the general understanding of mankind by the interposition of an arbitrary exception."

I see no reason why the usage proved in this case is not as reasonable as that sustained in the cases cited. Its application must necessarily be extremely limited, and can affect but a few persons. It has been recognized and acquiesced in for many years. It requires in the first taker the only act of appropriation that is possible in the nature of the case. Unless it is sustained, this branch of industry must necessarily cease, for no person would engage in it if the fruits of his labor could be appropriated by any chance finder. It gives reasonable salvage for securing or reporting the property. That the rule works well in practice is shown by the extent of the industry which has grown up under it, and the general acquiescence of a whole community interested to dispute it. It is by means clear that without regard to usage the common law would not reach the same result. That seems to be the effect of the decisions in *Taber v. Jenny* and *Bartlett v. Budd.* If the fisherman does all that is possible to do to make the animal his own, that would seem to be sufficient. Such a rule might well be applied in the interest of trade, there being no usage or custom to the contrary. OLIVER W. HOLMES, THE COMMON LAW 217. But be that as it may, I hold the usage to be valid, and that the property in the whale was in the libelant.

The rule of damages is the market value of the oil obtained from the whale, less the cost of trying it out and preparing it for the market, with interest on the amount so ascertained from the date of conversion. As the question is new and important, and the suit is contested on both sides, more for the purpose of having it settled than for the amount involved, I shall give no costs.

Decree for libellant for $71.05, without costs.

NOTES

(1) Is this holding consistent with *Pierson v. Post*? Does the court's reasoning suggest that Livingston was correct in his dissent in *Pierson* when he argued that the court should have deferred to the code of sportsmen? To the extent that the *Ghen* court deviated from the strict rule of capture in *Pierson*, why did it do so? Did the customary usage followed in *Ghen* provide adequate notice to the defendant (and similarly situated people) that the fin-backed whale that floated ashore was owned? Are there other shortcomings in the decision?

(2) What purpose is served by possession? One reading of the decision in *Pierson v. Post* is that the court adopts possession as the touchstone because it gives notice and thus reduces the likelihood of litigation. The waifs in the whaling cases arguably served the same function. *See also* Carol M. Rose, *Possession as the Origin of Property,* 52 U. CHI. L. REV. 73, 76 (1985). Alternatively, the court may have adopted possession because of the ease of applying possession to determine ownership. Which of these readings of *Pierson* is most consistent with *Ghen*?

(3) Note the cases discussed in *Ghen*. Which offers the most relaxed standard for gaining ownership rights in a whale? Are there problems with such a relaxed standard? In addition to these cases, consider the following decisions dealing with the capture of other species. Are the differences in these decisions due largely to differences in the species at issue and the particular difficulties of capturing them? Is it possible to formulate a single, general rule of capture that covers all of the cases?

(a) ***State v. Shaw*** involved a criminal prosecution for larceny for removing fish from a privately owned fish trap in Lake Erie. The trap consisted of a long tunnel that led to an enclosure. The opening where the tunnel joined the enclosure was nearly 3 feet in diameter. Although this was big enough for fish to leave the trap, fish behavior is such that few ever did. The trial court held that, because of the opening, the owner lacked complete possession, which was necessary to establish ownership of the fish. While acknowledging that fish in the trap could swim away, the Ohio Supreme Court reversed: "The possession of the owners of the nets was so complete and certain that the defendants went to the nets and raised them with absolute assurance that they could get the fish that were in them." *State v. Shaw,* 65 N.E. 875, 876 (Ohio 1902). Did the court simply choose to protect those who had invested time and money in constructing the traps?

(b) ***Liesner v. Wanie*** involved a wolf hunt in which plaintiffs wounded the animal and "had him so in their power that escape was highly improbable, if not impossible, before defendant appeared on the scene and with his gun pointed so as to reach within some three feet of the animal delivered a finishing shot." The trial court awarded the wolf to the plaintiffs and the Wisconsin Supreme Court affirmed: "The instant a wild animal is brought under the control of a person so that actual possession is practically inevitable, a vested property interest in it accrues which cannot be divested by anothers intervening and killing it. [ ] Such is the law of the chase by common law principles, differing from the more ancient civil law which postponed the point of vested interest to that of actual taking." *Liesner v. Wanie,* 145 N.W. 374, 376 (Wis.1914).

SECTION 2. LIMITS ON THE POWER TO CAPTURE

Pierson v. Post—at least in its official telling—presents the property-by-possession issue in its purest simplicity, unencumbered by questions of land ownership. By setting the *Pierson* case "upon a certain wild and uninhabited, unpossessed and waste land," the dispute avoided all questions of landowner rights. But even ignoring Indian populations, unpossessed land was a transient phase. As more and more land passed into private hands, wildlife issues became more complex. They also became more complex as game shortages led to the widespread regulation of hunting and fishing to conserve game populations.

a. PRIVATE OWNERSHIP OF LAND AS A LIMIT ON THE POWER TO CAPTURE

Fisher v. Steward

New Hampshire Supreme Court.
Smith 60 (1804).

TROVER for a swarm of bees. There was a second count for two hundred pounds of honey in the comb.

The case was, the plaintiffs found a swarm of bees in a tree on the (defendant's) land in Claremont, marked the tree, and notified the defendant, who cut down the tree, September, 1803, and converted the honey to his own use.

. . .

At the trial there was some dispute whether the plaintiffs or one of the defendant's family first discovered the bees, and whether the plaintiffs gave notice of the finding and marking the tree. The other parts of the case were proved.

THE COURT summed up, and observed that two questions had been made on the trial: first, whether the plaintiffs first discovered the bees; and, secondly, supposing they did, whether the property in the honey was in them.

The first is a question of evidence proper for the consideration of the jury.

The second is a question of law, and one about which the Court entertained no doubt. The plaintiffs do not pretend to have any property in the land or in the tree, nor had they any property in the bees. How then came they by a property in the honey? It must have been by occupancy. But how did they occupy, or appropriate the honey to themselves? They saw the bees enter the tree, they heard them make a noise near the tree, and they marked the tree. The two first gave no right; they do not amount to occupancy. The marking of the tree was a trespass, and consequently can avail the plaintiffs nothing. The doctrine contended for by plaintiffs is injurious to the rights of property. Till the bees occupied the tree in question, it is not pretended that plaintiffs had any right in it. What gave them a right? Having seen a swarm of bees, in which they had no property, occupying it? This circumstance, whether the effect of accident, or the result of labor and skill, cannot lessen the rights of the owner of the soil. Will it be pretended that plaintiffs thereby acquired a right to the tree? If they acquired a title to the honey, they must necessarily have a right to take it away, to cut down the tree, to pass over the defendant's land for the purpose, & c. Admitting that plaintiffs could acquire property in a swarm of bees, or in the honey, by finding, in some cases, they could not do so in the present case, because such right or property interferes with the rights and property clearly vested in defendant; it is inconsistent with it; it lessens its value at least. It is much more consonant to our ideas of property to say, that the bees and honey in the defendant's trees belong to him in the same manner and for the same reason as all mines and minerals belong to the owner of the soil.

Will it be pretended by the plaintiffs that they could have put, without defendant's permission, a swarm of bees into defendant's tree, and there kept them till they had made honey; and then, in case he cut down the tree, maintained trespass for the cutting, or trover for the honey? One would suppose the present case was not stronger than that; here they had no right to the bees.

It has been said, that, by the usage in this part of the State, the person who finds bees acquires a property in them wherever found. We recognize no such usage. We have no local customs or usages which are binding in one part of the State and not in another. If this be the law here, it must be so in every other part of the State.

Verdict for defendant.

NOTES

(1) Why was the usage of whalers relevant to the determination of rights in whales but the usage of bee-finders deemed immaterial? Is it because landed property rights were involved? Because the bee-finding custom was not universal? Because honeybees are more common than fin-back whales? Recall the discussion of bees in Bracton. How would the case have been decided under the common law?

(2) Property permutations: Bees have been a recurrent source of litigation and thus offer examples of several variations on the theme:

(a) Finder v. Landowner: In litigation between a finder and a landowner, other courts reached the same decision as the New Hampshire court in *Fisher v. Steward. See, e.g., Gillet v. Mason,* 7 Johns. 16 (N.Y.Sup. Ct.1810) (plaintiff's act of marking the bee tree conferred no property in either the bees or the honey against the owner of the land who has "a qualified property . . . in bees, in consideration of the soil whereon they are found, or an ownership, *ratione soli*"); *State v. Repp,* 73 N.W. 829 (Iowa 1898) ("By the law of nature, the person who hived the swarm would be entitled to it; but, under the regulation of property rights since the institution of civil society, the forest, as well as the cultivated field, belongs to the owner thereof, and he who invades it is a trespasser.")

(b) Finder v. Finder: When the dispute has been between two claimants who had no interest in the relevant land, courts have resolved the dispute by applying the rule of capture. *Ferguson v. Miller,* 1 Cow. 243 (N.Y.Sup.Ct.1823) (first to reduce bees to possession became owner, rather than first to discover). *See also Adams v. Burton,* 43 Vt. 36 (1870) (a plaintiff in the process of cutting down bee tree, with the permission of the landowner, had sufficient property in the bees to maintain an action against a third party who prevented him from finishing the job).

PERSPECTIVES

(1) Honeybees and humans: The importance of bees is difficult to appreciate given the widespread production of granulated sugar that has occurred during the past half-century. Although cane sugar has been available in small quantities in Europe since the Classic Age of Greece, honey remained the primary sweetener until World War II.

Initially, honey was obtained by raiding wild hives. At some point, humans began to keep bees, employing baskets or pots as hives. Until the development of the moveable frame hive by Lorenzo Langstroth in 1851, the process was essentially unchanged: in the early summer, the beekeeper caught and hived swarms of bees from his old hives; in late summer, he killed the bees in most hives, cut out the combs, and strained the honey from the wax; the remaining hives were overwintered to provide the swarms to repeat the process the following year. Langstroth's invention allowed individual frames to be removed without destroying the hive, which in turn meant that harvesting the honey no longer required killing the bees.

The honeybee (*Apis mellifera*) is indigenous to Europe, Africa, and Asia. It was brought to North America by early European colonizers. In his *Notes on Virginia,* Thomas Jefferson wrote:

> The honey-bee is not a native of our continent. . . . The Indians concur with us in the tradition that it was brought from Europe; but when, and by whom, we know not. The bees have generally extended themselves into the country, a little in advance of the settlers. The Indians, therefore, call them the white man's fly, and consider their approach as indicating the approach of the settlements of the whites.

THOMAS JEFFERSON, NOTES ON VIRGINIA *in* 2 THE WRITINGS OF THOMAS JEFFERSON 103 [query VI] (Library ed. 1903) (1784).

(2) Honeybees and parakeets: As an introduced species, the honeybee competed with indigenous species and may have played a part in the extinction of the Carolina Parakeet—the only representative of the parrot family in the United States. The species ranged from Florida and the Gulf Coast north to Virginia and occasionally into Pennsylvania and New York through the Great Lakes to eastern Colorado.

The parakeet was a conspicuous presence because it was gregarious, flocking in raucous groups of hundreds of birds, and because of its bright plumage, which generally resembled a larger version of the cage-bird currently sold in pet shops as parakeets: it had a green body with a yellow head and neck, and a reddish-orange forehead.

As early as 1831, Audubon noted that the species' numbers were declining. As the century progressed, its range gradually shrank. The last reliable wild sightings were in Florida in 1904; the last member of the species died in captivity at the Cincinnati Zoo in February, 1918. The human side of the bird's demise is recounted in CHRISTOPHER COKINOS, HOPE IS THE THING WITH FEATHERS 7–58 (2000).

As is often the case, the extinction of the parakeet was the result of a combination of factors. As seed eaters, the species developed a fondness for cultivated fruits and grains that made it unpopular with farmers who relentlessly killed them. The species was also hunted as a game bird, shot as a target, killed for its feathers, and netted for sale as a cage bird— despite Audubon's report that "their screams are so disagreeable as to render them at best very indifferent companions." Nonetheless, these actions appear not to account fully for the parakeet's rapid disappearance.

Between 1600 and 1859, farming often consisted of clearing land, farming the soil to exhaustion, and moving on to begin again. These practices were particularly common with the large tobacco, cotton, and rice plantations of the South—the parakeet's core range. Since settlers initially cultivated the valley floors, prime parakeet habitat was typically the first cleared. The volume of land cleared is noteworthy: while land clearing was relatively modest until 1800, almost 114,000,000 acres had been cleared by 1850; in the next decade, almost 40,000,000 more acres were cleared for agriculture.

Finally, the honeybee was a competitor—not for food, but for vital nesting spots. The bees nested in hollow trees, the roosting and nesting sites of parakeets. Thus, the bees may have prevented roosting. In addition, as one review noted, "the magnitude of destruction of hollow trees by 'bee hunters' in search of honey and wax is little appreciated." Daniel McKinley, *The Carolina Parakeet in Pioneer Missouri*, 72 WILSON BULL. 279, 283 (1960).

M'Conico v. Singleton

South Carolina Supreme Court.
9 S.C.L. (2 Mill) 244 (1818).

This was an action of trespass, *quare clausum fregit,* and to support it the plaintiff proved, that he had warned and ordered the defendant not to hunt on his lands, and that the defendant had notwithstanding, rode over, and hunted deer on his unenclosed and unimproved lands. The verdict of the jury was, that each party should pay their own costs; and the plaintiff now moves for a new trial on the grounds:

1st. Because the riding over the unenclosed and unimproved lands is in law a trespass, for which an action will lie, when it is contrary to the express orders of the owner.

2d. Because the verdict is in itself a nullity.

■ JOHNSON, J.:—Until the bringing of this action, the right to hunt on unenclosed and uncultivated lands has never been disputed, and it is well known that it has been universally exercised from the first settlement of the country up to the present time; and the time has been, when, in all probability, obedient as our ancestors were to the laws of the country, a civil war would have been the consequence of an attempt, even by the legislature, to enforce a restraint on this privilege. It was the source from whence a great portion of them derived their food and raiment, and was, to the devoted huntsman, (disreputable as the life now is,) a source of considerable profit. The forest was regarded as a common, in which they entered at pleasure, and exercised the privilege; and it will not be denied that animals, *feræ naturæ,* are common property, and belong to the first taker. If, therefore, usage can make law, none was ever better established.

This usage is also clearly recognized as a right by several acts of the legislature on the subject; particularly the act of 1769, (Pub. Laws, 276,) which restrains the right to hunt within seven miles of the residence of the hunter. Now if the right to hunt beyond that did not before exist this act was nugatory; and it cannot be believed that it was only intended to apply to such as owned a tract of land, the diameter of which would be fourteen miles.

It appears to me also, that there is no rule of the English common law, at variance with this principle; but, it is said, that every entry on the lands of another is a trespass, and the least injury, as treading down grass, and the like, will support it. [ ] But there must be some actual injury to support the action. Now it will not be pretended that riding over the soil is an injury; and the forest being the common, in which the cattle of all are used to range at large, the grass, if perchance there be any, may also be regarded as common property; and surely no action will lie against a commoner for barely riding over the common.

The right to hunt on unenclosed land, I think, therefore, clearly established; but if it were doubtful, I should be strongly inclined to support it. Large standing armies are, perhaps, wisely considered as dangerous to free institutions; the militia, therefore, necessarily constitutes our greatest security against aggression; our forest is the great field in which, in the pursuit of game, they learn the dexterous use and consequent certainty of firearms, the great and decided advantages of which have been seen and felt on too many occasions to be forgotten, or to require recurrence to.

Having come to the conclusion, that it is the right of inhabitants to hunt on unenclosed lands, I need not attempt to prove that the dissent or disapprobation of the owner cannot deprive him of it; for I am sure it never entered the mind of any man, that a right which the law gives, can be defeated at the mere will and caprice of an individual.

. . .

■ GRIMKE, COLCOCK, CHEVES, and NOTT, JJ., concurred. GANTT, J., dissented [without opinion].

Broughton v. Singleton

Constitutional Court of Appeals of South Carolina.
11 S.C.L. (2 Nott & McC.) 338 (1820).

This was an action of trespass, quare clausum fregit, in which the Jury found for the plaintiff, $300 damages.

The circumstances were substantially these: The defendant, and several others, were out on a hunting party, and rode into an old uncultivated field, around which there had been a fence, but which was then down in many places. The plaintiff came up, while they were in the field, and ordered them off. The defendant replied that he did not know the field belonged to him, and that they would go out, and did so accordingly. While they were yet in the field, and before they could get out, the plaintiff seized the gun of one of the party, (Mr. Moore,) and in the end, took it from him, but the witness did not know what led to it, as they were scuffling for it when he first saw them, and while they were engaged, the defendant cried out to some one to "shoot the plaintiff." The plaintiff then fled, as the witness said, in a great fright, and one of them pursued him a short distance. The plaintiff had before forbade the defendant to hunt on his land, but he had very recently purchased this place, and it was proved as clearly as negative evidence could make it, that all of the party were ignorant that he then owned it . . . .

The defendant [moved to dismiss] on the ground, that the hunting was on the uninclosed grounds of the plaintiff, and by law he was authorized to hunt there, and the plaintiff's forbidding him, did not take that right away.

■ JOHNSON, J.:—Our ideas of those injuries, for which the action of trespass will lie, are principally derived from English authorities, and I am disposed to think they are followed without a proper regard to the vast difference between the situation of the two countries, so that in pursuing the letter, we lose sight of the principle. There, almost every foot of soil is appropriated to some specific purpose—here, much the greater part consists in uninclosed and uncultivated forest, and a part in exhausted old fields, which have been abandoned, as unfit for further cultivation, in which the cattle of the citizens feed at will. There, it is as practicable as necessary to protect the occupant against those petty trespasses—here, it is wholly impracticable, and I think unnecessary. The attempt to give this protection to uninclosed land, would overwhelm us in a sea of petty litigation, destructive of the interests and peace of the community. Upon this principle, it was determined in the case of *M'Connico v. Singleton,* 9 S.C.L. (2 Mill) 244 (1818), that hunting on inclosed lands, was not such a trespass as would sustain an action . . . .

On the merits of the case, I am equally satisfied, that injustice has been done the defendant. The field in which the trespass was committed, if not wholly abandoned, was so exposed, and the dilapidated state of the fencing was such as to justify the belief that it was. And if he had a right to enter it, the [plaintiff's] forbidding him could not take it away; but all the injury complained of was the mere riding on the soil, and from the evidence, it appears he was ignorant, that it belonged to the plaintiff. If it be an injury, the damages given must strike every one at once as enormous and excessive. It is said however, that the personal insult offered to the plaintiff is a justification for this verdict. If one man wantonly entered on the lands of another for the purpose of insulting him, I would make it the means of punishing him, although he had not left his track on the soil. But in this case any insult which the plaintiff received was the consequence of his own indiscretion, and he ought not now to profit by it.

NOTT and HUGER, JJ., concurred; COLCOCK and GANTT, JJ., dissented.

Fripp v. Hasell

Court of Appeals of Law of South Carolina.
32 S.C.L. (1 Strob.) 173 (1847).

This was an action of trespass, *quare clausum fregit*. The alleged trespass consisted in this. The plaintiff is the owner of an island about eight miles long, and three quarters wide; surrounded by the sea, and deep, navigable waters. There is a house, with a small but dilapidated fence surrounding it, where the plaintiff has sometimes resided, but at the time of the trespass it was untenanted. The plaintiff, some years ago, had given a general license, but how, was not explained, to all persons to hunt on the island, on paying him $1.75 cents per day. But this license had been revoked by an advertisement in the Mercury, published for some months before, and at the time of the trespass. The defendants went upon the island, and hunted two days. They killed one deer, but never offered to pay the plaintiff any thing for the privilege.... [At trial, the judge,] with opinions leading him to maintain very strongly the propriety rights of the landlord against the inroads of the hunter, ... came to the conclusion, and so instructed the jury, that the plaintiff was entitled to recover.

. . .

■ EVANS, J.:—[T]he only question to be decided is, whether the defendants had a right to hunt on the plaintiff's land, under the authority of the cases of *M'Connico v. Singleton,* 9 S.C.L. (2 Mill) 244 (1818); and *Broughton v. Singleton,* 2 N. & M'C. 335 (1820). In these cases, it is conceded that no such right exists by the common law of England; but it is said to have become a right, by the immemorial usage of the State, commencing with its earliest settlement, common to all the people to hunt on any uninclosed grounds. The exact meaning of these words, or what kind of enclosure shall exclude the right of the hunter, it is perhaps very difficult to define. The word enclose, in common parlance, means to surround or to include, and the term close, means that which is surrounded. But does this mean surrounded by something, which the labor and skill of man has placed around it, such as fences, or deep ditches, or walls of wood or stone or brick; or does it not also mean such barriers as clearly separate it from adjoining lands, whether they are the works of nature or the industry of man. We have no express legislation on this subject, but may we not safely resort for a guide to the analogous case, of what shall be a sufficient enclosure to protect the planter against the inroads of horses, cattle and hogs, whose right to go at large in the range, is derived from the same common origin, the common law of South Carolina. By the fence law of 1827, 6 Stat., 331, a deep, navigable stream, is declared to be equivalent to a fence, or in other words, where a field is surrounded, in whole or in part, by a deep, navigable stream, it is a sufficient enclosure to authorize the owner to empound stock depredating on his fields, or to subject him to the payment of the damages committed by them; such a stream is sufficient for a cultivated field, and as was well said in the argument, it would be strange if such a cultivated field should be sufficiently enclosed by the natural boundary of a deep, navigable stream, whilst one not cultivated should require in addition, a fence constructed by human labor. In any view which I have been able to take of this case, I am satisfied with the instructions given to the jury [to rule in favor of the plaintiff landowner].

NOTES

(1) Note the progression of ideas within these three opinions, written over a 30–year period in a single state. What trends are taking place, and why?

Do these changes in the law reflect changes in human population densities? in game populations? in egalitarian sentiments?

(2) Hunting as a metaphor for freedom: One commenter has noted that the abundance of game and the equality of opportunity to kill it "were important symbols of liberty" during the colonial period. JAMES A. TOBER, WHO OWNS THE WILDLIFE? 4 (1981). Hostility to restrictions on hunting and fishing was a heritage of the hated English class-based game laws; restrictions thus conflicted with the American myths of egalitarianism. Antipathy to the English game laws and the class system that those laws supported provoked over-heated rhetoric in judicial opinions throughout the nineteenth century. A Georgia decision captures the ideology of the early federal period:

> [The Waltham Black Act—the English statute that made killing deer a capital offense—] never could have been in force [in Georgia], because that statute, as is discoverable from the preamble and the context, is founded upon a tender solicitude for the amusement and property of the aristocracy of England. It was made to protect from the violation or profanation of the people, the forest of his majesty or the park of the peer. How then could it apply to a country which was but one extended forest, in which the liberty of killing a deer, or cutting down a tree, was as unrestrained as the natural rights of the deer to rove, or the tree to grow; and where was the aristocracy whose privileges were to be secured?

State v. Campbell, T.U.P.C. 166, 167–68 (Ga.1808).

As social stratification increased in the United States, the rhetoric escalated. In an 1888 case pitting a hunting club against a duck hunter, both the majority and the dissent affirmed their allegiance to the principles that, "by the law of nature every man, of whatever rank or station, has an equal right of taking, for his own use, all creatures fit for food that are wild by nature, so long as they do no injury to another's rights." *Sterling v. Jackson,* 37 N.W. 845, 851 (Mich.1888).

The dissent was even more grandiloquent:

> Game and forestry laws are not in harmony with the American idea, and are of late origin in the history of our country. Such laws can only be supported and justified on the ground that the game is fast disappearing, and ought to and must be protected and preserved for the use and benefit of the people,—for the general public, and not for a specified few. Our fish and game laws have not been passed for the express benefit of clubs of wealthy sportsmen, who can afford to buy up or lease all the land along the navigable streams and lakes of this state, and thus shut out the poor man who loves the rod or gun as well as they do, and who, in the spirit of our institutions, has a common right with them in the "fowl of the air and the fish of the sea."
>
> The Pilgrim fathers, fleeing to the new world from the tyrannies of a despotic era in the history of the mother country, brought with them, not only religious ideas, but many other notions as to the rights of the common people not then prevalent or countenance in England; and the old colony of Massachusetts Bay early adopted laws looking towards

the establishment of a common right in the people to the fish and wild game then abounding in the waters and woods of the new world.

Id. at 855–56 (Morse, J., dissenting). *See also New England Trout & Salmon Club v. Mather,* 35 A. 323, 328 (Vt.1896) (Thompson, J., dissenting) (condemning "the iniquitous fish and game laws of England, enacted by the ruling class for their own enjoyment, and which led to a system under which the catching of a fish or the killing of a rabbit was deemed of more consequence than the happiness, liberty, or life of a human being"); *see also Hallock v. Dominy,* 7 Hun. 52, 55 (N.Y.App.Div.1876) (striking down county ordinance as analogous to English game laws, which "are contrary to the spirit of our institutions").

The heated rhetoric suggests that more was at stake than is immediately apparent. Limitations on taking game conflicted with American ideology. Repudiation of the English restrictions on hunting was a symbol of America's egalitarianism and its rejection of old world class structures— an ideology that was increasingly important as the nation became more economically stratified during the Gilded Age. Is something similar occurring during the current period of economic stratification?

(3) Constitutional protection for a "right to hunt": The importance of hunting—whether as a symbol of freedom or as a source of food—can be seen in its protection in colonial ordinances and early state constitutions. For example, the Massachusetts Bay Body of Liberties enacted in 1641 and 1647 guaranteed householders "free fishing and fowling in any great ponds [those of more than ten acres], and Bayes, Coves and Rivers, so farre as the sea ebbes and flowes," as well as access across private land. A COPPIE OF THE LIBERTIES OF THE MASSACHUSETS COLONIE IN NEW ENGLAND § 16, *reprinted in* SOURCES AND DOCUMENTS OF UNITED STATES CONSTITUTIONS 47, 49 (William F. Swindler, ed. 1975). Access was provided by guaranteeing the right to "pass and re-pass on foot through any man's property for that end so they trespass not upon any man's corn or meadow." *Barrows v. McDermott,* 73 Me. 441, 447 (1882). William Penn's Frame of Government of 1683 granted the colonists the "liberty to fowl and hunt upon the lands they hold, and all other lands therein not enclosed; and to fish, in all waters in the said lands." FRAME OF GOVERNMENT OF PENNSYLVANIA § XXII (1683), *reprinted in* 8 SOURCES AND DOCUMENTS OF UNITED STATES CONSTITUTIONS 263, 266 (William F. Swindler, ed. 1979).

Similar language can be found in early state constitutions. In a provision considered in several cases below, the Vermont Constitution provides that

the inhabitants of this state shall have liberty, in seasonable times, to hunt and fowl on the lands they hold, and on other lands not inclosed; and in like manner to fish in all boatable and other waters (not private property) under proper regulations, to be hereafter made and provided by the general assembly.

VT. CONST. OF 1793/6 ch. II, § 40, *reprinted in* 9 SOURCES AND DOCUMENTS OF UNITED STATES CONSTITUTIONS 507, 514 (William F. Swindler, ed. 1979). *See also* PA. CONST. OF 1776 art. II, § 43 (repealed 1790), *reprinted in* 8 SOURCES

AND DOCUMENTS OF UNITED STATES CONSTITUTIONS 277, 284 (William F. Swindler, ed. 1979).

(4) Hunting and the rise of private property in land: Inevitably the "common right" of free hunting and fishing came into conflict with another, much-cherished institution, the private ownership of land. As Americans understood private property in land, it included the right to exclude others, whether or not they interfered with an owner's use of the land. Landowners possessed the inherent power to close their lands to hunting. But as more lands were closed, hunting and fishing became less a public right and more a private privilege, much as in Britain. The public collectively might still own game until it was captured, but for the landless, opportunities to capture dwindled. How could these conflicting aims and institutions be reconciled? How could the law respect private property and still keep hunting an available pastime—and food source—for the average citizen?

One approach was to allow landowners to exclude, but to make exclusion difficult, particularly for unenclosed, uncultivated lands where most hunting took place. Hunters were also aided by a judicial inclination to resolve factual uncertainties in their favor. An example is *Payne v. Gould,* a case arising in Vermont—and thus covered by the constitutional provision quoted immediately above. Plaintiff sued in trespass under a statute providing that, "if the owner or occupant of inclosed lands, or cultivated land not inclosed, conspicuously posts notices on the same, as provided by law, a person who willfully enters thereupon without the permission of the owner or occupant for the purpose of fishing, trapping, or shooting thereon, shall forfeit $10, to be recovered by the owner thereof in an action of trespass, in addition to the damages sustained thereby." In finding for the defendant, the court concluded that the landowner had not taken adequate steps to exclude hunters:

> The facts found show that the boundary line ... is 3,636 1/2 feet long; that it is not marked by fence nor by anything equivalent thereto. The boundary consists of an imaginary line only. In the disposition of this case, it is not necessary to consider how the boundaries should be marked to make the land inclosed within the meaning of the law in question. It is enough to say that the land must be surrounded by visible objects, natural or artificial, except the premises be such that the owner is not required to fence them to make them inclosed, as is the case with occupied lands along the side of an open public highway, Vt. Stat. § 3567; [ ], and that an imaginary line only is not sufficient.

> The locus in quo, therefore, was not inclosed land, and no claim is made in the briefs that it was "cultivated land;" ...

> It is urged, however, that, if the plaintiff's land is neither inclosed nor cultivated, he is entitled to recover nominal damages for the breaking and entering, as in the ordinary case of trespass on the freehold. Herein the case is unlike the ordinary case of trespass. By the organic law of the state, the inhabitants thereof "shall have the liberty in seasonable times to hunt and fowl on the lands they hold, and on other lands not inclosed," under proper regulations made and provided by the General Assembly. CONST. ch. 2, § 40; *State v. Norton,* 45 Vt. 258

(1872). The facts found show that the defendant entered upon the land in question for the purpose of shooting, and that, being so entered, he did there shoot. . . . The land not being inclosed, the defendant was exercising the right guaranteed him by the constitution, and did not commit actionable trespass in so doing.

Payne v. Gould, 52 A. 421 (Vt.1902).

(5) Ownership rights in submerged lands: The tension between the rule of capture and private ownership of land has also frequently produced conflict when the land in question lies beneath *legally* nonnavigable bodies of water. Such lands are subject to private ownership even when the water body is sufficient to permit limited navigation by shallow-draft boats often used by hunters and fishers:

(a) *Marsh v. Colby:* Marsh brought a trespass action against Colby who had fished from a boat on a small lake. Defendant appealed. The court reversed in the following brief *per curiam* decision:

> The small lake or pond on which the alleged trespass was committed was almost entirely enclosed within the lines of plaintiff's farm. Whatever question might arise respecting the right to exclusive fisheries in larger bodies of water, the right of the land-owner to the exclusive control of small bodies thus situated would seem clear.
>
> It has always been customary, however, to permit the public to take fish in all the small lakes and ponds of the State, and in the absence of any notification to the contrary, we think any one may understand that he is licensed to do so. No such notification appears in this case, and we therefore hold that the defendant was not a trespasser in passing upon plaintiff's land with the intent to take fish, having no knowledge that objection existed to his doing so.

Marsh v. Colby, 39 Mich. 626 (1878).

(b) *McKee v. Gratz* involved title to mussels that defendant had harvested from water located on plaintiff's land. Plaintiff brought an action to recover the value of the mussels. The Supreme Court affirmed a judgment for plaintiff, but Justice Holmes offered a word of caution:

> it cannot be said as matter of law that those who took the mussels were trespassers; or even wrongdoers in appropriating the shells. The strict rule of the English common law as to entry upon a close must be taken to be mitigated by common understanding with regard to the large expanses of unenclosed and uncultivated land in many parts at least of this country. Over these it is customary to wander, shoot and fish at will until the owner sees fit to prohibit it. A license may be implied from the habits of the country. *Marsh v. Colby,* 39 Mich. 626 (1878). In Missouri the implication is fortified by the limit of statutory prohibitions to enclosed and cultivated land and private ponds. R.S. 1919, §§ 5662, 3654. There was evidence that the practice had prevailed in this region. Whether those who took these mussels were entitled to rely upon it, and whether, if entitled to rely upon it for occasional uses, they could do so to the extent of the considerable and systematic work that was done were questions for the jury. They could not be disposed of by the Court. . . .

McKee v. Gratz, 260 U.S. 127 (1922).

Landowner rights in submerged lands raise particularly knotty questions about public access and incidental use rights—such as fishing, fowling, or trapping—in stream banks and beds. We return to these issues in Chapter 3.

State v. Corbin

Court of Appeals of Minnesota.
343 N.W.2d 874 (1984).

■ LANSING, J.:—This is a case of first impression, construing the 1979 amendment to MINN. STAT. § 100.273, subd. 7 (1982) allowing a hunter to trespass on unposted agricultural land to retrieve a wounded animal without permission of the landowner....

The facts, as stipulated, are as follows. On November 6, 1982, Jay Corbin, Ronald Niebuhr and other members of their hunting party requested permission to hunt at the Soost farms. Wayne and Ed Soost told the hunters they could hunt in the woods but could not go "through the standing corn." The next day, the hunters returned and asked if they could get a wounded deer out of the corn field. Ed Soost refused to allow the retrieval of the deer until he got his corn picked. Later, Soost became suspicious and went to his corn field "to see what the Sam Hill was down on the other end of the field." Soost learned that Corbin and Niebuhr had entered the corn field to retrieve the wounded deer. The corn field was part of the Soost property that was not posted with "no trespassing" signs....

The sole issue on appeal is whether a hunter commits a trespass prohibited under MINN. STAT. § 100.273, subd. 3, by retrieving a wounded deer from unposted agricultural land after being told not to do so by the landowner. MINN. STAT. § 100.273, subd. 3, provides:

> No person shall enter upon any land not his own regardless if it is agricultural land with intent to take any wild animals after being notified not to do so, either orally by the owner, occupant or lessee, or by signs erected pursuant to subdivision 6.

This section, which applies both to agricultural and nonagricultural land, became effective in 1978. *See* LAWS OF MINNESOTA 1978, Chapter 794, Section 2. In 1979, the legislature made a number of changes to MINN. STAT. § 100.273. One of these changes, incorporated in subdivision 2, requires affirmative permission to hunt on agricultural land. This subdivision reads, in part:

> No person shall enter upon the agricultural lands of another with the intent of hunting big or small game * * * unless and until the permission of the owner, occupant, or lessee is obtained.

See LAWS OF MINNESOTA 1979, Chapter 291, Section 4.

As part of the same legislative act, subdivision 7 was amended to create a limited exception for entry without permission to retrieve a wounded animal from agricultural lands that are not posted:

During the season for taking big or small game, a hunter may on foot retrieve a wounded big or small game animal from agricultural land of another which is not posted pursuant to subdivision 6, without permission of the landowner, and shall then leave as soon as possible.

See LAWS OF MINNESOTA 1979, Chapter 291, Section 4.

Corbin and Niebuhr obtained the initial permission necessary to enter upon Soost's land to hunt deer. Whether their subsequent entry into the cornfield to retrieve the wounded deer constituted a trespass depends upon the interpretation of subdivision 7. This subdivision allows hunters to trespass in certain instances to retrieve a wounded animal without permission of the landowner. The State would interpret "without permission" to mean "without having received a refusal." The defendants, on the other hand, maintain that "without permission" allows entry even after a refusal has been received.

In construing the statute, we are aided by several principles. First, penal statutes must be construed strictly; any reasonable doubt must be interpreted in favor of the defendant. [ ] Second, specific provisions of an act prevail over prior, general provisions. [ ] Finally, we "cannot supply that which the legislature purposely omits or inadvertently overlooks." [ ]

In light of the misdemeanor penalty for violating subdivision 3, this statute is penal in nature. Second, subdivision 7 was enacted after subdivision 3 and is the more specific subdivision because it regulates a narrower range of activity. Finally, a plain reading of the entire statute suggests a purposeful omission of the construction urged by the State. The parallel subdivisions create gradations of protection and categories of notice, including written permission, oral permission, oral notice, and notice by posting signs. *See* MINN. STAT. § 100.273, subds. 2, 3, 5, 6. Subdivision 3 specifically provides two methods for a property owner to warn a hunter about trespassing—signs and oral notice. Subdivision 7, which is the subdivision at issue, includes only one method of notice: posting. Therefore, the inference exists that the legislature purposely omitted an oral notice provision in subdivision 7.

We note that this interpretation allows limited entry on unposted agricultural land to retrieve a wounded animal after an oral notice not to do so, but would prohibit a similar entry on unposted nonagricultural land. Because the statute generally defines a more protected status for agricultural lands, an anomaly is created.

The legislature may desire to address this by (a) requiring affirmative permission to enter agricultural land regardless of the presence of a wounded animal, or (b) placing greater weight on the refusal of permission to enter agricultural land, or (c) providing an additional limited exception for hunters to enter nonagricultural land to retrieve wounded animals. Until it does so, we believe that statutory construction requires the interpretation given by the trial court. If a landowner wishes to avoid this temporary intrusion on agricultural land, the owner should post the land, pursuant to MINN. STAT. § 100.273, subd. 6.

Affirmed.

NOTES

(1) In what way does *State v. Corbin*, and the statutes considered in it, show a continued evolution in thoughts about the rights of landowners versus the ideal of free public hunting? What change was made in the 1979 amendment? Would such a statute be constitutional in Vermont, given the constitutional provision in that state protecting public hunting rights in lands not "inclosed"?

Consider the Kansas statute on posting: It is unlawful to take wildlife on land that is posted "with signs stating that hunting, trapping or fishing on such land shall be by written permission only." KAN. STAT. ANN. § 32–1013(a). Nonetheless, "a person licensed to hunt . . . and following or pursuing a wounded animal on land so posted without written permission of the landowner . . . shall not be deemed to be in violation of this provision while in such pursuit, except that the provisions of this subsection shall not authorize a person to remain on such land if instructed to leave by the owner." *Id.* § (b). *See also* N.D. CENT. CODE § 20.1–01–17 to–19.

(2) The fact that a hunter has a hunting license does not, of course, itself confer any right to hunt on private land. *Hamilton v. Williams*, 200 So. 80 (1941).

(3) Hunting and posting: The Minnesota statute involved in *State v. Corbin* imposed criminal penalties for trespass. This is generally the situation in those states that have adopted posting statutes. These statutes thus do not directly affect state common-law remedies for civil trespass such as that involved in *M'Conico v. Singleton*.

State posting statutes are both widespread and various:

(a) General criminal trespass statutes: Some states have general criminal trespass statutes that are applicable to hunters as well as all other non-privileged entrants. Alaska, for example, criminalizes entering or remaining unlawfully on a premises but creates a privilege to enter for

(b) . . . a person who, without intent to commit a crime on the land, enters or remains upon unimproved and apparently unused land, which is neither fenced nor otherwise enclosed in a manner designed to exclude intruders . . . unless

(1) notice against trespass is personally communicated to that person . . . ; or

(2) notice against trespass is given by posting in a reasonably conspicuous manner under the circumstances.

(c) A notice against trespass is given if the notice

(1) is printed legibly in English;

(2) is at least 144 square inches in size;

(3) contains the name and address of the person under whose authority the property is posted and the name and address of the person who is authorized to grant permission to enter the property;

(4) is placed at each roadway and at each way of access onto the property that is known to the landowner;

(5) in the case of an island, is placed along the perimeter at each cardinal point of the island; and

(6) states any specific prohibition that the posting is directed against, such as "no trespassing," "no hunting," "no fishing," "no digging," or similar prohibitions.

ALASKA STAT. § 11.46.350(b). *See also* MONT. CODE. ANN. § 45–6–201; *Nev. Rev. Stat.* §§ 207.200, 503.240.

(b) No posting/prior permission: In some states, no posting is required and all entries to hunt are trespasses unless the entrant obtains permission. For example, a Colorado statute states: "It is unlawful for any person to enter upon privately owned land . . . to hunt or take any wildlife by hunting, trapping, or fishing without first obtaining permission from the owner or person in possession of such land." COLO. REV. STAT. § 33–6–116(1). *See also* CONN. GEN. STAT. § 53a–109(a); GA. CODE ANN. § 27–3–1. *See also* IDAHO CODE § 36–1603; OK. STAT. tit. 29, § 6–304; TENN. CODE ANN. § 70–4–106(a); UTAH CODE ANN. § 23–20–14.

(c) Posting to prohibit hunting: Some states authorize simple posting procedures. Arizona, for example, provides: "Landowners or lessees of private land desiring to prohibit hunting or shooting on their lands shall post such lands, using a notice or signboard not less than eight inches by eleven inches with the wording plainly legible." ARIZ. REV. STAT. § 17–304. *See also* MASS. GEN. LAWS 131 § 36; MISS. CODE ANN. § 49–7–79; N.D. CENT. CODE § 20.1–01–17 to–20; VT. CODE ANN. tit. 10, § 14; VA. CODE ANN. §§ 18.2–134,–134.1; W. VA. CODE §§ 20–2–7,–8. Other states imposed detailed posting requirements. *E.g.,* LA. REV. STAT. ANN. § 14:61.12; NEB. REV. STAT. §§ 37–723 to–726; N.H. REV. STAT. ANN. § 635:4; N.J. STAT. ANN. § 23:7–1; N.M. STAT. ANN. § 30–14–6; N.Y. ENVTL. CONSERV. §§ 11–2111,–2115; N.C. GEN. STAT. §§ 14–159.6 to .10; TENN. CODE ANN. § 70–4–106(b).

(d) Prohibiting posting: Some states make it illegal to post land when the poster is not authorized to do so by the owner. *E.g.,* CAL. FISH & GAME CODE § 2018; MICH. COMP. LAWS § 324.73105; WASH. REV. CODE. § 77.15.220; W. VA. CODE § 20–2–9.

(4) Landowner rights and the farm lobby: Note that the statute at issue in *State v. Corbin* was limited to agricultural lands. Other states also draw distinctions between different types of land. California, for example, criminalizes "[e]ntering any lands under cultivation or enclosed by fence." CAL. PENAL CODE § 602(k). *See also* IDAHO CODE § 36–1602 ("cultivated, posted, or enclosed by fences"); NEB. REV. STAT. § 37–723 ("farms and ranches"); N.J. STAT. ANN. § 4:17–2 ("agricultural or horticultural lands").

(5) Creating incentives to conserve habitat: As lawmakers have considered the conflict between landowner rights and free public hunting, have they given adequate thought to the desirability of encouraging landowners to manage their lands so as to improve wildlife habitat? Are landowners likely to manage lands to produce a "crop" of wildlife if they do not have rights to harvest that crop? Would the ability to sell the permission to hunt provide such an incentive?

We will return in Chapter 3 to consider landowner rights in more detail, with specific consideration of the legal issues raised by private game preserves and measures intended to encourage private action to improve wildlife habitat.

(6) Creating incentives to permit hunting: Vermont provides reimbursement for damages to "crops, fruit trees, or crop-bearing plants" caused by deer and black bear only "on land not posted against hunting." VT. CODE ANN. tit. 10, § 4829. *See also* WASH. REV. CODE. § 77.36.060.

(7) Hunting and easements in roadways: The public often has only an easement for a road with the abutting landowner retaining ownership of the underlying fee. Does the public easement include a right to hunt?

A North Dakota statute provided that "any person may enter upon legally posted land to recover game shot or killed on land where such person had a lawful right to hunt." In *Rutten v. Wood,* plaintiff sued a hunter who, while on a public road that crossed plaintiff's posted land, shot geese flying over the land and then left the highway to recover the geese. The court held that the road easement did not include a right to hunt. Defendant therefore had no lawful right to hunt on the road and thus was not within the statute authorizing entry on to posted land to retrieve lawfully killed game. *Rutten v. Wood,* 57 N.W.2d 112 (N.D.1953).

In *Reis v. Miller,* owners of land subject to public right-of-way easements for highways filed a declaratory judgment action against state officials, challenging constitutionality of statute allowing hunting, fishing and trapping on the easements. Plaintiffs argued that the applicable territorial and state statutes should not be construed to "include hunting, fishing, trapping and other recreational activities as part of the highway right-of-way." After reviewing several prior decisions recognizing the use of roads for hunting, the court concluded that "this court has liberally construed statutes defining public highways 'in favor of the right of the public to have access to, and use of, section lines.' [ ] We combine a broad reading of the easements for public use with legislative and judicial recognition of recreational use of public highways and conclude that hunting, fishing and trapping are included in the public right-of-way easements in South Dakota. We further conclude that it is the appropriate function of the South Dakota Legislature to determine the extent of the recreational easement." *Reis v. Miller,* 550 N.W.2d 78 (S.D.1996).

(8) Access for nonhunters? Given that today most people would prefer to watch and photograph wildlife rather than to hunt it, should birders and picture-takers have the same access rights to private lands as hunters? What about morel mushroom "hunters"?

b. STATE REGULATION AS A LIMIT ON THE POWER TO CAPTURE

Jones v. Metcalf

Supreme Court of Vermont.
119 A. 430 (1923).

■ TAYLOR, J.:—In October, 1919, the plaintiff set a bear trap in the "Sherwin pasture" in the town of Stratton, to which a chain and clog were attached. At some time before the 14th of October, the bear in question got into this trap, but had succeeded in getting away from the place where it was set, taking the trap, chain, and clog along with it. At some distance from the place where the trap was set the chain became entangled, so that the bear had been unable to make any further escape, when discovered by members of the defendant's party. The defendant was then the fish and game warden for Windham county. Having information that there were bear traps set in the vicinity of Stratton in violation of law, he set out in company with two deputy wardens and a guide to make an investigation. Their search brought them to the Sherwin pasture in the afternoon of October 14.

They discovered the place where the trap had been set, and indication on the ground that some animal had gotten into it and dragged it away. Continuing the search, one of the party, not the defendant, discovered the bear in the trap and had shot it before the defendant arrived on the scene. The latter directed his assistants to carry the bear to their automobile, some two or three miles away, he carrying the trap and chain. The bear and trap were taken to Brattleboro, where the defendant resides. He retained possession of the trap, and left the bear at a slaughterhouse to be properly dressed and await the appearance of a claimant. He caused a notice of the seizure to be published in the next issue of the *Brattleboro Reformer* with a view, as he testified, of discovering the owner. The notice reached the plaintiff, and on October 18th he went to Brattleboro, where he met the defendant and Mr. Gibson, the state's attorney of Windham county, at the office of the latter. He identified the trap as his and the one he had set in the Sherwin pasture. On his demand the trap was delivered to him, and the defendant went with him to the slaughterhouse, where he received the hide of the bear. The carcass was not taken, as the meat was found to have spoiled, so that it was unfit for food. The defendant made no claim of ownership of the trap or bear, and after the interview at the office of the state's attorney did nothing to keep the trap or any part of the bear from the plaintiff. The latter claimed that the hide and meat of the bear were spoiled through the fault of the defendant, and he was permitted to recover damages for the loss of the animal and compensation for time and expenses in securing his property after it was taken by the defendant.

. . .

It will be seen that the case presents two separate, though interrelated, questions: (1) The right of property in a wild animal captured in a manner forbidden by law, as against a fish and game warden, who, acting in his official capacity, has taken it into his possession with a view of securing evidence for a prosecution of the offender. (2) The right of such game warden to seize without a warrant property of the offender employed in the unlawful capture and retained for a like purpose. . . .

The plaintiff's right to maintain an action for damage on account of the bear stands differently than his right of action respecting the trap. His title to the trap was unquestioned, and his rights were those of unqualified ownership; while, if he had any property rights in the bear, they were such as arise from having reduced the animal to possession. The rule is every-where recognized that animals *feræ naturæ* at large in the state belong to the people of the state in their collective and sovereign capacity, and not in their individual and private capacity, except so far as private ownership may be acquired therein under the Constitution, subject always to such proper regulations as the Legislature may make. From this common property an inhabitant of the state has the right to appropriate to his own use such as he may capture and retain in conformity with reasonable regulations established by law for the common good. In such manner, and such only, he can acquire a qualified ownership in the animal which the law recognizes as private property. . . .

The precise question presented here has never before arisen in this court. It has been held in other jurisdictions, however, that the act of reducing a wild animal to possession, as affecting the question of ownership, must not be wrongful and that such animals captured in violation of law do not become the property of the capturer, such as will give him the right to maintain an action against a game warden, who seizes or releases the animal. *James v. Wood,* 19 A. 160 (Me.1889); *State v. Repp,* 73 N.W. 829 (Iowa 1998); *Rexroth v. Coon,* 23 A. 37 (R.I.1885). The question has usually arisen in actions between a trespasser and the owner of the land on which wild animals were taken, or one defending in the right of the latter.

Blades v. Higgs, 11 H.L. Cas. 621, 11 Eng. Rep. 1474 (H.L 1865), is a leading English case on the subject. The opinion by the Lord Chancellor reviews the earlier English cases and states the rule to be that title to property created merely by the act of reducing a thing into possession necessarily implies a reduction into possession effected by an act which is not in any way of a wrongful nature. The case holds that such an act effected by one who is at the moment a trespasser cannot create a title to property. *James v. Wood, supra,* may be regarded as a leading case in this country on the question, and is very much in point. The action was trespass for entering upon the plaintiff's land and liberating a moose and a deer confined there. The plaintiff had captured the moose and purchased the deer during the closed season. The defendant justified as a game warden. His act was not authorized by any provision of statute. It was held that the defendant had not justified the taking of the deer, as he failed to show that it had been captured in violation of law. But as to the moose it was held that the plaintiff's illegal act of capture out of season gave him no title to support the action-that the law protects the title or claim of no one that arises from a violation of law.

The argument in support of the holding is convincing. The law distinguishes between rights acquired in conformity with and arising under its provision, and claims originating in their clear and palpable violation. It will not enforce claims made in contravention of its mandates, nor protect property held against, and being used for, the deliberate purpose of disobeying its enactments. A different course would be suicidal. The law cannot lend its aid to the disobedience of its own commands and to the destruction of its own authority.

. . .

The question is unaffected by the fact that the bear was a noxious animal, for the destruction of which the state offered a bounty. The distinction found in some cases between wild animals of a "base" nature and those of a "generous" nature relates to the question whether the particular animal was the subject of larceny, and was probably made in favor of human life at a time when larceny was a capital offense. While it has been held that wild animals of a base nature, in contemplation of law, are not a subject of larceny, it seems that the distinction has never been made when the right of the owner to be protected by a civil action is involved. *Warren v. State*, 1 Greene 106 (Iowa 1848); *Norton v. Ladd*, 5 N.H. 203 (1830); 4 BLACKSTONE, COMMENTARIES *234–35. The general property in the bear when at large was in the people of the state in their sovereign capacity. They could protect it or invite its destruction as deemed for the common good. They could regulate the means of capture, likewise for the common good, though not for the protection of the animal. Such is the purpose and effect of the statute which it is claimed the plaintiff violated.

Reversed and remanded.

NOTES

(1) The wrongful hunter: One sign of the law's declining solicitude toward hunters—and its increasing embrace of English ideas—was its adoption of the legal rule that a hunter acting wrongfully had to relinquish captured wildlife. A hunter who trespassed or who violated game laws did not lawfully acquire title, and therefore could claim no ownership. No longer could the hunter merely pay nominal damages for the trespass or pay a nominal fine for violating game laws, while keeping the game.

The leading decision, discussed in *Jones v. Metcalf*, was an English case, *Blades v. Higgs*, 11 H.L. Cas. 621, 11 Eng. Rep. 1474 (H.L 1865), a ruling by the House of Lords sitting as a judicial body. In *Blades*, the Lords reasoned that a trespasser could not lawfully acquire title to a captured animal since the capture occurred without authorization, yet since the animal was dead (or otherwise controlled) it could no longer be unowned *feræ naturæ*. Someone had to own it, and the obvious candidate was the owner of the land where the trespass occurred.

The analysis was adopted in America, but not without eliciting criticism, both because of its alleged unfairness to hunters and because it deviated from the strict rule of capture. How could a landowner gain rights in wildlife without capturing it? To many judges, the new rule smacked of the hated English precedent that recognized privileged landowners as owners of roaming game on their private preserves. Dissenting in *Sterling v. Jackson*, Justice Campbell of the Michigan Supreme Court condemned *Blades v. Higgs* as a misguided "piece of new judicial legislation":

> The common law which we inherit is the common law, untainted by feudalism and royal prerogative; and, if we eliminate these elements and their statutory modifications, the case presents no difficulties.

> Even in the case of *Blades v. Higgs*, 13 C.B.N.S. 866, 143 Eng. Rep. 333 (Exch. Ch. 1863), which, after all, was decided on the strength of a previous exchequer chamber decision that had not been supposed

to go so far, that game killed on a man's land by a trespasser belonged to the land-owner, it was not pretended that this was not a long step forward, even under the game laws, and not sustainable except as a piece of new judicial legislation. It has not yet been carried far enough to make the property so complete that larceny will lie for the bird or animal killed and taken, and this of itself condemns the doctrine. But in that case it was practically admitted that the original common law did not vary from the civil law, and was conclusive against any ownership but that of the captor. According to all the elementary common-law writers, no one had any interest whatever in any wild creature of earth, air, or water, until he had taken it into his own keeping alive or dead, and then only so long as it did not escape from his custody.

Sterling v. Jackson, 37 N.W. 845, 859 (Mich.1888) (Campbell, J., dissenting). To give captured game to a landowner was to give it to a person who had not captured it, and to raise the ugly specter that a trespassing hunter might one day be charged with theft as well as trespass, perhaps leading to the onerous criminal penalties—including ''transport'' to the British colonies in North America—imposed on trespassing hunters in early modern England.

A variation of this theme was offered in *Rosenthal-Brown Fur Co. v. Jones–Frere Fur Co.,* 110 So. 630, 632 (La.1926), when the court concluded that a trespassing hunter ''must account to [the land] owner for all the fruits of his unlawful exercise ... this being in accord with the moral maxim of the law that 'no man ought to enrich himself at the expense of another.' ''

To the modern legal mind—less confined by the rigidity of property concepts—a better rationale for the holding in *Blades v. Higgs* is that trespassers and game-law violators are denied rights in their game as a means of deterring future wrongful acts. Unlawfully captured game goes to the landowner or to the state, not in recognition of their ownership rights, but simply as a means of implementing a policy of deterrence.

(2) Wrongful possession and the rise of police power regulations: James Magner, a retail dealer in game in Chicago, was charged with violating a state statute setting game seasons and prohibiting the sale of game out of season, including game obtained from other states. In upholding the conviction, the Court explained the state's power to restrict common law rights to capture and dispose of wild animals:

> No one has a property in the animals and fowls denominated ''game,'' until they are reduced to possession. 2 KENT'S COMMENTARIES 416 *et seq.* (8th ed.); COOLEY ON TORTS 435. Whilst they are untamed and at large, the ownership is said to be in the sovereign authority,—in Great Britain, the king,—2 BLACKSTONE'S COM. *409–10—but, with us, in the people of the State. The policy of the common law was to regulate and control the hunting and killing of game, for its better preservation; and such regulation and control, according to Blackstone, belong to the police power of the government. 4 *id.* *174.

So far as we are aware, it has never been judicially denied that the government, under its police powers, may make regulations for the preservation of game and fish, restricting their taking and molestation to certain seasons of the year, although laws to this effect, it is believed, have been in force, in many of the older States, since the organization of the Federal government. On the contrary, the constitutional right to enact such laws has been expressly affirmed, in regard to fish, by Massachusetts, in *Burnham v. Webster,* 5 Mass. 266 (1809); *Nickerson v. Brackett,* 10 Mass. 212 (1813); and by Indiana, in *Gentile v. State,* 29 Ind. 409 (1868)—and, in regard to game, by New York, in *Phelps v. Racey,* 60 N.Y. 10 (1875); and by Vermont, in *State v. Norton,* 45 Vt. 258 (1872). And, upon principle, the right is clear.

The ownership being in the people of the State—the repository of the sovereign authority—and no individual having any property rights to be affected, it necessarily results, that the legislature, as the representative of the people of the State, may withhold or grant to individuals the right to hunt and kill game, or qualify and restrict it, as, in the opinion of its members, will best subserve the public welfare.

Stated in other language, to hunt and kill game, is a boon or privilege granted, either expressly or impliedly, by the sovereign authority—not a right inhering in each individual; and, consequently, nothing is taken away from the individual when he is denied the privilege, at stated seasons, of hunting and killing game. It is, perhaps, accurate to say that the ownership of the sovereign authority is in trust for all the people of the State, and hence, by implication, it is the duty of the legislature to enact such laws as will best preserve the subject of the trust and secure its beneficial use, in the future, to the people of the State. But in any view, the question of individual enjoyment is one of public policy, and not of private right.

The Court also responded to defendant's claim that the state statute should be construed to exclude game obtained from outside the state, given that banning the sale of such game (in this case, 144 quail imported from Kansas) would not aid wildlife in Illinois:

But, it is argued this can not be the correct construction, because such a prohibition does not tend to protect the game of this State. To this there seem to be two answers: First, the language is clear and free of ambiguity, and, in such case, there is no room for construction—the language must be held to mean just what it says. Second, it cannot be said to be within judicial cognizance that such a prohibition does not tend to protect the game of this State. It being conceded, as it tacitly is, by the argument, that preventing the entrapping, netting, ensnaring, etc., of wild fowls, birds, etc., during certain seasons of the year, tends to the protection of wild fowls, birds, etc., we think it obvious that the prohibition of all possession and sales of such wild fowls or birds during the prohibited seasons would tend to their protection, in excluding the opportunity for the evasion of such law by clandestinely taking them, when secretly killed or captured here, beyond the State and afterwards bringing them into the State for sale, or by other subterfuges and evasions.

It is quite true that the mere act of allowing a quail netted in Kansas to be sold here does not injure or in anywise affect the game here; but a law which renders all sales and all possession unlawful, will more certainly prevent any possession or any sale of the game within the State, than will a law allowing possession or sales here of the game taken in other States. This is but one among many instances to be found in the law where acts, which in and of themselves alone are harmless enough, are condemned because of the facility they otherwise offer for a cover or disguise for the doing of that which is harmful.

Magner v. State, 97 Ill. 320 (1881).

(3) *State v. Norton:* According to the criminal indictment, the defendant, Solomon Norton, "did unlawfully, with guns, sticks, knives, and other instruments of death, chase, drive, worry, and kill a live animal called a deer, found running at large within said state," in violation of the following statute:

If any person shall hereafter, within the period of ten years, kill any animal of the deer kind, found running at large within this state, or assist therein, or shall hurt or worry any such animal, he shall be punished by a fine of fifty dollars, and costs of prosecution, to be recovered by a suit before a justice of the peace; one half of said fine to be paid to the complainant, and the other half to be paid into the treasury of the town in which such animal shall be so hurt, worried, or killed.

Defendant admitted the facts but claimed that the statute conflicted with a provision in the state constitution (section 40) protecting the rights of citizens to hunt: "[T]he inhabitants of this state shall have liberty, in seasonable times, to hunt and fowl on the lands they hold, and on other lands not inclosed; and in like manner to fish in all boatable and other waters (not private property), under proper regulations to be hereafter made and provided by the general assembly." Rejecting the argument, the court held the ban on deer hunting a "proper regulation":

The rights secured by this section of the constitution were not intended to be absolute and unconditional, but were to be governed and controlled by such proper regulations as might thereafter be made by the general assembly. The right was reserved to the general assembly to determine what were seasonable times in which to hunt and fowl, and having exercised this right, the court will not assume (certainly in the absence of proof) that it has been exercised in an unconstitutional manner. The numerous statutes which have been passed for the protection of game and fish, have been deemed necessary to the beneficial enjoyment of the constitutional right, and the court will not hold such laws unconstitutional, until it is clearly shown that they are so prohibitory as to virtually deprive the inhabitants of the right secured to them by the constitution.

State v. Norton, 45 Vt. 258 (1872). In light of this ruling, what is the legal impact of the state constitutional provision guaranteeing a right to hunt? Are hunters in Vermont better protected than hunters in Illinois under *Magner v. State*?

(4) The wrongful hunter (pt. II): Along with *Jones v. Metcalf*, consider the following materials addressing how the violation of game laws affects rights in captured animals:

(a) *James v. Wood*: A landowner brought a trespass action against defendant game warden, who came onto his land and freed moose and a deer. The release of the deer was held to be wrongful because the landowner had lawfully acquired it outside the state. The release of the moose, however, was proper because the landowner captured it in violation of state game laws:

> This court has said, in substance, that the law protects the title or claim of no one that arises from a violation of law.... Suppose a hunter has his rifle leveled at game in close time, and some one shoves it aside so that the game is missed. Shall the hunter have damages? He has only been prevented from continuing a criminal act.

> Suppose lobsters illegally taken are thrown overboard alive. Is he who does it a trespasser? Shall the taker of them have damages for his illegal catch? Or suppose one lands a salmon in violation of law, and a bystander, while it is yet alive, throws it back into the water. Shall the fisherman have the value of the salmon that the law forbids his having at all?

> When game is killed, it absolutely becomes property, but, when taken alive, only conditionally so; for, when released, property in it is gone. So long, then, as the possession of live game is illegal, qualified property in it is illegal also, and the releasing of such game interferes with no legal right or title of the person illegally holding it captive.

> . . .

> The plaintiff's illegal act prevented the moose from becoming property at all. Not so with the illegal act of a thief who may have stolen a coat; for the coat was already property, and had an owner, who alone could lawfully take it from the thief. The public, whose servant the defendant was, stands in the place of the owner of the coat. Care should be taken, therefore, not to confound the doctrine of this case with the well-settled rule of law that possession of property is a good title against everybody but the true owner.

James v. Wood, 19 A. 160 (Me.1889). Would this case have come out differently if the defendant had not been a game warden? What if he had been simply a private citizen concerned about animal welfare? Does the court's reasoning in any way depend on the exercise of governmental powers?

(b) *Dapson v. Daly*: Both plaintiff and defendant were hunting deer during open season. Plaintiff fired at the deer. While the deer was still "galloping," defendant also shot it, whereupon it died and was carried off by the defendant. The trial court concluded that the deer was not sufficiently wounded by the plaintiff for the plaintiff to claim ownership of it. The plaintiff was also denied relief, however, for an independent reason—because he failed to show that he was properly licensed to hunt deer:

The plaintiff in the case at bar failed to show that he was duly authorized by law to hunt. Unless so licensed, he was not entitled to the rights of a huntsman. It was an essential part of his case to show that he was a lawful huntsman before he could invoke in his own behalf the law of the chase. The plaintiff, in order to prevail, was bound to show title in himself and could not rely on the weakness of the defendant's rights. [ ] The plaintiff never acquired physical possession of the deer. The first step toward showing title in himself was to prove that he was licensed to hunt.

Dapson v. Daly, 153 N.E. 454 (Mass.1926). Would this case have turned out differently if the plaintiff had captured the deer and then had it taken away by the defendant? Does it matter whether the defendant was properly licensed to hunt?

See also State ex rel. Visser v. State Fish & Game Commission, 437 P.2d 373 (Mont.1968) (licensed elk hunters cannot claim elk killed by unlicensed guide; also, lawfully killed elk are subject to confiscation if game tags are not properly filled out and attached); *Fischer v. Knapp,* 332 N.W.2d 76 (N.D.1983) (foxes illegally dug out of den belong to state); *State v. Hastings,* 41 N.W.2d 305 (N.D.1950) (muskrats taken out of season are subject to seizure by the state as contraband; seller of pelts that were unlawfully trapped held guilty, at time of sale, of crime of obtaining money by false pretenses).

(c) Restatement of Property: Consider the following comment from the *Restatement of Property*:

By virtue of his possession, a possessor of land occupies a favored position with respect to some things which are for the time being within the space comprehended by his possession, but which may be regarded as not yet having been reduced to possession. Included among such things are those wild birds and wild animals which have not been appropriated and which are in general open to appropriation. If such things come within the space possessed by a possessor of land, his right of exclusive occupation of the land enables him to prevent, for the time being, an appropriation by others. Subject to such paramount authority as may be asserted by the state, he not only has this power to prevent appropriation by others, but an attempt at appropriation by others may be rendered ineffective by his right to claim the benefit of the attempt. Thus, if *B*, a trespasser, shoots wild game upon land possessed by *A*, *A* may claim the game or recover damages for its conversion. . . . One who catches fish or shoots game on the land of another is guilty of trespass. He is liable for the conversion of the fish and game so taken to the same extent he would be were the fish and game included in the possession of the land. The presence, however, on specific land of such things as fish and game is so fleeting and so uncontrollable that the possessor of the land is deemed to have, with respect to such things, but a prior right of appropriation rather than possession.

RESTATEMENT OF PROPERTY § 450, comment g, at 2906 (1944).

Along with *Jones v. Metcalf* and the comments of Justice Campbell of the Michigan Supreme Court criticizing *Blades v. Higgs*, consider the following case:

State v. Bartee

Texas Court of Appeals.
894 S.W.2d 34 (1994).

■ ONION, J.:—These appeals are taken by the State from pretrial orders setting aside indictments....

The[y] present rather novel and interesting legal questions and are possibly a case of first impression as to whether a white-tailed deer can be the subject of the theft and criminal mischief statutes, and whether the State of Texas may be alleged as an owner in such situations....

[Defendants each killed a deer out of season. The indictments charged that, "with intent to deprive the owner ... THE STATE OF TEXAS, of property ... ONE WHITE–TAILED DEER, [defendants] did unlawfully appropriate said property." Defendants filed a motion to set aside the indictment, arguing that "the indictments did not allege an offense ... against the laws of the State of Texas because a wild animal such as a white-tailed deer could not be subject of theft or criminal mischief statutes for the reason that there are no identifiable property rights in wild animals [and] the 'state of Texas' cannot legally be the owner of a white-tailed deer as alleged in the indictment."

[T]he real thrust of the [state's] argument ... is that the trial court erred in holding that under no circumstances could a white-tailed deer be property subject to the theft and criminal mischief statutes and that the State could not be alleged as an owner in such an indictment.

[The theft statute provides that a "person commits [theft] if he unlawfully appropriates property with intent to deprive the owner of property." The criminal mischief statute provides that a "person commits an offense if ... he intentionally or knowingly damages or destroys the tangible property."]

The property subject to [these statutes] includes "anything capable of being possessed or owned, whether tangible or intangible, and whether inherently valuable or merely representative of something of value." [ ] Thus, in dealing with property subject to theft, we are dealing with a broad general definition without exclusions.

In order to be the subject of [these statutes] the thing or property taken must be capable of individual ownership....

We find nothing in the Penal Code itself to exclude white-tailed deer and deer antlers from being the subject of the theft or criminal mischief statutes. We must examine other statutes, caselaw and authorities in pursuit of an answer to the questions presented.

We begin by flipping through the pages of time. History reveals a long recognition of common ownership in game and wild animals and its developing subjectivity to governmental authority. At one point the law of ancient Athens forbade the killing of game. Roman law recognized common ownership, but imposed its regulations on the taking of wild animals. There is a history of varying controls exercised by the lawgiving power over the right of a citizen to acquire a qualified ownership in animals *feræ naturæ* evidenced by the Salic law, exemplified by the legislation of Charlemagne, and later by the Napoleonic Code which permitted police regulations to direct the manner in which common ownership was to be enjoyed. *See Geer v. Connecticut*, 161 U.S. 519, 522–26 (1896).

The common law of England also based property in game upon the principle of common ownership, and therefore treated it as subject to governmental authority. *Geer*, 161 U.S. at 526. In *State v. Ward*, 40 S.W.2d 1074, 1077 (Mo.1931), the Supreme Court of Missouri wrote:

> At a very remote time the right and power of the sovereign authority to regulate and control the taking of wild animals were asserted and recognized. Originally, the title seems to have been regarded as vested in the sovereign as a personal prerogative; but, on the granting of Magna Charta and the Charter of the Forest by Henry III in 1225, the rights of the sovereign in unreclaimed wild animals were limited, and the rule of the Roman Law restricting the sovereign power to controlling and regulating the taking of such animals became the common law of England. The rule of the Civil Law recognizing the qualified title of the sovereign in wild animals, having been adopted by England, became the common law of the United States, and here the rule is that the general ownership of wild animals, as far as they are capable of ownership, is in the state, not as a proprietor, but in its collective sovereign capacity as the representative and for the benefit of all its citizens in common. [ ]

The attribute of government to control the taking of animals *feræ naturæ* (wild animals) which was recognized and enforced by the common law of England was vested in the American colonial governments where not denied by their characters or in conflict with grants of the royal prerogative. The power which the colonies possessed passed to the states with separation from the mother country, and remains in the states until the present time in so far as its exercise is not incompatible with rights which were conveyed to the federal government by the United States Constitution. *See Geer*, 161 U.S. at 528.

In Texas, it has been said that the common law provides that animals *feræ naturæ* belong to the state and no individual property rights exist as long as the animal remains wild, unconfined, and undomesticated. *Jones v. State*, 45 S.W.2d 612, 613–14 (1931); *Wiley v. Baker*, 597 S.W.2d 3, 5 (Tex.Civ.App.1980). Unqualified property rights in wild animals can arise when they are legally removed from their natural liberty and made the subjects of man's dominion. *Jones*, 45 S.W.2d at 614. This qualified right is lost, however, if the animal regains its natural liberty. *Wiley*, 597 S.W.2d at 5.

.   .   .

In *Runnels v. State,* 213 S.W.2d 545, 547 (Tex.Crim.App.1948), the Court of Criminal Appeals discussed when wild animals became subject to theft. The Court wrote:

> Wild animals are not subject to theft until they become the property of an owner. This they do immediately upon being reduced to possession. *Jones v. State,* 45 S.W.2d 612 [(Tex.Crim.App.1931)]. This seems to be the settled law in all jurisdictions. Mr. X captures a wildcat. It is a wildcat still, but it immediately becomes his property. The fisherman becomes the owner of his catch as soon as he secures possession. It is wild game still, but is the subject of theft. [ ]

The reason behind the principle expressed in *Runnels* is that the gist of the offense of theft consists in the misappropriation of another person's property. [ ] *Jones* recognized that when wild animals, including deer, become property it was such property that would pass to the executors and administrators of a deceased person's estate. *Jones,* 45 S.W.2d at 613–14; 1 HALSBURY'S LAW OF ENGLAND § 799. Thus, it is legally possible for an individual to have qualified property rights in a wild animal, particularly a deer. [ ]

. . .

Section 1.011(a) of the Texas Parks and Wildlife Code provides "(a) All wild[9] animals, fur-bearing animals, wild birds, and wild fowl inside the borders of this state are *the property of the people of this state.*" TEX. PARKS & WILDLIFE CODE ANN. § 1.011(a) (Vernon 1991) (Emphasis added). The emphasized phrase or the phrase "property of the public" are found in all the statutory forerunners of section 1.011 as far back as 1907. With regard to the ownership of wild animals, we do not find that the various statutes enacted over the years have departed from the common law. The statutory phrase "property of the people of this state" does not appear to have been interpreted by our courts. Despite its use in various statutes over the years, our courts have consistently referred to the ownership of wild animals as being in "the state" or belonging to "the state." *See Dobie,* 48 S.W.2d at 290; *Jones,* 45 S.W.2d at 613; *Wiley,* 597 S.W.2d at 5.

. . .

While the legislature has declared that all wild animals are property of the people of this state, these elected representatives of the people, in order to protect the common ownership and to properly regulate and protect wild animals and game, have entrusted a state agency with the power and responsibility to do so under statutes enacted, and by regulations adopted, as provided by law. The power of the state agency is to be exercised like all other powers of government as a trust for the benefit of the people and not as a prerogative for the advantage of the government or for the benefit of private individuals. . . .

9. " 'Wild,' when used in reference to an animal, means a species, including each individual of a species, that normally lives in a state of nature and is not ordinarily domes- ticated." TEX. PARKS & WILDLIFE CODE ANN. § 1.101 (Vernon 1991). A white-tailed deer is a game animal. *See* TEX. PARKS & WILDLIFE CODE ANN. § 63.001(a) (Vernon Supp. 1994).

In the Parks and Wildlife Code the legislature has provided for scientific breeders of white-tailed deer. Tex. Parks & Wildlife Code Ann. § 43.351 et seq. (Vernon 1991 & Supp. 1994). The Parks and Wildlife Department is authorized to issue permits to qualified persons to possess white-tailed deer for propagation, management, and scientific purposes. Tex. Parks & Wildlife Code Ann. § 43.352 (Vernon Supp. 1994). Among the privileges of the permit is the right of the scientific breeder to engage in the business of breeding white-tailed deer, and for that purpose to hold in possession and in captivity white-tailed deer for propagation or sale. Tex. Parks & Wildlife Code Ann. §§ 43.352, 43.357 (Vernon Supp. 1994). The implication is that the proceeds of any sale may be retained by the scientific breeder. Permits may also be granted to individuals by the department for the trapping, transportation and transplanting of "wild white-tailed deer" from areas overpopulated by such deer to other areas of the state, all without cost to the State government. Tex. Parks & Wildlife Code Ann. § 63.007 (Vernon 1991). There may be other examples, but clearly while acting under permits from the State, the scientific breeder and the transporter would legally have qualified rights of ownership or possession of the white-tailed deer. As we have already seen, wild animals legally reduced to possession may be the subject of theft. *Runnels,* 213 S.W.2d at 547. Likewise, the white-tailed deer in the legal possession of a scientific breeder or transporter with the consent of the State may be the subject of theft, and for that matter, criminal mischief as well. It must be recognized then that the prosecution may bring theft and criminal mischief charges concerning white-tailed deer but only in limited and very circumscribed situations. A white-tailed deer in its natural state of liberty cannot be the subject of the theft and criminal mischief statutes. *See Runnels,* 213 S.W.2d at 547. This is undoubtedly one of the reasons why we have been unable to find a single reported case in Texas involving the theft of deer from the State. The prosecutor in charging theft or criminal mischief involving a white-tailed deer must be extremely careful in choosing the proper allegations in the State's pleadings, but also keenly aware of the facts which will support those allegations. Otherwise, the prosecutor may be up the creek without the proverbial paddle.

. . .

SUMMARY

White-tailed deer in their natural state of liberty are not the proper subject of the criminal offenses of theft and criminal mischief. In limited and circumscribed situations, however, qualified property rights may be legally acquired in white-tailed deer and these deer may be the subject of theft and criminal mischief. White-tailed deer antlers legally acquired may also be the subject of theft....

■ Before Peeples, Rickhoff, and Onion, JJ.

■ Rickhoff, J., concurring:—I agree with the majority "that white-tailed deer in their natural state of liberty cannot be the subject of theft." As the majority observes, animals are either wild (*feræ naturæ*) or domestic (*domitæ naturæ*). No one, not even the state, "owns" wild animals, at least in the proprietary sense, when they are in their natural habitat.

. . .

The majority observes that white-tailed deer in the possession of a scientific breeder or transporter may be the subject of theft or criminal mischief, or that "[t]here may be other examples" that allow such qualified rights of ownership or possession of white-tailed deer. If this is so, then I believe there are many white-tailed deer that are privately owned in Texas that could be the subject of a theft or criminal mischief indictment and in the future there will be many thousands.

If the majority is merely holding that it is possible for a white-tailed deer to become personal property and that, accordingly, it will be difficult for the State to prove the deer in this case was owned by the State, then I agree. Here, the State was alleged in very general terms to be the owner of a particular deer. As the majority correctly notes, this may be sufficient for purposes of an indictment, but how is it going to prove this deer was reduced to possession by the State? This, I believe, is the "bridge too far." *See* CORNELIUS RYAN, A BRIDGE TOO FAR (1974).

Recognizing that this is not the case where ownership of white-tailed deer should be resolved, I want to follow on the majority's surmise that there may be "other examples."

While "wild" white-tailed deer meet the definition of "wildlife" found in the Texas Parks and Wildlife Code, *see, e.g.,* TEX. PARKS & WILDLIFE CODE ANN. § 61.005 (Vernon 1991), the ownership of any wild animal, as personal property, is easy enough to answer: no one owns wild animals.

Possibly the earliest case to address the issue of ownership of wild animals is *Pierson v. Post,* 3 Cai. 175 (N.Y.1805) which held that "property in [wild] animals is acquired by occupancy only." A century later, Justice Holmes agreed that occupancy, or possession, was a necessary prerequisite to obtaining a property interest in wild animals. He reaffirmed *Pierson* by stating that "[w]ild birds are not in the possession of anyone; and possession is the beginning of ownership." *Missouri v. Holland,* 252 U.S. 416, 434 (1920). The result is that "[a]s a general rule, wild fish, birds and animals are owned by no one. Property rights in them are obtained by reducing them to possession." *United States v. Long Cove Seafood, Inc.,* 582 F.2d 159, 163 (2d Cir.1978). Wild animals are not the property of the landowner, whether it be an individual, a neighborhood association or any other entity, but are common property whose control and regulation are to be exercised "as a trust for the benefit of the people." *Geer v. Connecticut,* 161 U.S. 519, 528–29 (1896). Federal and state authority over wildlife is not based on ownership, but upon the state's police power to preserve and regulate an important resource. *Toomer v. Witsell,* 334 U.S. 385, 402 (1948). As the Supreme Court declared, "[I]t is pure fantasy to talk of 'owning' wild fish, birds, or animals. Neither the States nor the Federal Government . . . has title to these creatures until they are reduced to possession by skillful capture." *Douglas v. Seacoast Products, Inc.,* 431 U.S. 265, 284 (1977).

In 1909, the Court of Criminal Appeals of Texas was faced with a constitutional challenge by an individual who was arrested for trying to sell two ducks he killed. He contended "that the right to alienate property is a natural and necessary consequence to the ownership of property, and is a fundamental right and privilege guaranteed by the Constitutions of the United States and the State of Texas,.... " The court recognized the police power of the state because "the absolute ownership of wild game is vested in the people of the state and that such is not the subject of private ownership." The court went on to recognize that individuals can only acquire ownership of wild animals in a qualified way, and the legislature therefore had the right to restrict the sale of the wild ducks that had been killed. *Ex parte Blardone,* 115 S.W. 838, 840 (Tex.Crim.App.1909). Previously, it was common law that an individual acquired an absolute interest in game he killed. [ ] If the state, through legislative enactment, has the police power to change the common law and subject individuals to restrictions and conditions on how they acquire wild animals, then it follows that it may control the acquisition of wild animals as they have with § 44.002 of the Parks and Wildlife Code, which prohibits the captivity or propagation of a game animal without a license. *See* TEX. PARKS & WILDLIFE CODE ANN. § 44.002 (Vernon 1991). However, it is the view of this writer that the state has not defined wild animals so as to absolutely exclude from ownership all white-tailed deer within the boundaries of the state.... Unless they are acquired unlawfully, wild animals confined by a landowner are no longer wild and may become property that could pass through executors, generate tort liability for their owners, or become the subject of conversion or theft under a similar indictment.

While we are across the bridge and beyond the record with our suppositions regarding how the state will satisfy their ownership under the indictment, I offer this example of deer as personalty.

Our state legislature has defined "wild" as any animal that "normally lives in a state of nature and is not ordinarily domesticated." TEX. PARKS & WILDLIFE CODE ANN. § 1.101 (Vernon 1991). Furthermore, the legislature declared that, a white-tailed deer is a game animal. *See* TEX. PARKS & WILDLIFE CODE ANN. § 63.001(a) (Vernon Supp. 1994). Any entity that acquires a white-tailed deer from a breeder and a permit from the state can confine that deer and the offspring, and reduce them to their care. TEX. PARKS & WILDLIFE CODE ANN. § 43.352 (Vernon Supp. 1995). The state, in an effort "that native species may be preserved," extended their regulations over all white-tailed deer, even when confined under permit, but in doing so the legislature specifically allowed the most common method of reducing wild game to man's domain—"high fences." TEX. PARKS & WILDLIFE CODE ANN. § 43.366 (Vernon Supp. 1995). I am aware of no challenge that has ever been brought in Texas to the prohibition against the captivity of game animals or the prohibition against containing them in areas larger than 320 acres. TEX. PARKS & WILDLIFE CODE ANN. § 43.360 (Vernon Supp. 1995). Nor am I aware of anyone who has been required to remove game-proof fencing. One would think that this provision prohibiting captivity would not apply to an area large enough to maintain a natural habitat. If there exists a high percentage of privately held lands in Texas with deer-proof fencing, many thousands of deer could become the property of landowners based on common law principles. In other words, if white-tailed deer are lawfully acquired by a licensed breeder from another state pursuant to the allowed exemption and sold to a permit-holding individual with a ranch with a deer-proof fence, and that deer remains so confined in this habitat (which is natural in all ways except that the animal and their increase cannot escape the landowner's domain), is it not the landowner's white-tailed deer? As the facts are developed in appropriate cases, we may find that an increasing number of white-tailed deer in Texas are privately owned and may be the subject of theft.

In given cases our courts could recognize the current reality in Texas that deer, and many other terrestrial game animals and fish, are held in private game-proof preserves, parks or lakes and ponds by landowners who have entirely reduced these creatures to their domain and have acquired ownership in them in a proprietary sense. While wildlife management has presented very difficult political issues for our legislature to balance it should be clear that once high fences were allowed, much of the responsibility for preserving and increasing our wildlife has fallen to the owners of these fenced preserves. With that responsibility should also come the rights, duties and liabilities of ownership.

The legislature has not clearly stated that individuals may not own white-tailed deer lawfully acquired, nor am I aware of any case that so holds. Until a case is presented with a sufficient record allowing us to properly rule, the status of confined but lawfully acquired and maintained white-tailed deer in Texas will be unclear.

NOTES

(1) State ownership of wildlife: In the end, the court in *Bartee* allows the State of Texas to proceed with a criminal prosecution for theft of a wild deer, but it defines the necessary interest so narrowly that the state will rarely succeed. For purposes of theft, the state apparently owns deer only under circumstances in which private parties would own them: that is, when they have been captured and kept in confinement. Free-roaming deer, it appears, are not subject to theft. *See State v. Lee,* 41 So.2d 662 (Fla.1949) (indictment charging theft for the taking of two captive deer held by state fish and game commission upheld).

Note that the court recognizes the state's sovereign ownership of wildlife, on behalf of the people, for certain purposes, but concludes that sovereign ownership is insufficient to sustain a theft prosecution. If it is insufficient for that purpose, what legal importance does it carry? We will return to this issue in Chapter 5. We shall also see how the state-ownership doctrine arose as a means of justifying state regulatory powers over wild animals.

(2) The variety of "ownership": In *Bartee,* the court uses various phrases when talking about ownership rights in wildlife: "common ownership" [¶¶ 9–10], state sovereign ownership [¶ 10], "animals *feræ naturæ* belong to the state" [¶ 12], "property of the people of this state" [¶ 15], private ownership through possession [¶ 12], the permitted ownership of "a scientific breeder or transporter" [¶ 17], "no one owns wildlife" [¶ 19], and ownership by confining within game-proof fencing [¶ 27]. Which of these are treated as synonyms and which describe different ideas? Are the ideas consistent with one another? How carefully is the court choosing its terminology?

(3) Theft and the private landowner: Does *Bartee* respond to Justice Campbell's worries in *Sterling v. Jackson* that a trespassing hunter could be charged with the theft of a wild animal killed on the land of a private landowner? If the state only owns wild animals that are under control, could a private landowner claim more extensive rights? In thinking about this issue, consider the next note.

(4) Capture revisited: The concurring opinion by Judge Rickhoff in *Bartee* returns us in useful ways to the issue of capture. In his view, deer that are confined behind high fences are adequately controlled so that the landowner owns them, even if the area is large enough to qualify as natural habitat for the animals. If this is so, would a successful hunter trespassing in the confined area be liable for theft as well as for trespass? Would the issue turn on how high the fences were? What if an occasional deer could jump out, but most could not, or if mature adults could escape but fawns could not? Might a hunter be guilty of theft for killing a fawn [*"ratione impotentiæ"*] but not an adult deer? If the application of theft statutes turns on such fine details, is this fair to criminal defendants?

Rickhoff's comments raise further questions, particularly pertinent to private game ranches:

(a) What about wild animals that move around only within small ranges? If the range of an animal population is entirely on the land of one owner, with an adequate surrounding buffer, and if the animals are almost certain not to leave, are they adequately confined? Is it sensible to insist that the landowner in such a case construct a useless fence to keep the animals in? Also, what about the private owner whose land completely surrounds a pond? Could the owner claim that wildlife limited to the pond (fish, muskrats, mink, etc.) are adequately confined to the pond, and thus privately owned, if they are highly unlikely to depart? Do these hypotheticals differ from *State v. Shaw* (*supra*), in which the court decided that fish were adequately captured in an incomplete enclosure, so long as their behavior was such that they were highly unlikely to escape? We return to the rights of landowners in nonnavigable water bodies in Chapter 3.

(b) Rickhoff seems to have in mind the case in which a landowner constructs a fence and then imports captured animals to stock the enclosed space. But what if the owner merely constructs a high fence and happens to surround wild animals already on the land? Have they been captured, even though never physically seized? If so, must the landowner be aware of their presence?

(c) *State v. Brogan:* Welch Brogan owned an elk farm composed of some 400 acres; at times he had up to 250 head of elk on the farm. His conviction for entrapping wild elk by opening gates and baiting his pastures with hay was upheld on appeal. The court also noted in passing that Brogan did not own the deer that had been inadvertently trapped on his ranch when the fences were closed. *State v. Brogan,* 862 P.2d 19 (Mont. 1993). Is *Brogan* another example of the proposition set forth in *Magner v.*

State that wrongful possession confers no right? Would Justice Rickhoff agree with either conclusion?

(d) Justice Rickhoff's speculations are hardly idle. Texas has more game ranches that any other state—and the state ownership doctrine has encouraged ranchers to raise exotic species: "Exotics were perfectly suited to the new climate [that focused on trophy hunting]. Unlike native deer, which belong to all the citizens of a state no matter where they roam, exotics can be privately bought, sold, or hunted anytime and in any numbers." Burkhard Bilger, *A Shot in the Ark*, NEW YORKER, Mar. 5, 2001, at 74, 75. The result are large enclosures surrounded by 8-foot high galvanized wire fences—and when the gates were shut there often were native deer inside. On the Diamond K Ranch, "[s]ome four thousand exotic animals, representing thirteen species, live on the ranch's five thousand acres, along with fifteen hundred white-tailed deer." *Id.* at 76. Is there any factual difference between the exotics and the deer? Of the 50 hunters a year that pay $1600 for a weekend hunt, half come for deer and half for exotics.

(5) Domestic by species? Consider *State v. Mierz.* The case arose out of an attempt by wildlife agents to remove two coyotes that the defendant had taken into captivity. The defendant (Mierz) responded by assaulting the officers, and sought to justify his actions as a permissible defense of property—the coyotes. The Washington Supreme Court rejected the defense because defendant did not own the coyotes:

> RCW 77.16.040 provides that "it is unlawful to bring into this state, offer for sale, sell, possess, exchange, buy, transport, or ship wildlife * * **" RCW 77.08.010(16) defines wildlife as
>
> > all species of the animal kingdom whose members exist in Washington in a wild state. This includes but is not limited to mammals, birds, reptiles, amphibians, fish, and invertebrates. The term "wildlife" does not include feral domestic mammals, [old world rats and mice], or * * * fish or shellfish* * **
>
> Mierz argues that his "domesticated" coyotes were "feral domestic mammals," and not wildlife, under this definition. This argument suggests that while RCW 77.16.040 bars possession of wild coyotes, there is an exception for Mierz's coyotes because he caught them and brought them to his home.
>
> Statutes are to be construed to effect their purposes, and to avoid an unlikely or strained consequence. [ ] A number of decisions broadly interpret various provisions of the wildlife laws so as to better protect wildlife.[14] Construing "feral domestic mammals" to include any animal reclaimed from the wild would defeat the purpose of the wildlife code to "preserve, protect, and perpetuate wildlife." RCW 77.12.010; [ ] We think it more likely . . . that "feral domestic mammals" refers to

---

14. *Silz v. Hesterberg,* 211 U.S. 31 (1908) (State prohibitions on possession apply to animals lawfully acquired in other states), *quoted in Graves v. Dunlap,* 152 P. 532 (Wash.1915); *State v. Walsh,* 870 P.2d 974 (Wash.1994) (defendants were engaged in a "hunt," though no animal was nearby, when they spotlighted and took aim at decoys); *State v. Rhodes,* 795 P.2d 724 (Wash. App.1990).

individual members of domestic species such as cats or dogs that have run away, species that the wildlife code is not intended to protect.[15] [ ]

Mierz's interpretation would lead to insuperable difficult in enforcing wildlife laws; individual "domesticated" members of a wild species would not be protected and could be possessed or taken with impunity. Wildlife agents would have to test the degree of domestication of a particular animal before concluding that the animal was wildlife. *Grave v. Dunlap*, 152 P. 532 (Wash.1915) (citing the "difficulty of determining whether a fowl killed and possessed during the closed season had been a reclaimed or wild bird"). This would be absurd. Wildlife agents must treat *all* members of wild species as wild. This is required to make the wildlife laws workable.

State v. Mierz, 901 P.2d 286 (Wash.1995). Recall also the notes following *Koop v. United States* in Chapter 1.

(6) Theft of animals *feræ naturæ*—a concurrence: The Second Circuit Court of Appeals reached a result consistent with *Bartee* in a criminal prosecution for interstate transportation of clams harvested in violation of state law. In addition to charging the defendants with misdemeanors under the Lacey Act, the indictment also alleged felony violations under the National Stolen Property Act. The indictments were predicated upon the theory that the state owned the wildlife in question pursuant to a statute providing that "[t]he State of New York owns all fish, game, wildlife, shellfish, crustacea and protected insects in the state." The court stated that the validity of the indictment turned on "whether New York has asserted a true ownership interest in wildlife." The court held that it had not done so; its claim of ownership was actually "for the purpose of regulating and controlling their use and disposition." *United States v. Long Cove Seafood, Inc.*, 582 F.2d 159 (2d Cir.1978).

(7) Theft of animals *feræ naturæ*—a dissent: In *State v. Fertterer*, the Montana Supreme Court affirmed the felony conviction of poachers under a statute criminalizing "public mischief" for knowingly destroying "public property." The court held that the state's interest in unconfined wildlife was sufficient to support a criminal conviction: "[W]e hold that Montana has an ownership interest in wild game held by it in its sovereign capacity for the use and benefit of the people.... We hold that wild animals are public property within the meaning of Montana's criminal mischief statute." *State v. Fertterer*, 841 P.2d 467 (Mont.1992).

PERSPECTIVES

Is there a justification for giving landowners broad rights to exclude hunters? What was the problem with allowing unrestricted public hunting

---

15. Our construction of "wildlife" to include recaptured wildlife is also mandated by precedent. At common law "all property rights in animals *feræ naturæ* [wild animals] was in the sovereign for the use and benefit of the people," *Cawsey v. Brickey*, 144 P. 938 (Wash.1914). One who caught and confined a wild animal was entitled to possess the "reclaimed" animals as long as it was confined. *Graves v. Dunlap*, 152 P. 532 (Wash.1915) [ ]. But the right to reclaim and keep a wild animal was abrogated in 1913 when the first game code was passed. *Graves*, ...

on uncultivated and unenclosed lands? From a different perspective: is the right to prevent others from killing wildlife a necessary stick in the bundle of landowner rights? Does the public own the stick labeled "wildlife"? (Is this the meaning of the state ownership doctrine?) Isn't the public in some real sense a co-owner of all property in land when there is wildlife upon the land? If it is, then why can't the public permit anyone to obtain property in wildlife under the terms the public sets—which might include free access to the wildlife as long as the hunter does no damage to the other resources that the land produces? Would such a regime of rights—which divided the bundle of sticks among a number of different owners and prohibited them from wasting the resources held by other owners—differ from earlier varieties of the English common law when pannage and estovers were divided among different holders?

Consider an alternative property rights regime:

William Cronon, Changes in the Land: Indians, Colonists, and the Ecology of New England
62–65 (1983).

When it came to land, ... there was less reason for gift giving or exchange. Southern New England Indian families enjoyed exclusive use of their planting fields and of the land on which their wigwams stood, and so might be said to have "owned" them. But neither of these were permanent possessions. Wigwams were moved every few months, and planting fields were abandoned after a number of years. Once abandoned, a field returned to brush until it was recleared by someone else, and no effort was made to set permanent boundaries around it that would hold it indefinitely for a single person. What families possessed in their fields was the *use* of them, the crops that were produced by a woman's labor upon them. When lands were traded or sold ... what were exchanged were usufruct rights, acknowledgments by one group that another might use an area for planting or hunting or gathering. Such rights were limited to the period of use, and they did not include many of the privileges Europeans commonly associated with ownership: a user could not (and saw no need to) prevent other village members from trespassing or gathering nonagricultural food on such lands, and had no conception of deriving rent from them. Planting fields were "possessed" by an Indian family only to the extent that it would return to them the following year. In this, they were not radically different in kind from other village lands; it was *European* rather than Indian definitions of land tenure that led the English to recognize agricultural land as the only legitimate Indian property. The Massachusetts Court made its ownership theories quite clear when it declared that "what landes any of the Indians, within this jurisdiction, have by possession or improvement, by subdueing of the same, they have just right thereunto, according to that Gen: 1:28, chap: 9:1, Psa: 115, 16."

The implication was that Indians did *not* own any other kind of land: clam banks, fishing ponds, berry-picking areas, hunting lands, the great bulk of a village's territory. (Since the nonagricultural Indians of the north had *only* these kinds of land, English theories assigned them no property rights at all.) Confusion was easy on this point, not only because of English ideologies, but because the Indians themselves had very flexible definitions of land tenure for such areas. Here again, the concept of usufruct right was crucial, since different groups of people could have different claims on the same tract of land depending on how they used it. Any village member, for instance, had the right to collect edible wild plants, cut birchbark or chestnut for canoes, or gather sedges for mats, wherever these things could be found. No special private right inhered in them. Since village lands were usually organized along a single watershed, the same was true of rivers and the coast: fish and shellfish could generally be taken anywhere, although the nets, harpoons, weirs, and tackle used to catch them—and hence sometimes the right to use the sites where these things were installed—might be owned by an individual or a kin group. Indeed, in the case of extraordinarily plentiful fishing sites—especially major inland waterfalls during the spawning runs—several villages might gather at a single spot to share the wealth. All of them acknowledged a mutual right to use the site for that specific purpose, even though it might otherwise lie within a single village's territory. Property rights, in other words, shifted with ecological use.

Hunting grounds are the most interesting case of this shifting, nonagricultural land tenure. The ecological habits of different animals were so various that their hunting required a wide range of techniques, and rights to land use had to differ accordingly. The migratory birds in the ponds and salt marshes, for example, were so abundant that they could be treated much like fish: whoever killed them owned them, and hunters could range over any tract of land to do so, much like the birds themselves. (In this, Indian practices bore some resemblance to European customs governing the right of hunters, when in pursuit of game, to cross boundaries which were otherwise legally protected.) Likewise, flocks of turkeys and the deer herds were so abundant in the fall that they were most efficiently hunted by collective drives involving anywhere from twenty to three hundred men. In such cases, the entire village territory was the logical hunting region, to which all those involved in the hunt had an equal right.

The same was not true, on the other hand, of hunting that involved the setting of snares or traps. The animals prey to such techniques were either less numerous, as in the case of winter deer or moose, or sedentary creatures, like the beaver, which lived in fixed locales. These were best hunted by spreading the village population over as broad a territory as possible, and so usufruct rights had to be designed to hold the overlap of trapped areas to a reasonable minimum. Roger Williams described how, after the harvest, ten or twenty men would go with their wives and children to hunting camps which were presumably organized by kin lineage groups. There, he said, "each man takes his bounds of two, three, or foure miles, where hee sets thirty, forty, or fiftie Traps, and baits his Traps with that food the Deere loves, and once in two dayes he walks his round to view his Traps."

At least for the duration of the winter hunt, the kin group inhabiting a camp probably had a clear if informal usufruct right to the animals caught in its immediate area. Certainly a man (or, in the north, his wife) owned the animals captured in the traps he set, though he might have obligations to share which created *de facto* limits to his claims on them. The collective activities of a camp thus tended to establish a set of rights which at least temporarily divided the village territory into hunting areas. The problem is to know how such rights were allocated, how permanent and exclusive they were, and—most crucially—how much their interaction with the European fur trade altered them. The full discussion of this issue, which anthropologists have debated for decades, must wait for the next chapter. For now, we can conclude that, however exclusive hunting territories originally were and however much the fur trade changed them, they represented a different kind of land use—and so probably a different set of usufruct rights than planting fields, gathering areas, or fishing sites.

What the Indians owned—or, more precisely, what their villages gave them claim to—was not the land but the things that were on the land during the various seasons of the year. It was a conception of property shared by many of the hunter-gatherer and agricultural peoples of the world, but radically different from that of the invading Europeans. In nothing is this more clear than in the names they attached to their landscape, the great bulk of which related not to possession but to use. In southern New England, some of these names were agricultural. Pokanoket, in Plymouth County, Massachusetts, was "at or near the cleared lands." Anitaash Pond, near New London, Connecticut, meant, literally, "rotten corn," referring to a swampy location where corn could be buried until it blackened to create a favorite Indian delicacy. Mittineag, in Hampden County, Massachusetts, meant "abandoned fields," probably a place where the soil had lost its fertility and a village had moved its summer encampment elsewhere.

Far more abundant than agricultural place-names, however, throughout New England, were names telling where plants could be gathered, shellfish collected, mammals hunted, and fish caught. Abessah, in Bar Harbor, Maine, was the "clam bake place." Wabaquasset, in Providence, Rhode Island, was where Indian women could find "flags or rushes for making mats." Azoiquoneset, also in the Narragansett Bay area, was the "small island where we get pitch," used to make torches for hunting sturgeon at night. The purpose of such names was to turn the landscape into a map which, if studied carefully, literally gave a village's inhabitants the information they needed to sustain themselves. Place-names were used to keep track of beaver dams, the rapids in rivers, oyster banks, egg-gathering spots, cranberry bogs, canoe-repairing places, and so on....

c.   THE RIGHT TO HUNT (PT. 2)

NOTES

The rule of capture and anti-hunting sentiment: Would-be capturers of *feræ naturæ* have had to contend with more than just game laws and landowner rights. Anti-hunting sentiment, widely shared by many Americans, has given rise to affirmative measures, physical as well as legal, to disrupt or limit hunting activities. These measures have in turn fueled a backlash in states where hunters have a strong political presence.

In the 1998 general election, two states adopted constitutional amendments that were intended to protect hunting. Minnesota adopted a section that stated:

> Hunting and fishing and the taking of game and fish are a valued part of our heritage that shall be forever preserved for the people and shall be managed by law and regulation for the public good.

MINN. CONST. Art. 13, § 12. Utah moved beyond the declaratory and imposed substantive restrictions on the power of the people to initiate legislation:

> Legislation initiated to allow, limit, or prohibit the taking of wildlife or the season for or method of taking wildlife shall be adopted upon approval of two-thirds of those voting.

UTAH CONST. Art. VI, § 1.

The most common example of the political tensions are the Hunter Harassment Statutes:

People v. Sanders

Supreme Court of Illinois.
696 N.E.2d 1144 (1998).

■ McMORROW, J.:—The State charged defendant Robert Sanders by information with violation of section 2(c) of the Illinois Hunter Interference Prohibition Act, [ ]. Pursuant to defendant's motion to dismiss, the circuit court of Lake County entered an order on February 20, 1997, dismissing the criminal charge against defendant. The court found section 2(c) impermissibly vague and overbroad, in violation of the United States Constitution. U.S. Const., amends. I, V . . . . We affirm.

BACKGROUND

Section 2 of the Illinois Hunter Interference Prohibition Act (Act) states:

> Any person who performs any of the following is guilty of a Class B misdemeanor:
>
> (a) Interferes with the lawful taking of a wild animal by another with intent to prevent the taking.
>
> (b) Disturbs or engages in an activity that will tend to disturb wild animals, with intent to prevent their lawful taking.
>
> (c) [D]isturbs another person who is engaged in the lawful taking of a wild animal or who is engaged in the process of taking, with intent to dissuade or otherwise prevent the taking.
>
> (d) [E]nters or remains upon public lands, or upon private lands without permission of the owner or his agent or a lessee, with intent to violate this Section.

720 ILCS 125/2.

The Act defines "wild animal" as "any wild creature the taking of which is authorized by the fish and game laws of the State." 720 ILCS 125/1(a). Under the Act, "taking" means "the capture or killing of a wild animal and includes travel, camping, and other acts preparatory to taking which occur on lands or waters upon which the affected person has the right or privilege to take such wild animal." 720 ILCS 125/1(b). No other terms are defined by the Act.

The State filed an information on November 19, 1996, charging defendant, Robert Sanders, with the offense of "Interference with lawful taking of wild animal." 720 ILCS 125/2. The State alleged that on February 16, 1996, defendant "disturbed Elizabeth B. Surge" with the intent to dissuade her, by yelling at her and taking her photograph as she attempted to shoot a deer.

In documents filed with the circuit court, defendant initially contended that the confrontation with Surge occurred "on a public street in a residential neighborhood relating to the capture of deer." The State's response to defendant's motion to dismiss stated that defendant approached Surge at a "deer relocation sight [sic] in Highland Park." On appeal, defendant apparently agrees with the State's characterization of the incident, since the defendant's appellee's brief concedes that "[d]efendant took a picture of, and spoke to a person working at a deer relocation center."

Defendant moved to dismiss the information. Defendant claimed that subsection (c) of section 2 is overbroad in violation of the first amendment to the United States Constitution and unconstitutionally vague in violation of the "Due Process Clause."

On February 20, 1997, the circuit court of Lake County entered a written finding granting defendant's motion to dismiss....

STANDARD OF REVIEW

We presume all statutes are constitutionally valid. [ ] In construing a statute, this court must affirm the enactment's validity and constitutionality if reasonably possible. [ ] The party challenging a statute's constitutionality bears the burden of clearly establishing its constitutional infirmity. [ ]

ANALYSIS

Before this court, the State contends the circuit court erroneously found section 2(c) of the Act unconstitutional. The State argues the statute is neither overbroad nor vague.

While defendant agrees with the result reached by the lower court, he suggests on appeal that we affirm by following a different analysis than that chosen by the circuit court. Defendant accurately argues that the term "intent to dissuade" in section 2(c) must be subjected to a separate, "content-neutrality" inquiry before this court confronts the basis employed by the circuit court for its ruling, i.e., whether the statute is unconstitutionally overbroad or vague. This is so because, logically, if section 2(c) is impermissibly content-based, then we need not reach the defendant's overbreadth or vagueness challenge with respect to that section. [ ]

A. Content–Neutrality

The government may not prohibit the expression of thoughts simply because society finds the expressed idea offensive or disagreeable. [ ] Under the content-neutrality principle, "the government may not proscribe any expression because of its content, and an otherwise valid regulation violates the first amendment if it differentiates between types of expression based on content." [ ] Thus, any enactment intended to silence an opinion is presumptively invalid, [ ], and may only survive if justified by a compelling state interest and if narrowly tailored to achieve that interest. [ ]

The government's purpose in enacting a prohibition on expression controls a "content-neutrality" inquiry. [ ] A restriction that applies impartially to all viewpoints is deemed content-neutral. [ ]

Defendant maintains that inclusion of the phrase "intent to dissuade" in section 2(c) renders the statute content-based, because the word "dissuade" means "advise" or "exhort." Defendant reasons further that, if the state proscribes conduct performed with an intent to dissuade, then the state commits the constitutionally impermissible act of penalizing a citizen for the content of his expression. By outlawing a viewpoint which is expressed with an intent to dissuade, defendant continues, the state implicitly "shut[s]-off one half of the debate" about hunting, and allows those who disturb a hunter without an intent to dissuade to avoid criminal liability.

In *State v. Miner,* 556 N.W.2d 578 (Minn.App.1996), the Minnesota Court of Appeals construed a "hunter harassment" statute which stated in part:

> "A person who has the intent to prevent, disrupt, or dissuade the taking of a wild animal or enjoyment of the out-of-doors may not disturb or interfere with another person who is lawfully taking a wild animal or preparing to take a wild animal."

[ ] The *Miner* court held that, to the extent the statute only applied to persons whose intent was to "dissuade the taking of a wild animal or enjoyment of the out-of-doors," the statute was impermissibly content-based. [ ] "Dissuade," the court explained, carries a connotation of using argument, reasoning, entreaty, admonition, advice or appeal to convey a message. [ ] The statute therefore discriminated between opposing points of view by attempting to silence persons intending to convey a particular message. [ ]

Further, the *Miner* court ruled that the State of Minnesota could not articulate a constitutionally sound argument in favor of the content-based law. Assuming *arguendo* that the state possessed a compelling interest in protecting the right of individuals to lawfully take wild animals, the state failed to explain why prohibiting disturbing speech only if the speaker intends to dissuade the taking of an animal was necessary to serve and protect that interest. *Miner,* 556 N.W.2d at 583; *Dorman v. Satti,* 862 F.2d 432, 437 (2d Cir.1988) (court stated that "[t]here is no showing that protecting hunters from harassment constitutes a compelling state interest").

In the case at bar, the State cites to *State v. Lilburn,* 875 P.2d 1036 (Mont.1994), and *Woodstock Hunt Club v. Hindi,* 684 N.E.2d 1089 (Ill.App. 1997), both of which construed the phrase "intent to dissuade" in hunter harassment statutes as content-neutral. In each case, the reviewing court read the phrase "intent to dissuade" as a nonessential element of a larger statutory scheme, designed to punish any interference with a taking, regardless of whether the offender intended to convey a particular message. [ ] Hence, the Montana Supreme Court and Illinois Appellate Court held that, while the statutes potentially outlawed verbal utterances by someone intending to prevent a taking of wildlife, they did not criminalize verbal utterances on the basis of content. [ ]

The *Lilburn* court decided that opponents of the statute placed errone-ous emphasis on the word "dissuade":

> Reading the statute as a whole, it is clear that the conduct proscribed is the "disturbance" of a hunter engaged in a lawful activity, when it is done with the intent to either dissuade the hunter or to prevent the taking of an animal. The fact that the speech or actions may disturb a hunter is not dependent on the content of what is expressed, or whether it is prompted by an anti-hunting sentiment. A person could blurt out anything at the moment a hunter is trying to shoot, and this could "disturb" the hunter by distracting him or her, or by scaring the animal away. The content of what was said would be irrelevant.

[ ] *See also Woodstock Hunt Club,* [ ] (the Act does not single out any particular thought or opinion for prohibition, but "merely prohibits inten-tional interference with the lawful taking of wild animals").

We agree that proper interpretation of the term "dissuade" demands that we place the term in its full context. [ ] However, we cannot ignore the plain meaning of "intent to dissuade," as employed in section 2(c). [ ] As explained in *Miner,* the word "dissuade" carries a specific meaning associ-ated with argument and with promoting a particular point of view. [ ] Subjecting to criminal liability expression which is made with an intent to dissuade, while failing to threaten punishment for expressions intended to encourage or persuade, constitutes an illegal legislative censure of opinion.

We note as well that, had the legislature intended to curb conduct without regard to any message conveyed by the conduct, it could have done so by limiting the criminal *scienter* in section 2(c) to the phrase "intent to prevent" and no more. Indeed, section 2(a) proscribes "interferences" with hunting when the interference is motivated by an intent to prevent. 720 ILCS 125/2(a). Thus, the inclusion of a separate subsection adding the words "intent to dissuade" substantiates our judgment that the legislature intentionally injected the concept of suasion into subsection (c). Section 2(c) is not content-neutral.

The prohibitions of section 2(c) do not serve a compelling state inter-est. While the Act furthers reasonable and legitimate state interests by permitting hunting within its borders, [ ], none of these considerations are of such magnitude as to constitute a compelling interest. Further, even if we did find that the state's concerns could be characterized as "compel-ling," the General Assembly's decision to protect that interest by targeting expression of an opinion, as opposed to intentional, disruptive behavior in general, is difficult to justify. [ ]

Nevertheless, inclusion of the term "intent to dissuade" in section 2(c) is not fatal to the validity of the entire Act. Mindful of our obligation to uphold legislative enactments whenever reasonably possible, [ ], we may excise the offending portion from the Act and preserve the remainder, [ ], provided the remainder is complete in and of itself, and is capable of being executed wholly independently of the severed portion. [ ]. . . .

Section 2 readily survives the severability test. As originally drafted, section 2 purports to prohibit four distinct means of interrupting a "taking" of wildlife. Each subsection stands independently of the others, so that the removal of one (such as subsection (c)) undermines neither the completeness nor the executability of the remaining subsections. We believe the legislature would endorse section 2 without subsection (c). The plain purpose of the statute is to outlaw any intentional hindrance of the taking of wildlife. Section 2 accomplishes that aim, with and without inclusion of "intent to dissuade." In particular, section 2(a) proscribes "[i]nterfer[ing] with the lawful taking of a wild animal by another with intent to prevent the taking." 720 ILCS 125/2(a). Section 2(a) is virtually identical to section 2(c), except for the inclusion of the "dissuade" aspect in the latter. By removing subsection (c), this court can neutralize a constitutional infirmity without altering any of the remaining prohibitions in the Act. [ ]

. . .

CONCLUSION

We find section 2(c) of the Illinois Hunter Interference Prohibition Act (720 ILCS 125/2(c) a content-based regulation not justified by a compelling state interest. Thus, we affirm the order of the circuit court finding section 2(c) unconstitutional. We also affirm the circuit court's order dismissing the criminal information filed against defendant.

Affirmed.

■ HARRISON, J., concurring in part and dissenting in part:—I agree that section 2(c) of the Illinois Hunter Interference Prohibition Act, [ ], is facially invalid under the first amendment to the United States Constitution. [ ] I write separately because I have come to that conclusion for somewhat different reasons from those advanced by the majority. In addition, I believe the majority is incorrect in upholding the remainder of the statute. In my view, the entire statute is constitutionally infirm and should be invalidated.

Hunter harassment statutes, such as Illinois' Hunter Interference Prohibition Act, proliferated during the years between 1981 and 1996. Through efforts of the Sportsman's Caucus and the Wildlife Legislative Fund of America, a prohunting lobby based in Washington, D.C., every state in the nation has enacted some version of the law. K. Hessler, *Where Do We Draw the Line Between Harassment and Free Speech?: An Analysis of Hunter Harassment Law,* 3 ANIMAL L. 129, 161 n.21 (1997). Most of the state statutes are based on model legislation drafted by the Wildlife

Legislative Fund. Comment, *The Right to Arm Bears: Activists' Protests Against Hunting*, 45 U. MIAMI L.REV. 1109, 1111 n.14 (1991).

The hunter harassment laws were enacted in response to a growth in antihunting protests by activists who regard hunting as cruel to animals, bad for the ecosystem, and morally wrong. [ ] Historically, the protests have taken a variety of forms. These include walking along with hunters in the field and speaking to them about the violence and cruelty of hunting (*see Dorman v. Satti*, 862 F.2d 432, 434 (2d Cir.1988)); standing in the hunters' way and engaging in other conduct, such as screaming and waving, that causes them to miss opportunities to shoot their prey (*see State v. Casey*, 876 P.2d 138, 139 (Idaho 1994)); forming a semicircle around a hunter and refusing to move from the line of fire after verbal entreaties to him to desist fail (*see State v. Ball*, 627 A.2d 892, 895 (Conn.1993)); staging demonstrations, with signs and chanting, at the entrances of wildlife refuges and other hunting sites; spreading deer repellant (*see* [ ]); and making loud noise with sirens or bullhorns in order to scare animals away from hunting areas (*see Woodstock Hunt Club v. Hindi*, 684 N.E.2d 1089 (Ill.App.1997)).

The constitutionality of hunter harassment laws has been the subject of a substantial amount of litigation (*see State v. Miner*, 556 N.W.2d 578 (Minn.App.1996); *State v. Casey*, 876 P.2d 138 (Idaho 1994); *State v. Lilburn*, 875 P.2d 1036 (Mont.1994); *State v. Ball*, 627 A.2d 892 (Conn. 1993); *State v. Bagley*, 474 N.W.2d 761 (Wis.App.1991); *Dorman v. Satti*, 862 F.2d 432 (2d Cir.1988); *Opinion of the Justices*, 509 A.2d 749 (N.H. 1986)), and academic commentary, [ ].

Although the courts and commentators are not uniform in their analysis of the statutes, there is no serious dispute that these laws implicate rights protected by the first amendment to the United States Constitution....

Section 2(c) is not the only portion of the statute applicable to traditional speech. The remaining subsections apply to verbal conduct too....

In addition, first amendment protection is no longer limited to expressive speech. It extends to expressive conduct as well. [ ] Accordingly, in analyzing the statute under the first amendment, we must be mindful of its relationship to what antihunting protestors do, not simply what they say.

   . . .

.... In its origins and application, the statute "clearly is designed to protect hunters from conduct-whether verbal or otherwise-by those opposed to hunting." *Dorman*, 862 F.2d at 437.

That the statute is intended to target an antihunting point of view is manifest in section 2(c)'s use of the word dissuade, as the majority points out. It is also apparent, however, in the remaining portions of the law. Although the other sections contain no explicit content-based limitation on the scope of prohibited conduct, the absence of such limitations will not save a statute from a first amendment challenge where it is nevertheless clear that the government's asserted interest is related to the suppression of free expression and concerned with the content of such expression. [ ] Such is the case here.

Under every section of the statute, not just section 2(c), culpability is limited to those whose intent is to prevent the taking of wild animals. While those in favor of hunting may very well disturb wild animals or their fellow sportsmen, it is difficult to envision a scenario where their aim is to prevent an animal from being taken. As a practical matter no one who favors recreational hunting is going to engage in conduct prohibited by the law. Correspondingly, no one in favor of recreational hunting is going to be found guilty of violating the statute. The law affects one group and one group only: those who are morally or philosophically opposed to capturing or killing animals. The proof is in the case law. The State has not cited and I have not found a single instance in any jurisdiction in which a hunter harassment law was enforced against anyone other than an antihunting protestor.

That the statute is specifically designed to silence those who oppose recreational hunting is further demonstrated by the liability provisions of the law. Those found guilty of violating the statute are not simply subject to criminal penalties. They also face the extraordinary prospect of having to pay civil damages, including punitive damages, to hunters whose efforts were thwarted by the protestor's efforts. Among compensable items of recovery are expenditures for travel, guides and special equipment and supplies. 720 ILCS 125/4(b). These penalties serve no governmental interest of any kind. Their only function is to protect the personal, pecuniary interests of sportsmen and quell dissent by those who oppose the hunt.

Because the Illinois statute is content-based, it can withstand first amendment scrutiny only if it "is necessary to serve a compelling state interest and * * * is narrowly drawn to achieve that end." [ ] The majority is right to hold that section 2(c) does not meet this exacting standard, but it should have reached the same conclusion with respect to the remainder of the statute.

Sportsmen may be entitled to engage in lawful hunting, but they do not have the right to do so free from annoyance, harassment and confrontation. Hunting and the treatment of animals present important moral, social and political issues. For some, those issues are every bit as compelling as racial equality, gender discrimination, and abortion. Under the first amendment, we cannot circumscribe the debate on those questions any more than we can limit the debate on the rights of women and minorities or the state's role in regulating reproduction. . . .

. . .

For the foregoing reasons, I would affirm the judgment of the circuit court, but declare section 2 of the Illinois Hunter Interference Prohibition Act to be unconstitutional in its entirety. In addition, I would overrule the appellate court's opinion in *Woodstock Hunt Club v. Hindi* upholding the statute's constitutionality.

■ BILANDIC, J., DISSENTING:—I respectfully dissent. I would find that section 2(c) of the Act meets constitutional standards.

I agree with the decision and reasoning of our appellate court in *Woodstock Hunt Club v. Hindi,* 684 N.E.2d 1089 (Ill.App.1997), which rejected overbreadth and vagueness challenges to the Hunter Interference Prohibition Act. That court correctly concluded that section 2(c) is not impermissibly content-based. Section 2(c) prohibits the disturbance of a hunter when that disturbance is intended to "dissuade or otherwise prevent" the taking of an animal. Although the disturbance may take the form of verbal expression, the commission of this offense is not dependent on the content of the expression. The *Woodstock Hunt Club* court aptly illustrated this distinction:

> A person may violate the Act by shouting "Fire!", by waving a placard proclaiming "Hunting is good!" in front of a hunter, or by playing the 1812 Overture on a stereo system, if any of these actions is done with the intent to dissuade or prevent the taking of a wild animal and disturbs either a hunter or his intended quarry.

[ ]

The majority reasons that the use of the term "dissuade" renders section 2(c) impermissibly content-based because that term connotes the conveyance of a message. Section 2(c), however, does not prevent antihunting advocates from attempting to convince hunters not to hunt. Rather, it merely prohibits disturbing a hunter who is engaged in the hunt if the intent of the disturbance is to dissuade or otherwise prevent the taking of the animal. It is the act of disturbing, not the act of dissuading, that is proscribed. The content of what is said to disturb the hunter is not relevant. As noted by the Montana Supreme Court in rejecting this precise argument, a person could wish to prevent the taking of an animal by a hunter for reasons other than opposition to hunting, such as a desire to shoot the animal himself. *State v. Lilburn,* 875 P.2d 1036, 1042–43 (Mont. 1994). Section 2(c) simply does not single out any particular thought or opinion for prohibition. It is therefore content-neutral.

. . .

NOTES

Harassment and the race to capture: In a provocative essay, Professor James Krier explores hunter harassment in the context of the rule of capture set forth classically in *Pierson v. Post.* Pierson was allowed to keep the fox because he was the first to capture it, even though his capture interfered with Post's lawful, almost-productive hunt. Pierson, that is, was viewed as a lawful competitor in the race to capture, and as the winner he was entitled to reap the rewards. Why not, asks Krier, view animal rights advocates in the same way—as competitors in the race to capture—when they scare animals away so that present-day Posts cannot capture them? Assuming that such advocates are not trespassing, should they not have the same right as hunters to interact with wildlife in their chosen ways? Should they not have the chance to be first? Two hundred years ago, society may have benefitted only by killing chicken-eating foxes, so perhaps it made sense to limit the race to capture to competing hunters. Today, however, with conservation an important interest, should not conservation advocates have an equal chance to pursue their interests, given that they are as much co-owners of wildlife as hunters? James E. Krier, *Capture and Counteraction: Self–Help by Environmental Zealots*, 30 U. RICH. L. REV. 1039 (1996).

As a counterbalance, should states enact statutes banning hunters from interfering with lawful wildlife-watching activities? Should birders watching geese be able to sue later-arriving hunters who shoot at the birds?

SECTION 3.   DURABILITY OF PRIVATE RIGHTS IN CAPTURED WILDLIFE

2 WILLIAM BLACKSTONE, COMMENTARIES ON THE LAWS OF ENGLAND
*393 (1st ed. 1776).

In all these creatures, reclaimed from the wildness of their nature, the property is not absolute, but defeasible: a property, that may be destroyed if they resume their ancient wildness and are found at large. For if the pheasants escape from the mew, or the fishes from the trunk, and are seen wandering at large in their proper element, they become *feræ naturæ* again; and are free and open to the first occupant that hath ability to seize them.

Brown v. Eckes
City Court of Yonkers, New York.
160 N.Y.S. 489 (1916).

■ BEALL, J.:—It appears from the evidence that the complainant, Brown, hived certain bees on Hamilton avenue in this city; that one of the hives swarmed and left Brown's place; that the defendant Eckes was doing some work on the house of a man named Deane, and, seeing a swarm of bees in the air, pounded upon tin and brought them down upon the Deane property, where they located upon a grapevine; that Mr. Deane did not wish any bees, and required Eckes to remove them; that Eckes upon that evening met the defendant Stevens, was claimed that he had lost a swarm of bees; and that Eckes delivered the bees to Stevens.

It has come to the hand of this court to decide all sorts of questions about all sorts of animals, reptiles, and insects. Cases of men, women, and children are constant; cases of those who have wronged others and of those who unjustly contest matters. Horses and their condition, habits, and relationship to their owners and strangers are perpetually with us. We are seldom lonely for the want of a dog case, and have expounded that law at great length, while matters of cats, goats, wild deer, pigeons, birds, including the usefulness of the highhold, otherwise known as the flicker, and as to whether he is a song-bird, and of hens and roosters and robins, and as to which of them chiefly annoys the tired man at dawn, are things with which the court is thoroughly familiar. But this is the first time it has had to dive into the interesting question of the law of bees. It is to be presumed that ultimately we shall have to deal with ants and flies and other varieties of insects. The law of snakes we know.

It is not the intention of the court to review the history of bees, of their origin in Asia, and of how they have followed man in the development of civilization, and have been tamed and used by him, and have contributed to his comfort and welfare, although it is an interesting study and one to be recommended. We shall pass without comment the fact that the claimant to these bees is a lawyer, and that no lawyer needs bees to assist him in stinging. The thing really turns on the question of identity, and at the preliminary hearing, when the courtroom was nearly filed with lawyers, I offered to appoint any one of them a referee to make personal examination of these bees for marks of identification, which offer they unanimously rejected, the first time in my experience with the law that a lawyer has refused to accept a reference.

The original proceeding was to determine whether or not the defendants here were guilty of larceny under that section of the Code which required a man to advertise lost property, and it was even contended that it was the duty of the finder to return this property to the owner—as one should keep a rattlesnake for a pet and allow it to stroll upon another's property, and that other be guilty of larceny unless he returned it; as one should house a tiger which might escape on another's domain, and hold that other guilty of larceny unless he returned it. The court refused to entertain the charge of larceny, and the parties hereto were generous enough to submit the question of ownership to the court as arbitrator.

The custom in London with respect to the trial of men charged with cruelty to animals is this: They are brought to a court, where there is a large yard, and a special judge examines the animals to determine their condition. I have followed the same custom, and nearly always examine the horses where men are brought before me for cruelty to them. The rule of this court for many years has been, in cases involving the ownership of dogs, to take the claimants into my big office, station them at opposite ends of the room, and allow the dog to choose his master. The ownership of pigeons and of chickens we have determined by releasing them at the roosting time and permitting them to decide upon their homes. But in this case I decline to deal personally with the subject-matter of this action, and, together with the lawyers, refuse to make any personal or private inspection of them.

Extensive research has been made into this question of bees by both counsel for the contendants and by the court, and I admit that the subject of the law of the busy bee is a fascinating one. It is admitted by both sides that bees are *feræ naturæ*, and as to the law of them Blackstone classifies them with wild animals; but Blackstone's law was taken from the Greeks and from the Romans, and, curiously enough, there has been practically no change in that law since the days of Plato, and an uninterrupted line of decisions through Greek, Roman, English, French, the Netherlands, and the English common law, down to late decisions in Iowa, are practically to the same effect—the probable reason for this set policy being the danger of touching the subject. For instance, it has been pointed out to me that

Gaius, whose *Commentaries* are supposed to have been written 160 A.D., states it thus:

> In those wild animals whose nature or custom it is to go away and return—as pigeons, bees, and deer, which habitually go into the forests and return—our rule is laid down that only the determination of the intent of returning marks the end of the property in them, and the property in them is acquired by the next one who take (or occupies) them; it is said that when their habit of returning ceases, their intent (or instinct) of returning also ceases.

And in Justinian's *Corpus Juris Civilis* it is put as follows:

> Bees are wild by nature; and so, if a swarm alight on your tree, it is not to be considered yours, until you have hived it, any more than the birds which build their nests there; and hence, if it be hived by another, it becomes his property. * * * A swarm which has flown from your hive is considered yours as long as it is in your sight, and not difficult to be pursued; otherwise, it belongs to the next person who takes it.

While Domat said:

> As we may possess living creatures, which it is not always possible to have in our power and custody, so we retain possession of them whilst we shut them up, whilst we have them under the care of a keeper, or if, being made tame, they return home without a keeper, as bees to their hives, and pigeons to their dove houses.

Civil Law, I, bk. 3, pt. 1, subd. 7, § 2133. Puffendorf, in his *Law of Nature*, expresses it thus:

> Yet bees are no doubt wild by nature, since their custom of returning to their hive doth not proceed from their familiarity with mankind, but from their own secret instinct; they being in all respects utterly unteachable. It is nevertheless one of Plato's laws—whosoever shall pursue the swarms which belong to others and by striking upon the brass shall draw them with the delightful sound to fix near himself, let him make restitution for the damage. Where he seems to presuppose that the owner of the bees did not follow them when they left his hives, Pliny will have the bees to be neither wild nor tame; others divide them into both kinds. But that, so long as they return to our hives, they are properly our own and cannot be hurt without our loss or damage, is very laboriously proved in that declamation of Quintilian, entitled "The Poor Man's Bees."

Volume 4, c. 6, § 5.

Of course, if the bees were Brown's, his title to them was not destroyed by the fact that they alighted on Deane's land, and there are pointed out to me many authorities in favor of this. Thibaut (*Syst. des Pandekten Rechts*) accepts it as the general law of the civilized world. The Code Napoleon (section 564) makes it the law of France and of Algiers. Louisiana, adopting the French Code, adopts it. Section 519, LA. CODE CIVILE. Bracton (liber 2, c. 1) recognizes man's qualified property in them both by the natural law as well as the civil law. *See also* PREUSS, ALLGEMEIN LANDRECHT, I, 9, § 118 f.

Oesterr; GESETZBUCH, § 384; DURANTON, COURS. DE DROIT, IV, No. 56; ORTOLAN, EXPLIQ. DES INST. No. 357; TOUILLIER, COURS. DE DROIT, 4, No. 50; PAND. 33, 7, 12, § 13; *also* FR. LOIS USUELLES, 4 ANVRIL, 1889, § 2, subd. 9:

> The proprietor of a swarm has the right to reclaim and repossess them so far as he can see them and follow them; otherwise, the swarm belongs to the owner of the land upon which they affix themselves.

See 3 KENT, COMMENTARIES 348; *Wallis v. Mease*, 3 Bin. 546 (Pa.1811); 4 BLACKSTONE, COMMENTARIES *236, note 18; *Merrils v. Goodwin*, 1 Root 209 (Conn. 1790); *State v. Repp*, 73 N.W. 829 (Iowa 1898); *The Case of Swans*, 7 Coke 15b, 77 Eng. Rep. 435 (K.B. 1592).

The act of reducing to possession wild animals must not be wrongful, and if it is done by one who is a trespasser he gets no title, which vests in the owner of the soil, and the wrongdoer is liable to the owner for the trespass and for conversion. *Harper v. Galloway*, 51 S. 226 (Fla. 1910); *Commonwealth v. Chace*, 26 Mass. (9 Pick.) 14 (1829); *Lonsdale v. Rigg*, 11 Exch. 654; *Blades v. Higgs*, 11 H.L. Cas. 621, 11 Eng. Rep. 1474 (H.L 1865),

> A mere temporary escape of the bees does not divest the title of the owner *per industriam*. They remain his property. A stranger cannot acquire title if they intend to return, or the owner promptly pursues or reclaims or can identify them, although they may flee to and alight upon the land of another, where the owner cannot get them without becoming a trespasser himself.

Merrils v. Goodwin, supra; Case of Swans, supra; Goff v. Kilts, 15 Wend. 550 (N.Y.1836).

> In a larceny case it was held:

> To acquire a right in an animal so that it may become a subject of larceny, the pursuer must bring it into his ownership and control, so that he may subject it to his own use at his pleasure, and must so maintain his possession and control as to indicate that he does not intend to abandon them again to the world at large; but in cases where larceny is charged, the law does not require absolute security against the possibility of escape.

And one who asserts a legal title to them once they have swarmed must have kept them in sight until they settled.

> If a swarm [bees] fly from a hive of another, his qualified property continues so long as he can keep them in sight, and possess the power to pursue them. Under these circumstances, no one else is entitled to take them.

2 BLACKSTONE COMMENTARIES *393; 2 KENT, COMMENTARIES *394. We moderns may wonder at the completeness of the law of bees, and at the attention and time that has been expended upon what we regard as a trivial subject. Nothing is trivial that involves human rights. Besides, it may be remembered that, in the days of those whom we term the ancients, the bee occupied a much more important place in the economy of the state than if does now. In Greece, in Egypt, in Judea, and to a somewhat less extent in the Roman provinces, honey was a most important article of commerce.

Upon the whole, I take it that the case turns upon the question of identity, and of whether the owner, and I shall take the liberty of enlarging the doctrine to include an employe of the owner, kept the bees in sight during the swarm until they alighted; this being really part of the question of identification. I determine that Brown has established the ownership of these bees, and is entitled to recover them, passing without comment the fact that this queen bee occasioned all of us a great deal of trouble by organizing the swarm. I make acknowledgment to counsel in the case, William A. Walsh on the one hand and Clarence Alexander on the other, for the ability and thoroughness with which they have briefed the case and helped me to this decision.

Shepard v. Leverson

New Jersey Supreme Court.
2 N.J.L. 391 (1808).

An action of trover and conversion was brought by Leverson against Shepard and Layton, ... for taking and converting to their use, one thousand oysters, the property of Leverson.... [T]he parties agreed to the following state of the case.... :

[T]hat the plaintiff had planted a bed or quantity of oysters in North river, ... a public navigable river and highway, where the tide flows and reflows, and in which fish and oysters are found and taken as of right; that in the particular spot where this bed or quantity of oysters were planted, there were no oysters to be found at the time of planting; that the plaintiff, Leverson, had no right of several fishery,[1] unless the planting said bed gave him one; that the plaintiff below, Leverson, was continually in the habit of taking oysters from said bed, in said river.

■ KIRKPATRICK, C.J.:—From this case it is manifest, the plaintiff below, sets up no claim to a several fishery in this river, by reason of any grant or purchase of soil, either adjacent to, or covered by its waters.

. . .

Here, the plaintiff has thrown his oysters into a public river, where all the inhabitants have a common right of fishery.

For the plaintiff, it is urged, that the property of the oysters having been once vested in him by occupancy, it could not be divested but by his own voluntary act, or by operation of law; by abandonment, with intent that it should fall again into the common stock. [ ]

The principle is correct enough; but how does it apply? How is the intent to be known? Certainly, in most cases, only by the act itself. Suppose a man was to take a deer in a forest, and be simple enough to let it go again in the same forest, saying to himself, this is my deer and no man shall

---

1. A "several fishery" is a common law property classification denoting that the holder of the fishery has an exclusive, private right to fish. The word "several" is used in a now-uncommon meaning of "Exclusive, indi- vidual, appropriated." 2 FRANCIS RAWLE, BOUVI- ER'S LAW DICTIONARY 989 (new ed. Boston 1897). The variety of common-law classifica- tions of fisheries will be examined in Chapter III.

touch it: I apprehend it would never be asked by the next taker, what was the intention of this simpleton. The very act of letting it go is an abandonment, in contemplation of law. It is returned to the common stock.

. . .

But it is said, that is not the case here; that in the particular sport where this bed or quantity of oysters was planted, there was no oysters to be found at the time of the planting; that these, therefore, could be resumed; that they were not thrown into the common stock. Let us examine this:

The oyster, like other animals, propagates its own species; it does so, particularly, as the case states, in this river. It does not appear when this bed was planted; it does not appear, whether the oysters taken by the defendant were of the old stock, or of the young brood, or whether of either one or the other; the spawn of another bed, higher up the stream, might have lodged here and formed these; they are in no way identified, *they have no ear mark*, they cannot be distinguished. To what purpose would it be for my simpleton to say, that there was no deer in that part of the forest where he let his loose.

Will it be said that the plaintiff is entitled not only to the old stock planted, but to the young brood also? and that he having first occupied the ground, all accessions belong to him? I apprehend not. The oyster, though once settled in the sand, is incapable of locomotion, yet from its mode of propagation, may people a whole river. Could it be said then, that the first planter might, by this means, secure to himself the oyster fishery in the whole extent of this water? And yet, if he can appropriate one spot, why not another, and another, and another?

I am informed that this business of planting oysters in these waters has been carried to great extent; that the beds now there, claimed by individuals on this principle, are numerous, and of great value; that this right has been recognized by a sort of tacit consent, and the property protected by mutual forbearance. And as it has a tendency to increase the quantity of oysters, and at the same time, with little or no injury to others, to promote the interest of those engaged in it, I wish it could have been supported and rendered permanent, but upon the whole case, I can see no principle upon which that can be done.

. . .

Judgement reversed.

NOTES

(1) The duration of rights in wildlife: The general rule of personal property law is that an owner's rights in a thing continue indefinitely, until the thing is abandoned, transferred or destroyed—and abandonment requires a showing that the owner intended to relinquish his or her rights to the thing. Why are wild animals different? Why might an owner's rights in a lawfully captured animal end if the animal gets away? Are there policy rationales that support such a rule? Is it chiefly a matter of notice or fairness to other capturers, who might not realize that a free-roaming animal is owned? Is it instead a way of encouraging re-capture—that is, rewarding the labor of the new capturer, without regard to matters of notice? Might it even be a way of punishing initial capturers who either fail to control the animals they possess or fail to pursue them vigorously once they escape? Finally, how might the answers to these questions affect the outcomes of various cases, in terms of deciding what an owner needs to do, before or after escape, to avoid losing rights?

(2) Hot pursuit? In *Brown v. Eckes* the court suggests that an owner of a swarm can retain ownership of it when it flies away either by pursuing it and keeping it in sight or by demonstrating that it has a habit of returning. Does it appear that Brown followed his swarm in hot pursuit? If not, did he adequately show that they had a habit of returning? Note the varied ideas expressed in the precedents cited by the court. At least one says that the owner need merely "possess the power to pursue them"—suggesting that actual pursuit is unnecessary—while another considers it sufficient if the owner "reclaims or can identify them." Does it matter that the swarm came down to Deane's property only because Eckes "pounded upon tin"? Is it relevant that, in a residential area of suburban New York City, swarms of bees are unlikely to be wild?

One precedent relied upon in *Brown* was *Goff v. Kilts,* 15 Wend. 550 (N.Y.Sup.Ct.1836), where the court endorsed the rule that "if a swarm fly from the hive of another, his qualified property continues in them so long as he can keep them in sight, and possesses the power to pursue them." In *Goff,* the swarm entered land owned by another person, and stayed there for two months, making honey in a tree. The owner of the swarm retained rights in the swarm, given that he kept them in sight and followed them to their new location. But he had no rights in the honey (or the tree), which belonged to the owner of the land, and could not enter the land to recapture the swarm without committing trespass. *See also Merrils v. Goodwin,* 1 Root 209 (Conn.1790).

(3) Propagating oysters: The court in *Shepard v. Leverson* seems sympathetic to the plaintiff's plight and to the desirability of protecting oyster operations such as the plaintiff's. Why, then, does the court ultimately decide that the plaintiff's oysters have returned to the "common stock" and are thus available for other people to capture? Notice the plaintiff's practical points: (i) the stretch of the river involved had no oysters in it until plaintiff planted them; (ii) because oysters do not move, plaintiff could recapture them at any time; (iii) other oyster beds are also claimed by individuals, who by "tacit consent" and "mutual forbearance" respect one another's rights. Why were these arguments not sufficient? Were Shepard and Layton unaware of plaintiff's rights? If not, why should they get the oysters, particularly given the ease of capturing them? If (as seems likely) the court's principal concern had to do not so much with the oysters as with plaintiff's exclusive use of a section of river, were there ways of addressing that concern, short of denying the plaintiff all property rights in the oysters? Might suitable, unused oyster beds be subject to a first-in-time rule of capture, much the same as wild foxes? Finally, in light of this ruling, what is likely to happen to private oyster operations in the North River? to the state's total harvest of oysters?

(4) *Mullett v. Bradley*: Plaintiff captured a sea lion near San Francisco and shipped it to New York on order. The purchaser refused to accept the animal because of wounds it received while being captured. The animal then escaped, was subsequently captured in a fish pound, and sold to defendant. A year after the escape, plaintiff discovered that defendant had the animal, demanded its return, and instituted this action when defendant refused. On an appeal from the dismissal of his claim, plaintiff argued that, since sea lions are found only on the west coast, the animal had not resumed its "natural liberty" because it was not in its native place. The court rejected the argument: "it may be said to have regained its natural liberty when, by its own volition, it has escaped from all artificial restraint, and is free to follow the bent of its natural inclinations." *Mullett v. Bradley,* 53 N.Y.S. 781, 783 (App.Div.1898).

(5) *Sollers v. Sollers*: Plaintiff fenced a natural cove off the Patuxent River and placed fish that he had caught within the fenced area; defendant took the fish. Plaintiff brought a trespass action, arguing in part that he owned the fish because he had caught and confined them. The court rejected this argument:

> to complete the right of property in fish, an actual appropriation or "mancupation" must be made. The possession must be complete; and if, when taken, they are voluntarily restored to their native element, so that they can only be regained in like manner to that by which they were originally taken, the right of property is lost.... [W]e do not think that it can properly be maintained that by the construction of a fence across the mouth of the cove the plaintiff has so confined the fish as to retain the title to those he had caught and placed therein. By so restoring them to their native element, he relinquished the possession of them, and thereby lost such right of property as he may have had in them.

Sollers v. Sollers, 26 A. 188, 188 (Md.1893). What policy rationale—if any—supports the court's ruling? Would it matter if the fence was lawfully constructed? If the fish had been placed in an artificial pond? How does the court's reasoning compare with that of Judge Rickoff in *Bartee v. State*?

(6) *State v. Taylor*: Consider *State v. Taylor,* a subsequent New Jersey case based on facts nearly identical to those in *Shepard* but reaching the opposite result. The decision more directly addressed the problems raised by allowing private citizens to make exclusive use of public waterways:

> The principle, as applied to animals *feræ naturæ,* is not questioned. But oysters, though usually included in that description of animals, do not come within the reason or operation of the rule. The owner has the same absolute property in them that he has in inanimate things or in domestic animals. Like domestic animals, they continue perpetually in his occupation, and will not stray from his house or person. Unlike animals *feræ naturæ,* they do not require to be reclaimed or made tame by art, industry, or education; nor to be confined, in order to be within the power of the owner. If at liberty, they have neither the inclination

nor the power to escape. For the purposes of the present inquiry, they are obviously more nearly assimilated to tame animals than to wild ones, and, perhaps, more nearly to inanimate objects that to animals of either description. . . .

It was held by the Chief Justice, in the case of *Shepard and Layton v. Leverson,* that the mere act of throwing the oysters into a public river, where all the inhabitants have a common right of fishery, was of itself an abandonment in law, on the ground that, where the subject is put without the power of the owner, where it is thrown into the common stock, from which it cannot be distinguished, there can be no question of intent. It was held analogous to the case of a deer taken in a forest, and turned loose again. But it was admitted that where the act relied on as an abandonment is in itself equivocal, and where the identical property may be known and resumed at pleasure, then the intention may be made a question. Now this case finds that the oysters in question could readily be identified; that no oysters grew naturally where they were planted, and that the spot where they were planted was designated. The subject of the property, having itself no power of locomotion, and being planted where no other oysters naturally grew, it was not (as in the case of the deer in a forest) put without the power of the owner, nor thrown into the common stock, from which it could not be distinguished.

. . .

It was earnestly urged, as an objection to sustaining the conviction in the present case, that the principle recognized by the court will, in effect, authorize the exclusive appropriation of public navigable waters to private purposes, and that it will virtually confer upon every individual who stakes off and plants an oyster bed a right of several fishery in the land thus appropriated, to the exclusion of the public. This difficulty manifestly embarrassed the court in the case of *Shepard v. Leverson,* and was adverted to in *Brinckerhoff v. Starkins.* But does any such consequence necessarily result from the instruction given to the jury? They were expressly told that, if these oysters were planted where oysters naturally grew, or if they could not be readily distinguished from the natural product of the waters by persons engaged in fishing, the defendant could not be convicted. If, then, the oysters interfered in any way with the defendant's right of fishing, or with the right of navigation, or any other right of the public in the waters, it is not claimed that the defendant had not a right to remove or destroy them. Clearly the legislature may, at their pleasure, prohibit the planting of oysters by individuals in navigable waters, or cause them to be removed when planted, whenever they become injurious to the public interests or are regarded as an encroachment upon the public rights. But admitting, as may be done, that the planting of the oysters in the public waters was a clear case of nuisance and encroachment upon the public right, it could give the defendant no right to steal them or appropriate them to his own use. The deposit of wood in the public highway is an encroachment on the right of way, and may and does necessarily prevent any other individual from availing himself of the same privilege upon the same spot. The wood may be removed as a nuisance, but a third party would not be justified in stealing it because it was a nuisance. It is not pretended, in the present case, that the defendant's right of fishing was in the least impaired, or that the oysters were taken in the fair exercise of his lawful right. The case presented is that of a willful and wanton appropriation of his neighbor's property, with intent to steal.

State v. Taylor, 27 N.J.L. 117 (1858). Is this a more satisfactory solution than the decision in *Shepard v. Leverson*?

(7) Two resolutions of the property conundrum, or: John Locke in two jurisdictions:

(a) A statutory resolution: New Jersey's solution to the problem of encouraging oyster production was to institute a state leasing program. At least as early as 1824, the legislature adopted a statute authorizing the leasing of tidelands for the planting of oysters. The statute created a commission to supervise the leasing program and allowed littoral owners to stake off lots adjacent to their lands for the beds. *See Martin v. Waddell*, 41 U.S. (16 Pet.) 367, 379 (1842). The constitutionality of this leasing program was upheld in *Gough v. Bell*, 21 N.J.L. 156 (1847), and *Wooley v. Campbell*, 37 N.J.L. 163 (1874).

(b) A common-law resolution: The New York courts reached a different conclusion on the question of ownership of planted oysters. In *Fleet v. Hegeman*, 14 Wend. 42 (N.Y.1835), plaintiff had staked and planted an oyster bed adjacent to littoral land that he owned fronting on Oyster Bay, Queens County. Defendant subsequently removed oysters from the bed and plaintiff brought an action in trespass for taking and carrying away some 600–700 oysters. Plaintiff argued that he "acquired a separate property in the oysters . . . by separating them from the common mass of things and reducing them to possession, designating his ownership by the stakes enclosing his bed." Defendant countered that it was settled law that a person owning land adjacent to navigable waters "has no exclusive right below high water mark, and can acquire none except by grant from the state." Furthermore, defendant noted, the court had previously decided that the mere marking of a bee tree "was not such a reclamation as to give property in them to the finder." *Ferguson v. Miller*, 1 Cowen. 243 (N.Y.Sup.Ct.1823); *Gillet v. Mason*, 7 Johns. 16 (N.Y.Sup.Ct.1810).

The court began with the proposition that plaintiff had acquired "a qualified property in the oysters" when he harvested them for replanting in the staked bed. Had he abandoned that property by planting them in the bay where there was a common right to fish? The court concluded that he had not.

In reaching this conclusion, the court began with the proposition that plaintiff had not intended to abandon the oysters. Thus, as to inanimate things—such as "goods, plate, [or] money"—defendant's argument would fail because intent was the crucial element. "Oysters have not the power of locomotion any more than inanimate things," the court noted, "and when property has once been acquired in them, no good reason is perceived why it should not be governed by the rules of law applicable to inanimate things.''

The court rejected defendant's argument that oysters ''fall within the rules of law applicable to animals denominated *feræ naturæ*'' and ''are the property of a man no longer than while they continue in his keeping or possession.'' But the law applicable to animals *feræ naturæ* has always recognized that if such animals

> have in fact been domesticated and possess the *animus revertendi*, they are not common property, and the occupant who takes them gets no title; and if he takes them, knowing their condition, he becomes a trespasser. This is clear upon well settled authority. The right of the plaintiff to the oysters is within the reason of these principles. They have been reclaimed, and are as entirely within his possession and control as his swans, or other fowl, that may float habitually in the bay. They were distinctly designated according to usage; and besides, the defendants had actual information of the ownership, and they can set up no greater right to take them, because found in their native element, than tame pigeons in the air, or a domesticated deer upon the mountain.

The court concluded by patting itself on the back: ''We certainly would have regretted if the law had given countenance to such depredations, and we are rejoiced to find that they are as gross a violation of the law as they are of the first principles of justice.''

Subsequent decisions crafted a common-law system consistent with the decision *Fleet*. Following two decisions that examined the implications of allowing a private person to use public lands for private gain, the court held

> oysters planted by an individual in a bed clearly marked out and defined in the tide waters of a bay or arm of the sea, which is a common fishery to all the inhabitants of the state where the bay or arm of the sea is situated, and where there are no oysters growing spontaneously at the time, are the property of the person who plants them, and the taking of them by another person is a trespass, for which an action lies.

The court emphasized that the bed must not interfere with the common right of fishing. *Lowndes v. Dickerson,* 34 Barb. 586 (N.Y.App.Div.1861). *See Decker v. Fisher,* 4 Barb. 592 (N.Y.Sup.Ct.1848); *Brinckerhoff v. Starkins,* 11 Barb. 248 (N.Y.Sup.Ct.1851).

(8) *Pierson v. Post,* a reprise: *Shepard* and *Fleet* present the same conflict between alternative bases of property raised in *Pierson v. Post*. Plaintiffs argued for a Lockean conception: By planting the oysters they had mingled their labor with them and thus they were property. The *Shepard* court rejected this argument in favor of the possession-as-notice theory adopted by the *Pierson* court. But if possession gives notice, why is notice not sufficient to give *de jure* possession? Note that the *Shepard* court states that the oysters ''are in no way identified, *they have no ear marks, they cannot be distinguished.*'' If marking is sufficient to establish ownership, *i.e.,* to serve as a substitute for actual physical possession, why is it not sufficient that the oyster bed be marked? Must individual animals be identifiable?

PERSPECTIVES

(1) The biology of oysters: The conflict between the alternative bases for property was particularly pressing in regard to oysters because of a combination of biology and economics.

An oyster is a bivalve mollusk found in warm, shallow bays and estuaries where the waters are less saline and food is more plentiful. While most species are too small for food, the American Oyster (*Ostrea virginica*) reaches a length of 2–6 inches. Oysters have a two-stage life cycle: Fertilized eggs develop into small, free-swimming/drifting larvae approximately 1/300th of an inch long. The larvae—called "veligers"—grow rapidly, doubling their size twice during the 3 to 3.5 weeks that they swim and drift with the tides. When they are approximately 1/75th of an inch long, the veligers settle to the bottom. If they find a suitable substrate such as rocks, shells, or roots, they glue their shell to the object and begin the second phase of their life cycle. These young, sessile oysters are known as "spats." They mature in 1.5 to 5 years depending upon water temperature.

Oyster farmers collect spat by providing clean firm surface for the veligers to set on. Because oysters do not move once they have attached themselves to a substrate, the spat can be moved to new locations and planted in beds to be harvested—terminology suggesting the analogy to a crop of wheat or corn. It is possible to plant spat into areas such as mud flats that had previously not supported beds due to lack of the necessary substrate.

(2) The economics of oysters: Oyster economics are far simpler than oyster biology. They have a high value and require little work once they were planted. The total amount of oysters could be increased by planting new beds. Given the economic value of the species, there was a strong incentive to do so *if* the person who invested the time and money in creating the new bed was reasonably certain of reaping what he had sowed.

E.A. Stephens & Co. v. Albers

Colorado Supreme Court.
256 P. 15 (1927).

■ BURKE, C.J.:—.... Plaintiff [Albers] brought this action in justice court for the value of a fox pelt and had judgment for $300. Appealed to the county court, and there tried as replevin[1] without a jury, it resulted in a judgment for the return of the property or the payment of its value, *i.e.,* $75. Defendant brings error....

We learn from the record that a certain subspecies of fox, having its habitat from Central United States "north to the treeless tundras," was a

---

1. Replevin is an action to regain possession of chattels which have been unlawfully taken or withheld from the plaintiff.

wild fur-bearing animal valuable only for its pelt; that the individuals thereof varied in color from dull yellow to black, and were known accordingly as "red," "cross," "silver," "silver-black," and "black." Of these the rarest, having fur the most difficult to imitate, and hence the most valuable, was the "silver," or "silver-black." Some 40 years ago silver foxes became very scarce, and enterprising trappers and traders founded the business of breeding them in captivity. At one time a single skin sold in London for $2,700. The industry was first established on Prince Edward Island and spread thence throughout Canada and the United States, until in 1922 there were, in this country alone, approximately 500 silver fox ranches, holding in captivity 15,000 animals, operating as stock ranches and farms for the breeding of domestic animals, representing an investment of $8,000,000, keeping registration books, issuing pedigrees, breeding for size, form, disposition, color and luster, wrestling with problems of housing, mating, inbreeding, feeding, weaning, culling, transporting, killing, skinning, and marketing, and classifying its products as "scrubs," "grades," and "thoroughbreds."

In January, 1926, plaintiff embarked in this business when she received, and installed at the ranch in Southern Morgan county where she and her husband lived, several silver foxes, among them one "McKenzie Duncan," whose pelt is the subject of this litigation. He was registered under No. 11335 of the Silver Fox Breeders' Association of Prince Edward Island. His pedigree shows him to have been bred by J.A. McKenzie of that place, tattoo marked "1" in the right ear and "335" in the left, and his ownership transferred by said McKenzie to the Windswept Farms of Henderson, N.Y. It is in evidence, and undisputed, that plaintiff purchased McKenzie Duncan from the last-mentioned owner for $750, and that a common method used by breeders to mark individuals for identification is tattooing in the ears. Duncan was of the second generation born in captivity and, although kept in an inclosure especially designed to guard against the admitted danger of escape and flight, was sufficiently domesticated to take food from the hand of his keeper. Within two weeks, however, he slipped through an inner gate, inadvertently left unfastened, at feeding time, and, excited by his owner's cry for aid, cleared the outer fence and disappeared. Nightfall soon put an end to pursuit, and the following evening he fell a victim to the shotgun of a ranchman, some six miles distant, who discovered him prowling near his chicken house. This man knew nothing of the name, nature, value, or ownership, of McKenzie Duncan, but took his pelt and intrusted it to a trapper to dispose of on commission. The trapper sold it to defendant for $75, pocketed the money, and passed out of the picture. Plaintiff later learned the fate of her fox, instituted an inquiry which located its pelt in defendant's possession, and this litigation ensued. The pelt in question was introduced in evidence, and, although then dried and wrinkled about the head, the tattoo marks were still distinguishable. Defendant's manager, who bought the skin from the trapper, testified that at that time it showed 10 or 12 shot punctures and that a part of the nose had been shot away, whereas the method of killing followed by those engaged in the industry is by crushing or poisoning. He further testified that at the time of the purchase he did not make an inspection for indicia of ownership; that he had been in the business nine years and was an expert in it; had handled over 30,000 skins; knew that he was buying this skin from a professional trapper; was advised that the seller was not the owner but represented a man who had killed the animal on a ranch in Eastern Colorado; and that this was the only skin bought that season which came from a fox that had been shot. He also said the price paid was due in part to the fact that the fur was black, which seems to have been the view of the county court, whereas plaintiff insisted it was silver-black, and apparently so convinced the justice court.

Defendant says McKenzie Duncan was a wild animal whose possession was essential to ownership, and that when he escaped and pursuit was abandoned plaintiff lost title which the ranchman obtained by slaughter and passed to defendant by sale. Plaintiff says the fox was domesticated; that his disposition to return to his pen (*animum revertendi*) must be presumed; that irrespective of such facts foxes are taxable in this state, hence the common-law rule as to domesticated animals applies; and that the common-law rule as to wild animals is not applicable here.

So far as we have been able to determine, the diligence of counsel has spread before us all "the law and the Gospels" touching the question at issue. Four chapters of the Bible, department bulletin No. 1151 of the United States Department of Agriculture, Belden on Fur Farming for Profit, Harding on Fox Raising, Darwin's Origin of Species, Shakespeare's Henry IV, St. John Lucas, Suteonius, Aesop's Fables, the Tale of the Spartan Youth, the Harvard Law Review, the Albany Law Journal, the Central Law Journal, the London Law Times, the Criminal Law Magazine, and certain anonymous writers, not to mention numerous statutes and court decisions, adorn and illuminate their briefs. Leaving with reluctance all these landmarks save the last two mentioned, we turn to the question here at issue, which is one of first impression in this jurisdiction.

For the common law we go to Blackstone, who says:

> [A qualified property may subsist in wild animals] by a man's reclaiming and making them tame by art, industry and education; or by so confining them within his own immediate power, that they cannot escape and use their natural liberty.* * * These are no longer the property of a man, than while they continue in his keeping or actual possession; but if at any time they regain their natural liberty, his property instantly ceases; unless they have *animum revertendi* (the intention of returning), which is only to be known by their usual custom of returning.* * *....

2 WILLIAM BLACKSTONE, COMMENTARIES ON THE LAWS OF ENGLAND *388–395; 2 JAMES KENT, COMMENTARIES ON THE LAWS OF AMERICA *348 (14th ed. 1884).

It should be borne in mind that when this common-law rule was formulated the great wild animal menageries of the present day, with their enormous collections and vast investments, were in embryo, and the business of raising fur-bearing animals in captivity was practically unknown in England.

Counsel for defendant insists that whether an animal be wild or domestic must be determined from the species, not from the individual. In this position the cases do not support him, even those at common law. The exception, which was a part of the rule, applied to animals having an intention to return (*animum revertendi*), was based upon characteristics of the individual. That exception was invoked in *Manning v. Mitcherson,* 69 Ga. 447 (1882), a suit over a canary bird, and *Ulery v. Jones,* 81 Ill. 403 (1876), an action involving a buffalo bull calf. But the exception was in each stretched until it cracked, because in each a single return was shown from which the "usual custom of returning" was inferred. We think these cases cannot be reconciled with *Mullett v. Bradley,* 53 N.Y.S. 781 (App.Div.1898), where a sea lion, whose native home was in the Pacific Ocean, escaped from captivity in New York and was awarded to a fisherman who caught it in the Atlantic, although such animals were never found in those waters. [ ] These authorities are rather confusing than enlightening, and even suggest that one modification of the rule would permit the owner to recover if he could identify his property. We know of no case so applying it (save those dealing with bees), and the injustice of its application to one who captures or kills ordinary wild animals which have escaped from restraint and returned to their natural habitat is apparent. Again, Mr. Black's definition of domestic animals as "such as contribute to the support of a family or the wealth of a community" would include all fur-bearing animals held in captivity, wherever born or however wild.

We take no notice of such cases as *State v. House,* 65 N.C. 315 (1871), involving larceny of a fur-bearing animal, dead or alive, from the trap of its captor; or *Goff v. Kilts,* 15 Wend. 550 (N.Y.Sup.Ct.1836), involving recovery of a swarm of bees which had been followed by their owner from their old to their new home; or *Haywood v. State,* 41 Ark. 479 (1883), involving the theft of a mocking bird in its cage; or the numerous cases involving the theft of dogs—as they seem to us wholly inapplicable.

It should also be observed that, contrary to the position taken by counsel for plaintiff, liability of the owner of a wild animal which escapes and does damage has no relation to that owner's property right in the animal after escape, notwithstanding the support which it finds in Note, *Property in Animals Feræ Naturæ,* 12 HARV. L. REV. 346 (1898). One who captures a rattlesnake and carries it into his neighbor's house, where it bites the neighbor's child, is liable in damages, not because it was his snake, but because he placed a dangerous reptile in a position to injure others. Having paid the damages, he thereby obtains no right of action against another neighbor who the following day killed the same snake in his potato patch, whence it had escaped from its captor. Nor has birth in captivity anything to do with the question. A wild cat may be just as wild if born in a cage as if born on a mountainside.

Counsel for defendant, by supplemental brief filed February 17, 1927, calls our attention to the fact that H.B. 367, by the terms of which this fox would be classed as domestic, had passed the lower house of the General Assembly then in session. This he urges as legislative recognition of the existence of the common-law rule in Colorado, and argues therefrom the relegation of those in plaintiff's position to that department of the government as their only source of relief. Counsel for plaintiff answering says: (a) McKenzie Duncan was a domestic animal, hence not included in the pending act; (b) if passed, the bill has no application here; (c) the bill may not pass. He is wrong as to (a), right as to (b), and too trustful as to (c). The bill passed with the emergency clause and "safety clutch" and was approved March 17, 1927. It declares all such fur-bearing animals as the one here in question domestic. As set out in counsel's brief, it protected title in them and their increase for two years after escape. As finally approved, it extends that protection ad infinitum. As the act apparently includes muskrats, which have been known to multiply at the rate of 1,500 per cent. per annum, contains no provision to prohibit the intermingling of the escaped with the wild, fails to indicate which line shall be deemed legitimate in determining the status of the offspring, and neglects to designate the official or agency to be charged with the duty of sorting, we are fortunate in being relieved of the necessity of construing or applying it in the instant case.

Counsel for defendant further says this common-law rule is in force in this jurisdiction by virtue of an act passed by our territorial Legislature in 1861:

The common law of England, so far as the same is applicable and of a general nature, * * * shall be the rule of decision, and shall be considered as of full force until repealed by legislative authority.

[ ]

Applicability as to past or to future conditions would often be difficult, if not impossible, of ascertainment. That it is to be determined when claimed is clearly indicated by the language of Mr. Justice Beck, who, speaking for the court 19 years after the passage of the statute, in a case where the common-law rule as to damage done by trespassing cattle was involved, said:

Such a rule of law is wholly unsuited and inapplicable to the present condition of the state and its citizens.

Morris v. Fraker, 5 Colo. 425, 428 (1880).

For the reasons hereinbefore pointed out, we think it equally clear that the common-law rule now invoked "is wholly unsuited and inapplicable to the present condition of the state," the transaction in question, and the industry out of which it grew.

Having then neither statute nor applicable common-law rule governing the case, we must so apply general principles in the light of custom, existing facts, and common knowledge, that justice will be done. So the courts of England and the United States have acted from time immemorial, and so the common law itself came into existence.

The thread is too frail to support its burden. McKenzie Duncan was held in captivity, semidomesticated, escaped by accident, fled against the will of his owner, and pursuit was abandoned by compulsion. This defendant in fact had, or is charged with, knowledge that the pelt purchased was the product of a vast, legitimate, and generally known industry; that it had a considerable and easily ascertainable value; that it bore the indicia of ownership; that it had been taken in an unusual way; that the seller was not the owner; that no right of innocent purchasers had intervened; and that it was from an animal taken in a locality where its kind *feræ naturæ* was unknown and in a state where large numbers were kept in captivity.

We are loath to believe that a man may capture a grizzly bear in the environs of New York or Chicago, or a seal in a millpond in Massachusetts, or an elephant in a cornfield in Iowa, or a silver fox on a ranch in Morgan county, Colo. and snap his fingers in the face of its former owner whose title had been acquired by a considerable expenditure of time, labor, and money; or that the rule, which requires that where one of two persons must suffer the loss falls upon him whose carelessness caused it, has any application here. If the owner was negligent in permitting the escape, the dealer was even more reckless in making the purchase.

Under all the circumstances of this case, we feel obliged to hold that the defendant obtained no title which it can maintain against the plaintiff.

The judgment is accordingly affirmed.

NOTES

(1) *Albers* is an unusual case from a jurisprudential perspective, and worthy of careful study. The court decides to set aside the common law rule governing escaping wild animals and to craft a new rule of law, more suited to the needs of a locale where citizens engage both in wild trapping and in raising fur-bearing animals in captivity. On the facts of the case the court could have decided in favor of the owner, Albers, on various grounds: by deciding that the particular fox had a habit of returning, or by deciding that it had not regained its natural liberty, given that silver foxes were not native to Colorado. The court declines to do so. Why? Recall that the New Jersey court in *Shepard v. Leverson* placed weight on the fact that the oysters at issue were not property because they were "in no way identified, *they have no ear marks,* they cannot be distinguished." Why were the markings on the fox here inadequate to resolve the dispute?

The court apparently based its ruling on the practical needs of the fur industry and on the likelihood that future cases would arise, not involving such peculiar animals as McKenzie Duncan. The court plainly disliked the idea of having to decide, on an animal-by-animal basis, whether a wild animal such as a fox is sufficiently tame that it will return to its owner. Having set that issue aside, what facts does it focus on, and what new rule does it embrace? Will the new rule adequately protect the fur industry? Is it fair to trappers, particularly the normal trapper who captures an animal without seeing it in advance? The court emphasizes that the defendant here had substantial notice that the late McKenzie Duncan was privately owned, but that notice arose, of course, only after the animal was dead. If we decide that Duncan remained privately owned, might the defendant be liable for killing the animal, or is it enough that the defendant has returned the carcass? What if the animal is chiefly valuable for breeding purposes, so that the return of the pelt does not make the owner whole?

Note the 1927 statute enacted by the Colorado legislature. Does it seem a sensible approach? Will it be fair to trappers?

(2) Is the Colorado court correct that such common-law concepts as *animum revertendi* are inadequate to strike an appropriate balance between trapping and commercial wildlife farming? Consider the several cases that the court cites and summarily distinguishes:

(a) *Manning v. Mitcherson* involved a canary that had escaped from its cage. On a previous occasion when it had escaped, the bird had returned. The court noted that plaintiff had the bird for two years, that it knew its name, would answer its owner, and that it had previously returned. It concluded "[u]nder this evidence, there does not seem to be any question of sufficient possession and dominion over this bird, to create a property right in the plaintiff." *Manning v. Mitcherson,* 69 Ga. 447 (1882).

(b) *Ulery v. Jones* concerned a bison plaintiff had acquired when it was six months old and which had been raised with livestock. The animal was "of a roving disposition, and annoyed the defendant very much by jumping over his fence and into his pasture." On its final excursion, defendant shot the bison. The court reversed a jury verdict for defendant because "it cannot be denied, under the evidence, the animal was so tame and gentle as to render it no longer of a wild nature. It was completely tamed, and, therefore, a subject of property." *Ulery v. Jones,* 81 Ill. 403 (1876).

(c) *Haywood v. State* arose from the larceny of a mockingbird and its cage. After reviewing the common law classifications, the court concluded: "The reclaimed mocking bird in question was no doubt personal property. The owner could have brought trespass against the thief, who invaded her portico at night, and deprived her of the possession of her songster, which she prized above price; and she could have maintained replevin against the person to whom he sold it, had he refused to surrender it to her.... To hold that larceny might be committed of the cage, but not of the bird, would be neither good law nor common sense." *Haywood v. State,* 41 Ark. 479 (1883).

(d) *State v. House* was an appeal from the dismissal of a larceny indictment for removing an otter from a trap. The dismissal was based on the common law: "[T]he thing stolen was not the subject of larceny" since it belonged to that "class of animals which, though they may be reclaimed, are not such of which larceny can be committed, by reason of the baseness of their nature." The appellate court reversed, rejecting the common-law rule:

> All of the distinctions as to animals *feræ naturæ* and as to their generous or base natures, which we find in the English books, will not hold good in this country. The English system of game laws seems to have been established more for princely diversion than for use or profit, and is not at all suited to the wants of our enterprising trappers.

> We take the true criterion to be, the *value* of the animals, whether for the food of man, for its fur, or otherwise.

State v. House, 65 N.C. 315 (1871). Does the court's rule in effect mean that *any* animal that someone values sufficiently to capture will support a conviction for larceny?

Does the Colorado court in *Stephens* implicitly agree with the statement in *State v. House* that "[t]he English system of game laws seems to have been established more for princely diversion than for use or profit, and is not at all suited to the wants of our enterprising" game farmers. Would the difference be more accurately expressed in terms of divergent economic systems, *e.g.,* feudal vs. market-based?

Graves v. Dunlap

Washington Supreme Court.
152 P. 532 (1915).

■ MAIN, J.:—The purpose of this action was to establish the plaintiff's ownership ... of certain game animals and birds, and to restrain the defendants, the game warden and the prosecuting attorney of Spokane county, from interfering with ... the plaintiff's ownership ... of the animals. [The trial court entered an order restraining the defendants from prosecuting the plaintiff for possession of the wild animals. The defendants appeal.]

The facts are not in dispute: [Plaintiff owned a dairy farm. During the winter of 1901, a doe with a broken leg began to feed with his dairy herd. The doe was placed in a box stall in the barn and cared for until she recovered; she was then placed in an inclosure. The following season, plaintiff was given a buck. Over the years, plaintiff cared for the herd and when the action was filed in 1913 it had grown to about 20 deer in an inclosure of 15 to 20 acres. Plaintiff also kept several pheasants in the same inclosure.]

[Defendants claim that plaintiff] has no right to keep the deer and the fowls in the inclosure, and that both the deer and the fowls are subject to the same regulation by the Legislature as is the wild game of the state. The [plaintiff] claims that he has a property right in the deer and the fowls, and that therefore it cannot be taken away by act of the Legislature without due compensation being first made. The question, therefore, is whether the [plaintiff] had acquired a property right in the deer and birds which he was entitled to have protected.

Animals *feræ naturæ* are known by the denomination of "game." 2 WILLIAM BLACKSTONE, COMMENTARIES ON THE LAWS OF ENGLAND *410–11. The [plaintiff's] deer and fowls come within the term "game," unless by the fact of their reclamation and confinement there has been acquired a property right therein which is not recognized in wild game. Without reviewing the early common law upon the subject of game, it may be said that the recognized doctrine is that the title to game belongs to the state in its sovereign capacity, and that the state holds this title in trust for the use and benefit of the people of the state. The state, through its Legislature, has the right to control for the common good the killing, taking, and use of game, so long as the rights guaranteed either by the state or federal Constitution are not encroached upon. In *Cawsey v. Brickey,* 144 P. 938 (Wash.1914), it was said:

Under the common law of England all property right in animals *feræ naturæ* was in the sovereign, for the use and benefit of the people. The killing, taking, and use of game was subject to absolute governmental control for the common good. This absolute power to control and regulate was vested in the colonial governments as a part of the common law. It passed with the title to game to the several states as an incident of their sovereignty, and was retained by the states for the use and benefit of the people of the states, subject only to any applicable provisions of the federal Constitution.

See also Geer v. Connecticut, 161 U.S. 519 (1896). Many other decisions to the same effect might be cited, but the multiplication of authorities upon this question is hardly necessary.

While animals *feræ naturæ* belong to the state, as indicated, yet, when they are reclaimed by the art and power of man, they are the subject of property, and a property right thereto may be acquired. . . .

In 2 JAMES KENT, COMMENTARIES ON AMERICAN LAW *348 (14th ed. 1884), upon the same question, the author observes:

Animals *feræ naturæ,* so long as they are reclaimed by the art and power of man, are also the subject of a qualified property; but when they are abandoned, or escape, and return to their natural liberty and ferocity, without the *animus revertendi,* the property in them ceases. While this qualified property continues, it is as much under protection of law as any other property, and every invasion of it is redressed in the same manner.

[ ]

It will be noticed from the excerpt quoted from Kent that the author uses the term "qualified property." Many of the decisions which discuss the question use the same term. The [defendants] contend that, since the property right is a qualified one, the state, in the exercise of its police power, can take it away with impunity. But the qualified property referred to is a property right which is defeasible upon a condition subsequent, which may or may not happen. This condition is that, if the animals return to their wild state, the property right ceases. . . .

Animals *feræ naturæ,* if reclaimed and kept in inclosed ground, are property which will pass to the executors and administrators of a deceased person. In *Dieterich v. Fargo,* 87 N.E. 518 (N.Y.1909), quoting with approval from 1 Halsbury's Laws of England, § 799, it was said:

Deer, though strictly speaking *feræ naturæ,* if reclaimed and kept in inclosed ground, are the subject of property, pass to the executors, and are liable to be taken in distress.

Animals *feræ naturæ* are also, while they are reclaimed, the subject of larceny. In *State v. Shaw,* 65 N. E. 875 (Ohio 1902), it is said:

To acquire a property right in animals *feræ naturæ,* the pursuer must bring them into his power and control, and so maintain his control as to show that he does not intend to abandon them again to the world at large. When he has confined them within his own private inclosure, where he may subject them to his own use at his pleasure, and maintains reasonable precautions to prevent escape, they are so impressed with his proprietorship that a felonious taking of them from his inclosure, whether trap, cage, park, net, or whatever it may be, will be larceny.

It would seem that if wild animals, when reclaimed, will pass to the executors or administrators of a deceased person, or may be the subject of larceny, that the possession of such animals would have such a right or title thereto that it could not be taken away without due compensation first made. If such property right can be taken away be the act of the Legislature, then it does not have the same protection of the law as any other property, which both Kent and Blackstone say it is entitled to.

The [defendant] cites the case of *Cawsey v. Brickey*, 144 P. 938 (Wash.1914), as sustaining his contention that the [plaintiff] had only a qualified property in the deer and fowls, and that such a property right could be destroyed by the Legislature at any time. In that case the court was considering the status of game which had not been reclaimed. The question whether the Legislature had the power to destroy the property right which exists in reclaimed game animals was not before the court and was not considered in the opinion.

At the legislative session for the year 1913 there was passed what is known as the Game Code. [ ] Section 21 of this Code provides that no person shall at any time or in any manner acquire any property in, or subject to his dominion or control, any of the game birds, game animals, or game fish mentioned in the act, but that such game animals, fish, and birds shall always and under all circumstances remain the property of the state. Section 33 provides:

> No person shall, within the state of Washington, hunt, catch, take, kill, ship, convey or cause to be shipped or transported by common or private carrier, to any person, either within or without the state, purchase, expose for sale, have in possession with intent to sell, sell to any person or have in possession or under control at any time, any elk, moose, caribou, deer, fawn, mountain sheep or mountain goat, or any part thereof, including the hides, horns or hoofs except as herein provided.

It will be noticed that this statute provides that no person shall "have in possession or under control at any time" any of the wild animals therein mentioned. It was under this statute that the [defendants] claimed that the [plaintiff] was unlawfully confining the deer and fowls mentioned. It may well be doubted whether, when all of the provisions of the act are considered, it was intended by the Legislature that it should be retroactive, in the sense that it should cover game animals and birds reclaimed prior to its passage, and confined as were those of the [plaintiff]. It is a rule of construction that a statute will not be given a retroactive effect, unless by its terms it is shown clearly that that was the legislative intent. [ ] But, if the statute were to be given a retroactive construction, it is plain that the [plaintiff] had acquired such a property right in the deer and fowls that it could not be taken away without due process of law, as provided in article 1, § 3, of the Constitution of this state, and the fourteenth amendment to the federal Constitution.

But the [defendants] contend that under the statutes of this state as they existed in 1901, and subsequent thereto, the [plaintiff's] possession of the deer and fowls has been at all times wrongful, and that therefore he could acquire no property right therein. [The game law of 1897, 1899, and 1901, however, made it unlawful for any person "hunt, pursue, take, kill, injure, or destroy any deer." It was not until 1903 that the game law included the term "possess" in its list of prohibited acts.] In these statutes we find nothing which would make the possession of game, such as that exercised by the [plaintiff], unlawful. It is true that both the laws of 1903 and 1911 use the term "possess." But reading this term in connection with the context it is plain that the Legislature meant to take possession during the prohibited season. In addition to this the [plaintiff's] herd of deer had its foundation some two years previous to the passage of the law of 1903. There can be no question that in none of the laws passed prior to the year 1913 were the terms used sufficiently broad to cover the possession of deer which were reclaimed and kept in an inclosure.

The [defendants] also complain of certain provisions of the judgment. This judgment provides that the [plaintiff] is not entitled to kill the deer, or any of them, during the closed season, except that, should any deer become wounded or crippled, and it should become necessary to kill it on that account, that this might be done, or if it should become necessary in the care and management of the herd of domesticated animals to kill one or more of them, this might be done. We do not think the decree went too far in this regard. To kill an animal wounded or crippled in a fight many times becomes a humane act. And since the [plaintiff] has a property right in the animals, if necessary in the care and management of the herd to kill, he may do so without offending the law.

The portion of the judgment relating to fowls, after providing that the [plaintiff] shall have the same ownership and right to possession thereof as he is given to the deer, concludes:

And to dispose of them in such manner as he sees fit.

The provision of the decree which gives the right to the [plaintiff] to dispose of the fowls in such manner as he sees fit is too broad. Acting thereunder the [plaintiff] would have the right to kill and sell such fowls during the closed season. If this may be done, it would seriously interfere with the enforcement of the game laws of the state, because of the difficulty of determining whether a fowl killed and possessed during the closed season had been a reclaimed or wild bird. For the protection of the game birds of the state, the state has the power to prohibit the killing and disposing of reclaimed game during the closed season. In *New York ex rel. Silz v. Hesterberg*, 211 U.S. 31 (1908), the relator, August Silz, a dealer in imported game, had been arrested and convicted for having in his possession in the city of New York one imported golden plover which had been lawfully taken, killed, and captured in England during the open season for such game birds there, and thereafter sold and consigned to Silz in the city of New York by a dealer in game in the city of London. He likewise had in his possession the body of one black cock, a member of the grouse family, which was lawfully taken, killed, and captured in Russia during the open season for such game there, and thereafter sold and consigned to Silz in

New York City by the same dealer in London. Such birds were imported by Silz in accordance with the tariff laws of the United States, during the open season for grouse and plover in New York. At the time Silz was arrested under the statutory law of New York, it was unlawful for him to have in his possession birds or fowl of the kind mentioned. The Supreme Court of the United States sustained the law and the conviction of Silz thereunder. In the course of the opinion it was said:

> In order to protect local game during the closed season it has been found expedient to make possession of all such game during that time, whether taken within or without the state, a misdemeanor. In other states of the Union such laws have been deemed essential, and have been sustained by the courts [citing authorities]. It has been provided that the possession of certain kinds of game during the closed season shall be prohibited, owing to the possibility that dealers in game may sell birds of the domestic kind under the claim that they were taken in another state or country. The object of such laws is not to affect the legality of the taking of game in other states, but to protect the local game in the interest of the food supply of the people of the state. We cannot say that such purpose, frequently recognized and acted upon, is an abuse of the police power of the state, and as such to be declared void because contrary to the fourteenth amendment of the Constitution.

The [plaintiff] claims that, since the plaintiff testified upon the trial that he had never killed any of his birds and never expected to, the question whether or not he would have a right to kill and dispose of the birds under the decree is simply a moot question. The future rights of the [plaintiff] under the decree are measured, not by the testimony which he gave upon the trial, but by the language of the judgment. Under the judgment as drawn he plainly would have the right to kill and dispose of any of his birds at any time. He does not claim that his property rights in either the game animals or the birds is beyond the police power of the state. In the course of his brief upon this question it is said:

> If the lower court had thought it proper to decide the moot question of plaintiff's right to kill his expensive birds, we should not have objected; and if your honors think it necessary to decide that question, we certainly do not object. Indeed, to be of as much assistance as we may, we expressly concede that plaintiff has no right to kill, sell, or have possession of the carcasses of his birds during the time when the law declares it illegal.

It cannot be successfully contended that the provision of the decree which gives the right, whether it is exercised or not, to kill, sell, or have in possession the carcasses of the birds during the closed season, covers a moot question. On the other hand, if the question of the right of the [plaintiff] to kill and dispose of his birds was not before the court, a provision in the judgment which gives him this right has no proper place therein.

The cause will be remanded, with direction to the superior court to eliminate that clause from the judgment which reads as follows: "And to dispose of them in such manner as he sees fit.'' In all other respects the judgment is

affirmed

■ MORRIS, C.J., and ELLIS and FULLERTON, JJ., concur.

NOTES

(1) Further limits on rights in captured wildlife: As *Graves* illustrates, those who capture wild animals face more than just the risk that an animal might escape back to the wild. Although game laws commonly limit prospectively a person's power to capture wild animals, the wildlife owner in *Graves* faced limits that arose after capture occurred. According to the court, the owner of a captured animal has a private property right in it, but states can still regulate the use and disposition of wild animals, dead or alive, and at least prospectively ban the possession of wild animals lawfully acquired. Note, though, how the court in *Graves* engages in creative statutory interpretation to accommodate both the state's interests that led to the new law and the interests of the landowner whose original game stock predated the law: by interpreting the ban on possessing animals as inapplicable to landowners who owned such animals before the law went into effect, the court was able to avoid the constitutional question as to whether the law effected an unconstitutional taking of private property without the payment of just compensation. On what statutory language or legislative history does the court base this interpretation? The court also states that the otherwise applicable ban on killing deer out of season does not apply to the killing of wounded or crippled animals. Again, on what does the court base this sensible, but not expressly authorized, exception? On the facts of this case the landowner was allowed to continue doing what he wanted to do, but note that the landowner did face significant limits on his private rights in captive wildlife. The ban on selling out of season limited his rights to transfer what he owned; the ban on killing (except for wounded or crippled animals) had the same effect.

Consider the impact of game laws such as those described in *Graves* on the private rights acquired by a lawful hunter. States typically ban the sale of wild game and limit its possession out of season. Thus, a hunter acquires only limited rights in captured game—the right to possess the deer, and consume it, during a brief period of time. Would a state likely prosecute a deer hunter whose lawfully acquired deer winds up in pieces in a home freezer? If not, might it nonetheless be sensible to promulgate a law that bans such conduct?

(2) *Dieterich v. Fargo:* The *Graves* court distinguished between ownership and possession, on the one hand, and commercial activity, on the other. What is the basis for this distinction? Does it turn on the difference between a taking of property and the regulating of the uses of that property?

Dieterich, cited with approval by the *Graves* court, involved a commercial deer-ranching operation. Dieterich owned a private deer park of approximately 2,400 acres. He regularly slaughtered deer and shipped them to market in New York City. Under the provisions of the state game code, shipment of venison killed in the state was prohibited outside of a specified open hunting season. When the American Express Company refused to accept Dieterich's venison for shipment outside the open season, he sought injunctive relief against the president of the company. Plaintiff argued that the game law was inapplicable to his deer, which he argued were domesticated.

The court agreed. It concluded that "there is no doubt that the deer of the plaintiff were as fully reclaimed as the animals mentioned in the English decisions." Commenting that no one could reasonably apply the game laws to domestic ducks, the court held that it was equally inapplicable to plaintiff's deer because the "purpose [the game law] so far as animals are concerned was to protect the wild animals of the state." Thus, "domesticated deer may lawfully be killed and the venison thereof may lawfully be accepted for transportation by an express company ... without restriction as to number, provided this is done only in the open season." *Dieterich v. Fargo,* 87 N.E. 518 (N.Y.1909). *See also Jones v. State,* 45 S.W.2d 612 (Tex.Crim.App.1931) (reversing conviction for possession of fish removed from a private pond).

(3) *Bilida v. McCleod*: In 1988, Claire Bilida found a raccoon that she named "Mia." Bilida and her family kept the raccoon as a pet; it lived in a cage at the back of the family's house in Warwick, Rhode Island. On August 8, 1995, a Warwick police officer entered Bilida's backyard in response to a security alarm signal. While investigating the alarm—which proved to be false—the officer saw Mia in her cage. Uncertain whether possession of the raccoon was legal, he called the city's animal control officer, and then left. A half hour later, the two officers returned to find Bilida at home. They seized the animal when it was determined that Bilida lacked the permit which is required under Rhode Island law for possession of raccoons and certain other animal species. The animal control officer contacted state officials who ordered the animal killed so that it could be tested for rabies. Bilida brought § 1983 action against State of Rhode Island, the Department of Environmental Management, and its employees for the destruction of her pet.

The trial court granted summary judgment for all defendants; plaintiff appealed. The First Circuit affirmed:

[T]he due process clause protects "property" interests; and while the notion of property interest has been stretched quite far in certain contexts, *e.g., Goldberg v. Kelly,* 397 U.S. 254 (1970), it depends importantly on what interests are recognized under state law. *See Board of Regents v. Roth,* 408 U.S. 564, 577 (1972); *Marrero-Garcia v. Irizarry,* 33 F.3d 117, 121 (1st Cir.1994). Citing these cases, the district court ruled that "even where additional process might be laudable," the court could not "create constitutional protection for objects that the state has declared illegal to possess." 41 F.Supp.2d at 151.

A number of cases hold, as the district court did here, that a claimant has no property interest in *"per se* contraband," *i.e.,* something that it is illegal merely to possess. *E.g., Boggs v. Rubin,* 161 F.3d 37, 40 (D.C.Cir.1998), *cert. denied,* 528 U.S. 811 (1999); *Lyon v.*

Farrier, 730 F.2d 525, 527 (8th Cir.1984). *Cf. One 1958 Plymouth Sedan v. Pennsylvania,* 380 U.S. 693, 699 (1965). Because a raccoon taken from the wild cannot lawfully be possessed in Rhode Island without a permit, the district court deemed Mia to fall into the same category. With little enthusiasm, we agree with the district court that state law undermines Bilida's claim of the required property interest.

Under Rhode Island law, "wild game within a state belongs to the people in their collective sovereign capacity" and is not subject to "private ownership except in so far as the people may elect to make it so." *State v. Kofines,* 80 A. 432, 440 (R.I.1911) (quoting *Ex Parte Maier,* 37 P. 402 (Cal.1894)). State law makes illegal possession of raccoons taken from the wild without a permit issued by the Department. [ ] This amounts to saying that, under state law, Mia could not be reduced to private ownership and lawfully possessed as property without a permit. . . .

Bilida v. McCleod, 211 F.3d 166 (1st Cir.2000).

(4) Pets: As *Bilida* demonstrates, a cat or a dog is not sufficiently exotic for some people. The regulation of the international and interstate trade in wildlife will be considered later.

The willingness in *Graves* to accommodate the property interests of the animal owner does not typically appear in cases involving inherently dangerous animals. New York City, for example, adopted an ordinance prohibiting the keeping of "an animal of a species which is wild, ferocious, dangerous or naturally inclined to do harm." An association of people who owned ferrets brought an action challenging the application of the ordinance to their pets. Although noting that ferrets have been bred in captivity since the fourth century B.C.E., the court deferred to the agency's decision to classify the ferret as a "wild" animal because it was based on a large body of evidence that ferrets were a danger to humans (particularly children and infants), that the rabies virus was highly adapted to ferrets and the progress of the disease was poorly understood in the species, and the threat that escaped ferrets would establish a feral population that could decimate some species of wildlife—a feral population of ferrets in New Zealand contributed to the extinction of 20 species of birds endemic to the islands. Based on the evidence presented by the city, the court rejected plaintiffs' equal protection and due process claims. *New York City Friends of Ferrets v. City of New York,* 876 F.Supp. 529 (S.D.N.Y.1995). *See also People v. Fabing,* 581 N.E.2d 248 (Ill.App.1991) (convictions under statute prohibiting possession of "life-threatening" reptiles for keeping four-foot alligator and two fifteen-to-twenty-foot pythons upheld as to pythons but reversed as to alligator; factual determination that a reptile is "life-threatening" is to be made "on a species-wide" rather than individual basis). *But see City of Rolling Meadows v. Kyle,* 494 N.E.2d 766 (Ill.App. 1986) (prosecution under statute prohibiting possession of animals "other than domesticated house pets" for keeping a monkey reversed because the city failed to provide a definition of "domesticated house pets"); *Kent v. Polk County Board of Supervisors,* 391 N.W.2d 220 (Iowa 1986) (county ban on possession of lion could be applied to lion kept as pet); *City of Warren v. Testa,* 461 N.E.2d 1354 (Ohio C.P.1983) (city can ban possession of full-grown lion and apply law to lion already privately owned).

CHAPTER 3

WILDLIFE AND PRIVATE PROPERTY IN LAND

Chapter 2 explored the limits that private ownership of land impose on the right to capture: a hunter has no right to capture wildlife on private lands when the owner properly exercises the right to exclude. That issue, however, only begins the examination of the links between wildlife and private property in land. Can landowners seek relief against other trespassory and nontrespassory invasions that disturb wildlife on their land? Do they have interests in the wildlife on their lands that are enforceable against the state? Do they have rights to protect their lands against destructive animals, and, if not, can they seek compensation from the state for the destruction? Do they have any special rights under state fish and game laws? And what about that special category of private lands—lands submerged beneath waterways? These and related issues occupy this chapter. Later chapters examine issues raised by restrictions on the ability of landowners to alter wildlife habitat on their lands.

SECTION 1. FAST LAND

a. THE ENGLISH COMMON–LAW BACKGROUND

(i) PROPERTY IN LAND AND WILDLIFE: THE ROLE OF THE SOVEREIGN

Sutton v. Moody

Kings Bench.
1 Ld. Raym. 250, 91 Eng. Rep. 1063 (1698).

Trespass quare clausum suum fregit et centum cuniculos suos adtunc et ibidem inventos venatus fuit occidit cepit et asportavit.[1] Upon not guilty pleaded, verdict for the plaintiff and intire damages.

Gould Serjeant moved in arrest of judgment, [that no action will lie for hunting *conies*,[2] which are *feræ naturæ*, as was decided in *Greenhill's case*] and therefore there is no property in them in any; therefore since the

---

1. Because he had broken the plaintiff's close and at that time and in that same place was hunting and he [the defendant] killed 100 of the plaintiff's conies, kept them, and carried them off.

2. "Coney" is the now-obsolete term for adult rabbits.

plaintiff has laid property in them by the word [*suos*] it is ill, and no damages ought to have been given for them. [As to deer in a park, and conies in a warren, the owner has a special property in them as long as they are in the warren or in park; but if they are not in a park or warren, he may not say *suas* [*i.e., "mine"*], unless he add, "that they were domestic:" thus] if the action had been for having hunted in *warenna sua*, and killed *cuniculos suos* there found, it had been good, for then he would have had a privileged property in them.... But generally there is no property in things which are *feræ naturæ*.....

Holt Chief Justice, a warren is a privilege, to use his land to such a purpose; and a man may have warren in his own land, and he may alien the land, and retain the privilege of warren. But this gives no greater property in the conies to the warrener, for the property arises ... from the possession; and therefore if a man keeps conies in his close (as he may) he has a possessory property in them, so long as they abide there; but if they run into the land of his neighbour, he [the neighbor] may kill them, for then he has the possessory property. [If a man start a hare in his own ground and course it to the close of another person, and there takes it, the hare belongs to the owner of the ground where it was first started; but if it was started in the close of another man and there killed, it is the hare of the owner of the close where it was killed; but if the hare starts in another man's ground and is coursed out of it, it is the hare of the captor, for the property rests in the owner of the soil, *ratione loci;* but if she runs beyond his (the captor's) ground (being *feræ naturæ*) he loseth his property; thus during the time they are in his soil the plaintiff may call them his conies; but if he starts a hare in my close, and kills her there, it is mine; and where started in a forest, and hunted and killed in another person's land, the property is in the owner of the forest.]

[In the present case the plaintiff declares, *quare clausum fregit & cuniculos suos ibidem invent', & c.* which shews the conies to have been in his close at the time of the takings.] And by the whole Court judgment was given for the plaintiff, because he had a property by the possession....

NOTES

In *The Case of Swans* [Chapter 2], the court outlined three types of property that a person might acquire in wild animals: (a) *per industriam,* by taking or taming them; (b) *ratione impotentiæ et loci,* when the animal is powerless to leave "by reason of inability and place"; and (c) *ratione privilegii,* through ownership of a franchise. This third category—and the distinction between the second and third categories—were the issues in *Sutton v. Moody.*

The distinction between the two categories is to be found in the three rules that Justice Holt lays down: (i) If *A* starts a hare on *B*'s land and kills it there, the property in the hare remains in *B.* (ii) If *A* starts a hare on *B*'s land and chases it onto *C*'s land, where he kills it, the property is in *A,* although a trespasser. (iii) If *A* starts a hare in *B*'s warren (or forest), and chases it onto *C*'s land, where he kills it, the property remains in *B.* The difference between (ii) and (iii) is the distinction between *ratione loci* (as it is now denominated) and *ratione privilegii*. In the case of a trespasser, the right of property which the owner of land has *ratione loci* ceases when the animal leaves his land; on the other hand, the property that the owner of a warren has *ratione privilegii* continues.

PERSPECTIVES

(1) A critical strand in the English law of wildlife involved the relationship between land tenure, private rights in wildlife, and the state's—initially, the King's—powers. Recall that the court in *The Case of Swans* argued that at least some animals are subject to special rules that vest greater powers in the state. *Sutton v. Moody* examines an additional point: a person might hold a special power from the King—a "franchise"—to take certain game animals. A franchise—be it a warren (as in *Sutton v. Moody*) or a park or chase—could be an interest in its owner's land or in the land of another. Although these concepts—and the language they are expressed in—seem arcane, the following materials demonstrate that they have a continuing influence on wildlife law.

(2) Property and sovereignty: As noted in Chapter 2, current distinctions between proprietary and sovereign powers were not recognized in medieval England—particularly in the centuries immediately following the Norman Conquest. The King not only headed what we now call the government (and thus exercised law-making powers), he also stood at the apex of a feudal land-holding system (and in that capacity exercised what we would now term property rights). Thus, when describing the common law during this period, it is anachronistic to distinguish between "property" rights and "government" power. Landowners generally possessed only those rights granted to them by their superiors in the feudal hierarchy— and those superiors, particularly the Crown, could withdraw rights and reassign them under many circumstances. It was—to use the proper term— a *tenurial* system of limited proprietary rights held subject to a higher lord, rather than the *allodial* system of rights that the modern age knows best. Similarly, many things that are now viewed as governmental were exercised by people holding certain tenures in land—for example, the right to hold court and hang criminals.

Another critical aspect of this period was the King's constant need for revenue and his concomitant inclination to raise money by selling a wide variety of "franchises." These included exclusive powers to hold markets, to manufacture certain goods, to undertake forms of trade, and to capture certain fish and game. The court in *The Case of Swans*, for example, examined the King's power to grant special rights in royal fowl. To solidify influence, gain favor, and raise money, the Crown often granted such exclusive franchises to private parties. In the process, the franchises disrupted the lives and livelihoods of many people. But, just as surely as the Crown was inclined to grant such franchises, disgruntled citizens were inclined to complain about them, to violate them, and ultimately to challenge the Crown's power to grant them. The Crown's push for greater authority, legal and proprietary, was thus challenged and eventually restrained by a popular force that sought more extensive—and more stable—

private rights. The Magna Carta is only one of the truces in this struggle between advocates of royal prerogative and proponents of what we now call the rule of law.

One piece of the landowner-wildlife relationship was considered in Chapter 2: landowners over time gained the right to exclude hunters, unless the hunter held a franchise to enter their land. A key case in the emergence of this idea was *Sutton v. Moody*, which recognized landowner rights while also acknowledging that the common landowner had only a right to try to capture wildlife—rather than a right in the wildlife itself—so that wildlife leaving his property was fair game for others. The court in *Sutton* expressed the view that wildlife captured by a trespasser belonged to the landowner—an issue that remained unsettled in England until the decision of the House of Lords in *Blades v. Higgs*, 11 H.C.L. 621, 11 Eng. Rep. 1474 (H.L. 1865).

The court in *Sutton* also discussed the King's ability to grant exclusive hunting rights in land—a warren, in the case before the court. By implication, only franchisees possessed secure hunting rights, and even they might be required to show title or lose the right. *See King v. Talbot*, Cro. Car. 311, 79 Eng. Rep. 871 (K.B. 1634) (a *quo warranto* action seeking to determine by "what warrant" defendant claims a free warren in the forest of S; defendant claimed the warren by prescription). Landowners who hunted their lands, based not on a franchise but merely on their right to exclude, faced the possibility that the right might be withdrawn or overridden at any time. *See Rex v. Chipp*, 2 Str. 711, 93 Eng. Rep. 800 (K.B. 1726) [discussed *infra*].

The notes that follow briefly examine key aspects of these relationships: (a) the King's claim of ownership in wildlife; (b) the King's power to grant exclusive franchises to hunt wildlife; (c) the special rules governing forests; (d) qualification statutes limiting who could hunt; (e) other statutory restrictions on how, when, and where animals might be captured; and (f) the duties imposed on landowners to accommodate wildlife on their lands. This is the basis for American wildlife law. We will return to the relationship between property and sovereignty in Chapter 5.

(3) The King's prerogative and wildlife: The nature and scope of the King's prerogative has bedeviled courts and commentators for centuries. One issue in this debate was whether the prerogative included ownership of all wildlife in the realm. As *The Case of Swans* indicates, there was a consensus from an early date that the King owned at least certain regal fish and fowl. But what of other animals? Did the King also own them—and if so, were the incidents of ownership as expansive as with royal animals? The King, of course, asserted ownership perhaps primarily so that he could sell or give away the right to hunt. But, if he did own all wildlife, was this prerogative ownership in some sense property-in-trust for the people, so that the King was limited in his power to create private interests in wildlife that would deprive his subjects of the chance to capture them? And a further complication: given the King's prerogative rights in wildlife, what powers did Parliament have to govern the use and capture of such animals?

For Roman jurists, animals were *res nullius*—a thing owned by no one. *See* THE INSTITUTES OF JUSTINIAN bk. II, tit. 1, § 12 (J.A.C. Thomas trans.

1975) (1st ed. 533) [Chapter 2 *supra*]. Although generally following Justinian, Henry de Bracton adopted a different perspective, writing that wild animals were an example of "things that are owned by no one [by natural law, but] do now belong to the king by the civil law." HENRY DE BRACTON, DE LEGIBUS ET CONSUETUDINIBUS ANGLIAE bk. 2, ch. 1, ff. 8b (ca. 1256). Bracton was not the first jurist to claim that the King owned the wild animals in his realm. This contention was also advanced by Justice Walmsley in *Bowlston v. Hardy,* Cro. Eliz. 547, 78 Eng. Rep. 794 (K.B. 1597) (no landowner owns unconfined wild animals "unless by grant from the King, or by prescription . . . for the Queen hath the royalty in such things whereof none can have any property.").

This skimpy precedent led Blackstone to assert: "Upon the whole it appears, that the king, by his prerogative, and [holders of royal franchises], are the *only* persons who may acquire any property, however fugitive and transitory, in these animals *feræ naturæ*, while living." 2 WILLIAM BLACKSTONE, COMMENTARIES *419. Blackstone based his conclusion on the fundamental proposition of feudalism: "[T]he king is the ultimate proprietor of all the lands in the kingdom . . . and that therefore he has the right of the universal soil, to enter thereon, and to chase and take such creatures as his pleasure." *Id.* at *415. This principle was buttressed by another: "[T]hese animals are *bona vacantia* [*i.e.,* unclaimed goods], and, having no other owner, belong to the king by his prerogative." *Id.*

But the record was not as clear as Blackstone suggested—and Blackstone's view was sharply contested by Edward Christian, editor of a common annotated edition of Blackstone and the author of an 1821 treatise on game laws.[3] Christian argued that "game does not belong to the King." As he noted,

> If all wild animals belonged to the crown, it would have been superfluous to have specified whales, sturgeons, and swans. Lord Coke tell us, that "a swan is a royal fowl; and all those the property whereof is not known, do belong to the king by his prerogative: and so whales and sturgeons are royal fish, and belong to the king by his prerogative:" *Case of swans,....* But these are the only animals which our law has conferred this honour upon.

2 WILLIAM BLACKSTONE, COMMENTARIES *419 n.9 (New York: W.E. Dean, Printer, 1832) (this edition, among others, includes Christian's notes). To bolster his argument, Christian cited an early case holding that the King had no property in deer that escaped from a forest, as well as *dicta* from *The Case of Monopolies*:

---

3. The chapter in the treatise titled "Game does not belong to the King" is a reprint of Christian's note in his edition of Blackstone. EDWARD CHRISTIAN, A TREATISE ON THE GAME LAWS 22–38 (London: J. & W.T. Clarke, 1821). The *Biographical Dictionary of the Common Law* reports that he was the brother of Fletcher Christian of *H.M.S.*

Bounty; that he was a "[f]ailure at the bar" but became a professor at Cambridge. Lord Ellenborough observed that he was "fit only to rule a copybook." He is reported to have died "[i]n the full vigour of his incapacity." BIOGRAPHICAL DICTIONARY OF THE COMMON LAW 114 (A.W.B. Simpson ed. 1984).

it is true, that none can make a park, chase, or warren, without the King's license, for that is *quodam modo*[4] to appropriate those creatures which are *feræ naturæ, et nullius in bonis*[5] to himself, and to restrain them in their natural liberty, which he cannot do without the King's license; but for hawking, hunting, & c. which are matters of pastime, pleasure, and recreation, there needs no license, but every one may, in his own land, use them at his pleasure, without any restraint to be made, unless by Parliament.

The Case of Monopolies, 11 Co. Rep. 84b, 87b, 77 Eng. Rep. 1260, 1264 (K.B. 1602). Might one resolution of Christian's conundrum be to note that the term "property" can be used to refer to a variety of different relationships between people in relation to things?

In part, the resolution of the dispute depends upon the concept of prerogative. *The Case of Swans* states that swans, whales, and sturgeons "belong to the King by his prerogative." Similarly, the court in *The Case of the Royal Fishery of Banne*, 56 Davis, 80 Eng. Rep. 540 (K.B. 1611), announced that "[e]very navigable river, so high as the sea flows and ebbs in it, is a royal river, ... and belongs to the king by his prerogative."

What is it that swans, whales, and navigable rivers share? The nature of the King's "prerogative"—and the type of "ownership" that that prerogative confers—are vexing questions.

(a) Bracton identified two broad categories of prerogative ownership:

[1] A thing which cannot be possessed [and] cannot be given, as a sacred thing ... or a *quasi*-sacred things, as one connected with the fisc [*i.e.*, the public treasury], or ... the walls and gates of a city. Such may neither be given nor possessed because they are the property of no one, that is, of no individual person, only that of God, or the fisc....
[2] There are also things that belong to the crown because of the king's privilege but do not so touch the common welfare that they may not be given and transferred to another, for if they are that will be to the damage of no one except the king or prince himself. If things of that kind, as wreck of the sea, treasure trove, and great fish, as whale, sturgeon and other royal fish, have been granted to another and a question arises thereon, he who claims such a liberty must show that it belongs to him, for if he has no special warrant he cannot maintain himself therein, even though he puts forward the prescription of long use, for here great length of time does not diminish the wrong but increases it; nor does time run against the king, in the case nor in this, nor need he [the king] prove that such things belong to him, since it must be clear to everyone that they belong to the crown by the *jus gentium*.

HENRY DE BRACTON, DE LEGIBUS ET CONSUETUDINIBUS ANGLIAE bk. 2, chs. 5, ff. 14 (ca. 1256). For Bracton, prerogative property existed both in things that "constitute the crown itself and concern the common welfare" and in things that "do not so touch the common welfare." Swans fall into the

---

4. ["in a certain way."]   5. ["and among the property of no person."]

latter category and thus may be the property of individuals if they can prove "special warrant." The position adopted by the judges of the King's Bench in *The Case of Swans* is consistent with this interpretation.

(b) Blackstone began with a definition of the term: "By the word prerogative we usually understand that special pre-eminence, which the king hath over an above all other persons, and out of the ordinary course of the common law, in right of his regal dignity." This definition was followed with an elaborate classification scheme.

Prerogatives, he wrote, were "either *direct* or *incidental*. The *direct* are such positive substantial parts of the royal character and authority as are rooted in and spring from the king's political person." These "direct prerogatives" were further divided "into three kinds: being such as re-gards, first, the king's royal *character*; secondly, his royal *authority;* and, lastly, his royal *income*."

The second category of prerogative—the King's "royal *authority*"—invested "our sovereign lord . . . with a number of authorities and powers; in the exertion whereof consists the executive part of government." This heading was in turn subdivided into two categories: foreign and domestic powers. The King's prerogatives in domestic affairs includes

the prerogative of appointing *ports* and *havens*, or such places only, for persons and merchandize to pass into and out of the realm, as he in his wisdom sees proper.

By the feudal law all navigable rivers and havens were computed among the *regalia* [royalties], and were subject to the sovereign of the state. And in England it hath always been holden, that the king is lord of the whole shore. . . .

In addition to "those branches of the king's prerogative, which contrib-ute to his royal dignity, and constitute the executive power of the govern-ment," Blackstone summarized a third category, the King's fiscal preroga-tives. These were a diverse group of feudal sources of revenue including:

A tenth branch of the king's ordinary revenue, said to be grounded on the consideration of his guarding and protecting the seas from pirates and robbers, is the right of *royal fish*, which are whale and sturgeon; and these, when either thrown ashore, or caught near the coast, are the property of the king, on account of their superior excellence.

1 WILLIAM BLACKSTONE, COMMENTARIES *239–*64, *281–*90.

Although Blackstone's classification scheme pigeon-holed many of the incidents of royal prerogative, it brought apparent order without a corre-sponding insight: What, for example, ties the control of navigable rivers to the right to sturgeons and whales? While both might produce revenue, so might a large and equally disparate list of things.

Does the anomalous—or at least heterogenous—nature of the list reflect a historical process rather than a rational allocation of powers? That is, does at least part of the difficulty lie in the fact that prerogative was political power before there was an attempt to conceptualize it? And further, that the conceptualization was largely an attempt to rationalize, in both senses of that word?

In addition to serving as the basis for the claim that the King owned wildlife in the realm, the King's prerogative played three additional roles in the evolution of wildlife law: (i) it was the basis for the claim that he owned the land beneath navigable rivers in trust for the people, a trust that included a right to fish; (ii) it was the source of the power to create "forests"; and (iii) it was the source of the power to create the hunting franchises of chase, park, and warren. The first role of prerogative is examined later in this chapter.

(4) Forests: Prerogative ownership was not the only type of claim by the Crown to special powers over wildlife. Following the Norman Conquest, William the Conqueror arrogated to himself the power to designate tracts of land as "forests." Writing more than 500 years later, John Manwood defined a "forest" as

> a certen Territorie of woody grounds & fruitfull pastures, privileged for wild beasts and fowles of, Forest, Chase, and Warren, to rest and abide in, in the safe protectio[n] of the King, for his princely delight and pleasure, which Territorie of grou[n]d, so privileged, is meered and bounded by unremoveable, marks, meeres, and boundaries ... and also replenished with wilde beasts of venerie or Chase, and with great coverts of vert, for the succour of the said wild beasts, to have their abode in: for the preservation and continuance of which said place, together with the vert and Venison, there are certen particuler Lawes, Priviledges and Officers, belonging to the same.

JOHN MANWOOD, A TREATISE AND DISCOURSE OF THE LAWES OF THE FOREST cap. i, § 1 (Thomas Wright & Bonham Wright, London 1598). Coke gave a more concise definition in the following century: "A Forest doth consist of eight things, *videlicet* of soil, covert, laws, courts, judges, officers, game, and certain bounds." EDWARD COKE, FOURTH PART OF THE INSTITUTES OF THE LAWS OF ENGLAND 289 (1628).

The crucial point in both definitions is that a "forest" was a legal classification of land rather than a physical description of that land: A forest might include villages and cultivated fields as well as tracts of trees and brush—and not all of the land within a forest was owned by the King. In more modern terminology, a forest was a land-use classification.

The forest law was, in the traditional phrase, intended to protect "the vert and Venison." The vert—the green plants—was protected by restricting the uses of lands within the forest; it was protected to preserve the "venison"—specified species of wildlife: The "five wild beasts of venerie, that are called beastes of Forest ... the *Hart*, the *Hynde*, the *Hare*, the *Boare*, and the *Wolfe*."[6] JOHN MANWOOD, *supra*, cap. iv, § 1.

---

6. In addition to the "beastes of Forest," there were the "5 wilde beasts, that are called beasts of Chase, the Buck, the Doe, the Fox, the Martron, and the Roe" and four "beasts and foules of Warren ..., the Hare, the Connie, the Phesant, and the Partridge." JOHN MANWOOD, *supra*, cap. iv, §§ 2–3. The lists include three species of deer: the hart and the hind were the male and female red

deer; the buck and doe were the male and female fallow deer; the roe is the third species. The "Martron" was the marten.

Turner questioned whether all of these animals were in fact protected in all forests, G.J. Turner, *Introduction* to SELECT PLEAS OF THE FOREST ix-xiv (G.J. Turner ed. & trans., 1901) (vol. 13 Selden Soc'y Pubs.); Man-

To protect the vert and venison, there was an administrative and law enforcement system staffed with unique officers—justices, wardens, verderers, gamekeepers, woodwards, agisters, and regarders—who acted under a distinct body of law in a series of judicial and prerogative courts—the courts of Swanimote, Attachment, Regard, the General and Special Inquisitions, and the Eyre.

Although the King had the power—the prerogative—to create the forest and, indeed, was seised of the *forest*, he was not necessarily seised of all of the lands within the forest because individuals could hold land within forests. The ability of such inholders to fully exploit their land was, however, restricted by its location within the forest. As Manwood put it, "by the lawes of the Forest, no man may cut downe his woods, nor destroy any coverts, within the Forest, without the view of the Forester, and license of the Lord Chief Justice in Eyre of the Forest, although that the soile, wherein those woods do grow, be a mans owne freehold." *Id.*, ch. 8, § 2.

The punishment for impermissibly intruding upon the forest was amercement (fine) at the next eyre in addition to an annual fine based on the crops sown: For every acre illegally planted, the fine was a shilling for winter corn (either wheat or rye) and sixpence for spring corn (generally oats). The tenant was allowed to remain—subject to the continuing payment of the fine at subsequent regards. Thus the administrative system effectively converted fines into a source of permanent, annual rent. While the hunt was the origin of the forest, the institution quickly acquired a financial component that often overshadowed the desire to prevent the destruction of habitat.

(5) The King's power to create hunting franchises: The King's prerogative not only was the basis of forests, but also supported his power to create the hunting franchises of chase, park, and warren; these franchises allowed a subject to hunt different classes of game.

Blackstone provided the following discussion of the hunting franchises:

> As to a *forest*; this, in the hands of a subject, is properly the same thing as a chase: being subject to the common law, and not to the forest laws. But a *chase* differs from a park, in that it is not enclosed, and also in that a man may have a chase in another man's ground as well as in his own, being indeed the liberty of keeping beasts of chase or royal game therein, protected even from the owner of the land, with a power of hunting them thereon. A *park* is an enclosed chase, extending only over a man's own grounds. The word *park* indeed properly signifies an enclosure; but yet it is not every field or common, which a gentleman pleases to surround with a wall or paling, and to stock with herd of deer, that is thereby constituted a legal park: for the king's grant, or at least immemorial prescription, is necessary to make it so. [I]t is unlawful at common law for any person to kill any beasts of park or chase, except such as possess these franchises of forest, chase or park.

wood's list is a handy point of reference for those species accorded at least some protec- tion.

> *Free-warren* is a similar franchise, erected for preservation or
> custody (which the word signifies) of beasts and fowls of warren;
> which, being *feræ naturæ,* every one had a natural right to kill as he
> could; but upon the introduction of the forest laws, at the Norman
> conquest ... these animals being looked upon as royal game and the
> sole property of our savage monarchs, this franchise of free-warren was
> invented to protect them; by giving the grantee a sole and exclusive
> power of killing such game so far as his warren extended, on condition
> of his preventing other persons. [N]o man, not even a lord of a manor,
> could by common law justify sporting on another's soil, or even on his
> own, unless he had the liberty of free-warren....

2 WILLIAM BLACKSTONE, COMMENTARIES *38–39. *See also* RICHARD BURN, THE
JUSTICE OF THE PEACE 437 (Henry Lintot, London: 1755).

The distinction between forests and chases is worthy of note. Blackstone wrote that "a *forest* ... in the hands of a subject, is properly ... a
chase" and that the distinction between the two was that a chase is
"subject to the common law, and not to the forest laws." As the previous
note explained, a central characteristic of a forest was a system of prerogative courts that existed independently of the common law. When the King
granted a subject a forest, the grantee was not vested with the Crown's
prerogative: when forests "passed by royal grant into the hands of subjects,
they were considered to have lost many of the incidents of a forest." G.J.
Turner, *Introduction* to SELECT PLEAS OF THE FOREST cix (G.J. Turner ed. &
trans., 1901) (vol. 13 Selden Soc'y Pubs.). Rather than a forest, the grantee
generally received a "chase." As the King's Bench stated in construing a
charter "to have a forrest within twenty manors,"

> It is a chase, and not a forrest, being in the hands of a subject, a
> swannymote court, a subject may have, but no subject can have a
> forrest, because none can make a justice in eyre[7] but the King....
> [because t]o make a justice in eyre, and such like, these are *jura
> regalia.* ... A forrest hath such immunities which are prerogatives
> Royall; and this is the reason why a subject cannot have a forrest, but
> a chase.

King v. Briggs, 2 Bulst. 295, 80 Eng. Rep. 1133 (K.B. 1615). *But see Case of
Leicester Forest,* Cro. Jac. 155, 79 Eng. Rep. 135 (K.B. 1608) (a subject may
have a forest "if the king gives authority by express words, [grants the]
commission ... to use and have officers of a forest ... otherwise, without
such liberties, it is but a chase, being in the hands of a common person").

Thus, as a general matter, when the King granted a royal forest to a
subject, some of the King's rights with respect to preservation of the vert
and venison "became vested in the new proprietor. The mere grant of the
forest effected no such disafforestment as to enable its inhabitants to hunt
and cut their timber at pleasure. In general, the restrictions under which
they had lived continued, and it was only the machinery by which they
were enforced that was altered." G.J. Turner, *supra,* at cx. But the
prerogative power to hold forest courts did not pass and owners of chases
were restricted to arresting trespassers as a prelude to an action in the

---

7. [The royal judicial official who presided over forest courts.]

common law courts. It thus was through the common law of trespass and the statutory prohibitions attached to it that the owners of the lesser hunting franchises protected their property.

Over time, Parliament and the courts responded to the social and economic changes associated with the rise of the gentry by reducing the role of the franchises and expanding the role of trespass. *See* G.J. Turner, *supra*, at cxviii-cxxii. The hunting franchises were freeholds, incorporeal hereditaments that allowed their owner to hunt for the types of wildlife covered by the franchise. The conception of hunting franchises as independent freeholds gradually withered, to be replaced by the perspective that regarded the various rights as incidents of the ownership of the soil. In other words, property *ratione loci/soli* came to replace property *ratione privilegii*—a transition that was still incomplete at the time of the American Revolution. *See Blades v. Higgs,* 11 H.C.L. 621, 11 Eng. Rep. 1474 (H.L. 1865).

For our purpose, one crucial point to note is what the King's prerogative power to create hunting franchises says about land ownership. Although it is common to think of property as the antithesis of regulation, property can also be a form of regulation. The hunting franchises are a case in point. When the King granted someone a park, chase, or warren, the person received a power to engage in specified activities on the land burdened by the franchise. The assertion of the power to grant franchises was an assertion of power over wildlife—an assertion that could form the basis for other, more traditional regulatory acts. The grant of a franchise also implicitly creates a limitation: that which is not granted is retained; a landowner who does not have a warren cannot "of right" hunt on his own property—the fee thus does not include a power to hunt. The granting of a franchise thus was effectively an assertion of royal power as both a positive and a negative.

(6) Warrens: The particular franchise involved in *Sutton v. Moody* was the right of "free warren." The word "warren" was used to denote either the exclusive right to hunt certain species of wildlife on a particular piece of land or the land on which the franchise was to be exercised. Royal grants of free warren were so common during the middle ages that it is probable that most lords of manors held such rights as incidents of their tenure by the middle of the fourteenth century. The charter granting a landowner a warren

> consisted of three principle clauses. The first was a formal grant of free warren in the demesne lands[8] of the person to whom the charter was granted. The second declared that the grant was subject to a proviso that the lands were not within the metes of the king's forest; and the third prescribed the mode in which the grant was to be enjoyed: namely, in such a way that no person might enter the land and hunt on it or to take anything which belonged to the warren without the

---

8. [Demesne lands were those lands of a manor—the basic unit of land held by a lord (generally, a baron) of the king—that were not *granted* out to tenants but were instead held by the lord for his own use and occupancy. Demesne lands included lands let for years or at will. *See* 2 BLACKSTONE, COMMENTARIES *90.]

license and will of the grantee or his heirs under pain of a forfeiture [to the king] of ten pounds.

G.J. Turner, *supra,* at cxxiii. Turner argues that the royal grants of free warren may be the source of the right to exclude others from hunting on one's land. *Id.*

Since warrens were a tenure (an incorporeal hereditament) they could be granted independently of the underlying tenure in the land or could be retained by the grantors when the burdened land was transferred. Thus, it was possible to own a warren on the land of another, as Chief Justice Holt recognized in his analysis in *Sutton v. Moody.* There is no evidence, however, that the King granted warrens to anyone other than the landholder.

(7) Qualification statutes: Beginning in 1390, Parliament enacted a series of statutes that established wealth qualifications that a person was required to satisfy in order to hunt game. The 1390 statute, for example, provided in part:

> That no Manner of Artificer, Labourer, nor any other Layman, which hath not Lands or Tenements to the Value of 40s. by Year, nor any Priest nor other Clerk, if he be not advanced to the value of 10. by Year, shall have or keep henceforth any Greyhound, Hound, nor other Dog to hunt; nor shall they use Fryets, Heys, Nets, Harepipes, nor Cords, nor other Engines for to take or destroy Deer, Hares, nor Conies, nor other Gentlemen's Game, upon Pain of One Year's Imprisonment.

13 Rich. 2, ch. 13 (1390).

Such statutes effectively prohibited landowners from hunting on their own land if they were insufficiently wealthy. *E.g., Rex v. Chipp,* 2 Str. 711, 93 Eng. Rep. 800 (K.B. 1726) ("the statutes forbid such persons as the defendant to hunt at all" and the fact that defendant owned the land was immaterial). Predictably, these restrictions were unpopular with the common people since they restricted hunting along class lines, allocating wild game—and the sport of hunting it—to the privileged elite.

Qualification statutes served various aims. As the 1390 statute indicates, the statutes restricted a recreational activity that could easily divert laborers from attending to their work for lords and employers. They also removed the prime reason for ordinary people to possess and carry weapons and thus reduced the risk of social unrest. *See* E.P. THOMPSON, WHIGS AND HUNTERS: THE ORIGINS OF THE BLACK ACT (1976).

(8) Statutory prohibitions on habitat destruction: On occasion, Parliament restricted private land uses to protect wildlife habitat and hence game populations. In 1692, for example, it passed *An Act for the More Easy Discovery and Conviction of Such as Shall Destroy the Game of this Kingdom*:

> Provided always, and be it enacted, That for the better preserving the red and black game of grouse, commonly called heath-cocks, or heath-polts, no person whatsoever, on any mountains, hills, heaths, moors, forests, chases, or other wastes, shall presume to burn, between the

second day of February and twenty-fourth of June, any grig, ling, heath, furze, goss, or fern, upon pain that the offender or offenders shall be committed to the house of correction, for any time not exceeding one month and not less than ten days, there to he whipt, and kept to hard labour.

3 & 4 Wm. & M., ch. 23, § 11 (1692). When this statute proved insufficient to deter illegal habitat destruction, Parliament prohibited unlicensed persons from selling fern ashes. AN ACT FOR THE BETTER PRESERVATION OF THE GAME, 5 Anne ch. 14, § 5 (1706). *See also* AN ACT FOR THE PREVENTING THE BURNING OR DESTROYING OF GOSS, FURZE OR FERNE, IN FORESTS OR CHACES, 28 Geo. 2, ch. 19, § 3 (1755).

Similarly, a statute enacted in 1393 required that all dams include weirs "of reasonable wideness" to permit spawning runs. JUSTICES OF THE PEACE SHALL BE CONSERVATORS OF THE STATUTES MADE TOUCHING SALMONS, 17 Rich. 2, ch. 9 (1393).

Such statutory provisions were rare; they were also unnecessary in a social system in which the upper classes devoted large tracts of land to wildlife habitat. The statutes—like the forest laws—do illustrate, nonetheless, that property in land was subject to direct use-restrictions when the King or Parliament deemed it necessary to protect wildlife habitat.

(9) Popular complaints: English game laws, qualification statutes, and the associated restrictions on owning firearm drew strong protest from advocates for the common people, particularly the small landowners who often could not hunt, could not own guns, and could do little legally about the crop damage caused by wild game. In a 1757 pamphlet, "A True–Born Englishman" complained bitterly that small farmers could not harvest the hares, partridges, and pheasants on their lands, including those that were destroying crops. As for restrictions on firearm ownership, he complained that they offered a "direct Road to arbitrary Government" by undercutting the ability of ordinary people to defend their homes. Most heinous was the fact that game laws robbed citizens of their right to enjoy the land's natural bounty, "the Blessings given by the All–Wise Creator." AN ALARM TO THE PEOPLE OF ENGLAND, SHEWING THEIR RIGHTS, LIBERTIES, AND PROPERTIES, TO BE IN THE UTMOST DANGER FROM THE PRESENT DESTRUCTIVE AND UNCONSTITUTIONAL ASSOCIATION FOR THE PRESERVATION OF THE GAME ALL OVER ENGLAND, WHICH IS PROVED TO BE ILLEGAL (London, 1757). A pamphleteer writing in the next century took a more sober approach. "Every one knows, that in those districts where pheasants and partridges are cautiously preserved, less rent can be obtained for the farms, on account of the depredations of those animals." He also argued, echoing a point made for generations, that landowners who could not harvest such game had no incentive to encourage their propagation: "It is a well known fact, though particular instances cannot easily be adduced that freeholders of small property, frequently destroy the nests of pheasants and partridges." William Elford, *A Few Cursory Remarks on the Obnoxious Parts of the Game Law, in* 10 THE PAMPHLETEER 19, 26, 27 (London, 1817).

The aristocratic side did not go undefended. In his many writings on the game laws, Joseph Chitty noted that it was "reckoned unsafe" sometimes "to trust the common people with arms." Then, too, he urged, "it will scarcely be denied, that the liberty of killing game, if given universally to the people, would encourage habits of dissipation and irregularity, tending to unfit them for the pursuits best suited to their condition." Chitty did recommend, however, that all landowners gain the right to hunt on their lands. Joseph Chitty, *Observations on the Game Laws, in* 9 THE PAMPHLETEER 171, 181, 184 (London, 1817).

(ii) FURTHER LIMITS ON LANDOWNER RIGHTS: VARMINTS

Geush v. Mynns

Kings Bench.
Cro. Jac. 321, 79 Eng. Rep. 274 (1614).

Trespass *quare vi et armis clausum fregit, & c.* The defendant justified upon the report that a vermin called a badger was found there *ad damnum inhabitantium;* by reason whereof he uncoupled his hounds in the place where, and hunted there, and found the badger, and chased him until he earthed him in the place where, and thereupon digged the ground and took the badger and killed him; that afterwards he stopped up the earth again, . . . and demands judgment.—Whereupon the plaintiff demurred.

The Court held, that the action well lay: for although the common law warrants the hunting of such ravenous beasts of prey in another man's land, because the destroying of such creatures is profitable for the public, yet the law requires that such things should be done in an ordinary and usual manner: and this is confirmed and explained by the statute of 8 Eliz. c. 15; for although the statute gives reward for killing of vermin, yet it saith it must be with consent, and with reasonable engines and devices; therefore there being an ordinary course, viz. hunting to kill the badger, the digging for him was unlawful.

NOTES

(1) Varmints and the limits of property in land: What does the decision in *Geush* suggest about the inviolability of property in land— particularly the right to exclude? An alternative report of the case records the following comment by one of the justices: "the digging here in this, or the like case may be lawful, if it be in pursuit of such a vermin, lawfully begun, and so doth earth him in another man's ground, as here it was, in the plaintiff's ground, he may well justify the digging him out (if by no other means he could come to take him) and this ought to have been shewed in pleading . . . for he might have got him out either by smoking him out, or by using of tarriers . . . and so as the case here is, the justification is not good." *Gedge v. Minne,* 2 Buls. 60, 62, 80 Eng. Rep. 958, 960 (K.B. 1614). What is the justification for permitting such trespasses— whether or not any digging is involved? Should the public good always trump property?

(2) Does the decision in *Geush* change your understanding of *Pierson v. Post* with its emphasis on foxes as "noxious beasts"?

Does *Geush* also suggest why fox hunting might have become such an important class ritual for the newly landed gentry in England? Note that there is no suggestion that a person must meet a wealth requirement to hunt such varmints—since they are not "game"—or that property boundaries are of much concern.

(3) Evolution of the law of trespass and varmints: The English law has gradually become more restrictive as concern for property in land has risen. *Gundry v. Feltham* was a trespass action "for breaking and entering the plaintiff's closes, with horses, dogs, & c. and for beating and hunting for game therein, and for breaking down, trampling down, and destroying the hedges of the plaintiff." Defendant justified his actions as "the only way and means" of hunting fox and claimed that the did "as little damage to ... plaintiff as he ... possibly could." The court granted judgment for defendant on the ground that plaintiff's pleadings admitted the truth of defendant's assertion that this was the only way to kill the fox. Chief Justice Mansfield summarily stated that "it is settled that a man may follow a fox into the grounds of another." Justice Buller, concurring in the decision, elaborated: "The demurrer admits ... that this was the only means of killing the fox. This case does not determine that a person may unnecessarily trample down another person's hedges, or maliciously ride over his grounds: if he do more than is absolutely necessary, he cannot justify it." *Gundry v. Feltham*, 1 T.R. 334, 337–38, 99 Eng. Rep. 1125, 1127 (K.B. 1786).

A century later in *Paul v. Summerhayes*, a landowner sought to prevent defendant from entering his land in pursuit of a fox. Chief Justice Coleridge for the Queen's Bench Division sided with the landowner:

> The sport of foxhunting must be carried on in subordination to the ordinary rights of property.... There is no principle of law that justifies trespassing over the lands of others for the purpose of fox-hunting. The case of *Gundry v. Feltham* is distinguishable from the present case, and can be supported, if it is to be supported at all, only on the grounds [that t]he demurrer admitted that what was done was the only means for destroying the fox.... [W]here any other object was involved than that of the destruction of a noxious animal, an entry on the land of another, against his will, could not be justified.

Paul v. Summerhayes, [1878] 4 Q.B.D. 9, 10–11.

(iii) PROTECTING WILDLIFE ON PRIVATE LANDS

Keeble v. Hickeringill

Queen's Bench.
11 East 574, 103 Eng. Rep. 1127 (1707).

Action upon the case. Plaintiff declares that he was, 8th November in the second year of the queen, lawfully possessed of a close land called Minott's Meadow, *et de quodam vivario, vocato* a decoy pond, to which divers wildfowl used to resort and come: and the plaintiff had at his own costs and charges prepared and procured divers decoy ducks, nets, machines, and other engines for the decoying and taking of the wildfowl, and enjoyed the benefit in taking them: the defendant, knowing which, and intending to damnify the plaintiff in his vivary, and to fright and drive away the wildfowl used to resort thither, and deprive him of his profit, did, on the 8th of November, resort to the head of the said pond and vivary, and did discharge six guns laden with gunpowder, and with the noise and stink of the gunpowder did drive away the wildfowl then being in the pond: and on the 11th and 12th days of November the defendant, with design to damnify the plaintiff and fright away the wildfowl, did place himself with gun near the vivary, and there did discharge the said gun several times that was then charged with the gunpowder against the said decoy pond, whereby the wildfowl was frighted away, and did forsake the said pond. Upon not guilty pleaded a verdict was found for the plaintiff and 20 damages.

■ HOLT, C.J.:—I am of opinion that this action doth lie. It seems to be new in its instance, but not new in the reason or principle of it. For 1st, this using or making a decoy is lawful. 2dly, this employment of his ground to that use is profitable to the plaintiff, as is the skill and management of that employment. As to the first, every man that hath a property may employ it for his pleasure and profit, as for alluring and procuring decoy ducks to come to his pond. To learn the trade of seducing other ducks to come here in order to be taken is not prohibited either by the law of the land or the moral law; but it is as lawful to use art to seduce them, to catch them, and destroy them for the use of mankind, as to kill and destroy wildfowl or tame cattle. Then when a man useth his art or his skill to take them, to sell and dispose of for his profit; this is his trade; and he that hinders another in his trade or livelihood is liable to an action for so hindering him.... [W]here a violent or malicious act is done to a man's occupation, profession, or way of getting a livelihood; there an action lies in all cases. But if a man doth him damage by using the same employment; as if Mr. Hickeringill had set up another decoy on his own ground near the plaintiff's, and that had spoiled the custom of the plaintiff, no action would lie because he had as much liberty to make and use a decoy as the plaintiff. This is like the case of 11 H. 4, 47. One schoolmaster sets up a new school to the damage of an antient school, and thereby the scholars are allured from the old school to come to his new. (The action there was held not to lie.) But suppose Mr. Hickeringill should lie in the way with his guns, and fright the boys from going to school, and their parents would let them go thither; sure that schoolmaster might have an action for the loss of his scholars. [ ] A man hath a market, to which he hath toll for horses sold: a man is bringing his horses to market to sell; a stranger hinders and obstructs him from going thither to the market; an action lies because it imports damage.... Now considering the nature of the case, it is not possible to declare of the number [of birds], that were frighted away; because the plaintiff had not possession of them, to count them. Where a man brings trespass for taking his goods, he must declare of the quantity, because he, by having had the possession, may know what he had, and therefore must know what he lost.... And when we do know that of long time in the kingdom these artificial contrivances of decoy ponds and decoy ducks have been used for enticing into those ponds wildfowl, in order to be taken for the profit of the owner of the pond, who is at the expense of servants, engines, and other management, whereby the markets of the nation may be furnished; there is great reason to give encouragement thereunto; that the people who are so instrumental by their skill and industry so to furnish the markets should reap the benefit and have their action. But in short, that which is the true reason, is, that this action is not brought to recover damage for the loss of the fowl, but for the disturbance. [ ] So is the usual and common way of declaring.

NOTES

(1) *Keeble* again raises the fundamental question of the relationship between ownership of land and rights in wildlife: what rights does a landowner have in relation to wild animals whose presence on her land is beneficial? Under the common law's property system as outlined in *The Case of Swans*, Samuel Keeble had no property in the ducks that defendant scared away since they were *feræ naturæ*, could and did fly away (and thus were not property *ratione impotentiæ et loci*), and had not been captured (and thus were not property *per industriam*). The problem thus was: How could plaintiff sue in the absence of some interest in the ducks?

(2) Fair competition in the race to capture: *Keeble* is also one of the classic cases of the English common law, important not just for wildlife law or property law but also for the entire field of fair versus unfair business competition. The court construed the plaintiff's claim to be that he was engaged in a lawful enterprise and, while so engaged, was maliciously disrupted by the defendant. Not only did the plaintiff have no property in the ducks, there also had been no trespass or physical damage to plaintiff's land. Thus for the court it was the fact that operating the decoy pond was Keeble's trade that gave him standing to sue despite the lack of entry onto his property and the fact that the ducks were not his. The essence of the wrong was depriving Keeble of the chance to capture the ducks with the intent merely of disrupting his efforts. Note the court's analogy to private schools: a defendant can set up a competing school and lure students away, but cannot scare students away from the plaintiff's school by lying in wait with his guns. The case thus raises a fundamental issue: to what extent should motive enter into the law? If the Reverend Edmund Hickeringill had discharged his guns while shooting at ducks, Samuel Keeble would have had no cognizable claim—why should the fact that the Reverend was motivated by malice make any difference?

Compare the outcome in *Keeble* with the classic capture case, *Pierson v. Post.* Could the theory of *Keeble* have been put to use on the facts of the *Pierson* case? Consider also the relevance of *Keeble* to the hunter harassment statute examined in Chapter 2.

PERSPECTIVES

(1) Duck decoys: As is apparent upon more than a cursory reading of the case, the "decoys" involved in *Keeble v. Hickeringill* were not the life-sized models that presently are known by the term. Rather, the decoys were traps that employed large ponds, radiating curved channels covered with nets, and dogs or tame ducks to lure the wild ducks to their destruction. The technology and art of decoying are discussed in detail in RALPH WILLIAM FRANKLAND PAYNE-GALLWEY, THE BOOK OF DUCK DECOYS: THEIR CONSTRUCTION, MANAGEMENT AND HISTORY (1886).

(2) The English background, in sum: What, then, was the English legal heritage that colonists brought with them when they journeyed to North America? What was the common-law understanding about the rights that landowners possessed vis-a-vis wildlife? Do the following basic points fairly cover the complex English story?

(a) Wildlife was owned by the King/state in a prerogative or sovereign sense (and, in the case of royal animals, in a proprietary sense as well). This ownership right was more than simply a power to regulate private activities by landowners and hunters. When the creators of English law—be it King, Parliament, or court—decided who could hunt and where, they were making a positive allocation of public property rather than simply regulating private conduct.

The state also held the power to protect wildlife, both by banning or limiting takes and by restricting habitat alteration. Though English courts did not use the term "easement" to describe the arrangement, the state as owner of wildlife in effect held an easement on lands used by wildlife since it held a power to prevent the landowner from interfering with its rights in the wildlife.[1] The scope of the easement—and the powers and duties it included—were far from clear.

(b) Landowners also had no right to hunt that they could assert against the state. Although landowners were normally permitted to take animals other than game—particularly those that caused harm—there is no evidence that they held protected rights to do so.

In addition, landowners were obligated to bear the costs of having wildlife on their lands. Protected wildlife was able not only to cross private land but also to live on it. Furthermore, the state had the power to require landowners to protect wildlife habitat as a means of sustaining game populations.

(c) Although it was generally acknowledged that the King had the power to authorize landowners to hunt on their holdings, the state's power to authorize one person to hunt on the lands of another was unclear. Initially, the King held the prerogative power to create forests and to permit others to hunt in them; the King also had the power to grant chases in the lands of other; there seems to have been no power—or the power

---

1. Technically, the interest is a special form of an easement known as a *profit a prendre*. A profit is "the right to take something which is the produce of the land." It includes the right to use lands to hunt and fish and the collateral power to prevent the owner of the land from taking actions that unreasonably interfere with the right. Unlike other easements, it may be held in gross, *i.e.*, not as an interest appurtenant to a dominant estate. When it is held in gross, it is techni-cally not an easement but rather an interest in the land itself. Hunting and fishing rights are traditional profits. *E.g., Figliuzzi v. Carcajou Shooting Club of Lake Koshkonong*, 516 N.W.2d 410 (Wis.1994) (enjoining a four-building, 26–unit condominium complex for constituting an unreasonable interference with a hunting and fishing profit a prendre possessed by 19 members of a hunting club). Profits are discussed in more detail below.

went unexercised—to grant warrens in another's land. These powers were resisted by land holders and had been curtailed if not abolished by the time of the American Revolution.

(d) By the time of the American Revolution the power to grant hunting franchises had fallen into desuetude as the landed gentry increasingly turned to the more flexible writ of trespass and to Parliament to define rights in wildlife on their lands. Thus, although they did not own any wildlife until lawful capture took place, they were able to exclude others from hunting on their lands—with the exception of persons pursuing varmints. Finally, landowners could seek redress against persons who engaged in nuisances that disrupted their lawful attempts to attract and capture wildlife.

b. PRIVATE LAND AND WILDLIFE IN THE NEW WORLD

(i) PROPERTY IN LAND AND WILDLIFE: THE ROLE OF THE SOVEREIGN

Cawsey v. Brickey

Supreme Court of Washington.
144 P. 938 (1914).

■ ELLIS, J.:—Action to enjoin the enforcement of an order creating a game preserve in Skagit county. The plaintiffs constitute a gun club, and have leased for a term of years certain lands as a shooting preserve, including lands of the interveners, and have for a long time maintained thereon a gun club, and have expended considerable sums in equipment. The defendants are the sheriff, prosecuting attorney, game warden, and the three members of the game commission, of Skagit county, appointed under the Game Code. [ ] Acting under section 4 of that law, the game commission selected certain lands as a game preserve, including the lands covered by the plaintiffs' lease as well as those owned by the interveners. The injunction was denied. The plaintiffs and interveners have appealed.

The appellants attack the law of 1913, and particularly subdivision 7, of section 4, claiming that it is unconstitutional [because it] deprives the appellants of valuable property rights and privileges without due process of law, bears unequally on different persons and communities, and is class legislation. . . .

Subdivision 7, section 4, of the act reads as follows:

The county game commission in their respective counties shall have the power and authority by giving notice thereof by publication for three successive weeks in a newspaper published at the county seat of such county describing such lands to be set aside as a game preserve, to set aside certain parts or portions of their respective counties as game preserves wherein no game bird or game animal or game fish can be caught or killed within the boundaries thereof, for such time and so long as they may see fit and proper: Providing, however, that no game preserve or preserves so set aside by said county game commission shall consist of more than three (3) townships in any one county. Laws of 1913, page 359.

Do these provisions tend to deprive any one of property rights or vested privileges? We think not. Under the common law of England all property right in animals *feræ naturæ* was in the sovereign for the use and benefit of the people. The killing, taking, and use of game was subject to absolute governmental control for the common good. This absolute power to control and regulate was vested in the colonial governments as a part of the common law. It passed with the title to game to the several states as an incident of their sovereignty, and was retained by the states for the use and benefit of the people of the states, subject only to any applicable provisions of the federal Constitution. *Geer v. Connecticut,* 161 U.S. 519, 527, 528 (1896); *Harper v. Galloway,* 51 So. 226, 228 (Fla.1910); *State v. Snowman,* 46 A. 815 (Me.1900); *Smith v. State,* 58 N.E. 1044 (Ind.1900); *Ex parte Maier,* 37 P. 402 (Cal.1894); *Magner v. People,* 97 Ill. 320 (1881); *State v. Hume,* 95 P. 808 (Or.1908); *Sherwood v. Stephens,* 90 P. 345 (Idaho 1907); *Hornbeke v. White,* 76 P. 926 (Colo. App. 1904); FREUND, POLICE POWER § 418. There is no private right in the citizen to take fish or game, except as either expressly given or inferentially suffered by the state. *State v. Tice,* 125 P. 168 (Wash.1912). Section 21 of the Game Code provides:

> No person shall at any time or in any manner acquire any property in, or subject to his dominion or control, any of the game birds, game animals, or game fish, or any parts thereof, of the game birds, game animals or game fish herein mentioned, but they shall always and under all circumstances be and remain the property of the state. Laws of 1913, p. 365.

This is but declaratory of the common law. Whatever special or qualified rights or, more correctly speaking, privileges, a landowner may have as to game, while it is on his own land, though protected by the laws of trespass as against other persons, have no protection, because they have no existence, as against the state. Since the title to game is in the state for the common good, the state's right to control, regulate, or prohibit the taking of game wheresoever found and on whosesoever land is an inherent incident of the police power of the state. TIEDEMAN'S LIMITATIONS OF POLICE POWER § 121f. It may be exercised *ad libitum* so long as the regulation or prohibition bears equally on all persons similarly situated with reference to the subject-matter and purpose to be served by the regulation. *Portland Fish Co. v. Benson,* 108 P. 122 (Or.1910).

Does the act here in question bear unequally on persons similarly situated so as to be obnoxious to the constitutional inhibition against class legislation? We think not. It is the universality of the operation of a law on all persons of the state similarly situated with reference to the subject-matter that determines its validity as a general and uniform law, not the extent of territory in which it operates. That its operation may not be at all times coextensive with the territorial limits of the state is usually an immaterial circumstance. [ ] The owner of land which from its location and character is peculiarly suited for a game preserve is not situated similarly to other landowners with reference to the subject-matter and purpose of a law creating a preserve. The subject-matter and purpose is protection and preservation of game. It is so declared in the title of the act. One whose land is thus peculiarly suited to meet those purposes obviously occupies a different relation to the purpose of the law from that occupied by one whose land is not so suited. When, therefore, the state authorizes the setting apart of his land for a game preserve and deprives him and all others of the privilege of taking game thereon, the law operates equally on all persons similarly situated, and is a proper exercise of the police power.

In this phase the case here is not distinguishable from *Hayes v. Territory,* 5 P. 927 (Wash.Terr.1884), where a territorial law restricted hunting in only five counties. Obviously owners of land in those counties were subjected to restricted hunting on their own land, while owners of land in other counties could hunt on their own land without restriction. The law was assailed as invalid on the ground that it granted special privileges. The Territorial Supreme Court, through Greene, C.J., tersely and soundly disposed of the question as follows:

> The game law in question restricted hunting in five counties only. It is contended that, for this reason, it is inconsistent with that inhibition in the Organic Act, which forbids the Legislature from granting special privileges. But the provisions of this game law fall without distinction upon all inhabitants of the territory. All are forbidden to hunt at certain seasons within the counties named. There is no special privilege, unless it be in favor of the brute life of the specified area, or those of human kind who are so happy as to be alive at the hunting season.

In both the *Hayes Case* and this case the circumscribed geographical operation of the law makes the difference in the relation of those owning land within and those owning land without the circumscribed area. Barring this difference, the law is absolutely uniform in its operation on all persons. No one can hunt or take game or fish within that area.

The case of *Harper v. Galloway,* 51 So. 226 (Fla.1910), which is more nearly apposite than any other case cited by appellants is not a parallel to the case here. It presents the antithesis of this and the case of *Hayes v. Territory.* The law of the state of Florida there involved regulated the taking of game in a single county. It required residents of the state, but not of that county, to give three days' notice to the game warden and pay a special license tax in order to be permitted to hunt in that county. Neither notice nor license tax was required of residents of that county. Obviously, since the game of the state belongs to the state for the benefit of all the people of the state, the requirement of a notice and license tax from other citizens, but not from residents of the county, was an unreasonable and unjust discrimination. It imposed a burden upon some of the residents of the state, not put upon other residents of the state with reference to the subject regulated, though all stood in the same relation to the subject regulated, barring the immaterial incident of geographical location. The court clearly recognized that fact as the basis of its decision. We hold that the section complained of deprives the appellants of no property right, bears equally upon all persons similarly situated, and is not void as class legislation.

Alford v. Finch

Florida Supreme Court.
155 So.2d 790 (1963).

■ CALDWELL, J.:—[The Game and Freshwater Fish Commission (defendant) entered into an agreement with a group of landowners to open their land to the public for hunting. In exchange, the Commission agreed to close other lands to all hunting "as a breeding ground." Plaintiff owned some 700 acres of land that was included within the closed hunting area. Defendant did not consult with plaintiff prior to closing his land to hunting.]

This cause necessitates the determination of whether, under Sec. 30 Art. IV, of the Florida Constitution,[1] the Commission has the power to close to hunting for a period of years, without consent or compensation, the private property of one owner, leaving unaffected in the same vicinity the private property of others. The Court can take judicial notice of the fact that vast acreages are maintained in Florida by owners for the principal, if not the sole, purpose of preserving, protecting and shooting game thereon.

The exclusive common law right of a landowner to take game on his land, known as property *ratione soli,* was defined by Lord Westberry in an early English case[3] as "the common law right which every owner of land has to kill and take such animals feræ naturæ as may from time to time be found on his land." This right has been recognized throughout the history of common law, with one exception: Following the Norman Conquest the King contended that he was lord paramount of the field, possessed of the right to the universal soil and of the exclusive right to take the game, but the irate landowners, vehemently objecting, quickly and decisively recaptured their rights and re-established the common law.[4]

American cases are in harmony with the common law rule. In *Hanson v. Fergus Falls National Bank & Trust Co.,* [65 N.W.2d 857, 863 (Minn. 1954)], the Minnesota court said:

> Summarized, the right of hunting on premises is an incorporeal right growing out of the soil, referred to in law as a profit *a prendre,* and may be segregated from the fee of the land and conveyed in gross to

1. *Fla. Const.*, Art. IV, § 30: powers, duties, etc.

(1) From and after January 1, 1943, the management, restoration, conservation, and regulation, of the birds, game, fur-bearing animals, and fresh-water fish, of the State of Florida, and the acquisition, establishment, control, and management, of hatcheries, sanctuaries, refuges, reservations, and all other property now or hereafter owned or used for such purposes by the State of Florida, shall be vested in a Commission to be known as the Game and Fresh Water Fish Commission.* * *

　　　* * *

(4) Among the powers granted by the Commission by this section shall be the power to fix bag limits and to fix open and closed seasons, on a statewide, regional or local basis, as it may find to be appropriate, and to regulate the manner and method of taking, transporting, storing and using birds, game, fur-bearing animals, fresh-water fish, reptiles, and amphibians. The Commission shall also have the power to acquire by purchase, gift, all property necessary, useful, or convenient, for the use of the Commission in the exercise of its powers hereunder.

3. *Blades v. Hicks*, 11 H.L. Cas. 621, 630 (1865).

4. 2 WILLIAM BLACKSTONE, COMMENTARIES ON THE LAWS OF ENGLAND *415.

one having no interest or ownership in the fee, and when so conveyed it is assignable and inheritable.

In *Hamilton v. Williams,* [200 So. 80, 81 (Fla.1941)] this Court said:

Wild game is vested in the State as trustee for all its citizens with full power and authority in the State to regulate and protect.* * *

The owner of the soil, however, has special and qualified interest in the wild game while it is thereon. Such special and qualified interest *is a property right incident to his ownership of the soil. That property right is the right to exclusively hunt such wild game upon the soil, subject to any lawful regulation by the State.* * *

While it is true this court held as contended by petitioner in the case of *State [ex rel. Spencer] v. Bryan,* 99 So. 327, 329 (Fla.1924), "The power and discretion of the Legislature to control * * * the subject of hunting game is not limited by the organic law, and the subject regulated may be as restricted in the manner and extent as the Legislature deems advisable," nevertheless *such holding in no sense of the word meant that the Legislature or any citizen could deprive another citizen of a vested property right such as defined above except by due process of law.*

(Emphasis added)

In a later case, this Court said the Legislature could provide by law for the conservation of game, "where such laws do not deny to any one having rights in the premises the due process of law or the equal protection of the laws that are guaranteed to all persons by the state and federal Constitutions."

The [defendant] has confused the ownership of the game in its wild state with the ownership of the right to pursue the game. The landowner is not the owner of the game, feræ naturæ, but he does own, as private property, the right to pursue game upon his own lands. That right is property, just as are the trees on the land and the ore in the ground, and is subject to lease, purchase and sale in like manner. The right to hunt on another's premises, the right of venery, is an interest in real estate in the nature of an incorporeal hereditament and as such is within the statute of frauds and requires a writing for its creation.

The predominant feature in the instant case is the taking, with neither consent nor compensation, by the [defendant] from the [plaintiffs], of a property right—the right to pursue the game on their land. It is our view that the Commission is empowered to regulate the taking of game and to acquire property, by purchase and gift, for its use but that under the authority delineated in the Constitution, it is not, under the guise of regulation or otherwise, empowered to take private property for public purpose without just compensation. There is no Florida precedent for a contrary view and such federal precedent as there may be is less than persuasive. We are not yet ready in this State to embrace the "managed economy" theory of government.

. . .

We find: (1) That the [plaintiffs] were the owners of a property right, an incorporeal hereditament which runs with the fee, to take the game on their lands under valid regulation, (2) That the [defendant] took the private property of the [plaintiffs] without just compensation, (3) That such taking cannot be justified under any theory, inherent power, *damnum absque injuria* or otherwise and (4) That [defendant] has no constitutional authority, express or otherwise, to exercise the police power to classify private property as a refuge without compensation to the owner.

Affirmed.

■ ROBERTS, C.J., and THOMAS and THORNAL, JJ., concur.

■ DREW, J. (dissenting):—. . . . The court below, in the course of its comprehensive decree in this cause, noted the express authority of the Commission under Art. IV, Sec. 30(4), Fla. Const., to "fix * * * closed seasons * * * on a * * * local basis," and recognized the "sound propagation, management, and conservation technique" evident in the order creating this refuge by maintaining closure in the subject area. It concluded, however, that the acknowledged public purpose and benefit did not warrant extinguishing appellees' hunting rights on their lands, and that such action constituted a taking of private property without compensation, a deprivation of property without due process, and denial of equal protection of the laws, contrary to Sec. 29, Art. XVI, and Sec. 1, 4 and 12, Decl. Rights, Fla. Const. and Amend. XIV, U.S. Const.

Considerable reliance, in support of this conclusion, is placed upon the statement in *Hamilton v. Williams*, 200 So. 80, 81 (Fla.1941):

> The owner of the soil, however, has a special and qualified interest in the wild game while it is thereon. Such special and qualified interest is a property right incident to his ownership of the soil. That property right is the right to exclusively hunt such wild game upon the soil, subject to any lawful regulation by the State. *L. Realty Co. v. Johnson,* 100 N.W. 94 (Minn.1904); *State v. Mallory,* 83 S.W. 955 (Ark.1904); *Schulte v. Warren,* 75 N.E. 783 (Ill.1905); *Lamprey v. Danz,* 90 N.W. 578 (Minn.1902).

The decision in that case was simply that the purchase of a hunting license does not authorize entry upon private lands to take game, such rights being exclusively in the owner. The purpose of the adjudication was, therefore, to determine the limited rights vested by a hunting license, rather than to define the nature of an owner's interest in wild game on his land except as a right to have exclusive access and to prevent access of others by trespass.[2] Neither this nor later cases can be regarded as authority for the existence of individual property interests of any description in game while it is still in the wild state, or for the limitation imposed below upon the well established sovereign trust title and right of control over the taking of wild game upon private lands in this State.

The contention is that decisions elsewhere sustaining sovereign authority in these circumstances are distinguishable because of the unique

---

2. The cases cited relate in the main to determination of rights between owners and third party individuals and not to state control of an owner's alleged rights in game.

character of the area involved and its particular relationship to the conservation program.[3] I believe, however, that such factors go only to the issue of the necessity for the regulation or its reasonable relationship to the preservation of public interests, and that so long as the designation of the area in question is in fact necessary to accomplish the Commission's lawful objectives, it may be sustained whether or not another area would serve as well. Inherent in any exercise of the power to establish closed seasons on a local basis, Art. IV, Sec. 30, *supra*, is a difference or 'inequality' of law, but this is an inequality between hunters as opposed to owners in one area and those in another. I conclude that the right regulated is one which, except for the law of trespass, may in any given locality be exercised in the same manner by all individuals, or which may in any given area be denied to all, including owners, so long as the prohibition is shown to be genuinely in the public interest.

In the instant case, the choice of appellees' property as a part of the refuge is not shown to have been made on any improper basis, and I think the record evidence is conclusive that the action of the Commission was within its constitutional powers. The appellees, by inclusion of their lands within the refuge, have not suffered the loss or invasion of private property rights cognizable at law, nor have they demonstrated on any objective standard that the regulation deprives them of the only use to which their lands are reasonably susceptible. They benefit, potentially at least, equally with members of the public at large in improved hunting conditions in the surrounding areas covered by the lease agreements above described.

The independent provisions in our laws for the acquisition by the Commission of title to lands for conservation purposes do not in may opinion foreclose the creation of a refuge area by maintaining hunting prohibitions within a specified locality in those instances when the public interests require only the regulation or prohibition of the taking of game therein without the exercise of proprietary control by the Commission....

With profound respect for the views of my colleagues, I must say that in my humble judgment the majority opinion emasculates the Commission in one of its most significant functions, the effective preservation of a vital but ever diminishing part of the public domain—its wildlife.

I would accordingly reverse the decision of the chancellor and remand the cause for the entry of a decree denying injunctive relief.

■ TERRELL and O'CONNELL, JJ., concur.

NOTES

(1) Ratione loci/soli: *Cawsey* presents the dominant American view: hunting even on one's own land is a privilege—which the state can extend or withhold at will—rather than a right. *E.g., State v. Herwig,* 117 N.W.2d 335, 337–38 (Wis.1962) ("It is ... well settled that hunting is a privilege as

---

3. *Lansden v. Hart,* 180 F.2d 679 (7th Cir.1950). *See also Platt v. Philbrick,* 47 P.2d 302 (Cal.App.1935); *State v. McKinnon,* 133 A.2d 885 (Me.1957); *Bauer v. State Game Comm.,* 293 N.W. 282 (Neb.1940); *Maitland v. People,* 23 P.2d 116 (Colo.1933); *Cook v. State,* 74 P.2d 199 (Wash.1937).

against the state (commonly called hunting rights in reference to land), which the state can grant, deny, or regulate."). According to these decisions, a landowner has a right to hunt only in relation to other individuals, not against the state. Thus, when a landowner transfers hunting rights to another person the rights transferred include only rights to enter the land and to enjoy protection against other private persons, not rights as against the state. Is this approach simply an application of the basic principles of English law, set forth above? Do the forest laws and qualification statutes of England provide direct precedents? Does it make sense to say that a landowner has protected rights against other private parties but not against the state? Does it make a difference in what capacity the state withdraws or limits the right to hunt? Would a state agency be liable for damages if its employees engaged in the conduct described in *Keeble*? If they trespassed upon the land, causing injury to wildlife located there?

In *Collopy v. Wildlife Commission*, the Colorado Supreme Court upheld a regulatory ban on hunting, similar to that in *Cawsey*, that established a 4–square mile preserve for wildlife. In doing so, the court expressly rejected the landowner's claim that he possessed a property right to hunt on his land:

> [R]elying on *Alford v. Finch*, 155 So.2d 790 (Fla.1963) and *Allen v. McClellan*, 405 P.2d 405 (N.M.1965), Collopy argues that state ownership of wild game does not extinguish a landowner's independent common law property right to hunt such game upon his own land. Although the state may, if reasonably necessary, regulate public hunting of state-owned game by establishing closed seasons in specific localities, see section 33–1–110(1)(a), Collopy contends that its power to enforce closure regulations against private landowners is circumscribed by the constitutional prohibition against taking private property here property ratione soli without just compensation.

> This constitutional claim is cognizable only if it is first acknowledged that a landowner's right to hunt on his own land is a "property right" under state law. We here decide that the right to hunt wild game upon one's own land is not a property right enforceable against the state under Art. II, Sec. 15 of the Colorado Constitution.[13]

> Although the issue now before us was not unequivocally decided in *Maitland v. People*, [23 P.2d 116 (Colo.1933)], this court there stated:

>> The right to kill game is a boon or privilege granted either expressly or impliedly, by the sovereign authority and *is not a right inhering in any individual.*

---

13. We note in passing that the Commission regulation does not wholly proscribe hunting on the Collopy farm; only goose hunting is prohibited. Thus, even if this state classified property *ratione soli* as a property right, it is questionable whether a ban on taking a single species would so substantially impair that right as to constitute a compensable taking. Cf. *Alford v. Finch, supra,* *Allen v. McClennan, supra.* Moreover, because a landowner's property *ratione soli* is subject to "lawful regulation," *Alford v. Finch, supra,* a closure affecting only a single species could well be deemed a reasonable police power regulation of a landowner's right to hunt on his land rather than a constitutionally impermissible appropriation of that right.

23 P.2d at 117 (emphasis added). Because *Maitland,* like the present case, dealt with a claim that the state had unconstitutionally taken a landowner's crops by forbidding him to kill game on his ranch, its characterization of the right to hunt game as a "boon or privilege" rather than an individual right suggests that this court has not heretofore classified property *ratione soli* as a distinct property right accompanying land ownership. *See also Game and Fish Commission v. Feast,* 402 P.2d 169 (Colo.1965).

Moreover, *Maitland's* characterization of the right to hunt as a privilege against the state rather than a property right comports with decisions in other jurisdictions which have rejected the argument that landowners enjoy a property right to take game on their own soil. See *Lansden v. Hart,* 180 F.2d 679 (7th Cir.1950); *Bishop v. United States,* 126 F.Supp. 449, 449 (Ct.Cl.1954) ("plaintiff's allegation ... that the right to hunt geese is a property right cannot be taken seriously in view of the Supreme Court's opinion in *Geer v. Connecticut,* 161 U.S. 519. . . . No citizen has a right to hunt wild game except as permitted by the state."); *State v. Herwig,* 117 N.W.2d 335, 337–38 (Wis.1962) ("Hunting is a privilege against the state (commonly called hunting rights in reference to land) which the state can grant, deny or regulate a privilege of reducing wild life, which the hunter did not own, to possession and to ownership by a means and at a time and place which are lawful."); *State v. McKinnon,* 133 A.2d 885 (Me.1957); *Holbrook Island Sanctuary v. Inhabitants of Town of Brooksville,* 214 A.2d 660 (Me.1965) (*dictum*); *Bauer v. Game, Forest Station and Parks Commission,* 293 N.W. 282 (Neb.1940); *but see Alford v. Finch, supra; Allen v. McClellan, supra.*

Collopy v. Wildlife Commission, 625 P.2d 994, 999–1000 (Colo.1981).

(2) *Alford* **and the right to hunt:** *Alford* is the leading—indeed, nearly the sole—case to adopt the view that a landowner, at least under some circumstances, might have a right to hunt enforceable against state regulatory agencies. *Alford* was followed in *Allen v. McClellan,* 405 P.2d 405 (N.M.1965), in which the court construed a state statute to deny a state agency the power to designate private land as a game preserve, thereby avoiding alleged takings of private property rights.

What was the actual holding in *Alford*? Is it possible to reconcile the decision with the other rulings given the facts of the case? Note that, in *Alford,* the court was concerned about the seemingly unequal treatment of similarly situated, nearby landowners. In the view of the trial court, the state agency failed to offer a "just basis" for distinguishing among the landowners. Would the court have reached the same decisions if the ban on hunting had been uniformly applied to all lands? if the game at issue was scarce and therefore in need of broad protection?

Note also how the court in *Alford* summarizes the English common-law. Is this an apt recitation of that complex history? It is worth noting that all of the citations offered by the court, including *Blades v. Hicks,* dealt with the rights of landowners in relation to other private parties, either trespassers or transferees of hunting easements, and that none considered the rights of landowners as against the state. Still, poor history (or, perhaps, poor history in particular) has a way of taking on life, as the following excerpt illustrates:

> At common law, a landowner traditionally had the right to hunt wild animals on his or her land. In fact, the commitment to this property right was so ingrained at common law that when the King, following the Norman Conquest, attempted to limit this right, the landowners, "vehemently objecting, quickly and decisively recaptured their rights and re-established the common law." *Alford v. Finch,* 155 So.2d 790, 792 (Fla.1963) (citing 2 *Blackstone, Commentaries* *415).

Clajon Production Corp. v. Petera, 70 F.3d 1566, 1575 (10th Cir.1995).

(3) *Clajon Production Corp. v. Petera:* Private landowners challenged—on a variety of constitutional grounds—the state's claim to ownership of wildlife located on private land. Before the trial court, plaintiffs alleged "that by virtue of the common law property doctrines of property *ratione soli,* profit a prendre and the right of venery, they own the exclusive right to hunt the wild animals that are present on their property." Because of that ownership, they contended, the state's entire wildlife regulatory system was invalid as applied to private land. The trial court rejected the claims based on federal constitutional law; it did not reach what rights landowners had to wildlife as a matter of state property law. *Clajon Production Corp. v. Petera,* 854 F.Supp. 843 (D.Wyo.1994). On appeal, plaintiffs dropped their novel claim that the state's mere assertion of ownership of wildlife violated their property rights. Instead, they argued that the state's regulatory system interfered with their property right "to hunt the 'harvestable surplus' from their land—*i.e.,* the excess animals available for hunting which were produced on their land." The appellate court rejected plaintiffs' constitutional argument without resolving the underlying state law question. Although the plaintiffs raised "an unclear and difficult issue" under state property law, the court held that they suffered no constitutional deprivation even if they possessed the property rights that they claimed. *Clajon Production Corp. v. Petera,* 70 F.3d 1566, 1575–76 (10th Cir.1995).

(4) *Schultz v. Morgan Sash & Door Co.:* Plaintiff corporation purchased deer from a zoo and enclosed them on its 160 acre parcel of land behind a "six foot fence ... with several strands of barbed wire on top." The deer were fed from a barn, sometimes by hand, and were petted and played with by corporate employees and visitors. The enclosed land also included buffalo, peacocks, and ducks all kept for "recreation, enjoyment and amusement." After 10 years, the deer population increased to 55 or 60, including some 40 bucks. Desirous of reducing the herd, plaintiff placed an advertisement in the Daily Oklahoman:

> "White deer. Season is open. Shoot your buck. $50.00 each. They are fat. Morgan Deer Farm, two miles east of Norman, Highway 9. Start shooting Saturday morning. Lasts one week."

State wildlife officials sought to apply state hunting laws to the activity, but the court rejected their asserted jurisdiction. Applicable state statutes expressly excluded from their coverage domesticated animals and pets. On the facts, the court determined that the deer herd qualified as "domesticated pets," and therefore were not covered by state game laws. *Schultz v. Morgan Sash & Door Co.*, 344 P.2d 253 (Okl.1959).

(5) Owning wildlife habitat—the public easement: Note the language in *Cawsey* holding that the factual inequality of land justifies legal inequality: "The owner of land which from its location and character is peculiarly suited for a game preserve is not situated similarly to other landowners with reference to the subject-matter and purpose of a law creating a preserve." [¶ 7]

The idea that landowner rights depend in part on the land's natural features is an idea with a long history in Anglo–American law. It came under assault in the late nineteenth century when pressures to make law more scientific led to the emergence of more abstract rhetoric about ownership entitlements. Legal scholars in particular began to theorize about the bundle of rights that ownership entailed, as if ownership rights could be defined without regard for the surrounding communal context. According to one scholar, the past half century has seen a counter-movement: a shift toward ownership rights that vary, at times significantly, based on factual differences among the land parcels. *See* Eric T. Freyfogle, *Context and Accommodation in Modern Property Law*, 41 STAN. L. REV. 1529 (1989); Eric T. Freyfogle, *The Particulars of Owning*, 25 ECOLOGY L.Q. 574, 585 (1999) ("Slowly, painfully, people are coming to think that landowner rights should somehow depend on the natural features of the parcel owned.")

The decision in *United States ex rel. Bergen v. Lawrence* is an example of how rights to the use of land may vary with the character of the land. Lawrence, a cattle rancher, constructed a 28–mile fence, enclosing his private ranch land and nearly 10,000 acres of public grazing lands, to protect it against migrating pronghorn. In the harsh winter of 1983, the fence kept pronghorn from reaching their winter feeding grounds and many starved. The court ordered the fence removed as a violation of the federal Unlawful Inclosures Act, which bans the enclosure of public lands. In affirming the ruling, the federal appellate court left open the issue as to whether, aside from the federal statute, private ranchlands might be subject to an easement for migrating antelope:

> Lawrence retains the right to exclude antelope [from his private land] at this time because the district court did not find any implied easement for antelope. If Lawrence attempts such an exclusion, an action might be brought claiming such an easement or servitude. At that time, the question would be proper for judicial consideration.

United States ex rel. Bergen v. Lawrence, 848 F.2d 1502 (10th Cir.1988). *See State v. Sour Mountain Realty, Inc.*, 714 N.Y.S.2d 78 (App.Div.2000) (erection of 3500 foot long, "snake proof" fence, intended to exclude migrating timber rattlesnakes—a state-listed threatened species—is an unlawful "taking" of the snakes under state endangered species act); *Department of Community Affairs v. Moorman*, 664 So.2d 930 (Fla.1995) (prohibition on construction of fence to permit endangered species of deer to cross land freely did not violate due process or result in taking). Recall also the decision in *Just v. Marinette County*, 201 N.W.2d 761 (Wis.1972), excerpted in Chapter 1.

We will return to this issue in Chapter 14.

(ii) DEFENDING LAND AGAINST WILDLIFE

Barrett v. State

New York Court of Appeals.
116 N.E. 99 (1917).

■ ANDREWS, J.:—At one time beaver were very numerous in this state. So important were they commercially that they were represented upon the seal of the New Netherlands and upon that of the colony as well as upon the seals of New Amsterdam and of New York. Because of their value, they were relentlessly killed, and by the year 1900 they were practically exterminated. But some 15 animals were left scattered through the southern portion of Franklin county. In that year the Legislature undertook to afford them complete protection, and there has been no open season for beaver since the enactment of chapter 20 of the Laws of 1900.

In 1904 it was further provided that:

No person shall molest or disturb any wild beaver or the dams, houses, homes or abiding places of same.

[ ]

This is still the law, although in 1912 the forest, fish, and game commission was authorized to permit protected animals which had become destructive to public or private property to be taken and disposed of. [ ]

By the act of 1904, $500 was appropriated for the purchase of wild beaver to restock the Adirondacks, and in 1906 $1,000 more was appropriated for the same purpose. The commission, after purchasing the animals, was authorized to liberate them. Under this authority 21 beaver have been purchased and freed by the commission. Of these 4 were placed upon Eagle creek, an inlet of the Fourth Lake of the Fulton Chain. There they seem to have remained and increased.

Beaver are naturally destructive to certain kinds of forest trees. During the fall and winter they live upon the bark of the twigs and smaller branches of poplar, birch, and alder. To obtain a supply they fell even trees of large size, cut the smaller branches into suitable lengths, and pull or float them to their houses. All this it must be assumed was known by the Legislature as early as 1900.

The claimants own a valuable tract of woodland upon Fourth Lake bounded in the rear by Eagle creek. Their land was held by them for building sites and was suitable for that purpose. Much of its attractiveness depended upon the forest grown upon it. In this forest were a number of poplar trees. In 1912 and during two or three years prior thereto 198 of these poplars were felled by beaver. Others were girdled and destroyed. The Court of Claims has found, upon evidence that fairly justifies the inference, that this destruction was caused by the four beaver liberated on Eagle creek and their descendants, and that by reason thereof the claimants have been damaged in the sum of $1,900. An award was made to them for that sum, and this award has been affirmed by the Appellate Division. To sustain it the respondents rely upon three propositions. It is said: First, that the state may not protect such an animal as the beaver which is known to be destructive; second, that the provision of the law of 1904 with regard to the molestation of beaver prohibits the claimants from protecting their property, and is therefore an unreasonable exercise of the police power; and, third, that the state was in actual physical possession of the beaver placed on Eagle creek, and that its act in freeing them, knowing their natural propensity to destroy trees, makes the state liable for the damage done by them.

We cannot agree with either of these propositions.

As to the first, the general right of the government to protect wild animals is too well established to be now called in question. Their ownership is in the state in its sovereign capacity, for the benefit of all the people. Their preservation is a matter of public interest. They are a species of natural wealth which without special protection would be destroyed. Everywhere and at all times governments have assumed the right to prescribe how and when they may be taken or killed. As early as 1705, New York passed such an act as to deer. [ ] A series of statutes has followed protecting more or less completely game, birds, and fish.

> The protection and preservation of game has been secured by law in all civilized countries, and may be justified on many grounds.* * * The measures best adapted to this end are for the Legislature to determine, and courts cannot review its discretion. If the regulations operate, in any respect, unjustly or oppressively, the proper remedy must be applied by that body.

Phelps v. Racey, 60 N.Y. 10, 14 (1875).

Wherever protection is accorded, harm may be done to the individual. Deer or moose may browse on his crops; mink or skunks kill his chickens; robins eat his cherries. In certain cases the Legislature may be mistaken in its belief that more good than harm is occasioned. But this is clearly a matter which is confided to its discretion. It exercises a governmental function for the benefit of the public at large, and no one can complain of the incidental injuries that may result.

It is sought to draw a distinction between such animals and birds as have ordinarily received protection and beaver, on the ground that the latter are unusually destructive and that to preserve them is an unreasonable exercise of the power of the state.

The state may exercise the police power "wherever the public interests demand it, and in this particular a large discretion is necessary vested in the Legislature to determine, not only what the interest of the public require, but what measures are necessary for the protection of such interests.* * * To justify the state in thus interposing its authority in behalf of the public, it must appear, first, that the interests of the public generally, as distinguished from those of a particular class, require such interference; and, second, that the means are reasonably necessary for the accomplishment of the purpose, and not unduly oppressive upon individuals." *Lawton v. Steele,* 152 U.S. 133, 136 (1894).

The police power is not to be limited to guarding merely the physical or material interests of the citizen. His moral, intellectual, and spiritual needs may also be considered. The eagle is preserved, not for its use, but for its beauty.

The same thing may be said of the beaver. They are one of the most valuable of the fur-bearing animals of the state. They may be used for food. But apart from these considerations, their habits and customs, their curious instincts and intelligence, place them in a class by themselves. Observation of the animals at work or play is a source of never-failing interest and instruction. If they are to be preserved experience has taught us that protection is required. If they cause more damage than deer or moose, the degree of the mischief done by them is not so much greater or so different as to require the application of a special rule. If the preservation of the former does not unduly oppress individuals, neither does the latter.

In the determination of what is a reasonable exercise of the powers of the government, the acts of other governments under similar circumstances have some bearing. In Wyoming, Utah, North Dakota, Wisconsin, Maine, Colorado, and Vermont, beaver are absolutely protected. In Michigan, they are protected except between November 1st and May 15th of each year. In South Dakota, except between November 15th and April 2d. In Quebec, for a number of years there was no open season. Lately there has been an open season for a short time in the autumn.

We therefore reach the conclusion that in protecting beaver the Legislature did not exceed its powers. Nor did it so do in prohibiting their molestation. It is possible that were the interpretation given by the respondents to this section right a different result might follow. If the claimants, finding beaver destroying their property, might not drive them away, then possibly their rights would be infringed. In *Aldrich v. Wright*, 53 N.H. 398 (1873), it was said in an elaborate opinion, although this question we do not decide, that a farmer might shoot mink even in the closed season should he find them threatening his geese.

But such an interpretation is too rigid and narrow. The claimants might have fenced their land without violation of the statute. They might have driven the beaver away, were they injuring their property. The prohibition against disturbing dams or houses built on or adjoining water courses is no greater or different exercise of power from that assumed by the Legislature when it prohibits the destruction of the nests and eggs of wild birds even when the latter are found upon private property.

The object is to protect the beaver. That object as we decide is within the power of the state. The destruction of dams and houses will result in driving away the beaver. The prohibition of such acts, being an apt means to the end desired, is not so unreasonable as to be beyond the legislative power.

We hold therefore that the acts referred to are constitutional....

Somewhat different considerations apply to the act of the state in purchasing and liberating beaver. The attempt to introduce life into a new environment does not always result happily. The rabbit in Australia, the mongoose in the West Indies, have become pests. The English sparrow is no longer welcome. Certain of our most troublesome weeds are foreign flowers.

Yet governments have made such experiments in the belief that the public good would be promoted. Sometimes they have been mistaken. Again, the attempt has succeeded. The English pheasant is a valuable addition to our stock of birds. But whether a success or failure, the attempt is well within governmental powers.

If this is so with regard to foreign life, still more is it true with regard to animals native to the state, still existing here, when the intent is to increase the stock upon what the Constitution declares shall remain forever wild forest lands. If the state may provide for the increase of beaver by prohibiting their destruction, it is difficult to see why it may not attain the same result by removing colonies to a more favorable locality or by replacing those destroyed by fresh importations.

Nor are the cases cited by the respondents controlling. It is true that one who keeps wild animals in captivity must see to it at his peril that they do no damage to others. But it is not true that whenever an individual is liable for a certain act the state is liable for the same act. In liberating these beaver the state was acting as a government. As a trustee for the people and as their representative, it was doing what it thought best for the interests of the public at large. Under such circumstances, we cannot hold that the rule of such cases as those cited is applicable.

We reach the conclusion that no recovery can be had under this claim. . . .

The judgment of the Appellate Division and the determination of the Court of Claims must be reversed, and the claim dismissed, with costs in Appellate Division and in this court.

■ HISCOCK, C.J., and CHASE, HOGAN, POUND, McLAUGHLIN, and CRANE, JJ., concur.

Cross v. State

Supreme Court of Wyoming.
370 P.2d 371 (1962).

■ BLUME, J.:—This case involves the question as to whether or not a man may protect his property against depredation by protected game animals.

Albert "Ab" Cross was charged on six counts for shooting two moose . . . in violation of the laws of the State of Wyoming. . . .

. . . Cross admitted the killing of the moose in question, admitted they were killed out of season and at a time when the defendant did not possess a proper license or permit, and admitted to all facts set forth in the complaint of the state, upon which the defendant was tried on appeal. Defendant, however, asserted and presently asserts that he is not guilty of any of the crimes charged against him despite such admission of fact by reason of the fact that such killing was done by him in defense of property.

[The stipulated facts were as follows:] Albert Cross, and his father before him, have owned about 7,200 acres of land on the Dunoir River in

Fremont County. George Cross, father of defendant, moved there in 1907. Wild game was non-existent there in 1907, but game animals started to appear in that area in 1915, avoiding the meadowlands. The big increase in game population and resultant trespass on meadowland became noticeable from 1937 onward.

There has been a large and increasing herd of wild game having its fall and winter range within and along the Dunoir and upper Wind River regions in Fremont County, near the town of Dubois, Wyoming, and adjacent to the Game and Fish Dennison Refuge. During the summer and fall months, these animals range and forage on the Shoshone National Forest, near the Refuge, staying well back in the mountains and away from the private lands of the defendant and his neighbors. As winter sets in, the annual migrations of wild animals begin, leading them to follow various natural courses, through the Forest Reserve, down creek bottoms, and along ridges, many of which natural trails converge and enter upon the "H-" Ranch, belonging to defendant.

This annual migration of wild game, including many head of moose, numbering one hundred twenty-five to two hundred head, has been observed yearly, commencing as early as 1915, and is induced by severe weather and the scarcity of natural feed for the animals at that period of the year. Because of the terrain and the area in, around and on the defendant's ranch, and because several streams flow out of the mountains onto the land of the defendant, it is inevitable that the migrating moose, elk, deer and other animals follow these water courses, and, consequently gather upon the ranch lands of the defendant, where they remain to graze until molested; and, when driven away, inevitably return to these grazing lands, making it their feeding grounds as long as they are able to do so.

These animals each year have done serious and substantial damage to the defendant's ranch, the extent of these damages ranging annually from fifteen hundred dollars to four thousand dollars; the principal items of damage are the consumption of pasture and other forage reserved for defendant's livestock, injury to the turf, curtailing the production of hay and other natural grasses growing on the ranch lands, serious and costly destruction of fences caused by the attempts of the moose, elk and other wild animals to jump over the fences, and either becoming entangled in the wires or breaking through them; the interference of the wild game, especially moose, with the normal ranching operations, due to the necessity for patrolling the areas which are constantly threatened by the moose in the destruction of the necessary reserves of winter and spring feed for the domestic animals, and the necessity for driving them away; the damage to fences requiring interruption of ranching operations; and finally, the disturbance caused by the moose themselves in driving them off the ranch, exciting domestic livestock thereon; and the refusal of domestic livestock to graze on, forage or eat hay or other edible substances after the same has been trampled, urinated upon and defecated upon by the moose; and the stench of moose offal, especially the urine, is so offensive to both domestic animals and humans, that it constitutes a serious menace.

It is virtually impossible to keep the moose and elk off the defendant's ranch property by fencing, for the reason that fences do not offer a serious enough obstacle to prevent entry by wild game.

The defendant has, over the years, done everything in his power to get assistance from the State Game and Fish Department to help solve his plight; he has hired and paid for riders to get the wild animals driven away; he has expended considerable sums of money hiring airplanes to "spook" the moose and elk away from his premises; he has been forced into long drawn out and expensive litigation with the Game and Fish Department over the years in an effort to induce the department to enforce sufficient control to protect the residents in this area; this defendant and various of his neighbors have been forced to support and maintain this ever-increasing herd of wild game species and have been helpless to prevent the wild game from virtually "taking over" the ranching operations by belligerently driving cattle from feed grounds, by chasing horses, by chasing hired help and their families indoors, by usurping and defending their usurpation of sheds, barns, hay corrals, etc.; children are permitted to carry firearms from ranches to school as a protection against the quarrelsome moose; and defendant has experienced perennial frustration in attempting to control the wild game herds and protect his property with insufficient help from the Game and Fish Department.

Defendant and the Game and Fish Department used guns and cherry bombs and other means to "spook" the moose away, but this was ineffective; on the 12th of February, 1959, two moose were in his meadow feeding; defendant had chased them out before; he had tried to "spook" them; one ran into his fence and became entangled in the wire, and, in her efforts to free herself, tore down considerable good fence belonging to defendant; defendant then shot the moose in defense of his property which was being damaged in his presence, and therefore pleads justification for the said offense.

It is argued by the state that the legislature has enacted a comprehensive game law with certain exceptions and that, hence, it cannot be contended that other exceptions may be made. If it is true that the legislature intended that constitutional rights of persons could not be asserted in this connection, then it clearly exceeded its authority. It is further argued that the legislature may modify the common law, which is true, and that it has modified the common law otherwise applicable herein. A lengthy argument as to the police power of the legislature has been made in the brief of counsel for the state. It is readily admitted that, as argued by the state, the rights of individuals are subject to certain reasonable regulations by the legislature under the police power, but the police power too has its limitations and cannot come in direct conflict with constitutional provisions. [ ] So we shall proceed to consider whether or not the legislature can, pursuant to police power, prohibit a man from protecting his property from the depredations of wild animals. The authorities are practically unanimous on that point.

It is stated in 38 C.J.S. *Game* § 10a, p. 12, as follows:

Legal justification may always be interposed as a defense by a person charged with killing a wild animal contrary to law. Hence the killing of game protected by the statute or regulations is not prevented by them when reasonably necessary for the protection of person or property * * *.

And in 24 AM. JUR. *Game and Game Laws* § 12, it is stated:

In general, a statute forbidding the killing of game under penalty does not apply to a killing which is necessary for the defense of person or property. To justify such a killing, it must be reasonably necessary for the protection of a person or property.* * *

The rule here stated is supported by the following cases: *Aldrich v. Wright,* 53 N.H. 398 (1873); *Cook v. State,* 74 P.2d 199 (Wash.1937); *State v. Burk,* 195 P. 16 (Wash.1921); *State v. Rathbone,* 100 P.2d 86 (Mont.1940); *State v. Ward,* 152 N.W. 501 (Iowa 1915); *Cotton v. State,* 17 So. 2d 590 (Ala.App. 1944); *Commonwealth v. Masden,* 175 S.W.2d 1004 (Ky. App. 1944); *Commonwealth v. Riggles,* 39 Pa. Dist. & Co. R. 188 (Pa. Qtr. Sess. 1940). Thus in *State v. Ward,* the court stated:

By way of analogy we may note that the plea of reasonable self-defense may always be interposed in justification of the killing of a human being. We see no fair reason for holding that the same plea may not be interposed in justification of the killing of a goat or a deer. The right of defense of person and property is a constitutional right (article 1, § 1, Const. Iowa), and is recognized in the construction of all statutes. If in this case it was reasonably necessary for the defendant to kill the deer in question in order to prevent substantial injury to his property, such fact, we have no doubt, would afford justification for the killing.* * *

In *State v. Rathbone,* 100 P.2d 90, the court stated as follows:

* * * Article III of the Constitution is "A Declaration Of Rights Of The People Of The State Of Montana." Section 3 thereof reads as follows: "All persons are born equally free, and have certain natural, essential, and inalienable rights, among which may be reckoned the right of enjoying and defending their lives and liberties, of acquiring, possessing, and protecting property, and of seeking and obtaining their safety and happiness in all lawful ways." * * *

These constitutional provisions enunciate natural, fundamental and inalienable rights enjoyed by and guaranteed to every person residing within the State of Montana. They are absolute and self-executing in so far as they limit the power of the legislature to restrict these rights of the people for the reason that sec. 29 of the same article provides: "The provisions of this constitution are mandatory and prohibitory, unless by express words they are declared to be otherwise." * * *

In *Aldrich v. Wright,* the court stated:

"All men have certain natural, essential and inherent rights, among which are the enjoying and defending life and liberty, acquiring, possessing and protecting property." Bill of Rights, art. 2. In this declaration of the right of defending life and liberty, and protecting property, the Bill of Rights, more properly called the Declaration of Rights, professes to set forth a mere recognition of a natural right. The right thus recognized is maintained by the elementary principles of the common law, which are, in general, adopted by the ninetieth article of the constitution, subject to legislative alteration and repeal; as a fundamental and essential right, the defense of life, liberty and property is here put, by a special guaranty, above the altering and repealing power of the legislature.

Counsel for the state claim that these cases are not in point. They say that they have been decided under a constitutional provision which directly gives the right to protect property. For instance, the Constitution of Pennsylvania, as also the constitutions of a number of other states, provides:

> All men are born equally free and independent, and have certain inherent and indefeasible rights, among which are those of enjoying and defending life and liberty, of acquiring, possessing and protecting property and reputation, and of pursuing their own happiness. Art. 1, § 1, CONST. PA.

Our Constitution does not have the exact wording of the Constitution of Pennsylvania and so counsel claim that the right to protect property is not a constitutional right. We think that the brief of counsel for the state does a grave injustice to the intelligence and statesmanship of the able framers of our Constitution, the memory of some of whom like that of the late Chief Justice Potter has not yet faded into the distant past. It is unbelievable that the inherent and inalienable right to protect property, as well as life and liberty, recognized long before the Declaration of Independence, was ignored or omitted from our Constitution or is nullified thereby. We discussed inalienable rights at some length in *State v. Langley,* 84 P.2d 767, 769, 770 (Wyo.1938), and stated as follows:

> * * * With the Renaissance began a new period in human history. Thoughts of liberty and freedom took possession of the minds of men, first in the field of religion, then of politics, later in the field of economics. It came to be a part of the legal philosophy of the times that each man has, as such, and because he is a human being, certain natural, inherent and indefeasible rights of which no government should, or has the right to, deprive him.* * * The doctrine of natural and inherent rights to life, liberty and property was announced in the Declaration of Independence, in the constitutions of New Hampshire, Virginia, and Pennsylvania in 1776, in the constitution of Vermont in 1777, in that of Massachusetts in 1780, in that of New Jersey in 1784. Other constitutions followed in the same vein. Section 3 of Article 1 of our own constitution refers to natural rights of man and section 2 of the same article provides that "in their inherent right to life, liberty and the pursuit of happiness, all members of the human race are equal." There are those who maintain that man has no natural rights; that none can exist except in society, and that whatever rights he has, he, accordingly, receives from society. However that may be theoretically, natural rights are recognized by our constitution. The doctrine is part of the positive law of the land, and section 6 of Article 1 of our constitution provides that no person shall be deprived of life, liberty or property without due process of law. The article evidently refers to the

natural and inherent rights otherwise mentioned, and so it becomes apparent, particularly in view of the history above outlined, that the framers of the constitution meant that the *protection* thereof is important and that they, though loosely defined, should not be unduly invaded.

(Emphasis supplied.) *See also* section 7, Article 1.

. . .

If any further authorities were necessary to show that counsel for the state are utterly wrong in the contention above mentioned, we need only to refer to the Washington cases above cited which hold that a person has a right to protect his property against the depredations of wild animals if reasonably necessary. We have examined the Constitution of Washington. It contains no such wording as the Constitution of Pennsylvania above quoted, but it contains the same provision as our Constitution that no person shall be deprived of life, liberty or property without due process of law. If he cannot be deprived thereof, he necessarily must have the right to protect it. The Washington court in *State v. Burk,* cited the Iowa case of *State v. Ward,* 152 N.W. 501 (Iowa 1917), and used the same quotation from that case as we have used heretofore in this opinion.

All the cases agree that before the wild game may be killed, it must be reasonably necessary to protect one's property. That matter has been discussed at length in the various cases which have been cited.

The situation as to wild animals is very much the same in the State of Montana as it is in this state. The court in the Rathbone case above cited stated that it would not undertake to state under what particular facts a killing of a wild animal would be justified and that each case must be decided on its own facts. We think that that should be true in this state. The Montana case further stated that to justify such killing it must be reasonably necessary and that all other remedies should be exhausted before killing such animals. The statement as to the exhaustion of remedies is indefinite and whether the remedies have been exhausted must depend on the facts in a particular case. The thought in that connection would seem to be implied in the rule that the killing must be reasonably necessary. The court in the Montana case referred to complaints made by the landowner so that the Game and Fish Department might be advised of the facts of the depredations. It held such complaints admissible in evidence for the purpose of determining as to whether or not the landowner had exhausted his remedies. The agreed statements in the case at bar show that a great many complaints have been made by the landowner so we need not consider that matter any further.

Counsel for the state argue that a remedy is available to the property owner whose property is damaged or destroyed by wild animals under the provisions of § 23–15, W.S. 1957. It provides that the Game and Fish Commission has power "To authorize the game warden to kill any of the wild life in this state when in the judgment of the commission said killing is necessary." We can see no force in the argument of the state if counsel refer to anything more than a general notice by the landowner heretofore mentioned.

Section 23–117, W.S. 1957, provides that a person whose property is damaged by wild animals may file a claim with the Game and Fish Commission for the amount of damages sustained. It is argued by the state that this gives such landowner an adequate remedy. We hardly think that a landowner should be compelled to waive his constitutional rights by filing a claim for damages, perhaps every month, every two months, every year, or at other intervals, and recover damages perhaps after protracted litigation. The argument of the state carried to its logical conclusion would mean that a person must, before killing a wild animal, permit his property, even his own home, to be invaded and destroyed. It would mean a relinquishment of his constitutional rights for money which may be recovered by a claim filed with the commission. Counsel for the state have cited us no authority, and the case of *Commonwealth v. Masden,* 175 S.W.2d 1004 (Ky. App. 1944), holds against the contention of the state.... Speaking of the landowner's constitutional rights the court stated:

> The appellee is of the opinion that by reason of the game laws he was deprived of his right to protect his crops against the depredations of the deer and thus to minimize his damages, but it is generally recognized that one has the constitutional right to defend his property against imminent and threatened injury by a protected animal even to the extent of killing the animal.* * *

In conclusion, though we may be guilty of tautology, we think that before a defendant can resort to force in protecting his property from wild animals protected by law he should use every remedy available to him before killing such animals. He should use only such force as may be reasonably necessary and suitable to protect his property and must use only such force and means as a reasonably prudent man would use under the circumstances.

NOTES

(1) Liability vs. protection: Although *Barrett* and *Cross* might at first glance seem inconsistent, notice the differences between the cases. *Barrett* was an attempt to obtain compensation from the government for damage done by wildlife; *Cross,* on the other hand, involved a landowner's defense to a criminal prosecution for killing game out of season and in defense of his property. Courts have traditionally been reluctant to impose liability on the state in the absence of express legislative authorization; indeed, sovereign immunity might preclude such liability for other than constitutionally based claims. On the other hand, they are prone to protect criminal defendants against seemingly unfair applications of criminal laws. On the issue of state liability, the conclusion in *Barrett* has long been the dominant rule:

> Of the courts that have considered whether damage to private property by protected wildlife constitutes a "taking," a clear majority have held that it does not and that the government thus does not owe compensation. The Court of Claims rejected such a claim for damage done to crops by geese protected under the Migratory Bird Treaty Act in *Bishop v. United States,* 126 F.Supp. 449, 452–53 (Ct.Cl.1954), *cert.*

denied, 349 U.S. 955 (1955). The United States Court of Appeals for the Seventh Circuit rejected a similar claim under the Federal Tort Claims Act in *Sickman v. United States,* 184 F.2d 616 (7th Cir.1950), *cert. denied,* 341 U.S. 939 (1951). Several state courts have also rejected claims for damage to property by wildlife protected under state laws. *See, e.g., Jordan v. State,* 681 P.2d 346, 350 n. 3 (Alaska App.1984) (defendants were not deprived of their property interest in a moose carcass by regulation prohibiting the killing of a bear that attacked the carcass because "their loss was incidental to the state regulation which was enacted to protect game"); *Leger v. Louisiana Department of Wildlife & Fisheries,* 306 So.2d 391 (La.Ct.App.), *writ of review denied,* 310 So.2d 640 (La.1975) (because wildlife is regulated by the state in its sovereign, as distinct from its proprietary capacity, the state has no duty to control its movements or prevent it from damaging private property); *Barrett v. State,* 116 N.E. 99 (N.Y.1917) (damage to timber by beavers not compensable because the state has a general right to protect wild animals as a matter of public interest, and incidental injury by them cannot be complained of); *see also Collopy v. Wildlife Commission, Department of Natural Resources,* 625 P.2d 994 (Colo.1981); *Maitland v. People,* 23 P.2d 116, 117 (Colo.1933); *Cook v. State,* 74 P.2d 199, 203 (Wash.1937); *Platt v. Philbrick,* 47 P.2d 302, 304 (Cal.App.1935). *But see State v. Herwig,* 117 N.W.2d 335 (Wis. 1962); *Shellnut v. Arkansas State Game & Fish Commission,* 258 S.W.2d 570 (Ark.1953).

Mountain States Legal Foundation v. Hodel, 799 F.2d 1423 (10th Cir.1986). Even the cases cited in *Mountain States* as contrary precedents did not involve the imposition of monetary liability on governments: in *Herwig,* the alleged taking was used successfully as a defense against a criminal prosecution for violating game laws; in *Shellnut* the taking was used to invalidate a regulatory restriction on private land.

A recent, prominent case adopting the no-taking rule is *Moerman v. State,* 21 Cal.Rptr.2d 329 (Cal.App.1993), *cert. denied sub nom. Moerman v. California,* 511 U.S. 1031 (1994) (no liability for damage caused by endangered tule elk, introduced into the area by the state).

(2) Statutory provisions authorizing recovery for wildlife damage: Although landowners generally do not have a common-law right to sue states for damage caused by wildlife, many states have statutory provisions authorizing compensation for damages caused by specific species—generally game animals.

Wisconsin, for example, operates a program that compensates landowners both for damage caused by wildlife in excess of $250 and for the costs of wildlife abatement efforts. WIS. STAT. § 29.889. The program protects landowners against "damage to commercial seedlings or crops growing on agricultural land, damage to crops that have been harvested for sale or further use but that have not been removed from the agricultural land, damage to orchard trees or nursery stock or damage to apiaries or livestock." *Id.* § 29.889(4), (6). To gain compensation, however, a landowner "shall permit hunting of the type of wild animals causing the wildlife damage on that land," subject to certain limitations (*e.g.,* hunters must provide advance notice, cannot use motor vehicles, may not erect hunting stands).

Wyoming allows recovery for damage done by "big or trophy game animals or game birds." WYO. STAT. ANN § 23–1–901 (1999). *See Parker Land & Cattle Co. v. Wyoming Game & Fish Commission*, 845 P.2d 1040 (Wyo.1993) (because bison is neither a big game animal nor a trophy game animal, no recovery for bison-caused livestock damage). As in Wisconsin, a landowner seeking recovery must permit public hunting during authorized hunting seasons. *See also* VT. CODE ANN. tit. 10, § 4829; WASH. REV. CODE. § 77.36.060.

(3) The right to defend property: As the court in *Cross* notes, landowners have been more successful in their claim of a right to defend their property by killing depredating wildlife when other means have proven unsuccessful. Although several of the decisions cited in *Cross* were based on state constitutional provisions, others rested on interpretations of the statutes at issue. *E.g., Cook v. State*, 74 P.2d 199 (Wash.1937) (construing statute restricting trapping of fur-bearing animals as inapplicable to animals destroying private dam). Note, too, that some states have require those seeking to use the defense to have exhausted other alternatives or to obtain a permit from the state wildlife agency. *E.g., State v. Webber*, 736 P.2d 220 (Or.App.1987).

The right to defend property is far from universally accepted. Recall, for example, *State v. Cleve*, 980 P.2d 23 (N.M.1999) [Chapter 1], in which Cleve was convicted of killing depredating game out of season. A more recent example is *State v. Thompson*, 33 P.3d 213 (Idaho App. 2001). Laura Thompson asked her son to shoot a deer that was eating plants in her garden; he did so. Both Thompsons were charged with misdemeanors. They filed motions to dismiss, claiming that the statute prohibiting killing of deer out of season "impermissibly placed limitations on the constitutional right to protect one's property." The court rejected this argument because the statute in question is designed to achieve "the preservation, protection, and perpetuation of wildlife," an objective that "serves the common welfare of the citizens of Idaho." The statute thus was a reasonable limitation on the right to protect property.

There also is no right to kill federally protected threatened or endangered species to protect property. The leading case is *Christy v. Hodel*, 857 F.2d 1324 (9th Cir.1988), *cert. denied sub nom., Christy v. Lujan*, 490 U.S. 1114 (1989). Christy was a sheep rancher with a lease to graze sheep on the east slope of the Rocky Mountains in Montana. After his flock had been repeatedly raided by grizzly bears, Christy shot and killed a bear that was attacking his flock. Prosecuted and fined $2500 under the Endangered Species Act, Christy argued that he had a constitutional right to protect his property. The Ninth Circuit Court of Appeals disagreed: "We simply hold that the right to kill federally protected wildlife in defense of property is not 'implicit in the concept of ordered liberty' nor so 'deeply rooted in this Nation's history and tradition' that it can be recognized by us as a fundamental right guaranteed by the fifth amendment." *Id.* at 1330. Citing *Barrett*, the court noted that "the regulations do not forbid plaintiffs from personally defending their property by means other than killing grizzly bears." *Id.* at 1331. *See also United States v. Darst,* 726 F.Supp. 286 (D.Kan.1989).

As *Christy* demonstrates, wildlife damage often arises because of the particular land-use choices made by a landowner—raising sheep in a landscape inhabited by grizzly bears, for instance. Grizzly bears pose no risk to the vast majority of human activities. Moreover, grizzly bears inhabit only a small part of the country, which means that sheep can be safely raised in many places. Given these facts, should property law protect an owner who wants to raise sheep in grizzly bear country? Is this case materially different from the landowner who might like to raise hogs in the middle of a residential area? As humans continue to encroach on remaining habitat and as conservation measures enable wildlife populations to increase, conflicts are likely to become more common. *See* Jim Robbins, *Man v. Beast: Whose Neighborhood Is It, Anyway?,* N.Y. TIMES, Jan. 27, 2000, at B14. *See also* Francis X. Clines, *At a National Park, White–Tail Deer Reign and Local Homeowners Are Irate,* N.Y. TIMES, Dec. 20, 1999, at A24.

(4) Statutory provisions authorizing defense of property: Many states have statutes authorizing landowners to kill or harass wildlife in defense of their property. The statutes are highly variable.

New York, for example, grants property owners broad statutory rights to kill bothersome animals. In some situations, permits are required in advance; in others, the landowner must notify state officials after taking the wildlife; sometimes the carcass must be delivered to the state. In the case of certain common animals, however, the authority to take is more or less unlimited (*e.g.,* "Skunks injuring property or which have become a nuisance may be taken at any time in any manner"). N.Y. ENVTL. CONSERV. LAW § 11–0521,–0523 (1999). With beaver populations far larger than in the era of *Barrett,* landowners can now obtain permits to take them. *Id.* § 11–0521(2).

Landowners in Rhode Island can kill bothersome fur bearers without advance permission but, except in the case of rabbits, must present the carcass to the state within 24 hours. R.I. GEN. LAWS § 20–16–2 (1999). Maine vests broad powers in landowners to kill animals, but requires that the animals be "found in the act" of causing damage. The landowner must report all relevant facts to a game warden within 12 hours. ME. REV. STAT. ANN. tit. 12, § 7501 (1999). Connecticut, in contrast, requires advance permits to control nuisance animals, limits takes to circumstances where damage is "unreasonable," and prescribes that licensed animal control businesses may kill animals only using methods that "conform to the recommendations of the 1993 report of the Veterinary Medical Association panel on euthanasia." CONN. GEN. STAT. § 26–47 (1999).

(5) Fencing statutes: Should it make any difference in defense-of-property cases whether the jurisdiction requires private owners to fence in their livestock or landowners to fence them out? Recall that the North Carolina Supreme Court in *McConico v. Singleton,* 9 S.C.L. (2 Mill) 244 (1818) [Chapter 2], thought that the fence-out provisions of state law were relevant to the issue of whether private individuals were entitled to hunt on unenclosed lands. Is there a justifiable basis for requiring landowners to fence out privately owned animals, such as cattle and sheep, to gain protection against their depredations while allowing landowners to kill trespassing publicly owned animals such as elk and moose?

PERSPECTIVES

Beaver as "a source of never-failing interest and instruction": The court in *Barrett* justified its decision not only on utilitarian grounds, but also on the ground that the state's power to guard the citizen's educational and aesthetic needs. Beaver, the court stated, are "in a class by themselves" because of "their habits and customs, their curious instincts and intelligence. Observation of the animals at work or play is a source of never-failing interest and instruction."

What sorts of justification should be sufficient when the state seeks to protect wildlife? David Ehrenfeld, a leading conservation biologist, has labeled this question "the conservation dilemma." Nature, he writes, is often viewed as "a gigantic toolshed" in which "everything that is not a tool or a raw material is probably refuse. This attitude, nearly universal in our time, creates a terrible dilemma for the conservation or for anyone who believes of Nature, as Goethe did, that 'each of her creations has its own being, each represents a special concept, yet together they are one.' The difficulty is that the humanistic world accepts the conservation of Nature only piecemeal and at a price: there must be a *logical, practical* reason for saving each and every part of the natural world that we wish to preserve. And the dilemma arises on the increasingly frequent occasions when we encounter a threatened part of Nature but can find no rational reason for keeping it." DAVID EHRENFELD, *The Conservation Dilemma, in* THE ARROGANCE OF HUMANISM 176 (1978).

This belief has led to the attempts to discover a variety of anthropocentric (ultimately economic) values that can justify the preservation of non-resources. Ehrenfeld provides a list of the usual suspects: recreational and aesthetic values, undiscovered or undeveloped values, ecosystem stabilization values, value as examples of survival, environmental baseline and monitoring values, scientific research values, habitat reconstruction values, and conservation value (avoidance of irreversible change). But as he notes, the reasons are rationalizations and their truthfulness in individual cases is often of little comfort because, "rationalizations being what they are, they are usually readily detected by nearly everyone and tend not to be very convincing, regardless of their truthfulness. In this case they are not nearly as convincing to most people as the short-term economic arguments used to justify the preservation of 'real' resources such as petroleum and timber." The problem, in Ehrenfeld's view, is that these "values" represent an attempt to find a way to compare the value of an intact salt marsh and a shopping center. The difficulty is the presumptuousness of the process, "the implication ... that both the valuable and the valueless qualities of the tidal marsh are all known and identified."

In place of this arrogant assumption of complete knowledge, Ehrenfeld urges the adoption of "the Noah Principle," the recognition that communities and species "should be conserved because they exist and because this existence is itself but the present expression of a continuing historical process of immense antiquity and majesty." Such an approach, he suggests, is a possible way out of "the humanists' trap": "Do you love Nature?" they ask. "Do you want to save it? Then tell us what it is good for." The only way out of this kind of trap, if there is a way, is to smash it, to reject it utterly. This is the final realism; we will come to it sooner or later—if sooner, then with less pain." *Id.*

(iii) PROTECTING WILDLIFE ON PRIVATE LANDS

Harrison v. Petroleum Surveys, Inc.

Court of Appeal of Louisiana.
80 So.2d 153 (1955).

■ TATE, J.:—Plaintiff-landowners appealed from judgment after trial on the merits dismissing their suit for muskrats killed and damages to muskrat lands allegedly caused by the geophysical explorations conducted thereon by Petroleum Surveys, Inc., defendant-Appellee.

Such geophysical exploration operations consist of recording the sub-terranean reactions to explosions set off about 200 feet beneath the ground at a certain predesignated pattern of points situated over certain territory. The skilled interpretation of these recorded reactions may approximately indicate the presence or absence of mineral potentialities. In marshy country such as is here involved, the surveying, explosion, and recording crews are transported on "marsh buggies"—huge, heavy vehicles which churn through the marsh on two sets of two broad (4' wide each) wheels leaving tracks from 18 inches to four feet deep, depending on the softness of the marsh, and approximately twelve feet in width.

By stipulation between the parties, it is admitted that Petroleum Surveys employees did actually trespass specifically without authorization from plaintiff-landowners (hereinafter designated as "the Harrisons") on their property by operating their marsh buggies on approximately two acres of marsh land at the northwest corner of their section, and by firing the shot in question at a depth of 172 feet, after sinking a pipe 190 feet deep. It is further expressly stipulated that this trespass was unintentional and was the result of an honest surveying error.

[The evidence taken as a whole] convinces us, as claimed, that Petroleum Surveys' operations completely crushed the two-acre tract in question and the muskrat-supporting 3–cornered grass growing thereon....

2.   The Muskrat

The evidence presented describes the muskrat as a small (2 lb.) fur-bearing animal, living in marshy areas. It feeds on the roots of certain grasses, which it eats from tunnels under the ground dug by itself. The muskrat lives underground in nests, and prefers areas with ground firm enough to support grass, but not so firm as to impede its digging processes. It also prefers areas upon which certain types of grass grow, such as "3–cornered" grass. The male inhabits the nest with the female. An external manifestation of this nest may be a "muskrat hill", which may also indicate four or five or more such combined nests. The muskrat breeds monthly a litter of 2–4 kittens, constructing a new chamber to its nest for each such litter.

The trapping of muskrats for their pelts on the four million marsh acres in southern Louisiana is an important economic activity of our State.

3. The Factual Consequences of the Trespass

The Harrisons' witnesses consisted of the owner, trapping supervisor, and trapper of the 2–acre tract in question, and several other experienced trappers and trapping superintendents. They testified that the operation of marsh buggies over muskrat lands such as are here involved will kill many of the muskrats and their litters in tunnels and nests, since the muskrat upon approach of danger hides in his underground tunnels (and since the marsh buggy trails go deeper than the tunnels of the muskrat hill). These operations also destroy the rich three-cornered grass upon which they feed. Because of this destruction and of the packing of the ground, they testified that such muskrat lands would not be good for trapping for from 8 to 15 or more years thereafter.

Most of these witnesses were also familiar with the land here involved. They testified that due to the plentiful 3–cornered grass and the right softness of the soil, it was good muskrat land. They estimated that approximately 600–1000 muskrats, including young, inhabited these two acres, and that several hundred would be killed by operation of the marsh buggies upon the land in question. While one of the three Petroleum Surveys crew members testified that it was not good muskrat land, and the other two also testified they did not see any muskrats, as admitted by these witnesses, their job was not to look for muskrats but to shoot many exploration points per day.

Petroleum Surveys sought to contradict this factual testimony mostly by the testimony of an expert biologist specializing in marsh ecology and fur animal habitats, who had published several works, made several surveys, and had engaged in trapping supervision and activities himself. While on direct examination the estimates of this witness were conservative as to the amount of muskrat produced by given acreages or the amount of damage caused by marsh buggies to muskrat potentialities of a given tract of land, on cross-examination approximately two months later based to a great degree upon disparate findings in his published works, it developed that one explanation for the discrepancies between his testimony and that of plaintiffs' witnesses was that the expert had based his measurements on extremely large tracts of land (say one hundred thousand acres) in which necessarily the major portion would be bayou, bay, or otherwise unsuited for muskrat operations.

Under cross-examination, this expert admitted that well-suited land could produce from 40–70 muskrats per acre in trapping operations. The Harrisons' witnesses directly concerned with trapping operations on these two acres testified that upon this tract were maintained 20–25 traps which produced an average of 100 muskrats per year, or an average of 50 muskrats per acre. The other trappers and trapping supervisor witnesses testified to the effect that good marshland such as this tract could reasonably be expected to produce approximately 50 muskrats per acre per year.

We feel that the plaintiffs have established by a preponderance of the evidence that two-acre tract damaged by Petroleum Surveys was good muskrat land and could reasonably have been expected to produce through trapping operations an average of 100 muskrats per year. It is not seriously denied that over the last several years the landowner's net profit per muskrat pelt would be 57–58 cents.

Defendant's expert testified that marsh lands can be restored to full production after marsh buggy destruction in at the latest 3–4 years. The Harrisons testified that from previous experience it took 15 or more years after the incident to restore the lands to full production. Two of plaintiff's witnesses, Eunice J. Vinet and Alidore Mahler, trapping operators with probably the most extensive practical experience concerning such marsh buggy damage of those testifying (aside possibly from the expert), stated that marshland similar to the present was generally restored to full muskrat production within 8–10 years. This latter estimate we will accept as fairest to all parties.

4.   Legal Cause of Action for Damage to Muskrat Lands

The chief defense to this action urged by Petroleum Surveys is its contention that by law the Harrisons had no cause of action for the damages alleged because as a matter of law the landowner has no property interest in the muskrats themselves while still untrapped. Muskrats, being wild animals, are owned by the State of Louisiana while still at large, LSA–R.S. 56:101, 56:102, 56:252; and wild beasts in general belong not to the landowner, but to the captor no matter upon whose land captured, Article 3415, LSA–C.C.

It was this contention the District Court sustained in dismissing the landowners' suit.

While the landowner does not own the muskrats situated on his property, he owns the exclusive right to take muskrats therefrom, *Esmele v. Violet Trapping Co.,* 175 So. 471 (La.1937); *Curran v. Jones,* 112 So. 492 (La.1927); *Rosenthal-Brown Fur Company v. Jones-Frere Fur Company,* 110 So. 630 (La.1926).

Defendant skillfully urges that these cases hold that only trespassers in bad faith are held liable for muskrats taken from another's land, and then only for the profits derived therefrom under the principle of restoring the fruits of unjust enrichment, Article 1963, LSA–Civil Code. Some language in these cases might be so construed. But the facts of the *Curran* and *Rosenthal-Brown* cases cited involve a determination of the measure to be used in the accounting by possessors under (what was subsequently held to be) inferior title to the true owners of the land for profits derived by the wrongful possessors during their possession thereof.

The Esmele case simply awards the true lessee the estimated profit on pelts taken by a wrongful trespasser (a trapping company) without discussion as to legal good or bad faith, *see Esmele v. Violet Trapping Company,* 166 So. 477 (La.1936), *on merits*. It is not authority for the proposition that the owner of muskrat lands cannot recover from the trespasser for damages occasioned thereby, but rather the contrary. The wrong or damage to the rightful possessor occasioned in the Esmele case was the wrongful trapping of muskrats by the trespasser on the lease-owner's muskrat land, and the trespasser was held in damages to the lease-owner for the estimated profits the lease-owner lost through the trespasser's wrongful act and not for profits on pelts taken by the trespasser. *See id.* at 479.

Negligence is a violation of a relative right, and trespass a violation of an absolute one: but, under Article 2315, LSA–C.C., either wrongful act entitles one injured thereby to recover the damages occasioned him thereby. Through this wrongful act (trespass) of Petroleum Surveys, the landowner has suffered provable damage and is entitled to recover therefor. While punitive damages may be recovered when the trespass is intentional or willful or wanton, [ ], only compensatory damages are awarded in unintentional trespasses as this. To this extent only in damage suits arising out of trespasses is considered the question of legal good or bad faith, so important in the sometimes related question of measuring recovery by the true owner from the possessor of fruits, profits, and revenues derived from the latter's wrongful possession.

The Harrisons sought recovery for (1) 500 muskrats killed in the ground by Petroleum Surveys' operations; (2) loss of 1,500 muskrats, over 15 years.

Petroleum Surveys correctly urge that the Harrisons cannot recover for the muskrats killed in the ground by defendant's operations. The property right of the landowners' damage is not the muskrats themselves (which do not belong to them) but the economic value of the right to trap muskrats on the land in question.

Petroleum Surveys also urge that for this same reason, at least as pleaded, the Harrisons cannot recover damages, since they are seeking payment for 1,500 muskrats to be captured in the future, over fifteen years. But the petition pleads, Article 21: "That because of the destruction of said muskrat hills and the damages to the surface of the land, the land has become valueless for trapping purposes for a period of 15 years." Under Article 22, the petition originally itemized this damage as "loss of fur revenues for 15 years and damages to the land." In response to defendant's exception of vagueness, this itemization was further explained as loss of profits from 100 muskrats a year for 15 years. (The evidence indicates that muskrat lands are leased, not at so many dollars per acre, but at so much per cent of the price received for each muskrat subsequently trapped thereon during the life of the lease.)

Contrary to the contention of Petroleum Surveys that any recoverable damages could only have been pleaded as the restoral cost for the acreage, or the value of 3–cornered grass on the tract, we feel that plaintiffs have adequately pleaded the damage sustained by them through defendant's trespass. This damage is not only the value of the grass destroyed, but is really the damage to the property right representing the chief economic value of this small tract—its ability to produce muskrats in trapping operations, measured by the loss of muskrat revenues reasonably to have been expected therefrom had the trespass not occurred.

5.   Award

In cases where although there is a legal right to recovery, an exact estimation of damages cannot be made, courts have discretion to assess same based upon all the facts and circumstances of the case, see, for instance, *Brantley v. Tremont & Gulf Railway Company*, 75 So. 2d 236 (La.1954), involving damages occasioned by causing overflow of minnow pond and loss of minnows therein. As previously discussed in detail, in evaluating the economic loss occasioned to the Harrisons by destruction temporarily of the value of this small tract for muskrat trapping purposes through defendant's unauthorized trespass, we feel an award based on loss of 100 muskrats per year, over a period of 8 years, at an average loss of profits to plaintiffs of 57 cents per muskrat, or $456 in all, will be a fair award under all the facts and circumstances as shown by the evidence herein.

NOTES

Trespass and damages: *Harrison* is a straight-forward case involving trespass to land. Just as landowners have the right to exclude hunters, so too they can exclude other people, including people whose actions harm their wildlife-related operations. To prove trespass, a plaintiff must demonstrate a direct, physical invasion of his land. No showing of damages is required (unlike in nuisance law, considered below), and the defendant is liable even for mistaken entries (as in *Harrison*) as long as the entry involved an intentional physical act and was not the result merely of a physical accident.

The question in *Harrison* had to do with the calculation of the plaintiff's damages. The plaintiff sought full recovery for the value of all muskrats that either were killed or that, as a result of the trespass, would never be born. The court rejects this approach: muskrats are wild animals, and the landowner does not own them. Yet, even though the landowner did not own the animals, what exactly was the theory of recovery? Was it based on the profits that the plaintiff would have earned by harvesting this natural crop of muskrats? Was it based instead on the slightly different theory that the land itself had decreased in value for a period of years because its rental value for trapping had declined? Note the court's phrases: "the economic value of the right to trap muskrats" and "the loss of muskrat revenues reasonably to have been expected." Are these ideas the same? Do they adequately take into account the labor and expenses that a landowner would incur in trapping the muskrats? Given the difficulty that the court has in calculating damages to a business, would a landowner who placed esthetic or other psychological value on wildlife be barred from recovering damages?

Note also the court's comments about possible punitive damages against trespassers: they can be recovered, the court says, "when the trespass is intentional or willful or wanton."

Lenk v. Spezia

California Court of Appeals.
213 P.2d 47 (1949).

■ THOMPSON, J.:—The plaintiff brought suit for damages against the defendants as individuals and as copartners for negligently killing 518 hives of bees and causing the loss of 14 tons of honey which would have otherwise been produced. It is alleged the bees were poisoned by the negligent dusting of crops of tomatoes with insecticide compound containing arsenic of trioxide, from an airplane, and thus permitting the poisonous dust to drift or lodge on plaintiff's hives and bees which were located near by, and by depositing the poisonous insecticide on the feeding fields of the bees.

The answer denies the material allegations of the complaint, except that it is admitted the defendants dusted tomato crops in that vicinity from their airplane with insecticide powder containing a small proportion of arsenic, for the necessary benefit and protection of said crops of tomatoes from prevalent insects, worms and pests. The answer specifically denies that defendants deposited or negligently permitted poisonous insecticide to be carried to or spread upon plaintiff's bees or feeding grounds, and affirmatively alleges that plaintiff's loss of bees and honey was due to his own contributory negligence in failing and refusing to remove the hives or to protect the bees from the poisonous dust in spite of the fact that he had previous knowledge of the defendants' intention to use that powder to dust the tomato crops in the vicinity of his hives.

The court found that plaintiff owned the hives and bees which he kept in several colonies in Lisbon and Clarksburg districts in Yolo County; that said bees ranged over a wide field at distances of five miles from their hives in search of nectar and pollen; that defendants did not spread or deposit insecticide powder negligently or at all upon plaintiff's bees or upon their feeding grounds; that the defendants were not negligent in dusting the crops of fruit or tomatoes in fields adjacent to the places where plaintiff's hives and bees were kept; that said bees were not poisoned and did not die as a result of defendants' negligence or carelessness in dusting the crops in that vicinity. On the contrary, the court affirmatively found that the bees were destroyed on account of the contributory negligence of plaintiff in failing and refusing to exercise any care for their protection in spite of the fact that plaintiff had full knowledge of defendants' intention to use the poisonous insecticide in dusting the tomato crops on fields in the immediate vicinity of his hives of bees.

The evident theory of the court was that the cause of the death of plaintiff's colonies of bees was his negligence in deliberately releasing his bees from their hives and permitting them to range over the surrounding fields for nectar and pollen, when he had full knowledge that crops in adjacent fields had been or were about to be dusted with insecticide powder containing arsenic which he knew to be poisonous to bees.

The appellant's theory of the cause of the death of his bees was that defendants released the poisonous insecticide powder from their airplane when the wind was blowing directly toward the place where their hives were stationed, and that the poisonous compound drifted to and upon his hives and bees. There is a conflict of evidence upon that issue. In effect the court found against the plaintiff on that theory by determining that the defendants did not negligently deposit insecticide dust or powder upon the hives or bees, or upon their feeding fields. There is substantial evidence to support that finding.

Honey bees often obtain the poison when feeding on blossoms in fields which have been dusted or sprayed for the protection of the crops and carry it back to the hives in the nectar or pollen, which sometimes results in the death of the entire colony of bees.

In Roy A. Grout's recent volume, *The Hive and the Honey Bee*, the author says that for many years toxic compounds have been used to protect fruit and vegetables from pests. The trees and vines are usually sprayed when they are in full bloom. That is the very time when the bees visit them in search of nectar and pollen. It is difficult to protect the fruit and vegetables from pests without detriment to the bees which usually get the poison from the blossoms after they have been sprayed or dusted. They sometimes die immediately or soon if they get sufficient poison. But they often take it back to the hive in the nectar or pollen or both, which sometimes results in the death of the entire colony of bees.

We are of the opinion that the evidence adequately supports the findings and judgment. We are convinced that large numbers of plaintiff's bees died in and about their apiaries, and probably they died from poisoned insecticide which they procured in other fields while they were ranging in search of coveted nectar or pollen, or from poisoned dust which drifted with the wind from other fields to the hives of plaintiff. But we are unable to say, as a matter of law, that they were poisoned by the insecticide which was released from defendants' airplane. There is some evidence that other farmers were dusting their crops in that vicinity about the same time. One of said crops was located just across the river from one of plaintiff's apiaries.

In the present case the burden was on plaintiff to prove, not only that it was the poisonous dust used by the defendants which killed his bees, but also that defendants were guilty of negligence on account of the manner in which they dusted the adjacent tomato fields, and that such negligence was the proximate cause of the death of the bees....

It is true that a defendant who is engaged in spraying or dusting fruit, vegetables or other products with the use of an airplane, or otherwise, by negligently spreading liquid or powder known to contain a dangerous proportion of arsenic or other poisons, in such a manner as to endanger the lives of bees, animals or property of another person in the immediate vicinity, may become liable for the damages resulting therefrom. *Miles v. A. Arena & Co.,* 73 P.2d 1260 (Cal.App.1938); *Lundberg v. Bolon,* 194 P.2d 454 (Ariz.1948); *S.A. Gerrard Co. v. Fricker,* 27 P.2d 678 (Ariz.1933); *Hammond Ranch Corp. v. Dodson,* 136 S.W.2d 484 (Ark.1940).

But in the *Miles* case, a judgment was rendered against the defendant for negligently dusting a field of honeydew melons by means of an airplane from which poisonous insecticide was spread while a wind was blowing directly toward plaintiff's land where the hives of bees were located. That judgment was affirmed on appeal because the evidence was completely satisfactory, if not undisputed, that the defendant knowingly released the poisonous dust from its airplane while the wind was blowing toward plaintiff's hives and the poison actually reached the hives and killed all the bees they contained, including the queen bees which are known to remain in their hives. That is some proof that the bees in and about the apiary died from the poisoned compound which drifted from the field dusted by the defendant. Specimens of the identical dust taken from the bees and the hives were procured and analyzed. The trial court adopted definite findings that it was the defendant's poisonous dust which drifted to and upon plaintiff's bees and killed them. In the present case the findings were just the contrary in that regard. The Appellate Court said:

> * * * He should not do the dusting, or have it done, under conditions which would indicate to a reasonably prudent person that damage to his neighbor would result.

. . .

If plaintiff's bees procured the poisonous compound from which they died while they were trespassing on the fields of other owners of land, it appears that the plaintiff could not recover damages unless the poison was distributed wantonly, maliciously, or with the deliberate intent to injure or destroy the bees. There is no evidence in this case of such wanton or malicious conduct. Under such circumstances there was no duty on the defendants or the owners of the land to protect plaintiff's trespassing bees from the danger of said poisonous compound. *Holt v. Mundell,* 112 P.2d 1039, 1043 (Colo.1941); *Jeanes v. Holtz,* 211 P.2d 925 (Cal.App.1949); [ ].

In the *Holt* case, defendant sprayed his crop of maize with a compound containing poison to protect the growing grain from grasshoppers which were prevalent and harmful to his crop. Plaintiff's cattle trespassed on that land and evidently procured some of the poisonous mixture, as a result of which several cows died. Plaintiff brought suit for damages and recovered judgment. On appeal the judgment was reversed. The court held that because the cattle were trespassing on the land at the time they procured the poisonous mixture from which they died, the plaintiff was precluded from recovering damages. Quoting with approval from the text in 33 A.L.R. at page 449, the court said in that regard: " * * * In general, it may be said that the owner of premises, inclosed or otherwise, is not bound to keep them safe for trespassing animals, and is not liable for injuries to such cattle resulting from eating or drinking poisonous or other substances on the premises; and this is true both in sections where stock are lawfully allowed to run at large, and in jurisdictions where the common-law rule as to keeping animals from straying is in force."

In 3 C.J.S., *Animals,* § 213(d)bb, at pp. 1329, 1330, it is said in that regard: "An owner is not liable for death to trespassing animals from poison on his premises where the poison was intended for another purpose, and he was not guilty of gross or wanton negligence."

We are of the opinion the same rule applies to trespassing bees.

. . . . Plaintiff was an experienced beekeeper, having been engaged in that industry for some thirty-eight years. Many farmers in that vicinity produced tomatoes, which they were accustomed to spray or dust in the months of August and September of each year to protect the crops from worms, insects and other detrimental pests. The plaintiff knew of that fact. He knew that the insecticide used by the defendants was poisonous to the bees. He was personally notified and knew that they intended to use that compound to dust the tomato crops. He had previously protected his bees on such occasions by either removing the hives or by screening them. But upon the occasions complained of in this suit, with knowledge of the intention of the defendants to dust the crops, he failed and refused to take any of said precautions to protect them. On the contrary, he removed the screens and permitted the bees to leave their hives and go at large.

The defendants were engaged in dusting tomato crops in the vicinity of plaintiff's apiaries by blowing the insecticide upon the vines and crops from an airplane. In July and August, 1946, defendants dusted the tomato crop of Mr. Pylman which was situated three-quarters of a mile northeast of plaintiff's home place. In August of that year he similarly treated the tomato crop of Mr. Fonts, situated about one-half mile northwest of plaintiff's Lisbon apiary. That same year they dusted the tomato crop of Mr. Silva situated one mile northwest of plaintiff's same premises. And in August of that year they dusted a large tomato crop belonging to Mr. Krull, which was located two miles southwest of plaintiff's home place. There is evidence that other operators also dusted other crops in that vicinity in a similar manner. Defendants testified that before dusting said crops they personally notified plaintiff for their intention to do so, and offered to use their trucks to assist him in removing his hives to a safe place, but that he refused to take any means of protecting his bees, saying, with respect to a particular crop, that, "If we dusted that job he would sue us." Mr. Borges, one of the defendants, testified that before proceeding to dust the crops, they flew their airplane along the border of the fields and released powder to determine whether it would be carried by the wind toward plaintiff's apiaries, and that if the wind was blowing in that direction they delayed the proceeding of dusting. He said that when they actually dusted the crops the wind was blowing "just the opposite direction." There is also evidence that just before dusting the tomato crop adjacent to plaintiff's home place, with knowledge of their intention to do so the plaintiff removed the screens which he had previously placed over the hives.

It is true that plaintiff lost many colonies of bees as the probable result of poisonous insecticide used by someone. He found many dead bees in his yard and about the hives. He testified that the powder which he found upon the hives and bees, and which was analyzed and found to be poisonous, was gray or green in color. But the defendant Spezia testified that the only insecticide which they used was pink in color. The evidence fails to show that any pink powder was found on plaintiff's bees, hives or premises.

The foregoing evidence not only fails to satisfactorily show that it was the insecticide which was used by the defendant to spray the crops of tomatoes that killed plaintiff's bees, but there is substantial proof that, with full knowledge on the part of plaintiff that it was to be used, he failed and neglected to exercise ordinary precaution to either remove his hives or to adequately screen them during the periods of dusting, for protection of the bees. We are of the opinion the evidence on that subject sustains the findings of the court that plaintiff lost his bees as a result of his own contributory negligence.

When the owner of animals or bees contributes proximately to their injury or death, he is thereby barred from recovery. . . .

We are constrained to hold there is ample evidence in this case to support the findings that plaintiff is barred from recovery by his contributory negligence.

The judgment is affirmed.

NOTES

(1) Negligence and nuisance: *Lenk* is usefully compared with *Keeble v. Hickeringill*. Both involved actions to obtain redress for nontrespassory invasions of the plaintiff's wildlife-related activities. *Keeble* illustrates the nuisance-based approach to such conflicts, although the case itself was not explicitly plead in nuisance. Nuisance involves a use of land that, under the circumstances, causes substantial harm to another landowner's use and enjoyment of her land. Smoke, odors, and noises are the classic examples of nuisances when they result from intentional, unreasonable or ultrahazardous conduct. Nuisance thus is a description of a result rather then the description of the quality of conduct. Scaring away ducks by maliciously discharging guns is an unreasonable land use.

It is a harder case when the defendant's actions are not malicious or unreasonable but nonetheless cause substantial harm, as was the case in *Lenk v. Spezia. Lenk* was brought as a negligence action and the plaintiff lost because the defendants used care in dusting their crops. Furthermore, the plaintiff's seemingly unreasonable behavior raised issues of contributory negligence. If *Lenk* had been brought as a nuisance action the key element of wrongdoing would have been slightly different: rather than being judged on whether defendants had failed to use due case to avoid harm (the negligence standard), the issue would have been whether defendants' conduct was an unreasonable activity; if the activity itself was unreasonable, then the fact that it was carried out carefully would have been irrelevant if it caused substantial harm to the plaintiff. Due care is a defense to a negligence action; it is not a defense in a nuisance action, at least where (as in *Lenk*) the defendant's conduct was intentional. Note also, the possibility of an action brought under a strict liability theory for ultrahazardous activities.

If *Lenk* arose today, could the plaintiff claim that pesticide spraying is ultrahazardous, so that the sprayer is liable for all damage caused, without regard for issues of reasonableness and due care? *See, e.g., Langan v. Valicopters, Inc.*, 567 P.2d 218 (Wash.1977) (crop duster strictly liable for damages caused to adjacent fields).

(2) Trespassing bees: Note the court's comments about the plight of bees who depart plaintiff's land and wander over the lands of others: plaintiff could recover for their death only if "the poison was distributed wantonly, maliciously, or with the deliberate intent to injure or destroy bees," *i.e.*, if the case were analogous to *Keeble*. Why should this be the limit on defendants' liability? If the entry of the bees onto defendants' lands was foreseeable (as it clearly was), should this alter the defendants' duties to exercise care? Is it relevant that bees provide invaluable services as plant pollinators?

Compare *Lenk* with *State v. Long*. Landowner Willis Long was convicted of first degree malicious mischief for killing two hunting dogs that were chasing a wild deer across his land. The owners of the dogs were in the area hunting bobcat. The court rejected Long's claim that he was merely protecting wildlife located on his property from harmful trespass:

> .... Long's right to exclude trespassing hunters from his property does not create a corresponding right to kill hunting dogs momentarily crossing his property. *See* OP. ATT'Y GEN. 711–12; *Zanotti v. Bolles,* 67 A. 818 (Vt.1907). Moreover, although Long's right to game on his property is superior to that of trespassers, the State's property right to regulate wildlife is superior to Long's: "Wildlife is the property of the state." RCW 77.12.010. "Game is not a property right appurtenant to land. Game belongs to the State." *State v. Quigley,* 324 P.2d 827 (Wash.1958). Long cannot successfully maintain that he killed Rowdy and Sparkle in defense of wildlife or of his property.

State v. Long, 991 P.2d 102 (Wash.App.2000). The court rejected as inapt Long's citations to precedents authorizing the protection of domestic animals. It also rejected his claim that he was empowered by statute to abate a public nuisance that was specially injurious to him: the dogs may have been injurious to the state's deer, the court held, but not to Long or his property. Might the case have turned out differently if Long had been engaged in hunting deer? Or was the the problem that as a landowner he had no legal interest in the deer? Would he have been justified in killing dogs harassing the deer if he ran a deer-farming operation?

(3) Migrating wildlife: What if a landowner's "use" of wildlife entails watching them or benefitting from their services as members of the ecosystem rather than trapping or shooting them as in *Harrison* and *Keeble*? Could a landowner complain if a neighbor blocked the free passage of wild animals that would otherwise migrate to his land? Consider the following, eloquent presentation by an English court in 1879, describing the landowner's rights to enjoy the land's natural features:

> What then is the right of land and its owner or occupier? It is to have all natural incidents and advantages, as nature would produce them; there is a right to all the light and heat that would come, to all the rain that would fall, to all the wind that would blow; a right that the rain, which would pass over the land, should not be stopped and made to fall on it; a right that the heat from the sun should not be stopped and reflected on it, a right that the wind should not be checked, but should be able to escape freely....

Bryant v. Lefever, 4 C.P.D. 172 (1879) (also reported, with a additional facts, at 48 Q.B.D. 380). *Bryant* does not specifically include wildlife in its list of the land's natural incidents, but is wildlife not as natural and as valuable as the sun and the rain? The court in *Bryant* went on to note that a landowner's rights to the natural incidents of his parcel are qualified by the rights of neighboring landowners to make reasonable use of their own lands. Neighbors could disrupt the land's natural incidents, but they could do so only if their actions qualified under the shifting, context-specific idea of reasonableness. Thus, a landowner retained the right to complain of unreasonable actions by neighbors that disrupted the land's natural features. Could a landowner, then, complain about unreasonable behavior by another landowner that blocked the free passage of animals? How different is this hypothetical from the facts of *Keeble*?

For a consideration of *Bryant* (and other cases) and their relevance in the contemporary land-use context, see Eric T. Freyfogle, *Eight Principles for Property Rights in the Anti–Sprawl Age,* 23 WM. & MARY ENVTL. L. & POL'Y REV. 777 (1999).

(iv) THE POWER TO TRANSFER ACCESS

Millbrook Hunt, Inc. v. Smith

New York Appellate Division.
670 N.Y.S.2d 907 (1998).

MEMORANDUM BY THE COURT:—In an action, *inter alia,* for a judgment declaring that the plaintiff has an easement over the defendant's property and to permanently enjoin the defendant from interfering with the plaintiff's use of that easement, the defendant appeals. . . .

ORDERED that the order and the interlocutory judgment are affirmed, without costs or disbursements.

The plaintiff, Millbrook Hunt, Inc. (hereinafter the Hunt), is an organization dedicated to the preservation and perpetuation of traditional fox hunting. The defendant Edgar O. Smith is the owner of a 285–acre parcel of land situated in the Town of Stanford, Dutchess County, which is subject to an agreement captioned "Lease and Easement Agreement" (hereinafter the Agreement), and which permits the Hunt to use the land for the purpose of fox hunting. The Agreement was entered into by the Hunt and Smith's predecessor in title in 1987, and was for a term of 75 years "unless terminated sooner pursuant to the terms of the Lease or pursuant to law". In 1995 Smith, who objected to hunting and who had undertaken measures to transform his property into a wildlife habitat and nature preserve, ejected members of the Hunt from his property while they were performing routine maintenance of their fox-hunting trails.

The Hunt thereafter commenced this action seeking, inter alia, a judgment declaring that it has an easement over Smith's property, and to permanently enjoin Smith from interfering with its use of that easement. Smith moved for summary judgment dismissing the complaint on the ground that at most the Agreement conferred a revocable license to the Hunt, which he had terminated. The Hunt cross-moved to dismiss the affirmative defenses and the counterclaims contained in Smith's answer. The Supreme Court denied Smith's motion and granted the Hunt's cross motion, and an interlocutory judgment was entered August 20, 1996.

To determine the true character of an interest, a court must examine the nature of the right rather than the name given to it by the parties. [ ] The mere labeling of an interest as an easement does not necessarily make it an easement; it may be a license. [ ] Easements and licenses in real property are distinct in principle, though it is sometimes difficult to distinguish them. [ ] An easement implies an interest in land ordinarily created by a grant, and is permanent in nature. [ ] A license does not imply an interest in land, but is a mere personal privilege to commit some act or series of acts on the land of another without possessing any estate therein.

Here, paragraph 1 of the Agreement indicates that the Hunt leased a particular one-quarter acre parcel of land for a period of 75 years. In addition, pursuant to paragraph 6 of the Agreement, the Hunt clearly reserved an absolute right to fox hunt on the remaining parcel of land. This right was for the benefit of the Hunt and attached to it without reference to use on any particular lands. Contrary to Smith's contentions, the fact that paragraph 10 of the Agreement reserves to the grantor the "absolute right to develop his land" and the right to redirect the Hunt's trails, does not render the grant a revocable license. Although the agreement provides that the grantor may "relocate" the Hunt's improvements, or redirect their trails "in order to make such improvements to the Land", the grantor does not have the right to completely exclude the Hunt from the property. Furthermore, an essential feature of the type of easement involved herein, which distinguishes it from a license, is that the interest in the land is for some definite period. [ ] Here, the agreement specifically provides that the Hunt's right to use the parcel was for a definite period of 75 years.

It is clear that the parties sufficiently expressed their intent to reserve to the Hunt a permanent right to fox-hunt on the parcel. Thus, the Hunt has an easement in the disputed area rather than a revocable license. Smith had both actual and constructive notice of this easement prior to the date that he bought the land and is estopped from denying its existence. [ ]

We have examined Smith's remaining contentions and find them to be without merit.

Central Oregon Fabricators, Inc. v. Hudspeth

Court of Appeals of Oregon.
977 P.2d 416 (1999).

■ HASELTON, J.:—Defendants appeal from a judgment quieting title to 24,000 acres of land in favor of plaintiffs and extinguishing an express profit a prendre[1] granting defendants the right to hunt and fish on plaintiffs' property. On de novo review ... we agree with defendants' principal contention that the trial court erred in concluding that defendants had abandoned their rights or, alternatively, that those rights had been extinguished by way of adverse possession. We further agree, in part, that the trial court erroneously construed the scope of defendants' rights

---

1. A profit a prendre is a species of easement that gives the holder or grantee an "interest in the land itself" and the right to enter the land of the servient owners to sever or remove things previously constituting part of the land. *Jackson County v. Compton,* 609 P.2d 1293 (Or.1980). As the court explained in *Bingham v. Salene,* 14 P. 523 (Or.1887):

The property in animals ferae naturae, while they are on the soil, belong to the owner of the soil, and he may grant a right to others to come and take them, by a grant of hunting, shooting, fowling, and so forth.* * * [S]uch a grant is a license of a profit a prendre.

The same general rules governing easements govern profits. *Jackson County,* 609 P.2d 1293.

under the deed. Accordingly, we affirm in part, reverse in part, and remand for further proceedings.

On August 7, 1964, Hudspeth Land and Livestock Company and Hudspeth Sawmill Company executed a deed conveying more than 24,000 acres of land in Wheeler County (the "Bald Mountain property") to plaintiff Central Oregon Fabricators, Inc. (COF). On the same day, and immediately after executing the deed, Fred Hudspeth, one of the principal owners of the Hudspeth companies, asked plaintiff Jack Rhoden, principal owner of COF, if he and his family could continue to hunt on the land. Rhoden agreed, and COF, for a payment of $10 and "other good and valuable consideration," subsequently executed a deed granting 11 individuals rights to hunt and fish on the Bald Mountain property. Among the grantees were defendants Alan and Barry Hudspeth and Fred Hudspeth, the predecessor-in-interest of defendant F & M Realty Company, Inc. (F & M). That deed, which is the focus of this dispute, provided that COF

> does hereby grant, bargain, sell and convey unto said Grantees, their heirs and assigns, and personal guests while accompanying the Grantees, the right, privilege, and easement to shoot, kill and take away wild fowl, including but not limited to wild duck, pheasant, grouse, sage hen, quail and other birds of every kind and nature; and wild game, including but not limited to deer, antelope and elk; and to fish in streams and ponds, all of which may be upon the following described real property, or in any and all lakes, and sloughs, and waters situated, lying and being upon said lands lying within Wheeler county, Oregon, as described [as the Bald Mountain Property].

The deed did not include a limitation on duration but provided, instead, that the conveyance was "to have and to hold said rights granted unto said Grantees, their heirs and assigns, and personal guests while accompanying the Grantees * * *."

Immediately after COF acquired the Bald Mountain property in 1964, Rhoden began constructing fences and trenches around the perimeter of the property, putting locked gates on all access roads, and employing guards to patrol the property during hunting season.

In 1989, Rhoden individually acquired an undivided one-half interest in the property from the trusts of the heirs of his former partner, John Crawford. That conveyance was explicitly "subject to" defendants' and the other grantees' rights under the 1964 hunting deed.

At about the time that Rhoden acquired his one-half interest in the property, he and his sons began operating a hunting recreation and guide service on the property, Bald Mountain Recreation, Inc., which charged hunters a fee of up to $5,000 per person for a five-day guided hunting trip. In operating that business, Rhoden modified the cattle and logging practices on the property in ways designed to enhance hunting. For example, Rhoden put out food and planted additional grass to encourage elk to come onto the property and reduced the number of cattle to compensate for the increase in elk.

From 1964 until the trial in 1997, defendant Barry Hudspeth and Fred Hudspeth, F & M's predecessor in interest, never exercised their rights to hunt or fish on the property. Only defendant Alan Hudspeth attempted to exercise rights under the 1964 deed. In 1968 or 1969, Alan hunted on the property after telling Rhoden his plans. In 1974, Alan again told Rhoden that he planned to hunt on the property; however, after Rhoden told him that there would be several other paying hunters in the area, Alan decided to hunt on other land that he owned.

In October 1988, Rhoden invited his grandchildren to hunt on a portion of the Bald Mountain property that had been conveyed to a neighbor. Todd Rhoden, one of Rhoden's grandsons, brought his friend, Todd Hudspeth, who was Alan's son, with him. Jack Rhoden told Todd Hudspeth that he could not stay and hunt. When Todd's grandfather, Fred Hudspeth learned what had happened, he directed his attorney to send Rhoden a copy of the deed, and an explanation of the rights it granted, so as to make it "perfectly clear that the rights existed and to restate the rights so that no one would forget them." Rhoden never responded to that letter. However, he later apologized to Alan Hudspeth about the incident.

In August 1994, Alan Hudspeth approached Rhoden at a golf course and told him that he would like the keys or combinations to the locked gates so that he could hunt during the upcoming season. Although the testimony at trial was disputed, Rhoden apparently told Alan that he did not want him hunting on the land because he had paying hunters coming. After that conversation, Rhoden went home and examined the 1964 deed. He became quite concerned after reading the deed and called his attorney for advice because he believed that the wording granted a broad right to hunt, and he could see that, "with the number of people that they might want to bring * * * because the[e] deed left it wide open for them to bring anybody," that it could "screw up" all the property.

[Over time, several Hudspeth family members conveyed their rights back to Rhoden. Unsold rights all ended up in F & M Realty Co. (F & M), which, desirous of making commercial use of the hunting rights,] began developing a plan to sell memberships to hunt on the property by assigning the rights on an annual basis to the members.

In September 1995, plaintiffs filed this action to quiet title, alleging that defendants had abandoned their rights under the 1964 deed or, in the alternative, for declaratory relief, seeking a declaration that defendants' rights under the deed were strictly personal and not "subject to commercialization, sale, or profit taking." . . . .

With respect to plaintiffs' principal claim of abandonment, the court determined that defendants' nonuse of the property after 1964, coupled with their failure to object to plaintiffs' action in fencing, gating, and patrolling the property and excluding uninvited guests, evinced an abandonment of the property by no later than 1988. The court further and alternatively determined that defendants' interests were extinguished through adverse possession:

> The Court finds that the Plaintiffs adversely possessed the Defendants' hunting rights. An interest in property, either in whole or in part, can be adversely possessed if the party satisfies the elements of adverse possession. The servient estate can adversely possess a right to use the

property away from the dominant holder. *Simpson v. Fowles,* [536 P.2d 499] (1975). The party must show that possession is (1) open, notorious and a hostile claim of right as against others; (2) continuous; (3) exclusive; and (4) the property was held for the statutory period of time, *i.e.* ten years. Although this legal theory was not claimed by the Plaintiffs, the Court believes that under the broad claim of declaratory judgment, the Court can make a finding regarding this theory to adjudicate the rights of the parties.

It is clear that after the August, 1964, conveyance, Plaintiffs fenced the property, gated and locked the property and patrolled the property in a manner open and notorious to all others. It is clear that Plaintiffs prohibited all parties, except permitted guests, from going onto the property. Plaintiffs also managed all incidents of ownership in Bald Mountain, including the hunting rights, to the exclusion of all others. Finally, Plaintiffs' exclusivity of ownership was continuous for well over ten (10) years and most definitely during the hunting season.

The court subsequently entered a judgment that incorporated its findings and dismissed defendants' counterclaims. . . .

We turn to the first assignment of error challenging the trial court's determination of abandonment. In *Abbott v. Thompson,* 641 P.2d 652 (Or.App.), *rev. denied* 648 P.2d 851 (Or.1982), we explained that the party claiming abandonment must show both nonuse and "either [a] verbal expression of an intent to abandon or conduct inconsistent with an intention to make further use." With respect to the second element, "conduct which is equivocal in character does not suffice." [ ] Rather, "[t]he intent to abandon must be clear and it must be accompanied by some specific act of abandonment." *Rich v. Runyon,* 627 P.2d 1265 (Or.App.1981).

Here, the trial court stated:

The Defendants, Fred, Alan and Barry Hudspeth, have made no attempt to use the property pursuant to the hunting rights since the conveyance in August, 1964. They did not hunt or fish on the property for approximately thirty (30) years. The only exception to this non-use was in 1968 or 1969, when Alan Hudspeth hunted on Bald Mountain, [with] Jack Rhoden's permission.

In addition to Defendants' non-use, Jack Rhoden began to fence the Bald Mountain property shortly after the August, 1964 conveyance. He placed locks and gates on the property and intensely patrolled the property during hunting season. He kept all parties, other than invited guests, off the property and did not allow anyone to hunt elk until somewhere between 1989 and 1990. Rhoden continued this action each year thereafter. [Defendants] failed to limit the Plaintiffs' actions, which were totally inconsistent with their hunting rights. Defendants' failure to curb Plaintiffs' actions continued from the time of the August, 1964 conveyance through 1994. Due to the extensive non-use and the other factors listed above, the Court finds that [defendants] have abandoned their hunting and fishing rights.

Defendants do not dispute the trial court's finding of the first required element, nonuse. They argue, however, that plaintiffs failed to prove that defendants intended to abandon their rights through evidence of either "a verbal expression" of such an intention or "conduct inconsistent with an intent to make further use." *Abbott,* 641 P.2d 652. Specifically, defendants contend that the trial court erroneously relied on plaintiffs' comments and conduct as proof of defendants' intent. . . .

We agree with defendants that plaintiffs failed to prove that defendants intended to abandon their rights under the 1964 deed. We so conclude for two related reasons. First, as a matter of law, defendants' passivity or acquiescence was, without more, insufficient to demonstrate an intent to abandon. Second, Rhoden's conduct in developing the Bald Mountain property's hunting and fishing potential and in excluding trespassers was not inconsistent with—and, indeed, enhanced—defendants' own interests. Thus, defendants' "failure to curb" those activities cannot be deemed to be inconsistent with retention of their rights.

As noted, the trial court concluded that the alleged abandonment occurred by no later than October 1988, before the incident involving Todd Hudspeth, and plaintiffs do not contend otherwise. The parties' only interactions pertaining to the property between 1964 and 1988 were in 1968 or 1969, when Alan Hudspeth hunted at Bald Mountain, and in 1974, when Alan told Rhoden he would like to hunt on the property but ultimately hunted elsewhere. Neither of those incidents involved Fred or Barry and, thus, could not be probative of their intent.

[The Court considered and rejected plaintiffs' claim that Alan Hudspeth only hunted with permission, suggesting that he had relinquished his vested rights to hunt:] Alan's conduct in 1968 or 1969 was, at best, "equivocal in character." Hunting on the property cannot be deemed an abandonment of the right to hunt on the property. Obtaining consent does not unequivocally evince the relinquishment of the right to act without consent. Certainly, Rhoden, who denied that Alan had ever hunted on Bald Mountain after 1964, did not attribute such significance to the alleged "permission."

We thus conclude that plaintiffs failed to prove that defendants either verbally expressed their intent to abandon their rights under the 1964 deed or engaged in conduct that was clearly inconsistent with those rights.

Defendants next assign error to the trial court's sua sponte determination that plaintiffs acquired title in fee simple by adverse possession, a theory that plaintiffs never pleaded or argued. Plaintiffs respond that the court properly addressed adverse possession because defendants' counterclaim, which generally sought a declaration of

> the interests, rights, and obligations of the parties in and to the property * * *, the nature of the rights granted to Defendants under the Deed, * * * and the terms and manner under which Defendants' rights may be exercised, utilized, assigned, or transferred, at least implicated that issue.

We agree with defendants that the trial court erred in granting plaintiff relief on an unpleaded theory. Plaintiffs never pleaded a claim for adverse possession; they never sought leave of the court to amend their pleadings to conform to any proof of adverse possession, [ ]; and they never otherwise contended that adverse possession was somehow apposite. . . . Thus, the trial court erred in granting relief on the basis of adverse possession. Given our disposition with respect to abandonment, we reverse the judgment quieting title in plaintiffs in fee simple and declaring the deed void.

We turn to defendants' fifth assignment, which contests the trial court's construction of the 1964 deed and consequent declaration of the parties' rights and interests under the deed. Defendants assert that the trial court erred in concluding that: (1) rights under the deed could be assigned only to "natural persons" and that any such assignment could not be to "more than one natural person"; (2) the hunting rights pertained only to the types of animals specifically identified in the deed; and (3) "personal guests" under the deed do not include persons who pay to hunt.

In *Tipperman v. Tsiatsos*, 964 P.2d 1015 (Or.1998), the court described the legal principles governing the proper construction of an instrument creating an easement by express grant. Because easements and profits are governed by the same general rules, [ ], in construing the 1964 deed, we first "declare the meaning of what is written in the instrument" and look beyond the wording to the intent of the original parties "only where there is an uncertainty or ambiguity." 964 P.2d 1015. Moreover, as we recently explained:

> In giving effect to an easement's purpose, general principles of reasonableness control. Ordinarily, an easement passes no rights to the grantee except those rights that are necessary for the easement's reasonable and proper enjoyment. Similarly, the grantor retains "full dominion and use of the land [subject to an easement], except so far as a limitation of the grantor's right is essential to the fair enjoyment of the easement that was granted."

Watson v. Banducci, 973 P.2d 395 (Or.App.1999), quoting *Miller v. Vaughn*, 8 Or. 333, 336 (1880) (citations omitted).

Defendants first contend that the phrase "to grantees, *their heirs and assigns*" (emphasis added) is unlimited both as to the nature and the number of potential heirs and assignees. In particular, defendants contend that, under the deed, grantees may assign their interests to entities as well as to natural persons and that hunting rights may be assigned to more than one individual or entity. Defendants are correct that that language, viewed in isolation, is broad. *See, e.g., Sunset Lake v. Remington*, 609 P.2d 896 (Or. 1980) (refusing to limit or restrict the term "assigns" after looking at the definition of "assigns" as "one to whom a right of property is legally transferred," and "generally comprehends all those who take * * * under the assignor, whether by conveyance, devise, descent or act of law"). However, the context of the deed compels a narrower construction. In particular, the deed refers to "personal guests" of the grantees—and at least implicitly by extension—of their heirs and assigns. People, individuals, have personal guests. Entities don't. Moreover, to the extent that any ambiguity remains, our assessment of the "circumstances existing at the time of the grant or easement," *Tipperman*, 964 P.2d 1015, particularly, including the discussion between Fred Hudspeth and Jack Rhoden, persuades us that assignees under the deed must be "natural persons." The trial court correctly so construed the deed.

Conversely, nothing in the deed's language or surrounding circumstances compels the construction, endorsed by the trial court, that any grantee's interest cannot be assigned to more than one person. Thus, the trial court erred in holding that "[a]ny assignment * * * cannot be divided, multiplied or assigned to more than one natural person." Nevertheless, we emphasize that a proliferation of assignments, impinging on the grantors' right to make reasonable use of the property, would exceed the scope of the easement. [ ]

Defendants next assert that the deed's language, "including but not limited to," followed by a list of the types of game that may be hunted, grants the right to hunt types of game other than those specifically listed. Defendants are correct. The plain language of the deed "clearly contemplates" that the rights extend to wild game other than those expressly listed. *See State ex rel Juvenile Dept. v. Ware,* 927 P.2d 1114 (Or.App.1996) (holding that "including but not limited to" language in a statute granting the juvenile court authority to impose conditions of probation "clearly contemplate[d]" that the juvenile court could impose conditions "other than those expressly listed in the statute").

Finally, defendants assert that the term "personal guests" in the context of the deed encompasses both paying and nonpaying guests, as long as they accompany the grantee or the grantee's successor in interest. Plaintiffs challenge that construction, asserting that "[a] purchaser of a hunting pass would be more accurately described as a business invitee rather than a personal guest." We agree with plaintiffs. "Personal guest" in common usage has a noncommercial connotation. Moreover, to the extent that that term could ever be understood, dubiously, to refer to paying customers or clients, such a construction cannot be squared with the circumstances surrounding the granting of the profit. We thus sustain the trial court's construction of the deed in that regard.

NOTES

(1) The landowner's power to permit others to hunt: As a general matter, landowners have the power to allow other people to come onto their lands to hunt and fish. As with other incidents of ownership, the power to permit use is subject to limitations: the hunter must, for example, comply with all state licensing, closed seasons, and bag limit laws. *Cf. Wickham v. Walker,* Barnes 125, 94 Eng. Rep. 838 (K.B. 1725) (court rejected defense that defendant had permission to hunt on the land because under the qualification statute defendant was not qualified to hunt and the permission of the landowner therefore was immaterial).

(2) Varieties of permission: Permission to enter can be granted in many ways and subject to almost an infinite variety of terms, from the casual oral permission to enter for a day to take a single species to a full-blown conveyance of perpetual, exclusive rights to engage in all lawful hunting. The practical issues are easy to list: How long does the right last? Who can enter the land, and when and where? What animals can be taken and how?

Is the right transferable or divisible? Is it exclusive? Is any rental or other fee due? Can the landowner unilaterally cancel the right or change its fundamental terms? When can the hunter complain about land-use practices by the owner that diminish the hunting right?

Given the nearly infinite flexibility of landowner-hunter arrangements, generalizations are difficult. The rights obtained by a particular hunter or fisher can only be determined by reference to the terms of the deal struck with the landowner. When these have been reduced to writing and cover all relevant issues, courts simply enforce the agreement as signed—assuming that no terms conflict with public policy. Often—as *Central Oregon Fabricators* illustrates—agreements are fragmentary, leaving critical issues unaddressed. When courts are required to fill in the gaps, they do so by drawing upon all evidence of the parties' intentions. They also tend to place the agreement into one of several familiar common-law categories, with legal consequences flowing from the category chosen.

(a) License vs. easement: When the parties' agreement is ambiguous, courts often ask whether the hunter obtained a durable easement or merely a license. Whether the parties intended one or the other (or, as in *Central Oregon Fabricators*, some mix of the two) is not determined solely—or even chiefly—by the labels that the parties choose since lay people often misuse and mix inconsistent legal terms. Instead, courts look to the arrangement that the parties seemed to envision. *E.g., David Lee Boykin Family Trust v. Boykin,* 661 So.2d 245 (Ala.Civ.App.1995) (interpreting document entitled "lease" as a license). Words of grant or conveyance, for example, suggest that the parties intended an easement, but an easement can be created without such language. *E.g., Thompson v. Finnerud,* 212 N.W. 497 (S.D.1927). On the other hand, the more informal, personal, and transient an agreement is, the more likely it is to be viewed as a license.

Traditionally, a durable property right to hunt or fish was termed a "profit" or, more technically, a "profit a prendre" rather than an easement. As the court in *Central Oregon Fabricators* notes in footnote 1, a profit is a particular type of property right that allows the holder to enter onto the land of another and take something from the land—in this case, wildlife. The *Restatement* defines "profit a prendre" as "an easement that confers the right to enter and remove timber, minerals, oil, gas, game or other substances from land in the possession of another." RESTATEMENT OF THE LAW OF PROPERTY: SERVITUDES § 1.2(2) (2000). In the context of hunting and fishing rights, commentators from time to time have objected to this terminology, arguing that a hunting right cannot technically be a profit given that the landowner does not own the wildlife; a hunting right, therefore, is merely a right to enter land for a specific purpose, much like a typical right-of-way. *E.g.,* JON W. BRUCE & JAMES W. ELY, JR., THE LAW OF EASEMENTS AND LICENSES IN LAND 1–21 (1988). Nonetheless, rights to hunt and fish were classed as profits at the common law and the profit terminology remains firmly entrenched. In any event, profits today are typically viewed as merely a particular type of easement, and governed by the same rules as other easements, rendering the terminology unimportant. *See Figliuzzi v. Carcajou Shooting Club of Lake Koshkonong,* 516 N.W.2d 410

(Wis.1994) (easement same as profit); *see also* RESTATEMENT OF THE LAW OF PROPERTY: SERVITUDES 6–8 (combining easements, profits, and covenants running with the land into a general category, "servitudes").

(b) The key differences: An easement is considered an interest in the land itself. A license, on the other hand, is merely a permissive right to enter property or, at most, a contract right; it does not give rise to a property interest. Important consequences flow from the category chosen. As the Supreme Court of Minnesota explained:

> While there are divers kinds of licenses, it is sufficient to now state that a license is not an estate but a permission giving the licensee a personal legal privilege enjoyable on the land of another. [ ] It is destroyed by an attempted transfer if the licensor so elects. [ ] It is revocable at the licensor's will, [ ], or by his death, [ ]. Normally payment of consideration does not render it irrevocable. [ ]
>
> A profit a prendre is more substantial. It gives a right enforceable against others. [ ] If in gross (*i.e.,* a profit which is held by one independently of his ownership of other land) it is generally transferable and inheritable. [ ] Since a profit a prendre is an interest in realty, it must be created, in contrast to a license, by a properly executed writing. [ ] One ancient form of profit a prendre is the granting of hunting rights. *Council v. Sanderlin,* 111 S.E. 365 (N.C.1922); *St. Helen Shooting Club v. Mogle,* 207 N.W. 915 (Mich.1926). While it is true that wild life is not part of the soil as many common forms of profits a prendre are, yet the right to hunt and take game appertains to the land and is a profit flowing from the ownership. It is an incorporeal right allied so closely to the fee, probably for historical reasons, that it justifiably can be regarded as a profit a prendre. This is true although wild life is a subject of ownership only when reduced to possession, *Liesner v. Wanie,* 145 N.W. 374 (Wis.1914); *see Missouri v. Holland,* 252 U.S. 416 (1920) (Holmes, J., "* * * possession is the beginning of ownership.") While title is in the state as trustee, [ ], the owner of the land has a qualified property interest in that it is he who has the exclusive right to reduce game to possession. *L. Realty Co. v. Johnson,* 100 N.W. 94 (Minn.1904); *Lamprey v. Danz,* 90 N.W. 578 (Minn.1902).

Minnesota Valley Gun Club v. Northline Corp., 290 N.W. 222, 224 (Minn. 1940).

Without regard for whether an interest is an easement or a license, the holder of the right is limited by its terms. *E.g., Thomas v. Weller,* 281 N.W.2d 790 (Neb.1979) (where easement contains specific geographic limits, hunter must abide by them). Unless otherwise specified, the holder of an easement or license has no right to erect permanent structures on the land. *Wechsler v. People,* 537 N.Y.S.2d 900 (N.Y.App.1989). On the other hand, the holder of a hunting easement can typically post lands under state posting laws. *E.g., Nelson v. State,* 883 S.W.2d 839 (Ark.1994) (construing holder of hunting easement as "lessee" of property for purposes of state posting statute).

(c) Assignment and division: Although hunting and fishing easements are typically held in gross, they can be attached (appurtenant) to a tract of land (the dominant estate) if the parties so intend; the dominant estate will usually be a parcel adjacent to the land subject to the easement. In such a case, the easement is held by the owner of the dominant estate and passes to subsequent owners of that estate whether by sale or inheritance. *E.g., Merriam v. First National Bank of Akron*, 587 So.2d 584 (Fla.App.1991). Easements in gross are also transferable and inheritable unless the parties either intended the right to be personal to the holder or otherwise limited it (as in *Central Oregon Fabricators*). *Compare Hanson v. Fergus Falls Natl. Bank*, 65 N.W.2d 857 (Minn.1954) (hunting rights, like other profits, are transferable) *with Maw v. Weber Basin Water Conservancy Dist.*, 436 P.2d 230 (Utah 1968) (on facts of case, hunting easement was personal to holders). An easement that is transferable can also be divided— that is, the holder of the easement can grant hunting rights to multiple others—when the hunting rights are exclusive or when the parties otherwise envisioned this power. In all cases, however, the total use of the easement must not overburden the servient estate. In the case of a nonexclusive easement, the landowner retains the power to grant the same hunting rights to others. When that is the case, courts typically assume that the easement holder has no rights to divide and thus cannot sell hunting rights to others in competition with the landowner. In contrast, licenses generally are not transferable or divisible unless the parties clearly intended otherwise, and indeed a few courts continue to show respect for the old rule that any attempt to transfer a license renders it void. *See* JON W. BRUCE & JAMES W. ELY, JR., *supra*, at §§ 1.04, 8.01–.04, 10.04.

(d) duration and termination. Perhaps the key difference between a license and an easement is that a license is revocable by the landowner at any time without advance notice, unless revocation would be so unfair that the landowner should be estopped from doing so (as when, perhaps, the licensee has made substantial, foreseeable expenditures in reliance on the license). Revocation is permitted even when the licensee pays consideration for the license. If the revocation breaches the license agreement the hunter may have contract remedies, but the revocation is valid. A landowner can properly terminate a license agreement upon a material breach by the hunter. In the event of a sale of the underlying land the license automatically terminates since it is not an interest in the land that binds a subsequent owner.

In contrast to the license, an easement cannot be terminated by the landowner except when a power is reserved to do so. Easements can be perpetual in duration, but can be limited by the parties to any chosen length of time. Nontransferable easements, of course, end upon the death of the holder. Easements are binding on subsequent owners of land so that the sale of the land does not affect the easement. An easement, however, is subject to statutory requirements for recordation and a subsequent purchaser who buys without actual or apparent notice of the easement can take free of it. *E.g., Reeves v. Alabama Land Locators, Inc.*, 514 So.2d 917 (Ala.1987). A further important limit on the duration of easements comes from state statutes that limit the enforceability of easements to a specified period (*e.g,* 40 years) unless the holder re-records the interest to keep it alive. *See Figliuzzi v. Carcajou Shooting Club of Lake Koshkonong,* 516 N.W.2d 410 (Wis.1994).

As *Central Oregon Fabricators* illustrates, easements can also be lost either by abandonment (nonuse plus intent to relinquish) or by the underlying landowner's adverse use of the easement area for the period necessary to establish adverse user.

(3) Landowner-hunter conflicts: One particularly awkward issue, that is often unaddressed even in written agreements, is how the owner of the underlying fee interest can use the land during the period of the easement or license. In a prominent decision, the Supreme Court of Wisconsin barred a landowner from constructing a 26–unit condominium project on 42 acres of land because the construction would unduly interfere with hunting and fishing rights held by a shooting club under a 1896 grant. *Figliuzzi v. Carcajou Shooting Club of Lake Koshkonong,* 516 N.W.2d 410 (Wis.1994) (holding that landowner may not unreasonably interfere with the use of the easement). *Accord Wechsler v. People,* 537 N.Y.S.2d 900 (N.Y.App.1989). In contrast, the Iowa Supreme Court refused to protect the holder of hunting and fishing rights on forested land when the landowner removed all the timber, planted the land in corn, and destroyed a pond used for fishing and turtling. *Mikesh v. Peters,* 284 N.W.2d 215, 219 (Iowa 1979) (holding that landowner can make free use of the property "absent an express covenant to the contrary or a malicious bad faith destruction of the clearly designated object (*i.e.,* game or its habitat) of the right").

Robert K. Davis, *A New Paradigm in Wildlife Conservation: Using Markets to Produce Big Game Hunting in* WILDLIFE IN THE MARKETPLACE

(Terry L. Anderson & Peter J. Hill, eds. 1995).

For many years a growing segment of the environmental and resource economics profession has been preoccupied with extramarket or nonmarket goods—those goods and services that are produced and consumed in the absence of normal, functioning markets. Wildlife-oriented recreation typically has fallen into that category. Traditionally a by-product of private agriculture and forestry, the wildlife has been the responsibility of governments. Public parks and refuges are set aside for certain species or acquired for hunting, but the main function of wildlife agencies is to regulate the take among licensed hunters and to reduce poaching and trespassing. With all this, the wildlife conservation movement has had to recognize the predominance of private land in the United States and that many species of primarily farmland and ranchland game are dependent for much of their habitat on private lands. [ ] If the landowner is not interested in the production or use of wildlife, then habitat may be destroyed and wildlife populations reduced. Much effort has been devoted by the state wildlife agencies and by organizations of hunters and fishermen to curry landowner favor so that wildlife habitat will be preserved, and wildlife recreationists—usually hunters and fishermen—will be tolerated on private land.

An Historical Perspective

In 1930, the American Game Policy Committee, under the chairmanship of Aldo Leopold, addressed the future of wildlife on private land. It considered the merits of establishing landowner property rights in game, and then resolved that the American system of state regulation and control could work if sportsmen would pay the landowner something for the privilege of hunting. [ ] In this way landowners would have an incentive to maintain populations of game animals.

Sixty years after the Leopold Committee delivered its findings, we find the practice of paying fees for hunting widespread in Texas, [ ], and on commercial timberlands of the southern states. [ ] Waterfowl hunting has long been subject to leases and fees, and there is evidence that goose hunting on Maryland's eastern shore is becoming a farm enterprise. [ ]

Fee and lease hunting has been slowly coming to the Rocky Mountain West. [ ] Despite large expanses of national forest and public grazing lands, hunters' willingness to pay for a place to hunt and landowners' willingness to sell access to hunting have created a market for access to hunting in western Colorado. This development creates a set of new parameters for wildlife management on lands where private management is dominant, as on private lands, or influential, as on public grazing lands.

On the private lands where private management holds full sway, producing access to wildlife for recreation can become an economic enterprise. On public lands where forage permits are held by private managers, there can be a shift in emphasis from livestock grazing to more use of the forage by wildlife provided the bureaucratic managers and the affected public interests will agree with the private managers who want to make this shift.

But enlarging the private interest in wildlife management through activities in markets challenges the American notion that wildlife is only to be managed by public agencies and calls for some innovations in policy if wildlife conservation on private and public lands is to benefit fully from private entrepreneurship. There are elements in the wildlife conservation movement that see only a public responsibility for wildlife and expect nothing good to come from the assertion of private interests in the production of wildlife on private or public lands. In part this view stems from a mistaken attribution of the decline of wildlife populations to private commercial exploitation rather than to the root cause, which is a lack of definite and secure property rights in wildlife. This view also stems from the bureaucratic self-interest of the public wildlife agencies in wanting to perpetuate their own central roles in wildlife affairs.

This paper reports on a series of investigation in western Colorado that sought a better understanding of the role of markets in (a) improving the quality of hunting; (b) providing access to landlocked public lands; and (c) creating incentives for private efforts to protect and manage wildlife....

Barriers to Private Wildlife Ranches

The picture that emerges from all these studies reveals the importance of private entrepreneurship in the production of hunting opportunities and game management. This development is the result of a resurgence of elk and deer populations in northwestern Colorado and an increasing demand for hunting in the region. It comes at a time when the livestock industry may be looking for alternative ranch enterprises and recreational demands for western lands are growing. [ ] The development of a private economic interest in game would appear to be a welcome turn of events given the mixed record of the attempts of state wildlife agencies and of public land managing agencies to motivate private operators to protect habitat, preserve wildlife, and tolerate hunters on private and public lands under their control. At last, economic motives provide the private land manager with the same wildlife production goals as the conservation agencies are given by their popular mandates.

In a situation that defies logic, Colorado's Ranching for Wildlife program [a program that gives private landowners a longer hunting season and an allocation of hunting licenses in exchange for limited public access and some wildlife management activities], which could restore wildlife to its former prominence in much of the state, has encountered political and philosophical opposition. [ ] Among some constituents of the public land agencies, private control of access to public land, which could improve hunting (and range condition), is generally abhorred. After years of insistence on public access to all public lands, these groups are slow to recognize controlled hunting as a desirable alternative to unlimited public access. Some are concerned that an enlarged private role will have ruinous effects if it depends upon commercialization, [ ], and privatization. [ ]

Acceptance by wildlife conservation groups of a role for private enterprise in wildlife production is carefully qualified to avoid support for privatization and for private activities on behalf of wildlife on public lands. [ ] In their attempts to maintain ethical purity, these observers add confusion to a set of issues that are clamoring for clarification.

The Question of Privatization

Wildlife entrepreneurship is complicated in America by the question of who owns the game. The rhetoric of the state wildlife agencies and their sportsmen clientele or a rancher who wants compensation for wildlife damages would have us believe that the state owns the game, but that is an overstatement. . . .

[One report] emphasizes that the landowner possess the exclusive right to hunt game animals that inhabit his land, subject to the right of the state to regulate such hunting. Possessing these rights, an owner may convey hunting rights to another by granting or leasing his property for such purposes.

Lueck,[2] who examines the economic nature of wildlife law, concludes that regardless of the legal status of wildlife, landowners always will be interested in controlling rights to wildlife if the rights have value. While Colorado's wildlife ranchers are behaving consistently with this idea by

---

2. Dean L. Lueck, *The Economic Na-*   (1989).
ture of Wildlife Law, 18 J. LEG. STUD. 291–324

selling access to the wildlife on the lands they control, Colorado's Ranching for Wildlife program is in jeopardy because of fears expressed by sportsmen and biologists that the program gives too many privileges or "rights" to landowners. [ ] Such fears appear to be more closely related to longstanding rivalries between sportsmen and landowners than to any objective changes in the property rights to wildlife or political influence over wildlife policy. The wildlife on the ranches continues to remain unowned until it is reduced to possession and the politics of wildlife policy continues to be a free-for-all.

In reality the Colorado program operates like any other government franchising program; the state agency retains responsibility for provision of the public service, in this case wildlife conservation and hunting, but contracts with private interests to produce the service. Fears of privatization in franchising are misplaced because franchising neatly separates the responsibility for provision, which is retained by the state, from responsibility for production, which may be contracted out. [ ] Thus, if private entities can produce a public service more efficiently than a public agency, franchising the private production of the service captures the private efficiency of production without sacrificing public control over the terms governing provision of the service. There can be little doubt that these private ranchers are producing higher-quality hunting opportunities with much greater efficiency that the state wildlife agency could if it controlled the identical tracts of land.

Compared to the spontaneous occurrence of fee hunting on private land, the franchising approach has several advantages:

1. Free public hunting is produced as a part of the franchise agreement.

2. Wildlife population-management objectives are jointly developed by the state and the private manager and hunting quotas are set to achieve them.

3. A commitment is obtained to improve habitat for wildlife and expert advice is devoted to this activity.

4. Wildlife management can be coordinated over much of the range of a game herd by combining ownership into a single management unit, as Colorado does. In contrast, there is no evidence that nonenfranchised operators coordinate their wildlife management actions in any way.

. . .

The Future of the Market

This research from northwestern Colorado introduces some possibilities worth exploring. Private landowners are turning to fee-hunting as an income alternative, and hunters are seeking controlled access as a means to higher-quality hunting. But before this market development can be a consistent force for improved land management, better game management, or community economic development, some amendments to custom are required. The state wildlife agencies need to provide more support and leadership to their programs for franchising private ranches to provide hunting and to manage wildlife. Given the mixture of public and private landownership, the BLM needs to find ways of making fee access to public lands more acceptable than an uncompromising policy of free, open access.

Lacking some more conducive policy changes, the entrepreneurial, market-based approach may not thrive, but it will not collapse. As long as the elk hold out, there will be a strong demand from hunters willing to pay access fees; but unless there is an expanding program of franchising, opportunities will be missed to enlist the private entrepreneurs to work for elk-management goals and better land management. Given the constraints under which state wildlife agencies work, they have little leverage on either the private or the public lands. They are forced to manage smaller herds than might otherwise be optimal, and their margins for error are slimmer than they might otherwise be. [ ] Presently, if herds expand beyond a safe margin and during a severe winter, the regional economy could be set back for as long as it takes for the herds to recover. In the interim, some ranchers might be forced to sell their lands to new owners less interested in the regional hunting business.

For their part, the BLM and its constituents could fashion a new policy toward public access through fee hunting on intermixed public lands. Such a policy could provide added leverage for improving range condition and wildlife management and could enhance regional incomes.

Alternatively, if open access to public lands is pushed to the limit and markets for hunting are discouraged, declining incomes may accompany a deterioration of hunting quality. This is not conjecture. One of the entrepreneurs who managed a wildlife ranch in this part of Colorado described guiding and outfitting as the "only game" in his little town. As the long-term economic fortunes of the livestock ranching industry continue to be bleak, the other extractive industries face tougher sledding on the public lands and the government in Washington continues to operate with tighter budgets, the small towns of the Rocky Mountain West must wonder where the future lies.

Conclusion

It may take an unusual measure of vision to see the linkage between community survival and wildlife entrepreneurship. The ranchers and hunters who are participating in the markets for big game hunting may have inadvertently found the vision. It remains for the agencies who control wildlife and public land policies, and their broader constituencies, to swing squarely behind the paradigm and begin to exploit it more fully. Until this happens, the prospects for improved wildlife management are tenuous.

NOTES

(1) Free-market approaches to conservation issues hold considerable appeal for people who place high value on individual liberty. In the case of wildlife, how persuasive is the claim that secure private rights in wildlife can adequately promote conservation? Consider the following issues raised by this approach:

(a) The example Davis uses involves a species with high market value. What of the species (well in excess of 99%, no doubt) that do not possess *any* market value?

(b) Managing land to promote one or a few species is often harmful to other species inhabiting the land, and indeed can quickly lead to their extinction.

(c) Those who seek to achieve maximum efficiency in the production of a favored species (whether wild or domestic) often find it useful to breed the species for desired traits; when this is done, the captive animal line can quickly differ genetically from wild versions, raising troubling problems when the captive animals escape or otherwise interbreed with fully wild animals.

(d) Finally, what are the ethics of transferring a publicly owned resource into private ownership? If such a transfer is to occur, should the public be paid?

(2) Free-market environmentalism and Aldo Leopold: To lend support to his claim, Davis cites the work of Aldo Leopold, who helped craft the 1930 American Game Policy which sought to promote conservation by making it easier for landowners to control hunting on their lands. If the posting of private lands became easier and more legitimate, owners could then charge hunters to come on and would have an economic incentive to protect or restore game habitat. What Davis does not mention is that Leopold's enthusiasm for this conservation approach faded within a few years. Management for a few game species, he decided, was often harmful to wildlife as a whole, particularly when game populations reached levels higher than those that would exist absent human intervention. Indeed, much of Leopold's time in later years was spent fighting with sportsmen and tourism groups that sought to maintain artificially high populations of white-tailed deer, despite the ecological damage they were causing. In his mature writings, Leopold urged that conservation measures (including wildlife-related ones) seek to promote the overall health of the land community, and he became quite critical of those who thought that landowner-profit alone could bring about sound conservation. *E.g.,* Aldo Leopold, *Conservation: In Whole or in Part? in* THE RIVER OF THE MOTHER OF GOD AND OTHER ESSAYS BY ALDO LEOPOLD 317 (Susan L. Flader & J. Baird Callicott eds. 1991) ("It follows that if conservation on private lands is to be motivated solely by profit, no unified conservation is even remotely possible."). Leopold's story is told in CURT MEINE, ALDO LEOPOLD: LIFE AND WORK (1988); SUSAN L. FLADER, THINKING LIKE A MOUNTAIN: ALDO LEOPOLD AND THE EVOLUTION OF AN ECOLOGICAL ATTITUDE TOWARD DEER, WOLVES, AND FORESTS (1974).

SECTION 2. SUBMERGED LAND

All of the legal issues involving wildlife and land are also present when the land is covered by water. But swamps, bogs, and wetlands, creeks, streams, and rivers, ponds and lakes, and the oceans—all of the numerous types of waterways and bodies—also give rise to a range of unique legal issues. These issues reflect two root questions: Who owns the lands submerged beneath waters? And what are the incidents of that ownership?

These issues can be seen in a range of more specific questions: Does ownership of the submerged land include a right to exclude people from traversing the surface? Does it matter whether a person may float across the surface of the water without touching the bottom or must walk down the stream? Is it a trespass in either case? Because of the historical importance of waterways as highways for commerce and access to land, a special set of rules have evolved that allows "navigable" waters to be used as highways. Is fishing including within the permissible uses if such highways? Is fowling? And how is the term "navigable" to be defined?

a. THE ENGLISH COMMON-LAW BACKGROUND

The Case of the Royal Fishery of Banne

King's Bench.
Davis 56, 80 Eng. Rep. 540 (1611)[1].

In the river *Banne* in *Ulster,* which divides the county of *Antrim* from the county of *Londonderry*, about two leagues from the sea, where the stream is navigable, there is a rich fishery in salmon, which was parcel of an ancient inheritance of the crown ... but now is granted by the king, to the city of *London,* in fee farm.[2] The profit of this fishery for the space of 200 years past, was taken and shared amongst the *Irish* lords, who made incursion and intrusion on the possessions of the crown in *Ulster,* and possessed by strong hand the territories adjoining the said river *Banne,* until the first year of the reign of our lord the king that now is [James I].

In the first year of this reign, Sir *Randall Mac Donnell* obtained a grant to him and his heirs, by letters patents, of the territory of *Rout* ... adjoining to the river *Banne,* in that part where the said fishery is, and hath at all times been. By these letters patents the king grants to him [all castles, messuages, tofts, mills, dove-houses, gardens, orchards, lands, meadows, grass grounds, pastures, woods, underwoods, rents, reversions and services, fisheries, fishings, waters, and water-course, etc. and all other hereditaments in or within the said territory of Rout, in the county of Antrim, excepting and reserving to ourselves, heirs and successors, three parts of the fishing of the river of Banne].

And upon this grant, Sir *Randall Mac Donell* made a petition to the lord deputy, to be put in quiet possession of the fourth part of the said fishery.... [T]he chief judges, being of the privy-council, in this matter ... certified their opinion and resolution, that no part of the said fishery passed to the said Sir *Randall Mac Donell,* by the letters patents aforesaid. And in this case divers points were considered and resolved.

---

1. This translation from the Law French into English is from JOSEPH ANGELL, A TREATISE ON THE RIGHT OF PROPERTY IN TIDE WATERS app. 35–42 (1826).

2. [Fee farm was an interest in land in which the land is held by the tenant and his heirs at an annual rent.]

First, Although the rule of the civil law be, that ["rivers and ports are public property, and therefore everyone has a right of fishing in ports and rivers"] which rule is found in *Bracton, lib. 2, cap. 12,* yet by the common law of *England,* a man may have a proper and several interest, as well in a water or river, as in a fishery; and therefore a water may be granted.... If one grants to another *aquam suam,* the fishery in it shall pass, because it is included in the word *aqua....* Also ... assize lieth of fishery ... for a man may have an estate freehold in a fishery.... In assize of nusance, the plaintiff counts that he is disturbed in his fishery; exception was taken to the county, for that no freehold was assigned, to which the fishery was appendant, and there it is said, that fishery is a freehold in itself, wherefore it is not necessary to shew to what freehold it is appendant....

Secondly, There are two kinds of rivers; navigable and not navigable. Every navigable river, so high as the sea flows and ebbs in it, is a royal river, and the fishery of it is a royal fishery, and belongs to the king by his prerogative; but in every other river not navigable, and in the fishery of such river, the tenants of the soil on each side have an interest of common right. The reason for which the king hath an interest in such navigable river, so high as the sea flows and ebbs in it, is, because such river participates of the nature of the sea, and is said to be a branch of the sea so far as it flows; ... and the sea is not only under the dominion of the king ... but it is also his proper inheritance; and therefore the king shall have the land which is gained out of the sea.... Also the king shall have the grand fishes of the sea, whales and sturgeons, & c. which are royal fishes, and no subject can have them without the king's special grant, ... and the king shall have wild swans, as royal fowls, on the sea and branches of it; the case of *Swans, 7 Co.* So wreck of the sea is a royal perquisite.... And for this reason before the statute of *18 Ed. 3.* no subject could pass over the sea, without the king's special licence; but there it is enacted, that the sea shall be open to all merchants.... And that the king hath the same prerogative and interest in the branches of the sea and navigable river, so high as the sea flows and ebbs in them, which he hath *in alto mari,* is manifest by several authorities....

[I]t was resolved, that the river *Banne,* so far as the sea flows and ebbs in it, is a royal river; and the fishery of salmon there is a royal fishery, which belongs to the king, as a several fishery, and not to those who have the soil on each side of the water. But on the other part it was agreed, that every inland river not navigable, appertains to the owners of the soil, where it hath its course, ... and if such river runneth between two manors, and is the ... boundary between them, the one moiety of the river and fishery belongeth to one lord, and the other moiety to the other....

Thirdly, It was resolved, that no part of this royal fishery of the *Banne* could pass by the grant of the land adjoining, by the general grant of all fisheries; for this royal fishery is not appurtenant to land, but is a fishery in gross, and parcel of the inheritance of the crown by itself; and general words in the king's grant shall not pass such special royalty, which belongeth to the crown by prerogative ...

Lastly, It was agreed, that where the king granted to Sir *Randall Mac Donnell* all the territory adjoining to this river, and all fisheries within this territory, *exceptis tribus partibus piscariæ de Banne,* that the fourth part of this fishery should not pass to him by this grant; for the king's grant shall pass nothing by implication . . . .

These points were resolved in this case, by the rules and authorities of the common law . . . .

NOTES

(1) As with *The Case of Swans, The Case of the Royal Fishery of Banne* amply repays a close reading. To a degree greater than commonly recognized, the decision is the foundation of Anglo–American fishing rights law. The case is also a cornerstone of a body of law that came to be known in the United States as the "public trust doctrine."

(2) Ownership of submerged lands, fishing rights, and navigability: In *The Case of the Royal Fishery,* the court frames the central issues—who can fish and where—that will be the continuing focus in these materials on waterways. According to the court, the right to fish in waterways is tied to a number of factual and legal issues—the navigability of the waterway, the relevance of tides to navigability, ownership of the underlying land, and the King's prerogative. Although the court did not resolve all the issues it raised, it did frame the discussion of several issues—not just on fishing rights, but also on the ownership of submerged lands and the proper interpretation of deeds concerning such lands—for centuries to come.

(a) The nature of an interest in a fishery: The first issue the court decided was that a fishery could be private property: "by the common law of England, a man may have a proper and several [*i.e.,* individual] interest . . . in a fishery." [¶ 4] As a corollary of this holding, the court noted that the right to fish could be held independently of the ownership of any land. As the court noted, "a man may have an estate of freehold in a fishery . . . wherefore it is not necessary to shew to what freehold it is appendant." [¶ 4] In more modern terminology, the fishery could either be appurtenant to a parcel of land or held in gross.

The separation of fishery and soil might occur in several ways. For example, the King could retain the fishing right when granting the riparian land; the landowner might transfer the two interests—land and fishery—separately or retain only one while granting the other; a person could acquire the right to fish through prescription; the public might gain rights through prescription or implied dedication.

As previously noted, the interest technically is a profit a prendre, the right to take something that was the produce of the land. The right to take fish is a piscary profit a prendre. *See generally* 8 THOMPSON ON REAL PROPERTY § 65.02(b), at 38 (David A. Thomas ed., 1994). Piscary profits a prendre were common at the common law. *See* 2 WILLIAM BLACKSTONE, COMMENTARIES *34.

(b) Presumptive fishing rights as an incident of the ownership of submerged lands: The court's second point was that fishing rights—as profit a prendre—presumptively belong to the owner of the submerged land. This decision, of course, merely shifted the question: who owns the land beneath a waterway? The court set out two presumptions on ownership of such lands:

First, the King is presumed to be the owner of the lands beneath tidal waters: "Every navigable river, so high as the tide flows and ebbs in it, is a royal river, and the fishery of it is a royal fishery." This ownership is an incident of royal prerogative: "the king hath an interest in such navigable river, so high as the sea flows and ebbs in it, ... because such river participates of the nature of the sea ... and the sea is not only under the dominion of the king ... but it is also his proper inheritance; ... the king hath the same prerogative and interest in the branches of the sea and navigable river, ... which he hath *in alto mari* [the high seas]." [¶ 5]

Second, the submerged soil of a nonnavigable stream is presumptively owned by "the tenants of the soil on each side" of the stream: "every inland river not navigable, appertains to the owners of the soil, where it hath its course, ... and if such river runneth between two manors, and is the ... boundary between them, the one moiety of the river and fishery belongeth to one lord, and the other moiety to the other...." [¶ 6]

The court's assignment of the fishery to the owner of the soil was simply a presumption because either the soil or the fishery itself might be held by another person. As a subsequent case noted,

In case of a private river, the lord's having the soil is good evidence to prove, that he hath the right of fishing; and it puts the proof upon them that claim *liberam piscariam*. But in the case of a river that flows and reflows, and is an arm of the sea, there, *prima facie,* it is common to all: and if any will appropriate a privilege to himself, the proof lieth on his side.

Lord Fitzwalter's Case, 1 Mod. 105, 86 Eng. Rep. 766 (K.B. 1674). Thus, the presumption is rebuttable and can be overcome by showing a grant or a prescriptive right that altered the default position.

(c) "Navigable": Finally, the court in *The Case of the Royal Fishery* decided that "There are two kinds of rivers; navigable and not navigable." [¶ 5] Assigning presumptive ownership based on the navigability of the waterway shifts the question to "navigability." What does the term mean? Was navigability the source of the King's title or merely a characteristic of it?

According to William Blackstone, navigable waters were owned as prerogative by the King. "By feudal law," Blackstone stated, "all navigable rivers and havens were computed among the *regalia* (royalties), and were subject to the sovereign of the state. And in England it hath always been holden, that the king is lord of the whole shore." 1 WILLIAM BLACKSTONE, COMMENTARIES *264. The court in *The Case of the Royal Fishery* announced a similar rule: "Every navigable river, so high as the sea flows and ebbs in it, is a royal river, ... and belongs to the king by his prerogative"; the fishery in such a river is "a royal fishery." Upon careful reading this language is ambiguous. The court's statement covers only one class of rivers: those that are navigable *and* subject to the influence of the tides.

Are there navigable rivers above the ebb and flow of the tide? Might there also be tidal waters that are not navigable?

When other decisions are added to the mix, the question becomes increasingly perplexing. In *Lord Fitzwalter's Case,* 1 Mod. 105, 86 Eng. Rep. 766 (K.B. 1673), Chief Justice Hale based fishing rights solely on ownership of the soil—without regard for navigability—apparently relying on *The Case of the Royal Fishery.* In private rivers—rivers, presumably, where the soil was privately owned—the landowner also owned the fishery. In tidal waters, however, the King owned the soil and hence the fishery. In a subsequent decision, however, Chief Justice Holt defined public fishing rights solely in terms of navigability—with no suggestion that tidal influence was crucial: "Every subject of common may fish with lawful nets, & c. in a *navigable river,* as well as in *the sea.*" *Warren v. Matthews,* 6 Mod. 73, 87 Eng. Rep. 831, *same case* 1 Salk. 357, 91 Eng. Rep. 312 (K.B. 1704). Later in the century, in *Carter v. Murcot,* 4 Burr. 2162, 98 Eng. Rep. 127 (K.B. 1768), Lord Mansfield repeated Holt's view, tying fishing rights to navigability and noting that, in navigable rivers that were "arms of the sea," a person could nonetheless claim an exclusive right to fish based on prescription.

Thus the questions: Although tidal influence seemed to play a role in defining navigability, are navigable waters solely waters that are subject to the ebb and flow of the tides? Or is land ownership the key issue, with tidal influence and navigability relevant only as guides to the identity of the landowner? And, most importantly, is navigability itself a unitary concept or simply a shorthand for several possible use rights such as transportation, fishing, and fowling?

The decisions in *Lord Fitzwalter's Case* and *Warren v. Matthews*—like the decision in *The Case of the Royal Fishery*—present difficulties because they shift back and forth in their reliance on navigability. Adding to the confusion was the reality that the expansion of trade and development led English citizens to use more and more rivers as highways for travel and commerce. This included rivers that were beyond the reach of the tides; inland rivers, in other words, were becoming "navigable in fact"—and English law recognized a public right to use such rivers for travel and commerce whenever a history of such use could be shown, notwithstanding private ownership of the bed and banks. *See* Glenn J. MacGrady, *The Navigability Concept in the Civil and Common Law Historical Development, Current Importance, and Some Doctrines that Don't Hold Water,* 3 FLA. ST. U.L. REV. 511, 571–75 (1975). Some courts and commentators apparently referred to such waterways as navigable; others limited the legal definition of navigability to tidal waters and used other terms (*e.g.,* public highways) to describe nontidal waters in which the public had rights of passage. In his treatise, Chief Justice Hale referred to them by various names, distinguishing them from legally navigable waters. He also discussed the status of streams made passable by private efforts:

> There be some streams or rivers, that are private not only in propriety or ownership, but also in use, as little streams and rivers that are not a common passage for the king's people. Against, there be other rivers, as well fresh as salt, that are of common or publick use for carriage of boats and lighters. And these, whether they are fresh or salt, whether

they flow and reflow or not, are *prima facie publici juris*, common highways for man or goods or both from one inland town to another. Thus the rivers of Wey, of Severn, of Thames, and divers others, as well above the bridges and ports as below, as well above the flowings of the sea as below, and as well where they are become to be of private propriety as in what parts they are of the king's propriety, are publick rivers *juris publici*. And therefore all nuisances and impediments of passages of boats and vessels, though in the private soil of any person, may be punished by indictments, and removed. . . . But if any person at his own charge makes his own private stream passage for boats or barges, either by making of locks or cuts, or drawing together other streams; and hereby that river, which was his own in point of propriety become now capable of carriage of vessels; yet this seems not to make it *juris publici*, and he may pull it down again, or apply it to his own private use. For it is not hereby made to be *juris publici*, unless it were done at a common charge, or by a publick authority, or that by long continuance of time it hath been freely devoted to a publick use. And so it seems also to be, if he that makes such a new river or passage doth it by way of recompence of compensation for some other publick stream that he hath stopped for his own conveniency. . . .

Sir Matthew Hale, *De Juris Maris, in* STUART A. MOORE, A HISTORY OF THE FORESHORE 374–75 (3d ed. 1888). Hale's comments remain good law in England. *See* 49(2) HALSBURY'S LAWS OF ENGLAND 742–43 (4th ed., reissue 1997) (citing Hale). *Cf.* R.H. Helmholz, *Magna Carta and the* jus commune, 66 U. CHI. L. REV. 297, 355–56 (1999) (interpreting chapter 33 of Magna Carta as aimed chiefly at keeping all waterways in England open to navigation, thus implementing an idea contained in continental law).

These questions remained alive in England for nearly three centuries. As a consequence, early Americans who looked to England for guidance met both a confusing record of judicial decisions and conflicting comments by treatise writers. It was not until the late nineteenth century that England clarified its fishing laws by limiting public fishing rights to tidal waters.[3] By then, however, American courts had reached their own conclusions on the various unresolved issues.

(3) The royal prerogative in navigable waters: In a part of the decision not included above, the court in *The Case of the Royal Fishery* surveyed at length precedents recognizing the King's ownership of all land beneath the high tide line ("so far as the sea flows and ebbs") and his concomitant power to control the activities conducted on and over them. The King owned these lands, however, not in the proprietary way that he owned his manors and other fast lands, but as a matter of royal prerogative. Prerogative status apparently had at least two significant consequences:

(a) Public use rights: The first incident of prerogative ownership of a fishery was that it was available to the public. The King, the courts concluded, held such fisheries in a trust-like capacity subject to public use

---

3. As so limited, *The Case of Royal Fishery of Banne* properly states current En-glish law. *See* 18 HALSBURY'S LAW OF ENGLAND 258–61 (4th ed. 1977).

rights. In *Lord Fitzwalter's Case,* 1 Mod. 105, 86 Eng. Rep. 766 (K.B. 1673), Chief Justice Hale noted that in tidal waters the King owned the soil and the general public could fish. In *Warren v. Matthews,* 6 Mod. 73, 87 Eng. Rep. 831, *same case* 1 Salk. 357, 91 Eng. Rep. 312 (K.B. 1704), Chief Justice Holt, like his predecessor Chief Justice Hale, equated the King's ownership of a fishery with the public's right to use it.

(b) Termination of public use by Royal grant: The public nature of the prerogative ownership meant that alienation of the property with the resulting loss of public rights was not to be presumed. As the court wrote in *The Case of the Royal Fishery*: "general words in the king's grant shall not pass such special royalty, which belongeth to the crown by prerogative" Thus, a general grant of land, even when it referred to fisheries, was insufficient to alienate the King's prerogative and the public's use rights.

(4) Classification of property in fisheries: In *The Case of the Royal Fishery,* the court decided that "the fishery of salmon there is a royal fishery, which belongs to the king, as a several fishery." A several fishery was one type of fishery recognized by the King's Bench. To understand the classification, it is helpful to recall that a fishery is a profit a prendre—a category of property that can exist either as part of another tenure (appendant) or as an independent interest (in gross).

Blackstone offered the following categorization of fisheries:

A *free fishery,* or exclusive right of fishing in a public river, is also a royal franchise; and is considered as such in all countries where the feudal polity has prevailed.... This differs from a *several* fishery; because he that has a several fishery must also be (or at least derive his right from) the owner of the soil, which in a free fishery is not requisite. It differs also from a *common* of piscary before mentioned, in that the free fishery is an exclusive right, the common of piscary is not so: and therefore, in a free fishery a man has a property in the fish before they are caught, in a common of piscary not till afterwards. [I]t must be acknowledged, that the rights and distinctions of the three species of fishery are very much confounded in our law-books; and that there are not wanting respectable authorities which maintain that a *several* fishery may exist distinct from the property of the soil, and that a *free* fishery implies no exclusive right, but is synonymous with *common* of piscary.

2 WILLIAM BLACKSTONE, COMMENTARIES *39–40. Types of fisheries are also examined in 2 HENRY P. FARNHAM, THE LAW OF WATERS AND WATER RIGHTS 1390–92 (1904).

The excerpt demonstrates the common-law penchant for classifying the potentially different categories of property interests. According to Blackstone, a fishery is several, common, or free:

(a) a several fishery is "exclusive of the right of all other persons." *Seymour v. Courtenay,* 5 Burr. 2814, 98 Eng. Rep. 478 (K.B. 1771). Common examples of a several fishery are a pond or a nonnavigable stream where both banks are owned by the same person. When such a stream is the boundary between two landowners, they each have a several fishery over their portion of the submerged land. A several fishery may be in gross rather than appendant if the landowner conveyed his interest to another person as an exclusive right.

   (b) a common fishery, or *communis piscaria*, is like other commons such as a common of pasture: it is a nonexclusive and limited right. *Smith v. Kemp*, 2 Salk. 637, 91 Eng. Rep. 537 (K.B. 1693) (*"Communis piscaria ... was to be resembled to the case of other commons"*). The most widespread common fishery is the public's right to fish in a navigable stream. A common fishery may also be created by a landowner's grant of a nonexclusive right to fish in what was originally a several fishery; some classification schemes—to split hairs even more finely—gave such a right a slightly different name: a common of fishery.

   (c) a free fishery, or *libera piscaria,* was defined by Blackstone as an "exclusive right of fishing in a public river"; it thus was "a royal franchise; and is considered as such in all countries where the feudal polity has prevailed." Under this definition, a free fishery is a subspecies of a several fishery in gross, distinguished by the critical fact that it is an interest in a public river; as such it can be based on either an express grant from the King or prescription. A different definition of a free fishery was offered by Chief Justice Holt in *Smith v. Kemp,* Carth 285, 90 Eng. Rep. 769 (K.B. 1693): *"Libera piscaria,* which is where the right of fishing is granted to the grantee, and such a grantee hath a property in the fish, and may bring a possessory action for them, without making any title [to land]." Holt's definition, however, does not distinguish a free fishery from a several fishery (if exclusive) or from a common fishery in gross (if non-exclusive); in fact, Holt defined several fishery as requiring ownership of the soil. Thus, in Holt's definitional scheme, a free fishery could exist in a nonnavigable waterway and would arise if the owner of a several fishery granted his interest to someone while retaining ownership of the land.

(5) Fisheries and fish: Does ownership of a fishery include ownership of the fish in the fishery or is it only a right to catch fish? Is it, in other words, a right to go fishing or a right to the free-swimming fish? English courts decided that it was the latter—at least in certain circumstances. Blackstone, for example, wrote that "in a free fishery a man has a property in the fish before they are caught." 2 WILLIAM BLACKSTONE, COMMENTARIES *40. And in *Smith v. Kemp,* Chief Justice Holt stated, *"Libera piscaria,* which is where the right of fishing is granted to the grantee, and such a grantee hath a property in the fish, and may bring a possessory action for them, without making any title [to land]." *Smith v. Kemp,* Carth 285, 90 Eng. Rep. 769 (K.B. 1693). The decision in *Greyes Case,* Owen 20, 74 Eng. Rep. 869 (K.B. 1594), makes the crucial point explicitly: there is property in fish in "a trunk, or some other narrow place where they be put to be taken at will and pleasure; but otherwise it is where they are put into a pond." Can this statement be squared with the general proposition that no one has property in animals *feræ naturæ* until they are reduced to possession? Does it reflect the unique characteristic of fish—that they are constrained by their need to remain in water? Is the property in the fish simply property by possession? To state the point more clearly: if I put a deer in a pen, is it in my possession—and thus my property? If I put a fish in a pond that has no inlet or outlet so that it cannot escape, is the fish in my possession?

(6) The King's power to grant exclusive fisheries in public waters: When the King granted a private fishery in a navigable waterway, he curtailed the public's right to fish in those waters. Whether he could lawfully do so depended upon the nature of the King's "ownership" of the beds and banks of such waterways.

The court in *The Case of the Royal Fishery* announced that "[e]very navigable river, so high as the sea flows and ebbs in it, is a royal river, . . . and belongs to the king by his prerogative." If the King's "ownership" is an incident of his prerogative, can it be alienated? The court in *The Case of the Royal Fishery* thought so, raising no questions about the validity of the grant of the fishery in fee farm to the City of London. Despite grants by Kings and Queens of individual rights to fisheries in navigable waters, the issue of the royal power to do so was still debated at the time of the American Revolution.

Blackstone, for example, although acknowledging the validity of fisheries previously granted, argued that the Magna Carta (1215) "prohibited for the future the grants of exclusive fisheries." 4 WILLIAM BLACKSTONE, COMMENTARIES *424. He referred to the thirty-third chapter of the Great Charter:

> All kydells[4] for the future shall be removed altogether from the Thames and Medway, and throughout all of England, except upon the sea shore.

MAGNA CARTA c. 33 (1215). Joseph Chitty in his *Treatise on the Game Laws* concurred: "the king's granting of such exclusive rights, was an usurpation of prerogative. . . . For by Magna Carta . . . the King is expressly precluded from making fresh grants." 1 JOSEPH CHITTY, A TREATISE ON THE GAME LAWS 271–72 (1812). Chief Justice Holt also agreed—at least in the result— noting "Every subject . . . may fish . . . in a *navigable river* . . . and the King's grant cannot bar them thereof." *Warren v. Matthews,* 6 Mod. 73, 87 Eng. Rep. 831 (K.B. 1704).

Nonetheless, in *Carter v. Murcot,* 4 Burr. 2162, 98 Eng. Rep. 127 (K.B. 1768), the King's bench held that "the Crown may grant a several fishery in a navigable river."[5] *Carter v. Murcot* was concerned with a further question: could an exclusive fishery in a navigable water be acquired through prescription. The court concluded that, since such a right could be created by grant, it could arise by prescription: "Now if it may be granted, it may be prescribed for. . . . But it can't be presumed; it must be proved." To the same effect is *Lord Fitzwalter's Case,* 1 Mod. 105, 86 Eng. Rep. 766 (K.B. 1674), and Hale's influential treatise.

---

4. A "kydell" was a fish-weir. *See* WILLIAM S. MCKECHNIE, MAGNA CARTA 343 (2d rev. ed. 1914).

5. It was subsequently decided that the Magna Carta did prevent the King from creating private rights in navigable waters that were inconsistent with the public right to fish. *Lord Fitzharding v. Purcell* [1908], 2 Ch. 139, 167; *Neill v. Duke of Devonshire,* [1882] 8 App.Cas. 135.

This position, however, was also subject to question. First, as a matter of prerogative, laches and other limitations do not run against the Crown. Second, a prescription "for a right common to all the subjects of the realm cannot be supported. A man might as well prescribe that he [has] a right to travel on the King's highway as appurtenant to his estate." *Ward v. Creswell*, Willes 267, 125 Eng. Rep. 1166 (C.P. 1742) (since every subject has a right to fish in the sea, plaintiff may not prescribe for such a right).

The uncertainty about the King's power to create private rights carried over into America, where courts continue to wrestle even now with questions on the power of the colonies and then the states to grant exclusive rights in navigable waterways. *See, e.g., Kraft v. Burr,* 476 S.E.2d 715 (Va.1996) (considering whether owner of land beneath navigable tidal waters, whose title traced back to the King, could claim an exclusive fishery, citing Magna Carta and Blackstone). By the late nineteenth century, this issue was wrapped up with both the public trust doctrine—which in various flexible ways imposed limits on the power of states to transfer submerged lands free of public rights—and the federal navigation servitude. The story continues in the next section of this chapter.

(7) The English background, in sum: What, then, was the English legal heritage that colonists brought with them to North America? Do the following points fairly cover the complex English story?

(a) A right to fish—technically a piscary profit a prendre—can be private property.

(b) The property in the fishery presumptively is an incident of the ownership of the submerged lands. The presumption may be overcome by proving a grant or prescription that changed the default position by severing the two estates (the soil and the fishery).

(c) Ownership of the submerged lands presumptively depends upon whether the water is navigable or nonnavigable. The king is the presumed owner of the lands beneath tidal waters and thus is the presumptive owner of the fishery in such waters. On the other hand, the riparian owner or owners are the presumptive owners of the submerged soil and the fishery in a nonnavigable stream.

(d) The definition of "navigable" was uncertain. On the one hand, there was case law and commentary suggesting that navigability at law was restricted to waters subject to the influence of the tides. On the other hand, other caselaw and commentary stated that navigable waters included all bodies of water that were navigable in fact. Finally, other precedent suggested that non-tidal streams were nonnavigable at law but subject to public use rights as highways for commerce.

(e) When the king owned the submerged land—when the waters were "navigable" however the term was defined—he held that land in a prerogative capacity that imposed a trust-like restriction on his powers and permitted public use of the waters. This trust-like restriction also imposed some restriction on the King's power to alienate such lands and cut off the public use.

b. RIGHTS IN WATERWAYS IN A NEW WORLD

NOTES

When American courts began issuing published decisions and searching more earnestly for English precedents around 1800, they extracted a clear rule from a distinctly unclear legal record: A river was navigable under the English common law, they concluded, when it was subject to the ebb and flow of the tides; furthermore, both title to submerged lands and fishing rights depended on a river's navigability under the tidal test. A leading American case was the opinion by James Kent in *Palmer v. Mulligan*, 3 Cai. R. 307 (N.Y.1805), which relied on *Banne, Carter,* and the views of Chief Justice Hale in his influential treatise, *De Jure Maris.* By 1826, American treatise writer Joseph Angell could assert, though not entirely accurately, that "no part of the law is more clearly settled, than that to determine, whether or not, a river is navigable, a regard must be had to the ebbing and flowing of the tide." JOSEPH K. ANGELL, A TREATISE ON THE RIGHT OF PROPERTY IN TIDE WATERS 61–62 (1826).

The equation of navigability with tidal influence created uncertainty about public rights to use other waterways for travel, commerce, and recreation. That uncertainty lingered because few cases arose in which public use rights were challenged. Cases instead dealt with the more economically potent issues of bed ownership, bank usage, and rights in fish, particularly rights to take shellfish. From the incomplete historical data that is available, it appears that the typical approach in the early United States was for jurisdictions to follow Hale's lead and recognize public travel rights in all inland waters that were usable by the public, without regard for tidal influence. Paradoxically, that is, navigability at law in many jurisdictions was important for purposes of land ownership and fishing, but not for navigation! In his treatise, Angell insisted that navigability at law was based on tidal influence, but nontidal waters, he acknowledged, could be "public highways" for travel and transport. *Id.* 62 (cited favorably in *Idaho v. Coeur d'Alene Tribe,* 521 U.S. 261, 285 (1997)). Angell's views, however, were challenged by other scholars studying the English legal record. Louis Houck asserted that fishing rights under English law (and, hence, under well-grounded American law) depended on navigability, and navigability was a question of factual usage rather than tidal influence. Holt and Mansfield had it right, Houck asserted, American courts had been misled by Hale and his treatise:

> Deprived of Lord Hale's great name, the law, as laid down in the treatise referred to, in relation to rivers, would hardly ever have been recognized in this country. It was the name of that great jurist that dazzled our judges, and caused some of them to disregard the plainest principles of common reason.

LOUIS HOUCK, A TREATISE ON THE LAW OF NAVIGABLE RIVERS 18–19 (1868). By the time Houck wrote, American jurisdictions were in the process of redefining navigability at law to include inland waterways that were navigable in fact. Houck viewed such decisions as correcting a misunderstanding by American courts; more accurately, however, these decisions merely shifted from one line of English precedent to another.

Adams v. Pease

Connecticut Supreme Court of Errors.
2 Conn. 481 (1818).

THIS was an action of trespass *quare clausum fregit*,[1] alleging, that the plaintiff was lawfully seised and possessed of a certain tract of land laying in the town of *Suffield*, bounded *North* on the plaintiff's own land in *Connecticut* River, *East* on the centre of the bed of *Connecticut* River, *South* on *John Wright's* land in said river, and *West* on the *West* bank of said river, containing five acres of land covered with the water flowing in said river; and that the defendants, during the plaintiff's seisin and possession, with force and arms, and against the peace, entered upon said land, and the water covering said land, with fish-boats, seines, & etc. and being so entered, did, then and there, with like force, catch and carry away 3,000 of the plaintiff's fish, called shad, then being and swimming in said water on said land, and converted the same to their own use, whereby the plaintiff wholly lost said fish.

The plaintiff owns a large farm in *Suffield*, bounded *East* on *Connecticut* River. The *locus in quo* lies between the shore and the centre of the river, against the farm. It is above Enfield falls; and is passable with flat-bottomed boats, carrying from five to thirty tons burden, up and down the river, but not with ships and vessels; though some vessels, built above, have been floated down. The waters there, and for a considerable distance below, are never affected by the rising and falling of the sea. The river, from its mouth to this place, and far above, is, and always has been, used for the purpose of transportation by water, and is, for that purpose, of great public importance; the right of such use being common to all the citizens of the state. The trespass complained of, was committed, by drawing a seine over the *locus in quo*, during the preceding fishing season, from the opposite shore, and hauling it back, thereby taking fish.

A case embracing this statement was reserved for the consideration and advise of the nine Judges.

. . .

■ SWIFT, C.J.:—By the common law, in the sea, in navigable rivers, and navigable arms of the sea, the right of fishing is common to all. In rivers not navigable, the adjoining proprietors have the exclusive right. Rivers are considered to be navigable as far as the sea flows and reflows; and thus far

---

1. ["*Trespass quare clausum fregit* . . ." is the opening phrase of the common law writ for trespass to real property, *i.e.*, the form of action which lies to recover damages for injuries to realty consequent upon defendant's entry without right onto plaintiff's land. The "close" is an interest in the soil, or in trees or growing crops. In every case where a person has a right to exclude another from land, the law encircles it, if not already inclosed, with an imaginary fence, and entitles him to compensation in damages for the injury sustained by the act of another passing through his boundary—denominating the injurious act a breaking of the inclosure. *See* 2 BOUVIER'S LAW DICTIONARY 1139 (Rawle's Rev. 1897); 1 *id.* at 336. The allegations were boilerplate. Other forms of the writ were used for unlawful taking of goods (*trespass de bonis asportatis*) and for injuries that were the immediate consequence of acts done to person or personal property (*trespass vi et armis*). On the development of the forms of actions and the common law system of writs, see FREDERIC W. MAITLAND, THE FORMS OF ACTION AT COMMON LAW (1936).]

the common right of fishing extends. Above the ebbing and flowing of the tide, the fishery belongs exclusively to the adjoining proprietors; and the public have a right or easement in such rivers, as common highways, for passing and repassing with vessels, boats, or any water-craft. *The Case of the Fishery on the Banne,* Davies' Rep. 56. A more perfect system of regulations on this subject could not be devised. It secures common rights, as far as the public interest requires; and furnishes a proper line of demarcation between them and private rights. As we have adopted the principal part of these regulations, I think we ought to take the whole, and decide, that above tide-water the adjoining proprietors on rivers have the exclusive right of fishery, and the community a right of passing in them, as highways, with every kind of water-craft.

I am of opinion, that the plaintiff is entitled to recover.

■ HOSMER, J.:— "In rivers not navigable," says *Lord Mansfield* in *Carter v. Murcot,* 4 Burr. 2164, "the proprietors of the land have the right of fishery on their respective sides, and it generally extends *ad filum medium aquae.*[2] But in navigable rivers, the proprietors of the land on each side have it not." These principles of common law have not been controverted, and indeed, are incontrovertible.

The case is reduced to this question merely, whether the river *Connecticut* is a navigable river, where the tide does not ebb and flow? If the term navigable is construed according to its popular import, every river capable of being sailed upon by boat, however small or shallow, is embraced by it. Many of the inconsiderable streams which fall into *Connecticut* River, are of this description. The same common law, however, which has established the principle, has furnished a definite explication of the disputed term. Every river, where the sea ebbs and flows, is, by the common law, considered as navigable; and all rivers not thus distinguished, are not navigable. [ ]

The distinction between rivers navigable and not navigable, that is, where the sea does, or does not, ebb and flow, is very ancient. [ ] The former are called *arms of the sea,* while the latter pass under the denomination of *private* or *inland rivers.* "That is called an arm of the sea where the tide flows and re-flows, and so far only, as the tide flows and re-flows." *Hale de jure maris, cap.* 4. "If a river runs contiguously between the land of two persons, each of them is owner of that part of the river, which is next his land, of common right." *Rex v. Wharton,* 12 Mod. 510.

The detriment, which, it has been argued, the public must derive from this doctrine, is entirely ideal; and rests on a misconception of the law. All rivers above the flow of the tide, in reference to the use of them, are public, and of consequence, are subservient to the public accommodation. Hence, the fisheries, ferries, bridges, and the internal navigation, are subject to the regulation of government.

The argument, from inconvenience, must be very powerful, to cast a shade on a long established principle. Here I discern no inconvenience. On the other hand, the doctrine of the common law, as I have stated it,

---

2.   ["To the thread of the stream."]

promotes the grand ends of civil society, by pursuing that wise and orderly maxim of assigning to every thing capable of ownership, a legal and determinate owner.

The other Judges were of the same opinion.

Pitkin v. Olmstead

Connecticut Supreme Court.
1 Root 217 (1790).

ACTION of trespass for interrupting the plaintiffs in their fishery in Connecticut river. Plea not guilty. The jury find the following facts on a special verdict, viz.

That Connecticut river is a public navigable river, and abounds with fish, salmon and shad in the season of them. That in A.D. 1774 [plaintiffs' predecessors in interest, "who had formed themselves into a fish company,"] with much expense and labor cleared a fish-place, opposite the lands of Nehemiah, Moses, and Samuel Olmstead, [which were upstream from the abutting land of Elisha Pitkin on the Connecticut River]. That said Olmsteads gave a lease to [plaintiffs' predecessors in interest] of said fish-place, ... with liberty to clear and draw seines on their land adjoining to said river, for the consideration of one-twentieth part of the fish, they should take: Which lease was sundry times renewed and continued down to the year 1788; ... that in A.D. 1787 [plaintiffs' predecessors in interest] were forbidden by said Olmsteads to fish any more at said place, opposite their lands; [plaintiffs' predecessors in interest] sold their seine, boat and all their fishing apparatus to [plaintiffs] who applied to ... Elisha Pitkin, Esq. for liberty to draw their seine upon his land adjoining to said river, south of said Olmsteads' land; which he granted, and also became one of their company; and the plaintiffs in the fall of the year A.D. 1787 cleared the bed of the river opposite said Elisha's land and also of said Olmsteads and in the spring of the year A.D. 1788, the plaintiffs constantly fished in the river opposite said Elisha's land, and also opposite the land of said Olmsteads and drew their seine on said Elisha's land; and in the fall of the year A.D. 1788 the defendants with design to prevent the plaintiffs from fishing in the bed of said river, opposite the lands of said Olmsteads, [constructed a log barrier extending into the river from their land for 100 feet] below the common low-water mark, ...; that the same is an obstruction to taking of fish; and that the plaintiffs were thereby obstructed and prevented from catching fish at said place in the year 1789, and the jury refer the question of law upon the facts aforesaid to the court, viz. Whether the defendants are guilty or not.

Judgment of the court—The law is so upon the facts aforesaid that the defendants are guilty.

BY THE COURT:—The river being a public navigable river, it is free for all the citizens, to navigate their vessels in and to draw seines for the purpose of taking fish—that the bed of the said river is the private property of no one, but remains as public as the waters that flow in it—whoever therefore by labor and expense, clears a fish-place in its bed, acquires a right to occupy and enjoy it, in preference to any other; and by a long-continued possession and occupation, in the proper season, the right is strengthened and confirmed; and the defendants had no right to disturb or interrupt the plaintiffs in the exercise of their right in their own proper fishing-place, so long as they [plaintiffs] did not go upon their [defendants'] land.

NOTES

(1) *Adams* and *Pitkin* examine the interaction of two elements: (1) the idea of navigability and (2) the nature of the public and private rights in waterways. How does the court define each concept? What is the relationship between the two concepts? The court in *Adams* notes that vessels carrying up to 30 tons use the river riparian to Adams' land. Why then is the river not navigable at that point? What is the general allocation of public and private rights? How did the fishers in *Pitkin* acquire a right to exclude the public from a stretch of the river that was—unlike the stretch at issue in *Adams*—"public"? Do either of the cases make sense from a policy perspective? What rationales do the courts offer? What rationales might you construct to justify the two decisions?

The remainder of the materials in this section on rights in waterways in the new world is divided between the two elements presented in the decisions in *Adams* and *Pitkin*. It begins with the question of how waters are divided between public and private and the attendant questions of the meaning of "navigable." It then examines the ability of an individual to acquire private rights in "public" waters and concludes with a brief discussion of private rights in private waters.

(2) ***Hunt v. Hitchcock:*** Consider the following entry in the case of *Hunt v. Hitchcock* (1773), in the Superior Court of the Colony of Connecticut:

> This was a Writ of Error but in fact little more than a Case stated relative to the Right of Fishing in Ousatonnock River. Two sets of Fishermen had each a fishing place for drawing a Seine on the Opposite sides of the River and nearly opposite to each other. Those on the East side were first in the use of their place, the others in drawing their Net came within a small part of the scoop of their Net, and by that means caught Fish, that might perhaps have been taken by the others, but did not give them any Actual Interruption in the use of their fishery. An Action of Trespass was [brought] by those on the East side against those on the West for thus coming within the sweep of their Net, and the Question was how far the Fishery is Common, and what right those who Clear fishing places on the River, gain. It was the Opinion of the Court that this was a public River, and that in such river the Fishery is common, and that the bare clearing of the Place did not give such an Exclusive Right as to prevent all others from fishing there in all cases, but no Interruption may be given to those Actually in Possession, to prevent their drawing their Net. In the present Case the Defendants in the Original Action were adjudged Not to have been Trespassers, and the Judgment of the lower Court was reversed.

THE SUPERIOR COURT DIARY OF WILLIAM SAMUEL JOHNSON 1772–1773 at 74 (John T. Farrell, ed. 1942). How does this ruling compare with *Pierson v. Post* [Chapter 2]? With *Keeble v. Hickeringill, supra*?

PERSPECTIVES

(1) The customs of fisheries: During the colonial and antebellum periods, men often fished in "companies" that claimed rights to specific fishing-places such as rocks at natural obstacles such as falls. "Patten Rock," for example, was located "on the west side of the west channel [of the Merrimack River.] It was a famous fishing right, and had been occupied for a great length of time." George E. Burnham, *Amoskeag's Old Fishing Rocks,* 4 MANCHESTER HISTORIC ASSOCIATION COLLECTIONS 60, 66 (1908). Such rights initially were based upon a combination of priority in time and work expended in "improving" the rocks for use as fishing platforms. In 1762, for example, Patten and three other men spent several days drilling holes, blasting, and chiselling a rock to serve as a platform. The rights were held by common agreement, were transferable, and could also be rented to others. *E.g.,* MATTHEW PATTEN, THE DIARY OF MATTHEW PATTEN OF BEDFORD, N.H. 51 (1903) (on June 8–9, 1758, "I got 4 shad and a small salmon for my part from the setting place Will[ia]m Peters fished for me by ye halves"). Similar fishing rights existed at all the falls on the Merrimack and on many of the nation's rivers. *E.g., Carson v. Blazer,* 2 Binn. 475 (Pa.1810) (Yeates, J.) ("the owners of lands on the margin of the Susquehanna . . . upon their clearing out a pool of *reasonable extent* immediately opposite their respective shores, had and exercised the sole right of drawing their seines therein."); *Freary v. Cooke,* 14 Mass. 488 (1779) (jury found that there was "an ancient custom among the inhabitants on said [Connecticut] river, that when any one of them cleared a place for seine-fishing, he held it against every body during the fishing season"); *McCullough v. Wall,* 38 S.C.L. (4 Rich.) 68 (1850) (upholding claim to property in fishing locations separate from riparian land ownership on the Catawba River). *Pitkin v. Olmstead* was reaffirmed in *Russell v. Stocking,* 8 Conn. 236 (1830); *see also Chalker v. Dickinson,* 1 Conn. 382 (1815).

> A contemporary analysis noted that
>
> The true foundation of these incorporeal interests is long continued occupation and enjoyment, under circumstances implying acquiescence on the part of those, who have other interests, which conflict either directly or by consequence with the newly assumed right. . . . [T]he foundation of prescription is the necessity of upholding an interest, which has been exercised as if enjoyed under an actual grant, from the policy of sustaining rather than destroying rights.

Acquisition of Title by Prescription, 19 AM. JURIST 96, 100–101 (1838).

(2) The social dimension of fisheries: Pre-industrial society was closely tied into natural rhythms. "It was a time of rejoicing," one early historian wrote, "when spring came and the salmon began to run." SAMUEL T. DOLE, WINDHAM IN THE PAST 276 (Frederick H. Dole ed., 1916). The return of the salmon brought the male population of the surrounding farms and towns to the rivers for a celebration of natural abundance. Matthew Patten's day book provides an often-laconic description of his trips to Amoskeag, a major fishing spot on the Merrimack River. While fishing was serious business, the falls must also have had a carnival air. Patten's day book has several entries such as the one for May 31, 1758: "a pint and a jill of rum and a mug of Cyder at Thos Halls and got 44 pounds of Salmon for my part." MATTHEW PATTEN, THE DIARY OF MATTHEW PATTEN OF BEDFORD, N.H. 51 (1903). He also noted on June 12: "went frolicking to Namaskeag with my wife."

The Merrimack River offers an example of the importance of fisheries during the period before industrialization destroyed the East Coast's anadromous fish runs. Formed from the joining of the Pemigewasset River and the Winnipesaukee River in central New Hampshire, the Merrimack drains a basin of some 5,000 square miles as it flows south out of the White Mountains of New Hampshire into Massachusetts before turning northeast and emptying into the Atlantic Ocean. When Europeans arrived in the area, the Merrimack supported annual runs of approximately 18,000 Atlantic Salmon; its American Shad, Alewives, and Lamprey Eel runs were even larger. Early writers attest to the abundance: "The rivers, rivulets and brooks were literally full of salmon, shad, alewives, and eels. These fish were so plentiful, as to be used for manure for corn." CHARLES E. POTTER, THE HISTORY OF MANCHESTER, FORMERLY DERRYFIELD, IN NEW-HAMPSHIRE 641 (Manchester, 1856). For an examination of the impacts of industrialization on the Merrimack River Basin, see THEODORE STEINBERG, NATURE INCORPORATED (1991).

Although the social importance of the fisheries declined as the society moved into an industrial, money-based economy, they remained significant and continued to be a source of litigation and legislation. For this reason, there are far more legal artifacts (cases and statutes) on the fisheries than on other aspects of wildlife law. The broad principles, however, were applicable not only to fish but more generally to all wildlife. Fish differ legally only in that they (and other water-based wildlife such as ducks) are affected by issues of navigability.

(3) Anadromy: Anadromous fish are born in fresh water, but spend most of their adult lives in the ocean before returning to fresh water to spawn; "catadromous" species reverse the process, spawning in salt water and maturing in fresh. Both anadromy and catadromy are evolutionary responses to seasonal variations in ecosystems and thus are similar to other forms of animal migration. These adaptations allow species to utilize the seasonal benefits of an ecosystem while avoiding its limitations during other seasons: the birds that fly north in the spring to mate and raise young rely upon the seasonal abundance of insects before returning south when the landscapes turn frigid and insect life becomes dormant. Anadromy allows fish to use rivers and streams despite the limitations on food in such habitats during fall and winter in temperate and northerly latitudes. Since riverine communities are largely dependent upon food produced outside of the river itself, the seasonally limited food supply limits the size of the year-round fish populations. Nevertheless, the riverine environment offers an extremely high oxygen content and relatively secure spawning and incubation conditions—because the low year-round population levels limit predator populations. Migration into rivers to reproduce makes use of these benefits, while migration into the ocean environment avoids the limitations and allows the species to mature in the far richer marine environment. *See generally* Rudolph J. Miller & Ernest L. Brannon, *The Origin and Development of Life History Patterns in Pacific Salmonids*, PROCEEDINGS OF THE SALMON AND TROUT MIGRATORY BEHAVIOR SYMPOSIUM 296–309 (E.L. Brannon and E.O. Salo, eds., 1982), pp. 296–309; Randall F. Schalk, *The Structure of an Anadromous Fish Resource, in* FOR THEORY BUILDING IN ARCHEOLOGY 207–49 (Lewis R. Binford, ed., 1977); DEANNA J. STOUDER, PETER A. BISSON, ROBERT J. NAIMAN ED., PACIFIC SALMON AND THEIR ECOSYSTEM (1997).

Although anadromy evolved as a way to overcome the limitations of nutrient-poor, seasonally limited freshwater ecosystems, that evolutionary strategy became a liability with the advent of hydro-power dams. As one conservation biologist has noted, "Migratory species are exposed to double jeopardy because they are subject to the pressures of change at both ends of their routes, and may have to run a gauntlet of polluted waterways and altered landscapes on the way." John Terbogh, *Preservation of Natural Diversity: The Problem of Extinction Prone Species*, 24 BIOSCI. 715, 721 (1974). Such is the case with the anadromous species: their migratory life histories place the species at risk from a variety of human actions on the high seas and on their spawning beds as well as in the rivers that link the two.

(i) PUBLIC WATERS / PRIVATE WATERS

NOTES

(1) "Navigability" as the divide between public and private: *Adams* and *Pitkin* provide a snapshot of the law at the beginning of the nineteenth century, a snapshot that reveals a judiciary honoring the institution of the common law as the members of the court understood it. For the court, common law recognized public rights to uses other than navigation—uses such as fishing and bathing—only when the water was "navigable"—a concept the court defined in terms of tidal ebb and flow. The court did acknowledge that the public had an easement to use non-tidal-but-navigable-in-fact waters as highways, but held that that easement did not include a right to fish. As we have seen, this understanding of the English common law was simplistic and arguably inaccurate. It also has a touch of irony: navigability at law was relevant only for non-navigation uses of the waterway. It is this assumption—*that only navigable waters are fully public*—that led to the emphasis on "navigability" and the continuing equation of "navigable" and "public."

Over the course of the two centuries since the decisions in *Adams* and *Pitkin*, there has been a substantial expansion of public rights. Initially, this occurred through changes in the definitions of navigability: courts recognized that inland waterways that were navigable-in-fact were also navigable-at-law. Such bodies of water therefore are encumbered with public use rights. More recently, some courts have concluded that navigability is a poor metaphor, that navigability is an element of public use rather than its touchstone.

The expansion of public use rights was given impetus by three groups of decisions by the United States Supreme Court. The first held that the states had special ownership rights in lands beneath navigable waterways. The second group of cases expanded the definition of "navigable" to include those bodies of water that are navigable in fact. The third group held that the state's ownership of submerged lands was a trust for the public.

(2) Expanding public use rights: Initially, state courts responded to questions about public use rights in a body of water with discussion of navigability. But the geographic differences between America and England soon presented difficulties.

(a) Changing definitions of navigability: As *Adams* and *Pitkin* illustrate, American courts generally began the nineteenth century by embracing the presumed law of England, which linked fishing rights to the ownership of the soil as determined by the navigability of the waterway as determined in turn by the reach of the tides. In *Adams v. Pease*, Pease contended that the Connecticut River was in fact navigable and "[i]t would be preposterous to say, that the *Mississippi*, above the flowing and ebbing of the tide, may be held and enjoyed as private property." However sensible this contention, the Connecticut court rejected it, as did several other states. *E.g., Cobb v. Davenport,* 32 N.J.L. 369 (1867) (lake 3 miles long and 1 mile wide was private because non-tidal). Courts adhering to this approach, however, often recognized the third category noted by the court in *Adams v. Pease* and by treatise writers such as Hale and Angell: "the public have a right or easement in such rivers, as common highways, for passing and repassing with vessels, boats, or any water-craft." *See also Hooker v. Cummings,* 20 Johns. 90 (N.Y.Sup.Ct.1822).

Courts in other states were more receptive to geographic realities. In *Carson v. Blazer,* 2 Binn. 475 (Pa.1810), the Pennsylvania Supreme Court noted that the common law was received in the state only to the extent "applicable to our local situation"—and its limitation of "navigability" to tidal waters was inapplicable: "the common law principle concerning rivers, even if extending to America, would not apply to a river such as the Susquehanna, which is a mile wide, ... and which is navigable and is actually navigated by large boats. If such a river had existed in England, no such law would ever have been applied to it." The riparian landowner's attempt to assert an exclusive fishery in the Susquehanna River was rejected. Pennsylvania was not alone in abrogating the tidal test. *See, e.g., Bullock v. Wilson,* 2 Port. 436 (1835); *McManus v. Carmichael,* 3 Iowa 1 (1856); *Collins v. Benbury,* 25 N.C. 277 (1842), *following remand,* 27 N.C. 118 (1844); *Ingram v. Threadgill,* 14 N.C. 59 (1831).

(b) "Navigable"—where we are now: Navigability in fact is the applicable legal standard: a waterbody that is navigable in fact is navigable at law. Of course, changing the standard simply shifted the question, requiring courts to decide what was required for factual navigability.

(i) "Commerce" as the touchstone: Perhaps under the influence of the federal test for navigability with its emphasis on commerce (discussed below), many states have adopted tests that focus on whether the water body can be used for commercial purposes. Most frequently this is a question of whether the body is capable of being used to float logs. In *Munninghoff v. Wisconsin Conservation Commission,* 38 N.W.2d 712 (Wis. 1949), for example, the court noted that a stream was navigable when it "has periods of navigable capacity ordinarily recurrent from year to year and continuing long enough to make the stream usable as a highway. *Willow River Club v. Wade,* 76 N.W. 273 (Wis.1898). The capacity for floating logs to market during the spring freshets which normally lasts six weeks was held to make a stream navigable. *Falls Mfg. Co. v. Oconto River Imp. Co.,* 58 N.W. 257 (Wis.1894)." *See also Ramsey River Road Property Owners Association v. Reeves,* 387 So.2d 1194 (La.App.1980); *Monroe Mill Co. v. Menzel,* 77 P. 813 (Wash.1904).

  (ii) Recreational use as the standard: Some jurisdictions have arguably gone further, holding that waterways capable of floating only small vessels such as an occasional canoe are also in fact navigable. The thrust of these decisions is captured in *People v. Mack*:

> It hardly needs citation of authorities that the rule is that a navigable stream may be used by the public for boating, swimming, fishing, hunting and all recreational purposes. *Munninghoff v. Wisconsin Conservation Commission,* 38 N.W.2d 712, 714–716 (Wis.1949); *Willow River Club v. Wade,* 76 N.W. 273 (Wis.1898); *see Diana Shooting Club v. Husting,* 145 N.W. 816 (Wis.1914) (which pointed out that at common law the rights of hunting and fishing were held to be incident to the right of navigation.)

> The modern tendency in several other states, as well as here, to hold for use of the public any stream capable of being used for recreational purposes is well expressed in *Lamprey v. State (Metcalf),* 53 N.W. 1139 (Minn.1893), where the court said: "But if, under present conditions of society, bodies of water are used for public uses other than mere commercial navigation, in its ordinary sense, we fail to see why they ought not to be held to be public waters, or navigable waters, if the old nomenclature is preferred. Certainly, we do not see why boating or sailing for pleasure should not be considered navigation, as well as boating for mere pecuniary profit." *Lamprey* points out that there are innumerable waters—lakes and streams—which will never be used for commercial purposes but which have been, or are capable of being used, "for sailing, rowing, fishing, fowling, bathing, skating" and other public purposes, and that it would be a great wrong upon the public for all time to deprive the public of those uses merely because the waters are either not used or not adaptable for commercial purposes. Cases from other states which cite with approval the test in *Lamprey v. State,* include *Coleman v. Schaeffer,* 126 N.E.2d 444, 446 (Ohio 1955); *Hillebrand v. Knapp,* 274 N.W. 821, 822 (S.D.1937); *Roberts v. Taylor,* 181 N.W. 622, 625–626 (N.D.1921); *see Muench v. Public Service Commission,* 53 N.W.2d 514, 519 (Wis.1952), wherein a Wisconsin statute now makes a stream navigable in fact which is capable of floating Any boat, skiff or canoe, of the shallowest draft used for recreation purposes.

People v. Mack, 97 Cal.Rptr. 448 (Cal.App.1971). *See also Southern Idaho Fish & Game Association v. Picabo Livestock, Inc.,* 528 P.2d 1295 (Idaho

1974); *Gwathmey v. State Department of Environment, Health, & Natural Resources,* 464 S.E.2d 674 (N.C.1995). The decisions are collected and considered in Harrison C. Dunning, *Waters Subject to the Public Right, in* 4 WATERS & WATER RIGHTS ch. 32 (Robert E. Beck ed., 1996).

Even states that phrase their navigability test in terms of commercial use are recognizing that recreational boating is a commercial enterprise, given the activities of boat rental companies, tour groups, and individual river guides; hence, recreational streams increasingly satisfy the requirement of suitability for commerce. *E.g., Adirondack League Club, Inc. v. Sierra Club,* 92 N.Y.2d 591 (1998).

(iii) Restricting "navigability": Although most states have adopted expansive definitions of navigability, a few continue to employ sharply restricted the standard. Some of these decisions have focused on the nature of public use rights that accompany a finding a waterbody to be navigable, other have adopted restrictive definitions of "navigability" itself. For example, Georgia limits navigability under state law to rivers capable of carrying large commercial barges. *See Givens v. Ichauway, Inc.,* 493 S.E.2d 148 (Ga.1997) (suggesting a river must be capable of floating a barge that is 245 feet long, 35 feet wide, with 7' 6' foot draft).

(c) Decoupling navigability and public rights: Although most states continue to base public use rights in a waterway on the navigability of the waterway, some have explicitly rejected the linkage, holding that public rights exist even in nonnavigable streams.

(i) Constitutional and quasi-constitutional protections of access: The Alaska Constitution reserves for "the public for common use" all naturally occurring "fish, wildlife, and waters"; this provision has been interpreted to vest in the public rights to "use the water itself" even in nonnavigable waterways. *Alaska Public Easement Defense Fund v. Andrus,* 435 F.Supp. 664 (D.Alaska 1977) (quoting ALASKA CONST., Art. VIII, § 3).

The California Constitution similarly guarantees "[t]he people shall have the right to fish upon and from the public lands of the state and in the waters thereof, excepting upon land set aside for fish hatcheries, and no land owned by the state shall ever be sold or transferred without reserving in the people the absolute right to fish thereupon." CAL. CONST. Art. I, § 25. *See State v. San Luis Obispo Sportsman's Association,* 584 P.2d 1088 (Cal.1978).

A different form of access guarantee is found in the Massachusetts Bay Body of Liberties enacted in 1641 and 1647. The Ordinance guarantees householders "free fishing and fowling in any great ponds [those of more than ten acres], and Bayes, Coves and Rivers, so farre as the sea ebbes and flowes," as well as access across private land to reach such bodies of water. A COPPIE OF THE LIBERTIES OF THE MASSACHUSETS COLONIE IN NEW ENGLAND § 16, *reprinted in* SOURCES AND DOCUMENTS OF UNITED STATES CONSTITUTIONS 47, 49 (William F. Swindler, ed. 1975). Access is provided by guaranteeing the right to "pass and re-pass on foot through any man's property for that end so they trespass not upon any man's corn or meadow." *Barrows v.*

McDermott, 73 Me. 441, 447 (1882). The Ordinance has been expanded to include many types of water recreation and is applicable to most fresh water lakes in Maine, Massachusetts, and New Hampshire. *See* Leighton L. Leighty, *Public Rights in Navigable State Waters—Some Statutory Approaches,* 6 LAND & WATER L. REV. 459, 471–72 (1971).

   (ii) Legislative declarations: Some state legislatures have declared that public use rights exist independently of the navigability of a waterbody. Indiana, for example, asserts that the public "has a vested right in . . . [t]he use of the public freshwater lakes for recreational purposes." IND. CODE ANN. § 14–26–2–5(c)(2)(B). "Public freshwater lake" is defined as any lake that "has been used by the public with the acquiescence of a riparian owner," *id.* 14–26–2–3–(a), and "recreational purpose" is defined to include fishing. *Id.* § 14–26–2–5(b)(1).

> Minnesota even more explicitly decouples navigability and public rights:

> Public waters are not determined exclusively by the proprietorship of the underlying, overlying, or surrounding land or by whether it is a body or stream of water that was navigable in fact or susceptible of being used as a highway for commerce at the time this state was admitted to the union.

MINN. STAT. ANN. § 103G.15(b).

(3) State sovereign ownership of river beds: The second element in the transformation of public use rights was the decision by the United States Supreme Court that states, upon entering the Union, took title to all lands beneath navigable waterways. Given the correlation in the common law between stream-bed ownership and fishing rights, the decision inevitably had profound effects on public rights to capture fish and other water-based wildlife.

   The story of state sovereign ownership begins with the New Jersey Supreme Court's decision in *Arnold v. Mundy,* a suit involving conflicting claims to oyster beds. The court upheld the state's ownership of lands beneath tidal waters against claims based on grants from the successors in interest of the colony's proprietors. Writing for the court, Chief Justice Kirkpatrick drew upon English precedent and the writings of jurists such as Emmerich de Vattel to explain the special terms on which the state held such lands:

> Upon the whole, therefore, I am of opinion, . . . that by the law of nature, which is the only true foundation of all the social rights; that by the civil law, which formerly governed almost the whole civilized world, and which is still the foundation of the polity of almost every nation in Europe; that by the common law of England, of which our ancestors boasted, and to which it were well if we ourselves paid a more sacred regard; I say I am of opinion, that by all these, the navigable rivers in which the tide ebbs and flows, the ports, the bays, the coasts of the sea, including both the water and the land under the water, for the purpose of passing and repassing, navigation, fishing, fowling, sustenance, and all the other uses of the water and its products (a Few things excepted) are common to all the citizens, and

that each has a right to use them according to his necessities, subject only to the laws which regulate that use; that the property, indeed, strictly speaking, is vested in the sovereign, but it is vested in him not for his own use, but for the use of the citizen, that is, for his direct and immediate enjoyment.

Arnold v. Mundy, 6 N.J.L. 1, 76–77 (1821). The doctrine of royal prerogative ownership of submerged lands thus was transformed in the transition from monarchy to republic into the doctrine of state sovereign ownership in which the state held the lands as trustee for the real sovereign, the people.

This reasoning subsequently was adopted by the United States Supreme Court in *Martin v. Waddell's Lessee,* 41 U.S. (16 Pet.) 367 (1842). *Martin* arose out of essentially identical facts involving oyster beds in Raritan Bay, New Jersey. Title to these beds, the Supreme Court held, passed to the State of New Jersey at the time of the Revolution because the state was the successor to the powers of the King and Parliament. The states held these lands, however, not in a proprietary capacity, but in a prerogative capacity that was intertwined with the political powers to govern, much as the King's Bench had explained the royal prerogative ownership in *The Royal Fishery of Banne.* The state held such lands, the Court wrote, "as a public trust, for the benefit of the whole community, to be freely used by all for navigation and fishing, as well for shell-fish as floating fish." 41 U.S. at 413.

Three years later, the Court held that new states also owned submerged lands since to decide otherwise would be to deny the new states "equal footing with the original thirteen states." *Pollard's Lessee v. Hagan,* 44 U.S. (3 How.) 212, 229 (1845). Thus, when a state joins the Union, it acquires title to lands beneath navigable waters—regardless of the ownership of the riparian lands—to the same extent as the original states and subject to the same trust limitations.

Martin and *Pollard's Lessee* left two key issues unresolved: what does "navigable" mean? And which sovereign—federal or state—has the final say on the definition of this crucial term?

(a) The federal definition of "navigability": The evolution of the federal definition of "navigable" has followed a path similar to that of state definitions. The Supreme Court began by embracing the tidal standard and ended with a navigable-in-fact test. Federal law, however, has an additional wrinkle since "navigability" is relevant not only for title under the state ownership doctrine announced in *Martin,* but also for Admiralty and Commerce Clause jurisdiction; hence, there is not a single, all-encompassing federal definition. *United States v. Appalachian Electric Power Co.,* 311 U.S. 377 (1941).

Initially, federal courts adhered to the common understanding of English precedent and held that only waters within the ebb and flow of the tide were navigable. *The Steamboat Thomas Jefferson,* 23 U.S. (10 Wheat.) 428, 429 (1825). In *The Propeller Genesee Chief v. Fitzhugh,* 53 U.S. (12 How.) 443, 453–54 (1851), however, the Court held that federal admiralty jurisdiction extended to the Great Lakes, justifying its decision with language that echoed ideas of equal footing. The abandonment of tidality as the test for admiralty jurisdiction was followed by its rejection for Commerce Clause jurisdiction in *The Daniel Ball*, 77 U.S. (10 Wall.) 557 (1870), where the Court held that rivers are navigable at law when they are navigable in fact, and they are navigable in fact "when they are used, or are susceptible of being used, in their ordinary condition, as highways for commerce, over which trade and travel are or may be conducted in the customary modes of trade and travel on water." *Id.* at 563.

(b) **Source of law—federal or state?:** The extension of *The Daniel Ball*'s navigable-in-fact test to the distinct legal issue of determining state title to the submerged lands occurred in passing in *Barney v. Keokuk*, 94 U.S. 324, 338 (1877). But it was not until a trilogy of cases decided between 1922 and 1931 that the Supreme Court made it clear that the federal test must be applied to determine which submerged lands passed to the state upon statehood. *See United States v. Utah*, 283 U.S. 64 (1931); *United States v. Holt State Bank*, 270 U.S. 49 (1926); *Brewer-Elliott Oil & Gas Co. v. United States*, 260 U.S. 77 (1922).

(c) **Navigability-for-title:** Subsequent navigability-for-title cases have established the following points:

"(1) Navigability for title is determined as of the date each state came into the Union.

"(2) Such navigability is determined by the natural and ordinary condition of the water at the time, not whether it could be made navigable by artificial improvements. However, the fact that rapids, rocks, or other obstructions make navigation difficult will not destroy title navigability so long as the waters were usable for a significant portion of the time.

"(3) Navigability in intrastate commerce is all that is required, not usability in interstate commerce.

"(4) The waters must be usable by the 'customary mode of trade or travel on water.' This may include waters usable for commercial log floating. This includes waters as little as three or four feet deep that are geographically located so they have been, or can be use by canoes or rowboats for commercial trade and travel (fur traders' canoes)...."

Ralph W. Johnson & Russell A. Austin, Jr., *Recreational Rights and Titles to Beds on Western Lakes and Streams*, 7 NAT. RESOURCES J. 1, 24–25 (1967). *See generally Utah v. United States*, 403 U.S. 9, 9–10 (1971); *United States v. Oregon*, 295 U.S. 1 (1935); *United States v. Utah*, 283 U.S. 64 (1931); *United States v. Holt State Bank*, 270 U.S. 49 (1926); *Brewer-Elliott Oil & Gas Co. v. United States*, 260 U.S. 77 (1922); *Oklahoma v. Texas*, 258 U.S. 574 (1922); *Packer v. Bird*, 137 U.S. 661 (1891).

(d) **Effect on state title:** By the time the source-of-law issue was resolved, many Eastern and Midwestern states had decided that owners of riparian lands on navigable waterways held title to the underlying bed. In such states, the effect of the navigability-for-title ruling was not to nullify those grants, nor to limit materially the power of states to continue granting riparian lands on such terms. Rather, its effect was to qualify private titles to such lands (and the public's title, in the case of lands still in public hands) with the public trust burdens recognized by the Supreme

Court in *Martin v. Waddell's Lessee*. Landowners could own such lands, but their use of them was subject to heightened restrictions aimed at preserving the public's use of navigable waterways for travel, fishing, and various other purposes.

In the West, the decisions had greater effect because the law was less settled. There, states typically chose to retain (or reassert) public ownership of all navigable river beds, recognizing riparian land titles as extending merely to high-or low-water marks rather than to the thread of the river. In such states, public fishing rights were secured by the continued public ownership of the underlying land.

These disparate results have been sanctioned by the Supreme Court. The Court has made it clear that once a state takes title to the beds of navigable waters, questions about ownership of the bed are governed by state law rather than federal common law. *Oregon ex rel. State Land Board v. Corvallis Sand and Gravel Co.*, 429 U.S. 363 (1977). The Court buttressed this conclusion in *Phillips Petroleum Co. v. Mississippi*, 484 U.S. 469, 475 (1988), when it stated that the states had the power "to recognize private rights in [trust] lands as they see fit." The state may, therefore, alienate title to the bed of a navigable stream. But ownership of the bed is a different question than use of the waterway for navigation, fishing, fowling, and other activities. While states may be free to alienate the beds of navigable waters, are they also free to cut off public use rights?

(3) Federal law as a source of public access rights: State law is not the only source of public rights in bodies of water. Many federal laws also guarantee public use of waterways. And, under the Supremacy Clause, a federal law recognizing public use rights supercedes state law so that bodies of water need not be navigable under state law to be "public" under federal law.

    (a) The navigation servitude: One important source of public rights is the federal navigation servitude, a doctrine that secures "the exercise of the public right of navigation" as well as "the governmental control and regulation necessary to give effect to that right." *United States v. W.R. Cress*, 243 U.S. 316, 320 (1917). The servitude "exists by virtue of the Commerce Clause." *Kaiser Aetna v. United States*, 444 U.S. 164, 177 (1979). It is more than simply a regulatory power. It is, as the Supreme Court has variously said, a "dominant servitude" on all submerged lands subject to it, *United States v. Rands*, 389 U.S. 121, 122–23 (1967); "a permanent easement that [is] a pre-existing limitation" upon the title of all such submerged lands, including lands held by private owners. *Lucas v. South Carolina Coastal Council*, 505 U.S. 1003, 1028 (1992). *See Phillips Petroleum Co. v. Mississippi*, 484 U.S. 469, 479 (1988) (lands beneath navigable waterways are "subject to the federal navigation easement and the power of Congress to control navigation on those streams under the Commerce Clause"). "When a navigational servitude exists, it gives rise to the right of the public to use those waterways" to which it applies. *Dardar v. Lafourche Realty Co.*, 985 F.2d 824, 832 (5th Cir.1993) (citing *Kaiser Aetna v. United States*, 444 U.S. 164 (1979)).

    The navigational servitude attaches to all waterways that are navigable in fact under the standard announced in *The Daniel Ball*, 77 U.S. (10

Wall.) 557 (1871) and *The Montello*, 87 U.S. (20 Wall.) 430 (1874). According to the decision in *The Montello*, a river is navigable if it is suitable for commerce conducted by "vessels of any kind that can float upon water," including those "propelled by animal power," and "no matter what mode the commerce may be conducted." *Id.* at 441–42 (finding the Fox River in Wisconsin navigable to its source even though travel required dragging shallow, flat-bottomed boats over rocks and portaging water falls). When the servitude applies, it overrides the property rights of the owner of the underlying land, just as other servitudes do:

> It is no answer to say that these private owners had interests in the water that were recognized by state law. We deal here with the federal domain, an area which Congress can completely pre-empt, leaving no vested private claims that constitute "private property" within the meaning of the Fifth Amendment.

United States v. Twin City Power Co., 350 U.S. 222, 227 (1956).

Although the dominance of the federal servitude is plain, the scope of the public rights it protects are far less clear. The few cases that have considered the issue have either concluded or assumed that the servitude protects not only public access rights but also public fishing rights—and that it does so notwithstanding the fact that a waterway is nonnavigable under state law. *Dardar v. Lafourche Realty Co.*, 985 F.2d 824 (5th Cir.1993); *Boone v. United States*, 944 F.2d 1489 (9th Cir.1991) (by implication); *United States v. Harrell*, 926 F.2d 1036 (11th Cir.1991) (by implication); *Loving v. Alexander*, 745 F.2d 861 (4th Cir.1984).

In the leading case, *Vaughn v. Vermilion Corp.*, 444 U.S. 206 (1979), commercial fishers sought access under the servitude to canals that, although connected to navigable waterways, were nonnavigable under state law and hence closed to public use. Some of the canals were entirely human constructed; others, although also constructed, were allegedly created "in part by means of diversion or destruction of a preexisting natural navigable waterway." *Id.* at 208. State courts denied access. Although agreeing that human-constructed canals generally were not covered by the servitude, the United States Supreme Court reversed the state court with respect to the canals that destroyed or diverted naturally navigable waterways, ruling that in such waterways the navigation servitude was a federal defense to a trespass action. *See also Atlanta School of Kayaking, Inc. v. Douglasville–Douglas County Water & Sewer Authority*, 981 F.Supp. 1469 (N.D.Ga.1997) (servitude provides a federal law right of access, despite state law, to whitewater river with rapids, rocks, and shifting currents, that is usable by kayaks after rains). *Cf. State v. Head*, 498 S.E.2d 389 (S.C.App.1997) (artificial lakes created on private land adjacent to navigable waters are open to public under state law); *Mentor Harbor Yachting Club v. Mentor Lagoons, Inc.*, 163 N.E.2d 373 (Ohio 1959) (artificial extensions of naturally navigable channels become a part thereof and are public waters under state law). Little if any litigation has considered to what extent the federal servitude protects public fowling rights. Such rights, however, were an integral part of public use rights in waterways navigable at law when the federal constitution was drafted.

(b) A potpourri of possible federal statutory access rights:
Numerous federal statutes protect the navigability of waterways in various

settings by ensuring that they remain unobstructed. The effect of such statutes on wildlife issues is uncertain, however, both because they make no mention of fishing, hunting, and trapping, and because there are few relevant decisions.

The Northwest Ordinance of 1787 is a potentially important source of access rights. Article IV of the Ordinance provides that navigable waterways flowing into either the Mississippi or St. Lawrence Rivers, together with portage routes between such rivers, "shall be common highways, and forever free." 1 Stat. 51, 52 note (1789), re-enacted at 1 Stat. 51 (1789). According to the chief interpretive decision, *Economy Light & Power Co. v. United States,* 256 U.S. 113, 122 (1921), the Ordinance remains valid and in effect to the extent that "it established public rights of highway in navigable waters"; to that extent (but not, apparently, in other ways), the Ordinance was "no more capable of repeal by one of the states than any other regulation of interstate commerce enacted by the Congress." *See Moore v. Sanborne,* 2 Mich. 519, 525 (1853) (Northwest Ordinance effected "a perpetual reservation of rights to the public"). On the continuing force of the Northwest Ordinance, *compare* W. HULL & R. HULL, *supra,* at 53–55 n.24 (arguing that it remains effective) and G. Graham Waite, *The Dilemma of Water Recreation and a Suggested Solution,* 1958 WIS. L. REV. 542, 553–58 (arguing that *Economy Light* should be narrowly construed and that the Ordinance did not survive entry of states into the Union).

The terms of the Ordinance were applied to the Southwest Territory on May 26, 1790, 1 Stat. 123, and in slightly different terms to all navigable rivers within the United States Territory "south of the state of Tennessee." 2 Stat. 229, 235 (1803). Language requiring that navigable waterways remain "forever free" was included in the enabling acts under which various states entered the Union, and presumably remains in force as a limit on the powers of such states. *See* WILLIAM J. HULL & ROBERT W. HULL, THE ORIGIN AND DEVELOPMENT OF THE WATERWAYS POLICY OF THE UNITED STATES 7 & n.28 (1967) (citing 12 states). Similar language was included in the Constitutions of several states. *Id.* at 7 & n. 27 (citing 8 states).

A codified statute, 33 U.S.C. § 10, provides that all navigable rivers in the region covered by the Louisiana Purchase "shall be and forever remain public highways." A similar provision, 43 U.S.C. § 931, applies broadly to all navigable rivers on public lands. The "forever free" language worked its way into various treaties with Indian tribes, in some instances covering all lakes and streams without regard for navigability. *E.g.,* Treaty of the Upper Missouri, § 8, 11 Stat 657 (1855). Finally and perhaps most significantly, the Rivers and Harbors Act bans all obstructions of navigable waterways except those permitted by federal law, implying that such waterways are open for public navigation. 33 U.S.C. § 403.

Do any of these statutes give rise to a federal law right to engage in fishing and hunting on navigable waterways? In many states the issue is academic since applicable state law provides such rights. In other jurisdictions, however, the issue is potentially important—yet it is little litigated, perhaps because many of the statutes are uncodified and little known.

Statutes that merely protect the use of rivers as public highways or common highways are unlikely to give rise to public fishing or hunting rights, given the English and early American tradition of using the term "public highway" to refer to waters open solely for public travel. *See, e.g., Adams v. Pease*, 2 Conn. 481 (1818) [*supra*]. Until authoritative rulings are given, however, the issue remains open. From a different perspective, even "public highway" statutes may have importance for the protection of wildlife habitat since transportation requires water—a resource that is becoming increasingly scarce.

Greater uncertainty surrounds the Rivers and Harbors Act, which speaks in terms of navigation generally, rather than use as highways. The Supreme Court has interpreted the statute in ways strongly protective of public rights. *E.g., United States v. Alaska*, 503 U.S. 569, 578 (1992); *United States v. Republic Steel Corp.*, 362 U.S. 482, 491 (1960). Motivated by that interpretive posture, several courts have assumed that rivers deemed navigable under the Act are open to public fishing, without regard for state law. *E.g., United States v. Harrell*, 926 F.2d 1036, 1038 (11th Cir.1991). Still, the issue has received little judicial—and even less scholarly—attention.

In enacting the Rivers and Harbors Act, Congress no doubt sought to protect fishing vessels as well as other vessels against obstructions to navigation. It is far less clear, however, that Congress sought to prescribe who had rights to fish, even if it had the power to do so. Nonetheless, given the Supreme Court's interpretive perspective when dealing with this statute and given also the close connection at common law between navigability and public rights to fish, a court could easily interpret the statute to protect public fishing rights. Far less likely is an interpretation protecting public fowling or trapping rights. Nor is it likely that the statute diminishes a state's general licensing and regulatory powers; its effect, rather, is to limit a state's power exclude the public by charging tolls or by treating public use as a trespass.

* * *

The effect of the evolution of navigability, state sovereign ownership, and the public trust doctrine is the subject of the remainder of this section. Our concern is with the public's right to use bodies of water: under what circumstances does the public have a right-to-use? What is included within the right? Does it include only navigation? Does is also fishing? fowling? hunting?

We begin with public use rights in public waters (regardless of how defined). What rights do the public have in such waters? May states cut off those rights if they choose to alienate the beds of such waters?

(ii) THE PUBLIC TRUST DOCTRINE AND PUBLIC RIGHTS IN PUBLIC WATERS

Illinois Central R.R. v. Illinois

Supreme Court of the United States.
146 U.S. 387 (1892).

■ FIELD, J.:—[In 1869, the Illinois legislature had given fee title to the land beneath Chicago's harbor for a distance of one mile from the shore to the

Illinois Central Railroad in exchange for an annual payment. In 1873, the legislature changed its mind and repealed the 1869 statute. The state brought a quiet title action and won. On appeal, the Supreme Court began with the source of Illinois's title to the lake bed:]

The state of Illinois was admitted into the Union in 1818 on an equal footing with the original states, in all respects. Such was one of the conditions of the cession from Virginia of the territory northwest of the Ohio river, out of which the state was formed. But the equality prescribed would have existed if it had not been thus stipulated. There can be no distinction between the several states of the Union in the character of th jurisdiction, sovereignty, and dominion which they may possess and exercise over persons and subjects within their respective limits. . . .

It is the settled law of this country that the ownership of and dominion and sovereignty over lands covered by tide waters, within the limits of the several states, belong to the respective states within which they are found, with the consequent right to use or dispose of any portion thereof, when that can be done without substantial impairment of the interest of the public in the waters, and subject always to the paramount right of congress to control their navigation so far as may be necessary for the regulation of commerce with foreign nations and among the states. This doctrine has been often announced by this court, and is not questioned by counsel of any of the parties. *Pollard's Lessee v. Hagan*, 44 U.S. (3 How.) 212 (1845); *Weber v. Commissioners*, 85 U.S. (18 Wall.) 57 (1873).

. . .

The question, therefore, to be considered, is whether the legislature was competent to thus deprive the state of its ownership of the submerged lands in the harbor of Chicago, and of the consequent control of its waters; or, in other words, whether the railroad corporation can hold the lands and control the waters by the grant, against any future exercise of power over them by the state.

That the state holds the title to the lands under the navigable waters of Lake Michigan, within its limits, in the same manner that the state holds title to soils under tide water, by the common law, we have already shown; and that title necessarily carries with it control over the waters above them, whenever the lands are subjected to use. But it is a title different in character from that which the state holds in lands intended for sale. It is different from the title which the United States hold in the public lands which are open to pre-emption and sale. It is a title held in trust for the people of the state, that they may enjoy the navigation of the waters, carry on commerce over them, and have liberty of fishing therein, freed from the obstruction or interference of private parties. The interest of the people in the navigation of the waters and in commerce over them may be improved in many instances by the erection of wharves, docks, and piers therein, for which purpose the state may grant parcels of the submerged lands; and, so long as their disposition is made for such purpose, no valid objections can be made to the grants. It is grants of parcels of lands under navigable waters that may afford foundation for wharves, piers, docks, and other structures in aid of commerce, and grants of parcels which, being occupied, do not substantially impair the public interest in the lands and waters remaining, that are chiefly considered and sustained in the adjudged cases as a valid exercise of legislative power consistently with the trust to the public upon which such lands are held by the state. But that is a very different doctrine from the one which would sanction the abdication of the general control of the state over lands under the navigable waters of an entire harbor or bay, or of a sea or lake. Such abdication is not consistent with the exercise of that trust which requires the government of the state to preserve such waters for the use of the public. The trust devolving upon the state for the public, and which can only be discharged by the management and control of property in which the public has an interest, cannot be relinquished by a transfer of the property. The control of the state for the purposes of the trust can never be lost, except as to such parcels as are used in promoting the interests of the public therein, or can be disposed of without any substantial impairment of the public interest in the lands and waters remaining. It is only by observing the distinction between a grant of such parcels for the improvement of the public interest, or which when occupied do not substantially impair the public interest in the lands and waters remaining, and a grant of the whole property in which the public is interested, that the language of the adjudged cases can be reconciled. General language sometimes found in opinions of the courts, expressive of absolute ownership and control by the state of lands under navigable waters, irrespective of any trust as to their use and disposition, must be read and construed with reference to the special facts of the particular cases. A grant of all the lands under the navigable waters of a state has never been adjudged to be within the legislative power; and any attempted grant of the kind would be held, if not absolutely void on its face, as subject to revocation. The state can no more abdicate its trust over property in which the whole people are interested, like navigable waters and soils under them, so as to leave them entirely under the use and control of private parties, except in the instance of parcels mentioned for the improvement of the navigation and use of the waters, or when parcels can be disposed of without impairment of the public interest in what remains, than it can abdicate its police powers in the administration of government and the preservation of the peace. In the administration of government the use of such powers may for a limited period be delegated to a municipality or other body, but there always remains with the state the right to revoke those powers and exercise them in a more direct manner, and one more conformable to its wishes. So with trusts connected with public property, or property of a special character, like lands under navigable waters; they cannot be placed entirely beyond the direction and control of the state.

The harbor of Chicago is of immense value to the people of the state of Illinois, in the facilities it affords to its vast and constantly increasing commerce; and the idea that its legislature can deprive the state of control over its bed and waters, and place the same in the hands of a private corporation, created for a different purpose,—one limited to transportation of passengers and freight between distant points and the city,—is a proposition that cannot be defended.

The area of the submerged lands proposed to be ceded by the act in question to the railroad company embraces something more than 1,000 acres, being, as stated by counsel, more than three times the area of the outer harbor, and not only including all of that harbor, but embracing adjoining submerged lands, which will, in all probability, be hereafter included in the harbor. It is as large as that embraced by all the merchandise docks along the Thames at London; is much larger than that included in the famous docks and basins at Liverpool; is twice that of the port of Marseilles, and nearly, if not quite, equal to the pier area along the water front of the city of New York. And the arrivals and clearings of vessels at the port exceed in number those of New York, and are equal to those of New York and Boston combined. Chicago has nearly 25 per cent. of the lake carrying trade, as compared with the arrivals and clearings of all the leading ports of our great inland seas. In the year ending June 30, 1886, the joint arrivals and clearances of vessels at that port amounted to 22,096, with a tonnage of over 7,000,000; and in 1890 the tonnage of the vessels reached nearly 9,000,000. As stated by counsel, since the passage of the lake front act, in 1869, the population of the city has increased nearly 1,000,000 souls, and the increase of commerce has kept pace with it. It is hardly conceivable that the legislature can divest the state of the control and management of this harbor, and vest it absolutely in a private corporation. Surely an act of the legislature transferring the title to its submerged lands and the power claimed by the railroad company to a foreign state or nation would be repudiated, without hesitation, as a gross perversion of the trust over the property under which it is held. So would a similar transfer to a corporation of another state. It would not be listened to that the control and management of the harbor of that great city—a subject of concern to the whole people of the state—should thus be placed elsewhere than in the state itself. All the objections which can be urged to such attempted transfer may be urged to a transfer to a private corporation like the railroad company in this case.

Any grant of the kind is necessarily revocable, and the exercise of the trust by which the property was held by the state can be resumed at any time. Undoubtedly there may be expenses incurred in improvements made under such a grant, which the state ought to pay; but, be that as it may, the power to resume the trust whenever the state judges best is, we think, incontrovertible. The position advanced by the railroad company in support of its claim to the ownership of the submerged lands, and the right to the erection of wharves, piers, and docks at its pleasure, or for its business in the harbor of Chicago, would place every harbor in the country at the mercy of a majority of the legislature of the state in which the harbor is situated.

We cannot, it is true, cite any authority where a grant of this kind has been held invalid, for we believe that no instance exists where the harbor of a great city and its commerce have been allowed to pass into the control of any private corporation. But the decisions are numerous which declare that such property is held by the state, by virtue of its sovereignty, in trust for the public. The ownership of the navigable waters of the harbor, and of the lands under them, is a subject of public concern to the whole people of the state. The trust with which they are held, therefore, is governmental, and cannot be alienated, except in those instances mentioned, of parcels used in the improvement of the interest thus held, or when parcels can be disposed of without detriment to the public interest in the lands and waters remaining.

This follows necessarily from the public character of the property, being held by the whole people for purposes in which the whole people are interested. As said by Chief Justice Taney in *Martin v. Waddell,* 41 U.S. (16 Pet.) 367, 410 (1842): "When the Revolution took place the people of each state became themselves sovereign, and in that character hold the absolute right to all their navigable waters, and the soils under them, for their own common use, subject only to the rights since surrendered by the constitution to the general government." In *Arnold v. Mundy,* 6 N.J.L. 1 (1821), which is cited by this court in *Martin v. Waddell,* and spoken of by Chief Justice Taney as entitled to great weight, and in which the decision was made "with great deliberation and research," the supreme court of New Jersey comments upon the rights of the state in the bed of navigable waters, and, after observing that the power exercised by the state over the lands and waters is nothing more than what is called the *"jus regium,"* the right of regulating, improving, and securing them for the benefit of every individual citizen, adds: "The sovereign power itself, therefore, cannot, consistently with the principles of the law of nature and the constitution of a well-ordered society, make a direct and absolute grant of the waters of the state, divesting all the citizens of their common right. It would be a grievance which never could be long borne by a free people." Necessarily must the control of the waters of a state over all lands under them pass when the lands are conveyed in fee to private parties, and are by them subjected to use.

. . .

. . . . The legislature could not give away nor sell the discretion of its successors in respect to matters, the government of which, from the very nature of things, must vary with varying circumstances. The legislation which may be needed one day for the harbor may be different from the legislation that may be required at another day. Every legislature must, at the time of its existence, exercise the power of the state in the execution of the trust devolved upon it. We hold, therefore, that any attempted cession of the ownership and control of the state in and over the submerged lands in Lake Michigan, by the act of April 16, 1869, was inoperative to affect, modify, or in any respect to control the sovereignty and dominion of the state over the lands, or its ownership thereof, and that any such attempted operation of the act was annulled by the repealing act of April 15, 1873, which to that extent was valid and effective. There can be no irrepealable contract in a conveyance of property by a grantor in disregard of a public trust, under which he was bound to hold and manage it.

NOTES

(1) What is the Court's holding? Does it establish a flat prohibition against transfers of trust property? Was the decision predicated upon the magnitude of the grant?

Was the decision instead predicated upon the belief that the state's transfer of the property precluded subsequent regulation of the property? Or that the state's traditional power to regulate in the public interest, *aka* the police power, was less expansive than the state's power over navigable waters under the public trust doctrine?

Professor Joseph Sax characterized the decision in these words:

The Court stated that the title under which Illinois held the navigable waters of Lake Michigan is

> different in character from that which the state holds in lands intended for sale.* * * It is a title held in trust for the people of the state, that they may enjoy the navigation of the waters, carry on commerce over them, and have liberty of fishing therein, freed from the obstruction or interference of private parties.

> With this language, the Court articulated a principle that has become the central substantive thought in public trust litigation. When a state holds a resource which is available for the free use of the general public, a court will look with considerable skepticism upon *any* governmental conduct which is calculated *either* to reallocate that resource to more restricted uses *or* to subject public uses to the self-interest of private parties.

Joseph L. Sax, *The Public Trust Doctrine in Natural Resource Law: Effective Judicial Intervention*, 68 MICH. L. REV. 471, 489–90 (1970).

(2) Public use rights in navigable waterways where the beds are state property: Recall that the initial consensus was that all members of the public had a right to fish in common in navigable waters. The rationale offered by the courts and treatise writers for the public right was that "the property of the coasts, bays, and arms of the sea, and of the fishery therein, was in the King; but in trust, as to fisheries, for all the king's subjects, except when otherwise especially granted." *Dill v. Wareham*, 48 Mass. (7 Metc.) 438, 445 (1844) (Shaw, C.J.); *see also Gough v. Bell*, 21 N.J.L. 156 (1847). *Cf. Yard v. Carman*, 3 N.J.L. 936, 944 (1812) (Pennington, J.) (an "exclusive right of fishing in the arms of the sea and great rivers, was thought by our English ancestors, a restraint on their natural rights, as odious and more injurious than the game laws"). To what extent has this understanding been modified?

As noted, the Supreme Court in *Illinois Central* stated that the state's title "is a title held in trust for the people of the state, that they may enjoy the navigation of the waters, carry on commerce over them, and have liberty of fishing therein, freed from the obstruction or interference of private parties." The traditional formulation of the public rights in the trust property generally adds "swimming"—or the more dated, "bathing"—to navigation and fishing.

When the state has retained sovereign ownership of the beds of navigable waterways, public access is unchallenged. Conflicts over public use rights therefore generally center on the collateral use of riparian fast land. For example, can a boater use fast land to portage around a non-navigable stretch of the river?

Consider the evolution of Montana law. In *Herrin v. Sutherland*, the plaintiff landowner brought a trespass action against a duck hunter. The state supreme court followed the common law rule which linked fishing and hunting rights to ownership of the soil. Since Montana had retained ownership of the bed of the stream, the public had the right to hunt and fish based on its ownership of the submerged lands. Hunters, however, had no right to walk along the bank above the low-water mark or to fire shotguns at waterfowl flying over private land because the public's ownership only extended to the mean low-water mark of the stream. *Herrin v. Sutherland*, 241 P. 328 (Mont.1925).

In a later decision, based primarily on the public trust doctrine, the court expanded public access rights to the high-water mark. It also decided that recreational users could enter private land to portage around barriers in navigable waterways, as long as they did so "in the least intrusive way possible, avoiding damage to the private property holder's rights." The court also decided that public access rights were not dependent upon ownership of the submerged land; they arose directly from the trust imposed on such lands when Montana became a state. In so ruling, the court implicitly set aside the common-law rule attaching fishing rights to ownership of (submerged) lands. *Montana Coalition for Stream Access, Inc. v. Curran*, 682 P.2d 163 (Mont.1984). *See also Montana Coalition for Stream Access v. Hildreth*, 684 P.2d 1088 (Mont.1984) (reaffirming *Curran*).

The Montana legislature responded by enacting the Stream Access Law to codify recreational use of Montana streams. The statute was promptly challenged by landowners. In *Galt v. State Department of Fish, Wildlife, & Parks*, the court upheld the majority of the statute provisions, noting that, although a riparian landowner might hold title to the bed of a non-navigable stream, the landowner's "fee [is] impressed with a dominant estate in favor of the public." The legislature went too far, however, when it sought to give recreational users a right to build duck blinds and to engage in big game hunting below the high-water mark because "[t]he public has a right of use up to the high water mark, but only such use as is necessary to utilization of the water itself. We hold that any use of the bed and banks must be of minimal impact." *Galt v. State Department of Fish, Wildlife, & Parks*, 731 P.2d 912 (Mont.1987). *See also Madison v. Graham*, 126 F.Supp.2d 1320 (D.Mont.2001).

(3) Public trust—federal or state law? What was the source of law that the Supreme Court applied in *Illinois Central*? Although the Court's language sounds like it is applying constitutional law, it has subsequently stated that the "conclusion reached was necessarily a statement of Illinois law." *Appleby v. City of New York*, 271 U.S. 364, 395 (1926). The Court buttressed this assertion in *Phillips Petroleum Co. v. Mississippi*, 484 U.S. 469, 475 (1988), when it stated that the states had the power "to recognize private right in [trust] lands as they see fit."

The Court has suggested, however, that there is some minimum body of rights that states must recognize as a matter of federal law. *E.g, Smith v. Maryland*, 59 U.S. (18 How.) 71, 74–75 (1855) (state has "duty to preserve unimpaired those public uses for which the [submerged] soil is held"); *Idaho v. Coeur d'Alene Tribe,* 521 U.S. 261, 283 (1997) (submerged lands within a state are "infused with a public trust that the State itself is bound to respect"). Recall the statement in *Illinois Central* that submerged lands were impressed with a trust that permits the public to "enjoy the navigation of waters, carry on commerce over them, and have liberty of fishing therein freed from the obstruction or interference of private parties." [¶ 5]

(4) Scholarly commentary on the public trust doctrine: In the years since Professor Sax's article was published, the literature on the public trust doctrine has mushroomed. *See, e.g.,* Michael C. Blumm, Harrison C. Dunning, and Scott W. Reed, *Renouncing the Public Trust Doctrine: An Assessment of the Validity of Idaho House Bill 794,* 24 ECOLOGY L.Q. 461 (1997) (doctrine is a fundamental attribute of sovereignty that draws substance from the Equal Footing Doctrine); Richard A. Epstein, *The Public Trust Doctrine,* 7 CATO 411 (1987) (doctrine finds support in the Due Process and Equal Protection Clauses); James R. Rasband, *The Disregarded Common Parentage of the Equal Footing and Public Trust Doctrines,* 32 LAND & WATER L. REV. 1 (1997) (public trust doctrine is a sibling of Equal Footing); Charles F. Wilkinson, *The Headwaters of the Public Trust: Some Thoughts on the Source and Scope of the Traditional Doctrine,* 19 ENVTL. L. 425 (1989) (doctrines is rooted in the Commerce Clause).

Others writers have raised questions: Richard Lazarus has suggested that the doctrine may be unnecessary given the expansion of standing, administrative law, and environmental law. Richard J. Lazarus, *Changing Conceptions of Property and Sovereignty in Natural Resources: Questioning the Public Trust Doctrine,* 71 IOWA L. REV. 631 (1986). Jim Huffman has argued that the doctrine is inherently anti-democratic in its assumption that judges better understand the public good than do legislators. James L. Huffman, *A Fish out of Water: The Public Trust Doctrine in a Constitutional Democracy,* 19 ENVTL. L. 527 (1989). *But see* RICHARD NEELY, HOW COURTS GOVERN AMERICA (1981) (arguing that judges are not tied to the search for campaign contributions and thus are more likely to serve the public interest than are legislators).

(iii) PUBLIC RIGHTS IN NAVIGABLE WATERS OVER PRIVATE LANDS

Munninghoff v. Wisconsin Conservation Commission

Supreme Court of Wisconsin.
38 N.W.2d 712 (1949).

This is an appeal from a judgment, entered January 25, 1949, which reversed the action of the conservation commission, and its director, dated November 15, 1947, denying the application of petitioner, Paul Munninghoff, for a muskrat farm license under § 29.575, Stats. The respondent, Munninghoff, seeks a muskrat farm license for lands owned and leased by him in Oneida county, which are under the navigable waters of the Wisconsin river.... The license was refused by the conservation commission and its director on the ground that § 29.575, Stats., does not authorize the granting of a license for navigable waters.

■ MARTIN, J.:— It is admitted that the lands upon which Munninghoff desires to operate a muskrat farm are his own lands, and are located under the navigable waters of the Wisconsin river. These waters became navigable by the erection by the Rhinelander Paper Company of a dam in the year 1906, which dam flooded the land in question and it has been flooded since that time. The issues in this case are whether the conservation commission, pursuant to § 29.575, Stats., can license privately owned lands lying under navigable waters, and whether such muskrat farming is an incident to navigation.

The muskrat farm law was originally passed in 1919. [As amended, § 29.575(1) provides:] "The owner or lessee of any lands within the state of Wisconsin suitable for the breeding and propagating of muskrats * * * shall have the right upon complying with the provisions of this section to establish, operate and maintain on such lands a muskrat * * * farm, for the purpose of breeding, propagating, trapping and dealing in muskrats."

. . .

[Under Wisconsin law, it] is not essential to the public easement [in navigable waterways] that the capacity for navigation be continuous throughout the year to make it navigable or public. It is sufficient that a stream has periods of navigable capacity ordinarily recurrent from year to year and continuing long enough to make the stream usable as a highway. *Willow River Club v. Wade*, 76 N.W. 273 (Wis.1898). The capacity for floating logs to market during the spring freshets which normally lasts six weeks was held to make a stream navigable. *Falls Mfg. Co. v. Oconto River Imp. Co.*, 58 N.W. 257 (Wis.1894). . . .

[T]he meaning of [§ 29.575(1) was] construed in *Krenz v. Nichols*, 222 N.W. 300, 303 (Wis.1928), wherein it was stated:

The state, under its police power, and to carry out its trust, passed the statute in question. So far as it affects the public, the statute is reasonable, and is not contrary to any provision of the federal or state Constitution. Nor do we think it is contrary to the decision of this court in *Diana Shooting Club v. Husting*, 145 N.W. 816 (Wis.1915). In that case the court upheld the right of a citizen of the state to hunt from a boat in the navigable inland streams of the state, notwithstanding that the boat should be on the waters over the lands of a private owner. The court there said that was a right incident to the right of navigation, and that the right of navigation was free to all the citizens of the state upon such waters, by virtue of the Ordinance of 1787, the Enabling Act of the state Constitution, and the constitutional provision thereto. . . .

In Wisconsin the owner of the banks of the stream is the owner of the bed, regardless of whether the stream is navigable or non-navigable. The owner of the submerged soil of a running stream does not own the running water, but he does have certain exclusive rights to make a reasonable use of the water as is passes over or along his land. For instance, he may erect a pier for navigation; he may pump part of the water out of the stream to irrigate his crops; his cattle may be permitted to drink of it; and his muskrats may use it to gather vegetation for the construction of muskrat houses or for food. . . .

In the present case the respondent would make use of the water flowing over or past his land in permitting the muskrats to swim in the water, gather feed found in the water or in the bed of the river, build muskrat houses on the bed where the water is shallow, and dig runways in the banks from underneath the surface of the water to their burrows in the banks above the water line.

In general, the rights of the public to the incidents of navigation are boating, bathing, fishing, hunting, and recreation. *See Doemel v. Jantz,* 193 N.W. 393 (Wis.1923). Trapping is not included for it is an incident of land use. *See Johnson v. Burghorn,* 179 N.W. 225, 228 (Mich.1920). Appellant asserts that float trapping does not require the use of the bottom. However, floats for float trapping are always anchored to the bottom and any method of anchoring or securing a float would, of necessity, require the use of the land or the bottom. The right to use the running water of the bed for float trapping is not included in the easement of navigation. To float trap in navigable water constitutes a trespass upon the submerged land for which the trespasser may be prosecuted by the owner of the soil and enjoined from using the public water for that purpose.

The muskrats on a muskrat farm have been bought and paid for by the licensee. They are his personal property whether they are swimming in the waters above his lands or running along on the dry land within the limits of his licensed premises. The presence of the muskrats in a navigable stream covering privately owned lands does not entitle a trespasser to take them any more than a trespasser would be entitled to seize domestic ducks in the same stream. But if a muskrat should leave a licensed area, he becomes *feræ naturæ,* and is legitimate prey for a neighboring trapper. [ ]

Appellant also asserts that the right of navigation includes the incidental use of the bottom. This is true where the use of the bottom is connected with navigation, such as walking as a trout fisherman does in a navigable stream, boating, standing on the bottom while bathing, casting an anchor from a boat in fishing, propelling a duck boat by poling against the bottom, walking on the ice if the river is frozen, etc. These have nothing in common with trapping because the latter involves the exercise of a property right in the land or the bottom.

The Ordinance of 1787, Art. IX, § 1, Wisconsin Constitution, is not involved in this case. There is no interference with the public's rights of navigation. The navigable waters are not licensed—land alone is licensed, and that land must be privately owned or leased.

The conservation department has authority to issue the license applied for.

Judgment affirmed.

NOTES

(1) Wisconsin's subsequent case law: Since its decision in *Munninghoff,* the Wisconsin Supreme Court has explained that private landowners hold only "qualified" title to land beneath navigable waterways, while the state's interest in protecting the public trust is so great as to amount to "paramount" title. *Town of Ashwaubenon v. Public Service Commission*, 125 N.W.2d 647 (Wis.1963). Indeed, in recent pronouncements the Court has sometimes failed even to mention these private ownership rights, *e.g., Wisconsin's Environmental Decade, Inc. v. Department of Natural Resources*, 271 N.W.2d 69 (Wis.1978). None of these later cases, however, cited or considered *Munninghoff*, and none involved material disruptions of the waterway bed. *Munninghoff* likely remains good law in Wisconsin on the issue of public rights to attach traps to the bottom of navigable waterways.

(2) Public use rights in navigable waterways where the beds are private property: As noted, although navigability for title is a federal question, states have discretion to grant at least a qualified title to submerged lands to private persons. As a result, there are two groups of states: those in which the beds of navigable waterways are private property of riparian landowners and those in which such lands are owned by the state. *Munninghoff* illustrates the now-prevailing division of public and private rights in navigable waterways in situations where the beds are owned by riparians.

Waterways that are navigable in fact are typically open to the public, not just for travel and commerce, but also for fishing, swimming, and—less frequently—hunting. *E.g., State v. Sorensen*, 436 N.W.2d 358 (Iowa 1989) (public use rights extend well beyond navigation and commerce); *State ex rel. Thompson v. Parker*, 200 S.W. 1014 (Ark.1917) (public right to hunt and fish on navigable waters). Uncertainties still arise, as *Munninghoff* illustrates, but they typically entail activities that disturb streambanks or submerged lands: by attaching traps to the river bottom as in *Munninghoff*, by raking the bottom for shellfish, or by standing or walking on stream beds and banks. *E.g., Sheftel v. Lebel*, 689 N.E.2d 500 (Mass.App.1998) (no public right to affix permanent structures to privately owned tidal lands between low-and high-tide marks); *Curry v. Hill*, 460 P.2d 933 (Ok.1969) (public can fish in navigable waterway but cannot fix trot lines on privately owned stream beds); *Gianoli v. Pfleiderer*, 563 N.W.2d 562 (Wis.App.1997) (no public right to walk dogs or beachcomb between ordinary low-and high-tide marks). State law often permits boaters on navigable waterways to portage around obstacles. *E.g., Elder v. Delcour*, 269 S.W.2d 17 (Mo.1954). Louisiana law includes a more extensive right for the public to make use of privately owned banks. *Nevels v. State*, 665 So.2d 26 (La.App.1995).

The general consensus on public use rights in such waters was reached through a variety of legal routes, which sometimes give rise to state-specific details in public and private rights. Moreover, a few states continue to conclude that navigability of inland waters under state law only gives the public rights of access for travel, with landowners retaining exclusive rights to capture wildlife. In such states, "navigability" at law remains a crucial issue.

How different is the law in Montana discussed above? Does ownership of the bed of a navigable waterway play a significant role?

(3) Shellfish: One activity that has caused sharp conflict in the use of submerged lands is the harvest and propagation of shellfish. Chapter 2 considered how the rule of capture applied to shellfish, both naturally occurring and artificially propagated. How do the access concerns that we have been examining in this chapter apply to shellfish? Should their more sedentary existence play a role in the law?

Cases arising out of digging shellfish on privately owned, submerged lands generally conclude that the conduct is a trespass, at least when lands are posted, even though under the rule of capture landowners have no ownership rights in naturally occurring shellfish. For example, in *People v. Johnson* clamdiggers were charged with trespass on posted private lands that apparently were subject to the ebb and flow of the tides. Such waterways were open to public fishing—but was clamming a form of fishing?

> [T]he question remains whether the right to take shellfish placed by nature in privately owned land is vested in the public as part of the common right of fishery or is reserved to the owner of the underlying land. The determination of this question must conform to the principle laid down by the Court of Appeals in *Hedges v. West Shore Realty Co.,* 44 N.E. 691, 693 (N.Y.1896), that,
>
>> Where two such rights or interests exist, with respect to the same portion of the earth's surface, each must be exercised and enjoyed in a reasonable way. Each right or interest in such a case is always subject to the qualification that it cannot be exercised or enjoyed in such a way as to destroy the other.
>
> While the public character of the waters is not affected by the ownership of the underlying land, neither does privately-owned land lose its character by the inflow of navigable waters, except to the extent that private rights must yield to dominant rights of the public. The source of the public rights is the navigable water, and the underlying land is open to those activities of the public that are closely connected with the water. . . .

But when an activity is more closely identified with the underlying land, when it entails some physical disturbance of that land not directly connected with the enjoyment of the waters, the character of the activity as private or public should be determined by the ownership of the lands. We think, therefore, that in the case of clamming, because of the relative lack of mobility of the shellfish, their way of living in the land, and the ability of a landowner to retain more than nominal dominion and control over them, the activity is more closely related to ownership of the underlying land than to utilization of the public waters. For this reason, we would hold, if the case were one of first impression, that the defendants had no right to rake for the shellfish in the private lands.

[Given the conflicting decisions, the court chose to follow] *McKee v. Gratz,* 260 U.S. 127 (1922), . . . holding that a good cause of action was stated by a complaint seeking to recover damages for the taking of mussels from the bed of a stream on the plaintiff's farm in Missouri. In so holding, the Court said, per Mr. Justice Holmes:

As to the plaintiff's title, it is not necessary to say that the mussels were part of the realty within the meaning of the Missouri Statutes or in such sense as to make the plaintiff an absolute owner. It is enough that there is a plain distinction between such creatures and game birds or freely moving fish, that may shift to another jurisdiction without regard to the will of land owner or State. Such birds and fishes are not even in the possession of man. [*Missouri v. Holland,*] 252 U.S. [416,] 434 (1919); 2 KENT, COMMENTARIES 349; *Young v. Hichens,* 6 Q.B. 606. On the other hand it seems not unreasonable to say that mussels having a practically fixed habitat and little ability to move are as truly in the possession of the owner of the land in which they are sunk as would be a pre-historic boat discovered under ground or unknown property at the bottom of a canal. [ ]

People v. Johnson, 166 N.Y.S.2d 732 (Suffolk County Police Ct. 1957). *Compare People v. Dunn,* 610 N.Y.S.2d 121 (Sup.Ct.1993) (clams naturally found on private lands under navigable waterways are not owned by the landowner, thus, clamdigger is not guilty of larceny; no consideration given to trespass issues). Does the decision in *Johnson* differ from *Munninghoff?* from *Harrison v. Petroleum Surveys, Inc.,* 80 So.2d 153 (La.App.1955) (the Louisiana muskrat case)?

(iv) PRIVATE RIGHTS IN PUBLIC WATERS

NOTES

(1) Judicial hostility to claims of private right: In retrospect, the cases that began this section—*Adams* and *Pitkin*—are illustrative of the era in which the courts showed their greatest respect for private rights in fisheries. Public fishing rights were limited to waterways subject to the ebb and flow of the tides, and even then, as *Pitkin* demonstrates, fishing groups could stake out territories in navigable waterways and over time gain exclusive rights to those territories. Private rights declined as the century progressed—although they did so more rapidly in some jurisdictions than others and along no predetermined path.

　　(a) (Another) rule of capture: The recognition of property interests based on long use (prescription) encourages economic risk-taking by rewarding the first user. Inevitably, however, the conservative and monopolistic tendencies of property became apparent. Rights based on "long-continued possession and occupation" increasingly came into conflict with newer technologies and changing social conditions. And when they did, the courts increasingly rejected claims to private rights in public resources. *E.g., Shrunk v. Schuylkill Navigation Co.,* 14 Serg. & Rawle 71 (Pa.1826) (denying protection for fisher on public river who claimed exclusive fishing rights based on "long continued usage"). *See also Delaware & Maryland R.R. v. Stump,* 8 G. & J. 479 (Md.1837); *Waters v. Lilley,* 21 Mass. (4 Pick.) 145, 145 (1827); *Jacobson v. Fountain,* 2 Johns. 170 (N.Y.Sup.Ct.1807); *Cortelyou v. Van Brundt,* 2 Johns. 357 (N.Y.Sup.Ct.1807); *Smith v. Miller,* 22 F. Cas. 603 (C.C.D.R.I.1828) (No. 13,080). *See generally Charles River Bridge v. Warren Bridge,* 36 U.S. (11 Pet.) 420 (1837).

(b) **Shifting norms and industrial development:** During the first half of the nineteenth century, courts in various settings curtailed or ignored claims of customary rights, particularly rights to hunt, fish, till the land, and graze livestock. It was the dawning era of steam power, industrialization, and expanding market economies. Americans for the most part were quick to embrace the latest technology, and they were prepared to welcome, and often to subsidize, rapid economic change. Many of the new enterprises—canals, railroads, steamships, factories, and the like—used nature more intensively and with greater disruption than did the settled, agrarian enterprises of the colonial era. Textile mills, for instance, blocked rivers to harness water power, diverted water flows through canals that nearly drained rivers dry, and dumped waste into streams to the detriment of human users and aquatic ecosystems. Legislatures often sought to soften the impacts of such activities on traditional land-and river-users by requiring compensation for injuries caused. Ultimately, however, customary property rights were eliminated; such interests were not allowed to halt industrial development. Courts did their part to facilitate this economic shift, often by redefining property rights through a refusal to recognize that traditional users had any interest that required compensation. *E.g., McFarlin v. Essex Co.,* 64 Mass. (10 Cush.) 304 (1852); *Shrunk v. Schuylkill Navigation Co.,* 14 Serg. & Rawle 71 (Pa.1826). As they did so, the courts necessarily diminished the legal protections enjoyed by the more sensitive, agrarian, traditional ways of drawing sustenance from nature.

Studying this era of history, legal scholars have seen in it an increasing willingness to use property law instrumentally—to use it, that is, as a tool to facilitate economic change. Growth was more important than protecting old, settled ways of living. As the legal historian James Willard Hurts noted, property law itself became "an institution of growth rather than merely security." JAMES W. HURST, LAW AND THE CONDITIONS OF FREEDOM IN THE NINETEENTH-CENTURY UNITED STATES 28 (1956). Property became an "instrumental value in the service of the paramount goal of promoting economic growth." MORTON HORWITZ, THE TRANSFORMATION OF AMERICAN LAW, 1780–1860 at 53 (1977). As Horwitz has also noted: "At its deepest level, the attack on prescription represented an effort to free American law from the restraints of economic development that had been molded by the common law's feudal conception of property." *Id.* at 47.

(2) **The resilience of custom:** By 1903, the California Supreme Court was willing to rule out all possibility that private parties could claim exclusive rights in a navigable waterway open to public fishing. *Pacific Steam Whaling Co. v. Alaska Packers' Ass'n,* 72 P. 161 (Cal.1903). Despite the judicial hostility to private rights in public rivers that characterized the nineteenth century, claims of right to exclusive fishing and hunting rights based on custom have proved remarkably resilient.

(a) *Harvat v. Clear Creek Drainage District:* Harvat and his hunting companions claimed a prescriptive right to hunt and fish off an island in the North Platte River. They claimed to have used the area from 1961 to 1973 but it was not until 1972 that Harvat "indicated the perimeters of his claim by stakes. Duck blinds and decoy sets were placed and moved up and down the river bank and in the river throughout the period to take advantage of good decoy water. Harvat hunted every day of duck season throughout the period except on weekends when 'kids were running all over the place.' " He resisted attempts of other hunters to move into the area, but there was testimony that at times other hunters used the area claimed by plaintiffs. The Nebraska Supreme Court affirmed the trial court's injunction barring plaintiff from further trespasses onto the island. *Harvat v. Clear Creek Drainage District*, 249 N.W.2d 209 (Neb.1977).

(b) The Altoona Snag Union was a group of drift-net fishers that had removed snags from a stretch of the Columbia River. Based on their effort, the members of the Union claimed an exclusive right to set their nets. "Membership in the Altoona Snag Union is evidenced by ownership of a 'drift right,' by which the union gives an exclusive right to fish a particular drift where snags have been removed. Drift rights have traditionally been treated as valuable personal property and have been passed to family members through probate and divorce proceedings. It is undisputed fishermen have paid valuable consideration for their drift rights.... Enforcement of drift rights occurs in a variety of ways, all of which include some degree of intimidation and, in some cases, threats to life and property." When the Union sought to add judicial action to their arsenal of enforcement methods, the Washington Supreme Court held that the union's members did not have an exclusive fishing right: "This court has previously held the State, in its sovereign capacity, owns the fish in its waters. [ ] As such, individual fishermen cannot assert a property right over fish until they are caught. [ ] These ... plaintiffs do not enjoy a legal right to portions of public waters to the exclusion of other citizens of this state." The court acknowledged that its decision might produce "chaos in the drifts[,] economic detriment to those holders of drift rights[, and] overcrowding," but concluded that it was powerless to provide the remedy sought by the union. *Marincovich v. Tarabochia*, 787 P.2d 562, 565 (Wash. 1990).

(3) Title by prescription and free-market environmentalism: Advocates of market-based solutions to conservation issues often endorse the creation of property rights as a means of integrating conservation into the broader markets for goods and services. *E.g.,* Roger A. Sedjo & R. David Simpson, *Property Rights Contracting and the Commericalization of Biodiversity, in* WILDLIFE IN THE MARKETPLACE 167 (Terry L. Anderson & Peter J. Hill eds. 1995). Would the recognition of the claims of the Altoona Snag Union have increased the likelihood that other economic actors would consider the effect of their actions on the fishery? That is, would recognition of the claims have forced other actors to internalize the costs of their decisions on the salmon runs?

Does the following decision represent a step toward a market-based decision?

Columbia River Fishermen's Protective Union v. City of St. Helens

Supreme Court of Oregon.
87 P.2d 195 (1939).

■ BEAN, J.:—[Plaintiffs are drift net fishers whose "drift" is located downstream from the outfall of defendant's sewers. Plaintiffs alleged that] defendants deposit said sewage, chemicals and waste matter in the waters of said Columbia river and the waters of the Willamette Slough, and by reason thereof the said waters are being destroyed for fishing purposes, and the fish and aquatic life are being destroyed, and the nets of plaintiffs are being destroyed, causing said nets to be rotted by the chemicals and foreign matter clinging to said nets, and salmon passing through said waters to the spawning grounds of the Willamette and Columbia rivers are so affected by the aforesaid wrongful acts of defendants in polluting said waters that the said salmon are unable to survive and pass through said waters and are killed, thus depleting the supply of salmon and the future supply of salmon, and causing irreparable injury to plaintiffs in their vocation as fishermen and the destruction of their nets. . . .

Defendants contend that the plaintiffs are not authorized to maintain this suit, but if there is any right to maintain such a suit, it inheres in the state of Oregon.

Plaintiffs, as gill net fishermen, have a special interest, distinct from the public in fishing their drift which will be protected in a court of equity against destruction by acts of the defendants, which destroy their nets and interfere with their fishing. . . . To delete the fish from the Columbia and Willamette rivers is to prevent the plaintiffs from pursuing their vocations and earning their livelihood fishing with gill nets in the portions of the rivers where they have been accustomed to fish.

Where the injury resulting from the nuisance is, in its nature, irreparable, as when destruction of the means of subsistence will ensue from the wrongful act, courts of equity will interfere by injunction, in furtherance of justice and in the interest of the violated rights of property. [ ]

There is a vital distinction between the rights of plaintiffs, who are accustomed to fishing in the river and have a license so to do, and the rights of other citizens of the state, who never fish in the river and do not intend to and are interested only in a general way in the benefit the state receives by the prosecution of a valuable industry, so that surely the plaintiffs have a special interest differing widely from the interest of the public in fishing in the portions of the river mentioned.

. . .

Numerous suits have been maintained in the courts of this state to prevent interference with the right of fishing. The difference between this case and the several others cited above is in degree. There is a greater degree of interference in the present case than in the cases heretofore prosecuted.

Enormous quantities of salmon are found in the Columbia and Willamette rivers and are of extensive commercial value. The salmon industry has grown to great proportions and has been one of the principal industries of the state of Oregon for many years. Thousands of citizens of Oregon earn their livelihood by catching salmon, and the business aggregates hundreds of thousands of dollars annually. All the citizens of Oregon have a common right to fish in the waters mentioned in the complaint, and to deprive any one citizen of that right is to violate the state constitution....

. . .

Section 39–603, Oregon Code Supplement 1935, prohibits the pollution of streams and public waters of the state by depositing any deleterious substance or any substances which do or may render the waters of a stream, or any other body of water, destructive of fish life. Section 40–213, Oregon Code 1930, prohibits depositing deleterious substances, explosives or poisons, or using the same in the waters of the state.

The regulatory power of a state extends not only to the taking of its fish, but also over the waters inhabited by the fish. Its care of the fish would be of no avail if it had no power to protect the waters from pollution. 11 R.C.L. 1047, § 35. *See Eagle Cliff Fishing Co. v. McGowan,* 137 P. 766 (Or.1914). We read in 11 R.C.L. 1039, § 26, as follows: "But, on the other hand, a member of the public who is specially injured by the maintenance of a nuisance, may abate it or maintain an equitable action for relief therefrom. Thus, if one exercising his right to take fish from a common fishery is obstructed by a nuisance, he may abate the obstruction."

. . .

The jurisdiction of equity courts to grant relief by injunction in a proper case against a nuisance, either public or private, is undoubted and well-settled, and wherever the circumstances of the case are such that adequate redress cannot be obtained elsewhere, equity will afford relief....

The provision for a statutory penalty for polluting a stream is not a bar to prosecuting a suit to prevent the same. [ ]

NOTES

(1) Rights against pollution and obstruction: Is *Fishermen's Protective Union* consistent with *Marincovich?* How can the drift fishers maintain an action if—as *Marincovich* decides—they have no rights in the fishery? Would the Union or its members be able to obtain damages?

As *Fishermen's Protective Union* demonstrates, people lawfully engaged in fishing, particularly on a commercial basis, have had little trouble convincing courts that they have valuable interests worthy of protection, whether under common law actions such as nuisance or under statutes that create causes of action for damages or injunctions. Fishers in public waters have typically only had to show interference with ongoing operations, to recover damages for lost income. *See, e.g., State of Louisiana ex rel. Guste v. M/V Testbank,* 752 F.2d 1019 (5th Cir.1985), *cert. denied sub. nom., White v. M/V Testbank,* 477 U.S. 903 (1986); *Union Oil Co. v. Oppen,* 501 F.2d 558 (9th Cir.1974).

(2) Riparian rights: When a person owns land that is riparian to a waterbody—that is, when the land abuts the waterbody—the landowner has a bundle of rights in the waterbody. These riparian rights exist in all states, although they are more restricted in the Western states that have adopted the prior appropriation doctrine to allocate consumptive uses of water.

Among the traditional, non-consumptive uses within the riparian's bundle of rights are the right to fish, hunt, boat, and swim; more recent cases add additional uses such as waterski, sunbath, and ice skate. *E.g., Miotke v. City of Spokane,* 678 P.2d 803 (Wash.1984). *See also People v. Mack,* 97 Cal.Rptr. 448 (Cal.App.1971); *Matto v. Dan Beard, Inc.,* 546 A.2d 854 (Conn.App.), *cert. denied,* 550 A.2d 1082 (Conn.1988); *Thies v. Howland,* 380 N.W.2d 463 (Mich.1985). Although these rights are shared with the general public under the public trust doctrine when the waters are navigable, riparian landowners may have rights in addition to those of the public because of their status as riparians. Some states, for example, permit riparians to farm oysters in submerged lands because of their ownership of riparian land. *E.g., Board of Public Works v. Larmar Corp.,* 277 A.2d 427 (Md.1971); *State ex rel. Rohrer v. Credle,* 369 S.E.2d 825 (N.C.1988); *City of Corpus Christi v. Davis,* 622 S.W.2d 640 (Tex.App.1981); *Sund v. Keating,* 259 P.2d 1113 (Wash.1953).

(v) PRIVATE RIGHTS IN PRIVATE WATERS

Harris v. Brooks

Supreme Court of Arkansas.
283 S.W.2d 129 (1955).

■ WARD, J.:—The issues presented by this appeal relate to the relative rights of riparian landowners to the use of a privately owned non-navigable lake and the water therein.

Appellant, Theo Mashburn, lessee of riparian landowners conducts a commercial boating and fishing enterprise. In this business he rents cabins, sells fishing bait and equipment, and rents boats to members of the general public who desire to use the lake for fishing and other recreational purposes. He and his lessors filed a complaint in chancery court on July 10, 1954 to enjoin appellees from pumping water from the lake to irrigate a rice crop, alleging that, as of that date, appellees had reduced the water level of the lake to such an extent as to make the lake unsuitable "for fishing, recreation, or other lawful purposes." After a lengthy hearing, the chancellor denied injunctive relief, and this appeal is prosecuted to reverse the chancellor's decision.

Factual Background. Horseshoe Lake, located about 3 miles south of Augusta, is approximately 3 miles long and 300 feet wide, and, as the name implies, resembles a horseshoe in shape. Appellees, John Brooks and John Brooks, Jr., are lessees of Ector Johnson who owns a large tract of land adjacent to the lake, including three-fourths of the lake bed.

For a number of years appellees have intermittently raised rice on Johnson's land and have each year, including 1954, irrigated the rice with water pumped from the lake. They pumped no more water in 1954 than they did in 1951 and 1952, no rice being raised in 1953. Approximately 190 acres were cultivated in rice in 1954.

.... In March 1954 Mashburn leased ... a relatively small camp site on the bank of the lake and installed the business above mentioned at a cost of approximately $8,000, including boats, cabins, and fishing equipment. Mashburn began operating his business about the first of April, 1954, and fishing and boat rentals were satisfactory from that time until about July 1st or 4th when, he says, the fish quit biting and his income from that source and boat rentals was reduced to practically nothing.

Appellees began pumping water with an 8 inch intake on May 25, 1954 and continued pumping until this suit was filed on July 10, and then until about August 20th. They quit pumping at this time because it was discovered fish life was being endangered. The trial was had September 28, 1954, and the decree was rendered December 29, 1954.

The Testimony. ... The years 1952, 1953 and 1954 were unusually dry and the water levels in similar lakes in the same general area were unusually low in August and September of 1954. During August 1954 Horseshoe Lake was below "normal," but it is not entirely clear from the testimony that this was true on July 10 when the suit was filed. It also appears that during the stated period the water had receded from the bank where Mashburn's boats were usually docked, making it impossible for him to rent them to the public. There is strong testimony, disputed by appellees, that the normal level of the lake is 189.67 feet above sea level and that the water was below this level on July 10. Unquestionably the water was below normal when this suit was tried the latter part of September, 1954.

On the part of appellees it was attempted to show that: they had used the water for irrigation several years dating back to 1931 and Mashburn knew this when he rented the camp site; although they had been pumping regularly since May 25, 1954 the water did not begin to fall in the lake until July 1st or 4th; an agent of the Arkansas Game and Fish Commission examined the lake and the water about July 2nd and found no condition endangering fish life, and similar examinations after suit was filed showed the same condition, and; they stopped pumping about August 20th when they first learned that fish life was being endangered.

Issues Clarified. In refusing to issue the injunction the chancellor made no finding of facts, and did not state the ground upon which his decision rested.... If it be conceded that the testimony does show and the chancellor should have found that the water in Horseshoe Lake was at or below the normal level when this suit was filed on July 10th, then appellants would have been entitled to an injunction provided this case was decided strictly under the uniform flow theory mentioned hereafter. However, as explained later we are not bound by this theory in this state. It appears to us there might have been some confusion as to the ground upon which appellants based their contention for relief. Under the pleadings it appears that they may be asking for relief on two separate grounds: (a) The right to fish and (b) The right to conduct a commercial boating enterprise. It was incumbent upon appellants to show that one or both rights were unreasonably interfered with when the water level sank below "normal." It is difficult to tell whether the testimony establishes this fact in either instance. (a) The only testimony in the first instance is that fish quit biting somewhere about the 4th of July but there was no conclusive evidence that this was caused by the lake being below "normal" level. It is common knowledge that fish quit biting some time for no apparent good reason. There was no testimony that fish life was endangered before July 10th but on the other hand there was positive testimony to the contrary. (b) Likewise there was no conclusive testimony showing that it was impractical to dock or run boats on the lake prior to July 10th. Moreover it would be pure conjecture to say that the same water level, whether normal or otherwise, controlled both fishing and boating. Certainly appellants made no attempt to make any distinction either in the pleadings or by the testimony between the two causes of action.

In view of the above situation it is urged by appellees that the case should therefore be affirmed, but we have concluded that the best interest of the parties hereto and the public in general will be served by concluding this case in the light of the announcements hereafter made and the conclusions hereafter reached. Before attempting such conclusion it appears proper to make some general observations relative to the law regulating the use of water in lakes and streams.

Two Basic Theories. Generally speaking two separate and distinct theories or doctrines regarding the right to use water are recognized. One is commonly called the "Appropriation Doctrine" and the other is the "Riparian Doctrine."

Appropriation Doctrine. Since it is unnecessary to do so we make no attempt to discuss the varied implications of this doctrine. Generally speaking, under this doctrine, some governmental agency, acting under constitutional or legislative authority, apportions water to contesting claimants. It has never been adopted in this state, but has been in about 17 western states. This doctrine is inconsistent with the common law relative to water rights in force in this and many other states. One principal distinction between this doctrine and the riparian doctrine is that under the former the use is not limited to riparian landowners.

Riparian Doctrine. This doctrine, long in force in this and many other states, is based on the old common law which gave to the owners of land bordering on streams the right to use the water therefrom for certain purposes, and this right was considered an incident to the ownership of land. Originally it apparently accorded the landowner the right to have the water maintained at its normal level, subject to use for strictly domestic purposes. Later it became evident that this strict limitation placed on the use of water was unreasonable and unutilitarian. Consequently it was not long before the demand for a greater use of water caused a relaxation of the strict limitations placed on its use and this doctrine came to be divided into (a) the natural flow theory and (b) the reasonable use theory.

(a) Natural Flow Theory. Generally speaking again, under the natural flow theory, a riparian owner can take water for domestic purposes only, such as water for the family, live stock, and gardening, and he is entitled to have the water in the stream or lake upon which he borders kept at the normal level. There are some expressions in the opinions of this court indicating that we have recognized this theory, at least to a certain extent.

Reasonable Use Theory. This theory appears to be based on the necessity and desirability of deriving greater benefits from the use of our abundant supply of water. It recognizes that there is no sound reason for maintaining our lakes and streams at a normal level when the water can be beneficially used without causing unreasonable damage to other riparian owners. The progress of civilization, particularly in regard to manufacturing, irrigation, and recreation, has forced the realization that a strict adherence to the uninterrupted flow doctrine placed an unwarranted limitation on the use of water, and consequently the court developed what we now call the reasonable use theory. This theory is of course subject to different interpretations and limitations. In 56 AM. JUR., page 728, it is stated that "The rights of riparian proprietors on both navigable and unnavigable streams are to a great extent mutual, common, or correlative. The use of the stream or water by each proprietor is therefore limited to what is reasonable, having due regard for the rights of others above, below, or on the opposite shore. In general, the special rights of a riparian owner are such as are necessary for the use and enjoyment of his abutting property and the business lawfully conducted thereon, qualified only by the correlative rights of other riparian owners, and by certain rights of the public, and they are to be so exercised as not to injure others in the enjoyment of their rights." It has been stated that each riparian owner has an equal right to make a reasonable use of waters subject to the equal rights of other owners to make the reasonable use, *United States v. Willow River Power Co.,* 324 U.S. 499 (1945). The purpose of the law is to secure to each riparian owner equality in the use of water as near as may be by requiring each to exercise his right reasonably and with due regard to the rights of others similarly situated. *Meng v. Coffey,* 93 N.W. 713 (Neb.1903).

This court has to some extent recognized the reasonable use theory, *Thomas v. La Cotts,* 257 S.W.2d 936 (Ark.1953); *Harrell v. City of Conway,* 271 S.W.2d 924 (Ark.1954), but we have also said in the *City of Conway* case that the uniform flow theory and the reasonable use theory are inconsistent and, further that we had not yet made a choice between them. It is not clear that we made a choice in that case. The nucleus of this opinion is, therefore, a definite acceptance of the reasonable use theory. We do not understand that the two theories will necessarily clash in every case, but where there is an inconsistency, and where vested rights may not prevent, it is our conclusion that the reasonable use theory should control.

In embracing the reasonable use theory we caution, however, that we are not necessarily adopting all the interpretations given it by the decisions of other states, and that our own interpretation will be developed in the future as occasions arise. Nor is it intended hereby that we will not in the future, under certain circumstances, possibly adhere to some phases of the uniform flow system. It is recognized that in some instances vested rights may have accrued to riparian landowners and we could not of course constitutionally negate those rights.

It should also be made clear that nothing in this opinion is intended to or can infringe upon the powers of the Arkansas State Game and Fish Commission as invested by Amendment No. 35 to the Constitution of this State. It is recognized that said Commission has the power to propagate, preserve, and protect fish in streams and lakes. In exercising this power the Commission will undoubtedly be interested in some instances in the amount of water that may be removed from lakes or streams where injury to fish life is involved.

The result of our examination of the decisions of this court and other authorities relative to the use by riparian proprietors of water in non-navigable lakes and streams justifies the enunciation of the following general rules and principles:

(a) The right to use water for strictly domestic purposes—such as for household use—is superior to many other uses of water—such as for fishing, recreation and irrigation.

(b) Other than the use mentioned above, all other lawful uses of water are equal. Some of the lawful uses of water recognized by this state are: fishing, swimming, recreation, and irrigation.

(c) When one lawful of water is destroyed by another lawful use the latter must yield, or it may be enjoined.

(d) When one lawful use of water interferes with or detracts from another lawful use, then a question arises as to whether, under all the facts and circumstances of that particular case, the interfering use shall be declared unreasonable and as such enjoined, or whether a reasonable and equitable adjustment should be made, having due regard to the reasonable rights of each.

Application To This Case. Some of the questions, therefore, which must be considered are these:

(a) Had appellees on July 10, 1954, by the continued use of water from Horseshoe Lake, destroyed appellants' right to fish and conduct the boating enterprise? If so, the injunction should be granted.

(b) If it is found however that appellants' rights had only been impaired at the stated time, then it must be judged, under all the facts and circumstances as before mentioned, whether such impairment is unreasonable. If it is so found then the injunction should issue. If it is found that appellants' rights have not been unreasonably impaired, having due regard to all the facts and circumstances and the injury which may be caused appellees as weighed against the benefits accruing to appellants, then the injunction should be denied.

We do not minimize the difficulties attendant upon an application of the reasonable use rule to any given set of facts and circumstances and particularly those present in this instance. It is obvious that there are no definite guide posts provided and that necessarily much must be left to judgment and discretion. The breadth and boundaries of this area of discretion are well stated in *Restatement of the Law, Torts,* § 852c in these words:

> The determination in a particular case of the unreasonableness of a particular use is not and should not be an unreasoned, intuitive conclusion on the part of the court or jury. It is rather an evaluating of the conflicting interests of each of the contestants before the court in accordance with the standards of society, and a weighing of those, one

against the other. The law accords equal protection to the interests of all the riparian proprietors in the use of water, and seeks to promote the greatest beneficial use of the water, and seeks to promote the greatest beneficial use by each with a minimum of harm to others. But when one riparian proprietor's use of the water harmfully invades another's interest in its use, there is an incompatibility of interest between the two parties to a greater or lesser extent depending on the extent of the invasion, and there is immediately a question whether such a use is legally permissible. It is axiomatic in the law that individuals in society must put up with a reasonable amount of annoyance and inconvenience resulting from the otherwise lawful activities of their neighbors in the use of their land. Hence it is only when one riparian proprietor's use of the water is unreasonable that another who is harmed by it can complain, even though the harm is intentional. Substantial intentional harm to another cannot be justified as reasonable unless the legal merit or utility of the activity which produces it outweighs the legal seriousness or gravity of the harm.

In all our consideration of the reasonable use theory as we have attempted to explain it we have accepted the view that the benefits accruing to society in general from a maximum utilization of our water resources should not be denied merely because of the difficulties that may arise in its application. In the absence of legislative directives, it appears that this rule or theory is the best that the courts can devise.

Our Conclusion. After careful consideration, an application of the rules above announced to the complicated fact situation set forth in this record leads us to conclude that the Chancellor should have issued an order enjoining appellees from pumping water out of Horseshoe Lake when the water level reaches 189.67 feet above sea level for as long as the material facts and circumstances are substantially the same as they appear in this record. We make it clear that this conclusion is not based on the fact that 189.67 is the normal level and that appellees would have no right to reduce such level. Our conclusion is based on the fact that we think the evidence shows this level happens to be the level below which appellants would be unreasonably interfered with. . . .

We think the conclusion we have reached is not only logical but practical. Although appellees had quit using water from the lake when this case was tried yet they testified that they intended to use water therefrom in 1955. We might assume that they would want to also use water in subsequent years, so it would seem to be to the best interest of all parties concerned to have a definite level fixed at which pumping for irrigation must cease in order to avoid useless litigation.

Appellees make the point that the Chancellor should be sustained because they have acquired a prescriptive right to the unlimited use of the water in Horseshoe Lake, and, to the same effect, that appellants are estopped from asserting any rights to the contrary. We cannot sustain this contention. Although appellees, according to the record, have used this water for irrigation purposes on several occasions in previous years, dating back for more than seven years, yet it appears that appellants had not been disturbed in the exercise of their riparian rights previous to 1954. Prior to that year appellees had merely been exercising their lawful rights as riparian owners and their exercise of those rights was in no way adverse to the rights of any one. [ ] In the *City of Conway* case, where the same contention was made that appellees here make the contention was denied, the court saying [271 S.W.2d 927]: "We are unable to find any act or acts on the part of Conway of an adverse claim or nature, or such as would put appellants on notice of any adverse claim." The court then followed with citations which are applicable here.

■ McFADDIN, J., concurs.

NOTES

(1) The opinion sets out the two different approaches courts have adopted in the absence of legislation, the natural flow theory and the reasonable use theory. In adopting the reasonable use theory, Justice Ward stressed that the court's objective was "to secure to each riparian owner equality in the use of water as near as may be." [¶ 15] How can a court assure equality when uses are as dissimilar as those in *Harris*? Do the court's four rules suggest that "equality of right" is chimerical in such cases? Do the first three rules have any application to the case? Note that the court does not discuss them, turning instead to the final rule and *The Restatement of Tort*'s discussion of "reasonableness." Does the court sufficiently explain why it chose to impose the limit that it did on the pumping? Does the court satisfactorily explain why the commercial boating and fishing are more reasonable uses of Horseshoe Lake than rice farming? More broadly, is "reasonableness" an inherently unstable standard because it will shift whenever the relative values of the competing uses change?

(2) Private waters/private rights: Recall that the initial consensus was that, in nonnavigable waters, the riparian landowner held title to the bed of the stream *ad filum medium aquæ*; she was, therefore, entitled to prevent others from fishing on her land, effectively creating an exclusive right to fish. *E.g., Moulton v. Libbey,* 37 Me. 472, 489 (1854); *Collins v. Benbury,* 25 N.C. 277, 283 (1842). Has this understanding been modified?

(3) Riparian rights: Much of the discussion on submerged lands has focused—albeit often only by negative implication—on questions of private rights in private waters, if only because that status is generally treated as the benchmark. As the decision in *Harris v. Brooks* demonstrates, there is also a range of potential use issues even when there are not public use rights at stake. This can also be the case when the use does not itself "consume" the water:

Beacham v. Lake Zurich Property Owners Association

Supreme Court of Illinois.
526 N.E.2d 154 (1988).

■ MILLER, J.:—The plaintiffs, Diana Beacham and Sandy Point Beach, Inc., brought an action in the circuit court of Lake County seeking a declaration that, as an owner of a part of the lake bed of Lake Zurich, Beacham and her licensees were entitled to the reasonable use of the entire lake, including the waters overlying those parts of the lake bed owned by members of the defendant, the Lake Zurich Property Owners Association (Property Owners Association or Association). The trial judge dismissed the plaintiffs' complaint, ruling that the Property Owners Association could exclude Beacham and her licensees from that part of the lake overlying the lake bed controlled by the Association. The appellate court ordered the plaintiffs' complaint reinstated, holding that ownership of a part of the bed of a private, nonnavigable lake entitles such owners and their licensees to the reasonable use and enjoyment of the surface waters of the entire lake provided they do not unduly interfere with the reasonable use of the waters by other owners and their licensees.

The subject of this dispute, Lake Zurich, is a private, nonnavigable body of water covering about 240 acres in Lake County. Plaintiff Diana Beacham owns about 15% to 20% of the lake bed of Lake Zurich, and she operates a business, Sandy Point Beach, Inc., that rents boats to the public for recreational use on the lake. Defendant Property Owners Association is an organization composed of a number of lake bed owners who executed license agreements granting the Association permission to use and regulate their lake bed properties. The Property Owners Association controls the greater part of the lake bed, and it has attempted to assert exclusive possession of the overlying waters by instituting a quota and permit system for various types of boats. The Association enforces its access controls by issuing written warnings to violators and by seeking to have persistent violators arrested and prosecuted for trespassing. Beacham and her licensees have received warnings from the Property Owners Association, and Beacham herself has been unsuccessfully prosecuted for criminal trespass.

. . .

This court has not previously determined the respective rights of lake bed owners in the use and enjoyment of the lake, and, as the appellate court did, we therefore turn to a consideration of the decisions of other States on this issue. Under the common law rule, the owner of a part of a lake bed has the right to the exclusive use and control of the waters above that property. This rule is a corollary of the traditional common law view that the ownership of a parcel of land entitles the owner to the exclusive use and enjoyment of anything above or below the property. *See Smoulter v. Boyd*, 58 A. 144 (Pa.1904). Courts following the common law principle have held that the owner of a part of a lake bed may exclude from the surface of the overlying water all other persons, including those who own other parts of the lake bed. *See Medlock v. Galbreath*, 187 S.W.2d 545 (Ark.1945); *Lanier v. Ocean Pond Fishing Club, Inc.*, 322 S.E.2d 494 (Ga.1984); *Sanders v. De Rose*, 191 N.E. 331 (Ind.1934); *Baker v. Normanoch Association, Inc.*, 136 A.2d 645 (N.H. 1957); *Commonwealth Water Co. v. Brunner*, 161 N.Y.S. 794 (App. Div. 1916); *Smoulter v. Boyd*, 58 A. 144 (Pa.1904); *Taylor Fishing Club v. Hammett*, 88 S.W.2d 127 (Tex.Civ.App. 1935); *Wickouski v. Swift*, 124 S.E.2d 892 (Va.1962). As the appellate court noted, however, in certain of those decisions the interest of the party challenging the restriction was quite small in comparison with the interest of the majority owner. *See Baker*, 136 A.2d 645; *Smoulter*, 58 A. 144; *Wickouski*, 124 S.E.2d 892.

In those States in which the civil law rule prevails, the owner of a part of a lake bed has a right to the reasonable use and enjoyment of the entire lake surface. *See Duval v. Thomas*, 114 So. 2d 791 (Fla.1959); *Beach v. Hayner*, 173 N.W. 487 (Mich.1919); *Johnson v. Seifert*, 100 N.W.2d 689 (Minn.1960); *Snively v. Jaber*, 296 P.2d 1015 (Wash.1956); Those courts rejecting the common law rule have noted the difficulties presented by attempts to establish and obey definite property lines, *Beach,* 173 N.W. at 488; *Snively,* 296 P.2d at 1019, and certain other impractical consequences of that rule, such as the erection of booms, fences, or barriers, *Duval,* 114 So. 2d at 795. Moreover, application of the civil law approach promotes rather than hinders the recreational use and enjoyment of lakes. *Duval,* 114 So. 2d at 795; *Johnson,* 100 N.W.2d at 695. We conclude that the arguments supporting the civil law rule warrant its adoption in Illinois. Restricting the use of a lake to the water overlying the owner's lake bed property can only frustrate the cooperative and mutually beneficial use of that important resource.

We, therefore, affirm the appellate court's holding that where there are multiple owners of the bed of a private, nonnavigable lake, such owners and their licensees have the right to the reasonable use and enjoyment of the surface waters of the entire lake provided they do not unduly interfere with the reasonable use of the waters by other owners and their licensees.

The question remains, however, whether the plaintiffs' use of the lake, including the renting of boats to members of the general public, is a reasonable one that does not unduly interfere with the reasonable use of the lake by other owners and their licensees. [ ] Because that question is not before us and remains for consideration by the trial court in the first instance, we express no view on it now.

NOTES

(1) Problems of lakes: *Beacham* sets forth the two approaches to access to nonnavigable lakes. As the court's citations display, both approaches enjoy support. The rule that nonnavigable lakes are closed to the public, even when a public road provides direct access to the lake, enjoys greater support. *E.g., Winans v. Willetts,* 163 N.W. 993 (Mich.1917); *Lembeck v. Nye,* 24 N.E. 686 (Ohio 1890). *Beacham* takes the view that the civil law rule will better promote efficient use of a nonnavigable lake, but is this so? Given the vagueness of the "reasonable use" limit that the court imposes, and given the high costs of litigating disputes, has the court perhaps created more conflict than it has eliminated? If the court had ruled in favor of the property owner's association, what would have happened next? Would Beacham perhaps have reached an agreement with the association governing her overall level of use? Does not the common law rule put greater pressure on landowners to resolve their differences without turning to the courts? What if a distinct majority of landowners prefer to close a lake to all motorboats? Should they have the power to do so over the objection of a single landowner?

Considered more broadly, *Beacham* illustrates the contentiousness of issues surrounding the use of private lakes with multiple owners, particularly in lake-studded states such as Michigan, which attract boating and fishing enthusiasts. Disputes often surround the interpretation of lake use rights under deeds, *e.g., Beach v. Hayner,* 173 N.W. 487 (Mich.1919), and whether the class of landowners with lake access rights can be expanded by excavating private canals, *e.g., Thompson v. Enz,* 154 N.W.2d 473 (Mich. 1967).

(2) Private fish ponds: Occasionally human-constructed lakes are so private and so cut off from other waterbodies that statutes or judicial rulings vest ownership rights in the fish in the private landowner rather than in the state. *E.g., Tyrrell Gravel Co. v. Carradus,* 619 N.E.2d 1367 (Ill.App.1993) (concluding that owner of land also owned the fish and that the fish were part of the realty so that title to them passed with the land). Recall that the English courts reached the same conclusion. *Smith v. Kemp,* Carth 285, 90 Eng. Rep. 769 (K.B. 1693); *Greyes Case,* Owen 20, 74 Eng. Rep. 869 (K.B. 1594) (individual has property in fish in "a trunk, or some other narrow place where they be put to be taken at will and pleasure").

Consider the case of the 25–member Diversion Lake Club, which purchased all of the land around an irrigation reservoir and expended some $125,000 stocking the land with deer, turkeys, and quail and the waters with fish for use as a hunting and fishing reserve. A nonmember claimed that the public had a right to hunt and fish on the waters of the reservoir; the Club sought to enjoin his continuing trespasses. The Texas appellate court affirmed an injunction:

> Of course, there is a general right in the public (or anyone with a license) to fish in the public streams and waters, but there is no such right inferred that permits a trespass upon the lands of another. [ ]
>
> In *Knudson v. Hall,* 148 P. 1070 (Utah), it is held that: "Although a person is entitled to fish in a river, that right does not entitle him to fish in waters which are on another's land because of overflows, or which are not a part of the natural channel of the river."

Heath v. Diversion Lake Club, 33 S.W.2d 479, 481 (Tex.Civ.App.1930). *See also Pleasant Lake Hills Corp. v. Eppinger,* 209 N.W. 152 (Mich.1926); *Gunter's Island Hunting Club v. Hucks,* 317 S.E.2d 470 (S.C.App.1984). Consider also the following statute:

> § 5210   Private ponds. A person owning a natural pond of not more than twenty acres or an artificial pond entirely upon his premises, stocked at his own expense with fish artificially hatched or reared, may take fish from such pond at any time for the purpose of propagation or consumption as food on his premises, provided that the sources of water supply for such pond are entirely upon his premises or that fish do not have access to such pond from waters not under his control or from waters stocked at the expense of the state.

Vt. Stat. Ann. tit. 10, § 5210.

(3) A riparian right to kill fish? In a prominent decision, *People v. Truckee Lumber Co.,* the California Supreme Court upheld the right of the state, acting on behalf of the people, to bring a public nuisance action against a riparian landowner who was polluting a nonnavigable river, killing the fish in it. The riparian defended with the claim that it possessed an exclusive fishery in all fish on its land because the river was nonnavigable and that it owned both banks of the river; if it chose, it could lawfully capture all of the fish, leaving none for other riparians. While admitting that the riparian could catch all the fish, the court rejected the argument that the right to catch included a right to kill:

> While the right of fishery upon his own land is exclusively in the riparian proprietor, this does not imply or carry the right to destroy what he does not take. He does not own the fish in the stream. His right of property attaches only to those he reduces to actual possession, and he cannot lawfully kill or obstruct the free passage of those not taken.

People v. Truckee Lumber Co., 48 P. 374 (Cal.1897). For a more extended discussion of the issue, see *State v. Haskell,* 79 A. 852 (Vt.1911).

(4) A riparian right to clean water: Riparian water rights law has long given landowners the power to complain of pollution that materially disturbs their use of adjacent waterways, whether or not navigable, including pollution that harms wildlife. Consider the following cases:

(a) *Snyder v. Callaghan:* Riparian landowners and a citizen watershed association sued the state for giving consent to an upstream construction activity that would degrade the waterway. Upholding their right to challenge the state, the West Virginia Supreme Court of Appeals explained the property rights of riparians:

> The riparian owner has a property interest in the flow of a natural watercourse through or adjacent to his property.... The obstruction or diversion of the natural watercourse or the introduction into it of sediment, sludge, refuse or other materials which corrupt the quality of the water by upper riparian owners or users constitutes an infringement of the lower riparian owner's property right, which may be enjoined or give rise to a cause of action for damages.

Snyder v. Callaghan, 284 S.E.2d 241 (W.Va.1981).

(b) *Springer v. Joseph Schlitz Brewing Co:* Plaintiffs, owners of a large farm on the Yadkin River, sued upstream brewery for pollution that "caused six unprecedented fish kills and otherwise impaired the quality" of the waterway, arguing that the pollution violated their riparian property rights. The court upheld the theory of liability:

> In North Carolina, a riparian landowner has a right to the agricultural, recreational, and scenic use and enjoyment of the stream bordering his land, subject, however, to the rights of upstream riparian owners to make reasonable use of the water without excessively diminishing its quality. Though he does not own the fish in the stream, the riparian owner's rights include the opportunity to catch them. Interference with riparian rights is an actionable tort, and a riparian landowner may join several polluters as joint tort-feasors.

The upstream brewery discharged its pollution, not directly into the river, but into a municipal waste treatment plant that was unable to process it properly. Ordinarily polluters are not liable for inadequacies in municipal treatment facilities. The court held, however, that the brewery would be liable if it violated the municipality's sewage ordinance or if it knew or should have known that the city's treatment plant could not adequately treat its sewage. *Springer v. Joseph Schlitz Brewing Co.*, 510 F.2d 468 (4th Cir.1975).

(5) A riparian right to unobstructed flow: Fish, of course, are often affected as much or more by obstructions in waterways, particularly dams, as they are by pollution. On the rights of riparian landowners to complain of obstructions that block fish, consider *State v. Haskell:*

> [A riparian landowner possesses only] a qualified or special right of property in the fish therein; that is, the exclusive right of fishing within the boundaries of his own territory. . . . He cannot lawfully kill, materially injure, or obstruct the free passage of, those which he does not take. . . . [H]e cannot divert [the waterway] from its course, nor pollute it, but leave it so the landowners on the stream above and below may enjoy a like use of the water, including taking fish therefrom; and [ ] this right carries with it the common right to have fish inhabit and spawn in the stream, for which purpose they must have a common passageway to and from their spawning and feeding grounds. It follows that the right to have fish, migratory in nature, pass up and down such a stream to and from their breeding or feeding grounds, is a public right which may be regulated and protected by the state.

State v. Haskell, 84 Vt. 429, 79 A. 852 (1911). *See also Holyoke Company v. Lyman,* 82 U.S. (15 Wall.) 500 (1872).

c. THE SPECIAL CASE OF WESTERN WATER LAW

NOTES

(1) A brief note on prior appropriation water rights: Under both riparian and prior appropriation systems of water law, a water right is a usufruct—a right to use water rather than the ownership of any molecules. As the court in *Harris v. Brooks*, 283 S.W.2d 129 (Ark.1955) [*supra*], noted, in those states that follow the riparian doctrine a riparian landowner has a right to make *reasonable use* of water. In those states that follow the prior appropriation doctrine, on the other hand, an appropriator has the right to make *beneficial use* of water.

For our purposes, it is sufficient to group water into three general categories: (a) "confined" surface water, *i.e.*, streams, lakes, and similar water; (b) diffused surface water, *i.e.*, storm run-off, bogs, swamps, and the like; and (c) groundwater, *i.e.*, underground water. Traditionally, each type of water has been subject to a different legal regime. For fish and wildlife, the two types of surface waters are crucial—particularly in the arid West. The division between riparian and prior appropriation legal regimes is most clearly applicable to confined surface waters.[1]

---

1. There is a third category of water rights regimes that is a hybrid of riparian and prior appropriation systems. The states of the humid West and the borderland states of the Midwest, *i.e.*, the Pacific Coast states and some of the states that straddle the 100th meridian, initially applied riparian law. They have all either shifted to prior appropri-

The prior appropriation doctrine evolved in the arid West. The basic assumptions implicit in this system are (1) that there is not enough water for all uses and (2) priority of use gives the better right. Historically, appropriation developed in the context of mining and irrigation; both of these uses remove water from the stream and move it to where it is needed either to mine or to irrigate crops. Since neither of these uses necessarily occurred on lands riparian to streams, water and land were not necessarily related: the appropriation doctrine thus focuses on the right to divert and beneficially use water. A traditional statement of the requirements for an appropriation is:

> To constitute a valid appropriation of water, three elements must always exist: (1) An intent to apply it to some existing or contemplated beneficial use; (2) an actual diversion from the natural stream channel by some mode sufficient for the purpose; and (3) an application of the water within a reasonable time to some beneficial use.

Simons v. Inyo Cerro Gordo Mining & Power Co., 192 P. 144 (Cal.App.), *review denied,* 192 P. 152 (Cal. 1920). The fundamental difference between the two systems of water law is summarized by Justice Stephen Field who, as a member of the California Supreme Court, played a crucial role in the development of appropriation law:

> By the custom which has obtained among miners in the Pacific States and Territories, where mining for the precious metals is had on the public lands of the United States, the first appropriator of mines, whether in placers, veins, or lodes, or of waters in the streams on such lands for mining purposes, is held to have a better right than others to work the mines or use the waters. The first appropriator who subjects the property to use, or takes the necessary steps for that purpose, is regarded, except as against the government, as the source of title in all controversies relating to the property. As respects the use of water for mining purposes, the doctrines of the common law declaratory of the rights of riparian owners were, at an early day, after the discovery of gold, found to be inapplicable or applicable only in a very limited extent to the necessities of miners, and inadequate to their protection. By the common law the riparian owner on a stream not navigable, takes the land to the centre of the stream, and such owner has the right to the use of the water flowing over the land as an incident to his estate. And as all such owners on the same stream have an equality of right to the use of the water, as it naturally flows, in quality, and without diminution in quantity, except so far as such diminution may be created by a reasonable use of the water for certain domestic, agricultural, or manufacturing purposes, there could not be, according to that law, any such diversion or use of the water by one owner as would work material detriment to any other owner below him. Nor could the water by one owner be so retarded in its flow as to be thrown back to the injury of another owner above him. . . . "This is the necessary result of the perfect equality of right among all the propri-

ation or have incorporated significant ele-   law.
ments of prior appropriation into their water

etors of that which is common to all." [*Tyler v. Wilkinson,* 24 F. Cas. 472 (D.R.I.1827) (No. 14,312)] "Every proprietor of lands on the banks of a river," says Kent, "has naturally an equal right to the use of the water which flows in the stream adjacent to his lands, as it was wont to run (*currere solebat*) without diminution or alteration. No proprietor has a right to use the water to the prejudice of other proprietors above or below him. . . . *Aqua currit et debet currere ut currere solebat. . . .*" 3 KENT'S COMMENTARIES 439.

This equality of right among all the proprietors on the same stream would have been incompatible with any extended diversion of the water by one proprietor, and its conveyance for mining purposes to points from which it could not be restored to the stream.

Atchison v. Peterson, 87 U.S. (20 Wall.) 507, 510–12 (1874).

(2) Diversions: Recall the statement by the California Court of Appeals in *Simons v. Inyo Cerro Gordo Mining & Power Co.,* 192 P. 144 (Cal.App.), *review denied,* 192 P. 152 (Cal. 1920), that "a valid appropriation of water" required three elements, including "an actual diversion from the natural stream channel." The implication of the diversion requirement are examined in

In re Application A–16642
Nebraska Game & Parks Commission v. The 25 Corporation

Supreme Court of Nebraska.
463 N.W.2d 591 (1990).

■ CAPORALE, J.:—This is a direct appeal from an order of the Director of Water Resources partially granting the permit requested by applicant-appellee, Nebraska Game and Parks Commission (applicant), for an instream flow appropriation at Long Pine Creek. . . .

After lengthy hearings, the director granted the application in part, as more particularly set forth in part II below. Together, the complaining objectors have lodged 32 assignments of error, which can be summarized as claiming that (1) the statutory scheme authorizing instream appropriations, NEB. REV. STAT. §§ 46–2,107 through 46–2,119 (Reissue 1988), is unconstitutional under NEB. CONST. art. XV, §§ 4, 5, and 6; . . . .

BACKGROUND

The application in question, A–16642, was filed on April 29, 1988. Therein, the applicant seeks a permit for an instream appropriation of water to maintain a naturally reproducing rainbow and brown trout fishery in Long Pine Creek. The creek is a 33–mile-long cold-water tributary of the Niobrara River and is the longest self-sustaining trout stream in Nebraska.

More specifically, the applicant seeks an instream flow appropriation for a segment of the creek between the confluence of Bone Creek and the boundary of Ranges 20 and 21 West, in Township 29 North, Brown County,

Nebraska. Three different flows were requested, to be measured at different points along the segment. The measuring points are referred to as the upper, middle, and lower study sites. The director denied an appropriation at the upper site but granted a 50–cubic-foot-per-second (cfs) appropriation at the middle site and a 60–cfs appropriation at the lower site, as the applicant requested. This is the first instream flow appropriation granted in this state.

ANALYSIS

1.   CONSTITUTIONALITY OF STATUTES

With the foregoing brief background, we reach the constitutional challenges presented by the first summarized assignment of error, namely, that the statutory scheme permitting instream flow appropriations, §§ 46–2,107 through 46–2,119, violates Neb. Const. art. XV, §§ 4, 5, and 6.

. . .

The complaining objectors essentially make two constitutional attacks: (a) that an instream flow appropriation, as authorized by the statutes, is not an "appropriation" within the meaning of the Nebraska Constitution; and (b) that certain features of the instream appropriations authorized "directly conflict with the constitutional provisions regulating appropriations." [ ] The relevant provisions of article XV are:

> The necessity of water for domestic use and for irrigation purposes in the State of Nebraska is hereby declared to be a natural want.

Neb. Const. art. XV, § 4.

> The use of the water of every natural stream within the State of Nebraska is hereby dedicated to the people of the state for beneficial purposes, subject to the provisions of the following section.

Neb. Const. art. XV, § 5.

> The right to divert unappropriated waters of every natural stream for beneficial use shall never be denied except when such denial is demanded by the public interest. Priority of appropriation shall give the better right as between those using the water for the same purpose, but when the waters of any natural stream are not sufficient for the use of all those desiring to use the same, those using the water for domestic purposes shall have preference over those claiming it for any other purpose, and those using the water for agricultural purposes shall have the preference over those using the same for manufacturing purposes. Provided, no inferior right to the use of the waters of this state shall be acquired by a superior right without just compensation therefor to the inferior user.

Neb. Const. art. XV, § 6.

(a) Appropriation without Physical Diversion

It is clear that nothing in these provisions expressly prohibits appropriations for instream use. The complaining objectors would imply a prohibition from the definition of appropriation. Although they realize that the Constitution does not define the word, they would have us read "[t]he right to divert unappropriated waters of every natural stream for beneficial use" as such a definition. From this, they would then have us conclude that a physical diversion is an essential element of any appropriation, and then reach the further conclusion that because of this, § 6 must be read as prohibiting instream appropriations.

.   .   .

The complaining objectors assert their reading of § 6 as limiting appropriations to out-of-stream uses reflects what the framers "plainly intended." [ ] To shore up their view, the complaining objectors turn to the customs of miners in the early days of water appropriations in the west. In that connection we are constrained to observe that there probably was not much mining going on in Nebraska and that the customs of miners in other jurisdictions are not a compelling ground for overturning a statute. Be that as it may, it appears that in those days an actual diversion of water away from the stream was considered necessary before a use could be perfected into a protected right. We recognize that there are many cases and authorities which still define an appropriation in terms of a physical diversion of water applied to a beneficial use. *See, e.g., Simons v. Inyo Cerro Gordo Co.,* 192 P. 144 (Cal.App.1920); 1 W. HUTCHINS, WATER RIGHTS LAWS IN THE NINETEEN WESTERN STATES 366 (1971). The complaining objectors urge that this was the view of the framers when § 6 was adopted and that § 6 must therefore be read as requiring such a diversion.

We agree with the complaining objectors' reading of § 6 so far as it recognizes the framers' intent to adopt the doctrine of prior appropriation. This does not, however, mean that we accept the argument that § 6 was intended to prohibit instream appropriations.

.   .   .

We have long recognized that §§ 4, 5, and 6 grant constitutional protection to the doctrine of prior appropriation. [ ] This doctrine was adopted by our Legislature via the irrigation act of 1895, parts of which were later incorporated into NEB. CONST. art. XV, §§ 4, 5, and 6. [ ]

Prior to the adoption of the appropriation system, water rights in Nebraska were governed by the common-law system of riparian rights. Under the riparian system, only those landowners whose property is adjacent to a body of water have a right to use that water. The rights of all riparians along a given body of water are equal, regardless of when they began using the water. Riparian proprietors could not divert significant flows out of the natural channel of a stream without returning that water to the channel, nor could they apply that water to nonriparian lands. [ ] While this doctrine was well suited to "England's green and pleasant land," where ample rains watered crops and most uses were nonconsumptive, it soon became apparent to settlers that pure riparianism would hinder development in the more arid regions of the American West. [ ] Nebraska responded to this "natural want" of water by adopting the doctrine of prior appropriation.

The attributes of the appropriative doctrine which distinguish it from riparianism are its focus on the application of the water to a beneficial use, rather than on the ownership of riparian land, and its use of a first-in-time, first-in-right approach to conflicts between users, as opposed to the riparian system's equality among riparians. The appropriative system permits water use on lands where the riparian system would deny it and protects senior, more established water uses in times of shortage. Adoption of the appropriative system permitted the acquisition of a right to the beneficial use of water based on the seniority of the use, independent of the riparian or nonriparian nature of the land.

Obviously, some type of diversion is necessary in order to use water on nonriparian land; the crucial question, however, is this: Do the laws of Nebraska require a diversion when one is not required by the laws of physics?

As this is the first instream flow appropriation granted, this is the first time this court has been asked to determine whether a diversion is a necessary prerequisite to a valid appropriation. Although a number of courts and authorities have stated that a diversion is a prerequisite, this view has been criticized as being obsolete. [ ] The diversion requirement traditionally served two functions. First, it provided notice to others of the intent to appropriate and, once the appropriation was perfected, of the existence of the appropriation. [ ] Second, the capacity of the diversion works established the maximum amount a user could claim to have appropriated. [ ]

Since the permit system provides a surer method of providing lasting notice of the existence and quantity of valid appropriative rights, requiring a diversion as a prerequisite serves no useful purpose. Nebraska's permit system predates the adoption of the constitutional provisions under discussion. Given the principle of constitutional interpretation that each and every clause in a constitution has been inserted for some useful purpose, [ ], we must conclude that the use in § 6 of the term "divert" serves some purpose other than to prohibit nondiversionary appropriations. It seems more likely that the framers chose to use "divert" in order to stress that the appropriative right was independent of riparian ownership. Since § 6 sets forth the other key aspects of the appropriative right, that the water must be put to beneficial use and that priority of appropriation gives the better right, it is reasonable to conclude that "divert" was intended to express the third aspect of the appropriative right, to wit, the ability to take the water away from the stream's locale.

Our conclusion that diversions are not constitutionally required for all appropriations is not aberrant. Of the nine other Western States with constitutional provisions protecting prior appropriation, only two mention diversion: Colorado and Idaho. [ ] Article 15, § 3, of the Idaho Constitution provides that "[t]he right to divert and appropriate the unappropriated waters of any natural stream to beneficial uses, shall never be denied, except that the state may regulate and limit the use thereof for power purposes." Article XVI, § 6, of the Colorado Constitution provides that "[t]he right to divert the unappropriated waters of any natural stream to beneficial uses shall never be denied."

Both Idaho and Colorado have faced the question now before us and have rejected the complaining objectors' argument. The Idaho Supreme

Court in *State, Department of Parks v. Idaho Department of Water Adminis-tration,* 530 P.2d 924 (Idaho 1974), upheld an instream appropriation against an identical challenge, as did the Colorado Supreme Court in *Colorado River Water v. Colorado Water,* 594 P.2d 570 (Colo.1979).

. . .

Even if we were to conclude that the framers of article XV, § 6, intended to give constitutional protection only to appropriations made by means of a physical diversion, we would not be forced to conclude that such protection prohibits the Legislature from creating other means of acquiring rights to water. There is nothing in the language of the Constitution which indicates that § 6 is the exclusive means of acquiring a water right. Indeed, we have long held that the adoption of § 6 did not do away with riparian rights. [ ] Just as Nebraska originally adopted the appropriation doctrine by statute, [ ], the Legislature can, subject to constitutional limitations, including those set forth in § 6, provide for the acquisition of nondiversion-ary appropriative rights to public water.

(b) Effects of Instream Appropriation

This brings us to the complaining objectors' second constitutional challenge to the instream appropriation statutes. They argue that the statutes work to deprive them of their constitutional right to divert unappropriated water. They base their argument on Justice McFadden's dissent in *State, Department of Parks v. Idaho Department of Water Administration,* 530 P.2d 924 (Idaho 1974), and on the similarities between the relevant provisions of the Nebraska and Idaho Constitutions.

The short and perhaps overly simplistic answer to that argument is that the Constitution only protects the right to divert unappropriated water, and once there has been an instream appropriation, that water is no longer "unappropriated." The more complete answer is that Justice McFadden's approach is inapplicable to Nebraska law.

The complaining objectors argue that the instream appropriation stat-utes permit the state to withdraw water from appropriation in violation of the command of § 6 that "[t]he right to divert unappropriated waters ... for beneficial use shall never be denied except when such denial is demand-ed by the public interest." They rely on the following language from Justice McFadden's dissent:

> I recognize that the state, acting in its proprietary capacity, may appropriate water without offending Article 15, section 3; but as in the case of private appropriators, the state's appropriative right depends upon the application of water to a "beneficial use." In this case, however, the state agency is directed to hold unappropriated waters "in trust for the people of the state" for "scenic beauty and recreation-al purposes." [ ] If the state were to hold unappropriated waters in trust for these purposes, it certainly would not be acting in a proprie-tary capacity; it would be doing nothing more than it already had a duty to do in its sovereign capacity. [ ]
>
> [T]he title to the public waters of the state is vested in the state for the use and benefit of all the citizens of the state * * *. This is not,

however, an interest or title in the proprietary sense, but rather in the sovereign capacity as representative of all the people for the purpose of guaranteeing that the common rights of all shall be equally protected and that no one shall be denied his proper use and benefit of this common necessity." [ ] In my view, the in-stream use of a natural stream for recreational purposes and for scenic beauty is a public beneficial use which inheres in the state's sovereign ownership of such water. Therefore, since the state already has the right to so use the water, it cannot acquire the right to "appropriate" the water for these purposes.

. . . To allow the state to in effect reserve water from appropriation in furtherance of non-proprietary, non-power purposes—when the framers of the Constitution contemplated that private beneficial users could appropriate water being held by the state in its sovereign capacity—amounts to nothing less than a denial of the constitutional right to appropriate the "unappropriated waters" of any natural stream. . . .

(Emphasis in original.)

This reasoning is inapplicable to Nebraska law for several reasons. First, the cases supporting the propositions upon which Justice McFadden relies are all Idaho cases and are not precedent in Nebraska. The complaining objectors have failed to demonstrate that there are any analogous Nebraska precedents. Second, the statutory scheme before us does not provide for the holding of "unappropriated waters 'in trust for the people of the state' " but, rather, authorizes an instream appropriation of the public water for particular beneficial uses. Third, and most important, Nebraska's Constitution expressly provides for a public interest exception to the right to divert. Justice McFadden's conclusion that the Idaho statute was unconstitutional was based on the fact that the Idaho Constitution, "[u]nlike the constitutions of some other western states . . . makes an exception [to the right to appropriate] only for power purposes—*not for the demands of the public interest*. . . ." (Emphasis supplied.) [ ]

Unlike that of Idaho, Nebraska's constitutional right to appropriate can and must be limited by the demands of the public interest. NEB. CONST. art. XV, § 6. The instream flow appropriation statutes can be viewed as a mechanism for determining whether the public interest demands that the right to appropriate water from a given stream should be denied. This view is supported by the fact that the statutory scheme includes a legislative finding that "the public interest demands the recognition of instream uses for fish, recreation, and wildlife," § 46–2,107, and requires the Director of Water Resources to find that the instream flow appropriation is in the public interest. §§ 46–2,115 and 46–2,116.

. . .

The view that § 6 demands individual, case-by-case determinations of the public interest for each new application is a narrow and parsimonious interpretation of the constitutional language and, as such, conflicts with the rule that constitutional provisions should receive a broad and liberal interpretation. [ ] The language of § 6 does not compel a continuing, case-by-case determination. The relevant clause of § 6 simply permits the state to deny appropriations based upon the dictates of the public interest. It does not prescribe the manner by which the public interest is to be determined nor the mechanisms by which it may be accomplished.

. . .

Finally, the complaining objectors assert that the public interest test of § 46–2,116 fails to meet the level of necessity required by the Constitution. It does not do so, in their view, because it does not require that the economic, social, and environmental value of the instream use exceed that of the reasonably foreseeable out-of-stream uses foregone or afforded to junior appropriators, but merely requires that the director consider these factors. This argument is unpersuasive. First, the Legislature has already found that the public interest demands the recognition of instream uses for piscatorial and other purposes. § 46–2,107. The complaining objectors do not challenge this finding. Second, the director must consider other factors besides the relative value of the uses; he must also consider whether the application is consistent with state goals for water resources use. § 46–2,116(3). The complaining objectors' interpretation ignores this consideration, even though it is a valid factor in determining the weight of the public interest in the appropriation.

For all the reasons set out above, the complaining objectors have failed to satisfy their burden of demonstrating the questioned statutes to be unconstitutional, and, therefore, their constitutional challenges fail.

AFFIRMED.

NOTES

(1) Is the court convincing? Is there need for a diversion given the state's permit system? Is it simply an historical anomaly? Or does the diversion requirement continue to satisfy notice concerns? Consider the following case.

The Montana Department of Fish, Wildlife and Parks (DFWP) asserted a "use" right under the Montana prior appropriation doctrine to the *in situ* waters of Bean Lake. The claimed use was "recreation" and "fish and wildlife" purposes. Since the early 1930s, DFWP had planted fish in Bean Lake and in 1964 the agency acquired land abutting the lake. It managed the lake to provide recreational fishing. Its claim to a water right was challenged by numerous parties:

> The arguments of DFWP in support of its claim may be summarized: in-stream, in-lake, or in-source recreational fish and wildlife uses without a diversion are beneficial uses which support appropriation by the Department on behalf of the public. . . .
>
> . . . . [T]he Department urges that the purpose of diversion is to give notice of the appropriated use by the appropriator and in this case the extensive efforts and expenditures by the Department in developing and managing the fishery clearly gave such notice though no

diversion occurred. In other words, the actual application of the water to a beneficial use meets the requirements of intent or notice.

The respondents ... claim that DFWP has not met the basic elements of a valid appropriation under the law prior to 1973.... Respondents ... contend that in the stocking and managing of Bean Lake, the Department had no intent at the time to make an appropriation on which to base a water right. The diversion requirement provides evidence of an intent that gives notice to other water users of the specifics of the appropriation. [ ]

These are the principal contentions of the parties....

We accept as given that the activities of the DFWP in stocking Bean Lake, maintaining the fishery resource, making studies of the Bean Lake surface levels and fish population, enforcing rules relating to motor boats, coupled with the general public use of Bean Lake for the purpose of recreation, wildlife, and fishing constituted a beneficial use of the waters within the meaning of the appropriation doctrine....

It is clear ... that under Montana law before 1973, no appropriation right was recognized for recreation, fish and wildlife, except through a [specific state] statute. The prevailing legal theory was that some form of diversion or capture was necessary for an appropriation even though some forms of non-diversionary water rights were given appropriation status.... Whatever the merits of the lack of diversion argument, the DFWP and the public could not have intended an appropriation where none was recognized by law, and for the same reason, adverse appropriators could not have had notice of such a claim. We therefore uphold the Water Court's decision that DFWP, for itself or for the public, had no appropriation right in Bean Lake....

In the Matter of the Adjudication of the Existing Rights to the Use of All the Water Both Surface and Underground, Within the Dearborn Drainage Area, 766 P.2d 228 (Mont.1988). In its opinion, the court cited an earlier case holding that the construction of fish ladders, a barrier dam, and a fish trap were a sufficient "diversion" to establish an appropriative right.

(2) Statutory and non-statutory instream appropriations: Like Colorado and Nebraska, several have enacted statutes that expressly authorize instream appropriations. *See, e.g.,* Idaho Code § 67–4307; Or. Rev. Stat. §§ 537.338 *et seq.*; Wyo. Stat. §§ 41–3–1001 *et seq.*

Some courts have also recognized the validity of instream rights despite the lack of an express statutory basis:

(a) *State v. Morros:* The Nevada State Engineer issued permits for water rights to the United States Bureau of Land Management and Forest Service for stock-and wildlife-watering, and a permit to appropriate the waters of Blue Lake for public recreation and fishery purposes. The Attorney General of Nevada, on behalf of the State Board of Agriculture, and other parties sought judicial review of the state engineer's decisions, arguing that state water law "absolutely requires a physical diversion of water to obtain a water right, and that the district court therefore erred in affirming the state engineer's grant of a right to the water of Blue Lake *in* *situ.*" The BLM contended that "under NRS 533.035, which provides that '[b]eneficial use shall be the basis, the measure and the limit of the right to the use of water,' beneficial use is the only essential requirement for water appropriation in Nevada."

Noting that "[m]any recreational uses of water.... do not demand a physical diversion of water," the court cited a 1969 statute declaring recreation to be a beneficial use of water and concluded

> Diversions are not needed for and are incompatible with many recreational uses of water. Therefore, enactment of NRS 533.030(2) [the 1969 statute] mandates recognition of in situ water appropriation for recreation. *See McClellan v. Jantzen,* 547 P.2d 494, 496 (Ariz.App. 1976) ("when 'wildlife, including fish' and ... when 'recreation' were added to the purposes for appropriation, the concept of in situ appropriation of water was introduced—it appearing to us that these purposes could be enjoyed without a diversion"). *See also State Department of Parks v. Idaho Department of Water Administration,* 530 P.2d 924, 929 (Idaho 1974).

Similarly, the court concluded that an appropriation of water for wildlife watering was permissible under state law:

> Wildlife watering is encompassed in the NRS 533.030(2) definition of recreation as a beneficial use of water. Nevada law recognizes the recreational value of wildlife, [ ], and the need to provide wildlife with water. [ ] Sport hunting, a common use of wildlife, is a form of recreation. The legislative history of NRS 533.030(2) indicates that the legislature intended the provision to include wildlife watering under the rubric of recreation as a beneficial use of water. [ ] It follows that providing water to wildlife is a beneficial use of water.

State v. Morros, 766 P.2d 263 (Nev.1988)

(b) *Dekay v. United States Fish & Wildlife Service***:** The United States Fish and Wildlife Service operates the LaCreek National Wildlife Refuge in South Dakota. In 1971, FWS purchased 6,665 acres of land contiguous to the Refuge and applied to the South Dakota Water Management Board for three water right permits. These included a new water right to the natural flow of water from six springs. FWS did not plan to divert or develop the springs; its application was filed solely to protect their continued flow, which was to be used to maintain 235 acres of marshes, sloughs, and wet meadows for wildlife habitat. Neighboring landowners challenged the granting of the permits.

Under applicable state law, only enumerated agencies were empowered to reserve *in situ* water rights—and FWS was not one of the enumerated agencies. FWS argued, however, that the spring's natural flow was intended for current use to maintain 235 acres of marshes and other waterfowl habitat. The court held that the permit was properly granted because the "[a]ppropriation of water for waterfowl habitat and other wildlife is a beneficial use. ARSD 74:03:04:01 ("All streams in South Dakota are assigned the beneficial uses of irrigation and wildlife propagation and stock watering."). *Dekay v. United States Fish & Wildlife Service,* 524 N.W.2d 855 (S.D.1994).

(3) Private instream appropriations and transfers to instream uses: As the Colorado and Nebraska statutes demonstrate, most states restrict the power to make instream appropriations to designated state agencies. Thus private individuals cannot make an instream appropriation. Should private entities be permitted to do so?

California does not permit instream appropriations. *See Fullerton v. State Water Resources Control Board*, 153 Cal.Rptr. 518 (Cal.App.1979) (holding that a diversion is required to make an appropriation); *California Trout, Ltd. v. State Water Resources Control Board*, 153 Cal.Rptr. 672 (Cal.App.1979) (same). The California Water Code, however, states that "[a]ny person entitled to the use of water.... may petition the board ... for a change for purposes of preserving or enhancing wetlands habitat, fish and wildlife resources, or recreation in, or on, the water." CAL. WATER CODE § 1707(a). What is the effect of such a policy?

PERSPECTIVES

Irrigated agriculture—water quantity and quality issues: Given its emphasis on using water out of the streambed, prior appropriation water law presents significant problems for fish and wildlife habitat. For example, irrigated agriculture was a cause of the listing of 50 of the 68 western fish species listed as endangered or threatened. Michael R. Moore et al., *Water Allocation in the American West: Endangered Fish Versus Irrigated Agriculture,* 36 NAT. RESOURCES J. 319, 321 (1996).

The prior appropriation doctrine produces an asymmetry: riparians in Western states have been able to challenge water pollution as a private nuisance, *e.g., Wilmore v. Chain O'Mines* 44 P.2d 1024 (Colo.1934); *Hill v. Standard Mining Co.,* 85 P. 907 (Idaho 1906), but those same landowners would generally be unable to complain of diversions that totally dried up the stream. Similarly, water pollution that kills fish is a public nuisance, *e.g., People v. Truckee Lumber Co.,* 48 P. 374 (Cal.1897), but diversions that kill fish probably are not. What is to account for this bias?

Shokal v. Dunn

Supreme Court of Idaho.
707 P.2d 441 (1985).

■ BISTLINE, J.:—On December 21, 1978, respondent Trout Co. applied for a permit to appropriate 100 c.f.s. of waters from Billingsley Creek near Hagerman, Idaho. Numerous protests were filed.... The Department of Water Resources (Water Resources) held a hearing on the application ... and issued Permit No. 36–7834....

[On appeal, the district court] determined that Water Resources had failed to properly evaluate the question of "local public interest," holding that the applicant had the ultimate burden of proving that a proposed water use was in the local public interest under I.C. § 42–203A.

In response ..., Resources held four days of hearing.... The Director conditionally granted the application upon a subsequent showing by the applicant, Trout Co., that the project would meet certain requirements and restrictions set forth in the [district court's] order. Accordingly, the Director again approved Permit No. 36–7834 for fish propagation and hydropower generation. . . .

Subsequently, Trout Co. submitted a new set of drawings of the facility, and a document entitled "Contemplated Operational Criteria for the Trout Co. Fishraising Facility" (hereinafter "Operational Criteria"). . . .

The protestants filed new protests raising many factual issues regarding the "Operational Criteria." After reviewing the "Operational Criteria" and considering the objections raised by the protestants and other parties, Water Resources, without further hearing, issued its final order on July 21, 1982, granting the application for Permit No. 36–7834. Appeal was again taken to the district court, [which again reversed and remanded the decision to issue the permit.]

. . .

III. THE LOCAL PUBLIC INTEREST

[T]he only matters for the agency to consider on remand are those which relate generally to the local public interest. I.C. § 42–203A(5)(e). We turn first to the interpretation of this provision, a question of first impression before this Court.[2]

A. *Defining the Local Public Interest*

Under I.C. § 42–203A(5)(e), if an applicant's appropriation of water "will conflict with the local public interest, where the local public interest is defined as the affairs of the people in the area directly affected by the proposed use," then the Director "may reject such application and refuse issuance of a permit therefor, or may partially approve and grant a permit for a smaller quantity of water than applied for, or may grant a permit upon conditions."

The Utah Supreme Court interpreted a similar provision [Utah Code Ann. § 100–8–1] to authorize the State Engineer "to reject or limit the priority of plaintiff's application [for a permit to appropriate water for a power project] in the interest of the public welfare." *Tanner v. Bacon*, 136

---

2. The requirement that Water Resources protect the public interest is related to the larger doctrine of the public trust, which Justice Huntley comprehensively discussed in *Kootenai Environmental Alliance v. Panhandle Yacht Club, Inc.*, 105 Idaho 622, 671 P.2d 1085 (1983). The state holds all waters in trust for the benefit of the public, and "does not have the power to abdicate its role as trustee in favor of private parties." *Id.* at 625, 671 P.2d at 1088. Any grant to use the state's waters is "subject to the trust and to action by the State necessary to fulfill its trust responsibilities." *Id.* at 631, 671 P.2d at 1094. Trust interests include property values,

"navigation, fish and wildlife habitat, aquatic life, recreation, aesthetic beauty and water quality." *Id.* at 632, 671 P.2d at 1095. Reviewing courts must "take a 'close look' at the action [of the legislature or of agencies such as Water Resources] to determine if it complies with the public trust doctrine and will not act merely as a rubber stamp for agency or legislative action." *Id.* at 629, 671 P.2d at 1092. Justice Huntley concluded, "The public trust at all times forms the outer boundaries of permissible government action with respect to public trust resources." *Id.* at 632, 671 P.2d at 1095.

P.2d 957, 964 (Utah 1943); *see also People v. Shirokow,* 605 P.2d 859, 866 (Cal.1980) (In the public interest, the Water Board may impose the condition that the applicant salvage the water required for his or her project.); *East Bay Municipal Utility District v. Department of Public Works,* 35 P.2d 1027, 1029 (Cal.1934) ("Where the facts justify the action, the water authority should be allowed to impose [on an application to appropriate water for a power project], in the public interest, the restrictions and conditions provided for in the act," or to reject the application "in its entirety."). Both the Utah and California Supreme Courts have upheld state water agencies which had granted appropriations subject to future appropriations for uses of greater importance—in effect prioritizing among uses according to the public interest. [ ] The Director of Water Resources has the same considerable flexibility and authority, which he has already implemented in earlier proceedings in this matter, to protect the public interest.

Indeed, I.C. § 42–203A places upon the Director the affirmative duty to assess and protect the public interest. . . .

The authority and duty of the Director to protect the public interest spring naturally from the statute; the more difficult task for us is to define "the local public interest." Public interest provisions appear frequently in the statutes of the prior appropriation states of the West, but are explicated rarely. *See, e.g.,* Cal. Water Code § 1253; *see generally* 1 R. CLARK, ED., WATERS AND WATER RIGHTS § 29.3 (1967). I.C. § 42–203A provides little guidance. Fortunately, however, the legislature did provide guidance in a related statute, I.C. § 42–1501. We also derive assistance from our sister states and from the academic community.

In I.C. § 42–1501, the legislature declared it "in the public interest" that:

the streams of this state and their environments be protected against loss of water supply to preserve the minimum stream flows required for the protection of fish and wildlife habitat, aquatic life, recreation, aesthetic beauty, transportation and navigation values, and water quality.

Not only is the term "public interest" common to both §§ 42–1501 and 42–203A, and the two sections common to the same title, [ ], but also the legislature approved the term "public interest" in both sections on the same day, March 29, 1978. [ ] Clearly, the legislature in § 42–203A must have intended the public interest on the local scale to include the public interest elements listed in § 42–1501: "fish and wildlife habitat, aquatic life, recreation, aesthetic beauty, transportation and navigation values, and water quality." *Accord* NATIONAL WATER COMMISSION, NEW DIRECTIONS IN U.S. WATER POLICY 5 (1973) ("The people of the United States give far greater weight to environmental and aesthetic values than they did when the nation was young and less settled."), *cited in* R. Robie, *The Public Interest in Water Rights Administration,* 23 ROCKY MTN. MIN. L. INST. 917, 933 (1977).

In so intending, the legislature was in good company. Unlike other state public interest statutes, the Alaska statute enumerates the elements of the public interest. The public interest elements of I.C. § 42–1501 are almost precisely duplicated within the Alaska statute, which is set out in the margin.[3] . . .

The Alaska statute contains other elements which common sense argues ought to be considered part of the local public interest. These include the proposed appropriation's benefit to the applicant, its economic effect, its effect "of loss of alternative uses of water that might be made within a reasonable time if not precluded or hindered by the proposed appropriation," its harm to others, its "effect upon access to navigable or public waters," and "the intent and ability of the applicant to complete the appropriation." Alaska Stat. § 46.5.080(b).

Several other public interest elements, though obvious, deserve specific mention. These are: assuring minimum stream flows, as specifically provided in I.C. § 42–1501, discouraging waste, and encouraging conservation. *See Shirokow,* 605 P.2d at 866 (The California Supreme Court found water salvage to be sufficiently in the public interest to require it of a permittee).

The above-mentioned elements of the public interest are not intended to be a comprehensive list. As observed long ago by the New Mexico Supreme Court, the "public interest" should be read broadly in order to "secure the greatest possible benefit from [the public waters] for the public." *Young & Norton v. Hinderlider,* 110 P. 1045, 1050 (N.M. 1910) (Rejects considering only public health and safety; considers relative costs of two projects.). By using the general term "the local public interest," the legislature intended to include any locally important factor impacted by proposed appropriations.

Of course, not every appropriation will impact every one of the above elements. Nor will the elements have equal weight in every situation. The relevant elements and their relative weights will vary with local needs, circumstances, and interests. For example, in an area heavily dependent on recreation and tourism or specifically devoted to preservation in its natural state, Water Resources may give great consideration to the aesthetic and

---

3. Alaska Stat. § 46.15.080 provides:

(b) In determining the public interest, the commissioner shall consider

(1) the benefit to the applicant resulting from the proposed appropriation;

(2) the effect of the economic activity resulting from the proposed appropriation;

(3) the effect on fish and game resources and on public recreational opportunities;

(4) the effect on public health;

(5) the effect of loss of alternate uses of water that might be made within a reasonable time if not pre-cluded or hindered by the proposed appropriation;

(6) harm to other persons resulting from the proposed appropriation;

(7) the intent and ability of the applicant to complete the appropriation; and

(8) the effect upon access to navigable or public waters.

See also Bank of America National Trust & Savings Association v. State Water Resources Control Board, 116 Cal. Rptr. 770, 771, 42 Cal. App. 3d 198, 201 (1974) (If supported by the record, the state water board can condition a permit for a reservoir on providing for the public interest element of public access for recreation).

environmental ramifications of granting a permit which calls for substantial modification of the landscape or the stream.

Those applying for permits and those challenging the application bear the burden of demonstrating which elements of the public interest are impacted and to what degree. As Judge Schroeder correctly noted below, this burden of production lies with the party

> that has knowledge peculiar to himself. For example, the designer of a fish facility has particularized knowledge of the safeguards or their lack concerning the numbers of fish that may escape and the amount of fecal material that will be discharged into the river. As to such information the applicant should have the burden of going forward and ultimately the burden of proof on the impact on the local public interest. On the other hand, a protestant who claims a harm peculiar to himself should have the burden of going forward to establish that harm.

However, the burden of proof in all cases as to where the public interest lies ... rests with the applicant:

> [I]t is not [the] protestant's burden of proof to establish that the project is not in the local public interest. The burden of proof is upon the applicant to show that the project is either in the local public interest or that there are factors that overweigh the local public interest in favor of the project.

The determination of what elements of the public interest are impacted, and what the public interest requires, is committed to Water Resources' sound discretion. *See* 1 R. CLARK, ED., WATERS AND WATER RIGHTS § 29.3, 170 (1967).

In light of the preceding discussion, the district court admirably established some of the public interest elements which Water Resources must consider in this case. Judge Schroeder observed:

> First, as previously outlined, if the Department gives weight to the economic benefits of the project, it should also give consideration to the economic detriments. The effect of the project on water quality should be considered. It is not clear to what extent that was done in this case. The effect of the project on alternative uses of the watercourse should be considered—e.g., the impact on recreational and scenic uses. The effect on vegetation, wildlife, and other fish should be considered. This is not a catalogue of all factors that may relate to the public interest element, but is a suggestion of factors to be weighed in determining whether the project will or will not be in the public interest.

> . . . .

The dewatering of Billingsley Creek raises significant public interest and public trust concerns. In his discussion of the issue Judge Smith simply declared that "the rights of an appropriator prevail over riparian rights." Such a statement on its face fails to account for the state's policy of providing for minimum stream flows, and for the public's legitimate interests in the stream environment, wildlife, aesthetics, recreation, and alternative uses. . . .

IV. CONCLUSION

The above elements of the public interest, together with other elements and factors which Water Resources deems relevant, will be considered at the hearing on the amended application. Water Resources should accept relevant testimony and other evidence providing additional information on the public interest.

The decision of the district court is reversed in part, affirmed in part, and remanded for further proceedings consonant herewith.

■ DONALDSON, C.J., and HUNTLEY, J., concur.

■ BAKES and SHEPARD, JJ., concur in the result.

NOTES

(1) Would the Director ever be justified in permitting a diversion that dewatered a stream segment? That is, what is the scope of the Director's discretion in determining the public interest? This can also be rephrased as a question of judicial review: to what extent should the court defer to agency "expertise" rather than independently evaluating the evidence? Under traditional administrative law principles, courts generally are unwilling to reweigh evidence.

Is the "local public interest" standard static or does it require consideration of an evolving list of interests and values? Is there anything that the Director could *not* consider?

(2) *Hardy v. Higginson*: In a subsequent decision, the Idaho Supreme Court held that an application to amend an existing permit was subject to the subsequently enacted "local public interest" standard. The court dismissed the claim that this violated his "vested right or ... contractual right to divert water," by noting that "water permits only give ... an inchoate or contingent right to put the water to a beneficial use." Among the conditions imposed on the permit was a requirement imposed on a previously approved diversion to protect a species of fish that requires cold, clean water. The modification permitted the diversion only "to the extent that such diversion can occur without increasing or decreasing the water levels, temperature, quality, and/or flow velocity within the natural sculpin pool located downstream." *Hardy v. Higginson*, 849 P.2d 946 (Idaho 1993).

For a history of the evolution of the public trust doctrine in Idaho, see Scott W. Reed, *The Public Trust Doctrine in Idaho*, 19 ENVTL. L. 655 (1989).

(3) Public and private: The Idaho Code provides: "All the waters of the state, when flowing in their natural channels, including the waters of all natural springs and lakes within the boundaries of the state are declared to be the property of the state." Idaho Code § 42–101. Similar provisions can be found in the constitutions and codes of other Western states. The Colorado Constitution, for example, provides: "The water of every natural stream, not heretofore appropriated, within the state of Colorado, is hereby declared to the property of the public, and the same is dedicated to the use of the people of the state." COLO. CONST. art. XVI, § 5. Recall also *Day v. Armstrong*, 362 P.2d 137 (Wyo.1961), in which the court held that the

Wyoming Constitution's declaration of public ownership created public rights in streams that flowed over private lands. To what extent ought such declarations to restrict private rights in waters?

Joseph Sax stated the question:

The problem is really quite simple, it does not require mastery of obtuse legal doctrines to appreciate what is going on. The heart of the matter is that public values have changed, and the use of water has reached some critical limits. One result is that we need to retrieve some water from traditional water users to sustain streams and lakes as natural systems and to protect water quality. Moreover, traditional sources of new supply—such as dams and transbasin transportation of water, on which convention users depend—are being closed off for a variety of familiar reasons, including both federal reluctance to finance new projects, and environmental objections. Thus, we have a potential head-on conflict between existing water users and their existing and future demands, and future demands of what may broadly be called instream uses.

Joseph Sax, *Limits on Private Rights,* 19 ENVTL. L. 973 (1989).

CHAPTER 4

LIABILITY FOR WILDLIFE

The law on liability for damages caused by wildlife is a jumble. In part, this reflects the infrequency of such cases and thus a certain novelty to the issues—particularly since the cases often have a whiff of the exotic. The confusion is often expressed as a tendency to make sweeping generalizations, *e.g., Collins v. Otto*, 369 P.2d 564, 566 (Colo.1962) ("The law is virtually universal that one who harbors a wild animal, which by its very nature is vicious and unpredictable, does so at his peril, and liability for injuries inflicted by such animal is absolute liability."), to create confused categories, *e.g., Candler v. Smith*, 179 S.E. 395, 397 (Ga.App.1935) ("When a person is injured by an attack of an animal *feræ naturæ*, the negligence of the owner or keeper thereof is presumed, because the dangerous and ferocious propensities of a wild beast"), or to lapse into overly broad *dicta*, *e.g., Gooding v. Chutes Co.*, 102 P. 819 (Cal.1909) (discussing the rule of liability applicable to a wild animal in a case involving a domestic animal).

These problems are compounded by the failure to distinguish among a variety of factual patterns as courts cite prior decisions indiscriminately. In fact, the range of possible cases is substantial and implicate a diverse range of legal policies. What follows is an overview of three topics: (1) liability for personal injuries where land ownership is and is not involved; (2) liability for property damage; and (3) liability of governmental entities.

Section 1. Liability for Personal Injuries

Edward Hoagland, *Wild Things*

57 GRANTA 39, 42 (Spring 1997).

[I]n 1951, at the age of eighteen, I got a job working with real tigers, elephants, monkeys and panthers in the menagerie at the Ringling Brothers and Barnum & Bailey Circus, crossing America from Connecticut to Nebraska for fourteen dollars a week....

Occasionally, some neophyte, one of the new workhands who had joined the circus because they were hungry (gulping that first meal down), would show off for the townie girls after the afternoon show. After prodding old Joe, the ruddy-maned lion, to roar, he might move a few feet on to silent, watchful Rajah, Joe's still bigger counterpart in the adjacent cage, and instead of tormenting him, might tentatively begin to pet that beautiful black-and-yellow coat through the bars, which were spaced wide enough to get even your elbow through. And—about once a year—when that young man, half-soused, did so, while the girls oohed and aahed, Rajah would wait till his hand moved up past his ribs to his magnificent shoulder, then whirl in a flash and grab and crunch it, pull the arm all the way in, rip it out of its socket and claw it off. The stump would be sewn up, and he'd get a free night in the hospital, then be put on a Greyhound bus for wherever his home was, still howling in agony at every jounce.

a. THE ENGLISH COMMON-LAW BACKGROUND

May v. Burdett

Queens Bench.
9 Q.B. 101 (1846).

■ LORD DENMAN, C.J.:—This was a motion to arrest the judgment in an action on the case for keeping a monkey which the defendant knew to be accustomed to bite people, and which bit the female plaintiff. The declaration stated that the defendant wrongfully kept a monkey, well knowing that it was of a mischievous and ferocious nature and used and accustomed to attack and bite mankind, and that it was dangerous to allow it to be at large; and that the monkey, whilst the defendant kept the same aforesaid, did attack, bite, and injure the female plaintiff, whereby, & c.

It is objected on the part of the defendant, that the declaration was bad for not alleging negligence or some default of the defendant in not properly or securely keeping the animal; and it was said that, consistently with this declaration, the monkey might have been kept with due and proper caution, and that the injury might have been entirely occasioned by the carelessness and want of caution of the plaintiff herself.

A great many cases and precedents were cited upon the argument: and the conclusion to be drawn from them appears to us to be that the declaration is good upon the face of it; and that whoever keeps an animal accustomed to attack and bite mankind, with knowledge that it is so accustomed, is prima facie liable in an action on the case at the suit of any person attacked and injured by the animal, without any averment of negligence or default in the securing or taking case of it. The gist of the action is the keeping of the animal after knowledge of its mischievous propensities.

The precedents, both ancient and modern, with scarcely an exception, merely state the ferocity of the animal and the knowledge of the defendant, without any allegation of negligence or want of care. A great many were referred to upon argument, commencing with the register and ending with *Thomas v. Morgan*, [ ], and all in the same form, or nearly so. . . .

[T]he conclusion to be drawn from an examination of all the authorities appears to us to be this: that a person keeping a mischievous animal with knowledge of its propensities is bound to keep it secure at his peril, and that, if it does mischief, negligence is presumed, without express averment. The precedents as well as the authorities fully warrant this conclusion. The negligence is in keeping such a animal after notice. The case of *Smith v. Pelah*, 2 Stra. 1264, 93 Eng. Rep. 1171 (K.B. 1746), and a passage in 1 HALE'S PLEAS OF THE CROWN, 430(b), put the liability on the true ground. It may be that, if the injury was solely occasioned by the wilfulness of the plaintiff after warning, that may be a ground of defence, by plea in confession and avoidance: but it is unnecessary to give any opinion as to this; for we think that the declaration is good upon the face of it, and shews a prima facie liability in the defendant.

It is said, indeed, further, on the part of the defendant, that, the monkey being an animal *feræ naturæ*, he would not be answerable for injuries committed by it, if it escaped and went at large without any default on the part of the defendant, during the time it had so escaped and was at large, because at that time it would not be in his keeping nor under his control: but we cannot allow any weight to this objection: for, in the first place, there is no statement in the declaration that the monkey had escaped, and it is expressly averred that the injury occurred whilst the defendant kept it: we are besides of opinion, as already stated, that the defendant, if he would keep it, was bound to keep it secure at all events.

The rule therefore will be discharged.

NOTES

(1) What is the basis of liability? Is it the introduction into the community of an unacceptable risk? Is it the control that the defendant has over the animal? If so, why doesn't the loss of control when the animal escapes end the defendant's potential liability? Or is defendant seeking to confuse property categories with civil liability categories?

(2) *Mitchil v. Alestree* was an action for damages suffered when plaintiff was struck by defendant's horse. The court upheld a verdict for plaintiff, noting "[i]t was the defendant's fault, to bring a wild horse into such a place where mischief might probably be done, by reason of the concourse of people." One judge posed an additional hypothetical: "If one hath kept a tame fox, which gets loose and grows wild, he that kept him before shall not answer for the damage the fox doth after he hath lost him, and he hath resumed his wild nature." *Mitchil v. Alestree*, 1 Vent. 295, 86 Eng. Rep. 190 (K.B. 1676).

Is *May v. Burdett* inconsistent with the hypothetical in *Mitchil*? Is there a difference between a fox and a monkey that might be relevant? Should an introduced species be treated differently than a species that naturally occurs in the jurisdiction? Or, is the point of the hypothetical that the fox "hath resumed his wild nature"?

(3) *Filburn v. The People's Palace & Aquarium Co.:* The court in *May v. Burdett* focused on the liability standard while treating the status of animal in a formulaic manner. That is, the statement in the plaintiff's declaration that the animal was "of a mischievous and ferocious nature" is treated as an unexamined category. What types of animals are "of a mischievous and ferocious nature"? Is it a question of fact or do species fall into categories set by law that are not subject to further challenge? Recall the prior discussion of the similar problem of characterizing animals as "wild" or "domestic" in Chapter 1.

These questions were addressed in *Filburn v. The People's Palace &
Aquarium Co.* The case was brought to recover damages for injuries caused
by an elephant which, while being exhibited by defendants, ran at the
plaintiff and injured him. The jury concluded that the elephant was not an
animal dangerous to man and that defendants had not known it to be
dangerous; they nonetheless awarded plaintiff 125£ in damages. In affirming the jury's verdict, the court offered the following analysis of the proper
classification of animals:

> There is no doubt that the law of England recognises two distinct
> classes of animals. With regard to one class, a person who keeps an
> animal of that class must keep it at his peril, and prevent it from doing
> injury; and whether he knows it to be dangerous or not is immaterial.
> There is another class of animals which the law assumes not to be of a
> dangerous nature, although individuals of that class may become
> dangerous, and a person who keeps an animal of that class is not liable
> for injury done unless he knew that the individual animal was danger-
> ous. What is the best formula for determining to which particular class
> a particular animal belongs?
>
> There are some animals which it is well known are not originally
> by nature dangerous, and it is immaterial whether they have become
> domesticated or not. Whether they are *feræ naturæ*, as not being the
> subject of property, is not the point. Thus, rabbits, hares, pheasants,
> partridges, and the like, are *feræ naturæ* in the sense that they do not
> belong to any one until they have been reduced to possession, but they
> are not *feræ naturæ* in the sense that they are dangerous. There is
> another set of animals which the law has recognised as not being of a
> dangerous nature in England; there are cows, oxen, horses, dogs,
> sheep, and many other, which I need not attempt to enumerate. How
> has that recognition come about?
>
> Some of these animals originally, whether in this country or
> elsewhere, in their wild state were dangerous, but a great many years
> ago the whole race of animals of that kind in this country was so tamed
> that it is known as a matter of fact that their progeny is not danger-
> ous. The animals I have mentioned are recognised by the law of
> England as not being of a dangerous nature because of such universal
> knowledge, and the law assumes without further proof that such
> animals are not of a dangerous nature.... Unless, therefore, an
> animal can be brought within one or other of those recognised
> classes—namely, animals which are nowhere dangerous, or animals
> which have come to be recognised in England as not being of a
> dangerous nature—it must be treated as an animal belonging to the
> class of animals which must be kept from doing mischief, and such
> animal would come within the first and not the second class.

Filburn v. The People's Palace & Aquarium Co., 59 Q.B.D. 471 (Ct. App.
1890).

Applying these standards to the elephant, Lord Esher concluded that
"[i]t certainly cannot be said that elephants are within the class of animals
which are not dangerous by nature; nor is it true to say that elephants have
been used in this country for such a length of time that it has come to be a

matter of universal knowledge that their progeny are not dangerous." Therefore, "a person who keeps an elephant on his land does so at his own risk, and must prevent it doing any injury, except where the person injured brings the injury on himself. Whether he knew the particular animal was dangerous or not is immaterial." *Id.*

Note that even "nondangerous" wild animals may cause injury. A common case in England involved the question of a landowner's liability for rabbits that he introduced and that escaped, causing damage to a neighbor's wheat crop. *See Boulston's Case,* 5 Co. Rep. 104b, 77 Eng. Rep. 216 (K.B. 1597) *infra.*

b. LIABILITY FOR PERSONAL INJURIES IN THE NEW WORLD

Irvine v. Rare Feline Breeding Center, Inc.

Court of Appeals of Indiana.
685 N.E.2d 120 (1997).

■ CHEZEM, J.:—For the past thirty years, Mosella Schaffer has lived on a fifty acre farm in Hamilton County, Indiana where she has raised and maintained exotic animals. These animals have included zebras, llamas, camels, kangaroos, and, beginning in 1970, Siberian tigers. Although her original intent was to breed and sell the animals, she soon found it difficult to part with many of them.

In 1993, Scott Bullington was renting a room in the garage area of Schaffer's house. Aware of his friend Irvine's interest in wild animals, Bullington informed Irvine of Schaffer's farm and the animals she kept there. Irvine, then in his late twenties, began to stop by and see the animals as per Schaffer's open invitation. Over the next two years, Irvine visited Schaffer's farm several dozen times. During these visits, people would occasionally pet the tigers through a fence.

On the afternoon of December 2, 1995, Irvine arrived at Schaffer's home to see Bullington. The two men drank alcohol and watched television until early evening when Bullington announced that he had to leave to attend his employer's Christmas party. Because Irvine had consumed a substantial amount of alcohol, Bullington told Irvine he could stay over night on the couch. Some time after Bullington had left, Irvine exited Bullington's apartment, walked to the front of Schaffer's property and visited with the llamas and zebras. As he was doing so, Schaffer drove up, stopped her car, had a brief, friendly conversation with Irvine, and went into her house.

Around 8:00 p.m., Irvine decided to visit the tigers before going to sleep. Thus, he went through Schaffer's garage, proceeded through the utility room, continued through the sun room, and ended up in the back yard. Irvine then approached the wire caging, as he and others had done in the past, placed a couple fingers inside the enclosure, and attempted to pet a male tiger. As he was scratching the male tiger, a female tiger made some commotion, which caused Irvine to look away from the male tiger. At that moment, the male tiger pulled Irvine's arm through the two inch by six inch opening of the wire fence.

Upon hearing Irvine's shouts, Schaffer came out of her house, banged an object against the fence, and freed Irvine. Schaffer immediately drove Irvine to the hospital. Irvine was treated and admitted to the hospital. Later, he was transferred to another hospital, and underwent six surgeries during a thirteen day hospital stay. Further surgeries are indicated though Irvine is uninsured.

On May 30, 1996, Irvine filed a complaint against Schaffer. [He subsequently filed a motion for partial summary judgment on several issues. After denying the majority of the motion, the trial court] granted Irvine's petition to certify three issues for interlocutory appeal: 1) whether incurred risk or other defenses are available in a strict liability animal case; 2) whether Irvine was an invitee as a matter of law; and 3) whether the defense of assumption of risk is available in a noncontractual case. We accepted jurisdiction of the interlocutory appeal.

Discussion and Decision

Irvine first argues that Indiana has historically adhered to strict tort liability in wild animal cases. He further argues that when the Indiana Comparative Fault Act (IND. CODE § 34–4–33–1 *et seq.*, the "Act") was adopted, it did not change the law in wild animal cases. Moreover, he claims that no exceptions to strict liability in wild animal cases have ever been applied in Indiana. He also argues that even if his status is somehow relevant, he was clearly an invitee. Thus, he asserts that the trial court should not have denied his summary judgment on the strict liability issue. In contrast, Schaffer argues that Indiana has not adopted, and should not adopt, strict liability in wild animal cases. In the alternative, Schaffer asserts that if strict liability is the general rule, an exception should apply here.

. . .

I. Liability in a Wild Animal Case

We first address whether strict liability is the common law rule for wild animal cases in Indiana. The parties have not cited and we have not found a case specifically applying strict liability to a true wild animal case in Indiana. However, the basic rule has been frequently stated in various contexts. *Holt v. Myers,* 93 N.E. 31 (Ind. App. 1910) (mentioning wild animal strict liability rule although case dealt with vicious dog); *Gordan v. Kaufman,* 89 N.E. 898 (Ind. App. 1909); *Bostock-Ferari Amusement Co. v. Brocksmith,* 73 N.E. 281 (Ind. App. 1904) (setting out wild animal rule and its rationale, but not applying it because bear's inherent dangerousness was not cause of harm); *Partlow v. Haggarty,* 35 Ind. 178 (1871); *see also Hill v. Rieth–Riley Construction Co.,* 670 N.E.2d 940, 945 (Ind.Ct.App.1996) ("The term 'inherently dangerous' is more properly applied to activities or instrumentalities which are, by their nature, always dangerous, *i.e.,* blasting or wild animals.") Accordingly, we have little difficulty concluding that Indiana's common law recognized the strict liability rule for wild animal cases—despite the fact that previously, Indiana courts have not had the opportunity to apply the rule.

We next address the issue of whether the adoption of the Act changed the common law rule of strict liability in wild animal cases. "We presume the legislature does not intend by the enactment of a statute to make any change in the common law beyond what it declares, either in express terms or by unmistakable implication." *Rocca v. Southern Hills Counseling Center, Inc.,* 671 N.E.2d 913, 920 (Ind.Ct.App.1996). An abrogation of the common law will be implied (1) where a statute is enacted which undertakes to cover the entire subject treated and was clearly designed as a substitute for the common law; or, (2) where the two laws are so repugnant that both in reason may not stand. *Id.* "As a statute in derogation of the existing common law, the Act must be strictly construed." *Indianapolis Power & Light Co. v. Brad Snodgrass, Inc.,* 578 N.E.2d 669, 673 (Ind.1991).

The Act, enacted in 1983 and effective in 1985, "governs any action based on fault[.]" IND. CODE § 34–4–33–1. Strict liability, by definition, is liability without fault. *Black's Law Dictionary* 991 (abridged 6th ed.1991). Thus, the Act would seem to be inapplicable to a strict liability action. The legislative history lends further support for this conclusion. The original version of IND. CODE § 34–4–33–2 provided that "Fault," for purposes of the Act, "include[d] any act or omission that [was] negligent, willful, wanton, reckless, or intentional toward the person or property of others, *or that subject[ed] a person to strict tort liability,* but [did] not include an intentional act. The term also include[d] breach of warranty, unreasonable assumption of risk not constituting an enforceable express consent, incurred risk, misuse of a product for which the defendant otherwise would be liable, and unreasonable failure to avoid injury or to mitigate damages." (Emphasis added).

By the time of its effective date, that same section had been changed to its current form: " '[f]ault' includes any act or omission that is negligent, willful, wanton, reckless, or intentional toward the person or property of others. The term also includes unreasonable assumption of risk not constituting an enforceable express consent, incurred risk, and unreasonable failure to avoid injury or to mitigate damages." IND. CODE § 34–4–33–2. The current form includes no reference to strict liability. Narrowly construing the Act, we conclude that it does not explicitly apply to a strict liability claim. *See Templin v. Fobes,* 617 N.E.2d 541, 544 n. 1 (Ind.1993) (products liability case in which our supreme court noted, "practical problems arise, at least in part, because of the operation of Indiana's Comparative Fault Act, which would apply in Templins' negligence claims against Fobes but not in the Templins' strict liability claim against Rockwood.").

II. Exceptions or Defenses

Having concluded that the Act has not changed common law strict liability in wild animal cases, we next address Irvine's contention that no exceptions to strict liability in wild animal cases have ever been applied in this state. While we agree with Irvine's contention, this fact is of no surprise in view of the lack of any true wild animal cases in Indiana. As this is an issue of first impression, we look to the reason behind the strict liability wild animal rule and consult other sources as necessary.

We have previously set out the rationale for imposing strict liability against owners for injuries caused by an attack by a naturally ferocious or dangerous animal. *See Hardin v. Christy*, 462 N.E.2d 256, 259, 262 (Ind. App.1984) (citing *W. Prosser, Law of Torts* (4th ed. 1971)). Strict liability is appropriately placed:

> upon those who, even with proper care, expose the community to the risk of a very dangerous thing.... The kind of "dangerous animal" that will subject the keeper to strict liability ... must pose some kind of an abnormal risk to the particular community where the animal is kept; hence, the keeper is engaged in an activity that subjects those in the vicinity, including those who come onto his property, to an abnormal risk ... The possessor of a wild animal is strictly liable for physical harm done to the person of another ... if that harm results from a dangerous propensity that is characteristic of wild animals of that class. Thus, strict liability has been imposed on keepers of lions and tigers, bears, elephants, wolves, monkeys, and other similar animals. No member of such a species, however domesticated, can ever be regarded as safe, and liability does not rest upon any experience with the particular animal.

W. Page Keeton et al., Prosser and Keeton on the Law of Torts § 76, at 541–42 (5th ed. 1984). Although having done so in an asbestos case and using slightly different terms, Judge Posner concisely set out the rationale for the wild animal strict liability rule using the following hypothetical:

> [k]eeping a tiger in one's backyard would be an example of an abnormally hazardous activity. The hazard is such, relative to the value of the activity, that we desire not just that the owner take all due care that the tiger not escape, but that he consider seriously the possibility of getting rid of the tiger altogether; and we give him an incentive to consider this course of action by declining to make the exercise of due care a defense to a suit based on an injury caused by the tiger—in other words, by making him strictly liable for any such injury.

G.J. Leasing Co. v. Union Electric Co., 54 F.3d 379, 386 (7th Cir.1995).

With the rationale for the rule in mind, we analyze whether any exceptions or defenses to the strict liability wild animal rule are appropriate. Like the sources previously cited, the *Restatement* provides:

> (1) A possessor of a wild animal is subject to liability to another for harm done by the animal to the other, his person, land or chattels, although the possessor has exercised the utmost care to confine the animal, or otherwise prevent it from doing harm.

> (2) This liability is limited to harm that results from a dangerous propensity that is characteristic of wild animals of the particular class, or of which the possessor knows or has reason to know.

Restatement (Second) of Torts § 507 (1977). However, because the general rule in § 507 is "subject to a number of exceptions and qualifications, which are too numerous to state in a single Section," § 507 should be read together with § 508, § 510, § 511, § 512, § 515, and § 517. *Restatement, supra* cmt. a, § 507. Thus, we look to those other sections to help flesh out the Restatement's rule.

Section 510(a) provides: "The possessor of a wild animal ... is subject to strict liability for the resulting harm, although it would not have occurred but for the unexpectable ... innocent, negligent or reckless conduct of a third person." However, "[a] possessor of land is not subject to strict liability to one who intentionally or negligently trespasses upon the land, for harm done to him by a wild animal ... that the possessor keeps on the land, even though the trespasser has no reason to know that the animal is kept there." *Restatement, supra* § 511. Invitees and licensees are dealt with in § 513, which states: "The possessor of a wild animal ... who keeps it upon land in his possession, is subject to strict liability to persons coming upon the land in the exercise of a privilege whether derived from his consent to their entry or otherwise." Yet, if the invitee or licensee "knows that the dangerous animal is permitted to run at large or has escaped from control they may be barred from recovery if they choose to act upon the possessor's consent or to exercise any other privilege and thus expose themselves to the risk of being harmed by the animal. (*See* § 515)." *Restatement, supra* cmt. a, § 513.

Section 515(2), in turn, provides: "The plaintiff's contributory negligence in knowingly and unreasonably subjecting himself to the risk that a wild animal ... will do harm to his person ... is a defense to the strict liability." Comment c. to § 515(2) explains:

> Although one harmed by a wild ... animal that has escaped from control of its possessor or harborer is not barred from recovery because he has not exercised ordinary care to observe the presence of the animal or to escape from its attack, he is barred if he intentionally and unreasonably subjects himself to the risk of harm by the animal. Thus *one who without any necessity for so doing that is commensurate with the risk involved knowingly puts himself in reach of an animal that is effectively chained or otherwise confined cannot recover against the possessor or harborer of the animal.* So, too, although a licensee or an invitee upon land of another upon which he knows that wild ... animals are kept under the possessor's control does not take the risk that they will escape and harm him, he does nonetheless take the risk of harm by the animals that he knows are roaming at large, so that he will to a reasonable certainty encounter them if he avails himself of the invitation or permission held out to him by the possessor of the land. (Emphasis added).

Comment d. to § 515(2) states: "This kind of contributory negligence, which consists of voluntarily and unreasonably encountering a known danger, is frequently called either contributory negligence or assumption of risk, or both."

Section 515(3) provides: "The plaintiff's assumption of the risk of harm from the animal is a defense to the strict liability." The comment to § 515(3) states that "one employed as a lion tamer in a circus may be barred from recovery by his assumption of the risk when he is clawed by a lion. In the same manner, *one who* voluntarily teases and provokes a chained bear, or *goes within reach of a vicious dog,* is barred from recovery if he does so with knowledge of the danger." (Emphases added).

As indicated by the extensive quotations above, the *Restatement* clearly recognizes exceptions or defenses[3] to wild animal strict liability. *Prosser and Keeton* also agree that defenses are available to a strict liability wild animal claim. "[C]ontributory negligence by way of knowingly and unreasonably subjecting oneself to a risk of harm from an abnormally dangerous animal will constitute a defense" to a strict liability claim. *Prosser and Keeton, supra* § 79, at 565. "Thus, a plaintiff who voluntarily and unreasonably comes within reach of an animal which he knows to be dangerous, . . . has no cause of action when it attacks him." *Id.* at 566; *see also Opelt v. Al. G. Barnes Co.,* 183 P. 241 (Cal.App.1918) (crawling under rope near leopard's cage); *Heidemann v. Wheaton,* 34 N.W.2d 492 (S.D.1948) (going within reach of bear).

Because we agree with the rationale of the exceptions and/or defenses set out in the *Restatement,* and because we find it to be in keeping with Indiana's recent policy regarding allocation of fault, we adopt the *Restatement*'s approach in wild animal cases.

III.   *Genuine Issues of Material Fact*

Finally, we address whether any genuine issues of material fact exist which would support the trial court's partial denial of summary judgment.

A.   *Irvine's Status*

In view of our adoption of the *Restatement*'s strict liability wild animal rule along with its exceptions and defenses, Irvine's status becomes important. In some circumstances, a party's status (as either an invitee, licensee, or trespasser) is a question of fact not determinable at the summary judgment level. [ ] However, where the operative facts are not in dispute, a party's status may be determined as a matter of law by the trial court. [ ]

In arguing that he was an invitee as a matter of law, Irvine relies upon the following evidence:

a) Irvine was invited by Schaffer to come any time (R. 153).

b) Schaffer's affidavit does not deny the above testimony; rather, she claimed that Irvine was specifically not invited by her on the day of the accident (R. 69).

c) Irvine was on the premises 80–100 times (R. 149–50).

d) Bullington testified that Irvine had specifically visited him at least 30 times (R. 218).

e) On several occasions, Irvine had gone through the passageway or breezeway between Schaffer's house and garage and Schaffer voiced no objection (R. 152).

---

3. Although some courts attempt to make distinctions, often times the various defenses are used interchangeably to describe virtually identical conduct. Thus, what one judge or commentator might call incurred risk, another might call assumed risk, or more generally, contributory negligence. To the extent that they recognize similar conduct, we too use the defenses interchangeably in this context.

f) On the day of the accident, Bullington had invited Irvine to stay (R. 227).

g) On December 2, 1995, and before the accident, Schaffer saw Irvine on her premises, chatted with him, and did not ask him to leave (R. 165).

In contrast, Schaffer has introduced her own affidavit which states that Irvine did not have permission to enter her house or the backyard containing the tiger enclosure. (R. 72). Her affidavit also states that Bullington did not have authority to give Irvine permission to enter her home or the backyard containing the tiger enclosure. *Id.* Accordingly, there is some conflicting evidence regarding Irvine's status, thus precluding summary judgment on this issue.

B. Defenses

In adopting the *Restatement*'s view that incurred risk/assumed risk may be a defense to a strict liability wild animal claim, we must next examine whether genuine issues of material fact exist regarding a defense in Irvine's case. Incurred risk requires a mental state of venturousness and a conscious, deliberate and intentional embarkation upon the course of conduct with knowledge of the circumstances. [ ] In other contexts, we have stated that the defense of incurred risk is generally a question of fact, and the party asserting it bears the burden of proving it by a preponderance of evidence. [ ]

Here, the parties designated conflicting evidence regarding whether Irvine knowingly and unreasonably put himself within reach of a wild animal that was effectively chained or otherwise confined. There was evidence that around the time of the accident, Irvine had been volunteering at the Indianapolis Zoo and had been told not to have contact with tigers. Moreover, there was evidence that Irvine was aware of a prior incident wherein the tiger which injured him grabbed another man's thumb. However, there was other evidence tending to indicate that Schaffer and others had petted the tiger safely in the past. Also, there was evidence that Irvine may have been rather intoxicated on the night in question. In view of the conflicting evidence and inferences, summary judgment was properly denied on the issue of whether a defense was appropriate in this case.

Affirmed.

NOTES

(1) Strict liability and its defenses: *Irvine* illustrates the approach courts often take in personal injury cases involving wild animals held in captivity. As recommended by *Prosser* and the *Restatement,* possessors of wild animals are held strictly liable for injuries, *i.e.,* they are held liable without regard for any showing of "fault" such as negligence. As *Irvine* also illustrates, strict liability is not absolute liability. As the court notes, there are various defenses based on factors such as the status of the plaintiff (*e.g.,* trespasser) and the plaintiff's conduct. *E.g., Whitefield v. Stewart,* 577 P.2d 1295 (Okla.1978) (provocation of animal by plaintiff is a defense); *Heidemann v. Wheaton,* 34 N.W.2d 492 (S.D.1948) (*Restatement of*

Torts exceptions applicable); *Mills v. Smith,* 673 P.2d 117 (Kan.App.1983) (statutory defense of comparative fault). How many defenses does the court in *Irvine* identify? On the facts as alleged, is the plaintiff likely to recover on remand?

(2) Wild animals that can be tamed: Should strict liability apply when a wild animal has been tamed and thus is no longer wild? Consider the following excerpt from *Abrevaya v. Palace Theatre & Realty Co.,* involving a performing theater monkey that inexplicably "left his perch" and attacked an infant in the audience:

> The plaintiffs' insistence that the monkey is and cannot be aught else but a wild animal is supported solely by a reference to a professor of law for authority: "A distinction has been made between animals which, by reason of their species, are by nature ferocious, mischievous or intractable, and those of a species normally harmless. In the first category are lions and tigers, bears, elephants, wolves and monkeys, and other similar animals. No individual of such a species, however domesticated, can ever be regarded as safe, and liability does not rest upon any experience with the particular animal. In the second class are cattle, sheep, horses, dogs and cats, and other creatures regarded as usually harmless. As to these, it must be shown that the defendant knew, or had reason to know, of a dangerous propensity in the one animal in question." WILLIAM PROSSER, LAW OF TORTS § 57, at 323 (2d ed. 1953). On the other hand, the defendant urges, with equal vehemence, that, unlike a tiger and a wolf, a monkey is not impervious to being domesticated, and in support of its case, the defendant cites as authority a compendium of the law which states that "an animal, although classed as ferae naturae, is susceptible of substantial domestication, as the bee, deer, and monkey" and that, "the owner is not liable in the absence of proof of negligence in the manner of keeping it, or of proof that it was of a vicious disposition, and was kept after the owner had knowledge thereof." 3 C.J., *Animals,* § 317, at 88; [ ].

> . . .

> It has not been suggested by the plaintiffs in so many words that I take judicial notice of the claimed vicious and refractory habits of the monkey. [ ] But that is what, in substance, its submission on this application comes down to. In any case, were I to assume to endeavor to proceed upon the doctrine of judicial notice, I could not say that the propensities of the monkey are of such "generalized knowledge as are so notorious as not to be the subject of reasonable dispute." Model Code of Evidence, rule 801. No scientific data were presented to support the taking of judicial notice, one way or the other. As I have said, legal authorities alone have been submitted—and they are in disagreement. In my view, judicial notice of such a matter must be bottomed upon more universal acceptance and based upon sterner stuff.

Abrevaya v. Palace Theatre & Realty Co., 197 N.Y.S.2d 27, 29–30 (Sup.Ct. 1960).

Faced with such a requirement, what evidence might the plaintiff introduce so that strict liability applies? Will evidence about monkeys as a group be sufficient? Must the evidence relate to the same species? To the exact animal? For a similar ruling, see *Pate v. Yeager*, 552 S.W.2d 513 (Tex.Civ.App.1977) (monkey that had been family pet for 26 years was "domesticated" so that plaintiff was required to prove "that defendants knew that the animal was accustomed to do mischief, or that the defendants committed acts of negligence").

In *Filburn*, Lord Esher seemed to place the burden on the owner of a non-domesticated and not-universally-recognized-as-safe *species* to establish that the individual animal was not vicious. What is the effect of *Abrevaya*?

(3) Escaped wild animals: Strict liability also applies to wild animals that have escaped and are roaming at large—at least until they have fully regained their liberty and natural habitat. *See Smith v. Jalbert*, 221 N.E.2d 744 (Mass.1966) (zebra on streets of West Springfield, Massachusetts); *Briley v. Mitchell*, 115 So.2d 851 (La.1959) (16–point antlered deer that gored police officer in residential section of city); *Candler v. Smith*, 179 S.E. 395 (Ga.App.1935) (baboon that escaped from zoo and entered private car); *Phillips v. Garner*, 64 So. 735 (Miss.1914) (monkey that entered private home and attacked girl). *See Hays v. Miller*, 43 So. 818 (Ala.1907) (strict liability for harm caused by wolf on chain being taken for walk).

Recall also the following passage from *E.A. Stephens & Co. v. Albers*, 256 P. 15 (Colo.1927) [Chapter 2], which distinguishes the law of property ownership from the law of tort liability in the case of an escape animal:

> It should also be observed that, contrary to the position taken by counsel for plaintiff, liability of the owner of a wild animal which escapes and does damage has no relation to that owner's property right in the animal after escape.... One who captures a rattlesnake and carries it into his neighbor's house, where it bites the neighbor's child, is liable in damages, not because it was his snake, but because he placed a dangerous reptile in a position to injure others. Having paid the damages, he thereby obtains no right of action against another neighbor who the following day killed the same snake in his potato patch, whence it had escaped from its captor. Nor has birth in captivity anything to do with the question. A wild cat may be just as wild if born in a cage as if born on a mountainside.

E.A. Stephens & Co. v. Albers, 256 P. 15 (Colo.1927).

(4) Statutory immunities for landowners: Most states have statutes that limit the liability for personal injuries of landowners who open their land without charge to recreational users. Commonly the statutes provide that there is liability only if the landowner has engaged in intentional or malicious conduct.

Wisconsin's statute includes an additional provision: "no owner and no officer, employe or agent of an owner is liable for any injury to, or any injury caused by, a person engaging in a recreational activity on the owner's property or for any injury resulting from an attack by a wild animal." The Wisconsin Supreme Court has interpreted this provision to eliminate nearly all liability of landowners for wild animals, whether or not in captivity and whether or not the plaintiff is a recreational user of the land. *Hudson v. Janesville Conservation Club,* 484 N.W.2d 132 (Wis.1992) (immunity where injured party was not recreating when injured); *Pichelman v. Barfknecht,* 539 N.W.2d 338 (Wis.App.1995) (immunity applicable to owner of pet raccoon). The ruling creates the anomalous situation that, in Wisconsin, landowners face greater liability for domesticated animals than for captive wild ones.

Brunelle v. Signore

California Court of Appeal.
263 Cal.Rptr. 415 (1989).

■ Per Curiam:—Plaintiff David Brunelle has appealed from a judgment entered following the trial court's granting of defendant's (Anthony Signore's) motion for summary judgment. On appeal, plaintiff contends that the trial court abused its discretion in granting summary judgment in favor of defendant. He argues that the questions of foreseeability and reasonableness of defendant's actions are questions of fact for the jury to decide. After consideration of the factors discussed in *Rowland v. Christian,* 443 P.2d 561 (Cal.1968), we have determined that defendant owed no duty of care to plaintiff to prevent his injury as a result of a spider bite, where (1) as a matter of law, injury to the plaintiff was unforeseeable by defendant, owner of a private residence; (2) the burden to the homeowner of preventing injury would be great; and (3) the task of defining the scope of the duty and the measures required of the homeowners would be extremely difficult. Therefore, we shall affirm the judgment.

FACTS & PROCEDURAL HISTORY

In September 1986, plaintiff spent the weekend at defendant's vacation home in Cathedral City, a structure which abutted the desert. During the weekend, plaintiff was bitten by a Brown Recluse Spider.[1] As a result of the spider bite, plaintiff was severely injured: The venom released by the spider bite destroyed tissue in plaintiff's right foot, his foot was swollen, infected and had ulcerated lesions. Within 24 hours plaintiff was unable to walk or even stand as a result of swelling and intense pain. Because of the severity of his injury, plaintiff was required to take a two-month medical leave from his work. He then returned to work part-time in a wheelchair for almost two months, before resuming work on a full-time basis. Approximately eighteen months after the bite, plaintiff described his foot as being totally fatigued after a day at the office, and stated that dress shoes aggravated his foot and caused swelling and discomfort.

. . .

DISCUSSION

. . .

---

1. The Brown Recluse Spider is a relatively small, tan to brown spider, which, with its legs extended, is approximately the size of a half dollar. It can be easily identified by a violin or fiddle-shaped marking on its back.

In order to maintain an action for negligence, plaintiff must be able to show that: (1) defendant owed a legal duty of care; (2) he breached that duty; and (3) defendant's breach was the proximate or legal cause of plaintiff's injury. [ ] Thus, in order to determine whether the trial court properly granted summary judgment in this case, we must first consider whether defendant owed plaintiff a duty of care to protect plaintiff from or prevent plaintiff's injury as a result of a spider bite in defendant's home.

The general rule in California is that all persons have a duty " 'to use ordinary care to prevent others being injured as a result of their conduct.' [Citations.]" *Rowland v. Christian*, 443 P.2d 561 (Cal.1968); Civ. Code, § 1714; *see Ballard v. Uribe*, 715 P.2d 624 (Cal.1986).

As explained by the California Supreme Court, " 'duty is not an immutable fact of nature', but only an expression of the sum total of those considerations of policy which lead the law to say that the particular plaintiff is entitled to protection." *Ballard v. Uribe*, 715 P.2d 624, citations omitted. Whether a duty of care exists "is a question of law to be determined on a case-by-case basis." *Isaacs v. Huntington Memorial Hospital*, 695 P.2d 653 (Cal.1985).

In making its determination, the court must weigh several factors: "[T]he foreseeability of harm to the plaintiff, the degree of certainty that the plaintiff suffered injury, the closeness of the connection between the defendant's conduct and the injury suffered, the moral blame attached to the defendant's conduct, the policy of preventing future harm, the extent of the burden to the defendant and consequences to the community of imposing a duty to exercise care with resulting liability for breach, and the availability, cost, and prevalence of insurance for the risk involved. [Citations.]" *Rowland v. Christian*, 443 P.2d 561; *Isaacs v. Huntington Memorial Hospital*, 695 P.2d 653.

Plaintiff has not cited nor has our research revealed any California case that discusses the issue of whether an owner or occupier of a residence, a business or a hotel/motel may be held liable for plaintiff's injury as a result of an insect or spider bite sustained on the premises. Our research has also failed to reveal any case in any jurisdiction within the United States in which an owner or occupier of a private residence was held liable for injuries sustained as a result of an insect or spider bite. In addition, we note that the very few out-of-state cases which have considered the issue of whether a owner of a business or a hotel/motel may be held liable for injury sustained as a result of an insect bite have split on the issue. [citations and discussion omitted]

Our consideration of the *Rowland* factors leads us to the conclusion in this case that a owner or occupier of a private residence does not have a duty to protect or prevent bites from harmful insects where: (1) it is not generally known that the specific insect is indigenous to the area; (2) the homeowner has no knowledge that a specific harmful insect is prevalent in the area where his residence is located; (3) the homeowner has on no occasion seen the specific type of harmful insect either outside or inside his home; and (4) neither the homeowner nor the injured guest has seen the specific insect that bit the guest either before or after the bite occurred. To impose a duty under these circumstances, where the owner or occupier of the premises had no reason to anticipate or guard against such an occurrence would be unfair and against public policy. Imposition of a duty even in those cases where the homeowner shared general knowledge with the public at large that a specific harmful insect was prevalent in the area but the homeowner had not seen the specific harmful insect either outside or inside his home would impose a duty on the owner or occupier of the premises that would also be unfair and against public policy.[5] In either of these instances, the burden on the landowner would be enormous and would border on establishing an absolute liability. Further, the task of defining the duty and the measures required of the owner or occupier of private residences to meet that duty would be difficult in the extreme.

Plaintiff argues that defendant had knowledge there were other dangerous insects, *i.e.*, black widow spiders and scorpions, on his property and thus should have taken precautions and/or warned plaintiff against the danger. This argument is not persuasive.

Here plaintiff urges imposition of a duty because defendant had general knowledge of the prevalence of other harmful insects around his home and also urges that defendant had a duty to use a professional exterminator and/or exterminate his house himself "more frequently" and also to hire a professional cleaning person or persons to clean defendant's home when he [defendant] was not in residence. However, that foreseeability which an owner or occupier of a residence shares with the public at large does not, *per se*, impose a duty on such owner or occupier to procure professional exterminators and/or cleaning crews to "de-bug" his residence, inside and out, on a periodic basis. An owner or occupier of property is not an insurer of the safety of persons on the premises. [ ] His responsibility is not absolute, or based on a duty to keep the premises absolutely safe. [ ] The law does not impose a duty of extraordinary care.

For the reasons stated, we conclude that defendant, as a matter of law, had no duty to protect against the risk that plaintiff would sustain injury as a result of a spider bite.

The judgment is affirmed.

NOTES

(1) Native wild animals at large: *Brunelle* represents the principal approach toward liability for unconfined native wild animals that are

---

5. In addition, there is some support for the conclusion that a landowner has no duty to protect against attacks by indigenous animals or insects. As noted by the Court of Appeals of Georgia " 'Generally, the law does not require the owner or possessor of land to anticipate [the] presence of, or guard [an] invitee against harm from animals *feræ naturæ*.' [Citations.]" *Williams v. Gibbs,* 182 S.E.2d 164, 165 (Ga.App.1971). Although there are no California cases which consider the issue, we note that the *Restatement Second of Torts* provides that an owner or occupier of land is not normally liable for injury to others as a result of an attack by wild animal indigenous to the area, even where the owner or occupier kept the animal and it later escaped. *Rest. 2d Torts,* § 508 [keeper of wild animal has no duty for injury of wild animal attack where animal breaks free from confinement, if animal indigenous to the area]; *see also Palumbo v. Game & Fresh Water Fish Com'n,* 487 So.2d 352 (Fla.App. 1986) [the court held that summary judgment was proper, stating that an owner or possessor of land is not liable for injury from wild animals [alligators] where he had not reduced the animal to possession before the attack and the animal was indigenous to the area].

present on private land. In such circumstances, landowner liability is based on negligence, chiefly the failure to warn of hidden dangers. In practice, this standard is often hard to satisfy, and it is difficult to find decisions in which landowners have been found liable for negligence. This may reflect a strong sense that landowners should rarely be liable for unpredictable natural conditions on their lands and the courts' disinclination to encourage landowners to exterminate native wildlife in an effort to make the outdoors safe. In addition to the decisions cited in note 5 of *Brunelle*, see *Robison v. Gantt*, 673 So.2d 441 (Ala.Civ.App.1995) (water moccasin at swimming pool); *Williams v. Gibbs*, 182 S.E.2d 164 (Ga.App.1971) (plaintiff was injured when she fell as she ran to get away from a rattlesnake that emerged from the grass beside her); *Nicholson v. Smith*, 986 S.W.2d 54 (Tex.App.1999) (plaintiff, a business invitee, is stung more than 1,000 times by fire ants and dies); *Overstreet v. Gibson Product Co.*, 558 S.W.2d 58 (Tex.Civ.App.1977) (plaintiff was bitten by a rattlesnake while shopping for groceries in defendant's store). Perhaps the most common case involves a rat bite. *See, e.g., DeLuce v. Fort Wayne Hotel*, 311 F.2d 853 (6th Cir.1962); *Williams v. Milner Hotels Co.*, 36 A.2d 20 (Conn.1944); *Harvey v. Hammer*, 249 N.Y.S.2d 1012 (Sup.Ct.1964).

SECTION 2.   LIABILITY FOR PROPERTY DAMAGE

a.   THE ENGLISH COMMON-LAW BACKGROUND

Boulston's Case

Kings Bench.
5 Co. Rep. 104b, 77 Eng. Rep. 216 (1597).
Cro. Eliz. 547, 78 Eng. Rep. 794 (1597).

Between Boulston and Hardy it was adjudged in the Common Pleas, that is a man makes coney-boroughs in his own land, which increase in so great number that they destroy his neighbours' land next adjoining, his neighbours cannot have an action on the case against him who makes the said coney-boroughs; for so soon as the coneys come on his neighbour's land he may kill them for they are *feræ naturæ,* and he who makes the coney-boroughs has no property in them, and he shall not be punished for the damage which the coneys do in which he has no property, and which the other may lawfully kill. [This cause is not like the cases put . . . of erecting lime-kiln, dye-houses, or the like; for there the annoyance is by the act of the parties who make them; but it is not so here, for the conies of themselves went onto plaintiff's land, and he might take them when they came upon his land, and make profit of them. . . . And [again:] this case is not like to other cases which were put of nuisances; for there the tort is by the party himself who doth it; but here the putting the conies into his own land is not any tort, and if there be any wrong it is by the conies themselves, who are *feræ naturæ.*]

NOTES

(1) Is *Boulston* consistent with *May v. Burdett*? Recall that in *May v. Burdett*, the court held that a person who keeps a wild animal "was bound to keep it secure at all events." Why is someone liable for a monkey that runs at large and bites a person but not for animals that leave his land to destroy his neighbor's crops? Why are property classifications relevant to one but not the other?

Recall also *Mitchil v. Alestree* [discussed in the notes following *May*]. The court in *Mitchil* argued that, "If one hath kept a tame fox, which gets loose and grows wild, he that kept him before shall not answer for the damage the fox doth after he hath lost him, and he hath resumed his wild nature." Should it make any difference if the species was not indigenous to the area? Rabbits were not indigenous to England, having been introduced to the island in the 11th or 12th century. Should it make any difference whether defendant himself introduced the nonindigenous animal? Should it make a difference whether the nonindigenous animal had been present for so long that "the mind of man runneth not to the contrary"?

(2) Why is the creation of a coney-warren different than the construction of a lime-kiln? A lime-kiln will foreseeably put out noxious vapors—and thus is a nuisance. Coneys that are not effectively confined within the warren will also foreseeably leave the land in search of food. Why is this not also a nuisance? Is there some relevant difference between the two?

Can the "independent agency" of the coneys—note the court's statement that "if there be any wrong it is by the conies themselves"—shield the person who introduces them from liability? Such an idea seems atavistic at best. *See* OLIVER WENDELL HOLMES, THE COMMON LAW 18–24 (Boston: 1881) (discussing early law holding animals and inanimate objects liable for injuries they "caused").

The court adopts an extremely restricted view of causation and foreseeability—one that is unlikely to be accepted by a modern court.

PERSPECTIVES

Rabbits and the question of introduced ("exotic") species: The coney, or, as it is now known, the rabbit (*Oryctolagus cuniculus*), was not indigenous to England. The species was initially introduced into England and Scotland from Spain, apparently in the late eleventh or early twelfth century.

The rabbit was ill-suited to the cold and wet English countryside and initially the species fared poorly. Establishing warrens[1] in which the species could survive was a costly and labor-intensive process. Most often, substantial amounts of earth would be piled into mounds for the rabbits to burrow into; the initial borrows for the animals often had to be dug by hand.

---

1. The early term was coneygarth, conyger, or conigree, "which were contractions or corruptions of the two words, coneys and earth." JOHN SHEAIL, RABBITS AND THEIR HISTORY

18. The current term—"warren"—initially referred to the franchise to hunt a group of animals that included both hares and rabbits.

Despite the difficulties, the species gradually evolved to survive the English weather and by the sixteenth century it was common.

Rabbits were prized as a source of both fur and fresh meat, which was scarce. In addition, they were a source of sport, being coursed by greyhounds and shot by hunters. Once a warren was established, rabbits were a source of substantial profit. One commentator in the 1650s calculated that "one acre of good land rightly ordered and well stockt" would produce an income of 20 and a profit of 18—which was a greater profit than any other livestock would provide. John Sheail, *Rabbits and Agriculture in Post–Medieval England*, 4 J. HIST. GEOGRAPHY 343, 347 (1978). As a result of such economics, many manors allocated substantial acreage to rabbit warrens. The economic significance of rabbits began to decline in the mid-eighteenth century as British agriculture went through a revolutionary transition to new crops, rotations, and technologies. By 1800, grain prices had risen to the point that warrens were being torn out so that land could be plowed.

In his history of the English countryside, Oliver Rackham noted,

> The rabbit was one of the most successful farming innovations; its commercial decline is part of the modern fashion for concentrating on only a few crops. Its history illustrates Darwinian evolution. The changes from the tender, expensive animal of the twelfth century to the self-reliant rabbit of the eighteenth and the ubiquitous pest of the nineteenth are almost certainly due to genetic change and adaptation to our climate. Since 1953, the terrible selection imposed by disease[2] has produced a different rabbit again, a tough and unsociable animal which lives on the surface and so does not infect its colleagues. The rabbits outside my college windows are solitary and survive the Cambridge winters without burrows.

OLIVER RACKHAM, THE HISTORY OF THE COUNTRYSIDE 48 (1986). *See generally* JOHN SHEAIL, RABBITS AND THEIR HISTORY (1971); Harry V. Thompson, *The Rabbit in Britain, in* THE EUROPEAN RABBIT 64–107 (Harry V. Thompson & Carolyn M. King eds. 1994); ELSPETH M. VEALE, THE ENGLISH FUR TRADE IN THE LATER MIDDLE AGES (1966); Elspeth M. Veale, *The Rabbit in England*, 5 AG. HIST. REV. 85 (1957).

b. PROPERTY DAMAGE IN THE NEW WORLD

King v. Blue Mountain Forest Association

New Hampshire Supreme Court.
123 A.2d 151 (1956).

■ KENISON, C.J.:—This case poses the problem as to what remedies exist in this state by statute or at common law for damage to property allegedly caused by wild animals. The four counts in each declaration present different grounds of liability but certain historical background is common to all counts.

---

2. [In 1953–1954, some 99% of the rabbit population in Britain was killed when   myxomatosis was introduced into the country from France.]

The defendant corporation was organized in 1891 by Austin Corbin, "under chapter 152 of the General Laws, for the purpose of enabling him to conveniently manage the park owned by him, consisting of about 25,000 acres of land, including Croydon and Grantham mountains, all fenced and stocked with wild animals, located in the towns of Newport, Cornish, Croydon, and Grantham, in establishing and maintaining which he expended in the vicinity of $500,000." [ ] Included among the animals imported into Corbin park were Prussian wild boar from the Black Forest of Germany. [ ] Generally the boar could survive the climate of this state only if fed in the winter. [ ] By special act of the Legislature the defendant was given special game privileges within the park upon the erection of a fence enclosing the entire area. Laws 1895, c. 258; [ ] Section 1 of that statute provided that "all fish, birds, and game of, in, or upon" the park "shall be the property" of the defendant, its successors or assigns. The Blue Mountain Forest Association is the only one to have imported wild boar into the northeastern part of the United States and they are not indigenous to the North American continent. According to Champollion, [*Blue Mountain Forest and Its Animals*] 61, "It is in looking for worms and roots that the boar tears up the ground with his snout. At the time when the boar were most numerous in the forest, there was hardly an acre in the open, that had not somewhere been rooted up or the grass trampled down by the boar." Champollion fixes the life span of the boar at 20 to 30 years, so that those boar presently inhabiting the Forest must be of the fourth or fifth generation of the animals originally imported into Corbin Park.

Beginning in 1938, and thereafter from time to time, some boar escaped from the park. It is alleged that the escaped boar and their progeny, bred and born during the period of their escape, caused damage to the plaintiffs' lands and crops, which damage was characteristic of wild boar as a class and normally expected of them if at large. It is also alleged that several years prior to the trespasses in September 1954, the boar and their progeny had from time to time passed back and forth from the defendant's park on to land of others, through holes in the fenced enclosure and that the boar habitually returned to defendant's enclosure for the winter or at seasons of food shortage to be fed or cared for by the defendant.

I. The first count in the declaration is in trespass predicated on the common-law liability of an owner or possessor for trespass to real estate by his livestock. [ ] At an early date it was firmly established in this state that the owner or possessor of livestock was liable for such trespass irrespective of negligence. [ ] . . . .

If a farmer who owns or possesses contented cows is held to strict liability for trespass to real estate it would be a strange doctrine that would not impose at least the same liability upon the owner of battering boar which were imported into the state for the purposes of exclusive and private hunting. Whether the damage to the plaintiffs' real estate was caused by a wild boar that escaped or by its progeny born after its escape, which also belonged to the defendant, Laws 1895, c. 258, is not determinative of its liability for trespass. Winfield on Tort (6th ed. 1954) p. 646, states that there is no English decision on the duration of an owner's liability but suggests that if the wild animal is not indigenous it should continue until some one assumes permanent control of it. [ ] The present situation has some parallel to *Brackett v. Bellows Falls Hydro–Electric Corporation,* 87 N.H. 173, 175 A. 822, where the defendant was held liable for trespass by flooding the plaintiff's land and the damages were increased by the breeding of muskrats thereon even though this may not have been strictly foreseeable. We conclude that the demurrer to the first count in the plaintiffs' declaration should be overruled.

II. The fourth count of the declaration is in case[1] but alleges no negligence. It is predicated on the theory that the possessor of wild animals is held to a standard of strict liability. It is conceded that there is no case in this jurisdiction imposing strict liability for damage to persons or property by escaped wild animals but it is urged that a rule should be adopted in this state following the *Restatement of Torts,* section 507, which reads as follows:

> Except as stated in §§ 508, 517, a possessor of a wild animal is subject to liability to others, except trespassers on his land, for such harm done by the animal to their persons, lands or chattels as results from a dangerous propensity which is characteristic of wild animals of its class or of which the possessor has reason to know, although he has exercised the utmost care to confine the animal or otherwise prevent it from doing harm.

Section 508 relates to indigenous wild animals after their escape and section 517 relates to wild animals kept in pursuance of a public duty, neither of which sections are applicable to this case.

It is true that strict liability for the keeping of dangerous wild animals is supported by a large number of jurisdictions and that the English courts have regarded this liability as a mere phase and specific application of the rule in *Rylands v. Fletcher,* (1868) LR 3 HL 330. *See* WILLIAM PROSSER, SELECTED TOPICS IN THE LAW OF TORTS 159, 160 (1953); [ ]. However some recent cases have shown a tendency to impose liability only for negligence. *Vaughan v. Miller Bros. "101" Ranch Wild West Show,* 109 W.Va. 170, 153 S.E. 289; *Panorama Resort v. Nichols,* 165 Va. 289, 182 S.E. 235. While some of the older text writers have summarized the law in favor of strict liability, [ ], it is significant that the most recent definitive treatise has criticized the rule of strict liability as it prevails in England. [ ] Likewise it has been pointed out in a careful analysis that many of the cases which have been decided on the basis of strict liability could have been decided on the basis of negligence. Mary Coate McNeely, *A Footnote on Dangerous Animals,* 37 MICH. L. REV. 1181 (1939).

An examination of the cases in this state definitely indicate a clear tendency to limit strict liability to those cases where the Legislature has provided for it, [ ], or to those situations where the common law of the state has imposed such liability and the Legislature has not seen fit to change

---

1. [That is, an "action on the case" or, more fully, "trespass on the case"; here, it is an action seeking relief for an interference with property rights that occurs in a manner that is not direct, physical, and immediate. *See* "Case," 1 BOUVIER'S LAW DICTIONARY 288–89 (Rawle's ed., Boston, 1897).]

it.... In view of the consistent policy evidenced by an unbroken line of decisions in this state which, with the exception of cases of cattle trespass to real estate, impose liability at common law for negligence only, we do not now adopt a rule of absolute liability for injuries to persons and property caused by wild animals, as a general principle of law. The demurrer to the fourth count of the declaration should be sustained.

III. The third count in the declaration is an action of trespass based on the statute, RSA 467:3–6. This statute which was Laws 1949, c. 294, an act relating to the extermination of wild boar in the counties of Sullivan and Grafton, reads as follows: [the statute recited the history of the introduction of wild boar into the state, how they had escaped and were now running at large. It declared them to be a public nuisance and required the owner to destroy all such wild boar before April 1, 1950; after that date anyone suffering injuries from the boar could recover her losses through a trespass action against the owner of the boar.]

.... This is not a retrospective law which is prohibited by Part I, Article 23rd of the New Hampshire Constitution. The police power of the state to control matters which are or may be considered nuisances is extremely broad. "The instances are numerous in which acts and things not nuisances at common law, and in themselves harmless and inoffensive, or even beneficial, and only liable to become offensive to the public health or comfort by improper use, have been, by statute, declared nuisances. Such legislation, whenever brought in question, has been sustained by the courts." [ ]

We do not know the number of wild boar that have escaped from Corbin Park or the number presently at large. The statute is not unconstitutional merely because the problem might have been solved by the state paying bounties for the capture of wild boar. Nor is the statute unconstitutional merely because a different remedy could have been devised such as directing the Fish & Game Department to kill wild boar as was done in the case of elk in the same general area to avoid "a potential threat to agriculture [sic] interests." Laws 1955, c. 43. The Legislature has decided that the defendant's actions, although originally lawful and authorized, have now disturbed the equilibrium of a section of the state and that the defendant is the responsible cause so that it should have the burden of correcting the situation. Contrary to the views of many jurisdictions we do not as a matter of judicial policy impose absolute liability for damage by wild animals. [ ] However, we cannot say that the state is powerless to adopt the view of absolute liability for damage by wild boar as a legislative policy. The statute, RSA 467:3–6, is constitutional and the demurrer to the third count in the declaration should be overruled.

IV. The second count in the plaintiffs' declaration is in trespass predicated on the theory that the wild boar are "reclaimed" wild animals for whose acts the defendant is responsible. Reliance is placed on the Irish case of *Brady v. Warren,* [1909] 2 Ir. Rep. 632, where the defendant was held liable for damage to adjoining property caused by a herd of deer which the defendant kept in an enclosure which had fallen in disrepair, so that the deer passed in and out of the enclosure. However, in that case the deer were tame and it is not authority for holding that boar which are both wild and dangerous, [ ], and to which title is not lost by their escape, are in the class of reclaimed animals. [ ] The demurrer to the second count of the declaration should be sustained.

The plaintiffs' declaration states a cause of action for trespass to real estate and for trespass under the statute. The demurrer to counts one and three should be overruled and to counts two and four should be sustained.

Remanded.

NOTES

(1) What role did the 1895 statute's declaration that "all fish, birds, and game of, in, or upon" the park "shall be the property" of the Association play in the decision? Could Counts 1 (trespass of livestock) and 2 (the animals had been "reclaimed") have been decided as they were in the absence of the statute? Did the statute merely recognize a property right that existed independently under the common law?

Is the court's treatment of Counts 1 (trespass of livestock) and 4 (strict liability for trespass of wild animals) consistent? Does the court offer a satisfactory distinction for its differing results? Are there, as implemented, any meaningful distinctions between these two actions since neither requires a showing of negligence?

(2) Recall the decision in *Barrett v. State,* 116 N.E. 99 (N.Y.1917), holding that the state was not liable for damages caused by beaver that it had reintroduced. Is *Barrett* distinguishable from *Blue Mountain*?

(3) Exotic vs. indigenous: Did the court's holding depend, more than it acknowledged, on the fact that the boars were an exotic species? That is, would the court have extended liability as far as it did if the animals were native to the area and, upon escaping, had mingled with existing populations of the same species? Note that, in discussing Count 1, suggested that "if the wild animal is not indigenous [the owner's liability] should continue until some one assumes permanent control of it." Note also, that the court seems willing to include within this rule the offspring of nonindigenous animals.

William Prosser argued that strict liability for damage caused by wild animals arises out of the abnormal nature of the risk. *William L. Prosser, Handbook of the Law of Torts* § 75 (3d ed. 1964). An exotic species is by definition an unusual risk in the community. In *King v. Blue Mountain Forest Association,* it was the Association that introduced wild boar into the forest and imposed a risk on the community that had not previously existed.

(4) *Andrews v. Andrews*: In *Andrews,* defendant excavated springs on his land to create a three-or four-acre pond and took steps to attract geese by scattering feed and placing "lame wild geese" on his land. Within two years, the pond was a winter home for some 3000 geese. The geese fed on plaintiff's adjacent land, destroying his crops and fields. Plaintiffs alleged that "defendant knew or should have known, before constructing the said pond at the location stated, placing lame wild geese thereon and bait thereon, that large numbers of wild geese would be attracted to the plaintiff's fields and destroy plaintiff's crops." The North Carolina Supreme Court sustained the complaint:

> While careful search fails to reveal a case based on similar facts, the application of well-established legal principles offers some help in pointing the way to a solution of the legal problem presented. The plaintiffs call to their aid an ancient maxim handed down to us from the time when Latin was the language of the courts: *Sic utere tuo ut alienum non laedas,* (to use your own so that you do not injure another). The law makes it a private nuisance when one by an improper use of his property does injury to the land, property, or rights of another. [ ]

> The plaintiff's cause of action is grounded in that field of tort liability designated as private nuisance. Private nuisance may be *per se* or *per accidens.* A private nuisance *per se* (by itself) or at law, is an act, occupation, or structure which is a nuisance at all times and under any circumstances, regardless of location or surroundings. A private nuisance *per accidens,* or, in fact, becomes a nuisance by reason of its location or the manner in which it is constructed, or maintained, or operated. [ ]

> The defendant . . . contends the complaint is insufficient by reason of the fact that negligence neither in the construction of the pond nor in the manner in which it is maintained and operated is alleged. The argument ignores the fact that negligence and nuisance are separate fields of tort liability. While the same act or ownership may constitute negligence and at the same time become a nuisance *per accidens,* and be practically inseparable, yet the latter may be created, or maintained, or operated without negligence.

> .   .   .

> We conclude the plaintiffs' complaint, when liberally construed, states a cause of action for nuisance *per accidens,* or in fact. Whether they can offer proof to support the allegations of the complaint will present a problem for another day and another tribunal.

One justice dissented:

> The general rule is, there is no individual property in wild animals, geese or fish so long as they remain wild, unconfined, and in a state of nature. [ ]

> The doctrine of liability attaching to one who owns or keeps insecurely confined on his premises wild animals causing injury has no application to the facts here. . . .

> *Sickman v. United States,* 184 F.2d 616, 618 (7th Cir.), *cert. denied,* 342 U.S. 843 (1950), is a case with strikingly similar facts, and was brought under the Federal Torts Claims Act, [ ], to recover $26,500 alleged damages to crops of corn and soybeans claimed to have been destroyed in 1946 and 1947 by migratory waterfowl, principally Canada geese. The Court said: " * * * a private person could not be held liable for the trespasses of animals which are *feræ naturæ,* and which have not been reduced to possession, but which exist in a state

of nature. The United States, considered as a private person, did not have any ownership, control or possession of these wild geese which imposed liability for their trespasses."

Andrews v. Andrews, 88 S.E.2d 88 (N.C.1955). Is the court's approach in *Andrews* more realistic than that of the court in *Boulston*?

SECTION 3. GOVERNMENTAL LIABILITY

NOTES

Property damage—torts and takings: Chapter 3 examined the reluctance of courts to hold governmental entities liable for damage to real property caused by wild animals—despite legal doctrines asserting that the state "owns" wildlife. Landowners such as the plaintiff in *Barrett v. State,* 116 N.E. 99 (N.Y.1917) [Chapter 3], who sought to recover for the trees destroyed by the beaver, have unsuccessfully brought tort claims. *See also Sickman v. United States*, 184 F.2d 616 (7th Cir.1950), *cert. denied,* 341 U.S. 939 (1951) (no liability under the Federal Tort Claims Act for damage done to crops by geese protected by the Migratory Bird Treaty Act); *Leger v. Louisiana Department of Wildlife & Fisheries*, 306 So.2d 391 (La.Ct. App.), *writ of review denied,* 310 So.2d 640 (La.1975) (because wildlife is regulated by the state in its sovereign, as distinct from its proprietary capacity, the state has no duty to control its movements or prevent it from damaging private property). Sovereign immunity often bars such claims without regard to their substantive merit.

Other plaintiffs have brought actions alleging that government wildlife-conservation programs are an unconstitutional taking of property without payment of just compensation. This claim arises in a variety of contexts: the ranchers in *Moerman v. State*, 21 Cal.Rptr.2d 329 (Cal.App. 1993), *cert. denied sub nom. Moerman v. California*, 511 U.S. 1031 (1994), who sought compensation for destruction of fences and forage caused by reintroduced elk; the rancher *Clajon Production Corp. v. Petera*, 70 F.3d 1566, 1575 (10th Cir.1995) [Chapter 3]), that claimed the state had taken his right to hunt game found on his land; and the developer in *Good v. United States*, 189 F.3d 1355 (Fed.Cir.1999), who argued that the presence of an endangered species denied him the most economically advantageous use of his land. These regulatory taking claims are examine in Chapter VI.

Owners of personal property enjoy no greater likelihood of success. *See, e.g., Molohon v. United States*, 206 F.Supp. 388 (D.Mont.1962) (owner of hunting dog that died after ingesting poison placed in a horse carcass as bait for predators failed to prove negligence); *Parker Land & Cattle Co. v. United States*, 796 F.Supp. 477 (D.Wyo.1992) (rancher failed to prove that his cattle had been infected with brucellosis from wild elk).

The following materials examine a related issue: when is a government liable for publicly owned wildlife that causes personal injuries.

Carlson v. State

Supreme Court of Alaska.
598 P.2d 969 (1979).

■ BURKE, J.:—This case involves a bear attack. The issue is whether the State of Alaska may be held liable for personal injuries inflicted by a bear, when the bear is attracted to the site of the attack by garbage that had accumulated on state-owned property. The superior court granted summary judgment in favor of the State on the ground that the State was immune from liability under the Alaska Tort Claims Act, AS 09.50.250. We conclude that the State was not immune under the Act and that, depending on the facts to be established, the State may be liable for personal injuries resulting from the attack. We therefore reverse the decision of the superior court and remand the case for further proceedings.

I. Facts

On the evening of October 22, 1975, appellant Julie Carlson was attacked and mauled by a bear at the Robe River turnout at Mile 2 of the Richardson Highway near Valdez. The Robe River turnout is a state-owned roadside area built and designed for tourist use. It was equipped with six to ten fifty-five gallon drums, without lids, for use as litter barrels. The Carlsons lived in a camper which had been removed from their pick-up and placed on the ground in a rented space. They had lived there for about six months. Every day the Carlsons drove the pick-up truck from the camper space and parked it at the Robe River turnout. From there they rode a bus into town. The turnout was the closest available parking area to the bus stop. In the mornings the turnout was usually full of cars belonging to people who caught the bus, but in the evenings, by the time the Carlsons returned from town, there were usually only one or two cars there. The State and the City of Valdez were apparently aware that the turnout was used for such parking.

On the day of the attack, the Carlsons had had to park some distance from the road, next to the litter barrels. The barrels were running over, and garbage and trash were scattered around on the ground. The attack occurred as the Carlsons were walking to their pick-up truck from the bus-stop in the evening. As they crossed the turnout toward their truck, a bear appeared. It threw James into the woods then attacked Julie. Julie was severely wounded, suffering a broken leg and lacerations on her back, and it appears that she now may be suffering permanent partial disability.

The Carlsons filed a suit for damages against the State of Alaska. Their basic contention was that the State was negligent in allowing garbage to accumulate at the turnout, since it knew that there were bears in the area, and it knew or should have known that garbage would attract bears and pose a danger to people who used the turnout. They also alleged that the State was negligent in failing either to warn users of the turnout of the danger of bears or to fence the area to keep bears out or to take other measures to protect the users of the turnout. The State pled as affirmative defenses (1) that Julie Carlson was comparatively negligent and (2) that the State was protected by sovereign immunity.

The superior court granted the State's motion for summary judgment. The court had before it undisputed evidence that it was the State's normal practice to cease all litter barrel pick-up at roadside turnouts around October 1 and that pick-ups at the Robe River turnout had been discontinued around October 1, 1975, in accordance with that practice. The court reasoned that the State's decision regarding maintenance of highway turnout areas was a discretionary function for which the State was immune from suit under AS 09.50.250(1). Following denial of their motion for reconsideration, the Carlsons filed this appeal.

II. Discretionary Act Exception

The first issue that we address is whether, on the undisputed facts of this case, the State was entitled to summary judgment as a matter of law. [ ]

The evidence which was before the trial court pertaining to the State's decision not to pick up trash at the Robe River turnout established the following facts: The State had entered into an agreement with the City of Valdez under which the City agreed to service the litter barrels at five locations, including the Robe River turnout. For this service the State agreed to pay the City one hundred fifty dollars per month for two pick-ups per week at each location. This agreement, however, terminated October 1, 1975, apparently in accordance with the State's normal practice....

The standards for applying the discretionary act exception of the Alaska Tort Claims Act have been extensively discussed in three cases: *Jennings v. State,* 566 P.2d 1304 (Alaska 1977); *State v. I'Anson,* 529 P.2d 188 (Alaska 1974); *State v. Abbott,* 498 P.2d 712 (Alaska 1972). In those cases we adopted and reaffirmed the planning-operational test, under which decisions that rise to the level of planning or policy-making are considered discretionary acts which do not give rise to tort liability, while decisions that are merely operational in nature are not considered to be discretionary acts and therefore are not immune from liability. *See, e.g., State v. I'Anson,* 529 P.2d at 193.

The distinction between planning decisions and operational decisions does not depend merely on *who* made the decision. Rather the distinction is based on the *type* of decision that is being made, examined "within an analytical framework which is sensitive to the policies underlying the discretionary function or duty exception." *Id.* The reason for preserving sovereign immunity for certain acts of the State is the necessity for judicial abstention in certain policy-making areas that have been committed to other branches of government. *Id.* In *I'Anson,* for example, we held that the State's failure to properly mark and stripe a portion of a highway at a campground entrance did *not* come within the discretionary act exception because "functions of this nature do not involve broad basic policy decisions which come within the 'planning' category of decisions which are expressly entrusted to a coordinate branch of government." *Id.* at 193–94. Similarly, in *Abbott* we held that the State's failure to maintain a highway adequately in the winter was *not* within the exception because decisions on how to maintain a highway "simply do not rise to the level of governmental policy decisions calling for judicial restraint." 498 P.2d at 722 (footnote omitted). We recognized that the initial decision whether to maintain highways in the winter at all is a policy determination but held that the subsequent decisions on how that policy was to be carried out were *operational* decisions, aimed at implementing the *policy* decision. *Id.*

We believe that the reasoning in *Abbott* is controlling here. The State's decision on the broad question of whether to maintain highway turnouts in the winter at all is indeed a policy determination that cannot give rise to tort liability. However, the decisions made pursuant to that policy, on how to implement it that is, decisions on how to *cease* maintenance are operational decisions. As to these the State is under a duty to act with reasonable care. Thus, for example, a decision not to remove the litter barrels from the turnout after October 1 when trash pick-up was discontinued was an operational decision, not a policy decision. If the State negligently implemented the decision to cease trash pick-up at the Robe River turnout, the discretionary act exception to the waiver of sovereign immunity does not shield the State from liability. We therefore reverse the decision of the superior court.

III. Another Possible Ground for Affirming Judgment

. . .

The ground urged by the State in support of its motion for summary judgment, both in the superior court and on appeal to this court, was stated as follows:

> It is clear that the only basis for a cause of action against the state of Alaska must come from a duty flowing from its inherent possession or control of all wild animals within its dominion, and for its failure to properly control such animals. However, liability for animals *feræ naturæ* has never been recognized unless, somehow, those animals have been reduced to the possession of a particular person or agency.

The State's statement of the law is probably correct, but it is inapplicable to this case. The State appears to have misconstrued the basis for the Carlsons' allegation of negligence. The Carlsons do not contend that the State was liable simply because of its "inherent possession or control" of wild animals; their theory of negligence is that the State created a dangerous situation, that it knew the situation was dangerous, and that it failed either to correct the situation or to warn people of the danger. The State's conceded lack of control over the attacking bear, therefore, provides no basis for affirming judgment in favor of the State.

IV. State's Liability for Damage Caused by Wild Animals

Since the State's conduct in this case is not within the discretionary act exception to the waiver of sovereign immunity in the Alaska Tort Claims Act, it is subject to review under the "ordinary principles of negligence." *See Webb v. City and Borough of Sitka,* 561 P.2d 731, 733 & n. 9 (Alaska 1977). In *Webb* we adopted the following rule:

> A landowner or owner of other property must act as a reasonable person in maintaining his property in a reasonably safe condition in view of all the circumstances, including the likelihood of injury to

others, the seriousness of the injury, and the burden on the respective parties of avoiding the risk.

Id. at 733 (footnote omitted). Whether particular conduct is reasonable under the circumstances is generally considered a question of fact for the jury. It is therefore ordinarily not an appropriate issue for determination on a motion for summary judgment. *Id.* at 735. Since the case at bar also presents several unresolved questions of fact,[7] it is particularly necessary that it be submitted to a jury for determination.

There is a surprising dearth of case law not only in Alaska but also in other states and in the federal courts on the issue of liability for damage caused by a wild animal when the animal is not under the control of the defendant. The parties have not cited and this court has been unable to locate *any* case with facts precisely analogous to those of the case at bar. The few cases that have considered similar facts, however, appear to agree that, if a landowner knows that a wild animal is creating a dangerous situation on his property, he has a duty either to remove the danger or to warn the people who may be threatened by the danger.

The most helpful case appears to be *Wamser v. City of St. Petersburg,* 339 So. 2d 244 (Fla.App.1976). *Wamser* involved a lawsuit against a city by a swimmer who had been attacked by a shark at a city-operated beach. The court held that, because the danger was not reasonably foreseeable, the city had no duty to guard the swimmer against a shark attack or to warn him of the possibility of such an attack. The city also was found to have no duty to seek information about the frequency of sharks in the beach area, since no shark attacks had ever occurred at the beach so as to indicate the necessity for obtaining such information.

Similarly, in *Mann v. State,* 47 N.Y.S.2d 553 (Ct.Cl.1944), the State was found not liable for damages to a car caused when a deer ran across the highway. The court held that the State could not be held liable for failure to erect fences or post warning signs where plaintiff did not allege that the State had actual or constructive notice of a dangerous situation. *See also Morrison v. State,* 123 N.Y.S.2d 105 (Ct. Cl. 1952) (where deer crossing highway creates hazard, State may have duty to post warning signs).

There are several cases involving visitors to national parks who were attacked by bears. *Claypool v. United States,* 98 F. Supp. 702 (S.D.Cal. 1951), involved a park visitor who was injured by a grizzly bear in Yellowstone National Park. The visitor had asked a park ranger if it was safe to camp in a particular campsite. Although a bear had raided that particular campsite only a few days earlier injuring several people, the ranger assured the visitor it was safe to camp there. *Id.* at 703. The court found that the government had a duty to warn under the circumstances. *Id.* at 706.

---

7. For example, the extent of the State's knowledge of the presence of bears at the Robe River turnout is in dispute. There was considerable evidence of bears in the general area. The State however, points out that there was no evidence that the State had specific knowledge of the presence of bears at the turnout itself.

In contrast, the government was found not liable for another Yellowstone bear attack in *Rubenstein v. United States,* 338 F. Supp. 654 (N.D.Cal.1972). In this instance the visitor had been given the usual warning brochures on the dangers of bears, and park officials had no specific knowledge of bears in the area of the campsite where the attack occurred. The court held that the government could not be held liable for the completely unforeseeable actions of wild animals. *See also Martin v. United States,* 564 F.2d 1355 (9th Cir. 1976), *cert. denied,* 432 U.S. 906 (1977); *Ashley v. United States,* 215 F. Supp. 39 (D.Neb.1963), *aff'd per curiam,* 326 F.2d 499 (8th Cir.1964).[8]

These cases suggest some of the factual questions which remain to be resolved in the case at bar. It will be necessary to decide, for example, the extent of the State's knowledge of the presence of bears at the Robe River turnout; whether it was reasonably foreseeable that a bear would attack a person who was using the turnout; and whether the State had sufficient knowledge of danger so as to give rise to a duty to post warning signs. These questions and possibly others must be resolved by the finder of fact.

REVERSED and REMANDED for trial.

NOTES

(1) Public liability for wild animals: As *Carlson* illustrates, courts are reluctant to hold states liable for injuries caused by wild animals—even on state-owned land—unless the state has materially exacerbated the danger (as it perhaps did in *Carlson*) or has failed to warn of hidden dangers of which the state has specific knowledge (as in the decision in *Claypool,* discussed in *Carlson*). What reasons exist for refusing to hold a state liable in the absence of such factors?

(2) *Wamser v. City of St. Petersburg*: Robert Wamser was severely injured when he was attacked by a shark while swimming in the waters of the Gulf of Mexico adjacent to a beach operated by the City of St. Petersburg. The District Recreation Supervisor for the city stated in his deposition that, to his knowledge, there had never been a shark attack at any of the city beaches in the 2 years he had worked for the City. A Marine Patrol captain of the Department of Natural Resources of Florida stated that prior to the attack, he had patrolled the waters along the beaches in the area and had observed that sharks inhabited the gulf waters off Treasure Island and that these sharks on occasion came within close proximity of the beach area. In another affidavit filed by appellants, a

---

8. For other cases involving injuries caused by wild animals, *see CeBuzz, Inc. v. Sniderman,* 466 P.2d 457 (Colo.1970) (customer bitten by spider in grocery store); *Williams v. Gibbs,* 182 S.E.2d 164 (Ga.App. 1971) (gasoline station customer injured while running from rattlesnake); *Overstreet v. Gibson Product Co.,* 558 S.W.2d 58 (Tex. 1977) (customer bitten by rattlesnake in grocery store).

These cases involve the liability of a business proprietor to a customer. This is a situation which, under traditional principles of tort law, imposes a stricter duty than mere reasonable behavior. Findings of liability in these cases, however, do not appear to depend on this higher duty, so these cases still provide some guidance in Alaska where the reasonable person standard applies in all cases. *See Webb v. City & Borough of Sitka,* 561 P.2d 731, 733 & n. 9 (Alaska 1977).

commercial fisherman stated that he had observed sharks swimming up and down the beaches and sandbars in the waters adjacent to Treasure Island. The court affirmed summary judgment for defendant:

> The rule is that generally the law does not require the owner or possessor of land to anticipate the presence of or guard an invitee against harm from animals *feræ naturæ* unless such owner or possessor has reduced the animals to possession, harbors such animals, or has introduced onto his premises wild animals not indigenous to the locality. *Gowen v. Willenborg*, 366 S.W.2d 695 (Tex. Civ. App. 1963); *Williams v. Gibbs*, 182 S.E.2d 164 (Ga.App.1971); [ ].

> In the instant case there was nothing to indicate that the city had knowledge of a shark hazard. To the contrary, the record shows that the attack at a previously safe beach was unexpected. In the absence of reasonable foreseeability of the danger, there was no duty on the part of the city to guard an invitee against an attack by an animal *feræ naturæ* or to warn of such an occurrence. *Williams v. Gibbs, supra*; *Rubenstein v. United States*, 338 F.Supp. 654 (N.D.Cal.1972). *Cf. Claypool v. United States*, 98 F.Supp. 702 (S.D.Cal.1951). Nor was the city under a duty to obtain information from local agencies to determine the frequency with which sharks appeared in and around the beach area, since there was no attack on record in the history of the beach to indicate the necessity for obtaining such information.

Wamser v. City of St. Petersburg, 339 So.2d 244 (Fla.App.1976).

(3) *Arroyo v. State:* A child mauled by a mountain lion in a state park sued for damages, alleging a failure to warn and general negligence. The court rejected the action on the ground that the lion was a "natural condition" in the park within the meaning of a state statute insulating the state from liability for all natural conditions. The court also concluded that lions were a natural condition as a matter of law, even though lion populations had increased due to a state mandated moratorium on lion hunting. *Arroyo v. State*, 40 Cal.Rptr.2d 627 (Cal.App.1995).

(4) Deer and cars: One recurrent group of cases involve the intersection of deer and cars. In addition to *Mann v. State* and *Morrison v. State* noted in *Carlson*, consider *Leslie v. State*. Plaintiff was driving on a two-lane highway. As she approached a railroad underpass, she saw two deer near the north side of the highway. She slowed down. An oncoming vehicle emerged from the underpass, struck one of the deer and veered into claimant's lane, causing her severe and permanent injuries. Plaintiffs contended that the state was negligent in failing to post a "deer crossing" sign. The New York Court of Claims rejected the argument. The court found that the state had established through the testimony of a biologist with the Department of Environmental Conservation that a deer crossing sign was not warranted because of the low deer population in the area and the lack of a defined deer crossing at the accident site. The Appellate Division affirmed:

> The purpose of a deer crossing sign is "to warn of reasonably well-defined locations where deer tend to cross a highway." [ ] Such a sign should be erected only where necessary. [ ] The posting of such a sign

is discretionary and, in regard thereto, the State enjoys a limited immunity from negligence. *Ufnal v. Cattaraugus County,* 463 N.Y.S.2d 342 (App.Div.), *leave to appeal denied,* 454 N.E.2d 1317 (N.Y.1983). Claimants have failed to show that the State's failure to erect a deer crossing sign was irrational. *Cf. Massar v. New York State Thruway Authority,* 228 N.Y.S.2d 777 (App.Div.1962).

Leslie v. State, 502 N.Y.S.2d 825 (App.Div.1986).

More recent cases include *Ryan v. New Mexico State Highway & Transportation Department,* 964 P.2d 149 (N.M.App.1998) (allegation of negligence in failing to post signs raises factual issue that precludes summary judgment for state); *Monzo v. Commonwealth,* 556 A.2d 493 (Pa.Cmwlth.1989) (same; plaintiff also alleged defects in road construction, which contributed to injury); *Rippy v. Fogel,* 529 A.2d 608 (Pa.Cmwlth. 1987) (complaint dismissed for failure to state claim when plaintiff alleged that deer on highway was "dangerous condition" within meaning of statute holding state liable for dangerous conditions).

(5) *Peterson v. Wyoming Game & Fish Commission:* While hunting elk, plaintiff was attacked and severely mauled by a grizzly bear. The animal, Bear 34, was part of a research project on grizzly bears in the Yellowstone ecosystem. The animal was initially captured and radio-collared in 1978. Over the next sixteen years, the bear was recaptured several times—three times during the period between July and September 1994. Researchers had determined that Bear 34 was killing livestock and was deaf. The Game and Fish personnel, however, did not classify Bear 34 as a nuisance bear so that it would be killed. Plaintiff's claim was that "Game and Fish personnel were negligent with respect to their maintenance and supervision of Bear 34." Defendant moved for summary judgment, contending that the agency was immune under the Wyoming Governmental Claims Act. The Wyoming act creates a presumption of immunity: "Under the Wyoming Governmental Claims Act, immunity is the rule, and liability is the exception. [ ] Liability exists only when the statute recognizes an exception to sovereign immunity. [ ] In the absence of a statutory exception, no liability attaches to the state or its employees." The court rejected plaintiff's contention that it should broadly construe a statutory exception for "peace officers" and held the state immune. *Peterson v. Wyoming Game & Fish Commission,* 989 P.2d 113 (Wyo.1999).

Oklahoma City v. Hudson

Supreme Court of Oklahoma.
405 P.2d 178 (1965).

■ BLACKBIRD, J.:—The [plaintiff] filed this action to recover damages for personal injuries. Plaintiff was an employee of the Oklahoma City Zoo. On the day in question he was engaged in cleaning out the pit used for housing lions. Prior to this operation he had closed the door shutting off the area where he was to work. While so working, two lions beat against the door, it opened, and the animals rushed into the place where he was working, mauling him severely. He recovered a verdict and judgment in the sum of

$57,300.00. After the overruling of its motion for a new trial, defendant perfected the present appeal.

The amended petition which plaintiff filed in this action contained general allegations of the defendant's failure to provide him a "reasonably" safe place to work and safe methods and safeguards for carrying out his duties in connection with cleaning the lion pit, and, in more detail, further alleged:

(f) Failure of the defendant to provide safe locks and/or catches on the restraining cage where lions were kept while plaintiff was engaged in cleaning said lion pit and moat; and, in this connection, plaintiff alleges that said locks were old, rusty, worn, defective and insecure and that while plaintiff was carrying out his duties, said lions were continually scratching, pawing, lunging and biting against the restraining cage door where said lions had been placed; that as a result of said old, worn and defective lock, it gave way under the constant pressure of said lions lunging, clawing, pawing and striking at said lock and said lions escaped into the enclosure where the plaintiff was carrying out his duties. Plaintiff alleges that said old, worn and defective locks were known by the defendant or should have been known by the exercise of reasonable care and diligence on the part of defendant and that the same was wholly unknown to this plaintiff.

The evidence at the trial established that plaintiff had worked at the zoo seven or eight months prior to the accident. Plaintiff testified, in substance, that his "training" during the early days of his employment had been as a "helper" to two other employees in cleaning the "run-around" used by hoofed animals and that he had cleaned the lion pit "not more than three times" previous to the date of his injury. When he was interrogated at length about whether, on the day of the accident, he had securely locked the safety doors closing off from the pit, the part of the zoo in which the lions customarily remained, while the pit was being cleaned, plaintiff testified to the effect that the last one of the door locks was "hard to lock." When asked whether he actually latched the safety doors, he, at one point, testified: "I am not one hundred percent positive."

Despite the fact that plaintiff's petition, as above indicated, purported to state a cause of action based upon defendant's negligence, and, at the pre-trial conference it was decreed that the general nature of the case, inter alia, was "negligence of defendant," the court submitted the case to the jury on the theory of defendant's absolute liability, by giving the following instructions:

No. 6.

You are further instructed that one who harbors a wild animal, such as a lion, which is by its very nature vicious and unpredictable does so at his peril, and liability for injuries inflicted by such animal is absolute.

No. 7.

You are further instructed while it is not in itself unlawful for a person to keep wild beasts, although they may be such as are of a nature vicious and dangerous, as a lion, yet it is the duty of those who own or keep them to do it in such a manner as will absolutely prevent the occurrence of an injury to others through the vicious acts of the animals as they are naturally inclined to commit; and for any injury they may do to others, the person keeping them is liable, irrespective of any questions of negligence or knowledge of previous acts showing a vicious disposition.

While defendant urges several grounds for reversing the order and/or judgment appealed from, it is necessary to deal only with its argument urging error in the above quoted instructions. It maintains that their common fallacy consisted of invoking the doctrine of absolute liability, while in truth such doctrine has no application to a case like the present one, where the plaintiff is defendant's employee, rather than a member of the public. Herein lies the distinction between this case and *City of Mangum v. Brownlee,* 75 P.2d 174 (Okl.1938), and *City of Tonkawa v. Danielson,* 27 P.2d 348 (Okl.1933), wherein the plaintiffs were members of the general public, not associated in any way with the care, keeping, or harboring of the animals involved. The distinction to which we allude was noted in *Haneman v. Western Meat Co.,* 97 P. 695, 696 (Cal.App.1908), wherein the court said:

> While it is true that the owner of a vicious animal, who knows that such animal is vicious, should be held liable to all persons for damages caused by the vicious acts of such animal, if the owner allows such persons to be subjected to danger without warning, yet it is not the policy of the law to make the master an insurer against accidents that may happen to an employee in the ordinary course of his employment.
>
> * * *
>
> To hold the owner of such animal liable it must be shown that such owner failed in some duty to the party injured.

In this case, it is unnecessary to become involved in, or to discuss, the various differences in the opinions of various courts as to whether the usual defenses in tort actions generally, such as contributory negligence, assumption of risk, etc., apply to actions by the patrons of a zoo or other places where wild animals are kept on exhibit for amusement or educational purposes (Notice *Hansen v. Brogan,* 400 P.2d 265 (Mont.1965), and the Annotation at 22 A.L.R. 610, 629, and 69 A.L.R. 500) or to actions by domestic servants (notice the Annotation at 49 A.L.R.2d 317, 350, et seq.) or employees generally, who were not hired to help keep, or care for, wild animals and who might only infrequently, or casually, come into contact with them during the performance of unrelated tasks of their employment. Here, plaintiff was not a spectator at the zoo, but the undisputed evidence is that he was employed specifically to assist in caring for wild animals on exhibit there, that he had undergone an apprenticeship or "training" period, and that he had had some previous experience in working in the lion pit. There can be no doubt in our opinion but that the rules applying to master and servant cases apply here, and that the doctrine of absolute liability has no application. The giving of the quoted instructions were the practical equivalent of an instructed verdict for the plaintiff, and constituted prejudicial error. This error was valid ground for a new trial. Therefore, the trial court's order overruling defendant's motion for such new trial is hereby reversed, and this cause is remanded to said court with instructions to set aside said order and enter a new one granting defendant a new trial.

NOTES

(1) Employees: As *Hudson* illustrates, strict liability for injuries caused by captive wild animals does not protect employees hired and trained to work with such animals. The relevant body of law in such cases is the worker's compensation laws, which provide remedies for on-the-job injuries. Worker's compensation statutes create insurance systems in which recovery is predicated upon an employment relationship rather than fault. Recovery, however, is limited to a specified figure rather than to actual damages as determined by a jury.

Worker's compensation statutes may also apply to an employee hired to work with animals who seeks recovery from an owner of the animal other than his employer. *See Rosenbloom v. Hanour Corp.*, 78 Cal.Rptr.2d 686 (Cal.App.1998) ("Shark Club," which owned aquarium and shark, was not liable for shark bite to employee of shark-handling company that was hired to move the shark to a larger tank).

(2) City zoos: Injuries to visitors at city zoos have proven a fruitful source of litigation. At one time, cases often turned on whether a zoo was considered a governmental function—for which the city enjoyed complete immunity—or whether it was a proprietary function—in which case no immunity existed. *Compare Grover v. City of Manhattan*, 424 P.2d 256 (Kan.1967) (government function, hence city immune) *with Moloney v. City of Columbus*, 208 N.E.2d 141 (Ohio 1965) (proprietary function, hence no immunity). Despite the declining importance of this distinction, the cases continue to evidence no clear rule. *See Sakach v. City of Pittsburgh*, 687 A.2d 34 (Pa.Cmwlth.1996) (city immune by statute when dolphin bites off tip of finger of volunteer); *Burns v. Gleason*, 819 F.2d 555 (5th Cir.1987) (city strictly liable for 9–year old boy mauled by jaguar); *Franken v. City of Sioux Center*, 272 N.W.2d 422 (Iowa 1978) (city strictly liable for tiger bite but defenses in Restatement are available); *City & County of Denver v. Kennedy*, 476 P.2d 762 (Colo.App.1970) (city liable only on showing of negligence).

CHAPTER 5

State Proprietary and Sovereign Powers

Wildlife law does not easily fit into familiar categories. On one hand, animals have always occupied a unique niche in human consciousness: they are often the symbols that people our thoughts—the Grimm Brother's wolf at the door, Reynard the crafty fox of medieval market dramas, and the magical, ambiguous coyote of so many Indian stories. Indeed, Paul Shepard has argued that "the human species emerged enacting, dreaming, and thinking animals and cannot be fully itself without them." PAUL SHEPARD, THE OTHERS: HOW ANIMALS MADE US HUMAN 4 (1996).

On the other hand, the law has viewed animals as potential property—recall the fox carcass that figured so prominently in *Pierson v. Post.* Wildlife excited the imagination of the continental jurists such as Hugo Grotius, Emerich de Vattel, and Samuel, Baron von Pufendorf because, as unowned stuff, wild animals were one of the few remaining examples of the "state of nature," that theoretical, mythical construct of the human world before society came into being. Wildlife thus was a speculation on the origin of property.

But wildlife is an uncommon sort of property. Not only is it alive, it is also dependent for its continued survival on a forbearance that history demonstrates is uncommon—for wildlife, as unowned, vagrant stuff subject to capture, requires the tolerance of everyone who might kill it or destroy its habitat. Hence the final component of wildlife law: the complex relationship between wildlife and the state—or, more accurately, the relationship between individuals and the state in relation to wildlife.

As common law judges explored and developed these relationships, they drew upon the language of property and sovereignty. Recall the decision of the King's Bench in *The Case of Swans.* Swans are royal fowl because they are pure and, therefore, all unbranded swans "do belong to the King by his prerogative." The court in *The Case of the Royal Fishery of Banne* offered a similar rationale: every river "is a royal river, and the fishery of it is a royal fishery, and belongs to the king by his prerogative" because "such river ... is said to be a branch of the sea so far as [the sea] flows" due to the fact that "the sea is not only under the dominion of the king ... but it is also his proper inheritance."

As these statements suggest, property and sovereignty were metaphorically and legally joined in wildlife. The King as sovereign was the owner of wildlife—at least, he owned all the wildlife that counted: those species that qualified as fish and game. Or so the common law was understood in America:

Under the common law of England all property right in animals *feræ naturæ* was in the sovereign, for the use and benefit of the people. The killing, taking, and use of game was subject to absolute governmental control for the common good. This absolute power to control and regulate was vested in the colonial governments as a part of the common law. It passed with the title to game to the several states as an incident of their sovereignty, and was retained by the states for the use and benefit of the people of the states, subject only to any applicable provisions of the federal Constitution.

Cawsey v. Brickey, 144 P. 938 (Wash.1914).

This passage reveals the difficulty the court had in describing the government's relationship to wildlife. In England, courts would have spoken in terms of the Crown's "prerogative," but royal prerogative was an anathema in America. Hence the struggle to find a different terminology. American courts were familiar with two ways to talk about power over things: there was *proprietary* power, embodied in concepts of property and title, and there was *sovereign* power, represented by the government's authority—granted by the sovereign people—to regulate conduct. In the case of wildlife, however, neither of these powers alone seemed quite right. Sensing that inadequacy—and searching for a better description—courts mingled the categories. As the decision in *Cawsey* illustrates, American courts recognized the expansive nature of government's role by vesting it with both "title to game" and "absolute governmental control." But this blended power also was not quite right; the combined categories gave government too much discretion. Unlike a private owner who might use wildlife solely for personal gain, when the government was the owner its powers were constrained by the public interest. Thus, its proprietary rights could be exercised only "for the use and benefit of the people of the states" and not for the benefit of an individual or special group. The government's "absolute regulatory power" was similarly limited by the public good. As the *Cawsey* decision demonstrates, the courts sought to confine the broad powers vested in government by impressing those powers with duties drawn from property law. The metaphor they employed to describe this mixture of sovereign and proprietary powers was the trust: the state was a trustee for the people and state sovereign ownership was a public trust.

This odd mixture of sovereign and proprietary power remains vitally relevant because it continues to undergird wildlife law. It also accounts—in part at least—for the law's unique structure. Consider: in what sense does government, on behalf of the people, "own" wildlife that has not passed into private hands? Is it still meaningful to speak of the government's powers as a form of ownership, or is such language anachronistic, the confusing baggage from a time before courts had developed the jurisprudence of regulatory power? If the state does in some sense own wildlife, is its authority limited beyond the ever-present obligation to act in the public interest? Can the state, for example, treat wildlife as it does other public property? States have nearly unlimited power over public property; do they have the same flexibility with respect to public property interests in animals? Consider also wildlife habitat and food. If the state owns wildlife what limits does its ownership impose on private landowners? Can landowners use their lands as they choose, displacing and indirectly killing wildlife by destroying habitat? Or, is the state's ownership an easement-like interest under which the state can limit a landowner's activities that unduly disturb state-owned animals? That is: when the government granted land to individuals while retaining ownership of wildlife, did it retain rights to continue using that land for wildlife, rights that it can enforce, not as a sovereign regulator, but as a wildlife proprietor?

This chapter explores these issues, examining the state's overlapping roles as sovereign and proprietor. To understand the state's role in managing wildlife, it is necessary to begin with a backward glance at first principles.

SECTION 1.   THE CONJUNCTION OF SOVEREIGN AND PROPRIETARY POWERS

PERSPECTIVES

(1) The English common law: In the decades after the Norman Conquest, the modern conceptions of sovereignty and property were as yet not formed. The King was both sovereign and proprietor and the distinction between the two was at best blurred. Indeed, sovereignty was a form of property—recall the decision in *The Case of Swans* that "all white swans not marked ... and ... swimming in an open and common river, might be seised to the King's use by his prerogative, because ... a swan is a Royal fowl; ... and so whales and sturgeons are Royal fish, and *belong to the King by his prerogative.*"

Over time, sovereignty and property came to be perceived as different things—and in both, the King's powers slowly declined.[1] Some were usurped by holders of private lands, who gradually transformed feudal tenurial relations into something approaching the fee simple. Other royal powers were seized by Parliament. By the time of the American Revolution, the line between sovereignty and property—although still contested—had been sufficiently clarified that people understood them to be different forms of power. The government (that is, the King, both alone and in Parliament) held powers to tax, regulate, and spend; private owners held powers to use their property and to exclude others.

Some royal powers, however, were not cleanly divisible. For example, the King owned navigable waterways as an aspect of his prerogative, but was this power primarily proprietary or sovereign? In Chapter 3, we examined the long-lasting controversies over fishing rights. The King owned such rights, but were they—like dry land—property that could be

---

1. The story is summarized in Charles Donahue, Jr., *The Future of the Concept of Property Predicted from Its Past, in* PROPERTY: NOMOS XXII 28, 34–47 (J. Pennock & J. Chapman eds, 1980). More detail on the early period, in which vassals in Norman England began to acquire identifiable property rights, is provided in Robert C. Palmer, *The Origins of Property in England,* 3 L. & HIST. REV. 1 (1985), and Robert C. Palmer, *The Economic and Cultural Impacts of the Origins of Property, 1180–1220,* 3 L. & HIST. REV. 375 (1985).

sold to raise revenues, or did the King own them in a different, more restricted sense? Why could the public fish in the King's rivers? Royal lands generally were not open to public use, and citizens could not seize swans or venison to fill the dinner plate. What was different about fishing that gave rise to such limits on royal power? During the first part of the nineteenth century, state court judges transformed this jumble of English precedent into coherent rules. They concluded that fishing rights depended upon title to lands beneath the waterway, which was determined by the navigability of the waterway; navigability, in turn, depended upon whether the waterway was subject to the ebb and flow of the tides. This conclusion reflected both a reading of the English precedent and a theory of popular sovereignty: the King had owned the lands beneath navigable waterways as a sovereign and upon the Revolution this sovereignty passed to the people, who lodged it in the states subject to any applicable provisions of the federal Constitution.

The American judges also confronted a distinctly ambiguous legal record on wildlife other than fish. What wildlife did the King own by prerogative? Recall that in the mid-thirteenth century Bracton wrote "wild beasts, birds and fish ... are ... the property of the prince by the *jus gentium* [human law]." HENRY DE BRACTON, DE LEGIBUS ET CONSUETUDINIBUS ANGLIAE bk. 2, ch. 1, ff. 8b (ca. 1256). At the end of the sixteenth century, the King's Bench decided in *The Case of the Swans* that unmarked swans were "seised to the King's use by his prerogative, because ... a swan is a Royal fowl." A century later, Chief Justice Holt began his analysis in *Sutton v. Moody* with the proposition that the King was empowered to create hunting franchises—and hence necessarily had some rights in wild game. Both Bracton and Holt concluded that the King had powers over wildlife that arose from his status as King. Given the property-based vision of the period, it was natural to view the King's claims as property: a grantor cannot, after all, grant something that he does not own. At the time of the Revolution, Blackstone echoed Bracton: "Upon the whole it appears, that the king, by his prerogative, and [holders of royal franchises], are the *only* persons who may acquire any property, however fugitive and transitory, in these animals *feræ naturæ*, while living." 2 WILLIAM BLACK-STONE, COMMENTARIES ON THE LAWS OF ENGLAND *419. For Blackstone, the conclusion was a rational deduction from the basic proposition that the King was the "the ultimate proprietor of all the lands in the kingdom." *Id.* at *415.

Blackstone's view was sharply contested by Edward Christian, editor of a common annotated edition of Blackstone and the author of an 1821 treatise on game laws. Christian argued that "game does not belong to the King":

> If all wild animals belonged to the crown, it would have been superfluous to have specified whales, sturgeons, and swans. Lord Coke tell us, that "a swan is a royal fowl; and all those the property whereof is not known, do belong to the king by his prerogative: and so whales and sturgeons are royal fish, and belong to the king by his prerogative:" *Case of swans,* 7 Co. 16. ... But these are the only animals which our law has conferred this honour upon.

2 WILLIAM BLACKSTONE, COMMENTARIES ON THE LAWS OF ENGLAND *419 n.9 (New York: W.E. Dean, Printer, 1832) (this edition among others includes Christian's notes).

(2) The transformation of the common law in a new world: The heated English debate on the powers of king and landed gentry over wildlife was not settled during the early years of America's independence. Through a process similar to that involving fisheries, early state court judges concluded that Blackstone was more compatible with the new democracies in America which shared his abhorrence of the hierarchical social structure embedded in the game laws. *See generally* THOMAS A. LUND, AMERICAN WILDLIFE LAW 21–24 (1980); JAMES A. TOBER, WHO OWNS THE WILDLIFE? 146–47 (1981).

Blackstone's monarchical views did, however, present problems. The leading case to confront these problems was *Arnold v. Mundy*, 6 N.J.L. 1 (1821), a cases discussed in Chapter 3 in connection with the emergence of the public trust doctrine in navigable waters. *Arnold* was a dispute over rights to harvest shellfish. Successors in title to the colony's proprietors claimed that their patents included title to submerged tidelands and thus the exclusive right to gather shellfish. Their claim was disputed by individuals who had leased the right to harvest oysters from the state. The issue before the New Jersey Supreme Court thus was who held title to tidelands.

Resolution of the dispute required the court to analyze the transactions between the King and the colony's proprietors. In the original patent, the King granted all rights—both sovereign and proprietary—to the proprietors. Decades later, the proprietors relinquished the rights of sovereignty back to the Crown, retaining only their proprietary rights. Thus, in a two-step process, sovereign and proprietary rights were starkly split. Inevitably, the question of ownership of the submerged lands arose. This question turned upon resolution of the further question: in what capacity had the King held submerged lands?

Under English law, the right to fish in navigable waters (as we saw in Chapter 3) was "a royal fishery, and belongs to the king by his prerogative" in the words of the Kings Bench in *The Case of the Royal Fishery of Banne*. The King's right thus was, in some sense, proprietary. But the public nonetheless had rights to fish in such fisheries without need of any grant from the King—a fact that suggests that the King did not "own" the submerged lands as a private person and that, in some sense, his rights were sovereign. Was the fishery a proprietary right, retained by the colonial proprietors, or was it a sovereign power, which the proprietors had returned to the King and which the state of New Jersey, in turn, assumed at the time of the Revolution?

The New Jersey Supreme Court concluded that it was an incident of the King's sovereign powers, which meant that the state held the power to decide who could fish and where. Even as the court was reaching this conclusion, however, it could describe the situation only by making extensive use of property terminology:

> Every thing susceptible of property is considered as belonging to the nation that possesses the country, and as forming the entire mass of its

wealth. But the nation does not possess all those things in the same manner. By far the greater part of them are divided among the individuals of the nation, and become *private property*. Those things not divided among the individuals still belong to the nation, and are called *public property*. Of these, again, some are reserved for the necessities of the state, and are used for the public benefit, and those are called *"the domain of the crown or of the republic;"* others remain common to all the citizens, who take of them and use them, each according to his necessities, and according to the laws which regulate their use, and are called *common property*. Of this latter kind, according to the writers upon the law of nature and of nations, and upon the civil law, are the air, the running water, the sea, the fish, and the wild beasts. VATTEL, Bk i, § 235; 2 BLACKSTONE, COMMENTARIES ON THE LAWS OF ENGLAND 14. But inasmuch as the things which constitute this *common property* are things in which a sort of transient usufructuary possession, only, can be had; and inasmuch as the title to them and to the soil by which they are supported, and to which they are appurtenant, cannot well, according to the common law notion of the title, be vested in all the people; therefore, the wisdom of that law has placed it in the hands of the sovereign power, to be held, protected, and regulated for the common use and benefit.

Arnold v. Mundy, 6 N.J.L. 1 (1821).

Two decades later, the United States Supreme Court employed similar language and reasoning in *Martin v. Waddell's Lessee*, 41 U.S. (16 Pet.) 367 (1842) [also considered in Chapter III], when it decided that title to the beds of navigable waterways was held by the state.

(3) From submerged lands to wildlife—the evolution of sovereign ownership and the public trust: The decisions in *The Royal Fishery of Banne*, Davis 56, 80 Eng. Rep. 540 (K.B. 1611), *Arnold v. Mundy*, 6 N.J.L. 1 (1821), and *Martin v. Waddell's Lessee*, 41 U.S. (16 Pet.) 367 (1842), were concerned with the right to harvest fish—finfish (salmon) in *Banne* and shellfish (oysters) in *Arnold* and *Martin*. As noted in Chapter 3, these decisions are the cornerstones of the public trust doctrine as that doctrine is applied to the beds and banks of navigable waterways. *See, e.g., National Audubon Society v. Superior Court*, 658 P.2d 709 (Cal.1983) [*infra*]. But these cases also are the seminal decisions in the evolution of another line of precedent, one concluding that sovereign ownership and the accompanying public trust extend not only to navigable waterways and fish, but to all wildlife.

Like most foundational conclusions, this one emerged gradually. An initial step was the recognition that the state's sovereign ownership of submerged lands gave it an interest at least akin to property in oysters growing in the soil:

> As to the ownership of property in oysters, while lying in the Bay of Delaware, ... the judge [in the decision below] did not say, that the property was in the state of New Jersey; his words are these: "It appears satisfactorily, that causes of complaint existed, some time, concerning the destruction of oysters, which are a valuable article of food bestowed upon us by Providence, and for the preservation of

which laws are usually made by states. *Although, perhaps, they may not have a right of absolute property in these articles, they do, and may, nevertheless, pass regulations for their preservation.*" To the law, thus laid down, certainly no objection can be made. The right of preventing the destruction of fish and oysters, is a most salutary one, and has been exercised by all states and nations.

Kean v. Rice, 12 Serg. & Rawle 203 (Pa.1824) (Tilghman, C.J.).

Sovereign ownership was next applied to swimming fish as well as shellfish. In *Dunham v. Lamphere,* for example, Chief Lemuel Justice Shaw[3] upheld a state statute prohibiting the use of seines within a mile of the Nantucket shore. Like his predecessors, Shaw drew upon Vattel: "like other valuable commodities, fish, *as well swimming as shell fish,* are susceptible of being property; and every such things, says Vattel, Bk. 1, §§ 234, 235, is considered as belonging to the nation that possesses the country, as forming part of the aggregate mass of its wealth; those not divided are called public property." *Dunham v. Lamphere,* 69 Mass. (3 Gray) 268 (1855) (emphasis added).

The final step was to extend state sovereign ownership to all wildlife— a step that seemed natural since fish and wildlife were treated the same by common-law, *e.g.,* 2 WILLIAM BLACKSTONE, COMMENTARIES ON THE LAWS OF ENGLAND *391–92, and civilian writers, *e.g.,* EMERICH DE VATTEL, THE LAW OF NATIONS bk.1, § 234 (Joseph Chitty trans., Philadelphia, 1876) (1758). The effect of this final step is apparent in a decision by the Minnesota Supreme Court. Defendant, who had been convicted of possessing game after the close of the open season even though the prosecutor acknowledged that it had been killed within the open season, argued that the statute was unconstitutional:

> It is claimed that the act in question proceeds upon the plan of first declaring all wild game and fish within the state to be its absolute property, and then, upon that basis, providing how, and under what limitations, persons may acquire a qualified right of property in them from the state. Counsel for defendants contend strenuously that the state has no proprietary right in animals *feræ naturæ,* and can acquire none by mere legislation; that such animals are *bona vacantia,* in which a right of property can be acquired only by reducing them to possession. If it was the intention of the legislature to declare all wild game the property of the state, in a proprietary sense, that feature of the law might be subject to counsel's criticism; but that question is not material here, for it is not necessary to resort to any such doctrine as the source of the power of the state to adopt police regulations for the preservation of wild game within its borders.

We take it to be the correct doctrine in this country that the ownership of wild animals, so far as they are capable of ownership, is

---

3. Lemuel Shaw (1781–1861) was one of the leading jurists of his day. After serving in the Massachusetts legislature, he served as Chief Justice of the Massachusetts Supreme Judicial Court from 1830–1860. Among his influential opinions was *Brown v. Kendall,* 60 Mass. (6 Cush.) 292 (1850), establishing negligence as the primary standard for liability in tort. *See generally* LEONARD W. LEVY, THE LAW OF THE COMMONWEALTH AND CHIEF JUSTICE SHAW (1957).

in the state, not as proprietor, but in its sovereign capacity, as the representative, and for the benefit, of all its people in common. The preservation of such animals as are adapted to consumption as food, or to any other useful purpose, is a matter of public interest; and it is within the police power of the state, as the representative of the people in their united sovereignty, to enact such laws as will best preserve such game, and secure its beneficial use in the future to the citizens, and to that end it may adopt any reasonable regulations, not only as to time and manner in which such game may be taken and killed, but also imposing limitations upon the right of property in such game after it has been reduced to possession. Such limitations deprive no person of his property, because he who takes or kills game had no previous right of property in it, and, when he acquires such right by reducing it to possession, he does so subject to such conditions and limitations as the legislature has seen fit to impose.

State v. Rodman, 59 N.W. 1098 (Minn.1894).

Rodman illustrates late nineteenth century judicial thinking about the legal basis of wildlife conservation. Note that, while the decision introduces a new phrase—the "police power"—it still blends language about sovereignty and property. And it is this blended power that buttresses the extraordinary power the state has over wildlife that has not passed into private ownership. It is the blending of sovereignty and property that authorizes the state to decide what property rights a person will acquire in wildlife once it has been captured. In *Rodman,* the state banned possession of lawfully killed game beyond the fifth day after the end of the open season. The court describes this, not as a subsequent restriction on rights previously acquired by a lawful hunter, but instead as integral to the property rights the hunter obtains in the first instance. A hunter, in other words, acquires something akin to a fee simple determinable, a limited possessory right in the captured game that terminates automatically five days into the closed season. The state as sovereign owner has the power to determine the interests that it will permit an individual to acquire. One reason for this approach may have been that states were ending market hunting—a step that would, in time, benefit wildlife as much or more than any other legal act. They did so by banning the sale of lawfully captured game by withholding the right to sell—a dramatic limit on property rights that would have been hard to justify as a traditional police power regulation during a period characterized by substantive due process limitations on state regulatory powers. *See, e.g., Lochner v. New York,* 198 U.S. 45 (1905); *Munn v. Illinois,* 94 U.S. 113 (1877).

The United States Supreme Court summarized much of this evolution at the close of the nineteenth century in

Geer v. Connecticut

United States Supreme Court.
161 U.S. 519 (1896).

■ WHITE, J.:—[Defendant was found guilty of possessing "with the wrongful and unlawful intent to procure transportation beyond the limits of the

State" woodcock, ruffed grouse, and quail. He appealed, arguing that the statutes prohibiting the transportation of game birds out of the state were unconstitutional. The Connecticut Supreme Court rejected his argument. T]he sole issue which the case presents is, was it lawful, under the Constitution of the United States (section 8, Article I), for the State of Connecticut to allow the killing of birds within the State during a designated open season, to allow such birds, when so killed, to be used, to be sold, and to be bought for use, within the State, and yet to forbid their transportation beyond the State? Or, to state it otherwise, had the State of Connecticut the power to regulate the killing of game within her borders so as to confine its use to the limits of the State, and forbid its transmission outside of the State?

. . . . The solution of the question involves a consideration of the nature of the property in game and the authority which the State had a right lawfully to exercise in relation thereto.

From the earliest traditions, the right to reduce animals *feræ naturæ* to possession has been subject to the control of the law-giving power.

The writer of a learned article in the *Repertoire of the Journal du Palais* mentions the fact that the law of Athens forbade the killing of game, [ ], and Merlin says, [ ], that "Solon, seeing that the Athenians gave themselves up to the chase, to the neglect of the mechanical arts, forbade the killing of game."

Among other subdivisions, things were classified by the Roman law into public and common. The latter embraced animals *feræ naturæ,* which, having no owner, were considered as belonging in common to all the citizens of the State. . . .

. . .

. . . . In the feudal as well as the ancient law of the continent of Europe, in all countries, the right to acquire animals *feræ naturæ* by possession was recognized as being subject to the governmental authority and under its power, not only as a matter of regulation, but also of absolute control. Merlin, [ ], mentions the fact that although tradition indicates that, from the earliest day in France, every citizen had a right to reduce a part of the common property in game to ownership by possession, yet it was also true that, as early as the Salic law, that right was regulated in certain particulars. . . .

. . .

In both the works of Merlin and Pothier, [ ], will be found a full reference to the history of the varying control exercised by the law-giving power over the right of a citizen to acquire a qualified ownership in animals *feræ naturæ,* evidenced by the regulation thereof by the Salic law, already referred to, exemplified by the legislation of Charlemagne, and continuing through all vicissitudes of governmental authority. This unbroken line of law and precedent is summed up by the provisions of the Napoleon Code, which declares, [ ]: "There are things which belong to no one, and the use of which is common to all. Police regulations direct the manner in which they may be enjoyed. The faculty of hunting and fishing is also regulated by special laws.'' Like recognition of the fundamental principle upon which the property in game rests has led to similar history and identical results in the common law of Germany, in the law of Austria, Italy, and, indeed, it may be safely said in the law of all the countries of Europe. [ ]

The common law of England also based property in game upon the principle of common ownership, and therefore treated it as subject to governmental authority.

Blackstone, while pointing out the distinction between things private and those which are common, rests the right of an individual to reduce a part of this common property to possession, and thus acquire a qualified ownership in it, on no other or different principle from that upon which the civilians based such right. 2 WILLIAM BLACKSTONE, COMMENTARIES ON THE LAWS OF ENGLAND *1, *12.

Referring especially to the common ownership of game, he says:

But, after all, there are some few things which, notwithstanding the general introduction and continuance of property, must still unavoidably remain in common, being such wherein nothing but an usufructuary property is capable of being had; and therefore they still belong to the first occupant during the time he holds possession of them, and no longer. Such (among others) are the elements of light, air, and water, which a man may occupy by means of his windows, his gardens, his mills, and other conveniences. Such, also, are the generality of those animals which are said to be *feræ naturæ* or of a wild and untamable disposition, which any man may seize upon or keep for his own use or pleasure.

Id. at *14.

A man may lastly have a qualified property in animals *feræ naturæ, propter privilegium*, that is, he may have the privilege of hunting, taking, and killing them in exclusion of other persons. Here he has a transient property in these animals usually called game so long as they continue within his liberty, and he may restrain any stranger from taking them therein; but, the instant they depart into another liberty, this qualified property ceases. * * * A man can have no absolute permanent property in these, as he may in the earth and land; since these are of a vague and fugitive nature, and therefore can only admit of a precarious and qualified ownership, which lasts so long as they are in actual use and occupation, but no longer.

Id. at *394.

In stating the existence and scope of the royal prerogative, Blackstone further says:

There still remains another species of prerogative property, founded upon a very different principle from any that have been mentioned before,—the property of such animals, *feræ naturæ*, as are known by the denomination of *game,* with the right of pursuing, taking, and destroying them, which is vested in the king alone, and from him derived to such of his subjects as have received the grants of a chase, a park, a free warren, or free fishery. * * * In the first place, then, we have already shown, and indeed it cannot be denied, that, by the law of nature, every man, from the prince to the peasant, has an equal of pursuing and taking to his own use all such creatures as are *feræ naturæ*, and therefore the property of nobody, but liable to be seized by the first occupant, and so it was held by the imperial law as late as Justinian's time. * * * But it follows from the very end and constitution of society that this natural right, as well as many others belonging to man as an individual, may be restrained by positive laws enacted for reasons of state or for the supposed benefit of the community.

Id. at *410.

The practice of the government of England from the earliest time to the present has put into execution the authority to control and regulate the taking of game.

Undoubtedly, this attribute of government to control the taking of animals *feræ naturæ*, which was thus recognized and enforced by the common law of England, was vested in the colonial governments, where not denied by their charters, or in conflict with grants of the royal prerogative. It is also certain that the power which the colonies thus possessed passed to the States with the separation from the mother country, and remains in them at the present day, in so far as its exercise may be not incompatible with, or restrained by, the rights conveyed to the federal government by the constitution. . . .

The adjudicated cases recognizing the right of the States to control and regulate the common property in game are numerous. In *McCready v. Virginia,* 94 U.S. 391 (1876), the power of the State of Virginia to prohibit citizens of other States from planting oysters within the tide waters of that State was upheld by this court. In *Manchester v. Massachusetts,* 139 U.S. 240 (1890), the authority of the State of Massachusetts to control and regulate the catching of fish within the bays of that State was also maintained. *See also Phelps v. Racey,* 60 N.Y. 10 (1875); *Magner v. People,* 97 Ill. 320 (1881); *American Express Co. v. People,* 24 N.E. 758 (Ill.1890); *State v. Northern Pacific Express Co.,* 59 N.W. 1100 (Minn.1894); *State v. Rodman,* 59 N.W. 1098 (Minn.1894); *Ex parte Maier,* 37 P. 402 (Cal.1894); *Organ v. State,* 19 S.W. 840 (Ark.1892); *Allen v. Wyckoff,* 2 A. 659 (N.J. 1886); *Roth v. State,* 37 N.E. 259 (Ohio 1894); *Gentile v. State,* 29 Ind. 409 (1868); *State v. Farrell,* 23 Mo. App. 176 (1886), and cases there cited; *State v. Saunders,* 19 Kan. 127 (1877); *Territory v. Evans,* 23 P. 115 (Idaho 1890).

Whilst the fundamental principles upon which the common property in game rest have undergone no change, the development of free institutions had led to the recognition of the fact that the power or control lodged in the State, resulting from this common ownership, is to be exercised, like all other powers of government, as a trust for the benefit of the people, and not as a prerogative for the advantage of the government as distinct from the people, or for the benefit of private individuals as distinguished from the public good. Therefore, for the purpose of exercising this power, the State, as held by this court in *Martin v. Waddell,* 41 U.S. (16 Pet.) 367 (1842), represents its people, and the ownership is that of the people in their united sovereignty. The common ownership, and its resulting responsibility in the State, is thus stated in a well-considered opinion of the supreme court of California:

> The wild game within a State belongs to the people in their collective sovereign capacity. It is not the subject of private ownership, except in so far as the people may elect to make it so; and they may, if they see fit, absolutely prohibit the taking of it, or traffic and commerce in it, if it is deemed necessary for the protection or preservation of the public good.

Ex parte Maier, 37 P. 402 (Cal.1894).

The same view has been expressed by the supreme court of Minnesota, as follows:

> We take it to be the correct doctrine in this country that the ownership of wild animals, so far as they are capable of ownership, is in the State, not as a proprietor, but in its sovereign capacity, as the representative and for the benefit of all its people in common.

State v. Rodman, 59 N.W. 1098 (Minn.1894).

The foregoing analysis of the principles upon which alone rests the right of an individual to acquire a qualified ownership in game, and the power of the State, deduced therefrom, to control such ownership for the common benefit, clearly demonstrates the validity of the statute of the State of Connecticut here in controversy. The sole consequence of the provision forbidding the transportation of game killed within the State, beyond the State, is to confine the use of such game to those who own it,— the people of that State. The proposition that the State may not forbid carrying it beyond her limits involves, therefore, the contention that a State cannot allow its own people the enjoyment of the benefits of the property belonging to them in common, without at the same time permitting the citizens of other States to participate in that which they do not own. It was said in the discussion at bar, although it be conceded that the State has an absolute right to control and regulate the killing of game as its judgment deems best in the interest of its people, inasmuch as the State has here chosen to allow the people within her borders to take game, to dispose of it, and thus cause it to become an object of State commerce, as a resulting necessity such property has become the subject of interstate commerce; hence controlled by the provisions of article 1, § 8, of the Constitution of the United States. But the errors which this argument involves are manifest. It presupposes that, where the killing of game and its sale within the State are allowed, it thereby becomes "commerce" in the legal meaning of that word. In view of the authority of the State to affix conditions to the killing and sale of game, predicated, as is this power, on the peculiar nature of such property and its common ownership by all the citizens of the State, it may well be doubted whether commerce is created by an authority given by a State to reduce game within its borders to possession, provided such game be not taken, when killed, without the jurisdiction of the State. The common ownership imports the right to keep the property, if the sovereign so chooses, always within its jurisdiction for every purpose. The qualification which forbids its removal from the State necessarily entered into and formed part of every transaction on the subject, and deprived the mere sale or exchange of these articles of that element of freedom of contract and of full ownership which is an essential attribute of commerce. Passing, however, as we do, the decision of this question, and granting that the dealing in game killed within the State, under the provision in question, created internal State commerce, it does not follow that such internal commerce became necessarily the subject-matter of interstate commerce, and therefore under the control of the Constitution of the United States. The distinction between internal and external commerce and interstate commerce is marked, and has always been recognized by this court . . .

The fact that internal commerce may be distinct from interstate commerce destroys the whole theory upon which the argument of the plaintiff in error proceeds. The power of the State to control the killing of and ownership in game being admitted, the commerce in game which the State law permitted was necessarily only internal commerce, since the restriction that it should not become the subject of external commerce went along with the grant, and was a part of it. All ownership in game killed within the State came under this condition, which the State had the lawful authority to impose; and no contracts made in relation to such property were exempt from the law of the State consenting that such contracts be made, provided only they were confined to internal, and did not extend to external, commerce.

The case in this respect is identical with *Kidd v. Pearson,* 128 U.S. 1 (1888). The facts there considered were, briefly, as follows: The State of Iowa permitted the distillation of intoxicating liquors for "mechanical, medicinal, culinary, and sacramental purposes." The right was asserted to send out of the State intoxicating liquors made therein, on the ground that, when manufactured in the State, such liquors became the subject of interstate commerce, and were thus protected by the constitution of the United States; but this court, through Mr. Justice Lamar, pointed out the vice in the reasoning, which consisted in presupposing that the State had authorized the manufacture of intoxicants, thereby overlooking the exceptional purpose for which alone such manufacture was permitted. So here the argument of the plaintiff in error substantially asserts that the State statute gives an unqualified right to kill game, when in fact it is only given upon the condition that the game killed be not transported beyond the State limits. It was upon this power of the State to qualify and restrict the ownership in game killed within its limits that the court below rested its conclusion, and similar views have been expressed by the courts of last resort of several of the States. . . .

. . . . It is, indeed, true that in *State v. Saunders,* 19 Kan. 127 (1877), and *Territory v. Evans,* 23 P. 115 (Idaho 1890), it was held that a State law prohibiting the shipment outside of the State of game killed therein violated the interstate commerce clause of the Constitution of the United States, but the reasoning which controlled the decision of these cases is, we think, inconclusive, from the fact that it did not consider the fundamental distinction between the qualified ownership in game and the perfect ownership in other property, and thus overlooked the authority of the State over property of game killed within its confines, and the consequent power of the State to follow such property into whatever hands it might pass with conditions and restrictions deemed necessary for the public interest.

Aside from the authority of the State, derived from the common ownership of game and the trust for the benefit of its people which the State exercises in relation thereto, there is another view of the power of the State in regard to the property in game, which is equally conclusive. The right to preserve game flows from the undoubted existence in the State of a police power to that end, which may be none the less efficiently called into play, because by doing so interstate commerce may be remotely and indirectly affected. [ ] Indeed, the source of the police power as to game birds (like those covered by the statute here called into question) flows from the duty of the State to preserve for its people a valuable food supply. *Phelps v. Racey,* 60 N.Y. 10 (1875); *Ex parte Maier,* 37 P. 402 (Cal.1894); *Magner v. People,* 97 Ill. 320 (1881). The exercise by the State of such power therefore comes directly within the principle of *Plumley v. Massachusetts,* 155 U.S. 461 (1894). The power of the State to protect by adequate police regulation, its people against the adulteration of articles of food (which was in that case maintained), although, in doing so, commerce might be remotely affected, necessarily carries with it the existence of a like power to preserve a food supply which belongs in common to all the people of the State, which can only become the subject of ownership in a qualified way, and which can never be the object of commerce except with the consent of the State, and subject to the conditions which it may deem best to impose for the public good.

Judgment affirmed.

■ BREWER and PECKHAM, JJ., not having heard the argument, took no part in the decision of this cause.

■ FIELD, J., dissenting:—.... When any animal, whether living in the waters of the State or in the air above, is lawfully killed for the purposes of food or other uses of man, it becomes an article of commerce, and its use cannot be limited to the citizens of one State to the exclusion of citizens of another State. Although there are declarations of some courts that the State possesses a property in its wild game, and, when it authorizes the game to be killed and sold as an article of food, it may limit the sale only for domestic consumption, and the Supreme Court of Errors of Connecticut, in deciding the present case, appears to have held that doctrine, I am unable to assent to its soundness, *where the State has never had the game in its possession or under its control or use.* I do not admit that in such case there is any specific property held by the State by which in the exercise of its rightful authority, it can lawfully limit the control and use of the animals killed to particular classes of persons or citizens, or to citizens of particular places or States. But, on the contrary, I hold that where animals within a State, whether living in its waters or in the air above, are, at the time, beyond the reach or control of man, so that they cannot be subjected to his use or that of the State in any respect, they are not the property of the State or of any one in a proper sense. I hold that, until they are brought into subjection or use by the labor or skill of man, they are not the property of any one, and that they only become the property of man according to the extent to which they are subjected by his labor or skill to his use and benefit. When man, by his labor or skill, brings any such animals under his control and subject to his use, he acquires to that extent a right of property in them, and the ownership of others in the animals is limited by the extent and right thus acquired. This is a generally recognized doctrine, acknowledged by all States of Christendom. It is the doctrine of law, both natural and positive. The Roman law, as stated in the Digest, cited in the opinion of the majority, expresses it as follows: "That which belongs to nobody is acquired by the natural law by the person who first possesses it." A bird may fly at such height as to be beyond the reach of man or his skill, and no one can then assert any right of property in such bird; it cannot, then, be said to belong to any one. But when, from any cause, the bird is brought within the reach and control or use of man, it becomes at that instant his property, and may be an article of commerce between him and citizens of the same or of other States.

In an opinion written by me some years since, I had occasion to speak of this rule of law. I there said that it was a general principle of law, both natural and positive, that where a subject, animate or inanimate, which otherwise could not be brought under the control or use of man, is reduced to such control or use by his individual labor or skill, a right of property in it is acquired. The wild bird in the air belongs to no one, but when the fowler brings it to the earth and takes it into his possession, it is his property. He has reduced it to his control by his own labor, and the law of nature and the law of society recognize his exclusive right to it. The pearl at the bottom of the sea belongs to no one, but the diver who enters the water and brings it to light has property in the gem. He has by his own labor reduced it to possession, and, in all communities and by all law, his right to it is recognized. So the trapper on the plains and the hunter in the North have a property in the furs they have gathered, though the animals from which they were taken roamed at large, and belonged to no one. They have added by their labor to the uses of man an article promoting his comfort, which, without that labor, would have been lost to him. They have a right, therefore, to the furs, and every court in Christendom would maintain it. So, when the fisherman drags by his net fish from the sea, he has a property in them, of which no one is permitted to despoil him. *Spring Valley Water Works v. Schottler,* 110 U.S. 347, 356 (1884) (Field, J., dissenting).

. . .

I do not doubt the right of the State, by its legislation, to provide for the protection of wild game, so far as such protection is necessary for their preservation, or for the comfort, health, or security of its citizens, and does not contravene the power of Congress in the regulation of interstate commerce. But I do deny the authority of the State, in its legislation for the protection and preservation of game, to interfere in any respect with the paramount control of Congress in prescribing the terms by which its transportation to another State, when killed, shall be restricted to such conditions as the State may impose. The absolute control of Congress in the regulation of interstate commerce, unimpeded by any State authority, is of much greater consequence that any regulation the State may prescribe with reference to the place where its wild game, when killed, may be consumed.

. . .

■ HARLAN, J., dissenting:—. . . . I do not question the power of the State to prescribe a period during which wild game within its limits may not be lawfully killed. The State, as we have seen, does not prohibit the killing of game altogether, but permits hunting and killing of woodcock, quail, ruffled grouse, and gray squirrels between the 1st day of October and the 1st day of January. The game in question having been lawfully killed, the person who killed it and took it into his possession became the rightful owner thereof. This, I take it, will not be questioned. As such owner he could dispose of it by gift or sale, at his discretion. So long as it was fit for use as food, the State could not interfere with his disposition of it, any more than it could interfere with the disposition by the owner of other personal property that was not noxious in its character. To hold that the person receiving personal property from the owner may not receive it with the intent to send it out of the State is to recognize an arbitrary power in the government which is inconsistent with the liberty belonging to every man, as well as with the rights which inhere in the ownership of property. Such a holding would also be inconsistent with the freedom of interstate commerce which has been established by the Constitution of the United States. . . .

NOTES

(1) Note how the majority distinguishes the state's proprietary interest in game and its sovereign authority to regulate in the public interest. Does the Court suggest differences in these legal bases, either in terms of state powers or state responsibilities?

When speaking of the proprietary interest, the Court explains that wildlife is owned by the people in common, with the state empowered to act on their behalf. Is this meaningfully different from the idea that the state itself owns wildlife, subject to duties to manage it in the public interest? Is the Court's language truer to the trust concept under which the people-in-common (the beneficiaries or cestui que trust) hold legal title to the corpus of the trust (the wildlife) which is managed by the trustee (the government) which holds legal title and which has a fiduciary responsibility to the cestui que trust?

Note also that the court describes the ownership arrangement as a "trust for the benefit of the people." [¶ 15] If we are to take this trust language seriously, who created this trust? The state is the trustee, and the people are the beneficiaries, but who is the settlor—that is, who created the trust, established its terms, and transferred property to it? Note that the Court refers to "[t]he common ownership, and *its resulting responsibility in the State*." [¶ 15 emphasis added] This language suggests that the Court viewed the people as themselves the settlor, placing the wildlife in trust for themselves. Does the lack of a clear settlor undercut the accuracy and value of the trust label? Or, is this "trust" simply a metaphor justifying restrictions on the state's power? Does the Court use the metaphor to suggest that there are trust-like obligations to act in the best interest of the beneficiary?

Are courts themselves empowered to flesh out the terms of the trust? If not, does the lack of clear terms also undercut the viability of the public trust in wildlife?

Finally, note the Court's use of *Martin v. Waddell* [¶ 15], the Supreme Court decision that is one of the bases of the public trust doctrine. Although *Martin* dealt with navigable waterways (and the shellfish in them), *Geer*'s use of it suggests that—like the Minnesota court in *State v. Rodman*—the Supreme Court understood its public trust principles to apply fully to all wildlife, terrestrial as well as aquatic.

(2) In their dissents, Justices Field and Harlan challenge the power of the state to define the specific property rights that a person gains upon capturing wildlife. In doing so, they suggest that such rights arise independently of any lawmaking by the state. How can that be? The Supreme Court has consistently held that property rights arise under state law and are protected constitutionally only to the extent recognized by a state's supreme court. *E.g., Board of Regents v. Roth,* 408 U.S. 564, 577 (1972) ("Property interests, *of course,* are not created by the Constitution. Rather, they are created and their dimensions are defined by existing rules or understandings that stem from an independent source such as state law") (emphasis added); *Fox River Paper Co. v. Railroad Commission,* 274 U.S. 651, 657 (1927) (Fourteenth Amendment "affords no protection to supposed rights of property which the state courts determine to be nonexistent"). Is there any reason to believe that property rights in wildlife differ from property rights in other chattels? Or that state lawmakers have any less power to alter state laws in the public interest, including state property laws. Are Field and Harlan asserting otherwise? Neither justice cited precedent in support of his reasoning and neither attempted to align his views with the longstanding linkage between property rights and state law. Can Field's and Harlan's dissents be reconciled with this rule of law? Are their opinions examples of the excesses of the substantive due process era?

We shall return to the fate of *Geer* later in the chapter.

SECTION 2.   CLARIFICATION OF SOVEREIGN POWERS: FROM A "WELL–REGULATED SOCIETY" TO THE "POLICE POWER" TO ADMINISTRATIVE EXPERTISE

As *Rodman* and *Geer* illustrate, by the end of the nineteenth century courts had developed new terminology to describe the sovereign power of states to act in the public interest. The chosen term was the "police power," a term that originally signified the state's inherent power to enact laws in furtherance of the public good. Such laws, of course, restricted private activities, including private efforts to acquire, use, and dispose of private property.

The transition to the "police power" as the dominant metaphor for discussions of the power of the state occurred during the middle of the nineteenth century. It raises a number of questions: how was this power integrated into the older regime of common-law rights? How did it affect longstanding notions about nuisance, trespass, and the like? Did it indeed represent an actual increase in public power or was it simply a repackaging of already-accepted ideas? Most pertinently: What did this transition mean for private rights in wildlife and the state's proprietary role over animals in the wild?

To answer these questions—and take another step toward understanding the link between state and wildlife—we need to consider briefly a vision that guided and shaped much early nineteenth century jurisprudence, the common-law vision of a "well-regulated society."

Inhabitants of the Towns of Stoughton, Sharon, & Canton v. Baker

Massachusetts Supreme Judicial Court.
4 Mass. 522 (1808).

This was a special action of the case, in which the plaintiffs declare than on the 15th day of March, 1805, the legislature ... appointed *N. Tillinghast, E. Loud,* and *E. Turner*, Esquires, a committee ... to repair the several dams on *Neponset* River, between the sea and *Paul's* bridge ... , and to order such alterations to be made in the fishways through the several dams aforesaid, or to cause such new fishways to be made around such dams ... as in their opinion ... should be sufficient for the passage of shad and alewives at the dams aforesaid. The expense of making the alterations, it was resolved, should be borne one fourth part by the towns of *Stoughton, Sharon,* and *Canton,* and three fourths parts by the respective owners of the dams where the alterations should be made. [The committee ordered alterations to the fishway on a dam owned by defendants; the alterations cost $274.53. The towns brought a successful action to recover three fourths of the costs and defendants appealed.]

[The appeal was heard upon an agreed statement of facts: T]hat the defendants are seised in fee simple of a water-mill and dam on *Neponset* River.... [T]he defendant's dam is an ancient dam, and their title thereto is derived from on *Israel Stoughton,* who acquired his right thereto in the year 1633, by grants to him from the town of *Dorchester* ... of a mill privilege, of a wear[1] adjoining his mill, and an exclusive right to take shad and alewives between the wear and the bridge, with a condition that he was to sell the alewives there taken to the plantation[2] at five shillings the thousand, and other fish at reasonable rates; that the said grant was confirmed by the General Court[3] in the year 1634; that no fishway was ever made through the said dam until the year 1789....

---

1. [That is, a "weir"—a fence or a net set in a stream to catch fish.]

2. [That is, the residents of the town of Dorchester.]

3. [The General Court is the Massachusetts legislature.]

■ PARSONS, C.J.:—.... The defendants ... object to the claim for the expenses of making the alterations in the sluice-way, arguing that the legislature had no authority to pass the said resolve; because their dam is an ancient dam, derived from a grant by the town of *Dorchester* in 1633, held by them and by those whose estate they have therein, without any sluice-way for the passage of fish from that time to the year 1789, when the legislature first directed that a passage be opened for fish;—because, in the year 1633, a wear for the taking of fish was granted as appurtenant to their mill, by which the grantee, his heirs and assigns, had a several fishery between the dam and the sea, and that this grant of a wear was, in the same year, confirmed by the colony legislature, so that the public have no right for the passage of fish above or through their wear; ... ;—because, if the public have not this right, but claim to take it for the public use, the commonwealth is bound by the constitution to make a reasonable compensation to the owners, and not charge them with the expense of making the sluice-way.

. . .

The ancient grants by towns are very loosely expressed, and when a fee was intended, words of inheritance are seldom use. When a long possession by the grantee, his heirs or assigns, has followed, the original grant has uniformly been considered as a grant of a fee. In this case, we are therefore of opinion that *Stoughton* took a fee in the *mill privilege,* as it is usually called in this state. And having a privilege to build a mill, he necessarily had a right to erect a dam, to raise water sufficient to drive his mill.

But the right to build a dam for the use of a mill was under several implied limitations. One was to protect private rights, by compelling him to make compensation to owners of land above, for, and damages occasioned by, overflowing their lands: another was to protect the rights of the public in the fishery; so that the dam must be so constructed that the fish should not be interrupted in their passage up the river to cast their spawn. Therefore every owner of a water-mill or dam holds it on the condition, or perhaps under the limitation, that a sufficient and reasonable passage-way shall be allowed for the fish. This limitation, being for the benefit of the public, is not extinguished by any inattention or neglect, in compelling the owner to comply with it. For no laches can be imputed to the government, and against it no time runs so as to bar its rights.

If the government should, in its grant of a *mill privilege,* expressly or by necessary implication, waive this limitation, it should be bound. But it would be an unreasonable construction of the grant by *Dorchester,* to admit that by it all the people are deprived of a free fishery in the river above the dam, to which, until the grant, they were unquestionably entitled.

The public, therefore, having a right to the benefits of this limitation, as to the mill and dam of the defendants, there must be some remedy by which this public benefit may be secured. But this remedy, say the defendants, cannot be obtained by any authority of the committee of the General Court, but should be sought for through the intervention of a jury.

The legislature may make all laws not repugnant to the constitution; and we do not know that this law is repugnant to it. And the usage of the

General Court to appoint committees to locate and describe the site and dimensions of passage-ways for fish is ancient, and has been long continued. But if a committee, thus appointed, should locate and describe a passage-way for fish unnecessary and unreasonable, by which the property of the owner of the mill was injured without any public benefit, we do not admit that he would be without remedy. The owner holds his privilege subject to the limitation, that a reasonable and sufficient passage-way should be allowed for fish. Any prostration of the dam by a committee, not within this limitation, would be an injury to the owner, for which he might appeal to his country,[4] and have a remedy by the verdict of a jury.

. . .

NOTES

(1) What is the basis of the court's decision in *Stoughton*? What is the source of "the right of the public to have a convenient passage-way for the fish"? Is it the common-law property interest, *i.e.*, a "common fishery"? Note the interaction between public and private rights and the adjustment of the two that the court strives to achieve.

(2) The common-law vision of a well-regulated society: Eighteenth- and nineteenth-century common-law judges viewed humans not as autonomous individuals but as members of a community, and, as members of the social order, they were dependent for their well-being on a healthy functioning community. Individuals held rights, but those rights arose out of and were constrained by the duty of all citizens to conduct their affairs to sustain the well-being of the whole.

In his important work on the subject, historian William Novak summarizes this time:

> Nineteenth-century America was a *public* society in ways hard to imagine after the invention of twentieth-century privacy. Its governance was predicated on the elemental assumption that public interest was superior to private interest. Government and society were not created to protect preexisting private rights, but to further the welfare of the whole people and community. [The then-widespread] public regulations ... were consistently and routinely legitimated by the principle canonized by New York Chancellor James Kent: "Private interest must be made subservient to the general interest of the community." Any reversal of that sentiment—any attempt to subsume public welfare in the private interest—was a perversion of republicanism and a reversion to that dark age when governance was captured by private lords and manors.

WILLIAM J. NOVAK, PEOPLE'S WELFARE: LAW & REGULATION IN NINETEENTH CENTURY AMERICA 9 (1996) (endnotes omitted). This well-regulated society was largely implemented and given content at the local level, where a wide variety of regulatory measures guided private conduct in an effort to maintain a harmonious whole.

---

4. ["Country" is a term used in pleading that usually signifies a jury, or the inhabitants of a district from which a jury is summoned.]

> [W]ithin communities, individuals were expected to conform their behavior to local rules and expectations. No community was deemed free without the power and right of members to govern themselves, *that is*, to determine the rules under which the locality as a whole would be organized and regulated. Such open-ended local regulatory power was simply a necessary attribute of any truly popular sovereignty.

Id. at 10. The liberty of the individual, so much cherished in early America, was intimately tied to this self-governance: the American citizen was free, not to act in isolation, but to join with neighbors in collective governing processes. Not the King alone, nor individuals acting in isolation, but the people as a collective entity held sovereign power. Individual rights, including the vitally important right of private property, were shaped and constrained by this popular power:

> Civil liberty consisted only in those freedoms consistent with the laws of the land. Such liberty was never absolute; it always had to conform to the superior power of self-governing communities to legislate and regulate in the public interest. From time immemorial, as the common law saying went, this liberty was subject to local bylaws for the promotion and maintenance of community order, comfort, safety, health, and well-being. Local police ordinances and regulations were seen as the foundation for the simultaneous freedom and order enjoyed in communities and associations such as the legendary Greek city-state, the English hundred, and the German mark. Freedom and regulation in this tradition were not viewed as antithetical but as complementary and mutually reinforcing. . . .
>
> Rights were thus not only social (as opposed to individual) and affirmative (as opposed to defensive), they were also distinctly relative (as opposed to absolute). In contrast to the Blackstonian notion of inviolable, individual guarantees against social or governmental intrusion, these nineteenth-century jurists emphasized the relation and qualified nature of rights. All rights were defined and subject to the larger society form which they sprang, particularly the coincident rights of others and the superior rights of the whole. Nathaniel Chipman argued that "man, sociable by the laws of his nature, has no right to pursue his own interest or happiness, to the exclusion of that of his fellow man." James Wilson elaborated that one had a right to exercise "intellectual" and "active powers" *provided* "he does no injury to others; and *provided* some public interests do not demand his labours."

Id. at 11, 34. The cornerstone of this well-regulated society, Novak recounts, was the law—particularly the common law—and the many detailed, regulatory measures that implemented basic common-law principles. At the core of the common law itself were two maxims that constrained private rights and guided popular lawmaking:

> The public vision of the common law was best expressed in two of its influential, commonly cited maxims: *salus populi suprema lex est* (the welfare of the people is the supreme law) and *sic utere tuo ut alienum non laedas* (use your own so as not to injury another). These two

maxims were the common law foundation for American police regulation. But to treat them as narrow legal rules would be a mistake. *Salus populi* and *sic utere tuo*, in fact, embodied complete and powerful moral and political philosophies. They were the common law blueprints for governance in a well-regulated society.

Id. at 42.

In his 1845 book, *A Selection of Legal Maxims,* Herbert Broom placed *salus populi* first because it was "of such universal application, and resulted so directly and manifestly from motives of public policy or simple principles on which our social relations depend." The maxim, Broom explained, rested on a firm foundation:

> There is an implied assent on the part of every member of society, that his own individual welfare shall, in cases of necessity, yield to that of the community; and that his property, liberty, and life shall, under certain circumstances, be placed in jeopardy or even sacrificed for the public good.

While *salus populi* applied most dramatically when buildings were pulled down "for the preservation and defence of the kingdom" or to "arrest the progress of a fire," the maxim "likewise applies to cases of more ordinary occurrence, in which the Legislature *ob publicam utilitatem,*[1] disturbs the possession or restricts the enjoyment of property by individuals." HERBERT BROOM, A SELECTION OF LEGAL MAXIMS 1–2, 3 (London, 1845).

Although *salus populi* provided the guiding principle, *sic utere tuo* was of more immediate relevance to land-use conflicts—and hence to wildlife issues. As Nathaniel Chipman explained in his 1833 treatise, *sic utere tuo* provided the particular standard for adjusting the interests of individual and community:

> The first rule for the attainment of [the general utility, the general interest and the happiness of man], is that rule of the civil law,—"so use your own right, that you injure no the rights of others." This is not only a rule of civil law, but is a general rule of the law of nature, subordinate to the more general rule, which requires that all actions of individuals be so directed as to promote the good of the whole.

NATHANIEL CHIPMAN, PRINCIPLES OF GOVERNMENT 164–65 (Burlington, Vt., 1833).

Sic utere tuo served as an all-purpose, flexible ideal that required citizens to bend their private activities so as not to disturb other citizens. This was the principle that gained expression in the remedies for nuisance, a body of law that in antebellum America was a very different creature than its pale, modern descendant. The law of public nuisance in particular provided strong remedies for a wide range of activities that, as Blackstone summarized, amounted to "offences against the public order and economical regimen of the state." 4 WILLIAM BLACKSTONE, COMMENTARIES ON THE LAWS OF ENGLAND *167.

---

1. ["for the public good."]

Although *sic utere tuo* did operate to constrain individual behavior in multiple ways, proponents of the well-regulated society did not view it chiefly as a restriction on individual liberty:

> By abating a nuisance or imprisoning a criminal, courts were not destroying liberties, they were defending the rights, actually expanding the liberty, of wronged citizens. The theorists of the well-regulated society, it is important to remember, saw themselves as champions, not critics, of liberty and rights. They merely pointed out that true freedom was always a product of reciprocal protection and respect. Liberty and the common good were not antagonistic in this formulation; they were mutually reinforcing.

William J. Novak, *supra*, at 45.

In short, *salus populi* and *sic utere tuo* together undergirded the common law as the central institution for communal governance:

> The common law rather than natural law, positivism, or constitutionalism was the legal foundation for the well-regulated society. But the common law that inspired these thinkers was not the private, static, or individualistic common law described by Roscoe Pound, Daniel Boorstin, and countless twentieth-century legal scholars. It was dynamic, social, and visionary. Its essence was a historical, organic understanding of the world in which public and private, individual and community, rights and duties were inextricably intertwined in a conception of a well-ordered, constantly changing, society.

Id. at 38 (endnotes omitted).

This communal vision guided not only common-law judges but also legislatures. One result was an abundance of land-use regulations that typified the era. This legislative outpouring included not just laws halting landowner activities deemed harmful, but also laws that obligated landowners to use their properties to foster to the common good:

> From 1776 to 1789, the use of private land in America was significantly constrained by legislation. Land use regulation was commonplace. Contrary to modern supposition, landowners were not free to do as they pleased so long as they refrained from causing injury. Many land use laws were intended not to protect health or safety but to extract positive benefits from landowners that would be useful to others in the community. Most striking, perhaps, were the aesthetic restrictions governing urban buildings and how to situate them. Other land use laws imposed or threatened substantial economic burdens. Some landowners were restrained from selling their land, or were obliged to accept the presence of mineral prospectors and mining operations on their land. Other landowners were obliged to permit entry by strangers and to endure the construction of extensive networks of dikes, ditches or fences on their land, and to contribute money and labor for constructing and maintaining them. Statutes requiring occupancy or use of land threatened landowners' entire ownership interests. Clearly, then, burdensome or invasive regulations restricting land use were common in America in 1789.

John F. Hart, *Land Use Law in the Early Republic and the Original Meaning of the Takings Clause,* 94 Nw. L. Rev. 1099, 1130–31 (2000) (citations omitted).

Although the well-regulated society was commonly discussed in legal terms, as a guiding social vision its coverage extended well beyond the courtroom and legislative chamber. In a country that was still overwhelmingly rural and agrarian, life moved in patterns that seemed ageless, guided by the seasons, and the harvests and fish runs that came with them. Customary ways of behavior—toward one another and toward the land—enjoyed widespread respect. Tillers of the soil in particular had no trouble accepting notions of dependence and interconnection. On the typical farm, many hands were needed for orderly and concerted work; in such a world, notions of individual autonomy were slow to take root. The household was an economic center as well as the base of family life and family governance. Just as the household had clear needs, so too did the larger social community. To the responsible farmer, the well-regulated town was but an expansion and diversification of the well-regulated family farm. In this world, status-based social and economic systems were both necessary and acceptable. Farmers and tradesmen exchanged commodities in an economic system of pervasively regulated prices; millers ground wheat and corn for regulated charges and opened their dams for the passage of fish during their "accustomed season."

PERSPECTIVES

HENRY DAVID THOREAU, A WEEK ON THE CONCORD AND MERRIMACK RIVERS

(1849).

Salmon, Shad, and Alewives were formerly abundant here, and taken in weirs by the Indians, who taught this method to the whites, by whom they were used as food and manure, until the dam and afterward the canal at Billerica, and the factories at Lowell, put an end to their migrations hitherward.... It is said, to account for the destruction of the fishery, that those who at that time represented the interests of the fishermen and the fishes, remembering between what dates they were accustomed to take the grown shad, stipulated, that the dams should be left open for that season only, and the fry, which go down a month later, were consequently stopped and destroyed by myriads. Others say that the fish-ways were not properly constructed. Perchance after a few thousand years, if the fishes will be patient, and pass their summers elsewhere, meanwhile, nature will have levelled the Billerica dam, and the Lowell factories, and the Grass-ground [Concord] River run clear again, to be explored by new migratory shoals, even as far as the Hopkinton pond and Westborough swamp.

.... Dim visions we still get of miraculous draughts of fishes, and heaps uncountable by the river-side, from the tales of our seniors sent on horseback in their childhood from the neighboring towns, perched on saddle-bags, with instruction to get one bag filled with shad, the other with alewives. . . .

. . . . Still patiently, almost pathetically, with instinct not to be discouraged, not to be *reasoned* with, revisiting their old haunts, as if their stern fates would relent, and still met by the Corporation with its dam. Poor shad! where is thy redress? When nature gave thee instinct, did she give thee the heart to bear thy fate? Still wandering the sea in thy scaly armor to inquire humbly at the mouths of rivers if man has perchance left them free for thee to enter. . . . I for one am with thee, and who knows what may avail a crow-bar against that Billerica dam?

NOTES

(1) Fisheries in the colonial and early republic eras: The communitarian norms central to the common-law vision of a well-regulated society incidentally protected wildlife—or, at least, that wildlife that the community valued. Thus, the fish runs that had so amazed the early settlers were the object of social concern. Since the grist-and saw-mills of the period were viewed as public utilities—private capital exercising certain governmental powers and subordinate to the community's needs—millers were expected to open their dams to permit the passage of fish during the appropriate seasons. Indeed, as part of the community, they were unlikely to interfere with fish runs given the importance of the resource to themselves and their neighbors. *See generally* 1 J. LEANDER BISHOP, A HISTORY OF AMERICAN MANUFACTURERS 122–32 (Philadelphia, 1861); WILLIAM E. NELSON, AMERICANIZATION OF THE COMMON LAW 46–63 (1975); Gary Kulik, *Dams, Fish, and Farmers: Defense of Public Rights in Eighteenth–Century Rhode Island, in* THE COUNTRYSIDE IN THE AGE OF CAPITALIST TRANSFORMATION 25, 29–34 (Steven Hahn & Jonathan Prude eds., 1985). Fishing itself was also restrained by the web of community values and limited markets. Matthew Patten, for example, consumed most of the fish he caught. While he did barter some fish for commodities such as salt (and a "jill of rum") that he could not produce, he did not fish to produce a marketable commodity. Thomas C. Thompson, *The Life Course and Labor of a Colonial Farmer,* 40 HIST. N.H. 135 (1985). The blast furnaces that were the first representatives of the industrial revolution were markedly different.

The agrarian-communitarian (the "well-regulated society") and the industrial-individualistic visions came into conflict with the erection of the first blast furnaces in the mid-eighteenth century. The furnaces, unlike earlier grist and sawmills, required a continuous supply of waterpower. Owners of the furnaces thus opposed statutory and common-law requirements that dams include fishways because fishways required spilling water and thus reduced the furnace's efficiency and output. Also unlike grist mills, the blast furnaces and the cotton mills that succeeded them were market concerns that employed wage workers, produced commodities for regional, national, or international markets, and were owned by capitalists who often lived outside the community. This struggle between farmers and dam owners was largely played out in the legislature as each sought statutes protecting their differing visions of the public good. Gary Kulik's study demonstrates that the farmers sought to maintain traditional, public rights to fish both because fish were an important subsistence food item and also because "they were defending a deeply felt definition of the public good and a sense of the proper balance between public and private rights," between "economic individualism and public virtue." Gary Kulik, *supra,* at 27.

As market relations increasingly supplanted the communitarian economic order based on subsistence, barter, and limited markets, economic liberalism was reflected in an increasing number of petitions signed not only by furnace and mill owners, but also by freemen of the community. The corporations gradually were successful in obtaining exemptions from statutes requiring dams to be constructed with suitable fish passage facilities. But it was not until the nineteenth century that the tide turned strongly in favor of the mill owners: just as they had been able to change the patterns of river use, so they were able to weaken the laws protecting fishing rights. In exempting the dams from the requirement of fishways, the legislature chose economic development and private gain; both farmers and fish lost. *See also* 2 CHARLES FRANCIS ADAMS, THREE EPISODES OF MASSACHUSETTS HISTORY 831 (1903); E.N. HARTLEY, IRONWORKS ON THE SAUGUS 262–63, 264–65 (1957); THEODORE STEINBERG, NATURE INCORPORATED 100–101 (1991).

(2) The common-law, activist state: From the earliest years of settlement, colonial and then state governments regulated not only the taking of fish but also their riverine habitat. Drawing upon nuisance principles, colonial and state legislatures enacted a large number of statutes intended to protect the public's interest in the fish runs. The demise of the Merrimack fish runs that Thoreau lamented is an example of a failed attempt to craft a well-regulated society. That the attempt failed is instructive—because it was not a result of governmental inaction: The Massachusetts General Court prohibited certain fishing methods,[2] mandated closed days,[3] required milldams to have fishways,[4] and licensed fishers.[5] In addition to these generally applicable statutes, the legislature enacted seventeen laws applicable to the Merrimack alone between 1783 and 1820. OSCAR HANDLIN & MARY FLUG HANDLIN, COMMONWEALTH 72 & n.80 (rev. ed. 1969). During the same period, New Hampshire enacted eleven laws to regulate its section of the river. THEODORE STEINBERG, NATURE INCORPORATED 171 & n.18 (1991).

(3) The minimalist state: Although the antebellum period was hardly a time of laissez faire libertarianism, it was a period with a minimal amount of permanent state government. For example, the plaintiffs in *Baker* were members of a committee appointed by the Massachusetts legislature. The case thus represents one method for handling a problem that would now be handled by an administrative agency. The failure of the citizen-committee method to prevent the extirpation of the fish runs points to the method's shortcoming: unlike an administrative agency with its staff of fisheries

---

2. *Nye v. Lamphere,* 68 Mass. (2 Gray) 295 (1854) (use of seine net prohibited).

3. *Commonwealth v. Wentworth,* 15 Mass. 188 (1818) (weirs must be removed three days per week).

4. *Commonwealth v. Chapin,* 22 Mass. (5 Pick.) 199 (1827); *Commonwealth v. Knowlton,* 2 Mass. 530 (1807).

5. *Nickerson v. Brackett,* 10 Mass. 212 (1813).

biologists and engineers, a citizen committee appointed by a legislature was likely to have political—rather than technical—expertise.

A similar approach can be seen in the prevalence of *qui tam* actions, a form of citizen-initiated law enforcement. In *Burnham v. Webster,* 5 Mass. 266 (1809), for example, the court states the case as

> The defendant was attached to answer to the plaintiff, one of the fish-wardens of the town of *Scarborough,* ... who sues as well for himself as for the poor of the said town, "in a plea of debt, for that said *Joseph* [Webster], at said *Scarborough,* on the first day of July last past, and on three other days and times between that day and the last day of said July, at the mouth of the *Little River,* ... did, by means and use of a seine or drag-net, take and catch thirty fish called bass, of the value of ten dollars, against the form of the statute in such cases made and provided; by force whereof the said *Joseph* hath forfeited for each and every of said offences, the sum of fifteen dollars, amounting in all to sixty dollars; and an action hath accrued to the plaintiff to sue for and recover the same as aforesaid, to be disposed of according to law. Yet though requested," & c.

Burnham was a *qui tam* informer.

The term *qui tam* is from *qui tam pro domino rege quam pro se ipso in hac parte sequitur*—"he who brings an action for the King as well as for himself." As the phrase indicates, a private person brings a civil proceeding on behalf of both herself and the state (or some other institution) to recover damages or to enforce penalties available under a statute; the private person shares any monetary recovery with the state or other institution. Technically, the action is a civil action of debt.

Qui tam provisions were common in wildlife statutes enacted during the antebellum period in the United States. *See, e.g., Curtis v. Hurlburt,* 2 Conn. 309 (1817); *Moulton v. Libbey,* 37 Me. 472 (1854); *Nye v. Lamphere,* 68 Mass. (2 Gray) 295 (1854); *Fagan v. Armistead,* 33 N.C. 433 (1850). *See generally* Harold J. Krent, *Executive Control over Criminal Law Enforcement: Some Lessons from History,* 38 AM. U.L. REV. 275, 296–302 (1989). In fact, in the reported American cases, *qui tam* actions are more common than direct prosecutions. Since many of the informers were—as Burnham—identified as fish or game wardens, it appears that the warden's salary often was dependent upon such prosecutions. This created an incentive for bribery. As Charles Potter noted, "The methods resorted to by the fishermen to elude the fish-wardens were various, the most common one doubtless being that of bribery." CHARLES E. POTTER, THE HISTORY OF MANCHESTER, FORMERLY DERRYFIELD IN NEW-HAMPSHIRE 651 (1856). Furthermore, the common reliance on *qui tam* actions—effectively placing bounties on bad guys—was also ineffective in areas where most of the population was engaged in the activity. "It was found that in the neighborhood of large fishing-places, all were more or less interested in the fishing-rights; as a consequence, the statute remained a dead letter." *Id.* at 650.

The prevalence of *qui tam* actions reflects the rudimentary nature of the state during the antebellum period. As Lawrence Friedman concluded, both the scope and administrative strength of regulation were limited. Regulation tended to be local, self-sustaining—as in the fee system— and conservative in the use of staff.... Basically, the law let private citizens enforce what regulation there was. If no one brought a lawsuit, or complained to the district attorney about some violation, nothing was done. The state did not seriously try to administer, or carry through independently, what the statutes decreed.

LAWRENCE M. FRIEDMAN, A HISTORY OF AMERICAN LAW 187 (2d ed. 1985).

The lack of salaried, professional enforcement staff contributed to flagrant poaching. A professional staff, however, would have imposed real costs on governments and taxpayers. The unwillingness to pay these costs suggests that the public did not view the problem as a significant one. Ultimately, laws against taking wildlife only stipulated and proposed penalties. George Bird Grinnell thought it all "merely an inheritance from English ancestors" that was never taken seriously. George Bird Grinnell, *American Game Protection: A Sketch, in* HUNTING AND CONSERVATION 201, 221 (George Bird Grinnell & Charles Sheldon eds., 1925). A history of New Hampshire wildlife—which found no prosecutions for poaching deer prior to 1878—indicates he may have been correct. *See* HELENETTE SILVER, A HISTORY OF NEW HAMPSHIRE GAME AND FURBEARERS 195 (1957).

(4) From well-regulated communities to police-powered states: As society changed in nineteenth-century America, particularly with increased industrialization and urbanization, lawmakers needed to act more forcefully to keep private actions in line with the common good. Increasingly, legislation became the primary method of making law; the courts—supplanted as the chief lawmakers—found themselves needing to explain the nature of the state's power to keep the society "well-regulated." A key decision, carrying forward old common-law ideals while giving shape to the new understandings of state power, was a decision by Chief Justice Shaw:

Commonwealth v. Alger

Supreme Judicial Court of Massachusetts.
61 Mass. 53 (1851).

■ SHAW, C.J.:—[Cyrus Alger was indicted for constructing a wharf that extended into Boston harbor beyond limits established pursuant to several statutes. The wharf, however, was constructed entirely within the bounds of land that Alger owned, and it apparently was not an actual obstruction to navigation. Alger defended his conduct by challenging the power of the state to restrict his use of private land. Chief Justice Shaw viewed the case a particularly important one, in light of "the magnitude and extent of the great public interests" and "the importance and value of the private rights." After an extended inquiry, Shaw concluded that the grant of land to Alger and similarly situated landowners passed the full fee interest to their lands beneath Boston harbor, subject to the limited right of way for boats and vessels. Since the riparian owner held the flats in fee, "it becomes necessary to inquire whether it was competent for the legislature to pass acts establishing the harbor lines."]

The manifest object of these statutes is to prevent injurious obstructions in the harbor of Boston, and to secure the free, common, and unobstructed use thereof, for the citizens of the commonwealth, and all other persons, for navigation with ships, boats, and vessels of all kinds, as a common and public right. If this can be done, without an unwarrantable encroachment on the rights of private property, it is an object of great importance, and one in which the holders of riparian rights, as well as all other holders of real estate, and the whole community, have a deep and abiding interest.

We think it is a settled principle, growing out of the nature of well ordered civil society, that every holder of property, however absolute and unqualified may be his title, holds it under the implied liability that his use of it may be so regulated, that it shall not be injurious to the equal enjoyment of others having an equal right to the enjoyment of their property, nor injurious to the rights of the community. All property in this commonwealth, as well that in the interior as that bordering on tide waters, is derived directly or indirectly from the government, and held subject to those general regulations, which are necessary to the common good and general welfare. Rights of property, like all other social and conventional rights, are subject to such reasonable limitations in their enjoyment, as shall prevent them from being injurious, and to such reasonable restraints and regulations established by law, as the legislature, under the governing and controlling power vested in them by the constitution, may think necessary and expedient.

This is very different from the right of eminent domain, the right of a government to take and appropriate private property to public use, whenever the public exigency requires it; which can be done only on condition of providing a reasonable compensation therefor. The power we allude to is rather the police power, the power vested in the legislature by the constitution, to make, ordain and establish all manner of wholesome and reasonable laws, statutes and ordinances, either with penalties or without, not repugnant to the constitution, as they shall judge to be for the good and welfare of the commonwealth, and of the subjects of the same.

It is much easier to perceive and realize the existence and sources of this power, than to mark its boundaries, or prescribe limits to its exercise. There are many cases in which such a power is exercised by all well ordered governments, and where its fitness is so obvious, that all well regulated minds will regard it as reasonable. Such are the laws to prohibit the use of warehouses for the storage of gunpowder near habitations or highways; to restrain the height to which wooden buildings may be erected in populous neighborhoods, and require them to be covered with slate or other incombustible material; to prohibit buildings from being used for hospitals for contagious diseases, or for the carrying on of noxious or offensive trades; to prohibit the raising of a dam, and causing stagnant water to spread over meadows, near inhabited villages, thereby raising noxious exhalations, injurious to health and dangerous to life.

Nor does the prohibition of such noxious use of property, a prohibition imposed because such use would be injurious to the public, although it may diminish the profits of the owner, make it an appropriation to a public use, so as to entitle the owner to compensation. If the owner of a vacant lot in the midst of a city could erect thereon a great wooden building, and cover it with shingles, he might obtain a larger profit of his land, than if obliged to build of stone or brick, with a slated roof. If the owner of a warehouse in a cluster of other buildings could store quantities of gunpowder in it for himself and others, he might be saved the great expense of transportation. If a landlord could let his building for a smallpox hospital, or a slaughter-house, he might obtain an increased rent. But he is restrained; not because the public have occasion to make the like use, or to make any use of the property, or to take any benefit or profit to themselves from it; but because it would be a noxious use, contrary to the maxim, *sic utere tuo, ut alienum non laedas.* It is not an appropriation of the property to a public use, but the restraint of an injurious private use by the owner, and is therefore not within the principle of property taken under the right of eminent domain. . . .

Supposing the principle itself to be well established, the great question then is, whether the act in question, fixing certain harbor lines, was within it; and we are of opinion that it is, although it may in some cases seem to trench somewhat largely on the profitable use of individual property. This opinion is founded on several considerations.

We have already alluded to the point, that a particular use of land, as well inland as on the sea-shore, which, in one situation, would be greatly injurious to common and public rights, in another position would be wholly harmless. A man having a hill of gravel on his farm, not constituting the embankment of a stream, may remove the earth at his pleasure, because such use can injure no one; when under other circumstances, it would be greatly injurious. Whether any restraint upon the use of land is necessary to the preservation of common rights and the public security, must depend upon circumstances, to be judged of by those to whom all legislative power is intrusted by the sovereign authority of the state, so to declare and regulate as to secure and preserve all public rights.

. . .

Wherever there is a general right on the part of the public, and a general duty on the part of a land owner, or any other person, to respect such right, we think it is competent for the legislature, by a specific enactment, to prescribe a precise, practical rule for declaring, establishing, and securing such right, and enforcing respect for it. It may be said in general terms, independently of any positive enactment, that it is the right of society, in the midst of a populous settlement, to be exempt from the proximity of dangerous and noxious trades, and that it is the duty of the owner of real estate, in the midst of many habitations, to abstain from erecting buildings thereon, or otherwise using it, for carrying on a trade dangerous to the lives, health, or comfort of the inhabitants of such dwellings; although a trade in itself useful and beneficial to the public. But such general duty and obligation not being fixed by a rule precise enough for practical purposes, we think it is competent for the legislature to interpose, and by a specific enactment to declare what shall be deemed a dangerous or noxious trade, under what circumstances and within what distance of habitations it may or shall not be set up, how the use of it shall be regulated, and to prohibit any other than such regulated use, by specific penalties.

This principle of legislation is of great importance and extensive use, and lies at the foundation of most enactments of positive law, which define and punish *mala prohibita*. Things done may or may not be wrong in themselves, or necessarily injurious and punishable as such at common law; but laws are passed declaring them offences, and making them punishable, because they tend to injurious consequences; but more especially for the sake of having a definite, known and authoritative rule which all can understand and obey. In the case already put, of erecting a powder magazine or slaughterhouse, it would be indictable at common law, and punishable as a nuisance, if in fact erected so near an inhabited village as to be actually dangerous or noxious to life or health. Without a positive law, every body might agree that two hundred feet would be too near, and that two thousand feet would not be too near; but within this wide margin, who shall say, who can know, what distance shall be too near or otherwise? An authoritative rule, carrying with it the character of certainty and precision, is needed. The tradesman needs to know, before incurring expense, how near he may build his works without violating the law or committing a nuisance; . . . . This requisite certainty and precision can only be obtained by a positive enactment. . . .

. . .

On the whole, the court are of opinion that the act fixing a line within the harbor of Boston, beyond which no riparian proprietor should erect a wharf or other permanent structure, although to some extent it prohibited him from building such structure on flats of which he owned the fee, was a constitutional law, and one which it was competent for the legislature to make; that it was binding on the defendant, and rendered him obnoxious to its penalties, if he violated its provisions.

NOTES

(1) How does Chief Justice Shaw explain the links between common law limits on property and police power regulation? What roles does he see the legislature playing in furthering basic common-law principles? Perhaps most critically, does he explain how far beyond the common law a legislature might go in restricting private conduct in the name of the public health, safety, and welfare?

Note that, for Shaw, it is not just the landowner who has rights that deserve protection: the community also has "public rights," and the task of lawmakers is to accommodate these different rights when conflicts arise. Indeed, as Shaw sees the law at issue, it is a law that states more expressly the "general right on the part of the public" and the corresponding "general duty on the part of a landowner." Those rights and duties exist, he states, as a matter of common law, apparently arising out of the *sic utere* doctrine; the legislature's task is to translate that doctrine into a specific rule that responds to the landowner's need for "requisite certainty and precision." Though *sic utere* today is sometimes viewed as a doctrine that protects individual landowners against interferences by their neighbors, Shaw views it as also embodying the public interest.

Note also that Shaw's decision explicitly echoed its heritage, stating that the legislature's power to regulate property "grow[s] out of the nature of *well ordered civil society*." [¶ 3 emphasis added] Property, he writes, may not be used in a manner that was "injurious to the rights of the community," *sic utere tuo ut alienum non laedas*. This "implied" limit on property reflected its "social and conventional" nature and the fact that it was subject to "reasonable" legislative regulation. In all of this, Shaw ratified and clarified the decisions in which states had regulated not only rivers to protect fisheries but subjects as diverse as highways, *People v. Cunningham*, 1 Den. 524 (N.Y.Sup.Ct.1845), graveyards, *Coates v. City of New York*, 7 Cow. 585 (N.Y.Sup.Ct.1827), and travelling on Sunday, *Mayo v. Wilson*, 1 N.H. 53 (1817).

While *Alger* is generally viewed as the most significant early statement of the police power—and remains one of the most-cited state court rulings from the nineteenth century—it was, of course, far from the only such decision. *See, e.g., Commonwealth v. Tewksbury*, 52 Mass. (11 Metc.) 55 (1846); *Vanderbilt v. Adams*, 7 Cow. 349 (N.Y.Sup.Ct.1827). *See generally* HENDRIK HARTOG, PUBLIC PROPERTY AND PRIVATE POWER 71–81 (1983); Scott M. Reznick, Comment, *Land Use Regulation and the Concept of Takings in Nineteenth Century America*, 40 U. CHI. L. REV. 854 (1973).

(2) Terminology: The "police power" is nothing more than the residual power of the state to govern. Blackstone wrote of

> the public *police* or *economy*. By the public police and economy I mean the due regulation and domestic order of the kingdom; whereby the individuals of the state, like members of a well-governed family, are bound to conform their general behaviour to the rules of propriety, good neighbourhood, and good manners; and to be decent, industrious and inoffensive in their respective stations. This head of offences must therefore be very miscellaneous, as it comprises all such crimes as especially affect public policy.

4 WILLIAM BLACKSTONE, COMMENTARIES ON THE LAWS OF ENGLAND *162. Among this "miscellaneous" group, Blackstone included nuisances and "destroying game."

During the late eighteenth and early nineteenth centuries, courts and lawmakers used phrases such as "internal police" and "police regulations" to describe Blackstone's miscellany of laws and regulations intended to promote public peace, order, safety, comfort, health, economy, morals, and general welfare; that is: The term was applied to laws regulating activities in the public interest. Although Chief Justice John Marshall may have coined the phrase "police power,"[1] it was a new generation of state court judges—most notably Chief Justice Shaw—who gave the doctrine its classic shape.

---

1. Marshall employed the term "police power" in *Brown v. Maryland*, 25 U.S. (12 Wheat.) 419 (1827).

(3) The "police power," separation of powers, and the common law's decline: The transition from the common-law vision of a "well-regulated society" to the police power carried important implications in terms of the allocation of power among government branches. Consider the following excerpt from *Commonwealth v. Chapin,* a Massachusetts decision that predated *Alger:*

> [I]t is plain that the mere erecting or continuing a dam whereby fish may be obstructed, is no longer an offence [as it was at the common law]. . . . The offence consists only in having a dam without providing a convenient passage for the fish during two or three months in the year, and the remedy where this requisition is not observed, is totally different from that which exists at common law for a nuisance. Instead of abating a dam which is found deficient, the statute provides a pecuniary mulct, and gives power to certain municipal officers to supervise the public interests, and see to the execution of the law.
>
> It follows, we think, that an indictment as at common law for a nuisance cannot be maintained; but that if the dam should be continued without opening through it, at the proper season, a passage way for fish, the proprietors will be subject to the penalty provided by the statute.

Commonwealth v. Chapin, 22 Mass. (5 Pick.) 199 (1827).

At common law, judges hearing nuisance actions decided whether a particular activity did or did not cause undue harm, and hence whether it was consistent with the public good. As statutes became more widespread and specific, the key issue in a judicial dispute increasingly was not whether the defendant's activity was a nuisance, but whether it complied with the governing statute. Statutes could be more precise than the common law, and hence could give clearer guidance, as the court in *Alger* recognized. When legislatures updated statutes they changed the law in a more clear-cut, abrupt way than did common law courts with their characteristically backward-looking, precedent-tied style of decision writing. Yet, once enacted, statutes also had a static quality that gave rise to potential problems of obsolescence. Moreover, statutes with all their detail often obscured the underlying principles—such as *sic utere* and *salus populi*—which emerged so clearly in common law decisions. *Sic utere* would remain alive in the legal consciousness, though confined largely to the law of nuisance. *Salus populi,* however, largely disappeared from memory, no longer serving as an overall check on assertions of individual rights. The police power, to be sure, gave legislatures sufficient authority to act in the public interest, but it became easier to see their work as invasions of private rights once *salus populi* faded and *sic utere* lost ground. The well-ordered common-law vision lost much of its force, particularly as a self-implementing limit on private rights. Its decline made way for new images of autonomous rights and new visions of land ownership, ones that defined private rights with little regard for social context and the common good.

(4) The police power and refrigeration: One change that tested the limits of the police power was a technological innovation: the development of refrigeration allowing iced game to be shipped long distances. On the development of the technology, *see* WILLIAM CRONON, NATURE'S METROPOLIS 230–35, 248–49 (1991).

A New York Court of Appeals' decision in a case involving the new technology became a key decision in the use of a broad understanding of the police power to conserve wildlife. The decision in *Phelps v. Racey* upheld the validity of a statute banning possession of game during the closed season. In doing so, the court offered a ringing endorsement of state power to conserve wildlife:

> The legislature may pass many laws the effect of which may be to impair or even destroy the right of property. Private interest must yield to the public advantage.... The protection and preservation of game has been secured by law in all civilized countries, and may be justified on many grounds, one of which is for purposes of food. The measures best adapted to this end are for the legislature to determine, and courts cannot review its discretion.

Phelps v. Racey, 60 N.Y. 10 (1875). *See also State v. Judy*, 7 Mo.App. 524 (1879) (to be effective, a game law must go further than merely prohibiting killing during specified seasons given the technological developments in refrigeration).

The plaintiff in the New York case, Royal Phelps, was a prominent conservationist, long active in the New York Association for the Protection of Game. The defendant was a game dealer in the city. According to historian James Tober, the New York Association was "particularly vigilant" in enforcing game laws against city game dealers as early as 1870:

> In December of that year, at the monthly meeting of the association, President Royal Phelps remarked that the good work of the club had had a great effect in halting the sale of illegal game and in encouraging high-class eating establishment to obey the law. "[Now] to invite guests to eat game out of season is to insult them." Using its membership fees and dues, the club employed a staff of detectives to roam the market stalls in search of violations. In 1873, for example, the association brought twenty-seven suits for violations of the game laws, all but three of which were decided in favor of the club. On March 1, 1877, the first day of the closed season, three detectives filed twenty-one complaints from which eighteen suits resulted. According to Charles Whitehead, counsel to the association, this represented the "usual number of delinquents engaged in selling game contrary to law." The most notable early victories of the association were in the cases against dealers Middleton and Carmen for possession of one hundred speckled trout in violation of the law, settled in the amount of $2,500 (or $25 per fish as specified by law), and against Joseph Racey for possession of quail beyond the legal date of sale. This latter case was appealed to the state appeals court, which upheld the conviction in a landmark decision supporting state authority to limit the sale of game.

JAMES A. TOBER, WHO OWNS WILDLIFE? THE POLITICAL ECONOMY OF CONSERVATION IN NINETEENTH-CENTURY AMERICA 216 (1981) (endnotes omitted).

West Point Water Power & Land Improvement Co. v. Moodie

Supreme Court of Nebraska.
66 N.W. 6 (1896).

■ POST, C.J.:—This was an application for a writ of mandamus ... to require [West Point Water Power] to construct a suitable fishway whereby fish may readily pass over or around a dam maintained by said respondent in the Elkhorn river. An answer was filed by the respondent, in which is contained the following admission: "It admits that the respondent owns and maintains a milldam across said Elkhorn river, at or near the city of West Point, and within said county of Cuming, and that the said respondent has never provided, and has not at the present time, a suitable fishway, nor any fishway whatever, whereby fish may pass over or around said milldam." The other allegations of the answer are, in substance, that the land upon which said dam is situated is private property; that the construction of said dam was authorized by the territorial legislature in the year 1867; that the respondent has acquired the right to maintain it, as at present constructed, by adverse user; that the Elkhorn river is a private, unnavigable stream, and to require the respondent to construct a fishway would be to damage its property, within the prohibition of the state constitution . .

The [statute involved provides:] "It shall also be unlawful for any person, association of persons, or corporation to place or establish any obstruction across any stream of water in this state that shall prevent the free passage of fish along said stream: provided, that all persons, associations of persons, or corporations erecting, owning, or maintaining a milldam across any stream in this state, shall at his or its own expense, construct and at all times maintain, subject to the approval of the fish commission, a suitable and substantial fishway whereby all fish passing along said stream can readily pass over or around said dam. Public waters within the meaning of this section shall embrace all lakes, ponds, rivers, creeks, bayous and streams except private artificial ponds or ponds subject to the exclusive dominion of a single ownership." [ ] The courts of the country have frequently been called upon to give effect to acts of this character, and have, it is believed, in every instance sustained the power of the legislature over the subject. *See Hooker v. Cummings,* 20 Johns. 90 (N.Y.Sup.Ct.1822); *Inhabitants of the Towns of Stoughton, Sharon, Canton v. Baker,* 4 Mass. 522 (1808); *Burnham v. Webster,* 5 Mass. 266 (1809); *Commonwealth v. M'Curdy,* 5 Mass. 324 (1809); *Nickerson v. Brackett,* 10 Mass. 212 (1813); *Commonwealth v. Chapin,* 22 Mass. (5 Pick.) 199 (1827); *Vinton v. Welsh,* 26 Mass. (9 Pick.) 87 (1829); *Commonwealth v. Essex Co.,* 79 Mass. (13 Gray) 239 (1859); *Cottrill v. Myrick,* 12 Me. 222 (1835); *Weller v. Snover,* 42 N.J.L. 341 (1880); *Parker v. People,* 111 Ill. 581 (1884); *Holyoke Co. v. Lyman,* 82 U.S. (15 Wall.) 500 (1872). In the case last cited, which involved a statute of Massachusetts, after which ours appears to have been modeled, the subject was considered in all its phases, resulting in the conclusion that, while a grant authorizing the use of the water of a stream for mill purposes is a vested right, such right is subject to legislative control, and that one erecting a dam in a stream annually frequented by fish, does so under the implied obligation to maintain sufficient openings to permit the passage of fish at all proper seasons. In that case Mr. Justice Clifford, after citing with approval the opinion of Chief Justice Shaw in *Commonwealth v. Essex Co.,* says: "From the earliest times the right of the public to the passage of fish in rivers, and the private rights of riparian proprietors, incident to and dependent on the public right, have been subject to regulation of the legislature. The mode adopted by the legislature, whether by public or private acts, to secure and preserve such rights, has been by requiring, in the erection of dams, such sluices and fishways as would enable these migratory fish, according to their known habits and instincts, to pass from the lower to the higher level of the water occasioned by such dam, so that, although their passage might be somewhat impeded, it would not be thereby essentially obstructed." And in *Commonwealth v. Chapin,* the same principle is recognized by Chief Justice Parker in the following language: "This common-law right of several fishery in the owners of lands bordering on rivers not navigable is subject to a reasonable qualification, in order to protect the rights of others, who, in virtue of owning the soil, have the same right, but might lose all advantage from it if their neighbors below them on a stream or river might, with impunity, wholly impede the passage of fish into the lakes or ponds where they, by instinct, prepare for the multiplication of the species. This restriction is founded upon that universal principle of every just code of laws: *'Sic utere tuo ut alienum non laedas.' " State v. Franklin Falls Co.,* 49 N.H. 240 (1870), to which we are referred in support of the opposing view, is not authority for the contention of the plaintiff in error. Indeed, it may be said to sustain the doctrine of the cases above cited since the propositions therein asserted are: (1) That the maintaining in an unnavigable river, which is the outlet of a large inland lake, of a dam without a fishway, so as to obstruct the passage of fish from the sea to the lake, is indictable at common law. (2) No right will be acquired, as against the state, by the obstruction of a public fishery for more than 20 years under a claim of right, where such obstruction originated without right.

Regarding the plaintiff in error's reliance upon a prescriptive right to maintain its dam without making provision for the passage of fish, and upon the fact that the construction of the dam was authorized by the territorial legislature, it is sufficient that the reserved powers of the state, including the right to conserve and promote the public welfare at the expense of private interests, denominated the "police power," is inalienable, and cannot be surrendered or bartered away by the legislature. [ ]; *Stone v. Mississippi,* 101 U.S. 814 (1879).

Lastly, it is urged that the law recognizes no common right of fishery in the streams of this state; that such right belongs exclusively to the owners of the soil; that it is, in short, a private right only, in which the state is not interested.... [T]he test of public utility is whether the particular regulation involved has some relation to the public welfare, and whether such is, in fact, the end sought to be attained. That the declared purpose of the act, *viz.* the preservation of the fish in our streams, is a proper function of the state government, as tending directly to promote the public welfare, is a proposition distinctly recognized by authority.... The provision for the construction of fishways must, therefore, be regarded as a duty enjoined upon persons and corporations maintaining dams in the streams of the state, in the interest of the public at large. . . .

NOTES

(1) The police power and private property: Cases such as *West Point Water Power* illustrate a longstanding willingness by courts to sustain regulatory measures aimed at keeping waterways open for fish, notwithstanding both private property rights and an express legislative authorization to block the waterway. The notes that follow explore aspects of that story, which has important implications for continuing efforts today to protect migratory fish runs. Note that, in *West Point Water Power*, the landowner's case was as strong as it could be: the waterway was nonnavigable; the public had no right to fish in it; the dam was authorized by statute and built entirely on private land; and the regulatory measure was enacted long after the dam was built. Still, the court had no trouble finding the statute valid.

Despite the willingness of courts to sustain such measures, however, many rivers were blocked and fish runs ended—the combined result of the strong political power of dam builders, private and public, and the often strong public support for development.

(2) The "public welfare": At the end of its decision in *West Point Water Power*, the court states, "the preservation of fish in our streams, is a proper function of the state government, *as tending directly to promote the public welfare*." [¶ 4 emphasis added] How does the preservation of fish promote the public welfare? Some contemporary cases tie the state's regulatory authority to a utilitarian calculus. *E.g., Parker v. People,* 111 Ill. 581 (1884) (state had power to order construction of fishways in private dam since otherwise "all the fish in our streams would soon be destroyed, and the production of food decreased perhaps million of dollars annually, and other food enhanced in price, so as to become oppressive to the poor and struggling masses."); *Commonwealth v. Manchester,* 25 N.E. 113 (Mass. 1890), *aff'd sub nom. Manchester v. Massachusetts,* 139 U.S. 240 (1891) ("The preservation of fish, even although they are not used as food for human beings, but as food for other fish which are so used, is for the common benefit"); *State v. Rodman,* 59 N.W. 1098 (Minn.1894) ("preservation of such animals as are adapted to consumption as food, or to any other useful purpose, is a matter of public interest; and it is within the police power of the state"); *Commonwealth v. Bender,* 7 Pa. Co. Ct. Rep. 620 (1887) (state may act "to increase the supply of fish and make this food cheaper and more abundant" even when the effect is to restrict defendant's right to use his property).

Other decisions take a more expansive view. Recall *Barrett v. State,* 116 N.E. 99 (N.Y.1917) [Chapter 3], in which defendant argued that the reintroduction of beaver was "an unreasonable exercise of the police power" because of the damage to plaintiff's property. The court rejected the contention categorically:

the general right of the government to protect wild animals is too well established to be now called in question. . . . Their preservation is a matter of public interest. They are a species of natural wealth which without special protection would be destroyed. Everywhere and at all times governments have assumed the right to prescribe how and when they may be taken or killed. As early as 1705, New York passed such an act as to deer. [ ] A series of statutes has followed protecting more or less completely game, birds, and fish.

See also Commonwealth v. Essex Co., 79 Mass. (13 Gray) 239 (1859) (the legislature has the power to balance competing public and private interests "[w]hether that public good, expected from the fishery, consisted in affording an additional article of food to the people, or ... otherwise"); *State v. Mrozinski,* 61 N.W. 560 (Minn.1894) (argument that police power is limited to measures that "are reasonably necessary to prevent the extermination or undue depletion of food fishes" rejected as too limited).

(3) Private rights, public rights, and the limits of the police power: *West Point* sits on the cusp of a fundamental transformation: the defendant argues "private property"; the court responds "police power." But defendant's private property argument is not the modern argument that the state's action is a taking of the private property. Rather, the defendant's argument is that the state lacks the power to act because all of the rights in the stream are private, *i.e.,* the fishery is a several rather than a common fishery and the banks are bed are privately owned. Thus, the upper riparian landowners are the only other entities with any interest in the proceeding and the state lacks the power to act. Had the court accepted this argument, the effect would have been to restrict the state's sovereign powers to common-law definitions of public property.

Defendant's argument thus reflects the earlier jurisprudence that mingled property and sovereignty. This perspective found strong (but highly unusual) support in a decision of the New York Supreme Court, *People v. Platt.* In 1819, the New York Supreme Court was faced with a challenge to an indictment of a dam owner for failing to alter its dam to allow the passage of salmon. The court concluded that the dam owner had the right to destroy the salmon run up the Saranac River. It predicated its conclusion on the fact that there was no common fishery in the river: In the absence of a public property right in the fishery, the state had no power to restrict the use of private property (*i.e.,* the land occupied by the milldam and the dam itself) or the destruction of private property (*i.e.,* the fish run). That is,

a. the river was nonnavigable at the common law;

b. therefore, the riparian landowner owned the soil beneath the river because it owned the land on both sides of the river;

c. therefore, the riparian landowner also owned the fishery in the river as a profit *a prendre* of the soil beneath the river;

d. therefore the defendant owned the fishery and it had a right to destroy the fish that annually swam through the fishery to reach their spawning grounds. *People v. Platt,* 17 Johns. 195 (N.Y.1819).

Does the final point follow from the preceding predicates? At the common law, did the owner of a fishery *own* the fish swimming in the fishery? Note also that the court ignored the fact that the salmon that spawn in the Saranac did not remain in that river but returned downstream where the public did have a right to fish. Should the fact that the fish spend part—even most—of their lives in a public fishery affect the court's property-based analysis?

(4) The inalienability of state power to regulate in the public interest: Defendant's argument in *West Point*—as well as in *People v. Platt*—can also be viewed as an assertion that the state could contract away its (sovereign) power to regulate in the public interest. In the terms of the period, can the government contract away the police power? The decision in *West Point* provided an answer to this issue: The state's power to restrict property for that purpose, the court declares, inheres in the state police power and is an inalienable source of state authority. Hence, one legislature cannot by express grant vest rights that enable a landowner to avoid later regulatory enactments.

The United States Supreme Court similarly decided the issue:

> If the legislature that granted this charter had the power to bind the people of the State and all succeeding legislatures to allow the corporation to continue its corporate business during the whole term of its authorized existence, there is no doubt about the sufficiency of the language employed to effect that object.... Whether the alleged contract exists, therefore, or not, depends on the authority of the legislature to bind the State and the people of the State in that way.

> All agree that the legislature cannot bargain away the police power of a State. "Irrevocable grants of property and franchises may be made if they do not impair the supreme authority to make laws for the right government of the State; but no legislature can curtail the power of its successors to make such laws as they may deem proper in matters of police." *Metropolitan Board of Excise v. Barrie,* 34 N.Y. 657 (1866); *Boyd v. Alabama,* 94 U.S. 645 (1876).

Stone v. Mississippi, 101 U.S. 814 (1879).

Washington Kelpers Association v. State

Washington Supreme Court.
502 P.2d 1170 (1972).
certiorari denied, 411 U.S. 982 (1973).

■ NEILL, J.:—Defendants State of Washington and the Director of Fisheries appeal from a judgment declaring RCW 75.12.650 unconstitutional and restraining the Department of Fisheries from enforcing the provisions of the statute.

. . .

The effect of the legislation is to prohibit the use of sports gear for commercial salmon fishing.

The record indicates that in 1969 there were nearly 2800 commercial salmon fishing licenses issued by the Department of Fisheries. Approximately one half of these licenses were commercial trolling licenses issued to fishermen using "angling" or sports gear rather than one of the various types of fixed trolling gear. Plaintiff is an association of these licensees who fish commercially with sports gear.

The trial court held that (1) RCW 75.12.650 is not a valid exercise of the police power in that it has no real or substantial relation to the objects stated to be accomplished by the Department of Fisheries; and (2) the statute discriminates within a class and violates both the state and federal constitutions.

In deciding the constitutional questions thus raised, it is necessary to view RCW 75.12.650 in the context of the comprehensive conservation and management programs for our salmon resource carried on by the state through the Department of Fisheries. Salmon in the waters of the state of Washington are a managed and protected resource from the time young salmon come out of their native spawning beds and move downstream to sea until the time they once again return from the ocean to these same beds to spawn their young and die. The Department of Fisheries' management program is quite complex. The department protects and improves habitat by regulating the taking of gravel and diversion of water from streams, initiating stream improvement cleanup work to insure that streams are suitable for salmon, constructing fish ladders and other devices which open up miles of Washington's streams which would otherwise be inaccessible to salmon, and maintaining hatcheries for the artificial propagation of salmon. As salmon go to sea, the department observes them and the conditions that affect them and predicts the survival expected in the oncoming harvest.

As there is a limited supply of salmon and high competition for them, the department must have a complex set of regulations so that salmon will be properly protected and managed as they return through the various intensive fisheries and so that a proper escapement will be obtained. Regulations are based on the expected size of salmon runs and the department's knowledge of the effectiveness of various types of fishing gear and the corresponding effect on the returning fish.

The ocean fishery, which includes the sport fishery and the commercial troll fishery, is the most difficult to regulate because the department cannot tell whether a particular fish caught is from a limited stock or an abundant stock. Heavy fishing may over fish limited stocks of fish while exploiting more abundant stocks. It is necessary to limit the ocean catch so that overutilization can be corrected by management of other fishing areas as the fish move to their home streams.

As the various runs of salmon move inland from the ocean, they begin to separate. The department, when these conditions are known, can apply regulations allowing for higher catches on abundant stocks and more stringent regulations to protect those stocks of fish which are weak. If an ocean catch is not tightly regulated and managed, it is impossible to properly protect weak stocks of fish.

The department has three management tools that are used in the regulation of fisheries. These are (1) regulation of the time of fishing, (2) the area of fishing, and (3) the type of gear that may be used for fishing. Management of the total fishing effort has necessitated the enactment of different regulations for sport fishing and for commercial fishing. Basically, the sports fisheries are managed to allow large numbers of fishermen to take a limited number of fish.... Under [administrative regulations] most rivers, streams, and ocean areas are open to angling with varying possession and bag limits for different areas. For the coastal fishery, the limit is three salmon of not less than 20 inches in length. [ ] No license is presently required for angling, but sport catches must be recorded upon salmon punch cards, which are returned to the Department of Fisheries. Fish taken by angling are for personal use only and may not be sold commercially.

Commercial fisheries, on the other hand, are managed to allow for proper escapement and maximum commercial take. The legislature has established license requirements for all segments of the commercial fishery. Areas open to commercial fishing are set by statute [ ] and permanent regulations [ ]. The legislature has also defined lawful gear for the various classes of licenses.

RCW 75.12.650 was enacted by the legislature as a part of the management and regulatory scheme of the Department of Fisheries as outlined above. The state asserts that the statute, by prohibiting the use of sports gear for commercial fishing, improves the Department of Fisheries' ability to manage both the sport and commercial ocean fisheries and furthers the overall conservation goals of the department.

In determining the constitutionality of RCW 75.12.650, we must remember that the state, in its sovereign capacity, owns the fish in the waters of the state. Fishermen have no private property rights in taking salmon. In regulating the fisheries, the state is merely enacting legislation concerning its own property and prescribing the methods which may be used in acquiring it by private persons.

. . .

The test, then, for determining whether RCW 75.12.650 is a valid exercise of the police power, is whether the statute has a reasonable and substantial relation to the accomplishment of some purpose fairly within the legitimate range or scope of the police power. Without exception, this court has found that the regulation of the salmon industry promotes the good order and welfare of the people of this state and is clearly within the legislative police power. [ ]

The precise objectives of RCW 75.12.650 are, as stated by representatives of the Department of Fisheries, to (1) make separate and distinct the sport and commercial fisheries and specifically to eliminate the abuse of purchasing a commercial license to circumvent sport catch limitations; (2) improve the policing of fishery violations and decrease the number of sport-caught fish illegally entering commercial channels; and (3) improve the management of the salmon industry. We believe each of these objectives to be fairly within the legitimate scope of the police power, as part of the comprehensive conservation and management program carried on by the state.

We turn to the second criterion for validity of the statute under the police power, *i.e.*, whether RCW 75.12.650 bears a reasonable relationship to the accomplishment of these goals.

The trial court was presented with substantial evidence tending to establish a relationship between RCW 75.12.650 and the stated objectives of the statute. Prior to the enactment of RCW 75.12.650, persons fishing with sport angling gear could fish commercially by purchasing a troll line license. [ ] The record indicates that during the last 10 years the number of persons purchasing troll line licenses and fishing with sport angling gear has rapidly increased and created problems in management of the salmon fishery and enforcement of existing conservation laws.

The Director and Assistant Director of the Department of Fisheries outlined at trial facts which would justify enactment of RCW 75.12.650. Both testified that RCW 75.12.650 was enacted to make sport and commercial ocean fisheries separate and distinct and to improve enforcement of sport and commercial fishery rules and regulations.

The director described the problem of identification of sport and commercial fishermen which RCW 75.12.650 should correct:

> There are several factors that concern us. Number one, a man holding a troller's license can fish either commercially or sportswise. In other words, he wears two hats. As an illustration, our patrol boat might spot a vessel in a preserve which he recognizes as belonging to comsport,[1] if I may use that term, and he will run over there to see what this commercial fisherman is doing in a preserve, and the holder of the troll license will say, "Well, I am not commercially fishing now; I am fishing sportswise."

. . .

In his testimony, the director emphasized that management and conservation are synonymous terms:

> Well, in the fishery management business, the terms "management" and "conservation" are synonymous. If you will read the literature which comes to us from other fisheries agencies, you will see that articles using the word "management" when they could very easily and more properly have used the word "conserve" or "conservation." Now, we can't conserve the fish unless we can properly manage it.

. . .

. . . . The trial court was presented with facts which can "reasonably be conceived to exist," and which demonstrate a reasonable and substantial relation between RCW 75.12.650 and a proper legislative purpose. We hold that RCW 75.12.650 is a valid exercise of the police power.

The trial court also concluded that RCW 75.12.650 discriminates within a class and violates both the state and federal constitutions. We

---

1. ["Comsport" refers to people licensed for commercial salmon trolling in vessels without fixed gear.]

have recognized that the state may classify its citizens for various purposes, treating some differently from others. In discussing class legislation, we said in *Clark v. Dwyer,* 353 P.2d at page 947:

> Article I, § 12 of the state constitution and the fourteenth amendment to the Federal constitution, prohibiting special privileges and immunities and guaranteeing equal protection of the laws, require that *class legislation must apply alike to all persons within a class, and reasonable ground must exist for making a distinction between those within, and those without, a designated class.* Within the limits of these restrictive rules, the legislature has a wide measure of discretion, and its determination, when expressed in statutory enactment, cannot be successfully attacked unless it is manifestly arbitrary, unreasonable, inequitable, and unjust.

(Italics ours.) [ ]

Clearly, RCW 75.12.650 applies equally to all persons within the statutory class. The law prohibits the use of "angling" or "personal use" gear for all commercial salmon fishing, and everyone who comes within the provisions of RCW 75.12.650 by the buying of a commercial license and fishing for commercial purposes is affected in the same way. [ ]

We move, therefore, to the second requirement for validity of class legislation—the existence of a reasonable ground for making a distinction between those who fall within the designated class and those who do not. A reasonable classification is one "which includes all (and only those) persons who are similarly situated with respect to the purpose of the law." [ ]

As noted above, RCW 75.12.650 was enacted to (1) make separate and distinct the sport and commercial fisheries and specifically to eliminate the abuse of purchasing a commercial license to circumvent sport catch limitations; (2) improve the policing of fishery violations and decrease the number of sport-caught fish illegally entering commercial channels; and (3) improve the management of the salmon fishery. We hold that the statutory class—all commercial fishermen—includes all and only those persons similarly situated with respect to the stated purposes of RCW 75.12.650; the classification is reasonable in light of its purpose.

Finally, this court has specifically rejected the contention that allowing only certain types of gear to be used for commercial fishing violates the equal protection clause of the federal constitution and Article 1, § 12 of the state constitution....

It is for the legislature—not this court—to determine which means of solving a particular problem is most appropriate and consistent with the overall conservation and management scheme for the salmon resource of this state. The concern of the judiciary is only whether—considering the established presumptions accorded to legislation in this area—the regulation in question has a reasonable and substantial relation to a legitimate object of the police power, and does not violate any direct or positive mandate of the state or federal constitutions.

RCW 75.12.650 is a valid exercise of the police power and violates neither the equal protection clause of the fourteenth amendment to the United States Constitution nor Article 1, § 12 of the state constitution.

The judgment of the trial court declaring RCW 75.12.650 to be unconstitutional is reversed. Remanded with directions to dismiss.

■ HAMILTON, C.J., FINLEY, STAFFORD, and UTTER, JJ., and SHORETT, J. pro tem., concur.

■ WRIGHT, J., not participating.

■ HUNTER, J., dissenting:—I agree with the majority that the state has broad power in regulating the taking of salmon for the purpose of preserving and enhancing the great salmon fishery resource of this state. The state's right and duty to accomplish this purpose cannot be questioned. The vital issue in this case, however, is whether the statute requiring the sports commercial fishermen to use more efficient equipment in the taking of salmon, and which is more destructive to the immature fish, has a reasonable and rational relationship to the objective of the preservation and conservation of the salmon fishery. The answer to me appears obvious on its face.

. . .

[T]he statute ... has a far-reaching and detrimental effect upon the sports commercial fishermen. The department admits the effect of this statute will be to reduce the number of commercial fishermen who now pursue this occupation of commercial fishing with sports gear. It is also clear from the record that the cost of converting from sports gear to fixed gear is considerable, which will force some commercial fishermen out of business, and that the risk and hazard of using fixed gear on the smaller boats, now adaptable to sports commercial fishing, is so great that others also will be forced out of business unless they are economically able to secure larger boats for the conversion. The drastic effect of this statute upon the ability of the sports commercial fisherman to stay in business in pursuing his occupation is therefore also of paramount consideration in determining the reasonableness of the new statute in the light of the purposes it purports to accomplish.

. . .

I cannot reasonably conceive from this record a state of facts to justify the required conversion of sports gear to fixed gear for commercial fishing to accomplish the objective intended by the statute, the conservation of the salmon fishery.

The judgment of the trial court should be affirmed.

■ ROSELLINI and HALE, JJ., concur.

NOTES

(1) What was the basis of the court's decision? Did the legislature actually make the decisions that the court ascribes to it? What role is played by the "expertise" of the Department of Fisheries?

(2) The apotheosis of management: The decision in *Kelpers Association* reflects the belief that it is possible for trained experts to manage a resource to provide the required escapement while allowing maximum harvests. This perspective is often associated with the Progressive movement. *See* Michael C. Blumm, *The Northwest's Hydroelectric Heritage, in* NORTHWEST LANDS, NORTHWEST PEOPLES 264, 265–66 (Dale D. Goble & Paul Hirt eds., 1999).

The director testified that "management" was a synonym for "conservation." Isn't a more accurate synonym "allocation"? As the assistant director testified, "This stock has been under full exploitation for some years, meaning that the total allowable harvest was already being taken."

Since the decision to restrict gear allocates fish among different groups of fishers, any restrictions will anger some identifiable group and generate political pressure on the agency. Pressure, in turn, may produce several different regulatory responses. The easiest is to seek increased funding to produce more salmon, since increasing the size of the pie pleases all users. The pie may not even need to grow to have the desired effect. The widespread use of hatcheries to "supplement" wild runs is an example of this approach. When cuts have to be made, an agency is likely to withdraw harvest rights from the politically weakest group. In the Pacific Northwest, the group most often singled out to bear the brunt of "conservation" reductions were Indian fishers—a topic that will be examined in more detail in Chapter 7.

The history of salmon fishing in the Pacific Northwest has been characterized as a series of "fish wars" as groups of users have battled one another for a share of a shrinking pie. Generally, the groups have marched to war wielding banners labeled "conservation."

PERSPECTIVES

(1) Management as religion: *Kelpers Association* demonstrates a belief that humans can affirmatively manage a wildlife population to produce a "harvestable surplus" in perpetuity. That belief is fundamentally mechanical in orientation. It views nature as a machine in which individual parts can be manipulated to produce desired products without affecting other parts of the machine that are producing other products. The fact that most Pacific Northwest populations of salmon have been listed as either threatened or endangered under the Endangered Species Act suggests that the belief is fundamentally inaccurate.

Daniel Botkin, an ecologist, has attempted to elucidate the problems inherent in the belief manifest in *Kelpers Association*. His basic point is simply stated:

> The changes that must take place in our perspective [on the nature of nature] are twofold: the recognition of the dynamic rather than static properties of the Earth and its life-support system, and the acceptance of a global view of life on the Earth. We have tended to view nature as a Kodachrome still-life ... but nature is a moving picture show.... [I]n the past decade, something new and important has been added to [our understanding of the Earth as a place strangely suited to support life]: a growing understanding of the extent to which life has influenced the environment at the planetary scale over the Earth's

history, and a growing recognition that our planetary life-support and life-containing system, now called the *biosphere,* is deeply complex. The biosphere is unlike the mechanical devices or our own construction, and its analysis requires the development of new scientific approaches.

We are accustomed to thinking of life as a characteristic of individual organisms. Individuals are alive, but an individual cannot sustain life. Life is sustained only by a group of organisms of many species—not simply a horde or mob, but a certain kind of system composed of many individuals of different species—and their environment, making together a network of living and nonliving parts that can maintain the flow of energy and the cycling of chemical elements that, in turn, support life. A system that can do this not only is rare, but also peculiar, peculiar from the perspective that we have become accustomed to in our methods of analyzing and constructing the physical trappings of our modern civilization.

DANIEL B. BOTKIN, DISCORDANT HARMONIES 7 (1990).

Botkin traces out the implications of his two proposed conceptual changes in the context of ecosystems as diverse as the moose and wolf populations on Isle Royale, Kirtland's warbler and the jack-pine forests of the upper midwest, and elephants in Tsavo National Park in East Africa. The examples seem to coalesce around the concept of scale: while change is natural, human change often is disruptive because it happens at a different scale—either of time or magnitude.

In the context of salmon, for example, the Washington Department of Fisheries was responsible for regulating only a small part of the total system. Regardless of how carefully they set escapement goals, the fishery was doomed to decline when dams closed off spawning habitat, turned rivers into lakes, and diced downstream-migrating smolts, when logging and grazing and suburban sprawl destroyed or degraded habitat, when toxic chemicals from pulp mills and aluminum smelters changed water chemistry.

(2) The conspiracy of optimism: One recurrent response to management failure is to manage more intensively. For example, the Forest Service justified above-sustainable-yield logging by projecting increased management: forests would be replanted with "better" trees which would be treated with herbicides to remove competitors and fertilizers to speed growth. When technology fails, apply more technology. "We have learned from our past mistakes" becomes a recurrent and often unjustified refrain. *See* PAUL W. HIRT, THE CONSPIRACY OF OPTIMISM (1994).

In the context of salmon, the conspiracy of optimism produced more hatcheries to supplement wild runs and lost habitat. Concerns with the resulting loss of genetic diversity was brushed aside; the scientists were engineering better fish. Problems with dams were met with removing downstream-migrating smolts from the river and barging them to the ocean. *See* Dale D. Goble, *Salmon in the Columbia Basin: From Abundance to Extinction, in* NORTHWEST LANDS, NORTHWEST PEOPLES 229 (Dale D. Goble & Paul W. Hirt eds., 1999).

SECTION 3. THE EVOLVING PROPRIETARY ROLE

Even as the Supreme Court in *Geer* was endorsing the idea that states own the wildlife within their borders, it was also embracing the idea that that ownership was best understood in terms of trust law so that the states held title, not for their own use, but for the benefit of the people. Trust terminology thereafter appeared regularly in judicial opinions. Often, as in *Geer*, it was found alongside language suggesting more traditional ownership. A typical example was provided by the Supreme Court of Washington in 1936:

> At the outset, we may repeat what has many times been held by this court, namely, that the food fish in the waters of this state belong to and are the sole property of the people thereof; that no person has any inherent or natural right to take such fish as against the state; that the state, in prescribing regulations with respect to taking fish from its waters, is dealing with its own property, over which its control is as absolute as that of any other owner over his property; and that any private right in that regard must be expressly or inferentially given by the state. *State v. Tice*, 125 P. 168 (Wash.1912); *Cawsey v. Brickey*, 144 P. 938 (Wash.1914); *Vail v. Seaborg*, 207 P. 15 (Wash. 1922); *McMillan v. Sims*, 231 P. 943 (Wash.1925); *State v. Cramer*, 8 P.2d 1004 (Wash.1932).
>
> But it is equally true, and is uniformly held, that, while the state owns the fish in its waters in its proprietary capacity, it nevertheless holds title thereto as trustee for all the people of the state and for the common good, and therefore regulations made for the use of this common property must bear equally on all persons similarly situated with reference to the subject-matter and purpose to be served by the regulation. *Cawsey v. Brickey*, 144 P. 938 (Wash.1914); *Barker v. State Fish Commission*, 152 P. 537 (Wash.1917); *State ex rel. Campbell v. Case*, 47 P.2d 24 (Wash.1935).

State ex rel. Bacich v. Huse, 59 P.2d 1101, 1103–04 (Wash.1936).

By late in the twentieth century, the overwhelming majority of states had embraced this perspective—typically by statute though at times through constitutional provisions. The statutory and constitutional provisions are collected in Oliver A. Houck, *Why Do We Protect Endangered Species, and What Does that Say About Whether Restrictions on Private Property to Protect Them Constitute "Takings"?*, 80 IOWA L. REV. 297, 310 & n.76 (1995).

a. THE PROPRIETOR AS TRUSTEE

While the state ownership doctrine was firmly entrenched in state law, the idea encountered criticism in the United States Supreme Court in certain constitutional-law contexts. In *Missouri v. Holland*, for example, Justice Holmes disposed of the state's claim "of exclusive authority" to regulate migratory waterfowl based "upon an assertion of title to migratory birds" with the biting comment, "To put the claim of the State upon title is to lean upon a slender reed. Wild birds are not in the possession of anyone; and possession is the beginning of ownership." *Missouri v. Holland*, 252 U.S. 416 (1920).

The Court's criticism grew increasingly frequent in a series of decisions on the constitutional permissibility of state laws under the dormant Commerce Clause. The line of cases eventually led to overruling *Geer* on the specific issue of state power to permit commerce in wildlife within the state while prohibiting its export:

Hughes v. Oklahoma

United States Supreme Court.
441 U.S. 322 (1979).

■ BRENNAN, J.:—The question presented for decision is whether [§ 4–115(B), an Oklahoma statute] violates the Commerce Clause, Art. I, § 8, cl. 3, of the United States Constitution, insofar as it provides that "[n]o person may transport or ship minnows for sale outside the state which were seined or procured within the waters of this state.... "[1]

Appellant William Hughes holds a Texas license to operate a commercial minnow business near Wichita Falls, Tex. An Oklahoma game ranger arrested him on a charge of violating § 4–115(B) by transporting from Oklahoma to Wichita Falls a load of natural minnows purchased from a minnow dealer licensed to do business in Oklahoma. Hughes' defense that § 4–115(B) was unconstitutional because it was repugnant to the Commerce Clause was rejected, and he was convicted and fined. The Oklahoma Court of Criminal Appeals affirmed, stating:

> The United States Supreme Court has held on numerous occasions that the wild animals and fish within a state's border are, so far as capable of ownership, owned by the state in its sovereign capacity for the common benefit of all its people. Because of such ownership, and in the exercise of its police power, the state may regulate and control the taking, subsequent use and property rights that may be acquired therein. *Lacoste v. Department of Conservation*, 263 U.S. 545 (1928); *Geer v. Connecticut*, 161 U.S. 519 (1896).... As stated in *Lacoste*, protection of the wildlife of a state is peculiarly within the police power of the state, and the state has great latitude in determining what means are appropriate for its protection.

1. [Quoted statute omitted].... The prohibition against transportation out of State for sale thus does not apply to hatchery-bred minnows, but only to "natural" minnows seined or procured from waters within the State. Section 4–115(B) is part of the Oklahoma Wildlife Conservation Code. Another provision of that Code requires that persons have a minnow dealer's license before they can lawfully seine or trap minnows within the State—except for their own use as bait—§ 4–116 (Supp. 1978), but no limit is imposed on the number of minnows a licensed dealer may take from state waters. Nor is there any regulation except § 4–115(B) concerning the disposition of lawfully acquired minnows; they may be sold within Oklahoma to any person and for any purpose, and may be taken out of the State for any purpose except sale.

Oklahoma law does not prohibit commercial minnow hatcheries within her borders from selling stock minnows to anyone, resident or nonresident, and minnows purchased therefrom may be freely exported. However, the law served to protect against the depletion of minnows in Oklahoma's natural streams through commercial exportation. No person is allowed to export natural minnows for sale outside of Oklahoma. Such a prohibition is not repugnant to the commerce clause.

Hughes v. State, 572 P.2d 573, 575 (Okla. Ct. Crim. App. 1977).

We noted probable jurisdiction, [ ]. We reverse. *Geer v. Connecticut,* 161 U.S. 519 (1896), on which the Court of Criminal Appeals relied, is overruled. In that circumstance, § 4–115(B) cannot survive appellant's Commerce Clause attack.

I

The few simple words of the Commerce Clause—"The Congress shall have Power ... To regulate Commerce ... among the several States...."—reflected a central concern of the Framers that was an immediate reason for calling the Constitutional Convention: the conviction that in order to succeed, the new Union would have to avoid the tendencies toward economic Balkanization that had plagued relations among the Colonies and later among the States under the Articles of Confederation. *See H.P. Hood & Sons, Inc. v. Du Mond,* 336 U.S. 525, 533–534 (1949). The Commerce Clause has accordingly been interpreted by this Court not only as an authorization for congressional action, but also, even in the absence of a conflicting federal statute, as a restriction on permissible state regulation. The cases defining the scope of permissible state regulation in areas of congressional silence reflect an often controversial evolution of rules to accommodate federal and state interests. *Geer v. Connecticut* was decided relatively early in that evolutionary process. We hold that time has revealed the error of the early resolution reached in that case, and accordingly *Geer* is today overruled.

A

Geer sustained against a Commerce Clause challenge a statute forbidding the transportation beyond the State of game birds that had been lawfully killed within the State. The decision rested on the holding that no interstate commerce was involved. This conclusion followed in turn from the view that the State had the power, as representative for its citizens, who "owned" in common all wild animals within the State, to control not only the *taking* of game but also the *ownership* of game that had been lawfully reduced to possession. By virtue of this power, Connecticut could qualify the ownership of wild game taken within the State by, for example, prohibiting its removal from the State: "The common ownership imports the right to keep the property, if the sovereign so chooses, always within its jurisdiction for every purpose." [ ] Accordingly, the State's power to qualify ownership raised serious doubts whether the sale or exchange of wild game constituted "commerce" at all; in any event the Court held that the qualification imposed by the challenged statute removed any transactions involving wild game killed in Connecticut from *interstate* commerce.[6]

Mr. Justice Field and the first Mr. Justice Harlan dissented, rejecting as artificial and formalistic the Court's analysis of "ownership" and "commerce" in wild game. They would have affirmed the State's power to provide for the protection of wild game, but only "so far as such protection ... does not contravene the power of Congress in the regulation of interstate commerce." Their view was that "[w]hen any animal ... is lawfully killed for the purposes of food or other uses of man, it becomes an article of commerce, and its use cannot be limited to the citizens of one State to the exclusion of citizens of another State."

B

The view of the *Geer* dissenters increasingly prevailed in subsequent cases. Indeed, not only has the *Geer* analysis been rejected when natural resources other than wild game were involved, but even state regulations of wild game have been held subject to the strictures of the Commerce Clause under the pretext of distinctions from *Geer*.

The erosion of *Geer* began only 15 years after it was decided....

The *Geer* analysis has also been eroded to the point of virtual extinction in cases involving regulation of wild animals. The first challenge to *Geer*'s theory of a State's power over wild animals came in *Missouri v. Holland*, 252 U.S. 416 (1920). The State of Missouri, relying on the theory of state ownership of wild animals, attacked the Migratory Bird Treaty Act on the ground that it interfered with the State's control over wild animals within its boundaries. Writing for the Court, Mr. Justice Holmes upheld the Act as a proper exercise of the treatymaking power. He commented in passing on the artificiality of the *Geer* rationale: "To put the claim of the State upon title is to lean upon a slender reed." 252 U.S. at 434.

Foster-Fountain Packing Co. v. Haydel, 278 U.S. 1 (1928), undermined *Geer* even more directly. A Louisiana statute forbade the transportation beyond the State of shrimp taken in Louisiana waters until the heads and

---

6. .... Our Brother REHNQUIST suggests that the Court in Geer offered as an "alternative basis for its decision" (in the final paragraph of its 15-page opinion) that the "State, in the exercise of its police power, could act to preserve for its people a valuable food supply, even though interstate commerce was remotely and indirectly affected." [ ] That this was not an "alternative basis," however, is made clear in a sentence not quoted by our Brother REHNQUIST:

The power of a State to protect by adequate police regulation its people against the adulteration of articles of food, ... although in doing so commerce might be remotely affected, necessarily carries with it the existence of a like power to preserve a food supply *which belongs in common to all the people of the State, which can only become the subject of ownership in a qualified way, and which can never be the object of commerce except with the consent of the State and subject to the conditions which it may deem best to impose for the public good.*

161 U.S. at 535 (emphasis added).

Thus, rather than an "alternative basis" independent of the "state ownership" and "no interstate commerce" rationales, this "preservation of a valuable resource" rationale was premised on those rationales. In any event, even if an "alternative basis," this rationale has met the same fate as *Geer*'s primary rationale.

shells had been removed.[10] The statute clearly relied on the *Geer* state-control-of-ownership rationale. Anyone lawfully taking shrimp from Louisiana waters was granted "a qualified interest which may be sold within the State." Only after the head and shell had been removed within the State did the taker or possessor acquire "title and the right to sell and ship the same 'beyond the limit[s] of the State, without restriction or reservation.' "
[ ]

Ignoring the niceties of "title" to the shrimp and concentrating instead on the purposes and effects of the statute, *Foster-Fountain Packing* struck down the statute as economic protectionism abhorrent to the Commerce Clause....

Foster-Fountain Packing's implicit shift away from *Geer*'s formalistic "ownership" analysis became explicit in *Toomer v. Witsell*, 334 U.S. 385 (1948), which struck down as violations of the Commerce Clause and the Privileges and Immunities Clause certain South Carolina laws discriminating against out-of-state commercial fishermen:

> The whole ownership theory, in fact, is now generally regarded as but a fiction expressive in legal shorthand of the importance to its people that a State have power to preserve and regulate the exploitation of an important resource. And there is no necessary conflict between that vital policy consideration and the constitutional command that the State exercise that power, like its other powers, so as not to discriminate without reason against citizens of other States.

431 U.S. at 284.

Although stated in reference to the Privileges and Immunities Clause challenge, this reasoning is equally applicable to the Commerce Clause challenge. *Douglas v. Seacoast Products, Inc.*, 431 U.S. 265 (1977), dispelled any doubts on that score....

C

The case before us is the first in modern times to present facts essentially on all fours with *Geer*. We now conclude that challenges under the Commerce Clause to state regulations of wild animals should be

---

10. .... The state legislature may have been encouraged to [pass the law challenged in *Foster-Fountain*] by certain language in *Lacoste v. Department of Conservation*, 263 U.S. 545 (1924), language also relied on by the Oklahoma Court of Criminal Appeals in this case. *Lacoste* upheld a Louisiana "severance" tax on the skins of all wild furbearing animals and alligators taken in the State. The Court cited *Geer* for the proposition that:

> The wild animals within its borders are, so far as capable of ownership, owned by the State in its sovereign capacity for the common benefit of all of its people. Because of such ownership, and in the exercise of its police power the State may regulate and control the taking, subse-

quent use and property rights that may be acquired therein.

Nevertheless, *Lacoste* expressly declined to uphold the tax "by virtue of the power of the State to prohibit, and therefore to condition, the removal of wild game from the State." [ ] Rather than reach this issue, the Court upheld the measure as a valid police regulation designed to conserve and protect wild animals, noting that the tax applied to all skins taken within the State, whether kept within the State or shipped out. [ ] Thus, despite its citation of *Geer*, *Lacoste* is actually more compatible with the cases following the views of the Justices dissenting in *Geer*.

considered according to the same general rule applied to state regulations of other natural resources, and therefore expressly overrule *Geer*. We thus bring our analytical framework into conformity with practical realities. Overruling *Geer* also eliminates the anomaly, created by the decisions distinguishing *Geer*, that statutes imposing the most extreme burdens on interstate commerce (essentially total embargoes) were the most immune from challenge. At the same time, the general rule we adopt in this case makes ample allowance for preserving, in ways not inconsistent with the Commerce Clause, the legitimate state concerns for conservation and protection of wild animals underlying the 19th-century legal fiction of state ownership.

II

We turn then to the question whether the burden imposed on interstate commerce in wild game by § 4–115(B) is permissible under the general rule articulated in our precedents governing other types of commerce. *See, e.g., Pike v. Bruce Church, Inc.*, 397 U.S. at 142. Under that general rule, we must inquire (1) whether the challenged statute regulates evenhandedly with only "incidental" effects on interstate commerce, or discriminates against interstate commerce either on its face or in practical effect; (2) whether the statute serves a legitimate local purpose; and, if so, (3) whether alternative means could promote this local purpose as well without discriminating against interstate commerce. The burden to show discrimination rests on the party challenging the validity of the statute, but "[w]hen discrimination against commerce . . . is demonstrated, the burden falls on the State to justify it both in terms of the local benefits flowing from the statute and the unavailability of nondiscriminatory alternatives adequate to preserve the local interests at stake." *Hunt v. Washington Apple Advertising Comm'n*, 432 U.S. 333, 353 (1977). . . .

Section 4–115(B) on its face discriminates against interstate commerce. It forbids the transportation of natural minnows out of the State for purposes of sale, and thus "overtly blocks the flow of interstate commerce at [the] State's borders." *Philadelphia v. New Jersey*, 437 U.S. at 624. . . . At a minimum such facial discrimination invokes the strictest scrutiny of any purported legitimate local purpose and of the absence of nondiscriminatory alternatives.

Oklahoma argues that § 4–115(B) serves a legitimate local purpose in that it is "readily apparent as a conservation measure." [ ] The State's interest in maintaining the ecological balance in state waters by avoiding the removal of inordinate numbers of minnows may well qualify as a legitimate local purpose. We consider the States' interests in conservation and protection of wild animals as legitimate local purposes similar to the States' interests in protecting the health and safety of their citizens. [ ] But the scope of legitimate state interests in "conservation" is narrower under this analysis than it was under *Geer*. A State may no longer "keep the property, if the sovereign so chooses, always within its jurisdiction for every purpose." *Geer v. Connecticut*, 161 U.S. at 530. The fiction of state ownership may no longer be used to force those outside the State to bear the full costs of "conserving" the wild animals within its borders when equally effective nondiscriminatory conservation measures are available.

Far from choosing the least discriminatory alternative, Oklahoma has chosen to "conserve" its minnows in the way that most overtly discriminates against interstate commerce. . . .

We therefore hold that § 4–115(B) is repugnant to the Commerce Clause.

III

The overruling of *Geer* does not leave the States powerless to protect and conserve wild animal life within their borders. Today's decision makes clear, however, that States may promote this legitimate purpose only in ways consistent with the basic principle that "our economic unit is the Nation," [ ], and that when a wild animal "becomes an article of commerce . . . its use cannot be limited to the citizens of one State to the exclusion of citizens of another State." *Geer v. Connecticut,* 161 U.S. at 538 (Field, J., dissenting).

Reversed.

■ REHNQUIST, J., with whom BURGER, C.J., joins, dissenting:—[The dissenters agreed that the minnows entered the stream of interstate commerce, but would nonetheless have upheld the statute because of the state's special relationship to wildlife:]

The Court in *Geer* expressed the view derived from Roman law that the wild fish and game located within the territorial limits of a State are the common property of its citizens and that the State, as a kind of trustee, may exercise this common "ownership" for the benefit of its citizens. [ ] Admittedly, a State does not "own" the wild creatures within its borders in any conventional sense of the word.[2] *Baldwin v. Montana Fish & Game Commission,* 436 U.S. 371, 386 (1978); *Douglas v. Seacoast Products, Inc.,* 431 U.S. 265, 284 (1977); *Toomer v. Witsell,* 334 U.S. 385, 401–402 (1948); *Missouri v. Holland,* 252 U.S. 416, 434 (1920). But the concept expressed by the "ownership" doctrine is not obsolete. *Baldwin v. Montana Fish & Game Commission,* 436 U.S. at 392 (BURGER, C.J., concurring). This Court long has recognized that the ownership language of *Geer* and similar cases is simply a shorthand way of describing a State's substantial interest in preserving and regulating the exploitation of the fish and game and other natural resources within its boundaries for the benefit of its citizens. *Douglas v. Seacoast Products, Inc.,* 431 U.S. at 284; *Toomer v. Witsell,* 334 U.S. at 402.

In recognition of this important state interest, the Court has upheld a variety of regulations designed to conserve and maintain the natural resources of a State. *See, e.g., Baldwin v. Montana Fish & Game Commission,* 436 U.S. 371; *Huron Portland Cement Co. v. Detroit,* 362 U.S. 440

---

2. The *Geer* Court itself did not use the term "ownership" in any proprietary sense. *See* 161 U.S. at 529 (" 'We take it to be the correct doctrine in this country, that the ownership of wild animals, so far as they are capable of ownership, is in the State, not as a proprietor but in its sovereign capacity as the representative and for the benefit of all its people in common.' ").

(1960); *Lacoste v. Department of Conservation,* 263 U.S. 545 (1924); *Patsone v. Pennsylvania,* 232 U.S.138 (1914); *Geer v. Connecticut,* 161 U.S. 519 (1896); *Manchester v. Massachusetts,* 139 U.S. 240 (1891); *McCready v. Virginia,* 94 U.S. 391 (1877); *Smith v. Maryland,* 59 U.S. (18 How.) 71 (1855). To be sure, a State's power to preserve and regulate wildlife within its borders is not absolute. But the State is accorded wide latitude in fashioning regulations appropriate for protection of its wildlife. Unless the regulation directly conflicts with a federal statute or treaty, *Douglas v. Seacoast Products, Inc.,* 431 U.S. at 284; *Kleppe v. New Mexico,* 426 U.S. 529, 546 (1976); *Missouri v. Holland,* 252 U.S. at 434; allocates access in a manner that violates the Fourteenth Amendment, *Takahashi v. Fish & Game Commission,* 334 U.S. 410 (1948); or represents a naked attempt to discriminate against out-of-state enterprises in favor of in-state businesses unrelated to any purpose of conservation, *Foster-Fountain Packing Co. v. Haydel,* 278 U.S. 1, 13 (1928), the State's special interest in preserving its wildlife should prevail. And this is true no matter how "Balkanized" the resulting pattern of commercial activity.

. . .

NOTES

(1) What concerns appear to motivate the Court in its decision to overrule *Geer*? Do these concerns extend beyond regulatory measures that expressly limit commerce in wildlife based on state boundaries? If the state's ownership of wildlife is merely a "legal fiction" under the federal commerce clause, might state ownership also be a legal fiction under other provisions of the Constitution, such as the takings clause and privileges and immunities clause?

What does it mean to say that a doctrine is a "legal fiction"? Does it mean that the doctrine is based on an error? Does it suggest that states do not retain special powers over unowned wildlife, powers that go beyond the general power that they possess to regulate the use of privately owned animals? Note that the majority states that state ownership is "a fiction expressive in legal shorthand of the importance to its people that a State have power to preserve and regulate the exploitation of an important resource." [¶ 12] Is "legal fiction" a term of art for "metaphor"?

Finally, is it the proper role of the United States Supreme Court to propose alterations to state laws rather than to invalidate them if they conflict with federal law?

(2) What is the disagreement between the majority and dissent? Do they disagree on the proposition that a state has a special interest in the conservation of wildlife? Do they disagree on whether that interest is different than the state's interest in conserving all natural "resources"? Does a state hold all resources in trust?

(3) The decision in *Hughes* raised an obvious question: What was its impact on the state ownership doctrine for other legal purposes? Where did states stand in terms of their powers to limit property rights that a hunter or fisher acquired upon capture? For example, could a state still prohibit *all* sales of wildlife? Could it do so on other, non-proprietary bases?

Shortly after *Hughes* was handed down states began considering its implications on state powers generally. The following decision illustrates what has become the common approach:

State v. Fertterer

Supreme Court of Montana.
841 P.2d 467 (1992).

■ WEBER, J.:—A jury in the Eighth Judicial District Court, Cascade County, Montana, convicted Richard J. Fertterer, Sr. of seven misdemeanor fish and game violations and two counts of felony criminal mischief. This jury also found David John Fertterer guilty of four misdemeanor fish and game violations and two counts of felony criminal mischief. Defendants appeal the felony convictions and the sentence imposed by the District Court. We affirm in part and reverse in part.

The Fertterers raise the following issues for our review:

1. Are wild animals "public property" within the purview of § 45–6–101, MCA?

. . .

From November 1989, through August 1990, the Department of Fish Wildlife and Parks (FWP) conducted an undercover investigation of a large scale poaching operation run by the Fertterers. During the investigation FWP agents, posing as out-of-state hunters, had extensive contact with the defendants. At trial, agents testified they were actively guided by the Fertterers during two separate five-day hunts. Neither defendant had an outfitter license. In addition, agents testified that during those hunts, Fertterers were spotlighting and killing game without proper tags, illegally trapping bear, soliciting the sale of an illegally killed mountain lion hide, and attempting to sell approximately 1000 pounds of deer and elk meat to an Illinois FWP agent posing as an owner of a meat market.

. . .

Fertterers contend they were wrongfully convicted of felony criminal mischief where wild animals are not properly classified as property or public property within Montana's criminal code. In the alternative defendants claim the criminal mischief statute is unconstitutionally vague as applied to Fertterers and violates the legislative intent of Title 87, MCA.

Are wild animals "public property" within the meaning of § 45–6–101, MCA?

Section 45–6–101(1)(a), MCA, provides:

(1) A person commits the offense of criminal mischief if he knowingly or purposely:

(a) injures, damages, or destroys any property of another or public property without consent;. . . .

In this instance, defendants contend the District Court incorrectly instructed the jury that wild animals in Montana are owned by the State and are public property. Fertterers argue that the State has no title ownership in the wild animals within its borders; thus, the animals are not owned by the State.

Although the criminal code fails to define "public property", it offers some other definitions regarding ownership which are helpful in defining "public property" under Montana's criminal code.

Section 45–2–101(46), MCA, defines owner as follows:

"Owner" means a person other than the offender who has possession of or any other interest in the property involved, even though such interest or possession is unlawful, and without whose consent the offender has no authority to exert control over the property.

Under this definition, ownership is not limited to title ownership such as that applied to the ownership of real property or to personal property such as cattle or other livestock. The statute recognizes that a lesser interest than title ownership is sufficient as an ownership interest in property crimes.

In *State v. Tome*, 228 Mont. 398, 742 P.2d 479 (1987), this Court recognized that an interest less than title ownership was sufficient to prove ownership for the purpose of Montana's criminal mischief statute. *Id.* at 401, 742 P.2d at 481. In that case, the defendant was charged with felony criminal mischief for $191 in vandalism damages to a city building and $359 in damages to a vending machine leased by a golf pro employed by the city. The defendant argued that the lower court incorrectly considered $359 in damages to the machine in convicting him of felony criminal mischief. This Court held that mere possessory ownership is sufficient to show ownership under the criminal mischief statute.

Similarly here, the State need not prove it had title ownership interest in wild game within its borders. As stated in § 45–2–101(46), MCA, the State is an owner of the property if, without the State's consent, the Fertterers had no authority to exert control over the game.

. . .

While the criminal code does not require the State to prove title ownership, the State must prove it possesses an interest superior to the interest of the Fertterers. We conclude that under the statutes and cases of Montana, the State has a superior interest under the ownership theory and also has such an interest by virtue of its police power to regulate the taking of game.

A brief historical analysis shows that beginning with *Geer v. Connecticut,* 161 U.S. 519 (1896), the United States Supreme Court recognized that the states had a right to regulate the taking of game within their borders. This regulatory power was derived from the states' "title ownership" in the game, and also from the states' police power. In *Geer,* the Court determined that a Connecticut law prohibiting the taking of game birds outside its borders did not violate interstate commerce. That court likewise relied on the title ownership theory in subsequent federal cases including *Baldwin v. Montana,* 436 U.S. 371 (1978). In *Baldwin,* the Court recognized Montana's interest in regulating the taking and preserving the game animals within its borders. It held that Montana's disparate licensing fees between resident hunters and non-resident hunters did not violate the privileges and immunities clause of the Constitution or the equal protection clause. In the 1979 case of *Hughes v. Oklahoma,* 441 U.S. 322 (1979), the United States Supreme Court concluded that an Oklahoma law which prohibited the transporting of live minnows across state lines into Texas violated the interstate commerce clause. As a part of that opinion, it expressly abandoned the title ownership theory as promulgated in *Geer.* The defendants argue that the *Hughes* decision effectively precludes Montana from convicting them of criminal mischief for destroying public property.

The State contends there are no federal constitutional questions of interstate commerce, equal protection, or privileges and immunities; and as a result, *Hughes* is not controlling. We agree with that contention. There is no federal constitutional issue or other federal question presented in the present case. As a result, the holding in *Hughes* is not controlling here. We do point out that as we compare *Hughes* to *Baldwin,* we are not certain the holding expressed in this case would be found to contradict *Hughes.*

Montana has long recognized that Montana has the power to regulate game animals under both a title ownership and police power theory. In *Rosenfeld v. Jakways,* 67 Mont. 558, 216 P. 776 (1923), this Court stated the rule very clearly.... The State's ownership in wild game for the use and benefit of its people was affirmed in *Heiser v. Severy,* 117 Mont. 105, 158 P.2d 501 (1945), and again in *State ex rel. Visser v. State Fish & Game Comm'n,* 150 Mont. 525, 437 P.2d 373 (1968). In *Visser,* this Court confirmed the State's ownership of wild game and its authority to regulate private ownership of game as long as those regulations do not violate the Constitution.

Montana's case law affirming the State's property interest in wild game is consistent with case law from other jurisdictions, including Washington, Colorado, Oregon, Indiana, Texas, Michigan and Alabama. In *State v. Gillette,* 27 Wash. App. 815, 621 P.2d 764 (1980), Washington sued and recovered damages from property owners whose reconstruction of a stream bank resulted in the killing of salmon. That court concluded that Washington had standing to sue. It held: "food fish of the state are the sole property of the people of the state.... " Likewise in *Collopy v. Wildlife Comm'n,* 625 P.2d 994 (Colo.1981), that court upheld a regulation prohibiting hunting within a specific area. The court recognized that the ownership of wild game is in the state for the benefit of all the people. Finally, in *Rogers v. State,* 491 So. 2d 987 (Ala. App. 1985), that court stated: "The authority of the state to regulate hunting ... derives from the long established and well recognized principle of law that ownership of wild animals is vested in the state." *See also Ridenour v. Furness,* 504 N.E.2d 336 (Ind.App.1987); *Wiley v. Baker,* 597 S.W.2d 3 (Tex. App. 1980); and *Glave v. Michigan Terminix Co.,* 159 Mich. App. 537, 407 N.W.2d 36 (1987).

In accordance with the above cited Montana cases, and consistent also with *Baldwin,* we hold that Montana has an ownership interest in wild game held by it in its sovereign capacity for the use and benefit of the people. We further hold that under its police powers, which extend to such wild game, the State may prohibit the killing of wild game and regulate the killing of the same. We hold that wild animals are public property within the meaning of Montana's criminal mischief statute, and that Montana's interest in such public property is superior to the interest of the Fertterers.

NOTES

(1) How does the Montana court interpret and limit *Hughes*? Has it read the case fairly? Given the United States Supreme Court's role in interpreting federal law—and its lack of power to interpret state law—is it appropriate for a state court to ignore pointed language in decisions by the United States Supreme Court? Does the decision simply reflect our federal system's allocation of power between the state and federal judiciary? That is, does *Hughes* stand for the proposition that the state ownership and public trust doctrines have no role in federal law, while *Fertterer* stands for the proposition that the doctrines have continuing vitality within a state? Consider the following summary of *Hughes*:

> [T]he majority [in *Hughes*] did not, and could not, overrule principles dating back to Roman law that wild animals are the common property of the citizens of a state. As noted above, the great majority of American states continue to regard wildlife as common property.... At a minimum, these assertions place wildlife in an exalted position in the pantheon of state interests; a state may not own wildlife in quite the same sense that it holds the deed to a state building, but it has always had a special interest in wildlife preservation that, for example, goes beyond state interests in protecting the facades of other people's buildings. The trust analogy announced in *Geer* was not overruled in *Hughes* and remains the most accurate expression of this state interest: Wildlife belongs to everyone and the state has a special authority, and obligation, to ensure its perpetuation.

Oliver A. Houck, *Why Do We Protect Endangered Species, and What Does That Say About Whether Restrictions on Private Property to Protect Them Constitute "Takings"?,* 80 Iowa L. Rev. 297, 311 n.77 (1995).

(2) *O'Brien v. State*: *Fertterer* presents the dominant interpretation of *Hughes* by state courts. The Wyoming Supreme Court, for example, embraced similar arguments:

> [w]ildlife within the borders of a state are owned by the state in its sovereign capacity for the common benefits of all its people. Because of such ownership and in the exercise of its police power, the state may regulate the taking and use thereof.... [T]he state has great latitude in determining what means are appropriate for the protection of wildlife. We hasten to [add] that the enlightened concept of this ownership is one of a trustee with the power and duty to protect, preserve and nurture wildlife.

O'Brien v. State, 711 P.2d 1144, 1148–49 (Wyo.1986).

PERSPECTIVES

Although decisions of the United States Supreme Court have not discouraged state courts from retaining the doctrine that states are trustee owners of wildlife, the Court also has not helped flesh out the application of trust doctrine to wildlife as it has in the case of the trust's application to navigable waterways. Although general, broad language is common in state decisions, explanations of the trust have been few and incomplete. This has left the door open for academic commentators to offer their own prescriptions of where the trust doctrine might head. The following excerpt illustrates ideas widely promoted by advocates of strong measures to protect wildlife:

Deborah G. Musiker, Tom France, & Lisa A. Hallenbeck, *The Public Trust and* Parens Patriae *Doctrines: Protecting Wildlife in Uncertain Political Times*

16 PUB. LAND L. REV. 87 (1995).

Wildlife occupies a unique place on the American landscape and in the American mind. It is both protected as a cherished treasure and exploited like many other resources. From almost any perspective, personal feeling and public debate over wildlife policy are grounded in a fundamental belief: Wildlife is a public resource. Even our literature and our art embody this belief. Nonetheless, wildlife populations have steadily declined for decades. Some species have gone quietly to extinction, while others remain only in fragile populations. The steady erosion and elimination of wildlife populations have occurred without public recompense, financial or otherwise, despite widespread acknowledgment of wildlife as a public resource.

Air, water, and wildlife are all resources of the commons, yet each presents distinct challenges in both legal construct and practical management. Unlike air and water, wildlife is bound to the land, and each species has special habitat needs. This attachment to the land has caused wildlife law to develop its own unique character....

State authority to regulate and conserve wildlife is well established. This article argues that states have not only the authority to regulate and conserve wildlife, but also an affirmative duty to do so. Under the public trust doctrine, the state serves as trustee of its wildlife resource. As trustee, the state must protect the corpus of its wildlife trust by preventing its unreasonable exploitation and by seeking compensation for unavoidable losses. This duty stems from the special relationship created by the state's ownership of its wildlife in its sovereign capacity, and the public's expectation that the state holds this common resource for the benefit of the people.

The public trust doctrine extends beyond the state's ordinary police power and requires the state to take affirmative action to protect its wildlife base. By affording judicial review of state actions affecting the wildlife resource, the public trust doctrine offers a means by which a court can place a "check" on legislative grants of public lands and other government conduct affecting wildlife. Moreover, under the public trust doctrine and the associated doctrine of *parens patriae,* the state may bring suit to recover for injury to wildlife. Legislation need not be in place for states to take action to protect their wildlife.

. . .

Under the public trust doctrine, the state holds natural resources in trust for the benefit of the people. The state may not destroy or relinquish its control over public resources except under certain, very narrow circumstances. The state's ownership of the resource as sovereign is the source of the state's public trust rights and obligations, and affords the state special authorities while imposing on it certain duties.

. . .

1. Duties Imposed by the Public Trust Doctrine

The common law public trust doctrine guides judicial review of state conduct. When courts apply the public trust doctrine, they generally view state conduct towards the trust resource with skepticism. When a state holds a resource which is available for the free use of the general public, a court will look with considerable skepticism upon any governmental conduct which is calculated either to reallocate that resource to more restricted uses or to subject public uses to the self-interest of private parties.

This skepticism, stemming from the U.S. Supreme Court decision in *Illinois Central*, suggests that the role of the public trust doctrine is to protect the public interest from "insufficiencies of the democratic process." Under the public trust doctrine, the courts place checks on the other branches of government. When the legislature or an administrative agency fails to fully consider the public interest in making a decision that affects a trust resource, or engages in "dubious governmental conduct," the public trust doctrine provides a mechanism by which the courts may intervene to protect the resource.

The state, as trustee, must prevent substantial impairment of the wildlife resource so as to preserve it for the beneficiaries—current and future generations. Under the public trust doctrine, the state must: (1) consider the potential adverse impacts of any proposed activity over which it has administrative authority; (2) allow only activities that do not substantially impair the state's wildlife resources; (3) continually monitor the impacts of an approved activity on the wildlife to ensure preservation of the corpus of the trust; and (4) bring suit under the *parens patriae* doctrine to enjoin harmful activities and/or to recover for damages to wildlife.

* * *

What powers and duties do the authors ascribe to the trustee? Are these powers and duties consistent with the cases applying the public trust doctrine to navigable waters? Are there public trusts or is there *a* public trust? That is, do the principles applicable to the public trust in navigable waters apply equally to the public trust in wildlife?

Consider these questions in conjunction with the next group of cases.

b. THE POWER TO SEEK COMPENSATION FOR DAMAGES TO THE CORPUS OF THE TRUST

State Department of Fisheries v. Gillette

Court of Appeals of Washington.
621 P.2d 764 (1980).

■ REED, C.J.:—Defendants Cyril and Sharon Gillette appeal a verdict and judgment awarding damages to the Washington State Department of Fisheries for loss of salmon caused when the Gillettes reconstructed the bank of a stream bordering their property. . . .

Defendants live on farm property bordering Cedar Creek, a salmon spawning stream in Clark County. Seasonal flooding of the creek left unwanted deposits of soil and gravel in Gillettes' adjoining pasture. In the spring of 1976, the flooding washed away so much of the bank that a utility pole was left dangling unsupported along the edge of the creek. Mr. Gillette appealed to the local Public Utility District for assistance in resetting the pole. Although P.U.D. officials did not help, they evidently suggested the Gillettes reconstruct the bank themselves. Accordingly, one of Gillettes' employees, Ricky Smith, was directed to rebuild the bank. Gillette and the employee testified the reconstruction took place in September 1976. Smith testified that, using a caterpillar tractor with an attached blade, he drove back and forth through the stream and pushed material from the creek bed and the adjacent field into the bank. The dike thus created rose as much as 20 feet above the creek.

RCW 75.20.100 provides that anyone wishing to construct a hydraulic project that will interfere with any river or stream bed must obtain written approval from both the Director of Fisheries and the Director of Game. The statute's purpose is to ensure that such projects include adequate protection for the fish life involved. Violation of the statute is a gross misdemeanor. Being unaware of the statute's requirements, the Gillettes did not obtain the necessary hydraulics project permit.

Representatives of both the Department of Game and the Department of Fisheries responded to reports of the construction and inspected the scene. The Department of Fisheries then filed this action in negligence for damages for the loss to the salmon fishery caused by the project.[2] At the close of the evidence, the court granted Fisheries a directed verdict on the issue of liability. The jury thus considered only proximate cause and damage issues and awarded the State $3,150. Defendants appeal.

CAPACITY AND STANDING

. . .

The second prong of defendants' argument opposing Department of Fisheries' standing raises a more significant question. Does the Department of Fisheries, or the State of Washington for that matter, have standing to bring a civil action for damage to fish, absent specific legislative authorization? Although no Washington cases have addressed this question, and other jurisdictions have divided on the issue,[4] we believe our statutes and court decisions provide the guidance necessary for its resolution.

First, the legislature has specifically charged the Department of Fisheries with the duty to preserve, protect, perpetuate and manage the food fish and shellfish in the waters of the state. . . . [T]he department shall

---

2. The Department of Fisheries dropped a connected claim for destruction of salmon spawning habitat because the creek rehabilitated itself.

4. See cases cited at footnote 6, *infra*

seek to maintain the economic well-being and stability of the commercial fishing industry in the state of Washington.

RCW 75.08.012. Our courts have long recognized the rule that

> when a statute contains a grant of authority to achieve a lawful objective there is included in the grant by implication the doing of such acts as are reasonably necessary to properly attain such objective.

State v. Melton, 41 Wash. 2d 298, 300, 248 P.2d 892 (1952); accord, [ ] There is no question that the Hydraulics Act furthers the lawful objectives outlined in RCW 75.08.012. Nor does it seem unreasonable for the Department to protect the fish in its charge through a damage action when individuals have caused a loss to the fishery.

Second, the state's proprietary interest in animals *feræ naturæ* dates at least from the common law of England. *See* 2 W. BLACKSTONE, COMMENTARIES *403. Our courts have incorporated this concept in cases upholding the state's authority to regulate fish and game. *State Department of Fisheries v. Chelan County P.U.D. 1,* 91 Wash. 2d 378, 588 P.2d 1146 (1979), and cases cited therein. Washington courts have emphasized that the food fish of the state are the sole property of the people and that the state, acting for the people, is dealing with its own property, "over which its control is as absolute as that of any other owner over his property." *State ex rel. Bacich v. Huse,* 187 Wash. 75, 79, 59 P.2d 1101 (1936). [ ] In addition to recognizing the state's proprietary interest in its fish, our courts have also held that the state holds its title as trustee for the common good. *State ex rel. Bacich v. Huse, supra.*

In bringing this action, the Department of Fisheries specifically relied on its capacity as trustee and its responsibilities under RCW Title 75 to protect the state's fisheries. Violation of a statute is negligence per se and an individual in the class protected by the statute has a cause of action for damages proximately caused by the violation. *Currie v. Union Oil Co.,* 49 Wash. 2d 898, 901, 307 P.2d 1056 (1957); *Engelker v. Seattle Electric Co.,* 50 Wash. 196, 96 P. 1039 (1908). Defendants admit they violated RCW 75.20.100, which is designed to protect society's interest in preserving the fishery and fish habitat. Representing the people of the state—the owners of the property destroyed by violation of the statute—the Department of Fisheries thus has a right of action for damages. In addition, the state, through the Department, has the fiduciary obligation of any trustee to seek damages for injury to the object of its trust. We note in passing that if the state were denied a right of recovery for the damage which the jury found this construction did to the state's fishery, no one would have standing to recover for the injury. *Department of Environmental Protection v. Jersey Central Power & Light Co.,* 133 N.J. Super. 375, 336 A.2d 750, 759 (1975), *rev'd on other grounds,* 69 N.J. 102, 351 A.2d 337 (1976) (questionable whether, absent special interest, anyone but state is proper party to sue for damages to environment); [ ] We therefore hold that where the violation of a statute designed to protect the state's property causes injury to that property, the state or a responsible executive agency of the state has standing to seek compensation for the injury.[6]

---

6. *See also Department of Environmental Protection v. Jersey Central Power &* *Light Co.,* 133 N.J. Super. 375, 336 A.2d 750 (1975), *rev'd on other grounds,* 69 N.J. 102,

DAMAGE ARGUMENTS

Addressing defendants' damage arguments, we turn first to their challenge to the sufficiency of the evidence that their activities caused any damage to fish at all. Defendants argue that the only way to show damage would be to compare the actual number of salmon hatched in Cedar Creek in years prior to the construction work with the actual number hatched in 1976. Defendants present no authority in support of this argument and we therefore need not consider it. *Roberts v. Atlantic Richfield Co.*, 88 Wash. 2d 887, 568 P.2d 764 (1977). We note, however, that our courts consider circumstantial evidence to be as competent as direct evidence. *State v. Gosby*, 85 Wash. 2d 758, 539 P.2d 680 (1975).

From the record, we glean the following summary of testimony which the jury was entitled to believe. Prior to the construction, the stream bed at the site was "one of the better spawning areas." Salmon spawning peaks in late October. There was no sign of construction as late as October 15. On October 25, fishermen noticed muddy water downstream from the site. The next day they visited the site and saw carcasses and dried salmon eggs in fresh tractor tracks on the Gillette bank. They also saw salmon trying to spawn in the area. The stream bottom appeared mushy and lacked the gravel necessary for nesting sites. Based on the number of salmon redds (nests) in the half-mile below the construction site, there should have been 30 redds in the affected area. Fisheries Department specialists saw no redds at all on December 1. The Department's expert witnesses concluded spawning had probably occurred in the area. Core samples taken in January indicated the stream bed had a percentage of fine materials significantly higher than would permit incubating salmon to survive. If salmon had spawned in the area before construction, most of the nests would have been destroyed. Any remaining eggs would have a poor chance of surviving. Spawning attempted after construction would have been unsuccessful because of the lack of gravel and the high percentage of silt. Fry counts in the spring of 1977 showed virtually no fry in the construction area, the counts being the second lowest of any stream in Southwest Washington. Thus, even accepting Gillettes' contention that the construction occurred in September, the jury had before it sufficient circumstantial evidence from which it could find actual damage. A reviewing court will not disturb a jury verdict supported by substantial evidence. *Hernandez v. Western Farmers Ass'n*, 76 Wash. 2d 422, 425, 456 P.2d 1020 (1969).

Defendants next challenge the trial court's adoption in its instructions of the measure of damages theory presented by the Department of Fisheries. The only evidence regarding the value of the fish lost derived from the testimony of Donald McIsaac, a biostatistician and fish production specialist from the Department of Fisheries. Working from the testimony of other witnesses as to the number of nests which should have been in the construction area, Mr. McIsaac referred to studies showing number of eggs

351 A.2d 337 (1976); *State v. Bowling Green*, 38 Ohio St. 2d 281, 313 N.E.2d 409 (1974); *contra, State v. Dickinson Cheese Co.*, 200 N.W.2d 59 (N.D.1972); *Commonwealth v. Ag-* *way, Inc.*, 210 Pa. Super. 150, 232 A.2d 69 (1967). *See generally*, Annot., 42 A.L.R. Fed. 23 (1979).

per nest and survival rates to predict the number of fish which would have survived to be caught. He concluded that the state's fishery lost 606 adult fish as a result of defendants' construction project.

According to his testimony, as summarized in the statement of facts, the value of these fish was

> basically the market value of the fish, which was the net economic value of the salmon to the public fishery. [H]e defined net economic value ... as essentially the amount of value or profits society made from the catch of the fish.

For the sports fishery, this figure was derived from a 1976 study adjusted for inflation and included the amount people would spend for the opportunity to catch fish. For the commercial fishery, Mr. McIsaac multiplied the ex-vessel price paid by a commercial processor by a factor of 2.1 to "reflect additional value to society for wages and income generated by further processing of fish." Under this theory, the value of the destroyed fish was $9,431.78. On cross examination, Mr. McIsaac admitted the ex-vessel price for all the fish would be $3,859.10. As indicated, the jury's award was $3,150.

Defendants challenge this measure of damages as too remote and speculative to provide a basis for recovery. Defendants, however, do not challenge the technical validity of the basis of Mr. McIsaac's valuation theory. Nor did they present evidence other than Mr. McIsaac's cross examination testimony as to any other theory for measuring damages to society. This court declines to assess the technical validity of a theory which was presented by expert testimony, a matter generally within the trial court's discretion. *See Myers v. Harter,* 76 Wash. 2d 772, 459 P.2d 25 (1969). In any event, we are reluctant to immunize a defendant once damage has been shown merely because "the extent or amount thereof cannot be ascertained with mathematical precision, provided the evidence is sufficient to afford a reasonable basis for estimating loss." *Jacqueline's Washington, Inc. v. Mercantile Stores Co.,* 80 Wash. 2d 784, 786, 498 P.2d 870 (1972); *accord, Lundgren v. Whitney's, Inc.,* 94 Wash. 2d 91, 614 P.2d 1272 (1980). Here, defendants do not deny their activity disrupted the bed of a salmon spawning stream. The Department presented ample evidence to justify a finding that damage did occur as a result of defendants' project. On this record, we believe Mr. McIsaac's testimony on direct and cross examination provided the jury with the requisite reasonable basis for estimating the loss.

Affirmed.

■ PEARSON and PETRICH, JJ., concur.

NOTES

(1) What is the source of the state's power to seek compensation? Is it the state's role as owner of the wildlife? As trustee?

(2) In *Gillette,* the court treated the public trust as a *source* of power: because the state was a trustee, it could recover compensation for damages to the corpus of the trust. This is the trust power that courts have most frequently considered.

As the Washington Court of Appeals notes in footnote 6, two relatively early judicial rulings (from Pennsylvania and North Dakota) denied a state the power to seek compensation for injury to wild animals. Other than these rulings, however, courts have uniformly upheld this power.

Most cases have involved wildlife killed by pollution. *E.g., State v. City of Bowling Green*, 313 N.E.2d 409 (Ohio 1974) (state can sue city for fish killed by negligent operation of municipal sewage treatment plant); *In re Steuart Transportation Co.*, 495 F.Supp. 38 (E.D.Va.1980) (both state and United States can obtain damages for pollution-killed waterfowl, under public trust doctrine and *parens patriae*). *See also Maryland Department of Natural Resources v. Amerada Hess Corp.*, 350 F.Supp. 1060 (D.Md.1972); *Maine v. M/V Tamano*, 357 F.Supp. 1097 (D.Me.1973). Other fact patterns, however, have also led to litigation. *E.g., United States v. Burlington Northern R.R.*, 710 F.Supp. 1286 (D.Neb.1989) (wildlife losses due to fire caused by locomotive); *Attorney General v. Hermes*, 339 N.W.2d 545 (Mich. App.1983) (damages recovered based on wholesale value of fish taken by commercial fisher in violation of fishing laws).

Although courts commonly allow governments to sue for damages, they have had difficulty settling upon liability standards and, even more, in selecting valuation methods. *E.g., State, Department of Environmental Protection v. Jersey Central Power & Light Co.*, 336 A.2d 750 (N.J.App.Div. 1975), *rev'd*, 351 A.2d 337 (N.J.1976). In an unusual action, the state styled its complaint in unjust enrichment and fraud—rather than the more typical nuisance or negligence—for the unlawful taking of fish; the court found no evidence of fraud, and determined that the defendant had not been unjustly enriched, but it did find that the state had adequately proven a case in conversion and awarded in damages the full wholesale value of the fish taken.

Finally, in addition to these difficulties, damage recoveries for injuries caused by interstate water pollution are limited by the preemptive impacts of the federal Clean Water Act. *Attorney General v. Hermes*, 339 N.W.2d 545 (Mich.App.1983).

(3) One of the arguments that the court in *Gillette* uses to justify the state's power to recover for wildlife damage is that, if the state lacked such power, no one would have standing to seek relief. But is this so, even in the case of a fishery that is open to all? Recall *Columbia River Fishermen's Protective Union v. St. Helens*, 87 P.2d 195 (Or.1939), and accompanying notes in Chapter 3.

(4) Powers vs. duties: Although the case focuses on the *power* of the state to sue as trustee, the court in *Gillette* also proclaims that "the state ... has the fiduciary obligation of any trustee to seek damages for injury to the object of its trust." [¶ 8] Similarly, in *State v. City of Bowling Green*, the court held:

> We conclude that where the state is deemed to be the trustee of property for the benefit of the public it has the obligation to bring suit not only to protect the corpus of the trust property but also to recoup

the public's loss occasioned by the negligent acts of those who damage such property.

State v. City of Bowling Green, 313 N.E.2d 409 (Ohio 1974). According to such decisions, the public trust imposes a duty on the state to take steps to conserve wildlife while also giving it the power to do so. Consider the following statement:

> [T]he ownership of the sovereign authority [of wildlife] is in trust for all the people of the state, and hence, by implication, it is the duty of the Legislature to enact such laws as will best preserve the subject of the trust and secure the beneficial use, in the future, to the people of the state.

State v. Hanlon, 82 N.E. 662, 663 (Ohio 1907) (quoting *Magner v. People,* 97 Ill. 320 (1881)). Do these considerations suggest that the real question is whether a court will enforce the trust in the face of inaction?

c. Duty of the Trustee to Conserve the Corpus of the Trust

National Audubon Society v. the Superior Court of Alpine County

Supreme Court of California.
658 P.2d 709 (1983).
certiorari denied, 464 U.S. 977 (1983).

■ Broussard, J.:—Mono Lake, the second largest lake in California, sits at the base of the Sierra Nevada escarpment near the eastern entrance to Yosemite National Park. The lake is saline; it contains no fish but supports a large population of brine shrimp which feed vast numbers of nesting and migratory birds. Islands in the lake protect a large breeding colony of California gulls, and the lake itself serves as a haven on the migration route for thousands of Northern Phalarope, Wilson's Phalarope, and Eared Grebe. Towers and spires of tufa on the north and south shores are matters of geological interest and a tourist attraction.

Although Mono Lake receives some water from rain and snow on the lake surface, historically most of its supply came from snowmelt in the Sierra Nevada. Five freshwater streams—Mill, Lee Vining, Walker, Parker and Rush Creeks—arise near the crest of the range and carry the annual runoff to the west shore of the lake. In 1940, however, the Division of Water Resources, the predecessor to the present California Water Resources Board, granted the Department of Water and Power of the City of Los Angeles (hereafter DWP) a permit to appropriate virtually the entire flow of four of the five streams flowing into the lake. DWP promptly constructed facilities to divert about half the flow of these streams into DWP's Owens Valley aqueduct. In 1970 DWP completed a second diversion tunnel, and since that time has taken virtually the entire flow of these streams.

As a result of these diversions, the level of the lake has dropped; the surface area has diminished by one-third; one of the two principal islands in the lake has become a peninsula, exposing the gull rookery there to coyotes and other predators and causing the gulls to abandon the former island. The ultimate effect of continued diversions is a matter of intense dispute, but there seems little doubt that both the scenic beauty and the ecological values of Mono Lake are imperiled.

. . .

This case brings together for the first time two systems of legal thought: the appropriative water rights system which since the days of the gold rush has dominated California water law, and the public trust doctrine which, after evolving as a shield for the protection of tidelands, now extends its protective scope to navigable lakes. Ever since we first recognized that the public trust protects environmental and recreational values, *Marks v. Whitney*, 491 P.2d 374 (Cal.1971), the two systems of legal thought have been on a collision course. Johnson, *Public Trust Protection for Stream Flows and Lake Levels*, 14 U.C. Davis L. Rev. 233 (1980). They meet in a unique and dramatic setting which highlights the clash of values. Mono Lake is a scenic and ecological treasure of national significance, imperiled by continued diversions of water; yet, the need of Los Angeles for water is apparent, its reliance on rights granted by the board evident, the cost of curtailing diversions substantial.

Attempting to integrate the teachings and values of both the public trust and the appropriative water rights system, we have arrived at certain conclusions which we briefly summarize here. In our opinion, the core of the public trust doctrine is the state's authority as sovereign to exercise a continuous supervision and control over the navigable waters of the state and the lands underlying those waters. This authority applies to the waters tributary to Mono Lake and bars DWP or any other party from claiming a vested right to divert waters once it becomes clear that such diversions harm the interests protected by the public trust. The corollary rule which evolved in tideland and lakeshore cases barring conveyance of rights free of the trust except to serve trust purposes cannot, however, apply without modification to flowing waters. The prosperity and habitability of much of this state requires the diversion of great quantities of water from its streams for purposes unconnected to any navigation, commerce, fishing, recreation, or ecological use relating to the source stream. The state must have the power to grant nonvested usufructuary rights to appropriate water even if diversions harm public trust uses. Approval of such diversion without considering public trust values, however, may result in needless destruction of those values. Accordingly, we believe that before state courts and agencies approve water diversions they should consider the effect of such diversions upon interests protected by the public trust, and attempt, so far as feasible, to avoid or minimize any harm to those interests.

The water rights enjoyed by DWP were granted, the diversion was commenced, and has continued to the present without any consideration of the impact upon the public trust. . . .

1.   Background and history of the Mono Lake litigation

DWP supplies water to the City of Los Angeles. . . .

After purchasing the riparian rights incident to Lee Vining, Walker, Parker and Rush Creeks, as well as the riparian rights pertaining to Mono Lake, the city applied to the Water Board in 1940 for permits to appropriate the waters of the four tributaries. At hearings before the board, various interested individuals protested that the city's proposed appropriations would lower the surface level of Mono Lake and thereby impair its commercial, recreational and scenic uses.

The board's primary authority to reject that application lay in a 1921 amendment to the Water Commission Act of 1913, which authorized the board to reject an application "when in its judgment the proposed appropriation would not best conserve the public interest." [ ] The 1921 enactment, however, also "declared to be the established policy of this state that the use of water for domestic purposes is the highest use of water," [ ], and directed the Water Board to be guided by this declaration of policy. Since DWP sought water for domestic use, the board concluded that it had to grant the application notwithstanding the harm to public trust uses of Mono Lake.

The board's decision states that "[i]t is indeed unfortunate that the City's proposed development will result in decreasing the aesthetic advantages of Mono Basin but *there is apparently nothing that this office can do to prevent it*. The use to which the City proposes to put the water under its Applications ... is defined by the Water Commission Act as the highest to which water may be applied and to make available unappropriated water for this use the City has, by the condemnation proceedings described above, acquired the littoral and riparian rights on Mono Lake and its tributaries south of Mill Creek. This office therefore has *no alternative but to dismiss all protests based upon the possible lowering of the water level in Mono Lake and the effect that the diversion of water from these streams may have upon the aesthetic and recreational value of the Basin.*" [ ]

By April of 1941, the city had completed the extension of its aqueduct system into the Mono Basin by construction of certain conduits, reservoirs at Grant and Crowley Lakes, and the Mono Craters Tunnel from the Mono Basin to the Owens River.... Between 1940 and 1970, the city diverted an average of 57,067 acre-feet of water per year from the Mono Basin. The impact of these diversions on Mono Lake was clear and immediate: the lake's surface level receded at an average of 1.1 feet per year.

In June of 1970, the city completed a second aqueduct designed to increase the total flow into the aqueduct by 50 percent. Between 1970 and 1980, the city diverted an average of 99,580 acre-feet per year from the Mono Basin. By October of 1979, the lake had shrunk from its prediversion area of 85 square miles to an area of 60.3 square miles. Its surface level had dropped to 6,373 feet above sea level, 43 feet below the prediversion level.

. . .

As noted above, Mono Lake has no outlets. The lake loses water only by evaporation and seepage. Natural salts do not evaporate with water, but are left behind. Prior to commencement of the DWP diversions, this naturally rising salinity was balanced by a constant and substantial supply of fresh water from the tributaries. Now, however, DWP diverts most of the fresh water inflow. The resultant imbalance between inflow and outflow not only diminishes the lake's size, but also drastically increases its salinity.

Plaintiffs predict that the lake's steadily increasing salinity, if unchecked, will wreck havoc throughout the local food chain. They contend that the lake's algae, and the brine shrimp and brine flies that feed on it, cannot survive the projected salinity increase. To support this assertion, plaintiffs point to a 50 percent reduction in the shrimp hatch for the spring of 1980 and a startling 95 percent reduction for the spring of 1981. These reductions affirm experimental evidence indicating that brine shrimp populations diminish as the salinity of the water surrounding them increases. [ ] DWP admits these substantial reductions, but blames them on factors other than salinity.

DWP's diversions also present several threats to the millions of local and migratory birds using the lake. First, since many species of birds feed on the lake's brine shrimp, any reduction in shrimp population allegedly caused by rising salinity endangers a major avian food source. The Task Force Report considered it "unlikely that any of Mono Lake's major bird species . . . will persist at the lake if populations of invertebrates disappear." [ ] Second, the increasing salinity makes it more difficult for the birds to maintain osmotic equilibrium with their environment.[10]

The California gull is especially endangered, both by the increase in salinity and by loss of nesting sites. Ninety-five percent of this state's gull population and 25 percent of the total species population nests at the lake. [ ] Most of the gulls nest on islands in the lake. As the lake recedes, land between the shore and some of the islands has been exposed, offering such predators as the coyote easy access to the gull nests and chicks. In 1979, coyotes reached Negrit Island, once the most popular nesting site, and the number of gull nests at the lake declined sharply. In 1981, 95 percent of the hatched chicks did not survive to maturity. Plaintiffs blame this decline and alarming mortality rate on the predator access created by the land bridges; DWP suggests numerous other causes, such as increased ambient temperatures and human activities, and claims that the joining of some islands with the mainland is offset by the emergence of new islands due to the lake's recession.

Plaintiffs allege that DWP's diversions adversely affect the human species and its activities as well. . . .

2.   The Public Trust Doctrine in California

"By the law of nature these things are common to mankind—the air, running water, the sea and consequently the shores of the sea." INSTITUTES

---

10. In the face of rising salinity, birds can maintain such equilibrium only by increasing either their secretion of salts or their intake of fresh water. The former option is foreclosed, however, because Mono Lake is already so salty that the birds have reached their limit of salt secretion. Thus, the birds must drink more fresh water to maintain the osmotic equilibrium necessary to their survival. As the Task Force predicts, "[t]he need for more time and energy to obtain fresh water will mean reduced energy and time for other vital activities such as feeding, nesting, etc. Birds attempting to breed at Mono Lake . . . are likely to suffer the most from direct salinity effects, since the adult birds must devote so much time to obtain fresh water that they may not be able to raise young successfully." [ ]

OF JUSTINIAN 2.1.1. From this origin in Roman law, the English common law evolved the concept of the public trust, under which the sovereign owns "all of its navigable waterways and the lands lying beneath them 'as trustee of a public trust for the benefit of the people.' " *Colberg, Inc. v. State of California ex rel. Dept. Pub. Works*, 432 P.2d 3 (Cal.1967). The State of California acquired title as trustee to such lands and waterways upon its admission to the union, *City of Berkeley v. Superior Court*, 606 P.2d 362 (Cal.1980); from the earliest days, *see Eldridge v. Cowell*, 4 Cal. 80, 87 (1854), its judicial decisions have recognized and enforced the trust obligation.

Three aspects of the public trust doctrine require consideration in this opinion: the purpose of the trust; the scope of the trust, particularly as it applies to the nonnavigable tributaries of a navigable lake; and the powers and duties of the state as trustee of the public trust. We discuss these questions in the order listed.

(a) The purpose of the public trust

The objective of the public trust has evolved in tandem with the changing public perception of the values and uses of waterways. As we observed in *Marks v. Whitney*, 491 P.2d 374, "[p]ublic trust easements [were] traditionally defined in terms of navigation, commerce and fisheries. They have been held to include the right to fish, hunt, bathe, swim, to use for boating and general recreation purposes the navigable waters of the state, and to use the bottom of the navigable waters for anchoring, standing, or other purposes." We went on, however, to hold that the traditional triad of uses—navigation, commerce and fishing—did not limit the public interest in the trust res. In language of special importance to the present setting, we stated that "[t]he public uses to which tidelands are subject are sufficiently flexible to encompass changing public needs. In administering the trust the state is not burdened with an outmoded classification favoring one mode of utilization over another. [Citation.] There is a growing public recognition that one of the most important public uses of the tidelands—a use encompassed within the tidelands trust—is the preservation of those lands in their natural state, so that they may serve as ecological units for scientific study, as open space, and as environments which provide food and habitat for birds and marine life, and which favorably affect the scenery and climate of the area." [ ]

Mono Lake is a navigable waterway. [ ] It supports a small local industry which harvests brine shrimp for sale as fish food, which endeavor probably qualifies the lake as a "fishery" under the traditional public trust cases. The principal values plaintiffs seek to protect, however, are recreational and ecological—the scenic views of the lake and its shore, the purity of the air, and the use of the lake for nesting and feeding by birds. Under *Marks v. Whitney*, 491 P.2d 374, it is clear that protection of these values is among the purposes of the public trust.

(b) The scope of the public trust

Early English decisions generally assumed the public trust was limited to tidal waters and the lands exposed and covered by the daily tides, [ ];

many American decisions, including the leading California cases, also concern tidelands. *See, e.g., City of Berkeley v. Superior Court*, 606 P.2d 362 (Cal.1980); *Marks v. Whitney*, 491 P.2d 374; *People v. California Fish Co.*, 138 P. 79 (Cal.1913). It is, however, well settled in the United States generally and in California that the public trust is not limited by the reach of the tides, but encompasses all navigable lakes and streams. *See Illinois Central Railroad Co. v. Illinois*, 146 U.S. 387 (1892) (Lake Michigan); [ ]

Mono Lake is, as we have said, a navigable waterway. The beds, shores and waters of the lake are without question protected by the public trust. The streams diverted by DWP, however, are not themselves navigable. Accordingly, we must address in this case a question not discussed in any recent public trust case—whether the public trust limits conduct affecting nonnavigable tributaries to navigable waterways.

This question was considered in two venerable California decisions. . . .

We conclude that the public trust doctrine, as recognized and developed in California decisions, protects navigable waters from harm caused by diversion of nonnavigable tributaries.[19]

(c) Duties and powers of the state as trustee

In the following review of the authority and obligations of the state as administrator of the public trust, the dominant theme is the state's sovereign power and duty to exercise continued supervision over the trust. One consequence, of importance to this and many other cases, is that parties acquiring rights in trust property generally hold those rights subject to the trust, and can assert no vested right to use those rights in a manner harmful to the trust.

As we noted recently in *City of Berkeley v. Superior Court,* 606 P.2d 362, the decision of the United States Supreme Court in *Illinois Central Railroad v. Illinois,* 146 U.S. 387, "remains the primary authority even today, almost nine decades after it was decided." [ ] The Illinois Legislature in 1886 had granted the railroad in fee simple 1,000 acres of submerged lands, virtually the entire Chicago waterfront. Four years later it sought to revoke that grant. The Supreme Court upheld the revocatory legislation. Its opinion explained that lands under navigable waters conveyed to private parties for wharves, docks, and other structures in furtherance of trust purposes could be granted free of the trust because the conveyance is consistent with the purpose of the trust. But the legislature, it held, did not have the power to convey the entire city waterfront free of trust, thus barring all future legislatures from protecting the public interest. The opinion declares that: "A grant of all the lands under the navigable waters of a State has never been adjudged to be within the legislative power; and any attempted grant of the kind would be held, if not absolutely void on its face, as subject to revocation. The State can no more abdicate its trust over

---

19. In view of the conclusion stated in the text, we need not consider the question whether the public trust extends for some purposes—such as protection of fishing, environmental values, and recreation interests— to nonnavigable streams. For discussion of this subject, see Walston, *The Public Trust Doctrine in the Water Rights Context: The Wrong Environmental Remedy*, 22 SANTA CLARA L. REV. 63, 85 (1982).

property in which the whole people are interested, like navigable waters and soils under them, * * * than it can abdicate its police powers in the administration of government and the preservation of the peace. In the administration of government the use of such powers may for a limited period be delegated to a municipality or other body, but there always remains with the State the right to revoke those powers and exercise them in a more direct manner, and one more conformable to its wishes. So with trusts connected with public property, or property of a special character, like lands under navigable waterways, they cannot be placed entirely beyond the direction and control of the State." 146 U.S. at 453–454.

Turning to the Illinois Central grant, the court stated that: "Any grant of the kind is necessarily revocable, and the exercise of the trust by which the property was held by the State can be resumed at any time. Undoubtedly there may be expenses incurred in improvements made under such a grant which the State ought to pay; but, be that as it may, the power to resume the trust whenever the State judges best is, we think, incontrovertible. * * * The ownership of the navigable waters of the harbor and of the lands under them is a subject of public concern to the whole people of the State. The trust with which they are held, therefore, is governmental and cannot be alienated, except in those instances mentioned of parcels used in the improvement of the interest thus held, or when parcels can be disposed of without detriment to the public interest in the lands and waters remaining." *Id.* at 455–456.

The California Supreme Court indorsed the Illinois Central principles in *People v. California Fish* 138 P. 79 (Cal.1913)....

In summary, the foregoing cases amply demonstrate the continuing power of the state as administrator of the public trust, a power which extends to the revocation of previously granted rights or to the enforcement of the trust against lands long thought free of the trust, *see City of Berkeley v. Superior Court,* 606 P.2d 362. Except for those rare instances in which a grantee may acquire a right to use former trust property free of trust restrictions, the grantee holds subject to the trust, and while he may assert a vested right to the servient estate (the right of use subject to the trust) and to any improvements he erects, he can claim no vested right to bar recognition of the trust or state action to carry out its purposes.

Since the public trust doctrine does not prevent the state from choosing between trust uses, *Colberg, Inc. v. State of California,* 432 P.2d 3; *County of Orange v. Heim,* 106 Cal. Rptr. 825 (Cal.App.1973), the Attorney General of California, seeking to maximize state power under the trust, argues for a broad concept of trust uses. In his view, "trust uses" encompass all public uses, so that in practical effect the doctrine would impose no restrictions on the state's ability to allocate trust property. We know of no authority which supports this view of the public trust, except perhaps the dissenting opinion in *Illinois Central R.R. v. Illinois,* 146 U.S. 387 (1892). Most decisions and commentators assume that "trust uses" relate to uses and activities in the vicinity of the lake, stream, or tidal reach at issue. [ ] The tideland cases make this point clear; after *City of Berkeley v. Superior Court,* 606 P.2d 362, no one could contend that the state could grant tidelands free of the trust merely because the grant served some public purpose, such as increasing tax revenues, or because the grantee might put the property to a commercial use.

Thus, the public trust is more than an affirmation of state power to use public property for public purposes. It is an affirmation of the duty of the state to protect the people's common heritage of streams, lakes, marshlands and tidelands, surrendering that right of protection only in rare cases when the abandonment of that right is consistent with the purposes of the trust.

3. The California Water Rights System

"It is laid down by our law writers, that the right of property in water is usufructuary, and consists not so much of the fluid itself as the advantage of its use." *Eddy v. Simpson*, 3 Cal. 249, 252 (1853). Hence, the cases do not speak of the ownership of water, but only of the right to its use. *Rancho Santa Margarita v. Vail*, 81 P.2d 533 (1938); [ ]. Accordingly, Water Code section 102 provides that "[a]ll water within the State is the property of the people of the State, but the right to the use of water may be acquired by appropriation in the manner provided by law."

Our recent decision in *People v. Shirokow*, 605 P.2d 859 (Cal.1980), described the early history of the appropriative water rights system in California. . . .

"[In 1913, the legislature enacted] the Water Commission Act, which created a Water Commission and provided a procedure for the appropriation of water for useful and beneficial purposes. The main purpose of the act was 'to provide an orderly method for the appropriation of [unappropriated] waters.' [ ] By amendment in 1923, the statutory procedure became the exclusive means of acquiring appropriative rights. [ ] The provisions of the Water Commission Act, as amended from time to time, have been codified in Water Code, divisions 1 and 2. [ ]"

The role of the Water Board under the 1913 act, as *Shirokow* indicated, was a very limited one. . . .

Judicial decisions confirmed this limited role. According to the courts, the function of the Water Board was restricted to determining if unappropriated water was available; if it was, and no competing appropriator submitted a claim, the grant of an appropriation was a ministerial act. [ ]

In 1926, however, a decision of this court led to a constitutional amendment which radically altered water law in California and led to an expansion of the powers of the board. . . .

[The] amendment . . . establishes state water policy. All uses of water, including public trust uses, must now conform to the standard of reasonable use. [ ]

The 1928 amendment itself did not expand the authority of the Water Board. The board remained, under controlling judicial decisions, a ministerial body with the limited task of determining priorities between claimants seeking to appropriate unclaimed water. More recent statutory and judicial developments, however, have greatly enhanced the power of the Water

Board to oversee the reasonable use of water and, in the process, made clear its authority to weigh and protect public trust values.

[T]he function of the Water Board has steadily evolved from the narrow role of deciding priorities between competing appropriators to the charge of comprehensive planning and allocation of waters. This change necessarily affects the board's responsibility with respect to the public trust. The board of limited powers of 1913 had neither the power nor duty to consider interests protected by the public trust; the present board, in undertaking planning and allocation of water resources, is required by statute to take those interests into account.

4. *The relationship between the Public Trust Doctrine and the California Water Rights System*

As we have seen, the public trust doctrine and the appropriative water rights system administered by the Water Board developed independently of each other. Each developed comprehensive rules and principles which, if applied to the full extent of their scope, would occupy the field of allocation of stream waters to the exclusion of any competing system of legal thought. Plaintiffs, for example, argues that the public trust is antecedent to and thus limits all appropriative water rights, an argument which implies that most appropriative water rights in California were acquired and are presently being used unlawfully. Defendant DWP, on the other hand, argues that the public trust doctrine as to stream waters has been "subsumed" into the appropriative water rights system and, absorbed by that body of law, quietly disappeared; according to DWP, the recipient of a board license enjoys a vested right in perpetuity to take water without concern for the consequences to the trust.

We are unable to accept either position. In our opinion, both the public trust doctrine and the water rights system embody important precepts which make the law more responsive to the diverse needs and interests involved in the planning and allocation of water resources. To embrace one system of thought and reject the other would lead to an unbalanced structure, one which would either decry as a breach of trust appropriations essential to the economic development of this state, or deny any duty to protect or even consider the values promoted by the public trust. Therefore, seeking an accommodation which will make use of the pertinent principles of both the public trust doctrine and the appropriative water rights system, and drawing upon the history of the public trust and the water rights system, the body of judicial precedent, and the views of expert commentators, we reach the following conclusions:

a. The state as sovereign retains continuing supervisory control over its navigable waters and the lands beneath those waters. This principle, fundamental to the concept of the public trust, applies to rights in flowing waters as well as to rights in tidelands and lakeshores; it prevents any party from acquiring a vested right to appropriate water in a manner harmful to the interests protected by the public trust.

b. As a matter of current and historical necessity, the Legislature, acting directly or through an authorized agency such as the Water Board, has the power to grant usufructuary licenses that will permit an appropriator to take water from flowing streams and use that water in a distant part of the state, even though this taking does not promote, and may unavoidably harm, the trust uses at the source stream. The population and economy of this state depend upon the appropriation of vast quantities of water for uses unrelated to in-stream trust values.... Now that the economy and population centers of this state have developed in reliance upon appropriated water, it would be disingenuous to hold that such appropriations are and have always been improper to the extent that they harm public trust uses, and can be justified only upon theories of reliance or estoppel.

c. The state has an affirmative duty to take the public trust into account in the planning and allocation of water resources, and to protect public trust uses whenever feasible. Just as the history of this state shows that appropriation may be necessary for efficient use of water despite unavoidable harm to public trust values, it demonstrates that an appropriative water rights system administered without consideration of the public trust may cause unnecessary and unjustified harm to trust interests. [ ] As a matter of practical necessity the state may have to approve appropriations despite foreseeable harm to public trust uses. In so doing, however, the state must bear in mind its duty as trustee to consider the effect of the taking on the public trust, *see United Plainsmen v. N.D. State Water Con. Commission*, 247 N.W.2d 457, 462–463 (N.D. 1976), and to preserve, so far as consistent with the public interest, the uses protected by the trust.

Once the state has approved an appropriation, the public trust imposes a duty of continuing supervision over the taking and use of the appropriated water. In exercising its sovereign power to allocate water resources in the public interest, the state is not confined by past allocation decisions which may be incorrect in light of current knowledge or inconsistent with current needs.

The state accordingly has the power to reconsider allocation decisions even though those decisions were made after due consideration of their effect on the public trust. The case for reconsidering a particular decision, however, is even stronger when that decision failed to weigh and consider public trust uses. In the case before us, the salient fact is that no responsible body has ever determined the impact of diverting the entire flow of the Mono Lake tributaries into the Los Angeles Aqueduct. This is not a case in which the Legislature, the Water Board, or any judicial body has determined that the needs of Los Angeles outweigh the needs of the Mono Basin, that the benefit gained is worth the price. Neither has any responsible body determined whether some lesser taking would better balance the diverse interests. Instead, DWP acquired rights to the entire flow in 1940 from a water board which believed it lacked both the power and the duty to protect the Mono Lake environment, and continues to exercise those rights in apparent disregard for the resulting damage to the scenery, ecology, and human uses of Mono Lake.

It is clear that some responsible body ought to reconsider the allocation of the waters of the Mono Basin. No vested rights bar such reconsideration. We recognize the substantial concerns voiced by Los Angeles—the city's need for water, its reliance upon the 1940 board decision, the cost both in terms of money and environmental impact of obtaining water elsewhere. Such concerns must enter into any allocation decision. We hold only that they do not preclude a reconsideration and reallocation which also takes into account the impact of water diversion on the Mono Lake environment.

. . .

This opinion is but one step in the eventual resolution of the Mono Lake controversy. We do not dictate any particular allocation of water. Our objective is to resolve a legal conundrum in which two competing systems of thought—the public trust doctrine and the appropriative water rights system—existed independently of each other, espousing principles which seemingly suggested opposite results. We hope by integrating these two doctrines to clear away the legal barriers which have so far prevented either the Water Board or the courts from taking a new and objective look at the water resources of the Mono Basin. The human and environmental uses of Mono Lake—uses protected by the public trust doctrine—deserve to be taken into account. Such uses should not be destroyed because the state mistakenly thought itself powerless to protect them.

NOTES

(1) What is the public trust resource in the *Mono Lake* decision? Is it the water, the wildlife, or both? Can water be separated from the wildlife that live in it or depend upon it? Recall that the traditional formulation of the trust: it is "a title held in trust for the people of the state, that they may enjoy the navigation of the waters, carry on commerce over them, and have liberty of fishing therein." *Illinois Central R.R. v. Illinois,* 146 U.S. 387, 452 (1892). Does the "liberty of fishing" include only a right to dangle a baited hook in a sterile body of water? Note, however, that the primary wildlife resources in Mono Lake were gulls, phalaropes, and grebes rather than fish.

(2) Public trust and wildlife: The intriguing questions surrounding the public trust concern the duties or limitations that the trust imposes. Is the state under an obligation to take affirmative steps to protect the wildlife that form the corpus of the trust? Is it prohibited from authorizing actions by others that would impinge upon the corpus? The California court decided that

> the public trust is more than an affirmation of state power to use public property for public purposes. It is an affirmation of the duty of the state to protect the people's common heritage of streams, lakes, marshlands and tidelands, surrendering that right of protection only in rare cases when the abandonment of that right is consistent with the purposes of the trust.

[¶ 32] This meant, the court said, that

> The state has an affirmative duty to take the public trust into account in the planning and allocation of water resources, and to protect public trust uses whenever feasible. Just as the history of this state shows that appropriation may be necessary for efficient use of water despite unavoidable harm to public trust values, it demonstrates that an

appropriative water rights system administered without consideration of the public trust may cause unnecessary and unjustified harm to trust interests. [ ] As a matter of practical necessity the state may have to approve appropriations despite foreseeable harm to public trust uses. In so doing, however, the state must bear in mind its duty as trustee to consider the effect of the taking on the public trust, *see United Plainsmen v. N.D. State Water Con. Commission*, 247 N.W.2d 457, 462–463 (N.D. 1976), and to preserve, so far as consistent with the public interest, the uses protected by the trust.

[¶ 46] "It is clear," the court concluded, "that some responsible body ought to reconsider the allocation of the waters of the Mono Basin. *No vested rights bar such reconsideration.*" [¶ 49]

These principles are easily applied directly to the public trust in wildlife. Just as the trust in navigable waters requires the state to protect "the scenery, ecology, and human uses of Mono Lake" [¶ 48] by reconsidering previously appropriated water rights, so the trustee's obligation to protect and preserve requires it to exercise "continuing supervisory control over" wildlife and its habitat—and "[n]o vested rights bar such reconsideration." As the court also notes, this does not mean that wildlife trumps all other land uses: "As a matter of practical necessity the state may have to approve appropriations despite foreseeable harm to public trust uses. In so doing, however, the state must bear in mind its duty as trustee to consider the effect of the taking on the public trust."

One example of such an approach is *Texas Eastern Transmission Corp. v. Wildlife Preserves, Inc.*, a decision of the New Jersey Supreme Court. Texas Eastern sought to condemn a right of way across four tracts of land that were part of Troy Meadows Wildlife Preserve, an area of over 1400 acres maintained by Wildlife Preserves. Because the landowner was a private entity, the doctrine of prior public use—which requires a "comparative evaluation of two public uses, one existing and one proposed, . . . in order to determine which should prevail as the paramount use"—was not available to the preserve. Nonetheless, the court felt that it could take into consideration the fact that

> defendant's devotion of its land to a purpose which is encouraged and often engaged in by government itself gives it a somewhat more potent claim to judicial protection against taking of its preserve or a portion of it by arbitrary action of a condemnor. In such unique cases courts realize that more than a dollar valuation is involved. The public service being rendered must be considered and it cannot be evaluated adequately only in dollars and cents. [ ] The difference is not in the principle [that the condemnor must act reasonably] but in its application; that is, the *quantum* of proof required of this defendant to show arbitrariness against it should not be as substantial as that to be assumed by the ordinary property owner who devotes his land to conventional uses.

To accomplish these objectives, the court instructed the trial court on remand that the ultimate burden of proving arbitrariness in the choice of route will be on Wildlife Preserves. Procedurally, however, if it introduces reasonable proof of (1) the serious damage claimed to result from installation of the pipeline on the path chosen by plaintiff, and (2) an apparently reasonably available alternate route or routes, which will avoid the serious damage referred to, the burden of going forward with the evidence will shift to plaintiff. A *prima facie* case of arbitrariness having been made out, Texas Eastern may present its evidence to the contrary, which it claims indicates that the location of the right of way selected represented a reasonable and not capricious choice, considering all the factors which may properly enter into the question of what course of action is reasonably required to serve the public convenience and necessity. In this connection plaintiff has suggested that the alternate route proposed by defendant will be much more costly than the one chosen. Of course, cost is a factor for consideration, but a relative one. Within reasonable limits the fact that an alternate route will be more expensive should not deter its selection by a utility, if the public convenience and necessity are better served thereby.

Texas Eastern Transmission Corp. v. Wildlife Preserves, Inc., 225 A.2d 130, 137, 138 (N.J.1966).

CHAPTER 6

STATE AND NATIONAL GOVERNMENTS IN THE FEDERAL SYSTEM

Chapter 5 examined the tangled relationship between sovereignty and property that found expression in the "state ownership doctrine"—a bundle of ideas that center on the concept that the state as sovereign "owned" the wildlife within its borders in trust for its citizens. As it developed, state sovereign ownership overlaps with public trust concepts. The materials in Chapter 5 examined these doctrines as a source of state power. Because the state owned the wildlife, it was empowered both to regulate private conduct—whether conduct intended to capture animals or to destroy their habitat—to conserve the trust property and to demand compensation when private conduct destroyed trust resources.

The states, of course, are situated in a federal system in which the national government is supreme within the reach of the powers delegated to it. To what extent does wildlife come within the scope of the powers delegated to the national government? For much of the history of the nation, the answer turned on the state ownership doctrine. Not only was the doctrine the source of affirmative powers to regulated, it also served as a shield against federal power: since the state owned the wildlife, it was beyond the constitutional limitations of the dormant Commerce Clause or the Privileges and Immunities Clause. It is with the state ownership doctrine as a shield that we begin the examination of the role of the national government.

SECTION 1. NATIONAL CONSTITUTIONAL LIMITS ON STATE POWER

NOTES

Federal power may override state law in two different ways. First, the Constitution itself (as construed by the courts, of course) may preclude states from acting in certain ways. In wildlife law, this is most likely to occur in situations involving the limitations imposed on states to protect interstate equality found in the Privileges and Immunities Clause and the Commerce Clause. After the Civil War, litigants might also press equal protection and due process claims.

Second, a federal lawmaker—most frequently, Congress—may exercise power delegated to it by the Constitution and thereby supplant inconsistent state law. This occurs most frequently when actions are taken by the federal government pursuant to the Treaty Clause, the Commerce Clause, and the Property Clause.

The materials in this section examine the first type of limitation—situations in which the language of the Constitution standing alone is asserted to supplant state powers.

a.   IN THE BEGINNING: STATE OWNERSHIP AS A SHIELD AGAINST FEDERAL POWER

How is legal responsibility for wildlife allocated under the federal system? Once again, the story begins with oysters—the most economically valuable wildlife resource of the early federal period.

As was discussed in both Chapter 3 and 5, the New Jersey Supreme Court decided that as between a state and private claimants, the state "owned" the submerged lands and the oysters growing on them. *Arnold v. Mundy*, 6 N.J.L. 1 (1821). That decision was subsequently ratified by the United States Supreme Court. *Martin v. Waddell's Lessee*, 41 U.S. (16 Pet.) 367 (1842).

But, as between state and national governments, who had the final say in the allocation, or regulation of access to, wildlife? *Corfield v. Coryell* is the beginning of the constitutional law of wildlife.

Corfield v. Coryell

Circuit Court for the Eastern District of Pennsylvania.
6 F. Cas. 546 (1823) (No. 3,230).

[Plaintiff's ship, the *Hiram*, was seized as it was being used to rake oysters at the oyster beds in Maurice River Cove, a navigable waterway in New Jersey. Defendant, acting as the prize master, sailed the ship to Leesburg, where a court was convened and the ship was condemned and ordered sold. Defendant argued that the seizure was justified under a New Jersey statute that prohibited non-residents from raking oysters. Plaintiff, in turn, alleged that the state statute was void under the federal constitution.]

■ WASHINGTON, CIRCUIT JUSTICE:—The points reserved present for the consideration of the court, many interesting and difficult questions, which will be examined in the shape of objections made by the plaintiff's counsel to the seizure of the Hiram, ... These objections are,—

First. That the [New Jersey statute] ... is repugnant to the constitution of the United States in the following particulars: 1. To the eighth section of the first article, which grants to congress the power to regulate commerce with foreign nations, and among the several states, and with the Indian tribes. 2. To the second section of the fourth article, which declares, that the citizens of each state shall be entitled to all privileges and immunities of citizens in the several states....

The first question then is, whether this act ... is repugnant to the power granted to congress to regulate commerce? Commerce ... among the several states, can mean nothing more than intercourse ... among those states, for purposes of trade, be the object of the trade what it may; and this intercourse must include all the means by which it can be carried on, whether by the free navigation of the waters of the several states, or by a passage over land through the states, where such passage becomes necessary to the commercial intercourse between the states. It is this intercourse which congress is invested with the power of regulating, and with which no state has a right to interfere. But this power, which comprehends the use of, and passage over the navigable waters of the several states, does by no means impair the right of the state government to legislate upon all subjects of internal police within their territorial limits, which is not forbidden by the constitution of the United States, even although such legislation may indirectly and remotely affect commerce, provided it do not interfere with the regulations of congress upon the same subject. Such are inspection, quarantine, and health laws; laws regulating the internal commerce of the state; laws establishing and regulating turnpike roads, ferries, canals, and the like.

In the case of *Gibbons v. Ogden,* 22 U.S. (9 Wheat.) 1 (1824), which we consider as full authority for the principles above stated, it is said, "that no direct power over these objects is granted to congress, and consequently they remain subject to state legislation. If the legislative power of the Union can reach them, it must be for national purposes; it must be when the power is expressly given for a specified purpose, or is clearly incident to some power which is expressly given." But if the power which congress possesses to regulate commerce does not interfere with that of the state to regulate its internal trade, ... much less can that power impair the right of the state governments to legislate, in such manner as in their wisdom may seem best, over the public property of the state, and to regulate the use of the same, where such regulations do not interfere with the free navigation of the waters of the state, for purposes of commercial intercourse, nor with the trade within the state, which the laws of the United States permit to be carried on. The grant to congress to regulate commerce on the navigable waters belonging to the several state, renders those waters the public property of the United States, for all the purposes of navigation and commercial intercourse; subject only to congressional regulation. But this grant contains no cession, either express or implied, of territory, or of public or private property. The *jus privatum* which a state has in the soil covered by its waters, is totally distinct from the *jus publicum* with which it belongs, to be used by them according to their necessities, or according to the laws which regulate their use.... If then the fisheries and oyster beds within the territorial limits of a state are the common property of the citizens of that state, and were not ceded to the United States by the power granted to congress to regulate commerce, it is difficult to perceive how a law of the state regulating the use of this common property, under such penalties and forfeitures as the state legislature may think proper to prescribe, can be said to interfere with the power granted....

It was insisted by the plaintiff's counsel, that as oysters constituted an article of trade, a law which abridges the right of the citizens of other states to take them ... amounts to a regulation of the external commerce of the state. But it is a manifest mistake to denominate that a commercial regulation which merely regulates the common property of the citizens of the state, by forbidding it to be taken at improper seasons, or with destructive instruments. The law does not inhibit the buying and selling of oysters after they are lawfully gathered, and have become articles of trade; but it forbids the removal of them from the beds in which they grow, (in which situation they cannot be considered articles of trade,) unless under the regulation which the law prescribes ...

2.   The next question is whether this act infringes that section of the constitution which declares that "the citizens of each state shall be entitled to all the privileges and immunities of citizens in the several states?" The inquiry is, what are the privileges and immunities of citizens in the several states? We feel no hesitation in confining these expressions to those privileges and immunities which are, in their nature, fundamental; which belong, of right, to the citizens of all free governments; and which have, at all times, been enjoyed by the citizens of the several states which compose this Union, from the time of their becoming free, independent, and sovereign. What these fundamental principles are, it would perhaps be more tedious that difficult to enumerate. They may, however, be all comprehended under the following general heads: Protection by the government; the enjoyment of life and liberty, with the right to acquire and possess property of every kind, and to pursue and obtain happiness and safety; subject nevertheless to such restraints as the government my justly prescribe for the general good of the whole. The right of a citizen of one state to pass through, or to reside in any other state for purposes of trade, agriculture, professional pursuits, or otherwise; to claim the benefit of the writ of habeas corpus; to institute and maintain actions of any kind in the courts of the state; to take, hold and dispose of property, either real or personal; and an exemption from higher taxes or impositions than are paid by the other citizens of the state; may be mentioned as some of the particular privileges and immunities of citizen which are clearly embraced by the general description of privileges deemed to be fundamental: to which may be added, the elective franchise, as regulated and established by the laws or constitution of the state in which it is to be exercised. These, and many others which might be mentioned, are strictly speaking, privileges and immunities.... But we cannot accede to the proposition which was insisted on by the counsel, that, under this provision of the constitution, the citizens of the several states are permitted to participate in all the rights which belong exclusively to the citizens of any other particular state, merely upon the ground that they are enjoyed by those citizens; much less, that in regulating the use of the common property of the citizens of such state, the legislature is bound to extend to the citizens of all the other states the same advantages as are secured to their own citizens. A several fishery, either as the right to it respects running fish, or such as are stationary, such as oysters, clams, and the like, is as much the property of the individual to whom it belongs, as dry land, or land covered by water; and is equally protected by the laws of the state against the aggressions of others, whether citizens or strangers. Where those private rights do not exist to the exclusion of the common right, that of fishing belongs to all the

citizens or subjects of the state. It is property of all; to be enjoyed by them in subordination to the laws which regulate its use. They may be considered as tenants in common of this property; and they are so exclusively entitled to the use of it, that it cannot be enjoyed by others without the tacit consent, or the express permission of the sovereign who has the power to regulate its use.

. . .

Let judgement be entered for the defendant.

NOTES

(1) The constitutional problems the state ownership doctrine solved: What constitutional problems did the court solve through the use of the idea that the state was the owner-as-sovereign of the wildlife?

In his list of fundamental privileges protected by the clause, Washington lists the right to engage in work. Why is the occupation of harvesting of oysters not "fundamental"? Similarly, Washington included in his short list of fundamental rights "the right to acquire and possess property of every kind." Why did this right not include the right to reduce an animal *feræ naturæ* to possession and thereby to acquire a property in it?

Might Justice Washington's careful list reflect the need of a slaveholder to protect the peculiar institution of slavery?

(2) The road from *Corfield* to *Geer*: Between the decision in *Corfield* in 1823 and *Geer* in 1896, the Supreme Court decided three wildlife cases. These decisions trace the rise of the state ownership doctrine as a shield against federal regulation:

(a) *Smith v. Maryland* involved the seizure of a sloop that was licensed under federal law to engage in fishing. It was seized and condemned by Maryland officials for dredging oysters in violation of state law. The sloop's owner argued that the federal license conferred an immunity. The Court disagreed, relying upon the state's ownership of the submerged lands:

> But this soil is held by the State, not only subject to, but in some sense in trust for, the enjoyment of certain public rights, among which is the common liberty of taking fish, as well shellfish as floating fish. [ ] The State holds the propriety of this soil for the conservation of the public rights of fishery thereon, and may regulate the modes of that enjoyment so as to prevent the destruction of the fishery. In other words, it may forbid all such acts as would render the public right less valuable, or destroy it altogether. This power results from the ownership of the soil, from the legislative jurisdiction of the State over it, and from its duty to preserve unimpaired those public uses for which the soil is held. [ ]; *Corfield v. Coryell*, 6 F. Cas. 546 (C.C.E.D.Pa.1823) (No. 3,230).

Smith v. Maryland, 59 U.S. (18 How.) 71 (1855).

(b) *McCready v. Virginia* also involved oysters. McCready, a citizen of Maryland, was indicted, convicted, and fined $500 by a Virginia circuit court for planting oysters in Ware River, a navigable stream. Again, the United States Supreme Court began with state ownership:

> The principle has long been settled in this court, that each State owns the beds of all tide-waters within its jurisdiction, unless they have been granted away. [ ] In like manner, the States own the tide-waters themselves, and the fish in them, so far as they are capable of ownership while running. For this purpose the State represents its people, and the ownership is that of the people in their united sovereignty. [ ] The title thus held is subject to the paramount right of navigation, the regulation of which, in respect to foreign and interstate commerce, has been granted to the United States. There has been, however, no such grant of power over the fisheries. These remain under the exclusive control of the State, which has consequently the right, in its discretion, to appropriate its tide-waters and their beds to be used by its people as a common for taking and cultivating fish, so far as it may be done without obstructing navigation. Such an appropriation is in effect nothing more than a regulation of the use by the people of their common property. The right which the people of the State thus acquire comes not from their citizenship alone, but from their citizenship and property combined. It is, in fact, a property right.

McCready v. Virginia, 94 U.S. 391 (1876).

(c) *Manchester v. Commonwealth* was an appeal from a conviction for using a prohibited purse seine within the territorial limits of Massachusetts. The Court held simply that Congress had not chosen to regulate the menhaden fishery and that Massachusetts therefore was free to do so "according to the principles declared in *Smith v. Maryland.*" *Manchester v. Commonwealth,* 139 U.S. 240 (1891).

(d) *Geer v. Connecticut* capped this line of cases in holding that the state, as owner of the wildlife within its borders, was free to regulate its taking and possession—even to the point of defining the nature of any property interests that might be acquired in the wildlife.

The remainder of this section traces the demise of the state ownership doctrine as a shield against federal power.

b. AT PRESENT: THE DEMISE OF STATE OWNERSHIP AS A SHIELD

NOTES

Interstate equality vs. local obligations: The Constitution both explicitly and implicitly limits the power of states to discriminate against residents of other states. The Privileges and Immunities Clause of Article IV explicitly bars state discrimination against citizens of other states. The grant of power to Congress in Article I to regulate interstate commerce has been understood to restrict implicitly state power to affect such commerce since the decision in *Cooley v. Board of Wardens,* 53 U.S. (12 How.) 299 (1851). This includes a limitation on state discrimination against interstate commercial relationships. The two clauses thus share overlapping objectives based on a broad concern for interstate equality.[1]

---

1. Despite their overlapping objectives, the two clauses differ in their focus: the Commerce Clause is concerned primarily with business that is carried on in more than

States generally may not discriminate against nonresident's access to privately owned resources located within the state. Thus, the Commerce Clause prohibits states from giving their residents a preference in purchasing commodities owned by private entities, *e.g., Pennsylvania v. West Virginia,* 262 U.S. 553 (1923) (state residents may not be given a preference to purchase natural gas produced in the state), and from denying nonresident firms a chance to compete for resident consumers, *e.g., Hunt v. Washington State Apple Advertising Commission,* 432 U.S. 333 (1977) (state law prohibiting non-resident apple growers from shipping apples into state in boxes marked with shipping state's grading system impermissibly restricts competition). Similarly, the Privileges and Immunities Clause prohibits a state from giving its residents a preference to employment with private entities, *e.g., Hicklin v. Orbeck,* 437 U.S. 518 (1978) (state statute giving preference to residents in all employment "resulting from" oil and gas development held unconstitutional), and from denying non-residents the right to acquire property on equal terms with residents, *e.g., Blake v. McClung,* 172 U.S. 239 (1898) (state statute giving preference to residents in distribution of assets of insolvent company impermissible).

The goal of interstate equality is not, however, the only relevant constitutional objective; state governments also have fundamental, if poorly defined, responsibilities to their residents. In meeting these obligations, a state may provide benefits to its residents that it withholds from nonresidents. A state, for example, may impose residency requirements for education, *Martinez v. Bynum,* 461 U.S. 321 (1983) (residence requirement for free public education permissible under Privileges and Immunities Clause), and charge nonresidents higher tuition to attend state universities, *Starns v. Malkerson,* 401 U.S. 985 (1971), *aff'g mem.* 326 F.Supp. 234 (D.Minn. 1970) (one-year residency requirement for reduced in-state tuition permissible under Privileges and Immunities Clause). A state may also provide direct subsidies to in-state businesses and deny them to out-of-state businesses, *e.g., Hughes v. Alexandria Scrap Corp.,* 426 U.S. 794 (1976), favor local contractors, *American Yearbook Co. v. Askew,* 409 U.S. 904, *aff'g mem.* 339 F.Supp. 719 (M.D.Fla.1972), create resident-hiring preferences for publicly funded construction projects, *White v. Massachusetts Council of Construction Employers, Inc.,* 460 U.S. 204 (1983), and prefer state residents in selling concrete from a state-owned plant, *Reeves, Inc. v. Stake,* 447 U.S. 429 (1980), without running afoul of the Commerce Clause.

As the examples suggest, although states may not regulate private conduct in ways that discriminate between residents and non-residents, they have much greater freedom to prefer their own citizens when they are distributing public resources and benefits—be it tax revenues, jobs, or concrete. But are all public resources created equal? Again, what is hidden in the term "property"? May a state prefer its own residents when it sells property such as trees and forage? May a state prefer its own residents when it leases public trust land beneath navigable waters? May a state prefer its own residents when it sells rights to wildlife within its borders?

one state while the Privileges and Immunities Clause is concerned primarily with how states treat nonresidents.

(i) THE PRIVILEGES AND IMMUNITIES CLAUSE

> The Citizens of each State shall be entitled to all Privileges and Immunities of Citizens in the several States.
>
> UNITED STATES CONSTITUTION art IV, § 2, cl. 1

NOTES

Post-*Corfield* developments: Professor Laurence Tribe places *Corfield* at the center of his examination of the "classic" Privileges and Immunities Clause doctrine. 1 LAURENCE TRIBE, AMERICAN CONSTITUTIONAL LAW 1250–55 (3d ed. 2000). Tribe's decision reflects not only the fact that *Corfield* was the first major analysis of the Clause, but also that Justice Washington's opinion embodied the natural law ethos of the period. The Clause, Washington wrote, encompassed those privileges and immunities "which are in their very nature, fundamental; which belong, of right, to the citizens of all free governments." [¶ 9]

This formulation, however, contained the potential to trump state law since, if a privilege or immunity were "fundamental," the state would be required to grant it to non-citizens even (perhaps) if it did not grant it to its own citizens. Furthermore, it was at most a small step beyond *Corfield's* formulation to a requirement that *all* state citizens be treated similarly in every state, thus forging a group of uniform national rights protected by the national government. Perhaps because of its broadly nationalizing potential, the Supreme Court never endorsed the expansive core of Washington's vision. Beginning with *Paul v. Virginia,* 75 U.S. (8 Wall.) 168 (1868), the post-Civil–War Court rejected the natural rights theory.

Paul involved a Virginia statute requiring non-resident insurance companies to post bonds and specified that the bonds were to be issued by the state. Samuel Paul was the Virginia agent for several New York insurance companies; he refused to comply with the requirement, was indicted, convicted, and fined. He appealed his conviction to the Supreme Court, alleging *inter alia* that the Virginia statute violated the Privileges and Immunities Clause. The Court disagreed:

> [T]he privileges and immunities secured to citizens of each State ... are those privileges and immunities which are common to the citizens in the latter States under their constitution and laws by virtue of their being citizens. Special privileges enjoyed by citizens in their own States are not secured in other States by this provision. It is not intended by the provision to give the laws of one State any operation in other States. They can have no such operation, except by the permission, express or implied, of those States.

Incorporation was a "special privilege"—and thus corporations were not protected by the Clause. *Paul v. Virginia,* 75 U.S. (8 Wall.) 168 (1868). *See also Downham v. Alexandria Council,* 77 U.S. (10 Wall.) 173 (1869).

While rejecting fundamental rights as an *trump* on state powers, the Court nonetheless retained the concept as a *limit* on the privileges and immunities accorded constitutional protection. In *The Slaughterhouse Cases,* the Court wrote

[The Privileges and Immunities Clause] did not create those rights, which it called privileges and immunities of citizens of the States. It threw around them in that clause no security for the citizen of the State in which they were claimed or exercised. Nor did it profess to control the power of the State governments over the rights of its own citizens.

Its sole purpose was to declare to the several States, that whatever those rights, as you grant or establish them to your own citizens, or as you limit or qualify, or impose restrictions on their exercise, the same, neither more nor less, shall be the measure of the rights of citizens of other States within your jurisdiction.

The Slaughter-House Cases, 83 U.S. (16 Wall.) 36 (1873).

The post-Civil War formulation of the Clause thus involved two elements: first, states might withhold "special privileges" from non-citizens while extending them to their own citizens, *i.e.,* the Clause only protected "fundamental rights"; second, states might withhold any rights—even fundamental rights—from non-citizens as long as they also withheld them from their own citizens. On the types of privileges that fell into each category, *see generally* W.J. Meyers, *The Privileges and Immunities of Citizens in the Several States,* 1 MICH. L. REV. 286, 364 (1902); *see also* Note, *The Equal Privileges and Immunities Clause of the Federal Constitution,* 28 COLUMBIA L. REV. 347 (1928).

* * *

Recall that the under the Court's analysis in *McCready v. Virginia,* 94 U.S. 391 (1876), hunting and fishing were "special privileges"—even when they were the individual's occupation—rather than "fundamental rights" because they involved the common property of the state's citizens. As such, states could deny equal treatment to noncitizens. This question—the constitutional status of fishing as an occupation—reached the Supreme Court a third time in

Toomer v. Witsell

United States Supreme Court.
334 U.S. 385 (1948).

■ VINSON, C.J.:—This is a suit to enjoin as unconstitutional the enforcement of several South Carolina statutes governing commercial shrimp fishing in the three-mile maritime belt off the coast of that State. Appellants, who initiated the action, are five individual fishermen, all citizens and residents of Georgia, and a non-profit fish dealers' organization incorporated in Florida. Appellees are South Carolina officials charged with enforcement of the statutes.

[The shrimp fishery at issue extended from North Carolina to Florida. Most of the shrimp in the region are migratory, swimming south in the late summer and fall and returning north in the spring. Given the nature of the resource, the commercial shrimpers wanted to start trawling off the Carolinas in the summer and follow the shrimp down the coast to Florida. There was, however, no federal regulation of the fishery and the four regional states had been unable to adopt a uniform regulatory scheme since some of the states sought to channel the income to their own residents. Restrictions on non-resident fishing led to retaliation and the fishery was effectively partitioned at the state lines.]

The statutes appellants challenge relate to shrimping during the open season in the three-mile belt: Section 3300 of the South Carolina Code provides that the waters in that area shall be "a common for the people of the State for the taking of fish." Section 3374 imposes a tax of 1/8 cents a pound on green, or raw, shrimp taken in those waters. Section 3379, as amended in 1947, requires payment of a license fee of $25 for each shrimp boat owned by a resident, and of $2,500 for each one owned by a non-resident. Another statute, not integrated in the Code, conditions the issuance of non-resident licenses for 1948 and the years thereafter on submission of proof that the applicants have paid South Carolina income taxes on all profits from operations in that State during the preceding year. And § 3414 requires that all boats licensed to trawl for shrimp in the State's waters dock at a South Carolina port and unload, pack, and stamp their catch "before shipping or transporting it to another State or the waters thereof." Violation of the fishing laws entails suspension of the violator's license as well as a maximum of a $1,000 fine, imprisonment for a year, or a combination of a $500 fine and a year's imprisonment.

. . .

Fourth. Appellants' most vigorous attack is directed at § 3379 which, as amended in 1947, requires non-residents of South Carolina to pay license fees one hundred times as great as those which residents must pay. The purpose and effect of this statute, they contend, is not to conserve shrimp, but to exclude non-residents and thereby create a commercial monopoly for South Carolina residents. As such, the statute is said to violate the privileges and immunities clause of Art. IV, § 2, of the Constitution and the equal protection clause of the Fourteenth Amendment.

Article IV, § 2, so far as relevant reads as follows:

The Citizens of each State shall be entitled to all Privileges and Immunities of Citizens in the several States.

The primary purpose of this clause, like the clauses between which it is located—those relating to full faith and credit and to interstate extradition of fugitives from justice—was to help fuse into one Nation a collection of independent, sovereign States. It was designed to insure to a citizen of State A who ventures into State B the same privileges which the citizens of State B enjoy. For protection of such equality the citizen of State A was not to be restricted to the uncertain remedies afforded by diplomatic processes and official retaliation. "Indeed, without some provision of the kind removing from the citizens of each State the disabilities of alienage in the other States, and giving them equality of privilege with citizens of those States, the Republic would have constituted little more than a league of States; it would not have constituted the Union which now exists." *Paul v. Virginia,* 75 U.S. (8 Wall.) 168, 180 (1869).

In line with this underlying purpose, it was long ago decided that one of the privileges which the clause guarantees to citizens of State A is that of doing business in State B on terms of substantial equality with the citizens of that State.

Like many other constitutional provisions, the privileges and immunities clause is not an absolute. It does bar discrimination against citizens of other States where there is no substantial reason for the discrimination beyond the mere fact that they are citizens of other States. But it does not preclude disparity of treatment in the many situations where there are perfectly valid independent reasons for it. Thus the inquiry in each case must be concerned with whether such reasons do exist and whether the degree of discrimination bears a close relation to them. The inquiry must also, of course, be conducted with due regard for the principle that the States should have considerable leeway in analyzing local evils and in prescribing appropriate cures.

With these factors in mind, we turn to a consideration of the constitutionality of § 3379.

By that statute South Carolina plainly and frankly discriminates against non-residents, and the record leaves little doubt but what the discrimination is so great that its practical effect is virtually exclusionary. This the appellees do not seriously dispute. . . .

As justification for the statute, appellees urge that the State's obvious purpose was to conserve its shrimp supply, and they suggest that it was designed to head off an impending threat of excessive trawling. The record casts some doubt on these statements. But in any event, appellees' argument assumes that any means adopted to attain valid objectives necessarily squares with the privileges and immunities clause. It overlooks the purpose of that clause, which, as indicated above, is to outlaw classifications based on the fact of non-citizenship unless there is something to indicate that non-citizens constitute a peculiar source of the evil at which the statute is aimed.

. . .

Thus, § 3379 must be held unconstitutional unless commercial shrimp fishing in the maritime belt falls within some unexpressed exception to the privileges and immunities clause.

Appellees strenuously urge that there is such an exception. Their argument runs as follows: Ever since Roman times, animals *feræ naturæ*, not having been reduced to individual possession and ownership, have been considered as *res nullius* or part of the "negative community of interests" and hence subject to control by the sovereign or other governmental authority. More recently this thought has been expressed by saying that fish and game are the common property of all citizens of the governmental unit and that the government, as a sort of trustee, exercises this "ownership" for the benefit of its citizens. In the case of fish, it has also been considered that each government "owned" both the beds of its lakes, streams, and tidewaters and the waters themselves; hence it must also "own" the fish within those waters. Each government may, the argument continues, regulate the corpus of the trust in the way best suited to the interests of the beneficial owners, its citizens, and may discriminate as it sees fit against persons lacking any beneficial interest. Finally, it is said that this special property interest, which nations and similar governmental bodies have traditionally had, in this country vested in the colonial governments and passed to the individual States.

Language frequently repeated by this Court appears to lend some support to this analysis.[33] But in only one case, *McCready v. Virginia*, 94 U.S. 391 (1876), has the Court actually upheld State action discriminating against commercial fishing or hunting by citizens of other States where there were advanced no persuasive independent reasons justifying the discrimination. In that case the Court sanctioned a Virginia statute applied so as to prohibit citizens of other States, but not Virginia citizens, from planting oysters in the tidal waters of the Ware River. The right of Virginians in Virginia waters, the Court said, was "a property right, and not a mere privilege or immunity of citizenship." And an analogy was drawn between planting oysters in a river bed and planting corn in state-owned land.

It will be noted that there are at least two factual distinctions between the present case and the *McCready* case. First, the *McCready* case related to fish which would remain in Virginia until removed by man. The present case, on the other hand, deals with free-swimming fish which migrate through the waters of several States and are off the coast of South Carolina only temporarily. Secondly, the *McCready* case involved regulation of fishing in inland waters, whereas the statute now questioned is directed at regulation of shrimping in the marginal sea.

Thus we have, on the one hand, a single precedent which might be taken as reading an exception into the privileges and immunities clause and, on the other, a case which does not fall directly within that exception. Viewed in this light, the question before us comes down to whether the reasons which evoked the exception call for its extension to a case involving the factual distinctions here presented.

However satisfactory the ownership theory explains the *McCready* case, the very factors which make the present case distinguishable render that theory but a weak prop for the South Carolina statute. That the shrimp are migratory makes apposite Mr. Justice Holmes' statement in *Missouri v. Holland*, 252 U.S. 416, 434 (1920), that "To put the claim of the State upon title is to lean upon a slender reed. Wild birds are not in the possession of anyone; and possession is the beginning of ownership." Indeed, only fifteen years after the *McCready* decision, a unanimous Court indicated that the rule of that case might not apply to free-swimming fish.[35] The fact that it is activity in the three-mile belt which the South Carolina statute regulates is of equal relevance in considering the applicability of the ownership doctrine. . . .

33. The most extended exposition appears in the majority opinion in *Geer v. Connecticut,* 161 U.S. 519 (1896).

35. *Manchester v. Massachusetts,* 139 U.S. 240, 265 (1891). In that case appellant, a citizen of Rhode Island, was convicted of violating a Massachusetts statute which regulated fishing in Buzzard's Bay. The Court upheld Massachusetts' power to enact the regulation, but pointed out that the statute "makes no discrimination in favor of citizens of Massachusetts and against citizens of other states."

The whole ownership theory, in fact, is now generally regarded as but a fiction expressive in legal shorthand of the importance to its people that a State have power to preserve and regulate the exploitation of an important resource.[37] And there is no necessary conflict between that vital policy consideration and the constitutional command that the State exercise that power, like its other powers, so as not to discriminate without reason against citizens of other States.

These considerations lead us to the conclusion that the *McCready* exception to the privileges and immunities clause, if such it be, should not be expanded to cover this case.

Thus we hold that commercial shrimping in the marginal sea, like other common callings, is within the purview of the privileges and immunities clause. And since we have previously concluded that the reasons advanced in support of the statute do not bear a reasonable relationship to the high degree of discrimination practiced upon citizens of other States, it follows that § 3379 violates Art. IV, § 2, of the Constitution.

. . .

Affirmed in part and reversed in part.

■ FRANKFURTER, J., with whom JACKSON, J., joins, concurring:—Barring the portion entitled Fourth, I join the Court's opinion. While I agree that South Carolina has exceeded her power to control fisheries within her waters, I rest the invalidity of her attempt to do so on the Commerce Clause. The Court reaches this result by what I deem to be a misapplication of the Privileges-and-Immunities Clause of Art. IV, § 2, of the Constitution.

To regard any limitation upon the Privileges-and-Immunities Clause as "some unexpressed exception" and not give any clue to the basis on which such an "exception" may be implied is to leave the matter too much at large. It deals with the Constitution as though its various clauses were discrete and not a coherent scheme for government. Specifically, the Privileges-and-Immunities Clause, like the Contract Clause, must be put "in its proper perspective in our constitutional framework." [ ]

Like other provisions of the Constitution, the Clause whereby "The Citizens of each State shall be entitled to all Privileges and Immunities of Citizens in the several States" must be read in conjunction with the Tenth Amendment to the Constitution. This clause presupposes the continued retention by the States of powers that historically belonged to the States, and were not explicitly given to the central government or withdrawn from the States. I think it is fair to summarize the decisions which have applied Art. IV, § 2, by saying that they bar a State from penalizing the citizens of other States by subjecting them to heavier taxation merely because they are such citizens or by discriminating against citizens of other States in the pursuit of ordinary livelihoods in competition with local citizens. It is not conceivable that the framers of the Constitution meant to obliterate all

---

37. *See, e.g.,* ROSCOE POUND, AN INTRODUCTION TO THE PHILOSOPHY OF LAW 197–202 (1922). The fiction apparently gained currency partly as a result of confusion between the Roman term *imperium* or governmental power to regulate, and *dominium*, or ownership. Power over fish and game was, in origin, *imperium.*

special relations between a State and its citizens. This Clause does not touch the right of a State to conserve or utilize its resources on behalf of its own citizens, provided it uses these resources within the State and does not attempt a control of the resources as part of a regulation of commerce between the States. A State may care for its own in utilizing the bounties of nature within her borders because it has technical ownership of such bounties or, when ownership is in no one, because the State may for the common good exercise all the authority that technical ownership ordinarily confers.

When the Constitution was adopted, such, no doubt, was the common understanding regarding the power of States over its fisheries, and it is this common understanding that was reflected in *McCready v. Virginia,* 94 U.S. 391 (1876). The *McCready* case is not an isolated decision to be looked at askance. It is the symbol of one of the weightiest doctrines in our law. It expressed the momentum of legal history that preceded it, and around it in turn has clustered a voluminous body of rulings. Not only has a host of State cases applied the *McCready* doctrine as to the power of States to control their game and fisheries for the benefit of their own citizens, but in our own day this Court formulated the amplitude of the *McCready* doctrine by referring to "the regulation or the distribution of the public domain, or of the common property or resources of the people of the state, the enjoyment of which may be limited to its citizens as against both aliens and the citizens of other states." *Truax v. Raich,* 239 U.S. 33, 39, 40 (1915).

But a State cannot project its powers over its own resources by seeking to control the channels of commerce among the States. It is one thing to say that a food supply that may be reduced to control by a State for feeding its own people should be only locally consumed. The State has that power and the Privileges-and-Immunities Clause is no restriction upon its exercise. It is a wholly different thing for the State to provide that only its citizens shall be engaged in commerce among the States, even though based on a locally available food supply. That is not the exercise of the basic right of a State to feed and maintain and give enjoyment to its own people. When a State regulates the sending of products across State lines we have commerce among the States as to which State intervention is subordinate to the Commerce Clause. That is the nub of the decision in *Foster-Fountain Packing Co. v. Haydel,* 278 U.S. 1 (1928). South Carolina has attempted such regulation of commerce in shrimp among the States. In doing so she has exceeded the restrictions of the Commerce Clause.

NOTES

(1) The Court in *Toomer* enunciated a new standard for evaluating state actions alleged to violate the Privileges and Immunities Clause. The Clause, the Court writes, "bar[s] discrimination against citizens of other States *where there is no substantial reason for the discrimination beyond the mere fact that they are citizens of other States.*" [¶ 8 emphasis added] State ownership, the Court continues, is not such a "substantial reason" because "[t]he whole ownership theory ... is now generally regarded as but a fiction expressive ... of the importance to its people that a State have

power to preserve and regulate the exploitation of an important resource.''
[¶ 18] Why would state ownership justify such discrimination when the
importance of the resource to citizens of the state will not?

(2) Although the Court was at pains to distinguish *McCready,* what is left
of the earlier decision's rationale? Does the distinction between free-
swimming and sessile distinguish the two cases?

(3) Is Frankfurter's distinction between the Commerce Clause and the
Privileges and Immunities useful? Consider whether a state could charge
differential rates for noncommercial hunting and fishing licenses under the
majority's and the dissent's approaches. Does the majority's two-step
analysis—is the privilege being regulated sufficiently fundamental to be
protected [¶ 7] and, if so, whether the restrictions are justified [¶ 11]—
provide a method for allowing differential rates for noncommercial licenses?
In other words, is the crucial element the conclusion that fishing is a
"common calling"? [¶ 20]

(4) *Takahashi v. Fish & Game Commission* was a companion case to
Toomer. A California statute prohibited aliens from holding commercial
fishing licenses. Since such licenses were a prerequisite to employment, the
statute effectively barred aliens from earning a living as commercial
fishers. The Supreme Court held that the statute violated the Equal
Protection Clause of the Fourteenth Amendment. The Court refused to
accept California's argument that the statute was justified by the state's
ownership of the fish within its tidal waters: "To whatever extent the fish
in the three-mile belt off California may be 'capable of ownership' by
California, we think that 'ownership' is inadequate to justify California in
excluding any or all aliens who are lawful residents of the State from
making a living by fishing in the ocean off its shores while permitting all
others to do so." *Takahashi v. Fish & Game Commission,* 334 U.S. 410
(1948).

(5) *United States v. California:* A case not cited by the Supreme Court
in *Toomer* may nonetheless have played a significant role in the decision. In
United States v. California—decided by the Court in 1947—the Supreme
Court held that the United States rather than California was "the owner in
fee simple of, or possessed of paramount rights in and powers over, the
lands, minerals and other things of value underlying the Pacific Ocean,
lying seaward of the ordinary low water mark." *United States v. California,*
332 U.S. 19, 22, 41 (1947).

After deciding that the United States rather than the coastal states
owned the land beneath the marginal ocean, what was left of the rationale
in *McCready*?

PERSPECTIVES

Imperium **and** *dominium:* The Court in *Toomer* cited Roscoe
Pound's[1] discussion of the confusion of *"imperium"* and *"dominium"*:

---

1. Roscoe Pound (1870–1964) was an
American jurist and botanist. He studied law

at Harvard but left without receiving a degree. He then practiced and taught law in

Roman jurists. . . . [u]nder the influence of the Stoic idea of *naturalis ratio* . . . conceived that most things were destined by nature to be controlled by man. Such control expressed their natural purpose. Some things, however, were not destined to be controlled by individuals. Individual control would run counter to their natural purpose. Hence they could not be subjects of private ownership. Such things were called *res extra commercium.* They might be excluded from the possibility of private ownership in any of three ways. It might be that from their nature they could only be used, not owned, and from their nature they were adapted to general use. These were *res communes.* Or it might be that they were made for or from their nature they were adapted to public use, that is use for public purposes by public functionaries or by the political community. These were *res publicæ.* Again it might be because they had been devoted to religious purposes or consecrated by religious acts inconsistent with private ownership. Such things were *res sanctæ, res sacræ,* and *res religiosæ.* In modern law, as a result of the medieval confusion of the power of sovereign to regulate the use of things (*imperium*) with ownership (*dominium*) and of the idea of the corporate personality of the state, we have made the second category into property of public corporations. And this has required modern systematic writers to distinguish between those things which cannot be owned at all, such as human beings, things which may be owned by public corporations but may not be transferred, and things which are owned by public corporations in full dominion. We are also tending to limit the idea of discovery and occupation by making *res nullius* (*e.g.,* wild game) into *res publicæ* and to justify a more stringent regulation of individual uses of *res communes* (*e.g.,* of the use of running water for irrigation or for power) by declaring that they are the property of the state or are "owned by the state in trust for the people." It should be said, however, that while in form our courts and legislatures seem thus to have reduced everything but the air and the high seas to ownership, in fact the so-called state ownership of *res communes* and *res nullius* is only a sort of guardianship for social purposes. It is *imperium,* not *dominium.* The state as a corporation does not own a river as it owns the furniture in the statehouse. It does not own wild game as it owns the cash in the vaults of the treasury. What is meant is that conservation of important social resources requires regulations of the use of *res communes* to eliminate friction and prevent waste, and requires limitation of the times when, place where and persons by whom *res nullius* may be acquired in order to prevent their extermination. Our modern way of putting it is only an incident of the nineteenth-century dogma that everything must be owned.

Roscoe Pound, An Introduction to the Philosophy of Law 197–99 (1922).

Nebraska while simultaneously serving as the director of the state's botanical survey. Pound subsequently was professor (1910–1937) and dean (1916–1936) at Harvard. He was a prolific writer and scholar. He argued for a theory of social interests, asserting that the law must respond to contemporary social conditions and the needs of society. Some people believe that his writings were the basis for much of the New Deal.

Do Pound's categories correspond to those that Bracton grouped under the term "prerogative"?

Baldwin v. Fish & Game Commission

United States Supreme Court.
436 U.S. 371 (1978).

■ BLACKMUN, J:—This case presents issues, under the Privileges and Immunities Clause of the Constitution's Art. IV, § 2, and the Equal Protection Clause of the Fourteenth Amendment, as to the constitutional validity of disparities, as between residents and nonresidents, in a State's hunting license system.

I

Appellant Lester Baldwin is a Montana resident. He also is an outfitter holding a state license as a hunting guide. The majority of his customers are nonresidents who come to Montana to hunt elk and other big game. Appellants Carlson, Huseby, Lee and Moris are residents of Minnesota. They have hunted big game, particularly elk, in Montana in past years and wish to continue to do so.

In 1975, the five appellants, disturbed by the difference in the kinds of Montana elk-hunting licenses available to nonresidents, as contrasted with those available to residents of the State, and by the difference in the fees the nonresident and the resident must pay for their respective licenses, instituted the present federal suit for declaratory and injunctive relief and for reimbursement, in part, of fees already paid. [ ] The defendants were the Fish and Game Commission of the State of Montana, the Commission's director, and its five commissioners. The complaint challenged the Montana elk-hunting licensing scheme specifically, and asserted that, as applied to nonresidents, it violated the Constitution's Privileges and Immunities Clause, Art. IV, § 2, and the Equal Protection Clause of the Fourteenth Amendment. A three-judge District Court was convened and, by a divided vote, entered judgment denying all relief to the plaintiff-appellants. *Montana Outfitters Action Group v. Fish & Game Commission*, 417 F. Supp. 1005 (D.Mont.1976). We noted probable jurisdiction. [ ]

II

The relevant facts are not in any real controversy.... [Montana's elk population is one of the largest in the United States. Big game hunting had grown remarkably in popularity: during the 10–year period from 1960 to 1970 licenses issued by Montana increased by approximately 67% for residents and by approximately 530% for nonresidents. A non-resident elk hunting license cost between 7.5 and 37 times the cost for a Montana resident.]

Elk management is expensive. In regions of the State with significant elk population, more personnel time of the Fish and Game Commission is spent on elk than on any other species of big game. [ ]

Montana has more than 400 outfitters who equip and guide hunting parties. [ ] These outfitters are regulated and licensed by the State and provide services to hunters and fishermen. It is estimated that as many as half the nonresidents who hunt elk in western Montana utilize outfitters. [ ] Three outfitter-witnesses testified that virtually all their clients were nonresidents. [ ]

. . .

III

In the District Court the majority ... noted that the appellants conceded that Montana constitutionally may charge nonresidents more for hunting privileges than residents. [ ] It concluded, however, that on the evidence presented the 7 1/2-to-1 ratio in favor of the resident cannot be justified on any basis of cost allocation. [ ]

[T]he court concluded that the State "has the power to manage and conserve the elk, and to that end to make such laws and regulations as are necessary to protect and preserve it." [ ] In reaching this result, the majority examined the nature of the rights asserted by the plaintiffs. It observed that there were just too many people and too few elk to enable everyone to hunt the animals. "If the elk is to survive as a species, the game herds must be managed, and a vital part of the management is the limitation of the annual kill." [ ].... The right asserted by the appellants was "no more than a chance to engage temporarily in a recreational activity in a sister state" and was "not fundamental." [ ] Thus, it was not protected as a privilege and an immunity under the Constitution's Art. IV, § 2. The majority contrasted the nature of the asserted right with educational needs at the primary and college levels, citing *San Antonio School District v. Rodriguez*, 411 U.S. 1 (1973), and [ ], and said: "There is simply no nexus between the right to hunt for sport and the right to speak, the right to vote, the right to travel, the right to pursue a calling." [ ] It followed that it was necessary only to determine whether the system bears some rational relationship to legitimate state purposes. Then:

> We conclude that where the opportunity to enjoy a recreational activity is created or supported by a state, where there is no nexus between the activity and any fundamental right, and where by its very nature the activity can be enjoyed by only a portion of those who would enjoy it, a state may prefer its residents over the residents of other states, or condition the enjoyment of the nonresident upon such terms as it sees fit.

The dissenting judge took issue with the "ownership theory," and with any "special public interest" theory, and emphasized the absence of any cost-allocation basis for the license fee differential. He described the majority's posture as one upholding discrimination because political support was thereby generated, and took the position that invidious discrimination was not to be justified by popular disapproval of equal treatment. [ ]

IV

Privileges and immunities. Appellants strongly urge here that the Montana licensing scheme for the hunting of elk violates the Privileges and

Immunities Clause of Art. IV, § 2, of our Constitution. That Clause is not one the contours of which have been precisely shaped by the process and wear of constant litigation and judicial interpretation over the years since 1789. If there is any significance in the fact, the Clause appears in the so-called States' Relations Article, the same Article that embraces the Full Faith and Credit Clause, the Extradition Clause (also in § 2), the provisions for the admission of new States, the Territory and Property Clause, and the Guarantee Clause. Historically, it has been overshadowed by the appearance in 1868 of similar language in § 1 of the Fourteenth Amendment, and by the continuing controversy and consequent litigation that attended that Amendment's enactment and its meaning and application.

The Privileges and Immunities Clause originally was not isolated from the Commerce Clause, now in the Constitution's Art. I, § 8. In the Articles of Confederation, where both Clauses have their source, the two concepts were together in the fourth Article. [ ] Their separation may have been an assurance against an anticipated narrow reading of the Commerce Clause. [ ]

Perhaps because of the imposition of the Fourteenth Amendment upon our constitutional consciousness and the extraordinary emphasis that the Amendment received, it is not surprising that the contours of Art. IV, § 2, cl. 1, are not well developed, and that the relationship, if any, between the Privileges and Immunities Clause and the "privileges or immunities" language of the Fourteenth Amendment is less than clear. We are, nevertheless, not without some pronouncements by this Court as to the Clause's significance and reach. There are at least three general comments that deserve mention:

[The Court reviewed the decisions in *Paul v. Virginia,* 75 U.S. (8 Wall.) 168 (1868), *Hague v. CIO,* 307 U.S. 496, 511 (1939), and *Austin v. New Hampshire,* 420 U.S. 656 (1975).]

When the Privileges and Immunities Clause has been applied to specific cases, it has been interpreted to prevent a State from imposing unreasonable burdens on citizens of other States in their pursuit of common callings within the State, *Ward v. Maryland,* 79 U.S. (12 Wall.) 418 (1871); in the ownership and disposition of privately held property within the State, *Blake v. McClung,* 172 U.S. 239 (1898); and in access to the courts of the State, *Canadian Northern R.R. v. Eggen,* 252 U.S. 553 (1920).

It has not been suggested, however, that state citizenship or residency may never be used by a State to distinguish among persons. Suffrage, for example, always has been understood to be tied to an individual's identification with a particular State. [ ] No one would suggest that the Privileges and Immunities Clause requires a State to open its polls to a person who declines to assert that the State is the only one where he claims a right to vote. The same is true as to qualification for an elective office of the State. [ ] Nor must a State always apply all its laws or all its services equally to anyone, resident or nonresident, who may request it so to do. [ ] Some distinctions between residents and nonresidents merely reflect the fact that this is a Nation composed of individual States, and are permitted; other distinctions are prohibited because they hinder the formation, the purpose, or the development of a single Union of those States. Only with respect to those "privileges" and "immunities" bearing upon the vitality of the Nation as a single entity must the State treat all citizens, resident and nonresident, equally. Here we must decide into which category falls a distinction with respect to access to recreational big-game hunting.

Many of the early cases embrace the concept that the States had complete ownership over wildlife within their boundaries, and, as well, the power to preserve this bounty for their citizens alone. It was enough to say "that in regulating the use of the common property of the citizens of [a] state, the legislature is [not] bound to extend to the citizens of all the other states the same advantages as are secured to their own citizens." *Corfield v. Coryell,* 6 F. Cas. 546, 552 (C.C.E.D.Pa.1825) (No. 3,230). It appears to have been generally accepted that although the States were obligated to treat all those within their territory equally in most respects, they were not obliged to share those things they held in trust for their own people. In *Corfield,* a case the Court has described as "the first, and long the leading, explication of the [Privileges and Immunities] Clause," [ ], Mr. Justice Washington, sitting as Circuit Justice, although recognizing that the States may not interfere with the "right of a citizen of one state to pass through, or to reside in any other state, for purposes of trade, agriculture, professional pursuits, or otherwise; to claim the benefit of the writ of habeas corpus; to institute and maintain actions of any kind in the courts of the state; to take, hold and dispose of property, either real or personal," [ ], nonetheless concluded that access to oyster beds determined to be owned by New Jersey could be limited to New Jersey residents. This holding, and the conception of state sovereignty upon which it relied, formed the basis for similar decisions during later years of the 19th century. *E.g., McCready v. Virginia,* 94 U.S. 391 (1877); *Geer v. Connecticut,* 161 U.S. 519 (1896). *See Rosenfeld v. Jakways,* 216 P. 776 (Mont.1923). In *Geer,* a case dealing with Connecticut's authority to limit the disposition of game birds taken within its boundaries, the Court roundly rejected the contention "that a State cannot allow its own people the enjoyment of the benefits of the property belonging to them in common, without at the same time permitting the citizens of other States to participate in that which they do not own." [ ]

In more recent years, however, the Court has recognized that the States' interest in regulating and controlling those things they claim to "own," including wildlife, is by no means absolute. States may not compel the confinement of the benefits of their resources, even their wildlife, to their own people whenever such hoarding and confinement impedes interstate commerce. *Foster-Fountain Packing Co. v. Haydel,* 278 U.S. 1 (1928); *Pennsylvania v. West Virginia,* 262 U.S. 553 (1923); *West v. Kansas Natural Gas Co.,* 221 U.S. 229 (1911). Nor does a State's control over its resources preclude the proper exercise of federal power. *Douglas v. Seacoast Products, Inc.,* 431 U.S. 265 (1977); *Kleppe v. New Mexico,* 426 U.S. 529 (1976); *Missouri v. Holland,* 252 U.S. 416 (1920). And a State's interest in its wildlife and other resources must yield when, without reason, it interferes with a nonresident's right to pursue a livelihood in a State other than his own, a right that is protected by the Privileges and Immunities Clause.

Toomer v. Witsell, 334 U.S. 385 (1948). *See Takahashi v. Fish & Game Commission*, 334 U.S. 410 (1948).

Appellants contend that the doctrine on which *Corfield, McCready,* and *Geer* all relied has no remaining vitality. We do not agree. Only last Term, in referring to the "ownership" or title language of those cases and characterizing it "as no more than a 19th-century legal fiction," the Court pointed out that that language nevertheless expressed " 'the importance to its people that a State have power to preserve and regulate the exploitation of an important resource.' " *Douglas v. Seacoast Products, Inc.*, 431 U.S. at 284, *citing Toomer v. Witsell*, 334 U.S. at 402. The fact that the State's control over wildlife is not exclusive and absolute in the face of federal regulation and certain federally protected interests does not compel the conclusion that it is meaningless in their absence.

We need look no further than decisions of this Court to know that this is so. It is true that in *Toomer v. Witsell* the Court in 1948 struck down a South Carolina statute requiring nonresidents of the State to pay a license fee of $2,500 for each commercial shrimp boat, and residents to pay a fee of only $25, and did so on the ground that the statute violated the Privileges and Immunities Clause. [ ] Less than three years, however, after the decision in *Toomer,* so heavily relied upon by appellants here, the Court dismissed for the want of a substantial federal question an appeal from a decision of the Supreme Court of South Dakota holding that the total exclusion from that State of nonresident hunters of migratory waterfowl was justified by the State's assertion of a special interest in wildlife that qualified as a substantial reason for the discrimination. *State v. Kemp,* 44 N.W.2d 214 (S.D.1950), *appeal dismissed,* 340 U.S. 923 (1951). In that case South Dakota had proved that there was real danger that the flyways, breeding grounds, and nursery for ducks and geese would be subject to excessive hunting and possible destruction by nonresident hunters lured to the State by an abundance of pheasants. [ ]

Appellants have demonstrated nothing to convince us that we should completely reject the Court's earlier decisions. . . .

Does the distinction made by Montana between residents and nonresidents in establishing access to elk hunting threaten a basic right in a way that offends the Privileges and Immunities Clause? Merely to ask the question seems to provide the answer. We repeat much of what already has been said above: Elk hunting by nonresidents in Montana is a recreation and a sport. In itself—wholly apart from license fees—it is costly and obviously available only to the wealthy nonresident or to the one so taken with the sport that he sacrifices other values in order to indulge in it and to enjoy what it offers. It is not a means to the nonresident's livelihood. The mastery of the animal and the trophy are the ends that are sought; appellants are not totally excluded from these. The elk supply, which has been entrusted to the care of the State by the people of Montana, is finite and must be carefully tended in order to be preserved.

Appellants' interest in sharing this limited resource on more equal terms with Montana residents simply does not fall within the purview of the Privileges and Immunities Clause. Equality in access to Montana elk is not basic to the maintenance or well-being of the Union. Appellants do not—and cannot—contend that they are deprived of a means of a livelihood by the system or of access to any part of the State to which they may seek to travel. . . .

. . .

The judgment of the District Court is affirmed.

■ BURGER, C.J., concurring:—In joining the Court's opinion I write separately only to emphasize the significance of Montana's special interest in its elk population and to point out the limits of the Court's holding.

The doctrine that a State "owns" the wildlife within its borders as trustee for its citizens, *see Geer v. Connecticut,* 161 U.S. 519 (1896), is admittedly a legal anachronism of sorts. *See Douglas v. Seacoast Products, Inc.,* 431 U.S. 265, 284 (1977). A State does not "own" wild birds and animals in the same way that it may own other natural resources such as land, oil, or timber. But, as noted in the Court's opinion, [ ], and contrary to the implications of the dissent, the doctrine is not completely obsolete. It manifests the State's special interest in regulating and preserving wildlife for the benefit of its citizens. *See Douglas v. Seacoast Products, Inc.,* 431 U.S at 284, 287. Whether we describe this interest as proprietary or otherwise is not significant.

. . .

It is the special interest of Montana citizens in its elk that permits Montana to charge nonresident hunters higher license fees without offending the Privileges and Immunities Clause. The Court does not hold that the Clause permits a State to give its residents preferred access to recreational activities offered for sale by private parties. Indeed it acknowledges that the Clause requires equality with respect to privileges "bearing upon the vitality of the Nation as a single entity." [ ] It seems clear that those basic privileges include "all the privileges of trade and commerce" which were protected in the fourth Article of the Articles of Confederation. [ ] The Clause assures noncitizens the opportunity to purchase goods and services on the same basis as citizens; it confers the same protection upon the buyer of luxury goods and services as upon the buyer of bread.

■ BRENNAN, J., with whom WHITE and MARSHALL, J.J., join, dissenting:—Far more troublesome than the Court's narrow holding—elk hunting in Montana is not a privilege or immunity entitled to protection under Art. IV, § 2, cl. 1, of the Constitution—is the rationale of the holding that Montana's elk-hunting licensing scheme passes constitutional muster. The Court concludes that because elk hunting is not a "basic and essential activit[y], interference with which would frustrate the purposes of the formation of the Union," [ ], the Privileges and Immunities Clause of Art. IV, § 2—"The Citizens of each State shall be entitled to all Privileges and Immunities of Citizens in the several States"—does not prevent Montana from irrationally, wantonly, and even invidiously discriminating against nonresidents seeking to enjoy natural treasures it alone among the 50 States possesses. I cannot agree that the Privileges and Immunities Clause is so impotent a guarantee that such discrimination remains wholly beyond the purview of that provision.

.   .   .

NOTES

(1) The *Toomer* decision shifted the focus of review under the Privileges and Immunities Clause from the question of whether a right was "fundamental" to the sufficiency of the state's justification for discriminating. Did the Court step backward in *Baldwin*? Would Montana's facially discriminatory fee structure have survived the application of *Toomer*'s "substantial reason" test?

Professor Jonathan Varat has argued that the "fundamental" rights standard seemingly resurrected in *Baldwin* is fundamentally empty:

> the fundamentality doctrine reaffirmed in *Baldwin* reflects neither an appreciation of the instances in which interstate divisiveness is likely to result from residence classifications, nor the fundamental interest or suspect classification approaches to equal protection, nor any other discernible concept that can be tied to the purposes of the privileges and immunities clause. It is, instead, an historical relic lacking independent content. Furthermore, it deflects attention from the real differences between a state's relationship to its own residents and its relationship to the residents of other states, differences that might justify deviation from a strict rule of equal treatment.

Jonathan D. Varat, *State "Citizenship" and Interstate Equality*, 48 U. CHI. L. REV. 487, 515–16 (1981).

(2) **State "ownership" of public resources—wildlife vs. other natural resources / recreational vs. commercial:** The Court offers two additional dichotomies. The first is an implicit distinction between wildlife and other natural resources. The Court begins with the proposition that there are some goods and services that a state may reserve to its citizens. [¶ 15] As the Court acknowledges, however, this merely restates the problem: why are elk included in the special class when most other natural resources are not? *Cf. Hicklin v. Orbeck*, 437 U.S. 518 (1978) (fact that state owned substantial oil and gas deposits did not justify preferential hiring requirement for state residents). Historically, one such category involved resources such as wildlife in which the state has "complete ownership." [¶ 16] More recently, however, the absoluteness of the state's "interest in regulating and controlling those things they claim to 'own'" has been reduced by the demands of interstate commerce. [¶ 17]

The Court then offers a distinction between "commercial" and "recreational." Does this distinction make sense? Note that Chief Justice Burger in his concurrence emphasizes that the category "recreational activities" is too broad since such activities when offered for sale by private parties is not covered by the exemption. Would the Clause would be offended if, for example, the state required nonresidents to pay three times the ticket price to see a movie or to ride a rollercoaster?

Does the decision instead reflect the continuing vitality of concerns once encapsulated in state public-trust ownership? Given that elk are public resources (*i.e.,* "owned by the state in trust for its citizens"), if the Privileges and Immunities Clause required equal sharing, is it likely that either many state residents would be denied a hunting license or that overhunting would occur? In other words, might the decision reflect a fear that Montana would no longer choose to conserve its elk population—*i.e.,* that its taxpayers would no longer choose to fund the conservation programs? The Court suggests such a rationale in its comments on *State v. Kemp,* 44 N.W.2d 214 (S.D.1950), *appeal dismissed,* 340 U.S. 923 (1951): "In that case South Dakota had proved that there was real danger that the flyways, breeding grounds, and nursery for ducks and geese would be subject to excessive hunting and possible destruction by nonresident hunters lured to the State by an abundance of pheasants." [¶ 19]

Does this reading explain the seeming anomaly that the Court, while acknowledging that state ownership of wildlife was "no more than a 19th-century legal fiction," appears nonetheless to rely upon those cases in support of its holding.

(3) *Tangier Sound Waterman's Association v. Pruitt* is an example of the current understanding of the Privileges and Immunities Clause. Virginia enacted a statute tripling the charge for a nonresident commercial fishing license. When it was challenged, the state argued that the increase was justified by the need to generate funds to enhance and conserve the fisheries. The fee had been set by dividing the total expenses for fisheries management and research for 1989–1990 by the number of nonresident commercial fishing licenses.

Relying on *Toomer,* the Fourth Circuit Court applied a two-step test: first, was the privilege sufficiently fundamental to fall within the scope of the Clause; second, if the privilege is protected, are the restrictions placed on it closely related to the advancement of a substantial state interest. Since the right to earn a living has long been recognized as fundamental under the Clause, the dispute focused on the second prong of the test. The state argued that the nonresident fee was set

> to prevent subsidy of nonresidents by Virginia taxpayers. Specifically, [the state argues] that the reason for the higher fee is "to recover from nonresidents their share of the expenses of managing the resource from which they are benefitting." [ ] Because these expenses from the general fund are paid by Virginia taxpayers, the argument continues, "it is unfair for Virginia's taxpayers to be taxed to provide benefits for residents of other states who do not pay Virginia taxes."

The Court in *Toomer* had recognized that it was permissible for states to impose higher fees on nonresidents; subsequent decisions have required the higher nonresident fees to equalize "as nearly as possible" the burden between residents and nonresidents. The Fourth Circuit concluded that Virginia had failed to "creat[e] any credible method for allocating the costs as between residents and nonresidents which places the burden equally or approximately equally upon residents and nonresidents":

In demonstrating that the nonresident harvester's license fee is not closely related to a substantial state interest, the [Waterman's Association] note[s] that the nonresident commercial fishermen are required to pay the fees that resident commercial fishermen pay, to pay sales and use taxes on supplies purchased or used in Virginia, and to pay the $1,150 additional fee. Thus, aside from the additional fee, nonresident commercial fishermen contribute to the funds of the Commonwealth. The appellees further point out that the nonresident harvester's license fee was derived by dividing what the state spends on all fishermen, recreational and commercial, by the number of resident commercial fishermen. Thus, the appellees claim that nonresident commercial fishermen are being charged unfairly for programs funded by all taxpayers to benefit all fishermen, whether commercial or sport fishermen. [ ] Therefore, the argument goes, assuming that preventing a subsidy to nonresident commercial fishermen is a "substantial state interest," the nonresident harvester's license fee is not closely related to that interest. We agree; it is patent from the record that [the Virginia statute] does not impose the burden of the fee equally or approximately equally on resident and nonresident commercial fishermen, for their respective shares of Virginia's expenses of managing her commercial fisheries.

Tangier Sound Waterman's Association v. Pruitt, 4 F.3d 264 (4th Cir.1993).

Tangier Sound reflects the current understanding that differential fees are permissible to the extent that they reflect actual cost differences. Under this approach, *Baldwin* is an aberration. The fee charged out-of-state residents was 25 times the fee charged in-state residents ($225 versus $9). The district court had determined that the state could justify a nonresident fee of no more than 2.5 times the resident fee ($22.50) based upon direct and indirect costs to the state of maintaining the elk herd. *Montana Outfitters Action Group v. Fish and Game Commission,* 417 F.Supp. 1005, 1008 (D.Mont.1976).

(ii) THE DORMANT COMMERCE CLAUSE: IMPERMISSIBLE BURDENS ON INTERSTATE COMMERCE

> The Congress shall have Power ... To regulate Commerce with foreign Nations, and among the several States, and with the Indian Tribes.
>
> UNITED STATES CONSTITUTION art. 1, § 8, cl. 3.

NOTES

(1) The two Commerce Clauses: The Commerce Clause has given rise to two different strands of jurisprudence. The first focuses on the reach of Congress' affirmative power to regulate activity that involves "Commerce ... among the several States." The Supreme Court's first Commerce Clause decision—*Gibbons v. Ogden,* 22 U.S. (9 Wheat.) 1 (1824)—laid the basis for this branch of the law by holding that a New York statute granting a steamboat monopoly was void for conflicting with a federal statute licensing steamboats for interstate commerce. It was not until the end of the nineteenth century, however, that congressional regulation of commerce became sufficiently common to produce a sustained body of litigation.

The second strand is the "dormant" or "negative" Commerce Clause. This body of caselaw reflects the conclusion that the Commerce Clause itself imposes limitations on the regulatory power of the states. The question is whether, in the absence of a federal statute, a state statute is void because of its disruptive impact on interstate commerce. In such cases, the Court has been guided by its interpretation of purpose of the Clause: the government under the Articles of Confederation had "failed" in part because the states had waged economic warfare against one another as state legislatures responded to their local constituents. In the Court's view, the Clause was intended to correct this problem by preventing internal trade barriers—by prohibiting the "economic Balkanization" of the country, in the common metaphor. Hence, the Commerce Clause is read as barring discrimination against interstate commercial relationships.

Until at least the 1970s, it was the dormant Commerce Clause that was the more important in wildlife law because Congress had enacted so few statutes regulating wildlife. It is, therefore, with the dormant clause that we begin.

(2) *Gibbons v. Ogden*: Recall that the first challenge to the constitutionality of the New Jersey statute at issue in *Corfield* was that it violated the Commerce Clause. When Justice Washington wrote *Corfield*, the Supreme Court had decided only the first significant Commerce Clause case, *Gibbons v. Ogden*, 22 U.S. (9 Wheat.) 1 (1824). *Gibbons* involved a challenge to a monopoly the New York legislature had granted to Robert Livingston and Robert Fulton to operate "boats moved by fire or steam" within the state; Aaron Ogden had purchased the franchise. He sought an injunction to prevent Thomas Gibbons from continuing to operate steamboats between Elizabethtown, New Jersey, and New York City. Gibbons responded that the New York statute violated the Commerce Clause by interfering with interstate commerce.

The Court agreed with Gibbons. Chief Justice Marshall's opinion gave the Clause a broad, fact-based reading: "commerce," he wrote, was "a general term, applicable to many objects.... Commerce, undoubtedly, is traffic, but it is something more—it is intercourse. It describes the commercial intercourse between nations, and parts of nations, in all its branches." *Id.* at 189–90. The word "comprehend[s] every species of commercial intercourse ... It has truly been said, that commerce, as the word is used in the constitution, is a unit, every part of which is indicated by the term." *Id.* at 193–94. But the Constitution gave the power "To regulate Commerce ... among the several States.... It is not intended to say, that these words comprehend commerce, which is completely internal, which is carried on between man and man in a state, or between different parts of the same state, and which does not extend to or *affect* other states.... Comprehensive as the word 'among' is, it may very properly be restricted to that commerce which concerns more states than one." *Id.* at 194 (emphasis added). This power extends to commerce wherever it was present so that "the power of congress may be exercised within a state." *Id.* at 195. This power "comprehends navigation, within the limits of every state in the Union; so far as that navigation may be, in any manner, connected with 'commerce with foreign nations, or among the several states, or with the Indian tribes.' " *Id.* at 196–97.

(3) Judicial response to a changing statutory landscape: The statutes that were the focus of the initial constitutional attacks generally prohibited non-citizens from taking wildlife within the state's jurisdiction. *E.g., Corfield v. Coryell,* 6 F. Cas. 546 (C.C.E.D.Pa.1823) (No. 3,230); *State v. Medbury,* 3 R.I. 138 (1855). In such cases, the state ownership doctrine was cited to establish that the statute did not violate the Commerce Clause because it regulated state property rather than commerce. As the century progressed, however, the constitutional challenges increasingly were to state statutes that sought to prohibit the possession or sale of game. These statutes had at least two objectives. First, restrictions on possession and sale reinforced taking prohibitions by making convictions easier to obtain since the state was no longer required to prove that the animals had been illegally killed. Second, prohibitions on shipping wildlife out of the state reserved the resource for state residents. Both types of statutes implicated federalism, but they raised different issues than the earlier statutes because in these cases the wildlife had been reduced to possession and thus was the property of the possessor under the rule of capture.

    (a) State statutes prohibiting possession or sale of game: In *Magner v. People,* 97 Ill. 320 (1881), defendant—a retail dealer in game in Chicago—appealed his conviction for violation of a statute prohibiting the possession or sale game. Defendant had purchased a box of 144 quail in Leavenworth, Kansas, and sold it at retail in Chicago. He argued that the statute was unconstitutional under the Commerce Clause. The Illinois Supreme Court rejected this argument, concluding that "[v]ery clearly [the challenged] law relates only to the internal commerce of the State in the article of game.... [I]t acts altogether upon the retail or domestic traffic within the State." *Magner v. People,* 97 Ill. 320 (1881). *See also Ex parte Maier,* 37 P. 402 (Cal.1894) ("It is true the law is intended to protect game within the state, but it by no means follows from that fact that it is not the intention, as a means to accomplish that very end, to prohibit the sale of meat of animals procured elsewhere."); *State v. Randolph,* 1 Mo.App. 15 (1876) ("The game law would be nugatory if, during the prohibited season, game could be imported from the neighboring States. It would be impossible to show, in most instances, where the game was caught. The State of Missouri has as much right to preserve its game as it has to preserve the health of its citizens."); *Roth v. State,* 37 N.E. 259 (Ohio 1894). *But see People v. O'Neil,* 39 N.W. 1 (Mich.1888) (statute that "punishes with severe penalties acts which are confessedly innocent in themselves," must be unambiguous); *Commonwealth v. Wilkenson,* 21 A. 14 (Pa.1891) ("The manifest object of this act was the preservation of game within this commonwealth. We cannot assume that it was intended to preserve game elsewhere, and it would be a forced construction to hold that it was intended to exclude from our markets quail and other game killed in other states, where by the laws of those states the killing of them was lawful.").

    (b) State statutes prohibiting sale of game lawfully taken within the state or prohibiting shipment of such game out of the state:

A second type of statute authorized the killing of game for personal use while criminalizing all sales. The American Express Company challenged the constitutionality of an Illinois statute which prohibited all sales of game killed within the state and all transportation of game killed in the state for subsequent sale. The company had received a shipment of quail that had been lawfully taken in the state during the open season on the species; the company argued that once the game had been killed it became absolute property and the act therefore violated due process by destroying this property.

The court disagreed, noting that the argument was predicated on a "fallacy": the assumption that the killer "has absolute an property in the dead animals." Since "ownership was in the people of the state," the legislature has the power to specify the incidents of ownership that could be acquired in the dead animals. "If the legislature of the state thought that a statute preventing a citizen from killing quail for sale in the market, and imposing penalties on a common carrier for shipping or transporting for sale, would result in protecting the game in the state, we perceive no valid reason why a statute of that character might not be enacted." *American Express Co. v. People*, 24 N.E. 758 (Ill.1890). *Accord Organ v. State*, 19 S.W. 840 (Ark.1892). *But see State v. Saunders*, 19 Kan. 127 (1877); *Territory v. Evans*, 23 P. 115 (Idaho 1890).

(5) *Geer v. Connecticut:* Look again at the Supreme Court's decision in *Geer* [Chapter 5]. How many rationales does the Court offer for its decision? Are the state ownership and police power rationales independent of each other? Note that the Court states that the police power to protect its citizens' food from adulteration "carries with it the existence of a like power to preserve a food supply which belongs in common to all the people of the State, [and] which can only become the subject of ownership in a qualified way." [¶ 21]

(6) The convergence of two strands of Commerce Clause jurisprudence: When it was decided, *Geer* reflected the intersection of two strands of nineteenth century Commerce Clause jurisprudence:

(a) Bright lines—inter vs. intra: The first was the judiciary's attempt to maintain rigid lines between "inter-" and "intrastate" commerce in order to preserve completely separate spheres of federal "commerce" power and state "police" power. A classic statement of the principles at work in this strand of Commerce Clause cases is *United States v. E.C. Knight Co.*, 156 U.S. 1 (1895). The case involved a suit under the Sherman Antitrust Act to prevent American Sugar Refining Company from acquiring four competing refineries and thereby gaining ownership of 98% of the sugar refining capacity in the country. The Court held that the Act did not reach this monopoly because the Constitution did not empower Congress to regulate "manufacturing"; it could only regulate commerce, which "succeeds to manufacture, and is not a part of it." "The fact," Chief Justice Fuller wrote, "that an article is manufactured for export to another State does not of itself make it an article of interstate commerce." *United States v. E.C. Knight Co.*, 156 U.S. 1 (1895). Since the Court viewed the issue as a zero sum game—the powers of both the state and Congress were "exclusive" so that if the states could regulate, Congress could not and vice versa—the increasing (factual) nationalization of commerce and the corresponding (legal) federalization of commercial regulation heralded a corresponding decrease in state power. Preservation of the states required the Court to ignore reality by crafting artificial and ultimately untenable constructions. *See generally* GEOFFREY R. STONE ET AL., CONSTITUTIONAL LAW 151–67 (2d ed. 1991).

Note that *Geer* was handed down little more than a year after the *Knight* decision.

(b) Common property: The second strand of *fin de siecle* Commerce Clause jurisprudence was the idea that natural resources—wildlife and water, earth and air—were owned in common by the people with the states acting as trustees. For example, in *Hudson County Water Co. v. McCarter* the state of New Jersey brought an action to enjoin the violation of a state statute prohibiting the export of water. The state supreme court upheld an injunction, concluding that there

> is a residuum of public ownership in the State [in the flow of nonnavigable streams, and this right was] reinforced . . . by the State's title to the bed of the stream where flowed by the tide [so] that, as against the rights of riparian owners . . . , the State was warranted in prohibiting the acquisition of the title to water on a larger scale.

The water company appealed. The United States Supreme Court acknowledged the state courts' rationale, but preferred "to put the authority which cannot be denied to the State upon a broader ground than that which was emphasized below, since in our opinion it is independent of the more or less attenuated residuum, of title that the State may be said to possess." This broader authority was the police power. While acknowledging that the line between private property and the police power was difficult to fix with precision, nonetheless

> it is recognized that the State as *quasi*-sovereign and representative of the interests of the public has a standing in court to protect the atmosphere, the water and the forests within its territory, irrespective of the assent or dissent of the private owners of the land most immediately concerned. *Kansas v. Colorado,* 185 U.S. 125 (1902), 206 U.S. 46 (1907); *Georgia v. Tennessee Copper Co.,* 206 U.S. 230 (1907). . . . On this principle of public interest and the police power, and not merely as the inheritor of a royal prerogative, the State may make laws for the preservation of game, which seems a stronger case. *Geer v. Connecticut,* 161 U.S. 519 (1896).

Hudson County Water Co. v. McCarter, 209 U.S. 349 (1908).

Hughes v. Oklahoma

United States Supreme Court.
441 U.S. 322 (1979).
[reprinted in Chapter 5].

NOTES

(1) Does the majority or the dissent offer the more accurate interpretation of the *holding* in *Geer*? Were there one or two independent rationales?

What is the disagreement between the two opinions? Do the majority and dissent disagree on the proposition that a state has a special interest in the conservation of wildlife? Is that interest different than the state's interest in conserving all natural "resources"?

Note that the majority and the dissent are essentially mirror images of one another: the majority, having determined that the Oklahoma statute was discriminatory on its face, imposed the burden on the state to demonstrate the absence of less discriminatory means of achieving its stated objectives; the dissent, on the other hand, would impose the burden on the person challenging the statute to demonstrate the absence of equally satisfactory means of avoiding its impact. Which is preferable? Which has the better basis in the Constitution?

(2) *Hughes* **in the state courts:** Recall the decision in *State v. Fertterer,* 841 P.2d 467 (Mont.1992) [excerpted in Chapter 5], in which the Montana Supreme Court held that *Hughes* had decided the application of the Commerce Clause to bans on interstate sales of game but had no effect on the power of states to regulate either the taking of game or to prohibit all sales. *Fertterer* is the dominant interpretation of *Hughes* by state courts. *See, e.g., O'Brien v. State,* 711 P.2d 1144, 1148–49 (Wyo.1986).

(3) The Black Bass Act: At the time that *Hughes* was decided, the Black Bass Act provided:

> It shall be unlawful for any person to deliver ... for transportation ... from any State ... any black bass or other fish, if (1) such transportation is contrary to the law of the State ... from which such ... fish ... is to be transported.... '

Black Bass Act of 1926, 44 Stat. 576, *amended by,* Act of July 30, 1947, ch. 348, 61 Stat. 517, *and,* Act of July 16, 1952, ch. 911, § 2, 66 Stat. 736, *repealed by* Lacey Act Amendments of 1981, Pub. L. 97–79, § 9(b)(1), 95 Stat. 1079. *Cf. United States v. Howard,* 352 U.S. 212 (1957) (holding that a state regulation was a "law of the State" and that defendant's indictment for shipping fish across states lines in violation of the state fish and game agency was good).

Did the Court err in reaching the constitutional issue given the statute?

(4) *Maine v. Taylor:* Robert Taylor operated a bait business in Maine. He imported live baitfish into Maine, despite a state statute prohibiting such importation. He was indicted under the Lacey Act Amendments of 1981[1] which makes it a federal crime to transport fish in interstate commerce in violation of state law. He moved to dismiss the indictment on the ground that the Maine statute unconstitutionally burdened interstate commerce; Maine intervened to defend the validity of its statute. After an evidentiary hearing, the District Court denied the motion to dismiss and held the state statute constitutional. Taylor appealed, and the Court of Appeals. This decision was in turn reversed by the Supreme Court.

---

1. The Lacy Act Amendments replaced the Black Bass Act discussed in the preceding note.

The Court began by noting that, while the Maine statute "restricts interstate trade in the most direct manner possible, blocking all inward shipments of live baitfish at the State's border," this fact alone did not make the statute unconstitutional. Citing *Hughes,* the Court stated the relevant test: "once a state law is shown to discriminate against interstate commerce 'either on its face or in practical effect,' the burden falls on the State to demonstrate both that the statute 'serves a legitimate local purpose,' and that this purpose could not be served as well by available nondiscriminatory means." At the evidentiary hearing, the state offered evidence from three scientific experts who

> testified that live baitfish imported into the State posed two significant threats to Maine's unique and fragile fisheries. First, Maine's population of wild fish—including its own indigenous golden shiners—would be placed at risk by three types of parasites prevalent in out-of-state baitfish, but not common to wild fish in Maine. Second, nonnative species inadvertently included in shipments of live baitfish could disturb Maine's aquatic ecology to an unpredictable extent by competing with native fish for food or habitat, by preying on native species, or by disrupting the environment in more subtle ways.
>
> The prosecution experts further testified that there was no satisfactory way to inspect shipments of live baitfish for parasites or commingled species. According to their testimony, the small size of baitfish and the large quantities in which they are shipped made inspection for commingled species "a physical impossibility." Parasite inspection posed a separate set of difficulties because the examination procedure required destruction of the fish. Although statistical sampling and inspection techniques had been developed for salmonids (*i.e.,* salmon and trout), so that a shipment could be certified parasite-free based on a standardized examination of only some of the fish, no scientifically accepted procedures of this sort were available for baitfish.

Defendant's expert disagreed, denying that "any scientific justification supported Maine's total ban on the importation of baitfish." Furthermore, none of the parasites "posed any significant threat to fish in the wild."

The Supreme Court concluded that "the District Court's finding that [scientifically accepted techniques for the sampling and inspection of live baitfish] have not been devised ... cannot be characterized as clearly erroneous." Furthermore, the state's ban was supported by the "substantial scientific uncertainty surround[ing] the effect that baitfish parasites and nonnative species could have on Maine's fisheries. Moreover, we agree with the District Court that Maine has a legitimate interest in guarding against imperfectly understood environmental risks, despite the possibility that they may ultimately prove to be negligible." *Maine v. Taylor,* 477 U.S. 131 (1986).

Justice Stevens demurred: "There is something fishy about this case." In his view, scientific uncertainties should have weighed again the state: "Since the State engages in obvious discrimination against out-of-state commerce, it should be put to its proof. Ambiguity about dangers and alternatives should actually defeat, rather than sustain, the discriminatory measure."

Taylor is the only recent case in which the Supreme Court has upheld a patently discriminatory statute. The state prevailed because it convinced the Court that the district court was correct in finding that (1) Maine's fisheries were unique and fragile; (2) that parasites and nonnative species in the shipments could introduce diseases that would disturb the state's aquatic ecology; and (3) there was no satisfactory alternative to the ban because no screening system existed. In sum, because the out-of-state products posed a unique harm to the state, Maine was permitted to discriminate on the basis of state-of-origin.

(5) Better safe than sorry: The decision in *Maine v. Taylor* can be viewed as an application of the "precautionary principle," the proposition that decisionmakers must take precautionary measures or avoid affirmative acts when there is some basis for concluding that the activity may have negative environmental impacts—*even in the absence of conclusive evidence on the causal relationship between the activity and the adverse environmental effect.* In its most rigorous form, the principle effectively shifts the burden of proof: those who propose an undertaking must demonstrate that the project will not cause environmental harm. One rationale for this approach in the human health context was summarized by Professor Sidney Shapiro:

> When a regulator makes a decision under conditions of uncertainty, there are two possible types of error. The regulator can overregulate a risk that turns out to be insignificant or the regulator can underregulate a risk that turns out to be significant. If the regulator erroneously underregulates, the burden of this mistake falls on those individuals who are injured or killed, and their families. If a regulator erroneously overregulates, the burden of this mistakes falls on the regulated industry which will pay for regulation that is not needed. This result, however, is fairer than setting the burden of uncertainty about a risk on potential victims.

Sidney Shapiro, *Keeping the Baby and Throwing Out the Bathwater: Justice Breyer's Critique of Regulation,* 8 ADMIN. L.J. 731, 732 (1995); *see also* Donald T. Hornstein, *Reclaiming Environmental Law: A Normative Critique of Comparative Risk Analysis,* 92 COLUM. L. REV. 562, 641 (1992) ("the danger of false positives [is] far less serious than the danger of false negatives"). Those who prefer market-based solutions are skeptical of the precautionary principle. *E.g.,* Frank B. Cross, *Paradoxical Perils of the Precautionary Principle,* 53 WASH. & LEE L. REV. 851 (1996).

Pacific Northwest Venison Producers v. Smitch

Ninth Circuit Court of Appeals.
20 F.3d 1008 (1994).
certiorari denied, 513 U.S. 918 (1994).

■ SKOPIL, J.:—Plaintiffs Pacific Northwest Venison Producers and several of its members (collectively, "PNVP") appeal the district court's summary judgment in favor of the Washington Department of Wildlife and the

Washington State Wildlife Commission (collectively, "Department of Wildlife" or "Department"), upholding the constitutionality of the Department's regulations banning the private ownership and exchange of several species of wildlife. We affirm.

FACTS AND PRIOR PROCEEDINGS

In January 1991, the Department of Wildlife promulgated regulations that prohibit the "importation, holding, possession, propagation, sale, transfer or release" of "deleterious exotic wildlife," including mouflon sheep. [ ] In June 1992, the Department promulgated emergency regulations which added fallow deer and sika deer to its list of prohibited deleterious exotic wildlife. [ ] At the same time, the Department promulgated emergency regulations that prohibit the same activities regarding certain native wildlife species, including elk. [ ] The purported reason for the emergency regulations was to guard against perceived dangers to native wildlife presented by captive herds of these animals.

Following the promulgation of the regulations, the Department invited several wildlife experts to speak at a workshop to determine whether these animals actually present risks to native wildlife. The Department invited only experts who had previously expressed concern about the risks that game farms pose to native wildlife. Neither experts who support game farms nor ranchers who raise the prohibited wildlife were allowed a hearing to present evidence to counter the concerns raised at this workshop.

The experts at the workshop identified several risks to native wildlife presented by game farms. First, the importation of any animals presents a risk of importing diseases such as tuberculosis and brucellosis. Animals carrying the disease can infect native wildlife either after escaping, or through fenceline transmission.

Second, importation of animals presents some risk of importing the parasitic meningeal worm. This parasite is fatal to all cervids except the white-tail deer, which acts as a carrier. Scientists have not conclusively established whether other cervids are able to carry and pass on the meningeal worm in low numbers that are difficult to detect. The meningeal worm has not yet been found west of the Great Plains, possibly because the drier interior of the continent is not amenable to its secondary hosts, snails and slugs. Some experts fear that if a white-tail deer were to pick up the meningeal worm from an animal imported from the East, the parasite could spread rapidly within the white-tail deer population, and eventually decimate populations of other cervids.

Third, captive herds present the possibility that groups of animals might escape and become free-ranging herds, competing with native wildlife for forage and habitat. Finally, game farms present risks that escaped animals will breed with wild animals and affect the genepool of Washington's native wildlife.

PNVP, an agricultural cooperative of commercial game farms in Washington, Oregon, and British Columbia, filed this lawsuit shortly after the emergency regulations were promulgated, challenging the regulations as applied to elk, mouflon sheep, sika deer, and fallow deer. On summary judgment, the district court held that the regulations do not violate the Commerce Clause, substantive due process, or equal protection, but that the Department violated plaintiffs' procedural due process rights by failing to provide them with a hearing. The court also ruled that the federal Endangered Species Act preempted the state regulation banning the propagation of subspecies of sika deer that are federally listed endangered species. PNVP appeals the district court's judgment on the Commerce Clause ground only.

DISCUSSION

. . . .

Discriminatory Versus Evenhanded Regulations

The United States Constitution gives Congress the power "[t]o regulate Commerce with foreign Nations, and among the several States * * * " U.S. CONST. Art. I, § 8. Even in areas where Congress has not exercised this authority, state regulations may violate the Commerce Clause either because the regulations discriminate against interstate or foreign commerce, or because they incidentally affect such commerce. If the regulations discriminate in favor of in-state interests, the state has the burden of establishing that a legitimate state interest unrelated to economic protectionism is served by the regulations that could not be served as well by less discriminatory alternatives. *See Maine v. Taylor*, 477 U.S. 131, 138 (1986). In contrast, if the regulations apply evenhandedly to in-state and out-of-state interests, the party challenging the regulations must establish that the incidental burdens on interstate and foreign commerce are clearly excessive in relation to the putative local benefits. [ ]

PNVP contends that two provisions demonstrate that the Department of Wildlife regulations are discriminatory. The first is the inclusion of "importation" in the list of prohibited activities. [ ] The second is the "grandfather clauses," which allow owners to keep animals already legally present within the state. [ ]

The Ban on Importation

PNVP argues that any state prohibition of imports or exports is per se discriminatory. The Supreme Court has stated that "where simple economic protectionism is effected by state legislation, a virtually per se rule of invalidity has been erected. The clearest example of such legislation is a law that overtly blocks the flow of interstate commerce at a State's borders." *City of Philadelphia v. New Jersey*, 437 U.S. 617, 624 (1978).

. . . . In practical effect, the importation ban adds nothing to the prohibitions that apply equally to in-state and out-of-state interests, because animals could not be imported if they are not allowed to be held, possessed, transferred, or sold once inside the state. An import ban that simply effectuates a complete ban on commerce in certain items is not discriminatory, as long as the ban on commerce does not make distinctions based on the origin of the items. [ ]

. . . . The regulations at issue here clearly are not fueled by economic protectionism, nor do they result in the citizens of Washington receiving benefits that are denied to others. The ban on importation thus does not make these regulations discriminatory.

. . .

The State's Interests

The state's putative interests to be served by these regulations are to protect its native wildlife from diseases and parasites, to maintain the genetic purity of its wildlife, to protect its wildlife from competition for forage and habitat, and to ensure that native wildlife will not be captured and added to captive herds. Clearly, the protection of wildlife is one of the state's most important interests. *See Hughes v. Oklahoma,* 441 U.S. 322, 337 (1979) (state interest in protection of wild animals is similar in importance to interest in protecting health and safety of citizens). PNVP argues, however, that this is not the real purpose behind the regulations, and speculates that the real reason for the regulations is traditional antipathy of wildlife biologists toward game farming.

PNVP has failed to offer evidence that could legally support an inference that the Department was not actually concerned about the health of Washington's wildlife. PNVP argues that other species that might as easily transmit the diseases and parasites that concern the Department have not been banned, and that from this fact, the district court was required to make the inference in PNVP's favor that the state's interest was not actually in the health of its wildlife. But the Supreme Court has long held that the fact that a state regulation addresses only one aspect of a problem does not alone cast doubt on the state's motivation. [ ] Thus, the district court could not infer that the state's purported interests were not its actual interests based on the state's failure to prohibit other carriers of diseases. [ ]

PNVP also argues that the Department could not actually be interested in genetic purity because the state formerly released animals imported from out of state to supplement its native herds. However, PNVP fails to present any reason, either legal or factual, why the court could reasonably disbelieve the Department simply because current policy makers disagree with past policy makers as to the desirability of releasing non-indigenous animals into the wild. PNVP has thus failed to offer legally sufficient evidence from which a factfinder could infer that the state's putative interests were not its actual interests.

Burdens On Interstate and Foreign Commerce

PNVP also argues that it has shown an issue of material fact as to whether the regulations' impacts on interstate and foreign commerce are clearly excessive in relation to the putative benefits. . . .

In *Pike v. Bruce Church,* 397 U.S. 137 (1970), the Supreme Court articulated the balancing test used to determine whether evenhanded state laws and regulations are valid under the Commerce Clause:

> Where the statute regulates evenhandedly to effectuate a legitimate local public interest, and its effects on interstate commerce are only incidental, it will be upheld unless the burden imposed on such commerce is clearly excessive in relation to the putative local bene-

fits.* * * If a legitimate local purpose is found, then the question
becomes one of degree. And the extent of the burden that will be
tolerated will of course depend on the nature of the local interest
involved, and on whether it could be promoted as well with a lesser
impact on interstate activities.

[ ]

Regulations promulgated pursuant to the state's interest in the preservation of its wildlife carry a strong presumption of validity. [ ] To defeat the
Department's motion for summary judgment, PNVP was required to show
that it could offer evidence at trial legally sufficient to support a determination that the impacts of the regulations on interstate and foreign commerce
are so great that they outweigh this vital state interest. Evidence that
interstate and foreign commerce is in some way affected by the regulations
is not enough to meet this burden; what is required is evidence that these
effects are of a type or an extent that could support a determination that
they are "clearly excessive" in relation to the state's interest in the health
of its native wildlife. [ ] PNVP has failed show that it could produce such
evidence.

. . .

Finally, PNVP argues that it has offered evidence that less burdensome alternatives would protect the state's wildlife as well as the regulations do. Because "the extent of the burden that will be tolerated" depends
in part on whether the state's interest "could be promoted as well with a
lesser impact on interstate activities," [ ], such evidence may create a
material dispute as to whether the burden on interstate commerce outweighs the state's interest. . . .

PNVP's suggested alternatives include testing for diseases and parasites, quarantine for the length of time that it takes to establish whether an
animal has a particular disease or parasite, tagging to ensure that animals
are not imported from the East, heavy fencing to prevent escapes, and
increased law enforcement. PNVP has offered evidence in the form of
expert opinions that these alternatives combined with the alleged propensity of animals to return after escaping can adequately reduce the risks to
native wildlife.

The bulk of the evidence offered by PNVP consists of expert affidavits
stating that the increase in risks present in its proposed alternatives is
acceptable when considered against the regulations' effect of foreclosing the
commercial movement of these animals in and out of Washington. How
much risk to wildlife is acceptable, however, is quintessentially a legislative
determination. It is the role of the state, and not of the courts, to determine
how much risk to the state's wildlife is acceptable in the balance with
private economic interests. Nonetheless, we assume that at some point the
risks presented by proposed alternatives as compared to challenged regulations would be so small that courts should not give them credence. PNVP
has arguably offered evidence that could support a finding that its proposed
alternatives would reduce the risks to that point.

There are significant gaps in PNVP's offering, however. In particular,
PNVP has produced very little to counter the Department's expert affida-

vits stating that alternatives similar to those proposed by PNVP have proven ineffective in other states and provinces due to accidents and illegal activity. In response to the Department's expert affidavits alleging extensive and specific facts showing that these animals have a tendency to escape regardless of the measures taken to secure them, and that they often are never recovered, PNVP offered an expert's unsupported opinion that animals have a propensity to return to their captive herds and to a ready supply of food. In response to the Department's affidavits describing illegal activity that has occurred in other states and provinces, including the alteration of tags in order to bring animals in from the East and the capture of wild free-ranging elk to supplement captive herds, PNVP experts opine that increased law enforcement efforts would eliminate the threat of such activity.

. . . . We need not decide whether the offered evidence could support a determination that the proposed alternatives would serve the state's interests as well as the Department's regulations, however, because the evidence is too inconclusive to have a significant effect on the balance between the burdens on interstate commerce and the state's putative interests. If the determination could not, as a matter of law, tip the balance against the Department, the issue is not material to the outcome of the case.

. . .

CONCLUSION

Plaintiffs in this case have expended considerable time and money in an economic endeavor, only to have their state government subsequently deem that endeavor to be potentially harmful, and therefore prohibited. We note that the district court held that the federal constitution provides some protection in such a situation through its guarantees of procedural due process and of just compensation for the taking of property. In the absence of evidence either of economic protectionism on the part of the state, or of substantial burdens on interstate or foreign commerce, however, we must conclude that the Commerce Clause does not protect their economic investment against legitimate state regulations protecting native wildlife.

NOTES

(1) *Maine v. Taylor* demonstrates that the demise of the state ownership doctrine as a shield against the application of standard Commerce Clause analysis does not mean that importation or exportation prohibitions are facially impermissible. Is the court in *Venison Producers* correct that the state has the power to ban all commerce in wildlife if it chooses to do so? Are there limits on the state's power in this area? Recall that in *Hughes v. Oklahoma,* 441 U.S. 322, 337 (1979), the Supreme Court equated the state interest in protection of wildlife with its interest in protecting the health and safety of citizens.

(2) A subsequent challenge to the regulation at issue in *Venison Producers* on taking grounds led to a decision by the Washington Court of Appeals that there had been no taking because the elk owners had not been deprived of all economically viable uses. *Schreiner Farms v. Smitch*, 940 P.2d 274 (Wash.App.1997).

PERSPECTIVES

Health and genetic issues: In *Venison Producers*, the state defended its prohibitions by pointing to health risks.

(a) Elk farming operations—to provide canned hunts for trophy bulls, meat, and velvet antlers for traditional Asian medicines—are a booming industry in the West. But the operations impose a risk of disease: in 1994, an epidemic of bovine tuberculosis broke out on a game farm in Alberta. The government shot 2700 elk and paid $24,000,000 in compensation to protect wild herds; Canada's livestock industry lost its tuberculosis-free status. The fear that tuberculosis will spread to wild populations appears to have some basis: in 1992, the disease was found in a wild deer shot outside a game farm in Hardin, Montana, that was under quarantine. Hal Herring, *On a Montana Ranch, Big Game and Big Problems*, HIGH COUNTRY NEWS, Nov. 10, 1997, at 4–5.; *Mule Deer Infected by Imported Elk*, WILDLIFE L. NEWS. Q., Fall, 1994, at 11.

(b) Genetic testing in Norway shows that more that a quarter of all salmon returning to spawn in the country's rivers are escapees from fish farms. Even though only about 1% of the captive population escaped from the farms in 1995, that still amounted to some 200,000 to 650,000 fish. Geneticists fear that the escapees will overwhelm the wild population. Crossbreeding between wild and pen-reared stocks are problematic for several reasons. The pen-reared salmon, for example, have been bred for rapid growth and high fat content. In addition, fish-farmed salmon lack the river-specific characteristics that are necessary for the long-term survival of wild stocks. Preliminary American and Canadian research indicates that escapees have begun to interbreed with the remaining wild stocks. Walter Gibbs, *Fish-Farm Escapees Threaten Wild Salmon*, N.Y. TIMES, Science, Oct. 1, 1996, at B7. Salmon farming along Scotland's coasts have been implicated in the near-demise of wild salmon. Alan Cowell, *Invercreran Journal: Fish Farms Spawn Trouble for Salmon Anglers*, N.Y. TIMES, July 17, 2001. Nor is the problem confined to the Atlantic Ocean: between 1994 and 1997, more than 9,000 Atlantic salmon were caught in the Pacific Ocean between Washington and Alaska—escapees of West coast fish farming operations. Rosamond L. Naylor, *et al.*, *Nature's Subsidies to Shrimp and Salmon Farming*, 282 SCI. 883–84 (1998).

(iii) VESTED RIGHTS AND THE FIFTH AND FOURTEENTH AMENDMENTS

States have broad power to protect wildlife. As with other types of governmental regulation, however, state actions cannot go so far as to amount to a taking of private property without just compensation.

Several cases have already considered this issue. In *Barrett v. State*, 116 N.E. 99 (N.Y.1917) [Chapter 3], the New York Court of Appeals held that the state was not liable for damage to land caused by beavers that it had reintroduced into the watershed. The United States Supreme Court in

Geer v. Connecticut, 161 U.S. 519 (1896), upheld the power of a state to limit the property rights that a person might acquire in captured animals—a decision foreshadowed by *Phelps v. Racey,* 60 N.Y. 10 (1875), in which the New York Court of Appeals held that the state had power to prohibit possession beyond the end of open season. Numerous other decisions reached similar results. In *Commonwealth v. Gilbert,* 35 N.E. 454 (Mass. 1893), the court upheld the state's power to apply similar bans to captive-raised wild animals. *See also Farris v. State Game & Fish Commission,* 310 S.W.2d 231 (Ark.1958) (upholding power of state to prohibit sale of game fish raised by fish farmers in their privately owned reservoirs but striking down regulation banning a person from permitting the edible portion of a game fish to go to waste). Recall, however, *Graves v. Dunlap,* 152 P. 532 (Wash.1915) [Chapter 2], in which the court construed a ban on possession of certain game animals as inapplicable to animals held in captivity before the law took effect, chiefly to avoid the serious issue as to whether the ban would have amounted to an uncompensated taking of private property.

Vested property rights cases most often arise when states restrict the use of private land to conserve wildlife, commonly by restricting alteration of valuable wildlife habitat. Recall *Meredith v. Talbot County,* 560 A.2d 599 (Md.App.1989) [Chapter 3], in which the Maryland Court of Appeals upheld zoning restrictions designed to protect bald eagle habitat and *Just v. Marinette County,* 201 N.W.2d 761 (Wis.1972) [Chapter 1], in which the Wisconsin Supreme Court upheld restrictions on the development of wetlands. Although such cases are more common, we begin with a quick look at personal rather than real property.

(A) Personal Property

Andrus v. Allard

United States Supreme Court.
444 U.S. 51 (1979).

■ BRENNAN, J.:—The Eagle Protection Act and the Migratory Bird Treaty Act are conservation statutes designed to prevent the destruction of certain species of birds. Challenged in this case is the validity of regulations promulgated by appellant Secretary of the Interior that prohibit commercial transactions in parts of birds legally killed before the birds came under the protection of the statutes. The regulations provide [that species protected by the respective acts,]

> their parts, nests, or eggs, lawfully acquired prior to the effective date of Federal protection.... may not be imported, exported, purchased, sold, bartered, or offered for purchase, sale, trade, or barter.

Appellees are engaged in the trade of Indian artifacts: several own commercial enterprises, one is employed by such an enterprise, and one is a professional appraiser. A number of the artifacts are partly composed of the feathers of currently protected birds, but these artifacts existed before the statutory protections came into force. After two of the appellees who had sold "pre-existing" artifacts were prosecuted for violations of the Eagle Protection Act and the Migratory Bird Treaty Act, appellees brought this suit for declaratory and injunctive relief in the District Court for the District of Colorado. The complaint alleged that the statutes do not forbid the sale of appellees' artifacts insofar as the constituent birds' parts were obtained prior to the effective dates of the statutes. It further alleged that if the statutes and regulations do apply to such property, they violate the Fifth Amendment.

[A three-judge court voided the regulations because of "grave doubts whether these two acts would be constitutional if they were construed to apply to pre-act bird products."] We reverse.

I

Appellant Secretary of the Interior contends that both the Eagle Protection and Migratory Bird Treaty Acts contemplate regulatory prohibition of commerce in the parts of protected birds, without regard to when those birds were originally taken. Appellees respond that such a prohibition serves no purpose, arguing that statutory protection of wildlife is not furthered by an embargo upon traffic in avian artifacts that existed before the statutory safeguards came into effect.

A

Our point of departure in statutory analysis is the language of the enactment....

The terms of the Eagle Protection Act plainly must be read as appellant Secretary argues. The sweepingly framed prohibition in § 668(a) makes it unlawful to "take, possess, sell, purchase, barter, offer to sell, purchase or barter, transport, export or import" protected birds. Congress expressly dealt with the problem of pre-existing bird products by qualifying that general prohibition with the proviso that "nothing herein shall be construed to prohibit *possession or transportation*" of bald or golden eagle parts taken prior to the effective date of coverage under the Act.

In view of the exhaustive and careful enumeration of forbidden acts in § 668(a), the narrow limitation of the proviso to "possession or transportation" compels the conclusion that, with respect to pre-existing artifacts, Congress specifically declined to except any activities other than *possession* and *transportation* from the general statutory ban. To read a further exemption for pre-existing artifacts into the Eagle Protection Act, "we would be forced to ignore the ordinary meaning of plain language." *TVA v. Hill,* 437 U.S. 153, 173 (1978). Nor can there be any question of oversight or drafting error. Throughout the statute the distinct concepts of possession, transportation, taking, and sale or purchase are treated with precision....

. . .

B

The fundamental prohibition in the Migratory Bird Treaty Act is couched in language as expansive as that employed in the Eagle Protection Act. Title 16 U.S.C. § 703 provides that

[u]nless and except as permitted by regulations made as hereinafter provided in this subchapter, it shall be unlawful * * * to pursue, hunt, take, capture, kill, attempt to take, capture, or kill, possess, offer for sale, sell, offer to barter, barter, offer to purchase, purchase, deliver for shipment, ship, export, import, cause to be shipped, exported, or imported, deliver for transportation, transport or cause to be transported, carry or cause to be carried, or receive for shipment, transportation, carriage, or export

protected birds.... [T]he text, context, and purpose of the Migratory Bird Treaty Act support the Secretary's interpretative regulations of that enactment.

On its face, the comprehensive statutory prohibition is naturally read as forbidding transactions in all bird parts, including those that compose pre-existing artifacts. While there is no doubt that regulations may exempt transactions from the general ban, nothing in the statute *requires* an exception for the sale of pre-existing artifacts. And no such statutory exception can be implied. When Congress wanted an exemption from the statutory prohibition, it provided so in unmistakable terms. [ ]

. . .

We are therefore persuaded that the Migratory Bird Treaty Act empowers the Secretary of the Interior to bar commercial transactions in covered bird parts in spite of the fact that the parts were lawfully taken before the onset of federal protection. We see no indication to the contrary. It follows that the Secretary could properly permit the possession or transportation, and not the sale or purchase, of pre-existing bird artifacts. Accordingly, we disagree with the District Court's interpretation of the Act as inapplicable to pre-existing legally obtained bird parts.

II

We also disagree with the District Court's holding that, as construed to authorize the prohibition of commercial transactions in pre-existing avian artifacts, the Eagle Protection and Migratory Bird Treaty Acts violate appellees' Fifth Amendment property rights because the prohibition wholly deprives them of the opportunity to earn a profit from those relics.

Penn Central Transportation Co. v. New York City, 438 U.S. 104, 123–128 (1978), is our most recent exposition on the Takings Clause. That exposition need not be repeated at length here. Suffice it to say that government regulation—by definition—involves the adjustment of rights for the public good. Often this adjustment curtails some potential for the use or economic exploitation of private property. To require compensation in all such circumstances would effectively compel the government to regulate by purchase. "Government hardly could go on if to some extent values incident to property could not be diminished without paying for every such change in the general law." *Pennsylvania Coal Co. v. Mahon*, 260 U.S. 393, 413 (1922); [ ]

The Takings Clause, therefore, preserves governmental power to regulate, subject only to the dictates of " 'justice and fairness.' " [ ] There is no abstract or fixed point at which judicial intervention under the Takings

Clause becomes appropriate. Formulas and factors have been developed in a variety of settings. [ ] Resolution of each case, however, ultimately calls as much for the exercise of judgment as for the application of logic.

The regulations challenged here do not compel the surrender of the artifacts, and there is no physical invasion or restraint upon them. Rather, a significant restriction has been imposed on one means of disposing of the artifacts. But the denial of one traditional property right does not always amount to a taking. At least where an owner possesses a full "bundle" of property rights, the destruction of one "strand" of the bundle is not a taking, because the aggregate must be viewed in its entirety. [ ] In this case, it is crucial that appellees retain the rights to possess and transport their property, and to donate or devise the protected birds.

It is, to be sure, undeniable that the regulations here prevent the most profitable use of appellees' property. Again, however, that is not dispositive. When we review regulation, a reduction in the value of property is not necessarily equated with a taking. [ ] In the instant case, it is not clear that appellees will be unable to derive economic benefit from the artifacts; for example, they might exhibit the artifacts for an admissions charge. At any rate, loss of future profits—unaccompanied by any physical property restriction—provides a slender reed upon which to rest a takings claim. Prediction of profitability is essentially a matter of reasoned speculation that courts are not especially competent to perform. Further, perhaps because of its very uncertainty, the interest in anticipated gains has traditionally been viewed as less compelling than other property-related interests. [ ]

Regulations that bar trade in certain goods have been upheld against claims of unconstitutional taking. For example, the Court has sustained regulations prohibiting the sale of alcoholic beverages despite the fact that individuals were left with previously acquired stocks.... Similarly, ... a federal law that extended a domestic sales ban from intoxicating to nonintoxicating alcoholic beverages "on hand at the time of the passage of the act," [ ], was upheld. Mr. Justice Brandeis dismissed the takings challenge, stating that "there was no appropriation of private property, but merely a lessening of value due to a permissible restriction imposed upon its use." [ ]

It is true that appellees must bear the costs of these regulations. But, within limits, that is a burden borne to secure "the advantage of living and doing business in a civilized community." *Pennsylvania Coal Co. v. Mahon*, 260 U.S. at 422 (Brandeis, J., dissenting). We hold that the simple prohibition of the sale of lawfully acquired property in this case does not effect a taking in violation of the Fifth Amendment.

Reversed.

NOTES

(1) *Sammons v. Commissioner of Internal Revenue:* Does the case simply reflect the general conclusion that some reduction in value is not automatically a taking? Although the owner cannot, perhaps, obtain full market value for the artifacts, she has not been deprived of all economic value. Consider the decision in *Sammons v. Commissioner of Internal Revenue.*

In *Sammons,* the taxpayer sought to take a deduction for the donation of artifacts to the Museum of Native American Cultures. Among the artifacts were thirty-five pieces made with Bald Eagle feathers, claws or other body parts. The Commissioner argued that no deduction should be allowed for the artifacts because public policy forbid a tax deduction: "To allow the Sammons a deduction for donating the artifacts to the museum," the director contended, "would encourage a violation of the federal law by subsidizing, through tax benefits flowing from the donation, an illegal transaction." The court found the argument "unpersuasive" and concluded that allowing the deduction would not

> severely or immediately frustrate national or state policy[because n]o evidence was presented tending to prove that allowance of the deduction would encourage the killing or acquisition of protected bird species. It may be true that persons who presently own artifacts of this nature might be encouraged to donate the items to a museum so that they could claim a deduction on their tax returns, but we do not view this as a threat to the national policy of protecting endangered bird species. Nor do we find anything in the record to suggest that by permitting a deduction for the contribution of the Eagle artifacts, unscrupulous sellers of Indian art are likely to hunt, capture and kill protected eagle species in an effort to manufacture "ancient" artifacts that can be sold to collectors, unsuspecting or not, for spurious donations to charitable organizations.

Sammons v. Commissioner of Internal Revenue, 838 F.2d 330 (9th Cir. 1988). Is the court's final conclusion consistent with the apparent statutory of banning all sales of eagle parts?

(2) *Lawton v. Steele:* Or, does the opinion reflect the fact that personal property is subject to greater regulatory control than is real property? Consider *Lawton v. Steele.*

Lawton brought an action for conversion against a state game warden, alleging that defendant had unconstitutionally forfeited nets that plaintiff was using to fish illegally because the state forfeiture statute provided for summary seizure and forfeiture.

> The ... only real, difficulty connected with the act ... is in its declaration that any net, etc., maintained in violation of any law for the protection of fisheries is to be treated as a public nuisance, "and may be abated and summarily destroyed by any person; and it shall be the duty of each and every protector aforesaid and every game constable, to seize, remove, and forthwith destroy the same." The legislature, however, undoubtedly possessed the power, not only to prohibit fishing by nets in these waters, but to make it a criminal offense, and to take such measures as were reasonable and necessary to prevent such offenses in the future. It certainly could not do this more effectually than by destroying the means of the offense. If the nets were being used in a manner detrimental to the interests of the public, we think it was within the power of the legislature to declare them to be nui-

sances, and to authorize the officers of the State to abate them.... In this case there can be no doubt of the right of the legislature to authorize judicial proceedings to be taken for the condemnation of the nets in question, and their sale or destruction by process of law.... But where the property is of little value, and its use for the illegal purpose is clear, the legislature may declare it to be a nuisance, and subject to summary abatement....

It is not easy to draw the line between cases where property illegally used may be destroyed summarily and where judicial proceedings are necessary for its condemnation. If the property were of great value, as, for instance, if it were a vessel employed for smuggling or other illegal purposes, it would be putting a dangerous power in the hands of a custom officer to permit him to sell or destroy it as a public nuisance, and the owner would have good reason to complain of such act as depriving him of his property without due process of law. But where the property is of trifling value, and its destruction is necessary to effect the object of a certain statute, we think it is within the power of the legislature to order its summary abatement....

Lawton v. Steele, 152 U.S. 133 (1894).

(3) Taking personal property: In *Lucas v. South Carolina Coastal Commission,* Justice Scalia wrote:

[I]n the case of personal property, by reason of the State's traditionally high degree of control over commercial dealings, [the owner] ought to be aware of the possibility that new regulation might even render his property economically worthless (at least if the property's only economically productive use is sale or manufacture for sale). *See Andrus v. Allard,* 444 U.S. 51, 66–67 (1979) (prohibition on sale of eagle feathers).

Lucas v. South Carolina Coastal Council, 505 U.S. 1003, 1027–28 (1992).

(B) Real Property

NOTES

(1) Currently, the primary federal restriction on state power to regulate property is found in the Taking Clause of the Fifth Amendment. The prohibition, however, originally was not applicable to the states. *See Barron v. Mayor & City Council of Baltimore,* 32 U.S. (7 Pet.) 243 (1833).

Before the Taking Clause was held to limit state action, the primary federal protection for vested interests was under the Contract Clause. When the Supreme Court held that land grants were contracts, *Fletcher v. Peck,* 10 U.S. (6 Cranch.) 87 (1810), some state courts concluded that the failure of a state to reserve the power to regulate land uses in the grant meant that subsequent restrictions impaired the contract. *People v. Platt,* 17 Johns. 195 (N.Y.1819). Recognition of the effects of this expansive interpretation, led the Court to retreat. In language echoing the *salus populi* maxim, the Court noted that the object and end of all government is to promote the happiness and prosperity of the community by which it is established; and it can never be assumed, that the government intended to diminish its powers of accomplishing the end for which it was created.... While the rights of private property are sacredly guarded, we must not forget, that the community also have rights, and that the happiness and well-being of every citizen depends on their faithful preservation.... We cannot ... by ... mere technical reasoning, take away from [the states] any portion of that power over their own internal police and improvements, which is so necessary to their well-being and prosperity.

Charles River Bridge v. Warren Bridge, 36 U.S. (11 Pet.) 420 (1837). *See* STANLEY I. KUTLER, PRIVILEGE AND CREATIVE DESTRUCTION (1971); Charles Warren, *The Charles River Bridge Case,* 20 GREEN BAG 284, 346 (1908); *see generally* BENJAMIN F. WRIGHT, THE CONTRACT CLAUSE OF THE CONSTITUTION at iii, 95 (1938). The inalienability of state power to act for the common good was reaffirmed and emphasized in *West River Bridge Co. v. Dix,* 47 U.S. (6 How.) 507 (1848) (legislature cannot convey its power of eminent domain), and *Stone v. Mississippi,* 101 U.S. 814 (1880) (legislature cannot bargain away police power).

(2) Land-use restrictions—antecedents: Although the bulk of land use regulation came with the increasing urbanization of the twentieth century, precedent for controlling land uses to protect wildlife extends far back into the English common law. Recall that in 1692, Parliament prohibited burning of heaths and moors to protect grouse habitat. An Act for the More Easy Discovery of Such as Shall Destroy the Game of this Kingdom, 3 & 4 Wm. & Mary, ch. 23, § 11 (1692).

Land uses were also pervasively regulated in America during the colonial period. Colonial legislatures and local governmental units imposed restrictions on the use of private property to ensure that wildlife habitat was not destroyed. *Cf.* John F. Hart, *Colonial Land Use Law and Its Significance for Modern Takings Doctrine,* 109 HARV. L. REV. 1252 (1996). That regulatory tradition continued after the Revolution. John F. Hart, *Land Use in the Early Republic and The Original Meaning of the Takings Clause,* 94 NW. U.L. REV. 1099, 1130–31 (2000). The most frequent examples involved anadromous fish runs—a fact that reflects biology rather than power: anadromous fish runs are both recurrent and restricted to well-defined areas. Nonaquatic wildlife, on the other hand, did not present such a restricted biological pattern.

The result of this lengthy history of regulating land uses to protect wildlife habitat is the lack of modern challenges to the *power* of the state to do so.

(3) Regulatory takings under the Fourteenth Amendment: It was not until the adoption of the Fourteenth Amendment, that the Supreme Court applied that Amendment's due process clause to prohibit a state from taking property without paying just compensation. *Chicago B. & Q.R.R. v. Chicago,* 166 U.S. 226 (1897).

(a) Taking as a restriction on use: Originally, the Taking Clause prohibited only physical seizure of property. FRED BOSSELMAN ET AL., THE

TAKING ISSUE 51–123 (1973). In 1923, however, the United States Supreme Court decided that, in another of Justice Holmes's famous phrases, "while property may be regulated to a certain extent, if regulation goes too far it will be recognized as a taking." *Pennsylvania Coal Co. v. Mahon,* 260 U.S. 393, 415 (1922). It may be, as the authors of *The Taking Issue* put it that "Holmes rewr[ote] the Constitution," FRED BOSSELMAN, *supra,* 124, but it is, nonetheless, now settled that property can be "taken" even when it is physically untouched. The difficulty with Justice Holmes's aphoristic phrase is, of course, the question of how far is "too far."

The early cases suggest that the Court thought that "too far" was quite far. Four years after *Mahon,* the Court for the first time faced a comprehensive zoning ordinance that restricted the location of commercial, industrial, apartment, single-family, and other land uses, as well as specifying the size of lots and the size and height of buildings. The Court upheld the ordinance as a valid exercise of the government's power to protect the public; the public interest in segregating inconsistent land uses was sufficient to justify the resulting diminution in value of 75%. *Village of Euclid v. Ambler Realty Co.,* 272 U.S. 365 (1926).

Two years later, the Court went even further. In *Miller v. Schoene,* 276 U.S. 272 (1928), the owner of several red cedars challenged a state statute requiring cedars to be removed in order to control a disease that destroyed apple trees. The cedar owner contended that his property had been taken. The Court held that it was not:

> the state was under the necessity of making a choice between the preservation of one class of property and that of the other wherever both existed in dangerous proximity. It would have been none the less a choice if, instead of enacting the present statute, the state, by doing nothing, had permitted serious injury to the apple orchards within its borders to go on unchecked. When forced to such a choice the state does not exceed its constitutional powers by deciding upon the destruction of one class of property in order to save another which, in the judgment of the legislature, is of greater value to the public. It will not do to say that the case is merely one of a conflict of two private interests and that the misfortune of apple growers may not be shifted to cedar owners by ordering the destruction of their property; for it is obvious that there may be, and that here there is, a preponderant public concern in the preservation of the one interest over the other.

Id. at 279.

(b) The modern era: The modern era in taking jurisprudence began with the Court's next important regulatory taking decision—*Penn Central Transportation Co. v. City of New York,* 438 U.S. 104 (1978). The railroad's application for a permit to build a 55–story office complex on top of Grand Central Station was denied and it challenged the decision. Acknowledging that there was no " 'set formula' for determining when 'justice and fairness' require that economic injuries caused by public action be compensated by the government, rather than remain disproportionately concentrated on a few persons," *id.* at 124, the Court listed three factors to be considered in balancing the public and private interests at stake: (1) the economic impact on the applicant, (2) the extent to which the regulation interfered with "distinct investment-backed expectations," and (3) the "character" of the government action. *Id.*

The imprecision of the *Penn Central* factors was not significantly ameliorated when the Court rephrased it as a two-part test in *Agins v. City of Tiburon*, 447 U.S. 255 (1980):

> The application of a general zoning law to particular property effects a taking if the ordinance does not substantially advance legitimate states interests, [ ] or denies an owner economically viable use of his land [*Penn Central*]. . . . [T]he question necessarily requires a weighing of private and public interests.

Id. at 260–61. The Court has continued to cite this language from *Agins*. *E.g., Lucas v. South Carolina Coastal Council*, 505 U.S. 1003, 1016 (1992). Its two criteria thus provide the overall structure in the following discussion.

    (i) "substantial nexus": The Court first examined *Agins*'s requirement that "the ordinance [must] substantially advance legitimate states interests" in *Nollan v. California Coastal Commission*, 483 U.S. 825 (1987)—the first decision since *Pennsylvania Coal* in which the Court found a taking. In *Nollan*, the owners of a small beachfront bungalow sought to replace it with a substantially larger house. The Coastal Commission granted approval conditioned on the landowners granting an easement to allow the public to walk along the beach. The state asserted that the easement was necessary to protect the public's ability to see the beach and to offset increased privatization and congestion. The Court stated that a proposed condition would not be a taking if (a) an outright denial of the permit would not be and (b) the condition serves the same purpose as would the denial. *Id.* at 836. Focusing on the second requirement, Justice Scalia stated that it was "quite impossible" that the commission's concerns would be met by allowing people to walk along the Nollan's property; the asserted state interest therefore lacked a "substantial nexus" with the permit condition, and the condition was a taking. *Id.* at 838–39, 841–42.

    In 1997, the Supreme Court returned to the "substantial nexus" standard in *Dolan v. City of Tigard*, 512 U.S. 374 (1994). The owner of a store sought a permit to double its size and pave its parking lot. The city conditioned the permit on the owner's grant of an easement covering the 100–year floodplain plus an additional 15–foot strip of land for a bicycle and pedestrian path. The Supreme Court held that the conditions satisfied the "essential nexus" test enunciated in *Nollan*—the expansion of impervious surfaces on the lot would increase run-off into the stream and increased traffic to a larger store would be offset by providing alternative means of transportation. But the Court added an additional requirement: when the government goes beyond regulatory restrictions to "exact" cash or property from the landowner, the degree of exactions must "bear[] the required relationship to the projected impact of petitioner's proposed development." *Id.* at 388. The city's exaction failed this additional requirement because physical access was not necessary to satisfy the flood control objectives, *id.* at 393, and the justification for the path was insufficiently quantified, *id.* at 395–96. What is required, the Court stated, is "rough proportionality": "No precise mathematical calculation is required, but the city must make some sort of individualized determination that the required dedication is related both in nature and extent to the impact of the proposed development." *Id.* at 391.

(ii) **economic impact:** In both *Pennsylvania Coal* and *Penn Central*, the Court treated the economic impact of the regulation as an important factor in determining whether a taking had occurred. In a decision handed down in the same term as *Nollan,* the Court again addressed the relevance of economic impact of regulation. In *Keystone Bituminous Coal Ass'n v. DeBenedictis,* 480 U.S. 470 (1987), the Court cited the *Agins*'s test and held that a Pennsylvania statute requiring coal mine operators to leave at least 50% of the coal located beneath public buildings, dwellings, and cemeteries was not a taking because it did not render coal mining unprofitable.

(iii) *Lucas:* In 1992, the Supreme Court sought to clarify this jumble of precedents in *Lucas v. South Carolina Coastal Council,* 505 U.S. 1003 (1992). Plaintiff had purchased two ocean-front lots on a barrier island off the coast of South Carolina. The state legislature subsequently enacted the Beachfront Management Act which effectively prevented Lucas from erecting permanent structures on his lots. The trial court held that the Act rendered Lucas's land worthless, and ordered the state to pay compensation; the state supreme court reversed—and was reversed in turn by the United States Supreme Court.

Writing for the majority, Justice Scalia began by acknowledging the difficulty in determining how far was "too far." He noted, however, that there are

> two discrete categories of regulatory action [that are] compensable without case-specific inquiry into the public interest advanced in support of the restraint. The first encompasses regulations that compel the property owner to suffer a physical "invasion" of his property.... The second situation in which we have found categorical treatment appropriate is where regulation denies all economically beneficial or productive use of land.... As we have said on numerous occasions, the Fifth Amendment is violated when land-use regulation "does not substantially advance legitimate state interests *or denies an owner economically viable use of his land." Agins,* 447 U.S. 260.

Lucas, 505 U.S. at 1015–16. Despite the statement that "categorical treatment [is] appropriate ... where regulation denies all economically beneficial or productive use of land," the Court quickly noted an exception: when "the proscribed use interest was not part of [the owner's] title to begin with." *Id.* at 1027. That is, as the Court subsequently explained,

> regulations that prohibit all economically beneficial use of land ... cannot be newly legislated or decreed (without compensation), but must inhere in the title itself, in the restrictions that background principles of the State's law of property and nuisance already place upon landownership. A law or decree with such an effect must, in other words, do no more that duplicate the result that could have been achieved in the courts—by adjacent landowners (or other uniquely affected persons) under the State's law of private nuisance, or by the

State under its complementary power to abate nuisances that affect the general public, or otherwise.

Id. at 1029.

(iv) a working summary: In *Lucas*, the Court effectively reshuffled the cases:

(A) if a landowner can prove that the challenged regulation results in either a physical invasion of the property or the deprivation of "all economically beneficial or productive use of land," compensation is due *unless* the government can show that the restriction inheres in the "background principles of the State's law of property" or in restrictions traceable to public or private nuisance law.

(B) in all other cases, the regulation is a taking if it does not "substantially advance legitimate state interests," an inquiry that "necessarily requires a weighing of private and public interests." If the governmental action involves the imposition of a permit condition, the government must demonstrate a "substantial nexus" between the permit condition and the public purposes; this showing must demonstrate that there is a "roughly proportional" relationship between the condition and the impact of the private activity.

How will this approach affect regulation of private property to protect wildlife habitat? Consider the following cases.

(4) *Palazzolo v. Rhode Island*: In 1978, plaintiff acquired a tract of coastal land largely covered by salt-water marsh. Although the state regulatory agency expressed willingness to approve development on the small portion of tract that was dry upland, Palazzolo's applications to fill and develop the marsh were uniformly denied, based on state wetlands-protection regulations that predated his land acquisition. Plaintiff challenged the denial as an unlawful taking of his property, claiming that the restriction amounted to a total deprivation of all economic value.

The Rhode Island Supreme Court denied the claim. First, the court reasoned that, since plaintiff acquired the property subject to all existing regulations, including wetlands protection, he could not challenge them. Second, the court held that plaintiff had not been deprived of all value because Palazzolo could develop the upland. Although the plaintiff's taking argument was based entirely on the *Lucas* total-deprivation test, the state court also opined that the plaintiff could not succeed with a multiple-factors taking argument based on *Penn Central*, and for the same reason: Because the plaintiff acquired the land after the regulations went into effect, he had no "reasonable investment-backed expectations" that were dashed by the state's refusal to permit development.

The United State Supreme Court reversed and remanded. The Court agreed that the plaintiff's total-deprivation claim under *Lucas* failed because of the value of the dry upland. The Court reversed on the effect of the timing of the land acquisition on the taking claim. The state court erred, the Supreme Court decided, when it refused to allow plaintiff to attack regulations that predated his land acquisition and in its related ruling that such regulations undercut any reasonable, investment-backed expectation of being able to develop. The legal right to challenge a regulation, the Court held, does not end when the land changes hands; expectations and legal rights based on prior law can be passed along to new owners. In separate opinions, Justices O'Connor and Breyer urged that, while a landowner could attack a land-use regulation in existence at the time of acquisition, the timing and circumstances of acquisition, as well as the mere passage of time, were relevant factors in determining the reasonableness of landowner expectations; Justice Scalia, in turn, wrote separately to express an opposing view. *Palazzolo v. Rhode Island,* ___ U.S. ___, 121 S.Ct. 2448 (2001).

Sierra Club v. Department of Forestry & Fire Protection

California Court of Appeals.
26 Cal.Rptr.2d 338 (1993).
review denied (1994).[1]

■ PETERSON, P.J.:—In these consolidated appeals, we conclude the trial court properly invalidated two timber harvest plans (THP's), which were approved by the California Department of Forestry and Fire Protection (Forestry) in 1988 in order to allow the logging of two similar plots of virgin old-growth forest, and which have been the subject of extensive previous legal proceedings over the past five years. As Forestry subsequently conceded before the trial court, its decision to approve these THP's was a prejudicial abuse of discretion, and was not supported by applicable law or substantial evidence in the record showing adequate consideration of mitigation measures proposed by the California Department of Fish and Game (Fish and Game), which measures were designed to protect certain rare animal species shown to be dependent on old-growth forests. We also reject, on the sole ground that it is not yet ripe for review, the claim made in this appeal that the state would effect an unconstitutional taking of private property by protecting those species. We, therefore, affirm the trial court's decisions invalidating the THP's in issue.

I. FACTS AND PROCEDURAL HISTORY

The procedural history of these cases, which we have seen on many occasions in the past, has been much more extensive than one might wish. In briefest summary, we are concerned here with two THP's which were submitted for approval by appellant Pacific Lumber Company (P–L) in 1988. One THP ... concerned P–L's attempt to log more than 220 acres of virgin, old-growth forest in the area of Owl Creek in Humboldt County. [A]t about the same time ... P–L ... submitted another similar THP in Humboldt County ... for another parcel of roughly equal size near Salmon Creek in the Headwaters Forest.

[The THPs were initially submitted to Forestry for approval. Forestry is required to solicit the views of Fish and Game on wildlife issues. For both THPs, Fish and Game proposed mitigation measures designed to reduce

---

1. [In denying review, the California   not officially published.]
Supreme Court ordered that the opinion be

the effect of the logging on wildlife species, especially six relatively rare animal species which are dependent on old-growth forests for their continued survival. These species are: (1) the marbled murrelet, a bird related to puffins and auks which feed at sea, but nests in fully-mature or overmature trees in old-growth forests situated, like the two parcels in question here, within easy flying distance of the California coastline; (2) the spotted owl, a raptor which also is highly dependent upon old-growth forests for its habitat; (3) the northern goshawk, another raptor which inhabits such forests; (4) the red tree vole, a small mammal native to these forests; (5) the Olympic salamander, an amphibian which inhabits springs and small brooks in deep forests; and (6) the tailed frog, a frog with a tail-like protuberance, which needs clear, cold forest streams to survive. Forestry approved the THPs without ordering the mitigation measures specified by Fish and Game; Fish and Game filed a formal nonconcurrence statement as to the Owl Creek THP. Litigation ensued. Following an initial appeal to the Court of Appeals in which the decisions were reversed, two trials were held. In both, the approval of the THP was reversed on the ground that it had been erroneous.]

II.   DISCUSSION

We conclude we must affirm the trial court's rulings in both cases. The trial court properly ruled Forestry had committed a prejudicial abuse of discretion in approving the THP's to log Owl Creek and Salmon Creek, since Forestry did not follow applicable law and there was no substantial evidence to support Forestry's initial rejection of the mitigation measures, designed to protect rare or endangered wildlife, which had been specified by Fish and Game officials. Our reasons for reaching this conclusion are as follows.

. . .

B.   The Possible Conflict Between Wildlife Protection and the Takings Clause

It appears that P–L's arguments regarding the protection of private property from unconstitutional takings did play a large role in initially motivating Forestry to reject the mitigation measures suggested by Fish and Game as not *economically* feasible. Significantly, P–L's constitutional argument concerning a regulatory taking is both misplaced in the context of these particular administrative actions and appeals, and is inconsistent with precedents dealing with wildlife protection in general. We address this inconsistency, and the problem it creates in this case, in order to clarify the issues.

First, as we will explain, the takings issue is not properly joined and ripe for review here. We do not know what the economic effect of the mitigation measures to be imposed upon P–L will be; nor do we have here a final administrative determination as to mitigation measures, so we may decide whether such regulatory decision deprives P–L of all of the value of its property, thereby constituting a regulatory taking. [ ] P–L contends only that it might not be allowed to harvest 80 percent of its timber, or perhaps all the timber on some particular parcels (rather than the roughly 50 percent it had initially sought to harvest); but the final economic effect of the regulatory action on these parcels and its lands as a whole remains unclear. P–L "thus does not state a ripe claim for regulatory taking." [ ] The administrative process is not final; the mitigation measures suggested by Fish and Game have not been finally adopted as a condition to issuance of the THP's. Until that is done, a determination of claimed economic loss and its effect on P–L's lands is premature, bottomed on speculation unsupported by an adequate record.

If these particular parcels (but not P–L's other lands which do not have old-growth characteristics or are not the habitats of threatened species) were to be protected wholly or in part from logging operations in order to save threatened wildlife species, we note that this district, the federal courts of appeals, and appellate courts in our sister states have generally rejected the claim that a state or federal statute enacted in the interest of protecting wildlife is unconstitutional because it curtails the uses to which real property may be put.

There is, however, an interesting dichotomy between those cases which have endorsed a state's attempts to protect wildlife on private lands, and more recent intimations from federal precedents involving the takings clause of the Fifth Amendment to the U.S. Constitution as applied to regulation of land use, usually through zoning or planning. We, therefore, review the relevant case law first as to wildlife protection and secondly as to issues arising under a constitutional takings analysis.

1. Wildlife Protection Cases

In the landmark case of *Platt v. Philbrick,* 47 P.2d 302 (Cal.App.1935), Presiding Justice Nourse rejected such a claim: "The complaint that the statute [protecting wildlife on private property] as a whole is unconstitutional because it might permit an injury to appellant's property without compensation is without any foundation. All private property within the state is held subject to the general police powers. [Citation] It is conceivable that private property in every fish and game district in the state might suffer some damage through the restrictions of the Fish and Game Code generally, but this is a damage which the property owner must bear in the interest of the public welfare." *See also Terminals Equipment Co. v. City and County of San Francisco,* 270 Cal. Rptr. 329 (Cal.App.1990) ("Generally, the adoption of zoning ordinances or land use plans such as the one at issue in this case is a matter within the police power of the state and its subdivisions.")

Similarly, in *Christy v. Hodel,* 857 F.2d 1324, 1326–1327, 1334–1335 (9th Cir.1988), the Ninth Circuit found no unconstitutional taking from government actions which protected endangered species, even though the government thereby prevented a sheepherder from protecting his sheep by shooting marauding Montana grizzly bears. The Ninth Circuit in reaching this conclusion cited numerous decisions, including the opinion of this district in *Platt*; the opinion of the Tenth Circuit in *Mountain States Legal Foundation v. Hodel,* 799 F.2d 1423, 1428–1429 (10th Cir.1986) (The damage caused by federally protected wild jackasses was not a compensable taking); and the early decision of the New York Court of Appeals in *Barrett v. State,* 116 N.E. 99 (1917) (The damage to timber stands caused by state-protected beavers was not a compensable taking).

A landowner whose valuable stands of old-growth forest are infested with protected species is subject to state regulations designed for the legitimate purpose of such protection. The cases cited above clearly indicate that the federal and state governments may regulate and protect rare species on private lands without, *ipso facto,* triggering an unconstitutional taking of private property on which such species are present. P–L's contrary argument, based upon the fact that the several species in question actually physically occupy the habitat afforded by its property, presents a distinction without a difference in light of the cases cited above. That authority necessarily upholds governmental protection of such species while on the land of an unconsenting landowner or leaseholder. In particular, we note that *Barrett,* upheld such state regulation in order to protect beavers which occupied the land in question and denuded it of the standing timber constituting its only real economic asset. [ ]

Further, if governments may constitutionally protect wildlife species occupying private land, whose activities arguably interfere with the land's market value during such occupancy, it would seem certain that such protection may be equally afforded to the relatively innocuous and endangered species in question here. Contemporary wildlife management and environmental regulation, as we currently know them, would seem difficult if not impossible if the exercise of that police power of the states to preserve and protect endangered species automatically triggered a partial or whole unconstitutional taking of the private land on which those species are situate.

2. Federal Jurisprudence Concerning the Constitutionality of Regulatory Takings

In contrast, however, to the cases cited above, in which the courts have generally endorsed wildlife regulation by the states and federal governments—and have rejected attempts to challenge wildlife laws as effecting unconstitutional takings, the recent jurisprudence of the federal Supreme Court may indicate the high court will in the future take a new course on takings issues generally, with a conceivable future impact on wildlife regulation. In *Lucas v. South Carolina Coastal Council,* 505 U.S. 1003 (1992), the justices of the Supreme Court expressed a surprising diversity of views upon the proper analysis of a takings clause issue which arose when the state of South Carolina passed a statutory scheme of land protection which forbade a landowner to build houses on his land, in a development on a barrier island off the coast of South Carolina which was subject to erosion, and which for half of the past 40 years had been subject to daily flooding by the ebb and flow of the tides. [ ]

From this factual situation in *Lucas*—which the six justices in the majority apparently accepted as a clear case of a total diminution of the value of the property, for purposes decreed by the state and, thus, seemingly an unconstitutional taking unless compensated, the justices nevertheless derived four separate opinions. Even the opinion of the court by Justice Scalia appears less than a totally resounding statement of principle, since it merely remands the matter for further proceedings in the state courts as to whether, under South Carolina's preexisting state common law of nuisance and property use, the construction of homes on Lucas's property could have been enjoined: "The question, however, is one of state law to be dealt with on remand.* * * [A]s it would be required to do if it sought to restrain Lucas in a common-law action for public nuisance, South Carolina must identify background principles of nuisance and property law that prohibit the uses he now intends in the circumstances in which the property is presently found. Only on this showing can the State fairly claim that, in proscribing all such beneficial uses, the Beachfront Management Act is taking nothing." *Lucas v. South Carolina Coastal Council*, 505 U.S. at 1031–32.

As Professor Epstein suggests, "Although anticipated before its arrival, last term's decision in *Lucas v. South Carolina Coastal Council* has been rightly regarded as anticlimactic." [ ] Indeed, the commentary on *Lucas* from academic and legal commentators seems more concerned with what the high court left undone and ought to have done, rather than what the *Lucas* opinion actually did. As Professor Fisher observes, "Several features of the Supreme Court's opinion in *Lucas* are highly problematic.* * * The problem of defining the [limits of the] property whose 'economic value' is at issue has not been solved by the Court and does not seem susceptible to any satisfactory solution. The nuisance exception that the Court builds into its new test will contribute to the already infamous vagueness of the takings doctrine and may lead to inconsistency in the vulnerability of similar tracts of land to severe land-use regulation. Finally, if the cynical view of state legislators on which the opinion seems to be founded is realistic, the decision will be wholly ineffectual." [ ]

Nevertheless, we do discern from *Lucas* certain principles which are relevant here. If indeed California were to promulgate laws or regulations which would forbid P–L from logging all of its extensive acreage in the state, thereby effecting a total loss of all economical or productive use of the land, and if the logging of land would not have been subject to preexisting regulation by the state's laws of property or nuisance, then Lucas arguably indicates a taking has occurred. One problem in applying a *Lucas* analysis to the facts of this case, however, is that wildlife regulation of some sort has been historically a part of the preexisting law of property, as the cases cited above either presuppose or assume; and thus, we are left with a circular argument. *See also Agins v. City of Tiburon*, 598 P.2d 25 (Cal.1979) (California state courts may not entertain claims of compensation for a regulatory taking), *aff'd on other grounds*, 447 U.S. 255, 263 n. 9 (1980) ("Mere fluctuations in value during the process of governmental decisionmaking" are not a taking); *First Lutheran Church v. Los Angeles County*, 482 U.S. 304, 321 (1987) (The takings clause requires payment "where the government's activities have already worked a taking of all use of property.* * * ").

Two recent cases from this district have also rejected similar challenges, based on a takings argument, to state wildlife regulations. *See Sierra Club v. California Coastal Commission*, 15 Cal. Rptr. 2d 779 (Cal. App.1993), *review denied* (. . . rejected, as unripe and unsubstantiated by the record, a similar takings clause argument where the administrative action in question would have protected certain forest lands from cutting or development); *accord, Moerman v. State of California,* 21 Cal. Rptr. 2d 329 (Cal.App.1993), *review denied* (. . . there was no unconstitutional taking of private property where wild wapitis wandered).

As our Supreme Court has denied review in these two cases arising from our own district, we do not believe a different approach is warranted here (as P–L urges relying, *inter alia,* on *Lucas*) since it is questionable whether on this record a result inapposite to *Sierra Club* and *Moerman* could be reached. We simply do not know the financial effect which this state's wildlife regulation in issue here will have on the land to which the THP's involved in these appeals apply, or on other forested lands of P–L in this state.[4]

Our conclusion is required by the standards set by the *Lucas* opinion itself. *Lucas* recognizes that the evolving federal law, regarding the constitutional limits of governmental regulations concerning land use, springs from *Pennsylvania Coal Co. v. Mahon,* 260 U.S. 393, 415 (1922), authored by Justice Holmes: "[W]hile property may be regulated to a certain extent, *if regulation goes too far it will be recognized as a taking.*" (Emphasis added.) Following *Mahon,* "In 70–odd years of succeeding regulatory takings jurisprudence, we have generally eschewed any set formula for determining *how far is too far,* preferring to engage in * * * essentially ad hoc, factual inquiries [citation]." *Lucas v. South Carolina Coastal Council,* 505 U.S. at 1015.

These "ad hoc, factual inquiries" demand an adequate record, which we do not possess here, in order to determine whether a taking has occurred. Justice Scalia in *Lucas* analyzed two "discrete categories" of regulatory actions constituting a Fifth Amendment taking and compensable without case specific inquiry "into the public interest advanced in support of the restraint" imposed by such action. 505 U.S. at 1015–16. They are: (1) regulations compelling a property owner "to suffer a physical 'invasion' of his property," and (2) regulations denying "*all* economically beneficial or productive use of the land." (*Id.*, emphasis added.)

P–L does not contend that an unconstitutional taking is implicated in these cases because California's regulation of its land use fails to advance legitimate state interests in the protection of endangered species, or because of any claimed constitutional defects in the statutory and regulatory process by which the THP applications are considered by Forestry. P–L simply suggests that such state regulation of the use of its land, albeit expressing a legitimate state concern, might nonetheless fall within the second *Lucas* category of compensable taking through regulatory action by

---

4. Even, for example, if state regulation kept the two small and separated parcels at issue here totally unlogged in perpetuity, as seems unlikely, this would not likely establish a total diminution of the value of P–L's timber throughout the state. *See City & County of San Francisco v. Golden Gate Heights Investments,* 18 Cal. Rptr. 2d 467 (Cal.App.1993), *review denied* (. . . rejected takings argument based upon *Lucas,* where the appellant could not show that the government action would have taken all the value of the extensive property in issue, and the action would only have reduced the value of a portion of it); *accord,* [ ].

denying all economically beneficial or productive use of P–L's parcels here implicated, zoned exclusively for timber production.

It is, first, obvious that whether any state regulation of land use will deny all economic or productive use of the land to which applied must continue to be decided on an ad hoc basis, dependent on the extent of regulation and whether application thereof does, in fact, deny all such economic and productive use.

This issue of compensable Fifth Amendment taking by state regulatory action is not ripe for decision in the case at bench, and we decline to enter an advisory opinion thereon. We do not, as did the state court in *Lucas,* reject the possibility (in this case the virtual reality) of "further administrative and trial proceedings," [ ], and proceed to the merits on the apparent assumption (made by the lower court in *Lucas*) that a categorical taking has in fact occurred.

On the contrary, we deem the record before us inadequate for the purpose of categorically disposing of P–L's Fifth Amendment takings claim. It does not permit an answer to the Holmes query of how far the state regulations go, *Pennsylvania Coal Co. v. Mahon,* [ ], since their application to P–L's land will be established in the future. P–L is free to seek a new THP from Forestry consistent with the trial court's decision we have affirmed. The nature and extent of timber harvest to be allowed on the subject parcels must be further determined by Forestry subject to judicial review. Whether P–L will be denied all economic or productive use of its land is dependent on Forestry's action in responding to P–L's THP applications if made after remand. In sum, the nature and extent of permitted timber harvest on P–L's parcels must necessarily be known "before adjudicating the constitutionality of the regulations that purport to limit it." *MacDonald, Sommer & Frates v. Yolo County,* 477 U.S. 340, 351 (1986).

. . .

D. Conclusion

The trial court judges correctly resolved the legal issues in these cases—in light of the applicable legal principles, the evidence, and the explicit and implicit concessions by Forestry made upon the record. We find no basis for reaching a different result here.

NOTES

(1) Is the court's analysis persuasive? Does its statement that there is "an interesting dichotomy between those cases which have endorsed a state's attempts to protect wildlife on private lands, and more recent intimations from federal precedents involving the takings clause of the Fifth Amendment," [¶ 9], misstate the relationship between the two bodies of law? That is, do the "cases which have endorsed a state's attempts to protect wildlife on private lands" constitute a background principle that is relevant to the resolution of questions involving "the takings clause of the Fifth Amendment"?

Recall that in *Lawton v. Steele* the Court stated: "The preservation of game and fish . . . has always been treated as within the proper domain of the police power." Recall also that in *Hughes v. Oklahoma,* 441 U.S. 322, 337 (1979), the Supreme Court equated the state interest in protection of wildlife with its interest in protecting health and safety of citizens. Does this suggest that protection of wildlife is a background principle? If not, what would count as a background principle?

(2) The public trust as a "background principle": Does the public trust serve as an exception to the taking prohibition? In *Illinois Central R.R. v. Illinois,* 146 U.S. 387 (1892) [Chapter 3], the state legislature had sold the land beneath Chicago's harbor to the Illinois Central Railroad. A subsequent legislature sought to revoke the grant. The Supreme Court held that the state had the power to do so because the state's title to lands beneath navigable waters was impressed with a trust:

> It is a title held in trust for the people of the state, that they may enjoy the navigation of the waters, carry on commerce over them, and have liberty of fishing therein, freed from the obstruction or interference of private parties. The interest of the people in the navigation of the waters and in commerce over them may be improved in many instances by the erection of wharves, docks, and piers therein, for which purpose the state may grant parcels of the submerged lands; and, so long as their disposition is made for such purpose, no valid objections can be made to the grants. . . . But that is a very different doctrine from the one which would sanction the abdication of the general control of the state over lands under the navigable waters of an entire harbor or bay, or of a sea or lake. Such abdication is not consistent with the exercise of that trust which requires the government of the state to preserve such waters for the use of the public. The trust devolving upon the state for the public, and which can only be discharged by the management and control of property in which the public has an interest, cannot be relinquished by a transfer of the property. The control of the state for the purposes of the trust can never be lost, except as to such parcels as are used in promoting the interests of the public therein, or can be disposed of without any substantial impairment of the public interest in the lands and waters remaining. . . . The state can no more abdicate its trust over property in which the whole people are interested, like navigable waters and soils under them, . . . than it can abdicate its police powers in the administration of government and the preservation of the peace. . . .

Furthermore, the state not only had the constitutional power to resume title and management over the submerged lands, it had the power to do so without the payment of compensation for the submerged lands since the original grant did not convey the land free from the public trust:

> Any grant of the kind is necessarily revocable, and the exercise of the trust by which the property was held by the state can be resumed at any time. Undoubtedly there may be expenses incurred in *improvements made under such a grant,* which the state ought to pay; but, be that as it may, the power to resume the trust whenever the state judges best is, we think, incontrovertible. . . .

.... We hold, therefore, that any attempted cession of the ownership and control of the state in and over the submerged lands in Lake Michigan, by the act of April 16, 1869, was inoperative to affect, modify, or in any respect to control the sovereignty and dominion of the state over the lands, or its ownership thereof, and that any such attempted operation of the act was annulled by the repealing act of April 15, 1873, which to that extent was valid and effective. There can be no irrepealable contract in a conveyance of property by a grantor in disregard of a public trust, under which he was bound to hold and manage it.

Illinois Central R.R. v. Illinois, 146 U.S. 387 (1892).

In the language of *Lucas,* does *Illinois Central* hold the public trust to be one of the "background principles of the State's law of property and nuisance already place[d] upon landownership"? When a private entity acquires submerged lands, its title is impressed with the public trust and state actions to protect the trust do not result in a taking. *E.g., National Audubon Society v. Superior Court,* 658 P.2d 709 (Cal.), *cert. denied,* 464 U.S. 977 (1983) [Chapter 5]; *Orion Corp. v. State,* 747 P.2d 1062 (Wash. 1987), *cert. denied,* 486 U.S. 1022 (1988).

Does the trust in wildlife impose similar restrictions on private lands?

Is the public-trust-as-background-principle simply a reformulation of the state-ownership-as-limit-on-federal-regulation?

(3) Oliver Wendell Holmes on wildlife conservation as a "background principle": In *Missouri v. Holland*—one of the most frequently cited United States Supreme Court cases on wildlife—Justice Holmes concluded that, in "matters of the sharpest exigency for the national well being," a treaty could supply the basis for congressional action despite the lack of an express power. He then turned to the matter before the Court, the protection of migratory birds:

Here a national interest of very nearly the first magnitude is involved. It can be protected only by national action in concert with that of another power. The subject matter is only transitorily within the State and has no permanent habitat therein. But for the treaty and the statute there soon might be no birds for any powers to deal with. We see nothing in the Constitution that compels the Government to sit by while a food supply is cut off and the protectors of our forests and our crops are destroyed.

Missouri v. Holland, 252 U.S. 416, 433, 435 (1920) [*infra*].

(4) One commentator, reviewing the extensive legal history on the subject, concludes that wildlife-related restrictions on private land qualify as "background principles" of property law within the meaning of *Lucas:*

The historical antecedents of modern property law in this country and of the laws protecting wildlife reveal that the use of private property has always been constrained by transcendent social or communal obligations, including the obligation to avoid harming wild animals and the lands upon which they depend. Laws protecting wildlife resources have historically been part of the preexisting common law of most states, and state courts, relying on the common law doctrines of state wildlife trust and public trust, have repeatedly sustained those laws in the face of assertions of contrary individual private rights. "To a layman, and even to a lawyer who has not had occasion to deal with the subject, the extent of the power of the states with reference to fish, game, and all wild life within their borders is perfectly astounding."[210] State laws protecting wild animals and the lands that sustain them, therefore, reflect long-held background principles of common law, under which a state's authority to regulate and protect wildlife resources is seen as superior to any conflicting private right or interest in the land on which wildlife roams.[211] These laws, therefore, are the paradigmatic example of laws that *"inhere [themselves], in the restrictions that the background principles of the State's law of property and nuisance already place on land ownership."*[212]

Hope M. Babcock, *Should* Lucas v. South Carolina Coastal Council *Protect Where the Wild Things Are? Of Beavers, Bob-o-Links, and Other Things That Go Bump in the Night,* 85 IOWA L. REV. 849 (2000); *see also* Oliver A. Houck, *Why Do We Protect Endangered Species, and What Does that Say About Whether Restrictions on Private Property to Protect Them Constitute "Takings?",* 80 IOWA L. REV. 297 (1995).

SECTION 2.   PREEMPTING STATE LAW: THE USES OF FEDERAL POWER

a.   THE TREATY CLAUSE

[The President] shall have Power, by and with the Advice and Consent of the Senate, to make Treaties, provided two-thirds of the Senators present concur.

UNITED STATES CONSTITUTION art. II, § 2.

This Constitution, and the Laws of the United States which shall be made in Pursuance thereof; and all Treaties made, or which shall be made, under the Authority of the United States, shall be the supreme law of the Land; . . . .

UNITED STATES CONSTITUTION art. VI, cl. 2.

---

210. *Cook v. State,* 74 P.2d 199, 201 (Wash.1937).

211. Although beyond the scope of this Article's focus on background principles of property law, it is also worth pointing out that laws protecting wildlife and wildlife habitat also fit within a state's common law parens patriae authority to abate nuisances which injure the public health and comfort. The parens patriae doctrine has long applied to the protection of natural resources, authorizing states to seek injunctive relief for a collective injury to a substantial number of its citizens where no private individual has standing to proceed. *See, e.g., North Dakota v. Minnesota,* 263 U.S. 365 (1923) (flooding caused by change in drainage system); *New York v. New Jersey,* 256 U.S. 296 (1921) (discharge of sewage); *Georgia v. Tennessee Copper,* 206 U.S. 230 (1907) (air pollution); *Missouri v. Illinois,* 180 U.S. 208 (1901) (discharge of sewage).

212. *Lucas v. South Carolina Coastal Council,* 505 U.S. 1003, 1029 (1992) (emphasis added).

NOTES

The Weeks–McLean Migratory Bird Act: In 1913, Congress added a rider to a statute appropriating funds for the Department of Agriculture:

> All ... migratory game and insectivorous birds which in their northern and southern migrations ... do not remain ... the entire year within the borders of any State or Territory, shall hereafter be deemed to be within the custody and protection of the Government of the United States, and shall not be destroyed or taken contrary to regulations [adopted by the Department of Agriculture].... *Provided, however,* that nothing herein contained shall be deemed to ... interfere with the local laws of the States and Territories for the protection of nonmigratory game or other birds resident and breeding within their borders, nor to prevent the States and Territories from enacting laws and regulations to promote and render efficient the regulations of the Department of Agriculture provided under this statute.

Act of Mar. 4, 1913, ch. 145, 37 Stat. 828, 847 [commonly known as the Weeks–McLean Migratory Bird Act]. The Weeks–McLean Act was quickly challenged as unconstitutional:

United States v. Shauver

District Court for the Eastern District of Arkansas.
214 F. 154 (1914).

■ TRIEBER, D.J.:—The defendant demurs to the indictment in this cause, which charges him with a violation of that part of the Appropriation Act for the Department of Agriculture, [ ], known as the "migratory birds" provision, and the regulations made by the Department of Agriculture in pursuance thereof, and which have been approved by the President. [The court quoted in its entirety the relevant provisions of the Act.]

In pursuance of this authority the Department of Agriculture has adopted suitable regulations, which have been approved by the President. The only ground of the demurrer is that the act is unconstitutional.

That the national Constitution is an enabling instrument, and therefore Congress possesses only such powers as are expressly or by necessary implication granted by that instrument, is not questioned. Unless, therefore, there is some provision in the national Constitution granting to Congress either expressly or by necessary implication the power to legislate on this subject, the act cannot be sustained.

. . .

It is ... well settled that as to all internal affairs the states retained their police power, which they, as sovereign nations, possessed prior to the adoption of the national Constitution, and no such powers were granted to the nation. [ ]

But it is now equally well settled that the United States does possess what is analogous to the police power, which every sovereign nation possesses, as to its own property, *Camfield v. United States,* 167 U.S. 518 (1897), and to carry into effect those powers which the Constitution has conferred upon it, *In re Debs,* 158 U.S. 564 (1895); *Light v. United States,* 220 U.S. 523 (1911); [ ]. It is not claimed by counsel for the government that the power to enact such legislation exists under the commerce clause of the Constitution, but it is claimed that subsection 2 of section 3, art. 4, of the Constitution, which is as follows, grants the necessary power:

> The Congress shall have power to dispose of and make all needful rules and regulations respecting the territory or other property belonging to the United States; and nothing in this Constitution shall be so construed as to prejudice any claims of the United States, or of any particular state.

It is also claimed that it is one of those implied attributes of sovereignty in which the national government has concurrent jurisdiction with the states; that it is a dormant right in the national government; and, where the state is clearly incompetent to save itself, the national government has the right to aid. To sustain the latter proposition stress is laid on the fact that it is impossible for any state to enact laws for the protection of migratory wild game, and only the national government can do it with any fair degree of success; consequently the power must be national and vested in the Congress of the United States. A similar argument was presented to the court in *Kansas v. Colorado,* 206 U.S. 46 (1907), but held untenable. Mr. Justice Brewer, speaking for the court, disposed of it by saying:

> But the proposition that there are legislative powers affecting the nation as a whole, which belong to, although not expressed in, the grant of powers, is in direct conflict with the doctrine that this is a government of enumerated powers. That this is such a government clearly appears from the Constitution, independently of the amendment, for otherwise there would be an instrument granting certain specified things made operative to grant other and distinct things. This natural construction of the original body of the Constitution is made absolutely certain by the tenth amendment. This amendment, which was seemingly adopted with prescience of just such a contention as the present, disclosed the wide-spread fear that the national government might, under the pressure of a supposed general welfare, attempt to exercise powers which had not been granted. With equal determination the framers intended that no such assumption should ever find justification in the organic act, and that, if in the future further powers seemed necessary, they should be granted by the people in the manner they had provided for amending that act.* * * Its principal purpose was not the distribution of power between the United States and the states, but a reservation of the people of all powers not granted.

> This disposes of that contention.

Are migratory birds, when in a state on their usual migration, the property of the United States or of the states where they are found? If they are the property of the nation, the states would have no power to regulate, control, or prohibit the hunting or killing of them. But the rule of law which all the American courts have recognized is that animals feræ naturæ, denominated as game, are owned by the states, not as proprietors, but in their sovereign capacity as the representatives and for the benefit of all their people in common. This principle has not only been maintained by all the highest courts of the states in which the question has arisen, but has had the approval of the Supreme Court of the United States in every case which has come before it. *Martin v. Waddell,* 41 U.S. (16 Pet.) 367 (1842); *McCready v. Virginia,* 94 U.S. 391 (1876); *Smith v. Maryland,* 59 U.S. (18 How.) 71 (1855); *Manchester v. Massachusetts,* 139 U.S. 240 (1890); *Lawton v. Steele,* 152 U.S. 133 (1894); *Geer v. Connecticut,* 161 U.S. 519 (1896); *The Abby Dodge,* 223 U.S. 166 (1912).

. . .

Even after the game has been reduced to possession there is but a qualified ownership in it, subject to the control of the state. *Phelps v. Racey,* 60 N.Y. 10 (1875); *Commonwealth v. Savage,* 29 N.E. 468 (Mass. 1892); *Organ v. State,* 19 S.W. 840 (Ark.1892); *State v. Geer,* 22 A. 1012 (Conn.1891), *aff'd sub nom., Geer v. Connecticut,* 161 U.S. 519 (1896); *State v. Northern Pacific Express Co.,* 59 N.W. 1100 (Minn.1894); *State v. Rodman,* 59 N.W. 1098 (Minn.1894); *American Express Co. v. People,* 24 N.E. 758 (Ill.1890); *Ex parte Maier,* 37 P. 402 (Cal.1894); *People v. Collison,* 48 N.W. 292 (Mich.1891); *In re Deininger,* 108 F. 623 (D. Or. 1901).

The . . . Lacey Act, the constitutionality of which has been sustained, *Rupert v. United States,* 181 F. 87 (8th Cir.1910), in effect legalizes the statutes of the states for the control of wild game within their borders whether migratory or not, *People ex rel. Hill v. Hesterberg,* 76 N.E. 1032 (N.Y.1906). The claim that the migratory birds are the property of the United States must therefore be held untenable.

. . .

It may be, as contended on behalf of the government, that only by national legislation can migratory wild game and fish be preserved to the people, but that is not a matter for the courts. It is the people who alone can amend the Constitution to grant Congress the power to enact such legislation as they deem necessary. All the courts are authorized to do when the constitutionality of a legislative act is questioned is to determine whether Congress, under the Constitution as it is, possesses the power to enact the legislation in controversy; their power does not extend to the matter of expediency. If Congress has not the power, the duty of the court is to declare the act void. The court is unable to find any provision in the Constitution authorizing Congress, either expressly or by necessary implication, to protect or regulate the shooting of migratory wild game when in a state, and is therefore forced to the conclusion that the act is unconstitutional.

The demurrer to the indictment will be sustained.

On Motion for Rehearing

■ TRIEBER, D.J.:—. . . . It is claimed that the act is authorized by the commerce clause of the Constitution.

. . .

This same contention was made in *Geer v. Connecticut,* 161 U.S. 519 (1896), and was decided adversely. The court there said:

But the errors which this argument involves are manifest. It presupposes that, where the killing of game and its sale within the state is allowed, it thereby becomes commerce in the legal meaning of that word. In view of the authority of the state to affix conditions to the killing and sale of game, predicated as is this power on the peculiar nature of such property and its common ownership by all the citizens of the state, it may well be doubted whether commerce is created by an authority given by a state to reduce game within its borders to possession, provided such game be not taken, when killed, without the jurisdiction of the state. The common ownership imports the right to keep the property, if the sovereign so chooses, always within its jurisdiction for every purpose.* * * Passing, however, as we do, the decision of this question, and granting that the dealing in game killed within the state, under the provision in question, created internal state commerce, it does not follow that such internal commerce became necessarily the subject-matter of interstate commerce, and therefore under the control of the Constitution of the United States.

After quoting from *Gibbons v. Ogden,* 22 U.S. (9 Wheat.) 1 (1824), and *The Daniel Ball,* 77 U.S. (10 Wall.) 557 (1870), it proceeds: "The fact that internal commerce may be distinct from interstate commerce destroys the whole theory upon which the argument of the plaintiff in error proceeds."

The principle there established has never been questioned nor modified by any later decisions of that court. . . .

NOTES

(1) The federal government advanced three different theories to justify the statute: a "Tragedy of the Commons" rationale, the Property Clause, and (on motion for rehearing) the Commerce Clause.

The government's first argument—"where the state is clearly incompetent to save itself, the national government has the right to aid" [¶ 6]—was predicated upon the fact that migratory birds did not remain long within the jurisdiction of any state and thus there was little incentive for any state to restrict its hunters. Why did the court find this argument unpersuasive?

The court's dismissal of the Property Clause rationale was predicated upon the conclusion that the state "owned" wildlife and thus the federal government did not. What is the basis of the state's claim of ownership? Is the state's claim more convincing than the federal government's claim? How is the division of property and sovereignty—which were both held by the King—to be understood in a nation where political power is divided between national and local? Is it inconsistent to hold that states owned *resident* wildlife while the federal government owned *migratory* or transboundary wildlife?

Note that the court states that "[i]f they are the property of the nation, the states would have no power to regulate, control, or prohibit the hunting or killing of them." [¶ 8] This proposition reflects the then-current understanding that the federal and state spheres were mutually exclusive. When we examine the Property Clause below consider whether the exclusivity principle has ever been true in regard to the regulation of federal property.

(2) Weeks–McLean in the lower federal courts: The federal district court for Kansas also held the act unconstitutional. *United States v. McCullagh*, 221 F. 288 (D.Kan.1915). Two state courts reached the same result—from the opposite side of the issue. In each, defendants prosecuted for violating *state* game laws argued that state laws had been nullified by the federal statute; the state courts held that the federal statute was unconstitutional and the prosecution for violation of state law could proceed unimpeded. *See State v. McCullagh*, 153 P. 557 (Kan.1915); *State v. Sawyer*, 94 A. 886 (Me.1915). The statute was upheld in an unreported decision of the federal district court for South Dakota. Edward W. Bourne, *Comment, Treaty-making Power as Support for Federal Legislation*, 29 YALE L.J. 445, 445 n.2 (1920). *See also United States v. Selkirk*, 258 F. 775 (S.D.Tex.1919).

(3) Weeks–McLean in the Supreme Court: *Shauver* was appealed to the Supreme Court, where it was argued twice—the first time before a bench of only six justices. Following the ratification of the Migratory Bird Treaty and enactment of implementing legislation, the Court dismissed the appeal as moot at the suggestion of the Solicitor General. 248 U.S. 594 (1919). Subsequently and without discussing the constitutionality of the Act, the Supreme Court held that the Weeks–McLean Migratory Bird Act did not prevent a state from passing statutes prohibiting the shipping of wildlife by common carriers. *Carey v. South Dakota*, 250 U.S. 118 (1919).

Although the constitutionality of the Act was never decided by the Supreme Court, it is clear that it is constitutional under current Commerce Clause jurisprudence. This conclusion was implicitly reached in two decisions holding the subsequently enacted Migratory Bird Treaty Act constitutional under the Commerce Clause. *See Cochrane v. United States*, 92 F.2d 623 (7th Cir.1937), and *Cerritos Gun Club v. Hall*, 96 F.2d 620 (9th Cir.1938). In 1979, the Supreme Court also upheld the Treaty Act under the Commerce Clause. *Andrus v. Allard*, 444 U.S. 51 (1979).

(4) The Migratory Bird Treaty and the Migratory Bird Treaty Act: While *Shauver* was pending before the Supreme Court, the United States negotiated a treaty with Great Britain (acting for Canada) to protect migratory birds. Convention for the Protection of Migratory Birds, Aug. 16, 1916, United States–Great Britain, 39 Stat. 1702, T.S. No. 628. The 1916 Convention established three categories of migratory birds: migratory game birds, migratory insectivorous birds, and migratory nongame birds. *Id.*, art. I. The Convention established closed seasons on birds in each category. For migratory game birds, the closed season is between March 10 and September 1 with "the High Contracting Powers" further agreeing that the actual open season will be for no more than three and one-half months as each party "may severally deem appropriate and define by law or regulation." *Id.*, art. II, ¶ 1. For the final two categories, the closed season is year round. *Id.*, art. II, ¶¶ 2, 3. On the political background to the treaty, *see* KURKPA-TRICK DORSEY, THE DAWN OF CONSERVATION DIPLOMACY (1998).

Congress enacted implementing legislation on July 3, 1918. Migratory Bird Treaty Act, Act of July 3, 1918, ch. 128, 40 Stat. 755 (codified as amended at 16 U.S.C. §§ 703–711 (1988)). The MBTA provides in part:

> Sec. 2. That unless and except as permitted by regulations made as hereinafter provided, it shall be unlawful to hunt, take, capture, kill, attempt to take, capture or kill, possess, offer for sale, sell, offer to purchase, purchase, deliver for shipment, ship, cause to be shipped, deliver for transportation, transport, cause to be transported, carry or cause to be carried by any means whatever, receive for shipment, transportation or carriage, or export, at any time or in any manner, any migratory bird, included in the terms of the convention between the United States and Great Britain for the protection of migratory birds concluded August sixteenth, nineteen hundred and sixteen, or any part, nest, or egg of any such bird.

The constitutionality of the Act was quickly challenged and affirmed.[1] The first decision was by District Court Judge Trieber who distinguished his prior decision in *Shauver* on the ground that the Treaty Clause meant that the Tenth Amendment was simply inapplicable. *United States v. Thompson,* 258 F. 257 (E.D.Ark.1919). Other district courts reached the same conclusion. *See United States v. Rockefeller,* 260 F. 346 (D.Mont. 1919); *United States v. Samples,* 258 F. 479 (W.D.Mo.1919); *United States v. Selkirk,* 258 F. 775 (S.D.Tex.1919). One of the cases (consolidated in the district court as *United States v. Samples*) was appealed to the United States Supreme Court:

Missouri v. Holland

United States Supreme Court.
252 U.S. 416 (1920).

■ HOLMES, J.:—This is a bill in equity brought by the State of Missouri to prevent a game warden of the United States from attempting to enforce the Migratory Bird Treaty Act, [ ], and the regulations made by the Secretary of Agriculture in pursuance of the same. The ground of the bill is that the statute is an unconstitutional interference with the rights reserved to the States by the Tenth Amendment, and that the acts of the defendant done and threatened under that authority invade the sovereign right of the State and contravene its will manifested in statutes. The State also alleges a pecuniary interest, as owner of the wild birds within its borders and otherwise, admitted by the Government to be sufficient, but it is enough that the bill is a reasonable and proper means to assert the alleged quasi sovereign rights of a State. [ ] A motion to dismiss was sustained by the District Court on the ground that the Act of Congress is constitutional. *United States v. Samples,* 258 F. 479 (W.D.Mo.1919); *accord United States v. Thompson,* 258 F. 257 (E.D.Ark.1919); *United States v. Rockefeller,* 260 F. 346 (D.Mont.1919). The State appeals.

On December 8, 1916, a treaty between the United States and Great Britain was proclaimed by the President. It recited that many species of

---

1. We will examine the substance of the Act in Chapter 10.

birds in their annual migrations traversed many parts of the United States and of Canada, that they were of great value as a source of food and in destroying insects injurious to vegetation, but were in danger of extermination through lack of adequate protection. It therefore provided for specified closed seasons and protection in other forms, and agreed that the two powers would take or propose to their lawmaking bodies the necessary measures for carrying the treaty out. [ ] The above mentioned act of July 3, 1918, entitled an act to give effect to the convention, prohibited the killing, capturing or selling any of the migratory birds included in the terms of the treaty except as permitted by regulations compatible with those terms, to be made by the Secretary of Agriculture. Regulations were proclaimed on July 31, and October 25, 1918. [ ] It is unnecessary to go into any details, because, as we have said, the question raised is the general one whether the treaty and statute are void as an interference with the rights reserved to the States.

To answer this question it is not enough to refer to the Tenth Amendment, reserving the powers not delegated to the United States, because by Article II, § 2, the power to make treaties is delegated expressly, and by Article VI treaties made under the authority of the United States, along with the Constitution and laws of the United States made in pursuance thereof, are declared the supreme law of the land. If the treaty is valid there can be no dispute about the validity of the statute under Article I, § 8, as a necessary and proper means to execute the powers of the Government. The language of the Constitution as to the supremacy of treaties being general, the question before us is narrowed to an inquiry into the ground upon which the present supposed exception is placed.

It is said that a treaty cannot be valid if it infringes the Constitution, that there are limits, therefore, to the treaty-making power, and that one such limit is that what an act of Congress could not do unaided, in derogation of the powers reserved to the States, a treaty cannot do. An earlier act of Congress that attempted by itself and not in pursuance of a treaty to regulate the killing of migratory birds within the States had been held bad in the District Court. *United States v. Shauver*, 214 F. 154 (E.D.Ark.1914); *United States v. McCullagh*, 221 F. 288 (D.Kan.1915). Those decisions were supported by arguments that migratory birds were owned by the States in their sovereign capacity for the benefit of their people, and that under cases like *Geer v. Connecticut*, 161 U.S. 519 (1896), this control was one that Congress had no power to displace. The same argument is supposed to apply now with equal force.

Whether the two cases cited were decided rightly or not they cannot be accepted as a test of the treaty power. Acts of Congress are the supreme law of the land only when made in pursuance of the Constitution, while treaties are declared to be so when made under the authority of the United States. It is open to question whether the authority of the United States means more than the formal acts prescribed to make the convention. We do not mean to imply that there are no qualifications to the treaty-making power; but they must be ascertained in a different way. It is obvious that there may be matters of the sharpest exigency for the national well being that an act of Congress could not deal with but that a treaty followed by such an act could, and it is not lightly to be assumed that, in matters requiring national action, "a power which must belong to and somewhere reside in every civilized government" is not to be found. *Andrews v. Andrews,* 188 U.S. 14, 33 (1903). What was said in that case with regard to the powers of the States applies with equal force to the powers of the nation in cases where the States individually are incompetent to act. We are not yet discussing the particular case before us but only are considering the validity of the test proposed. With regard to that we may add that when we are dealing with words that also are a constituent act, like the Constitution of the United States, we must realize that they have called into life a being the development of which could not have been foreseen completely by the most gifted of its begetters. It was enough for them to realize or to hope that they had created an organism; it has taken a century and has cost their successors much sweat and blood to prove that they created a nation. The case before us must be considered in the light of out whole experience and not merely in that of what was said a hundred years ago. The treaty in question does not contravene any prohibitory words to be found in the Constitution. The only question is whether it is forbidden by some invisible radiation from the general terms of the Tenth Amendment. We must consider what this country has become in deciding what that amendment has reserved.

The State as we have intimated founds its claim of exclusive authority upon an assertion of title to migratory birds, an assertion that is embodied in statute. No doubt it is true that as between a State and its inhabitants the State may regulate the killing and sale of such birds, but it does not follow that its authority is exclusive of paramount powers. To put the claim of the State upon title is to lean upon a slender reed. Wild birds are not in the possession of anyone; and possession is the beginning of ownership. The whole foundation of the State's rights is the presence within their jurisdiction of birds that yesterday had not arrived, tomorrow may be in another State and in a week a thousand miles away. If we are to be accurate we cannot put the case of the State upon higher ground than that the treaty deals with creatures that for the moment are within the state borders, that it must be carried out by officers of the United States within the same territory, and that but for the treaty the State would be free to regulate this subject itself.

As most of the laws of the United States are carried out within the States and as many of them deal with matters which in the silence of such laws the State might regulate, such general grounds are not enough to support Missouri's claim. Valid treaties of course "are as binding within the territorial limits of the States as they are elsewhere throughout the dominion of the United States." *Baldwin v. Franks,* 120 U.S. 678, 683 (1887). No doubt the great body of private relations usually fall within the control of the State, but a treaty may override its power. We do not have to invoke the later developments of constitutional law for this proposition; it was recognized as early as *Hopkirk v. Bell,* 7 U.S. (3 Cranch) 454 (1806), with regard to statutes of limitation, and even earlier, as to confiscation, in *Ware v. Hylton,* 3 U.S. (3 Dall.) 199 (1796). It was assumed by Chief Justice Marshall with regard to the escheat of land to the State in *Chirac v. Chirac,* 15 U.S. (2 Wheat.) 259, 275 (1817). [ ] Further illustration seems unnecessary, and it only remains to consider the application of established rules to the present case.

Here a national interest of very nearly the first magnitude is involved. It can be protected only by national action in concert with that of another power. The subject matter is only transitorily within the State and has no permanent habitat therein. But for the treaty and the statute there soon might be no birds for any powers to deal with. We see nothing in the Constitution that compels the Government to sit by while a food supply is cut off and the protectors of our forests and our crops are destroyed. It is not sufficient to rely upon the States. The reliance is vain, and were it otherwise, the question is whether the United States is forbidden to act. We are of opinion that the treaty and statute must be upheld. [ ]

> *Decree affirmed.*

■ VAN DEVANTER and PITNEY dissent [without opinion].

NOTES

(1) Holmes' opinion initially seems concise and straightforward: he simply explores the possible tests for the constitutional validity of treaties, concludes that they must involve matters of national interest and must not contravene any specific constitutional prohibition, and then applies these standards to the treaty before the Court. The conciseness of the opinion should not, however, obscure its complexity.

Why is the Tenth Amendment, which figured so prominently in *United States v. Shauver*, irrelevant? The Court repeatedly decided during this period—in *Geer, Ward v. Race Horse,* 163 U.S. 504, 510 (1896) ("the complete power to regulate the killing of game within its borders" is "a necessary incident of [state] authority"), *The Vessel "Abby Dodge" v. United States,* 223 U.S. 166 (1912) (unconstitutionality of federal statute regulating sponge harvest within state waters "obvious"), *Patsone v. Pennsylvania,* 232 U.S. 138, 143 (1914), and *New York ex rel. Kennedy v. Becker,* 241 U.S. 556, 562 (1916) ("It is not to be doubted that the power to preserve fish and game within its borders is inherent in the sovereignty of the state")—states own wildlife within their borders. Why is this property interest not protected by the Tenth Amendment?

If the Tenth Amendment provides no limit, what are the limitations on the power of the United States to enter into treaties?

Could a treaty authorize the federal government to do something contrary to the text of the Constitution? For example, could Congress rely upon a treaty to seize physical possession of real property without paying compensation? Are birds the property of the state? Although the decision in *Missouri v. Holland* is aphoristic and suggestive rather than definitive on such questions, Holmes does state, "The treaty in question does not contravene any prohibitory words to be found in the Constitution." [¶ 5] In *Geofroy v. Riggs,* the Supreme Court offered the following *dicta* description of the power thus conferred:

> The treaty power, as expressed in the Constitution, is in terms unlimited except by those restraints which are found in that instrument

against the action of the government or of its departments, and those arising from the nature of the government itself and of that of the States. It would not be contended that it extends so far as to authorize what the Constitution forbids, or a change in the character of the government or in that of one of the States, or a cession of any portion of the territory of the latter, without its consent. [ ] But with these exceptions, it is not perceived that there is any limit to the questions which can be adjusted touching any matter which is properly the subject of negotiations with a foreign country.

De Geofroy v. Riggs, 133 U.S. 258 (1890) (Field, J.). In short, according to Justice Field, the treaty power is subject to the constitutional limitations that apply to *all* exercise of federal power—a position ultimately adopted in a case decided nearly forty years after *Missouri v. Holland:*

> no agreement with a foreign nation can confer power on Congress, or on any other branch of Government, which is free from the restraints of the Constitution.
>
> ... The prohibitions of the Constitution were designed to apply to all branches of the National Government and they cannot be nullified by the Executive or by the Executive and the Senate combined.

Reid v. Covert, 354 U.S. 1 (1957).

(2) The Treaty Clause and the Commerce Clause: Did the Supreme Court's subsequent, more expansive interpretation of Congress's power under the Commerce Clause deprive *Missouri v. Holland* of its significance? That is, given that the Weeks–McLean Migratory Bird Act would now be constitutional, is the treaty power moot? Keep this question in mind when reading the following materials on the more recent shifts in the Court's federalism decisions.

(3) The treaty-making power and Indian tribes: Although the effect of treaties with Indian tribes is examined in detail in Chapter 7, you should note that the power to make treaties with Indian tribes is constitutionally coextensive with the power to make treaties with foreign nations. *E.g., Holden v. Joy*, 84 U.S. (17 Wall.) 211, 242 (1872); *Worcester v. Georgia*, 31 U.S. (6 Pet.) 515, 558 (1832).

b.   THE AFFIRMATIVE COMMERCE CLAUSE: WHEN CONGRESS ACTS

> The Congress shall have Power ... To regulate Commerce with foreign Nations, and among the several States, and with the Indian Tribes.
>
> UNITED STATES CONSTITUTION art. 1, § 8, cl. 3.

Douglas v. Seacoast Products, Inc.

United States Supreme Court.
431 U.S. 265 (1977).

■ MARSHALL, J.:—The issue in this case is the validity of two Virginia statutes that limit the right of nonresidents and aliens to catch fish in the territorial waters of the Commonwealth.

I

[Persons or corporations wishing to fish commercially in Virginia must obtain licenses. Section 60 of the applicable statute governs licensing of nonresidents of Virginia to fish for menhaden. The section prohibits nonresidents from catching menhaden in the Virginia portion of Chesapeake Bay. A second section, § 81.1, limits licenses to United States citizens. Seacoast Products, Inc., is one of three companies that dominate the menhaden industry. The other two firms, unlike Seacoast, have fish-processing plants in Virginia and are owned by American citizens. In 1973, the family of Seacoast's founder sold the business to Hanson Trust, Ltd., a United Kingdom company. Seacoast continued its operations unchanged after the sale. All of its officers, directors, boat captains and crews are American citizens, as are over 95% of its plant employees.]

At the time of its sale, Seacoast's fishing vessels were enrolled and licensed American-flag ships. [ ] Under 46 U.S.C. §§ 808, 835, the transfer of these vessels to a foreign-controlled corporation required the approval of the Department of Commerce. This was granted unconditionally over the opposition of Seacoast's competitors after a full public hearing that considered the effect of the transfer on fish conservation and management, on American workers and consumers, and on competition and other social and economic concerns. [ ] Following this approval, appellees' fishing vessels were re-enrolled and relicensed pursuant to 46 U.S.C. §§ 251–252, 263. They remain subject to all United States laws governing maritime commerce.

[Because of its foreign ownership and because it did not operate processing plants in Virginia, Seacoast was barred by state law from fishing in Virginia waters.] Appellees accordingly filed a complaint in the District Court for the Eastern District of Virginia, seeking to have §§ 60 and 81.1 declared unconstitutional and their enforcement enjoined. A three-judge court was convened and it struck down both statutes. It held that the citizenship requirement of § 81.1 was pre-empted by the Bartlett Act, 16 U.S.C. § 1081 *et seq.*, and that the residency restriction of § 60 violated the Equal Protection Clause of the Fourteenth Amendment. We noted probable jurisdiction of the Commissioner's appeal, [ ], and we affirm.

II

Seacoast advances a number of theories to support affirmance of the judgment below. [ ] Among these is the claim that the Virginia statutes are pre-empted by federal enrollment and licensing laws for fishing vessels. The United States has filed a brief as *amicus curiae* supporting this contention. Although the claim is basically constitutional in nature, deriving its force from the operation of the Supremacy Clause, Art. VI, cl. 2, it is treated as "statutory" for purposes of our practice of deciding statutory claims first to avoid unnecessary constitutional adjudications. [ ] Since we decide the case on this ground, we do not reach the constitutional issues raised by the parties.

The well-known principles of pre-emption have been rehearsed only recently in our decisions. [ ] No purpose would be served by repeating them here. It is enough to note that we deal in this case with federal legislation arguably superseding state law in a "field which . . . has been traditionally occupied by the States." *Jones v. Rath Packing Co.,* 430 U.S. 519 (1977). Preemption accordingly will be found only if " 'that was the clear and manifest purpose of Congress.' *Rice v. Santa Fe Elevator Corp.,* 331 U.S. 218, 230 (1947)." We turn our focus, then, to the congressional intent embodied in the enrollment and licensing laws.

A

The basic form for the comprehensive federal regulation of trading and fishing vessels was established in the earliest days of the Nation and has changed little since. [The Court traced the history of federal registration and licensing of vessels from a statute enacted in the First Congress in 1789.] Appellees' vessels were granted licenses for the "mackerel fishery"[10] after their transfer was approved by the Department of Commerce.

. . .

B

Deciphering the intent of Congress is often a difficult task, and to do so with a law the vintage of the Enrollment and Licensing Act verges on the impossible. There is virtually no surviving legislative history for the act. What we do have, however, is the historic decision of Mr. Chief Justice John Marshall in *Gibbons v. Ogden,* 22 U.S. (9 Wheat.) 1 (1824), rendered only three decades after passage of the Act. *Gibbons* invalidated a discriminatory state regulation of shipping as applied to vessels federally licensed to engage in the coasting trade. Although its historic importance lies in its general discussion of the commerce power, *Gibbons* also provides substantial illumination on the narrower question of the intended meaning of the Licensing Act.

The case challenged a New York law intended to encourage development of steamboats by granting Robert Fulton and Robert Livingston the exclusive right to operate steam-powered vessels in all of the State's territorial waters. The right to navigate steamboats between Elizabethtown Point, N.J., and New York City was, by assignment from Fulton and Livingston, granted to Aaron Ogden. Thomas Gibbons began operating two passenger ferries in violation of Ogden's submonopoly. Gibbons' steamboats had been enrolled and granted "license . . . to be employed in carrying on the coasting trade" under the Enrollment and Licensing Act. [ ]

Ogden nevertheless obtained an injunction from the New York courts enforcing the monopoly by restraining Gibbons from running his ferries in New York waters. Chancellor James Kent rejected Gibbons' pre-emption claim based upon his federal licenses. Kent found that the sole purpose of the license was to "giv[e] to the vessel an *American* character," *i.e.,* to

---

10. The quaint categories of the statute have remained unchanged since the "mackerel fishery" was added by the Act of May 24, 1828, [ ]. They seem to correspond to the only three types of sea creatures sought by organized fishing fleets at that time. [ ]

A license for the "mackerel fishery" entitles the holder to catch "cod or fish of any other description whatever." Act of Apr. 20, 1836, [ ].

establish its nationality as an American-flag ship. This would have reduced various duties and taxes assessed under federal law, but in Kent's view, it did not oust the power of the State to regulate the use of chattels within its borders. [ ] The highest state court affirmed, ruling that "the only effect" of the license was "to determine [the vessel's] national character, and the rate of duties which she is to pay." [ ]

On appeal to this Court, Mr. Chief Justice Marshall held that the rights granted to Gibbons by federal law superseded the conflicting state-created rights asserted by Ogden. Marshall first considered the power of Congress under the Commerce Clause. He concluded that "[c]ommerce among the States, cannot stop at the external boundary line of each State, but may be introduced into the interior," [ ], and that "[t]he power of Congress . . . , whatever it may be, must be exercised within the territorial jurisdiction of the several States." [ ] The Court next defined the nature of the commerce power: "the power to regulate; that is, to prescribe the rule by which commerce is to be governed." [ ] Ogden's claim that the States may exercise concurrent power over commerce, or even exercise their police powers, where that exercise conflicts with express federal law was rejected. [ ]

The Court then turned to the question whether "the laws of New–York" did "come into collision with an act of Congress" so that "the acts of New–York must yield to the law of Congress." [ ] Mr. Chief Justice Marshall found the conflict unquestionable: "To the Court it seems very clear, that the whole act on the subject of the coasting trade, according to those principles which govern the construction of statutes, implies, un-equivocally, an authority to licensed vessels to carry on the coasting trade." [ ] The license granted to Gibbons under the Act "must be understood to be what it purports to be, a legislative authority to [Gibbons'] steamboat . . . 'to be employed in carrying on the coasting trade, for one year from this date.'" [ ] The Court rejected Ogden's argument and the holding of the New York courts that the license "gives no right to trade; and that its sole purpose is to confer the American character." [ ] Finally, the Court decided that the statutory phrase "coasting trade" encompassed the carriage of passengers for hire as well as the transport of goods. [ ]

Although *Gibbons* is written in broad language which might suggest that the sweep of the Enrollment and Licensing Act ousts all state regulatory power over federally licensed vessels, neither the facts before the Court nor later interpretations extended that far. *Gibbons* did not involve an absolute ban on steamboats in New York waters. Rather, the monopoly law allowed some steam vessels to ply their trade while excluding others that were federally licensed. The case struck down this discriminatory treatment. Subsequent decisions spelled out the negative implication of *Gibbons*: that States may impose upon federal licensees reasonable, nondiscriminatory conservation and environmental protection measures otherwise within their police power.

For example, in *Smith v. Maryland,* 59 U.S. (18 How.) 71 (1855), the Court upheld a conservation law which limited the fishing implements that could be used by a federally licensed vessel to take oysters from state waters. The Court held that an "enrollment and license confer no immunity from the operation of valid laws of a State," [ ], and that the law was valid because the State "may forbid all such acts as would render the public right [of fishery] less valuable, or destroy it altogether," [ ]. At the same time, the Court explicitly reserved the question of the validity of a statute discriminating against nonresidents. [ ] To the same effect is the holding in *Manchester v. Massachusetts,* 139 U.S. 240 (1891). There, state law prohibited the use by any person of certain types of fishing tackle in specified areas. Though Manchester was a Rhode Island resident basing a claim on his federal fisheries license, the Court held that the statute

> was evidently passed for the preservation of the fish, and makes no discrimination in favor of citizens of Massachusetts and against citizens of other States.... [T]he statute may well be considered as an impartial and reasonable regulation ... and the subject is one which a State may well be permitted to regulate within its territory, in the absence of any regulation by the United States. The preservation of fish ... is for the common benefit; and we are of opinion that the statute is not repugnant to the Constitution and the laws of the United States.

[ ]

. . .

Although it is true that the Court's view in Gibbons of the intent of the Second Congress in passing the Enrollment and Licensing Act is considered incorrect by commentators, its provisions have been repeatedly re-enacted in substantially the same form. We can safely assume that Congress was aware of the holding, as well as the criticism, of a case so renowned as *Gibbons.* We have no doubt that Congress has ratified the statutory interpretation of *Gibbons* and its progeny. [ ] We consider, then, its impact on the Virginia statutes challenged in this case.

C

The federal licenses granted to Seacoast are, as noted above, identical in pertinent part to Gibbons' licenses except that they cover the "mackerel fishery" rather than the "coasting trade." Appellant [state] contends that because of the difference this case is distinguishable from *Gibbons.* He argues that *Gibbons* upheld only the right of the federal licensee, as an American-flag vessel, to navigate freely in state territorial waters. He urges that Congress could not have intended to grant an additional right to take fish from the waters of an unconsenting State. Appellant points out that the challenged statutes in no way interfere with the navigation of Seacoast's fishing boats. They are free to cross the State's waters in search of fish in jurisdictions where they may lawfully catch them, and they may transport fish through the State's waters with equal impunity.

Appellant's reading of *Gibbons* is too narrow. *Gibbons* emphatically rejects the argument that the license merely establishes the nationality of the vessel. That function is performed by the enrollment. [ ] Rather, the license "implies, unequivocally, an authority to licensed vessels to carry on" the activity for which they are licensed. [ ] In *Gibbons,* the "authority ... to carry on" the licensed activity included not only the right to navigate in, or to travel across, state waters, but also the right to land passengers in New York and thereby provide an economically valuable service. The right to perform that additional act of landing cargo in the State which gave the license its real value was part of the grant of the right to engage in the "coasting trade." [ ]

The same analysis applies to a license to engage in the mackerel fishery. Concededly, it implies a grant of the right to navigate in state waters. But, like the trading license, it must give something more. It must grant "authority ... to carry on" the "mackerel *fishery*." And just as *Gibbons* and its progeny found a grant of the right to trade in a State without discrimination, we conclude that appellees have been granted the right to fish in Virginia waters on the same terms as Virginia residents.

. . .

Finally, our interpretation of the license is reaffirmed by the specific discussion in *Gibbons* of the section granting the license, [ ]. The Court pointed out that "a license to do any particular thing, is a permission or authority to do that thing; and if granted by a person having power to grant it, transfers to the grantee the right to do whatever it purports to authorize. It certainly transfers to him all the right which the grantor can transfer, to do what is within the terms of the license." [ ] *Gibbons* recognized that the "grantor" was Congress. [ ] Thus *Gibbons* expressly holds that the words used by Congress in the vessel license transfer to the licensee "all the right" which Congress has the power to convey. While appellant may be correct in arguing that at earlier times in our history there was some doubt whether Congress had power under the Commerce Clause to regulate the taking of fish in state waters,[16] there can be no question today that such power exists where there is some effect on interstate commerce. *Perez v. United States,* 402 U.S. 146 (1971); *Heart of Atlanta Motel v. United States,* 379 U.S. 241 (1964); *Wickard v. Filburn,* 317 U.S. 111 (1942). The movement of vessels from one State to another in search of fish, and back again to processing plants, is certainly activity which Congress could conclude affects interstate commerce. *Cf. Toomer v. Witsell,* 334 U.S. 385, 403–406 (1948). Accordingly, we hold that, at the least, when Congress re-enacted the license form in 1936, using language which, according to *Gibbons,* gave licensees "all the right which the grantor can transfer," it necessarily extended the license to cover the taking of fish in state waters, subject to valid state conservation regulations.[19]

---

16. *See, e.g., McCready v. Virginia,* 94 U.S. 391, 395 (1877) ("There has been ... no ... grant of power over the fisheries [to the United States]. These remain under the exclusive control of the State ... "); *Manchester v. Massachusetts,* 139 U.S. 240, 258–260 (1891); *Geer v. Connecticut,* 161 U.S. 519 (1896); 17 CONG. REC. 4734 (1886) (conservation amendment to fisheries license, Act of Feb. 28, 1887, c. 288, 24 Stat. 435, ... , believed not to apply to state territorial waters).

19. Indeed, an amendment to the license form made at the time of the 1936 re-enactment specifically authorizes "the taking of fish." Acting to reverse a Circuit Court of Appeals decision, *The Pueblos,* 77 F.2d 618 (2d Cir.1935), Congress authorized issuance of licenses for the "coasting trade and mackerel fishery." The amendment explains that vessels so documented "shall be deemed to have sufficient license for engaging in the coasting trade and the taking of fish of every description, including shellfish." 49 Stat.

D

Application of the foregoing principles to the present case is straight-forward. Section 60 prohibits federally licensed vessels owned by nonresidents of Virginia from fishing in the Chesapeake Bay. Licensed ships owned by noncitizens are prevented by § 81.1 from catching fish anywhere in the Commonwealth. On the other hand, Virginia residents are permitted to fish commercially for menhaden subject only to seasonal and other conservation restrictions not at issue here. The challenged statutes thus deny appellees their federally granted right to engage in fishing activities on the same terms as Virginia residents. They violate the "indisputable" precept that "no State may completely exclude federally licensed commerce." *Florida Lime & Avocado Growers, Inc. v. Paul,* 373 U.S. 132, 142 (1963). They must fall under the Supremacy Clause.

[The state argued that it had title to the submerged lands pursuant to the Submerged Lands Act, 43 U.S. §§ 1301–1315. The Court noted that, pursuant to the Act, Congress had made the grant "expressly" conditioned upon the retention by the United States of "all constitutional powers of regulation and control" over the lands and waters ceded to the states "for purposes of commerce, navigation, national defense, and international affairs."]

In any event, "[t]o put the claim of the State upon title is," in Mr. Justice Holmes' words, "to lean upon a slender reed." *Missouri v. Holland,* 252 U.S. 416, 434 (1920). A State does not stand in the same position as the owner of a private game preserve and it is pure fantasy to talk of "owning" wild fish, birds, or animals. Neither the States nor the Federal Government, any more than a hopeful fisherman or hunter, has title to these creatures until they are reduced to possession by skillful capture. *Ibid.; Geer v. Connecticut,* 161 U.S. 519, 539–540 (1896) (Field, J., dissenting). The "ownership" language of cases such as those cited by appellant must be understood as no more than a 19th-century legal fiction expressing "the importance to its people that a State have power to preserve and regulate the exploitation of an important resource." *Toomer v. Witsell,* 334 U.S., at 402; *see also Takahashi v. Fish & Game Commission,* 334 U.S. 410, 420–421 (1948). Under modern analysis, the question is simply whether the State has exercised its police power in conformity with the federal laws and Constitution. As we have demonstrated above, Virginia has failed to do so here.

III

Our decision is very much in keeping with sound policy considerations of federalism. The business of commercial fishing must be conducted by peripatetic entrepreneurs moving, like their quarry, without regard for state boundary lines. Menhaden that spawn in the open ocean or in coastal waters of a Southern State may swim into Chesapeake Bay and live there for their first summer, migrate south for the following winter, and appear off the shores of New York or Massachusetts in succeeding years. A number

1368, 46 U.S.C. § 263. *See also* S. REP. No. 83, 24th Cong., 1st Sess. (1836), describing the modification in the Enrollment and Licensing Act, [ ], as intended "to enable those engaged in the mackerel fishery to take other fish without incurring a penalty."

of coastal States have discriminatory fisheries laws, and with all natural resources becoming increasingly scarce and more valuable, more such restrictions would be a likely prospect, as both protective and retaliatory measures. Each State's fishermen eventually might be effectively limited to working in the territorial waters of their residence, or in the federally controlled fishery beyond the three-mile limit. Such proliferation of residency requirements for commercial fishermen would create precisely the sort of Balkanization of interstate commercial activity that the Constitution was intended to prevent. [ ] We cannot find that Congress intended to allow any such result given the well-known construction of federal vessel licenses in *Gibbons*.

For these reasons, we conclude that §§ 60 and 81.1 are preempted by the federal Enrollment and Licensing Act. Insofar as these state laws subject federally licensed vessels owned by nonresidents or aliens to restrictions different from those applicable to Virginia residents and American citizens, they must fall under the Supremacy Clause. As we have noted above, however, reasonable and evenhanded conservation measures, so essential to the preservation of our vital marine sources of food supply, stand unaffected by our decision.

The judgment of the District Court is

Affirmed.

■ REHNQUIST, J., with whom POWELL, J. joins, concurring in the judgment and concurring in part and dissenting in part:—I concur in the judgment of the Court and join in all but Parts II–D, and III of its opinion. As the Court states, it appears that licenses issued to appellees' ships under the federal licensing statute, [ ], confer upon their grantees an affirmative right to engage in fishing activities in the coastal waters of the United States on the same terms as any other fishermen. I also agree that the federal statute pre-empts similar state licensing legislation which would allow some to engage in the fishery while absolutely excluding any federal licensees. This, I believe, is as much as need be said to decide the case before us. Rather than stopping there, however, the Court embroiders upon this holding a patchwork of broader language whose purpose is almost as uncertain as its long-run effect.

The Court's treatment of the States' interests in their coastal fisheries appears to me to cut a somewhat broader swath than is justifiable in this context. True enough, the States do not "own" free-swimming creatures within their territorial limits in any conventional sense of that term *Missouri v. Holland,* 252 U.S. 416, 434 (1920); *Pierson v. Post,* 3 Cai. 175 (N.Y.1805). It is therefore no answer to an assertion of federal pre-emptive power that such action amounts to an unconstitutional appropriation of state property. But it is also clear that the States have a substantial proprietary interest sometimes described as "common ownership," *Geer v. Connecticut,* 161 U.S. 519, 529 (1896), in the fish and game within their boundaries. This is worthy of mention not because it is inconsistent with anything contained in the Court's opinion, but because I am not sure that the States' substantial regulatory interests are given adequate shift by a single sentence casting the issue of state regulation as "simply whether the State has exercised its police power in conformity with the federal laws and

Constitution." [ ] The precedents of this Court, none of which are disputed today, have upheld a variety of regulations designed to conserve and maintain the collective natural resources of the State. *Huron Portland Cement Co. v. Detroit,* 362 U.S. 440 (1960); *Patsone v. Pennsylvania,* 232 U.S. 138 (1914); *Geer v. Connecticut,* 161 U.S. 519 (1896); *Manchester v. Massachusetts,* 139 U.S. 240 (1891); *McCready v. Virginia,* 94 U.S. 391 (1877); *Smith v. Maryland,* 59 U.S. (18 How.) 71 (1855); *see Takahashi v. Fish & Game Commission,* 334 U.S. 410, 420–421 (1948). The exact bases for these decisions vary, but the cases are consistent in recognizing that the retained interests of States in such common resources as fish and game are of substantial legal moment, whether or not they rise to the level of a traditional property right. The range of regulations which a State may invoke under these circumstances is extremely broad. Neither mere displeasure with the asymmetry of the pattern of state regulation, nor a sensed tension with a federal statute will suffice to override a state enactment affecting exploitation of such a resource. Barring constitutional infirmities, only a direct conflict with the operation of federal law such as exists here will bar the state regulatory action. [ ] This is true no matter how "peripatetic" the objects of the regulation or however "Balkanized" the resulting pattern of commercial activity. [ ]

. . .

NOTES

(1) What is the justification for the Court's decision that Congress intended to preclude state regulation that discriminates between residents and nonresidents? Does the fact that Congress can overrule the Court on matters of statutory construction justify a more policy-based decisionmaking style? Note that the policy concerns cited by the Court are similar to those that underlie the dormant Commerce Clause—an antipathy towards discrimination against nonresidents (who will lack political means of redressing grievances) and a fear that such discrimination will lead to economic Balkanization as other states respond with similar protective legislation.

Why might the majority have ignored Justice Rehnquist's spirited defense of the state ownership doctrine? Might the doctrine carry more weight in a dormant Commerce Clause case than in an affirmative Commerce Clause case such as *Douglas*?

(2) Preemption: The Supreme Court typically divides its preemption analysis into three general categories:

(a) express preemption where Congress has explicitly stated its intent to preclude state regulation in a given area.

(b) implied preemption where the structure or objectives of the congressional enactment are such that Congress has impliedly precluded all state regulation of the area.

(c) conflict preemption where the Congress did not intend to preempt all state regulation, but where the particular state law conflicts with the federal statute.

A concise statement of preemption law is found in *Pacific Gas &
Electric Co. v. State Energy Resources Conservation & Development Commission*, 461 U.S. 190 (1983):

> It is well-established that within Constitutional limits Congress may
> preempt state authority by so stating in express terms. *Jones v. Rath
> Packing Co.*, 430 U.S. 519, 525 (1977). Absent explicit preemptive
> language, Congress' intent to supersede state law altogether may be
> found from a "scheme of federal regulation so pervasive as to make
> reasonable the inference that Congress left no room to supplement it,"
> "because the Act of Congress may touch a field in which the federal
> interest is so dominant that the federal system will be assumed to
> preclude enforcement of state laws on the same subject," or because
> "the object sought to be obtained by the federal law and the character
> of obligations imposed by it may reveal the same purpose." *Fidelity
> Federal Savings & Loan Ass'n v. de la Cuesta*,——U.S.——,——(1982);
> *Rice v. Santa Fe Elevator Corp.*, 331 U.S. 218, 230 (1947). Even where
> Congress has not entirely displaced state regulation in a specific area,
> state law is preempted to the extent that it actually conflicts with
> federal law. Such a conflict arises when "compliance with both federal
> and state regulations is a physical impossibility," *Florida Lime &
> Avocado Growers, Inc. v. Paul*, 373 U.S. 132, 142–143 (1963), or where
> state law "stands as an obstacle to the accomplishment and execution
> of the full purposes and objectives of Congress." *Hines v. Davidowitz*,
> 312 U.S. 52, 67 (1941).

**(3) Why there have been no big affirmative Commerce Clause
cases in wildlife law:** The history of federal regulation of wildlife has
occurred in a manner that largely obviated the affirmative Commerce
Clause as a source of constitutional dispute. Following the district decisions
holding the Weeks–McLean Migratory Bird Act to be unconstitutional, the
active Commerce Clause has figured only peripherally in wildlife law.

In 1918, Congress enacted the Migratory Bird Treaty Act (MBTA)—
which was a significant expansion of federal authority. But, as its title
attests, that statute was predicated upon the Treaty Clause.

Between the enactment of the MBTA and the mid-1960s, Congress did
little in regard to wildlife that challenged state preeminence: it established
grants-in-aid programs to assist state agencies in acquiring wildlife habitat,
e.g., Pittman–Robertson Act of 1937, 16 U.S.C. §§ 669–669i (1988); Dingell–Johnson Act of 1950, 16 U.S.C. §§ 777–777*l* (1988); created a federal
program for the acquisition of wildlife refuges, Migratory Bird Conservation Act of 1929, 16 U.S.C. §§ 715a–715r (1988); Migratory Bird Hunting
Stamp Act of 1934, 16 U.S.C. §§ 718–718j (1988); imposed minimal and
generally ignored habitat planning requirements on federal water projects,
Fish & Wildlife Coordination Act of 1934, 16 U.S.C. §§ 661–667e (1988);
and enacted a statute protecting the national symbol, the Bald Eagle, Bald
Eagle Protection Act of 1940, 16 U.S.C. §§ 668–668d (1988).

By the time that Congress again became actively involved in wildlife
conservation, the scope of the active Commerce Clause had apparently been
resolved in favor of broad federal power. The Court's recent turn to the
belief that the political process is not sufficiently solicitous of state inter-

ests may be a harbinger of changes to come—as the isolated wetlands case at the end of this section suggests.

National Association of Home Builders v. Babbitt

District of Columbia Circuit Court of Appeals.
130 F.3d 1041 (1997).
certiorari denied, 524 U.S. 937 (1998).

■ WALD, J.—The National Association of Home Builders of the United States, the Building Industry Legal Defense Fund, the County of San Bernardino, and the City of Colton, California brought this action in the United States District Court for the District of Columbia to challenge an application of section 9(a)(1) of the Endangered Species Act ("ESA"), 16 U.S.C. § 1538(a)(1), which makes it unlawful for any person to "take"—*i.e.,* "to harass, harm, pursue, hunt, shoot, wound, kill, trap, capture, or collect, or attempt to engage in any such conduct," 16 U.S.C. § 1532(19)—any endangered species. The plaintiffs sought a declaration that the application of section 9 of the ESA to the Delhi Sands Flower–Loving Fly ("the Fly"), which is located only in California, exceeds Congress' Commerce Clause power and an injunction against application of the section to the plaintiff's construction activities in areas containing Fly habitat.

[The Delhi Sands Flower–Loving Fly was listed by the Fish and Wildlife Service ("FWS") as an endangered species. The Fly's habitat is located entirely within an eight mile radius in southwestern San Bernardino County and northwestern Riverside County, California. Listing the Fly forced San Bernardino County to alter plans to construct a new hospital on a site that contained Fly habitat. The FWS and the County] agreed on a plan that would allow the County to build the hospital and a power plant in the area designated as Fly habitat in return for modification of the construction plans and purchase and set aside of nearby land as Fly habitat. In November 1995, FWS issued a permit to allow construction of the power plant. During the same month, however, the County notified the FWS that it planned to redesign a nearby intersection to improve emergency vehicle access to the hospital. The FWS informed the County that expansion of the intersection as planned would likely lead to a "taking" of the Fly in violation of ESA section 9(a). After brief unsuccessful negotiations between the County and FWS, the County filed suit in district court challenging the application of section 9(a)(1) to the Fly.

[The district court granted summary judgment to the government. The court of appeals affirmed.]

I. FACTUAL AND PROCEDURAL BACKGROUND

The Delhi Sands Flower–Loving Fly, which lives only in the "Delhi series" soils found in southwestern San Bernardino County and northwestern Riverside County, California, is the only remaining subspecies of its species. The other subspecies, the El Segundo Flower–Loving Fly, is believed to be extinct due to destruction of its habitat through urban development. [ ] The Fly is also one of only a few North American species in the "mydas flies" family and one of only a few species in that family that visit flowers in search of nectar, thereby pollinating native plant species. [ ]

Over 97 percent of the historic habitat of the Fly has been eliminated, and, prior to its listing as endangered, its remaining habitat was threatened by urban development, unauthorized trash dumping, and off-road vehicle use. [ ] There are currently 11 known populations of the Fly, all of which occur within an eight mile radius of one another. [ ] The size of the entire population of Flies was recently estimated in the low hundreds. [ ]

[In 1990, FWS was petitioned to list the species as endangered. Following a two-year investigation, the agency determined that the Fly is "in imminent danger of extinction due to extensive habitat loss and degradation that has reduced its range by 97 percent" and added it to the endangered species list.]

II. DISCUSSION

Appellants challenge the application of section 9(a)(1) of the ESA, which makes it unlawful for any person to "take any [endangered or threatened] species within the United States or the territorial sea of the United States," 16 U.S.C. § 1538(a)(1), to the Delhi Sands Flower–Loving Fly. *See also Babbitt v. Sweet Home Chapter of Communities for a Great Oregon*, 515 U.S. 687 (1995) (upholding agency's interpretation of the term "take" to include significant habitat degradation). Appellants argue that the federal government does not have the authority to regulate the use of non-federal lands in order to protect the Fly, which is found only within a single state. Indeed, they claim that "the Constitution of the United States does not grant the federal government the authority to regulate wildlife, nor does it authorize federal regulation of nonfederal lands." [ ]

. . .

Appellants' Commerce Clause challenge to the application of section 9(a)(1) of the ESA to the Fly rests on the Supreme Court's decision in *United States v. Lopez*, 514 U.S. 549 (1995). In *Lopez*, the Court held that the Gun–Free School Zones Act of 1990, 18 U.S.C. § 922(q), which made possession of a gun within a school zone a federal offense, exceeded Congress' Commerce Clause authority. Drawing on its earlier Commerce Clause jurisprudence, *see especially Perez v. United States*, 402 U.S. 146, 150 (1971), the *Lopez* Court explained that Congress could regulate three broad categories of activity: (1) "the use of the channels of interstate commerce," (2) "the instrumentalities of interstate commerce, or persons or things in interstate commerce, even though the threat may come only from intrastate activities," and (3) "those activities having a substantial relation to interstate commerce * * *, *i.e.*, those activities that substantially affect interstate commerce." *Lopez*, 514 U.S. at 558–59. Possession of a gun within 1000 feet of a school, the Court explained, clearly did not fit the first two categories. In addition, it could not be regulated under the third category as an activity that "substantially affects" interstate commerce because it was not commercial in nature and was not an essential part of a larger regulation of economic activity. Moreover, the Court explained, Congress had made no findings about the effect of gun possession in school zones on interstate commerce. Thus, concluding that Congress had no rational basis for finding that gun possession within school zones had a substantial effect on interstate commerce, the Court declared the statute unconstitutional. [ ]

It is clear that, in this instance, section 9(a)(1) of the ESA is not a regulation of the instrumentalities of interstate commerce or of persons or things in interstate commerce. As a result, only the first and the third categories of activity discussed in Lopez will be examined. In evaluating whether ESA section 9(a)(1) is a regulation of the use of the channels of interstate commerce or of activity that substantially affects interstate commerce, we may look not only to the effect of the extinction of the individual endangered species at issue in this case, but also to the aggregate effect of the extinction of all similarly situated endangered species. As the *Lopez* Court explained, " *'where a general regulatory statute bears a substantial relation to commerce,* the *de minimis* character of individual instances arising under the statute is of no consequence.' " *Lopez*, 514 U.S. at 558 (quoting *Maryland v. Wirtz*, 392 U.S. 183, 196 n. 27 (1968), overruled on other grounds, *National League of Cities v. Usery*, 426 U.S. 833 (1976), overruled by *Garcia v. San Antonio Metro. Transit Auth.*, 469 U.S. 528 (1985) (first emphasis added)). If a statute regulates "a class of activities * * * within reach of the federal power," *Perez*, 402 U.S. at 154, the courts have "no power 'to excise, as trivial, individual instances' of the class," *id.* Because section 9(a)(1) of the ESA regulates a class of activities—takings of endangered species—that is within Congress' Commerce Clause power under both the first and third Lopez categories, application of section 9(a)(1) to the Fly is constitutional.[3]

A.   *Channels of Interstate Commerce*

Application of section 9(a)(1) of the ESA to the Fly can be viewed as a proper exercise of Congress' Commerce Clause power over the first category of activity that the *Lopez* Court identified: the use of the "channels of interstate commerce." *Lopez*, 514 U.S. at 558. Although this category is commonly used to uphold regulations of interstate transport of persons or goods, it need not be so limited. Indeed, the power of Congress to regulate the channels of interstate commerce provides a justification for section 9(a)(1) of the ESA for two reasons. First, the prohibition against takings of an endangered species is necessary to enable the government to control the transport of the endangered species in interstate commerce. Second, the prohibition on takings of endangered animals falls under Congress' authority " 'to keep the channels of interstate commerce free from immoral and

---

3. Judge Henderson's concurring opinion expresses the view that the first *Lopez* category does not apply; as to the third *Lopez* category, however, I find our reasoning to be substantially similar. We agree that "the loss of biodiversity itself has a substantial effect on our ecosystem and likewise on interstate commerce," [ ], and that "at the time it passed ESA the Congress contemplated protecting endangered species through regulation of land and its development, which is precisely what the Department has attempted to do here. Such regulation, apart from the characteristics or range of the specific endangered species involved, has a plain and substantial effect on interstate commerce," [ ].

injurious uses.' " *Id.* (quoting *Heart of Atlanta Motel Inc. v. United States,* 379 U.S. 241, 256 (1964)).[4]

The ESA's prohibition on takings of endangered species can be justified as a necessary aid to the prohibitions in the ESA on transporting and selling endangered species in interstate commerce. In this sense, the prohibition against takings of endangered species is analogous to the prohibition against transfer and possession of machine guns (including purely intrastate possession) of 18 U.S.C. § 922(*o*), which has been upheld by the Fifth, Sixth, Ninth, and Eleventh Circuits as a regulation of the channels of interstate commerce. In *United States v. Rambo,* 74 F.3d 948, 951 (9th Cir.), *cert. denied,*——U.S.——(1996), for instance, the Ninth Circuit upheld section 922(*o*) against a *Lopez*-inspired Commerce Clause challenge. The court held that the statute was a " 'regulation of the use of the channels of interstate commerce' " because "[b]y regulating the market in machineguns, including regulating intrastate machinegun possession, Congress has effectively regulated the interstate trafficking in machineguns." [ ] Thus, section 922(*o*) is properly classified as a first category regulation because " 'federal regulation of intrastate incidents of transfer and possession is essential to effective control of the interstate incidents of such traffic.' " [ ] In other words, it is necessary to regulate possession of machineguns in order to effectively regulate the interstate traffic in machineguns because it is impossible to sell machineguns in interstate commerce without first possessing them. Similarly, the prohibition on "taking" endangered species is properly classified as a first category regulation because one of the most effective ways to prevent traffic in endangered species is to secure the habitat of the species from predatory invasion and destruction. Therefore, like section 922(*o*), section 9(a)(1) of the ESA can be properly upheld as a regulation of the use of the channels of interstate commerce.

The prohibition on takings of endangered animals also falls under Congress' authority to prevent the channels of interstate commerce from being used for immoral or injurious purposes. This authority was perhaps best described by the Supreme Court in *Heart of Atlanta,* 379 U.S. 241,

---

4. Judge Sentelle unsuccessfully attempts to draw a parallel between the statute at issue in *Lopez,* which the Supreme Court determined was not a regulation of the use of the channels of interstate commerce, and the statute at issue in this case. In fact, the two statutes are different in material respects. First, § 922(q)'s prohibition against possession of a firearm in a school zone clearly was not necessary to enable the government to control the transportation of firearms in interstate commerce. Yet, as noted above and discussed in greater depth below, the ESA's prohibition against taking endangered species is necessary to enable the government to control the transport of endangered species in interstate commerce. Thus, in this respect, ESA section 9(a)(1) is much more similar to the prohibition against transfer and posses-

sion of machine guns of 18 U.S.C. § 922(*o*), which has been repeatedly found constitutional, than it is to § 922(q). [ ] Second, § 922(q)'s prohibition against possession of a firearm in a school zone clearly did not fall under Congress' authority " 'to keep the channels of interstate commerce free from immoral and injurious uses,' " *Heart of Atlanta,* 379 U.S. at 256, because it regulated possession of firearms within only a very limited area. However, as is again discussed in greater depth below, the ESA's prohibition on taking endangered animals clearly does fall under Congress' authority to keep the channels of interstate commerce free from immoral and injurious uses in cases where the pressures of interstate commerce place the existence of species in peril.

which the *Lopez* Court cited and quoted in its reference to Congress' power to regulate the use of the "channels of interstate commerce." In *Heart of Atlanta,* the Supreme Court upheld a prohibition on racial discrimination in places of public accommodation serving interstate travelers against a Commerce Clause challenge. The Court explained that " 'the authority of Congress to keep the channels of interstate commerce free from immoral and injurious uses has been frequently sustained, and is no longer open to question.' " [ ] It does not matter if the activities that are regulated are of a "purely local character," the Court elaborated, " '[i]f it is interstate commerce that feels the pinch, it does not matter how local the operation which applies the squeeze.' " [ ] Thus, the power of Congress over interstate commerce "also includes the power to regulate the local incidents thereof, including local activities in both the States of origin and destination, which might have a substantial and harmful effect upon that commerce." [ ] This same principle was elaborated in the seminal case of *United States v. Darby,* 312 U.S. 100 (1941), which was the only other case cited by the *Lopez* Court in its description of the first category of activity that Congress can regulate under its commerce power. In *Darby,* the Court upheld federal wage and hour regulations against a Commerce Clause challenge, noting that such regulations were necessary to prevent states with higher regulatory standards from being disadvantaged vis-a-vis states with lower regulatory standards. In upholding the regulation, the Court explained that "Congress, following its own conception of public policy concerning the restrictions which may appropriately be imposed on interstate commerce," is free to exclude from commerce goods that will have injurious effects in the state in which they are produced or to which they are destined. [ ] This is true even though the activity prohibited by the regulation at issue in *Darby*—failure to meet minimum wage and maximum hour requirements— might have had little or no direct effect outside the state in which the goods were produced.

This same reasoning that the Supreme Court applied in *Darby* and *Heart of Atlanta* is applicable to the case at hand. In those cases as well as here, Congress used its authority to rid the channels of interstate commerce of injurious uses to regulate the conditions under which goods are produced for interstate commerce. In *Darby,* Congress used this authority to prevent labor exploitation of employees producing lumber for interstate commerce. In *Heart of Atlanta,* Congress used this authority to prevent racial discrimination by a hotel serving an interstate clientele. Similarly, in this case, Congress used this authority to prevent the eradication of an endangered species by a hospital that is presumably being constructed using materials and people from outside the state and which will attract employees, patients, and students from both inside and outside the state. Thus, like regulations preventing racial discrimination or labor exploitation, regulations preventing the taking of endangered species prohibit interstate actors from using the channels of interstate commerce to "promot[e] or spread[ ] evil, whether of a physical, moral or economic nature." *North American Co. v. S.E.C.,* 327 U.S. 686, 705 (1946). Congress is therefore empowered by its authority to regulate the channels of interstate commerce to prevent the taking of endangered species in cases like this where the pressures of interstate commerce place the existence of species in peril.

. . .

B.   *Substantially Affects Interstate Commerce*

The takings clause in the ESA can also be viewed as a regulation of the third category of activity that Congress may regulate under its commerce power. According to *Lopez*, the test of whether section 9(a)(1) of the ESA is within this category of activity "requires an analysis of whether the regulated activity 'substantially affects' interstate commerce." [ ] A class of activities can substantially affect interstate commerce regardless of whether the activity at issue—in this case the taking of endangered species—is commercial or noncommercial. As the *Lopez* Court, quoting *Wickard v. Filburn,* 317 U.S. 111 (1942), noted:

> [E]ven if appellee's activity be local and though it may not be regarded as commerce, it may still, whatever its nature, be reached by Congress if it exerts a substantial economic effect on interstate commerce, and this irrespective of whether such effect is what might at some earlier time have been defined as "direct" or "indirect."

Lopez, 514 U.S. at 556 (quoting *Wickard,* 317 U.S. at 125).[7]

This interpretation of the *Lopez* decision is consistent with this court's recent decision in *Terry v. Reno,* 101 F.3d 1412 (D.C.Cir.1996), *cert. denied,*——U.S.——(1997). In *Terry,* we upheld the Freedom of Access to Clinic Entrances Act against a Commerce Clause challenge, concluding that the *Lopez* decision did not restrict Congress' Commerce Clause power to activity that is "commercial." We rejected the argument that Congress could not regulate protest in front of abortion clinics because protest is an intrastate, noncommercial activity, explaining that "Congress has authority to regulate '*activities* that substantially affect interstate commerce.' " [ ] We further explained that in order to be subject to Congress' Commerce Clause power, "[t]he regulated activity—in this case, interfering with abortion clinics—need not be commercial, so long as its effect on interstate commerce is substantial." [ ]

Other circuits have also held that a statute need not regulate economic activity directly in order to fall under Congress' Commerce Clause power. . . .

In evaluating the effect of the regulated activity on interstate commerce, I begin, as we did in *Terry,* [ ], with the legislative history of the Act under challenge. As we explained in *Terry,* "we consider 'even congressional committee findings' regarding the effect on interstate commerce of the regulated activity." 101 F.3d at 1415 (quoting *Lopez,* 514 U.S. at 562).

---

7.   Indeed, the case at hand is in many ways directly analogous to *Wickard.* In both cases, the appellee's activity, growing wheat for personal consumption and taking endangered species, is local and is not "regarded as commerce." *Wickard,* 317 U.S. at 125. However, in both cases, the activity exerts a substantial economic effect on interstate commerce—by affecting the quantity of wheat in one case, and by affecting the quantity of species in the other.

The Committee Reports on the ESA reveal that one of the primary reasons that Congress sought to protect endangered species from "takings" was the importance of the continuing availability of a wide variety of species to interstate commerce. As the House Report explained:

> As we homogenize the habitats in which these plants and animals evolved, and as we increase the pressure for products that they are in a position to supply (usually unwillingly) we threaten their—and our own—genetic heritage.

> The value of this genetic heritage is, quite literally, incalculable. . . .

>   . . .

> From the most narrow possible point of view, it is in the best interests of mankind to minimize the losses of genetic variations. The reason is simple: they are potential resources. They are keys to puzzles which we cannot solve, and may provide answers to questions which we have not yet learned to ask.

>   . . .

> Who knows, or can say, what potential cures for cancer or other scourges, present or future, may lie locked up in the structures of plants which may yet be undiscovered, much less analyzed? More to the point, who is prepared to risk being [sic] those potential cures by eliminating those plants for all time? Sheer self interest impels us to be cautious.

H.R. REP. No. 93–412, at 4–5 (1973). Similarly, the Senate Report on the precursor to the ESA, noted:

> * * * From a pragmatic point of view, the protection of an endangered species of wildlife with some commercial value may permit the regeneration of that species to a level where controlled exploitation of that species can be resumed. In such a case businessmen may profit from the trading and marketing of that species for an indefinite number of years, where otherwise it would have been completely eliminated from commercial channels in a very brief span of time. Potentially more important, however, is the fact that with each species we eliminate, we reduce the [genetic] pool . . . available for use by man in future years. Since each living species and subspecies has developed in a unique way to adapt itself to the difficulty of living in the world's environment, as a species is lost, its distinctive gene material, which may subsequently prove invaluable to mankind in improving domestic animals or increasing resistance to disease or environmental contaminant, is also irretrievably lost.

S. REP. No. 91–526, at 3 (1969).

This legislative history distinguishes the ESA from the statute at issue in *Lopez*. In *Lopez*, the Court noted that "as part of our independent evaluation of constitutionality under the Commerce Clause we of course consider legislative findings, and indeed even congressional committee findings regarding effect on interstate commerce." [ ] The *Lopez* Court found, however, that there were no "congressional findings [that] would enable [it] to evaluate the legislative judgment that the activity in question substantially affected interstate commerce." [ ] In this case, in contrast, the committee reports on the ESA discuss the value of preserving genetic diversity and the potential for future commerce related to that diversity. *See also Tennessee Valley Auth. v. Hill,* 437 U.S. 153, 178–79 (1978) (recognizing that one of the primary concerns underlying the Endangered Species Act was concern "about the *unknown* uses that endangered species might have and about the *unforeseeable* place such creatures may have in the chain of life on this planet").

. . .

Congress could rationally conclude that the intrastate activity regulated by section 9 of the ESA substantially affects interstate commerce for two primary reasons. First, the provision prevents the destruction of biodiversity and thereby protects the current and future interstate commerce that relies upon it. Second, the provision controls adverse effects of interstate competition.[10]

1. BIODIVERSITY

Approximately 521 of the 1082 species in the United States currently designated as threatened or endangered are found in only one state. [ ] The elimination of all or even some of these endangered species would have a staggering effect on biodiversity—defined as the presence of a large number of species of animals and plants—in the United States and, thereby, on the current and future interstate commerce that relies on the availability of a diverse array of species.

The variety of plants and animals in this country are, in a sense, a natural resource that commercial actors can use to produce marketable products. In the most narrow view of economic value, endangered plants and animals are valuable as sources of medicine and genes.[11] Fifty percent

---

10. Judge Sentelle asserts that these rationales have "no stopping point." [ ] In fact, however, they have very clear and obvious limits. In the case of the first rationale, the argument stops at endangered species. Activities that threaten a species' existence threaten to reduce biodiversity and thereby have a substantial negative effect on interstate commerce. Thus, the biodiversity rationale offered here provides support for the Endangered Species Act only insofar as the Act prevents activities that are likely to cause the elimination of species. In the case of the second rationale, the argument stops at activities that are the product of destructive interstate competition. Under this rationale, interstate competition that is likely to produce destructive results, such as elimination of endangered species' habitat, environmental degradation, or exploitation of labor, can be regulated by Congress. Thus, the destructive interstate competition rationale provides support for the Endangered Species Act only insofar as the Act prevents a bidding down of regulatory standards that is likely to result in the elimination of endangered species' habitat.

11. This is a necessarily constrained view of the "value" of biodiversity. Endangered species of course have value beyond the profit they can produce as sources of medicine and genes. For example, tourists travel to see them, scientists study and learn from them, and people get aesthetic pleasure from them. In addition, every species offers some clues to the path of the evolutionary chain that produced it and to the role of certain genes also found in humans. For instance, researchers have recently concluded that basic research into the genes of the common

of the most frequently prescribed medicines are derived from wild plant and animal species.[12] Such medicines were estimated in 1983 to be worth over $15 billion a year. [ ] In addition, the genetic material of wild species of plants and animals is inbred into domestic crops and animals to improve their commercial value and productivity. As Amici Curiae explained: "Fortifying the genetic diversity of U.S. crops played a large part in the explosive growth in farm production since the 1930s, accounting for at least one-half of the doubling in yields of rice, soybeans, wheat, and sugarcane, and a three-fold increase in corn and potatoes. Genetic diversity provided by wild plants also protects domestic crops from disease and pest damage." [ ] Similar genetic engineering can be used with animals. For instance, it is not beyond the realm of possibility that the genes of a wild pollinator species like the Fly might be inbred with the honeybee, which currently pollinates most major U.S. crops, to produce a pollinator that is more disease resistant.

Each time a species becomes extinct, the pool of wild species diminishes. This, in turn, has a substantial effect on interstate commerce by diminishing a natural resource that could otherwise be used for present and future commercial purposes. Unlike most other natural resources, however, the full value of the variety of plant and animal life that currently exists is uncertain. Plants and animals that are lost through extinction undoubtedly have economic uses that are, in some cases, as yet unknown but which could prove vitally important in the future.[13] A species whose worth is still unmeasured has what economists call an "option value"—the value of the possibility that a future discovery will make useful a species

---

fruit fly " 'can yield crucial clues to human development.' " Jennifer Ackerman, *Journey to the Center of the Egg*, N.Y. TIMES, Oct. 12, 1997, § 6, at 45 (quoting biologist Christiane Nusslein–Volhard). Moreover, every species has a place in the ecosystem. Extinction of a species can therefore have an important effect on the larger system of which it is a part. As biologist Edward O. Wilson explained:

> ... The traditional econometric approach, weighing market price and tourist dollars, will always underestimate the true value of wild species. None has been totally assayed for all of the commercial profit, scientific knowledge, and aesthetic pleasure it can yield. Furthermore, none exists in the wild all by itself. Every species is part of an ecosystem, an expert specialist of its kind, tested relentlessly as it spreads its influence through the food web. To remove it is to entrain changes in other species, raising the populations of some, reducing or even extinguishing others, risking a downward spiral of the larger assemblage.

EDWARD O. WILSON, THE DIVERSITY OF LIFE 308 (1992).

12.   For example, the venom of a species of South American pit viper led to the discovery of the angiotension system that regulates blood pressure in human beings. This helped scientists devise a molecule that alters blood pressure and is the preferred prescription drug for hypertension, bringing the pharmaceutical company that manufactures it $1.3 billion a year in sales. BIODIVERSITY II: UNDERSTANDING AND PROTECTING OUR BIOLOGICAL RESOURCES 9 (Marjoie L. Reaka–Kudla et al. eds. 1997). Similarly, the saliva of the leech led to the development of the anticoagulant hirudin, which is used to treat hemorrhoids, rheumatism, thrombosis, and contusions and to dissolve blood clots that threaten skin transplants, and a substance derived from the saliva of the vampire bat of Central and South America is being developed to open clogged arteries and thereby prevent heart attacks. *See* WILSON, *supra* note 11, at 285–86.

13.   Some of the most important medical products derive from organisms that were once considered worthless or nearly so. For example, *Penicillium* mold, which "sparked the concept of antibiotics," was at one time valued only for the flavor it added to blue cheeses. [ ]

that is currently thought of as useless. *See* Bryan Nolan, *Commodity, Amenity, and Morality: The Limits of Quantification in Valuing Biodiversity, in* BIODIVERSITY 200, 202 (Edward O. Wilson ed., 1988). To allow even a single species whose value is not currently apparent to become extinct therefore deprives the economy of the option value of that species. Because our current knowledge of each species and its possible uses is limited, it is impossible to calculate the exact impact that the loss of the option value of a single species might have on interstate commerce.[14] *See* Alan Randall, *What Mainstream Economists Have to Say about the Value of Biodiversity, in* BIODIVERSITY, *supra,* at 217. In the aggregate, however, we can be certain that the extinction of species and the attendant decline in biodiversity will have a real and predictable effect on interstate commerce.

The few federal courts that have considered post-*Lopez* Commerce Clause challenges to federal wildlife protection have found that the extinction of animals substantially affects interstate commerce. In *United States v. Bramble,* 103 F.3d 1475 (9th Cir.1996), the Ninth Circuit held that the Eagle Protection Act was a valid exercise of Congress' Commerce Clause power because "[e]xtinction of the eagle would substantially affect interstate commerce by foreclosing any possibility of several types of commercial activity." [ ]; *see also United States v. Lundquist,* 932 F.Supp. 1237, 1245 (D.Or.1996) (holding that "the possession of eagle parts is an activity which affects a broad regulatory scheme relating to commercial transactions and which, when viewed in the aggregate with similar activities nationwide, substantially affects interstate commerce") (citing *Lopez,* 514 U.S. at 561). Similarly, in *United States v. Romano,* 929 F.Supp. 502, 507–09 (D.Mass. 1996), the District Court of Massachusetts upheld the Lacey Act, 16 U.S.C. §§ 3371–78, which prohibits any person from importing, exporting, transporting, selling, receiving, acquiring, or purchasing in interstate or foreign commerce any fish or wildlife taken, possessed, transported, or sold in violation of state or foreign law. Citing Congress' findings that the protection of endangered species protects future commercial activity, the court held that the Act was within Congress' Commerce Clause power. [ ][16]

---

14. Both Judge Sentelle and Judge Henderson appear to misunderstand this argument. [ ] Although both quote the statement it is "impossible to calculate the exact impact" of the extinction of a single species, both ignore the second half of the argument: that in the aggregate we can be certain that a decline in biodiversity will have a *"real and predictable"* effect on interstate commerce. As a result of this omission, both misportray the argument as claiming that the extinction of a single endangered species, by itself, has a substantial effect on interstate commerce.... To the contrary, the argument is that because biodiversity has a real, substantial, and predictable effect on both the current and future interstate commerce, "the de minimis character of individual instances arising under [the ESA] is of no consequence." *Lopez,* 514 U.S. at 558. In other words, because we

know that in the aggregate the extinction of endangered species will have a substantial effect on interstate commerce, it does not matter that it is "impossible to calculate the exact impact" of the extinction of a single species such as the Fly.

16. The District Court of Hawaii relied on a similar reasoning in an earlier case involving a Commerce Clause challenge to the ESA, *Palila v. Hawaii Dept. of Land and Natural Resources,* 471 F.Supp. 985 (D.Haw. 1979), *aff'd,* 639 F.2d 495 (9th Cir.1981). In that case, the court pointed to the interstate commerce effects of protecting endangered species to support its decision to uphold the Endangered Species Act. The court explained: "In this context, a national program to protect and improve the natural habitats of endangered species preserves the possibilities of interstate commerce in these species and of

I join these courts in concluding that the extinction of animals substantially affects interstate commerce. . . .

2. DESTRUCTIVE INTERSTATE COMPETITION

The taking of the Fly and other endangered animals can also be regulated by Congress as an activity that substantially affects interstate commerce because it is the product of destructive interstate competition. It is a principle deeply rooted in Commerce Clause jurisprudence that Congress is empowered to act to prevent destructive interstate competition. As the Supreme Court explained in *Hodel v. Virginia Surface Mining & Reclamation Ass'n*, 452 U.S. 264 (1981) (*"Hodel v. Virginia"*), a case that the *Lopez* Court cited repeatedly, "prevention of * * * destructive interstate competition is a traditional role for congressional action under the Commerce Clause." [ ]

The case at hand bears a substantial similarity to the three cases in which the Supreme Court best articulated the principle that Congress may act to prevent interstate competition that has a destructive effect: *Hodel v. Virginia*, 452 U.S. 264, *Hodel v. Indiana*, 452 U.S. 314 (1981), and *United States v. Darby*, 312 U.S. 100 (1941). . . .

The parallels between *Hodel v. Virginia* and the case at hand are obvious. The ESA and the Surface Mining Act both regulate activities—destruction of endangered species and destruction of the natural landscape—that are carried out entirely within a State and which are not themselves commercial in character. The activities, however, may be regulated because they have destructive effects, on environmental quality in one case and on the availability of a variety of species in the other, that are likely to affect more than one State. In each case, moreover, interstate competition provides incentives to states to adopt lower standards to gain an advantage vis-a-vis other states: In *Hodel v. Virginia*, 452 U.S. 264, the states were motivated to adopt lower environmental standards to improve the competitiveness of their coal production facilities, and in this case, the states are motivated to adopt lower standards of endangered species protection in order to attract development.[18]

. . .

interstate movement of persons, such as amateur students of nature or professional scientists who come to a state to observe and study these species, that would otherwise be lost by state inaction." *Id.* at 995. The court thus concluded that the state's program of preserving herds of "wild" sheep and goats which destroyed the habitat of an endangered bird constituted an unlawful "taking" of the bird by the state. *Id.*

18. In his dissent, Judge Sentelle attempts to distinguish *Hodel v. Virginia*, 452 U.S. 264, *Hodel v. Indiana*, 452 U.S. 314, and *United States v. Darby*, 312 U.S. 100, from the case at hand by asserting that "[i]n the present case neither Congress nor the litigants, nor for that matter Judge Wald, has pointed to any commercial activity being regulated, any commercial competition being unfairly challenged, or any other sort of commerce being destroyed by the taking of the fly." [ ] Again, this is inaccurate. In addition to arguing that a decline in biodiversity would have a substantial and predictable destructive effect on interstate commerce, [ ], this section of the opinion refers repeatedly to the fact that the ESA regulates the conditions under which development takes place, and thereby prevents states from adopting lower standards of endangered species protection in order to attract development (*e.g.*, construction of a hospital, power plant, and

Like *Darby,* 312 U.S. 100, the case at hand involves a regulation of the conditions under which commercial activity takes place. The statute in *Darby* regulated the wages and hours of workers in Georgia who were engaged in producing lumber for interstate commerce. Similarly, the statute in this case regulates the taking of endangered species in the process of constructing a hospital, power plant, and intersection that will likely serve an interstate population. In both cases, Congress passed the statute in part to prevent states from gaining a competitive advantage by enacting lower regulatory standards than other states. Congress was aware that no state could be expected to require significantly more rigorous labor standards or endangered species protection than other states, because for each individual state, the cost of providing better working conditions or preserving a species outweighs the benefits even though in aggregate, the benefits of better labor standards and biodiversity outweigh the costs.

As the cases discussed above illustrate, the Court has long held that Congress has the power under the Commerce Clause to prevent destructive interstate commerce similar to that at issue in this case. I therefore find that Congress has the power to prevent interstate competition that will result in the destruction of endangered species just as it has the power to prevent interstate competition that will result in harm to the environment, *Hodel v. Virginia,* 452 U.S. 264, the destruction of "prime farm land," *Hodel v. Indiana,* 452 U.S. at 324, or the employment of people under substandard labor conditions, *Darby,* 312 U.S. 100.

III. CONCLUSION

We hold that the section 9(a)(1) of the Endangered Species Act is within Congress' Commerce Clause power and that the Fish and Wildlife Service's application of the provision to the Delhi Sands Flower–Loving Fly was therefore constitutional. The district court's decision granting the Government's motion for summary judgment is therefore

Affirmed.

■ HENDERSON, J., concurring:—I agree with Judge Wald's conclusion that the "taking" prohibition in section 9(a)(1) of the Endangered Species Act (ESA) constitutes a valid exercise of the Congress's authority to regulate interstate commerce under the Commerce Clause.[1] I cannot, however, agree entirely with either of her grounds for reaching the result and instead arrive by a different route.

intersection)—activity that even Judge Sentelle presumably would admit is commercial in nature.

1. It is beyond question that the development San Bernardino County proposes is not only a "discomfit[ure]"of the Delhi Sands Flower–Loving Fly, *see* Dissent, but also a "taking" within the meaning of ESA, *see Babbitt v. Sweet Home Chapter of Communities for a Great Oregon,* 515 U.S. 687, 691 (1995) (upholding Department of Interior's interpretation in 50 C.F.R. § 17.3 of statutory definition of "take" to include "an act which actually kills or injures wildlife," which "may include significant habitat modification or degradation where it actually kills or injures wildlife by significantly impairing essential behavioral patterns, including breeding, feeding, or sheltering"). Further, the extent of inconvenience the County experiences if the unlawful taking is prevented, *see* Dissent, is irrelevant so long as the prevention is authorized under the Commerce Clause.

Judge Wald first asserts that section 9(a)(1) is a proper regulation of the "channels of commerce." In support she cites decisions upholding regulation of commercially marketable goods, such as machine guns and lumber, and public accommodations. In each case, the object of regulation was necessarily connected to movement of persons or things interstate and could therefore be characterized as regulation of the channels of commerce. Not so with an endangered species, as the facts here graphically demonstrate. The Delhi Sands Flower–Loving Flies the Department of the Interior seeks to protect are (along with many other species no doubt) entirely *intra*state creatures. They do not move among states either on their own or through human agency. As a result, like the Gun–Free School Zones Act in *Lopez*, the statutory protection of the flies "is not a regulation of the use of the channels of interstate commerce." [ ]

Judge Wald also justifies the protection of endangered species on the ground that the loss of biodiversity "substantially affects" interstate commerce because of the resulting loss of potential medical or economic benefit. Yet her opinion acknowledges that it is "impossible to calculate the exact impact" of the economic loss of an endangered species. [ ] As far as I can tell, it is equally impossible to ascertain that there will be any such impact at all. It may well be that no species endangered now or in the future will have any of the economic value proposed. Given that possibility, I do not see how we can say that the protection of an endangered species has any effect on interstate commerce (much less a substantial one) by virtue of an uncertain potential medical or economic value. Nevertheless, I believe that the loss of biodiversity itself has a substantial effect on our ecosystem and likewise on interstate commerce. In addition, I would uphold section 9(a)(1) as applied here because the Department's protection of the flies regulates and substantially affects commercial development activity which is plainly interstate.

First, I agree with Judge Wald that biodiversity is important to our understanding of ESA and its relation to interstate commerce. As Judge Wald's opinion notes:

> Every species is part of an ecosystem, an expert specialist of its kind, tested relentlessly as it spreads its influence through the food web. To remove it is to entrain changes in other species, raising the populations of some, reducing or even extinguishing others, risking a downward spiral of a larger assemblage.

[ ] The effect of a species' continued existence on the health of other species within the ecosystem seems to be generally recognized among scientists. *See* Stephen M. Johnson, *United States v. Lopez: A Misstep, but Hardly Epochal for Federal Environmental Regulation*, 5 N.Y.U. ENVTL. L.J. 33, 79 (1996) ("It is a fundamental principle of ecology that ecosystems are composed of interdependent parts that play vital roles in preserving the ecosystem. As an ecosystem becomes less diverse, it becomes less adaptable to stresses that are placed on it.") (footnotes omitted); Myrl L. Duncan, *Property as a Public Conversation, Not a Lockean Soliloquy: A Role for Intellectual and Legal History in Takings Analysis*, 26 ENVTL. L. 1095, 1129 (1996) ("[S]cientists have rediscovered that the world cannot meaningfully be broken down into isolated parts, that every part is connected to every other part. Perhaps the strongest statements about interconnectedness

come from scientists, scholars, and regulators working in the field of conservation biology who are critical of the species-by-species, reaction-to-crisis approach taken by the Endangered Species Act. They understand that species protection issues cannot be separated from those of ecosystem health.") (footnotes omitted). Some studies show, for example, that the mere presence of diverse species within an ecosystem (biodiversity) by itself contributes to the ecosystem's fecundity. *See* Yvonne Baskin, *Ecologists Dare to Ask: How Much Does Diversity Matter?* 264 SCI. 202 (1994). The Congress recognized the interconnection of the various species and the ecosystems when it declared that the "essential purpose" of ESA, which protects endangered species, is in fact "to protect the ecosystem upon which we and other species depend." H.R. REP. No. 93–412, at 10 (1973); [ ] Given the interconnectedness of species and ecosystems, it is reasonable to conclude that the extinction of one species affects others and their ecosystems and that the protection of a purely intrastate species (like the Delhi Sands Flower–Loving Fly) will therefore substantially affect land and objects that are involved in interstate commerce. There is, therefore, "a rational basis" for concluding that the "taking" of endangered species "substantially affects" interstate commerce so that section 9(a)(1) is within the Congress's Commerce Clause authority. *See Lopez*, 514 U.S. at 557–59.

The interstate effect of a taking is particularly obvious here given the nature of the taking the County proposes. In enacting ESA, the Congress expressed an intent to protect not only endangered species but also the habitats that they, and we, occupy. [ ] At the same time, the Congress expressly found that "economic growth and development untempered by adequate concern and conservation" was the cause for "various species of fish, wildlife, and plants in the United States hav[ing] been rendered extinct." [ ] It is plain, then, that at the time it passed ESA the Congress contemplated protecting endangered species through regulation of land and its development, which is precisely what the Department has attempted to do here. Such regulation, apart from the characteristics or range of the specific endangered species involved, has a plain and substantial effect on interstate commerce. In this case the regulation relates to both the proposed redesigned traffic intersection and the hospital it is intended to serve, each of which has an obvious connection with interstate commerce. [ ][5] Insofar as application of section 9(a)(1) of ESA here acts to regulate commercial development of the land inhabited by the endangered species, "it may ... be reached by Congress" because "it asserts a substantial economic effect on interstate commerce." *Wickard v. Filburn*, 317 U.S. 111, 125 (1942), quoted in *United States v. Lopez*, 514 U.S. 549, 556 (1995).[6]

For the preceding reasons I believe that the Department of the Interior's regulation of the County's proposed "taking" of the endangered

---

5. In light of these authorities I cannot agree with my dissenting colleague that "[t]he activity regulated in the present case involves" only "local land use."

6. The dissent suggests this justification has no "stopping point" as required by *Lopez*. [ ] In *Lopez* the Court was concerned that the "theories" offered by the government would authorize regulation of "all activities that might lead to violent crime, regardless of how tenuously they relate to interstate commerce" and "any activity that it found was related to the economic productivity of individual citizens." *Id.* The rationale on which I rely permits regulation only of activities (including land use) that adversely affect species that affect, or are involved in, interstate commerce.

Delhi Sands Flower–Loving Fly, pursuant to section 9(a)(1) of ESA, is a lawful exercise of governmental authority under the Commerce Clause.

■ SENTELLE, J., dissenting:—. . . . The Department of Interior asserts that section 9(a)(1)(B) of the ESA, and specifically its use of that section to prohibit activities in southern California which might disturb a fly existing only in southern California, are constitutional under the Commerce Clause. U.S. CONST. Art. I, § 8, cl. 3. That clause empowers Congress to "regulate commerce with foreign nations, and among the several states, and with the Indian tribes." This brings the next question: Can Congress under the Interstate Commerce Clause regulate the killing of flies, which is not commerce, in southern California, which is not interstate? Because I think the answer is "no," I can not join my colleagues' decision to affirm the district court's conclusion that it can.

NOTES

(1) Forty bushels of wheat and the nature of biodiversity: Is the Delhi Flower–Loving Sandfly like the forty bushels of wheat that characterizes *Wickard v. Filburn*? Is the cumulative effect of hundreds of small decisions—the rationale for the decision in *Wickard*—analogous to biodiversity where each individual species might be expendable but the cumulative effect of the loss of hundreds of species might be disastrous?

For an extended examination of the case, see John Copeland Nagle, *The Commerce Clause Meets the Delhi Sands Flower–Loving Fly*, 97 MICH. L. REV. 174 (1998).

(2) *United States v. Bramble*: Ronald Bramble advertised sea otter pelts for sale. Two undercover federal wildlife agents responded to the advertisement and Bramble invited them into his home to negotiate the sale. During the negotiations, Bramble showed the agents parts of eagles, hawks, and owls. Possession of the bird parts violated two federal statutes, the Eagle Protection Act and the Migratory Bird Treaty Act [MBTA]. On appeal from his conviction, Bramble challenged the constitutionality of the statutes under the Commerce Clause. Since the Supreme Court held the MBTA to be constitutional under the Treaty Clause in *Missouri v. Holland* [*supra*], the appeals court focused its attention on the Eagle Protection Act. Noting that the Act

> was passed to protect eagles from extinction. [ ] To serve that end, the Act prohibits all traffic in eagles or eagle parts. [ ]
>
> The Act forbids not only commerce or attempted commerce in eagle parts, but also simple possession of them. [ ] Both commerce in and possession of eagle parts, each taken as a class, have substantial effects on interstate commerce, because both activities, even when conducted purely intrastate, threaten the eagle with extinction. [ ]
>
> Extinction of the eagle would substantially affect interstate commerce by foreclosing any possibility of several types of commercial activity: future commerce in eagles or their parts; future interstate travel for the purpose of observing or studying eagles; or future

commerce in beneficial products derived either from eagles or from analysis of their genetic material. As the court explained in *Palila v. Hawaii Dep't of Land & Natural Resources,* 471 F.Supp. 985 (D.Hawai'i 1979), *aff'd,* 639 F.2d 495 (9th Cir.1981), . . . :

> [A] national program to protect and improve the natural habitats of endangered species preserves the possibilities of interstate commerce in these species and of interstate movement of persons, such as amateur students of nature or professional scientists who come to a state to observe and study these species, that would otherwise be lost by state inaction.

United States v. Bramble, 103 F.3d 1475, 1481 (9th Cir.1996).

(3) *Gibbs v. Babbitt:* The provision of the Endangered Species Act similar to the one challenged in *Home Builders* also produced a Commerce Clause challenge in *Gibbs v. Babbitt,* 214 F.3d 483 (4th Cir.2000), *cert. denied sub nom.,* ___ U.S. ___, 121 S.Ct. 1081 (2001). The dispute arose out of successful efforts to reintroduce the red wolf in North Carolina. Private landowners complained about restrictions on their ability to protect their property against wolves that wandered off federal lands. As in *Home Builders,* a divided panel sustained the validity of the provision under the Commerce Clause. In the majority's view, the challenged law did not regulate "channels of interstate commerce" nor did it protect things in interstate commerce. It did, however, regulate activities that had a substantial relation to interstate commerce: "The relationship between red wolf takings and interstate commerce is quite direct—with no red wolves, there will be no red wolf related tourism, no scientific research, and no commercial trade in pelts." 214 F.3d at 492. The court also noted that red wolves affect commerce through their impacts on livestock raising and other farming enterprises, whether the impacts are beneficial or deleterious. 214 F.3d at 495. *See* Dave Owen, Note, *Gibbs v. Babbitt,* 28 ECOLOGY L.Q. 377 (2001).

(4) Regulating a fly? Although Judge Sentelle in his dissent claimed that the "taking" at issue in the case was "not commerce," the particular activity being regulated was a major new hospital, both the construction and the operation of which was very much embedded in interstate commerce. Indeed, presumably many federal laws applied to the construction effort, from labor and occupational safety standards to a wide array of environmental statutes. Once constructed, of course, the hospital would be subject to extensive federal control. That being so, why was there even a serious question as to whether the statute regulated interstate commerce? Was there a reason why Judge Wald talking about "takings" in the abstract? On this issue, consider the final part of Justice Steven's dissenting opinion in the following case.

Solid Waste Agency of Northern Cook County v. United States Army Corps of Engineers

United States Supreme Court.
531 U.S. 159 (2001).

■ REHNQUIST, C.J.:—Section 404(a) of the Clean Water Act (CWA or Act), 86 Stat. 884, as amended, 33 U.S.C. § 1344(a), regulates the discharge of dredged or fill material into "navigable waters." The United States Army Corps of Engineers (Corps), has interpreted § 404(a) to confer federal authority over an abandoned sand and gravel pit in northern Illinois which provides habitat for migratory birds. We are asked to decide whether the provisions of § 404(a) may be fairly extended to these waters, and, if so, whether Congress could exercise such authority consistent with the Commerce Clause, U.S. Const., Art. I, § 8, cl. 3. We answer the first question in the negative and therefore do not reach the second.

Petitioner, the Solid Waste Agency of Northern Cook County (SWANCC), is a consortium of 23 suburban Chicago cities and villages that united in an effort to locate and develop a disposal site for baled nonhazardous solid waste. The Chicago Gravel Company informed the municipalities of the availability of a 533–acre parcel, bestriding the Illinois counties Cook and Kane, which had been the site of a sand and gravel pit mining operation for three decades up until about 1960. Long since abandoned, the old mining site eventually gave way to a successional stage forest, with its remnant excavation trenches evolving into a scattering of permanent and seasonal ponds of varying size (from under one-tenth of an acre to several acres) and depth (from several inches to several feet).

The municipalities decided to purchase the site for disposal of their baled nonhazardous solid waste. . . .

Section 404(a) grants the Corps authority to issue permits "for the discharge of dredged or fill material into the navigable waters at specified disposal sites." 33 U.S.C. § 1344(a). The term "navigable waters" is defined under the Act as "the waters of the United States, including the territorial seas." § 1362(7). The Corps has issued regulations defining the term "waters of the United States" to include

> waters such as intrastate lakes, rivers, streams (including intermittent streams), mudflats, sandflats, wetlands, sloughs, prairie potholes, wet meadows, playa lakes, or natural ponds, the use, degradation or destruction of which could affect interstate or foreign commerce * * *.

33 C.F.R. § 328.3(a)(3) (1999).

In 1986, in an attempt to "clarify" the reach of its jurisdiction, the Corps stated that § 404(a) extends to intrastate waters:

> a.   Which are or would be used as habitat by birds protected by Migratory Bird Treaties; or
>
> b.   Which are or would be used as habitat by other migratory birds which cross state lines; or
>
> c.   Which are or would be used as habitat for endangered species; or
>
> d.   Used to irrigate crops sold in interstate commerce.

51 *Fed. Reg.* 41217.

This last promulgation has been dubbed the "Migratory Bird Rule."

The Corps initially concluded that it had no jurisdiction over the site because it contained no "wetlands," or areas which support "vegetation typically adapted for life in saturated soil conditions," 33 C.F.R. § 328.3(b) (1999). However, after the Illinois Nature Preserves Commission informed the Corps that a number of migratory bird species had been observed at the site, the Corps reconsidered and ultimately asserted jurisdiction over the balefill site pursuant to subpart (b) of the "Migratory Bird Rule." The Corps found that approximately 121 bird species had been observed at the site, including several known to depend upon aquatic environments for a significant portion of their life requirements. . . .

. . .

Congress passed the CWA for the stated purpose of "restor[ing] and maintain[ing] the chemical, physical, and biological integrity of the Nation's waters." 33 U.S.C. § 1251(a). In so doing, Congress chose to "recognize, preserve, and protect the primary responsibilities and rights of States to prevent, reduce, and eliminate pollution, to plan the development and use (including restoration, preservation, and enhancement) of land and water resources, and to consult with the Administrator in the exercise of his authority under this chapter." § 1251(b). Relevant here, § 404(a) authorizes respondents to regulate the discharge of fill material into "navigable waters," 33 U.S.C. § 1344(a), which the statute defines as "the waters of the United States, including the territorial seas," § 1362(7). Respondents have interpreted these words to cover the abandoned gravel pit at issue here because it is used as habitat for migratory birds. We conclude that the "Migratory Bird Rule" is not fairly supported by the CWA.

This is not the first time we have been called upon to evaluate the meaning of § 404(a). In *United States v. Riverside Bayview Homes, Inc.,* 474 U.S. 121 (1985), we held that the Corps had § 404(a) jurisdiction over wetlands that actually abutted on a navigable waterway. In so doing, we noted that the term "navigable" is of "limited import" and that Congress evidenced its intent to "regulate at least some waters that would not be deemed 'navigable' under the classical understanding of that term." *Id.* at 133. But our holding was based in large measure upon Congress' unequivocal acquiescence to, and approval of, the Corps' regulations interpreting the CWA to cover wetlands adjacent to navigable waters. *See id.* at 135–139. We found that Congress' concern for the protection of water quality and aquatic ecosystems indicated its intent to regulate wetlands "inseparably bound up with the 'waters' of the United States." *Id.,* at 134.

It was the significant nexus between the wetlands and "navigable waters" that informed our reading of the CWA in *Riverside Bayview Homes.* Indeed, we did not "express any opinion" on the "question of the authority of the Corps to regulate discharges of fill material into wetlands that are not adjacent to bodies of open water * * *." *Id.,* at 131–132 n.8. In order to rule for respondents here, we would have to hold that the jurisdiction of the Corps extends to ponds that are *not* adjacent to open water. But we conclude that the text of the statute will not allow this.

. . .

Where an administrative interpretation of a statute invokes the outer limits of Congress' power, we expect a clear indication that Congress intended that result. *See Edward J. DeBartolo Corp. v. Florida Gulf Coast Building & Constr. Trades Council,* 485 U.S. 568, 575 (1988). This requirement stems from our prudential desire not to needlessly reach constitutional issues and our assumption that Congress does not casually authorize administrative agencies to interpret a statute to push the limit of congressional authority. *See ibid.* This concern is heightened where the administrative interpretation alters the federal-state framework by permitting federal encroachment upon a traditional state power. *See United States v. Bass,* 404 U.S. 336, 349 (1971) ("[U]nless Congress conveys its purpose clearly, it will not be deemed to have significantly changed the federal-state balance"). Thus, "where an otherwise acceptable construction of a statute would raise serious constitutional problems, the Court will construe the statute to avoid such problems unless such construction is plainly contrary to the intent of Congress." *DeBartolo,* at 575.

Twice in the past six years we have reaffirmed the proposition that the grant of authority to Congress under the Commerce Clause, though broad, is not unlimited. *See United States v. Morrison,* 529 U.S. 598 (2000); *United States v. Lopez,* 514 U.S. 549 (1995). Respondents argue that the "Migratory Bird Rule" falls within Congress' power to regulate intrastate activities that "substantially affect" interstate commerce. They note that the protection of migratory birds is a "national interest of very nearly the first magnitude," *Missouri v. Holland,* 252 U.S. 416, 435 (1920), and that, as the Court of Appeals found, millions of people spend over a billion dollars annually on recreational pursuits relating to migratory birds. These arguments raise significant constitutional questions. For example, we would have to evaluate the precise object or activity that, in the aggregate, substantially affects interstate commerce. This is not clear, for although the Corps has claimed jurisdiction over petitioner's land because it contains water areas used as habitat by migratory birds, respondents now, *post litem motam,* focus upon the fact that the regulated activity is petitioner's municipal landfill, which is "plainly of a commercial nature." [ ] But this is a far cry, indeed, from the "navigable waters" and "waters of the United States" to which the statute by its terms extends.

. . .

We hold that 33 CFR § 328.3(a)(3) (1999), as clarified and applied to petitioner's balefill site pursuant to the "Migratory Bird Rule," 51 *Fed. Reg.* 41217 (1986), exceeds the authority granted to respondents under § 404(a) of the CWA. The judgment of the Court of Appeals for the Seventh Circuit is therefore

Reversed.

■ STEVENS, J., with whom SOUTER, GINSBURG, and BREYER, JJ., join, dissenting:—In 1969, the Cuyahoga River in Cleveland, Ohio, coated with a slick of industrial waste, caught fire. Congress responded to that dramatic event, and to others like it, by enacting the Federal Water Pollution Control Act (FWPCA) Amendments of 1972, 86 Stat. 817, as amended 33 U.S.C. § 1251 *et seq.,* commonly known as the Clean Water Act (Clean Water Act, CWA, or Act). The Act proclaimed the ambitious goal of ending water pollution by 1985. § 1251(a). The Court's past interpretations of the CWA have been fully consistent with that goal. Although Congress' vision of zero pollution remains unfulfilled, its pursuit has unquestionably retarded the destruction of the aquatic environment. Our Nation's waters no longer burn. Today, however, the Court takes an unfortunate step that needlessly weakens our principal safeguard against toxic water.

It is fair to characterize the Clean Water Act as "watershed" legislation. The statute endorsed fundamental changes in both the purpose and the scope of federal regulation of the Nation's waters. In § 13 of the Rivers and Harbors Appropriation Act of 1899 (RHA), 30 Stat. 1152, as amended, 33 U.S.C. § 407, Congress had assigned to the Army Corps of Engineers (Corps) the mission of regulating discharges into certain waters in order to protect their use as highways for the transportation of interstate and foreign commerce; the scope of the Corps' jurisdiction under the RHA accordingly extended only to waters that were "navigable." In the CWA, however, Congress broadened the Corps' mission to include the purpose of protecting the quality of our Nation's waters for esthetic, health, recreational, and environmental uses. The scope of its jurisdiction was therefore redefined to encompass all of "the waters of the United States, including the territorial seas." § 1362(7). That definition requires neither actual nor potential navigability.

The Court has previously held that the Corps' broadened jurisdiction under the CWA properly included an 80–acre parcel of low-lying marshy land that was not itself navigable, directly adjacent to navigable water, or even hydrologically connected to navigable water, but which was part of a larger area, characterized by poor drainage, that ultimately abutted a navigable creek. *United States v. Riverside Bayview Homes, Inc.,* 474 U.S. 121 (1985). Our broad finding in *Riverside Bayview* that the 1977 Congress had acquiesced in the Corps' understanding of its jurisdiction applies equally to the 410–acre parcel at issue here. Moreover, once Congress crossed the legal watershed that separates navigable streams of commerce from marshes and inland lakes, there is no principled reason for limiting the statute's protection to those waters or wetlands that happen to lie near a navigable stream.

In its decision today, the Court draws a new jurisdictional line, one that invalidates the 1986 migratory bird regulation as well as the Corps' assertion of jurisdiction over all waters except for actually navigable waters, their tributaries, and wetlands adjacent to each. Its holding rests on two equally untenable premises: (1) that when Congress passed the 1972 CWA, it did not intend "to exert anything more than its commerce power over navigation," *ante,* at 680, n. 3; and (2) that in 1972 Congress drew the boundary defining the Corps' jurisdiction at the odd line on which the Court today settles.

As I shall explain, the text of the 1972 amendments affords no support for the Court's holding, and amendments Congress adopted in 1977 do support the Corps' present interpretation of its mission as extending to so-called "isolated" waters. Indeed, simple common sense cuts against the particular definition of the Corps' jurisdiction favored by the majority.

I

The significance of the FWPCA Amendments of 1972 is illuminated by a reference to the history of federal water regulation, a history that the majority largely ignores. Federal regulation of the Nation's waters began in the 19th century with efforts targeted exclusively at "promot[ing] water transportation and commerce." Kalen, *Commerce to Conservation: The Call for a National Water Policy and the Evolution of Federal Jurisdiction Over Wetlands,* 69 N.D.L. REV. 873, 877 (1993). This goal was pursued through the various Rivers and Harbors Acts, the most comprehensive of which was the RHA of 1899. Section 13 of the 1899 RHA, commonly known as the Refuse Act, prohibited the discharge of "refuse" into any "navigable water" or its tributaries, as well as the deposit of "refuse" on the bank of a navigable water "whereby navigation shall or may be impeded or obstructed" without first obtaining a permit from the Secretary of the Army. [ ]

During the middle of the 20th century, the goals of federal water regulation began to shift away from an exclusive focus on protecting navigability and toward a concern for preventing environmental degradation. Kalen, 69 N.D.L. REV. at 877–879, and n.30. This awakening of interest in the use of federal power to protect the aquatic environment was helped along by efforts to reinterpret § 13 of the RHA in order to apply its permit requirement to industrial discharges into navigable waters, even when such discharges did nothing to impede navigability. *See, e.g., United States v. Republic Steel Corp.,* 362 U.S. 482, 490–491 (1960) (noting that the term "refuse" in § 13 was broad enough to include industrial waste). Seeds of this nascent concern with pollution control can also be found in the FWPCA, which was first enacted in 1948 and then incrementally expanded in the following years.

The shift in the focus of federal water regulation from protecting navigability toward environmental protection reached a dramatic climax in 1972, with the passage of the CWA. The Act, which was passed as an amendment to the existing FWPCA, was universally described by its supporters as the first truly comprehensive federal water pollution legislation. The "major purpose" of the CWA was "to establish a *comprehensive* long-range policy for the elimination of water pollution." S. Rep. No. 92–414 at 95 (1971). And "[n]o Congressman's remarks on the legislation were complete without reference to [its] 'comprehensive' nature * * *." *Milwaukee v. Illinois,* 451 U.S. 304, 318 (1981) (Rehnquist, J.). A House sponsor described the bill as "the most comprehensive and far-reaching water pollution bill we have ever drafted," [ ], and Senator Randolph, Chairman of the Committee on Public Works, stated: "It is perhaps the most comprehensive legislation that the Congress of the United States has ever developed in this particular field of the environment." [ ] This Court was therefore undoubtedly correct when it described the 1972 amendments as establishing "a comprehensive program for controlling and abating water pollution." *Train v. City of New York,* 420 U.S. 35, 37 (1975).

Section 404 of the CWA resembles § 13 of the RHA, but, unlike the earlier statute, the primary purpose of which is the maintenance of navigability, § 404 was principally intended as a pollution control measure....

. . .

Because of the statute's ambitious and comprehensive goals, it was, of course, necessary to expand its jurisdictional scope. Thus, although Congress opted to carry over the traditional jurisdictional term "navigable waters" from the RHA and prior versions of the FWPCA, it broadened the *definition* of that term to encompass all "waters of the United States." § 1362(7). Indeed, the 1972 conferees arrived at the final formulation by specifically deleting the word "navigable" from the definition that had originally appeared in the House version of the Act. The majority today undoes that deletion.

The Conference Report explained that the definition in § 502(7) was intended to "be given the broadest possible constitutional interpretation." [ ] The Court dismisses this clear assertion of legislative intent with the back of its hand. [ ] The statement, it claims, "signifies that Congress intended to exert [nothing] more than its commerce power over navigation." [ ]

The majority's reading drains all meaning from the conference amendment. By 1972, Congress' Commerce Clause power over "navigation" had long since been established. *The Daniel Ball,* 10 Wall. 557 (1871); *Gilman v. Philadelphia,* 3 Wall. 713 (1866); *Gibbons v. Ogden,* 9 Wheat. 1 (1824). Why should Congress intend that its assertion of federal jurisdiction be given the "broadest possible constitutional interpretation" if it did not intend to reach beyond the very heartland of its commerce power? The activities regulated by the CWA have nothing to do with Congress' "commerce power over navigation." Indeed, the goals of the 1972 statute have nothing to do with *navigation* at all.

As we recognized in *Riverside Bayview,* the interests served by the statute embrace the protection of " 'significant natural biological functions, including food chain production, general habitat, and nesting, spawning, rearing and resting sites' " for various species of aquatic wildlife. 474 U.S. at 134–135. For wetlands and "isolated" inland lakes, that interest is equally powerful, regardless of the proximity of the swamp or the water to a navigable stream. Nothing in the text, the stated purposes, or the legislative history of the CWA supports the conclusion that in 1972 Congress contemplated—much less commanded—the odd jurisdictional line that the Court has drawn today.

. . .

IV

Because I am convinced that the Court's miserly construction of the statute is incorrect, I shall comment briefly on petitioner's argument that Congress is without power to prohibit it from filling any part of the 31 acres of ponds on its property in Cook County, Illinois. The Corps' exercise of its § 404 permitting power over "isolated" waters that serve as habitat for migratory birds falls well within the boundaries set by this Court's Commerce Clause jurisprudence.

In *United States v. Lopez,* 514 U.S. 549, 558–559 (1995), this Court identified "three broad categories of activity that Congress may regulate under its commerce power": (1) channels of interstate commerce; (2) instrumentalities of interstate commerce, or persons and things in interstate commerce; and (3) activities that "substantially affect" interstate commerce. *Ibid.* The migratory bird rule at issue here is properly analyzed under the third category. In order to constitute a proper exercise of Congress' power over intrastate activities that "substantially affect" interstate commerce, it is not necessary that each individual instance of the activity substantially affect commerce; it is enough that, taken in the aggregate, the *class of activities* in question has such an effect. *Perez v. United States,* 402 U.S. 146 (1971) (noting that it is the "class" of regulated activities, not the individual instance, that is to be considered in the "affects" commerce analysis); *see also Hodel v. Virginia Surface Mining & Reclamation Association, Inc.,* 452 U.S. 264, 277 (1981); *Wickard v. Filburn,* 317 U.S. 111, 127–128 (1942).

The activity being regulated in this case (and by the Corps' § 404 regulations in general) is the discharge of fill material into water. The Corps did not assert jurisdiction over petitioner's land simply because the waters were "used as habitat by migratory birds." It asserted jurisdiction because petitioner planned to *discharge fill* into waters "used as habitat by migratory birds." Had petitioner intended to engage in some other activity besides discharging fill (*i.e.,* had there been no activity to regulate), or, conversely, had the waters not been habitat for migratory birds (*i.e.,* had there been no basis for federal jurisdiction), the Corps would never have become involved in petitioner's use of its land. There can be no doubt that, unlike the class of activities Congress was attempting to regulate in *United States v. Morrison,* 529 U.S. 598, 613 (2000) ("[g]ender-motivated crimes"), *Lopez,* 514 U.S. at 561 (possession of guns near school property), the discharge of fill material into the Nation's waters is almost always undertaken for economic reasons. *See* V. Albrecht & B. Goode, *Wetland Regulation in the Real World,* EXH. 3 (Feb. 1994) (demonstrating that the overwhelming majority of acreage for which § 404 permits are sought is intended for commercial, industrial, or other economic use).[15]

Moreover, no one disputes that the discharge of fill into "isolated" waters that serve as migratory bird habitat will, in the aggregate, adversely affect migratory bird populations. *See, e.g.,* 1 SECRETARY OF THE INTERIOR, REPORT TO CONGRESS, THE IMPACT OF FEDERAL PROGRAMS ON WETLANDS: THE LOWER MISSISSIPPI ALLUVIAL PLAIN AND THE PRAIRIE POTHOLE REGION 79–80 (Oct. 1988) (noting that "isolated," phase 3 waters "are among [the] most important and also the most threatened ecosystems in the United States" because "[t]hey are prime nesting grounds for many species of North American waterfowl * * *" and provide "[u]p to 50 percent of the [U.S.] production of migratory waterfowl"). Nor does petitioner dispute that the particular waters it seeks to fill are home to many important species of migratory birds, including the second-largest breeding colony of Great Blue Herons in northeastern Illinois, [ ], and several species of waterfowl protected by international treaty and Illinois endangered species laws, [ ].[16]

In addition to the intrinsic value of migratory birds, *see Missouri v. Holland,* 252 U.S. 416, 435 (1920) (noting the importance of migratory

15. The fact that petitioner can conceive of some people who may discharge fill for noneconomic reasons does not weaken the legitimacy of the Corps' jurisdictional claims. As we observed in *Perez v. United States,* 402 U.S. 146 (1971), "[w]here the *class of activities* is regulated and that *class* is within the reach of federal power, the courts have no power to excise, as trivial, individual instances of the class." *Id.,* at 154.

16. Other bird species using petitioner's site as habitat include the "Great Egret, Green-backed Heron, Black-crowned Night

birds as "protectors of our forests and our crops" and as "a food supply"), it is undisputed that literally millions of people regularly participate in birdwatching and hunting and that those activities generate a host of commercial activities of great value. The causal connection between the filling of wetlands and the decline of commercial activities associated with migratory birds is not "attenuated," *Morrison,* 529 U.S. at 612; it is direct and concrete. *Cf. Gibbs v. Babbitt,* 214 F.3d 483, 492–493 (4th Cir.2000) ("The relationship between red wolf takings and interstate commerce is quite direct—with no red wolves, there will be no red wolf related tourism * * * ").

Finally, the migratory bird rule does not blur the "distinction between what is truly national and what is truly local." *Morrison,* 529 U.S., at 617–618, 120 S.Ct. 1740. Justice Holmes cogently observed in *Missouri v. Holland* that the protection of migratory birds is a textbook example of a *national* problem. 252 U.S. at 435 ("It is not sufficient to rely upon the States [to protect migratory birds]. The reliance is vain * * * "). The destruction of aquatic migratory bird habitat, like so many other environmental problems, is an action in which the benefits (*e.g.,* a new landfill) are disproportionately local, while many of the costs (*e.g.,* fewer migratory birds) are widely dispersed and often borne by citizens living in other States. . . .

The power to regulate commerce among the several States necessarily and properly includes the power to preserve the natural resources that generate such commerce. *Cf. Sporhase v. Nebraska ex rel. Douglas,* 458 U.S. 941, 953 (1982) (holding water to be an "article of commerce"). Migratory birds, and the waters on which they rely, are such resources. Moreover, the protection of migratory birds is a well-established federal responsibility. As Justice Holmes noted in *Missouri v. Holland,* the federal interest in protecting these birds is of "the first magnitude." 252 U.S. at 435. Because of their transitory nature, they "can be protected only by national action." *Ibid.*

. . .

Because I would affirm the judgment of the Court of Appeals, I respectfully dissent.

NOTES

(1) How does the majority characterize the regulated activity? Is that characterization accurate? Does the characterization reside in the eye of the beholder? Do migratory birds significantly effect interstate commerce? Does solid waste disposal substantially effect interstate commerce? Do isolated wetlands—at least in the aggregate—significantly affect interstate commerce?

Is the Commerce Clause limited to economic effects? May Congress, in other words, regulate commerce to achieve other objectives—such as envi-

Heron, Canada Goose, Wood Duck, Mallard, Greater Yellowlegs, Belted Kingfisher, Northern Waterthrush, Louisiana Waterthrush, Swamp Sparrow, and Red-winged Blackbird." [ ]

ronmental protection? And, since the answer to that question seems quite clear, why is there any constitutional question about regulating wetlands that are used by migratory birds?

(2) A recent review of the Supreme Court's Commerce Clause cases concluded:

> Present day Commerce Clause jurisprudence seems nothing more than a struggle between two branches of government, with neither Congress nor the Court willing to give up power they perceive they are entitled to under the Constitution. Probably the Commerce Clause has been interpreted more broadly in the period after *Jones & Laughlin* that the Framers intended.[225] However, by articulating an incoherent standard in *Lopez* and reinforcing it in *Morrison,* the Court has overstepped its *own* boundaries of constitutional authority. With a new, unworkable and imprecise standard, there is a real danger of courts reaching too far and striking down statutes that, under modern jurisprudence, fall well within Congress' power to regulate pursuant to the Commerce Clause. As observed in *Gibbs,* "[t]he irony of disregarding limits on ourselves in the course of enforcing limits upon others will assuredly not be lost on those who look to courts to respect restraints imposed by rules of law."[227]

Christy H. Dral & Jerry J. Phillips, *Commerce by Another Name:* Lopez, Morrison, SWANCC, *and* Gibbs, 31 Envtl. L. Rep. (Envtl. L. Inst.) 10413, 10424 (2001).

SECTION 3.   FEDERAL AND STATE POWER OVER FEDERAL LANDS

a.   FEDERAL POWER OVER FEDERAL LANDS: THE PROPERTY CLAUSE

> The Congress shall have Power to dispose of and make all needful Rules and Regulations respecting the Territory or other Property belonging to the United States.
>
>   UNITED STATES CONSTITUTION art. IV, § 3, ¶ 2

Hunt v. United States

United States Supreme Court.
278 U.S. 96 (1928).

■ SUTHERLAND, J.:—The Kaibab National Forest and the Grand Canyon National Game Preserve, covering practically the same area, are situated

---

225. However, it is difficult to satisfactorily return to the Framer's understanding of a constitutional clause in present day circumstances because the times and indeed the very meaning of words have dramatically changed. For an excellent illustration of this proposition, see Thomas Y. Davies, *Recovering the Original Fourth Amendment,* 98 MICH. L. REV. 547 (1999).

227. *Gibbs v. Babbitt,* 214 F.3d 483, 492 (4th Cir.2000).

north of the Colorado River in Arizona. They were created by proclamations of the President under authority of Congress. During the last few years deer on these reserves have increased in such large numbers that the forage is insufficient for their subsistence. The result has been that these deer have greatly injured the lands in the reserves by over-browsing upon and killing valuable young trees, shrubs, bushes and forage plants. Thousands of deer have died because of insufficient forage. Attempts were made under the direction of the Secretary of Agriculture to remove some of the deer from the reserves to other lands, but these entirely failed, as did other means. The district forester, acting under the direction of the Secretary of Agriculture, proceeded to kill large numbers of the deer and ship the carcasses outside the limits of the reserves. That this was necessary to protect the lands of the United States within the reserves from serious injury is made clear by the evidence. The direction given by the Secretary of Agriculture was within the authority conferred upon him by act of Congress. And the power of the United States thus to protect its lands and property does not admit of doubt, *Camfield v. United States*, 167 U.S. 518, 525–26 (1897); *Utah Power & Light Co. v. United States*, 243 U.S. 389 (1917); *McKelvey v. United States*, 260 U.S. 353, 359 (1922); *United States v. Alford*, 274 U.S. 264 (1927), the game laws or any other statute of the state to the contrary notwithstanding.

Appellants interfered with these acts of the United States officials and threatened to arrest and prosecute any person or persons attempting to kill or possess or transport such deer, under the claim that such officials were proceeding in violation of the game laws of the State of Arizona, the observance of which would have so restricted the number of deer to be killed as to render futile the attempt to protect the reserves. Three persons who had killed deer under the authority of the United States were actually arrested. Thereupon suit was brought to enjoin appellants from continuing or threatening such interference, arrest or prosecution. The court below, after trial, found for the United States and entered a decree in accordance with the prayer of the bill, with the limitation, however, that the decree should not be construed to permit the licensing of hunters to kill deer within said reserves in violation of the state game laws. *United States v. Hunt*, 19 F.2d 634 (D.Ariz.1927).

While the Solicitor General does not concede the authority of the court to make this limitation, he is content to let the decree stand. We, therefore, pass the matter without consideration and accept the opinion and decree below, with the modification that all carcasses of deer and parts thereof shipped outside the boundaries of the reserve shall be plainly marked by tags or otherwise, in such manner as the Secretary of Agriculture may by regulation prescribe, to show that the deer were killed under his authority within the limits of the reserves.

Thus modified the decree is affirmed.

NOTES

(1) The scope of the power delegated by the Property Clause has been a point of contention between states with public lands and the federal government since the earliest days of the republic. The historical pattern in the Supreme Court's interpretation of the scope of the clause has moved in tandem with the policies adopted by Congress. When federal policy was disposition of the public domain, the Supreme Court upheld the exclusivity of federal law in determining when title passed. *E.g., Bagnell v. Broderick*, 38 U.S. (13 Pet.) 436, 450 (1839); *Wilcox v. McConnel*, 38 U.S. (13 Pet.) 498, 516–17 (1839). When Congress decided to lease rather than sell lead mines, the Court again upheld its decision. *United States v. Gratiot*, 39 U.S. (14 Pet.) 526 (1840). *See generally* Dale D. Goble, *The Myth of the Classic Property Clause Doctrine*, 63 DENV. U.L. REV. 495 (1986). And when Congress began to direct its delegatees to manage the lands and conserve their resources, the Court again upheld its power to do so:

(a) *Camfield v. United States:* In 1885, Congress enacted "An act to prevent unlawful occupancy of the public lands"—commonly known as the Unlawful Enclosure Act because it prohibited "all enclosures of any public lands" by any person without color of title. Camfield purchased a group of alternate sections of lands from the Union Pacific Railroad. (The railroad and public lands formed a checkerboard.) Camfield carefully constructed a fence on his lands that effectively enclosed 20,000 acres of contiguous public lands. When prosecuted for violating the Unlawful Enclosure Act, he argued that, if it applied to fences constructed on private property, it was unconstitutional. The Supreme Court disagreed. Analogizing the fences to nuisances, the Court quoted "the familiar maxim: *Sic utere tuo ut alienum non lædas*," and noted "[n]o person maintaining such a nuisance can shelter himself behind the sanctity of private property." In addition, the United States was not like a private property owner and need not rely upon the state courts to protect its interests:

> [W]e think the fence is clearly a nuisance, and that it is within the constitutional power of Congress to order its abatement, notwithstanding such action may involve an entry upon the lands of a private individual. The general government doubtless has a power over its own property analogous to the police power of the several States, and the extent to which it may go in the exercise of such power is measured by the exigencies of the particular case.... The inconvenience, or even damage, to the individual proprietor does not authorize an act which is in its nature a purpresture of government lands.

Camfield v. United States, 167 U.S. 518, 525–26 (1897).

(b) *Utah Power & Light Co. v. United States:* In compliance with state—but not federal—law, the power company had constructed diversion works and other facilities on federal lands in Utah. The company argued that this was sufficient because the "rights and powers of the United States as the owner of land within a State which is not used or needed for a governmental purpose, are the same as those of other owners of similar land within the same State." The Court rejected this argument:

> Not only does the Constitution (Art. IV, § 3, cl. 2) commit to Congress the Power "to dispose of and make all needful rules and regulations respecting" the lands of the United States, but the settled course of legislation, congressional and state, and repeated decisions of this court have gone upon the their that the power of Congress is exclusive and

that only through its exercise in some form can rights in lands belonging to the United States to be acquired. True, for many purposes a State has civil an criminal jurisdiction over lands within its limits belonging to the United States, but this jurisdiction does not extend to any matter that is not consistent with full power in the United States to protect its lands, to control their use and to prescribe in what manner others may acquire rights in them. Thus while the State may punish public offenses, such as murder or larceny, committed on such lands, and may tax private property, such a live stock, located thereon, it may not tax the lands themselves or invest others with any right whatever in them

Utah Power & Light Co. v. United States, 243 U.S. 389, 403–04 (1917).

(c) *United States v. Alford:* Alford was indicted for failing to extinguish a fire that he had built on his lands; the fire was built near inflammable materials located on lands owned by the United States. He demurred to the indictment on the ground that if it was applied to any lands other than National Forest lands it was unconstitutional. The Supreme Court rejected his argument, construing the statute as intended "to prevent forest fires which have been one of the great economic misfortunes of the country. The danger depends on the nearness of the fire, not upon the ownership of the land where it is built." As thus construed, the statute is constitutional because "Congress may prohibit the doing of acts upon privately owned lands that imperil the publicly owned forests." *United States v. Alford,* 274 U.S. 264 (1927).

Kleppe v. New Mexico

Supreme Court of the United States.
426 U.S. 529 (1976).

■ MARSHALL, J.:—At issue in this case is whether Congress exceeded its powers under the Constitution in enacting the Wild Free-roaming Horses and Burros Act.

I

The Wild Free-roaming Horses and Burros Act, [16 U.S.C. §§ 1331–1340], was enacted in 1971 to protect "all unbranded and unclaimed horses and burros on public lands of the United States," [ ], from "capture, branding, harassment, or death." [ ] The Act [directs the Secretary of the Interior acting through the Bureau of Land Management (BLM) and the Secretary of Agriculture acting through the Forest Service] "to protect and manage [the animals] as components of the public lands * * * in a manner that is designed to achieve and maintain a thriving natural ecological balance on the public lands." . . .

[After initially entering into a cooperative agreement with BLM on the management of the wild free-roaming horses and burros on the public lands, the New Mexico Livestock Board—the state agency charged with enforcing the New Mexico Estray Law—terminated the agreement, "[a]sserting that the Federal Government lacked power to control wild horses and burros on the public lands of the United States unless the animals were moving in interstate commerce or damaging the public lands."]

The differences between the Livestock Board and the Secretaries came to a head in February 1974. On February 1, 1974, a New Mexico rancher, Kelley Stephenson, was informed by the BLM that several unbranded burros had been seen near Taylor Well, where Stephenson watered his cattle. Taylor Well is on federal property, and Stephenson had access to it and some 8,000 surrounding acres only through a grazing permit issued pursuant to § 3 of the Taylor Grazing Act, [ ]. After the BLM made it clear to Stephenson that it would not remove the burros and after he personally inspected the Taylor Well area, Stephenson complained to the Livestock Board that the burros were interfering with his livestock operation by molesting his cattle and eating their feed.

Thereupon the Board rounded up and removed 19 unbranded and unclaimed burros pursuant to the New Mexico Estray Law. Each burro was seized on the public lands of the United States and, as the director of the Board conceded, each burro fit the definition of a wild free-roaming burro under § 2(b) of the Act. [ ] On February 18, 1974, the Livestock Board, pursuant to its usual practice, sold the burros at a public auction. After the sale, the BLM asserted jurisdiction under the Act and demanded that the Board recover the animals and return them to the public lands.

. . .

[The District Court held the Act unconstitutional on the ground that it "conflicts with * * * the traditional doctrines concerning wild animals," and is in excess of Congress' power under the Property Clause of the Constitution.]

II

The Property Clause of the Constitution provides that "Congress shall have Power to dispose of and make all needful Rules and Regulations respecting the Territory or other Property belonging to the United States." U.S. CONST., Art. IV, § 3, cl. 2. In passing the Wild Free-roaming Horses and Burros Act, Congress deemed the regulated animals "an integral part of the natural system of the public lands" of the United States, [ ], and found that their management was necessary "for achievement of an ecological balance on the public lands." [ ] According to Congress, these animals, if preserved in their native habitats, "contribute to the diversity of life forms within the Nation and enrich the lives of the American people." [ ] Indeed, Congress concluded, the wild free-roaming horses and burros "are living symbols of the historic and pioneer spirit of the West." [ ] Despite their importance, the Senate committee found:

> [These animals] have been cruelly captured and slain and their carcasses used in the production of pet food and fertilizer. They have been used for target practice and harassed for "sport" and profit. In spite of public outrage, this bloody traffic continues unabated, and it is the firm belief of the committee that this senseless slaughter must be brought to an end. [ ]

For these reasons, Congress determined to preserve and protect the wild free-roaming horses and burros on the public lands of the United States. The question under the Property Clause is whether this determination can be sustained as a "needful" regulation "respecting" the public lands. In answering this question, we must remain mindful that, while courts must eventually pass upon them, determinations under the Property Clause are entrusted primarily to the judgment of Congress. *United States v. San Francisco,* 310 U.S. 16, 29–30 (1940); *Light v. United States,* 220 U.S. 523, 537 (1911); *United States v. Gratiot,* 39 U.S. (14 Pet.) 526, 537–38 (1840).

Appellees argue that the Act cannot be supported by the Property Clause. They contend that the Clause grants Congress essentially two kinds of power: (1) the power to dispose of and make incidental rules regarding the use of federal property; and (2) the power to protect federal property. According to appellees, the first power is not broad enough to support legislation protecting wild animals that live on federal property; and the second power is not implicated since the Act is designed to protect the animals, which are not themselves federal property, and not the public lands. As an initial matter, it is far from clear that the Act was not passed in part to protect the public lands of the United States[7] or that Congress cannot assert a property interest in the regulated horses and burros superior to that of the State.[8] But we need not consider whether the Act can be upheld on either of these grounds, for we reject appellees' narrow reading of the Property Clause.

Appellees ground their argument on a number of cases that, upon analysis, provide no support for their position. Like the District Court, appellees cite *Hunt v. United States,* 278 U.S. 96 (1928), for the proposition that the Property Clause gives Congress only the limited power to regulate wild animals in order to protect the public lands from damage. But *Hunt,* which upheld the Government's right to kill deer that were damaging foliage in the national forests, only holds that damage to the land is a sufficient basis for regulation; it contains no suggestion that it is a necessary one.

Next, appellees refer to *Kansas v. Colorado,* 206 U.S. 46, 89 (1907). The referenced passage in that case states that the Property Clause "clearly * * * does not grant to Congress any legislative control over the states, and must, so far as they are concerned, be limited to authority over the property belonging to the United States within their limits." But this does no more than articulate the obvious: The Property Clause is a grant of power only over federal property. It gives no indication of the kind of "authority" the Clause gives Congress over its property.

Camfield v. United States, 167 U.S. 518 (1897), is of even less help to appellees. Appellees rely upon the following language from *Camfield:*

7. Congress expressly ordered that the animals were to be managed and protected in order "to achieve and maintain a thriving natural ecological balance on the public lands." [ ] *Cf. Hunt v. United States,* 278 U.S. 96 (1928).

8. .... The Secretary makes no claim here, however, that the United States owns the wild free-roaming horses and burros found on public land.

While we do not undertake to say that Congress has the unlimited power to legislate against nuisances within a State which it would have within a Territory, we do not think the admission of a Territory as a State deprives it of the power of legislating for the protection of the public lands, though it may thereby involve the exercise of what is ordinarily known as the police power, *so long as such power is directed solely to its own protection.* [ ] (emphasis added).

Appellees mistakenly read this language to limit Congress' power to regulate activity on the public lands; in fact, the quoted passage refers to the scope of congressional power to regulate conduct on *private* land that affects the public lands. And *Camfield* holds that the Property Clause is broad enough to permit federal regulation of fences built on private land adjoining public land when the regulation is for the protection of the federal property. *Camfield* contains no suggestion of any limitation on Congress' power over conduct on its own property; its sole message is that the power granted by the Property Clause is broad enough to reach beyond territorial limits.

Lastly, appellees point to dicta in two cases to the effect that, unless the State has agreed to the exercise of federal jurisdiction, Congress' rights in its land are "only the rights of an ordinary proprietor * * **" *Fort Leavenworth R.R. v. Lowe,* 114 U.S. 525, 527 (1885). *See also Paul v. United States,* 371 U.S. 245, 264 (1963). In neither case was the power of Congress under the Property Clause at issue or considered and, as we shall see, these dicta fail to account for the raft of cases in which the Clause has been given a broader construction.[9]

In brief, beyond the *Fort Leavenworth* and *Paul* dicta, appellees have presented no support for their position that the Clause grants Congress only the power to dispose of, to make incidental rules regarding the use of, and to protect federal property. This failure is hardly surprising, for the Clause, in broad terms, gives Congress the power to determine what are "needful" rules "respecting" the public lands. [ ] And while the furthest reaches of the power granted by the Property Clause have not yet been definitively resolved, we have repeatedly observed that "[t]he power over the public land thus entrusted to Congress is without limitations." *United States v. San Francisco,* 310 U.S. at 29. [ ]

The decided cases have supported this expansive reading. It is the Property Clause, for instance, that provides the basis for governing the Territories of the United States. [ ] And even over public land within the States, "[t]he general government doubtless has a power over its own property analogous to the police power of the several states, and the extent to which it may go in the exercise of such power is measured by the exigencies of the particular case." *Camfield v. United States,* [ ]. We have noted, for example, that the Property Clause gives Congress the power over

---

9. Indeed, *Hunt v. United States,* [ ], and *Camfield v. United States,* [ ], both relied upon by appellees, are inconsistent with the notion that the United States has only the rights of an ordinary proprietor with respect to its land. An ordinary proprietor may not, contrary to state law, kill game that is damaging his land, as the Government did in *Hunt;* nor may he prohibit the fencing in of his property without the assistance of state law, as the Government was able to do in *Camfield.*

the public lands "to control their occupancy and use, to protect them from trespass and injury, and to prescribe the conditions upon which others may obtain rights in them * * **" *Utah Power & Light Co. v. United States,* [ ]. And we have approved legislation respecting the public lands "[i]f it be found to be necessary, for the protection of the public or of intending settlers [on the public lands]." *Camfield v. United States,* [ ]. In short, Congress exercises the powers both of a proprietor and of a legislature over the public domain. [ ] Although the Property Clause does not authorize "an exercise of a general control over public policy in a State," it does permit "an exercise of the complete power which Congress has over particular public property entrusted to it." [ ] In our view, the "complete power" that Congress has over public lands necessarily includes the power to regulate and protect the wildlife living there.

III

Appellees argue that if we approve the Wild Free-roaming Horses and Burros Act as a valid exercise of Congress' power under the Property Clause, then we have sanctioned an impermissible intrusion on the sovereignty, legislative authority, and police power of the State and have wrongly infringed upon the State's traditional trustee powers over wild animals. The argument appears to be that Congress could obtain exclusive legislative jurisdiction over the public lands in the State only by state consent, and that in the absence of such consent Congress lacks the power to act contrary to state law. This argument is without merit.

Appellees' claim confuses Congress' derivative legislative powers, which are not involved in this case, with its powers under the Property Clause. Congress may acquire derivative legislative power from a State pursuant to Art. I, § 8, cl. 17, of the Constitution by consensual acquisition of land, or by nonconsensual acquisition followed by the State's subsequent cession of legislative authority over the land. [ ][11] In either case, the legislative jurisdiction acquired may range from exclusive federal jurisdiction with no residual state police power, [ ], to concurrent, or partial, federal legislative jurisdiction, which may allow the State to exercise certain authority. [ ]

But while Congress can acquire exclusive or partial jurisdiction over lands within a State by the State's consent or cession, the presence or absence of such jurisdiction has nothing to do with Congress' powers under the Property Clause. Absent consent or cession a State undoubtedly retains jurisdiction over federal lands within its territory, but Congress equally surely retains the power to enact legislation respecting those lands pursu-

---

11. Article I, § 8, cl. 17, of the Constitution provides that Congress shall have the power:

To exercise exclusive Legislation in all Cases whatsoever, over such District (not exceeding ten Miles square) as may, by Cession of Particular States, and the Acceptance of Congress, become the Seat of the Government of the United States, and to exercise like Authority over all Places purchased by the Consent of the Legislature of the State in which the Same shall be, for the Erection of Forts, Magazines, Arsenals, dock-Yards, and other needful Buildings * * **

The Clause has been broadly construed, and the acquisition by consent or cession of exclusive or partial jurisdiction over properties for any legitimate governmental purpose beyond those itemized is permissible. [ ]

ant the Property Clause. [ ] And when Congress so acts, the federal legislation necessarily overrides conflicting state laws under the Supremacy Clause. U.S. Const., Art. VI, cl. 2. [ ] As we said in *Camfield v. United States*, [ ], in response to a somewhat different claim: "A different rule would place the public domain of the United States completely at the mercy of state legislation."

Thus, appellees' assertion that "[a]bsent state consent by complete cession of jurisdiction of lands to the United States, exclusive jurisdiction does not accrue to the federal landowner with regard to federal lands within the borders of the state," [ ], is completely beside the point; and appellees' fear that the Secretary's position is that "the Property Clause totally exempts federal lands within state borders from state legislative powers, state police powers, and all rights and powers of local sovereignty and jurisdiction of the states," [ ], is totally unfounded. The Federal Government does not assert exclusive jurisdiction over the public lands in New Mexico, and the State is free to enforce its criminal and civil laws on those lands. But where those state laws conflict with the Wild Free-roaming Horses and Burros Act, or with other legislation passed pursuant to the Property Clause, the law is clear: The state laws must recede. [ ]

Again none of the cases relied upon by appellees are to the contrary. . . .

In short, these cases do not support appellees' claim that upholding the Act would sanction an impermissible intrusion upon state sovereignty. The Act does not establish exclusive federal jurisdiction over the public lands in New Mexico; it merely overrides the New Mexico Estray Law insofar as it attempts to regulate federally protected animals. And that is but the necessary consequence of valid legislation under the Property Clause.

Appellees' contention that the Act violates traditional state power over wild animals stands on no different footing. Unquestionably the States have broad trustee and police powers over wild animals within their jurisdictions. [ ]; *Geer v. Connecticut,* 161 U.S. 519, 528 (1896). But, as *Geer v. Connecticut* cautions, those powers exist only "in so far as [their] exercise may be not incompatible with, or restrained by, the rights conveyed to the federal government by the constitution." [ ] "No doubt it is true that as between a State and its inhabitants the State may regulate the killing and sale of [wildlife], but it does not follow that its authority is exclusive of paramount powers." *Missouri v. Holland,* 252 U.S. 416, 434 (1920). Thus, the Privileges and Immunities Clause, U.S. Const., Art. IV, § 2, cl. 1, precludes a State from imposing prohibitory licensing fees on nonresidents shrimping in its waters, *Toomer v. Witsell,* 334 U.S. 385 (1948); the Treaty Clause, U.S. Const., Art. II, § 2, permits Congress to enter into and enforce a treaty to protect migratory birds despite state objections, *Missouri v. Holland,* 252 U.S. 416, 434 (1920); and the Property Clause gives Congress the power to thin overpopulated herds of deer on federal lands contrary to state law. *Hunt v. United States,* 278 U.S. 96 (1928). We hold today that the Property Clause also gives Congress the power to protect wildlife on the public lands, state law notwithstanding.

IV

. . .

Appellees are concerned that the Act's extension of protection to wild free-roaming horses and burros that stray from public land onto private land, [ ], will be read to provide federal jurisdiction over every wild horse or burro that at any time sets foot upon federal land. While it is clear that regulations under the Property Clause may have some effect on private lands not otherwise under federal control, [ ], we do not think it appropriate in this declaratory judgment proceeding to determine the extent, if any, to which the Property Clause empowers Congress to protect animals on private lands or the extent to which such regulation is attempted by the Act. We have often declined to decide important questions regarding "the scope and constitutionality of legislation in advance of its immediate adverse effect in the context of a concrete case", [ ], or in the absence of "an adequate and full-bodied record." [ ] We follow that course in this case and leave open the question of the permissible reach of the Act over private lands under the Property Clause.

NOTES

(1) The state ownership doctrine: What impact does *Kleppe* have on the state ownership doctrine for wildlife that spend at least part of their time on federal lands? Note that the Court began its analysis by stating, "As an initial matter, it is far from clear . . . that Congress cannot assert a property interest in the regulated horses and burros superior to that of the State." Recall the argument by the United States in *United States v. Shauver* that the Property Clause was a source of power justifying the enactment of the Weeks–McLean Migratory Bird Act. Does the Court's dicta in *Kleppe* justify a federal claim of ownership of migratory birds? Does the Court's dicta instead refer to an interest *ratione soli*? Note also that the Court is careful to refrain from deciding the constitutionality of the Act under the Property Clause as applied to horses and burros found on private lands.

(2) The extraterritoriality of the Property Clause: Carl Brown was hunting ducks within the boundaries of Voyageurs National Park. Although the fast land within the Park were federal, the submerged lands were state because the waters were navigable. The state permitted hunting at the location; the federal government did not. Brown appealed his conviction by the magistrate to the district court; the state participated as *amicus*. The issue, as the court of appeals framed it, was whether the Property Clause delegated the federal government sufficient power to regulate the uses of non-federal lands to protect nearby federal lands. That issue, in turn, depended on whether the federal hunting regulations "can be deemed 'needful' prescriptions 'respecting' the public lands." The court decided that they could, and sustained the conviction: "[B]ecause duck hunting occurs in close proximity to adjacent lands, there is potential danger of unwarranted intrusion on public lands, injury to park users, and disruption of wildlife migration patterns." *United States v. Brown*, 552 F.2d 817 (8th Cir.), *cert. denied*, 431 U.S. 949 (1977). *See also Stupak–Thrall v.*

United States, 843 F.Supp. 327 (W.D.Mich.1994) (Property Clause empowers federal government to promulgate regulations prohibiting the use of electronic fish-finders on navigable waters within wilderness area). The decision in *Brown* is placed in its larger context in Eugene R. Gaetke, *The Boundary Waters Canoe Area Wilderness Act of 1978: Regulating Nonfederal Property under the Property Clause,* 60 OR. L. REV. 157 (1981).

(3) *Bailey v. Holland*: Congress is not limited to relying upon the Property Clause when it seeks to protect federal lands. In *Bailey v. Holland,* an owner of land adjacent to a National Wildlife Refuge challenged a federal regulation closing his private land to hunting, alleging that it exceeded the federal government's power and was a taking of his property. The court upheld the restriction on the authority of the Migratory Bird Treaty Act and hence the Treaty Clause. *Bailey v. Holland,* 126 F.2d 317 (4th Cir.1942).

b. THE STATE ROLE ON FEDERAL LANDS

(i) GENERAL PRINCIPLES

NOTES

(1) *Omaechevarria v. Idaho*: Secundino Omaechevarria was convicted of pasturing sheep on a cattle range, in violation of an Idaho statute. The land in question was owned by the federal government. He appealed his conviction to the Supreme Court, arguing that the state statute denied him equal protection of the laws. The Supreme Court, in a decision written by Justice Brandeis, affirmed the conviction. The Court began with the general principle: "The police power of the state extends over the federal public domain, at least when there is no legislation by Congress on the subject." *Omaechevarria v. Idaho,* 246 U.S. 343 (1918).

Omaechevarria remains the law: in the absence of federal legislation preempting state law, state law is applicable on the federal lands. Stated from a different perspective: there is no dormant Property Clause.

(2) *Granite Rock*: The Supreme Court's most recent extended discussion of state power on federal land involved a company that held unpatented mining claims to limestone deposits on federally owned land in the Big Sur region of the Los Padres National Forest in California. Following analysis of the deposit, the company prepared a plan for the development of the mine. The Forest Service prepared an environmental assessment pursuant to NEPA. The District Ranger approved the plan of operations with modifications, taking into account likely environmental impacts on the federal lands but ignoring impacts elsewhere. Shortly after the federal approval, the California Coastal Commission informed the company that it needed a state permit for mining since the mine was located within the state's coastal zone. Granite Rock responded by filing an action in federal court seeking to enjoin the state officials.

The Supreme Court began its analysis with the proposition announced in *Omaechevarria* and reaffirmed in *Kleppe v. New Mexico,* 426 U.S. 529, 543 (1976): " 'the State is free to enforce its criminal and civil laws' on

federal land so long as those laws do not conflict with federal law."
California Coastal Commission v. Granite Rock Co., 480 U.S. 572, 580
(1987). The issue thus was whether the federal statutory and regulatory
scheme preempted state regulation. The Court concluded that it did not,
basing its decision in part on a distinction between land use planning and
environmental regulation. The Court characterized the federal action as
land use planning—a description that it drew from the federal statutes
involved, the Federal Land Policy and Management Act of 1976 (FLPMA)
and the National Forest Management Act (NFMA). "For purposes of this
discussion and without deciding this issue, we may assume that the
combination of the NFMA and the FLPMA pre-empts the extension of state
land use plans onto unpatented mining claims in national forest lands." *Id.*
at 585. On the other hand, the Coastal Commission's characterized its
activities as environmental regulation—and the Court accepted this characterization:

> The line between environmental regulation and land use planning will
> not always be bright; for example, one may hypothesize a state envi-
> ronmental regulation so severe that a particular land use would
> become commercially impracticable. However, the core activity de-
> scribed by each phrase is undoubtedly different. Land use planning in
> essence chooses particular uses for the land; environmental regulation,
> at its core, does not mandate particular uses of the land but requires
> only that, however the land is used, damage to the environment is kept
> within prescribed limits. . . . Congress clearly envisioned that although
> environmental regulation and land use planning may hypothetically
> overlap in some instances, these two types of activity would in most
> cases be capable of differentiation. Considering the legislative under-
> standing of environmental regulation and land use planning as distinct
> activities, it would be anomalous to maintain that Congress intended
> any state environmental regulation of unpatented mining claims in
> national forests to be per se pre-empted as an impermissible exercise of
> state land use planning. Congress' treatment of environmental regula-
> tion and land use planning as generally distinguishable calls for this
> Court to treat them as distinct, until an actual overlap between the
> two is demonstrated in a particular case.

Id. at 587–88.

Is the protection of wildlife habitat "environmental regulation" or
"land use planning"? If the state were to specify that certain classes of
habitat were to the protected, would this be "land use regulation"? If so, is
it pre-empted? Note that the Court actually does not decide the issue—
"without deciding this issue, we may assume that the combination of the
NFMA and the FLPMA pre-empts the extension of state land use plans
onto unpatented mining claims in national forest lands." *Id.* at 585. *See
generally* Eric T. Freyfogle, Granite Rock: *Institutional Competence and the
State Role in Federal Land Planning*, 59 U. Colo. L. Rev. 465 (1988); John
D. Leshy, Granite Rock *and the States' Influence over Federal Land Use*, 18
Envtl. L. 99, 109–12 (1987).

(ii) A SPECIAL NOTE: HUNTING AND FISHING ON FEDERAL LANDS

Defenders of Wildlife v. Andrus

District of Columbia Circuit Court of Appeals.
627 F.2d 1238 (1980).

■ McGOWAN, C.J.:—This is an appeal from an order of the District Court granting a preliminary injunction against the Secretary of the Interior. It raises the question of whether, under the circumstances of this case, the National Environmental Policy Act obligates the Secretary to prepare and circulate an environmental impact statement when he does not act to prevent the State of Alaska from conducting, as part of a wildlife-management program, a wolf hunt on certain federal land. Because the Secretary's conduct here does not constitute a "major Federal action" within the meaning of the Act, we hold that the Secretary is not so obligated, and we reverse.

I *The Background of this Action*

On February 16, 1979, the Alaska Department of Fish and Game (ADFG) announced a program whose aim was to kill from aircraft 170 wolves (approximately sixty percent of the wolf population) in an area of 35,000 square miles in the interior part of the state. Many, perhaps most, of the wolves were to be killed on federal lands for which the Department of the Interior is responsible. On February 23, counsel for one of the appellees, Natural Resources Defense Counsel, Inc., asked the Department to prepare an environmental impact statement for Alaska's program before allowing it to begin. The Department, however, did not exercise whatever authority it may have to stop the program and did not prepare an impact statement. On March 12, appellees organizations and individuals interested in the preservation of the environment in general and of wildlife in particular filed a complaint asking for declaratory and injunctive relief against appellants the Secretary and two other officials of the Department of the Interior.

The complaint predicted that, although the wolf hunt was proposed in order to increase the number of moose in the region by decreasing the numbers of their major predator, it would in fact weaken the moose herds by ending a "culling process [which] is natural selection in action, and [which] assures survival of the fittest moose * * *" and would devastate the wolf packs even beyond the ADFG's estimates. This interference with these two major species, the complaint continued, would disrupt the ecology of the entire area.

The complaint asserted that the Federal Land Policy and Management Act (FLPMA), [ ], authorizes the Secretary of the Interior to prevent the killing of wildlife on federal lands and requires him to evaluate whether he must intervene if he is fully to serve the environmental concerns of the Act. The complaint claimed as one of its "Violations of Law" that appellants failed to make that evaluation. The other violation of law the complaint alleged is that appellants had, but failed to meet, an obligation under

[NEPA] to prepare an environmental impact statement before deciding not to prevent Alaska from killing wolves on Federal land.

On March 13, 1979, the United States District Court for the District of Columbia issued a temporary restraining order which enjoined appellants to "take all steps necessary to halt the aerial killing of wolves by agents of the State of Alaska" on the relevant federal lands. Although Alaska has apparently continued to kill wolves on its own lands, it has discontinued doing so on federal lands.

. . .

[T]he District Court believed it was "confronted with a simple question: Does NEPA require the Secretary of the Interior to prepare an EIS prior to permitting an extensive wolf kill to take place on federal lands?" The District Court reasoned that FLPMA requires the Secretary "to *manage* and *plan* the use of federal lands" and that "[c]learly, an environmental assessment of the wolf elimination program must be part of the decisionmaking process." The District Court therefore issued a preliminary injunction which required appellants "to prevent any such killing of wolves pending preparation of an environmental impact statement on the potential effects of the wolf control program."

II *Earlier Related Cases*

This is not the first time a federal court has been asked to order the Secretary of the Interior to keep Alaska from killing wolves on federal land. In 1976, the Alaska Department of Fish and Game announced that it proposed to kill about eighty percent of the wolves in three of its game-management units. Many of the plaintiffs in the case presently before us asked the District Court for the District of Columbia . . . for an injunction similar to the one we are now reviewing. *Defenders of Wildlife v. Andrus,* 9 Envtl. Rep. Cas. 2111 (Feb. 14, 1977). They contended that the Secretary of the Interior had violated FLPMA, the Alaska Native Claims Settlement Act (ANCSA), [ ], and NEPA by failing (1) to assess the environmental consequences of killing wolves and (2) to prepare an environmental impact statement. The Secretary responded that he lacked authority to close federal land to state wildlife-management programs.

Judge Gasch decided, after examining the language and legislative history of FLPMA and ANCSA, that the Secretary does have that authority. . . . *Defenders of Wildlife v. Andrus,* 9 Envtl. Rep. Cas. at 2118. Judge Gasch therefore granted the request for a preliminary injunction.

After that injunction issued, the Secretary ordered the Governor of Alaska, by telegram, not to kill wolves on the relevant federal land. Alaska complied, but brought an action in the District Court for Alaska . . . which asked the court to declare the Secretary's order a violation of the Alaska Statehood Act, [ ], and to enjoin the Secretary to withdraw that order. *Alaska v. Andrus,* 429 F. Supp. 958 (D.C.Alaska 1977). Plaintiffs in the action over which Judge Gasch presided intervened in the Alaska suit. Like Judge Gasch before him, Judge von der Heydt found that the Secretary had the power to close federal lands to state wildlife-management programs, but he held that the Secretary need not exercise that power, since the

Secretary's failure to prevent the state from carrying out its program did not convert that program into "a major federal action triggering NEPA requirements." *Id.* at 962....

The state and the intervenors appealed to the Court of Appeals for the Ninth Circuit.[3] *Alaska v. Andrus,* 591 F.2d 537 (9th Cir.1979). That court affirmed, holding that, "even if the Secretary had some power under a delegation by Congress to stop the wolf-kill program, his failure to exercise that power in effect, his inaction was not the type of conduct that requires an environmental impact statement." *Id.* at 540. The court noted that it has always hesitated to describe as "federal" programs in which federal funds are not spent and federal agents are not employed.

Meanwhile, the Secretary had appealed from Judge Gasch's grant of a preliminary injunction. *Defenders of Wildlife v. Andrus,* 593 F.2d 1371. On March 16, 1979, after the Ninth Circuit had handed down its decision, we vacated the injunction and directed that the complaint be dismissed "for want of equity." In an unpublished memorandum accompanying our order, we said that "[s]ound principles of comity dictate that this court should not undertake an independent examination of the issues resolved by the Ninth Circuit ruling." We also noted that recent developments in the case had infected it with a staleness which made the grant of equitable relief, always a matter within the court's discretion, inappropriate.

. . .

IV *The Secretary's Obligations Under NEPA*

. . .

[W]e turn to the specific issue we must resolve. Does NEPA require that the Secretary prepare and circulate an environmental impact statement in the circumstances of this case?

Our discussion of that question must center around the fact that, while the plain language of the statute calls for an impact statement when there is "major Federal action," here it is the Secretary's inaction which is complained of....

[A]s it is written, NEPA only refers to decisions which the agency anticipates will lead to actions. This common-sense reading of the statute is confirmed by the statutory directive that the impact statement is to be part of a "recommendation or report" on a "proposal" for action. That is, only when an agency reaches the point in its deliberations when it is ready to propose a course of action need it be ready to produce an impact statement....

None of this is to say that agencies may, by manipulating the time at which they actually develop recommendations or reports on proposals, seek to avoid or perniciously to delay preparing an impact statement. It is

---

3. The Secretary also appealed. Before the case was decided, however, he reversed his earlier stand by concluding he had au- thority to close federal lands to Alaska's wolf hunt. He therefore withdrew his appeal.

simply to confirm that Congress did not expect agencies to prepare statements if there is to be no action.

. . .

V *The Relationship of NEPA and FLPMA*

The District Court and appellees believe that the above analysis of the Secretary's duty under NEPA is insufficient. They reason that FLPMA imposes such supervisory duties on the Secretary that every failure to prohibit a state wildlife program which is carried out on Federal land and which may have significant environmental consequences must be accounted for with an impact statement. The District Court decided

> that the Secretary has a nondiscretionary duty to plan for and manage federal land and resources. In view of this responsibility, the Secretary must prohibit any major actions significantly affecting the human environment from occurring on federal lands until an environmental impact statement has been prepared and circulated. Accordingly, until an EIS has been prepared, the Secretary must take appropriate action to prevent aerial wolf killing on federal lands by the State of Alaska and its agents.

[ ]

FLPMA . . . was enacted "to provide the first comprehensive, statutory statement of purposes, goals, and authority for the use and management of about 448 million acres of federally-owned lands administered by the Secretary of the Interior through the Bureau of Land Management." S. Rep. No. 94–583, 94th Cong., 1st Sess. 24 (1975). As such, it certainly imposes on the Secretary a general duty "to plan for and manage federal land and resources." However, the District Court's reasoning seems to us to upset an allocation of functions Congress carefully and explicitly made in FLPMA, for Congress there assigned the states the primary responsibility for the management of wildlife programs within their boundaries.

It is unquestioned that "the States have broad trustee and police powers over wild animals within their jurisdictions," *Kleppe v. New Mexico,* 426 U.S. 529, 545 (1976). Neither is it questioned that, because the Property Clause of the Constitution provides that "Congress shall have Power to dispose of and make all needful Rules and Regulations respecting the Territory or other Property belonging to the United States," U.S. Const., Art. IV, § 3, cl. 2, Congress may, if it wishes, pre-empt state management of wildlife on federal lands. *Kleppe v. New Mexico,* 426 U.S. at 539–41. Despite its ability to take control into its own hands, Congress has traditionally allotted the authority to manage wildlife to the states. For instance, in the Multiple Use–Sustained Yield Act of 1960, Congress declared:

> It is the policy of the Congress that the national forests are established and shall be administered for outdoor recreation, range, timber, watershed, and wildlife and fish purposes.* * * Nothing herein shall be construed as affecting the jurisdiction or responsibilities of the several States with respect to wildlife and fish on the national forests.* * *

16 U.S.C. § 528.

Even in writing specifically "environmental" legislation, Congress has adhered to that allocation. Thus, Congress stated in the National Wildlife Refuge System Administration Act,

> The Provisions of this Act shall not be construed as affecting the authority, jurisdiction, or responsibility of the several States to manage, control, or regulate fish and resident wildlife under State law or regulations in any area within the System.

16 U.S.C. § 668dd(c). Similarly, the Wild and Scenic Rivers Act provides that

> [n]othing in this chapter shall affect the jurisdiction or responsibilities of the States with respect to fish and wildlife.

16 U.S.C. § 1284(a).[7]

Far from attempting to alter the traditional division of authority over wildlife management, FLPMA broadly and explicitly reaffirms it. Section 302(b) of FLPMA begins by directing that the Secretary shall regulate "the use, occupancy, and development of the public lands." After a proviso relating to the use of lands by federal agencies, section 302(b) continues:

> *Provided further,* That *nothing in this Act* shall be construed as authorizing the Secretary concerned to require Federal permits to hunt and fish on public lands or on lands in the National Forest System and adjacent waters *or as enlarging or diminishing the responsibility and authority of the States for management of fish and resident wildlife.* However, the Secretary concerned *may* designate areas of public land and of lands in the National Forest System where, and establish periods when, no hunting or fishing will be permitted for reasons of public safety, administration, or compliance with provisions of applicable law. Except in emergencies, any regulations of the Secretary concerned relating to hunting and fishing pursuant to this section shall

---

7. When Congress has wished to change this traditional allocation of tasks, it has done so self-consciously and precisely, as the Endangered Species Act of 1973, [ ], demonstrates. The House Committee responsible for the bill carefully noted that coherent national and international policies were needed adequately to protect endangered species. [ ] In the Act itself, Congress specifically provided:

> Any State law or regulation which applies with respect to the importation or exportation of, or interstate or foreign commerce in, endangered species or threatened species is void to the extent that it may effectively (1) permit what is prohibited by this chapter or by any regulation which implements this chapter, or (2) prohibit what is authorized pursuant to an exemption or permit provided for in this chapter or in any regulation which implements this chapter. This chapter shall not otherwise be construed

to void any State law or regulation which is intended to conserve migratory, resident, or introduced fish or wildlife, or to permit or prohibit sale of such fish or wildlife.

16 U.S.C. § 1535(f). Even in this Act, however, the House Committee report continued the comments quoted above by reaffirming the importance of state management of wildlife:

> [T]he states are far better equipped to handle the problems of day-to-day management and enforcement of laws and regulations for the protection of endangered species than is the Federal government. It is true, and indeed desirable, that there are more fish and game enforcement agents in the state system than there are in the Federal government.

H. Rep. No. 93–412, 93d Cong., 1st Sess. 7 (1973).

be put into effect only after consultation with the appropriate State fish and game department.

43 U.S.C. § 1732(b) (emphasis added).[8]

The first quoted sentence of section 302(b) self-evidently places the "responsibility and authority" for state wildlife management precisely where Congress has traditionally placed it—in the hands of the states. The second quoted sentence of the section arguably permits ("may"), but certainly does not require ("shall"), the Secretary to supersede a state program, and even when he does so, it must be after consulting state authorities. We are simply unable to read this cautious and limited permission to intervene in an area of state responsibility and authority as imposing such supervisory duties on the Secretary that each state action he fails to prevent becomes a "Federal action." A state wildlife-management agency which must seek federal approval for each program it initiates can hardly be said to have "responsibility and authority" for its own affairs.

Appellees remind us that FLPMA directs the Secretary to "manage the public lands under principles of multiple use and sustained yield," 43 U.S.C. s 1732(a), and that

> "multiple use" means * * * a combination of balanced and diverse resource uses that takes into account the long-term needs of future generations for renewable and nonrenewable resources, including, but not limited to, recreation, range, timber, minerals, watershed, wildlife and fish, and natural scenic, scientific and historical values * * *.

43 U.S.C. § 1702(c). Appellees also remind us that, pursuant to his authority under FLPMA, 43 U.S.C. § 1714(e), the Secretary has ordered that some of the lands on which wolves are to be killed

> are withdrawn from settlement, sale, location, entry or selection under the operation of the public land laws, including but not limited to the mining laws * * * and are reserved and appropriated for the public purpose of preserving, protecting, and maintaining the resource values of said lands which would otherwise be lost * * *.

8. A glance at the legislative history confirms what is plain enough on the face of the statute—Congress intended that the primary responsibility for wildlife management would lie with the states. The Committee report on the House version of the bill explained that the bill

> provides that hunting and fishing will be permitted in accordance with Federal and State laws and that no Federal permits for hunting or fishing are authorized by this section. It permits the Secretaries to close areas to hunting and fishing for reasons of public safety. The Secretaries are expected to use the authority granted by the bill to close areas only if essential to the public safety, and then only for the shortest periods needed to accomplish this purpose. Protection of the public safety includes prevention and

avoidance of hazards to persons, animals, and property.

H. Rep. No.94–1163, 94th Cong., 2d Sess. 6 (1976), 1976 U.S.C.C.A.N. 6175, 6180. The Conference Report makes the point even more clearly.

> The conferees authorize the two Bureaus to ban hunting and fishing for reasons of public safety, administration, and compliance with applicable law. The word "administration" authorizes exclusion of hunting and fishing from an area in order to maintain supervision. It does not authorize exclusions simply because hunting and fishing would interfere with resource-management goals.

H. Rep. No. 94–1724, 94th Cong., 2d Sess. 60 (1976), 1976 U.S.C.C.A.N. 6231.

43 *Fed. Reg.* 59756 (December 21, 1978).

Nevertheless, the statutory provisions of which appellees remind us are all part of FLPMA. Section 302(b) of that Act expressly commands that "nothing in this Act" enlarges or diminishes the state's responsibility for managing wildlife. We are therefore unable to conclude that appellees' citations to FLPMA should alter our understanding of the Secretary's obligation to prepare an environmental impact statement when he declines to exercise the power which FLPMA arguably gives him to preempt state wildlife-management programs.[10]

The order of the District Court granting a preliminary injunction is reversed.

NOTES

(1) Does the Secretary have the authority under FLPMA to halt the wolf kill? The statutes gives the Secretary power to close federal lands to hunting "for reasons of public safety, administration, or compliance with provisions of applicable law." What are examples of each of these? What does "administration" mean?

(2) What does the court mean by the final footnote? Other provisions in FLPMA provide general management standards: "The Secretary shall manage the public lands under the principles of multiple use and sustained yield." 43 U.S.C. § 1732(a) "In managing the public lands the Secretary shall, by regulation, or otherwise take any action necessary to prevent unnecessary or undue degradation of the lands." *Id.* § 1732(b). Could the Secretary violate these provisions by failing to halt a wolf kill under some circumstances?

(3) Is the state's objective (increasing moose and caribou populations) a hunting and fishing regulation? Is it habitat management? Recall the irruptive nature of wild ungulate populations and the habitat damage caused by a population explosion. If the state proposed to kill *all* predators, would the Secretary be obliged to wait for habitat degradation before acting? Is the line between the two as sharp as Congress—and the court—seem to feel?

Consider the prairie dog. Hated by cattle ranchers because it eats grass and shot by "varmint" hunters just because, the species has long been the target of extermination. But prairie dogs are keystone species whose burrowing and grazing structure the prairie ecosystem. Prairie dog burrows provide homes for burrowing owls, rattlesnakes, and black-footed ferrets; mountain plovers require the grazed-over towns to nest; the animals themselves are food for the ferrets, ferruginous hawks, and swift foxes. Thus, it is not surprising that the drive to exterminate prairie dogs has

---

10. It is possible to read appellees' complaint as alleging that the Secretary has violated duties under FLPMA quite apart from FLPMA's effect on his obligation to prepare an environmental impact statement. However, we do not understand the District Court to have done more than instruct the Secretary to halt the killing of wolves until he has prepared an environmental impact statement. Therefore, although our discussion of FLPMA has necessarily touched on the limited nature of the Secretary's obligations under the Act, we do not otherwise reach the question of whether he has violated it.

pushed black-footed ferrets to the brink of extinction and have threatened burrowing owls, swift foxes, and a host of other species: some 158 species of animals live in, feed off, or rely upon prairie dog towns. Mark Matthews, *"Nobody Gives a Damn About the Prairie Dog,"* HIGH COUNTRY N., Nov. 11, 1996. Could a federal land managing agency simply do nothing and claim that it had no obligation to account for the known impacts of its deliberate inaction?

(4) Congressional reassurances: Despite the increasingly pervasive federal role in wildlife conservation since the Lacey Act, the national government has retained a formal policy of deference to traditional state prerogatives. Congress has repeatedly sought to reassure the states that it is they who have the responsibility and authority to manage resident wildlife. *E.g.,* Migratory Bird Conservation Act, 16 U.S.C. §§ 715h (state may set bag limits more restrictive than federal limits), 718c (state may require hunting license); the Multiple Use–Sustained Yield Act of 1960, 16 U.S.C. § 528 (1988) ("Nothing herein shall be construed as affecting the jurisdiction or responsibilities of the several States with respect to wildlife and fish on the national forests."); National Wildlife Refuge System Administration Act, 16 U.S.C. § 668dd(c) (1988) ("The Provisions of this Act shall not be construed as affecting the authority, jurisdiction, or responsibility of the several States to manage, control, or regulate fish and resident wildlife under State law or regulations in any area within the System."); National Wild & Scenic Rivers Act, 16 U.S.C. § 1284(a) (1988) ("Nothing in this Act shall affect the jurisdiction or responsibilities of the States with respect to fish and wildlife."); Federal Land Policy & Management Act, 43 U.S.C. § 1732(b) (1988) ("[N]othing in this Act shall be construed as authorizing the Secretary concerned to require Federal permits to hunt and fish ion public lands or on lands in the National Forest System and adjacent waters or as enlarging or diminishing the responsibility and authority of the States for management of fish and resident wildlife."). What do these various statutes suggest in the context of the *Granite Rock* distinctions?

Given this record of deference, courts have not hesitated, not only to allow states to enforce their wildlife laws on federal lands, but also to allow federal agencies to defer to state management decisions when they choose to do so. *E.g., Totemoff v. State,* 905 P.2d 954 (Alaska 1995) (sustaining conviction of subsistence hunter on federal lands who used spotlight in violation of state law); *O'Brien v. State,* 711 P.2d 1144 (Wyo.1986) (sustaining conviction for hunting in federal wilderness area without state-licensed guide as required by state law); *Fund for Animals, Inc. v. Thomas,* 932 F.Supp. 368 (D.D.C.1996) (Forest Service can allow states to decide whether and how to regulate the baiting of game on federal land without preparing environmental impact statement).

SECTION 4.   A CHRONOLOGICAL PERSPECTIVE

This chapter has examined the evolution of federal constitutional authority over wildlife by examining the various clauses of the Constitution that empower the federal government to regulate wildlife. This perspective highlights the separate fields of federal authority—a traditional view of federal power. Examining the cases chronologically, on the other hand, highlights the similarities in the courts' analysis and the gradual evolution of the rationales.

Corfield v. Coryell, 6 F. Cas. 546 (C.C.E.D.Pa.1823) (No. 3,230), is the beginning. Defendant challenged the constitutionality of a New Jersey statute prohibiting non-residents from harvesting oysters. The court held that the statute violated neither the Privileges and Immunities Clause nor the dormant Commerce Clause because the state owned the oysters and thus it was merely allocating common property among its citizens. This conclusion was accepted by the Supreme Court in three decisions decided over the course of the nineteenth century. *Smith v. Maryland*, 59 U.S. (18 How.) 71 (1855); *McCready v. Virginia*, 94 U.S. 391 (1876); *Manchester v. Commonwealth*, 139 U.S. 240 (1891).

Corfield led to *Geer v. Connecticut*, 161 U.S. 519 (1896), the apogee of the state ownership doctrine as a shield against federal law. In *Geer*, the Court held that the state's power as owner was such that it could determine what property interests an individual acquired when she captured wildlife. Although the Court was careful to note that the state had the power to regulate wildlife only "in so far as its exercise may be not incompatible with, or restrained by, the rights conveyed to the federal government by the constitution," the caveat—like the similar language in *Smith*, *McCready*, and *Manchester*—was ignored. The caveat, however, became the rule in the twentieth century.

The change was signalled by *Missouri v. Holland*, 252 U.S. 416 (1920), in which the Court held that the Treaty Clause empowered Congress to regulate migratory birds—something that it has previously been unable to do under the Commerce or Property Clauses. The transformation was captured in the phrase from Justice Holmes' decision that the Court quoted repeatedly: "To put the claim of the State upon title is to lean upon a slender reed."

The erosion of *Geer* began in earnest in 1928 when the Court limited the decision to situations in which the state entirely banned export; if the state chose to allow commerce in wildlife, it lost its power to restrict that commerce under the dormant Commerce Clause. *Foster-Fountain Packing Co. v. Haydel*, 278 U.S. 1 (1928).

In the same term, the Court held that the Property Clause gave a federal land manager the power to order the killing of wildlife contrary to state statutes when the wildlife was damaging federal property. *Hunt v. United States*, 278 U.S. 96 (1928).

In *Toomer v. Witsell*, 334 U.S. 385 (1948), the Court returned to the Privileges and Immunities Clause. The Clause, the Court held, precluded states from imposing licensing barriers to the pursuit of one's occupation. A North Carolina statute imposing discriminatory licensing fees on non-resident shrimp fishers thus was unconstitutional.

The decisions then came in a rush. In *Kleppe v. New Mexico*, 426 U.S. 529 (1976), the Court held that the Property Clause empowered Congress to preempt state law managing feral horses and burros on the public lands. The next year the Court decided that a state could not prohibit nonresidents from fishing in its coastal waters when they held federal licenses. *Douglas v. Seacoast Products, Inc.,* 431 U.S. 265 (1977). *Douglas* undercut—if it did not overrule—the decisions in *Smith v. Maryland* and *Manchester v. Commonwealth.* In 1978, the Court refused to extend *Toomer* to recreational hunting, holding that the Privilege and Immunities did not require states to treat non-residents on par with residents in the allocation of hunting licenses. *Baldwin v. Fish & Game Commission,* 436 U.S. 371 (1978). Finally, in *Hughes v. Oklahoma,* 441 U.S. 322 (1979), the Court formally overruled *Geer,* while "mak[ing] ample allowance for preserving . . . the legitimate state concerns for conservation and protection of wild animals underlying the 19th-century legal fiction of state ownership."

The trajectory of the Court decisions has been to bring wildlife law into conformity with general constitutional principles: although a state's special interest in wildlife cannot be used to shield its allocational decisions when those decisions favor its own citizens' commercial activities, a state retains broad powers to regulate "noncommercial" access to wildlife—even to the point of being able to discriminate in favor of its own citizens.

CHAPTER 7

THE THIRD SOVEREIGN: INDIAN TREATY RIGHTS IN THE FEDERAL SYSTEM

In many regions of the United States—particularly the Great Lakes, the northern Great Plains, the Southwest and the Pacific Northwest—it is impossible to understand wildlife law without understanding the importance of a third sovereign: the Indian tribes and nations. Indian law is an amalgam of constitutional law, federal jurisdiction, sovereign immunity, and intergovernmental relations as well as topics such as property, torts, contracts, and taxation.

In this chapter, we are concerned with Indian rights to hunt and fish. The source of these rights lies in aboriginal use:

> Indian possession or occupation was considered with reference to their habits and modes of life; their hunting grounds were as much in their actual possession as the cleared fields of the whites; and their rights to its exclusive enjoyment in their own way and for their own purposes were as much respected, until they abandoned them, made a cession to the government, or an authorized sale to individuals.

Mitchel v. United States, 34 U.S. (9 Pet.) 711, 746 (1835). *See also Sac & Fox Tribe v. Licklider*, 576 F.2d 145 (8th Cir.), *cert. denied*, 439 U.S. 955 (1978) (aboriginal rights remain in Indians unless ceded by treaty, abandoned, or extinguished by statute). The importance of traditional practices often led tribes to reserve continuing rights to hunt and fish in treaties with the United States. The impact of these rights outside of reservations has produced disputes with private landowners who seek to restrict access to traditional hunting or fishing sites as well as frequent clashes with state governments over the power of states to regulate the treaty rights.

We begin with a brief look at the nature of the treaty right.

SECTION 1. CONSTRUING TREATIES: GENERAL PRINCIPLES

Felix Cohen's Handbook of Federal Indian Law

ch. 3, § C2(a)–(b) (rev. ed. 1982).

The concept of a federal trust responsibility to Indians evolved judicially. It first appeared in Chief Justice Marshall's decision in *Cherokee Nation v. Georgia.*[24] *Cherokee Nation* was an original action filed by the tribe in the Supreme Court to enjoin enforcement of state laws on lands guaranteed to the tribe by treaties. The Court decided that it lacked original jurisdiction because the tribe, although a "distinct political society" and thus generically a "state," was neither a state of the United States nor a foreign state and therefore was not entitled to bring the suit initially in the Court. Chief Justice Marshall concluded that Indian tribes "may, more correctly, perhaps, be denominated domestic dependent nations ... in a state of pupilage" and that "[t]heir relation to the United States resembles that of a ward to his guardian."

The Court's subsequent decision in *Worcester v. Georgia*[29] reaffirmed the status of Indian tribes as self-governing entities without, however, elaborating on the nature or meaning of the guardian-ward relationship....

As the following sections indicate, during the twentieth century the trust principles articulated in *Cherokee Nation v. Georgia* have been applied in many specific situations to establish and protect rights of Indian tribes and many specific situations to establish and protect rights of Indian tribes and individuals. Trust obligations define the required standard of conduct for federal officials and Congress. Fiduciary duties form the substantive basis for various claims against the federal government. Even more broadly, federal action toward Indians as expressed in treaties, agreements, statutes, executive orders, and administrative regulations is construed in light of the trust responsibility. As a result, the trust relationship is one of the primary cornerstones of Indian law.

   . . .

The trust obligation of the United States also constrains congressional power in a procedural manner. Since Congress is exercising a trust responsibility when dealing with Indians, courts presume that Congress' intent toward them is benevolent and have developed canons of construction that treaties and other federal action should when possible be read as protecting Indian rights and in a manner favorable to Indians.

The primary canons of construction in Indian law were first developed in cases involving treaties. In construing Indian treaties, the courts have required that treaties be liberally construed to favor Indians, that ambiguous expressions in treaties must be resolved in favor of the Indians, and that treaties should be construed as the Indians would have understood them. These precepts represent an acknowledgment of the unequal bargaining position, based partially on the United States' superior negotiating skills and knowledge of the language. One consequence of this is that many important protections have been held by the courts to be reserved implicitly by treaties. For example, important resource rights such as reserved water rights and the right to hunt and fish are implied from treaties and agreements by which Indian reservations were created. Similarly, the

---

24. 30 U.S. (5 Pet.) 1 (1831).   **29.** 31 U.S. (6 Pet.) 515 (1832).

reservation of tribal self-government free of state jurisdiction was initially derived by implication from treaties.

. . .

Similar rules of construction have been applied to situations which do not involve treaties. The essential policy for the development of the canons in treaty cases was not based on the form of the transaction, a treaty, but rather was rooted in the special trust relationship between the United States and Indian tribes. In addition, in implementing the federal-tribal relationship Congress has not drawn distinctions between treaty tribes and nontreaty tribes.

Statutes, agreements, and executive orders dealing with Indian affairs have been construed liberally in favor of establishing Indian rights. This applies, for example, to the recognition of hunting and fishing rights and water rights, and to exemptions from exercises of state taxing authority.

Once powers of tribal self-government or other Indian rights are shown to exist, by treaty or otherwise, later federal action which might arguably abridge them is construed narrowly in favor of retaining Indian rights. The principle of a "clear and plain statement" before Indian treaty rights can be abrogated also applies in nontreaty contexts. . . .

. . .

The rules for construing federal statutes in Indian affairs have a pervasive influence in Indian law. The cannons are variously phrased in different contexts, but generally they provide for a broad construction when the issue is whether Indian rights are reserved or established, and for a narrow construction when Indian rights are to be abrogated or limited. These canons play an essential role in implementing the trust relationship between the United States and Indian tribes and are involved in most of the subject matter of Indian law.

NOTES

(1) This excerpt from the standard treatise on Indian law sets out the key concepts that underlie the materials in the remainder of this chapter—the trust responsibility. The relationship between the tribes and the federal government imposes fiduciary obligations on the government to act as a trustee—an obligation that is often stated as an interpretive strategy to be employed to resolve ambiguities in federal actions.

(2) Some examples: In *Menominee Tribe v. United States*, 391 U.S. 404 (1968), the Court held that, despite the fact that the treaty did not specifically mention hunting or fishing, the words "to be held as Indian lands are held" was effective to reserve the rights to hunt and fish. An 1891 statute setting aside the Annette Islands as a reservation for the Metlakatla Indians was held to impliedly reserve the adjacent waters exclusively for Indian fishing since the purpose of the reservation was to make the Indian self-sufficient—something that was impossible without the exclusive rights to the fishing grounds adjacent to the islands. *Alaska*

Pacific Fisheries v. United States, 248 U.S. 78 (1918). *See also Antoine v. Washington*, 420 U.S. 194 (1975).

SECTION 2.   THE NATURE OF THE TREATY RIGHT

Whitefoot v. United States

United States Court of Claims.
293 F.2d 658 (1961).
certiorari denied, 369 U.S. 818 (1962).

■ REED, J. (Retired), sitting by designation:—This is a suit to recover compensation for the taking by destruction through inundation of certain fishing rights and other rights claimed as the individual property of plaintiffs in the Columbia River near Celilo Falls in the States of Washington and Oregon by the construction by the United States of The Dalles Dam, completed in 1956.

The plaintiffs are Indians enrolled in the Yakima Nation,[1] a confederation created and granted a reservation by the Treaty between the United States and the Yakima Nation, June 9, 1855, [ ]. By the treaty the various tribes composing the Nation gave up their claim by Indian title to a large expanse of territory over which they roamed in return for the United States' recognition of a portion of the area claimed under Indian title as a reservation for the Yakima Nation and [for other compensation]. By this treaty the Yakima Nation secured rights recognized by the United States which could not be infringed without compensation.

Then, as now, fishing in the Columbia for anadromous fish was important to the Indians and provided them their food, fresh and dried, and a medium for acquiring other commodities. In the treaty, therefore, this provision was made in article III:

> The exclusive right of taking fish in all the streams, where running through or bordering said reservation, is further secured to said confederated tribes and bands of Indians, as also the right of taking fish at all usual and accustomed places, in common with citizens of the Territory, and of erecting temporary buildings for curing them; together with the privilege of hunting, gathering roots and berries, and pasturing their horses and cattle upon open and unclaimed land.

[ ]

Under this authority both Yakima Reservation Indians and Indians who live off the Reservation and around Celilo Falls have continued to fish at the Falls. [ ] Many of them, including plaintiff Minnie Whitefoot, claimed the exclusive right to fish at certain points or rocks away from their reservation called fishing stations. As the Commissioner found,

---

1. [The Yakama Nation has decided to adopt the spelling of its name that was used in the Treaty between the Nation and the United States. The spelling "Yakima" was used for several years and has not been changed in original documents.]

* * * the right of particular families in the tribe to use, occupy and fish from certain of the tribally owned fishing stations was a right which was respected and recognized by the Indians from remote times. This right of individual Indian families to use, occupy, and fish from specific fishing stations amounted primarily to a right, infrequently exercised, to exclude others from using the same stations. It was a right which the Indians recognized by custom and usage as passing down from one generation to the next through the family line. The right could not be sold or transferred by its immediate holder.

With the growth of commercial fishing for canning purposes and the appearance of Indian fishermen without ancestral fishing stations, disputes arose as to the use of the stations. There were no records of the claimed rights. To meet this situation the Celilo Fish Committee, composed of three Indians from each of the affected reservations, plus representatives of nonreservation Indians, was organized through the local Indian Superintendents in 1935. Frequently the Committee used the "ancient Indian custom of inheritance and succession," to determine rights of fishing at stations.

The growth of the Northwest and the increasing need for power and flood control caused Congress to enact water power legislation. The construction that is involved in this case is The Dalles Dam on the Columbia River between Washington and Oregon. Appropriation was made in 1950. [ ] Previously Congress had been advised of the fishery situation at Celilo Falls.[4] In an appropriation act for the civil functions of the Army, [ ], authority for compensation for the loss of the fishing rights in question was made. The act provided that, except in the case of Indians not enrolled in tribes, the payments were to be made to the respective tribes, not to the individual fishermen. Pursuant to this authority an agreement was reached between the United States and the Yakima Tribe on December 17, 1954. Paragraph 2 of the agreement provided for payment to the Tribe of some fifteen million dollars for all of its fishing privileges,

Minnie and Ambrose Whitefoot, members of the Yakima Tribe and residing on the Reservation, protested the per-capita distribution of the fifteen million dollar payment which gave $3,270 to each enrolled tribal member, including children of which the Whitefoots had five, on the ground

---

4. Property right in the fish—The Indians contend that they have a property right in the fish which migrate up the river, a right which may not be infringed upon without the payment of just compensation. The best that can be said for this question at the present time is that it is moot since the decision of the courts to date have pertained to easements in real property upon which the usual and accustomed fishing sites were located. * * * The Indian Service believe that the courts will hold that the treaties vested a property right in the annual fish migrations similar to that in the real estate upon which the fishing sites are located. The import and ramifications of such a holding are manifest. It is not believed that the treaties guarantee, or were intended to guarantee, annual fish migrations in the river, in perpetuity, or that damages will be paid by the Federal Government for any diminution of these runs from whatever cause ensuing. * * *

Report of Chief of Engineers, United States Army, in H. Doc. No. 531, 81st Cong., 2d Sess., vol. 7, 2868, 2951–2952 (June 28, 1949).

of inadequacy, but accepted those portions of the money on the basis of economic necessity and without prejudice to this litigation. [ ]

. . .

The basis of plaintiff Minnie Whitefoot's claim is that she was the owner of six "usual and accustomed fishing stations" descended to her as heir of her father, recognized as hers by tribal custom and used by her through the years. Defendant denies that the right to use these stations exclusively rested in Minnie Whitefoot. The issue is whether the right to use these six fishing stations, with easements on the public lands at Celilo Falls no different from those of other similar stations, were her individual private property or a part of the communal property of the tribe. If Minnie's claim of private ownership is found correct, she would, she argues, be entitled to a payment for the value of the use of these stations.

We have heretofore called attention to the fact that the appropriation acts authorized payments to the tribes. Here it is the Yakima Tribe. The agreement of December 17, 1954, for payment of the fifteen million dollars . . . was for the destruction of the usual and accustomed fishing stations preserved to the Yakimas by the treaty of June 9, 1855, Article III. . . . Paragraph 5 of that agreement of 1954 . . . subordinated the rights of "the Tribe to take fish." One cannot conclude from the Act authorizing payment and the contract otherwise than that the Congress, the Engineers and the Yakima Nation looked upon the fishing stations as the latter's property to be used as it might determine for its own benefit.

Such communal holding of property is in accord with normal Indian custom. Land is so held whether by Indian title or after creation of a reservation.[7] The general rights of the individual in tribal property are discussed in *Federal Indian Law* (1958), a revision and updating through the year 1956 of FELIX S. COHEN'S HANDBOOK OF FEDERAL INDIAN LAW. A few excerpts will show the theory.

In Powers of Indian Tribes, 55 INTERIOR DEC. 14, 50, tribal powers over property are considered at length.

The powers of an Indian tribe with respect to tribal land are not limited by any rights of occupancy which the tribe itself may grant to its members. The proposition that occupancy of tribal land does not create any vested rights in the occupant as against the tribe is supported by a long line of court decisions: * * *.

[ ]

7. *Prairie Band of Potawatomi Indians v. United States*, 165 F. Supp. 139, 147 (Ct.Cl. 1959), *cert. denied*, 359 U.S. 908 (1959): "The unbroken rule of law from *Johnson v. M'Intosh*, 21 U.S. (8 Wheat.) 543 (1823), to date is that Indian title, unrecognized by the United States by treaty or patent, covers the right to use only, a right that may be withdrawn by the Government at any time without liability for compensation. * * * This right to use the land is, however, the property of the band, tribe, or nation of Indians that occupies the land, either by Indian title or a right of occupancy that is recognized by the United States by treaty. The individual's right to use depends upon tribal law or custom. The tribal right to use is communal. No instance is known of individual ownership of tribal lands."

While property is vested in a tribe, it is the individual member who enjoys the use of the property. *Federal Indian Law,* [ ]. As to fishing, this is true.[10] But, like the lands, the interests in the fisheries are communal, subject to tribal regulation.

We hold that the use of accustomed fishing places, whether on or off the reservation, is a tribal right for adjustment by the tribe and that the fact that certain Indians have been allowed to have sole use of a particular spot by the Tribe gives that individual no property right against the Tribe and does not limit the Tribe's right to collect the damages for obliteration of fishing spots by the dam. We hold further that Minnie Whitefoot has no claim against the United States.

. . .

The petition must be dismissed.

NOTES

(1) Despite the court's ruling—which drew upon a long line of precedent—individual Yakama in 1855 apparently did have private interests in fishing spots analogous to private profits a prendre at the common law. As Minnie Whitefoot expressed it, she was the owner of six "usual and accustomed fishing stations' descended to her as heir of her father, recognized as hers by tribal custom and used by her through the years." A subsequent decision, however, suggests that such facts are legally irrelevant. In *United States v. Washington,* 520 F.2d 676 (9th Cir.1975), the court found that the Lummi Indians had individually owned their reef net sites at the time the treaty was signed, but nonetheless held that the fishing rights belonged to the tribe rather than to individual Indians.

What is the nature of the treaty right? What right does the tribe have? Was the description by the Army Corps of Engineers in footnote 4 an accurate description of the tribe's interest?

What was the nature of Lightfoot's interest? Does the decision simply hold that such questions cannot be litigated in the federal courts because they must be decided by the tribe as a governmental entity? That is, is the decision a comity-based result that draws a boundary around the tribe as a

---

10. It is plain that there are only a comparatively small number of fishing locations upon the river within the reservation, and that, broadly speaking, the fishing rights upon the river belong to the tribe; but there can be fishing in the river without granting exclusive rights to defined locations.

It does not follow, from the described conditions, that the individual Indian who wants to fish in that stream can be denied in order that, to his exclusion, fishing may be carried on for commercial purposes, in part, for the benefit of Indians of the tribe who do not care or who are not able to fish. The treaty was with the tribe; but the right of taking fish at all places within the reservation, and usual and accustomed grounds and stations outside the reservation, was plainly a right common to the members of the tribe—a right to a common is the right of an individual of the community.

Mason v. Sams, 5 F.2d 255, 258 (W.D.Wash. 1925). *See United States v. Brookfield Fisheries,* 24 F. Supp. 712, 716 (D.Or.1938); *Seufert Brothers Co. v. United States,* 249 U.S. 194 (1919); [ ].

governmental entity, leaving individual tribal members who feel wronged to seek redress from the tribe itself?

Is the treaty right similar to the conception of state sovereign ownership? Is any analogy to a private property regime likely to capture the nature of an interest in a communal property regime?

(2) The United States Supreme Court has described this communal ownership as follows:

> The distinctive characteristic of communal property is that every member of the community is an owner of it as such. He does not take as heir, or purchaser, or grantee; if he dies his right of property **does** not descend; if he removes from the community it expires; if he wishes to dispose of it he has nothing which he can convey; and yet he has a right of property in the land as perfect as that of any other person; and his children after him will enjoy all that he enjoyed, not as heirs but as communal owners.

Cherokee Nation v. Journeycake, 155 U.S. 196 (1894). Does this description accurately capture Whitefoot's interest in the fishing stations?

The communal ownership recognized by the court was at least partially an artifact of the treaty-making process and did not fully reflect relationships among Indians either in 1855 or now. Whatever its virtues in simplifying land titles and augmenting tribal powers, the court's ruling remains a simplified, external perspective on a complex set of cultural and legal relationships.

It is also important to note that "the land use and allocation concepts of the American Indian varied considerably from tribe to tribe." Julian C. Juergensmeyer & James B. Wadley, *The Common Lands Concept: A "Commons" Solution to a Common Environmental Problem*, 14 NAT. RESOURCES J. 361, 371–72 (1974). Recall on this point the excerpt from Bill Cronon's book, *Changes in the Land: Indians, Colonists, and the Ecology of New England*, comparing the Indian and English land tenure systems.

PERSPECTIVES

How Coyote made the Columbia River: Long ago, the country of the Colville people was covered by a large lake. A long ridge of mountains on the west prevented the waters of the lake from reaching to ocean. Coyote knew that if he could make a passage through the mountains, the salmon would swim up the river and the people would have food. Coyote used his power to dig a hole through the mountains. The waters of the lake drained through the hole and the Columbia River flowed to the ocean as it does today. Coyote was right: The salmon were able to swim up the river and the people had plenty to eat. The hole that Coyote dug formed a bridge that allowed the people to walk across the Columbia River. Later, an earthquake collapsed the bridge and it fell into the river where the Cascades of the Columbia are now located. ELLA CLARK, INDIAN LEGENDS OF THE PACIFIC NORTHWEST 88 (1953).

Section 3.   Treaty Rights as Limitations on Private Rights

NOTES

(1) The Indian fisheries of the Columbia Basin: The salmon that spawned in the Columbia Basin were exploited by three distinct cultural groups: (1) the Northwest Coast cultural area west of the Cascades, peopled primarily by the Kalapuya and Chinook; (2) the Plateau cultural area east of the Cascades extending into the Salmon River drainage in Idaho, peopled by a large number of groups including the Wishram, Umatilla, Walla Walla, Yakama, and Nez Perce; and (3) the Great Basin cultural area covering the Snake River and its tributaries below the Salmon River as well as the headwaters of the Salmon, which was peopled by the Paiute, Shoshoni, and Bannock.

While divided by many cultural elements, these people shared a dependence upon salmon. For at least 10,000 years they had annually harvested millions of pounds of fish without depleting the runs. They often travelled great distances to fishing sites. Celilo Falls on the Columbia, for example, drew fishers from all of the Plateau groups as well as traders from west of the Cascades. Similarly, Washington Irving reported that at Salmon Falls on the Snake River a group of explorers employed by John Jacob Astor had in 1811 come upon

> about one hundred lodges of Shoshonies busily engaging in killing and drying fish. The salmon begin to leap shortly after sunrise. At this time the Indians swim to the centre of the falls, where some station themselves on rocks, and others stand to their waists in the water, all armed with spears, with which they assail the salmon as they attempt to leap, or fall back exhausted. It is an incessant slaughter, so great is the throng of fish.

Washington Irving, Astoria or Anecdotes of an Enterprise Beyond the Rocky Mountains 373 (E. Todd ed., 1964) (1st ed. 1836). Irving noted that "salmon are taken here in incredible quantities" and reported that one explorer "had seen several thousand salmon taken in the course of one afternoon." The journals of the Lewis and Clark expedition report villages of fishers and racks of drying salmon along nearly the entire length of the Clearwater, Snake, and Columbia.

(2) The Stevens Treaties: Rapid white settlement in the mid–1850s created conflict between settlers and the indigenous peoples. Congress directed Isaac Stevens, Superintendent of Indian Affairs and Governor of the Washington Territory, to negotiate treaties to avoid war. Over a seven-month period in late 1854 and 1855, Stevens in the company of Joel Palmer, Superintendent of Indian Affairs for the Oregon Territory, negotiated treaties with more than 17,000 Indians, extinguishing Indian title to more than 64 million acres.

Stevens was not a disinterested participant in the negotiations. As an ambitious politician, he favored rapid settlement of the region. To facilitate this goal, Stevens organized small bands of Indians into "tribes," creating new political entities under the leadership of "chiefs" of Stevens' choosing. Furthermore, the negotiations were conducted in Chinook trade jargon—a simple language of approximately 300 words. Stevens did not understand Chinook nor (apparently) did many of the Indians. Finally, the treaties were drafted in English—and largely before meetings with the Indians.

Despite these various impediments, the tribes insisted upon guarantees for their traditional fishing practices. The Stevens treaties therefore guaranteed

> The exclusive right of taking fish in all the streams, where running through or bordering said reservation, is ... secured to said confederated tribes and bands of Indians, as also the right of taking fish at all usual and accustomed places, in common with citizens of the Territory, and of erecting temporary buildings for curing them; together with the privilege of hunting, gathering roots and berries, and pasturing their horses and cattle upon open and unclaimed land.[1]

Treaty with the Yakama Nation, art. III, June 11, 1855, 12 Stat. 951, 953. The same language appeared in the treaties with the Umatilla, Nez Perce, and Warm Springs Tribes of the Columbia Plateau as well as the nations of the Puget Sound and Washington Coast.

The meaning of this simple phrase has been a subject of litigation and dispute almost since the signing ceremony.

United States v. Taylor

Washington Territorial Supreme Court.
13 P. 333 (Wash.Terr.1887).

■ HOYT, J.:—This suit was brought by the United States, R.H. Milroy, as Indian agent, and several Indian plaintiffs, for themselves and for the Yakima Nation or Tribe of Indians, of which they are alleged to be members, to restrain the appellee, Frank Taylor, from maintaining a fence around a large body of land abutting upon "Tum Water Fishery," in the Columbia river, which fence, the complaint alleges, obstructs the land approaches to said fishery, and thus prevents the whole enjoyment thereof claimed by said Indians under their treaty with the United States entered into June 9, 1855, and ratified by the senate of the United States, March 8, 1859. By his answer the appellee admits the making and ratification of said treaty, and the inclosing of said land by a fence upon a portion thereof over which said Indians had been accustomed to travel in going to and from said fishery; that there was no fence built upon the side next to the river, the river itself being the only means of inclosure on that side, but avers that he had the right, as owner in fee of said land, to thus inclose the same to protect his crops growing thereon, notwithstanding said treaty. Appellants

---

1. The quoted language appears with slight variation in the phrasing in all of the treaties with the Columbia Plateau nations as well as the Washington coastal and Puget Sound tribes. As a result, the courts construe the treaties *in pari materia*.

replied, and the cause was tried upon these pleadings. There are other issues raised by the pleadings, but they are immaterial on this appeal, under the stipulation upon which the decree was given from which this appeal is prosecuted.

The stipulation referred to is as follows:

First. That the treaty mentioned in the complaint in this action was made and concluded as therein alleged, and that the plaintiffs are members of the Yakima Tribe or Nation of Indians, as alleged in the complaint. *Second.* That, prior to and at the time of entering into said treaty, the 'Tum Water Fishery,' mentioned and described in the pleadings, was one of the ancient, usual, and accustomed fisheries of said Yakima Tribe or Nation of Indians, and referred to in said treaty; was used and enjoyed as such by the Indians of said tribe in the manner in the complaint alleged, and continued to be so used and enjoyed therefor, except as hereinafter stated; and that said Indian plaintiffs, as members of said tribe or nation, so used and enjoyed the same. *Third.* That subsequent to the conclusion and ratification of said treaty, and before the commencement of this action, the said defendant, Frank Taylor, and his several grantors, obtained patents from the United States to the lands in the complaint and answer described, under the homestead, pre-emption, and other land laws of the United States, and said Taylor is still the owner thereof. *Fourth.* That said lands extend to and border upon the Columbia river at the site of said fishery, and are the same lands over and upon which said Indians have heretofore been accustomed to go and return from said fishery, and upon which they had landed and cured the fish taken by them from said fishery, and where they have been accustomed, during the fishing season, to make their temporary abode, and pasture their ponies. *Fifth.* That since his acquirement of said land, said Frank Taylor, as owner thereof, has caused the same to be inclosed by lawful fences for the purpose of utilizing the same for agricultural purposes, thereby preventing said Indians from entering upon the same, as before they had been accustomed to do, under the claim that the United States, by means of the said grantor, invested him and his said grantors with absolute title to said lands, and the exclusive right to use the same. . . .

From the above stipulation it will at once be seen that the single question now to be determined is that of the rights of the appellants under said treaty, as against the appellee, as owner of the land by title acquired from the United States subsequent to said treaty, under the homestead law and other acts of congress.

The portion of said treaty under which appellants claim their right to relief herein is as follows: "The exclusive right of taking fish in all streams, where running through or bordering said reservation, is further secured to said confederated tribes and bands of Indians, as also the right of taking fish at all usual and accustomed places in common with citizens of the territory, and of erecting temporary buildings for curing them, together with the privilege of hunting, gathering roots and berries, and pasturing their horses and cattle upon open and unclaimed land."

Both parties invoke the aid of the rule laid down by the supreme court of the United States, that a treaty of this kind is to be liberally construed in favor of the Indians; and that, in so far as the language used will allow, that construction will be adopted which will best subserve the object which the Indians, at the time of the treaty was made, would have been most likely to have desired and understood. We must, then, investigate the treaty in question in the light of this rule.

The appellants contend that this clause was a reservation, from the force and effect of other portions of the treaty, of certain rights therein specified, while the appellee insists that it should be construed as a specific grant of rights by the United States. We think the contention of the appellants must prevail, as it seems to us that the Indians, in making the treaty, would have been more likely to have intended to grant only such rights as they were to part with, rather than to have conveyed all, with the understanding that certain were to be at once reconveyed to them.

What did the Indians intend to reserve to themselves by the words, "as also the right of taking fish at all usual and accustomed places, in common with citizens of the territory?" It will be seen by the statement of facts above set out that, at the time this treaty was made, there existed within the territory, which was the subject-matter of the treaty, certain ancient fisheries which had for generations been used as such by said Indians, who had certain well-defined habits and methods connected with such use; and it is contended, on the part of appellant, that the effect of the words above quoted was to reserve to the Indians the right to enjoy all of these fisheries as they had heretofore; while, on the other side, it is claimed that the liberal interpretation of the words in the interest of the Indians would make them apply, not to any particular places of fishing then in use, but to all places which in the future might become usual and accustomed places of fishing, and that, as to such places, they had the same rights as other citizens, and, in addition thereto, the right to use the shore for the purpose of curing their fish. Many arguments can be and have been made in favor of each of these positions. But when we take into consideration the facts disclosed by this record, and the further fact, which the court knows as a matter of common knowledge, that these Indians were always tenacious in adhering to past customs and traditions, we think the contention of appellant must prevail, as we think it much more natural that these Indians should have desired to preserve as fully as possible a right then and for a long time before enjoyed by them, rather than to have provided for a right to be enjoyed in unknown ways, and under new conditions, even although such new rights might possibly be of more avail than the old. Besides, the construction contended for by appellee would make the right to use the shore for the purpose of erecting houses and drying fish a servitude imposed upon all the shore line of the territory, so that every person occupying the same would be liable to have his occupancy disturbed by such floating servitude, though, at the time he purchased, the water in front of the land had never been a place used for taking fish. And it seems to us that this servitude would, when viewed from the standpoint of the United States as a contradicting party, have been much more objectionable than the other one, though in the minds of the Indians, as the other contradicting party therein, old places and methods would doubtless seem, and would probably be, to them of much greater value.

The appellee further claims that even if the above position is correct, and the Indians were entitled by said treaty to the rights claimed, still that such rights do not now exist as against the defendant, as by the act of congress subsequently passed, under which he has taken this land, such treaty has, as to him, been repealed. But with this position we cannot agree, as these laws simply authorize the appropriation by the settler of unappropriated lands, and only authorize the extinguishment of the title which the government holds at the time of the appropriation; and, if the land selected by the settler has at such time any servitude or easement impressed upon it, he takes subject thereto.

It follows from what has been said, and from the agreement of the parties, that the judgment of the district court must be reversed, and the cause remanded for further proceedings in accordance with such stipulation and this opinion.

■ GREENE, C.J., and LANGFORD, J., concur.

NOTES

What is the nature of the fishing right reserved in the treaty? Is it best understood as a private property right or is some other legal categorization more apt? Are there analogous common-law rights? To whom does the right seem to belong, the user or the tribe?

United States v. Winans

United States Supreme Court.
198 U.S. 371 (1905).

■ McKENNA, J.:—This suit was brought to enjoin the respondents from obstructing certain Indians of the Yakima Nation, in the state of Washington, from exercising fishing rights and privileges on the Columbia river, in that state, claimed under the provisions of the treaty between the United States and the Indians, made in 1859.

There is no substantial dispute of facts, or none that is important to our inquiry.

The treaty is as follows:

.   .   .

"The exclusive right of taking fish in all the streams where running through or bordering said reservation is further secured to said confederated tribes and bands of Indians, as also the right of taking fish at all usual and accustomed places, in common with citizens of the territory, and of erecting temporary buildings for curing them, together with the privilege of hunting, gathering roots and berries, and pasturing their horses and cattle upon open and unclaimed land. . . . "

.   .   .

The respondents or their predecessors in title claim under patents of the United States the lands bordering on the Columbia river, and under grants from the state of Washington to the shore land which, it is alleged, fronts on the patented land. They also introduced in evidence licenses from the state to maintain devices for taking fish, called fish wheels.

At the time the treaty was made the fishing places were part of the Indian country, subject to the occupancy of the Indians, with all the rights such occupancy gave. The object of the treaty was to limit the occupancy to certain lands, and to define rights outside of them.

The pivot of the controversy is the construction of the second paragraph. Respondents contend that the words "the right of taking fish at all usual and accustomed places in common with the citizens of the territory" confer only such rights as a white man would have under the conditions of ownership of the lands bordering on the river, and under the laws of the state, and, such being the rights conferred, the respondents further contend that they have the power to exclude the Indians from the river by reason of such ownership. Before filing their answer respondents demurred to the bill. The court overruled the demurrer, holding that the bill stated facts sufficient to show that the Indians were excluded from the exercise of the rights given them by the treaty. The court further found, however, that it would "not be justified in issuing process to compel the defendants to permit the Indians to make a camping ground of their property while engaged in fishing." [ ] The injunction that had been granted upon the filing of the bill was modified by stipulation in accordance with the view of the court.

Testimony was taken on the issues made by the bill and answer, and upon the submission of the case the bill was dismissed, the court ... expressing its views as follows:

> ... [t]he only issue left for determination in this case is as to whether the defendants have interfered or threatened to interfere with the rights of the Indians to share in the common right of the public of taking fish from the Columbia river and I have given careful consideration to the testimony bearing upon this question. I find from the evidence that the defendants have excluded the Indians from their own lands, to which a perfect, absolute title has been acquired from the United States government by patents, and they have more than once instituted legal proceedings against the Indians for trespassing, and the defendants have placed in the river in front of their lands fishing wheels for which licenses were granted to them by the state of Washington, and they claim the right to operate these fishing wheels, which necessitates the exclusive possession of the space occupied by the wheels. Otherwise the defendants have not molested the Indians nor threatened to do so. The Indians are at the present time on an equal footing with the citizens of the United States who have not acquired exclusive proprietary rights, and this it seems to me is all that they can legally demand with respect to fishing privileges in waters outside the limits of Indian reservations under the terms of their treaty with the United States.

The remarks of the court clearly stated the issue and the grounds of decision[:] it was decided that the Indians acquired no rights but what any inhabitant of the territory or state would have. Indeed, acquired no rights but such as they would have without the treaty. This is certainly an impotent outcome to negotiations and a convention which seemed to promise more, and give the word of the nation for more. And we have said we will construe a treaty with the Indians as "that unlettered people" understood it, and "as justice and reason demand, in all cases where power is exerted by the strong over those to whom they owe care and protection," and counterpoise the inequality "by the superior justice which looks only to the substance of the right, without regard to technical rules." [ ] How the treaty in question was understood may be gathered from the circumstances.

The right to resort to the fishing places in controversy was a part of larger rights possessed by the Indians, upon the exercise of which there was not a shadow of impediment, and which were not much less necessary to the existence of the Indians than the atmosphere they breathed. New conditions came into existence, to which those rights had to be accommodated. Only a limitation of them, however, was necessary and intended, not a taking away. In other words, the treaty was not a grant of rights to the Indians, but a grant of right from them,—a reservation of those not granted. And the form of the instrument and its language was adapted to that purpose. Reservations were not of particular parcels of land, and could not be expressed in deeds, as dealings between private individuals. The reservations were in large areas of territory, and the negotiations were with the tribe. They reserved rights, however, to every individual Indian, as though named therein. They imposed a servitude upon every piece of land as though described therein. There was an exclusive right of fishing reserved within certain boundaries. There was a right outside of those boundaries reserved "in common with citizens of the territory." As a mere right, it was not exclusive in the Indians. Citizens might share it, but the Indians were secured in its enjoyment by a special provision of means for its exercise. They were given "the right of taking fish at all usual and accustomed places," and the right "of erecting temporary buildings for curing them." The contingency of the future ownership of the lands, therefore, was foreseen and provided for; in other words, the Indians were given a right in the land,—the right of crossing it to the river,—the right to occupy it to the extent and for the purpose mentioned. No other conclusion would give effect to the treaty. And the right was intended to be continuing against the United States and its grantees as well as against the state and its grantees.

The respondents urge an argument based upon the different capacities of white men and Indians to devise and make use of instrumentalities to enjoy the common right. Counsel say: "The fishing right was in common, and aside from the right of the state to license fish wheels, the wheel fishing is one of the civilized man's methods, as legitimate as the substitution of the modern combined harvester for the ancient sickle and flail." But the result does not follow that the Indians may be absolutely excluded. It needs no argument to show that the superiority of a combined harvester over the ancient sickle neither increased nor decreased rights to the use of land held in common. In the actual taking of fish white men may not be confined to a spear or crude net, but it does not follow that they may construct and use a device which gives them exclusive possession of the fishing places, as it is admitted a fish wheel does. Besides, the fish wheel is not relied on alone. Its monopoly is made complete by a license from the state. The argument based on the inferiority of the Indians is peculiar. If the Indians had not been inferior in capacity and power, what the treaty would have been, or that there would have been any treaty, would be hard to guess.

. . .

It is further contended that the rights conferred upon the Indians are subordinate to the powers acquired by the state upon its admission into the Union. In other words, it is contended that the state acquired by its admission into the Union "upon an equal footing with the original states," the power to grant rights in or to dispose of the shore lands upon navigable streams, and such power is subject only to the paramount authority of Congress with regard to public navigation and commerce. The United States, therefore, it is contended, could neither grant nor retain rights in the shore or to the lands under water.

The elements of this contention and the answer to it are expressed in *Shively v. Bowlby,* 152 U.S. 1 (1894). It is unnecessary, and it would be difficult, to add anything to the reasoning of that case. The power and rights of the states in and over shore lands were carefully defined, but the power of the United States, while it held the country as a territory, to create rights which would be binding on the states, was also announced, opposing the dicta scattered through the cases, which seemed to assert a contrary view. It was said by the court, through Mr. Justice Gray:

> Notwithstanding the dicta contained in some of the opinions of this court, already quoted, to the effect that Congress has no power to grant any land below high-water mark of navigable waters in a territory of the United States, it is evident that this is not strictly true.
>
>   * * *
>
> By the Constitution, as is now well settled, the United States having rightfully acquired the territories, and being the only government which can impose laws upon them, have the entire dominion and sovereignty, national and municipal, Federal and state, over all the territories, so long as they remain in a territorial condition. [ ]

Many cases were cited. And it was further said:

> We cannot doubt, therefore, that Congress has the power to make grants of lands below high-water mark of navigable waters in any territory of the United States, whenever it becomes necessary to do so in order to perform international obligations, or to effect the improvement of such lands for the promotion and convenience of commerce with foreign nations and among the several states, or to carry out other public purposes appropriate to the objects for which the United States hold the territory.

The extinguishment of the Indian title, opening the land for settlement, and preparing the way for future states, were appropriate to the objects for which the United States held the territory. And surely it was within the competency of the nation to secure to the Indians such a remnant of the great rights they possessed as "taking fish at all usual and accustomed places." Nor does it restrain the state unreasonably, if at all, in the regulation of the right. It only fixes in the land such easements as enable the right to be exercised.

The license from the state, which respondents plead, to maintain a fishing wheel, gives no power to them to exclude the Indians, nor was it intended to give such power. It was the permission of the state to use a particular device. What rights the Indians had were not determined or limited. This was a matter for judicial determination regarding the rights of the Indians and rights of the respondents. And that there may be an adjustment and accommodation of them the Solicitor General concedes and points out the way. We think, however, that such adjustment and accommodation are more within the province of the circuit court in the first instance than of this court.

NOTES

(1) Again, what is the nature of the fishing right reserved by the treaty? Is it a right that Congress could eliminate by repealing the treaty or is it a vested property right that can be eliminated only upon payment of just compensation?

What was the origin of the right to fish? Was it granted by the United States or reserved by the Indians? When a treaty is silent, where does the right reside? In *Menominee Tribe v. United States*, 391 U.S. 404 (1968), the Court held that a treaty that was silent on hunting and fishing rights impliedly reserved the rights for the tribe.

Note that *Winans* addressed not only the rights of treaty fishers versus private landowners, but also resolved the question of the status of treaty rights versus state power.

(2) ***Seufert Brothers Co. v. United States***: Seufert Brothers operated a fish wheel (a device that operated like a waterwheel and scooped fish into storage nets) on the Oregon shore of the Columbia River at The Dalles to supply its cannery. The company constructed the wheel at a location claimed by Sam Williams, a Yakama. The lands ceded by the Yakama, however, were located across the river in Washington. The company argued that the Yakama had no treaty right to fish or to construct buildings for drying salmon at the location of its fish wheel since the wheel was located within the lands ceded by a different tribe. Relying upon the evidence that the Yakama traditionally had fished at the location and its decision in *Winans*, the Court concluded:

> To restrain the Yakima Nation to fishing on the north side and shore of the river would greatly restrict the comprehensive language of the treaty, which gives them the right "of taking fish at all usual and accustomed places, * * * and of erecting temporary buildings for

curing them," and would substitute for the natural meaning of the expression used,—for the meaning which it is proved the Indians, for more than fifty years derived from it,—the artificial meaning which might be given to it by the law and by lawyers.

The suggestion, so impressively urged, that this construction "imposes a servitude upon the Oregon soil" is not alarming from the point of view of the public, and private owners not only had notice of these Indian customary rights by the reservation of them in the treaty, but the "servitude" is one existing only where there was an habitual and customary use of the premises, which must have been so open and notorious during a considerable portion of each year, that any person, not negligently or wilfully blind to the conditions of the property he was purchasing, must have known of them.

Seufert Brothers Co. v. United States, 249 U.S. 194 (1919).

SECTION 4.   TREATY RIGHTS AS LIMITATIONS ON STATE POWERS

NOTES

On-and off-reservation: The fisheries clause of the Stevens Treaties provides:

The exclusive right of taking fish in all the streams, where running through or bordering said reservation, is ... secured to said confederated tribes and bands of Indians, as also the right of taking fish at all usual and accustomed places, in common with citizens of the Territory, and of erecting temporary buildings for curing them.

Treaty with the Yakama Nation, art. III, June 9, 1855, 12 Stat. 951, 953. The treaties thus reserved two different rights: An "exclusive right" to take fish from streams on and bordering the reservation and a right "in common with citizens of the United States" to fish at all "usual and accustomed stations" off the reservation.

The history of federal Indian policy has made it difficult in many instances to determine what is "on-reservation" rather than "off-reservation." At various points in the past century and a quarter, federal policy has promoted the "allotment" of tribal lands to individual Indians with the result that communal/tribal ownership of large tracts of land was replaced by the individual ownership of smaller parcels. Not infrequently, individual allotments quickly wound up in non-Indian ownership. As a result, much land within the exterior boundaries of many Indian reservations is in non-Indian ownership. Regulation of such lands and of their owners has proved contentious.

For example, in *Montana v. United States,* 450 U.S. 544 (1981), the Crow Tribe sought to regulate hunting and fishing by non-Indians on lands within the reservation owned in fee simple by non-Indians. While holding that "the Tribe may prohibit nonmembers from hunting or fishing on land belonging to the Tribe or held by the United States in trust for the Tribe," and that, "if the Tribe permits nonmembers to fish or hunt on such lands, it may condition their entry by charging a fee or establishing bag and creel limits," the Court also held that such regulatory authority did not extend to non-Indian fee lands within the reservation.

Similarly, in *Puyallup Tribe, Inc. v. Department of Game*, 433 U.S. 165 (1977), the Court held that the Tribe could not regulate fishing in the Puyallup River where it was within the exterior boundaries of the Tribe's reservation since, in part, most of the land had passed into non-Indian ownership.

PERSPECTIVES

Euro-Americans, canning, and the Columbia River salmon: Prior to the opening of the first cannery on the Columbia in 1866, the Euro–American invasion of the Pacific Northwest had little effect on the salmon runs. Canning quickly changed this. After the first year's production of less than 6,000 pounds, the number of canneries and their output expanded rapidly.

The canneries' demand for fish fostered technological innovation. Traps and fishwheels replaced the dipnets, harpoons, and weirs that had served the Indians for millennia and were, in turn, replaced by gillnetters, purse seiners, and, most recently, ocean trollers. The canneries' demand also fostered overfishing: the chinook catch peaked in 1883 when 40 canneries packed 43,000,000 pounds. Total production reached its maximum in 1911 when almost 50,000,000 pounds of salmon were packed. By 1975, the amount of Columbia salmon which was canned dropped to less than that in 1867, the second year of cannery operations. The problem has long been recognized; in 1894 the Oregon Fish and Game Protector wrote:

> It does not require a study of the statistics to convince one that the salmon industry has suffered a great decline during the past decade, and that it is only a matter of a few years under the present conditions when the chinook of the Columbia will be as scarce as the beaver that once was so plentiful in our streams.... For a third of a century Oregon has drawn wealth from her streams, but now, by reason of her wastefulness and a lack of intelligent provision for the future, the source of that wealth is disappearing and is threatened with annihilation.

ANTHONY NETBOY, THE COLUMBIA RIVER SALMON AND STEELHEAD TROUT 36 (1980).

Concurrent with the decrease in the size of the runs was an increase in competition among groups of fishers for control over access to the resource. Gillnetters fought trappers and fishwheel operators; upriver fishers fought downriver fishers; recreational fishers fought commercial fishers. While the competitors employed the rhetoric of conservation, the real issue was one of allocation: Who would be allowed to take the fish? *See generally* Dale D. Goble, *The Road to the Endangered Species Act, in* NORTHWEST LANDS AND

PEOPLES: READINGS IN ENVIRONMENTAL HISTORY 229–63 (Dale D. Goble & Paul W. Hirt eds., 1999).

a. STATE REGULATION OF ON–RESERVATION HUNTING AND FISHING

NOTES

(1) *New Mexico v. Mescalero Apache Tribe:*

. . . . The decision in *Worcester v. Georgia*, 31 U.S. (6 Pet.) 515, 561 (1832), reflected the view that Indian tribes were wholly distinct nations within whose boundaries "the laws of [a State] can have no force." We long ago departed from the "conceptual clarity of Mr. Chief Justice Marshall's view in *Worcester*," *Mescalero Apache Tribe v. Jones*, 411 U.S. 145, 148 (1973), and have acknowledged certain limitations on tribal sovereignty. For instance, we have held that Indian tribes have been implicitly divested of their sovereignty in certain respects by virtue of their dependent status, that under certain circumstances a State may validly assert authority over the activities of nonmembers on a reservation, and that in exceptional circumstances a State may assert jurisdiction over the on-reservation activities of tribal members.

Nevertheless, in demarcating the respective spheres of State and tribal authority over Indian reservations, we have continued to stress that "Indian tribes are unique aggregations possessing attributes of sovereignty over both their members and their territory," *White Mountain Apache Tribe v. Bracker*, 448 U.S. 136, 142 (1980), *quoting United States v. Mazurie*, 419 U.S. 544, 557 (1975). Because of their sovereign status, tribes and their reservation lands are insulated in some respects by an "historic immunity from state and local control," *Mescalero Apache Tribe v. Jones*, 411 U.S. at 152, and tribes retain any aspect of their historical sovereignty not "inconsistent with the overriding interests of the National Government." *Washington v. Confederated Tribes*, 447 U.S. 134, 153 (1980).

New Mexico v. Mescalero Apache Tribe, 462 U.S. 324 (1983).

(2) *Pioneer Packing Co. v. Winslow* involved the "exclusive right" under the Stevens Treaties to take fish from streams on reservation. Pioneer Packing purchased steelhead from Quinault Indians for shipment to New York City. The shipment was seized by the county game warden under a state statute that prohibited shipment of steelhead out of the state. The packing company sought an injunction to require the warden to return the shipment and to restrain him from interfering with shipments in the future. The Washington Supreme Court began its analysis by stating: "The first question is whether the Indians have title to the fish in the river on the reservation, or whether title thereto is in the state in trust for all the people thereof, with merely a license on the part of the Indians to catch them." Following an extended examination of the events leading to the creation of the Quinault reservation and the applicable federal caselaw, the Court concluded that the tribe held title to the fish in the river. As such, they had a right to sell the fish for shipment in interstate commerce that could not be regulated by the state government: "The case of *Geer v. Connecticut,* 161 U.S. 519 (1896), is not in point, because in that case there was only a qualified ownership in the game which the defendant was charged with unlawfully . . . inten[ding] to procure the transportation of the same beyond the limits of the state, while in the case now before us, the Indians had an unqualified right to sell them [that] was protected by the interstate commerce clause of the Federal Constitution." *Pioneer Packing v. Winslow,* 294 P. 557 (Wash.1930).

b.   STATE REGULATION OF OFF-RESERVATION HUNTING AND FISHING

(i) THE RIGHT TO HUNT AND FISH

NOTES

(1) *Ward v. Race Horse:* Race Horse was a Bannock living on the Fort Hall Reservation in Southeastern Idaho. The treaty between the United States and the Bannocks was negotiated at Fort Bridger and ratified by Congress in 1868. The treaty guaranteed the Indians "the right to hunt on the unoccupied lands of the United States so long as game may be found thereon, and so long as peace subsists among the whites and Indians on the borders of hunting districts." On July 1, 1895, Race Horse killed seven elk in western Wyoming. Prosecuted by the state for violating its game laws, he sought a writ of habeas corpus from the federal circuit court. The court granted the writ and ordered the prisoner discharged. The state appealed to the Supreme Court.

The Supreme Court began with *Geer v. Connecticut* and the conclusion that "[t]he power of a State to control and regulate the taking of game cannot be questioned." But the treaty language, if given a literal reading (the construction suggested by the defendant), would undercut the state's power to control game within its borders: "It would also render necessary the assumption that Congress, wilst preparing the way, by treaty, for new settlements and new States, yet created a provision not only detrimental to their future well-being, but also irreconcilably in conflict with the powers of the States already existing." The equal footing doctrine enunciated in *Pollard v. Hagan,* 44 U.S. (3 How.) 212 (1845), precluded Congress from depriving Wyoming of a power held by Connecticut. Thus the admission of Wyoming implicitly abrogated the treaty right to hunt:

> The power of all the States to regulate the killing of game within their borders will not be gainsaid, yet, if the treaty applies to the unoccupied land of the United States in the State of Wyoming, that State would be bereft of such power, since every isolated piece of land belonging to the United States as a private owner, would be exempt in this regard from the authority of the State. Wyoming, then, will have been admitted into the Union, not as an equal member, but as one shorn of a legislative power vested in all other States of the Union, a power

resulting from the fact of statehood and incident to its plenary existence.

Ward v. Race Horse, 163 U.S. 504 (1896).

(2) *United States v. Winans:* Does the decision in *Race Horse* survive the decision in *Winans* [*supra*]? Recall that the Court in *Winans* stated:

> It is further contended that the rights conferred upon the Indians are subordinate to the powers acquired by the state upon its admission into the Union. In other words, it is contended that the state acquired by its admission into the Union "upon an equal footing with the original states," the power to grant rights in or to dispose of the shore lands upon navigable streams, and such power is subject only to the paramount authority of Congress with regard to public navigation and commerce. The United States, therefore, it is contended, could neither grant nor retain rights in the shore or to the lands under water.

> The elements of this contention and the answer to it are expressed in *Shively v. Bowlby,* 152 U.S. 1 (1894). It is unnecessary, and it would be difficult, to add anything to the reasoning of that case. The power and rights of the states in and over shore lands were carefully defined, but the power of the United States, while it held the country as a territory, to create rights which would be binding on the states, was also announced, opposing the dicta scattered through the cases, which seemed to assert a contrary view.

United States v. Winans, 198 U.S. 371 (1905).

(3) *State v. Tulee:* Tulee, a Yakama, was convicted of catching and selling salmon without having obtained a state license to do so. He claimed that he did not need a license because he had a treaty right to fish without interference of the state. The Washington Supreme Court affirmed the conviction, relying upon *Race Horse*:

> Upon admission to the Union, a state assumes all the rights and powers the exercise of which is enjoyed by her sister commonwealths, each state, regardless of the date of its admission to the Union, standing on a basis of equality with the other states. [ ]

After an extended quotation from *Race Horse,* the court characterized *Winans* simply as holding that the treaties created "a perpetual servitude on the lands necessary for their use in taking fish at their accustomed fishing places." Thus, the treaties affected only private off-reservation interests. The state's governmental powers were undiminished:

> Under the authorities, it is clear that the state of Washington enjoys to the full the exercise of its police power, as an equal of the other states making up our federal Union.... Under the treaty, the members of the Yakima Tribe are entitled to an easement to cross and use lands necessary to the enjoyment of their fishing rights at their old accustomed fishing places.

State v. Tulee, 109 P.2d 280, 287 (Wash.1941).

Tulee appealed:

Tulee v. Washington

United States Supreme Court.
315 U.S. 681 (1942).

■ BLACK, J.:—The appellant, Sampson Tulee, a member of the Yakima tribe of Indians, was convicted in the Superior Court for Klickitat County, Washington, on a charge of catching salmon with a net without first having obtained a license as required by state law.[1] The Supreme Court of Washington affirmed. [ ] The . . . appellant challenging the validity of the Washington statute as applied to him on the ground that it was repugnant to a treaty made between the United States and the Yakima Indians.

The appellant claims that the Washington statute compelling him to obtain a license in order to fish for salmon violates the [fishing rights] provision of Article III of the treaty:

. . .

The state does not claim power to regulate fishing by the Indians in their own reservation. *Pioneer Packing Co. v. Winslow*, 294 P. 557 (Wash. 1930). Nor does it deny that treaty rights of Indians, whatever their scope, were preserved by Congress in the act which created the Washington Territory and the enabling act which admitted Washington as a state. [ ] Relying upon its broad powers to conserve game and fish within its borders,[2] however, the state asserts that its right to regulate fishing may be exercised at places like the scene of the alleged offense which, although within the territory originally ceded by the Yakimas, is outside of their reservation. It argues that the treaty should not be construed as an impairment of this right and that since its license laws do not discriminate against the Indians, they do not conflict with the treaty. The appellant, on the other hand, claims that the treaty gives him an unrestricted right to fish in the "usual and accustomed places," free from state regulation of any kind. We think the state's construction of the treaty is too narrow and the appellant's too broad; that while the treaty leaves the state with power to impose on Indians equally with others such restrictions of a purely regulatory nature concerning the time and manner of fishing outside the reservation as are necessary for the conservation of fish,[3] it forecloses the state from charging the Indians a fee of the kind in question here.

In determining the scope of the reserved rights of hunting and fishing, we must not give the treaty the narrowest construction it will bear. In *United States v. Winans*, 198 U.S. 371 (1905), this Court held that, despite the phrase "in common with citizens of the territory," Article III conferred upon the Yakimas continuing rights, beyond those which other citizens

---

1. "It shall be unlawful to catch, take or fish for food fish with any appliance or by any means whatsoever except with hook and line * * * unless license so to do has been first obtained * * *." REMINGTON'S REVISED STATUTES OF WASHINGTON § 5693. "For each dip bag net license for the taking of salmon on the Columbia River, (the license fee shall be) five dollars * * *." *Id.* § 5703.

2. *Geer v. Connecticut*, 161 U.S. 519 (1896); *Ward v. Race Horse*, 163 U.S. 504, 507 (1896); *Patsone v. Pennsylvania*, 232 U.S. 138 (1914); *Lacoste v. Department of Conservation*, 263 U.S. 545, 549 (1924).

3. Cf. *People ex rel. Kennedy v. Becker*, 241 U.S. 556 (1916). See *United States v. Winans*, 198 U.S. at 384.

may enjoy, to fish at their "usual and accustomed places" in the ceded area; and in *Seufert Brothers Co. v. United States,* 249 U.S. 194 (1918), a similar conclusion was reached even with respect to places outside the ceded area. From the report set out in the record before us of the proceedings in the long council at which the treaty agreement was reached, we are impressed by the strong desire the Indians had to retain the right to hunt and fish in accordance with the immemorial customs of their tribes. It is our responsibility to see that the terms of the treaty are carried out, so far as possible, in accordance with the meaning they were understood to have by the tribal representatives at the council and in a spirit which generously recognizes the full obligation of this nation to protect the interests of a dependent people. *United States v. Kagama,* 118 U.S. 375, 384 (1886); *Seufert Brothers Co. v. United States,* 249 U.S. at 198, 199.

Viewing the treaty in this light we are of the opinion that the state is without power to charge the Yakimas a fee for fishing. A stated purpose of the licensing act was to provide for "the support of the state government and its existing public institutions." [ ] The license fees prescribed are regulatory as well as revenue producing. But it is clear that their regulatory purpose could be accomplished otherwise, that the imposition of license fees is not indispensable to the effectiveness of a state conservation program. Even though this method may be both convenient and, in its general impact fair, it acts upon the Indians as a charge for exercising the very right their ancestors intended to reserve. We believe that such exaction of fees as a prerequisite to the enjoyment of fishing in the "usual and accustomed places" cannot be reconciled with a fair construction of the treaty. We therefore hold the state statute invalid as applied in this case.

The judgment of the Supreme Court of Washington is reversed.

NOTES

(1) To what extent may the state regulate fishing at "usual and accustomed places"? *Why* is the license an impermissible intrusion into the treaty right? Is it the revenue-producing aspect of the license that is problematic? If the state were to institute a regulatory program that involved issuing a limited number of licenses to control the total number of fish taken, could it apply that regulatory program to the Yakama off-reservation fishery if it did so in a way that gave all applicants an equal opportunity to acquire a license?

(2) In *Tulee,* the state made arguments that it would continue to press for at least forty years: "Relying upon its broad powers to conserve game and fish within its borders ... , the state asserts that its right to regulate fishing may be exercised ... outside of their reservation. It argues that the treaty should not be construed as an impairment of this right and that since its license laws do not discriminate against the Indians, they do not conflict with the treaty." *Does* the state's regulatory system discriminate against treaty fishers? Can facially neutral statutes discriminate by failing to consider relevant categories or to uphold existing rights?

Implicit in the state's argument, is the proposition that "conservation" is not "allocation," that is, that its actions are driven by a desire to conserve the resource rather than to allocate the resource among different fishers. This argument surfaced next in the *Puyallup Trilogy* discussed below.

(3) The *Puyallup* Trilogy:

(a) *Puyallup I*: In the mid–1960s, the Washington Department of Game brought a declaratory judgment action, challenging the immunity of Puyallup, Nisqually, and Muckleshoot tribal members from regulation by the Department. It argued that "the Indians never had, as against the United States, any right to the 'use and occupancy' of any land; that they were and are a conquered people without right or title to anything. Having nothing to cede, there was no consideration for any promises made to them, and there is no necessity to respect these promises even though they were labeled 'treaties.'" The Washington Supreme Court rejected this contention: "[R]egardless of whether treaties with Indian tribes were necessary, they were deemed desirable by the United States and those entered into by it cannot be repudiated by this state or its courts." The court further held: "The burden of proof, once the defendant has established that he is a member of a tribe having a treaty right to take fish at all 'usual and accustomed grounds and stations,' is on the state to show that its regulations, which limit the Indian fishing rights either as to the time or manner of fishing, are reasonable and necessary to conserve the fishery." *Department of Game v. Puyallup Tribe, Inc.*, 422 P.2d 754 (Wash.1967).

The decision was brought to the United States Supreme Court on a writ of certiorari; the Court affirmed the decision, but introduced new distinctions that would prove troublesome:

> The treaty right is in terms the rights to fish "at all usual and accustomed places." We assume that fishing by nets was customary at the time of the Treaty; and we also assume that there were commercial aspects to that fishing as there are at present. But the *manner* in which the fishing may be done and its purpose, whether or not commercial, are not mentioned in the Treaty. We would have quite a different case if the Treaty had preserved the right to fish at the "usual and accustomed places" *in the "usual and accustomed" manner*. But the Treaty is silent as to the mode or modes of fishing that are guaranteed.... And we see no reason why the right of the Indians may not also be regulated by an appropriate exercise of the police power of the State. The right to fish "at all usual and accustomed" places may, of course, not be qualified by the State, even though all Indians born in the United States are now citizens of the United States. [ ] But the manner of fishing, the size of the take, the restriction of commercial fishing, and the like may be regulated by the State in the interest of conservation, provided the regulation meets appropriate standards and does not discriminate against the Indians.

Puyallup Tribe v. Department of Game, 391 U.S. 392 (1968).

The conclusion that the state could regulate the technology employed by treaty fishers required the Court to remand the case to resolve the resulting factual issues:

Whether the prohibition of the use of set nets in these fresh waters was a "reasonable and necessary" conservation measure was left for determination by the trial court when the Supreme Court, deeming the injunction ... too broad, remanded the case for further findings. When the case was argued here, much was said about the pros and the cons of that issue. Since the state court has given us no authoritative answer to the question, we leave it unanswered and only add that any ultimate findings on the conservation issue must also cover the issue of equal protection implicit in the phrase "in common with."

Is the Court's decision on technology consistent with the interpretive canon that a treaty is to be construed as the Indians would have understood it— given that net fishing was a traditional fishing technology?

These two decisions came to be known as *Puyallup I.*

(b) *Puyallup II:* Following remand of *Puyallup I* from the Supreme Court, the trial court took evidence and upheld the Department of Game's regulation of the treaty fishery. The Department permitted only a sports fishery for steelhead, prohibiting the use of nets on the ground that "a commercial net fishery would be inconsistent with the conservation of the steelhead fishery." With minor modifications, the Department's actions were upheld by the Washington Supreme Court. *Department of Game v. Puyallup Tribe, Inc.,* 497 P.2d 171 (Wash.1972).

On certiorari, the United States Supreme Court began by succinctly stating the issue: "The ban on all net fishing in the Puyallup River for steelhead grants, in effect, the entire run to the sports fishermen. Whether that amounts to discrimination under the Treaty is the central question in these cases." The Court had little difficulty in concluding that it was discriminatory:

> If hook-and-line fishermen now catch all the steelhead which can be caught within the limits needed for escapement, then that number must in some manner be fairly apportioned between Indian net fishing and non-Indian sports fishing so far as that particular species is concerned. What formula is not for us to propose....
>
> The aim is to accommodate the rights of Indians under the Treaty and the rights of other people.
>
> We do not imply that their fishing rights persist down to the very last steelhead in the river. Rights can be controlled by the need to conserve a species; and the time may come when the life of a steelhead is so precious in a particular stream that all fishing should be banned until the species regains assurance of survival. The police power of the State is adequate to prevent the steelhead from following the fate of the passenger pigeon; and the Treaty does not give the Indians a federal right to pursue the last living steelhead until it enters their nets.

Department of Game v. Puyallup Tribe, 414 U.S. 44 (1973).

(c) *Puyallup III:* Following remand, the trial court upheld new regulations allocating 45% of the harvestable run of steelhead to the treaty fishery. On review, the Washington Supreme Court entered into an extended analysis of the treaty language that demonstrated, to the court's satisfaction, that "in common with" meant "like everybody else" so that the treaty right amounted to little: "We conclude ... that a proper interpretation of the Treaty of Medicine Creek permits the state to promulgate conservation regulations meeting appropriate standards that affect all citizens, Indian and non-Indian, equally." The treaty, the court stated, put Indians "on an equal footing with" non-Indians, something that, the court candidly acknowledged, was "superfluous today." Having construed the treaty to provide no right to fish beyond that available to all citizens, the court affirmed the trial court's allocation on the ground that it was not an abuse of discretion—based on the law of the case.

On certiorari, the United States Supreme Court did not note or comment on the Washington court's extended brief. Instead, the Court affirmed the allocation of fish between treaty and non-treaty fishers. *Puyallup Tribe, Inc. v. Department of Game,* 433 U.S. 165 (1977).

The *Puyallup trilogy* ultimately settled little. The Washington Supreme Court's conclusion that the treaty gave Indians no rights beyond those of the general public reflected the escalating struggle for the dwindling resource. The decision was only one of several in which the court provided support for the state's intransigent regulators.

By the time that *Puyallup III* was decided, however, two other cases: *Sohappy v. Smith*—which became *United States v. Oregon*—and *United States v. Washington* had become the primary vehicle for resolving the dispute. *Sohappy/United States v. Oregon* concerned the allocation of fish among the various fishers in the Columbia Basin; *United States v. Washington* concerned the fishers in the Puget Sound and Washington coast. These decisions and the on-going saga are considered below.

(4) The Lacey Act is the primary federal statute regulating commercial transactions in wildlife. It makes it unlawful "to import, export, transport, sell, receive, acquire or purchase" any wildlife or plant in violation of federal, state, or tribal law. 16 U.S.C. §§ 3372(a)(1), 3373(d)(1)(B). The interaction of treaty rights, tribal law, and the Lacey Act have produced three recurrent types of cases: (a) Lacey Act violation predicated upon violation of state law; Indian defendant claiming a treaty right; (b) Lacey Act violation predicated upon violation of federal law; Indian defendant claiming a treaty right; and (c) Lacey Act violation predicated upon violation of tribal law. The latter two situations will be examined below.

In *United States v. Williams,* a Nez Perce was prosecuted under the Lacey Act for selling moose in violation of state law which prohibited all sales. Defendant appealed his conviction, contending that the trial court had erred in determining that the state law was "reasonably necessary for conservation of wildlife" and thus had appropriately been applied to a tribal member. *United States v. Williams,* 898 F.2d 727, 728 (9th Cir.1990). The United States, on the other hand, argued that it was not necessary to prove that state law had a conservation basis for it to be applied through the Lacey Act to a tribal member. The court rejected both arguments. On the one hand, before state fish and game laws can be applied to treaty hunters, "the state must establish that its laws are necessary for conservation purposes. *Antoine v. Washington,* 420 U.S. 194, 207 (1975); *United*

States v. Sohappy, 770 F.2d 816 (9th Cir.1985), *cert. denied,* 477 U.S. 906 (1986). Thus, before convicting Williams, the district court [properly] held a hearing to determine the conservation necessity of the Montana and Idaho laws, applied to Williams through the Lacey Act." *Id.* at 729. On the other hand, "[t]he purpose of requiring the government to prove the conservation necessity before imposing its wildlife laws on tribe members is to safeguard the hunting and fishing rights held by the tribes while pursuing the important goal of conservation.... The argument of the United States would essentially lead to the loss of tribal treaty rights in hunting." *Id.* Thus, state law can be a predicate violation for prosecution under the Lacey Act as long as the state law is necessary for the conservation of the species.

PERSPECTIVES

(1) Declining runs and the "allocation" of "conservation": During the 1960s and early 1970s, the ocean trollers and the coastal communities dependent on the commercial and recreational salmon fishery held political power on fishery issues in Oregon and Washington. The ocean fishery was largely unregulated: It was not until 1976, that Oregon and Washington imposed any regulation of catch, gear, or seasons within the three-mile territorial limit; regulation was entirely nonexistent beyond the territorial limit. Ocean trollers could evade any individual state's restriction simply by unloading elsewhere, and thus there was little incentive for any state to regulate. The result was the imposition of increasingly severe restrictions on river and estuary fishing. By the mid–1970s, ocean fishers were taking two-thirds of the total chinook and coho catch.

The Supreme Court in *Puyallup I* briefly outlined the resulting regulatory system. Washington divided the anadromous fish species into two groups, steelhead and all other species. "Steelhead may be taken only by hook and not commercially. Salmon may be taken commercially with nets of a certain type in certain areas." *Puyallup Tribe v. Department of Game,* 391 U.S. 392 (1968). Although salmon could be commercially harvested with nets on the ocean, set nets—a traditional tribal fishing method—were prohibited in the shallow estuaries and rivers. Furthermore, the state established "salmon preserves" at the mouths of most rivers; all nets were prohibited in these preserves. Only the recreational, hook-and-line fishing was permitted in the "preserves."

Professor Ralph Johnson described the allocational results of *Puyallup I*: State "conservation" regulations were

> also designed to allocate the salmon among various user groups. There are two principal means of accomplishing this: by a "zoning" system under which the state determines where fishing can take place, and by regulations determining the type of fishing gear that can be used. As for the zoning system, unfortunately the Indians find themselves in the worst possible zone. Under the zone system, generally only sports fishermen and commercial trollers are permitted to fish at sea.... Gill netters, reef netters, and purse seiners are permitted in the Straits of Juan de Fuca. Sportsmen and gill netters can fish in Puget Sound,

with each type of fishermen excluded from certain areas and all fishermen excluded from waters near the river mouths. Most of the Indians' usual and accustomed fishing sites are on or very near the rivers. As the fish move toward the river each of the non-Indian groups take part of the run. The zoning system permits the non-Indian commercial and sports fishermen to get the first crack at the fish. By the time the fish enter the rivers and move toward the Indian fishing sites, there are few left to catch; those remaining are needed for spawning.

Ralph Johnson, *The States Versus Indian Off–Reservation Fishing: A United States Supreme Court Error*, 47 WASH. L. REV. 207, 234 (1972). Similarly, by restricting fishing gear and establishing catch limitations, the Washington Department of Game effectively allocated the entire steelhead run to non-treaty sportfishers—as the Court acknowledged in *Puyallup II*. See *Department of Game v. Puyallup Tribe*, 414 U.S. 44, 46–47 (1973).

(2) Steelhead and salmon: The regulatory system at issue in the *Puyallup Trilogy* distinguished steelhead and salmon. The distinction is full of meaning—most significantly, it reflected the distinction between game (the steelhead) and non-game species (salmon). In England, "angling" was a sport for "those that are virtuous, gentle, and freeborn" who had the time to pursue "the sport or game" of angling rather than participating in the "toilsome and unpleasant" forms of fishing with nets for commercial purposes—or so the first English book on the field sports, *The Treatise of Fishing with an Angle* (1496), posed the dichotomy. See JOHN McDONALD, THE ORIGINS OF ANGLING AND A NEW PRINTING OF THE TREATISE OF FISHING WITH AN ANGLE (1963). Both the treatise and its more famous successor, Izaak Walton's *The Compleat Angler, or the Contemplative Man's Recreation* (1653), praised the Atlantic salmon as "the goodliest fish that a man can angle for." And the goodliest way to angle for the fish was with flies. This virtuous angling tradition eventually crossed the Atlantic in the early nineteenth century. When Euro–Americans reached the Pacific coast, they encountered new species that caused confusion: how should the anadromous and non-anadromous salmonids be classified scientifically. But—as Thomas Kuhn noted in *The Structure of Scientific Revolutions*—scientists are creatures of their time. The anadromous steelhead and the non-anadromous rainbow trout were both classified as *Salmo*, the genus of the Atlantic salmon, while the other anadromous species were classified as *Oncorhynchus*. Physical characteristics that were inconsistent with this classification were ignored: the steelhead—like the rainbow trout and unlike the other salmon—rose to flies and thus was a proper fish to angle for. Thus,

> salmon were a food fish, a commodity, a means to a livelihood. Trout, however, were a sports fish. The long-standing social conventions behind this meant that their role for humans was to provide pleasure and character-building recreation; despite anglers enjoying their catch at mealtime, consumption was not the primary reason for catching trout. Tradition, and then laws ... dictated the tools of procurement and denied the use of nets in sport. This was consistent with how anglers treated Atlantic salmon; for steelhead, the scientific linkage of

the *Salmo* genus reinforced the cultural affinity. To promote their notion of proper relations to *Salmo*, anglers borrowed the tactic used earlier to curb market hunting of game and fowl. This meant affirming that steelhead were *Salmo*, with its sporting traditions, and supporting legislation to ban the commercial sale of steelhead.

Timothy M. Rawson, *What's in a Name? Of* Salmo, Oncorhynchus, *and Our Perception of Fish* (paper presented at American Society for Environmental History Annual Conference, Tacoma, Washington, Mar. 16, 2000). Washington's regulatory scheme reflected this cultural tradition: the treaty fishers transgressed a fundamental divide by taking steelhead with nets and offering their catch for sale.

In 1988, studies of morphology, behavior, biochemistry, and genetics led the Committee on Names of Fishes of the American Fisheries Society to reclassify steelhead, rainbow, cutthroat, and golden trout as *Oncorhynchus*. There are now officially no *Salmo* in the Pacific. One Seattle writer captured the issues that led anglers to object to the reclassification:

> [C]hanging a time-honored, smooth, and esthetically pleasing name like *Salmo* to an awkward, clunky, tongue-sticking name like *Oncorhynchus* ... one cannot help but wish anglers had been given a vote. The fact that for every similarity cited by scientists between Pacific salmon and steelhead, anglers can cite a difference—and those differences are important enough, at least from the fisherman's point of view, to forever hold salmon and steelhead separate and apart, no matter what their evolutionary history.... [T]he most obvious of these differences is that steelhead remain bright and strong long after they return to the rivers, and thus remain desirable to catch, while salmon ... turn rusty and ugly and break out with blotches of fungus that make them look like piscatorial lepers.... Steelhead always have been much less numerous than salmon and therefore are more highly prized by anglers.... [T]he most important difference of all is the salmon's unwillingness ... to take an artificial fly ... while the steelhead is wondrously responsive.

STEVE RAYMOND, STEELHEAD COUNTRY 21–22 (1991). The differences in perspective, of course, reflect long-standing questions on the relative value of different types of knowledge. *Cf.* RICHARD WHITE, THE ORGANIC MACHINE (1995).

Sohappy v. Smith

District Court for the District of Oregon.
302 F.Supp. 899 (1969).

■ BELLONI, J.:—Fourteen individual members of the Confederated Tribes and Bands of the Yakima Indian Nation filed case No. 68–409 against the members and director of the Fish Commission of the State of Oregon and the Oregon State Game Commission. They seek a decree of this court defining their treaty right "of taking fish at all usual and accustomed places'' on the Columbia River and its tributaries and the manner and extent of the State of Oregon may regulate Indian fishing.

. . .

Most of the argument has centered around the state's interpretation of that provision. It believes that it gives the treaty Indians only the same rights as given to all other citizens. Such a reading would not seem unreasonable if all history, anthropology, biology, prior case law and the intention of the parties to the treaty were to be ignored.

. . .

From the earliest known times, up to and beyond the time of the treaties, the Indians comprising each of the intervenor tribes were primarily a fishing, hunting and gathering people dependent almost entirely upon the natural animal and vegetative resources of the region for their subsistence and culture. They were heavily dependent upon such fish for their subsistence and for trade with other tribes and later with the settlers. They cured and dried large quantities for year around use. With the advent of canning technology in the latter half of the 19th Century the commercial exploitation of the salmonid resource by non-Indians increased tremendously. Indians, fishing under their treaty-secured rights, also participated in this expanded commercial fishery and sold many fish to non-Indian packers and dealers.

During the negotiations which led to the signing of the treaties the tribal leaders expressed great concern over their right to continue to resort to their fishing places and hunting grounds. They were reluctant to sign the treaties until given assurances that they could continue to go to such places and take fish and game there. The official records of the treaty negotiations prepared by the United States representatives reflect this concern and also the assurances given to the Indians on this point as inducement for their acceptance of the treaties.

The Supreme Court has recently restated the nature of the non-exclusive off-reservation fishing rights secured by these Indian treaties. In *Puyallup Tribe v. Department of Game,* 391 U.S. 392 (1968), it declared:

> The right to fish "at all usual and accustomed" places may, of course, not be qualified by the State, even though all Indians born in the United States are now citizens of the United States. * * * But the manner of fishing, the size of the take, the restriction of commercial fishing, and the like may be regulated by the State in the interest of conservation, provided the regulation meets appropriate standards and does not discriminate against the Indians.

The Court . . . affirmed the view that to the extent "necessary for the conservation of the fish" the state could exercise its police power to impose appropriate restrictions on the time and manner of fishing that did not discriminate against the Indians.

. . .

The issue in these cases concerns the limitation on the state's power to regulate the exercise of the Indians' federal treaty right. At least three such limitations are indicated by the Supreme Court in its Puyallup decision. First, the regulation must be "necessary for the conservation of the fish." Second, the state restrictions on Indian Treaty fishing must "not discriminate against the Indians." And third, they must meet "appropriate standards."

The regulations and policies heretofore applied by the state's regulatory and enforcement agencies have been premised upon the belief that, except for a right of access over private lands and exemption from the payment of license fees, the treaties afforded the Indians no rights beyond those accorded under the Fourteenth Amendment of the United States Constitution and under Article 1, Section 20, of the Oregon Constitution. The state argues that its regulatory scheme complies with the treaty requirements so long as the specific regulations applicable at any particular time or place impose no greater restriction on Indians fishing at such time or place than are imposed upon others fishing there. The state contends that the Indians' right to take fish at their usual and accustomed places is not a right that must be given any separate recognition or protection or be separately dealt with in the state's regulatory scheme. It argues that it may, in the interest of conservation, impose any restriction on treaty Indians fishing at their usual and accustomed places which it may impose upon non-Indians fishing at those same locations, even to the point of completely closing certain such areas to all forms of commercial fishing. It further argues, on the basis of its reading of a number of federal court decisions, including *Puyallup Tribe v. Department of Game,* that it may not allow Indians to fish at their usual and accustomed places in any manner or at any time that it does not similarly allow non-Indians to fish at those same locations. There is no support in any of these federal cases for any such narrow interpretation of the state's authority to distinguish between the regulation of Indian treaty-protected fishing and that of fishing by others.

The plaintiffs and intervenor tribes contend that before Oregon may regulate the taking and disposition of fish by treaty Indians at their usual and accustomed fishing places:

(a) It must establish preliminary to regulation that the specific proposed regulation is both reasonable and necessary for the conservation of the fish resource. In order to be necessary, such regulations must be the least restrictive which can be imposed consistent with assuring the necessary escapement of fish for conservation purposes; the burden of establishing such facts is on the state.

(b) Its regulatory agencies must deal with the matter of the Indians' treaty fishing as a subject separate and distinct from that of fishing by others. As one method of accomplishing conservation objectives it may lawfully restrict or prohibit non-Indians fishing at the Indians' usual and accustomed fishing places without imposing similar restrictions on treaty Indians.

(c) It must so regulate the taking of fish that the treaty tribes and their members will be accorded an opportunity to take, at their usual and accustomed fishing places, by reasonable means feasible to them, a fair and equitable share of all fish which it permits to be taken from any given run.

They also contend that ORS 511.106(1), 506.006(4), and certain orders of the Fish Commission establishing closed areas or seasons above Bonneville Dam may not be applied so as to prevent Indians from taking fish at their usual and accustomed places east of the confluence of the Columbia and Deschutes Rivers under their treaty rights because such application is not reasonable and necessary for conservation and constitutes an arbitrary and unreasonable total prohibition against the exercise of such treaty rights. In addition, they contend that such application of the regulations violates ORS 506.045.

[T]hese contentions of the plaintiffs and the tribes correctly state the law applicable to state regulation of the Indians' federal treaty right.

. . .

The parties place differing interpretations on the limitations on state authority inherent in the requirement that the state restriction on treaty-referenced fishing must be "necessary for the conservation of the fish."

By this reference the Supreme Court was undoubtedly speaking of conservation in the sense of perpetuation or improvement of the size and reliability of the fish runs. It was not endorsing any particular state management program which is based not only upon that factor but also upon allocation of fish among particular user groups or harvest areas, or classification of fish to particular uses or modes of taking.

The state may regulate fishing by non-Indians to achieve a wide variety of management or "conservation" objectives. Its selection of regulations to achieve these objectives is limited only by its own organic law and the standards of reasonableness required by the Fourteenth Amendment. But when it is regulating the federal right of Indians to take fish at their usual and accustomed places it does not have the same latitude in prescribing the management objectives and the regulatory means of achieving them. The state may not qualify the federal right by subordinating it to some other state objective or policy. It may use its police power only to the extent it is necessary to prevent the exercise of that right in a manner that will imperil the continued existence of the fish resource. The measure of the legal propriety of a regulation concerning the time and manner of exercising this "federal right" is, therefore, "distinct from the federal constitutional standard concerning the scope of the police power of the state." *Puyallup Tribe v. Department of Game*, 391 U.S. at 402 n.14. To prove necessity, the state must show there is a need to limit the taking of fish and that the particular regulation sought to be imposed upon the exercise of the treaty right is necessary to the accomplishment of the needed limitation. This applies to regulations restricting the type of gear which Indians may use as much as it does to restrictions on the time at which Indians may fish.

Oregon's conservation policies are concerned with allocation and use of the state's fish resource as well as with their perpetuation. . . .

. . .

The parties also place widely differing interpretations upon the Supreme Court's criteria that the state's restriction on the time and manner of fishing by treaty Indians must not discriminate against the Indians. The state believes that this means only that each law or regulation must be equally applicable to Indian and non-Indian. The United States, on the hand, contends that the state's over-all regulation of the fishery must not discriminate against the Indians' exercise of their treaty rights in favor of the taking of fish by others at other locations—that it is the treaty right which must be given equal protection with other interests in the state's regulatory scheme. It says that in the case of anadromous fish the total impact of the state's regulations on the entire run as it proceeds through the area of the state's jurisdiction must be considered; that a nondiscriminatory set of regulations requires that treaty Indians be given an opportunity to catch fish at their usual and accustomed places equal to that of other users to catch fish at locations preferred by them or by the state.

In considering the problem of salmon and steelhead conservation in the Columbia River and its tributaries, it is necessary to consider the entire Columbia River system. The off-shore fishery in the Pacific Ocean has some effect on the numbers of fish that enter the river. The salmon and steelhead that enter the Columbia River are anadromous fish and spend much of their adult life in the Pacific Ocean. Therefore, they must pass as fingerlings down the Columbia River to the sea; and as adults they must pass up the Columbia River into the particular tributary or area where they spawn.

One of the principal tools which the states of Oregon and Washington use for managing most runs of the anadromous fish resources of the Columbia River system is the "escapement goal." This goal is set by the Fish Commission, generally in conjunction with the Washington Department of Fisheries, as being the estimated numbers of fish which must escape above all commercial fishing in order that, considering all factors which influence the matter above that point, the greatest aggregate numbers of fish from such fish run will be produced and return down the Columbia to the Pacific Ocean. In establishing the escapement goal for a particular run the Fish Commission and its biological staff consider the losses which will occur above the escapement goal point from all causes, including natural causes, losses at dams and the sports catch on the upstream and tributaries in Oregon, Washington and Idaho. All the estimated numbers of fish in a given run in excess of the escapement goal are regarded by the Fish Commission as harvestable.

The state regulates fishing within its borders from the Continental Shelf to the upper limits of the river and its tributaries. It manages its resources to allow the harvest to be taken on whatever portions of the river it desires. It must manage the over-all fish run in a way that does not discriminate against the treaty Indians as it has heretofore been doing. Oregon recognizes sports fishermen and commercial fishermen and seems to attempt to make an equitable division between the two. But the state seems to have ignored the rights of the Indians who acquired a treaty right to fish at their historic off-reservation fishing stations. If Oregon intends to maintain a separate status of commercial and sports fisheries, it is obvious a third must be added, the Indian fishery. The treaty Indians, having an absolute right to that fishery, are entitled to a fair share of the fish produced by the Columbia River system.

The Supreme Court has said that the right to fish at all usual and accustomed places may not be qualified by the state. *Puyallup Tribe v. Department of Game,* 391 U.S. at 398. I interpret this to mean that the state cannot so manage the fishery that little or no harvestable portion of the run remains to reach the upper portions of the stream where the historic Indian places are mostly located.

It is clear that the state has the full and complete power to regulate all kinds of fishing, including the Indian fishery, to the end that the resource is preserved. There is no reason to believe that a ruling which grants the Indians their full treaty rights will affect the necessary escapement of fish in the least. The only effect will be that some of the fish now taken by sportsmen and commercial fishermen must be shared with the treaty Indians, as our forefathers promised over a hundred years ago.

. . .

NOTES

(1) *United States v. Washington:* Following the decision in *Sohappy,* the United States on its own behalf and as trustee for several Tribes with treaty fishing rights in Puget Sound and on the Washington coast filed suit against the state of Washington seeking a judicial determination of the tribe's rights to the anadromous fish resource and the state's authority to regulate the treaty rights. Judge Boldt's decision in *United States v. Washington,* 384 F.Supp. 312 (W.D.Wash.1974), paralleled Judge Belloni's decision in *Sohappy.* In addition, however, the Boldt decision provided a more detailed description of the allocation:

> In *Arizona [v. California,* 373 U.S. 546 (1963)] the United States Supreme Court held that irrigation water rights reserved by implication in an Indian treaty could only be limited in amount to the total reasonably required by the needs of the treaty tribe as determined from time to time indefinitely in the future. That holding cannot be distinguished in principle or application from the fishing rights specifically reserved by the plaintiff tribes and recognized by the United States in the treaties. Since tribal on reservation treaty right fishing is exclusive, fish taken on reservation shall not be included in any allocation of fish between treaty and non-treaty fishermen. Therefore, the *amount* or *quantity* of any species of fish that may be taken off reservation by treaty right fishing during a particular fishing period can only be limited by either:
>
> > (a) The number of fish required for spawning escapement and any other requirements established to be reasonable and necessary for conservation, and
> >
> > (b) The number of harvestable fish non-treaty fishermen may take at the tribes' "usual and accustomed grounds and stations" while fishing "in common with" treaty right fishermen.

As used above, "harvestable" means the number of fish remaining to be taken by any and all fishermen, at usual and accustomed grounds and stations, after deducting the number of fish required for spawning escapement and tribal needs.

Arizona was concerned with the amount of water impliedly reserved for the use of the treaty tribe and it was held they were entitled to the full amount required to serve their needs. In the present case a basic question is the amount of fish the plaintiff tribes may take in off reservation fishing under the express reservation of fishing rights recorded in their treaties. The evidence shows beyond doubt that at treaty time the opportunity to take fish for personal subsistence and religious ceremonies [ ] was the single matter of utmost concern to all treaty tribes and their members. The extent of taking fish by tribal members for these purposes is now less than in former times but for a substantial number of tribal members at or near poverty level their need in these particulars is little, if any, less than it was for their ancestors. For these reasons the court finds that the taking of fish for ceremonial and subsistence purposes has a special treaty significance distinct from and superior to the taking of fish for commercial purposes and therefore fish taken to serve ceremonial and subsistence needs shall not be counted in the share of fish that treaty right fishermen have the opportunity to take. Such needs shall be limited to the number of fish actually used for: (a) Traditional tribal ceremonies; and (b) Personal subsistence consumption by tribal members and their immediate families.

By dictionary definition and as intended and used in the Indian treaties and in this decision "in common with" means sharing equally the opportunity to take fish at "usual and accustomed grounds and stations"; therefore, nontreaty fishermen shall have the opportunity to take up to 50% of the harvestable number of fish that may be taken by all fishermen at usual and accustomed grounds and stations and treaty right fishermen shall have the opportunity to take up to the same percentage of harvestable fish, as stated above. While emphasizing the basic principle of sharing equally in the opportunity to take fish at usual and accustomed grounds and stations, the court recognizes that innumerable difficulties will arise in the application of this principle to the fisheries resource. . . .

United States v. Washington, 384 F.Supp. 312, 342–43 (W.D.Wash.1974), *aff'd,* 520 F.2d 676 (9th Cir.1975), *cert. denied,* 423 U.S. 1086 (1976).

(2) *Sohappy v. Smith:* In 1974, Judge Belloni amended the 1969 order in *Sohappy* to conform to the 50/50 allocation that Judge Boldt had ordered. The order was promptly appealed to the Ninth Circuit Court of Appeals, which affirmed the District Court in a *per curiam* decision:

The 1969 decree established that these Indians are entitled under their treaty rights to their opportunity for a fair share of the Columbia River fishery, within the broad guidelines set by the court. The same decree permitted the States to regulate fishing "to the extent that [they] can establish that such regulations are reasonable and necessary for conservation of the fish resources and do not discriminate against the Indians." Thus, the decree did not permit the States to regulate Indian treaty fishing unless the States fulfilled their burden in respect to any such regulation by establishing that the particular regulation was (1) reasonable, and (2) necessary to conserve fish resources, and (3) did not discriminate against these Indians.

The States vigorously argue that the 50 percent allocation provision in the 1974 amending order was a substantial departure from the 1969 decree, that they had no adequate notice that any such allocation was in issue, and that the provision cannot be justified or substantiated by the record before the district court in the 1974 proceedings.

We do not think that the 1974 order was a departure from the 1969 decree. That decree established the Indians' right to a fair share of the salmon harvest, if any harvest there was to be. The 1974 order did no more than define "fair share" in the context of the spring Chinook Salmon run, after the States had failed to promulgate any regulations that complied with the 1969 decree. Although the order was prompted by the controversy over the 1974 spring run, the district court obviously intended the order to apply to future spring Chinook Salmon runs. If its intention were otherwise, the court would have expressly restricted the amending order. Nothing on the face of the order or in the skimpy record suggests that the allocation is either inequitable or impracticable. [ ] We note, in passing, the merit in the States' contention that they should have an opportunity to make a record concerning the propriety of the district court's apportionment of spring Chinook Salmon runs yet to occur. Evidence directed to that issue, which the States could muster and present, would no doubt prove useful to the district court. The states, not the Indians, have the burden of establishing the respects, if any, in which the proposed allocation of future spring Chinook Salmon runs is inequitable or impracticable and of offering alternative allocation proposals which will as well or better protect the Indians' treaty rights as defined by the 1969 decree and conserve this fish resource.

Sohappy v. Smith, 529 F.2d 570 (9th Cir.1976). *Sohappy* has become *United States v. Oregon*—a still-continuing jurisdictional vehicle for resolving the conflicting interests in the Columbia Basin anadromous fish runs.

The Supreme Court denied certiorari in both *Sohappy* and *United States v. Washington*. Continued state and individual resistance to district court decisions, however, finally pushed the Court to confront the issues presented in these cases:

Washington v. Washington State Commercial Passenger Fishing Vessel Association

United States Supreme Court.
443 U.S. 658 (1979).

■ STEVENS, J.:—To extinguish the last group of conflicting claims to lands lying west of the Cascade Mountains and north of the Columbia River in what is now the State of Washington, the United States entered into a series of treaties with Indian tribes in 1854 and 1855. The Indians relinquished their interest in most of the Territory in exchange for monetary payments. In addition, certain relatively small parcels of land were reserved for their exclusive use, and they were afforded other guarantees, including protection of their "right of taking fish, at all usual and accustomed grounds and stations * * * in common with all citizens of the Territory." 10 Stat. 1133.

The principal question presented by this litigation concerns the character of that treaty right to take fish. . . .

II

One hundred and twenty-five years ago when the relevant treaties were signed, anadromous fish were even more important to most of the population of western Washington than they are today. At that time, about three-fourths of the approximately 10,000 inhabitants of the area were Indians. Although in some respects the cultures of the different tribes varied—some bands of Indians, for example, had little or no tribal organization while others, such as the Makah and the Yakima, were highly organized—all of them shared a vital and unifying dependence on anadromous fish. [ ]

Religious rites were intended to insure the continual return of the salmon and the trout; the seasonal and geographic variations in the runs of the different species determined the movements of the largely nomadic tribes. [ ] Fish constituted a major part of the Indian diet, was used for commercial purposes, and indeed was traded in substantial volume. The Indians developed food-preservation techniques that enabled them to store fish throughout the year and to transport it over great distances. [ ] They used a wide variety of methods to catch fish, including the precursors of all modern netting techniques. [ ] Their usual and accustomed fishing places were numerous and were scattered throughout the area, and included marine as well as fresh-water areas. [ ]

All of the treaties were negotiated by Isaac Stevens, the first Governor and first Superintendent of Indian Affairs of the Washington Territory, and a small group of advisers. Contemporaneous documents make it clear that these people recognized the vital importance of the fisheries to the Indians and wanted to protect them from the risk that non-Indian settlers might seek to monopolize their fisheries. [ ] There is no evidence of the precise understanding the Indians had of any of the specific English terms and phrases in the treaty. [ ] It is perfectly clear, however, that the Indians were vitally interested in protecting their right to take fish at usual and accustomed places, whether on or off the reservations, [ ], and that they were invited by the white negotiators to rely and in fact did rely heavily on the good faith of the United States to protect that right.

Referring to the negotiations with the Yakima Nation, by far the largest of the Indian tribes, the District Court found:

At the treaty council the United States negotiators promised, and the Indians understood, that the Yakimas would forever be able to continue the same off-reservation food gathering and fishing practices as to time, place, method, species and extent as they had or were exercising. The Yakimas relied on these promises and they formed a material and basic part of the treaty and of the Indians' understanding of the meaning of the treaty. [ ]

The Indians understood that non-Indians would also have the right to fish at their off-reservation fishing sites. But this was not understood as a significant limitation on their right to take fish. Because of the great abundance of fish and the limited population of the area, it simply was not contemplated that either party would interfere with the other's fishing rights. The parties accordingly did not see the need and did not intend to regulate the taking of fish by either Indians or non-Indians, nor was future regulation foreseen. [ ]

Indeed, for several decades after the treaties were signed, Indians continued to harvest most of the fish taken from the waters of Washington, and they moved freely about the Territory and later the State in search of that resource. [ ] The size of the fishery resource continued to obviate the need during the period to regulate the taking of fish by either Indians or non-Indians. [ ] Not until major economic developments in canning and processing occurred in the last few years of the 19th century did a significant non-Indian fishery develop. It was as a consequence of these developments, rather than of the treaty, that non-Indians began to dominate the fisheries and eventually to exclude most Indians from participating in it—a trend that was encouraged by the onset of often discriminatory state regulation in the early decades of the 20th century. [ ]

In sum, it is fair to conclude that when the treaties were negotiated, neither party realized or intended that their agreement would determine whether, and if so how, a resource that had always been thought inexhaustible would be allocated between the native Indians and the incoming settlers when it later became scarce.

III

Unfortunately, that resource has now become scarce, and the meaning of the Indians' treaty right to take fish has accordingly become critical. The United States Court of Appeals for the Ninth Circuit and the Supreme Court of the State of Washington have issued conflicting decisions on its meaning. In addition, their holdings raise important ancillary questions that will appear from a brief review of this extensive litigation.

The federal litigation was commenced in the United States District Court for the Western District of Washington in 1970. The United States, on its own behalf and as trustee for seven Indian tribes, brought suit against the State of Washington seeking an interpretation of the treaties and an injunction requiring the State to protect the Indians' share of the anadromous fish runs. Additional Indian tribes, the State's Fisheries and Game Departments, and one commercial fishing group, were joined as parties at various stages of the proceedings, while various other agencies and groups, including all of the commercial fishing associations that are parties here, participated as amici curiae. [ ]

During the extensive pretrial proceedings, four different interpretations of the critical treaty language were advanced. Of those, three proceeded from the assumption that the language required some allocation to the Indians of a share of the runs of fish passing through their traditional fishing areas each year. The tribes themselves contended that the treaties had reserved a pre-existing right to as many fish as their commercial and subsistence needs dictated. The United States argued that the Indians were entitled either to a 50% share of the "harvestable" fish that originated in and returned to the "case area" and passed through their fishing places, or to their needs, whichever was less. The Department of Fisheries agreed that the Indians were entitled to "a fair and equitable share" stated in terms of a percentage of the harvestable salmon in the area; ultimately it proposed a share of "one-third."

Only the Game Department thought the treaties provided no assurance to the Indians that they could take some portion of each run of fish. That agency instead argued that the treaties gave the Indians no fishing rights not enjoyed by non-treaty fishermen except the two rights previously recognized by decisions of this Court—the right of access over private lands to their usual and accustomed fishing grounds, [ ], and an exemption from the payment of license fees. [ ]

The District Court agreed with the parties who advocated an allocation to the Indians, and it essentially agreed with the United States as to what that allocation should be. It held that the Indians were then entitled to a 45% to 50% share of the harvestable fish that will at some point pass through recognized tribal fishing grounds in the case area. The share was to be calculated on a river-by-river, run-by-run basis, subject to certain adjustments. Fish caught by Indians for ceremonial and subsistence purposes as well as fish caught within a reservation were excluded from the calculation of the tribes' share. In addition, in order to compensate for fish caught outside of the case area, *i.e.,* beyond the State's jurisdiction, the court made an "equitable adjustment" to increase the allocation to the Indians. The court left it to the individual tribes involved to agree among themselves on how best to divide the Indian share of runs that pass through the usual and accustomed grounds of more than one tribe, and it postponed until a later date the proper accounting for hatchery-bred fish. [ ] With a slight modification, the Court of Appeals for the Ninth Circuit affirmed, [ ], and we denied certiorari, [ ].

The injunction entered by the District Court required the Department of Fisheries (Fisheries) to adopt regulations protecting the Indians' treaty rights. [ ] After the new regulations were promulgated, however, they were immediately challenged by private citizens in suits commenced in the Washington state courts. The State Supreme Court, in two cases that are here in consolidated form in No. 77–983, ultimately held that Fisheries could not comply with the federal injunction. [ ]

As a matter of federal law, the state court first accepted the Game Department's and rejected the District Court's interpretation of the treaties and held that it did not give the Indians a right to a share of the fish runs, and second concluded that recognizing special rights for the Indians would violate the Equal Protection Clause of the Fourteenth Amendment.

The opinions might also be read to hold, as a matter of state law, that Fisheries had no authority to issue the regulations because they had a purpose other than conservation of the resource. In this Court, however, the Attorney General of the State disclaims the adequacy and independence of the state-law ground and argues that the state-law authority of Fisheries is dependent on the answers to the two federal-law questions discussed above. [ ] We defer to that interpretation, subject, of course, to later clarification by the State Supreme Court. Because we are also satisfied that the constitutional holding is without merit,[20] our review of the state court's judgment will be limited to the treaty issue.

When Fisheries was ordered by the state courts to abandon its attempt to promulgate and enforce regulations in compliance with the federal court's decree—and when the Game Department simply refused to comply—the District Court entered a series of orders enabling it, with the aid of the United States Attorney for the Western District of Washington and various federal law enforcement agencies, directly to supervise those aspects of the State's fisheries necessary to the preservation of treaty fishing rights. [ ] The District Court's power to take such direct action and, in doing so, to enjoin persons who were not parties to the proceeding was affirmed by the United States Court of Appeals for the Ninth Circuit. [ ] That court, in a separate opinion, [ ], also held that regulations of the International Pacific Salmon Fisheries Commission posed no impediment to the District Court's interpretation of the treaty language and to its enforcement of that interpretation. Subsequently, the District Court entered an enforcement order regarding the salmon fisheries for the 1978 and subsequent seasons, which, prior to our issuance of a writ of certiorari to review the case, was pending on appeal in the Court of Appeals. [ ]

Because of the widespread defiance of the District Court's orders, this litigation has assumed unusual significance. We granted certiorari in the state and federal cases to interpret this important treaty provision and thereby to resolve the conflict between the state and federal courts regarding what, if any, right the Indians have to a share of the fish, to address the implications of international regulation of the fisheries in the area, and to remove any doubts about the federal court's power to enforce its orders. [ ]

IV

The treaties secure a "right of taking fish." The pertinent articles provide:

> The right of taking fish, at all usual and accustomed grounds and stations, is further secured to said Indians, in common with all citizens of the Territory, and of erecting temporary houses for the purpose of curing, together with the privilege of hunting, gathering roots and

---

20. The Washington Supreme Court held that the treaties would violate equal protection principles if they provided fishing rights to Indians that were not also available to non-Indians. The simplest answer to this argument is that this Court has already held that these treaties confer enforceable special benefits on signatory Indian tribes, [ ], and has repeatedly held that the peculiar semi-sovereign and constitutionally recognized status of Indians justifies special treatment on their behalf when rationally related to the Government's "unique obligation toward the Indians." [ ]

berries, and pasturing their horses on open and unclaimed lands: *Provided, however,* That they shall not take shell fish from any beds staked or cultivated by citizens."

At the time the treaties were executed there was a great abundance of fish and a relative scarcity of people. No one had any doubt about the Indians' capacity to take as many fish as they might need. Their right to take fish could therefore be adequately protected by guaranteeing them access to usual and accustomed fishing sites which could be—and which for decades after the treaties were signed were—comfortably shared with the incoming settlers.

Because the sparse contemporaneous written materials refer primarily to assuring access to fishing sites "in common with all citizens of the Territory," the State of Washington and the commercial fishing associations, having all adopted the Game Department's original position, argue that it was merely access that the negotiators guaranteed. It is equally plausible to conclude, however, that the specific provision for access was intended to secure a greater right—a right to harvest a share of the runs of anadromous fish that at the time the treaties were signed were so plentiful that no one could question the Indians' capacity to take whatever quantity they needed. Indeed, a fair appraisal of the purpose of the treaty negotiations, the language of the treaties, and this Court's prior construction of the treaties, mandates that conclusion.

A treaty, including one between the United States and an Indian tribe, is essentially a contract between two sovereign nations. [ ] When the signatory nations have not been at war and neither is the vanquished, it is reasonable to assume that they negotiated as equals at arm's length. There is no reason to doubt that this assumption applies to the treaties at issue here. [ ]

Accordingly, it is the intention of the parties, and not solely that of the superior side, that must control any attempt to interpret the treaties. When Indians are involved, this Court has long given special meaning to this rule. It has held that the United States, as the party with the presumptively superior negotiating skills and superior knowledge of the language in which the treaty is recorded, has a responsibility to avoid taking advantage of the other side. "[T]he treaty must therefore be construed, not according to the technical meaning of its words to learned lawyers, but in the sense in which they would naturally be understood by the Indians." [ ] This rule, in fact, has thrice been explicitly relied on by the Court in broadly interpreting these very treaties in the Indians' favor. *Tulee v. Washington,* 315 U.S. 681 (1942); *Seufert Brothers Co. v. United States,* 249 U.S. 194 (1919); *United States v. Winans,* 198 U.S. 371 (1905). [ ]

Governor Stevens and his associates were well aware of the "sense" in which the Indians were likely to view assurances regarding their fishing rights. During the negotiations, the vital importance of the fish to the Indians was repeatedly emphasized by both sides, and the Governor's promises that the treaties would protect that source of food and commerce were crucial in obtaining the Indians' assent. [ ] It is absolutely clear, as Governor Stevens himself said, that neither he nor the Indians intended that the latter "should be excluded from their ancient fisheries," [ ], and it is accordingly inconceivable that either party deliberately agreed to authorize future settlers to crowd the Indians out of any meaningful use of their accustomed places to fish. That each individual Indian would share an "equal opportunity" with thousands of newly arrived individual settlers is totally foreign to the spirit of the negotiations. Such a "right," along with the $207,500 paid the Indians, would hardly have been sufficient to compensate them for the millions of acres they ceded to the Territory.

It is true that the words "in common with" may be read either as nothing more than a guarantee that individual Indians would have the same right as individual non-Indians or as securing an interest in the fish runs themselves. If we were to construe these words by reference to 19th-century property concepts, we might accept the former interpretation, although even "learned lawyers" of the day would probably have offered differing interpretations of the three words. But we think greater importance should be given to the Indians' likely understanding of the other words in the treaties and especially the reference to the "right of taking fish"—a right that had no special meaning at common law but that must have had obvious significance to the tribes relinquishing a portion of their pre-existing rights to the United States in return for this promise. This language is particularly meaningful in the context of anadromous fisheries—which were not the focus of the common law—because of the relative predictability of the "harvest." In this context, it makes sense to say that a party has a right to "take"—rather than merely the "opportunity" to try to catch—some of the large quantities of fish that will almost certainly be available at a given place at a given time.

This interpretation is confirmed by additional language in the treaties. The fishing clause speaks of "securing" certain fishing rights, a term the Court has previously interpreted as synonymous with "reserving" rights previously exercised. [ ] Because the Indians had always exercised the right to meet their subsistence and commercial needs by taking fish from treaty area waters, they would be unlikely to perceive a "reservation" of that right as merely the chance, shared with millions of other citizens, occasionally to dip their nets into the territorial waters. Moreover, the phrasing of the clause quite clearly avoids placing each individual Indian on an equal footing with each individual citizen of the State. The referent of the "said Indians" who are to share the right of taking fish with "all citizens of the Territory" is not the individual Indians but the various signatory "tribes and bands of Indians" listed in the opening article of each treaty. Because it was the tribes that were given a right in common with non-Indian citizens, it is especially likely that a class right to a share of fish, rather than a personal right to attempt to land fish, was intended.

In our view, the purpose and language of the treaties are unambiguous; they secure the Indians' right to take a share of each run of fish that passes through tribal fishing areas. But our prior decisions provide an even more persuasive reason why this interpretation is not open to question. For notwithstanding the bitterness that this litigation has engendered, the principal issue involved is virtually a "matter decided" by our previous holdings.

The Court has interpreted the fishing clause in these treaties on six prior occasions. In all of these cases the Court placed a relatively broad gloss on the Indians' fishing rights and—more or less explicitly—rejected the State's "equal opportunity" approach;....

. . .

The purport of our cases is clear. Nontreaty fishermen may not rely on property law concepts, devices such as the fish wheel, license fees, or general regulations to deprive the Indians of a fair share of the relevant runs of anadromous fish in the case area. Nor may treaty fishermen rely on their exclusive right of access to the reservations to destroy the rights of other "citizens of the Territory." Both sides have a right, secured by treaty, to take a fair share of the available fish. That, we think, is what the parties to the treaty intended when they secured to the Indians the right of taking fish in common with other citizens.

V

We also agree with the Government that an equitable measure of the common right should initially divide the harvestable portion of each run that passes through a "usual and accustomed" place into approximately equal treaty and nontreaty shares, and should then reduce the treaty share if tribal needs may be satisfied by a lesser amount. Although this method of dividing the resource, unlike the right to some division, is not mandated by our prior cases, it is consistent with the 45%–55% division arrived at by the Washington state courts, and affirmed by this Court, in *Puyallup III* with respect to the steelhead run on the Puyallup River. The trial court in the *Puyallup* litigation reached those figures essentially by starting with a 50% allocation based on the Indians' reliance on the fish for their livelihoods and then adjusting slightly downward due to other relevant factors. [ ] The District Court took a similar tack in this case, *i.e.,* by starting with a 50–50 division and adjusting slightly downward on the Indians' side when it became clear that they did not need a full 50%. [ ]

The division arrived at by the District Court is also consistent with our earlier decisions concerning Indian treaty rights to scarce natural re-sources. In those cases, after determining that at the time of the treaties the resource involved was necessary to the Indians' welfare, the Court typically ordered a trial judge or special master, in his discretion, to devise some apportionment that assured that the Indians' reasonable livelihood needs would be met. [ ] This is precisely what the District Court did here, except that it realized that some ceiling should be placed on the Indians' apportionment to prevent their needs from exhausting the entire resource and thereby frustrating the treaty right of "all [other] citizens of the Territory."

Thus, it first concluded that at the time the treaties were signed, the Indians, who comprised three-fourths of the territorial population, depend-ed heavily on anadromous fish as a source of food, commerce, and cultural cohesion. Indeed, it found that the non-Indian population depended on Indians to catch the fish that the former consumed. [ ] Only then did it determine that the Indians' present-day subsistence and commercial needs should be met, subject, of course, to the 50% ceiling. [ ]

It bears repeating, however, that the 50% figure imposes a maximum but not a minimum allocation. As in *Arizona v. California* and its predecessor cases, the central principle here must be that Indian treaty rights to a natural resource that once was thoroughly and exclusively exploited by the Indians secures so much as, but no more than, is necessary to provide the Indians with a livelihood—that is to say, a moderate living. Accordingly, while the maximum possible allocation to the Indians is fixed at 50%, the minimum is not; the latter will, upon proper submissions to the District Court, be modified in response to changing circumstances. If, for example, a tribe should dwindle to just a few members, or if it should find other sources of support that lead it to abandon its fisheries, a 45% or 50% allocation of an entire run that passes through its customary fishing grounds would be manifestly inappropriate because the livelihood of the tribe under those circumstances could not reasonably require an allotment of a large number of fish.

. . .

Accordingly, any fish (1) taken in Washington waters or in United States waters off the coast of Washington, (2) taken from runs of fish that pass through the Indians' usual and accustomed fishing grounds, and (3) taken by either members of the Indian tribes that are parties to this litigation, on the one hand, or by non-Indian citizens of Washington, on the other hand, shall count against that party's respective share of the fish.

. . .

The judgments of the Court of Appeals for the Ninth Circuit, and the Supreme Court of the State of Washington are vacated and the respective causes remanded to those courts for further proceedings not inconsistent with this opinion....

■ POWELL, J., with whom STEWART and REHNQUIST, JJ., join, dissenting in part. . . .

NOTES

(1) Is there a sound legal basis for the 50/50 allocation? The Ninth Circuit Court of Appeals offered the following analogy by way of explanation:

> [T]he treaties established something analogous to a cotenancy in the off-reservation fishery.[3] The treaty fishers derive their rights from one of the cotenants, the tribes. The nontreaty fishers derive their rights from the other, the state as the successor to the United States. The

---

3. We refer to the cotenancy analogy only because it is helpful in explaining the rights of the parties, not because all the rights and incidents of a common law cotenancy necessarily follow. The shared interest in a yearly run which is apportioned on a yearly basis between two parties, each having equal rights in it. It is this equality of right between two quasi-sovereigns which we expressed by analogy [as a cotenancy]. Obviously, not all the rules of cotenancy in land can apply to an interest in the nature of a profit....

population-head-count disparity is the unremarkable result of normal principles of property law applied to the changing numbers within cotenant classes.

Puget Sound Gillnetters Association v. United States District Court, 573 F.2d 1123 (9th Cir.1978).

(2) *United States v. Washington (Phase II)*—**hatchery fish:** The Supreme Court's 1979 decision in *Washington v. Washington State Commercial Passenger Fishing Vessel Association* resolved the key issue of how to allocate fish between treaty and non-treaty fishers. The decision did not, however, resolve all of the issues. The initial *United States v. Washington* series of decisions had explicitly set aside two additional issues: Did the tribes' share (whatever it might be) apply to hatchery-raised as well wild fish? Did the treaties include an implicit right to habitat protection? Once the allocation issue had been resolved, the district court turned to these issues. We will consider the habitat question below.

The hatchery issue was of great importance given the heavy reliance on hatcheries to supplement declining wild populations. Reviewing the history of the applicable treaties and Supreme Court decisions, the district quickly concluded that the tribes were entitled to share in the hatchery-raised fish:

> The inescapable conclusion is that if hatchery fish were to be excluded from the allocation, the Indians' treaty-secured right to an adequate supply of fish—the right for which they traded millions of acres of valuable land and resources—would be placed in jeopardy. The tribes' share would steadily dwindle and the paramount purpose of the treaties would be subverted. Contrary to what the Supreme Court held to be the parties' intentions, nontreaty fishermen would ultimately "crowd the Indians out of any meaningful use of their accustomed places to fish." *Washington Phase I.*

In reaching this conclusion, the court expressly rejected the state's claim that its proprietary interests in the fish and regulatory powers over them made hatchery fish different from wild fish:

> [T]he State contends that it has regulatory and ownership interests in hatchery fish and that neither the treaties nor any subsequent enactment has preempted such interests. With respect to the State's asserted regulatory interest, it has been firmly established that the State's authority to regulate treaty fishing extends no further than the imposition of nondiscriminatory, necessary conservation measures. *See Puyallup Trilogy,* [ ]. The State has not claimed that it seeks to regulate the allocation of hatchery fish in order to conserve the resource. Rather, the State believes that because it provides funding for (at least part of) its hatchery program, its authority to regulate hatchery fish is not limited to conservation measures. The crux of the State's argument is that it has bought its way out of the obligation to respect the tribes' treaty rights. Both the premise and the conclusion of this argument are fallacious. First, the State's use of the term "regulate" is inappropriate. The State does not seek to control the time, manner, location, or extent of hatchery-fish fishing; it wishes to control the allocation of

hatchery fish. Second, it is too late in the day to challenge the fact, recently reaffirmed in Phase I, that the treaty governs the allocation of fish. Under the Supremacy Clause of the Constitution, the State is bound by the allocation decreed pursuant to the treaty. In the absence of a claim that hatchery fish must be excluded from the allocation in order to preserve the resource, the State's police powers are not implicated in the determination whether hatchery fish are "fish" for purposes of the treaty allocation.

United States v. Washington (Phase II), 506 F.Supp. 187 (W.D.Wash.1980).

PERSPECTIVES

(1) Hatchery fish and the mechanization of nature: Initial attempts to propagate fish artificially often only depleted the wild runs which provided the eggs for the hatchery. But the belief that human could outperform nature persisted. Hatcheries were touted as the solution to "the fisherman's problem": Spawning habitat could be closed off by dams or damaged by logging, grazing, and development while the take of the species could continue to increase because hatcheries would produced far more fish than nature could provided without human assistance. We could indeed have it all.

The belief was predicated on the idea that hatcheries could reduce substantially juvenile mortality, thus increasing the number of smolts sent out to the ocean. And hatcheries have achieved this goal to a significant extent: More than a billion artificially reared juveniles were released by hatcheries in the Pacific Northwest in 1981.

Nonetheless, hatcheries have been at best a mixed blessing. First, hatcheries have failed to compensate for overfishing and habitat loss; indeed, hatchery stocking often contributes to the decline of wild stocks because now-favored ocean fisheries do not distinguish between the two sources. Second, hatchery fish released into the wild are far less likely to survive than are wild stocks; hatchery production thus produces fewer returning fish than wild runs. Third, the presence of hatchery fish is destructive to wild stocks that run into the same watershed because some hatchery stock interbreed with wild runs and produce less viable offspring.

The belief in the ability of hatcheries to replace wild runs was also—though less consciously—predicated upon assumptions that nature was a machine in which the individual components could be manipulated to produce the outputs that we as a species desired. *See generally* Dale D. Goble, *The Road to the Endangered Species Act, in* Northwest Lands and Peoples: Readings in Environmental History 229–63 (Dale D. Goble & Paul W. Hirt eds., 1999); Gary K. Meffe, *Techno-Arrogance and Halfway Technologies: Salmon Hatcheries on the Pacific Coast of North America*, 6 *Conservation Bio.* 351 (1992).

(2) The civil rights movement of the Pacific Northwest: As the Ninth Circuit Court of Appeals wrote with extraordinary candor:

Except for some desegregation cases, [ ], the district court has faced the most concerted official and private efforts to frustrate a decree of a federal court witnessed in this century.

Puget Sound Gillnetters Association v. District Court, 573 F.2d 1123, 1126 (9th Cir.1978). And an exasperated judge commented:

The record in this case ... among others, make it crystal clear that it has been the recalcitrance of Washington State officials (and their vocal non-Indian commercial and sports fishing allies) which produced the denial of Indian rights requiring intervention by the district court. This responsibility should neither escape notice nor be forgotten.

United States v. Washington, 520 F.2d 676, 693 (9th Cir.1975), *cert. denied,* 423 U.S. 1086 (1976) (Burns, J., concurring). The recalcitrance of which Judge Burns wrote is demonstrated by the state's response to the "Boldt decision," *United States v. Washington,* 384 F.Supp. 312 (W.D.Wash.1974). In a classic example of state interposition—much touted in the nearly contemporaneous South—the Washington Supreme Court issued a counter-manding order to the applicable state agency. *Puget Sound Gillnetters Association v. Moos,* 565 P.2d 1151, 1158–59 (Wash.1977). *Cf. United States v. Crookshanks,* 441 F.Supp. 268 (D.Or.1977) (similar countermanding order issued by state trial court). As a result, the District Court for Western Washington took over operation of the state fish and game departments, an action upheld by the court of appeals. *Puget Sound Gillnetters Association v. United States District Court,* 573 F.2d 1123 (9th Cir.1978), *vacated on other grounds,* 443 U.S. 658 (1979). The lawlessness of the state officials fed the lawlessness of the non-treaty commercial and sport fishers; six shootings were reported in the ten days after the Boldt decision was handed down. Schmidbauser, *The Struggle for Cultural Survival: The Fishing Rights of the Treaty Tribes of the Pacific Northwest,* 52 NOTRE DAME LAW. 30, 39 (1976). There also was massive illegal fishing by non-Indians; in 1976 it was estimated that 34% of the runs was harvested illegally. UNITED STATES CIVIL RIGHTS COMMISSION, INDIAN TRIBES 72 (1981). *See generally United States v. Baker,* 641 F.2d 1311 (9th Cir.1981); *United States v. Olander,* 584 F.2d 876 (9th Cir.1978); *United States v. Crookshanks,* 441 F.Supp. 268 (D.Or. 1977).

The dispute has strong racist overtones. As the Supreme Court noted, the exclusion of Indians from the salmon fisheries was fostered in part "by the onset of often-discriminatory state regulation in the early decades of the twentieth century." *Washington v. Washington State Commercial Passenger Fishing Vessel Association,* 443 U.S. 658, 669 (1979); *see also id.* at 673 n.20. For one example of such racially discriminatory attitudes, see *State v. Towessnute,* 154 P. 805, 807 (Wash.1916). *See generally* AMERICAN FRIENDS SERVICE COMMITTEE, UNCOMMON CONTROVERSY (1970); Burnett, *Indian Hunting, Fishing and Trapping Rights: The Record and the Controversy,* 7 IDAHO L. REV. 49 (1970).

NOTES

(1) Wisconsin Chippewa litigation: The Pacific Northwest was not the only region to witness an intense struggle over Indian treaty rights to fish and hunt off-reservation. Six bands of Chippewa entered into treaties with the United States in 1837, 1842, and 1854, ceding roughly 27 million acres and, *inter alia*, reserving "[t]he privilege of hunting, fishing, and gathering the wild rice, upon the lands, the rivers and the lakes included in the territory ceded." In 1908, the Wisconsin Supreme Court held that these treaty rights were abrogated by the state's admission into the Union. *State v. Morrin*, 117 N.W. 1006 (Wis.1908).

In the late 1970s, the bands brought a federal claim to reassert their rights. In the first round of decisions, the district court held that the treaty rights had been extinguished; the Seventh Circuit reversed. *United States v. Bouchard*, 464 F.Supp. 1316 (W.D.Wis.1978), *rev'd sub nom.*, *Lac Courte Oreilles Band v. Voigt*, 700 F.2d 341 (7th Cir.), *cert. denied*, 464 U.S. 805 (1983) [*LCO I*]. On remand, the district court held that *LCO I* applied only to property that had not been sold to private parties after the decision. The Seventh Circuit again reversed, holding that the treaty rights applied to all public lands in the state. *Lac Courte Oreilles Band v. Wisconsin*, 760 F.2d 177 (7th Cir.1985) [*LCO II*].

On remand, the district court held that the treaty rights extended to all forms of animal and plant life that the bands had historically used. The court refused to allocate the resources on a percentage basis, holding that they were not scarce. The state could impose restrictions on the bands' use of resources only to the extent that the restrictions were necessary and reasonable. *Lac Courte Oreilles Band v. Wisconsin*, 653 F.Supp. 1420 (W.D.Wis.1987) [*LCO III*]. A subsequent decision allowed the state to regulate not only for conservation but also for health and safety reasons. The court also concluded that the treaty rights were restricted to providing a "modest" livelihood. *Lac Courte Oreilles Band v. Wisconsin*, 668 F.Supp. 1233 (W.D.Wis.1987).

The next issue brought before the court was whether the bands could regulate the take of muskellunge and walleye. The court held that the bands could do so if they adopted regulations that would preserve the species. *Lac Courte Oreilles Band v. Wisconsin*, 707 F.Supp. 1034 (W.D.Wis. 1989). The allocation of hunting rights to deer, small game, and fur-bearers was the subject of *LCO VI*. The district court held that the resources were to be apportioned 50/50, relying on the Supreme Court's decision in *Washington v. Washington State. Commercial Passenger Fishing Vessel Association. Lac Courte Oreilles Band v. Wisconsin*, 740 F.Supp. 1400 (W.D.Wis.1990). The court imposed taking restrictions, such as a prohibition on using lights to hunt deer.

For the history and background of the *Lac Courte Oreilles Band* litigation, see Charles F. Wilkinson, *To Feel the Summer in the Spring: The Treaty Fishing Rights of the Wisconsin Chippewa*, 1991 Wis. L. Rev. 375.

(2) *United States v. Michigan:* There has also been an intense dispute over off-reservation fishing rights in Michigan. *See United States v. Michigan*, 471 F.Supp. 192 (W.D.Mich.1979), *vacated*, 623 F.2d 448 (6th Cir. 1980), *United States v. Michigan*, 653 F.2d 277 (6th Cir.1981), *on remand*, 520 F.Supp. 207 (W.D.Mich.), *cert. denied*, 454 U.S. 1124 (1981). *See also* Diane H. Delekta, Comment, *State Regulation of Treaty Indians' Hunting and Fishing Rights in Michigan*, 1980 Det. C.L. Rev. 1097.

Minnesota v. Mille Lacs Band of Chippewa Indians

Supreme Court of the United States.
526 U.S. 172 (1999).

■ O'CONNOR, J.:—In 1837, the United States entered into a Treaty with several Bands of Chippewa Indians. Under the terms of this Treaty, the Indians ceded land in present-day Wisconsin and Minnesota to the United States, and the United States guaranteed to the Indians certain hunting, fishing, and gathering rights on the ceded land. We must decide whether the Chippewa Indians retain these usufructuary rights today. The State of Minnesota argues that the Indians lost these rights through an Executive Order in 1850, an 1855 Treaty, and the admission of Minnesota into the Union in 1858. After an examination of the historical record, we conclude that the Chippewa retain the usufructuary rights guaranteed to them under the 1837 Treaty.

I

A

[In 1837, several Chippewa Bands were summoned to Fort Snelling to negotiate a treaty ceding their land to the United States. The Chippewa agreed to sell land to the United States, but insisted on preserving their right to hunt, fish, and gather in the ceded territory. In response to this request, the fifth article of the Treaty guaranteed the Chippewa the right to hunt, fish, and gather on the ceded lands:

> The privilege of hunting, fishing, and gathering the wild rice, upon the lands, the rivers and the lakes included in the territory ceded, is guarantied [sic] to the Indians, during the pleasure of the President of the United States.

1837 Treaty with the Chippewa, 7 Stat. 537. In 1842, there were additional land cessions. The 1842 treaty also reserved usufructuary rights on the ceded lands.

[In the late 1840's, pressure mounted to remove the Chippewa to their unceded lands in the Minnesota Territory.] President Taylor responded to this pressure by issuing an Executive Order on February 6, 1850. The order provided:

> The privileges granted temporarily to the Chippewa Indians of the Mississippi, by the Fifth Article of the Treaty made with them on the 29th of July 1837, "of hunting, fishing and gathering the wild rice, upon the lands, the rivers and the lakes included in the territory ceded" by that treaty to the United States; and the right granted to the Chippewa Indians of the Mississippi and Lake Superior, by the Second Article of the treaty with them of October 4th 1842, of hunting on the territory which they ceded by that treaty, "with the other usual privileges of occupancy until required to remove by the President of the United States," are hereby revoked; and all of the said Indians remaining on the lands ceded as aforesaid, are required to remove to their unceded lands.

The officials charged with implementing this order understood it primarily as a removal order, and they proceeded to implement it accordingly. [ ]

[The Government sought to encourage the Chippewa to remove to Minnesota by changing the location where the payments for the land cessions would be made. The first annuity payment under this plan ended in disaster: around 150 Chippewa died in an outbreak of measles and dysentery; another 230 Chippewas died on the winter trip home to Wisconsin. The experience intensified opposition to the removal order among the Chippewa as well as among non-Indian residents of the area. The Secretary of the Interior approved a request "to suspend the removal of these Indians."

[Although the United States abandoned its removal policy, it did not abandon its attempts to acquire more Chippewa land. To this end, the Commissioner of Indian Affairs summoned representatives of the Mississippi, Pillager, and Lake Winnibigoshish Bands of Chippewa Indians to Washington, D.C., for the treaty negotiations. The result was the sale of additional Chippewa lands to the United States.] To this end, the first article of the 1855 Treaty contains two sentences:

> The Mississippi, Pillager, and Lake Winnibigoshish bands of Chippewa Indians hereby cede, sell, and convey to the United States all their right, title, and interest in, and to, the lands now owned and claimed by them, in the Territory of Minnesota, and included within the following boundaries, viz: [describing territorial boundaries]. And the said Indians do further fully and entirely relinquish and convey to the United States, any and all right, title, and interest, of whatsoever nature the same may be, which they may now have in, and to any other lands in the Territory of Minnesota or elsewhere.

[ ]

Article 2 set aside lands in the area as reservations for the signatory tribes. [ ] The Treaty, however, makes no mention of hunting and fishing rights, whether to reserve new usufructuary rights or to abolish rights guaranteed by previous treaties. The Treaty Journal also reveals no discussion of hunting and fishing rights. [ ]

A little over three years after the 1855 Treaty was signed, Minnesota was admitted to the Union. [ ] The admission Act is silent with respect to Indian treaty rights.

B

In 1990, the Mille Lacs Band of Chippewa Indians and several of its members filed suit in the Federal District Court for the District of Minnesota against the State of Minnesota, the Minnesota Department of Natural Resources, and various state officers (collectively State) seeking, among other things, a declaratory judgment that they retained their usufructuary rights under the 1837 Treaty and an injunction to prevent the State's interference with those rights. The United States intervened as a plaintiff in the suit; nine counties and six private landowners intervened as defendants. The District Court bifurcated the case into two phases. Phase I of the litigation would determine whether, and to what extent, the Mille Lacs Band retained any usufructuary rights under the 1837 Treaty, while Phase II would determine the validity of particular state measures regulating any retained rights.

[The District Court rejected the State's arguments that the 1837 Treaty rights were extinguished by the 1850 Executive Order or by the 1855 Treaty with the Chippewa, holding that the order was unlawful because the President had no authority to order removal of the Chippewa without their consent and that the parties to the 1855 Treaty did not intend to abrogate the usufructuary privileges guaranteed by the 1837 Treaty. In Phase II, the State and the Bands agreed to a Conservation Code and Management Plan to regulate hunting, fishing, and gathering in the Minnesota portion of the territory ceded in the 1837 Treaty. This did not, however, resolve all of the resource allocation and regulation issues.]

[On appeal, the Court of Appeals for the Eighth Circuit affirmed. 124 F.3d 904 (1997). The Eighth Circuit held: (1) President Taylor lacked the authority to issue the 1850 Executive Order abrogating the Indians' hunting, fishing, and gathering rights; (2) the 1855 Treaty did not extinguish the Mille Lacs Band's usufructuary privileges; and (3) under the "equal footing doctrine," Minnesota's entrance into the Union did not extinguish any Indian treaty rights.]

In sum, the Court of Appeals held that the Chippewa retained their usufructuary rights under the 1837 Treaty with respect to land located in the State of Minnesota. This conclusion is consistent with the Seventh Circuit Court of Appeals' earlier decision holding that the Chippewa retained those same rights with respect to the ceded land located in Wisconsin. *Lac Courte Oreilles Band of Lake Superior Chippewa Indians v. Voigt*, 700 F.2d 341, *appeal dismissed and cert. denied sub nom. Besadny v. Lac Courte Oreilles Band of Lake Superior Chippewa Indians*, 464 U.S. 805 (1983) (Brennan, Marshall, and Stevens, JJ., would affirm)....

II

We are first asked to decide whether President Taylor's Executive Order of February 6, 1850, terminated Chippewa hunting, fishing, and gathering rights under the 1837 Treaty. The Court of Appeals began its analysis of this question with a statement of black letter law: " 'The President's power, if any, to issue the order must stem either from an act of Congress or from the Constitution itself.' " 124 F.3d, at 915 (*quoting Youngstown Sheet & Tube Co. v. Sawyer*, 343 U.S. 579, 585 (1952)). The court considered whether the President had authority to issue the removal order under the 1830 Removal Act (hereinafter Removal Act), 4 Stat. 411. The Removal Act authorized the President to convey land west of the Mississippi to Indian tribes that chose to "exchange the lands where they now reside, and remove there." [ ] According to the Court of Appeals, the Removal Act only allowed the removal of Indians who had consented to removal. [ ] Because the Chippewa had not consented to removal, according to the court, the Removal Act could not provide authority for the President's 1850 removal order. [ ]

In this Court, no party challenges the Court of Appeals' conclusion that the Removal Act did not authorize the President's removal order.... We agree that the Removal Act did not forbid the President's removal order, but as noted by the Court of Appeals, it also did not authorize that order.

Because the Removal Act did not authorize the 1850 removal order, we must look elsewhere for a constitutional or statutory authorization for the order. In this Court, only the landowners argue for an alternative source of authority; they argue that the President's removal order was authorized by the 1837 Treaty itself. [ ] There is no support for this proposition, however. The Treaty makes no mention of removal, and there was no discussion of removal during the Treaty negotiations. Although the United States could have negotiated a treaty in 1837 providing for removal of the Chippewa— and it negotiated several such removal treaties with Indian tribes in 1837— the 1837 Treaty with the Chippewa did not contain any provisions authorizing a removal order.... Based on the record before us, the proposition that the 1837 Treaty authorized the President's 1850 removal order is unfounded. Because the parties have pointed to no colorable source of authority for the President's removal order, we agree with the Court of Appeals' conclusion that the 1850 removal order was unauthorized.

. . .

We conclude that President Taylor's 1850 Executive Order was ineffective to terminate Chippewa usufructuary rights under the 1837 Treaty. The State has pointed to no statutory or constitutional authority for the President's removal order, and the Executive Order, embodying as it did one coherent policy, is inseverable. We do not mean to suggest that a President, now or in the future, cannot revoke the Chippewa usufructuary rights in accordance with the terms of the 1837 Treaty. All we conclude today is that the President's 1850 Executive Order was insufficient to accomplish this revocation because it was not severable from the invalid removal order.

III

The State argues that the Mille Lacs Band of Chippewa Indians relinquished its usufructuary rights under the 1855 Treaty with the Chippewa. Specifically, the State argues that the Band unambiguously relinquished its usufructuary rights by agreeing to the second sentence of Article 1 in that Treaty:

> And the said Indians do further fully and entirely relinquish and convey to the United States, any and all right, title, and interest, of whatsoever nature the same may be, which they may now have in, and to any other lands in the Territory of Minnesota or elsewhere.

10 Stat. 1166.

This sentence, however, does not mention the 1837 Treaty, and it does not mention hunting, fishing, and gathering rights. The entire 1855 Treaty, in fact, is devoid of any language expressly mentioning—much less abrogating—usufructuary rights. Similarly, the Treaty contains no language providing money for the abrogation of previously held rights. These omissions are telling because the United States treaty drafters had the sophistication and experience to use express language for the abrogation of treaty rights. In fact, just a few months after Commissioner Manypenny completed the 1855 Treaty, he negotiated a Treaty with the Chippewa of Sault Ste. Marie that expressly revoked fishing rights that had been reserved in an earlier Treaty. *See* Treaty with the Chippewa of Sault Ste. Marie, Art. 1, 11 Stat. 631 ("The said Chippewa Indians surrender to the United States the right of fishing at the falls of St. Mary's . . . secured to them by the treaty of June 16, 1820"). [ ]

. . .

The 1855 Treaty was designed primarily to transfer Chippewa land to the United States, not to terminate Chippewa usufructuary rights. It was negotiated under the authority of the Act of December 19, 1854. This Act authorized treaty negotiations with the Chippewa "for the extinguishment of their title to all the lands owned and claimed by them in the Territory of Minnesota and State of Wisconsin." [ ] The Act is silent with respect to authorizing agreements to terminate Indian usufructuary privileges, and this silence was likely not accidental. During Senate debate on the Act, Senator Sebastian, the chairman of the Committee on Indian Affairs, stated that the treaties to be negotiated under the Act would "reserv[e] to them [i.e., the Chippewa] those rights which are secured by former treaties." [ ]

. . .

To summarize, the historical record provides no support for the theory that the second sentence of Article 1 was designed to abrogate the usufructuary privileges guaranteed under the 1837 Treaty, but it does support the theory that the Treaty, and Article 1 in particular, was designed to transfer Chippewa land to the United States. At the very least, the historical record refutes the State's assertion that the 1855 Treaty "unambiguously" abrogated the 1837 hunting, fishing, and gathering privileges. Given this plausible ambiguity, we cannot agree with the State that the 1855 Treaty abrogated Chippewa usufructuary rights. We have held that Indian treaties are to be interpreted liberally in favor of the Indians, *Washington v. Washington State Commercial Passenger Fishing Vessel Assn.*, 443 U.S., at 675–676; [ ], and that any ambiguities are to be resolved in their favor, *Winters v. United States*, 207 U.S. 564, 576–577 (1908). [ ]

IV

Finally, the State argues that the Chippewa's usufructuary rights under the 1837 Treaty were extinguished when Minnesota was admitted to the Union in 1858. In making this argument, the State faces an uphill battle. Congress may abrogate Indian treaty rights, but it must clearly express its intent to do so. *United States v. Dion*, 476 U.S. 734, 738–740 (1986); *see also Washington v. Washington State Commercial Passenger Fishing Vessel Assn.*, 443 U.S. at 690; *Menominee Tribe v. United States*, 391 U.S. 404, 413 (1968). There must be "clear evidence that Congress actually considered the conflict between its intended action on the one hand and Indian treaty rights on the other, and chose to resolve that conflict by abrogating the treaty." *United States v. Dion*, 476 at 740. There is no such "clear evidence" of congressional intent to abrogate the Chippewa Treaty rights here. The relevant statute—Minnesota's enabling Act—provides in relevant part:

> [T]he State of Minnesota shall be one, and is hereby declared to be one, of the United States of America, and admitted into the Union on an equal footing with the original States in all respects whatever.

Act of May 11, 1858, 11 Stat. 285.

This language, like the rest of the Act, makes no mention of Indian treaty rights; it provides no clue that Congress considered the reserved rights of the Chippewa and decided to abrogate those rights when it passed the Act. The State concedes that the Act is silent in this regard, [ ], and the State does not point to any legislative history describing the effect of the Act on Indian treaty rights.

With no direct support for its argument, the State relies principally on this Court's decision in *Ward v. Race Horse,* 163 U.S. 504 (1896). In *Race Horse,* we held that a Treaty reserving to a Tribe " 'the right to hunt on the unoccupied lands of the United States, so long as game may be found thereon, and so long as peace subsists among the whites and Indians on the borders of the hunting districts' " terminated when Wyoming became a State in 1890. [ ] This case does not bear the weight the State places on it, however, because it has been qualified by later decisions of this Court.

The first part of the holding in *Race Horse* was based on the "equal footing doctrine," the constitutional principle that all States are admitted to the Union with the same attributes of sovereignty (*i.e.,* on equal footing) as the original 13 States. [ ] As relevant here, it prevents the Federal Government from impairing fundamental attributes of state sovereignty when it admits new States into the Union. [ ] According to the *Race Horse* Court, because the Treaty rights conflicted irreconcilably with state regulation of natural resources—"an essential attribute of its governmental existence," *Race Horse,* [ ]—the Treaty rights were held an invalid impairment of Wyoming's sovereignty. Thus, those rights could not survive Wyoming's admission to the Union on "equal footing" with the original States.

But *Race Horse* rested on a false premise. As this Court's subsequent cases have made clear, an Indian tribe's treaty rights to hunt, fish, and gather on state land are not irreconcilable with a State's sovereignty over the natural resources in the State. *See, e.g., Washington v. Washington State Commercial Passenger Fishing Vessel Assn.,* 443 U.S. 658 (1979); *see also Antoine v. Washington,* 420 U.S. 194 (1975). Rather, Indian treaty rights can coexist with state management of natural resources. Although States have important interests in regulating wildlife and natural resources within their borders, this authority is shared with the Federal Government when the Federal Government exercises one of its enumerated constitutional powers, such as treaty making. U.S. CONST., Art. VI, cl. 2. *See, e.g., Missouri v. Holland,* 252 U.S. 416 (1920); *Kleppe v. New Mexico,* 426 U.S. 529 (1976); *United States v. Winans,* 198 U.S. at 382–384; [ ] Here, the 1837 Treaty gave the Chippewa the right to hunt, fish, and gather in the ceded territory free of territorial, and later state, regulation, a privilege that others did not enjoy. Today, this freedom from state regulation curtails the State's ability to regulate hunting, fishing, and gathering by the Chippewa in the ceded lands. But this Court's cases have also recognized that Indian treaty-based usufructuary rights do not guarantee the Indians "absolute freedom" from state regulation. *Oregon Dept. of Fish and Wildlife v. Klamath Tribe*, 473 U.S. at 765, n.16. We have repeatedly reaffirmed state authority to impose reasonable and necessary nondiscriminatory regulations on Indian hunting, fishing, and gathering rights in the interest of conservation. *See Puyallup Tribe v. Department of Game of Wash.*, 391 U.S. 392, 398 (1968); *Washington v. Washington State Commercial Passenger Fishing Vessel Assn.*, 443 U.S. at 682; *Antoine v. Washington*, 420 U.S. at 207–208. This "conservation necessity" standard accommodates both the State's interest in management of its natural resources and the Chippewa's federally guaranteed treaty rights. Thus, because treaty rights are reconcilable with state sovereignty over natural resources, statehood by itself is insufficient to extinguish Indian treaty rights to hunt, fish, and gather on land within state boundaries.

. . .

The Chief Justice reads *Race Horse* to establish a rule that "temporary and precarious" treaty rights, as opposed to treaty rights "which were 'of such a nature as to imply their perpetuity,'" are not intended to survive statehood. [ ] But the "temporary and precarious" language in *Race Horse* is too broad to be useful in distinguishing rights that survive statehood from those that do not. In *Race Horse,* the Court concluded that the right to hunt on federal lands was temporary because Congress could terminate the right at any time by selling the lands. 163 U.S. at 510. Under this line of reasoning, any right created by operation of federal law could be described as "temporary and precarious," because Congress could eliminate the right whenever it wished. In other words, the line suggested by *Race Horse* is simply too broad to be useful as a guide to whether treaty rights were intended to survive statehood.

The focus of the *Race Horse* inquiry is whether Congress (more precisely, because this is a treaty, the Senate) intended the rights secured by the 1837 Treaty to survive statehood. [ ] The 1837 Treaty itself defines the circumstances under which the rights would terminate: when the exercise of those rights was no longer the "pleasure of the President." There is no suggestion in the Treaty that the President would have to conclude that the privileges should end when a State was established in the area. Moreover, unlike the rights at issue in *Race Horse*, there is no fixed termination point to the 1837 Treaty rights. The Treaty in *Race Horse* contemplated that the rights would continue only so long as the hunting grounds remained unoccupied and owned by the United States; the happening of these conditions was "clearly contemplated" when the Treaty was ratified. [ ] By contrast, the 1837 Treaty does not tie the duration of the rights to the occurrence of some clearly contemplated event. Finally, we note that there is nothing inherent in the nature of reserved treaty rights to suggest that they can be extinguished by implication at statehood. Treaty rights are not impliedly terminated upon statehood. *Wisconsin v. Hitchcock*, 201 U.S. 202, 213–214 (1906); *Johnson v. Gearlds*, 234 U.S. 422,

439–440 (1914). The *Race Horse* Court's decision to the contrary—that Indian treaty rights were impliedly repealed by Wyoming's statehood Act—was informed by that Court's conclusion that the Indian treaty rights were inconsistent with state sovereignty over natural resources and thus that Congress (the Senate) could not have intended the rights to survive statehood. But as we described above, Indian treaty-based usufructuary rights are not inconsistent with state sovereignty over natural resources. [ ] Thus, contrary to the State's contentions, *Race Horse* does not compel the conclusion that Minnesota's admission to the Union extinguished Chippewa usufructuary rights guaranteed by the 1837 Treaty.

Accordingly, the judgment of the United States Court of Appeals for the Eighth Circuit is affirmed.

■ REHNQUIST, C.J., with whom SCALIA, KENNEDY and THOMAS, JJ., join, dissenting:—. . . . Rather than engage in the flawed analysis put forward by the Court, I would instead hold that the Executive Order constituted a valid revocation of the Chippewa's hunting and fishing privileges. Pursuant to a Treaty, the President terminated the Indians' hunting and fishing privileges in an Executive Order which stated, in effect, that the privilege to come onto federal lands and hunt was terminated, and that the Indians move themselves from those lands.

No party has questioned the President's power to terminate the hunting privilege. . . .

. . . . And because the 1837 Treaty, in conjunction with the Presidential power over public lands gave the President the power to order removal in conjunction with his termination of the hunting rights, the Court's severability analysis is unnecessary. In sum, there is simply no principled reason to invalidate the 150–year-old Executive Order, particularly in view of the heightened deference and wide latitude that we are required to give orders of this sort.

III

Although I believe that the clear meaning of the Executive Order is sufficient to resolve this case, and that it is unnecessary to address the Court's treatment of the 1855 Treaty and the 1858 admission of Minnesota to the Union, I shall briefly express my strong disagreement with the Court's analysis on these issues also.

As the Court notes, in 1855, several of the Chippewa Bands agreed, in exchange for further annuity payments of money and goods, to "fully and entirely relinquish and convey to the United States, any and all right, title, and interest, of whatsoever nature the same may be, which they now have in, and to any other lands in the Territory of Minnesota or elsewhere." 10 Stat. 1166. The plain meaning of this provision is a relinquishment of the Indians of "all" rights to the land. The Court, however, interprets this provision in a manner contrary to its plain meaning by first noting that the provision does not mention "usufructuary" rights. It argues, citing examples, that since the United States "had the sophistication and experience to use express language for the abrogation of treaty rights," but did not mention the 1837 Treaty rights in drafting this language, it perhaps did not intend to extinguish those rights, thus creating an interpretation at odds with the Treaty's language. Then, using our canons of construction that ambiguities in treaties are often resolved in favor of the Indians, it concludes that the Treaty did not apply to the hunting rights.

I think this conclusion strained, indeed. First, the language of the Treaty is so broad as to encompass "all" interests in land possessed or claimed by the Indians. Second, while it is important to the Court that the Treaty "is devoid of any language expressly mentioning—much less abrogating—usufructuary rights," [ ], the definition of "usufructuary rights" explains further why this is so. Usufructuary rights are "a real right of limited duration on the property of another." *See* BLACK'S LAW DICTIONARY 1544 (6th ed. 1990). It seems to me that such a right would fall clearly under the sweeping language of the Treaty under any reasonable interpretation, and that this is not a case where "even 'learned lawyers' of the day would probably have offered differing interpretations of the [treaty language]." *Cf. Washington v. Washington State Commercial Passenger Fishing Vessel Assn.,* 443 U.S. 658, 677 (1979). And third, although the Court notes that in other treaties the United States sometimes expressly mentioned cessions of usufructuary rights, there was no need to do so in this case, because the settled expectation of the United States was that the 1850 Executive Order had terminated the hunting rights of the Chippewa. Thus, rather than applying the plain and unequivocal language of the 1855 Treaty, the Court holds that "all" does not in fact mean "all."

IV

Finally, I note my disagreement with the Court's treatment of the equal footing doctrine, and its apparent overruling sub silentio of a precedent of 103 years' vintage. . . .

[T]he Court, in a feat of jurisprudential legerdemain, effectively overrules *Ward* sub silentio. First, the Court notes that Congress may only abrogate Indian treaty rights if it clearly expresses its intent to do so. Next, it asserts that Indian hunting rights are not irreconcilable with state sovereignty, and determines that "because treaty rights are reconcilable with state sovereignty over natural resources, statehood by itself is insufficient to extinguish Indian treaty rights to hunt, fish, and gather on land within state boundaries." [ ] And finally, the Court hints that *Ward* rested on an incorrect premise—that Indian rights were inconsistent with state sovereignty.

Without saying so, this jurisprudential bait-and-switch effectively overrules *Ward,* a case which we reaffirmed as recently as 1985 in *Oregon Dept. of Fish and Wildlife v. Klamath Tribe,* 473 U.S. 753 (1985). *Ward* held merely that treaty rights which were only "temporary and precarious," as opposed to those which were "of such a nature as to imply their perpetuity," do not survive statehood. 163 U.S. at 515. Here, the hunting privileges were clearly, like those invalidated in *Ward,* temporary and precarious: The privilege was only guaranteed "during the pleasure of the President"; the legally enforceable annuity payments themselves were to terminate after 20 years; and the Indians were on actual notice that the President might end the rights in the future, [ ].

Perhaps the strongest indication of the temporary nature of the Treaty rights is presented unwittingly by the Court in its repeated (and correct) characterizations of the rights as "usufructuary." As noted, usufructuary rights are by definition "of limited duration." BLACK'S LAW DICTIONARY 1544 (6th ed. 1991). Thus, even if the Executive Order is invalid; and even if the 1855 Treaty did not cover the usufructuary rights: Under *Ward*, the temporary and precarious Treaty privileges were eliminated by the admission of Minnesota to the Union on an equal footing in 1858. Today the Court appears to invalidate (or at least substantially limit) *Ward*, without offering any principled reason to do so.

NOTES

(1) How secure are the hunting and fishing rights of the Mille Lacs in light of the Supreme Court's decision? Can the President at any time revoke them by unilateral action? If so, is revocation likely as a political matter? Would the President have the power to undertake a partial revocation—such as revoking them for all lands and waters not in public ownership, or for lands (such as wildlife refuges) where hunting is generally banned—or must the revocation be either all or nothing?

(2) In light of *Mille Lacs*, is there any continuing validity to the nineteenth-century decision in *Race Horse*? That is, could a state still claim that certain reserved tribal rights were so temporary that they expired automatically when the state entered the union, or has *Race Horse* been so limited that it has no application beyond its immediate facts? Note that, according to the majority, "the *Race Horse* inquiry is whether Congress (more precisely, because this is a treaty, the Senate) intended the rights secured by the 1837 Treaty to survive statehood." If the issue is now solely one of intent, should not the intent of the tribe count as well?

(3) *Mille Lacs* illustrates how off-reservation hunting and fishing rights often turn, not on a single treaty or statutory provision, but on the interplay of several such provisions. It also further illustrates why generalizations about tribal rights are so difficult to make; the rights of each tribe vary depending upon the treaties they signed and the actions taken under those treaties.

(4) On the choice of dictionaries and decisionmakers: Chief Justice Rehnquist relies upon BLACK'S to argue that usufructuary rights are "of limited duration." [¶ 38] The Chief Justice fails to note that the definition upon which he relies is applicable "[i]n [the] civil law" rather than the common law. Recall the discussion in Chapter 3 of the common law usufructuary right to hunt or fish on another's property. Such rights were well-established incorporeal hereditaments, *i.e.,* inheritable, intangible property interests that were *not* temporally limited. *See, e.g.,* RESTATEMENT (THIRD) OF PROPERTY: SERVITUDES xxi (Tentative Draft No. 1, 1989) ("A profit [the specific type of usufructuary right at issue] creates the right to enter on and remove a physical substance from land in the possession of another. It imposes a duty on the owner and possessor of the land not to interfere with removal of the substance."); *see also* 8 THOMPSON ON REAL PROPERTY § 65.01(a), at 33–34 (David A. Thomas ed., 1994); 3 HERBERT T. TIFFANY,

THE LAW OF REAL PROPERTY § 839, at 427 (3d ed. 1939). *See generally* Michael C. Blumm, *et al., Judicial Termination of Treaty Water Rights: The Snake River Case,* 36 IDAHO L. REV. 449 (2000).

(ii) THE ENVIRONMENTAL SERVITUDE: THE RIGHT TO HAVE SOMETHING TO HUNT AND FISH

United States v. Washington (Phase II)
District Court for the Western District of Washington.
506 F.Supp. 187 (1980).

■ ORRICK, D.J.:—[The first part of the *Phase II Decision* is discussed in the notes following *Washington v. Washington State Commercial Passenger Fishing Vessel Association*; this part of the decision addresses the final issue:] whether the right of taking fish incorporates the right to have treaty fish protected from environmental degradation.

IV

A

From the numerous opinions rendered in Phase I, and the application of the principles enunciated therein to the hatchery issue, flows the resolution of the remaining issue in Phase II the environmental issue. As previously noted, the only aspect of this issue presently before the Court is the legal question whether the tribes' fishing right includes the right to have treaty fish protected from environmental degradation. . . .

At the outset, the Court holds that implicitly incorporated in the treaties' fishing clause is the right to have the fishery habitat protected from man-made despoliation. Virtually every case construing this fishing clause has recognized it to be the cornerstone of the treaties and has emphasized its overriding importance to the tribes. *See Washington Phase I.* The Indians understood, and were led by Governor Stevens to believe, that the treaties entitled them to continue fishing in perpetuity and that the settlers would not qualify, restrict, or interfere with their right to take fish. [ ]

The most fundamental prerequisite to exercising the right to take fish is the existence of fish to be taken. In order for salmon and steelhead trout to survive, specific environmental conditions must be present. A fisheries study prepared jointly by the State and the federal government identifies at least five such conditions: "(1) access to and from the sea, (2) an adequate supply of good-quality water, (3) a sufficient amount of suitable gravel for spawning and egg incubation, (4) an ample supply of food, and (5) sufficient shelter." It is undisputed that "alteration of even one of these essential, finely-balanced requirements will affect the production potential." It is also undisputed that these conditions have been altered and that human activities have seriously degraded the quality of the fishery habitat.

. . .

The conclusion that the treaty-secured fishing right incorporates an environmental right is consonant with the implied-reservation-of-water doctrine that is often employed in the construction of Indian treaties. In *Winters v. United States*, 207 U.S. 564 (1908), the seminal case in this area, the Supreme Court held that when the treaty creating the Fort Belknap Indian Reservation was signed, the parties impliedly reserved a sufficient quantity of water to irrigate the arid reservation land. Without that water, the purpose of creating the Reservation to enable the tribe to give up its nomadic existence and sustain itself on a relatively small tract of land would be incapable of fulfillment. [ ] Thus, the construction of dams or reservoirs or the undertaking of any other activities that would prevent water from flowing to the Reservation was enjoined. [ ]

In this case, there can be no doubt that one of the paramount purposes of the treaties in question was to reserve to the tribes the right to continue fishing as an economic and cultural way of life. It is equally beyond doubt that the existence of an environmentally-acceptable habitat is essential to the survival of the fish, without which the expressly-reserved right to take fish would be meaningless and valueless. Thus, it is necessary to recognize an implied environmental right in order to fulfill the purposes of the fishing clause. Indeed, courts have already recognized implied water rights for the specific purpose of preserving fish. . . .

C

The more difficult issues pertaining to the State's duty involve its nature and scope. Several guiding considerations emerge from the numerous cases involving disputes between states and treaty tribes. First, the treaty-secured right to take fish at usual and accustomed places may not be qualified or conditioned by the State. *Puyallup I*, 391 U.S. at 398–399. *See also Tulee v. Washington*, [ ]; *Winans*, [ ]; *Final Decision I*, [ ]. Second, the State may not subordinate the fishing right to any other objectives or purposes it may prefer.

> It [the state] may not force treaty Indians to yield their own protected interests in order to promote the welfare of the state's other citizens.

United States v. State of Washington, 520 F.2d at 686. *See also Final Decision I*, [ ]; *Sohappy v. Smith*, 302 F.Supp. 899, 908 (D.Or.1969). Third, the State may affirmatively regulate treaty fishing solely for the purpose of conserving the resource. *Puyallup Trilogy*, [ ]; *Final Decision I*, [ ]; *Sohappy v. Smith*, [ ]. It would virtually obliterate these narrowly-drawn limitations on the State's authority were this Court to rule, by denying plaintiffs' pending motion, that the State may now regulate treaty fishing for two purposes: to conserve the resource or to destroy it.

Unlike many of the preceding cases, this case does not (at this stage of this litigation) involve an attempt by the State affirmatively to regulate the fishery. Contrary to the State's apprehensions, neither does this case involve an attempt by plaintiffs to impose an affirmative duty on the State to protect the fish habitat. Rather, plaintiffs seek the recognition of a negative duty such that when the State exercises its broad regulatory powers it does not impair the environmental conditions necessary for the survival of the treaty fish. According to the United States:

> [T]he duty here is the duty to refrain from taking or approving actions which have a significant adverse impact on the treaty right fishery.

Plaintiff is not seeking any new legislation or expenditure of resources by the State. It is merely asking that the State, in carrying out its regulatory authority over public or private actions with environmental impact, not authorize actions that will significantly damage or destroy the treaty guaranteed fishery.

In light of this characterization of the duty sought to be imposed, the State's claim that recognition of an environmental right will require it to make additional expenditures in violation of the Tenth Amendment ... is ill-founded. The State need not make any additional expenditures, the treaty right from which the State's duty arises is not based on the commerce clause, and the question of the appropriate scope of any relief to be granted is not yet in issue. Moreover, the State already purports to act as if it has voluntarily assumed the very duty which it here resists.

The [Washington Fisheries] Department's habitat protection functions include evaluating potential effects of public or private projects or activities that may affect salmon production. Reports and recommendations concerning these activities are made to the appropriate agencies. * * *

Departmental functions that relate directly to habitat protection include setting restrictions for hydraulic permits, inspecting hydraulic projects, developing recommendations regarding water right applications, and establishing fish use flows for salmon production streams. * * *

In concert with the Department of Fisheries, the Department of Game inspects and issues joint permits for hydraulic permits. * * * [A]ctivities affecting stream beds are directed to be conducted at a time and in a manner that minimize adverse effects on the stream environment for fish. The two departments review all plans for major projects affecting stream habitat and develop appropriate recommendations. All water right applications are similarly reviewed for their possible impact on fishery resources and commented upon where needed. Recently, annual logging plans of several major timber owners have come under detailed review and comment by personnel of both departments.

Whether the State effectively carries out these activities, and whether they are adequate, are questions to be addressed at the relief stage of this litigation. For present purposes it is sufficient to note that the State has at least implicitly acknowledged that it has a duty not to impair or permit the impairment of the fish habitat.

As the parties approach the relief stage, of critical concern will be the precise scope of the State's environmental duty. Plaintiffs urge the Court to hold the State to a standard of "no significant deterioration," which would preclude the State from appreciably reducing the environmental quality of the fish habitat. The State responds by arguing that the cases cited by plaintiffs do not support their position. The Court finds a more fundamental flaw in plaintiffs' proposal. The "no significant deterioration" standard was articulated by courts and expressly adopted by Congress in order to effectuate the goals of various environmental statutes. [ ] The standard reflects Congress' legislative judgment, arrived at after weighing competing environmental and economic considerations. In each of the above-cited statutes, Congress indicated that the nondegradation standard was necessary in order to realize the statutory objectives. In contrast, here the Court rather than Congress is called upon to impose a nondegradation standard. It is well established that the scope of an impliedly-reserved right may not be broader than the minimal need which gives rise to the implied right. [ ] Thus, the scope of the State's environmental duty must be ascertained by examining the treaty-secured fishing right rather than by selecting a desirable standard that has been imposed by Congress in a different context.

. . .

The tribes' treaty allocation is currently set at 50 percent of each harvestable run. Id. That the ceiling has been applied creates the presumption that the tribes' moderate living needs exceed 50 percent and are not being fully satisfied under the treaties. As the burden is upon the State to demonstrate to the Phase I court that the tribes' needs may be satisfied by a lesser allocation, the State must also bear the burden in Phase II to demonstrate that any environmental degradation of the fish habitat proximately caused by the State's actions (including the authorization of third parties' activities) will not impair the tribes' ability to satisfy their moderate living needs. Naturally, the plaintiffs must shoulder the initial burden of proving that the challenged action(s) will proximately cause the fish habitat to be degraded such that the rearing or production potential of the fish will be impaired or the size or quality of the run will be diminished.

NOTES

(1) What is the nature of the right claimed by the tribe? Is the court correct that the remedy is the more problematic issue? How would you characterize the remedial standard? Should the treaty fishers be given a veto over all land-use decisions in the Columbia Basin? Given the history of this litigation—recall that the district court was required to manage the state department of game to ensure that the orders in Phase I were carried out—was the environmental decision manageable?

(2) Phase II in the Ninth Circuit: The magnitude of the potential changes may explain the fate of Judge Orrick's decision on appeal to the Ninth Circuit. The initial decision, *United States v. Washington*, 694 F.2d 1374 (9th Cir.1982), reversed Orrick's environmental-right holding. That decision was vacated and rehearing en banc granted. The en banc decision held that the Circuit Court lacked jurisdiction because the district court's ruling on the motions for partial summary judgment was not a final reviewable decision under the Federal Rules of Civil Procedure:

> In determining whether the decision to grant declaratory relief is proper, we consider both the circumstances of the parties and the sound jurisprudence of the court. Declaratory relief should be denied when prudential considerations counsel against its use, [ ], and the decision to grant declaratory relief should always be made with reference to the public interest. [ ] Declaratory relief should be denied when it will neither serve a useful purpose in clarifying and settling the legal relations in issue nor terminate the proceedings and afford relief from the uncertainty and controversy faced by the parties. [ ]

The limitations upon issuance of a declaratory judgment, expressed as a doctrine of judicial discretion, reflect concerns similar to
those underlying the case and controversy limitation of Article III, [ ],
though the principles of sound discretion are more comprehensive and
are subject to more flexible elaboration by the court. We choose to rest
our decision in this case on the proposition that issuance of the
declaratory judgment on the environmental issue is contrary to the
exercise of sound judicial discretion. The legal standards that will
govern the State's precise obligations and duties under the treaty with
respect to the myriad State actions that may affect the environment of
the treaty area will depend for their definition and articulation upon
concrete facts which underlie a dispute in a particular case. Legal rules
of general applicability are announced when their consequences are
known and understood in the case before the court, not when the
subject parties and the court giving judgment are left to guess at their
meaning. It serves neither the needs of the parties, nor the jurisprudence of the court, nor the interests of the public for the judiciary to
employ the declaratory judgment procedure to announce legal rules
imprecise in definition and uncertain in dimension. Precise resolution,
not general admonition, is the function of declaratory relief. These
necessary predicates for a declaratory judgment have not been met
with respect to the environmental issue in this case.

The State of Washington is bound by the treaty. If the State acts
for the primary purpose or object of affecting or regulating the fish
supply or catch in noncompliance with the treaty as interpreted by past
decisions, it will be subject to immediate correction and remedial action
by the courts. In other instances, the measure of the State's obligation
will depend for its precise legal formulation on all of the facts presented by a particular dispute. The trial court is instructed to vacate its
judgment with reference to the environmental aspect of the case. The
declaratory judgment resolving the separate issue relating to hatchery
fish does not suffer from similar infirmities. In this context, the state
of the record provides a sufficient basis upon which the court may
exercise its discretion. Further, a declaratory judgment on the issue
clarifies and settles the legal relations of the parties and affords relief
from a precise dispute identified in the proceedings.

United States v. Washington, 759 F.2d 1353 (9th Cir.), *cert. denied,* 474
U.S. 994 (1985).

PERSPECTIVES

Mary Christina Wood, *The Tribal Property Right to Wildlife Capital (Part II): Asserting a Sovereign Servitude to Protect Habitat of Imperiled Species*
25 VT. L. REV. 357, 387–88 (2001).

Common law is replete with judicial implication of corollary rights
necessary to the full enjoyment of property. When dealing with Indian

property, the Supreme Court has invoked the reserved rights doctrine to imply such rights. The landmark case of *Winters v. United States,* for example, found an implied reservation of water necessary to irrigate an arid Indian reservation.[144] . . .

Courts have made clear that the reserved rights doctrine reaches beyond merely the land interests of tribes to the tribal hunting and fishing rights as well.[146] Clauses reserving usufructuary harvest rights in ceded lands constitute separate reservation of property rights which are distinct from reservation lands. The Supreme Court in *Winans* recognized the fishing property right and upheld an implied tribal right of access to traditional sites, noting that the treaty "fixes in the [ceded] land such easements as enables the [fishing] right to be exercised."[148]

The reserved rights doctrine provides a sound basis for implying a negative conservation easement to protect the natural production areas of salmon. Such an easement, like the access easement in *Winans* and the water rights in *Winters,* is a necessary corollary to the enjoyment of a tribal property interest. Ninth Circuit precedent already recognizes a major component of such a conservation easement. In *United States v. Adair,*[149] the court found that an 1864 treaty with the Klamath Tribe entitled the tribe to an instream flow necessary to support its treaty fishing and hunting activities—in essence, a water right to support habitat. . . . Courts have recognized the instream habitat water right in the contest of several other tribal fisheries as well.[152] . . .

* * *

(1) In addition to the cases cited by Professor Wood, *see also Kittitas Reclamation District v. Sunnyside Valley Irrigation District,* 763 F.2d 1032 (9th Cir.1985); *Confederated Tribes of the Umatilla Indian Reservation v. Alexander,* 440 F.Supp. 553 (D.Or.1977). *See generally* Michael C. Blumm & Brett M. Swift, *The Indian Treaty Piscary Profit and Habitat Protection in the Pacific Northwest: A Property Rights Approach,* 69 U. COLO. L. REV. 407, 462–502 (1998).

(2) Euro–Americans, habitat alteration, and the Columbia River salmon: Rivers sit at the bottom of watersheds with the result that whatever happens on the land eventually affects the river. Thus the health of the riverine environment is intimately dependent upon the surrounding land. As a result, all land use decisions that affect the physical structure of

144. *Winters v. United States,* 207 U.S. 564, ___ (1908).

146. *United States v. Winans,* 198 U.S. 371, 381 (1905); *Washington v. Washington State Commercial Passenger Fishing Vessel Ass'n,* 443 U.S. 658, 679–80 (1979) (citing *Winans*).

148. *Winans,* 198 U.S. at 384.

149. *United States v. Adair,* 723 F.2d 1394 (9th Cir.1983).

152. *See, e.g., Colville Confederated Tribes v. Walton,* 647 F.2d 42, 48 (9th Cir. 1981) (recognizing the Colville Tribe's "right to water to establish and maintain the Omak Lake replacement fishery includes the right to sufficient water to permit natural spawning of the trout"): *Flathead Irrigation Dist. v. United States,* 832 F.2d 1127, 1132 (9th Cir. 1987), *cert. denied,* 486 U.S. 1007 (1988) (recognizing the Flathead Tribe's right to instream flows to preserve tribal fisheries); *United States v. Anderson,* 591 F.Supp. 1, 5 (E.D.Wash.1982) (holding that the Spokane Tribe "has reserved rights to sufficient water to preserve fishing in the Chamokane Creek"); [ ]

the riparian environment or the quantity or quality of the river's water affect the fish dependent upon that water.

(a) Allocating habitat: Salmonids evolved in cold, clean, highly oxygenated water. Changes to streams that impact these conditions also impact salmon.

(i) Water quantity: Fish require water. The over-appropriation of many streams in the Columbia Basin has made the availability of water a major problem. Some stretches of former salmon-producing streams, such as the Lemhi River on the Idaho–Montana border and the Umatilla River in Oregon, are now drained dry by irrigators during all but the wettest years. Even where streams continue to flow, salmon habitat is often reduced by flow alteration or water level fluctuation caused by irrigation withdrawals. While irrigation is the major cause, insufficient water may also result from land uses which do not directly consume water. Removal of vegetation, for example, accelerates runoff and increases the likelihood that a stream will dry up in the summer.

(ii) Water quality: The quality of the available water is as important as its quantity. The most important quality parameters are: (A) temperature—the most important determinant of the type of fishery a river supports, because it directly affects fish metabolic rates. Salmonids are cold-water species which are adversely affected by temperatures above 62°–68° F. Logging, grazing, and agricultural activities which remove tree cover or riparian vegetation expose the stream to direct sunlight and increase water temperature; irrigation return water is also warmer than stream water; (B) chemistry—alteration of the chemical balance may seriously affect the fishery. The impacts of mining are often the most dramatic, but the herbicides, pesticides, and fertilizers used in agriculture, forest, and range management may be even more damaging. Reduced oxygen content is also a significant problem and a river's oxygen content may be reduced as a result of increased water temperature, reduced water flow, increased productivity (eutrophication) caused by the leaching of nutrients and fertilizers, or increased oxygen consumption from the breakdown of organic wastes; (C) sediment—turbidity and siltation adversely affect each stage of a salmon's life cycle. Land-disturbing activities such as agriculture, logging, mining, and construction all produce sediment.

(b) The Columbia River hydroelectric system: Perhaps the most important source of the problems facing anadromous fish within the Columbia Basin is the region's hydroelectric system. Development of hydropower in the Columbia Basin began in 1888 with the construction of the T.M. Sullivan Dam at Willamette Falls on the Willamette River. Within twenty years, fourteen more hydroelectric facilities had been constructed on the Snake, Boise, and Spokane Rivers in Idaho; on the Similkameen, Naches, Spokane, and Wenatchee Rivers in Washington; on the Rock Creek and the Clackamas and Deschutes Rivers in Oregon. These early facilities had low dams with relatively small storage capacity; construction of major dams did not begin until the 1930s when Rock Island, Bonneville, and Grand Coulee Dams were begun. There are now almost 130 hydroelectric or multipurpose dams on the Columbia and its tributaries.

The most obviously destructive effect of dam building has been to close off or drown spawning and rearing habitat. In 1941, the Bureau of Reclamation closed the gates on Grand Coulee Dam, thus blocking more than 1,100 river miles of spawning and rearing habitat. Idaho Power's Brownlee Dam and Portland General Electric's Pelton Dam each destroyed a major run. In addition, mainstem Columbia and Snake River dams drowned spawning and rearing habitat beneath their impoundments. The cumulative result has been a reduction in accessible spawning habitat by more than one-half.

The habitat losses vary by species since different species have different ranges and habitat requirements. Thus steelhead habitat fell from 12,935 river miles in 1850 to 8,915 in 1975; spring chinook habitat decreased from 10,618 to 5,417; the summer chinook's range was reduced from 4,972 to 2,268 miles; fall chinook habitat was reduced from 1,825 to 1,658; chum habitat fell from 309 to 194 miles; sockeye lost all but 794 of its previous 2,268 miles of habitat. Coho, on the other hand, actually gained 654 miles of habitat as a result of removal of natural blockages, primarily on the Willamette River.

In addition to reducing the Basin's aggregate capacity to produce salmon, shutting off habitat funnels the fish into smaller and smaller areas, which increases the species' vulnerability to a local environmental catastrophe.

Even when equipped with fish passage facilities, dams kill by changing the river environment. Salmon and steelhead evolved in free-flowing streams. The dams have completely destroyed this environment: a free-flowing river has been replaced by a series of computer controlled, slack-water ponds. The impoundments have deleterious effects on salmonids. The warmer, slack-water environment of the impoundments is conducive to native and exotic predators and hostile to salmon and steelhead. The impoundments expose migrating salmon to increased water temperatures and altered water chemistry, thus enhancing their susceptibility to disease. In addition, the current in the impoundments is substantially reduced from that of a free-flowing river. Downstream migration coincides with spring runoff when the high flow volumes allow the smolts to move quickly downstream into the estuary. Prior to the impoundments, smolts migrated from the Snake, Salmon, and Clearwater drainages into saltwater in ten to fourteen days; the same trip now requires more than fifty days. The increased time required for migration has severe effects on the smolts, actually stopping the migration of some individuals. Delayed migration also exposes the juveniles to greater predation. Each dam exacts its toll with a staggering cumulative effect. As a result of the radically altered river environment, the present salmon and steelhead runs in the upper Columbia Basin are mere remnants of historic runs.

See generally Michael C. Blumm, *Hydropower v. Salmon: The Struggle of the Pacific Northwest's Anadromous Fish Resources for a Peaceful Coexistence with the Federal Columbia River Power System,* 11 ENVTL. L. 211 (1981); Michael C. Blumm & Andy Simrin, *The Unraveling of the Parity Promise: Hydropower, Salmon, and Endangered Species in the Columbia Basin,* 21 ENVTL. L. 657 (1991); Dale D. Goble, *Introduction to the*

Symposium on Legal Structures for Managing the Pacific Northwest Salmon and Steelhead: The Biological and Historical Context, 22 IDAHO L. REV. 417 (1986).

SECTION 5.   FEDERAL POWER TO LIMIT TREATY RIGHTS

United States v. Dion

United States Supreme Court.
476 U.S. 734 (1986).

■ MARSHALL, J.:—Respondent Dwight Dion, Sr., a member of the Yankton Sioux Tribe, was convicted of shooting four bald eagles on the Yankton Sioux Reservation in South Dakota in violation of the Endangered Species Act, [ ]. The District Court dismissed before trial a charge of shooting a golden eagle in violation of the Bald Eagle Protection Act, [ ] (Eagle Protection Act). Dion was also convicted of selling carcasses and parts of eagles and other birds in violation of the Eagle Protection Act and the Migratory Bird Treaty Act, [ ]. The Court of Appeals for the Eighth Circuit affirmed all of Dion's convictions except those for shooting bald eagles in violation of the Endangered Species Act. [ ] As to those, it stated that Dion could be convicted only upon a jury determination that the birds were killed for commercial purposes. [ ] It also affirmed the District Court's dismissal of the charge of shooting a golden eagle in violation of the Eagle Protection Act. [ ] We granted *certiorari,* [ ], and we now reverse the judgment of the Court of Appeals insofar as it reversed Dion's convictions under the Endangered Species Act and affirmed the dismissal of the charge against him under the Eagle Protection Act.

I

The Eagle Protection Act by its terms prohibits the hunting of the bald or golden eagle anywhere within the United States, except pursuant to a permit issued by the Secretary of the Interior. The Endangered Species Act imposes an equally stringent ban on the hunting of the bald eagle. The Court of Appeals for the Eighth Circuit, however, sitting en banc, held that members of the Yankton Sioux Tribe have a treaty right to hunt bald and golden eagles within the Yankton Reservation for noncommercial purposes. It further held that the Eagle Protection Act and Endangered Species Act did not abrogate this treaty right. It therefore directed that Dion's convictions for shooting bald eagles be vacated, since neither the District Court nor the jury made any explicit finding whether the killings were for commercial or noncommercial purposes.[3]

The Court of Appeals relied on an 1858 treaty signed by the United States and by representatives of the Yankton Tribe. Treaty with the Yancton (1858 spelling) Sioux, Apr. 19, 1858, 11 Stat. 743. Under that

---

3. On remand from the *en banc* court, an Eighth Circuit panel rejected a religious freedom claim raised by Dion. Dion does not pursue that claim here, and accordingly we do not consider it.

treaty, the Yankton ceded to the United States all but 400,000 acres of the land then held by the Tribe. The treaty bound the Yanktons to remove to, and settle on, their reserved land within one year. The United States in turn agreed to guarantee the Yanktons quiet and undisturbed possession of their reserved land, and to pay to the Yanktons, or expend for their benefit, various moneys in the years to come. The area thus reserved for the Tribe was a legally constituted Indian reservation, [ ]. The treaty did not place any restriction on the Yanktons' hunting rights on their reserved land.

All parties to this litigation agree that the treaty rights reserved by the Yankton included the exclusive right to hunt and fish on their land. [ ][4] As a general rule, Indians enjoy exclusive treaty rights to hunt and fish on lands reserved to them, unless such rights were clearly relinquished by treaty or have been modified by Congress. F. COHEN, HANDBOOK OF FEDERAL INDIAN LAW 449 (1982) (hereinafter COHEN). These rights need not be expressly mentioned in the treaty. *See Menominee Tribe v. United States,* 391 U.S. 404 (1968); *Alaska Pacific Fisheries v. United States,* 248 U.S. 78 (1918). Those treaty rights, however, little avail Dion if, as the Solicitor General argues, they were subsequently abrogated by Congress. We find that they were.

II

It is long settled that "the provisions of an act of Congress, passed in the exercise of its constitutional authority, * * * if clear and explicit, must be upheld by the courts, even in contravention of express stipulations in an earlier treaty" with a foreign power. *Fong Yue Ting v. United States,* 149 U.S. 698, 720 (1893); *cf. Goldwater v. Carter,* 444 U.S. 996 (1979). This Court applied that rule to congressional abrogation of Indian treaties in *Lone Wolf v. Hitchcock,* 187 U.S. 553, 566 (1903). Congress, the Court concluded, has the power "to abrogate the provisions of an Indian treaty, though presumably such power will be exercised only when circumstances arise which will not only justify the government in disregarding the stipulations of the treaty, but may demand, in the interest of the country and the Indians themselves, that it should do so." [ ]

We have required that Congress' intention to abrogate Indian treaty rights be clear and plain. COHEN 223; *see also United States v. Santa Fe Pacific R.R.,* 314 U.S. 339, 353 (1941). "Absent explicit statutory language, we have been extremely reluctant to find congressional abrogation of treaty rights. * * * " *Washington v. Washington Commercial Passenger Fishing Vessel Association,* 443 U.S. 658, 690 (1979). We do not construe statutes as abrogating treaty rights in "a backhanded way," *Menominee Tribe v. United States,* 391 U.S. at 412; in the absence of explicit statement, " 'the intention to abrogate or modify a treaty is not to be lightly imputed to the Congress.' " *Id.* at 413, *quoting Pigeon River Co. v. Cox Co.,* 291 U.S. 138, 160 (1934). Indian treaty rights are too fundamental to be easily cast aside.

We have enunciated, however, different standards over the years for determining how such a clear and plain intent must be demonstrated. In

---

4. Such treaty rights can be asserted by Dion as an individual member of the Tribe.   *See United States v. Winans,* 198 U.S. 371, 381 (1905); [ ].

some cases, we have required that Congress make "express declaration" of its intent to abrogate treaty rights. *See Leavenworth, L., & G. R.R. v. United States,* 92 U.S. 733, 741–742 (1876); [ ]. In other cases, we have looked to the statute's " 'legislative history' " and " 'surrounding circumstances' " as well as to " 'the face of the Act.' " *Rosebud Sioux Tribe v. Kneip,* 430 U.S. 584, 587 (1977), *quoting Mattz v. Arnett,* 412 U.S. 481, 505 (1973). Explicit statement by Congress is preferable for the purpose of ensuring legislative accountability for the abrogation of treaty rights, *cf. Seminole Nation v. United States,* 316 U.S. 286, 296–297 (1942). We have not rigidly interpreted that preference, however, as a per se rule; where the evidence of congressional intent to abrogate is sufficiently compelling, "the weight of authority indicates that such an intent can also be found by a reviewing court from clear and reliable evidence in the legislative history of a statute." COHEN 223. What is essential is clear evidence that Congress actually considered the conflict between its intended action on the one hand and Indian treaty rights on the other, and chose to resolve that conflict by abrogating the treaty.

A

The Eagle Protection Act renders it a federal crime to "take, possess, sell, purchase, barter, offer to sell, purchase or barter, transport, export or import, at any time or in any manner any bald eagle commonly known as the American eagle or any golden eagle, alive or dead, or any part, nest, or egg thereof." 16 U.S.C. § 668(a). The prohibition is "sweepingly framed"; the enumeration of forbidden acts is "exhaustive and careful." *Andrus v. Allard,* 444 U.S. 51, 56 (1979). The Act, however, authorizes the Secretary of the Interior to permit the taking, possession, and transportation of eagles "for the religious purposes of Indian tribes," and for certain other narrow purposes, upon a determination that such taking, possession, or transportation is compatible with the preservation of the bald eagle or the golden eagle. 16 U.S.C. § 668a.

Congressional intent to abrogate Indian treaty rights to hunt bald and golden eagles is certainly strongly suggested on the face of the Eagle Protection Act. The provision allowing taking of eagles under permit for the religious purposes of Indian tribes is difficult to explain except as a reflection of an understanding that the statute otherwise bans the taking of eagles by Indians, a recognition that such a prohibition would cause hardship for the Indians, and a decision that that problem should be solved not by exempting Indians from the coverage of the statute, but by authorizing the Secretary to issue permits to Indians where appropriate.

The legislative history of the statute supports that view. The Eagle Protection Act was originally passed in 1940, and did not contain any explicit reference to Indians. Its prohibitions related only to bald eagles; it cast no shadow on hunting of the more plentiful golden eagle. In 1962, however, Congress considered amendments to the Eagle Protection Act extending its ban to the golden eagle as well. As originally drafted by the staff of the Subcommittee on Fisheries and Wildlife Conservation of the House Committee on Merchant Marine and Fisheries, the amendments simply would have added the words "or any golden eagle" at two places in the Act where prohibitions relating to the bald eagle were described. [ ]

Before the start of hearings on the bill, however, the Subcommittee received a letter from Assistant Secretary of the Interior Frank Briggs on behalf of the Interior Department. The Interior Department supported the proposed bill. It noted, however, the following concern:

> The golden eagle is important in enabling many Indian tribes, particularly those in the Southwest, to continue ancient customs and ceremonies that are of deep religious or emotional significance to them. We note that the Handbook of American Indians (Smithsonian Institution, 1912) volume I, page 409, states in part, as follows:
>
>> Among the many birds held in superstitious and appreciative regard by the aborigines of North America, the eagle, by reason of its majestic, solitary, and mysterious nature, became an especial object of worship. This is expressed in the employment of the eagle by the Indian for religious and esthetic purposes only.
>>
>> * * *
>
> There are frequent reports of the continued veneration of eagles and of the use of eagle feathers in religious ceremonies of tribal rites. The Hopi, Zuni, and several of the Pueblo groups of Indians in the Southwest have great interest in and strong feelings concerning eagles. In the circumstances, it is evident that the Indians are deeply interested in the preservation of both the golden and the bald eagle. If enacted, the bill should therefore permit the Secretary of the Interior, by regulation, to allow the use of eagles for religious purposes by Indian tribes.

[ ]

The House Committee reported out the bill. In setting out the need for the legislation, it explained in part:

> Certain feathers of the golden eagle are important in religious ceremonies of some Indian tribes and a large number of the birds are killed to obtain these feathers, as well as to provide souvenirs for tourists in the Indian country. In addition, they are actively hunted by bounty hunters in Texas and some other States. As a result of these activities if steps are not taken as contemplated in this legislation, there is grave danger that the golden eagle will completely disappear.

[ ]

The Committee also reprinted Assistant Secretary Briggs' letter in its Report, [ ], and adopted an exception for Indian religious use drafted by the Interior Department. The bill as reported out of the House Committee thus made three major changes in the law, along with other more technical ones. It extended the law's ban to golden eagles. It provided that the Secretary may exempt, by permit, takings of bald or golden eagles "for the religious purposes of Indian tribes." And it added a final proviso: "Provided, That bald eagles may not be taken for any purpose unless, prior to such taking, a permit to do so is procured from the Secretary of the Interior." [ ] The bill, as amended, passed the House and was reported to the Senate Committee on Commerce.

At the Senate hearings, representatives of the Interior Department reiterated their position that, because "the golden eagle is an important part of the ceremonies and religion of many Indian tribes," the Secretary should be authorized to allow the use of eagles for religious purposes by Indian tribes. [ ] The Senate Committee agreed, and passed the House bill with an additional amendment allowing the Secretary to authorize permits for the taking of golden eagles that were preying on livestock. That Committee again reprinted Assistant Secretary Briggs' letter, [ ], and summarized the bill as follows: "The resolution as hereby reported would bring the golden eagle under the 1940 act, allow their taking under permit for the religious use of the various Indian tribes (their feathers are an important part of Indian religious rituals) and upon request of a Governor of any State, be taken for the protection of livestock and game." [ ] The bill passed the Senate, and was concurred in by the House, with little further discussion.

It seems plain to us, upon reading the legislative history as a whole, that Congress in 1962 believed that it was abrogating the rights of Indians to take eagles. Indeed, the House Report cited the demand for eagle feathers for Indian religious ceremonies as one of the threats to the continued survival of the golden eagle that necessitated passage of the bill. [ ] Congress expressly chose to set in place a regime in which the Secretary of the Interior had control over Indian hunting, rather than one in which Indian on-reservation hunting was unrestricted. Congress thus considered the special cultural and religious interests of Indians, balanced those needs against the conservation purposes of the statute, and provided a specific, narrow exception that delineated the extent to which Indians would be permitted to hunt the bald and golden eagle.

Respondent argues that the 1962 Congress did not in fact view the Eagle Protection Act as restricting Indian on-reservation hunting. He points to an internal Interior Department memorandum circulated in 1962 stating, with little analysis, that the Eagle Protection Act did not apply within Indian reservations. [ ] We have no reason to believe that Congress was aware of the contents of the Vaughn memorandum. More importantly, however, we find respondent's contention that the 1962 Congress did not understand the Act to ban all Indian hunting of eagles simply irreconcilable with the statute on its face.

Respondent argues, and the Eighth Circuit agreed, that the provision of the statute granting permit authority is not necessarily inconsistent with an intention that Indians would have unrestricted ability to hunt eagles while on reservations. Respondent construes that provision to allow the Secretary to issue permits to non-Indians to hunt eagles "for Indian religious purposes," and supports this interpretation by pointing out testimony during the hearings to the effect that large-scale eagle bounty hunters sometimes sold eagle feathers to Indian tribes. We do not find respondent's argument credible. Congress could have felt such a provision necessary only if it believed that Indians, if left free to hunt eagles on reservations, would nonetheless be unable to satisfy their own needs and would be forced to call on non-Indians to hunt on their behalf. Yet there is nothing in the legislative history that even remotely supports that patronizing and strained view. Indeed, the Interior Department immediately after the passage of the 1962 amendments adopted regulations authorizing permits only to "individual Indians who are authentic, bona fide practitioners of such religion." [ ]

Congress' 1962 action, we conclude, reflected an unmistakable and explicit legislative policy choice that Indian hunting of the bald or golden eagle, except pursuant to permit, is inconsistent with the need to preserve those species. We therefore read the statute as having abrogated that treaty right.

B

Dion also asserts a treaty right to take bald eagles as a defense to his Endangered Species Act prosecution. He argues that the evidence that Congress intended to abrogate treaty rights when it passed the Endangered Species Act is considerably more slim than that relating to the Eagle Protection Act. The Endangered Species Act and its legislative history, he points out, are to a great extent silent regarding Indian hunting rights. In this case, however, we need not resolve the question of whether the Congress in the Endangered Species Act abrogated Indian treaty rights. We conclude that Dion's asserted treaty defense is barred in any event.

Dion asserts that he is immune from Endangered Species Act prosecution because he possesses a treaty right to hunt and kill bald eagles. We have held, however, that Congress in passing and amending the Eagle Protection Act divested Dion of his treaty right to hunt bald eagles. He therefore has no treaty right to hunt bald eagles that he can assert as a defense to an Endangered Species Act charge.

. . .

III

We hold that the Court of Appeals erred in recognizing Dion's treaty defense to his Eagle Protection Act and Endangered Species Act prosecutions.... The judgment of the Court of Appeals is reversed in part, and the case is remanded for further proceedings consistent with this opinion.

It is so ordered.

NOTES

(1) What standard did the Court establish for abrogation of treaty rights? What justification did the Court offer for this standard?

Does the ruling in *Dion* answer the question of the legal status of tribal rights to hunt and fish? Could Congress terminate all such rights by abrogating all treaties recognizing them, or would that raise issues of the taking of private property without just compensation? Does the Court's ruling suggest how it might respond to tribal claims based on private property rights? Recall that Congress has commonly compensated tribes for hunting and fishing rights destroyed as a result of federal development projects. Are such payments optional?

In the international arena, each party to a treaty is able to revoke it, subject only to such limitations and such consequences as might be set forth in the treaty itself. Are there settings in which an Indian tribe might have the power to revoke a treaty made with the United States? If not, why the imbalance?

(2) *United States v. Peterson:* The Blackfoot reservation is located in northwestern Montana. During the treaty negotiations in 1895 leading to the establishment of the reservation, the Tribe insisted on retaining hunting and fishing rights in the lands being ceded. Fifteen years after the treaty was negotiated, Congress set aside the Glacier National Park from ceded lands abutting the Tribe's reservation. In 2000, two Blackfeet were observed killing bighorn sheep within the Park. At their trial for unlawful hunting, they claimed the right to hunt within the Park based on the rights the Tribe had reserved in the treaty. The court acknowledged that "[a]brogation is a troubling question because there is scant evidence contemporary with the creation of Glacier National Park that Congress *'actually considered* the conflict between its intended action on the one hand and Indian treaty rights on the other, and chose to resolve that conflict by abrogating the treaty.' *United States v. Dion,* [ ]." Nonetheless, the court concluded that—with respect to hunting rights within the Park boundaries—the treaty had been abrogated because Congress specified that "[a]ll hunting or the killing, wounding, or capturing at any time of any bird or wild animal . . . is prohibited within the limits of [Glacier] park." 16 U.S.C. § 170. This language and the surrounding events were sufficiently "clear evidence" of the requisite intent to abrogate. *United States v. Peterson,* 121 F.Supp.2d 1309, 1318 (D.Mont.2000).

(3) George Coggins offered the following analysis of the intersection between Indian treaty rights and federal wildlife regulations:

> [The] blithe and unexamined assumption that application of federal law would work an abrogation [of treaty rights is a fundamental error.] Just as there is a fundamental distinction in eminent domain law between regulation and taking, so too are there distinctions between the destruction, modification, or regulation of a right. [Whatever the impact of] the general application of state fish and game laws to Indians . . . the federal statutes arise out of population crises, are limited to certain species, and relax protection as the crisis is surmounted.

> The thesis that federal wildlife law was intended to regulate but not abrogate Indian treaty rights is also supported by the principles and canons established in the state cases. Most pertinent is the concept that states may restrict the exercise of hunting and fishing rights guaranteed by supreme federal law,[285] on as well as off the reservation,[286] when necessary for the conservation of the wildlife resource. . . .

---

285. *Puyallup Tribe v. Department of Game,* 391 U.S. 392 (1968) (*Puyallup I*).

286. *Puyallup Tribe, Inc. v. Department of Game,* 433 U.S. 165 (1977) (*Puyallup III*).

Courts should attempt to reconcile seemingly conflicting enactments before totally superceding one or the other.... To achieve a better balance, it must first be held that federal wildlife statues do apply to Indians, for the necessary conservation can be effected in no other way, and it is possible to go on to devise methods for ameliorating the possible harshness of such a rule.

George C. Coggins & William Modricin, *Native American Indians and Federal Wildlife Law,* 31 STAN. L. REV. 375 (1979).

Coggins suggests that there is a fundamental difference between state and federal wildlife law. Is he correct? If the Eagle Protection Act were repealed and eagles were delisted under the Endangered Species Act, would tribal rights to hunt eagles revive, despite the ruling in *Dion?* That is, is Coggins correct that tribal rights have not been abrogated but suspended during the pendency of the restrictive federal statutes? Are there settings in which the abrogation v. suspension distinction might have considerable importance?

In 1970, FWS listed the gray whale as endangered under the Endangered Species Conservation Act of 1969; the species was therefore included on the endangered species list following enactment of the Endangered Species Act in 1973. In 1993, FWS concluded that the eastern North Pacific population of gray whales had recovered to near its estimated original population and removed the species from the list. 58 FED. REG. 3121, 3135 (1993). Following this decision, the Makah Nation of Neah Bay sought to resume whaling pursuant to their version of the Stevens treaties which guaranteed "[t]he right of taking fish and of whaling or sealing at usual and accustomed grounds and stations." Treaty of Neah Bay, 12 Stat. 939, 940 (1855). The federal government supported the Makah's treaty right to take whales—thus also supporting Coggins' argument that treaties are suspended rather than abrogated.

The Makah decision to whale produced widespread opposition among animal rights and anti-whaling groups. For various perspectives, see Richard K. Eichstaedt, *"Save the Whales" v. "Save the Makah": The Makah and the Struggle for Native Whaling,* 4 ANIMAL L. 145 (1998); Keith A. Johnson, *The Makah Manifesto,* SEATTLE TIMES, Aug. 23, 1998 (statement by president of the Makah Whaling Commission); *Gray Whales in Peril in Neah Bay,* 39 PAWS N. 4 (Fall 1998) (Progressive Animal Welfare Society position statement). *See also Metcalf v. Daley,* 214 F.3d 1135 (9th Cir.2000) (holding that agencies had failed to comply with NEPA before supporting Makah before the International Whaling Commission). We return to the conservation of whales in Chapter 8.

(4) The Lacey Act and treaty rights—violation of federal law: Yurok Indians of the Hoopa Valley Reservation were charged with violating a Department of the Interior moratorium on their treaty right to harvest salmon runs on the Klamath River. Their convictions were upheld against an assertion of treaty rights because the Ninth Circuit felt that the regulation was promulgated to protect the fisheries—a power that the Department necessarily had as trustee of the tribe: "We hold that the general trust statutes of Title 25 do furnish Interior with broad authority to supervise and manage Indian affairs and property commensurate with the trust obligations of the United States." *United States v. Eberhardt,* 789 F.2d 1354, 1360 (9th Cir.1986). This is sufficient authority "to regulate Indian fishing on the Hoopa Valley Reservation consistent with its obligations to manage and conserve Indian resources." *Id.* at 1361.

Two federal statutes that are considered in detail in Chapter 10—the Migratory Bird Treaty Act and the Bald and Golden Eagle Protection Act— served as the predicate statutes for the indictment of a Jemez Pueblo, who was convicted of selling golden eagle parts to an undercover federal agent. In *United States v. Sandia,* the defendant argued that he had not violated the predicate statutes because the killing of the eagle was imbued with religious significance and thus was protected under the Religious Freedom Restoration Act. The Tenth Circuit rejected this defense:

> We do not decide whether Mr. Sandia's taking of the birds was, in the first instance, legal under RFRA because Mr. Sandia subsequently sold the birds he claims to have taken for religious purposes. This subsequent sale of the birds destroys defendant's claim that he engaged in protected religious activity. When defendant decided to sell the birds, he no longer possessed them for religious purpose and therefore possessed them in violation of federal law.

United States v. Sandia, 188 F.3d 1215, 1218 (10th Cir.1999). Defendant's conviction under the Lacey Act was, therefore, upheld.

SECTION 6.   INDIAN NATIONS AS WILDLIFE MANAGERS

a.   ON-RESERVATION TRIBAL MANAGEMENT

New Mexico v. Mescalero Apache Tribe

United States Supreme Court.
462 U.S. 324 (1983).

■ MARSHALL, J.:—We are called upon to decide in this case whether a State may restrict an Indian Tribe's regulation of hunting and fishing on its reservation. With extensive federal assistance and supervision, the Mescalero Apache Tribe has established a comprehensive scheme for managing the reservation's fish and wildlife resources. Federally approved Tribal ordinances regulate in detail the conditions under which both members of the Tribe and nonmembers may hunt and fish. New Mexico seeks to apply its own laws to hunting and fishing by nonmembers on the reservation. We hold that this application of New Mexico's hunting and fishing laws is preempted by the operation of federal law.

I

The Mescalero Apache Tribe (Tribe) resides on a reservation located within Otero County in south central New Mexico. The reservation, which represents only a small portion of the aboriginal Mescalero domain, was created by a succession of Executive Orders promulgated in the 1870's and 1880's. The present reservation comprises more than 460,000 acres, of which the Tribe owns all but 193.85 acres. Approximately 2,000 members of the Tribe reside on the reservation, along with 179 non-Indians, including resident federal employees of the Bureau of Indian Affairs and the Indian Health Service.

. . .

Anticipating a decline in the sale of lumber which has been the largest income-producing activity within the reservation, the Tribe has recently committed substantial time and resources to the development of other sources of income. The Tribe has constructed a resort complex financed principally by federal funds, and has undertaken a substantial development of the reservation's hunting and fishing resources. These efforts provide employment opportunities for members of the Tribe, and the sale of hunting and fishing licenses and related services generates income which is used to maintain the Tribal government and provide services to Tribe members.[4]

Development of the reservation's fish and wildlife resources has involved a sustained, cooperative effort by the Tribe and the Federal Government. Indeed, the reservation's fishing resources are wholly attributable to these recent efforts. Using federal funds, the Tribe has established eight artificial lakes which, together with the reservation's streams, are stocked by the Bureau of Sport Fisheries and Wildlife of the U.S. Fish and Wildlife Service, Department of the Interior, which operates a federal hatchery located on the reservation. None of the waters are stocked by the State. The United States has also contributed substantially to the creation of the reservation's game resources. Prior to 1966 there were only 13 elk in the vicinity of the reservation. In 1966 and 1967 the National Park Service donated a herd of 162 elk which was released on the reservation. Through its management and range development[6] the Tribe has dramatically increased the elk population, which by 1977 numbered approximately 1,200. New Mexico has not contributed significantly to the development of the elk herd or the other game on the reservation, which includes antelope, bear and deer.[7]

The Tribe and the Federal Government jointly conduct a comprehensive fish and game management program. Pursuant to its Constitution and to an agreement with the Bureau of Sport Fisheries and Wildlife, the Tribal Council adopts hunting and fishing ordinances each year. The tribal ordinances, which establish bag limits and seasons and provide for licensing of hunting and fishing, are subject to approval by the Secretary under the

---

4. Income from the sale of hunting and fishing licenses, "package hunts" which combine hunting and fishing with use of the facilities at the Inn, and campground and picnicking permits totalled $269,140 in 1976 and $271,520 in 1977. The vast majority of the nonmember hunters and fishermen on the reservation are not residents of the State of New Mexico.

6. These efforts have included controlling and reducing the population of other animals, such as wild horses and cattle, which compete for the available forage on the reservation.

7. The New Mexico Department of Game and Fish issued a permit for the importation of the elk from Wyoming into New Mexico. The Department has provided the Tribe with any management assistance which the Tribe has requested; such requests have been limited. [ ]

Tribal Constitution and have been so approved. The Tribal Council adopts the game ordinances on the basis of recommendations submitted by a Bureau of Indian Affairs range conservationist who is assisted by full-time conservation officers employed by the Tribe. The recommendations are made in light of the conservation needs of the reservation, which are determined on the basis of annual game counts and surveys. Through the Bureau of Fish and Wildlife, the Secretary also determines the stocking of the reservation's waters based upon periodic surveys of the reservation.

Numerous conflicts exist between State and tribal hunting regulations. For instance, tribal seasons and bag limits for both hunting and fishing often do not coincide with those imposed by the State. The Tribe permits a hunter to kill both a buck and a doe; the State permits only buck to be killed. Unlike the State, the Tribe permits a person to purchase an elk license in two consecutive years. Moreover, since 1977, the Tribe's ordinances have specified that State hunting and fishing licenses are not required for Indians or non-Indians who hunt or fish on the reservation. The New Mexico Department of Game and Fish has enforced the State's regulations by arresting non-Indian hunters for illegal possession of game killed on the reservation in accordance with tribal ordinances but not in accordance with State hunting regulations.

. . .

II

New Mexico concedes that on the reservation the Tribe exercises exclusive jurisdiction over hunting and fishing by members of the Tribe and may also regulate the hunting and fishing by nonmembers. New Mexico contends, however, that it may exercise concurrent jurisdiction over nonmembers and that therefore its regulations governing hunting and fishing throughout the State should also apply to hunting and fishing by nonmembers on the reservation. Although New Mexico does not claim that it can require the Tribe to permit nonmembers to hunt and fish on the reservation, it claims that, once the Tribe chooses to permit hunting and fishing by nonmembers, such hunting and fishing is subject to any State-imposed conditions. Under this view the State would be free to impose conditions more restrictive than the Tribe's own regulations, including an outright prohibition. The question in this case is whether the State may so restrict the Tribe's exercise of its authority.

Our decision in *Montana v. United States,* does not resolve this question. Unlike this case, *Montana* concerned lands located within the reservation but *not* owned by the Tribe or its members. We held that the Crow Tribe could not as a general matter regulate hunting and fishing on those lands. [ ][12] But as to "lands belonging to the Tribe or held by the

---

12. Even so, the Court acknowledged that "Indian tribes retain inherent sovereign power to exercise some forms of civil jurisdiction over non-Indians on their reservations, even on non-Indian fee lands." [ ] The Court stressed that in *Montana* the pleadings "did not allege that non-Indian hunting and fish-ing on [non-Indian] reservation lands [had] impaired [the Tribe's reserved hunting and fishing privileges]," [ ], or "that non-Indian hunting and fishing on fee lands imperil the subsistence or welfare of the Tribe," [ ], and that the existing record failed to suggested "that such non-Indian hunting and fishing

United States in trust for the Tribe," we "readily agree[d]" that a Tribe may "prohibit nonmembers from hunting or fishing * * * [or] condition their entry by charging a fee or establish bag and creel limits." [ ] We had no occasion to decide whether a Tribe may only exercise this authority in a manner permitted by a State.

On numerous occasions this Court has considered the question whether a State may assert authority over a reservation. The decision in *Worcester v. Georgia*, 31 U.S. (6 Pet.) 515, 561 (1832), reflected the view that Indian tribes were wholly distinct nations within whose boundaries "the laws of [a State] can have no force." We long ago departed from the "conceptual clarity of Mr. Chief Justice Marshall's view in *Worcester*," *Mescalero Apache Tribe v. Jones*, 411 U.S. 145, 148 (1973), and have acknowledged certain limitations on tribal sovereignty. For instance, we have held that Indian tribes have been implicitly divested of their sovereignty in certain respects by virtue of their dependent status, that under certain circumstances a State may validly assert authority over the activities of nonmembers on a reservation, and that in exceptional circumstances a State may assert jurisdiction over the on-reservation activities of tribal members.[15]

Nevertheless, in demarcating the respective spheres of State and tribal authority over Indian reservations, we have continued to stress that "Indian tribes are unique aggregations possessing attributes of sovereignty over both their members and their territory," *White Mountain Apache Tribe v. Bracker*, 448 U.S. 136, 142 (1980), *quoting United States v. Mazurie*, 419 U.S. 544, 557 (1975). Because of their sovereign status, tribes and their reservation lands are insulated in some respects by an "historic immunity from state and local control," *Mescalero Apache Tribe v. Jones*, 411 U.S. 145, 152 (1973), and tribes retain any aspect of their historical sovereignty not "inconsistent with the overriding interests of the National Government." *Washington v. Confederated Tribes*, 447 U.S. 134, 153 (1980).

The sovereignty retained by tribes includes "the power of regulating their internal and social relations," *United States v. Kagama*, 118 U.S. 375, 381–382 (1886), cited in *United States v. Wheeler*, 435 U.S. 313, 322 (1978). A tribe's power to prescribe the conduct of tribal members has never been doubted, and our cases establish that "absent governing Acts of Congress," a State may not act in a manner that "infringed on the right of reservation Indians to make their own laws and be ruled by them." *McClanahan v. Arizona State Tax Commission*, 411 U.S. 164, 171–172 (1973), quoting *Williams v. Lee*, 358 U.S. 217, 219–220 (1959). [ ]

---

* * * threaten the Tribe's political or economic security." [ ]

15. *See Puyallup Tribe v. Washington Game Department*, 433 U.S. 165 (1977). *Puyallup* upheld the State of Washington's authority to regulate on-reservation fishing by tribal members. Like *Montana v. United States*, the decision in *Puyallup* rested in part on the fact that the dispute centered on lands which, although located within the reserva-

tion boundaries, no longer belonged to the tribe; all but 22 of the 18,000 acres had been alienated in fee simple. The Court also relied on a provision of the Indian treaty which qualified the Indians' fishing rights by requiring that they be exercised "in common with all citizens of the Territory," [ ], and on the State's interest in conserving a scarce, common resource. [ ]

A tribe's power to exclude nonmembers entirely or to condition their presence on the reservation is equally well established. *See, e.g., Montana v. United States,* [ ]. Whether a State may also assert its authority over the on-reservation activities of nonmembers raises "[m]ore difficult questions," *Bracker,* 448 U.S. at 144. While under some circumstances a State may exercise concurrent jurisdiction over non-Indians acting on tribal reservations, [ ], such authority may be asserted only if not preempted by the operation of federal law. [ ]

In *Bracker* we reviewed our prior decisions concerning tribal and State authority over Indian reservations and extracted certain principles governing the determination whether federal law preempts the assertion of State authority over nonmembers on a reservation. We stated that that determination does not depend "on mechanical or absolute conceptions of state or tribal sovereignty, but calls for a particularized inquiry into the nature of the state, federal, and tribal interests at stake." [ ]

We also emphasized the special sense in which the doctrine of preemption is applied in this context. [ ] Although a State will certainly be without jurisdiction if its authority is preempted under familiar principles of preemption, we cautioned that our prior cases did not limit preemption of State laws affecting Indian tribes to only those circumstances. "The unique historical origins of tribal sovereignty" and the federal commitment to tribal self-sufficiency and self-determination make it "treacherous to import * * * notions of preemption that are properly applied to other contexts." [ ] By resting preemption analysis principally on a consideration of the nature of the competing interests at stake, our cases have rejected a narrow focus on congressional intent to preempt State law as the sole touchstone. They have also rejected the proposition that preemption requires "an express congressional statement to that effect." [ ] State jurisdiction is preempted by the operation of federal law if it interferes or is incompatible with federal and tribal interests reflected in federal law, unless the State interests at stake are sufficient to justify the assertion of State authority. [ ][16]

Certain broad considerations guide our assessment of the federal and tribal interests. The traditional notions of Indian sovereignty provide a crucial "backdrop," [ ], against which any assertion of State authority must be assessed. Moreover, both the tribes and the Federal Government are firmly committed to the goal of promoting tribal self-government, a goal embodied in numerous federal statutes. We have stressed that Congress' objective of furthering tribal self-government encompasses far more than encouraging tribal management of disputes between members, but includes Congress' overriding goal of encouraging "tribal self-sufficiency and economic development." [ ] In part as a necessary implication of this broad federal commitment, we have held that tribes have the power to manage the use of its territory and resources by both members and nonmembers, [ ], to undertake and regulate economic activity within the reservation, [ ],

---

16. The exercise of State authority may also be barred by an independent barrier—inherent tribal sovereignty—if it "unlawfully infringe[s] 'on the right of reservation Indians to make their own laws and be ruled by them.'" *White Mountain Apache Tribe v. Bracker,* 448 U.S. at 142, quoting *Williams v. Lee,* 358 U.S. 217, 220 (1959). [ ]

and to defray the cost of governmental services by levying taxes. [ ] Thus, when a tribe undertakes an enterprise under the authority of federal law, an assertion of State authority must be viewed against any interference with the successful accomplishment of the federal purpose. [ ]

Our prior decisions also guides our assessment of the state interest asserted to justify State jurisdiction over a reservation. The exercise of State authority which imposes additional burdens on a tribal enterprise must ordinarily be justified by functions or services performed by the State in connection with the on-reservation activity. [ ] Thus a State seeking to impose a tax on a transaction between a Tribe and nonmembers must point to more than its general interest in raising revenues. [ ] A State's regulatory interest will be particularly substantial if the State can point to off-reservation effects that necessitate State intervention. *Cf. Puyallup Tribe v. Washington Game Department,* 433 U.S. 165 (1977).

III

With these principles in mind, we turn to New Mexico's claim that it may superimpose its own hunting and fishing regulations on the Mescalero Apache Tribe's regulatory scheme.

A

It is beyond doubt that the Mescalero Apache Tribe lawfully exercises substantial control over the lands and resources of its reservation, including its wildlife. As noted above, supra, at 2384, and as conceded by New Mexico, the sovereignty retained by the Tribe under the Treaty of 1852 includes its right to regulate the use of its resources by members as well as non-members. In *Montana v. United States,* we specifically recognized that tribes in general retain this authority.

Moreover, this aspect of tribal sovereignty has been expressly confirmed by numerous federal statutes. Pub. L. 280 specifically confirms the power of tribes to regulate on-reservation hunting and fishing. [ ] This authority is afforded the protection of the federal criminal law by 18 U.S.C. § 1165, which makes it a violation of federal law to enter Indian land to hunt, trap or fish without the consent of the tribe. [ ] The 1981 amendments to the Lacey Act, [ ], further accord tribal hunting and fishing regulations the force of federal law by making it a federal offense "to import, export, transport, sell, receive, acquire, or purchase any fish or wildlife ... taken or possessed in violation of any * * * Indian tribal law." [ ]

B

Several considerations strongly support the Court of Appeals' conclusion that the Tribe's authority to regulate hunting and fishing preempts State jurisdiction. It is important to emphasize that concurrent jurisdiction would effectively nullify the Tribe's authority to control hunting and fishing on the reservation. Concurrent jurisdiction would empower New Mexico wholly to supplant tribal regulations. The State would be able to dictate the terms on which nonmembers are permitted to utilize the reservation's resources. The Tribe would thus exercise its authority over the reservation only at the sufferance of the State. The tribal authority to regulate hunting and fishing by nonmembers, which has been repeatedly confirmed by federal treaties and laws and which we explicitly recognized in *Montana v. United States,* would have a rather hollow ring if tribal authority amounted to no more than this.

Furthermore, the exercise of concurrent State jurisdiction in this case would completely "disturb and disarrange," [ ], the comprehensive scheme of federal and tribal management established pursuant to federal law....

Concurrent State jurisdiction would supplant this regulatory scheme with an inconsistent dual system: members would be governed by Tribal ordinances, while nonmembers would be regulated by general State hunting and fishing laws. This could severely hinder the ability of the Tribe to conduct a sound management program. Tribal ordinances reflect the specific needs of the reservation by establishing the optimal level of hunting and fishing that should occur, not simply a maximum level that should not be exceeded. State laws in contrast are based on considerations not necessarily relevant to, and possibly hostile to, the needs of the reservation. For instance, the ordinance permitting a hunter to kill a buck and a doe was designed to curb excessive growth of the deer population on the reservation. [ ] Enforcement of the State regulation permitting only buck to be killed would frustrate that objective. Similarly, by determining the Tribal hunting seasons, bag limits, and permit availability, the Tribe regulates the duration and intensity of hunting. These determinations take into account numerous factors, including the game capacity of the terrain, the range utilization of the game animals, and the availability of tribal personnel to monitor the hunts. Permitting the State to enforce different restrictions simply because they have been determined to be appropriate for the State as a whole would impose on the Tribe the possibly insurmountable task of ensuring that the patchwork application of State and Tribal regulations remains consistent with sound management of the reservation's resources.

Federal law commits to the Secretary and the Tribal Council the responsibility to manage the reservation's resources. It is most unlikely that Congress would have authorized, and the Secretary would have established, financed, and participated in Tribal management if it were thought that New Mexico was free to nullify the entire arrangement. Requiring Tribal ordinances to yield whenever State law is more restrictive would seriously "undermine the Secretary's [and the Tribe's] ability to make the wide range of determinations committed to [their] authority." [ ]

The assertion of concurrent jurisdiction by New Mexico not only would threaten to disrupt the federal and tribal regulatory scheme, but would also threaten Congress' overriding objective of encouraging tribal self-government and economic development. The Tribe has engaged in a concerted and sustained undertaking to develop and manage the reservation's wildlife and land resources specifically for the benefit of its members. The project generates funds for essential tribal services and provides employment for members who reside on the reservation. This case is thus far removed from those situations, such as on-reservation sales outlets which market to nonmembers goods not manufactured by the tribe or its members, in which the tribal contribution to an enterprise is *de minimis.* [ ] The Tribal enterprise in this case clearly involves "value generated on the reservation by activities involving the Trib[e]." [ ] The disruptive effect that would result from the assertion of concurrent jurisdiction by New Mexico would plainly "stan[d] as an obstacle to the accomplishment of the full purposes and objectives of Congress," [ ].

C

The State has failed to "identify any regulatory function or service * * * that would justify" the assertion of concurrent regulatory authority. [ ] The hunting and fishing permitted by the Tribe occur entirely on the reservation. The fish and wildlife resources are either native to the reservation or were created by the joint efforts of the Tribe and the Federal Government. New Mexico does not contribute in any significant respect to the maintenance of these resources, and can point to no other "governmental functions it provides," [ ], in connection with hunting and fishing on the reservation by nonmembers that would justify the assertion of its authority.

The State also cannot point to any off-reservation effects that warrant State intervention. Some species of game never leave tribal lands, and the State points to no specific interest concerning those that occasionally do. Unlike *Puyallup Tribe v. Washington Game Department,* this is not a case in which a Treaty expressly subjects a tribe's hunting and fishing rights to the common rights of nonmembers and in which a State's interest in conserving a scarce, common supply justifies State intervention. [ ] The State concedes that the Tribe's management has not had an adverse impact on fish and wildlife outside the reservation." [ ]

We recognize that New Mexico may be deprived of the sale of state licenses to nonmembers who hunt and fish on the reservation, as well as some federal matching funds calculated in part on the basis of the number of State licenses sold. However, any financial interest the State might have in this case is simply insufficient to justify the assertion of concurrent jurisdiction. . . .

IV

In this case the governing body of an Indian Tribe, working closely with the Federal Government and under the authority of federal law, has exercised its lawful authority to develop and manage the reservation's resources for the benefit of its members. The exercise of concurrent jurisdiction by the State would effectively nullify the Tribe's unquestioned authority to regulate the use of its resources by members and nonmembers, interfere with the comprehensive tribal regulatory scheme, and threaten Congress' firm commitment to the encouragement of tribal self-sufficiency and economic development. Given the strong interests favoring exclusive tribal jurisdiction and the absence of State interests which justify the assertion of concurrent authority, we conclude that the application of the State's hunting and fishing laws to the reservation is preempted.

Accordingly, the judgment of the Court of Appeals is *Affirmed.*

NOTES

(1) Of the many facts the Court presented, which are relevant to its ultimate ruling? The Court emphasized, *inter alia*, how comprehensive the tribal regulatory scheme was and how the state alleged no adverse impacts of tribal management on adjacent nontribal lands. How far would we need to change the facts before reaching a point of uncertainty as to the power of states to regulate? Could a state ban the introduction on tribal lands of exotic game species? What if a tribe sought to maintain deer populations at artificially high levels, thereby adversely affecting vegetation? Would a state have the power to regulate tribal lands in the interests of conservation in the event that tribal laws were inadequate for the purpose? What if the state sought to protect a species under a state endangered species law? Does the Court's ruling suggest how it would resolve such questions?

Recall early decisions on the difficulties states face in enforcing game laws. Did the Court here adequately consider the impact on the state's power to enforce its state-wide laws when tribes allow hunting during a state's closed season? Might a state legitimately insist that any animal killed during the closed season be marked by tribal officials so that state inspectors know that it was lawfully taken on tribal lands?

(2) Tribes as landowners: If the Tribe were simply a private landowner, could it be prohibited by state law from operating a fishing operation on its lands if the fish were privately stocked in ponds? If the Tribe were a private landowner, could it fence its land, introduce a game species, and allow private individuals to hunt the stocked animals without interference from state law?

(3) On-and off-reservation, redux: The same on-and off-reservation issues noted above are also present in the context of tribal regulatory authority.

(a) *Montana v. United States* arose out of an attempt by the Crow Tribe to regulate fishing on the Big Horn River within the external boundaries of the Tribe's reservation. The Court began by deciding that the Treaties of Fort Laramie had not reserved the bed of the river. Thus, title to the bed passed to the state upon its admission into the Union—and the Tribe therefore was seeking to regulate the use of non-Tribal lands. The Court then turned to the question of the authority of the Tribe to regulate hunting and fishing on such non-Tribal lands within the boundaries of its reservation. The general principle, the Court stated, was that "exercise of tribal powers beyond what is necessary to protect tribal self-government or to control internal relations is inconsistent with the dependent status of the tribes, and so cannot survive without express congressional delegation." Applying these principles to the case, the Court concluded:

> [N]othing in this case suggests that ... non-Indian hunting and fishing so threatens the Tribe's political or economic security as to justify tribal regulation. The complaint in the District Court did not allege that non-Indian hunting and fishing on fee lands imperil the subsistence or welfare of the Tribe. Furthermore, the District Court made express findings, left unaltered by the Court of Appeals, that the Crow Tribe has traditionally accommodated itself to the State's "near exclu-

sive" regulation of hunting and fishing on fee lands within the reservation. [ ] And the District Court found that Montana's statutory and regulatory scheme does nor prevent the Crow Tribe from limiting or forbidding non-Indian hunting and fishing on lands still owned by or held in trust for the Tribe or its members.

Montana v. United States, 450 U.S. 544 (1981). *See Nevada v. Hicks*, ____ U.S. ____, 121 S.Ct. 2304 (2001) (when "state interests outside the reservation are implicated, States may regulate the activities even of tribe members on tribal land").

(b) *South Dakota v. Bourland* involved an attempt by the Cheyenne Sioux Tribe to exclude non-Indians from hunting on land within its reservation that had been taken by the United States to construct the Oahe Dam and Reservoir Project on the Missouri River. The Court held that the project act had abrogated the Tribe's power to regulate non-Indians because it had opened them to public use and had subjected hunting and fishing on the reservoir to federal regulation. *South Dakota v. Bourland*, 508 U.S. 679 (1993).

b.   OFF-RESERVATION TRIBAL MANAGEMENT

Settler v. Lameer

Ninth Circuit Court of Appeals.
507 F.2d 231 (1974).

■ JAMESON, D.J.:—Three actions involving the validity of fishing regulations promulgated by the Tribal Council of the Yakima Indian Nation are joined in this appeal. . . .

I.   BACKGROUND

. . . . In 1966, the Yakima Tribal Council enacted regulations deemed necessary to promote the conservation of the fishing resources which were reserved in the Treaty of 1855. Resolution T–90–66 among other things established fishing seasons, prohibited fishing in certain areas, allocated fishing sites, established a tribal identification system, and specified the methods of fishing that were permissible and the type of boats and gear that could be used. In addition it provided methods of enforcement and penalties. Although purporting to regulate fishing activities of tribal members outside of the reservation, the resolution provided for arrest, seizure of equipment and punishment *only within the boundaries of the reservation.*

Resolution T–90–66 was amended in 1968 by T–48–68. That resolution provided for off-reservation enforcement of tribal fishing regulations in the following language:

> Any Tribal Game Warden or any Tribal Law Enforcement Officer shall be *authorized to enforce the provisions of this and any other regulation of the Yakima Tribe governing the exercise of Treaty fishing rights whether on or off the Yakima Reservation* and where violations are committed in his presence, he shall arrest the offender, take him into

custody, and seize all fishing gear, boats or motors used by said offender.

The enforcement of these resolutions with respect to off-reservation tribal fishing is the basis of the three actions.

A. *Cause No. 71–2364*

Alvin Settler, an enrolled member of the Confederated Tribes and Bands of the Yakima Indian Nation, was convicted ... by the Yakima Tribal Court of twice violating Tribal Resolution T–90–66.... It is conceded that on both occasions, Settler was fishing at "usual and accustomed fishing sites" off the reservation. Although given citations at the site of the violations, Settler was not arrested until he was found within the exterior boundaries of the reservation.

In the habeas corpus proceedings instituted by Settler following his conviction, the district court dismissed the petition for lack of jurisdiction. This court reversed and remanded for a hearing on the merits. *Settler v. Yakima Tribal Court,* 419 F.2d 486 (9th Cir.1969).

On remand, the district court held:

(1) "[T]he regulation of the right to fish in the 'usual and accustomed places' off of the reservation granted by the Treaty is an internal affair of the Yakima Indian Tribe * * ** Such tribal fishing regulations are binding upon tribal members and are enforceable in the Yakima Indian Tribal Court."

(2) The state has certain limited rights to regulate off-reservation fishing by Indians, but "such regulation must be necessary for the conservation of the fishery resources."

(3) "Any right the state may have to impose restrictions on off-reservation fishing activities does not preclude the Yakima Indian Tribe from placing restrictions on its own members to control their fishing activities [off reservation] where state regulations are inapplicable, unenforceable, or nonexistent."

B. *Causes Nos. 74–1627 and 74–1656*

Mary Settler, also a member of the Yakima Indian Nation, was convicted by the Yakima Tribal Court ... for a violation of Tribal Resolution T–90–66.... Tribal officers ... arrested Mary at a "usual and accustomed" fishing site approximately 56 miles outside the confines of the Yakima Reservation....

As a result of the same incident, Alvin Settler was convicted of a violation of T–90–66, as amended, for knowingly allowing his fishing crew to fish during the Yakima Tribe's closed season and to use illegal fishing gear registered in his name. Unlike Mary, Alvin was arrested *within* the external boundaries of the reservation.

Petitions for writ of habeas corpus filed by both Mary and Alvin were denied for lack of jurisdiction. On appeal, this court reversed, *Settler v. Lameer,* 419 F.2d 1311 (9th Cir.1969), and remanded for proceedings on the merits.

On remand, the district court, ruling on cross motions for summary judgment in the case of Mary Settler, held that:

(1) the arrest of Mary Settler some 56 miles outside of the Reservation was unauthorized and unlawful. The *enforcement* of Tribal fishing regulations "is limited to arrest and seizure on the reservation, * * * even though the Tribe has the authority to govern the exercise of the Indian's right to take fish at the 'usual and accustomed places' located off of the reservation."

(2) "* * * because the Tribal authorities lacked jurisdiction to enforce Tribal Regulations off the reservation, the seizure of petitioner's personal property incident to petitioner's arrest was unlawful."

The court denied Alvin Settler's petition, noting that the issues were the same as those in No. 71–2364.

Issues on Appeal

The two primary issues presented on appeal are:

(1) Whether the Yakima Indian Nation may enforce its fishing regulations with respect to violations committed by Tribal members outside the reservation by arresting and trying violators upon their return to the reservation;

(2) Whether and under what circumstances the Yakima Indian Nation may enforce tribal fishing regulations by physically arresting violators and seizing their fishing gear at the usual and accustomed fishing places off the Yakima Reservation.

. . .

II.   APPLICATION OF FISHING REGULATIONS TO OFF RESERVATION TO OFF RESERVATION FISHING

Mary and Alvin Settler and the State of Washington[9] contend that the Yakima Indian Nation may not regulate off-reservation Tribal fishing activities because (a) in the Yakima Treaty of 1855, the Confederated Tribes of the Yakima Nation did not reserve the right to exercise criminal jurisdiction beyond the territorial confines of the reservation; (b) Congress has not subsequently authorized the Yakima Nation to exercise criminal jurisdiction beyond the territorial confines of the reservation; and (c) any Tribal exercise of criminal jurisdiction outside of the reservation would be in derogation of the sovereignty of the State of Washington.

. . .

(b) Extent of Treaty Fishing Rights

The Settlers and the State of Washington do not question the existence of Tribal fishing rights or the right of the Yakima Nation to regulate

---

9. The State of Washington filed a brief amicus curiae in 71–2364 in support of its position that the "state possesses the sole and exclusive authority to regulate fishing activities in off-reservation waters." The United States filed amicus curiae briefs in 71–2364 and 74–1656 in support of the position of the Chief of Police and Chief Judge of the Yakima Tribal Court.

fishing activities within the reservation boundaries. The Settlers expressly recognize also that the Tribal Council may *"enact* regulations concerning the fishing by tribal members at the usual and accustomed off reservation treaty sites." They contend, however, that the Treaty constituted a relinquishment of all Tribal jurisdiction beyond the confines of the reservation; that Congress has never subsequently authorized the Yakima Nation to exert such jurisdiction; and that the State of Washington has exclusive *enforcement* powers off the reservation. The State of Washington claims "sole and exclusive authority to regulate fishing activities in off-reservation waters."

In interpreting the language of treaties with the Indians, the court must consider "[h]ow the words of the treaty were understood by the unlettered people, rather than their critical meaning." *Worcester v. Georgia,* 31 U.S. (6 Pet.) 515, 582 (1832); *Winans,* 198 U.S. at 380–381. Moreover, in interpreting Indian treaties the Supreme Court has consistently followed the general rule that "Doubtful expressions are to be resolved in favor of the weak and defenseless people who are the wards of the nation, dependent upon its protection and good faith." [ ]

The Treaty expressly reserved to the confederated tribes and bands of Indians "the right of taking fish at all usual and accustomed places, in common with citizens of the Territory." It would be unreasonable to conclude that in reserving these vital rights, the Indians intended to divest themselves of all control over the exercise of those rights. Prior to the Treaty the regulations for fishing had been established by the Tribe through its customs and tradition. The Indians must surely have understood that Tribal control would continue after the Treaty.

In addition, the Treaty of 1855 does not expressly state that the Yakima Nation relinquished its jurisdiction over matters pertaining to fishing rights. As the treaty constitutes a grant of rights from the Indians to the Government, *Winans,* 198 U.S. at 381, any rights not granted must be considered retained by the Tribe. Here, the Indians qualified their fishing right *only* to the extent of permitting citizens of the territory to fish "in common" with them at "usual and accustomed fishing places" off the reservation. Given this fact and the vital role of fishing in the Yakima culture, we conclude that the Yakima Nation did reserve the authority to regulate Tribal fishing at "all usual and accustomed places," whether on or off the reservation.

This conclusion is supported by the nature of the fishing rights. As set forth in *Whitefoot v. United States,* 293 F.2d 658, 663 (Ct.Cl.1961), *cert. denied,* 369 U.S. 818 (1962), the fishing rights reserved in the Treaty of 1855 are communal rights of the Tribe, even though the individual members benefit from those rights. The determination of when and how the rights may be exercised is an "internal affair" of the Tribe. As the district court correctly pointed out, "one of the last remnants of sovereignty retained by the Yakima Indian Tribe is the power to regulate their internal and social relations." This was recognized in *Williams v. Lee,* 358 U.S. 217, 221–222 (1959), with reference to the Treaty with the Navajo Tribe:

> implicit in these treaty terms, as it was in the treaties with the Cherokees involved in *Worcester v. Georgia,* was the understanding

that the internal affairs of the Indians remained exclusively within the jurisdiction of whatever tribal government existed.

The mere fact that the fishing may take place off the reservation does not make the regulation of treaty fishing any less an internal matter. The locus of the act is not conclusive. [ ] The Tribe has the authority to regulate the exercise of the fishing rights it retained at "all usual and accustomed places," even those off the reservation.

This does not mean that the State of Washington is without any authority to regulate off-reservation fishing. That power has been expressly recognized, but it has been strictly limited.

[The court discussed *Tulee v. Washington,* noting that "any regulations which are imposed by the state on off-reservation fishing by Yakima Indians must be reasonable and 'necessary to the conservation of fish.' "]

We agree with the district court in cause No. 71–2364 that "once the limits of state authority have been reached there remain significant areas of fishing activities which are not necessarily subject to state regulation. Among the fishing activities particularly susceptible to regulation by the Tribe are: (1) the use of accustomed fishing places; (2) the allocation of fishing time among individual members of the Tribe; (3) the type of gear; (4) the time of taking fish; (5) the determination of preference among fishing purposes, *i.e.,* subsistence, commercial, or ceremonial."

We conclude that the regulation of these activities with respect to off-reservation fishing is within the scope of the rights retained by the Yakima Nation in the Treaty of 1855. Appellees had the authority to arrest and prosecute tribal members for violation of the Tribal fishing regulations. The district court correctly held in 71–2364 and 74–1627 that an arrest on the reservation for violation of fishing regulations off the reservation is valid.

III. OFF–RESERVATION ARREST AND SEIZURE

We turn now to the question presented in the Mary Settler case: whether the Yakima Nation has the right under its Tribal Resolution T–48–68 to enforce tribal fishing regulations by arrest and seizure at "usual and accustomed" fishing places off the reservation.

The district court concluded that, "The incidents of sovereignty retained by the Indian tribes on the reservation do not include the authority to make an arrest outside of the territorial limits and confines of the Reservation to enforce an Indian Tribal regulation." . . .

. . . . The only case we have found which discusses the question of off-reservation regulation by a tribe is *United States v. Washington.* There the court held that, "The Yakima Nation and the Quinault Tribe are presently qualified to self-regulate the off-reservation fishing of their tribal members." The court, however, did not deal specifically with the question of off-reservation arrest and seizures by tribal law enforcement officers.

In resolving this issue, we must again look to the intention of the Indians at the time of the Treaty. Having determined that the Yakima Nation by the Treaty of 1855 intended to retain not only their ancient fishing rights but also the power to regulate the exercise of those rights regardless of location, it would be inconsistent to narrowly limit the *enforcement* of those rights to arrest and seizure on the reservation. The power to regulate is only meaningful when combined with the power to enforce.

The district court has suggested two alternative methods of enforcing the tribal regulations: (1) withholding "the rights or benefits of the protection of Treaty created immunities"; and (2) "wait until a transgressor has returned to the reservation and then make an arrest and confine that person or cause him to be present in court." Either method at best affords only a partial solution to the enforcement problem. For either to be effective, it would be necessary for the Yakima Nation to have its game wardens or other enforcement officers patrol "usual and accustomed" fishing places off the reservation and check licenses, fishing gear, and the quantity and nature of a catch in order to establish violations for which the Tribe may impose criminal penalties.

The second suggested method would of course be available only in the event the violators came voluntarily to the reservation. Many members of the Tribe, including the Settlers, do not reside on the reservation and could easily avoid arrest by staying away from the reservation. Sanctions imposed upon non-reservation members by withholding fishing privileges would also be difficult to enforce in the absence of the power to arrest.

The regulatory authority retained by the Yakima Nation with respect to the exercise of its off-reservation fishing rights can be truly effective only through off-reservation enforcement powers at the "usual and accustomed" fishing places. In *United States v. Winans,* 198 U.S. at 381, the Supreme Court characterized the fishing rights secured by the Treaty of 1855 as constituting "a servitude upon every piece of land as though described therein." Tribal jurisdiction extends to such land for the limited purpose of preserving tribal fishing rights connected therewith.

Throughout their briefs, the Settlers and the State of Washington contend that any recognition of tribal jurisdiction outside the confines of the reservation violates the sovereignty of the State of Washington. In support of this argument reliance is placed on the "equal footing" doctrine enunciated in *Ward v. Race Horse.* In *Race Horse,* the Court held that the Enabling Act admitting Wyoming to the Union, [ ], invalidated certain off-reservation hunting provisions in the Bannock Indian Treaty of 1869. According to the Court, to hold these hunting provisions of the treaty viable would be to deny Wyoming "equal footing" with the other states.

The strict construction and application of the "equal footing" doctrine in *Race Horse* has been modified by implication. *See Johnson v. Gearlds,* 234 U.S. 422, 438–440 (1914); *Donnelly v. United States,* 228 U.S. 243, 259–264 (1913); and *United States v. Winans,* 198 U.S. at 381–384. Every state entering the Union is admitted subject to all treaties currently in effect. In the event of a conflict between state law and a prior treaty, the prior treaty must take precedence. Only Congress may modify or abrogate a treaty.

We conclude that by the Treaty of 1855 the Yakima Indian Nation retained regulatory and enforcement powers with respect to tribal fishing at all "usual and accustomed places" off the reservation. No act of Congress, including the Washington Enabling Act, [ ], has qualified these reserved powers. The powers therefore continue to exist.

In so holding, we are not blind to the potential for both regulatory and enforcement problems. Any problems which may arise, however, are a product of the vast changes that have taken place in the almost 120 years since the signing of the Yakima Treaty in 1855. These changed conditions may necessitate a modification of the treaty. Obviously, the courts may not re-write treaties or qualify the Indian rights thereunder. If Treaty changes should be required, that is a matter for Congress.

Our holding that the Yakima Indian Nation may enforce its fishing regulations by making arrests and seizures off the reservation is a very narrow one. Off-reservation enforcement is limited strictly to violations of tribal fishing regulations. The arrest and seizure of fishing gear must be made at "usual and accustomed places" of fishing, and only when violations are committed in the presence of the arresting officer. Tribal officers patrolling off-reservation sites are subject to all reasonable regulations that may be imposed by the State of Washington for the orderly conduct of inspections, arrests and seizures. Cooperation between state, local and Tribal officials is encouraged. Ultimately, effective regulation of the fishing resource is of benefit to both Indian and non-Indian.

. . .

NOTES

(1) What is the basis of the court's decision in *Settler*? Does the tribe have power—as a sovereign—to regulate the conduct of its members regardless of their location within or without the reservation? Was the court concerned that there was a potential regulatory gap, *i.e.*, conduct that could not be regulated by the state?

(2) *United States v. Washington:* Although there is a large body of caselaw on state regulation of off-reservation treaty fishers and hunters, there are few cases addressing the power of tribes to regulate treaty fishers and hunters off-reservation. In *United States v. Washington,* the district court concluded that the tribe was "entitled to exercise its governmental powers by regulating the treaty right fishing of its members, without any state regulation thereof" if the tribe met specified qualifications, including appropriate tribal regulations, an enforcement staff, and a professional fishery staff. *United States v. Washington,* 384 F.Supp. 312, 340–42 (W.D.Wash.1974), *aff'd,* 520 F.2d 676 (9th Cir.1975), *cert. denied,* 423 U.S. 1086 (1976).

(3) The Lacey Act—violation of tribal law: The Lacey Act states that "[i]t is unlawful for any person to ... export, sell, receive, acquire, or purchase any fish or wildlife ... taken or possessed ... in violation of any Indian tribal law." 16 U.S.C. § 3371(a)(1). The term "Indian tribal law" is defined as "any regulation of, or other rule of conduct enforceable by, any Indian tribe, band, or group but only to the extent that such regulation or rule applies within Indian country as defined in" the federal code. *Id.*

§ 3371(c). The Act also specifies that "[n]othing in this act shall be construed as ... repealing, superseding, or modifying any right, privilege, or immunity granted, reserved, or established pursuant to treaty, statute, or executive order pertaining to any Indian tribe, band, or community." *Id.* § 3378(c)(2).

United States v. Sohappy was a prosecution of tribal members for selling salmon in violation of tribal regulations. The defendants challenged their convictions, claiming that the application of the Lacey Act was precluded by the Act's disclaimer provisions. The Ninth Circuit rejected this argument. The court began with the proposition that federal laws generally apply to Indian violations of tribal law unless the tribe has retained exclusive jurisdiction over the offense. Such exclusivity occurs when the crime is committed against another tribal member. This was not the case in *Sohappy,* the court concluded, because the tribal law was "designed to preserve fishing opportunities of Indians *and* non-Indians.... Therefore, ... Indian fishing offenses are not purely intra-Indian matters, but impact upon federal and state interests." *United States v. Sohappy,* 770 F.2d 816, 819 (9th Cir.1985), *cert. denied,* 477 U.S. 906 (1986). Lacking such exclusivity, the court held that defendants could be prosecuted under the Lacey Act. This conclusion was buttressed by the repeated statements in the legislative history of a congressional intent to apply the Act to violations of tribal regulations.

United States v. Big Eagle involved the prosecution of Indians who were not members of the tribe for harvesting fish in violation of tribal regulations. Defendant argued that, because the tribe lacked jurisdiction over him since he was not a tribal member, he did not violate the regulations. The Eighth Circuit rejected the argument: "the crucial inquiry is whether the acts complained of took place within the reservation and not, as Big Eagle insists, whether the Lower Brule Tribe itself has the power to prosecute.... Whether the Indian tribe maintains complete jurisdiction to enforce or not—so long as the land is within the Reservation—it is also within the jurisdiction of the United States Government." *United States v. Big Eagle,* 881 F.2d 539, 541 (8th Cir.1989), *cert. denied,* 493 U.S. 1084 (1990). The only issues, therefore, were whether the conduct violated the tribal regulation and, if so, whether the violation occurred within the boundaries of the reservation.

Tribal regulations can also serve as the basis for prosecution of non-Indians under the Lacey Act. In *United States v. Gardner,* defendant was convicted of killing an elk on the Uintah and Ouray Reservation in violation of the Ute Tribe's fish and game regulations. His argument that he could not be prosecuted for violating tribal regulations because he was not an Indian was rejected by the court: "the non-Indian status of the defendant is not an essential element of jurisdiction for a [Lacey Act] violation." *United States v. Gardner,* 244 F.3d 784, 788 (10th Cir.2001).

(4) Tribal management authority under federal statute: *Settler* involved tribal management authority arising under the Yakama Tribe's treaty of 1855. Federal resource management statutes have increasingly recognized tribal entities as managers on par with state fish and wildlife departments. *See generally* Charles Wilkinson, *The Role of Bilateralism in*

Fulfilling the Federal–Tribal Relationship: The Tribal Rights–Endangered Species Secretarial Order, 72 WASH. L. REV. 1063 (1997).

The Pacific Northwest Electric Power Planning & Conservation Act established a comprehensive regulatory structure to oversee the operation of the federal Columbia River hydroelectric system. The Northwest Power Planning Council created by the Act was required to develop a "program to protect, mitigate, and enhance fish and wildlife, including related spawning grounds and habitat, on the Columbia River and its tributaries." 16 U.S.C. § 839b(h)(1)(A). The fish and wildlife program was to be developed based on recommendations "from the Federal, and the region's State, fish and wildlife agencies and from the region's appropriate Indian tribes." *Id.* § 839b(h)(2). *See also id.* § 839b(h)(3), (4)(A), (5), (6)(A), (7), 12(A).

CHAPTER 8

INTERNATIONAL WILDLIFE LAW

In Chapter 6, we examined the decision in *Missouri v. Holland*, 252 U.S. 416 (1920), in which the United States Supreme Court held that a treaty negotiated with Great Britain pursuant to the Treaty Clause of the Constitution gave the national government the power to regulate the killing of migratory birds. In this Chapter, we examine the other side of the equation: the legal effect of international agreements at the international level.

International wildlife law is a relatively recent phenomenon. The first wildlife treaties were the Berne Convention Establishing Uniform Regulations Concerning Fishing in the Rhine (Germany–Switzerland) (1869), the Basle Convention Establishing Uniform Regulations Concerning Fishing in the Rhine (France, Germany, Switzerland) (1875), and the Treaty Concerning the Regulation of Salmon Fishing in the Rhine River (Germany, Luxembourg, the Netherlands, and Switzerland) (1886). As their titles suggest, these conventions sought to allocate rather than to preserve. The first wildlife treaty (1911) to which the United States was a party also concerned a transboundary species, the North Pacific fur seal, and shared the same objective.

International wildlife law has grown dramatically over the past thirty years. This Chapter is at best an introduction to the issues. Perhaps not surprisingly, however, many of the issues will be familiar.

SECTION 1. INTRODUCTION

International law raises a basic question: what *is* law?

Within nation-States, there generally is a well-defined system for creating and enforcing law. In the more stable States, this system includes legislative, executive, and judicial powers to be exercised in accord with constitutions. The legislative, executive, and judicial entities in such States create laws of general applicability that are enforced against all residents. In these States, at least, the question "what is law?" has a generally positivist answer: law is the statement of legislative, executive, and judicial powers that are made in compliance with the procedural and substantive standards specified in the State's constitution. Even in such States, of course, there are gray areas where ambiguity dominates—as any student of administrative law can attest. But the gray is relatively marginal.

Applying the same standards to international law, however, raises far-from-trivial questions. Most fundamentally, there is no well-defined system for creating international law, no legislative, executive, or judicial entities empowered to act and limited by a constitution. As a general matter, international law is a question of agreement among States, binding only those who agree to be bound.

Is this law? "Sometimes international law is viewed as a rather strange breed of law to which the term 'law' is applied only by courtesy if at all. A number of great legal philosophers—Hobbes, Pufendorf, Bentham, and Austin are example—have all doubted the legal character of international law.... Clearly some definitions of law would exclude international law. Disputes, for example, are not routinely decided by an international judiciary, and there exists no coercive agency of formal international status which can effectively enforce the law. Rules do not emanate from any single 'sovereign.'" Morton A. Kaplan & Nicholas deB. Katzenbach, The Political Foundations of International Law 5 (1961). Or is it simply Humpty Dumpty in *Alice in Wonderland*: words have whatever meaning we choose to give them at the moment?

This question generally is discussed as a debate between the proponents of positivism, on the one hand, and those of natural law, on the other. This dichotomy no longer adequately describes the international legal system:

Gregory Maggio & Owen J. Lynch, Human Rights, Environment, and Economic Development
6–19 (1996).

Classical Theories: Natural Law and Positivism

"Classical" theories of international law generally fall into one of two categories. The first, which is Natural Law, is based on the premise that there are certain normative principles or postulates that are true or "self-evident" and which exist independently of their codification or enforcement by human beings. As Allott notes [in *International Law and International Revolution* (1989)], exponents of Natural Law include Francisco de Vitoria and other Spanish theologian jurists of the sixteenth century, and the seventeenth century Dutch Protestant jurist Hugo Grotius.... [1]

The other major category is Positivism, which holds that norms are valid only insofar as they have been created according to a definite and discernible rule. [According to Hans Kelsen in *General Theory of Law and State* (trans. 1943),] all norms can be traced back to an "ultimate rule, ... according to which the norms of this order are established and annulled, receive or lose their validity." Positivists arrange all norms hierarchically in their relation to the "ultimate rule." For positivists, law is independent of morality....

Positivism has had a major impact on the development of the current state-centric system of international law and its supporting legal structure. In particular, positivism has promoted the dominant view that international law consists only of "subjects" (nation-states) and "objects" (everything else).... The dichotomy between nation states and everything else ... has

---

1. [Recall the discussion following *Pierson v. Post* in Chapter II.]

constrained the ability of international law and law making processes to accommodate input from a broader spectrum of participants, and thereby to be more responsive to a wide diversity of interests that often arise and operate independently of nation-states and the governments that regulate and serve them. . . .

The Classical Statist Approach

The classical view of international law, a view wherein states are the only recognized subjects, arguably still predominates. . . . Because states are the only players in the paradigm, only states can create and employ international law. Individuals and or other non-state actors which suffer harm from another state or the citizens of the other state must rely upon their own state to employ international law on their behalf.

The classical view is deeply embedded among the dominant political and economic attitudes of those who head nation-states, and in the international legal structures and institutions which they have created and maintained. It is premised on ideas regarding the "sovereign equality of states," a duty of non-intervention on the part of states in the internal affairs of other states, and state consent to international obligations. It effectively excludes the direct and official participation of other types of actors with expertise and concerns that can help make the international system more broad-based, democratic, fair, and responsive to concerns and issues outside of the official purview of nation states and national governments. For example, the classical view would preclude indigenous and other tribal societies from seeking redress before the International Court of Justice or other official international judicial fora when their respective national governments deny them recognition of legal rights over natural resources they directly depend on, and may have occupied and utilized for many generations. The rationale is that these communities do not qualify under the law of nations as states.

It is increasingly obvious that global society is not the exclusive domain of nation states. Since the end of the Second World war, international organizations, namely the organs of the United Nations system, as well as regional political and economic entities such as the Organization of American States (OAS), the European Communities (now European Union) and military/security bodies such as NATO have emerged as supra-national legal personalities on the international plane.

International organizations, in particular the multilateral financial development institutions, as well as transnational commercial enterprises, religious movements, and non-governmental organizations (NGOs) also play a major role in shaping international society and the attitudes and behaviors of states. For example, much global economic activity, and many resulting environmental and human rights controversies involve transnational commercial enterprises, both legal and illegal, which have a major impact on global stability and security. Additionally, . . . other non-state personalities are increasingly acknowledged as having an important role to play in facilitating international legal and political objectives.

Still, the classic state-centric view endures and continues to predominate. The only parties which are recognized for purposes of bringing an action before the International Court of Justice are nation states. Also, all members of the United Nations Organization must be nation states. Furthermore, according to the classical view, although a state may owe a duty to its own citizens and those of neighboring states which may be harmed by its activities, arguably it does not yet formally owe any duty to international society as a whole. Such a viewpoint imposes serious handicaps on efforts to create legal incentives and otherwise promote the sustainable development and management of natural resources.

Challenges to the Classical Approach

Prevailing notions of international law also appear ill-suited to finding adequate solutions for the myriad problems which are transnational in scope. Among these are global warming, ozone depletion, over-fishing, deforestation, marine pollution, narcotics and contraband armaments traffic, illegal trade in endangered species of flora and fauna, and unregulated financial transfers. These phenomena are in large measure supra-national in scope and exceed the capacities of any individual state or even any bloc of states to control effectively. The current seemingly futile attempts by the United States and the European Community to control cross-border drugs-trafficking provide telling examples. . . .

Increased demands—and increased successes—by indigenous peoples advocating for rights to self-determination, including the right to be recognized as distinct autonomous actors in international law, are reflected in international instruments. . . . These documents reflect awareness by human rights advocates that securing recognition of the rights of indigenous communities encompasses protection of their cultural values and knowledge, including local knowledge related to biodiversity conservation and sustainable use. . . .

The emergence of international institutions, including the United Nations Organization and its political organs such as the FAO, UNESCO, UNDP, UNEP, ILO, and UNICEF, and the multilateral development institutions of the Bretton Woods system, constitutes another major inroad into the classical approach to international law. . . . The political organs of the United Nations, for example, have recognized international legal personalities, *i.e.,* are deemed to be subjects, and the laws which govern their operations are part of the corpus of international law.

Organizations such as UNEP and the ILO have, in addition, also played a major role in developing treaties and other international legal instruments. For example, its Regional Seas Programme, UNEP has facilitated the creation of several important environmental protection conventions for protecting marine bodies of water. The ILO is responsible for drafting of two of the major international conventions concerning the rights and interests of indigenous and tribal peoples.

NGOs too are playing an increasingly significant role in the development of international law, and some international NGOs have been characterized as actual international actors based on their transnational focus and membership. Some NGOs such as IUCN, through its Environmental Law centre, and WWF have participated in drafting recent international conventions such as the Convention on Biological Diversity. IUCN also has drafted a proposed International Covenant on Environment and Development, which is intended to be a major effort at the progressive development of international environmental law. . . . The position of the majority of G–77 countries in the *Request for an Advisory Opinion* from the ICJ in 1995 on the legality of the use of nuclear weapons, was prepared and guided largely by the World Court Project, an NGO umbrella organization. In that opinion, NGOs substantially influenced the arguments and subject matter before the Court, even though the ICJ's Statute does not recognize their existence as parties to the cases. [Judge Rosalyn Higgins of the International Court of Justice] and others have even gone so far as to argue that individuals are international actors as well, and that existing international legal structures must be reevaluated in order to accommodate this reality. In Higgins' opinion

> [I]nternational law is not only "rules"; moreover, its norms are not fixed indefinitely and are thus wholly responsive to the needs of the system. . . . [T]he notion of "subjects" and "objects" has no credible reality and . . . no functional purpose. . . . It is more helpful, and closer to perceived reality, to return to the view of international law as a particular decision-making process. Within that process (which is a dynamic and not a static one) there are a variety of participants, making claims across state lines, with the object of maximizing various values. . . . [I]n this model, there are no "subject" and "objects", but only participants. Individuals are participants, along with states, international organizations . . . multinational corporations, and indeed non-governmental groups. . . .

The Emerging Order

An alternative perspective is emerging that reflects contemporary international realities more accurately by calling for recognition of non-state entities as legitimate participants in international law and policy making. . . . Nevertheless, non-state actors still suffer under a "procedural disability" in protecting their rights and interests and in contributing to the development of the international legal order. Allott contends that current structures are impediments to the progressive development of an international legal system, what he refers to as the "international public realm."

Hard Law vs. Soft Law

Positivist approaches to law generally define a norm as a law if its breach is followed by some sanction or other means of enforcement. The generally accepted categories of international law are treaties, "general principles of law," and customary international law. Article 38(1) of the International Court of Justice identifies the above three categories as sources of international law and also adds " . . . judicial decisions and the teachings of the most highly qualified publicists of the various nations, as subsidiary means for the determination of rules of law."

Treaties and other conventions are obligatory upon the states signing them. By their nature, they are intended to be agreements governing the legal relations between the signatories, and in theory Parties can enforce their noncompliance through arbitration, an action before the International Court of Justice or other institutionalized dispute resolution mechanisms.

During the last 40 years, a new range of international commitments have developed and been confirmed by a range of instruments that do not fall into the traditional categories of "treaty" or "custom" or "general principles." The legal status of these instruments, which are often referred to as "soft law," has been a major subject of discussion among legal scholars. Dupuy has fittingly described soft law as "... either not yet or not only law." The instruments include declarations, codes of conduct, guidelines and other promulgations of the political organs of the United nations system, operational directives of the multilateral development institutions, and resolutions and other statements by non-governmental organizations. Although they do not possess the strict characteristic of recognized enforceability as commonly understood for law, depending on the circumstances, they may possess significant normative weight....

In contemporary international environmental law ... there appears to be a blurring between "soft law" law and formal "hard law" legal sources. This may be characteristic of international law regarding environmental issues or a trend emerging in international law in general. This tendency with regard to issues concerning sustainable development and environmental protection can be observed in current state practice....

Section 2.   Sources and Principles of International Law

a.   Sources of International Law

The primary judicial body of the United Nations (UN) is the International Court of Justice (ICJ). The court plays a central role in the development of international law. Article 38 of the Statute of the International Court of Justice—the court's "constitution"—sets out four sources of law:

1.   The Court, whose function is to decide in accordance with international law such disputes as are submitted to it, shall apply:

(a) international conventions, whether general or particular, establishing rules expressly recognized by the contesting states;

(b) international custom, as evidence of a general practice accepted as law;

(c) the general principles of law recognized by civilized nations; and

(d) subject to the provisions of Article 59,[1] judicial decisions and the teachings of the most highly qualified publicists of the various nations, as subsidiary means for the determination of rules of law.

Note that the first three sources—treaties, customs, and general principles—are binding legal obligations. The fourth source—judicial decisions and the writing of scholars—are only means of discovering the law and

---

1.   Article 59 reads: "The decision of the Court has no binding force except between   the parties and in respect of that particular case."

thus do not create binding obligations. Note also that the ICJ statute does not take into account the more recent development of "soft law."

Finally, note a pedagogical corollary of paragraph (d): there are no "cases" to structure the materials in this chapter. International law owes more to the civil-law than to the common-law tradition.

(i) TREATIES

Treaties are the first source of international law; it is also the strongest source because it is a formal document containing the mutual promises of the signatory States. This is the primary function of a treaty: to create or restate specific legal obligations between the parties to it. A treaty may be defined—as it is defined in article 2 of the 1969 Vienna Convention on the Law of Treaties—as "an international agreement concluded between States in written form and governed by international law, whether embodied in a single instrument or in two or more related instruments and whatever its particular designation." The crucial element is the intent to create a legal relationship between the contracting parties. The only formal requirement is that it be written. Treaties may be bilateral—between two parties—or multilateral—among more than two parties.

There is no required process for drafting treaties. As a general matter, however, treaties result from the identification of an objective, negotiations among the parties, adoption and signature by the drafters, and ratification by the respective States. Once ratified, treaties must be implemented; in many settings, to be effective, compliance must be monitored.

(ii) CUSTOM

The second source of law listed in Article 38 of the ICJ Statute is "international custom, as evidence of a general practice *accepted as law*." (emphasis added) That is, the customary practices of States create international law when the States act under the belief that the actions are required by law (*opinio juris*). Custom thus requires both an objective element (the practice) and a subjective element (*opinio juris*). Consider the following example of the evolution of custom:

> The Conference of the Law of the Sea which met between 1973 and 1982 adopted one of the most important modern international treaties. During the long process of its elaboration, in which all states of the world participated, a certain number of existing rules were codified, but there also arose a consensus on several new norms. On the basis of this consensus an international practice formed, even before the adoption of the new treaty. This was particularly the case with the exclusive economic zone, now codified in part V of the [United Nations Convention on the Law of the Sea], where it was recognized from the beginning that coastal states have sovereign rights for the purpose of conserving and managing living and non-living natural resources and have jurisdiction to preserve the marine environment. It was also accepted that coastal state jurisdiction to legislate regarding ships in innocent passage through the territorial sea includes measures to

conserve marine biological resources and preserve the marine environment and to prevent, reduce and control marine pollution.

ALEXANDRE KISS & DINAH SHELTON, INTERNATIONAL ENVIRONMENTAL LAW 105 (1991). As the United States Supreme Court noted, customary law is binding "not because it was prescribed by any superior power, but because it has been generally accepted as a rule of conduct." *The Scotia,* 81 U.S. (14 Wall.) 170, 187 (1871).

Custom obviously raises a variety of proof questions.

(iii) GENERAL PRINCIPLES OF LAW

The substance of the third source of international law—"the general principles of law recognized by civilized nations"—is subject to substantial debate. "What has happened is that international tribunals have employed elements of legal reasoning and private law analogies in order to make the law of nations a viable system for application in a judicial process." IAN BROWNLIE, PRINCIPLES OF PUBLIC INTERNATIONAL LAW 16 (4th ed. 1990). Others have argued that the term "general principles" embraces natural law concepts of justice and equity.

If the question piques your curiosity, you might consider *Case Concerning the Gabcikovo–Nagymaros Project (Hungary v. Slovakia), I.C.J.* (1997) <http://www.icj-cij.org>, in which the ICJ struggled with the concept of sustainable development and its role in resolving a dispute between Hungary and Slovakia over an environmentally damaging lock-construction project on the Danube River.

(iv) JUDICIAL DECISION AND THE TEACHINGS OF HIGHLY QUALIFIED PUBLICISTS

International courts can turn to the judicial decisions of State courts, other international judicial bodies, and the writings of "highly qualified publicists" to assist them in determining international law. Although scholarly writings play a more explicit role in the development of international than in "domestic" law—the internal law of a nation-State—such writings are not themselves law; these sources are "subsidiary" and non-binding.

The Paquete Habana

Supreme Court.
175 U.S. 677, 700 (1900).

International law is part of our law, and must be ascertained and administered by the courts of justice of appropriate jurisdiction, as often as questions of right depending upon it are duly presented for their determination. For this purpose, where there is no treaty, and no controlling executive or legislative act or judicial decision, resort must be had to the customs and usages of civilized nations; and, as evidence of these, to the works of jurists and commentators, who by years of labor, research and experience, have made themselves peculiarly well acquainted with the subjects they treat. Such works are resorted to by judicial tribunals, not for the speculations of their authors concerning what the law ought to be, but for trustworthy evidence of what the law really is.

(v) "SOFT" LAW

Recall the excerpt from Maggio and Lynch that discussed the rise of "soft" law. Maggio and Lynch noted Dupuy's "fitting" description of soft law as either "not yet law or not only law":

> "Soft" law is a paradoxical term for defining an ambiguous phenomenon. Paradoxical because, from a general and classical point of view, the rule of law is usually considered "hard," *i.e.*, compulsory, or it simply does not exist. Ambiguous because the reality thus designated, considering its legal effects as well as its manifestations, is often difficult to identify clearly.

> Nevertheless, a new process of normative creation which jurists feel uncomfortable analyzing does exist and has been developing for more or less twenty years. "Soft" law certainly constitutes part of the contemporary law-making process but, as a social phenomenon, it evidently overflows the classical and familiar legal categories by which scholars usually describe and explain both the creation and the legal authority of international norms. In other words, "soft" law is a trouble maker because it is either not yet law or not only law.

Pierre–Marie Dupuy, *Soft Law and the International Law of the Environment,* 12 MICH. J. INT'L L. 420, 420 (1991).

Dupuy suggests three reasons for the development. First, the proliferation of a permanent network of international governmental organizations (IGOs) and non-governmental organizations (NGOs) at both a regional and universal level. Second, the diversification of States primarily as a result of the emergence of the underdeveloped countries which hold a majority but lack the power of the developed States. Third—and most importantly—the world economy has rapidly integrated to create a level of interdependence necessitating new types of international law—including international environmental law.

The most common source of soft law is the repetitive statement of norms in resolutions and recommendations by international bodies.

* * *

Although both custom and "soft" law are becoming increasingly important, international wildlife law remains primarily treaty law.

b. FUNDAMENTAL PRINCIPLES OF INTERNATIONAL WILDLIFE LAW

(i) THE CENTRAL PRINCIPLE OF INTERNATIONAL WILDLIFE LAW: NATION-STATE SOVEREIGNTY OVER NATURAL RESOURCES

The fundamental principle of international wildlife law is that a nation-State is sovereign over the resources within its borders. This principle was incorporated into the Stockholm Declaration of the United Nations Conference on the Human Environment (UNCHE) (1972) as Principle 21:

> States have, in accordance with the Charter of the United Nations and the principles of international law, the sovereign right to exploit their own resources pursuant to their own environmental policies, and the responsibility to ensure that activities within their jurisdiction or control do not cause damage to the environment of other States or of areas beyond the limits of national jurisdiction.

Note that the "sovereign right to exploit" is matched against, and is in tension with, the clearest customary rule of international environmental law: the prohibition on transboundary harm. *See also* Rio Declaration on Environment and Development, Principle 2, 3 I.L.M. 874 (1992) (reiteration of Principle 21 from Stockholm Declaration).

This provision of the Stockholm Declaration was also incorporated verbatim as Article 3 of the Convention on Biological Diversity (entered in force, 1993) (CBD). The Preamble to the CBD affirmed even more specifically a State's power over its living natural resources, stating: "States have sovereign rights over their own biological resources." Posed against this prefatory statement, however, are others with much different messages: "[T]he conservation of biological diversity is a common concern of humankind"; and "States are responsible for conserving their biological diversity and for using their biological resources in a sustainable manner." The Convention defines "sustainable use" as "use of components of biological diversity in a way and at a rate that does not lead to the long-term decline of biological diversity, thereby maintaining its potential to meet the needs and aspirations of present and future generations." Thus, State sovereignty is paired against, not just a legal duty to avoid transboundary harm, but a softer obligation to conserve resources and to avoid long-term biodiversity declines. Similarly, while a single State may have sovereign control over its biological resources, outsiders—indeed, all of humankind—have legitimate interests in how those resources are put to use.

The following excerpt explores these tensions:

CYRILLE DE KLEMM WITH CLARE SHINE, BIOLOGICAL DIVERSITY CONSERVATION AND THE LAW

1–4 (1993).

The most fundamental rule in international relations is that States are sovereign entities and that, subject to international law, they may conduct their business as they please. States exercise sovereign rights over all natural resources on their territory, which means that they may conserve, exploit or destroy them, or allow them to be destroyed as they wish.

The conservation of natural resources and habitats is, in consequence, a matter which comes under the exclusive jurisdiction of the States on whose territory they are situated. The State also has sovereignty over marine resources found in the Exclusive Economic Zone (EEZ) and on the continental shelf, as well as in its inland waters and territorial sea. In contrast, the rule applicable to the high seas, beyond the jurisdictional limits of any State, is that of the freedom of the high sea which includes the freedom of fishing. However, pursuant to the Law of the Sea Convention of

1982, the extension of the EEZ to 200 miles has in fact probably brought more than 95% of marine species under national sovereignty.

The principle of national sovereignty over natural resources, which include all living resources, is restated in several international instruments relating to the conservation of species.

Principle 21 of the Stockholm Declaration, adopted by the United Nations Conference on the Human Environment which was held in Stockholm in 1972, states that

> States have, in accordance with the Charter of the United Nations and the principles of international law, the sovereign right to exploit their own resources pursuant to their own environmental policies. . . .

This principle is reproduced word for word in article 3 of the Convention on Biological Diversity of 1992. It also appears in Principle 2 of the Rio Declaration, adopted by the United Nations Conference on Environment and Development in Rio de Janeiro in June 1992 (UNCED), but has been altered to refer to "environmental and developmental policies."

The sovereign right to destroy is qualified, however, by another general rule of law, also embodied in Principle 21 of the Stockholm Declaration and in the new Convention on Biological Diversity, which is that states have

> the responsibility to ensure that activities within their jurisdiction or control do not cause damage to the environment or other States or of areas beyond the limits of national jurisdiction.

Subject to this restriction, the sovereign right to destroy nature is in theory absolute. However, as in any other area, states may of course always voluntarily accept limitations of their sovereign rights by treaty.

. . .

Concern has rapidly grown about the need to conserve species and natural habitats in the face of rapidly-developing threats of all kinds. There are two very different stands to this concern about the loss of biological diversity. Firstly, the anthropocentric views is centred on a loss to science and the economy, as well as a more general loss of potential benefits for both present and future generations. Secondly, what is now referred to as the "ecocentric" view is concerned with the intrinsic value of biological diversity, which humanity may use but which it has no moral right to destroy, as well as with its fundamental role in maintaining the life-sustaining systems of the biosphere and the evolutionary potential of the Earth.

Over recent decades, the idea has taken shape that all States, and the international community in general, have at the every least an interest in the conservation of wild species and the habitats in which they live. Widespread disquiet at environmental degradation has slowly crystallised in the form of a consensus to establish rules of international law intended to achieve a better balance between sovereign rights over natural resources . . . and the need to preserve wild species. . . .

The above consensus has been formalized over the years in three different spheres, namely scientific, political and legal.

The scientific community was instrumental in this process through the International Biological Programme in the 1960s, as was the International Union for the Conservation of Nature and Natural Resources (IUCN)....

In 1980, a document of major importance for the development of world conservation policies was published by the IUCN in cooperation with the United Nations Environment Programme and the World Wide Fund for Nature (WWF).... This document, entitled, the World Conservation Strategy (WCS), laid down three major conservation goals. These were respectively:

* The maintenance of essential ecological processes;

* the preservation of genetic diversity;

* the sustainable use of species and ecosystems.

. . .

Political consensus on the need to conserve biological diversity was achieved at the United Nations Conference on the Human Environment in 1972, which resulted in the creation of UNEP and the adoption of the Stockholm Declaration.... This consensus formed the foundation for the development of a number of international instruments laying down certain general conservation objectives and sometimes very specific conservation rules. The very fact that these instruments could be adopted confirmed the evolution of the principle of national sovereignty over natural resources, as well as the recognition that the absolute character of this principle must be tempered because the international community was acknowledged to have a real interest in the conservation of certain of these resources.

* * *

(ii) A COROLLARY TO THE CENTRAL PRINCIPLE: NATION-STATE SOVEREIGNTY STOPS AT THE BORDER

When the United States acquired Alaska from Russia in 1867, it acquired the Pribilof Islands, including St. Paul and St. George Islands. The islands were important as the rookery for the North Pacific fur seals. While numbers are difficult to pin down, it is likely that there were about 2.5 million seals on the two islands when the United States acquired title.

The life cycle of the fur seal begins with the seals return to the rookeries beginning in April. The large adult males arrive first to establish territories; the mature females return to give birth and to mate again. Males acquire harems of from 30 to 50 females. Pups are born in June or July, and remain in the rookery until November; during this period the young are fed by their mothers, who must forage in the off-shore waters for fish.

Two aspects of this life cycle are crucial to the story. First, males and females are born in roughly even numbers, but only one male is needed for every 30 females. Thus, biologically, a high percentage of males are a harvestable surplus. Second, females with pups and immature females are far more likely to be in the ocean during the summer than are non-breeding males, which haul out on the off chance that they might be able to breed.

The United States chose to manage the Pribilof herds by leasing the islands to a private company subject to the condition that they harvest no more than 100,000 young male seals each year. This was, in theory, a sustainable approach. The lessee, however, overharvested and by 1889 was unable to fulfill the quota in its lease.

A contributing factor was the rise of pelagic—high seas—sealing. Pelagic sealing was problematic for two reasons. First, between 50 and 80% of the seals sank after being shot. Second, females made up 80–90% of the harvest. The combination was such that 1000 seal pelts meant that 1,000–5,000 seals had been shot and several thousand more pups died of starvation.

The principle antagonists were Great Britain (on behalf of Canada) and the United States. The United States claimed that the Bering Sea was under its jurisdiction as a result of the cession from Russia; Great Britain asserted the traditional freedom of seas. In 1886 and 1887, the United States seized British Columbia sealing vessels and imprisoned and fined the crews. During negotiations on a treaty to arbitrate the dispute, both parties agreed to a cessation of sealing. The treaty was signed in February 1892. Following briefing and argument, the arbitral panel handed down its decision in August 1893:

Behring Sea Fur–Seals Case (Great Britain/United States)

Award and Declaration of Arbitral Tribunal, 15 August 1893.
1 Int'l Envtl. L. Rep. 67–70.

Whereas by a Treaty between the United States of America and Great Britain, ... it was ... agreed and concluded that the questions which had arisen between the Government of the United States of America and the Government of Her Britannic Majesty, concerning the jurisdictional rights of the United States in the waters of Behring's Sea, and concerning also the preservation of the fur-seal in or habitually resorting to said sea, and the rights of the citizens and subjects of either Country as regards the taking of fur-seals...., should be submitted to a Tribunal of Arbitration....

[The treaty posed five questions for the tribunal:]

"1. What exclusive jurisdiction in the sea now known as the Behring's Sea, and what exclusive rights in the seal fisheries therein, did Russia assert and exercise prior and up to the time of the cession of Alaska to the United States?

"2. How far were these claims of jurisdiction as to the seal fisheries recognized and conceded by Great Britain?

"3. Was the body of water now known as the Behring's Sea included in the phrase *Pacific Ocean*, as used in the Treaty of 1825 between Great Britain and Russia; and what rights, if any, in the Behring's Sea were held and exclusively exercised by Russia after said Treaty?

"4.   Did not all the rights of Russia as to jurisdiction and as to the seal fisheries in Behring's Sea east of the water boundary [under the cession of Alaska by Russia], pass unimpaired to the United States under that Treaty [of cession]?

"5.   Has the United States any right, and if so, what right of protection or property in the fur-seals frequenting the islands of the United States in Behring Sea when such seals are found outside the ordinary three-mile limit?"

. . .

Now we, the said Arbitrators, . . . decide and determine[:]

As to the first of the said five points, [by a 6–1 majority:]

By the *Ukase* of 1821, Russia claimed jurisdiction in the sea now known as the Behring's Sea, to the extent of 100 Italian miles from the coasts and islands belonging to her, but, in the course of the negotiations which led to the Treaties of 1824 with the United States and of 1825 with Great Britain, Russia admitted that her jurisdiction in the said sea should be restricted to the reach of cannon shot from shore, and it appears that, from that time up to the time of the cession of Alaska to the United States, Russia never asserted in fact or exercised any exclusive jurisdiction in Behring's Sea or any exclusive rights in the sea fisheries therein beyond the ordinary limits of territorial waters.

As to the second of the said five points, [by a 6–1 majority,] do decide and determine that Great Britain did not recognize or concede any claim, upon the part of Russia, to exclusive jurisdiction as to the seal fisheries in Behring Sea, outside of ordinary territorial waters.

As to the third of the said five points, as to so much thereof as requires us to decide whether the body of water now known as the Behring Sea was included in the phrase "Pacific Ocean" as used in the Treaty of 1825 between Great Britain and Russia, We, the said Arbitrators, do unanimously decide and determine that the body of water now known as the Behring Sea was included in the phrase "Pacific Ocean" as used in the said Treaty.

As to so much of the third point as requires us to decide what rights, if any, in the Behring Sea were held and exclusively exercised by Russia after the said Treaty of 1825, We, [by a 6–1 majority], do decide and determine that no exclusive rights of jurisdiction in Behring Sea and no exclusive rights as to the seal fisheries therein, were held or exercised by Russia outside of ordinary territorial waters after the Treaty of 1825.

As to the fourth of the said five points, We, the said Arbitrators, do unanimously decide and determine that all the rights of Russia as to jurisdiction and as to the seal fisheries in Behring Sea, east [of the cession line] did pass unimpaired to the United States. . . .

As to the fifth of the said five points, We, [by a 5–2 majority], do decide and determine that the United States has not any rights of protection or property in the fur-seals frequenting the islands of the United States in the Behring Sea, when such seals are found outside the ordinary three-mile limit.

NOTES

(1) Into which of the four categories discussed in Section 1 does the decision fall? What is the status of the decision as precedent, either for resolving other disputes or establishing general principles of law?

(2) After years of reading common-law cases, the *Fur-Seals Case* probably seems unenlightening, stripped as it is of all analysis. Are there any general principles embedded in the decision? Which of the decided points involve legal questions? Which are factual?

(3) Migration and *animum revertendi*: In its brief, the United States argued that

> the Alaskan fur seal, begotten, born, and reared on the Pribilof Islands, within the territory of the United States, is essentially a land animal, which resorts to the water only for food and to avoid the rigor of winter, and cannot propagate its species or live except in a fixed home upon land . . . , a residence of several months on shore being necessary for propagation; that it is domestic in its habits and readily controlled by man while on land; that it is an animal of great value to the United States and to Great Britain; that the only home of the Alaskan seal herd is on the Pribilof Islands; . . . that its course when absent from these islands is uniform and confined principally to waters adjacent to the coast of the United States; that it never mingles with any other herd, and if driven from these islands would probably perish; that at all times, when in the water, the identity of each individual can be established with certainty, and that at all times, whether during its short excursions from the islands in search of food or its longer winter migration, it has fixed intention, or instinct, which induces it to return thereto.

54 Int'l Envtl. L. Rep. 54. Are fur seals domestic because they have *animum revertendi*? Must *animum revertendi* be instilled into the animal before it can be considered tame or is a natural migratory cycle sufficient?

Associate Supreme Court Justice Harlan, one of two United States arbitrators, found the argument offered by the United States persuasive. In exercising his right to submit a separate opinion, Harlan—relying upon the law of nature—argued that the law will "recognize a right of property in [animals *feræ naturæ*] in favor of one who, by acting upon their natural instincts, and by care, watchfulness, self-denial, and industry, induces or causes them to *abide*, for stated periods in each year, upon his premises." Hence, the fact that the United States chose not to drive the seals from its land, meant that it had a property in them. *Id.* at 81. Are you convinced?

(4) The tragedy of the commons / The tragedy of the market, redux: Fur seals were a classic example of the tragedy of the commons discussed in the notes following *Pierson v. Post* [Chapter 2]: Because sealers from any one country gained nothing by conserving the species—given that sealers from other countries were likely to kill those left unharvested—killing proceeded apace and the seal population crashed, dropping from at least 2.5 million to fewer than 400,000 in less than a decade. The crash convinced the interested states that "mutual coercion, mutually agreed upon"—in Garrett Hardin's famous phrase—was the only alternative to the economic—if not biological—extinction of the species.

Following the decision—and after nearly 20 years of confrontation and short-term bilateral agreements—a treaty was finally negotiated among Great Britain (for Canada), Japan, Russia, and the United States in 1911. *Interim Convention on the Conservation of North Pacific Fur Seals*, July 7, 1911, 37 Stat. 1542 (no longer in force). The treaty banned all pelagic sealing. In exchange, the treaty allocated a percentage of each of the Bearing Sea herds to the various parties.

See generally KURKPATRICK DORSEY, THE DAWN OF CONSERVATION DIPLOMACY 105–65 (1998); SIMON LYSTER, INTERNATIONAL WILDLIFE LAW 40–48 (1985).

(5) Limiting the global commons: International law has increasingly limited the global commons, particularly the high seas. The traditional 3–mile seaward boundary of State sovereignty—the "territorial sea"—has been replaced by a 200–mile exclusive economic zone (EEZ) within which the coastal State has "sovereign rights for the purpose of exploring and exploiting, conserving and managing the natural resources, whether living or non-living, of the waters superjacent to the sea-bed" and "jurisdiction ... with regard to ... the protection and preservation of the marine environment." United Nations Convention on the Law of the Sea, Art. 56(1), 21 I.L.M. 1261 (1982) (entered into force, November 16, 1994) (UNCLOS). In addition to exclusive sovereignty and jurisdiction within the EEZ, UNCLOS limits the high seas fisheries of anadromous fish such as salmon by giving the "State of origin" the power to set "total allowable catch for stocks originating in its rivers"—a catch-limit applicable both within and without the EEZ. *Id.* Art. 66(2).

(iii) CUSTOMARY LAW PROHIBITION ON TRANSBOUNDARY HARM

International environmental law has given rise to very little binding customary law—largely because it is relatively new. Perhaps the only clearly established customary rule bans States from using their resources in ways that cause harm beyond their borders. The rule was incorporating in Principle 21 of the Stockholm Declaration, quoted above, and has been repeated in various other conventions, including the Convention on Biological Diversity. Catherine Tinker, *Responsibility for Biological Diversity Conservation Under International Law*, 28 VAND. J. TRANSNAT'L L. 777, 806–09 (1995). Transboundary harm is easy to perceive in the instance of pollution. Far less clear, however, is the extent to which transboundary harm might result from resource-use practices. For example, does transboundary harm include the destruction of wildlife habitat that harms populations of animals such as migratory birds that cross State boundaries? If the United States permits or subsidizes the destruction of wetlands used by migratory waterfowl has it harmed Canada or Mexico?

As noted below, the special challenges of migratory or other transboundary wildlife have led not only to the various migratory bird treaties between the United States and Great Britain (Canada), Japan, Mexico, and the Soviet Union, but also to treaties such as the Convention on the Conservation of Migratory Species of Wild Animals (signed 1979; in force

1980; amended in 1985 and 1988), commonly known as the Bonn Convention.

International rivers are another example of the principle prohibiting transboundary harm. *See* The United Nations Convention on the Law of the Non–Navigational Uses of International Watercourses, 36 I.L.M. 700 (1997). The Convention provides in part that "[w]atercourse States shall, individually and, where appropriate, jointly, protect and preserve the ecosystem of international watercourses." *Id.* Art. 20.

c. EMERGING PRINCIPLES OF INTERNATIONAL WILDLIFE LAW

Although the prohibition of transboundary harm is perhaps the only generally accepted principle of customary international environmental law, several other principles are increasingly recognized. One or more of these principles may, in time, shift from "soft law" to the status as customary law. Among the more important, in terms of wildlife, are:

(i) THE PRECAUTIONARY PRINCIPLE

The precautionary principle is a response to uncertainty. Traditionally, environmental harms were regulated through tort systems—and hence did not operate until after harm had occurred. The decision to regulate conduct before harm occurs reflects a recognition that waiting for harm to occur before acting is often far more costly to society than is regulating or even banning the harmful conduct. The precautionary principle speaks to when regulation should be undertaken. It is an attempt to shift the burden of proof: those who seek to continue a questionable activity or policy have the burden of demonstrating that prohibitory or ameliorating policy responses are unneeded, rather than requiring advocates of prohibition or amelioration to prove that regulation is required to avoid environmental harm. In the words of the Principle 15 of the Rio Declaration on Environment and Development (1992):

> In order to protect the environment, the precautionary approach shall be widely applied by States according to their capabilities. Where there are threats of serious or irreversible damage, lack of full scientific certainty shall not be used as a reason for postponing cost-effective measures to prevent environmental degradation.

The principle has been subject to challenge as simply impractical. Consider Chris Stone's objections:

> Humankind has been dealing with perils from the beginning. Indeed, much of the activity that characterizes civilization can be conceived as response to uncertainties: the family, irrigation projects, city walls, agriculture, savings and insurance. Risk management is nothing new. But some of the new threats, mostly technology-driven, are potentially more far-reaching in space and time, more serious in magnitude, and the means of containing them less well understood. Caution should be high on everyone's agenda. The proponents of the precautionary principle deserve credit for their effective and insistent advocacy.

Yet, the precautionary principle—both the law and the literature taken together—is in disarray. To begin with, there is no "the" precautionary principle there. There are droves of differing versions, none of which is particularly helpful. Some sound downright wrong.... Are its ambitions restricted to informing when inaction is not justified, such as in its widely held but largely sterile triple negative: not having absolute causal proof of harm is not a justification for not acting? Or is the aim to stipulate when risk-reducing action *is* justified? The principle is so shapeless it has even been offered as a basis for penalizing those who were not sufficiently cautious or caring in the past....

Certainly more clarity is possible. But there are several reasons to doubt that any single principle can be fashioned more trenchant than "take care."

Christopher D. Stone, *Is There a Precautionary Principle?*, 31 Envtl. L. Rep. (Envtl. L. Inst.) 10790, 10799 (2001).

A more positive endorsement of the precautionary principle—and a call for its embrace as customary law—is offered by Catherine Tinker, *Responsibility for Biological Diversity Conservation Under International Law*, 28 Vand. J. Transnat'l L. 777, 806–09 (1995). Details about the principle's appearance in various international agreements pertaining to wildlife are contained in Chris W. Backes & Jonathan M. Vershuuren, *The Precautionary Principle in International, European, and Dutch Wildlife Law*, 9 Colo. J. Int'l Envtl. L & Pol'y 43 (1998).

Is Stone demanding more certainty than can reasonably be expected of any emerging norm? Would his standard be satisfied by many common law principles during their early evolution? Doesn't the common law stand for the fundamental proposition that law can be given content over time?

The United States has objected to the inclusion of the precautionary principles in such documents as the United Nations Framework Convention on Climate Change (1992). *See* Philippe Sands, *The "Greening" of International Law: Emerging Principles and Rules*, 1 Ind. J. Global Legal Stud. 293 (1994).

(ii) SUSTAINABLE USE AND DEVELOPMENT

International conventions and declarations have increasingly spoken in terms of "sustainable utilization" or "sustainable development." The Convention on Wetlands of International Importance, Especially as Waterfowl Habitat, T.I.A.S. No. 11084, 996 U.N.T.S. 245 (entered into force, December 21, 1975), for example, requires the Parties "to promote the conservation of the wetlands included in the List, and as far as possible the wise use of wetlands in their territory." Art. 3(1). In 1987, the Conference of Parties defined "wise use" as "[t]he wise use of wetlands is their sustainable utilization for the benefit of mankind in a way compatible with the maintenance of the natural properties of the ecosystem." Similarly, the Convention on Biological Diversity, 31 I.L.M. 818 (1992), states the "objectives of this Convention ... are the conservation of biological diversity, the sustainable use of its components and a fair and equitable sharing of the benefits arising out of the utilization of genetic resources." Art. 1.

The Stockholm Declaration of the United Nations Conference on the Human Environment, June 16, 1972, 11 I.L.M. 1416 (1972), for example, speaks broadly of "a special responsibility to safeguard and wisely manage the heritage of wildlife and its habitat which are now gravely imperilled by a combination of adverse factors." Principle 4. The World Charter for Nature, Oct. 28, 1982, 22 I.L.M. 455 (1983), goes further, stating that "[l]iving resources shall not be utilized in excess of their natural capacity for regeneration." Art. II(10)(a). And both the "Brundtland Report" [WORLD COMMISSION ON ENVIRONMENT AND DEVELOPMENT, OUR COMMON FUTURE (1987)] and the Rio Declaration on Environment and Development, June 13, 1992, 31 I.L.M. 874 (1992), repeatedly stresses the centrality of sustainable development.

While these instruments indicate that sustainable use is emerging as a principle of international law, what is lacking is a consensus on the meaning of the concept or how to apply it in specific cases. *See Case Concerning the Gabcikovo–Nagymaros Project (Hungary v. Slovakia,* I.C.J. <http://www.icj-cij.org> (Sept. 1997), particularly the Separate Opinion of Vice–President Weeramantry. *See generally* Philippe Sands, *The "Greening" of International Law: Emerging Principles and Rules,* 1 IND. J. GLOBAL LEGAL STUD. 293 (1994).

(iii) CONVENTION ON BIOLOGICAL DIVERSITY: A GLIMPSE AHEAD?

One of the chief products of the Rio Earth Summit in 1992 was the Convention on Biological Diversity (entered in force, 1993), 31 I.L.M. 818 (1992) (CBD), which now binds over 150 parties—with the conspicuous exception of the United States.[2] The CBD contains numerous, "hard law" obligations that the parties to it have assumed, but in each instance the obligation has been greatly diminished by the qualification that a party is committed to act only "as far as possible and as appropriate"—except the obligation in Article 6 to "[d]evelop national strategies, plans or programmes for the conservation and sustainable use of biological diversity," which is a duty that is qualified by the statement that each State is to act "in accordance with its particular conditions and capabilities." Given these limiting qualifications, the CBD places only minimal restrictions on the ability of States to exercise their sovereign rights to exploit national resources. Nonetheless, the CBD is a revealing and important document because it brings together—and in important ways clarifies—key emerging principles of international environmental law. Thus, it offers a sense of how current conflicts may eventually be resolved.

While recognizing that States "have sovereign rights over their biological resources," the CBD Preamble also states that "States are responsible for conserving their biological diversity and for using their biological

---

2. President Clinton signed the convention in 1993 but the Senate has not ratified it; the concerns of the United States have focused on intellectual property issues, rather than conservation duties.

resources in a sustainable manner." Conservation and sustainable use give rise to a certain tension, but that tension is reduced—in favor of conservation—by the definition given to "sustainable use" as "the use of components of biological diversity in a way and at a rate that does not lead to the long-term decline of biological diversity." Thus, use patterns are sustainable only if they do not, over the long term, diminish biological diversity (which is defined as including "diversity within species, between species and of ecosystems"). The CBD does not directly define "conservation," but it does define the two types of conservation: *in-situ* conservation, which means "the conservation of ecosystems and natural habitats and the maintenance and recovery of viable populations of species in their natural surroundings" and *ex-situ* conservation, which is "conservation of components of biological diversity outside their natural habitats," *i.e.*, in zoos, captive-breeding centers, and gene banks.

The Preamble's express embrace of the precautionary principle is also relevant: "[I]t is vital to anticipate, prevent and attack the causes of significant reduction or loss of biological diversity at the source," and "where there is a threat of significant reduction or loss of biological diversity, lack of full scientific certainty should not be used as a reason for postponing measures to avoid or minimize such threat."

While sanctioning the "sustainable use" of biological resources (and insisting upon the "fair and equitable sharing" of the benefits of genetic resources), the CBD nonetheless declares firmly the overall obligation of States to conserve biological diversity. The "fundamental requirement" of that obligation, the Preface states, "is the *in-situ* conservation of ecosystems and natural habitats and the maintenance and recovery of viable populations of species in their natural surroundings."

In addition to specific requirements to identify and monitor important components of biological diversity, the CBD obligates parties (in Article 8) to establish "protected areas or areas where special measures need to be taken to conserve biological diversity"; to "[r]egulate or manage biological resources important for the conservation of biological diversity whether within or outside protected areas"; to "[p]romote the protection of ecosystems, natural habitats and the maintenance of viable populations of species in natural surroundings"; to "[r]ehabilitate and restore degraded ecosystems and promote the recovery of threatened species"; and to "[p]revent the introduction of, control or eradicate those alien species which threaten ecosystems, habitats or species."

No doubt States were quick to sign the CBD because its many obligations are so qualified by the recurrent "as far as possible and as appropriate" language. Nonetheless, the Convention does propose a reconciliation of the exploitation-conservation conflict by encouraging States to limit their resource use practices to those that do not lead to long-term declines in diversity "within species, between species and of ecosystems." It also declares plainly the common interest of humankind in biological resources everywhere, emphasizing the central role of precaution when humans interact with nature's vast complexity.

(iv) HUMAN RIGHTS AND HEALTHY ENVIRONMENTS

One additional emerging area of international law that may come to play a significant role in wildlife conservation is international human rights law. The first principle of the Stockholm Declaration of the United Nations Conference on the Human Environment provides:

> Man has the fundamental right to freedom, equality and adequate conditions of life, in an environment of a quality that permits a life of dignity and well-being, and he bears a solemn responsibility to protect and improve the environment for present and future generations.

11 I.L.M. 1416 (1972). Twenty years later, the Rio Declaration on Environment and Development set out as its first principle that "Human beings ... are entitled to a healthy and productive life in harmony with nature." 31 I.L.M. 874 (1992).

In addition to these soft law principles, the right to a healthy environment has also been recognized in positive international law by regional human rights treaties, including the Protocol of San Salvador:

> 1.   Everyone shall have the right to live in a healthy environment and to have access to basic public services.

> 2.   The States Parties shall promote the protection, preservation and improvement of the environment.

Additional Protocol to the American Convention on Human Rights in the Area of Economic, Social and Cultural Rights, Art. 11 (November 14, 1988), 28 I.L.M. 161, 165 (1989). *See generally* Alexandre Kiss, *An Introductory Note on a Human Right to Environment, in* ENVIRONMENTAL CHANGE AND INTERNATIONAL LAW 199 (Edith Brown Weiss ed. 1992). Nonetheless, the existence as well as the content of a human right to a healthy environment is disputed. *See, e.g.,* Neil A.F. Popovic, *Pursuing Environmental Justice with International Human Rights and State Constitutions,* 15 STAN. ENVTL. L.J. 338 (1996); Dinah Shelton, *Human Rights, Environmental Rights, and the Right to Environment,* 28 STAN. INT'L L.J. 103 (1991).

The potential significance of a right to a *healthy* environment is that human rights are an exception to the general principle of international law that only States have standing to enforce international legal norms. As one commenter has noted, "The parallel evolutions of human rights protection and environmental protection disclose some affinities that should not pass unnoticed. They both witness, and precipitate, the gradual erosion of so-called domestic jurisdiction. The treatment by the state of its own nationals becomes a matter of international concern." A.A. Cancado Trindade, *The Contribution of International Human Rights Law to Environmental Protection, With Special Reference to Global Environmental Change, in* ENVIRONMENTAL CHANGE AND INTERNATIONAL LAW 244, 245 (Edith Brown Weiss ed. 1992). Thus, human rights are limits on State sovereignty—and individuals may assert these rights in a variety of international legal fora such as the Inter–American Court of Human Rights as well as in domestic courts. *E.g., Sterling v. Cupp,* 625 P.2d 123 (Or.1981) (consideration of wide range of international human rights documents in determining rights of prisoners in state prison). *See also* Raul M. Sanchez, *Mexico's El Cuchillo Dam Project,* 28 U. MIAMI INTER-AM. L. REV. 425 (1996–97).

SECTION 3.   SPECIES-BASED CONSERVATION: WHALES

> The moot point is, whether Leviathan can long endure so wide a chase, and so remorseless a havoc; whether he must not at last be exterminated from the waters, and the last whale, like the last man, smoke his last pipe, and then himself evaporate in the final puff.
>
>   HERMAN MELVILLE, MOBY-DICK (1st ed. 1851).

International agreements to conserve wildlife in order to maintain sustainable harvests began with treaties designed to protect either single species or a groups of related species. A current example of such a convention is presented by international attempts to regulate whaling. Whales and whaling present a particularly provocative subject of inquiry for various reasons: the considerable (and uncommon) success of regulation in aiding recovery of whale populations; the strong emotional attachment that many people have to the animals (leading to senses that they possess intrinsic moral value); and the fact that, for the most part, whales today are like trees in the National Forests—they are, for the most part, more economically valuable alive—for human recreation—than dead.

a.   A BRIEF HISTORY OF WHALING TO 1946

Industrial whaling began with the Basques, who started hunting right whales in Biscay Bay in the eleventh or twelfth century. As their technology improved and the inshore whale populations declined, the whalers moved further and further from shore. By the late sixteenth century, the Basques were whaling off the coast of Newfoundland. Basque whalers were replaced by the British and Dutch, and right whales were nearly extinct in the North Atlantic within a century. This has been the recurrent pattern:

> The history of whaling is made up of a number of chapters each covering a few centuries and all more or less repeating the same pattern.... Each began with new discovery and hopeful enterprise, passed through a phase of fierce competition and ruthless exploitation, with improving techniques and ended at length in diminishing resources, exhaustion and failure.

F.D. OMMANNEY, LOST LEVIATHAN 69 (1971).

With the passing of the right-whale as the industry's mainstay, the Dutch industry declined. The British, however, shifted their focus to the Greenland right—or bowhead—whale and were joined by French and German whalers. The availability of bowhead whales meant, however, that right whales continued to be harvested, "subsidized" by the bowhead harvest. The near-extinction of the bowhead followed. Americans began whaling in earnest in the eighteenth and nineteenth centuries, initially in the inshore waters off Massachusetts, Connecticut, New York, and California. With the depletion of the in-shore stocks, the whalers moved on to South America, Australia, and New Zealand. The Civil War—which led to the destruction of the whaling fleet—followed by the rise of petroleum—a substitute for whale oil—led to the industry's gradual decline at the beginning of the twentieth century.

During the period of American decline, whaling moved into the Arctic and Antarctic Oceans. Norwegians developed more effective harpoons and equipped their ships with steam power. In 1904, Norway established the first Antarctic whaling station to facilitate processing. Factory ships that allowed whales to be processed on the high seas were added to the fleets. The number of whales killed rose dramatically: in 1910, more than 10,000 whales were slaughtered; in 1914–15, Norway alone killed 14,917 whales just in Antarctica; in 1931, the number reached 43,129 whales.

The doctrine of freedom of the high seas as recognized in the *Behring Sea Fur–Seals Case* made regulation possible only if the whaling nations agreed. Agreement was initially produced not by the overharvest of whales but by the glut of whale oil: the processing companies sought to "stabilize" the market by allocating production among themselves. The attempt was only partially successful.

The first formal step toward international regulation of whaling was the Convention for the Regulation of Whaling, 49 Stat. 3079, T.S. No. 880 (Sept. 24, 1931), negotiated under the auspices of the League of Nation at the encouragement of the International Council for the Exploration of the Sea (ICES). The Convention was only a tentative step. Proposals to adopt a common ownership approach to whales were rejected in favor of the traditional free seas principle. Nonetheless, the Convention did apply to "all waters of the world." Similarly, although it prohibited the taking of right whales, it did not create either an enforcement mechanism or specify penalties. Instead, the focus was on licensing whaling ships and other steps to preserve the industry.

The 1931 Convention led to a series of protocols that in turn produced to the International Agreement for the Regulation of Whaling in 1937. 52 Stat. 1460, T.S. No. 933. The Agreement prohibited taking both right and gray whales, established closed seasons and closed areas. The formal agreement had little effect on the high seas, where whaling continued unabated. By the time World War II broke out, it was apparent that the existing international management regime was a failure. The end of the war provided a more hospitable climate:

> The period following World War II marked a tremendous opportunity for whale conservation. The drastic overcapitalization of the whaling industry that had occurred during the 1930s had been eradicated due to losses from the war. The two countries that had resisted international regulation most adamantly, Germany and Japan, were no longer capable of resisting regulation; the willingness of all whaling nations to establish international regulatory agencies was at its peak.

James E. Scarff, *The International Management of Whales, Dolphins, and Porpoises: An Interdisciplinary Assessment*, pt. 1, 6 ECOLOGY L.Q. 323, 351 (1977). The International Convention for Regulation of Whaling (ICRW) was concluded in 1946. *See generally* Anthony D'Amato & Sudhir K. Chopra, *Whales: Their Emerging Right to Life*, 85 AM. J. INT'L L. 21, 28–32

(1991); Judith Berger–Eforo, Note, *Sanctuary for Whales: Will This Be the Demise of the International Whaling Commission or A Viable Strategy for the Twenty-first Century?*, 8 PACE INT'L L. REV. 439, 451–63 (1996); James E. Scarff, *supra*, at 343–58.

International Convention for the Regulation of Whaling

10 U.S.T. 952; 161 U.N.T.S. 72.
signed: 2 December 1946.
entered into force: 10 November 1948.

The Governments whose duly authorised representatives have subscribed hereto,

Recognizing the interest of the nations of the world in safeguarding for future generations the great natural resources represented by the whale stocks;

Considering that the history of whaling has seen over-fishing of one area after another and of one species of whale after another to such a degree that it is essential to protect all species of whales from further over-fishing;

Recognizing that the whale stocks are susceptible of natural increases if whaling is properly regulated, and that increases in the size of whale stocks will permit increases in the number of whales which may be captured without endangering these natural resources;

Recognizing that it is in the common interest to achieve the optimum level of whale stocks as rapidly as possible without causing widespread economic and nutritional distress;

Recognizing that in the course of achieving these objectives, whaling operations should be confined to those species best able to sustain exploitation in order to give an interval for recovery to certain species of whales now depleted in numbers;

Desiring to establish a system of international regulation for the whale fisheries to ensure proper and effective conservation and development of whale stocks . . . ; and

Having decided to conclude a convention to provide for the proper conservation of whale stocks and thus make possible the orderly development of the whaling industry;

Have Agreed as follows:

Article I

1. This Convention includes the Schedule attached thereto which forms an integral part thereof. All references to "Convention" shall be understood as including the said Schedule either in its present terms or as amended in accordance with the provisions of Article V.

2. This Convention applies to factory ships, land stations, and whale catchers under the jurisdiction of the Contracting Governments and to all waters in which whaling is prosecuted by such factory ships, land stations, and whale catchers.

Article II

As used in this Convention:

1. "Factory ship" means a ship in which or on which whales are treated either wholly or in part;

2. "Land station" means a factory on the land at which whales are treated whether wholly or in part;

3. "Whale catcher" means a ship used for the purpose of hunting, taking, towing, holding on to, or scouting for whales;

4. "Contracting Government" means any Government which has deposited an instrument of ratification or has given notice of adherence to this Convention.

Article III

1. The Contracting Governments agree to establish an International Whaling Commission, hereinafter referred to as the Commission, to be composed of one member from each Contracting Government. Each member shall have one vote and may be accompanied by one or more experts and advisers.

2. The Commission shall elect from its own members a Chairman and Vice–Chairman and shall determine its own Rules of Procedure. Decisions of the Commission shall be taken by a simple majority of those members voting except that a three-fourths majority of those members voting shall be required for action in pursuance of Article V. . . .

.   .   .

4. The Commission may set up, from among its own members and experts or advisers, such committees as it considers desirable to perform such functions as it may authorize.

.   .   .

Article IV

1. The Commission may either in collaboration with or through independent agencies of the Contracting Governments or other public or private agencies, establishments, or organizations, or independently

(a) encourage, recommend, or if necessary, organize studies and investigations relating to whales and whaling;

(b) collect and analyze statistical information concerning the current condition and trend of the whale stocks and the effects of whaling activities thereon;

(c) study, appraise, and disseminate information concerning methods of maintaining and increasing the populations of whale stocks.

2. The Commission shall arrange for the publication of reports of its activities, and it may publish independently or in collaboration with the International Bureau for Whaling Statistics at Sandefjord in Norway and other organizations and agencies such reports as it deems appropriate, as

well as statistical, scientific, and other pertinent information relating to whales and whaling.

Article V

1.   The Commission may amend from time to time the provisions of the Schedule by adopting regulations with respect to the conservation and utilization of whale resources, fixing (a) protected and unprotected species; (b) open and closed seasons; (c) open and closed waters, including the designation of sanctuary areas; (d) size limits for each species; (e) time, methods, and intensity of whaling (including the maximum catch of whales to be taken in any one season); (f) types and specifications of gear and apparatus and appliances which may be used; (g) methods of measurement; and (h) catch returns and other statistical and biological records.

2.   These amendments of the Schedule (a) shall be such as are necessary to carry out the objectives and purposes of this Convention and to provide for the conservation, development, and optimum utilization of the whale resources; (b) shall be based on scientific findings; (c) shall not involve restrictions on the number or nationality of factory ships or land stations, nor allocate specific quotas to any factory or ship or land station or to any group of factory ships or land stations; and (d) shall take into consideration the interests of the consumers of whale products and the whaling industry.

.   .   .

Article VIII

1.   Notwithstanding anything contained in this Convention any Contracting Government may grant to any of its nationals a special permit authorizing that national to kill, take and treat whales for purposes of scientific research subject to such restrictions as to number and subject to such other conditions as the Contracting Government thinks fit, and the killing, taking, and treating of whales in accordance with the provisions of this Article shall be exempt from the operation of this Convention. Each Contracting Government shall report at once to the Commission all such authorizations which it has granted. Each Contracting Government may at any time revoke any such special permit which it has granted.

.   .   .

Article XI

Any Contracting Government may withdraw from this Convention on 30th June, of any year by giving notice on or before 1st January, of the same year to the depository Government, which upon receipt of such a notice shall at once communicate it to the other Contracting Governments. Any other Contracting Government may, in like manner, within one month of the receipt of a copy of such a notice from the depository Government give notice of withdrawal, so that the Convention shall cease to be in force on 30th June, of the same year with respect to the Government giving such notice of withdrawal.

NOTES

(1) Are the Convention's various goals incompatible? Note the first goal: "safeguarding for future generations the great natural resources represented by the whale stocks." What is to be safeguarded "for future generations"—whale stocks or natural resources? Or, are whale stocks simply natural resources? Does the term "natural resources" imply certain perspectives on whales?

Similarly, is there an inconsistency in the preamble's statement that the contracting nations "decided to conclude a convention to provide for the proper conservation of whale stocks and thus make possible the orderly development of the whaling industry"? Presumably, the "orderly development of the industry" is to be understood against the backdrop of overfishing and the statement that "it is essential to protect all species of whales from further over-fishing."

Note the fourth goal, which states, "it is in the common interest to achieve the optimum level of whale stocks as rapidly as possible without causing widespread economic and nutritional distress." The term "optimum level" is not defined in the Convention. What is "the optimum level"? The maximum numbers of whales? The maximum number of whalers? What would have to be specified to determine the optimum?

Finally, note the language in the fourth preambulatory statement: conservation was to be achieved without "widespread economic and nutritional distress." Note the similar language in Article V. What balance does the Convention seek between economics and conservation? Does the language suggest an optimism—or naivete—about economic actors' willingness to endure short-term constraints for long-term stability?

(2) Are the preamble's problems cured by the governance structure the Convention created? For example, does the International Whaling Commission (IWC) have sufficient authority to resolve any ambiguities in its founding document? What powers does the IWC have? Examine Article V carefully. What conservation actions is the IWC empowered to adopt? Are there limits on when it may act? If a whaling vessels violates the Schedule (the Convention's term for regulations), who is to enforce the Schedule? Does the IWC have any enforcement authority?

(3) What types of conduct are authorized by Article VII? What limits are placed on the Scientific Permit? Can the IWC exercise any control over the issuance of permits under Article VII?

(4) Does the ICRW have procedures to incorporate advances in scientific knowledge about whales?

(5) Who may join the IWC? Is membership limited to nations engaged in whaling? Might non-whaling nations wish to join? If so, for what purpose might they ratify the Convention and become a member?

(6) May the IWC permanently end whaling, whether for conservation or moral reasons?

b.   A BRIEF HISTORY OF WHALING FROM 1946 TO THE PRESENT

The ICRW came into force in November 1948. During its early history, the Commission was dominated by whaling States. This period was marked by frequent conflicts and threats of withdrawal from the Commission as nations competed for larger quotas. As a result, the IWC consistently set catch limits in excess of sustainable use. Simultaneously, the whaling nations increased their capital investment as they raced to kill whales, each attempting to catch a larger share of the permitted harvest. The combination of the politics at the IWC and escalation of technology on the seas was the commercial and near-biological extinction of several species.

At its first meeting in 1949, the IWC set the Antarctic baleen whale quota at 16,000 BWU.[1] As the season progressed, each factory ship would call in its weekly catch; when the catch neared the preestablished quota, the Bureau of International Whaling Statistics would set a closing date. The quota system thus created an incentive to catch whales as quickly as possible—and the whaling nations responded by increasing the number, size, and speed of the catcher boats.

Despite mounting evidence that whale populations could not withstand exploitation at a rate of 16,000 BWU, the IWC was unable to achieve consensus to reduce the harvest because major whaling powers formally objected. By 1959, the situation had deteriorated to the point that no quota could be set. An attempt to resolve the impasse through the creation of a scientific commission also failed when its recommendation of a total ban on hunting blue and humpback whales and a quota of no more than 7,000 fin whales was rejected by the major whaling States.

This history can be traced in the population of blue whales. Originally, blue whales are estimated to have numbered about 150,000 animals. At a population between 100,000 and 125,000, a sustainable harvest of approximately 6,000 whales should be possible. Blue whales were, however, be killed at a rate of 30,000 per year and the population dropped to only 10,000 animals by the early 1950s. In 1963, when the scientific committee presented its subsequently rejected findings, the total population was estimated at between 650 and 3,790 animals. The scientific committee also concluded that the population decreases of some species were inexplicable if whalers were honestly reporting their catch. A proposal adopted in principle in 1963 to require international observers on whaling vessels subsequently lapsed, however, when it proved to be impossible to reach an agreement to implement the proposal.

By the late 1960s, the Antarctic stocks had declined to the point that the industry largely abandoned the region and shifted its focus to the North Pacific. In December 1970, the United States Department of the Interior listed the eight largest whales species as endangered. 35 Fed. Reg. 18,319 (1970). In 1972, the UNCHE unanimously adopted a proposal calling on the IWC to establish a 10-year moratorium on all commercial whaling. Over the course of the 1970s, the pro-whaling nations increasingly were fighting a rear-guard action. Although UNCHE provided the impetus for change, change when it finally came came as much through the addition

---

1. The BWU was a Blue Whale Unit based nominally on the oil value of the species. One BWU equaled one blue whale or two fin whales or two-and-one-half humpback whales or six sei whales. *See generally* R. Michael M'Gonigle, *The "Economizing of Ecology: Why Big Rare Whales Still Die"*, 9 Ecology L.Q. 119, 137–41 (1980).

of new members to the IWC as through the transformation of the perspectives of traditional members.

The IWC responded to UNCHE's call by defeating a United States-sponsored resolution to impose the requested moratorium. The next five years produced escalating conflict. Proposals for moratoria became more frequent and expansive. In 1974, the United States again proposed a ten-year moratorium on whaling. In 1979, Australia and the United States proposed complete bans on commercial whaling. In 1980, three moratoria proposals were introduced: a total ban on all whaling, a ban on commercial whaling, and a ban on sperm whaling. Finally, in 1982, Seychelles proposed a "cessation" of all commercial[2] whaling to go into effect in 1986. The three-year period was designed to give whaling nations time to gradually phase out the commercial activities and to buffer the economic impacts. A detailed examination of the history of the IWC during this period concluded:

> With membership increased to thirty-nine by new recruits from the developing states, thirty-seven IWC members attended the thirty-fourth meeting in 1982. This meeting proved to be an historic occasion. The new members provided the three-quarters majority necessary to impose zero quotas on all commercially exploited stocks for the 1986 coastal and 1985–86 pelagic seasons.

Patricia Birnie, *The Role of Developing Countries in Nudging the International Whaling Commission from Regulating Whaling to Encouraging Nonconsumptive Uses of Whales,* 12 ECOLOGY L.Q. 937, 964 (1985). Formal objections were filed by Japan, Norway, and the Soviet Union. The "cessation" was reviewed and extended in 1990; it remains in effect today. In addition, in 1994 the IWC created an Antarctic whale sanctuary. The sanctuary covers some 8 million square miles and includes 90% of the feeding grounds.

Following the IWC's extension of the moratorium in 1990, Iceland formally withdrew from the Commission. Norway and Japan have threatened to do so, contending that the ban on whaling is a flagrant abuse of the objectives of the ICRW because the ban lacks scientific justification. The focus of dispute is the minke whale. The Scientific Committee estimates that there are more than 900,000 minkes—a population clearly capable of supporting a sustainable harvest. Norway unilaterally resumed commercial whaling in 1993, setting a quota of 296 minke whales; it has subsequently expanded its self-set quota; in 1999, Norway increased its quota to 750 whales. Norway also took the lead in creating a new international whaling commission, the North Atlantic Marine Mammal Commission (NAMMCO) composed of Norway, Iceland, Greenland, and the Faero Islands. *See* David D. Caron, *The International Whaling Commission and the North Atlantic Marine Mammal Commission: The Institutional Risks of Coercion in Consensual Structures,* 89 AM. J. INT'L L. 154 (1995).

Japan has taken a different tack, engaging in "scientific" whaling:

---

2. "Commercial" whaling was understood to exempt aboriginal whaling, particularly by the Inuit in the circumpolar Arctic.

[Japan has issued itself two scientific permits.] One is an extension of its existing programme in the Southern Hemisphere (now 400 +/- minke whales from the Antarctic). The second is for a two-year feasibility study primarily aimed at feeding ecology in the context of contributing to the "conservation and sustainable use of marine living resources in the western North Pacific, especially within Japan's EEZ." The programme proposes the taking of 100 minke whale, 50 Bryde's whales, and 10 sperm whales in the western North Pacific. The issuance of such permits is a sovereign right under the Convention. The Commission adopted Resolutions by majority calling on the Government of Japan to refrain from issuing these permits and reiterated that in reviewing scientific permits, the Scientific Committee should examine whether research is required for management or could be carried out using nonlethal means.

52nd Meeting of the International Whaling Commission, Final Press Release (6 July 2000), 3 J. INT'L WILDLIFE L. & POL'Y 174, 176 (2000).

Critics have argued that the scientific permits are simply a cover for continued commercial whaling, pointing to the fact that the research could be carried out using nonlethal methods and that the whales are processed and sold in Japan. William C. Burns, *The International Whaling Commission and the Future of Cetaceans: Problems and Prospects,* 8 COLO. J. INT'L ENVTL. L. & POL'Y 31, 46–50 (1997). A leading Japanese international law scholar rejects these charges:

Certainly, whales taken under special permits will be processed after conducting scientific investigations, and whale meat and by-products will come into the market. However, the sale of meat and by-products is not for avaricious business purposes, but for supporting research efforts, especially financing research cruises to the Antarctic. Under contract with the Japanese Government, it is conditioned that any profit resulting from the sale of whale products should revert back to the research program.

Kazuo Sumi, *The "Whale War" Between Japan and the United States: Problems and Prospects,* 17 DEN. J. INT'L L. & POL'Y 317, 321 (1989). In 1993, Japan presented two petitions to the IWC. The first sought to have Japan's whaling industry classified as "aboriginal" so that it would be exempt from IWC regulation; the second sought an increase in the number of scientific permits. Both requests were denied. Recall also the discussion of the Makah Nation's decision to resume subsistence whaling in Chapter 7—a decision that was attacked as providing cover for Japanese and Norwegian whalers.

See generally Pat W. Birnie, *International Legal Issues in the Management and Protection of the Whale: A Review of Four Decades of Experience,* 29 NAT. RESOURCES J. 903, 921–29 (1989); Anthony D'Amato & Sudhir K. Chopra, *supra,* at 32–48; Judith Berger–Eforo, *supra*; Sidney Holt, *Whale Mining, Whale Saving,* 9 MARINE POL'Y 192 (1995); SIMON LYSTER, *supra,* at 17–38; James E. Scarff, *supra,* at 358–71.

NOTES

(1) At the 51st Annual meeting, the pro-whaling nations sarcastically described the IWC as "an anachronism, a slow organisation that pretends to manage whaling while actually doing no management at all. As a management regime, the IWC has been stone dead for many years, but as the world's leading hypocritical, double-standard forum it is still jetting around." Quoted in Karen Simpson, *supra,* at 352. The underlying argument is that the ICRW has been subverted from a document intended to manage commercial whaling into one that serves to protect animal rights by banning whaling without regard to the species populations. Is the argument accurate?

What is the basis for the IWC's power? Recall the language in Article V(2): "amendments [to harvest quotas] (a) shall be such as are necessary to carry out the objectives and purposes of this Convention and to provide for the conservation, development, and optimum utilization of the whale resources; (b) shall be based on scientific findings." What justification is there for a moratorium on taking minke whales given the scientific data showing populations at or near pre-whaling levels? The following is the most recent population estimates:

Population	Year(s) of survey	Size	95% confidence limits
Minke Whales			
-Southern Hemisphere	1982–1989	761,000	510,000–1,140,000
-North Atlantic	1987–1995	149,000	120,000–182,000
-Northwest Pacific	1989–1990	25,000	12,800–48,600
Fin Whales			
-North Atlantic	1969–1989	47,300	27,700–82,000
Gray Whales			
-Eastern North Pacific	1987/88	21,000	19,800–22,500
Bowhead Whales			
-Bering, Beaufort Seas	1988	7,500	6,400–9,200
Humpback Whales			
-Western North Atlantic	1979–1986	5,500	2,890–8,120
Blue Whales			
-Southern Hemisphere	1985–1991	460	210–1,000
Pilot Whales			
-Central and Eastern North Atlantic	1989	780,000	440,000–1,370,000

INTERNATIONAL WHALING COMMISSION, WHALE POPULATION ESTIMATES <http://ourworld.compuserve.com/homepages/iwcoffice/Estimate.htm>.

Consider the following analysis:

The perception of legitimacy of ... an organization [such as the IWC] rests (1) on the integrity and accuracy of its science, and (2) on the political integrity and managerial accuracy of decisions taken on the basis of that science. Both of these aspects of institutional legitimacy have been suspect throughout the history of the IWC. For years prowhaling and antiwhaling states have debated what the scientific data indicate about the viability of whale stocks. During the first twenty-five years of the IWC's existence, the organization oversaw the continued overexploitation and depletion of whale stocks. The recommendations of the IWC Scientific Committee at that time, environmentalists allege, were distorted and ignored by the whaling states, a powerful allegation calling into question the integrity of the organization. Today the situation is reversed; the prowhaling nations, particularly Japan, Norway and Iceland, charge that the IWC is ignoring scientific findings in setting its policies. These nations allege that the IWC prohibits *all* whaling, even though the scientific community has concluded that some hunting of minke whales would be sustainable. The whaling states claim that the views of the Scientific Committee are distorted or ignored by nonwhaling states in order to prevent all whaling. They argue that the issue is not the conservation of whales— all parties involved have stated their acceptance of the importance of "conservation" and "sustainability." They contend instead that, under the guise of conservation, the IWC is attempting to grant whales an entitlement to life, absolute protection from further utilization.

Caron, *supra,* at 159–60. Within a nation-State, shifting consensus generally leads to legal change. Is this possible at the international level? Given that States are bound only when they choose to be bound, what tools are available to a global majority in the face of a refusal by a State to conform to a new consensus?

(2) Domestic law and international law: As noted, the ICRW does not contain direct enforcement or sanction provisions. This has been partially remedied by two United States statutes, the Pelly Amendment to the Fisherman's Protective Act of 1971, 22 U.S.C. ¶¶ 1978–1980, and the Packwood–Magnuson Amendment to the Magnuson Fishery Conservation and Management Act, 16 U.S.C. ¶ 1821(e)(2).

The Pelly Amendment creates a certification process that can lead to the imposition of trade sanctions. When the Secretary of Commerce determines that foreign nationals are conducting fishing operations that diminish the effectiveness of an international fishery conservation program, he is to certify his finding to the President. The President may then direct the Secretary to prohibit the importation of fish products from the offending country. If the President decides not to impose an import ban, he is required to inform Congress of his reasons for refusing to do so. The Amendment has been amended several times so that it now applies not only to fisheries but also to "the living resources of the sea," including marine mammals. After eight years without the imposition of sanctions under the Pelly Amendment, Congress enacted the Packwood–Magnuson Amendment. It imposed mandatory sanctions by specifying that a certification by the Secretary of Commerce that foreign nationals were engaged in conduct that diminished the effectiveness of the ICRW required the Secretary to reduce the fishing quota of the offending nation.

Foreign countries have been certified several times for diminishing the effectiveness of the ICRW. No Pelly sanctions have been applied and only a handful of Packwood–Magnuson sanctions have been imposed. Nonetheless, the threat of the certification process has been effective in inducing foreign States to modify their conduct. For an extended discussion of certifications, see Gene S. Martin, Jr. & James W. Brennan, *Enforcing the International Convention for the Regulation of Whaling: The Pelly and Packwood–*

Magnuson Amendments, 17 DEN. J. INT'L L. & POL'Y 293 (1989). We will return to the issues raised by the extraterritorial application of domestic law.

(3) Aboriginal whaling: The whaling group's statement that the IWC is "the world's leading hypocritical, double-standard forum" refers to the aboriginal exceptions to the moratorium on whaling. Several indigenous groups continue to rely upon whales for cultural or spiritual subsistence as well as food. Although the ICRW does not explicitly recognize aboriginal whaling rights, there has been a quota for such takings since before the adoption of the Convention. The aboriginal quota for the period through 2002 is:

> Bering–Chukchi–Beaufort Seas stock of bowhead whales (taken by Alaskan Eskimos and native peoples of Chukotka)—The total number of landed whales for the years 1998, 1999, 2000, 2001 and 2002 shall not exceed 280 whales, with no more than 67 whales struck in any year (up to 15 unused strikes may be carried over each year).

> Eastern North Pacific gray whales (taken by those whose "traditional, aboriginal and subsistence needs have been recognised"[3])—A total catch of 620 whales is allowed for the years 1998, 1999, 2000, 2001 and 2002 with a maximum of 140 in any one year.

> West Greenland fin whales (taken by Greenlanders)—An annual catch of 19 whales is allowed for the years 1998, 1999, 2000, 2001 and 2002.

> West Greenland minke whales (taken by Greenlanders)—The annual of whales struck for the years 1998, 1999, 2000, 2001 and 2002, shall not exceed 175 (up to 15 unused strikes may be carried over each year).

> East Greenland minke whales (taken by Greenlanders)—An annual catch of 12 whales is allowed for the years 1998, 1999, 2000, 2001 and 2002 (up to 3 unused strikes may be carried over each year).

> Humpback whales taken by St Vincent and The Grenadines—for the seasons 2000 to 2002, the annual catch shall not exceed two whales.

<http://ourworld.compuserve/com/homepag-es/iwcoffice/Catches.htm#Aboriginal>

Is the United States' position as an anti-whaling nation and as a defender of the aboriginal exception defensible? As you consider the aboriginal exception, keep in mind that many countries such as Japan have long, unbroken histories of subsistence-whaling by residents of coastal communities. Are the Japanese citizens who continue that tradition less deserving of protection than native whalers in Alaska or Canada? If so, why?

Note the careful phrasing in regard to Eastern North Pacific gray whales which may be "taken by those whose 'traditional, aboriginal and subsistence needs have been recognised.' " This phrasing reflects the fact that the term "aborigine" is not defined. Japan has argued, for example,

---

3. This includes the Makah Nation.

that its coastal villages ought to be permitted to take whales as they "traditionally" have. It also argues that the fact that the villages sell whale products should not preclude their designation as aboriginal.

(4) Other international conventions: The ICRW is not the only international convention potentially applicable to whales. In addition, the following conventions may also apply: (1) international conventions: Convention on International Trade in Endangered Species (CITES) (1973), Conservation of Antarctic Marine Living Resources (1979), Conservation of Migratory Species of Wild Animals (1979), and the United National Convention of the Law of the Sea (UNCLOS) (1982); (2) regional conventions: Convention on Nature Protection and Wildlife Preservation in the Western Hemisphere (1940), African Convention on the Conservation of Nature and Natural Resources (1968), and Berne Convention on the Conservation of Wild Life and Natural Habitat (1979). A variety of general principles and guidelines are also potentially applicable. These include UNEP in Shared Natural Resources, the IUCN in the World Conservation Strategy, and the UN in the World Charter for Nature.

The most important of these is CITES, which is discussed in the next section.

PERSPECTIVES

Anthony D'Amato and Sudhir K. Chopra, *Whales: Their Emerging Right to Life*
85 Am. J. Int'l L. 21 (1991).

Writers of science fiction have often speculated what it would be like to discover, on a planet in outer space, a much higher form of intelligence. How would we react to those creatures? Would we be so fearful of them that we would try to kill them? Or would we welcome the opportunity to attempt to understand their language and culture? Stranger than fiction is the fact that there already exists a species of animal life on earth that scientists speculate has higher than human intelligence. The whale has a brain that in some instances is six times bigger than the human brain and its neocortex is more convoluted. Discussing the creative processes of whales, Dr. John Lilly says that a researcher "is struck with the fact that one's current expectations determine, within certain limits, the results attained with a particular animal at that particular time." Whales speak to other whales in a language that appears to include abstruse mathematical poetry. They have also developed interspecies communication with dolphins. Whales are the most specialized of all mammals. They are sentient, they are intelligent, they have their own community, and they can suffer. Yet because they have no hands to fashion tools or construct weapons for self-defense—because they "do not have the ability to drive harpoons through living flesh"—they are vulnerable to human predation. Many species of whales have been savagely hunted to near extinction. Even today, despite the international restrictions that have made the outfitting of new whaling vessels unprofitable, whalers already in the business-using their sunk capital investments-continue to search out and destroy these magnificent creatures.

Professor Richard Falk writes that "it is a late hour on the biological clock that controls cetacean destiny, but hopefully not too late." Australia, a nation that in years past had engaged heavily in whaling, declared in 1979 that "the harpooning of these animals is offensive to many people who regard killing these special and intelligent animals as inconsistent with the ideals of mankind, and without any valid economic purpose in mitigation." Yet national policies do not automatically transmute into international legal restrictions. Neither the present opposition to whaling of an overwhelming number of states nor the ethical revulsion of many people throughout the world protects whales from the whale-hunting minority of states or gives them an international legal entitlement to survive. Even if some observers feel that the burgeoning international law of "human rights" should in principle include the preservation of whales, that very label seems inappropriate because it connotes species chauvinism.

. . .

I. The Moral Claim

[There is a strong] claim of environmental awareness—that we owe to living creatures in the environment *per se*, without calculating their utility to future generations of human beings. The dawning of such a sense of duty involves a broadening of humanistic consciousness comparable to the Copernican revolution that changed the Ptolemaic earth-centered conception of the universe to the modern realization that ours is but a minor planet revolving around a minor star in only one of billions of galaxies. We may be at the brink of replacing the view that "nature" exists only to serve people, with a larger ecological awareness that people share and ought to share the planet with many other sentient creatures.

This strong environmental claim requires at a minimum that we pause to consider the effect of certain human activities upon other living creatures. . . .

[D'Amato and Chopra make an argument similar to that set out in the excerpt from Peter Singer in Chapter 1:]

[T]here can be little physiological doubt what whales feel pain; indeed, the real question is whether they perceive acute pain to an even greater degree than humans. This latter possibility is evidenced by the far wider range of skin sensations apparently registered by the complex cerebral cortex of the whale.

Anyone who has watched an animal in intense pain—a dog, a cat, a rabbit, a horse—knows that the animal is suffering. When we consider whales, whose intelligence may be superior to our own it is nearly impossible to avoid concluding that these majestic creatures are capable of a degree of suffering that we may not be able to fathom.

. . .

. . . . To be sure, whales are not human, but are they "less" than human? The mind set that exults in the killing of whales and the "sports" hunting of endangered wildlife species overlaps with the mind set that accepts genocide of "inferior" human beings. Conversely, the extension of rights to whales resonates deeply with the historical-legal extensions of equal rights to women and to minority groups. We believe that the phrase "human rights" is only superficially species chauvinistic. In a profound sense, whales and some other sentient mammals are entitled to humans rights or at least to *humanist rights*—to the most fundamental entitlements that we regard as part of the humanitarian tradition. They are entitled to those fundamental rights not because they are "less" than human but because they are "different" from humans in various respects that do not affect or qualify the rights in question. In this article we argue only for extending the single most fundamental of all human-rights—the right to life—to whales.

. . .

II. The International Law Claim

The entitlement of whales to live and be left alone has arguably resulted from the developing practices of various institutions—international, conventional and national—concerned with whaling.

[D'Amato and Chopra trace the history of whaling, emphasizing the number and variety of international agreements, principles, and statements that reflect an increasing awareness of the need to protect wildlife in general and whales in particular. These include the conventions noted above. Following this lengthy discussion, they conclude:] The six stages we have recapitulated—free resource [up to World War I], regulation [1918–1931], conservation [1931–1945], protection [1945–1977], preservation [1977–1982], entitlement—may be viewed as a progression from self-interest to altruism, or from individualism to communalism, but we suggest that there are better conceptualized as a broadening of international cultural consciousness. The whalers of the early twentieth century were persuaded to accept the second stage—regulation—even though many of them found that it hindered their individual freedom. They accepted it on the rational ground that they themselves might destroy their livelihood as a whole unless certain common restrictions were placed on the whaling enterprise. This rational conclusion constituted an increase in breadth of consciousness, from "do anything we want," to "don't do some things that might hurt other whalers and eventually ourselves." Similarly, the step from regulation to conservation met resistance; whalers had to be persuaded that long-term conservation would benefit the industry as a whole, which in turn would enhance the economic interests, or at least prospects, of each whaler. Again, consciousness was broadened. And so it has continued with each of our six analytic stages. In the fifth and sixth stages, whalers face the loss of their entire enterprise, yet the increase in consciousness now embraces the environment as a whole, the planet on which we all live. In this respect, whalers should be no different from anyone else; everyone's self-interest is in a stable and viable ecosystem. Hence, it would be a mistake to conclude that the transition from the first stage to the second, or for that matter from any one stage to the next, has been more difficult or historically important than any other.

Although the distance covered between stage one and stage six amounts to a catastrophic change—from uninhibited freedom to prohibition—the change from any one stage to the next was incremental, depicting the same underlying psychological and philosophical process of increasing breadth of consciousness. For this reason, we contend that what we have denominated as the last stage—entitlement—is not qualitatively different from the others. Rather, it is part of a relentless, historically necessary progression. We may or may not be in the final entitlement stage today—different people think differently—but its seeds were planted in each of the five preceding stages.

Readers who are familiar with international jurisprudence will recognize that in our discussion of the changing psychology and breadth of consciousness, we have implicitly been sketching trends in the component of international law called *opinio juris*. The development of international custom is inevitably a dynamic process, and the seeds of a future conflict-resolving synthesis are always present in the clash of thesis and antithesis that constitutes the claim conflicts among states. To anticipate a customary trend is to argue that, in a sense, it already exists. We have already seen, in the history we have recounted, the practice of states (reflected through their whaling activities) moving through six stages that are best characterized as increases in international breadth of consciousness. This combination of practice and consciousness formally constitutes the material and psychological elements of general custom. What states *do* becomes what whey legally *ought* to do, by virtue of a growing sense that what they do is right, proper and natural. The dawning sense of duty to the environment-to protect the ability of our small, green planet to sustain life-is evidence of a sense of obligation that constitutes the *opinio juris* component of binding customary international law.

Hence, if our argument in this section is accepted, we have sketched more than a political-cultural history of a relentless increase in breadth of consciousness about whales. We have suggested an *opinio juris*—a growing sense of international legal obligation toward whales. In the current stage of that progression, nearly all nations accept the obligation of preservation. And in this consensus of preservation, we suggest that there is the incipient formation of the final, decisive stage—the entitlement of whales to life. Whether that final stage has already arrived cannot be definitively determined. But we argue that in its inevitability it has already been anticipated in the law.

* * *

(1) Are D'Amato and Chopra arguing that there is an emerging soft law entitling whales to life? Or are they arguing that various hard and soft law instruments have achieved—or have nearly achieved—the status of law? Have the events that have occurred since their article was written buttressed or undercut their argument?

(2) The Japanese have argued that the drive to preserve whales reflects culturally specific values. The imposition of these values on States and cultures that do not share them is a form of imperialism:

The research whaling dispute is part of a long-pending whaling question between both countries and is only the tip of the iceberg. In the background of this controversy lies a perception gap concerning the whale and whaling. Owing to differences in dietary customs, religious beliefs, cultural backgrounds and emotional sensibilities, this perception gap remains wide and appears to be growing.

.... At present, Americans have no direct economic interests in whaling. For this reason, the United States has evolved its national position on whales along the lines of a protectionist approach.

On the other hand, the Japanese have been heavily dependent upon the whale as a source of food and for other purposes from days immemorial. The fact that many whale bones have been excavated from Japanese archaeological mounds demonstrates that whale meat and bones were used by ancient Japanese. The whale is mentioned in the "Manyoshu," the oldest anthology of poems in Japan, which was compiled at the end of the eighth century. For the Japanese people, the whale is not only a food source, but also a basis of culture. All parts of the whale have been used most effectively, and have become part of the daily life of the Japanese and contributed to the formation of a unique traditional culture. To cite one example, baleens of the right whale have been used as an essential part of "Bunraku," Japan's traditional puppet theater. However, nowadays, it is difficult to obtain them because the catch of this species is completely prohibited.

. . .

[I]t must be pointed out that so-called "structural violence of the majority" prevails in the IWC. Respect for minority views is the fundamental principle of democracy. However, this principle has been trampled down by the majority....

The only real aim of the majority countries seems to be the choking off of any type of commercial whaling. They attempt to achieve this aim by fair means or foul. That is the reason they have little interest in scientific research of whale stocks. Prevailing in the IWC is no longer the scientific approach, but rather what can only be called "missionary zeal." Even the exercise of the legitimate right of a member country under the ICRW to file an objection to an amendment of the Schedule or to conduct scientific whaling is under political and economic pressure. By the threat or use of "sanctions," the United States has played a leading role as an international enforcer in forcing the majority's value system upon the minority.

Kazuo Sumi, *The "Whale War" Between Japan and the United States: Problems and Prospects*, 17 DEN. J. INT'L L. & POL'Y 317, 318 (1989).

(3) Watching whales bigger business than hunting whales: The *New York Times* recently reported that the whale-watching industry was far larger than the whale hunting industry: whale watchers spent more than $300 million on tour tickets while Japan's total sales of whale meat was only $32 million. James Brooke, *The Watch for Whales Is Outpacing the Hunts*, N.Y. TIMES, Aug. 19, 2001, at 11.

(4) The IWC has a web site at <http://ourworld.compuserve.com/homepages/iwcoffice>.

Section 4.   Species-Based Preservation: Elephants

In 1969, Congress enacted the second iteration of endangered species legislation, the Endangered Species Conservation Act (ESCA). Among other provisions was a directive to the Secretaries of the Interior and State to call an international meeting on protecting endangered species. It was nearly four years before representatives from some eighty nations finally met in Washington, D.C. in February 1973.

The conference reflected a convergence of interests between wildlife exporting-and importing-States. Exporting States recognized that conservation measures were necessary to prevent the extermination of an economically valuable resource; many importing nations were responding to public opinion that favored protection of wildlife, as well as utilitarian concerns for the protection of genetic resources for potential exploitation. The International Union for the Conservation of Nature and Natural Resources (IUCN) circulated draft proposals beginning in 1967; Kenya and the United States also subsequently prepared drafts. Discussions among the three drafters produced a Unified Working Paper that became the basis for the conference and a multilateral treaty:

Convention on International Trade in Endangered Species of Wild Fauna and Flora

27 U.S.T. 1087; 993 U.N.T.S. 243.
signed: 3 March 1973.
entered into force: 1 July 1975.
amended: 22 June 1979.

The Contracting States,

Recognizing that wild fauna and flora in their many beautiful and varied forms are an irreplaceable part of the natural systems of the earth which must be protected for this and the generations to come;

Conscious of the ever-growing value of wild fauna and flora from aesthetic, scientific, cultural, recreational and economic points of view;

Recognizing that peoples and States are and should be the best protectors of their own wild fauna and flora;

Recognizing, in addition, that international co-operation is essential for the protection of certain species of wild fauna and flora against over-exploitation through international trade;

Convinced of the urgency of taking appropriate measures to this end;

Have agreed as follows:

Article I

Definitions

For the purpose of the present Convention, unless the context otherwise requires:

(a) "Species" means any species, subspecies, or geographically separate population thereof;

(b) "Specimen" means:

(i) any animal or plant, whether alive or dead;

(ii) in the case of an animal: for species included in Appendices I and II, any readily recognizable part or derivative thereof; and for species included in Appendix III, any readily recognizable part or derivative thereof specified in Appendix III in relation to the species; and

(iii) in the case of a plant: for species included in Appendix I, any readily recognizable part or derivative thereof; and for species included in Appendices II and III, any readily recognizable part or derivative thereof specified in Appendices II and III in relation to the species;

(c) "Trade" means export, re-export, import and introduction from the sea;

. . .

Article II

Fundamental Principles

1. Appendix I shall include all species threatened with extinction which are or may be affected by trade. Trade in specimens of these species must be subject to particularly strict regulation in order not to endanger further their survival and must only be authorized in exceptional circumstances.

2. Appendix II shall include:

(a) all species which although not necessarily now threatened with extinction may become so unless trade in specimens of such species is subject to strict regulation in order to avoid utilization incompatible with their survival; and

(b) other species which must be subject to regulation in order that trade in specimens of certain species referred to in sub-paragraph (a) of this paragraph may be brought under effective control.

3. Appendix III shall include all species which any Party identifies as being subject to regulation within its jurisdiction for the purpose of preventing or restricting exploitation, and as needing the co-operation of other Parties in the control of trade.

4. The Parties shall not allow trade in specimens of species included in Appendices I, II and III except in accordance with the provisions of the present Convention.

Article III

Regulation of Trade in Specimens of Species Included in Appendix I

1. All trade in specimens of species included in Appendix I shall be in accordance with the provisions of this Article.

2. The export of any specimen of a species included in Appendix I shall require the prior grant and presentation of an export permit. An export permit shall only be granted when the following conditions have been met:

(a) a Scientific Authority of the State of export has advised that such export will not be detrimental to the survival of that species;

(b) a Management Authority of the State of export is satisfied that the specimen was not obtained in contravention of the laws of that State for the protection of fauna and flora;

(c) a Management Authority of the State of export is satisfied that any living specimen will be so prepared and shipped as to minimize the risk of injury, damage to health or cruel treatment; and

(d) a Management Authority of the State of export is satisfied that an import permit has been granted for the specimen.

3. The import of any specimen of a species included in Appendix I shall require the prior grant and presentation of an import permit and either an export permit or a re-export certificate. An import permit shall only be granted when the following conditions have been met:

(a) a Scientific Authority of the State of import has advised that the import will be for purposes which are not detrimental to the survival of the species involved;

(b) a Scientific Authority of the State of import is satisfied that the proposed recipient of a living specimen is suitably equipped to house and care for it; and

(c) a Management Authority of the State of import is satisfied that the specimen is not to be used for primarily commercial purposes.

.   .   .

Article IV

Regulation of Trade in Specimens of Species Included in Appendix II

1. All trade in specimens of species included in Appendix II shall be in accordance with the provisions of this Article.

2. The export of any specimen of a species included in Appendix II shall require the prior grant and presentation of an export permit. An export permit shall only be granted when the following conditions have been met:

(a) a Scientific Authority of the State of export has advised that such export will not be detrimental to the survival of that species;

(b) a Management Authority of the State of export is satisfied that the specimen was not obtained in contravention of the laws of that State for the protection of fauna and flora; and

(c) a Management Authority of the State of export is satisfied that any living specimen will be so prepared and shipped as to minimize the risk of injury, damage to health or cruel treatment.

3. A Scientific Authority in each Party shall monitor both the export permits granted by that State for specimens of species included in Appendix II and the actual exports of such specimens.

Whenever a Scientific Authority determines that the export of specimens of any such species should be limited in order to maintain that species throughout its range at a level consistent with its role in the ecosystems in which it occurs and well above the level at which that species might become eligible for inclusion in Appendix I, the Scientific Authority shall advise the appropriate Management Authority of suitable measures to be taken to limit the grant of export permits for specimens of that species.

4.   The import of any specimen of a species included in Appendix II shall require the prior presentation of either an export permit or a re-export certificate.

. . .

Article V

Regulation of Trade in Specimens of Species Included in Appendix III

1.   All trade in specimens of species included in Appendix III shall be in accordance with the provisions of this Article.

2.   The export of any specimen of a species included in Appendix III from any State which has included that species in Appendix III shall require the prior grant and presentation of an export permit. An export permit shall only be granted when the following conditions have been met:

(a) a Management Authority of the State of export is satisfied that the specimen was not obtained in contravention of the laws of that State for the protection of fauna and flora; and

(b) a Management Authority of the State of export is satisfied that any living specimen will be so prepared and shipped as to minimize the risk of injury, damage to health or cruel treatment.

3.   The import of any specimen of a species included in Appendix III shall require, except in circumstances to which paragraph 4 [on the re-export of specimens] of this Article applies, the prior presentation of a certificate of origin and, where the import is from a State which has included that species in Appendix III, an export permit.

. . .

Article VI

Permits and Certificates

1.   Permits and certificates granted under the provisions of Articles III, IV, and V shall be in accordance with the provisions of this Article.

2.   An export permit shall contain the information specified in the model set forth in Appendix IV, and may only be used for export within a period of six months from the date on which it was granted.

3.   Each permit or certificate shall contain the title of the present Convention, the name and any identifying stamp of the Management Authority granting it and a control number assigned by the Management Authority.

. . .

Article VII

Exemptions and Other Special Provisions Relating to Trade

1. The provisions of Articles III, IV and V shall not apply to the transit or transhipment of specimens through or in the territory of a Party while the specimens remain in Customs control.

2. Where a Management Authority of the State of export or re-export is satisfied that a specimen was acquired before the provisions of the present Convention applied to that specimen, the provisions of Articles III, IV and V shall not apply to that specimen where the Management Authority issues a certificate to that effect.

3. The provisions of Articles III, IV and V shall not apply to specimens that are personal or household effects. This exemption shall not apply where:

(a) in the case of specimens of a species included in Appendix I, they were acquired by the owner outside his State of usual residence, and are being imported into that State; or

(b) in the case of specimens of species included in Appendix II:

(i) they were acquired by the owner outside his State of usual residence and in a State where removal from the wild occurred;

(ii) they are being imported into the owner's State of usual residence; and

(iii) the State where removal from the wild occurred requires the prior grant of export permits before any export of such specimens;

unless a Management Authority is satisfied that the specimens were acquired before the provisions of the present Convention applied to such specimens.

4. Specimens of an animal species included in Appendix I bred in captivity for commercial purposes, or of a plant species included in Appendix I artificially propagated for commercial purposes, shall be deemed to be specimens of species included in Appendix II.

5. Where a Management Authority of the State of export is satisfied that any specimen of an animal species was bred in captivity or any specimen of a plant species was artificially propagated, or is a part of such an animal or plant or was derived therefrom, a certificate by that Management Authority to that effect shall be accepted in lieu of any of the permits or certificates required under the provisions of Article III, IV or V.

6. The provisions of Articles III, IV and V shall not apply to the non-commercial loan, donation or exchange between scientists or scientific institutions registered by a Management Authority of their State, of herbarium specimens, other preserved, dried or embedded museum specimens, and live plant material which carry a label issued or approved by a Management Authority.

7. A Management Authority of any State may waive the requirements of Articles III, IV and V and allow the movement without permits or certificates of specimens which form part of a travelling zoo, circus, menagerie, plant exhibition or other travelling exhibition provided that:

(a) the exporter or importer registers full details of such specimens with that Management Authority;

(b) the specimens are in either of the categories specified in paragraph 2 or 5 of this Article; and (c) the Management Authority is satisfied that any living specimen will be so transported and cared for as to minimize the risk of injury, damage to health or cruel treatment.

Article VIII

Measures to Be Taken by the Parties

1. The Parties shall take appropriate measures to enforce the provisions of the present Convention and to prohibit trade in specimens in violation thereof. These shall include measures:

(a) to penalize trade in, or possession of, such specimens, or both; and

(b) to provide for the confiscation or return to the State of export of such specimens.

. . .

3. As far as possible, the Parties shall ensure that specimens shall pass through any formalities required for trade with a minimum of delay. To facilitate such passage, a Party may designate ports of exit and ports of entry at which specimens must be presented for clearance. The Parties shall ensure further that all living specimens, during any period of transit, holding or shipment, are properly cared for so as to minimize the risk of injury, damage to health or cruel treatment.

. . .

6. Each Party shall maintain records of trade in specimens of species included in Appendices I, II and III which shall cover:

(a) the names and addresses of exporters and importers; and

(b) the number and type of permits and certificates granted; the States with which such trade occurred; the numbers or quantities and types of specimens, names of species as included in Appendices I, II and III and, where applicable, the size and sex of the specimens in question.

7. Each Party shall prepare periodic reports on its implementation of the present Convention and shall transmit [them] to the Secretariat. . . .

Article IX

Management and Scientific Authorities

1. Each Party shall designate for the purposes of the present Convention:

(a) one or more Management Authorities competent to grant permits or certificates on behalf of that Party; and

(b) one or more Scientific Authorities.

. . .

Article X

Trade with States not Party to the Convention

Where export or re-export is to, or import is from, a State not a Party to the present Convention, comparable documentation issued by the competent authorities in that State which substantially conforms with the requirements of the present Convention for permits and certificates may be accepted in lieu thereof by any Party.

. . .

Article XIV

Effect on Domestic Legislation and International Conventions

1. The provisions of the present Convention shall in no way affect the right of Parties to adopt:

(a) stricter domestic measures regarding the conditions for trade, taking, possession or transport of specimens of species included in Appendices I, II and III, or the complete prohibition thereof; or

(b) domestic measures restricting or prohibiting trade, taking, possession or transport of species not included in Appendix I, II or III.

. . .

Article XV

Amendments to Appendices I and II

1. The following provisions shall apply in relation to amendments to Appendices I and II at meetings of the Conference of the Parties:

(a) Any Party may propose an amendment to Appendix I or II for consideration at the next meeting. . . .

(b) Amendments shall be adopted by a two-thirds majority of Parties present and voting. For these purposes "Parties present and voting" means Parties present and casting an affirmative or negative vote. Parties abstaining from voting shall not be counted among the two-thirds required for adopting an amendment.

(c) Amendments adopted at a meeting shall enter into force 90 days after that meeting for all Parties except those which make a reservation in accordance with paragraph 3 of this Article.

. . .

3. During the period of 90 days provided for by sub-paragraph (c) of paragraph 1 or sub-paragraph (*l*) of paragraph 2 of this Article any Party may by notification in writing to the Depositary Government make a reservation with respect to the amendment. Until such reservation is withdrawn the Party shall be treated as a State not a Party to the present Convention with respect to trade in the species concerned.

Article XVI

Appendix III and Amendments thereto

1. Any Party may at any time submit to the Secretariat a list of species which it identifies as being subject to regulation within its jurisdiction for

the purpose mentioned in paragraph 3 of Article II. Appendix III shall include the names of the Parties submitting the species for inclusion therein, the scientific names of the species so submitted, and any parts or derivatives of the animals or plants concerned that are specified in relation to the species for the purposes of sub-paragraph (b) of Article I.

2. Each list submitted under the provisions of paragraph 1 of this Article shall be communicated to the Parties by the Secretariat as soon as possible after receiving it. The list shall take effect as part of Appendix III 90 days after the date of such communication. At any time after the communication of such list, any Party may by notification in writing to the Depositary Government enter a reservation with respect to any species or any parts or derivatives, and until such reservation is withdrawn, the State shall be treated as a State not a Party to the present Convention with respect to trade in the species or part or derivative concerned.

. . .

Article XXIII

Reservations

1. The provisions of the present Convention shall not be subject to general reservations. Specific reservations may be entered in accordance with the provisions of this Article and Articles XV and XVI.

2. Any State may, on depositing its instrument of ratification, acceptance, approval or accession, enter a specific reservation with regard to:

(a) any species included in Appendix I, II or III; or

(b) any parts or derivatives specified in relation to a species included in Appendix III.

3. Until a Party withdraws its reservation entered under the provisions of this Article, it shall be treated as a State not a Party to the present Convention with respect to trade in the particular species or parts or derivatives specified in such reservation.

Article XXIV

Denunciation

Any Party may denounce the present Convention by written notification to the Depositary Government at any time. The denunciation shall take effect twelve months after the Depositary Government has received the notification.

NOTES

(1) Appendix I lists "all species threatened with extinction which are or may be affected by trade." CITES, Art. II(1). Approximately 830 species are listed in Appendix I, including all whales covered by the IWC moratorium (the remainder are listed in Appendix II), the great apes, tigers, sea turtles, pandas, some orchids and cacti. *See* 50 C.F.R. ¶ ¶ 23.23.

Appendix I species may be traded only if *both* the exporting and the importing States issue permits authorizing the transaction. Note that the requirement for an import permit in addition to an export permit is the primary distinction between Appendix I and Appendices II and III. A second distinction is that, in the case of species listed in Appendix I, specimens must not be used "for primarily commercial purposes"—that is, they cannot be incorporated into products for sale or be sold as food or medicine. As stated in the first CITES fundamental principle (Article II(1)), trade in Appendix I species "must be subject to particularly strict regulation" and "must only be authorized in exceptional circumstances."

What standards must be met before a permit may be issued by the importing country? *See* CITES Art. III(3). What must the respective Scientific Authorities find? *See id.* (2)(a) and (3)(a)–(b). What must the respective Management Authorities find? *See id.* (2)(b)–(d) and (3)(c).

Is the line between commercial and noncommercial uses of specimens always clear? Is a zoo that charges admission to see an endangered animal engaged in a commercial activity? Is an animal part used in a religious ceremony properly imported if the importer is a commercial business that sells such items, at a profit, to local religious communities?

Consider also: can a State opposed to trade in endangered species simply refuse all requests for import or export permits, without regard for whether the request meets the requirements of CITES (*see* Article XIV)?

(2) Appendix II lists two types of species: those that, "although not necessarily now threatened with extinction may become so unless trade in specimens of such species is subject to strict regulation" and those "must be subject to regulation in order that trade in specimens of [the first type] may be brought under effective control." CITES, Art. II(2). Over 25,000 species are included in Appendix II. Note that, by implication, a species may be listed in Appendix II only if it is subject to existing trade; in the case of a species in Appendix I, it is sufficient if the species merely is or "may be" "affected by trade."

Appendix II species may be traded if accompanied by an export permit. What findings must be made before the exporting country is authorized to issue a permit? *See id.* IV(2). What is the role of the importing state? *See id.* IV(3).

(3) Appendix III lists "all species which any Party identifies as being subject to regulation within its jurisdiction for the purpose of preventing or restricting exploitation, and as needing the co-operation of other Parties in the control of trade." *Id.* II(3). Appendix III species may be traded if accompanied by an export permit. What findings must be made before the exporting country is authorized to issue a permit? *See id.* V.

Note that, in effect, the restrictions of Appendix III exist only as an aid to States that voluntarily seek it. No species is listed unless a State specifically asks to have it listed. Even then, an export permit is required only to take a specimen out of the State that has asked to have the species listed—not from all States in which the species might be found. In practice, then, the export-permit requirement is intended to help the State of export control the illegal flow of specimens out of that State.

(4) Exceptions and reservations: Article VII contains several exceptions to the permitting requirements. Several of these should be or will become familiar to you since they reappear—or parties to lawsuits argue that they should appear—in United States domestic law. Note that one of the CITES exceptions is for "pre-existing stocks," an exception that was asserted to be constitutionally required despite the silence of the Eagle Protection Act and the Migratory Bird Treaty Act in *Andrus v. Allard*, 444 U.S. 51 (1979) [Chapter 6]. Similarly, CITES largely excepts specimens captively bred, artificially propagated, or ranched—an issue that was first discussed in *Cayman Turtle Farm, Ltd. v. Andrus*, 478 F.Supp. 125 (D.D.C.1979) [Chapter 1] (*see* Art. VII(4)). Recall that in both cases, concern about poaching was an important rationale for rejecting the exceptions.

In addition, Article XXIII authorizes parties to enter "reservations" with respect to any species and thereby to opt out of the Convention with respect to that listing. What is the status of a Party that enters a reservation as to a particular listing?

(5) Since CITES is not self-executing, enforcement is the responsibility of party States. *See* CITES, Art. VIII, ¶ 1. The need for legislation to implement CITES was one impetus that led to the enactment of the Endangered Species Act of 1973. The Secretary of the Interior acting through the United States Fish and Wildlife Service is both the Scientific Authority and the Management Authority. 16 U.S.C. ¶ 1537a(a)

PERSPECTIVES

(1) At the 1989 biennial meeting of the parties to CITES, the parties voted to list the African elephant in Appendix I, thus effectively banning trade in elephant ivory. The listing decision was the result of a confluence of events.

In 1978, the United States Secretary of the Interior listed the elephant as threatened under the Endangered Species Act. 43 Fed. Reg. 20,504 (1978). Subsequently, the Secretary imposed restrictions on importations of ivory. Congress responded by enacting the African Elephant Protection Act, Pub. L. No. 100–478, § 2001, 102 Stat. 2306, 2315 (1988) (codified at 16 U.S.C. §§ 4201–4245). The Act required a country-by-country review of elephant management practices and imposed restrictions on ivory importation. In quick succession, the Department of the Interior, Kenya, Great Britain, France, and the European Community announced bans on all trade in ivory—between Jun 5 and 9, 1989, nations accounting for nearly half of the market for ivory banned its import.

These events reflected the dramatic decline in elephant populations. The availability of automatic weapons, unstable and often-corrupt governments, and high prices for ivory led to dramatic increases in poaching. Although numbers are imprecise, the population of African elephants dropped from around 1.2 million individuals in 1980 to fewer than 600,000 in 1989. Some east African nations lost 3/4 of their elephants.

Not all nations banned ivory imports, however. Japan, for example, did not ban imports from countries that were members of CITES or from States—such as South Africa, Botswana, and Zimbabwe—that had refused to join the ban. *See generally* Michael J. Glennon, *Has International Law Failed the Elephant?*, 84 Am. J. Int'l L. 1 (1990).

(2) Following the addition of the elephant to Appendix I, Botswana, Malawi, South Africa, Zambia, and Zimbabwe entered reservations to the listing and thus could lawfully continue to trade in ivory. Since 1989, these countries have sought to move the African elephant from Appendix I to Appendix II. The following documents provide a variety of perspectives on the issues:

Recognition of the Benefits of Trade in Wildlife, Document 8.48

PROCEEDINGS OF THE EIGHTH CONFERENCE OF THE PARTIES TO CITES (1992), submitted by Botswana, Malawi, Namibia, and Zimbabwe.

CITES recognizes the economic value of wildlife (*Preamble to the Convention*, ¶ 2) and the principle of sustainable use as an option for management of populations of wild species. However, commercial trade in wildlife and wildlife products has been increasingly portrayed in some quarters as having only negative effects on the conservation of species.

The attached draft resolution seeks to provide a distinction between trade which has a detrimental effect on the survival of a species and trade which is beneficial to conservation.

The overwhelming majority of species of wild flora and fauna which CITES seeks to protect and enhance occur in the developing countries of the world. Many of these countries are characterized by poor economies, low agricultural production and rural poverty.

It is unreasonable to expect human populations, particularly in the most impoverished countries, to neglect an available source of food or money to tolerate dangerous and destructive wild animals in the name of conservation. Conservation programmes need to be developed which take into account the needs of local people, which provide incentives for sustainable management of wildlife and which, where appropriate, ensure economic benefits to them.

With the exception of fisheries, the importance of wildlife as a food source has never received the consideration it deserves. Consequently, its economic value is generally not recognized. This is of particular significance when areas are newly set aside for crop or cattle production in regions where wildlife (or a combination of wildlife and domestic stock) could be economically competitive if properly managed and sustainably used. In many cases wildlife can provide an attractive alternative land use *provided its products are not undervalued*. Where wildlife is properly valued, it is increasing on both private and communal lands in many developing countries and is to some extent replacing lower-valued uses such as cattle production and subsistence agriculture. Whenever such beneficial forms of wildlife use lead to international trade, CITES should not prevent their development.

Total prohibition of the use of wild flora and fauna, whilst appearing superficially to provide a quick answer to many conservation problems, may in practice be totally ineffective in achieving conservation goals. Such imposed "solutions" both alienate local people, who have the greatest influence over the survival of species, and preclude any legal economic return to them. In these circumstances, it should not be surprising if they do not support the actions taken.

When a programme of sustainable use of wild flora and fauna is implemented, the economic benefits that are derived ensure the maintenance of the habitat. All the species sharing that habitat are beneficiaries, thus contributing to the maintenance of biodiversity.

Whether the use of wildlife is beneficial or detrimental depends entirely on the conservation policies and practices in the states concerned. Trade should be viewed as beneficial when it is based upon sustainable use and the financial returns are used to:

a) provide income to rural wildlife producer communities; or

b) to meet the costs of protected-area maintenance by government agencies; or

c) further invest in wildlife development by landholders; or

d) provide income at the national level to developing countries.

It might be argued that providing national income to developing countries is neutral or only slightly beneficial. In the long term it greatly influences the government attitude to land allocated to wildlife and may be very important.

Trade may be viewed as negative in its influence or wild flora and fauna when it is conducted by persons or agencies who return none of the benefits to conservation of the resource and when producer countries have no institutions or mechanisms to ensure that rural peoples benefit from sustainable use of their wild resources.

Trade is too often viewed in the CITES context as a simple matter of harvesting wild resources for financial gain. In practice, many of the most valuable wildlife products available for international trade from developing countries do not result from deliberate exploitation policies to obtain the products. They may result from natural mortality or they may arise as a *by-product* of management of species populations to maintain habitats. Legal trade in such products can be used to enhance species populations.

CITES frequently fails to distinguish between illegal trade and legal trade which is supported by developing countries Scientific and Management Authorities. When illegal trade has appeared to be excessive, CITES Parties have frequently voted to prohibit all trade. The paradox is that the returns from legal trade often provide funds and incentive to contain the illegal trade in developing countries.

In submitting this draft resolution, the proponents are aware that trade must benefit conservation. Only in this way will a growing criticism of wildlife use for commercial purposes be stemmed.

The proponents are further aware of the fundamental problem that many Parties to the Convention do no allocate adequate resources for wildlife conservation, including CITES implementation. Wildlife conservation does not receive sufficient priority, either in relation to other spheres or interest or in relation to other international commitments to the environment. The solution lies in ensuring a high economic value for wildlife coupled with enlightened policies to allow rural peoples to realize that value.

* * *

(a) The producer States arguments are based on economics: international trade in ivory provides a financial incentive to conserve elephants. Are you persuaded?

Consider the following dissenting vote:

In 1961 Milton Friedman argued that Yellowstone National Park should be sold to private enterprise. If enough people wanted to preserve it as a park, he contended, they would vote with their dollars and gate receipts would dictate its continued use as a park—rather than, say, as a source of lumber. If the public wants this kind of activity enough to pay for it, "private enterprises will have every incentive to provide such parks." Essentially this same argument has been made with respect to other natural resources such as wildlife.

Why not leave the future of the elephant to the market? If its greater utility lies in its appeal to tourists, the argument would go, the elephant will and should be preserved by gate receipts at parks; if its greater value lies in its ivory, the ivory will be harvested. Let the market decide.

The trouble with this argument, as applied to either Yellowstone or the elephant, is that it assumes a perfect market, one that will accurately measure all demand for alternative uses (ivory versus protection). But the market does not accurately measure demand for protection. Many people who have never been to Yellowstone nonetheless want it preserved as a park and are willing to pay tax dollars for its preservation merely because they like knowing Yellowstone is there. These preferences for preservation are not measured by gate receipts; the market that reflects conservationist demand is not an economic market—it is a political one. In voting for or against one's congressional representative, one considers whether the representative has voted for or against preservation of Yellowstone. Similarly, tourist revenues in Africa do not accurately reflect the total demand for preservation of the elephant. Many people who have never been to Africa would wish their governments to support elephant conservation simply because they like knowing that the elephant is still there.

Stated in traditional economic terms, the ivory market represents a classic case of market failure. The ivory market produces effects external to the exchange that occurs between a buyer of ivory and a poacher/seller. This "externality" is the cost imposed upon those who prefer that the elephant remain alive—a cost comparable to that imposed upon townspeople by a factory that belches pollutants. The market in both situations fails, for the generator of the externality does not have to pay for harming others. One might object that no market failure occurs because the victims could simply bargain with the poachers (or polluters) and offer them a higher price for stopping than they could get for continuing. But—aside from practical difficulties (such as figuring out whom to pay to stop shooting elephants and how to monitor contractual compliance)—such an approach overlooks the problem of the free rider: not all who benefit from the negotiated restriction will contribute. Private solutions thus fail. What is required, it becomes evident, is a public solution—regulation.

Michael J. Glennon, *Has International Law Failed the Elephant?*, 84 Am. J. Int'l L. 1, 5–6 (1990).

(b) The producer States also argue that ranching wildlife protects biodiversity. Is this correct? Does it depend upon the intensity of the ranching operation? Of the nature of the ranched species? Keep in mind that managing land for one species valued by the market—whether wild or domesticated—can often be harmful to other life forms and lead to considerable ecosystem degradation. Recall the discussion on elk ranching in Chapter 3.

David Favre, *Debate Within the CITES Community: What Direction for the Future?*
33 Nat. Resources J. 875 (1993).

The [Convention on International Trade in Endangered Species of Fauna and Flora (CITES)] is based upon 1960s perceptions of wildlife issues, as seen by North American and European drafters. With the passage of time new ideas and perceptions have developed. Many of the developing countries have a different perspective about wildlife management arising out of their own philosophy, economic reality and social needs. At the 1992 Conference of the Parties in Kyoto, Japan, developing countries began a serious debate about their permitting and management responsibilities under CITES. The buzzword of the halls, as well as of the formal meetings of the Party States, was "sustainable utilization." Was CITES outmoded? Should there be a major overhaul of CITES? Is it working at all? During a two week conference it was impossible for the debate to come to closure, but many issues were fairly raised. The degree to which new issues are satisfactorily resolved will determine the continued viability of the treaty.

Origins of the Current Debate

The present debate is the result of two threads which have become intertwined. The first is a concept. The second is the debate over the fate of the African elephant. There is an interesting historical irony that the same organization which sponsored the initial drafting of CITES is also the promoter of a concept which now represents a threat to the viability of CITES. The World Conservation Union (IUCN), sponsor of CITES in the late 1960s, during the 1980s fostered the concept of "sustainable development." In 1980 the IUCN adopted the World Conservation Strategy, which seeks to establish a plan by which preservation of the ecosystems and the needs of humans can coexist. The plan promotes sustainable use of natural resources, including wildlife.

The second thread began in 1989 at the 7th Conference of the Parties. After a long and emotional debate, the Conference of the Parties listed the African elephant on Appendix I, prohibiting the international commercial sale of ivory. This decision was disputed at the time by a block of South African countries, who ultimately took reservations on the listing. The group, lead primarily by Zimbabwe, came to the Kyoto Conference in 1992 with a number of draft resolutions dealing with basic policy issues, as well as a proposal for downlisting the elephant to Appendix II within their countries. The downlisting would have allowed the resumption of commercial export of ivory from their countries.

Concepts and Context for the Debate

To understand the richness and the fundamental nature of the debate within the international CITES community it is important to break out the mixture of beliefs, attitudes and concepts which are held by the debaters. The nature of the debate, occurring in a two-week meeting every two or so years, does not allow a reflective examination of all the premises held by the debaters. Outcome has to be the focus of efforts, not a understanding of other perspectives, or the seeking of accommodation and compromise on points of belief and principle. . . .

. . .

B.   Sustainable Utilization

"[S]ustainable utilization" is a concept first promoted in the international arena by the IUCN's World Conservation Strategy and more recently in the document referred to as the Brundtland Report as well as *Caring for the Earth: A Strategy for Sustainable Living*. The definition of the term appears simple, yet may vary when more details are sought or policy implemented. While the concept is familiar to wildlife managers, what is new is its application to all human development activities. By the time of the Earth Summit in June of 1992, sustainable development was the accepted principle from which all international environmental discussions started. The Rio Declaration and its 27 Principles focused on how to achieve the goal, not whether the concept ought to be a goal. For example, Principle 3 states, "the right to development must be fulfilled so as to equitably meet development and environmental needs of present and future generations."

Wildlife as a renewable resource is generally within the concept of sustainable use. However, the concept itself is neutral on the issue of whether to use wildlife at all. It merely suggest parameters that ought to used if wildlife are removed from their natural setting. At the Kyoto Conference the "Consumptive Use Block" with its series of proposed resolutions [excerpted above] went a step beyond sustainable use. They promoted the view that the economic value of wildlife, as realized through international trade, must be fostered and encouraged by the CITES process in order to realize the goal of protection and recovery of listed species. In their view the value of wildlife is perceived almost entirely within the framework of removal of individual specimens for purposes of trade. The tenor of the documents submitted by the Consumptive Use Block suggest that economic value, as realized through international trade, is the only value of wildlife that will help conserve species.

A broader view of the use of wildlife has been set out by John Robinson and Kent Redford:

> [W]e and most other authors agree that unless wildlife has some use to people, then wildlife will not be valued by people. If wildlife has no value, then wildlife and its habitat will be destroyed to make way for other land uses. That use of wildlife can be consumptive or nonconsumptive. People can value wildlife for commercial, recreational, scientific, aesthetic or spiritual reasons. But people must use and therefore value wildlife, otherwise wildlife will be lost.

> The pragmatic debate is concerned with whether the use of wildlife furthers or hinders its conservation.... It is unclear, however, what uses will further conservation.... Accepting use as a means to conserve wildlife is not the same as providing economic justifications for conserving wildlife. We do equate value with use, but not all value can be measured using economic indices. To the extent that the use of wildlife brings animals or their products into the marketplace, wildlife will also have economic value, but economic value does not supersede other values, it augments them.... Value cannot be completely discredited in economic terms. Value transcends economics.

This suggests the core of the present debate within CITES. All agree that wildlife must have value to people. However, some seem to be pushing an agenda that focuses exclusively on consumptive economic value. Since CITES does deal with trade issues, they seek to have CITES adopt the policy of saving or conserving specimens through economic exploitation. Some within the CITES community fear that this line of argument is being pursued by exploiters in disguise, that under the pretense of consumptive use programs specimens will be consumed in ever greater numbers to the ultimate detriment of the entire species.

A key premise for those promoting consumptive use of wildlife is that it would be done only within the context of "sustainable use." Initially this seems logical and unassailable; if a use is sustainable, then by definition it can not threaten the population of a species. However, closer examination reveals it is not all that simple.

Representative of those seeking to focus on the economic utilization of wildlife is the IUCN subgroup referred to as the IUCN/SSC Specialist Group on Sustainable Use of Wild Species ("Sustainable Use Committee"). While there is no formal tie between CITES and this IUCN group, there is significant crossover of participants, and the policy document developed by this organization will most likely be the base point for discussions within the CITES community as well.

The Sustainable Use Committee has produced a draft document, *Criteria and Requirements for Sustainable Use of Wild Species*. The drafters of this document seem to hold the same view as that of the Consumptive Use Block at the Kyoto Conference. "The social and economic benefits from sustainable use can provide a powerful incentive to conserve wild species and their supporting ecosystem, provided the people most likely to have an impact on the species and ecosystems concerned receive an adequate share of those benefits." The factual basis for such a statement has been contested by at least one reviewer of the document.

This document is an example of how a logical proposition can be twisted when specific policies are adopted. The logical start point for a sustainable use management program is the determination that a particular use is sustainable. Yet in the specifics of the 2nd Draft of the *Guideline,* it is quite clear that use of wildlife can proceed without that determination, and indeed that only upon a showing of declining populations would the use of a species be reduced or stopped. This reversal of position has been accomplished by a shift of the burden of proof. In this document the burden is placed on those who seek to stop exploitation, rather than on those who wish to engage in the exploitation.

CITES is not silent on the issue of sustainable use, although that term is not used. It is fundamental to the permit granting process that an export permit may be granted only so long as the Scientific Authority of the exporting country advises "that such export will not be detrimental to the survival of that species." Therefore, any State program or practice that is sustainable should also be non-detrimental and allowable under the treaty. Given that CITES accommodates the practice of sustainable use, it is not clear why so many Party States and individuals are attacking CITES as inadequate. Like the concept of sustainable use, CITES is silent on the necessity or appropriateness of engaging in international trade.

* * *

Professor Favre is skeptical of the concept of "sustainable use." What would he prefer as a guiding management philosophy? Consider the following point of view from a conservation biologist:

DANIEL BOTKIN, *Why The Elephants Died: Breakdown in the Management of Living Resources in* DISCORDANT HARMONIES

15–19 (1990).

A Landsat satellite image taken in the late 1970s from 140 miles above the Earth over East Africa shows a curious geometric feature—two straight lines, each stretching 50 miles or more, one north and the other south-southeast, meeting at an obtuse angle, as though a planetary engineer had sketched the lines with a triangle and pencil at a drafting table. To the east of the lines, a dull brown indicates an area so thinly vegetated that an almost bare soil dominates the reflectance of light from the surface. To the west, a garish red indicates dense vegetation in infrared wavelengths, which are invisible to the naked human eye.

About the same time that the satellite orbited silently far overhead, I flew a few hundred feet above the ground in a single-engine aircraft ... from whose noisy cockpit one of the boundaries was clearly visible. What appears as one line in the satellite view was revealed from this nearer vantage point as four: a railroad, a highway, and two fire breaks stretching into the blue haze, of the horizon toward Nairobi. On the east of the line lay one of two parts of Tsavo, one of Kenya's largest national parks, covering approximately 5,000 square miles. It was the park land that appeared brown from the satellite and could be seen now as a desertlike dusty soil with a thin scattering of live and dead shrubs and trees, among which almost no game was visible. The land outside the park, to the west, which is red in the Landsat image, contained dense thickets of dark green trees and shrubs. The scene was strange from this elevation, just as it was from the satellite, appearing as a photographic negative of one's expectation of a park. Rather than an island of green in a wasted landscape, Tsavo appeared as a wasted island amid a green land.

The character of Tsavo was the result of 30 years of interplay between people and nature; of vagaries of climate, including a major drought that persisted through 1969 and 1970; and of a controversy over management that involved issues as old as Western civilization—the character of nature undisturbed by human influence and the proper role of human beings in nature. Perhaps nowhere else was the impact of well-meaning management of wild nature so visible from a planetary perspective. Something had failed at Tsavo, in spite of the best intentions, and the failure of management of living resources was an example of a breakdown not merely in management, but also in myths, beliefs, and fundamental paradigms that modern technological civilization held about nature.

The Elephants and Lessons of Tsavo

Tsavo became a park in 1948. Its first-warden, David Sheldrick, looked at its dry flat landscape, thickly vegetated by *Commiphora* trees and wild sisal, and knew that the park could attract tourists only to see wild game, not other scenic beauty. But much of the big game had been shot around the turn of the century by European settlers, and of the remaining wildlife, black rhinoceros and elephant were under intense pressure from poachers.

Sheldrick devoted years to building roads, providing year-round water for the wildlife, and eradicating poaching by catching and driving off poachers through a kind of antiguerrilla effort using Land Rovers, aircraft, and World War II repeating rifles. A thousand miles of roads were built to increase tourists' access. The Galena River was dammed, and artesian wells were dug. These measures resulted in a rapid buildup of elephants that took their toll on the vegetation, knocking down and killing trees and shrubs. The land seemed on its way to becoming desert. By 1959, areas where the vegetation had once been so thick that elephants were visible only if they actually crossed a road in front of tourists began to resemble a "lunar landscape," Sheldrick's wife, Daphne, wrote years later. Sheldrick became concerned. He wrote in a report that

> during the past few years, the destruction of vegetation by elephant has reached serious proportions. If present trends continue, it is doubtful if the Park can continue to support the existing population much longer. What effect this will have on other species remains to be seen, but I think it is important that we should seek scientific advice regarding this problem as soon as possible.

As with so many of these cases, the effects of human actions and the vagaries of the natural environment, including recurrent droughts, were confounded, and it was difficult to decide what to do. By 1966, most people believed that the park could be saved only by removing many elephants, and for a while Sheldrick agreed.

But the rains came again, and the park seemed to recover; instead of the thicket of trees and shrubs, grasses sprouted and seemed to promise better food for the wildlife. The elephant population continued to grow, and the resource-management controversy worsened. The Ford Foundation agreed to sponsor a scientific study, and Richard Laws, one of the world's foremost experts on elephants and other large mammals, who had been studying elephants in Uganda, agreed to head the project. He and other scientists and some conservationists soon concluded that about 3,000 elephants should be shot to keep the population within its food supply and protect the game from the dangerous effects of its intrinsic capacities for growth. Sheldrick at first favored such action, but in the end reversed himself and returned to the very old idea that nature can take care of itself and that human interference is undesirable. He decided that "the conservation policy for Tsavo should be directed towards the attainment of a natural ecological climax, and that our participation towards this aim should be restricted to such measures as the control of fires, poaching, and other forms of human interference." At that time, the phrase "natural ecological climax" was taken to mean nature in a mature condition, the result of a long series of stages that occurs after a catastrophic clearing of the landscape and, once attained, persists indefinitely without change. Many, like Sheldrick, accepted the "climax" condition as the truly natural and most desirable state of wilderness. When the trustees of the park sided with Sheldrick and concluded that more studies, especially of the vegetation, were needed, Laws resigned and returned to England.

Sheldrick had come to believe that the die-offs of elephants during the droughts could be regarded as a natural culling, bringing the number of elephants "in line with the carrying capacity of their particular dry weather feeding grounds," producing a selective death of the weaker, ensuring a healthier population, and allowing the regeneration of vegetation. In short, he believed that nature used the droughts to maintain or restore its proper balance. But the drought of 1969 and 1970 was much worse than previous ones of the century, and as an estimated 6,000 elephants starved to death, they destroyed the vegetation, producing the scene still visible a decade later from the air and from space. Elephants and human beings together had drafted the lines on the Landsat image.

Here was a controversy very different from the better publicized environmental issues of the 1960s. Then, as environmentalism was achieving worldwide recognition, most environmental issues seemed to produce two extreme camps that disagreed on goals: the environmentalists seeming to argue that the salvation of civilization and the human spirit lay in the preservation of nature, and their opponents seeming to respond that environmentalism threatened industry, economics, progress, and perhaps civilization. In a quite different way, the disagreement at Tsavo was among conservationists who shared basic goals and a fundamental love of wild nature: they wished to conserve in perpetuity fine examples of wild nature for their own sake and for people to view. But they disagreed on methods.

. . . .

The story of Tsavo illustrates several important issues. The idea of the character of nature undisturbed by human influence is complex and open to numerous interpretations. There were two dominant opinions about what had happened at Tsavo. One was that undisturbed nature always achieves a balance, a constancy, a stability—the "natural ecological climax" ... —and human beings only interfere with and destroy that balance. Therefore, the proper role for people is hands off. The other interpretation was that nature varies greatly, and human actions are required to create a balance. In regard to Tsavo, as with most other environmental issues of our century, the former belief won out, and the devastation of Tsavo was a product, at least in part, of this policy.

There is a third possibility: even Tsavo, large as it is, is too small to sustain an elephant population "naturally," and before the European colonization of Africa and the establishment of modem African nations, the elephants, when subjected to one of the recurrent droughts, would have migrated from Tsavo to another part of Africa. This possibility accepts change as intrinsic at a scale as large as Tsavo and is not consistent with the old idea of a balance of nature at that scale, but is consistent with the new perspective toward which we are moving. Even so, one who insisted that a balance of nature must exist could still argue that at the scale of the entire African continent, the elephant population must have achieved a constancy over time before the imposition of a political geography over an ecological geography.

Twenty years after the great Tsavo drought, elephants in Africa are in great danger from rampant illegal poaching that is reducing them to a threatened fraction of their former abundance. Clearly, the direct control of poaching, as Sheldrick did so well, is necessary if elephants are to survive. But the lesson of Tsavo is that wise management cannot stop simply with the eradication of poaching. Wise management in the future might require harvesting excess elephant populations when or if they occur again in parks and preserves, but would also control killings that impose a rate of decline that exceeds the reproductive capacities of elephant populations, a rate that is occurring because of the illegal poaching. The rate of change is the problem, not the harvesting per se. In the last analysis, the survival of elephants will depend on our perception of them within the context of their total, variable environment.

* * *

(a) If management of elephant populations is required by increased human populations is there any reason why the valuable parts of the elephants that must be killed should not become items of commerce?

The 1997 CITES conference of parties created a special listing in Appendix II for elephants from Botswana, Namibia, and Zimbabwe; all other elephants remain on Appendix I. The three nations were permitted to sell an "experiment" quota of 59 tons of ivory to Japan—subject to several conditions, including correction of enforcement and control problems and an earmarking of the receipts from the sale to elephant conservation. *See* Stephen Kass, *Corporate Brief: Environmental Law,* NAT. L.J., Aug. 11, 1997.

(b) Aldo Leopold and the Wisconsin deer wars: Over-populations of particular animals have posed recurring problems and have often led to conflicting views of how and whether wildlife managers should intervene to cull the perceived excess. Botkin, using Tsavo by way of illustration, is quick to conclude that the anti-culling position has been the one embraced by "environmentalists" and that they have embraced it out of a mistaken belief that "undisturbed nature always achieves a balance, a constancy, a stability." His simple story, however, can be refined, particularly as a generalization.

Excessive deer populations in Wisconsin in the 1930s and 1940s led Aldo Leopold and other conservationists to propose culling deer herds in parts of that state where browse damage and winter starvation were occurring. Opposition to the culling came from various quarters: hunting groups who enjoyed high game populations, chambers of commerce that believed high deer populations would draw tourists, and citizens repulsed by the idea of slaughtering "innocent" deer (the movie *Bambi* was released at the height of the controversy). Professional wildlife managers did not then (or at any time since) embrace the "balance of nature" view that Botkin describes—indeed, Leopold himself, author of the nation's leading text (*Game Management* (1933)), was quite pointed in describing its flaws. Although popular opposition to deer culling was in many instances infused with a sense that nature on its own would achieve a balance, opponents were motivated far more by economic and moral concerns. At the time, the term "environmentalist" was not yet in common usage; if it had been, the label would have been attached, not to the anti-culling side, but to Leopold and his pro-culling colleagues. The story of Leopold and the deer wars is related in detail in Curt Meine, *Aldo Leopold: His Life and Work* (1988).

As the Wisconsin tale reveals, conflicts over excessive populations can turn on far more than ecological models. Good science of the type that Botkin promotes will not prevail simply by banishing popular misunderstandings about nature's innate tendency to achieve a "balance." More potent, in the case of elephants, whales, and deer, are the moral and economic implications of human intervention—which typically have little to do with ecological models, good or bad. The precautionary principle is also potentially relevant: a person may agree that human intervention is appropriate, but oppose action in a given setting—particularly the wide-spread slaughter of large mammals—until greater confidence is achieved in human understanding. Finally, there is the issue of institutional competence: a person may agree that intervention is needed, but oppose intervention in a given setting due to distrust of the agency or entity that will undertake the action. For a nuanced and comprehensive examination of the multitude of positions on a more recent controversy over the culling of a deer herd, see JAN E. DIZARD, GOING WILD: HUNTING, ANIMAL RIGHTS, AND THE CONTESTED MEANING OF NATURE (1994).

(c) Protecting species that cross international boundaries: The African elephant is listed as a species of concern not just under CITES but also under the Convention on the Conservation of Migratory Species of Wild Animals (in force, 1983), commonly known as the Bonn Convention. The Bonn Convention provides direct legal protection, in the form of distinct obligations imposed on Party States, for a small number of listed endangered species that "cyclically and predictably" cross international boundaries ("endangered" is defined as "in danger of extinction throughout all or a significant portion of its range"). In the case of listed species, Parties "shall endeavor" (i) "to conserve and, where feasible and appropriate, restore ... habitats"; (ii) "to prevent, remove, compensate for or minimize, as appropriate, the adverse effects of activities or obstacles that seriously impede or prevent the migration of the species"; and (iii), "to the extent feasible and appropriate, to prevent, reduce or control factors that are endangering ... the species." Article III(4). In addition, parties are obligated to prohibit the taking of animals belong to such species except in narrowly tailored circumstances. Article III(5).

African elephants are listed under the Bonn Convention, not as an endangered species, but among the far more numerous species that have an "unfavourable conservation status" (as complexly defined). Species on this list (Appendix II) are not directly protected. Instead, the Convention provides a framework in which individual States can enter into agreements for the protection of such species. Progress in protecting Appendix II species was slow during the Convention's first decade, largely because Parties sought to protect species only through the cumbersome process of negotiating formal treaties. By 1994 only four such treaties had taken effect. Since then, the Conference of the Parties has encouraged States to develop informal Memoranda of Understandings (MOUs), setting forth the plans and expectations of the signatories to the MOUs. Because they are not legally binding MOUs can be developed more rapidly and with less political disruption. Many MOUs have been negotiated since the mid–1990s. The documents can readily be turned into treaties; in the meantime, however, and so long as the signing parties adhere to them, they offer protection for the species covered.

Few nations in the Western Hemisphere have become parties to the Bonn Convention; none in North America. The principal migratory animals in North America—birds—are covered by existing treaties, but other species do cross national boundaries, including several large predators.

(d) An informative web site is maintained by the Secretariat at <http://www.cites.-org>.

Section 5.   Habitat-Based Preservation: Wetlands

International conventions protecting wildlife are the most common form of international wildlife law. Far less common are treaties protecting wildlife habitat.

NOTES

(1) Convention on Nature Protection and Wildlife Preservation in the Western Hemisphere: The first international agreement to seek the conservation of wildlife habitat was the Convention on Nature Protection and Wildlife Preservation in the Western Hemisphere, 56 Stat. 1354,

U.S.T.S. 981 (entered into force, April 30, 1942). One treatise calls the treaty "a visionary document, well ahead of its time in terms of the concepts it espouses. The protection of species from man-induced extinction, the establishment of protected areas, the regulation of international trade in wildlife, special measures for migratory birds and the need for international cooperation are all elements of wildlife conservation which are covered by the Convention—many of them for the first time by an international treaty." SIMON LYSTER, *supra,* at 97–98. The Convention's emphasis on habitat protection as a means of protecting wildlife species, while farsighted, suffered from a basic flaw: the Convention "fail[ed] to set up an administrative structure to review and promote enforcement of its terms. In consequence . . . it has become a 'Sleeping Convention'. . . . " *Id.* at 98. Nonetheless, the Parties did commit themselves to establishing "national parks, national reserves, nature monuments and strict wilderness reserves."

(2) Convention on Wetlands of International Importance, Especially as Waterfowl Habitat: A more recent and comprehensive treaty is the Convention on Wetlands of International Importance, Especially as Waterfowl Habitat, T.I.A.S. No. 11084, 996 U.N.T.S. 245 (entered into force, December 21, 1975). The Convention was signed at Ramsar, Iran in 1971— and hence is commonly known as the Ramsar Convention. The Convention grew out of concerns about declining waterfowl populations—a condition highlighted by a NGO, International Waterfowl Resources Bureau (now, Wetlands International). But the importance of wetlands extends beyond waterfowl:

> Wetlands are amongst the most productive life-support systems on Earth, and their conservation is important for biological, hydrological and economic reasons. They provide essential habitat for hundreds of species of waterfowl, fish, amphibians, reptiles, mammals and plants. They act as natural sponges which control flood and droughts. A subtropical saltmarsh may produce organic material at more than twice the rate of the most fertile hayfield, and two thirds of the commercially important fish and shellfish harvested along the U.S. Atlantic seaboard—and 98% of those harvested in the Gulf of Mexico—depend on estuaries and associated wetlands for food, spawning grounds and nurseries for their fry. In spite of their valuable functions, wetlands in many parts of the world have been destroyed at an alarming rate in recent decades by drainage, land reclamation and pollution.

SIMON LYSTER, *supra,* at 183. Despite the crucial values of wetlands, they are among the most threatened habitat types. In the United States, for example, legal protection for wetlands face stiff opposition from those who claim that any restriction on development is an invasion of property rights.

"*Desiring* to stem the progressive encroachment on and loss of wetlands now and in the future," the Ramsar Convention established a framework for funding and monitoring wetlands conservation; it also created a process for obtaining commitments from Parties for wetlands conservation.

(a) "Wetlands" is defined by the Convention as "areas of marsh, fen, peatland or water, whether natural or artificial, permanent or temporary, with water that is static or flowing, fresh, brackish or salt, including areas of marine water the depth of which at low tide does not exceed six metres." Art. 1(1). This is a broad definition, including habitats as diverse as mangrove swamps, wet meadows, peat bogs, coastal beaches, tidal flats, tropical rivers, and coral reefs.

(b) The List of Wetlands of International Importance: Application of the Convention is triggered by the listing of a wetland. To become a signatory, a country must designate "suitable wetlands within its territory." *Id.* 2(1). The Convention provides only very general criteria for "suitability": "Wetlands should be selected for the List on account of their international significance in terms of ecology, botany, zoology, limnology or hydrology." *Id.* 2(2). Given the generality of the criteria, the Parties to the Convention in 1980 adopted the "Cagliari criteria" that established soft law standards in three areas: quantitative criteria for wetlands important for waterfowl; criteria for wetlands important to plants and animals; and criteria for wetlands that are representative or unique. The criteria for wetlands of international importance for waterfowl are:

> a) regularly supports 10,000 ducks, geese and swans, or 10,000 coots, or 20,000 waders; or
>
> b) regularly supports 1% of the individuals in a population or one species or sub-species of waterfowl; or
>
> c) regularly supports 1% of the breeding pairs in a population of one species or sub-species of waterfowl.

SIMON LYSTER, *supra,* at 188. The criteria for wetlands that should be considered of international importance for plants or animals are:

> a) supports an appreciable number of rare, vulnerable or endangered species or subspecies of plant or animal; or
>
> b) is of special value for maintaining the genetic or ecological diversity of a region because of the quality and peculiarities of its flora and fauna; or
>
> c) is of special value as the habitat of plants or animals at a critical stage of their biological cycles; or
>
> d) is of special value for its endemic plant or animal species or communities.

Id.

As of August, 2001, the Parties have designated some 1079 wetlands comprising 82.1 million hectares (ha).[1] Canada has designated 36 sites totalling 13,051,501 ha; Japan has 11 listed wetlands with a combined area of 83,725 ha; the United Kingdom has listed 162 sites with an area of 841,093 ha; the United States has designated 17 wetlands totalling 1,177,-980 ha.

(c) The Montreux Record, established by Resolution 4.8 (1990), is the "record of Ramsar sites where changes in ecological character have occurred, are occurring or are likely to occur as a result of technological

---

1. A hectare is 2.47 acres.

developments, pollution or other human interference." The List is maintained by the Ramsar Bureau in consultation with the Contracting Parties concerned. Resolution 5.4 (1993) specified that the purpose of the Montreux Record is to identify priority sites for positive national and international conservation attention, including applications of the Ramsar Advisory Mission and allocation of resources available under financial mechanisms. The Everglades in the United States is on the Montreux Record.

(d) Site management: Ramsar requires the Parties "to promote the conservation of the wetlands included in the List, and as far as possible the wise use of wetlands in their territory." Art. 3(1). Although "wise use" is not defined in the Convention, the Parties have subsequently given the term substantive content. In 1987, the Conference of Parties in Regina, Canada defined "wise use": "[t]he wise use of wetlands is their sustainable utilization for the benefit of mankind in a way compatible with the maintenance of the natural properties of the ecosystem." "Sustainable utilization" is defined as "[h]uman use of wetland so that it may yield the greatest continuous benefit to present generations while maintaining its potential to meet the need of and aspirations of future generations."

(e) The legal consequence of inclusion on the list are minimal. The Convention specifies that Parties are "to promote the conservation of the wetlands included in the List," in part, by "establishing nature reserves" on the wetlands. Arts. 3(1), 4(1). An obligation to "promote" conservation imposes no obligation to ensure that listed wetlands are actually protected. One international law treatise commented that, "[a]mong the treaties providing for an international list of protected sites, the Ramsar Convention is the least demanding." CYRILLE DE KLEMM, *supra,* at 149. Nonetheless, the Convention has been instrumental in protecting a number of significant wetlands from degradation or destruction. *See* SIMON LYSTER, *supra,* at 192–93.

(f) An informative web site is located at <http://www.ramsar.org>.

SECTION 6.   TRADE AND WILDLIFE: SEA TURTLES AND SHRIMP, DOLPHINS AND TUNA

a.   "FREE TRADE," "DEREGULATED INTERNATIONAL COMMERCE," AND THE ENVIRONMENT

NOTES

(1) "Free trade" has become a foundational principle in American foreign policy. The primary arguments offered for liberalizing international trade focus on increasing efficiency in the use of resources and the (presumed) concomitant economic growth and wealth creation. Proponents contend that these effects will in turn lead to increased environmental protection:

> Is economic growth, driven by trade, part of the problem or part of the solution? One reason why environmental protection is lagging in many countries is low incomes. Countries that live on the margin may simply

not be able to afford to set aside resources for pollution abatement, nor may they think that they should sacrifice their growth prospects to help solve global pollution problems that in large part have been caused by the consuming life style of richer countries. If poverty is at the core of the problem, economic growth will be part of the solution, to the extent that it allows countries to shift gear from more immediate concerns to long run sustainability issues. Indeed, at least some empirical evidence suggests that pollution increases at the early stages of development but decreases after a certain income level has been reached, an observation that has become known in academic circles as the Environmental Kuznets Curve (EKC).[1]

Trade Liberalization Reinforces the Need for Environmental Cooperation, World Trade Organization Press Release (Oct. 8, 1999).

Opponents of liberalized trading regimes often question the underlying assumption that economic growth is paramount: achieving social goals, mitigating environmental impacts, and protecting national sovereignty are often cited as competing objectives. Herman Daly—a leading "ecological"economist—captures the dissent:

> The correct name for "free trade" (who can oppose freedom?) is "deregulated international commerce," which should serve to remind us that deregulation is not always a good policy. Recall recent experience with the deregulation of the savings and loan institutions, the junk bond financed leveraged buyouts, [etc.] Any profit-making entity has an interest in externalizing costs. Regulation is needed to keep costs internal, so that cost reductions come from true efficiency, rather than simply throwing the costs onto others in the form of lowered standards.

Herman E. Daly, *Problems with Free Trade: Neoclassical and Steady–State Perspectives, in* TRADE AND THE ENVIRONMENT 147, 151 (Durwood Zaelke *et al.,* eds, 1993).

(2) Tension points between trade and environmental protection: Environmental regulations with direct impacts on international trade tend to fall into four categories. The two most common are (a) regulations that restrict the characteristics of products that can be sold (*e.g.,* rules governing the permissible lead content of gasoline or mandating particular pollution control features on cars), and (b) regulations that specify how products are made or raw materials produced (*e.g.,* rules restricting pollution generated by manufacturing plants, or requiring coal miners to restore mining sites). The former are commonly called "product standards"; the latter, "process standards." The other two categories are (c) rules governing the

---

1. The Kuznets Curve is the name applied to the conclusion of a World Health Organization (WHO) study that found that pollution levels tended to rise until a certain level of gross domestic product (GDP) was achieved. After that pollution declined. *See* GENE GROSSMAN AND ALAN KRUEGER, ENVIRONMENTAL IMPACTS OF A NORTH AMERICAN FREE TRADE AGREEMENT (1991). Unfortunately, not all pollutants follow Kuznets Curves; some continue to rise with increases in GDP. In addition, the report demonstrates correlation rather then causation. Finally, much of the pollution reduction results from shifting polluting activities (*e.g.,* manufacturing, mining, and chemical processing) to other locations, often in other countries.

handling and disposal of waste and (c) rules limiting the flow of wildlife and wildlife products. Rules in the final category plainly affect wildlife. But as the following materials illustrate, wildlife may also be involved in product and process standards.

This section centers around a single, dominant question: Is it permissible for a State to close or restrict its domestic markets to imported products that are produced in ways that are harmful to wildlife outside that State? States plainly have the power and right to exclude products that are harmful in themselves—at least so long as they are not discriminating against or among international sources of such products. But what of products that are both safe and physically identical to products sold within the State? Can a State exclude timber that has been harvested by clearcutting the habitat of an endangered species while allowing sale of identical timber produced in other, less damaging ways? Can it exclude manufactured goods if the manufacturer dumped toxic wastes in a river? Such questions are inextricably linked to another: Is a person who buys such timber or manufactured goods morally implicated in their production?

Individuals acting alone clearly may refuse to buy goods produced in ways they find morally or prudentially wrong. If individuals can do so, why should communities or States be barred from acting collectively? If knowledgeable individuals view two products (two physically identical pine boards, for example) as different simply because of how they are produced, should international trade law also view them as different products? That is, might differences in production processes alone be sufficient—in at least some instances—to differentiate two physically identical products, and thus to blur the distinction between product standards and process standards?

Process-focused bans on importing products into a large market such as the United States can have a powerful effect on how such products are produced. Thus, import restrictions can be tools to mitigate environmental harms taking place elsewhere. In addition, such bans can help level the playing field of international competition. If producers of a given good in the United States face costly environmental restrictions on production methods, is it fair for them to be undercut by foreign producers who do not face such restrictions? If the answer to this question is "no," United States producers gain a powerful argument (international competitiveness) when they approach lawmakers seeking to weaken environmental laws. If the answer is "yes," however, note that producers (and lawmakers seeking to please them) gain a powerful argument to justify trade restrictions that protect United States businesses. Finally, there is the question of how far a country such as the United States can rightfully go in insisting that other States take better care of their environments—over which, according to international law, those foreign States have sovereign powers. Is the United States in such instances improperly imposing its own values on other countries? Recall Japan's similar argument that the United States is engaging in cultural imperialism when it seeks to ban the commercial harvest of whales. Is it a sufficient response to argue that United States laws only apply to goods coming into the United States, and that other States are free to do as they please so long as they do not try to sell their products in the United States?

b. THE INTERNATIONAL TRADING REGIME: GATT AND THE WTO

One component of the post-World War II drive to create international organizations to deal with international problems was the General Agreement on Tariffs and Trade (GATT). GATT negotiations were concluded in 1947; negotiations on the administrative institution—the International Trade Organization—were abandoned when it became apparent that the United States Senate would not ratify the agreement. GATT has evolved primarily through multilateral negotiating "rounds," the most recent of which was the Uruguay Round. The Uruguay Round created the administrative and legal structure envisioned in the 1940s, the Word Trade Organization (WTO).

GATT is designed to produce progressive reductions in trade barriers among Parties. As such, GATT is prohibitory; its core principles each prohibit some form of discrimination.

(i) GATT'S CORE PRINCIPLES

GATT has three core principles.

First, the Most Favored Nation obligation prohibits discrimination between products of other Party states:

Article I

General Most–Favoured–Nation Treatment

1. With respect to customs duties and charges of any kind imposed on or in connection with importation or exportation or imposed on the international transfer of payments for imports or exports, and with respect to the method of levying such duties and charges, and with respect to all rules and formalities in connection with importation and exportation, and with respect to all matters referred to in paragraphs 2 and 4 of Article III,* any advantage, favour, privilege or immunity granted by any contracting party to any product originating in or destined for any other country shall be accorded immediately and unconditionally to the like product originating in or destined for the territories of all other contracting parties.

The second core principle prohibits discrimination between imported and domestically produced goods:

Article III

National Treatment on Internal Taxation and Regulation

1. The contracting parties recognize that internal taxes and other internal charges, and laws, regulations and requirements affecting the internal sale, offering for sale, purchase, transportation, distribution or use of products, and internal quantitative regulations requiring the mixture, processing or use of products in specified amounts or proportions, should not be applied to imported or domestic products so as to afford protection to domestic production.

2.   The products of the territory of any contracting party imported into the territory of any other contracting party shall not be subject, directly or indirectly, to internal taxes or other internal charges of any kind in excess of those applied, directly or indirectly, to like domestic products. Moreover, no contracting party shall otherwise apply internal taxes or other internal charges to imported or domestic products in a manner contrary to the principles set forth in paragraph 1.

. . .

4.   The products of the territory of any contracting party imported into the territory of any other contracting party shall be accorded treatment no less favourable than that accorded to like products of national origin in respect of all laws, regulations and requirements affecting their internal sale, offering for sale, purchase, transportation, distribution or use. . . .

The third and final fundamental principle prohibits quantitative restrictions on imported goods:

Article XI

General Elimination of Quantitative Restrictions

1.   No prohibitions or restrictions other than duties, taxes or other charges, whether made effective through quotas, import or export licences or other measures, shall be instituted or maintained by any contracting party on the importation of any product of the territory of any other contracting party or on the exportation or sale for export of any product destined for the territory of any other contracting party.

NOTES

(1) "like products"—"dolphin safe tuna": The crucial term in these provision obviously is "like product"—if the products are "like products," discrimination is prohibited; if the products are not "like products," distinctions are permissible. As noted above, a crucial question from an environmental perspective is whether two products are "like products" if they are produced using different processes or production methods (PPM). Is physical similarity alone the touchstone? For example, is tuna that is produced by setting nets on dolphins like tuna that is not captured by killing dolphins? Does "dolphin-safe tuna," in other words, differ sufficiently from "not-dolphin-safe tuna"?

Under the United States Marine Mammal Protection Act (MMPA) countries exporting tuna to the United States were required either (1) to establish that they had a regulatory program equivalent to that of the United States and that their incidental take of dolphins while fishing for tuna was no more than 125% of that of the United States, or (2) agree to ban purse seining for dolphins, require observers on all tuna boats, and reduce their incidental take of dolphins. Mexico challenged these requirements, contending that the tuna in the can was a like product to all other canned tuna. The GATT Panel agreed:

Article III:4 calls for a comparison of the treatment of imported tuna *as a product* with that of domestic tuna *as a product*. Regulations governing the taking of dolphins incidental to the taking of tuna could not possibly affect tuna as a product. Article III:4 therefore obliges the United States to accord treatment to Mexican tuna no less favourable than that accorded to United States tuna, whether or not the incidental taking of dolphins by Mexican vessels corresponds to that of United States vessels.

GATT Dispute Panel Report on Mexican Complaint Concerning United States Restrictions on Imports of Tuna, Aug. 16, 1991, 30 I.L.M. 1594, § 5.14 at 1618 (1991) (*Tuna/Dolphin I*). *See also* GATT Dispute Panel Report on European Economic Community Complaint Concerning United States Restrictions on Imports of Tuna, June 1994, 33 I.L.M. 839 (1994) (*Tuna/Dolphin II*).[2] Or, as Gertrude Stein might have put it, tuna-in-a-can is tuna-in-a-can is tuna-in-a-can.

Note that in the dolphin-tuna controversy both protectionist and preservationist motives were present: the domestic tuna-fishing industry want a level playing field (to shield it from foreign competition) and environmentalists wanted to "save the dolphins." Is it possible to tease out the contributing factors in the policy decision? Should an importing State that is seeking to impose trade restrictions bear the burden of doing so?

(2) "Eco-imperialism"?: The tuna-dolphin cases can be seen as raising the issue that we also saw in the whaling context: recall the Japanese argument that the attempt to prohibit it from killing whales was cultural imperialism:

> Behind the environmental argument against free trade is also the zeal to impose one's ethical preferences on other communities and nations. But the use of *state power* in the shape of trade sanctions to force others into accepting one's own idiosyncratic choice of ethical concerns seems wholly inappropriate....

> For instance, one can appreciate that Americans are particularly touched by dolphins being caught cruelly in purse seine nets set for tuna. But I wonder.... If Americans have their dolphins, Indians have their sacred cows. Animal rights activists object to American slaughterhouses .....

> ... [T]he poor countries ... see "eco-imperialism" when the strong nations use trade power to force their preferred values on the weaker nations .....

Jagdish Bhagwati, *Trade and the Environment: The False Conflict?, in* TRADE AND THE ENVIRONMENT 159, 170–71 (Durwood Zaelke *et al.,* eds, 1993).

Furthermore, proponents of unregulated trade argue that allowing nations to distinguish between good based on production processes threatens unconstrained protectionism:

> ... it is difficult to think of a way to effectively contain the cross-border assertion of priorities. If governments suspend the trading

---

2. Neither of the *Tuna/Dolphin* decisions has been adopted GATT.

rights of other nations because they unilaterally assert that their environmental priorities are superior to those of others, then the same approach can be employed on any number of grounds. . . .

Changing the world trading rules so as to permit the suspension of trading rights of others by individual contracting parties, based simply on the unilateral and extraterritorial assertion of their environmental priorities, undoubtedly would be difficult because many countries would view such a change to be a big step down a slippery slope.

GATT, *Trade and Environment Report* 33–34 (1992). Should the lowest common denominator prevail? Can these arguments be distinguished from a race to the bottom in which environmental restrictions are abandoned as an impediment to the only relevant value, wealth creation?

(ii) GATT'S ENVIRONMENTAL EXCEPTIONS

Article XX

General Exceptions

Subject to the requirement that such measures are not applied in a manner which would constitute a means of arbitrary or unjustifiable discrimination between countries where the same conditions prevail, or a disguised restriction on international trade, nothing in this Agreement shall be construed to prevent the adoption or enforcement by any contracting party of measures:

. . .

(*b*)   necessary to protect human, animal or plant life or health;

. . .

(*g*)   relating to the conservation of exhaustible natural resources if such measures are made effective in conjunction with restrictions on domestic production or consumption;

NOTES

(1) Article XX(b): What types of State-enforced discrimination are permitted by Article XX(b)? At least two issues have arisen. First, what is the meaning of the term "necessary"? Second, may the section be applied to protect animals outside the jurisdiction of the State applying the sanction?

In *Tuna/Dolphin I*, the United States argued that its embargo of Mexican-caught tuna was permitted under XX(b) because the action was "necessary" in that "there was no alternative measure reasonably available" to achieve the objective of reducing dolphin mortality. *Tuna/Dolphin I*, 30 I.L.M. § 5.24 at 1618. Mexico disagreed, contending (a) that the provision did not apply "outside the jurisdiction of the contracting party" taking the challenged action and (b) that the action was not necessary "because alternative means consistent with the General Agreement were available to [the United States] to protect dolphin lives or health, namely international cooperation between the countries concerned." *Id.* At this initial stage of the dispute, the panel agreed with Mexico:

[I]f the broad interpretation of Article XX(b) suggested by the United States were accepted, each contracting party could unilaterally determine the life or health protection policies from which other contracting parties could not deviate without jeopardizing their rights under the General Agreement. The General Agreement would then no longer constitute a multilateral framework for trade among all contracting parties but would provide legal security only in respect of trade between a limited number of contracting parties with identical internal regulations.

The Panel considered that the United States' measures, even if Article XX(b) were interpreted to permit extrajudicial protection of life and health, would not meet the requirement of necessity set out in that provision. The United States had not demonstrated to the Panel—as required of the party invoking an Article XX exception—that it had exhausted all options reasonably available to it to pursue its dolphin protection objectives through measures consistent with the General Agreement, in particular through the negotiation of international cooperative arrangements, which would seem to be desirable in view of the fact that dolphins roam the waters of many states and the high seas.

Id. ¶ ¶ 5.27–.28.

Should the fact that the United States had attempted unsuccessfully for twenty years to negotiate an agreement through the Inter–American Tropical Tuna Commission have carried more weight with the panel? If the decision is read to require negotiated settlements rather than good faith efforts, are dolphins effectively sacrificed to "free" trade?

The *Tuna/Dolphin II* panel reached a similar decision:

a contracting party cannot justify a measure inconsistent with another GATT provision as "necessary" ... if an alternative measure which it could reasonably be expected to employ and which is not inconsistent with other GATT provisions is available to it. By the same token, in cases where a measure consistent with other GATT provisions is not reasonably available, a contracting party is bound to use, among the measures reasonably available to it, that which entails the least degree of inconsistency with other GATT provisions.

Tuna/Dolphin II, 33 I.L.M. ¶ 5.35 at 896–97.

Note that, once again, the fear is that protectionism is disguised as preservation. But is the definition of "necessary" as the "least trade restrictive" alternative consistent with the general understanding of the term? Recall the jurisprudence of the Necessary and Proper Clause in the United States Constitution. *E.g., McCulloch v. Maryland,* 17 U.S. (4 Wheat.) 316 (1819). Similarly, doesn't this definition elevate trade over all other interests—an approach that it is arguably inconsistent with the underlying purposes of Article XX. Finally, isn't a requirement that negotiations always be a precondition to action inconsistent with Article XX's authorization of unilateral action? We will return to this story in the shrimp dispute discussed below.

(2) Article XX(g): What types of State-enforced discrimination are permitted by Article XX(g)? Dolphins—as well as other wildlife species—clearly are an "exhaustible natural resource." But what measures "relate to" the protection of such resources? Presumably this is a less-restrictive standard than the "necessity" standard of Article XX(b), but the matter is uncertain. Article XX(g), rather than XX(b), gained center stage in the dispute over shrimp that is examined below.

(3) Eco-labelling: The Dolphin Protection Consumer Information Act, 16 U.S.C. § 1385 note, imposes the "dolphin-safe tuna" labeling standards on cans of tuna. Mexico challenged these labeling requirements:

> The Panel noted that the labelling provisions ... do not restrict the sale of tuna products; ... Nor do these provisions establish requirements that have to be met in order to obtain an advantage from the government. Any advantage which might possibly result from access to this label depends on the free choice by consumers to give preference to tuna carrying the "Dolphin Safe" label.

Tuna/Dolphin I, 30 I.L.M. ¶ 5.42 at 1622. Despite the panel decision, the issue continues to be disputed internationally.

United States—Import Prohibition of Certain Shrimp & Shrimp Products

World Trade Organization, Report of the Appellate Body.
Oct. 12, 1998.
38 I.L.M. 121 (1999).

I. Introduction: Statement of the Appeal

1. This is an appeal by the United States from certain issues of law and legal interpretations in the Panel Report, United States—Import Prohibition of Certain Shrimp and Shrimp Products. [In 1996, India, Malaysia, Pakistan and Thailand initiated proceedings regarding a prohibition imposed by the United States on the importation of shrimp; Malaysia and Thailand initiated proceedings the following year. The Dispute Settlement Body (the "DSB") responded by establishing a panel to examine the complaints. The Dispute Resolution Panel Report was circulated to the Members of the World Trade Organization (the "WTO") on 15 May 1998.

2. [Under the Endangered Species Act of 1973, the United States promulgated regulations requiring all United States shrimp trawl vessels to use approved Turtle Excluder Devices ("TEDs") at all times and in all areas where there is a likelihood that trawling will interact with sea turtles. In 1989, Congress enacted Pub. L. No. 101–162, 103 Stat. 988 making appropriations for several agencies. The statute included § 609, which directed the Secretary of State, in consultation with the Secretary of Commerce to "initiate negotiations as soon as possible for the development of bilateral or multilateral agreements with other nations for the protection and conservation of ... sea turtles" and to "initiate negotiations as soon as possible with all foreign governments which are engaged in, or which have persons or companies engaged in, commercial fishing operations which, as determined by the Secretary of Commerce, may affect adversely such species of

sea turtles, for the purpose of entering into bilateral and multilateral treaties with such countries to protect such species of sea turtles." 16 U.S.C. § 1537 note. The section imposed an import ban on shrimp unless the harvesting nation is "certified." Certification is available when sea turtles are not present in the harvesting nation's jurisdiction or the nation has adopted a regulatory program governing the incidental taking of sea turtles that is comparable to the United States program and where the average rate of incidental taking of sea turtles by their vessels is comparable to that of United States vessels.]

7. In the Panel Report, the Panel reached the following conclusions:

In the light of the findings above, we conclude that the import ban on shrimp and shrimp products as applied by the United States on the basis of Section 609 of Public Law 101–162 is not consistent with Article XI:1 of GATT 1994, and cannot be justified under Article XX of GATT 1994.

. . .

[The United States appealed the panel decision.]

IV. Issues Raised in This Appeal

98. The issues raised in this appeal by the appellant, the United States, are the following:

. . .

(b) whether the Panel erred in finding that the measure at issue constitutes unjustifiable discrimination between countries where the same conditions prevail and thus is not within the scope of measures permitted under Article XX of the GATT 1994.

. . .

VI. Appraising Section 609 Under Article XX of the GATT 1994

111. We turn to the second issue raised by the appellant, the United States, which is whether the Panel erred in finding that the measure at issue constitutes unjustifiable discrimination between countries where the same conditions prevail and, thus, is not within the scope of measures permitted under Article XX of the GATT 1994.

A. The Panel's Findings and Interpretative Analysis

112. [The Panel relied upon the chapeau—the introductory clause—of Article XX to mean that] "Members [may] derogate from GATT provisions so long as, in doing so, they do not undermine the WTO multilateral trading system, thus also abusing the exceptions contained in Article XX. Such undermining and abuse would occur when a Member jeopardizes the operation of the WTO Agreement in such a way that guaranteed market access and nondiscriminatory treatment within a multilateral framework would no longer be possible.... Section 609, as applied, is a measure conditioning access to the US market for a given product on the adoption by exporting Members of conservation policies that the United States considers to be comparable to its own in terms of regulatory programmes

and incidental taking.... [I]t appears to us that, in light of the context of the term "unjustifiable" and the object and purpose of the WTO Agreement, the US measure at issue constitutes unjustifiable discrimination between countries where the same conditions prevail and thus is not within the scope of measures permitted under Article XX."

. . .

114.   The Panel did not follow all of the steps of applying the "customary rules of interpretation of public international law" as required by Article 3.2 of the DSU. As we have emphasized numerous times, these rules call for an examination of the ordinary meaning of the words of a treaty, read in their context, and in the light of the object and purpose of the treaty involved. A treaty interpreter must begin with, and focus upon, the text of the particular provision to be interpreted. It is in the words constituting that provision, read in their context, that the object and purpose of the states parties to the treaty must first be sought. Where the meaning imparted by the text itself is equivocal or inconclusive, or where confirmation of the correctness of the reading of the text itself is desired, light from the object and purpose of the treaty as a whole may usefully be sought.

. . .

118.   In *United States—Gasoline,* [May 20, 1996, 35 I.L.M. 603 (1996),] we enunciated the appropriate method for applying Article XX of the GATT 1994:

> In order that the justifying protection of Article XX may be extended to it, the measure at issue must not only come under one or another of the particular exceptions—paragraphs (a) to (j)—listed under Article XX; it must also satisfy the requirements imposed by the opening clauses of Article XX. The analysis is, in other words, *two-tiered: first, provisional justification by reason of characterization of the measure under XX(g); second, further appraisal of the same measure under the introductory clauses of Article XX.* (emphasis added)

119.   The sequence of steps indicated above in the analysis of a claim of justification under Article XX reflects, not inadvertence or random choice, but rather the fundamental structure and logic of Article XX....

. . .

122.   We hold that the findings of the Panel quoted in paragraph 112 above, and the interpretative analysis embodied therein, constitute error in legal interpretation and accordingly reverse them.

123.   Having reversed the Panel's legal conclusion that the United States measure at issue "is not within the scope of measures permitted under the chapeau of Article XX," we believe that it is our duty and our responsibility to complete the legal analysis in this case in order to determine whether Section 609 qualifies for justification under Article XX....

B.   Article XX(g): Provisional Justification of Section 609

125.   In claiming justification for its measure, the United States primarily invokes Article XX(g)....

126.   Paragraph (g) of Article XX covers measures:

> relating to the conservation of exhaustible natural resources if such
> measures are made effective in conjunction with restrictions on domes-
> tic production or consumption;

1.   "Exhaustible Natural Resources"

127.   We begin with the threshold question of whether Section 609 is a
measure concerned with the conservation of "exhaustible natural resources" within the meaning of Article XX(g).... In the proceedings before
the Panel, ... the parties to the dispute argued this issue vigorously and
extensively. India, Pakistan and Thailand contended that a "reasonable
interpretation" of the term "exhaustible" is that the term refers to "finite
resources such as minerals, rather than biological or renewable resources."
In their view, such finite resources were exhaustible "because there was a
limited supply which could and would be depleted unit for unit as the
resources were consumed." Moreover, they argued, if "all" natural resources were considered to be exhaustible, the term "exhaustible" would
become superfluous. They also referred to the drafting history of Article
XX(g), and, in particular, to the mention of minerals, such as manganese,
in the context of arguments made by some delegations that "export
restrictions" should be permitted for the preservation of scarce natural
resources. For its part, Malaysia added that sea turtles, being living
creatures, could only be considered under Article XX(b), since Article XX(g)
was meant for "nonliving exhaustible natural resources." It followed,
according to Malaysia, that the United States cannot invoke both the
Article XX(b) and the Article XX(g) exceptions simultaneously.

128.   We are not convinced by these arguments. Textually, Article XX(g) is
not limited to the conservation of "mineral" or "non-living" natural
resources. The complainants' principal argument is rooted in the notion
that "living" natural resources are "renewable" and therefore cannot be
"exhaustible" natural resources. We do not believe that "exhaustible"
natural resources and "renewable" natural resources are mutually exclusive. One lesson that modern biological sciences teach us is that living
species, though in principle, capable of reproduction and, in that sense,
"renewable," are in certain circumstances indeed susceptible of depletion,
exhaustion and extinction, frequently because of human activities. Living
resources are just as "finite" as petroleum, iron ore and other non-living
resources.

129.   The words of Article XX(g), "exhaustible natural resources," were
actually crafted more than 50 years ago. They must be read by a treaty
interpreter in the light of contemporary concerns of the community of
nations about the protection and conservation of the environment. While
Article XX was not modified in the Uruguay Round, the preamble attached
to the WTO Agreement shows that the signatories to that Agreement were,
in 1994, fully aware of the importance and legitimacy of environmental
protection as a goal of national and international policy. The preamble of
the WTO Agreement—which informs not only the GATT 1994, but also the
other covered agreements—explicitly acknowledges "the objective of sustainable development":

The *Parties* to this Agreement,

Recognizing that their relations in the field of trade and economic endeavour should be conducted *with a view to raising standards of living, ensuring full employment and a large and steadily growing volume of real income and effective demand, and expanding the production of and trade in goods and services,* while allowing for the optimal use of the world's resources in accordance with the *objective of sustainable development, seeking both to protect and preserve the environment and to enhance the means for doing so* in a manner consistent with their respective needs and concerns at different levels of economic development, . . .

(emphasis added).

130. From the perspective embodied in the preamble of the WTO Agreement, we note that the generic term "natural resources" in Article XX(g) is not "static" in its content or reference but is rather "by definition, evolutionary." It is, therefore, pertinent to note that modern international conventions and declarations make frequent references to natural resources as embracing both living and non-living resources. . . .

. . .

132. We turn next to the issue of whether the living natural resources sought to be conserved by the measure are "exhaustible" under Article XX(g). That this element is present in respect of the five species of sea turtles here involved appears to be conceded by all the participants and third participants in this case. The exhaustibility of sea turtles would in fact have been very difficult to controvert since all of the seven recognized species of sea turtles are today listed in Appendix 1 of the Convention on International Trade in Endangered Species of Wild Fauna and Flora ("CITES"). The list in Appendix 1 includes "all species *threatened with extinction* which are or may be affected by trade." (emphasis added)

. . .

134. For all the foregoing reasons, we find that the sea turtles here involved constitute "exhaustible natural resources" for purposes of Article XX(g) of the GATT 1994.

2. "Relating to the Conservation of [Exhaustible Natural Resources]"

135. Article XX(g) requires that the measure sought to be justified be one which "relat[es] to" the conservation of exhaustible natural resources. In making this determination, the treaty interpreter essentially looks into the relationship between the measure at stake and the legitimate policy of conserving exhaustible natural resources. . . .

137. In the present case, we must examine the relationship between the general structure and design of the measure here at stake, Section 609, and the policy goal it purports to serve, that is, the conservation of sea turtles.

138. Section 609(b)(1) imposes an import ban on shrimp that have been harvested with commercial fishing technology which may adversely affect sea turtles. This provision is designed to influence countries to adopt

national regulatory programs requiring the use of TEDs by their shrimp fishermen. In this connection, it is important to note that the general structure and design of Section 609 cum implementing guidelines is fairly narrowly focused. There are two basic exemptions from the import ban, both of which relate clearly and directly to the policy goal of conserving sea turtles. First, Section 609, as elaborated in the 1996 Guidelines, excludes from the import ban shrimp harvested "under conditions that do not adversely affect sea turtles." Thus, the measure, by its terms, excludes from the import ban: aquaculture shrimp; shrimp species (such as pandalid shrimp) harvested in water areas where sea turtles do not normally occur; and shrimp harvested exclusively by artisanal methods, even from non-certified countries. The harvesting of such shrimp clearly does not affect sea turtles. Second, under Section 609(b)(2), the measure exempts from the import ban shrimp caught in waters subject to the jurisdiction of certified countries.

139.   [There are two types of certification. First, a country may be certified as having a fishing environment that does not pose a threat of incidental taking of sea turtles in the course of commercial shrimp trawl harvesting.

140.   [Second, a country may be certified if it has a regulatory program that is comparable to that of the United States program and to have a rate of incidental take of sea turtles that is comparable to the average rate of United States' vessels.] This requirement is, in our view, directly connected with the policy of conservation of sea turtles. It is undisputed among the participants, and recognized by the experts consulted by the Panel, that the harvesting of shrimp by commercial shrimp trawling vessels with mechanical retrieval devices in waters where shrimp and sea turtles coincide is a significant cause of sea turtle mortality. Moreover, the Panel did "not question ... the fact generally acknowledged by the experts that TEDs, when properly installed and adapted to the local area, would be an effective tool for the preservation of sea turtles."

141.   In its general design and structure, therefore, Section 609 is not a simple, blanket prohibition of the importation of shrimp imposed without regard to the consequences (or lack thereof) of the mode of harvesting employed upon the incidental capture and mortality of sea turtles. Focusing on the design of the measure here at stake, it appears to us that Section 609, cum implementing guidelines, is not disproportionately wide in its scope and reach in relation to the policy objective of protection and conservation of sea turtle species. The means are, in principle, reasonably related to the ends. The means and ends relationship between Section 609 and the legitimate policy of conserving an exhaustible, and, in fact, endangered species, is observably a close and real one, a relationship that is every bit as substantial as that which we found in *United States—Gasoline* between the EPA baseline establishment rules and the conservation of clean air in the United States.

142.   In our view, therefore, Section 609 is a measure "relating to" the conservation of an exhaustible natural resource within the meaning of Article XX(g) of the GATT 1994.

3. "If Such Measures are Made Effective in conjunction with Restrictions on Domestic Production or Consumption"

143. In *United States—Gasoline,* we held that the above-captioned clause of Article XX(g),

> ... is appropriately read as a requirement that the measures concerned impose restrictions, not just in respect of imported gasoline but also with respect to domestic gasoline. The clause is a requirement of even-handedness in the imposition of restrictions, in the name of conservation, upon the production or consumption of exhaustible natural resources.

In this case, we need to examine whether the restrictions imposed by Section 609 with respect to imported shrimp are also imposed in respect of shrimp caught by United States shrimp trawl vessels.

144. [Although Section 609 addresses only the mode of harvesting of imported shrimp, it simply extended to non-domestic vessels regulations that had previously been applied to domestic shrimp trawl vessels under the Endangered Species Act.] We believe that, in principle, Section 609 is an even-handed measure.

145. Accordingly, we hold that Section 609 is a measure made effective in conjunction with the restrictions on domestic harvesting of shrimp, as required by Article XX(g).

C. The Introductory Clauses of Article XX: Characterizing Section 609 under the Chapeau's Standards

147. Although provisionally justified under Article XX(g), Section 609, if it is ultimately to be justified as an exception under Article XX, must also satisfy the requirements of the introductory clauses—the "chapeau"—of Article XX, that is,

> Subject to the requirement that such measures are *not applied in a manner which would constitute a means of arbitrary or unjustifiable discrimination between countries where the same conditions prevail, or a disguised restriction on international trade,* nothing in this Agreement shall be construed to prevent the adoption or enforcement by any Member of measures:

(emphasis added) We turn, hence, to the task of appraising Section 609, and specifically the manner in which it is applied under the chapeau of Article XX; that is, to the second part of the two-tier analysis required under Article XX.

1. General Considerations

. . .

150. We commence the second tier of our analysis with an examination of the ordinary meaning of the words of the chapeau. The precise language of the chapeau requires that a measure not be applied in a manner which would constitute a means of "arbitrary or unjustifiable discrimination between countries where the same conditions prevail" or a "disguised restriction on international trade." There are three standards contained in

the chapeau: first, arbitrary discrimination between countries where the same conditions prevail; second, unjustifiable discrimination between countries where the same conditions prevail; and third, a disguised restriction on international trade. In order for a measure to be applied in a manner which would constitute "arbitrary or unjustifiable discrimination between countries where the same conditions prevail", three elements must exist. First, the application of the measure must result in *discrimination*.... Second, the discrimination must be *arbitrary or unjustifiable* in character. We will examine this element of *arbitrariness or unjustifiability* in detail below. Third, this discrimination must occur *between countries where the same conditions prevail*. ...

151. In *United States—Gasoline,* we stated that "the purpose and object of the introductory clauses of Article XX is generally the prevention of 'abuse of the exceptions of [Article XX].' " ...

[The Appellate Body examined several developments within the WTO, including "most significant[ly]" the decision to create a permanent Committee on Trade and the Environment (CTE) within the WTO.]

158. The chapeau of Article XX is, in fact, but one expression of the principle of good faith. This principle, at once a general principle of law and a general principle of international law, controls the exercise of rights by states....

159. The task of interpreting and applying the chapeau is, hence, essentially the delicate one of locating and marking out a line of equilibrium between the right of a Member to invoke an exception under Article XX and the rights of the other Members under varying substantive provisions ... of the GATT 1994, so that neither of the competing rights will cancel out the other and thereby distort and nullify or impair the balance of rights and obligations constructed by the Members themselves in that Agreement. The location of the line of equilibrium, as expressed in the chapeau, is not fixed and unchanging; the line moves as the kind and the shape of the measures at stake vary and as the facts making up specific cases differ.

160. With these general considerations in mind, we address now the issue of whether the application of the United States measure, although the measure itself falls within the terms of Article XX(g), nevertheless constitutes "a means of arbitrary or unjustifiable discrimination between countries where the same conditions prevail" or "a disguised restriction on international trade." We address, in other words, whether the application of this measure constitutes an abuse or misuse of the provisional justification made available by Article XX(g)....

2. "Unjustifiable Discrimination"

161. We scrutinize first whether Section 609 has been applied in a manner constituting "unjustifiable discrimination between countries where the same conditions prevail." Perhaps the most conspicuous flaw in this measure's application relates to its intended and actual coercive effect on the specific policy decisions made by foreign governments, Members of the WTO. Section 609, in its application, is, in effect, an economic embargo which requires *all other exporting Members,* if they wish to exercise their

GATT rights, to adopt *essentially the same* policy (together with an approved enforcement program) as that applied to, and enforced on, United States domestic shrimp trawlers. As enacted by the Congress of the United States, the *statutory* provisions of Section 609(b)(2)(A) and (B) do not, in themselves, *require* that other WTO Members adopt *essentially the same* policies and enforcement practices as the United States. Viewed alone, the statute appears to permit a degree of discretion or flexibility in how the standards for determining comparability might be applied, in practice, to other countries. However, any flexibility that may have been intended by Congress when it enacted the statutory provision has been effectively eliminated in the implementation of that policy through the 1996 Guidelines promulgated by the Department of State and through the practice of the administrators in making certification determinations.

. . .

163. The actual *application* of the measure, through the implementation of the 1996 Guidelines and the regulatory practice of administrators, *requires* other WTO Members to adopt a regulatory program that is not merely *comparable,* but rather *essentially the same,* as that applied to the United States shrimp trawl vessels. Thus, the effect of the application of Section 609 is to establish a rigid and unbending standard by which United States officials determine whether or not countries will be certified, thus granting or refusing other countries the right to export shrimp to the United States. Other specific policies and measures that an exporting country may have adopted for the protection and conservation of sea turtles are not taken into account, in practice, by the administrators making the comparability determination.

164. [I]t is not acceptable, in international trade relations, for one WTO Member to use an economic embargo to *require* other Members to adopt essentially the same comprehensive regulatory program, to achieve a certain policy goal, as that in force within that Member's territory, *without* taking into consideration different conditions which may occur in the territories of those other Members.

165. Furthermore, when this dispute was before the Panel and before us, the United States did not permit imports of shrimp harvested by commercial shrimp trawl vessels using TEDs comparable in effectiveness to those required in the United States if those shrimp originated in waters of countries not certified under Section 609. In other words, *shrimp caught using methods identical to those employed in the United States have been excluded from the United States market solely because they have been caught in waters of countries that have not been certified by the United States.* The resulting situation is difficult to reconcile with the declared policy objective of protecting and conserving sea turtles. This suggests to us that this measure, in its application, is more concerned with effectively influencing WTO Members to adopt essentially the same comprehensive regulatory regime as that applied by the United States to its domestic shrimp trawlers, even though many of those Members may be differently situated. We believe that discrimination results not only when countries in which the same conditions prevail are differently treated, but also when the application of the measure at issue does not allow for any inquiry into the

appropriateness of the regulatory program for the conditions prevailing in those exporting countries.

166.   Another aspect of the application of Section 609 that bears heavily in any appraisal of justifiable or unjustifiable discrimination is the failure of the United States to engage the appellees, as well as other Members exporting shrimp to the United States, in serious, across-the-board negotiations with the objective of concluding bilateral or multilateral agreements for the protection and conservation of sea turtles, before enforcing the import prohibition against the shrimp exports of those other Members. . . .

168.   [T]he protection and conservation of highly migratory species of sea turtles, that is, the very policy objective of the measure, demands concerted and cooperative efforts on the part of the many countries whose waters are traversed in the course of recurrent sea turtle migrations. The need for, and the appropriateness of, such efforts have been recognized in the WTO itself as well as in a significant number of other international instruments and declarations. As stated earlier, the Decision on Trade and Environment, which provided for the establishment of the CTE and set out its terms of reference, refers to both the Rio Declaration on Environment and Development and Agenda 21. Of particular relevance is Principle 12 of the Rio Declaration on Environment and Development, which states, in part:

> Unilateral actions to deal with environmental challenges outside the jurisdiction of the importing country should be avoided. *Environmental measures addressing transboundary or global environmental problems should, as far as possible, be based on international consensus.*

(emphasis added). . . .

. . .

173.   The application of Section 609, through the implementing guidelines together with administrative practice, also resulted in other differential treatment among various countries desiring certification. Under the 1991 and 1993 Guidelines, to be certifiable, fourteen countries in the wider Caribbean/western Atlantic region had to commit themselves to require the use of TEDs on all commercial shrimp trawling vessels by 1 May 1994. These fourteen countries had a "phase-in" period of three years during which their respective shrimp trawling sectors could adjust to the requirement of the use of TEDs. With respect to all other countries exporting shrimp to the United States (including the appellees, India, Malaysia, Pakistan and Thailand), on 29 December 1995, the United States Court of International Trade directed the Department of State to apply the import ban on a world-wide basis not later than 1 May 1996. On 19 April 1996, the 1996 Guidelines were issued by the Department of State bringing shrimp harvested in all foreign countries within the scope of Section 609, effective 1 May 1996. Thus, all countries that were not among the fourteen in the wider Caribbean/western Atlantic region had only four months to implement the requirement of compulsory use of TEDs. We acknowledge that the greatly differing periods for putting into operation the requirement for use of TEDs resulted from decisions of the Court of International Trade. Even so, this does not relieve the United States of the legal consequences of the discriminatory impact of the decisions of that Court. The United States,

like all other Members of the WTO and of the general community of states, bears responsibility for acts of all its departments of government, including its judiciary.

174.   The length of the "phase-in" period is not inconsequential for exporting countries desiring certification. . . .

175.   Differing treatment of different countries desiring certification is also observable in the differences in the levels of effort made by the United States in transferring the required TED technology to specific countries. . . .

176.   When the foregoing differences in the means of application of Section 609 to various shrimp exporting countries are considered in their cumulative effect, we find, and so hold, that those differences in treatment constitute "unjustifiable discrimination" between exporting countries desiring certification in order to gain access to the United States shrimp market within the meaning of the chapeau of Article XX.

3.   "Arbitrary Discrimination"

177.   We next consider whether Section 609 has been applied in a manner constituting "arbitrary discrimination between countries where the same conditions prevail." We have already observed that Section 609, in its application, imposes a single, rigid and unbending requirement that countries applying for certification under Section 609(b)(2)(A) and (B) adopt a comprehensive regulatory program that is essentially the same as the United States' program, without inquiring into the appropriateness of that program for the conditions prevailing in the exporting countries. Furthermore, there is little or no flexibility in how officials make the determination for certification pursuant to these provisions. In our view, this rigidity and inflexibility also constitute "arbitrary discrimination" within the meaning of the chapeau.

. . .

185.   In reaching these conclusions, we wish to underscore what we have not decided in this appeal. We have not decided that the protection and preservation of the environment is of no significance to the Members of the WTO. Clearly, it is. We have not decided that the sovereign nations that are Members of the WTO cannot adopt effective measures to protect endangered species, such as sea turtles. Clearly, they can and should. And we have not decided that sovereign states should not act together bilaterally, plurilaterally or multilaterally, either within the WTO or in other international fora, to protect endangered species or to otherwise protect the environment. Clearly, they should and do.

186.   What we have decided in this appeal is simply this: although the measure of the United States in dispute in this appeal serves an environmental objective that is recognized as legitimate under paragraph (g) of Article XX of the GATT 1994, this measure has been applied by the United States in a manner which constitutes arbitrary and unjustifiable discrimination between Members of the WTO, contrary to the requirements of the chapeau of Article XX. For all of the specific reasons outlined in this Report, this measure does not qualify for the exemption that Article XX of

the GATT 1994 affords to measures which serve certain recognized, legitimate environmental purposes but which, at the same time, are not applied in a manner that constitutes a means of arbitrary or unjustifiable discrimination between countries where the same conditions prevail or a disguised restriction on international trade. . . .

VII. Findings and Conclusions

187. For the reasons set out in this Report, the Appellate Body:

(a) reverses the Panel's finding that accepting non-requested information from non-governmental sources is incompatible with the provisions of the DSU;

(b) reverses the Panel's finding that the United States measure at issue is not within the scope of measures permitted under the chapeau of Article XX of the GATT 1994, and

(c) concludes that the United States measure, while qualifying for provisional justification under Article XX(g), fails to meet the requirements of the chapeau of Article XX, and, therefore, is not justified under Article XX of the GATT 1994.

NOTES

(1) A step toward environmental protection? The Appellate Body's Report is an intriguing document. Although it ultimately ruled against the United States, the Appellate Body did uphold the power of individual States to use trade laws to achieve environmental goals. First, it implicitly acknowledged the power of States to regulate trade based on process and production methods. If the Report is accepted as governing precedent on this issue, it could have wide-spread effects. In addition, the Report is quick to conclude that the measure under scrutiny was sufficiently related to the conservation of "exhaustible natural resources." Finally, since the resources at issue (sea turtles) lived outside the United States, the Appellate Body—by implication—concluded that the GATT does not categorically prohibit trade-restrictive measures intended to protect the environment outside a State's territory—at least in the case of migratory endangered species in international waters. Note, however, that it is less clear that a State could take unilateral action to protect an endangered species located entirely within another nation.

The troubles that the United States encountered were, on the surface at least, matters of implementation: the adequacy of its efforts to negotiate bilateral and multilateral agreements protecting sea turtles; the sufficiency of the flexibility it accorded other States in developing their own, equally effective regulatory and enforcement measures; the even-handedness of the application of its regulations to other States; the adequacy of its efforts to transfer technology to other States; and the reasonableness of its prohibition of the importation of shrimp caught by TED-using boats in waters controlled by noncertified States. The United States could have complied with all of these requirements; had it done so, the statute and its regulatory scheme presumably would have passed muster. Consider: could the

United States, by complying with Article XX as interpreted in this ruling, ban the importation of goods from countries that do not have water pollution laws protecting aquatic species that are comparable to those in place in the United States?

On the other hand, consider the Report's criticism that the United States failed to invest sufficient time and effort in negotiating agreements to protect sea turtles before taking unilateral action. How fair is this criticism, given the endangered status of the turtles? How consistent is it with the precautionary principle? Would it not be wiser to act first and talk later; that is, take immediately action to protect the turtles, and then work out refinements to minimize the ill effects on free trade? One commentator summarized the efforts of the United States as follows:

> The United States unsuccessfully argued that it had tried in good faith to enter into bilateral and multilateral negotiations to protect sea turtles and had succeeded in doing so with 19 other countries but not the complainants in this case. The United States additionally contended that it had successfully negotiated the Inter–American Convention on the Protection and Conservation of Sea Turtles in 1996 and proposed to other Asian nations, including the complainants, that they should also enter into multilateral negotiations, but were turned down by the complainants.

Lakshman Guruswamy, *The Annihilation of Sea Turtles: World Trade Organization Intransigence and U.S. Equivocation,* 30 Envtl. L. Rptr. (Envtl. L. Inst.) 10261, 10266 (2000). Is it sound environmental policy to have demanded even this much effort—and delay? Does the Appellate Body's decision reflect the tunnel vision of those who are trained to think of the environment exclusively as a "resource"?

(2) Forgoing all talk? As noted, the Appellate Body characterized the United States' actions as "arbitrary or unjustifiable discrimination" because it did not hold discussion or offer assistance to all countries. What if the United States had simply imposed its import ban without any discussion or assistance? Would this have avoided the discrimination claim? Or might discrimination nonetheless take place because an import ban might have differential impacts based on the differing circumstances of other nations?

(3) The WTO and the primacy of free trade: Overall, does the Appellate Body's Report seem a fair and balanced ruling on an issue involving important, conflicting principles of environmental protection and free trade? By design, the WTO was set up specifically to promote free trade; it thus is not a neutral body. Is it reasonable to expect such a body to give sufficient weight to non-trade concerns? Is it even competent to do so?

One specific criticism leveled at the WTO is that its adjudications only pay attention to trade laws, ignoring, *inter alia,* the more than 900 treaties dealing with environmental protection. *E.g.,* Lakshman Guruswamy, *supra,* at 10263–64. Note that, in the shrimp dispute case, the Report makes no substantive use of the Convention on the Conservation of Migratory Species of Wild Animals, the Convention on Biological Diversity, the customary ban on transboundary harm, and numerous other "hard law" elements of international environmental law—yet the dispute fundamentally concerned whether or not the United States acted arbitrarily in protecting critically endangered species. The Report contains no hint that the States bringing the action had "dirty hands" because they permitted conduct that was obviously harmful to endangered species, nor any sense that the dire plight of sea turtles might warrant emergency action—and be relevant in deciding how "arbitrary" and "unjustified" the United States was.

Is the answer (at least tactically) to set up an environmental tribunal that is equally narrow in focus, one that decides whether particular trade practices are arbitrary and violative of environmental treaties without mentioning the GATT and giving little or no weight to the value of free trade? Should environmental protection come first, with free trade left for lengthy negotiations?

(4) Implications of the lack of deference: Ultimately, the key charge against the United States was that its conduct in distinguishing among foreign sources of shrimp was arbitrary (and, as such, unjustified). In interpreting that term in Article XX, the Appellate Body subjected the United States' conduct to particularly close scrutiny, questioning at each point whether it could have accomplished its aims in ways more specifically tailored to reduce adverse effects on trade. In practice, then, "arbitrary" meant conduct that was not narrowly and specifically drawn to protect trade. Under United States law, governmental conduct that is challenged as "arbitrary" is accorded a high degree of deference; indeed, the "arbitrary and capricious standard" is among the most deferential of standards. In the hands of the Appellate Body, however, "arbitrary" was far closer to the least deferential standard used in United States law—strict scrutiny.

Consider the possible effects if such scrutiny were employed in applying environmental treaties. For instance, the Bonn Convention states that parties must "endeavour" to conserve the habitats of listed migratory endangered species. Under ordinary review standards, nearly any conservation effort would likely comply with this vague obligation. But consider: Article XX of the GATT does not so much as mention a State obligation to negotiate multilateral treaties, yet the Appellate Body found United States' negotiation efforts (agreements with 19 countries) inadequate. Might conservationists, then, be heartened by this ruling, hoping that similar rigor might be brought to bear in the case of environmental obligations?

(5) The United States responds: The United States responded to the Appellate Body Report by revising its regulations and certification processes, by attempting to reach additional agreements, particularly with Asian nations, and by taking further efforts to distribute TED technology. While it undertook these efforts—and in accordance with a strict agreed-upon timetable—the import restriction remained in place. Once United States' efforts were concluded, Malaysia challenged them. The WTO panel hearing the challenge limited its inquiry to whether United States efforts complied with the requirements of the Appellate Body Report. While concluding that the United States had done so, the panel elaborated on the duty of the United States (and similarly situated nations seeking to take unilateral action) to negotiate bilateral and multilateral agreements. That duty of "serious good faith" negotiation included an obligation to negotiate with every nation that exported shrimp to the United States, in each instance taking into account the peculiar circumstances and needs of that nation, and to do so before taking any unilateral action. *United States—Import Prohibition of Certain Shrimp and Shrimp Products*, 2001 WL 671012 (W.T.O.) (June 15, 2001), *upheld* WT/DS58/AB/RW (Oct. 22, 2001).

(6) Would a revised dolphin/tuna embargo survive under the standards as construed in the shrimp case?

(7) The WTO maintains a web site at <http://wto.org>.

c. NORTH AMERICAN FREE TRADE AGREEMENT

NOTES

(1) In December 1992, Canada, Mexico, and the United States concluded the North American Free Trade Agreement (NAFTA), 32 I.L.M. 289 (1993). Environmental concerns appear very selectively in the Treaty as negotiated by President Bush I. Bill Clinton made NAFTA's environmental and labor shortcomings a major campaign issue and, following his election, he negotiated environmental and labor "side agreements." *See generally* PIERRE MARC JOHNSON & ANDRE BEAULIEU, THE ENVIRONMENT AND NAFTA (1996).

(2) NAFTA (proper)'s environmental provisions: When the apparent lack of environmental protection in the negotiation drafts became a political issue, additions were made to incorporate some concerns. Thus, for example, NAFTA's preamble specifies that the treaty's goal is to

> CONTRIBUTE to the harmonious development and expansion of world trade ... in a manner consistent with environmental protection and conservation; PROMOTE sustainable development ... [and] STRENGTHEN the development and enforcement of environmental laws and regulations.

NAFTA, Preamble, 32 I.L.M. at 297. To this end, NAFTA is subordinated to the "specific trade obligations" of five conservation agreements, including CITES. *Id.* Art. 104. The parties—by unanimous consent—have subsequently added two additional bilateral treaties to the list of subordinating agreements, the 1916 Convention on the Protection of Migratory Birds (Great Britain [for Canada]-United States) and the 1936 Convention for the Protection of Migratory Birds and Game mammals (Mexico–United States) [implemented in the United States through the Migratory Bird Treaty Act, *see* Chapters 6 and 10]. *See generally* Robert Housman, *The North American Free Trade Agreement's Lessons for Reconciling Trade and the Environment*, 30 STANFORD J. INT'L L. 379 (1994).

(2) The environmental "side agreements": The more significant changes were incorporated in "side agreements" negotiated among the parties. The most important of these was the North American Agreement on Environmental Cooperation (NAAEC), Sept. 8, 1993, 32 I.L.M. 1480 (1993). The agreement is regarded as a landmark because it is not restricted to specific regions, species, media, or pollutants, but instead is applicable whenever the Parties feel that environmental protection can be increased by cooperation.

(3) The Commission on Environmental Cooperation: NAAEC creates the trilateral Commission on Environmental Cooperation (CEC) as a continuing, centralized forum for environmental cooperation. The CEC is composed of three entities: the Council, the Secretariat, and the Joint Public Advisory Committee.

The Council of Ministers is composed of cabinet-level officers from each member State, Canada's Minister of the Environment, Mexico's Secretary of the Environment, and the United States' Administrator of the Environmental Protection Agency. It is the political, governing body of the CEC. It serves as a general forum for discussion of environmental issues and is empowered to settle environmental disputes by consensus.

The Secretariat is the side agreement's administrative component. Its duties include investigating and reporting to the Council.

The Joint Public Advisory Committee (JPAC) provides a formal mechanism through which NGOs and individuals may influence the decisionmaking of the CEC. *See* NAAEC, Art. 16(4)-(7), 32 I.L.M. at 1489.

(4) Article 13 reports: Article 13 empowers the Secretariat on it own initiative to investigate and report on any matter "within the scope of the annual program." *Id.* Art. 13(1). It may also investigate and report on any matter "related to the cooperative functions of this Agreement," provided two of the Parties do not object. *Id.*

NGOs and individuals may file petitions the Secretariat to investigate and report on environmental problems. Among the first Article 13 reports—triggered by a petition from the Group of 100 (Mexico) and the National Audubon Society (United States)—concerned the death of some 40,000 migratory birds at an agricultural reservoir in Guanajuato, Mexico. The Secretariat sent an international team of experts to investigate. They concluded that the die-off was caused by avian botulism, but suggested that several pollutants present at the reservoir might have been the initial cause. The CEC Secretariat's report on the matter concluded that Canada and the United States should help Mexico continue its attempts to clean up the watershed flowing into the reservoir. CEC Secretariat Report on the Death of Migratory Birds at the Silva Reservoir (1994–95) [available at <http://www.cec.org>].

(5) Articles 14 and 15: NGO and individual participation in environmental protection under the NAAEC is most apparent in Article 14 and 15, which create a process allowing any citizen of the three countries who believes that "a Party is failing to effectively enforce its environmental law" to file a complaint. NAAEC, Art. 14(1), 32 I.L.M. at 1488. If the Secretariat concludes that the submission meets certain requirements—alleges harm to the complainant, raises a matter that would advance the goals of the NAAEC, demonstrates that private remedies under domestic law are not available, and establishes that the information comes from mass media reports—the Secretariat forwards the submission to the Party who must respond promptly. *Id.* Art. 14(2)-(3). The Secretariat is to evaluate the Party's response and determine whether a factual record should be developed. *Id.* Art. 15(1). If the Secretariat concludes that a record should be created, it is to inform the Council and, if two Parties concur, it is to proceed. *Id.* Art. 15(2).

Although there is no enforcement provision associated with the provisions—and hence they are referred to as the citizen "spotlight" process—there is some indication that the process can serve to protect the environment. For example, the third submission complained that the Mexican government had failed to conduct an environmental impact review before authorizing the construction of a cruise ship pier at Cozumel Island. SEM–96–001.[3] Following publication of the factual record, Mexico abandoned the project. *But see* Submission of the Biodiversity Legal Foundation, SEM–95–01 (creating a "legislative exception" when the United States Congress rescinded a large portion of the funding for the Endangered Species Act).

The utility of the spotlight process is the subject of debate. *Compare* David L. Markell, *The Citizen Spotlight Process,* ENVTL. FORUM, Mar./Apr. 2001, at 32, *with* Jay Tuchton, *The Citizen Petition Process Under NAFTA's Environmental Side Agreement: It's Easy to Use, But Does it Work?,* 26 Envtl. L. Rep. (Envtl. L. Inst.) 10018 (1996).

---

3. SEM stands for Submissions on Enforcement Matters. Guidelines for submission have been issued and can be found at <http://www.cec.org>.

CHAPTER 9

State Game Laws

As the materials in Chapter 3 demonstrated, a landowner's power to take wildlife on her land or to alter wildlife habitat on that land are wispy reeds in the bundle of rights recognized at common law. Chapter 3 treated these issues from the landowner side of the equation. This chapter examines some of these issues from the flip side: as questions of the power of government to regulate conduct. That is, what constraints do states face as they seek to protect wildlife?

As we have seen, states have traditionally been the primary regulators of access to wildlife. Historically, that primacy has focused almost exclusively on the taking of a limited number of species—those that fall into the imprecise categories "game" and "sport fish." Although the focus has broadened over time, the majority of states remain reticent to move beyond a "hook-and-bullet" perspective and fully to fulfill the trust in *wildlife*. As the materials in Chapter 5 demonstrated—and as is highlighted in section 2 of this chapter—this is a question of political choice rather than of legal compulsion: states have extremely broad constitutional power to protect wildlife.

States commonly exercise this power by enacting fish and game codes. Although these vary widely in detail, they generally

(a) create an agency: Each state has established an agency (or agencies) with the power to manage the state's wildlife resources. The structure of these agencies vary widely as do the powers delegated to them. For example, maritime states frequently have a fisheries agency as well as a separate game agency. Some of the issues surrounding state fish and game agencies are examined in sections 3 and 4.

(b) adopt a classification scheme for wildlife: As we touched upon in Chapter 1, states classify wildlife. Frequently, this involves enumerating a list of game animals and another of "vermin"—with a residual, "everything else" category.

(c) mandate a regulatory scheme: The code often provides that game may be taken subject to specified conditions, that vermin may be killed at anytime, and that the species in the residual category are protected. These provisions raise basic criminal law issues that are examined in section 5.

SECTION 1. ENGLISH AND EARLY AMERICAN REGULATION OF THE TAKING OF WILDLIFE

a. THE COMMON-LAW BACKGROUND

NOTES

(1) Governmental regulation to conserve wildlife has a long lineage. In addition to prohibitions on habitat modification—recall the forest laws and statute prohibiting the burning of furse noted in Chapter 3—there were three types of English game laws: (1) statutes directly regulating the taking of wildlife, (2) qualification statutes specifying who might hunt, and (3) statutes imposing penalties on those who "stole" deer and other game from the landed gentry's parks and warrens.

(2) Direct regulation of taking in Great Britain: In 1285, Parliament enacted the Statute of Westminster II, Chapter 47 of which provided:

> That ... all ... Waters wherein Salmons be taken, shall be in Defence[1] for taking Salmons from the Nativity of our Lady unto St. Martin's Day; and that likewise young Salmons shall not be taken nor destroyed by Nets, nor by other Engines at Millpools, from the midst of April unto the Nativity of St. John Baptist. And in Places whereas such Waters be, there shall be assigned Conservators of this Statute, which being sworn, shall oftentimes see and inquire of the Offenders. And for the first Trespass, they shall be punished by burning of their Nets and Engines. And for the second Time, they shall have Imprisonment for a Quarter of a Year. And for the third Trespass, they shall be Imprisoned a whole Year; and as their Trespass increaseth, so shall their Punishment.

Note that the statute not only established closed seasons on taking salmon, it also established a rudimentary enforcement structure. English game conservation statutes fell into at least four general categories:

(a) closed periods: In 1523, Parliament passed a statute to prohibit hunting hares when there was snow on the ground because this allowed them to be "traced" and killed. The Penalty for Unlawfully Hunting the Hare, 14 & 15 Hen. 8, ch. 10 (1523). Ten years later, it imposed a closed season on wildfowl "between the last day of May, and the last day of August ... upon pain of one year's imprisonment." To Avoid Destroying of Wild–Fowl, 25 Hen. 8, ch. 11, § 2 (1533). Similarly, a statute enacted in 1604 prohibited the taking of pheasants and partridges other than "betwixt the Feast of St. Michael the Archangel and the Feast of the Birth of Our Lord God." An Act for the Better Execution of the Intent and Meaning of Former Statutes Made Against Shooting in Guns, and for the Preservation of the Game in Pheasants and Partridges, and against the Destroying of

---

1. "Defence" means "prohibition, denial, or refusal." Here, the statute prohibits the taking of salmon during the specified period.

Hares with Hare–Pipes and Tracing Hares in the Snow, 2 Jac. 1, ch. 27, § 6 (1604).

(b) gear restrictions: In 1423, Parliament prohibited "the standing of nets and engines, called trinks, and all other nets which be and were wont to be fastened and hanged continually day and night . . . overthwart the . . . rivers of the realm, which standing is a cause of . . . great . . . destruction of the brood and fry of fish." No Man Shall Fasten Nets to Any Thing over Rivers, 2 Hen. 6, ch. 15 (1423). A subsequent act "for preservation of spawn and fry of fish" prohibited the use of "any manner of net, trammell, kepe, wore, hivie, crele, or by another engine, device, ways of means whatsoever .. but only with a net or trammel, whereof every mesh or mask shall be two inches and a half broad." An Act for Preservation of Spawn and Fry of Fish, 1 Eliz., ch. 17, § 3 (1558).

(c) bag limits: The act "for preservation of spawn and fry of fish" also prohibited taking fish smaller than certain minimum sizes: pike, for example, had to be at least ten inches long and salmon at least 16 inches. An Act for Preservation of Spawn and Fry of Fish, 1 Eliz., ch. 17, § 2 (1558). Other statutes prohibited taking eggs from the nests of birds or the taking of molting birds. *See, e.g.,* To Avoid Destroying of Wild–Fowl, 25 Hen. 8, ch. 11, §§ 1, 2 (1533); 10 Geo. II, ch. 32, § 10 (1737).

(d) prohibitions on commerce in wildlife: In 1540, Parliament enacted a statute imposing a penalty on anyone buying or selling a pheasant or partridge. 32 Hen. 8, ch. 8 (1540). A statute adopted in 1604 imposed penalties on anyone who "shall sell, or buy to sell again, any deer, hare, partridge, or pheasant." An Act for the Better Execution of the Intent and Meaning of Former Statutes Made Against Shooting in Guns, and for the Preservation of the Game in Pheasants and Partridges, and against the Destroying of Hares with Hare–Pipes and Tracing Hares in the Snow, 2 Jac. 1, ch. 27, § 4 (1604). A subsequent statute imposed a 5£ fine on "any higlar, chapman, carrier, inn-keeper, victualler, or alehouse keeper" for the possession of "any hare, pheasant, partridge, moor, heath-game, or grouse." An Act for the Better Preservation of the Game, 5 Anne, ch. 14, § 2 (1706). In 1755, all sales of game were prohibited. An Act to Explain and Amend a Clause in an Act Made. . . ., 28 Geo. 2, ch. 12 § 1 (1755).

(3) Qualification statutes: In Chapter 3, the qualification statute of 1390 was noted as evidence of the fact that a landowner did not have a right to hunt on his land. But the "qualification statutes"—so-called because they imposed qualifications on the privilege of hunting—played a far broader role in the British social structure. As they evolved, these statutes came to prohibit the ownership of certain species of dogs, the possession of guns, nets, and other "engines for destroying game," as well as hunting by individuals not meeting specified wealth requirements. The various statutes culminated in 1671 in An Act for the Better Preservation of the Game, and for Securing Warrens not Inclosed, and the Several Fishings of the Realm, 22 & 23 Car. 2, ch. 25 (1671). The 1671 statute formed the basis of the English game laws until 1831.

The 1671 Act had two primary provisions. First, it established property qualifications for hunters: "every person . . . not having . . . some . . . estate of inheritance, in his own or his wife's right, of the clear yearly value of one hundred pounds per annum, ... other than the son and heir apparent of an esquire, or other person of higher degree, and the owners and keepers of forests, parks, chases, or warrens ... in respect of the said forests, parks, chases, or warrens, are hereby declared to be persons ... not allowed to have or keep ... guns, [dogs], or other engines [for the taking and killing of game]." *Id.* § 3.

Second, although the statute did not impose penalties for hunting by unqualified persons, it did authorize "all lords of manors, or other royalties, (not under the degree of an esquire,)" to permit their gamekeepers to "take and seize all such guns, bows, greyhounds, setting-dogs, lurchers, or other dogs, ... ferrets, tramels, lowbels, hays, or other nets, hare-pipes, snares, or other engines, for taking and killing conies, hares, pheasants, partridges, or other game" and to "search the houses, out-houses, or other places of any such person ... by this act prohibited to keep or use" the specified hunting devices. *Id.* § 2. The effect was to create a new, privatized system of law enforcement in which the landed gentry was delegated governmental powers. For example, in *Barrington v. Turner,* 3 Lev. 28, 83 Eng. Rep. 560 (K.B. 1693), the court upheld defendant's demurrer to plaintiff's trespass action for killing two greyhounds. The dogs had chased a deer from plaintiff's land into defendant's park from where it had strayed to eat the grass on plaintiff's land. The court held the defendant's action justified since plaintiff was not qualified to hunt.

(4) The Waltham Black Act: The most notorious of all English game laws was the Waltham Black Act, 9 Geo. I, ch. 22, § 1 (1723). The Black Act was a truly remarkable statute: it imposed capital punishment for between 200 and 250 separate offenses—depending upon how one parses the commas—including death for those who "wilfully hunt, wound, kill, destroy, or steal any red or fallow deer, or unlawfully rob any warren or place where conies or hares are usually kept, or shall unlawfully steal or take away any fish out of any river or pond." The Black Act was the favorite example when American judges wished to remind their readers of the tyranny that game laws could produce. Recall, for example, *State v. Campbell,* T.U.P.C. 166 (Ga.1808) [Chapter 2].

PERSPECTIVES

Robin Hood and the romance of poaching: One of the enduring English stories is the tale of Robin Hood. In the *Gest of Robyn Hode,*[3] our hero's means of sustenance troubles the king who has set out to capture him because "good Robin.... always slew the king's deer And did with them as he liked." *A Gest of Robyn Hode* verses 364–65, *reprinted in* R.B. DOBSON & J. TAYLOR, RYMES OF ROBYN HOOD 105 (1976). While Robin alone has survived in the popular imagination, he was only one of several, now-forgotten outlaws who were also the subject of gests. Like Robin and his

---

3. *A Gest of Robyn Hode* and *A Lyttell Geste of Robyn Hode* were first published in the late fifteenth or early sixteenth century; they were drawn from an earlier text—written perhaps as early as 1400—that has not survived and that was itself based on an oral tradition dating to an even earlier period. The man himself probably lived in the late thirteenth or early fourteenth century.

men, Adam Bell, Clim of the Clough, and William of Cloudesley "were outlawed for venyson." ADAM BELL, CLIM OF THE CLOUGH, AND WILLIAM CLOUDESLE (c. 1680), *reprinted in* J.C. HOLT, ROBIN HOOD 66 (1982). For another, less romantic, perspective on the politics of poaching, *see* C.J. RIBTON-TURNER, A HISTORY OF VAGRANTS AND VAGRANCY AND BEGGARS AND BEGGING 30–31 (1887).

b. THE COMMON LAW IN A NEW WORLD

NOTES

American abundance and taking restrictions: Initially, the abundance of fish and game made taking restrictions appear unnecessary and a policy of free access was simply assumed. Experience demonstrated, however, that wildlife, while renewable, was not infinite. Closed seasons and other restrictions began to appear at the end of the seventeenth century. By the Revolution, every colony except Georgia had restricted killing deer. As population increased, so did legislative output.

(a) closed periods: Massachusetts, for example, required all weirs to be removed three days each week, *Commonwealth v. Wentworth*, 15 Mass. 188 (1818); New York prohibited fishing on Sunday, *Sickles v. Sharp*, 13 Johns. 497 (N.Y.Sup.Ct.1816); and North Carolina closed fishing 48 hours a week, *Fagan v. Armistead*, 33 N.C. 433 (1850). Virginia prohibited killing deer between January and August. St. George Tucker, *Notes to* 3 BLACKSTONE'S COMMENTARIES 394 n.2 (Philadelphia, 1803). Thomas Lund cites other colonial and state statutes establishing closed periods on the taking of waterfowl, fish, oysters, and deer. Thomas A. Lund, *Early American Wildlife Law*, 51 N.Y.U.L. REV. 703, 719–21 (1976).

(b) gear restrictions: Connecticut prohibited the use of brush weirs for taking fish, *Eastman v. Curtis*, 1 Conn. 323 (1815); Massachusetts prohibited the use of seine or drag nets in Falmouth, *Nye v. Lamphere*, 68 Mass. (2 Gray) 295 (1854); and Queens, New York outlawed dredging for oysters, *Smith v. Levinus*, 8 N.Y. 472 (1853).

(c) bag limits: Connecticut prohibited taking more than six bushels of oysters per week, *Hayden v. Noyes*, 5 Conn. 391 (1824), and Maine placed the limit at seven bushels, "including shells." *Moulton v. Libbey*, 37 Me. 472 (1854).

(d) prohibitions on commerce in wildlife: As the nineteenth century drew to a close, states also began to impose restrictions on the sale of game. A variety of prohibitions were adopted with differing legal results. Some states prohibited all sales of game, *e.g., American Express Co. v. People*, 24 N.E. 758 (Ill.1890); some banned all sales of out-of-season game, *e.g., Phelps v. Racey*, 60 N.Y. 10 (1875); others banned all sales of in-state-and-out-of-season wildlife, *e.g., Commonwealth v. Hall*, 128 Mass. 410 (1880); some banned shipping game out of state, *e.g., State v. Geer*, 22 A. 1012 (Conn.1891), *aff'd sub nom. Geer v. Connecticut*, 161 U.S. 519 (1896).

(e) **licenses:** Fishing licenses were required by Connecticut, *Hayden v. Noyes,* 5 Conn. 391 (1824), Maine, *Moulton v. Libbey,* 37 Me. 472 (1854), and Massachusetts, *Nickerson v. Brackett,* 10 Mass. 212 (1813).

J.W. MEADER, THE MERRIMACK RIVER

248–49 (Boston, 1869).

It may not be supposed that fishing was altogether confined to legitimate days; on the contrary, though perhaps for the purpose of keeping the officials busy and zealous in the discharge of their duties, attempts were constantly made at surreptitious fishing and violation of the law, which, however, generally involved no more serious consequences than bloody noses, and engendered irritation and ill-feeling between the officials and the fishermen. The fish clandestinely obtained seemed to possess a peculiar flavor, or possibly the sport was so attractive to many that legal restraint was impossible. On one occasion, as the disciples of Walton were playing an unlawful business on Long Island (opposite the Lawrence corporation), an obnoxious and officious official from Haverhill (named Vincent), with his posse, pounced upon them, and the scene that ensued may be imagined. Donneybrook was outdone, the official and his party were repeatedly fished out of the river, after unceremonious baptisms by the faithful, and soon as possible beat a precipitate retreat without making any arrests, but with a wholesome lesson in prudence to guide them in the future enforcement of obnoxious laws.

PERSPECTIVES

The mythology of poaching in a new world: Although the evidence is necessarily anecdotal, the prevalence of poaching is uniformly acknowledged. As one historian of the Merrimack River Valley commented, "a history of the unlawful fishing at the [Amoskeag] Falls would be more voluminous than interesting." CHARLES E. POTTER, THE HISTORY OF MANCHESTER, FORMERLY DERRYFIELD IN NEW-HAMPSHIRE 651 (1856). J.W. Meader offers a "boys-will-be-boys" air—a still-prevalent attitude: "other than the fact that it's against the law, what's wrong with . . . poaching?" RAGNAR BENSON, SURVIVAL POACHING 8 (1980). Such an attitude is a short step from support. Claude Dallas, for example, became something of a folk hero after shooting two Idaho Fish and Game agents who caught him poaching. JEFF LONG, OUTLAW (1985); JACK OLSEN, GIVE A BOY A GUN (1985).

Tacit support for poaching reflected a widespread attitude that crept into judicial opinions. The Georgia Supreme Court, for example, opined that English game laws were "productive of tyranny." The game laws were

> founded upon a tender solicitude for the amusement and property of the aristocracy of England. It was made to protect from the violation or profanation of the people, the forest of his majesty or the park of a peer. How then could it apply to a country which was but one extended forest, in which the liberty if killing a deer, or cutting down a tree, was as unrestrained as the natural rights of the deer to rove, or the tree to grow?

State v. Campbell, T.U.P.C. 166, 168 (Ga.Sup.Ct.1808). Another court stated that game laws were "contrary to the spirit of our institutions." *Hallock v. Dominy,* 7 Hun. 52, 55 (N.Y.App.Div.1876).

Furthermore, Meader's conclusion that "surreptitious fishing and violation of the law . . . generally involved no more serious consequences than bloody noses, and . . . irritation," ignores the simple fact that fish runs and game animals were depleted by poaching. *See, e.g.,* HELENETTE SILVER, A HISTORY OF NEW HAMPSHIRE GAME AND FURBEARERS 195 (1957) (overhunting was the prime cause of the extermination of white-tailed deer in New Hampshire). Once again, wildlife was a given, simply stage props for the human drama.

This cavalier attitude supports an observation by Lawrence Friedman that "a group may be less severe on its own forms of deviance than on the deviance of outsiders. . . . Juries in America were more tolerant of violations of game laws than the king and his servants would have been." LAWRENCE M. FRIEDMAN, A HISTORY OF AMERICAN LAW 284 (2d ed. 1985). Furthermore, there is reason to believe that poachers were—and are— capable of more than bloody noses. *See, e.g.,* Thomas A. Lund, *Early American Wildlife Law,* 51 NEW YORK UNIVERSITY LAW REVIEW 703, 723–24 (1976); JACK OLSEN, GIVE A BOY A GUN (1985); Michael A. Scialfa, An Ethnographic Analysis of Poachers and Poaching in Northern Idaho and Eastern Washington 19–20 (1992) (unpublished M.S. thesis, University of Idaho).

SECTION 2.   STATE COMMISSIONS AND THEIR POWERS

a.   COMMISSION COMPOSITION AND THE CONTROL OF POWER

Humane Society v. New Jersey State Fish & Game Council

New Jersey Supreme Court.
70 N.J. 565, 362 A.2d 20 (1976).

■ CLIFFORD, J.—This case presents a challenge, on equal protection and due process grounds, to the constitutionality of N.J.S.A. 13:1B–24. That enactment sets forth the qualifications and recommendation procedures for appointment to the Fish and Game Council, an appointive eleven member body within the Division of Fish, Game and Shell Fisheries of the Department of Environmental Protection. The trial court (which heard the case on what it called "a limited stipulation of facts and legal argument"), in a formal opinion later clarified by a supplemental letter to counsel and subsequent order, held the statute unconstitutional, [ ]. While defendants' appeal was pending in the Appellate Division, this Court granted certification directly to the Chancery Division, [ ]. We conclude the statute survives the constitutional attack made here and therefore we reverse.

I

The Fish and Game Council is invested with certain regulatory powers aimed at protecting and developing an adequate supply of fish and game for recreational and commercial purposes. These powers are expressed primarily by the Council's determinations as to when and where in the state hunting and fishing shall take place, and which fresh water fish, game birds, game animals, and fur bearing animals may be taken and in what numbers. The wildlife thus regulated are those animals which are the focus of the sports of hunting and fishing.[4] In addition, the Council supervises a program of wildlife propagation, the expenses of which are supported by fees for hunting and fishing licenses paid for by sportsmen and commercial fishermen.

Plaintiffs are two non-profit organizations, the Humane Society, New Jersey Branch, and the Sierra Club, and two individuals who are taxpayers and citizens of New Jersey. They contend that the Fish and Game Council membership statute is constitutionally defective because it enumerates three classes of appointees to the Council—sportsmen, farmers, and commercial fishermen—and excludes from appointment any person who is not recommended to the Governor by either the State Agricultural Convention or the New Jersey State Federation of Sportsmen's Clubs (hereafter Sportsmen's Federation).

The statutory provisions for membership and appointment are as follows:

13:1B–24. Fish and Game Council; members; terms.

There shall be within the Division of Fish and Game, a Fish and Game Council which shall consist of eleven members, each of whom shall be chosen with due regard to his knowledge of and interest in the conservation of fish and game. Each member of the council shall be appointed by the Governor, with the advice and consent of the Senate. Three of such members shall be farmers, recommended to the Governor for appointment to the council by the agricultural convention held pursuant to the provisions of article two of chapter one of Title 4 of the Revised Statutes; six of such members shall be sportsmen, recommended to the Governor for appointment to the council by the New Jersey State Federation of Sportsmen's Clubs; and two of such members shall be commercial fishermen.

It is stipulated that the individual plaintiffs, the members of the Humane Society, New Jersey Branch, and the Sierra Club are all interested in and knowledgeable about the conservation of fish and game. As the statute indicates, although sponsorship by the Sportsmen's Federation and the State Agricultural Convention is essential to appointment to the Fish and Game Council, membership in those organizations is not. Plaintiffs enjoy the state's lands and wildlife for purposes other than hunting, fishing, and farming. For personal and policy reasons they cannot or will not become affiliated with or seek membership in the Sportsmen's Federation, nor do they at all suggest that they qualify, by occupation or

4. Endangered species are separately regulated by statute, see N.J.S.A. 23:2A–1 *et* *seq.* and do not come within the scope of the Council's power and duties.

otherwise, as farmers.[5] Plaintiffs contend, moreover, that any such affiliation would not serve to give them an effective voice in making or becoming the subject of recommendations to the Governor. In fact, the State conceded at oral argument that as a practical matter all appointees to the Council have been members of either the Sportsmen's Federation or the Agricultural Convention.

The essence of plaintiffs' challenge is that they are practically barred from participating in the Fish and Game Council's decisions which affect plaintiffs' recreational and educational activities. They characterize their exclusion from the ranks of those eligible for appointment as a denial of equal protection. Additionally, they contend that the statutory delegation of the power of appointment to a private organization such as the Sportsmen's Federation violates due process. The trial court's opinion upheld plaintiffs' position and ruled that a person otherwise qualified may not statutorily be excluded from appointment to the Fish and Game Council on the grounds that he or she is not either a sportsman, a farmer, or a commercial fisherman. [ ] By the order following this formal opinion and supplemental letter, referred to above, the trial judge also declared unconstitutional those provisions of N.J.S.A. 13:1B–24 which channel appointments to the Council through the Sportsmen's Federation and the Agricultural Convention. Finally, he enjoined defendants from acting pursuant to the membership statute, with the result that the terms of five of the eleven Council members have expired and are being filled by holdover appointees.

II

It must be stressed here that plaintiffs have not alleged malefaction on the part of the Council members, past or present, nor has the inherent subject of their activities—namely, hunting and fishing in their recreational and commercial aspects—come under attack. Nor do plaintiffs condemn the qualifications the statute articulates for appointment to the Council, for they agree Council members should be chosen "with due regard to [their] knowledge of and interest in the conservation of fish and game." What rankles is the selection process, which operates so that the individual plaintiffs and the members of the organizational plaintiffs, all of whom possess the statutory qualifications for appointment, are excluded.

The trial court correctly applied to the Council membership statute the minimum scrutiny, rational basis test, which looks to whether a state of

---

5. Although neither side contends that the term 'sportsman' per se excludes environmentalists from its scope, plaintiffs point out that of fifteen Sportsmen's Federation officers or former officers responding to interrogatories, only one did not engage in hunting or fishing activities. Of 316 member clubs listed in response to interrogatories, 212 were named Rod and Gun Club or Trap Shooting Club. Only five of the listed clubs had titles suggesting purposes unrelated to hunting and fishing. One response by the Federation states that many member clubs include campers, hikers, and backpackers in their numbers but that no records are kept with reference to these non-hunting and fishing activities.

The State Agriculture Convention, held pursuant to statute, N.J.S.A. 4:1–5, is an annual meeting of delegates from county agricultural boards and private agricultural groups. Its membership elects by majority vote three farmers for recommendation to the Fish and Game Council. As such, the Agricultural Convention would not be the appropriate means for plaintiffs to seek access to the Council.

facts exists that can reasonably justify the legislative scheme. *Salyer Land Co. v. Tulare Lake Basin Water Storage District*, 410 U.S. 719 (1973). There the Supreme Court rejected an equal protection challenge directed against provisions in the California Water Code which established voter qualifications for electing the directors of water storage districts in the state. Only landowners were eligible to vote, and the votes were apportioned according to the assessed valuation of the land. The classification was found acceptable despite the fact that it impinged on the franchise, because landowners as a class bore the entire burden of the costs of the water district and California "could rationally conclude that they, to the exclusion of residents, should be charged with responsibility for [the district's] operation." 410 U.S. at 731.

Here, as in *Salyer*, a particularized unit of government is implicated and the persons who achieve office do not have plenary powers. The Fish and Game Council is a specialized body, with statutorily prescribed duties and statutory limits on its powers and activities. Its members serve by appointment, not by election. Access to the Council cannot be said to be entwined with the fundamental right to vote, which would call for this Court to use the stricter, close scrutiny standard of review and would rebut the presumption of validity the statute now enjoys. *Bullock v. Carter*, 405 U.S. 134 (1972); *Kramer v. Union Free School District*, 395 U.S. 621 (1969).

The burden, then, is on plaintiffs to demonstrate that the impact upon them of the Fish and Game Council's decisions is so significant and substantial as to render a statutory scheme which effectively bars them from appointment to the Council patently arbitrary and unreasonable. Only upon such a showing can their non-membership in this specialized body assume the dimensions of a constitutional deprivation.

III

It is axiomatic that the Fourteenth Amendment does not forbid classifications per se.

Equal protection does not require that all persons be dealt with identically. If there is some reasonable basis for the recognition of separate classes, and the disparate treatment of the classes has a rational relation to the object sought to be achieved by the lawmakers, the constitution is not offended. *N.J. Chapter, American Inst. of Planners v. N.J. State Bd. of Planners*, 227 A.2d 313, 323 (N.J.), *appeal dismissed*, 389 U.S. 8 (1967).

The Legislature may prescribe such qualifications as reasonably relate to the demands of a specialized office. [ ] Logic is not offended by the classes included in the challenged statute. We have already stressed the discrete character of the Fish and Game Council, charged as it is with certain responsibilities and powers pertinent to ensuring the statutory objective of an abundant supply of game for recreational and commercial hunting and fishing. Sportsmen, farmers, and commercial fishermen feel directly the impact of decision-making in this area and are likely to have the necessary expertise to make the required decisions competently.

The statute specifies that six of the eleven Council members must be sportsmen. Assuming this category consists of the hunters and fishermen of the state, it is difficult to conceive of a group with a keener interest in maintaining a plentiful supply of game, in developing regulations to insure safety in hunting, and in overseeing the operations of the state's hatching and game farm and its stocking activities. Farmers, who are represented by three Council members, own the major part of the hunting lands in the State. Thus, as property owners, they are directly affected by the Council's activities. They are also in an advantageous position to recognize the point at which overpopulation in a species of game animal has become a matter of concern. The Council's power to regulate animals which menace agricultural crops, see N.J.S.A. 23:4–63.3, further justifies representation by farmers. To the extent that sportsmen and farmers have special interests which may at times conflict, the presence of both groups on the Council is at once a rational legislative decision and a desirable one. For the same reason it is appropriate that these Council members be recommended to the Governor by organizations consisting of their peers.

Two commercial fishermen are appointed to the Council directly by the Governor, and their method of selection cannot be said to offend the due process principles plaintiffs advance. Regarding this classification, however, plaintiffs point out that inasmuch as the Council has jurisdiction over fresh water fishing and there is little commercial fresh water fishing in New Jersey, commercial fishermen therefore have only a tenuous connection with the purposes of the statutory scheme. That appointment is specified from this group rather than from the general public, however, is not necessarily arbitrary and capricious: the Council issues licenses to fishermen who wish to fish commercially in those waters of the Atlantic Ocean that are within the state's jurisdiction, see N.J.S.A. 23:3–41 and N.J.S.A. 23:3–47. Additionally, it is logical to assume that commercial fishermen have, by virtue of their trade, an overall expertise that commends their membership on the Fish and Game Council. The fact that the Council's minimal control of salt-water fishing has no significant commercial impact obviates any suggestion that the two commercial fishermen who serve on it could use their office to promote directly their own or the industry's economic well-being over the public interest.

VI

Having determined that there is a reasonable basis for the statutory inclusion of sportsmen, farmers, and commercial fishermen, and giving all due regard to plaintiffs' articulated concerns, we cannot find that plaintiffs' exclusion is of sufficient import to offend the Fourteenth Amendment. While neither side evinced any certainty at oral argument that the term "sportsman" does not include an environmentalist, nevertheless even if we assume that the classification contemplates only hunters and fishermen, the statutory scheme is not unduly stringent. The legislative arrangement suggests that the numbers of sportsmen for purposes of the appointment process should be substantial, inasmuch as eligibility for membership in the Sportsmen's Federation is provided to every duly organized sportsmen's club in the state with twenty-five or more members specifically for the purpose of permitting "the broadest possible representation of sportsmen in the making of recommendations for appointment of sportsmen to membership in the council * * *." N.J.S.A. 13:1B–25.

Plaintiffs have elected not to align themselves with the Sportsmen's Federation, a choice that assuredly is theirs to make. However, they have neither alleged nor proven that their interests are antithetical to the Federation or that, should they attempt to join, they would be rejected. It is perfectly reasonable, therefore, to view their continued absence from the Council as a product of plaintiffs' own alienation rather than as the result of a statutory exclusion.

More compelling, however, is the fact that the dominion of the Fish and Game Council is so confined. The wildlife it regulates, as indicated, are limited specifically to those species which are commonly the subjects of hunting and fishing, and even then the regulatory power is restricted. *See, e.g.,* N.J.S.A. 23:4–49, defining game birds to include twenty-two species; N.J.S.A. 23:4–1, prohibiting hunting of most of these birds except in open season fixed by federal regulations. *See also* N.J.S.A. 23:4–18. The hunting season and, where applicable, the bag limits for certain birds and small game, N.J.S.A. 23:4–1, N.J.S.A. 23:4–2, and N.J.S.A. 23:3–32, certain fur-bearing animals, N.J.S.A. 23:4–39, deer, N.J.S.A. 23:4–43, foxes, N.J.S.A. 23:4–58.1, and certain fish, N.J.S.A. 23:5–1, are set forth by statute where no provision in these instances otherwise appears in the State Fish and Game Code. The Council is responsible for issuing the regulations which comprise the Code, N.J.S.A. 13:1B–30. While it enjoys, in the discharge of this function, a certain flexibility permitting enlargement or limitation of the statutory designations, nevertheless the Council at all times must condition such departures on the essential purpose its regulations are designed to serve—the maintenance of a plentiful supply of game and fish for recreational hunting and fishing. Notice and public hearings as well as scientific investigation and research must precede adoption of and any changes in Code regulations and amendments thereto, N.J.S.A. 13:1B–31 *et seq.* The statutory scheme expressly subjects "[a]ny regulation, or amendment thereto, or repealer thereof" to appropriate judicial review. N.J.S.A. 13:1B–35.

The Council does not have unfettered authority to decide that hunting or fishing will take place on private property, see N.J.S.A. 23:7–1, or on state-owned lands. As to the latter, co-existing with the Division of Fish, Game and Shell Fisheries in the Department of Environmental Protection is the Division of Parks, Forestry and Recreation, N.J.S.A. 13:1B–15.100 *et seq.,* which has its own Council. This likewise is made up of eleven members, who recommend programs and policies concerning the acquisition, development, use and improvement of state parks, forests, and recreation areas. N.J.S.A. 13:1B–15.104. The competitive interests of the respective Councils are served by the legislative scheme, and it is fair to say that the interests of plaintiffs in enjoying the state's lands and wildlife for purposes other than hunting and fishing are represented in part by the Parks, Forestry and Recreation Council.

In summary, what authority the Fish and Game Council has been given by N.J.S.A. 13:1B–30, empowering that body to determine "under what circumstances, when and in what localities, by what means and in what amounts and numbers" fish and game may be taken, must be said to be circumscribed by other agencies, [ ], and existing statutory norms. That authority is limited as well by the mandate that the Council direct its regulations toward providing "an adequate and flexible system of protection, propagation, increase, control and conservation" of fish and game birds and animals. The consignment of the specialized powers and duties flowing from this legislative scheme to so-called special interest groups has a rational basis, because these entities are most directly affected by the Council's regulations and possess the requisite expertise for achievement of the statutory objective.

Furthermore, the statute passes muster even were we to go beyond the traditional rational basis test and apply the means focused test, which this Court has used to determine constitutional challenges asserting interests more fundamental than the ones advanced by these plaintiffs. [ ] The governmental interest in establishing regulations to ensure a plentiful supply of game animals for consumption and sport is suitably furthered by placing a degree of regulatory control in the hands of a Fish and Game Council composed of sportsmen, farmers, and commercial fishermen. Opening the Council's membership to persons with differing philosophies might reflect the art of public relations, but it is not a constitutional necessity.

V

Finally, plaintiffs contend that the role played by the Agricultural Convention and the Sportsmen's Federation in recommending nine of the eleven appointees amounts to an "inbred nominating process" offensive to due process because it produces a Council incompletely representative of the public interest. [ ]

The delegation of nominating authority to private persons is not in derogation of the constitution where that document is silent as to the appointment of public officials. [ ] Even delegation of legislative authority to private parties may withstand constitutional challenge if sufficient safeguards exist to prevent an arbitrary concentration of power in persons or groups motivated by self interest. "The test is whether the particular delegation is reasonable under the circumstances considering the purpose and aim of the statute. [ ]

. . .

Finally, we record our recognition of the fact that the Council's operations bear on the public interest. That being so, the present composition of the Council may be perceived as less than ideal. While the cure does not lie in opening up Council membership to other public interest groups in addition to farmers, sportsmen and commercial fishermen, we acknowledge that a better balance would be achieved by the presence of some public members. Legislative action towards that end would be salutary.

VI

The judgment of the trial court is reversed. The injunction is dissolved, and appointments to fill the vacancies now held by holdover appointees may be made forthwith consistent with the existing legislative formula.

For reversal: CHIEF JUSTICE HUGHES, JUSTICES MOUNTAIN, SULLIVAN, CLIFFORD and SCHREIBER and JUDGE CONFORD—6.

For affirmance: JUSTICE PASHMAN—1.

■ PASHMAN, J., dissenting:.... Because I find the discriminatory impact of this statutory scheme to be arbitrary and unreasonable and because I feel that plaintiffs deserve independent representation on the Council, I dissociate myself from the majority and would affirm the trial court's decision.

. . .

I fully agree with the trial judge's statement of the issue and with his conclusion that the classification in the statute is arbitrary. The majority today, however, rejects this rational and just result. In part, the Court bases its decision on plaintiffs' failure to demonstrate that "the term 'sportsman' does not include an environmentalist." [ ] While information clearly within the realm of judicial notice should suggest the basis for this distinction, differences between the interests advanced by plaintiffs and those of the Sportsmen's Federation were clearly established at trial. In fact, not only are plaintiffs' concerns distinguishable from those of the groups which are represented on the Council, but in certain instances they may be diametrically opposed. Sportsmen and environmentalists often (though not always) operate from different premises. The Council through its component organizations, for example, attempts to meet its conservation mandate solely by the regulation of hunting and the propagation of different species of animals. Plaintiffs, on the other hand, view conservation in terms of a broader ecosystem within which game animals and their relative numbers are merely singular components. This broader view of conservation is reflected in the greater range of activities in which plaintiffs participate. These activities, which include backpacking, camping and birdwatching are clearly affected both by the decisions of the Fish and Game Council and by the often adverse interests of the groups which are now represented on the Council. Thus, it would be meaningless for plaintiffs to affiliate themselves with groups whose interests they do not share.

NOTES

(1) The state fish and game council allocates a public resource—wildlife that resides within the state—among potential recipients. Why is it permissible for the state legislature to give allocational authority to a body comprised of individuals with a stake in the allocation process?

In *Reynolds v. Sims,* 377 U.S. 533 (1964), the Supreme Court established the one-person one-vote principle as a core element of equal protection. Why is this principle inapplicable to the Fish and Game Council? Is it simply that the council is not selected through an election? Is it sufficient that the individual plaintiffs in *Humane Society* are equal participants in the election of state legislators—who ultimately determine the process for selecting the fish and game council?

(2) Agency capture: New Jersey is far from alone in favoring sportsmen and farmers when selecting citizens to run state fish and game or wildlife commissions. What impacts might such favoritism have in terms of the policy decisions made by these commissions? Are hunters likely to have the same idea of desired game populations as would conservationists more concerned about maintaining the health of ecosystems? Might the membership of a state commission in some manner affect the degree of deference that a court gives to commission decisions when considering a challenge to their validity?

Assuming that state wildlife agencies could be de-politicized, should they? Is your answer affected by your perspective on the agency's job? Traditionally, agencies have allocated wildlife by setting seasons and bag limits. Is that function appropriate for politicians? To the extent that you conceive wildlife management to include conservation of non-game species, does your answer change? What steps might be taken to reduce the role of politics?

(3) Animal rights: According to public opinion polls, a majority of Americans favor bans on hunting, largely out of concerns over the welfare of individual animals. Should citizens who hold such views be represented on the boards of state commissions, or has a legislature, by expressly permitting hunting of certain species, effectively decided as a matter of state policy that anti-hunting sentiment is properly ignored? If animal rights advocates did gain membership on such a board, would they be obligated to support hunting of game species as part of their larger duty to uphold and enforce state laws?

(4) Solidifying political control: Citizen groups dismayed with the policy predispositions of state commissions have at times undertaken successfully to change wildlife laws by means of initiatives and referenda, especially by pushing measures such as bans on leg-hold traps. Recall, for example, the discussion in Chapter 1 on California's ban on leg-hold traps. To ward off such moves, agency defenders have proposed amendments to state constitutions to require super-majority votes to sustain wildlife-related initiatives. Voters in Utah in 1998 amended the state's constitutional provision on initiatives to require a two-thirds majority for any "legislation initiated to allow, limit, or prohibit the taking of wildlife or the season for or method of taking wildlife"; in the case of legislation on any other subject, a simple majority is sufficient. UTAH CONST. Art. VI, sec. 1(2)(a)(ii). Though largely opposed by wildlife conservation organizations (and unanimously opposed by animal welfare groups), the amendment was presented to voters as a pro-wildlife measure.

Several states in recent years have also debated constitutional provisions guaranteeing citizens the right to hunt—measures supported by similar coalitions of traditional, game-focused approaches to wildlife management. In 1998, Minnesota added the following provision to its constitution: "Hunting and fishing and the taking of game and fish are a valued part of our heritage that shall be forever preserved to the people and shall be managed by law and regulation for the public good." MINN. CONST. Art. 13, sec. 12. Virginia voters in 2000 embraced an alternative phrasing: "The people have a right to hunt, fish, and harvest game, subject to such regulations and restrictions as the General Assembly may prescribe by general law." VA. CONST. Art. XI, sec. 4. What effects, if any, are such provisions likely to have on the lawmaking powers of state legislatures and on the regulatory powers of state commissions? Do they limit lawmaking powers with enough specificity for courts to enforce them? Are they anything more than symbolic gestures? Keep in mind that several states included such provisions in their initial constitutions in the eighteenth and nineteenth centuries. As noted in chapter 3, even the Vermont provision, which expressly opens all "unenclosed" private land to public hunting, has been construed so as offer scant protection for public hunters. Notice also that both the Minnesota and Virginia provisions distinguish between the hunting of game (protected) and nongame (not protected). Has the term "game" in these states now become a constitutional issue for state courts to decide?

b.   Delegation of the Power to Make Law

Bean v. McWherter

Supreme Court of Tennessee.
953 S.W.2d 197 (1997).

■ HOLDER, J.:—This appeal addresses the General Assembly's power to delegate rule-making authority to administrative agencies. The Court of Appeals held that the General Assembly could not constitutionally delegate power to the Tennessee Wildlife Resources Commission ("TWRC") to add or delete animals from the dangerous species list. We reverse and hold that the legislature may delegate power to add and delete items from a statutory schedule absent explicit guidance standards. The legislature, however, must provide a basic standard accompanied by a general policy when delegating in areas concerning public health, safety, and general welfare.

BACKGROUND

The plaintiffs, Robert Bean *et al.*, claimed to be owners, dealers, or licensed propagators of various wildlife species. They filed a complaint seeking a declaratory judgment against the defendants, the TWRC and the Director of the Tennessee Wildlife Resources Agency ("Director"). The plaintiffs alleged that Tenn. Code Ann. § 70–4–403(1) & (3) violated the Tennessee Constitution by unlawfully delegating legislative authority to both the TWRC and to the Director.

The trial court granted the plaintiffs' petition. The trial court held the delegation unconstitutional because "the legislature did not provide the agencies with any standards by which they were to proceed in deleting or adding species under [the statute]." The Court of Appeals affirmed the trial court and held that the delegation was unconstitutional due to the absence of specific standards. The appellate court reasoned that, absent specific standards, the statute vests the TWRC and the Director with "the discretion to determine what the law shall be as opposed to discretion as to the law's execution."

We find the delegation of power constitutionally valid. For the reasons stated below, we reverse the Court of Appeals and dismiss the case.

STATUTORY LANGUAGE

The issue in controversy concerns the statutory provisions in Tenn. Code Ann. § 70–4–403(1) & (3). This statute classifies Tennessee wildlife into five (5) general classes. Class I includes "all species inherently dangerous to humans." Class II includes all native species ("presently occurring in the wild") not listed in another class. Class III is a domestic or semi-domestic class of animals that: (1) is not listed in other classifications; and (2) requires "no permits except those required by the department of agriculture." Class IV includes native species that may only be possessed by zoos and temporary exhibitors. Class V includes species that are injurious to the environment.

This appeal focuses on Class I and Class III. Class I provides that "[t]he commission, in conjunction with the commissioner of agriculture, may add or delete species from the list of Class I wildlife by promulgating rules and regulations." Tenn. Code Ann. § 70–4–403(1). Class III permits "[t]he commission, in conjunction with the commissioner of agriculture, [to] add or delete species from the list of Class III wildlife by promulgating rules and regulations." The delegation of the authority to add and delete species from Class I and Class III is the focus of this appeal by the defendants. Tenn. Code Ann. § 70–4–403(3).

ANALYSIS

The General Assembly may grant an administrative agency the power to promulgate rules and regulations which have the effect of law in the agency's area of operation. [ ] This grant of power, however, should be limited and defined in such a manner that administrative officials can discern and implement the legislature's will. [ ] An administrative agency may be afforded discretion as to implementation of legislative policy but not as to determination of that policy. [ ]

Our review of previous case law reveals that this Court has never succinctly stated a test for determining whether a delegation of power is constitutional. In *Lobelville Special School District v. McCanless,* 381 S.W.2d 273 (Tenn.1964), this Court quoted 16 C.J.S. *Constitutional Law* § 133, 560–61 for the proposition that lawful delegations require a "sufficient basic standard" accompanied by "a definite and certain policy and rule of action." *Id.* at 274. Legislative delegations must also contain sufficient safeguards to prevent agencies from acting in an arbitrary manner. [ ] Prior case law, however, has not enunciated criteria for analyzing whether the legislature's guidelines or standards are adequate to prevent arbitrary action.

We are mindful of the need for guidance in this area. We have reexamined *Tasco [v. Long,* 368 S.W.2d 65 (1963)] and its progeny and have created a test for analyzing the adequacy of the standards or guidelines contained in a statute alleged to have unlawfully delegated legislative power. We, therefore, hold that the test for determining whether a statute is an unlawful delegation is whether the statute contains sufficient standards or guidelines to enable both the agency and the courts to determine if the agency is carrying out the legislature's intent.

Governing standards need not be expressed provided such standards can be reasonably ascertained from the statutory scheme as a whole. The necessity of expressed standards is contingent upon the statute's subject matter and on the degree of difficulty involved in articulating finite standards. Detailed or specific legislation may be neither required nor feasible when the subject matter requires an agency's expertise and flexibility to deal with complex and changing conditions.

The requirement of expressed standards may also be relaxed when the discretion to be exercised relates to or regulates for the protection of the public's health, safety, and welfare. In *Tasco v. Long,* 368 S.W.2d 65 (1963), this Court was confronted with a statute that delegated powers to a board to grant general contractor licenses. The statute stated that the board

> shall have the power to make such by-laws, rules, and regulations as it shall deem best, providing the same are not in conflict with the laws of Tennessee.

Id. at 67. We interpreted the statute's standard as one of reasonableness. *Id.* at 67–69. The board, therefore, was given the discretion to act provided its decisions were neither arbitrary nor capricious and were in harmony with the laws of this state. *Id.* Although these guidelines were vague, they were held sufficient under the circumstances.

In *Tasco,* we found that the policy behind the statute was "to protect the general public from contractors who are not qualified to perform work which they have contracted * * *." *Id.* at 68. Accordingly, *Tasco* teaches us that minutely detailed standards are not required when the statute's policy relates to public health, safety, or welfare and when flexibility is necessary for practical legislation.

The legislative policy of the present statute is clear. The statute outlines a general scheme designed to protect the public from dangerous animals. If the agency adds a non-enumerated animal to one of the legislative classes, that species is regulated pursuant to the legislative scheme. The mere adding or deleting of animals from a nonexclusive list or moving an animal from one classification to another does not alter the legislative policy of providing public protection. *See State v. Edwards,* 572 S.W.2d 917 (Tenn.1978) (holding adding and deleting items from a non-exclusive list permissible).

Because the present statute concerns issues of public safety and welfare, the requirement of expressed or specific standards is relaxed. The legislative standard for adding an animal to Class I is whether the animal is "inherently dangerous." The legislature has also provided a non-exclusive list, in both Class I and Class III, of animals falling within the legislatively-created categories or classifications. These lists provide the agency with additional criteria for classifying animals.

We have carefully considered the entire statutory scheme and find that the statute implies a standard of reasonableness. We further find that the statute's guidelines are that animals possessing characteristics consistent with the legislature's listed examples and statutory definitions are to be classified pursuant to the legislative scheme. These standards are clearly adequate to allow both us and the TWRC to determine whether the legislature's intent is being furthered.

We hold the present delegation of power constitutional. We reverse the Court of Appeals judgment and remand for further proceedings consistent with this opinion. Costs of this appeal are taxed to the appellees, Robert Bean *et al.,* for which execution may issue if necessary.

■ ANDERSON, C.J., and DROWOTA, REID and BIRCH, JJ., concur.

NOTES

(1) State agencies are creatures of statute. As such, they have only those powers delegated to them by the legislature. Commonly legislatures delegate agencies the power to set policy and to promulgate regulations that have the force and effect of law. There are, however, limits on the power that can be delegated to an agency. Different courts phrase these limits differently. Sometimes the limitation is stated as a prohibition on delegating legislative powers. More realistic courts, on the other hand, acknowledge that such phrases are empty—how does a regulation differ from a statute?—and look instead to determine whether the legislature has imposed meaningful limits on the power delegated. Those limits might be either substantive or procedural. How did the court in *Bean* resolve this issue?

(2) *Wyoming Coalition v. Wyoming Game & Fish Commission*: A coalition of local businesses, guides and outfitters challenged a decision by the Game and Fish Commission to reduce the bull elk hunting season in Teton County. Plaintiffs argued that the "Commission's authority ... is not constrained by any identifiable legislative standards and is therefore violative of the Wyoming Constitution." The Wyoming Supreme Court disagreed:

> We recognize the proposition that a legislature must define standards in as reasonably precise a fashion as the subject matter permits. The will of the legislature must be clear, which we find it is in this case. The agency is not permitted to follow its own course in articulating rules. The standards found in the Wyoming Game and Fish Act in the statement of its purpose are sufficient to support the delegation challenged by the Coalition. It is incumbent upon the Commission "to provide an adequate and flexible system for control, propagation, management, protection and regulation of all Wyoming wildlife." Wyo. Stat. § 23–1–103.

Wyoming Coalition v. Wyoming Game & Fish Commission, 875 P.2d 729 (Wyo.1994). *See also Westervelt v. Natural Resources Comm'n*, 263 N.W.2d 564 (Mich.1978) (standards and adequate procedural safeguards held sufficient); *Adams v. North Carolina Dep't of Natural and Economic Resources*, 249 S.E.2d 402 (N.C.1978) (general standards accompanied by procedural safeguards sufficient); *Northwest Gillnetters Ass'n v. Sandison*, 628 P.2d 800, 804 (Wash.1981) (legislative delegation upheld because the statute defined "what is to be done and who is to do it, and procedural safeguards exist to control arbitrary administrative action").

SECTION 3. CONSTITUTIONAL LIMITATIONS ON REGULATORY ACTIONS: CONSTITUTIONALLY *ULTRA VIRES*

Statutes that regulate hunting and fishing are often highly detailed, full of finely drawn lines and sometimes surprising distinctions—recall that frogs are fish in Maryland. State regulatory powers may be broad, but do they give state legislatures free rein to draw distinctions as they see fit? Can they apply laws to one part of the state and not another? To one category of land and not another? Recall the decisions in *Cawsey v. Brickey,* 144 P. 938 (Wash.1914), and *Alford v. Finch,* 155 So.2d 790 (Fla.1963) [Chapter III].

As the following decision illustrates, it is possible to challenge particular wildlife statutes by claiming that they run afoul of basic principles of due process and equal protection, as well as by arguing that a given statute amounts to a special (that is, local) law, in violation of state constitutional provisions that commonly ban such law. Courts hearing such challenges, however, tend to show considerable deference to legislative determinations—even when it seems obvious that politics is at play. In practice, successful challenges thus are rare.

State v. Bonnewell

Court of Appeals of Arizona.
196 Ariz. 592, 2 P.3d 682 (1999).

■ RYAN, J.:—Kurt Bonnewell, Lauralu Harkins, Lee P. Hulsey, and Walter John Randall ("Defendants") were convicted of setting a leghold trap on public land in violation of Arizona Revised Statutes Annotated ("A.R.S.") section 17–301(D)(1), a class two misdemeanor. On appeal, they argue that the statute is a special or local law in violation of the Arizona Constitution and that it violates the equal protection clauses of the Arizona and United States Constitutions.

We hold that A.R.S. section 17–301(D) is not an unconstitutional local or special law because it rationally furthers a legitimate governmental purpose, applies to all persons in Arizona, and benefits no static class of individuals. We also hold that the statute does not violate the equal protection clauses of either the Arizona Constitution or the United States Constitution because it is rationally related to a legitimate governmental purpose. We therefore affirm.

Background

In the November 1994 general election, voters passed Proposition 201, which was codified as A.R.S. section 17–301(D). The pertinent part of the statute made unlawful the taking of wildlife on public lands by leghold trap. The statute makes exceptions for the use of traps by government officials to protect against threats to human health or safety, or for research, falconry, relocation of wildlife, or rodent control. *See* A.R.S. § 17–301(D)(1), (3), (4), and (5). According to the pamphlet issued by the Secretary of State on the 1994 Ballot Propositions, the purposes of the initiative were, among others, to prevent cruelty to wildlife on public lands and to prevent injuries to pets, children, and adults using public lands for recreation.

Defendants were each charged with setting a leghold trap in violation of A.R.S. section 17–301(D). Each filed a motion to dismiss the charges, arguing that the statute constituted a local or special law that violated

article 4, part 2, section 19 of the Arizona Constitution and violated the
equal protection guarantees of the Arizona and United States Constitutions
because it made criminal behavior on public land that remained legal when
practiced on private land. At an evidentiary hearing, each Defendant
admitted setting a prohibited leghold trap on public land, but presented
evidence that leghold traps were humane, that they did not indiscriminately injure people or nontarget species, and that the law provided a benefit to
private landowners at the expense of those who trapped on public land. The
State presented no evidence. The trial court denied the motion to dismiss,
ruling that voters could have rationally determined that characteristics of
leghold traps justified banning them from public lands and that the
distinction between public and private lands was legitimate. [ ]

Discussion

. . .

Special or Local Law

Defendants argue that section 17–301(D) constitutes a special or local
law prohibited by the Arizona Constitution. Defendants contend that the
statute conveys benefits to private landowners who can still use leghold
traps to control predation of their livestock and game and to trap fur-
bearing animals for financial gain. We conclude, however, that A.R.S.
section 17–301(D) is not a special law because its classification furthers a
legitimate government objective, it encompasses all members of the relevant class, and the class is flexible.

The Arizona Constitution prohibits any special or local law "granting
any individual any special or exclusive privilege or immunities," or "when
a general law can be made applicable." Art. 4, part 2, § 19(13), (20). The
prohibition against special legislation is intended to prevent the legislature
from providing special benefits and favors to certain groups or locations. [ ]
A law is not a "special" law if (1) the classification is rationally related to a
legitimate government objective, (2) the classification encompasses all
members of the relevant class, and (3) the class is flexible, allowing
members to move into and out of the class. [ ] If a law treats all members of
a class alike and the classification is reasonable, the law is not special
legislation. [ ] Also, the classification must be accepted as reasonable unless
"palpably arbitrary." [ ]

We first consider whether section 17–301(D)'s classification based on
location is rationally related to a legitimate purpose. The statute establishes classifications based on location; it prohibits the use of leghold traps
on public land but not on private land. The information pamphlet on
Proposition 201 indicates that among the purposes of the law are the
prevention of cruelty to animals on public land and the protection from
injury of pets, children, and adults on public land. We believe the statute
rationally furthers these legitimate governmental interests.

Defendants agree that prevention of cruelty to animals on public lands
is a legitimate State interest, but argue that the classification does not
rationally further that interest. Defendants assert that the only rational
means of furthering the State's interest in preventing cruelty to animals,

assuming that leghold traps are cruel, would be to enact a general law prohibiting the use of leghold traps throughout the State on both public and private land. However, to be general, a law need not apply to every person, place, or thing within the State; the law must apply uniformly to those cases and members within the circumstances provided for by the law. [ ] While a law governing all land throughout the State would certainly further the State's interest in preventing cruelty to animals, it does not necessarily follow that the approach taken by the initiative does not further the State's interests. Legislation can be enacted one step at a time, addressing first what is perceived as the most acute aspect of a problem. [ ] Consequently, Defendants are mistaken in assuming that only a statute prohibiting all leghold trapping could further the interest involved.

We do not believe the classification here to be palpably arbitrary. The people of Arizona could legitimately determine that cruelty to animals should be eliminated on land belonging to the people of the State and that the State should prohibit the use of devices perceived to be inhumane and cruel. The statute furthers that purpose.

The statute also furthers the State's interest in preventing injury to people who use public lands for recreation. The classification between private and public lands is reasonably related to this purpose of the statute. Unlike private land, in which the owner has control over the access of individuals onto the property, public lands are accessible to and used by the general public. The private owner, being responsible for his property, would presumably know of the presence of traps that might pose a danger and be able to warn anyone admitted on the property to avoid injury. Such is not the case on public lands, where anyone using the land might accidentally and unexpectedly place a foot in one of the traps, causing injury. Prohibiting the placement of leghold traps on public lands furthers the purpose of the statute to protect users of public lands from injury caused by the traps.

We next consider whether the statute meets the second requirement of a general law. This requirement mandates that the classification encompass all members of the relevant class. The statute precludes use of leghold traps on public lands. It thus creates a class of all persons wishing to trap on public land throughout the State—this class is prohibited from using leghold traps. The restriction is equally applicable to all members of the class, that is, all people using public lands. Thus, the statute meets this requirement.

The third requirement of a general law is that the class be flexible. Defendants argue that because of the limited amount of private land available in Arizona, the class is static. The existing private land, although limited, can be sold and purchased or leased, allowing movement in and out of the class. Thus, a person who buys or leases private land may use leghold traps on that property. But if that person then sells or surrenders his or her lease to that private property, that person cannot then use leghold traps on public lands. Therefore, we conclude that the class created here is elastic.

In their reply brief, Defendants assert that the statute gives a special class of landowners the privilege of harvesting publicly owned wildlife. Defendants argue this privilege is a significant right, but they fail to demonstrate how it impacts the three-part test to determine whether the statute is a general or special law. Furthermore, we note that persons using public rather than private lands are not precluded from harvesting the State's wildlife. They are simply precluded from using a specific method, deemed cruel and dangerous, to do so.

Equal Protection

Defendants also claim that A.R.S. section 17–301(D) violates the equal protection clauses of the United States and Arizona Constitutions. *See* U.S. Const. amend. XIV, § 1; Ariz. Const. art. 2, § 13. The effects of the two provisions are essentially the same. [ ] Because the statute implicates neither a fundamental right nor a suspect class, we apply a rational basis test. [ ] Under the rational basis test, the statute must be rationally related to furthering some legitimate governmental interest. [ ] A classification can be based on rational speculation unsupported by evidence. [ ] An equal protection analysis of whether the statute is rationally related to a legitimate State interest is similar to the initial analysis conducted in determining if the statute constitutes a special or general law. [ ] As part of our decision that section 17–301(D) is not a special law, we concluded that it is rationally related to a legitimate purpose. Thus, we also conclude that the statute does not violate the equal protection clauses of the Arizona and United States Constitutions.

Defendants argue that the statute is not rationally related to a legitimate state interest because A.R.S. section 17–301(D) is a wildlife statute that "frustrates" sound wildlife management and impedes "professional game management objectives." Therefore, according to Defendants, the statute cannot be considered as furthering a legitimate State interest.

. . .

We acknowledge that wildlife management certainly could be one of the State interests addressed by A.R.S. section 17–301(D). But other State interests are also implicated. The State has a legitimate interest in preventing cruelty to animals. *See, e.g.,* A.R.S. § 13–2910 (prohibiting cruelty to animals on either public or private property). The State also has a legitimate interest in protecting users of public lands from injuries. Thus, Defendants are mistaken in contending that only wildlife management can be considered a legitimate State interest in analyzing the validity of the statute.

We therefore conclude that the prohibition of leghold traps on public lands is rationally related to the purposes of the statute. The drafters of the legislation and those voting for it could have concluded that the statute would achieve the purposes intended. Defendants have not shown otherwise.

Conclusion

Defendants' convictions are affirmed.

NOTES

(1) The court claims that public lands and private lands are somehow meaningfully different when it comes to preventing cruelty to animals. Has it made a convincing showing on the question? Are wildlife on private lands any less deserving of protection? Do leg traps on private land hurt animals any less? Presumably the statute was written as it was for political reasons; private landowners—ranchers in particular, one might guess—had enough political power to get themselves excluded from the ban. Might there also be issues of the right of landowners to protect their property against wildlife? As the court explains, the state constitutional ban on special legislation is intended "to prevent the legislature from providing special benefits and favors to certain groups or locations." Does the challenged law in this case grant special benefits to landowners? Are there legitimate private-property concerns that somehow take the statute out of the "special benefit" category?

(2) The needs of wildlife management—most dramatically the variety of habitats—often cause state legislatures and game commissions to establish different rules for different geographic areas, including rules that prohibit hunting in some places while allowing it in others. Claims that such laws are "special legislation" are routinely rejected. *E.g., Maitland v. People,* 23 P.2d 116 (Colo.1933); *Bauer v. Game, Forestation & Parks Commission,* 293 N.W. 282 (Neb.1940). Such laws can still be attacked as arbitrary and hence invalid exercises of the police power—an issue taken up below. And as illustrated by *Alford v. Finch* [Chapter 3], landowners in rare situations have successfully argued that differential bans on hunting are an unlawful taking of private property.

(3) *Tennessee Conservation League v. Cody:* A conservation group challenged the state statute governing hunting raccoons with dogs, which provided differing rules for various parts of the state and which the legislature amended regularly in response to intense political pressure. According to the plaintiff association, (i) the differing rules for different parts of the state ran afoul of the state constitutional ban on special legislation, and (ii) the provision as a whole was an arbitrary exercise of state power. Reviewing the record, the court was quick to admit that politics was at work:

> TCL [Tennessee Conservation League] contends the frequent changes in the law relative to raccoons is evidence of a careless disregard of this Constitutional mandate. If the Court has counted correctly, there have been 51 Acts of the Legislature affecting raccoons since 1955. During approximately one-half of the intervening time the Legislature met every other year. Perhaps the Federal Internal Revenue Code is the only other law so often amended.

Though the court was troubled by the repeated changes, it was also mindful of the need for laws to keep up with the times:

> As our society becomes more populous, sophisticated and affluent, our values change, as has been true for all of recorded history. The people of this State, assembled in the Constitutional Convention in 1870, invested the Legislature with the power and discretion to implement these values from time to time. For this Court to impose its judgment or discretion in this case would be a usurpation of a judgmental act specifically granted to the Legislature.

We know of no other discipline where it is insisted the Legislature is bound to follow the opinions of the best experts in the given field. This certainly is not true in taxation, finances, public health, schools, or other areas of governmental regulation, all of which seem to be responsive to more exact standards. Difficulty or the impossibility of enforcement or the general public's acceptance or perception of laws are all valid conditions which the Legislature must or may consider.

The earnest and almost persuasive arguments of TCL have been seriously and deliberately weighed but this Court has concluded sound Constitutional principles compel it to leave the protection of the raccoon population and training of coon dogs in the hands of the Legislature so long as there is a viable causal connection between their action and this Constitutional provision.

Tennessee Conservation League v. Cody, 745 S.W.2d 854 (Tenn.1987).

(4) *Bruce v. Director, Department of Chesapeake Bay Affairs*: Residents of Somerset County, Maryland, challenged state statutes banning residents of one county from harvesting crabs and oysters within another county. Somerset County, long an active center for such harvesting, was suffering drastically lowered harvests, chiefly due to disease and environmental conditions, so much so that commercial harvesters were losing their livelihood. *Held:* the statutes were an unreasonable and unlawful exercise of the police power, given that they failed in any discernible way to further "the safety, health, moral, social or economic welfare of the 'body politic.'" In reaching its conclusion, the court placed weight on the fact that the statutes undercut longstanding economic livelihoods rather than simply recreational activities. *Bruce v. Director, Department of Chesapeake Bay Affairs,* 276 A.2d 200 (Md.App.1971).

Arkansas Game & Fish Commission v. Murders

Arkansas Supreme Court.
938 S.W.2d 854 (1997).

■ ARNOLD, C.J.:—The appellant, Arkansas Game and Fish Commission, appeals a ruling of the Garland County Circuit Court declaring that amended code 18.04, which prohibits road hunting, is void. Because we agree that the amended portion of the Commission's rule is unconstitutionally overbroad and exceeds the scope of the Commission's constitutional authority, we affirm the ruling of the trial court.

The appellees are licensed hunters who reside in Garland County, Arkansas. Pursuant to Ark. Code Ann. § 25–15–207(a) (1987), they brought a declaratory judgment action against the Commission and its Director, Steve N. Wilson, challenging amended code provision 18.04. The provision generally prohibits hunting from or shooting across any city, county, state, or federally maintained road or right-of-way. It further prohibits hunting within fifty yards from the center of any city, county, state, or federally-maintained road or right-of-way during any modern gun deer season. The penalty for violation of the rule ranges from a $100.00 to a $1,000.00 fine.

The amendatory language at issue, added by the Commission in April of 1995, reads as follows:

> NOTE: It shall be prima facie evidence during modern gun and muzzleloading deer season that a person is hunting if the person is in possession of a loaded firearm on any city, county, state, or federally-maintained road or the right-of-way thereof in an area in which wild game is likely to be present. Firearms being carried in a motor vehicle or conveyance must be unloaded and enclosed in a case or placed in a gun rack (unloaded) while on any city, county, state or federally-maintained road or the right-of-way thereof in an area in which wild game is likely to be present.
>
> . . .
>
> EXCEPTIONS: (1) Handguns carried in motor vehicle for purpose other than hunting.
>
> (2) Persons engaged in a lawful action to protect their livestock or property.
>
> (3) Law enforcement officials in respect to the official job duties.

The appellees filed this action on August 10, 1995, challenging the amended code 18.04 on many grounds, including that it was arbitrary and capricious and unconstitutionally vague and overbroad. They also claimed that the amendment violated the American Disabilities Act, the equal protection clause, the constitutional right to bear arms, the presumption of innocence, and the separation-of-powers doctrine. Finally, the appellees claimed that the amendment was contrary to statute, particularly Ark. Code Ann. § 5–73–120. Following a trial, the trial court entered an order declaring that the amended portion of regulation 18.04 was void. The trial court's order adopted the appellees' findings and conclusions, with the exception of their arguments regarding the ADA. On appeal, the Commission challenges each of the trial court's rulings.

The appellees maintain, and the trial court agreed, that amended code 18.04 is unconstitutionally overbroad because its wording is so inclusive that it may affect the rights of non-hunters who possess loaded or uncased firearms on city, county, state, or federally-maintained roads or rights-of-way. In turn, the Commission urges that amended code 18.04 bears a rational relationship to the legitimate objective of suppressing illegal road hunting, an activity which, pursuant to Amendment 35 of the Arkansas Constitution, the Commission has the authority to regulate. According to the Commission, the fact that some persons who have no intention of hunting may travel the highways during deer season with loaded or uncased firearms does not undermine the rule's legitimate sweep.

We agree that the Commission, under Amendment 35, has plenary authority over the "control, management, restoration, conservation and regulation of birds, fish, game and wildlife resources of the State." Section 8 of Amendment 35 also grants the Commission "the exclusive power and authority to regulate the manner of taking game, to regulate seasons, and to fix penalties for violation of the regulations." However, while we have said that the Commission has broad discretion in carrying out its powers,

[ ], its discretion is not unfettered. The Commission's power to regulate the manner of taking game certainly does not translate into a general power to regulate the general possession of all firearms on city, county, state, or federally maintained roads or rights-of-way.

An overbroad statute is one that is designed to punish conduct which the state may rightfully punish, but which includes within its sweep constitutionally protected conduct. [ ] The Commission's rule, as amended, essentially shifts the burden to non-hunters who possess loaded or uncased firearms on city, county, state, or federally maintained roads or rights-of-way, to prove that he or she is not engaged in the prohibited act of road hunting. When examining amended rule 18.04, we conclude that it may include within its sweep innocent and legitimate conduct. For example, it is an affirmative defense to the charge of carrying a weapon that the person charged was carrying the weapon upon a journey. *See* Ark.Code Ann. § 5–73–120(c)(4). The amended rule is thus overbroad, and exceeds the Commission's authority granted under Amendment 35 to regulate the manner of taking game.

.... Based upon the foregoing, the decision of the trial court is affirmed.

State v. Walsh

Washington Supreme Court, *en banc.*
870 P.2d 974 (Wash.1994).

■ GUY, J.:—In 1947, the Legislature passed the present Game Code of the State of Washington which reorganized the Department of Game and the State Game Commission. Laws of 1947, ch. 275. This comprehensive regulation of the state's wildlife devoted an entire chapter to prohibited acts and penalties. Among its many provisions, the game code outlawed hunting while intoxicated; using dogs of any kind to hunt deer or elk; constructing dams or other obstructions across any river or stream which inhibit the free passage of all game fish; and, the subject of this appeal, using artificial light after sunset to hunt deer and other big game. This is commonly known as "spotlighting."

Under RCW 77.16.050 (the "spotlighting statute"),

[i]t is unlawful to hunt big game with a spotlight or other artificial light. It is prima facie evidence of a violation of this section to be found with a spotlight or other artificial light and with a firearm, bow and arrow, or crossbow, after sunset, in a place where big game may reasonably be expected.

The Department of Wildlife often attempts to enforce the spotlighting statute by planting a styrofoam deer at sunset in a field by the side of a rural road. When cars drive by the decoy at night, their headlights illuminate the decoy's reflective eyes.

Defendants in these two consolidated appeals allegedly either aimed at the decoy (Osborn), or shot it (Walsh). At trial, the two district courts dismissed the charges against defendants, ruling the use of the decoy made it impossible for defendants to commit the crime of spotlighting. On appeal, the respective superior courts reversed and remanded the cases for trial, holding the State had presented evidence sufficient to prove illegal spotlighting. Defendants now appeal, claiming because it is impossible to hunt a decoy deer, the charges against them for spotlighting big game should be dismissed.

BACKGROUND

Defendants Walsh and Reeves

The State presented the following evidence at trial: On November 16, 1990, defendant Reeves and defendant Walsh were riding in an automobile down a gravel road in southern Thurston County. It was approximately 6 p.m., an hour after sunset, and they were in an area known to attract deer. As their automobile turned onto Johnson Creek Road, out of the darkness appeared two eyes shining in their car's headlights. Defendant Reeves, who was driving, immediately stopped the car, reversed it, and aimed the headlights where he had first seen the eyes illuminated. He turned off the motor and defendant Walsh got out of the car with a rifle.

Not far away waited Department of Wildlife Agents Mann and Furrer seated in their patrol car, listening for sounds of game poachers at work. This was not an unwarranted expectation or accidental surveillance, for earlier in the day the agents had placed this antlered, decoy deer, complete with reflective eyes, in the clearcut. Defendant Walsh fired her rifle at the decoy, nicking its right ear but not otherwise imperiling the lifeless replica. This action by defendant Walsh was observed by the agents and admitted to by defendant Walsh.

Recognizing the ruse, defendants Reeves and Walsh began to drive out of the area when they were stopped by the Department of Wildlife agents and read their *Miranda* rights. The agents found a .243 caliber hunting rifle in the automobile and a spent shell on the roadway matching the caliber of that rifle. Defendant Walsh, when asked what she thought she had shot at that night, answered "a two point buck." She recognized it was a decoy immediately after taking her shot.

Defendant Osborn

On October 20, 1990, Agent Neal from the Department of Wildlife and Sergeant Predmore from the Buckley Police Department watched as defendant Osborn stopped his automobile on Forest Service Road 194 near Sunset Lake in Pierce County. The time was approximately 7:25 p.m., after sunset, and the area was known to contain deer. Agent Neal and Sergeant Predmore were observing this area because earlier that day they had set up a decoy deer in an open area. While so observing, Agent Neal and Sergeant Predmore saw defendant Osborn first drive by the decoy, stop his automobile, put it in reverse, and then aim the automobile's headlights so as to pick up the reflective eyes of the decoy. Defendant Osborn then exited his automobile, stood on the driver's side in front of the windshield and brought his rifle to his shoulder, sighting the decoy through the rifle's scope. Osborn was then observed bringing the rifle down, pausing, and sighting again. Ultimately, Osborn put the rifle down and threw a rock at the decoy. Agent Neal, through hand signals, motioned to Sergeant Predmore to pull the decoy down with the line attached to it. However, the decoy snagged on a stump and, in Agent Neal's words, "looked real fake at that time".

Defendant Osborn then returned to his automobile and started the engine. Agent Neal and Sergeant Predmore arrived in their patrol car, signalling with blue lights for defendant Osborn to stop. Agent Neal recognized defendant Osborn as Officer James Osborn, a member of the Buckley Police Department. Agent Neal also found a high-powered rifle with a scope sitting on the front seat of defendant Osborn's automobile.

A day or two later, defendant Osborn allegedly joked to other members of the Buckley Police Department he had almost shot the game department deer, and for a moment it looked like a real deer. However, the testimony at trial conflicted over whether defendant Osborn had loaded his gun and had intended to shoot the decoy, believing it to be a live deer.

All defendants were charged with spotlighting in violation of RCW 77.16.050. The defendants went to trial in their respective district courts, and in both cases the district courts dismissed the charges before reaching a verdict. In defendants Reeves' and Walsh's case, the district judge ruled in favor of defendants' impossibility defense, stating:

> Given the facts of this case, I find that it is factually impossible for the defendants to have killed big game in violation of RCW 77.16.050. If it was factually impossible for the defendants to have killed big game, then it was just as factually impossible for defendants to have hunted big game or to have made an "effort" to kill big game. I reference RCW 77.08.010(7) wherein the term "[t]o hunt" is defined as an "effort to kill, injure, capture or harass [a] wild animal or wild bird."

[ ] The district court, while dismissing the citation against defendants Reeves and Walsh, also granted the prosecutor leave to charge defendants with attempted spotlighting.

The district judge in defendant Osborn's trial dismissed the charge against Osborn at the close of the prosecutor's case, finding:

> I can't see how we can say that this is an effort to hunt. That's how the statute reads. An effort to kill—actually, not to hunt, an effort to kill, injure, capture, or harass a wild animal or wild bird. I don't see how we can say that what we have heard today—there was no wild animal involved in any of this.

[ ]

On appeal to the respective county superior courts, the State won reversal of the dismissals, with the superior courts rejecting defendants' impossibility defenses. The courts ruled because the State presented sufficient evidence of defendants' intent to hunt big game, the fact defendants actually hunted a decoy was not grounds for dismissal. Both cases were remanded for trial.

ISSUES

The primary issue is whether the defense of impossibility applies to the crime of spotlighting big game under RCW 77.16.050. Defendant Osborn also attacks RCW 77.16.050 as being unconstitutionally vague and unconstitutionally overbroad.

ANALYSIS

Impossibility

Traditionally, legal impossibility was a defense to criminal charges of attempt while factual impossibility was not. The distinction between the two proved extremely elusive, though, and the Model Penal Code, as well as most courts, no longer recognize impossibility as a valid defense to crimes of attempt. [ ] Instead, the courts aim their telescopic sights at whether a defendant completed the crime charged regardless of the impossibility, or whether the defendant committed an attempt. [ ]

We begin our analysis with the plain words of the spotlighting statute. They are straightforward—the statute requires proof of three elements: (1) hunting, (2) big game, and (3) artificial light. RCW 77.08.010(7) defines the first element, "[t]o hunt", as "an effort to kill, injure, capture, or harass a wild animal or wild bird." Next, RCW 77.08.030 defines "big game", the second element, as elk, blacktail deer, whitetail deer, moose, mountain goat, caribou, mountain sheep, pronghorn antelope, cougar, black bear, or grizzly bear. Finally, as agreed, "artificial light" includes a car's headlights.

Defendants argue they sighted a deer decoy in their rifles, not big game and, therefore, the State failed to prove at trial defendants hunted big game. Instead, according to defendants, the State proved they hunted styrofoam, an act which is not illegal. Defendants conclude the existence of the decoy made it impossible for defendants to complete the crime of spotlighting.

This argument camouflages an incorrect assumption: that to hunt big game, defendants must actually encounter big game. Hunting, however, is an activity involving effort. From 1947 to the present, the Legislature has defined hunting as "an *effort* to kill [or] injure" a wild animal or wild bird. RCW 77.08.010(7). (Italics ours.) Every fall, thousands of Washington residents journey deep into the woods in search of game. To say that they do not hunt until they actually encounter game defines the activity far too narrowly. Like hunting, when we take rod and reel to a mountain lake and dip our line in its waters, we begin to fish. Effort defines these activities.

Hunters begin to "hunt big game," not when they actually encounter big game, but rather when they make an effort to kill or injure big game in an area where such animals may reasonably be expected. The spotlighting statute outlaws making this effort with the aid of artificial light. We find, therefore, the State presented evidence sufficient to show defendants completed the crime of spotlighting. When defendants allegedly took aim at the decoy in their headlights, believing it to be a deer, they hunted big game with artificial light. Whether a defendant fires a shot may be evidence of intent, but it is not essential to prosecuting the charge.

. . .

We therefore affirm the superior courts' rulings. The superior courts held correctly the cases against defendants Reeves, Walsh and Osborn should have gone to the trier of fact.

Vagueness

Defendant Osborn contends the spotlighting statute does not draw a clear line between innocent and criminal behavior and thus is unconstitutionally vague. Defendant Osborn argues the police could use the statute to charge anyone who drives at night with an unloaded firearm through an area populated with deer. The spotlighting statute does not implicate First Amendment rights. Therefore, the court evaluates the vagueness statute "in light of how the statute has been applied in [defendants'] individual cases." [ ] No charges were placed against the defendant for spotlighting until he allegedly aimed his headlights at the decoy, exited the automobile and sighted his rifle. The statute requires evidence of hunting, a requirement which both defines the statute sufficiently so that "ordinary people can understand what conduct is proscribed" and provides "ascertainable standards of guilt to protect against arbitrary enforcement." [ ] The defendant's challenge to vagueness is without merit.

Overbreadth

Defendant Osborn argues that the spotlighting statute infringes impermissibly on his Second Amendment right to bear arms and is therefore unconstitutionally overbroad. Because the spotlighting statute regulates behavior, not speech, we will not overturn it unless the overbreadth is both real and substantial in relation to the ordinance's plainly legitimate sweep. [ ]

We find the spotlighting statute does not excessively burden defendant's right to bear arms and is rather a reasonable regulation of conduct under the State's police power. Defendant's argument is without merit.

CONCLUSION

The superior courts of Pierce and Thurston County are affirmed, and the cases are remanded to the trial district courts.

NOTES

(1) Were the defendants in *Walsh* correct in arguing that the state statute made it a crime simply to drive at night through an area where game was present with an unloaded rifle in the vehicle? In response to defendant Osborn's claim of vagueness, the court notes that he was not arrested until he "exited the automobile and sighted his rifle." But were these latter facts needed to prove Osborn's guilt? If not, should the court consider them when assessing Osborn's claim that the statute as written was vague or overbroad? Is it relevant that, under the specific statute at issue, spotlighting while possessed of a rifle was only prima facie evidence of hunting rather than conclusive?

(2) Fairness v. enforceability: The statutes and regulations at issue in *Murders* and *Walsh* are illustrative of how state lawmakers have sought to reconcile the need for fairness—in the form of banning only conduct that is culpable—with the need to craft criminal statutes that can be enforced, given that the state's burden in a criminal case is to prove each element of an offense beyond a reasonable doubt. Game officers are simply too few and too scattered to catch hunters in the act of poaching. They also have trouble proving mental state of hunters engaged in questionable acts. Because of these enforcement challenges, many state fish and game laws merely require a showing of circumstantial acts—actions that are suggestive of an intent to engage in wrongdoing but that could be entirely innocent. Constitutional challenges to such statutes typically entail claims that they are unacceptably vague or overbroad; other challenges are that they are not rationally related to game protection or otherwise substantially linked to public health, safety, and welfare. Courts considering such claims face predictable dilemmas: Should they narrow an overbroad statute by construing a statutory term narrowly (*e.g.,* construing a statutory reference to "animal" to mean "game animal") or by inserting a mental state requirement into a statute that does not expressly contain one (*e.g.,* construing a statute that bans spotlighting to require a showing of intent to take game)? Similarly, should courts allow a defendant who is clearly engaged in wrongful hunting to avoid conviction by pointing to the statute's possible unfair application to others who are engaged in innocent behavior? As the following materials indicate, answers vary.

(a) *Singleton v. Commonwealth*: Defendants challenged as overbroad a spotlighting statute similar to the one in *Walsh.* The statute required no showing that defendants were hunting or attempting to find game; the mere casting of light while possessing a firearm was sufficient. *Held*: Statute is unconstitutionally overbroad, and defendant can challenge it without regard to whether he was taking game by artificial light. *Singleton v. Commonwealth,* 740 S.W.2d 159 (Ky.App.1986).

(b) *State v. McAffry*: Defendant challenged spotlighting statute that made it a crime to cast light "for the purpose of spotting, locating or taking any animal" while possessing a gun. *Held:* Statute is unconstitutionally overbroad because "animal" could include livestock; defendant can raise this objection without any showing that he was in fact looking for livestock. *State v. McAffry,* 949 P.2d 1137 (Kan.1997).

(c) *State v. Morrison*: Defendant challenged spotlighting statute that was essentially identical to the one in *McAffry. Held:* Statute is not unconstitutionally vague or overbroad. Defendant cannot object to the statute's possible application to ranchers looking for livestock without evidence that defendant was engaged in that activity. Court construed "any animal" in the statute to mean "any game animal," thereby reducing its breadth. *State v. Morrison,* 341 N.W.2d 635 (S.D.1983).

Such issues are, of course, not limited to state statutes. In *United States v. Jarrell,* 143 F.Supp.2d 605 (W.D.Va.2001), defendant challenged his conviction for hunting in a national park, arguing that he was simply passing through the park on the way to hunt on private land.

(3) **Other constitutional challenges:** Although vagueness and overbreadth have been the most common grounds of constitutional attack on game statutes and regulations (*e.g., Russell v. Department of Natural Resources,* 701 N.E.2d 1056 (Ill.1998) (hunting license revocation statute not vague); *Corry v. State,* 710 So.2d 853 (Miss.1998) (term "bait" in hunting over bait statute not vague); *State v. Davis,* 448 So.2d 645 (La.1984) (statute prohibiting the taking of "illegal deer" is not overbroad

because it covers the accidental killing of doe); *State v. Stewart*, 253 S.E.2d 638 (N.C.App.1979) (statute not overbroad); *State v. Rudolph*, 289 N.W.2d 484 (Minn.1979) (not overbroad); *State v. Barber*, 581 P.2d 27 (N.M.App. 1978) (not vague)), other constitutional objections have occasionally been raised. *E.g., State v. Austin*, 704 P.2d 55 (Mont.1985) (spotlight statute is arbitrary and not related to the protection of wildlife when the defined offense includes no mental state requirement (such as intent to take game) and provides an exemption for landowners on their own lands); *State v. Saurman*, 413 N.E.2d 1197 (Ohio 1980) (upholding similar statute as rationally related to the protection of game); *Clajon Production Corp. v. Petera*, 70 F.3d 1566 (10th Cir.1995) (statute granting two supplemental hunting permits to owners of 160 acres or more without distinguishing among sizes of holdings (plaintiff owned 90,000 acres) is not void for failing to substantially advance a legitimate governmental interest); *State v. Duranleau*, 260 A.2d 383 (Vt.1969) (prohibition on carrying loaded rifle or shotgun in vehicle on public highway is not violation of constitutional right to bear arms); *State v. Bontrager*, 683 N.E.2d 126 (Ohio App.1996) (hunter orange requirement not a violation of freedom of religion when applied to Amish hunter who opposed wearing bright colors on religious grounds).

(4) Private game farming: Game farming—whether of native (*e.g.*, elk) or exotic species (*e.g.*, fallow and sika deer)—is a topic that we encountered from several different perspectives. On the one hand, farming and ranching operations are touted as methods of conserving wildlife populations by providing landowners with incentives to protect habitat. *E.g., Cayman Turtle Farm, Ltd. v. Andrus*, 478 F.Supp. 125 (D.D.C.1979) [Chapter 1] (ranching operation would help to conserve endangered sea turtles). On the other hand, there are risks such as the possibility that the wildlife will escape. *E.g., King v. Blue Mountain Forest Association*, 123 A.2d 151 (N.H.1956) [Chapter 4] (private liability for damages to property—a remedy that would be less than satisfactory if the escape involved the transmission of a disease to wild populations).

The question of escapes—whether of genes or diseases—is one of the problems cited by critics of game ranching and farming operations. The issue is generally at the center of state responses to such operations—as the decision in *Pacific Northwest Venison Producers v. Smitch*, 20 F.3d 1008 (9th Cir.), *cert. denied*, 513 U.S. 918 (1994) [Chapter 6], illustrates. But there is a self-definitional component as well. A hunting guide recently complained that "wild animals [have] ceased being public property in North America and [have] entered the domain of chattel." Game farming, he argued, is an abdication of the "public trust of wildlife," an abdication that "marked a point in this country when we gave up something, a turning away from a defining characteristic of American life.... Ownership of animals represents a return to feudalism." Furthermore, "[i]n going from public ownership to game ranching," he writes, "we go from participation, whether hunting or bird watching—to something perilously close to domination.... [A]ll you have to do is go to a bull sale and see those blocky black Angus that can hardly walk and you know that game ranching breeds out wildness." Samuel Western, *Born Caged: A New "Wild" West*, High Country News 20 (Apr. 27, 1998).

Given the risks and the emotion, it is hardly surprising that state responses to the game farming have varied dramatically. Wyoming and Colorado, like Washington, have banned importation of exotics. *Courts, States Shoot Down Exotic Big Game Ranching,* WILDLIFE L. NEWS Q., Summer 1993, at 1, 3. And at least a dozen states have banned "canned hunts"—where hunters pay to kill wildlife on fenced private lands. Texas is dramatically different:

> People here [in Texas] have a preternatural respect for private property, and their state is capacious enough to accommodate any vision of the landscape. During the past seventy years, Texas has become a vast experimental station for exotic-animal breeding, a land of miniature Africas and Asias nested within what was once wide-open country.... [A]t last count, the state has almost two hundred thousand "exotics, ... representing some sixty-five species, and ranchers are said to drastically underreport their stock. Texas may have as many Indian blackbuck antelope as India, more Arabian oryx that Saudi Arabia, more scimitar-horned oryx that Africa.

Burkhard Bilger, *A Shot in the Ark,* THE NEW YORKER, Mar. 5, 2001, at 74, 74. *See generally* ELIZABETH CARY MUNGALL & WILLIAM J. SHEFFIELD, EXOTICS ON THE RANGE (1994).

SECTION 4.   DELEGATED POWERS AS LIMITATIONS ON COMMISSION ACTIONS: STATUTORILY *ULTRA VIRES*

Armstrong v. State

Washington Court of Appeals.
958 P.2d 1010 (1998).

■ HOUGHTON, C.J.:—Ronald and Melvin Armstrong (the Armstrongs) filed a class action lawsuit against the Department of Fish and Wildlife (Department) seeking to enjoin enforcement of a regulation requiring modern gun hunters to wear fluorescent orange clothing while hunting. The Armstrongs argued that the Department did not have statutory authority to adopt and enforce the regulation.... The Armstrongs appeal from the superior court's ruling that the regulation was valid. We hold that the Department acted within its delegated authority in promulgating the regulation, and therefore affirm.

FACTS

In November 1993, a Department enforcement officer issued Ron Armstrong a citation for failing to wear hunter orange clothing in violation of WAC 232-12-055. A Grays Harbor district court judge dismissed the criminal proceeding, ruling that the Department lacked the authority to adopt the regulation. The Superior Court upheld the District Court's decision on appeal.

The Department then adopted a policy *not* to enforce the hunter orange regulation in Grays Harbor County, although the Department urged residents to continue wearing hunting orange when hunting. The Department did not alter enforcement of the regulation for the rest of the state.[3]

The Armstrongs filed a class action lawsuit seeking injunctive relief enjoining enforcement of the hunter orange regulation. Specifically, they challenged the Wildlife Department's authority to require hunter orange clothing under WAC 232–12–055. Upon cross-motions for summary judgment, the trial court issued an oral ruling declaring the regulation was constitutional and a proper exercise of the agency's authority.

Trial Court's Decision and Reasoning

The trial court relied upon *Hartman v. State Game Comm'n,* 532 P.2d 614 (Wash.1975), in determining that the regulation was correctly promulgated. According to *Hartman,* a court determines the extent of regulatory authority granted by determining the legislative intent as derived from the supporting statute and prefatory language. Using these standards, the trial court noted that RCW 77.12.010[6] and 77.12.040,[7] when read together, signify that the "manner of taking" is not limited to the method by which an animal is killed. According to the trial court, the "plain meaning" of the "manner of taking encompasses more than just the method used for killing wildlife."

The trial court also determined that the Legislature intended to expand the Department's rule-making power by amending RCW 77.12.010 to include the phrase "maximizes public recreational opportunities," which, the court stated, "constituted a broad expansion of the Commission's rule-making power." Under this "broad grant of discretion" to implement regulations, the court ruled that the Department has the right to regulate for public safety and the hunter orange requirement was "in every sense a proper rule."

The trial court accordingly granted summary judgment in favor of the Department. The Armstrongs appeal.

---

3. During the 1995 legislative session, the Department supported the adoption of SB 5171 codifying the hunter orange regulation as statute. The Legislature did not pass the bill.

6. RCW 77.12.010, Policy of protection of wildlife, provides in pertinent part that:

> Wildlife is the property of the state. The department shall preserve, protect, and perpetuate wildlife. Game animals, game birds, and game fish may be taken only at times or places, or in manners or quantities as in the judgment of the commission *maximizes public recreational opportunities* without impairing the supply of wildlife.

(Emphasis added.)

7. RCW 77.12.040, Regulating the taking or possessing of game, provides in pertinent part that:

> The commission shall adopt, amend, or repeal, and enforce reasonable rules prohibiting or governing the time, place, and *manner of taking or possessing game* animals, game birds, or game fish. The commission may specify the quantities, species, sex, and size of game animals, game birds, or game fish that may be taken or possessed. The commission shall regulate the taking, sale, possession, and distribution of wildlife and deleterious exotic wildlife. The director may adopt emergency rules under RCW 77.12.150.

(Emphasis added.)

ANALYSIS

Promulgation of the Rule

In adopting the hunter orange regulation, WAC 232–12–55, the Department issued a statement of the regulation's purpose. The Department explained that the agency adopted this rule in response to a statistically high number of firearm-related hunting accidents in Washington occurring because of misidentification and other vision-related causes. According to the Department, these types of accidents comprise the majority of firearm-related hunting accidents, and so the use of fluorescent hunter orange clothing "serve[s] as a valuable aid in increasing hunter visibility while in the field." In the Department's view, the hunter orange requirement will reduce these types of firearm-related accidents, a conclusion that is supported by evidence of fewer similar accidents occurring in other states following the implementation of similar regulations.

The Armstrongs contend that neither express nor implied statutory authority supports the Department's hunter orange regulation. They assert that reference to the subject of hunter safety is "conspicuously absent" from the Department's statutory authority and cannot be implied as necessary to effectuate its duties.

There is no express reference to safety in either RCW 77.12.010 or RCW 77.12.040. Thus, we must determine whether "manner of taking" read in connection with "maximizes public recreational opportunities" grants the Department an implied power to regulate hunter safety by requiring hunters to wear fluorescent orange.

The extent of the Department's rule-making authority is a question of law reviewed de novo. [ ] A party asserting the regulation's invalidity bears the burden of proving that the action was invalid. [ ] The regulation is invalid if the court concludes the rule either: (1) violates constitutional provisions; (2) exceeds the agency's statutory authority; (3) was adopted without compliance to statutory rule-making procedures; or (4) that it could not have been the product of a rational decision-maker. [ ]

Furthermore, where the Legislature has specifically delegated rule-making authority to an agency, the agency's regulations are presumed valid, and only compelling reasons demonstrating that the regulation conflicts with the intent and purpose of the legislation warrant striking down a challenged regulation. [ ] Thus, the regulation will be upheld if reasonably consistent with the statute being implemented. [ ] The wisdom or desirability of the rule is not a question for the court's review, [ ], although the court's purpose is to ascertain and give effect to the Legislature's intent. [ ]

To this end, the declaration of purpose is an important guide to understanding the breadth of authority the Legislature has delegated to the Department. [ ] Thus, if an operative statute can be construed in a manner consistent with its broad statement of purpose, it should be so construed. [ ]

Here, the Legislature charged the Department with two duties: (1) the duty to "preserve, protect, and perpetuate" the State's wildlife resources; *and* (2) the duty to "maximize" hunting and fishing "recreational opportunities." RCW 77.04.055(1)(b) and 77.12.010. The Legislature also granted the Department authority to adopt and enforce "reasonable rules prohibiting or governing the time, place, and manner of taking or possessing game animals." RCW 77.12.040. The Department's authority includes powers that are expressly delegated by statute and those necessarily implied from statutory grants of authority. [ ] Appropriate rules may be adopted to "fill in the gaps" in legislation if such rules are "necessary to the effectuation of a general statutory scheme." [ ]

Statutory Construction and Context

Neither "manner" nor "taking" is specifically defined in the Department regulations or statutes governing hunting. When words are not defined by statute, the court may refer to dictionary definitions and to common usage in light of the context in which the word is used. [ ]

The Department urges us to define "manner" as "a way of doing something or the way in which a thing is done or takes place" and "takes" as "to catch or get * * * by killing." The Armstrongs emphasize that "taking" is the operative word and provide a similar definition for "taking."

We agree with the trial court that "manner of taking," when read together with "maximiz[ing] public recreational opportunities," connotes more than just killing game. The plain meaning of the words suggests the definition encompasses not only the method of killing, but also the "manner" of hunting in general. The "manner" of hunting involves the way in which hunting is conducted, which not only includes the physical act by which a hunter kills an animal, but also supervision and oversight of the hunter's conduct relative to other hunters within the surrounding vicinity engaged in similar activity.

Further, in determining the meaning of a word used in a particular instance, we consider the subject matter within which the word is used and the statutory context in which it appears. [ ]

In this regard, we note that the Department's supervision of and concern for hunter safety as an implied agency power is consistent with other statutes and regulations regarding wildlife and game. *See e.g.,* RCW 77.16.070 (prohibition against hunting while intoxicated); RCW 77.32.155 (requiring hunting education program for hunting license, which includes instruction on safety); RCW 77.32.197 (requirement for training program for trappers, which includes instruction on trapper safety); WAC 232–12–054 (safety regulations regarding bow and arrow hunting); WAC 232–12–227 (and hunter education training program requirements, which include instruction on safety); WAC 232–12–807 (Department operations and procedures include the responsibilities of the information and education division that is charged with planning and development of hunter education and safety training). These statutes and regulations imply that the Department has the authority to ensure that hunting is conducted safely. They indicate that the Department may be properly concerned for the safety of the hunter as well for other hunters and individuals within the hunting area.

Case Law

[O]n point is *RSB v. State,* 632 So.2d 24 (Ala.Crim.App.1993), where the court addressed a challenge to the authority of the Alabama Department of Conservation and Natural Resources to require hunter orange clothing using an agency regulation. The Alabama regulation was based upon statutes similar to ours. In pertinent part, the Alabama statutes provided that the state agency's duties were to "protect, conserve and increase the wildlife of the state," and that it had the authority to "regulate the manner, means and devices for catching or taking game." Ala. Code § 9–2–2(1); § 9–2–7(a)(6).

Based upon these statutes and the Alabama Department of Conservation and Natural Resource's general authority to promulgate rules to implement its statutory directives, the *RSB* court held that the department commissioner "did not exceed his authority when he enacted the 'hunter orange' requirement for hunters." *RSB,* 632 So.2d at 28; [ ]

Based upon the statutory context of the hunter orange regulation and based upon case law discussed above, the regulation is reasonably consistent with the Department's statutory directives. Courts have long recognized that the Legislature may enact statutes in broad outline, leaving to administrative agencies the duty to arrange the details of the statute's effectuation and enforcement. [ ] Regulating hunter safety, thus, is an implied power that is necessary to the Department's effectuation of its duty to maximize public hunting recreational opportunities, a responsibility which the Legislature left in broad scope to the Department's discretion and oversight. [ ]

Affirmed.

NOTES

Agency powers, express and implied: State fish and game agencies operate under powers granted by state statutes. In many instances, they rely upon powers implicit in statutes written in broad terms. *Armstrong* illustrates a typical approach courts follow when assessing claims that agencies have acted *ultra vires*: they construe the agency's powers broadly in light of the goals set by the legislature. What significance should be attached to the legislature's rejection of a statute mandating that hunters wear orange—that the legislature did not favor the requirement? Or, that the legislature preferred to leave the issue to the agency's experts to whom they had delegated sufficient authority?

Massachusetts Society for the Prevention of Cruelty to Animals v. Division of Fisheries and Wildlife

Supreme Judicial Court of Massachusetts.
651 N.E.2d 388 (1995).

■ O'CONNOR, J.:—The plaintiffs brought these actions in the Superior Court to obtain judgments declaring that a certain regulation that had been promulgated by the defendant division of fisheries and wildlife (division) is inconsistent with G.L. c. 131, § 80A (1992 ed.), and is, therefore, invalid. The regulation, set forth at 321 Code Mass. Regs. § 3.02(5) (1989), governs the use of so-called "padded jaw traps" to trap fur-bearing mammals in Massachusetts. A judge allowed a motion to "fuse" [consolidate] the two actions. Thereafter, the plaintiffs in the two cases filed a single motion for summary judgment. The division and its director also filed a motion for summary judgment. A judge allowed the plaintiffs' motion and denied that of the defendants. The judge ordered the entry of a declaratory judgment stating, "The regulation set forth at 321 [Code Mass. Regs.] § 3.02(5) is invalid to the extent said regulation permits padded jaw traps to be used, set, placed or maintained on land, because it contravenes G.L. c. 131, § 80A." The defendants appealed and we allowed the division's application for direct appellate review. We vacate the judgment and order the entry of a judgment declaring that the regulation set forth at 321 Code Mass. Regs. § 3.02(5) is not inconsistent with G.L. c. 131, § 80A, and is valid.

General Laws c. 131, § 80A provides in relevant part:

No person shall use, set, place or maintain any steel jaw leghold trap on land for the capture of fur-bearing mammals except in or under buildings on land owned, leased or rented by him. The steel jaw leghold trap may be used for the capture of fur-bearing mammals in water only if set in such a manner that all reasonable care is taken to insure that the mammal dies by drowning in a minimum length of time. No other device which is set in such a manner that it will knowingly cause continued suffering to such a mammal caught therein, or which is not designed to kill such a mammal at once or take it alive unhurt shall be used, set, placed or maintained for the capture of fur-bearing mammals
* * **

Whoever violates any provision of this section, or of any rule or regulation made under the authority thereof, shall be punished by a fine of not less than fifty nor more than one hundred dollars, or by imprisonment for not more than thirty days, or by both such fine and imprisonment.

The division promulgated 321 Code Mass. Regs. § 3.02(5) on September 1, 1989, following this court's holding in *Commonwealth v. Black,* 532 N.E.2d 43 (Mass.1989), that the "Woodstream Soft Catch Trapping System" was not a "steel jaw leghold trap" within the meaning of G.L. c. 131, § 80A. Title 321 Code Mass. Regs. § 3.02(5)(b)(14) provides that, under specified conditions and with specified limitations, "[p]added jaw traps may be used for the taking of fur-bearing mammals when set in water or on land * * *." Section 3.02(5)(a) defines the term "[p]added jaw trap" in material part as:

only those padded jaw traps patented and marketed as the Woodstream "Soft–Catch"—model Numbers 1, 1–1/2 ("Fox") and 3 ("Coyote"), or padded jaw traps of a similar type, design, and construction which conform to the following specifications. Such padded jaw traps shall be a trap of the spring-loaded type with offset jaws designed to capture a fur-bearing mammal by closing upon one of its legs and which is so constructed that the edges designed to touch the mammal are composed of a non-metallic substance which eliminates or substantially mitigates injury to the trapped mammal and which in its overall design and manufacture is designed and intended to capture fur-bearing mammals alive and unhurt when set in the manner and used for the purpose for which it is intended.

We quote representative portions of the judge's memorandum of decision in support of his order for judgment in the Superior Court:

> Here, the plain language of G.L. c. 131, § 80A shows a legislative intent to prevent injury and suffering to animals. The statute prohibits the use of traps unless those traps immediately kill the animal or take the animal "alive unhurt" without inflicting "suffering." The defendants urge this court to hold that the statute does not prohibit the use of padded jaw traps because the designers of these traps "intended" to construct a trap which would take the animal unhurt. There is nothing in the statutory language of G.L. c. 131, § 80A, however, which suggests such a narrow legislative intent. The word "designed," when considered along with the words to take the animal "alive unhurt," must be construed to mean that in a workable, practical sense the trap's design takes animals unhurt.* * * Holding that a trap which was intended by its designers to take the animal unhurt, but that in actuality hurts animals, is a trap which G.L. c. 131, § 80A does not prohibit, would clearly defeat the Legislature's expressed intent as evidenced in the plain language of the statute. Accordingly, if the padded jaw traps authorized by the Regulation take animals alive but hurt, even though those injuries may not be severe or easily detected, its use is prohibited by G.L. c. 131, § 80A.

> In the present case, the plaintiffs have presented uncontradicted evidence, including scientific studies, that the padded jaw traps authorized by the Regulation hurt animals.* * * Indeed, it is manifest from the content of the Regulation that its drafters contemplated the use of traps which would capture animals alive hurt as opposed to "alive unhurt" as required by G.L. c. 131, § 80A. The Regulation specifically authorizes a trap "which eliminates or substantially mitigates injury to the trapped mammal.* * *" On this point, the defendants do not contest that, on occasion, animals are hurt by the traps. Although the padded jaw traps authorized by the Regulation may very well reduce injury to animals when compared to steel jaw traps, padded jaw traps do not capture the animals uninjured.* * * [ ]

We disagree with the judge's reasoning in a critical respect. We do not agree with the judge's premise, on which his ultimate conclusion is substantially or entirely based, that "[t]he statute prohibits the use of traps unless those traps immediately kill the animal or take the animal 'alive unhurt' without inflicting 'suffering.' " The Legislature did not choose such sweeping and unforgiving language. Instead, the Legislature expressly prohibited the "setting" of devices in a way that would "knowingly" produce continuing animal suffering, and also prohibited devices that are "designed" to produce such a result. The statute does not express a zero tolerance of traps that may occasionally result in fur-bearing mammals being taken alive but hurt, nor does the statute prohibit the use of a trap solely because it, or a similarly designed trap, has previously caused an animal to suffer continuing pain.

We agree with the judge that the word "designed" in the provision that "[n]o other device * * * which is not designed to kill * * * a mammal at once or take it alive unhurt shall be used, set, placed or maintained for the capture of fur-bearing mammals" does not refer to the trap designer's subjective intent but instead refers, in an objective sense, to the way in which the trap works and the results it achieves as a practical matter. The defendants, in this court at least, agree. Thus, we read the statute effectively to say, "No other device which is set in such a manner that it will knowingly cause continued suffering to * * * a mammal caught therein, or which is not [fit, adapted, prepared, suitable or appropriate] to kill * * * a mammal at once or take it alive unhurt shall be used, set, placed or maintained for the capture of fur-bearing mammals." *See* BLACK'S LAW DICTIONARY 447 (6th ed. 1990). A device that is "fit, adapted, prepared, suitable or appropriate" (*i.e.,* designed) to kill a mammal at once or take it alive unhurt need not have a one hundred per cent success rate however. It is enough that, in the ordinary course, the desired result is accomplished. The result is that, in addition to steel jaw leghold traps, G.L. c. 131, § 80A, prohibits any other device which is (1) set in such a manner that it will knowingly cause continued suffering to a mammal caught therein or (2) is not fit, adapted, prepared, suitable or appropriate in the ordinary course of events to kill such a mammal at once or take it alive unhurt. [ ]

The division filed numerous affidavits of trappers affirming that they had caught "thousands" of animals alive and unhurt by using padded jaw traps. The division also submitted materials describing the objective features of padded jaw traps and explaining how those features tended to make likely the catching of animals alive and unhurt. The materials show that padded jaw traps are realistically designed to accomplish that objective. The materials also provided proof that, when set properly, a padded jaw trap is not a device that will knowingly cause continued suffering to a trapped animal. These assertions of fact were not contradicted or challenged either by the defendants' admission that occasionally padded jaw traps have caught animals alive and hurt or by any other materials made available to the judge in connection with the motions for summary judgment. We conclude, therefore, that the declaratory judgment entered in the Superior Court must be vacated and that a new judgment shall enter declaring that the regulation set forth in 321 Code Mass. Regs. § 3.02(5) is consistent with G.L. c. 131, § 80A, and is valid.

So ordered.

NOTES

(1) The court determines that padded leghold traps are "designed" to take animals "alive unhurt" even though in many cases they do hurt animals without killing them. What incidence of animals taken alive and hurt is tolerable before a trap is barred by the statute? Has the state commission been faithful to the legislature's intent?

(2) As *Massachusetts SPCA* illustrates, state game commissions are obligated to exercise their delegated powers in compliance with specific state statutes. Quite often, cases arise in which disgruntled citizens claim that they have not done so. For a variety of prudential reasons, courts tend to defer to agency interpretations of their governing statutes. Might deference be less justified in a case such as this, given the tendency of state commissions to favor hunting and trapping interests and to denigrate concerns about animal welfare? Once again, does the case reflect capture of the agency by its constituency?

Fund for Animals v. Oregon Department of Fish & Wildlife

Oregon Court of Appeals.
765 P.2d 215 (1988).

■ WARDEN, J.:—Petitioners seek a determination of the validity of a rule by which the State Fish and Wildlife Commission set seasons and numbers of tags for hunting cougar in various wildlife units throughout Oregon. ORS 183.400(1). The seasons begin no earlier than November 15, 1988, and end no later than January 31, 1989. OAR 635–67–015. Petitioners assert that the record does not show that the Commission adequately investigated the supply and condition of cougars before adopting the rule. We uphold the rule.

We may invalidate a rule only if it violates constitutional provisions, exceeds the statutory authority of the agency or was adopted without compliance with applicable rulemaking procedures. ORS 183.400(4). The Commission's authority to adopt these rules comes from ORS 496.162(1), which provides, in pertinent part:

(1) *After investigation of the supply and condition of wildlife,* the commission, at appropriate times each year, shall by rule:

(a) Prescribe the times, places and manner in which wildlife may be taken by angling, hunting or trapping and the amounts of each of those wildlife species that may be taken and possessed."

(Emphasis supplied.)

Petitioners argue that the Commission did not conduct the investigation that the statute requires, because the information available to it was inadequate to determine either the number of cougars or their condition. In support of their arguments, they refer to statements presented at an earlier hearing in which the Commission adopted a Cougar Management Plan, one purpose of which was to begin to acquire better information on those subjects.

In *Bassett v. Fish and Wildlife Comm.,* 556 P.2d 1382 (Or.App.1976), we held that, even assuming that an investigation is a prerequisite to the Commission's authority to issue rules, it did not need to place the factual basis for its decision on the record. Rather, a factual inquiry into the issue of its compliance with the investigation requirement had to await a different proceeding. However, in *Kids Against the Cut v. Wage and Hour Comm.,* 597 P.2d 1264 (Or.App.1979), we held that a rule allowing a subminimum wage for minors was invalid when the record affirmatively showed that those members of the Wage and Hour Commission who voted for it did not believe that failure to adopt it would substantially curtail opportunities for the employment of minors. ORS 653.030, we held, authorized the Commission to permit a subminimum wage only when it could find that failure to do so would have such an effect.

These cases require us to invalidate a rule, in a proceeding under ORS 183.400(1), when the agency's power to act depends on certain prerequisites and the record affirmatively shows that the agency did not comply with those prerequisites. In such circumstances, the agency would have adopted the rule in excess of its statutory authority. ORS 183.400(4)(b). In this case, the record does not show such a failure.

The information before the Commission when it adopted the challenged rule indicates that cougars are particularly difficult to observe and that the Department of Fish and Wildlife has never performed a comprehensive survey of their numbers or condition. However, the record also shows that the Department has kept careful count of the number of cougars taken each year and of the number of complaints of cougar damage it has received, each broken down by management unit. The Department's recommendations for the dates and areas of permitted hunting and for the number of tags, recommendations that the Commission accepted, were based on that information and on general knowledge of cougar habits and habitats. Assuming that an investigation was a statutory prerequisite for the adoption of this rule, petitioners have not shown that the Commission did not conduct the requisite investigation.

RULE UPHELD.

NOTES

Courts have nearly uniformly rejected claims that agency decisions are insufficiently supported, at least when challengers have not introduced substantial contrary evidence. *E.g., Strong v. Bostick,* 420 So.2d 1356 (Miss.1982) (evidence on record of low deer populations in certain parts of state is sufficient to sustain regulation banning use of dogs as aids in deer hunting in those regions). Courts are more demanding when statutes contain express requirements that agencies prepare studies or make particularized findings. *E.g., Mountain Lion Coalition v. California Fish and Game Commission,* 263 Cal.Rptr. 104 (Cal.App.1990) (setting aside regulation allowing sport hunting of mountain lions for failure to prepare and circulate for public comment an adequate draft Environmental Impact Document as required by the state Environmental Quality Act).

SECTION 5. ENFORCEMENT METHODS AND ACTIONS

Game laws can be categorized in a variety ways. For example, Thomas Harelson, a game warden, divided his state's statutes into three groups:

(a) *social* statutes such as those prohibiting hunting on Sunday;

(b) *traditional* laws such as the rule against hunting waterfowl with a shotgun that has too many shells in the chamber; and

(c) *resource protection* statutes such as bag limits.

Thomas Harelson, *Streamlining Waterfowl Enforcement,* PROCEEDINGS OF THE INTERNATIONAL CONFERENCE ON IMPROVING HUNTER COMPLIANCE WITH WILDLIFE LAWS 153 (1992).

Alternatively, the *State Wildlife Laws Handbook* notes that there are several common types of statutes:

(a) *taking restrictions*, including closed seasons, bag limits, gear restrictions, baiting prohibitions;

(b) *waste statutes* generally prohibit permitting game to go to waste once it has been taken;

(c) *spotlighting laws* prohibit hunting at night with artificial lights;

(d) *commercial transactions* are often restricted, although there is substantial variance among the states;

(e) *transportation restrictions* may apply to individual hunters or to common carriers; and

(f) *regulation of businesses* such as guides, outfitters, fur dealers, and taxidermists.

RUTH S. MUSGRAVE *ET AL.,* STATE WILDLIFE LAWS HANDBOOK 26–29 (1993).

Regardless of how one categorizes game laws, they are criminal laws that raise traditional criminal law issues.

a.   CRIMINAL LAW 101: AN OVERVIEW

State v. Thompson

Idaho Court of Appeals.
948 P.2d 174 (1997).

■ SCHWARTZMAN, J.:—Charley Thompson Jr. appeals from a district court decision affirming the magistrate's conviction of Thompson under I.C. § 36–1402(d) for hunting while his license to hunt was revoked. Thompson argues that the evidence was insufficient to support his conviction. For the reasons stated below, we affirm.

I

FACTS AND PROCEDURAL BACKGROUND

Charley Thompson was convicted on January 23, 1995, of possessing unlawfully taken game, I.C. § 36–502. As part of the sentencing under that conviction, Thompson's hunting license was revoked and he was not allowed to hunt or purchase a hunting license until January 1, 1996. In late August of 1995, Officer Lester McDonald of the Idaho Fish and Game Department, stationed in the Council area, heard from a fellow conservation officer that Thompson was currently working in McDonald's area, and further, that if Thompson was working there he was probably hunting as well.

Following this lead, Officer McDonald discovered that Thompson was working for a logging company, building a road in the mountains. In the early afternoon hours of September 9, 1995, Officer McDonald came across Thompson at a logging camp, sitting in the back of a pickup truck. McDonald, dressed in plain clothes, passed himself off as a hunter and engaged Thompson in conversation. Thompson stated that he was waiting for some of his co-workers to return to the camp so that they could all go elk hunting together, but that he wasn't sure if he would be hunting himself, or if he was just going to go along to "call" for his friends. Thompson also described in detail his past hunting exploits as well as the particulars of the type of compound bow and arrows he used. Thompson mentioned that he had seen and heard a lot of elk during the time period he had been working in the logging camp. Towards the end of the conversation Thompson advised that, if his co-workers didn't arrive soon, he was going to go hunting without them. After the conversation ended, McDonald proceeded down the road for about a quarter mile and then stopped and walked to an area where he could conduct surveillance.

After about half an hour, one of Thompson's companions arrived at the camp and both men began to get their hunting gear together and change into camouflage clothing. Thompson changed from a light-colored t-shirt to a darker colored one. He put on a camouflage baseball cap and a camouflage jacket, and obtained his compound bow and arrows from the cab of his pickup. After the men were dressed and ready, they began to walk hurriedly down the road.

Officer McDonald then came up from behind and surprised the men. Thompson was wearing the aforementioned camouflage clothing, carrying his compound bow and arrows,[1] had a string release aid wrapped around his wrist and there was an elk bugle call in his mouth. McDonald asked the men for their hunting licenses.

After some initial confusion, Thompson admitted that he did not have a hunting license, but protested that he was not hunting. Thompson told Officer McDonald that he had borrowed the compound bow for target practice because he was thinking of purchasing it, and that he had borrowed the camouflage jacket and the elk call. McDonald then issued Thompson a citation under I.C. § 36–1402(d) for hunting while his license to hunt was revoked.

After a court trial, the magistrate found Thompson guilty, fined him $1000 plus court costs and sentenced him to 180 days in jail with 150 suspended. Thompson appealed to the district court which affirmed the decision of the magistrate. Thompson timely appeals.

II

ANALYSIS

On appeal, Thompson asserts that there was insufficient evidence for the magistrate to have found the essential elements of the crime beyond a

---

1. In his quiver Thompson was carrying four arrows, two of which were twenty-seven- inch-long broadhead arrows used to kill elk.

reasonable doubt. If the evidence is insufficient to support a guilty verdict, the conviction must be set aside. [ ] Thompson does not contest the fact that his hunting license had been revoked for earlier violations, but specifically argues that the state did not prove beyond a reasonable doubt that Thompson was engaging in "hunting."

I.C. § 36–1402(d) states, in pertinent part: "It shall be a misdemeanor for any person to hunt, fish, or trap or purchase a license to do so during the period of time for which such privilege is revoked." An explicit statutory definition of "hunting" is provided in I.C. § 36–202(i):

"Hunting" shall mean chasing, driving, flushing, attacking, pursuing, worrying, following after or on the trail of, shooting at, stalking, or lying in wait for, any wildlife whether or not such wildlife is then or subsequently captured, killed, taken, or wounded. Such term does not include stalking, attracting, searching for, or lying in wait for, any wildlife by an unarmed person solely for the purpose of watching wildlife or taking pictures thereof.

Thompson argues that the state failed to present any evidence that, at the time of his citation, he was engaging in any activity which would fall under the statutory definition of "hunting." Thompson contends that there was no evidence of chasing, driving, flushing, worrying, shooting at, stalking, or lying in wait for, wildlife. This contention is based upon the following facts: (1) that the officer did not see Thompson use the elk call; (2) that there was no indication that Thompson's actions had any effect on local wildlife; and (3) that the logging road upon which Thompson was apprehended did not contain any elk trails or any other wildlife.

Thompson makes much of the following statement made by the state at trial:

[I]t's the State's contention that he was pursuing elk. He indicated that he was going to go hunting and did leave the camp. He was 60 or 70 yards away with all the gear and in the area where elk were, and it's our contention that he was pursuing elk.

Quoting from Webster's Dictionary, Thompson maintains that the state improperly stretched the definition of "pursuing" in order to convict him and that his actions in no way rise to the level of "hunting."

We disagree. Thompson was apprehended hiking quickly down a road in the woods dressed in camouflage clothing, carrying nearly all the necessary accoutrements of a hunter, including an elk call which protruded from his lips. Furthermore, just half an hour prior, Thompson had freely stated that he was waiting for his co-workers so that he could go hunting, but that, if the co-workers didn't arrive soon, that he was going hunting without them.

Thus, although the record reveals conflicting evidence in this case, there was sufficient evidence for the magistrate to conclude that Thompson was, indeed, "hunting" within the statutory meaning of the term.[3] Thompson's judgment of conviction is, accordingly, affirmed.

---

3. We note that in construing a statute,   a court should take into consideration the

State v. Neilson

Louisiana Court of Appeal.
660 So.2d 130 (1995).

■ BROWN, J.:—Defendants, Dale Neilson and Reggie Scott, were found guilty of hunting deer during illegal hours. Neilson was also found guilty of operating a motor vehicle while intoxicated ("OMVI"). Both defendants appeal, challenging the sufficiency of the evidence upon which they were convicted. We reverse the hunting violation and affirm the conviction for OMVI.

FACTS

During the night of November 17, 1990, in a heavily hunted area of DeSoto Parish, agents for the Louisiana Department of Wildlife and Fisheries were looking for night hunters. They were notified by the DeSoto Parish Sheriff's Office that a small red vehicle was seen in the area. Agent Dalton Green drove to the location where the vehicle was spotted and saw the taillights of a car entering a parking area in front of a hunting campsite. It was shortly after midnight when Agent Green pulled in behind the vehicle, a small red Nissan. Dale Neilson was driving and Reggie Scott was in the front passenger seat. Neilson's uncle came out of the deer camp.

At this time, Agents Randy Greer and Kitt Carson arrived. In response to questioning, defendants stated that they had driven from Houma, Louisiana, and had been cruising nearby logging roads scouting for deer in anticipation of hunting the next morning. As the questioning progressed, defendants grew belligerent and displayed signs of intoxication. Agent Carson attempted to administer a field sobriety test to Neilson, who refused to cooperate after failing the initial part of the test. Meanwhile, Agents Green and Greer conducted a limited search of the vehicle, in which they found several empty beer cans, hunting clothes, camping equipment and two high-powered hunting rifles.

Both defendants were charged with hunting deer during illegal hours and hunting deer from a public road. Neilson was also charged with hunting deer from a moving vehicle, driving with a suspended license and second offense operating a motor vehicle while intoxicated. Defendants' cases were consolidated and tried before a judge. Neilson and Scott were both found guilty of hunting during illegal hours. Defendants, however, were acquitted of hunting from a public road and hunting from a moving vehicle. Each defendant was fined $1,500 and given a 30 day suspended jail sentence. [ ] On appeal, defendants argue that the evidence presented at trial was insufficient to support their convictions.

reason for the law, that is, the object and the purpose of the law should be analyzed, as well as the legislative intention in its enactment. [ ] I.C. § 36–202(i) when read in conjunction with § 36–1402(d) does not require that a person must actually be apprehended in the act of shooting at an animal in order to be considered "hunting." In construing the statute defining "hunting" we aim to give it a sensible construction as will effectuate legislative intent, and, if possible, avoid an absurd conclusion. [ ] Perhaps the magistrate recalled the familiar aphorism (here paraphrased): *If he looks like a hunter, walks like a hunter, talks like a hunter and has an elk bugle call in his mouth, chances are he's a hunter.*

DISCUSSION

. . .

Hunting During Illegal Hours

At the time of the offense, the relevant statutory provision was LSA–R.S. 56:123 . . . which stated in part that "game quadrupeds may be taken in the open season * * * only from one half hour before official sunrise to one half hour after official sunset." LSA–R.S. 56:123(C). The statute's penalty provision assessed fines and/or incarceration for the "hunting or taking of deer after one-half hour after official sunset and before one-half hour before official sunrise." LSA–R.S. 56:123(E)(3)(a). A reading of these provisions makes it clear that "hunting or taking" is an essential element of the offense. *State v. Crawford,* 403 So. 2d 1221 (La.1981).

The evidence presented at trial consisted solely of testimony from Wildlife and Fisheries Agents Green, Greer and Carson. The agents testified that they received various reports regarding a suspicious red vehicle. Agent Green observed a red vehicle turning down a dirt road in the direction of a remote deer camp. The car stopped at the camp, Agent Green pulled in behind it, and almost immediately the other agents arrived. Statements given by defendants indicated that they had been traveling logging roads looking for deer to hunt the next day. Two high-powered rifles were found on the middle of the car's front seat.

On the other hand, the agents testified that they did not hear any shots fired from defendants' car, nor was the barrel of any weapon seen protruding from the car's windows. No spotlight was found in the car and there was no evidence of a freshly killed deer. Agent Greer testified that he removed the rifles from the car, but could not state whether they were loaded or whether any ammunition was found.

In his oral reasons for judgment, the trial judge discussed the definition of the term "hunting":

> Hunting is a broad, broad term. And in this case, there is no testimony that the guns were loaded. The officer could not remember whether they were loaded or not. There was no evidence that there was ammunition. The only testimony is from the Defendants, that they were looking for deer with the headlights of the vehicle. They planned to hunt the next day with two (2) high powered rifles in the vehicle. * * * However, taking hunting within the definition of *State versus Crawford,* as defined in several other cases, the term hunting has been defined as "the act of pursuing and taking of wild game" or more simply as "the search for game or other wild animals." And that was *State versus Bass* they were citing * * *. [B]y the Defendants' own statements, *they were obviously looking for deer during illegal hours* and the Court finds them both Guilty of the offense of Hunting during Illegal Hours.

(emphasis added).

The court in *Crawford,* defined the term hunting with reference to its earlier decision of *State v. Bass,* 321 So. 2d 520 (La.1975). In *Bass,* the court relied upon the *Random House Dictionary of the English Language* and *Corpus Juris Secundum* to lend meaning to the terms "hunting" and "hunt." The judicially crafted definitions in *Crawford* and *Bass,* however, were superseded on September 11, 1981, when the definitions contained in LSA–R.S. 56:8 became effective. Therein, the term " '[h]unt' means, in different tenses, attempting to take." LSA–R.S. 56:8(55). " 'Take' means, in its different tenses, the attempt or act of hooking, pursuing, netting, capturing, snaring, trapping, shooting, hunting, wounding, or killing by any means or device." LSA–R.S. 56:8(95).

The term "hunt" has been legislatively defined with reference to the term "take." Terms such as the attempt to trap, shoot, hunt, wound, kill, etc. are used to define "take."

We view the evidence in the light most favorable to sustain the convictions. The state did not show that the rifles were loaded and readied for shooting if a deer was spotted. The evidence upon which defendants' convictions were based does not exclude reasonable doubt that they merely "looked" for the location of deer to improve their chances for a successful hunt the following day. In fact, the trial court concluded that defendants by their own statements were looking for deer during illegal hours and that alone was sufficient under the statute. We conclude that the statutory definitions for "hunting" and "taking" are not so broad as to encompass the limited, relatively passive activity of merely looking for wild game to hunt at a later legal hour. Accordingly, on these facts, defendants' convictions for hunting deer during illegal hours are reversed.

NOTES

(1) *Thompson* and *Nielson* are examples of the types of issues that commonly arise in criminal enforcement actions brought under fish and game laws. What actions are violations of particular statutes or regulations? Has the government sustained its burden of proving each element of the offense beyond a reasonable doubt?

Typically, statutes and regulations are drafted with an eye toward ease of enforcement, with the predicable effect that cases sometimes arise in which charges are brought for behavior that appears innocuous. Courts in such instances find themselves torn: Should they enforce a statute as written, so as not to hamper enforcement efforts in clearly legitimate settings, or should they find ways to protect seemingly innocent defendants from occasionally overzealous prosecutors? In both *Thompson* and *Nielson,* the courts seem to focus on the evidence relating to behavior and whether it amounted to "hunting" within the relevant statutes—and appropriately so, given that in neither case did the crime alleged require a showing of intent to hunt or take game. Yet were the courts really disinterested in probing subjective intent? When such a case goes to a jury, are jury members likely to separate a defendant's actions from the apparent reasons for it? That is, are juries and judges ever really indifferent to the issue of intent? We examine *mens rea* in the next subsection—but note how the concept is tied into the questions presented in the two cases.

(2) ***State v. Pollock***: Defendant captured a fawn and kept it temporarily as a pet. He contacted the state department of conservation to inquire about obtaining a permit to keep the animal and was told that, since the deer was captured during the closed season, possession of it was unlawful. When game officials arrived to recover the animal, defendant claimed that he had "put it on an airplane" and "sent it to Tennessee," chiefly so that the game warden would not take it. *Held*: The crime of possessing a deer taken in closed season requires no showing that the deer was killed or wounded by an act of hunting; defendant's conviction sustained. *State v. Pollock*, 914 S.W.2d 1 (Mo.App.1995).

(3) Waste—*State v. Huebner*: One common type of game law is a prohibition against wasting game. Such statutes reflect popular disapproval of hunting practices in which hunters slaughter game simply for the pleasure of it, leaving the meat to rot. Today, a more important rationale today is the value of such statutes in aiding enforcement, particularly in addressing poaching in which hunters take animals simply to acquire particular parts that have high black-market value, such as horns or internal or reproductive organs. A typical case is *State v. Huebner*:

> Huebner shot a mountain goat in the Avalanche Lake area of Madison County in the early evening of September 15, 1989. According to him, by the time he was able to retrieve the animal the next day, the meat was not fit for human consumption. This was disputed by other hunters in the area, who testified at trial as witnesses for the State. Huebner took only the head, horns, and cape of the animal and left the rest. He was charged with violation of § 87–3–102, MCA (1989):
>
>> Waste of fish or game. It shall be unlawful and a misdemeanor for any person responsible for the death of any game animal of this state, excepting grizzly, black, and brown bear and mountain lion, to detach or remove from the carcass only the head, hide, antlers, tusks, or teeth or any or all of aforesaid parts or to waste any part of any game animal, game bird, or game fish suitable for food or to abandon the carcass of any game animal in the field[.]

Huebner challenged his conviction on the ground that the waste statute was unconstitutionally vague:

> Section 87–3–102, MCA (1989), establishes that the wasting of game meat other than grizzly, brown, or black bear or mountain lion is illegal. A person commits "waste" by doing any of the following: (1) removing *only* the head, hide, antlers, tusks, or teeth of any game animal other than the three trophy animals listed; (2) wasting any part of any game animal, bird, or fish, other than the three trophy animals listed, which is suitable for food; or (3) abandoning in the field the carcass of any game animal other than the three trophy animals listed. The statute gives a person of ordinary intelligence reasonable notice of what is prohibited. We hold that it is not unconstitutionally vague.

Huebner also claimed that the statute implicitly required a showing of criminal intent. The court rejected this argument:

> The statute prohibiting a person from shooting a game animal and abandoning the meat, or as in this case, removing only those parts suitable for a trophy mount, is obviously intended to preserve game resources for the benefit of the public. Numerous Montana cases have

recognized the State's duty to protect public wildlife resources through regulations designed for that purpose. *E.g., State v. Jack* 539 P.2d 726 (Mont.1975). Hunters are an identifiable group of persons exercising their right to utilize the State's game resources for food and other purposes. They are responsible for knowing the laws pertaining to their sport. We hold that § 87–3–102, MCA (1989), indicates a legislative purpose to impose absolute liability for wasting game meat other than grizzly, brown, or black bear, or mountain lion.

State v. Huebner, 827 P.2d 1260 (Mont.1992).

b.   THE QUESTION OF *MENS REA*: INTENT, KNOWLEDGE, AND STRICT LIABILITY

State v. Mobbs

Vermont Supreme Court.
740 A.2d 1288 (1999).

■ Before AMESTOY, C.J., and DOOLEY, MORSE, JOHNSON, and SKOGLUND, JJ.

ENTRY ORDER

Defendant Scott Mobbs appeals his conviction of taking a moose in closed season in violation of 10 V.S.A. App. § 31(f). On appeal from Chittenden District Court defendant argues (1) the court erred in not requiring the State to prove specific intent to take a moose as an element of the offense.... We affirm.

On October 12, 1997, defendant was bow hunting for deer in the Richmond area. While in the woods, defendant heard a noise, looked up, and glimpsed what he thought was a deer. From approximately twenty-five yards, defendant shot his arrow hitting the hind quarters of the animal. As the animal ran away, defendant realized he had shot a moose, not a deer. For the entire year of 1997, there was no open season for moose in Richmond.

Later that day, the owner of the property on which defendant was hunting found the wounded moose bleeding from its hind quarters. The owner recorded the license plate numbers of the vehicles on the property and contacted the Richmond police. Several days later, the property owner and state game warden searched the area for the injured moose and found the moose dead. Based on the vehicle information obtained from the landowner, the game warden located defendant and questioned him about the moose. Defendant admitted to the warden that he had mistakenly shot the moose thinking it was a deer.

Defendant was charged with taking a moose in closed season in violation of 10 V.S.A. App. § 31(f). Read *in pari materia* with the definitions of "taking" and big game violations, § 31(f) states, "game animals * * * may be taken only during the period specified." As defined by 10 V.S.A. § 4001(23), "taking" an animal means "pursuing, shooting, hunting, killing, capturing, trapping [or] snaring." Because a moose is defined as "big game," 10 V.S.A. § 4001(31), defendant was sentenced pursuant to

10 V.S.A. § 4518 (providing penalties for violations of provisions relating to taking big game).

Defendant filed two motions to dismiss. In the first, defendant argued that the State would be unable to prove that he was motivated by any criminal intent when he shot at the moose.... The court denied both motions. After a finding of guilty by the court, defendant renewed his pretrial motions. The court again denied the motions and imposed a $300.00 fine and a $250.00 restitution payment. The sentence was stayed pending this appeal.

Defendant's central claim is that the court erred in not requiring the State to prove that defendant had the specific intent to shoot a moose. Defendant argues that because he intended to perform a lawful activity in taking a deer, he cannot be guilty of taking a moose. The "starting point in the search for the mental element required for conviction of any particular crime is the intent to do the deed which constitutes the actus reus of that offense." [ ] Here, defendant argues that the deed which constituted the actus reus for a violation of § 31(f) was the intent to take a moose. We disagree. The "deed" was the shooting of the game, an act defendant conceded he intended to do. [ ] (defendant charged with sending letter in violation of abuse prevention order need possess only intent to send letter, not intent to violate order).

Defendant argues that he did not know the animal was not a deer. However, his knowledge regarding whether the animal was a moose or a deer is immaterial. *See State v. Ward,* 56 A. 85 (Vt.1903) (if statute makes offense criminal without regard to knowledge, then ignorance of fact no excuse). The defendant in *Ward* shot at an animal he believed was a deer with antlers—a lawful activity—but which in fact was a deer without antlers—an unlawful activity. We affirmed defendant's conviction in *Ward,* holding that defendant's error did not eradicate his culpability. We noted defendant "had it in his power to find out what the fact was, or to refrain from acting until he had found out." *Id.* at 85.

Here too, defendant had the ability to make certain that he was shooting at a deer. During trial, defendant admitted to taking quick aim and shooting. After only a glimpse of the animal, defendant shot through a small pocket in the trees, intending to kill the animal he was aiming at. He did not attempt to ascertain the facts before shooting. Defendant's actions, characterized by the trial court as "shooting on the blind," resulted in the very activity the legislature sought to prohibit—the killing of moose in prohibited season. Defendant's presence in the woods with the intent to take game exposed him to a risk of liability if he failed to ensure he was shooting at the correct animal.

Allowing defendant to prevail on the argument that specific intent was required to be culpable for killing the moose would nullify the statute. Although the statute must be construed in a light most favorable to the accused, it should not frustrate the statutory purpose or lead to absurd consequences. [ ] If the defense were allowed, every violation of the statute could be defended on the ground that the thing killed was not the thing intended to be killed. Proof beyond a reasonable doubt that defendant knew he was killing prohibited wildlife rather than wildlife in season would be nearly impossible. *See Ward,* 56 A. at 85 (rejecting defendant's argument that a hunter cannot possibly know whether the deer he intended to shoot had horns).

. . .

Affirmed.

Commonwealth v. Sellinger

Pennsylvania Commonwealth Court.
763 A.2d 525 (2000).

■ LEDERER, SENIOR J.:—The Appellants were members of a group of ten individuals charged with violating 34 Pa. C.S. § 2308(8) relating to hunting in areas that had been baited. A District Justice found the five Appellants guilty and their convictions were upheld on appeal to the Court of Common Pleas of Lycoming County. This appeal followed. We affirm the trial court.

On November 23, 1998, Wildlife Conservation Officers of the Pennsylvania Game Commission observed a group of people hunting on the grounds of the Elbow Hunting Club in Lycoming County. The area in which they were hunting contained three game feeders each of which contained shelled corn and each of which was surrounded by bear droppings. All of the Appellants were observed to be close enough to the feeders to be aware of them at the time they were cited, each admitted knowledge of the existence of the feeders and each was carrying a loaded firearm. They were found guilty of violating the statute prohibiting hunting with bait because the trial court determined that the Appellants knew or should have known that they were violating the statute.

The issues addressed on appeal are whether the Commonwealth's evidence establishing beyond a reasonable doubt that the Appellants were hunting and that they knew or should have known of the existence of the bait was sufficient to sustain their convictions and whether the statute under which they were convicted is unconstitutionally vague.

Under the Game and Wildlife Code the possession of a firearm suitable for hunting is prima facie evidence that a person is engaged in the act of hunting. 34 Pa. C.S. § 2301. The Commonwealth charged the Appellants with hunting by the use of bait after they were observed in possession of loaded firearms in an area that was baited.

At trial the Commonwealth argued a standard of strict liability. It said that a conviction should follow from a mere showing that the Appellants were hunting in a baited area, regardless of whether they intended to take advantage of the bait or whether they even knew of its existence.

The Appellants contend that this is not enough to prove a violation of the statute. They argue that a violation of the Game Law is a criminal offense and that the Commonwealth must, therefore, prove that they committed a voluntary act before they can be convicted. What they argue, as the Trial Court recognized, is that "the Commonwealth has not proven that they *intended* to hunt through the use of bait," [ ] (emphasis added), and that the "central issue * * * [is] the standard of culpability the

Commonwealth [is] required to establish to prove Defendant's acts constituted violations of 34 Pa. C.S. § 2308(a)(8)." [ ]

Intent, however, need not be demonstrated to prove a violation of the Game Laws. "Title 18 (relating to crimes and offenses) is inapplicable to this title insofar as it relates to: (1) intent, willfulness of conduct * * *." 34 Pa. C.S. § 925(j).

The trial court recognized this but believed as we do that the Legislature intended that some voluntary act must be proved before there is a violation of the Game Laws. The trial court found that the voluntary act in this case was the Commonwealth's evidence that the Appellants were hunting in knowing proximity of the feeders. "The actions by the Defendants of hunting near the bait constituted the voluntary acts for which they were found to be in violation of the statute." [ ]

The Court called this the "reasonable hunter" or "negligent hunter" standard and found that it was essentially the standard followed by the enforcement officers on the day of the incident in question. One of the Wildlife Officers described the policy they followed on the morning they cited the Appellants this way: "We all had agreed that if a hunter was within view of it or if a hunter knew where the feeder was, had knowledge of it, and if the firearm was loaded, they would be charged." [ ] The Court found this approach "realistic" and "reasonable" and "consistent with effective enforcement of the law in question."

We agree with the trial court. To impose the Commonwealth's strict liability standard would be unjust. It is possible to attract game to an area by the use of bait that is not apparent to anyone but the person who set it out. Shelled corn or salt spread in high grass or underbrush and certain commercial liquids are but two ways to do this. These are undetectable to the lawful hunter who happens to find himself in the area in which they have been set. If we were to apply strict liability to this statute then a completely innocent hunter, exercising the utmost of good citizenship and sportsmanship might unknowingly hunt in a baited area. Such a person cannot fairly or reasonably be found guilty of unlawful hunting.

The Appellants' argument goes too far in the other direction. It would be an exceedingly difficult burden for the Commonwealth to carry if it had to prove that a hunter acted with the intent to violate the statute. We note again that our legislature specifically removed the element of intent from the Game Laws, 34 Pa. C.S. § 925(j). To require the Commonwealth to prove it here would thwart the legislative purpose behind the enactment of the statute by making the enforcement of it almost impossible.

The trial court's decision in this matter follows a clear, well-reasoned and persuasive path between the thickets of strict liability and criminal intent. We adopt it here in finding that a violation of 34 Pa. C.S. 2308(a)(8) occurs regardless of whether the hunter actually intends to take advantage of the bait if he continues to hunt in an area after he knows or has reason to know that it is a baited area; even if he proceeds to hunt by walking away from the bait rather than toward it, so long as he continues to hunt. A hunter who becomes aware of the existence of bait and unloads his weapon is no longer hunting.

The Appellants next argue that the law is unconstitutionally vague because it does not set forth a specific distance a person must be from a bait or a baited area before they can lawfully hunt.

The United States Court of Appeals for the Fourth Circuit addressed a similar challenge to a federal statute prohibiting hunting with bait[2] in *United States v. Chandler*, 753 F.2d 360 (4th Cir.1985). The court refused to define the limits of a baited area by a specific distance that a hunter must maintain from the bait. In doing so the court held that:

> The extent of a "baited area" is defined only by the capacity of bait placed anywhere within it to act as an effective lure for the particular hunter charged. An arbitrary spatial limitation would fail to protect those [animals] that are attracted within shooting range by bait in areas just outside any arbitrary limitation that may be set.

Id. at 362.

We find this reasoning to be persuasive and adopt it here in defining a baited area by its capacity to act as an effective lure for the particular hunter charged with a violation of the statute. In doing so we find that the statute is not unconstitutionally vague.

NOTES

(1) *Mobbs* and *Sellinger* are illustrative of the many cases in which courts must determine what showing of knowledge or intent is required to convict a defendant of a particular offense? Note that, in *Mobbs*, the court rejects on legal grounds defendants claim that he mistook a moose for a deer. What justification can you provide for the conclusion that defendant's mistake was "immaterial"? Note the differing mental states considered in *Sellinger*—the one proposed by the state, the one proposed by the appellant, and the one ultimately embraced by the court. How different would they likely be in practice? In ruling as it did has the court been fair to the legislature's policy determination as set forth in the criminal statute? Has it, on its own, crafted a reasonable compromise between the interests of the individual and the needs of the state to enforce game laws effectively?

(2) Hunting over bait: Aside from the crime of spotlighting, perhaps no game-related crime has produced more litigation than the crime of hunting over bait. *Sellinger* presents some of the common issues: Must a hunter subjectively know that the bait is present? Note that the court in *Sellinger* adopts an objective, has-reason-to-know standard. How near the bait can a person hunt? Another common issue: Do unharvested crops in a field qualify as bait? In recent decades, conservation groups such as Pheasants Forever have successfully encouraged many landowners to plant crops specifically to sustain game birds over the winter. Should such food plots be considered "bait"? (Generally they are excluded.)

Although most hunting-over-bait statutes contain no *mens rea* requirement, the approach taken in *Sellinger* has become increasingly common. *E.g., Ex parte Phillips*, 771 So.2d 1066 (Ala.2000); *People v. Schneider*, 673

---

2. Migratory Bird Treaty Act § 2, 16 U.S.C. § 703.

N.Y.S.2d 845 (N.Y.App.1998). As a matter of fairness, courts seem inclined to want proof that a defendant knew or should have known that bait was in the area, even when the governing statute contains no such requirement.

(3) *Mens rea* **in general:** Recent decisions on hunting over bait provide evidence of a larger shift by courts toward requiring evidence of at least civil negligence to sustain criminal violations of fish and game laws. Although courts do still insist that some statutes require no showing of *mens rea (e.g., State v. Fowler,* 676 A.2d 43 (Me.1996) (conviction for hunting or possessing deer during closed season requires no showing of intent to engage in these activities)), prosecutors are increasingly finding that cases are hard to sustain on appeal without evidence of something more than a technical violation. *E.g., Ford v. State,* 344 S.E.2d 514 (Ga.App.1986) (conviction of elderly woman for possessing illegal game taken by her companion who hunted on an improperly issued license overturned for lack of showing that the woman knew or should have known that the license was improperly issued). The Supreme Court of Oregon has decided that misdemeanor and felony violations of fish and game laws always require demonstration of "a culpable mental state." *State v. Cho,* 681 P.2d 1152 (Or.1984) (purchasing gall bladder of bear); *State v. Holt,* 681 P.2d 1158 (Or.1984) (illegal killing of buck deer). *See Orr–Hickey v. State,* 973 P.2d 612 (Alaska App.1999) (hunting offenses as general rule require showing that defendant knew or should have known—in this instance, that area was closed to hunting and that a particular sheep was taken in violation of state hunting law); *State v. Bucheger,* 440 N.W.2d 366 (Wis.App.1989) (requirement that defendant knew or should have known inferred from regulation that lacks one).

c.   CONSTITUTIONAL LIMITS ON ENFORCEMENT METHODS: A MISCELLANY

Mollica v. Volker

Second Circuit Court of Appeals.
229 F.3d 366 (2000).

■ LEVAL, J.:—Plaintiff-appellant Paul Mollica appeals from the district court's grant of summary judgment to the defendant. Mollica brought suit ... pursuant to 42 U.S.C. § 1983, complaining that defendant James Volker, an officer of the New York State Department of Environmental Conservation, had violated his Fourth Amendment right to be free from unreasonable search and seizure by stopping him at a checkpoint during hunting season to make deer tag and weapon safety checks. The district court granted summary judgment to Volker. The court found no violation of Mollica's Fourth Amendment rights and, in any event, that Volker was entitled to qualified immunity. We affirm on the ground that Volker was entitled to qualified immunity.

BACKGROUND

On November 23, 1997, during hunting season, on County Road 2 in Greene County, at its intersection with Ski Run Road (also referred to by the parties as Bearpen or Bear Pen Road), environmental conservation officer Volker set up a checkpoint. He had received no specific instruction from superiors at the Department of Environmental Conservation to do so, but testified that his "assignment was to conduct a patrol for deer season checking deer hunters." Ski Run Road is a dirt road providing access to a State-owned hunting ground. Volker's purpose was to stop all vehicles leaving the hunting ground on Ski Run Road to make routine deer tag and weapons safety checks. That evening at approximately 7:00 P.M., sometime after dark, Mollica drove down Ski Run Road after hunting for several days. Mollica saw Volker's official, marked vehicle parked at the intersection. Mollica contends that Volker ordered him to exit his vehicle. Volker contends Mollica stopped and exited his vehicle without having been told to do so. Because, on appeal from a grant of summary judgment, we review the evidence in the light most favorable to the non-moving party, [ ], we assume for purposes of our discussion that Volker ordered Mollica to stop and exit his vehicle. Volker in any event does not dispute that he intended to stop Mollica's vehicle.

Upon exiting his vehicle, Mollica approached Volker's vehicle and expressed his refusal to consent to any search. At this time, Volker's partner, a Greene County Deputy Sheriff, shone his flashlight into Mollica's car and looked in it from the outside. Once Volker ascertained Mollica had no deer, he told Mollica he was not being detained. Mollica returned to his vehicle and drove away. He then brought this suit.

DISCUSSION

Mollica's primary contention is that Volker's stopping him and ordering him out of his vehicle as part of a "checkpoint" and then supervising his partner's shining a light in Mollica's vehicle, without justification based on any particularized suspicion, violated his Fourth Amendment right to be free from unreasonable seizure and search.

We focus first on the constitutionality of the initial stop because if a stop is lawful, passengers and drivers have no Fourth Amendment interest in not being ordered out of the stopped vehicle. [ ] Moreover, once a vehicle is lawfully stopped, a police officer's looking through the windows into the vehicle from outside, even when shining a flashlight to illuminate the inside of the vehicle, does not constitute a "search" of the vehicle within the meaning of the Fourth Amendment. [ ]

The Supreme Court first addressed the Fourth Amendment implications of motor vehicle checkpoints in *United States v. Ortiz*, 422 U.S. 891 (1975). *Ortiz* held that absent probable cause or consent, border patrol officers could not search vehicles at a traffic checkpoint about 65 miles away from the border, but did not address the question whether the checkpoint itself (and any stoppage, slowdown, or other detention arising out of the checkpoint's operation) was permissible. The next year, in *United States v. Martinez–Fuerte*, 428 U.S. 543 (1976), the Court reached the question it had previously reserved; it held that although a stop at a fixed checkpoint some distance from the border between Mexico and the United States for brief questioning of the vehicle's occupants, to determine if the vehicle might be carrying illegal aliens, constituted a "seizure" for

Fourth Amendment purposes, it was lawful. More recently, the Court applied the analysis of *Martinez-Fuerte* to a temporary checkpoint used to check drivers briefly for signs of intoxication, *see Michigan Dept. of State Police v. Sitz*, 496 U.S. 444 (1990), and again, found the checkpoint constitutional.

The *Sitz* Court explained that a motor vehicle checkpoint's reasonableness, and thus its constitutionality, is determined by evaluating and balancing three broad factors—the magnitude of the State's interest in operating the checkpoint, the intrusion inflicted upon motorists by the operation of the checkpoint, and the degree to which the operation of the checkpoint (the seizure) advances the State's interest, also referred to as "effectiveness." [ ]

. . .

Volker contends that the district court's judgment must be affirmed as there can be no doubt he is entitled to qualified immunity. We agree. Qualified immunity "shields [police officers] from personal liability for damages 'insofar as their conduct does not violate clearly established statutory or constitutional rights of which a reasonable person would have known,' or insofar as it was objectively reasonable for them to believe that their acts did not violate those rights." [ ] For a constitutional right to be "clearly established" for purposes of determining whether an officer is entitled to qualified immunity, the

> contours of the right must be sufficiently clear that a reasonable official would understand that what he is doing violates that right. This is not to say that an official action is protected by qualified immunity unless the very action in question has previously been held unlawful, but it is to say that *in the light of pre-existing law the unlawfulness must be apparent.*

. . .

The determinative question therefore becomes "whether under preexisting law [Volker] * * * would have understood * * * his * * * acts [to be] unlawful." [ ] Neither we nor the Supreme Court have ever found the brief detention and inquiry incidental to the operation of a particular motor vehicle checkpoint to be unconstitutional. There is no caselaw clearly establishing that what Volker did was unreasonable or violated the Constitution. We think that any unlawfulness in Volker's checkpoint would not have been apparent to a reasonable officer. We therefore must affirm the district court's grant of summary judgment on the basis of qualified immunity.

The more troublesome question is whether, having recognized that the suit must be dismissed by reason of immunity, we should push further to announce a view as to whether Volker's operation of the checkpoint did or did not violate the Constitution. The Supreme Court has urged lower courts to answer the ultimate constitutional question, rather than rely solely on qualified immunity, lest the "standards of official conduct * * * tend to remain uncertain." *County of Sacramento v. Lewis*, 523 U.S. 833, 841 n. 5 (1998) ("[T]he better approach to resolving cases in which the defense of qualified immunity is raised is to determine first whether the plaintiff has alleged a deprivation of a constitutional right.''); [ ]. In *Horne v. Coughlin,* 191 F.3d 244 (2d Cir.1999), we considered whether the *Sacramento* dictum should be regarded as having mandated a procedure to be followed in all cases, or as guidance to be followed in suitable cases but not in cases where the disadvantages of the procedure would outweigh the benefits. We observed that, while in some circumstances it would be highly desirable for a court to reach the constitutional question, in others, it could be quite harmful. [ ]

. . .

We are inclined to believe that, were it required to be decided, Volker's checkpoint should probably be sustained. Some of the factors that have influenced the Supreme Court clearly favor upholding the checkpoint. First, Volker's checkpoint was in one way actually less intrusive than those approved in *Sitz* and *Martinez-Fuerte.* According to the implications of Volker's testimony, it was situated so as to stop few cars, the majority of which were likely to be hunters. Hunters, having chosen to participate in a highly regulated activity, have a lesser expectation of freedom from such intrusions than citizens not engaged in regulated activity. [ ] Secondly, as the district court pointed out:

> It would be impossible for environmental conservation officers to perform their regulatory functions without stopping hunters as they leave known public hunting areas. The only other way they could enforce their mandate would be to go into the woods to search for hunters actively engaged in hunting. Such a course of action would not only be absurd but it would also be extremely (and unreasonably) dangerous. Furthermore, it is impossible to determine whether game is properly tagged until after the hunter ha[s] secured the game and ha[s] departed the area.

Volker, furthermore, could not have proceeded by attempting to spot drivers whose particular characteristics gave rise to a reasonable suspicion. Unlike driving under the influence of alcohol, the possession of improperly tagged deer cannot be readily identified by the manner of driving, or other features ascertainable without stopping a motor vehicle. Use of a checkpoint under such circumstances could even serve as a means of preventing individual officers from making stops based on illegitimate criteria. These factors tend to support the defendant as to the "effectiveness" inquiry.

In some respects, however, the constitutionality of Volker's checkpoint is less clear than the constitutionality of the checkpoints in *Martinez-Fuerte, Sitz,* and *Maxwell.* The dominant governmental interest Volker points to is the State's interest in regulating the taking of deer—arguably less weighty than the interests at stake in *Sitz, Martinez–Fuerte,* and *Maxwell.* It is true, Volker testified he intended also to conduct checks for weapons safety, which would serve the interest of protecting human life. On the other hand, there was no corroboration from any higher state authority that it was state policy to establish checkpoints to check for weapons safety. And, while Mollica did not dispute Volker's assertion, it is somewhat undermined by the fact that Volker did not undertake a safety check of Mollica's weapons. Moreover, whereas in the previously cited cases, superior officials had established policy and directed subordinate officers to establish official checkpoints, to be operated at specific locations and in accordance with specific guidelines, Volker was acting pursuant to his own discretion. He was instructed only to "conduct a patrol for deer season checking deer hunters." The ad hoc, unsupervised nature of Volker's checkpoint is a factor the Supreme Court has identified as tending to undermine a finding of reasonableness. *See Sitz,* 496 U.S. at 447, 452–53; *Martinez-Fuerte,* 428 U.S. at 553, 559. Finally, unlike the large, official checkpoints at issue in *Sitz* and *Martinez-Fuerte,* the checkpoint established by Volker at night on a presumably seldom-traveled road may have had the same capacity to frighten motorists that caused the Supreme Court in *Sitz* and *Martinez-Fuerte* to frown on roving patrols.

Because the district court's decision was made on summary judgment, as is common with dismissals based on qualified immunity, the record is quite scanty. The only evidence of the state's interest in establishing Volker's checkpoint is supplied by defendant Volker's own brief deposition testimony. The record includes no assertion by any higher authority as to whether Volker's superiors encouraged the establishment of such checkpoints, whether they believe it is a desirable way to enforce the law, how checkpoint sites should be selected, or how efficacy in enforcing the law should be balanced against inconvenience to or other impositions on motorists. While Volker testified, as noted above, that his objective included not only monitoring to see that deer were taken only in conformity with state law, but also monitoring weapons safety, there was no evidence as to whether weapons safety was within the scope of his duties, or within the Department's policies. Furthermore, the evidentiary record with respect to efficacy and intrusiveness to non-hunter motorists is very thin. Thus, while we are inclined to think that Volker's checkpoint would be found permissible under the Supreme Court's standards, expressing such a conclusion would involve some speculation and would require us to make assumptions to fill the gaps in a scanty record.

.   .   .

Given the scant record before us (as is common in appeals from summary judgment based on qualified immunity), we are faced with three possible courses of action: (1) reach out on an inadequate record to announce a view, in dictum, on a constitutional question whose resolution is unnecessary to decide the case, (2) remand to the district court and direct the district court to require the parties to participate in further proceedings that will have no bearing on the result of their case, or (3) decline to express a view on the underlying constitutional question since we lack adequate information to do so. We think it clear that the third option is the preferable one. [ ] We conclude that Volker is entitled to qualified immunity and do not reach out to answer whether Volker's checkpoint was constitutional.

NOTES

Is the court in *Mollica* correct in asserting that the state's interest "in regulating the taking of deer" was "arguably less weighty" than the governmental interests in discovering illegal immigrants or preventing intoxicated individuals from driving? [§ 13] The weight of the governmental interest in wildlife conservation has been a recurrent question. Recall that Justice Holmes in *Missouri v. Holland*, 252 U.S. 416 (1920), spoke of the protection of migratory birds as involving "a national interest of very nearly the first magnitude." Nearly 60 years later, Justice Brennan went a step further: "We consider the States' interests in conservation and protection of wild animals as legitimate local purposes similar to the States' interests in protecting the health and safety of their citizens." *Hughes v. Oklahoma*, 441 U.S. 322 (1979). Can a line be drawn between wildlife conservation (*Holland*) and ecosystem preservation (*Hughes*) and game management (*Mollica*)?

Rainey v. Hartness

Arkansas Supreme Court.
5 S.W.3d 410 (1999).

■ CORBIN, J.:—Appellants Jerry Rainey and James Harton filed a civil-rights suit in the Grant County Circuit Court against Appellee James Hartness, a wildlife enforcement officer with the Arkansas Game and Fish Commission. The suit alleged that Hartness (1) entered their property without authority; (2) seized Harton's rifle through an illegal search and converted it without due process of law and just compensation; and (3) damaged their crops by driving over them on a four-wheel, all-terrain vehicle. The trial court granted summary judgment to Hartness, and Appellants appealed. [ ]

Appellants' claims involve actions that occurred on the morning of October 21, 1995, during muzzleloading deer season. The record reflects that Appellants were engaged in hunting on wooded land owned by Rainey and leased by Harton. Appellants were situated at deer stands in different areas of the land. Hartness was patrolling the area that morning, when he noticed unattended vehicles on Rainey's property, leading him to believe that people were hunting there. Hartness rode his four-wheel vehicle onto the property, where he first encountered Rainey at his deer stand. When Hartness asked to see Rainey's hunting license, Rainey initially produced the license of someone else. Hartness issued Rainey a citation, pursuant to Regulation 03.06 of the Arkansas Game and Fish Commission Regulations (the Regulations), for being in possession of the hunting license of another person.

Hartness then followed the path to another deer stand, where he encountered Harton. According to Hartness, Harton came down from his deer stand without being asked to do so. Hartness considered this strange because it was a cold morning and because hunters normally wait for him to come up to them. Harton stated that he was muzzleload hunting, and he produced a license to do so. After viewing the license, Hartness climbed up the ladder and looked through the opening in the deer stand. There, he saw a Marlin Lever Action .22 caliber rifle with a scope. Hartness took possession of the rifle and issued Harton a citation for violating Regulation 07.03, which provides that it is "unlawful to have in immediate possession a centerfire or rimfire weapon while participating in muzzleloading deer seasons."

Appellants were found guilty of the violations in municipal court. Harton, however, appealed his conviction to circuit court. [ ]

Appellants brought their suit pursuant to the Arkansas Civil Rights Act of 1993, [ ], and 42 U.S.C. §§ 1983 and 1988. Appellants alleged that Hartness's actions ... violated their constitutional right to be free from unreasonable searches and seizures. They alleged further that the seizure of Harton's rifle violated his right to bear arms and was a taking without due process and just compensation. Lastly, they alleged that Hartness damaged their crops by driving over them on his four-wheel vehicle.

. . .

The Fourth Amendment to the United States Constitution provides:

The right of the people to be secure in their persons, houses, papers, and effects, against unreasonable searches and seizures, shall not be violated, and no warrants shall issue, but upon probable cause, supported by oath or affirmation, and particularly describing the place to be searched, and the persons or things to be seized.

Article 2, § 15, of the Arkansas Constitution is virtually identical to the Fourth Amendment, and we interpret it in the same manner as the United States Supreme Court interprets the Fourth Amendment. [ ]

The Supreme Court has recognized that the protection afforded by the Fourth Amendment does not extend to open fields or lands. [ ] This court has also recognized the "open fields" doctrine. [ ] Additionally, Rule 14.2 of the Arkansas Rules of Criminal Procedure provides: "An officer may, without a search warrant, search open lands and seize things which he reasonably believes subject to seizure."

Here, the evidence showed that Rainey's property was open, wooded land. Appellants admit in their complaint that the land was used for the recreational purpose of hunting deer and other game. Regulation 01.00–B provides in pertinent part that wildlife officers have authority to "go upon any property outside of private dwellings, posted or otherwise, in the performance of their duties," and that they "may with or without a warrant according to law, conduct searches." In their memorandum below, Appellants essentially concede that if Hartness was a properly elected wildlife officer, he had authority to come onto Rainey's land. Thus, Hartness's entry onto the property on his four-wheel vehicle did not violate the Fourth Amendment or Article 2, § 15. The question then is whether Hartness's actions in climbing up the ladder to look into Harton's deer stand violated those constitutional provisions. Appellants urge that Harton enjoyed a legitimate expectation of privacy in his deer stand, and that, therefore, the warrantless search of the stand's interior violated the Fourth Amendment. We disagree.

Within the meaning of the Fourth Amendment, a search "occurs when an expectation of privacy that society is prepared to consider reasonable is infringed." [ ] A person who knowingly exposes an object to the public cannot expect the protection from unreasonable search and seizure provided by the Fourth Amendment. [ ] "[E]ven a property interest in premises may not be sufficient to establish a legitimate expectation of privacy with respect to particular items located on the premises or activity conducted thereon." [ ] When an expectation of privacy is claimed, the trial court must determine: (1) Whether the defendant has asserted or manifested a subjective expectation of privacy, and (2) whether that expectation is objectively reasonable. [ ] Although the first prong is a question of fact, the second is one of law. [ ] Thus, even assuming that the defendant has proven a *subjective* expectation of privacy, in the final analysis, that expectation must be objectively reasonable. [ ] After reviewing the evidence in this case, we conclude that the trial court did not err in finding that, as a matter of law, Harton enjoyed no legitimate expectation of privacy in the deer stand.

The evidence presented below demonstrates that the stand was little more than a metal box, with sides three to four feet high and a roof elevated on poles at each corner of the box. Persons standing inside the box were exposed to the public's view, as Hartness testified that he observed Harton on the stand as he approached the area. There was no evidence that Harton used the stand to engage in private activity, other than eating meals, or that he attempted to shield his activities from the public. Moreover, Harton employed no apparent means of restricting access to the stand. [ ] There was no evidence that the structure was inaccessible to other persons (*i.e.*, that the hatch door was locked or that the ladder was removed whenever he was not using the stand), only Harton's claim that it was not open to use by other persons unless he invited them. Accordingly, there was a "theoretical possibility" that "animals, children, scavengers, snoops, and other members of the public" would happen onto the stand, thus rendering any claimed expectation of privacy objectively unreasonable. [ ]

Furthermore, contrary to Appellants' assertion, there is no evidence that the deer stand was within the curtilage of the temporary residences (*i.e.*, campers on blocks) located on the property. Assuming, *arguendo*, that the campers qualify as "houses" under the Fourth Amendment, we nonetheless conclude that the stand was not within the curtilage. The Supreme Court has held that curtilage questions should be resolved with reference to four factors: (1) the proximity of the area to the home; (2) whether the area is included within an enclosure surrounding the home; (3) the nature of the uses to which the area is put; and (4) the steps taken to protect the area from observation by people passing by. [ ] Here, the evidence showed that Rainey's stand was approximately one-quarter mile away from the campers, and that Harton's stand was approximately one-quarter mile from Rainey's stand. Thus, the area sought to be protected (the deer stand) was approximately one-half mile away from the campers. There was no evidence of a fence or other enclosure surrounding the campers and the stand. Nor was there any evidence that the stand was used for the "intimate activities of the home." [ ] Finally, as explained above, Harton did little, if anything, to restrict access to the stand by other persons. Accordingly, the stand was not a part of the curtilage.

Based on the foregoing, we conclude that Hartness was entitled to qualified immunity from Appellants' federal civil-rights claims. Hartness's conduct on October 21, 1995, did not violate any clearly established constitutional rights possessed by Appellants. Appellants enjoyed no rights under the Fourth Amendment that would protect them from (1) Hartness's entry onto their property and (2) Hartness's search of Harton's deer stand. Because Hartness's search of the stand was legal under the Fourth Amendment, his seizure of the rifle as evidence was valid. Rule 10.2 of the Arkansas Rules of Criminal Procedure provides that a permissible object of seizure includes evidence of a criminal offense or other violation of the law. Accordingly, seizure of the gun was not a "taking" proscribed by Article 2, §§ 21 and 22, of the Arkansas Constitution.

NOTES

(1) *State v. McHugh*: Defendants were charged with possession of an untagged deer. The case, in the court's words, presented

> the question of whether a wildlife law enforcement officer may make a suspicionless stop of a hunter leaving a wildlife habitat during hunting season and detain him briefly to ascertain whether he has a valid hunting license, to ask whether he has game in his possession, and, if so, to request to inspect the game. After being subjected to such a stop, the defendants freely and voluntarily acknowledged their possession of game and allowed a wildlife officer to inspect a dressed and quartered buck deer in their ice chest. Because the divided deer portions were not tagged as required by law, La.R.S. 56:125, the officer charged the defendants with statutory violations.

The court began its assessment of the search by summarizing the general search-and-seizure law and rejecting the state's claim that the search was justified as an "investigatory stop":

> Subject only to a few exceptions that were specifically established and well-defined prior to the adoption of our state constitution, a search, seizure or invasion of privacy conducted without a warrant issued upon probable cause is constitutionally prohibited. [ ] Once a defendant makes an initial showing that a warrantless search or seizure occurred, the burden of proof shifts to the state to affirmatively show that it was justified under one of the narrow exceptions to the rule requiring a search warrant. [ ]

> It is undisputed that the stop in the present case was not authorized by a warrant. The state contends, however, that the stop was justified and came within an established exception to the warrant requirement, *viz.*, the "investigatory stop" exception. A law enforcement officer may stop a person in a public place whom he reasonably suspects is committing, has committed, or is about to commit an offense and may demand of him his name, address, and an explanation of his actions. [ ] Therefore, an investigatory stop must be justified by some objective manifestation that the person stopped is, or is about to be engaged in criminal activity, or there must be reasonable grounds to believe that the person has committed or is wanted for past criminal conduct. [ ]

The state failed to carry its burden of showing that the wildlife agents' detention of the defendants came within the "investigatory stop" exception. The record clearly indicates that when the defendants arrived, the officers were still engaged in the process they had begun the previous day of indiscriminately stopping as many boats as possible to check licenses and inquire about game in hunters' possession.

Although the stops did not qualify as lawful investigatory stops, they were permissible, the court decided, as routine suspicionless stops of persons engaged in hunting activities, given the state's strong needs to use such stops for game enforcement:

It is impossible for agents to tell whether a hunter is licensed without stopping him for a license check. Without the prospect of suspicionless license check stops, hunters would have little incentive to purchase and carry hunting licenses. Unlike an unlicensed motor vehicle operator who incurs a substantial risk of being found out as an unauthorized driver by getting a traffic ticket or becoming involved in an accident, an unlicensed hunter runs only a small risk if agents cannot make suspicionless stops to check licenses. Further, because a hunting license lacks the utility of a driver's license as a means of identity and credibility, a hunter does not have the same incentive as a driver to maintain a valid license.

An extremely important aspect of wildlife law enforcement involves the conservation of game by detecting and apprehending violators who take or possess game in excess of the limits legally permitted. Because the taking or possession of game per se is not illegal, however, an agent's observation of a hunter killing or carrying game usually does not give rise to reasonable suspicion or probable cause that there has been a violation. Unlike drugs or drunk drivers, dead ducks evince no telltale signs, smells or behavior plainly indicating criminal activity. Consequently, if agents were not entitled to make suspicionless stops of hunters for license checks and brief questioning, the enforcement of the game limit laws would be retrenched to an unacceptable level.

The court emphasized, however, that its ruling was a narrow one:

[W]e hold that a game agent's stop of a hunter in or departing from a wildlife habitat in open season and detention of him for the limited purposes of a license check and requests for game information and inspection does not violate the state or federal constitution. Our holding today is limited to the type of stop described in this opinion. Any further detention must be based on consent, probable cause or reasonable suspicion.

State v. McHugh, 630 So.2d 1259 (La.1994).

(2) *Mollica, Rainey,* and *McHugh* examine the general powers game wardens typically possess to undertake searches and seizures in the course of law enforcement efforts. In all cases an inquiry into the power to undertake searches must begin by reviewing state statutes vesting power in the wardens; only if they have such power is it necessary to determine whether a particular search is consistent with federal and state constitutional requirements.

As *Mollica* and *McHugh* illustrate, courts are willing to uphold suspicionless game checkpoints as long as they are set up in areas where the people stopped are likely to be hunters and as long as the stop and questioning are minor in duration and intrusiveness. Of course, under the constitution wardens also have the full range of powers to search based on probable cause or incident to an arrest. *See also State v. Thurman,* 996 P.2d 309 (Idaho App.1999) (routine stop constitutional where limited to determining whether automobile occupant had been hunting or fishing).

(3) Open field: Many enforcement efforts fit within the "open field" exception to the warrant requirement, an exception that applies to outdoor areas generally (not just fields) except those that are within the "curtilage" of a dwelling or other space where tenants have reasonable expectations of privacy. *E.g., State v. Sorenson,* 441 N.W.2d 455 (Minn.1989); *Betchart v. California State Dept. of Fish and Game,* 205 Cal.Rptr. 135 (Cal.App.1984); *State v. Hoagland,* 270 N.W.2d 778 (Minn.1978). As the leading treatise explains:

> Courts never took the word "open" in the [open-fields] rule too seriously; the rule was applied even when the land was fenced, even when it was posted with no trespassing signs, and even when the evidence discovered was not itself in plain view. Similarly, the word "fields" was never restricted to a literal or technical definition of a place suitable for pasture or tillage. [Open-field] analysis has been applied to police intrusions into wooded areas, desert, vacant lots in urban areas, open beaches, reservoirs, and open waters.

1 WAYNE R. LaFAVE, SEARCH AND SEIZURE: A TREATISE ON THE FOURTH AMENDMENT 523 (3d ed. 1996) (citations omitted).

As Professor LaFave notes, courts have typically been willing to allow law enforcement officials to enter any land outside the "curtilage" of a home, even when probable cause for an arrest or search is absent and even where these exists no reasonable suspicion. *Id.* at 524–25. No precise answer can be given on how much space around a home is within the curtilage. The Supreme Court in *United States v. Dunn,* 480 U.S. 294 (1987), explained that questions having to do with the extent of the curtilage "should be resolved with particular reference to four factors: the proximity of the area claimed to be curtilage to the home, whether the area is included within an enclosure surrounding the home, the nature of the uses to which the area is put, and the steps taken by the resident to protect the area from observation by people passing by."

(4) State constitutional limits: Although the federal constitution permits warrantless searches of open fields, state constitutions may provide landowners greater protection. In *State v. Romain,* 983 P.2d 322 (Mont. 1999), the Montana Supreme Court ruled that landowners may have a reasonable expectation of property over outdoor areas not within the curtilage. In *Romain,* the defendant's rural tract was fenced, posted with no trespassing signs, and largely screened by brush from public sight along the adjacent road. Game wardens acting on an anonymous tip of poaching drove over defendant's quarter-mile driveway, entering through an open gate, parked and knocked on the front door. As they drove in, they saw evidence of an illegally taken elk. The court suppressed all evidence obtained by the wardens on the ground that the wardens' mere entry on to the land without warrant or permission was an unlawful search. *See also State v. Bullock,* 901 P.2d 61 (Mont.1995) (defendant had reasonable expectations of privacy regardless of whether elk carcass was within curtilage; evidence of poaching should have been suppressed).

In *Corry v. State,* 710 So.2d 853 (Miss.1998), hunters were charged with violations by a warden who had crossed a privately owned open field. The court held that the warden's powers were limited by state trespass law. Only the owner or tenant of the land could raise that objection, however, and on the facts, even the owner could not complain about the entry because the warden had observed a violation of law before entering the land.

(5) Forfeiture: Many state statutory schemes include provisions permitting state to seize personal property—such as fishing gear, nets, and rifles—used in violating fish and game laws. Forfeiture provisions differ widely as to when forfeiture can occur, what property can be seized and by whom, and what legal process, if any, is required.

(a) Constitutional and statutory limits on forfeiture: In assessing the legality of a forfeiture, the first step is to review the applicable statute because forfeiture must be is expressly authorized. If the statute authorizes forfeiture, the next issue is the limits imposed by the federal constitution. The primary constitutional hurdles are the Due Process Clause—which protects citizens from being deprived of property without due process of law—and the Eighth Amendment—which prohibits excessive fines. Recall that in *Lawton v. Steele,* 152 U.S. 133 (1894) [Chapter 6], the United States Supreme Court upheld the power of a state to enact forfeiture laws, including summary forfeiture.

A treatise on constitutional law summarizes the issues:

> The Supreme Court of the United States has long upheld the power of the government to seize and take title to property that has been used ... to commit "wrongs" to society or persons. However, the Court has not provided clear constitutional guidelines regarding the government's ability to require the forfeiture of such property to the government.

> Forfeiture actions might present problems under the Eight Amendment prohibition against excessive fines, due process clauses of the Fifth and Fourteenth Amendments, or the principles established by the taking of property clause of the Fifth Amendment. To the extent that the forfeiture is a punishment for a crime, the Eighth Amendment prohibition against excessive fines might provide the easiest basis for such analysis. Analysis of forfeiture problems under the procedural due process principles would focus on the "fairness" of the procedures provided to the owner of the property. Analysis of forfeiture issues under the takings clause of the Fifth Amendment, which applies to state and local actions though the Fourteenth Amendment, would focus on whether the government action was so unfair and unjust as to require the payment of compensation to the property owner.

In *Bennis v. Michigan*, [516 U.S. 442 (1996)], the Supreme Court, by a five-to-four vote of the Justices, upheld a state law requiring forfeiture of an automobile, owned by a husband and wife in joint tenancy, solely on the basis that the husband had procured the services of a prostitute in the car, without the knowledge of his co-owner spouse. The majority opinion in *Bennis*, by Chief Justice Rehnquist, relied on earlier decisions ... in rejecting the so-called "innocent-owner defense." ...

2 RONALD D. ROTUNDA & JOHN E. NOWAK, TREATISE ON CONSTITUTIONAL LAW 691–92 (3d. ed. 1999). The Supreme Court has recently subjected criminal forfeitures to a fairness principle of proportionality under the Eighth Amendment excessive fines clause, but forfeitures of instrumentalities of crime have traditional been, and apparently remain, excluded from that clause. *United States v. Bajakajian*, 524 U.S. 321 (1998).

(b) *One 1992 Toyota 4–Runner v. Mississippi Dept. of Wildlife Fisheries & Parks*: Jon and Linda Devine were convicted of illegally fishing with the aid of an electrical device and possession of the illegally acquired fish. A law enforcement officer (Carr) had observed them in their boat "shocking up fish, a method of fishing in which a person drags an electrical wire over the edge of the boat. The weighted wire carries a current which shocks motley catfish on the bottom of the river, causing them to rise to the surface." The officer did not arrest them until three hours later, when the Devines brought their boat to the boat ramp and loaded it onto their trailer, pulled by a Toyota 4–Runner. After they had pulled away from the ramp, officers arrested the defendants and searched their vehicle and possessions. The officers seized not only their dip net and other equipment used to catch the fish but also their boat, motor, trailer, ice chest (which contained the fish), and the Toyota. The Devines challenged the forfeiture, arguing that the forfeiture should be limited to property being used when they were observed shocking the fish.

This argument is predicated on the presumption that Officer Carr could have only lawfully arrested the Devines at the time that he was observing them; had he done it then, the State would have been entitled to seize the boat, motor, fishing gear, chains over the side of the boat, and the shocking device. Since he illegally arrested them after a three hour delay, the Devines reiterate that all of the evidence he obtained must be suppressed, they must be released, and all personal property that was seized must be returned to them. Finally, they suggest without support that Officer Carr delayed his arrest in order to subject the greatest amount of personal and real property to forfeiture.

The Devines' argument is without merit. First, there is absolutely no evidence in the record in this appeal that Officer Carr deliberately waited to arrest the Devines until he could seize the boat trailer and the Toyota 4–Runner, as well as the properties he had observed on the river. Second, to the extent that the appellant properties argue that the only items seizable were those that were observed at the time when a lawful arrest could have been made, which they theorize could have only occurred while Officer Carr was actually observing their conduct, we have held that the arrests in this case were lawful when made, as were the searches; thus, the seizures were incident to lawful arrests. Finally, as the State notes, the plain text of the statute authorized the forfeiture of all of the properties since they were directly and indirectly used to obtain the fish through shocking, and transport the contraband fish and illegal equipment away from the river. The fish were found in the boat, which was towed on the trailer attached to the Toyota 4–Runner, in which the shocking device was found. Although the seizures are additionally subject to the constitutional constraints of the Excessive Fines Clause of the Eighth Amendment ... all of the defendant properties were properly *subject* to forfeiture under the statutory definition of § 49–7–103.

The Devines also challenged the forfeiture on the ground that the statute authorizing it did not articulate a standard by which law enforcement agents could determine what property was seizable—an omission that arguably conflicted with the state constitution. The court rejected this argument, but only after construing the applicable forfeiture statute "to require law enforcement agents to have probable cause to believe that the subject property has been used, directly or indirectly, to accomplish the various violations that are enumerated." On the record, the court had no trouble finding that probable cause did exist.

Under the Eighth Amendment, the Devines urged that the forfeiture of the Toyota should be treated as an excessive fine because it was not an instrument of criminal activity within the Eighth Amendment. This argument was also rejected, although only because the Devines had failed to raise it at the trial court. Nonetheless, the court reversed the order forfeiting the vehicle based on a state statute, enacted two years after the illegal fishing, that banned forfeitures of motor vehicles; although forfeiture was proper at the time of the crime, the court nonetheless applied the new statute to the case. *One Toyota 4–Runner v. Mississippi Department of Wildlife Fisheries & Parks,* 721 So.2d 609 (Miss.1998). *See also Baum v. State,* 24 P.3d 577 (Alaska App.2001) (forfeiture of airplane valued at $40,000 and owned by defendant's brother did not violate the Excessive Fines Clause).

CHAPTER 10

FEDERAL PROTECTION FOR SPECIES

Wildlife conservation laws fall into two broad categories. The more common restricts killing—"taking"—wildlife. State fish and game laws governing seasons, bag limits, and gear restrictions on hunters and fishers are examples. This category is characterized by its focus on species: game regulations are species-specific. The second group of conservation statutes regulate the use of land to protect wildlife habitat. Although laws in this category are less common than taking restrictions, they are equally crucial since wildlife cannot survive without suitable habitat. This chapter examines federal law on species protection other than the Endangered Species Act, which is covered in Chapter 13. Federal habitat protection law—again with the exception of the Endangered Species Act—is considered in Chapter 11.

SECTION 1.   THE LACEY ACT

PERSPECTIVES

(1) The constitutional context of the Lacey Act: Recall that in *Geer v. Connecticut,* 161 U.S. 519 (1896) [Chapters 5 and 6], the Supreme Court held that the state as sovereign proprietor had the power to prohibit the out-of-state shipment of lawfully taken wildlife. *Geer* did not consider the related question of whether a state had the power to prohibit the importation of game lawfully killed outside the state. Could Connecticut prohibit the shipment of game killed in New York? In current constitutional jurisprudence, the question would be: does a state statute that facially discriminates against commerce originating in another state violate the dormant Commerce Clause? In the constitutional jurisprudence at the end of the nineteenth century, however, the answer was far from clear.

In *Gibbons v. Ogden,* 22 U.S. (9 Wheat.) 1 (1824), Chief Justice Marshall sought to define two separate spheres by drawing a line between the regulation of *interstate* commerce (which was exclusively a federal prerogative) and the regulation of *intrastate* activities that might "have a remote and inconsiderable influence on commerce." Subsequent Courts struggled to distinguish between permissible state police power statutes and impermissible commerce power statutes, with results that generally appear conclusory: statutes that the Court upheld were police power regulations, those that it struck down regulated commerce.

The Court shifted its focus in *Cooley v. Board of Wardens,* 53 U.S. (12 How.) 299 (1851), distinguishing between those subjects of commerce that require a uniform national rule and those which permit a diversity of treatment to meet local needs. Not surprisingly, the line between local and national also proved elusive.

The application of these constitutional principles to wildlife produced differing opinions. Could Connecticut, for example, prohibit the shipment of game killed in New York? In *In re Davenport,* the court granted a writ of habeas corpus after concluding that a state statute prohibiting the sale of game was unconstitutional as applied to game imported from another state. The state's asserted justification—to make it easier to enforce the game laws—was rejected as overbroad: "It would certainly be much easier to enforce our local inspection laws ... if our markets might be closed to importers of these commodities. But the unconstitutionality of all such local laws in restraint of interstate commerce has been definitely pronounced by the supreme court." *In re Davenport,* 102 F. 540 (E.D.Wash. 1900). On essentially similar facts, the district court for Oregon reached the opposite conclusion. *In re Deininger,* 108 F. 623 (D.Or.1901). Congress resolved the issue by enacting the Lacey Act criminalizing the shipment of wildlife and fish in interstate commerce if it was illegal under the laws of either the exporting or importing state. Lacey Act, §§ 3, 5, 31 Stat. 187, 188–89 (1900). *See also* Black Bass Act of 1926, 44 Stat. 576, *amended by,* Act of July 30, 1947, ch. 348, 61 Stat. 517, *and,* Act of July 16, 1952, ch. 911, § 2, 66 Stat. 736.

(2) The genesis of the Lacey Act: The Lacey Act reflected the confluence of two concerns: the rapid depletion of game as a result of market hunting for food and the equally dramatic destruction of many non-game bird species for millinery decoration—the "plume trade." Both concerns reveal a recurrent difficulty with federalism—particularly in regard to transboundary resources such as wildlife. One result of multiple jurisdictions is parochialism: hunters in one state are prone to consume as much of the resource as possible since others "downstream" may prevent its return in the future: a duck not shot today may be shot tomorrow in a different state. Each state thus was under pressure from its hunters (and hence its voters) to allow them to take as many ducks as possible. No state acting alone could conserve migratory species and thus none had an incentive to reduce the take of its own citizens. Although these perverse incentives— often misleadingly called the "tragedy of the commons"—were exacerbated by the now-abandoned constitutional jurisprudence of the period, they remain a source of recurrent problems in managing transboundary resources. *See* George C. Coggins, *Grizzly Bears Don't Stop at Customs: A Preface to Transboundary Problems in Natural Resources Law,* 32 KAN. L. REV. 1 (1983); Dale D. Goble, *Introduction to the Symposium on Legal Structures for Managing the Pacific Northwest Salmon and Steelhead: The Biological and Historical Context,* 22 IDAHO L. REV. 417 (1986).

The Act was also a response to a broad coalition of hunters, scientific naturalists, nature lovers, and humanitarians. *See* Theodore W. Cart, *The Lacey Act: America's First Nationwide Wildlife Statute,* FOREST HIST., Oct. 1973, at 4; Joseph Kastner, *Long before Furs, It was Feathers that Stirred Reformist Ire,* SMITHSONIAN, July 1994, at 97. The history of the Act is brought up through the 1981 and 1988 amendments in Robert D.

Anderson, *The Lacey Act: America's Premier Weapon in the Fight Against Unlawful Wildlife Trafficking,* 16 Pub. Land L. Rev. 27 (1995).

NOTES

(1) The Lacey Act of 1900: The Lacey Act was the first federal wildlife conservation statute with a national scope. The Act prohibited specific categories of interstate commerce in wildlife "or parts thereof." Act of May 25, 1900, ch. 553, §§ 3, 5, 31 Stat. 187, 188–89. As originally enacted, the Act contained three types of provisions. First, it added federal criminal penalties to interstate shipments of wildlife that violated state law; second, it imposed labeling requirements on interstate shipments of wildlife; and, third, it created an affirmative federal duty to conserve wildlife.

(a) Interstate shipment of wildlife illegally taken or possessed: The original version of the Lacey Act was intended primarily to supplement *state* law—it was a "tool to aid the States in enforcing their own laws concerning wildlife." S. Rep. No. 123, 97th Cong., 1st Sess. 2 (1981), *reprinted in* 1981 U.S.C.C.A.N. 1748, 1749. It did so by criminalizing two types of conduct. First, it prohibited delivery to a common carrier and the interstate transportation by a carrier of wildlife taken in violation of *state* law. Act of May 25, 1900, ch. 553, § 3, 31 Stat. 187, 188 (codified as amended at 16 U.S.C. § 3372). Second, it subjected interstate shippers to the laws of the state into which the game was transported. *Id.* § 5. Thus, a shipper was liable if possession of the wildlife was illegal under the law of either the shipping or the receiving state. Note the crucial two-step requirement: there must be a violation of a state law—the "predicate violation"—before there can be a violation of the Lacey Act.

The types of statutes that would serve as a predicate violation has steadily expanded since 1900. Certain foreign laws were covered in the 1930 Tariff Act, in which Congress prohibited importation into the United States of any animal or any product manufactured from any animal if the laws of the exporting country restricted the taking or exportation of the animal. Act of June 17, 1930, ch. 497, § 527, 46 Stat. 590, 741 (codified at 19 U.S.C. § 1527). A further expansion in 1935 brought the Lacey Act into conformity by including violations of federal or foreign law. Act of June 15, 1935, ch. 261, § 201, 49 Stat. 380, (codified as amended at 16 U.S.C. § 3372(a)(2)(A)).

The Act was also expanded in other ways: a restrictive administrative definition of "wildlife" was effectively reversed when the prohibition against interstate commerce was extended by the Black Bass Act of 1926 to include certain species of fish. Act of May 20, 1926, ch. 346, 44 Stat. 576. In 1947, the Bass Act was amended to include all "game" fish, Act of July 30, 1947, ch. 348, 61 Stat. 517; five years later, it was extended to cover all fish. Act of July 16, 1952, ch. 911, § 2, 66 Stat. 736.

By 1952, it thus was illegal to ship wildlife—including mammals, birds, and fish—in interstate commerce if the wildlife had been taken in violation of the law of a state, the federal government, or foreign nation or if possession of the wildlife would be illegal in the receiving state.

(b) Labeling requirements: The second type of conduct regulated by the original Act was the labeling of interstate shipments of wildlife. Section 4 of the Act required all packages containing wildlife to be "plainly and clearly marked, so that . . . the nature of the contents may be readily ascertained on inspection of the outside of such packages." Act of May 25, 1900, ch. 553, § 4, 31 Stat. 187, 188 (codified as amended at 16 U.S.C. § 3373).

(c) Affirmative conservation duties: The Act also included an affirmative conservation component. The Secretary of Agriculture was authorized to adopt courses of action for "the preservation, distribution, introduction, and restoration of game birds and other wild birds." Act of May 25, 1900, ch. 553, § 1, 31 Stat. 187 (codified at 16 U.S.C. § 701).

(2) The Lacey Act Amendments of 1981: In 1981, Congress substantially reworked the Lacey Act. *See* Lacey Act Amendments of 1981, Pub. L. 97–79, 95 Stat. 1079 (currently codified at 16 U.S.C. §§ 3371–3378). The statute was amended again in 1988. Act of Nov. 14, 1988, Pub. L. 100–653, 102 Stat. 3826. The original Act with its eighty years of accretions was replaced with a modern statutory scheme. As amended, the Lacey Act prohibits two categories of activities. First, it requires marking of shipments and provides civil and criminal penalties for failure to mark and for falsification of documents for shipments of wildlife. 16 U.S.C. §§ 3372–3373. Second, the Act prohibits interstate and foreign commerce in wildlife and plants that have been illegally, taken, possessed, transported, or sold. *Id.* The Act also includes a section containing definitions, *id.* § 3371, another creating a forfeiture scheme, *id.* § 3374, and four sections outlining enforcement powers, administrative responsibilities, and exceptions, *id.* §§ 3375–3378. The amendments left the affirmative conservation duties unchanged. *Id.* § 701.

As modified by the amendments of 1981 and 1988, the Act remains the centerpiece of federal regulation of commercial activities in wildlife.

a.   COVERAGE: DEFINITIONS

NOTES

(1) "Fish or wildlife": The Act's central definition is "fish or wildlife"[1]:

> The term "fish or wildlife" means any wild animal, whether alive or dead, including without limitation any wild mammal, bird, reptile, amphibian, fish, mollusk, crustacean, arthropod, coelenterate, or other invertebrate, whether or not bred, hatched, or born in captivity, and includes any part, product, egg, or offspring thereof.

16 U.S.C. § 3371(a). As thus defined, the terms are expansive; they include all vertebrate and nearly all invertebrate wild animals and parts or products made from such animals. *E.g., United States v. Parker*, 991 F.2d 1493,

---

1. In passing, you should note that the Lacey Act's definition of "plant" is far more restrictive than that of "fish or wildlife." Only plants that are listed pursuant to the Convention on International Trade in Endangered Species of Wild Fauna and Flora (CITES) or under a state statute fall within the definition. *See* 16 U.S.C. § 3371(f).

1497 (9th Cir.), *cert. denied,* 510 U.S. 839 (1993) (cockatoo eggs). Furthermore, the terms apply regardless of whether the animal is wild-or captive-born. *See United States v. Bernal,* 90 F.3d 465, 467 n. 4 (11th Cir.1996) (claim that Act does not apply to captive-bred endangered species "wholly meritless"). The definition does, however, distinguish between "wild" and "not-wild." Recall the discussion in Chapter 1 on the categories wild, tame, domestic, and feral. How do these four categories fit within the Lacey Act's two categories? Does the Act appear to adopt a species-based approach— rather than an animal-by-animal approach—since it rejects birth in captivity as a relevant factor? Does an elk born and raised on a game farm fit within the definition?

(2) "Taken": The definition of "taken," on the other hand, is narrower than that in many wildlife statutes. The Act defines the term as "captured, killed, or collected." *Id.* § 3371(i).

(3) "Transport" is broadly defined to include not only "move, convey, carry or ship by any means," but also "to deliver or receive for the purpose of movement, conveyance, carriage, or shipment." *Id.* § 3371(j). Thus, placing illegal wildlife into the stream of interstate commerce is sufficient. For example, in *United States v. Gay–Lord,* a North Carolina resident purchased fish that had been taken illegally in Virginia; he intended to market the fish in New York and Maryland and sold it to a North Carolina company that he knew would transport the fish to those markets. His conviction was upheld because he "knew that the rockfish would be shipped in interstate commerce and he took steps that began their travel to interstate markets." *United States v. Gay–Lord,* 799 F.2d 124, 126 (4th Cir.1986). *See also United States v. Atkinson,* 966 F.2d 1270, 1275 (9th Cir.1992), *cert. denied* 507 U.S. 1004 (1993) (defendant "either arranged to ship the deer carcasses to hunters' homes outside the State of Montana, or assisted the hunters in these shipments").

(4) "Sale" and "purchase": Two terms—"sale" and "purchase"—that had been left undefined in the 1981 Amendments have also proved significant. Prior to 1981, there was disagreement on whether the purchase of professional guide services on hunts where the hunter violated an applicable hunting law or regulation made the guide liable under the Lacey Act. In the legislative history of the 1981 Amendments, the Senate Report stated: "a commercial arrangement whereby a professional guide offers his services to illegally obtain wildlife is, in effect, an offer to sell wildlife. When such an offer is made with the requisite knowledge of the illegal nature of the act, [the statute] will apply." S. REP. No. 123, 97th Cong., 1st Sess. 12 (1981), *reprinted in* 1981 U.S.C.C.A.N. 1743, 1759. This interpretation was adopted by the Fifth Circuit in *United States v. Todd,* 735 F.2d 146, 152 (5th Cir.1984), *cert. denied,* 469 U.S. 1189 (1985), but was rejected by the Ninth, *United States v. Stenberg,* 803 F.2d 422, 435–36 (9th Cir.1986), and Tenth Circuit, *United States v. DeMasters,* 866 F.2d 327, 330 (10th Cir. 1989).

Congress resolved the issue in 1988 by amending the Act to define both "sale" and "purchase":

Sale. It is deemed to be a sale of fish or wildlife in violation of this Act for a person for money or other consideration to offer or provide—

(A) guiding, outfitting, or other services; or

(B) a hunting or fishing license or permit;

for the illegal taking, acquiring, receiving, transporting or possessing of fish or wildlife.

Purchase. It is deemed to be a purchase of fish or wildlife in violation of this Act for a person to obtain for money or other consideration—

(A) guiding, outfitting, or other services; or

(B) a hunting or fishing license or permit;

for the illegal taking, acquiring, receiving, transporting or possession of fish or wildlife.

16 U.S.C. § 3372(c).

The effect of the definitions can be seen in *United States v. Fejes.* Fejes, a licensed hunting guide, was indicted for violating the Lacey Act because two hunters who had employed him illegally killed caribou. On appeal, Fejes argued that "the district court erred by failing to instruct the jury that the illegal taking of wildlife must precede the sale of guide services to fall within the criminal provisions of the Lacey Act" because he could not know at the time that he sold his services that his prospective clients would engage in illegal conduct. The court rejected this argument:

> The Lacey Act defines a sale of wildlife to encompass the situation where "a person for money or other consideration to offer or *provide ... guiding, outfitting, or other services ... for the illegal taking* [of wildlife]." 16 U.S.C. § 3372(c)(1)(A) (emphasis added). The plain language of the statute indicates that the provision of guide services for the illegal taking of wildlife constitutes a sale, not merely making financial arrangements for such services.... [B]oth the plain language of the statute and the legislative history indicate that the provision of guiding or outfitting services for the illegal taking of game unambiguously falls within the criminal enforcement provisions of the Lacey Act.
>
> Moreover, Fejes's proposed construction would lead to absurd results. For example, if we were to construe the word "sale" as suggested by Fejes, guides and outfitters would be immune from criminal liability even if they became aware before a hunt, but after financial arrangements were made, that their customers intended to take game illegally. We must reject this construction because nothing in the statute or its legislative history suggests that Congress intended such an absurd result. [ ]
>
> Accordingly, we hold that "sale" for purposes of 16 U.S.C. § 3373(d)(1)(B) includes both the agreement to receive consideration for guiding or outfitting services and the actual provision of such guiding or outfitting services.

United States v. Fejes, 232 F.3d 696, 701 (9th Cir.2000). *Compare United States v. Romano,* 137 F.3d 677 (1st Cir.1998).

b.   OFFENSES

NOTES

(1) An outline of the marking offenses: The Lacey Act creates two distinct marking requirements. Unlike the other provisions of the Act— which require the violation of some other statute as a predicate of the Lacey Act violation—the marking requirements directly proscribe other- wise legal conduct.

(a) The failure to "plainly mark" containers: The first states: "It is unlawful for any person to import, export, or transport in interstate commerce any container or package containing any fish or wildlife unless the container or package has . . . been plainly marked" as prescribed by regulations. 16 U.S.C. § 3372(b). The marking regulations are found at 50 C.F.R. §§ 14.81–.82 and require, *inter alia,* that a package "conspicuously . . . list . . . its contents by species." *Id.* § 14.81. Violation of this provision subjects the violator to a civil penalty of up to $250; no criminal penalties are provided. 16 U.S.C. § 3373(a)(2). What *mens rea* is applicable to prosecutions for violation of the "plainly marked" requirement?

(b) Preparing false shipping documents: The second marking requirement states: "It is unlawful for any person to make or submit any false record, account, or label for, or any false identification of any fish, wildlife, or plant" that has been or intended to be shipped in interstate or foreign commerce. 16 U.S.C. § 3372(d). Any person who "knowingly" violates these provisions is subject to civil penalties of up to $10,000. *Id.* § 3373(a)(1). Any person who "knowingly" violates the shipping docu- ments requirement is also subject to criminal penalties. If the false docu- ments involves *either* the importation or exportation of the fish or wildlife *or* the sale or purchase of fish or wildlife valued at more than $350, the defendant faces fines of up to $10,000 and imprisonment for up to 5 years per offense. *Id.* § 3373(d)(3)(A). If neither of these alternatives is satisfied, the maximum penalties are fines and imprisonment of not more than 1 year. *Id.* § 3373(d)(3)(B). Finally, the fish or wildlife is subject to forfeiture "not withstanding any culpability requirements for civil penalty assess- ment or criminal prosecution." *Id.* § 3374(a). What *mens rea* is applicable to each of the potential sanction? What must the government prove to satisfy the *mens rea* requirement of each sanction?

United States v. Carpenter

Ninth Circuit Court of Appeals.
933 F.2d 748 (1991).

■ NOONAN, J.:—Marvin Carpenter (Carpenter) and Carpenter's Gold Fish Farm, Inc. (the company) were convicted of making false statements to the United States Fish and Wildlife Service (the Service) in violation of 18 U.S.C. § 1001; of killing migratory birds in violation of the Migratory Bird Treaty Act, 16 U.S.C. § 701; and, of violating the Lacey Act, 16 U.S.C. § 3372 by acquiring migratory birds killed in violation of federal law. They appeal.

The case poses a farming culture in which birds are threats to the farmer's livelihood against a national standard protective of migratory birds. The national standard must prevail but no more oppressively upon the farmer than Congress has provided. We affirm the convictions of violating the False Statement Act. We reverse the convictions of violating the Lacey Act and remand for sentencing under the Migratory Bird Treaty Act.

THE EVIDENCE

Carpenter began his goldfish farm in 1970 on 20 acres of farm land a few miles south of the city of Merced, California. The operation grew steadily and by 1988 consisted of approximately 450 acres of ponds breeding some 2 million fish per month. Birds were a problem.

According to the evidence at trial, Carpenter employed persons whose sole function was to shoot birds. The employees also poisoned the birds with sodium cyanide and trapped them in leg traps in which the birds died. The exact number of birds killed during the period of the indictment, 1983 to 1988, was not proved, but according to testimony at the trial Carpenter conceded that there had been "a massacre." Between 1983 and 1988 the company bought over 60,000 rounds of ammunition. The evidence of the lethal "birdmen," hired by Carpenter, indicated that thousands of birds were dispatched each year by shooting, poisoning or trapping. Most of the birds either decomposed in the ponds, were buried in pits, or were burned in an incinerator on the company's property.

In 1984 a state game warden advised an employee that a complaint had been received about wounded birds and that the shooting would have to stop. As a result, Carpenter decided to obtain a federal permit to kill a limited number of specified birds. On March 1, 1984 the first of these permits was issued by the Service. It permitted the company to take, by shooting only, a total of 50 of any combination of great and snowy egrets and great blue and black crowned night herons during the year 1984. Carpenter's purpose in obtaining the permit was to enable employees to tell inquiring game wardens that the company had a permit to kill birds. In practice, no attention was paid to the limits or specifications of the permit. In December 1984 the company reported that it had killed exactly 50 migratory birds of the four named species. The report was false. Carpenter obtained a second permit from the Service in November of 1986. A similar report in regard to this permit, signed by Carpenter in 1987, was also false.

A federal wildlife agent went to the farm in February 1988 to investigate complaints about killed birds. The agent ordered the company to cease all lethal means of bird control. After the agent's visit, Carpenter told an employee to "pick up all the traps, hide the chemicals and get rid of the cyanide" because "the feds would be coming in." Federal agents returned to search the farm in April pursuant to warrants.

PROCEEDINGS

The foregoing evidence was presented by the government to a jury which convicted the company on two false statement counts, Lacey Act counts and Migratory Bird Treaty Act counts. Carpenter was convicted on one false statement count and on the same Lacey Act and Migratory Bird Treaty Act violations.

The court construed the Migratory Bird Treaty Act offenses to be lesser-included offenses within the Lacey Act and sentenced Carpenter and the company on the Lacey Act violations and on the false statement violations. The company received a fine and probation. Carpenter was sentenced to 13 months in prison, fined and put on probation for five years.

Carpenter and the company challenge their convictions on various grounds.

ANALYSIS

The Lacey Act

The Lacey Act provides that it is unlawful for any person "to import, export, transport, sell, receive, acquire, or purchase any fish or wildlife or plant taken or possessed in violation of any law, treaty, or regulation of the United States or in violation of any Indian tribal law." 16 U.S.C. § 3372(a)(1) (1988). The government's position is that Carpenter and the company violated this statute by acquiring birds taken in violation of the Migratory Bird Treaty Act, 16 U.S.C. § 703.

The government's position is contrary to the plain words of the statute. In order to violate the Lacey Act a person must do something to wildlife that has already been "taken or possessed" in violation of law. The government's position collapses the two steps required by the statute into a single step—the very act of knowingly taking the bird in violation of laws is, in the government's view, the act of acquiring the bird. That is not the meaning of the statute. The bird must be taken before acquiring it violates the Lacey Act.

The government's position also is contrary to the usual rule of statutory interpretation that words are to be judged by their context and that words in a series are to be understood by neighboring words in the series. Here the statute enumerates a variety of ways in which birds, unlawfully shot, could be made a subject of acquisition. The verb "to acquire" is *ejusdem generis* as "sell," "receive," "purchase." The verb "acquire" has no similarity to "to shoot." The kind of acquiring condemned is of a bird already taken.

If there were ambiguity in the statute we would reach the same result by the general rule of lenity in interpreting a criminal statute. [ ] The statute, however, is not ambiguous, and we do not need to invoke the sensible rule of construing criminal statutes in favor of the defendant charged with the crime.

Again, if there were ambiguity in the statute, its purpose as set out in its legislative history would make crystal-clear that the government has found an entirely inappropriate way of convicting the defendants here. The government quotes a single sentence out of context stating that in 1981 protection for migratory birds was "restored to provide a more adequate remedy for some violations involving massive numbers of birds." S. REP. No. 123, 97th Cong., 1st Sess. 4, *reprinted in* 1981 U.S.C.C.A.N. 1748, 1751.

But the same report makes clear that the purpose of the original Lacey Act was "to outlaw interstate traffic in birds and other animals illegally killed in their State of origin." *Id.* at 1749. The purpose of the 1981 amendments was to deal with "a massive illegal trade in fish and wildlife and their parts and products." *Id.* at 1748. The Lacey Act, as amended, did not intend to duplicate the Migratory Bird Treaty Act by making the very act of killing a bird a crime because the bird when shot fell on the property of the shooter. The Lacey Act convictions are accordingly reversed.

. . .

AFFIRMED, in part, REVERSED, in part, and REMANDED.

NOTES

(1) An outline of trafficking offenses: The trafficking offenses are set forth in 16 U.S.C. § 3372(a), which makes it unlawful to

(a) import, export, transport, sell, receive, acquire, or purchase

(b) wildlife

(c) that has been taken, possessed, transported, or sold

(d) in violation of a state, tribal, federal, or foreign law or regulation.

Thus, there must be sufficient proof of (1) the predicate violation, *i.e.,* a taking, possessing, transporting, or selling of wildlife in violation of state, tribal, federal, or foreign law or regulation, as well as (2) activity that amounts to the importing, exporting, transporting, selling, receiving, acquiring, or purchasing of such wildlife.

One additional point: if the predicate violation is a violation of state or foreign law, the Lacey Act violation must involve interstate or foreign commerce. *Id.* § 3372(a)(2). On the other hand, if the predicate violation is a violation of federal or tribal law, any transportation or sale is sufficient. *Id.* § 3372(a)(1).

(2) *Carpenter* illustrates the crucial point: successful prosecution under the Lacey Act's trafficking offenses requires proof that the defendant trafficked in "illegal wildlife." This requires proof of two elements: that the wildlife is illegal and that the defendant engaged in a prohibited trafficking in the illegal wildlife. As the court in *Carpenter* concludes, the dead migratory birds at issue were illegal wildlife, but there was no trafficking in them.

Since the predicate violation in *Carpenter* was a violation of a federal rather than a state statute, trafficking can simply be the "transport" such wildlife. If Carpenter had moved the dead birds off his property for disposal, would he have satisfied the transport requirement? Or, given the court's concern about unduly restricting "farmers," might it have required the "transport" element to have some commercial aspect?

If Carpenter had hired a waste disposal company to haul the dead birds to a landfill, would the waste disposal company have violated the Lacey Act? Would the owner of a landfill, who received the birds from the waste disposal company?

(3) Defining crimes: As you may recall from your criminal law class, crimes generally have both a physical element—the *actus reus*—and a mental element—the *mens rea*. The bad act and the bad thought must concur: a person who unintentionally kills another person is not guilty of murder. The following simplified refresher may be helpful.

(a) **Actus reus** literally means "guilty act." The *actus reus* of an offense consists of a voluntary act that causes an invasion of the legally protected interest, *i.e.*, legal "harm." For example, when Carpenter's employees shouldered their shotguns and killed snowy egrets the *actus reus* of a violation of the Migratory Bird Treaty Act had been met: the employee had performed a voluntary act (pulling the trigger) that caused the egret's death (the harm). *Actus reus* has not proved conceptually difficult in most wildlife crimes—though recall *State v. Neilson*, 660 So.2d 130 (La.App. 1995) [Chapter 9], where the issue was whether driving slowly along a country road at night with rifles in the vehicle was "hunting."

(b) **Mens rea** literally means "guilty mind" and refers to the mental state necessary to the commission of a particular crime. "Scienter" is a synonym for *mens rea*. Criminal statutes employ a wide variety of words to specify the requisite *mens rea*: "intentionally," "wilfully," "knowingly," "recklessly", and "negligently" are perhaps the most common. Wildlife statutes most frequently employ "intentionally," "wilfully," and "knowingly," or their variants such as "with intent to ..." or "with knowledge of...."

(i) **Intentionally** can usefully be defined as desiring to cause the prohibited legal harm. The Model Penal Code defines the concept as the "conscious object [is] to cause such a result." MODEL PENAL CODE § 2.02(2)(a)(i).

(ii) **Wilfully** is an ambiguous term that most generally is a synonym for "intentionally."

(iii) **Knowingly** is being aware that one's conduct is substantially certain to cause the proscribed harm. *See* MODEL PENAL CODE § 2.02(2)(b)(ii).

See generally WAYNE R. LAFAVE, CRIMINAL LAW §§ 3.1–.2, 3.4–.5 (3d ed. 2000).

(4) *Mens rea* **and the Lacey Act:** Section 3372 provides in part:

(a) It is unlawful for any person—

(1) to transport, [etc.] ... any ... wildlife ... taken, [etc.] ... in violation of any law....

(b) It is unlawful for any person to import, [etc.] ... any container ... containing any ... wildlife unless the container ... has ... been plainly marked....

. . .

(d) It is unlawful for any person to make ... any false record ... of, any ... wildlife, which has been, or is intended to be ...

(1) imported ...

(2) transported in interstate commerce....

What *mens rea* requirements, if any, are applicable to each of the acts prohibited by the Lacey Act? Note, as you consider these questions, that § 3372 defines prohibited acts but does not impose any penalties.

(5) "Interstate"—*United States v. Dove*: Ray Dove, a resident of West Virginia, was licensed by the state to deal in wild animal parts, including bear gall bladders. W.K. Stump, an agent of the Virginia Department of Game and Inland Fisheries, began investigating Dove for allegedly selling gall bladders in Virginia, where sales were illegal under state law. In late 1998, Dove agreed to sell bladders to Stump; Dove delivered some bladders personally by driving into Virginia, other bladders were shipped from West Virginia to Stump in Virginia. In January 1999, following a series of telephone calls between Stump in Virginia and Dove in West Virginia, Dove agreed to sell yet additional bladders, which Stump was to pick up in West Virginia where sales were legal. Dove was convicted of violating the Lacey Act based on all of the transactions. The initial sales—in which Dove delivered or shipped the bladders into Virginia—clearly violated Virginia law; that violation, together with the interstate commerce element of the transaction, established the violation of the Lacey Act. Dove claimed, however, that the final transaction did not violate the Lacey Act because the sale did not violate Virginia law. The district court rejected the argument, concluding that the sale had a sufficient nexus with Virginia to violate Virginia law: Stump was present in Virginia, his telephone calls were made from Virginia, and he planned, as Dove knew, to return to Virginia with the bladders. *United States v. Dove,* 70 F.Supp.2d 634 (W.D.Va.1999). On appeal, the Fourth Circuit reversed the conviction for the final transaction. The sale took place under West Virginia law, the court concluded; hence the wildlife was not illegal wildlife based on the sale. Virginia law also prohibited "offers to sell" gall bladders, but that provision, the court held (as a matter of Virginia criminal law), only prohibited offers where the sale itself would have been illegal. On these facts, given the West Virginia connection, the sale would have been legal. Because no state law was violated, the final transaction did not violate the Lacey Act. *United States v. Dove,* 247 F.3d 152 (4th Cir.2001).

(6) Timing—*United States v. Sylvester*: Must the illegality of the wildlife exist before it is shipped in interstate commerce? In a decision under the original Lacey Act—but one that should be unaffected by the subsequent amendments—the Ninth Circuit upheld a conviction where the wildlife was not illegal at the time that it was transported in interstate commerce because the act that made it illegal—its sale—had not been completed at the time that it was shipped. All that was required, the court held, was "a situation such as this where the sale is an integral part of the interstate transfer of wildlife products." *United States v. Sylvester,* 605 F.2d 474, 475 (9th Cir.1979).

c.   PENALTIES

United States v. Lee

Ninth Circuit Court of Appeals.
937 F.2d 1388 (1991).

■ WALLACE, C.J.:—Lee, Chu, Wesley Hsu, Meng Hsu, Lin, and Wang (the fishermen) were indicted on various charges related to the illegal acquisition, sale and importation of salmon caught in Northern Pacific waters. Each of the fishermen filed pretrial motions to dismiss the charges on the grounds that the Lacey Act (Act), 16 U.S.C. §§ 3371–3378, was inapplicable and unconstitutional. The district court denied these motions, and the fishermen then pleaded guilty. . . . We affirm.

I

After receiving information that Lee was advertising salmon caught by vessels from the Republic of China (also referred to as Taiwan) for sale in the United States, the National Marine Fisheries Service (Service) of the Department of Commerce initiated an undercover investigative operation in early 1989. In connection with this operation, an undercover Service agent negotiated with Lee to purchase 500 metric tons of salmon that had been taken illegally by Taiwanese squid fishing vessels in the Northern Pacific waters. Lee agreed to transfer the salmon on the high seas from Taiwanese vessels to an American carrier, the Redfin, which was chartered by the Service for this operation. The salmon were then to be smuggled into the United States at Seattle, Washington, with their true origin masked through the use of fraudulent United States Certificates of Origin. In return for the salmon, the agent agreed to pay Lee $1.3 million in a series of transactions, including payments of cash, cashier's checks and monetary wire transfers. Each of the remaining five defendants were involved along with Lee in this operation, providing various services related to either the salmon transfer or the payment of funds.

On July 18, 1989, Taiwanese fishing vessels rendezvoused with the Redfin in international waters. Meng Hsu, Lin, and Chu went aboard the Redfin to await word of payment before transferring the salmon, and were arrested by government officials there. Meanwhile, Lee and Wesley Hsu accompanied the Service agent to a Seattle bank, where they received $330,000 for the first 129 metric tons of salmon. Both men were arrested before leaving the bank. Wang was arrested on the same date in his Seattle hotel room.

The government charged the fishermen with various crimes in a seven-count indictment. Principal among these allegations was the charge that the fishermen had violated the Act by engaging in a conspiracy to import salmon into the United States, while knowing that it had been taken in violation of the laws of Taiwan. Although the fishermen pleaded guilty, they reserved the right to challenge on appeal the applicability and constitutionality of the Act.

II

The section of the Act under which the fishermen were charged makes it unlawful for any person "to import, export, transport, sell, receive, acquire, or purchase . . . any fish or wildlife taken, possessed, transported, or sold in violation of any law or regulation of any State or in violation of *any foreign law*." 16 U.S.C. § 3372(a)(2) (emphasis added). A portion of the indictment charged that the fishermen imported salmon into the United States, while knowing that the salmon had been taken in violation of a Taiwanese regulation that prohibits Taiwanese squid fishing vessels from catching salmon. The fisherman contend that their unlawful taking of salmon cannot result in an Act violation, because the Taiwanese regulation at issue does not constitute a "foreign law" under section 3372(a)(2)(A). The district court rejected this argument. We review de novo the district court's interpretation of the Act. [ ]

The fishermen argue that the term "any foreign law" encompasses only foreign statutes, not foreign regulations. They point out that, prior to its amendment in 1981, the Act prohibited trade in wildlife taken in violation of "any law or regulation of any State or foreign country," 18 U.S.C. § 43(a)(2) (1976) (repealed by Lacey Act Amendment of 1981), but now does not mention "regulation," *see* 16 U.S.C. § 3372(a)(2). Moreover, they focus on the fact that the present section 3372(a)(2)(A) makes reference to "any law or regulation" in the context of state law, but does not mention "regulation" when referring to foreign law. In effect, they argue that because the Act no longer makes reference to foreign "regulations," the term "any foreign law" cannot include such regulations.

When presented with similar arguments in *United States v. 594,464 Pounds of Salmon,* 871 F.2d 824 (9th Cir.1989) (*594,464 Pounds*), however, we ruled that a Taiwanese regulation prohibiting the export of salmon without a permit constituted a "foreign law" under section 3372(a)(2)(A) and thereby supported an Act violation. That regulation was issued, as in this case, by a body of the Executive Yuan of the Republic of China, and we concluded that "the Act's term 'any foreign law' necessarily encompasses the Taiwanese regulation." *Id.* at 828. We first focused on the generally broad definition of the word "law" as " 'a body of rules of action or conduct prescribed by controlling authority, and having binding legal force.' " *Id.* at 826, *quoting Black's Law Dictionary* (5th ed. 1979). In response to the arguments regarding the significance of the failure to mention "regulation" when referring to foreign law, we observed that the 1981 Act Amendments "were passed in response to Congress's frustration at the inadequacy" of prior laws. [ ] Because Congress desired to expand the scope of the Act, we concluded that the term "any foreign law" was used not to limit the Act's applicability, but instead to encompass the wide range of laws passed by "the world's regimes that possess systems of law and government that defy easy definition or categorization." *594,464 Pounds,* 871 F.2d at 828. A narrow interpretation that did not include at least foreign regulations as grounds for violations would only serve to "gut[ ] the statute." *Id.*

Thus, circuit precedent indicates that this Taiwanese regulation, almost identical to the one in *594,464 Pounds,* constitutes a "foreign law." The fishermen urge a different result, however, because this action involves criminal penalties rather than the forfeiture action at issue in *594,464 Pounds*. The Act provides for civil penalties, criminal penalties, and forfeiture of illegally taken fish and wildlife. *See* 16 U.S.C. §§ 3373(a) (civil), 3373(d) (criminal), 3374 (forfeiture). All of these penalties are meant to apply to those who engage in conduct in violation of section 3372. *See id.* No reason exists to suppose that Congress intended "any foreign law" to mean something different in the criminal context than in the forfeiture context. Thus, the interpretation set forth in *594,464 Pounds* is applicable in this case.

. . . .

III

The fishermen next contend that Congress did not intend to impose criminal penalties under the Act for violations of a regulation that itself carries no criminal sanctions. They observe that the regulation at issue here provides only for the suspension of the licenses of the offending fishing vessel and the offending captain; it imposes no criminal penalties. Thus, the fisherman argue, to base criminal penalties on violations of this regulation is an unjustifiable, absurd result. [ ]

In *594,464 Pounds,* we rejected the argument that the Act did not encompass a Taiwanese salmon regulation because that regulation only provided for the imposition of civil sanctions. We concluded that the legislative history clearly demonstrated that "Congress intended the 1981 Amendments to apply to 'laws' that have nothing more than civil fines for penalties." [ ] Because that holding was in the context of a forfeiture proceeding, however, the fisherman argue that it does not control in the present case.

The fishermen's interpretation is contrary to both the language and legislative history of the Act, and has been rejected by this court. In imposing criminal punishment for wildlife takings in violation of any underlying foreign law, the Act draws no distinction based on the type of sanction imposed by the underlying law. *See* 16 U.S.C. § 3373(d); *see also id.* § 3371(d) (defining "law" broadly for purposes of the Act, as any law "which regulate[s] the taking, possession, importation, exportation, transportation, or sale of fish or wildlife or plants") . . . .

The fishermen argue the "inherent unfairness of applying criminal penalties to conduct that does not carry a criminal sanction in the relevant foreign country." They rely on *United States v. Gordon,* 464 F.2d 357 (9th Cir.1972), in which a federal gambling statute criminalized violations of "the law of a State." When confronted with uncertainty over whether Congress intended to refer only to state criminal laws or to refer also to civil laws, we resolved the ambiguity in favor of the defendant, holding that the federal crime could not be based on state civil violations. [ ]

More on point, however, is *United States v. Cameron,* 888 F.2d 1279 (9th Cir.1989), in which we upheld a criminal Act charge that was based on the taking of halibut in violation of the federal Halibut Act, even though the Halibut Act only provided for civil penalties. [ ] We observed that criminal sanctions under the Act require an element of scienter. [ ] This was inserted by Congress in response to fears that a simple general intent statute "would contain too much potential for abuse." S. REP. No. 123, 97th Cong., 1st Sess. 12, *reprinted in* 1981 U.S.C.C.A.N. 1748, 1759. This indicates that Congress foresaw the consequences of imposing criminal sanctions under the Act on those who would only suffer civil penalties for violations of the underlying law, and decided to mitigate these consequences by including the higher criminal culpability requirement. We conclude that the statutory language, the legislative history, and our holding in *Cameron* all support the position that criminal penalties under the Act can be predicated on foreign regulations imposing only civil sanctions.

IV

Of the six fishermen, only Meng Hsu was the captain of a squid fishing vessel, so only he could be penalized in the Republic of China under the salmon regulation at issue. Because they were not subject to any sanction in the Republic of China, the other five fishermen contend that the regulation cannot support Act criminal sanctions against them. This argument, however, mistakes what action the Act penalizes. As demonstrated above, it is irrelevant under the Act whether the fishermen would be exposed only to civil sanctions under the regulation. Similarly, it is irrelevant whether the fishermen would be liable at all under the regulation. The Act's criminal penalty provision does not require that the fishermen violated the regulation, but only that they took part in importing the salmon when they knew, or should have known, that the salmon had been taken in violation of the regulation. 16 U.S.C. § 3373(d)(1)-(2). Thus, all six fishermen, whether or not they occupied the position of captain on the ship, are equally subject to the Act's criminal penalties.

. . .

VI

The fishermen next contend that the Act is unconstitutionally vague because it fails to satisfy the due process requirements of fair notice and fair enforcement.

A

With regard to fair notice, " 'because we assume that man is free to steer between lawful and unlawful conduct, we insist that laws give the person of ordinary intelligence a reasonable opportunity to know what is prohibited, so that he may act accordingly.' " *Village of Hoffman Estates v. Flipside, Hoffman Estates, Inc.,* 455 U.S. 489, 498 (1982) (*Hoffman Estates*), *quoting Grayned v. City of Rockford,* 408 U.S. 104, 108 (1972) (*Grayned*). The fishermen argue that the Act's proscriptions do not clearly encompass the salmon regulation, and that therefore the Act fails to "give a person of ordinary intelligence adequate notice of the conduct it proscribes." *594,464 Pounds,* 871 F.2d at 829.

We confronted this issue in *594,464 Pounds,* and held that the term "any foreign law" was sufficiently clear to provide fair warning that the Act proscribes violations of the Republic of China regulation at issue in that case. [ ] Thus, we ruled that the use of that term to define Act violations satisfied the constitutional standards of due process. [ ] The fishermen argue, however, that our previous determination is applicable only to the civil forfeiture context under section 3374. Because "[a] statute providing for civil sanctions is reviewed for vagueness with somewhat greater tolerance than one involving criminal penalties," they contend that the Act is not sufficiently clear to justify the imposition of criminal penalties. *594,464 Pounds,* 871 F.2d at 829, *citing Hoffman Estates,* 455 U.S. at 498–99. They would have us hold that although section 3372 defines violations precisely enough to justify forfeiture proceedings, it is too vague to support criminal sanctions under section 3373.

This argument fails to recognize, however, "that a scienter require-ment may mitigate a law's vagueness, especially with respect to the adequacy of notice to the complainant that his conduct is proscribed." *Hoffman Estates,* 455 U.S. at 499. Significantly, in enacting the criminal penalty provisions in 1981, Congress acknowledged the potential for abuse if it criminally punished conduct that was simply a violation of foreign law. "[A]s a simple general intent statute, the Lacey Act Amendments of 1981 would contain too much potential for abuse and indiscriminate enforcement efforts." S. Rep. No. 123, 97th Cong., 1st Sess. 12, *reprinted in* 1981 U.S.C.C.A.N. 1748, 1759. Thus, Congress inserted a culpability requirement when defining the violations that are subject to criminal penalty. As a result, although civil forfeiture penalties may be imposed solely upon proof that a defendant has violated section 3372, as when he or she has imported fish in violation of a foreign law, criminal penalties are imposed less freely. In order to be subject to criminal sanction, one must engage in conduct violative of section 3372, *and* must know or, in the exercise of due care, should know that "the fish or wildlife or plants were taken, possessed, transported, or sold in violation of, or in a manner unlawful under, any underlying law, treaty or regulation." 16 U.S.C. § 3373(d)(1)-(2). Thus, although one may be held strictly liable under the forfeiture provision for section 3372 violations, one must be significantly more blameworthy to be subject to the Act's criminal penalties.

This added scienter element prevents the Act from criminally punish-ing those who violate the Act's provisions but are reasonably unaware that they are doing so. . . .

.   .   .

AFFIRMED.

NOTES

(1) Is the court's recurrent argument—that the culpability standards of the penalty provisions resolve the statute's ambiguities—satisfactory? Does it satisfactorily answer the various constitutional challenges?

Should the different culpability standards for forfeiture proceedings and felony prosecutions produce different results if the statutory language is "ambiguous"?

(2) An outline of the penalty provisions: The Lacey Act contains three categories of penalties: civil penalties, misdemeanor criminal penalties, and felony criminal penalties. 16 U.S.C. § 3373. In addition, the Act provides for the forfeiture of the illegal wildlife as well as equipment used in aid of the violation. *Id.* § 3374.

(a) Civil penalties for trafficking offenses may be imposed if the violator "in the exercise of due care should know" that the wildlife is illegal under "any underlying law, treaty, or regulation." *Id.* § 3373(a)(1). If the market value of the fish and wildlife is less than $350 and the Lacey Act violation involves only transportation, acquisition, or receipt of the illegal wildlife, the civil penalty is the lesser of $10,000 or the penalty attached to the conduct making the wildlife illegal, *i.e.,* if the animal is killed illegally under state law and the state law imposes a fine of $500, that is the maximum fine. In all other cases, a civil penalty of up to $10,000 can be assessed for each violation.

(b) "Misdemeanor" penalties involve both a negligence and a "knowing" requirement. Conviction requires proof (1) that the person "knowingly engages in conduct prohibited by the [Act]"—*i.e.,* "import[s], export[s], transport[s], sell[s], receive[s], acquire[s], or purchase[s]" wildlife—(2) that the wildlife was illegal pursuant to a predicate statute, and (3) that the person, "in the exercise of due care should know" that the wildlife is illegal. Upon conviction, the person can be fined up to $10,000 and imprisoned for up to one year. 16 U.S.C. § 3372(d)(2).

(c) "Felony" penalties are based upon "knowing" violations and are divided into two general classes: those involving import or export and those involving other types of trafficking.

> *Import/export felonies* require proof (1) that the violator "knowingly imports or exports" the wildlife (or attempts to do so), (2) that the wildlife was illegal pursuant to a predicate statute, and (3) that the violator knows that the wildlife is illegal. 16 U.S.C. § 3373(d)(1)(A). Thus, a person who enters the United States with an animal that he knowingly obtained in violation of a foreign law has violated the felony provisions of the Lacey Act.

> *Other trafficking offenses* punish sales of wildlife. These offenses require proof (1) that the person "violates any provision of this Act . . . by knowingly engaging in conduct that involves the sale or purchase" of wildlife, (2) that the wildlife was taken, possessed, transported or sold in violation of a predicate statute, (3) that the violator knows that the wildlife was taken, possessed, transported or sold in violation of the predicate statute, and (4) that the wildlife has a value of more than $350. *Id.* § 3373(d)(1)(B). Thus, a person who purchases guide services valued at $500 and illegally kills elk that he transports out of state has committed a felony violation since the purchase of the guide services satisfies both element (1) and (4).

Conviction of either type offense subjects the violator to a fine of up to $20,000 and imprisonment of up to five years. *Id.* § 3373(d)(1).

The *Lee* case demonstrates the interaction of the prohibition and penalty provisions of the Act.

(d) Permit revocations: The Departments of the Interior, Commerce, and Agriculture issue a variety of permits. The Lacey Act empowers the agencies to revoke any permits, license, or stamp (except a permit issued under the Magnuson Fishery Conservation and Management Act) held by any person convicted of a felony or misdemeanor under the Lacey Act. *Id.* § 3373(e).

(e) Forfeitures: The Lacey Act authorizes the forfeiture of the wild-life involved in both trafficking and fraudulent marking[2] violations. "The legislative history establishes that the forfeiture statute provides for strict liability, thereby eliminating any 'innocent owner' defense." *United States v. One Afghan Urial Ovis Orientalis Blanfordi Fully Mounted Sheep,* 964 F.2d 474, 476 (5th Cir.1992). *See also United States v. Proceeds from Sale,* 834 F.Supp. 385, 390–91 (S.D.Fla.1993).

Vehicles, aircraft, vessels, and other equipment may also be forfeited when they have been used in aid of the unlawful import, export, transport, sale, receipt, acquisition or purchase. These forfeitures are subject to two limitations. First, they may occur only after conviction for a felony. Second, an "innocent owner" defense is available and the United States thus is required to prove that the owner of the item knew or should have known that it would be used illegally.

(3) *United States v. Mitchell* raised the issue of whether the defendant had to violate the underlying statute or only have knowledge of its violation. (Note the discussion of this issue in *Lee,* where it was raised by the fishermen other than the captain.) Mitchell was indicted for importing the hides and horns of a Punjab urial and a Chinkara gazelle from Pakistan knowing that the animals had been taken in violation of Pakistani law. The Fourth Circuit reversed a dismissal of the indictment, holding that

> Under the Lacey Act, the government need not prove that Mitchell actually hunted or exported the animal trophies in violation of a foreign law himself, but only that he received and acquired them in interstate and foreign commerce knowing that they had been hunted, possessed or transported in violation of foreign law. Whether the portion of the Punjab Wildlife Act purporting to restrict the export of protected animal trophies from the Punjab to another province is constitutional or not, there still remains the factual question of whether or not he violated the portions of the law prohibiting possession of the animals without a permit. The government has submitted evidence that Mitchell knew it was illegal to hunt Punjab urial in the Province of Punjab. The government has asserted that it can prove that the animals were illegally hunted, that Mitchell knew that, and that he nevertheless acquired and transported them. Whether he exported them from Punjab itself is inconsequential—and thus whether that portion of the law prohibiting export from Punjab is constitutional is not dispositive.

United States v. Mitchell, 985 F.2d 1275 (4th Cir.1993).

(4) *United States v. Todd* involved helicopter hunting packages offered by the defendants in violation of the Airborne Hunting Act, 18 U.S.C. § 371, which prohibits hunting from aircraft. Defendants argued that the government had failed to prove that he had "knowingly" violated the Lacey Act. The Fifth Circuit rejected this contention:

> The government need not prove that the appellants knew of the existence of the Lacey Act itself, only that they knew of the illegal

---

2. Only wildlife shipments with false document are subject forfeiture; a wildlife shipment that is not marked is not subject to forfeiture. *Id.* § 3374(a)(1).

nature of the game. [ ] Todd testified that he knew that hunting from a helicopter was a violation of federal law. Short's knowledge may be inferred from the totality of the circumstances of the case. [ ] Short had a permit to hunt coyotes from the air and had extensive experience as a hunter. From these facts the jury could reasonably have inferred that Short was aware that hunting animals from an aircraft violated federal law. We see no deficiency in the proof of this element.

United States v. Todd, 735 F.2d 146 (5th Cir.1984), *cert. denied,* 469 U.S. 1189 (1985).

Section 2.   Wild Birds

Federal wildlife law does not treat all taxa—much less all species—equally. The current bias in protecting ''charismatic megafauna'' at the expense of less glamorous taxa such as insects or amphibians is not a new phenomenon. The Lacey Act, for example, initially protected ''wild animals or birds.'' The Act was construed by the Department of the Interior, however, to apply only to fur-bearing mammals and game birds. Similarly, Congress responded to outcries of birdwatchers when it enacted the first federal statute that itself protected wildlife.

PERSPECTIVES

Guy A. Baldassarre & Eric G. Bolen, Waterfowl Ecology and Management
517–20 (1994).

EARLY DAYS

Simply stated, waterfowl resources in North America experienced harsh exploitation in the years preceding passage of the Migratory Bird Treaty. Market hunting was commonplace, taking untold numbers of birds at any time and by any means, events that are discussed here in some detail. Nowhere was market hunting more widespread than on the eastern seaboard, where burgeoning cities were the outlets for fresh meat and immense flocks of waterfowl existed in fabled places such as Chesapeake Bay and Long Island Sound. Many market hunters used ''punt guns,'' which were little more than homemade cannons mounted on the bows of small, flat-bottomed boats. The bores of the punt guns varied in size according to the fortitude of their makers, but each was capable of holding large amounts of shot. Indeed, amounts equivalent to 10 or more modern shotgun shells were loaded as a single charge in the larger punt guns. One firing of such a weapon into a flock of ducks easily killed or wounded scores of birds, which often were attracted to the site with bait. With two or more guns per boat, market hunters might launch a deadly fusillade, firing first on a flock on the water, and then unloosing a second salvo as the remaining birds took flight. Pochards such as the Canvasback *(Aythya valisineria)* were particularly vulnerable to attacks of this sort because they run across the water before taking flight and hence presented highly susceptible targets. The only factors limiting market hunting were the skill of the operator, his supply of powder and shot, and the seasonal availability of waterfowl—neither regulations nor any tinge of conservation ethics curtailed the unchecked slaughter.

Day[1] summarized some of the excesses of the era, including one dealer's shipment from Virginia of as many as 1,000 ducks at a time throughout a 6–month season each year—and his marketing career spanned 30 years. Waterfowl shot on Currituck Sound, North Carolina, provided at least $100,000 each year to the local economy of duck hunters between 1903 and 1909. Among these transactions was the sale, for $1,700, of 2,300 Ruddy Ducks *(Oxyura jamaicensis)* killed in 1 month by four hunters. One hunter's daily bag once reached 282 Ruddy Ducks.

The slaughter by no means was limited to the eastern seaboard. A market hunter in Louisiana boasted of a day's kill of 430 ducks, and two others in California killed 218 geese in an hour, taking a total of about 450 geese for the day. Similar tallies are known from choice hunting areas on the Mississippi River, including 122 Wood Ducks *(Aix sponsa)* shot by a lone hunter before 0900 hrs. In Iowa, Musgrove[2] reported that one group of market hunters shot an average of 1,000 ducks/wk, or 14,000 ducks and shorebirds during a season. The ducks sold for $6–15/dozen, depending on the species, but others sometimes sold for only 10 cents apiece. Another operation in Iowa coupled market hunting with the hardware business; in some seasons, 75,000 ducks were marketed and ammunition sales reached 250,000 shells.

The last-known Labrador Duck *(Camptorhynchus labradorius)* fell to a hunter during the autumn of 1875 on Long Island Sound.[3] The extinction of this species can be blamed, in part, on market hunting within its limited range on the northern coastline of North America. Despite allegations of their poor-tasting flesh, Labrador Ducks appeared in the markets of New York, New Jersey, Maryland, and most likely, in other eastern cities. Without the modern-day convenience of refrigeration, shipments of Labrador Ducks and other waterfowl often spoiled before reaching the marketplace. A full explanation for the Labrador Duck's disappearance remains uncertain, but whatever the reasons were, the extinction of this species occurred during an era of exploitation and utter disregard for the welfare of waterfowl populations. And to it goes the ignominious distinction of being the only extinct species of waterfowl in North America, remembered today by a scant collection of fewer than 50 museum specimens.

Spring hunting also was legal, or at least it was not illegal to shoot waterfowl enroute to their breeding grounds. Only nine states protected waterfowl from spring hunting in 1900. Bag limits also were either nonexis-

1. A.M. Day, North American Waterfowl (1949).

2. J.W. Musgrove, *in* Wildfowling in the Mississippi Flyway 192 (E.V. Connett ed. 1949).

3. J.C. Greenway, Extinct and Vanishing Birds of the World (1958).

tent or so liberal as to be meaningless, thereby abetting the carnage of market hunting.

Plume hunting was another activity of the day, wantonly supporting the needs of a lucrative millinery trade with the slaughter of herons and egrets (*Ardeidae*) as well as other water birds. The demand for feathers led to the decimation of entire colonies of nesting water birds. Nonetheless, waterfowl also were part of the feather trade. The skins of more than 17,500 swans, mostly Trumpeter Swans *(Olor buccinator)* were sold for their plumage between 1853 and 1877, bringing a drastic reduction to the population; only 57 skins were sold between 1888 and 1897 as the availability of swans diminished over much of their former range.[4] More than 100,000 swan skins had been marketed by the Hudson's Bay Company by the time overhunting forced trade to a close.[5] Regrettably, most of the market hunting took place in Canada where swan colonies were accessible during the nesting season; hence, plume hunting claimed large numbers of breeding birds. The colorful plumage of male Wood Ducks also added a bonus to their value as table fare, thereby increasing the impetus for overshooting Wood Ducks throughout their range in the eastern United States. Indeed, naturalists of the day predicted that Wood Ducks easily might follow the Labrador Duck into extinction because of relentless year-long hunting pressure.[6]

In addition to waterfowl, other birds were diminishing rapidly under unacceptable levels of market hunting. Traps and nets, as well as guns, steadily eroded wildlife populations. During the slaughter of Passenger Pigeons (*Ectopistes migratorius*), as many as 3,500 birds were captured with the snap of a single trap, and netters in Michigan marketed more than 1 billion pigeons within the space of a few weeks, destroying forever one of the last great nesting colonies of that now-extinct species.[7] Greater Prairie Chickens *(Clipido pinnatits)* also were killed wholesale by market hunters; Swift and Lawrence[8] reported that one poultry dealer in New York City received 20 tons of Prairie Chicken meat in a single shipment.

Unremitting exploitation of wildlife—with little thought of conservation—clearly prevailed until the dawn of the 20th century.

a. THE MIGRATORY BIRD TREATY ACT OF 1918

NOTES

(1) While the Lacey Act was the first federal wildlife statute national in scope, it did not provide any additional protection for wildlife since its provisions were triggered only when possession of the wildlife was already illegal under state law. With the enactment of the Migratory Bird Treaty

---

4. W.E. BANKO, THE TRUMPETER SWAN (1960).

5. W.E. Banko & R.H. Mackay, *Our Native Swans, in* WATERFOWL TOMORROW 155 (J.P. Linduska ed. 1964).

6. *See* F.C. BELLROSE, THE COMEBACK OF THE WOOD DUCK (1976).

7. J.B. TREFETHEN, AN AMERICAN CRUSADE FOR WILDLIFE (1975).

8. E. Swift & C.H. Lawrence, *Laws that Protect, in* BIRDS IN OUR LIVES 468 (A. Steffrud ed. 1966).

Act (MBTA) in 1918, 16 U.S.C. §§ 703–711, Congress for the first time sought to play an independent role in wildlife conservation.

As discussed in Chapter 6, the MBTA was enacted to implement the Convention with Great Britain (on behalf of Canada). The Act also fulfills the country's obligations under the subsequent treaties with Mexico (1936), Japan (1972), and the Soviet Union (1976). As the materials in this section demonstrate, whether migratory birds are adequately protected under the MBTA and the four treaties remains uncertain—in part because the hazards facing migratory birds have changed over time. *See generally* George C. Coggins & Sebastian T. Patti, *The Resurrection and Expansion of the Migratory Bird Treaty Act,* 50 U. Colo. L. Rev. 165 (1979).

(2) The historical context: The rise of the progressives during the last decade of the nineteenth century produced the first sustained drive for the conservation of natural resources in the United States. Conservation of wildlife was one aspect of this broader of movement:

> As a movement, conservationism arose in opposition to the myth of superabundance widely held in American society. From the days of the first European settlement of North America, nature's bounty seemed unlimited, especially in contrast to depleted Europe. For centuries, Americans had found more resources whenever the need arose. Over the next ridge or beyond the next river, one could always discover more land, more trees, or more game. The existence of a vast area of unclaimed frontier discouraged resource users from showing prudence. Loggers removed huge swaths of trees, industrialists polluted air and water, and farmers and ranchers pushed the land beyond its productive capacity, usually without any sense that their practices were not sustainable. . . .

> Improved transportation and technology, inseparable from industrialization and population growth, compounded the problems caused by the belief in unlimited resources. Railroad expansion opened once pristine wilderness to economic activity and hunting, and improved engines gave sealing and fishing vessels greater range and power. Better firearms and fishing apparatus allowed people to take more resources for the same effort. . . . The biologist Aldo Leopold summed up the situation well: "The conquest of nature by machines has led to much unnecessary destruction of resources. Our tools improve faster than we do."

> The combination of optimism, improved technology, and economic competition led to what economists call "the fisherman's problem." Fish, seals, birds, and many other types of natural resources are common property—a resource used by many but owned by no one until killed, captured, or extracted. Because there is no sole owner, common property has, almost by definition, many users. These users have no economic incentive to show forbearance in their harvesting. . . .

> The demise of two species of highly mobile, formerly countless animals served as the alarm that roused the wildlife protection impulse in the American conservation movement. The extermination of the

passenger pigeon and the destruction of the bison herds caused many people to rethink their attitudes toward the environment. When hunters and scientists could no longer find species once thought to be indestructible, it was a clear signal that nature could no longer take the beating that Americans were dishing out. One writer expressed the hope that the extinction of the passenger pigeon "should forever teach us that our wildlife is ours only in trust and that we owe much to succeeding generations." ...

The destruction of these and other species indicated that, in a radical change in earth's history, the market determined which species became extinct. As John Burnham assessed the situation, "The buffalo and the wild pigeon went because of commercialism." Nature continued to eliminate species that could not adapt to a changing environment; now the market removed those that had more value dead than alive, including food animals, fur bearers, and predators....

Therefore, conservationists searched for alternatives to these market forces in an effort to regulate shared resources. They sought to safeguard natural resources by combining scientific knowledge with government power....

In a culture that enriched, or at least tolerated, those who ruined common resources, the only recourse for conservationists was government action. Beginning in the 1880s, a small group of dedicated people lobbied state legislatures to protect wildlife, but for a variety of reasons they gradually concluded that only the federal government could do an adequate job. First, state regulators were often no better than the unregulated market. Like individuals, states saw themselves as competing with each other. A state that restricted the hunting of migratory animals only left more in the pool for other states' hunters. Second, in order to get complete, uniform coverage throughout the United States, conservationists had to pound laws through more than forty state legislatures instead of one Congress. Third, some resources, such as fur seals, did not fall under any state's jurisdiction.

The next step, then, was to legitimize federal control over those species that, because of their range, migratory movements, or economic value, the states could not protect.... [C]onservationists wanted Washington's intervention into tradition states' rights areas. The first step in this direction was the Lacey Act of 1900, which used federal police powers to regulate interstate commerce in game birds. From that point on, conservationists waged a steady battle to broaden federal authority.

KURKPATRICK DORSEY, THE DAWN OF CONSERVATION DIPLOMACY: U.S.-CANADIAN WILDLIFE PROTECTION TREATIES IN THE PROGRESSIVE ERA 12, 13–14 (1998). *See also* SAMUEL HAYS, CONSERVATION AND THE GOSPEL OF EFFICIENCY (1959).

The result of these efforts were traced in Chapter 6. In 1913, Congress enacted the Weeks–McLean Migratory Bird Act, Act of Mar. 4, 1913, ch. 145, 37 Stat. 828, 847. It was promptly declared unconstitutional. *See United States v. Shauver,* 214 F. 154 (E.D.Ark.1914); *United States v. McCullagh,* 221 F. 288 (D.Kan.1915). While the government's appeal of

Shauver was pending in the Supreme Court, the United States and Great Britain (acting on behalf of Canada) negotiated the Convention for the Protection of Migratory Birds, Aug. 16, 1916, United States–Great Britain, 39 Stat. 1702, T.S. No. 628. Following ratification of the Treaty, Congress enacted legislation implementing the Convention and repealing the Weeks–McLean Act; the Supreme Court then dismissed the appeal as moot at the suggestion of the Solicitor General. 248 U.S. 594 (1919). The Migratory Bird Treaty Act of 1918 subsequently was upheld by the Supreme Court in *Missouri v. Holland,* 252 U.S. 416 (1920) [Chapter 6].

On the treaty negotiations, *see* KURKPATRICK DORSEY, *supra,* at 165–237.

(3) The migratory bird treaties: The 1916 Convention with Canada was the first of four treaties that the United States has negotiated to protect migratory birds. The scope of protection accorded by the succeeding treaties has broadened.

The agreement with Canada established three categories of migratory birds: migratory game birds, migratory insectivorous birds, and migratory nongame birds. Convention with Great Britain for the Protection of Migratory Birds, art. I. The Convention established closed seasons on birds in each category. For the final two categories, the closed season is year round—effectively prohibiting any killing of such species except pursuant to a scientific permit. *Id.* art. II. For migratory game birds, the closed season is between March 10 and September 1 with "the High Contracting Powers" further agreeing that the actual open season will be for no more than three and one-half months as each party "may severally deem appropriate and define by law or regulation." *Id.* art. II, § 1. Article V prohibits the taking of nests or eggs except for scientific research or propagation.

The subsequent treaties with Mexico, Japan, and the Soviet Union are patterned on the 1916 Convention, though each has its variations and idiosyncracies. Convention for the Protection of Migratory Birds and Game Mammals, Feb. 7, 1936, United States–Mexico, 50 Stat. 1311, T.S. No. 912; Convention for the Protection of Migratory Birds and Birds in Danger of Extinction, and their Environment, Mar. 4, 1972, United States–Japan, 25 U.S.T. 3329; Convention Concerning the Conservation of Migratory Birds and their Environment, Nov. 18. 1976, United States–U.S.S.R., 29 U.S.T. 4647, T.I.A.S. No. 9073. The combined coverage of the various treaties is such that all migratory species[1]—except the European Starling (*Sturnus vulgaris*) and the House Sparrow (*Passer domesticus*)[2]—are protected under the Act. A list of the species covered by the various conventions is at 50 C.F.R. § 10.13 (1993).

There is substantial overlap among the treaties; there is also some inconsistency among the provisions. For example, Article VII of the treaty

---

1. Non-migratory species such as quail, grouse, ptarmigan, and pheasant are not covered by the conventions or the Act.

2. The starling and house sparrow may be excluded from the list because they were viewed as agricultural pests. For example, the importation of either species was specifically prohibited by the Lacey Act as "injurious to the interest of agriculture or horticulture." Lacey Act, ch. 553, § 2, 31 Stat. 187, 188 (codified as amended at 18 U.S.C. § 42).

with Canada authorizes the issuance of permits to kill birds that, "under extraordinary circumstances, may become seriously injurious to agriculture or other interests in any particular community." Article II(E) of the Mexican convention, on the other hand, authorizes taking of birds "when they become injurious to agriculture and constitute plagues." The Japanese (art. III, § 1(b)) and Soviet (art. II, § 1(d)) conventions are far broader, authorizing taking to protect persons and property. *See generally* MICHAEL J. BEAN & MELANIE J. ROWLAND, THE EVOLUTION OF NATIONAL WILDLIFE LAW 65–69 (3d ed. 1997); George C. Coggins & Sebastian T. Patti, *supra,* at 170–74; Donell R. Grubbs, *Of Spotted Owls and Bald Eagles: Raptor Conservation Soars in to the '90s,* 19 CAP. U.L. REV. 451, 468–69 (1990).

(4) An outline of the MBTA: Following promulgation of the Treaty, Congress enacted the Migratory Bird Treaty Act of 1918 (MBTA). The current version of the Act, 16 U.S.C. §§ 703–711, implements all four of the migratory bird treaties. Despite the additional treaties, the MBTA has remained largely unchanged since 1918—in part, perhaps, because the 1918 Act was broadly drafted.

The Act begins with an expansive declaration that

> Unless and except as permitted by regulations . . . it shall be unlawful at any time, by any means or in any manner, to pursue, hunt, take, capture, kill, . . . possess, offer for sale, sell, purchase, ship, export, import, . . . transport or cause to be transported, . . . any migratory bird, or any product, . . . of any such bird or any part, nest, or egg thereof.

16 U.S.C. § 703.[3] The Secretary of the Interior is subsequently delegated power to promulgate regulations "to determine when, to what extent, if at all, and by what means . . . to allow hunting, taking, . . . possession, sale, purchase, shipment, . . . or export" of any bird covered by the conventions. *Id.* § 704. The basic structure of the Act thus is somewhat unusual: rather than prohibiting specific conduct, the MBTA prohibits *all* killing or possession and *all* commercial activity in migratory birds and authorizes the Secretary to promulgate regulations exempting conduct from this general prohibition.

The Act initially provided only misdemeanor penalties: "any person . . . who shall violate any provisions of said conventions or of this Act, or who shall violate or fail to comply with any regulation made pursuant to this Act shall be deemed guilty of a misdemeanor." *Id.* § 707(a). In 1960, Congress amended the Act, adding a provision making the sale of protected species a felony. Act of Sept. 8, 1960, Pub. L. No. 86–732, 74 Stat. 866 (codified as amended at 16 U.S.C. § 707 (1988)). The objective, Congress stated, was to impose "heavier penalties" on "commercial hunters" who "slaughte[r] these wildfowl for commercial purposes." S. REP. NO. 1779, 86th Cong., 2d Sess. (1960), *reprinted in* 1960 U.S.C.C.A.N. 3459, 3459–60. While the amendment authorized felony prosecutions, it mirrored the

---

3. This prohibition was broader than the Convention with Great Britain, which—while expansive—nonetheless covered less than all migratory bird species because it listed only a limited number of non-game, non-insectivorous species. The Convention did not apply to such seed-eating species as crossbills.

previous, misdemeanor provisions by not explicitly requiring scienter as an element of the crime: "Whoever ... shall (1) take by any manner whatsoever any migratory bird with intent to sell ... or (2) sell, offer for sale, barter or offer to barter, any migratory bird shall be guilty of a felony." 16 U.S.C. § 707(b).

(i) LIABILITY STANDARDS

United States v. Boynton

Fourth Circuit Court of Appeals.
63 F.3d 337 (1995).

■ MURNAGHAN, J.:—Defendants were convicted of hunting migratory birds over a baited area, a strict liability crime. Defendants admitted at a bench trial that they were hunting migratory birds over bait, but claimed that the grain which constituted the bait was scattered as the result of "normal agricultural planting or harvesting" or "*bona fide* agricultural operations and procedures" and thus that their hunting was lawful pursuant to the exceptions in the migratory bird hunting regulations for such situations. The magistrate judge conducting the bench trial decided that the scattered grain did not fall into either exception, and found the defendants guilty. The district court affirmed. Defendants now appeal. Finding no error in the convictions below, we affirm.

Hunting migratory birds over an area where seed or other bait is scattered is generally prohibited by the Migratory Bird Treaty Act ("MBTA"). [ ] Two exceptions to this rule are set forth in a regulation promulgated by the Fish and Wildlife Service pursuant to the Act, 50 C.F.R. § 20.21(i), as follows:

[N]othing in this paragraph shall prohibit:

(1) The taking of all migratory game birds, including waterfowl, on or over ... grains found scattered solely as the result of normal agricultural planting or harvesting; and

(2) The taking of all migratory game birds, except waterfowl, on or over any lands where ... wheat or other grain ... has been distributed or scattered as the result of bona fide agricultural operations or procedures....

[Defendants were hunting mourning doves over an area where a low-quality mixture of wheat seeds and chaff that had been scattered. Because the ground was dry and the grain had not been tilled into the soil, it had not sprouted. Agents from the United States Fish and Wildlife Service cited defendants under the MBTA and its implementing regulations for hunting in a baited area.

[Evidence at trial conflicted on the question of whether the manner in which the grain was scattered was the result of "normal agricultural planting or harvesting" or "*bona fide* agricultural operations or procedures" as those terms are defined by farmers in the region, experts in agronomy, and the Fish and Wildlife Service. Jay Quimby, the landowner, claimed that his intent was to grow the wheat to retard leakage from an nearby pond. An employee of the local Soil Conservation Service ("SCS")—which had paid for part of the cost of the pond—testified that the pond was not leaking; he also testified that the manner in which Quimby had spread the wheat at the pond was not a recognized method of erosion control and did not meet SCS standards for planting in eroding areas. An agronomist testified that putting wheat screenings on unprepared ground in the middle of summer without incorporating the seed into the soil was not a normal agricultural planting because wheat screenings planted in this manner could not be expected to grow. The defense introduced testimony of one of the defendants, who had taken a one-day class in erosion and who testified that broadcasting seed was a method of erosion control.

[The magistrate found as a matter of fact that the landowner who scattered the grain did not have the intent to harvest the grain and concluded that the first regulatory exception for "normal agricultural planting or harvesting" was therefore inapplicable. The magistrate next concluded that, viewing the facts surrounding the scattering objectively, the scattering did not fall into the second regulatory exception for "*bona fide* agricultural operations or procedures" because there had to be some "mixing into the soil of the seed and not just laying [the screenings] on top." The magistrate found the defendants guilty and fined each of them $190 with a $10 special assessment.]

Defendants argue that "normal" and "*bona fide*" should be construed so as to require proof of the intent of the person who scattered the grain, as an element of the crime. Defendants argue that the definitions of the words "normal" and "*bona fide*" require that when the subjective intent of the person who scattered the grain was to engage in an agricultural planting, harvesting, operation or procedure, hunting over the grain falls within the exception. . . .

.   .   .

Since the inception of the Migratory Bird Treaty in the early part of this century, misdemeanor violations of the MBTA, including hunting in a baited area, have been interpreted by the majority of the courts as strict liability crimes, not requiring the government to prove any intent element. [ ] As noted in a 1939 decision: "Congress deliberately omitted scienter as an essential ingredient of the minor offense [of violating the MBTA]. This concept is logical in light of the known practicality of the National Legislature in its enactments in support of the Migratory Bird Treaty." *United States v. Reese,* 27 F. Supp. 833, 835 (W.D.Tenn.1939). In 1986, Congress reiterated its continuing intent that misdemeanor violations of the MBTA are strict liability crimes. [ ] All circuits which have been faced with the question save one—the Fifth—have now held that the misdemeanor crimes created by the MBTA are strict liability crimes. [ ]

.   .   .

Bearing in mind that each defendant was fined $200, an interpretation of the regulations which would create a requirement that the government must prove the intent of the person who scattered the grain in order to prosecute successfully is absurd, and thwarts the purpose of Congress in creating a strict liability crime for hunting over a baited area. As noted in another 1939 opinion:

> [I]t was not the intention of Congress to require any guilty knowledge or intent to complete the commission of the offense, and ... accordingly scienter is not necessary. The beneficial purpose of the [Migratory Bird] treaty and the act would be largely nullified if it was necessary on the part of the government to prove the existence of scienter on the part of defendants accused of violating the provisions of the act.

United States v. Schultze, 28 F. Supp. 234, 236 (W.D.Ky.1939). To require the government to prove the intent of the person who scattered the grain in every case charging a misdemeanor violation of the MBTA would produce the absurd result, clearly not contemplated by Congress, of nullifying the ease of prosecution created by the designation of hunting over a baited area as a strict liability crime. The person who scattered the grain would have to be subpoenaed and questioned, along with corroborating witnesses, thus placing a burden on the prosecution and on third parties not even charged. As explained by the Supreme Court in reference to strict liability crimes generally:

> While the general rule at common law was that the *scienter* was a necessary element in the indictment and proof of every crime, ... there has been a modification of this view in respect to prosecutions under statutes the purpose of which would be obstructed by such a requirement. It is a question of legislative intent to be construed by the court.

United States v. Balint, 258 U.S. 250, 251 (1922). Therefore, we do not adopt the reading of the statute suggested by the defendants, and instead hold that the exceptions for "normal" planting and "*bona fide*" procedures both refer to an objective measure of the agricultural practices of the community.

. . .

We now turn to the defendants' contention that the evidence was insufficient to support the district court's finding that Jay Quimby's spreading of screenings was not the "normal" and "*bona fide*" practice in the area. Because the proper standard is an objective rather than subjective one, the defendants' attack on the sufficiency of the evidence of intent does not provide a basis for challenging the convictions. Reviewing the sufficiency of the evidence under the proper objective standard, we find that the evidence was sufficient to convict.

NOTES

(1) The ban on hunting "[b]y the aid of baiting, or on or over any baited area," 50 C.F.R. § 20.21(i), has been the most controversial regulation under the MBTA. What is the *mens rea* requirement? Is the court's explanation for the rule in *Boynton* satisfactory?

(2) Strict liability offenses (in general): Although most criminal statutes require that a person's acts be accompanied by some degree of fault—

such as intent, wilfulness, or knowledge—legislatures in the early nineteenth century began to enact a new type of criminal statute that regulated natural resources, business practices, and similar problems. These new offenses differed from traditional crimes (such as murder, rape, burglary, and the like) that involved immoral conduct. The new "public welfare offenses" were not, according to the then-prevailing perspective, inherently immoral; they could, however, be performed improperly and it was this that the new statutes sought to prohibit. The enactment of these offenses thus reflected a "shift of emphasis from protection of individual interests" to the "protection of public and social interests." Francis B. Sayre, *Public Welfare Offenses*, 33 COLUM. L. REV. 55, 67 (1933).

(3) Baiting, *mens rea*, and congressional intervention: *Boynton* involves perhaps the most contentious regulation, the ban on hunting with the use of (or "over") bait—particularly when penalties were imposed without regard for whether the hunter knew or even should reasonably have known that bait was nearby. The leading early case on *mens rea* and baiting is *United States v. Reese,* 27 F.Supp. 833 (W.D.Tenn.1939). Most courts have followed *Reese* and read the statutory provisions in the context of a prosecution for a misdemeanor as imposing strict liability: "it is not necessary to prove that a defendant violated the . . . Act with specific intent or guilty knowledge." *United States v. Manning,* 787 F.2d 431, 435 n. 4 (8th Cir.1986); *see also United States v. Pitrone,* 115 F.3d 1 (1st Cir.1997); *United States v. FMC Corp.,* 572 F.2d 902, 905–08 (2d Cir.1978); *United States v. Engler,* 806 F.2d 425 (3d Cir.1986); *United States v. Chandler,* 753 F.2d 360, 363 (4th Cir.1985); *United States v. Ireland,* 493 F.2d 1208 (4th Cir.1973) *(per curiam)*; *United States v. Catlett,* 747 F.2d 1102, 1104 (6th Cir.1984), *cert. denied,* 471 U.S. 1074 (1985); *United States v. Green,* 571 F.2d 1, 2 (6th Cir.1977) *(per curiam)*; *United States v. Smith,* 29 F.3d 270 (7th Cir.1994); *Rogers v. United States,* 367 F.2d 998, 1001 (8th Cir.1966), *cert. denied,* 386 U.S. 943 (1967); *United States v. Corbin Farm Service,* 444 F.Supp. 510, 536 (E.D.Cal.1978), *aff'd,* 578 F.2d 259 (9th Cir.1978); *United States v. Corrow,* 119 F.3d 796 (10th Cir.1997). The breadth of the prohibitory language has, however, caused some judicial unease; the Fifth Circuit has adopted the objective, "should have known" standard. *United States v. Delahoussaye,* 573 F.2d 910, 912 (5th Cir.1978).

Congress responded to criticisms of the strict liability standard rule by amending the MBTA in 1998 to incorporate a "knew or reasonably should have known" standard as applied to hunting over bait:

(b) It shall be unlawful for any person to—

(1) take any migratory game bird by the aid of baiting, or on or over any baited area, if the person knows or reasonably should know that the area is a baited area; or

(2) place or direct the placement of bait on or adjacent to an area for the purpose of causing, inducing, or allowing any person to take or attempt to take any migratory game bird by the aid of baiting on or over the baited area.

16 U.S.C. § 704(b). Recall that both the baiting and *mens rea* issues have arisen in state game regulation as well. *See* Chapter 9.

(4) Hunting methods: The regulations governing hunting methods—entitled "What hunting methods are illegal?"—are set forth at 50 C.F.R. § 20.21. These regulations—which were at issue in *Boynton*—provide, in part:

Migratory birds on which open seasons are prescribed in this part may be taken by any method except those prohibited in this section. No person shall take migratory game birds:

(a) With a trap, snare, net, rifle, pistol, swivel gun, shotgun larger than 10 gauge, punt gun, battery gun, machine gun, fish hook, poison, drug, explosive, or stupefying substance;

(b) With a shotgun of any description capable of holding more than three shells, unless it is plugged with a one-piece filler, incapable of removal without disassembling the gun, so its total capacity does not exceed three shells. . . .

(c) From or by means, aid, or use of a sinkbox or any other type of low floating device, having a depression affording the hunter a means of concealment beneath the surface of the water;

(d) From or by means, aid, or use of any motor vehicle, motor-driven land conveyance, or aircraft of any kind, except that paraplegics and persons missing one or both legs may take from any stationary motor vehicle or stationary motor-driven land conveyance;

(e) From or by means of any motorboat or other craft having a motor attached, or any sailboat, unless the motor has been completely shut off and/or the sails furled, and its progress therefrom has ceased: Provided, That a craft under power may be used to retrieve dead or crippled birds; however, crippled birds may not be shot from such craft under power except in the seaduck area as permitted in Subpart K of this part;

(f) By the use or aid of live birds as decoys; although not limited to, it shall be a violation of this paragraph for any person to take migratory waterfowl on an area where tame or captive live ducks or geese are present unless such birds are and have been for a period of 10 consecutive days prior to such taking, confined within an enclosure which substantially reduces the audibility of their calls and totally conceals such birds from the sight of wild migratory waterfowl;

(g) By the use or aid of recorded or electrically amplified bird calls or sounds, or recorded or electrically amplified imitations of bird calls or sounds . . . . .

(h) By means or aid of any motordriven land, water, or air conveyance, or any sailboat used for the purpose of or resulting in the concentrating, driving, rallying, or stirring up of any migratory bird;

(i) By the aid of baiting, or on or over any baited area, where a person knows or reasonably should know that the area is or has been baited. However, nothing in this paragraph prohibits:

(1) the taking of any migratory game bird, including waterfowl, coots, and cranes, on or over the following lands or areas that are not otherwise baited areas—

(i) Standing crops or flooded standing crops (including aquatics); standing, flooded, or manipulated natural vegetation; flooded harvested croplands; or lands or areas where seeds or grains have been scattered solely as the result of a normal agricultural planting, harvesting, post-harvest manipulation or normal soil stabilization practice;

(ii) From a blind or other place of concealment camouflaged with natural vegetation;

(iii) From a blind or other place of concealment camouflaged with vegetation from agricultural crops, as long as such camouflaging does not result in the exposing, depositing, distributing or scattering of grain or other feed; or

(iv) Standing or flooded standing agricultural crops where grain is inadvertently scattered solely as a result of a hunter entering or exiting a hunting area, placing decoys, or retrieving downed birds.

(2) The taking of any migratory game bird, except waterfowl, coots and cranes, on or over lands or areas that are not otherwise baited areas, and where grain or other feed has been distributed or scattered solely as the result of manipulation of an agricultural crop or other feed on the land where grown, or solely as the result of a normal agricultural operation.

Note that the MBTA prohibition includes possessing any parts of a migratory bird, including feathers, which is to say a person who takes possession of the feather of a robin, cardinal or bluejay (all listed birds, though largely nonmigratory) violates the Act. Applicable regulations do allow the possession of feathers of lawfully taken migratory game birds. 50 C.F.R. § 20.92.

* * *

Given the breadth of the term "take" and the strict liability standard, does killing of migratory birds as an unintended consequence of other activities result in liability under the MBTA?

United States v. FMC Corporation

Second Circuit Court of Appeals.
572 F.2d 902 (1978).

◼ MOORE, J.:—This is an appeal from a judgment of conviction entered after a jury trial against FMC Corporation ("FMC"), for violation of the Migratory Bird Treaty Act, by killing 92 migratory birds in violation of 16 U.S.C. § 703. The jury convicted defendant FMC of 18 counts of the 36 counts in the indictment.

The indictment charged that FMC between April 23, 1975 and June 25, 1975 ... "did unlawfully by means of toxic and noxious waters kill migratory birds included in the terms of the conventions between (specifically naming treaties between the United States of America and Great

Britain (1916), the United Mexican States (1936), and the Government of Japan (1972)), all in violation of Title 16, United States Code, section 703."

. . .

So far as pertinent, the Migratory Bird Treaty Act ("MBTA") provides:

* * * it shall be unlawful at any time, by any means or in any manner, to * * * kill * * * any migratory bird * * * included in the terms of the conventions between the United States and Great Britain * * * (Mexico) * * * (and Japan) * * **"

16 U.S.C. § 703.[1] A separate section provides for the penalties under the MBTA:

(a) * * * any person * * * or corporation who shall violate * * * section 703 * * * shall be deemed guilty of a misdemeanor and upon conviction thereof shall be fined not more than $500 or be imprisoned not more than six months, or both."

16 U.S.C. § 707.

The issue before us, as it was before the trial court and as charged to the jury, is clearly framed: does the statute require that the violation be intentional or in other words, where a crime is involved and a criminal penalty imposed for the violation thereof, must the violator have a *mens rea*.

I.   THE CHARGE OF THE COURT

With the undisputed fact that the birds died as a result of the noxious waters in the pond, the Court's charge was virtually a directed verdict. The Court charged:

Such legislation (the statute here in issue) dispenses with the conventional requirement for criminal conduct; namely, awareness of wrongdoing and the specific intent to violate the law.

. . .

In order to protect this public interest has lead (sic) to the creation of this particular statute which prohibits the killing of birds regardless of the means or manner. Therefore, under the law good will and good intention and measures taken to prevent the killing of the birds are not a defense. Therefore, if you find that the birds were killed by the products emitted from the FMC plant then you must return a verdict of guilty * * **

To make doubly sure that intent was not a factor to be considered, the charge continued:

The Government in this case does not have to prove that the defendant intended to kill the birds. You may convict the corporation even if you find that the killing of the birds was accidental or

---

1. The statute declares as unlawful "to pursue, hunt, capture, attempt to take, capture or kill * * **" Query, whether the word "kill" must be read in connection with the surrounding words and whether it is only mentioned as the usual result of pursuing, hunting or capturing.

unintentional provided that you find that the FMC Corporation did kill the birds as charged in the indictment * * **

Lack of necessity for establishing intent is further emphasized by the court's feeling of an obligation to tell the jury that the remedial steps taken by FMC to avoid the casualties are "under the Law * * * not a defense."

The Government argues that the statute makes it "unlawful at any time, by any means or in any manner, to * * * kill, [or] attempt to * * * kill * * * any migratory bird * * * *" and that there is no requirement of intent. FMC on the other hand, claims that the very use of the word "kill" imports an intentional act and that this interpretation is buttressed by the word "attempt" which, of necessity, would require an affirmative voluntary act.

II. FACTS

[FMC manufactures various pesticides including carbofuran and dithiocarbamates. Production of the dithiocarbamates produces large amounts of wastewater which was stored in a ten acre pond that held some 12 million gallons. The pond also held small amounts of wash water from the production of carbofuran. Before the wash water from carbofuran operation went into the pond, it was chemically treated to breakdown the carbofuran into safe constituents. Thus, no carbofuran should have been present in the pond.

[The pond attracted waterfowl during migration. Beginning in mid-April 1975, dead birds were discovered at the pond. A chemist from the state Department of Environmental Conservation visited FMC on May 7 in an effort to determine the cause of death. As the number of dead birds grew, FMC attempted to keep birds away from the pond. At the end of May, FMC was notified that carbofuran was the suspected cause of death. Analysis of the water in the pond indicated concentrations of carbofuran roughly 200 times greater than the level which could cause death to birds. By the end of June, FMC had determined that the process it employed to breakdown carbofuran was ineffective and that the pesticide was being pumped directly into the pond.

[On July 30, the indictment was handed down. Subsequent measures proved more effective in stopping the bird kills. An effective guard system was installed, avalarms were installed (loud pitched alarms which stimulate the distress cry of a bird), chemicals were added to the pond to break down the carbofuran, and nets were installed over the pond. By the time of trial, the pond had been graded over and a wastewater treatment facility had been constructed.]

III. DISCUSSION

Where there is no help to be had from legislative history or decisional authority, as in this specific situation, resort must be had to a rule of reason or even better, common sense. That the penalty is only a $500 fine or imprisonment for not more than six months, or both, does not affect the propriety of a criminal conviction. Were a corporate officer to have been added as a defendant he would not regard as *de minimis* a sentence of only six-months which, if consecutive on 36 counts, would be 18 years. Of course, this is a *reductio ad absurdum* argument but so is the Government's claim that the statute as to killing is "without limitation." [ ] Certainly construction that would bring every killing within the statute, such as deaths caused by automobiles, airplanes, plate glass modern office buildings or picture windows in residential dwellings into which birds fly, would offend reason and common sense. As stated in one of the early decisions under the Act, "[a]n innocent technical violation on the part of any defendant can be taken care of by the imposition of a small or nominal fine." *United States v. Schultze,* 28 F. Supp. 234, 236 (W.D.Ky.1939). Such situations properly can be left to the sound discretion of prosecutors and the courts.

Although in search for analogies the hunting cases are not entirely apposite, they may be considered in attempting to balance public policy in support of the protection of migratory birds with a reluctance to charge anyone with a crime which he does not know he is committing.

These cases involving hunters have consistently held that " * * * it is not necessary that the government prove that a defendant violated its provisions with guilty knowledge or specific intent to commit the violation." [ ] In *Shultze,* for example, defendants were convicted of violating the MBTA and regulations by taking morning doves lured to a field by the use of wheat "bait." The court rejected defendants' contention that they had not baited the field and had no knowledge that the field was baited. The court found each defendant guilty "even though there was no evidence of any guilty knowledge or intent upon his part at the time of the commission of the offense." [ ]

FMC was manufacturing a powerful pesticide. For the protection of its employees it had to wash down the areas where carbofuran was manufactured. The washwater was pumped into a sump where it was to decompose into safe constituents before entering the pond. As a result of more frequent washdown procedures, instituted in the prior few months to protect workers, the carbofuran did not remain in the sump long enough to decompose. The washwater was pumped into the pond and in such quantities that migratory birds were killed. It can be assumed that FMC did not know for some weeks that carbofuran was the cause of the deaths; that it took remedial measures in an effort to keep the birds from the pond; that it conferred with State and Federal Conservation agencies and gave them full cooperation as to ways and means of avoiding the danger. Yet the fact remains that it was FMC's product which killed the birds.

FMC contends that even if "the killing of migratory birds need not be accompanied by knowledgeable violation of the law" (as in the hunter cases), there must be "an intent to harm birds culminating in their death for there to be a conviction." [ ] FMC argues that it had no intention to kill birds, that it took no affirmative act to do so, possessed no scienter, and thus should not be held liable under the Act. It argues that, even in public welfare offenses, some "act" must be intended. In the hunter cases the act was pulling the trigger. In the case of *United States v. Dotterweich,* 320 U.S. 277 (1943) (holding president of drug company liable for shipping misbranded drugs in interstate commerce), the act was the shipping of the drugs. However, the term "act" itself is ambiguous, and a person failing to act when he has a duty to do so may be held to be criminally liable just as one who has acted improperly. *See* G. Hughes, *Criminal Omissions,* 67 YALE L.J. 590 (1958). In the most recent Supreme Court case imposing criminal liability for violation of the Food, Drug and Cosmetic Act, the Supreme Court held that the president of a national retail food chain was criminally liable because food being held for sale in a warehouse was allowed to be exposed to contamination by rodents, notwithstanding his lack of knowledge of the situation. *United States v. Park,* 421 U.S. 658 (1975)....

Here FMC did perform an affirmative act—it engaged in the manufacture of a pesticide known to be highly toxic. Then it failed to act to prevent this dangerous chemical from reaching the pond where it was dangerous to birds and other living organisms that ingested, or came into close contact with, the chemical. Such a situation is analogous to the situations in the various tort notions of strict liability which have insinuated themselves into American law since the English case of *Rylands v. Fletcher,* 3 Hurl. & C. 774 (1865), L.R. 1 Ex. 265 (1866), L.R. 3 H.L. 330 (1868)....

As civilization advances so have other protections for individuals against convictions without scienter or even knowledge that a crime is being committed. But as science, with its technological achievements, produces an ever widening array of poisonous pesticides for the destruction of food-and-grain destroying insects, so the manufacturers of such products will have to be ever on guard lest the waste created in the manufacturing process causes damage. The vast areas of our national industry, including pesticide manufacturing, which have come under the scrutiny of the Environmental Protection Agency, attest to the difficulty of avoiding conflict between crop destruction by insects and the dangers to wildlife resulting from noxious pesticides, designed to avoid such destruction.

Although FMC was not aware of the lethal-to-birds quality of the water in its pond (and in fairness to FMC this may be assumed) nevertheless it was aware of the danger of carbofuran to humans, a fact which caused FMC to wash down the carbofuran areas more frequently, which activity in turn pumped contaminated water into the pond. Imposing strict liability on FMC in this case does not dictate that every death of a bird will result in imposing strict criminal liability on some party. However, here the statute does not include as an element of the offense "wilfully, knowingly, recklessly, or negligently"; implementation of the statute will involve only relatively minor fines; Congress recognized the important public policy behind protecting migratory birds; FMC engaged in an activity involving the manufacture of a highly toxic chemical; and FMC failed to prevent this chemical from escaping into the pond and killing birds. This is sufficient to impose strict liability on FMC.

Accordingly, we affirm.

NOTES

(1) Is the court's analogy to strict liability for ultrahazardous activities persuasive? Is it appropriate to extend a standard applicable to civil liability into an area of criminal liability? Is the court's reliance on prosecutorial discretion reassuring?

(2) Unintentional poisoning: The baiting cases such as *United States v. Boynton* are the traditional type of prosecution under the MBTA; the hunters clearly intended to take ducks. In the mid–1970s, however, the Fish and Wildlife Service (FWS) began to prosecute people who killed migratory birds without expressly intending to do so. *United States v. FMC Corp.* is one example. *See also United States v. Moon Lake Electric Association,* 45 F.Supp.2d 1070, 1072 (D.Colo.1999) (strict liability standard applied to inadvertent electrocution). Other unintentional poisoning cases have reached similar results though sometimes from different rationales. For example, in *United States v. Corbin Farm Service,* 444 F.Supp. 510, 532–36 (E.D.Cal.1978), *aff'd on other grounds per curiam,* 578 F.2d 259 (9th Cir.1978), an employee of a pesticide distributor, an aerial applicator, and the owner of the alfalfa field were indicted for violating the MBTA when the spraying of a field killed several birds. The defendant's motion to dismiss on the ground that they had not intended to kill any birds was denied. The court stated that the issue was not intent but negligence— whether the defendants had acted with reasonable care under the circumstances. *See also United States v. Rollins,* 706 F.Supp. 742, 744–45 (D.Idaho 1989) (applying the due care standard and reversing a conviction for killing geese by spraying an alfalfa field); *United States v. Van Fossan,* 899 F.2d 636, 638–39 (7th Cir.1990) (defendant intended to kill an unprotected species (pigeons) and inadvertently killed protected species as well (grackles and mourning doves); conviction affirmed, liability standard specifically undecided). The issue is discussed in Conrad A. Fjetland, *Possibilities for Expansion of the Migratory Bird Treaty Act for the Protection of Migratory Birds,* 40 NAT. RESOURCES J. 47 (2000).

(3) Felony liability: While the majority of circuits upheld strict liability for misdemeanors, there has been more concern when this standard is used in felony prosecutions. In 1960, Congress amended the MBTA to add a felony provision. The amendment mirrored the previous, misdemeanor provisions by not explicitly requiring scienter as an element of the crime: "Whoever, in violation of this Act, shall (1) take by any manner whatsoever any migratory bird with intent to sell, ... or (2) sell ... any migratory bird shall be guilty of a felony." *Id.* § 707(b).

In 1985, the Sixth Circuit Court of Appeals held that the standard violated due process, stating "in order for one to be convicted of a felony ... Congress must require the prosecution to prove the defendant acted with some degree of scienter." *United States v. Wulff,* 758 F.2d 1121, 1125 (6th Cir.1985). Congress responded by amending the felony provisions in 1986 to read, "Whoever, in violation of this Act, shall *knowingly....* " Act of Nov. 10, 1986, Pub. L. No. 99–645, § 501, 100 Stat. 3590 (codified at 16 U.S.C. § 707(b)). Thus, the person who hunts migratory birds for recreation is strictly liable for a misdemeanor if he violates the Act's restrictions; the person who sells migratory birds in violation of the Act's provisions is subject to prosecution for a felony if her actions were "knowing." What does this standard require?

United States v. Pitrone was a prosecution of a taxidermist for selling mounted harlequin ducks that he had shot on a trip to Alaska. The trial judge instructed the jury that "knowingly" meant that "he was conscious and aware of his actions, realized what he was doing and what was happening around him, and did not act because of ignorance, mistake, or accident." The government, she added, did not need "to prove that the defendant knew that his actions were unlawful," but he "must know within the meaning of the statute that he was selling a bird." *United States v. Pitrone*, 115 F.3d 1, 4 (1st Cir.1997). On appeal, Pitrone challenged this instruction, contending that the government was required to prove that he knew he was violating the law. The First Circuit rejected his argument.

(ii) "EXCEPT AS PERMITTED BY REGULATIONS"

Questions about the breadth of the MBTA have focused, not just on *mens rea* and indirect takes, but also on the provision in § 703 allowing takes "as permitted by regulations."

United States v. Darst

District Court for the District of Kansas.
726 F.Supp. 286 (1989).

■ Crow, J.:—On October 1, 1988, Jerry Almquist, a conservation officer with the State of Kansas, visited the defendant's residence and observed a great horned owl in a leg trap. Mr. Almquist told defendant that taking or killing great horned owls is illegal and that he should call Mr. Case Vendel, a federal game officer, to inquire about a permit for trapping owls if they were killing his chickens. On February 20, 1989, Mr. Almquist returned to defendant's residence and saw another great horned owl trapped on a different pole. Defendant informed Mr. Almquist that he had set four traps on four different poles in order to protect his chickens and that the federal agent was never contacted about a permit.

Defendant represented himself at the trial held on May 12, 1989. He admitted in his testimony that he trapped and killed the great horned owls on both occasions and that he had not contacted federal agent Vendel nor obtained a permit from him. Defendant stated that his authority for killing the owls came from his constitutional right to defend his property.

The Magistrate found defendant guilty and fined him $125 and assessed costs of $25. Defendant appeals on the following legal issues: (a) whether the great horned owl is a properly designated migratory bird; (b) whether the statute is unconstitutionally broad for including as violations the defendant's actions taken in defense of his property; and (c) whether 16 U.S.C. § 703 is unconstitutionally vague in that the term, "migratory bird," is not adequately defined except by regulation, 50 C.F.R. § 10.13, which is excessively broad.

The Migratory Bird Treaty Act (MBTA), 16 U.S.C. § 703 *et seq.,* was passed in 1918 to give force and effect to a 1916 treaty between the United States and Great Britain entered "for the protection of migratory birds." The Supreme Court upheld the constitutionality of the MBTA in 1920.

Missouri v. Holland, 252 U.S. 416 (1920). The MBTA was later expanded to include conventions for the protection of birds entered by the United States with the countries of Mexico and Japan. The convention with Mexico provides that other migratory birds may be added later upon the agreement of the Presidents of both countries. *United States v. Richards,* 583 F.2d 491, 493 (10th Cir.1978); *United States v. Blanket,* 391 F.Supp. 15, 18 (W.D.Okla.1975). The protected migratory birds are listed in 50 C.F.R. § 10.13 which "does not enlarge or purport to enlarge the Conventions or extend the scope of the Act to any bird not included in the Conventions." *Blanket,* 391 F. Supp. at 19. Among the list of protected birds is the great horned owl.

Defendant first contends that the great horned owl is not a migratory bird and, therefore, he did not know it was protected under the MBTA. This contention is also tied into defendant's other issue of whether 16 U.S.C. § 703 is unconstitutionally vague in not defining a migratory bird except by regulation. [ ]

The Secretary of Interior is authorized by 16 U.S.C. § 704 to promulgate regulations regarding who may take or possess migratory birds and under what circumstances. Section 703 is prefaced with correlating language, as follows: "[u]nless and except as permitted by regulations made as hereinafter provided. . . . " By reading § 703 in conjunction with § 704, a person is adequately alerted that applicable regulations specify what conduct is prohibited and what migratory birds are protected. Neither the MBTA nor its attendant regulations are so vague that a person of ordinary intelligence would not reasonably know what conduct is prohibited under these provisions. *See United States v. Brandt,* 717 F.2d 955, 957 (6th Cir.1983).

A defendant in a criminal case cannot collaterally attack the Secretary's determination that a given species of birds needs protection, as long as the regulation promulgated to that end is facially valid. *United States v. Gigstead,* 528 F.2d 314, 317 (8th Cir.1976). The term, "migratory bird," is defined in 50 C.F.R. § 10.12 as any bird which belongs to a species listed in § 10.13. The court has not been provided any reason to question the listing of the great horned owl in § 10.13 as the proper designation of a species protected by the terms of the controlling treaties. Defendant's legal issues (a) and (c) are without merit.

NOTES

(1) As *Darst* suggests, several key terms in the MBTA are not defined in the statute. Many birds included on the protected list, such as the great horned owl, are migratory only in parts of their ranges, yet are protected everywhere—that is, a bird is deemed "migratory" based, not on whether it actually migrates, but whether the species of which it is a part is so designated. Owls generally, and great horned owls in particular, are almost entirely nonmigratory in fact. Owls living at the northern reaches of the species range do sometimes move south in winter when prey is scarce, but otherwise they are permanent residents. 2 ARTHUR C. BENT, LIFE HISTORIES OF NORTH AMERICAN BIRDS OF PREY 318 (Dover repr. 1961). Thus, the defendant in *Darst* had reason—factually, at least—to be surprised that great horned owls in Kansas were protected by the MBTA.

The MBTA also has no definitions of "pursue," "take," or other key terms, a problem that can complicate factual determinations in many cases. As the court notes, "migratory bird" is defined by regulation (50 C.F.R. § 10.13). The FWS has also defined various other terms in its regulations. Thus, "*Take* means to pursue, hunt, shoot, kill, trap, capture, or collect, or attempt to pursue, hunt, shoot, wound, kill, trap, capture, or collect." *Id.* Given this definition, might a bird watcher out to observe a member of a covered species be guilty of "taking" the bird because she was "pursu[ing]" it? Is *harm* implicit in the definition?

(2) Hunting regulations: As *Darst* demonstrates, the FWS has authority within limits set by treaties and the MBTA to regulate the taking of migratory birds. Recall that § 703 states, "*except as permitted by regulations* ... it shall be unlawful ... to hunt ... any migratory bird.*" The Secretary has relied upon this language to promulgate regulations specifying not only open seasons but also to regulate in detail all aspects relating to the hunting of such birds.

(3) Preemption: The MBTA's prohibitions on taking migratory birds except as permitted by the Secretary's regulations clearly preempt state law. The drafters of the Act, however, explicitly chose not to preempt all state law. The Act permits states to enact and enforce laws that are either consistent with the Secretary's regulations or which provide "further protection" for the species covered by the Act. 16 U.S.C. § 708. *See Carey v. South Dakota,* 250 U.S. 118 (1919) (state statute forbidding export of ducks upheld as not inconsistent with MBTA).

Humane Society v. Glickman

District of Columbia Circuit Court of Appeals.
217 F.3d 882 (2000).

■ RANDOLPH, J.:—The "International Convention for the Protection of Migratory Birds," 39 Stat. 1702 (1916), between the United States and Great Britain (acting for Canada) sought to preserve, in the words of Justice Holmes, "a national interest of very nearly the first magnitude," *Missouri v. Holland,* 252 U.S. 416, 435 (1920). The Treaty "recited that many species of birds in their annual migrations traversed certain parts of the United States and of Canada, that they were of great value as a source of food and in destroying insects injurious to vegetation, but were in danger of extermination through lack of adequate protection." *Id.* at 431. Legislation implementing the Treaty—the Migratory Bird Treaty Act of 1918— "prohibited the killing, capturing or selling any of the migratory birds included in the terms of the treaty except as permitted by regulations" now administered by the Department of the Interior. 252 U.S. at 431. In this appeal from the district court's order enjoining the Department of Agriculture from violating the statute, the question is whether the Migratory Bird Treaty Act prohibits federal agencies from killing or taking migratory birds without a permit from the Interior Department.

I

At the center of the controversy is the Canada goose—*Branta canadensis*. With its black-stockinged neck and head and distinctive white cheek patch, its loud resonant honking calls, and its V-shaped flight formations, the Canada goose is a familiar sight throughout most of North America. *See* FRANK C. BELLROSE, DUCKS, GEESE AND SWANS OF NORTH AMERICA 142 (3d ed. 1980). The Mid–Atlantic population of Canada geese, one of eleven recognized races, winters in the coastal areas of Virginia, Maryland, Delaware, and New Jersey, and returns in the spring to the tundra zone of the Ungava Peninsula in Quebec, its traditional summer breeding grounds. [ ] In recent years, however, large flocks of Canada geese have stopped migrating, preferring to breed, nest and rear their young in the coastal states of the middle Atlantic region. The Commonwealth of Virginia has become a host to many of these full-time residents. In 1991, an estimated 66,169 Canada geese lived year round in Virginia. By 1998 Virginia's resident goose population had quadrupled to 254,000. *See Wildlife Services, Animal and Plant Health Inspection Service, U.S. Dep't of Agriculture, Environmental Assessment for the Management of Conflicts Associated with Non–Migratory (Resident) Canada Geese, Migratory Canada Geese, and Urban/Suburban Ducks in the Commonwealth of Virginia* § 2.1, at 6 (Mar. 30, 1999) (*"Environmental Assessment"*). In the same year, only 70,000 migratory Canada geese wintered over in Virginia, *see id.* tbl.5, at 18, a number not much larger than the migratory population in the 1970s, *see* BELLROSE, *supra*, at 148.

Residential owners, farmers, government officials and many others are deeply concerned about the exploding population of Canada geese. Browsing by Virginia's resident geese has reduced state-wide yields of cereal grains, peanuts, soybeans and corn. Goose droppings have spoiled water quality around beaches and wetlands, and interfered with the enjoyment of parks and ball fields. The geese have damaged gardens, lawns and golf courses. Their fecal deposits threaten to contaminate drinking water supplies. *See Environmental Assessment*, [ ]. And they pose a hazard to aircraft. Resident geese are found at most of Virginia's airports and military bases. In 1995, a passenger jet hit ten Canada geese at Dulles International Airport, causing $1.7 million of wing and engine damage. *See id.* [ ]. Collisions have also occurred at other Virginia airports. And "Langley Air Force Base and Norfolk Naval Air Station have altered, delayed, aborted, and ceased flight operations because of Canada geese on their field." *Id.*[2]

In response to these problems and others, the Department of Agriculture, through its Animal Health and Inspection Service's Wildlife Services Division, instituted an "Integrated Goose Management Program" in conjunction with Virginia state agencies. The plan called for various measures such as harassment, biological control, habitat alteration, repellents, nest

---

2. Resident Canada geese and the problems they cause are not confined to the east coast. The Washington Post reported that the Agriculture Department, having obtained a permit from FWS, is rounding up resident Canada geese and killing them in twelve counties surrounding Puget Sound in Washington State. *See* Ben White, *Honk if You Hate Goose Droppings*, WASH. POST, June 29, 2000, at A29.

and egg destruction, and capture and killing. The killings were to take place during the "summer molt"—between mid-June and late-July—when the resident geese cannot fly (the migratory geese are in Canada at this time of year). An Environmental Assessment, issued on January 29, 1997, reflected the Interior Department's longstanding position that the Migratory Bird Treaty Act restricted not only private parties and states, but also federal agencies. Hence a "federal Migratory Bird Depredation Permit ... would be required and obtained for the proposed action." *Animal Damage Control, Animal and Plant Health Inspection Service, U.S. Dep't of Agriculture, Environmental Assessment for the Management of Conflicts Associated with Nonmigratory (Resident) Canada Geese and Urban/Suburban Mallard Ducks in the State of Virginia* 22 (Jan. 29, 1997). Interior's Fish and Wildlife Service (FWS) is authorized to issue such depredation permits for migratory birds that "bec[o]me seriously injurious to the agricultural or other interests in any particular community." International Convention for the Protection of Migratory Birds, art. VII, 39 Stat. 1702, 1704 (1916) ("International Convention"), *referenced in* 16 U.S.C. § 704; *see also* 50 C.F.R. pt. 21.

In 1997, the Director of FWS issued a memorandum to regional directors stating that federal agencies no longer needed to obtain a permit before taking or killing migratory birds. The Humane Society of the United States, Citizens for the Preservation of Wildlife, the Animal Protection Institute, and three individuals thereupon filed suit against the Secretaries of Agriculture and Interior and other officials in those departments seeking to enjoin implementation of the Goose Management Plan. The district court ruled that § 703 of the Migratory Bird Treaty Act restricted federal agencies. The court therefore enjoined the defendants "from conducting the Canada Goose Plan until such time as they shall obtain valid permits to do so pursuant to the" Act. *Humane Soc'y v. Glickman,* No. 98CV–1510, memorandum opinion at 21–22 (D.D.C. July 6, 1999).

II

Although Virginia's Canada geese are year-long residents, they are members of a species that migrates and therefore fall within the category of "migratory birds" protected by the 1916 Treaty and the Act. See 50 C.F.R. § 10.13. Protected from whom? The district court thought § 703 of the Act gave the answer—from everyone in the United States, including federal agencies. The provision reads:

> Unless and except as permitted by regulations made as hereinafter provided in this subchapter, it shall be unlawful at any time, by any means or in any manner, to pursue, hunt, take, capture, kill, ... any migratory bird, ...

16 U.S.C. § 703. As legislation goes, § 703 contains broad and unqualified language—"at any time," "by any means," "in any manner," "any migratory bird," "any part, nest, or egg of any such bird," "any product ... comprised in whole or part, of any such bird." The one exception to the prohibition is in the opening clause—"Unless and except as permitted by regulations made as hereinafter provided in this subchapter.... " For migratory game birds, of which the Canada goose is one, the exception

gives the Interior Department authority to regulate hunting seasons and bag limits. Article II of the Treaty itself required a closed season—no hunting of these birds—between March 10 and September 1, the typical period when the birds breed, molt and raise their young. In addition to issuing hunting regulations, [ ], the Secretary of the Interior may issue permits for killing Canada geese and other migratory birds if this is shown to be "compatible with the terms of the [Migratory Bird] conventions." 16 U.S.C. § 704. As we have said, Article VII of the Treaty contemplated that permits allowing the killing of migratory birds would be available in "extraordinary conditions" when the birds have "become seriously injurious to the agricultural or other interests in any particular community," International Convention, art. VII, 39 Stat. 1704.

As § 703 is written, what matters is whether someone has killed or is attempting to kill or capture or take a protected bird, without a permit and outside of any designated hunting season. Nothing in § 703 turns on the identity of the perpetrator. There is no exemption in § 703 for farmers, or golf course superintendents, or ornithologists, or airport officials, or state officers, or federal agencies. . . .

The defendants here, in order to promote their position that federal agencies are exempt from § 703, seek to introduce structural ambiguity into the Act, citing the criminal penalty provision of § 707(a):

> Except as otherwise provided in this section, any person, association, partnership, or corporation who shall violate any provisions of said conventions or of this subchapter, or who shall violate or fail to comply with any regulation made pursuant to this subchapter shall be deemed guilty of a misdemeanor and upon conviction thereof shall be fined not more than $15,000 or be imprisoned not more than six months, or both.

16 U.S.C. § 707(a). Federal agencies, they say, cannot be considered "persons" who may be held criminally liable for violating the Act or the Treaty. (They do not discuss whether federal officers carrying out the extermination of migratory birds could be considered "persons.") The defendants' reading of § 707(a) gains support from the canon that the term "person" does not ordinarily include the sovereign. *See United States v. Cooper Corp.,* 312 U.S. 600, 604 (1941). And so we are willing to assume that the criminal enforcement provision could not be used against federal agencies. From this the defendants reason that Congress could not have intended to have § 703 restrict federal agencies because there would have been no means to enforce the restrictions; at the time of its enactment, they tell us, there was no provision in the Migratory Bird Treaty Act for injunctive relief.[5]

The argument goes nowhere. Even without a specific review provision, there still could have been a suit against the appropriate federal officer for injunctive relief to enforce § 703. *Missouri v. Holland,* for instance, was a "bill in equity brought by the State of Missouri to prevent a game warden of the United States from attempting to enforce the Migratory Bird Treaty

---

5. Today, the Administrative Procedure Act, 5 U.S.C. § 702, authorizes suits in federal courts naming the United States as a defendant and specifying in any injunctive decree the federal officers "personally responsible" for compliance.

Act." 252 U.S. at 430. The Supreme Court had already recognized the "equity injunction as a method for review of administrative action" in *Noble v. Union River Logging R.R.*, 147 U.S. 165 (1893), affirming an injunction against the Secretary of the Interior although the underlying statute contained no provision for judicial review. . . .

Defendants' argument, and our assumption, that federal agencies are not "persons" within § 707(a)'s meaning therefore does not lead to the conclusion that Congress meant to exempt federal agencies from § 703. Indeed it would be odd if they were exempt. The Migratory Bird Treaty Act implements the Treaty of 1916. Treaties are undertakings between nations; the terms of a treaty bind the contracting powers. After ratification of the Treaty, President Woodrow Wilson affixed his signature to it and made it public, "to the end that the same and every article and clause thereof may be observed and fulfilled with good faith *by the United States* and the citizens thereof." 39 Stat. 1705 (italics added). If one year later, in 1917, Canadian authorities had started slaughtering eider ducks, no one would doubt that Canada would be guilty of violating Article IV of the Treaty, which protects these ducks. If some agency of the federal government did the same in Alaska, the United States too would be in violation of the Treaty. . . .

. . .

This too had been the longstanding conclusion of the Department of the Interior, which until 1997 had "historically interpreted the provisions of the MBTA as applying to actions of FWS employees themselves." Letter from Frank K. Richardson, Solicitor, U.S. Dep't of the Interior, to the Secretary of the Interior at 3 (May 31, 1985); [ ]. . . .

For many of the reasons we have mentioned, we disagree with the "tentative conclusion" in *Newton County Wildlife Ass'n v. United States Forest Service*, 113 F.3d 110, 115 (8th Cir.1997), and the holding in *Sierra Club v. Martin*, 110 F.3d 1551, 1555 (11th Cir.1997), that § 703 does not apply to federal agencies. Both opinions rest on the mistaken idea that in 1918, § 703 could be enforced only through the criminal penalty provision in § 707(a). The *Martin* opinion adds the thought that Congress could not have wanted the Act to apply to the Forest Service in the early 1900s because whenever it cut trees it might be destroying migratory birds or their nests, in violation of the Act. *See* 110 F.3d at 1555. The *Martin* court's assumption that timber harvesting could violate the Migratory Bird Treaty Act is not shared by others. The Eighth Circuit in *Newton County*, following the lead of the Ninth Circuit in *Seattle Audubon Society v. Evans*, 952 F.2d 297, 302 (1991), held that § 703 does not prohibit "conduct, such as timber harvesting, that indirectly results in the death of migratory birds." 113 F.3d at 114. Even if the *Martin* court were correct about timber harvesting, its observation about the Forest Service ignores the facts that it was not until 1997 that the Interior Department asserted immunity for federal agencies; that before then the Fish and Wildlife Service interpreted the Act to apply to all federal agencies; that during the pre–1997 period the Forest Service, like other federal agencies, could obtain permits; and that—as the documents submitted in this case show—it was the *Martin* case and other pending litigation that "spurred" Interior to adopt the "new" interpretation.[7]

We conclude that because the Wildlife Services division of the Department of Agriculture did not obtain a permit from the Department of the Interior, its implementation of the Integrated Goose Management Plan by taking and killing Canada Geese violates § 703 of the Migratory Bird Treaty Act.

Affirmed.

NOTES

(1) Does the court offer a reasonable interpretation of the very broad statutory language? Does the presence of the exception to § 703—"except as permitted by regulations"—suggest that the court's should err on the side of inclusivity? Are the facts in *Glickman* distinguishable from those presented in *Newton County Wildlife Ass'n v. United States Forest Service*, 113 F.3d 110, 115 (8th Cir.1997), *Sierra Club v. Martin*, 110 F.3d 1551, 1555 (11th Cir.1997), and *Seattle Audubon Society v. Evans*, 952 F.2d 297, 302 (9th Cir.1991)?

(2) The MBTA and habitat destruction: Litigation on the applicability of the MBTA to habitat alteration—most frequently, logging activities such as that at issue in the *Newton County, Martin,* and *Seattle Audubon* cases discussed briefly in the *Glickman* court's penultimate paragraph—will be examined in Chapter 14.

b. Bald and Golden Eagle Protection Act

NOTES

(1) An outline of the Bald and Golden Eagle Protection Act: The genesis of the Bald and Golden Eagle Protection Act (BGEPA), 16 U.S.C. §§ 668–668d, is in the Bald Eagle Protection Act, adopted by Congress in 1940 to protect the "symbol of American ideals of freedom" by making it illegal to "take, possess, sell, purchase, barter, offer to sell, purchase or barter, transport, export or import, at any time or in any manner" the protected species. 16 U.S.C. §§ 668–668d. The Act criminalized the taking or possession of the species, its parts, nests, or eggs. Unlike the MBTA, the Act defined "take" as "[t]o pursue, shoot, shoot at, wound, kill, capture, trap, collect, or otherwise *willfully* molest or disturb," 16 U.S.C. § 668(a) (emphasis added); scienter thus is an element of the crime. The Act granted the Secretary of the Interior discretion to permit the taking and possession of eagles "for scientific or exhibition purposes" and "for the protection of wildlife or agricultural or other interests in any particular locality" if, "after investigation," the Secretary determines that the taking "is compati-

---

7. Nor did the *Martin* court acknowledge the Supreme Court's dictum in *Robertson v. Seattle Audubon Society*, 503 U.S. 429 (1992), that the Act applies to federal agencies.

ble with the preservation of the bald eagle." *Id.* § 668a. The Act has been amended three times.

In 1962, Congress added golden eagles to the Act's prohibitions. Act of Oct. 24, 1962, Pub. L. No. 87–884, 76 Stat. 1246. The prohibitions were subject to the proviso that they did not "prohibit possession or transportation of [either protected species], alive or dead, or any part, nest, or egg thereof, lawfully taken" prior to the enactment of the Act. The amendment added two additional exceptions. First, the Secretary was authorized to permit takings of bald and golden eagles "for the religious purposes of Indian tribes." *Id.* Second, when requested by the governor of any state, the Secretary "shall authorize" taking golden eagles "for the purpose of seasonally protecting domesticated flocks and herds ... in such part or parts of such State and for such periods as the Secretary determines to be necessary to protect such interests." *Id.*

Congress amended the Act again in 1972 in response to the highly publicized poisoning of several dozen eagles and the aerial gunning of several hundred eagles by Wyoming ranchers. The Department of the Interior, adopting a narrow interpretation of its powers under the Act, concluded that the government could not prosecute anyone for the poisonings without proof that the person intended to kill eagles. The amendment reduced the degree of culpability required for a conviction: anyone who "shall knowingly, or with wanton disregard for the consequences of his act," take an eagle was subject to criminal penalties. *Id.* § 668(a). The definition of "take" was also amended specifically to include poisoning. Finally, the 1972 amendments increased the penalties for violations of the Act. Not only were the maximum fines and periods of imprisonment for criminal violations increased, the amendment also added civil fines and grazing permit forfeiture to the range of potential sanctions.

In 1978, Congress carved out another exception by permitting the Secretary to permit "the taking of golden eagle nests which interfere with resource development or recovery operations." *Id.* § 668a. Although the legislative history is focused on coal development in the West, the Act neither defines the term "resource development or recovery," nor provides any standards to guide the Secretary's exercise of this authority.

Although the Supreme Court has described the Act as containing "sweepingly framed prohibitions," *Andrus v. Allard,* 444 U.S. 51, 56 (1979), the various exceptions, taken together, are substantial. In addition, the Act has been marked by lax enforcement—particularly against Western ranching interests. *See* S. REP. NO. 1159, 92d Cong., 2d Sess. 3 (1972), *reprinted in* 1972 U.S.C.C.A.N. 4285, 4286–88 (quoting a *Washington Post* story); DONALD G. SCHUELER, INCIDENT AT EAGLE RANCH (1980). Some measure of the Act's failings is suggested by the fact that, despite the Act, the bald eagle was listed in 1967 as endangered under the Endangered Species Preservation Act of 1966. Office of the Secretary, Dept. of the Interior, *Endangered Species,* 32 Fed. Reg. 4001 (1967).[1]

---

1. In 1978, the species was downlisted to threatened in 5 of the conterminous 48 states. Fish & Wildlife Service, Dep't of the Interior, *Determination of Certain Bald Eagle Populations as Endangered or Threatened,* 43

(2) *The Case of Swans* **redux?** BGEPA was predicated in part on the belief that the bald eagle was "no longer a mere bird of biological interest but a symbol of American ideals of freedom," 16 U.S.C. § 668 note.[2] Recall that the King's Bench in *Case of the Swans* [Chapter 2] stated that "the law [of swans] is founded on a reason in nature; for the cock swan is an emblem or representation of an affectionate and true husband to his wife above all other fowls." As such, swans are "royal" because they are the peak of perfection. Is the bald eagle—like the swan—a symbolic animal? Does symbolism serve as a constitutional justification for the statutory protection accorded the species?

(3) The BGEPA and the MBTA: Since both bald and golden eagles are migratory species, they are protected under both the MBTA and the BGEPA. Both statutes may also serve as predicate crimes under the Lacey Act. *See, e.g., United States v. Sandia,* 188 F.3d 1215 (10th Cir.1999) (prosecution under the Lacey Act, the MBTA, and the BGEPA for selling a golden eagle skin). Since BGEPA does not include a minimum value provisions as does the Lacey Act, a prosecution under BGEPA may succeed even where it might fail under the Lacey Act. *E.g., United States v. Todd,* 735 F.2d 146 (5th Cir.1984).

There are, however, important differences between the two statutes. Perhaps the most significant is the role of scienter:

United States v. Allard

United States District Court, District of Montana.
397 F.Supp. 429 (1975).

■ SMITH, C.J.:—Defendant was found guilty by a jury of Counts I and III of an information charging him with selling golden eagle feathers in violation of 16 U.S.C. § 668(a).

A motion in arrest of judgment and a motion for a new trial raise problems relating to the laws protecting bald and golden eagles and the effect of those laws on reservation Indians.

[The court concluded that defendant's treaty hunting rights were abrogated by the 1962 amendments to the BGEPA.]

At the trial, the court . . . instructed the jury that it was necessary that the jury find that the defendant knew that the sale of eagle feathers was illegal. If this instruction was correct, then the court's order, denying an

---

Fed. Reg. 6230, 6233 (1978). *See* 50 C.F.R. § 17.11(h) (1993).

2. Benjamin Franklin had a different perspective on the Continental Congress' adoption of the Bald Eagle as the national symbol: "the Bald Eagle . . . is a Bird of bad moral Character; like those among Men who live by Sharping and Robbing, he is generally poor, and often very lousy." Letter from Benjamin Franklin to Sarah Bache (Jan. 26, 1784) *(quoted in United States v. Hetzel,* 385 F.Supp. 1311, 1315 n. 1 (W.D.Mo.1974).

Franklin may have been a far better ornithologist than the United States Congress, but, as George Coggins has noted about the national buzzard, "There are things that just are, that are accepted as such without analysis, and that appear necessary, though incidental to the life of the republic." George C. Coggins & William H. Hensley, *Constitutional Limits on Federal Power to Protect and Manage Wildlife: Is the Endangered Species Endangered?,* 61 IOWA L. REV. 1099, 1142 (1976).

offer to prove by the witness Ward that in the Indian artifact business it was the usage and custom to sell eagle feather bonnets and that it was unknown in the industry that such sales were illegal, was erroneous. The witness was well-qualified to state the custom in the trade, and the evidence, if given, would have corroborated defendant's claim that he had no knowledge of the law. Hence, if the instruction was correct, the court committed error in rejecting the evidence. On a further consideration of the matter, I conclude that the instruction should not have been given.

16 U.S.C. § 668(a) reads in pertinent part:

> Whoever ... shall knowingly, or with wanton disregard for the consequences of his act ... sell ... any golden eagle ... or any part. ...

The effect of the word "knowingly" is to require that the Government prove that the defendant knew that the feathers were golden eagle feathers, and I think it clear that a conviction would not be had were a person to sell golden eagle feathers thinking them to be turkey feathers. The motions here posed no problems in this regard. The Act does not, and no statute that I recall seeing, makes the defendant's knowledge of the law an element of the crime.

I find nothing in 16 U.S.C. § 668(a) which sheds much light upon the congressional intent, and the legislative history tells me no more than that Congress was greatly concerned about the preservation of the bald and golden eagles and was anxious to do something about it.

The rule of general application seems to be that in "regulatory measures ... where the emphasis of the statute is evidently upon ... social, betterment rather than the punishment of the crimes as in cases of *mala in se* ... " a specific intent is not required. In this area the axiom that ignorance of the law is no excuse seems to be true. [ ] In *Morissette v. United States,* 342 U.S. 246 (1952), the Court distinguished between knowledge of law and fact and said:

> But knowing conversion requires more than knowledge that defendant was taking the property into his possession. He must have had knowledge of the facts, though not necessarily the law, that made the taking a conversion.

.   .   .

When the Act of June 8, 1940, [the Bald Eagle Protection Act] was enacted to protect the bald eagle, the penalties were $500.00 and six months imprisonment. The Act of October 24, 1962, 76 Stat. 1246, added the golden eagle to the protected list and left the punishment provisions unchanged. The present rather severe penalties of one year imprisonment and $5,000.00 for a first offense, provided by the Act of October 23, 1972, [ ], were the result of reaction to the widespread publicity given acts of wanton destruction—the wholesale killing of eagles. In light of this history, I do not think that the penalty indicates a congressional intent to make knowledge of the law an element of the crime. The fact is that in protection of wildlife hosts of laws have been enacted and seldom if ever is intent made an element of the offense. Since the law is regulatory, since the penalties initially were moderate, since the crime at the first offense level is still a misdemeanor, since the taking of wildlife is traditionally regulated by laws not requiring specific intent, I am unable to find a congressional intent that knowledge of the law is an element of the offense. That being so, the exclusion of the evidence of custom was proper. Though the giving of the instruction was error, it was favorable to the defendant and he cannot now complain.

. . .

The motion in arrest of judgment and the motion for a new trial are denied.

NOTES

(1) The BGEPA requires that the violation be "knowing" and the *Allard* decision holds that this requires proof that the person knew the requisite facts to make the action a crime but that he need not know that it was a crime. This construction of the Act is consistent with *United States v. Pitrone*, 115 F.3d 1, 4 (1st Cir.1997), a prosecution under the felony provisions of the MBTA discussed above.

A contrary conclusion is reached in *United States v. Hetzel*, 385 F.Supp. 1311 (W.D.Mo.1974), a prosecution of a Boy Scout leader. Michael Bean and Melanie Rowland describe the decision as "a good example of the axiom that bad cases make bad law." MICHAEL J. BEAN & MELANIE J. ROWLAND, *supra*, at 98.

(2) The BGEPA and the MBTA: Can the government prosecute a person for taking, possessing, or selling eagles under the strict liability standard of the MBTA or must it proceed under the "knowingly" requirement of the BGEPA? In *United States v. Mackie*, the defendants were convicted under the MBTA for selling whole eagle and eagle parts to undercover agents. On appeal from their conviction, they argued that the United States was required to prosecute them under the more specific provisions of the BGEPA. The Ninth Circuit disagreed:

> When an act is proscribed by more than one criminal statute, the government may elect to prosecute under either so long as it does not discriminate against any class of defendants, [ ], and so long as the legislative history does not indicate that Congress intended to prohibit prosecution under the more general statute. [ ]

United States v. Mackie, 681 F.2d 1121 (9th Cir.1982). Concluding that "nothing in the legislative history of the MBTA or the BGEPA indicates a congressional intent to prohibit prosecution under the MBTA," the court held that "the government properly elected to proceed under the MBTA." *Id.*

United States v. Moon Lake Electric Association, Inc.

United States District Court, District of Colorado.
45 F.Supp.2d 1070 (1999).

■ BABCOCK, D.J.:—On June 9, 1998, the United States of America ("the government") filed an Information charging defendant, Moon Lake Electric

Association, Inc. ("Moon Lake"), with seven violations of the Bald and Golden Eagle Protection Act ("the BGEPA"), 16 U.S.C. § 668 (1997), and six violations of the Migratory Bird Treaty Act ("the MBTA"), 16 U.S.C. §§ 703 & 707(a) (1997) (collectively, "the Acts"), in connection with the deaths of 12 Golden Eagles, 4 Ferruginous Hawks, and 1 Great Horned Owl. Moon Lake moves for dismissal of the charges, arguing that the Acts do not apply to unintentional conduct that is not the sort of physical conduct normally exhibited by hunters and poachers. Moon Lake also argues that § 707(a) of the MBTA is unconstitutional as applied under the circumstances of this case. The issues are fully briefed and the parties presented oral argument on November 13, 1998. For the reasons set forth below, I deny Moon Lake's motion.

I.   BACKGROUND

I glean the following from the parties' briefs and oral arguments. Moon Lake is a "rural electrical distribution cooperative" that provides electricity to customers in northeastern Utah and northwestern Colorado. At issue in this case is Moon Lake's supply of electricity to an oil field near Rangely, Colorado. The electricity is conveyed by power lines strung across 3,096 power poles. The oil field is located near the White River in an area that is home to several species of protected birds, including Bald Eagles, Golden Eagles, Ferruginous Hawks, and Great Horned Owls. The oil field is mostly treeless, making Moon Lake's power poles preferred locations for perching, roosting, and hunting by birds of prey. The government alleges that Moon Lake has failed to install inexpensive equipment on 2,450 power poles, causing the death or injury of 38 birds of prey during the 29 month period commencing January 1996 and concluding June 1998.

As noted above, the Information charges Moon Lake with causing the deaths of 12 Golden Eagles, 4 Ferruginous Hawks, and 1 Great Horned Owl. Specifically, the Information alleges that Moon Lake did "take and kill" those 17 protected birds.

. . .

III.   WHETHER DEFENDANT'S ALLEGED CONDUCT CONSTITUTES A VIOLATION OF THE MBTA OR THE BGEPA

Moon Lake argues that the electrocutions, even if they occurred as alleged, do not constitute violations of the MBTA or the BGEPA because the electrocutions were unintentional and not caused by the sort of conduct normally exhibited by hunters and poachers. Moon Lake contends that, in proscribing the taking or killing of protected birds, Congress intended to target only poaching, hunting, trapping, and other "intentionally harmful" acts directed toward protected birds. In contending that its alleged conduct was unintentional, Moon Lake focuses on the *mens rea,* or mental state, required for conviction. By arguing that Congress intended to punish only conduct normally exhibited by hunters and poachers, Moon Lake directs my attention to the *actus reus,* or the physical act, required for conviction.

When courts interpret statutes, the initial inquiry focuses on the language of the statute itself. . . .

The BGEPA states, in relevant part:

Whoever, within the United States or any place subject to the jurisdiction thereof, without being permitted to do so as provided in this subchapter, shall knowingly, or with wanton disregard for the consequences of his act take, possess, sell, purchase, barter, offer to sell, purchase or barter, transport, export or import, at any time or in any manner, any bald eagle commonly known as the American eagle, or any golden eagle, alive or dead, or any part, nest, or egg thereof of the foregoing eagles, or whoever violates any permit or regulation issued pursuant to this subchapter, shall be fined not more than $5,000 or imprisoned not more than one year or both....

16 U.S.C. § 668. "Take" under the BGEPA "includes also pursue, shoot, shoot at, poison, wound, kill, capture, trap, collect, or molest or disturb...." 16 U.S.C. § 668c.

a. Whether the Acts Proscribe Only "Intentionally Harmful" Conduct

The plain language of the Acts belies Moon Lake's contention that the Acts regulate only "intentionally harmful" conduct....

The BGEPA, in contrast to § 707(a) of the MBTA, is not a strict liability crime. The BGEPA applies only to those who act "knowingly, or with wanton disregard for the consequences" of their acts. 16 U.S.C. § 668c; *see also* S. Rep. No. 92–1159, at 5, *reprinted in* 1972 U.S.C.C.A.N. 4285, 4289 (the defendant "must be conscious from his knowledge of surrounding circumstances and conditions that conduct will naturally and probably result in injury" to a protected bird). Accordingly, I reject Moon Lake's contention that the MBTA and the BGEPA prohibit only intentionally harmful conduct. Whether Moon Lake took or killed protected birds knowingly, or with wanton disregard for the consequences of its acts, is a question of fact for the jury's determination....

b. Whether the Acts Proscribe Only Physical Conduct Normally Associated with Hunting or Poaching

Moon Lake next argues that the Acts prohibit only physical conduct normally exhibited by hunters or poachers. After reviewing the plain language of the Acts, their respective legislative histories, and their designs as a whole, I disagree.

Congress modeled the BGEPA after the MBTA. Similar to the MBTA, the BGEPA proscribes taking, possessing, selling, purchasing, bartering, transporting, exporting, importing, pursuing, shooting, shooting at, poisoning, wounding, killing, capturing, trapping, collecting, molesting, and disturbing. 16 U.S.C. §§ 668(a) & 668c. Only taking, shooting, shooting at, capturing, and trapping constitute acts normally associated with hunting and poaching. By prohibiting "poisoning," "killing," "possessing," "molesting," and "disturbing" in addition to the acts normally associated with hunting, the BGEPA, like the MBTA, suggests that Congress intended to regulate conduct beyond the sort engaged in by hunters and poachers. And, as does the MBTA, the BGEPA proscribes taking or killing "at any time or in any manner." 16 U.S.C. § 668(a). I conclude, therefore, that the plain language of the Acts prohibits the alleged conduct of Moon Lake. *See Andrus,* 444 U.S. at 56 (describing the statutory prohibitions of the BGEPA as "comprehensive," "exhaustive," "carefully enumerated," "expansive," and "sweepingly framed"); *Mountain States Legal Foundation v. Hodel,* 799 F.2d 1423, 1427 (10th Cir.1986) (describing provisions of the BGEPA as "sweeping").

The BGEPA's legislative history, although sparse in comparison that of the MBTA, is less equivocal. In 1940, Congress passed, with little debate, "An Act for the Protection of the Bald Eagle." ... Congress amended the Act in 1962, extending protection to Golden Eagles.... Congress further amended the BGEPA in 1972, increasing its criminal penalties and reducing the *mens rea* required for conviction. [ ] Notably, during congressional hearings on the 1972 amendments, eagle electrocution was discussed before the Senate Committee on Commerce.... The following opinion letter was subsequently submitted for the record:

> We have your memorandum of July 19, 1972, inquiring as to the liability of power companies under the provisions of H.R.12186.
>
> The proposed legislation, in accordance with the protection provided by the third clause of Section 9 of Article I of the United States Constitution, could not be interpreted as operating ex post facto. This means that the power companies would not be liable for acts committed prior to the date of enactment. However, since power lines have a tendency to destroy eagles, such lines erected after the date of enactment should provide such safeguards as are available in order for the power companies to avoid the charge of acting with "negligent disregard for the consequences" of their acts. This obligation would be no more of a burden upon power companies than upon any other person or organization performing operations which had a tendency to destroy wildlife. In every case, reasonable precautions would have to be taken to prevent the killing of eagles.

(Ltr. from C. Brewster Chapman, Jr., Associate Solicitor, U.S. Department of the Interior, to Spencer H. Smith of 7/20/92, *reprinted in Hearings* at 24.) Thus, even if I did not regard the plain language of the BGEPA as conclusive, its legislative history suggests that it proscribes conduct beyond the sort typically exhibited by hunters and poachers.

In summary, I reject Moon Lake's argument that the Acts prohibit only physical conduct normally exhibited by hunters or poachers. After reviewing the plain language of the Acts, their respective legislative histories, and the judicial opinions cited by the parties, I conclude that the Acts must be interpreted as the government suggests....

Accordingly, I ORDER that defendant's motion to dismiss is DENIED.

NOTES

(1) Is the court's analysis persuasive? What was Moon Lake required to "know"? Did the *actus reus* in this situation involve an affirmative act or a failure to act despite a duty to do so? If mere knowledge of some likelihood of death is sufficient, does a foreseeable death violate the Act even if the defendant took all reasonable precautions?

(2) Zapped:

Of all the ways humans accidentally kill birds of prey, none of them is more needless than electrocuting them with ill-designed, poorly insulated power lines. . . .

Transmission towers—those marching giants hefting lines of at least 115,000 volts that hum and buzz and make your car radio sputter when you drive underneath—are rarely a problem, because the long insulators and wide gaps between wires prevent even eagles from completing circuits. The bird killers are the less-sinister looking distribution facilities—*i.e.,* lines that carry 34,500 volts or less. They can be made safe for birds by intelligent design or by retrofitting old poles with plastic insulators that slip over bare wires and conductors and by bolting triangular "perch guards," which prevent birds from touching down on the dangerous parts of crossarms. . . .

It wasn't until 1993 that the [Fish and Wildlife S]ervice finally cited a utility for violating the Migratory Bird Treaty Act. Special agents [Roger] Gephart and Frank Kuncir had investigated the electrocution of 10 raptors . . . by a single power pole owned by Pacific Gas and Electric in California's San Joaquin Valley. Under other poles Kuncir had discovered four golden eagles and 32 red-tails, barn owls, and ravens. Eventually, the company paid $1,500 in fines and agreed to retrofit. The only other ticket was issued on May 1, 1998, to Jack Mager, owner of Sand Point Electric, which serves a fishing village in southwest Alaska and whose lines had been killing about a dozen bald eagles a year. Mager paid a $500 fine and agreed to retrofit. . . .

While tickets may work for small companies, they don't always get the attention of the big ones. That is because if a ticket is paid, the violation is treated as a petty offense, with no admission of guilt. So the industry has been content to pursue business as usual, retrofitting when it gets yelled at and pounding itself on the chest for its work and awards. Now, however, it has been badly frightened by the example of Moon Lake.

Ted Williams, *Zapped!,* AUDUBON, Jan.-Feb. 2000 at 32, 32, 34, 41–42. Following the denial of its motion to dismiss the information, Moon Lake pleaded guilty and agreed to pay $100,000 in fines, to retrofit its poles, and to serve three years probation. *Id.* at 34.

c.   WILD BIRD CONSERVATION ACT OF 1992

NOTES

An outline of the Wild Bird Conservation Act: The Migratory Bird Treaty Act and the Bald and Golden Eagle Protection Act protect birds that are indigenous to the United States. The Wild Bird Conservation Act (WBCA), 16 U.S.C. §§ 4901–4916, on the other hand, protects "exotic birds"; that is, birds that are not naturally found within this country. 16 U.S.C. § 4903(2)(A).

(a) Findings and objectives: Congress found that "[p]opulations of many species of exotic wild birds ... have declined dramatically due to habitat loss and the public's demand for pet birds." H.R. REP. No. 102–749(II), 102d Cong., 2d Sess. 7 (1992), *reprinted in* 1992 U.S.C.C.A.N. 1592, 1610. These problems are compounded by the "unacceptably high" mortality rates of birds following capture: 30 to 50% die before leaving their country of origin and another 15% die during transit. *Id.* Since the United States is "the world's largest importer of exotic birds[, it] should play a substantial role in finding effective solutions to these problems." 16 U.S.C. § 4901(2). Enactment of the WBCA also reflected congressional recognition that the Convention on International Trade in Endangered Species of Fauna and Flora (CITES) had proven ineffective, in part because many exporting countries "lack the means to develop or effectively implement scientifically based management plans." *Id.* § 4901(7).

Congress therefore enacted the WBCA to promote the conservation of exotic birds by—

(1) assisting wild bird conservation and management programs in the countries of origin of wild birds;

(2) ensuring that all trade in species of exotic birds involving the United States is biologically sustainable and is not detrimental to the species;

(3) limiting or prohibiting imports of exotic birds when necessary to ensure that—

(A) wild exotic bird populations are not harmed by removal of exotic birds from the wild for the trade; or

(B) exotic birds in trade are not subject to inhumane treatment.

Id. § 4902.

(b) Moratoria and quotas on imports: To achieve these objectives, the WBCA seeks to regulate trade in wild-captured birds. It does so by statutorily establishing a moratorium on the importation of any species of exotic bird listed in any appendix of CITES.[1] *Id.* § 4904(c).

The WBCA also authorizes the Secretary to establish moratoria or import quotas on any species not listed under CITES. *Id.* § 4907. The Secretary may either establish a moratorium on the importation on any species of bird or on the importation of all species from any country. To bar the importation (or establish quotas) of birds by species, the Secretary must find that there is no "scientifically-based management plan" as required by § 4905(c)(2)-(3) and that the action is "necessary for the conservation of the species or is otherwise consistent with the purposes of this Act." *Id.* § 4907(a)(2)(A). He may prohibit the importation of all birds from a country if it "has not developed and implemented a management program

---

1. The Convention has three appendices that list species of birds. The first two appendices contain lists of endangered birds upon which the Convention signatories agree as a group; in the third appendix, individual nations may unilaterally list endangered birds. *Humane Society v. Babbitt*, 849 F.Supp. 814 (D.D.C.1994).

for exotic birds ... that ensures both the conservation and the humane treatment" of the birds. *Id.* § 4907(a)(2)(B).

(c) The Secretary's authority to lift moratoria: The Act authorizes the Secretary of the Interior to lift the moratorium on the importation of any species listed under CITES by including the species on the list of approved species. *Id.* § 4905. Two categories of birds may be included on the list. First, captive-bred birds may be included if "no wild-caught birds ... are in the trade" or the species "is bred in a qualifying facility."[2] *Id.* § 4905(b) Second, the moratorium on wild-caught birds may be lifted if the Secretary finds that CITES "is being effectively implemented with respect to that species [by e]ach country of origin for which the species is listed [based on a] scientifically-based management plan for the species." *Id.* § 4905(c).

(d) Prohibitions and penalties: The importation moratoria are enforced with both civil and criminal sanctions. The Act makes it unlawful to "import any exotic birds in violation of any prohibition, suspension, or quota." *Id.* § 4910(a)(1)(A). The Act establishes a two-tiered scienter requirement: a "person engaged in business as an importer of exotic birds" is strictly liable for civil penalties up to $25,000 for violating the act; other persons are liable only for "knowingly" violating the Act. *Id.* § 4912(a)(1)(A). The criminal penalty provisions follow the same pattern: strict liability for commercial importers and "knowing" liability for other persons. *Id.* § 4912(a)(2).

PERSPECTIVES

Free-market environmentalism: Among the congressional findings was one that explicitly reflected a free-market environmentalism perspective: "Sustainable utilization of exotic birds has the potential to create economic value in them and their habitats, which will contribute to their conservation and promote the maintenance of biological diversity generally." 16 U.S.C. § 4901(3).

The Act similarly requires as a condition of waiving importation moratoria that the exporting country must have a "scientifically-based management plan," which requires in part that the plan "provides for the conservation of the species and its habitat and *includes incentives for conservation.*" *Id.* § 4906(c)(2)(A).

d. NEOTROPICAL BIRD CONSERVATION ACT OF 1999

NOTES

An outline of the Neotropical Bird Conservation Act of 1999: Nearly two-thirds of the bird species that occur in the United States winter in Latin America and the Caribbean. The populations of many of these

---

2. Standards for determining whether a facility is a "qualifying facility" are set out in § 4906 and include a requirement that the Secretary find that "[t]he facility is operated in a manner that is not detrimental to the survival of the species in the wild" and that it is "operated in a humane manner." *Id.* § 4906(b)(2), (3).

species are in decline, primarily because of habitat loss and degradation. Recognizing these facts, Congress enacted the Neotropical Bird Conservation Act of 1999 (NBCA), 16 U.S.C. § 6101–6109. The Act seeks to "perpetuate healthy populations of neotropical migratory birds," to assist in the conservation of such birds "by supporting conservation efforts in the United States, Latin America, and the Caribbean," and to provide "financial resources and to foster international cooperation." *Id.* § 6102.

The Act seeks to achieve these objectives by directing the Secretary of the Interior to establish a program for funding projects to promote conservation of neotropical species. *Id.* § 6103. The federal share of the costs of projects cannot exceed 25%, although the non-federal share of projects outside the United States can be paid "in cash or in kind." *Id.* § 6104.

No monies have been appropriated to implement the statute.

SECTION 3.   PROTECTING FERAL HORSES AND BURROS

NOTES

The fight to save a memory: Following a letter-writing campaign by school children protesting the use of wild horses for dog food, Congress in 1959 adopted the Act Prohibiting the Use of Aircraft and Motor Vehicles to Hunt Feral Horse & Burros. This was followed a dozen years later with the Wild Free–Roaming Horses and Burros Act (WF–RHBA). For Congress, the feral horses and burros were swans: "living symbols of the historic and pioneer spirit of the West." 16 U.S.C. § 1331. Perhaps the pioneer rhetoric was appropriate since neither horses nor burros are indigenous to North America in the post-pleistocene era. *E.g.,* Kenneth A. Pitt, *The Wild Free–Roaming Horses and Burros Act: A Western Melodrama,* 15 ENVTL. L. 503 (1985). Regardless of its ironic aptness, the congressional rhetoric did accurately embody the perspective of those who pushed to have the feral horses and burros protected:

> On a memorable day in 1950, I came upon a truckload of mutilated horses as I was driving from our ranch to nearby Reno, where I work. I discovered that they were wild horses, captured in an airborne round-up. Their destination was a slaughter house, where the sole requirement was that the horses be ambulatory and plentiful. Their captors received six and one-half cents per pound. Because net profit depended upon quantity rather than upon condition, injury to the animals was of minimal concern.

> . . .

> At that time, twenty-one years ago, the practice of harvesting wild horses for use in commercial products had reached its peak. Their numbers had been reduced from two million to 25,000 in half a century, and the methods of gathering were ruthless and indiscriminate. If the exploitation had continued, these horses—so dramatically linked with our pioneer past—would literally have been wiped from the face of the earth. Burros, though not commercially exploited, fare no

better than horses. Claims of overpopulation and possible competition with native desert bighorn sheep led to systematic extermination programs.

The pet food industry had created a ready market for all the horses that could be caught, and exploiters were quick to take advantage of it. Since the old methods of running the horses by mounted horsemen was much too slow, cowboys took to the air. Low-flying airplanes drove the wild horses by the thousands at breakneck speed from their meager shelters in the rim rocks and canyons into the dry and barren flats below. To force the horses to turn or run faster, the airborne cowboys blasted them with sawed-off shotguns—never fatally, but sufficiently to terrify and maim. Injured and exhausted by their flight through the rugged terrain, the horses were no match for the fast trucks that continued the chase, the ropers, lashed to the cabs of the trucks, easily lassoed them. Tied to the end of the short were heavy truck tires, which the exhausted and frightened horses would drag around attempting to escape until they could fight no longer. Finally, thrown and tied by the feet, they were dragged up rough board ramps onto trucks where they were prodded to their feet and packed in tightly, their weight against each other often being all that held them on their feet. On the way to processing centers they were rarely, if ever, fed or watered. Because they weighed less, colts were often left to die from starvation or to become victims of predators.... Other methods of capture were conceived—all cruel. The operation was big business.

. . .

For most Americans, the mere knowledge that the Wild Ones still exist somewhere in the West instills a warm, comfortable feeling that not all of America as it used to be is lost and that they still have a link with the colorful past. Perhaps they remember, too, that the forebears of these animals were as alien to the shores of the New World as were our own forefathers and that together they settled the trackless wilderness, drove off Indian attacks, enforced law and order, brought civilization to this raw and young country, and carried the mail by Pony Express from Saint Jo to Sacramento and back again....

See Velma B. Johnson, *Review: The Fight to Save A Memory*, 50 TEX. L. REV. 1055, 1055–56 (1972) ("Wild Horse Annie" who led the efforts to protect wild horses).

a. ACT PROHIBITING THE USE OF AIRCRAFT & MOTOR VEHICLES TO HUNT FERAL HORSE & BURROS

NOTES

An outline of the Act: In 1959, Congress took the first steps to protect feral horses and burros by enacting a statute prohibiting the use of aircraft and motor vehicles "to hunt, for the purpose of capturing or killing" any wild horse or burro "running at large on any of the public lands." 18 U.S.C. § 47(a). The Act also prohibited the "pollution of any watering hole ... for the purpose of trapping, killing, wounding, or maiming" horses and burros. *Id.* § 47(b). Both offenses are punishable by fines, imprisonment for up to 6 months, or both.

The Act has been among the most successful federal criminal statutes since it apparently led to a complete cessation of the prohibited conduct—or, at least, it has produced no reported prosecutions.

b. WILD FREE–ROAMING HORSES & BURROS ACT OF 1971

NOTES

(1) The Wild Free–Roaming Horses & Burros Act of 1971, 16 U.S.C. §§ 1331–1340, provided two different types of management. First, the Act imposed an ambiguous land-management standard, which will be considered in the next chapter. Second—and most reflective of the animal welfare position of the backers of the legislation such as Wild Horse Annie—the Act placed all wild free-roaming horses and burros under federal "jurisdiction" and significantly restricted how the animals could be managed.

(2) An outline of the animal welfare provisions of the 1971 Act: The Act's substantive provisions begin with the assertion that "[a]ll wild free-roaming horses and burros are hereby declared to be under the jurisdiction of the Secretary of the Interior for the purpose of management and protection." 16 U.S.C. § 1333(a). Although the Secretary was directed to "manage wild free-roaming horses and burros ... to achieve and maintain a thriving natural ecological balance," *id.,* the Act nonetheless restricted the Secretary's power to destroy horses and burros. When an area was overpopulated, the Secretary could destroy "old, sick or lame animals ... in the most humane manner possible," and could have excess healthy animals "captured and removed for private maintenance under humane conditions and care." Wild Free–Roaming Horses & Burros Act of 1971, Pub. L. No. 92–195, § 3(b), 85 Stat. 649, 650. Furthermore, no healthy animals were to be destroyed because of overpopulation unless that was "the only practical way to remove excess animals." *Id.* § 3(c).

The Act also protected horses and burros against private individuals. It was made illegal for any person "willfully" to remove a wild free-roaming horse or burro from public lands, to convert a wild free-roaming horse or burro to private use, to "maliciously" cause the death or harassment of a wild free-roaming horse or burro, to process a wild free-roaming horse or burro "into commercial products," or to sell a wild free-roaming horse or burro. 16 U.S.C. § 1338(a).

(3) The 1978 amendments: In 1978, Congress amended the animal welfare provisions of the WF–RHBA. The Secretary was ordered to remove excess animals following a specified priority:

(A) The Secretary shall order old, sick, or lame animals to be destroyed in the most humane manner possible;

(B) The Secretary shall cause such number of additional excess wild free-roaming horses and burros to be humanely captured and removed for private maintenance and care for which he determines an adoption demand exists by qualified individuals, and for which he determines he can assure humane treatment and care . . .; and

(C) The Secretary shall cause additional excess wild free-roaming horses and burros for which an adoption demand by qualified individuals does not exist to be destroyed in the most humane and cost efficient manner possible.

Id. § 1333(b)(2).

The adoption program has been plagued with problems and controversy:

Animal Protection Institute, Inc. v. Hodel

Ninth Circuit Court of Appeals.
860 F.2d 920 (1988).

■ CHOY, J.:—The United States Secretary of the Interior and subordinate officials ("Secretary") appeal from the district court's grant of summary judgment for the Animal Protection Institute of America, Inc. and the Fund for Animals, Inc. ("the API"). The district court enjoined the Secretary from transferring the titles of wild horses and burros to persons who the Secretary knows intend to use the animals for commercial purposes upon receiving title. [ ] We affirm.

In 1971, Congress passed the Wild Free–Roaming Horses and Burros Act ("WHA") to preserve from "capture, branding, harassment, or death" wild horses and burros found on public lands as these animals were considered "living symbols of the historic and pioneer spirit of the West" that "enrich[ed] the lives of the American people." 16 U.S.C. § 1331. The WHA authorized the removal of excess wild horses and animals from public lands for private maintenance under humane conditions and care. 16 U.S.C. § 1333(b) (amended 1978). Under this grant of authority, the Secretary instituted its "adopt-a-horse" program by which individuals could "adopt" wild horses or burros. *See* 43 C.F.R. § 4740.2(b) (1977).

In 1978, as part of the Public Rangelands Improvement Act, Congress amended the WHA. The amendments set a limit of four on the number of excess animals an individual could adopt, absent a written finding by the Secretary that the individual could humanely care for more than four animals. 16 U.S.C. § 1333(b)(2)(B). The amendments specified that an adopter must be a "qualified individual" who could "assure humane treatment and care" for his animals. *Id.* The amendments also authorized the Secretary to grant adopters title to animals if the adopters were "qualified individuals" and had humanely treated the animal or animals in their care for a year. *Id.* § 1333(c).

In May 1984, the Bureau of Land Management ("BLM") published regulations that allowed it to waive adoption fees for wild horses or burros that were considered "unadoptable" at the adoption fee of $125 per horse or $75 per burro. [ ]

On September 11, 1985, the API filed a complaint in district court seeking declaratory and injunctive relief against the Secretary. The API claimed that the Secretary was violating the WHA in its roundup practices and maintenance of excess wild horses and burros, and in its adoption procedures for excess animals. The API alleged a statutory basis for its lawsuit under the Administrative Procedure Act, which allows a party "suffering legal wrong because of agency action, or adversely affected or aggrieved by agency action" to seek judicial review. [ ]

The parties eventually signed a stipulation settling the claims concerning the roundup and maintenance of wild equids. The dispute concerning adoption procedures remained unresolved. The API alleged that the Secretary's fee-waiver adoption program violated congressional intent under the WHA by facilitating the commercial exploitation of wild horses and burros. Specifically, the API claimed that entrepreneurs used the fee-waiver program in conjunction with the granting of powers of attorney to secure title to wild equids for commercial purposes. On cross-motions for summary judgment, however, the API limited its claim for relief to situations in which the Secretary transfers title to adopters knowing that they intend to use the animals for commercial purposes once they receive title. The district court subsequently granted the API injunctive relief, holding that when the Secretary has actual knowledge that an adopter intends to commercially exploit animals upon receipt of legal title, the Secretary may not transfer title to that adopter. The Secretary timely appeals.

. . .

To prevent the ruinous overpopulation of public lands by wild horses and burros, Congress has authorized the Secretary to remove "excess animals from the range." 16 U.S.C. § 1333(b)(2). The Secretary must humanely destroy "old, sick, or lame" excess animals. *Id.* § 1333(b)(2)(A). The healthy excess animals remain eligible for adoption by private parties if the Secretary determines that the prospective adopters are "qualified individuals" and the Secretary determines that these individuals "can assure humane treatment and care" for the animals. *Id.* § 1333(b)(2)(B). After taking care of the animals for a year, adopters may receive legal title to the animals if the Secretary determines that in the interim the adopters have remained "qualified individuals" and have provided "humane conditions, treatment and care" for the animals. *Id.* § 1333(c). Upon transfer of title, the animals no longer fall within the provisions of the WHA. *Id.* § 1333(d)(1).

The Secretary interprets this statutory scheme as imposing only one precondition on adopters for receiving title: adopters must provide humane treatment and care for one year. After this year period, the Secretary may transfer title even if he knows beforehand that once the adopters receive title, they will put the animals to commercial use.

However, section 1333(b)(2)(B) instructs the Secretary to make the initial determination that adopters are both "qualified individuals" and persons who "can assure humane treatment and care." Section 1333(c), in authorizing the transfer of title to adopters, requires the Secretary to insure that an adopter who seeks title remains a "qualified individual" and one who "has provided humane conditions, treatment and care" for the animals he has maintained. This language indicates that an adopter's assurance of humane treatment and care is not enough to warrant transfer of title; the adopter must also be a qualified individual. Viewed in light of the WHA's other statutory provisions that explicitly forbid the commercial exploitation of wild equids, *see id.* §§ 1333(d)(5); 1338(a)(4), and strive to insure their humane treatment, *see id.* §§ 1333(b)(2), 1333(c), 1338(a)(3), 1338a, it would be unreasonable to maintain that Congress intended a qualified individual to include a person who has expressed an intent to commercially exploit these "living symbols of the historic and pioneer spirit" that "enrich the lives of the American people." *See id.* § 1331.

A review of the legislative history confirms the assessment that the Secretary's position contravenes congressional intent....

Legislative history thus reveals that Congress intended the one-year wait for title transfer to act as a probationary period that would weed out unfit adopters. The Secretary's disregard for the announced future intentions of adopters undercuts Congress' desire to insure humane treatment for wild horses and burros. In fact, it renders the adoption process a farce, for the one-year requirement of humane treatment and care serves no purpose if on the day the one-year period expires, the adopter can proceed to the slaughterhouse with his horses or burros.

. . .

[T]he Secretary's practice of transferring title to adopters who the Secretary knows will commercially exploit the animals they adopt contravenes congressional intent.... Accordingly, we AFFIRM the district court's judgment.

NOTES

(1) Does the management structure that has evolved for feral equids make sense ecologically and morally? Are the ethics of turning captured feral horses into pet food different in any meaningful way from the ethics of using domestic horses or cattle for the same purpose? If large mammals are to be used for pet food—and the idea of vegetarian cats and dogs seems an oxymoron—is it better to raise the animals in the wild or in captivity?

(2) *Mens rea*: The Act imposes criminal sanctions on any person who

(1) willfully removes or attempts to remove a wild free-roaming horse or burro from the public land ... , or

(2) converts a wild free-roaming horse or burro to private use ... , or

(3) maliciously causes the death or harassment of any wild free-roaming horse or burro, or

(4) processes ... into commercial products the remains of a wild free-roaming horse or burro, or

(5) sells ... a wild free-roaming horse or burro ... , or

(6) willfully violates a regulation issued pursuant to this Act.

16 U.S.C. § 1338(a). What is the *mens rea* requirement for each offense?

PERSPECTIVES

(1) The Bambi syndrome: Susan M. Schectman examined several controversies involving wild deer and feral burros in national parks. Because of their reproductive and behavioral patterns, such species tend to be "irruptive"—their populations explode and then crash. Ms. Schectman's conclusions are a challenge to those who urge the protection of wild horses and burros:

> .... Non-native burros and native deer have increased in important scenic areas to the point where severe impacts are occurring to flora, fauna, and soil. Proper wildlife management requires reduction, and as a practical matter this can only be accomplished by shooting. Since there is an overpopulation of burros on southwestern public lands, there is a shortage of facilities which will accept burros relocated from crowded areas. But attempts to reduce herds have been delayed by NEPA actions and lengthy public involvement procedures....
>
> · · ·
>
> [When NPS determined that it was necessary to reduce the population of burros in one national park by shooting them,] media response was quick, severe, and emotional. Indicative of media coverage were reports that NPS rangers sought park personnel without the "Bambi Syndrome," a tendency to sympathize with and anthropomorphize burros instead of maintaining a professional and technical viewpoint. One radio station defined the "Bambi Syndrome" as a "reluctance to shoot harmless creatures." ...
>
> [T]he "Bambi Syndrome" subverted the [public] involvement process [required by NEPA]. The public was concerned with individual animals and not their ecosystem as a whole, and seemed to respond more to emotional media presentations than technical assessments prepared by the managers. Skepticism towards the managers and emotionalism created by Walt Disney-like misconceptions of wildlife jeopardized the information function [of the NEPA process]. The sentimental value of individual wildlife to the public became clear, but the decision-makers obtained few valuable comments or feasible alternatives: many suggested alternatives ranged from the emotional to the fanciful to the irrational.[105] While the information function was partially served, managers felt that the public was often not interested in staff assessments.... In no case did the public suggest a feasible alternative that the staff had not previously considered. The public's "Bambi Syndrome" was simply incompatible with sound resource management.

105. Suggested alternatives have included: shipment of burros to Mexico for food; use of burros for children's rides; continuous artificial feeding; maintenance of a burro herd despite adverse conditions to allow "survival of the fittest;" maintenance of a burro herd since the burro saved many pioneer lives; maintenance of a burro herd since the burro was ridden by Jesus and its dorsal/ventral stripe resembles a cross; retention of exotic burros since most Americans are also non-native; shipment of burros back to Somaliland, their native habitat. [ ]

Susan M. Schectman, *The "Bambi Syndrome:" How NEPA's Public Participation in Wildlife Management is Hurting the Environment*, 8 ENVTL. L. 611, 613, 630, 633 (1978).

(2) Animal rights and ecosystem management: The initial version of the Wild Free–Roaming Horses and Burros Act contained "obscure and arguably conflicting management standards." MICHAEL J. BEAN & MELANIE J. ROWLAND, THE EVOLUTION OF NATIONAL WILDLIFE LAW 395 (3d ed. 1997). On the one hand, Congress stated that the horses and burros were "to be considered in the area where presently found as an integral part of the natural system of the public lands." 16 U.S.C. § 1331. This suggests that the animals were to be treated as other types of resources under multiple use-management. On the other hand, the Act reduced management discretion—for example, horses and burros could be destroyed only if "such action is necessary to preserve and maintain the habitat in a suitable condition for continued use" and destruction is "the only practical way to remove excess animals from the area." Pub. L. 92–195, § 3, 85 Stat. 649 (current version at 16 U.S.C. § 1333(b)).

One result were two cases that highlighted the Act's ambiguities. In *American Horse Protection Association, Inc. v. Frizzell*, the court rejected the argument that "wild horses were given a higher priority on the public lands than other grazers" under the Act. 403 F.Supp. 1206 (D.Nev.1975). Since wild horses had no special status, the Secretary had broad discretion to remove animals determined to be in excess of the forage previously allocated to wildlife. In contrast, the decision in *American Horse Protection Association v. Kleppe* adopted a far more restrictive view of the Secretary's discretion. The court found a proposed roundup of horses to be arbitrary and capricious because the agency's estimates of the number of horses were "unreliable." 6 Envtl. L. Rep. (Envtl. L. Inst.) 20802, 20803 (D.D.C.1976). Furthermore, the Act mandated that the agency give "careful and detailed consideration . . . to *all* alternative courses of action that would have less severe impact on the wild horse population." *Id.* at 20804. Finally, the agency's failure to have a veterinarian on hand or on call during the roundup violated the Act's requirements that removals be carried out under "humane conditions and care." *Id.* In the court's view, wild horses were, at least, the first among equals.

Congress significantly amended the Act in 1978. First, it struck a new balance—or, perhaps, clarified the balance it intended to strike in 1971—between protecting wild horses and competing resources on the public lands. Second, Congress concluded that prompt action was needed to redress the imbalance that had developed and directed that excess horses be removed expeditiously. The main thrust of the 1978 amendments thus was to reduce the protection afforded wild horses and to reemphasize other uses of the resources wild horses consume. To this end, the amendments defined "excess" horses: horses are "excess" if they "must be removed from an area in order to preserve and maintain a thriving natural ecological balance and multiple-use relationship in that area." 16 U.S.C. § 1332(f). This definition makes explicit what was, at most, implicit in the 1971 Act: public ranges are to be managed for multiple uses, not merely for the maximum protection of wild horses. *See generally American Horse Protection Association v. Watt,* 694 F.2d 1310 (D.C.Cir.1982).

The management decisions facing the BLM involve an allocation of existing forage among livestock, wildlife (generally big game species), and wild horses. Whether a given population of horses is excess depends significantly on whether, under the applicable management plan, wild animals (including horses) are allocated 1%, 10% or 50% of a range's total forage (for many years they were often allocated just 1%). Does the definition of "excess" in the 1978 amendments provide a standard for determining proper forage allocations or does the reference to "multiple use relationship" give the managing agency nearly unlimited discretion? Might BLM remove all wild horses from an area as "excess" if that action were consistent with the agency's selected multiple-use goals?

SECTION 4.   MANAGING COMMERCIAL SPECIES

NOTES

Maximum sustainable yield: Wildlife species that are commercially valuable have customarily been managed to achieve "maximum sustainable yield" (MSY). The logic of this objective is beguiling since it is nearly a restatement of the utilitarian objective of the greatest good for the greatest number. MSY is simply the largest catch that can be harvested on a sustainable basis. It is a concept rooted in a mechanistic, economic view of nature.

> Sustainable harvests can be taken from a range of population densities but, in theory, the greatest harvest can be taken when net recruitment [*i.e.*, additions to the stock] is at its maximum. This must always be at some density below K [carrying capacity, *i.e.*, the maximum population that will exists in equilibrium with its environment] because at K deaths cancel births and there is zero net recruitment. Once a population at K has been reduced by an initial harvest, a subsequent sustainable yield (SY) can be calculated as a fraction of the reduced size.... [Mathematically,] the maximum sustainable yield (MSY) would be from the density at half the carrying capacity ($1/2\ K$) but in real populations the [maximum yield] may occur at a density which is much higher than 50% of carrying capacity. Values from 0.65 K to 0.9 K have been suggested for animals which breed slowly, such as marine mammals.

M.   Bolton, *Sustainability, in* CONSERVATION AND THE USE OF WILDLIFE RESOURCES 35, 39 (M. Bolton ed., 1997). *See generally* FRANCIS T. CHRISTY & ANTHONY SCOTT, THE COMMON WEALTH IN OCEAN FISHERIES 7–15, 215–21 (1965).

Although MSY is seductive, it has proved remarkably unsuccessful as a wildlife management strategy:

> Estimates of allowable catches—those that were believed to be sustainable—were made from a well-known equation developed in the study of populations, the S-shaped logistic growth curve. First proposed

in 1849 by Pierre–Francois Verhulst, a Belgian scientist, the curve is a description of how a population grows from a small number to its final limiting and sustaining abundance, which is known as the *carrying capacity*. In the twentieth century, several experiments demonstrated that populations of bacteria or certain insects grow according to Verhulst's equation if they are maintained under constant environmental conditions and provided with a constant supply of food.... The mathematics that generates this curve includes the idea that the population is stable in a classic sense: it will achieve an abundance that will remain constant forever unless disturbed, and once disturbed (increased above or decreased below its carrying capacity), the population will return to the same abundance. Scientists extrapolated from these experiments to the world outside the laboratory windows and assumed that the logistic could describe the growth of populations in the wilderness.

The logistic equation leads to a simple calculation of the population size that has the maximum growth, which turns out to be the population that is exactly one-half as large as the carrying capacity. This population size is known as the *maximum-sustainable-yield* population. If the mathematics were a true description of nature, the population could be allowed to grow each year above the maximum-sustainable yield level and then be harvested down to it. Like clockwork, the population would grow back exactly the same amount each year, and a precisely sustainable harvest could be obtained year after year.

For the maximum-sustainable-yield concept to work, several things must be true. The population must have an exact and single carrying capacity, and its growth must follow exactly the logistic curve. It must be possible to know precisely both the carrying capacity and the present population size. It must be possible to obtain complete cooperation from all harvesters so that exactly the right number is harvested each year.

For the maximum-sustainable-yield concept to be employed successfully a measurement problem must be solved. But this is rarely solved in the management of wild populations to the level of precision required....

The ideas underlying the maximum-sustainable-yield concept are ... the belief that nature undisturbed by human beings achieves a constancy that remains indefinitely, and that if disturbed, nature recovers its former status. The formal management of marine fisheries was based on the belief that nature undisturbed is constant and stable.

. . .

Managing fisheries exemplifies the challenge of managing a population that varies over time, and about which we always know too little. This presents an economic problem because fishermen would like to have a reliable, high, profitable, and constant harvest every year. However, fish populations vary in an apparently random fashion. Under the old management, the approach was to manage for a maximum sustainable yield or an optimum sustainable yield as calculated from the logistic growth equation. Under the old perspective, the optimum harvest simply took into account the uncertainty in measurements, but did not consider complexity or inherent random variations in populations.

DANIEL B. BOTKIN, DISCORDANT HARMONIES 20–21, 22, 199 (1990).

a.   MARINE MAMMAL PROTECTION ACT OF 1972

NOTES

(1) The Treaty for the Preservation and Protection of Fur Seals (1911), the Interim Convention on the Conservation of North Pacific Fur Seals (1957), and beyond: One of the first federal conservation efforts sought to protect a marine mammal, the North Pacific fur seal. The species life history raised issues similar to those presented by migratory birds: born on American-owned islands, the fur seals spent much of their lives in international waters. The United States asserted ownership over the valuable fur-bearers because of their place of birth; Canada and Britain responded with claims of freedom of the high seas. While the parties argued, the seal population collapsed 90%. The crash had a sobering effect and in 1911 the three parties, Japan, and Russia agreed upon a treaty that outlawed pelagic sealing and divided the land-based harvest among the signatories. The Treaty for the Preservation and Protection of Fur Seals, July 7, 1911, 37 Stat. 1542, T.S. No. 564. *See* Chapter 8.

Japan withdrew from the treaty in 1940 and it expired. Between 1941 and 1957, an agreement between the United States and Canada governed the harvest. In 1957, a new agreement between Canada, Japan, the Soviet Union, and the United States went into effect. The Interim Convention on the Conservation of North Pacific Fur Seals, Feb. 9, 1957, 8 U.S.T. 2283, T.I.A.S. No. 3948, 314 U.N.T.S. 105, reaffirmed the basic tenets of the 1911 Treaty. The Interim Convention was extended until 1988 when a steep decline in the population of fur seals plus a strong effort by animal welfare groups prevented United States' ratification of the protocol to extend the agreement. The seals are now covered by the Marine Mammal Protection Act.

(2) An introduction to the MMPA: The Marine Mammal Protection Act of 1972, 16 U.S.C. §§ 1361–1407, marked a transition in federal wildlife law. Previously, the federal government had not created comprehensive conservation programs for any wildlife other than migratory waterfowl—and even then, the program focused primarily on the regulation of hunting. Other federal statutes either reinforced state law—the Lacey Act, for example—protected individual species—for example, the Bald and Golden Eagle Protection Act—or prohibited certain types of conduct—the Airborne Hunting Act of 1971, for example.

Adoption of the Endangered Species Preservation Act of 1966, the Endangered Species Conservation Act of 1969, and the Wild Free–Roaming Horses and Burros Act of 1972 reflected the emergence of a new consensus that a broader perspective was necessary, but the programs that these acts established were tentative and unassuming. The MMPA's focus on populations and ecosystems was an ambitious break with the past. George Coggins has described it with admirable economy as "a technical and complex effort to restore and protect a variety of wildlife populations living in differing biological communities under a variety of legal conditions." George C. Coggins, *Federal Wildlife Law Achieves Adolescence: Developments in the 1970s,* 1978 DUKE L.J. 753, 786.

The MMPA had a number of features that were distinctive at the time it was adopted. While most previous federal legislation had at least employed language deferential to state management of wildlife, the MMPA expressly preempted all state law "relating to the taking of any species . . . of marine mammal," 16 U.S.C. § 1379(a), and substituted a comprehensive federal program based on the preservation of population stocks. *Id.* §§ 1372, 1362(10). While it preempted state law, the MMPA also established procedures and standards whereby a state could resume management authority over marine mammals. *Id.* § 1379. Central to the federal program was a moratorium of indefinite duration "on the taking and importation of marine mammals and marine mammal products." *Id.* § 1371(a). The Act provided for lifting the moratorium on takings when a population achieved certain levels. *Id.* §§ 1373, 1374.

The management standard of the MMPA thus focuses on populations. But, as one early review of the Act stated, although "[t]he population policy of the MMPA is its most substantial and innovative component," it was also "the most intricate and the most poorly articulated component of the Act: poorly articulated in its purpose, intricate in its implementation." Sanford E. Gaines & Dale R. Schmidt, *Wildlife Population Management under the Marine Mammal Protection Act of 1972,* 6 Envtl. L. Rep. (Envtl. L. Inst.) 50,096, 50,101 (1976).

Beyond all of its details, the MMPA was the most important piece of wildlife legislation before the Endangered Species Act because of its audacity: it was an ambitious attempt to protect and restore the populations of a diverse group of species including whales, porpoises, seals, walruses, manatees, polar bears, and sea otters. A brief review of the various species can be found in George C. Coggins, *Legal Protection for Marine Mammals: An Overview of Innovative Resource Conservation Legislation,* 6 ENVTL. L. 1, 3–10 (1975).

PERSPECTIVES

(1) Conflicting and overlapping interests: The legislative history of the MMPA is complicated by the large number of bills that were introduced—six in the House and seven in the Senate. The various bills reflected three of the recurrent positions on wildlife that we have examined: the utilitarian, ecological-conservationist, and animal welfare-animal rights. Michael Bean and Melanie Rowland offer a concise description of the three positions:

> By the early 1970s, pressure from many diverse interests had grown for a comprehensive and coordinated program to conserve the world's marine mammals. The pressures arose out of diverse perspectives.

Commercial interests, some scientists, and traditionalists in the conservation community believed that marine mammals were an important commercial and food resource that, with proper management, could be used indefinitely through sustained harvests. Other members of the scientific and conservation communities believed that because marine mammals played an important ecological role in marine systems, the first priority of federal policy ought to be to maintain their populations for ecological reasons. A third group comprised those who believed that marine mammals, because of their apparent intelligence and highly developed social systems, ought to be left undisturbed and made off-limits to human use. This group was motivated primarily by their concern for the welfare of individual animals.

MICHAEL J. BEAN & MELANIE J. ROWLAND, *supra,* at 109–10. *See generally* Sanford E. Gaines & Dale R. Schmidt, *supra,* at 50,103–08.

(2) The animal welfare/animal rights perspective: The animal welfare/animal rights perspective is well and passionately presented in an article that was published while Congress was debating the bills:

Ocean mammals everywhere are being subjected to slaughter and suffering at the hand of man. Two species—Stellar's Sea Cow and the sea mink—have already been rendered extinct. Stellar, in his journal, described the former animal as having shown "signs of a wonderful intelligence . . . indeed, an uncommon love for one another, which even extended so far that, when one of them was hooked, all the others were intent upon saving it." The biological cousins of Stellar's Sea Cow, the Manatee and the Dugong, exhibit similar human qualities and are noted particularly for their ostensible affection for man. Such behavior has, of course, facilitated not only their study but their killing as well, as the few of these mammals are rapidly being destroyed.

All of the other species of ocean mammals, including seals, sea otters, cetaceans (whales, dolphins, and porpoises), walruses, sea lions, and polar bears, are either nearing extinction or are in a seriously depleted state. None of the killing of these animals can be justified; all of it is being done for frivolous commercial reasons or unnecessary "scientific research." Many scientists are now questioning whether these animals will be able to survive the increasing pollution of the oceans. But one thing is clear: if these unique creatures are to be preserved for future generations, the killing must be stopped and stopped soon.

Persons with a humane interest in ocean mammals reject theories of "conservation" that are based on "sustained yield," "harvest," and "wildlife management." "Management" is as fraudulent and cruel a concept of conservation as "benevolent dictatorship" is of government. The killing of wildlife by harvesters and managers is no less bloody than that done by hunters and poachers. What is wanted by those who are "friends of the animals" is very simple: that ocean mammals be left alone. They should be neither harassed, killed, managed, nor harvested.

Alice Herrington & Lewis Regenstein, *The Plight of Ocean Mammals,* 1 ENVTL. AFFAIRS 792, 792–93 (1972).

(i) A NOTE ON STRUCTURE

NOTES

(1) Division of responsibility between Departments of the Interior and Commerce: Responsibility for implementation of the MMPA is divided between the Secretary of Commerce—acting through the National Marine Fisheries Service (NMFS), an agency in the National Oceanic and Atmospheric Agency (NOAA)—and the Secretary of the Interior—acting through the Fish and Wildlife Service (FWS). Commerce is responsible for "members of the order Cetacea [whales and porpoises] and members, other than walruses, of the order Pinipeda [seals]." 16 U.S.C. § 1362(12)(A)(i). It is also responsible for regulating the taking of all marine mammals (except sea otters) incidental to commercial fishing operations. *Id.* §§ 1362(12)(B), 1387(a)(4). Interior has responsibility for "all other marine mammals." *Id.* § 1362(12)(A)(ii); these are manatees, dugongs, polar bears, sea otters, and walruses.

(2) The Marine Mammal Commission: The Act also establishes an independent advisory board, the Marine Mammal Commission. *Id.* § 1401(a). The Commission is composed of three members appointed by the President with the advice and consent of the Senate. The appointees are selected from a list unanimously adopted by the Chair of the Council on Environmental Quality, the Secretary of the Smithsonian Institution, the Director of the National Science Foundation, and the Chair of the National Academy of Sciences; the list is to include only individuals "knowledgeable in the fields of marine ecology and resource management, and who are not in a position to profit from the taking of marine mammals," *id.* § 1401(b)(1).

The Commission is to "undertake a review and study of the activities of the United States pursuant to existing laws and international agreements relating to marine mammals" and to "conduct a continuing review of the stocks of marine mammals, [and] methods for their protection and conservation." *Id.* § 1402(a)(1)-(2). Based on these reviews and supporting studies, the Commission is to consult with the Secretaries, *id.* § 1402(b), and to recommend steps "necessary or desirable for the protection and conservation of marine mammals," *id.* § 1402(a)(4). Although the Commission is restricted to a consultative role, the Act requires the Secretaries to respond within 120 days to any recommendations made by the Commission; if the Secretary does not adopt the recommendation, he is required to send the Commission "a detailed explanation of the reasons why those recommendations were not followed or adopted." *Id.* § 1402(d).

In structuring the Commission, Congress sought to create an independent advisory body whose members would be insulated from partisan politics so that they could provide expert scientific advice to the Secretaries—two political appointees. The structure is intended to ensure the scientific integrity of the Commission. In requiring the Secretaries to respond within a specific time to all recommendations, Congress removed one of the bureaucracy's most frequently employed tools: delay. By requiring the Secretaries to provide "a detailed explanation" for refusing to follow Commission recommendations, Congress gave science a greater role in decisionmaking since agency "expertise" is removed as a trump card in challenges to decisions in which the Secretary has chosen not to follow a recommendation.

Courts that have faced this issue properly have given deference to the Commission rather than the Secretary. *Animal Welfare Institute v. Kreps,* 561 F.2d 1002 (D.C.Cir.1977) (setting aside regulation permitting import of seal skins as contrary to statute and, relying upon statements by Marine Mammal Commission, as lacking in any biological basis); *Committee for Humane Legislation, Inc. v. Richardson,* 414 F.Supp. 297 (D.D.C.1976) (relying upon Commission testimony and statements in evaluating agency decision to grant permits allowing incidental taking of yellowfin tuna).

(ii) "OPTIMUM SUSTAINABLE POPULATION"

NOTES

(1) The "primary objective" and MSY v. OSP: The "primary objective" of the MMPA is "to maintain the health and stability of the marine ecosystem." 16 U.S.C. § 1361(6). The Act thus seeks to broaden the perspective that has traditionally been used to manage commercially valuable wildlife by moving beyond "maximum sustainable yield" (MSY). Although Congress rejected MSY as the appropriate management standard, it struggled to define an alternative, more biologically based standard. Eventually, it settled on "optimum sustainable population" (OSP). The Act defined OSP as "the number of animals which will result in the maximum productivity of the population or species, keeping in mind the optimum carrying capacity of the habitat and the health of the ecosystem of which they form a constituent element." 16 U.S.C. § 1362(8) (current amended version). The standard thus is an amalgam of protectionist and utilitarian/managerial perspectives:

> The use of "population" rather than the conventional management term "yield" as the basic criterion reflects the protectionist focus on the maintenance of live animals in their natural state. Yet the implicit assumption that a certain population level for each species is optimal, and that the populations should be actively managed for that level, adopts the managerial view that positive control is preferable to abstention from human interference and is often necessary to protect the integrity of the ecosystem.

Sanford E. Gaines & Dale R. Schmidt, *supra,* at 50,101.

The term "OSP" has been defined by regulation as "a population size which falls within range from the population level of a given species or stock which is the largest supportable within the ecosystem to the population level that results in the maximum net productivity. Maximum net productivity is the greatest net annual increment in population numbers or biomass resulting from additions to the population due to reproduction and/or growth less losses due to natural mortality." 50 C.F.R. § 216.3. Does this approach differ from the logistic curve approach embedded in MSY? Daniel Botkin concluded that it did not: "the scientists [advising the agency on the meaning of OSP] returned to the same logistic growth curve that they had used in fisheries management, defining optimum sustainable population in terms of this curve.... This choice of a meaning for optimum sustainable population retained the assumption that the population follows the classic logistic curve and that it does in fact have a fixed carrying-capacity and absolute maximum-sustainable-yield level." DANIEL B. BOTKIN, DISCORDANT HARMONIES 23 (1990). In practice, the OSP has been set at 60% of the carrying capacity population—a figure 10% higher than the MSY level.

It should be noted that OSP focuses on populations independently of habitat. As a result, the primary management tool is a moratorium—a "complete cessation," 16 U.S.C. § 1362(7)—of indefinite duration "on the taking and importation of marine mammals and marine mammal products." *Id.* § 1371(a).

(2) "Depleted": The Act's prohibitions on taking and importing marine mammals can be waived in certain circumstances that often turn on whether the species is "depleted." This term is defined by the Act as "a species or population stock [that] is below its optimum sustainable population" or "a species or population stock [that] is listed as an endangered species or a threatened species under the Endangered Species Act." 16 U.S.C. § 1362(1)(A)-(C).

(iii) PROHIBITIONS AND PENALTIES

(A) The Taking Prohibition

Strong v. United States

Fifth Circuit Court of Appeals.
5 F.3d 905 (1993).
[Chapter 1].

United States v. Hayashi

Ninth Circuit Court of Appeals.
22 F.3d 859 (1993).

■ REINHARDT, J.:—David Hayashi appeals his conviction of taking a marine mammal in violation of 16 U.S.C. § 1372(a)(2)(A). We hold that the Marine Mammal Protection Act (MMPA) and the regulations implementing the act do not make it a crime to take reasonable steps to deter porpoises from eating fish or bait off a fisherman's line. Therefore, we conclude that insufficient evidence supported Hayashi's conviction, and we reverse.

I

On the morning of January 24, 1991, Hayashi, a part-time commercial fisherman, and his son were fishing for Ahi off the coast of Waianae, Hawaii. A group of four porpoises began to eat the tuna off Hayashi's and his son's lines. Hoping the impact of the bullets hitting the water would scare the porpoises away from their catch, Hayashi fired two rifle shots into the water behind the porpoises. The shots did not hit the porpoises. When the Hayashis reeled in their lines, they discovered that a porpoise had in fact eaten a part of at least one of the tuna.

A state enforcement officer reported to the National Marine Fisheries Service (NMFS) that occupants of Hayashi's vessel had fired at dolphins. In February 1991, NMFS agents interviewed Hayashi and his son, taking written statements from each. An April 22, 1991 information charged Hayashi with knowingly taking a marine mammal in violation of the MMPA, 16 U.S.C. § 1372(a)(2)(A).

[Hayashi was tried and convicted by a magistrate judge tried and convicted on stipulated facts; without oral argument, the district court affirmed the conviction.]

II

The MMPA declares it unlawful for any person to "take" a marine mammal in United States waters. See 16 U.S.C. § 1372(a)(2)(A). "The term 'take' means to harass, hunt, capture, or kill, or attempt to harass, hunt, capture, or kill any marine mammal." 16 U.S.C. § 1362(13). The MMPA prescribes both civil and criminal penalties, but the latter apply only to persons who "knowingly" violate any provision of the act. See 16 U.S.C. § 1375(b).

The government agrees that the only definition of "take" with possible application to Hayashi is "to harass" or "attempt to harass." The statute itself fails to define "harass." Various agencies of the federal government have promulgated regulations implementing the MMPA. The regulations applicable to porpoises, issued by the NMFS, do not define "harass" but further define "take" as including:

> The collection of dead animals, or parts thereof; the restraint or detention of a marine mammal, no matter how temporary; tagging a marine mammal; the negligent or intentional operation of an aircraft or vessel, or the doing of any other negligent or intentional act which results in disturbing or molesting a marine mammal; and feeding or attempting to feed a marine mammal in the wild.

50 C.F.R. § 216.3.[3] The "disturbing or molesting" example is the only regulatory definition potentially applicable to Hayashi's act of firing a rifle into the water behind a group of porpoises to scare them away from his fishing lines. We conclude that the regulation does not reach the conduct underlying Hayashi's conviction.

. . .

Following the "familiar principle of statutory construction that words grouped in a list should be given related meaning," we look to the other

---

3. The final "feeding" clause was added to section 216.3 by an amendment effective April 19, 1991. [ ] The amendment was therefore not in effect, although it had been proposed, when Hayashi committed the charged acts. It was in effect, however, when the information charging Hayashi was filed, and when he was tried.

statutory and regulatory examples of "taking." [ ] The statute groups "harass" with "hunt," "capture," and "kill" as forms of prohibited "taking." The latter three each involve direct and significant intrusions upon the normal, life-sustaining activities of a marine mammal; killing is a direct and permanent intrusion, while hunting and capturing cause significant disruptions of a marine mammal's natural state. Consistent with these other terms, "harassment," to constitute a "taking" under the MMPA, must entail a similar level of direct intrusion.

Interpreting "harassment" under the MMPA to involve a direct and significant intrusion also comports with a common understanding of the term "take," of which "harass" is simply one form. To "take" a marine mammal strongly suggests a serious diversion of the mammal from its natural routine. Congressional concern in passing the MMPA about marine mammals "in danger of extinction or depletion as a result of man's activities" supports this conception of "take." MMPA § 2(1). Killing, capturing, and hunting fit the common understanding of the term. "Harassment" under the MMPA, to constitute a "taking," must entail a similarly significant level of intrusiveness.

The NMFS regulatory definition of "take," as applied to porpoises, also supports this interpretation. . . .

The case for our interpretation is even stronger if we refer to 50 C.F.R. § 17.3, the regulatory definition of "harass" urged by the government and upon which the district court exclusively relied. . . . Section 17.3 specifically requires significant disruption of "normal" behavioral patterns. Deterrence of abnormal marine mammal activity is not proscribed.

This emphasis upon protecting natural animal behavior comports with the MMPA emphasis upon marine mammals as essential components of the natural marine ecosystem. *See* MMPA § 2(2), Pub.L. 92–522, 86 Stat. 1027 (1972) (marine mammals "should not be permitted to diminish beyond the point at which they cease to be a significant functioning element in the ecosystem of which they are a part"). The concern that underlies the prohibition against disturbing mammals was for mammals *as a part of nature,* not for mammals acting in ways that endanger human life or property.

Interpreting the act and regulations otherwise, as prohibiting *isolated* interference with *abnormal* marine mammal activity, would lead to absurdity. Under such a broad interpretation, anyone who acted to prevent or in any way interfered with *any* marine mammal activity would face potential criminal prosecution. Nothing could legally be done to save a modern-day Jonah from the devouring whale, or to deter a rampaging polar bear from mauling a child. Neither could a porpoise intent on swimming into severely contaminated waters, or into the propellers of a motorized boat, be diverted by the selfless actions of a good Samaritan. These are but examples of what the unreasonably broad interpretation advocated by the government would lead us to. Our conclusion that only direct and serious disruptions of normal mammal behavior fall under the term "harass" comports with a more reasonable understanding of the extent and scope of the MMPA.

Applying our interpretation to the act for which Hayashi was convicted, we conclude that there was insufficient evidence to find a criminal "taking" by "harassment." The stipulated facts, consisting almost entirely of Hayashi's and his son's statements to the NMFS investigator, show that Hayashi did not fire at the porpoises, nor did he hit them. He simply fired two successive shots behind and outside the area of the porpoises to discourage them from eating bait and hooked tuna from his fishing lines—an act that is not a part of the porpoise's normal eating habits. Even if the shots succeeded in scaring away the porpoises—and the stipulated facts do not tell us whether the porpoises were aware of, or reacted to, the shots—any diversion from eating off the fisherman's lines is not of the significance required for a "taking" under the MMPA. Hayashi's conduct was not the kind of direct, serious disruption of a porpoise's customary pursuits required to find a criminal "taking." Reasonable acts to deter porpoises from eating fish or bait off a fisherman's line are not criminal under the MMPA.

. . .

III

We hold that reasonable actions—those not resulting in severe disruption of the mammal's normal routine—to deter porpoises from eating fish or bait off a fishing line are not rendered criminal by the MMPA or its regulations. Because the evidence shows that Hayashi's action was reasonable, we conclude that insufficient evidence supported his conviction. We reverse.

■ BROWNING, J., dissenting:—The majority unjustifiably restricts the breadth of the Marine Mammal Protection Act to avoid subjecting Hayashi to a criminal prosecution the majority regards as unreasonable. The gloss imposed by the majority to limit the scope of "taking," a key jurisdictional term in the Act, has no source in the language, structure or legislative history of the Act and derives little support from the various circumstances collected to sustain it. It ignores the structure and purpose of the Act and substantially weakens it as an instrument for effectuating the public policy determined by Congress.

Much more is at stake in defining the statutory term "taking" than Hayashi's freedom to fire his rifle at dolphins to protect a tuna caught by his son. The meaning assigned to this term defines the authority of the Secretary of Interior and the Secretary of Commerce to regulate private and public activities affecting marine mammals. The authority granted the Secretary by the Act to prohibit acts harmful to marine mammals and to develop and encourage means of ensuring their survival is keyed directly or indirectly to the concept of "taking." A cramped construction of the term "taking" will therefore restrict most aspects of the scheme envisioned by Congress for the protection of marine mammals, from the monitoring of marine mammal populations to research into more humane fishing techniques.

The references in the Act to the term "taking" confirm its importance. The substantive provisions of the Act open with a moratorium on the "taking and importation of marine mammals and marine mammal products." 16 U.S.C. § 1371(a). The Secretary is authorized to allow exceptions to the moratorium by issuing permits "for taking and importation" of marine mammals, as detailed in the Act. 16 U.S.C. §§ 1371, 1374. What is prohibited and what is permitted are stated in terms of "taking" and will be fixed by the definition of that term. 16 U.S.C. §§ 1372, 1375, 1376. The Secretary's regulatory judgments are to be based upon the past and projected impact of "taking" upon the well-being of the species or stocks and the purposes and policies of the Act. 16 U.S.C. § 1373(a). The Act requires the Secretary to fund research into methods of fishing that minimize the incidental "taking" of marine mammals. 16 U.S.C. §§ 1380, 1381. Vessels receiving exemptions are required to report incidental "taking" of marine mammals, to provide information useful in the study of the effect of certain fishing techniques on marine mammal populations. 16 U.S.C. § 1383a(c), (g). The Act establishes a Marine Mammal Commission, one of whose duties is to conduct a "continuing review ... of humane means of taking marine mammals." 16 U.S.C. § 1402(a)(2).

. . .

NOTES

(1) Which court offers the more persuasive interpretation of the term "take"? Is the difference between the two decisions traceable to the presence of a regulation in one case and not in the other?

Is there any basis in the Act for the Ninth Circuit's focus on "direct," "sustained," or "significant" as a justification for a distinction between permissible and impermissible? For the court's distinction between "normal" and "abnormal"? Is there any scientific basis for the distinction? What effect would this line of reasoning have on the practical effectiveness of law enforcement?

(2) "Harassment": Inclusion of "harass" in the definition of "take" was a significant extension the over previous definitions such as those in the MBTA or the BGEPA. Following *Hayashi,* Congress amended the MMPA by adding a definition of "harassment":

any act of pursuit, torment, or annoyance which

(i) has the potential to injure ... ; or

(ii) has the potential to disturb a marine mammal ... by causing disruption of behavioral patterns, including, but not limited to, migration, breathing, nursing, feeding, or sheltering.

16 U.S.C. § 1362(18)(A). Is Hayashi's conduct "harassment" under the new definition?

(3) Prohibitions and penalties: The Act makes it unlawful "for any person subject to the jurisdiction of the United States ... to take any marine mammal on the high seas" or "in waters or lands subject to the jurisdiction of the United States." 16 U.S.C. § 1372(a)(1)-(2). It is also unlawful to possess, transport, purchase, sell, export, or import any marine mammal taken in violation of the Act. *Id.* (3)-(4), (c).

As with the MBTA, the *mens rea* element is used to distinguish among the potential penalties. "Any person who violates any provision of this Act or of any permit or regulation issued thereunder . . . may be assessed a civil penalty . . . of not more than $10,000 for each such violation." *Id.* § 1375(a)(1). "Any person who knowingly violated any provision of this Act or of any permit or regulation issued thereunder . . . shall . . . . . be fined not more than $20,000 for each such violation, or imprisoned for not more than one year, or both." *Id.* § (b).

(B) Exceptions to the Taking Prohibition

NOTES

Takings incidental to commercial fishing operations: The taking prohibition is the primary mechanism for implementing the moratorium imposed by the MMPA. The Act, however, includes several exceptions to the taking prohibition. The most complex is the exception for marine mammals "incidentally taken in the course of commercial fishing operations." 16 U.S.C. § 1371(a)(2). "Incidental" is a term of art under the MMPA—a statement that means, of course, that it has an aberrant definition. In fact, an "incidental" take may result from situations in which the taker's *mens rea* is intent.

Earth Island Institute v. Brown

United States District Court, Northern District of California.
865 F.Supp. 1364 (1994).

■ HENDERSON, C.J.:— . . . .

I.   BACKGROUND

. . . . The focal point of the instant dispute is one particular marine mammal: the northeastern offshore spotted dolphin. Plaintiffs contend that the Secretary of Commerce must, under the MMPA, prohibit the further killing of these dolphins in the course of commercial fishing for yellowfin tuna, given his recent ruling that their population levels are now "depleted." According to defendants, however, the MMPA does not require that the Secretary's finding of depletion be given this effect.

Congress enacted the MMPA in 1972 to protect dolphins and other marine mammals. In particular, Congress was concerned with the high dolphin mortality rates caused by the yellowfin tuna fishing industry in the eastern tropical Pacific Ocean ("ETP"). *Earth Island Institute v. Mosbacher,* 929 F.2d 1449 (9th Cir.1991). Because tuna tend to swim underneath dolphins, tuna fleets in the ETP typically set large "purse seine nets" on groups of dolphins. Although this effectively catches the tuna, it also maims or kills the dolphins who become entangled in the nets. Between 1959, when purse seine nets became widely used and 1972, millions of dolphins were killed by tuna fishermen in the ETP. [ ]

The MMPA addressed this problem by imposing a general moratorium on the killing or "taking" of all marine mammals, including dolphins. 16 U.S.C. § 1371; *American Tunaboat Ass'n v. Baldrige,* 738 F.2d 1013, 1014 (9th Cir.1984). The moratorium is subject to certain limited exceptions, one of which allows the Secretary of Commerce ("Secretary") to issue permits for the "incidental taking" of marine mammals during commercial fishing operations. 16 U.S.C. § 1371(a)(2). Congress added, however, that "it shall be the immediate goal" that the incidental kill rates in commercial fishing operations be reduced to "insignificant levels approaching zero." *Id.* In the case of purse seine fishing for yellowfin tuna, this goal shall be satisfied by "a continuation of the application of the best marine mammal safety techniques and equipment that are economically and technologically practicable." *Id.*

Pursuant to the commercial fishing exception, the Secretary issued the American Tunaboat Association ("ATA") a general permit which, *inter alia,* imposed a quota on the number of dolphins killed in the domestic yellowfin tuna fishery in the ETP. In 1984, Congress statutorily extended this permit, subject to certain additional conditions and quotas. 16 U.S.C. § 1374(b)(2). Thus, the ATA permit is now codified in the MMPA.

On November 1, 1993, the National Marine Fisheries Service ("NMFS") listed the northeastern offshore spotted dolphin as "depleted" in response to a 1991 petition filed by Environmental Solutions International, Greenpeace, and other organizations. [ ] "Depleted" is a term of art under the MMPA, and means that a species or population stock has fallen "below its optimum sustainable population ("OSP")." 16 U.S.C. § 1362(1)(A). Under agency regulations, a species is considered to have fallen below its OSP—and is therefore "depleted"—if its population level is **less than 60 percent** of its estimated "historic" levels, before purse seine fishing became prevalent. [ ]

In the case of the northeastern offshore spotted dolphin, the Secretary found that its population has diminished 77 percent from its historic population level of over 3 million in the 1950s. Thus, the current stock level is estimated to be at only **23 percent** of its OSP—a figure "far below" the 60 percent standard for triggering a finding of "depletion." [ ]

Plaintiffs argue that the Secretary is not permitted, under the terms of the ATA permit and the MMPA, to allow the ATA to continue killing dolphins that have been listed as depleted. Therefore, the Secretary must prohibit the ATA from continuing to set nets on, and kill, northeastern offshore spotted dolphins. Defendants, however, contend that such actions are permissible under the current ATA permit, and that the MMPA provisions relied on by plaintiffs are irrelevant to the instant dispute.[3]

Accordingly, plaintiffs filed the instant motion seeking an injunction against the further incidental taking of northeastern offshore spotted dolphin under the ATA permit.[4] In addition, plaintiffs request similar relief

3. The Secretary has also taken the position that no other steps, such as a "conservation plan," are needed to encourage the rebound of this severely depleted stock. A provision of the MMPA requires the NMFS to prepare a "conservation plan" for any species or stock designated as depleted, unless it determines that such a plan "will not promote the conservation of the species or stock." 16 U.S.C. § 1383b(b)(1)(C). In this case, the NMFS has concluded that such a plan is not necessary because "[i]nternational and U.S. efforts to reduce dolphin mortality in the purse-seine fishery for tuna, and to promote dolphin conservation have been, or are being, implemented." [ ]

4. Under the comparability standards developed   pursuant   to   16   U.S.C.

with respect to the western/southern stock of offshore spotted dolphins. While this stock is under continued study, it has not been listed by the Secretary as depleted. Nonetheless, plaintiffs urge us to extend relief to this stock as well, until and unless the NMFS issues a finding that it is *not* depleted because (1) the stock is potentially depleted, and (2) the setting of purse seine nets on western/southern offshore spotted dolphins may result in the killing of northeastern offshore spotted dolphins because the stock sometimes swim together and are difficult to differentiate.

.   .   .

II.   DISCUSSION

Resolution of this motion requires us to address the following issu[e]. [W]hether the incidental killing of northeastern offshore spotted dolphins in the ETP must cease, now that the Secretary has listed this stock as depleted, and if so, whether the western/southern stock should also be afforded this same protection. . . .

> A.   *Whether commercial tuna fishermen, operating under the ATA permit, are prohibited from killing northeastern offshore spotted dolphins, now that their population is depleted*

Under the MMPA, the Secretary normally issues a permit for commercial fishing operations after notice and hearing. In the case of the ATA permit, this process was protracted and complex, and often precipitated litigation. [ ] Thus, once domestic dolphin mortality rates declined significantly, Congress decided that a more streamlined approach was merited. [ ] Accordingly, in 1984, Congress bypassed the process for administratively renewing the ATA permit and instead statutorily extended the permit that had been issued to the ATA by the Secretary in 1980. At the same time, Congress added several additional restrictions. 16 U.S.C. § 1374(h)(2).

These 1984 amendments to the MMPA read, in pertinent part, as follows:

> (A) Subject to subparagraph (B) [below], *the general permit issued under paragraph (1) on December 1, 1980 to the American Tunaboat Association is extended* to authorize and *govern* the taking of marine mammals incidental to commercial purse seine fishing for yellowfin tuna during each year after December 31, 1984.

> (B) The extension granted under subparagraph (A) is subject to the following conditions. . . .

> (iii) *During the period of the extension, the terms and conditions of the general permit that are in effect on the date of the enactment of this paragraph shall apply, except that—*

§ 1371(a)(2)(B), the Secretary agrees that any such relief would also affect foreign fleets, which in recent years have become the larger source of dolphin mortality in the ETP. *Earth Island Institute v. Mosbacher*, 746 F. Supp. 964, 967–68 (N.D.Cal.1990), *aff'd*, 929 F.2d 1449 (9th Cir.1991). This factor is particularly significant here because domestic fishermen are responsible for only a small fraction of the number of northeastern offshore spotted dolphins killed each year. [ ]

(I) the Secretary may make such adjustments as may be appropriate to those terms and conditions that pertain to fishing gear and fishing practice requirements and to permit administration;

(II) *any such term and condition may be amended or terminated if the amendment or termination is based on the best scientific information available,* including that obtained under the monitoring program required under paragraph (3)(A); and

(III) during each year of the extension, not to exceed 250 coastal spotted dolphin (*Stenella attenuata*) and not to exceed 2,750 eastern spinner dolphin (*Stenella longirostris*) may be incidentally taken under the general permit, and no accidental taking of either species is authorized at any time when incidental taking of that species is permitted.

(C) The quota on the incidental taking of coastal spotted dolphin and eastern spinner dolphin under paragraph (2)(B)(iii)(III) shall be treated—

(i) as within, and not in addition to, the overall annual quota under the general permit on the incidental taking of marine mammals....

16 U.S.C. § 1374(h)(2) (emphasis added). In 1992, Congress further restricted total dolphin mortalities under the ATA permit to 1,000 for the year January 1, 1992 and 800 for the period January 1, 1993 through March 1, 1994, and prohibited any setting of nets on eastern spinner or coastal spotted dolphins. 16 U.S.C. § 1416(a).

When the above provisions of section 1374(h)(2) are taken together with other provisions of the MMPA, the terms of the 1980 permit, prior agency constructions, and legislative history, there is no doubt that Congress did not intend to allow, under the ATA permit, the continued killing of dolphins that the Secretary has listed as depleted.

First, as quoted above, the 1984 amendments **expressly extend** the terms of the permit issued to the ATA by the Secretary in 1980, and **expressly** state that such terms shall "govern" and "apply," subject to certain additional conditions simultaneously added by Congress in 1984. Section 1374(h)(2)(A) provides that the 1980 permit is "extended to authorize and govern" further takings. Similarly, section 1374(h)(2)(B)(iii) clearly states that "[d]uring the period of the extension, the terms and conditions of the general permit that are in effect on the date of the enactment of this paragraph shall apply [except for certain specified conditions]."

Second, it is equally clear that, under the 1980 ATA permit, the taking of depleted species was not allowed. As the parties agree, the 1980 permit was issued by the Secretary pursuant to sections 1371(a)(2) and 1374. Section 1371(a)(2) authorized the Secretary to issue a permit to the ATA for commercial fishing under section 1374, which expressly requires that any such permit be "consistent with the requirements of § 1371." Section 1371, in turn, forbids the Secretary from issuing any permit for the taking of depleted species, except for purposes of scientific research:

Except for scientific research purposes as provided for in paragraph (1) of this subsection, during the moratorium *no* permit may be issued for the taking of any marine mammal which has been designated by the Secretary as depleted, and no importation may be made of any such mammal.

16 U.S.C. § 1371(a)(3)(B) (emph. added). The 1980 ATA permit issued by the Secretary was necessarily subject to this explicit restriction. Defendants essentially concede as much when they admit that "[i]f this issue had arisen ten years ago [before the 1984 amendments] the defendants would agree that the Secretary could not then have issued a permit that authorized the ATA to take a depleted marine mammal." [ ]

The 1980 ATA permit itself confirms this point. It explicitly states that "[t]his permit . . . [is] issued *under the authority of and shall be valid only for takings consistent with the terms and conditions set forth in 50 C.F.R. 216.24* and the terms of this permit." (emphasis added). Under part 216–216.24 of the Code of Federal Regulations, the Secretary has repeatedly stated that the MMPA does not permit the taking of depleted marine mammals, and has limited the ATA permit to preclude the taking of any dolphin stock or species found to be depleted.

. . .

[T]he federal regulations referenced by the 1980 ATA permit, and which provide the authority for that permit, make it quite clear that the 1980 ATA general permit did not permit the taking of dolphins that belonged to a depleted species or stock. Indeed, defendants do not appear to seriously contest this point.

We further observe that the 1980 ATA permit ban on the taking of depleted dolphins is entirely consistent with Congressional intent. The unquestionable primary purpose of the MMPA is to prevent marine mammals from falling below their optimum sustainable population or OSP, and to replenish any depleted species. The introduction to the MMPA states that:

The Congress finds that—

(1) certain species and population stocks of marine mammals are, or may be, in danger of extinction or depletion as a result of man's activities;

(2) [such mammals] should not be permitted to diminish below their optimum sustainable population. Further measures should be immediately taken to replenish any species or population stock which has already diminished below that population

16 U.S.C. § 1361. [ ]

The Ninth Circuit Court of Appeals also underscored this point when it summarized the central scheme of the MMPA in 1984:

The MMPA generally imposes a moratorium on intentional takings of porpoise species most often associated with yellowfin tuna. Recognizing, however, that certain of the species exist in abundance, the MMPA delegates to the Secretary of Commerce the duty to issue permits for the taking of these porpoise incidental to commercial fishing. The Secretary of Commerce, in turn, delegates to [the National Oceanic &

Atmospheric Administration] the duty of determining which species of porpoise are "disadvantaged" or "depleted" within the meaning of the MMPA. *The basic approach of the statute and regulations has been to impose yearly quotas on the taking of abundant porpoise species by tuna fishermen, and to prohibit the taking of any species deemed depleted.*

American Tunaboat Association v. Baldrige, 738 F.2d 1013, 1014–15 (9th Cir.1984) (emphasis added); *see also Committee for Humane Legislation, Inc. v. Richardson,* 540 F.2d 1141, 1148 (D.C.Cir.1976) ("[The MMPA] was to be administered for the benefit of the protected species rather than for the benefit of commercial exploitation").[8]

Given all of the above, we readily find that the 1980 ATA permit prohibited the taking of depleted species in the ETP. This brings us back to the current ATA permit, which as described above, consists of an extension of this 1980 permit, "subject to" a number of additional conditions provided by Congress in 1984, 1988 and 1992. *See* 16 U.S.C. §§ 1374(h)(2), 1416(a). If any of these new permit terms contradicted, conflicted with, or otherwise modified the limitation on taking depleted species, that aspect of the 1980 ATA permit would, of course, yield to the new terms set by Congress. However, none of these additional conditions—all of which are designed to enhance the protection of dolphins—state that killing depleted species in the ETP is permissible. As such, the intent of Congress is clear. The Secretary may not, consistent with the MMPA, allow the ATA to continue killing northern offshore spotted dolphins, given their depleted status.

. . .

B. *Whether the western/southern offshore spotted dolphin is entitled to protection*

Although the western/southern offshore spotted dolphin is under continued study, it has not yet been listed by the Secretary as depleted. Plaintiffs, however, seek a prohibition against the incidental taking of this stock as well, until and unless the NMFS issues a finding that it is *not* depleted because (1) the stock is potentially depleted, and (2) the setting of purse seine nets on western/southern offshore spotted dolphins may result in the killing of northeastern offshore spotted dolphins because the stock sometimes swim together and are difficult to differentiate.

We are not persuaded that the ATA permit or the MMPA requires a ban on the incidental taking of species or stock that are not listed as depleted by the Secretary. Thus, the fact that the western/southern offshore spotted dolphin may be potentially depleted, does not provide adequate legal grounds to support the relief requested. Accordingly, this aspect of plaintiffs' motion shall be denied.

However, the record before the Court does indicate that northeastern and western/southern offshore spotted dolphins are closely related and have

8. In 1988, Congress amended the MMPA to allow the incidental take of small numbers of marine mammals from a depleted stock or species during the course of commercial fishing operations. 16 U.S.C. § 1383a. This amendment, however, does not apply to the ATA permit. [ ]

a similar outward appearance. [ ] In addition, as both defendants' and plaintiffs' experts agree, "stock boundaries in the ocean environment are well-recognized as being fluid in time and space." [ ] Thus, those northeastern offshore spotted dolphins that swim on the boundary between the northern and western/southern stocks are particularly vulnerable to further takings. Defendants have offered to propose ways to minimize the taking of northeastern offshore spotted dolphins in the boundary area, such as the use of buffer zones. Accordingly, and in order to fully effectuate the relief granted with respect to the northeastern offshore spotted dolphin, we shall require the parties to meet and confer regarding this matter.

. . .

NOTES

(1) What is the scope of the Secretary's discretion to permit incidental takings of depleted species?

(2) Dolphins and tuna: The "virtual genocide" produced by the practice of setting purse seines on dolphins in order to capture the tuna that frequently swim beneath the dolphins was a primary impetus for the enactment of the MMPA in 1972. H.R. REP. No. 707, 92d Cong., 2d Sess. 11 (1971), *reprinted in* 1972 U.S.C.C.A.N. 4144.

Michael Bean and Melanie Rowland have examined the history of the tuna-dolphin conflict and have concluded that it has progressed through three phases:

(a) 1972–1976—technological optimism: Initially, Congress believed that a quick, technological fix could be found to the problem. It therefore exempted takings incidental to fishing operations from the general prohibition against taking marine mammal for two years and appropriated $2 million to improve fishing methods and gear. There was little progress and the Act's "immediate goal"—reducing "the incidental kill or incidental serious injury of marine mammals permitted in the course of commercial fishing operations . . . to insignificant levels approaching zero mortality and serious injury rate," 16 U.S.C. § 1371(a)(2)—had not been achieved. The National Marine Fisheries Service (NMFS) therefore adopted regulations to implement the "immediate goal"; it did so by requiring the best available technology and fishing practices. The agency did not, however, set a ceiling on the number of dolphins that could be killed. In *Committee for Humane Legislation, Inc. v. Richardson*, 414 F.Supp. 297 (D.D.C.), *aff'd*, 540 F.2d 1141 (D.C.Cir.1976), the court rejected the agency's argument that it lacked the data necessary to evaluate the take on OSP.

(b) 1976–1984—ratcheting down: Responding to the district court's order, NMFS adopted regulations for 1977 that set a quota on the number of dolphins that could be killed by the United States tuna fleet. The initial annual quota of 78,000 dolphins was announced in mid-June and reached in about four months. The quotas dropped each year until they reached 20,500 in 1980. The quotas were met primarily through a shrinkage in the size of the tuna fleet:

At the time it appeared that remarkable progress had been made in solving a challenging environmental problem. The U.S. tuna fleet's incidental mortality had declined from several hundred thousand annually to fewer than 20,000. This dramatic decline, however, was largely attributable to the fact that fewer U.S. boats fished the waters of the eastern tropical Pacific Ocean. In the mid–1970s, more than 150 U.S. purse seine vessels plied these waters. They accounted for nearly 70 percent of the fishing capacity of the region. By 1987, however, the size the U.S. fleet in the eastern tropical Pacific was sharply reduced. Many boats had shifted their effort to the western Pacific while others now operated under foreign flags. The foreign fleet, with seventy vessels, was roughly twice the size of the U.S. fleet. A fishery that had long been dominated by the U.S. fleet had been transformed to one dominated by foreign boats. Eventually, nearly all U.S. boats disappeared from the region.

MICHAEL J. BEAN & MELANIE J. ROWLAND, *supra,* at 126.

(c) 1984–present—the international problem: With the decline in the size the U.S. fleet, the conservation gains were significantly undercut since Congress had no direct control over foreign-flagged vessels. The 1972 Act had directed the Secretaries of State and Commerce to begin negotiations with the Inter–American Tropical Tuna Commission to reduce incidental take. The Act also authorized the imposition of embargoes against tuna exported by countries whose fishers used methods prohibited to U.S. fishers or that resulted in the mortality of marine mammals in excess of U.S. standard. When neither approach proved particularly effective, Congress changed the standards to authorize embargoes against any fishing fleet whose average rate of dolphin deaths exceeded that of the U.S. fleet. NMFS, fearing a major trade dispute with Mexico, delayed promulgating regulations until faced with congressional hearings in 1988. In the same year, Congress again increased the requirements governing tuna imports. The new requirements included observers, specified kill rates, limits on mortality by species, and prohibitions against certain fishing practices.

In early 1990, Starkist Seafood announced that it would no longer process any tuna caught in association with dolphins and that it would label its products "dolphins safe." The move dramatically altered the domestic market for tuna when two other processors followed suit. Congress quickly endorsed the changes by enacting the Dolphin Protection Consumer Information Act to define the term "dolphin safe." 16 U.S.C. § 1385. Mexico, whose fleet dominated the eastern tropical Pacific Ocean, responded by challenging the MMPA's requirements as violation of the General Agreement on Tariffs and Trade (GATT). The panel that heard Mexico's complaint agreed; action beyond the hearing panel was suspended while Mexico and the United States attempted to resolve the dispute diplomatically. The MMPA was amended in 1992 to include a proposed "global moratorium" of at least five years on fishing by setting purse seines on dolphins. No other nation agreed, and the U.S. market was effectively closed to all tuna caught in association with dolphins by the International Dolphin Conservation Act of 1992, Pub. L. No. 102–523, 106 Stat. 3425.

Simultaneously, the incidental take by foreign fleets dropped from more than 80,000 in 1989 to less than 4,000 in 1993.

The international trade aspects of the dolphin-tuna controversy is examined in more detail in Chapter 8.

(3) Compliance monitoring: Compliance with quotas and other fishing regulations can only be determined by placing observers on board fishing vessels. Fishing captains and boat owners, however, objected to being required to carry federal monitors whose job is the collection of data to be used in enforcement actions. The program was challenged as violative of the Fourth Amendment's prohibitions against unreasonable searches. The Ninth Circuit *en banc* upheld the constitutionality of the program in *Balelo v. Baldrige,* 724 F.2d 753 (9th Cir.), *cert. denied,* 467 U.S. 1252 (1984). The court held that commercial fishing was a closely regulated industry and that fishing boat captains thus had no expectations of privacy that were protected by the Constitution.

* * *

Although the dolphin-tuna controversy has proved the most durable, it is not the only incidental take problem associated with commercial fishing operations.

Kokechik Fishermen's Association v. Secretary of Commerce

District of Columbia Circuit Court of Appeals.
839 F.2d 795 (1988).
certiorari denied sub nomine, Verity v. Center for Environmental Education, 488 U.S. 1004 (1989).

■ GESELL, D.J.:—This case requires us to examine an aspect of this nation's announced policy to protect, in waters under its jurisdiction, marine mammal populations that are in danger of depletion or extinction.

Following formal rulemaking proceedings, the Secretary of Commerce issued a regulation pursuant to the Marine Mammal Protection Act of 1972 ("MMPA"), 16 U.S.C. §§ 1361–1407, authorizing a group of Japanese commercial fishermen known as the Federation of Japan Salmon Fisheries Cooperative Association ("Federation") to take a fixed number of Dall's porpoise incidental to commercial fishing for salmon in U.S. conservation waters. The permit application was opposed at the administrative level by environmentalists, the Center for Environmental Education, *et al.* ("CEE") and by a group of Alaskan commercial fishermen, Kokechik Fishermen's Association, *et al.* ("Kokechik"). As finally authorized on May 22, 1987 after several amendments, the permit failed to meet objections advanced during the rulemaking process by Kokechik and CEE, on one side, and the Federation on the other side.

Shortly after the Secretary's final decision, the Federation, Kokechik and CEE filed petitions for review of the permit.... [T]he District Court ... preliminarily enjoined the Secretary of Commerce from issuing a permit to the Federation....

.... [W]e affirm and remand to the District Court only for such further proceedings consistent with this decision as may be required.

BACKGROUND

In 1952, the United States, Japan and Canada signed the International Convention for the High Seas Fisheries of the North Pacific Ocean ("INPFC"). 4 U.S.T. 380, T.I.A.S. No. 2786. Under this treaty, Japan agreed to refrain from fishing for salmon in certain areas of the North Pacific Ocean and in the Bering Sea. In 1978, the INPFC was renegotiated to bring the treaty in conformity with the recent adoption by the United States of a 200 mile Fisheries Conservation Zone, now known as the Exclusive Enterprise Zone ("EEZ"). 30 U.S.T. 1095, T.I.A.S. No. 9242. The protocol amending the treaty permitted the Japanese to fish for salmon inside the U.S. EEZ. *Id.* The North Pacific Fisheries Act of 1954 ("NPFA"), implementing the INPFC, was also amended in 1978 and exempted Japanese commercial salmon fishing from the strictures of the MMPA until June 9, 1981. 16 U.S.C. § 1034(b). The NPFA further provided that after June 9, 1981 the restrictions of the MMPA would apply with full force and effect to Japanese salmon fishing within the EEZ. *Id.* § 1034(c).

In 1981, the National Oceanic and Atmospheric Administration ("NOAA"), acting pursuant to section 1374 of the MMPA, issued the Federation a three year general permit allowing its members an annual take of 5,500 Dall's porpoise, 450 northern fur seals, and 25 northern sea lions incidental to their commercial salmon fishing. [ ] Congress then extended this permit in 1982 by amendments to the North Pacific Fisheries Act on the condition that further research be performed examining ways to reduce or avoid incidental takings of marine mammals during salmon gillnet fishing. 16 U.S.C. § 1034(b). The permit was scheduled to expire on June 9, 1987 and without either Congressional extension of the permit or the issuance of a new general permit, the Federation's commercial salmon fishing within the U.S. EEZ would effectively cease at that time.

[In July 1986 the Federation applied to the National Marine Fisheries Service ("NMFS") for a five-year extension of the previous permit's terms. NMFS published notice in the Federal Register as required by the MMPA; the notice included the status of each marine mammal stock affected and the effects of any permitted taking on its optimum sustainable population ("OSP"). The statement was restricted to the status of Dall's porpoise. The statement did not discuss either northern sea lions or northern fur seals. Because only one northern sea lion had been taken under the previous permit, NMFS considered the probability of other incidental takings too remote. Because northern fur seals from the Pribilof Islands were depleted, the MMPA precluded the agency from issuing a permit to take them.

[At the formal rulemaking hearing, the Administrative Law Judge ("ALJ") noted that northern fur seals, sea lions, harbor porpoise, Pacific white-sided dolphin, northern right whale dolphin, and killer whales are incidentally, although infrequently, taken during salmon gillnet fishing. The Secretary reviewed the record developed during the hearing, the ALJ's recommended decision, the exceptions filed thereto, and the Final Environmental Impact Statement, and issued a final rule that authorized the issuance of a permit allowing "an aggregate taking during the three year permit period of no more than 789 Dall's porpoise in the Bering Sea and 5,250 in the North Pacific Ocean, of which no more than 448 may be taken in the Bering Sea and no more than 2,494 may be taken from the North Pacific Ocean in any single calendar year." With regard to the northern fur seals, the Secretary ruled that the "incidental taking of northern fur seals, like the taking of northern (Steller) sea lions, harbor porpoise, Pacific white-sided dolphin, northern right whale dolphin, and killer whales is prohibited by the Marine Mammal Protection Act."]

ANALYSIS

The Federation's commercial salmon fishing in the U.S. EEZ is conducted with the use of gillnets. Gillnet fishing involves setting out nylon nets approximately nine miles long and 26 feet deep at dusk using small fleets of motor boats. The nets drift freely near the surface where salmon and marine mammals, primarily Dall's porpoise, feed during the night. These fish and mammals become ensnared in the drifting nets. The next morning motor boats retrieve the nets and haul in whatever catch has been ensnared in the nets.

As is readily apparent, this method of fishing does not permit discrimination between which species of fish and mammals will be ensnared and which will not. Consequently, although the Federation actively seeks to catch only salmon, marine mammals protected by the MMPA end up as unintentional victims of salmon gillnet fishing because of the nature of the fishing gear and techniques used. This result is absolutely prohibited by the MMPA unless, pursuant to the requirements of the Act, the Secretary of Commerce specifically grants permission for the taking of marine mammals incidental to commercial fishing.[10] 16 U.S.C. § 1371(a)(2).

The permit at issue here grants the Federation permission to take a specified quota of Dall's porpoise incidental to commercial gillnet salmon fishing. No other marine mammal species are included within the permit. Although Dall's porpoise is the protected marine mammal primarily affected by the Federation's fishing, it is foreseeable that takes of northern fur seals, northern sea lions, harbor porpoises, Pacific white-sided dolphins and killer whales will occur. Since the taking of any of these other marine mammals without a permit is absolutely prohibited by the MMPA, the legitimacy of the permit issued here comes under scrutiny. The MMPA must be analyzed to determine whether the Secretary of Commerce may legally issue a permit allowing incidental taking of one protected marine mammal species knowing that other protected marine mammal species will be taken as well.

Congress, by enacting the MMPA, put into effect a moratorium on the taking of marine mammals.[11] The term "moratorium" is defined by the Act

---

10. The Secretary defines the term "incidental catch" to include the taking of a marine mammal "as a consequence of the steps used to secure the fish in connection with commercial fishing operations," 50 C.F.R. § 216.3.

11. In turn, the Act defines "take" to mean "to harass, hunt, capture, or kill, or attempt to harass, hunt, capture, or kill any

to mean "a complete cessation of the taking of marine mammals.... " 16 U.S.C. § 1362(7) (emphasis added). Since June 9, 1981, this moratorium has applied to Japanese commercial fishing in the U.S. EEZ. Section 1377 of the MMPA requires the Secretary of Commerce to enforce the provisions of the Act and implementing regulations promulgated thereunder.

Under a limited exception to this moratorium, the taking of marine mammals incidental to commercial fishing operations may be allowed. 16 U.S.C. § 1371(a)(2). Before such a permissible taking can occur under this exception, two statutory requirements must be met: the taking must be authorized by regulations promulgated through formal rulemaking proceedings and a permit issued by the Secretary of Commerce; the taking must meet the requirements of the MMPA and be consistent with the primary goal of protecting marine mammals. *See id.*

Under the MMPA, before a permit authorizing a taking may be issued, the Secretary "must be assured that the taking ... is in accordance with sound principles of resource protection and conservation as provided in the purposes and policies of this chapter.... " 16 U.S.C. § 1371(a)(3)(A). The guiding principles of resource protection and conservation are set out in 16 U.S.C. §§ 1361(2) and 1361(6). Section 1361(2) provides:

> [Marine mammal] species and population stocks should not be permitted to diminish beyond the point at which they cease to be a significant functioning element in the ecosystem of which they are a part, and, consistent with this major objective, they should not be permitted to diminish below their optimum sustainable population....

Section 1361(6) reads in relevant part as follows:

> [I]t is the sense of Congress that [marine mammals] should be protected and encouraged to develop to the greatest extent feasible commensurate with sound policies of resource management and that the primary objective of their management should be to maintain the health and stability of the marine eco-system. Whenever consistent with this primary objective, it should be the goal to obtain an optimum sustainable population keeping in mind the carrying capacity of the habitat.

Thus, it is clear that "[t]he Act was to be administered for the benefit of the protected species rather than for the benefit of commercial exploitation." *Committee for Humane Legislation, Inc. v. Richardson,* 540 F.2d 1141, 1148 (D.C.Cir.1976).

Consonant with these principles, the MMPA provides a scheme to determine the number and kind of marine mammals which can be taken incidental to commercial fishing operations. Under this scheme, the Secretary is obligated to determine that the permit applicant has carried its burden of proving that the taking sought does not disadvantage the species involved and is consistent with the policies and purposes of the Act. The Secretary, thus, must first determine that the requested taking will not be

marine mammal." 16 U.S.C. § 1362(12). The Secretary further interprets the term "harass" to include "the restraint or detention of a marine mammal, no matter how temporary." 50 C.F.R. § 216.3.

to the disadvantage of the affected species and population stocks. 16 U.S.C. § 1373(a). Pursuant to this determination and in conjunction with the formal rulemaking proceedings, the Secretary must publish statements on population levels and the expected impact of the proposed regulations on the optimum sustainable population of the affected marine mammal species. 16 U.S.C. § 1373(d). Any decision the Secretary makes must be consistent with the MMPA "immediate goal" that

> the incidental kill or incidental serious injury of marine mammals permitted in the course of commercial fishery operations be reduced to insignificant levels approaching zero mortality and serious injury rate. . . .

16 U.S.C. § 1371(a)(2).

While the Act may not prohibit issuance of a permit where there is only a very remote possibility that marine mammals for which an optimum sustainable population has not been determined may be taken incidental to commercial fishing, such a situation is clearly not the case here. In its original permit application the Federation requested that 450 fur seals be allowed to be taken annually incidental to commercial salmon fishing in the U.S. EEZ. Although there were indications the taking might be less, it is readily apparent that the taking of these marine mammals is not merely a remote possibility but a certainty.[13]

In his final decision, the Secretary concluded that it was not possible to make the required finding that the northern fur seal population from the Commander Island stock is within its optimum sustainable population level. The Secretary found the evidence unclear and that a "significant dispute" existed as to whether it was above the minimum level of its optimum sustainable population. It could not be determined, therefore, that this protected stock would not be disadvantaged by takings incidental to the Federation's fishing operations in the U.S. EEZ. As to the Pribilof Island population, the Secretary found it was depleted. Thus, in neither case could findings which are an absolute requirement for the issuance of a permit and waiver of the MMPA be made.[14] Yet the Secretary, despite his inability to determine whether and to what extent northern fur seals would be disadvantaged by the Federation's fishing operations, issued the permit taking the position that as long as it did not authorize the taking of northern fur seals he had complied with the MMPA. The result was, in effect, that the permit allowed the Federation to take protected marine mammals for a price—the civil penalties imposed for such takings.

---

13. When he granted the permit to the Federation the Secretary was informed and knew that species of marine mammals other than Dall's porpoise, a species at the OSP level, would inevitably be taken incidental to the Federation's salmon fishing operations. These included northern fur seals from the Pribilof Island stock, a depleted species protected under the MMPA, as well as other species as to which no OSP finding one way or the other had been made—northern fur seals from the Commander Island stock, har-

bor porpoise, northern right whole dolphin, Pacific white-sided dolphin, and other dolphin, as well as various sea lions.

14. It is necessary to know the OSP in order to determine whether or not an activity will "disadvantage" the marine mammals involved. Therefore, Congress required the Secretary to act only on the basis of the very knowledge which he admits is unknown: the effect of any proposed taking on optimum sustainable population levels.

This is a result that the MMPA does not countenance. The MMPA effects a moratorium on the taking of marine mammals. Congress decided to undertake this decisive action because it was greatly concerned about the maintenance of healthy populations of all species of marine mammals within the ecosystems they inhabit. Exceptions to this moratorium clearly evidence a concern with the relationship between the activity engaged in and its effect on marine mammals and their ecosystem. It is the duty of the Secretary to take a systemic view of an activity's effect on marine mammals. A view that the permit process functions merely to determine which takes will be exempted from civil penalties is inconsistent with this duty because it allows—subject to the civil penalty price—illegal takings of other protected marine mammals.

The Secretary has no authority, by regulation or any other action, to issue a permit that allows conduct prohibited by that Act. Nonetheless, the Secretary chose to disregard these incidental takings as "negligible," an undefined and ambiguous standard at best. The MMPA, however, does not provide for a "negligible impact" exception to its permitting requirements where incidental takings are not merely a remote possibility but a certainty.

As enacted, section 1371(a)(4) creates a narrow exception for incidental, but not intentional, takings having a negligible impact on the species involved "by citizens of the United States while engaging in commercial fishing operations, ... " The Secretary is not authorized to extend this flexibility to the Japanese nor is he authorized to create a new undefined statutory exception under the heading of "negligible," which clearly has the effect of avoiding the strictures of the MMPA and congressional intent. Practical considerations or unavailability of information is no excuse. If the Secretary believes the Act needs amendment, then it is Congress he must address. The horse must stay ahead of the cart.

. . .

CONCLUSION

Thus, we hold that the permit, as granted to the Federation, is contrary to the requirements of the MMPA in that it allowed incidental taking of various species of protected marine mammals without first ascertaining as to each such species whether or not the population of that species was at the OSP level. If it is appropriate to grant foreign commercial fishermen some leeway to take marine mammals incidentally in carrying out their commercial fishing operations for salmon, it is for the Congress, not the Secretary to decide. Past administrative practice that is inconsistent with the purpose of an act of Congress cannot provide an exception and the moratorium must still be fully upheld in this situation. [ ]

Affirmed and remanded for further proceedings consistent with this decision.

■ STARR, J., dissenting:—. . . . [T]he question presented to us is the workaday one of statutory construction. In rejecting the common-sense reading of the statute adopted by the agency charged with administering it, the court reaches a result that, in my judgment, Congress never contemplated. In my view, today's decision is unsupported by the text, structure, or legislative history of the statute. I therefore respectfully dissent.

Under now-familiar principles, the task before us in construing a statute administered by an agency of the Executive Branch is clear. First, if Congress has addressed the precise issue in question, and the intent of Congress is clear, it is the judiciary's duty to give effect to that Congressional determination. [ ]; *Chevron, U.S.A. v. NRDC*, 467 U.S. 837, 842–43 (1984). If, on the other hand, the statute is silent or ambiguous with respect to the inquiry at issue, we are obliged under settled principles of law to defer to the agency's construction, if reasonable, of that statute. [ ]; *Chevron*, 467 U.S. at 844.

It is abundantly clear that Congress did not speak in so many words to the precise issue that the court decides today: whether the National Oceanic and Atmospheric Administration ("NOAA"), which is charged with administering the Marine Mammal Protection Act, [ ], is prevented from issuing a permit for one species because other species, for which a permit cannot lawfully issue, would inevitably be taken. Although the text of the statute does not provide a definitive answer to this question, the overall statutory scheme contemplates precisely the construction given by NOAA. In the MMPA, Congress created a species-based permit system that would enable fishing operations to carry on. The court's critical interpretive error, I believe, lies in its failure to give meaningful content to the species-based permit system established by Congress as an essential part of the legislative compromise embodied in the MMPA, a compromise evidenced by, on the one hand, the moratorium on the taking of marine mammals and, on the other hand, the system of permits for taking marine mammals in the course of fishing operations....

[T]he court has today created another hoop, nowhere to be found in the statute, through which NOAA must jump before it can issue a permit for the taking of marine mammals. But this hoop is singular in its difficulty. The court's construction of the MMPA effectively requires that no permit for any species issue until a permit for all mammals likely to be entangled can lawfully issue. This far-reaching construction fails, I believe, to account for NOAA's obligation under the Act to fashion a workable permit system on a species-by-species basis.

. . .

[T]he MMPA did not prohibit salmon gillnet fishing; rather, it allowed fishing to continue while at the same time placing a prohibition on marine mammal takings except to the extent that permits could be issued in accordance with statutory criteria for each species.... At the very least, Congress enacted a statutory scheme that places in tension the goal of total elimination of marine mammal takings and the need for a workable permit system administered in accordance with statutory criteria. *Chevron* and its progeny teach that we should defer to the reasonable resolution of that tension by the agency charged by Congress with the task of resolving it.

In my view, NOAA's interpretation and administration of the MMPA is eminently reasonable....

NOTES

(1) The precise legal issue in *Kokechik* was whether the Secretary of Commerce could issue an incidental take permit covering the killing of Dall's porpoises. Behind that issue, however, was another: what rights did the salmon-fishing Federation acquire by receiving a permit since it covered the incidental taking of one mammal species but not others that would also be taken? And there is yet another, related issue: what would have been the legal consequences had the Federation gone ahead with its fishing without bothering to obtain any permits? Is it possible, from the opinions in the case, to determine how the various parties—the litigants, the majority, and the dissent—would have answered these questions?

According to the opinion, the Federation sought, but was denied, a permit to take 450 northern fur seals. Lacking the permit, did it have the right to begin fishing that would certainly lead to the death of seals? The Federation seemed to think that it did, and so did the groups challenging the Dall's porpoise permit. But is this so? Would not a court have been willing to enjoin the fishing, given that the takings of the fur seals would clearly have been unlawful? If not, why not?

Injunction aside, there is the question of applicable penalties under the MMPA itself. The court seemed to think that the only penalties would have been the civil fines. But what of the stiffer fines and prison terms for knowing violations? Would not fishing that was sure to kill fur seals qualify as knowing violations?

Judge Kenneth Starr in his dissent seemed to assume that the Federation could unashamedly violate the law as long as it was willing to pay any penalties assessed; the fines would simply be a cost of doing business. Is this a respectable attitude toward the law, particularly for a federal judge? That is, is the law properly viewed as nothing more than a contract that a party might violate as long as it is willing to pay damages? Is Starr suggesting that illegal behavior has no moral overtones, or is his suggestion perhaps narrower: that some laws have moral implications, but laws prohibiting the killing of endangered mammals are not among them? If it is the latter, is Starr right in entertaining that assumption, given the congressional intent in enacting the MMPA and given opinion poll evidence [cited in Chapter 1] showing widespread public belief that species extinction is immoral?

On the other hand, if the killing of endangered seals is permissible as long as fines are paid, will not the Federation then have an economic incentive to reduce the killing (assuming, of course, that enforcement takes place)? Could such a market-based approach in practice achieve the best conservation outcome? Note that the civil penalties prescribed in the MMPA are "not more than $10,000 per violation." What should be considered a violation? Each seal killed? And what factors should be considered in setting the amount of the fine?

(2) *Committee for Humane Legislation v. Richardson:* The Secretary granted permits allowing fishers to take dolphins while fishing for tuna. The Secretary, however, lacked the scientific data necessary to determine the effect of the permitted takings on the OSP for the dolphins. The data was "critical," the court said, and its absence prevented the Secretary from making the findings mandated by the statute. Hence, the permit was invalid. *Committee for Humane Legislation v. Richardson*, 414 F.Supp. 297, 310 (D.D.C.) *aff'd*, 540 F.2d 1141 (D.C.Cir.1976). Is *Richardson* distinguishable from *Kokechik*?

(3) 1994 amendments: Congress responded to *Kokechik* by adopting an interim solution that waived the prohibition against incidental taking for any vessel that agreed to participate in a project to determine the effects of fishing on marine mammals. The interim provisions were extended twice before Congress developed a comprehensive regime for regulating incidental takes.

The amendments introduced a new order of complexity to the population approach that is the Act's centerpiece: If, after a stock assessment, the Secretary determines that the direct human-caused mortality exceeds the potential biological removal level of the stock and that the stock is affected by a commercial fishery that either causes frequent or occasional—as opposed to remote—incidental mortality, the Secretary is required to prepare a "take reduction plan." Thus, the 1994 amendments

(a) required the Secretary to prepare a "stock assessment" that summarizes the biological, distributional, and commercial factors affecting the marine mammal stock, 16 U.S.C. § 1386.

(b) the assessment is the basis for determining the "potential biological removal level," an estimate of the "maximum number of animals ... that may be removed from a marine mammal stock while still allowing that stock to reach or maintain its optimum sustainable population," *id.* § 1362(20).

(c) a stock is a "strategic stock" if the "direct human-caused mortality" of any stock exceeds its potential biological removal level, if the stock is listed as depleted under the MMPA or as threatened or endangered under the Endangered Species act, or if the stock "is declining and is likely to be listed as threatened," *id.* § 1362(19).

(d) the Secretary was directed to classify all commercial fisheries as having either "(i) frequent incidental mortality and serious injury of marine mammals; (ii) occasional incidental mortality and serious injury of marine mammals; or (iii) a remote likelihood of or no known incidental mortality or serious injury of marine mammals," *id.* § 1387(c)(1)(A).

(e) if a strategic stock "interacts" with a fishery that causes either frequent or occasional incidental takings, the Secretary is required to develop a "take reduction plan," *id.* § 1387(f)(1). The take reduction plan is to specify the methods to achieve both an "immediate goal"—"to reduce, within six months of its implementation, the incidental mortality ... to levels less than the potential biological removal level"—and a "long-term goal"—"to reduce, within 5 years of its implementation, the incidental mortality ... to insignificant levels approaching zero morality." *Id.*

For a fishery subject to a take reduction plan, compliance with the plan satisfies the requirements of the MMPA.

The 1994 amendments are a significant departure from the principles established in the original MMPA. The 1972 law imposed a blanket moratorium on taking marine mammals and a virtual bar against waiving the moratorium for depleted stocks. The 1994 amendments grew out of a recognition that these requirements could not be enforced and probably were unnecessary in any event to achieve the law's conservation objectives. Although somewhat ambiguous, the amendments reflect the ascendancy of the view that rather than seeking to eliminate incidental deaths of marine mammals, it is sufficient to keep mortality within acceptable limits.

MICHAEL J. BEAN & MELANIE J. ROWLAND, *supra,* at 134–35.

Consider the assumptions implicit in the amendments' interlocking definitions. Does the idea of "potential biological removal level" suffer from the same shortcomings that plagued "maximum sustained yield"?

(3) Takings incidental to other activities: Commercial fisheries are not the only types of human activities that incidentally take marine mammals. Motorboats have proved highly lethal to manatees in Florida. Off-shore oil and gas activities disrupt migration, feeding, and breeding. Under the original MMPA, civil and criminal sanctions were potentially applicable to such activities. In 1981, Congress authorized taking of marine mammals incidental to such activities pursuant to regulations designed to minimize the impact. The authority to permit such incidental taking was subject to the requirement that the Secretary determine that only "small numbers" of animals would be taken and that "the total . . . taking during each five-year . . . period will have a negligible impact" on the stock. 16 U.S.C. § 1371(a)(5)(A)-(C).

(C) The Importation Prohibition

NOTES

It is unlawful

to import into the United States . . . [a]ny marine mammal . . . taken in violation of this Act; or taken in another country in violation of the law of that country[; and a]ny marine mammal product if . . . the importation into the United States of the marine mammal from which such product is made is unlawful . . .; or . . . the sale in commerce of such product in the country of origin of the product is illegal; [and a]ny fish . . . if such fish was caught in a manner which the Secretary has proscribed for persons subject to the jurisdiction of the United States.

16 U.S.C. § 1372(c). The Act reinforces this language by explicitly stating that the Act imposes a "complete ban on the importation of marine mammals and marine mammal products." *Id.* § 1362(8).

The Act also prohibits the importation of any marine mammal if it was pregnant, nursing, or less than eight months old at the time of taking or was "taken in a manner deemed inhumane by the Secretary." *Id.* § 1372(b). *See generally Globe Fur Dyeing Corp. v. United States,* 467 F.Supp. 177 (D.D.C.1978), *aff'd,* 612 F.2d 586 (D.C.Cir.1980); *Animal*

Welfare Institute v. Kreps, 561 F.2d 1002 (D.C.Cir.1977), *cert. denied sub nom. Fouke Co. v. Animal Welfare Institute*, 434 U.S. 1013 (1978).

b.   MAGNUSON FISHERIES CONSERVATION AND MANAGEMENT ACT OF 1976

Ocean fisheries have long been a major source of protein for humans. The end of market hunting has left commercial fishing as the most significant continuing harvest of wildlife. Carl Safina provides an apt description: "Fishermen are the last major hunter-gatherers in modern culture, pursuing wildlife on an industrial scale with all the tools of the space age brought to bear." CARL SAFINA, SONG FOR THE BLUE OCEAN 16 (1997).

NOTES

(1) The oceans as the last great commons: The legal structure of the ocean fisheries is complex because the high seas represent the last of the commons, the final portion of the earth largely beyond the jurisdiction of any nation state. This reflects in part the sanctity of the belief in the freedom of the seas; in part the futility of attempts to regulate a vast and empty place. There have been two paths to the creation of regulation of ocean fisheries. On the one hand, there is the recurring assertion by coastal nations that what previously was "high seas" are in fact "territorial seas" or "conservation zones" subject to the dominion of the coastal nations. Thus the assertion of sovereignty over territorial seas has expanded from 3, to 12, to 200 miles. On the other hand, there have been a series of bi- and multi-lateral treaties that have sought to bring law to specific areas or species. For example, the United States is party to half a dozen treaties attempting to regulate the harvest of the anadromous salmonids of the Pacific Northwest. *See generally* Dale D. Goble, *Introduction to the Symposium on Legal Structures for Managing the Pacific Northwest Salmon and Steelhead: The Biological and Historical Context*, 22 IDAHO L. REV.417 (1986).

By the 1970s, many ocean fisheries were in decline as a result of overfishing—a decline often cited as a clear example of the "tragedy of the commons" in which individually (economically) "rational" action leads to tragedy. *E.g.*, Garrett Hardin, *The Tragedy of the Commons*, 162 SCI. 1243 (1968). Enforcement of conservation measures was difficult at best given the traditional freedom to fish on the high seas. When progress at the United Nations Law of the Sea Conference in the mid–1970s proved too slow, Congress fundamentally restructured fisheries policy by enacting the Magnuson Fishery Conservation and Management Act (FCMA), 16 U.S.C. §§ 1801–1883. *See generally* MICHAEL J. BEAN & MELANIE J. ROWLAND, *supra*, at 148–92; Eldon V.C. Greenberg, *Ocean Fisheries, in* ENVIRONMENTAL LAW 258–95 (Celia Campbell–Mohn *et al.* eds, 1993).

(2) State management of ocean fisheries: Traditionally, states regulated ocean fisheries—to the limited extent that they were regulated. Early United Supreme Court decisions upheld such regulation as an incident of the state's ownership of the land or resources involved or as an example of its power to promote public health and welfare. *E.g., Martin v. Waddell*, 41

U.S. (16 Pet.) 367 (1842); *Manchester v. Massachusetts,* 139 U.S. 240 (1890); *see also Alaska v. Arctic Maid,* 366 U.S. 199 (1961).

Some states went further and sought to regulate fishing on the high seas. Such regulation was held to be constitutional if the state could establish a "legitimate interest" in regulating the conduct. The case law has recognized two categories of legitimate interests in regulating the high seas fisheries. First, states have a legitimate interest in the conservation of fish, which often ignore the three-mile boundary so that fishing outside the line effects fish populations within the line. Second, regulation is permissible as a necessary adjunct of its power to regulate fishing within the territorial sea since fishers would otherwise be able to fish in the territorial seas and claim that the fish had been caught on the high seas.

As examined in Chapter 6, state regulation of fishing is subject to constitutional limitations imposed by the Commerce Clause, *e.g., Douglas v. Seacoast Products, Inc.,* 431 U.S. 265 (1977) (affirmative Commerce Clause); *Toomer v. Witsell,* 334 U.S. 385 (1948) (dormant Commerce Clause), the Privileges and Immunities Clause, *e.g., Toomer v. Witsell,* 334 U.S. 385 (1948), and the Equal Protection Clause, *e.g., Takahashi v. Fish & Game Commission,* 334 U.S. 410 (1948).

(3) International agreements as a regulatory regime: Although international agreements had been used to manage high seas fisheries since the early twentieth century, this approach became the primary mechanism in attempting to conserve fishery stocks during the period following World War II. The management strategies and regulatory tools varied widely. The Convention for the Establishment of an Inter–American Tropical Tuna Commission, for example, created an international commission that was authorized only to make recommendations to the signatories. May 31, 1949, 1 U.S.T. 230, T.I.A.S. No. 2044; *see also* Tuna Convention Act of 1950, 16 U.S.C. §§ 951–961 (implementing the Convention). The International Convention for the High Seas Fisheries of the North Pacific Ocean required some nations not to harvest certain species. May 9, 1952, United States–Canada–Japan, 4 U.S.T. 380, T.I.A.S. No. 2786. And the International Convention for the Northwest Atlantic Fisheries sought to allocate the take of several species among more than a dozen signatories. Feb. 8, 1949, 1 U.S.T. 477, T.I.A.S. No. 2089. By the mid–1970s, the United States was a party to 22 agreements. S. REP. No. 416, 94th Cong., 1st Sess. app. 1 (1975).

By the mid–1970s it was also clear that many of the agreements were failing to conserve the fisheries. In part this reflected the difficulties in enforcing restrictions on take. As the Senate Commerce Committee noted in 1975, "Most international agreements fail to provide for strong enforcement mechanisms and they are only as powerful as the signatory nations that make them." *Id.* at 10. Regardless of their variety, all of the agreements sought to limit the traditional freedom of fishing on the high seas— and the agreements thus bound only the parties to them; enforcement was impossible against non-signatories. Not only was conservation difficult because of a lack of enforcement, but the scientific data necessary to manage the resource was often lacking—recall the excerpt from Daniel Botkin on the problems with the logistic curve. *See generally* Wilbert

McLeod Chapman, *The Theory and Practice of International Fishery Development–Management,* 7 SAN DIEGO L. REV. 408 (1970).

(4) Extending national authority seaward: In 1964, Congress enacted the Bartlett Act, Pub. L. No. 88–308, 78 Stat. 194 (1964) (repealed 1977). The Act prohibited foreign-flagged fishing vessels from fishing within the territorial sea and from harvesting resources from the continental shelf. This was followed in 1966 by the Contiguous Fisheries Zone Act, Pub. L. No. 89–658, 80 Stat. 908 (1966) (repealed 1977), which created a new classification: the "contiguous zone" defined as the 9 miles seaward of the territorial sea. Foreign fishing was excluded from the contiguous zone. Neither the Bartlett Act nor the Contiguous Fisheries Zone Act included any management authority. By 1975, there was a consensus at the ongoing Law of the Sea Conference in favor of a 12–mile territorial sea and a 200–mile resource conservation zone; thirty-six nations had declared exclusive fishing zones greater than 12 miles.

(5) State ownership/federal ownership: State regulation of the three-mile wide territorial sea was predicated on ownership: the land beneath this band of waters was long assumed to be the property of the coastal states. In *United States v. California,* 332 U.S. 19 (1947), however, the Supreme Court held that the lands in fact belonged to the United States. The United States ceded these lands to the coastal states in the Submerged Lands Act of 1953, 43 U.S.C. §§ 1301–1315. Shortly thereafter, Congress asserted federal "jurisdiction, control, and power of disposition" over the "subsoil and seabed of the outer Continental Shelf" beyond the 3–mile band ceded to the states. Outer Continental Shelf Lands Act of 1953, 43 U.S.C. §§ 1331–1343, at § 1332(a).

(6) An introduction to the Magnuson Fisheries Management and Conservation Act (FCMA): The FCMA fundamentally restructured fisheries management off the coasts of the United States. It does so by establishing the authority for "the preparation and implementation, in accordance with National Standards, of fishery management plans that will achieve and maintain, on a continuing basis, the optimum yield from each fishery." 16 U.S.C. § 1801(b)(4).

(a) **The "exclusive economic zone" and beyond:** The Act established an "exclusive economic zone" (EEZ), a 197–mile-wide zone the boundary of which is "a line coterminous with the seaward boundary of each of the coastal States." *Id.* § 1802(11). Within the EEZ, "the United States claims, and will exercise rights in the manner provided in this Act, sovereign rights and exclusive fishery management authority over all fish, and all Continental Shelf fishery resources." *Id.* § 1811(a). Beyond the EEZ, the Act asserts "exclusive fishery management authority" over anadromous species[1] and all Continental Shelf fishery resources.[2] *Id.*

---

1. "Anadromous species" are "species of fish which spawn in fresh or estuarine waters of the United States and which migrate to ocean waters." *Id.* § 1802(1).

2. The term "Continental Shelf fishery resources" is defined to include a specific list of corals, crustaceans (crabs and lobsters), mollusks (abalones, conches and clams), and sponges as well as "any other sedentary species" added to the term by the Secretary upon finding that "at the harvestable stage" the species are either "(A) immobile on or

§ 1811(b). The Act also pledged that the United States will "cooperate directly or through appropriate international organizations" with nations involved in fisheries for "highly migratory species"[3] with a goal of "ensuring conservation" and promoting "the achievement of optimum yield" of such species. *Id.* § 1812.

(b) Controls on foreign fishers: Title II of the FCMA contains procedures and standards for the regulation of fishing by foreign-flagged vessels in the EEZ. The central provision is a prohibition unless (1) the fishing is permitted pursuant to a treaty in effect when the FCMA was enacted or under a "governing international fishery agreement" negotiated pursuant to the FCMA, *id.* §§ 1821(a)(1), (b), (c); (2) an "allocation" of fish is available, *id.* § 1812(e); and (3) a permit has been issued, *id.* § 1821(a)(3); *see also id.* § 1824 (permit procedures and requirements). Although foreign fishing has been phased out in the United States EEZ, it remains "hypothetically possible." Eldon V.C. Greenberg, *supra,* at 279.

(c) Regional fishery councils: To manage the fisheries in the EEZ and beyond, the FCMA established regional Fishery Management Councils (FMC) for (1) New England, (2) Mid–Atlantic, (3) South Atlantic, (4) Caribbean, (5) Gulf of Mexico, (6) Pacific, (7) North Pacific, and (8) Western Pacific. *Id.* § 1852(a)(1)-(8). The councils are composed of the state officer with responsibility for marine fisheries, the regional director of the National Marine Fisheries Service (NMFS), and four to twelve "qualified" individuals[4] appointed by the Secretary of Commerce from names submitted by the governors of the regional states. *Id.* § 1852(b). There are additional nonvoting members representing several federal agencies. *Id.* § 1852(c).

(d) Fishery Management Plans (FMPs): The regional councils are responsible for developing plans for managing each fishery[5] in the EEZ seaward of the states that make up the council. *Id.* § 1852(h)(1). These FMPs and a proposed regulation implementing the plan are submitted to the Secretary of Commerce, who has final authority to approve the plan. *Id.* § 1854(a)(3). The Secretary's approval or rejection is to be based on a review of the plan to determine that it complies with "the national standards, the other provisions of this Act, and any other applicable law." *Id.* § 1854(a)(1)(A). If, "after a reasonable period of time," a council fails to

---

under the seabed, or (B) unable to move except in constant physical contact with the seabed or subsoil." 16 U.S.C. § 1802(7).

3. The term "highly migratory species" means "tuna species, marlin ... , oceanic sharks, sailfishes ... , and swordfish." *Id.* § 1802(20). "Tuna species" is separately defined. *Id.* § 1802(39).

4. The FCMA specifies that the appointees

must be individuals who, by reason of their occupational or other experience, scientific expertise, or training, are knowledgeable regarding the conservation and management, or the commercial

or recreational harvest, of the fishery resources of the geographical area concerned.

16 U.S.C. § 1852(b)(2)(A). The Pacific Council also has "one representative of an Indian tribe with Federally recognized fishing rights." *Id.* § 1852(b)(5)(A).

5. "Fishery" means both the "stocks of fish which can be treated as a unit for purposes of conservation and management" based on "geographical, scientific, technical, recreational and economic characteristics," *and* the act of "fishing for such stocks." *Id.* § 1802(13).

submit a plan for any fishery that "requires conservation and management," the Secretary may develop the FMP. *Id.* § 1854(c). Similarly, the Secretary may develop the FMP when the council fails to submit a revised plan after the Secretary has disapproved its prior submission. *Id.* When the Secretary develops the plan, it is submitted to the regional council for comment. *Id.* § 1854(c)(4)(A).

(e) Emergency authority: If the Secretary finds that there is an emergency, he is empowered to promulgate regulations to respond to the emergency "without regard to whether a fishery management plan exists for such fishery." *Id.* § 1855(c)(1). The Secretary may exercise this power to promulgate "interim measures" to address overfishing. *Id.* The council may force the Secretary to adopt emergency regulations by unanimously requesting that he do so. *Id.* § 1855(c)(2)(A).

(f) Implementation and enforcement: Once an FMP has been approved, the Secretary is responsible for its implementation. *Id.* § 1855(d). He has available a range of both civil and criminal penalties for violations of the "Act or any regulation or permit issued pursuant to this Act." *Id.* § 1857(1)(A). Civil penalties of up to $100,000 may be assessed for any violation. *Id.* § 1858(a). Criminal penalties range from $100,000 and 6 months imprisonment up to $200,000 and ten years. *Id.* §§ 1859(a), (b).

(i) NATIONAL STANDARDS

NOTES

The FCMA originally contained seven "national standards"; three additional standards were added to the Act in 1996. The current ten standards require that "conservation and management" measures:[6] (1) "shall prevent overfishing while achieving, on a continuing basis, the optimum yield from each fishery"; (2) "shall be based upon the best scientific information available"; (3) "[t]o the extent practicable," shall manage a fish stock as a unit "throughout its range"; (4) "shall not discriminate between residents of different States"; (5) "shall, where practicable, consider efficiency"; (6) "shall take into account and allow for . . . contingencies in, fisheries, fishery resources, and catches"; (7) "shall, where practicable, minimize costs"; (8) "shall, consistent with the conservation requirements of this Act (including the prevention of overfishing and rebuilding of overfished stocks), take into account the importance of fishery resources to fishing communities"; (9) "shall, to the extent practicable, . . . minimize bycatch"; and (10) "shall, to the extent practicable, promote the safety of human life at sea." *Id.* § 1851(a)(1)-(10).

---

6. The term "conservation and management" refers to "all of the rules, regulations, conditions, methods, and other measures" that are required or useful in "rebuilding, restoring, or maintaining, any fishery resource and the marine environment"; and which are intended to secure a harvest of marine resources "on a continuing basis," to avoid "long-term adverse effects on fishery resources and the marine environment," and to assure options on the "future uses of these resources." *Id.* § 1802(5).

Note that the word "shall," which is used in all of the standards, is qualified by the phrase "to the extent practicable" in standards 3, 5, 7, 9, and 10. Does this suggest that there are two categories of standards, those that are commands and those that are limited by practicalities? Are the standards—despite their nominally imperative character—so imbued with discretion and uncertainty that they are all but unenforceable?

* * *

National standards 1 and 2—particularly as they have been reinforced by subsequent legislation—are the centerpiece of the Act's management requirements:

(A) National Standard One: "Overfishing" and "Optimum Yield"

NOTES

(1) The first standard requires that "[a]ny fishery management plan ... shall prevent overfishing while achieving, on a continuing basis, the optimum yield from each fishery." *Id.* § 1851(a)(1). This requirement is reinforced in section 303 of the Act, which states that the required provisions of an FMP include "conservation measures ... to prevent overfishing and rebuild overfished stocks." *Id.* 1853(a)(1)(A). Preventing overfishing is "the most basic objective of fishery management." S. Rep. No. 416, 94th Cong., 1st Sess. 31 (1975).

(a) "Overfishing" was defined by Congress in 1996 as "a rate or level of fishing mortality that jeopardizes the capacity of a fishery to produce the maximum sustainable yield on a continuing basis." 16 U.S.C. § 1802(29).

(b) "Optimum yield" (OY) is defined broadly: "The term 'optimum,' with respect to the yield from a fishery, means the amount of fish" which (A) "will provide the greatest overall benefit to the Nation ... taking into account the protection of marine ecosystems" and (B) "is prescribed ... on the basis of the maximum sustainable yield from the fishery, *as reduced by* any relevant social, economic, or ecological factor." As applied to an overfished fishery, the optimum yield is one that "provides for rebuilding to a level consistent with producing the maximum sustainable yield in such fishery." *Id.* § 1802(28) (emphasis added).

(c) "Maximum sustainable yield" (MSY) is defined by regulation as "the largest average annual catch or yield that can be taken over a significant period of time from each stock under prevailing ecological and environmental conditions." 50 C.F.R. § 602.11(d)(1).

As defined following the 1996 amendments, MSY thus is a ceiling. Actual catches are to be "reduced by any relevant social, economic, or ecological factor."

The 1996 amendments also contained additional provisions designed to require FMCs to address overfishing problems. A new mandatory provision was added: henceforth, all FMPs must "specify objective and measurable criteria for identifying when the fishery to which the plan applies is overfished (with an analysis of how the criteria were determined and the relationship of the criteria to the reproductive potential of stocks of fish in that fishery)." 16 U.S.C. § 1853(a)(10). When the fishery "is approaching an overfished condition or is overfished, [the plan shall] contain conservation and management measures designed to prevent overfishing or end overfishing and rebuild the fishery." *Id.* Finally, the 1996 amendments added reporting requirements, set a timetable, and established procedures to incorporate measures to prevent overfishing and rebuild overfished fisheries. *Id.* § 1854(e).

(2) Linking the definitions: Once optimum yield (OY) has been established in a specific Fishery Management Plan, it determines the amount of fish of a species that may be taken from the fishery in a particular year. Optimum, thus, does not mean "ideal under the best of all circumstances"; it merely means the amount of fish that the decisionmaker believes can be caught on an annual basis, considering the factors to be taken into account.

Predictably, OY calculations are highly contentious. Conservation interests generally favor lower numbers to help increase populations; fishing interests often (though not always) favor higher numbers, both because they are concerned with their current income and because of uncertainty over the extent to which they would be able to increase their catch if populations rose. When disputes spill over into the courtroom, the resulting legal issues are predictable: What does OY mean as a matter of law? How much discretion does a regional council (or the Secretary) have in setting it? And has the Council (or Secretary) in a given case made a determination that is (i) consistent with the legal meaning, (ii) adequately grounded in factual evidence, and (iii) within the range of discretion vested in it by law? These issues arise in the next case.

Although OY is, in the end, the key number, it is highly dependent on a fishery's maximum sustainable yield (MSY). So, too, is the determination as to whether a particular fishery is "overfished." Under the definitions, OY calculations begin with a determination of a fishery's MSY, which is then adjusted downward to OY based on "social, economic, or ecological factor[s]." Proper downward adjustments are debatable and contentious (as the next case also illustrates), but just as, if not more, important is the starting number—the MSY.

Similarly, "overfishing" occurs, according to the regulations, "whenever a stock or stock complex is subjected to a rate of level of fishing mortality that jeopardizes the capacity of a stock or stock complex to produce MSY on a continuing basis." 50 C.F.R. § 600.310(d)(ii). Thus, the determination that a fishery is overfished also depends directly on a fishery's MSY.

This interlinking of definitions would not be problematic if MSY were clearly defined and easily established—but it is not, as the next note explains.

(3) The messiness of MSY: On its face, MSY would seem to be a number based entirely on science since it ought to reflect the largest yield that a fishery could sustain if the fishery were fully healthy (*i.e.,* not depleted). Applicable regulations, however, confuse the issue, giving decisionmakers flexibility in determining MSY. MSY is defined as "the largest long-term average catch or yield" that a fishery can sustain, 50 C.F.R. § 600.310(c)(1)(i), and the proper "MSY control rule" is a harvesting strategy "which, if implemented, would be expected to result in a long-term average catch approximating MSY." *Id.,* § 600.310(c)(1)(ii). So far so good. But the regulations then go on to state that, because "MSY is a theoretical concept" (*i.e.,* a harvesting level based on hypothetical and uncertain circumstances), "its estimation in practice is conditional on the choice of an MSY control rule," *id.,* § 600.310(c)(2), which is to say, that a harvesting strategy for a fishery is set first, and then the MSY of the fishery is then based on it!

The regulations proceed to specify various ways in which harvesting strategies might be set, but in the end give decisionmakers room to make their own determinations. In the case of each harvesting method illustrated in the applicable regulation, the strategic aim is to "maximize the resulting long-term average yield," but the illustrations apparently are not binding. Even if a harvesting strategy does aim at maximizing long-term average yield, it remains unclear whether this "maximizing" requirement means the maximum yield that a fishery could produce under ideal circumstances, or whether it means the highest yield reasonably possible starting from current, depleted conditions and taking into account factors of practicality. In the end, the whole string of definitions might just be circular: a yield is the highest maximum when it is based on—and hence can sustain—a harvesting strategy that achieves the highest maximum. As if to emphasize and sum-up the underlying confusion, the regulation on MSY ends with the following sentence: "In any MSY control rule, a given stock size is associated with a given level of fishing mortality and a given level of potential harvest, where the long-term average of these potential harvests provides an estimate of MSY."

(4) Overfishing, again: Even setting to one side the challenges of setting MSY, the definitions of overfishing and overfished show similar room for political maneuvering. One might suppose that a fishery is overfished if its fish population is insufficient to yield a harvest equal to MSY—but not so. A fishery is overfished only when "a change in management practices is required in order to achieve an appropriate level and rate of rebuilding." 50 C.F.R. § 600.310(d)(1). Thus, if a management plan for a depleted fishery is, in theory, adequate over time to rebuild the stock to a point where it would achieve MSY, then it is not overfished, however depleted it might be. As for "overfishing," note again its precise meaning: fishing "at a rate or level that jeopardizes the capacity of a stock or stock complex to produce MSY on a continuing basis." Continuing harvesting of a seriously depleted fishery might not amount to overfishing under this definition if a factual determination is made that the stock nonetheless retains the "capacity" in time to rebound to levels that would produce MSY.

Return to the language of standard 1. Is the requirement that plans "prevent overfishing" a legal limit that exists independently of the requirement that the plans provide for harvesting the "optimum yield"? Given how both are linked to the political determination of MSY, can they be construed to have independent force?

* * *

The following case immerses us in the factually complex world of fisheries management. Note carefully, as you read it, exactly what legal challenges are being presented. Does the court offer its own interpretation of optimum yield? Does it view the restriction on overfishing as having independent force? And how rigorously does it question the factual determinations made by the government?

Blue Water Fisherman's Association v. Mineta

District Court for the District of Columbia.
122 F.Supp.2d 150 (2000).

■ ROBERTS, D.J.:—Plaintiffs, individuals and associations involved in the pelagic longline fishing industry, brought this challenge to the Commerce Secretary's ("Secretary's") regulations implementing the final 1999 Highly Migratory Species Fishery Management Plan.... Because I find that the Secretary acted within his authority ... , defendant's motion for summary judgment will be granted....

I. Introduction

Pelagic longline fishers catch species such as tuna, shark and swordfish. [ ] These species are known as Highly Migratory Species ("HMS"). [ ] Pelagic longline fishers catch HMS with long fishing lines attached to "a series of leaders that connect to individual hooks in the ocean at specific depths." [ ] There are less than 300 pelagic longline fishing boats currently in operation "over wide areas of the Atlantic Ocean, the Caribbean Sea, and the Gulf of Mexico," [ ], and the number of longline boats has remained constant since 1987. [ ] Pelagic longline fishers earn an average yearly income of $53,064, before paying fixed operating and maintenance costs. [ ]

Pelagic longline fishing and pelagic fish are subject to statutory and regulatory regimes, as well as international agreements, designed to protect HMS. [ ] The focus of this litigation is the final 1999 Highly Migratory Species Fishery Management Plan for Atlantic Tunas, Swordfish and Sharks ("HMS FMP"), promulgated by the National Marine Fisheries Service ("NMFS"), pursuant to its authority delegated by the Secretary of Commerce ("Secretary") under the Magnuson–Stevens Fishery Conservation and Management Act ("Magnuson–Stevens Act"), 16 U.S.C. §§ 1801–1883.

Plaintiffs claim that four of the HMS FMP's regulations are arbitrary and capricious, including (1) limits on Atlantic bluefin tuna ("ABT") that can be caught and kept per fishing trip, [ ]; (2) an area ban on fishing during the month of June, [ ]; (3) annual quotas for blue sharks and subquotas for porbeagle sharks, [ ]; and (4) a requirement that all pelagic longline fishers install a VMS [vessel monitoring system] unit on their vessels, [ ]. Specifically, the plaintiffs claim that each regulation violates certain National Standards set forth in the Magnuson–Stevens Act. *See* 16 U.S.C. §§ 1851(a)(1)-(10), 1853(a)(1)(C).

. . .

II. Legal Framework

A. The Magnuson–Stevens Act

The purpose of the Magnuson–Stevens Act is to protect HMS in waters extending two hundred (200) miles from the United States coast through conservation and management measures. *See* 16 U.S.C. §§ 1801(a), (b). Congress found that many HMS were "overfished"[3] and that as a result of "increased fishing pressure" and "the inadequacy of fishery resource conservation and management practices," the survival of HMS "is threatened." 16 U.S.C. § 1801(a)(2). Congress also found that other species, while not technically overfished, were "so substantially reduced in number that they could become similarly threatened." *Id.*

The Magnuson–Stevens Act directs the Secretary to prepare "fishery management plans which will achieve and maintain, on a continuing basis, the optimum yield from each fishery," 16 U.S.C. § 1801(b)(4), including HMS. *See* 16 U.S.C. § 1854(g)(1). That responsibility is delegated to NMFS. *Id.*

A plan issued pursuant to the Magnuson–Stevens Act must be consistent with ten National Standards. *See* 16 U.S.C. § 1851(a). Plaintiffs raise five of these standards in their claims, arguing that each of the 1999 HMS FMP regulations at issue violated one or all of them. The standards at issue are:

(1) Conservation and management measures shall prevent overfishing while achieving, on a continuing basis, the optimum yield from each fishery for the United States fishing industry.

(2) Conservation and management measures shall be based upon the best scientific information available.

(7) Conservation and management measures shall, where practicable, minimize costs and avoid unnecessary duplication.

(8) Conservation and management measures shall, consistent with the conservation requirements of this chapter (including the prevention of overfishing and rebuilding of overfished stocks), take into account the importance of fishery resources to fishing communities in order to (A) provide for the sustained participation of such communities, and (B) to the extent practicable, minimize adverse economic impacts on such communities.

(9) Conservation and management measures shall, to the extent practicable, (A) minimize bycatch and (B) to the extent bycatch cannot be avoided, minimize the mortality of such bycatch.

---

3. ....

Maximum Sustainable Yield ("MSY") is "the largest long-term average catch or yield that can be taken from a stock or stock complex under prevailing ecological and environmental conditions." 50 C.F.R. § 600.310(c)(1)(i). The Code recognizes that "[a]ny MSY values used in determining [optimum yield] will necessarily be estimates, and these will typically be associated with some level of uncertainty. Such estimates must be based on the best scientific information available (*see* § 600.315) and must incorporate appropriate consideration of risk (*see* § 600.335). Beyond these requirements, however, Councils have a reasonable degree of latitude in determining which estimates to use and how these estimates are to be expressed." 50 C.F.R. § 600.310(c)(2)(ii).

16 U.S.C. §§ 1851(a)(1), (2), (7)–(9).

Bycatch is defined as "fish which are harvested in a fishery, but which are not sold or kept for personal use, and includes economic discards and regulatory discards. Such term does not include fish released alive under a recreational catch and release fishery management program." 16 U.S.C. § 1802(2). In other words, bycatch is those fish that fishers catch but throw back into the ocean, either because they are not the kind of fish that people will buy (being too small, of the wrong gender or of bad quality), or because a regulation dictates that the fish cannot be kept. *See* 50 C.F.R. § 600.350(c). This second kind of bycatch is referred to as a regulatory discard. Regulatory discards may occur where certain fish species are so overfished that they cannot be kept or sold. *See* 50 C.F.R. § 622.32 (describing those species of fish which may not be harvested or possessed). For example, the 1999 HMS FMP allows pelagic longline fishers fishing south of a certain latitude to retain only one large or medium bluefin tuna per fishing trip. *See* 50 C.F.R. § 635.23(f)(1). All fish caught in excess of that limit must be discarded.

. . .

C. Standard of Review

The Magnuson–Stevens Act provides for judicial review of an HMS FMP under the same standards as those set forth in the Administrative Procedure Act ("APA"), 5 U.S.C. §§ 706(2)(A)-(D) (1994). *See* 16 U.S.C. § 1855(f). The APA directs that "the reviewing court shall ... hold unlawful and set aside agency action, findings, and conclusions found to be ... arbitrary, capricious, an abuse of discretion, or otherwise not in accordance with law." 5 U.S.C. § 706(2)(A).

. . .

III. Substantive Disputes

A. Atlantic Bluefin Tuna [ABT] Trip Limits

Plaintiffs challenge the limits on ABT that a longline fisher may catch and keep on any given fishing trip (referred to as the "ABT Trip Limit"). *See* 50 C.F.R. § 635.23(f). Plaintiffs argue that this provision is arbitrary and capricious because it violates the Magnuson–Stevens Act's National Standards One, Eight and Nine. I find that the defendant has described a sufficiently rational basis to support the need for ABT trip limits.

1. Background

ABT is an overfished species. [ ] To aid conservation, [the International Convention for the Conservation of Atlantic Tuna] ICCAT recommended per-nation ABT quotas under a twenty-year ABT fishery rebuilding program, beginning in 1999. [ ][5] NMFS in turn sets annual ABT quotas for each category of fishing vessel. *See* 50 C.F.R. § 635.27(a). Pelagic longliners currently are allocated 8.1% of the total United States quota. *Id.*

---

5. The total allowable ABT catch is 2,500 metric tons per year. Of this total, the United States is allotted 1,387 metric tons per year (or 55.48%). [ ] The total amount of ABT that the United States is permitted to land changes periodically according to ICCAT recommendations. [ ]

As a further conservation measure, NMFS does not allow pelagic longline fishers to target ABT. Longliners are allowed to catch and keep ABT only "incidentally." 50 C.F.R. § 635.23(f). This means that longliners may keep an ABT only if it is caught by accident when a longliner is fishing for other species. [ ] NMFS first imposed this "incidental-only" restriction on the longliners in 1981. [ ] The parties agree that current ABT catches are purely incidental and not a result of targeted fishing. [ ] At oral argument, plaintiffs stated that longline boats do not encounter ABT at all on ninety percent of their fishing trips.

In addition to the incidental-only restriction, pelagic longline fishers are not allowed to catch and keep more than a certain number of ABT during the course of each fishing trip. [ ] Pelagic longliners must discard any ABT caught above the limit. NMFS also has imposed a regulation that subtracts longliners' dead discards from their yearly quota. [ ] This means that whenever a longliner catches an ABT that is killed, the weight of that ABT is subtracted from the total yearly quota, whether that fish is kept or thrown back. Any ABT caught in excess of the yearly quota are subtracted from the following year's quota. *See* 50 C.F.R. § 635.27(a)(9)(i). Consistently, if the annual quota has not been reached for a particular year, NMFS increases the following year's quota. *Id.* Plaintiffs assert that the trip limits in combination with the discard penalties is arbitrary and capricious.

Plaintiffs argue that the trip limits do not achieve any conservation benefits because longliners catch ABT only incidentally and, therefore, imposing trip limits will not change the amount of ABT actually caught. The trip limits merely guarantee that ABT will have to be discarded. In combination with the requirement to subtract discards from the longliners' total quota, the trip limits all but ensure that longliners will never be able to harvest their allotted quota. Plaintiffs refer to this as a "death-spiral" effect: that is, the trip limits will cause discards, and the discards make it more likely that longliners will exceed their ABT quota, which in turn will cause the following year's quota to be reduced, only to start the cycle again.

Plaintiffs also point out that in past years, when they have been unable to harvest their allotted quota, NMFS has reallocated the unused portion of the longliners' quota to the "General Category,"[7] thus allowing fishers in the General Category to catch ABT in place of those that the longliners were unable to catch and keep. Plaintiffs do not argue that trip limits should be abolished; they merely argue that the current trip limits are so restrictive as to be arbitrary and capricious. Given that there is no evidence that longliners are targeting ABT, plaintiffs argue that the trip limits have no positive effect on conservation and may have a negative effect insofar as the limits encourage discards. In addition, plaintiffs state that the trip limits have a substantial negative economic effect on the pelagic longline fishing industry.

Defendant argues that NMFS's main objective in maintaining the trip limits is to ensure that longliners do not begin targeting ABT. Defendant

---

7. The "General Category" consists of fishers who catch and sell ABT over 73 inches long, and it includes both commercial and recreational fishers. [ ] Currently, NMFS allocates 47.1% of the annual ABT quota to the General Category and 8.1% to Longliners. [ ]

points out that a single ABT may "be worth thousands of dollars." [ ] In an industry where the average income is $53,064, the financial incentive to catch these fish is quite strong. [ ] Defendants maintain that the lack of a statistical relationship between target fish landed and ABT caught merely demonstrates that the current trip limits are having the desired effect of assuring that longliners catch ABT only incidentally.

Defendant states that NMFS was aware that the regulations might produce bycatch and might also produce a burden on the longline industry. NMFS decided, however, that it did not want to risk creating an incentive to target ABT by increasing the trip limits. Plaintiffs counter by stating that an *overall* yearly ABT quota achieves that result without having the trip limits' adverse economic effects. Defendant asserts that it has minimized adverse economic impacts to the extent practicable in light of its primary conservation purposes.

2. Discussion

a) National Standard One

Plaintiffs contend that the trip limits violate National Standard One by interfering with fishers' ability to catch their allotted quota, and preventing fishers from "achieving, on a continuing basis, the optimum yield from each fishery for the United States fishing industry." 16 U.S.C. § 1851(a)(1). They appear to reason that because optimum yield involves, in part, "maintaining an economically viable fishery together with its attendant contributions to the national, regional and local economies, and utilizing the capacity of the Nation's fishing resources," 50 C.F.R. § 600.310(f)(2)(i), there is a "requirement that the fishery provide an economic return to fishermen and fishing communities. . . . " [ ] Plaintiffs conclude that any regulation that detracts from their ability to catch and sell their portion of the ABT quota violates National Standard One, because the fishery as a whole would not be able to achieve optimum yield each year.

This argument is unavailing. NMFS is statutorily required to set out a plan that stops overfishing and rebuilds the stock of fish as quickly as possible. *See* 16 U.S.C. § 1854(e)(4)(A)(i). The statutory "optimum yield" definition recognizes that optimum yield is a standard that should be achieved over the long-run, not necessarily a standard that must be achieved with precision each year. *See* 50 C.F.R. § 600.310(f)(1)(ii) ("[i]n national standard 1, . . . 'achieving, on a continuing basis, the [optimum yield] from each fishery' means producing, from each fishery, a long-term series of catches such that the average catch is equal to the average [optimum yield]").

Plaintiffs' argument on this point does not adequately address the fact that National Standard One is meant to achieve optimum yield *while preventing overfishing.* Nor do the plaintiffs adequately address the requirement that NMFS take action to rebuild overfished stock. Nothing in the regulations presumes that longliners are *entitled* to catch their allotted quota. As defendant points out, even if applicable statutes and regulations required the HMS FMP to allow fishers to catch the optimum yield of ABT every year, such a requirement would not necessarily translate to a right vested in the pelagic longline industry to catch its annual allotted quota; rather, it would run to the rights of United States fishers as a whole.

The United States Court of Appeals for the District of Columbia Circuit has held that "an FMP can comply with [National] Standard 1 if there are social, economic or ecological factors that justify the pursuit of a yield less than the maximum sustainable yield." *C & W Fish Co. v. Fox,* 931 F.2d 1556, 1563 (D.C.Cir.1991). In this case, optimum yield, which is determined by the maximum sustainable yield in cases of overfished fisheries, *see* 16 U.S.C. § 1802(28), does not have to be a primary imperative in light of NMFS's statutorily-mandated conservation objectives. The ABT trip limits, 50 C.F.R. § 635.23(f), do not violate National Standard One.

b) National Standard Eight

Plaintiffs argue that the trip limits do not achieve significant conservation benefits, and the economic costs are not justified under National Standard Eight's requirement that defendant must, "to the extent practicable, minimize adverse economic impacts on such communities." 16 U.S.C. § 1851(a)(8). Defendant argues that, while economic effects must be taken into account, such effects were not meant to trump the real purpose of the Magnuson–Stevens Act, which is to preserve and protect United States fisheries. He emphasizes that minimizing adverse impacts on fishing communities need be achieved only "to the extent practicable." 16 U.S.C. § 1851(a)(8). NMFS is and has been concerned that the ABT fishery cannot withstand any additional fishing pressure. [ ] Apparently, a surge of ABT catches by pelagic longliners occurred in 1980, and the high prices received for the ABT encouraged fishers to consider targeting ABT. [ ] As a result, in 1981, NMFS imposed the first trip limits. [ ]

Because NMFS is still concerned that the financial rewards of selling ABT will encourage fishers to target ABT, NMFS decided that the current trip limits should be maintained. Further, the HMS FMP points out that the problem with excessive discards would not be addressed by changing the trip limits. [ ] Increasing the trip limit would ensure only that longliners meet their quota earlier in the season, because the overall ABT quota would remain the same. After the overall quota has been met, all subsequent catches would have to be discarded, and, since ABT are caught only incidentally, the ultimate discard rate would be substantially the same.

NMFS determined that increasing the trip limits would risk creating an incentive for fishers to target ABT which could impair ABT conservation efforts. Plaintiffs have not provided sufficient evidence from the record to support their claim that the current trip limits fail to minimize adverse economic impacts on the longline fishing community to the extent practicable. Defendant's bases for maintaining the current trip limits to further its conservation purposes were ample and not unreasonable. The ABT trip limits, 50 C.F.R. § 635.23(f), do not violate National Standard Eight.

c) National Standard Nine

In claiming that the trip limits fail to "minimize bycatch" to the extent practicable, as National Standard Nine requires, 16 U.S.C. § 1851(a)(9), plaintiffs argue that the trip limits not only "require[ ] us to discard dead fish" and create more bycatch, but the limits penalize longliners because bycatch is subtracted from the longliners' yearly quota. [ ]

NMFS is required to minimize bycatch only "to the extent practicable." 16 U.S.C. § 1851(a)(9). Defendant maintains that it has minimized bycatch "to the extent practicable" by closing off a certain area of the Atlantic to pelagic longline fishers for the month of June, which is known for its high concentrations of ABT.

Again, NMFS determined that the current trip limits were necessary to prevent fishers from targeting ABT. It is well within the agency's discretion to make this determination, and defendant was justified in maintaining the current trip limits to further its conservation purposes. *See National Fisheries Inst. v. Mosbacher,* 732 F. Supp. 210, 223 (D.D.C.1990) ("this question of whether certain billfish conservation and management measures would be in the nation's 'best interest' is 'a classic example of a factual dispute the resolution of which implicates substantial agency expertise.... It is therefore especially appropriate for me to defer to the expertise and experience of [the agency].' ") (internal citations omitted). The ABT trip limits, 50 C.F.R. § 635.23(f), do not violate National Standard Nine.

B.   The June Closure

[NMFS issued a regulation stating that "no person may deploy a pelagic longline" in a specified area off the Northeastern United States coast from June 1 through June 30 each year. The regulation was intended to prevent pelagic longline fishers from landing ABT or swordfish. Challenges to the closure under National Standards 1 and 8 were rejected by the court.]

C.   Pelagic Shark Quotas

[NMFS issued a regulation setting annual quotas for all pelagic sharks as well as separate quotas on blue sharks and porbeagle sharks. If longliners exceed the yearly quotas, the excess is subtracted from the following year's quota. Pelagic sharks are encountered only incidentally by longline fishers. Fishers sometimes encounter "anomalously large concentrations of pelagic sharks" by chance, causing the catch-rate on pelagic sharks to vary widely from year to year.

[Plaintiffs argue that porbeagle and blue sharks are healthy, resilient species which are not overfished; that NMFS failed to gather enough information about these sharks; and that the agency's information does not justify the quota regulations. Defendant agrees that the porbeagle and blue sharks are not overfished but states that their biological status is unknown and not "relatively healthy." Both species take a relatively long time to rebuild their stock because they breed slowly. Defendant also agrees that NMFS does not have sufficient data on the domestic pelagic shark fishery for stock evaluation purposes. Therefore, NMFS did not change the overall pelagic shark quota but rather established separate quotas for porbeagle and blue shark quotas.

[Plaintiffs argued that the regulation violated National Standards 1, 2, 8, and 9. The court rejected the challenge under National Standard 1:]

Nor does the fact that neither porbeagle nor blue sharks are overfished at the present time mean that the quotas and subquotas are improper. National Standard One requires that "[c]onservation and management measures shall *prevent* overfishing.... " 16 U.S.C. § 1851(a)(1) (emphasis added). The Magnuson–Stevens Act does not purport to protect only overfished species. The record shows that NMFS has cause to be concerned that porbeagle and blue sharks may become overfished. [ ] ("Generally, sharks are vulnerable to overfishing because they produce few offspring, mature late in life, and live many years."); [ ] (blue shark species may be "vulnerable to overfishing because it is caught in tremendous numbers as bycatch in numerous longline fisheries" and preliminary catch rates suggest that the blue shark population "may be declining"); [ ] (porbeagle sharks, "like most other sharks, can not withstand heavy fishing pressure"). NMFS has justified the blue shark quota and the porbeagle shark subquota with evidence that the regulations will prevent overfishing, as National Standard One requires. Accordingly, the pelagic shark quotas, 50 C.F.R. §§ 635.27(b)(1)(iii)(A), (C), do not violate National Standard One.

b) National Standard Two

Plaintiffs argue that NMFS does not have enough data and scientific information to justify the blue shark quota or the porbeagle shark subquota. To the extent that NMFS does have relevant data, plaintiffs argue that the data show that these restrictions are unwarranted. Specifically, NMFS stated that "[t]here is little evidence from the catch rate data that supports the need for more restrictive management measures at this time." [ ]

Defendant maintained that the pelagic shark quotas and subquotas are based on the best available scientific evidence for domestic pelagic shark fisheries. Although NMFS does not have sufficient data for stock evaluation purposes, defendant explained that, because "certain pelagic shark species are transoceanic and subject to exploitation by many nations, a comprehensive stock evaluation would require the cooperation of many nations." [ ] NMFS therefore determined that the "available information on catch, landings, and catch rates, while informative of general trends, is insufficient to modify current estimates of maximum sustainable yield or quota levels of pelagic sharks." [ ]

NMFS used the best information available to establish quotas separate from the overall quota, *not* to "modify" the current overall pelagic shark quota levels. An agency must base its determinations on information available at the time of preparing the HMS FMP or implementing the regulations. *See* 50 C.F.R. § 600.315(b)(2). I cannot demand more. [ ] NMFS established the blue shark quota and the porbeagle shark subquota to prevent these species from becoming overfished, and to reduce dead blue shark discards. [ ] NMFS may use the available information on porbeagle and blue sharks to create the conservation-based regulations. *See* 50 C.F.R. § 600.315(b) ("The fact that scientific information concerning a fishery is incomplete does not prevent the preparation and implementation of an FMP"); [ ]; *Parravano v. Babbitt,* 837 F. Supp. 1034, 1046 (N.D.Cal.1993) ("By requiring that decisions be based on the best scientific information available, the [Magnuson–Stevens] Act acknowledges that such information may not be exact or totally complete"), *aff'd,* 70 F.3d 539 (9th Cir.1995), *cert. denied,* 518 U.S. 1016 (1996); [ ] Accordingly, the pelagic shark quotas, 50 C.F.R. §§ 635.27(b)(1)(iii)(A), (C), do not violate National Standard Two.

. . .

d) National Standard Nine

Plaintiffs contend that the shark quotas require pelagic longline fishers to discard a substantial number of porbeagle and blue sharks caught incidentally, which effectively increases bycatch in violation of National Standard Nine. This Standard, however, provides that NMFS's regulations must minimize bycatch "to the extent practicable," and, "to the extent bycatch cannot be avoided, minimize the mortality of such bycatch." 16 U.S.C. §§ 1851(a)(9)(A), (B). "Fish that are bycatch and cannot be avoided must, to the extent practicable, be returned to the sea alive." 50 C.F.R. § 600.350(d).

Given that pelagic sharks are caught only incidentally, NMFS would have to eliminate *all* pelagic shark quotas to guarantee a reduction in bycatch. NMFS has established that this is not a reasonable alternative which would further conservation objectives. Even though a certain amount of bycatch cannot be avoided when there are pelagic shark quotas and subquotas, NMFS has minimized bycatch mortality with regulations that count dead (but not live) discards against the applicable shark quota. *See* 50 C.F.R. § 635.27(b)(1)(iv)(C) ("Sharks discarded dead are counted against the applicable directed fishery quota."). NMFS has established strong regulatory incentives for fishers to refrain from killing pelagic sharks and ensure that the sharks "be returned to the sea alive." 50 C.F.R. § 600.350(d). The pelagic shark quotas, 50 C.F.R. §§ 635.27(b)(1)(iii)(A), (C), do not violate National Standard Nine.

. . .

IV.   Conclusion

Based on the evidence in the administrative record, the ABT trip limit, June Closure and pelagic shark quota regulations are consistent with the Magnuson–Stevens Act, 16 U.S.C. §§ 1851(a)(1), (2), (7)-(9), 1853(a)(12), (14), 1854(g)(1)(C). The Secretary duly considered plaintiffs' arguments and comments, but acted within his discretion when he promulgated these final rules. . . .

NOTES

(1) Note how the plaintiffs framed their challenge to the ABT limits under National Standard 1. They did not challenge the determination of MSY; they questioned only the adjustments made to it to reach OY. Although the statutory definition of OY explains that "social, economic, or ecological factors" can justify *reductions* in optimum yield below the MSY, the plaintiffs here sought to use economic and social factors to *increase* the OY—or, perhaps more exactly, they argued that a full consideration of all social, economic, and ecological factors should have led the NMFS to make a lesser reduction in setting OY. As plaintiffs correctly note, the OY calculations are to take into account food production issues, including the need to maintain economically viable fishing operations. How does the court respond to this point? Is its response chiefly a legal response; that is, did the court disagree with the plaintiffs' interpretation of the law? Is its response instead one that arises out of deference to the policy expertise and factual findings of the NMFS? Is it clear from the opinion how the requirement to prevent overfishing fits into the calculation of OY? Is it important, on this issue, that economic and social conditions are relevant in setting OY but not in determining whether overfishing is taking place (which is based solely on MSY)?

As you consider these questions, consider the court's response to plaintiffs' argument that the quotas for porbeagle and blue sharks violated National Standard 1. Once again, the court upholds the agency's action based on the prevention of overfishing, rather than on the issue of OY. Should this outcome provide a signal to the agency as to how it might justify tight fishing limits under National Standard 1? If it routinely justifies its actions based on overfishing rather than on complex calculations of OY, will it likely receive more deference? On the other hand, is not the multi-factor OY calculation so complex and fact-dependent that a court is unlikely to second guess a final agency determination?

Questions about the court's application of National Standard 2 are set forth below.

(2) ***Northwest Environmental Defense Center v. Brennen*** was a challenge to the harvest quota for Oregon coastal, naturally spawning (OCN)[1] coho salmon. Coho are an anadromous species that hatch in freshwater, migrate to the ocean to mature, and then return to spawn in their natal stream. Most coho spend three years in the ocean; hence, there are three "cycles" of coho that are effectively linked across time. The Pacific Fishery Management Council (composed of state representatives from California, Idaho, Oregon, and Washington) has denominated the group that spawned in 1983, 1986, and 1989 as "Cycle 2." Because of adverse climatic conditions, only 57,000 OCN salmon spawned in 1983.

The Pacific Council manages anadromous species by setting annual "escapement goals" that specify the number of salmon that must escape harvest—generally ocean fishing—to spawn. The Council set an escapement goal of 170,000 for 1986 and 200,000 for 1989. When it published the final salmon management regulations for 1986, however, the Council set harvest quotas that were expected to result in escapement of only 142,800 OCN coho. In 1987, the Council changed its method of setting escapement goals to an "abundance-dependent" method. Under an abundance-dependent method, the escapement goal varies with the estimated stock size: for stock sizes under 270,000 fish, the escapement goal was 135,000 fish; for stock sizes between 270,000 and 400,000 fish, the escapement goal was one-half the stock; for stocks greater than 400,000, the goal was 200,000 fish.

The Northwest Environmental Defense Center (NEDC) challenged the abundance-dependent method for setting escapement goals as a violation of National Standard 1 because—as the Secretary acknowledged—an escape-

---

1. In addition to naturally spawning coho, there are also hatchery-reared coho.

ment of 200,000 was needed to produce the MSY. The court upheld the new method:

> NEDC has not produced any evidence that abundance-dependent escapement goals are inconsistent with the long-term ability of the OCN coho stocks to attain maximum sustainable yield. Both sides agree that spawning escapement of 200,000 OCN coho represents the maximum sustainable yield. The abundance-dependent method allows a harvest in excess of maximum sustainable yield whenever the run dips below 400,000 fish. The Secretary has set an escapement floor of 135,000, however, so that if the run falls to or below this number no harvest is allowed. The floor escapement level was established after review of the past history of the stock, stock recruitment analysis, and review of the expected geographic distribution of spawners. It includes a built-in margin of safety and conservatism. NEDC has not pointed to any evidence that a spawning escapement of 135,000, whether in one year or in several, is inconsistent with the long-term health of the OCN coho stock.

Northwest Environmental Defense Center v. Brennen, 958 F.2d 930, 935 (9th Cir.1992).

Brennen was primarily concerned with a claim that the harvesting plan (*i.e.,* the OY) violated the ban on overfishing, which *at the time* was defined by regulation rather than by statute. The court upheld the regulation, which then served as the basis for the 1996 statutory amendment. Because the language of the regulation is now in the statute, the case remains instructive on the meaning of overfishing. No overfishing took place in *Brennen,* the court held, because the stock (Cycle 2) was recovering and would in a few years (or so the Council predicted) return to a level where it could produce the MSY. The definition of overfishing proposed by plaintiffs and rejected by the court was that overfishing took place whenever an annual harvest failed to leave a breeding stock large enough to produce the MSY the following year. Had that interpretation been sustained, no fishing at all would be permitted in several fisheries.

Brennen is also useful in illustrating how easy it is to become confused about the terms OY, MSY, and overfishing. As the court noted, the statute (at the time) allowed OY to be set above MSY based on social, economic, and ecological factors; currently, OY must be less than MSY. On the facts of the case, however, it appears that OY for Cycle 2 was not set above MSY—despite the apparent assumption of some or all of the parties to the contrary (in the court's handling of the case, the issue never became important).

(3) *North Carolina Fisheries Association, Inc. v. Daley*: In 1995, NMFS determined that North Carolina commercial fishers caught 592,748 pounds of summer flounder in excess of their annual quota. The agency therefore reduced the quota for the succeeding year. The industry appealed the decision, arguing in part that

> that Defendant violated the APA because the 1997 summer flounder quota does not allow for the achievement of "optimum yield" on a

continuing basis contrary to the requirements of National Standard 1 of the Magnuson–Stevens Act, 16 U.S.C. § 1851(a)(1). [ ]

The crux of Plaintiffs argument seems to be that because less fish will be fished than the initial quota allows (because of the subtraction of the overages from the quota), optimum yield is not being achieved. Plaintiffs', however, misconstrue the term "optimum yield." The District of Columbia Circuit has defined optimum yield as "maximum yield *less* whatever amount need be conserved for economic, social or ecological reasons." *C & W Fish Co. v. Fox*, 931 F.2d 1556, 1563 (D.C.Cir.1991). This Court has also held that " 'optimum yield' is not the same as 'maximum yield.' " *J.H. Miles & Co. v. Brown*, 910 F.Supp. 1138, 1148 (E.D.Va.1995). Furthermore, optimum yield is measured on a continuing basis, therefore "management measures must aim to achieve, on a continuing basis, the optimum yield from each fishery, not the optimum yield in a single year." *Id.*

The Court finds that the Secretary did not violate National Standard 1.

North Carolina Fisheries Association, Inc. v. Daley, 16 F.Supp.2d 647 (E.D.Va.1997).

PERSPECTIVES

Bluefin tuna and globalization: On January 6, 2001, the Associated Press reported that a 444–pound bluefin tuna sold for over $175,000 at the Tsukiji Central Fish Market in Tokyo, Japan. Although the fish is unlikely to have come from the North Atlantic, the fish that are caught off Maine and Massachusetts during the summer tuna season are also wholesaled through Tsukiji:

A 40–minute drive from Bath, Maine, down a winding two-lane highway, the last mile on a dirt road, a ramshackle wooden fish pier stands beside an empty parking lot. At 6:00 p.m. nothing much is happening. Three bluefin tuna sit in a huge tub of ice on the loading dock.

Between 6:45 and 7:00, the parking lot fills up with cars and trucks with license plates from New Jersey, New York, Massachusetts, New Hampshire, and Maine. Twenty tuna buyers clamber out, half of them Japanese. The three bluefin, ranging from 270 to 610 pounds, are winched out of the tub, and buyers crowd around them, extracting tiny core samples to examine their color, fingering the flesh to assess the fat content, sizing up the curve of the body.

After about 20 minutes of eyeing the goods, many of the buyers return to their trucks to call Japan by cellphone and get the morning prices from Tokyo's Tsukiji market—the fishing industry's answer to Wall Street—where the daily tuna auctions have just concluded. The buyers look over the tuna one last time and give written bids to the dock manager, who passes the top bid for each fish to the crew that landed it.

The auction bids are secret. Each bid is examined anxiously by a cluster of young men, some with a father or uncle looking on to give advice, others with a young woman and a couple of toddlers trying to see Daddy's fish. Fragments of concerned conversation float above the parking lot: "That's all?" "Couldn't we do better if we shipped it ourselves?" "Yeah, but my pickup needs a new transmission now!" After a few minutes, deals are closed and the fish are quickly loaded onto the backs of trucks in crates of crushed ice, known in the trade as "tuna coffins." As rapidly as they arrived, the flotilla of buyers sails out of the parking lot—three bound for New York's John F. Kennedy Airport, where their tuna will be airfreighted to Tokyo for sale the day after next.

Bluefin tuna may seem at first an unlikely case study in globalization. But as the world rearranges itself—around silicon chips, Starbucks coffee, or sashimi-grade tuna—new channels for global flows of capital and commodities link far-flung individuals and communities in unexpected new relationships. The tuna trade is a prime example of the globalization of a regional industry, with intense international competition and thorny environmental regulations; centuries-old practices combined with high technology; realignments of labor and capital in response to international regulation; shifting markets; and the diffusion of culinary culture as tastes for sushi, and bluefin tuna, spread worldwide.

. . .

Japan remains the world's primary market for fresh tuna for sushi and sashimi; demand in other countries is a product of Japanese influence and the creation of new markets by domestic producers looking to expand their reach. Perhaps not surprisingly, sushi's global popularity as an emblem of a sophisticated, cosmopolitan consumer class more or less coincided with a profound transformation in the international role of the Japanese fishing industry. From the 1970s onward, the expansion of 200–mile fishing limits around the world excluded foreign fleets from the prime fishing grounds of many coastal nations. And international environmental campaigns forced many countries, Japan among them, to scale back their distant water fleets. With their fishing operations curtailed and their yen for sushi still growing, Japanese had to turn to foreign suppliers.

Jumbo jets brought New England's bluefin tuna into easy reach of Tokyo, just as Japan's consumer economy—a byproduct of the now disparaged "bubble" years—went into hyperdrive. The sushi business boomed. During the 1980s, total Japanese imports of fresh bluefin tuna worldwide increased from 957 metric tons (531 from the United States) in 1984 to 5,235 metric tons (857 from the United States) in 1993. The average wholesale price peaked in 1990 at 4,900 yen (U.S.$34) per kilogram, bones and all, which trimmed out to approximately U.S.$33 wholesale per edible pound.

Not surprisingly, Japanese demand for prime bluefin tuna—which yields a firm red meat, lightly marbled with veins of fat, highly prized (and priced) in Japanese cuisine—created a gold-rush mentality on fishing grounds across the globe wherever bluefin tuna could be found.

Theodore C. Bestor, *How Sushi Went Global*, FOREIGN POL'Y 54, 54–55, 57–58 (Nov./Dec. 2000).

(B) National Standard Two: "best available scientific information"

NOTES

(1) National Standard Two states: "Conservation and management measures shall be based upon the best available scientific evidence." 16 U.S.C. § 1851(a)(2).

The discussion of this standard in *Blue Water Fisherman's Association v. Mineta* is fairly typical. The court noted that this meant that the "agency must base its determinations on [the best] information available at the time" it makes the decision. This has at least two components. First, the standard recognizes that uncertainty may well be unavoidable. As the *Blue Water* court noted, "information may not be exact or totally complete." In upholding a closure of the commercial fishery for red drum, the same court acknowledged that the agency's decision was based on "imperfect information"—in part because the fishery had developed so rapidly that information simply was not available. *Southeastern Fisheries Association v. Mosbacher*, 773 F.Supp. 435, 442 (D.D.C.1991).

Second, in most regulatory contexts, one party benefits from inaction. The "best available" standard precludes the agency from relying upon partial ignorance as the basis for inaction. The "fact that scientific information concerning a fishery is incomplete does not prevent the preparation and implementation of an FMP," in the words of the *Blue Water* decision. In *National Fisheries Institute v. Mosbacher,* the court made the same point: the Act "does not force the Secretary and Councils to sit idly by, powerless to conserve and manage a fishery resource, simply because they are somewhat uncertain about the accuracy of relevant information." *National Fisheries Institute v. Mosbacher,* 732 F.Supp. 210, 220 (D.D.C. 1990).

On the other side, is it reasonable to conclude that "best available" should always refer only to scientific information that is already in existence, particularly when available information is clearly incomplete and additional information could be acquired quickly and without undue expense. That is, should "available" sometimes mean "easily obtainable" rather than just "already at hand"? What if the most recent scientific information shows a fish population in good shape, but unscientific harvesting data and anecdotal information suggest that the population has taken a sudden turn downward? Should a decisionmaker be able—or even obligated—to ignore data that do not rise to the level of being scientific? Might an agency act arbitrarily if it considered only existing, but dated scientific data when new data could be acquired within a reasonable time?

(2) "optimum yield" and "the best available scientific information": Recall that "optimum yield" is to be "prescribed . . . on the basis of the maximum sustainable yield from the fishery, as reduced by any relevant social, economic, or ecological factor." *Id.* § 1802(28). In *Northwest Environmental Defense Center v. Brennen,* plaintiff argued that the agency had impermissibly strayed from the requirements of the best available standard by relying upon socioeconomic factors. The court rejected this argument, noting that the definition of "optimum yield" authorized the consideration of such factors. 958 F.2d at 936.

(ii) FEDERALISM AND FISHERIES

NOTES

As previously noted, the FCMA created eight regional councils to manage the fisheries in the EEZ: (1) New England, (2) Mid–Atlantic, (3) South Atlantic, (4) Caribbean, (5) Gulf of Mexico, (6) Pacific, (7) North Pacific, and (8) Western Pacific. *Id.* § 1852(a)(1)-(8). The councils are a unique combination of state and federal actors:[1] the state officer with responsibility for marine fisheries, the regional director of the National Marine Fisheries Service (NMFS), and four to twelve "qualified" individuals[2] appointed by the Secretary of Commerce from names submitted by the governors of the regional states. *Id.* § 1852(b).

16 U.S.C. § 1852(b)(2)(A). The Pacific Council also has "one representative of an Indian tribe with Federally recognized fishing rights." *Id.* § 1852(b)(5)(A).

(a) State regulation of fisheries within the territorial sea: Unlike the Marine Mammal Protection Act, the FCMA does not preempt state law. In fact—with only one exception—the Act explicitly preserves the power of the states to regulate all fishing within their boundaries. *Id.* § 1856(a)(1). The exception is narrowly drawn, both procedurally and substantively. Procedurally, the Secretary is required to proceed under the formal adjudication provisions of the Administrative Procedure Act. *Id.* § 1856(b)(1). At the hearing, the Secretary has the burden of proving two substantive points: (1) that the fishing in the fishery is "engaged in predominantly within the [EEZ] and beyond," and (2) that the state has acted or failed to act with results that would "substantially and adversely affect the carrying out" of an FMP developed under the Act. *Id.* § 1856(b)(1)(A)-(B). The state may resume management of the fishery at anytime if "the reasons for which [the Secretary] assumed such regulation no longer prevail." *Id.* § 1856(b)(2).

(b) State regulation of fisheries in the EEZ and beyond: A state may also regulate a fishing vessel outside the boundaries of the State [if]

---

1. The constitutionality of the combination under the Appointments Clause and the principle of separation of powers has been raised but not decided. *Northwest Environmental Defense Center v. Brennen,* 958 F.2d 930, 937–38 (9th Cir.1992) (plaintiffs lacked standing to raise the constitutional issues).

2. The FCMA specifies that the appointees must be individuals who, by reason of their occupational or other experience, scientific expertise, or training, are knowledgeable regarding the conservation and management, or the commercial or recreational harvest, of the fishery resources of the geographical area concerned.

(A) The fishing vessel is registered under the laws of that State and (i) there is no fishery management plan ... for the fishery ... ; or (ii) the State's laws and regulations are consistent with the fishery management plan and applicable Federal fishing regulations for the fishery....

(B) The fishery management plan ... delegates management of the fishery to a State and the State's laws and regulations are consistent with such fishery management plan....

Id. § 1586(a)(3)(A)–(B).

Southeastern Fisheries Association, Inc. v. Mosbacher

United States District Court, District of Columbia.
773 F.Supp. 435 (1991).

■ HARRIS, D.J.:—Plaintiffs filed this action challenging certain provisions of the Secretarial Fishery Management Plan for the Red Drum Fishery of the Gulf of Mexico, as amended by Amendment Number One, and its implementing regulations....

Background

The Gulf of Mexico red drum fishery encompasses the internal waters and territorial seas of the Gulf states, and the Exclusive Economic Zone (EEZ).[1] Redfish spawn in the estuaries of the Gulf of Mexico, and the juvenile fish mature in the bays and territorial seas. As they reach sexual maturity, they migrate offshore to deeper waters where they live for most of the remainder of their lives, returning annually to the estuaries to spawn before returning again to deeper waters. Redfish are a long-lived species and, thus, are particularly susceptible to increases in fishing mortality.

Prior to 1984, most of the commercial and recreational redfish harvest occurred in state waters, and the fishery was primarily recreational.[3] As a result, there was no federal regulation and little state regulation of the fishery. However, in the early 1980's, cajun cuisine became popular and the demand, and, consequently, the price, for what ultimately would become "blackened redfish" increased rapidly. As a result, a commercial purse seine fishery for large redfish developed quickly in the EEZ. Historic harvest levels of the spawning stock in the EEZ prompted a work group of state, federal, and academic fisheries scientists to conclude that recruitment overfishing was a real possibility.[5] While the potential for harm was recognized, the degree of the potential harm was unknown.

. . .

1. The internal waters of the states are those brackish waters (*e.g.,* bays and rivers) shoreward of the states' baselines. As for the territorial seas, for Mississippi, Louisiana, and Alabama, they extend three miles from the states' baselines. The territorial waters of the Gulf Coasts of Florida and Texas extend three leagues (approximately nine miles) from the baseline....

3. In 1980, less than 50,000 pounds of redfish were harvested in the EEZ. In 1986, the EEZ catch was 8.1 million pounds.

5. Recruitment overfishing occurs when the spawning stock is reduced to a level too low to assure adequate levels of young fish.

Prior to 1986, the Gulf of Mexico Fishery Management Council, the Regional Council vested with authority for developing FMPs for Gulf resources, had not developed an FMP for redfish. Based on the growth of the fishery and scientific observations pertaining thereto, and at the request of plaintiffs and others, the Secretary decided to prepare an FMP for redfish in the Gulf. However, to provide for protection in the interim, emergency regulations were issued on June 30, 1986, for an effective period of 90 days. The regulations established a one-million-pound quota for the harvest of redfish in the EEZ and preserved the landing and possession laws of the Gulf states.[7] In addition, the Secretary initiated a Secretarial Plan that would permanently replace the emergency regulations. He also established a scientific research program to assess the health and future of the stock.

On September 26, 1986, with the concurrence of the Gulf Council, the Secretary extended the emergency regulations for an additional 90 days. However, the regulations were modified to prohibit the retention of redfish taken from the EEZ by all persons.

After a period of review and comments, on December 24, 1986, defendants announced the completion of the Secretarial FMP and issued final implementing regulations. The Secretarial FMP and regulations provided for a ban on harvesting redfish in the directed commercial fishery in the EEZ in 1987, with an annual review of commercial quota levels based on an assessment of offshore stock thereafter. The Secretarial FMP also allowed for an incidental by-catch of 100,000 pounds in the indirect redfish fishery and superseded the states' landing and possession laws for the purpose of landing the by-catch. It established a recreational bag limit of one red drum per person per trip in the EEZ, subject to state landing and possession laws if those laws were more restrictive. Finally, the regulations established a scientific program and a licensing scheme for the by-caught fish.

While the Secretary was preparing the Secretarial FMP, the Gulf Council began the preparation of an Amendment to the FMP. After a review and comment period, the Gulf Council adopted the Amendment in its final form on April 30, 1987, and submitted it to the Secretary for formal review on May 20, 1987. After another review and comment period, the Secretary approved the Amendment (Amendment One) in its entirety on August 28, 1987, and issued implementing regulations on September 16, 1987. The regulations (1) divided the EEZ in the Gulf into a primary area (off the coasts of Mississippi, Alabama, and Louisiana) and a secondary area (off the coasts of Florida and Texas), and permanently closed the EEZ in the secondary area, (2) closed the directed commercial red drum fishery in the primary area until a goal of 20% escapement of juvenile fish from inshore waters was achieved, (3) retained the 100,000 pound quota for the indirect redfish fishery in the primary area, (4) provided for application of state landing and possession laws to redfish harvested in the indirect fishery, and (5) restricted the recreational fishery to one fish per person.

This can occur through overfishing of adult spawners or juvenile fish, or a combination of both.

7.   The state laws allowed for the landing of the one million pounds in Mississippi, Alabama, and Louisiana.

The Amendment also provided for an annual scientific assessment of the red drum stock by the National Marine Fisheries Service (NMFS), and for an adjustment of the quotas by the Gulf Council.

Plaintiffs, associations of commercial fishermen and canning, processing, and other related interests, filed their original complaint on July 14, 1986....

Discussion

In their amended complaint, plaintiffs challenge (1) defendants' failure to supersede state laws in the adoption of the implementing regulations for Amendment One to the FMP.... They seek a declaratory judgment, as well as injunctive relief. All parties have moved for summary judgment.

. . .

The issue of defendants' failure to supersede state law in promulgating the implementing regulations goes to the Agency's interpretation of the MFCA [Magnuson Fishery and Conservation Act], a question of law. Giving proper deference to the Agency, the Court must determine "whether the agency's [interpretation] is based on a permissible construction of the statute." *Chevron, U.S.A., Inc. v. Natural Resources Defense Council, Inc.*, 467 U.S. 837, 843 (1984). The MFCA does not expressly preempt state regulation of the fishery. However, preemption will be implied if there is an actual conflict between state and federal law, such that dual compliance is impossible, *Florida Lime & Avocado Growers, Inc. v. Paul*, 373 U.S. 132, 142–43 (1963), or would thwart the objectives of Congress. *Silkwood v. Kerr–McGee Corp.*, 464 U.S. 238, 248 (1984). It is clear that federal regulations, no less than federal statutes, may have a preemptive effect. *Fidelity Federal Savings & Loan Ass'n v. De la Cuesta*, 458 U.S. 141, 153 (1982). Indeed, the Agency's own guidelines interpreting National Standard 3 of the MFCA provide that "[f]ederal regulations supersede any conflicting State regulation of EEZ fishing." [ ]

The Court finds that defendants' failure to supersede state law with respect to the indirect red drum fishery was arbitrary and an abuse of Agency discretion. Under the MFCA, the federal government has exclusive management authority over fisheries in the EEZ. 16 U.S.C. § 1811(a). Consistent with this tenet, "a State may not directly or indirectly regulate any fishing vessel outside its boundaries, unless the vessel is registered under the law of that state." 16 U.S.C. § 1856(a)(3).

Defendants' red drum regulations provide for a 100,000–pound quota for the indirect red drum fishery. However, they also provide that commercial fishermen landing red drum from an indirect fishery must comply with state landing and possession laws. Because at least four of the five Gulf states prohibit or restrict the landing, possession, or sale of redfish, the state laws conflict with the federally imposed quota. Defendants, in effect, have told commercial fishermen that they may catch the fish, but that they may not land them. This makes no sense, and creates a conflict that is impermissible under the MFCA. Defendants' and intervenors' arguments to the contrary are wholly unpersuasive.

In adopting the Secretarial FMP, defendants themselves stated that "state laws and regulations which prohibit the landing, sale or interstate commerce of red drum harvested commercially outside State waters are in conflict with measures in the FMP." In accordance with that conclusion, defendants expressly superseded conflicting state laws in the Secretarial FMP. Less than a year later, the Secretary approved the Amendment to the FMP and issued the implementing regulations, reversing his position and expressly choosing not to supersede state landing laws.

While a reversal of position in and of itself would not necessarily be considered arbitrary, defendants must provide a reasoned analysis supporting the change. *See Motor Vehicle Mfrs.*, 463 U.S. at 42. However, Amendment One simply provides that supersession "would adversely impact the cooperative state/federal approach to restoration/maintenance of the stock proposed under this amendment" and then discusses the costs of enforcement. Likewise, the explanation defendants now provide is that the reversal on the supersession issue reflects a new policy of cooperative management between the states and the federal government. Certainly cooperation between state and federal governments is permissible, as well as desirable, as long as the management schemes do not conflict and the objectives of the MFCA are accomplished. However, defendants emphasize the state-federal cooperation as if it were an end, indeed the most important end, unto itself. In so doing, they appear to have overlooked the fact that under the MFCA, effective fishery conservation and management, according to national standards, is the goal. If that can be accomplished through cooperative federal and state initiatives, a court would not interfere with the Secretary's scheme. However, in this case, the Secretary has allowed continued enforcement of state laws, which he has in the past acknowledged to be in conflict with federal regulations that he has promulgated. The Court, too, finds that a conflict exists and concludes, therefore, that the state laws cannot coexist in the federal scheme.

Additionally, the regulations require compliance with state laws, even if a vessel is not registered in the state where the catch is landed. Thus, the regulations go beyond what is authorized by the MFCA. *See* 16 U.S.C. § 1856(a)(3). In their Memorandum of Points and Authorities, defendants state that "[i]t is * * * obvious that those state laws to which the Secretary has deferred, are valid only to the extent they apply to vessels registered in the state which is seeking to apply them." The Court agrees that the regulations would only be valid in that limited context. However, if defendants are arguing that the regulation may stand and will simply be applied as stated above, the Court must disagree. As written, defendants' regulation is invalid, as it provides that "a person landing red drum other than from a directed commercial red drum fishery, must comply with the landing and possession laws of the State where landed." It does not include a clause limiting the states to enforcement of its laws only as to fishing vessels registered in the state seeking enforcement. Although the Court must give deference to the Agency's interpretation and application of its own regulations, where, as in this instance, the regulation so clearly violates the Agency's enabling statute, the Court may not allow the regulation to stand. In addition, there is no evidence that the Agency has adopted a lawful interpretation of the regulation's reach or that it has applied the regulation narrowly. Instead, the Court has only what may be characterized as a litigation-generated rationale for the regulation.

. . .

For all of the above reasons, it is appropriate to enter summary judgment in favor of plaintiffs and against defendants and defendant-intervenors as to supersession. . . .

NOTES

Given the lengths that the FCMA goes to preserve a state role in fishery management, why did the court give so little deference to the agency's decision to allow a continuing role for state law? Were the state and federal laws as much in conflict as the court believed? What political forces might have been behind the state laws?

(iii) CODA: THE COLLAPSING OCEAN FISHERIES

Implementation of the nation's most important fisheries law, the Magnuson–Stevens Fishery Conservation and Management Act, has reached a critical stage. Most U.S. fish stocks are in a state full exploitation or overutilization. The relative proportion of fish species have been drastically altered in some regions (*e.g.,* Georges Bank), with populations of dominant species collapsing and less abundant groups becoming dominant. The harvesting and processing capacity in many U.S. fisheries far exceeds levels that are consistent with sustainable fisheries.

Although there have been several successes in U.S. fisheries management in terms of maintaining or restoring stocks—examples include Atlantic striped bass, Pacific halibut, Atlantic surf clam, and North Pacific pollock—there have been many serious failures. Reasons include noncompliance with management regulations, the lack of sufficient data and appropriate models for stock assessments, a complex interplay of fluctuating marine populations and a political economy that tends to subsidize or overinvest in fishing capacity, and an inclination to make risk-prone rather than risk-averse decisions in the presence of uncertainty. Some analyses of fishery systems suggest that overinvestment and the inclination toward risk-prone decisionmaking result from the "common-pool" nature of most fishery resources and the "open-access" nature of the rules regarding how these resources can be used. . . .

The stressed nature of many fisheries is apparent from scientific reports of decreasing numbers of spawning fish, reduced overall biomass and population levels, and lower catch per unit effort (CPUE) in commercial fisheries. . . .

NATIONAL ACADEMY OF SCIENCES, SHARING THE FISH: TOWARD A NATIONAL POLICY ON INDIVIDUAL FISHING QUOTAS 13–14 (1999).

More troubling is the fact that humans are increasingly taking fish at lower trophic levels, *i.e.,* lower on the food chain. Rather than harvesting the top-level predators, increasingly the fish at the fish-market or in the frozen fish sticks are the fish that the predators previously fed on. As an article in *Science* reported, "landings from global fisheries have shifted in the last 45 years from large piscivorous fishes toward smaller invertebrates and planktivorous fishes, especially in the Northern Hemisphere." Daniel Pauly, *et al.*, *Fishing Down Marine Food Webs*, 279 Sci. 860, 860 (1998). The article concluded that "continuation of present trends will lead to widespread fisheries collapses" unless fisheries management shifts "to emphasize the rebuilding of fish populations ... within large 'no-take' marine protected areas." *Id.* at 863.

NOTES

Politics, self-interest, and decisionmaking structures: One reason for the failure of the FCMA to prevent overfishing and collapsing fish stocks is structural. Although no decisionmaking structure can guarantee good decisions, some come close to guaranteeing bad decisions—and the decisionmaking structure of the FCMA is among the worst. The regional councils have primary responsibility for preparing the FMPs. 16 U.S.C. § 1852(h). Those plans are submitted to the Secretary where the issue is whether the plan "is consistent with" the national standards and other applicable law. *Id.* § 1854(a)(1)(A). "Consistency" is a flexible standard that accords a substantial amount of discretion to the regional councils since there are a range of possible choices that are consistent—particularly with standards that are broadly drafted.

The Secretary's decision in turn is also subject to substantial discretion since it will be reversed only if it is "arbitrary, capricious, an abuse of discretion, or otherwise not in accordance with law." *Id.* § 1855(f)(1) (making 5 U.S.C. § 706(2)(A) applicable). As one former general counsel for NOAA has commented,

> regulations under the Magnuson Act are essentially impervious to judicial review.... [T]he joint actions of council and the Secretary command enormous deference. Courts will not usually second-guess the Secretary's interpretation of the National Standards ... and approved FMPS are "presumed valid"....
>
> [T]he case law construing the Magnuson Act grants what is probably the maximum deference to the Secretary, while the statute itself requires the Secretary, in turn, to grant maximum deference to the industry-dominated councils.

Robert J. McManus, *America's Saltwater Fisheries: So Few Fish, So Many Fishermen*, 9 NAT. RESOURCES & ENVT. 13, 15, 16 (Spring 1995). The councils are "industry-dominated" because of the definition of "qualifications":

> council members must be "knowledgeable about fisheries management, [ ], with the predictable result that industry participants, over time, have filled almost all council seats.
>
> The Magnuson Act condones this state of affairs: as long as they file specially tailored financial disclosure forms, council members are exempted from ... the section of the criminal code generally prohibit-

ing official acts that advance a personal financial interest. . . . Notwithstanding loud complaints, three members of the North Pacific Fishery Management Council (responsible for Alaskan fisheries) recently voted with a 9–2 majority that reserved increased amounts of groundfish to shore-based Alaska processors and the smaller inshore vessels that service them, even though two of the three owned such boats and the third soon became a paid lobbyist for the processors.

Id. at 13.

The result is that science can get lost or be employed as a justificatory veneer. As we have previously seen, "conservation" is often a cover for allocation. For a discussion of the politics of fisheries management, see CARL SAFINA, SONG FOR THE BLUE OCEAN 78–116 (1997).

* * *

Given the collapsing fisheries, what are the alternatives? Two approaches are currently generating the most discussion:

(A) *Individual Fishing Quotas: Privatizing a Fishery*

Sea Watch International v. Mosbacher

United States District Court, District of Columbia.
762 F.Supp. 370 (1991).

■ BOUDIN, D.J.:—Plaintiffs filed these actions on July 13, 1990, seeking judicial review of administrative actions taken by defendant Bryson in his capacity as Executive Director of the Mid–Atlantic Regional Fishery Management Council and approved by defendant Mosbacher, the Secretary of Commerce ("the Secretary"), under the Magnuson Fishery Conservation and Management Act of 1976, 16 U.S.C. §§ 1802–1882 ("the Magnuson Act" or "the Act"). . . .

In 1977, the Mid–Atlantic Regional Fishery Management Council ("the Council") began to regulate the surf clam and ocean quahog fisheries. The original FMP for these fisheries has been amended several times. In 1979, the surf clam fishery was divided into the Mid–Atlantic and New England surf clam fisheries. The Mid–Atlantic Council retained primary authority over both fisheries, as well as over the ocean quahog fishery. In each of the three fisheries, the Council established an aggregate annual catch quota, attainment of which would result in closure of that fishery for the year.

The Council regulated the three fisheries under different plans. Access to the Mid–Atlantic surf clam fishery was limited by a moratorium on the entry of new vessels, coupled with a system of permits restricted to 184 vessels with a history of surf clam fishing in the region. The permits were tied to the individual vessels for which they were issued, and could only be transferred together with those vessels. The vessels could not be replaced unless they sank, were destroyed by fire or otherwise left the fishery involuntarily. Thus, only vessels originally awarded permits could fish in the Mid–Atlantic surf clam fishery, a scheme which remained unchanged from 1977 to 1990. Additionally, access to the fishery was controlled by "effort restrictions" limiting the number of hours each vessel could fish.

There were, however, no limitations on the quantity of surf clams that could be harvested on a fishing trip.

The New England surf clam fishery was less restricted, with no permit system, and effort restrictions imposed only if a certain percentage of the annual aggregate catch quota was harvested. This fishery was further divided into two sub-areas, and separate quotas and quarterly sub-quotas were established for each. Finally, the quahog fishery essentially went unrestricted, except for the annual aggregate quota. Access to the fishery was unlimited, and effort restrictions were imposed only briefly in 1984. While the FMP authorized quarterly quotas, these quotas were never established. The annual aggregate quotas were set at levels above those actually reached, and the fishery thus was never closed.

In 1988, the Council proposed Amendment 8 to the Fishery Management Plan for Surf Clams and Ocean Quahogs ("Amendment 8"). This Amendment was the culmination of several years of work by the Council, and reflected numerous concerns about the viability of existing regulations, the migration of vessels from the surf clam fishery to the less-regulated quahog fishery, and the resultant increase in the quahog harvest. Amendment 8 was approved by the Secretary and implemented by regulations published in the Federal Register on June 14, 1990. The regulations became effective on September 30, 1990. Amendment 8 brought the three fisheries under a single limited access scheme built around individual transferable quotas ("ITQs"), which are transferable permits to fish for a fixed percentage of the annual aggregate catch quota for the species and area. Thus, although the annual quota for all fishermen may vary from year to year depending on the Council's determination of an optimum yield, the holder of, e.g., a 5% ITQ would be entitled to catch up to 5% of that quota.

For each of the fisheries, ITQs were allocated on the basis of vessel fishing history, although the data used to calculate that history and the weight assigned to it varied between the fisheries. For example, in the Mid–Atlantic surf clam fishery, eighty percent of the ITQ was derived by averaging vessel catch history from 1979 to 1988, with the last four years counted twice, and the lowest two years deleted. The other twenty percent was based upon the vessel's dimensions, as a proxy for the owner's capital investment. The results were divided by the total for all vessels in the fleet, producing an ITQ expressed as a percentage of the annual quota.[1]

After Amendment 8 went into effect, two groups of fishermen and seafood processing companies brought these actions, alleging serious economic harm from the ITQ assignments. Their most salient arguments are, first, that the ITQ system exceeded the defendants' statutory authority and, second, that the decision to limit access to the quahog fishery was unsupported by the administrative record. In each case, there are addition-

---

1. In the New England surf clam and the ocean quahog fisheries, the ITQ was the average of a vessel's catch history for every year between 1979 and 1988 that the vessel actually participated in the fishery, excluding the lowest year for vessels that participated for more than one year. These calculations were then divided by the total for all vessels to obtain a percentage figure.

al arguments that the challenged action also violated the National Standards for the other applicable provisions of the Magnuson Act.

. . .

1. *The ITQ System*

"Property Rights" Claim. Plaintiffs argue that implementation of the ITQ system for the three fisheries exceeds the Council's and the Secretary's statutory authority, and should therefore be set aside under Section 706(2)(C) of the Administrative Procedure Act, 5 U.S.C. § 706(2)(C), as incorporated into the Magnuson Act by 16 U.S.C. § 1855(d). Where Congress has spoken with precision on an issue, its determination resolves the matter; where the issue is less clearly determined by the statute, an agency interpretation ordinarily is upheld if it represents a reasonable construction of the statute. *Chevron U.S.A. v. Natural Resources Defense Council,* 467 U.S. 837, 842–43 (1984). The gist of plaintiffs' claim on this point is that an ITQ system "amount[s] to privatization of the surf clam and quahog resource," and that such a "transfer of private ownership interests in a fishery" is both unauthorized by the Magnuson Act and in conflict with an express prohibition on the assessment of fees in excess of costs. *See* 16 U.S.C. § 1854(d).

The difficulty with plaintiffs' argument is that Congress did authorize the creation of quotas. The Act expressly authorizes the Council and the Secretary to impose permit requirements and to establish limited access systems. 16 U.S.C. §§ 1853(b)(1), (6). The legislative history of this section refers specifically to the possibility of dividing "the total allowable catch into shares or quotas which are then distributed among the fishermen." S. REP. NO. 416, 94th Cong., 1st Sess. (1975), *reprinted in Legislative History of the Fishery Conservation and Management Act of 1976* at 691–92 (1976). Even without this legislative history, the language of the section broadly embraces the possibility of quotas. Nothing in its terms, and nothing else in the Magnuson Act cited to this Court, precludes making quotas transferable. Indeed, transferable permits were precisely the method utilized in the Mid-Atlantic surf clam fishery prior to adoption of Amendment 8, although transfer was linked to sale of the vessel.[8] The present ITQ system differs only in degree from the system of aggregate quotas and transferable permits previously in use and unchallenged by plaintiffs, and the interests created by it fall short of actual full-scale ownership.

The quota under the prior system indeed was derived somewhat differently, being expressed in terms of a given number of hours fishing rather than a percentage of the aggregate catch. However, plaintiffs fail to explain why this difference is significant.[9] The new quotas do not become

---

8. Defendants assert that under the previous system, sale of a vessel in the Mid–Atlantic surf clam fishery commanded a premium of anywhere from $50,000 to $150,000 over and above the value of the vessel itself. While plaintiffs' statement of material facts in dispute questions the Council's estimates of the value of that premium, it does not

dispute its existence. It is thus unsurprising that the surf clam and quahog ITQs also sell at a premium.

9. Although plaintiffs argue that the ITQ system grants those fishermen who hold ITQs the right to "leave their share of fish in the sea" and exclude other fishermen from it, it is hard to see why this should alter the permanent possessions of those who hold them, any more than landing rights at slot-constrained airports become the property of airlines, or radio frequencies become the property of broadcasters. These interests remain subject to the control of the federal government which, in the exercise of its regulatory authority, can alter and revise such schemes, just as the Council and the Secretary have done in this instance.[10] An arrangement of this kind is not such a drastic departure from ordinary regulation, nor is it so akin to the sale of government property, that the Court must require a more precise expression of congressional intent to uphold it.

There is even less to be said about plaintiffs' claim that the ITQ plan violates the prohibition on assessment of fees in excess of costs found in 16 U.S.C. § 1854(d). Plaintiffs complain that, because the ITQs are transferable, one fishermen must pay another for an ITQ. The statutory limitation on fees in excess of costs seemingly is designed to prevent the government from using quotas as a revenue-raising measure. That purpose is in no way frustrated by ITQ payments between fishermen. Certainly the payments are a barrier to a fisherman who wants to fish but does not possess an ITQ, but an even greater barrier would be provided by quotas that were not transferable at any price. Neither regime involves the agency in raising revenues in excess of costs.

. . .

2. *Limitation of Access to the Quahog Fishery*

Aside from the general challenges to the ITQ system described above, plaintiffs make several specific challenges to the decision to limit access to the ocean quahog fishery by bringing it under the same regulatory scheme as the two surf clam fisheries. They argue that the decision lacks support in the administrative record; that it does not comply with the Act's express requirements for a limited access management scheme; and that it violates applicable National Standards. The Court will address each claim in turn.

The Administrative Record. Plaintiffs contend that the decision to include ocean quahogs in the ITQ system lacks support in the administrative record and was arbitrary and capricious. . . .

In brief, plaintiffs' argument is that any regulation of the resource is responding to a "problem that does not exist." They dispute the Council's claim of an upward trend in the ocean quahog harvest data, and its prediction that the same "overcapitalization" that required restriction of

outcome. For the most part, the ITQ owners have ample incentive to use their rights to the fullest extent. If the Council and the Secretary determine that the quotas are not being used, nothing prevents them from altering the present regime to allow distribution and use of any unused quotas.

10. Plaintiffs have selected excerpts from statements made during the administrative proceedings in which defendants themselves have applied the term "property right" or similar labels to the ITQs. [ ] When examined in full, most of these quotations indicate that the property analogy was employed with an appropriate qualification. *E.g.,* [ ] ("Amendment 8 implies that [ITQs] are property in that they are 'owned' and can be sold, similar to a share of stock, *at least so long as the management scheme creating the rights is in place*") (emphasis added). Further, the Council's mere expressions of hope that the Amendment 8 regime would provide a lasting solution do not in themselves exclude the possibility of later re-evaluation and revision of the regulations.

access to the surf clam fisheries eventually will occur in this fishery. They cite the lower market demand for quahogs, and the undisputed fact that the annual quahog catch quota has never been reached. . . .

However, the administrative record shows that the Council's Scientific and Statistical Committee recommended the inclusion of quahogs in a comprehensive fishery management plan for several years prior to adoption of Amendment 8, [ ], and that the Council considered other alternatives, [ ]. The ultimate decision to adopt this recommendation was based on several related grounds, including the fact that surf clams and quahogs had become substitute goods for certain uses, [ ], that existing surf clam restrictions had already resulted in movement of vessels from that fishery into the quahog fishery, [ ]; and that the potential for further migration to and increased catches in the quahog fishery would be heightened by placing the surf clam fishery under the ITQ system while leaving the quahog fishery unregulated, [ ]. The Council coupled these long-term concerns with evidence of a recent increase in the quahog harvest.

In sum, the threat to the ocean quahog resource is reflected in the need for the existing annual quotas. An increase in this threat is posed by the diversion of ships from the surf clam to the quahog fishery as surf clam restrictions tighten. Both regulators and fishermen have an interest in having ground rules established before any problem matures. Contrary to plaintiffs' arguments, the Act does not mandate any finding of necessity before fishery access can be limited. The accompanying regulations state that "[i]n an unutilized or underutilized fishery, [limited access] may be used to reduce the chance that [overfishing or overcapitalization] will adversely affect the fishery in the future." 50 C.F.R. § 602.15(c). The issue thus turns on predictions about the future in an area of technical and scientific expertise, where special deference is due to regulatory agencies. [ ] Although plaintiffs' attack on this determination is by no means a frivolous one, the Court holds that the Council and the Secretary did have a rational basis for their action.

. . .

The National Standards. Plaintiffs argue that Amendment 8 creates incentives for consolidation of the quahog fishery, and has in fact resulted in consolidation, contrary to National Standard 4 and its prohibition of "excessive shares." They allege that two fishermen now hold ITQs totalling forty percent of the annual catch quota for ocean quahogs, and that fragmentation of the remaining shares will necessarily result in further consolidation, as holders of smaller shares sell their interest. This figure does give pause, although the raw number may not be economically significant. The defendants have acknowledged that increased efficiency due to consolidation was one of the explicit objectives of Amendment 8. However, the Act contains no definition of "excessive shares," and the Secretary's judgment of what is excessive in this context deserves weight, especially where the regulations can be changed without permission of the ITQ holders. The record reflects that the Council and the Secretary considered the problem, and addressed it by providing for an annual review of industry concentration, with the possibility of referral to the Department of Justice. [ ]

. . .

For all the reasons detailed above, the Court finds that the Secretary's decision to limit access to the ocean quahog fishery was not arbitrary and capricious or an abuse of discretion within the meaning of the Magnuson Act.

NOTES

(1) What rights and interests are necessary to property? Note the interests that the holders of an ITQ possess: a right to attempt to harvest a specified percentage of the quota—but not a right to harvest a specified amount of clams annually; a right to exclude unpermitted harvesters; a right to sell the permit—a right that, according to the Council is worth between $50,000 and $150,000. But, do permit holders have a right against the government to prevent an uncompensated taking of the ITQ—as long as the government's decision is not arbitrary or capricious as defined by the Administrative Procedure Act? If not, why might market prices for the permits be as high as they are? If the permits are worth so much, should the government be selling them, rather than giving them away?

(2) Petitioners argued in part that the ITQ system created the possibility that a fisher would choose to leave his share of the quota uncaught—an argument based (again) on the assumption that the FCMA *requires* that the optimum yield be harvested. Although the court does not address the issue directly, should it be possible for a conservation group to purchase a permit for the express purpose of leaving the fish in the ocean? (In the case of federal grazing permits, they cannot save the grass for wildlife.) Such possibilities are among the ideas that are often suggested by individuals advocating free-market environmentalism.

(3) *Alliance Against IFQs v. Brown:* A subsequent decision by the Ninth Circuit in a case arising from a challenge to a similar regulatory system of "individual fishing quotas" (IFQs) in the sablefish and halibut fishery off the coast of Alaska began with the following concise statement of the policy issue raised in both cases:

> Commercial ocean fishing combines difficult and risky labor with large capital investments to make money from a resource owned by no one, the fish. Unlimited access tends to cause declining fisheries. The reason is that to get title to a fish, a fisherman has to catch it before someone else does. *Pierson v. Post*, 3 Caines 175 (N.Y.1805). This gives each fishermen an incentive to invest in a fast, large boat and to fish as fast as possible. As boats and crews get more efficient, fewer fish escape the fishermen and live to reproduce. "The result is lower profits for the too many fishermen investing in too much capital to catch too few fish." TERRY L. ANDERSON & DONALD R. LEAL, FREE MARKET ENVIRON-MENTALISM 123 (1991).

Alliance Against IFQs v. Brown, 84 F.3d 343, 344 (9th Cir.1996). In upholding the privatization of the fishery, the court concluded:

This is a troubling case. Perfectly innocent people going about their legitimate business in a productive industry have suffered great economic harm because the federal regulatory scheme changed. Alternative schemes can easily be imagined. The old way could have been left in place, where whoever caught the fish first, kept them, and seasons were shortened to allow enough fish to escape and reproduce. Allocation of quota shares could have been on a more current basis, so that fishermen in 1996 would not have their income based upon the fish they had caught before 1991. Quota shares could have been allocated to all fishermen, instead of to vessel owners and lessees, so that the nonowning fishermen would have something valuable to sell to vessel owners. But we are not the regulators of the north Pacific halibut and sablefish industry. The Secretary of Commerce is. We cannot overturn the Secretary's decision on the ground that some parties' interests are injured. Government regulation of an industry necessarily transfers economic rewards from some who are more efficient and hardworking to others who are favored by the regulatory scheme. We have authority to overturn the Secretary's decisions only if they are arbitrary and capricious, or contrary to law. In this case, they are not.

Id. at 352.

(4) The IFQ moratorium: Congress responded to *Sea Watch* and *Alliance Against IFQs* by suspending authority to implement limited access systems: "A Council may not submit and the Secretary may not approve or implement before October 1, 2002, any fishery management plan ... which creates a new individual fishing quota program." 16 U.S.C. § 1853(d)(1)(A). The term "individual fishing quota" is defined as "a Federal permit under a limited access system to harvest a quantity of fish, expressed by a unit or units representing a percentage of the total allowable catch of a fishery that may be received or held for exclusive use by a person." *Id.* § 1802(21).

Note that the moratorium does not prohibit the development of IFQ regulatory systems. The National Academy of Sciences is directed to produce a report on IFQs by October, 1998, and the Secretary and Councils are directed to "consider" the report before submitting such regulatory schemes after the end of the moratorium. *Id.* 1853(d)(5). In addition, any proposed IFQ systems "shall ensure" that the program provides for the "review and revision" of the system including, "if appropriate, [procedures] for the renewal, reallocation, or reissuance of the" IFQ; provides for adequate enforcement; and "provides for a fair and equitable initial allocation of the individual fishing quotas, prevents any person from acquiring an excessive share of the individual fishing quotas issued, and considers the allocation of a portion of the annual harvest in the fishery for entry-level fishermen, small vessel owners, and crew members who do not hold or qualify for individual fishing quotas." *Id.*

(5) National Academy of Science report on transferable quotas: The traditional method of regulating fisheries is to set a total allowable catch (TAC), allow open fishing in the fishery until TAC has been reached, and then to close the fishery. Under an open access regime—that is, when any individual may choose to begin fishing—with reliance on TAC-based controls alone there are recurrent problems, most commonly a tendency for fishers to employ excessive labor and capital investments in the competition for a share of the fish:

> For example, in Alaska's halibut fishery prior to implementation of the IFQ programs, the season was progressively reduced in an attempt to maintain the annual catch of halibut with the TAC. In response, fishermen increased the number of vessels in their fleets, and used larger and larger vessels, with more and more gear. The frenzied *derbies* sometimes forced the fishing fleet to operate in dangerous weather, exacerbated *ghost fishing* from gear lost in the race for fish and created incentives to waste other species caught in the process. The cyclical nature of the fishery left consumers facing gluts of fresh halibut for a few weeks each year and buying frozen fish for the remainder of the year.

> The Alaskan IFQ programs for halibut and sablefish addressed and reduced these problems. Evidence from the Alaskan IFQ programs suggest that the derby has been eliminated, safety has improved, and ghost fishing has been reduced. At the same time, these programs have left the halibut and sablefish fisheries with fewer fishermen (as intended) and have enriched many of those whose catch history qualifies them for quota shares.

> The capacity of IFQs for transferability, consolidation, and leasing has led to a general concern that independent owner-operators of fishing vessels or crew members will be led into economic dependence on absentee owners as quota shares increase in value and small investors are excluded from the field. Consequently some programs (*e.g.,* Alaskan halibut and sablefish) have adopted owner-on-board and other provisions intended to prevent absentee ownership.

>   . . .

> The IFQ is one means to limit entry in order to reduce overcapitalization and the wasteful practices that occur under other systems. A major intended effect of IFQs is to create economic incentives for owners of vessels to decrease their inputs of labor and capital to the fishery. Thus, in fisheries with excess harvesting or processing capacity, vessels may be laid up and some crew members may lose their jobs, although others may increase their employment from a few days to several months per year. Processing plants may require fewer workers when processing is spread across a longer period of time. On the other hand, with IFQs, economic resources are no longer wasted through overinvestment in capital and labor. Changes in the harvesting and processing patterns resulting from IFQs could be beneficial to consumers favor year-round fresh products. Decreased cost and increased profitability can benefit consumers and the nation.

>   . . .

> ***** *Advantages*— IFQ programs are widely identified as being a highly effective way of dealing with overcapitalization in the fishing industry. Removing the race for fish has reduced the incentives to buy ever-larger vessels and more equipment and to fish during unsafe

conditions. Consumers have been able to purchase fresh fish during longer periods of the year. Many fishermen testified that IFQs provided the opportunity to utilize better fishing and handling methods, reducing bycatch of nontargeted species and maintaining higher product quality. Gear conflicts may also be reduced by IFQs.

* *Concerns*— A number of problems were identified in operative IFQ programs during the committee's work. Prominent among them are concerns about the fairness of the initial allocations, effects of IFQs on processors, increased costs for new fishermen to gain entry, consolidation of quota shares (and thus economic power), effects of leasing, confusion about the nature of the privilege involved, elimination of vessels and reduction in crews, and the equity of gifting a public trust resource.

NATIONAL ACADEMY OF SCIENCES, SHARING THE FISH: TOWARD A NATIONAL POLICY ON INDIVIDUAL FISHING QUOTAS 2–3, 4 (1999).

(6) Public trust and privatization: An important aspect of the legal and political framework shaping the management of fisheries is the public trust doctrine, the concept that the fish in the oceans belong to the public and the government holds them in trust for the public. As applied in the context of proposed IFQ systems, the public trust gives rise to several clusters of questions:

Can public trust resources be alienated?

If so, *should* they be?

If alienation is permissible, does the trust status of the resource impose continuing oversight obligations on the government? Does it impose obligations on the government to choose alternative management strategies that do the least harm to the public nature of the resource?

Does it strengthen the conclusion that IFQs are not property but a privilege held for the public good?

PERSPECTIVES

A free market perspective: Free-market environmentalists—who believe that properly structured markets largely can resolve environmental problems—generally favor property-based approaches to resource issues. Terry Anderson and Donald Leal offer a property-rights solution to the problem of overfishing.

"Ocean fisheries provide the classic case of the tragedy of the commons," they argue, because the rule of capture is coupled with a lack of restrictions on access: fish left by one fisherman are available to another so that there is an incentive to harvest the stock before others do. Since all fishers face this incentive, the result is overharvest of the fishery. This problem is exacerbated by the fact that there are no entry restrictions: anyone can become a fisher by buying a boat and heading out to sea.

Historically, the response to the open-access problem has been to "fence" ocean resources—a history outlined at the beginning of this section that led to the current management regime under which coastal states have an EEZ extending 200 miles seaward. Anderson and Leal argue, however, that "extending territorial limits is not the final solution to the problem of open access to ocean resources" because this is "only a first step for removing the inefficiencies that result from communal rights."

Extending national jurisdiction is only the first step because, Anderson and Leal argue, regulation has failed: "Unfortunately, there are inherent problems with regulation, because the regulators do not own the resource and do not face economic incentives to manage it efficiently." The Magnuson Fishery Conservation and Management Act of 1976, although an attempt to remove regulatory inefficiencies, has also failed because restricted entry in itself is insufficient to control the intensity of effort: fishers "substitut[e] fewer larger boats for more smaller sized boats. The result is that 'rising fish prices constrained by a limited number of vessels, and unconstrained by any sort of territorial limit, has led to vastly increased individual fishing capacity.' Even with licensing, regulators find that a few powerful fishing vessels can do in a few minutes what used to take days."

"The preferred free market environmentalism approach to the fishery problem," they contend, "is to allow the establishment of property rights." They find support for this contention in a study of oyster fisheries:

> Oyster fisheries along the United States coast offer a useful contrast of how property rights can improve resource allocation. Using data from oyster fisheries in Maryland, Virginia, Louisiana, and Mississippi from 1945 to 1970, economists Agnello and Donnelley tested the hypotheses that private ownership of oyster beds would generate more conservation and higher returns for fishermen than open-access beds.[11] Under open access, we would expect fishermen to take as many oysters as early as possible, with the result being diminishing returns later in the-season. Agnello and Donnelley found that the ratio of harvest during the earlier part of the season to the later part was 1.35 for open-access oyster beds and 1.01 for private beds. After controlling for other variables, they also found that fishermen in the private leasing state of Louisiana earned $3,207, while their counterparts in the common-property state of Mississippi earned $807. These findings support the expectation that private property rights solve the open-access problem.

They also find support in the attempts by informal associations such as that involved in *Marincovich v. Tarabochia*, 787 P.2d 562, 565 (Wash.1990) [Chapter 3], to restrict access—to create private property in the public domain. These attempts failed, not because they were inefficient, but because courts held them to be illegal:

> A cooperative association of boat owners is not freed from the restrictive provisions of the Sherman Antitrust Act * * * because it professes, in the interest of the conservation of important food fish, to regulate the price and the manner of taking fish unauthorized by legislation and uncontrolled by proper authority.

11. Richard J. Agnello & Lawrence P. Donnelley, *Prices and Property Rights in the Fisheries*, 42 S. Econ. J. 253 (1979).

Gulf Coast Shrimpers & Oystermans Association v. United States, 236 F.2d 658 (5th Cir.1956). As Anderson and Leal note, "any agreement establishing property rights to resources is difficult to maintain if the government declares it illegal."

There are two promising approaches to creating property rights in fisheries. The first is aquaculture, particularly of species such as oysters—which do not move—or salmon—which can be reared in pens. In such situations, the rights holder has direct control over the resource and can determine the efficient use of resources. But aquaculture has difficulties. Poaching of oysters from leased beds, for example, is a recurrent problem. Hence, Anderson and Leal argue, "the defense of private property rights must be strengthened," *i.e.,* the state must police and enforce the private rights against trespassers.

A second alternative is to establish individual tradable quotas, or ITQs:

This system is attractive for several reasons. First, each quota holder faces greater certainty that his share of the catch will not be taken by someone else. Under the current system, total allowable catch is established, but the share is determined by who is best at capturing the fugitive resources. With ITQs, holders do not compete for the shares, so there is less incentive to race other fishermen. Second, transferability allows quotas to end up in the hands of the most efficient fishermen—that is, those with the lowest costs and who can pay the highest price for the ITQs. Less efficient producers and inputs move to other industries. As a corollary, ITQs encourage progress in reducing the cost of catching fish. Fishermen who adopt new cost-reducing methods make more money with their quotas and are in a better position to purchase quotas from those who are less efficient. This is in marked contrast to the current regulatory system, which encourages over-investment in the race for fugitive resources.

Although ITQs offer numerous advantages, they also require continuing governmental involvement because it still is necessary to determine year by year the total allowable catch—and regulators are susceptible to political pressures from the special interest groups they regulate. (David Dana considers why this occurs in *Overcoming the Political Tragedy of the Commons: Lessons Learned from the Reauthorization of the Magnuson Act,* 24 ECOL. L. Q. 833 (1997).) In addition, questions still arise about harvesting methods, the incidental take of nontarget species, and conflicts between fishers harvesting different fish stocks—all of which can only be resolved by some type of collective decisionmaking. Given the number of vital questions that must be addressed on an on-going basis—whether in the form of evolving limits on private property rights or in the form of more traditional regulations—how different in practice would the "free-market" approach be from the "regulatory approach"? Nonetheless, Anderson and Leal, are optimistic: "Removing judicial roadblocks to collective action by voluntary fishing associations, implementing ITQ systems, and refraining from further governmental redistribution of fishing rights can move us a long way toward a free market environmental solution to the ocean commons problem." TERRY L. ANDERSON & DONALD R. LEAL, FREE MARKET ENVIRONMENTALISM 121–32 (1991).

Recall the judicial hostility to claims of property in navigable water discussed in Chapter 3. Morton Horwitz characterized these decision in the following comment: "At its deepest level, the attack on prescription represented an effort to free American law from the restraints of economic development that had been molded by the common law's feudal conception of property." MORTON HORWITZ, THE TRANSFORMATION OF AMERICAN LAW, 1780–1860 at 47 (1977). Do Anderson and Leal answer this charge?

(B) Managing the Marine Ecosystem

One of the complaints against traditional fisheries management is that its focus on particular fish stocks fails to attend adequately to the overall well-being of the ecosystems of which the fish are a part. Whether the population of a given fish species rises or falls can be dramatically affected by ecological conditions that are unrelated to harvesting pressures. Many reformers call for heightened attention to fisheries as ecological communities, communities that yield many benefits and yet that are so complex, and so little known, that scientists are only beginning to unravel their intricacies. Human ignorance is best handled by acting cautiously, by attending closely to how ecosystems respond to intervention, and by quickly revising patterns of interaction based on those responses. *E.g.,* Shi–Ling Hsu & James E. Wilen, *Ecosystem Management and the 1996 Sustainable Fisheries Act,* 24 ECOL. L.Q. 99 (1997); Marian Macpherson, *Integrating Ecosystem Management Approaches into Federal Fishery Management through the Magnuson–Stevens Fishery Conservation and Management Act,* 6 OCEANS & COASTAL L.J. 1 (2001); Alison Rieser, *Property Rights and Ecosystem Management in U.S. Fisheries: Contracting for the Commons?,* 24 ECOL. L.Q. 813 (1997). According to advocates of a more ecological, habitat-focused approach, ITQs or IFQs alone would accomplish very little: They could reduce costs incurred by fishers in harvesting their shares, but are unlikely to lead to improvements in fish populations or in ecological conditions unless accompanied by on-going, extensive, flexible controls on how, when, and where quota holders can exercise their rights—controls that could be harder to impose and update if private rights were recognized.

The author of the following section, Alison Rieser, has been among the most vocal advocates for an ecosystem approach to fisheries management. Although she sees virtue in the creation of private rights, such rights in her view should be allocated, not to individual fishers, but to entire communities of fishers, whose powers and responsibilities would be tailored based on the lessons learned from studies of fishing communities that have over time successfully managed shared ocean resources. Only with strong, continuing communal guidance, she argues, are individual fishers likely to embrace practices that sustain a fishery's overall health.

Alison Rieser, *Prescriptions for the Commons: Environmental Scholarship and the Fishing Quotas Debate*

23 HARV. ENVTL. L. REV. 393 (1999).

The hallmarks of "ecosystem management" include the twin goals of sustaining the integrity of an entire ecosystem over the long term and the adaptive and precautionary use of science to achieve that reality. The approach includes recognition of the complexity of ecosystems and their resilient, dynamic, and self-organizing features that can be supported to achieve sustainability. Humans are an integral part of ecosystems, but the management of ecosystems requires transcending political boundaries in order to take account of the complex spatial and temporal scales at which ecosystem processes occur.

. . .

The trend toward ecosystem-based management reflects recognition of two ideas crucial to the debate over ITQs. The first is that good fishing returns require management that ensures the health of the larger ecosystem of which the fish stock is a part. Even if humans only value the fish actually taken from the environment, humans still need to attend to the ecosystem effects of fishing to guarantee sustainable yields. Effective management of a marine ecosystem requires scientific data beyond the population dynamics of the commercially harvested fish stock and how much "surplus" fish those populations can produce. The second idea is that ecosystems have valuable components beyond the fish caught, marketed, and consumed. The other valuable CPRs [common-pool resources] of the ocean include the diversity of species and habitats. Fishing can harm other species and habitats and alter marine ecosystems in ways not fully understood. To protect the health and productivity of a marine ecosystem, restraints are needed to supplement total catch limits, including fish size limits, measures to prevent or minimize bycatch, restrictions on damaging fishing gears, and finally, closed areas to protect vital habitats.

Catching a species of fish for sale realizes one value of a rich and diverse marine ecosystem. If the right to engage in this activity is held exclusively by a group of individuals in the form of an ITQ, and these are traded actively in a market, there is a serious risk that all other valuable components of the ecosystem, which have no direct market value and whose contribution to the ecosystem's productivity is not understood, will be ignored. The value of the ecosystem itself is likely to be discounted by managers when setting regulations such as the total catch limit from which the annual, individual harvesting rights will be calculated.

. . .

[T]he need for management sensitive to the broader ecosystem may suggest, that, if property rights approaches are to be used to prevent resource depletion and spillover effects, these rights should take a particular form. These approaches should emphasize less the individual nature of the property right and more the community nature of the right. In fisheries management, for example, property rights could be allocated to a community, rather than an individual. Communities are more likely to embody a broader range of values and will therefore balance harvesting decisions against broader spatial and temporal views of the ecosystem. Communities can also enforce limits on individual appropriators through informal norms and sanctions.

III.   THE DEBATE OVER ITQS

. . .

Awarding fishermen usufructuary rights is not enough to guarantee they will become good stewards. Once ITQ programs are in place, they will be extremely costly to change, as the New Zealand experience has shown.[107] Moreover, ITQs are a form of individualized property that would tend to prevent fishermen from forming alternative production arrangements in which they could collect and share information[108] and adopt their own rules to address the appropriation and technological externalities described by Elinor Ostrom and Edella Schlager.[109] ITQs do not give fishermen a vehicle for collectively advancing their common concern for the future value of their property.[110]

Perhaps the most important shortcoming of ITQs arises with ecosystem management. ITQs alone do not create an institutional framework within which fishermen must work with other groups and individuals who depend upon and are concerned with a healthy, functioning marine ecosystem. In this way ITQs may run counter to the trend in environmental policy generally and, in particular, the new mandates of the Sustainable Fisheries Act that require fisheries management to take account of the inter-relatedness of species and their habitats, as well as the ecological ramifications of heavy fishing pressure on increasingly lower trophic levels.[111] These changes in the law, which reflect the growing global concern for preserving biological and ecological diversity, may mean the ITQ with its emphasis on achieving efficiency is already an obsolete policy instrument.

IV.   LESSONS FOR SCHOLARSHIP FROM THE ITQ DEBATE

. . .

The end of the ocean resource frontier is signaled by the increasing number of spillover effects between users, including fisheries bycatch

107. *See* Christopher Dewees, *Fishing for Profits: New Zealand Fishing Industry Changes for "Pakeha" and Maori With Individual Transferable Quotas, in* SOCIAL IMPLICATIONS OF QUOTA SYSTEMS IN FISHERIES 91 (Gísli Pálsson & Gudrún Pétursdóttir, eds., 1997); Basil M.H. Sharp, *From Regulated Access to Transferable Harvesting Rights: Policy Insights From New Zealand,* 21 MARINE POL'Y 501 (1997).

108. *See* Anthony D. Scott, *The ITQ as a Property Right: Where it Came From, How It Works, and Where It Is Going, in* TAKING OWNERSHIP: PROPERTY RIGHTS AND FISHERY MANAGEMENT IN THE ATLANTIC COAST 79–80 (Brian Lee Crowley, ed., 1996).

109. [Ed: In their studies of actual common-pool fisheries, summarized by Rieser in her article, these scholars found that fishers on their own tended to organize themselves and to develop rules that addressed technological externalities (problems that arise when vessels and different fishing gear

types conflict physically) and assignment problems (problems that arise when fishers do not coordinate their choice of fishing grounds), but they do not tend to solve appropriations externalities—problems of excessive harvesting by fishers, individually and collectively.]

110. *See* Scott, supra note 108, at 85.

111. *See* John Beddington, *Fisheries: The Primary Requirements,* 374 NATURE 213, 214 (1995); Carl Safina, *The World's Imperiled Fish,* 9 SCI. AM. PRESENTS 58, 60 (1998); Dick Russell, *Fishing Down the Food Chain,* AMICUS J. Fall, 1995 at 16. The Magnuson–Stevens Act requires fishery management regulations to minimize bycatch and mortality of fish caught incidentally, to include measures to protect habitat essential to exploited fish species, and to achieve the level of fishing that is consistent with the protection of marine ecosystems. *See* 16 U.S.C. §§ 1802(28), 1851(a)(1), 1851(a)(9) (1994 & Supp. II 1996).

levels, habitat destruction, and changes in biological relations among trophic levels (such as predator-prey relations) that now threaten the integrity of
whole marine ecosystem.[121] Having reached the end of the frontier, environmental law scholars and policymakers must recognize that property
rights accorded any one individual cannot adequately take account of the
entire ecosystem. Nor can one individual acting alone, even when given
incentives through a permanent property right, take sufficient actions to
ensure that all of the interconnecting components of a functioning ecosystem remain intact.[122] Even a large number of individuals with the same
new incentives, acting independently, cannot collectively address and account for all of these interacting components. Therefore, the individual
property right seems more consistent with the previous era of resource use,
a time when the policy goal was to design incentives to capture the flow of
benefits from fish populations without an excess investment in physical
capital.

The collapse of fish stocks and the subsequent cascading effects that
have been felt throughout the marine environment have made it apparent
that fisheries must also be managed on the basis of the entire ecosystem.
The institutions of management must abandon the frontier mentality and
emphasize common resource approaches. . . .

If new management approaches use property rights, those property
rights must be created in a manner informed by a wider sense of social
justice. The new property rights must acknowledge the importance of the
distribution of benefits as well as endangered species, endangered cultures,
and all groups dependent upon and affected by the condition of the natural
environment. In the modern fisheries commons, property rights should not
be designed to alienate fishermen and free them from the interference of
the community. Instead, a link should be established between rights and
responsibilities.

NOTES

(1) Community coherence: Rieser bases her call for allocating rights to
communities rather than individuals by drawing upon studies of communi-
ty-run fisheries (and other communally managed resources) that functioned
well for long periods of time. These communities, however, were typically
close-knit, often geographically isolated and ethnically homogenous groups
of people who typically interacted with one another in multiple ways—as
neighbors, relatives, church members, and the like, and not just as colleagues in fishing. Under the FCMA and other fishing regulatory regimes,
communal fishing rights have typically been recognized only in the case of
native tribal groups with high degrees of coherence. Is it feasible to
consider that such arrangements would work in other settings, particularly
among fishers who, for decades, have openly competed with one another?

---

121. *See* Susan Hanna, *The New Fron-*
tier of American Fisheries Governance, 20
ECOLOGICAL ECON. 221, 223 (1997).

122. *Id.* at 228–31.

Has the competitive spirit permeated such fishing areas to such an extent that a sudden shift to collegiality and mutual aid might seem unrealistic?

(2) Essential fish habitat: The 1996 amendments to the FCMA not only imposed a moratorium on new IFQ regulatory systems, the Act also added an additional required provision to FMPs: plans are required to "describe and identify essential fish habitat for the fishery." 16 U.S.C. § 1853(a)(7). "Essential fish habitat" was defined as "those waters and substrate necessary to fish spawning, breeding, feeding, or growth to maturity." *Id.* § 1802(10). Finally, the amendments required the Secretary to "establish by regulation guidelines to assist the Councils in the description and identification of essential fish habitat." *Id.* § 1855(b)(1)(A).

The amendments also require "[e]ach federal agency [to] consult with the Secretary with respect to any action authorized, funded, or undertaken, or proposed ... by such agency that may adversely affect any essential fish habitat." *Id.* § 1855(b)(2). If the Secretary determines that the proposed action would adversely affect the habitat, "the Secretary shall recommend ... measures that can be taken by such agency to conserve such habitat." *Id.* § 1855(b)(4)(A). The agency is required to respond to the recommendations, including a "description of the measures proposed by the agency for avoiding, mitigating, or offsetting the impact of the activity"; if the agency decides not to following the Secretary's recommendations, the agency "shall explain its reasons." *Id.* § 1855(b)(4)(B).

Although the added provisions are likely to increase awareness of fish habitat, the actual impact may well be minimal. The only substantive requirements are that (1) FMPs must "minimize *to the extent practicable* adverse effects on such habitat caused by fishing," *id.* § 1853(a)(7) (emphasis added), and (2) the Secretary must "ensure" that Commerce Department programs "further the conservation and enhancement of essential fish habitat," *id.* § 1855(b)(1)(C). As Michael Bean and Melanie Rowland note, "Both provisions allow for substantial ... discretion. Councils may determine what is 'practicable,' and the Secretary may determine what furthers habitat conservation and what does not." MICHAEL J. BEAN & MELANIE J. ROWLAND, *supra,* at 167. Similarly, the only enforceable provisions in the consult and comment requirements are procedural: the section mandates no substantive outcome, only consideration.

(3) Fishery management systems and the precautionary principle: One of the central elements of ecosystem management, as Rieser points out, is an attitude of caution in interacting with marine environments. Traditional fishery management tended to focus exclusively on assessments of fish stocks to set total allowable catches, ignoring many complex, little-know ecological interactions and ignoring, too, the reality that stock assessments were often severely flawed. According to critics, since the IFQ/ITQ approach retains the fundamental aspects of traditional fishery management—reliance upon stock assessments to set total allowable catch—it would perpetuate the problems caused by such blindness and arrogance. What is called for is management guided by an overriding precautionary principle.

> Many scientists believe that a primary cause of fishery management failures is the inherent uncertainty in stock assessments. This

uncertainty contributes to ineffective or untimely management actions and the reluctance of fishers to accept the economic costs of reducing effort even when stocks are in decline or their status is uncertain. To provide insurance against stock collapse, scientists have proposed establishing fishery reserves when the lack of accuracy in stock assessments and lack of resolve to fish conservatively make it difficult to achieve sustainable fishing levels under conventional management. The specific causes leading to collapse of a fishery are controversial because of the difficulty in discerning the relative contributions of fishing pressure, environmental forces, and management does not account for the effect of environmental degradation on MSY. Fishing fleets are ever more efficient at locating and catching remaining fish aggregations, with the result that once the fishery collapses, it may require long periods of time to recover, on the order of a decade or more, even in the absence of fishing. Ensuring against collapse is a primary but elusive goal of marine fishery management.

Central to the problem of uncertainty in fishery science and management is our difficulty in confronting it. Conventional fishery management relies on science, particularly our ability to determine appropriate target catches and out ability to estimate actual fishing mortality or stock size as a basis for recommending effort or catch controls to meet those targets. Even when science is adequate, the effectiveness of management to achieve desired control (*I.e.,* control the exploitation rate) may be uncertain. Experience and simulation analyses have shown that stock assessment methods sometimes are prone to errors exceeding 50% even when costly monitoring programs are in place. Worse, errors tend to be correlated from year to year, compounding their effects over time. Retrospective analysis often reveal biases, with stock size initially overestimated or underestimated for several consecutive years. When scientists and managers depend on catch data from the fishery itself (*i.e.,* fishery-dependent data), levels of bycatch and discards at sea often are unknown and those sources of fishing mortality may not be included properly in assessments. Fundamental parameters, such as the rate of natural mortality, can only be specified in a rather broad range, but they too can be imprecise, or in many fisheries, simply unavailable.

It has been argued that uncertainty in stock assessments is simply too large to manage a fishery sustainably using conventional tools. Establishing marine reserves is one alternative.

NATIONAL ACADEMY OF SCIENCES, MARINE PROTECTED AREAS: TOOLS FOR SUSTAINING OCEAN ECOSYSTEMS 32–33 (2001).

(4) Borrowing from the Endangered Species Act: As fisheries scholars have pondered how best to deal with low fish populations and declining marine ecosystems, many have turned to other bodies of law for ideas. One model that has drawn attention is the habitat-conservation planning provisions of the Endangered Species Act (which will be considered in Chapter 13). One scholar has considered at length how habitat conservation planning principles might be incorporated into the FCMA, largely under the national standards contained in the current law. Sharon R. Siegel, Note,

Applying the Habitat Conservation Model to Fisheries Management: A Proposal for a Modified Fisheries Planning Requirement, 25 COLUM. J. ENVTL. L. 141 (2000).

SECTION 5.   INJURIOUS WILDLIFE

The federal statutes examined to this point have sought to conserve populations of wildlife by restricting takings and commercial transactions in specimens. All of the species protected under these statutes have been deemed to be beneficial—because they are a commodity for market (marine fisheries and mammals) or for hunters (game birds), because they confer an indirect economic benefit (insectivorous birds), or because they have symbolic value (bald eagles and the feral horses and burros). Not all wildlife, however, is beneficial.

a.   THE LACEY ACT

NOTES

As discussed above, the Lacey Act is the primary federal statute supplementing state and federal wildlife conservation statutes by regulating the interstate and international shipment of wildlife. The Act as originally enacted also prohibited importation of fruit bats, mongooses, English sparrows, starlings, and "other birds and animals as the Secretary of Agriculture may from time to time declare injurious to the interest of agriculture or horticulture." 18 U.S.C. § 42 (current version). The statutory language has since been expanded substantially:

> The importation . . . of the mongoose of the species *Herpestes auropunctatus*; of the species of so-called "flying foxes" or fruit bats of the genus *Pteropus*; of the zebra mussel of the species *Dreissena polymorpha*; and such other species of wild mammals, wild[1] birds, fish (including mollusks and crustacea), amphibians, reptiles, brown tree snakes, or the offspring or eggs of any of the foregoing which the Secretary of the Interior may prescribe by regulation to be injurious to human beings, to the interests of agriculture, horticulture, forestry, or to wildlife or the wildlife resources[2] of the United States, is hereby prohibited.

Id. § 42(a)(1).

The most important change for wildlife conservation was the inclusion of the authority to ban the importation of wildlife that is "injurious . . . to wildlife or the wildlife resources of the United States." A recent review of the causes of endangerment among imperiled species in the United States found that "[c]ompetition with or predation by alien species is the second-

---

1. [The term "wild" is defined by the Act as "any creatures that, whether or not raised in captivity, normally are found in a wild state." *Id.* § 42(a)(2).]

2. [The terms "wildlife" and "wildlife resources" include "all . . . classes of wild creatures whatsoever, and all types of aquatic and land vegetation upon which such wildlife resources are dependent." *Id.*]

ranked threat ... affecting 49% of imperiled species." David S. Wilcove *et al., Quantifying Threats to Imperiled Species in the United States*, 48 BioSci. 607, 609 (1998).

Violation of the importation ban is subject to imposition of a fine, imprisonment of up to six months, or both. *Id.* § 42(b). The statute does not contain a scienter requirement; all that is required is the "importation" of the prohibited species. Would the owners of a vessel entering the United States with zebra mussel larvae in its ballast water be subject to prosecution?

b.   THE NONINDIGENOUS AQUATIC NUISANCE PREVENTION AND CONTROL ACT OF 1990

NOTES

Finding that "the potential economic disruption to communities affected by the zebra mussel due to its colonization of water pipes, boat hulls and other hard surfaces has been estimated at $5,000,000,000 by the year 2000, and the potential disruption to diversity and abundance of native fish and other species ... could be severe," Congress in 1990 enacted The Nonindigenous Aquatic Nuisance Prevention and Control Act, 16 U.S.C. § 4701–4751. The Act's coverage is extremely broad: "nonindigenous species" is defined as "any species or other viable biological material that enters an ecosystem beyond its historic range." *Id.* § 4702(11). The definition thus includes HIV/AIDS and the West Nile Virus since both are "viable biological material." The species must, however, also be a "nuisance," which the Act implicitly and ambiguously defines as a species that "threatens the diversity or abundance of native species or the ecological stability of infested waters, or commercial, agricultural, aquacultural or recreational activities dependent upon such waters." *Id.* § 4702(1).

While acknowledging the potential economic and ecological costs of introduced species, the Act itself does not detail any specific steps to be taken to deal with the threat. Rather, it establishes a task force—the Aquatic Nuisance Species Task Force—co-chaired by the Director of the Fish and Wildlife Service and the Undersecretary of Commerce for Oceans and Atmosphere with the Administrator of the Environmental Protection Agency, the Commandant of the Coast Guard, the Assistant Secretary of the Army, and the Secretary of Agriculture as members. *Id.* § 4721(b). The Task Force is to develop and implement a program to "identify the goals, priorities, and approaches" for preventing introduction of aquatic nuisance species and "describe the specific prevention, monitoring, control, education and research activities" to accomplish these goals. *Id.* § 4722(b).

c.   "ANIMAL DAMAGE CONTROL"

There is also an additional and quite different type of takings regulation: the eradication of species deemed to be "noxious animals." Attempts to eradicate animals—primarily predators—began almost simultaneously with the arrival of Europeans in North America. The federal government did not become involved in predator control programs until 1909 when

Congress enacted a statute appropriating money for "experiments and demonstrations in destroying noxious animals." Act of Mar. 4, 1909, ch. 301, 35 Stat. 1051.[1] The program was given a permanent structure in 1931 when Congress directed the Secretary of Agriculture to "promulgate the best methods of eradication ... mountain lions, wolves, coyotes, bobcats, prairie dogs, gophers, ground squirrels, jack rabbits, and other animals injurious to agriculture, horticulture, forestry, animal husbandry, wild game animals, fur-bearing animals, and birds." 7 U.S.C. § 426. Despite strong scientific challenges to the program in reports to Secretary in 1964, 1971, and 1978, Animal Damage Control (ADC) was reinvigorated by the Reagan administration. *See* MICHAEL J. BEAN, THE EVOLUTION OF NATIONAL WILDLIFE LAW 236–39 (rev. & expanded ed. 1983).

The success of ADC has contributed several species to the current endangered species list: the Gray Wolf, the Grizzly Bear, the Utah Prairie Dog, and the Black-footed Ferret have all been direct or indirect targets of animal damage control programs.

Southern Utah Wilderness Alliance v. Thompson

United States District Court for the District of Utah.
811 F.Supp. 635 (1993).

■ ANDERSON, SENIOR D.J.:—This matter came before the court on Plaintiffs' Motion for a Preliminary Injunction.... The court, having reviewed the voluminous record and the applicable law, hereby denies Plaintiffs' Motion for a Preliminary Injunction.

I. BACKGROUND

The Dixie and Fishlake National Forests support numerous types of wildlife and serve as grazing areas for livestock. Historically, Animal Damage Management ("ADM") decisions in these forests have led to conflicts between the supporters of the wildlife and of the domestic populations, especially because the ADMs authorize Animal Damage Control ("ADC"), which involves the control and reduction of predator species population, such as cougars and coyotes, through non-lethal and lethal control methods. Despite these conflicts, ADC programs have been conducted successfully since 1973, excluding 1991 and 1992.

Various statutes, regulations, and plans guide the implementation of ADC programs. Federal authority for ADM programs emanates from the Animal Damage Control Act of 1931, 7 U.S.C. §§ 426–426b (the "ADCA"), which directs the Secretary of Agriculture to "conduct campaigns for the destruction" of animals injurious to agriculture and livestock on the national forest and the public domain. Authority to conduct ADC programs currently resides with the Animal and Plant Health Inspection Service–Animal Damage Control ("APHIS–ADC").

---

1. Although states were challenging the constitutionality of federal efforts to protect migratory waterfowl, federal efforts to de- stroy predators aroused no righteous indignation or appeals to "states rights."

The National Forest Management Act, 16 U.S.C. § 1604(i) (1988) ("NFMA"), authorizes the Forest Service to manage land designated as National Forests and assess the environmental impact of ADC programs. The Forest Service Manual ("FSM") prepared under authority of the NFMA provides further guidance for implementation of ADM programs. In the FSM, the forest service recognizes the authority of the APHIS–ADC to conduct animal damage management services. The FSM requires both the forest service and the APHIS–ADC to reduce the damage done to wildlife by predation and to conduct ADM activities when predation causes or threatens to cause damage to livestock. [ ]

This shared responsibility and coordinated effort is memorialized in a Memorandum of Understanding ("MOU") prepared at the national level between the forest service and the APHIS–ADC. The MOU details the respective authority of each division. Generally, the APHIS–ADC is responsible for documenting predation loss and conducting the actual predation control pursuant to the ADCA, and the Forest Service is responsible for managing the land under its jurisdiction and for insuring compliance with environmental statutes.

Notwithstanding federal jurisdiction in this area, the states retain a significant amount of authority. State law authorizes ranchers with livestock on national forest allotments to protect their herds from predation. State law plays an important role in predator control in other ways. For example, federal statutes provide that state civil and criminal jurisdiction extends to forest reserves. [ ] This jurisdiction includes the application of state wildlife and game laws to hunting, trapping, and fishing activities on the national forests. [ ]

Under its authority, the State of Utah has protected two predators: (1) cougars and (2) black bears. The state, however, has not protected coyotes, but rather regulates coyotes as a predatory animal. [ ] Coyote regulation extends to federal lands, including national forest land. [ ] Because coyotes are a non-protected predatory animal, ranchers suffering predation loss may practice predator control methods against them. Consequently, because of this overlapping authority and of the possible conflict in state and federal predator control programs, both the Dixie and the Fishlake National Forest Plans call for cooperation between the state and federal agencies responsible for predator control.

In establishing an ADC program, the forest service is subject to other statutory constraints. First, as provided in the MOU, the forest service must comply with the National Environmental Policy Act, [ ], ("NEPA"), by analyzing the environmental effects of a proposed ADC program. If the program involves serious environmental impact, the agency must prepare an Environmental Impact Statement ("EIS"). If, however, the agency determines that the proposed program will involve minimal environmental impact, referred to as a Decision Notice and Finding of No Significant Injury ("FONSI"), the agency fulfills its NEPA mandate by preparing a less comprehensive environmental assessment ("EA").

In addition to its environmental obligations, the Forest Service must comply with its forest management obligations under the NFMA and the Administrative Procedures Act, [ ] ("APA"). The NFMA requires the forest service to limit management decisions to those consistent with its forest plan. The APA requires that the forest service base its decision on the administrative record that it has compiled. Any agency decision coming under the APA must not be arbitrary or capricious or in violation of other applicable law, in this case NEPA or the NFMA.

On April 25, 1991, Thompson, the supervisor of the Dixie National Forest, issued a FONSI and EA, which authorized a full range of non-lethal and lethal control methods, including aerial gunning, a type of lethal predator control in which predators are tracked and shot from a helicopter. The decision requires ranchers to use a combination of the following non-lethal control measures: using of guard dogs; changing bed grounds daily; having the herder camp with the herd; disposing of dead sheep at least one-half mile away from the grazing band; using more than one herder with the band; avoiding areas where historically predation has been high; using experienced herders; and using more and better quality dogs. Under the EA, the rancher must diligently apply non-lethal control measures before the forest service will authorize lethal control. When non-lethal measures prove ineffective, the forest supervisor then has available a full range of lethal control measures, including leghold traps and snares, hunting by calling and shooting, denning,[1] the use of hunting dogs, M–44s,[2] and the most objectionable measure, aerial gunning.[3]

Six separate appeals of Thompson's decision were filed with Regional Forester....

On January 15, 1992, three public interest groups, the Southern Utah Wilderness Alliance, The Wilderness Society, and the Humane Society of America; and three private individuals, Sharon and David Hatfield and Tina Marie Ekker [hereinafter collectively referred to as Plaintiffs], brought suit against the forest service, alleging that the proposed Dixie ADC program violates the APA, NEPA, and the NFMA. Plaintiffs seek injunctive and declaratory relief.

. . .

Similar events occurred with respect to ADC on the Fishlake National Forest....

II. DISCUSSION

. . .

B. *Balance of Harms*

In establishing the need for injunctive relief, the court balances the last three requirements: (1) whether, in the absence of injunctive relief, Plaintiffs are threatened with irreparable injury; (2) whether Plaintiffs' potential injury outweighs any damage to Defendants; and (3) whether an injunction will be adverse to the public interest. [ ] Plaintiffs assert three

---

1. Denning involves the killing of coyote pups in the den.

2. M–44s eject a cloud of sodium cyanide gas when activated by the coyote.

3. Aerial gunning is authorized only in the winter months and only in areas where other lethal methods have been unsuccessful.

types of irreparable harm: (1) that the ADCs threaten the viability of the coyote population; (2) that they lose enjoyment of recreational land and suffer psychological pain when lethal predator control is occurring; and (3) that the forest supervisors failed to follow NEPA, *see Sierra Club v. Marsh,* 872 F.2d 497 (1st Cir.1989) (agency failure to follow NEPA constitutes irreparable harm). Plaintiffs further contend that the permittees will suffer no further harm until spring because sheep predation ceases during the winter months. Contrariwise, the government asserts a long list of potential harms, including the threat to permittees' economic viability and the danger to wildlife from permittees' self-help efforts.

The court finds that the balance of harms does not "tip decidedly" in favor of Plaintiffs, but rather that it tips in favor of the permittees and the public. Injunctive relief would threaten permittees' interests in three ways. First, although predation loss varies from permittee to permittee, the record reveals a trend toward increased predation loss. This is evidenced by the fact that permittees are experiencing losses in allotments that have never suffered predation before. Second, actual losses to predation are much greater than confirmed losses. Various factors, including terrain and herd movement, make it impossible to assess the actual loss, but the court finds that predation loss is much greater than confirmed losses. Third, increased predation loss, the predominant reason why ranchers leave the sheep business, threatens the economic viability of the permittees.

Further, injunctive relief would not serve the public interest. The ADCA directs the Secretary of Agriculture to "conduct campaigns for the destruction" of animals injurious to agriculture and livestock on the national forest and the public domain. [ ] By contrast, the State of Utah has protected two predators: (1) cougars and (2) black bears. The state, however, has not protected coyotes, but rather regulates coyotes as a predatory animal. [ ] Coyote regulation extends to federal lands, including national forest land. [ ] Because coyotes are a non-protected predatory animal, ranchers suffering predation loss may practice predatory control methods against them. Thus, even if the court were to grant the injunction, the permittees may, by law, exterminate predators in order to protect their livestock. Therefore, injunctive relief could become a two-edged sword cutting against the public interest: first, by restricting the government from achieving its statutory objective; and second, by transferring the authority to conduct predator control to those ill-suited to conduct it, the permittees. This self-help situation would create a substantial risk of irreparable harm to the public interest.

Finally, Plaintiffs will suffer no irreparable injury because, despite its contrary contention, even with the ADC programs, the coyote population will remain viable. Nothing in the record supports Plaintiffs' contention that the ADCs threaten the coyote population. This is not to say that the injuries Plaintiffs assert are not real, but rather that this court finds that the injury is not irreparable. Accordingly, the court finds that the comparative harm weighs in favor of denying Plaintiffs' Motion for Preliminary Injunction. Having failed to establish irreparable harm, Plaintiffs, to prevail on their claim for injunctive relief, must establish with reasonable probability that they would prevail on the merits of its claim. [ ]

C. *Substantial Likelihood of Success on the Merits*

1. Do the EAs Violate the APA?—Plaintiffs argue that the ADCs violate the APA because the forest service did not objectively address the economic damage to the permittees, but rather based its decision on the permittees' self-interested statements. Consequently, Plaintiffs contend that the ADCs violate the APA because they are not based on relevant factors. The court finds that Plaintiffs' APA arguments are without merit, and therefore, as fully set forth herein, concludes that Plaintiffs do not have a substantial likelihood of success on their APA claims.

. . .

Plaintiffs argue that the EAs violate the APA because the respective forest supervisors have not established the need for the ADC program. Each forest supervisor must determine need based on studies conducted concerning that forest. Here, Plaintiffs contend, the forest supervisors have not assessed need beyond the word of the permittees.

Even then, Plaintiffs argue that the supervisors should establish some objective criteria for establishing need. For example, need for predator control might exist when the economic viability of the permittees is threatened by predation or when loss to predation reaches some percentage, such as five percent. Plaintiffs also assert that the ADCs have no rational basis because the need for the ADCs was never studied and is, therefore, uncertain, and because the effectiveness of the ADCs is open to dispute. In response, the government contends that the ADC programs are both necessary and effective.

Turning first to the need for the ADCs, the agency need not show that a certain level of damage is occurring before it implements an ADC program. In other words, it is not necessary to establish a criteria, such as economic viability of the permittees or percentage loss of a herd, to justify the need for an ADC. Chapter 2650.3 of the Forest Service Manual establishes a policy of animal damage management "when necessary to accomplish multiple-use objectives." [ ] This policy allows for control activities in two circumstances: (1) when predators threaten "public health or safety"; and (2) when predators "cause or threaten to cause damage to threatened or endangered animals or plants, other wildlife, permitted livestock, or other resources, on National Forest System lands or private property." [ ] "In evaluating the need for and in conducting animal damage management programs", the forest supervisor is instructed to "weigh the social, esthetic [sic], and other values of wildlife along with economic considerations." [ ] Hence, to establish need for an ADC, the forest supervisors need only show that damage from predators is threatened.

In this case, the record indicates that actual predation damage was occurring in both the Dixie and Fishlake National Forests. [ ] Consequently, the need for the ADC program is established. Moreover, the forest supervisors sought public comment and considered the competing social and economic values in evaluating the need for an ADC. [ ] Therefore, Plaintiffs have failed to show that the ADC was not needed.

Similarly, although disagreement exists concerning the effectiveness of predator control programs, the record establishes a rational basis for effectiveness. *See Marsh v. Oregon Natural Resources Council, Inc.,* 490 U.S. 360, 378 (1989) (when specialists express differing views, the agency has discretion to rely on the reasonable opinion of its own qualified expert). The supervisors have consulted numerous studies that establish the effectiveness of ADC programs. [ ] Further, they have discretion to decide when enough information has been gathered. [ ] Accordingly, this court will not second-guess the assessment of the forest supervisors concerning the effectiveness of the ADCs.

Finally, Plaintiffs argue that the ADCs violate the APA because they are contrary to the NFMA. [ ] Under the NFMA, the Forest Service must act in accordance with the forest plan promulgated for each forest. The respective forest plans permit predator control if needed. Plaintiffs assert that the ADCs violate the forest plans because they contain no objective analysis of the need for predator control. The court, however, has already found that the need for the ADCs was established because of actual and threatened damage to livestock. [ ] Therefore, Plaintiffs have failed to show that the ADCs are inconsistent with the respective forest plans or that the programs endanger the diversity of wildlife in the forests.

The record supports the hardiness of the coyote and attributes this hardiness to the coyotes adaptability and rapid reproductive capability. [ ] To jeopardize the viability of the coyote population, seventy-five percent of that population would have to be eradicated yearly for fifty years. [ ] Under the worst case scenario, the cumulative impact on the coyote population will be no more than a forty percent loss. [ ] Such losses will not endanger the coyote population. Therefore, the court finds that the ADCs as embodied in the EAs do not violate the APA.

2. Do the EAs Violate NEPA?—Plaintiffs next argue that the EAs are inadequate and in violation of NEPA....

III. CONCLUSION

The court denies Plaintiffs' Motion for a Preliminary Injunction. In assessing the requirements for injunctive relief, the court finds that Plaintiffs fail on all points....

NOTES

Might assigning APHIS–ADC responsibility "for documenting predation loss and conducting the actual predation control" affect the objectivity of the information, given the understandable desire to remain employed? Do not both graziers and control officers have an incentive to pad the numbers?

PERSPECTIVES

(1) Bounties in the New World: Placing bounties on the heads of varmints has been a governmental function from the earliest days of European settlement. These settlers and their descendants presumed that government had a responsibility to kill predators to protect private property and remove barriers to private economic activity. Bounties were a subsidy to stock raisers.

The most common object of bounties were wolves. In 1630, Massachusetts Bay Colony offered the first bounty: one penny per wolf. *See* 1 RECORDS OF THE GOVERNOR AND COMPANY OF MASSACHUSETTS BAY IN NEW ENGLAND 81 (Nathaniel B. Shurtleff ed., Boston, William White 1853). Virginia subsequently sought to combine a number of goals by offering Native Americans a cow for every eight wolves they killed, thus "introducing among them the idea of separate property" as a "step to civilizing them and to making them Christians." The Act of Mar. 10, 1656, 1 Va. Stat. 393 (W. Hening, ed., New York, N.Y. 1823). The Rhode Island government went one better in 1654, requiring each Indian to pay a tax of two wolf skins. 1 SAMUEL G. ARNOLD, HISTORY OF THE STATE OF RHODE ISLAND AND PLYMOUTH PLANTATION 315 (New York, Providence, Preston & Rands 1859). By the end of the eighteenth century, bounties were offered for wolves in most colonies. The bounties spread west with the livestock industry and were continued into the 1980s: Alaska had a bounty on wolves until 1984. ALASKA STAT. § 16.35.050 note (1990).

The wolf, of course, was not the only species with a reward on its head. A 1697 statute enacted by the General Assembly of West Jersey provided that "whatsoever Christian shall kill and bring the head of a wolf of prey or panther to any magistrate" was entitled to a bounty of twenty shillings; Afro–Americans and Native Americans were entitled to only ten shillings. SAMUEL N. RHOADS, THE MAMMALS OF PENNSYLVANIA AND NEW JERSEY 132–33 (1903). The practice of offering bounties extended beyond the English. In the 1500s, Jesuits in California offered a bounty of a bull for each Puma killed. But bounties have also been offered for killing bobcats, bears, coyotes, as well as various insect, bird, and mammal species classified as pests because of the economic harm they can cause. These bounty statutes share a common perspective with Blackstone since they spring from a simple calculus: What is the economic impact of the species on our species. *See generally* George C. Coggins & Parthenia B. Evans, *Predators Rights and American Wildlife Law,* 24 ARIZ. L. REV. 821 (1982).

Despite its widespread use, a bounty system is an extremely inefficient method of killing varmints. It not only creates an incentive to leave breeding stock for subsequent years but is also subject to widespread fraud. As a Senior Biologist for the Fish and Wildlife Service commented, "the bounty as a measure of control not only creates opportunities for fraud, but is usually ineffective and a waste of funds." STANLEY P. YOUNG, THE BOBCAT OF NORTH AMERICA 128 (1958). For example, bounty programs frequently required the claimant to present scalps or skins of the animal to a judge who was to certify that the claimant was entitled to the bounty. *See, e.g., Johns v. County Commissioners,* 10 So. 96 (Fla.1891). While the reliance upon the local judge was understandable in a period with few public employees, it opened the door to fraud since judges had no special expertise in the area. Once again, the rudimentary nature of state regulatory structures substantially undercut regulatory goals.

George Coggins has noted another effect:

Bounty systems were curious anomalies. In form they were economic incentives: the taxpayers at large agreed to reward those who rid the community of a menace. In practice they subsidized those on the fringes of civilization and thus had an additional virtue in keeping the rougher human element out in the forests were they belonged. Bounties were a simple answer to what people long thought was a simple, single problem, but the problem was not so simple and the solution did not work.

George C. Coggins & Parthenia B. Evans, *supra*, at 829.

Despite these shortcomings, bounties were employed for over 350 years in this country. The fact that the practice survived despite its recognized shortcomings suggests that this type of subsidy, by rewarding private initiative, reinforced the prevailing *laissez faire* myths of individual autonomy and self-reliance. JAMES WILLARD HURST, LAW AND THE CONDITIONS OF FREEDOM IN THE NINETEENTH-CENTURY UNITED STATES 7–8 (1956).

(2) The hired gun: A second and generally more effective method of killing predators is the professional hunter employed by a government. William Penn hired a professional wolf hunter in 1705, and the federal government still employs "Animal Damage Control Specialists." Employing individuals to kill predators ameliorates the perverse incentive to protect a breeding stock of varmints. It also embodies a fundamentally different perception of the proper role of government than does offering bounties to private persons. When the government hires a hunter, killing varmints becomes a governmental service like police and fire protection.

The approach is also more likely to eliminate the target species because of the changed nature of the economic incentive: a bounty will lead to kills only as long as the amount of the bounty exceeds the costs of killing. A government hunter, on the other hand, will be paid regardless of the number of predators killed and thus is more likely to "control" the last wolf.

(3) Making the country safe for sheep: Bounties, professional trappers, and habitat destruction led to the extermination of most large predators. As Barry Lopez noted, "The history of economic expansion in the West was characterized by the change or destruction of much that lay in its way. Dead wolves were what Manifest Destiny cost." BARRY H. LOPEZ, OF WOLVES AND MEN 184 (1978).

The cost, however, must be measured in more than just dead wolves. During the decade of the final slaughter of the American Bison, for example, the strychnine that wolfers used to kill wolves also killed millions of other animals: coyotes, kit foxes, badgers, vultures, ravens, and several species of raptors such as bald and golden eagles and red-tailed hawks. *See, e.g,* TOM MCHUGH, THE TIME OF THE BUFFALO 278–79 (1972). The killing of "non-target" wildlife has not stopped with the professionalization of the industry under APHIS–ADC: in 1977, of the 44,982 animals killed with steel traps only 25,026 were coyotes that the traps were set to capture. Some of the other animals killed were: 2,698 opossums, 1,367 porcupines, 3,345 raccoons, 6,348 skunks, 11 armadillo, 682 beaver, 20 deer, 273 dogs, 73 cats, 49 goats, 4 groundhogs, 100 kit foxes, 52 muskrat, 154 nutria, 98 rabbits, and 14 swift foxes. George C. Coggins & Parthenia B. Evans, *supra,* at 834, n.115.

(4) A free market approach: If the extermination of particular species is needed chiefly or entirely to meet the needs of livestock owners, should not the costs of extermination be internalized by making owners bear them? Why should taxpayers be the ones to bear the costs? One possible benefit: It livestock owners bore the costs, they might either find less costly means of dealing with the problem or shift their operations to locations in which predation was not a problem.

(5) Tailoring land uses to the land: Similarly, why should landowners be able to raise livestock in areas and using methods that create conflicts with native predators, given that conflicts are unknown or easily avoided in many parts of the country? Just as the pig belongs in the barnyard and is a nuisance in the parlor, might sheep be considered a nuisance in wolf or lion country, or in areas where nonlethal methods of predator control are inadequate? Landowners in cities are often banned by zoning ordinances from raising sheep on the ground that it is a land use that belongs elsewhere; could not the same be said for sheep in prime predator habitat?

CHAPTER 11

FEDERAL PROTECTION OF WILDLIFE HABITAT: THE TRADITIONAL PARADIGM

In 1933, Aldo Leopold began his influential text, *Game Management*, by charting the typical progression in public policies intended to protect game species. First came restrictions on hunting; next were efforts to control predators. Third, Leopold believed, were measures to set aside refuges or game preserves, either to serve as public hunting ranges or as protected breeding grounds. The typical fourth step, he asserted, was artificial replenishment—the fish hatchery approach. Only after these measures had been tried—and, frequently, failed—did societies move to the most sensible, yet challenging approach: managing landscapes that humans used so that wildlife might live on them. ALDO LEOPOLD, GAME MANAGEMENT 4 (1933). This chapter considers steps that fall into the third of Leopold's categories—setting aside lands as wildlife habitat.

We begin by looking at federal programs that give states financial incentives to acquire and manage lands as habitat. We then turn to the National Wildlife Refuge System—federally owned lands specifically acquired or reserved for habitat. Finally, we examine several federal land management systems—wilderness areas, wild and scenic rivers, and national parks—that are designed to preserve lands in relatively unaltered conditions.[1] Although such lands are not specifically reserved as wildlife habitat, wildlife does benefit from the restrictions on land alteration. In each instance, a recurrent issue is the extent to which other uses of these lands are permitted and the extent to which those uses are compatible with wildlife conservation goals.

As Leopold knew, wildlife often benefit from the creation of islands of high-quality habitat in otherwise-altered landscapes. Yet as he also knew, even large islands of habitat are insufficient, standing alone, to protect all types of wildlife. Migratory species, for example, pay no attention to the boundaries of such islands of habitat; and many sedentary species require larger or differently configured islands than the wildlife refuges that have been and continue to be set aside. Chapter 12 explores some of the biological needs of imperiled species and the implications of those needs in terms of landscape-scale planning. Chapters 13 and 14 build on those biological necessities, considering the federal Endangered Species Act and,

---

1. The final chapter considers the federal multiple-use lands—national forests and Bureau of Land Management (BLM) lands—that have wildlife protection as one of several, often conflicting aims.

ultimately, turning to the challenges posed by Leopold's fifth step: promoting wildlife in human-occupied spaces by making wildlife part of our working landscapes.

SECTION 1. FEDERAL FUNDING FOR STATE ACQUISITION OF WILDLIFE HABITAT

a. STATUTORY AUTHORITIES: EXPANDING COVERAGE

NOTES

(1) The Pittman–Robertson Act of 1937: The Pittman–Robertson Act—also known more formally as the "Federal Aid in Wildlife Restoration Act," 16 U.S.C. §§ 669–669i—is the primary program of federal assistance to states for "the selection, restoration, rehabilitation, and improvement" of wildlife habitat. *Id.* § 669a. As with many federal programs funding state activities, the Pittman–Robertson Act has been used to encourage states to act consistently with a national perspective on an issue. Initially, the Act was designed to ensure that state funding of wildlife programs was insulated from the political vagaries of the appropriation process. To that end, the Act encouraged states to prohibit "the diversion of license fees paid by hunters for any other purpose than the administration of [the] State fish and game department" by making such a prohibition a condition of receiving federal funds. *Id.* § 669.

In 1970, increasing federal emphasis on planning led Congress to amend the Act to allow states to participate either by submitting "projects" or "programs." Act of Oct. 23, 1970, Pub. L. No. 91–503, §§ 101–102, 84 Stat. 1097. Prior to the 1970 amendment, states were required to "submi[t] to the Secretary of the Interior full and detailed statements of any wildlife restoration projects" for which it was seeking funding. 16 U.S.C. § 669e(2). The term "wildlife-restoration project" is defined to "include the selection, restoration, rehabilitation, and improvement of areas of land or water adaptable as feeding, resting, or breeding places for wildlife, including [acquisition] of such areas ... and the construction ... of such works as may be necessary to make them available" for wildlife. *Id.* § 669a. In addition to this project-by-project approach, the 1970 amendment allowed states to submit "a comprehensive fish and wildlife resource management plan which shall insure the perpetuation of these resources"; the plan is to cover not less than five years. *Id.* § 669e(a).

Under either alternative, the Secretary is authorized to fund up to 75% of the proposal. *Id.* § 669e(a), (b). After allowances for certain federal administrative costs, funds are apportioned among the states based on geographic area, paid hunting-license holders, and total population. *Id.* § 669c. The monies are drawn from a fund created from taxes imposed on firearms, shells, and cartridges. 16 U.S.C. § 669b(a); 26 U.S.C. § 4161(b), 4181.

(2) Dingell–Johnson Act of 1950: The Dingell–Johnson Act—or, the Federal Aid in Fish Restoration Act, 16 U.S.C. §§ 777–777*l*—is a statute largely identical to the Pittman–Robertson Act that applies to fish. Funding comes from a federal excise tax on fishing equipment and baits. 16 U.S.C. § 777b; 26 U.S.C. § 9504(a).

(3) The Land and Water Conservation Fund Act of 1963: The Land and Water Conservation Fund Act, 16 U.S.C. § 460*l* to 460*l*–11, was enacted for "preserving, developing and assuring accessibility to ... outdoor recreation resources." 16 U.S.C. § 460*l*. Although not designed specifically to acquire wildlife habitat, the Act has proved to be "an important device for generating and distributing revenues for outdoor recreation purposes, including many of substantial direct or indirect benefit to wildlife." MICHAEL J. BEAN, THE EVOLUTION OF NATIONAL WILDLIFE LAW 233 (rev. & expanded ed. 1983).

Like the other federal funding sources, the Land and Water Conservation Fund is a special account in the Treasury for revenues from earmarked taxes and license fees. Unlike the other funds, however, the Land and Water Conservation Fund draws upon a wide variety of sources. 16 U.S.C. §§ 460*l*–5. Also unlike the other funds, the Land and Water Conservation Fund is available for both state and federal land acquisitions. The Act specifies no more than 60% of the funds are available for states. *Id.* §§ 460*l*–7. Federal funds may pay for no more than 50% of any project. *Id.* §§ 460*l*–8(d).

(4) The Fish and Wildlife Conservation Act of 1980: Both Pittman–Robertson[2] and Dingell–Johnson[3] are focused on games species. In 1980, Congress enacted the Fish and Wildlife Conservation Act—commonly known as the Non-game Act, 16 U.S.C. §§ 2901–2911. The Act actually has a broader reach than its common name might indicate: it emphasizes comprehensive planning for all wildlife species. It is a complicated statute with ten requirements for conservation plans, a multi-step process for approving the state conservation plans, and five federal reimbursement options. States were to inventory the nongame fish and wildlife within the state, determine "the size, range, and distribution" of populations and the "extent, condition, and location" of "significant habitat," evaluate potential problems facing the species and their habitat, and determine the steps to conserve the species in the face of those problems. *Id.* § 2903.

The Act's broad definition of "conservation," *id.* § 2902(3), and its emphasis on habitat echo the Endangered Species Act—in fact, the Act is designed to operate like a pre-Endangered Species Act: the conservation plans are to identify species at risk and take steps to prevent their slide toward endangerment.

There has, however, been one problem: the Act does not include independent funding provisions like those found in both Pittman–Robert-

---

2. Although Pittman–Robertson contains the undefined term "wildlife" that is not limited to game species, the Fish and Wildlife Service in 1982 implicitly defined the term as "wild birds and wild mammals" by specifying that eligible conservation projects were those that had "as their purpose the restoration, conservation, management, and enhancement of wild birds and wild mammals." 50 C.F.R. § 80.5(a)(1).

3. Dingell-Johnson applies only to "fish which have material value in connection with sport or recreation in the marine and/or fresh waters of the United States." 16 U.S.C. § 777a.

son and Dingell–Johnson and Congress has never appropriated funds to reimburse the states.

(5) Who pays the piper, calls the tune: Federal grant-in-aid measures have been a significant source of funds for the acquisition by the states of wildlife habitat. Since most of the funding for habitat acquisition comes either from earmarked excise taxes or the sale of Duck Stamps, the Migratory Bird Conservation Act, Pittman–Robertson, and Dingell–Johnson have been largely insulated from the vagaries of annual funding with its recurrent boom-bust cycles. At the same time, however, tying habitat acquisition into consumptive uses of wildlife has resulted in a system of state and federal wildlife areas that focuses on providing game for hunters. While nongame species do benefit from refuges, adoption of a comprehensive program to acquire lands to protect nongame species could have prevented the need to list some species as threatened or endangered.

b.   Judicial Construction: A Deferential Perspective

NOTES

Pittman–Robertson, Dingell–Johnson, and the Land and Water Conservation Fund Act each prohibit states from "converting" property acquired with federal assistance under the respective acts to uses other than that specified by the act unless the Secretary of the Interior approves the conversion. The Secretary generally is restricted to approving changes only if there is a substitution of other property of at least equal value.

What is a "conversion"? To what extent is the Secretary constrained in approving conversions? *See, e.g., Sierra Club v. Davies,* 955 F.2d 1188 (8th Cir.1992); *Friends of Shawangunks, Inc. v. Clark,* 754 F.2d 446 (2d Cir.1985).

Sportsmen's Wildlife Defense Fund v. Romer

District Court for the District of Colorado.
29 F.Supp.2d 1199 (1998).

■ Babcock, D.J.—In this environmental dispute, plaintiffs, Sportsmen's Wildlife Defense Fund (SWDF), Western Slope Environmental Resource Council (WSERC), Richard Saxton, and David Huerkamp (collectively, Plaintiffs) assert [a] violation of the Pittman–Robertson Wildlife Restoration Act (P–R Act), 16 U.S.C. § 669 *et seq.,* against defendants Roy Romer, in his official capacity as the Governor of the State of Colorado, John Mumma, in his official capacity as Director of the Colorado Division of Wildlife (DOW), Aristede Zavaras, in his official capacity as Director of the Colorado Department of Corrections (DOC) (collectively, State Defendants)....

.   .   .

II

Background

This action was filed by Plaintiffs to: 1) force the State Defendants to replace the portion of the Escalante State Wildlife Area (Wildlife Area) on which the DOC built a prison facility located near Delta, Colorado (Delta prison); and 2) prevent future misuses of state wildlife areas. [ ]

In 1955, the State of Colorado proposed the creation of the Wildlife Area located on the eastern flank of the Uncompahgre Plateau in Delta and Montrose Counties in western Colorado. The Wildlife Area, comprised of 10 separate tracts of land totaling more than 7,000 acres, is scattered along the Gunnison River, and its two main western tributaries, Escalante and Roubideau Creeks. It consists of nearly 200 square miles of desert and forest acquired over a 20 year period. [ ]

The Delta prison, originally known as the Delta Honor Camp, was built in the mid–1960's on approximately 80 acres of the 2,480 acre Lower Roubideau Tract of the Wildlife Area, the largest of the Wildlife Area's 10 tracts. Situated five miles west of Delta, Colorado, at the confluence of Roubideau Creek and the Gunnison River, the Delta prison, currently known as the Delta Correctional Center, functions as a minimum security correctional facility. [ ]

In 1994, the SWDF initiated an inquiry into how a prison came to be located in a state wildlife area. [ ] As a result, the State of Colorado entered into certain agreements with the State and Federal defendants to avoid or remedy any possible improprieties. Unsatisfied with the Defendants' actions, Plaintiffs filed suit in 1997 claiming that the State Defendants are violating the P–R Act and the Federal Defendants have violated the APA by allowing them to continue to violate the P–R Act.

III

A. *The Property At Issue*

This case involves the following parcels of land within the Lower Roubideau Tract of the Wildlife Area:

1. *82.74 acres (82.74 acre tract or prison compound)*

This tract is located in the southeast corner of the Lower Roubideau Tract where the DOC has constructed the Delta prison. [ ]

> *Funding:* The parties disagree whether the money to purchase this property came from federal aid monies or license fee monies.

2. *13.5 acres (13.5 acre tract)*

This tract is located directly north of the prison compound at the confluence of Cottonwood and Roubideau Creeks. [ ] This land was fenced by DOC from 1964 through 1996. Apparently, DOC plans to continue to use the 13.5 acre tract for certain purposes including "ingress and egress to DOC, for placement of signs, and for placement of security devices." [ ]

> *Funding:* The parties agree that this parcel was purchased with federal aid monies.

3. *31 acres (31 acre tract)*

This tract is located directly south of the prison compound along the west bank of Roubideau Creek. [ ] DOC acquired the 31 acre tract from DOW. [ ]

Funding: The parties disagree whether the funds to acquire this property came from federal aid monies or license fee monies.

4. *Buffer zone around the prison (buffer zone)*

    Funding: The parties disagree about the source of the funds used to purchase this property, although they agree that some portion of the buffer zone was acquired with federal aid monies.

. . .

The crux of this case, assuming there have been violations of the P–R Act, is:

1. whether federal monies or state license monies were used to purchase the pertinent property;

2. whether the State Defendants have a right to cure the violations and, if so;

3. what actions are required to cure any violations depending on whether there was a "diversion" of state license monies or a "misuse" of federal monies.

Each of these questions is resolved with reference to the P–R Act.

B. *Pittman-Robertson Act, 16 U.S.C. § 669, et seq.*

    The P–R Act provides in part:

    [t]he Secretary of the Interior is authorized to cooperate with the States, through their respective State fish and game departments, in wildlife-restoration projects . . . ; but no money apportioned under this chapter to any State shall be expended . . . until [the State] shall have assented to the provision (sic) of this chapter and shall have passed laws . . . which shall include a prohibition against the diversion of license fees paid by hunters for any other purpose than the administration of said State fish and game department. . . . The Secretary of the Interior and the State fish and game department of each State accepting the benefits of this chapter, shall agree upon the wildlife-restoration projects to be aided in such State under the terms of this chapter. . . .

16 U.S.C. § 669. Thus, the P–R Act provides federal matching grants to states for wildlife restoration projects funded jointly by a state and the USFWS. To qualify for federal matching funds, commonly referred to as "federal aid monies" or "P–R monies," a recipient state must agree to use its state hunting license fees solely for wildlife purposes. 16 U.S.C. § 669. The P–R Act further requires the state to enact legislation making it unlawful for the state to use its own license fee monies for any purpose other than wildlife.

P–R Act federal aid monies can be used only for wildlife restoration projects defined to mean:

    [t]he selection, restoration, rehabilitation, and improvement of areas of land or water adaptable as feeding, resting, or breeding places for wildlife, including acquisition by purchase, condemnation, lease, or gift of such areas or estates or interests therein as are suitable or capable

of being made suitable therefore, and the *construction thereon or therein of such works as may be necessary to make them available for such purposes.*

16 U.S.C. § 669a (emphasis added).

The P–R Act further restricts how state license fee revenues can be spent. The term "license revenues" is defined to include income from the "sale, lease, rental, or other granting of rights of real or personal property acquired or produced with license fee revenues." 50 C.F.R. § 80.4(a)(2). A state, like Colorado, that has assented to the P–R Act's terms may use its license fee monies only for the administration of its fish and game department. *See* § 669; 50 C.F.R. § 80.14. Thus, the P–R Act places mandatory restrictions on a recipient state's use of its own state monies and state wildlife areas for non-wildlife purposes such as highways, prisons, or schools.

Pursuant to 16 U.S.C. § 669i, the Secretary of the Interior has promulgated rules and regulations for carrying out the P–R Act's provisions. *See generally* 50 C.F.R. part 80. These regulations treat real property in the same manner, whether acquired or constructed with federal aid monies. Consequently, just as a state cannot spend matching federal aid monies on a non-approved project, a state cannot use real property acquired with federal aid monies for any purpose other than that previously approved by the USFWS. According to the regulations, real property acquired or constructed with federal aid funds must continue to serve the purpose for which it was acquired or constructed. *See* § 80.14(b). Therefore, if a state purchases real property for use as a wildlife area with any federal aid monies, the property must continue to be used as a wildlife area.

The regulations also restrict a state's use of real property acquired with state license fee monies. As discussed above, the regulations secure this restriction by defining the term "license fee revenue" broadly to include income from the sale, lease, or other granting of rights in real property acquired with license revenues. *See* § 80.4(a)(2).

If a state uses land acquired with federal aid monies for a non-approved purpose, the state is considered to have "misused" the federal aid monies, pursuant to § 80.14. If a state spends license fee monies on a non-approved purpose or uses land acquired with license fee monies for a non-approved purpose, the state is said to have "diverted" those license fee monies pursuant to § 80.4. The regulations contain explicit, separate remedies for "diversion" or "misuse." This distinction is important in this case.

1. *Diversion*

"A diversion of state license fee revenues occurs when any portion of license revenues is used for any purpose other than the administration of the State fish and wildlife agency." 50 CFR § 80.4(c). If a diversion occurs, the state becomes ineligible to participate under the . . . Act from the date the diversion is declared by the Director until:

1. adequate legislative prohibitions are in place to prevent diversion of license revenue, and;

2. all license revenues or assets acquired with license revenues are restored, or an amount equal to license revenue diverted or current market value of assets diverted (whichever is greater) is returned and properly available for use for the administration of the State fish and wildlife agency.

See 50 C.F.R. § 80.4(d)(2).

2. *Misuse*

"Misuse" of federal aid monies occurs when such funds are not "applied only to activities or purposes approved by the regional director. If otherwise applied, such funds must be replaced or the State becomes ineligible to participate." 50 CFR § 80.14(a). Section 80.14 provides further:

(b) real property acquired or constructed with Federal Aid funds must continue to serve the purpose for which it was acquired or constructed.

(1) When such property passes from management control of the fish and wildlife agency, the control must be fully restored to the State fish and wildlife agency or the real property must be replaced using non-Federal funds. Replacement property must be of equal value at current market prices and with equal benefits as the original property. The State may have a reasonable time, up to three years from the date of notification by the regional director, to acquire replacement property before becoming ineligible.

(2) When such property is used for purposes which interfere with the accomplishment of approved purposes, the violating activities must cease and any adverse effects resulting must be remedied....

50 CFR § 80.14. To establish misuse of federal aid monies requires proof that either: 1) P–R Act funds were used to acquire the land in question; or 2) the property was constructed or maintained with P–R Act funds.

C. *Acquisition of the Escalante State Wildlife Area*

On October 20, 1955, the State of Colorado submitted a financing request, "Project W–92–L" titled "Federal Aid in Fish and Wildlife Restoration Preliminary Project Statement Fish and/or Land Acquisition Project" to the United States Department of Interior (the Project). [ ] In the Project, Colorado proposed creating the Escalante State Wildlife Area by buying two large cattle ranches owned by the Huffington and Lockhart families. [ ] In compliance with the regulations in effect in 1955, the USFWS and the Secretary of Interior reviewed the project statement to determine if the Project was "substantial in character and design" and therefore suitable for federal aid. [ ] In November 1955, the USFWS and the Secretary of the Interior approved the Project including the acquisition of all the land at issue in this case. [ ] In December 1955, the USFWS prepared a federal aid appraisal report describing and appraising the entire Lockhart Ranch as a federal aid tract.

Upon approval of the Project, Colorado entered into negotiations with the Huffingtons and the Lockharts to purchase their ranches. For tax reasons, the owners requested that they receive payments for their land over three years. [ ] On November 1, 1956, Colorado and the Lockharts entered into an "Option to Purchase" in which the state agreed to purchase "Tract One" of the Lockhart Ranch in 1957 and Tracts Two and Three thereafter. [ ]

Although the State of Colorado made the first payment to Lockhart in 1957, for reasons unknown, it waited almost two years before submitting its project plans, specifications and estimates, required by 16 U.S.C. § 669e(a)(2) to obtain federal aid reimbursement. In October 1958, after the state had made two of three scheduled payments to the Lockharts, DOW submitted its plans, specifications, and estimates for the Project to USFWS for approval requesting reimbursement for the entire Lockhart ranch. [ ]

On November 21, 1958, the Secretary of the Interior conditionally approved the plans, specifications and estimates for the Project, but denied federal aid reimbursement for Lockhart Tract I because the state had delayed making its reimbursement request for more than a year, and federal aid reimbursement funds were no longer available for expenditures made in 1957. [ ] The USFWS reimbursed Colorado for the second two payments to the Lockharts.

Based on these undisputed facts, the State Defendants contend that no P–R Act funds were used to acquire the portion of the Lower Roubideau Tract where the Delta prison is located. As to the 82.74 acre tract, the State Defendants submit the affidavit of Mary Gessner, USFWS assistant regional director for federal aid stating that "based on [her] review of the [USFWS] files and [her] personal knowledge of the facts of this case:

1.   The Delta Correctional Center occupies approximately 80 acres of the Lower Roubideau Tract of the Escalante State Wildlife Area;

2.   None of the 80 acres was purchased with federal aid monies; and

3.   Some parcels within the Lower Roubideau Tract of the Escalante State Wildlife Area were purchased with federal aid funds provided to DOW by USFWS under the P–R Act.

[ ] Likewise, Robert Towry, Habitat Section Manager for the DOW, testified that he has no knowledge that federal aid monies were used to purchase the 31 acre tract directly south of the prison. [ ]

Plaintiffs, who do not genuinely dispute Gessner's affidavit or Towry's testimony, nevertheless argue that because a portion of the Lockhart Ranch was purchased using federal aid monies, I should hold that for purposes of the P–R Act, the entire Lockhart Ranch was paid for with P–R Act funds. I disagree.

The "cardinal canon" of statutory construction is that "courts must presume that the legislature says in the statute what it means and means in the statute what it says there." *Connecticut Nat'l Bank v. Germain,* 503 U.S. 249, 254 (1992). I further presume that Congress is aware of other existing law when it passes legislation. *Miles v. Apex Marine Corp.,* 498 U.S. 19, 32 (1990).

The P–R Act and its associated regulations, 50 C.F.R. § 80.4 and 80.14, contain no explicit language supporting Plaintiffs' fictive view or any language which could be construed to reach the result urged by Plaintiffs. I find and conclude that there is no genuine dispute that the 82.74 acre and the 31 acre tracts containing the Delta prison were not purchased with federal aid monies. Accordingly, I hold as a matter of law that as to these tracts there is no "misuse" of federal aid monies pursuant to § 80.14.

1. *Federal Aid Development of Lower Roubideau Tract*

Plaintiffs may also establish a P–R Act violation by showing that P–R Act monies were used to develop and maintain land subject to the P–R Act which is being used for a purpose other than for wildlife. Thus, Plaintiffs argue that even if the property transferred to the DOC was not "acquired with federal funds," it was "constructed with federal funds" which constitutes a "misuse" pursuant to § 80.14(b). Again, I disagree.

It is undisputed that even before the purchase of the Lockhart and Huffington Ranches was completed, Colorado incorporated the newly created Escalante State Wildlife Area into its annual statewide Federal Aid Fish and Wildlife Habitat Improvement Project, Project FW–6–D. [ ] Also, between 1958 and 1964, all wildlife development activities on the Lockhart Ranch were done using federal aid monies under Project FW–6–D. According to Claude E. White, former land manager of DOW's Southwest Region, Project FW–6–D used federal aid monies to construct improvements on the Lockhart Ranch. [ ] This was accomplished pursuant to the original management plan for the Wildlife Area, including the entire Lockhart Ranch. Id. at § 2–3. Also, all wildlife development on the Lockhart Ranch from 1958 through 1964 was conducted with federal aid monies. [ ] Federal aid monies were used in the Lower Roubideau Tract, including land currently part of the Prison Compound to:

1. hire seasonal labor who constructed and maintained fences and an irrigation system;

2. purchase fencing materials for use on the Lower Roubideau Tract, including land currently part of the Prison Compound; and

3. plant lure crops for wildlife on lands that later became part of the Prison Compound.

[ ]

. . .

Assuming arguendo, that P–R Act funds were spent on the 82.74 acre or the 31 acre tract to construct and maintain fences, construct and maintain irrigation ditches, and plant annual wildlife food plots, the Defendants contend that these expenditures are insufficient to constitute "misuse" pursuant to § 80.14(b)(1). I agree.

According to Defendants, the term "constructed" in the phrase "real property acquired or constructed with federal aid funds" contained in § 80.14(b)(1) refers to expensive major structures with long useful lives, such as buildings. Section 80.17 suggests that the term "constructed" applies only to capital improvements, and that less substantial and less permanent improvements are not covered by the term "constructed." 50 C.F.R. § 80.17 provides:

The State is responsible for maintenance of all capital improvements acquired or constructed with Federal Aid funds throughout the useful life of each such improvement.

50 C.F.R. § 80.17. The State bears no such responsibility where the improvement is something less than a "capital improvement." 50 C.F.R. § 80.17 provides further that the useful life of the improvement determines whether the improvement is a "capital improvement." Once the useful life of the improvement has expired, the P–R Act restrictions on use of the improvement also expire. 50 C.F.R. § 80.17.

50 C.F.R. § 80.20 provides that "[t]he State must control lands or waters on which capital improvements are made with Federal Aid funds." There is no such state control requirement where improvements do not rise to the level of "capital improvements." I conclude that the term "constructed" in § 80.14(b)(1) does not include expenditures for construction, operation, and maintenance of the fencing, earthen irrigation ditches, or wildlife food plots. The expenditures encompassed by the term "constructed" are similar in permanence and magnitude to the acquisition of land, the other word that appears in the phrase "real property acquired or constructed with Federal funds" in § 80.14(b)(1). In any event, Plaintiffs rely on expenditures made between 1958 and 1964 for the: 1) construction and maintenance of irrigation ditches, fences and corrals; and 2) planting alfalfa, barley and other wildlife food fields. [ ] Even if these activities could be viewed as "construction," pursuant to § 80.17, after more than 30 years, I conclude, as a matter of law, that any "useful life" of these improvements has expired. [ ] Consequently, the 82.74 acre and 31 acre tracts were not "real property . . . constructed with Federal funds" so as to constitute "misuse" of Federal Aid monies pursuant to § 80.14(b).

Instead, pursuant to § 80.4, a "diversion" of state license fee monies occurred in connection with the 82.74 acre and the 31 acre tracts comprising the prison compound. I turn then to the actions taken by State Defendants to remedy or "cure" this diversion.

D. *Right to "cure"*

As an initial matter, Defendants argue that the State Defendants have a right to cure any diversion or misuse. Although Plaintiffs take exception to the sufficiency of the actions to cure, they agree that the pertinent regulations allow a cure. [ ] However, Plaintiffs argue that a diversion cure pursuant to § 80.4(d)(2) is permissible only if the circumstances leading to the "diversion" are unintentional or accidental. [ ] I disagree.

Section 80.14(b) provides expressly for a cure of misuse of federal aid monies:

> (1) When such property passes from management control of the fish and wildlife agency, the control must be fully restored to the State fish and wildlife agency or the real property must be replaced using non-Federal funds. Replacement property must be of equal value at current market prices and with equal benefits as the original property. *The State may have a reasonable time, up to three years from the date of*

notification by the regional director, to acquire replacement property before becoming ineligible.

50 C.F.R. § 80.14(b)(1) (emphasis added).

Section 80.4(d)(2), pertaining to diversions of state license fee revenues, provides:

"If a diversion of license revenues occurs, the State becomes ineligible to participate under the pertinent Act from the date the diversion is declared by the Director [of USFWS] *until*:

All license revenues or assets acquired with license revenues are restored, or an amount equal to license revenue diverted or current market value of assets diverted (whichever is greater) is returned and properly available for use for the administration of the State fish and wildlife agency."

50 C.F.R. § 80.4(d)(2) (emphasis added).

Under the unambiguous language in these regulations, the state has an absolute right to cure a diversion or a misuse. To hold here that there is no right to cure a diversion could render a state perpetually ineligible to receive federal aid funds under the P–R Act, a result which Congress could not have intended. Accordingly, I conclude that Colorado has the right to cure: 1) any diversion pursuant to § 80.4 after a declaration of diversion; and 2) any misuse pursuant to § 80.14 within three years of notification. Furthermore, § 80.4 contains no requirement that the state's right to cure a diversion or, for that matter a misuse under § 80.14, be limited to unintentional or accidental diversions. Here, there has been neither a declaration of diversion nor notice of misuse, pursuant to these regulations.

E. *Sufficiency of "cure"*

In early 1995, the USFWS informed the DOW it had determined there was a diversion of assets in connection with the use of the 82.74 acre tract of the Escalante State Wildlife Area as the site for the Delta prison. [ ] In response, on February 28, 1995, the USFWS entered into a Memorandum of Agreement ("MOA") pursuant to which USFWS agreed not to declare Colorado in diversion under the P–R Act in exchange for DOW's agreement to "evaluate all potentially feasible options, select an action plan, and complete implementation by March 1, 1996, in compliance with 50 C.F.R. § 80.4(d)(2) and 50 C.F.R. § 80.14(b)(1) and (b)(2)." [ ]

According to Plaintiffs, on March 1, 1996, DOC continued to use all the parcels at issue in this case and no monies had been transferred to DOW. Yet, USFWS still did not declare Colorado in diversion. However, on March 1, 1996, DOC, DOW and the Colorado Division of Parks and Outdoor Recreation entered into a Memorandum of Understanding (MOU) pursuant to which the DOW agreed to transfer to the DOC the prison compound, along with a number of additional parcels and associated water rights. [ ]

Pursuant to the terms of the MOU, on or about June 18, 1996, DOC transferred $60,287.44 for the use of the DOW, and DOW quit-claimed the 82.74 acre tract and associated water rights to the DOC. [ ] On March 31, 1998, DOW also quit-claimed the 31 acre tract to the DOC for $29,500.00.

[ ] The parties agree that the 82.74 acre and 31 acre tracts may be treated similarly for purposes of these motions.

Defendants contend that all violations of the P–R Act at the Escalante State Wildlife Area have been cured. Plaintiffs respond that the sale price for the two tracts is "substantially less" than their current market value. Further, Plaintiffs contend that the Defendants have ignored the DOC's use of the 13.5 acre tract, the access road, and the buffer zone and, thus, there has been no cure with respect to these properties.

Plaintiffs argue further that no cure is possible because § 33–1–117, C.R.S., enacted by Colorado to comply with the P–R Act requirements, is not in compliance with 50 C.F.R. § 80.4's provision that "adequate legislative prohibitions [must be] in place to prevent diversion of license revenue" before a state declared to be in diversion is eligible to resume participation in the P–R Act. 50 C.F.R. § 80.4(d)(1). Thus, according to Plaintiffs, any § 80.4 cure cannot be effective until Colorado enacts a statute containing a specific prohibition of diversion of license revenues. I am not persuaded.

Section 33–1–117, C.R.S. titled "Assent of state to Pittman–Robertson act," provides:

> The state of Colorado through the division assents to the provisions of the act of congress entitled "An Act to provide that the United States shall aid the states in wildlife restoration projects, and for other purposes.... " The division is authorized to perform such acts as may be necessary to conduct and establish cooperative wildlife restoration projects, as defined in such act, in compliance with such act and the rules and regulations promulgated by the secretary of the interior thereunder. *No moneys or funds accruing to the division pursuant to such act shall be used for any purpose other than for such projects* and the administration of the division....

Section 33–1–117, C.R.S. (emphasis added). According to the State Defendants, there is no substantive problem with § 33–1–117.

The parties provide no authority for their respective positions. However, the plain language of the statute requires the DOW to act "in compliance with the [P–R Act] and the rules and regulations promulgated by the secretary of the interior thereunder." [ ] The provision thus incorporates by reference all statutory and regulatory requirements of the P–R Act. To require Colorado to include all possible violations of the P–R Act and its supporting rules and regulations would encourage "legislative loopholes." And, in this case, any P-R violation was a result of the DOW's actions in managing the property rather than the broad language of § 33–1–117.

1. *82.74 acre tract*

Plaintiffs submit the appraisal of its MAI appraiser showing a fair market value of the prison compound at more than $270,000. [ ] Under these circumstances, there is a genuine factual dispute about the sufficiency of the price paid by DOC to DOW for the 82.74 acre tract to cure the diversion.

2. *31 acre tract*

On March 31, 1998, pursuant to the MOU, DOW quitclaimed to DOC the 31 acre tract south of the prison compound for $29,500.00. [ ] Defendants agree that there is a material factual issue as to the fair market value of this tract and, thus, the sufficiency of the price paid by DOC to DOW for the 31 acre tract to cure the diversion.

I deny the motion and cross-motion for summary judgment on claim one as to the sufficiency of the cure for the 82.74 acre and 31 acre tracts.

. . .

4. *13.5 acre tract*

The 13.5 acre tract is located directly north of the Prison Compound at the confluence of Cottonwood and Roubideau Creeks. [ ] It is undisputed that: 1) the 13.5 acre tract was purchased with federal aid monies; and 2) the State Defendants violated the P–R Act in its use of the 13.5 acre tract. Thus, pursuant to § 80.14, there has been a misuse of federal aid monies.

In an attempt to cure its misuse, pursuant to § 80.14(b)(1), DOC restored this parcel to DOW's control. Plaintiffs respond that the P–R Act not only requires that the property be restored to DOW's control, but the property must "continue to serve the purpose for which it was acquired or constructed." [ ] I agree.

It is undisputed that the 13.5 acre tract was originally acquired to serve as winter range for deer, to provide water fowl resting area, and to provide hunting opportunities. [ ] DOC admits, however, that it "intends to use the land for ingress [to] and egress [from] the [Delta Prison], for placement of signs, and for placement of security devices." [ ] In addition, Plaintiffs present evidence that SWDF members have been stopped by prison guards while attempting to use the tract. [ ] In opposition, State Defendants present evidence that the "13.5 acre parcel is available for use by wildlife and members of the general public." [ ] Thus, there is a genuine factual dispute whether the 13.5 acre tract "continues to serve the purpose for which it was acquired. . . . " 50 C.F.R. § 80.14(b). Before there can be a determination of the sufficiency of the cure, at trial, I must resolve this factual dispute. Consequently, I deny the parties' summary judgment motions on claim one as to the 13.5 acre tract.

5. *Buffer Zone*

The fourth parcel at issue is a buffer zone extending 1000 feet in all directions from the boundary of the prison compound. According to the Defendants, this land was acquired with state license fees and with federal aid monies but the record does not reflect whether these monies were pooled or used separately to acquire definable portions of the buffer zone. Plaintiffs do not address the source of funds used to acquire this land. Because the consequences of a misuse or a diversion differ, evaluation of the sufficiency of an asserted "cure" is premature. At trial, I must determine how and which funds were used to acquire the buffer zone. I can then apply the proper cure provision to evaluate the sufficiency of any asserted cure. Moreover, assuming pooled funds were used to acquire the buffer zone, the parties have not adequately briefed the effect pooling has on remedy and cure.

Also, there is a factual dispute about whether this land has been rendered useless for wildlife purposes by the presence of the Delta Prison. [ ] In direct contradiction to Boyle's report, DOW wildlife biologist John Ellenberger states that "the area immediately surrounding the [Delta prison] is available for use by members of the general public for wildlife related recreational activities such as wildlife viewing, small game and waterfowl hunting, and big game hunting." [ ] Under these circumstances, I deny the parties' summary judgment motions on claim one as to the buffer zone.

IV

A. *Federal Defendants' Summary Judgment Motion and Plaintiffs' Cross-Motion*

The USFWS moves for summary judgment on Plaintiffs' claim two that it violated the APA by failing to enforce 50 C.F.R. § 80.4 against the State Defendants and claim three for violating the APA by failing to enforce § 80.14. Plaintiffs cross-move for summary judgment on these claims.

The following undisputed facts form the basis of the parties' motions: 1) placing and operating a prison on the 82.74 acre and the 31 acre tracts constituted a diversion pursuant to § 80.4; 2) the USFWS did not cease paying P–R Act federal aid funds to the State; 3) the USFWS has never officially declared Colorado to be in diversion; and 4) Colorado misused federal aid funds in its use of the 13.5 acre tract.

According to Plaintiffs, under these facts, pursuant to § 80.4, the USFWS was required to declare the State of Colorado in diversion and should have cut off federal funding to the state. And, if there was a misuse under § 80.14, the USFWS should have notified Colorado that it was ineligible to participate in federal funding.

In support of its motion, the USFWS states that its decision to delay making a decision whether to declare a diversion or give notice of a misuse under the P–R Act was not arbitrary or capricious pursuant to the Administrative Procedures Act, 5 U.S.C. § 706(2)(A) (APA).

.... Plaintiffs' cross-motion is more properly viewed as an appeal of the USFWS' decision to not declare a diversion or a misuse with respect to Colorado's use of a portion of the Escalante Wildlife Area as prison.

. . .

Under an APA review of agency action, the district court is required to affirm the final agency action unless that action is "arbitrary, capricious, an abuse of discretion, or otherwise not in accordance with law." ...

The USFWS may declare a state to be in diversion on account of its use of state license fee revenues if "any portion of license revenues is used for any purpose other than the administration of the State fish and wildlife agency.... " 50 C.F.R. § 80.4(c). If a declaration of diversion is made by the USFWS, the entire state is ineligible to receive further P–R Act federal aid funds from the USFWS until the state cures the diversion. 50 C.F.R. § 80.4(d). Also, a diversion declaration is an all or nothing proposition. If the Director of the USFWS declares a state to be in diversion, all future P–R Act federal aid funds are cut off until the diversion is remedied, regardless how much or little state license revenues were used by the state for nonwildlife purposes.

The Federal Defendants state that under the P–R Act and its supporting regulations, the USFWS's decision whether to declare the State of Colorado in diversion was discretionary. 50 C.F.R. § 80.4(d); 50 C.F.R. § 80.7. I agree.

Section 80.14(d)(2) sets out actions a state must take in order to cure a misuse of federal aid monies. It is silent, however, with respect to the actions the USFWS may or must take in response to the misuse. In contrast, § 80.4(d) provides that if a diversion of state license fee revenues occurs, the state "becomes ineligible to participate under the ... Act from the date the diversion is declared by the [USFWS] Director" until § 80.4(d)(2)'s requirements are fulfilled. The regulation contains no guidance concerning when or if a diversion must be declared. Thus, § 80.14 and 80.4 may be interpreted to grant the USFWS broad discretion whether to give notice of misuse or declare a diversion.

In this case, the record before me shows that USFWS reviewed and approved DOW's proposed actions to remedy any violations at the Escalante State Wildlife Area. According to the USFWS, it's choice not to give notice of misuse or declare a diversion facilitated Colorado's actions to cure the improprieties in this case. Thus, it was able to avoid the harsh remedy of cutting off all P–R Act funding to Colorado and placing wildlife at risk. [ ]

Upon consideration of all relevant factors, including USFWS' articulated reasons for its decision not to give notice of a misuse or declare a diversion, I cannot state, as a matter of law, that the exercise of discretion by the USFWS here was arbitrary, capricious, an abuse of discretion, or contrary to law. *See Citizens to Preserve Overton Park v. Volpe,* 401 U.S. 402, 416 (1971). Therefore, I will grant judgment for the Federal Defendants as a matter of law. [ ] I deny Plaintiffs' cross-motion on claims two and three.

NOTES

(1) The Pittman–Robertson Act refers to "wildlife-restoration projects." If the buffer zone and the 13.5 acre parcel are suitable for habitat, has the Act been violated if it simply is not open to hunting? Is there any requirement that the species for which the habitat is purchased be "huntable"?

(2) State politics: Note the alignment of the parties in the main case: various conservation groups brought the action to insist that the Colorado Division of Wildlife receive more money for the lands taken from it; among the defendants opposing this demand was the Colorado Division of Wildlife.

Plainly, high officials within the state had decided upon a unified state position on the issue. Perhaps in internal state discussions the Division of Wildlife objected and lost. Privately, state wildlife officials may have hoped that the state would lose the case.

c. MONEY AND STRINGS: FEDERAL MANAGEMENT STANDARDS

NOTES

(1) In addition to funding the acquisition of wildlife habitat, federal statutes not surprisingly also impose management mandates on state lands acquired with federal funds for wildlife habitat. The prohibition against converting such lands to other uses is one example. More generally, lands acquired for wildlife habitat with federal funds are required to be managed with wildlife as the dominant use. That is, the management directives seek to protect the public's investment.

(2) Pittman–Robertson Act of 1937 and Dingell–Johnson Act of 1950 are the primary source of federal funds for the acquisition of wildlife habitat by state fish and game agencies. While federal funds often bring federal control, neither Acts impose more than minimal restrictions on management of areas acquired with their funds. The most explicit management mandate contained in the two acts simply specifies that "[m]aintenance of wildlife-restoration projects established under the provisions of this Act shall be the duty of the States." Pittman–Robertson, 16 U.S.C. § 669g(a); Dingell–Johnson, *id.* § 777g(a) (identical except in its application to "fish-restoration and management projects").

Most wildlife statutes delegate broad discretion to the federal agency involved. Pittman–Robertson and Dingell–Johnson are no exception, granting the Secretary of the Interior the open-ended authority to specify standards for projects. Pittman–Robertson, 16 U.S.C. § 669; Dingell–Johnson, *id.* § 777. Since "wildlife restoration project" is defined to include "maintenance of completed projects," *id.* § 669g(a) (Pittman–Robertson); *id.* § 777g(a) (Dingell–Johnson), the Secretary has authority to specify management standards for areas acquired with funds provided under the acts.

In 1970, both acts were amended to encourage the states to develop "a comprehensive fish and wildlife resource management plan." Pittman–Robertson, *id.* § 669e(a)(1); Dingell–Johnson, *id.* § 777e(a)(1). The statutes specify that the plan is to "insure the perpetuation of these resources for the economic, scientific, and recreational enrichment of the people." Pittman–Robertson, *id.* § 669e(a)(1) (1988); Dingell–Johnson, *id.* § 777e(a)(1). The amendment, however, did not make comprehensive plans a prerequisite for further funds.

SECTION 2. ACQUISITION OF THE NATIONAL WILDLIFE REFUGE SYSTEM

For more than a century, the federal government has created land management systems to administer the land it owns. The first was the

National Forest System; but the idea proved fertile and there now is a National Park System, a National Wilderness System, a Wild and Scenic River System, and a Marine Sanctuary System. These systems share two characteristics: (1) a process for designating lands for inclusion within the system and (2) a set of standards to guide the management of each category of land. In this section we consider the first of these characteristics.

The most significant federal wildlife habitat acquisition program is the National Wildlife Refuge System. In its founding myth, the first refuge was created by President Theodore Roosevelt in 1903, when he issued an Executive Order that the federally owned "Pelican Island in Indian River ... State of Florida, be, and it is hereby, reserved and set apart ... as a preserve and breeding ground for native birds."[1] In 1905, 1906, and 1908, Congress authorized the President to set aside additional, specific refuges, Act of Jan. 24, 1905, ch. 137, 33 Stat. 614 (lands within the Wichita Forest Reserve); Act of June 29, 1906, ch. 3593, 34 Stat. 607 (lands within the Grand Canyon Forest Reserve); Act of May 23, 1908, ch. 192, 35 Stat. 267 (National Bison Range in Montana) (codified as amended at 16 U.S.C. § 671); in 1909, it appropriated funds to acquire unspecified lands for refuges. Act of Mar. 4, 1909, ch. 301, 35 Stat. 1051.

Despite the century that has elapsed since the designation of Pelican Island as a Refuge, the National Wildlife Refuge System has long been an anomaly among the federal land management systems. Rather than a single method for designating land for inclusion within the System, a refuge may be added to the system in any of at least five ways: through executive withdrawal of land owned by the federal government and managed by the Department of the Interior; through an exchange or purchase funded by statutes such as the Migratory Bird Conservation Act, the Land and Water Conservation Fund, or the Endangered Species Act; through an independent act of Congress; through transfers from other land managing agencies such as the Army Corps of Engineers; and through a donation from a non-federal landowner. NATHANIEL P. REED & DENNIS DRABELLE, THE UNITED STATES FISH AND WILDLIFE SERVICE (1984). The land classifications that resulted from this variety of transfers have been known as wildlife refuges, wildlife ranges, game ranges, wildlife management areas, waterfowl production areas, and the like. Since 1903, the Refuge System has grown to more than 500 refuges totalling some 90.8 million acres. Although nearly one-third of refuge lands are wetland habitat, the system contains a diverse range of habitat types from dwarf tundra in arctic Alaska to sub-tropical forests in Hawaii and Puerto Rico. *See* UNITED STATES FISH & WILDLIFE

---

1. Quoted in NATHANIEL P. REED & DENNIS DRABELLE, THE UNITED STATES FISH AND WILDLIFE SERVICE 7 (1984). The agency's founding myth is set out by Reed and Drabelle, *id.* at 5–8, and in Lynn Greenwalt, *The National Wildlife Refuge System, in* WILDLIFE IN AMERICA 399 (Howard P. Brokaw ed., 1978). As Michael Bean has noted, the first refuge might in fact be the reservation of Afognak Island in Alaska by President Benjamin Harrison in 1892 "in order that salmon fisheries in the waters of the Island, and salmon and other fish and sea animals, and other animals and birds ... may be protected and preserved unimpaired." Proclamation No. 39, 27 Stat. 1052 (1892); MICHAEL J. BEAN, THE EVOLUTION OF NATIONAL WILDLIFE LAW 22 n.59 (rev. & expanded ed. 1983). Benjamin Harrison, however, lacks the romantic cache of Teddy Roosevelt.

SERVICE, UNITED STATES DEPARTMENT OF THE INTERIOR, REFUGES 2003 at 3–1 to–16 (1993) [Draft Programmatic EIS].

A particularly useful source on the law governing wildlife refuges is Richard J. Fink, *The National Wildlife Refuges: Theory, Practice, and Prospect,* 18 HARV. ENVTL. L. REV. 1 (1994).

a.   STATUTORY AUTHORITIES: AN EVOLUTION OF RATIONALES

NOTES

(1) The limits of the Migratory Bird Treaty Act: As discussed in Chapter 10, the federal government got into the business of protecting migratory birds with the enactment of the Migratory Bird Treaty Act (MBTA) to implement the treaty negotiated with Great Britain in 1916. The MBTA sought to conserve migratory birds by regulating taking, possession, and sale of protected species. The Act was a logical response to the perceived problem of largely unregulated hunting, particularly for the market. It soon became apparent, however, that regulating taking was insufficient by itself because it addressed only part of the problem. Successful conservation of migratory birds required conservation of their habitats as well.

The Act's genesis in the drive to end market hunting and the plume trade led a focus on waterfowl habitat—swamps, in the terminology of the day. Historically, such lands had been viewed as waste areas that needed to be "reclaimed" and made productive. This perspective lay behind the Swamp Land Acts of 1849, 1850, and 1860 which had transferred federally owned wetlands to the states for reclamation. The result was a loss of habitat and declining numbers of ducks and geese. Congress responded by enacting a series of statutes that sought to conserve wetland habitats.

(2) The Migratory Bird Conservation Act of 1929: The Migratory Bird Conservation Act, 16 U.S.C. §§ 715–715k, was the first of these habitat-conservation statutes. It established a procedure through which the Secretary of the Interior is authorized to acquire lands and waters "suitable for use as an inviolate sanctuary ... for migratory birds." *Id.* § 715d. Since the acquisition of land by the federal government removes it from the tax base and otherwise restricts applicable state and local laws, the Act is solicitous of state and local interests.

(a) The Migratory Bird Conservation Commission: The Act creates a Commission "to consider and pass upon" land recommended for purchase or lease. *Id.* § 715a. It is an unusual body whose members are the Secretary of the Interior, the Administrator of the Environmental Protection Agency, the Secretary of Agriculture, two members of the Senate (selected by the President of the Senate), two members of the House of Representatives (selected by the Speaker of the House), and a state representative.[2] *Id.*

---

2.   The state representative is either the head of the state department with responsibility for administering its game laws or, if there is no such department, the governor of the state. 16 U.S.C. § 715a.

(b) State consent provisions: In addition to the inclusion of a state representative on the Commission, the Act contains other provisions intended to ensure that a state has a substantial voice in the decision. First, the Act specifies that no land can be acquired "in fee . . . unless the State in which the area lies shall have consented by law to the acquisition by the United States of lands in that State." *Id.* § 715f. Second, the Secretary of the Interior may not recommend a parcel for acquisition unless he has "consulted" with the county in which the land is located as well as the governor or the appropriate state wildlife agency. *Id.* § 715c.

(c) Saving state law: The Act also provides that state civil and criminal jurisdiction is "not affected" by the acquisition of the land by the United States, *id.* § 715g, and state fish and game laws are also not affected "in so far as they do not permit what is forbidden by Federal law." *Id.* § 715h.

Thus, the Act requires (1) the state to give general consent to the acquisition of land within its borders; (2) the Secretary to consult with the local government and state before acquiring any specific parcel of land; and (3) the Secretary to obtain approval of the Migratory Bird Conservation Commission.

(3) The Migratory Bird Stamp Act of 1934: While the Conservation Act provided a mechanism for authorizing purchases of land, it did not create a permanent funding mechanism. That occurred five years later when Congress enacted the Migratory Bird Hunting Stamp Act of 1934, the "Duck Stamp," 16 U.S.C. §§ 718–718j. The Act was adopted

> to supplement and support the Migratory Bird Conservation Act by providing funds for the acquisition of areas for use a migratory-bird sanctuaries, refuges, and breeding grounds, for developing and administering such areas, for the protection of certain migratory birds, for enforcement of the Migratory Bird Treaty Act . . . and for other purposes.

Act of March 16, 1934, ch. 71, 48 Stat. 452.

(a) License requirement: To accomplish these purposes, the Act imposed a license requirement: "No person who has attained the age of sixteen years shall take any migratory waterfowl unless at the time of the taking he carries on his person an unexpired Federal migratory-bird hunting and conservation stamp." 16 U.S.C. § 718a. Although possession of a stamp is necessary to hunt, it is itself insufficient: hunters are also required to comply both with any federal seasons or bags limits adopted pursuant to any treaty and with the game laws of the individual states. *Id.* § 718b(a), 718c. Violation of the Act subjects the violator to the penalties imposed by the Migratory Bird Treaty Act, including $500 fines, six months imprisonment, and forfeiture of hunting equipment. *Id.* § 718g, 707.

(b) Costs of stamp: Originally stamps cost $1. The cost was raised to $2 in 1949 and to $3 in 1958. In 1986, Congress enacted three stepped increases: $10 for 1987 and 1988, $12.50 for 1989 and 1990, and $15.00 thereafter. *Id.* § 718b(b). The stamps are issued and sold by the Postal Service. *Id.*

(c) Disposition of funds: All money received from the sale of the stamps is paid into the Migratory Bird Conservation Fund, a special account in the Treasury. Until 1958, most of the funds were actually expended for refuge development and administration rather than refuge acquisition. In 1958, Congress amended the Stamp Act to require that, after paying the production costs of the stamps, the remaining funds are to be used "for the location, ascertainment, and acquisition of suitable areas for migratory bird refuges under the Migratory Bird Conservation Act." *Id.* § 718d.

While the Duck Stamp has provided a source of continuing monies for refuge acquisition, the requirement that the funds be expended on the "acquisition of suitable areas for migratory bird refuges" and "waterfowl production areas," *id.* § 718d(b), (c), has created a National Wildlife Refuge System that is geared primarily to the production of waterfowl for hunters.

(4) "Waterfowl production areas": The 1958 amendments to the Stamp Act also authorized the acquisition of "Waterfowl Production Areas," which are defined as "small wetland and pothole areas." *Id.* § 718d. The Eighth Circuit has described these areas and their value as waterfowl habitat:

> Each square mile of such land is dotted by approximately 70 to 80 potholes of three to four feet deep.... [T]he potholes usually retain water through July or August, and therefore, provide an excellent environment for the production of aquatic invertebrates and aquatic plants, the basic foods for breeding adult ducks and their offspring. Essential to the maintenance of the land as a waterfowl production area is the availability of shallow water in these numerous potholes during the usually drier summer months.

United States v. Albrecht, 496 F.2d 906, 908 (8th Cir.1974).

The nature of waterfowl production areas led Congress to treat them differently. First, since they were not formal refuges, there was no need to acquire a fee in the land. The FWS was, therefore, authorized to acquire easements that protected the wetland values on the parcel. 16 U.S.C. § 718d(c). Second, Congress concluded that Waterfowl Production Areas "may be acquired without regard to the limitations and requirements of the Migratory Bird Conservation Act," *i.e.,* without the approval of either the state or the Migratory Bird Conservation Commission. *Id.*

(5) The Wetlands Loan Act of 1961: The revenue produced by the Stamp Act failed to keep pace with rising land costs or with the loss of wetlands. Congress responded in 1961 by enacting the Wetlands Loan Act, 16 U.S.C. § 715k–3 to 715k–5. The Act originally was a loan to the Department of the Interior against future receipts from the sale of Duck Stamps to "prevent the serious loss of important wetlands and other waterfowl habitat." *Id.* § 715k–3. After increasing the appropriation from $105 to $200 million and extending the repayment date four times,[3]

---

3. Funding was increased in 1976 (Act of Feb. 17, 1976, Pub. L. No. 94–215, § 2(a), 90 Stat. 189), and repayment was extended in 1967 (Act of Dec. 15, 1967, Pub. L. No. 90–205, § 1(b), 81 Stat. 612), 1976 (Act of Feb. 17, 1976, Pub. L. No. 94–215, § 2(b), 90 Stat.

Congress forgave the repayment obligation in 1986. Act of Nov. 10, 1986, Pub. L. No. 99–645, § 101(b), 100 Stat. 3584.

The Act specifies that "[n]o land shall be acquired with moneys from the migratory bird conservation fund unless the acquisition thereof has been approved by the Governor of the State or appropriate State agency." 16 U.S.C. § 715k–5. Thus, although the 1958 amendments to the Stamp Act that authorized the acquisition of Waterfowl Production Areas exempted them from the state approval requirements, the Wetlands Loan Act swept them back under these requirements.

(6) The Land and Water Conservation Fund Act of 1963: As noted above in the materials on federal funding of state habitat acquisition, the Land and Water Conservation Fund Act, 16 U.S.C. § 460*l* to 460*l*–11, provides funds for land acquisition by both federal and state entities. The Act specifies that "[n]ot less than 40 per centum of [the] appropriations shall be available for Federal purposes." *Id.* § 460*l*–7.

The federal funding is limited to "the acquisition of land, waters, or interests in land or waters" three general categories: (1) "[w]ithin the exterior boundaries of areas of the National Park System," (2) National Forest System inholdings or contiguous areas; and (3) for the National Wildlife Refuge System,

(a) for endangered or threatened species habitat;

(b) for "incidental fish and wildlife-oriented recreational development" or for "the protection of natural resources" pursuant to the Refuge Recreation Act, 16 U.S.C. § 406k–1(1)–(2);

(c) for "the development, advancement, conservation, and protection of fish and wildlife resources";[4] and

(d) for "any areas authorized for the National Wildlife Refuge System by specific Acts"

Id. § 460*l*–9(a)(1). The breadth of the authorization to the Secretary to acquire lands for wildlife habitat seems sufficient to allow the acquisition of any significant habitat. Furthermore, there is no requirement that the lands acquired need to be made available for outdoor recreation.

(7) Endangered Species Preservation Act of 1966: The first federal endangered species statute, the Endangered Species Preservation Act of 1966 (ESPA), Pub. L. No. 89–669, 80 Stat. 926, did little more than authorize the acquisition of habitat. The ESPA authorized the Secretary of the Interior to acquire lands "to carry out a program . . . of conserving, protecting, restoring, and propagating selected species of native fish and wildlife that are threatened with extinction." *Id.* § 3(a), (b). The Act's objectives, however, were modest: it permitted the Secretary to use up to $15,000,000 from funds available under the Land and Water Conservation Fund Act. *Id.* § 2(c).

189), 1983 (Act of Dec. 2, 1983, Pub. L. No. 98–200, § 2, 97 Stat. 1378), and 1984 (Act of Oct. 26, 1984, Pub. L. No. 98–548, § 102, 98 Stat. 2774).

4. Under the authority of 16 U.S.C. § 742f(a)(4).

(8) The Endangered Species Act of 1973: The Endangered Species Act of 1973 (ESA), 16 U.S.C. §§ 1531–1544, goes beyond the limited approach of the ESPA. Section 1534 requires the Secretaries of the Interior and Agriculture to "establish and implement a program to conserve fish, wildlife, and plants, including those which are listed" as threatened or endangered. *Id.* § 1534(a). To carry out the program, the Secretaries are "authorized to acquire ... lands, waters, or interest therein." *Id.* § 1534(a)(1). Funds from the Land and Water Conservation Fund are made available to fund the purchases. *Id.* § 1534(2).

b.   CONSTRUING FEDERAL ACQUISITION AUTHORITY

NOTES

(1) Land acquisition and federalism: Federal acquisition of land is often a politically sensitive issue—for a variety of reasons. Federal land is not subject to taxation by state or local governments; acquisition of land for a refuge thus reduces the county's property tax base. Although there are provisions for payments in lieu of taxes,[5] there are disputes about the economic impacts of the presence of federal lands within local taxing authorities. Similarly, state and local governments are alert to potential loss of jurisdictional powers such as land-use regulation or criminal laws. For example, what is the effect of the acquisition of land for a wildlife refuge on state hunting and fishing laws? Do state open range laws apply to refuges? *See United States v. Travis,* 66 F.Supp. 413 (W.D.Ky.1946) (Secretary's adoption of regulations prohibiting grazing on a refuge upheld despite the fact that the surrounding area was open range). Furthermore, federal restrictions may extend beyond the boundaries of federal lands when activities on those adjacent lands affects the federal lands. *See Bailey v. Holland,* 126 F.2d 317, 324 (4th Cir.1942) (closure to hunting of lands adjacent to refuge upheld as permissible: "to make this refuge more effective, the Secretary may prohibit all hunting in the immediate vicinity."). Thus, a recurrent issue both in the acquisition and the management of refuges—as well as other federal lands—is the role that the state will play. What role did Congress provide for the states in the various statutes that authorize the acquisition of lands for refuges?

(2) *United States v. Little Lake Misere Land Co.* was a quiet title action involving two parcels land that the United States acquired under the Migratory Bird Conservation Act in 1937 and 1939. In both transfers, mineral rights had been reserved for ten years to the Little Lake Misere Land Company. Defendant undertook no exploration activity during the

---

5. To address this problem, Congress has provided for a payment in lieu of taxes in the Refuge Revenue Sharing Act. The Secretary is directed to pay counties in which refuge lands are located the greater of 75 cents per acre or .75% of the fair market value of the land. 16 U.S.C. § 715s(c)(1)(A)–(B). In 1976, Congress enacted the Payment in Lieu of Taxes Act, 31 U.S.C. § 6901 *et seq.* adopted a similar provision applicable to all other federal lands. For a discussion of the costs and benefits of federal lands to the states in which they are located, see John D. Leshy, *Sharing Federal Multiple–Use Lands: Historic Lessons and Speculations for the Future, in* RETHINKING THE FEDERAL LANDS 235 (Sterling Brubaker ed. 1984).

ten year period and in 1955 the United States issued oil and gas leases to the lands. In 1940, Louisiana enacted a statute providing that mineral reservations contained in lands transferred to the United States were not terminated by the passage of time. The Land Company argued that it, therefore, was the owner of the mineral interests.

The Supreme Court began by characterizing the land transfers as "arising from and bearing heavily upon a federal regulatory program." While refusing to hold that federal law always governed land acquisition agreements to which the United States was a party, the Court also refused to apply the Louisiana statute to the transfer before it:

> Under Louisiana's Act 315, land acquisitions of the United States, explicitly authorized by the Migratory Bird Conservation Act, are made subject to a rule of retroactive imprescriptibility, a rule that is plainly hostile to the interests of the United States. As applied to a consummated land transaction under a contract which specifically defined conditions for prolonging the vendor's mineral reservation, retroactive application of Act 315 to the United States deprives it of bargained-for-contractual interests.

United States v. Little Lake Misere Land Co., 412 U.S. 580, 597 (1973).

(3) *United States v. Albrecht* arose out of a dispute involving the draining of a pothole wetland in North Dakota. Defendant's predecessor in interest in the fee (his parents-in-law) had conveyed an "easement" to the federal government obligating themselves, "their heirs, successors and assigns" to "cooperate in the maintenance of the aforesaid lands as a waterfowl production area by not draining or permitting the draining" of the lands. After defendant acquired the lands, an unidentified person mysteriously ditched them. When the government sought to force defendant to restore the lands by filling the ditch, he argued that "North Dakota statutory law does not specifically allow the type of easement, servitude, or right to property conveyed ... to the Government." Although noting that "[t]he classification of the interest in land conveyed in this case according to the traditional analysis of easements is difficult," the court nonetheless concluded that whatever North Dakota law might be that law

> is not controlling, particularly if viewed as aberrant or hostile to federal property rights. Assuming *arguendo* that North Dakota law would not permit the conveyance of the right to the United States in this case, the specific federal governmental interest in acquiring rights to property for waterfowl production areas is stronger than any possible "aberrant" or "hostile" North Dakota law that would preclude the conveyance granted in this case. *Little Lake Misere Land Co. v. United States,* 412 U.S. 580 (1973). We fully recognize that laws of real property are usually governed by the particular states; yet the reasonable property right conveyed to the United States in this case effectuates an important national concern, the acquisition of necessary land for waterfowl production areas, and should not be defeated by any possible North Dakota law barring the conveyance of this property right. To hold otherwise would be to permit the possibility that state could rely upon local property laws to defeat the acquisition of reasonable rights to their citizens' property pursuant to 16 U.S.C. § 718(c)

and to destroy a national program of acquiring property to aid in the breeding of migratory birds. We, therefore, specifically hold that the property right conveyed to the United States in this case, whether or not deemed a valid easement or other property right under North Dakota law, was a valid conveyance under federal law and vested in the United States the rights as stated therein.

United States v. Albrecht, 496 F.2d 906, 911 (8th Cir.1974).

North Dakota v. United States

United States Supreme Court.
460 U.S. 300 (1983).

■ BLACKMUN, J.:Under the federal Migratory Bird Hunting Stamp Act, the Secretary of the Interior is authorized to acquire easements over small wetland areas suitable for migratory waterfowl breeding and nesting grounds. Although the State of North Dakota initially consented to the Secretary's acquisition of easements over certain wetlands, the State now seeks to withdraw its consent and to impose conditions on any future acquisitions. This has led to the present litigation, for the State's present posture raises the question whether the Secretary may proceed to acquire easements pursuant to North Dakota's prior consent.

I

A

In 1929, the Migratory Bird Conservation Act [Conservation Act], 45 Stat. 1222, ch. 257, 16 U.S.C. §§ 715–715r, became law. By § 5 of that Act [§ 715d], the Secretary of the Interior was authorized to acquire land "for use as inviolate sanctuaries for migratory birds." Land acquisitions under the Conservation Act are subject to certain conditions: they must be approved in advance by the Migratory Bird Conservation Commission, 16 U.S.C. § 715a and 715d, and the State in which the land is located must "have consented by law to the acquisition," 16 U.S.C. § 715f.

In 1934, in order to provide funding for land acquisitions under the Conservation Act, the Migratory Bird Hunting Stamp Act [Stamp Act], 16 U.S.C. §§ 718a–718j, was enacted. Section 1 of the Stamp Act, 16 U.S.C. § 718a, required waterfowl hunters to purchase migratory bird hunting stamps, commonly known as duck stamps. By § 4, 16 U.S.C. § 718d, the proceeds from the sale of the stamps were to form a special "migratory bird conservation fund" [conservation fund] to be used primarily to pay for "the location, ascertainment, acquisition, administration, maintenance, and development" of bird sanctuaries pursuant to the Conservation Act.

To hasten the acquisition of land suitable for waterfowl habitats, Congress amended the Stamp Act in 1958. The price of a duck stamp was increased, and, most important for our present purposes, the Secretary of the Interior was authorized to expend money from the conservation fund for a new type of property: "small wetland and pothole areas, interests therein, and rights-of-way to provide access thereto," the small areas "to be designated as 'Waterfowl Production Areas.' " Pub. L. No. 85–585, § 3, 72

Stat. 487, 16 U.S.C. § 718d(c). Such waterfowl production areas could be "acquired without regard to the limitations and requirements of the Migratory Bird Conservation Act." *Id.* Because these waterfowl production areas did not have to be maintained as sanctuaries, there was no need for them to be purchased outright; the Secretary was authorized to acquire easements prohibiting fee owners from draining their wetlands or otherwise destroying the wetlands' suitability as breeding grounds.

Despite the 1958 amendments, however, the proceeds from duck stamp sales proved insufficient to acquire land at the rate Congress deemed necessary. Accordingly, a new source of income was provided through the Wetlands Act of 1961 (Loan Act), [ ]. Section 1 of this new Act originally authorized sums for appropriation not to exceed $105 million for a seven-year period. These sums were to be added to the conservation fund in the form of interest-free loans that were to be repaid out of duck stamp proceeds. In addition, § 3 of the Loan Act provided that no land could be acquired with money from the conservation fund unless consent had been obtained from the Governor or an appropriate agency of the State in which the land was located.

B

The principal waterfowl breeding grounds in the continental United States are located in four States of the northern Great Plains—North Dakota, South Dakota, Minnesota, and Montana.[4] North Dakota, in particular, is rich in wetlands suitable for waterfowl breeding, and the Government's acquisition of North Dakota land has been given high priority. [ ]

For the most part, North Dakota has cooperated with federal efforts to preserve waterfowl habitats. [Two years after the Conservation Act went into effect, the State gave its consent to the acquisition of migratory bird habitat. By 1958, the United States had acquired more than 276,000 acres of North Dakota land for use as migratory bird refuges. Similarly when the Loan Act was passed, gubernatorial consent was promptly forthcoming. Between 1961 and 1977, the governors consented to the acquisition of easements covering approximately 1.5 million acres of wetlands. The consents specified the maximum acreage to be acquired within each county in

---

4. When the glaciers retreated from the northern Great Plains at the end of the last ice age, they left in their wake thousands of shallow depressions. These depressions, known as prairie potholes, provide excellent breeding grounds for migratory ducks. In *United States v. Albrecht,* 496 F.2d 906 (8th Cir.1974), the Court of Appeals described the characteristics of a prairie pothole region and its advantages for breeding ducks:

> Each square mile of such land is dotted by approximately 70 to 80 potholes of three to four feet deep.... [On certain types of land] the potholes usually retain water through July or August, and therefore, provide an excellent environment for the production of aquatic inverte-

brates and aquatic plants, the basic foods for breeding adult ducks and their offspring. Essential to the maintenance of the land as a waterfowl production area is the availability of shallow water in these numerous potholes during the usually drier summer months. On the other hand, too much water, as a lake area with its deeper waters, does not provide the proper habitat for many species of duck to rear their young. Also, for the protection of their young, many species of duck prefer to be isolated in a small pothole, rather than to share a large lake.

[ ]

the State, but did not list particular parcels. By 1977, the Fish and Wildlife Service had obtained easements covering about half of the total wetlands acreage authorized by the consents. In the mid–1970's, cooperation between North Dakota and the United States began to break down and North Dakota enacted legislation in 1977 restricting the United States' ability to acquire easements over wetlands.]

The 1977 legislation affects the acquisition of wetlands easements in three major ways. First, § 2 of ch. 204, [ ], requires the Governor to submit proposed wetlands acquisitions for approval by the board of county commissioners of the county in which the land is located. The "federal agency involved"—here, the United States Fish and Wildlife Service—must provide the county with a "detailed impact analysis," and the county, as well, is directed to prepare an impact analysis at federal expense. If the county does not recommend the acquisition, the Governor may not approve it. Next, § 3 of ch. 204, [ ], authorizes the landowner to negotiate the terms and time period of the easement acquired by the United States, to restrict the easement "by legal description to the land, wetland, or water areas being sought," and to "drain any after-expanded wetland or water area in excess of the legal description." Finally, § 1 of ch. 426, [ ], restricts all easements to a maximum duration of 99 years. Because these restrictions have cast doubt upon the sufficiency of its title, the United States has acquired no easement over North Dakota wetlands since 1977.

In 1979, the United States brought suit in the United States District Court for the District of North Dakota, seeking a declaratory judgment that the 1977 state statutes were hostile to federal law in certain respects and could not be applied.... The District Court granted summary judgment for the United States, [ ], and the United States Court of Appeals for the Eighth Circuit affirmed. [ ] We noted probable jurisdiction over North Dakota's appeal. [ ]

II

The protection of migratory birds has long been recognized as "a national interest of very nearly the first magnitude." *Missouri v. Holland,* 252 U.S. 416, 435 (1920). Since the turn of the century, the Secretaries of Agriculture and of Interior successively have been charged with responsibility for "the preservation, distribution, introduction, and restoration of game birds and other wild birds." [Lacey Act,] 16 U.S.C. § 701. A series of treaties dating back to 1916 obligates the United States to preserve and protect migratory birds through the regulation of hunting, the establishment of refuges, and the protection of bird habitats. By providing for the acquisition of sanctuaries and waterfowl production areas, the Conservation Act and the Stamp Act play a central role in assuring that our Nation's migratory birds will continue to flourish.

In the absence of federal legislation to the contrary, the United States unquestionably has the power to acquire wetlands for waterfowl production areas, by purchase or condemnation, without state consent. [ ] Here, however, Congress has conditioned any such acquisition upon the United States' obtaining the consent of the Governor of the State in which the land is located. North Dakota concedes that its governors, at various times since 1961, have consented to the acquisition of easements over 1.5 million acres of North Dakota wetlands. The issue before us is whether North Dakota may revoke its consent to the acquisition of further easements in the State, and whether North Dakota by statute may impose conditions and restrictions on the United States' power to acquire easements.

A

North Dakota's central argument is that the gubernatorial consent required by 16 U.S.C. § 715k–5, once given, may be revoked by the State at will. North Dakota reads § 715k–5 to require not only that the Governor have consented to the acquisition of land for waterfowl production areas, but also that the Governor (and his successors in office) must continue to consent until the moment the land is actually acquired. Thus, although the United States has acquired easements over only half the acreage authorized by Governors Guy and Link, North Dakota asserts that it can terminate the United States' power to acquire the remainder. The United States takes the position that § 715k–5 does not permit a State to revoke its consent at will; once consent has been given, "the role assigned to the state by Congress has been exhausted." [ ]

As with any case involving statutory interpretation, "we state once again the obvious when we note that, in determining the scope of a statute, one is to look first at its language." [ ] "Absent a clearly expressed legislative intention to the contrary, that language must ordinarily be regarded as conclusive." [ ] The language of § 715k–5 is uncomplicated; it provides that money from the conservation fund shall not be used to acquire land "unless the acquisition thereof has been approved" by the Governor or the appropriate state agency. In this case, the acquisition of approximately 1.5 million acres of wetlands clearly "has been approved" by North Dakota's Governors. Nothing in the statute authorizes the withdrawal of approval previously given.

Nor does the legislative history of § 715k–5 suggest that Congress intended to permit Governors to revoke their consent. Before 1961, neither legislative nor gubernatorial consent was required prior to the acquisition of wetlands for waterfowl production areas. State legislative consent was a prerequisite to the acquisition of bird sanctuaries, § 715f, but waterfowl production areas were expressly exempted from this requirement, § 718d(c). Nonetheless, the United States followed an informal practice of obtaining agreement from the Governor or appropriate State agency before acquisition. The gubernatorial consent provision was intended simply to incorporate this practice. [ ] There is no indication in the legislative history or elsewhere that under this prior practice a Governor could withdraw consent already given.

In the absence of any evidence to the contrary, we must conclude that the consent required by § 715k–5 cannot be revoked at the will of an incumbent Governor. To hold otherwise would be inconsistent with the very purpose behind the Loan Act of which § 715k–5 is a part. The Loan Act was expressly intended to facilitate the acquisition of wetlands by making available an additional source of funds. The legislative history is replete with references to the need to preserve the Nation's wetlands by bringing four to five million additional acres under federal control. [ ] Obviously, this acquisition could not take place overnight; careful planning over many years was anticipated. [ ] If consent under § 715k–5 were revocable, the United States' ability to engage in such planning would be severely hampered. A detailed federal program involving the estimate of needs, setting of priorities, allocation of funds, and negotiations with landowners could be negated in an instant by a Governor's decision that the politics of the moment made further federal acquisitions undesirable.

Our conclusion in this regard is strengthened by the fact that, at the time of its enactment, the gubernatorial consent provision was not at all controversial. It was added by the Senate Committee on Commerce without explanation, [ ], and was accepted by the House of Representatives without explanation or discussion, [ ]. . . .

Although it has been intimated that a Governor's consent might become revocable if the United States were to delay unreasonably its land acquisitions pursuant to the consent, [ ], we need not reach that issue here. In this case, there has been no unreasonable delay. Until North Dakota's legislation interfered in 1977, the United States had pursued diligently its program of acquiring wetlands easements in North Dakota. The acreage fluctuated somewhat from year to year, but the acquisitions each year were substantial. In 1958, when Congress first authorized the Secretary of the Interior to acquire waterfowl production areas, it was generally anticipated that the United States' acquisition program would take a minimum of 20 to 25 years to complete. The acquisition program had been underway for only 16 years in 1977, a time span well within the limits contemplated by Congress.

B

We next consider North Dakota's 1977 legislation, which purports to impose conditions on the United States' power to acquire further wetlands easements. Because the statutes at issue raise somewhat different concerns, we discuss each in turn.

. . .

2. N.D. Cent. Code § 20.1–02–18.2. The United States does not challenge those portions of § 20.1–02–18.2 that permit a landowner to negotiate the conditions of an easement and restrict the scope of the easement to a particular legal description. The United States does object, however, to that part of § 20.1–02–18.2(2) that permits a landowner to "drain any after-expanded wetland or water area in excess of the legal description in the . . . easement. . . . " The United States' standard easement agreement contains a clause prohibiting the draining of after-expanded wetlands, [ ], and §§ 20.1–02–18.2(2) might be read to void such clauses even when agreed to by the landowner.

[Relying upon *United States v. Little Lake Misere Land Co.*, 412 U.S. 580 (1973), the Court held that the choice of applicable law presents a federal question. Although state law may be borrowed if appropriate, "specific aberrant or hostile state rules do not provide appropriate standards for federal law."]

Because the Louisiana statute at issue in *Little Lake Misere* was "plainly hostile to the interests of the United States," [ ], the Court refused to apply it. In language equally applicable to the present case, the Court said:

> To permit state abrogation of the explicit terms of a federal land acquisition would deal a serious blow to the congressional scheme contemplated by the Migratory Bird Conservation Act and indeed all other federal land acquisition programs. These programs are national in scope. They anticipate acute and active bargaining by officials of the United States charged with making the best possible use of limited federal conservation appropriations. Certainty and finality are indispensable in any land transaction, but they are especially critical when, as here, the federal officials carrying out the mandate of Congress irrevocably commit scarce funds.

[ ]

To the extent that § 20.1–02–18.2(2) authorizes landowners to drain after-expanded wetlands contrary to the terms of their easement agreements, we must conclude that it is equally hostile to federal interests and may not be applied to easements acquired under previously-given consents. The United States is authorized to incorporate into easement agreements such rules and regulations as the Secretary of the Interior deems necessary for the protection of wildlife, 16 U.S.C. § 715e, and these rules and regulations may include restrictions on land outside the legal description of the easement. *See Kleppe v. New Mexico,* 426 U.S. 529, 546 (1976); *Camfield v. United States,* 167 U.S. 518, 525–526 (1897). To respond to the inherently fluctuating nature of wetlands, the Secretary has chosen to negotiate easement agreements imposing restrictions on after-expanded wetlands as well as those described in the easement itself. As long as North Dakota landowners are willing to negotiate such agreements, the agreements may not be abrogated by state law.

3. *N.D. Cent. Code § 47–05–02.1.* Much the same analysis persuades us that this statute, which limits nonappurtenant easements to a maximum term of 99 years, may not be applied to wetlands easements acquired by the United States under consents previously given pursuant to the Stamp Act. The United States' commitment to the protection of migratory birds will not cease after 99 years have passed. This commitment has been incorporated into law for over 80 years and has been expressed in treaties since 1916, and the need to preserve migratory bird habitats is now no less than before.

To ensure that essential habitats will remain protected, the United States has adopted the practice of acquiring permanent easements whenever possible. Permanent easements are authorized by the gubernatorial consents given from 1961 to 1977, and the United States apparently has had no difficulty in negotiating permanent easements with North Dakota landowners. The automatic termination of federal wetlands easements after 99 years would make impossible the "[c]ertainty and finality" that we have regarded as "critical when . . . federal officials carrying out the mandate of Congress irrevocably commit scarce funds." *United States v. Little Lake*

Misere, 412 U.S. at 597. We conclude that § 47–05–02.1 is hostile to federal interests and may not be applied. [ ]

■ O'CONNOR, J., with whom REHNQUIST, J., joins, concurring in part, and dissenting in part—I agree with the Court that gubernatorial consent is required for the acquisition of wetlands easements, that the required consent was given in this case, and that North Dakota may not simply revoke its consent at will. I disagree with the Court, however, in its holding that the United States acquired its easements pursuant to the consents within a reasonable time as a matter of law. I would remand this case in order to allow the lower courts an opportunity to determine whether the federal Government delayed unreasonably in making its acquisitions. Because I would remand, and because I believe that the Court decides another issue that is not properly before the Court, I dissent in part.

NOTES

(1) What would be the result of a state repeal of its statutory consent to the acquisition of lands? Can the state impose conditions on acquisitions pursuant to subsequent gubernatorial consent? Is consent, in short, a yes/no proposition?

Is consent constitutionally required?

(2) ***United States v. Vesterso:*** In 1964 and 1965, the Fish and Wildlife Service purchased easements in Towner County, North Dakota. In 1983, the County Water Resource District Board began considering two drainage projects. The parcels affected by the proposed projects were subject to federal easements protecting wetlands on the properties. Without notifying the Fish and Wildlife Service, the Board constructed two ditches that meandered through parcels subject to the wetland easements. The Board members were found guilty of damaging a federal easement and placed on probation. They appealed their convictions, arguing in part that their conduct was permitted under state law and that state law controlled. North Dakota, they asserted, had an ownership interest in all watercourses within the state.[5] Since FWS only purchased the interest held by the private landowners, the state's regulatory powers—including its power to authorize draining—remained unaffected. The court rejected this claim: Because the watercourse was nonnavigable, the state's interest did not include the bed of the watercourse. The bed had been conveyed and the drainage caused damage to it. "Although the United States may not have exclusive ownership rights to the water contained in these features [the 'lakes, ponds, marshes, sloughs, swales, swamps, or potholes' covered by the easements], it clearly has a property interest which permits it to maintain the beds and banks of these features." *United States v. Vesterso,* 828 F.2d 1234, 1239 (8th Cir.1987).

---

5. This argument was based on a North Dakota statute expressing the public trust doctrine: "Waters on the surface of the earth excluding diffused surface waters but including surface waters whether flowing in well defined channels or flowing through lakes, ponds, or marshes which constitute integral parts of a stream system * * * belong to the public." *United States v. Vesterso,* 828 F.2d at 1239 (quoting N.D. Cent. Code § 61–01–01).

SECTION 3. MANAGEMENT STANDARDS FOR THE NATIONAL WILDLIFE REFUGE SYSTEM

NOTES

As noted above, the Refuge System has differed from other federal land management systems because there has been no single procedure for adding lands to the System. This section addresses another anomaly. When President Theodore Roosevelt issued an executive order on March 14, 1903, reserving Pelican Island in Florida, he specified only that it was to be "a preserve and breeding ground for native birds." Over time, the ad hoc, refuge-by-refuge designation process produced a variety of management standards, which were often as enigmatic as those for Pelican Island. The act establishing the National Bison Range in 1908, for example, merely directed the Secretary to take the steps necessary for the "proper care and maintenance" of the bison. Since each document creating a refuge—whether an Executive Order, an Act of Congress, or a donation—might specify particular management requirements or limitations, the Refuge "System" is managed under a framework of statutes that apply to the entire system—the statutes that are the focus of this section—, acts governing individual refuges or groups of refuges,[6] or particular species[7] or habitat.[8]

The following materials trace the evolution of the statutes that apply to the entire system, the statutes that have established a dominant-use land management system.

a. STATUTORY AUTHORITIES: EVOLVING TOWARD A *NATIONAL* SYSTEM

NOTES

(1) The management provisions of the Migratory Bird Conservation Act of 1929: The initial steps toward a management standard were taken in the Migratory Bird Conservation Act of 1929. Although the focus of the Act was on the procedure through which the Secretary of the Interior could acquire lands and waters, the Act set out only the sketchiest of management standards. First, to be included within a refuge, the land had to be "suitable for use as an inviolate sanctuary . . . for migratory birds." 16 U.S.C. 715d. Presumably, the "inviolate sanctuary" language

---

6. *See, e.g.,* 16 U.S.C. §§ 689–689d (Tahquitz National Game Preserve); *id.* §§ 690–690h (Bear River Migratory Bird Refuge); *id.* §§ 695–695r (California refuge areas).

7. *E.g.,* 16 U.S.C. § 696 (creating the National Key Deer Refuge to preserve that species).

8. *E.g.,* 16 U.S.C. § 1536(a)(2) (ESA provision imposing strict limitation on uses of refuge lands determined to be the critical habitat of a listed species).

imposes some minimal requirements. This is reinforced by a second provision of the 1929 Act that set out a series of prohibitions on private activities on refuge lands: "knowingly disturb, injure, or destroy any . . . improvement or property . . . or cut, burn, or destroy any timber grass, or other natural growth . . . ; nor shall any person take any bird, or nest or egg thereon" except as permitted by regulation. Migratory Bird Conservation Act, § 10, 45 Stat. 1224 (previously codified at 16 U.S.C. § 715i).

(2) The 1966 amendments to the Conservation Act: In 1966, Congress replaced the list of prohibitions with affirmative management standards that authorized the Secretary to administer the areas "to conserve and protect migratory birds . . . and other species of wildlife . . . and to restore or develop adequate wildlife habitat." 16 U.S.C. § 715i(a). This management authority includes the power "to manage timber, range, and agricultural crops; to manage other species of animals, including but not limited to fenced range animals, with the objectives of perpetuating, distributing, and utilizing the resources." *Id.* § 715i(b).

(3) The Refuge Revenue Sharing Act of 1935: Although the Migratory Bird Conservation Act specified that refuge lands were to be "inviolate sanctuar[ies]," the prospect of private economic gain proved irresistible. Six years later in 1935 Congress provided that 25% "of all money received . . . from the sale or other disposition of surplus wildlife, or of timber, hay, grass, or other spontaneous products of the soil . . . and from other privileges on refuges established under the Migratory Bird Conservation Act . . . shall be paid . . . to the county or counties in which such refuge is situated, to be expended for the benefit of the public schools and roads." Act of June 15, 1935, ch. 261, § 401, 49 Stat. 383. These provisions—the Refuge Revenue Sharing Act—created a constituency that could be expected to push for greater uses and therefore greater revenues.

(4) The Refuge Recreation Act of 1962: In 1962, Congress—"recogni[zing] mounting public demands for recreational opportunities on areas within the National Wildlife Refuge System"—enacted the first general administrative standards for the Refuge System. Act of Sept. 28, 1962, Pub. L. No. 87–714, 76 Stat. 653. In the Refuge Recreation Act of 1962, 16 U.S.C. §§ 460k to 460k–4, Congress sought to drive home a point by stating it seven times in a single section:

> In recognition of . . . resulting imperative need, if such recreational opportunities are to be provided, to assure that any . . . recreational use *will be compatible with, and will not prevent the accomplishment of, the primary purposes* for which [the refuge was] acquired or established, the Secretary of the Interior is authorized, *as an appropriate incidental or secondary use*, to administer such areas for public recreation when in his judgment public recreation can be *an appropriate incidental or secondary use*: Provided, That such public recreation use shall be permitted only to the extent that is practicable and *not inconsistent with . . . the primary objectives for which each particular area is established*; Provided further, That in order to insure accomplishment of such *primary objectives,* the Secretary . . . shall curtail public recreation use . . . whenever he considers such action to be necessary: and provided further, That none of the aforesaid refuges . . .

shall be used during any fiscal year for those forms of *recreation that are not directly related to the primary purposes and functions of the individual areas* until the Secretary shall have determined

(a) that such recreational use will not interfere with *the primary purposes for which the areas were established....*

Id. § 460k. The potential difficulty with repetition is that slight variations can appear important. Does this language create one or two or even three standards? Is it possible for an activity to be "not inconsistent" but also not "compatible"?

(5) The Refuge Revenue Sharing Act of 1964: The 1935 provisions were replaced by the current statute in 1964. Act of Aug. 30, 1964, Pub. L. No. 88–523, 78 Stat. 701 (codified as 16 U.S.C. § 715s). The current statute provides that revenues from "the sale or other disposition of animals, salmonoid cascassas [sic], timber, hay, grass, or other produce of the soil, minerals, shells, sand, or gravel" are to be paid to the counties in which refuges are located. *Id.* § 715s(a). Like its predecessor, the current Revenue Sharing Act embodies an assumption that such uses are permissible—and increased political pressure to open refuges to such income-producing activities. The 1966 Act did, however, add an important qualification by specifying that such commercial transactions were to be "incidental to but not in conflict with the basic purposes" of the refuge. *Id.*

(6) Malheur National Wildlife Refuge: The Malheur NWR is located at the bottom of the Harney Basin in eastern Oregon. Malheur Lake—the centerpiece of the Refuge—is one of the largest freshwater marshes in the western United States, ranging in surface area from 10,000 acres in dry years to more than 60,000 acres in wet years. A review of the waterfowl production on the refuge reveals a clear correlation between the amount of grazing permitted and the "precipitous decline" in waterfowl: between 1942 and 1950, an average of 111,352 ducks, geese, and swans were produced on the refuge; between 1951 and 1960 this dropped to 43,667; production continued to drop during the 1960s, averaging on 24,209. Grazing went from less than 4,000 AUMs[9] in 1942 when the Refuge was established to more than 10,000 AUMs in the 1950s and more than 12,000 AUMs in the 1960s. As a refuge employee noted, "Numerous authors have suggested that annual grazing and/or mowing [to produce hay] reduced water fowl production. [ ] A study conducted at Malheur NWR in 1964 provided indirect evidence that annual mowing and grazing reduced vegetation density and waterfowl production. [ ] More recent studies [ ] have substantiated this relationship." John E. Cornely, *Waterfowl Production at Malheur National Wildlife Refuge, 1942–1980,* TRANSACTIONS OF THE FORTY-SEVENTH NORTH AMERICAN WILDLIFE AND NATURAL RESOURCES CONFERENCE 559–71 (1982).

A non-employee was far blunter: "For most of its history, southeast Oregon's Malheur National Wildlife Refuge was a refuge in name only.... [S]tock damage caused duck production at the refuge to plunge from 151,000 to 21,300 between 1948 and 1974, a period during which federal

---

9. An Animal Unit Month (AUM) is a cow and calf grazing for one month.

grazing permits on the refuge doubled." Kathie Durbin, *Malheur Wildlife Refuge Discovers Desert Fish*, CASCADIA TIMES (1999).

(7) Opening refuges to hunting: The next intrusion upon the "inviolate sanctuary" concept occurred in 1949 when Congress raised the price of a Duck Stamp from $1 to $2 and in exchange agreed to allow hunting on up to 25% of each refuge. Act of Aug. 12, 1949, ch. 421, 63 Stat. 599. When the cost of a stamp was increased to $3 in 1958, hunting was allowed on up to 40% of each refuge. Act of Aug. 1, 1958, Pub. L. No. 85–585, 72 Stat. 486.

(8) The National Wildlife Refuge System Administration Act of 1966: Until the enactment of the Refuge Administration Act of 1966,[10] 16 U.S.C. § 668dd–668ee, there was no single law governing the administration of the federal wildlife refuges. Indeed, it was the Administration Act that created the National Wildlife Refuge System from a hodge podge of variously named entities—in addition to "wildlife refuges," there were "waterfowl production areas," "game ranges," "wildlife ranges," and "wildlife management areas"—under a variety of jurisdictions. All of these were consolidated into the "National Wildlife Refuge System." *Id.* § 668dd(a)(1).

While consolidation produced some consistency in the administration of the lands, the Administration Act actually contains little guidance on how the system's units are to be administered.

(a) The fundamental management standard: The Act does establish a basic management standard:

> The Secretary is authorized, under such regulations as he may prescribe, to permit the use of any area within the System for any purpose, including but not limited to hunting, fishing, public recreation and accommodations, and access whenever he determines that *such uses are compatible with the major purpose for which such areas are established.*

Id. § 668dd(d)(1)(A) (emphasis added). Beyond this compatibility limit, the Secretary's broad discretion is only minimally restricted: he may, for example, allow hunting on no more than 40% of a refuge, *id.*; his power to transfer lands out of the system is circumscribed by fair market value requirements for sales and equal value requirements for exchanges, *id.* § 668dd(a)(2)-(3), (b)(3). Is there a unified management standard applicable to all refuges or does "the purposes for which the refuge was created" continue to control management decisions?

(b) Penalties: The Act also imposes criminal sanctions on individuals using refuges:

> No person shall knowingly disturb, injure, cut, burn, remove, destroy, or possess any real or personal property of the United States, including natural growth, in any area of the System; or take or possess any fish,

---

10. The Refuge Administration Act was enacted as sections 4 and 5 of the Endangered Species Preservation Act of 1966, Pub. L. No. 89–669, § 4–5, 80 Stat. 926, 927; it was not denominated the National Wildlife Refuge System Administration Act until the Endangered Species Conservation Act of 1969. *See* Endangered Species Conservation Act of 1969, Pub. L. No. 91–137, § 12(f), 83 Stat. 275, 283.

bird, mammal, or other wild vertebrate or invertebrate animals or part or nest or egg thereof within any such area; or enter, use, or otherwise occupy any such area for any purpose.

Id. § 668dd(c).

b. DETERMINING THE APPLICABLE STANDARD

Schwenke v. Secretary of the Interior

Ninth Circuit Court of Appeals.
720 F.2d 571 (1983).

■ NORRIS, J.:   This case involves a series of executive orders and statutes dealing with livestock grazing and wildlife preservation on the Charles M. Russell National Wildlife Range (Russell Range or Range), an area of approximately 823,456 acres in northeastern Montana owned by the United States. We are called upon first to decide the relative priorities of wildlife and livestock in access to the natural forage resources of the Range. Second, we must decide whether livestock grazing on the Russell Range is to be administered under the Taylor Grazing Act or the National Wildlife Refuge System Administration Act (Wildlife Refuge Act).

I

Plaintiffs are ranchers holding permits for grazing on the Russell Range. They brought this action against the Secretary of the Interior and officials of the Department of the Interior's Fish and Wildlife Service seeking a declaratory judgment that livestock grazing on the Russell Range should be administered under the Taylor Grazing Act, rather than the Wildlife Refuge Act, as a use entitled to equal status with wildlife preservation, and that the Fish and Wildlife Service had unlawfully subordinated livestock grazing on the Russell Range to wildlife protection.

The district court granted partial summary judgment in favor of the ranchers, holding that livestock grazing and wildlife conservation are of coequal priority and that grazing is to be administered under the Taylor Grazing Act. On appeal, the Secretary argues that the land constituting the Russell Range was set aside by the government in 1936 primarily for wildlife preservation and that livestock grazing was to be only an incidental use. Alternatively, the Secretary argues that if the government ever intended to accord livestock grazing and wildlife protection equal status, Congress changed that priority scheme by legislation passed in 1976. Finally, the Secretary contends that legislation passed by Congress in 1976 mandates that grazing on the Russell Range be administered under the Wildlife Refuge Act, not the Taylor Grazing Act.

II

The first important legislation dealing with livestock grazing in the Western States was the Taylor Grazing Act, 43 U.S.C. § 315, enacted in 1934. The Act authorized the Secretary of the Interior "in his discretion, by order to establish grazing districts * * * [on public lands], which * * * in his opinion are chiefly valuable for grazing and raising forage crops." *Id.*

The Act also established a system for administering the grazing districts, through the issuance of grazing permits and the collection of grazing fees. Shortly after passage of the Act, several grazing districts were created under the Taylor Grazing Act, including districts on the land that later became the Russell Range.

In 1936, two years after passage of the Taylor Grazing Act, President Roosevelt issued Executive Order No. 7509, [ ]. That order contained several important provisions. First, it created the Fort Peck Game Range on the land that is now the Charles M. Russell Range and ordered that the Range was to be "withdrawn from settlement, location, sale or entry and reserved and set apart for the conservation and development of natural wildlife resources and for the protection and improvement of public grazing land and natural forage resources." *Id.*

Second, E.O. 7509 directed that conservation and development of wildlife on the Range were to be under the joint jurisdiction of the Secretary of the Interior and the Secretary of Agriculture and that grazing and natural forage resources on the Range were to be under the sole jurisdiction of the Secretary of the Interior.[3]

Third, the order specifically provided for a wildlife use. Since it is this part of E.O. 7509 that is at the heart of the present controversy, we set it out in full:

> [T]he natural forage resources [on the Range] shall be first utilized for the purpose of sustaining in a healthy condition a maximum of four hundred thousand (400,000) sharptail grouse, and one thousand five hundred (1,500) antelope, the primary species, and such nonpredatory secondary species in such numbers as may be necessary to maintain a balanced wildlife population, but in no case shall the consumption of forage by the combined population of the wildlife species be allowed to increase the burden of the range dedicated to the primary species.

Id.

Finally, the order provided that "all the forage resources within this range or preserve shall be available, except as herein otherwise provided with respect to wildlife, for domestic livestock" under rules and regulations promulgated by the Secretary of the Interior under the authority of the Taylor Grazing Act. *Id.*

E.O. 7509 can be read in several ways. It is possible, as the Secretary argues, to read the order as establishing an absolute priority for wildlife over livestock. E.O. 7509 specifically provides that "the natural forage resources [of the Russell Range] shall be *first* utilized" for the purpose of maintaining primary and nonpredatory secondary species of wildlife in such numbers as necessary to maintain a balanced wildlife population. While forage resources within the Range are available for livestock grazing, they are available "*except* as * * * otherwise provided [in the order] with respect

---

3. In 1936, when EO 7509 was issued, the Bureau of Land Management was a part of the Department of the Interior while the Fish and Wildlife Service was a part of the Department of Agriculture. It was not until three years later, in 1939, that Fish and Wildlife Service was moved to the Department of the Interior and the Secretary of the Interior thereby became responsible for the administration of the entire Range.

to wildlife." The "first utilized" language applies to (1) primary species; (2) secondary species; and (3) a balanced wildlife population. It is not unreasonable to argue that the numbers set out in the order establish priority among types of wildlife and that the first utilized language, referring as it does to both "primary" and "secondary species," establishes an absolute priority for wildlife over livestock.

It is also possible to read E.O. 7509, as do the ranchers, as making no distinction between wildlife and livestock in terms of access to the resources of the Range. The preamble to E.O. 7509 provides that the Range is withdrawn from settlement and sale "for the conservation and development of natural wildlife resources and for the protection and improvement of public grazing lands and natural forage resources." [ ] This passage, at least, does not distinguish between wildlife and livestock. Moreover, it is undisputed that from 1936 until 1976, the Bureau of Land Management and the Fish and Wildlife Service administered the Russell Range on the premise that wildlife and livestock had equal priority in access to the resources of the Range.

Neither the ranchers' nor the Secretary's position, however, is ultimately convincing. The ranchers' position—that grazing and wildlife preservation enjoy equal status on the Range—altogether ignores the language commanding that the resources of the Range shall be "first utilized" for the support of certain types of wildlife. The argument of the Secretary—that wildlife has absolute priority on the Range—ignores forty years of administration of the Range by the Fish and Wildlife Service and the Bureau of Land Management. It also ignores the language of the order itself. E.O. 7509 refers to a *"maximum"* of 400,000 sharptail grouse and 1500 antelope. Had an absolute wildlife priority been intended, it is hard to see why such limits were established. Moreover, the last portion of E.O. 7509 provides that land

> acquired and to be acquired by the United States for the use of the Department of Agriculture for the conservation of migratory birds and other wildlife, shall be and remain under the exclusive administration of the Secretary of Agriculture and may be utilized for public grazing purposes only to such extent as may be determined by the said Secretary to be compatible with the utilization of said lands for the purposes for which they were acquired as aforesaid under regulations prescribed by him.

This language clearly established an absolute priority for wildlife on any lands that may be acquired by the Department of Agriculture for conservation of birds and wildlife. If such a priority had been intended on the entire Range, we would expect similarly explicit language to have been employed. Finally, if an absolute priority for wildlife had been intended on the entire Range there would have been no need then to carve out a priority for wildlife on particular parts of the Range.

We therefore reject both of these extreme positions. We instead are persuaded by an intermediate position that seems to us to represent a fairer reading of E.O. 7509 than that advanced by either the ranchers or the Secretary. We believe E.O. 7509 establishes a limited priority for wildlife beyond which grazing and wildlife preservation have equal status.

It is clear that some priority for wildlife was intended. E.O. 7509 specifically provides that the resources of the Range shall be "first utilized" to support the primary and secondary species. It is equally clear, however, that that priority was limited. The order provides that the Range shall be first utilized for wildlife up to a maximum of 400,000 sharptail grouse, 1500 antelope, and that number of secondary species necessary to maintain a balanced wildlife population. We thus hold that E.O. 7509 established a priority in access to the forage resources of the Range for, in numbers within the Secretary's discretion, a maximum of 400,000 sharptail grouse, 1500 antelope, and that number of secondary species reasonably necessary to maintain a balanced wildlife population. Beyond those limits, wildlife and livestock have equal priority in access to the forage resources of the Range.

We do not believe the Secretary would vigorously dispute our reading of E.O. 7509. Fundamentally, our reading is that of the Secretary tempered by the numerical limits on priority for wildlife set out explicitly in the order. The Secretary does, however, argue that E.O. 7509, regardless of how it is read, is irrelevant to the priority scheme that must currently be employed on the Range because legislation passed by Congress in 1976 revoked E.O. 7509 and set forth a new priority scheme for access to the forage resources of the Range. It is to that argument that we now turn.

III

On October 15, 1966, Congress enacted the National Wildlife Refuge System Administration Act, 16 U.S.C. § 668dd–668ee, establishing the National Wildlife Refuge System. Then, in 1976 Congress enacted the Wildlife Refuge Act Amendments, Pub. L. 94–223, 90 Stat. 199 (codified at 16 U.S.C. § 668dd). That legislation provided that

[f]or the purpose of consolidating the authorities relating to the various categories of areas that are administered by the Secretary of the Interior for the conservation of fish and wildlife, * * * all lands, waters, and interests therein administered by the Secretary as wildlife refuges, * * * wildlife ranges, game ranges, wildlife management areas, or waterfowl production areas are hereby designated as the "National Wildlife Refuge System" [referred to herein as the "System"], which shall be * * * administered by the Secretary through the United States Fish and Wildlife Service.

The legislation thus transferred control of the Russell Range from the Bureau of Land Management and the Fish and Wildlife Service jointly to the Fish and Wildlife Service alone. The Secretary argues that P.L. 94–223 was passed to assure that wildlife would have absolute priority in access to the forage resources of the Range and that the priority scheme it mandated superseded any scheme that may have been effected by E.O. 7509. Pursuant to this interpretation of the 1976 Amendments, on May 3, 1978 the Secretary issued Public Land Order 5635, [ ], which transferred control of the Russell Range to the Fish and Wildlife Service, decreed that the Range was to be administered under the Wildlife Refuge Act, and declared that E.O. 7509 had been modified to the extent necessary to conform to these two orders.

The district court declared P.L.O. 5635 invalid. It held that the 1976 Amendments neither revoked the priority scheme set out in E.O. 7509 nor changed the statute under which the Range was to be administered. The district court held further that the only effect P.L. 94–223 had in regard to the Russell Range was to transfer administrative responsibility for the Range to the Fish and Wildlife Service. On appeal, the Secretary argues that we should reverse the district court and hold P.L.O. 5635 a valid exercise of his power.

The district court based its holding on the fact that the language of P.L. 94–223 did not explicitly revoke E.O. 7509 with respect to access to the forage resources of the Range. It refused to consider the legislative history of P.L. 94–223, relying on the "plain meaning" doctrine of statutory construction. The court reasoned that because P.L. 94–223 was not "ambiguous"—because its meaning was plain—there was no need to resort to legislative history. This, we believe, was error.

First, the district court misapplied the plain meaning rule. As stated by the Supreme Court less than two years ago, "the plain-meaning rule is 'rather an axiom of experience than a rule of law, and does not preclude consideration of persuasive evidence if it exists.' " [ ] "[E]ven the most basic general principles of statutory construction," the Court stated, "must yield to clear contrary evidence of legislative intent." [ ]

Second, the meaning of P.L. 94–223 is not altogether clear. It is true that the language of the statute only transfers control of the Range to the Fish and Wildlife Service and does not mention the relative priorities of livestock and wildlife in access to the forage resources of the Range. However, the primary mission of the Fish and Wildlife Service is wildlife preservation. Fish and Wildlife Act of 1956, § 2, 16 U.S.C. § 742a (1976). It is certainly possible to argue that when Congress transferred administrative responsibility for the Range to the Fish and Wildlife Service it had in mind the primary mission of the agency and intended to change the relative priority between livestock and wildlife on the Range. In short, P.L. 94–223 is sufficiently ambiguous to justify resort to its legislative history.

When we consider the legislative history of P.L. 94–223, it is clear that both legislators and members of the Department of the Interior instrumental in the passage of P.L. 94–223 believed that wildlife either already had or would, after passage of the 1976 Amendments, have priority on the Range. The Assistant Secretary of the Interior noted during the hearings on the Amendments that "[the] BLM will continue to manage the areas for the dominant use of wildlife." [ ] One Congressman stated that the ranges under discussion "have been set aside primarily to protect the resident wildlife and their habitat * * ** All acknowledge that the law requires that fish and wildlife be first priority on these three ranges." [ ] The Senate Floor Manager of the bill explained that

> [t]he Executive Order which created the game ranges specified that grazing would be permitted only when compatible with wildlife needs.

* * *

[The Fish and Wildlife Service intention is] to permit continuation of grazing on the game ranges where it does not interfere with the wildlife for which the areas were created.

* * *

What the bill does, simply is to say to the Fish and Wildlife Service "You administer this for the preservation of the wildlife and to the extent that it is compatible therewith, continue to issue grazing permits or whatever reasonable use there is of public lands."

* * *

[I]t is the legislative intent, so far as this bill is concerned, that the Fish and Wildlife Service will continue to manage these ranges to be utilized to whatever extent possible for other uses besides preservation of the fish and wildlife, so long as it does not impinge upon it and make it impossible to preserve those values.

[ ]

Were we to consider only the statute, read in light of its legislative history, we would rule that P.L. 94–223 commands that wildlife have priority in access to the forage resources of the Range and that the Range is to be administered under the Wildlife Refuge Act. We cannot consider the statute alone, however, for in determining its effect we must not only determine the meaning of P.L. 94–223 but must also determine whether the statute effectively revoked the contrary commands of E.O. 7509.

It is the law of our circuit that revocation or modification of an existing withdrawal should be express to be effective. [ ] Repeal of a statute or order by implication is not favored. [ ] We believe, given this rule, the priority scheme established by E.O. 7509 has not been revoked. Nowhere in the 1976 Amendments is anything said about priority in access to the forage resources of the Range. There is simply no mention of livestock, grazing, or E.O. 7509. Furthermore, the legislative history on this point is more indicative of confusion regarding the existing priority scheme than of an intent to change priorities. Many legislators seemed to think E.O. 7509 had established an absolute wildlife priority. Such confusion is not sufficient to revoke E.O. 7509. We thus hold that P.L. 94–223 did not revoke the priority scheme for access to the resources of the Range established by E.O. 7509.

IV

The Secretary contends also that P.L. 94–223 mandates that any grazing activity on the Russell Range be administered under the Wildlife Refuge Act rather than the Taylor Grazing Act, under which the Range was previously administered. The district court, however, held that P.L. 94–223 did not change the statute under which the Range is to be administered. We agree with the Secretary.

While the language of P.L. 94–223 does not explicitly change administration of the Range from the Taylor Grazing Act to the Wildlife Refuge Act, when the statute is read in conjunction with its legislative history the intention to change Range management to the Wildlife Refuge Act is clear.

The Wildlife Refuge Act is the statute under which the Fish and Wildlife Service manages the National Wildlife Refuge System. It defies reason to suggest that Congress merely liked the personnel of the Fish and Wildlife Service more than those of the Bureau of Land Management. Congress clearly wanted the Russell Range administered by the Fish and Wildlife Service because of its underlying mission to protect wildlife. The Wildlife Refuge Act is an integral part of that mission and, we believe, was part of the change Congress intended in transferring administrative responsibility for the Russell Range from the Bureau of Land Management to the Fish and Wildlife Service.

Moreover, the legislative history of the 1976 Amendments indicates that at least some leading legislators believed that transfer of management from the Bureau of Land Management to the Fish and Wildlife Service changed the statute under which the Range was to be administered from the Taylor Grazing Act to the Wildlife Refuge Act. Senator Moss noted:

> On behalf of the Committee on Commerce I would like to assure the Senator from Montana that sole administration of the Kofa, Russell, and Sheldon Game Ranges by the Fish and Wildlife Service will not result in the instantaneous termination of existing grazing privileges on these areas. Rather, it is the committee's understanding that the Service will continue to honor valid existing grazing permits that were issued by BLM under the Taylor Grazing Act. When these permits expire, the Service will then reexamine them to determine if continued grazing is compatible with wildlife needs. Grazing will be permitted to the extent compatible and will be administered by the Service pursuant to the National Wildlife Refuge Administration Act. I might note that the Service is currently administering over 1 million acres of refuge lands in 31 States for grazing purposes.

[ ]

We thus hold that, while P.L. 94–223 did not change the relative priorities of wildlife and livestock on the Charles M. Russell National Wildlife Range, it did change the statute under which the Range is to be administered from the Taylor Grazing Act to the National Wildlife Refuge System Administration Act.

NOTES

(1) *Schwenke* demonstrates the difficulties that must often be faced in determining what the primary purpose of any refuge is. It also suggests some of the difficulties that the FWS faces in attempting to manage the refuges as a *system* rather than as an accumulation of individual units. What could Congress have done to create a unified system with a unitary management standard? Would such a standard be a good idea? Leaving aside the apparent conflicts between cows and wildlife, should a refuge that was acquired for migratory waterfowl be managed under the same standard as a refuge that was acquired to protect the critical habitat of an endangered species?

(2) Consolidation: The Administration Act begins with the statements that its purpose is "consolidating the authorities relating to the various categories of areas that are administered by the Secretary of the Interior for the conservation of fish and wildlife," designating the various previous categories as the "National Wildlife Refuge System." 16 U.S.C. § 668dd(a)(1). *Schwenke* examines one part of this "consolidation"—the issue of whether the management standards that previously governed the diverse categories were replaced by the Administration Act's management standard.

The Administration Act, however, also consolidated the administration of the refuges in the Fish and Wildlife Service. In 1975, the Secretary sought to transfer management of the game ranges to the Bureau of Land Management. A challenge to the proposal by the Wilderness Society blocked the transfer and Congress responded by amending the Administration Act to add that the Refuge System "shall be administered by the Secretary through the United States Fish and Wildlife Service." 16 U.S.C. § 668dd(a)(1). The limits of this requirement were tested in *Trustees for Alaska v. Watt*, 524 F.Supp. 1303 (D.Alaska 1981), *aff'd mem.*, 690 F.2d 1279 (9th Cir.1982). In 1981, the Secretary designated the United States Geological Survey (USGS) as the lead agency on a study of the oil development potential of the Arctic National Wildlife Refuge. Relying upon the Administration Act's requirement that the Refuge System "shall be administered by . . . the United States Fish and Wildlife Service," the court held that the Act meant that "in administering the Arctic National Wildlife Refuge, FWS is required to control and direct the Refuge by regulating human access in order to conserve the entire spectrum of wildlife found in the Refuge." The Secretary's attempt to designate USGS as lead agency thus was contrary to the Administration Act.

c.   DOMINANT USE AND "COMPATIBILITY"

Defenders of Wildlife v. Andrus

District Court for the District of Columbia.
11 Env't Rep. Cas. (BNA) 2098 (1978).

■ PRATT, D.J.:[In April 1978, the Fish and Wildlife Service promulgated regulations governing recreational boating and water skiing at the Ruby Lake National Wildlife Refuge in Nevada. Petitioners brought suit in June, arguing that the regulations violated the Refuge Recreation Act.]

Findings of Fact

I.   *Ruby Lake National Wildlife Refuge*

1.1   On July 2, 1938, by Executive Order No. 7923, President Franklin Roosevelt "reserved and set apart" the Refuge "as a refuge and breeding ground for migratory birds and other wildlife," in order to effectuate further the purposes of the Migratory Bird Conservation Act. The area so reserved and set apart, which was then denominated the Ruby Lake Migratory Waterfowl Refuge, comprised all land and waters within a described area of approximately 37,640 acres in Elko and White Pine Counties, Nevada. [ ]

1.2   Section 5 of the Migratory Bird Conservation Act, [ ], authorizes the United States to purchase, rent or otherwise reserve areas "for use as inviolate sanctuaries for migratory birds * * ** " Section 6 of this Act, [ ], requires that easements and reservations retained by any grantor from whom the United States received title "shall be subject to rules and regulations prescribed by the Secretary of [Interior] for the occupation, use, operation, protection and administration of the areas as inviolate sanctuaries for migratory birds * * ** "

1.3   The primary purpose for which the Refuge was established is for use as a refuge, breeding ground and inviolate sanctuary for migratory birds.

. . .

1.6   The Refuge consists of 25,150 acres of wetlands and 12,468 acres of surrounding uplands. The wetland portion of the Refuge consist of the 7,000–acre South Sump, which is the primary waterfowl nest area, and the North and East Sumps, which are all maintained by a complex and intricate flowage of waters throughout the marsh basin. The average depth of water in the South Sump is approximately four feet, and in the North and East Sumps considerably less. [ ]

1.7   The management objectives of the Refuge are (1) to preserve, restore and enhance in their natural eco-systems all species of animals and plants that are endangered or threatened with becoming endangered on lands of the National Wildlife Refuge System; (2) to perpetuate the migratory bird resource for the benefit of people—to manage the refuge for an annual production of 5,000 canvasbacks and 5,000 redheads; (3) to preserve natural diversity and abundance of mammals and non-migratory birds on refuge lands; and (4) to provide an understanding and appreciation of fish and wildlife ecology and man's role in his environment, and to provide visitors with high quality, safe, wholesome, and enjoyable recreation which is fully compatible and consistent with, and which in no way harms or interferes with the area's primary purpose as a refuge and breeding ground for migratory birds and other wildlife. [ ]

1.8   All national wildlife refuges are maintained for the primary purpose of preserving, protecting and enhancing wildlife and other natural resources and of developing a national program of wildlife and ecological conservation and rehabilitation. These refuges are established for the restoration, preservation, development and management of wildlife and wildlands habitat; for the protection and preservation of endangered or threatened species and their habitat; and for the management of wildlife and wildlands to obtain the maximum benefits of these resources.

II.   *The Refuge Supports Canvasback and Redhead Ducks and a*
Diverse Population of Other Migratory Birds and Wildlife

2.1   The Refuge provides one of the most important habitats and nesting areas for over-water nesting waterfowl in the United States. The Refuge is particularly valuable to the canvasback and redhead duck, which use the area in approximately equal numbers for nesting and broodrearing during the spring, summer and early fall. [ ]

2.2   Continental populations of both redhead and canvasback duck are low and both species have suffered throughout their respective ranges from encroachment and habitat loss. In 1972, the annual winter waterfowl inventory conducted by the United States Fish and Wildlife Service showed an all time low of 179,000 canvasbacks. The redhead has faced intensive drainage programs in the prairie-parkland region of central North America, the major breeding area of this species. A more comprehensive program oriented towards habitat protection is necessary to conserve and protect these species. [ ]

2.3   The canvasback duck and the redhead duck have been listed as "migratory birds," as defined by Section 11 of the Migratory Bird Conservation Act, [ ], and are protected by [treaties between the United States and Canada, Mexico, and Japan.]

2.4   In addition to the canvasback and redhead duck, numerous species of waterfowl and other birds using the Refuge have been so designated as "migratory birds," including the prairie falcon, the peregrine falcon, the bald eagle, the golden eagle, the trumpeter swan, the white-faced ibis, the snowy egret, the great blue heron, the black-crowned night heron, the ruddy duck, the ringed-neck duck, the sandhill crane, the Canada goose, the coot and the cinnamon teal. [ ]

Conclusions of Law

III.   *The Ruby Lake Regulations are Invalid in That*
They Do Not Include Appropriate Findings
Necessary to Their Promulgation

3.1   On April 21, 1978, the Secretary of Interior promulgated the Ruby Lake Special Regulations, [ ].

3.2   These regulations permit year-round boating in an area designated as Zone 1 in the South Sump by boats without motors or boats with electric motors .

3.3   Beginning on July 1 on the east side and July 15 on the west side of an area designated as Zone 2 of the South Sump, and extending until December 31, boats without motors, boats with electric motors and boats with internal combustion motors of unlimited horsepower are permitted. No boat may exceed 20 miles per hour in an area or 5 miles per hour in areas so designated by the Refuge Manager.

3.4   Beginning on July 1 and extending until December 31, waterskiing is permitted on a designated area from 10 a.m. to 5 p.m. daily.

3.5   Beginning on August 1 and extending until December 31, boats without motors, boats with electric motors and boats with internal combustion motors of unlimited horsepower are permitted in an area designated as Zone 3 of the South Sump. No boat may exceed 20 miles per hour in any area or 5 miles per hour in areas so designated.

3.6   The Refuge Recreation Act of 1962, [ ], governs the Secretary's authority to permit recreation within the Ruby Lake National Wildlife

Refuge and all other areas within the National Wildlife Refuge System, national fish hatcheries and other conservation areas administered by the Secretary for fish and wildlife purposes. The Refuge Recreation Act provides in pertinent part that:

> In recognition of mounting public demands for recreational opportunities on areas within the National Wildlife Refuge System, national fish hatcheries, and other conservation area administered by the Secretary of the Interior for fish and wildlife proposes; and in recognition also of the resulting imperative need, if such recreational opportunities are provided, to assure that any present or future recreational use will be compatible with, and will not prevent accomplishment of, the primary purposes for which the said conservation areas were acquired or established, the Secretary of the Interior is authorized, as an appropriate incidental or secondary use, to administer such areas or parts thereof for public recreation when in his judgment public recreation can be an appropriate incidental or secondary use: *Provided,* That such public recreation use shall be permitted only to the extent that is practicable and not inconsistent with other previously authorized Federal operations or with the primary objectives for which each particular area is established; *Provided further,* That in order to insure accomplishment of such primary objectives, the Secretary, after consideration of all authorized uses, purposes, and other pertinent factors relating to individual area, shall curtail public recreation use within individual areas or in portions thereof whenever he considers such action to be necessary; *And provided further,* That none of the aforesaid refuges, hatcheries, game ranges, or other conservation areas shall be used during any fiscal year for those forms of recreation that are not directly related to the primary purposes and functions of the individual area *until the Secretary shall have determined—*

> (a) *that such recreational use will not interfere with the primary purposes for which the areas were established,* and

> . . .

[ ]

3.7   In supporting enactment, Congressman Dingell stated on the floor of the House:

> The Secretary must make certain findings before he throws these areas open to public use; the bill requires him to find, for example, that there is sufficient money available to administer and protect these areas, and *he must find that the utilization for recreational use will not be harmful to the basic purpose of the refuges.*

[ ]

3.8   In determining to permit recreational use of a National Wildlife Refuge, the burden of proof is necessarily on the Secretary to demonstrate that such use is incidental to, compatible with, and does not interfere with the primary purpose of the refuge as "an inviolate sanctuary for migratory birds."

3.9   The regulations violate the statutory standard because the Secretary failed to make the determination required by the statute that the permitted recreational use would not interfere with the Refuge's primary purpose an [sic] an "inviolate sanctuary for migratory birds."

3.10   The Refuge Recreation Act does not permit the Secretary to weigh or balance economic, political or recreational interests again the primary purpose of the Refuge.

3.11   When Congress has sought to authorize the weighing or balancing of competing interests it has done so explicitly. [ ]

3.12   Neither poor administration of the Refuge in the past, nor prior interferences with its primary purposes, nor past recreational uses, or deterioration of its wildlife resource since its establishment, nor administrative custom or tradition alters the statutory standard. The Refuge Recreation Act permits recreational use only when it will not interfere with the primary purpose for which the Refuge "was established." The prior operation of the Refuge in a manner inconsistent with that purpose does not change the base point for applying the statute's standard. Past recreational use is irrelevant to the statutory standard except insofar as deterioration of the wildlife resource from prior recreation use serves to increase the need to protect, enhance and preserve the resource. Past recreational abuses may indeed require the Secretary to curtail recreational use to an even greater degree than mandated by the Refuge Recreation Act, in order to restore and rehabilitate the area promptly as required by the Secretary's existing regulations. [ ]

IV.   *This Court Will Not Supply Findings to Support the Regulations on Behalf of the Secretary*

4.1   It is not the function of this Court to make findings, on behalf of the Secretary, that the regulations will not be harmful to the primary purpose of the refuge. [ ]

4.2   In the background material preceding the regulations in the Federal Register, the Secretary through his assistants cited problems "directly attributable to the continued use of large powerboats at Ruby Lake."

4.3   The legislative history of the Refuge Recreation Act indicates that motorboating is inconsistent with refuge purposes. [ ]

4.4   In adopting these regulations the Assistant Secretary balanced economic, political and recreational interests against the primary wildlife purpose of the refuge and reached a compromise. [ ]

4.5   The compromise reached by the Assistant Secretary in adopting these regulations was not supported by certain members of his staff. The former Refuge Manager, an expert in wildlife biology and management, testified in opposition to the regulation. The Deputy Associate Director for Wildlife refused to surname the regulation because in his opinion the regulations were not in the best interest of the Refuge and the resources for which it was established.

. . .

1.   The Ruby Lake Special Regulations, [ ], are declared unlawful.

2.   Defendant Secretary of the Interior is hereby permanently enjoined from acting pursuant to the above cited regulations.

. . .

Defenders of Wildlife v. Andrus

District Court for the District of Columbia.
455 F.Supp. 446 (1978).

■ PRATT, D.J.: [Five days after the regulations were enjoined, the Secretary promulgated essentially identical regulations accompanied by an express determination that the permitted uses were compatible with the purposes for which the refuge was established.]

Findings of Fact

1.   Public use of the Refuge currently exceeds 50,000 visitors each year. Approximately 30,000 boaters annually are now using the 7,000–acre South Sump that makes up the southern portion of the Refuge. [ ] In recent years the annual increase in boating has exceeded 19% And is projected to increase in the Elko County portion of the Refuge by over 300% by the year 2020. [ ]

2.   The preferred nesting habitat for migratory birds is located in the South Sump. Although some nesting takes place outside this area, approximately 85% of canvasback and redhead production would occur in the South Sump. [ ]

3.   The reproductive cycle of over-water nesting ducks at the Refuge consists of four distinct stages: nest site selection, initial nesting, late nesting and re-nesting, and broodrearing. Waterfowl production on the Refuge for any given year is determined by the breeding population density, nesting success, and duckling survival. [ ]

4.   Hens flush easily when disturbed by either canoe or powerboat even after nesting is well underway, [ ], but this disturbance decreases as incubation proceeds.

5.   Powerboating may cause abandonment of established nests. [ ]

6.   Re-nesting may occur when the first nest is lost through predation, destruction or abandonment. Re-nesting is an ordinary occurrence for canvasback and redhead ducks and re-nesting success is essential to the maintenance of production levels of the Refuge. Approximately once every four years canvasback and redhead ducks nest later than usual due to climatic conditions. Late nesting and re-nesting ducks go through both nest site selection and actual nesting stages, which together extend from May 15 through September 1. [ ] Even in normal years delayed nesting is typical of redheads throughout their range. [ ] Re-nesting may account for up to 46% of the total nesting of redhead ducks in a given season. [ ]

7.   Broodrearing is the period from the hatching of the egg until the hen abandons the brood. During broodrearing, ducklings are dependent upon the hen for safety, and their vulnerability to predators is increased in her absence. Disturbances caused by internal combustion powerboats may

separate hens from ducklings. Broodrearing continues from about April 25 to September 30 in each season. [ ]

8. Mechanical cutting action of propellers on aquatic vegetation and increased turbidity caused by motors decreases vegetative productivity of the Refuge. Emergent vegetation such as hard-stem bulrush, used by migratory waterfowl for nesting, may be removed by motorboats creating new channels. [ ]

9. Samples taken on the Refuge demonstrate that where no boating was permitted the marsh produced 328% more submergent vegetation than in areas of heavy boating. [ ]

10. Nesting ducks on the Refuge may be flushed from their nests by the noise of a 25 horsepower boat passing at full throttle within 300 yards of the nest. [ ]

11. Total Refuge waterfowl use days show a steady downward trend over the past twenty years and it appears that the most obvious cause for the decline in waterfowl use is human disturbance. [ ]

12. Unlimited horsepower powerboating without appropriate regulation has had unavoidable adverse impacts on over-water nesting waterfowl and has resulted in lower waterfowl production and less wildlife diversity. [ ]

13. The annual loss of waterfowl production in any particular year due to boating activities is an irretrievable loss to the continental waterfowl population. [ ]

14. When boats of unlimited horsepower are permitted without appropriate regulation, the long-term effects of boating are cumulative and will ultimately determine the number of birds returning to nest at the Refuge in future years. [ ]

15. The impacts of boating under the circumstances described in paragraph 14 above, extend to other wildlife species found on the Refuge and may be essentially similar to those on canvasbacks and redheads for other over-water nesting waterfowl including the ruddy duck. [ ]

16. Waterskiing in a waterfowl nesting area within a migratory bird sanctuary does not promote or enhance, and may harm, waterfowl habitat, nest site selection, nesting, re-nesting, late nesting, or broodrearing.

17. The use of unlimited horsepower internal combustion motors in a waterfowl nesting area within a migratory bird sanctuary does not promote or enhance, and may harm, waterfowl habitat, nest site selection, nesting, re-nesting, late nesting or broodrearing.

18. On July 19, 1978, the Director, Fish and Wildlife Service, signed special regulations which permit powerboating, motorless boating, and waterskiing within the Ruby Lake National Wildlife Refuge (the "Refuge"). These July 19, 1978 regulations are in large part the same as the April 21, 1978 special regulations which this Court held to be unlawful in *Defenders of Wildlife v. Andrus,* [ ].

19. If the regulations are permitted to continue in effect they will immediately and irreparably damage plaintiff's interests and the wildlife resources of the Refuge. The use of powerboats of unlimited horsepower on the

Refuge (including for waterskiing) will directly and immediately harm the wildlife resources of the Refuge (i) by reducing submergent aquatic vegetation which is the principal food source for migratory waterfowl, [ ]; (ii) by reducing macroinvertebrate populations which are the principal food sources for ducklings, [ ]; (iii) by breaking up broods, by separating ducklings from their hen, by forcing broods out of brooding areas, and thereby reducing brood size, [ ]; and (iv) by reducing the reproductive success of late nesting and re-nesting hens. [ ]

20.   Late nesting and re-nesting extends through September 1 of each season and occurs with sufficient frequency to be significant to the immediate and long-term productivity of the Refuge. [ ]

21(a) The level of boating use permitted by these regulations is not incidental to or compatible with, and will interfere with the primary purpose of the Refuge.

(b).   The suggestion that horsepower limitations would not be appropriate, and would not aid the primary purpose of the Refuge, is completely contrary to all reason and the facts of the record.

(c).   The proposed speed limitations to be used in conjunction with horsepower are so obviously unenforceable that to rely on a speed limitation, even as high as twenty miles an hour, is unrealistic because of its very unenforceability.

Conclusions of Law

22.   The regulations violate the statutory standard of the Refuge Recreation Act because the degree and manner of boating use which they would permit is not incidental or secondary use, is inconsistent, and would interfere with the Refuge's primary purpose.

23.   The regulations violate the statutory standard of the Refuge Recreation Act because the degree and manner of boating use which they would permit is not practicable because of their unenforceability.

24.   The Secretary's determination that the level of boating permitted by the regulations does not interfere with the Refuge's primary purpose is arbitrary and capricious.

25.   Based on the record in this action, the use of boats with unlimited horsepower in the South Sump of the Refuge is inconsistent and interferes with its primary purpose as a refuge and breeding ground for migratory birds and wildlife.

An Order consistent with the foregoing Findings of Fact and Conclusions of Law has been entered this day.

NOTES

(1) What is the applicable legal standard under the Refuge Recreation Act? Is the standard the same as the "compatibility" standard under the Refuge Administration Act?

(2) The court's first opinion states that the Assistant Secretary had balanced the competing interests. Is that unlawful or only unwise? Is it relevant that some of the Assistant Secretary's professional staff opposed the regulation as too lax? Is it relevant that the Assistant Secretary is a political appointee?

(3) For a review of the history behind the case written by an employee at the Ruby Lake Refuge, see Stephen H. Bouffard, *Wildlife Values Versus Human Recreation: Ruby Lake National Wildlife Refuge,* TRANSACTIONS OF THE FORTY-SEVENTH NORTH AMERICAN WILDLIFE AND NATURAL RESOURCES CONFERENCE 553–58 (1982). Bouffard concludes his review: "As at Ruby Lake NWR, the Refuge Recreation Act will continue to be used to protect wildlife objectives should recreational programs conflicts with these objectives."

Humane Society v. Lujan

District Court for the District of Columbia.
768 F.Supp. 360 (1991).

■ JACKSON, D.J.:This case is brought by ... the Humane Society of the United States, and various coalitions of homeowner/citizens, against the United States Secretary of the Interior and the Director of the Fish and Wildlife Service ("FWS" or "the Service") to prevent the implementation of defendants' decision to permit limited public deer hunting on a national wildlife refuge in Fairfax County, Virginia. . . .

In August, 1989, the FWS issued a final rule, 54 Fed.Reg. 36032 (Aug. 31, 1989), opening the Mason Neck National Wildlife Refuge ("the Refuge") for deer hunting during the fall hunting season in Virginia. The Refuge, comprising approximately 2300 acres of Mason Neck, an 8000–acre peninsula on the south shore of the Potomac River 18 miles downstream from Washington, D.C., was established in 1969 as a habitat and sanctuary for bald eagles. It has been altogether closed to hunting for the first 20 years of its existence. The decision in 1989 to open it to deer hunting was impelled, in principal part, by FWS' desire to find an expedient to control the Refuge's burgeoning white-tailed deer population.

The Humane Society questions the legitimacy of the Service's justification for the hunt, as well as its refusal to acknowledge the potential for harm to the wildlife species to which the Refuge is dedicated, the bald eagle. The homeowner organizations are primarily fearful of injury to people and property in the vicinity, although some individuals apparently share the Humane Society's abhorrence of animal hunting generally.

Plaintiffs bring this action under [the Bald and Golden Eagle Protection Act of 1940, the Migratory Bird Treaty Act of 1918, the Endangered Species Act of 1973, the National Environmental Policy Act of 1969, the National Wildlife Refuge System Administration Act of 1966, and the Refuge Recreation Act of 1962. The court dismissed the Endangered Species Act claim on procedural grounds.]

The National Wildlife Refuge System Administration Act of 1966, [ ], and the Refuge Recreation Act of 1962, [ ], authorize the Secretary of the Interior to permit "appropriate incidental or secondary use[s]" of wildlife refuges, even though "recreational" in character, including hunting, which are "compatible with, and will not prevent accomplishment of, the primary purpose for which the[se] areas were established." [ ] The applicable regulation provides that any action the Secretary takes must be "consistent with principles of sound wildlife management, and must otherwise be in the public interest." [ ]

The parties are in voluble disagreement as to how to ascertain whether a secondary use of a wildlife refuge is "compatible" with its primary purpose. Plaintiffs postulate the existence of an "almost absolute presumption" against secondary uses of wildlife refuges, a phrase derived from the case of *Defenders of Wildlife v. Administrator, Environmental Protection Agency,* 688 F. Supp. 1334, 1355 (D.Minn.1988), *aff'd in relevant part,* 882 F.2d 1294, 1299–1301 (8th Cir.1989). They also cite an earlier decision of another judge of this district court in *Defenders of Wildlife v. Andrus,* [ ] (*"Ruby Lake"*), permanently enjoining the FWS from permitting recreational motorboating at the Ruby Lake National Wildlife Refuge in Nevada. The *Ruby Lake* court declared that the "burden of proof is necessarily on [the Service] to demonstrate that [recreational] use is incidental to, compatible with, and does not interfere with the primary purpose of the refuge," and that the RRA "does not permit [FWS] to weigh or balance * * * recreational interests against [that] purpose." [ ]

Defendants reject plaintiffs' suggestion that anything resembling a formal "presumption" against secondary uses is to be found in the legislation. They submit that the Act requires only that the Secretary make a "finding" that the proposed secondary use is "compatible" with the primary purpose of the Refuge, as he has in this case, and this Court must review that finding under the familiar inhibitions of APA review. *See Humane Society of the United States v. Hodel,* 840 F.2d 45 (D.C.Cir.1988); *Friends of Animals, Inc. v. Hodel,* 1988 WL 236545 (D.D.C. Nov.10, 1988).

The Service has contended throughout these proceedings that the hunt is actually part of an overall "refuge management plan," and that the hunt will, in fact, further the primary purpose of the Refuge in providing an authentic natural habitat for bald eagles. FWS asserts that deer overpopulation in the Refuge is causing its degradation; excessive browsing has shorn away much ground level new growth. Plaintiffs argue that the relevant data on the deer population at Mason Neck is too sparse, dated, and sporadic to provide a reliable indication of the size of the deer herd. Further, because deer are nomadic and can be found throughout the Mason Neck peninsula, including other parklands adjacent to the Refuge, it is far from certain that reducing the herd indigenous to or found in the Refuge itself will solve the problem of overbrowsing. The hunt may not, therefore, significantly reduce the foraging deer population in the Refuge.[9]

Nevertheless, the administrative record reflects that the FWS has monitored the deer presence in the Refuge since the 1970's by several methods, all of which, flawed or not, showed it to be steadily increasing. By

---

9. Plaintiffs actually find nothing about the decision to allow the hunt to be defensible. Not only is the ostensible justification offered for it specious, they contend, but the precautions taken by FWS against injuries to persons or property are inadequate or futile; the disturbance of the bald eagles' tranquility, not to mention their health, a virtual certainty; and the hunt as a means to an end, *i.e.,* a reduction of the deer herd, as cruel as it is inefficient.

1988 the size of the herd was estimated to be roughly double the number the land area could comfortably support. Inspection of the vegetation reinforced the population estimates; browsing to excess was, at least in the Service's opinion, apparent, to knowledgeable observers. Examination of deer carcasses disclosed evidence of malnutrition, a sign, the Service said, that the deer, as well as the flora upon which they fed, were suffering as a result of their overabundance.

Having concluded that the deer population must be reduced, the record shows, the FWS did give thought to alternative means of doing so. Trapping and transportation were rejected as too time-consuming, labor-intensive, and costly, as was chemical sterilization of the deer. The introduction of predators was contraindicated by the proximity of human habitation. FWS was without sufficient personnel at the Refuge to do the job in-house by itself. A well-controlled public hunt was in its judgment, the optimum solution. That it would simultaneously gratify the desire of some local sportsmen for the opportunity to hunt Mason Neck was merely a felicitous by-product.

FWS then turned to the matters of the eagles' and public safety during the hunt. The hunt territory was to be limited to the inland areas, away from the eagles' preferred roosting sites near the river shore. The single extant eagles' nest would be circumscribed by a buffer zone in which neither hunting nor transit would be permitted.[10] And boundaries would be fixed, and well-marked, to keep hunters away from dwellings and roads adjacent to the Refuge.[11]

This Court need only conclude that the agency took account of the relevant factors, and that the decision was not arbitrary and capricious, in order to sustain it. FWS appears to have done as it was obliged to do here, as this district court has concluded in other cases challenging similar decisions by the Service to open other wildlife refuges to deer hunting. [ ] As was true in those cases, this controversy, too, it appears, is animated

---

10. Several studies contained in the record suggest that any human presence, and, in particular, gunfire, disturb eagles, causing them to "flush", or fly out of their roosts and flee from the disturbance. At the preliminary injunction hearing in November, 1990, the Court received extrinsic evidence regarding eagles' sensitivity to the presence of humans, and it concurred with the Secretary's finding that the shotgun hunt would not unduly disturb the eagles. Experience with the 1990 shotgun hunt has not disproved that conclusion.

11. Plaintiffs contend that the proximity of private dwellings to the Refuge, as well as a major thoroughfare which is traversed daily by school buses, makes the hunt inordinately dangerous to humans. Plaintiffs assert that the buffer zones which the FWS has established are inadequate to assure safety, because shotgun blasts can, according to plaintiffs, travel distances in excess of the buffer zones, and because certain hunters will "inevitably" either not see or will ignore the markers delineating the buffer zones.

As the Court observed upon its own visit to the premises of the hunt, the hunt area is separated from homes and from the road by buffer zones of a minimum of 275 and 100 yards, respectively. The boundaries are well-marked by swatches of brightly colored material every several yards, each visible from its nearest neighbor. Additionally, all hunters wishing to participate in the hunt must attend a safety orientation session.

It is possible that some hunters may disregard the markers or disrespect the rules, but as the Court has previously observed, the fact that some people will break the rules does not demonstrate the folly of promulgating such rules in the first place. And again, experience with the 1990 shotgun hunt is reassuring.

primarily by the plaintiffs' fundamental philosophical and public policy disagreement with the government over the wisdom, and perhaps the morality, of the sanctioned killing of wild game on public lands ironically denominated a "wildlife refuge." Neither wisdom nor morality, however, is countenanced as a ground upon which this Court may substitute its judgment as to the proper uses to be made of the Refuge for that of the defendants, even were it wholly in sympathy with plaintiffs.

NOTES

(1) Is *Humane Society* consistent with *Defenders of Wildlife* (the Ruby Lake case)?

(2) Congress has foreclosed uses until the Secretary determines that "such uses are compatible with the major purposes for which such areas were established," Refuge Administration Act, 16 U.S.C. § 668dd(d)(1), or that "such recreational uses will not interfere with the primary purposes for the areas were established," Refuge Recreation Act, 16 U.S.C. § 460K. There are several possible positions on what incidental uses of Refuges are permissible under the standard. For example, must an incidental use be demonstrated to be necessary for the management of wildlife? Is an incidental use permissible if it is neutral? If it is at least not harmful?

Consider the following possibilities:

(a) No deer hunting is permitted despite demonstrable harm to other wildlife caused by their browsing.

(b) No deer hunting is permitted despite demonstrable habitat damage caused by their browsing.

(c) Deer hunting is permitted to reduce deer populations to prevent damage to habitat.

(d) Deer hunting is permitted as long as it has no discernible effect on other wildlife.

(e) Deer hunting is permitted when it is not shown to be actually harmful to other wildlife.

(f) The refuge is managed to produce "surplus" deer for hunters as long as it has no discernible effect on other wildlife.

(g) The refuge is managed to produce "surplus" deer for hunters when it is not shown to be actually harmful to other wildlife.

(h) The refuge is managed to produce deer despite demonstrable harm to other wildlife.

Which is the most analogous to the *Defenders of Wildlife* case? To *Humane Society*? Consider also:

(a) ***Fund for Animals v. Clark***: The National Elk Range abuts Grand Teton National Park on the east; it was reserved to provide winter range for elk. As part of its management of the range, FWS has routinely provided supplemental feed for the elk. As part of a larger dispute with the FWS over its management of the Range, the Fund argued that FWS had violated the Administration Act "by not conducting a compatibility study to determine if the supplemental feeding programs for elk and bison are 'uses' that are compatible with the purpose of the [Elk Range]." The court rejected this argument, holding that the feeding program was not a "use":

> The statute grants the Secretary of the Interior the authority to permit any "use" of a refuge area that is compatible with the major purposes for which the refuge was founded. [ ] The statute gives examples of these "uses" which include hunting, fishing, public recreation and accommodation, and access, [ ], as well as easements for powerlines, telephone lines, canals, ditches, pipelines, and roads. [ ] Although it is clear that, while the listed "uses" are not meant to be all inclusive of the types of activities the Secretary may permit on a refuge, they do encompass a common ingredient. That is, they are all "uses" meant to be performed by third parties or the public. This definition of "use" is further bolstered by the fact that the statute specifically exempts from the compatibility requirement actions taken by "persons authorized to manage" the refuge area. [ ] Clearly, the setting out of feed lines for elk and bison on the NER is not the type of "use" contemplated by the statute as it is performed by "persons authorized to manage" the NER. Since Congress has not spoken unambiguously with respect to whether "uses" include or exclude supplemental feeding programs conducted by persons charged with managing the NER, the court must "defer to the agency's interpretation if it represents a permissible construction of the statute." [ ]

Fund for Animals v. Clark, 27 F.Supp.2d 8 (D.D.C.1998). If the court is correct, was the decision in *Humane Society v. Lujan* correct?

(b) ***Animal Lovers Volunteer Association, Inc. v. Cheney:*** In 1986, the Fish and Wildlife Service (FWS) began trapping red fox at Seal Beach National Wildlife Refuge in order to protect two endangered species, the California least tern and the light-footed clapper rail. The Animal Lovers Volunteer Association brought suit, alleging inter alia that defendant was violating the Administration Act because the trapping program was incompatible with the major purpose of the refuge:

> Plaintiffs contend ... that the decision to control the red fox population in order to save the rare birds is an abuse of discretion since there is no proof that red foxes are preying on the birds.
>
> Plaintiffs further contend that the manner in which the decision is implemented is an abuse of discretion. They contend that the defendants unnecessarily chose to kill the red foxes instead of using alternative methods of controlling the species and that their use of traps that catch animals results in the unnecessary death of animals other than red foxes that are caught in them. They make various additional accusations regarding the inhumane and cruel treatment of the red foxes by the defendants.

The court summarily rejected plaintiffs arguments: "The administrative record demonstrates that the defendants considered all the relevant factors and came to a decision that is rationally supported by substantial evidence." *Animal Lovers Volunteer Association, Inc. v. Cheney,* 795 F.Supp. 994, 999 (C.D.Cal.1992). Is this a "use" of the refuge? If it is not, is the decision nonetheless judicially reviewable as an abuse of discretion under the Administrative Procedure Act?

Recall also the discussion in Chapter 1 of the utilitarian trade-offs in protecting foxes and rails.

(c) *Wilderness Society v. Babbitt*: The Society brought an action challenging the agency's refusal to prepare an EIS on refuge management at the Hart Mountain Wildlife Refuge and alleging a violation of the Administration Act by continuing to allow cattle to graze on the refuge. The court concluded that the FWS had violated the Administration Act by failing to make the requisite determination that grazing was compatible with the refuge's primary purpose:

> In the present case, the Service renewed annual grazing permits without regard to the incompatibility of grazing to the Refuge's purposes. As early as December 1989, the Service was aware that its grazing practices were damaging the Refuge. The Refuge Manager warned that "there is no question that current grazing practices causing this damage are negatively impacting fish and wildlife habitats and are (1) in violation of the refuge's executive orders and (2) currently not compatible with the uses for which the refuges were established."
>
> The Refuge Manager's report did not foreclose the possibility that the Service could formulate a grazing plan that would be compatible with purposes of the Refuge. Based upon this report, however, the Service had a duty to investigate the compatibility of grazing with the Refuge's purposes prior to permitting grazing on the Refuge. Nonetheless, the Service continued its same practices, issuing grazing permits for 1990 without any compatibility determination.

Wilderness Society v. Babbitt, 5 F.3d 383 (9th Cir.1993). The dissenting judge argued that the Administration Act applied only prospectively: "The Refuge Act does not specify that the Service has a duty to make a compatibility determination to permit the continuation of a preexisting use of the Refuge. *See* 16 U.S.C. § 668dd(d)(1)(A). The majority holds that the Act *required* the Service to complete a compatibility analysis before permitting any more grazing, a practice that had been permitted on the Refuge since 1936. I find a complete absence of authority to support the requirement." *Id.*

(3) **"compatibility with . . . "**: Despite the Administration Act's compatibility standard—which was applicable nation-wide—it was the individual purposes of each refuge (as set forth in the statute, Executive Order, or other document creating it) that remained the management touchstone. That is, the uniformity nominally legislated by the Administration Act was more apparent than real since the "compatibility" of a particular, non-wildlife use depended upon the major purposes for which the refuge was established: a refuge that was acquired to protect an endangered species, for example, was likely to have a dramatically different set of compatible uses than was a migratory waterfowl refuge. *Cf. New England Naturist Association v. Larsen*, 692 F.Supp. 75 (D.R.I.1988) (upholding decision to close refuge entirely to protect endangered species).

PERSPECTIVES

A humane alternative: In *Humane Society v. Lujan*, plaintiff sought to prevent the killing of deer. A recent article in the Humane Society newsletter offers the group's perspective on a humane solution to burgeoning deer populations:

> Pushing each plunger one hundred times, Rick Naugle, HSUS research associate for Wildlife and Habitat Protection, patiently blends the contents of two connected syringes. He squirts the mixture into an orange dart, places the dart in a blowpipe, and moves the blowpipe to his lips. With a puff, the dart soars across space, strikes the hip of a surprised female deer, injects its contents, and falls to the ground. After a few seconds, the does resumes feeding, but next spring she probably will not produce a fawn.

> This scene has been repeated hundreds of times since September 1993, when HSUS began a daring experiment at Fire Island National Seashore in New York.... The unique challenge was to administer the vaccine without capturing, handling, or even touching the animals—a requirement established by the National Park Service (NPS), which manages most of Fire Island.

> What brought The HSUS and the contraception research team to Fire Island? In the late 1980s, deer were becoming increasingly frequent visitors to the backyards and boardwalks of the Fires Island communities. The deer became remarkably tame, tolerating the approach of people within a few yards, and sometimes seeking handouts. Although the animals endeared themselves to may of the human residents, complaints about the deer began to increase. Concerns were also raised—probably not well-founded—about the impact of deer on the unique barrier island ecology. In response, the NPS and the New York State Department of Environmental Services (NYSDEC) organized a recreational hunt of these tame creatures.

> Not surprisingly, the hunt was a disaster, for both the animals and the people. To the horror of residents, wounded animals struggled in pain on the community boardwalks.... In its wake, the hunt left a community torn apart and a deer population whose numbers would be fully restored—and then some—by the next fawning season.

> [The search for an alternative led to Jay Kirkpatrick, Ph.D. and John Turner, Ph.D.] who had recently demonstrated that porcine zona pellucida (PZP) immunocontraceptive vaccine prevented pregnancies in captive white-tailed deer. Equally important, Drs. Kirkpatrick and Turner had successfully delivered the vaccine in the field to the famous ponies of Assateague Island National Seashore in Maryland. If it could be done with wild ponies, why not wild deer?

> Drs. Kirkpatrick and Turner were attracted by the opportunity to conduct a novel experiment on an accessible population of free-ranging wildlife and to help a community live peaceably with its wild neighbors. But what sealed the deal was an extraordinary offer from the residents of Fire Island: they would not only fully fund the field research but

also organize a network of volunteers to identify and attract individual does for PZP vaccine treatment. . . .

We treated seventy-four does that first fall, each one receiving the two injections necessary to maximize effectiveness. During the following spring and summer, the deer monitors searched for fawns and found that the treated animals had produced 62 percent fewer fawns that they had the year before.

. . .

We have learned an enormous amount since then. We have treated deer at Fire Island every autumn since 1993. The effectiveness of the vaccine has increased with successive annual booster shots, so that, on average, only 18 percent of the treated deer become pregnant.

Allen T. Rutberg, *Darting Does*, ALL ANIMALS (ANIMAL UPDATE) 2, 2–3 (Summer 1999) [Humane Society of United States newsletter]. What concerns might there be about the effects of deer "on the unique barrier island ecology"? What are the potential limitations of the approach?

The problem confronting residents of Fire Island is being repeated across the country as wildlife habitat is increasingly suburbanized and as some species—such as deer—have increasingly adapted to life among humans. Deer-control campaigns are increasingly divisive as animal rights proponents battle landowners who view deer increasingly as nuisances if not threats. In Millford, New Jersey, for example, there were over 100 deer-automobile collisions in 1999 as the town's deer population has increased dramatically. Rather than hiring sharpshooters and face the divisiveness that follows, the town chose instead to adopt a costly plan of trapping the deer and shipping them to an upstate New York farm—where they will be sold to venison ranches or slaughterhouses since New York prohibits releasing them into the wild. Andrew Jacobs, *New Jersey Town Exports Unwanted Deer out of State*, N.Y. TIMES, Apr. 23, 2000. Recall also the discussion in Chapter 3 on the power of landowners to kill wildlife to protect their land.

d. NATIONAL WILDLIFE REFUGE SYSTEM IMPROVEMENT ACT OF 1997

Congress revised the management provisions applicable to the Refuge System when it enacted the National Wildlife Refuge System Improvement Act of 1997, Pub. L. No. 105–57, 111 Stat. 1254 (codified into the Refuge Administration Act at 16 U.S.C. § 668dd–668ee). The Act modifies the previous management laws in three ways: it announces a mission for the entire Refuge System, defines compatibility for non-wildlife uses of refuge lands, and requires the FWS to engage in land and resource planning.

(1) The mission statement: The Refuge Improvement Act enunciates a new, systemwide Mission Statement to guide the management of refuges:

The mission of the System is to administer a national network of lands and waters for the conservation, management, and where appropriate, restoration of the fish, wildlife and plant resources and their habitats

within the United States for the benefit of present and future generations of Americans.

16 U.S.C. § 668dd(a)(2).

The Act defines the crucial term "conservation"—as well as its statutory synonym "management"—as "to sustain and, where appropriate, restore and enhance, healthy populations of fish, wildlife, and plants utilizing
. . . methods and procedures associated with modern scientific resource
programs." *Id.* § 668ee(4). The statement thus requires refuge managers to
focus on "protection, research, census, law enforcement, habitat management, propagation, live trapping and transplantation, and regulated taking" as necessary to at least sustain healthy populations and the habitats
on which they depend. Furthermore, under some unstated circumstances
(*i.e.,* "where appropriate") there is a further mission to "restore and
enhance, healthy populations." § 4(3).

The Mission Statement is fleshed out in several directives that the
FWS is required to satisfy in administering the System. On the one hand,
the Act mandates that the Secretary shall:

> * * * "provide for the conservation of fish, wildlife, and plants, and
> their habitats within the System;"

> * * * "ensure that the biological integrity, diversity, and environmen-
> tal health of the System are maintained for the benefit of present and
> future generations;"

> * * * "plan and direct the continued growth of the System in a
> manner that is best designed to accomplish the mission of the System,
> to contribute to the conservation of the ecosystems of the United
> States, to complement efforts of States and other Federal agencies to
> conserve fish and wildlife and their habitats, and to increase support
> for the System and participation from conservation partners and the
> public;"

> * * * "monitor the status and trends of fish, wildlife, and plants in
> each refuge."

Id. § 668dd(4)(A)-(C), (N). On the other hand, the Act also mandates that
the Secretary shall:

> * * * "recognize compatible wildlife-dependent recreational uses as the
> priority general public uses of the System through which the American
> public can develop an appreciation for fish and wildlife;"

> * * * "ensure that opportunities are provided within the System for
> compatible wildlife-dependent recreational uses;"

> * * * "ensure that priority general public uses of the System receive
> enhanced consideration over other general public uses in planning and
> management of the System;"

> * * * "provide increased opportunities for families to experience com-
> patible wildlife-dependent recreation, particularly opportunities for
> parents and their children to safely engage in traditional outdoor
> activities, such as fishing and hunting;"

* * * "continue, consistent with existing laws and interagency agreements, authorized or permitted uses of units of the System by other Federal agencies, including those necessary to facilitate military preparedness."

Id. § (H)-(L).

As is often the case, Congress has crafted a wish list of potentially incompatible objectives and turned the problem over to an agency. The challenge facing FWS is to craft regulations and guidelines that provide additional clarity and guidance for the managers of individual refuges who will be faced with the difficult problems of balancing such potentially conflicting mandates.

The initial indications are that the FWS views the Refuge Improvement Act as fundamentally redefining its mandate by unequivocally establishing conservation as the dominant management criterion and by clarifying the hierarchy of potential uses of refuges. In the agency's initial statements on the Act, it has offered a "new vision" of the Refuge System: "The vision stresses the basic principles that *wildlife comes first,* that *ecosystems, biodiversity and Wilderness* are vital concepts in refuge management, that refuges must be *healthy,* and that growth of the System must be *strategic.*" U.S. FISH & WILDLIFE SERVICE, FULFILLING THE PROMISE: VISIONS FOR WILDLIFE, HABITAT, PEOPLE AND LEADERSHIP IN PREPARATION FOR THE NATIONAL WILDLIFE REFUGE SYSTEM CONFERENCE, KEYSTONE, COLORADO, OCTOBER 18–22, 1998 (2d draft 1998). FWS thus has chosen to emphasize the ecological standards the Act imposes on refuge acquisition and administration: to "ensure that the biological integrity, diversity, and environmental health of the System is maintained for the benefit of present and future generations of Americans." *Id.* § 668(a)(4)(B).

(a) **Biological integrity:** The concept of "integrity" has come to have a fairly distinct meaning among conservation biologists: "integrity" refers to a system's "wholeness," particularly with regard to evolutionary and interdependent biogeographic processes; it is "the capability of supporting and maintaining a balanced, integrated, adaptive community of organisms having a species composition, diversity, and functional organization comparable to that of natural habitat of the region." J.R. Karr & D.R. Dudley, *Ecological Perspective on Water Quality Goals,* 5 ENVIRONMENTAL MANAGEMENT 55–68 (1981); *see also* P.L. Angermeier & J.R. Karr, *Biological Integrity Versus Biological Diversity as Policy Directives,* 44 BIOSCIENCE 690–697 (1994). The difficulty is that this definition contrasts sharply with the highly manipulated impoundments that characterize many of the waterfowl refuges. Such refuges almost certainly do not have the species composition, diversity, or functional organization that they would have in their unimpounded state. On the other hand, they may reproduce a now-missing composition, diversity, and functional organization—and perhaps this is what Congress meant since it clearly did not intend to produce a massive realignment in refuge operations.

(b) **Biodiversity:** Managing for biodiversity provides a similar range of challenges. The term refers to the variety and variability among living organisms and the ecological complex in which these organisms occur. The term encompasses different levels of biological organization—including communities, species, populations, individual organisms and genes—and different spatial contexts—ranging from home ranges to the biosphere. Refuge managers must decide what this mandate means, given a pre-existing set of refuges with ongoing uses and historically diverse purposes. As the FWS recently noted, "No clear guidance has been forthcoming on how to prioritize efforts to maintain biodiversity compared to other programs aimed at conservation of trust resources." U.S. FISH & WILDLIFE SERVICE, FULFILLING THE PROMISE: VISIONS FOR WILDLIFE, HABITAT, PEOPLE AND LEADERSHIP IN PREPARATION FOR THE NATIONAL WILDLIFE REFUGE SYSTEM CONFERENCE, KEYSTONE, COLORADO, OCTOBER 18–22, 1998 (2d draft 1998).

(c) **Ecosystem health:** Ecosystem or environmental health is a value-laden metaphor that links the condition of an ecosystem to the condition of an individual organism. *E.g.,* G.N. Norton, *Ecological Health and Sustainable Resource Management, in* ECOLOGICAL ECONOMICS (R. Costanza ed. 1991); D. Wicklum & R.W. Davies, *Ecosystem Health and Integrity?,* 73 CANADIAN J. BOTANY 997–1000 (1995). "Health" is a symbol for a complex set of ecological realities that are thought to be desirable, rather than a condition that can be measured or defined precisely in value-free ways. R.J. Steedman, *Ecosystem Health as a Management Goal,* 13 J.N. AM. BENTHOLOGICAL SOC'Y 605–610 (1994). Accordingly, efforts to measure or prescribe ecosystem health must begin by recognizing the values and judgments—including both ecological and cultural components—that are to be employed.

(2) **Compatibility determinations:** The second significant change contained in the Refuge Improvement Act involves the creation of procedures and the elaboration of the standard for making "compatibility" determinations. Under the Administration Act, refuge managers were provided no statutory guidance beyond the term "compatible." The Refuge Improvement Act modifies the compatibility determination requirement in three ways. First, it amplifies the previous guidance on what non-wildlife uses are to be permitted on refuges. Second, the Act also establishes a procedure for making compatibility determinations. Third, the Act creates a hierarchy of three categories of uses of refuge lands.

(a) **Additional guidance on "compatibility":** Under the compatibility standard established by the Administration Act, uses such as hunting, fishing, mining, and grazing have been permitted on refuges. The Refuge Improvement Act continues this tradition—with a shift in emphasis. Recall the language of the Administration Act: FWS may permit the "use of any area ... for any purpose ... compatible with the major purposes for which [the area] was established." 16 U.S.C. § 460k. Two points to note: first, "compatible" is entirely undefined; second, as *Schwenke* demonstrated, the standard focuses on individual units.

The Refuge Improvement Act addresses both points. First, it defines "compatible use" as a use that "will not materially interfere with or detract from the fulfillment of the mission of the System or the purposes of the refuge." *Id.* § 668ee(1). The "not materially interfere with or detract from" language provides additional guidance both to refuge managers and to courts. Furthermore, by incorporating the Mission Statement's conservation mandate, the new compatibility standard increases the emphasis on sustaining and restoring fish and wildlife populations. Whether it will restrain some of the more egregious uses of refuges remains to be seen.

Second, the Improvement Act also affects the *Schwenke* problem. Not only does the Act require compatibility with *both* the mission statement *and* the purposes of the refuge, it also states that "each refuge shall be managed to fulfill the mission of the System, as well as the specific purposes for which that refuge was established." *Id.* § 668dd(a)(3)(A). This movement toward a systemwide perspective is muted by the requirement that "if a conflict exists between the purposes of a refuge and the mission of the System, the conflict shall be resolved in a manner that first protects the purposes of the refuge." *Id.* § 668dd(a)(4)(D). Nonetheless, although Congress did not choose to consolidate completely the system's management requirements, the Improvement Act is a step toward a national system.

(b) Making compatibility determinations: In addition to the guidance on the meaning of the term "compatible," the Act also sets out a procedure for making compatibility determinations. The Act requires refuge managers to prepare a written evaluation of non-wildlife uses, to solicit public comment on the evaluation, and expeditiously to terminate non-compatible uses. *Id.* § 668dd(d)(3).

(c) Priority uses: Finally, the Act emphasizes that some wildlife-related human uses are "priority" uses. *Id.* § 668dd(a)(3)(C). The Act establishes a hierarchy of uses: (1) the dominant, wildlife-conservation uses; (2) "wildlife-dependent recreation," which is defined as "hunting, fishing, wildlife observation and photography, or environmental education and interpretation," *id.* § 668ee(2); recreational use must be "compatible," *id.* § 668ee(1); and (3) any new or renewed use that is determined to be a "compatible use," *id.* § 668dd(d)(3). Wildlife remains the dominant use, but "compatible wildlife-dependent recreational uses" are designated as "the priority general public uses of the System," are to receive "priority consideration in refuge planning and management" and "should be facilitated," *id.* § 668dd(a)(3)(C). All other "compatible uses" are at the bottom of the hierarchy—they are to be permitted but not facilitated.

The congressional report accompanying the Improvement Act makes it clear that the use of the term "facilitated" in describing the agency's obligation with regard to wildlife-dependent recreation was carefully chosen. H.R. Rep. No. 106, 105th Congress, 1st Session. (1997). The phrase "should be facilitated" falls short of a definite requirement; in the language of the Report, it is an "encouragement, but not a requirement." *Id.* Read together, the Report and the statute indicate that wildlife-dependent recreation is an important use of refuges—but "wildlife and wildlife conservation must come first." Thus, the Act reinforces the "dominant use" concept that has historically characterized the system.

But: Is "compatibility" a suitable standard for decisions on managing biological systems? What is the focus of a compatibility determination? Will the decisionmaker focus on the affirmative conservation mandate? Will the decisionmaker focus on predicting and mitigating impacts? Does the standard permit consideration of intensities—that is, of the fact that even low-impact recreation has an impact that may become incompatible if the number of recreationists increases sufficiently?

(3) Comprehensive conservation plans: The third change mandated by the Improvement Act is a planning process that is intended to guide the management of individual refuges. The planning process is the core of the Improvement Act. The plans are an example of the increasing emphasis on land and resource planning in the management of federal land systems. For example, the National Forest Management Act required the Forest Service to prepare land management plans for each forest, *id.* § 1600–1614; the Federal Land Policy and Management Act imposed similar planning obligations on the Bureau of Land Management, *id.* § 1701–1781.

Federal land and resource planning is a three-step process. *See, e.g.,* George C. Coggins & Parthenia B. Evans, *Multiple Use, Sustained Yield Planning on the Public Lands,* 53 U. COLO. L. REV. 411 (1982); Charles F. Wilkinson & H. Michael Anderson, *Land and Resource Planning in the National Forests,* 64 OR. L. REV. 1 (1985). First, the agency collects data to determine the inventory of resources present within the planning unit. Second, the agency prepares an integrated plan that is developed with public participation. The plan assesses resources and addresses competing uses. Third, the plan is implemented through a series of agency actions.

The Refuge Improvement Act imposes a similar planning mandate on the FWS. In drafting the plans, the FWS is required to consider the resources present on the refuge—"the distribution, migration patterns, and abundance of fish, wildlife, and plant populations and related habitats," 16 U.S.C. § 668dd(e)(2)(B), and "the archeological and cultural values of the planning unit," *id.* § 668(e)(2)(C), for example—as well as the purposes of the refuge, *id.* § 668dd(e)(2)(A). The agency is required to solicit public comment on draft plans and to consult with adjacent landowners and state wildlife agencies. *Id.* § 668dd(e)(3)(A)-(b). Once a plan is adopted, the agency is required to manage each refuge "in a manner consistent with the plan." *Id.* § 668dd(e)(1)(E). The Act's Mission Statement as well as its compatibility determinations are to be implemented primarily through the development of "comprehensive conservation plans." *Id.* § 668dd(e).

The Comprehensive Conservation Plans thus are the documents through which the conservation mandate of the Mission Statement and the compatibility of non-wildlife uses are to be balanced and implemented on individual refuges.

For a general overview and assessment of the Improvement Act, see Robert L. Fischman, *The National Wildlife Refuge System and the Hallmarks of Modern Organic Legislation,* 29 *Ecology L.Q.* ___ (forthcoming 2002); Kevin Gergely, J. Michael Scott, & Dale Goble, *A New Direction for the U.S. National Wildlife Refuges: The National Wildlife Refuge System Improvement Act of 1997,* 20 NATURAL AREAS J. 107 (2000).

Wyoming v. United States

District Court for the District of Wyoming.
61 F.Supp.2d 1209 (1999).

■ BRIMMER, D.J.:—.... This case is the result of a dispute between the State of Wyoming ("Wyoming") and the United States Fish and Wildlife

Service ("FWS") over the proper management of brucellosis on the National Elk Refuge ("Elk Refuge") outside of Jackson, Wyoming. Brucellosis is a bacterial borne pathogen, strains of which may infect the mammary glands and reproductive tracts of many ungulates, including elk and cattle. Brucellosis often results in spontaneous abortions among newly infected animals. This contagious disease is spread when infected animals come into contact with uninfected animals. Studies are inconclusive whether the disease is spread between species, such as from elk to cattle, or vice versa. The efficacy of vaccinating elk against brucellosis with a cattle-specific vaccine is also disputed.

In the winter, Wyoming vaccinates elk against brucellosis on several state-operated feeding grounds. Wyoming filed this lawsuit when the FWS refused to allow Wyoming Game and Fish personnel to enter the Elk Refuge for the purpose of vaccinating elk. Wyoming argues that although the Elk Refuge is Federal public land, it is nevertheless entitled to vaccinate the elk on the Refuge regardless of whether the FWS objects to this type of management.

. . .

[The court initially considered and dismissed the state's claims based on its inherent sovereignty and on the Tenth Amendment because the state was unable to establish that the federal government had waived its sovereign immunity from suit as to those claims.]

D.   Count III: Review of Agency Action

Plaintiffs' third Count, plead in the alternative, asks this Court for a review of agency action under the provisions of the Administrative Procedure Act, 5 U.S.C. § 703. . . .

The provision of the Refuge Act upon which Plaintiffs rely states:

Nothing in this Act shall be construed as affecting the authority, jurisdiction, or responsibility of the several States to manage, control, or regulate fish and resident wildlife under State law or regulations in any area within the System. Regulations permitting hunting or fishing of fish and resident wildlife within the System shall be, to the extent practicable, consistent with State fish and wildlife laws, regulations, and management plans.

16 U.S.C. § 668dd(m).

. . . . As stated above, the mission of the Refuge Act is to provide a national network of lands whereby wildlife can be managed and preserved for future generations. According to this mission statement, Plaintiffs' interests do not appear to be among those that Congress intended to protect or benefit through the Refuge Act. In fact, Plaintiffs' alleged sovereign interest in managing wildlife appears to be at odds with the Refuge Act's mission of creating a "national network" of management. Allowing each state to manage wildlife on the national refuges within its borders would thwart the goal of creating a nationwide network of lands to be managed by one entity. . . .

2. The Refuge Act Does Not Give Wyoming Mutual Rights to Manage Wildlife on Federal Lands

Plaintiffs argue that the Court may hold unlawful Defendant Babbitt's ultra vires actions found to be not in accordance with law and in excess of statutory limitation. [ ] The crux of Plaintiffs' claims is that Wyoming has "sovereign authority" to manage and control wildlife on the Elk Refuge. Thus, Plaintiffs contend that Defendant Babbitt's actions infringing upon that authority are ultra vires. The Court agrees that § 706(2)(A) and (C) of the APA allow the Court to review ultra vires actions. However, for the reasons stated below, the Court finds that Defendant Babbitt did not act in excess of his authority: Wyoming does not have mutual rights to manage wildlife on the Elk Refuge.

Plaintiffs rely almost exclusively on the Refuge Act's "saving clause," *supra,* as evidence that Congress intended to leave the "sovereign authority" to manage wildlife on the Refuges with the States. However, as discussed in Section C, the States do not have sovereign authority to manage wildlife on Refuge lands. The Property Clause gives the Federal Government complete power over particular public property that Congress has entrusted to it. *See Kleppe v. New Mexico,* 426 U.S. 529, 540 (1976). This "complete power * * * necessarily includes the power to regulate and protect the wildlife living there." *Id.* at 540–41. Thus, Wyoming does not have "authority, jurisdiction, or responsibility" to manage elk on the Refuge. To interpret the decision of the Secretary that is being challenged in this matter as "affecting" such "authority, jurisdiction, or responsibility" would be erroneous. 16 U.S.C. § 668dd(m).

Even if the Court were to find that Plaintiffs, at one time, possessed the sovereign authority to manage wildlife on federal lands (which the Court does not), Plaintiffs no longer possess such authority because the Refuge Act grants the authority to manage wildlife on refuge lands to the Secretary of the Interior. Congress has intended, through the sweeping and general language of the Refuge Act, to vest such authority in the Secretary. The "scheme of federal regulation is so comprehensive [in this case] as to make it a reasonable inference that Congress intended to occupy the field." [ ] Several provisions of the Refuge Act express Congress's intention in this regard. . . .

Congress created the National Wildlife Refuge System for the "purpose of consolidating the authorities relating to the various categories of areas that are administered by the Secretary for the conservation of fish and wildlife, * * * including * * * all lands, waters, and interests therein administered by the Secretary * * *" through the FWS. 16 U.S.C. § 668dd(a)(1). The mission of the Refuge System is to "administer a national network of lands and waters for the conservation, *management,* and where appropriate, restoration of the fish, wildlife, and plant resources and their habitats within the United States." 16 U.S.C. § 668dd(a)(2) (emphasis added). Through these provisions, Congress undoubtedly envisioned a nationwide, cohesively administered network of lands and waters where wildlife would be managed and conserved under the direction of the Secretary. There is no indication in these provisions that Congress intended to curtail the Secretary's power or leave any residual power to the States.

Congress also provided that in administering the Refuge System, "the Secretary *shall*," "provide for the conservation of * * * wildlife," and "ensure the biological integrity, diversity, and environmental health of the System." 16 U.S.C. § 668dd(a)(4) (emphasis added). The Secretary is also authorized, "under such regulations as he may prescribe, to * * * permit the use of any area within the System for any purpose, including but not limited to hunting, fishing, * * * and access whenever he determines that such uses are compatible with the major purposes" of the Refuge System. 16 U.S.C. § 668dd(d)(1)(A). To give teeth to the Secretary's power to limit activities on refuge lands, Congress made it criminal for any person to knowingly "enter, use, or otherwise occupy any such area for any purpose; unless such activities are performed by persons authorized to manage such area." 16 U.S.C. § 668dd(c).

To the Court, this broad language surely indicates that Congress meant to give the Secretary complete administrative and management authority over national refuges. For example, Section (d)(1)(A) indicates that the Secretary has sole discretion to decide who may have access to the Elk Refuge and what activities may be conducted there.[8] When this language is given its full and expansive plain meaning, it is evident that Congress left little room for any other entity to exert management control over national refuges. Indeed, the Court cannot conceive how a program to vaccinate elk on a national refuge would not fall within the scope of the Secretary's duties of "conservation of fish and wildlife," § 668dd(a)(1), "conservation [and] management * * * of fish, wildlife and plant resources and their habitats," § 668dd(a)(2), or providing for the "biological integrity, diversity, and environmental health of the System." 16 U.S.C. § 668dd(a)(4)(B).

The "saving clause" relied upon by Plaintiffs does not alter the conclusion that the Secretary has complete authority to manage the wildlife on national refuges. Again, that provision, entitled "State authority," provides:

> Nothing in this Act shall be construed as affecting the authority, jurisdiction, or responsibility of the several States to manage, control, or regulate fish and resident wildlife under State law or regulations in any area within the System. Regulations permitting hunting or fishing of fish and resident wildlife within the System shall be, to the extent practicable, consistent with State fish and wildlife laws, regulations, and management plans.

16 U.S.C. § 668dd(m).

First, to interpret this provision as allowing the mere existence of a State statute or regulation to dictate policies and activities on a federal refuge, where Congress has already carefully crafted a system for its administration by the Secretary, would be at odds with the vast majority of the Refuge Act's other provisions. It is a well accepted rule of statutory

---

8. This section alone supports the position that Defendant Babbitts' actions were not ultra vires; the Secretary had discretion to decide what activities may be conducted on the Refuge.

interpretation that the provisions of a statute should not be interpreted in a manner that renders one part of the statute inoperative. [ ] In this case, adopting Plaintiffs' interpretation of the "State authority" provision would render a large part of the Refuge Act inoperative.

A more reasonable interpretation of the "saving clause" is that it reflects a Congressional intent for states to retain their role as primary managers of hunting and fishing of resident wildlife within their borders as consistent with federal law. The second sentence of § 668dd(m) lends credence to this interpretation when it directs that regulations promulgated by the Secretary "permitting hunting or fishing of fish and resident wildlife within the System shall be, to the extent practicable, consistent with State fish and wildlife laws, regulations, and management plans." Indeed, this second sentence supports the proposition that Congress intended the Secretary's authority to be paramount—the Secretary only needs to be consistent with State law "to the extent practicable."

Plaintiffs' exclusive reliance upon the first sentence of this provision is misplaced. They cannot latch on to one sentence of an entire statute and ignore the rest, especially when the remainder of the statute (indeed, even the remainder of their specific provision) strongly supports a contrary position. The Court's interpretation of the "State authority" provision gives it a meaning consistent with the entire Refuge Act, a result dictated by principles of statutory interpretation.

Plaintiffs also argue that Congress intended, by the savings clause, to maintain the "status quo" with regard to management authority on the Refuge. The status quo, according to Plaintiffs, was that the States traditionally managed the wildlife, even on federal lands. Plaintiffs refer the Court to the legislative history associated with the provision that would ultimately become 16 U.S.C. § 668dd(m). They cite the following language:

> This amendment added a new provision to section 4(c) of the House bill stating that this legislation shall not be construed to affect the authority, jurisdiction, or responsibility of the States relating to fish and resident wildlife in any area within the National Wildlife Refuge System. This provision is designed to maintain the status quo with respect to the dispute between the States and the Department of the Interior over the issue of which entity has authority to regulate fish and resident wildlife in such areas. Both parties to the dispute have agreed that it does maintain the status quo. It will permit them to resolve the dispute through future negotiations.

Although the Plaintiffs argue that the legislative history cited above supports their position, the Court finds the opposite to be true. Granted, this language refers to maintaining the "status quo." However, the status quo refers not to the authority of the several States to manage wildlife on federal lands, but to the *dispute* that state agencies and the Department of Interior had over which entity should manage the wildlife in these areas. Congress acknowledged that dispute. So, rather than shifting the authority over federal lands away from the federal government, Congress intended to "maintain the status quo relative to the dispute," so as to permit the parties involved in the dispute "to negotiate and resolve the problem at a future date." S. Rep. No. 1463 (1966), *reprinted in* 1966 U.S.C.C.A.N. 3348....

Congress recognized the ongoing conflict between the state and federal entities and encouraged the parties, in the language of the Refuge Act, to negotiate a resolution to their disputes. For example, Congress directed the Secretary to "ensure effective coordination, interaction, and cooperation with owners of land adjoining refuges and the fish and wildlife agency of the States in which the units of the System are located." 16 U.S.C. § 668dd(a)(4)(E). Nowhere in this language does Congress indicate that the States either have or retain a sovereign right to manage wildlife on federal lands. Congress recognized an ongoing dispute between the entities and instructed the Secretary to work cooperatively to resolve any disputes to the extent practicable. Neither this Congressional instruction nor the saving clause require the Secretary to yield to the management policies of the States. To so read the Refuge Act would violate both its plain language and intent.

. . .

. . . . Because the Refuge Act does not give Plaintiffs a right to manage wildlife on the Elk Refuge, the Court can fashion no remedy and has no jurisdiction over their claims. Plaintiffs have failed to state a claim upon which relief may be granted. Defendants' motion to dismiss Count III is thus **GRANTED.** Count III of Plaintiffs' Amended Complaint is **DISMISSED.**

. . .

NOTES

(1) Was the Improvement Act a necessary component of the court's decision? That is, would the result have been different under the Administration Act?

Although the court resolved the controversy through traditional statutory interpretation, it could have phrased the issue in terms of preemption: Did federal law directly or indirectly preempt the application of state law. Ordinarily, state and local laws apply on federal lands, and wildlife management is a field in which the federal government has traditionally deferred to state decisionmaking. Preemption analysis in the federal lands setting is considered in Chapter 6, Section 3(b).

(2) Would the Improvement Act have changed any of the other decisions in this section?

SECTION 4. RESTRICTED-USE LAND MANAGEMENT SYSTEMS: INDIRECTLY PROTECTING WILDLIFE HABITAT

The National Wildlife Refuge system is the only federal land management system with wildlife protection as its primary purpose. Other land management systems, however, also indirectly benefit wildlife. In this section, we look at three systems—the Wilderness Preservation System, the Wild and Scenic River System, and the National Park System. Each system comprises a collection of widely dispersed islands of wildlife habitat. Each system is also governed by organic statutes that contain congressional guidance, although, as with the National Wildlife Refuge System, individual units in the systems are often subject to idiosyncratic management requirements.

There are other variations as well. Units in the National Park System are governed by a single federal agency, the National Park Service, an agency in the Department of the Interior. Wilderness areas, on the other hand, are subjected to more fragmented control. One of the compromises in the Wilderness Act of 1964 was the congressional decision not to create a new agency to manage wilderness areas—as had been done to manage the national forests, national parks, and wildlife refuges. Instead, lands designated for wilderness protection were to be managed by the agency that had managed the lands before their selection for wilderness status. The National Wild and Scenic River System operates in an analogous manner. No single agency manages designated waterways. The federally owned lands along designated waterways continue to be managed by the land-managing agency, subject to the special rules applicable to the System. For many designated rivers, however, much of the riparian land is not owned by the federal government, and restrictions on these lands result from the Wild and Scenic Rivers Act and its implementing regulations.

a.   THE WILDERNESS PRESERVATION SYSTEM

A wilderness, in contrast with those areas where man and his own works dominate the landscape, is hereby recognized as an area where the earth and its community of life are untrammeled by man, where man himself is a visitor who does not remain. An area of wilderness is further defined to mean in this chapter an area of undeveloped Federal land retaining its primeval character and influence, without permanent improvements or human habitation, which is protected and managed so as to preserve its natural conditions and which (1) generally appears to have been affected primarily by the forces of nature, with the imprint of man's work substantially unnoticeable; (2) has outstanding opportunities for solitude or a primitive and unconfined type of recreation; (3) has at least five thousand acres of land or is of sufficient size as to make practicable its preservation and use in an unimpaired condition; and (4) may also contain ecological, geological, or other features of scientific, educational, scenic, or historical value.

16 U.S.C. § 1131(c).

NOTES

(1) The Wilderness Act of 1964: When Congress enacted the Wilderness Act, 16 U.S.C. § 1131–1136, it enunciated a clear preservation policy:

In order to assure that an increasing population, accompanied by expanding settlement and growing mechanization, does not occupy and modify all areas within the United States ... leaving no lands designated for preservation and protection in their natural condition, it is hereby declared to be the policy of the Congress to secure for the American people of present and future generations the benefits of an enduring resource of wilderness.

Id. § 1131(a). Implementation of this policy has led to the designation of some 94 million acres (almost 57 million of which are in Alaska) of public lands as wilderness.

(a) Designation process: Unlike the National Wildlife Refuge System with its multiple methods for designating land for inclusion in the system, land can be included in a wilderness area only if Congress so chooses. The Wilderness Act established a process under which the Secretary of Agriculture (as to lands in the National Forest System) and the Secretary of the Interior (as to the National Park System and the National Wildlife Refuge System) were to propose areas under their jurisdiction to the President who would in turn recommend them to Congress for inclusion in the system. The presidential recommendations "shall become effective only if so provided by an Act of Congress." *Id.* § 1132(b), (c). In 1976, Congress extended the wilderness review and recommendation requirements to lands managed by the Bureau of Land Management. 43 U.S.C. § 1782(c). On the designation process, see *Parker v. United States,* 309 F.Supp. 593 (D.Colo.1970), *aff'd,* 448 F.2d 793 (10th Cir.1971), *cert. denied,* 405 U.S. 989 (1972).

(b) Management requirements: When an area is designated for inclusion in the system, the agency administering the area "shall be responsible for preserving the wilderness character of the area." 16 U.S.C. § 1133(b). Congress specifically provided, "there shall be no commercial enterprise and . . . no temporary road, no use of motor vehicles, motorized equipment or motorboats, no landing of aircraft, no other forms of mechanized transport, and no structure or installation within any such area." *Id* § 1133(c). These prohibitions are "subject to existing rights," *id.,* to continued mining and mineral leasing (initiated prior to 1984), *id.* § 1133(d)(2)-(3), to the possibility of water resource development projects, and continued livestock grazing, *id.* § 1133(d)(4).

(2) The Wilderness Act and Wildlife: The Act barely mentions wildlife. The celebratory definition of "wilderness" does speak of "the earth and its community of life." *Id.* § 1131(c). And Congress was careful to state, "Nothing in this Act shall be construed as affecting the jurisdiction or responsibilities of the several States with respect to wildlife and fish in the national forests." *Id.* § 1133(c)(7). Nonetheless, the Act is an important source of habitat protection because of the size of the blocks of land that are protected against development. Such large, relatively undisturbed tracts are essential, particularly for large mammals such as grizzly bears.

* * *

The difference between the restrictions imposed by the Wilderness Act and the discretion accorded the National Park Service (NPS) under its Organic Act are the subject of the following case:

Alaska Wildlife Alliance v. Jensen

Ninth Circuit Court of Appeals.
108 F.3d 1065 (1997).

■ WRIGHT, C.J.:—We must decide the extent to which federal statutes restrict commercial fishing in Alaska's Glacier Bay National Park (the

Park). We hold that ... commercial fishing is statutorily prohibited in the Park's designated wilderness areas, but not in its non-wilderness areas.

I

Plaintiffs sued the Secretary of the Interior and officials of the National Park Service, claiming that commercial fishing in the Park violates certain federal statutes. Plaintiffs interpret the [National Park Service] Organic Act ... and the Alaska National Interest Lands Conservation Act ("ANILCA") to prohibit commercial fishing throughout the Park. The Park Service concedes that commercial fishing is prohibited by statute in the Park's wilderness areas. It maintains, however, that the statutes give it discretion to permit commercial fishing in non-wilderness areas. The Allied Fishermen of Southeast Alaska (the Fishermen), an association of commercial fishers, intervened to defend its interests. It argues that ... that commercial fishing is permitted throughout the Park.

The district court concluded that ... that commercial fishing is statutorily prohibited only in wilderness areas of the Park. Plaintiffs appeal the determination that commercial fishing is permitted in non-wilderness areas of the Park. The Fishermen cross-appeal the court's findings that ... federal law prohibits commercial fishing in the Park's wilderness areas. ...

II

. . .

B.   *Commercial Fishing in Glacier Bay Wilderness*

We review questions of statutory interpretation de novo, but will defer to the agency's interpretation unless it contravenes the express language of the statute or clear congressional intent. *Chevron U.S.A. v. Natural Resources Defense Council,* 467 U.S. 837, 843 (1984); [ ]

ANILCA designates roughly 2.77 million acres of the Park as "wilderness" to be administered under the Wilderness Act, [ ], unless otherwise provided by ANILCA. Greater protections apply to wilderness areas than to ordinary park lands. In pertinent part, the Wilderness Act bans commercial enterprise from wilderness areas: "Except as specifically provided for in this chapter, and subject to existing private rights, there shall be no commercial enterprise * * * within any wilderness area designated by this chapter.... " 16 U.S.C. § 1133(c). The court held that this provision bans commercial fishing in Glacier Bay's wilderness areas, and the Park Service agrees with this interpretation.

The Fishermen argue that two provisions exempt commercial fishing from the Wilderness Act's ban on commercial activity. The first is a section of the Wilderness Act that allows motorized vessels in wilderness areas "where these uses have already become established." 16 U.S.C. § 1133(d)(1). This provision is of no use to the Fishermen. Their use of motorboats is not at issue; it is fishing for profit that the Wilderness Act prohibits. This they may not do, whether from motorized vessels or otherwise.

Next, the Fishermen cite a section of ANILCA that provides:

On all public lands where the taking of fish and wildlife is permitted in accordance with the provisions of this Act or other applicable State and Federal law, the Secretary shall permit * * * the continuance of existing uses, and the future establishment, and use, of temporary campsites, tent platforms, shelters, and other temporary facilities and equipment directly and necessarily related to such activities.

[ ] The Fishermen interpret this provision to require that all "existing uses" of park resources be allowed to continue. The plain language of ANILCA does not support this interpretation, and the Park Service's contrary interpretation requires deference.

The court correctly held that ANILCA and the Wilderness Act prohibit commercial fishing in the Park's wilderness areas.

C. *Commercial Fishing in the Park Non–Wilderness Areas*

Plaintiffs argue that the Organic Act and ANILCA prohibit commercial fishing throughout the Park. The Park Service and the Fishermen interpret the statutes to give the Park Service discretion to permit or to prohibit commercial fishing in non-wilderness areas of the Park. In the absence of an explicit statutory directive, we must defer to the Park Service's interpretation if it is "permissible" in light of the available evidence of congressional intent. *Chevron,* [ ]. The question before us is not which interpretation we prefer, but whether the Park Service's interpretation is reasonable. [ ] Because the Park Service is charged with administering the statutes at issue, we must find its interpretation reasonable "unless there are compelling indications that it is wrong, especially when Congress has refused to alter the administrative construction." [ ]

1. *Statutory Directive*

No statute expressly prohibits commercial fishing in the Park's non-wilderness areas or demonstrates clear congressional intent to restrict the Park Service's discretion to permit commercial fishing. We discuss each of the statutes on which plaintiffs rely for their contrary view.

a. Organic Act

The Organic Act, 16 U.S.C. § 1 *et seq.,* governs all national parks. The Act gives the Secretary of the Interior authority to "make and publish such rules and regulations as he may deem necessary or proper for the management of the parks, monuments, and reservations under the jurisdiction of the National Park Service." [ ] The Act defines the scope of the Secretary's delegated authority as follows:

The authorization of activities shall be construed and the protection, management, and administration of these areas shall be conducted in light of the high public value and integrity of the National Park System and shall not be exercised in derogation of the values and purposes for which these various areas have been established, except as may have been or shall be directly and specifically provided by Congress.

[ ] Thus, the Secretary may not exercise his authority to the detriment of the Act's purpose, which is "to conserve the scenery and the natural and historic objects and the wild life therein and to provide for the enjoyment of the same in such manner and by such means as will leave them unimpaired for the enjoyment of future generations." [ ]

Plaintiffs argue that the Secretary's failure to prevent commercial fishing in the Park derogates the Act's purpose of conservation and therefore violates an express statutory directive. We disagree. Whether conduct derogates long-term goals of conservation is a factual question that we are not prepared to reach. In the absence of a specific congressional statement that commercial fishing derogates the Act's goals, there is no reason to conclude that the Secretary's failure to prohibit commercial fishing violates the Act. Had Congress intended to prohibit commercial activity in national parks, it could have used the same clear language used in the Wilderness Act when it amended the Organic Act in 1970 and 1978. [ ]

. . .

2. Congressional Intent

Other indicia of congressional intent support the Park Service's interpretations of the Organic Act and ANILCA. . . .

Plaintiffs argue that Congress's 1978 amendment to the Organic Act was intended to reprimand the Park Service for permitting commercial fishing in national parks. See Pub. L. 95–250 (Mar. 27, 1978) (prohibiting the Secretary from authorizing activities "in derogation of the values and purposes for which" the parks were created), codified at 16 U.S.C. § 1a–1. The legislative history does not support plaintiffs' reading. Congress added the "derogation" language when it expanded the Redwood National Park. The House Report describes this language as assuring that "management of these areas shall not compromise these resource values except as Congress may have specifically provided. Thus, the Secretary is to afford the highest standard of protection and care to the lands within the Redwood National Forest." [ ] The legislative history therefore refutes plaintiffs' assertion that Congress had fish in mind when it added that language.[10]

We need not establish conclusively that Congress intended to delegate the authority to regulate commercial fishing. We need only search for "compelling indications" that it did not, [ ], for only then may we reject the Park Service's interpretation.

3. Deference to Agency Interpretation

Having found the Park Service's interpretation reasonable, we must defer to it. . . .

4. Case Law

Contrary to plaintiffs' assertion, no case has held that the Organic Act prohibits hunting, trapping or fishing in national parks. Some cases have

---

10. Plaintiffs base several other arguments on legislative history. The probative value of such arguments is extremely limited. . . .

held that the Organic Act permits the Secretary to prohibit these activities. *See Michigan United Conservation Clubs v. Lujan,* 949 F.2d 202 (6th Cir.1991) (upholding Park Service regulation against trapping in national park; the agency's decision that trapping would derogate park purposes not arbitrary and capricious); *Organized Fishermen of Florida v. Hodel,* 775 F.2d 1544 (11th Cir.1985) (upholding regulatory restriction on fishing in Everglades National Park; no statute expressly permitted fishing in that park, so Congress had not limited Secretary's discretion to prohibit it), *cert. denied,* 476 U.S. 1169 (1986); *National Rifle Association v. Potter,* 628 F. Supp. 903 (D.D.C.1986) (finding that regulatory ban on hunting and trapping in particular parks was not arbitrary and capricious because nothing in the Act clearly permits hunting and trapping in all national parks).

These cases support the result we reach by recognizing the broad discretion that the Organic Act confers on the Park Service and the deference courts owe to the Park Service's interpretation of the statute it administers. *See also Bicycle Trails Council of Marin v. Babbitt,* 82 F.3d 1445, 1452 (9th Cir.1996) (interpreting Organic Act to give Park Service authority to close mountain bike trails; agency finding that trails would endanger park values was not arbitrary and capricious); *Conservation Law Foundation v. Secretary of the Interior,* 864 F.2d 954 (1st Cir.1989) (holding that Park Service could permit limited use of offroad vehicles on national seashore); *Wilderness Public Rights Fund v. Kleppe,* 608 F.2d 1250, 1254 (9th Cir.1979) (holding that Park Service could allocate more permits to commercial river guides than to users experienced enough to run river on their own), *cert. denied,* 446 U.S. 982 (1980); *Sierra Club v. Andrus,* 487 F. Supp. 443, 448 (D.D.C.1980) (finding that Park Service enjoys discretion to determine how to protect park resources, so that his failure to exercise water rights is subject to deferential review), *aff'd,* 659 F.2d 203 (D.C.Cir. 1981).

III

The district court properly held that plaintiffs have standing to challenge commercial fishing in the Park. Moreover, it properly held that commercial fishing is statutorily prohibited only in the Park's designated wilderness areas. Neither an express statutory directive nor compelling evidence of clear congressional intent contradicts the Park Service's interpretations of the statutes at issue. AFFIRMED.

■ SCHROEDER, C.J., concurring: I concur in all of the majority opinion except Part II.C.2, dealing with Congressional Intent. With respect to the non-wilderness areas of Glacier Bay National Park, we today decide only that commercial fishing is not expressly prohibited by statute. The Secretary's proposed regulations are not before us, nor is any question of the limits of the Secretary's discretion to permit commercial fishing.

In my view, the legislative history contains strong indications that Congress considered consumptive use of resources to be generally prohibited in national parks, and that by making Glacier Bay a national park in 1980, Congress intended that commercial fishing be phased out in the park. The key committee report noted that "[s]ince the establishment of the

National Park System in 1916, the consumptive use of wildlife resources within National Parks and National Monuments has been prohibited. Such units have traditionally been viewed as wildlife sanctuaries for the nonconsumptive enjoyment of the American public." [ ]

Consistent with this background understanding, the committee stated that "Glacier Bay National Park [is] intended to be [a] large sanctuar[y] where fish and wildlife may roam freely, developing their social structures and evolving over long periods of time as nearly as possible without the changes that extensive human activities would cause." [ ] Continued commercial fishing is inconsistent with the concept of a sanctuary.

Congress' treatment of the Dry Bay area, where it explicitly intended commercial fishing to continue, is also instructive. Congress designated those units where commercial fishing was to continue as "preserves," rather than as part of the Park itself, indicating congressional understanding that commercial fishing is inconsistent with those uses generally permitted in national parks. [ ] ("The preserve is to be managed in the same manner as the park, except that hunting and trapping may be allowed * * * [and] the existing commercial fishing operations are allowed to continue."); *see also* [ ] (noting that the House committee excluded Dry Bay from the proposed park addition "so that active commercial fishing operations would be located outside the Park boundaries."). Speaking of the three areas where commercial fishing was to be permitted to continue, including Dry Bay, the Senate committee noted that "[i]n all three units the actual fishing takes place offshore in the ocean, outside of the units." [ ] By referring to "all three units" where commercial fishing was "to continue," the committee indicated its understanding that commercial fishing would not continue elsewhere.

Notwithstanding its understanding that commercial fishing was inconsistent with the values and purposes of national parks, however, Congress also indicated its intent that existing uses, where inconsistent, be phased out rather than abruptly terminated. The committee noted that

> [w]hen establishing new units of the National Park System the Congress has had a long-standing traditional practice of reviewing those values and activities within new units which, if immediately curtailed, might result in substantial hardships to the local residents of the area. Consequently, in appropriate instances certain * * * activities have been phased out of such units gradually, rather than terminated immediately at the time of establishment of the unit.

[ ] Congress' intent that existing uses be phased out to avoid hardship, as well as its intent that certain subsistence and sport uses be permitted to continue, [ ], explain the absence of an immediate statutory ban on commercial fishing within the Park.

Today's decision is limited to the question the district court decided, whether federal statutes contain an immediate prohibition on all commercial fishing in the park. It should not be interpreted as an endorsement of unfettered agency discretion to permit commercial fishing in the Park.

NOTES

(1) The case demonstrates the difference between the broad discretion accorded the National Park Service (NPS) under its Organic Act and the reduced discretion of the land-managing agency under the Wilderness Act.

The case also demonstrates once again that general management mandates are subject to specific provisions of the statute designating an area for inclusion in a particular land management system. A further illustration is *Isle Royale Boaters Ass'n v. Norton,* 154 F.Supp.2d 1098 (W.D.Mich.2001).

(2) Managing for wilderness: Wilderness areas might seem the easiest of all lands to manage: simply leave them alone and let nature take its course. That approach is often followed, and with good results. For the most part, however, even large areas of wilderness show signs of human actions, not because of what humans have done within the area but because of what they have done elsewhere. Inevitably, human activities on surrounding lands disrupt ecological processes and disturbance regimes (*e.g.,* forest fires) that would otherwise affect the wilderness enclaves. Similarly, the plants and wildlife living in many wilderness areas continue to be affected by human activities elsewhere. Such disruptions raise inevitable questions: Should a managing agency deliberately intervene in a wilderness area to attempt to counteract these disruptions, by starting fires, for instance, or culling animal populations that are excessively high because human actions elsewhere have eliminated natural predators or competitors? Note the guiding language contained in the definition of wilderness: a wilderness area should be "untrammeled by man" with "the imprint of man's work substantially unnoticeable," yet it should also "retain[ ] its primeval character" and be "managed so as to preserve its natural conditions." What happens when "primeval character" and "natural conditions" can only be maintained through management actions that display vividly "the imprint of man's work"?

(3) The Omnibus Consolidated and Emergency Supplemental Appropriations Act for FY 1999: In section 123 of the Omnibus Consolidated and Emergency Supplemental Appropriations Act for FY 1999, Pub. L. No. 105–277, 112 Stat. 2681, Congress responded to the decision of the NPS to close all of Glacier Bay to commercial fishing. The section contained four sets of directives: (1) it closed specific non-wilderness waters to commercial fishing and reaffirmed the ban on commercial fishing in wilderness waters; (2) it established a procedure to "grandfather" certain fishers who would be eligible to receive lifetime fishing permits; (3) it specified that marine waters outside Glacier Bay would remain open to commercial fishing; and (4) it directed a cooperative State–Federal fisheries management plan be developed for the grandfathered fishing. In addition, the Act provided substantial monetary compensation for fishers who would no longer be permitted to fish in the Park.

The evolution of the controversy—of which the decision in *Alaska Wildlife Alliance v. Jensen* was only one component—is traced in the preamble to proposed regulations implementing the legislative solution. *See* 64 FED. REG. 41,854 (1999).

b. THE WILD AND SCENIC RIVER SYSTEM

NOTES

The Wild and Scenic Rivers Act of 1968: Congress enacted the Wild and Scenic River Act (WSRA), 16 U.S.C. § 1271–1287, to preserve free-flowing rivers. Unlike other systems, the Wild and Scenic River System focuses on a single resource—segments of rivers.

(a) Designation of river segments for inclusion in the Wild and Scenic River System: River segments can be designated for inclusion in the system in either of two ways:

Congressional designation begins with the enactment of a statute naming a river segment as a "potential addition" and directing the Secretary whose agency has jurisdiction over the land to study the segment and report back to Congress. *Id.* § 1275(a), 1276(a), (b). In preparing the reports, the Secretary is to give priority to those rivers facing the greatest threats from development and which include largest proportion of private lands. *Id.* § 1275(a). The reports are to discuss the costs and "potential uses of the land and water which would be enhanced, foreclosed, or curtailed if the area were included in the ... system," *id.*, as well as the qualifying characteristics: "possess[ing] outstandingly remarkable scenic, recreational, geologic, fish and wildlife, historic, cultural, or other similar values" and a "free-flowing condition." *Id.* § 1271. The report is circulated among designated federal and state officials; notice is published in the *Federal Register*; and the report, together with comments from the federal and state officials, is submitted to the President and Congress. *Id.* § 1275(b), (c). Congress decides whether to designate the river segment as a component of the system. *Id.* § 1274(a).

State/Federal designation allows river segments to be added to the system through state initiative and federal concurrence. This alternative requires three steps: First, the river must be designated "by or pursuant to an act of the legislature of the State." *Id.* § 1273(a). Second, the governor of the state must apply to the Secretary of the Interior to have the river segment included in the system. *Id.* Third, the Secretary must find that the segment "meet[s] the criteria established in this Act," and must notify other federal agencies and publish notice in the *Federal Register. Id.*

(b) Management mandates for river components: Different management requirements are applicable to river segments listed as potential system additions and those that are included within the system:

Protection of potential system additions: The WSRA prohibits the Federal Energy Regulatory Commission (FERC) and all other federal agencies from licensing or otherwise assisting any project "on or directly affecting" any river listed for potential inclusion in the system for three years after the river is listed. *Id.* § 1278(b). Water development projects above or below the segment are not prohibited as long as they will not "invade the area or diminish the scenic or recreational, and fish and wildlife values present" in the segment. *Id.* Listing a segment as a potential addition also withdraws the land within a quarter mile of each bank from "entry, sale, or other disposition under public land laws," *id.* § 1279(b), and the minerals "from all forms of appropriation under the mining laws," although mineral leasing may continue subject to conditions "appropriate to safeguard the area in the event it is subsequently included in the system," *id.* § 1280(b). Finally, rivers listed as potential additions are protected by a requirement that, "[i]n all planning for the use and development of water and related land resources, consideration shall be given by all Federal agencies involved to potential national wild, scenic and recreational river areas." *Id.* § 1276(d)(1).

Protections for river segments included within the system depend upon the status of the segment as a wild, scenic, or recreational river. This is the first and most important decision that the managing agency must make once Congress has designated the river for inclusion in the system. *Id.* § 1274(b). A "wild river" is "free of impoundments and generally inaccessible except by trail, with watersheds or shorelines essentially primitive and waters unpolluted"; like wilderness areas, they are "vestiges of primitive America." *Id.* § 1273(b)(1). a "scenic river" is "free of impoundments, with shorelines or watersheds still largely primitive and shorelines largely undeveloped, but accessible in places by roads." *Id.* § 1273(b)(2). Finally, "recreational rivers" are "readily accessible by road or railroad, . . . may have some development along their shorelines, and . . . may have undergone some impoundment or diversion in the past." *Id.* § 1273(b)(3). Although Congress generally did not distinguish among the categories in defining management standards, the Act does require that "[e]ach component of the national wild and scenic river system shall be administered in such manner as to protect and enhance the values which caused it to be included." *Id.* § 1281(a). Hence, the defining characteristics of the three categories necessarily limit the types of activities that can occur within the river and its protected corridor.

In addition to determining the status of the river segment, the managing agency must also establish "detailed boundaries" limited only by the requirement that it include no more than 320 acres of land per river mile. *Id.* § 1274(b). Finally, the managing agency is required to prepare a "comprehensive management plan . . . to provide for the protection of the river values." *Id.* § 1274(c).

Rivers included within the system are subject to the same general protection accorded rivers listed for possible inclusion in the system. *E.g., id.* § 1278(a) (FERC and other federal agencies may not license or otherwise assist a water development project directly affecting the segment); *id.* § 1279(a) (federal land within the segment boundaries is withdrawn from "entry, sale, or other disposition").

(3) "outstandingly remarkable ... fish and wildlife ... values": Although the WSRA is more than thirty years old, it has only recently become a significant potential factor in wildlife law because only recently have litigants sought to force land managing agencies to implement the Act's management requirements. As noted, the agency's report to Congress is required to identify the river's "outstandingly remarkable values" (ORVs); Congress then includes a statement of ORVs in the enabling act designating the segment for inclusion in the system, the Act itself requires the managing agency to give "primary emphasis" to "esthetic, scenic, historic, archaeological, and scientific" values, or the managing agency may designate ORVs in the comprehensive planning document. Regardless of the source of the ORV, the Act requires that a river segment "shall be administered in such manner as to protect and enhance the values which caused it to be included" in the system. *Id.* § 1281(a). One of the ORVs is "fish and wildlife."

(a) The Donner und Blitzen River: Congress designated the Donner und Blitzen River in eastern Oregon as a wild river in 1988. The enabling act specified that the river's ORVs were geology, recreation, scenery, fisheries and vegetation. In 1991, the Bureau of Land Management (BLM) hired a group of scientists to inventory the river corridor; their report concluded that the river corridor contained rare plant communities and recommended that the agency prohibit grazing in the corridor. In 1993, BLM issued an EA under NEPA evaluating a proposed river plan under the WSRA. The Oregon Natural Desert Association challenged the plan, alleging that "BLM violated the WSRA by adopting, without any rational basis, a management plan for the river that fails to protect and enhance native plants, plant communities and fisheries." *Oregon Natural Desert Association v. Green,* 953 F.Supp. 1133, 1143–44 (D.Or.1997). The court agreed, noting *inter alia* that "nearly half of the surveyed aquatic habitat remains in 'poor' or 'fair' condition due to poor water quality and riparian vegetation. It is undisputed that the health of the coldwater fish in the river area is linked to the vitality of water and vegetation" which was being destroyed by continued grazing with the resulting "overheated water and siltation." *Id.* at 1145. Concluding that the record before it established that the ORVs were being degraded by continued cattle grazing, the court held that the river plan violated the WSRA. *Id.* at 1146.

(b) The John Day River: Congress also added the John Day River in eastern Oregon to the Wild and Scenic River System in 1988. In doing so, Congress specified that the river's ORVs included fisheries. As the court noted, "It is one of the most important river systems in the Columbia River Basin for wild salmon, especially spring chinook and winter steelhead. The genetic integrity of these wild salmon runs is enhanced because there are no fish hatcheries in the Basin." *National Wildlife Federation v. Cosgriffe,* 21 F.Supp.2d 1211, 1215 (D.Or.1998). The BLM did not release a draft river plan until October 1993, nearly five years after the river's designation—a delay that violated the Act's requirement that a plan be completed within three years. While acknowledging that the ORVs were degraded, the court concluded that plaintiff had failed to present evidence tying current grazing practices to the degradation. The court therefore ordered BLM to prepare the river plan, but did not enjoin continued grazing during the preparation. *Id.* at 1220, 1222.

(c) The Owyhee River: Segments of the Owyhee River were designated for inclusion in the Wild and Scenic River System in 1984 and 1988. Fish and wildlife were specified as ORVs. The court noted that the redband trout, a species petitioned for listing under the Endangered Species Act, was found in the corridor. *Oregon Natural Desert Association v. Singleton,* 47 F.Supp.2d 1182, 1185 (D.Or.1998). The BLM river management plan noted that grazing negatively impacted the ORVs, but contained no proposals to remove cattle from the corridor. The court ordered BLM to conduct a second environmental review that considered alternatives to continued grazing in the corridor. One year later, the court issued an injunction requiring BLM to remove cattle from the riparian zone and to eliminate the grazing permits involved. 75 F.Supp.2d 1139, 1145 (D.Or.1999).

This trilogy of cases has dramatically raised the profile of the WSRA as a potential source of protection for wildlife habitat. Since riparian habitat is the most important habitat particularly in the arid west, judicial enforcement of the requirement that the managing agency "protect and enhance" riparian values is singularly important.

c. THE NATIONAL PARK SYSTEM

The National Park Service (NPS) administers a land management system that includes lands that fall within a variety of different classifications. The more than fifty National Parks are only the most visible of the lands. In addition, Congress has created designations such as national monuments, national seashores, national lakeshores, national parkways, national recreation areas, national wild rivers, national preserves—a variety of classifications *almost* too numerous to catalogue. For a list, see 36 C.F.R. § 1.2(g)-(i).

This section examines the two most important lands for wildlife habitat: National Monuments created by the President under the authority of the Antiquities Act and the National Parks designated by Congress.

(i) THE ANTIQUITIES ACT

NOTES

(1) The Antiquities Act, 16 U.S.C. § 431–433, provides in part:

> The President of the United States is authorized, in his discretion, to declare by public proclamation historic landmarks, historic and prehistoric structures, and other objects of historic or scientific interest that are situated upon the lands owned or controlled by the Government of the United States to be national monuments, and may reserve as a part thereof parcels of land, the limits of which in all cases shall be confined to the smallest area compatible with the proper care and management of the objects to be protected....

Id. § 431. As the recent designation of several new national monuments demonstrated, the power granted by the Act has frequently been controversial.

(2) "objects of historic or scientific interest": What is included within the statutory phrase "objects of historic or scientific interest"? In 1941, President Roosevelt used the Antiquities Act to create a 220,000–acre Jackson Hole National Monument in western Wyoming. When challenged by the state as "barren" of any of the features listed in the Act, the United States introduced evidence of trails and historic spots in connection with the early trapping and hunting of animals formulating the early fur industry of the West, structures of glacial formation and peculiar mineral deposits and plant life indigenous to the particular area, a biological field for research of wild life in its particular habitat within the area, involving the study of the origin, life, habits and perpetuation of the different species of wild animals. . . .

Wyoming v. Franke, 58 F.Supp. 890 (D.Wyo.1945). This was sufficient:

If there be evidence in the case of a substantial character upon which the President may have acted in declaring that there were objects of historic or scientific interest included within the area, it is sufficient upon which he may have based a discretion. For example, if a monument were to be created on a bare stretch of sage-brush prairie in regard to which there was no substantial evidence that it contained objects of historic or scientific interest, the action in attempting to establish it by proclamation as a monument, would undoubtedly be arbitrary and capricious and clearly outside the scope and purpose of the Monument Act.

Id.

(3) *Cappaert v. United States:* Although the Antiquities Act is not explicitly a wildlife habitat protection statute, wildlife do come within the "other objects of . . . scientific interest" that justify the designation of a monument. In 1952, President Truman withdrew from the public domain a 40–acre tract of land surrounding Devil's Hole, a deep limestone cavern in Nevada. Approximately 50 feet below the opening of the cavern is a pool 65 feet long, 10 feet wide, and at least 200 feet deep. The Proclamation establishing the monument noted that "the geologic evidence that this subterranean pool is an integral part of the hydrographic history of the Death Valley region is further confirmed by the presence in this pool of a peculiar race of desert fish, and zoologists have demonstrated that this race of fish, which is found nowhere else in the world, evolved only after the gradual drying up of the Death Valley Lake System isolated this fish population from the original ancestral stock that in Pleistocene times was common to the entire region."

In 1968, the Cappaerts—who own a 12,000–acre ranch near Devil's Hole—began pumping groundwater on their ranch. As a result of the pumping, the summer water level of the pool in Devil's Hole began to decrease. When the water dropped below a specified level, the Devil's Hole pupfish was unable to spawn. When the state granted a permit to continue the pumping, the Department of the Interior sought an injunction to prevent the Cappaerts from lowering the pool level below that needed to maintain a viable population of the fish.

The Supreme Court affirmed the injunction:

This Court has long held that when the Federal Government withdraws its land from the public domain and reserves it for a federal purpose, the Government, by implication, reserves appurtenant water then unappropriated to the extent needed to accomplish the purpose of the reservation. In so doing the United States acquires a reserved right in unappropriated water which vests on the date of the reservation and is superior to the rights of future appropriators. . . .

In determining whether there is a federally reserved water right implicit in a federal reservation of public land, the issue is whether the Government intended to reserve unappropriated and thus available water. Intent is inferred if the previously unappropriated waters are necessary to accomplish the purposes for which the reservation was created. [ ] Both the District Court and the Court of Appeals held that the 1952 Proclamation expressed an intention to reserve unappropriated water, and we agree. The Proclamation discussed the pool in Devil's Hole in four of the five preambles and recited that the "pool * * * should be given special protection." Since a pool is a body of water, the protection contemplated is meaningful only if the water remains; the water right reserved by the 1952 Proclamation was thus explicit, not implied.

. . .

[T]he purpose of reserving Devil's Hole Monument is preservation of the pool. Devil's Hole was reserved "for the preservation of the unusual features of scenic, scientific, and educational interest." The Proclamation notes that the pool contains "a peculiar race of desert fish * * * which is found nowhere else in the world" and that the "pool is of * * * outstanding scientific importance * * *." The pool need only be preserved, consistent with the intention expressed in the Proclamation, to the extent necessary to preserve its scientific interest. The fish are one of the features of scientific interest. The preamble noting the scientific interest of the pool follows the preamble describing the fish as unique; the Proclamation must be read in its entirety. Thus, as the District Court has correctly determined, the level of the pool may be permitted to drop to the extent that the drop does not impair the scientific value of the pool as the natural habitat of the species sought to be preserved.

Cappaert v. United States, 426 U.S. 128 (1976).

(ii) NATIONAL PARK SERVICE ORGANIC ACT OF 1916

NOTES

(1) Congress created the first national park in 1872 when it set aside land in Yellowstone "as a public park or pleasuring-ground for the benefit and enjoyment of the people." Act of Mar. 1, 1872, ch. 24, § 1, 17 Stat. 32 (codified at 16 U.S.C. § 21). By 1916, Congress had created thirteen national parks and an additional nineteen national monuments. The administrative responsibility for the various entities was parceled out among a number of agencies. JOSEPH L. SAX, MOUNTAINS WITHOUT HANDRAILS 5–15 (1980). It was not until forty-four years after the establishment of Yellowstone that Congress finally enacted a formal management mandate and an agency to implement it.

(2) National Park Service Act: In 1916, Congress enacted the National Park Service Organic Act, 16 U.S.C. § 1, 2–4. The statute created the National Park Service (NPS) and directed it "to promote and regulate the use" of the Parks to "conform to the fundamental purpose of said parks[:] to conserve the scenery and the natural and historic objects and the wild life therein and to provide for the enjoyment of the same in such manner and by such means as will leave them unimpaired for the enjoyment of future generations." National Park Service Organic Act, Act of Aug. 25, 1916, ch. 408, § 1, 39 Stat. 535 (codified as amended at 16 U.S.C. § 1).

(A) Duties and Powers: The Issues of Management Discretion

NOTES

"to promote and regulate"—recreation and conservation: The mandate given the NPS—"to promote and regulate"—involves an almost inevitable conflict. It is a mandate that has produced an agency that generally prefers recreation to conservation, that promotes tourism rather than preservation. The mandate of an unimpaired park has produced a natural-appearing facade over a depleted ecosystem. An example: the Service's desire to maintain peaceful scenes led it to exterminate animals that were "detrimental to the use" of the parks. RICHARD WEST SELLARS, PRESERVING NATURE IN THE NATIONAL PARKS 71 (1997). Predators such as cougars, wolves, coyotes, lynx, bobcats, foxes, badgers, mink, weasels, fishers, otters, and martens were unnatural impairments to the natural grandeur that the Service sought to "leave unimpaired." Similarly, the Service suppressed fire, culled big game populations, applied pesticides, and fed garbage to bears and hay to elk. This reflects the dominant element of Park management: the Service has always been far more heavily staffed with landscape architects—a discipline that seeks to create landscape to match the people—than with biologists: in the post-World War II years, the Service employed 6 biologists and "about 140" landscape architects. *Id.* 165–66. The NPS is an agency that struggles to escape its initial assumptions that the National Parks should provide breathtaking views from roadside turnouts. As such it has intensively manipulated wildlife populations:

> The continuous interplay between two competing conceptions of managing the park's biota forms an enduring theme in the history of Yellowstone. Active intervention is as old as the park itself. Early park administrations manipulated wildlife conditions, shooting predators and feeding elk during cold winters to protect and enhance wildlife populations that park visitors wanted to see. Yellowstone rangers actually herded elk back into the protective enclave of the park. Fisheries experts and park authorities encouraged the type of fish that anglers preferred, going so far as to destroy pelican eggs on Molly Island. Though some sources discuss this period as merely protection of big game, portraying management as passive, we can see that protection involved vigorous action on the part of managers.

> During the 1930s the Wildlife Division brought an ecological awareness to the park. Because division personnel had been students of

Joseph Grinnell, their university training prepared them not only for work in systematics but also to see the park wildlife in ecological terms, rather than in terms of protective custody. They set up guiding principles for wildlife management that have remained largely intact, including protection for all native species. At the same time that they brought their ecological vision of wildlife relationships, the Wildlife Division also continued an active management approach in Yellowstone, but in this version of intervention they intended managers to limits actions to reestablishing original ecological conditions altered by human hand. The Wildlife Division was willing to shoot crows, trap small predators, or alter lake levels if it meant the endangered trumpeter swan would survive. They also believed it necessary to limit the number of elk on the northern range. Scientists and range managers continued that active management stance throughout the 1940s and 1950s, most conspicuously by controlling the number of elk within the park border, and in less dramatic fashion by suppressing wildfires. Today, the most obvious forms of active management include efforts to sustain native fisheries against exotic invaders. The reintroduction of the wolf, moreover, is clearly an active and interventionist strategy. While justified and rationalized in very modern ways, wolves howling once again in Yellowstone also recall to mind Charles C. Adam's appeal for preserving the primitive conditions found in the national parks.

JAMES A. PRITCHARD, PRESERVING YELLOWSTONE'S NATURAL CONDITIONS 307–08 (1999).

The tension between "promote and regulate" is central to the following cases.

Sierra Club v. Babbitt

District Court for the Eastern District of California.
69 F.Supp.2d 1202 (1999).

■ ISHII, D.J.:—This action challenges the reconstruction project by the National Park Service ("NPS") regarding Highway 140 from Yosemite National Park's western border to the Pohono Bridge ("the El Portal Road" or "the Road"). Plaintiffs originally sought to enjoin Defendants from taking any steps towards the continuation of the El Portal Road reconstruction project ("the Project") until the NPS provides necessary consideration of all significant environmental effects in compliance with the National Environmental Policy Act, 42 U.S.C. § 4321 *et seq.* ("NEPA"), the Wild and Scenic Rivers Act, 16 U.S.C. § 1271 *et seq.* ("WSRA"), the National Park Organic Act, 16 U.S.C. § 1 *et seq.*, and the Administrative Procedures Act ("APA"), 5 U.S.C. § 701 *et seq.* Plaintiffs also seek various related types of declaratory relief.

. . . .

[In January 1997, a winter storm damaged the El Portal Road in Yosemite National Park. The National Park Service ("NPS") began the planning process to repair the road, including compliance with NEPA. For part of its length, the road ran along the Merced River, sometimes encroaching upon the riparian zone.

[The NPS prepared an Environmental Assessment (EA) on the project. Following public comment, the agency issued a Finding of No Significant Impact (FONSI) after concluding that it would be able to mitigate impacts to the point that they would no longer be "significant." In reviewing the agency's decision on this point, the court held that the agency had "failed to identify and evaluate significant adverse impacts" on a range of biological resources such as nesting bats and rainbow trout. Upon concluding that "Defendants' decision not to prepare an EIS was arbitrary and capricious," the court granted plaintiffs motion for injunctive relief.

[The court then turned to plaintiff's claim under the National Park Service Organic Act:]

III.   NATIONAL PARK SERVICE ORGANIC ACT

A.   Background

The National Park Service Organic Act ("the Organic Act") of 1916 establishes the National Park Service to "promote and regulate the use of the Federal areas known as national parks, monuments and reservations hereinafter specified, * * * to conserve the scenery and the natural and historic objects and the wild life therein and to provide for the enjoyment of the same in such manner and by such means as will leave them unimpaired for the enjoyment of future generations." 16 U.S.C. § 1. Plaintiffs allege Defendants have violated the Organic Act because "construction involved in expanding the El Portal Road is permanently altering the Merced River Canyon, within the boundaries of Yosemite National Park, inconsistent with the mandates and limitations imposed on the National Park Service by the Organic Act, 16 U.S.C. § 1 *et seq.* and by the regulations and policies promulgated thereunder." [ ]

B.   Analysis

The Organic Act commits the NPS to the protection and furtherance of two fundamentally competing values; the preservation of natural and cultural resources and the facilitation of public use and enjoyment. These competing values of conservation and public use have been actively in conflict since before the establishment of the NPS. The Organic Act did not resolve the conflict in favor of one side or the other. *See* Nathan L. Scheg, *Preservationists vs. Recreationists in Our National Parks,* HASTINGS W.-N.W.J.ENVTL.L. & POL'Y 47 (1998). Rather, the Organic Act acknowledges the conflict and, saying nothing about how to achieve resolution, grants deference to NPS in balancing the competing and conflicting values.

. . .

The Organic Act is set forth in Section 1, Section 1 notes 2–4, and Sections 22, and 43 of Subchapter I of Title 16 of the United States Code. Taken together, the provisions of the Organic Act establish the National Park Service and provide that the national parks be administered so as to "*conserve* the scenery and the natural and historic objects and the wild life therein *and* to *provide for the enjoyment* of the same in such a manner and by such means as will leave them unimpaired to [sic] the enjoyment of future generations." 16 U.S.C. § 1 (emphasis added). Section I recognizes, both implicitly and explicitly the tension between conservation and providing for public enjoyment. Courts have consistently recognized the discretion that the Organic Act accords NPS. *See Bicycle Trails Council of Marin v. Babbitt* 82 F.3d 1445, 1454 (9th Cir.1996) (noting several courts have accorded NPS authority to determine what uses of park resources are proper and which avenues best achieve the Organic Act's mandates). The Organic Act itself does not mandate that the balance in any particular decision reflect one value over the other. For that reason, the Organic Act does not serve as basis for a cause of action when the issue is confined to the Agency's exercise of discretion in attempting to balance valid, competing values. The Organic Act would serve as a basis for a cause of action were the NPS to allow use of a national park in a way that was not in the interests of either conservation or public enjoyment or in a way that was clearly against the interests of future generations. The current action does not fall in either category. The current action concerns how best to preserve access to the park while at the same time preserving the values for which the Yosemite Valley and the Merced River corridor were declared a national park. How NPS does that is within its discretion and the Organic Act offers no basis for the court to conclude that Defendants have violated the Act on the basis of NPS's exercise of discretion to decide that El Portal Road should be repaired in a certain manner.

. . .

Therefore, the court concludes Plaintiffs are not entitled to injunctive relief under the National Parks Organic Act and their motion for summary adjudication on this issue will be denied.

NOTES

(1) Is the court correct that the discretion accorded the agency is such that it has completely unreviewable discretion to choose between any degree of preservation and any degree of recreation? Does the mandate "to promote and regulate" mean simply that any balance between promotion and regulation is permissible? Doesn't the NPS have an enforceable duty to protect a Park's resources "unimpaired for the enjoyment of future generations"?

Is the NPS dual mandate significantly different than the FWS mandate under the Refuge Improvement Act [*supra*] to conserve animals and plants on wildlife refuges while facilitating wildlife-dependent recreation (including hunting and fishing)?

(2) The duty to protect: While the court's language in the *Portal Road Case* that "the Organic Act does not serve as basis for a cause of action when the issue is confined to the Agency's exercise of discretion in attempting to balance valid, competing values" of preservation and recreation is striking, its decision itself is the norm. The courts have rarely found the balance struck by the agency between promotion and regulation to be illegal:

(a) *National Wildlife Federation v. National Park Service*: Plaintiffs challenged the NPS decision to leave Fishing Bridge Campground open despite increasing human-grizzly bear interactions. Plaintiffs alleged that the agency's decision violated both the Endangered Species Act and the Organic Act. The court disagreed:

> The Park Service carries out a multiple charge under the Organic Act. While the Park Service is clearly responsible for the preservation of grizzly bears, it is also charged with "promoting" and "providing for the enjoyment" of park resources. . . .
>
> Defendants correctly note that the Organic Act is silent as to how the protection of park resources and their administration are to be effected. Under such circumstances, the Park Service has broad discretion in determining which avenues best achieve the Organic Act's mandate. *Organized Fishermen of Florida v. Hodel,* 775 F.2d 1544, 1550 (11th Cir.1985); *Sierra Club v. Andrus,* 487 F.Supp. 443, 448 (D.D.C.1980), *aff'd Sierra Club v. Watt,* 659 F.2d 203, (D.C.Cir.1981); *Universal Interpretive Shuttle Corp. v. Washington Metropolitan Area Transit Comm.,* 393 U.S. 186, 187 (1968). Further, the Park Service is empowered with the authority to determine what uses of park resources are proper and what proportion of the park's resources are available for such use. 16 U.S.C. § 3; [ ]

National Wildlife Federation v. National Park Service, 669 F.Supp. 384 (D.Wyo.1987).

(b) *Conservation Law Foundation v. Clark:* Plaintiffs brought action seeking a permanent injunction barring all off-road vehicle use on the Cape Cod National Seashore until adoption of an off-road vehicle management plan that adequately prevented damage to the seashore. They claimed that the Plan, as adopted and implemented, violated several statutes including the National Park Service Act. The court offered the following description of the requirements of the Park Service Act:

> The Park Service Act, [ ], is a law of general applicability which governs the National Park Service's management of the National Park System including the Seashore. The Park Service Act provides in pertinent part that the National Park Service must administer park lands so as "to conserve the scenery and the natural and historic objects and the wildlife therein and to provide for the enjoyment of the same in such manner and by such means as will leave them unimpaired for the enjoyment of future generations." The Park Service Act thus emphasizes the preservation of park lands in their natural, scenic, and historic condition. . . . [The Act] allows for a balancing of preservation and development only to the extent that such development does not derogate from the overriding preservation mandate.[7]

Conservation Law Foundation v. Clark, 590 F.Supp. 1467 (D.Mass.1984), *aff'd,* 864 F.2d 954 (1st Cir.1989). Despite this "overriding preservation mandate," the court found the Secretary's decision not to be arbitrary and

---

7. Thus the statutes require a level of protection greater than that generally extended to National Forest lands under the "multiple use" concept of 16 U.S.C. § 528 *et seq.* ("Multiple Use Sustained Yield Act") (national forests to be "administered for out-door recreation, range, timber, wildlife, and fish purposes"), but less than that afforded to National Wilderness lands under 16 U.S.C. § 1131 *et seq.* ("Wilderness Act") (national wilderness lands to "be administered * * * in such manner as will leave them unimpaired

capricious "[i]n the face of such radically different opinions [by the experts] on the success of the Plan."

(c) ***Southern Utah Wilderness Alliance v. Dabney:*** The NPS prepared a Backcounty Management Plan (BMP) that continued the agency's previous policy of allowing the use of four-wheel-drive vehicles on rough jeep tracks or trails traversing Canyonlands National Park and portions of the adjoining Glen Canyon National Recreation Area. The Wilderness Alliance challenged the BMP as it applied to trails in Salt Creek Canyon, Horse Canyon, and Lavender Canyon. Salt Creek is the only year-round, fresh water creek in the Park other than the Colorado and Green Rivers and the Salt Creek Jeep Trail runs in and out of the creek bed. At various points, the creek bed is the trail; there is no practical way to reroute the trail to keep it out of the water course. "In the years preceding the BMP's development, the Park Service had received numerous requests for assistance in removing vehicles that had broken down or become stuck in the trail. Instances where vehicles lost transmission, engine, or crankcase fluids in the water also occurred several times a year." The district court held that the agency's decision to allow continued use of Salt Creek as a highway was impermissible under the Organic Act and the enabling legislation creating Canyonlands National Park:

> the Park Service's mandate is to permit forms of enjoyment and access that are *consistent* with preservation and *inconsistent* with significant, permanent impairment.
>
> Continued use of vehicles on the Salt Creek Jeep Trial beyond Peekaboo Spring is inconsistent with this clear legislative directive. The administrative record shows both that the riparian areas in Salt Creek Canyon are unique and that the effects of vehicular traffic beyond Peekaboo Spring are inherently and fundamentally inimical to their continued existence. The presence of the jeep trails eliminates areas that would otherwise support rare riparian vegetation and provide a rare habitat for a diverse array of small mammals and birds. Driving vehicles through the water kills aquatic species by increasing turbidity, churning pool bottoms, breaking down banks, and decreasing fish habitat.

Southern Utah Wilderness Alliance v. Dabney, 7 F.Supp.2d 1205, 1211 (D.Utah 1998). On appeal, the Tenth Circuit reversed:

> The Organic Act mandates that the NPS provide for the conservation and enjoyment of the scenery and natural historic objects and the wildlife therein *"in such manner and by such means as will leave them unimpaired for the enjoyment of future generations."* 16 U.S.C. § 1 (emphasis added). Neither the word "unimpaired" nor the phrase "unimpaired for the enjoyment of future generations" is defined in the Act. It is unclear from the statute itself what constitutes impairment, and how both the duration and severity of the impairment are to be evaluated or weighed against the other value of public use of the park.
>
> Although the Act and the Canyonlands enabling legislation place an overarching concern on preservation of resources, we read the Act

as permitting the NPS to balance the sometimes conflicting policies of resource conservation and visitor enjoyment in determining what activities should be permitted or prohibited. *See* 16 U.S.C. § 1 ("to conserve * * * and to provide for the enjoyment of * * *."); 16 U.S.C. § 271 ("to preserve * * * for the inspiration, benefit, and use of the public * * *."); *see also Bicycle Trails Council v. Babbitt*, 82 F.3d 1445, 1468 (9th Cir.1996) (finding that the NPS "struck a reasoned balance among the sometimes competing goals of recreation, safety, and resource protection as well as among the sometimes competing recreational interests of bicyclists and other park visitors" and that the authority of the NPS to strike such balances "inheres in the Organic Act and the [Golden Gate National Recreation Area] Act"); *Sierra Club v. Babbitt*, 69 F. Supp. 2d 1202, 1246–47 (E.D.Cal.1999) ("The Organic Act commits the NPS to the protection and furtherance of two fundamentally competing values; the preservation of natural and cultural resources and the facilitation of public use and enjoyment"). The test for whether the NPS has performed its balancing properly is whether the resulting action leaves the resources "unimpaired for the enjoyment of future generations." Because of the ambiguity inherent in that phrase, we cannot resolve the issue before us. . . .

Southern Utah Wilderness Alliance v. Dabney, 222 F.3d 819 (10th Cir. 2000).

Is the term "unimpaired" as ambiguous as the Tenth Circuit asserts? If Salt Creek would return to its pre-highway condition after a "generation" of non-use, has it been left "unimpaired"? Is there a "recreational carrying capacity" beyond which additional users impair the park? For example, if it were conclusively established that additional use as a highway would permanently alter the creek and riparian area, is it "unimpaired"? Is the court asserting that the term is sufficiently empty of content that a highway may be an improvement and therefore not an impairment of the creek habitat?

(3) Recreational carrying capacity: If there is a recreational carrying capacity, the problem confronting the NPS is one of allocating the limited resource. The BMP at the center of the dispute in *Wilderness Alliance* was partially allocative in that it established a limited permit system for part of the trails. *See also Wilderness Public Rights Fund v. Kleppe*, 608 F.2d 1250 (9th Cir.1979), *cert. denied*, 446 U.S. 982 (1980) (holding that a permit system limiting the number of rafters allowed on the Colorado River through Grand Canyon was permissible).

PERSPECTIVES

William J. Lockhart, *New Nonimpairment Policy Projected for the National Park System,*

30 Envtl. L. Rep. (Envtl. L. Inst.) 10704 (2000).

Textually, it is hard to dispute that the Organic Act's directive to leave parks "unimpaired" sets a rigorous standard to be met in the NPS' fulfillment of its primary duty "to conserve the scenery and the natural and historic objects and the wildlife" of the parks. That no-impairment standard is clearly framed as the controlling requirement of the Act, despite the further and potentially conflicting directive to "provide for the enjoyment." The text clearly makes the "enjoyment" directive subsidiary: it is expressly subordinated to the no-impairment prohibition by the Act's directive to provide for enjoyment only "in such manner and by such means as will leave them [the park resources] unimpaired for the enjoyment of future generations."

The unqualified prohibition against impairment strongly suggests an uncompromising standard that would bar all but *de minimis* adverse impacts, an interpretation that is well supported by dictionary definitions. Webster's says that to impair is "to make worse: diminish in quantity, value, excellence or strength."[15] Not only does that definition apply without regard for the degree, extent, or significance of any "worsening" or "diminution," but illustrations accompanying the definition also make clear that the term properly includes qualitative changes that are subtle, experiential, and not readily quantified, as in "impair their health by wild living" or "his pleasure was impaired by worry about money."[16] Moreover, this widely applicable interpretation of "impairment" is fully supported by the Redwoods Amendment's strong reaffirmation of the Organic Act standard, which prohibited any "derogation" of the "values or purposes" of the parks—a similarly qualitative standard of broadly applicable rigor.[17]

Undoubtedly, then, the Organic Act directive that the NPS must leave park resources "unimpaired" sets a confining limit on the extent and character of permissible adverse effects, regardless of source—whether from internal park management actions or from the transboundary impacts of external activities. Indeed, the no-impairment/no-derogation standard, if understood as applying to the subtle sort of adverse changes suggested by the dictionary definitions, sets an extremely strict standard and would seem to bar virtually any actions that would have more than de minimis adverse effects on park resources.[18]

Despite the textual rigor and primacy of the impairment prohibition, however, the Organic Act's accompanying statutory directive to provide for visitor "enjoyment" has provoked continuing debate over the proper role of the NPS in authorizing activities and developments in the parks whose

---

15. WEBSTER'S THIRD NEW INTERNATIONAL DICTIONARY OF THE ENGLISH LANGUAGE UNABRIDGED (1976). *See also* THE AMERICAN HERITAGE DICTIONARY OF THE ENGLISH LANGUAGE 644 (2d College ed., 1985) ("to diminish in strength, value, quantity or quality").

16. *Id.*

17. "Derogate" is defined by WEBSTER'S, *supra* note 15, at 608–09, as "to make to seem inferior; lower in esteem"; "to place something at a disadvantage or in disesteem esp. by taking part of it away"; or (archaic) "to take away (a part or quality of something) so as to do injury to the whole." THE AMERICAN HERITAGE COLLEGE EDITION, supra

note 15, at 356, defines derogate as "to detract; take away"; or "to deviate from a standard or expectation."

18. Traditional forms of legislative history offer little insight into the meaning or level of protection intended by this provision. But Yale emeritus historian Robin W. Winks finds considerable contemporaneous evidence that the key figures in drafting the Act intended a very high level of protection. *See* Robin W. Winks, *The National Park Service Act of 1916: "A Contradictory Mandate"?*, 74 DENV. U.L. REV. 575 (1997).

impacts inevitably involve some degree of "impairment." In view of the Act's explicit, albeit subsidiary, directive to "provide for the enjoyment" of park resources, it can be argued that the Act's "impairment" prohibition could not have been intended to adopt the dictionary meaning of the term in full rigor. Virtually any step taken within a park to provide for visitor enjoyment must, to some degree, "impair" affected resources within the meaning of the dictionary definition by diminish[ing] them in quantity, value, excellence, or strength. Illustrative are the very ordinary examples offered by the NPS' memorandum to the district court in [*Southern Wilderness Alliance v. Dabney*] in support of the NPS' contention that a literal interpretation prohibiting "any impairment" would unworkably bar even traditional low-impact visitor activities:

> [I]t is clear that hiking and backpacking in Canyonlands can and do result in damage to portions of the fragile cryptobiotic crusts which overlay [the surface of] relatively rare soils within the Park and which are essential to the Park's ecology.* * * Under [a standard prohibiting "any impairment," the Act] would prohibit the creation or mainte-nance of foot trails as well as most hiking and camping in * * * any * * * area * * * that contains desert soils. This reasoning could be extended to virtually any use which has an impact of any substance in the back-country and could virtually prohibit public access of any kind to the attractions which led to the creation of the Park. Such a result is clearly not within the intent of Congress.[20]

In short, the NPS argued that the "impairment" prohibition, if applied at full rigor (of the dictionary definition) would preclude the NPS from making even minimal provision "for enjoyment," despite that aspect of the statutory mandate. Similarly, the NPS later argued that a standard pre-cluding "any impairment" "could effectively preclude visitor use in all units of the National Park System." If, indeed, that were the result of a rigorous interpretation of "impairment," it would undoubtedly violate the well-established axiom of statutory interpretation requiring that, ordinari-ly, all terms of a statute must be given meaning. Thus, while a high level of protection for park resources was undoubtedly intended, the Act provides confusing guidance for park managers who must try to determine the point at which the adverse effects of visitor facilities or activities may become prohibited impairments. Lacking more detailed guidance, the Act neverthe-less demands highly refined management judgments in walking that fine and heretofore largely invisible line. The Solomons counted on to make these refined judgments—NPS park superintendents and their staffs—daily confront the real-world dilemma that virtually any step they may take to accommodate visitors' needs or preferences has the potential for adverse impacts on park resources. Indeed, it is reasonable to speculate that practical decisionmakers may tend to devalue the impairment prohibition as hortatory—and impossible to apply literally—because virtually any ser-

---

20. U.S. Memorandum (1) In Opposi-tion to Plaintiffs Motion for Summary Judg-ment and (2) In Support of U.S. Cross-Mo-tion for Summary Judgment in *Southern Utah Wilderness Alliance v. Dabney & Utah Trail Machine Ass'n et al.*, at 57–58 (United States District Court, District of Utah, Civ. No. 2:95CV 0559B) (quoting Declaration of Walt Dabney, Superintendent, Canyonlands National Park) (hereinafter U.S. Summary Judgment Memorandum).

vices or facilities provided for visitors' "enjoyment" will inevitably cause some adverse impacts on preexisting "natural" park conditions, and could thus fall within the rigorous dictionary definition of "impair." Since the Act's internal contradiction forecloses literal application, it may be argued, it is open to an interpretation recognizing a wide range of discretion to "balance" the two main goals of resource protection and provision for visitor enjoyment. Yet, "balancing" seems clearly contrary to the explicit statutory priority given to the impairment prohibition, leaving park managers at risk of straying beyond the murky but mandatory line drawn by the statute.

* * *

Confusion created by the Organic Act's twin management aims is exacerbated by the fact that individual units of the National Park System are established by documents (presidential proclamations in the case of National Monuments and statutes in the case of National Parks) that impose special management requirements.[1] The following article highlights the importance, collectively, of these many establishment documents, both in terms of current management decisions and in terms of how wildlife-related reform might best be undertaken:

Robert L. Fischman, *The Problem of Statutory Detail in National Park Establishment Legislation and Its Relationship to Pollution Control Law*
74 DENV. U.L. REV. 779 (1997).

Legal scholarship examining national park management focuses almost exclusively on the so-called "Organic Act" describing the overarching mandate for the National Park Service ("NPS" or "Service")....

But the bright fame of this broad statement of purpose has blinded many scholars to several hundred sections that follow it in Title 16. These are the sections that establish to which lands the overarching mandate will apply and, increasingly in recent years, detail how the Organic Act will apply to the specifically reserved units managed by the Service. The Organic Act would be nothing more than a distant vision, with no on-the-ground application, were it not for the establishment statutes that have created 54 national parks, 73 national monuments, and a variety of other reservations in the 374–unit national park system.

There are good reasons why the literature on national park management focuses on the Organic Act. Certainly, the overarching mandate is one of the most important statements of American cultural values enacted as environmental law. Also, it is the fundamental interpretive rule in exercising and reviewing the proprietary management discretion of the Service. The Organic Act, unlike establishment legislation, applies comprehensively to the entire geographic sweep of the national park system. Finally, the

---

1. Note, in the *Wilderness Alliance* decision excerpted above, the consideration given to the Canyonlands enabling legislation.

Organic Act sets up an elegant tension between providing for enjoyment (often interpreted as recreation) and leaving units unimpaired (often interpreted as preservation). This tension has stoked the furnace of countless heated arguments over management direction for the Service.

Unfortunately, this deserved interest in the NPS organic legislation has almost completely eclipsed searching analysis of establishment legislation....

. . .

A. The Role of Congress in the Management of the National Park System

Any single statute is a snapshot of the congressional landscape at the time of its enactment. Important legislation, such as the Organic Act, conveys a great deal about the compromises and accommodations necessary to secure enactment. However, because Congress seldom amends overarching legislation, these statutes have limited use as indicators of trends. Establishment statutes, because Congress regularly enacts them, serve well as indicators of the expanding role of congressional involvement in national park system management. Perhaps the most important trend revealed by establishment legislation over the past few decades is the expansion in the number of units composing the national park system.

Less noted but equally important, however, is the tendency in recent decades for Congress to specify in greater detail the management tasks for newly established units of the national park system. In its simplest form, establishment legislation would specify the metes and bounds of an area to be reserved or acquired for management by the Service under the Organic Act. However, during the past twenty-five years, Congress has rarely limited its lawmaking to simple area designation in establishment legislation. As the discussion [below] will show, Congress increasingly tailors management instructions to the Service for each unit established. Congress may specify management constraints on park administration with respect to visitor activities such as fishing, hunting, or grazing. It also may set out a particular process for planning, involving public hearings and consultations; and, it may require the management plan itself to address certain issues.

The greater congressional attention to management detail in establishment legislation gives rise to an increasingly important but frequently overlooked source of law for management of the national park system. Although the Organic Act remains an important interpretive tool, Service decision-makers must look first to establishment legislation to determine whether it speaks to an issue that an NPS unit needs to deal with. In the past decade, commentators have increasingly called for management reform to strengthen the Service's efforts in preservation. As the biological diversity of the United States continues to erode, for instance, the national park system becomes ever more valuable to maintain the biological integrity of representative ecosystems throughout the country. An examination of establishment legislation reveals that simple clarification of the Organic Act to stress the preservation prong of the Service's dual mandate, or even amending the Organic Act to embrace explicitly biological diversity, would not be sufficient to achieve comprehensive reform. Establishment legislation, which guides the management and planning for individual parks would also need to be revisited.

* * *

The potential diversity of uses within areas managed by the NPS is highlighted by the following decision:

National Rifle Association v. Potter

District Court for the District of Columbia.
628 F.Supp. 903 (1986).

■ JACKSON, D.J.: In this action for declaratory and injunctive relief plaintiff National Rifle Association of America ("NRA") and plaintiff-intervenor Wildlife Legislative Fund of America ask the Court to set aside a certain regulation promulgated under the aegis of the Secretary of the Interior which prohibit hunting and trapping in the National Park System except where specifically contemplated by Congress. Upon consideration of cross-motions for summary judgment—the principal legal issue being the accuracy of the Secretary's divination of legislative intent and the material facts largely matters of history—the Court finds that the regulation is not "arbitrary, capricious, an abuse of discretion, or otherwise not in accordance with law," 5 U.S.C. § 706, and defendants' motions for summary judgment will, accordingly, be granted and that of plaintiff denied.

I

The first national park, Yellowstone, was created by Congress in 1872 as a "public park or pleasuring ground for the benefit and enjoyment of the people." 16 U.S.C. § 21. By 1916, 13 national parks and 19 national monuments had been established, responsibility for their administration, however, having been dispersed among a number of government agencies, including the Departments of Interior, Agriculture and War. To provide more cohesive management for this expanding corpus of publicly-owned repositories of the nation's natural and historic heritage, Congress in that year created the National Park Service ("NPS"), whose mission, it said, was:

> [To] promote and regulate the use of the Federal areas known as national parks, monuments, and reservations hereinafter specified * * * by such means and measures as conform to the fundamental purpose of the said parks, monuments, and reservations, which purpose is to conserve the scenery and the natural and historic objects and the wild life therein and to provide for the enjoyment of the same in such manner and by such means as will leave them unimpaired for the enjoyment of future generations.

16 U.S.C. § 1 [hereinafter, the "Organic Act"]. The Secretary of the Interior was authorized to "make and publish such rules and regulations as he may deem necessary or proper for the use and management of the parks.* * *" 16 U.S.C. § 3. Although the Secretary was permitted in his discretion to provide "for the destruction of such animals and of such plant

life as may be detrimental to the use of any of said parks, monuments, or reservations," *id.*, the paramount objective of the park system with respect to its indigenous wildlife, and the philosophy which came to pervade the new Park Service to whom it was entrusted, was, from the beginning, one of protectionism. Witness an early directive from the Secretary of the Interior to NPS' first director: "[h]unting will not be permitted in any national park." [ ]

Beginning in the late 1930's, Congress began to add to the system a number of "nontraditional" park areas, such as national seashores, lakeshores and scenic riverways, in many of which Congress itself specifically undertook to authorize hunting, trapping and fishing as permitted recreational activities. In the 1960's, in recognition of the heterogeneous character of the territories it was now overseeing, the Park Service evolved on its own a concept of "management categories" as a means to differentiate the administration required for them. Under the new taxonomy, outlined in a memorandum in July of 1964 from then-Secretary of the Interior Udall to the Director of the Park Service, the park system was divided into three categories—natural, historical and recreational—with the policies for their governance to reflect the nature of the areas and the uses to which they had historically been put. [ ] Thus, in the case of recreation areas, which had traditionally accommodated multiple uses, the Park Service began to allow hunting, trapping and fishing on its own initiative if otherwise in accordance with federal, state and local laws. [ ]

Two subsequent amendments to the Organic Act, however, caused the Park Service to doubt the extent of its autonomy in the matter. In a 1970 amendment, known as the General Authorities Act, 16 U.S.C. § 1a–1, 1c, Congress declared:

> [T]hat the national park system, which began with establishment of Yellowstone National Park in 1872, has since grown to include superlative natural, historic, and recreation areas in every major region of the United States * * *; that these areas, though distinct in character, are united through their inter-related purposes and resources into one national park system as cumulative expressions of a single national heritage; * * * and that *it is the purpose of this Act to include all such areas in the System and to clarify the authorities applicable to the system.*

16 U.S.C. § 1a–1 (emphasis added). The Act continued: "[e]ach area within the national park system shall be administered in accordance with the provisions of any statute made specifically applicable to that area," as well as any other applicable authorities, "including, but not limited to the [Organic Act]." 16 U.S.C. § 1c. Eight years later, in a rider to the Redwood National Park Expansion Act, Pub. L. No. 95–250, 92 Stat. 163, Congress reiterated its intention that:

> [T]he promotion and regulation of the various areas of the National Park System * * * shall be consistent with and founded in the purpose established by [the Organic Act], to the common benefit of all the people of the United States. The authorization of activities shall be construed and the protection, management, and administration of these areas shall be conducted in light of the high public value and

integrity of the National Park System and shall not be exercised in derogation of the values and purposes for which these various areas have been established, *except as may have been or shall be directly and specifically provided by Congress.*

16 U.S.C. § 1a–1 (emphasis added). Perceiving in these amendments an implied reproof for having strayed from the true purpose of the Organic Act (and, specifically, for its "management categories" system), NPS concluded that Congress conceived of the park system as an integrated whole, wherein the Park Service was to permit hunting and trapping only where it had been specifically authorized, or discretion given it to do so, by Congress in the applicable enabling act. [ ]

Shortly thereafter NPS began the task of revising its regulations to bring them into harmony with the revealed congressional will by abandoning the "management categories." Proposed regulations were first published in the Federal Register on March 17, 1982, 47 Fed. Reg. 11,598 (1982), and, after consideration of the comments received, final regulations, including that presently in dispute, were published on June 30, 1983, to take effect on October 3, 1983. [ ] The contested regulation reads as follows:

§ 2.2 Wildlife protection.

(a) The following are prohibited:

(1) The taking of wildlife, except by authorized hunting and trapping activities conducted in accordance with paragraph (b) of this section.

* * *

(b) *Hunting and trapping*

(1) *Hunting shall be allowed in park areas where such activity is specifically mandated by Federal statutory law.*

(2) Hunting may be allowed in park areas where such activity is specifically authorized as a discretionary activity under Federal statutory law if the superintendent determines that such activity is consistent with public safety and enjoyment, and sound resource management principles. Such hunting shall be allowed pursuant to special regulations.

(3) *Trapping shall be allowed in park areas where such activity is specifically mandated by Federal statutory law.** * *

(4) Where hunting or trapping or both are authorized, such activities shall be conducted in accordance with Federal law and the laws of the State within whose exterior boundaries a park area or a portion thereof is located. Nonconflicting State laws are adopted as a part of these regulations.

* * *

36 C.F.R. § 2.2 (1985) (emphasis added).[4]

---

4. The regulations apply to all 338 units of the National Park System (including four areas administered by the Park Service under cooperative agreements with other agencies), of which 44 are considered recreation areas. *See* 36 C.F.R. § 1.2(1) (1985). Of

II

Plaintiff NRA filed this action on April 30, 1984, contending that the regulation arbitrarily and capriciously reverses a by-now venerable, and beneficent, Park Service policy of permitting hunting and trapping in recreational areas of the park system in the sound, *i.e.*, conservation-conscious, discretion of individual park superintendents, and that no express congressional command is, or has ever been, necessary to empower it to do so. Defendants respond that the philosophy of the Park Service, since its first expression in the Organic Act, has always been exclusively protectionist; that hunting and trapping have never been permitted in traditional parks and monuments; and that, while the Service may have succumbed to error in the late 1960's and 1970's, it has now acted to restore itself to grace by conforming its policy to a constant congressional intent of which it was pointedly reminded by the 1970 and 1978 amendments to the Organic Act.

. . .

In the instant case, it is the intent of Congress, as expressed in the Organic Act, the amendments, and the enabling acts creating the individual park units, which is to be ascertained. Specifically, the Court must determine whether the Park Service has made a "permissible construction" of them as precluding hunting and trapping unless Congress says otherwise, or whether, as plaintiff argues, the absence of a direct prohibition should be construed as authorizing the Secretary to exercise his own good judgment in the matter.

"The starting point in every case involving construction of a statute is the language itself." [ ] The Organic Act directs the Park Service to promote and regulate the use of the national parks "by such means and measures as conform to [their] fundamental purpose * * * *which purpose is to conserve the scenery and the natural and historic objects and the wild life therein* and to provide for the enjoyment of the same in such manner and by such means as will leave them unimpaired for the enjoyment of future generations." 16 U.S.C. § 1 (emphasis added). Plaintiff contends that this language is certainly not inconsistent with properly regulated hunting and trapping, while defendants argue that "conservation" of wildlife means just that: safeguarding it from harm, whether from natural or human causes.

Although the language of the Organic Act, standing alone, may not be plainly inconsistent with the concept of limited hunting and trapping, plaintiff's interpretation of it is nevertheless inconsistent with that principle of statutory interpretation known as *expressio unius est exclusio alterius, i.e.,* that omissions from enumerated specifics are generally presumed to

---

these, 40 were established by federal enabling acts, 31 of which expressly permit hunting, and three of which leave the matter to the Secretary's discretion. Six units have enabling acts which are silent as to hunting:.... In one of these, Padre Island National Seashore, the Park Service permits hunting because it reads the legislative history to evince Congress' intent to allow it. In another, Chattahoochee River National Recreation Area, hunting is not permitted, but plaintiff concedes that the legislative history indicates Congress' intent to prohibit it.

be deliberate exclusions from the general unless otherwise indicated. [ ] In the Organic Act Congress speaks of but a single purpose, namely, conservation; and the fact that Congress thereafter saw fit in the various acts creating individual units of the Park System to authorize hunting and/or trapping expressly (or to leave such matters to NPS' discretion) leads to a supposition that it expected that they would not be allowed to take place elsewhere.

It may also be significant that section three of the Organic Act permits the Secretary to "provide in his discretion for the destruction of such animals and of such plant life as may be detrimental to the use of any * * * parks, monuments, or reservations." 16 U.S.C. § 3. Had Congress intended section one of the Act to allow the Secretary discretion to permit hunting and trapping—certainly a most efficient form of destruction of undesirable wildlife—it would hardly have been necessary to grant him specific authority elsewhere to destroy for purpose of preventing "detriment." Finally, in its 1978 rider to the Redwood National Park Expansion Act, Congress reiterated its intention that the National Park System be administered in furtherance of the "purpose" (not "purposes") of the Organic Act, that being, of course, the conservation of, *inter alia,* wildlife resources. *See* 16 U.S.C. § 1a–1, 1c.

Nonetheless, if the statutory language may still be thought to be inconclusive (which it may in truth be; Congress is surely able to say "no hunting or trapping" in the park system unless it ordains) the Court must therefore turn to other sources, including the legislative histories of the various acts, for such light as they may shed on the issue.

Although the legislative history of the Organic Act itself is not teeming with references to the taking of fauna, such as there are lead to the conclusion that Congress did not contemplate any so-called "consumptive" uses of the new park system it was creating. For example, there is a House Report that states that the overriding purpose of the bill was to preserve "nature as it exists." [ ] Another speaks of a unit of the park system as a "game preserve." [ ]. . . .

Moreover, the interpretations given the Organic Act and the first enabling acts by those officials initially charged with their implementation in the early days of the park system reveals that they understood hunting and trapping were not to be permitted. . . .

The language and legislative histories of the several enabling acts creating park areas which are "silent" as to hunting are similarly subversive of plaintiff's position. . . .

Finally, with respect to the extent trapping must be regarded as a discrete predatory activity, plaintiff submits that the use of the word "hunting" in the relevant legislation implicitly subsumes trapping as a subset. However, although the enabling acts for two parks do contain provisions allowing hunting, fishing *and trapping* despite titles reading simply "Hunting and Fishing," [ ], when Congress has intended to provide for trapping, it has generally done so explicitly, and its omission in other statutes must be presumed to be intentional. Thus, hunting *and trapping* have been expressly authorized in 20 park areas, but in 25 others Congress authorized only hunting. On this record, the Court cannot but find that Congress considers the two activities to be distinct.

In sum, upon review of the relevant legislative histories and the statutes themselves, the Court is satisfied that the Park Service's reading of the statutory law comports with the apparent legislative intent; its interpretation is at least a reasonable one, and that is all it need be in the circumstances. The Secretary and the Park Service have been charged by Congress with the responsibility for achieving the sometimes conflicting goals of preserving the country's natural resources for future generations while ensuring their enjoyment by current users. Notwithstanding his recent predecessors may have permitted hunting and trapping in selected park areas of their choosing, the present Secretary has re-examined the subject in the light of recent amendments to the Organic Act and has concluded that his primary management function with respect to Park wildlife is its preservation unless Congress has declared otherwise. The regulation thus issues rationally from that conclusion, and if relief is to be forthcoming, plaintiff must look to Congress for it, not the courts.

NOTES

(1) Is the court's analysis persuasive? Under *Chevron* should the court simply have determined that the statutory language and legislative history were not conclusive and thus deferred to the agency's interpretation? Could the agency reverse itself?

(2) The discretion to protect: Although *Sierra Club v. Babbitt* (the *Portal Road case*) and *National Rifle Association v. Potter* are on opposite ends of the recreation/preservation continuum, in both decisions the court upholds the Secretary's discretion under the Organic Act to determine the balance. Thus, although the duty to leave the parks and their resources "unimpaired for future generations" imposes no significant restrictions on the Secretary's ability to promote recreational use of the parks even when doing so negatively affects park resources, that duty is the source of affirmative authority to act. Recall the similar caselaw concerning the public trust doctrine, which serves as a source of affirmative power to protect wildlife but imposes few restrictions on the trustee's ability to exploit trust resources. Does this reflect the lack of any judicially enforceable standards in both areas? A healthy balance between the political and the judicial branches?

Consider the following cases in which the NPS relied upon its Organic Act to protect park resources:

(a) *Michigan United Conservation Clubs v. Lujan* involved the distinction between hunting and trapping. In the legislation establishing the Pictured Rocks National Lakeshore and Sleeping Bear Dunes National Lakeshore, Congress required the Secretary to permit "hunting and fishing" but was silent on "trapping." Under the regulation at issue in *National Rifle Association v. Potter,* trapping was, therefore, prohibited. The trappers' challenge to the regulation was rejected by the Sixth Circuit:

we agree with and adopt the findings in *Potter* supporting the view that, unlike national forests, Congress did not regard the National Park System to be compatible with consumptive uses. Rather, Congress intended the Park Service to manage the system in order "to conserve the scenery and the natural and historic objects and the wild life therein * * * in such manner and by such means as will leave them unimpaired for the enjoyment of future generations[,]" 16 U.S.C. § 1, "except as may have been or shall be directly and specifically provided by Congress." 16 U.S.C. § 1a–1. Notwithstanding that the goals of user enjoyment and natural preservation may sometimes conflict, the NPS may rationally conclude, in light of the Organic Act and its amendments, that its primary management function with respect to wildlife is preservation unless Congress has declared otherwise.

Michigan United Conservation Clubs v. Lujan, 949 F.2d 202, 207 (6th Cir.1991).

(b) ***Organized Fishermen v. Hodel***: Unlike hunting and trapping, recreational fishing is generally permitted in parks. Commercial fishing, on the other hand, is treated like hunting and trapping: it is prohibited unless authorized by statute. Thus, a challenge by commercial fishers to regulations imposing bag limits on fish caught in the Everglades National Park, establishing sanctuaries in the Park for endangered species, and prohibiting all commercial fishing in the Park as of December 31, 1985, was rejected by the Eleventh Circuit. The court noted that:

> Where Congress has intended to permit commercial fishing in a national park, it has done so expressly by statute. *See, e.g.,* 16 U.S.C. § 459a–1 (1982) (regarding the Cape Hatteras National Seashore) ("the legal residents of villages [within the Seashore] shall have a right to earn a livelihood by fishing within the boundaries [of the Seashore], subject to such rules and regulations as the * * * Secretary may deem necessary * * *."); 16 U.S.C. § 230d (1982) (regarding the Barataria Marsh Unit of Jean Lafitte National Historical Park) ("Within the Barataria Marsh Unit, the Secretary shall permit hunting, fishing (including commercial fishing) * * *."); 16 U.S.C. § 410hh–4 (1982) (regarding the Malaspina Glacier Forelands Area of Wrangell–Saint Elias National Preserve, Cape Krusenstern National Monument, and the Dry Bay Area of Glacier Bay National Preserve) ("the Secretary may take no action to restrict unreasonably the exercise of valid commercial fishing rights or privileges obtained pursuant to existing law * * *.").

Organized Fishermen v. Hodel, 775 F.2d 1544 (11th Cir.1985), *cert. denied*, 476 U.S. 1169 (1986).

(3) Protection through removal: The NPS administers the Gettysburg National Military Park and Eisenhower National Historic Site, two contiguous parcels of in Pennsylvania. By the early 1980s, the NPS became concerned that the number of deer in the parks was negatively affecting the historical appearance of the land. Through a lengthy process under the National Historic Preservation Act, 16 U.S.C. § 470 *et seq.*, and NEPA, the agency developed a plan to restore a more historic landscape to the battleground by cutting 576 acres of non-historic woodlands, altering 278 acres of non-historic woodlands to reflect historic woodlots, shifting the agriculture to historical field patterns, and reducing deer populations to 25 per forested square mile. Among the alternatives considered for reducing the deer population were capture and transfer and contraception. The agency decided, however, that shooting the deer was the preferable alternative. Animal rights advocates challenged the decision, alleging in part that the decision violated the Organic Act. The District of Columbia Circuit Court of Appeals rejected the claims:

> Under the National Park Service Organic Act, the Secretary of the Interior "may * * * provide in his discretion for the destruction of such animals and of such plant life as may be detrimental to the use of any said parks, monuments, or reservations." 16 U.S.C. § 3. Because the Organic Act is silent as to the specifics of park management, the Secretary has especially broad discretion on how to implement his statutory mandate. *See Daingerfield Island Protective Soc'y v. Babbitt,* 40 F.3d 442, 446 (D.C.Cir.1994); *see also Bicycle Trails Council v. Babbitt,* 82 F.3d 1445, 1454 (9th Cir.1996) (adopting the district court's opinion); *Intertribal Bison Cooperative v. Babbitt,* 25 F.Supp.2d 1135 (D.Mont.1998). Still, a "finding of detriment" is necessary before the Park Service may engage in a "controlled harvest" such as the one proposed by the Park Service in its deer management program....

> The Park Service claims that it made a sufficient "finding of detriment" to justify the destruction of the deer under the Organic Act when it concluded that overbrowsing by deer in the historic woodlots and cropfields was detrimental to the purposes of the parks. As is reflected at several points in the record, the Park Service determined that the overbrowsing was preventing it from achieving the parks' objectives of preserving the historic appearance of the woodlots and cropfields, components of the landscape critical to the understanding and interpretation of the historic events that took place in each park. [ ] For example, in its Record of Decision initiating the deer management program, the Park Service concluded that

>> [d]ata from the [Storm Report] showed that the woodlots and cropfields could not be maintained in a way necessary to achieve park objectives. The high level of deer browsing was preventing a sufficient number of tree seedlings from becoming established, which is needed to perpetuate the historic woodlots. The agricultural program was unable to grow historical crops to maturity in Eisenhower NHS and the southern part of Gettysburg NMP due to deer browsing.

> [ ] The Court concludes that Park Service made a sufficient "finding of detriment" on the record to satisfy the requirements of the Organic Act.

Davis v. Latschar, 202 F.3d 359 (D.C.Cir.2000).

(B) The Problem of Edges

NOTES

(1) "External" threats: One of the recurrent issues in federal land management is the extent of the federal government's power to protect its lands from actions on adjacent parcels. In *Cappaert v. United States* (noted in the discussion of the Antiquities Act), groundwater pumping on a neighboring ranch was draining the aquifer that surfaced in Devil's Hole and threatening the Devil's Hole pupfish. The Supreme Court held that the United States had the power to protect the fish. Similarly, in *Bailey v. Holland,* 126 F.2d 317, 324 (4th Cir.1942), the court of appeals held that the federal government had the power to close lands adjacent to a national wildlife refuge to hunting: "to make this refuge more effective, the Secretary may prohibit all hunting in the immediate vicinity." And in *United States v. Brown,* 552 F.2d 817 (8th Cir.), *cert. denied,* 431 U.S. 949 (1977), the court upheld federal prohibitions against hunting within the boundaries of Voyageurs National Park despite the fact that the hunter was on state land at the time. *See also United States v. Southern Florida Water Management District,* 28 F.3d 1563 (11th Cir.1994) (suit against local water district for contamination of national wildlife refuge and national park that resulted in an agreement that specified steps would be taken to restore and preserve the federal land).

The record is not, however, entirely favorable. The government failed, for example, to enjoin an asserted nuisance from the construction of four, 300–foot high office buildings in *United States v. Arlington County,* 487 F.Supp. 137 (E.D.Va.1979). And the gap between the power to protect and the willingness to do so is often even more striking. In the 1980s, for example, the NPS was prohibited from any interference with land uses external to park by the politicians running the Department. *See* George C. Coggins, *Protecting Wildlife Resources of National Parks from External Threats,* 22 LAND & WATER L. REV. 1, 18 n.145 (1987); *see generally* Robert B. Keiter, *On Protecting the National Parks from the External Threats Dilemma,* 20 LAND & WATER L. REV. 355 (1984); William J. Lockhart, *External Threats to Our National Parks: An Argument for Substantive Protection,* 16 STAN. ENVTL. L.J. 3 (1997).

(2) Bison, elk, brucellosis, and domestic cows: Things not only leak into parks, they also leak out. The dispute in *Wyoming v. United States*— the case that closed the materials on the National Wildlife Refuge System— was grounded in the fact that elk wander out of the National Elk Range and thus might infect domestic cattle with *brucella abortus,* the bacterium that can cause the disease brucellosis.

The dispute over bison, elk, brucellosis, and domestic cattle provides a perspective on several important issues: the relationship between the long-dominant livestock industry and the emerging recognition of the value of wildlife on the public domain; the problem of islands, or more formally, the biological irrelevance of legal boundaries in the management of wildlife; the propriety of the NPS "natural regulation" management on an island surrounded by private property; the ethics of killing animals deemed surplus because their population is larger than we desire.

(3) *Fund for Animals v. Hodel* was filed in 1985 to stop the NPS "from taking any action which would allow migrating bison to be killed," seeking an injunction requiring the NPS to contain the bison within the park, and requiring the agency to prepare an EIS on bison management. The Montana federal district court rejected all of plaintiff's claims, holding that the

NPS decisions were not arbitrary and did not constitute major federal action significantly affecting the human environment so as to require an EIS. *Fund for Animals v. Hodel,* CV 85–250–BU (D.Mont.1985), discussed in *Fund for Animals, Inc. v. Lujan,* 794 F.Supp. 1015 (D.Mont.1991).

(4) *Fund for Animals, Inc. v. Lujan* was a challenge to an interim bison management plan predicated upon claims that the NPS had violated NEPA and the Organic Act. The court again rejected plaintiff's claims, entering elaborate findings of fact:

12. Brucellosis is a serious disease both in livestock and in humans. The disease causes sterility and fetal abortions in livestock and undulant fever in humans. . . .

13. Prior to the 1940's, undulant fever was a significant health risk. Five percent of those who contracted it died. Since eradication, the incident rate of undulant fever has declined 99%.

14. The brucellosis organism can survive 10–57 days in tap water; 5–78 days in cloth or fabric; 100 days in untreated manure; 43 days in dry soil; and 66 days in damp soil. Moreover, the bacteria can indefinitely survive freezing. The disease is transmitted through raw milk, through fluids surrounding the animal fetus, and through the aborted fetus itself.

15. Montana has only recently (1985) achieved status as a brucellosis-free state, after 30 years of effort and expenditure of $30 million. Nationally, $1 billion has been spent on eradication of brucellosis.

16. Montana exports substantial numbers of beef cattle nationally and internationally. In 1989, 800,000 cattle were shipped out of state. Montana cattle producers depend upon the ability to freely ship livestock in interstate commerce.

17. The brucellosis-free status achieved by Montana directly affects the ability of cattle producers to ship livestock in interstate commerce and saves $1 to $2 million per year by allowing cattle to be shipped without testing.

18. Brucellosis can exist in two types of hosts, dead-end hosts and preferential hosts. . . . Ungulates such as bison, cattle, and elk are preferential hosts of which the disease can take advantage and leave to infect other species.

19. Elk do not presently pose a significant risk of transmission of the disease due to their low rate of infection (1.4% in Yellowstone elk), and their different social behavior patterns.

20. Fifty-four percent of the Yellowstone bison tested in 1988 (465 animals) tested positive for brucellosis and are therefore infected. Tissue tests of Yellowstone bison have isolated or cultured the brucellosis bacteria. The court finds that about half the Yellowstone bison herd is infected with brucellosis.

21. Results from a study conducted at the Texas A & M School of Veterinary Medicine conclusively show that bison are susceptible to brucellosis, as are domestic livestock. The court finds that bison and livestock readily transmit the disease to each other.

22. Bison migrate out of Yellowstone Park onto private and public land used by cattle.

Fund for Animals, Inc. v. Lujan, 794 F.Supp. 1015, 1019 (D.Mont.1991). Based upon these findings, the court denied plaintiff's motion: "stopping the interim control actions would not be in the public interest given the serious threat of brucellosis, the large number of excess bison, and the lack of feasible alternatives to control bison migrating out of the Park." *Id.* at 1020.

On appeal,

[t]he Fund contends that the district court abused its discretion in denying preliminary injunctive relief because it relied on clearly erroneous factual findings. The Fund specifically challenges the district court's findings that the migrating bison pose a serious risk of transmitting brucellosis to Montana cattle. . . .

In challenging the district court's finding that bison infected with brucellosis pose a risk to domestic cattle, the Fund relied on the uncontested fact that no case has been reported of the transmission of brucellosis from Yellowstone bison to domestic cattle. The Fund's argument ignores the evidence in the record which supports the district court's finding that the "[u]ncontrolled migration of potentially brucellosis-infected bison into Montana causes a real and present danger to the livestock industry of Montana as well as a significant health risk to humans."

The record shows that brucellosis is a serious disease that causes miscarriages in cattle and can result in death to humans who contract undulant fever from infected cattle. The district court received evidence of a study conducted at the Texas A & M School of Veterinary Medicine that demonstrated infected bison could transmit brucellosis to cattle in a controlled environment. The record also shows that approximately half of the Yellowstone bison herd have tested positive for brucellosis. The court's expert, Dr. David Cameron, testified that bison have a greater possibility of transmitting brucellosis to cattle if the two species come into close contact. Domestic cattle are most likely to be infected with brucellosis by ingestion, either directly by contact with a newborn bison calf or fetus, or indirectly through ingesting contaminated feed.

The district court did not clearly err in finding that the migrating Yellowstone bison pose a serious health risk. Although no documented case of transmission from infected Yellowstone bison to cattle has been verified, the evidence presented at the hearing supports the district court's finding that a serious potential for such transmission exists.

Fund for Animals, Inc. v. Lujan, 962 F.2d 1391, 1400–01 (9th Cir.1992).

PERSPECTIVES

(1) Burdens of proof (*aka,* a preponderance of the evidence) and scientific uncertainty, pt. 1: The district court in *Fund for Animals, Inc. v. Lujan* made several "factual" findings that arguably pushed a fuzzy grey into a sharply etched black-and-white. Compare a more nuanced examination of the science where the dominant theme is uncertainty:

Brucellosis is endemic in Greater Yellowstone's wildlife populations. The disease was first detected in Yellowstone bison in 1917, which was also the first time wildlife were definitively identified as brucellosis carriers. In 1930, brucellosis was discovered in elk at the National Elk Refuge; three years later, it was detected in elk inside Yellowstone National Park. Ironically, scientists generally agree that brucellosis was first passed to bison and elk by infected livestock. Blood tests conducted on the 569 Yellowstone bison shot during the 1988–89 winter in Montana revealed that fifty-four percent of them carried the brucellosis organism.[171] But recent culture of tissue samples—a much more reliable method of identifying active infection than blood sampling—taken from 213 bison killed during the 1991–92 winter indicate that only twelve percent were infected with brucellosis, and only one of the nine infected females tested positive for brucellosis in her reproductive tract. In 1989, eleven of the sixteen bison shot from the Grand Teton population also tested positive from blood samples for brucellosis. Moreover, recent blood tests confirm that elk from herds utilizing 18 of the 23 feedgrounds maintained in western Wyoming carry brucellosis, which means approximately 18,000 elk may have been exposed to the disease. The tests also indicate that the brucellosis organism found in bison and elk is the same one that is responsible for brucellosis in cattle.

The brucellosis organism is transmitted between animals primarily by contact with infected reproductive materials. Infection can occur when a brucellosis-free animal consumes forage contaminated by the organism after an infected animal has expelled an aborted fetus, or when a susceptible animal directly ingests the organism from fetal material, or when it licks the reproductive organs of an infected animal. Brucellosis transmission, therefore, mainly occurs during late pregnancy in association with abortion or parturition. In Greater Yellowstone, elk usually give birth from late-May through mid-June, while bison usually begin birthing one month earlier. Under appropriate conditions, the brucellosis organism can survive for many days in aborted material.[178]

---

171. E. Tom Thorne *et al., Brucellosis in Free–Ranging Bison: Three Perspectives,* *in* THE GREATER YELLOWSTONE ECOSYSTEM: REDEFINING AMERICA'S WILDERNESS HERITAGE 275 (R. Keiter & M. Boyce eds., 1991). Although Montana officials extracted blood samples that showed approximately fifty percent of the bison were exposed to the brucellosis organism, blood sampling does not reveal whether the bison can transmit the disease. Montana officials were sharply criticized for not conducting thorough studies of tissue samples from the 569 bison slain during the 1988–89 public hunt. Jay F. Kirkpatrick,

Trouble Where the Bison Roam, 2 ENDANGERED SPECIES 4, 8 (Winter 1992).

178. IVAL AUTHUR MERCHANT, AN OUTLINE OF INFECTIOUS DISEASES OF DOMESTIC ANIMALS 252, 254 (1951). Outside an animal body, the *Brucella abortus* organism will survive "four hours in direct sunlight, four days in bovine urine, 5 days dried in burlap and room temperature, 30 days in an unheated cellar, 37 days when dried slowly in soil, and 75 days in an aborted fetus in cool weather." *Id. See also The Fund for Animals, Inc. v. Lujan,* 794 F.Supp. 1015 (D.Mont.1991), Memorandum and Order, at 6. However, predators roam

Brucellosis is more likely to be transmitted when animals are in close contact with one another. University researchers have determined that bison in a controlled setting can pass the organism to previously uninfected cattle.[179] In Greater Yellowstone, researchers had believed brucellosis persisted in the bison population because of their herding instincts, but one expert has now suggested that the organism is passed from female bison to their nursing calves through "mother's milk." In the case of elk, the winter feedgrounds in western Wyoming are prime locations for transmission of brucellosis. With elk and bison freely intermingling during late pregnancy on the National Elk Refuge, they are undoubtedly passing the disease back and forth to one another. Wildlife allegedly have been responsible for several brucellosis outbreaks in western Wyoming cattle, but they have never been proven to be the actual source.

Indeed, science has not definitively answered whether brucellosis can be transmitted from wildlife to cattle in the wild. There is no confirmed instance where free roaming wildlife have infected domestic livestock with brucellosis on the open range. After reviewing years of bison-brucellosis research, a respected scientist specializing in brucellosis recently concluded that because Yellowstone's wild bison are not affected by brucellosis in the same manner as cattle, they are not a threat to transmit brucellosis to cattle. In a controlled setting, however, where bison and cattle were held in close proximity to one another, researchers observed that brucellosis-infected bison passed the disease to the cattle at the same rate as cattle passed it to one another. Relying largely upon this study, the Ninth Circuit Court of Appeals recently affirmed a Montana federal district court's finding that "bison and livestock readily transmit the disease to each other."[186] . . .

Significantly, Yellowstone's bison do not appear to be adversely affected by the brucellosis organism. Although nearly half of the Yellowstone bison population tests positive for brucellosis in blood samples, there is very little fetal loss. Recent tissue samples taken from 213 bison, shot during the 1991–92 winter, revealed that only one cow bison was culture positive for brucellosis in her reproductive tract. The brucellosis-infected Yellowstone bison herd has been completely closed to other bison for 77 years, yet it has continued to reproduce at a rate comparable to uninfected Montana cattle herds. Researchers speculate that these bison may test positive for exposure to the disease, but

the Greater Yellowstone region widely, and they generally consume aborted material rather quickly. Margaret M. Meyer, *Brucella Abortus in the Yellowstone National Park Bison Herd* 3, 16 (Report to the Department of the Interior, Yellowstone National Park, Mar. 18, 1992).

179. Donald S. Davis et al., *Brucella Abortus in Captive Bison. I. Serology, Bacteriology, Pathogenesis, and Transmission to Cattle*, 26 J. WILDLIFE DISEASES 366 (July 1990). The one confirmed case of brucellosis

transmission from bison to cattle outside of a rigidly controlled setting occurred on a ranch where domestic bison were being raised with cattle. [ ]

186. *Fund for Animals, Inc. v. Lujan*, 962 F.2d 1391 (9th Cir.1992). . . . This same district court, however, concluded that "elk do not presently pose a significant risk of transmission of the disease due to their low rate of infection * * * and their different social behavior patterns." [ ]

nevertheless be immune to it and incapable of transmitting it through reproductive materials. One respected veterinary scientist has concluded that "brucellosis in bison, most certainly as now manifested in the Yellowstone National Park bison herd, is decidedly not a carbon copy of bovine brucellosis." . . .

Scientists believe that vaccination against brucellosis generally protects livestock from the disease. Scientific studies have established a seventy percent effectiveness rate in preventing brucellosis in cattle vaccinated against the disease. Teton County ranchers on the west side of the Continental Divide in Wyoming routinely vaccinate their calves against brucellosis, and they have never experienced a wildlife-related brucellosis outbreak despite the intermingling that occurs between cattle and wildlife on their public domain grazing leases. In fact, most scientists are convinced that vaccination of cattle against brucellosis provides substantial—but not complete—protection against the risk of disease transmission in the wild, where cattle and wildlife are not regularly in close contact with one another.

. . .

Because elk and bison regularly commingle on the National Elk Refuge and come in contact elsewhere in Greater Yellowstone, an elk vaccination program would only succeed in eradicating brucellosis if the disease was also eliminated in bison. However, recent experiments with bison vaccination have not been encouraging, which means there is yet no effective means for protecting bison from brucellosis. In other words, current scientific research suggests that the only way to eliminate brucellosis in bison is to kill every one with the disease. But the only way to test bison for the disease is to trap them, and then to hold and test them over an extended time. Not only is this process quite difficult, expensive, and harmful to the animals, but it would violate the Park Service's commitment to the herd's free ranging status. While this type of intensive management is precisely how the livestock industry handles the disease in domestic livestock, it may not be appropriate for managing Greater Yellowstone's wildlife, particularly when the risk of transmission is quite low.

Robert B. Keiter & Peter H. Froelicher, *Bison, Brucellosis, and Law in the Greater Yellowstone Ecosystem,* 28 LAND & WATER L. REV. 1 (1993).

(2) Burdens of proof (*aka,* a preponderance of the evidence) and scientific uncertainty, pt. 2: The information presented by Keiter and Froelicher is far more complex and nuanced than that found by the federal district court in *Fund for Animals, Inc. v. Lujan,* 794 F.Supp. 1015 (D.Mont.1991). How to explain the differences? Consider the following:

As formal systems of inquiry, law and science have several important features in common. Each tradition claims an authoritative capacity to sift evidence and derive rational and persuasive conclusions from it. The reliability of observers (or witnesses) and the credibility of their observations are of critical concern to both legal and scientific decision-making. Unlike organized religion, neither science nor law owes allegiance to a single dogmatic authority. In both fields, rules governing the assessment of facts occasionally undergo massive shifts—in science through the work of paradigm-transforming pioneers and in the law (ordinarily but not always) through the actions of legislatures. Normal progress within each discipline occurs through a decentralized, silent revolution brought about by individuals making decisions at the frontiers of established doctrine in accordance with their personal understanding of the existing tradition.

The considerable differences between scientific and legal thinking are most apparent in their approaches to fact-finding. Science, as conventionally understood, is primarily concerned with getting the facts "right"—at least to the extent permitted by the existing research paradigm or tradition. The law also seeks to establish facts correctly, but only as an adjunct to its transcendent objective of settling disputes fairly and efficiently. This basic dichotomy accounts for a number of secondary contrasts. Because the law needs closure, the process of legal fact-finding is always bounded in time: inquiry has to stop when the evidence is exhausted. The judicial inquirer cannot postpone a decision by choosing to wait for more evidence. As John Ziman, British physicist and sociologist of science, has noted, "If we are forced to a premature opinion on a scientific question, we are bound to give the Scottish verdict *Not Proven,* or say that the jury have disagreed, and a new trial is needed." The law, by contrast, must take a position based on the facts at hand, however premature such a decision may appear in the eyes of scientists.

Fact-finding in law proceeds through a form of ritualized courtroom discourse that subjects the scientist's firsthand reporting of observation and experiment to additional conceptual and rhetorical filters. What the legal fact-finder "knows" is a function of what the witnesses in a proceeding choose to relate in court in answer to questions posed by lawyers. British mystery writer R. Austin Freeman wryly commented on this highly restricted form of knowing in a 1911 novel: "The scientific outlook is radically different from the legal. The man of science relies on his own knowledge and observation and judgment, and disregards testimony.* * * A court of law must decide according to the evidence which is before it; and that evidence is of the nature of sworn testimony. If a witness is prepared to swear that black is white and no evidence to the contrary is offered, the evidence before the Court is that black is white, and the Court must decide accordingly." Freeman satirized, but around a kernel of truth. "Science," for the law's purposes, is simply the composite of testimony presented in and around an adjudicatory proceeding, and its quality depends heavily on the skill and intentions of the lawyers who elicit the presentation. The facts that the law constructs (or reconstructs) are thus necessarily different from the facts that scientists construct to persuade their peers in their own rhetorically and procedurally distinctive surroundings.

To serve its need for decisive endings, the law has devised a complex system of rules and practices for choosing what to believe when facts are uncertain; these rules and practices by definition are not "scientific." They include, to start with, the rules by which the legal system determines what evidence and which witnesses are relevant to the dispute at hand. Another body of legal rules addresses the problem of making decisions on the basis of conflicting evidence. For example, in civil cases the legal system places the "burden of proof" on the plaintiff. In order to prevail the plaintiff must prove his claim by a "preponderance of the evidence"—in other words, more than 50 percent of the evidence must be in the plaintiff's favor. This requirement is a way of ensuring that even in those borderline cases in which the evidence is perfectly balanced the legal fact-finder will have an orderly basis for deciding between the disputants. Science under the same circumstances would be neither willing nor able to declare a winner. Administrative decisions generally call for a lower standard of proof, whereas criminal trials demand something closer to scientific certainty ("beyond reasonable doubt"). A contrafactual or contra-scientific conclusion can, in appropriate circumstances, be declared the "right" conclusion from the standpoint of the law. In criminal proceedings, for instance, evidence deemed highly relevant to a scientifically "correct" determination of guilt or innocence might be excluded in order to protect individuals against coercion by the state, thereby producing a technically "incorrect" but morally just outcome.

Even in civil cases, the legal system's allegiance to values other than those of science may open the way to decisions that look like sheer irrationality. For example, in a 1946 paternity case against Charlie Chaplin, a jury held the actor liable, and the court ordered him to pay child support, even though blood-group evidence showed he could not have been the father. Francisco Ayala, a distinguished biologist, and Bert Black, an engineer-lawyer, cite this as a bizarre decision that flies in the face of scientific knowledge. Michael Saks, a social psychologist and expert on evidence, takes a more moderate stance, pointing out that "the jury may have doubted the manner in which the blood test was carried out, the underlying science, or the honesty of the expert witnesses." Equally, Saks notes, the jury's sense of justice could have affected the outcome. Biological relationships, after all, do not always control in determining an adult's financial or custodial responsibility for a child. To ensure support for children, state laws have traditionally presumed that a child born to a married woman is her husband's legitimate offspring. Perhaps the jury analogized Chaplin's position to that of the canonical husband, taking into account his vastly superior economic standing in comparison with the child's mother. Under any of these readings, the jury's refusal to accept the scientific denial of Chaplin's paternity could properly be characterized as social wisdom rather than scientific illiteracy.

SHEILA JASANOFF, SCIENCE AT THE BAR: LAW, SCIENCE, AND TECHNOLOGY IN AMERICA 8–11 (1995).

Greater Yellowstone Coalition v. Babbitt

District Court for the District of Montana.
952 F.Supp. 1435 (1996).
affirmed by memorandum, 108 F.3d 1385 (9th Cir.1997).

■ LOVELL, D.J.:—In this case, several conservation groups and an individual challenge a federal action under the Administrative Procedure Act (the

"APA") and the National Environmental Policy Act ("NEPA"). The Plaintiffs currently seek to enjoin implementation of the Interim Bison Management Plan (the "1996 Interim Plan"), which in 1995 was drafted jointly by the State of Montana ("Montana"), the National Park Service ("NPS"), and the Animal and Plant Inspection Service ("APHIS"), and has since been revised and finalized in 1996. This matter is before the court on Plaintiffs' motion for preliminary injunction. . . .

I. BACKGROUND

In 1995, Montana, NPS, and APHIS agreed upon a draft of the Interim Bison Management Operating Procedures (the "1996 Interim Plan") for managing Yellowstone bison that leave Yellowstone National Park (the "Park") and enter public and private lands in Montana. The NPS and Montana prepared a Draft Environmental Assessment ("EA") on the 1996 Interim Plan, and released it on December 20, 1995, for public comment. Over 260 comments on the EA were received from state and federal agencies, Native American tribes, various organizations, and individuals. The 1996 Interim Plan was corrected and revised based upon public comments. On August 5, 1996, a Finding of No Significant Impact ("FONSI") was issued by NPS which stated that pursuant to federal statutes and regulations no environmental impact statement need be prepared for the 1996 Interim Plan. On August 9, 1996, Montana issued a Decision Notice, which announced its intention to implement the 1996 Interim Plan. After the issuance of the NPS FONSI and Montana's Decision Notice, all parties to the 1996 Interim Plan approved the plan.

In 1902, there were approximately 23 bison ranging in Yellowstone National Park. [ ] In order to increase the herd, domestic bison from Montana and Texas were brought to Yellowstone. [ ] In order to further improve the herd, bison were herded by cowboys and managed as livestock, and a ranch was established in the Lamar Valley of the Park, with corrals and barns. [ ] In 1954, there were approximately 1,477 bison in the park. [ ] NPS decided to reduce the herd, however, and by 1967 the number of bison had dropped to 397. [ ]

In 1967, NPS changed its policy regarding the Yellowstone bison by deciding to discontinue its overt management of the bison. By 1988 there were 2,800 bison in the Park. [ ] In 1992 there were 3,400 bison in the Park. [ ] In 1995 there were approximately 3,900 bison in the Park. [ ]

Thus, the Yellowstone bison herd has steadily increased over the years, and with these increases the herd has required more and more land for forage, causing the northern herd to wander out of the Park in winter months to seek additional forage in Montana. In 1968, the NPS began a program of boundary protection involving park personnel shooting bison approaching boundary areas. [ ] NPS subsequently discontinued its boundary protection program.

However, because the Yellowstone herd is infected with brucellosis, and because bison have damaged private property and carry a health risk to humans, the State of Montana has had little choice but to destroy Yellowstone bison entering the state. Neither Montana nor the NPS has been satisfied with this state of affairs, which under the 1992 Interim Plan essentially required Montana to manage the Yellowstone herd for NPS by culling some 450 bison from the herd each winter, as these bison enter the State of Montana. It is important to note, however, that this annual culling of the herd by the State of Montana has had no impact upon the integrity of the herd, and in fact the herd has rebounded to even higher numbers despite Montana's removal of bison each winter.

Recognizing that the Yellowstone bison, if they are to remain free-ranging, must be jointly managed by state and federal governments, the NPS and the State of Montana entered into a Settlement Agreement in *State of Montana v. United States,* Cause No. CV 95–6 (D. Mont., Nov. 20, 1995), whereby NPS and Montana agreed to prepare an interim joint operations plan (the 1996 Interim Plan), to prepare an Environmental Assessment of the 1996 Interim Plan (the "EA") to determine whether an environmental impact statement ("EIS") need also be prepared, and to take public comments on the 1996 Interim Plan and the EA. All of these steps have been accomplished, and the Environmental Assessment and Response to Public Comments formed the basis of a Finding of No Significant Impact ("FONSI") by the Superintendent of the Park and the NPS Director of the Intermountain Field Area. [ ] Accordingly, NPS and Montana have jointly determined that an EIS need not be prepared. The 1996 Interim Plan is now being implemented within and without the Park, and Plaintiffs seek to enjoin certain parts of this plan.

1996 Interim Plan

The 1996 Interim Plan deals with an area north and west of Yellowstone National Park, in Park and Gallatin counties of the State of Montana, wherein 87% of the land is federally owned, 1% of the land is state owned, and 12% of the land is privately owned. During certain times of the year, cattle graze on private and public lands north and west of the Park. [ ]

Eagle Creek/Bear Creek

The Montana Department of Livestock ("DOL") has the responsibility to remove bison that leave the Eagle Creek/Bear Creek area. DOL may request that NPS personnel assist in shooting operations outside of the Park. This procedure is intended to prevent bison moving onto private lands. No capture facilities are contemplated in the Eagle Creek/Bear Creek area.

Reese Creek Area

Capture operations in the Stephens Creek area of the Park are intended to prevent bison from leaving the Park in the Reese Creek boundary area and entering private lands. Bison that enter private lands are to be shot, with the permission of the private landowner. DOL is to conduct these removals, but NPS personnel are to assist in shooting these bison. The capture operations will be conducted within the Park in the Reese Creek area (the sole siting of a capture operation in the Park), and the captured animals will be shipped to slaughter. The Reese Creek area is not considered to be critical winter range for bison. [ ] Bison are not known to be a springtime food source for grizzly bears hibernating in the Reese Creek area. [ ] Gray wolves do not use the habitat in Reese Creek. *Id.*

West Boundary Area

In this area there will be portable capture facilities outside of the Park, and bison moving onto private lands will be shot with the permission of the private landowner. All captured bison will be field tested for brucella antibodies, and all bison testing positive will be shipped to a slaughter facility. Male and non-pregnant female bison that test negative for brucella antibodies will be permitted to move onto public lands adjacent to the Park. It is estimated that about 40% of the migrating bison in the West Yellowstone area will be saved under the 1996 Interim Plan, as opposed to having potentially all of the Yellowstone bison in this area being shot under the previous interim plan. [ ] The West Yellowstone area only provides marginal winter habitat, and was not used by bison prior to the 1980s. [ ] Bison are not known to be a significant springtime food source for grizzly bears hibernating in the West Yellowstone area, but it is expected that bison winterkill will continue unaffected by the 1996 Interim Plan and such carrion will continue to be available for grizzly bear consumption. [ ] Gray wolves do not use the habitat at West Yellowstone. [ ]

Other Areas

Bison sometimes move into remote public lands adjacent to the Park, such as Hellroaring Creek, Slough Creek, and portions of the Lee Metcalf/Cabin Creek area. These bison will be monitored and allowed to remain on these outlying public lands.

. . .

Organic Act Claims. Title 16 of the United States Code, section one, requires NPS to conform its actions to its purpose, which "purpose is to conserve the scenery and the natural and historic objects and the wildlife therein and to provide for their enjoyment and leave them unimpaired for future generations." 16 U.S.C. § 1. Plaintiffs argue that by this statutory language Congress has clearly required NPS to leave the Yellowstone bison absolutely untouched. But the statutory purpose language obviously gives park managers broad discretion in determining how best to conserve wildlife and to leave them unimpaired for future generations. *See, e.g., Bicycle Trails Council of Marin v. Babbitt,* 82 F.3d 1445, 1454 (9th Cir.1996).

In the case at hand, for example, how best to conserve a bison herd infected with a serious disease, which disease has been the subject of a nation-wide eradication program for some fifty years? How best to leave the herd unimpaired for future generations when the neighboring governmental entity can legally, and will in fact, shoot members of the herd stepping over the political boundary line? How best to conserve and protect this particular herd under these particular circumstances?

This is just the type of question that the APA contemplates when it permits an agency to make a well-reasoned discretionary decision based upon its expertise. In this case, federal regulation mandates that the NPS administer the park in accordance with approved general management and resource management plans, or in emergency operations involving threats to life, property, or park resources. [ ] The 1996 Interim Plan is an approved resource management plan that was created within the discretionary powers of the NPS.

In their next argument, Plaintiffs assert that the Organic Act requires a finding of "detriment" before NPS may destroy park resources. The statute cited by Plaintiffs provides that

> [t]he Secretary of the Interior * * * may also provide in his discretion for the destruction of such animals and of such plant life as may be detrimental to the use of any of said parks, monuments, or reservations.

16 U.S.C. § 3. Plaintiffs couple this statute with an NPS policy requiring an explicit finding of detriment by a park superintendent when a controlled harvest program is contemplated, i.e., a program designed to kill a percentage of a herd for no other reason than the desire to reduce the size of the herd. [ ] However, the very language of this policy limits it to situations involving a controlled harvest. [ ] This "explicit finding" policy is inapplicable on these facts, therefore, because the 1996 Interim Bison Plan does not authorize a controlled harvest program but a boundary protection program.

In any event, the obvious purpose of the policy is to require a park superintendent to make the decision to reduce the size of a wildlife population in writing and to make that decision based upon scientific documentation. Although in this case the Yellowstone Superintendent's decision is not a decision to reduce the size of a wildlife population, it is a written program decision based on scientific documentation. Accordingly, Plaintiffs' "explicit finding of detriment" argument under 16 U.S.C. § 3 is not likely to succeed on the merits.

As Defendant–Intervenors point out, Montana has been forced periodically to thin and cull the Park's bison herd, with the result that the herd has produced maximum numbers of bison for public enjoyment. *Fund for Animals v. Lujan,* 794 F. Supp. 1015, 1021 (D.Mont.1991). Had Montana not performed this function for the NPS but instead fenced certain Park boundaries, hundreds of bison might starve within the Park each winter. [ ] Additionally, given the infectious disease within the herd and Montana's stringent removal program, NPS might reasonably consider that its failure to cooperate with Montana would be detrimental to the use of the Park.

Defendants also point out that they have statutory authorization to cooperate with states in the enforcement of state laws. 16 U.S.C. § 1a–6 provides that "[t]he Secretary of the Interior is authorized to—* * * (2) cooperate, within the National Park System, with any State or political subdivision thereof in the enforcement of supervision of the laws or ordinances of that State or subdivision* * *." In this case, Montana law requires that wild bison exposed to brucella be hazed out of the state or captured and destroyed. Mont. Code Ann. § 81–2–201(1). Clearly, the NPS has a rational interest in cooperating with Montana both to reduce the total annual number of Yellowstone bison destroyed and also to reduce the herd's population of brucella-exposed bison. NPS policies clearly authorize

NPS cooperation with Montana to control brucellosis in the Yellowstone herd and migration of the herd out of the Park. [ ]

Generally, Plaintiffs' arguments call for the NPS to take an extremely myopic view of the Yellowstone bison herd, such that when members of the herd step over the (invisible) political boundary line, Plaintiffs would have the NPS pretend that these Yellowstone bison have simply disappeared. Such a myopic view does not square with an ecosystems approach to the Yellowstone bison herd. In responding to public comments on the Draft Environmental Assessment, the NPS states that its policy is to manage park resources and activities within a regional and ecosystems context:

> Park activities also may have effects outside the boundaries of the parks. Pertinent policies guide park involvement in planning in a regional context and working cooperatively to address mutual problems or issues that cross boundaries. NPS units strive to work with adjacent federal, state, local agencies, and adjacent landowners in cooperative planning and management. Because parks are integral parts of larger regional environments (ecosystems), the NPS works cooperatively with others to anticipate, avoid, and resolve potential conflicts, and to protect park resources.

[ ]

Because the NPS has statutory authorization to cooperate with Montana in prohibiting the entrance of brucellosis-infected bison to the state and because NPS policy calls for an ecosystems approach to managing park resources, it appears that Plaintiffs' are not likely to succeed on the merits of their Organic Act claims.

NOTES

(1) *Intertribal Bison Cooperative v. Babbitt* was the decision on the merits of *Greater Yellowstone Coalition v. Babbitt.* Relying upon the finding of facts in its earlier decision in *Fund for Animals, Inc. v. Lujan,* the court found the 1996 and 1997 interim management plans to be both reasonable and legal under the National Park Service Organic Act, the Yellowstone Park Organic Act, and NEPA:

> The court concludes that neither the decision to implement the 1996 Interim Plan nor the decision to implement the 1997 Interim Plan was arbitrary or capricious or otherwise not in accordance with the law. Neither were the Interim Plans implemented in violation of NEPA. Both plans were prepared and implemented well within the discretion and statutory authority of the NPS to manage the Park bison.

Intertribal Bison Cooperative v. Babbitt, 25 F.Supp.2d 1135, 1140 (D.Mont. 1998).

(2) *Fund for Animals v. Clark* involved a shift in jurisdiction and a corresponding shift in fortunes for plaintiff. Fund for Animals sought to enjoin a proposed hunt planned by NPS and FWS designed to thin the bison herd located on federal lands in northwestern Wyoming. The hunt was to be held pursuant to a bison management plan developed by the Fish and Wildlife Service (which manages the National Elk Range), the National

Park Service (which administers Grand Teton National Park), and the Forest Service (which manages the Bridger–Teton National Forest). The plan discussed size of the herd, methods of reducing the herd size, winter distribution of the bison, and disease management. Plaintiff argued that defendants had failed to evaluate a supplemental winter-feeding program. The court agreed that defendants had failed to evaluate the feeding program as required by NEPA. In determining whether to grant an injunction, the court evaluated the likelihood of harm to other interested persons, and concluded that

> [t]he record in this case indicates that no other interested parties would suffer substantial harm should the court issue an injunction enjoining the federal defendants from going forward with their plan to reduce the bison herd. All of the supposed consequences that the federal defendants urge would occur should the bison hunt not go forward are speculative. First, the danger of the bison likely causing an outbreak of brucellosis is not supported by the record. Dr. Margaret Meyer, a respected expert in the field of veterinary public health and brucellosis infection who is familiar with the history and disease status of the Jackson Hole bison, states in her declaration that the risk of the bison herd infecting other livestock is "remote" and there is "virtually no risk" of infection to humans. [ ] Second, the safety issues outlined by defendants such as the bison moving onto roads and into populated areas are entirely speculative. Given the small number of animals that were scheduled to be taken in the bison hunt, the court cannot conclude that having 35–40 "extra" bison in the herd will increase the already tolerable risks associated with the inevitable interplay between humans and bison that will occur so long as a bison herd of any size remains in this area. Consequently, the court concludes that other interested parties will not be subjected to substantial harm should the court issue the injunctive relief sought by plaintiffs.

Fund for Animals v. Clark, 27 F.Supp.2d 8, 14–15 (D.D.C.1998).

PERSPECTIVES

(1) The Fund for Animals is an "animal protection organization" that was founded by Cleveland Armory in 1967. Its motto, " 'We speak for those who can't,' illustrates a mission of speaking out against egregious forms of animal cruelty. [It is] a leading opponent of sport hunting, commercial trapping, and other acts of egregious cruelty to wild animals. . . . The Fund for Animals believes that every individual wild animal deserves protection form pain, suffering, and death—whether that animal's species is endangered or thriving." The Fund for Animals, Mission Statement [http://fund.org/about/n5_mission.asp; visited Mar. 19, 2001].

Following the NPS decision to approve the Bison Management Plan, The Fund issued the following statement:

> Despite ten years of effort, millions of tax dollars, and overwhelming public opinion opposed to the ongoing slaughter of Yellowstone's bison, the federal government has authorized the implementation of a scientifically fraudulent, inhumane, unnecessary, and costly bison

management strategy. The Joint Management Plan will continue to permit the shooting and inhumane slaughter of America's bison to protect slightly more than 2,000 cows at an annual cost of 1.7 million taxpayer dollars. The government's complete failure to develop a sensible, humane, scientifically credible, and cost-effective plan undermines the interests of the American public and the integrity of the National Park System. The National Park Service's (NPS) desire to capitulate to the preposterous demands of Montana has caused it to abandon its mandate to protect Yellowstone and all of its wild inhabitants.

The NPS ignored more than 70,000 comments it received demanding increased protection for Yellowstone bison both inside and outside of the park. Instead, it has capitulated to the preposterous demands of the livestock industry and state livestock agencies, and in doing so, has abandoned its mandate to protect Yellowstone and all of its wild inhabitants.

Establishing a dangerous precedent for wildlife management in and outside of national parks, the bison management plan is not based on the best available scientific evidence and is entirely focused on bison instead of imposing any new requirements on Montana's cattle producers. Given the overwhelming evidence of a lack of any measurable risk of *Brucella abortus* transmission from bison to cattle, the 1.7 million dollar annual price tag on the Joint Management Plan represents an enormous fleecing of the American taxpayer and is antithetical to the protection of a wild and free-roaming bison population in America's most famous national park.

Statement of The Fund for Animals in Response to Record of Decision for the Final Environmental Impact Statement and Bison Management Plan for the State of Montana and Yellowstone National Park [http://fundforanimals.ctsg.com/library/documentViewer.-asp?ID=271&table=documents; visited Mar. 19, 2001]

Leaving aside the dispute over the risk of transmission of brucellosis from bison to domestic cattle, how does the bison issue differ from the question of the overpopulation of deer at stake in *Humane Society v. Lujan*? Consider the following note.

(2) **Public and private:** A fundamental transformation is occurring in the West. The traditionally dominant livestock industry is no longer seen as cowboys in white hats. Wildlife is now valued not only as a consumptive resource but also as both an end in itself and for its biodiversity value. The bison-elk-and-brucellosis controversy is only one example of the intensifying conflict between livestock and wildlife. Federal protection of wild horses, the reintroduction of wolves, and limitations on predator control programs are other examples of a fundamental shift. Livestock are no longer automatically accorded priority on the public domain:

In the Yellowstone region, few people question the priority given to bison and other wildlife inside the national parks and wildlife refuges. On the public lands outside the parks, though, the question of priority is still subject to debate. Ranchers have historically enjoyed considerable influence over multiple-use policies, enjoying ready access to the national forest lands for livestock grazing purposes. But wildlife is now recognized as an important resource across the public domain, and it is clear that Greater Yellowstone's wildlife populations cannot exist solely inside the parks. As a national political matter as well as a regional socio-economic matter, the fact is that wildlife—particularly large charismatic species like the bison and elk—have greater value on the Greater Yellowstone public domain than cattle. None of the bison-brucellosis court cases have suggested otherwise. In short, political, legal, and ecological realities are such that cattle must make room for bison on the Greater Yellowstone public domain. This same answer is increasingly emerging elsewhere, too.

Robert B. Keiter & Peter H. Froelicher, *Bison, Brucellosis, and Law in the Greater Yellowstone Ecosystem,* 28 LAND & WATER L. REV. 1 (1993).

(3) The problem with islands—the parable of the prairie chicken: In the mid-nineteenth century, there were millions of Greater Prairie-Chickens *(Typanuchus cupido)* in the tall grass prairie of Illinois. But the invention of the steel plow allowed farmers to slice through the dense root systems of the grasslands. By the end of the nineteenth century, the Illinois prairie had become a scattering of remnant parcels and the millions of birds had dropped to thousands. In 1933, when the state banned hunting of the species that had once been shipped to markets in Chicago by the thousands, there were 25,000 birds in Illinois. But the population continued its collapse: there were 2,000 birds in 1962 when the state established a sanctuary; a Nature Conservancy sanctuary was established five years later. But privately owned grasslands continued to be converted and the two populations of the birds were isolated from each other. By 1993, there were only 46 birds in Illinois. Hatching rates—the percentage of eggs in a nest that hatch—dropped from 91–100% to 38% at the state sanctuary. DNA testing on the remaining birds and on specimens collected in the 1930s and 1960s indicated that the remaining birds had lost one third of their genetic diversity. Birds were brought into the state from existing and genetically more diverse populations elsewhere; hatching rates climbed back to 94%. There were no significant changes in environmental or climatic factors that would account for the dramatic changes.

In a report in *Science,* the sanctuary and state game managers concluded that the population collapse was an example of

the general scenario predicted by "extinction vortex" models. [ ] These models predict that demographic and genetic effects reinforce each other in small populations to increase the probability of local extinction. We believe that the near complete loss of suitable grasslands and satellite populations in the region drove the greater prairie chicken toward this scenario. Small population size and isolation then led to low genetic diversity and decreased fitness.... Isolated relict populations, such as greater prairie chickens in Illinois, cannot be conserved indefinitely with inadequate habitat and small size.

Ronald L. Westmeier, *et al., Tracking the Long–Term Decline and Recovery of an Isolated Population,* 282 SCI. 1695, 1697 (1998).

The parable of the prairie chicken is that habitat fragmentation that isolates breeding populations leads to a decrease in the genetic variation among the remaining individuals as they become increasingly inbred. This in turn decreases the fitness of the birds and a collapse into extinction. As Michael Soule, a father of conservation biology, noted in a commentary on the Westmeier study:

> the most sinister actor in the extinction melodrama is neither genetics nor random population fluctuations; it is the loss of habitat and habitat quality, accompanied by overexploitation of biological resources, the increasing number of exotic species, pollution, and climate change.

Michael E. Soule & L. Scott Mills, *No Need to Isolate Genetics, id.* at 1658, 1659.

When everything becomes an island, many animals become prairie chickens—and prairie chickens are only a short step from a famous inhabitant of the island of Mauritius: the dodo (*Raphus cucullatus*).

* * *

J. Michael Scott, *et al.*, *Nature Reserves: Do They Capture the Full Range of America's Biodiversity?*

11 ECOLOGICAL APPLICATIONS 999, 999, 1004, 1005 (2001).

Human transformation of the world's landscapes is increasing at an ever accelerating pace. [ ] These changes have led, in turn, to the extinction and endangerment of a growing number of species [ ] and loss of their natural areas. The U.S. endangered species list has increased from 178 species in 1976 to 1742 species in 1999. [ ] The Nature Conservancy lists 267 species in the United States as extinct or presumably extinct and 3170 species as imperiled. [ ] In the United States 126 ecosystems have been identified as being threatened or endangered. [ ]

These problems are occurring in spite of the fact that the United States has an extensive system of nature reserves in national parks, national wildlife refuges, and designated wilderness areas. In addition, large areas of lands administered by the Bureau of Land Management, Forest Service, and various states are managed, at least in part, for the protection of biodiversity. These public lands have management restrictions that provide some protection from anthropogenic change, assist in maintenance of ecosystem functions, serve as population sources and reserves, and provide areas in which ecosystems may be restored. Existing reserves and other public lands may well be inadequate for protecting biodiversity against excessive habitat loss, simply because many of the resources at risk occur preferentially on multiple-use public or privately owned lands. Preliminary assessments of the distribution of threatened and endangered species suggest that >90% of such species occur on private lands, with 66% having >60% of their area on private lands. [ ]

. . .

The distribution of nature reserves, whether examined across the entire landscape of the coterminous United States or by ecological zone, shows the same pattern. Nature reserves are largely limited to sites of higher than average elevation and less productive soils. Most of the larger nature reserves included in our analysis have been in existence for a relatively long time period. Many of the largest national parks were created in the early 1900s. Similarly, the national forests, which contain most of the legally designated wilderness areas, date from th early decades of the 20th century. It has been argued that, at the time these lands were set aside, they were considered "the lands nobody wanted." In other words, they were often opportunistically established because of their relative lack of value for commercial uses, human habitat, or because of their scenic attributes or recreational value. Sullivan and Shaffer [*Biogeography of the Megazoo,* 189 SCI. 13 (1975)] predicted that the result of such a reserve selection and establishment process would be a network of reserves that is very inefficient in terms of preserving a diversity of ecosystems and their associated resources.

.... To preserve the full range of ecological and genetic variation in species, and thus maintain their potential to respond to varying conditions, we must establish a set of nature reserves that is representative of the natural variation found in the United States. The current system of nature reserves fails to do so.

CHAPTER 12

BIODIVERSITY: A PRIMER ON SCIENCE, VALUES, AND POLICY

Thus far our inquiry has focused on individual organisms and, in the last chapter, on enclaves of land managed for wildlife habitat. In this chapter and the two that follow, our focus shifts from individual animals to species and populations. The inquiry widens to include a broad range of species that the law, until recently, has deemed valueless. Even more significant is the focus on landscapes and ecological processes—on the entire interconnected web of life.

The dominant conservation challenge of our time is the disruption of biological diversity—or "biodiversity," as the concept has come to be termed. What biodiversity is, and why it is important, are the subjects of this chapter. The materials also survey the causes of the loss of native biodiversity and the scientific and policy responses to these losses. This chapter is the background for the book's final two chapters—Chapter 13, which examines the federal Endangered Species Act, and Chapter 14, which considers the legal bases for managing landscapes to promote biodiversity.

SECTION 1. A STATUS REPORT ON BIODIVERSITY

DAVID QUAMMEN, THE SONG OF THE DODO
11–12 (1996).

Let's start indoors. Let's start by imagining a fine Persian carpet and a hunting knife. The carpet is twelve feet by eighteen, say. That gives us 216 square feet of continuous woven material. Is the knife razor-sharp? If not, we hone it. We set about cutting the carpet into thirty-six equal pieces, each one a rectangle, two feet by three. Never mind the hardwood floor. The severing fibers release small tweaky noises, like the muted yelps of outraged Persian weavers. Never mind the weavers. When we're finished cutting, we measure the individual pieces, total them up—and find that, lo, there's still nearly 216 square feet of recognizably carpetlike stuff. But what does it amount to? Have we got thirty-six nice Persian throw rugs? No. All we're left with is three dozen ragged fragments, each one worthless and commencing to come apart.

Now take the same logic outdoors and it begins to explain why the tiger, *Panthera tigris*, has disappeared from the island of Bali. It casts light on the fact that the red fox, *Vulpes vulpes*, is missing from Bryce Canyon National Park. It suggests why the jaguar, the puma, and forty-five species of birds have been extirpated from a place called Barro Colorado Island—and why myriad other creatures are mysteriously absent from myriad other sites. An ecosystem is a tapestry of species and relationships. Chop away a section, isolate that section, and there arises the problem of unraveling.

.... Thomas E. Lovejoy, a tropical ecologist at the Smithsonian Institution, has ... coin[ed] his own term. Lovejoy's term is *ecosystem decay.*

His metaphor is more scientific in tone than mine of the sliced-apart Persian carpet. What he means is that an ecosystem—under certain specifiable conditions—loses diversity the way a mass of uranium sheds neutrons. Plink, plink, plink, extinctions occur, steadily but without any evident cause. Species disappear. Whole categories of plants and animals vanish.

a. WHAT IS BIODIVERSITY?

REED F. NOSS & ALLEN Y. COOPERRIDER, SAVING NATURE'S LEGACY
3–12 (1994).

In little more than a decade, biodiversity progressed from a short-hand expression for species diversity into a powerful symbol for the full richness of life on earth. Biodiversity is now a major driving force behind efforts to reform land management and development practices worldwide and to establish a more harmonious relationship between people and nature.

Biodiversity. A symbol? An issue? A driving force? It would be easier if biodiversity could be measured by the quantity of bird species in a forest, wildflowers in a meadow, or beetles in a log. But simplicity is not one of the virtues of biodiversity. Ecosystems are more complex than we can imagine. Our most intricate machines—say, a space shuttle and all its ground-control computers—are simple toys compared to an old-growth forest, its myriad known and unknown species, and their intricate genetic codes and ecological interactions. Just identifying and counting species is difficult enough. The almost infinite complexity of nature defies our best efforts to classify, categorize, or even describe.

A common misconception is that biodiversity is equivalent to species diversity—the more species in an area, the greater its biodiversity. However, biodiversity is not just a numbers game. On a global scale, maintaining maximal species richness is a legitimate goal and requires keeping global extinction rates low enough that they are balanced or surpassed by speciation. When we consider species richness at any scale smaller than the biosphere, quality is more important than quantity. It is not so much the number of species that we are interested in, it is their identity. Fragmenting an old-growth forest with clearcuts, for example, would increase species richness at a local scale but would not contribute to species richness at a broader scale if sensitive species were lost from the landscape.

Diversification can all too easily become homogenization. The greatest cause of homogenization worldwide is the introduction of nonnative plants and animals, often called exotics. Exotics are species that have invaded new areas due to accidental or deliberate transport by humans. Although species naturally disperse and colonize new areas, so that floras and faunas change continually over long periods of time, human transport and habitat disturbance have greatly increased the rate and scale of invasions. Many regions have nearly as many exotic as native species today. Introductions of exotics may increase species richness locally or even regionally, but they contribute nothing positive to biodiversity. Rather, they pollute the integrity of regional floras and faunas and often alter fundamental ecological processes, such as fire frequency and intensity, and nutrient cycles. Thus, whole ecosystems are changed. Regions invaded by exotics lose their distinctive characters. Every place begins to look the same. The result is global impoverishment. For these reasons, we emphasize *native biodiversity*, not diversity per se.

The important task is not to define biodiversity, but rather to determine the components of biodiversity in a region, their distribution and interrelationships, what threatens them, how we measure and monitor them, and what can be done to conserve them....

> Biodiversity is the variety of life and its processes. It includes the variety of living organisms, the genetic differences among them, the communities and ecosystems in which they occur, and the ecological and evolutionary processes that keep them functioning, yet ever changing and adapting.

This definition recognizes variety at several levels of biological organization. Four levels of organization commonly considered are genetic, population/species, community/ecosystem, and landscape or regional. Each of these levels can be further divided into compositional, structural, and functional components of a nested hierarchy. Composition includes the genetic constitution of populations, the identity and relative abundance of species in a natural community, and the kinds of habitats and communities distributed across the landscape. Structure includes the sequence of pools and riffles in a stream, down logs and snags in a forest, the dispersion and vertical layering of plants, and the horizontal patchiness of vegetation at many spatial scales. Function includes the climatic, geological, hydrological, ecological, and evolutionary processes that generate and maintain biodiversity in ever-changing patterns over time.

. . .

Conserving biodiversity, then, involves much more than saving species from extinction. As implied by our characterization of biodiversity, biotic impoverishment can take many forms and occur at several levels of biological organization....

GENETIC LEVEL

Genes, sequences of the DNA (deoxyribonucleic acid) molecule, are the functional units of heredity. Species differ from one another and individuals within species vary largely because they are unique combinations of genes. Gene frequencies and genotypes (individual organisms with a particular genetic make-up) within a population change over time as a consequence of both random and deterministic forces. Random changes include mutations that create new genes or sequences of genes, and loss of genes by change in small populations (called sampling error or genetic drift). Deterministic changes include natural and artificial selection, where some genotypes are more successful reproducers than others. In the long run, genetic change leads to evolutionary change as individuals adapt to different situations and pass on their new traits to offspring. Genetic diversity is fundamental to the variety of life and is the raw material for evolution of new species. . . .

Conservation goals at the genetic level include maintaining genetic variation within and among populations of species, and assuring that processes such as genetic differentiation and gene flow continue at normal rates. . . .

. . .

SPECIES LEVEL

The species level of diversity is probably what most people think of when they hear the term *biodiversity*. Although in some ways species diversity is the best known aspect of biodiversity, we should bear in mind that the vast majority of species in the world are still unknown. Of an estimated 10 to 100 million species on Earth, we have named only about 1.8 million. Known species are dominated by insects, half of them beetles. But many invertebrates, bacteria, and other organisms remain to be discovered, even in the United States. Hundreds of invertebrate species can be found in one square meter of soil and litter in old-growth temperate forest. Even more amazing, Norwegian microbiologists found between 4000 and 5000 species of bacteria in a single gram of soil from a beech forest. . . .

A population is a local occurrence of a species and is the unit that we usually manage. Conservation goals at the population/species level include maintaining viable populations of all native species in natural patterns of abundance and distribution. These goals grade into community-level goals of maintaining native species richness and composition.

Despite the problems and biases of single-species management, many species require individual attention, particularly when they have become so rare that heroic measures are needed to save them. In addition, certain kinds of species warrant management emphasis because their protection will conserve more than themselves. Especially important in this regard are keystone species, which play pivotal roles in their ecosystems and upon which a large part of the community depends. The importance of a keystone species is often disproportionate to its abundance. The beaver, for instance, creates habitats used by many species and also regulates hydrology and other ecosystem functions. If we reduce beaver numbers through heavy trapping, then all else being equal, we impoverish the landscape. The beaver is not an endangered species, but it is greatly reduced or even absent from many regions where it was once abundant. . . .

Some kinds of species have great pragmatic value for conservation, especially those we can characterize as "umbrellas" or "flagships." To illustrate the umbrella concept, consider a carnivore (such as a grizzly bear or wolf) that requires millions of acres of land to maintain a viable population. If we secure enough wild habitat for these large predators, many other less-demanding species will be carried under the umbrella of protection. Umbrella species are often charismatic, so they also function as flagships or symbols for major conservation efforts. The grizzly bear, for instance, is a potent symbol for wilderness preservation in the northern Rocky Mountains. No umbrella is complete, however. Some endemic plant species have very small ranges—perhaps restricted to a single rock out-crop—that might not be protected in an ideal wilderness network estab-lished for grizzlies.

. . .

COMMUNITY OR ECOSYSTEM LEVEL

In many cases, conservation is most efficient when focused directly on the community or ecosystem. A community is an interacting assemblage of species in an area. Terrestrial communities are usually defined by their dominant plants (for instance, the beech-maple forest), but functional or taxonomic groups of animals (for example, bird communities, lizard com-munities, herbivore communities) are also recognized. Functional groups of organisms (species that use a set of resources in similar ways, such as bark-gleaning birds) are often called *guilds*. Similarly, aquatic communities may be taxonomically or functionally defined, for example fish communities or littoral (shoreline) vegetation.

An ecosystem is a biotic community plus its abiotic environment. Ecosystems range in scale from microcosms, such as a vernal pool, to the entire biosphere. Many ecologists equate the terms *ecosystem* and *commu-nity*, except that ecosystem ecologists emphasize processes more than species and other entities. . . .

LANDSCAPE AND REGIONAL LEVELS

If biodiversity occurs at multiple levels of organization, it is worth protecting at all levels. Forman and Godron defined a landscape as "a heterogeneous land area composed of a cluster of interacting ecosystems that is repeated in similar form throughout." . . .

A primary conservation goal at the landscape or regional level is to maintain complete, unfragmented environmental gradients. This extends the representation goal beyond traditional ecosystem boundaries. Species richness and composition are known to vary along environmental gradi-ents. The most commonly studied gradient is elevation. In the western Cascades of Oregon, the number of species and amphibians, reptiles, and mammals declines sharply with increasing elevation. This presents a prob-lem for conservation, because generally speaking, the low-elevation, high-diversity sites are private lands which are often heavily exploited and have few natural areas left. Mid-elevation sites are commodity-production public lands, and large protected areas (such as designated wilderness) occupy the high-elevation, lowest diversify sites. This biased pattern of habitat protec-tion is common throughout the western Untied States.

NOTES

(1) Keystones and umbrellas: Although Noss and Cooperrider neither propose to reduce the task nor offer any shortcuts that might allow us to focus our efforts on small parts of biodiversity while ignoring others, they do claim that some parts are more important than others in sustaining the overall diversity and health of an ecosystem. Keystone species such as beaver exercise disproportionate influence so that conserving such species can promote the well being of many other species. [Recall the discussion on beavers as keystone species in Chapter 2 following *Pierson v. Post.*]

Similarly, "umbrella" species are useful management targets, not because they affect the well being of many other species, but because efforts to protect them—for example, by conserving large tracts of grizzly bear habitat—will conserve other species, if not entire ecological communities.

(2) What is an ecosystem? Noss and Cooperrider make extensive use of the term "ecosystem," as do most biologists writing about landscape-level ecological functioning. They define it as "a biotic community plus its abiotic environment"—which is to say, as the entire interconnected web of living organisms plus the nonliving parts of nature that they inhabit. The following excerpt comments further on what the term means and what it does not. The author, a widely published curator at the American Museum of Natural History, continues to find it useful to use spatial terms to describe ecosystems to general audiences—an ecosystem is a place—though he emphasizes that ecosystem boundaries are "fuzzy" and ecosystems can be defined and selected on widely varied spatial scales. Note also how Eldredge focuses on processes such as energy flows among the components of the ecosystem:

> An ecosystem is a place, an arena where energy flows constantly from one living component to another. These living components are not species, but rather *local populations* of various different species. It is, in large measure, the local population of squirrels living in a patch of forest, dependent on the acorns produced by oak trees, and being eaten by local red foxes and broad-winged hawks. But the local ecosystem is much more than the organisms in it. It is, in addition, the flowing energy itself, plus the inorganic components—the chemical composition and temperature of the sediment, soil, water, or atmosphere, depending on the nature of the system, be it a lake, a section of prairie or a montane meadowland. It is the nutrients—various organic and inorganic compounds, such as vitamins—that are found locally. Finally, the local ecosystem is a place, a pond, say, or a beach. All these components go into the mix and define the dynamic web of life that *is* a local ecosystem.
>
> Where are the boundaries of local ecosystems? A lake might have a distinct shoreline, but the plants fringing its edges—those in the shallow waters as well as those living down close to the edge—are invariably different from plants (like water lilies) living in deeper waters or the trees and shrubs living on drier ground farther away from the shoreline itself. How do we recognize the boundaries between ecosystems?
>
> Ecosystem boundaries are inherently fuzzy. If we say a pond is an ecosystem, and its surrounding forest is an ecosystem, what do we make of the osprey—a fish-eating hawk—that perches, rests, and nests

in forest trees, but plunges feet first into the lake to get its food, its all-important energy source? Clearly local ecosystems are connected, and they are connected by energy flowing across their blurred boundaries.

NILES ELDREDGE, LIFE IN THE BALANCE 55–56 (1998).

b.   THE VALUES OF BIODIVERSITY

Numerous writers have undertaken to survey the reasons why we ought to be concerned about losses of biodiversity. Some are widely accepted; others—particularly those that rely on the intrinsic values in other life forms—are more contentious. Noss and Cooperrider survey the basic rationales for protecting biodiversity in the following excerpt:

REED F. NOSS & ALLEN Y. COOPERRIDER, SAVING NATURE'S LEGACY
17–23 (1994).

Aldo Leopold observed: "The last word in ignorance is the man who says of an animal or plant: 'What good is it?' If the land mechanism as a whole is good, then every part is good, whether we understand it or not. If the biota, in the course of aeons, has built something we like but do not understand, then who but a fool would discard seemingly useless parts? To keep every cog and wheel is the first precaution of intelligent tinkering."

.   .   .

The value of biodiversity is our fundamental assumption. . . . However, it is worth reviewing briefly the types of value that humans ascribe to nature. Often arguments about what is proper management of natural resources can be put in perspective, if not totally resolved, by understanding how people value nature in different ways.

DIRECT UTILITARIAN VALUES

The kind of value easiest to appreciate, for many people, is the utilitarian or instrumental value of a species or other natural resource. That the "what good is it" question is so often asked suggests that many people value things largely for their direct utility for humans. Though incomplete as a justification for saving biodiversity, such values are real.

The medicinal value of certain plants and invertebrates provides a powerful argument for conservation, as does the value of wild gene pools for agriculture and wild populations for food. Wild species provide an estimated 4.5 percent of the Gross Domestic Product of the United States, worth $87 billion annually in the late 1970s. Fisheries contributed 100 million tons of food to people worldwide in 1988. One-fourth of all prescription drugs in the United States contain active ingredients extracted from plants, and nearly 3000 antibiotics are derived from microorganisms. . . . By one estimate, only about 5000 (2 percent) of the 250,000 described species of vascular plants have been screened for their chemical compounds. We are driving species to extinction without even trying to learn what they might contribute to human society.

Arguments based on utility are limited, however. Leopold observed that "one basic weakness in a conservation system based wholly on economic motives is that most members of the land community have no economic value." Similarly, Ehrenfeld lamented, "what biologist is willing to find a value—conventional or ecological—for all 600,000–plus species of beetles?" What happens if we thoroughly screen a plant for medicinal compounds and conclude that it has none? Do we then say it is permissible to extinguish that species? Conservationists often fall into the trap of justifying species preservation for utilitarian purposes, thereby sanctioning the humanistic attitude that is responsible for the biodiversity crisis. The attitude implied by economic valuations is that the worth of a species depends on its direct utility to humans. If a species does not benefit us, it is worthless.

. . .

INDIRECT UTILITARIAN VALUES

Natural ecosystems and biodiversity also provide benefits to humans that are indirect, yet essential. Paul and Anne Ehrlich call these benefits "ecosystem services." Every habitat on Earth, including urban and agricultural environments, is an ecosystem that receives and transforms energy, produces and recycles wastes, and relies on complex interactions among species to carry out these functions. But urban and agricultural ecosystems are dependent on natural ecosystems for their sustenance. Solar energy is the basis of virtually all food chains (rare exceptions include chemically based communities in deep-sea vents) and is converted to chemical energy by photosynthetic plants. Plants, including crops, often depend on animals to pollinate their flowers and disperse their seeds, on nitrogen-fixing bacteria to convert molecular oxygen to a form that can be assembled into proteins, and on microorganisms to convert complex organic compounds into inorganic nutrients that can be taken up by their roots. Animals, fungi, and microbes in an ecosystem have comparable interdependencies. Thus, an ecosystem is a richly interconnected well of relationships greater than the sum of its parts.

But how does a natural ecosystem benefit humans, besides providing pharmaceuticals and other products? An entire book could be written on this subject. Ehrlich and Ehrlich describe ecosystem services upon which human civilization is entirely dependent, including: (1) maintaining atmospheric quality by regulating gas ratios and filtering dust and pollutants; (2) controlling and ameliorating climate through the carbon cycle and effects of vegetation in stimulating local and regional rainfall; (3) regulating freshwater supplies and controlling flooding (wetlands, for example, can act as giant sponges to soak up moisture during rainy periods and release water slowly during dry periods); (4) generating and maintaining soils through the decomposition of organic matter and the relationships between plant roots and mycorrhizal fungi; (5) disposing of wastes, including domestic sewage and wastes produced by industry and agriculture, and cycling of nutrients; (6) controlling pests and diseases, for example through predation and parasitism on herbivorous insects; and (7) pollinating crops and useful wild plant species by insects, bats, hummingbirds, and other pollinators.

RECREATIONAL AND ESTHETIC VALUES

Probably most people who care about the environment are motivated primarily by their personal appreciation of nature's beauty. John Muir, founder of the Sierra Club and a leading force in the creation of the U.S. national park system, firmly believed that exposure of ordinary people to wild places would foster an attitude to save these places. Leopold, too, noted that people will behave ethically only toward something they can experience and have faith in. Recreational and esthetic enjoyment of nature often leads directly to appreciation of nature for its own sake, that is, to a spiritual or ethical appreciation of biodiversity. Without people motivated by their experiences of wild places, we would arguably have fewer wild areas remaining and the status of biodiversity in North America would be even more precarious.

Despite the critical role of these kinds of human experience in promoting conservation, areas set aside to fulfill recreational or esthetic objectives do not necessarily meet biodiversity conservation goals. Many national parks, wilderness areas, and other large reserves selected on the basis of esthetic criteria are relatively depauperate biologically. . . .

INTRINSIC, SPIRITUAL, AND ETHICAL VALUES

The limitations of utilitarian arguments for conserving biodiversity leave an alternative: the appreciation of wild creatures and wild places for themselves. We believe that nature of biodiversity possess *all* the kinds of value reviewed above, but that intrinsic values (or the spiritual and ethical appreciation of nature for its own sake) offer the least biased and ultimately most secure arguments for conservation. Virtually all religious traditions recognize the value of a human being—for example, a newborn baby—as at least partially independent of what that person might do for us. Why shouldn't we feel the same way about other creatures? The acknowledgment that natural objects and processes are valuable in themselves reflects a basic intuition of many people. Science cannot prove or disprove intrinsic value. Yet as scientists, we see no objective reason for believing that humans are fundamentally superior to any other organism. If we have value, then all natural things have value.

NOTES

(1) Ecological processes and biodiversity: As the preceding excerpt explains, humans are interwoven into a complex of living systems. We draw our sustenance from these systems, and in the long run are dependent on their continuing fertility and health. In the case of individual components of nature that humans use directly—whether specific minerals or specific life forms—the scarcity of one component might be offset by the discovery of another that is equally useful. But all life depends on certain basic ecological processes, for which there are no substitutes. These processes not only sustain life, but are themselves largely the outcome of the complex interactions of that life. As Noss and Cooperrider urge, "[c]onserving ecological processes is essential to conserving biodiversity." *Id.* at 42. Ecological processes, they conclude, are usefully organized into six interrelated categories: "(1) energy flows, (2) nutrient cycles, (3) hydrological cycles, (4) disturbance regimes, (5) equilibrium processes, and (6) feedback effects." *Id.*

For the most part, the roles of these processes are easy to perceive. In the case of the energy and nutrient cycles, for instance, nearly all terrestrial life depends upon plant growth and the success of plants in capturing and using sunlight. Plants draw nutrients from the soil; some nutrients return to the soil when the plants die; some nutrients are consumed by animals or, increasingly, harvested by humans. In time, those nutrients return to the earth, but they are often returned in ways and to places that make them relatively inaccessible for future plant growth (in the bottoms of rivers and lakes or buried in landfills). For nutrient cycles to remain healthy, nutrients taken from the soil need to be returned to the soil. According to many conservation writers, one of the most grave environmental problems of the current age is the loss and degradation of soil, due in large part to disruptions of natural processes for maintaining fertility. *E.g.*, JAMES GLANZ, SAVING OUR SOIL: SOLUTIONS FOR SUSTAINING EARTH'S VITAL RESOURCE (1995); WES JACKSON, NEW ROOTS FOR AGRICULTURE (1985).

The ecological process that many people understand least—and one that figures significantly in the declines and possible recovery of many imperilled species—is the suite of natural forces termed "disturbance regimes."

> [M]ost ecosystems are subject to regularly or sporadically recurring events such as fires, windstorms, landslides, or floods. These events are often called catastrophic, but historical records show that they have always occurred and that ecosystems have complex responses to them. What appears to devastate a natural community at a local scale or in the short term by causing death and destruction may actually be essential to rejuvenation and persistence at a broader spatiotemporal scale.

> Many plant and animal species are not only adapted to disturbances, but depend on them for survival. A well-studied example is the Kirtland's warbler, which requires homogeneous thickets of five-and six-year-old jack pines interspersed with grassy clearings for breeding. This kind of habitat is created and maintained by intense fires. If fires are suppressed, as is usually the case in managed forests, habitat for Kirtland's warbler would disappear. Restoring and maintaining a regular pattern of fires has helped conserve this endangered species.

> Prairies, other grasslands, oak savannas, and ponderosa and longleaf pine forests often depend on frequent, low-intensity ground fires. These fires recurred historically at intervals of 1 to 25 years, depending on the particular community and site conditions. The life histories of the dominant species in these communities have been shaped evolutionarily by fire. Without fire, these communities gradually change to other types that may be less diverse or healthy. . . .

> . . .

> [S]pecies in any region have adapted, through evolution, to a particular disturbance regime. If we radically alter that regime, many

species will be unable to cope with the change and will be eliminated. For example, the patchwork created by clearcutting differs from the mosaic created by fire or windthrow in fundamental ways. A landscape of dispersed clearcuts and tree plantations—a common pattern across much of the United States—has less dead wood and other structure within patches, greater contrast between patches, and more pronounced edge effects than a naturally disturbed landscape....

Human actions that mimic natural disturbances are much less likely to interfere with ecosystem function and threaten biodiversity than human actions that impose novel disturbance regimes on an ecosystem. Consider, for instance, livestock grazing in the northern Great Plains, which once supported bison. Restoring free-ranging bison would be the ideal management strategy from a biodiversity perspective. Short of this ideal, a livestock grazing systems that mimics bison grazing patterns is more likely to be compatible with the region's remaining biodiversity than some grazing patterns based on English pasture management.

REED F. NOSS & ALLEN Y. COOPERRIDER, SAVING NATURE'S LEGACY 43–46 (1994).

(2) Biodiversity, Leopold, and land health: Ecological processes have gained increased attention in recent years in legal literature. In discussing them, many scholars prefer to follow the lead of the Ehrlichs and use the term "ecosystem services," by way of emphasizing the direct benefits humans receive from healthy natural processes. *See, e.g.,* 20 STAN. ENVTL. L.J. 309–536 (2001) (special issue on ecosystem services). Today's interest builds upon the work of leading conservation scientists and writers, extending back for several generations. As so often is the case, Aldo Leopold was one of the first to develop conservation policies specifically grounded on the maintenance of such processes. In various writings in the 1930s and 1940s, he identified disruptions of such processes as evidence that the land community as a whole was in ill health. Over time, Leopold refined his thoughts on ecological functioning into what he termed a "biotic view of land," with "land" defined, as he regularly defined it, to include the entire community of life that inhabited a given place. Conservation policy, Leopold concluded, was most likely to succeed if it focused on a single, overall goal, phrased in ecological terms. Leopold spent much of the final decade of his life attempting to piece together such a goal, working as best he could with what he well knew was a fragmentary understanding of how nature functioned and what human activity was doing to it. The goal that Leopold proposed to his conservation colleagues during and just after World War II was the goal he summed up with the term "land health." The following excerpt considers what Leopold meant by land health, with particular attention to the role of native species:

"Land-health," Leopold wrote in 1944, "is the capacity for self-renewal in the soils, waters, plants, and animals that collectively comprise the land."[1] "Health expresses the cooperation of the interde-

---

1. *Conservation: In Whole or in Part, in* THE RIVER OF THE MOTHER OF GOD AND OTHER ESSAYS BY ALDO LEOPOLD 311, 318 (Susan L. Flader & J. Baird Callicott, eds., 1991) (essay originally written in 1944) (hereinafter RMG).

pendent parts: soil, water, plants, animals, and people. It implies collective self-renewal and collective self-maintenance."[2] Health, of course, was a characteristic commonly associated with a single organism. Leopold used the term in much the same way and with the same good connotations, but without asserting that land operated as tightly and coherently as an organism. Whenever he spoke of land health, he chose his words with care:

> The land consists of soil, water, plants, and animals, but health is more than a sufficiency of these components. It is a state of vigorous self-renewal in each of them, and in all collectively. Such a collective functioning of interdependent parts for the maintenance of the whole is characteristic of an organism. In this sense land is an organism, and conservation deals with its functional integrity, or health.[3]

Like human health for physicians today, land health for Leopold the land doctor was easiest to explain by identifying symptoms of disease, and Leopold did so in many writings. A concise list appeared at the beginning of one of his most important essays on the subject, "The Land–Health Concept and Conservation":

> The symptoms of disorganization, or land sickness, are well known. They include abnormal erosion, abnormal intensity of floods, decline of yields in crops and forests, decline of carrying capacity in pastures and ranges, outbreak of some species as pests and the disappearance of others without visible cause, a general tendency toward the shortening of species lists and of food chains, and a world-wide dominance of plant and animal weeds. With hardly a single exception, these phenomena of disorganization are only superficially understood.[4]

Leopold's understanding of land health was shaped by his early days in the Southwest, where overgrazing and other misdeeds caused visible erosion, waterway degradation, and declines in the productivity of native grasslands. Once in Wisconsin, he remained painfully aware of soil issues, both erosion and declines in tilth and fertility, so much so that whenever he wrote about land sickness he always began with soil. Hydrologic modification typically appeared second on his list of symptoms, whether the visible evidence took the form of unnatural floods, droughts, or declining water tables. Other issues followed in line: disruptions of species lists and food webs, the emergence of particular species as pests, declines in the quantity and quality of the land's yield, and others.

In another essay that displayed his intellectual progress, Leopold illustrated land sickness by citing the problems that remained, in two

---

2. *Land-Use and Democracy, in* RMG, *supra* note 1, at 295, 300 (originally published in 1942).

3. *Conservation: In Whole or in Part, supra* note 1, at 310.

4. *The Land–Health Concept and Conservation, in* ALDO LEOPOLD, FOR THE HEALTH OF THE LAND: UNPUBLISHED ESSAYS AND OTHER WRITINGS 218, 219 (J. Baird Callicott & Eric T. Freyfogle eds., 1999) (originally written 1946; first published 1999) [hereinafter *Land-Health Concept*].

specific settings, despite the best efforts of conservationists. One example came from southwestern Wisconsin, an area where federal conservation bureaus had worked for years. Though their various efforts had achieved successes, full health remained illusive:

> [T]his region still displays flashy streams, loss of topsoil, silting of reservoirs, migration of plowland from upland to marshes and flood-channels, irruption of white grubs and weed pests, exaggerated drouth damage, falling water table[s], and scarcity of upland game.[5]

His other example came from a place he also knew well, the Southwest. There, control measures had largely come too late, "after erosion due to early overgrazing had gained momentum." Leopold wrote:

> The result: silted reservoirs, tearing out of valleys, widespread drainage of already dry soils by gullies, wholesale conversion of grass to chaparral, wholesale replacement of palatable by unpalatable range plants, irruption of rodent pests, loss of vulnerable and predacious wild species, falling water tables, dust storms.[6]

Leopold also focused on the land's ability to recycle nutrients efficiently and endlessly. Only if this happened, would the soil—"the repository of food between its successive trips through the chains"—retain its fertility and produce abundant, nutritious yields. Land was healthy "when its food chains are so organized as to be able to circulate the same food an indefinite number of times."[7]

Land sickness, Leopold knew, was not a fatal ailment. The land would not fully succumb and no longer sustain life. The outcome was less dire but nonetheless disturbing, and in the long run, just as unacceptable. He addressed the issue toward the end of his essay "The Land Ethic":

> This almost world-wide display of disorganization in the land seems to be similar to disease in an animal, except that it never culminates in complete disorganization or death. The land recovers, but at some reduced level of complexity, and with a reduced carrying capacity for people, plants, and animals.[8]

. . .

As he thought about land health, Leopold was perplexed most by the matter of preserving native species. To what extent were native species needed to sustain the land's health, and in what numbers were they needed? No living person could answer that question, Leopold believed, and he doubted an answer would soon emerge. A full complement of native species was apparently needed to keep a place functioning, but did that mean every species? Probably not, Leopold guessed. But who was to decide which species were dispensable? Who knew

---

5. *Biotic Land–Use, in* FOR THE HEALTH OF THE LAND, *supra* note 4, at 198, 201 (originally written circa 1942; first published 1999) [hereinafter *Biotic Land–Use*].

6. *Id.* at 202.

7. *Id.* at 205.

8. ALDO LEOPOLD, A SAND COUNTY ALMANAC AND SKETCHES HERE AND THERE 219 (1949).

which species held keystone positions in an ecosystem so that their removal or disappearance might cause decline?

Leopold's thoughts about this issue progressed along two lines, even as he and his students actively studied the systemic roles of particular species. One line of thought centered on the roles of species in keeping food webs intact and returning nutrients to the soil. The land's functioning was threatened by the shortening and simplification of food webs. Its health, accordingly, required "not only characteristic kinds, but also characteristic numbers of each species in the food chains."[9] Leopold's other line of thought centered on community functioning in general and on the vast human ignorance about how land worked. For Leopold, these intertwined lines of thought justified the retention of as many native species as possible—not because they were all clearly essential, but because errors could be costly. "As far as we know," he observed cautiously in 1942, "the state of health depends on the retention in each part of the full gamut of species and materials comprising its evolutionary equipment."[10] "No species can be 'rated' without the tongue in the cheek," he observed three years before:

> [T]he old categories of "useful" and "harmful" have validity only as conditioned by time, place, and circumstance. The only sure conclusion is that the biota as a whole is useful, and biota includes not only plants and animals, but soils and waters as well.[11]

"We must assume, therefore," he added in his important 1946 essay,

> that some causal connection exists between the integrity of the native communities and their ability for self-renewal. To assume otherwise is to assume that we understand the biotic mechanisms. The absurdity of such an assumption hardly needs comment, especially to ecologists.[12]

Eric T. Freyfogle, A Sand County Almanac *at 50: Leopold in the New Century*, 30 Envtl. L. Rptr. (Envtl L. Inst.) 10058 (2000).

c.   ESTIMATING SPECIES AND RATES OF LOSS

It comes as a surprise to many people to hear that even the most knowledgeable scientists have only a vague idea how many living species reside on earth—to say nothing of our ignorance about genetic variation within species and about the varied composition of ecological communities. The following excerpt examines this uncertainty and why it exists. It also surveys current estimates of the rate at which species are being eliminated as a result of human activities. According to most biologists, species loss is occurring rapidly today: we are undergoing an extinction crisis, the sixth— so far as we can tell—in the history of the planet.

---

9. *Biotic Land–Use, supra* note 5, at 205.

10. *Land-Use and Democracy, supra* note 2, at 300.

11. *A Biotic View of Land, in* RMG, *supra* note 1, at 267.

12. *Land-Health Concept, supra* note 4, at 221.

NILES ELDREDGE, LIFE IN THE BALANCE

171–73 (1998).

Biologists do not know exactly how many species are currently on the planet. Science has recorded and named some 1.6 million species, but we know this can only be some small fraction—no more than 10% to 15%—of the true number. Some biologists believe we have identified only 1% to 3%, and that there may be as many as 100 million species on the planet. Because concern over the accelerating loss of species has been mounting, biologists have turned in earnest to the key question, How many species are on Earth? They have begun to converge on an estimate of some 14 million species, but opinions still sharply differ on this vital issue.

Why are we so ignorant of the biotic riches of Earth? Scientific survey of the world's species began in the seventeenth century, but did not switch into high gear until the mid-nineteenth century, when the heyday of European colonialism mixed with the Industrial Revolution, producing a blossoming of exploration and scientific inquiry. Naturalists like Alfred Russell Wallace and Henry Walter Bates traveled to the then-exotic destinations such as the Amazon Basin and the Spice Islands (part of present-day Indonesia) to amass vast collections of plants, insects, spiders, aquatic invertebrates, fish, amphibians, reptiles, birds, and mammals. The collections of such as intrepid explorers found their way at first into privately held "cabinets" of natural history and increasingly into the large natural history museums that were founded in the mid-nineteenth century—museums such as the British Museum of Natural History in London, the Natural History Museum of the Smithsonian Institution in Washington, D.C., and my own favorite treasure trove, the American Museum of Natural History in New York. . . .

Needless to say, there are far more species than experts to identify them. For some groups, there are few (sometimes no) experts actively working to inventory the world's stock. One way biologists frame accurate guesstimates of how many species probably exist in the world is to assess what we know we have found already, observe the rate that new species are turning up, evaluate how concerted the effort is to find new species for a given group, and derive some sense of what might still be out there, as yet unidentified.

Ornithologists think that they have found most of the world's bird species, as the number has begun to level off at around 9,000, and mammalogists also think they have described and named well over 90% of the world's mammal species. [But] even large species of mammals still turn up on a regular basis, such as the large antelope and deer recently discovered in recently war-ravaged Vietnam and the several species of lemur discovered over the past decade on Madagascar. New bird species also turn up regularly. Because so many systematists have focused on birds and mammals—big and obvious, the charismatic megafauna—and because much more numerous groups, such as insects, have received relatively much less attention, the ratio of named to as-yet-undiscovered species varies widely from group to group.

There is yet another major source of inference for assessing the actual number of species on Earth, one that is tied into the very critical question, How do we know that we are in the midst of a sixth, major global mass extinction? The connecting link is *habitat*, by now familiar as the essential ingredient in species loss, but one which, quite obviously, underlies the sheer existence of species.

In an elegant series of studies, Smithsonian coelopterist Terry Erwin came to his by-now famous—and still controversial—estimate that there are some 30 million species of insects in the Tropics alone. Erwin carefully sampled the insect (especially beetle) faunas of various forest canopies in Panama, Brazil, and Amazonian Peru. Erwin's goal was to determine how limited beetle species were, on average, to particular types of trees. Then, taking into account the total aerial extent and canopy diversity of the tropical rain forest, he was able to derive an estimate of the total number of beetle species currently in existence, and from that estimate extrapolated an estimate for the total number of insects.

Coming as it did when most of the world's biologists were still thinking that there are at most only a few million species on Earth, Erwin's analysis shocked a lot of biologists into attention. More recent work, including similar in-depth, total assaying of a region's biotic riches, have tempered his estimates somewhat, but we now are accustomed to thinking that there are at least 10 million species of insects, rather than 1 to 2 million species, a 10-fold increase in our estimates of Earth's living species diversity. If so rich a percentage of the world's species is yet undiscovered, then their loss, their undocumented extinction, becomes more critical.

NOTES

(1) Rates of loss: Given how little we know about the number of species on earth, estimates of ongoing extinctions are little more than calculated guesses. Species losses are assumed to be greatest in tropical rain forests, and the disappearing species are largely ones unknown to science. The most prominent estimate of planetary losses was made by biologist E.O Wilson. Chiefly based on calculations of rates of deforestation and other habitat alteration, Wilson estimated that the planet was losing species at a rate of 27,000 per years, or 3 per hour. His estimate, he claimed, was based on "cautious parameters, selected in a biased manner to draw a maximally optimistic conclusion." E.O. WILSON, THE DIVERSITY OF LIFE 280 (1992). According to Niles Eldredge, "[s]ome biologists think Wilson's figure is too high, but plenty more think he has underestimated the situation." NILES ELDREDGE, LIFE IN THE BALANCE 174 (1998).

In September 2000, the World Conservation Union (IUCN) released its latest "Red List" of global threatened species. Issued every four years, the report documents only the status of known species, including more than 800 listed as having gone extinct or extinct in the wild since 1500. The 2000 report lists 18,276 species and subspecies known to be threatened, including, in the most imperiled category ("critically endangered") 180 mammal species (up from 169 in 1996) and 182 bird species (up from 168). Worldwide, approximately 25 percent of all reptile species, 20 percent of all amphibians, and 30 percent of all fishes (chiefly freshwater) are listed as threatened, though the report notes that actual percentages could be higher since none of the categories has been fully assessed. The IUCN Red List is available at <www.redlist.org>. *See also* World Biodiversity Database <www.eti.uva.nl/Database/WBD.-html>.

(2) The situation in the United States: In a useful 1999 survey of the status of American wildlife, ecologist David Wilcove offered the following summary of where things stand in the United States:

> Somewhat in excess of 100,000 native species (terrestrial and freshwater) have been identified in the Untied States, including over 16,000 ferns, conifers, and flowering plants, 2,500 vertebrates (mammals, birds, reptiles, amphibians, and fishes), and roughly 75,000 insects. These 100,000 or more species represent an unknown fraction of the nation's total flora and fauna—unknown because scientists have no idea how many insects, mites, fungi, and other little creatures remain undiscovered and undescribed in wildlands and backyards across the country. The actual number of species in the United States is probably several times the known number.
>
> Only for a few well-studied groups, such as flowering plants, vertebrates, and butterflies, do scientists have enough information to assess how well they are faring. Based on its studies of these better-known groups, The Nature Conservancy estimates that approximately 1 percent of America's plant and animal species have vanished over the past two to three centuries. An additional 16 percent are in immediate danger of extinction, and another 15 percent are considered vulnerable. Thus, about a third of America's species are "of conservation concern," according to the Conservancy. The remaining two-thirds "appear to be relatively secure at present."

DAVID S. WILCOVE, THE CONDOR'S SHADOW: THE LOSS AND RECOVERY OF WILDLIFE IN AMERICA 7–8 (1999). Wilcove's prediction that the actual number considerably exceeds 100,000 was supported by a detailed survey released the following year, PRECIOUS HERITAGE: THE STATUS OF BIODIVERSITY IN THE UNITED STATES (Bruce A. Stein, Lynn S. Kutner & Jonathan S. Adams, eds., 2000). Written by scientists from The Nature Conservancy and the Association for Biodiversity Information, the survey represented the first effort to assemble species data gathered by the National Heritage programs of all 50 states. The report documents the presence of more than 200,000 native species in the United States. Some one third of the species are at risk, the report concludes, and at least 500 species have already gone extinct or are missing. The report also concludes that the United States supports a broader variety of large-scale ecosystems than any other nation on Earth.

Detailed information on biodiversity in the United States, contained in a searchable data base, is available at <www.abi.org>.

(3) Freshwater fauna: Different categories of wildlife vary widely in their sensitivity to human-induced changes in habitat. Of all wildlife categories, birds have tended to be most resilient because of their mobility and the fact that few of them—in their North American ranges—are entirely dependent on highly specific habitat types. (For this reasons, writers out to challenge endangered species protections often use birds to convey the suggestion that "things aren't so bad." *See, e.g.,* CHARLES C. MANN & MARK L. PLUMMER, NOAH'S CHOICE: THE FUTURE OF ENDANGERED SPECIES 71–78 (1995).) At the other end of the spectrum are the life forms that live in rivers and lakes—the freshwater fauna, which are perhaps the most imperiled. Wilcove offers the following summary of the far greater threats facing such wildlife:

> In 1990, The Nature Conservancy published a remarkable analysis of the status of various types of animals. It revealed, perhaps for the first time, the extent to which freshwater species were disappearing in the United States. According to the Conservancy, more than a third (40 percent) of North American fishes are extinct or vulnerable to extinction. The comparable figure for North American crayfishes is 51 percent, while for freshwater mussels it jumps to a staggering 67 percent. In contrast, the percentage of birds considered extinct or at risk is only 15 percent; the figure for mammals is 17 percent, and for reptiles 18 percent. Aquatic species, in short, are suffering much higher losses than terrestrial species. Even more ominous, perhaps, is the accelerating rate of loss. Among fishes, for example, the rate of extinction has doubled over the course of the twentieth century.

> Such high percentages of imperiled species would be troubling under any circumstances, but they are especially so in this case because they represent the loss of an extraordinarily diverse assortment of species. Over 800 different kinds of fish inhabit North America's fresh waters; the Mississippi River drainage alone contains nearly as many fish species as are found in all of Europe. And no other place on earth could match the diversity of native snails that once occurred in the Coosa River drainage or the numbers of species of freshwater mollusks in the Tennessee River drainage. For all sorts of freshwater animals from crayfish to caddisflies—the United States is the center of diversity. To an extraterrestrial ecologist visiting this planet at the end of the nineteenth century, the most notable feature of the American landscape might well have been its rich assortment of freshwater animals.

> Driving these changes in our aquatic ecosystems has been a suite of activities as vast as the scale of human enterprise itself. People have altered the physical structure of rivers by constructing everything from simple weirs to massive dams. They have straightened streambeds, smoothed bottom contours, constructed dikes, inserted culverts, and otherwise rebuilt hundreds and hundreds of rivers to suit their fancy. Pollutants, both organic and inorganic, pour into our waters from cities, industrial complexes, power plants, farmlands, pasturelands, mines, and quarries. Many are what are called "point-source pollutants," traceable to individual factories, sewage treatment plants, strip mines, and the like. Others, such as pesticides, silt, and fertilizers, fall into the category of "nonpoint-source" pollutants, which wash into rivers from sources spread across the landscape. Water is diverted and drained from lakes and rivers for drinking and irrigation, while throughout the country new species of plants and animals are introduced, some to entertain anglers, some to control imagined or real pests, and some by accident or carelessness. All these activities (and

many others) have been harming fishes, mussels, and other aquatic species for a long-long time.

We tend to think of water pollution and overfishing as the primary culprits behind the loss of freshwater biodiversity, but in fact, neither problem has endangered as many species of fish, mussels, amphibians, and crayfish as has habitat destruction. It is only because our terrestrial imaginations prevent us from perceiving the extent to which we have damaged rivers as habitats—by altering their shapes, their flows, and their flood-plains, and by filling them with alien species—that we overlook the leading role that habitat destruction has played in the loss of freshwater life.

DAVID S. WILCOVE, THE CONDOR'S SHADOW: THE LOSS AND RECOVERY OF WILDLIFE IN AMERICA 106–08 (1999).

SECTION 2.   THE CAUSES OF SPECIES LOSS

a.   CAUSES OF BIOLOGICAL IMPOVERISHMENT

A population of a species increases as a result of births (natality) and immigration and decreases because of deaths (mortality) and emigration. The elementary truism is that extinction occurs when mortality consistently exceeds natality. More helpful is the richer statement that extinction occurs when a species is unable to persist in the face of environmental change. *See generally* Geerat J. Vermeij, *The Biology of Human–Caused Extinction, in* THE PRESERVATION OF SPECIES 28 (Bryan G. Norton ed., 1986). The change may be either physical (*e.g.*, habitat destruction, weather, pollution, soil erosion) or biological (*e.g.*, the introduction or elimination of diseases, parasites, symbionts, predators, prey, competitors).

Humans are the most important cause of both physical and biological changes in the environment. In fact, a leading conservation biologist has concluded that there is no documented case of an extinction "caused solely by nonhuman agencies." Michael E. Soule, *What Do We Really Know about Extinction?, in* GENETICS AND CONSERVATION 111, 112 (Christine M. Schonewald–Cox *et al.* eds., 1983). Two categories of human actions have historically been the leading causes of extinction. The more important is the indirect mortality caused by habitat alteration and the introduction of exotic species. The other is direct human-caused mortality, primarily hunting. VINZENZ ZISWILER, EXTINCT AND VANISHING ANIMALS app. I, at 106–14 (Fred & Pille Bunnell trans., 1967) (hunting has caused the extinction of at least 27 species of birds and 70 species of mammals). The following excerpt categorizes and quantifies the various causes of endangerment and extinction today.

David S. Wilcove *et al.*, *Quantifying Threats to Imperiled Species in the United States*
48 BIOSCI. 607 (1998).

Biologists are nearly unanimous in their belief that humanity is in the process of extirpating a significant portion of the earth's species. The ways in which we are doing so reflect the magnitude and scale of human enterprise. Everything from highway construction to cattle ranching to leaky bait buckets has been implicated in the demise or endangerment of particular species. According to Wilson,[1] most of these activities fall into four major categories, which he terms "the mindless horsemen of the environmental apocalypse": overexploitation, habitat destruction, the introduction of non-native (alien) species, and the spread of diseases carried by alien species. To these categories may be added a fifth, pollution, although it can also be considered a form of habitat destruction.

. . .

In this article, we quantify the extent to which various human activities are imperiling plant and animal species in the United States. . . .

To obtain an overview of the threats to biodiversity in the United States, we tabulated the number of species threatened by five categories of threats: habitat destruction, the spread of alien species, overharvest, pollution (including siltation), and disease (caused either by alien or native pathogens). [The authors constructed their data set with information drawn from The Nature Conservancy, the Network of Natural Heritage Programs and Data Centers, and the federal list of threatened and endangered species.] A total of 2490 imperiled species, subspecies, and populations fit these criteria.

Information on the threats to each of these species, subspecies, and populations was obtained from a number of sources, including [the listing documents under the ESA, published surveys, and interviews.] We included only known threats and excluded potential or hypothetical ones. . . .

We were able to obtain information on threats for 1880 (75%) of the 2490 imperiled species, subspecies, and populations that met out criteria for inclusion in this study. [Of the 2490 imperiled species, 1478 were plants; of the 2019 animals, 1578 were vertebrates and 471 were invertebrates.] (For 52 of the species, we could not identify any anthropogenic threats.) We used the resulting database to determine the relative significance of the major threats categories and to investigate differences between species groups in their vulnerability to particular threats. We compare the distribution of threats among plants and animals, among vertebrate and invertebrate animals, and within vertebrate classes. . . .

Ranking the threats

Table 2 presents a summary of the percentages of species that are imperiled by habitat loss, alien species, pollution, overexploitation, and disease. Not surprisingly, habitat destruction and degradation emerged as the most pervasive threat to biodiversity, contributing to the endangerment of 85% of the species we analyzed. Indeed, habitat loss is the top-ranked threat (in terms of the number of species it affects) for all species groups. Competition with or predation by alien species is the second-ranked threat in the overall analysis, affecting 49% of the imperiled species.

1. E.O. WILSON, THE DIVERSITY OF LIFE (1992).

Alien species affect a higher proportion of imperiled plants (57%) than animals (39%).... However, certain groups of animals (most notably birds and fish) appear to be as broadly affected as plants by alien species....

For all aquatic animal groups (amphibians, fish, dragonflies and damselflies, freshwater mussels, and crayfish), pollution is second only to habitat loss as a cause of endangerment. Our finding that a large number of aquatic species are threatened by pollution may reflect the fact that our definition of pollution includes siltation, which is one of the leading threats to aquatic biodiversity in North America.

Table 2. Percentages of species in different groups that are imperiled by habitat degradation and loss, alien species, pollution, overexploitation, and disease. Categories are nonexclusive and therefore do not sum to 100.

Cause	All species (1880)	Vertebrates (494)	Invertebrates (331)	Plants (1055)	Mammals (85)	Birds (98)	Reptiles (38)	Amphibians (60)	Fishes (213)	Freshwater mussels (102)	Crayfish (67)	Tiger beetles (6)	Butterflies and skippers (33)	Other invertebrates (104)
Habitat degradation/loss	85	92	87	81	89	90	97	87	94	97	52	100	97	94
Alien species	49	47	27	57	27	69	37	27	53	17	4	0	36	52
Pollution	24	46	45	7	19	22	53	45	66	90	28	0	24	19
Overexploitation	17	27	23	10	45	33	66	17	13	15	0	33	30	46
Disease	3	11	0	1	8	37	8	5	1	0	0	0	0	0

A closer look at habitat destruction

Given the primacy of habitat destruction as a threat to biodiversity, we examined its causes in greater detail. For this fine-scale analysis, we focused exclusively on US species, subspecies, and populations that have been added to the federal endangered species list or have been formally proposed for such listing by USFWS as of 1 January 1996. We focused on listed species because more information is usually available for them than for imperiled but unlisted species....

Categorizing habitat destruction. For the fine-scale analysis, we divided habitat destruction and degradation into 11 major categories:

* Agriculture (including agricultural practices, land conversion and water diversion for agriculture, pesticides and fertilizers; excluding livestock grazing).

* Livestock grazing (including range management activities).

* Mining, oil and gas, and geothermal exploration and development (including roads constructed for and pollutants generated by these activities).

* Logging (including impacts of logging roads and forest management practices).

* Infrastructure development (including bridges, dredging for navigation, and road construction and maintenance).

* Military activities.

* Outdoor recreation (including swimming, hiking, skiing,camping, and mining roads).

* Off-road vehicles specifically.

* Water development (including diversion for agriculture, livestock, residential use, industry, and irrigation; dams reservoirs, impoundments, and other barriers to water flow; flood control; drainage projects; aquaculture; navigational access and maintenance).

* Dams, impoundments, and other barriers to water flow specifically.

* Pollutants (including siltation and mining pollutants).

* Land conversion for urban and commercial development.

* Disruption of fire ecology (including fire suppression).

As in the coarse-scale analysis, we did not distinguish between current and historical threats or between major and minor threats. In many instances, the apparent threat to a species was actually spawned by another threat. Wherever possible, we attributed threats to their ultimate cause, based on the information in the *Federal Register*. For example, logging operations near a stream can lead to siltation, which is harmful to certain rare fishes and mussels. Thus, logging rather than siltation would have been scored as the threat to those fishes and mussels.

Table 3. Percentages of imperiled birds and plants in Hawaii and in the continental United States that are threatened by habitat degradation and loss, alien species, pollution, overexploitation, and disease. Categories are nonexclusive and therefore do not sum to 100.

Cause	Continental US birds (56)	Hawaiian birds (42)	Continental US plants (641)	Hawaiian plants (414)
Habitat degradation/loss	88	93	90	66
Alien species	48	98	30	99
Pollution	38	2	12	0
Overexploitation	39	24	13	6
Disease	4	81	1	0

Ranking the causes of habitat destruction. The most overt and widespread forms of habitat alteration were, as might be expected, the leading threats to species that are either listed or proposed for listing (hereafter referred to collectively as "endangered" species), as measured by the number of species they affect. These forms include agriculture (affecting 38% of endangered species), commercial development (35%), water development (30% when agricultural diversion is included; 17% for just dams, impoundments, and other barriers), and infrastructure development (17%). Not surprisingly, the impacts of water development are felt most acutely by aquatic species. Ninety-one percent of endangered fish and 99% of endangered mussels are affected by water development, in contrast to 10% of mammals and 22% of birds. Within the category of infrastructure development, roads affect a wide array of species (15% of all endangered species), confirming their reputation as "a leading threat to biodiversity."

Outdoor recreation also harms a large number of endangered species (27%). It affects a significantly higher proportion of plants than animals (33% vs. 17%). Within the category of outdoor recreation, the use of off-road vehicles is implicated in the demise of approximately 13% of endangered species.

Among extractive land uses, logging, mining, and grazing have contributed to the demise of 12%, 11%, and 22%, respectively, of the endangered species we analyzed. Both logging and mining are especially serious threats to freshwater mussels, probably because they result in increased amounts of silt, in the cases of both logging and mining, and of toxic pollutants, in the case of mining. Livestock grazing, on the other hand, is particularly harmful to plants, affecting 33% of endangered plant species compared to 14% of endangered animals; the difference is highly significant.

Finally, 168 species (14%) are threatened by disruption of fire regimes in the ecosystems in which they live. Of these, 85 (7%) are threatened by fire suppression and 83 (7%) are threatened by controlled or uncontrolled fires.

Conservation implications

The major findings of this study confirm what most conservation biologists have long suspected: Habitat loss is the single greatest threat to biodiversity, followed by the spread of alien species. However, the discovery that nearly half of the imperiled species in the United States are threatened by alien species—combined with the growing numbers of alien species—suggests that this particular threat may be far more serious than many people have heretofore believed. . . .

Pollution (including siltation) ranks well below alien species as a threat to imperiled species in general, but it exceeds alien species as a threat to aquatic taxa. As [one study points] out, the pollutants affecting the largest number of aquatic species are agricultural pollutants, such as silt and nutrients, that enter lakes and rivers as runoff from farming operations. These non-point source pollutants have proved to be exceedingly difficult to regulate and control.

Finally, this study . . . raise[s] troubling questions about the future of imperiled species in the United States. [This study] found that a high proportion of imperiled species is threatened by either fire suppression within their fire-maintained habitats or alien species. Both types of threats must be addressed through active, "hands-on" management of the habitat, such as pulling up alien plants and trapping alien animals or using prescribed fire to regenerate early successional habitats. Although the ESA prohibits actions that directly harm listed animals and, to a lesser extent, listed plants, it does not require landowners to take affirmative actions to maintain or restore habitats for listed species. Thus, a landowner is under no obligation to control exotic weeds, undertake a program of prescribed burning, or do any of the other things that may be absolutely necessary for the long term survival of many imperiled species. In fact, it may be possible for a landowner to rid himself of an endangered species "problem" by literally doing nothing and waiting until the habitat is no longer suitable for the species in question. Even those landowners who care deeply about endangered species and wish to protect them face a daunting burden: The costs of undertaking these management actions can be considerable and, at present, are usually not tax deductible.

NOTES

(1) Habitat fragmentation: As David Quammen illustrates so vividly with his story of the Persian carpet that began this Chapter, habitat fragmentation can harm species, even when the total amount of apparently suitable habitat remains large. The detailed research of David Wilcove and his associates starkly confirms the overall impacts of human-induced habitat alteration, including fragmentation.

Fragmentation has been most studied in forest habitats; only recently has attention been paid to the adverse effects that are caused the fragmentation of grasslands:

> In the Midwest ... prairie fragments smaller than 75 acres are unlikely to be occupied by grasshopper sparrows, and those smaller than about 150 acres are ignored by bobolinks and Henslow's sparrows. Not surprisingly, the problem is most serious in the tallgrass region, where over 96 percent of the native prairie has been destroyed. In Illinois, for instance, fewer than a fifth of the state's 245 remaining patches of prairie are larger than 25 acres, and only 9 are larger than 100 acres. Small wonder, then, that the little Henslow's sparrow is now classified as a threatened species in a state where its population numbered in the hundreds of thousands earlier in the century.
>
> Exactly why fragmentation is harmful to these birds remains something of a mystery, but a few studies suggest that rates of nest predation and parasitism are much higher in the smaller fragments than in the larger ones—precisely the pattern we saw with respect to forest-dwelling songbirds in the East. With their high proportions of edge to interior, small patches of prairie may be overrun by nest-plundering birds and mammals living along their borders.

DAVID S. WILCOVE, THE CONDOR'S SHADOW: THE LOSS AND RECOVERY OF WILDLIFE IN AMERICA 100–01 (1999). Recall the parable of the prairie chicken discussed at the end of Chapter 10.

(2) K-selection and r-selection: One theory that seeks to explain the particular vulnerability of certain species to extinction as a result of environmental changes emphasizes the role of natural selection in creating alternative life history patterns and characteristics. *See generally* ROBERT H. MACARTHUR & EDWARD O. WILSON, THE THEORY OF ISLAND BIOGEOGRAPHY 145–80 (1967); Eric R. Pianka, *On r-and K–Selection*, 104 AM. NATURALIST 592 (1970); Lawrence B. Slobodkin, *On the Susceptibility of Different Species to Extinction: Elementary Instructions for Owners of a World, in* THE PRESERVATION OF SPECIES 226 (Bryan G. Norton ed., 1986); John Terborgh, *Preservation of Natural Diversity: The Problem of Extinction Prone Species*, 24 BIOSCI. 715 (1974). This theory has two core points. The first is the recognition that different environmental factors impose different selective pressures and that adaptation is therefore largely a matter of compromises in the allocation of time and energy among competing environmental demands. The second point is that different life history adaptations are favored by different population densities relative to the carrying capacity of the relevant environment. At low population densities, adaptations that promote rapid population increase are selected. This extreme is found in short-lived habitats such as pools of rainwater or new forest openings. The most successful individual will be one that discovers the new habitat and reproduces rapidly before the habitat either deteriorates or is discovered by competitors; lengthy lifespans have little value because the habitats are relatively ephemeral. At the other extreme are habitats characterized by high population densities. This extreme is found in long lasting, stable habitats such as coral reefs or old-growth forests. In such habitats, selection favors adaptations that allow the individual to survive and reproduce on few resources; lengthy lifespans and the production of competitive offspring are characteristics that are selected in such situations.

In other words, the vulnerability of a particular species to environmental change is related to that species' strategy for perpetuating itself. The strategies form a continuum between alternative approaches: a species may either produce large numbers of offspring as quickly as possible or it may invest more time in each of a small number of offspring. The environment imposes pressures on a species that move it toward one or the other of these basic strategies. In an uncertain environment, an individual's best chance of passing its genes onto the future is by producing large numbers of offspring; in a relatively predictable environment, on the other hand, an individual's best chance comes from producing fewer offspring—since producing many offspring will exhaust the habitat's resources—and investing more time in each. These two endpoints are known respectively as an r-strategy[2] (a "weedy," opportunistic reproductive strategy adapted to an unpredictable environment) and a K-strategy[3] (an equilibrium-based strategy for predictable, steady-state environments). Obviously, all species arrive at some compromise on the continuum between these endpoints since it is impossible to invest everything in either reproduction or growth.

Species that share adaptive strategies can also be expected to share other traits. *See* ROBERT E. RICKLEFS, ECOLOGY 577–79 (3d ed. 1990); JAMES F. WITTENBERGER, ANIMAL SOCIAL BEHAVIOR 352–53 (1981); Eric R. Pianka, *supra*, at 593. Similarly, the two strategies are related to distinct climates and mortality patterns: r-selection is associated with variable or unpredictable climates and often-catastrophic mortality, *e.g.*, large winter die offs; K-selection, on the other hand, is associated with fairly constant or at least predictable weather and more directed mortality, *e.g.*, predator-prey relationships, that tend to select for greater efficiency. Since r-strategy species tend to be invasive, opportunistic species that do well in disturbed habitats—its economy is the boom-bust cycle of the resource rush—r-selection favors high production of offspring, rapid individual development, early reproduction, small body size, a short lifespan, and single reproduction. K-strategy species, on the other hand, tend to live in stable ecosystems—its economy is a steady state that fluctuates minimally around equilibrium

---

2. "r" refers to the maximum intrinsic rate of natural increase [r_{max}].

3. "K" refers to a habitat's carrying capacity.

with its habitat—and *K*-selection favors production of few offspring, slow individual development, delayed reproduction, large body size, a long lifespan, and repeated reproduction.

Examples may be helpful. The California condor offers a classic example of a *K*-selection strategy. It is the largest land bird in North America, 4 to 4.5 feet long with an 8.5 to 9.5 foot wingspan and weighing 18 to 22 pounds. Condors form monogamous, long-term pair bonds. They lay a single egg in alternate years. The young requires six months to fledge and remains dependent upon its parents for an additional six months. An individual does not sexually mature until it is 6 to 8 years old and may live for 45 years. *See generally* PAUL R. EHRLICH *ET AL.*, BIRDS IN JEOPARDY 24–25 (1992); PAUL R. EHRLICH *ET AL.*, THE BIRDER'S HANDBOOK 218 (1988); CARL B. KOFORD, THE CALIFORNIA CONDOR (1953); John Ogden, *The California Condor,* AUDUBON WILDLIFE REPORT 1985 at 288 (Roger L. Di Silvestro ed., 1985).

In comparison, an *r*-strategy species is the English or house sparrow. The house sparrow is a small (6.25 inch) European bird that was initially introduced in Brooklyn shortly after 1850; it had become the most abundant bird around human habitations by the early twentieth century. It is a prolific breeder, producing several broods each year. It is able to do so because less than six weeks elapse between the laying of eggs and the independence of the young. *See generally* NATIONAL GEOGRAPHIC SOCIETY, FIELD GUIDE TO THE BIRDS OF NORTH AMERICA 432 (2d ed. 1987); PAUL R. EHRLICH *ET AL., supra,* at 632–35; 1 DONALD STOKES, A GUIDE TO BIRD BEHAVIOR 261–73 (1979). Other examples of *r*-strategy species are game birds such as ducks and pheasants which have very large broods.

As is apparent from these descriptions, *K*-strategy species are more extinction prone than are *r*-strategy species. The very efficiency with which *K*-strategy species exploit their environment is a liability *during periods of rapid or chaotic change.* The larger body size of individuals of a *K*-strategy species—while giving an advantage in interspecific competition and in defense against predators and allowing individuals to exploit a larger area—means that there are fewer individuals. Similarly, lower reproduction rates (which keep the population of a species in equilibrium with its environment) and a greater investment in individual offspring (which reduces the mortality of individual offspring) are more efficient uses of available energy because little is wasted on offspring that are unlikely to live to reproduce and because maintenance of population at carrying capacity prevents habitat degradation while allowing the species to exploit available resources. At the same time, lower reproduction rates make it more difficult both for the species to recover if its population becomes depressed and for it to adapt to a changed environment because fewer offspring contain less genetic variability. Thus, the very "fittedness" of *K*-strategy species to a particular environment—which is advantageous during periods of stability—becomes a serious handicap when the habitat changes more rapidly than genes can be substituted in a population—and in species that reproduce slowly, genes are substituted slowly.

Perhaps not surprisingly, the California Condor is listed as an endangered species, while the House Sparrow is a "pest." More generally, *K*-strategy species are more likely to become endangered or threatened and thus require more careful monitoring during periods of rapid habitat modification.

b.   EXOTICS, DISEASE, AND OTHER THREATS

The overview report by David Wilcove and associates identifies a variety of causes of biodiversity decline. Next to habitat alteration in overall importance is the complex of factors commonly labeled as "invasive species" or "exotics." The following article by Martin Enserink provides details on that complex. Following Enserink, is an excerpt by Tim Palmer that focuses on forests in the United States. As its author notes, the changes brought on by logging are obvious for all to see. Harder for the untrained eye to see are the changes brought on by atmospheric pollution, the degradation of forest soils, and the disruption of the various ecosystem processes that sustain forest health. As he explains, declines in forest health have direct affects on forest-dwelling wildlife.

Martin Enserink, *Biological Invaders Sweep In*

285 SCI. 1834 (1999).

One spring morning in 1995, ecologist Jayne Belnap walked into a dry grassland in Canyonlands National Park, Utah, an area that she had been studying for more than 15 years. "I literally stopped and went, 'Oh my God!'" she recalls. The natural grassland—with needle grass, Indian rice grass, saltbush, and the occasional pinyon-juniper tree—that Belnap had seen the year before no longer existed; it had become overgrown with 2-foot-high Eurasian cheatgrass. "I was stunned. It was like the aliens had landed," says Belnap, a researcher with the U.S. Geological Survey (USGS) in Moab. "Now, we've lost this ecosystem forever."

A few years earlier and a continent away, as Yugoslavia fell apart in a series of wars, Serbian scientists discovered a new enemy in a field near Belgrade airport: the western corn rootworm, apparently flown in from the United States. Vigorous international action might have curbed this pest's first known venture outside North America, says entomologist József Kiss of the University of Agricultural Sciences in Gödöllô, Hungary, but the turmoil of war prevented such a collaboration. Now it's too late....

Meanwhile, in South Africa, ecologists are bracing for the rise of Varroa, a mite that parasitizes honeybees. After sweeping through Europe and North America for decades, Varroa was found near the Cape Town harbor in 1997; now it's all over South Africa, and the first colonies have died, says Mike Allsopp, who heads the honeybee section of the Plant Protection Research Institute in Stellenbosch. What worries Allsopp most is the fact that between 50% and 80% of South Africa's native flower species are pollinated by bees—a much higher percentage than in Europe or the United States. "Commercial keepers can keep their colonies alive with chemical treatments," says Allsopp. "But if Varroa wipes out 99% of the natural colonies, as it has done elsewhere, what effect is that going to have on the indigenous flora? No one really knows."

These are just three examples on a list that could be extended almost endlessly. As the world shrinks and travel and trade boom, plant and animal species have become globetrotters too, sometimes because humans decide to take them along, sometimes by accident. And whereas globalization may be the mantra of the new economy, for the environment it may spell disaster. The innocent-looking zebra mussel, a Eurasian invader that entered U.S. waters in the late 1980s and clings by the thousands to every hard surface it finds, does tens of millions of dollars worth of damage each year by clogging U.S. water pipes. Even worse, exotic species can devour or outcompete species that have called an ecosystem home for tens of thousands of years. Biological invasions are the second biggest cause of biodiversity loss in the United States, after habitat destruction, according to a 1998 study; they could soon become the first.

Ecologists are paying more and more attention, if only because they increasingly find themselves studying not primordial ecosystems but collections of microbes, plants, and animals from around the world, flung together in an ecological melting pot. "It's the fate of all ecology," says marine ecologist Jeb Byers of the University of California, Santa Barbara. Some ecologists have suggested, only half-jokingly, that the field should start calling itself "mixoecology" or "recombination ecology." Many fear that another century or so of frenetic international traffic will lead to an "ecological homogenization" of the world, with a small number of immensely successful species, like the zebra mussel, cheatgrass, the European house sparrow, and the Argentine ant dominating nature everywhere—a global McEcosystem.

Hopes of arresting this process are spurring new studies. Policy-makers trying to restrict traffic in exotic species and prevent invaders from running rampant are hampered by not knowing exactly where the danger will spring up next. If ecologists could identify likely invaders, governments could simply restrict imports of those treacherous species, and managers could mercilessly weed them out or trap them. But making such predictions has been devilishly difficult; the few predictive models are still hotly debated, and they apply to only a narrow range of organisms at best. Some past invasions seem to fit no pattern at all. A true theory of prediction—what several researchers call the "Holy Grail of invasion biology"—still proves elusive. "It will always be very difficult to predict," says ecologist Ted Case of the University of California, San Diego.

Portrait of an invader

For most of human history, shipping animals and plants around has been considered a good thing. New World colonists brought in seeds, plants, and livestock and took other species back to Europe; 19th century "acclimatization societies" strived to populate America and Australia with European plants, birds, and mammals, including every bird mentioned in Shakespeare's work. Most such imports quickly die, but others—perhaps one in 10—settle into their new home. Of those, perhaps another 10% spread unchecked. As early as the late 19th century, when imported rabbits started ravaging Australian vegetation it became clear that newcomers could be dangerous. Now, the U.S. Department of Agriculture (USDA) intercepts about 3000 potential pests at the border every year, but many others make it through, and thousands of exotics are firmly established. In a lush state like Florida, one in every three or four plant species is non-native; in parts of San Francisco Bay, a staggering 99% of all biomass is thought to belong to non-native species.

After a slow start, the field of invasion biology is at last taking off. The journal *Biological Invasions* was launched just last month, and invasion biologists suddenly find themselves attracting more and more grants, students, and postdocs. Hundreds of scientists are staging plant takeovers in the lab or fencing off patches of sea floor to watch competition between marine critters in action. "People who worked on invasions used to feel like bastard children," says ecologist Sarah Reichard of the University of Washington, Seattle. "Like we had said something dirty. Now, all of a sudden everybody is interested. It's great!"

. . .

Vulnerable territory

Even if the stereotypical invader's signature is still uncertain, is there a typical ecosystem that easily gets invaded? Many researchers have found that exotic species move in more easily amid other types of ecological disruption. That was the common denominator Case identified in a set of invasions by ants, birds, and geckoes. Argentine ants are abundant in Californian towns and suburbs, says Case, and although they sometimes spread into the surrounding coastal sage scrub, they are never farther than 50 or 100 meters from the humanmade landscape.

Case also studied why native, asexually reproducing geckoes were driven out of Pacific islands by a sexual species from Southeast Asia. Turning Hawaiian aircraft hangars into makeshift laboratories, he watched how well the two species do under different circumstances and found that the newcomers are good at snapping insects on smooth surfaces with abundant light—in other words, on the walls of buildings. The invaders don't do nearly as well in forests, and without urbanization, Case says, they wouldn't have made it.

Another long-standing theory is that ecosystems rich in species, with their dense, interconnected webs of ecological relationships, can resist invasions, while those with fewer species succumb. For example, islands—which usually have fewer species than comparable areas of mainland—are often also the most heavily invaded. Models and lab experiments seem to support the idea; in an as-yet-unpublished study, for instance, a team led by John Stachowicz of the University of Connecticut, Groton, created artificial marine ecosystems with anywhere from zero to three North Atlantic species and then seeded each with a known invader, a Pacific tunicate called *Botrylloides diegensis*. The more species there were, the smaller the tunicate's chance of survival.

But a growing number of researchers think it's exactly the other way around. "To those small-scale experimenters and modelers I say: Go take a hike," says ecologist Tom Stohlgren of Colorado State University in Fort Collins—and he means it literally. His team recently sampled 100 plots in nine natural grasslands, national parks, and wildlands throughout the central United States. The number of exotic species in each, he reported at an ecological meeting last month, was positively correlated with the number of native species. The very circumstances that favor a wealth of native species, says Stohlgren, such as light, water, and nitrogen, also make a place attractive to newcomers. And experiments with just a few species don't remotely resemble real life, he adds.

There's yet another shadow on the prospects of prediction. Scientists have repeatedly witnessed exotic species living inconspicuously in their new habitat for decades—until the population suddenly explodes like Teletubbies in a toy store. In some cases, the reasons were obvious: Three species of exotic fig trees grown in Florida gardens for a century started spreading only 20 years or so ago—after the arrival of the fig wasp species that pollinate them. But often, such lag times are "quite mysterious," says ecologist Daniel Simberloff of the University of Tennessee, Knoxville. Take Brazilian pepper, "an incredibly awful" invader in south Florida, Simberloff says. "It sat around in people's yards as a harmless ornamental for many years, doing nothing. And suddenly in the late '40s, early '50s, it exploded"—and nobody knows why.

.   .   .

Given all this uncertainty, many ecologists are quite modest about their power to predict. For now, just forecasting the advance of a limited group of species in a number of habitats is difficult enough. Belnap, for instance, discovered that at least in Utah soils, cheatgrass often strikes where the potassium/magnesium ratio in the soil is high, suggesting that potassium uptake may be limiting for this species. She's now looking to see if the same holds true for other annual weeds and for other soils. Such studies are arduous, but they may be the only way to go. Says Case of UCSD: "The best approach is case by case." It's scant comfort that there will be many more cases to study.

TIM PALMER, THE HEART OF AMERICA: Our Landscape, Our Future
85–88 (1999).

Just as deer and owls depend on the forest, so is the forest dependent on good soil and air. But as a result of unregulated logging, the soil and nutrient base that the trees need has been diminished. Meanwhile, air pollution, including acid rain and ozone, has destroyed forest health and attacked the ability of trees to grow and resist disease. With the trees' immune systems crippled, invasions of exotic plants, fungi, and insects now strike down one tree species after another, with no end in sight.

The vulnerability of our woodlands to these impoverishments and vectors is what really defines the term *forest health*. This understanding recognizes forest health not just as a prerequisite for production of lumber and pulp but as a condition that supports a full complement of native plant and animal species and offers productive habitat to nurture them. Forest health requires plant life that builds soil and protects it from erosion; that moderates the effects of floods, droughts, and the weather; and that provides for people's needs without a loss of ability to provide for those needs in the future.

In *The Dying of the Trees*, which may be the most important book ever written about the forests of America, Charles Little reports on the current forest pandemic—an epidemic occurring everywhere. The problem is not just that we've cut the original forest down, and not just that the replacement forest is commercially managed as sterile tree farms. The new problem is that our trees are dying on a massive scale without ever seeing the logger's saw.

From the time of the first white settlement until the 20th century, the only tree known to become extinct in the wild was the white-blossomed franklinia, in 1803. Curiously, the next passing was not until an Asian fungus struck the American chestnut in the early 1900s, killing all adults of the species. But now insects, fungi, and blights are diminishing many key species, including hemlocks, white pines, beeches, dogwoods, and sugar maples. Hickories, ashes, and oaks of the central Appalachians unexplainably topple over in the prime of their lives. The beautiful butternut that my father pointed out to me as a child in the Allegheny Mountains of Pennsylvania may become extinct—it is the first tree to be named a candidate for the endangered species list. The problems stem from acid rain, air pollution, and weakened ecosystems in the wake of logging that leveled the original forest and tampered in unfathomed ways with its soils.

Acid rain invades the Northeast, where clouds with the pH of vinegar can be found for a hundred days a year in some places. Unpolluted rain has a pH of 5.6, but the forests subject to the greatest acid outfall, in a broad belt from New York to Tennessee, test at 4.2—dramatically lower on the scale of tolerance. Half of the red spruces of Camels Hump in Vermont's Green Mountains show dead or diseased foliage from acid rain. In Allegheny National Forest in Pennsylvania, 28 percent of the sugar maples were dead in 1994. Fish and amphibians succumb to poisoning as the pH of streams and lakes plummets. Primary sources of the acid are coal-burning power plants, which are fueled by the strip mines, long-tunnel mines, and mountaintop removals of Appalachia.

Excessive ozone in the lower atmosphere, caused by our burning of oil, gas, and coal, destroys trees in other ways, damaging leaves and fatally restricting photosynthesis. Even seedlings of the giant sequoia show ozone damage. Fifty-five percent of the trees in national forests of the southern Sierra Nevada have been ozone poisoned by smog wafting up to the mountains from the suburban and agribusiness maw of California. Ninety different plant species in the Great Smoky Mountains suffer from excessive ozone. Even the Forest Service, an agency that long resisted such warnings, released a study indicating that timber mortality national-wide had increased by 24 percent between 1986 and 1991. Worst hit were the hardwoods, whose mortality jumped by 37 percent. In 1998, the Lucy Braun Association reported Appalachian trees dying at two to four times the expected rate; the areas of greatest mortality coincided with the worst acid rain and ozone pollution.

Biologists maintain that damage from acid rain and air pollution makes the trees more susceptible to invasion by pathogens that can normally be resisted. Acid destroys the waxy surface of leaves; open wounds are then vulnerable to fungi and bacteria. The woolly adelgid, which is killing off hemlocks wholesale in the East, thrives on excess nitrogen in the polluted atmosphere of the Appalachians. Moreover, in an effect that is longer lasting, the pollution affects the forest floor. Acid rain dissolves aluminum, nickel, zinc, and lead in the soil, enabling trees to take up these toxic elements. The leaching of calcium from soils, probably caused by frequent logging and acid rain, could result in a 50 percent reduction of forest bio-mass in about 120 years.

. . .

While soil damage from logging and air pollution from fossil fuels stand as two formidable threats for the habitat of forests, other problems also diminish the wooded elegance of our country. The cottonwoods on flood-plains through the West and the Great Plains turn into skeletons and are not being replaced along many rivers because the germination of new trees requires flood flows that scour shorelines or deposit silt. Dams have controlled the rivers so much that we seldom have floods, silt, or cotton-wood regeneration on waterways as significant as the Missouri and Snake Rivers.

Affecting every region, the invasion of exotic species, from tamarisks on floodplains of the Southwest to scotch broom in the Northwest to kudzu in the Southeast, preempts the space needed by our native trees. In California, the majestic blue and valley oaks of the Central Valley and surrounding hills fail to regenerate and grow, suffering from the invasion of annual grasses that mat the soil and make it inhospitable to acorns and oak seedlings.

Yet another monumental reason for collapse in many types of forest has been our misguided compulsion to suppress all natural forest fires. . . .

At the turn of the 21st century, members of Congress fumbled with legislative bills that would ostensibly improve forest health. In fact, they offered little but increased logging and failed to address the real forest health crisis. It's a crisis of habitat for the trees themselves, and it involves the quality of our air, invasions of exotic species, loss of soil due to erosion from clear-cuts and road building, and the shackling of natural processes such as floods and natural forest necessary for ecosystems to function.

NOTES

The dangers of genetic engineering: The blending of genes and species recounted by the above two excerpts could well be on the verge of a massive expansion with the emergence (and, so far, modest regulatory control) of new tools of genetic engineering. One challenge posed by the technology: It "provides the illusion that humanity can be weaned off its historic dependence on wild plants and animals as the raw material for selective breeding of its food crops and for a large share of its medicines. Were this illusion to become embodied in policy, efforts to save habitat and biodiversity would be even more impeded than they are today." John Harte, *Land Use, Biodiversity, and Ecosystem Integrity: The Challenge of*

Preserving Earth's Life Support System, 27 ECOLOGY L.Q. 929, 955 (2001). *See also* John Charles Kunich, *Mother Frankenstein, Doctor Nature, and the Environmental Law of Genetic Engineering*, 74 S. CAL. L. REV. 807 (2001).

Aside from this general fear, genetically modified organisms pose specific dangers. One is that, when modified organisms are introduced into the wild, they will harm existing, native life forms (in addition to the specific life forms that they might be intended to harm). A related danger: The new organisms themselves, like other alien species, will enter natural communities and disrupt or outcompete native species. Finally, there is the possibility (or near certainty, some scientists would assert) that modified genetic material used intentionally in an engineered organism can in one way or another "escape" and affect the genetic makeup of other species. The first of these dangers is highlighted by a study of the unintended effects of genetically modified corn. A.R. Zangerl, *et al.*, *Effects of exposure of event 176 Bacillus thuringiensis corn pollen on monarch and black swallowtail caterpillars under field conditions*, ___ PROC. NATL. ACAD. SCIS. ___ (2001) (pollen from Bt corn engineered with "Norvatis event 176" (carrying insecticidal protein toxins designed to resist damage by European corn borer) caused significant reduction in growth rates of black swallowtail butterfly larvae under field conditions).

c. THE MECHANICS OF EXTINCTION

When the population of a species declines to some level, it will ineluctably be driven to extinction. How extinction occurs and the special dangers facing small populations have become a major focus of scientific research. From such research, scientists hope to be able to evaluate the dangers faced by particular species. Generally, species with low numbers (and isolated populations of more populous species) confront four types of risks that do not typically cause long-term harm to more numerous and wide-spread species: demographic stochasticity, social dysfunction, genetic deterioration, and extrinsic forces. *See generally* John A. Beardmore, *Extinction, Survival, and Genetic Variation, in* GENETICS AND CONSERVATION 125 (Christine M. Schonewald–Cox *et al.* eds., 1983); Jared M. Diamond, *"Normal" Extinctions of Isolated Populations, in* EXTINCTIONS 191 (Matthew H. Nitecki ed., 1984); Mark L. Shaffer, *Minimum Population Sizes for Species Conservation*, 31 BIOSCI. 131 (1981); D. Simberloff, *The Proximate Causes of Extinction, in* PATTERNS AND PROCESSES IN THE HISTORY OF LIFE 259 (D.M. Raup & D. Jablonski eds., 1986); Michael E. Soule, *What Do We Really Know About Extinction?, in* GENETICS AND CONSERVATION 111 (Christine M. Schonewald–Cox *et al.* eds., 1983).

Demographic stochasticity is the random variation in population variables: sex ratio, birth and death rates, age distribution of individuals, and the like. Variations in these factors in turn cause variations in population size. Skewed sex ratios, for example, lead to inbreeding or directly to extinction if all of a species are a single sex.[1] Demographic stochasticity is unlikely to cause extinction except in the smallest of populations.

---

1. This occurred with the dusky seaside sparrow whose last generation consisted sole-ly of males. Paul W. Sykes, *Decline and Disappearance of the Dusky Seaside Sparrow*

Social dysfunction can give rise to two distinct types of liability. First, social behavior may itself increase the risk to a species. Group mating rituals such as the lekking behavior of the heath hen and group defensive or flocking behaviors such as those of the Carolina parakeet are examples of behaviors that increase the ease of hunting a species. Sociality itself also increases the potential for epidemics and local catastrophic events. TIM HALLIDAY, VANISHING BIRDS 101–02 (1978); Michael E. Soule, *supra,* at 117; Jared M. Diamond, *supra,* at 200. Second, social behavior required for reproduction may become impossible when populations drop below certain levels. There is evidence, for example, that breeding among social animals may require the synchronization that is triggered by social stimuli. The passenger pigeon may be an example of a species whose demise was immediately caused by the inability to congregate in groups large enough to facilitate breeding. TIM HALLIDAY, *supra,* at 94.

Genetic deterioration was discussed in the parable of the prairie chick-en [Chapter 11], noted above: the small, isolated populations lacked the genetic diversity necessary for survival and were rescued from extinction (for the moment) only when birds from different populations were introduced. Genetic deterioration has two elements. The first is inbreeding depression—a "decrease in vigor, viability, and fecundity" that results when rates of inbreeding are greater than 1% to 2% per generation. Michael E. Soule, *supra,* at 118. Inbreeding causes an increase in the number of individuals who are homozygous, that is, which have the same form of a gene. When the gene controls an otherwise-unexpressed and deleterious trait, homozygosity can lead not only to gross abnormalities but also lower viability and fertility. D. Simberloff, *supra,* at 263–65. The second type of genetic deterioration is a decrease in the genetic variation in a population. Decrease in genetic variation reduces a species potential adaptability to environmental changes. This is unlikely to be a serious problem since "it is likely that other factors will eliminate a small population before failure to evolve endangers it." D. Simberloff, *supra,* at 263.

Extrinsic forces are random events such as extreme weather conditions (extended drought, tornadoes, and the like) and other random catastrophes (fires, floods, epidemics, and the like). Each of these events can cause the extinction of a small localized population of a species.

These factors are of more than academic concern since they are crucial to a determination of the "minimum viable population"—a concern that underlies many of the current debates on protection of endangered or threatened species. It is also a concern that turns on toleration of uncertainty: how certain does society wish to be that a species will still be present at some point in the future? *E.g.,* Mark L. Shaffer, *Minimum Population Sizes for Species Conservation,* 31 BIOSCI. 131 (1981); Mark L.

from Merritt Island, Florida, 34 AM. BIRDS 378 (1980). Demographic stochasticity and genetic deterioration act synergistically because skewed sex ratios are one result of inbreeding. D. Simberloff, *The Proximate Causes of Extinction, in* PATTERNS AND PROCESSES IN THE HISTORY OF LIFE 259, 263 (D.M. Raup & D.

Jablonski eds., 1986). *Cf.* Jared M. Diamond, *"Normal" Extinctions of Isolated Populations, in* EXTINCTIONS 191, 193–96 (Matthew H. Nitecki ed., 1984) (the major cause of population fluctuations is environmental fluctuations rather than demographic accidents).

Shaffer & Fred B. Samson, *Population Size and Extinction: A Note on Determining Critical Population Sizes,* 125 AM. NATURALIST 144 (1985).

d.   DISRUPTING THE FLOW OF EVOLUTION

Norm Myers & Andrew H. Kroll, *The Biotic Crisis and the Future of Evolution*

98 PROC. NAT'L ACAD. SCIS. 5389 (2001).

Human activities have brought the Earth to the brink of biotic crisis. Many biologists consider that coming decades will see the loss of large numbers of species. Fewer scientists—witness the lack of professional papers addressing the issue—appear to have recognized that, in the longer term, these extinctions will alter not only biological diversity but also the evolutionary processes by which diversity is generated. Thus, current and predicted environmental perturbations form a double-edged sword that will slice into both the legacy and future of evolution.

. . .

One of the first truisms absorbed by biologists is that evolution is not predictable. We can no more predict the future composition of communities than some Ordovician ecologist could have foreseen the Great Barrier Reef. However, despite our inability to predict the products of evolution the trajectories of future morphologies or the innovations of future physiologies we can make meaningful estimates about evolutionary processes as they will be affected by the depletion of biological diversity. We may have little basis for predicting what large mammals might look like two million years from now, but much better reason to suppose that there will be very few of them.

The evolutionary dimension to the current biotic crisis has been vividly expressed by Michael Soule: "Death is one thing, an end to birth is something else." In other words, impending extinctions will be far from the full final outcome of current environmental disruption. At least as important will be the alteration of evolutionary process, and for a period that is difficult to estimate but must surely measure in millions of years.

First-Order Effects. There will be several first-order effects stemming from the biotic crisis: (i) a major extinction of species within the foreseeable future, estimated by some to remove between one-third and two-thirds of all species now extant; (ii) a mega-mass extinction of populations, proportionately greater than the mass extinction of species, within the foreseeable future; (iii) alien invasions and other mixings of biotas; (iv) progressive depletion and homogenization of biotas, with potential threshold effects on ecosystems; (v) biotic impoverishment generally, possibly including a decline of global biomass; and (vi) gross reduction if not virtual elimination of entire sectors of some biomes, notably tropical forests, coral reefs, and wetlands, all of which have served as centers of diversification in the past.

Further Evolutionary Effects. These first-order impacts will likely engender a series of further consequences, including although not limited to: (i) fragmentation of species' ranges, with disruption of gene flow; (ii) decline in effective population sizes, with depletion of gene reservoirs/pools; and (iii) biotic interchanges introducing species and even biotas into new areas, with multiple founder effects and novel competitive and other ecological interactions. These impacts, in turn, might disrupt food chains/webs, symbioses, or other biological associations.

These consequences could lead to further repercussions such as the following six:

An outburst of speciation. As large numbers of niches are vacated, in conjunction with a splitting off of disjunct populations through habitat fragmentation, there may well be an outburst of speciation, even of adaptive radiation, albeit not remotely on a scale to match the extinction spasm. It is unlikely that speciation will be evenly distributed among surviving lineages; it may be concentrated among particular clades or ecological types that thrive in human-dominated ecosystems.

Proliferation of opportunistic species. r-selected and generalist species, often appearing as opportunistic species, may proliferate, especially if there is preferential elimination of K-selected species that include natural controls of r-selected populations. Could this proliferation lead to what has been characterized as a "pest and weed" ecology?

Depletion of "evolutionary powerhouses" in the tropics. Virtually every major group of vertebrates and many large categories of invertebrates and plants originated in spacious zones with warm, equable climates. In addition, tropical species appear to have persisted for relatively brief periods of geologic time, implying high rates of evolutionary turnover and episodes of explosive speciation. According to Jablonski, the tropics have been "the engine of biodiversity" for at least 250 million years. Today, we face the prospect of severe depletion if not virtual elimination of tropical forests, wetlands, estuaries, coral reefs, and other biomes, with their exceptional biodiversity and ecological complexity. Because some of these biomes appear, in some senses at least, to have served in the past as preeminent "powerhouses" of evolution, their decline could entail severe consequences for rediversification as the biosphere emerges from environmental crisis.

Decline of biodisparity. Elimination of species is not the only measure of an extinction event. There can be declines, as well, in biodisparity, the biota's manifest morphological and physiological variety. Biodisparity impoverishment can be assessed through the surrogate measure of loss of higher taxa or guilds, and, over the past 2000 years, the preferential elimination of species-poor genera has reduced biodisparity at rates even greater than those of species loss. Will the same pattern of non-random culling persist in the future?

An end to speciation of large vertebrates. Even our largest protected areas will prove far too small for further speciation of elephants, rhinoceroses, apes, bears, and big cats, among other large vertebrates. What knock-on consequences and ripple effects could there be for smaller species, indeed for biotas as a whole given, for example, the depauperizing impacts of the present-day decline of elephants?

Emergent novelties. There may be many emergent novelties, although these are especially difficult to predict. For instance, there could be an explosive radiation within certain higher taxa, notably small mammals and insects able to thrive in human-dominated ecosystems. The question is not whether persistent lineages can evolve in unexpected ways, but rather to what extent the environmental constraints humans place on surviving populations will channel innovations toward properties we associate with pests.

SECTION 3. THE CHALLENGES OF CONSERVATION

a. THE FUNDAMENTALS OF CONSERVATION BIOLOGY

Concerns about the loss of biodiversity led to the creation of a new field of biological science, conservation biology. Conservation biology studies the causes of species declines and seeks to develop tools to protect and restore. The following excerpt discusses the basic lessons that conservation biologists have learned and the core ideas that they believe should guide landscape-scale or ecosystem management.

Reed F. Noss, *Some Principles of Conservation Biology, As They Apply to Environmental Law*
69 CHI.-KENT L. REV. 893 (1994).

Conservation is not as simple today as in the past. One hundred years ago it seemed that if we could just stop the plume hunters from shooting egrets to decorate ladies' hats, and if we could only save a few areas of spectacular scenery in national parks, we were doing well. Somewhat later it became apparent that we had to protect many kinds of habitats— wetlands, grasslands, deserts, forests of all kinds—to save wildlife....

As ecology, genetics, and other biological sciences matured, they slowly began to have more influence on conservation philosophy, and in the last two decades they have begun to inform conservation practice. But as the influence of scientists on environmental policy increased, so did doubts about our ability to comprehend nature.

Ecological science has undergone significant changes in recent years. Among the new paradigms in ecology, none is more revolutionary than the idea that nature is not delicately balanced in equilibrium, but rather is dynamic, often unpredictable, and perhaps even chaotic. It follows that classical preservationist approaches to conservation, to the extent that they attempt to hold nature static, do not reflect realities of nature. A related idea is that ecological phenomena operate across vast landscapes, and that parks and other areas set aside for their natural qualities are inevitably buffeted by exotic species invasions, uncontrolled human activities, disruptions of hydrology, and other cross-boundary effects.

Nature cannot be expected to manage itself and maintain all of its components in a world where natural processes have been dramatically altered. Even the largest wild areas on earth are changing inexorably due to natural forces and are now being affected by long-distance transport of pollutants, thinning of the ozone layer, and probably global warming....

I. Conservation Biology and Values

The emergence of conservation biology as a distinct discipline in the late 1970s and its flowering in the mid–80s with the founding of the Society for Conservation Biology can be traced to the increasing interest of ecologists, geneticists, and other "basic" biological scientists in conservation problems and the dissatisfaction of these scientists with wildlife management, forestry, fisheries, and other traditional natural resource disciplines. The resource disciplines were concerned with mostly utilitarian ends and focused on a narrow range of the biological spectrum, chiefly game birds and mammals, edible fish, commercial trees, and livestock forage. Although the resource disciplines had already begun to broaden in the 1970s with more attention to "nongame" and endangered species, the broadening was not great or fast enough for conservationists interested in biodiversity, the total variety of life on earth. Moreover, it was quickly recognized that because conservation problems are inherently transdisciplinary, conservation biology must involve not only biologists, but also geographers, sociologists, economists, philosophers, lawyers, political scientists, educators, artists, and other professionals.

A distinguishing feature of conservation biology is that it is mission oriented. Underlying any mission is a set of values. Philosophers of science now recognize that no science is value free, despite all we were taught in school about the strict objectivity of the scientific method. Conservation biology is more value-laden than most sciences because it is not concerned with knowledge for its own sake but rather is directed toward particular goals. Maintaining biodiversity is an unquestioned goal of conservation biologists....

. . .

The philosophy underlying conservation biology and other applied sciences is one of prudence: in the face of uncertainty, applied scientists have an ethical obligation to risk erring on the side of preservation. Thus, anyone attempting to modify a natural environment and put biodiversity at risk is guilty until proven innocent. This shift in burden of proof is consistent with the precautionary principle, which is gaining increased support in many professions....

II. Principles of Conservation Biology

.... Like ecology, conservation biology has so far been largely a science of case studies. Whatever generalities exist, like "everything is connected to everything else," seem trite. But despite the anecdotal nature of much of our knowledge in conservation biology, some principles or empirical generalizations are becoming clear. These principles will hopefully be useful to policy makers, legal scholars, land-use planners, land managers, and conservationists in general, and they can be adapted to scales ranging from local land-use plans to global strategies. I begin with some general principles and then move to specific tasks such as reserve design and ecosystem management. Although any principle is a generalization and will have exceptions, taken together these principles provide a robust basis for conservation planning.

A. General Principles

The general principles of conservation biology emerge from an appreciation of the complexity of nature, and an understanding that we will never know precisely how nature works. Thus, we had better be as cautious and gentle as possible in our manipulations.

"Ecosystems are not only more complex than we think, but more complex than we can think." This quote from ecologist Frank Egler was probably based on a 1927 statement by evolutionary biologist J.B.S. Haldane, who said "[m]y suspicion is that the universe is not only queerer than we suppose, but queerer than we can suppose." In any case, the proper response to this situation is humility. Humility demands that we prefer erring on the side of preservation to erring on the side of development. Thus, humility demands a shift in burden of proof [on whether development should occur].

The less data or more uncertainty involved, the more conservative a conservation plan must be. Some non-trivial level of uncertainty accompanies all planning decisions. When information on species locations, population sizes and trends, interspecific interactions, responses to disturbance, and other factors is scarce or questionable, the best interim strategy is one that minimizes development and other human disturbance during the time needed to gather the necessary biological information. . . .

Natural is not an absolute, but a relative concept. Because human impacts penetrate all boundaries, no purely natural areas exist anywhere in the world today. Yet few would disagree that a remnant of virgin forest or tallgrass prairie is more natural than a clearcut or a shopping mall.

Conservation biology is highly value-laden. No science is value-free, but values and ethics play a more prominent role in applied, mission-oriented sciences like conservation biology than in basic research. The greatest objectivity follows from stating biases, values, interests, predilections, and goals straightforwardly. Such openness may not seem appropriate in a courtroom, where the assumption seems to be that science is only concerned with facts, but is entirely consistent with the oath of honesty.

Conservation must be goal-directed. Explicit (though not necessarily quantitative) goals are better than vague goals, and ambitious goals are usually preferable to weak goals. Without stated goals, conservation programs flounder. In an apparent effort to appear reasonable, some conservationists begin their bargaining with goals that are already highly compromised. Because few goals are ever fully attained, starting with a compromise may mean ending up with nothing.

In order to be comprehensive, biodiversity conservation must be concerned with multiple levels of biological organization and many different spatial and temporal scales. There is no one best scale or level of organization for conservation research or action. The trick is finding the best scale for solving each specific problem, then integrating across scales for the overall conservation strategy.

Conservation biology is interdisciplinary, but biology must determine the bottom line. Human cultural systems are far more adaptable than biological systems. Thus, although sociological and economic concerns must enter into any conservation planning exercise, the vital needs of nonhuman species must not be compromised. Furthermore, because a healthy economy ultimately depends on a healthy ecosystem, human actions that are not compatible with the integrity of the ecosystem should not be permitted.

B.   Principles of Reserve Design and Management for Target Species

Although ecosystem management is the buzzword of the day, management of individual species on a population or metapopulation level remains a necessary part of any conservation strategy. Without individual attention, many species that have declined due to human activity are likely to become extinct in the near future. Besides, we know much more about managing species than managing ecosystems. The Interagency Scientific Committee that developed a conservation strategy for the northern spotted owl offered five general principles for reserve design that they characterized as "widely accepted" within the community of conservation biologists. Few scientists have disagreed with their bold statement. I paraphrase these five reserve design principles below, then add several of my own that apply to species especially sensitive to human activity.

Species well distributed across their native range are less susceptible to extinction than species confined to small portions of their range. The idea here is that a widely distributed species will be unlikely to experience a catastrophe, disturbance, or other negative influence across its entire range at once. For instance, a severe drought may dry up the breeding ponds used by a species of salamander for several years in a row across two or three states. If that salamander occurs nowhere else, it may become extinct. However, if the salamander is distributed broadly, at least some areas within its range are likely to contain breeding ponds that do not dry out completely. From those refugia, the species can slowly recolonize areas where it had been eliminated....

Large blocks of habitat, containing large populations of a target species, are superior to small blocks of habitat containing small populations. The principle of "bigness" is another of the universally accepted generalizations of conservation biology. All else being equal, large populations are less vulnerable than small populations to extinction. A larger block of suitable habitat will usually contain a larger population. In line with the preceding principle, large blocks of habitat are also less likely to experience a disturbance throughout their area. Thus, refugia and recolonization sources are more likely to occur in large blocks of habitat than in small blocks, thus enhancing population persistence.

Blocks of habitat close together are better than blocks far apart. Many organisms are capable of crossing narrow swaths of unsuitable habitat, such as a trail, a narrow road, or a vacant lot; far fewer are able to successfully traverse a six-lane highway or the City of Chicago. In the absence of impenetrable barriers, habitat blocks that are close together will experience more interchange of individuals of a target species than will blocks far apart. If enough interchange occurs between habitat blocks, they are functionally united into a larger population that is less vulnerable to extinction for any number of reasons.

Habitat in continuous blocks is better than fragmented habitat. This rule follows logically from the previous two but also brings in some new considerations. Fragmentation involves a reduction in size and an increase in isolation of habitats. The theory of island biogeography predicts that either of these processes will lead to lower species richness due to decreased immigration rates (in the case of isolation) and increased extinction rates (in the case of small size). Thus, a small island far from the mainland is predicted to have the lowest species richness. . . .

Interconnected blocks of habitat are better than isolated blocks. Connectivity—the opposite of fragmentation—has become one of the best accepted principles of conservation planning. Despite continuing arguments over benefits versus costs of particular corridor designs, few conservation biologists would disagree that habitats functionally connected by natural movements of organisms are less subject to extinctions than habitats artificially isolated by human activity. . . .

Blocks of habitat that are roadless or otherwise inaccessible to humans are better than roaded and accessible habitat blocks. Roads and other providers of human access often lead to high mortality rates for large carnivores, furbearers, desert tortoises, commercially valuable plants such as cacti, and other species exploited or persecuted by people. Although the ultimate solution to these problems must involve education and change in human values and behavior, the immediate need is to restrict access to habitats of sensitive species . . . . .

"[C]onservation strategy should not treat all species as equal but must focus on species and habitats threatened by human activities." This statement from Jared Diamond seems logical enough, but it is amazing how much time and money has been spent studying and managing species that do not really require human assistance (*e.g.*, white-tailed deer). Similarly, high species diversity in clearcuts and other human-disturbed habitats has been used to justify intensive forestry and other forms of manipulative management, even though the species that thrive in such habitats are mostly opportunistic weeds. The most appropriate target species for conservation are generally those most sensitive to human disturbance.

Populations that fluctuate widely are more likely to go extinct than populations that are more stable over time. Mean population size is sometimes a poor indicator of vulnerability. A population with a relatively large mean size but high variance may be more likely to go extinct than a smaller but more stable population. Large-bodied animal species, although more vulnerable to many specific threats, generally fluctuate less and therefore can probably be viable with smaller populations.

Disjunct or peripheral populations of species are more likely to be genetically impoverished but also genetically distinct than are central populations. This well-documented pattern is a direct consequence of reduced gene flow to isolated or marginal populations. The pattern presents a dilemma because populations with lower heterozygosity are likely to be less adaptable to future environmental change and therefore might be seen as less important to conserve. Marginal populations are also likely to be in suboptimal habitat. Thus, conservation at the species level may be more effective when directed to the central portion of each species' range. On the other hand, disjunct or peripheral populations are likely to have diverged genetically from central populations due to genetic drift, adaptation to local environments, or both. Directional selective pressures can be expected to be intense for these populations. If we are concerned with maintaining opportunities for speciation—future biodiversity—then conservation of peripheral and disjunct populations is critical. . . .

C.   Ecosystem Management

The idea that we can manage ecosystems is arrogant and misleading. However, management based on some understanding of ecosystems and aimed at protecting whole communities or habitat mosaics is certainly sensible. . . .

Maintaining viable ecosystems is usually more efficient, economical, and effective than a species-by-species approach. Although, as noted earlier, many sensitive species require individual attention in order to avoid extinction, focusing on every species individually is impossible. There are likely to be thousands of species inhabiting any given region, if we include microbes, soil invertebrates, and other poorly known groups. The "coarse filter" approach of representing all types of habitats and communities in areas managed for their natural values is probably the most inclusive of all conservation strategies. The goal of the Gap Analysis project of the National Biological Survey is to evaluate how well native vegetation types and associated species are represented in protected areas.

Biodiversity is not distributed randomly or uniformly across the landscape. In establishing protection priorities, focus on "hot spots." Hot spots are areas of concentrated conservation value, such as centers of endemism or areas of high species richness. Hot spots can be recognized at many spatial scales. For example, globally, the humid tropics stand out as hot spots of species richness, with the greatest diversity for most taxa in Central and South America. But within an area such as the Amazon Basin, biologists have identified hot spots of endemism. Some kinds of organisms, such as coniferous trees, are most diverse in North America. Looking more closely, the greatest diversity of conifers appears to be the seventeen species in the Russian Peak area of northern California. Every landscape has areas of concentrated biodiversity. Map overlays that display multiple conservation criteria can show the locations of these hot spots.

Ecosystem boundaries should be determined by reference to ecology, not politics. Ecosystems do not respect property and jurisdictional lines. Ecologists often say that the boundaries of all ecosystems—even the biosphere—are open, exchanging energy and materials with other systems. But of course boundaries are not entirely arbitrary. Topography, geology, soils, and other factors often create discontinuities on the landscape. Ecosystems can be delimited by vegetation, watersheds, or physiography, all of which are hierarchically organized but mappable. . . .

Because conservation value varies across a regional landscape, zoning is a useful approach to land-use planning and reserve network design. Some advocates of ecosystem management favor a "landscape without lines" approach, where human activities are spread throughout a landscape. This approach is not likely to offer sufficient protection to hot spots and areas especially sensitive to human disturbances. A concentric zoning model with protection increasing inward and intensity of human use increasing outward is recommended.

Ecosystem health and integrity depend on the maintenance of ecological processes. Flow of energy and cycling of nutrients are fundamental processes of all ecosystems. Photosynthesis, herbivory, predation, disease, decomposition, competition, cooperation, disturbance, succession, erosion, deposition, and other biotic and abiotic processes assure that energy keeps flowing and nutrients keep cycling. Disruption of the characteristic processes of any ecosystem will likely lead to biotic impoverishment. Although even grossly impoverished ecosystems (for instance, an abandoned strip mine or sewage lagoon) continue to function, they cannot be said to have integrity.

Human disturbances that mimic or simulate natural disturbances are less likely to threaten species than are disturbances radically different from the natural regime. Species have evolved along with disturbances. Natural selection has provided species with ways to escape, tolerate, or exploit natural disturbances, so that life histories of species are often closely tied to a specific disturbance regime. . . .

Ecosystem management requires cooperation among agencies and landowners and coordination of inventory, research, monitoring, and management activities. Because political and landownership boundaries do not conform to ecological boundaries, agencies and landowners will need to cooperate in order to manage resources and conserve biodiversity effectively. Both within and among agencies, the usually separate functions of biological inventory, research, monitoring, and management should be united into one holistic scheme.

Management must be adaptive. Much land management in the past has been trial and error, with errors often not recognized until long after damage was done. Even then, destructive practices often continued because no rigorous studies linked degradation of habitats to specific management practices. Recognizing that every land management practice is an experiment with an uncertain outcome, research and monitoring should be coordinated to test hypotheses about the effects of management treatments on biodiversity and ecological integrity. The information gained from these experiments should be used to adjust management in a desirable direction.

Natural areas have a critical role to play as benchmarks or control areas for management experiments. This value was recognized by Aldo Leopold, who pointed out that wilderness provides a "base-datum of normality" for a "science of land health." Scientists shudder to think of experiments without controls, but this is the case for much land management today. Existing natural areas are imperfect baselines for many reasons, but they are the best we have. Ecosystem management, because it is essentially experimental and adaptive, requires natural areas as controls. Unfortunately, many of the proponents of ecosystem management today propose it as an alternative to protected areas, rather than as a necessary complement.

b. LANDSCAPE MANAGEMENT: BIODIVERSITY PLANNING AT THE LANDSCAPE LEVEL

As Noss observes, principles of conservation biology can be the basis for action only when land management takes place at large spatial scales, well above the size of the typical parcel. Even large areas of federal land are often too small to manage apart from surrounding nonfederal lands with which they are ecologically interconnected. Chapter 11 considered some of the particular legal settings in which federal agencies have undertaken to manage lands at the ecosystem or landscape scale. Here our focus is on the fundamental policy issues. Is ecosystem management simply a way for more people to have a voice in how a landscape is used, or is it really a goal-drive enterprise of the type that Noss advocates—an enterprise that maintains a sharp focus on managing lands to sustain viable populations of all species of concern?

The following excerpt comes from the Overview of the 1995 Report of the Interagency Ecosystem Management Task Force, the product of a team representing numerous federal agencies. As one would expect from a committee product, it reflects widely differing perspectives, all brought together in seemingly harmonious language. The commentary that follows contains a critical probing of the federal document, noting its internal conflicts and speculating as to why the agency report, on its face, seems so contradictory. The final excerpt is from a provocative essay by Professor Oliver Houck, who asks whether humans should be viewed as parts of the ecosystems that they manage.

REPORT OF INTERAGENCY ECOSYSTEM MANAGEMENT TASK FORCE (1995)

THE ECOSYSTEM APPROACH

Definitions

An ecosystem is an interconnected community of living things, including humans, and the physical environment within which they interact.

The ecosystem approach is a method of sustaining or restoring natural systems and their functions and values. It is goal driven, and it is based on a collaboratively developed vision of desired future conditions that integrates ecological, economic, and social factors. It is applied within a geographic framework defined primarily by ecological boundaries.

The goal of the ecosystem approach is to restore and sustain the health, productivity, and biological diversity of ecosystems and the overall quality of life through a natural resource management approach that is fully integrated with social and economic goals.

Characteristics of the Ecosystem Approach

The ecosystem approach is a comprehensive regional approach to protecting, restoring, and sustaining our ecological resources and the communities and economics that they support. Past efforts have been fragmented, and have produced mixed results. Evidence of the stress that has been placed upon ecological resources can be seen in the decline of the salmon populations in the Pacific Northwest and the oyster stock in the Chesapeake Bay, the decline in migratory bird populations, and degraded coral reef systems. The causes of these problems are as varied as human activity itself: the way we farm, work, travel, and spend our leisure hours.

The ecosystem approach integrates ecological protection and restoration with human needs to strengthen the essential connection between economic prosperity and environmental well being. The ecosystem approach provides the framework that draws together federal, state, local, and tribal governments, and the public, to achieve the ultimate goal of healthy, sustainable ecosystems that provide us with food, shelter, clean air and water, and a multitude of other goods and services.

. . .

Principles of the Ecosystem Approach

Federal agencies should adopt a set of common principles to guide them in implementing and participating in ecosystem efforts. The principles below are intended to provide such guidance. Because there are so many types of agencies with such varying missions, agencies will need to tailor these principles to their own mandates and circumstances.

* Develop a shared vision of the desired ecosystem condition that takes into account existing social and economic conditions in the ecosystem, and identify ways in which area parties can contribute to, and benefit from, achieving ecosystem goals.

* Develop coordinated approaches among federal agencies to accomplish ecosystem objectives, collaborating on a continuous basis with state, local, and tribal governments, and other stakeholders to address mutual concerns.

* Use ecological approaches that restore or maintain the biological diversity and sustainability of the ecosystem.

* Support actions that incorporated sustained economic, sociocultural, and community goals.

* Respect and ensure private property rights and work cooperatively with private landowners to accomplish shared goals.

* Recognize that ecosystems and institutions are complex, dynamic, characteristically heterogeneous over space and time, and constantly changing.

* Use an adaptive approach to management to achieve both desired goals and a new understanding of ecosystems.

* Integrate the best science available into the decision-making process, while continuing scientific research to improve the knowledge base.

* Establish baseline conditions for ecosystem functioning and sustainability against which change can be measured; monitor and evaluate actions to determine if goals and objectives are being achieved.

Benefits of the Ecosystem Approach

The goal of the ecosystem approach is to restore and maintain the health of ecological resources together with the communities and economics that they support. The inclusion of people and their economic needs is a fundamental part of the approach....

. . .

The following discussion outlines some of the most important benefits that may be realized by individuals and interest groups in the private sector, and by units of government.

Consensus-building. Under the ecosystem approach, governmental decision-making processes are more open to the public, and the public is involved early in the process. Interested parties are encouraged to help establish goals and identify ways to achieve them. The consensus-based orientation of the ecosystem approach benefits the public because people are more likely to get what they want with regard to ecological and economic goals.

NOTES

(1) Unraveling substance and process: To what extent does ecosystem management, as described in the federal report, measure up to the visions set forth by Reed Noss? Is it aimed at promoting the restoration of native species in something close to native numbers and ranges? Does it have, instead, other goals? Indeed, to what extent is it management aimed at a pre-determined goal, and to what extent is it, instead, simply a framework that brings people together and allows them, once assembled, to select their own goals (which, if the process is unfettered, could well conflict with the maintenance of biodiversity)? Consider the following critical commentary on the Report:

The *Interagency Ecosystem Report* is a political document, aimed mostly at audiences outside the federal government and designed to quell fears that ecosystem management will mean a surge in intrusive federal power. Like most political documents, this one contains inconsistencies, calculated inconsistencies in this case, intended to make the document palatable to readers with differing views. The Interagency Ecosystem Report's inner tensions are nowhere more plain than in its expressed goal for ecosystem management. The ecosystem approach, we are told at one point, is merely "a process," the neutral aim of which is to achieve the "desired ecosystem outcome" that has been set collectively by the people and entities (including federal agencies) whose lives and activities are bound with and to the ecosystem. Federal agencies interested in the ecosystem are encouraged "to play the role of facilitator and assistant in the development of a (desired, shared) vision; they should avoid imposition of a solely federal vision upon local communities." The shared ecosystem vision that comes out of this "process" is expected to "tak[e] into account existing social and economic conditions in the ecosystem, and identify ways in which all parties can contribute to, and benefit from, achieving ecosystem goals."

This soothing language is aimed, evidently enough, at calming the fears of critics of expansive federal power. It allows them to hope that ecosystem management, in practice, might be just a modified version of business-as-usual exploitation. Here and in other places, the Inter-agency Ecosystem Report suggests that affected ecosystem members are free to set whatever goals they like, whether or not consistent with lasting ecological health. Elsewhere, however, the Report contains far different language, intended probably for consumption by the agencies themselves and revealing much more about the real hopes of the people who did the drafting. Notwithstanding the process language, the eco-system approach, we are told, is a "goal driven" enterprise; it is "a method for sustaining and restoring natural systems and their func-tions and values"; it has an established, background goal—"to restore and sustain the health, productivity, and biological diversity of ecosys-tems...." Federal agencies are instructed to "[u]se ecological ap-proaches that restore or maintain the biological diversity and sustain-ability of the ecosystem." They are to generate "protocols establishing ecological indicators for monitoring ecosystem sustainability," as if ecosystem sustainability were an assumed element of every "desired ecosystem outcome." Volume One of the Interagency Ecosystem Re-port draws to a close with a further critical point, quietly slipped in: the "shared vision," we are told, "should be consistent with the overarching goal of sustaining biological diversity of the ecosys-tem...."

On first reading, the Interagency Ecosystem Report seems incon-sistent, pushing both a process model that allows local people to set their own goals and an alternative management method that comes with a goal already outlined—a quickly sketched goal that includes not just the maintenance but the restoration of the "health" and "biologi-cal diversity" of ecosystems. Is it possible to bring these sentences together, to reduce or eliminate the seeming inconsistency? Are they more artfully written than first meets the eye?

What the authors of the Interagency Ecosystem Report knew all too well is that many people across the land know little about matters of ecological health and, for that reason and others, value it rather little. They are out to make a living, whether meager or opulent, and want little interference from a meddling, distant government. Vast numbers of businesses are adamantly opposed to environmental protec-tion and to anything that smacks of land-use regulation, without regard for long-term communal well-being. For people concerned about land health, these are tough nuts to crack; they are potent obstacles that have to be dealt with, and cannot simply be bypassed.

They cannot be bypassed, but they can be pushed and cajoled and educated and encouraged to reflect on the long-term good of the land and its human inhabitants; they can, that is, be moved along, step by step, lesson by lesson, in the direction of valuing the land more highly and considering longer-term perspectives. In the short term, resistant voices need to speak out, or the resistance and backlash can bring everything to a halt. In the long-run, there is less need to accept views inconsistent with land health. Short-term planning processes largely take people as they are, hoping to educate them a bit and draw upon their more virtuous natures, but in the end letting them express and act upon their antecedent, exogenous views. Over time, more flexibility is possible. A well-constructed strategy has more room to maneuver, more chances to accentuate some views over others and shape public understanding and values. It offers the opportunity, that is, to lead.

The surface inconsistencies in the Interagency Ecosystem Report exist largely because the Report deliberately consolidates the long term with the short term, to the confusion of both. In the short term, ecosystem management is a process-based system of communal decisionmaking, aimed at getting people together, sharing ecological data with them, and hoping that as a group they can think and act more virtuously than they would as individuals. But as the process continues, federal agencies are expected to keep pushing and working to promote the substantive parts of the Report, the parts that speak to land health as an established goal and to biodiversity maintenance as a central element of that goal. These, it seems, are the goals that the federal actors are to promote in the many ways listed in the Report— by gathering and disseminating data, by making research capabilities available, by convening study groups, by issuing reports, by public education measures, by working closely with nonfederal groups with similar ecological aims, and so forth.

Over time, this effort is expected to pay off in the form of increased influence in the ecosystem management process. Step by step, the journey toward land health is expected to continue, as people become more familiar with the environmental degradation around them and more aware of the causes of that degradation; as they see the costs and limitations of old ways of living; as people out for quick exploitation move to other places, taking their destructive attitudes with them; and as the people who stay see the benefits, to them and their children, of a land that is healthy and aesthetically pleasing.

Eric T. Freyfogle, *Repairing the Waters of the National Parks: Notes on a Long–Term Strategy*, 74 DENV. L. REV. 815, 818–21 (1997).

(2) Humans and ecosystems: In the following excerpt, Oliver Houck raises—and undertakes to answer—a question that undergirds all efforts at ecosystem management: are people parts of the ecosystems the manage, or are they best thought of as living outside of them?

Oliver A. Houck, *Are Humans Part of Ecosystems?*
28 ENVTL. L. 1 (1998).

Neither answer, people-are-in ecosystems or people-are-out, seems to work. Taking the question as a little more legitimate than it first appears, then, let me surface three points of view on the human role in the environment that probably everyone at some point has embraced or embraces to some degree. Their history parallels the conservation history of the country at large.

The first point of view you could call "humans as God's engineers." People are not only parts of ecosystems; we improve them daily. From the time we were kicked out of the Garden of Eden, the Earth has been a pretty terrible place, full of plagues, fires, and floods—until we began to set things right. When I would go to the auditorium in grade school we would see films with titles like "Nature on the Rampage" about the Mississippi River or the Wild Colorado. To the rescue came the Army Corps of Engineers. On other days, to the rescue would come the Standard Oil Company or the Federal Highway Program. If I had grown up in Arizona, I might have been rescued by cattlemen or the Bureau of Reclamation....

Only recently, the excesses of the God's engineers point of view have sent us in search of others. At the opposite pole is a different view of people and nature. Always latent in the background of America, as early as the writings of Emerson and Thoreau, it has emerged in recent decades as a second major point of view: humans in the environment are, basically, Earth's virus. This point of view features the sprawl of shopping malls, cul-de-sacs, and crumbling cities from Maine to Florida, California so done in by humans it is spinning them back out to Oregon and Montana, and the Colorado front range now building at a rate of ten acres per hour. It takes to heart a recent Canadian study concluding that, over the next fifty years, it will take four Earths and ten Earth atmospheres to perpetuate the American way of life, and this was before the latest sales figures on Chevrolet Suburbans and the enlarged Ford Explorer....

It is the very darkness of this second point of view that triggers its demise. It is simply a dead end. You cannot hold on to it, personally or professionally, and function. You cannot apply it to basic transactions in your life....

The despair of point of view two has led to a third point of view, very much in vogue these days. The human role in ecosystems is as ecosystem steward. If we just manage nature right, we will have a win-win situation. This is the predicate of something called the New Ecology, a movement that has apparently discovered that everything changes in nature, and, therefore, we do not really need to try and preserve anything because, after all, it is going to change. Quoting from Daniel Botkin's *Discordant Harmonies:* "Nature in the 21st century will be a nature that we make ... a more comfortable home, for each of us individually and for all of us collectively in our civilizations."[13] This win-win ethic is all around us. In Louisiana we have advertisements with happy egrets on tops of oil rigs, multiple-purpose structures serving birds and man. Here in the West, a recent Weyerhaeuser advertisement shows a wizard spreading trees from its arms, growing forests ahead of a happy couple who are walking hand in hand, escorted by

13. DANIEL BOTKIN, DISCORDANT HARMO-   CENTURY 189, 193 (1990).
NIES: A NEW ECOLOGY FOR THE TWENTY-FIRST

Bambi-like deer and rabbits, into the win-win woods land. It is certainly an ethic fueling all of those trucks now carrying salmon around the dams on the Columbia River, a process the National Marine Fisheries Service refers to as "smolt facilitation."[14] They too, are win-winning. . . .

The thesis that man is part of nature not as its conqueror but as its companion is now at the heart of ecosystem management. Let me demonstrate to you how ecosystem management is being defined in many journals and planning documents today. "Ecosystem management reflects a stage in the continuing evolution of social values and priorities. It is neither a beginning nor an end. . . . *[It] should maintain ecosystems in the appropriate condition to achieve desired social benefits.*"[19] According to proposed Forest Service regulations, ecosystem management is "a concept of natural resources management, wherein natural forest activities are considered *in the context of economic, ecological and social interactions.*"[20] What I suggest we have here is large-case Human and lower-case everything else. Ecosystem management is whatever we want to do. Stripped of its gloss, we are back to point of view one.

What I suggest is that there is another point of view, a fourth view. In my thesis, in which I am not completely confident but in which I am sufficiently convinced to ask for a response, we must split the concept of ecosystem from the concept of management. I start with the proposition that human actions and impacts cannot define what a ecosystem is—not because humans are a virus and are intrinsically destructive, and not because as God's engineers we make colossal mistakes (although both cases could certainly be argued). Rather, once you put people in the equation, there is no equation. Humans come in and consume it. So we have to start by defining an ecosystem apart from people. Where humans come in is next on the management side. The exercise is two-step.

We have some experience in environmental law both in fusing these two steps and in treating them separately. Let me offer two examples. The bedrock principle of natural resources management for much of this century has been "multiple use," which is, of course, management for the use of human beings; in the words of Gifford Pinchot, the greatest good for the greatest number of people. The failure of this principle to provide even for the bare survival of natural resources—something far short of their perpetuation in a sustainable state—has become one of the better known lessons of environmental law. . . .

Suppose now, for a contrasting example, we bifurcate the inquiry and separate humans from the initial stage, as we have with the protection of endangered species. Under the Endangered Species Act (ESA), we take habitats most threatened by human activity and, in effect, create safety

---

14. Endangered Species, Permits, 63 Fed. Reg. 8435 (1998) (to be codified at 50 C.F.R. pts. 217–227).

19. Robert T. Lackey, *Ecosystem Management: Paradigms and Prattle, People and Prizes, in* AMERICAN INSTITUTE OF FISHERY RESEARCH BIOLOGISTS, PROCEEDINGS OF THE CONFERENCE, "FORTY YEARS OF CONTROVERSY AND ACHIEVEMENT IN NORTH AMERICAN FISHERIES," 8, 9 (1997) (emphasis added).

20. National Forest System Land and Resource Management Planning, 60 Fed. Reg. 18,886, 18,920 (1995) (to be codified at 36 C.F.R. pt. 215, 217, 219) (emphasis added).

zones around them. The measures of these zones are not what people need or desire; they are the biological needs of the species themselves. Whatever else might be said about the ESA, from the standpoint of arriving at alternatives that better protect these habitats, it has worked. The Act did not dictate what had to be done to save the Texas blind salamander or the delta smelt, but it said what could not be done, and required humans to come up with step two, a better answer. The first step was a scientific one: how much does the species need? The second step was human and political: how are we going to provide it? Across the country, agonizingly at times because the political steps here are difficult, the conclusion emerges that this approach works. It has begun to change management and development practices that, although long recognized as net-destructive and unsustainable, were beyond the reach of politics or law.

With these examples in mind, we may return to the issue of ecosystem management. Its rationale is unassailably logical. We cannot go around this world trying to save each individual creature. It is more cost effective, efficient, and just plain possible to save ecosystems and, thereby, all the life within them. Which begs our original question: what defines the ecosystem? Does any definition tell us what mix of timber and owls to have in the Pacific Northwest old growth forests? Could it determine on any objective basis just how much run of the river we should have in the Columbia? Can it say how many oil and gas canals should be cut through the Louisiana coastal zone? Haven't we been having these and similar conversations for the last thirty years? With bottom lines based on human needs and desires and not on species, where have these conversations gone? Not very far. Sadly, these conversations continue today under the heading of ecosystem management. In a recent decision approving timber harvests in the George Washington National Forest in West Virginia, a court explained: "[T]he forest service does not manage ecosystems just for the sake of managing them or for some notion of intrinsic ecosystem values.... For the Forest Service, ecosystem management means to produce desired resource values, uses, products or services in ways that also sustain the diversity and productivity of ecosystems."[30] So defined, the ecosystem is basically up for grabs....

The same conclusion emerges from our recent experience with ecosystem management on the public range....

Now, to their credit, conservation biologists have seen this problem coming and have tried to develop principles for ecosystem management, an objective, scientifically supportable bottom line. In fact, two quite different approaches have emerged. The first, spearheaded by several Pacific Northwest researchers and scientists, is quite direct. There is no mystery to saving ecosystems; you just set them aside and leave them alone. The bigger the better. Do you want rules for ecosystem management? Here is one: the bigger the better. Here is another: the less intrusion the better. The difficulty with this approach is, how does one apply it? Is it saying that everything that is going to be ecosystem-managed is now treated as

30. *Krichbaum v. Kelley,* 844 F.Supp.   (4th Cir.1995). 1107, 1115 (W.D.Va.1994), *aff'd,* 61 F.3d 900

wilderness? Lots of luck. If it is not saying that, then how much intrusion will be allowed? May we put a few cows out? May we take a few trees? A few more? What I am suggesting is that even if you go with this model, it does not give you a baseline. It gives you an aspirational goal: large tracts of unfragmented habitat.

The second approach to ecosystem management is indirect and works in exactly the opposite direction, from the bottom up. The lead here came, again, out of the Pacific Northwest forests, in an effort made famous by Dr. Jack Ward Thomas, later to become Chief of the U.S. Forest Service. Faced with the question of how much Pacific old growth forest needed to remain unlogged, he began drawing those owl circles and determining minimum habitat requirements for the survival of the species over time, which led to the Forest Ecosystem Management Assessment Team (FEMAT) plan, based on multiple indicator species and setting aside even larger tracts of the Pacific Northwest as biological reserves. The species defined the ecosystem, and have gone a long way towards saving it. The next acid test was the Tongass, still at war with the largest clearcut production in the United States. Changing management of the Tongass would be changing thirty years of history and planning based on heavy federal subsidies. Biologists began with the northern goshawk, the spotted owl, a species of trout, and several other genuine, indicator species, and started mapping out their needs. What was left could be timbered. After a long struggle, their approach has led to a reduction in the proposed harvest on the Tongass by about one-half, and the creation of large, unfragmented, biological reserves. The same story is playing out in coastal California, where habitat conservation plans are being built from the ground up from the needs of the California gnatcatcher, coastal cactus wren, and orange-throated whiptail lizard for conservation of some of the most expensive real estate in America. It is playing out in the Sacramento Delta, where massive irrigation systems are being modified upstream to protect the delta smelt. All of these dramatic results and more arise not from defining an ecosystem as something left over after human use, but rather by, first, defining the needs of its individual parts.

The danger in ecosystem management, as it is currently emerging in government planning, is that it tends to put—indeed, it intends to put—humans back into step one, into the definition of the ecosystem itself. The ecosystem management goal is not predicated on a natural system; it is predicated on human needs and desires....

.... As a matter of science and logic, there is no way we can save creatures without their ecosystems. But as a matter of law and policy, the way that works best so far is to work from the creatures on up. In my opinion, that is the real lesson of the spotted owl. That is the lesson of what is going on with development planning along the southern California coast, in the Sacramento Delta, in the Tongass Forest, and in red-cockaded woodpecker habitats across the American south. Why is it so? Why does this approach work? I suggest it works because what you obtain from species is a number that can be defended in science and in court and that does not have humans in it. It is an equation that we do not consume.

So, are humans part of ecosystems? Obviously so, but if we manage ecosystems that way we will lose them. We are part of ecosystems, but we are not their measure. In order to measure an ecosystem and its management goals we need to look at species other than the human species. What other species need is the bottom line, step one. Then, we manage it through people. Humans are step two.

. . . . [S]pecies themselves are not the issue in ecosystem management. I am not contending that we ought to manage ecosystems from species up, rather than the top down (and certainly not from people down) because I love all creatures great and small. For purposes of this thesis, I do not care about the snail darter. . . . It is not because I love the miner's canary that I like the idea of miner's canaries. I like the idea of what it does when we put it down in the mine: it will die first, which tells me something about that ecosystem. In ecosystem management, species are valuable because of their indicator-ness, not because of their species-ness. I think that there is a certain truth-in-advertising here. When you think of why you sided with the spotted owl, if you did, was it not because of the ecosystem it occupied? I think this is intuitively what we all do. I prefer law that matches our intuition. It is more honest.

SECTION 4. SOBER PROSPECTS

This final section offers two perspectives on the conservation challenges that lie ahead. The first perspective is an historic one: a look at efforts a century ago to protect a much publicized subspecies that was on the brink of extinction. The second presents the personal perspective of a scientist who has spent years engaged in the work of protecting biodiversity.

a. THE FATE OF THE HEATH HEN: A PRECAUTIONARY TALE

The dominant American ethic of land exploitation has occasionally been tempered with a concern about the fate of certain species, particularly those that possessed economic value or that appealed to people emotionally or aesthetically. By the Progressive Era of the late nineteenth and early twentieth centuries, organized efforts were undertaken to aid a few species on the brink of extinction. One such preservation effort focused on the Heath Hen, the eastern race of the species *Tympanuchus cupido*. (The midwestern and western race, greatly imperiled today in many parts of its range, is the greater prairie chicken; its plight in Illinois was considered in Chapter 11.) Heath hens inhabited dry, brushy habitat dominated by low trees such as stunted scrub-oak, as well as grassy clearings and meadows. Its prime range centered on the mid-Atlantic coast, from Pennsylvania and New Jersey to Massachusetts, though it was encountered from Maine to as far south as the Carolinas. The heath hen was so numerous when the first English-speaking settlers arrived that the Puritans ate it regularly. By the late nineteenth century, however, numbers had declined significantly and the hen was in grave trouble.

The tale of the heath hen's decline, and of the efforts made to reverse it, is recounted by natural history writer Christopher Cokinos in *Hope Is the Thing with Feathers*, from which the excerpts that follow are taken. Numerous lessons emerge from this tale, about fluctuating species populations, the dangers facing imperilled populations, minimum viable populations, and, on the human side, about the scientific, political, and social difficulties of planning and implementing a sound recovery plan.

The heath hen was a ground-nesting bird, typically constructing its well-camouflaged nests among the leaves, grasses and ferns beneath scrub oaks and berry bushes. At least on Martha's Vineyard—its last holdout, and the place where the first scientific study of the bird was undertaken—it "laid yellow brown eggs sometimes marked with dark splotches. Hatching out in June or July after three and a half weeks of incubation, the Heath Hen's precocial broods averaged between 5 and 10." [p.129] "In the spring, Heath Hens favored grasses, clover, sorrel and other new growth. In summer, they would eat insects and berries, including bayberry and blueberry. Heath Hens especially liked the leaves and fruit of partridge berry, so much so the plant came to be called Heath Hen plum." [p.133] The Heath Hen required occasional fires in its range to maintain favorable habitat conditions. "Set by lightening strikes, Native Americans and, on Martha's Vineyard, blueberry farmers, fire kept forests from establishing themselves, thus generating the brushy scrub-oak and berry-bush barrens Heath Hens needed for foraging and nesting, as well as the meadows needed for booming grounds or leks." [p.130].

As human numbers increased, habitats changed, and firearms became more accurate, Heath Hen numbers suffered a steady decline. Although in retrospect it is difficult to allocate responsibility among these causes, over-hunting is viewed today as the prime culprit. By the early eighteenth century the Hen's decline was noticeable enough in places to stimulate action. Conservation efforts arose to counteract the waxing forces pressing against the Hen. A battle, that is, had been joined, between preservation and exploitation, with the Heath Hen caught in the middle.

So the Heath Hen began to fall to a killing frenzy that provided tremendous numbers of birds to colonies and settlements, then to the growing markets of eastern cities, where prices fluctuated wildly according to supply and interest. In 1821, two Long Island Heath Hens fetched a hefty $5, with the price doubling within five years. Even if some people did not care for the taste of Heath Hens, they could be easily obtained. The birds filled up the wooden market stalls in Boston, New York and elsewhere. When local populations of Heath Hens dwindled, commercial hunters turned to the western Greater Prairie–Chickens to fill the void, so deluging the market that by 1861 a pair typically cost just 50 cents.

The massacre of Heath Hens caught the attention of the New York State Legislature as early as 1708, when some public officials sought to protect the birds on the Long Island plains. In 1791, that assembly considered a bill that some representatives had understood to offer protection to *heathens*. After the misunderstanding cleared up, the bill passed.

These and other state attempts to protect Heath Hens proved useless. Consider Massachusetts, which in 1831 declared spring off-limits for hunting the birds. Even if enforcement existed—which it didn't—the fine amounted to only $2, typically less than the market value of two Heath Hens. Massachusetts continued, off and on, to make utterly ineffectual attempts to preserve the bird. The state, in fact, permitted towns to exempt themselves from the closed-season regulation; so in 1842 the village of Tisbury, on Martha's Vineyard, voted to allow a Heath Hen hunt in early December, provided no dogs were used. (This was the same village that, years before, had voted to protect the birds.) When the fine had been raised to $20, in 1850, Tisbury again exempted itself and allowed a November hunt, without dogs—apparently an attempt to ensure good eats for Thanksgiving. In 1855, however, the state lifted all protections for the Heath Hen—only to reinstate them a few years later. Regulations in other states were equally pointless. The Heath Hen was "ruthlessly persecuted ... by thoughtless hunters" who defied regulations and faced no serious threat of punishment, wrote ornithologist Alfred Gross.

In 1851, hunter and writer E. J. Lewis bemoaned that New Jersey gunners shot out whole flocks of Heath Hens, "these scarce and beautiful birds [being] butchered long before the time sanctioned by the strong or rather the weak arm of the law." He continued: "Thus it is that the destructive hand of the would-be respectable poacher, as well as the greedy gun of the pot-hunter, hastens to seal the fate of the doomed prairie hen in these eastern regions."

Despite such forecasts and explicit pleas for better laws and enforcement, state governments tragically never fulfilled their own protective regulations, and, at that time, the federal government had no role in wildlife oversight.

Poaching of Heath Hens had, therefore, a long history, which continued well into the twentieth century. In his report on the Martha's Vineyard Heath Hens for 1899, Deputy Game Warden John E. Howland wrote, "I am convinced that more or less [i.e., some] of these birds are shot each year, but as yet I have not been able to get the proper evidence to convict any one." According to Martha's Vineyard resident Charles Brown, writing in 1932, "A few persons shipped bootleg heath hens to Boston, receiving for them $5 per pair," through much of the nineteenth century, in defiance of the law. "This was considered a great price," he noted. Massachusetts's own fish and game report for 1912–14 noted that "the price secured was sufficiently attractive to encourage violations."

Poaching, at least on Martha's Vineyard, may have been more than financial motivations behind it. In the Massachusetts state fish and game report for 1907, we find this curious statement: "It has been even stated that sentiments well-nigh voodoolike in tendency were current on the island, e.g., that a boy must eat heath hen before reaching a certain age."

Collectors also took their toll on the Heath Hen. Well-known collector C.E. Hoyle offered 80 Heath Hen specimens for sale in 1904 at the bargain price of $700 for the lot—and this was but a minuscule portion of the Heath Hen specimens he had procured for individuals and museums. Working in the 1890s, Hoyle shot most of the world museum specimens of the Heath Hen, doubtless having a significant impact on the already diminishing population.

As overhunting and the other causes of decline reduced Heath Hen populations, the range inhabited by the bird shrunk rapidly:

Altering habitat, in conjunction with relentless overhunting, doomed the Heath Hen—at least on the mainland United States. As early as 1792, Heath Hens had disappeared from New Hampshire. Humans had extirpated them from the Connecticut Valley shortly after the War of 1812. By that time, Heath Hens had vanished from mainland Massachusetts. On Long Island—a favored habitat—the bird was gone by the mid–1840s. There is no evidence the race lasted on the American mainland much beyond 1870, when Heath Hens had been exterminated from Pennsylvania and New Jersey. From then on, the Heath Hen lived only on Martha's Vineyard, where a flock had flown of its own accord at some time in the distant past.

It was not long before people realized that the heath hen was found only on Martha's Vineyard. One home. One population. One opportunity to preserve it.

Local game warden John Howland knew that Martha's Vineyard [had become] the last holdout for the Heath Hen. That made matters all the more frustrating. . . .

On July 21, 1905, Howland wrote to the Massachusetts Fisheries and Game Commission, urging the members to realize the likelihood that the Heath Hen would go extinct if the state didn't take drastic action and soon. Suddenly, the State of Massachusetts got serious and began to enforce a new, five-year closed season with the threat of $100 fines. Almost as if to underscore the dangers a fire in 1906 raged on Martha's Vineyard, and the Heath Hen population dropped to 80 birds.

Two years after Howland's letter, in 1907, the Massachusetts Legislature set aside a refuge for Heath Hens on Martha's Vineyard, having acted on a bill introduced by legislator Ulysses Mayhew. The chair of the state Fisheries and Game Commission, the National Audubon Society, and even the U.S. Department of Agriculture had all weighed in, urging an increase in the poaching fine, retention of the closed season and some kind of protection and breeding program, all of which happened. Now the Heath Hen would have a protected home, a reservation of its own encompassing 1,600 acres within the island's interior.

In 1908, the state bought another 600 acres, complete with a barn and house serving as refuge headquarters. The state then rented another 1,000 acres, and additional money flowed in from private contributions. In a flurry of ethically enlightened behavior, Massachusetts sought to undo decades of malignant neglect and destruction of the Heath Hen.

The legislature outlined key issues to be confronted in the effort to save the bird: the extent and types of plantings on the refuge; protections against poaching, disease and fire; and a breeding program to increase the Heath Hen's numbers. In 1907, the year of the refuge's opening, someone located nine Heath Hen eggs and gave them to a bantam hen to incubate. But on June 20, as a Heath Hen chick began to hatch out, the bantam hen struck repeatedly at the egg until the chick died. None of the other eggs hatched. The same experiment occurred with Ring-necked Pheasant eggs and, in that case, the barnyard hen treated the chicks as her own.

The Heath Hen population by 1908 had fallen to between just 45 and 60 birds on the entire island, despite the fact that 10 birds had been hatched the year before. Then the Heath Hens began to rebound, with 200 birds in 1909 and 300 birds in 1910. The next year, though, the population plummeted to 150. The Heath Hens recovered again in 1912, doubling back to 300 birds. The factors behind these tremendous fluctuations were not clear, because no one had organized a scientific field study of the Heath Hen—the only glaring omission in Massachusetts's plan of action.

In 1913, the state appointed William Day as refuge warden, the caretaker for the some 400 Heath Hens now living on the reserve and elsewhere on the island. Day cut down shrubs and trees to create firebreaks, guarded against poachers, planted winter crops to supplement the Heath Hen's diet and shot creatures suspected of eating Heath Hens: 15 Northern Harriers (then called Marsh Hawks), 3 Sharp-shinned Hawks, 5 Redtailed Hawks, 23 feral cats (the summer people often abandoned hundreds of mousers upon leaving the island), and 18 rats. Day also planted trees, 7,000 pines in one year alone, as part of an effort to develop a timber economy on the Vineyard—an effort that could not have helped the Heath Hen, which needed meadow and scrub oaks, not pines.

When, in April 1916, the state ornithologist for Massachusetts, the distinguished E.H. Forbush, visited the island he counted 800 Heath Hens on the refuge. No one disputed Day's contention that the birds now lived not only on the reservation but virtually everywhere on the island, number about 2,000. On any given afternoon, William Day could roust 300 Heath Hens at once. Finally, it seemed, the effort to save the Heath Hen had succeeded.

Although the Heath Hen for several years enjoyed a rise in numbers, its troubles were far from over. In May 1916, a deadly fire ran through much of its range, right during the breeding season. Many hens stayed close to their nests and were burned alive. Those that escaped had trouble nesting again that year, given the lack of plant cover to hide their nests. By the following year, the extent of the damage became painfully clear. The population of some 2,000 birds had declined to a mere 126.

The May 1916 disaster highlighted the danger of keeping all of the Heath Hens in a single, interbreeding population. Coincidentally, at a meeting less than a month before the fire, state officials and leading ornithologist had decided to remove some of the Heath Hens from the island and to try to establish a population on the mainland. Despite the much-lowered numbers caused by the fire, the decision was made to proceed with the plan.

[D]espite the population plunge, Massachusetts officials went ahead with their plans and captured some Heath Hens. The state dispersed the birds to New York conservation authorities on Long Island and to a game-bird breeder in Wenham, Massachusetts. The hope was that the captive birds would soon begin to breed.

Ornithology's shoot 'em-and-tag 'em days weren't over yet, but this experiment likely marked the first high-stakes meeting of ornithology and poker: a conservation gamble. The experiment failed. Nature called its bluff. None of the birds bred successfully. The captured Heath Hens—16 males and 10 females—died in captivity, representing a substantial portion of the world's remaining Heath Hen population.

One of the defects of efforts to conserve the Hen was the lack of a sound scientific study of its behaviors and needs. Such a study was finally begun in April of 1923, when ornithologist Alfred Gross arrived on the island to conduct it. He began by undertaking a comprehensive survey of the bird, only to find that its numbers had declined to 46. By the following year the population had risen to 54 birds, but there was a shocking sex imbalance; Gross could find no more than 3 females at any time. Fearing that the males would harass the females in ways that would disrupt their ability to nest, Gross decided to remove some of the excess males, at a rate of 5 per year.

By the following year—predictably, given the sex imbalance—the overall population was once again down:

May 12, 1925, was a lovely day—the air became warm and pleasant—but Alfred Gross found just two Heath Hens on the refuge property. At James Green's farm near West Tisbury, there lived just one Heath Hen, who had probably always frequented the farm in a group separate from those that preferred to stay on the reservation. For a while this lone male constituted the entire "flock" on Green's property.

Three birds seen. All males. Gross estimated that there were just 25 Heath Hens living on Martha's Vineyard.

While humans worried over the grim numbers—the population had virtually been halved in just one year—some unseen females managed, almost miraculously, to raise chicks on three separate broods. Keniston watched a half-dozen chicks gamboling in a field between the refuge fire tower and the house.

Then the rains came. More than two inches of rain fell in 72 hours, drowning the chicks, washing them into road ruts and muddy puddles or else chilling them beyond a saving warmth. No reliable observers ever saw Heath Hen chicks again.

The same month that the chicks vanished, Alfred Gross spoke to about four dozen people gathered in a conference room at the State House in Boston. It was June 4, 1925. On that day, some cultural threshold was passed. In years prior, news of the Heath Hen crisis would have set off a fierce round of shooting, the last frenzy of museum and private collection, to get the rare and valuable skins. Not this time. Science had taken a stand against collecting and urged conservation management instead. The conference participants—officials from the Federation of New England Bird Clubs, the State of Massachusetts, Massachusetts Audubon and others—drew up a list of desperate emergency measures to stave off further losses.

A new state warden would be hired to patrol the refuge from October to March—"a complete patrol ... rigidly enforced," an edict that suggests winter poaching had persisted to some degree. Additionally, James Green, the farmer, would be deputized as a warden, because of the Heath Hen present on his property. A third warden, Edward F. McLeod—to be paid for by the Federation of New England Bird Clubs—would be hired to shoot "vermin" and assist in patrols; that organization immediately began to raise funds to supplement the state budget. Feeding and baiting of the birds would continue, in order to encourage their presence on the protected reservation ground. Finally, the Federation paid Pennsylvania's Chief of Vermin Control, J.J. Slauterback, to offer advice on how best to trap, poison and shoot hawks, rats and feral cats.

All of these steps came at a time when the Heath Hen had become something of a star. Newspaper and magazine stories had sensitized people across the country to the plight of this bird. Local opposition to the Heath Hen appeared, over the last two years, to have moderated, at least publicly. . . .

By late 1926, with Hen populations perilously low, the actors involved in preserving it were increasingly at one another's throats, trading charges and countercharges of bad faith, incompetence, and lack of commitment. Arthur Clark, one of the participants, continued to claim that "vermin-control" efforts were the key to success, even though Gross's research and showing that predation was not a major cause of species decline. Clark among others continued to believe that recovery could be brought about. Gross, however,

> knew better. In both his public and private statements the ornithologist betrayed a fatalism about the Heath Hen race; he felt nothing could save the birds. . . .

> The foremost reason for Gross's bleak assessment was the confirmation that the birds were indeed showing signs of disease. Studies found Heath Hens with tumor—like growths caused by the blackhead parasite, a disease of domestic poultry communicable to Heath Hens, and infections of the gizzard caused by the *Dispharynx* parasite, which also affects Ruffed Grouse.

> Aware that a do-nothing approach was politically infeasible, Gross advised the state to remove all domestic poultry from the Reservation, even though Heath Hens had all but disappeared from the public land.

By the spring of 1927, the picture had become even more bleak. The field census that March turned up only 13 Hens.

Ill-timed fire. Plunderous goshawks. Unquantifiable, suspected predation by other hawks and cats. Rains. Frosts. Poaching. Suspected sterility among males. Phone lines that tangled up the birds. Too many males. Too few females. Inbreeding. Disease.

Thirteen Heath Hens seen, no more than 30 conjectured.

. . .

Thirteen Heath Hens fed among sweet fern and blueberry. They idled in James Green's fields as the farmer stirred a pot of soup or wrote down a list of the month's groceries. The birds continued their ancient rhythms. The humans bickered. Apologized. Then bickered some more.

. . .

When, between April 5 and 9, 1928, another census took place, the counters outnumbered the counted. Local interest in and support for the Heath Hen had never been higher, and mistakes yielded alchemic conversions of one species to another. Transformations of Bobwhite Quail into Heath Hens were never more numerous. Readers delivered photos of alleged Heath Hens to newspaper editors, who politely explained that the birds pictured were Ruffed Grouse. Heath Hens were everywhere! But the Heath Hens were three, all males.

With three males remaining, the fate of the Heath Hen was sealed. For those tending it, the recovery effort had become a death watch. In early May, 1928, one of the remaining three Hens died, its body found among blackberry bushes. The suspected cause of death: a collision with telephone wires. Late in the year another one of the Hens disappeared without a trace, leaving the final survivor, a Hen given the nickname "Booming Ben."

Booming Ben proved remarkably hardy, and as each winter came and watchers thought it would be his last, he surprised them by showing up in the spring.

The Heath Hen showed himself three times in May 1931, then vanished until February 9, 1932, when he reappeared at the Green homestead. The bird had weathered another turn of the year, but he now behaved oddly, avoiding the field where he had eaten so freely of corn and grain. Instead, he lurked at the edge of the scrub oaks, and, for nearly the next month, Green watched the newly wary bird.

March 11, 1932, was a cool day—in the 40s—and it was the last day that James Green ever saw the bird. Ornithologists now consider that to be the final confirmed sighting of the Heath Hen. Alfred Gross, in his privately printed autobiography, wrote that the last sighting was on April 6, 1932.

Despite the close attention paid to Ben, his date of death was never known, nor is it clear that his body was ever found.

Reports of sightings continued into July when someone saw what he called a "somewhat ragged-looking" Heath Hen. These summer sightings were never confirmed, and Gross's subsequent view in the published literature was that all later reports of the bird, extending into 1933, were of female Ring-necked Pheasants. Ludicrously, reported sightings of "Heath Hens" occurred as late as the 1960s.

No one ever found the remains of Booming Ben. But in 1997, Alita Prada, of Locke Mills, Maine, came forward to say that in 1932, her mother and a friend names Estenna Norton had hit the bird while Norton was driving on a foggy Vineyard night. The two women were so mortified that one of them flung the corpse as far as she could into the woods. Fearing prosecution, they never said a word about it except to relatives, years later. Of course, it's quite possible that the bird they killed was a Ruffed Grouse or a Ring-necked Pheasant and, Prada tells me, the two women never mentioned the identification bands.

CHRISTOPHER COKINOS, HOPE IS THE THING WITH FEATHERS 136–38, 140–42, 161–62, 168–70 (2000).

b.   WHERE WE STAND

DAVID S. WILCOVE, THE CONDOR'S SHADOW
232–38 (1999).

Musings about the theoretical feasibility of protecting the nation's vanishing wildlife bear little resemblance to the current situation. According to the most recent assessment by the U.S. Fish and Wildlife Service, fewer than 10 percent of the plants and animals protected by the Endangered Species Act are actually increasing in numbers and on the road to recovery. An additional 27 percent are judged to be stable, indicating that the decline in numbers or the loss of habitat that earned them a place on the endangered list has been halted at least temporarily; 33 percent are still declining, despite protection under the act; and for an additional 31 percent, the Fish and Wildlife Service lacks enough data to determine trends. One can quibble with the accuracy of some of these numbers, inasmuch as they are based on professional judgment rather than hard data and analysis, but the overall picture they provide is clear: Despite a number of heartening success stories, a distressingly large fraction of America's imperiled wildlife continues to slip closer to extinction.

There are almost as many explanations for this apparent lack of success as there are interest groups fighting over control of the nation's land and water. That said, four factors in particular strike me as especially significant contributors to the problem. First, across the nation, efforts to monitor trends in wildlife populations are woefully inadequate. Most of our game animals fall under the watchful eye of state and federal agencies, but game animals constitute only a tiny fraction of our total fauna. The nation's birdwatchers do a reasonably good job of tracking population trends among songbirds, adding a few hundred more species to the watch list. But for the vast majority of species—from minnows to mice to mussels—monitoring programs are fragmentary, inconsistent, and often nonexistent. This ignorance is for the most part self-imposed: Proposals to expand the monitoring capabilities of agencies like the Fish and Wildlife

Service inevitably draw fire from anti-environmental ideologues and their allies in Congress, who would rather not know about a problem affecting wildlife, lest it necessitate a costly or controversial solution.

Second, by the time a trend becomes too obvious to ignore and the institutions charged with safeguarding the nation's wildlife are jostled awake, it is often too late to take effective action. The plants and animals that end up on the federal endangered species list typically are added to that list only after their populations have dropped to critically low levels. A 1993 study found that the median population size of an animal species when it is finally placed on the endangered species list is approximately 1,000 individuals; the corresponding value for plants is less than 120. Such small populations are easily erased by random events, such as a hurricane (Schaus' swallowtail) or industrial accident (Clinch River mussels), or even by random fluctuations in birth and death rates. A number of plants have been added to the endangered list when only open or two individuals were known to be left.

Third, when the relevant institutions and agencies finally step forward to protect vanishing species, they usually do so with inadequate resources. A strong case can be made that the amount of money available for endangered species recovery programs (which was never enough to begin with) has not kept pace with the growing number of species now recognized as imperiled.... Further compounding this disparity is the fact that throughout the history of the Endangered Species Act, a disproportionately large share of the money has been spent on a handful of charismatic species....

Finally, until recently, we have failed to give landowners any incentive to help endangered species. The Endangered Species Act relies on the threat of fines and jail sentences to discourage people from engaging in conduct harmful to vanishing wildlife. Such measures are an important and necessary step toward saving these species, but they do little to motivate people to go beyond the basic requirements of the law and actively assist endangered wildlife. Many landowners, for example, are capable of aiding in the recovery of endangered species by creating or restoring habitats on their land, but are unwilling to do so. Their unwillingness stems from a fear that if they take actions that attract endangered species to their property or increase the populations of endangered species that are already there, their "reward" for doing so will be more regulatory restrictions on the use of that property....

Given these obstacles to effective conservation—a lack of information, a tendency to ignore a problem until it becomes a crisis, a failure to commit adequate resources, and a failure to reward landowners who aid in the restoration and imperiled wildlife—and given the steadily increasing population and growing economy of the Untied States, the future seems clear: shrinking pieces of nature harboring a growing roster of endangered species and demanding ever more intensive and expensive management. The need for intensive management follows ineluctably from the reduction in the amount of habitat. Many of the small, isolated scraps of undeveloped land that are set aside as nature reserves eventually will be overrun by alien plants and animals unless some sort of control program is put in place. . . .

By one estimate, over 60 percent of the plants and animals on the endangered species list are vulnerable to either alien species or fire suppression. The uncomfortable implication of this finding is that many of these species could disappear even if every single acre of their habitat were protected from development, unless that habitat was managed property. Management takes money (someone must be paid to pull up the melaleuca, trap the feral pigs, or carefully burn the jack pines), and no federal or state agency has created a permanent endowment for this sort of stewardship. We are, in short, running up a hefty stewardship bill with little thought as to how we shall pay it. And pay it we must, for not to do so would defeat the purpose behind laws like the Endangered Species Act and our investment in our national wildlife refuges and national parks.

We are, for better or worse, the guardians of a significant share of the nation's flora and fauna. The extent of that responsibility grows with every species added to the endangered list and with every foreign plant or animal that gains a foothold in this country due to our negligence or stupidity. I know of only two way to reduce the magnitude of that burden. One is to walk away form it—to decide that a nation without whooping cranes, red wolves, Colorado squawfish, and thousands of other rare plants and animals is no poorer for their absence. The other is to grow out of it—to increase the amount of habitat available to these species through the science and art of ecological restoration. Doing so will not only boost populations of many imperiled species, it will also provide them with larger blocks of habitat that may be better able to sustain fires and other natural disturbances or withstand the onslaught of alien species.

In the past, we have been the beneficiaries of nature's own remarkable recuperative abilities. The eastern forests (and the wildlife within them) returned to life with relatively little assistance from us after they were cleared in the eighteenth and nineteenth centuries. To an increasing degree, however, the restoration of degraded ecosystems and missing species will require our active involvement. Not all ecosystems can be restored, and not all species can be reintroduced to restored habitats, but enough can to prompt the question, will we rise to the challenge? To some extent we already have, as evidenced by the landowners eagerly enrolling in the Fish and Wildlife Service's safe harbor program, or the popular support for projects such as the restoration of the Everglades or the reestablishment of wolves within Yellowstone.

In the long run, however, even our best efforts at ecological restoration could be veiled by our failure to control a potentially sinister and pervasive threat to wildlife: global climate change. Atmospheric concentrations of greenhouse gases such as carbon dioxide and methane are increasing due to the burning of fossil fuels, the destruction of forests, the spread of intensive agriculture, and other changes in land use. Many scientists now predict that a continuation of these activities will result in a rise in average global temperatures of between 0.9 and 3.5 degrees Celsius over the course of the next century. That increase could trigger a significant rise in sea level as well as changes in weather patterns, including droughts and floods.

How all of this will affect wildlife is unknown, but the possible effects are enormous. The habitats of some species may simply disappear, as could happen if a rising ocean submerges the nesting beaches of sea turtles an other coastal species. In other cases, the changes are likely to be more subtle but no less disruptive. An increase or decrease in precipitation or the length of the growing season could be enough to alter the vegetation in a given region of the country, favoring the growth of certain type of trees, shrubs, or grasses over other types, thereby scrambling and rearranging the habitats of many animals. . . .

As the causes of species endangerment have expanded, so too has the range of issues that must be addressed by conservationists. What we eat, how we farm, where we build houses and highways, the energy we use to fuel our economy, even the kinds of animals we allow to be sold as pets—all these factors and many more will determine the future of wildlife in America. The fact that we are increasingly aware of these linkages is a positive sign. So too are the growing number of people who have joined in efforts to restore degraded ecosystems and conserve imperiled species. But it remains to be seen whether enough people will speak out on behalf of wildlife to have an impact comparable to that of the men and women who first rose to defend our embattled fauna more than a century ago.

CHAPTER 13

ENDANGERED SPECIES: AN OVERVIEW

In 1962, the Department of the Interior established a Committee on Rare and Endangered Wildlife Species. Two years later, the Committee published a preliminary list of 63 species that it considered to be threatened with extinction. COMMITTEE ON RARE & ENDANGERED WILDLIFE SPECIES, BUREAU OF SPORT FISHERIES & WILDLIFE, U.S. DEPT. OF THE INTERIOR, RARE AND ENDANGERED FISH AND WILDLIFE OF THE UNITED STATES at i (Resource Pub. No. 34, July 1966). This list—known as the "Redbook"—lacked any legal status; indeed, it contained one species, the Utah prairie dog, that another federal agency was trying to eradicate. The Redbook did, however, increase awareness of the loss of species at a time when a broadly based environmental consciousness was beginning to stir in America.

The first legal response to increasing public concern for protecting endangered wildlife came in 1964. Recognizing that species loss was due largely to habitat loss, Congress included a provision in the Land and Water Conservation Fund Act, 16 U.S.C. §§ 460*l* through 460*l*–11, allowing monies to be used in "the acquisition of land, waters, or interests in land or waters ... [f]or any national area which may be authorized for the preservation of species of fish or wildlife that are threatened with extinction." This statutory beginning reflected two fundamental changes that grew out of the increased scientific and popular awareness of ecology: first, it provided for the *protection* of wildlife rather than the *management* of game species and, second, that protection was to be accomplished through *habitat* preservation rather than *taking* restrictions. Zoo specimens—like the Victorian curio cabinet—were no longer sufficient: wildlife was to be protected in the wild.

SECTION 1. ENDANGERED SPECIES ACTS: THE EVOLUTION OF ENDANGERED SPECIES PROTECTION

NOTES

(1) Endangered Species Preservation Act of 1966 (ESPA): The core element of the Endangered Species Preservation Act of 1966 (ESPA), Pub. L. No. 89–669, 80 Stat. 926, was habitat protection. Acknowledging that "one of the unfortunate consequences of growth and development" is the extermination of native species of fish and wildlife, Congress declared a national policy for the "conservation, protection, restoration, and propagation" of native fish and wildlife "that are threatened with extinction." *Id.* § 1(a). As is often the case, the grand sweep of the Act's policy statement gave way to a more modest implementation scheme: Congress established a relatively small program of habitat acquisition, authorizing the Secretary to spend up to $15,000,000 from funds available under the Land and Water Conservation Fund Act. *Id.* § 2(c). The ESPA, however, did contain at least one idea that was to prove fruitful: it directed the Secretary of the Interior to publish a list of endangered "species of native fish and wildlife." *Id.* § 1(c).

Perhaps most importantly, however, the enactment of the ESPA redefined extinction as a national issue. It henceforth was a problem for the federal government.

(2) Endangered Species Conservation Act of 1969 (ESCA): The ESPA's focus on habitat ignored the impact of taking and commercial activities on wildlife. The failure to regulate these activities was partially remedied in 1969 when Congress extensively supplemented the ESPA and named the combined provisions the Endangered Species Conservation Act (ESCA), Pub. L. No. 91–135, 83 Stat. 275, 283. The ESCA provided a more comprehensive but still limited program that emphasized the regulation of interstate and foreign commerce in species listed as endangered.

(3) Convention on International Trade in Endangered Species of Wild Fauna & Flora (CITES): In the ESCA, Congress instructed the Secretaries of the Interior and State to call an international meeting on protecting endangered species. The instructions led eventually to the signing of CITES. As discussed in Chapter 8, CITES created a system of import and export permits that establish a control structure to regulate international commerce in species designated for protection. Since the Convention was not self-executing, enforcement is the responsibility of party states. The need for legislation to implement CITES was a primary impetus that led to the enactment of the ESA in 1973.

(4) State Endangered Species Legislation: Congress was not alone in responding to public interest in endangered species. State lawmakers also acted. In part, this was a response to the implicit invitation contained in the 1969 Act: in amending the Lacey Act, Congress signalled a willingness to continue its traditional policy of deference to state regulation of the taking of wildlife. In part, increased state activity was also a response to the perceived inadequacies of the federal legislation. As one commenter noted, the federal endangered species list was "more commemorative than protective." Philip Weinberg, *Practice Commentary, in* N.Y. ENVTL. CONSERV. LAW § 11–0536 (McKinney 1984). Critics in particular pointed to the fact that it was possible legally to kill a species that had been listed as endangered because neither the ESPA nor the ESCA prohibited takings of listed species. As a result, eleven states enacted endangered species legislation between 1969 and 1973.

Although Nevada was the first state to enact legislation,[1] it was the two statutes that New York adopted in 1970 that became the model for

---

1.   Nevada's statute is, in fact, an example of why state law proved insufficient to the task. While the act provided that if a species or subspecies was threatened with extinction

most other states. The first was the Mason Law, which prohibited the sale of enumerated species or of products made from those species. N.Y. ENVTL. CONSERV. LAW § 11–0536 (McKinney 1984). The Mason Law in several cases provided protection to species not on the federal list. For example, the statute listed the tiger while the federal list included only four subspecies of tigers.

The second New York statute was the Harris Law. N.Y. ENVTL. CONSERV. LAW § 11–0535 (McKinney 1984). Unlike the Mason Law, which is wholly independent of federal law, the Harris Law was intended to complement and supplement the ESCA by prohibiting "the importation, transportation, possession or sale . . . or possession with intent to sell" any species listed either by the federal or state government as endangered. *Id.* § 11–0535(2).

The two statutes not only closed the New York market to products made from listed species by prohibiting possession and sale, the statutes also forced businesses such as furriers who dealt in listed species out of the state. Not surprisingly, the two statutes were immediately challenged under a variety of constitutional theories; also not surprisingly, both were held to be constitutional. *See A.E. Nettleton Co. v. Diamond,* 264 N.E.2d 118 (N.Y.1970), *appeal denied sub nom., Reptile Products Ass'n v. Diamond,* 401 U.S. 969 (1971) (Mason Act constitutional); *Palladio, Inc. v. Diamond,* 321 F.Supp. 630 (S.D.N.Y.1970), *aff'd,* 440 F.2d 1319 (2d Cir.) (*per curiam*), *cert. denied,* 404 U.S. 983 (1971) (Harris Law constitutional); *see generally* Robert C. Davis, Note, *Constitutional Problems in Environmental Legislation—The Mason Law,* 12 B.C. INDUS. & COMM. L. REV. 657 (1971).

For a more recent, detailed examination of state endangered species legislation, *see* Dale D. Goble *et al., Local and National Protection of Endangered Species: An Assessment,* 2 ENVTL. SCI. & POL'Y 43 (1999).

(5) The Endangered Species Act of 1973: An Overview of The First Endangered Species Act of 1973: The Endangered Species Act of 1973, following the standard structural pattern for modern federal statutes, can be divided into three parts: (1) a preliminary part that gives the Act's title, sets out Congress' findings, and defines a series of important terms; (2) the major substantive and procedural requirements that form the core of the Act; and (3) a concluding, administrative part containing conforming amendments, repeals of previous statutes, and the statute's effective date.

The central substantive and procedural requirements are found in five sections:

> * * *   *section 4,* which establishes procedures for listing species as either threatened or endangered, for designating critical habitat, and for preparing recovery plans for listed species;

it was to be placed on a list of "fully protected species, and no member of its kind may be captured, removed or destroyed," NEV. REV. STAT. ANN. § 503.585 Michie 1986), any listed species "found to be destructive of domestic animals or fowl or a menace to health" may be destroyed. *Id.* § 503.586.

* * *   *section 7,* which requires federal action agencies to consult with the federal fish and wildlife agencies to "insure that actions authorized, funded or carried out by them do not jeopardize the continued existence" of the species;

* * *   *section 9,* which prohibits any person from taking or engaging in commerce in endangered species;

* * *   *section 11,* which specifies the civil and criminal penalties applicable to the violations set out in section 9; and

* * *   *section 10,* which provides specific exemptions, permits, and exceptions to the prohibitions in section 9.

Although the Act has been amended several times, these five sections remain the basic components of its mechanism for protecting species faced with extinction.[2]

As the brief description of these sections suggests, the ESA envisions a linear process: when a species is listed as endangered or threatened and its critical habitat is designated under section 4, the FWS prepares a recovery plan for the species that specifies how the threat to the species's continued existence will be removed or mitigated so that the species no longer requires protection under the ESA. In the interim, the species is protected by the provisions of sections 7 and 9 unless the activity is exempted or permitted pursuant to sections 10 and 11.

* * *

The initial decisions under the Act reached inconsistent results. In *National Wildlife Federation v. Coleman,* 529 F.2d 359 (5th Cir.1976), the court enjoined the Federal Highway Administration's decision to proceed with project that would lead to private development that would destroy habitat of listed sandhill cranes. In *Sierra Club v. Froehlke,* 534 F.2d 1289 (8th Cir.1976), on the other hand, the court permitted the Corps of Engineers to balance biological data against the value of the project and to proceed with a development that would destroy the habitat of a listed species of bat. These decisions set the stage for the Supreme Court decision that captured the attention of the nation:

Tennessee Valley Authority v. Hill

Supreme Court of the United States.
437 U.S. 153 (1978).

■ BURGER, C.J.:—[The Tennessee Valley Authority (TVA), a federal agency created to produce and market hydroelectric power, began constructing the Tellico Dam on the Little Tennessee River in 1967. In 1973, a University of Tennessee ichthyologist found a previously unknown species of perch, the snail darter, in the Little Tennessee River. Following a petition by plaintiff, the Secretary of the Interior listed the snail darter as an endangered species in 1975, declared the area of the Little Tennessee which would be

---

2. In addition, the Act provides authority to acquire land (§ 5), establishes a federal-   state cooperative program (§ 6), and implements CITES (§ 8).

affected by the Tellico Dam to be its critical habitat, and concluded that the impoundment would destroy the species entire habitat. TVA took the position that the only available alternative was to attempt relocating the snail darter population to another suitable location; to this end, it conducted a search of alternative sites which might sustain the fish and transplanted of a number of snail darters to the nearby Hiwassee River.

[In February 1976, plaintiffs brought an action to enjoin completion of the dam on the ground that it would violate the Act by causing the extinction of the species. Following trial, the district court denied relief, stating that it would be "absurd" to grant relief against a project that was essentially complete. The court of appeals reversed, remanding "with instructions that a permanent injunction issue halting all activities incident to the Tellico Project which may destroy or modify the critical habitat of the snail darter" "until Congress, by appropriate legislation, exempts Tellico from compliance with the Act or the snail darter has been deleted from the list of endangered species or its critical habitat materially redefined."]

II

We begin with the premise that operation of the Tellico Dam will either eradicate the known population of snail darters or destroy their critical habitat. Petitioner does not now seriously dispute this fact. . . .

Starting from the above premise, two questions are presented: (a) Would TVA be in violation of the Act if it completed and operated the Tellico Dam as planned? (b) If TVA's actions would offend the Act, is an injunction the appropriate remedy for the violation? For the reasons stated hereinafter, we hold that both questions must be answered in the affirmative.

(A)

It may seem curious to some that the survival of a relatively small number of three-inch fish among all the countless millions of species extant would require the permanent halting of a virtually completed dam for which Congress has expended more than $100 million. The paradox is not minimized by the fact that Congress continued to appropriate large sums of public money for the project, even after congressional Appropriations Committees were apprised of its apparent impact upon the survival of the snail darter. We conclude, however, that the explicit provisions of the Endangered Species Act require precisely that result.

One would be hard pressed to find a statutory provision whose terms were any plainer than those in § 7 of the Endangered Species Act. Its very words affirmatively command all federal agencies "to insure that actions *authorized, funded, or carried out* by them do not *jeopardize* the continued existence" of an endangered species or "*result* in the destruction or modification of habitat of such species * * ** " 16 U.S.C. § 1536 (emphasis added). This language admits of no exception. Nonetheless, petitioner urges, as do the dissenters, that the Act cannot reasonably be interpreted as applying to a federal project which was well under way when Congress passed the Endangered Species Act of 1973. To sustain that position, however, we would be forced to ignore the ordinary meaning of plain language. It has not been shown, for example, how TVA can close the gates of the Tellico Dam without "carrying out" an action that has been "authorized" and "funded" by a federal agency. Nor can we understand how such action will *"insure"* that the snail darter's habitat is not disrupted.[18] Accepting the Secretary's determinations, as we must, it is clear that TVA's proposed operation of the dam will have precisely the opposite effect, namely the *eradication* of an endangered species.

Concededly, this view of the Act will produce results requiring the sacrifice of the anticipated benefits of the project and of many millions of dollars in public funds. But examination of the language, history, and structure of the legislation under review here indicates beyond doubt that Congress intended endangered species to be afforded the highest of priorities.

When Congress passed the Act in 1973, it was not legislating on a clean slate. [The court reviewed the major provisions of the Endangered Species Conservation Act of 1966 and the Endangered Species Conservation Act of 1969.]

Despite the fact that the 1966 and 1969 legislation represented "the most comprehensive of its type to be enacted by any nation" up to that time, Congress was soon persuaded that a more expansive approach was needed if the newly declared national policy of preserving endangered species was to be realized. By 1973, when Congress held hearings on what would later become the Endangered Species Act of 1973, it was informed that species were still being lost at the rate of about one per year, [ ], and "the pace of disappearance of species" appeared to be "accelerating." [ ] Moreover, Congress was also told that the primary cause of this trend was something other than the normal process of natural selection:

> [M]an and his technology has [sic] continued at any ever-increasing rate to disrupt the natural ecosystem. This has resulted in a dramatic rise in the number and severity of the threats faced by the world's wildlife. The truth in this is apparent when one realizes that half of the recorded extinctions of mammals over the past 2,000 years have occurred in the most recent 50–year period.

---

18. In dissent, Mr. Justice Powell argues that the meaning of "actions" in § 7 is "far from 'plain,'" and that "it seems evident that the 'actions' referred to are not all actions that an agency can ever take, but rather actions that the agency is *deciding whether* to authorize, to fund, or to carry out." [ ] Aside from this bare assertion, however, no explanation is given to support the proffered interpretation. This recalls Lewis Carroll's classic advice on the construction of language:

> "When *I* use a word," Humpty Dumpty said, in rather a scornful tone, "it means just what I choose it to mean—neither more nor less."

Through the Looking Glass, in THE COMPLETE WORKS OF LEWIS CARROLL 196 (1939). Aside from being unexplicated, the dissent's reading of § 7 is flawed on several counts. First, under its view, the words "or carry out" in § 7 would be superfluous since all prospective actions of an agency remain to be "authorized" or "funded." Second, the dissent's position logically means that an agency would be obligated to comply with § 7 only when a project is in the planning stage. But if Congress had meant to so limit the Act, it surely would have used words to that effect, as it did in the National Environmental Policy Act, 42 U.S.C. §§ 4332(2)(A), (C).

[ ] That Congress did not view these developments lightly was stressed by one commentator:

> The dominant theme pervading all Congressional discussion of the proposed [Endangered Species Act of 1973] was the overriding need *to devote whatever effort and resources were necessary* to avoid further diminution of national and worldwide wildlife resources. Much of the testimony at the hearings and much debate was devoted to the biological problem of extinction. Senators and Congressmen uniformly deplored the irreplaceable loss to aesthetics, science, ecology, and the national heritage should more species disappear.

Coggins, *Conserving Wildlife Resources: An Overview of the Endangered Species Act of 1973*, 51 N.D.L. REV. 315, 321 (1975) (emphasis added).

The legislative proceedings in 1973 are, in fact, replete with expressions of concern over the risk that might lie in the loss of any endangered species....

> As we homogenize the habitats in which these plants and animals evolved, and as we increase the pressure for products that they are in a position to supply (usually unwillingly) we threaten their—and our own—genetic heritage.
>
> *The value of this genetic heritage is, quite literally, incalculable.*
>
>   . . .

As the examples cited here demonstrate, Congress was concerned about the *unknown* uses that endangered species might have and about the *unforeseeable* place such creatures may have in the chain of life on this planet.

In shaping legislation to deal with the problem thus presented, Congress started from the finding that "[t]he two major causes of extinction are hunting and destruction of natural habitat." S. REP. No. 93–307 at 2 (1973). Of these twin threats, Congress was informed that the greatest was destruction of natural habitats. [ ] Witnesses recommended, among other things, that Congress require all land-managing agencies "to avoid damaging critical habitat for endangered species and to take positive steps to improve such habitat." [ ] Virtually every bill introduced in Congress during the 1973 session responded to this concern by incorporating language similar, if not identical, to that found in the present § 7 of the Act. These provisions were designed, in the words of an administration witness, "for the first time [to] prohibit [a] federal agency from taking action which does jeopardize the status of endangered species." [ ]

As it was finally passed, the Endangered Species Act of 1973 represented the most comprehensive legislation for the preservation of endangered species ever enacted by any nation....

Section 7 of the Act, which of course is relied upon by respondents in this case, provides a particularly good gauge of congressional intent. As we have seen, this provision had its genesis in the Endangered Species Act of 1966, but that legislation qualified the obligation of federal agencies by stating that they should seek to preserve endangered species only "*insofar as is practicable and consistent with the[ir] primary purposes* * * **"

Likewise, every bill introduced in 1973 contained a qualification similar to that found in the earlier statutes....

What is very significant in this sequence is that the final version of the 1973 Act carefully omitted all of the reservations described above....

It is against this legislative background that we must measure TVA's claim that the Act was not intended to stop operation of a project which, like Tellico Dam, was near completion when an endangered species was discovered in its path. While there is no discussion in the legislative history of precisely this problem, the totality of congressional action makes it abundantly clear that the result we reach today is wholly in accord with both the words of the statute and the intent of Congress. The plain intent of Congress in enacting this statute was to halt and reverse the trend toward species extinction, whatever the cost. This is reflected not only in the stated policies of the Act, but in literally every section of the statute. All persons, including federal agencies, are specifically instructed not to "take" endangered species, meaning that no one is "to harass, harm,[30] pursue, hunt, shoot, wound, kill, trap, capture, or collect" such life forms. 16 U.S.C. §§ 1532(14), 1538(a)(1)(B). Agencies in particular are directed by §§ 2(c) and 3(2) of the Act to "use * * * all *methods* and procedures which are necessary" to preserve endangered species. 16 U.S.C. §§ 1531(c), 1532(2) (emphasis added). In addition, the legislative history undergirding § 7 reveals an explicit congressional decision to require agencies to afford first priority to the declared national policy of saving endangered species. The pointed omission of the type of qualifying language previously included in endangered species legislation reveals a conscious decision by Congress to give endangered species priority over the "primary missions" of federal agencies.

It is not for us to speculate, much less act, on whether Congress would have altered its stance had the specific events of this case been anticipated. In any event, we discern no hint in the deliberations of Congress relating to the 1973 Act that would compel a different result than we reach here. Indeed, the repeated expressions of congressional concern over what it saw as the potentially enormous danger presented by the eradication of any endangered species suggest how the balance would have been struck had the issue been presented to Congress in 1973.

Furthermore, it is clear Congress foresaw that § 7 would, on occasion, require agencies to alter ongoing projects in order to fulfill the goals of the Act.[32] ...

---

30. We do not understand how TVA intends to operate Tellico Dam without "harming" the snail darter. The Secretary of the Interior has defined the term "harm" to mean "an act or omission which actually injures or kills wildlife, including acts which annoy it to such an extent as to significantly disrupt essential behavioral patterns, which include, but are not limited to, breeding, feeding or sheltering; *significant environmental modification or degradation which has such effects is included within the meaning of* 'harm.'" 50 C.F.R. § 17.3 (1976) (emphasis added).

32. Mr. Justice Powell characterizes the result reached here as giving "retroactive" effect to the Endangered Species Act of 1973. We cannot accept that contention. Our holding merely gives effect to the plain words of the statute, namely, that § 7 affects all projects which remain to be authorized, funded, or carried out. Indeed, under the Act there could be no "retroactive" application

One might dispute the applicability of these examples to the Tellico Dam by saying that in this case the burden on the public through the loss of millions of unrecoverable dollars would greatly outweigh the loss of the snail darter. But neither the Endangered Species Act nor Art. III of the Constitution provides federal courts with authority to make such fine utilitarian calculations. On the contrary, the plain language of the Act, buttressed by its legislative history, shows clearly that Congress viewed the value of endangered species as "incalculable." Quite obviously, it would be difficult for a court to balance the loss of a sum certain—even $100 million—against a congressionally declared "incalculable" value, even assuming we had the power to engage in such a weighing process, which we emphatically do not.

In passing the Endangered Species Act of 1973, Congress was also aware of certain instances in which exceptions to the statute's broad sweep would be necessary. Thus, § 10, 16 U.S.C. § 1539, creates a number of limited "hardship exemptions," none of which would even remotely apply to the Tellico Project. In fact, there are no exemptions in the Endangered Species Act for federal agencies, meaning that under the maxim *expressio unius est exclusio alterius,* we must presume that these were the only "hardship cases" Congress intended to exempt.

. . .

(B)

Having determined that there is an irreconcilable conflict between operation of the Tellico Dam and the explicit provisions of § 7 of the Endangered Species Act, we must now consider what remedy, if any, is appropriate. It is correct, of course, that a federal judge sitting as a chancellor is not mechanically obligated to grant an injunction for every violation of law.... As a general matter it may be said that "[s]ince all or almost all equitable remedies are discretionary, the balancing of equities and hardships is appropriate in almost any case as a guide to the chancellor's discretion." [ ]

But these principles take a court only so far. Our system of government is, after all, a tripartite one, with each branch having certain defined functions delegated to it by the Constitution. While "[i]t is emphatically the province and duty of the judicial department to say what the law is," *Marbury v. Madison,* 1 Cranch 137, 177 (1803), it is equally—and emphatically—the exclusive province of the Congress not only to formulate legislative policies and mandate programs and projects, but also to establish their relative priority for the Nation. Once Congress, exercising its delegated powers, has decided the order of priorities in a given area, it is for the Executive to administer the laws and for the courts to enforce them when enforcement is sought.

Here we are urged to view the Endangered Species Act "reasonably," and hence shape a remedy "that accords with some modicum of common

since, by definition, any *prior* action of a federal agency which would have come under the scope of the Act must have already *resulted* in the destruction of an endangered species or its critical habitat. In that circumstance the species would have already been extirpated or its habitat destroyed; the Act would then have no subject matter to which it might apply.

sense and the public weal." [ ] But is that our function? We have no expert knowledge on the subject of endangered species, much less do we have a mandate from the people to strike a balance of equities on the side of the Tellico Dam. Congress has spoken in the plainest of words, making it abundantly clear that the balance has been struck in favor of affording endangered species the highest of priorities, thereby adopting a policy which it described as "institutionalized caution."

Our individual appraisal of the wisdom or unwisdom of a particular course consciously selected by the Congress is to be put aside in the process of interpreting a statute. Once the meaning of an enactment is discerned and its constitutionality determined, the judicial process comes to an end. We do not sit as a committee of review, nor are we vested with the power of veto. . . .

We agree with the Court of Appeals that in our constitutional system the commitment to the separation of powers is too fundamental for us to pre-empt congressional action by judicially decreeing what accords with "common sense and the public weal." Our Constitution vests such responsibilities in the political branches.

Affirmed.

■ POWELL, with whom Blackmun joins, dissenting: The Court today holds that § 7 of the Endangered Species Act requires a federal court, for the purpose of protecting an endangered species or its habitat, to enjoin permanently the operation of any federal project, whether completed or substantially completed. This decision casts a long shadow over the operation of even the most important projects, serving vital needs of society and national defense, whenever it is determined that continued operation would threaten extinction of an endangered species or its habitat. This result is said to be required by the "plain intent of Congress" as well as by the language of the statute.

In my view § 7 cannot reasonably be interpreted as applying to a project that is completed or substantially completed when its threat to an endangered species is discovered. Nor can I believe that Congress could have intended this Act to produce the "absurd result"—in the words of the District Court—of this case. If it were clear from the language of the Act and its legislative history that Congress intended to authorize this result, this Court would be compelled to enforce it. It is not our province to rectify policy or political judgments by the Legislative Branch, however egregiously they may disserve the public interest. But where the statutory language and legislative history, as in this case, need not be construed to reach such a result, I view it as the duty of this Court to adopt a permissible construction that accords with some modicum of common sense and the public weal.

. . .

NOTES

(1) What rationales does the Court cite for conserving endangered and threatened species? Is the decision justifiable on ethical, scientific, cultural, or economic grounds?

(2) Retroactivity: One point of dispute between the majority and the dissent is the application of the Act to ongoing actions. Chief Justice Burger writes:

> Mr. Justice Powell characterizes the result reached here as giving "retroactive" effect to the Endangered Species Act of 1973. We cannot accept that contention. [U]nder the Act there could be no "retroactive" application since, by definition, any *prior* action of a federal agency which would have come under the scope of the Act must have already *resulted* in the destruction of an endangered species or its critical habitat. In that circumstance the species would have already been extirpated or its habitat destroyed; the Act would then have no subject matter to which it might apply.

Supra n.32. Justice Powell, on the other hand, writes:

> The critical word in § 7 is "actions" and its meaning is far from "plain." It is part of the phrase: "actions authorized, funded or carried out." In terms of planning and executing various activities, it seems evident that the "actions" referred to are not all actions that an agency can ever take, but rather actions that the agency is deciding whether to authorize, to fund, or to carry out. In short, these words reasonably may be read as applying only to prospective actions, *i.e.*, actions with respect to which the agency has reasonable decisionmaking alternatives still available, actions not yet carried out.

Is either statement entirely accurate? Which approach is most in accord with the legislative history?

(a) Columbia River Basin hydroelectric system: Consider, for example, the operation of the Columbia River Basin hydroelectric system, a series of large dams that generate hydroelectricity and kill salmon. Contrary to Justice Burger's assertion, the dams effects are cumulative rather than instantaneous: the basin's salmon runs have dwindled over time to the point where many have gone extinct and many others are listed under the ESA. How should the ESA apply to such ongoing actions? Is Justice Powell's formulation—whether there are "reasonable decisionmaking alternative still available"—satisfactory? Is Justice Powell's understanding of "reasonable" consistent with the Act? Would the application of the ESA to an agency's ten-year plan for logging be retroactive for Justice Powell?

(b) *Sierra Club v. Babbitt*: When Congress granted lands to railroads, it frequently created a checkerboard pattern of federal and private lands by granting the railroad alternate one-mile-square sections. Access is a recurrent problem on such lands. In 1962, the Bureau of Land Management (BLM) entered into a reciprocal right-of-way agreement with Seneca Sawmill Company permitting both parties to construct roads across the other's land to reach their property. In September 1990, Seneca submitted a proposed right of way; a BLM biologist concluded that the road (or perhaps the logging) might affect spotted owls and recommended the initiation of consultation with FWS. The Department's regional solicitor issued an opinion letter concluding that consultation was unnecessary because the agency lacked discretion under the 1962 agreement. The Sierra

Club challenged the road-building activity. On appeal, the Ninth Circuit offered a brief review of the prior decisions:

> after enactment of the ESA the execution of a reciprocal right-of-way agreement clearly would implicate section 7(a)(2). *See, e.g., Conner v. Burford,* 848 F.2d 1441, 1454–58 (9th Cir.1988) (holding that the BLM must comply with section 7 by identifying all the potential impacts on a protected species of all post-leasing activities before entering into lease agreements), *cert. denied,* 489 U.S. 1012 (1989). Similarly, a project undertaken pursuant to a preexisting agreement could not avoid the procedural requirements of section 7(a)(2) if the project's implementation depended on an additional agency action. *See, e.g., O'Neill v. United States,* 50 F.3d 677, 680–81 (9th Cir.1995) (explaining why section 7(a)(2) of the ESA applies to a preexisting water service contract where the United States must act each year to supply the water); *Conservation Law Found. v. Andrus,* 623 F.2d 712, 715 (1st Cir.1979) (holding that the ESA will apply to any contract the Secretary enters into which requires a future action on the Secretary's part);
> [ ].

Sierra Club v. Babbitt, 65 F.3d 1502, 1508 (9th Cir.1995). The agreement in the present case, the court stated, presented an unresolved issue: "To what extent does section 7 apply where the BLM granted right-of-way by contract to a private entity *before* passage of the ESA *and* the agency's continuing ability to influence the private conduct is limited to three factors unrelated to the conservation of the threatened spotted owl." *Id.* The court held that the ESA was inapplicable in such situations: "where, as here, the federal agency lacks the discretion to influence the private action, consultation would be a meaningless exercise; the agency simply does not possess the ability to implement measures that inure to the benefit of the protected species." *Id.* at 1509. *See also Pacific Rivers Council v. Thomas,* 30 F.3d 1050 (9th Cir.1994) (agency enjoined from continuing on ongoing projects such as roadbuilding and livestock grazing until completing consultation following listing of species).

PERSPECTIVES

(1) "Little fish stops big dam": Predictably the media treated the case as a "man bites dog" story, ignoring the broader issues of conserving biodiversity or protecting free-flowing streams in the face of an economically wasteful water project. The media version of the case with its emphasis on environmental extremism raises the question of whether *Hill* helped or hurt the conservation movement.

(2) The problem of economic valuation of non-commodities: In *Hill,* the Supreme Court held that "Congress viewed the value of endangered species as 'incalculable'" and denied the judiciary the power "to balance the loss of a sum certain—even $100 million—against [this] congressionally declared 'incalculable' value." The snail darter revealed that this ethic could have a cost.

How can an economic value be placed on snail darters? More generally, how can dollar values be placed on non-market resources and values? These issues have arisen recurrently in two types of cases: those involving statutory provisions requiring polluters to pay damages for the destruction of natural resources such as wildlife and cases such as *In re Steuart Transportation Co.,* 495 F.Supp. 38 (E.D.Va.1980), in which the state asserts its role as trustee for its citizens seeking damages for injuries to the corpus of the trust.

The Comprehensive Environmental Response, Compensation and Liability Act (CERCLA) of 1980 is perhaps the most prominent statute to include a provisions making entities that release hazardous substances liable for "damages for injury to, destruction of, or loss of natural resources." 42 U.S.C. § 9607(a)(4)(C). *See also* Oil Pollution Act of 1990, 33 U.S.C. § 2702(b)(2)(A); Clean Water Act, 33 U.S.C. § 1321(f)(4). In 1986, the Department of the Interior promulgated regulations governing "natural resource damage assessments" under CERCLA and the Clean Water Act. The regulations specified that natural resource damages were the lesser of either (a) the restoration or replacement costs or (b) the value of lost use of the resources. When the regulations were challenged, Interior argued that its approach optimized social utility:

> [I]f use value is higher than the cost of restoration or replacement, then it would be more rational for society to be compensated for the cost to restore or replace the lost resource than to be compensated for the lost use. Conversely, if restoration or replacement costs are higher than the value of uses foregone, it is rational for society to compensate individuals for their lost uses rather than the cost to restore or replace the injured natural resource.

Ohio v. Department of the Interior, 880 F.2d 432, 456 (D.C.Cir.1989) (quoting 50 FED. REG. 52,126, 52,141 (1985)). The court rejected this argument, concluding that the regulations were contrary to congressional intent:

> The fatal flaw of Interior's approach . . . is that it assumes that natural resources are fungible goods, just like any other, and the value to society generated by a particular resource can be accurately measured in every case—assumptions that Congress apparently rejected. As the foregoing examination of CERCLA's text, structure and legislative history illustrates, Congress saw restoration as the presumptively correct remedy for injury to natural resources. To say that Congress placed a thumb on the scales in favor of restoration is not to say that it forswore the goal of efficiency. "Efficiency," standing alone, simply means that the chosen policy will dictate a result that achieves the greatest value for society. Whether a particular choice is efficient depends on *how the various alternatives are valued. Our reading of CERCLA does not attribute to Congress an irrational dislike of* "efficiency"; rather, it suggests that Congress was skeptical of the ability of human beings to measure the true "value" of a natural resource. . . . Congress' refusal to view use value and restoration cost as having equal presumptive legitimacy merely recognizes that natural resources have value that is not readily measured by traditional means.

Id. at 456–57 (footnotes omitted).

What is the use value of the snail darter? If something has no use value, how should damages be assessed in an economically rational world?

(3) Ethics and useless species: The snail darter produced a crisis that continues to reverberate in American politics. From the time that Europeans first arrived on the continent, a simple utilitarianism had been the dominant perspective: the land and its resources were for the taking. Long after Frederick Jackson Turner chronicled the closing of the frontier, the pioneer spirit continued to dominate resource decisionmaking. In Patty Limerick's telling phrase, it was an "Empire of Innocence," we destroyed—Indians and buffalo and countless other snail darters—while remaining fundamentally innocent. PATRICIA N. LIMERICK, THE LEGACY OF CONQUEST 36–54 (1987). It is this innocent certainty that can be heard in the perplexed arguments that followed in the wake of the snail darter.

Although all of the disputants professed a desire to protect species, not all senators placed the same ethical value on this objective. The species-preservation goal was of distinctly secondary importance for the group of senators that included William Scott, John Stennis, and Jake Garn. This group's rhetoric disparaged "useless," "esoteric," and "insignificant" species;[1] they believed that animals exist only to "serv[e] mankind"[2] and should be protected only to the extent that they were "of a substantial benefit to mankind."[3] The idea that a small fish that "has no use at all" could stop a major water development project was more than unfathomable, it was heresy: quoting *Genesis*, Senator Scott argued, "People should have dominion over fish, wildlife, and plants. Only where the lower species are of benefit to mankind are they important."[4] While Senator Scott was conspicuous in his reliance upon Christian theology, other members of this group shared his fundamental perspective when they challenged the ESA's paramount policy that all species of plants and animals are entitled to protection.[5] Ultimately, these senators believed that "considerations of

1. *E.g.*, 124 CONG. REC. 21,146 (1978) (statement of Sen. Stennis) (complaining that a dam in Maine was being delayed by "the existence of a useless plant known as the Furbish lousewort"; any federal project "could be stopped cold if it impacted on the most insignificant, most obscure and most worthless" plant or animal); *id.* at 21,330 (statement of Sen. Garn) ("some rare weed"); *id.* at 21,333 (statement of Sen. McClure) (only "significant species" should be protected); *id.* at 21,573 (statement of Sen. Garn) ("preserving esoteric species"); *id.* at 21,580 (statement of Sen. Scott) ("some obscure form of life").

2. *Id.* at 21,356 (statement of Sen. Scott).

3. Senator Scott offered an amendment to the definition of "endangered species" specifically incorporating this requirement. *Id.* at 21,356.

4. *Id.* at 21,356 (statement of Sen. Scott). The Senator from Virginia also con-

tended, "we should segregate those [species] which are beneficial to mankind from those which do not serve any known beneficial purpose." *Id.* Senator Culver, speaking in opposition to the amendment, argued that "we can never know ... at any given point in time what the particular value a species hay or may not have for humans." *Id.* at 21,356 (statement of Sen. Culver). Senator Scott's "presently utilitarian" outlook was shared by the other senators in this group. *E.g.*, *id.* at 21,331 (statement of Sen. Garn) ("undertaking tremendous costs ... is out of proportion to the value of the woundfin minnow, or the snail darter, or the lousewort, or the waterbug"); *id.* at 21,333 (statement of Sen. McClure) (only "significant species" deserve protection).

5. *See, e.g.*, *id.* at 21,330 (statement of Sen. Garn) (man is "endowed by his Creator with rationality").

convenience and comfort . . . should take precedence" over the preservation of species.[6]

The first ESA had enacted a distinctly different ethic—the ethical decision that, in the Court's words, "the value of endangered species [is] 'incalculable' " and thus in excess of any "sum certain" such as the $100 million sunk in the Tellico Dam. As Senator Culver stated during the 1978 debate, "we have an ethical and moral responsibility to pass on to future generations, in as pristine a state as possible, what we in turn have inherited."[7] The decision to protect all species from human actions reflected a recognition "that we do not have the wisdom to decide what species shall live and what species shall die."[8] While counseling humility, these senators also offered a utilitarian justification—albeit utilitarianism with a longer perspective: as Senator Patrick Leahy noted, "*Homo sapiens* is perceived to stand at the top of the pyramid of life, but the pinnacle is a precarious station [sustained only by] the web of life . . . that forms the foundation of our total environment."[9] Since the ESA sought to protect all of the bricks in the foundation, it was "[i]n the last analysis . . . addressed much more to our concern over the future of man than to our concern over anything else."[10]

NOTES

(1) The Endangered Species Act Amendments of 1978 and 1979— An Overview of The Second Endangered Species Act of 1973: Despite Justice Powell's assured assertion—"I have little doubt that Congress will amend the Endangered Species Act to prevent the grave consequences made possible by today's decision"—Congress did not repeal the ESA. Rather, as Professor Bill Rogers commented, "The congressional reaction to the *Hill* decision was swift, immediate and indecisive." WILLIAM D. RODGERS, ENERGY AND NATURAL RESOURCES LAW 467 n.5 (1979).

The problem was that *TVA v. Hill* pitted two popular species against one another: endangered species versus pork. *See generally* George C. Coggins & Irma S. Russell, *Beyond Shooting Snail Darters in Pork Barrels: Endangered Species and Land Use in America*, 70 GEO. L.J. 1433 (1982). The Supreme Court's resolution of the conflict presented Congress with a dilemma: how to preserve the ESA while also protecting the pork barrel. The congressional watchword became "flexibility." Congress decided upon an approach that offered something for both species: while retaining section 7's central substantive standard with only minor modifications, the Endangered Species Act Amendments of 1978 added a new entity—the Endangered Species Committee, *aka* "The God Squad"—that was empowered to grant exemptions from the Act's prohibitions.

6. *Id.* at 21,573 (statement of Sen. Garn).

7. *Id.* at 21,287 (statement of Sen. Culver).

8. *Id.* at 21,142 (statement of Sen. Nelson).

9. *Id.* at 21,286 (statement of Sen. Leahy).

10. *Id.* at 21,142 (statement of Sen. Nelson).

These amendments—and the fine tuning that occurred the following year—formalized the consultation processes under section 7: the slightly more than 100 words in the original section became the first subsection of a section that had expanded to nearly 8 pages in the Statutes at Large. There also were changes to section 4: the Amendments required that critical habitat generally be designated at the time a species is listed; they also substantially expanded the procedure for listing a species and designating its critical habitat was substantially elaborated by requiring a status review and additional notice and public comment opportunities.

(2) Tellico Dam, pts 2 and 3: As part of the 1978 Amendments, the Tellico Dam was put on fast-track consideration by the Endangered Species Committee. Following a review of reports on the project, Charles Schultze, Chair of the Council of Economic Advisors, noted, "The project is 95 percent complete, and if one takes just the cost of finishing it against the benefits, and does it properly, it doesn't pay, which says something about the original design." The Committee voted unanimously to deny the TVA an exemption for the Project. Following the vote, Secretary of the Interior and Chair of the Endangered Species Committee Cecil Andrus commented, "I hate to see the snail darter get the credit for stopping a project that was ill-conceived and uneconomic in the first place." *Species Panel Denies Exemption to Tellico Dam, But Exempts Grayrocks Dam,* 9 ENV'T REP. (BNA) 1776 (Jan. 26, 1979).

Despite the Committee's decision, maneuvering by Tennessee Senator Howard Baker led to a congressional exemption of the project in 1979.

(3) The Endangered Species Act Amendments of 1982—An Overview of the Third Endangered Species Act of 1973: If the theme of the 1978 Amendments was flexibility, the dominant concern in 1982 was a tension between more and less administrative discretion. On the one hand, evidence indicated that the complex procedural steps introduced by the 1978 and 1979 Amendments had significantly reduced the effectiveness of the Act. At the same time, however, Congress was concerned with the actions of James G. Watt, a Secretary of the Interior openly hostile to conservation.

To that end, the Amendments specified that the listing determination was to be made "*solely* on the basis of the best scientific and commercial data available"; economics were not to be considered. Designation of critical habitat, on the other hand, was a more open-ended question in which economic impacts were relevant—but in which biology remained the trump card. Section 4 was also amended to restructure the listing procedure into a three-step process and the linkage between listing a species and designating its critical habitat was relaxed. The consultation and exemption procedures were also substantially rewritten: steps were deleted, deadlines shortened. But again, the rewrite left the substantive standard unaffected: federal agencies remained obligated both to use their authorities to carry out programs for the conservation of listed species and to insure that actions they authorized, funded, or carried out did not jeopardize the continued existence of a listed species or adversely modify its critical habitat. Finally, the 1982 Amendments also expanded the incidental take permit that had initially been created under the 1978 Amendments.

The ESA was also amended in several details in 1984, 1986, and 1988.

(5) The Administrative Amendment of the Endangered Species Act, 1994–?—An Overview of the Fourth Endangered Species Act of 1973: Following Republican congressional victories in 1994, Secretary of the Interior Babbitt "resolve[d] to save the Endangered Species Act by implementing a series of reforms on the implementation of the Act from top to bottom, particularly as it applied to private lands." This objective was pursued through "incentive-based strategies to try and reconcile endangered species conservation with economic development." Donald J. Berry, *Keynote Speech—Opportunity in the Face of Danger: The Pragmatic Development of Habitat Conservation Plans,* 4 HASTINGS WEST-NORTHWEST J. ENVTL. L. & POL'Y 129, 131 (1998). The centerpiece of the initiative was an expanded emphasis on habitat conservation planning as a mechanism for permitting land development within the habitat of listed species. The HCP process seeks to balance two competing goals: flexibility (to adopt to changing circumstances and information) and certainty (to allow the permittee to make economic decisions). In practice the trade-offs require the developer to obtain approval for a habitat conservation plan (HCP)—which requires a commitment to long-term funding, habitat set asides, and other mitigation measures; if it is approved, the fish and wildlife agencies issue an "incidental take permit" authorizing the developer—in J.B. Ruhl's phrase—to kill listed species, legally. *See* J.B. Ruhl, *How to Kill Endangered Species, Legally: The Nuts and Bolts of Endangered Species Act "HCP" Permits for Real Estate Development,* 5 ENVTL. L. 345 (1999). At the end of 1996, the fish and wildlife agencies published *Endangered Species Habitat Conservation Planning Handbook* that specified procedures and set out timetables for decisionmaking.

Significantly the *Handbook* endorsed both a "safe harbors" and a "no surprises" policy. Under a safe harbor program, landowners who undertake voluntary conservation measures can obtain a permit authorizing the future take of listed species above a background level. The no-surprises policy goes even further: the fish and wildlife agency agrees not to impose additional mitigation requirements except in narrowly defined instances. In 1998, the agencies promulgated a final rule adopting the no-surprises policy. 63 *Fed. Reg.* 8859 (1998). The following year, a final safe harbor regulation was promulgated. 64 *Fed. Reg.* 32706 (1999). Both policies produced intense controversy. A judicial challenge to the no-surprises regulation is currently pending. *Spirit of the Sage Council v. Babbitt,* No. 1:98CV01873 (D.D.C. filed July, 29, 1998).

(6) The ban on balancing: On the surface, *TVA v. Hill* remains good law: once an action is found to jeopardize a species an injunction must follow, regardless of economic consequences, unless an exemption is obtained. Note, though, that few cases present facts as stark as those assumed in *Hill*: a species comprising one population that a single federal action would destroy. Several observers have detected comments in later Supreme Court opinions that portend a relaxation of this firm rule when the danger to a species is less clear. Federico Cheever, *Butterflies, Cave Spiders, Milk–Vetch, Bunchgrass, Sedges, Lilies, Checker–Mallows and Why the Prohibition Against Judicial Balancing of Harm Under the Endan-*

gered Species Act is a Good Idea, 22 WM. & MARY ENVTL. L. & POL'Y REV. 313 (1998).

SECTION 2.   COVERAGE

NOTES

(1) The ESA—like most statutes—creates categories and specifies legal results that are to flow from inclusion within those categories. Under the ESA, there are three classifications of species—"endangered," "threatened," and "proposed to be listed"—and one classification of geographic areas—"critical habitat." The results that follow from categorizing a species and a geographic area are expressed in the fundamental legal mandate—"conserve"—and in the various management requirements contained in the Act—the most important being the consultation mandate of section 7 and the taking prohibitions of section 9.

(2) **"endangered species," "threatened species," "proposed to be listed," and "warranted but precluded":** The Act defines three terms that effectively specify the level of protection to be accorded a species:

(a) The Act defines the term "endangered species" as "any species which is in danger of extinction throughout all or a significant portion of its range other than a species of the Class Insecta determined by the Secretary to constitute a pest whose protection under the provisions of this Act would present an overwhelming and overriding risk to man." 16 U.S.C. § 1332(6). Note a critical issue presented by this definition: how should a species that flourishes in certain places but that (i) has disappeared from much of its historic habitat and (ii) is imperiled in part of the remaining habitat be treated? Could it be listed as "endangered" in the parts of its range where it is absent or scarce? The issue is considered in *Defenders of Wildlife v. Norton,* below.

(b) The term "threatened species" is defined as "any species which is likely to become an endangered species within the foreseeable future throughout all or a significant portion of its range." *Id.* § 1332(20).

The distinction between the categories "endangered" and "threatened" is captured in a footnote in a case involving a challenge to a decision not to list the Alexander Archipelago wolf:

> Defendants [Fish and Wildlife Service] contend that the Archipelago wolf is not endangered or threatened at this time. At the same time they admit that under the current Forest Service plan, the wolf will be "seriously imperiled" in the future. [ ] Clearly, in passing the ESA, Congress did not intend the Secretary to wait until a particular species is on the verge of extinction before taking action. If, with the continuation of current circumstances, the wolf will be "endangered" in the future, it is clearly "threatened" today.

Biodiversity Legal Foundation v. Babbitt, 943 F.Supp. 23, 26 n. 5 (D.D.C. 1996).

(c) The original version of the ESA included only two categories—threatened and endangered. In the 1978 amendments, Congress added a third category, "proposed to be listed." *Id.* § 1536(a)(4). The category is self-defining.

(d) The final category of species was added in 1988 when Congress created the "warranted but precluded" status. *Id.* § 1533(b)(3)(B)(iii). The amendment added a third category of possible findings on a petition to list a species. In addition to finding that a petition was either warranted or not, the Secretary could determine that listing was warranted but that "the immediate ... promulgation of a ... regulation ... is precluded by [other] pending proposals to determine whether [another] species [should be listed] and expeditious progress is being made" on the determination of the status of the other species. *Id.*

(3) "species": The Act's coverage is more expansive than it might initially appear because of the definition of "species" to include "any subspecies of fish or wildlife or plants, and any distinct population segment of any species of vertebrate fish or wildlife which interbreeds when mature." *Id.* § 1532(16). Were there a truth-in-titling requirement for federal statutes, the Endangered Species Act would be titled the Endangered Subspecies and Vertebrate–Distinct–Populations Act.

The inclusion of "subspecies" and "populations" within the definition is important in part because of the flexibility it provided. The Secretary is able to vary the classification of distinct populations of a single species. The grey wolf, for example, is not listed in Alaska, is listed as threatened in Minnesota, and as endangered in the northern Rocky Mountains.

FWS and NMFS published a final policy on February 1, 1996. The policy stated that the agencies will consider three factors in determining whether a group of vertebrates is a distinct population segment:

1. Discreteness of the population segment in relation to the remainder of the species to which it belongs;

2. The significance of the population segment to the species to which it belongs; and

3. The population segment's conservation status in relation to the Act's standards for listing (*i.e.,* is the population segment, when treated as if it were a species, endangered or threatened?).

61 Fed. Reg. 4722 (Feb. 7, 1996). As a policy statement rather than a regulation, the factors do not have the force and effect of law. The history of FWS's sometimes-inconsistent application of the term "distinct population segment" is examined in *Southwest Center for Biological Diversity v. Babbitt*, 926 F.Supp. 920 (D.Ariz.1996).

(4) "conserve" is the central management standard in the Act. It—and its cognates "conserving" and "conservation"—are defined to mean "to use and the use of all methods and procedures which are necessary to bring any endangered species or threatened species to the point at which the measures provided pursuant to this Act are no longer necessary. Such methods and procedures include, but are not limited to, all activities associated with scientific resources management such as research, census, law enforcement, habitat acquisition and maintenance, propagation, live trapping, and transplantation, and, in the extraordinary case where population pressures within a given ecosystem cannot be otherwise relieved, may include regulated taking." *Id.* § 1332(3).

Note that "conserve" is essentially a synonym for "recovery": To conserve is not merely to stabilize a species, it is to improve its plight. At first glance, conserve would seem to mean improve a species chances to the point where it no longer qualifies for listing; that is, "delisting" a species would seem to turn on the same standard (in reverse) as listing. On close reading, however, the standards differ slightly. It is not enough, for delisting, that a species no longer be threatened (that is, no longer likely to become endangered): It must be able to maintain that status even after ESA protections are withdrawn.

(5) "critical habitat": The Supreme Court's decision in *TVA v. Hill* demonstrated the crucial importance of the concept of "critical habitat." Congress responded by defining the previously undefined term in the 1978 Amendments: "critical habitat" is "(i) the specific areas within the geographical area occupied by the species, at the time it is listed ... on which are found those physical or biological features (I) essential to the conservation of the species and (II) which may require special management considerations of protection; and (ii) specific areas outside the geographical area occupied by the species at the time it is listed ... upon a determination by the Secretary that such areas are essential for the conservation of the species." 16 U.S.C. § 1532(5).

Note that this definition links directly to the definition of "conservation." In many—probably most—instances a listed species can be conserved (that is, can be recovered) only if it expands both its numbers and its physical range. If it loses part of its existing habitat, then it has even greater need to expand into unoccupied areas. Given this reality, what habitat, in terms of quantity and location, is "essential" to recovery? Has the listing agency manifestly failed to comply with the statute if the habitat it designates is plainly insufficient, standing alone, to provide adequate space for recovery? Or, can an agency designate little or no habitat on the theory that, while a given species needs adequate habitat, such habitat might be found or restored in various places—which is to say that no particular acre (or waterway segment) is truly essential?

(6) "Secretary": A final jurisdictional term is "Secretary" which can be the Secretary of the Interior, the Secretary of Commerce, or the Secretary of Agriculture depending upon the context. Primary administrative responsibilities are divided between the Secretary of the Interior and Secretary of Commerce "as program responsibilities are vested pursuant to the provisions of Reorganization Plan Numbered 4 of 1970." *Id.* § 1332(15). Under the Reorganization Plan and prior statutes, the Secretary of Commerce has responsibility for *most* marine species, including anadromous fish (*e.g.,* salmon). The Secretary of the Interior has responsibility for all marine mammals *except* whales, seals, and sea lions (*e.g.,* sea otters and polar bears) as well as marine birds. The Secretary of the Interior has responsibility for all other plant and animal species. *See* Reorganization Plan No. 4 of 1970, 35 Fed. Reg. 15,627 (1970); Fish and Wildlife Act of 1956, Pub. L.

No. 1024, § 3, 70 Stat. 1119, 1120; Pub. L. No. 86–359, 73 Stat. 642 (1959). The "Secretary" is the Secretary of Agriculture "with respect to the enforcement of the provisions of this Act and [CITES] which pertain to the importation or exportation of terrestrial plants." *Id.*

The Fish and Wildlife Service (FWS) administers the programs for the Secretary of the Interior; the National Marine Fisheries Service (NMFS) administers the responsibilities of the Secretary of Commerce; the Animal and Plant Health Inspection Service (APHIS) acts for the Secretary of Agriculture.

SECTION 3.   LISTING DETERMINATIONS AND CRITICAL HABITAT DESIGNATIONS

a.   LISTING DETERMINATIONS

Holly Doremus, *Listing Decisions Under the Endangered Species Act: Why Better Science Isn't Always Better Policy*
75 WASH. U.L.Q. 1029 (1997).

The decision to list a species under the ESA presents the listing agency with two difficult problems. The "taxonomy problem" requires the agency to determine whether a particular group of organisms constitutes a "species" within the meaning of the statute. The "viability problem" requires it to decide whether a species is "endangered" or "threatened." Superficially, each of these problems appears amenable to a strictly scientific solution. Indeed most commentators, as well as participants on both sides of the ESA reauthorization debate, agree that listing determinations are scientific. In fact, however, both prongs of the listing decision force the agencies to look beyond scientific information. As a result, agency practices inevitably fail to measure up to the legislative and public vision of value-neutral scientific decisions.

. . .

1.   The Meaning of "Species"

The ESA's definition of "species" is singularly uninformative. It is merely a list masquerading as a definition: "The term "species' includes any subspecies of fish or wildlife or plants, and any distinct population segment of any species of vertebrate fish or wildlife which interbreeds when mature." The legislature's failure to further define "species," "subspecies," and "distinct population segment" could indicate either that it assumed the terms were unambiguous or that it could not devise acceptable definitions. The absence of any discussion of these terms in the early legislative history supports the former explanation, at least with respect to "species" and "subspecies". At the same time, the deliberate expansion of the statutory term to include lower taxonomic categories suggests an intent to reject narrow technical interpretations of the groups within the law's scope.

At the conceptual level, the meaning of species is reasonably clear: the term refers to a natural grouping or kind distinguishable from others. Nonscientists recognize two major grounds for differentiating between groups of creatures: differences in physical form, or morphology; and the boundaries of sexual compatibility, the ability to mate and produce fertile offspring. Both these bases for classification are consistent with an "essentialist" view of species as invariant and fundamentally distinct from one another, as in the Platonic ideal of unchanging forms or the biblical concept of unvarying kinds created by God....

Most scientific species classification schemes also rely on morphological and reproductive distinctions, albeit largely stripped of their essentialist connotations. The earliest taxonomic classification systems relied almost entirely on morphological differences to distinguish essential, invariant natural kinds. The development of evolutionary theory, however, undercut the essentialist view by showing that species are capable of gradual transformation to entirely new forms. This revelation led Darwin to conclude that all species classification schemes are inherently arbitrary....

Nonetheless, scientists did not abandon the pursuit of classification. Taxonomic systems remained useful for indexing information, and continued to reflect readily observable differences between natural groups. But taxonomists did add an evolutionary focus: they searched for classification schemes which would both recognize obvious morphological distinctions and account for evolutionary relationships.

This search culminated in 1940 with the proposal by Ernst Mayr of the biological species concept ("BSC"), which relies on sexual isolation to distinguish natural groups. Mayr's BSC defines a species as a group of actually or potentially interbreeding populations reproductively isolated from other such groups. Mayr focused on reproductive isolation because of its vital role in speciation, the process by which new species evolve. Groups which regularly exchange genes through interbreeding tend to remain alike because adaptive traits can spread throughout the group....

In the half-century since Mayr proposed it, the BSC has become the most widely known and utilized biological definition of species. It is not universally accepted, however, because it is not universally applicable. Its emphasis on interbreeding, for example, makes it inapplicable to organisms like the common dandelion which reproduce primarily through asexual methods. It is equally awkward to apply the BSC to organisms which are able to interbreed readily with other groups while still maintaining their own distinct morphological and genetic identity. These difficulties have led biologists to develop a host of competing species concepts, each based on the authors' perception of evolutionary relationships, but varying in accordance with the authors' choice of organisms to study....

. . .

2.   Is the Identification of Endangered and Threatened Species Scientific?

Like the delineation of protectable groups, the identification of groups sufficiently at risk to warrant protection requires defining those categories and then applying them. Like "species," the terms "endangered" and "threatened" cannot be defined strictly on the basis of scientific information as that term is understood by the public, scientists and the legislature. Furthermore, because the science involved is often highly uncertain, application of any chosen definition leaves substantial room for discretionary choices.

a. Category Definition

As a necessary prerequisite to implementing the ESA, the listing agencies must supply the content Congress omitted from the statutory terms "endangered" and "threatened." Congress neglected to specify, in even the most general terms, either the relevant degree of extinction risk, or the relevant time period over which extinction risks should be evaluated.

The statute's vagueness is not unusual; Congress often leaves large policy gaps for implementing agencies to fill. The ESA's strictly science mandate, however, makes this particular gap problematic. It is impossible to specify a viability level which will qualify species for protection without looking beyond the realm of science. Like acceptable health risks from toxic substances, acceptable risks of species extinction are social policy decisions. Determining those acceptable risks requires value judgments which the agencies cannot make without stepping out of their assigned "scientific" role.

Once the choice of acceptable risk has been made, science is essential to achieving the goal of limiting extinction risks to that level. . . .

* * *

Professor Doremus concludes that, in the case of both of the issues she discusses, decisions would be more honest and consistent if Congress identified clearly why species were being protected; that is, if Congress explained what values it sought to promote and how much weight it gave to each. She agrees that economic factors should be excluded from the process, but the basic decisions, she urges, are still so interwoven with questions of value that science alone cannot lead (and has not led) to coherent decisions. Doremus proposes that the Act be amended to define "species" as follows:

> The term "species" includes any recognized taxonomic species, and any other identifiable group of fish or wildlife or plants which provides esthetic, ecological, educational, genetic, historical, recreational, scientific or other value significantly distinct from, or substantially additional to, that provided by other identifiable groups.

As for decisions on whether a species is endangered or threatened, she concludes that Congress should "add content" to the existing definitions by expressing, "in general qualitative terms," the "acceptable degree of risk." She advises against any move to express acceptable degree of risk in terms of specific probabilities of extinction (as in a 10% risk over a 100–year period) or in terms of minimum numbers for viability (*e.g.*, 500) set without regard for species and context.

NOTES

(1) Doremus criticizes Congress for not being more exact in its definitions, but realistically how clear could it be? Would any language put an end to variations in listing decisions, considering the problems that she highlights in gathering data and making predictions? How much delay and cost would be added to listing processes if agency decisions were subject to challenge on the ground that the agency made arbitrary and capricious decisions on basic questions of value?

(2) The listing process: Although the listing decision and the decision to designate critical habitat are generally to be made "concurrently," the process is easier to understand if the procedural steps for each decision are initially outlined separately.

The decision to list a species may be initiated either by a petition filed by any "interested person" or by the Secretary[1] on his own motion. 16 U.S.C. § 1533(b)(3)(A). Once a species has been listed, its status may be changed or it may be delisted as a result of a similar petition, the Secretary's motion, *id.* § 1533(b)(3)(A), or the Act's requirement that the Secretary review the lists of endangered and threatened species at least every five years to determine whether the status of a listed species has changed. *Id.* § 1533(c)(2).

The decision to list a species involves three procedural steps:

(a) the 90–day determination: "To the maximum extent practicable," the agency "shall make" a preliminary evaluation of all petitions it receives within 90 days. The Secretary is to determine either that the petition presents "substantial scientific or commercial information" that the petitioned action "may be warranted" or that it fails to do so. *Id.* § 1533(b)(3)(A). In *Biodiversity Legal Foundation v. Babbitt,* 146 F.3d 1249 (10th Cir.1998), the court held that the ESA does not impose a nondiscretionary duty on FWS to evaluate all petitions within 90 days. The Ninth Circuit's contrary—and better reasoned—view is below in *Center for Biological Diversity v. Norton. See also Save Our Springs v. Babbitt,* 27 F.Supp.2d 739, 747–48 (W.D.Tex.1997) (holding that the Secretary had violated the ESA when he failed to make a finding within 90 days).

(b) the status review: If the evidence presented by the petition satisfies substantial evidence threshold, the Secretary must "promptly commence" a review of the status of the species. 16 U.S.C. § 1533(b)(3)(A). The status review is to be completed within twelve months after receipt of the petition. *Id.* § 1533(b)(3)(B). The status review is the basis for a decision (which the Secretary "shall make") that the petitioned action is either (i) not warranted, (ii) warranted but precluded, or (iii) warranted. *Id.* If listing is warranted, the Secretary is to propose a regulation doing so. *Id.*

(c) the final decision: If the Secretary determines that the action is warranted and the species should be listed, delisted, or reclassified, he is required to publish notice of his conclusion and a text of a proposed rule. 16 U.S.C. §§ 1533(b)(4), (5). The publication initiates a public comment peri-

---

1. When a species falls within the jurisdiction of the Secretary of Commerce, the decision to list a species of change its status from threatened to endangered lies within the discretion of the Secretary of Commerce. *Id.* § 1533(a)(2)(A). A decision to delist a species or to reclassify a species from endangered to threatened is subject to additional procedural requirements since the Secretary of the Interior must concur in the decision before it becomes final. *Id.* § 1533(a)(2)(B).

od. The Secretary is to make a final decision "[w]ithin the one-year period" beginning with the publication of the proposed rule. *Id.* § 1533(b)(6)(A). The rule is either to be promulgated, withdrawn if the Secretary finds that there is insufficient information, or, in the event that "there is substantial disagreement regarding the sufficiency or accuracy of the available data," extended for an additional six months. *Id.* § 1533(b)(5)(B)(i).

(3) Substantive basis for the listing decision: Substantively, the decision to list, delist, or reclassify a species must to be based "*solely* upon the best scientific and commercial data available." *Id.* § 1533(b)(1)(A). The decision, in other words, is to be a biological decision; the economic impact of the decision *is not* to be considered. *See, e.g., Save Our Springs v. Babbitt,* 27 F.Supp.2d 739 (W.D.Tex.1997).

Center for Biological Diversity v. Norton

Court of Appeals for the Ninth Circuit.
254 F.3d 833 (2001).

■ BERZON, J.:—The Center for Biological Diversity (the "Center") appeals the district court's grant of summary judgment in favor of the Secretary of the Interior (the "Secretary"). The district court rejected the Center's effort to compel the Secretary to issue certain findings in response to petitions to list two species for protection under the Endangered Species Act ("ESA"). [ ] We find that the Secretary improperly refused to make the necessary findings and therefore reverse the district court's decision.

I. Background

The Endangered Species Act, enacted in 1973, provides "a means whereby the ecosystems upon which endangered species and threatened species depend may be conserved," and "a program for the conservation of such endangered species and threatened species." 16 U.S.C. § 1531(b). An "endangered species" is "any species which is in danger of extinction throughout all or a significant portion of its range," while a "threatened species" is one "which is likely to become an endangered species within the foreseeable future." *Id.* § 1532(6), (20).

At the heart of the present case is the relationship between two methods prescribed in the statute for listing species for protection as endangered or threatened under the ESA. One method allows the Secretary to act on her own initiative to identify species for protection. The second allows interested citizens to compel the Secretary's consideration of a species by filing a petition. The end result in either case is the same: the Secretary must issue a final determination stating whether circumstances warrant listing a species as endangered or threatened. There are, however, important differences between the two methods that dictate how (and when) the Secretary reaches that conclusion.

A. *Species Identified by the Secretary*

Under the first method, the Secretary may, on her own accord, consider whether a species is eligible for protection as endangered or threatened because of:

(A) the present or threatened destruction, modification, or curtailment of its habitat or range;

(B) overutilization for commercial, recreational, scientific, or educational purposes;

(C) disease or predation;

(D) the inadequacy of existing regulatory mechanisms; or

(E) other natural or manmade factors affecting its continued existence.

Id. § 1533(a)(1). If the Secretary finds that the "best scientific and commercial data available to [her]" demonstrates that a species is endangered or threatened because of the presence of one or more of these factors, *id.* § 1533(b)(1)(A), she must publish a proposed rule identifying the species as such. 50 C.F.R. § 424.11(c). A period of public comment follows. Within one year, the Secretary must either publish a final rule designating the species for protection or withdraw the proposed rule upon a finding "that available evidence does not justify the action." 50 C.F.R. § 424.17(a); *see also* 16 U.S.C. § 1533(b)(6)(A).[1]

Although not expressly provided in the statute, the regulations implementing the ESA also permit the Secretary to find that listing of a species *may* be warranted "but that the available evidence is not sufficiently definitive to justify proposing the action at that time." 50 C.F.R. § 424.15(a). The Secretary typically does not provide an explanation for this decision but instead publishes a brief, one-line notice in the Federal Register identifying the species as a "candidate" for protection under the ESA.[2] *See, e.g.,* 64 Fed. Reg. 57,534 (Oct. 25, 1999) (listing candidate species). Candidates are "any species being considered by the Secretary for listing as an endangered or a threatened species, but not yet the subject of a proposed rule." 50 C.F.R. § 424.02(b). From time to time, the Secretary may publish updates of the review status of species that are candidates for listing. 50 C.F.R. § 424.15(b). There is, however, no specific time frame during which the Secretary must act on candidate species. *See id.* (noting that "none of the substantive or procedural provisions of the Act apply to a species that is designated as a candidate for listing").

B.   *Species Identified by Petition*

The second method for listing species allows interested persons to petition the Secretary to add (or remove) species from either the endangered or threatened species lists. Once the Secretary receives such a petition, she has 90 days to decide whether it presents "substantial scientific or commercial information indicating that the petitioned action may be warranted." 16 U.S.C. § 1533(b)(3)(A). If so, the Secretary must

---

1. The Secretary may also delay a final decision for up to six months in order to solicit additional data because of "substantial disagreement" in the scientific community regarding the "sufficiency or accuracy of the available data relevant to the determination or revision concerned." 16 U.S.C. § 1533(b)(6)(B)(i).

2. The regulations explain that the purpose of candidate notices is to "invite comment from all interested parties regarding the status of the species named." 50 C.F.R. § 424.15(c).

"promptly commence a review of the status of the species concerned." *Id.* Within 12 months after the petition is filed, the Secretary must determine that either (1) the petitioned action is warranted, in which case she must publish a proposed rule designating the species for protection; (2) the petitioned action is not warranted; or (3) the petitioned action is warranted but immediate promulgation of a rule is precluded by other pending proposals. 16 U.S.C. § 1533(b)(3)(B). If the Secretary finds that action is "warranted but precluded," she must promptly publish that finding along with "a description and evaluation of the reasons and data on which the finding is based." *Id.* Findings that a petitioned action is not warranted or is "warranted but precluded" are subject to judicial review. 16 U.S.C. § 1533(b)(3)(C)(ii).

C.　The Petition Management Guidance Policy

In 1996, the Fish and Wildlife Service ("FWS") adopted a new policy governing its treatment of citizen-sponsored petitions. (The policy is described in the 1996 "Petition Management Guidance" manual and is hereafter referred to as the "PMG policy".) The policy provides that "[a] petition for an action on a species or critical habitat 'identical' or 'equivalent' to a petition *still pending (or active)* requires only a prompt (*i.e.,* within 30 days) response informing the submitter of the prior petition and its status; Federal Register publication of this response is not required." (Emphasis in the original.) The PMG policy equates species identified as candidates for listing with those designated "warranted but precluded" under 16 U.S.C. § 1533(b)(3)(B)(iii). Candidate species are thus "consider[ed] . . . as under petition," and a petition to list a candidate species is deemed "redundant." Consequently, the Secretary now treats petitions to list species already identified as candidates for protection as second petitions and does not—ever—fulfill the statutory obligations described above that ordinarily attach to initial petitions.

Several significant consequences for petitions to list species already designated by the Secretary as candidates for protection follow from the PMG policy. First, the Secretary may avoid publishing an explanation for her decision not to take more immediate action on a petition to protect a species. Second, because the Secretary's decision to designate a species as a candidate does not require any explanation, there is no basis to review the decision not to take prompt action on a petition to list a candidate species. Third, the timetable requirements that normally govern petitions do not apply. The Center's position in this case is that, taken together, these consequences substantially and impermissibly compromise the statutory scheme for considering petitions to list a species as endangered or threatened.

II.　The Chiricahua Leopard Frog and the Gila Chub

The particular species at issue in this case are the Chiricahua leopard frog (the "frog") and the Gila chub (the "chub").[3] Their histories under the

---

3. The Center offers the following descriptions of the species, which do not differ materially from the Secretary's: "The Gila chub (*Gila intermedia*) is a dark steel grey, chunky-bodied minnow, which averages 5–8 inches in length. It is endemic to the Gila

ESA demonstrate both the importance of the petition process and the statutory problems created by the PMG policy.

The chub appeared as a candidate for listing as early as 1982 and the frog as early as 1991. *See* 47 Fed. Reg. 58,454, 58,455 (Dec. 30, 1982) (chub); 56 Fed. Reg. 58,804, 58,806 (Nov. 21, 1991) (frog). Although the Secretary identified both species as candidates for listing, she had taken no action on either as of June 1998. At that time, the Center filed two petitions requesting that the Secretary extend ESA protection to both species. The Secretary did not, however, issue 90–day statements or 12–month findings in response to either petition, as required by 16 U.S.C. § 1533(b)(3)(A) and (B). Rather, the FWS sent a pair of letters to the Center explaining that it had already designated both the chub and the frog as candidate species. Citing the PMG policy, the FWS further noted that

> candidate species are considered to be under petition and covered by a "warranted but precluded" finding under section 4(b)(3)(B)(iii) of the [ESA]. Since listing of candidates is, by definition, already warranted, petitions on candidates are redundant and treated as second petitions. Preparation of a 90 day finding is considered superfluous and would add undue work to an already heavily burdened listing program. Therefore, the Service will not make a 90–day finding on your petition to list the Gila chub.

The same language was used in the letter denying action on the frog petition.

In August 1999, after the 12–month deadline passed, the Center filed suit to compel the Secretary to issue findings as required by the ESA.... [4]

III. Analysis

The Center is challenging the district court's conclusion that the PMG policy is consistent with the requirements of the ESA and the court's subsequent decision granting summary judgment in favor of the Secretary. We review that decision de novo. *Swanson v. United States Forest Serv.*, 87 F.3d 339, 343 (9th Cir.1996).

At issue here is the validity of the PMG policy. If that policy is supported by the clear intent of Congress under the ESA, "that is the end of the matter; for the court, as well as the agency, must give effect to the unambiguously expressed intent of Congress." *Chevron U.S.A., Inc. v. Natural Resources Defense Council*, 467 U.S. 837, 842–43 (1984). But if the

River basin in Arizona and New Mexico, although it has been extirpated from New Mexico. It is currently limited to fewer than 15 streams of the Gila River basin in central and southeastern Arizona." "The Chiricahua leopard frog (*Rana chiricahuensis*) is a stout leopard frog with a broad head and a short snout, averaging 3–4 inches in length, with a unique snore-like mating call. It historically occurred on the Mogollon Plateau in Arizona and New Mexico, the Sky Islands of southeastern Arizona, southwestern New Mexico, and northern Mexico. Today the Chiricahua leopard frog occupies fewer than 87 sites range wide."

4. In June 2000, the Secretary published a proposed rule to list the frog as a threatened species. 65 Fed. Reg. 37,343 (June 14, 2000). This action renders moot the Center's appeal as it relates to the frog petition. The status of the chub, however, is unchanged, and the validity of the PMG policy as it pertains to the chub is still properly before us.

ESA "is silent or ambiguous with respect to the specific issue, the question for the court is whether the agency's [policy] is based on a permissible construction of the statute." *Id.* at 843. The Secretary argues that the statute is silent or ambiguous on how she should handle petitions to list species already under consideration as candidates.

We disagree. The statute is not at all ambiguous, but instead is exquisitely clear, concerning what the Secretary must do when she receives a petition requesting action on a species.

First, "[t]o the maximum extent practicable, within 90 days after receiving the petition . . . the Secretary *shall* make a finding as to whether the petition presents substantial scientific or commercial information indicating that the petitioned action may be warranted." 16 U.S.C. § 1533(b)(3)(A) (emphasis added); *see also Forest Guardians v. Babbitt,* 174 F.3d 1178, 1187 (10th Cir.1999) (noting that when interpreting the listing requirements of the ESA, " '[s]hall' means shall"). Under the PMG policy, "candidate species" include those "for which sufficient information is available to indicate that a listing proposal is appropriate." Thus, designation of candidate status arguably constitutes a finding that the petitioned action "may be warranted" and might satisfy this initial requirement.

The ESA further provides, however, that within 12 months after receipt of the petition, "the Secretary *shall* make one of the following findings": (1) the petitioned action is warranted; (2) the petitioned action is not warranted; or (3) the petitioned action is "warranted but precluded." 16 U.S.C. § 1533(b)(3)(B) (emphasis added). Designating a species as a candidate for listing does not satisfy either of the first two options, and the Secretary makes no such claim. She does contend, however, that designation of candidate status fulfills the third option and thus fulfills her obligations under the ESA. For the following three reasons, the Secretary is wrong.

A.   Candidate status does not satisfy the findings requirements

While the Secretary's designation of candidate status may fulfill the requirements for a finding of "warranted but precluded" in spirit, it certainly does not satisfy them in deed. If the Secretary finds that listing of a species is "warranted but precluded," the ESA requires her to "promptly publish such findings in the Federal Register, together with *a description and evaluation of the reasons and data on which the finding is based.*" 16 U.S.C. § 1533(b)(3)(B)(iii) (emphasis added). A one-line notice in the Federal Register that a species has been designated a candidate does not fulfill this obligation.

A "warranted but precluded" finding has two components. First, it is an admission by the Secretary that a species qualifies for protection—and that protection is "warranted"—under the ESA, an admission which, as noted, might be met by a candidate designation under the PMG policy's revised definition of candidate species. Second, the finding also states that a final rule cannot be issued right away, for administrative reasons, thereby temporarily excusing the Secretary from issuing a final rule. The circumstances under which the Secretary may invoke that excuse, however, are narrowly defined; Congress emphasized that providing for the "warranted but precluded" designation was not designed to justify "the foot-dragging efforts of a delinquent agency." H. Conf. Rep. No. 97–835, at 22 (1982), *reprinted in* 1982 U.S.C.C.A.N. 2860, 2863. Specifically, the Secretary must show that she is "actively working on other listings and delistings and must determine and publish a finding that such other work has resulted in pending proposals which *actually* preclude[d] [her] proposing the petitioned action at that time." *Id.* (emphasis added). For that reason, "the Secretary must determine and present evidence that [s]he is, in fact, making expeditious progress in the process of listing and delisting other species." *Id.; see also* 16 U.S.C. § 1533(b)(3)(B)(iii) (requiring the Secretary to show that "expeditious progress is being made to add qualified species to either [the endangered or threatened species lists] and to remove from such lists species for which the protections of [the ESA] are no longer necessary").

When the Secretary, acting on her own initiative, designates a species for candidate status, she need not—and does not—explain why more immediate action is not appropriate. *Compare* 64 Fed. Reg. 57,534, 57,538 (Oct. 25, 1999) (including the chub in a list of candidate species) *with* 60 Fed. Reg. 15,281, 15,283 (Mar. 23, 1995) (providing a detailed explanation of the Secretary's finding that immediate action on the boreal toad was "precluded"). To the extent the PMG policy allows the Secretary to avoid this explanation in response to a citizen-sponsored petition, it is inconsistent with the express requirements of the ESA.

B. *Candidate status does not provide an adequate basis for judicial review*

The published findings supporting a determination that listing is "warranted but precluded" are important to the petition process. They provide public notice of species that are likely to become the subject of proposed rules and allow public agencies, private landowners, and other interested parties to respond appropriately. They also provide the basis for review of the Secretary's decision by the court.

The ESA specifically provides that the Secretary's "warranted but precluded" findings are subject to judicial review. 16 U.S.C. § 1533(b)(3)(C)(ii). Were this court to accept the Secretary's unexplained contention that her designation of the chub as candidate species was equivalent to a finding that listing was "warranted but precluded," judicial review would become meaningless. We would have no basis to evaluate the Secretary's conclusion that immediate action is precluded by other more urgent matters. *See Friends of the Wild Swan v. United States Fish & Wildlife Serv.*, 945 F.Supp. 1388, 1396–1400 (D.Or.1996) (holding that Secretary's finding that listing is "warranted but precluded" is arbitrary and capricious if not supported by the reasons provided); [ ].

Accordingly, the Secretary failed to fulfill her obligations under the ESA when she made no 12-month findings in response to the Center's petition. . . .

C. *Candidate status does not satisfy the ESA's mandatory deadlines*

The final significant statutory shortfall of the PMG policy is its lack of deadlines for action on species subject to petitions. As the legislative history of the ESA and its subsequent amendments demonstrate, Congress from the outset recognized that timeliness in the listing process is essential. . . .

As noted, the ESA now instructs the Secretary to determine if a petitioned request likely has merit within 90 days of its receipt; within 12 months, she must decide whether or not action is warranted or "warranted but precluded." 16 U.S.C. § 1533(b)(3). If the Secretary finds that action is "warranted but precluded," the cycle repeats: Within 12 months of that determination, she must again decide whether or not action is warranted or "warranted but precluded" and publish appropriate supporting findings. 16 U.S.C. § 1533(b)(3)(C)(i); *see also* H. Conf. Rep. 97–385, at 22 (1982), *reprinted in* 1982 U.S.C.C.A.N. 2860, 2863 (noting that within 12 months after filing a "warranted but precluded" finding, the Secretary again "must (a) publish a proposed regulation to implement the petitioned action, or (b) make a finding that the petitioned action is not warranted, or (c) make a new finding that [s]he is unable to propose such action at that time or to make a final determination within the statutorily specified time frame and evidence that [s]he is continuing to make progress in the process of listing and delisting other species"). By imposing these deadlines, Congress "replace[d] the Secretary's discretion with mandatory, nondiscretionary duties." *Id.* at 20, *reprinted in* 1982 U.S.C.C.A.N. 2860, 2861. The statutory deadlines thus assure that species tagged for protection are not forgotten in an administrative quagmire, but instead are periodically monitored and reconsidered for listing.

Candidate status does not guarantee a similar time frame for administrative action. . . . Because the PMG policy allows the Secretary to sidestep the prescribed time requirements, it is inconsistent with the ESA. . . .

IV.   Conclusion

For the foregoing reasons, we conclude that the PMG policy violates the plain terms of the ESA and that the Secretary improperly relied upon it when she refused to issue 12-month findings in response to the Center's petitions.

NOTES

(1) Listing and agency discretion: Because the number of species that likely deserve listing far exceeds the resources available to evaluate them, listing agencies (FWS and NMFS) have long sought to set listing priorities free of outside scrutiny. Their oft-repeated argument has been that, given flexibility, they can attend to those species most at risk and to those whose protection might yield collateral benefits. Critics have feared that politics would wield a heavy hand: Given flexibility, agencies would avoid listing species (such as the spotted owl) that would engender political hostility. The record over the years has confirmed that listing agencies often give in to such pressure, at times drawing harsh criticism from reviewing courts. At the same time, the call for flexibility does have obvious merit.

(2) Candidate conservation agreements: Although the court in *Center for Biological Diversity v. Norton* does not mention the fact, the Petition Management Guidelines it struck down were part of a larger effort by the

FWS to gain flexibility in managing at-risk species. Once a species is listed, various restrictions and consequences (explored below) follow—as does, quite often, political criticism, particularly in the case of species located in whole or in part on private land. To avoid those consequences, the FWS has begun identifying particular species as "candidates" for listing. Species so designated become the subject of "candidate conservation agreements," worked out with various parties—other federal agencies, states, and private landowners—in an effort to protect the species so that listing becomes unnecessary. The Petition Management Guidelines at issue in the above case were part of that overall strategy: The FWS wanted the authority to delay acting on citizen petitions to list species designated as candidates so that it had time (and resources) to work out such agreements. As the court concludes, however, the ESA does not permit this flexibility, which is—like listing flexibility generally—subject to abuse. A qualified defense of the FWS approach is offered in Francesca Ortiz, *Candidate Conservation Agreements as a Devolutionary Response to Extinction*, 33 GEORGIA L. REV. 413 (1999).

(3) The "warranted but precluded" process: When the Secretary determines a petitioned action—most commonly a petition to list a species—is warranted but precluded, the Act requires him to treat the finding as though it were a new petition submitted on the date of the finding. *Id.* § 1533(b)(3)(C)(i). Thus, the Secretary is required to make annual findings on such species until the listing backlog is reduced or the status of the species changes. The Secretary is also required to "implement a system to monitor effectively the status of all species [listed as warranted but precluded] and shall make prompt use of the authority [to promulgate emergency regulations] to prevent a significant risk to the well being of such species." *Id.* § 1533(b)(3)(C)(iii). Emergency listing are discussed below.

Defenders of Wildlife v. Norton

Court of Appeals for the Ninth Circuit.
258 F.3d 1136 (2001).

■ BERZON, J.:—The Defenders of Wildlife ("Defenders") appeal from an order of the district court granting summary judgment in favor of the Secretary of the Interior (the "Secretary"). The order upheld a decision by the Secretary not to designate the flat-tailed horned lizard for protection as a threatened species under the Endangered Species Act ("ESA"). 16 U.S.C. § 1531 et seq. We find that, in making that decision, the Secretary both relied on an improper standard and failed to consider important factors relevant to the listing process. Accordingly, we find her decision arbitrary and capricious and reverse the district court's order.

I. Background

The Endangered Species Act protects species of fish, wildlife and plants which the Secretary identifies as either "endangered" or "threatened." A species is "endangered" if it "is in danger of extinction throughout all or a significant portion of its range." 16 U.S.C. § 1532(6). Similarly, a species is "threatened" if it "is likely to become an endangered species within the foreseeable future throughout all or a significant portion of its range." 16 U.S.C. § 1532(20).

If the Secretary decides that, based on "the best scientific and commercial data available," one or more of five statutorily defined factors demonstrates that a species is endangered or threatened, she must issue a proposed rule recommending that species for ESA protection. 16 U.S.C. § 1533(b)(1)(A). A period of public comment follows. Within one year, the Secretary must either publish a final rule designating the species for protection or, if she finds "that available evidence does not justify the action," withdraw the proposed rule. 50 C.F.R. § 424.17(a)(iii); *see also* 16 U.S.C. § 1533(b)(6)(A).[2]

A.   The Flat–Tailed Horned Lizard

At issue in this case is the flat-tailed horned lizard (*Phrynosoma mcallii*) (the "lizard"), "a small, cryptically colored iguanid" that has adapted to the harsh conditions of the western Sonoran desert. 58 Fed. Reg. 62,624, 62,625 (Nov. 29, 1993). "It has the typically flattened body shape of horned lizards, a dark mid-vertebral stripe, a somewhat flattened tail, relatively long head spines or horns, and two rows of fringed scales on each side of the body. Dorsally, the flat-tailed horned lizard is pale gray to light rusty brown; the animal's ventral surface is white and unmarked." *Id.*

The lizard's natural habitat stretches across parts of southern California (namely, Imperial and eastern San Diego counties), southwestern Arizona and northwestern Mexico. *Id.* at 62,626. Over the last century, human activity has markedly affected this habitat. The filling of the Salton Sea, the conversion of arid desert into productive agricultural land, and the development of urban areas around Yuma, Arizona and El Centro, California have resulted in the disappearance of approximately 34% of the lizard's historic range. *Id.* As a result, animal conservation groups, including Defenders, have expressed concerns about the lizard's continued viability, and the United States Fish and Wildlife Service ("FWS") had targeted the lizard for ESA protection for much of the past two decades. 62 Fed. Reg. 37,852, 37,854 (July 15, 1997).

B.   The Lizard's Listing History

The Secretary first identified the lizard as a category 2 candidate for listing under the ESA in 1982. Candidates are "any species being considered by the Secretary for listing as an endangered or threatened species, but not yet the subject of a proposed rule." 50 C.F.R. § 424.02(b). At that time,[3] FWS regulations defined candidates designated category 2 as "taxa for which information in the possession of the Service indicated that proposing to list as endangered or threatened was possibly appropriate, but for which sufficient data on biological vulnerability and threats were not

---

2. The Secretary may also delay a final decision for up to six months because of "substantial disagreement" in the scientific community regarding the "sufficiency or accuracy of the available data relevant to the determination or revision concerned." 16 U.S.C. § 1533(b)(6)(B)(i).

3. The FWS dropped the sub-categorization of candidates in 1996. 61 Fed.Reg. 7596, 7597–98 (Feb. 28, 1996).

currently available to support proposed rules." 61 Fed.Reg. 7596, 7597 (Feb. 28, 1996).

The lizard remained a category 2 candidate until 1989, when the Secretary elevated it to category 1 status. Category 1 included species "for which the Service has on file sufficient information on biological vulnerability and threat(s) to support issuance of a proposed rule." *Id.* It was not until November 29, 1993, however, that the Secretary finally published a proposed rule listing the lizard as a threatened species. 58 Fed. Reg. at 62,624. Pursuant to the statutory requirements, the Secretary should have completed her review of the lizard and issued her final order by November 29, 1994. 16 U.S.C. § 1533(b)(6)(A)(i) (requiring action within one year of publication of the proposed rule). That day passed, however, without further action by the Secretary.

The passage of Public Law No. 104–6, 109 Stat. 73 (1995), in April 1995 interrupted progress on the lizard and other species awaiting listing decisions [by imposing a moratorium on making final listing decisions]. . . .

The moratorium remained in effect until April 26, 1996, when President Clinton signed an executive waiver allowing the Secretary to once again list species for protection. Another year passed, however, without a final decision on the lizard. Finally, on May 16, 1997, in response to a lawsuit brought by Defenders to compel action on the lizard, the district court in Arizona ordered the Secretary to issue a final decision within 60 days.

One month after the court's order, a group of federal and state agencies signed a Conservation Agreement ("CA") implementing a recently completed rangewide management strategy to protect the lizard, developed by representatives of the Federal Bureau of Land Management ("BLM"), the FWS, and state and local agencies. Pursuant to the CA, cooperating parties agreed to take voluntary steps aimed at "reducing threats to the species, stabilizing the species' populations, and maintaining its ecosystem." The underlying management strategy was based on an earlier effort by the BLM and the California Department of Fish and Game to provide protections for the lizard after it had been elevated to category 1 candidate status by the FWS in 1989.

Critical to the implementation of the CA was the designation of five "management areas" (MAs) subject to protective measures, including the monitoring of lizard populations, limitation of habitat disturbance including off-highway vehicle use, and acquisition of private inholdings. Some of the measures included in the CA had been in place for years, long before the Secretary published the initial proposed rule recommending the lizard for protection. Many of the actions and the overall scope of the MAs effected by the conservation effort, however, were new.

The Secretary issued her final decision on July 15, 1997 (the "Notice") withdrawing the proposed rule that had earlier recommended the lizard for listing as a threatened species. The Notice was premised on three factors: (1) that population trend data did not conclusively demonstrate significant population declines; (2) that some of the threats to the lizard's habitat had grown less serious since the proposed rule was issued; and (3) that the recently devised "conservation agreement w[ould] ensure further reductions in threats." 62 Fed. Reg. 37852. The Secretary's ultimate conclusion also turned on her determination that, however serious the threats to the lizard on private land, "[l]arge blocks of habitat with few anticipated impacts exist on public lands throughout the range of this species...." 62 Fed. Reg. 37860. The Secretary did not, however, separately consider whether the lizard is or will become extinct in "a significant portion of its range," as that term is used in the statute.

Six months after the Secretary withdrew the proposed rule, Defenders filed the instant suit challenging that decision....

II. Analysis

Defenders claims that "the best scientific evidence" available on the lizard and its habitat demonstrates the presence of as many as four of the five statutory factors indicating that a species is either threatened or endangered and thus eligible for ESA protection. The Secretary's answer to this claim is twofold: First, although the Secretary does not dispute that these factors may evidence threats to the lizard on *private land,* she contends that adequate habitat exists on *public land* to ensure the species' viability. Second, the Secretary relies on the newly introduced Conservation Agreement, which she contends will establish added protections for the lizard's public land habitat and thus remove the threat of extinction throughout all or a significant portion of its range in the foreseeable future. Both parts of this analysis, we conclude, are faulty.

A.   "Extinction throughout ... a significant portion of its range"

The distinction between public and private land explains much of the dispute between the Secretary and Defenders. Defenders' arguments in support of its claim that listing is warranted focus primarily on the loss of lizard habitat on *private* land. The Secretary, on the other hand, emphasizes the conservation efforts on *public* land to support her conclusion that the lizard is not threatened with extinction. 62 Fed. Reg. at 37,858 ("Because of the large amount of flat-tailed horned lizard habitat located on *public lands* within the United States and the reduction of threats on *these lands* due to changing land-use patterns and conservation efforts of public agencies, threats due to habitat modification and loss do not warrant listing of the species at this time." (Emphasis added)). The distinction also explains, in large part, the shift between the Secretary's initial findings that accompanied the proposed rule, recommending the lizard for protection based on concern about habitat loss on private land, and her findings that accompanied the withdrawal decision, emphasizing that available public lands are sufficient to support the species.

Whether the lizard's potential survival in its public land habitat is sufficient to preclude ESA protection depends largely on the meaning of the phrase "in danger of extinction *throughout ... a significant portion of its range.*" 16 U.S.C. § 1532(6) (emphasis added). Assuming the lizard's population remains viable on public land, it is not in danger of extinction throughout *all* its range. Defenders argue, however, that if the lizard's private land habitat constitutes "a significant portion of its range" and its survival there, as Defenders allege, is in jeopardy, the ESA requires the Secretary to designate the lizard for protection.

Standing alone, the phrase "in danger of extinction throughout ... a significant portion of its range" is puzzling. According to the Oxford English Dictionary, "extinct" means "has died out or come to an end.... Of a family, class of persons, a race of species of animals or plants: Having no living representative." Thus, the phrase "extinc[t] throughout ... a significant portion of its range" is something of an oxymoron. Similarly, to speak of a species that is "in danger of extinction" throughout "a significant portion of its range" may seem internally inconsistent, since "extinction" suggests total rather than partial disappearance. The statute is therefore inherently ambiguous, as it appears to use language in a manner in some tension with ordinary usage.

1.   *The Secretary's Explanation*

The Secretary's explanation of this odd phraseology is of no assistance in puzzling out the meaning of the phrase, since her interpretation simply cannot be squared with the statute's language and structure. The Secretary in her brief interprets the enigmatic phrase to mean that a species is eligible for protection under the ESA if it "faces threats in enough key portions of its range that the *entire species* is in danger of extinction, or will be within the foreseeable future." She therefore assumes that a species is in danger of extinction in "a significant portion of its range" only if it is in danger of extinction everywhere.[7]

If, however, the effect of extinction throughout "a significant portion of its range" is the threat of extinction everywhere, then the threat of extinction throughout "a significant portion of its range" is equivalent to the threat of extinction throughout *all* its range. Because the statute already defines "endangered species" as those that are "in danger of extinction throughout all ... of [their] range," the Secretary's interpretation of "a significant portion of its range" has the effect of rendering the phrase superfluous.

Such a redundant reading of a significant statutory phrase is unacceptable. When interpreting a statute, we must follow a "natural reading ... , which would give effect to *all* of [the statute's] provisions." *United Food & Commercial Workers Union Local 751 v. Brown Group, Inc.,* 517 U.S. 544, 549 (1996) (emphasis added). By reading "all" and "a significant portion of its range" as functional equivalents, the Secretary's construction violates that rule.

The Secretary tries to distinguish her definition of a species in danger "throughout ... a significant portion of its range" from a species in danger "throughout all" its range by noting Congress' expressed commitment to long-term conservation and its hope that the ESA would protect species well before they reached the brink of extinction. The extension of ESA protections to a species in danger "throughout ... a significant portion of

---

7. As we explain later, the Secretary has at other times applied the statute incon-   sistently with her current interpretation.

its range," the Secretary asserts, offers protection to species not yet faced with imminent extinction and therefore reflects the incremental approach Congress intended the ESA to provide. But this function too is fulfilled elsewhere in the statute.

As noted, the ESA provides protection to both "endangered species" and "threatened species." While an "endangered species" is a species "in danger of extinction throughout all or a significant portion of its range," 16 U.S.C. § 1532(6), "threatened species" include those "which [are] likely to become . . . endangered species within the foreseeable future throughout all or a significant portion of [their] range." 16 U.S.C. § 1532(20). The Secretary's interpretation thus conflates the distinct ESA protections for species facing extinction throughout "all" and throughout "a significant portion" of their range with the separate protections for "threatened" and for "endangered species." As such, the Secretary's construction once again views the statute as saying the same thing twice.

This understanding of the statutory language not only clashes with the rule against surplusage we have already discussed, but also runs up against the statute's legislative history. . . .

2.   Defenders' Explanation

Defenders' interpretation of the phrase "extinction throughout . . . a significant portion of its range" is similarly unsatisfactory. Defenders takes a more quantitative approach to the phrase, arguing that the projected loss of 82% of the lizard's habitat in this case constitutes "a substantial portion of its range." Appellants then cite to other cases in which courts found listing of species warranted after the loss of even smaller amounts of habitat. *Federation of Fly Fishers v. Daley,* 131 F. Supp. 2d 1158 (N.D.Cal. 2000) (finding listing of the steelhead trout warranted despite protections covering 64% of its range); *ONRC v. Daley,* 6 F. Supp. 2d 1139, 1157 (D.Or.1998) (finding the coho salmon in danger of extinction despite federal forest land protections extending over 35% of its range); 45 Fed. Reg. 63,812, 63,817–18 (Sept. 25, 1980) (listing the Coachella Valley fringe-toed lizard as a threatened species although 50% of its historical habitat remained).

There are two problems with Defenders' quantitative approach. First, it simply does not make sense to assume that the loss of a predetermined percentage of habitat or range would necessarily qualify a species for listing. A species with an exceptionally large historical range may continue to enjoy healthy population levels despite the loss of a substantial amount of suitable habitat. . . .

In the absence of a fixed percentage, Defenders' suggested interpretation of the phrase begins to look a lot like the faulty definition offered by the Secretary, *i.e.,* "a substantial portion of its range" means an amount of habitat loss such that total extinction is likely in the near future. As noted above, this reading does not comport with the other terms of the statute.

3.   Insight from the Legislative History

The legislative history of the ESA suggests an entirely different meaning of the inherently ambiguous phrase "extinction throughout . . . a significant portion of its range." [The court examined the legislative history, noting in particular the following statement by Senator Tunney in 1973:]

> An animal might be "endangered" in most States but overpopulated in some. In a State in which a species is overpopulated, the Secretary would have the discretion to list that animal as merely threatened or to remove it from the endangered species listing entirely while still providing protection in areas where it was threatened with extinction. In that portion of its range where it was not threatened with extinction, the States would have full authority to use their management skills to insure the proper conservation of the species.

. . .

The historical application of the Act is consistent with this interpretation of the statute, not with the interpretation suggested by the Secretary in her briefs in this case. Grizzly bears, for example, are listed as threatened species within the contiguous 48 states, but not in Alaska. Similarly, only the California, Oregon and Washington populations of the marbled murrelet, whose range in North America extends from the Aleutian Archipelago in Alaska to Central California, are listed as threatened. 57 Fed. Reg. 45,328 (Oct. 1, 1992) [other examples omitted].[10]

We conclude, consistently with the Secretary's historical practice, that a species can be extinct "throughout . . . a significant portion of its range" if there are major geographical areas in which it is no longer viable but once was. Those areas need not coincide with national or state political boundaries, although they can. The Secretary necessarily has a wide degree of discretion in delineating "a significant portion of its range," since the term is not defined in the statute. But where, as here, it is on the record apparent that the area in which the lizard is expected to survive is much smaller than its historical range, the Secretary must at least explain her conclusion that the area in which the species can no longer live is not a "significant portion of its range." *Asarco, Inc. v. EPA*, 616 F.2d 1153, 1159 (9th Cir.1980) ("A satisfactory explanation of agency action is essential for adequate judicial review, because the focus of judicial review is not on the wisdom of the agency's decision, but on whether the process employed by the agency to reach its decision took into consideration all the relevant factors.").

4.   *Application to This Case*

As noted, the Secretary did not, in her Notice, expressly consider the "extinction throughout . . . a significant portion of its range" issue at all. Had she applied the flexible standard we have adopted to the instant case,

---

10.   The text of the ESA and its subsequent application seems to have been guided by the following maxim:

> There seems to be a tacit assumption that if grizzlies survive in Canada and Alaska, that is good enough. It is not good enough for me. . . . Relegating grizzlies to Alaska is about like relegating happiness to heaven; one may never get there.

ALDO LEOPOLD, A SAND COUNTY ALMANAC 277 (1966).

she might have determined that the lizard is indeed in danger of "extinction throughout ... a significant portion of its range."

First, the habitat on private land may constitute "a significant portion of its range" demanding enhanced protections not required on public lands; alternatively, the inverse may be true. Second, and perhaps more persuasively given this interpretation of the statute, the lizard may face unique threats in either California or Arizona, or in major subportions of either state. Notably, the California Department of Fish and Game initially declined to sign the Conservation Agreement relied upon by the Secretary, suggesting perhaps that the lizard's habitat in the two states may require different degrees of protection.

The Secretary does not address at all in the Notice whether, on either of these bases, the lizard was "extinc[t] throughout ... a significant portion of its range." This omission with respect to a significant legal issue raised by the factual circumstances would itself be a sufficient basis for remanding the case to the Secretary to consider the question....

Nor did the Secretary address the lizard's viability in a site-specific manner with regard to the putative benefits of the CA. Although the Notice asserts that "MAs have been designated in the" five areas identified in the CA, [ ], there is evidence that, in at least three of those areas, the designation process was either incomplete or wholly unstarted at the time the Notice was issued. *See* 63 Fed. Reg. 16272; 63 Fed. Reg. 66561, 66561–62. Nowhere does the Secretary account for the effects of failure to implement the CA immediately in those areas where delay was expected. Thus, it is unclear how the benefits assertedly flowing from the CA affected any particular portion of the lizard's habitats, and accordingly unclear how the CA could have mitigated threats to the lizard throughout "a significant portion of its range." We therefore conclude that the Secretary's decision to withdraw the proposed rule designating the lizard as protected cannot be enforced on the basis of the Notice.

III.   Conclusion

For the foregoing reasons, we conclude that the Secretary's decision to withdraw the proposed rule recommending the lizard for ESA protection was arbitrary and capricious.

NOTES

(1) Avoiding private lands: Underlying the conduct of the FWS in the case is a worry about imposing restrictions on private land—a consequence that would follow if the species were listed and it inhabited private land. However politically wise such action might be, is it consistent with the letter and spirit of the ESA? Even if it is not, might it help further the aims of the Act by muting criticism of it? Is it legitimate for the FWS to consider that possibility?

(2) "Endangered" revisited: *Defenders of Wildlife v. Norton* interprets "endangered" in a way that could materially alter implementation of the ESA. The court suggests that a species is endangered when it is absent or in danger of disappearing from significant portions of its original range, even if it flourishes elsewhere. How would such a definition apply to, for instance, the bison or elk, which once inhabited the Midwest? Would the FWS be obligated to list such animals if a citizen petitioned for it? What values would be served by such listings if populations introduced there were not isolated from the numerous populations present elsewhere? In interpreting "endangered," did the court give inadequate weight to the power of the FWS to list distinct population segments of vertebrates?

(3) Promises of future action: The fish and wildlife agencies have increasingly based decisions not to list species on claims that another governmental entity will take steps to protect the species. In *Biodiversity Legal Foundation v. Babbitt,* 943 F.Supp. 23 (D.D.C.1996), FWS asserted that listing the Alexander Archipelago wolf was not warranted because "we believe that the Forest Service's TLMP [Tongass Land Management Plan] revision process together with subsequent implementation of the revised TLMP will provide sufficient opportunity to reverse the declining population trend which we believe would occur under continued implementation of the current TLMP." The court remanded the decision, noting "the Secretary ... cannot use promises of proposed future actions as an excuse for not making a determination based on the existing record." *Id.* at 26.

In *Oregon Natural Resources Council v. Daley,* 6 F.Supp.2d 1139 (D.Or.1998), plaintiffs challenged a decision by NMFS not to list an evolutionary significant unit (ESU) of coho salmon as threatened. A biological review led to the conclusion that listing was warranted. While a proposal to list was pending, however, Oregon adopted the Oregon Coastal Salmon Restoration Initiative, a mixture of conservation measures—many voluntary—designed to improve coho salmon habitat. The Initiative included a pledge by the state Department of Forestry to develop "proposals" to improve timber harvesting practices in the state. The state's planned actions were set forth in a Memorandum of Understanding, which the state reserved the right to terminate upon 30 days' notice. In response, the NMFS decided not to list the ESU on the ground that it was not likely to become endangered during the estimated two-year implementation period for the habitat-protection measures. The court overturned this decision, holding that (i) NFMS used the wrong listing standard by failing to determine whether the ESU was likely to become endangered "during the foreseeable future" (at least 30 years, rather than the 2–year time horizon actually used); and (ii) the NFMS improperly considered promises of future conservation measures as well as voluntary measures; instead, the court held, the agency should have considered only measures that were "currently operational" and legally binding. Although NFMS did properly consider the conservation benefits of the binding Northwest Forest Plan, that plan only applied to 35% of the salmon habitat and was not sufficient to protect the salmon. NMFS' refusal to list was therefore arbitrary and capricious. *See also Federation of Fly Fishers v. Daley,* 131 F.Supp.2d 1158 (N.D.Cal. 2000); *Save Our Springs Legal Defense Fund, Inc. v. Babbitt,* 27 F.Supp.2d 739 (W.D.Tex.1997); *Friends of Wild Swan, Inc. v. U.S. Fish & Wildlife Service,* 945 F.Supp. 1388 (D.Or.1996); *Southwest Center for Biological Diversity v. Babbitt,* 939 F.Supp. 49 (D.D.C.1996), *rev'd on other grounds,* 215 F.3d 58 (D.C.Cir.2000).

(4) Reviewing listing decisions: Listing decisions often lead to judicial challenges. Consider three recent decisions:

(a) *Defenders of Wildlife v. Babbitt*: Plaintiffs challenged the refusal of FWS to list the Canada lynx as either threatened or endangered. The district court set aside the agency action because it used the wrong standard: the FWS required "conclusive evidence" of danger, when the statute clearly obligated the agency to act based on the "best available" evidence, and to do so even when that evidence was incomplete. The court also overturned, as arbitrary and capricious, numerous factual findings made by the agency, including: that hunting and trapping posed no current threat; that the lynx currently occupied much of its historic range; and that the decline in overall population had been reversed. These findings were all "contradicted by overwhelming record evidence." *Defenders of Wildlife v. Babbitt*, 958 F.Supp. 670 (D.D.C.1997).

(b) *Southwest Center for Biological Diversity v. Babbitt*: Plaintiff brought suit against FWS for failing to list the Queen Charlotte goshawk, a large, elusive subspecies. The agency concluded that available data on the goshawk did not warrant a finding that it was threatened. To resolve the factual dispute, the district court ordered FWS to conduct a field count of the goshawk population. The circuit court reversed, holding that the district court had exceeded its authority. Under § 4 of the ESA, FWS is to make its determination based on "the best scientific and commercial data available"; the court cannot order the agency to perform additional scientific studies, particular when they are not requested by the plaintiff. *Southwest Center for Biological Diversity v. Babbitt*, 215 F.3d 58 (D.C.Cir.2000).

(c) *San Luis & Delta–Mendota Water Authority v. Badgley*: FWS acted improperly in listing Sacramento splittail fish as threatened species when it failed to take into account substantial scientific data on the fish before making its decision, even though the data were "submitted at the close of the third comment period and less than two weeks prior to the judicially-imposed deadline for USFWS to publish its listing decision." *San Luis & Delta–Mendota Water Authority v. Badgley*, 136 F.Supp.2d 1136 (E.D.Cal.2000).

(5) Emergency listings: Among the powers delegated to the Secretary in 1973, was the explicit authority to promulgate regulations that were immediately effective if she determined that there was "an emergency posing a significant risk to the well-being of any species." 16 U.S.C. § 1533(b)(7). Congress has subsequently amended the provision to reflect changes in the listing process—for example, doubling the original 120–day life of emergency regulations and requiring the Secretary to withdraw an emergency listing if he determined, "on the basis of the best scientific and commercial data available to him, that substantial evidence does not exist to warrant such regulation." *Id.* When it added the "warranted but precluded" category to the Act in 1987, Congress also required the Secretary to implement a system to monitor the status of species determined to be "warranted but precluded" and to "make prompt use" of the emergency listing authority "to prevent significant risk to the well being" of such species. *Id.* § 1533(b)(3)(C)(iii).

(6) Noncompliance with procedural requirements as a basis for invalidating a decision to list a species: In 1985, FWS proposed to list the Bruneau Hot Springsnail as endangered by a loss of habitat caused by irrigation withdrawals from groundwater. As a result of intense political pressure, FWS delayed reaching a final decision of listing until 1993; in reaching the decision, FWS made several procedural errors. Despite these errors, the Ninth Circuit Court of Appeals upheld the action. Under the Act, the Secretary has one year within which to reach a decision following publication of a proposed listing rule; this may be extended by six months if there is substantial disagreement regarding the existing data. 16 U.S.C. § 1533(b)(6)(A)(i)(I)-(IV). The Secretary's seven-year delay, however, did not void the listing because the time limits did not divest the Secretary of power to act: "As in *Brock* [*v. Pierce County,* 476 U.S. 253 (1986)], the time requirements are designed to be an impetus to act rather than a prohibition on action taken after the time expires." *Idaho Farm Bureau Federation v. Babbitt,* 58 F.3d 1392, 1401 (9th Cir.1995). The Ninth Circuit also held that the agency's procedural errors did not render the listing void.

The District Court for the District of Columbia reached similar conclusions in a case involving the listing of the California gnatcatcher as a threatened species. *See Endangered Species Committee of the Building Industry Association v. Babbitt,* 852 F.Supp. 32 (D.D.C.1994).

(7) Listing determinations and NEPA: NEPA requires an evaluation of the "environmental impacts of proposed actions" by federal agencies that will "significantly affect[] the quality of the human environment." 42 U.S.C. § 4332(1)(C). Is the Secretary required to prepare an EIS as part of the listing determination? In *Pacific Legal Foundation v. Andrus,* 657 F.2d 829 (6th Cir.1981), the court concluded that an EIS was not required because the decisions were insufficiently discretionary: "The Secretary is required to list whether any species is endangered or threatened based on the give factors listed in ESA. The Secretary does not have the discretion to consider the five factors required to be considered in filing an impact statement." *Id.* at 835. *See also Glover River Organization v. Department of the Interior,* 675 F.2d 251 (10th Cir.1982).

b.   Critical Habitat Designations

NOTES

(1) The evolution of "critical habitat": Section 7 of the 1973 Act contained a simple statement:

> All ... Federal ... agencies shall ... insure that actions authorized, funded, or carried out by them do not ... result in the destruction or modification of habitat ... determined by the Secretary ... to be critical.

Endangered Species Act of 1973, Pub. L. No. 93–205, § 7, 87 Stat. 884, 892. The Act did not, however, provide either procedural or substantive requirements beyond those implicit in the terms "determine" and "critical." When the Supreme Court in *TVA v. Hill* highlighted the importance of "habitat ... determined ... to be critical," Congress responded in 1978 by adding both substantive and procedural elements. The 1978 Amendments defined the term for the first time and crafted both substantive and procedural requirements for designating critical habitat. The most significant procedural requirement was the mandate that the Secretary, "to the maximum extent prudent," designate critical habitat concurrently with listing a species.

By 1982, it had become apparent that the linkage between listing determinations and habitat designations was too rigid and Congress again amended the provisions, this time loosening the linkage: habitat was to be designated concurrently with listing only "to the maximum extent prudent and *determinable.*" The conference report on the bill stated that the inclusion of the term "determinable" was intended to require the Secretary to designate habitat except when it was either not prudent or when the information was lacking. H.R. CONF. REP. No. 835, 97th Cong., 2d Sess. 19–20 (1982), *reprinted in* 1982 U.S.C.C.A.N. 2860, 2860–61. Thus, although the Amendments tempered the linkage, they did not sever the connection—and, indeed, Congress twice stated that it intended the Secretary generally to designate a species critical habitat "concurrently with making a determination . . . that a species is an endangered . . . or a threatened species." 16 U.S.C. §§ 1533(a)(3), 1533(a)(3)(A).

(2) The critical habitat designation process: As noted, the Secretary generally is to designate a species' critical habitat concurrently with the determination that a species is either endangered or threatened. 16 U.S.C. §§ 1533(a)(3), (b)(6)(C). In the first statement of the obligation, the ESA requires the Secretary to designate critical habitat concurrently with the listing determination "to the maximum extent prudent and determinable." *Id.* § 1533(a)(3). The second iteration of the requirement (later in the same section) focuses more exclusively on timing: a final habitat designation regulation must be published concurrently with the final listing regulation unless "it is essential to the conservation of such species that the regulation implementing [the listing] determination be promptly published" or "critical habitat of such species is not then determinable." *Id.* § 1533(b)(6)(C). If habitat is not determinable at the time of listing, the Secretary is required to continue to collect information and, by the end of a one-year period, to publish a final regulation "designating, to the maximum extent prudent, such habitat." *Id.* § 1533(b)(6)(C)(ii).

The Act thus envisions four possible situations:

1. most commonly, habitat is to be designated at the time a species is listed. *Id.* §§ 1533(a)(3), (b)(6)(C).

2. the listing determination and the habitat designation decisions may be separated when there is a conservation-based need to list the species before the habitat designation has been completed. *Id.* § 1533(b)(6)(C)(i).

3. the Secretary may delay the designation when the habitat is not determinable because of a lack of information. *Id.* § 1533(b)(6)(C)(ii). When the Secretary decides that the habitat is not then determinable, he may extend the decisionmaking period for an additional year. The Secretary is required, however, to

publish a final designation within two years of the publication of the general notice on listing "based on such data as may be available at that time." *Id.* § 1533(b)(6)(C)(ii).

4. the final situation is the only one in which the Secretary was not required to designate critical habitat. When it was not "prudent" to designate habitat—that is, when it would not be beneficial to the species—the Act excuses the Secretary from doing so. *Id.* The wildlife agencies had previously interpreted the term "prudent" to apply to two situations: (1) when designation would lead to increased illegal taking of the species by informing potential takers of the species' location, and (2) when designation "would not be beneficial to the species." *See* 45 *Fed. Reg.* 13,010, 13,023 (1980) (codified as amended at 50 C.F.R. § 424.12(a)). When Congress amended the Act's critical habitat provisions in 1982, it noted this definition with approval.

Habitat designation is to be made "on the basis of the best scientific data available and after taking into consideration the economic impact, and any other relevant impact, of specifying any particular area as critical habitat." *Id.* § 1533(b)(2). The Secretary is required to publish the critical habitat designation as a rule, *id.* § 1533(b)(6)(C), and to include "a summary ... of the data on which such regulation is based and [to] show the relationship of such data to such regulation." *Id.* § 1533(b)(8).

A much-cited and still useful study of critical habitat designations is Katherine Simmons Yagerman, *Protecting Critical Habitat under the Federal Endangered Species Act*, 20 ENVTL. L. 811 (1990). More recent studies include Thomas F. Darin, *Designating Critical Habitat Under the Endangered Species Act: Habitat Protection Versus Agency Discretion*, 24 HARV. ENVTL. L. REV. 209 (2000); Jack McDonald, *Critical Habitat Designation Under the Endangered Species Act: A Road to Recovery?*, 28 ENVTL. L. 671 (1998).

New Mexico Cattle Growers Association v. U.S. Fish & Wildlife Service

Court of Appeals for the Tenth Circuit.
248 F.3d 1277 (2001).

■ TACHA, C.J.:—The New Mexico Cattle Growers Association, New Mexico Farm & Livestock Bureau, New Mexico Wool Growers, Inc., New Mexico Wheat Growers Association, New Mexico Public Lands Council, Albuquerque Production Credit Association, Coalition of Arizona/New Mexico Counties for Stable Economic Growth, and Hidalgo County Cattle Growers Association (collectively "Appellants") all represent, in some fashion, elements of New Mexico's agricultural industry. Appellants appeal an order of the district court dismissing their suit against Appellee U.S. Fish & Wildlife Service ("FWS"). We exercise jurisdiction pursuant to the Administration Procedures Act ("APA"), [ ], and reverse.

I

The Southwestern Willow Flycatcher ("flycatcher"), *empidonax traillii extimus,* is one of four sub-species of the willow flycatcher, a small bird that nests in riparian areas along river beds. On July 23, 1993, the FWS published its "Proposed Rule to List the Southwestern Willow Flycatcher as Endangered With Critical Habitat." 58 Fed. Reg. 39495. On February 27, 1995, the FWS issued its "Final Rule Determining Endangered Status for the Southwestern Willow Flycatcher." 60 Fed. Reg. 10694. The Final Rule listed the flycatcher as endangered, but deferred the critical habitat designation ("CHD") in order to gather more information. However, the FWS did not, on its own initiative, move forward with the CHD for the flycatcher.

On March 20, 1997, the U.S. District Court for the District of Arizona, in the case *Southwest Ctr. for Biological Diversity v. Babbitt,* Civ. No. 96–1874–PHX–RGS (D. Ariz. March 20, 1997), ordered the FWS to complete the CHD for the flycatcher within 120 days. Pursuant to the court order, the FWS issued its CHD for the flycatcher on July 22, 1997. At that time, the known population of the flycatcher was between 300 and 500 nesting pairs spread across seven states and parts of Mexico. The CHD designated eighteen critical habitat units, including four in New Mexico, totaling 599 miles of stream and river beds.

The Endangered Species Act ("ESA"), which controls CHDs, requires the FWS to perform an economic analysis of the effects of the CHD before making a final designation. 16 U.S.C. § 1533(b)(2). In order to determine what the "economic impact" of a CHD will be, the FWS has adopted an incremental baseline approach (the "baseline approach"). The baseline approach utilized by the FWS is premised on the idea that the listing of the species (which will occur prior to or simultaneously with the CHD) will have economic impacts that are not to be considered. The primary statutory rationale for this position comes from 16 U.S.C. § 1533(b)(1)(A), which states that listing determinations be made "solely on the basis of the best scientific and commercial data available." Thus, the baseline approach moves any economic impact that can be attributed to listing below the baseline and, when making the CHD, takes into account only those economic impacts rising above the baseline. Using the baseline approach, the FWS determined that the flycatcher CHD resulted in no economic impact, stating that "[c]ritical habitat designation will ... result in no additional protection for the flycatcher nor have any additional economic effects beyond those that may have been caused by listing and by other statutes." Division of Economics, U.S. Fish & Wildlife Service, *Economic Analysis of Critical Habitat Designation for the Southwestern Flycatcher,* S3 (1997).

The appellants filed suit in district court in March 1998, challenging the flycatcher designation and alleging that the FWS had violated various provisions of both the ESA and the National Environmental Protection Act ("NEPA")....

. . .

[T]he appellants make the following arguments on appeal: (1) that the FWS's adoption of the baseline approach to measuring the economic impact of the flycatcher CHD is an erroneous construction and, thus, a violation of the ESA; (2) ... ; (3) that the FWS misapplied the critical habitat definition set forth in the ESA; (4) ... ; (5) that the FWS failed to address adequate alternatives to the CHD pursuant to NEPA; and (6) that the FWS, in making the flycatcher CHD, failed to properly cooperate with state and local agencies as required by NEPA. Because we rule in favor of the appellants on the first issue raised by holding that the baseline approach to economic impact analysis is not permitted by the ESA, thus setting aside the flycatcher CHD, we need not address any of the other issues raised.

II

This case is before us on review pursuant to the APA. Our standard of review of the lower court's decision in an APA case is de novo. [ ]

Normally, when the agency decision at issue involves interpretations of federal statutes, we owe deference to that decision as set forth in *Chevron, U.S.A., Inc. v. Natural Resources Def. Council, Inc.*, 467 U.S. 837, 842–43 (1984). Indeed, the district court in this case, applying *Chevron* deference to the FWS's use of the baseline approach, did not find it to be a violation of the ESA. The appellants, however, argue that *Chevron* deference is not applicable in this case. We agree.

The FWS concedes, in fact, that *Chevron* deference is not due the FWS's use of the baseline approach in making CHDs. Because the statutory interpretation resulting in the baseline approach has never undergone the formal rulemaking process, it remains an informal interpretation not entitled to deference. *Hunnicutt v. Hawk*, 229 F.3d 997, 1000 (10th Cir. 2000).... Instead, we simply ask if the agency's interpretation is "well reasoned" and has the "power to persuade." *Fristoe v. Thompson*, 144 F.3d 627, 631 (10th Cir.1998)....

III

. . .

The process set forth in the ESA for the protection of endangered and threatened species and the conservation of their ecosystem begins by granting the Secretary of the Interior, through the FWS, authority to list species in need of protection as either endangered or threatened. *Id.* § 1533(a). The ESA enumerates the factors to be considered by the agency when making a listing decision, including "the present or threatened destruction, modification, or curtailment of its habitat or range." *Id.* § 1533(a)(1). Further, the ESA specifically requires that the listing determination be based "solely on the basis of the best scientific and commercial data available." *Id.* § 1533(b)(1)(A). Thus, economic analysis is not a factor in the listing determination. Once a species is listed, all federal agencies are required to consult with the FWS to "insure that any action authorized, funded, or carried out by such agency ... is not likely to jeopardize the continued existence of any endangered species or threatened species." *Id.* § 1536(a)(2).

In addition to the protections afforded listed species by the ESA, the Act requires the agency to designate "critical habitat" for all listed species, to the extent determinable. *Id.* § 1533(a)(3). Critical habitat is defined as:

> (i) the specific areas within the geographic area occupied by the species, at the time it is listed ... on which are found those physical or biological features (I) essential to the conservation of the species and (II) which may require special management considerations or protection; and (ii) specific areas outside the geographic area occupied by the species at the time it is listed ... upon a determination by the Secretary that such areas are essential for the conservation of the species.

Id. § 1532(5)(A). Thus, the CHD may include specific areas found both inside of and outside of the geographic area occupied by the species.

The CHD is required to be based on "the best scientific data available" considering "the economic impact, and any other relevant impact, of specifying any particular area as critical habitat." *Id.* § 1533(b)(2). The agency "may exclude" a particular area from the CHD if the agency determines that "the benefits of such exclusion outweigh the benefits of specifying such area as part of the critical habitat, unless ... the failure to designate such area ... will result in the extinction of the species concerned." *Id.* § 1533(b)(2). Once critical habitat is designated, federal agencies must consult with the FWS to "insure that any action authorized, funded, or carried out by such agency ... is not likely to ... result in the destruction or adverse modification of [designated critical] habitat." *Id.* § 1536(a)(2). Thus, agency action that is prohibited is both (1) action that is likely to jeopardize the existence of a listed species and (2) action that is likely to result in the adverse modification of any area within a CHD.

The crux of the statutory dispute is in determining the meaning of "economic impact" in 16 U.S.C. § 1533(b)(2). The baseline approach adopted by the FWS utilizes a "but for" method for determining what economic impacts flow from the CHD. Thus, unless an economic impact would not result but for the CHD, that impact is attributable to a different cause (typically listing) and is not an "economic impact ... of specifying any particular area as critical habitat." Conversely, the approach advocated by the appellants would take into account all of the economic impact of the CHD, regardless of whether those impacts are caused co-extensively by any other agency action (such as listing) and even if those impacts would remain in the absence of the CHD. The issue presented is a question of first impression in this circuit and, to our knowledge, has not been decided by any of our sister circuits.

The root of the problem lies in the FWS's long held policy position that CHDs are unhelpful, duplicative, and unnecessary. Between April 1996 and July 1999, more than 250 species had been listed pursuant to the ESA, yet CHDs had been made for only two. S. Rep. No. 106–126, at 2 (1999). Further, while we have held that making a CHD is mandatory once a species is listed, *Forest Guardians v. Babbitt,* 174 F.3d 1178, 1186 (10th Cir.1999), the FWS has typically put off doing so until forced to do so by court order. S. Rep. No. 106–126, at 2 (1999).

In turn, the policy position of the FWS finds its root in the regulations promulgated by the FWS in 1986 defining the meaning of both the "jeopardy standard" (applied in the context of listing) and the "adverse modification standard" (applied in the context of designated critical habitat). Action violating the jeopardy standard is action reasonably expected "to reduce appreciably the likelihood of both the survival and recovery of a listed species." 50 C.F.R. § 402.02. Action violating the adverse modification standard is action "that appreciably diminishes the value of critical habitat for both the survival and recovery of a listed species." *Id.* Thus, the standards are defined as virtually identical, or, if not identical, one (adverse modification) is subsumed by the other (jeopardy). *See Am. Rivers v. Nat'l Marine Fisheries Serv.*, 1999 U.S. App. LEXIS 3860 *5 (9th Cir. Jan. 11, 1999) (agreeing with the agency that " 'jeopardy' and 'critical habitat' . . . are 'closely related,' and [thus] the jeopardy discussion properly 'encompasses' the critical habitat analysis"). While these regulatory definitions are not before us today, they have been the cause of much confusion in that they inform the FWS's interpretation of the ESA's economic impact language.[11]

Consistent with its long standing position, the FWS argues in the instant case that the impacts of the flycatcher listing and the flycatcher CHD are co-extensive. The FWS stated in its economic analysis that, because all actions "that result in adverse modification of critical habitat will also result in a jeopardy decision, designation of critical habitat for the flycatcher is not expected to result in any incremental restrictions on agency activities." Division of Economics, U.S. Fish & Wildlife Service, *Economic Analysis of Critical Habitat Designation for the Southwestern Flycatcher,* S3 (1997). The CHD itself states that "[c]ommon to both [the jeopardy standard and the adverse modification standard] is an appreciable detrimental effect on both survival and recovery of a listed species," and thus "actions satisfying the standard for adverse modification are nearly always found to also jeopardize the species concerned, and the existence of a critical habitat designation does not materially affect the outcome of consultation." 60 Fed. Reg. 39,131 (July 22, 1997). Moreover, the FWS continues to assert that agency action that is "likely to adversely modify critical habitat but not to jeopardize the species for which it is designated are extremely rare historically, and none have been issued in recent years." Appellee's Brief at 31.

However, as we have previously said, the fact that the FWS says that no real impact flows from the CHD does not make it so. *Catron County Bd. of Comm'rs v. United States Fish & Wildlife Serv.*, 75 F.3d 1429, 1436 (10th Cir.1996) ("[W]e disagree with the [Ninth Circuit] that no actual impact flows from the critical habitat designation. Merely because the Secretary says it does not make it so. The record in this case suggests that the impact will be immediate and the consequences could be disastrous.").

---

11. Though these regulatory definitions are not before us today, federal courts have begun to recognize that the results they produce are inconsistent with the intent and language of the ESA. *See, e.g., Sierra Club v.* *U.S. Fish & Wildlife Service,* 245 F.3d 434 (5th Cir.2001) (holding that the adverse modification standard of 50 C.F.R. 402.02 is inconsistent with the ESA).

Because *Catron County* dealt with whether an environmental impact statement had to be prepared pursuant to NEPA when the FWS made a CHD, the court was dealing specifically with the environmental impacts of the CHD rather than its economic impacts. However, our holding in that case casts doubt on the FWS's position in this case.

In fact, the district court in this case, by granting the appellants standing to challenge the CHD, implicitly acknowledged that they have been impacted by the flycatcher CHD. *N.M. Cattle Growers Ass'n v. United States Fish & Wildlife Serv.*, 81 F. Supp. 2d 1141, 1153 (D.N.M.1999) (holding that the appellants had alleged an injury in fact flowing from the flycatcher CHD). If none of the impacts of the CHD are actually attributable to the CHD, the district court's standing decision is rendered incoherent. If the injury alleged is attributable wholly to listing, then the appellants suffer no injury from the CHD, and cannot establish standing to challenge it. The district court's standing determination further points to the inconsistency between the policy position of the FWS and the language of the ESA itself. But the question of whether the impacts of listing and a CHD are co-extensive is not the precise question before us. Rather, the question is whether the FWS must analyze all of the economic impacts of critical habitat designation (regardless of whether the impacts are co-extensive with other causes), or only those impacts that are a "but for" result of the CHD.

It is true that the ESA clearly bars economic considerations from having a seat at the table when the listing determination is being made.... However, Congress clearly intended that economic factors were to be considered in connection with the CHD. 16 U.S.C. § 1533(b)(2).

The statutory language is plain in requiring some kind of consideration of economic impact in the CHD phase. Although 50 C.F.R. § 402.02 is not at issue here, the regulation's definition of the jeopardy standard as fully encompassing the adverse modification standard renders any purported economic analysis done utilizing the baseline approach virtually meaningless. We are compelled by the canons of statutory interpretation to give some effect to the congressional directive that economic impacts be considered at the time of critical habitat designation. [ ] Because economic analysis done using the FWS's baseline model is rendered essentially without meaning by 50 C.F.R. § 402.02, we conclude Congress intended that the FWS conduct a full analysis of all of the economic impacts of a critical habitat designation, regardless of whether those impacts are attributable co-extensively to other causes. Thus, we hold the baseline approach to economic analysis is not in accord with the language or intent of the ESA.

The FWS contends that should they be forced to abandon the baseline approach and consider all of the economic impact of a CHD, even if that impact is attributable co-extensively to another cause, they will be injecting economic analysis improperly into the listing process. The only two federal courts to consider this question come to essentially the same conclusion. *N.M. Cattle Growers Ass'n*, 81 F. Supp. 2d at 1158; *Trinity County Concerned Citizens v. Babbitt*, 1993 WL 650393 *4 (D.D.C. Sept.20, 1993) (holding that absent the baseline approach, "the Secretary would be required to include ... certain costs that might have already been incurred as a result of the listing of the species, for example, through the ESA's jeopardy and take provisions," even though "the Secretary is expressly forbidden from considering such economic costs in making the decision to list species"). We cannot agree.

Requiring that the FWS comply with the intent of the legislative body by considering economic impacts at a point subsequent to listing does not inject economic considerations into the listing process, but rather, situates those considerations in precisely the spot intended by Congress. Moreover, should this ruling result in certain areas being excluded from future CHDs, it will not undermine congressional intent that economic factors be excluded from the listing decision. The listing of the species will remain in effect and the significant protections afforded a species by listing will not be undermined. Indeed, if the FWS's position that the protections afforded by a CHD are subsumed by the protections of listing is accepted, this ruling will result in no decreased protection for endangered species or their habitat.

IV

As set forth above, the baseline approach to economic analysis pursuant the 16 U.S.C. § 1533(b)(2) is expressly rejected. The flycatcher CHD is thus set aside and the FWS is instructed to issue a new flycatcher CHD in compliance with this opinion as required by the ESA.

NOTES

(1) The effects of designating habitat: Although this case was overtly about the proper method of calculating the economic costs of habitat designation, lurking beneath the surface was another, more vital issue: what legal effect does that designation have? The FWS took the view that designation imposed no economic costs because the designation of critical habitat accorded a species no greater protection than listing the species. As it interpreted the statute, designation had essentially no *legal* effect (in that it did not restrict economic activity), and because it had no legal effect, it had no *economic* effect. The court disagreed.

As the Court explains, critical habitat is important most clearly under § 7(a)(2), the "no jeopardy" requirement, which obligates federal agencies to ensure that their actions do not jeopardize the continued existence of listed species and do not destroy or adversely modify designated critical habitat. In a controversial move, the FWS decided that the destruction or adverse modification of critical habitat only violated § 7 when it was so severe as to jeopardize the continued existence of a species; that is, the FWS essentially treated the entire requirement to protect critical habitat as surplus. Although much criticized by observers, the FWS position was not formally challenged until *Sierra Club v. U.S. Fish & Wildlife Service*, 245 F.3d 434 (5th Cir.2001), mentioned in the footnote above. In *Sierra Club*, the Fifth Circuit held that this interpretation was facially inconsistent with the ESA. Although the issue was not formally presented in *Cattle Growers*, the Tenth Circuit makes little effort to conceal its agreement with the Fifth Circuit. *Sierra Club* is excerpted below.

If these appellate court rulings stand, the FWS will need to alter significantly its interpretation of the ESA in major respects. In the case of critical habitat, the FWS may be obligated to implement more literally the statutory requirement that federal agencies not destroy or adversely modify any part of it. If this happens, the designation of critical habitat will likely become far more important and, hence, controversial. One specific consequence of such a development: the FWS will need to spend more effort estimating the economic costs of designating new critical habitat.

As noted below, critical habitat also plays a role in the application of the "no taking" rule to habitat alteration that kills or injures listed species. Although that ban (contained in § 9) is not limited to designated habitat (it protects occupied habitat, whether or not designated), courts have shown far greater willingness to uphold a taking determination if the habitat being altered has been formally designated. In practice, that is, habitat designation plays a role under § 9 as well as under § 7.

(2) Mandatory duty: As the court also notes, the designation of critical habitat is a mandatory, rather than a discretionary, duty. In *Forest Guardians v. Babbitt*, 174 F.3d 1178 (10th Cir.1999), the court concluded that an injunction was generally available to force an agency to make a habitat designation. The duty extended to situations in which the Secretary lacked resources to make the required designations.

(3) "prudent" and "determinable": Recall that the ESA requires the Secretary to designate critical habitat concurrently with the listing determination "to the maximum extent prudent and determinable." 16 U.S.C. § 1533(a)(3). The Secretary interpreted the term "prudent" to refer two narrow situations: (1) when designation would lead to increased illegal taking of the species by informing those who would take the species of its location, and (2) when designation "would not be beneficial to the species." *See Rules for Listing Endangered and Threatened Species, Designating Critical Habitat, and Maintaining the Lists*, 45 Fed. Reg. 13,010, 13,023 (1980) (codified as amended at 50 C.F.R. § 424.12(a)).[12]

"Determinable" was added in 1982 to reduce the tight linkage between listing determinations and habitat designations. The reports state that the inclusion of the term "determinable"—in conjunction with the requirement that the listing determination be based "solely" on biological factors, 16 U.S.C. § 1533(b)(1)(A)—was intended to insure that the Secretary was not forced to withdraw a proposed listing because he was unable to complete the economic analyses required for the designation of critical habitat within the prescribed time limits. H.R. REP. No. 567, 97th Cong., 2d Sess. 20 (1982), *reprinted in* 1982 U.S.C.C.A.N. 2807, 2810; *see also* S. REP. No. 418, 97th Cong., 2d Sess. 11 (1982).

The Secretary subsequently defined "determinable" by specifying that:

---

12. The House Report noted and approved the definition of "prudent" to refer to "to situations where the designation of critical habitat would inform those who would take the species illegally of the location of the species." H.R. REP. No. 567, 97th Cong., 2d Sess. 20 (1982), *reprinted in* 1982 U.S.C.C.A.N. 2807, 2820.

Critical habitat is not determinable when one or both of the following situations exist:

(i) Information sufficient to perform required analyses of the impacts of the designation is lacking, or

(ii) The biological needs of the species are not sufficiently well known to permit identification of an area as critical habitat.

50 C.F.R. § 424.12(2).

(4) Critical habitat and private property in land: The FWS determined that designating habitat for the coastal California gnatcatcher would be imprudent because (i) designation would cause more landowners to destroy the habitat, in order to circumvent the limitations imposed by the ESA, and (ii) designation "would not appreciably benefit" the gnatcatcher because its habitat was largely on private lands to which the protections of § 7 did not apply. The Ninth Circuit, reviewing a challenge to the agency's action, found both rationales unpersuasive. As for the claim that landowners would destroy designated habitat, the court noted that habitat studies were already publicly available; in addition, it ruled, the agency failed to determine whether, overall, the benefits of designation would exceed such harms. As for the "no benefit" claim, the court noted that § 7 applies to private land when landowners seek federal permits or federal funding; moreover, some 20 percent of the habitat was located on public land. Ultimately, the court concluded, the FWS was attempting improperly to expand the imprudence exception. Designation was not prudent, the agency argued, unless it would be beneficial to "most of the species." The court disagreed: the issue was whether designation would be "beneficial to the species," and designation could be beneficial even if it aided only part of a population. *Natural Resources Defense Council v. U.S. Dept. of Interior*, 113 F.3d 1121 (9th Cir.1997).

(5) Critical habitat designations and NEPA: Is an agency decision on critical habitat subject to NEPA? In *Douglas County v. Babbitt*, 48 F.3d 1495 (9th Cir. 1995), *cert. denied*, the court decided that the critical habitat designation process replaced NEPA study requirements so as to make them "superfluous." Furthermore, the court held, NEPA does not require an EIS for actions that preserve the physical environment:

> The district court found that the argument—that EISs are not required for federal actions that maintain the environmental status quo—could not be determinative, no matter its merits, because it assumed a fact not in evidence. That fact was, that the environment would remain unchanged if designated a critical habitat. The court offered as an example the possibility that the area could acquire more old growth characteristics if it were left alone.
>
> The district court missed the point. Of course a forest, free from all human interferences, changes all the time—saplings grow, mature trees die, dead trees decay. The touchstone is not *any* change in the status quo, but change effected by humans. [Intervenor] argues, and we agree, that when a federal agency takes an action that prevents human interference with the environment, it need not prepare an EIS.

The environment, of its own accord, will shift, change, and evolve as it naturally does.

Id. at 1506.

The Tenth Circuit reached the opposite conclusion in *Catron County Board of Commissioners v. U.S. Fish & Wildlife Service*, 75 F.3d 1429 (10th Cir.1996). The court noted the Ninth Circuit's decision and rejected it:

> The Ninth Circuit [held] that ... NEPA did not apply. *Douglas County*, 48 F.3d at 1507–08. We disagree with the panel's reasoning. First, given the focus of the ESA together with the rather cursory directive that the Secretary is to take into account 'economic and other relevant impacts,' we do not believe that the ESA procedures have displaced NEPA requirements. Secondly, we likewise disagree with the panel that no actual impact flows from the critical habitat designation. Merely because the Secretary says it does not make it so. The record in this case suggests that the impact will be immediate and the consequences could be disastrous. The preparation of an EA will enable all involved to determine what the effect will be....

Id. at 1436. *See also Southwest Center for Biological Diversity v. Rogers*, 950 F.Supp. 278 (D.Ariz.1996).

Which set of conclusory statements is more accurate? Does the designation of critical habitat impact values that NEPA requires to be considered? Note that the Tenth Circuit ruling in *Catron County* was relied upon in *New Mexico Cattle Growers* and strengthened by it. If the ban on adversely modifying critical habitat does carry force, independent of the no-jeopardy requirement, then designating habitat will affect how humans use the land—if only by halting activities that would otherwise take place.

SECTION 4.   RESTRICTIONS ON FEDERAL ACTIONS: THE CONSULTATION REQUIREMENT

NOTES

(1) Listing is the threshold: once a species is listed, the Act's protections become applicable. The first protective measure—found in section 7—applies to "any action authorized, funded, or carried out by" any federal agency. 16 U.S.C. § 1536(a)(2). When a federal agency proposes such an action, it is required to insure that the action is not "likely to jeopardize the continued existence of" a listed species or to "result in the destruction or adverse modification of" its critical habitat. *Id.* Section 9 contains the second protective measure: prohibitions on commercial activity in listed species and on taking such species. *Id.* § 1538(a). These prohibitions are backed by substantial criminal and civil sanctions. *Id.* § 1540(a)-(b).

(2) The evolution of consideration: The idea that an agency must consider the effects of its proposed actions on fish and wildlife and its habitat has a lengthy history.

(a) **Fish & Wildlife Coordination Act:** Perhaps the classic example of a statute that mandates consideration is the Fish & Wildlife Coordination Act, 16 U.S.C. §§ 661–666c. The Act is an equally classic example of the limitations of this approach. Among provisions calling for "development of a program for the maintenance of an adequate supply of wildlife," the original Act required consultation with the Bureau of Fisheries before the construction of any dam to determine whether fish ladders were "necessary." Act of Mar. 10, 1934, ch. 55, §§ 5, 3(b) 48 Stat. 401, 402, 401. The Act, however, included a significant qualification: if consultation produced suggestions for modifications to proposed water-development projects, modifications were to be made "if economically practicable." *Id.*

In 1946, Congress recognized that the Act had "proved to be inadequate in many respects," H.R. Rep. No. 1944, 79th Cong., 2d Sess. 1 (1946), and amended it to require consultation between the federal action agency, the Fish and Wildlife Service (FWS), and the state wildlife agency. Act of Aug. 14, 1946, ch. 965, § 2, 60 Stat. 1080. Consultation was to produce results: the action agency was to "make adequate provision consistent with the primary purposes of such impoundment . . . for the conservation . . . of wildlife." *Id.* § 3. The amendment also expanded the Act's coverage by extending the consultation and conservation requirements to include non-federal actions subject to federal permit requirements. *Id.* § 2.

A dozen years later Congress again noted that implementation of the Act "had fallen far short of the results anticipated." S. Rep. No. 1981, 85th Cong., 2d Sess. 4 (1958), *reprinted in* 1958 U.S.C.C.A.N. 3446, 3449. The Act was again substantially amended, most significantly by requiring that wildlife be given "equal consideration" with other features of the project. Act of Aug. 12, 1958, Pub. L. No. 85–624, 72 Stat. 563.

The current version of the Act states as its objective "to provide that wildlife conservation shall receive equal consideration . . . with other features of water-resource development." 16 U.S.C. § 661. To that end,

> whenever the waters of any stream . . . are proposed . . . to be . . . modified for any purpose whatever . . . by any . . . agency of the United States, or by any public or private agency under Federal permit . . . such agency shall first consult with the United States Fish and Wildlife Service. . . . [T]he Federal agencies shall give full consideration to the . . . recommendations of the [FWS].

Id. § 662.

Despite these efforts by Congress, Act has proved a failure—and, with the enactment of the National Environmental Policy Act (NEPA), the Coordination Act was swallowed up by NEPA's procedural examination requirements. *See, e.g., Missouri ex rel. Ashcroft v. Department of Army*, 526 F.Supp. 660, 677 (W.D.Mo.1980), *aff'd*, 672 F.2d 1297 (8th Cir.1982). *See also Texas Committee on Natural Resources v. Marsh*, 736 F.2d 262, 269 (5th Cir.1984) (the action agency must only "giv[e] serious consideration to the views expressed by the USFWS").

(b) **"Consideration" and the road to extinction:** If the road to hell is paved with good intentions, the road to extinction is often paved with statutes requiring "equal consideration." The Fish and Wildlife Coordination Act is only one of several statutes that impose "equal consideration" requirements on water development and permitting agencies:

(i) The Federal Power Act, 16 U.S.C. §§ 791a–825u, for example, requires the Federal Energy Regulatory Commission (FERC) to ensure that dams it licenses "adequately and equitably protect, mitigate damages to, and enhance fish and wildlife (including related spawning grounds and habitat)." *Id.* § 803(j).

(ii) The Anadromous Fish Act, 16 U.S.C. §§ 757a–757b, authorizes the Secretary of the Interior to enter into cooperative agreements with states and to undertake studies and fish restoration activities.

(iii) The Pacific Northwest Electric Power Planning & Conservation Act, 16 U.S.C. §§ 839–839h, goes further, requiring that federal agencies

> shall ... exercise [their] responsibilities [for managing, operating or regulating hydroelectric facilities] consistent with the purposes of this Act and other applicable laws, to adequately protect, mitigate, and enhance fish and wildlife, including related spawning grounds and habitat, affected by such projects or facilities in a manner that provides equitable treatment for such fish and wildlife with other purposes for which such system and facilities are managed and operated.

Id. § 839b(h)(11)(A)(i).

Despite these statutory requirements, several runs of Columbia River salmon have been listed as endangered. Requiring single-vision agencies such as the Army Corps of Engineers, the Federal Energy Regulatory Commission, or the Bonneville Power Administration to "consider" a different purpose leads to eminently predictable results. *See, e.g., Confederated Tribes & Bands of the Yakima Indian Nation v. Federal Energy Regulatory Commission,* 746 F.2d 466 (9th Cir.1984). As the Circuit Court of Appeals for the District of Columbia has noted, there often is a "lack of neutrality of government agencies in evaluating the risks and benefits of their ... programs" that may lead an agency "which has a statutory mandate ... [to] minimize the possible adverse effects of its programs." *Scientists' Institute for Public Information, Inc. v. AEC,* 481 F.2d 1079, 1089 n. 43 (D.C.Cir.1973).

We will return to this issue in Chapter 14 in the context of dam relicensing and efforts to restore the natural flow of waterways.

(c) National Environmental Policy Act: The best-known example of a statute requiring consideration of impacts is the National Environmental Policy Act (NEPA), 42 U.S.C. §§ 4321, 4331–4335. Section 102 is the heart of the Act. It requires "all agencies" to use "a systematic, interdisciplinary approach which will insure the integrated use of the natural and social sciences and the environmental design arts in planning and in decisionmaking which may have an impact on man's environment." *Id.* § 4332(A). To implement this mandate, the Act imposes a procedure on agency decisionmaking—this is, of course, the Environmental Impact Statement or EIS process.

The Act is succinct. If a proposed action is a "major Federal actio[n] significantly affecting the quality of the human environment," the agency proposing the action is required to prepare

a detailed statement . . . on

(i) the environmental impact of the proposed action,

(ii) any adverse environmental effects which cannot be avoided should the proposal be implemented,

(iii) alternatives to the proposed action,

(iv) the relationship between local short-term uses of man's environment and the maintenance and enhancement of long-term productivity, and

(v) any irreversible and irretrievable commitments of resources which would be involved in the proposed action should it be implemented.

Id. § 4332(C). The statement must be made available to federal and state officials as well as the general public. *Id.*

The process as it has evolved has embroidered additional details on this spare frame. The NEPA process generally begins with an Environmental Assessment (EA) rather than a "full-blown" EIS. The EA is prepared to determine whether the proposed action is a "major Federal actio[n] significantly affecting the quality of the human environment." The EA leads to (1) a Finding of No Significant Impact (FONSI) and a Record of Decision (ROD) if the proposed action is not a major action either because it does not cause significant environmental impacts or because those impacts may be sufficiently mitigated or (2) to an EIS if it is a major action. For a more detailed overview of NEPA, see Dinah Bear, *NEPA at 19: A Primer on an "Old" Law with Solutions to New Problems*, 19 ENVTL. L. REP. (ENVTL. L. INST) 10,061 (1989).

Impacts on wildlife are clearly within those that must be evaluated by the action agency. *E.g., Natural Resources Defense Council v. Grant,* 341 F.Supp. 356 (E.D.N.C.1972). Since permitting activities fall within NEPA's definition of agency action, its reach is expansive.

NEPA, however, is purely procedural. If the agency prepares a sufficient analysis of the impacts of the proposal it may proceed regardless of the devastation likely to result: "In this case, for example, it would not have violated NEPA if the Forest Service, after complying with the Act's procedural prerequisites, had decided that the benefits to be derived from downhill skiing at Sandy Butte justified the issuance of a special use permit, notwithstanding the loss of 15 percent, 50 percent, or even 100 percent of the mule deer herd." *See, e.g., Robertson v. Methow Valley Citizens Council,* 490 U.S. 332 (1989). At what point, however, might an agency's procedurally proper decision become arbitrary? Would total destruction of the deer herd to produce minimal benefits be a rational decision? Doesn't the arbitrariness standard of judicial review import some minimal substantive standards?

(d) The importance of procedure: Despite its purely procedural scope and the fact that it nowhere mentions wildlife, Michael Bean has written that NEPA "may . . . be among the most important federal statutes for the protection of wildlife." MICHAEL BEAN, THE EVOLUTION OF NATIONAL WILDLIFE LAW 195 (rev'd ed. 1983). Is Bean's assessment still accurate? Might Bean be referring to the following possible effects:

> **(a)** the action agency upon evaluation of the impacts may modify the project or decision, may develop alternatives to the project, or may abandon the project entirely;

> **(b)** the EIS may generate pressure from other federal agencies that cause the action agency to modify or abandon the project;

> **(c)** public reaction to the mandated disclosures may force the action agency to modify or abandon the project;

> **(d)** the disclosures may trigger the application of other statutes that do have substantive bite;

> **(e)** the process may be used to tie up the agency in court until the political climate changes; or

> **(f)** the EIS may present facts that, on review, transform a plausible agency plan into one that appears arbitrary and capricious.

The ESA is more than procedural.

a.   PROCEDURAL REQUIREMENTS

NOTES

The consultation process: Like the NEPA, the ESA requires agencies to take specified procedural steps before entering into any contracts or making "any irreversible or irretrievable commitment of resources." 16 U.S.C. §§ 1536(c)(1), (d). The Act imposes three procedural requirements:

(a) information gathering: an agency proposing "any action authorized, funded, or carried out by" the agency[1] is required to request information from the Secretary on whether any listed or proposed-to-be-listed species may be present in the area to be affected by the proposed action. *Id.* § 1536(c)(1).

At this stage, the action agency may initiate what has come to be called "informal" consultation. The joint FWS–NMFS consultation regulations offer informal consultation as "an optional process that includes all discussions, correspondence, etc., between the Service and the Federal [action] agency ... designed to assist the Federal agency in determining whether formal consultation or a conference is required." 50 C.F.R. § 402.13.

(b) biological assessment: if a species may be present, the action agency is required to conduct a "biological assessment" to determine whether that species is "likely to be affected" by the proposed action. 16 U.S.C. § 1536(c)(1); *see also* 50 C.F.R. § 402.12.

(c)(i) "formal" consultation: if the action agency concludes that the proposal is likely to affect a listed species, it must engage in formal

---

1. This is the implicit statutory definition of "agency action." *See* 16 U.S.C. § 1536(a)(2). FWS and NMFS have defined "action" as "all activities or programs of any kind." 50 C.F.R. § 402.02.

consultation with the Secretary to determine whether the proposal is "likely to jeopardize the continued existence of" the species or "result in the destruction or adverse modification of" its critical habitat. 16 U.S.C. § 1536(a)(2); *see also* 50 C.F.R. § 402.14.

Consultation results in the preparation by the Secretary of a "biological opinion" assessing the likely effect of the proposed action on the listed species. If the Secretary concludes that the proposed action would jeopardize a species or adversely modify its critical habitat, the Secretary is to suggest "reasonable and prudent alternatives" to the proposal that will not jeopardize the species of its habitat. 16 U.S.C. § 1536(b)(3). If the Secretary concludes that the proposed action would not violate the prohibitions or that his reasonable and prudent alternatives to the proposed action would not, and that any taking of the species incidental to the action will not jeopardize the species, the Secretary is to provide an "incidental take statement" as part of the biological opinion. *Id.* § 1536(b)(4). Incidental take statements are discussed below in section 8.

(ii) conference: if the action agency concludes that the proposal is likely to affect an unlisted species that is proposed to be listed, the agency "shall confer with the Secretary." *Id.* § 1536(a)(4). Although the Act does not specify what the outcome of conferring is to be, it does state that, unlike consulting, the prohibition against committing resources to the proposed action does not apply to conferring. *Id.* The joint FWS–NMFS regulations on consultation procedures state:

> A conference ... shall consist of informal discussions concerning an action that is likely to jeopardize the continued existence of the proposed species or result in the destruction or adverse modification of the proposed critical habitat.... During the conference, the Service [FWS or NMFS] will make advisory recommendations, if any, on ways to minimize or avoid adverse effects. If the proposed species is subsequently listed or the proposed habitat is designated prior to completion of the action, the Federal [action] agency must review the action to determine whether formal consultation is required.

50 C.F.R. § 402.10(c). If the action agency is unwilling to modify its proposal to avoid jeopardy, the Secretary does have the authority to promulgate an emergency regulation to protect the species.

Thomas v. Peterson

Ninth Circuit Court of Appeals.
753 F.2d 754 (1985).

■ SNEED, J.: Plaintiffs sought to enjoin construction of a timber road in a former National Forest roadless area. The District Court granted summary judgment in favor of defendant R. Max Peterson, Chief of the Forest Service, and plaintiffs appealed. We affirm in part, reverse in part, and remand for further proceedings consistent with this opinion.

. . .

This is another environmental case pitting groups concerned with preserving a specific undeveloped area against an agency of the United States attempting to obey the commands given it by a Congress which is mindful of both environmentalists and those who seek to develop the nation's resources. Our task is to discern as best we can what Congress intended to be done under the facts before us.

Plaintiffs—landowners, ranchers, outfitters, miners, hunters, fishermen, recreational users, and conservation and recreation organizations—challenge actions of the United States Forest Service in planning and approving a timber road in the Jersey Jack area of the Nezperce National Forest in Idaho. The area is adjacent to the Salmon River, a congressionally-designated Wild and Scenic River, and is bounded on the west by the designated Gospel Hump Wilderness and on the east by the River of No Return Wilderness. The area lies in a "recovery corridor" identified by the U.S. Fish & Wildlife Service for the Rocky Mountain Gray Wolf, an endangered species.

. . .

After the passage of the Central Idaho Wilderness Act, the Forest Service, in keeping with its earlier expressed intention, proceeded to plan timber development in the Jersey Jack area. In November, 1980, the Forest Service solicited public comments and held a public hearing on a proposed gravel road that would provide access to timber to be sold. The Forest Service prepared an environmental assessment (EA), [ ], to determine whether an EIS would be required for the road. Based on the EA, the Forest Service concluded that no EIS was required, and issued a Finding of No Significant Impact (FONSI), [ ]. The FONSI and the notice of the Forest Supervisor's decision to go ahead with the road were issued in a single document on February 9, 1981. The decision notice stated that "no known threatened or endangered plant or animal species have been found" within the area, but the EA contained no discussion of endangered species.

[The plaintiffs appealed the decision on the road to the Regional Forester, who affirmed the decision. The Regional Forester's decision was then appealed to the Chief of the Forest Service, who also affirmed the decision. The plaintiffs then filed this appeal, contending in part that]

(3) The road is likely to affect the Rocky Mountain Gray Wolf, an endangered species, and the Forest Service has failed to follow procedures mandated by the Endangered Species Act, [ ].

. . .

The plaintiffs' third claim concerns the Forest Service's alleged failure to comply with the Endangered Species Act (ESA) in considering the effects of the road and timber sales on the endangered Rocky Mountain Gray Wolf.

The ESA contains both substantive and procedural provisions. Substantively, the Act prohibits the taking or importation of endangered species, see 16 U.S.C. § 1538, and requires federal agencies to ensure that their actions are not "likely to jeopardize the continued existence of any endangered species or threatened species or result in the destruction or adverse modification" of critical habitat of such species, see 16 U.S.C. s 1536(a)(2).

The Act prescribes a three-step process to ensure compliance with its substantive provisions by federal agencies. Each of the first two steps serves a screening function to determine if the successive steps are required. The steps are:

(1) An agency proposing to take an action must inquire of the Fish & Wildlife Service (FWS) whether any threatened or endangered species "may be present" in the area of the proposed action. *See* 16 U.S.C. § 1536(c)(1).

(2) If the answer is affirmative, the agency must prepare a "biological assessment" to determine whether such species "is likely to be affected" by the action. *Id.* The biological assessment may be part of an environmental impact statement or environmental assessment. *Id.*

(3) If the assessment determines that a threatened or endangered species "is likely to be affected," the agency must formally consult with the FWS. *Id.* § 1536(a)(2). The formal consultation results in a "biological opinion" issued by the FWS. *See id.* § 1536(b). If the biological opinion concludes that the proposed action would jeopardize the species or destroy or adversely modify critical habitat, see id. s 1536(a)(2), then the action may not go forward unless the FWS can suggest an alternative that avoids such jeopardization, destruction, or adverse modification. *Id.* § 1536(b)(3)(A). If the opinion concludes that the action will not violate the Act, the FWS may still require measures to minimize its impact. *Id.* § 1536(b)(4)(ii)-(iii).

Plaintiffs first allege that, with respect to the Jersey Jack road, the Forest Service did not undertake step (1), a formal request to the FWS. The district court found that to be the case, but concluded that the procedural violation was insignificant because the Forest Service was already aware that wolves may be present in the area. The court therefore refused to enjoin the construction of the road. Plaintiffs insist, based on *TVA v. Hill*, 437 U.S. 153 (1978), that an injunction is mandatory once any ESA violation is found. Defendants respond, citing *Village of False Pass v. Clark*, 733 F.2d 605 (9th Cir.1984), that TVA applies only to substantive violations of the ESA, and that a court has discretion to deny an injunction when it finds a procedural violation to be *de minimis*.

We need not reach this issue. The Forest Service's failure goes beyond the technical violation cited by the district court, and is not *de minimis*.

Once an agency is aware that an endangered species may be present in the area of its proposed action, the ESA requires it to prepare a biological assessment to determine whether the proposed action "is likely to affect" the species and therefore requires formal consultation with the FWS. The Forest Service did not prepare such an assessment prior to its decision to build the Jersey Jack road. Without a biological assessment, it cannot be determined whether the proposed project will result in a violation of the ESA's substantive provisions. A failure to prepare a biological assessment for a project in an area in which it has been determined that an endangered species may be present cannot be considered a *de minimis* violation of the ESA.

The district court found that the Forest Service had "undertaken sufficient study and action to further the purposes of the ESA," [ ]. Its finding was based on affidavits submitted by the Forest Service for the litigation.[7] These do not constitute a substitute for the preparation of the biological assessment required by the ESA.

Given a substantial procedural violation of the ESA in connection with a federal project, the remedy must be an injunction of the project pending compliance with the ESA. The procedural requirements of the ESA are analogous to those of NEPA: under NEPA, agencies are required to evaluate the environmental impact of federal projects "significantly affecting the quality of the human environment," 42 U.S.C. § 4332(2)(C); under the ESA, agencies are required to assess the effect on endangered species of projects in areas where such species may be present. 16 U.S.C. § 1536(c). A failure to prepare a biological assessment is comparable to a failure to prepare an environmental impact statement.

Our cases repeatedly have held that, absent "unusual circumstances," an injunction is the appropriate remedy for a violation of NEPA's procedural requirements." [ ] Irreparable damage is presumed to flow from a failure properly to evaluate the environmental impact of a major federal action. [ ] We see no reason that the same principle should not apply to procedural violations of the ESA.

The Forest Service argues that the procedural requirements of the ESA should be enforced less stringently than those of NEPA because, unlike NEPA, the ESA also contains substantive provisions. We acknowledge that the ESA's substantive provisions distinguish it from NEPA, but the distinction acts the other way. If anything, the strict substantive provisions of the ESA justify more stringent enforcement of its procedural requirements, because the procedural requirements are designed to ensure compliance with the substantive provisions. . . .

The Forest Service would require the district court, absent proof by the plaintiffs to the contrary, to make a finding that the Jersey Jack road is not likely to effect [sic] the Rocky Mountain Gray Wolf, and that therefore any failure to comply with ESA procedures is harmless. This is not a finding appropriate to the district court at the present time. Congress has assigned to the agencies and to the Fish & Wildlife Service the responsibility for evaluation of the impact of agency actions on endangered species, and has prescribed procedures for such evaluation. Only by following the procedures can proper evaluations be made. It is not the responsibility of the plaintiffs to prove, nor the function of the courts to judge, the effect of a proposed action on an endangered species when proper procedures have not been followed. [ ]

---

7. The district court relied on the Forest Service's assertion that it had worked in "close cooperation" with the FWS, but that assertion is undermined by letters in the record from the FWS indicating that the Forest Service had not consulted with the FWS on the impact of the road and the timber sales on the gray wolf, and that the FWS felt that the Forest Service was not giving the wolf adequate consideration. [ ]

We therefore hold that the district court erred in declining to enjoin construction of the Jersey Jack road pending compliance with the ESA.

   . . .

NOTES

(1) How do the ESA procedures compare with the NEPA procedures? Is the biological assessment comparable to an EIS?

To what extent should NEPA caselaw inform decisions on consultation under the ESA? Note that there are several similarities: segmented decisions, programmatic decisions, cumulative impacts, etc.

(2) How does the court allocate the burden of going forward? Does the allocation further the purposes of the ESA?

(3) Biological assessments: Read literally, § 7 is both clear and broad in imposing a duty on agencies to prepare biological assessments. For any agency action proposed for an area where listed species "may be present," the agency "shall conduct" a biological assessment. "Any action" would seem to mean "any action"—regardless of its size. The regulations implementing this requirement, however, attempt to reduce this duty substantially. Under 50 C.F.R. § 402.12(b), an assessment is required only if the Federal action qualifies as a "major construction activity," which the regulations define (in § 402.02) as "a major Federal action significantly affecting the quality of the human environment as referred to in the National Environmental Policy Act." That is, the regulations equate the duty to prepare a BA with the duty to prepare an EIS.

Furthermore, the regulations state that the content of a BA is "at the discretion of the Federal agency." *Id.* § 402.12(f). In effect, the regulations treat the statutory requirement to prepare a BA as duplicative of NEPA, and hence of no independent effect. Are these regulations even plausibly consistent with § 7 of the ESA? Can they be made consistent by arguing that any federal action undertaken within any area in which listed species "may be present" is, from that fact alone, deemed a major federal action for which a full-scale EIS is needed? Why might the FWS and NMFS, in preparing the regulations, have been so anxious to diminish the duties Congress imposed on other agencies? *See Water Keeper Alliance v. U.S. Department of Defense,* 271 F.3d 21 (1st Cir. 2001) (applying "major construction activity" regulation, which was not challenged by plaintiff).

(4) Resource commitments: Section 7(d) prohibits "any irreversible or irretrievable commitment of resources . . . which has the effect of foreclosing formulation or implementation of any reasonable and prudent alternative measures" once consultation has been initiated. 16 U.S.C. § 1536(d).

In *Pacific Rivers Council v. Thomas,* the listing of chinook salmon led the USFS to evaluate more than 3500 ongoing projects such as timber sales and road construction to determine whether they might affect the salmon. USFS concluded that some 1700 projects were "not likely to adversely affect" the species. It submitted these projects to NMFS for informal consultation. USFS decided to allow these projects to continue during the informal consultation process because they were not irreversible or irretrievable commitments of resources under § 7(d). The district court concurred, and refused to enjoin the projects. The Ninth Circuit reversed: "We have previously made it clear that § 7(d) does not serve as a basis for *any* governmental action unless and until consultation has been initiated." Thus, the agency's decision

> that the timber, road, and range projects are not irreversible or irretrievable commitments of resources is of no moment. . . . Its conclusion that these activities "may affect" the protected salmon is sufficient reason to enjoin these projects. Only after the Forest Service complies with § 7(a)(2) can any activity that may affect the protected salmon go forward.

Pacific Rivers Council v. Thomas, 30 F.3d 1050, 1056 (9th Cir.1994). Does it make sense to prevent an agency from doing *anything* on a project that might affect a listed species until after it has initiated consultation? Presumably the project must be sufficiently far into the planning process that it has jelled enough to determine that it may affect a species. Is it that decision that precludes any additional action?

(5) Consultation and discretion: Recall the discussion following *TVA v. Hill* on "retroactivity" and the need for agency discretion as a trigger for the application of the ESA's consultation requirements.

(6) *Thomas v. Peterson* involved a federal action that was a discrete event: while the construction of the road would take time, the decision to construct it was a unitary event. The same can be said of the decision in *TVA v. Hill:* TVA would shut the flood gates and the reservoir would fill. While the dam construction and the reservoir filling took time, the decision to construct was the crucial event. Not all decisions are unitary. Often federal action is segmented:

Conner v. Burford

Ninth Circuit United States Court of Appeals.
848 F.2d 1441 (1988).
certiorari denied sub nomine, Sun Exploration & Production Co. v. Lujan,
489 U.S. 1012 (1989).

■ NORRIS, J.: This appeal presents the question whether federal agencies violated the National Environmental Policy Act of 1969 (NEPA), [ ], or the Endangered Species Act of 1973 (ESA), [ ], by selling oil and gas leases on 1,300,000 acres of national forest land in Montana without preparing either an environmental impact statement (EIS) or a comprehensive biological opinion encompassing the impact of post-leasing activities on threatened or endangered species. The district court ruled that the sale of the leases without an EIS or a comprehensive biological opinion violated both NEPA and the ESA. We affirm the judgment of the district court in part, reverse in part, and remand for further proceedings.

I

FACTS AND PROCEDURAL HISTORY

The Flathead National Forest in northwestern Montana is a vast tract of rugged mountainous wilderness. Its many lakes and rivers provide exceptionally pure surface water, prized for trout fishing, and its undisturbed ecosystem is a sustaining habitat not only for game animals, but also for the bald eagle, the peregrine falcon, the gray wolf, and the grizzly bear—all listed as threatened or endangered species under the ESA. The Gallatin National Forest in south-central Montana provides a tremendous diversity of natural resources. Its rugged landscape of mountains, valleys, and rivers supports abundant fish and wildlife populations, while portions of the forest also provide important timber reserves for the local logging industry. Bordered on the south by Yellowstone National Park, the Gallatin is the watershed for some of the nation's most important trout waters, including the blue-ribbon Madison River. Big game populations also teem in the wilds of the Gallatin, and 30,000 acres there have been identified as essential grizzly bear habitat.

Beneath the surface of these vast and beautiful national forests lies the reason for this litigation. Both forests are located in the geologic zone known as the Overthrust Belt, a formation running north-south from Canada to Mexico and thought to be a rich source of petroleum deposits. Since 1970, preliminary seismic explorations as well as oil seeps discovered in the area have triggered an avalanche of applications to the Bureau of Land Management (BLM) for oil and gas leases within the boundaries of the two forests.

In February and March of 1981, the United States Forest Service issued environmental assessments (EAs) recommending that a total of 1,300,000 acres of land in the Flathead and Gallatin National Forests be leased for oil and gas development. Based on these EAs, the Forest Service also issued Decision Notices and Findings of No Significant Impact (FONSIs), which conclude that the mere sale of oil and gas leases in the forests will have no significant impact on the human environment. The issuance of the FONSIs obviated the need for EISs at the lease sale phase of the project. [ ]

Following the preparation of the EAs and the FONSIs, the BLM sold over 700 leases for oil and gas exploration, development, and production on 1,350,000 acres within the two forests. The leases fall into two basic categories depending on the nature of the stipulations written into the lease to ameliorate the environmental impact of oil and gas activities. Some of the leases contain "no surface occupancy" (NSO) stipulations. On their face, these NSO stipulations appear to prohibit lessees from occupying or using the surface of the leased land without further specific approval from the BLM. Leases fully governed by an NSO stipulation are referred to herein as "NSO leases." Leases not governed by an NSO stipulation, which we refer to as "non-NSO leases," contain the Forest Service's standard stipulations for environmental protection and, in some cases, special stipulations to protect particularly sensitive areas. These standard and special stipulations, which we refer to collectively as "mitigation stipulations," authorize the government to impose reasonable conditions on drilling, construction, and other surface-disturbing activities; unlike NSO stipulations, however, they do not authorize the government to preclude such activities altogether.

In addition to issuing the EAs and FONSIs under NEPA, the Forest Service also initiated formal consultations with the Fish and Wildlife Service (FWS), as required under the ESA, 16 U.S.C. § 1536(b), for the purpose of determining whether the surface-disturbing activities of the oil and gas lessees might jeopardize the continued existence of threatened or endangered species. Both the Forest Service and the FWS decided there was insufficient information about the nature of post-leasing oil and gas activities to render a comprehensive biological opinion considering anything more than the lease sale itself. Instead the FWS proposed ongoing consultation and preparation of additional biological opinions at various stages of post-leasing activities.

Following the issuance of the FONSIs, the EAs, and the biological opinions, administrative appeals were filed by James Conner, the Montana Wildlife Federation, and the Madison–Gallatin Alliance (appellees). [ ] . . . . These appeals . . . were rejected and in 1982 leasing began in both the Flathead and Gallatin Forests.

Having exhausted their administrative remedies, the appellees then filed this action in federal district court in Montana, claiming that the sale of the leases without an EIS violated NEPA and that the sale of the leases without a biological opinion assessing the impact of post-leasing activities on the threatened and endangered species violated the ESA.

The district court granted appellees summary judgment on both their NEPA and ESA claims. *Conner v. Burford,* 605 F. Supp. 107 (D.Mont. 1985). . . . [T]he court ruled that the biological opinions of the FWS were inadequate to satisfy the ESA because they failed to address the effects of oil and gas activities beyond the lease sale phase. The court reasoned this failure would lead to a piecemeal evaluation of the project consequences and a progressive "chipping away" of important habitat. *Id.* at 109.

. . .

[On appeal, the court reversed the district court's decision that the government violated NEPA when it sold NSO leases without preparing an EIS; it affirmed the decision that the government violated NEPA when it sold non-NSO leases without an EIS.] We further agree with the district court that the government violated the ESA when it sold leases without preparing a comprehensive biological opinion on the effect of oil and gas activities on threatened and endangered species. . . . We therefore affirm in part, reverse in part, and remand with instructions.

. . .

III

THE ENDANGERED SPECIES ACT ISSUES

Section 7(a)(2) of the ESA, 16 U.S.C. § 1536(a)(2), requires the Secretary of the Interior to ensure that an action of a federal agency is not likely to jeopardize the continued existence[24] of any threatened or endangered

---

24. " 'Jeopardize the continued existence of' means to engage in an action that   reasonably would be expected, directly or indirectly, to reduce appreciably the likelihood

species. Section 7(b) sets out a process of consultation whereby the agency with jurisdiction over the protected species issues to the Secretary a "biological opinion" evaluating the nature and extent of jeopardy posed to that species by the agency action. 16 U.S.C. § 1536(b). The agency proposing the action (action agency) must provide the Secretary with "the best scientific and commercial data available." 16 U.S.C. § 1536(a)(2). If the biological opinion concludes that the proposed action is likely to jeopardize a protected species, the action agency must modify its proposal. In addition, section 7(d) forbids "irreversible or irretrievable commitment of resources" during the consultation process.

In this case, the ESA consultation process was triggered when the Forest Service notified the Secretary that the sale of oil and gas leases in the Flathead and Gallatin National Forests, proposed pursuant to the Mineral Leasing Act of 1920 (MLA), [ ], might affect threatened and endangered species living there, including the grizzly bear, the bald eagle, the peregrine falcon, and the gray wolf. The Secretary, through the FWS, issued biological opinions assessing the environmental effects of the lease sales. The FWS divided the oil and gas activities into stages and addressed the effects of only the leasing stage, concluding that there was "insufficient information available to render a comprehensive biological opinion beyond the initial lease phase." [ ] Thus, the biological opinions of the FWS, which concluded that leasing itself was not likely to jeopardize the protected species, did not assess the potential impact that post-leasing oil and gas activities might have on protected species. Rather the FWS opinions relied on "incremental-step consultation," contemplating that additional biological evaluations would be prepared prior to all subsequent activities and that lessees' development proposals would be modified to protect species: "[A]dditional consultation will be required for each of the subsequent phases of oil and gas activities." [ ]

The district court rejected the biological opinions because they were limited to the lease sale stage, holding that the FWS "violated ESA by failing to analyze the consequences of all stages of oil and gas activity on the forests." *Conner v. Burford,* 605 F. Supp. at 109 . . . .

. . . . On this record, we agree with the district court that the FWS' decision was not in accordance with the law.

A.   The Limited Scope of the Biological Opinions

The parties agree that before any leases could be sold, the FWS was required to prepare a biological opinion. *See, e.g. Thomas v. Peterson,* 753 F.2d 754, 763 (9th Cir.1985) (Forest Service's failure to prepare biological assessment *prior* to decision to build road violated ESA). The ESA requires that the biological opinion detail "how the *agency action* affects the species or its critical habitat." 16 U.S.C. § 1536(b)(3)(A) (emphasis added). Thus, the scope of the agency action is crucial because the ESA requires the biological opinion to analyze the effect of the entire agency action. *North*

---

of both the survival and recovery of a listed species in the wild by reducing the reproduction, numbers, or distribution of that species." Interagency Cooperation—Endangered

Species Act of 1973, as amended, 51 Fed. Reg. 19,958 (1986) (codified at 50 C.F.R. § 402.02 (1986)).

Slope Borough v. Andrus, 642 F.2d 589, 608 (D.C.Cir.1980), *aff'g in part, rev'g in part,* 486 F. Supp. 332 (D.D.C.1980) (legal adequacy of a "biological opinion" tested by matching the meaning of "agency action" with a legal definition of term). We interpret the term "agency action" broadly. *TVA v. Hill,* 437 U.S. 153, 173 & n. 18 (1978). As the District of Columbia Circuit has noted, "[c]aution can only be exercised if the agency takes a look at all the possible ramifications of the agency action." *North Slope,* [ ].

In *North Slope,* which involved an offshore oil lease sale under the Outer Continental Shelf Lands Act (OCSLA), [ ], the District of Columbia Circuit held that the "agency action" encompassed the entire leasing project, from the issuance of the leases through post-leasing development and production: " '[P]umping oil' and not 'leasing tracts' is the aim of congressional [mineral leasing] policy." *North Slope,* [ ]. Following the District of Columbia Circuit, we hold that agency action in this case entails not only leasing but leasing and all post-leasing activities through production and abandonment. Thus, section 7 of the ESA on its face requires the FWS in this case to consider all phases of the agency action, which includes post-leasing activities, in its biological opinion. Therefore the FWS was required to prepare, at the leasing stage, a comprehensive biological opinion assessing whether or not the agency action was likely to jeopardize the continued existence of protected species, based on "the best scientific and commercial data available." 16 U.S.C. § 1536(a)(2).

Both the Flathead and Gallatin biological opinions pay lip service to this statutory duty. Each contains the statement that the "action" being considered "includes not just final lease issuance but all resulting subsequent activities." [ ] However, as noted above, both biological opinions concluded that there was insufficient information pertaining to the specific location and extent of post-leasing oil and gas activities to render a comprehensive biological opinion beyond the initial lease stage.

Appellees argue that the FWS failed to prepare biological opinions based on the best data available. We agree. The FWS took the position that there was insufficient information on post-leasing activities to prepare comprehensive biological opinions. Although we recognize that the precise location and extent of future oil and gas activities were unknown at the time, extensive information about the behavior and habitat of the species in the areas covered by the leases was available. For example, appellees point out that three-fourths of the area studied in the forests had been designated "essential" or "occupied" habitat for protected species. [ ] Indeed, the environmental assessments prepared by the Forest Service contained detailed information on the behavior and habitats of the species, and discussed the likely impact of various stages of oil and gas activities. [ ]

We agree with appellees that incomplete information about post-leasing activities does not excuse the failure to comply with the statutory requirement of a comprehensive biological opinion using the best information available. 16 U.S.C. § 1536(a)(2). With the post-leasing and biological information that was available, the FWS could have determined whether post-leasing activities in particular areas were fundamentally incompatible with the continued existence of the species. . . .

Furthermore, although the FWS justified the decision to delay completing comprehensive biological opinions on the inexact information about post-leasing activities. Congress, in enacting the ESA, did not create an exception to the statutory requirement of a comprehensive biological opinion on that basis. The First Circuit, for example, has recognized that the Secretary may be required to make projections, based on potential locations and levels oil and gas activity, of the impact of production on protected species. *See Roosevelt Campobello Int'l Park Comm'n v. EPA,* 684 F.2d 1041, 1052–55 (1st Cir.1982) (EPA must prepare "real time simulation" studies of low risk oil spills despite the fact that study will only produce informed estimate of potential environmental effects).

In light of the ESA requirement that the agencies use the best scientific and commercial data available to insure that protected species are not jeopardized, 16 U.S.C. § 1536(a)(2), the FWS cannot ignore available biological information or fail to develop projections of oil and gas activities which may indicate potential conflicts between development and the preservation of protected species. We hold that the FWS violated the ESA by failing to use the best information available to prepare comprehensive biological opinions considering all stages of the agency action, and thus failing to adequately assess whether the agency action was likely to jeopardize the continued existence of any threatened or endangered species, as required by section 7(a)(2). To hold otherwise would eviscerate Congress' intent to "give the benefit of the doubt to the species."

B.   Incremental–Step Consultation as a Substitute for Comprehensive Biological Opinions

Appellants argue that the ESA's mandate to protect species is satisfied without a comprehensive biological opinion if an incremental-step consultation process is written into the leases. Specifically, appellants argue that the requirements of the ESA are satisfied by Threatened and Endangered Species (T & E) stipulations contained in each lease which provide:

> The Federal surface management agency is responsible for assuring that the leased land is examined prior to undertaking any surface-disturbing activities to determine effects upon any plant or animal species, listed or proposed for listing as endangered or threatened, or their habitats. The findings of this examination may result in some restrictions to the operator's plans or even disallow use and occupancy that would be in violation of the Endangered Species Act of 1973 by detrimentally affecting endangered or threatened species or their habitats. ,

Appellants reason that the T & E stipulations ensure that there will be adequate environmental review prior to the initiation of any activity which might jeopardize protected species. They argue that since the T & E stipulations reserve to the government the authority to absolutely preclude any activity likely to jeopardize a species, the need for a comprehensive biological opinion at the initial lease phase is obviated.

Appellants ask us, in essence, to carve out a judicial exception to ESA's clear mandate that a comprehensive biological opinion—in this case one addressing the effects of leasing and all post-leasing activities—be completed before initiation of the agency action. They would have us read into the ESA language to the effect that a federal agency may be excused from this requirement if, in its judgment, there is insufficient information available to complete a comprehensive opinion and it takes upon itself incremental-step consultation such as that embodied in the T & E stipulations. We reject this invitation to amend the ESA. That it is the role of Congress, not the courts.

. . .

NOTES

(1) How should potentially segmentable actions be treated? Under federal oil and gas leasing programs, most leases will never even be visited by the lessee (the cost of the lease is low relative to the potential return if oil is discovered so that purchasing numerous leases and exploring only a few is economically rational). If early exploration determines that the area is unlikely to overlie a field, no surface disturbance will occur and a full-scale ESA analysis would be wasted. Should the fact that more information will be available later affect the decisionmaking process? *See* 16 U.S.C. § 1536(a)(2) ("In fulfilling the requirements of this paragraph each agency shall use the best scientific and commercial data available.") Consider this question again in the note below discussing the decision in *Roosevelt Campobello International Park Commission v. United States Environmental Protection Agency,* 684 F.2d 1041, 1044 (1st Cir.1982).

On the other hand, the sale of a lease—even if it includes an NSO and T&E stipulation—creates pressure to open land for actions that might jeopardize a listed species. If early exploration determines that oil is likely, the existence of leases might lead pressure to produce a jeopardy determination that is less objective than would otherwise be the case. *See id.* § 1536(d) ("After initiation of consultation required under section [7(a)(2)], the Federal agency and the permit or license applicant shall not make any irreversible or irretrievable commitment of resources ... which has the effect of foreclosing the formulation or implementation of any reasonable and prudent alternative measures.")

(2) Planning vs. implementing: The fundamental issues raised in *Conner v. Buford* arise in many settings. A government agency prepares a policy document of general applicability that is later used as the basis for developing specific land-use activities. How meaningful is consultation at the initial, policy-setting stage, when site-specific details are as yet unknown? But as a practical matter, will consultation at the implementation stage be sufficient to protect the listed species? Consider:

(a) ***Swan View Coalition, Inc. v. Turner:*** In the early 1980s, the Forest Service began preparation of the Flathead National Plan pursuant to the National Forest Management Act (NMFA). Consultation on the proposed plan was initiated in March 1983; in May 1985, FWS issued a biological opinion concluding that "implementation of the proposed Flathead Forest Plan is not likely to jeopardize the continued existence of the grizzly bear, gray wolf, bald eagle or peregrine falcon." The final plan was published in December 1985 and FWS supplemented its biological opinion in January 1986, noting that the changes to the proposed plan did not alter the no jeopardy opinion. In December 1988, the Forest Service issued proposed amendments to the plan and reinitiated consultation; FWS issued a biological opinion in February 1989 concluding that the amendments would not jeopardize the listed species and stating that "[d]ue to the general nature of forest plans, ... formal consultation will be required on specific project activities that the Forest determines may affect threatened/endangered species."

Swan View Coalition challenged the adequacy of the biological opinion issued by FWS on a forest plan. Relying on *Conner v. Burford*, it argued that the biological opinion was inadequate because FWS failed to analyze the impacts of many of the decisions made in the Plan. Of particular concern were the Plan's provisions on timber harvesting, which provided guidance on the overall scale of harvesting even though they did not specify which tracts would be logged. The court rejected the argument, concluding that *Conner* was distinguishable:

> First, whereas the sale of a lease as in *Conner* is no more than a simple transaction which grants certain rights to the lessees and directly leads to development, the Forest Plan is a broad framework for the management of a National Forest which does not directly commit to development. Allowing for additional review at each subsequent stage of development recognizes both the managerial purpose of a Forest Plan to provide mechanisms for monitoring and regulating future development as well as its inherent limitations in predicting what development will actually occur.
>
> Second, FWS's review of the agency action in *Conner* gave no consideration to future development and relied entirely on future consultations. In this case, however, FWS has already given ample consideration to the standards and guidelines under which all future development will be undertaken. Therefore, any future consultation in this case would be in *addition* to the analysis already done at the Plan stage rather than the only review as was the case in *Conner*. ...

Swan View Coalition v. Turner, 824 F.Supp. 923, 935 (D.Mont.1992).

(b) *Lane County Audubon Society v. Jamison:* Following listing of the spotted owl, BLM developed a document—the "Jamison Strategy"—setting forth criteria for selection of land for logging in the millions of acres administered by the BLM in Washington, Oregon and California. BLM did not submit the Strategy for consultation, but it did submit 174 proposed timber sales selected under the strategy. Plaintiff sought to enjoin any sales until the Strategy itself had undergone consultation. On appeal, the Ninth Circuit held that the Jamison Strategy was an "action" subject to consultation under the ESA because it "establishes total allowable harvests" without the knowledge of which "[t]he impact of each individual sale on owl habitat cannot be measured." *Lane County Audubon Society v. Jamison,* 958 F.2d 290, 294 (9th Cir.1992). Thus, the district court properly enjoined the implementation of the Strategy prior to consultation.

Why should the overall strategy require consultation if all of the implementation actions—that is, the individual timber sales or oil-drilling projects—will be initiated only after consultation?

(3) Segmented actions and reinitiation of consultation—retroactivity redux: Note that the segmented action problem is similar to the problem created by a new listing. For example, assume that consultation leads to a determination that no listed species occupy a proposed action area and action is begun. A new species is then listed. What does the ESA require? What is the responsibility of the action agency? Of the wildlife agency?

In 1990, the Forest Service finalized Land and Resource Management Plans (LRMP) for two national forests in the Columbia Basin. In 1992, chinook salmon were listed as a threatened species. USFS responded by evaluating more than 3500 ongoing projects to determine whether they might affect the salmon, but did not reopen consultation on the Plan as a whole. In an action brought by Pacific Rivers Council, the district court enjoined the FS to consult on the LRMP, but refused to enjoin other continuing actions. On appeal, the Ninth Circuit affirmed the granting of the injunction requiring the FS to consult on the LRMP:

> The LRMPs are comprehensive management plans governing a multitude of individual projects. Indeed, every individual project planned in both national forests involved in this case is implemented according to the LRMPs. Thus, because the LRMPs have an ongoing and long-lasting effect even after adoption, we hold that the LRMPs represent ongoing agency action [and] the Forest Service [therefore is required] to consult with the NMFS as required under the ESA, 16 U.S.C. § 1536(a)(2).

Pacific Rivers Council v. Thomas, 30 F.3d 1050, 1053 (9th Cir.1994).

b. SUBSTANTIVE STANDARDS

NOTES

(1) Who decides?: What is the decisionmaking relationship between the action agency and the Secretary when it comes to determining whether a particular action will jeopardize a listed species or adversely modify its habitat? The action agency must consult with the Secretary, but is the agency bound by the Secretary's opinion? On the other hand, if it accepts the opinion, is it immune from legal challenge?

The Ninth Circuit offered the following summary of its prior decisions in an action brought against Bonneville Power Administration when the agency decided to act upon a jeopardy ruling that it received:

> We have previously addressed situations in which a consulting agency has issued a "no jeopardy" opinion and the action agency has adopted it. Although no bright line emerges from those cases, we have concluded that an action agency may not escape its responsibility under the Endangered Species Act by simply rubber stamping the consulting agency's analysis. *See Resources Ltd., Inc. v. Robertson,* 35

F.3d 1300, 1304 (9th Cir.1993); *Pyramid Lake,* 898 F.2d at 1415 ("A federal agency cannot abrogate its responsibility to ensure that its actions will not jeopardize a listed species. . . . "). On the other hand, we have held that an action agency need not undertake a separate, independent analysis in the absence of new information not considered by the consulting agency in reaching its "no jeopardy" conclusion. *See Stop H–3 Ass'n v. Dole,* 740 F.2d 1442, 1460 (9th Cir.1984). Finally, we have upheld an action agency's adoption of a "no jeopardy" finding even when based on admittedly "weak" best available evidence. *See Greenpeace Action v. Franklin,* 14 F.3d 1324, 1336 (9th Cir.1992).

In contrast, we now face a situation in which the consulting agency has issued a "jeopardy" finding. In considering the nature of our review of the action agency's adoption of the "jeopardy" determination, we are guided by the Supreme Court's decision in *Bennett v. Spear,* 520 U.S. 154 (1997). In *Bennett,* the Court observed that when a consulting agency issues a "jeopardy" opinion, its decision has a "powerful coercive effect." *Id.* at 169. The Court warned that an action agency disregards a "jeopardy" finding "at its own peril," and bears the burden of articulating in its administrative record the reasons for reaching the opposite result. *Id.* at 169–70. Acknowledging the expertise of a consulting agency, the Court explained that an action agency "runs a substantial risk if its (inexpert) reasons turn out to be wrong . . . for 'any person' [including an agency employee] who knowingly 'takes' an endangered or threatened species is subject to substantial civil and criminal penalties, including imprisonment." *Id.* (citing 16 U.S.C. § 1540).

In light of the action agency's obligations and risks as underscored by the Supreme Court, we decline the [ ] invitation [of industrial users of electricity from the Bonneville Power Administration] to scrutinize the BPA's adoption of NMFS's "jeopardy" finding more critically than we would an action agency's reliance on a consulting agency's "no jeopardy" opinion. To the extent the [industrial customers] seek to impose on the adoption of a "jeopardy" determination a higher evidentiary burden than that applied with respect to a "no jeopardy" finding, such attempt is contrary to the purposes and spirit of the Endangered Species Act. *See* 16 U.S.C. §§ 1531(a)(3), (b), & (c). Likewise, we will not require that an action agency reinvent the wheel and conduct an independent jeopardy analysis when nothing more is offered than evidence and arguments already considered by the consulting agency. Review under the APA's arbitrary and capricious standard is well developed in our precedent and we see no reason to refine it further here.

Aluminum Company of America v. Administrator, Bonneville Power Administration, 175 F.3d 1156 (9th Cir.1999). The court held that a party seeking to challenge the content of a biological opinion must do so by suing the agency that prepared it; it cannot challenge the opinion by suing only the agency that received it.

The Ninth Circuit has also held that a biological opinion is a final agency action for purposes of judicial review; a party seeking to challenge it need not wait to see whether the agency receiving it intends to act on it. *Pacific Coast Federation of Fishermen's Associations, Inc. v. National Marine Fisheries Service,* 265 F.3d 1028 (9th Cir.2001) (setting aside BO for failure to consider the full range of anticipated impacts); *American Rivers v. National Marine Fisheries Service,* 126 F.3d 1118 (9th Cir.1997).

(2) Challenges to agency actions: In *Resources Ltd., Inc. v. Robertson,* 35 F.3d 1300, 1304 (9th Cir.1993), the court ruled that an action agency cannot rely on a no-jeopardy finding when it failed to supply the FWS with substantial information relevant to the biological opinion. *See Bensman v. United States Forest Service,* 984 F.Supp. 1242 (W.D.Mo.1997) (Forest Service cannot rely on informal determination that timber harvest was "not likely to affect" species when it failed to study the action area and determine whether listed species actually used it). In *Greenpeace v. National Marine Fisheries Service,* 80 F.Supp.2d 1137 (W.D.Wash.2000), the court found that the NMFS violated the ESA by failing to prepare a comprehensive BO analyzing the full scope of a fishery Management Plan; in a subsequent ruling the court enjoined all fishing until the opinion was completed. *Greenpeace v. National Marine Fisheries Service,* 106 F.Supp.2d 1066 (W.D.Wash.2000).

(3) "the best scientific and commercial data available": Recall that the decision to list a species is to be made "solely on the basis of the best scientific and commercial data available." 16 U.S.C. § 1533(b)(1)(A). This standard is also the basis for the decision to promulgate an emergency regulation: "on the basis of the best scientific and commercial data available to him, that substantial evidence does not exist to warrant such regulation." *Id.* § 1533(b)(7). And critical habitat is to be designated "on the basis of the best scientific data available and after taking into consideration the economic impact, and any other relevant impact." *Id.* § 1533(b)(2). The standard appears again in the consultation provisions: "In fulfilling the requirements of this paragraph each agency shall use the best scientific and commercial data available." *Id.* § 1536(a)(2). What does this phrase mean? Can an agency use only the data on hand, or might "available" sometimes mean data that can be readily obtained? Consider the following dispute:

In 1973, Pittston Co. began the permitting process necessary to construct an oil refinery and marine terminal in Eastport, Maine, "a relatively pristine area of great natural beauty near the Canadian border." *Roosevelt Campobello International Park Commission v. United States Environmental Protection Agency,* 684 F.2d 1041, 1044 (1st Cir.1982). Among other requirements, the company sought a National Pollutant Discharge Elimination System (NPDES) permit under the Clean Water Act. In June 1978, the final EIS was issued on the project by the Environmental Protection Agency (EPA). Later that year, EPA initiated consultation with FWS and NMFS to assess the proposed refinery's impact on the right and humpback whales, and the northern bald eagle—listed species known to be in the area. In November, the NMFS issued a threshold determination that there were insufficient data to conclude that the project was not likely to jeopardize the continued existence of the endangered whales. In December, the FWS concluded that the project was likely to jeopardize the bald eagle.

The regional EPA office issued a notice of determination to deny Pittston's application for an NPDES permit in January 1979 and Pittston sought an adjudicatory hearing and administrative review of this decision.[1] Following extensive consultations, the fish and wildlife agencies issued jeopardy opinions, concluding that "on the basis of the best scientific data available that EPA was unable to comply with the statutory mandate that it 'insure that [the project] is not likely to jeopardize the continued existence of' endangered whales." *Id.* at 1045. Following the hearing, the ALJ rejected the biological opinions issued by NMFS and FWS, and ordered the NPDES permit be issued. The EPA Administrator denied review. Plaintiffs sought judicial review.

According to the First Circuit, whether the EPA had complied with its obligations under § 7(a)(2) turned upon its evaluation of the risk of a major oil spill. The ALJ concluded that the risk was "minute." After evaluating the evidence upon which the ALJ relied, the court concluded that it was not the "best available data" because the real time simulation studies that EPA, the state, and the Coast Guard "view as being necessary to a final determination of safety" had not been performed. Thus,

> Were the issue whether, by a preponderance of the evidence, it had been established that [tankers] could make the transit through Head Harbor Passage to Eastport with reasonable safety, the ALJ's decision might be accepted. But the issue is a harder one: whether, after using the best data available, it is established that the risk of significant oil spills from the proposed tanker traffic is so small as to insure that there is no likelihood of jeopardizing the two endangered species. All witnesses have agreed that real time simulation studies would contribute a more precise appreciation of risks of collision and grounding. We think the same could be said of a hydrographic survey of the depth of the channel, and perhaps of trial runs by [tankers] in ballast. If so, such methodologies obviously represent as yet untapped sources of "best scientific and commercial data."

Id. at 1054–55.

In what sense were the real time studies "available"? Because they could be readily performed? Because they were necessary and possible? Consider the governing regulations on the subject: "The federal agency requesting consultation shall provide the Service with the best scientific and commercial data available *or which can be obtained during the consultation.* . . . " 50 C.F.R. § 402.14(d).

Contrast the court's decision with the recent decision of the D.C. Circuit. Plaintiff brought suit against FWS for failing to list the Queen Charlotte goshawk, a large, elusive subspecies. The agency concluded that available data on the goshawk did not warrant a finding that it was threatened. To resolve the factual dispute, the district court ordered FWS to conduct a field count of the goshawk population. The circuit court

---

1. Pittston also sought an exemption from the God Squad pursuant to 16 U.S.C. § 1536(g)(1). The application was ruled not ripe for review until final action by EPA denying a permit. *Pittston Co. v. Endangered Species Comm.*, 14 Env't Rep. Cas. (BNA) 1257 (D.D.C.1980).

reversed, holding that the district court had exceeded its authority. Under § 4 of the ESA, FWS is to make its determination based on "the best scientific and commercial data available"; the court cannot order further scientific studies. *Southwest Center for Biological Diversity v. Babbitt,* 215 F.3d 58 (D.C.Cir.2000).

(4) Direct or foreseeable consequences?: In *National Wildlife Federation v. Coleman,* the Secretary of the Interior had consistently maintained that a project would jeopardize a listed species unless an interchange was moved and certain design features were altered; the DoT equally consistently maintained that the problems were created by secondary development, prompted by the highway rather than by the highway itself, and that these effects were beyond the scope of consultation. The Fifth Circuit disagreed: "The fact that the private development surrounding the highway and the Earl Bond Road interchange does not result from direct federal action does not lessen the appellee's duty under § 7 [because t]he appellees do control this development to the extent that they control the placement of the highway and interchanges." *National Wildlife Federation v. Coleman,* 529 F.2d 359, 375 (5th Cir.1976). *See also Riverside Irrigation District v. Andrews,* 758 F.2d 508, 512 (10th Cir.1985) (the "Corps is required to consider all effects, direct and indirect, of the discharge for which authorization was sought").

(i) JEOPARDIZE THE CONTINUED EXISTENCE OF A LISTED SPECIES

Defenders of Wildlife v. Babbitt

District Court for the District of Columbia.
130 F.Supp.2d 121 (2001).

■ HUVELLE, D.J.:—Plaintiffs, Defenders of Wildlife and Paul Huddy, bring this suit against defendants in their official capacities as the Secretaries and Directors of the Department of the Interior, Fish and Wildlife Service, Bureau of Land Management, National Park Service, Department of Defense, United States Air Force, United States Navy, United States Army, United States Army National Guard, United States Marine Corps, Department of Justice, Immigration and Naturalization Services, and the United States Border Patrol, alleging failure to comply with the Endangered Species Act of 1973, [ ], the National Environmental Policy Act ("NEPA"), [ ], and the Administrative Procedure Act ("APA"), [ ], with respect to the survival of the Sonoran pronghorn.

As grounds for their motion for summary judgment, plaintiffs argue (1) that the Biological Assessments ("BA") and Biological Opinions ("BO") prepared by defendants pursuant to the consultation process set forth in Section 7(a)(2) of the ESA, 16 U.S.C. § 1536(a)(2), are deficient because they fail to analyze the cumulative impacts or effects of other federal agency activities on the survival of the Sonoran pronghorn; (2) that the December 1998 Final Revised Sonoran Pronghorn Recovery Plan ("Plan" or "Recovery Plan") prepared by the Fish and Wildlife Service ("FWS") fails to comply with Section 4(f) of the ESA, 16 U.S.C. § 1533(f), for its failure to set forth required site-specific management actions; objective, measurable criteria; and estimates of the time required to carry out those measures, and to provide for appropriate notice and public comment; ... and (4) that defendants are failing to utilize their authority to implement programs for the conservation and recovery of the Sonoran pronghorn, in violation of Section 7(a)(1) of the ESA, 16 U.S.C. § 1536(a)(1)....

Both plaintiffs and defendants move for summary judgment....

BACKGROUND

The Sonoran pronghorn (*Antilocapra americana sonoriensis*), one of five subspecies of pronghorn, evolved in a unique desert environment and have distinct adaptations to this environment which distinguish it from other subspecies. [ ] In 1967, the FWS designated the Sonoran subspecies as endangered. [ ] While there is uncertainty as to the current population of Sonoran pronghorn in the United States, the most recent estimates range between 120 and 250 pronghorn. [ ] The only habitat in which Sonoran pronghorn currently remain in the United States is federally-owned land in Southwest Arizona. [ ] In Arizona, pronghorn inhabit the Barry M. Goldwater Range ("BMGR" or "Goldwater Range"), the Cabeza Prieta National Wildlife Refuge ("CPNWR" or "Cabeza Prieta NWR"), the Organ Pipe Cactus National Monument ("OPCNM" or "Organ Pipe Cactus NM"), and to a lesser extent, nearby Bureau of Land Management ("BLM") grazing allotments. [ ] The Goldwater Range is reserved for the use of the United States Air Force ("USAF") and United States Marine Corps ("USMC"), and is also used by the United States Army National Guard ("ARNG"). The CPNWR is administered by FWS and OPCNM is administered by the National Park Service ("NPS"). The Immigration and Naturalization Service ("INS") and United States Border Patrol ("BP") also operate in the area of the pronghorn habitat, primarily along the United States–Mexico border.

Factors threatening the continued survival of the Sonoran subspecies include lack of recruitment (survival of fawns), insufficient forage and/or water, drought coupled with predation, physical manmade barriers to historical habitat, illegal hunting, degradation of habitat from livestock grazing, diminishing size of the Gila and Sonoyta rivers, and human encroachment. [ ] Plaintiffs contend that the various military activities taking place in the pronghorn habitat are contributing significantly to the threat of extinction. Defendants claim that although the military activities "must be monitored and controlled, they do not constitute a survival threat to the Sonoran pronghorn." [ ] Plaintiffs also contend that INS/BP activities, grazing on BLM lands, and recreational activities in Cabeza Prieta NWR and Organ Pipe Cactus NM are adversely impacting the pronghorn. Defendants argue that these activities do not jeopardize the continued survival of the species.

. . .

I.   ENDANGERED SPECIES ACT CLAIMS

A.   Statutory Framework

. . .

Under Section 7 of the ESA, when a federal agency undertakes or permits actions that may affect a listed species, the agency must consult with FWS to "insure" that their activities are "not likely to jeopardize the continued existence of any endangered species or threatened species or result in the destruction or adverse modification of [critical] habitat of such species." 16 U.S.C. § 1536(a)(2). Under the formal consultation process, the agency prepares a Biological Assessment ("BA") that evaluates the impact of its activities on the listed species, and the FWS, after evaluation of the BA and "the best scientific and commercial data available," issues a Biological Opinion ("BO") detailing "how the agency action affects the species" and whether the action is "likely to jeopardize the continued existence" of the species. 16 U.S.C. § 1536(a)(2), (b)(3)(A), (c) . . . .

B.   Section 7(a)(2)—Consideration of Other Agency Activities

Under Section 7 of the ESA, each defendant agency "shall * * * insure that" its activities are "not likely to jeopardize the continued existence" of the Sonoran pronghorn. 16 U.S.C. § 1536(a)(2). Plaintiffs argue that defendants have failed to comply with this mandate because they have not taken into account the cumulative effects of all of the federal activities that affect pronghorn in preparing the BAs and BOs, and therefore, the BAs and BOs have incorrectly concluded that each defendant agency's activities would not jeopardize the continued survival of the pronghorn. Plaintiffs move the Court to remand the BAs and BOs to the defendant agencies for consultation about and consideration of these cumulative effects. Defendants contend that the BAs prepared by the consulting agencies need not evaluate cumulative effects. Defendants also contend that the consideration of "cumulative effects" in the BOs prepared by FWS need not include a discussion of other federal agency activities under the regulations implementing the ESA, but instead they are to be evaluated within the context of the "environmental baseline." Defendants argue that the BO's prepared by FWS have adequately addressed the other federal activities in the "action area" that constitute the "environmental baseline." Plaintiffs respond by arguing that defendants have, in certain cases, used an overly narrow definition of the action area of a particular agency's activities so as to exclude consideration of other federal activities, and that while some of the BO's list or acknowledge other federal activities affecting pronghorn, none of the BO's provides an *analysis* of the impacts of all the federal activities on the species or analyzes the proposed actions in the context of that aggregate impact.

Contrary to defendant's argument, . . . FWS must analyze the effects of the action in conjunction with the effects of other agencies' actions on the pronghorn, and that this has not been adequately done with respect to the BOs at issue here. The purpose of Section 7(a)(2)'s consultation requirement is to insure that an agency's activities do not jeopardize endangered species such as the pronghorn. For this reason, applicable regulations require an agency to analyze the effects of its activities when added to the past and present impacts of all federal activities in the action area on an endangered species, as well as certain anticipated actions that have already undergone formal or early consultation. An agency cannot fulfill this duty by simply listing the relevant activities or by narrowly defining the action area to exclude federal activities that are impacting the pronghorn. By limiting their analysis in such a manner, defendants avoid their statutory duty under the ESA to insure that their activities do not jeopardize the existence of the pronghorn. Therefore, the Court will grant summary judgment to plaintiffs on their Section 7(a)(2) claims relating to the BOs prepared by FWS in consultation with defendants, and remand those BOs for further consideration consistent with the regulations and the Court's opinion.[4]

1.   Environmental Baseline

The applicable regulations mandate that FWS address the following pursuant to formal consultation:

(1) Review all relevant information provided by the Federal agency or otherwise available. Such review may include an on-site inspection of the action area with representatives of the Federal agency and the applicant.

(2) Evaluate the current status of the listed species or critical habitat.

(3) *Evaluate the effects of the action and cumulative effects on the listed species or critical habitat.*

(4) Formulate its biological opinion as to whether the action, taken together with cumulative effects, is likely to jeopardize the continued existence of listed species or result in the destruction or adverse modification of critical habitat.

50 C.F.R. § 402.14(g) (emphasis added).[5]

The " '[e]ffects of the action' refers to the *direct and indirect effects of an action on the species* or critical habitat, together with the effects of other activities that are interrelated or interdependent with that action, *that will be added to the environmental baseline.*" 50 C.F.R. § 402.02 (emphasis added).[6] In turn, "[t]he environmental baseline includes *the past and present impacts* of all *Federal,* State, or private actions and other human activities in the action area, *the anticipated impacts of all proposed Federal*

4. By contrast, the Court finds that the consulting agencies do not have the duty to evaluate the cumulative effects in the BAs they prepare. Under 50 C.F.R. § 402.12(f), "[t]he contents of a biological assessment are at the discretion of the Federal agency and will depend on the nature of the Federal action." The regulation further provides that "[t]he following *may be considered* for inclusion: * * * [a]n analysis of the effects of the action on the species and habitat, including consideration of cumulative effects, and the results of any related studies." *Id.* (emphasis added). The Court therefore will grant summary judgment in favor of the consulting agency defendants with respect to the BAs.

5. Under the ESA, " '[c]umulative effects' are those effects of future State or private activities, *not involving Federal activ-*

ities, that are reasonably certain to occur within the action area of the Federal action subject to consultation." 50 C.F.R. § 402.02 (emphasis added). Therefore, defendants are correct that an analysis of "cumulative effects," as defined by the regulations, need not incorporate an analysis of the effects of other federal agency activities on the pronghorn.

6. "Interrelated actions are those that are part of a larger action and depend on the larger action for their justification. Interdependent actions are those that have no independent utility apart from the action under consideration." *Id.* Plaintiffs do not argue that the activities of the defendants which are the subjects of separate BOs are interrelated or interdependent.

projects in the action area that have already undergone formal or early section 7 consultation, and the impact of State or private actions which are contemporaneous with the consultation in process." *Id.* (emphasis added). It is therefore in the analysis of the environmental baseline that other federal activities in the action area that impact pronghorn must be taken into account by FWS. In turn, the analysis of the effects of the action must address these effects in conjunction with the impacts that constitute the baseline.... As illustrated below, the BOs prepared with respect to the activities of defendants do not contain this required analysis. Therefore, the Court will remand the BOs to the FWS to complete an analysis of the environmental baseline in each opinion and the effects of the action when added to that baseline. Such analysis should also address any take authorized with respect to the pronghorn, as an anticipated future impact.

For example, the September 5, 2000, INS/Border Patrol BO for "United States Border Patrol Activities in the Yuma Sector, Wellton Station, Yuma, Arizona," which is the most recent of the BOs at issue, concludes that agency action is not likely to jeopardize the continued existence of the pronghorn.... [ ] As required by the regulations, in its discussion of the environmental baseline, the BO sets forth all of the federal activities in the action area, which is broadly defined, that have past, present, or future anticipated impact on the pronghorn.[8] [ ] The BO notes activities of CPNWR, BLM, USAF, USMC, and OPCNM, and indicates the amount of take authorized, if any, with respect to each activity. [ ] The BO also sets forth the anticipated effects of the Border Patrol activities on the pronghorn. [ ] The BO is deficient, however, in that it does not analyze the effects of the activity in light of the environmental baseline. Simply reciting the activities and impacts that constitute the baseline and then separately addressing only the impacts of the particular agency action in isolation is not sufficient. *See Greenpeace v. National Marine Fisheries Service,* 80 F.Supp.2d 1137, 1149 (W.D.Wash.2000) ("Although [the BO] states that its conclusions are based on a 'cumulative effects analysis,' and even contains a section titled 'Cumulative Effects,' in fact this section contains no analysis whatsoever and is nothing more than a list * * ** The section contains no explanation of how the various groundfish fisheries and fishery management measures interrelate and how the overall management regime may or may not affect Steller sea lions.") (citations omitted); *see also Natural Resources Defense Council v. Hodel,* 865 F.2d 288, 298 (D.C.Cir. 1988) (under NEPA, finding insufficient "conclusory remarks [and] statements that do not equip a decisionmaker to make an informed decision about alternative courses of action, or a court to review the Secretary's reasoning"). There must be an analysis of the status of the environmental

---

8. The BO includes all the federal activities impacting pronghorn which have been the subject of consultation between an agency and FWS. None of the other BOs even contains a comprehensive list of these activities, let alone an analysis of their impacts on the pronghorn or an analysis of the effect of the proposed action when added to those impacts.... But a mere listing of activities does not constitute an analysis of the *impacts* of these activities, which is what is required by the regulation defining the baseline. 50 C.F.R. § 402.02 ("[t]he environmental baseline includes the past and present *impacts* of all Federal, State, or private actions * * * [and] the anticipated *impacts* * * *) (emphasis added). The USAF, BLM and NPS BOs do not even mention certain of the other federal activities that impact pronghorn in the action area.

baseline given the listed impacts, not simply a recitation of the activities of the agencies. *See Greenpeace*, 80 F.Supp.2d at 1149. The BO must also include an analysis of the effects of the action on the species when "added to" the environmental baseline—in other words, an analysis of the *total* impact on the species. 50 C.F.R. § 402.02. Moreover, there must be analysis of the impact of the total amount of take authorized, not simply a listing of those numbers. Such a critical analysis is missing from the INS BO, as well as the other BOs at issue here.

NOTES

(**1**) Aren't the cumulative impacts of *all* the activities in the area the source of the endangerment of the species? What justification might FWS offer for ignoring such synergistic effects? Should the analysis also consider the impacts of non-federal actions even though those actions are not subject to consultation under § 7(a)(2)?

(**2**) **Cumulative impacts and the right to take:** Does a cumulative impact analysis create a grandfathering system where initial activities are permitted to continue but new activities—because they increase the cumulative impact beyond acceptable levels—are prohibited? What alternatives might be crafted that would allow adjustment between existing and new uses?

(ii) DESTRUCTION OR ADVERSE MODIFICATION OF CRITICAL HABITAT

Sierra Club v. U.S. Fish & Wildlife Service

Fifth Circuit Court of Appeals.
245 F.3d 434 (2001).

■ HIGGINBOTHAM, J.:—This case requires us to assess the validity of agency action under the Endangered Species Act (ESA). Appellant challenges the refusal of the U.S. Fish and Wildlife Service (FWS) and the National Marine Fisheries Service (NMFS) to designate "critical habitat" for the Gulf sturgeon. Appellant contends that this decision relied on an invalid regulation and is therefore arbitrary and capricious. We agree and now reverse.

I

The Gulf sturgeon is a large, wide-ranging fish that can reach up to fifty years of age and five-hundred pounds in size. The sturgeon is one of the few anadromous species in the Gulf of Mexico, migrating between fresh and salt water. The sturgeon spends spring and summer in the Gulf Coast rivers from Louisiana to Florida. In the winter months, the sturgeon returns to the waters of the Gulf of Mexico to feed. Although the sturgeon once supported a major commercial fishery, habitat destruction and over-fishing conspired to bring about a population collapse. This alarming decrease in population led to the sturgeon's listing as a threatened species in 1991.

[Generally, the Secretary is required to designate critical habitat concurrently with the listing of a species. The Secretary, however, invoked two one-year statutory extensions from the listing date. Nonetheless, no critical habitat had been designated for the sturgeon by the deadline. In 1994, the Orleans Audubon Society filed suit to compel FWS to decide whether to designate critical habitat. While the litigation was pending, the agency informed the district court that it was in the process of designating critical habitat. The agency prepared a draft proposal which found that critical habitat designation would provide additional benefit to the species. The court ordered the Department on August 9, 1995, to "take all appropriate action," prompting the Department to render a decision. Two weeks later, however, the agency abruptly change direction and decided that it would not be prudent to designate critical habitat because the designation would not provide additional benefit to the species beyond other statutory regimes and conservation programs in place. After this decision, the Gulf States Marine Fisheries Commission approved a comprehensive Recovery/Management Plan for the species.

[The Orleans Audubon Society amended its complaint to challenge the refusal to designate critical habitat. The district court found that the agency had failed to articulate a rational basis for the finding that designation was "not prudent" because there was no evidence in the record to support the conclusion that the various programs would in fact benefit the sturgeon. Following remand to the agency, it decided on February 27, 1998, that critical habitat designation remained "not prudent" because designation would provide no additional benefit to the sturgeon. The Sierra Club challenged this decision.]

II

In 1973, Congress enacted the ESA as a "means whereby the ecosystems upon which endangered species and threatened species depend may be conserved," and "to provide a program for the conservation of such endangered species and threatened species." The ESA defines "conservation" as "the use of all methods and procedures which are necessary to bring any endangered species or threatened species to the point at which the measures provided [by the ESA] are no longer necessary." As the district court observed, the objective of the ESA is to enable listed species not merely to survive, but to recover from their endangered or threatened status.

To achieve this objective, Congress required the Secretary of the Interior to designate a "critical habitat" for all listed species. The ESA defines occupied critical habitat as "the specific areas within the geographic area occupied by the species, at the time it is listed * * * on which are found those physical or biological features (I) essential to the conservation of the species and (II) which may require special management considerations or protection." In addition to "occupied habitat," the ESA contemplates the designation of "unoccupied critical habitat." Unoccupied habitat is composed of the "specific areas outside the geographical area occupied by the species at the time it is listed * * * upon a determination by the Secretary that such areas are essential for the conservation of the species."

Once a species has been listed as endangered or threatened, the ESA states that the Secretary "shall" designate a critical habitat "to the maximum extent prudent or determinable." . . .

Critical habitat designation primarily benefits listed species through the ESA's consultation mechanism. Section 7(a)(2) of the statute requires federal agencies to consult with the Secretary to "insure that any action authorized, funded, or carried out by such agency * * * is not likely to jeopardize the continued existence of any endangered species or threatened species or result in the destruction or adverse modification" of that species's critical habitat. Thus, regardless of whether critical habitat is designated, an agency must consult with the Secretary where an action will "jeopardize the continued existence" of a species. If critical habitat has been designated, the statute imposes an additional consultation requirement where an action will result in the "destruction or adverse modification" of critical habitat.

Although the ESA does not elaborate on the two consultation scenarios discussed above, 50 C.F.R. § 402.02 defines each in terms of the effects of agency action on both the survival and recovery of the species. Thus, to "jeopardize the continued existence of" a species is "to engage in an action that reasonably would be expected, directly or indirectly, to reduce appreciably the likelihood of *both the survival and recovery* of a listed species in the wild." This "jeopardy standard" is similar to the regulation's description of "destruction or adverse modification" of critical habitat. The regulation defines "destruction or adverse modification" as "a direct or indirect alteration that appreciably diminishes the value of critical habitat for *both the survival and recovery* of a listed species."

III

The 1998 critical habitat decision by the Services relied on the "not prudent" exception to the ESA. The Services noted, first, that "[c]ritical habitat, by definition, applies only to Federal agency actions." They observed that agencies would have to engage in "jeopardy consultation" under the ESA where agency action could jeopardize the existence of a listed species. The Services reasoned that virtually any federal action that would adversely modify or destroy the Gulf sturgeon's critical habitat would also jeopardize the species' existence and trigger jeopardy consultation. Relying on the definitions of the destruction/adverse modification and jeopardy standards in 50 C.F.R. § 402.02, the Services concluded that designation of critical habitat would provide no additional benefit to the sturgeon beyond the protections currently available through jeopardy consultation.

. . .

The Services further noted that it was rare for agency action to adversely modify or destroy critical habitat without also jeopardizing the existence of the species. The Services concluded that these rare instances might involve federal action in the unoccupied critical habitat of an endangered species. Because critical habitat designation would protect the survival and recovery of the endangered species in a manner not afforded by jeopardy consultation, designation would be beneficial in those instances. Since the sturgeon is merely a *threatened* species, however, the Services reasoned that expansion of its population into unoccupied critical habitat would not be necessary for both survival and recovery. Later in the decision, the Services stated: "Protection of unoccupied habitat is * * * essential for full recovery, but not for survival of the Gulf sturgeon." Designation of unoccupied habitat was therefore deemed not prudent.

IV

A

Sierra Club contends that the regulation which informs much of the Services' 1998 decision facially conflicts with the ESA. We review a regulation interpreting the ESA under *Chevron, U.S.A., Inc. v. Natural Resources Defense Council, Inc.,* [467 U.S. 837 (1984)]. . . .

With the appropriate standard of review in mind, we turn to the merits of Sierra Club's challenge to 50 C.F.R. § 402.02. Sierra Club observes that the regulation defines the jeopardy and destruction/adverse modification standards in terms of both survival and recovery. Arguing that the regulation consequently equates the two consultation standards, Sierra Club asserts that 50 C.F.R. § 402.02 violates a cardinal principle of statutory construction—*i.e.,* "to give effect, if possible, to every clause and word of a statute * * * rather than to emasculate an entire section."[44] Sierra Club argues that the ESA contemplates two separate standards and that the regulation impermissibly conflates the two consultation standards.

We are unpersuaded by this argument. The mere fact that both definitions are framed in terms of survival and recovery does not render them equivalent. Significantly, the destruction/adverse modification standard is defined in terms of actions that diminish the *"value of critical habitat "*for survival and recovery.[45] Such actions conceivably possess a more attenuated relationship to the survival and recovery of the species. The destruction/adverse modification standard focuses on the action's effects on critical habitat. In contrast, the jeopardy standard addresses the effect of the action itself on the survival and recovery of the species. The language of the ESA itself indicates two distinct standards;[46] the regulation does not efface this distinction.

Sierra Club also contends that the regulation "sets the bar too high" for the destruction/adverse modification standard. Sierra Club argues that the regulation's requirement that an action affect both survival and recovery conflicts with the ESA. According to Sierra Club, the ESA requires consultation where an action affects recovery alone; it is not necessary for an action to affect the survival of a species.

44. *Bennett v. Spear,* 520 U.S. 154, 173 (1997).

45. 50 C.F.R. § 402.02 (emphasis added).

46. *See Greenpeace v. National Marine Fisheries Serv.,* 55 F. Supp. 2d 1248, 1265 (W.D.Wash.1999) ("Although there is considerable overlap between the two, the Act established two separate standards to be considered."); *Conservation Council for Hawai'i v. Babbitt,* 2 F. Supp. 2d 1280, 1287 (D.Hawai'i 1998) ("[T]he ESA clearly established two separate considerations, jeopardy and adverse modification, but recognizes * * * that these standards overlap to some degree.").

On this point, we are in agreement with Sierra Club. The ESA defines "critical habitat" as areas which are "essential to the conservation" of listed species. "Conservation" is a much broader concept than mere survival. The ESA's definition of "conservation" speaks to the recovery of a threatened or endangered species.[47] Indeed, in a different section of the ESA, the statute distinguishes between "conservation" and "survival." Requiring consultation only where an action affects the value of critical habitat to both the recovery *and* survival of a species imposes a higher threshold than the statutory language permits.[50]

The legislative history of the ESA affirms the inconsistency of 50 C.F.R. § 402.02 with the statute. A 1978 regulation defined "critical habitat" for purposes of the ESA as "any air, land or water area * * * the loss of which would appreciably decrease the likelihood of the *survival and recovery* of a listed species or a distinct segment of its population* * *."[52] Although Congress was aware of this regulatory interpretation of the statute, it chose not to adopt this approach when it amended the ESA in 1978 to define critical habitat. Instead, Congress employed the current statutory definition, which is grounded in the concept of "conservation." As a House Report accompanying a subsequent appropriations bill indicated, the 1978 amendments "significantly altered" the agency definition of critical habitat, which was phrased in terms of effects on both survival and recovery. The Services' definition of the destruction/adverse modification standard in terms of survival and recovery is consequently an attempt to revive an interpretation that was rejected by Congress.

. . .

B

We now turn to the substance of the 1998 decision. The district court found the 1998 decision to be valid, despite the facial conflict between 50 C.F.R. § 402.02 and the ESA. The court found that the decision was not arbitrary and capricious because "the agencies considered all of the neces-

---

47. *Compare* 16 U.S.C. § 1532(3) (defining "conservation" as "the use of all methods and procedures which are necessary to bring any endangered species or threatened species to the point at which the measures provided pursuant to this chapter are no longer necessary"), *with* 50 C.F.R. § 402.02 (" 'Recovery' means improvement in the status of listed species to the point at which listing is no longer appropriate under the criteria set out in" the ESA).

50. Admittedly, survival is a necessary condition for recovery; a species cannot recover without survival. The mere fact that a concept such as survival is a precondition of or implicit in a statutory term does not grant it independent significance. Consider a hypothetical law protecting the rights of individuals to swim in rivers and streams of their choosing. One who prevents such activity violates the ordinance. Although the concept of

"swimming" implies action by a live human being, one does not have to both stop the swimming *and* terminate the life of the swimmer to violate the statute. Yet this is the logic employed by the Services in interpreting the ESA.

52. 50 C.F.R. § 402.02 (1978) (emphasis added). The 1978 regulation also contained a definition of "destruction or adverse modification" that is virtually identical to the current definition. The 1978 definition read: "a direct or indirect alteration of critical habitat which appreciably diminishes the value of that habitat for survival and recovery of a listed species." *Id.* The only salient difference between the two definitions is that the current definition refers to "*both* survival and recovery." *See* 50 C.F.R. § 402.02 (2000) (emphasis added).

sary factors, which extend beyond the scope of the regulation, and articulated minimally rational conclusions that are supported by the factual record." The court further noted that the decision was based on the best scientific data available.

Sierra Club contests the court's findings, arguing that the Services' reliance on 50 C.F.R. § 402.02 went to the heart of its decision. Sierra Club contends that the agency further misinterpreted the ESA by concluding that designation of unoccupied habitat is never beneficial for threatened species.... We address each of these contentions in turn.

1

In addition to our power to review agency interpretations under *Chevron,* we may review the reasonableness of an agency's decision-making process under the Administrative Procedure Act (APA). We reverse agency action that is "arbitrary, capricious, an abuse of discretion, or otherwise not in accordance with law." Review is generally limited to the record in existence at the time the agency made its decision....

.... The Services expressly found that designation of unoccupied critical habitat was necessary to the recovery, but not the survival, of the sturgeon. In this instance, the invalid regulation directly informed the Services' conclusion that designation was not warranted. Moreover, the Services' evaluation of the merits of critical habitat designation was premised on the view that jeopardy consultation was "functionally equivalent" to consultation under the destruction/adverse modification standard. This position was based on the fact that 50 C.F.R. § 402.02 defined both standards in terms of survival and recovery. As we have concluded that the regulatory definition of the destruction/adverse modification standard is flawed, this "functional equivalence" argument is untenable.[73] The 1998 decision also considered the benefits of designation in light of existing protections outside the ESA consultation mechanism (*e.g.,* state and federal clean water laws). However, this analysis was further guided by the "survival and recovery" threshold.

2

We note that the Services' reliance on 50 C.F.R. § 402.02 also led them to erroneous conclusions regarding the benefit of designation for threatened species. Submerged in the 1998 decision is the contention that designation would only be "beneficial" in relation to the unoccupied habitat of certain endangered species. The Services reasoned that "[s]ince *threatened* species such as the Gulf sturgeon are, by definition, not currently at risk of extinction, but are rather anticipated to become so in the

---

73. We also question the rationale underlying the entire 1998 decision—*i.e.,* that designation is not "beneficial" to a species where it is less beneficial than other existing protections. As the Ninth Circuit observed in a recent opinion, "[n]either the Act nor the implementing regulations sanctions nondesignation of habitat when designation would be merely *less* beneficial to the species than another type of protection." *Natural Resources Defense Council v. Department of Interior,* 113 F.3d 1121, 1127 (9th Cir.1997). However, as the ESA is ambiguous on this point, we are unprepared to conclude that the Services' interpretation is an impermissible construction of the statute. *See Chevron U.S.A., Inc. v. Natural Resources Defense Council, Inc.,* 467 U.S. 837, 843 (1984).

foreseeable future, unoccupied critical habitat would not be immediately required for their survival." This conclusion was based, in part, on the regulation's definition of the destruction/adverse modification standard in terms of both survival and recovery.

Although we find the Services' reasoning to be flawed on the preceding basis alone, we note an additional source of error: the Services' argument would effectively prevent all threatened species from receiving critical habitat designation. It is difficult to reconcile this result with the ESA, which states that critical habitat "shall" be designated for threatened, as well as endangered, species. The agency's interpretation would read these provisions out of the statute. In light of the preceding errors, it is of no moment that the Services may have based their conclusions on the "best scientific data available." Given the extent of the Services' reliance on an invalid regulation, we conclude that the 1998 decision was arbitrary and capricious.

. . .

As the Services relied on an invalid regulation, however, we find that the 1998 decision was arbitrary and capricious. On remand, the Services will be given the opportunity to reconsider their decision in light of the appropriate legal standards.

NOTES

(1) A new era? *Sierra Club* could prove to be the most influential ESA ruling since *TVA v. Hill.* Practically speaking, the most important part of the ESA is § 7(a)(2) and the restrictions it imposes on federal agencies. The "no jeopardy" portion of 7(a)(2) has long been important, but it does not halt all activities that worsen the plight of listed species, much less activities that merely interfere with recovery. As implemented, it generally restricts only individual actions that, taken alone, would actually jeopardize the "continued existence" of a species (though recall the discussion above of cumulative effects). As interpreted in *Sierra Club,* the § 7(a)(2) ban on destroying or adversely modifying critical habitat could offer significantly greater protection—but only for those species for which habitat has been designated. Read literally, the statute bans all actions that would "adversely modify" critical habitat, no matter how modest the modification. Given the statute's clear focus on conservation (that is, recovery), a modification would be adverse if it interfered with conservation, whether or not in diminished a species' current plight.

(2) Designating habitat, revisited: As noted above, the Tenth Circuit in *New Mexico Cattle Growers* agreed with the decision in *Sierra Club.* The Tenth Circuit decision, you will recall, dealt with the designation of habitat, and whether the FWS had adequately fulfilled its mandatory duty to designate. Under these two rulings, the designation of critical habitat has become significantly more important. Critical habitat has been shifted, in terms of its purpose, from protecting against near-term extinction (jeopardy) to the promotion of conservation (recovery). In addition, the protection offered designated habitat under 7(a)(2) has been significantly increased—so much so that 7(a)(2) "no jeopardy" rulings might need to be renamed "no adverse modification" rulings to recognize the new, greater importance of the habitat-based standard.

Defenders of Wildlife v. Babbitt

District Court for the District of Columbia.
130 F.Supp.2d 121 (2001).

■ HUVELLE, D.J.:—[The procedural and factual background is set out *supra.*]

2.   Action Area

The BOs [biological opinions] of several of the defendant agencies are also deficient because of their overly narrow definition of action area, which results in the exclusion of certain relevant impacts from the environmental baseline. The environmental baseline includes, *inter alia,* "the past and present impacts of all Federal, State, or private actions and other human activities *in the action area,* [and] the anticipated impacts of all proposed Federal projects *in the action area* that have already undergone formal or early section 7 consultation." 50 C.F.R. § 402.02. The regulations define "action area" as "all areas to be affected directly or indirectly by the Federal action and not merely the immediate area involved in the action." [ ] In certain BOs, defendants have defined the action area in a manner inconsistent with this definition.

Defendants attempt to argue that their analysis need not consider other federal activities, since the action area is limited to the federal lands under the control of that agency and/or the immediate area of that agency's action. For example, defendants claim the USMC BO went further than necessary in noting the USAF use of the Gila Bend segment of the BMGR, because USMC "has no direct authority" there. [ ] That is not the test of whether an area is part of the action area. If pronghorn there will be directly or indirectly affected by USMC activity, the impacts of other activities there must be included as part of the environmental baseline. *See* 50 C.F.R. § 402.02. Similarly, with respect to the BLM grazing allotments BO, defendants argue that the action area consists solely of the grazing allotment lands, in other words, the immediate area involved.[10] [ ] The regulations explicitly reject such a definition of the action area. *See* 50 C.F.R. § 402.02.

---

10. Similarly, defendants argue that the action area at issue in the NPS "Organ Pipe Cactus National Monument General Management" BO consists only of the national monument area, which is the immediate area, without acknowledging indirect affects on pronghorn outside that immediate area. [ ] However, in the section labeled "Effects of the Action," the BO notes the possibility that traffic along State Road 85, which is located in part within the monument, "may act as a barrier to the pronghorn, restricting their movements to east of the highway," [ ], which is separate from the present range of most pronghorn, which is west of the high-way. [ ] The opinion notes that "[n]ot only is the highway a possible deterrent to expanding pronghorn populations, but the resulting modified behavior patterns may lead to a reduction in genetic exchange, reduced viability, and the ability to adapt to environmental change." [ ] Notwithstanding these possible direct and indirect effects from activities in Organ Pipe, including the potential isolation of pronghorn east of SR 85 from the rest of the population, and restriction of the remainder of the population to areas west of SR 85, the BO contains no discussion of past, present, or anticipated future impacts of federal

The Court cannot accept these overly narrow applications of the definition of an "action area," since they are inconsistent with both the broad purpose of the statute and the definition of "action area" set forth in 50 C.F.R. § 402.02. Pronghorn move across this relatively discreet area of land entirely under federal management without regard to which federal agency is responsible for administering a particular area. Given the unambiguous definition of an "action area," it cannot be narrowly applied so as to avoid taking into account the impacts of other federal activities on the pronghorn. Such an application would undermine the Act's requirement that agencies "insure" that their actions do not jeopardize the continued existence of endangered species.

Such a narrow approach to defining the action area in these three BOs is also inconsistent with the broader the definition of action area correctly applied in the INS and USMC BOs. . . .

The Court therefore remands the USAF, BLM, and NPS BOs for an analysis of the past and present impacts of the additional activities in the action area where pronghorn may be indirectly affected, as well as any anticipated impacts of activities in that area which have begun Section 7 consultation. *See* 50 C.F.R. § 402.02.

NOTES

(1) What is the relationship between "action area" and critical habitat? Would the Sonoran pronghorn have benefitted from having critical habitat designated for it? Does the fact that its existing habitat is exclusively on federally owned lands reduce or increase the need for such a designation? To what extent does the court's cumulative impact analysis implicate critical habitat?

(2) "Conservation": Recall that the ESA defines "conservation" as "the use of all methods and procedures which are necessary to bring any [listed] species to the point at which the measures provided in pursuant to this Act are no longer necessary." *Id.* § 1332(3). Is the decision in *Sierra Club* most accurately described as an example of an agency failing to "conserve" a listed species?

SECTION 5.   AFFIRMATIVE OBLIGATIONS

a.   AFFIRMATIVE OBLIGATIONS TO RECOVER LISTED SPECIES

NOTES

(1) The duty to conserve: Section 7(a)(1) contains two provisions. The first requires the Secretaries of the Interior and Commerce to review the

activities in the pronghorn range north and west of Organ Pipe, including BLM grazing lands, the Goldwater Range, and Cabeza Prieta. These lands should be considered part of the action area, as they were by USMC and INS, as the pronghorn there will be indirectly affected by the activities in the immediate area (Organ Pipe) if their range is restricted by such activities. *See* 50 C.F.R. § 402.02.

programs they administer and to "utilize such programs in furtherance of the purposes of this Act." 16 U.S.C. § 1536(a)(1). Three early cases applying § 7(a)(1) involved the Secretary of the Interior's regulation of migratory waterfowl. *See National Wildlife Federation v. Hodel,* 23 Env't Rep. Cas. (BNA) 1089 (E.D.Cal.1985); *Connor v. Andrus,* 453 F.Supp. 1037 (W.D.Tex.1978); *Defenders of Wildlife v. Andrus,* 428 F.Supp. 167 (D.D.C. 1977). None of the decisions place great emphasis on the language of § 7(a)(1)—or, indeed, employ an analysis or arrive at a decision that diverges from the general principles of judicial review of agency decision-making.

The second sentence in § 7(a)(1) states, "[a]ll other federal agencies shall, in consultation with and with the assistance of the Secretary, utilize their authorities in furtherance of the purposes of this Act by carrying out programs for the conservation of [listed] species." 16 U.S.C. § 1536(a)(1). These requirements are the substantive embodiment of the Act's policy declaration: "It is further declared to be the policy of Congress that all Federal departments and agencies shall seek to conserve [listed] species and shall utilize their authorities in furtherance of the purposes of this Act." *Id.* § 1531(c)(1).

The fundamental question, of course, is: what *does* section 7(a)(1) do? Does it do any more than authorize an agency to exercise discretion delegated to it by another statute to conserve a listed species? That is, does it simply give an agency another mission in addition to those contained in its enabling legislation?

The first case to examine the duty to conserve was *Carson-Truckee Water Conservancy District v. Watt.* The case was an action to force the Secretary of the Interior to store water for the irrigation district behind a federal dam. The Secretary argued, in part, that he was obligated by § 7(a)(1) to use the available water to conserve a species of fish, the cui-ui. The fish required "natural" flows to spawn and the lack of such flows led to its listing as an endangered species in 1976. The irrigation district argued that the ESA required only those flows necessary to maintain a population of cui-ui; the Secretary argued that he was required to provide flows sufficient "to get the species off the threatened and endangered lists." The court rejected the irrigators argument "the Secretary is required to give the Pyramid Lake fishery priority over all other purposes of Stampede until the cui-ui fish and Lahontan cutthroat trout are no longer classified as endangered or threatened." *Carson-Truckee Water Conservancy District v. Watt,* 549 F.Supp. 704 (D.Nev.1982), *aff'd sub nom., Carson–Truckee Water Conservancy District v. Clark,* 741 F.2d 257 (9th Cir.1984), *cert. denied sub nomine, Nevada v. Hodel,* 470 U.S. 1083 (1985).

The issue not raised in *Carson-Truckee* was, if the Secretary had lacked discretion to allocate the project water—if, for example, the statute had specified how all of the water was to be allocated—would he have been able to rely upon § 7(a)(1) to impose a different allocation? Recall again the discussion following *TVA v. Hill* on "retroactivity" and the need for agency discretion as a trigger for the application of the ESA's consultation requirements. Is discretion also the prerequisite to the obligations of § 7(a)(1)?

The court in *Platte River Whooping Crane Trust v. FERC* addressed these issues. Plaintiff challenged the relicensing of hydroelectric facilities on the Platte River. It sought to have the licensing agency—the Federal Energy Regulatory Commission—impose conditions on the licensee to insure adequate flows to maintain whooping crane habitat. Plaintiff relied in part on § 7(a)(1). The court rejected this argument:

> The Trust reads section 7 essentially to oblige the Commission to do "whatever it takes" to protect the threatened and endangered species that inhabit the Platte River basin; any limitation on FERC's authority contained in the [Federal Power Act] are implicitly superseded by this general command.... We think that Trust's interpretation of the ESA is far-fetched. As the Commission explained, the statute directs the agencies to "utilize their authorities" to carry out the ESA's objectives; it does not *expand* the powers conferred on an agency by its enabling act.

Platte River Whooping Crane Critical Habitat Maintenance Trust v. FERC, 962 F.2d 27 (D.C.Cir.1992).

(2) Section 7(a)(1) and the public trust: In *Carson-Truckee,* the Secretary used his § (7)(a)(1) duties as a shield to defend his decision on the allocation of water from the Stampede Reservoir. Given the statutory language—the Secretary "shall ... utilize such programs in furtherance of the purposes of this Act"—this is a straightforward interpretation. Can the section also be used as a sword? That is, would § 7(a)(1) have required the Secretary to adopt the alternative that he chose?

Note that this question is similar those raised by the public trust in wildlife examined in Chapters 3 and 5: does the trust serve only as a source of power that states may use to justify decisions to conserve wildlife, or does it also impose obligations on the trustee? Does § 7(a)(1) designate at least the Secretaries of the Interior and Commerce as trustees for threatened and endangered wildlife?

Pyramid Lake Paiute Tribe of Indians v. United States Department of Navy

Ninth Circuit Court of Appeals.
898 F.2d 1410 (1990).

■ O'SCANNLAIN, J.: We must determine whether certain practices of the Department of the Navy in leasing acreage and contiguous water rights to local farmers in Nevada violate federal law. The Pyramid Lake Paiute Tribe of Indians alleges that these practices seriously threaten the continued viability of an endangered species of fish, the cui-ui, in violation of the Endangered Species Act....

The Department of the Navy (the "Navy") owns and operates Fallon Naval Air Station ("Fallon") in Nevada. Located within the Carson Division of the Newlands Reclamation Project (the "Project"), Fallon contains nearly 3,000 acres of Project water right land.

The Navy conducts extensive flight training throughout most of the year at Fallon. As a result, the station is the site for hundreds of aircraft and repeated takeoffs and landings. The remote desert location of Fallon provides the Navy with certain training capabilities not available at any other naval facility. Fallon faces certain unique dangers, however, because of the desert conditions. For example, the Navy must contend with poor visibility caused by dust storms, damage to aircraft engines from foreign objects, and an increased risk of fire.

To diminish the risk of these dangers occurring, the Navy has surrounded the runways with "buffer zones" containing irrigated vegetation. These zones work to minimize the dangerous conditions and therefore lessen the risk of injury or death to Navy pilots. To maintain vegetation in the zones, the Navy has leased out since the 1950s approximately 2,200 acres of its Project water right land to local farmers (the "outlease program"). This land typically has been used as pasture land or to grow alfalfa, wheat grass, fescue "or other low water use crops."

The diversion of water used to irrigate the land involved in the outlease program is not controlled by the Navy, but rather, by the Truckee–Carson Irrigation District ("TCID")....

Before the upstream diversions for the Project as well as for other irrigation and municipal and industrial uses began, the Truckee River maintained the lake's level and provided river spawning flows for the cui-ui, a species of fish which has as its exclusive habitat Pyramid Lake. The Secretary of the Interior (the "Secretary") has categorized the cui-ui (pronounced "kwee-wee") as an endangered species under the Endangered Species Act (the "Act" or "ESA"). [ ] The parties do not dispute this categorization; indeed, they stipulate that "inadequate flows" of the Truckee River into Pyramid Lake have led to a "precarious condition" for the cui-ui.

In an effort to improve the cui-ui's condition, the United States Fish & Wildlife Service (the "FWS") developed a Cui–Ui Restoration Program aimed at generating a self-sustaining population of the fish through natural reproduction. The key goal of the Restoration Program is to increase the water level of Pyramid Lake. The parties recognize that "[a]dditional flows in the lower Truckee River and into Pyramid Lake are required to insure the survival of the cui-ui as a species" and that "greater flows are required to conserve and recover the cui-ui and to bring them to the point where they are no longer endangered or threatened." [ ]

In March 1986, the Tribe filed a complaint in federal district court seeking to enjoin the Navy's outlease program at Fallon. The Tribe alleges that the Navy's program imperils the continued viability of the cui-ui by contributing to a significant decrease in the water level of Pyramid Lake. The Tribe argues that the Navy's acts violate not only various provisions of the ESA, but also the National Environmental Policy Act ("NEPA") and the federal government's fiduciary obligation to the Tribe. The Tribe therefore urges that injunctive relief to protect the cui-ui as well as the Tribe's own interests is appropriate. After the court denied the Tribe's motion for a preliminary injunction, and before trial, the parties stipulated to most of the facts pertinent to decision in this case.

Based on these stipulations and its own findings of fact, the district court held that the Navy's actions do not place the cui-ui in "jeopardy" under section 7(a)(2) of the Act. The court further held that because the Navy was not jeopardizing the continued viability of the cui-ui, its failure to develop an environmental impact statement ("EIS") analyzing the outlease program does not violate the NEPA. For the same reasons, the court held that the Navy did not breach its fiduciary obligations to the Tribe. Finally, the court found that while section 7(a)(1) of the Act imposes an affirmative duty on non-Interior federal agencies to use their authority to conserve endangered species, that duty does not rise to the level of duty imposed upon the Interior Department. The court held that non-Interior agencies are entitled to "some discretion." It then ruled that the Navy did not abuse this discretion so as to violate section 7(a)(1) in refusing to adopt the conservation measures the Tribe proposed, finding that the proposals would be not only costly to implement but also largely ineffectual. The district court thus entered judgment for the Navy.

The Tribe timely appeals.

. . .

The [ESA] provides, in section 7(a)(1), that federal agencies outside the Interior Department shall execute their programs in a manner consistent with the conservation of endangered and threatened species. ESA § 7(a)(1), 16 U.S.C. § 1536(a)(1). In full, section 7(a)(1) provides:

> The Secretary shall review other programs administered by him and utilize such programs in furtherance of the purposes of this chapter. *All other federal agencies* shall, in consultation with and with the assistance of the Secretary, utilize their authorities in furtherance of the purposes of [the Act] by carrying out programs for the conservation of endangered species and threatened species listed pursuant to section 1553 of this title.

16 U.S.C. § 1536(a)(1) (emphasis added). Similar mandates are laid down in other sections of the Act. *See Carson–Truckee Water Conservancy Dist. v. Clark,* 741 F.2d 257, 261–62 & n. 3 (9th Cir.1984), *cert. denied,* 470 U.S. 1083 (1985) (hereinafter *"Carson-Truckee WCD"*); ESA §§ 2(b), (c), & 3(3), 16 U.S.C. §§ 1531(b), (c), & 1532(3). The key term in these sections, "conservation," means "to use and the use of all methods and procedures which are necessary to bring any endangered species or threatened species to the point at which the measures provided pursuant to [the Act] are no longer necessary." ESA § 3(3), 16 U.S.C. § 1532(3). This court has recognized that agencies have affirmative obligations to conserve under section 7(a)(1), but has not had occasion to consider the scope of those obligations. *Carson-Truckee WCD,* 741 F.2d at 262 n. 5.

The Tribe asserts that if an alternative to the challenged action would be equally as effective at serving the government's interest, and at the same time would enhance conservation to an equal or greater degree than does the challenged action, then the agency must adopt the alternative. The Tribe suggests in essence that section 7(a)(1) requires an agency to adopt the "least burdensome alternative," to borrow a phrase from constitutional law. The Tribe notes that it proposed an alternative to the current outlease program that would both require the use of less Project water and further the Navy's interest in pilot safety to the same degree. The Navy's refusal to adopt the proposal, the Tribe argues, violates the Navy's affirmative obligation to conserve under section 7(a)(1). The Navy responds that while section 7(a)(1) requires agencies to develop programs that will operate to conserve listed species, the agencies need do so only in a manner consistent with the accomplishment of the agencies' primary goals.

In construing a statute, this court first looks to the plain meaning of the language in question. [ ] If the language is unambiguous, its plain meaning controls unless Congress has "clearly expressed" a contrary legislative intent. [ ]

In *Tennessee Valley Authority v. Hill,* 437 U.S. 153 (1978), the Supreme Court examined the legislative history of the ESA. There, to conserve an endangered species of fish, the Court enjoined the TVA from completing construction of a dam which had commenced before the enactment of the latest version of the ESA and on which the federal government had spent over $50 million. [ ] In so doing, the Court stated that "[t]he plain intent of Congress in enacting [the ESA] was to halt *and reverse* the trend toward species extinction, *whatever the cost.*" [ ] (emphases added); [ ]

The Court's discussion of the Act in *TVA* makes clear that, on the one hand, the Navy's "primary mission" construction is not viable because it understates the Navy's duty to conserve. The Navy concedes that section 7(a)(1) contains a congressional directive that agencies must act affirmatively in the interest of listed species, but qualifies the declaration by stating that the section was not "intended to frustrate the agencies' accomplishment of their primary missions." [ ] The Court in *TVA* rejected such a proposition as being inconsistent with congressional intent. [ ] (noting that Congress "carefully omitted" from the final version of the Act all proposed language which tempered federal agencies' duty to conserve (*e.g.,* language which extended the duty only *"insofar as is practicable and consistent with the[ir] primary purposes"*)) (emphasis, brackets in original).

On the other hand, the Tribe's interpretation overstates the Navy's duty, for it would work to divest an agency of virtually all discretion in deciding how to fulfill its duty to conserve. We have recognized that the Secretary is to be afforded some discretion in ascertaining how best to fulfill the mandate to conserve under section 7(a)(1). *See Carson–Truckee WCD,* 741 F.2d at 262. That some discretion should be allowed is also evident from the regulations promulgated under the Act. For example, a non-Interior agency is given discretion to decide whether to implement conservation recommendations put forth by the FWS. 50 C.F.R. § 402.14(j) (1988). The interpretation of a statute by the agency charged with its administration is entitled to deference. *Chevron U.S.A., Inc.[v. Natural Resources Defense Council],* 467 U.S. [837,] 844 [(1984)].

In addition, we do not read *TVA* to compel adoption of the Tribe's interpretation of section 7(a)(1). As the Court's only comprehensive discussion of the ESA, *TVA* is undoubtedly instructive to our analysis. We see, however, at least one crucial difference between the situation the TVA faced and that which the Navy faces here. In *TVA,* it was indisputable that the challenged agency action, completion of the Tellico Dam, "would result in total destruction of the snail darter's habitat." [ ] Here, the FWS predicts no such grave danger. To the contrary, the FWS reports that the Navy's operation of the outlease program will not jeopardize the cui-ui. Moreover, while the Court in *TVA* referred to section 7(a)(1), its holding was premised upon section 7(a)(2).

Even were we to adopt the stringent standard of duty the Tribe would impose, we would be hard-pressed to rule that the Navy has violated section 7(a)(1) given the district court's findings of fact....

Given the district court's findings, the Navy did not abuse its discretion or act arbitrarily, capriciously, or otherwise not in accordance with law in its rejection of the Tribe's alternative plans specifically, or in its operation of the outlease program generally. [ ] The Navy has foregone plans to lease out the full portion of land with appurtenant water rights since entering into the 1985 agreement with the Tribe. The Navy has begun consultations with the FWS concerning a long-term outlease program and has hired experts to conduct a study of water conservation alternatives, which has now been completed. Moreover, the Navy represents to this court that it "will reduce its planned consumption of irrigation water and require improvements such as leveling and ditch lining to increase efficiency and reduce water loss." [ ]

We hold that the district court's finding relating to the insignificant impact of the conservation measures the Tribe has proposed is not clearly erroneous. We therefore affirm the court's holding that the Navy has not violated section 7(a)(1).

NOTES

To what extent does section 7(a)(1) act as a sword to compel agency action to conserve a species? How much discretion is the agency to be accorded in carrying out its conservation mandate?

Note the Tribe's characterization of its claim: "[I]f an alternative to the challenged action would be equally as effective at serving the government's interest, and at the same time would enhance conservation to an equal or greater degree than does the challenged action, then the agency must adopt the alternative." [¶ 12] Does the court adopt this standard?

Note the Navy's position: although "section 7(a)(1) contains a congressional directive that agencies must act affirmatively in the interest of listed species, ... the section was not 'intended to frustrate the agencies' accomplishment of their primary missions.'" [¶ 15] Does the court adopt this standard? Is it consistent with *TVA v. Hill*?

House v. United States Forest Service

United States District Court, Eastern District of Kentucky.
974 F.Supp. 1022 (1997).

■ FORESTER, D.J.: Before the Court are the parties' cross motions for summary judgment, as well as several procedural motions. All matters have been fully briefed and are ripe for review.

I. INTRODUCTION

This is a civil case brought against the United States Forest Service ... for declaratory and injunctive relief to prevent the Forest Service from proceeding with a proposed timber sale on Leatherwood Fork....

Plaintiffs, Bob House, Chris Schimmoeller, and Kentucky Heartwood, Inc., allege that defendants have violated or failed to adhere to procedures set forth in the Endangered Species Act, [ ] ("ESA"), the National Forest Management Act, [ ] ("NFMA"), the National Environmental Policy Act, [ ] ("NEPA"), and the Administrative Procedure Act, [ ] ("APA"), by authorizing the Leatherwood Fork timber sale, which plaintiffs submit will harm the Indiana bat, an endangered species.

. . .

II. FACTUAL BACKGROUND

[The 690,000–acre Daniel Boone National Forest is located in eastern Kentucky. The Forest Service began planning to log the Leatherwood Fork area (approximately 2,793 acres) in 1992. As the proposal was finalized, the project included seven separate cutting units of approximately 199 acres. The logging operations were structured to account for the presence of the Indiana bat, an endangered species,[1] that lives in the forest: at least three potential roost trees were to be left on each acre harvested, large old beech or sugar maple trees will be retained as den trees wherever possible, and all standing dead trees will be left intact. Additionally, 3 to 4 live trees will be left around each snag that is at least 16 inches in diameter within one mile of the Indiana bat hibernation cave. In addition, 16 seasonal wildlife ponds at the ridgetop area of the sale and four waterholes were to be constructed.

[The Forest Service prepared the environmental analysis documents required by NEPA, NFMA, and the ESA. These included a biological evaluation ("BE") regarding the effects, if any, the proposed project would have on threatened and endangered species, including the endangered Indiana bat. The Forest Service concluded that the project was "not likely to adversely affect" any endangered species including the Indiana bat. At the end of October 1995, the Forest Service gave the BE to the FWS as part of the formal consultation process. In mid-March 1996, FWS concurred in writing with the Forest Service's conclusion that the proposed action was "not likely to adversely affect threatened or endangered species." The Forest Service gave notice of the proposed sale; plaintiffs responded by providing comments critical of the sale. When the Forest Service approved

---

1. The Indiana bat was listed as an endangered species on March 11, 1967. Between 1960 and 1975, the bat's population decreased by 28%. In 1983, subsequent in time to the passage of the ESA, the U.S. Fish and Wildlife Service ("Fish & Wildlife") issued a recovery plan for the Indiana bat. Fish & Wildlife then designated seven (7) "Priority 1 hibernacula" where 85% of the Indiana bats currently hibernate. Despite the recovery plan's goal of halting the decline of the Indiana bat, the bat's population has contin-

ued to fall. Between 1960 and 1987 there was a 55% population decline at Priority 1 hibernacula, and a generally similar decline at Priority 2 hibernacula. [ ] According to the defendants' Indiana Bat Summer Habitat Management Strategy, "[i]f the present rate of decline continues, the Indiana Bat Recovery Team projects that the species will be extirpated from Priority 1 caves, and perhaps become extinct, by the year 2040." [ ]

. . .

the sale, plaintiffs filed an administrative appeal, which was rejected by the Regional Forester. Having exhausted their administrative remedies, plaintiffs sought judicial review.]

IV. ANALYSIS

A. Whether Defendants Violated the Endangered Species Act, 16 U.S.C. § 1531 et seq.

. . .

[P]laintiffs claim that defendants violated the ESA by: (1) failing to place top priority on the conservation of the Indiana bat; (2) failing to enter into formal consultations with Fish & Wildlife prior to approving the timber sale; and (3) sanctioning the timber sale which will "harm" the Indiana bat, thus constituting a "taking."

1. Whether defendants violated the ESA by failing to place top priority on the conservation of the Indiana bat

The Court does not find persuasive defendants' "balancing interests" argument.[8] Rather, the Court finds that the ESA mandates that defendants place conservation above any of the agency's competing interests. The Supreme Court, in *Tennessee Valley Authority v. Hill*, 437 U.S. 153 (1978), found that,

> [t]he plain intent of Congress in enacting [the ESA] was to halt and reverse the trend toward species extinction, whatever the cost.* * * [T]he legislative history undergirding Sec. 7 reveals an explicit congressional decision to require agencies to afford first priority to the declared national policy of saving endangered species. The pointed omission of the type of qualifying language previously included in endangered species legislation reveals a conscious decision by Congress to give endangered species priority over the "primary missions" of

---

8. Defendants argue that the ESA grants defendants some discretion among conservation measures for the benefit of listed species and that the case law behind the ESA provides that the defendants may balance their obligations to conserve with competing agency interests. For these premises, defendants cite the following distinguishable cases: *Pyramid Lake Paiute Tribe v. US. Dept. of Navy*, 898 F.2d 1410, 1417–18 (9th Cir.1990) (found no difference in the duties imposed by the ESA on agencies under the umbrella of the Department of the Interior and "Non–Interior" agencies; upheld the Department of the Navy's reliance on opinions of Fish and Wildlife Service in executing its program as it was not arbitrary or capricious because the program did not violate the ESA, as it would not "take" an endangered species); *Carson-Truckee Water Conservancy Dist. v. Clark*, 741 F.2d 257 (9th Cir.1984), *cert. denied, sub nom. Nevada v. Hodel*, 470 U.S. 1083 (1985) (upheld the Secretary of the Interior's decision to give priority to an endangered species of fish until such time as they no longer needed the protection of the ESA because such decision was in accordance with the ESA); *National Wildlife Federation v. National Park Service*, 669 F. Supp. 384 (D.Wyo.1987) (held continuing operation of campground under interim management plan pending results of EIS with regard to effects on endangered species of grizzly bear did not violate ESA). *While the Court agrees that defendants have some discretionary powers as to the methods of conservation it desires to implement, it does not agree with defendants' assertion that defendants may balance competing agency interests with the conservation of an endangered species, as this flies smack in the face of the Supreme Court's holding in* Tennessee Valley Authority v. Hill, *437 U.S. 153 (1978).*

federal agencies.* * * [T]he plain language of the Act, buttressed by its legislative history, shows clearly that Congress viewed the value of endangered species as "incalculable."

Id. at 184–86. *See also* 16 U.S.C. § 1531(c)(1) ("all Federal departments and agencies shall seek to conserve endangered species and threatened species and shall utilize their authorities in furtherance of the purpose of this Act.") Moreover, defendants' Forest Plan provides:

> Conservation and recovery of federally endangered, threatened, and proposed species is given top priority in management. All adverse impacts on federally listed species will be avoided except when it is possible to compensate adverse impacts totally through alternatives.

[ ]

Furthermore, defendants' Forest Plan provides, "all adverse impacts on federally listed species will be avoided except when it is possible to compensate adverse impacts totally through alternatives." [ ] Thus the Court concludes that defendants are bound by the ESA and their own Forest Plan, to place the Indiana bat, an endangered species, at the top of its priority list. It will become apparent to the reader of this Opinion and Order that defendants have failed to comply with its affirmative duty by placing the sale of 199 acres worth of trees before the protection of an endangered species.

NOTES

(1) What was the basis of the court's decision? Who has the more persuasive analysis—the court in *Pyramid Lake* or in *House*?

(2) Doing little vs. doing nothing: In *Pyramid Lake*, the Navy had taken steps to reduce its water use to benefit cui-ui restoration efforts. The petitioners thus were seeking to have the agency required to do more. *Florida Key Deer v. Stickney* involved the failure of the Federal Emergency Management Agency (FEMA) to do anything to protect listed species when deciding whether to provide flood insurance under the National Flood Insurance Program. Since the program provides insurance in areas that are unlikely otherwise to qualify for insurance, FEMA's management decisions have potentially significant impacts on wildlife habitat. This was the case on Big Pine Key which is the core remaining habitat of the Florida Key Deer. Evidence indicated that development would be substantially reduced if flood insurance was not made available. The district court held that FEMA's failure "to consider or undertake *any* action [violated] its mandatory obligation under section 7(a)(1)." *Florida Key Deer v. Stickney,* 864 F.Supp. 1222, 1237–38 (S.D.Fla.1994).

(3) National programs and local impacts: Section 7(a)(1) states that federal agencies "shall ... utilize their authorities" to conserve listed species. How should this affect programs that are national in scope given that listed species are—almost by definition—highly local in range? Should national programs be applied differently when they impact listed species in some areas? In *Sierra Club v. Glickman,* the Fifth Circuit held that § 7(a)(1) of the ESA required the Department of Agriculture to "develop an organized program utilizing USDA's authorities for the conservation" of listed species. *Sierra Club v. Glickman*, 156 F.3d 606, 612 (5th Cir.1998).

PERSPECTIVES

J.B. Ruhl, *Section 7(a)(1) of the "New" Endangered Species Act: Rediscovering and Redefining the Untapped Power of Federal Agencies Duty to Conserve,*

25 ENVTL. L 1107, 1149–52 (1995).

1. *An Antibacksliding Approach—Duty to Avoid Impeding Recovery*

The minimum approach the agencies could take, without completely eradicating the duty to conserve as an independent duty under the ESA, would be to bar federal agencies from taking action that would prevent or impede recovery of listed species. Such a criterion would offer advantages over the take and jeopardy prohibitions[in section 9 and 7(a)(2)], because many actions falling short of those all-or-nothing conditions nonetheless may impede or prevent recovery. For example,a minimum viable population of a particular listed species may be capable of existing indefinitely in a defined habitat area, albeit in permanent endangered or threatened status. Federal agency actions, either project-specific or program wide, which either reduce the amount of occupiable habitat to that minimum viable population size or prevent the area of occupiable habitat from enlarging, may not cause direct take or jeopardy to the species, but would very likely prevent that species from recovering.

Under such an approach, therefore, some additional conservation impacts would be felt beyond those caused by the take and jeopardy prohibitions. Federal programs promoting land use development would need to consider whether such development would have the effect of cutting off suitable recovery opportunities for species in adjacent habitats. Any suitable habitat area that is currently unoccupied, but potentially occupiable by a species in need of expanded range for recovery, could gain significant protections not provided by any of the take or jeopardy provisions. Hence, even in its most passive form, section 7(a)(1) offers something not currently being provided by the core ESA programs.

On the other hand, using section 7(a)(1) only for the limited purpose of not impeding recovery fails to capture the action-forcing, meaning of the provision,and clearly falls short of the ESA's definition of "conserving" as bringing species out of endangered or threatened status....

2. *An Alternatives Analysis Approach—A Duty to Adopt Recovery–Friendly Actions*

An approach more faithful to section 7(a)(1) than simply requiring no recovery-impeding actions would be to adopt the calculus the Pyramid Lake Paiute Tribe proposed in *Pyramid Lake*: federal agencies must adopt the most recovery-friendly of any viable action alternatives. However, that formula still provides little action-forcing effect; it also fails to respond to the need to define both how friendly is the minimum acceptable under section 7(a)(1) and how much agencies are required to consider cost and convenience.

To further develop the action-forcing feature of section 7(a)(1), therefore, the Tribe's approach could be amended to require that agencies must always generate a maximally recovery-friendly alternative for any proposed action. In other words, any time a federal agency contemplates an action, the agency would have to apply its authorities to develop an option that satisfies the agency's primary mission and at the same time provides the maximum amount of species conservation within the agency's authority, even if that means integrating components into the project that do not directly serve the primary mission of the project. The conservation consultation procedure would then require that the action agency select that "best conservation case" alternative unless it is demonstrated to be technologically or economically impracticable in light of the alternatives available to the agency. An agency wishing to depart from the best conservation case alternative would have to demonstrate it selected the practicable option that came closest to meeting that ideal level of conservation.

Although such an approach would create a benchmark for weighing agency compliance with the duty to conserve, and would inject some degree of action-forcing thought into the conservation consultation procedure, that approach would nonetheless fall short of satisfying section 7(a)(1). By hinging the best conservation case analysis on the presence of an agency action, the ESA would not take full advantage of the focus in section 7(a)(1) on action-forcing at the agency program level. Hence, while the best conservation case approach may effectively implement section 7(a)(1) for project-specific consultations, some additional benchmark would be needed for program-wide consultations. Moreover, the best conservation case option itself would be subject to no objective benchmark by which to compare the performance within an agency among different projects, and between agencies generally in how each responds to the duty to conserve. Thus, some broadly applicable notion of what constitutes conservation is needed.

3.   An Action–Forcing Approach—An Affirmative Duty to Advance Recovery Plans

The most aggressive approach FWS and NMFS could take under section 7(a)(1) would respond to the gaps described for the passive and moderate approach models: require all federal agencies to maximize their use of programmatic and project-specific authorities to implement recovery plans. Under this approach, not only would agencies choose recovery-friendly alternatives for each agency project, but they would use their authorities to develop recovery-friendly programs. These programs would be developed within or independent of (but not inconsistent with) each agency's primary mission actions, and would implement listed species recovery plans. FWS and NMFS would coordinate agencies' respective efforts through the programmatic consultations, and through project-specific consultations would ensure that those program-wide measures were being implemented. The only benchmarks needed for such analysis would be straightforward—what are the agencies' authorities and what do the pertinent recovery plans require?

On the one hand,such an approach appears to be the most faithful to the ESA's overall structure. Recovery plans are to be "develop[ed] and implement[ed] * * * for the conservation and survival of endangered species and threatened species." [16 U.S.C. § 1533(f)(1).] Section 7(a)(1) imposes on federal agencies the duty to "carry[ ] out programs for the conservation of endangered species and threatened species." [*Id.* § 1536(a)(1).] Those provisions all but expressly reference each other....

As the practice is now, however, recovery planning and the duty to conserve barely know each other, much less act like family. Indeed, the sad fate of recovery planning is that, because there is no realistic prospect of plans being implemented, these plans have become fanciful, unrealistically expensive propositions. Recovery planning is not grounded in reality, because there is no reality to its implementation. The duty to conserve and recovery planning, however, could dovetail and ground each other in reality within the ESA family. With recovery planning as its benchmark, the duty to conserve would have substance and force. With the duty to conserve as its benchmark, recovery planning would have a real design and would likely come back down to earth.

b. RECOVERY PLANNING

NOTES

(1) The evolution of recovery planning: Recovery planning was added to the Act in the 1978 Amendments. The concise provision specified first that the Secretary "shall develop and implement plans for the conservation and survival" of listed species, "unless he finds that such a plan will not promote the conservation of the species." 16 U.S.C. § 1533(f)(1). Second, it authorized the wildlife agencies, "in developing and implementing recovery plans," to "procure the services ... of qualified persons." *Id.* Both provisions ratified the existing agency practice. Both FWS and NMFS had been developing recovery plans in conjunction with "recovery teams" composed of both agency and non-agency personnel.

In 1979, Congress directed the Secretary to establish a ranking system "to ensure that species facing a high degree of threat receive priority review for listing" and a priority scheme for developing recovery plans. *Id.* § 1533(h).

The provisions were largely rewritten and substantially expanded in 1988. The general duty to "develop and implement" recovery plans became the introductory language to new procedural standards that substantially expanded the mandate to recover listed species. Congress began by instructing the Secretary to give priority to "those species, without regard to taxonomic classification, that are most likely to benefit from such plans, particularly those species that are, or may be, in conflict with ... economic activity." *Id.* § 1533(f)(1)(A).

The Amendments also set out a list of required information to be included in all recovery plans. These statutory criteria reflect a desire for certainty in an uncertain world: recovery plans are to include (i) "a description of such site-specific management actions ... necessary to achieve" the conservation and survival of the species, (ii) "objective, measurable criteria which, when met, would result" in delisting of the species, and (iii) "estimates of the time ... and the cost needed" to carry out the recovery plan. *Id.* § 1533(f)(1)(B).

Finally, the amendments required the plans to be developed following an opportunity for public comment. *Id.* § 1533(f)(4).

(2) Recovery planning and conservation: Neither the 1978 nor the 1988 Amendments defined the term "recovery." Implicitly, however, the term is defined by the requirement that "[t]he Secretary shall develop and implement plans (hereinafter ... referred to as "recovery plans") for the conservation and survival of [listed] species." *Id.* § 1533(f)(1). Recall that conservation is defined in terms of delisting species—a focus that is buttressed by the requirement that plans include "objective, measurable criteria which, when met, would result in a determination ... that the species be removed from the list." *Id.* § 1533(f)(1)(B)(ii).

FWS and NMFS have promulgated joint regulations that define "recovery" as "improvement in the status of listed species to the point at which listing is no longer appropriate under the criteria set out in section 4(a)(1) [16 U.S.C. § 1533(a)(1)] of the Act." 50 C.F.R. § 402.02.

Defenders of Wildlife v. Babbitt

District Court for the District of Columbia.
130 F.Supp.2d 121 (2001).

■ HUVELLE, D.J.:—[The procedural and factual background is set out *supra.*]

C.   Section 4(f)—Sufficiency of the Recovery Plan

The FWS is responsible for the formulation of a recovery plan pursuant to a delegation of authority from the Secretary under the ESA. *See* 50 C.F.R. § 402.01(b). Under the ESA, FWS is required to develop and implement a recovery plan "for the conservation and survival of" the Sonoran pronghorn. 16 U.S.C. § 1533(f)(1). "Any such [recovery] plan is supposed to be a basic road map to recovery, *i.e.*, the process that stops or reverses the decline of a species and neutralizes threats to its existence." *Fund for Animals v. Babbitt*, 903 F. Supp. 96, 103 (D.D.C.1995). Such a plan "shall, to the maximum extent practicable * * * incorporate in each plan":

> (i) a description of such site-specific management actions as may be necessary to achieve the plan's goal for the conservation and survival of the species;

> (ii) objective, measurable criteria which, when met, would result in a determination, in accordance with the provisions of this section, that the species be removed from the list; and

(iii) estimates of the time required and the cost to carry out those measures needed to achieve the plan's goal and to achieve intermediate steps toward that goal.

16 U.S.C. § 1533(f)(1)(B)(i)-(iii). "[T]he phrase 'to the maximum extent practicable' does not permit an agency unbridled discretion. It imposes a clear duty on the agency to fulfill the statutory command to the extent that it is feasible or possible." *Fund for Animals,* 903 F. Supp. at 107 (citations omitted). Plaintiffs allege that the "Final Revised Sonoran Pronghorn Recovery Plan" ("the Plan") issued by FWS in December 1998 is deficient in all three respects.

1. Site–Specific Management Actions

The ESA provides that "in developing and implementing recovery plans," the Secretary and the FWS shall "to the maximum extent practicable" incorporate into each recovery plan "a description of such site-specific management actions as may be necessary to achieve the plan's goal for the conservation and survival of the species." 16 U.S.C. § 1533(f)(1)(B)(i). "[W]hile the legislative history suggests that incorporation of 'site-specific management objectives' is supposed to assure that recovery plans 'are as explicit as possible in describing steps to be taken in the recovery of a species,' * * * the FWS has the flexibility under the ESA to recommend a wide range of 'management actions' on a site-specific basis." *Fund for Animals,* 903 F. Supp. at 106 (citations omitted). Plaintiffs argue that the Plan does not contain site-specific management *actions,* but provides only for further research and sets broad, unspecific goals.

The plan proposes four main categories of recovery actions: (1) "Enhance present population of Sonoran pronghorn to reach recovery goal of 300 adults. Decrease factors that are potentially limiting growth"; (2) "Establish and monitor new, separate herd[s]"; (3) "Continue monitoring the Sonoran pronghorn population. Maintain a protocol for a repeatable, comparable and justifiable survey technique"; and (4) "Verify taxonomic status of the species." [ ] Under each action is a series of steps or tasks to be undertaken to accomplish the action. "What the ESA requires is the identification of management actions necessary to achieve the Plan's goals for the conservation and survival of the species. A recovery plan that recognizes specific threats to the conservation and survival of a threatened or endangered species, but fails to recommend corrective action or explain why it is impracticable or unnecessary to recommend such action, would not meet the ESA's standard." *Fund for Animals,* 903 F. Supp. at 108.

The Court finds that the Plan does "recommend actions or * * * steps that could ultimately lead to actions" to address the threats identified. *Id.* While some of the tasks and interim steps merely provide for further investigation or research, others are concrete, specific actions. The Court cannot say that too many of them involve only research or investigation, or that alternative or additional actions should be implemented. *See id.* ("The choice of one particular action over another is not arbitrary, capricious or an abuse of discretion simply because one may happen to think it ill-considered, or to represent the less appealing alternative solution available. The Court will not impose plaintiffs' or its own view of a better way to stem the threat posed * * * than the methods chosen by the FWS.") (citations and internal quotation marks omitted).

The Plan also states that "[t]his plan is to be short-term (about 7 years) as critical survival information is not sufficiently understood about this animal. Annual updates, rather than a new plan or major revision, will be the concept for maintaining an up-to-date recovery plan. Implementation plans will be written for each major recovery project and will provide necessary details of the project." [ ] *See Fund for Animals,* 903 F. Supp. at 107–08 ("Because science and circumstances change, however, the FWS needs, and the statute provides, some flexibility as it implements the recovery plan."). The Court will defer to the agency's discretion that critical information is not sufficiently known to implement an exhaustively detailed plan at this time, and that annual updates for the short-term duration of the plan are the best method to insure that the plan is current and up-to-date. *Id.* at 107 ("It is not feasible for the FWS to attempt to address each possibility. By the time an exhaustively detailed recovery plan is completed and ready for publication, science or circumstances could have changed and the plan might no longer be suitable. Thus, the FWS recognized in the Plan that it would be reviewed every five years and revised as necessary. In these circumstances, the Court concludes that the FWS has provided sufficient detail to satisfy the statute.").

2. Objective Measurable Criteria

The ESA states that the FWS "shall, to the maximum extent practicable," incorporate into the recovery plan "objective, measurable criteria which, when met, would result in a determination * * * that the species be removed from the list." 16 U.S.C. § 1533(f)(1)(B)(ii). "Congress has spoken in clarion terms: the objective, measurable criteria must be directed towards the goal of removing the endangered or threatened species from the list. Since the same five statutory factors must be considered in delisting as in listing, the Court necessarily concludes that the FWS, in designing objective, measurable criteria, must address each of the five statutory delisting factors and measure whether threats to the [species] have been ameliorated." *Fund for Animals,* 903 F. Supp. at 111 (citations omitted). Pursuant to the ESA, the five delisting factors are:

(A) the present or threatened destruction, modification, or curtailment of its habitat or range;

(B) overutilization for commercial, recreational, scientific, or educational purposes;

(C) disease or predation;

(D) the inadequacy of existing regulatory mechanisms; or

(E) other natural or manmade factors affecting its continued existence* * **

16 U.S.C. § 1533(a)(1). The Plan sets forth a program and certain criteria for downlisting the species from endangered to threatened, rather than delisting altogether. [ ] ("The recovery objective is to remove the Sonoran pronghorn from the list of endangered species. This revision addresses first downlisting the subspecies to threatened."). The criteria set forth in the

Plan for consideration of reclassifying the Sonoran pronghorn as "threatened" rather than "endangered" are either 1) when there are "an estimated 300 adult Sonoran pronghorn in one U.S. population and a second separate population is established in the U.S. and remains stable over a five year period," or 2) "numbers are determined to be adequate to sustain the population through time." [ ] These criteria plainly do not address the five delisting factors. . . .

Defendants cite *Southwest Center for Biological Diversity v. Babbitt,* Civ. 98–372 TUC JMR (D. Ariz. Aug. 18, 1999), slip. op. at 12, where the court deferred to the FWS's determination that it was not practicable to incorporate the five statutory delisting factors into the objective, measurable delisting criteria in the recovery plan at issue. The court found that FWS had outlined where the record "supports the conclusion that development of delisting criteria was not practicable without first satisfying downlisting criteria," and outlined plans to research the delisting factors. [ ] Here, however, defendant FWS has simply stated that the plan will first address downlisting the pronghorn to threatened, [ ], without explaining the reasoning behind that determination or outlining where the record supports that determination. The court in *Southwest Center for Biological Diversity* found that such a "conclusory statement does not alone constitute an adequate justification for the failure to incorporate delisting criteria." [ ] Here, FWS has provided little more than its conclusion. This is insufficient to excuse compliance with the requirement to incorporate the five statutory delisting factors into the objective, measurable criteria. *See* [ ]; *Greenpeace,* 80 F. Supp. 2d at 1147 ("A biological opinion is arbitrary and capricious and will be set aside when it has failed to articulate a satisfactory explanation for its conclusions * * ** ").

The Court will therefore remand the Plan to FWS to incorporate the criteria, or alternatively, to provide an adequate explanation as to why the delisting criteria cannot practicably be incorporated at this time.

3. Time Estimates

The recovery plan is required "to the maximum extent practicable" to incorporate "estimates of the time required and the cost to carry out those measures needed to achieve the plan's goal and to achieve intermediate steps toward that goal." 16 U.S.C. § 1533(f)(1)(B)(iii). The Plan contains an "Implementation Schedule," which is a chart of the tasks listed under each of the four categories of management actions. [ ] However, of the 23 tasks listed, only 5 have a specific estimate of the time required to carry out that task. [ ] The other 19 are described simply as "ongoing." [ ] No time estimates are provided for the intermediate steps that are listed below certain tasks. *All* of the tasks implementing actions (2) "[e]stablish and monitor new, separate herd[s]" and (3) "[c]ontinue monitoring the Sonoran pronghorn population[, m]aintain a protocol for a repeatable, comparable and justifiable survey technique" are listed as ongoing without any specific time estimates. [ ]

Undoubtedly, certain measures cannot be completed by a time certain, for they are by definition ongoing. For example, "protect present range" (task 1.5) will presumably continue indefinitely into the future. [ ] However, time estimates could be provided for certain interim measures listed under that task which are not even included on the chart, such as "[i]nvestigate preferred habitat[, d]etermine areas preferred for pronghorn activities * * * [,] investigate preferred forage species * * * [, c]omplete a vegetation map that includes all pronghorn habitat." *Id.* (task 1.52). That such measures will be subject to ongoing revision and updating does not mean that it is not practicable to provide a time estimate within which they could initially be completed. . . .

NOTES

(1) What function do the various statutory requirements play? For example, since none of the dates are binding, should the court force the agency to supply them?

(2) Defining recovery: Recall the comments of Professor Holly Doremus early in the chapter on the difficulty of defining, as a scientific matter, when a species is threatened or endangered. Would the same challenges arise in the context of determining, in advance—in a forward-looking recovery plan—when a particular species has recovered to the point where it can be delisted? In a later article, Doremus explores the challenges of delisting, and hence of setting recovery targets. Delisting, she concludes, "is not just about biology." A key element—perhaps the central element—has to do with the various human activities that imperiled the species in the first instance. Unless those human activities are halted (and perhaps reversed), a species is likely to remain at risk, even if its numbers and range have improved. Delisting, she believes, is likely to occur frequently only if alternative regulatory restrictions are imposed that continue protecting at-risk species against adverse human activities. Thus, a key element in defining "recovery" for a species may entail the identification of specific regulatory measures that can remain in place indefinitely. Holly Doremus, *Delisting Endangered Species: An Aspirational Goal, Not a Realistic Expectation,* 30 Envtl. L. Rptr. (Envtl L. Institute) 10434 (2000).

(3) *Fund for Animals v. Babbitt:* The grizzly bear was listed as threatened in 1975. In 1993, FWS issued a Grizzly Bear Recovery Plan, which was challenged by several conservation organizations that contended it failed "adequately to set forth 'site-specific management actions' or 'objective, measurable criteria' " as required by the ESA. *Fund for Animals v. Babbitt,* 903 F.Supp. 96, 103 (D.D.C.1995).

Plaintiffs argued that there was a "lack of detail in the recommended management actions." Indeed, they argued, the management actions recommended in the recovery plan "are largely the same [for the various ecosystems] and are described in boilerplate statements." *Id.* at 107. Although acknowledging that "[o]bviously, the phrase 'to the maximum extent practicable' does not permit an agency unbridled discretion[but rather] imposes a clear duty on the agency to fulfill the statutory command to the extent that it is feasible or possible," the court concluded that the complexity was simply too great to expect detailed permit "exhaustive detail." *Id.*

It is not necessary for a recovery plan to be an exhaustively detailed document. Several other ESA provisions, some of which do not afford the FWS much discretion, already place limits on activities that may affect the grizzlies or empower the FWS to restrict threatening activities as needed. *See, e.g.,* 16 U.S.C. §§ 1532(a)(3)(A), 1536(a)(2), 1536(b)(4)(B)(iii), 1539(a)(2)(A). It is true that the recovery plan provision places a separate obligation on the FWS aside from those imposed by other provisions of the ESA. *See Idaho Dep't of Fish and Game v. National Marine Fisheries Service,* 850 F.Supp. 886, 895 (D.Or.1994). But the Plan's recommendations are implemented through FWS programs, cooperation and consultation with states, and the obligation of federal agencies to consult with the FWS or to implement conservation programs. *See* 16 U.S.C. §§ 1535, 1536(a)(1), (2). These programs may in many cases require the development of detailed and possibly site or situation specific restrictions to protect the grizzly bear. Because science and circumstances change, however, the FWS needs, and the statute provides, some flexibility as it implements the recovery plan.

Id. at 107–08. Turning to the specific plan elements challenged by plaintiffs, the court held that FWS had met its statutory obligations in regard to the plan's recommendations on hunting, road densities, commodity uses, and linkage corridors between isolated populations. The conclusion on commodity uses captures the flavor of the plan and the judicial review of it:

The GBRP [Grizzly Bear Recovery Plan] *identifies* the threats to grizzly habitat posed by logging, mining, oil and gas development, livestock grazing, interference with grizzly dens and recreation. [ ] The IGB [Interagency Grizzly Bear] Guidelines respond to each of these threats. [ ] In addition, the Plan *recommends* that land managers *consider* the needs of the grizzlies in making management decisions and provides for ongoing monitoring of the effect of threatening activities on the grizzly bear. [ ] By directly and specifically addressing the threats posed by human activities and resource development, the FWS has met its obligation under the ESA.

Id. at 109 (emphasis added).

In contrast, the court found that the recovery plan was deficient because FWS failed to comply with the statutory requirement that the agency " '*shall,* to the *maximum extent practicable,*' incorporate into the recovery plan 'objective, measurable criteria which, when met, *would* result in a determination * * * that the species be removed from the list.' 16 U.S.C. § 1533(f)(1)(B)(ii)." *Id.* at 111. With these requirements, Congress spoke

in clarion terms: the objective, measurable criteria must be directed towards the goal of removing the endangered or threatened species from the list. Since the same five statutory factors must be considered in delisting as in listing, 16 U.S.C. § 1533(a), (b), (c), the Court necessarily concludes that the FWS, in designing objective, measurable criteria, must address each of the five statutory delisting factors and measure whether threats to the grizzly bear have been ameliorated.

Id.

Is a recovery plan a framework for subsequent decisions or an action document that specifies steps leading to delisting of a species? Note that this decision is highly deferential to the agency in regard to the conservation-related components of the plan—most fundamentally, the court defers to the agency's conclusion that the plan contains only recommendations rather than management requirements—while simultaneously giving little deference to the plan's lack of "objective, measurable criteria" for delisting. Does the decision reflect the respective areas of expertise of agency and court? Is this exalting form over substance? Which of these questions are legal and which are factual/judgmental?

(4) Enforceability of recovery plans:

(a) *Sierra Club v. Lujan*: One of the major battles over the ESA has focused on the Edwards Aquifer, a 175–mile long underground aquifer that covers about 3600 square miles beneath eight counties in central Texas. The aquifer is recharged primarily from surface waters and rainfall seeping through porous earth. It discharges through a series of springs on the eastern edge of the aquifer, which are the only habitat of five federally endangered and threatened species: the fountain darter, the San Marcos gambusia (which may now be extinct), the San Marcos salamander, the Texas blind salamander, and Texas wild rice. Pumping from the aquifer has reduced the flow of the springs; during drought years, some of the springs ceased to flow. When FWS failed to implement a recovery plan for the endemic species, Sierra Club brought suit. The district court held:

> At least in the circumstances of this case, the ESA § 4 duty to develop and implement a plan is mandatory, not discretionary. The ESA says that he "shall" develop and implement such recovery plans. 16 U.S.C. § 1533(f). There is one stated exception: "Unless he finds that such a plan will not promote the conservation of the [endangered] species." *Id.* The Federal Defendants have never claimed that this exception applies to the present case. The Secretary's failure to develop and implement recovery plans permits this Court to review whether the USFWS has acted in accordance with Congress' wishes.

> Both the Federal Defendants and the Defendant–Intervenors argue the Secretary has discretion to set priorities and determine whether recovery plans will conserve the species. [However, f]or eight years, the Federal Defendants failed to implement the existing San Marcos Recovery Plan, and they failed to develop a plan for Comal Springs. They never identified the necessary springflow requirements of the species. The Federal Defendants argue that "particularly in light of the severe budget constraints" their duty to develop and implement a recovery plan should be discretionary. [ ] This Court refuses to legislate a new exception reading: "the Secretary shall develop and implement a recovery plan unless he claims, or suspects, that 'tight budget constraints' make develop or implementation of a recovery plan inconvenient or difficult to reconcile with the needs of other species, in which case he may or may not develop and implement a plan, when and if he pleases." . . .

. . .

The Court does not conclude the Federal Defendants must, without exception, immediately implement every step in every recovery plan. The Court concludes, however, the Federal Defendants may not arbitrarily, for no reason or for inadequate or improper reasons, choose to remain idle. . . .

Sierra Club v. Lujan, 36 Envt'l Rep. Cas. 1533 (W.D.Tex.1993), *appeal dismissed,* 995 F.2d 571 (5th Cir.1993).

(b) *National Wildlife Federation v. National Parks Service*: In the *National Wildlife Federation v. National Parks Service* decision discussed in the case, the Wildlife Federation challenged a decision by the Parks Service to keep the Fishing Bridge Campground open pending completion of an environmental impact statement. Plaintiffs sought closure of the campground—which was in grizzly bear habitat—to reduce the number of bears killed following human-bear encounters. Plaintiffs argued that closure was mandated by the *Grizzly Bear Recovery Plan:*

> Plaintiffs would urge upon this Court that the language of § 1533(f) obligates the Secretary to develop and implement a recovery plan, and that, once developed, all concerned agencies must adhere to it. The language does not so say. The Secretary is required to initiate a recovery plan "unless he finds that such a plan will not promote the conservation of the species." [ ]

> Plaintiffs further argue that since a grizzly bear recovery plan was already developed, the Park Service and the Secretary cannot later selectively decide which provisions to go forward with. To adopt such a position completely misconstrues congressional intent. . . . [T]he Secretary is required to develop a recovery plan only insofar as he reasonably believes that it would promote conservation. This Court will not attempt to second guess the Secretary's motives for not following the recovery plan. The Court finds that, confronted with newer and more sophisticated methods available to determine the effect that continued operation of Fishing Bridge would have upon the grizzly bear, the Secretary could reasonably have concluded that the implementation of such a plan should be stayed until the results of this new analysis become available through an EIS.

National Wildlife Federation v. National Park Service, 669 F.Supp. 384 (D.Wyo.1987).

(c) *National Audubon Society v. Hester*: In *National Audubon Society v. Hester,* the court refused to prohibit the agency from directly contradicting a recovery plan. FWS had developed a recovery plan for the California condor that adopted a strategy of keeping the remaining population in the wild rather than capturing them for a captive-breeding program. In 1985, increasing mortality in the wild population led the agency to change tactics; Audubon sued to prevent the policy reversal and obtained a preliminary injunction. The district court concluded, "In this proceeding, the record offers no reasoned analysis nor any strong justification for FWS' abrupt policy reversal." *National Audubon Society v. Hester,* 627 F.Supp. 1419, 1421 (D.D.C.1986). The Court of Appeals reversed without discussing the recovery plan:

We believe the Wildlife Service's decision to capture the remaining wild condors was manifestly defensible. That decision represented a reevaluation by the responsible agency of the costs and benefits associated with the existence of captive and wild condor flocks. Contrary to the plaintiff's assertion, the decision was not markedly at odds with previous policy.... [T]he agency reconsidered its policy after learning of recent developments, including the lead poisoning suffered by a bird inhabiting what was thought to be one of the safest locations.

National Audubon Society v. Hester, 801 F.2d 405, 408 (D.C.Cir.1986).

(d) ***Defenders of Wildlife v. Lujan:*** A similar result was reached in a suit brought to force FWS to implement the Northern Rocky Mountain Wolf Recovery Plan. The district court denied the request:

The Recovery Plan itself has never been an action document. [ ] It left open different approaches and contemplated that when an agency or group made specific proposals for achieving a particular objective of the plan, there would be a need for further study. [ ] Indeed, from the outset, the Fish and Wildlife Service noted that only when an actual action plan was in hand could the environmental impact of the recovery effort in Yellowstone be determined. [ ]

Defenders of Wildlife v. Lujan, 792 F.Supp. 834, 835 (D.D.C.1992).

The courts in *National Wildlife Federation, National Audubon Society,* and *Defenders of Wildlife* each delivered the same message: recovery plans do not in themselves restrict an agency's discretion. The court in *Oregon Natural Resource Council v. Turner* noted in passing that "the development and publication of a recovery plan in and of itself would not have afforded the endangered species any additional protection. The recovery plan presents a guideline for future goals but does not mandate any actions, at any particular time, to obtain those goals." *Oregon Natural Resource Council v. Turner,* 863 F.Supp. 1277, 1284 (D.Or.1994).

Are the cases distinguishable from *Sierra Club v. Lujan, supra*? If the nonimplementation of the plan causes listed species to be taken, does discretion give way to nondiscretionary duties?

PERSPECTIVES

Federico Cheever, *The Road to Recovery: A New Way of Thinking About the Endangered Species Act,*
23 ECOLOGY L.Q. 1, 73–75, 77–78 (1996).

A.   *The Recovery Concept as the Key to Interpretation*

First, we should accept that impact on recovery prospects play a central role in interpreting other provisions of the Endangered Species Act: (1) harm to recovery prospects may constitute harm to a species within the meaning of the section 9 taking prohibition; (2) harm to recovery prospects may constitute jeopardy to a species within the meaning of section 7(a)(2); (3) harm to recovery prospects may, constitute "adverse modification" of critical habitat within the meaning, of section 7(a)(2); and (4) recovery prospects should play a central role in the designation of critical habitat.

If we accept the central interpretive role of the recovery concept in determining what the Endangered Species Act does and does not allow, the Act, as a whole, suddenly begins to make more sense. The various enforcement mechanisms, so long divorced from the Act's stated purpose of conserving species and the ecosystems on which they depend, become methods of furthering that goal by furthering, or at least not foreclosing, recovery and conservation. If we view the substantive provisions of section 7 and 9 as paths to the ultimate goal of recovery, we will discourage formalistic readings of enforceable provisions of the Act, which construe the words of the Act to the long-term detriment of the species it was intended to protect, and encourage interpretation of the Act more in accord with the spirit in which it was enacted.

Emphasizing the central role of recovery would force us to move a few more steps away from the unhelpful "one threat model" of species protection and a little closer to the "probabilities model." Thinking in terms of recovery prevents us from limiting our focus to the effects of the proposed project or threat and forces us to ponder how the particular enforcement decision will likely affect the probable status of the species in the long run.

. . .

B. *Recovery Planning as the Key to Coordination*

Just as the concept of recovery should become the key to interpreting other provisions of the Endangered Species Act, so should the process of recovery planning coordinate the use of those provisions to conserve species. Currently, recovery plans describe the status of the species to be recovered and identify a recovery objective and a series of recovery tasks, arranged in a schedule, intended to achieve the identified objective. The value of recovery plans would be enhanced if they considered how application of other provisions of the Endangered Species Act could further, or at least not frustrate, recovery.

Recovery plans currently discuss a broad range of topics from the purely scientific to the political and legal. On occasion, they will refer to enforcement of other sections of the Act. However, additional analysis of the role of other provisions of the Act could be fruitful. The process might begin with a relatively simple set of questions: how will section 7(a)(2) consultation further recovery of the species? How will enforcement of the section 9 taking prohibition further recovery of the species? How will designation of critical habitat further recovery of the species? How will the issuance of section 7(b)(4) incidental take statements or section 10(a) incidental take permits further recovery of the species?

The National Research Council Committee on Scientific Issues in the Endangered Species Act recently offered what it calls "recovery plan guidance":

We recommend * * * that all recovery planning include an element of "recovery plan guidance" particularly with regard to activities to be reviewed under section 7, 9 and 10 of the ESA. To the extent feasible, the guidance should identify activities that can be assumed to be consistent with the requirements of those sections, activities that can be assumed to be inconsistent with them, and activities that require case by case evaluation.[344]

Specific consideration of the relationship between the recovery process and other provisions of the Act would strengthen the recovery process by giving it new credibility. A searching analysis of this relationship should demonstrate that recovery objectives are achievable with the regulatory tools available. The various mechanisms for indirectly enforcing recovery planning provisions would add to the available range of legal options.

The specific consideration of the relationship between the recovery process and other provisions of the Act would facilitate acceptance of enforcement of other provisions of the Act by linking their enforcement with a long-term positive goal-recovery and eventual delisting of the species. Some people currently opposed to endangered species protection might be swayed by the explanation that the burdens they see imposed upon landowners are part of a well thought out plan to nurse a species back to health. While this argument would not persuade everyone, it would certainly be more compelling than the more generalized arguments we must now use to justify enforcement.

.   .   .

CONCLUSION

In 1962, Thomas Kuhn used the phrase "paradigm change" to identify those revolutions in the nature of scientific thought when an old way of thinking becomes an inadequate tool for dealing with reality and a new way of thinking must replace it.[348] Such paradigm changes also occur in our understanding of law.[349] The Endangered Species Act is due for such a change. The "prohibitive" perception of the Act has become inadequate for dealing with biological and political reality. The needed change in our thinking can begin if we accept the central role of the concept of recovery in all aspects of the Endangered Species Act.

The Endangered Species Act's power and simplicity have made it effective in protecting biological diversity, while allowing flexibility to protect human economic interests through the reasonable and prudent alternatives process and the various exceptions to the taking prohibition. Like Ptolemaic astronomers, who did an excellent job of predicting the movement of the stars and planets despite the handicaps created by their assumption that the Sun revolved around the Earth, those charged with enforcing the Endangered Species Act have done much to mitigate the effects of their assumption that the Act is fundamentally prohibitive in nature. However, the connection between the enforcement of the Act's

---

344. COMMITTEE ON SCIENTIFIC ISSUES IN THE ENDANGERED SPECIES ACT, SCIENCE AND THE ENDANGERED SPECIES ACT 83 (1995).

348. *See* THOMAS S. KUHN, THE STRUCTURE OF SCIENTIFIC REVOLUTIONS 10, 68 (1970).

349. George Coggins notes that "paradigms are like tight ends in football; they seem to shift a lot." George C. Coggins, *Eleven Reasons to Disregard This Commentary on the Brave New Era in Western Public Land Law*, 65 U. COLO. L. REV. 401, 402 n.10 (1994).

substantive provisions and the Act's goal of furthering conservation and recovery of species has been tenuous. The authors of the Act understood that preventing extinction was not enough. They understood that any effective species preservation law must "conserve" or "recover" protected Species. A new focus on the concept of recovery and the recovery planning process might strengthen that connection to the benefit of protected species and begin the process of altering the way we think about the Endangered Species Act.

c. REINTRODUCING LISTED SPECIES

NOTES

(1) The evolution of reintroduction as a conservation tool: In 1973, Congress defined "conserve" as "the use of all methods and procedures which are necessary to bring any [listed] species to the point at which the measures provided pursuant to this Act are no longer necessary. Such methods and procedures include, but are not limited to, ... transplantation." 16 U.S.C. § 1532(3). Reintroduction—translocating members of a species into suitable habitat from which the species has been extirpated—is a valuable management tool for conserving species because it can be used to reduce some types of risks that small populations face as a result of their limited numbers. A geographically separate population provides some insurance against catastrophic changes to crucial environmental factors; a hurricane or an oil spill, for example, might extirpate a small or restricted population. Nonetheless, there has often been significant opposition to translocating populations. In part this is due to the fear of landowners that land-use restrictions will accompany the reintroduced species. To overcome such opposition, wildlife managers and conservation groups proposed the "experimental population" idea to Congress in 1982. Sponsors of the legislation hoped that federal agencies, state officials, and private landowners would be willing to "host" populations of listed species if they were assured that doing so would not restrict their land-management options. The 1982 amendments to the Endangered Species Act sought to provide these assurances by reducing the protection accorded reintroduced, "experimental" populations.

The increased management flexibility that Congress sought was achieved by allowing the Secretary to shift some members (the experimental population) of listed species between statutorily crucial categories—effectively to downlist or delist the members of the experimental population—and thus to reduce the stringency of the applicable management standards. Thus, § 10(j) treats most experimental populations as "threatened" species for purposes of the § 9 taking prohibitions—which allows the Secretary to determine which of the § 9 prohibitions are applicable to the population—and as a "species proposed to be listed" for purposes of the § 7 consultation requirements—which means that action agencies are required only to "confer" rather than to "consult" under § 7.

(2) The experimental population process: The Acts defines the term "experimental population" as "any population (including offspring arising solely therefore) authorized by the Secretary for release ... but only when, and at such times as, the population is wholly separate geographically from nonexperimental populations of the same species." 16 U.S.C. § 1539(j)(1). The defining characteristics of an experimental population thus are: [1] it is composed of individuals released under the authorization of the Secretary and [2] it is "wholly separate geographically from nonexperimental populations of the same species." *Id.* § 1539(j)(1).

Before he may authorize the release of an experimental population, the Secretary is required to make two findings: first, he must find that the release "will further the conservation" of the species, *id.* § 1539(j)(2)(A); and second, he must determine whether the population "is essential to the continued existence" of the species. *Id.* § 1539(j)(2)(B). The Secretary is required to make the finding on essentiality through the promulgation of a regulation. *Id.* The decision to release an experimental population thus requires the notice-and-comment procedures set out in the Administrative Procedures Act. *See* 5 U.S.C. § 553. The purpose for adopting this procedural mechanism was twofold: to ensure that the Secretary "will receive the benefit of public comment on such determinations [and] to provide a vehicle for the development of special regulations for each experimental population that will address the particular needs of that populations." H.R. Conf. Rep. No. 835, 97th Cong., 2d Sess. 34, *reprinted in* 1982 U.S.C.C.A.N. 2860, 2875.

If the population *is* essential, members of the species are to be treated as threatened species. *Id.* § 1539(j)(2)(C). If the population is determined to be nonessential, it is to be treated as a threatened species with two significant exceptions:

For the purposes of § 7, if the population is determined to be nonessential, it is to be treated as if it were a species that had only been proposed to be listed unless it is found on land within the National Wildlife Refuge or National Park System. *Id.* § 1539(j)(2)(C)(i). Thus, when the nonessential population is located outside Refuges and Parks, federal agencies are required only to "confer" rather than to "consult" with the Secretary, *id.*, and are not required to "insure" that actions they authorize, fund, or carry out do not jeopardize the species.[1] *Id.* § 1536(a)(2). Furthermore, the

---

1. Recall that § 7 generally draws a line between species that have been listed and those that have only been proposed for listing. The line begins in § 7(a). Section 7(a)(2) requires all federal agencies to "insure" that "any action authorized, funded or carried out by" the agency "is not likely to jeopardize the continued existence" of a listed species. 16 U.S.C. § 1536(a)(2). Section 7(a)(4), on the other hand, requires federal agencies only to "confer" on "any action which is likely to jeopardize the continued existence of any species proposed to be listed under section 4 of this Act." *Id.* § 1536(a)(4); *see also id.* § 1536(c)(1) (including proposed species within the biological assessment requirement). The subsection does not contain the requirement that agencies "insure" that

they do not jeopardize listed species. Furthermore, section 7(a)(4) explicitly exempts projects affecting proposed species from the prohibition against committing resources during consultation: the action agency, in other words, is not prohibited from proceeding with the proposed action while conferring. The courts concluded that section 7(a)(4) did not offer much protection. For example, the Corps of Engineers is permitted to construct a harbor project despite destruction of plants proposed to be listed as endangered since it had conferred with FWS. Enos v. Marsh, 769 F.2d 1363, 1368–69 (9th Cir.1985); *see also* Wilson v. Block, 708 F.2d 735, 750–51 (D.C. Cir.), *cert. denied,* 464 U.S. 956 (1983); County of Bergen v. Dole, 620 F.Supp. 1009, 1047–48, 1063 (D.N.J.1985).

Secretary is prohibited from designating critical habitat for nonessential populations. *Id.* § 1539(j)(2)(C)(ii). A nonessential population, in other words, is largely exempted from the protection provided by § 7.

On the other hand, if the population is determined to be "essential" or is located within a Refuge or Park, it is to be treated as though it is listed as a threatened species, *id.* § 1539(j)(2)(C), and, as such, is subject to normal interagency consultation requirements.

For purposes of § 9, both essential and nonessential experimental populations are to be treated as though they are listed as a threatened species. *Id.* § 1539(j)(2)(C). The § 9 prohibitions on taking and commerce therefore are applicable to the populations only to the extent that they are expressly extended to the species by regulation. The regulation governing the release of the species thus is to specify what commercial and taking restrictions are applicable to the population.

For a perceptive overview, see Federico Cheever, *From Population Segregation to Species Zoning: The Evolution of Introduction Law Under Section 10(j) of the Endangered Species Act,* 1 WYO. L. REV. 287 (2001).

(3) The first precaution of intelligent tinkering: One of Aldo Leopold's most famous metaphors on land health can serve as the basis for the ESA's reintroduction provisions: "If the land mechanism as a whole is good, then every part is good, whether we understand it or not. If the biota, in the course of aeons, has built something we like but do not understand, then who but a fool would discard seemingly useless parts? To keep every cog and wheel is the first precaution of intelligent tinkering." ALDO LEOPOLD, *Conservation, in* ROUND RIVER 145, 146–47 (1953).

Wyoming Farm Bureau Federation v. Babbitt

Tenth Circuit Court of Appeals.
199 F.3d 1224 (2000).

■ BRORBY, J.—These consolidated appeals stem from three separate challenges to the Department of Interior's ("Department") final rules governing the reintroduction of a nonessential experimental population of gray wolves in Yellowstone National Park ("Yellowstone") and central Idaho. The district court consolidated the challenges and struck down the wolf reintroduction rules, concluding they (1) are contrary to Congress' clear intent under section 10(j) of the Endangered Species Act, 16 U.S.C. § 1539(j), to prevent lessening the protection afforded to naturally occurring, individual members of the same species; (2) are contrary to the Department's own regulations extending Endangered Species Act protections to all individual animals within an area where experimental and nonexperimental populations may overlap; and (3) conflict with section 4 of the Endangered Species Act, 16 U.S.C. § 1533, by operating as a de facto "delisting" of naturally occurring wolves. *Wyoming Farm Bureau Federation v. Babbitt,* 987 F. Supp. 1349, 1372–76 (D.Wyo.1997). The district court ordered the reintroduced non-native wolves and their offspring removed from the identified experimental population areas, but stayed its own judgment pending this appeal. *Id.* at 1376. Discerning no conflict between the challenged experimental population rules and the Endangered Species Act, we reverse the district court's order and judgment.

I. Background

A. *Factual Summary*

. . .

The Secretary of Interior ("Secretary") listed the Northern Rocky Mountain Wolf, an alleged subspecies of the gray wolf, as an endangered species under the Endangered Species Act of 1973. 43 Fed. Reg. 9607 (March 9, 1978) ("Reclassification of the Gray Wolf in the United States and Mexico, with Determination of Critical Habitat in Michigan and Minnesota"). In 1978, the Secretary listed the entire gray wolf species as endangered in the lower forty-eight states, except Minnesota. [ ] In 1980, a team organized by the Department of Interior completed its Northern Rocky Mountain Wolf Recovery Plan ("Recovery Plan"), pursuant to the Endangered Species Act. The Department updated the Recovery Plan in 1987 to recommend the introduction of at least ten breeding pairs of wolves for three consecutive years in each of three identified recovery areas (Yellowstone National Park, central Idaho and northwestern Montana).

Based on the 1987 recommendation, and at Congress' direction, the Fish and Wildlife Service, in cooperation with the National Park Service and the United States Forest Service ("Forest Service"), prepared an environmental impact statement in accordance with the National Environmental Policy Act, 43 U.S.C. § 4332(2)(C). The final environmental impact statement analyzed the environmental effects of five wolf recovery alternatives. The proposed action alternative the Fish and Wildlife Service adopted called for the annual reintroduction of fifteen wolves in two nonessential experimental population areas—Yellowstone National Park and central Idaho—beginning in 1994. Section 10(j) of the Endangered Species Act, 16 U.S.C. § 1539(j), expressly authorizes the establishment of such nonessential experimental populations.

In June 1994, Secretary Bruce Babbitt adopted the proposed action alternative subject to certain conditions intended to "minimize or avoid the environmental impacts and public concerns identified during the environmental review process." One condition was the promulgation of nonessential experimental population rules to implement a wolf management program under section 10(j). The Department published its final experimental population rules in November 1994. 59 Fed. Reg. 60252 (Nov. 22, 1994). The Recovery Plan and final rules prescribe the release of 90–150 wolves from Canada into designated areas of Yellowstone and central Idaho over a three-to five-year period, [ ], notwithstanding the Department's acknowledgment (1) a colony of naturally occurring wolves exists in Montana which, as the number of wolves increases, eventually will recolonize areas of Yellowstone and Idaho; and (2) lone wolves have been confirmed to exist in or near the designated experimental population areas in Yellowstone and Idaho. The final experimental population rules expressly authorize persons coming into contact with wolves to take actions otherwise prohibited under the Endangered Species Act. For example, a livestock producer can "take" any wolf caught in the act of killing, wounding or biting livestock on his land so long as the incident is reported within twenty-four hours. [ ] The rules also provide a framework within which the Fish and Wildlife Service can manage "problem" wolves. [ ]

. . .

D.   *The Issues*

. . .

The Wolf Reintroduction Rules

The crux of this case, and hence this opinion, is the validity of the final rules governing the introduction of a nonessential experimental population of gray wolves in the entirety of Yellowstone and in central Idaho. The district court struck down the challenged rules as violative of section 4(f) and section 10(j) of the Endangered Species Act, 16 U.S.C. §§ 1533(f), 1539(j). . . . We afford the district court's decision no particular deference, but rather, review the rules and administrative record independently. [ ]

II.   Legal Analysis

. . .

B.   *Statutory Context*

Congress enacted the Endangered Species Act in 1973 to "provide for the conservation, protection, restoration, and propagation of species of fish, wildlife, and plants facing extinction." S. Rep. No. 93–307, at 1 (1973), *reprinted in* 1982 U.S.C.C.A.N. 2989 (emphasis added); *see also* 16 U.S.C. § 1531(b). Toward that end, the Endangered Species Act authorizes the Secretary of the Interior to list domestic or foreign species as endangered or threatened. 16 U.S.C. § 1533(a)-(b). Once a species is so listed, it is afforded certain protections, and federal agencies assume special obligations to conserve, recover and protect that species. For example, section 4(f), 16 U.S.C. § 1533(f), directs the Secretary to develop and implement recovery plans for the "conservation and survival" of listed species "unless he finds that such a plan will not promote the conservation of the species." In addition, section 7(a)(1) authorizes the Secretary to "live" trap and "transplant" (reintroduce) rare species, if necessary, to bring an endangered or threatened species to the point at which the protective measures of the Endangered Species Act are no longer necessary. *See* 16 U.S.C. §§ 1536(a)(1) and 1532(3) (definition of "conservation").

Congress added section 10(j) to the Endangered Species Act in 1982 to address the Fish and Wildlife Service's and other affected agencies' frustration over political opposition to reintroduction efforts perceived to conflict with human activity. Although the Secretary already had authority to conserve a species by introducing it in areas outside its current range, Congress hoped the provisions of section 10(j) would mitigate industry's fears experimental populations would halt development projects, and, with the clarification of the legal responsibilities incumbent with the experimental populations, actually encourage private parties to host such populations on their lands. H.R. Rep. No. 97–567, at 8 (1982), *reprinted in* 1982 U.S.C.C.A.N. 2807, 2808, 2817; *see also* 16 U.S.C. § 1539(j).

. . .

As the language of [§ 10(j)] makes clear, Congress contemplated the Secretary would promulgate special rules to identify each experimental population. As Congress explained:

> The purpose of requiring the Secretary to proceed by regulation, apart from ensuring that he will receive the benefit of public comment on such determinations, is to provide a vehicle for the development of special regulations for each experimental population that will address the particular needs of that population. Among the regulations that must be promulgated are regulations to provide for the identification of experimental populations. Such regulations may identify a population on the basis of location, migration pattern, or any other criteria that would provide notice as to which populations of endangered or threatened species are experimental.

H.R. Conf. Rep. No. 97–835 (1982), *reprinted in* 1982 U.S.C.C.A.N. 2860, 2875. In other words, Congress purposely designed section 10(j) to provide the Secretary flexibility and discretion in managing the reintroduction of endangered species. By regulation, the Secretary can identify experimental populations, determine whether such populations are essential or nonessential, and, consistent with that determination, provide control mechanisms (*i.e.*, controlled takings) where the Act would not otherwise permit the exercise of such control measures against listed species.

C. *Alleged Violations*

1. Geographic Separation

The Agencies do not dispute individual wolves may leave (and, from time to time, have left) Canada and Montana and enter the experimental population areas in central Idaho and Yellowstone. The Farm Bureaus and the Urbigkits argue, and the district court agreed, that this possibility establishes an overlap of wolf "populations," or the overlap of the experimental areas and the "current range" of naturally occurring wolf populations in contravention of the requirement in section 10(j)(1) that experimental populations of an endangered species must be wholly separate geographically from nonexperimental populations of the same species. We do not accept that contention.

Plaintiffs base their argument on a single piece of legislative history they claim demonstrates Congress never intended section 10(j) to lessen the Endangered Species Act protections afforded individual members of a natural population of a listed species, or to create law enforcement problems. *See Wyoming Farm Bureau Fed'n*, 987 F. Supp. at 1372–73. The 1982 House Report they rely on states the House Committee:

> carefully considered how to treat introduced populations that overlap, in whole or in part, natural populations of the same species. To protect natural populations and to avoid potentially complicated problems of law enforcement, the definition [of "experimental population"] is limit-

ed to those introduced populations that are wholly separate geographically from nonexperimental populations of the same species. Thus, for example, in the case of the introduction of individuals of a listed fish species into a portion of a stream where the same species already occurs, the introduced specimens would not be treated as an "experimental population" separate from the non-introduced specimens. . . . If an introduced population overlaps with natural populations of the same species during a portion of the year, but is wholly separate at other times, the introduced population is to be treated as an experimental population at such time as it is wholly separate. The Committee intends, however, that such a population be treated as experimental only when the times of geographic separation are reasonably predictable and not when separation occurs as a result of random and unpredictable events.

H.R. Rep. No. 97–567, at 33 (1982), *reprinted in* 1982 U.S.C.C.A.N. 2807, 2833. According to the Farm Bureaus, this passage "specifically prohibits the overlap of 'individuals' and/or 'specimens' of a species, not just the overlap of *entire* populations of a species," and demonstrates Congress' intent that an "experimental population" should exist "only when there is no possibility that members of the 'experimental population' could overlap with members of naturally occurring populations." They claim the Agencies erroneously fail to recognize that populations are necessarily made up of individuals; thus, the wolf reintroduction rules reflect an impermissible construction of section 10(j).

The Farm Bureaus further argue the reintroduction program creates law enforcement problems by characterizing naturally occurring individual wolves that wander into the experimental population as "experimental" rather than "endangered." According to the Farm Bureaus, naturally occurring individual wolves are entitled to full Endangered Species Act protection regardless of location, and because it is virtually impossible to differentiate between a naturally occurring wolf and a reintroduced wolf, officials will not be able to enforce those protections as Congress intended.

We begin our analysis by reviewing the statute itself, the extent to which Congress expressly defined relevant terms or otherwise clearly spoke to this issue, and conversely, the degree to which Congress delegated authority over the matter to the Agencies, in particular the Department of Interior. *See Chevron U.S.A.,* 467 U.S. at 842–43; *see also United States v. McKittrick,* 142 F.3d 1170, 1173 (9th Cir.1998), *cert. denied,* 525 U.S. 1072 (1999). As the district court recognized, the Endangered Species Act does not define the relevant terms or otherwise address the precise question at issue—whether the phrase "wholly separate geographically from nonexperimental populations" means that a reintroduced population of animals must be separate from every naturally occurring individual animal. *Wyoming Farm Bureau Fed'n,* 987 F. Supp. at 1371–74. Instead, as the statutory language and legislative history make clear, Congress deliberately left the resolution of this type management/conservation issue to the Department. *See McKittrick,* 142 F.3d at 1174 ("Congress' specific purpose in enacting section 10(j) was to give greater flexibility to the Secretary. Thus, each experimental population has its own set of special rules so that the

Secretary has more managerial discretion. This flexibility allows the Secretary to better conserve and recover endangered species." (Quotation marks and citations omitted.)); *see also* H.R. Rep. No. 97–567 at 33 (1982), *reprinted in* 1982 U.S.C.C.A.N. 2807, 2833. We therefore defer to the Department's interpretation of the phrase "wholly separate geographically from nonexperimental populations," so long as its interpretation does not conflict with the plain language of the Endangered Species Act. [ ] We perceive no conflict.

The Department defines "population" as a potentially self-sustaining group "in common spatial arrangement,"[3] and thus determined a "geographic separation" is any area outside the area in which a particular *population* sustains itself. *See Wyoming Farm Bureau Fed'n*, 987 F. Supp. at 1373; 59 Fed. Reg. at 60256. These definitions preclude the possibility of population overlap as a result of the presence of individual dispersing wolves—by definition lone dispersers do not constitute a population or even part of a population, since they are not in "common spatial arrangement" sufficient to interbreed with other members of a population. Moreover, since it is highly unlikely a lone wolf will encounter another solitary wolf of the opposite sex and reproduce for two years running, the populations left behind by the lone wolves do not expand simply because they travel away.

This interpretation of the "geographic separation" requirement of section 10(j) is consistent with the language and objectives of the Endangered Species Act as a whole. Congress defined "species," as used throughout the Act, to represent subspecies or "any distinct population segment" of an interbreeding species. 16 U.S.C. § 1532(16). This reference to species *vis a vis* populations or population segments, as opposed to individual specimens, is repeated throughout the text of section 10(j), thus reflecting the paramount objective of the Endangered Species Act to conserve and recover species, not just individual animals. *See McKittrick*, 142 F.3d at 1174 (citing H.R. Conf. Rep. No. 97–835 at 30 (1982), *reprinted in* 1982 U.S.C.C.A.N. 2860, 2871). This broader objective is further evidenced by the well-established fact individual animals can and do lose Endangered Species Act protection simply by moving about the landscape. Moreover, we find nothing in the Endangered Species Act that precludes steps to conserve a species in order to protect isolated individuals.[5] Nor are we

---

3. The Department generally defines "population" as "a group of fish or wildlife ... in common spatial arrangement that interbreed when mature." 50 C.F.R. § 17.3. It refined that definition in the context of the wolf reintroduction regulations to mean "at least two breeding pairs of gray wolves that each successfully raise at least two young" yearly for two consecutive years. 59 *Fed. Reg.* at 60256.

5. This conclusion represents our major departure from the district court's reasoning, and eliminates the premise on which the district court held the Department had violated its own regulations. *Wyoming Farm Bureau Fed'n*, 987 F. Supp. at 1373–74. As

explained more fully in section II.C.2 of this opinion, we hold the Department may, consistent with the plain language of section 10(j) and the context of the Endangered Species Act as a whole, treat all wolves found within the boundaries of the designated experimental population areas, including any lone dispersing wolves that may enter those areas, as nonessential experimental animals. Moreover, we hold the district court erred to the extent it suggested there is a temporal constraint on when and how long the Department may maintain an experimental population. While the regulations require an analysis of the degree to which experimental and natural populations might overlap at predict-

convinced the challenged rules present complicated law enforcement obstacles. The Department specifically determined "the experimental population area does not currently support any reproducing pairs of wolves;" thus, the legal protection afforded any particular wolf is clearly known, depending entirely on where the wolf is, not where it might once have been. For these reasons, we hold the Department's interpretation of the "geographic separation" provision reflects the goals of the Endangered Species Act "to protect natural populations" and "to avoid potentially complicated problems of law enforcement," H. Rep. No. 97-567, 97th Cong., 2d Sess. at 33 (1982), *reprinted in* 1982 U.S.C.C.A.N. at 2833, and is well within the scope of agency discretion granted by Congress and licensed by the Supreme Court. *See McKittrick,* 142 F.3d at 1174-75.

Plaintiffs' argument that the Agencies failed to release the Canadian wolves outside the "current range" of naturally occurring wolves is similarly flawed since Plaintiffs rigidly define "current range" as it is used in section 10(j) to be that territory occupied by an individual wolf. The plain language of the statute does not support their interpretation. Although the statute does not define "current range," section 10(j)(2)(A) requires that an "experimental population" must be established "outside the current range of such *species.*" 16 U.S.C. § 1539(j)(2)(A) (emphasis added). As discussed above, Congress defined "species," consistent with its broad conservation and recovery goals, to constitute distinct, interbreeding population segments or subspecies, not individual animals. By definition, then, an individual animal does not a species, population or population segment make. Therefore, the Department, exercising its discretion under section 10(j), reasonably interpreted the phrase "current range" to be the combined scope of territories defended by the breeding pairs of an identifiable wolf pack or population.

2. Protection of Naturally Occurring Wolves

The district court determined, at the behest of the Farm Bureaus and the Predator Project, that the Department must accord full endangered species protections to any naturally occurring wolf found within the experimental areas. Accordingly, the district court held the final reintroduction rules, which provide that "[a]ll wolves found in the wild within the boundaries of [the experimental areas] after the first releases will be considered nonessential experimental animals," (1) constitute a "de facto 'delisting'" of naturally occurring lone dispersers, and (2) illegally deny full Endangered Species Act protections to offspring of naturally dispersing wolves, and to offspring of naturally dispersing and introduced wolves, within the designated experimental areas. *Wyoming Farm Bureau Fed'n,* 987 F. Supp. at 1374-76. We believe this holding unnecessarily limits the administrative discretion and flexibility Congress intentionally incorporat-

able periodic times in order to determine when an introduced population is experimental, they do not require experimental and natural populations be forever kept distinct. To hold otherwise would be to undermine the recovery objective of section 10(j) altogether.

See 59 *Fed. Reg.* at 60261, 60276 (the Department designed the reintroduction program in part to expedite gray wolf recovery by encouraging interbreeding between experimental and native populations).

ed into section 10(j), ignores biological reality, and misconstrues the larger purpose of the Endangered Species Act.

Pursuant to section 10(j)(2)(B), 16 U.S.C. § 1539(j)(2)(B), the Secretary must, prior to authorizing a release, identify by regulation the population to be deemed experimental. As discussed above, this statutory requirement confers broad discretion to the Secretary to manage populations to better conserve and recover endangered species. Based on the facts (1) there were no reproducing wolf pairs and no pack activity within the designated experimental areas, (2) wolves can and do roam for hundreds of miles, and (3) it would be virtually impossible to preclude naturally occurring individual gray wolves from intermingling with the experimental population, 59 *Fed. Reg.* at 60256, 60261, the Secretary intentionally identified the experimental population as all wolves found within the experimental areas, including imported wolves and any lone dispersers and their offspring. The Department determined it could best manage the wolf reintroduction program to achieve species recovery in this manner. *Id.* at 60261. We find nothing in the Act that invalidates this approach by requiring the protection of individuals to the exclusion or detriment of overall species recovery, or otherwise limiting the Department's flexibility and discretion to define and manage an experimental population pursuant to section 10(j).

. . . .

The restrictive interpretation the Predator Project and Farm Bureaus advocate could actually undermine the Department's ability to address biological reality (*i.e.,* wolves can and do roam for hundreds of miles and cannot be precluded from intermingling with the released experimental population), and thus handicap its ability to effectuate species recovery. The Endangered Species Act simply does not countenance that result. . . .

NOTES

(1) Is the court's deference to the agency's definition of "wholly separate population" convincing? Is it justifiable under the legislative history? Does the Act focus on individuals or on populations? Recall the definition of "species" as a "distinct population segment." Similarly, the jeopardy standard focuses on populations. But the Act also seeks to protect individuals—as we will see when we consider the take prohibitions of § 9. More fundamentally, does the ESA protect individuals as individuals or as members of a species?

(2) Experimental for how long? The court decides that a population can be experimental, even if it is introduced into an area where wild members of the species occasionally stray, at least so long as the wild members do not breed. But what happens if, in time, the experimental populations and wild populations do intermingle? In the case of wolves, what happens if naturally wild wolves move next to an introduced pack, and establish an adjoining territory? How much contact is needed before it is proper to say that the experimental population is no longer distinct? Must evidence of interbreeding be shown? Is regular physical contact enough? Is it enough if the wild animals have taken up residence in the area, and are not merely passing through? Does the FWS have an enforceable obligation to remove the "experimental" label attached to a reintroduced population once it is no longer isolated?

(3) The perils of litigation strategies: Note the difficulties confronting both environmental groups and industry/land-user groups in deciding what position to take on the issues in this case. At the district court level, environmental groups appeared on both sides; the National Audubon Society appeared on the side of the Farm Bureau at the district court level—and won. It then switched sides on appeal—and won again! *See* Michael J. Bean, *Major Endangered Species Act Developments in 2000*, 31 Entl. L. Rptr. (Envtl. L. Inst.) 10283, 10284 (2001).

The Farm Bureau's aim was clear enough: to halt the reintroduction. But note that, if it succeeded on its legal theory and the reintroduction nonetheless went ahead (as a general recovery action, not under Section 10(j)), the situation for the Farm Bureau would have been far worse: The wolves would have been brought in, and they would have been fully protected as an endangered population. That latter possibility was precisely what several environmental groups, including the National Audubon Society, hoped would happen. Other environmental groups believed that reintroduction would be possible politically only if the introduced wolves were not treated as endangered.

(4) Experimental populations: Despite the passage of more than a decade since the enactment of the experimental population provision, it remains a relatively little-used conservation method: The Secretary has authorized the release of only 14 nonessential experimental populations of 11 species. In chronological order, the populations authorized for release are:

(a) Delmarva Peninsula fox squirrel—reintroduction approved in 1984;

(b) Colorado squawfish—reintroduction approved in 1985;

(c) woundfin—reintroduction approved in 1985;

(d) red wolf [2 populations]—reintroduction approved in 1986 and 1991;

(e) southern sea otter—reintroduction approved in 1987;

(f) yellowfin madtom—reintroduction approved in 1988;

(g) Guam rail—reintroduction approved in 1989;

(h) black-footed ferret [2 populations]—reintroduction approved in 1991 and 1994;

(i) whooping crane—reintroduction approved in 1993;

(j) gray wolf [2 populations]—reintroduction approved in 1994 and 1998;

(k) California condor—reintroduction approved in 1996.

The experimental populations released to date fall into broadly similar biological and political categories. Many, for example, involve species whose continued existence is due primarily to captive breeding programs; black-footed ferrets, Mexican wolves, red wolves, California condors, and Guam rails are not extinct only because they have been successfully bred in captivity. Other species are limited to isolated populations subject to a significant risk of a catastrophic event—southern sea otters and whooping cranes, for example, are both at risk from oil spills. Finally, the reintroduced species also tend to be politically controversial—because they compete directly with human activities such as fishing (Southern Sea Otters), because their presence may intrude upon land-use activities (Guam rails, whooping cranes, California condors, black-footed ferrets, Colorado squawfish, and woundfin), or because they are carnivores whose taste for meat may impact the range-beef industry (gray wolves).

Finally, both the whooping crane and California condor experimental populations were released outside of their historic ranges.

PERSPECTIVES

(1) The rapacious wolf: Wolves are the beasts of myth and magic, of lore and gore. Europeans brought an image of the wolf with them to this new world. It was an image expressed in a set of myths that reflected their history as herders, their religion's symbolic glorification of sheep, their fears of all things wild: the wolf of Aesop, of Little Red Riding Hood, of Peter and the Wolf; Beowulf and werewolves and Fenris, who will devour heaven and earth at the end of time. This "hidious and desolate wildernes, full of wild beasts and willd men" was a wildness that was their birthright and manifest destiny to subdue; the Bible made it moral, their belief in their own specialness made it natural. It required the domination of the wilderness and the destruction of the wolf, that "beast of waste and desolation," the ultimate symbol of the wildness both in the wilderness and in human psyches. It was the Christian thing to do, for the wolf was the devil in disguise and the conquest of the wilderness a morality tale in which the European played the hero's role.

(2) The exemplary wolf: The rapacious wolf is now paired with a rival image: a devoted family man, monogamous and playing with pups beside the den entrance. There is the nightly family sing-along. They are "God's dogs" who keep wild ungulate populations healthy by culling the weak, the sick, the old and the crippled; they are a valued part of the ecosystem.

(3) The non-symbolic wolf: In a famous passage, Aldo Leopold recounts killing a wolf in New Mexico, an event that, after-the-fact, led him to the conclusion that "[o]ny a mountain has lived long enough to listen objectively to the howl of a wolf":

> We were eating lunch on a high rimrock, at the foot of which a turbulent river elbowed its way. We saw what we thought was a doe fording the torrent, her breast awash in white water. When she climbed the bank toward us and shot out her tail, we realized our error: it was a wolf. A half-dozen others, evidently grown pups, sprang from the willows . . . .
>
> In those days we had never heard of passing up a chance to kill a wolf. In a second we were pumping lead into the pack, but with more

excitement than accuracy. . . . When our rifles were empty, the old wolf was down, and a pup was dragging a leg into impassable slide rocks.

We reached the old wolf in time to watch a fierce green fire dying in her eyes. I realized then, and have known ever since, that there was something new to me in those eyes—something known only to her and to the mountain. I was young then, and full of trigger itch; I thought that because fewer wolves meant more deer, that no wolves would mean a hunters' paradise. But seeing the green fire die, I sensed that neither the wolf nor the mountain agreed with such a view.

Since then I have lived to see state after state extirpate its wolves. I have watched the face of many a newly wolfless mountain, and seen the south-facing slopes wrinkle with a maze of new deer trails. I have seen every edible bush and seedling browsed, first to anaemic desuetude, and then to death. I have seen every edible tree defoliated to the height of a saddlehorn. Such a mountain looks as if someone had given God a new pruning shears, and forbidden Him all other exercise. . . .

I now suspect that just as a deer herd lives in mortal fear of its wolves, so does a mountain live in mortal fear of its deer.

ALDO LEOPOLD, *Thinking Like a Mountain, in* SAND COUNTY ALMANAC 129 (1949).

As with so many of his other ideas, Leopold's understanding of mountains has been borne out. The reintroduction of wolves into Yellowstone National Park and central Idaho has produced cascading changes in the ecosystems. As one report noted, the wolves "have killed half the coyotes in the area, forced elk to become more vigilant and provided many opportunities for scavengers to share their kills. Because there are fewer coyotes, rodents are more plentiful, a boon for predators like hawks and bald eagles, and overall biodiversity has sharply increased." Jim Robbins, *In Two Years, Wolves Reshaped Yellowstone,* N.Y. TIMES, Dec. 30, 1997, at B13. Grizzly bears, ravens, foxes, bald and golden eagles, owls, badgers, and pine martens have all benefitted from the presence of wolves. But the ripples extend even more broadly: the evidence suggests that aspen have been in decline because the absence of wolves allowed elk and moose to browse aspen stands more aggressively. William J. Ripple & Eric J. Larsen, *Historic Aspen Recruitment, Elk, and Wolves in Yellowstone National Park, USA,* 95 BIOLOGICAL CONSERVATION 361 (2000). *See generally* William K. Stevens, *Debating Nature of Nature in Yellowstone,* N.Y. TIMES, June 23, 1998, at B9; Yellowstone Ecosystem Studies <www.yellowstone.org>.

SECTION 6.   PROHIBITIONS AND PENALTIES

a.   PROHIBITIONS

NOTES

(1) Section 9 (16 U.S.C. § 1538) contains a comprehensive list of prohibited acts. Section 11 (16 U.S.C. § 1540) specifies a range of civil and criminal penalties applicable to those who commit prohibited acts. Before turning to the details of these two sections, it is helpful to examine their basic structures.

(2) Prohibited acts: Section 9 contains several different types of prohibitions:

(a) Prohibitions generally applicable to listed species of fish and wildlife: Section 9 contains an all-encompassing prohibition against conduct that harms an *endangered* species of *fish or wildlife* or that involves commercial transactions in such species. 16 U.S.C. § 1538(1)(A)-(F). Although endangered species are protected directly by the Act, *threatened* species of *fish or wildlife* are protected only through regulations adopted by the Secretary. That is, the ESA prohibits commercial activity and taking of endangered species, but specifies only that it is illegal to "violate any regulation pertaining ... to any threatened species of fish or wildlife ... and promulgated by the Secretary pursuant" to the Act. *Id.* § 1538(a)(1)(G). The Secretary has exercised the authority granted by these provisions to extend the prohibitions applicable to endangered species to threatened species generally, *see* 50 C.F.R. § 17.31, but the regulation listing a species as threatened may specify less restrictive prohibitions. The regulations applicable to threatened species—known as 4(d) regulations—are considered below.

(b) Prohibitions generally applicable to listed species of plants: A separate subsection contains prohibitions applicable to listed species of plants. The prohibitions broadly proscribe interstate and foreign commerce in listed species. There is no general prohibitions against taking listed species, presumably because plants are part of the real estate and steps to protect plants are therefore far more likely to raise taking concerns. The Act does distinguish between "areas under Federal jurisdiction"—where it is illegal to "remove and reduce to possession" or to "maliciously damage or destroy" an endangered species of plant—and any other area—where it is impermissible to "remove, cut, dig up, or damage or destroy" any endangered species "in knowing violation of any law or regulation of any State" or to do so "in the course of any violation of a State criminal trespass law." *Id.* § 1538(a)(2)(B).

(c) Prohibitions applicable to captive specimens: The general prohibitions are inapplicable to any specimen held in captivity on the date on which the final regulation listing that species is published in the *Federal Register*—as long as that holding was not "in the course of a commercial activity." *Id.* § 1538(b)(1). The meaning of this crucial term is discussed below. The exemption from the prohibitions applies only to the individual specimen and not to any offspring—except for raptors and their offspring held in captivity on November 10, 1978. *Id.* § 1538(2)(A). Falconers are required to maintain documents on these birds. *Id.* § 1538(2)(B).

(d) Prohibitions applicable to international trade pursuant to the Convention on International Trade in Endangered Species of Fauna and Flora (CITES): As discussed in Chapter 8, the ESA implements CITES. The prohibitions for violations of CITES are found in section 9. *Id.* § 1538(c).

(e) Regulation of imports and exports: Section 9 establishes a mandatory permit system for individuals seeking to engage in the business of importing and exporting fish, wildlife, or plants. *Id.* § 1538(d).

(f) Miscellaneous provisions: Finally, § 9 imposes reporting obligations, *id.* § 1538(e), and prohibits the importation or exportation of fish, wildlife, or plants except through ports designated by the Secretary. *Id.* § 1538(f).

(i) PROHIBITIONS ON "COMMERCIAL ACTIVITY"

NOTES

(1) The prohibitions on commercial activities: The Endangered Species Act specifies that "it is unlawful for any person subject to the jurisdiction of the United States to—

(A) import any such species into, or export any [endangered] species from the United States;

. . .

(D) possess, sell, deliver, carry, transport, or ship, by any means whatsoever, any such species taken in violation of [the Act];

(E) deliver, receive, carry, transport, or ship in interstate or foreign commerce, by any means whatsoever and in the course of a commercial activity, any such species; [or]

(F) sell or offer for sale in interstate or foreign commerce any such species.

16 U.S.C. § 1538(a)(1).

The breadth of the prohibition comes from the definitions of many of the included terms. Thus, the Act broadly defines the term "commercial activity" to mean "all activities of industry and trade, including, but not limited to, "the buying or selling . . . and activities conducted for the purpose of facilitating such buying and selling." *Id.* § 1532(2). Similarly, the term "species" includes "any subspecies of fish or wildlife or plants, and any distinct population segment of any species of vertebrate fish or wildlife which interbreeds when mature." *Id.* § 1532(16). Finally, the term "fish or wildlife" is defined to mean "any member of the animal kingdom, including without limitation any mammal, fish, bird (including any migratory, nonmigratory, or endangered bird for which protection is also afforded by treaty or other international agreement), amphibian, reptile, mollusk, crustacean, arthropod or other invertebrate, and includes any part, product, egg, or offspring thereof, or the dead body or parts thereof." *Id.* § 1532(8).

Thus, the importation or exportation and the transportation or sale in interstate or foreign commerce "in the course of a commercial activity" of "any part, product, egg, or offspring thereof, or the dead body or parts thereof" are all prohibited.

(2) The ESA's commercial prohibitions and state law: Section 6(f) contains three sentences that address areas of potential federal-state conflict: interstate and foreign commerce, state wildlife conservation laws, and prohibitions on taking listed wildlife. Unfortunately, little beyond this listing of topics is unambiguous. These sentences were the subject of intense debate during the legislative drafting process. Despite—or perhaps because of—this focus, "subsection (f) does not perhaps reach that level of clarity of which the English language is capable." *H.J. Justin & Sons, Inc. v. Brown,* 519 F.Supp. 1383 (E.D.Cal.1981), *aff'd in part, rev'd in part sub nom. H.J. Justin & Sons, Inc. v. Deukmejian,* 702 F.2d 758 (9th Cir.), *cert. denied* 464 U.S. 823 (1983).

The first sentence expressly preempts two categories of state commercial laws:

> *Any State law* or regulation *which applies* with respect *to* the importation or exportation of, or *interstate or foreign commerce* in, endangered species or threatened species *is void to the extent that it may* [1] effectively *permit what is prohibited* by this Act or by any regulation which implements this Act, or [2] *prohibit what is authorized* pursuant to an exemption or permit provided for in this Act or in any regulation which implements this Act.

16 U.S.C. § 1535(f) (emphasis added). The second and third sentences focus on state conservation and anti-taking laws.

What is preempted by the first sentence?

First, the sentence applies only to state laws regulating commerce. Other state wildlife laws—including those regulating takings of listed species—are unaffected.[1]

Second, the sentence concerns only species listed as endangered or threatened under the ESA; state regulation of commerce in other species is unaffected. For example, Justin Boot Company manufactured cowboy boots, some of which were made from exotic leathers. California prohibited the sale of products made from a variety of animals, including African elephant, Indonesian python, and wallaby kangaroo. While the African elephant was listed as a threatened species, the python and wallaby were not on the federal list. The district court held that, since the first sentence in § 6(f) applied only to commerce in federally listed species, the ESA was simply inapplicable and therefore without preemptive effect. *H.J. Justin & Sons, Inc. v. Brown,* 519 F.Supp. 1383, 1387 (E.D.Cal.1981), *rev'd on other grounds sub. nom., H.J. Justin & Sons, Inc. v. Deukmejian,* 702 F.2d 758, 759–60 (9th Cir.). *See also* Man Hing Ivory & Imports, Inc. v. Deukmejian, 702 F.2d 760, 765 n. 4 (9th Cir.1983).

(a) The ESA as a floor: The first category—"Any State law ... which applies ... to ... interstate or foreign commerce in, [listed] species is void to the extent that it may ... permit what is prohibited by this Act"—has not proved problematic; it is simply another example of the

---

1. Although state laws regulating the taking of listed species may *affect* commerce, the section draws a distinction between regulating commerce and regulating takings. The third sentence in § 6(f) applies to takings. This distinction between interstate and foreign commerce, on the one hand, and taking regulations, on the other, was the central point in the exchange of letters between Representative Dingell and Assistant Secretary Reed. *See 1973 House Hearings* 386–88 (1973); *see also* § 8.2.1(b) *supra*.

general proposition that the ESA provides a floor of protection for listed species.

(b) The ESA as a ceiling: The second clause—"Any State law ... which applies ... to ... interstate or foreign commerce in, [listed] species is void to the extent that it may prohibit what is authorized pursuant to an exemption or permit provided for in this Act"—has proved troublesome: are state statutes that are more protective of listed species preempted? Neither statutes that regulate *intrastate* commerce (such as intrastate sales) nor statutes that *affect* interstate commerce are expressly preempted. The degree to which the sentence should be read implicitly to void such statutes is the source of dispute—both as a result of the Protean term "commerce" and the financial stakes involved. The issue has been litigated in the context of permits issued to allow commerce in threatened species. *Compare Man Hing Ivory & Imports, Inc. v. Deukmejian,* 702 F.2d 760 (9th Cir.1983) (intrastate ban on sales of listed species preempted by § 6(f)) *with Cresenzi Bird Importers, Inc. v. New York,* 658 F.Supp. 1441 (S.D.N.Y. 1987), *aff'd,* 831 F.2d 410 (2d Cir.1987) (*per curiam*) (intrastate ban on sales of listed species not preempted by § 6(f)).

(3) The ESA and the Lacey Act: As the next case demonstrates, the ESA can serve as the predicate federal law for a violation of the Lacey Act.

(ii) PROHIBITIONS ON "TAKING"

NOTES

(1) The issues—"taking" and culpability: The Endangered Species Act contains an expansive definition of "take" that is the culmination of the two intertwined concepts that have marked the development of federal wildlife law's criminal prohibitions. The first is the list of the types of prohibited conduct—most commonly defined by the term "take." The ESA, for example, specifies that "it is unlawful for any person subject to the jurisdiction of the United States to ... take any [endangered] species within the United States or the territorial sea of the United States." 16 U.S.C. § 1538(a)(1)(B). The Act in turn defines " 'take' [as] to harass, harm, pursue, hunt, shoot, wound, kill, trap, capture, or collect, or to attempt to engage in any such conduct." *Id.* § 1532(19).

The second concept is culpability—what degree of culpability is required to support a conviction for a prohibited taking; culpability can range from willful through recklessness to negligence and on to strict liability. As with other federal wildlife statutes, the ESA's explicit culpability standards are contained in the section setting out the penalties and sanctions for violating the prohibitions against commerce and taking in § 9. These are discussed in the next section.

Does the definition of "take" in itself impose some culpability requirement? Do the terms in the definition implicitly require some type of "intent" to do harm?

(2) The evolution of "taking": National regulation of the taking of wildlife by the federal government began with the Migratory Bird Treaty

Act (MBTA) of 1918. The Act made it "unlawful to hunt, take, capture, kill, attempt to take, capture or kill, [or] possess" any migratory bird. Act of July 3, 1918, ch. 128, § 2, 40 Stat. 755, 755 (currently codified as amended at 16 U.S.C. § 702)). It did not, however, define what constituted a "take" beyond the content supplied by the other words in the prohibition. That is, the term presumably meant something other than "hunt," "capture," or "kill." The prohibition has been construed to impose liability for conduct that results in the unintended death of migratory birds—recall the decision in *United States v. FMC Corp.*, 572 F.2d 902 (2d Cir.1978), excerpted in Chapter 10.

The second federal statute to include a prohibition on taking wildlife was the Bald Eagle Protection Act of 1940, which criminalized the taking or possession of the species, its parts, nests, or eggs. Act of June 8, 1940, ch. 278, § 1, 54 Stat. 250, 250–51 (currently codified as amended at 16 U.S.C. § 668(a)). The Act defined "take" as "includ[ing] also pursue, shoot, shoot at, wound, kill, capture, trap, collect, or otherwise willfully molest or disturb." With the inclusion of the term "pursue" Congress began the expansion of the term to include nonlethal acts.

The next significant expansion came in 1971 when Congress enacted the Airborne Hunting Act of 1971, Pub. L. No. 92–159, § 1, 85 Stat. 481 (currently codified at 16 U.S.C. § 742j–1) and the Wild and Free–Roaming Horses and Burros Act, Pub. L. No. 92–195, 85 Stat. 649 (currently codified as amended at 16 U.S.C. § 1331–1340). While neither act employed the term "take," both statutes did nonetheless contribute to the expansion of the taking concept by prohibiting conduct that "harasses" wildlife. The Airborne Hunting Act imposes fines and imprisonment for the use of an aircraft "to shoot for the purpose of capturing or killing ... or ... to harass any bird, fish, or other animal." 16 U.S.C. § 742j–1. Similarly, the Horse and Burros Act proscribes conduct that "maliciously causes the death or harassment of any wild free-roaming horse or burro." 16 U.S.C. § 1338(a).

The various strands of federal taking law came together in the Marine Mammal Protection Act of 1972, Pub. L. No. 95–522, 86 Stat. 1029 (currently codified as amended at 16 U.S.C. §§ 1361–1407). Its definition of "take"—"to harass, hunt, capture, or kill, or attempt to harass, hunt, capture or kill"—reflects the gradual accretion of types of conduct that had come to be understood as a "taking" of wildlife. In addition to the paradigm "killing," lawmakers have increasingly come to understand that a variety of different types of conduct were potentially detrimental to the well being of wildlife. The most expansive of these was the concept of "harassment." For example, the term was included in the Horses and Burros Act in recognition that conduct not immediately detrimental might nonetheless have cumulative or long-term effects. The Conference Report stated that the House language that had required "substantial harm" was rejected in favor of the Senate language prohibiting "harassment" in order "to widen the scope of prohibited activities. Concern was expressed by the conferees for activities which although not immediately causing substantial harm, would have a cumulatively detrimental effect on the health and welfare of the animals." CONF. REP. NO. 681, 92d Cong., 1st Sess. (1971), *reprinted in* 1971 U.S.C.C.A.N. 2159, 2160. The term was chosen, in other words, to describe conduct that did not necessarily cause a measurable or immediate injury. *See, e.g.,* United States v. One Bell Jet Ranger II Helicopter, 943 F.2d 1121, 1124–25 (9th Cir.1991) (discussing the use of the term "harass" in the Airborne Hunting Act).

On the historical development of the taking concept, see generally Michael E. Field, *The Evolution of the Wildlife Taking Concept from its Beginning to Its Culmination in the Endangered Species Act,* 21 HOUSTON L. REV. 457 (1984).

Babbitt v. Sweet Home Chapter

United States Supreme Court.
515 U.S. 687 (1995).

■ STEVENS, J.:—The Endangered Species Act of 1973, [ ], (ESA or Act), contains a variety of protections designed to save from extinction species that the Secretary of the Interior designates as endangered or threatened. Section 9 of the Act makes it unlawful for any person to "take" any endangered or threatened species. The Secretary has promulgated a regulation that defines the statute's prohibition on takings to include "significant habitat modification or degradation where it actually kills or injures wildlife." This case presents the question whether the Secretary exceeded his authority under the Act by promulgating that regulation.

I

Section 9(a)(1) of the Endangered Species Act provides the following protection for endangered species:

> Except as provided in sections 1535(g)(2) and 1539 of this title, with respect to any endangered species of fish or wildlife listed pursuant to section 1533 of this title it is unlawful for any person subject to the jurisdiction of the United States to—
>
>   * * *
>
> (B) take any such species within the United States or the territorial sea of the United States[.]

16 U.S.C. § 1538(a)(1). Section 3(19) of the Act defines the statutory term "take":

> The term "take" means to harass, harm, pursue, hunt, shoot, wound, kill, trap, capture, or collect, or to attempt to engage in any such conduct.

16 U.S.C. § 1532(19). The Act does not further define the terms it uses to define "take." The Interior Department regulations that implement the statute, however, define the statutory term "harm":

> Harm in the definition of "take" in the Act means an act which actually kills or injures wildlife. Such act may include significant habitat modification or degradation where it actually kills or injures wildlife by significantly impairing essential behavioral patterns, including breeding, feeding, or sheltering.

50 CFR § 17.3 (1994). This regulation has been in place since 1975.

A limitation on the § 9 "take" prohibition appears in § 10(a)(1)(B) of the Act, which Congress added by amendment in 1982. That section authorizes the Secretary to grant a permit for any taking otherwise prohibited by § 9(a)(1)(B) "if such taking is incidental to, and not the purpose of, the carrying out of an otherwise lawful activity." 16 U.S.C. § 1539(a)(1)(B).

In addition to the prohibition on takings, the Act provides several other protections for endangered species. . . .

Respondents . . . brought this declaratory judgment action against petitioners, the Secretary of the Interior and the Director of the Fish and Wildlife Service, in the United States District Court for the District of Columbia to challenge the statutory validity of the Secretary's regulation defining "harm," particularly the inclusion of habitat modification and degradation in the definition. Respondents challenged the regulation on its face. Their complaint alleged that application of the "harm" regulation to the red-cockaded woodpecker, an endangered species, and the northern spotted owl, a threatened species, had injured them economically. [ ]

Respondents advanced three arguments to support their submission that Congress did not intend the word "take" in § 9 to include habitat modification, as the Secretary's "harm" regulation provides. First, they correctly noted that language in the Senate's original version of the ESA would have defined "take" to include "destruction, modification, or curtailment of [the] habitat or range" of fish or wildlife, but the Senate deleted that language from the bill before enacting it. Second, respondents argued that Congress intended the Act's express authorization for the Federal Government to buy private land in order to prevent habitat degradation in § 5 to be the exclusive check against habitat modification on private property. Third, because the Senate added the term "harm" to the definition of "take" in a floor amendment without debate, respondents argued that the court should not interpret the term so expansively as to include habitat modification.

The District Court considered and rejected each of respondents' arguments, finding "that Congress intended an expansive interpretation of the word 'take,' an interpretation that encompasses habitat modification." [ ]. . . .

A divided panel of the Court of Appeals initially affirmed the judgment of the District Court. [ ] After granting a petition for rehearing, however, the panel reversed. [ ]. . . .

The Court of Appeals' decision created a square conflict with a 1988 decision of the Ninth Circuit that had upheld the Secretary's definition of "harm." *See Palila v. Hawaii Department of Land & Natural Resources*, 852 F.2d 1106 (1988) (*Palila II*). The Court of Appeals neither cited nor distinguished *Palila II*, despite the stark contrast between the Ninth Circuit's holding and its own. We granted *certiorari* to resolve the conflict. [ ] Our consideration of the text and structure of the Act, its legislative history, and the significance of the 1982 amendment persuades us that the Court of Appeals' judgment should be reversed.

II

Because this case was decided on motions for summary judgment, we may appropriately make certain factual assumptions in order to frame the legal issue. First, we assume respondents have no desire to harm either the red-cockaded woodpecker or the spotted owl; they merely wish to continue logging activities that would be entirely proper if not prohibited by the ESA. On the other hand, we must assume arguendo that those activities will have the effect, even though unintended, of detrimentally changing the natural habitat of both listed species and that, as a consequence, members of those species will be killed or injured. Under respondents' view of the law, the Secretary's only means of forestalling that grave result—even when the actor knows it is certain to occur[9]—is to use his § 5 authority to purchase the lands on which the survival of the species depends. The Secretary, on the other hand, submits that the § 9 prohibition on takings, which Congress defined to include "harm," places on respondents a duty to avoid harm that habitat alteration will cause the birds unless respondents first obtain a permit pursuant to § 10.

The text of the Act provides three reasons for concluding that the Secretary's interpretation is reasonable. First, an ordinary understanding of the word "harm" supports it. The dictionary definition of the verb form of "harm" is "to cause hurt or damage to: injure." *Webster's Third New International Dictionary* 1034 (1966). In the context of the ESA, that definition naturally encompasses habitat modification that results in actual injury or death to members of an endangered or threatened species.

Respondents argue that the Secretary should have limited the purview of "harm" to direct applications of force against protected species, but the dictionary definition does not include the word "directly" or suggest in any way that only direct or willful action that leads to injury constitutes "harm."[10] Moreover, unless the statutory term "harm" encompasses indi-

---

9. [T]he Secretary's definition of "harm" is limited to "act[s] which actually kil[l] or injur[e] wildlife." [ ] In addition, in order to be subject to the Act's criminal penalties or the more severe of its civil penalties, one must "knowingly violat[e]" the Act or its implementing regulations. [ ] Congress added "knowingly" in place of "willfully" in 1978 to make "criminal violations of the act a general rather than a specific intent crime." [ ] The Act does authorize up to a $500 civil fine for "[a]ny person who otherwise violates" the Act or its implementing regulations. [ ] That provision is potentially sweeping, but it would be so with or without the Secretary's "harm" regulation, making it unhelpful in assessing the reasonableness of the regulation. We have imputed scienter requirements to criminal statutes that impose sanctions without expressly requiring scienter, [ ], but the proper case in which we might consider whether to do so in the § 9 provision for a $500 civil penalty would be a challenge to enforcement of that provision itself, not a challenge to a regulation that merely defines a statutory term. We do not agree with the dissent that the regulation covers results that are not "even foreseeable * * * no matter how long the chain of causality between modification and injury." [ ] Respondents have suggested no reason why either the "knowingly violates" or the "otherwise violates" provision of the statute—or the "harm" regulation itself—should not be read to incorporate ordinary requirements of proximate causation and foreseeability. In any event, neither respondents nor their *amici* have suggested that the Secretary employs the "otherwise violates" provision with any frequency.

10. Respondents and the dissent emphasize what they portray as the "established meaning" of "take" in the sense of a "wildlife take," a meaning respondents argue extends only to "the effort to exercise dominion

rect as well as direct injuries, the word has no meaning that does not duplicate the meaning of other words that § 3 uses to define "take." A reluctance to treat statutory terms as surplusage supports the reasonableness of the Secretary's interpretation. [ ][11]

Second, the broad purpose of the ESA supports the Secretary's decision to extend protection against activities that cause the precise harms Congress enacted the statute to avoid. In *TVA v. Hill,* 437 U.S. 153 (1978), we described the Act as "the most comprehensive legislation for the preservation of endangered species ever enacted by any nation." [ ] Whereas predecessor statutes enacted in 1966 and 1969 had not contained any sweeping prohibition against the taking of endangered species except on federal lands, [ ], the 1973 Act applied to all land in the United States and to the Nation's territorial seas. As stated in § 2 of the Act, among its central purposes is "to provide a means whereby the ecosystems upon which endangered species and threatened species depend may be conserved.* * * " [ ]

In *Hill,* we construed § 7 as precluding the completion of the Tellico Dam because of its predicted impact on the survival of the snail darter. [ ] Both our holding and the language in our opinion stressed the importance of the statutory policy. "The plain intent of Congress in enacting this statute," we recognized, "was to halt and reverse the trend toward species extinction, whatever the cost. This is reflected not only in the stated policies of the Act, but in literally every section of the statute." [ ] Although the § 9 "take" prohibition was not at issue in *Hill,* we took note of that prohibition, placing particular emphasis on the Secretary's inclusion of habitat modification in his definition of "harm." In light of that provision for habitat protection, we could "not understand how TVA intends to operate Tellico Dam without 'harming' the snail darter." [ ] Congress' intent to provide comprehensive protection for endangered and threatened species supports the permissibility of the Secretary's "harm" regulation.

over some creature, and the concrete effect of [sic] that creature." [ ] This limitation ill serves the statutory text, which forbids not taking "some creature" but "tak[ing] any [endangered] species"—a formidable task for even the most rapacious feudal lord. More importantly, Congress explicitly defined the operative term "take" in the ESA, no matter how much the dissent wishes otherwise, [ ], thereby obviating the need for us to probe its meaning as we must probe the meaning of the undefined subsidiary term "harm." Finally, Congress' definition of "take" includes several words—most obviously "harass," "pursue," and "wound," in addition to "harm" itself—that fit respondents' and the dissent's definition of "take" no better than does "significant habitat modification or degradation."

11. In contrast, if the statutory term "harm" encompasses such indirect means of killing and injuring wildlife as habitat modification, the other terms listed in § 3—"harass," "pursue," "hunt," "shoot," "wound," "kill," "trap," "capture," and "collect"— generally retain independent meanings. Most of those terms refer to deliberate actions more frequently than does "harm," and they therefore do not duplicate the sense of indirect causation that "harm" adds to the statute. In addition, most of the other words in the definition describe either actions from which habitat modification does not usually result (*e.g.,* "pursue," "harass") or effects to which activities that modify habitat do not usually lead (*e.g.,* "trap," "collect"). To the extent the Secretary's definition of "harm" may have applications that overlap with other words in the definition, that overlap reflects the broad purpose of the Act. [ ]

Respondents advance strong arguments that activities that cause minimal or unforeseeable harm will not violate the Act as construed in the "harm" regulation. Respondents, however, present a facial challenge to the regulation. [ ] Thus, they ask us to invalidate the Secretary's understanding of "harm" in every circumstance, even when an actor knows that an activity, such as draining a pond, would actually result in the extinction of a listed species by destroying its habitat. Given Congress' clear expression of the ESA's broad purpose to protect endangered and threatened wildlife, the Secretary's definition of "harm" is reasonable.

Third, the fact that Congress in 1982 authorized the Secretary to issue permits for takings that § 9(a)(1)(B) would otherwise prohibit, "if such taking is incidental to, and not the purpose of, the carrying out of an otherwise lawful activity," [ ], strongly suggests that Congress understood § 9(a)(1)(B) to prohibit indirect as well as deliberate takings. [ ] The permit process requires the applicant to prepare a "conservation plan" that specifies how he intends to "minimize and mitigate" the "impact" of his activity on endangered and threatened species, [ ], making clear that Congress had in mind foreseeable rather than merely accidental effects on listed species. No one could seriously request an "incidental" take permit to avert § 9 liability for direct, deliberate action against a member of an endangered or threatened species, but respondents would read "harm" so narrowly that the permit procedure would have little more than that absurd purpose. "When Congress acts to amend a statute, we presume it intends its amendment to have real and substantial effect." [ ] Congress' addition of the § 10 permit provision supports the Secretary's conclusion that activities not intended to harm an endangered species, such as habitat modification, may constitute unlawful takings under the ESA unless the Secretary permits them.

. . .

Nor does the Act's inclusion of the § 5 land acquisition authority and the § 7 directive to federal agencies to avoid destruction or adverse modification of critical habitat alter our conclusion. Respondents' argument that the Government lacks any incentive to purchase land under § 5 when it can simply prohibit takings under § 9 ignores the practical considerations that attend enforcement of the ESA. Purchasing habitat lands may well cost the Government less in many circumstances than pursuing civil or criminal penalties. In addition, the § 5 procedure allows for protection of habitat before the seller's activity has harmed any endangered animal, whereas the Government cannot enforce the § 9 prohibition until an animal has actually been killed or injured. The Secretary may also find the § 5 authority useful for preventing modification of land that is not yet but may in the future become habitat for an endangered or threatened species. The § 7 directive applies only to the Federal Government, whereas the § 9 prohibition applies to "any person." Section 7 imposes a broad, affirmative duty to avoid adverse habitat modifications that § 9 does not replicate, and § 7 does not limit its admonition to habitat modification that "actually kills or injures wildlife." Conversely, § 7 contains limitations that § 9 does not, applying only to actions "likely to jeopardize the continued existence of any endangered species or threatened species," [ ], and to modifications of habitat that has been designated "critical" pursuant to § 4, [ ]. Any overlap that § 5 or § 7 may have with § 9 in particular cases is unexceptional, [ ], and simply reflects the broad purpose of the Act set out in § 2 and acknowledged in *TVA v. Hill.*

We need not decide whether the statutory definition of "take" compels the Secretary's interpretation of "harm," because our conclusions that Congress did not unambiguously manifest its intent to adopt respondents' view and that the Secretary's interpretation is reasonable suffice to decide this case. *See generally Chevron U.S.A. Inc. v. Natural Resources Defense Council, Inc.,* 467 U.S. 837 (1984). The latitude the ESA gives the Secretary in enforcing the statute, together with the degree of regulatory expertise necessary to its enforcement, establishes that we owe some degree of deference to the Secretary's reasonable interpretation. [ ]

III

Our conclusion that the Secretary's definition of "harm" rests on a permissible construction of the ESA gains further support from the legislative history of the statute. . . .

IV

When it enacted the ESA, Congress delegated broad administrative and interpretive power to the Secretary. [ ] The task of defining and listing endangered and threatened species requires an expertise and attention to detail that exceeds the normal province of Congress. Fashioning appropriate standards for issuing permits under § 10 for takings that would otherwise violate § 9 necessarily requires the exercise of broad discretion. The proper interpretation of a term such as "harm" involves a complex policy choice. When Congress has entrusted the Secretary with broad discretion, we are especially reluctant to substitute our views of wise policy for his. *See Chevron,* [ ]. In this case, that reluctance accords with our conclusion, based on the text, structure, and legislative history of the ESA, that the Secretary reasonably construed the intent of Congress when he defined "harm" to include "significant habitat modification or degradation that actually kills or injures wildlife."

In the elaboration and enforcement of the ESA, the Secretary and all persons who must comply with the law will confront difficult questions of proximity and degree; for, as all recognize, the Act encompasses a vast range of economic and social enterprises and endeavors. These questions must be addressed in the usual course of the law, through case-by-case resolution and adjudication.

The judgment of the Court of Appeals is reversed.

It is so ordered.

■ O'CONNOR, J., concurring:—My agreement with the Court is founded on two understandings. First, the challenged regulation is limited to significant habitat modification that causes actual, as opposed to hypothetical or speculative, death or injury to identifiable protected animals. Second, even setting aside difficult questions of scienter, the regulation's application is limited by ordinary principles of proximate causation, which introduce notions of foreseeability. These limitations, in my view, call into question *Palila v. Hawaii Department of Land & Natural Resources,* 852 F.2d 1106 (9th Cir.1988) (*Palila II*), and with it, many of the applications derided by the dissent. Because there is no need to strike a regulation on a facial challenge out of concern that it is susceptible of erroneous application, however, and because there are many habitat-related circumstances in which the regulation might validly apply, I join the opinion of the Court.

[Following an extended rebuttal of Justice Scalia's dissent, Justice O'Connor concludes:] In my view, then, the "harm" regulation applies where significant habitat modification, by impairing essential behaviors, proximately (foreseeably) causes actual death or injury to identifiable animals that are protected under the Endangered Species Act. Pursuant to my interpretation, *Palila II*—under which the Court of Appeals held that a state agency committed a "taking" by permitting feral sheep to eat mamane-naio seedlings that, when full-grown, might have fed and sheltered endangered palila—was wrongly decided according to the regulation's own terms. Destruction of the seedlings did not proximately cause actual death or injury to identifiable birds; it merely prevented the regeneration of forest land not currently inhabited by actual birds.

. . .

With this understanding, I join the Court's opinion.

■ SCALIA, J., with whom The Chief Justice and THOMAS, J., join, dissenting: I think it unmistakably clear that the legislation at issue here (1) forbade the hunting and killing of endangered animals, and (2) provided federal lands and federal funds for the acquisition of private lands, to preserve the habitat of endangered animals. The Court's holding that the hunting and killing prohibition incidentally preserves habitat on private lands imposes unfairness to the point of financial ruin—not just upon the rich, but upon the simplest farmer who finds his land conscripted to national zoological use. I respectfully dissent.

I

The Endangered Species Act of 1973, [ ], provides that "it is unlawful for any person subject to the jurisdiction of the United States to take any [protected] species within the United States." [ ] The term "take" is defined as "to harass, *harm,* pursue, hunt, shoot, wound, kill, trap, capture, or collect, or to attempt to engage in any such conduct." [ ] The challenged regulation defines "harm" thus:

> "Harm" in the definition of "take" in the Act means an act which actually kills or injures wildlife. Such act may include significant habitat modification or degradation where it actually kills or injures wildlife by significantly impairing essential behavioral patterns, including breeding, feeding or sheltering.

[ ] In my view petitioners must lose—the regulation must fall—even under the test of *Chevron U.S.A. Inc. v. Natural Resources Defense Council, Inc.,* 467 U.S. 837 (1984), so I shall assume that the Court is correct to apply *Chevron.*

The regulation has three features which, for reasons I shall discuss at length below, do not comport with the statute. First, it interprets the statute to prohibit habitat modification that is no more than the cause-in-fact of death or injury to wildlife. Any "significant habitat modification" that in fact produces that result by "impairing essential behavioral patterns" is made unlawful, regardless of whether that result is intended or even foreseeable, and no matter how long the chain of causality between modification and injury. *See, e.g., Palila v. Hawaii Department of Land & Natural Resources (Palila II)*, 852 F.2d 1106, 1108–1109 (9th Cir.1988) (sheep grazing constituted "taking" of palila birds, since although sheep do not destroy full-grown mamane trees, they do destroy mamane seedlings, which will not grow to full-grown trees, on which the palila feeds and nests). [ ]

Second, the regulation does not require an "act": the Secretary's officially stated position is that an omission will do. The previous version of the regulation made this explicit. [ ] (" 'Harm' in the definition of 'take' in the Act means an act or omission which actually kills or injures wildlife * * * "). When the regulation was modified in 1981 the phrase "or omission" was taken out, but only because (as the final publication of the rule advised) "the [Fish and Wildlife] Service feels that 'act' is inclusive of either commissions or omissions which would be prohibited by section [1538(a)(1)(B)]." [ ] In its brief here the Government agrees that the regulation covers omissions, [ ] (although it argues that "[a]n 'omission' constitutes an 'act' * * * only if there is a legal duty to act").

The third and most important unlawful feature of the regulation is that it encompasses injury inflicted, not only upon individual animals, but upon populations of the protected species. "Injury" in the regulation includes "significantly impairing essential behavioral patterns, including *breeding*," [ ]. Impairment of breeding does not "injure" living creatures; it prevents them from propagating, thus "injuring" a population of animals which would otherwise have maintained or increased its numbers. What the face of the regulation shows, the Secretary's official pronouncements confirm. The Final Redefinition of "Harm" accompanying publication of the regulation said that "harm" is not limited to "direct physical injury to an individual member of the wildlife species," [ ], and refers to "injury *to a population*," [ ].

None of these three features of the regulation can be found in the statutory provisions supposed to authorize it. . . .

The Act's definition of "take" does expand the word slightly (and not unusually), so as to make clear that it includes not just a completed taking, but the process of taking, and all of the acts that are customarily identified with or accompany that process ("to harass, harm, pursue, hunt, shoot, wound, kill, trap, capture, or collect"); and so as to include attempts. § 1532(19). The tempting fallacy—which the Court commits with abandon, [ ]—is to assume that once defined, "take" loses any significance, and it is only the definition that matters. The Court treats the statute as though Congress had directly enacted the § 1532(19) definition as a self-executing prohibition, and had not enacted § 1538(a)(1)(B) at all. But § 1538(a)(1)(B) is there, and if the terms contained in the definitional section are susceptible of two readings, one of which comports with the standard meaning of "take" as used in application to wildlife, and one of which does not, an agency regulation that adopts the latter reading is necessarily unreasonable, for it reads the defined term "take"—the only operative term—out of the statute altogether.

. . .

* * *

The Endangered Species Act is a carefully considered piece of legislation that forbids all persons to hunt or harm endangered animals, but places upon the public at large, rather than upon fortuitously accountable individual landowners, the cost of preserving the habitat of endangered species. There is neither textual support for, nor even evidence of congressional consideration of, the radically different disposition contained in the regulation that the Court sustains. For these reasons, I respectfully dissent.

NOTES

(1) Is there any suggestion that Congress was prohibited from defining the term as the agency did? Or that Congress lacked the power, by amending the Act, to reject the agency's definition?

(2) *Mens rea:* The issue that divides the court is the role of intent: Must an activity be *intended to affect listed wildlife* to constitute "harm" and thus a "take"?

Justice Scalia argued that the statute required a specific intent because all of the other verbs in the definition "are affirmative acts ... which are directed immediately and *intentionally* against a *particular animal*." Is Scalia correct? That is, are "harass, pursue, hunt, shoot, wound, kill, trap, capture, or collect" acts directed "*intentionally* against a *particular animal*"? Does "kill" require specific intent or does it merely refer to the result? Consider the next note.

In part of the opinion not excerpted, Scalia created an example involving a turtle: "the Court's contention that 'harm' in the narrow sense adds nothing to the other words underestimates the ingenuity of our own species in a way that Congress did not. To ... destroy [an animal's] entire habitat in order to take it (as by draining a pond to *get at* a turtle), might neither wound nor kill, but would directly and intentionally harm." What does Scalia mean by the phrase "get at"? If he means "capture" or "kill," then those are in themselves violations of the Act. If he means leaving the animal without cover or food, then the harm comes not directly from draining the pond but indirectly through predation or starvation—precisely the type of indirect injuries that Scalia insists cannot fall within the term "harm."

(3) *Mens rea*, **redux:** In the winter of 1988–89, three Burlington Northern trains carrying grain derailed on a stretch of track south of Glacier National Park in northwestern Montana. The derailment spilled nearly 10,000 tons of corn which attracted grizzly bears to the site to feed. By October 1990, five grizzly bears had fatal encounters with BN trains in the immediate vicinity of the corn spills. The Ninth Circuit held that "the bear fatalities constituted a prohibited 'taking' within the meaning of the ESA." *National Wildlife Federation v. Burlington Northern Railroad,* 23 F.3d 1508, 1509 (9th Cir.1994).

The Glenn–Colusa Irrigation District pumps water from the Sacramento River to provide irrigation water for the Central Valley in California. For more than fifty years, the District had failed to install screening to prevent fish from being sucked into its pumps. The California Fish and Game Department finally installed screening in 1972. The screens turned out to be less than completely effective, particularly during peak irrigation periods when the District pumped at an average rate of 2,000 cubic feet per second. In 1990, the winter-run Chinook Salmon in the Sacramento River were listed as threatened. The district court held that the District's refusal to provide effective screening of its intake structure was a taking. *United States v. Glenn–Colusa Irrigation District,* 788 F.Supp. 1126, 1133 (E.D.Cal. 1992).

Did the defendants in either *Burlington Northern* or *Glenn-Colusa* perform acts directed *"intentionally* against a *particular animal"*?

(4) The varieties of takings: Given the wide variety of ways that human activities can kill or otherwise harm listed species, it is unsurprising that alleged takings have arisen on disparate facts. Consider the following decisions:

  (a) *Defenders of Wildlife v. Bernal*: In 1994, the Amphitheater School District purchased a 73–acre parcel in northwest Tucson to construct a high school. The site was within the subsequently designated critical habitat of the cactus ferruginous pygmy-owl. Within the parcel are three "arroyos" or "ephemeral desert waterways." The U.S. Army Corps of Engineers designated the arroyos as "jurisdictional waters" pursuant to the Clean Water Act. The original design of the school complex called for some construction within the arroyos, thereby requiring the school district to obtain a permit under the Clean Water Act. Because a federal permit was required, the FWS informed the Corps that consultation was required to assess the impact of the proposed project on the pygmy-owl. The school district, however, withdrew its application for the permit and redesigned the project so that construction would not affect the arroyos. When the district began construction preparation, Defenders filed suit alleging that the construction would take pygmy-owls. Following a three-day trial, the court found that pygmy-owls used territory to the north of the boundary and the west of the boundary of the school site and that no pygmy-owl had been detected anywhere within the school site itself. Although the construction site was suitable habitat, the trial judge also found that there was insufficient evidence to prove that a pygmy-owl used any portion of the construction site. Since the site was not *used* by owls, there was no taking. *Defenders of Wildlife v. Bernal,* 204 F.3d 920 (9th Cir.2000).

  (b) *United States v. Town of Plymouth*: FWS sued the Town of Plymouth for its failure to control off-road vehicles on public beach, which were harming piping plovers, a listed species. The court held that failure to protect habitat amounted to an unlawful take; court enjoined use of vehicles on beach unless the town followed certain requirements drawn from federal and state guidelines to protect the plovers. *United States v. Town of Plymouth,* 6 F.Supp.2d 81 (D.Mass.1998).

(c) *Strahan v. Coxe*: Environmentalist challenged a state's continued granting of permits for gillnet and lobster pot fishing in an area frequented by northern right whales, a listed species. Entanglement with the gear used in such fishing was a major cause of human-caused injury or death to the whales. The Circuit Court affirmed a verdict holding the state guilty of an unlawful take, even though it merely issued permits for the fishing; a government entity can be held liable for the harm caused by private parties whose activities it licenses or permits. *Strahan v. Coxe,* 127 F.3d 155 (1st Cir.1997).

(d) *Forest Conservation Council v. Rosboro Lumber Co.*: Conservation group challenged the proposed clearcutting of 40 acres of private forest adjacent to the breeding site of a single pair of spotted owls under § 9. The Ninth Circuit enjoined the logging as a likely taking. The lumber company must obtain an incidental take permit to proceed. In so ruling, the court expressly rejected the district court's conclusion that habitat modification amounted to a taking only when it threatened a listed species with extinction. *Forest Conservation Council v. Rosboro Lumber Co.,* 50 F.3d 781 (9th Cir.1995).

See also Loggerhead Turtle v. County Council of Volusia County, 148 F.3d 1231 (11th Cir.1998) (artificial beachfront lighting that disrupts listed sea turtles subject to control as unlawful take); *Marbled Murrelet v. Babbitt,* 83 F.3d 1060 (9th Cir.1996) (timber harvesting on private land is take when it harms listed bird); *Sierra Club v. Yeutter,* 926 F.2d 429 (5th Cir.1991) (even-aged timber management by Forest Service amounts to take when it disrupts breeding of red-cockaded woodpecker).

b.   CIVIL AND CRIMINAL PENALTIES

NOTES

(1) Penalties and enforcement: Like § 9, § 10 of the ESA contains a variety of provisions relating to penalties and the mechanics of enforcing the Act.

(a) Civil and criminal penalties: The section authorizes the imposition of both civil and criminal sanctions for violations of the prohibitions contained in § 9. The severity of the sanctions vary in relation to three factors: (1) whether the violation involves an endangered or a threatened species, *id.* § 1540(a)(1), (b)(1); (2) the violator's knowledge, *id.* § 1540(a)(1); and, (3) for some purposes, the violator's occupation, *id.* § 1540(a)(1). These provisions are discussed in detail in the next notes.

(b) Forfeitures: Section 10 authorizes two categories of forfeitures. First, "[a]ll fish or wildlife or plants taken, possessed, sold, purchased, offered for sale or purchase, transported, delivered, received, carried, shipped, exported, or imported contrary to the provisions of this Act" are subject to forfeiture. *Id.* § 1540(e)(4)(A). Second, "[a]ll guns, traps, nets, and other equipment, vessels, vehicles, aircraft, and other means of transportation used to aid the taking, possessing, selling, purchasing, offering for sale or purchase, transporting, delivering, receiving, carrying, shipping, exporting, or importing of any fish or wildlife or plants in violation of this Act" are subject to forfeiture upon conviction for a criminal offense. *Id.* § 1540(e)(4)(B).

(c) **Citizen suits:** The ESA contains extremely broad citizen suit provisions. "[A]ny person may commence a civil suit on his own behalf" to "enjoin any person, including the United States and any other governmental instrumentality or agency" allegedly violating the Act, *id.* 1540(g)(1)(A), and against the Secretary "where there is alleged a failure of the Secretary to perform any act or duty under section 1533 of this title which is not discretionary with the Secretary," *id.* 1540(g)(1)(C). Prior to commencing the action, the individual must give 60 days notice. *Id.* § 1540(g)(2)(A), (2)(C).

(d) **Miscellaneous provisions:** In addition, section 10 (1) grants jurisdiction to the federal district courts over action arising under the ESA, *id.* § 1540(c); (2) authorizes payment of rewards for information leading to prosecution under the Act, *id.* § 1540(d); (3) obligates the Secretary to enforce the Act, *id.* § 1540(e); and (4) authorizes the Secretary to promulgate regulations, *id.* § 1540(f).

(2) **Civil and criminal sanctions—the relevant factors:** As noted, the Act's sanctions vary in relation to three factors:

(a) **Endangered vs. threatened species:** Both civil and criminal sanctions are more stringent when the violation involves an endangered rather than a threatened species. *Id.* § 1540(a)(1), (b)(1).

(b) **"Knowingly":** Similarly, civil sanctions are more stringent when the individual "knowingly violates" the Act's prohibitions. *Id.* § 1540(a)(1). All criminal sanctions require knowing violations. *Id.* § 1540(b)(1).

(c) **The violator's occupation:** Finally, the Act imposes strict civil liability on "any person engaged in business as an importer or exporter of fish, wildlife, or plants." *Id.* § 1540(a)(1).

(3) **Civil penalties:** The most stringent civil penalties are reserved for individuals who either knowingly violate or are importers/exporters who violate the prohibitions applicable to endangered species. Such individuals who violate the prohibitions against taking, importing, exporting, transporting or selling and endangered species are subject to civil penalties of not more than $25,000. *Id.* § 1540(a)(1). Such persons who violate any other regulations issued under the Act—which includes the prohibitions applicable to threatened species—are subject to civil penalties of up to $12,000. *Id.* Finally, any person "who otherwise violates" any provision of the Act—that is, a person other than an importer/exporter who violates the Act without knowing she is doing so—is subject to a civil penalty of up to $500. *Id.*

(4) **Criminal sanctions:** Unlike the Act's civil penalties, all criminal sanctions are predicated upon "knowing" violations of the Act. *Id.* § 1540(b)(1). Knowing violators of the prohibitions against taking, importing, exporting, transporting or selling and endangered species are subject to criminal sanctions of not more than $50,000 and a year in jail. *Id.* Knowing

violators of a regulation applicable to a threatened species face criminal penalties of not more than $25,000 and imprisonment of not more than 6 months. *Id.* § 1540(b)(1). In addition, all individuals convicted of criminal violations face the loss of federal licenses, leases, and hunting permits, *id.* § 1540(b)(2), and forfeiture of all equipment and means of transportation involved in the violation, *id.* § 1540(e)(4)(B).

(5) Theory and practice: Don Barry—at the time the Deputy Assistant Secretary for Fish and Wildlife and Parks in the Department of the Interior—has aptly summarized the effect of § 9:

> You can probably count on two hands the number of prosecutions, either civilly or criminally, that have been brought by the federal government over the past 23 years because of an alleged take on private lands. So to that extent, [§ 9] has not been a readily and frequently utilized tool. And in fact we've had the loss of thousands and thousands of acres of endangered and threatened species habitat in the interim. On the other hand, I think it's fair to say that the mere threat of a section 9 prosecution is a very intimidating thing. And so even though the cases themselves have not been brought, just the mere existence of that threat and the fact that there's a citizen suit provision, which can allow third parties to enforce section 9, has been a very intimidating feature of the act, and it's one reason why perhaps it's had an effect above and beyond just the number of cases that have actually been brought.

Donald J. Barry, *Keynote Speech—Opportunity in the Face of Danger: The Pragmatic Development of Conservation Plans*, 4 HASTINGS WEST-NORTHWEST J. ENVTL. L. & POL'Y 129, 130–31 (1998).

United States v. McKittrick

Ninth Circuit Court of Appeals.
142 F.3d 1170 (1998).

■ SKOPIL, SENIOR J.:—The gray wolf, or Canis Lupus, is listed as endangered under the Endangered Species Act (ESA) throughout the coterminous United States, except in Minnesota, where it is listed as threatened. 50 C.F.R. § 17.11(h). Gray wolf populations in Canada, however, are plentiful. Pursuant to ESA section 10(j), the Fish and Wildlife Service (FWS) captured Canadian gray wolves and released them in Yellowstone National Park as an "experimental population" designed to replenish wolves in Wyoming and parts of Montana and Idaho, where they had been all but eradicated by about 1930. *See* 59 *Fed. Reg.* 60,251, 60,252 (Nov. 22, 1994). One of these wolves migrated from Yellowstone to the Red Lodge, Montana area, where it had a fatal encounter with Chad McKittrick. After shooting and killing the wolf, McKittrick skinned and decapitated it, taking the hide and head to his home.

The government charged McKittrick with three counts: one, taking the wolf in violation of 16 U.S.C. §§ 1538(a)(1)(G), 1540(b)(1), and 50 C.F.R. § 17.84(i)(3); two, possessing the wolf in violation of 16 U.S.C. §§ 1538(a)(1)(G), 1540(b)(1), and 50 C.F.R. § 17.84(i)(5); and three, transporting the wolf in violation of the Lacey Act, 16 U.S.C. §§ 3372(a)(1), 3373(d)(2).[1] Magistrate Judge Anderson conducted a trial and then sentenced McKittrick to six months' imprisonment after a jury convicted him on all counts. District Judge Shanstrom affirmed the conviction and sentence.

On appeal, McKittrick argues ... that his taking of the wolf was not "knowing" because he did not realize what he was shooting.... We reject each of these challenges and affirm the conviction .....

. . .

C. Degree of Intent

McKittrick argues that a violation of ESA section 11 requires the government to prove that he knew he was shooting a wolf, and that the jury instructions misled the jury about the requisite intent. We review for an abuse of discretion whether the magistrate judge's "precise formulation" of the intent element was sufficient. [ ] Whether the instructions actually misstated an element of the crime is subject to de novo review. [ ]

The instructions were accurate. McKittrick need not have known he was shooting a wolf to "knowingly violate[ ]" the regulations protecting the experimental population. 16 U.S.C. § 1540(b)(1). In 1978, Congress changed the wording of section 11 to "reduce[ ] the standard for criminal violations from 'willfully' to 'knowingly.'" H.R. REP. No. 95–1625, at 26 (1978), *reprinted in* 1978 U.S.C.C.A.N. 9453, 9476. It did this to "make[ ] criminal violations of the act a general rather than a specific intent crime." *Id.* As the magistrate judge recognized, the District of Montana had already decided the intent issue in the government's favor, holding on similar facts that "[t]he critical issue is whether the act was done knowingly, not whether the defendant recognized what he was shooting." *United States v. St. Onge*, 676 F. Supp. 1044, 1045 (D.Mont.1988); *see also United States v. Billie*, 667 F. Supp. 1485, 1493 (S.D.Fla.1987) ("[T]he Government need prove only that the defendant acted with general intent when he shot the animal in question."). The Fifth Circuit has reached the same conclusion in related situations. *See United States v. Nguyen*, 916 F.2d 1016, 1017–18 (5th Cir.1990) (sustaining possession conviction did not require that defendant know animal's ESA-protected status); *United States v. Ivey*, 949 F.2d 759, 766 (5th Cir.1991) (citing *St. Onge* and *Billie* in holding that, like § 1540(b)(1), § 1538(c) is a general intent statute). The Eleventh Circuit has expressed its agreement with the reasoning of these cases in holding that an analogous provision of the African Elephant Conservation Act requires only general intent. *See United States v. Grigsby*, 111 F.3d 806, 817 (11th Cir.1997). As these cases and the legislative history indicate,

---

1. Section 9 of the ESA, 16 U.S.C. § 1538(a)(1)(G), makes it illegal to violate any regulations issued under the statute. Section 11(b), 16 U.S.C. § 1540(b)(1), provides criminal penalties for knowing violations of any such regulation. The applicable regulations, promulgated by FWS, are found in section 17.84(i), the special rules pertaining to the gray wolf experimental population. See 50 C.F.R. § 17.84(i). The Lacey Act makes it illegal "to transport ... any wildlife ... taken in violation of any law, treaty, or regulation of the United States." 16 U.S.C. § 3372(a)(1).

section 11 requires only that McKittrick knew he was shooting an animal, and that the animal turned out to be a protected gray wolf.

. . .

We hold that ... that there was no error in ... the jury instructions. Accordingly, we affirm McKittrick's conviction for taking, possessing, and transporting a gray wolf in violation of the ESA and the Lacey Act. . . .

NOTES

What must McKittrick know to "knowingly" take a listed species? Recall the earlier discussion of the distinction between strict liability and knowing.

c.   DEFENSES

Section 11 contains one defense: neither criminal nor civil penalties may be imposed if the violator shows that he acted in a good faith belief that he "was acting to protect himself or herself, a member of his or her family, or any other individual from bodily harm" from the listed species. 16 U.S.C. § 1540(a)(3), (b)(3).

United States v. Clavette

United States Court of Appeals for the Ninth Circuit.
135 F.3d 1308 (1998).

■ REAVLEY, J.:—This is an appeal from the conviction of Paul Clavette for killing a grizzly bear in violation of the Endangered Species Act, 16 U.S.C. §§ 1538(a)(1)(G) and 1540(b)(1). We affirm.

I.   Background

On September 20, 1995, U.S. Fish and Wildlife Service Special Agent Tim Eicher began investigating the killing of a grizzly bear at a campsite southwest of Big Sky, Montana. At the campsite, Eicher discovered two pine trees with a pole suspended by rope between them. This was a "meat pole," used for stringing up and skinning large game animals. Underneath it, Eicher found traces of moose blood and hair, indicating that a moose had recently been dressed there. Eicher found the dead grizzly bear approximately 170 yards away, lying in a large pool of blood. The bear had been shot at least four times. Looking for bullets or spent shell casings, Eicher searched a conical area extending about 25 yards beyond the bear toward the campsite; he found one .7 mm casing by the meat pole and two bullets, one buried about two inches in the dirt at the base of a tree near the bear, and one on the surface of the ground next to the pool of the bear's blood.

Eicher located two bowhunters who had stopped at the campsite on September 17, 1995, to visit with an Oregon man skinning a freshly killed moose. The man seemed to be in a hurry and did not say anything about confronting or killing a grizzly. He did ask the bowhunters what would happen to someone who shot a grizzly bear. The bowhunters told him he had better be prepared to prove it was in self-defense.

Through these bowhunters and Montana hunting license records, Eicher identified the defendant, Paul Clavette, as the man at the campsite on September 17, 1995. Agents of the U.S. Fish and Wildlife Service in Portland, Oregon, obtained and executed a search warrant in defendant's home on November 2, 1995. During the course of that search, and after full Miranda warnings, Clavette admitted to killing the grizzly, claiming that it was in self-defense.

After a bench trial, the district court found Clavette guilty of illegally killing a grizzly bear. Clavette was sentenced to three years' probation. Additionally, Clavette was ordered to pay a fine of $2,000 and restitution of $6,250 to the United States Fish & Wildlife Service.

. . .

III.   Sufficiency of the Evidence

Because Clavette moved to dismiss at the close of the Government's case-in-chief, the sufficiency of the evidence is reviewed de novo. If any reasonable person could have found each of the essential elements of the offense charged beyond a reasonable doubt, the evidence is sufficient to convict.

To find Clavette guilty of knowingly taking an endangered species, the Government must prove, beyond a reasonable doubt, that: (1) Clavette knowingly killed a bear; (2) the bear was a grizzly; (3) Clavette had no permit from the United States Fish & Wildlife Service to kill a grizzly bear; and (4) Clavette did not act in self-defense or in the defense of others. Pursuant to the regulations, a grizzly bear may be taken in self-defense or defense of others, but any such taking must be reported within five days to the U.S. Fish and Wildlife Service.[24]

There is no dispute that Clavette knowingly killed a grizzly bear without first obtaining a permit from the Fish & Wildlife Service. The only issue at trial was whether he acted in self-defense or in defense of his wife. Because Clavette presented evidence that he acted in self-defense, the Government must disprove self-defense beyond a reasonable doubt.

Clavette and his wife changed their story multiple times. Clavette initially described his trip to Montana to Agent Earl Kisler as follows. Clavette said that as he was skinning a moose he had killed, he sensed something was wrong. He looked up and saw a seven-or eight-foot bear standing on its hind legs about 25 yards away from him, across a creek that ran past the campsite. He made noises to try to drive the bear away and fired a warning shot with his .7 mm rifle. Then, Clavette said, the bear began to circle the campsite, and Clavette was sure it was going to come forward. He told Kisler that he was terrified. Clavette's wife had retreated into the pickup truck. Clavette stated that when the bear was 40 to 75 yards away from the campsite, he shot it. The first shot hit the bear on the left side and appeared to paralyze its hindquarters, but it kept struggling, trying to get up, and so he emptied his rifle into it, reloaded, and fired more rounds into the bear.

---

24. 50 C.F.R. § 17.40(b)(i)(B) (1996).

Clavette later stated that there were two bears, although his wife still said that there had been one bear. Then, at trial, Clavette's wife testified that not only were there two bears, but that the second one charged her husband at a dead run. When asked why she had not mentioned two bears before, she explained that only one bear was shot. Clavette himself testified at trial that he had in fact told Agent Kisler about the second bear during their first discussion; Clavette surmised that it must have slipped their minds. He also testified that the second bear charged straight at him and that he crippled it with his first shot at 33 yards. Clavette said he saw the bear spin 180 degrees and dig with its front paws, trying to move away from him. The bear looked as if it was paralyzed in its hindquarters but actually ran another hundred yards away from him, without bleeding, so as to die in the spot where the bear was found by the agents.

Although he could not identify the order in which the shots occurred, Keith Aune, a wildlife laboratory supervisor for the Montana Department of Fish, Wildlife and Parks, testified that the shots Clavette described were inconsistent with his own observations and measurements gathered during the necropsy. No entry wounds appeared on the head, chest or front legs, as would be expected if the bear had been approaching at high speed; all the entry wounds were in the rear portion. The stories were also inconsistent with the physical evidence found by Agent Eicher at the site.

Given the physical evidence and the inconsistencies in the Clavettes' stories, a reasonable person could have found beyond a reasonable doubt that Clavette had not killed the bear in self-defense.

NOTES

(1) What must the government prove to sustain a conviction for "knowingly" taking a listed species? Must defendant know that the species is listed? Must know that he or she is taking the animal but not necessarily that it is listed?

What must defendant prove to establish the defense of persons defense? What mental standard is applicable to the defense?

(2) Defense of property: In Chapter 3, we looked at several cases in which a person sought to justify killing a protected species by asserting that he was protecting his property. The ESA does not contain an explicit defense-of-property defense. Is such a defense implicit in the statute or required by the Constitution? The Ninth Circuit decided that defense of property was no defense to a prosecution under the Act.

Christy was a sheep rancher with a lease to graze sheep on the east slope of the Rocky Mountains in Montana. After his flock had been repeatedly raided by grizzly bears, Christy shot and killed a bear that was attacking his flock. Prosecuted and fined $2500 under the Endangered Species Act, Christy argued that he had a constitutional right to protect his property. The Ninth Circuit Court of Appeals disagreed: "We simply hold that the right to kill federally protected wildlife in defense of property is not "implicit in the concept of ordered liberty" nor so "deeply rooted in this Nation's history and tradition" that it can be recognized by us as a fundamental right guaranteed by the fifth amendment." *Christy v. Hodel*, 857 F.2d 1324, 1330 (9th Cir.1988), *cert. denied sub nom., Christy v. Lujan*, 490 U.S. 1114 (1989). The court noted that "the regulations do not forbid plaintiffs from personally defending their property by means other than killing grizzly bears." *Id.* at 1331.

SECTION 7. EXCEPTIONS AND EXEMPTIONS

a. THE EXEMPTION PROCESS: THE GOD SQUAD

NOTES

(1) The exemption process: As originally enacted, the ESA contained an absolute prohibition on activities detrimental to the continued survival of a listed species. One congressional response to the Supreme Court's decision in *TVA v. Hill* was the creation of the Endangered Species Committee—the so-called "God Squad"—and create an elaborate mechanism for exempting federal projects from the prohibitions of § 7. 16 U.S.C. § 1536(g)-(*l*). The exemption process is a last resort: an exemption may be sought only after a species has been listed, the interagency consultation process has been completed, a finding has been made that the proposed action will violate the jeopardy or habitat modification prohibitions, and it is determined that there are no reasonable and prudent alternatives to the proposal. *Id.* § 1536(g)(1).

The Committee is composed of six cabinet-level officers and the governor of the state in which the proposed action was to occur. The stated rationale for the officers chosen—the Secretaries of the Interior, Agriculture, and the Army, the Chair of the Council of Economic Advisors, the Administrators of the Environmental Protection Agency and the National Oceanic and Atmospheric Administration, and a presidentially appointed representative from each affected state, 16 U.S.C. § 1536(e)—was that they offered "the broadest array of expertise and the greatest potential for a balancing of viewpoints concerning all of the alternatives to be considered." S. REP. No. 874, 95th Cong., 2d Sess. 4 (1978).[1]

Once the consultation process has been exhausted without producing any reasonable and prudent alternatives,

(a) the exemption process is initiated by filing a written application with the Secretary within 90 days of the completion of the consultation or the final denial of a permit application. 16 U.S.C. § 1536(g)(2)(A). The federal agency proposing the action, the governor of the state in which the action was to have occurred, or the "permit or license applicant" may apply for the exemption. *Id.* § 1536(g)(1).

---

1. *See also* 124 CONG. REC. 21,135 (1978) (statement of Sen. Randolph) ("Since this panel includes individuals with expertise in both environment and development matters, its decisions are likely to be balanced and fair."). Actually, the Committee members primary expertise is politics since that is the requirement for a position as a cabinet-level federal officer.

(b) Upon receipt of the application, the Secretary is required to notify the governor of any affected state and publish notice in the *Federal Register. Id.* § 1536(g)(2)(B). The *Federal Register* notice is to include "a summary of the information contained in the application and a description of the agency action" that led to the exemption application. *Id.*

(c) Within 20 days of receipt of the application, the Secretary is required to determine whether the federal action agency meets three threshold requirements: (i) the applicant must have carried out its consultation responsibilities "in good faith and made a reasonable and responsible effort to develop and fairly consider modifications or other reasonable and prudent alternatives to the proposed agency action"; (ii) it must have conducted the required biological assessments; and (iii) it must not have made "any irreversible or irretrievable commitment of resources."[2] *Id.* § 1536(g)(3)(A)(i)-(iii). If the applicant has does not satisfy all of these requirements, the Secretary is to deny the application. *Id.* § 1536(g)(3)(B).

(d) If the applicant satisfies these threshold requirements, the Secretary is to hold a formal hearing under the APA on the application.[3] *Id.* § 1536(g)(4).

(e) Within 140 days of determining that the federal action agency has met the three threshold criteria, the Secretary is to prepare a report for the Endangered Species Committee summarizing the evidence presented at the hearing on the various factors the Committee is to consider in reaching its decision. *Id.* § 1536(g)(5).

(f) The Committee has ultimate responsibility for granting or denying all exemptions. It may grant an exemption only if, by a vote of five of it members *voting in person, id.* § 1536(e)(5)(A), (e)(10), the Committee "determines on the record, based on the report of the Secretary [of the Interior], the record of the [formal] hearing, and on such other testimony or evidence as it may receive," *id.* § 1536(h)(1)(A), that

   (i) there are no reasonable and prudent alternatives to the agency action;

   (ii) the benefits of such action clearly outweigh the benefits of alternative courses of action consistent with conserving the listed species or its critical habitat, and such action is in the public interest;

   (iii) the action is of regional or national significance; and

   (iv) neither the Federal agency concerned nor the exemption applicant made any irreversible or irretrievable commitment of resources.

Id.

Finally, if the Committee grants an exemption, it must also establish "reasonable mitigation and enhancement measures" to "minimize the adverse effects" on the listed species. *Id.* § 1536(h)(1)(B).

---

2. The 20–day decision period may be extended with the agreement of the applicant. *Id.* § 1536(g)(3).

3. The Act specifies that the hearing is to be held under the formal adjudicatory hearing procedures set out in the Administrative Procedures Act §§ 554, 555, and 556. *Id.* § 1536(g)(4).

The exemption process thus is narrowly tailored: the decision is to be based upon a record created at a formal hearing, the Committee is required to find that the benefits of the proposal "clearly outweighs" the benefits of alternative courses, and it must do so through a procedure—the formality of the process and the requirement of a super-majority—that favors a decision to deny exemption requests. A decision to grant an exemption is, therefore, likely be a rare occurrence.

(2) *Portland Audubon Society v. The Endangered Species Committee:* Following litigation that forced the FWS to list the northern spotted owl as a threatened species and to designate critical habitat, the Bureau of Land Management sought an exemption for 13 timber sales in western Oregon. The exemptions were granted; conservation groups filed suit, challenging the procedure. They noted press reports that "according to two anonymous administration sources, at least three Committee members had been 'summoned' to the White House and pressured to vote for the exemption." The allegations required the court to decide "whether the ex parte contacts ... would be impermissible if they occurred in the manner alleged." The Court concluded that the APA's prohibition on ex parte contacts during the course of a "hearing on the record" were applicable and included the President and White House staff. The court, therefore, remanded the decision. *Portland Audubon Society v. Endangered Species Committee*, 984 F.2d 1534 (9th Cir.1993).

The BLM subsequently withdrew the exemption application and the proposed timber sales as a result of the changes following the defeat of the first Bush administration.

(3) Grayrocks Dam: The only other project to obtain an exemption was the Grayrocks Dam. The Grayrocks Project—part of a regional power-development program known as the Missouri Basin Power Project—was a three-unit, 1500–megawatt, coal-fired electric generating plant and the Grayrocks Dam and Reservoir on the Laramie River near Wheatland, Wyoming. Two federal agencies were involved in the project: the Rural Electrification Administration (REA) made commitments and loan guarantees to the sponsors of the project; the Army Corps of Engineers had issued a permit to allow construction of the dam.

Despite repeated requests by FWS, the REA refused to initiate consultation on the project. Conservation groups challenged both actions, contending that the flow regime associated with the dam would detrimentally affect the habitat of the endangered Whooping Crane on the Platte River downstream from the project. The REA's response to the lawsuit is a classic example of the mindset that the Act sought to rectify. It argued "that no adverse impact on the habitat had been demonstrated at the time REA decided to proceed." The district court rejected this contention:

> the Endangered Species Act places the burden upon the agencies who are authorizing, funding, or carrying out programs to insure that those programs do not jeopardize endangered species or habitats of the species. The burden is not upon someone else to demonstrate that there will be an adverse impact.... [T]he question is whether [REA] has met its burden of *insuring* that there will be no jeopardy.

Nebraska v. Rural Electrification Admin., 12 Env't Rep. Cas. (BNA) 1156, 1171 (D.Neb.1978). The court enjoined REA from guaranteeing loans for the project.

The Supreme Court's decision in *TVA v. Hill* ended the hopes of action agencies that further judicial review was likely to produce a different conclusion. An out-of-court settlement that included establishment of a trust fund to acquire additional habitat—one of the alternatives that FWS suggested in a biological opinion it had issued on the project—was negotiated among the parties. The Endangered Species Committee concluded that the settlement provisions were "reasonable mitigation and enhancement measures" that satisfied the ESA's requirements. It therefore voted to exempt the project from the ESA if constructed and operated in compliance with the settlement.

b. PERMISSIBLE TAKING OF LISTED SPECIES

The ESA authorizes the "knowing take" of a listed species in certain situations: the Secretary may (1) include an "incidental take statement" in the biological opinion at the end of the formal consultation procedures of § 7; (2) issue "incidental take permits" under § 10; and (3) permit takings of threatened species under § 4(d).

(i) INCIDENTAL TAKE STATEMENTS

NOTES

(1) "Jeopardy" and "taking": Both § 7 (which requires that a proposed federal action not "jeopardize the continued existence" of a listed species) and § 9 (which prohibits any activity that harms or harasses an endangered species) are applicable to actions that are funded, authorized, or carried out by a federal agency. The taking prohibition in § 9, however, is potentially more restrictive than the no-jeopardy requirement in § 7 since some actions that will not jeopardize the continued existence of a listed species might nonetheless result in the taking of individual members of the species.

In 1982, Congress amended the ESA to address this overlap by authorizing the fish and wildlife agency to permit the federal action agency to take listed species incidental to the proposed action.

(2) Formal consultation and incidental take statements: As previously discussed, when a federal agency proposes to "authorize, fund, or carry out" an activity, the agency is required to engage in consultation with the appropriate wildlife agency if any listed species may be present in the area to be affected by the proposed action. The action agency is required to prepare a "biological assessment" to determine whether that species is "likely to be affected" by the proposed action. 16 U.S.C. § 1536(c)(1). If the biological assessment concludes that the proposed action is likely to affect the species, the action agency must engage in formal consultation with the Secretary to determine whether the proposal is "likely to jeopardize the continued existence of" the species or "result in the destruction or adverse modification of" its critical habitat. *Id.* § 1536(a)(2). Consultation leads to the preparation by the Secretary of a "biological opinion" assessing the likely effect of the proposed action on the listed species. If the Secretary concludes that the proposed action would jeopardize a species or adversely modify its critical habitat, he is to suggest "reasonable and prudent alternatives" to the proposal that will not jeopardize the species of its habitat. *Id.* § 1536(b)(3). Finally, if the Secretary concludes

> (1)(a) that the action as proposed "is not likely to jeopardize the continued existence of any [listed] species or result in the destruction or adverse modification of [critical] habitat of such species" *or*

> (b) that reasonable and prudent alternatives to the proposed action he has suggested will prevent a violation of the prohibitions, *and*

> (2) that any taking of the species "incidental to the agency action" will not jeopardize the species,

the Secretary is to provide the action agency and the applicant with an "incidental take statement." *Id.* § 1536(b)(4). The incidental take statement is to specify "the impact of such incidental takings on the species," the "reasonable and prudent measures ... necessary to minimize such impact," and "the terms and conditions ... that must be complied with." *Id.* These terms and conditions are important because the Act states that "any taking that is in compliance with the terms and conditions ... shall not be considered to be a prohibited taking of the species concerned." *Id.* § 1536(*o*).

(3) *Bennett v. Spear*: The Supreme Court has offered the following discussion of the nature of incidental take statements:

> A Biological Opinion of the sort rendered here alters the legal regime to which the action agency is subject. When it "offers reasonable and prudent alternatives" to the proposed action, a Biological Opinion must include a so-called "Incidental Take Statement"—a written statement specifying, among other things, those "measures that the [Service] considers necessary or appropriate to minimize [the action's impact on the affected species]" and the "terms and conditions * * * that must be complied with by the Federal agency * * * to implement [such] measures." 16 U.S.C. § 1536(b)(4). Any taking that is in compliance with these terms and conditions "shall not be considered to be a prohibited taking of the species concerned." § 1536(*o*)(2). Thus, the Biological Opinion's Incidental Take Statement constitutes a permit authorizing the action agency to "take" the endangered or threatened species so long as it respects the Service's "terms and conditions." The action agency is technically free to disregard the Biological Opinion and proceed with its proposed action, but it does so at its own peril (and that of its employees), for "any person" who knowingly "takes" an endangered or threatened species is subject to substantial civil and criminal penalties, including imprisonment. *See* §§ 1540(a) and (b) (authorizing civil fines of up to $25,000 per violation and criminal penalties of up to $50,000 and imprisonment for one year); *see also Babbitt v. Sweet Home Chapter of Communities for Great Oregon*, 515 U.S. 687, 708 (1995) (upholding interpretation of the term "take" to include significant habitat degradation).

Bennett v. Spear, 520 U.S. 154 (1997).

(4) ***Arizona Cattle Growers' Assn. v. U.S. Fish & Wildlife Service:***
The ranchers' association challenged an incidental take statement (ITS)
issued by the FWS, which precluded cattle grazing in certain areas and
under certain conditions to protect listed species, including pygmy owls and
razorback suckers. FWS issued the statement to local offices of the BLM
(on whose land the private ranchers held grazing permits) based on its
conclusion that the listed species were likely to be in the area and would be
harmed by the grazing. The district court held that the ITS were improperly issued absent convincing evidence from FWS that the listed species were
present in the area, given that habitat modification amounts to an unlawful
take only if it kills or injures individual members of the species. *Arizona
Cattle Growers' Assn. v. U.S. Fish & Wildlife Service,* 63 F.Supp.2d 1034
(D.Ariz.1998).

Note that, although the ranchers won—thus freeing themselves from
the restrictions imposed by the ITS—the victory puts them in a dangerous
position. With the ITS, they would have been immune from liability if an
incidental take took place. With the ITS struck down, they open themselves
up to liability should species be present in the area and be harmed by their
grazing.

(ii) INCIDENTAL TAKE PERMITS

NOTES

Incidental taking by non-federal entities: Although many major
development projects undertaken by non-governmental entities require a
federal license or permit—and thus become "agency actions" subject to § 7
consultation—some private developmental activities that might affect listed
species do not require federal permission. Such non-federal actions are
ineligible for the incidental taking exemption provided through § 7's incidental take statement. To meet the perceived need permit development
while also conserving habitat for listed species, Congress also amended § 10
in 1982 to authorize the Secretary to permit an otherwise prohibited taking
if it "is incidental to, and not the purpose of, the carrying out of an
otherwise lawful activity." 16 U.S.C. § 1539(a)(1)(B). The conference report's stated objective was to provide developers with increased certainty:

> significant development projects often take many years to complete and
> permit applicants may need long-term permits. In this situation, and in
> order to provide sufficient incentives for the private sector to partici-
> pate in the development of such long-term conservation plans, ...
> adequate assurances must be made to the financial and development
> communities that a section 10(a) permit can be made available for the
> life of the project. Thus, the Secretary should have the discretion to
> issue section 10(a) permits that run for periods significantly longer
> than are commonly provided for under current administrative prac-
> tices.

H.R. CONF. REP. No. 835, 97th Cong., 2d Sess. 31 (1982), *reprinted in* 1982
U.S.C.C.A.N. 2860, 2872. While noting that permits of "30 or more years

duration may be appropriate," the committee also recognized that "circumstances and information may change over time." *Id.* Thus, the committee expected the plans to include "procedures by which the parties will deal with unforeseen circumstances." *Id.* These expectations reflected the committee's view of the habitat conservation plans (HCPs) as "creative partnerships between the public and private sectors and among governmental agencies in the interest of species and habitat conservation." *Id.* at 30 (1982), *reprinted in* 1982 U.S.C.C.A.N. at 2871.

The habitat-conservation-plan process was explicitly modeled on the then-recently developed San Bruno Mountain HCP, which had been negotiated to allow development of one of the last remaining blocks of open space in the San Francisco Bay area while also protecting much of the remaining habitat of the mission blue and San Bruno elfin butterflies. Prior to the discovery of the two species on the tract, the landowner had planned to develop the 3,800–acre site by building 8,500 residential units and some 2,000,000 square feet of commercial space. Following a two-year biological study and extended negotiations, a HCP was agreed upon by the landowner, the county, three surrounding municipalities, and a citizens group that opposed development of the mountain. The plan protected in perpetuity 87% of the habitat of the listed species, created a permanent institutional structure to insure protection of this habitat across the various jurisdictional boundaries, and established a funding program for habitat management through annual fees imposed on the developed property. *See Friends of Endangered Species, Inc. v. Jantzen,* 760 F.2d 976 (9th Cir.1985) (upholding the San Bruno HCP); TIMOTHY BEATLEY, HABITAT CONSERVATION PLANNING 23–26 (1994).

The Secretary had approved San Bruno HCP under § 10(a) which— before the 1982 Amendments—empowered him to "permit, under such terms and conditions as he may prescribe, any act otherwise prohibited by section 9 of this Act . . . to enhance the propagation or survival of the affected species." To clarify and limit the Secretary's powers in this area, the section was amended to authorize the issuance of a permit for any taking prohibited by § 9 "if such taking is incidental to, and not the purpose of, the carrying out of an otherwise lawful activity." 16 U.S.C. § 1539(a)(1)(B). To obtain a permit, the applicant is required to prepare a "conservation plan" that specifies the likely impact of the taking, the steps taken to "minimize and mitigate" the impact, and the funding available for the mitigation measures. *Id.* § 1539(a)(2)(A). Following opportunity for public comment, the Secretary may approve the permit if he finds that the proposed taking would be "incidental," that the applicant would minimize and mitigate takings "to the maximum extent practicable," that the applicant would "ensure . . . adequate funding for the plan," and—ultimately—that the taking would not "appreciably reduce the likelihood of the survival and recovery of the species in the wild." *Id.* § 1539(a)(2)(B). If the Secretary made the requisite findings, he was authorized the issue the permit subject to the terms and conditions he concluded were necessary.

* * *

The following excerpt examines how a little used provision of the ESA became the center piece of the Clinton-era approach toward endangered species enforcement, leading up to the important 2000 district court case (*NWF v. Babbitt*) that follows. The author of the article, a senior counsel of the National Wildlife Federation, served as lead counsel for the plaintiffs in the case:

John Kostyack, NWF v. Babbitt: *Victory for Smart Growth and Imperiled Wildlife,*
31 Envtl. L. Rep. (Envtl. L. Inst.) 10712 (2001).

Congress added the HCP tool to the ESA in 1982, in an effort to conserve imperiled species facing the risk of habitat destruction due to nonfederal economic activities. It viewed HCPs as a win-win situation for imperiled species and development interests: in return for securing ITPs (Incidental Take Permits) allowing development interests to take a limited amount of habitat, they would commit in an HCP to protect and manage other habitat areas, thus enhancing the species' overall recovery chances.

Upon assuming office in 1993, the Clinton Administration made HCPs one of its top ESA priorities, pushing federal wildlife agencies to get deals done as a strategy for countering criticism of the law as insufficiently user-friendly. Prior to 1993, the FWS had issued a mere 14 ITPs in connection with HCPs. Today, approximately 290 ITPs governing the management of over 20 million acres of land have been issued, and many more are under development. Many of the largest HCPs, in terms of acreage, are those that have been prepared by local governments to address proposed development in and around the habitats of listed species.

The Clinton-era expansion of HCPs has been controversial among environmentalists and independent scientists who have shown how the plans allow substantial amounts of habitat destruction while providing few reliable mitigation measures in exchange.[5] In response to these criticisms, the FWS and the National Marine Fisheries Service (NMFS)—the two agencies responsible for the administration of the ESA—recently amended their HCP handbook to include new guidelines on five key features of conservation planning: biological goals, monitoring, adaptive management, limits on permit duration, and citizen participation.[6]

These suggestions from the federal wildlife agencies on how local governments, developers, and others can effectively incorporate wildlife considerations into their land use planning were a positive step forward. However, the guidelines did not fully address the concerns of environmental groups and other critics of the HCP program. The new guidelines are completely voluntary and, thus, leave open the possibility that the glaring

---

5. *See, e.g.,* PETER KAREIVA ET AL., USING SCIENCE IN HABITAT CONSERVATION PLANS (American Institute of Biological Sciences and National Center for Ecological Analysis and Synthesis, 1999); LAURA HOOD ET AL., FRAYED SAFETY NETS: CONSERVATION PLANNING UNDER THE ENDANGERED SPECIES ACT (Defenders of Wildlife, 1998).

6. *See* Final Addendum to the Handbook for Habitat Conservation Planning and Incidental Take Permitting Process, 65 Fed. Reg. 35241 (June 1, 2000). The NMFS has only recently begun to play a prominent role in reviewing and approving HCPs and in setting HCP policy. Prior to the recent listings of various Pacific salmon species, it had little involvement with the issue.

gaps in species protection found in past plans will be built into future plans and continue to place imperiled species at risk. Rejecting the advice of conservationists, the FWS and the NMFS refused to issue any "bottom line" regulatory standards to help ensure that harmful HCPs are no longer approved.

Thus, to date, the only enforceable obligations placed on ITP applicants are the statutory standards themselves, of which there are six. Under ESA § 10(a)(2)(B), before issuing an ITP, the FWS or the NMFS must find that:

(1) the taking will be incidental;

(2) the applicant will, to the maximum extent practicable, minimize and mitigate the impacts of the taking (the "(B)(ii) finding");

(3) the applicant will ensure that adequate funding for the plan and procedures to deal with unforeseen circumstances will be provided (the "(B) (iii) finding"); and

(4) the taking will not appreciably reduce the likelihood of the survival and recovery of the species in the wild (the "(B)(iv) finding").

In addition, under ESA § 7(a)(2), the FWS or the NMFS must find that:

(5) the ITP will not jeopardize the existence of the species covered by the plan; and

(6) the ITP will not destroy or adversely modify the critical habitat of such species, if any critical habitat has been designated.

Although these standards may appear rigorous to some, they have not (as discussed above) generally produced scientifically rigorous HCPs. The FWS' spotty implementation of these standards, and the reluctance of either the FWS or the NMFS to take regulatory steps to prevent such poor implementation in the future, continues to put imperiled species at unnecessary risk.

Citizen Enforcement of HCP Approval Standards Prior to NWF v. Babbitt

Over the past 27 years since the enactment of the ESA, when the FWS had failed repeatedly to meet one of its other ESA mandates, conservationists succeeded in forcing compliance through court action. However, citizen enforcement to ensure FWS compliance with HCP approval standards is a different story.

Prior to the arrival of the Clinton Administration, the courts had issued only one ruling concerning HCP approval standards. In *Friends of Endangered Species v. Jantzen*,[11] the U.S. Court of Appeals for the Ninth Circuit rejected a challenge to the first HCP ever approved, a plan that addressed real estate development in and around the habitats of two listed butterflies on San Bruno Mountain in northern California. Because this HCP protected a substantial percentage of the remaining habitats of the two species (87% and 92%, respectively), provided for restoration of degraded habitats, and had earlier been deemed by Congress to be a "model" of

---

11. 760 F.2d 976 (9th Cir.1985).

endangered species conservation, this ruling does not provide much of a road map for evaluating the more controversial HCPs of the 1990s.

From 1985 to August 2000, only two additional rulings on HCP approval standards were issued. In *Sierra Club v. Babbitt*,[12] a federal court struck down two HCPs allowing development in the habitat of the endangered Alabama beach mouse. The court focused solely on the FWS' ESA § 10(a)(2)(B)(ii) finding, *i.e.,* that the applicants would minimize and mitigate takings of the species to the maximum extent practicable. According to the court, this finding was arbitrary because the promised mitigation measures were to be funded in part by voluntary contributions from unidentified third parties. This holding went to the heart of the conservation community's concerns with Clinton-era HCPs. The ruling highlighted how the FWS was allowing HCPs to go forward despite a high degree of uncertainty about whether developers would succeed in mitigating the harm to be caused by their proposed activity, and despite the developers' failure to take financial responsibility for addressing the inevitable challenges of achieving the mitigation goal.

In *Loggerhead Turtle v. County Council of Volusia County, Florida*,[14] a federal district court upheld an HCP allowing motor vehicles to be driven in and around the nesting areas of endangered sea turtles. Refusing "to become bogged down in the minutiae of each of the permit's measures," the court addressed only a handful of plaintiffs' concerns about the HCP. However, one of the court's findings was noteworthy, considering the recurring questions about the reliability of HCP conservation measures. The court upheld the FWS' ESA § 10(a)(2)(B)(iii) finding, *i.e.,* that the county would ensure adequate funding, because the FWS had an opportunity prior to the HCP to observe the county's commitment to funding the HCP's contemplated programs, and because the ITP was made conditional upon the FWS' approval of the county's future budget allocations. This language raises important questions, addressed again in *NWF v. Babbitt*, about whether permit revocation authority provides a sufficient safeguard for species to justify allowing an HCP with highly uncertain conservation measures to go forward.

On August 15, 2000, U.S. District Judge David Levi of the Eastern District of California issued his ruling in *NWF v. Babbitt*. Because this was just the fourth ruling on HCP approval standards since the HCP provisions were added to the ESA in 1982 and the first in the West since the HCP boom began there in the early 1990s, Judge Levi's detailed opinion provides important guidance to anyone seeking to design and influence HCPs and similar negotiated arrangements under the ESA.

National Wildlife Federation v. Babbitt

District Court for the Eastern District of California.
128 F.Supp.2d 1274 (2000).

■ LEVI, J.:—Plaintiffs challenge the United States Fish and Wildlife Service's issuance of an incidental take permit to allow development in the Natomas Basin....

---

12. 15 F.Supp.2d 1274 (S.D.Ala.1998).   **14.** 120 F.Supp.2d 1005 (M.D.Fla.2000).

I. Background and Procedural History

A. *The Natomas Basin*

The Natomas Basin ("Basin") is a low-lying region of predominately agricultural lands in the Sacramento Valley consisting of approximately 53,000 acres.... Because the area was subject until recently to frequent flooding, the Basin has remained relatively immune from development despite its proximity to a growing metropolitan region. The Basin provides habitat or potential habitat for a number of species listed as endangered or threatened under federal or state law....

In 1986, heavy spring rains caused significant flood damage in the Sacramento area[and led the Army Corps of Engineers to study proposals to improve flood control measures. In 1991, the Corps issued a feasibility report that proposed construction of the Auburn Dam and a series of levee improvements.]

The United States Fish and Wildlife Service ("the Service") reacted to the Corps' proposal with concern, noting the importance of the Basin to waterfowl using the Pacific Flyway for migration and to certain native species listed as endangered or threatened under federal or state law.... The 1991 Report found that the biological effects of th[e] degree of urbanization in the Basin [that would follow the flood control proposals] would be a dramatic loss of wildlife habitat. [ ]

. . .

In 1991, the Sacramento Area Flood Control Authority ("SAFCA") began the process of applying for an incidental take permit ("ITP") under § 10 of the Endangered Species Act ("ESA"), 16 U.S.C. §§ 1531 *et seq.* The ITP application was intended to permit implementation of the Corps' proposed ... flood control project.... In 1992, however, [Congress discontinued funding for study of the proposed dam and] SAFCA redirected its energies toward a more modest flood control project.... In order to implement the flood control project, SAFCA applied to the Corps for a permit under § 404 of the Clean Water Act, 33 U.S.C. §§ 1251 *et seq.,* to permit the discharge of fill material into certain wetlands and waterways in the basin....

In 1993, the Service listed the Giant Garter Snake ("GGS") as a threatened species under the ESA.... In [response to the listing] the Natomas Basin Habitat Conservation Plan Working Group ("Working Group") was formed, and began development of a habitat conservation plan ("Plan," or "HCP"), as required to qualify for an ITP. The Working Group was comprised of "representatives of land owners of a large proportion of the affected area." [ ]

In March 1994, the Service issued a Biological Opinion ("1994 Biological Opinion") regarding SAFCA's proposed flood control project.[2] [ ] The

---

2. Under § 7 of the ESA, the Service may not undertake action that may affect a listed species unless it first finds that the action "is not likely to jeopardize the continued existence of" a protected species, or result in the destruction or adverse modification of critical habitat. 16 U.S.C. § 1536(a)(2); *see also* 50 C.F.R. § 402.01(b).

1994 Biological Opinion noted that "nine of the twelve other extant populations [of the GGS are] on the verge of extinction," and expressed the Service's opinion that, given "the severe, declining trends in habitat suitability/availability and population levels throughout 75 percent of the range of the species," the American Basin population of GGS was "vital to the survival of the species." [ ] In addition, the 1994 Biological Opinion noted that, absent measures to mitigate the expected urbanization of existing GGS habitat, "this flood control project and consequent urban development could extirpate the giant garter snake from the American Basin." [ ] The 1994 Biological Opinion nevertheless concluded that the project would not likely "reduce appreciably the likelihood of the survival and recovery of the giant garter snake by adversely affecting reproduction, numbers and distribution of the species." [ ] This conclusion was premised on five conditions proposed by the Corps as limitations on any permit to be issued to SAFCA: (i) preconstruction surveys for the GGS; (ii) the use of measures to minimize incidental take; (iii) compensation for any direct losses of GGS habitat; (iv) completion of a habitat management plan that ensures the conservation needs of the GGS; and (v) execution of an agreement by the City, Sacramento and Sutter Counties, and the Service, to guarantee implementation of the plan. [ ] Most important among these conditions were numbers (iv) and (v), which the 1994 Biological Opinion characterized as

> a special permit condition that would establish a multispecies habitat conservation plan for the 55,000–acre lower American Basin, scheduled for completion prior to the start of construction of the proposed pumping station. An element of this habitat management plan would include an agreement among local governments and the Service that guarantees the conservation needs of the giant garter snake.

[ ]

In May 1994, landowners in the Working Group responded to the 1994 Biological Opinion by commissioning a team of consultants to begin preparing a draft HCP and an accompanying application for an ITP under ESA § 10. SAFCA subsequently released a draft HCP for public comment in March 1995. . . . The Service also provided comments in response to the 1995 draft HCP, and expressed concern over certain provisions of the Plan. The Service did, however, accept certain significant provisions of the Plan, including its proposed mitigation ratio of 0.5:1, whereby one-half acre of land would be acquired and conserved for each acre that was developed, and the Plan's estimate that only 17,500 acres in the basin would be developed over the 50 year life of the Plan.

. . . . Subsequently, the City of Sacramento took over for SAFCA as the prospective permittee, and in December 1996, the City submitted its application for an ITP, consisting of a draft HCP, draft Implementation Agreement and other supporting documents. [The Service prepared a draft Environmental Assessment ("EA") and leased the permit package for

---

This finding is typically made in a "biological opinion," which addresses whether jeopardy is likely to occur for any protected species, and if so, whether "reasonable and prudent alternatives" exist to avoid jeopardy. [ ]

public comment. In response, the Service proposed changes to the Plan and the City issued an amended version of the permit application, including a revised HCP; the Service prepared a revised EA. In December 1997, both parties executed the Implementation Agreement and, on December 31, 1997, the Service issued the permit to the City.]

B.   The Final HCP

The Natomas Basin HCP is intended "to promote biological conservation along with economic development and the continuation of agriculture within the Natomas Basin." [ ] The HCP lists 26 species that are "potentially subject to take," [ ], and which are to "be included in the state and federal permits issued in accordance with the Plan."[3] [ ] The proposed permit authorizes incidental take resulting from urban development, as well as any incidental take that may occur through rice-farming or result from management of the Plan's reserve lands. The HCP was developed as a regional conservation plan for the entire Natomas Basin, and was intended for use in connection with ITP applications for each of the municipalities and water companies with interests in the Basin:

> [t]he following agencies or jurisdictions will be seeking, or are expected to seek, Section 10(a)(1)(B) and [California Fish and Game Code] Section 2081 permits for their activities under this Plan: (1) the City of Sacramento; (2) Sacramento County; (3) Sutter County; (4) Reclamation District No. 1000; and (5) the Natomas Central Mutual Water Company.* * * These agencies will be seeking their respective permits for any incidental take that may occur as a result of their activities (*e.g.,* maintenance and public works), or, in the case of the local land use authorities, for any incidental take that may result from actions by third parties acting under existing zoning regulations or future land use permits.

[ ]

The Plan is administered by the Natomas Basin Conservancy ("NBC") which has the responsibility to establish and oversee "a concerted Basin-wide program for acquiring and managing mitigation lands on behalf of the permittees. Specifically, the NBC will be responsible for collecting and managing mitigation fees required by the City and Counties, for using the fees to establish mitigation lands, and for managing the mitigation lands for the benefit of the covered species." [ ] The Plan provides for a Technical Advisory Committee ("TAC"), comprised of representatives from the Service, the California Department of Fish and Game, and any permittee, as well as outside experts, "to advise the NBC in implementing" the HCP. [ ] The TAC's role is:

> to advise the NBC in making technical and biological decisions with respect to reserve land selection, enhancement, and management; monitoring programs and needs; species relocation or reintroduction

---

3. The Plan seeks permit coverage for a number of species that are not now protected under the ESA, to protect the City's interests in the event any of those species acquire statutory protection during the term of the ITP. The Plan also seeks permit coverage for certain species whose presence in the Basin is unconfirmed, to protect the City's interests in the event those species are later found to exist in the Basin.

plans; and other issues pertaining to technical implementation of the Plan.

[ ]

The Plan calls upon the NBC to assemble connected 400 acre blocks of reserve lands—with one block of at least 2500 acres—for the benefit of the Giant Garter Snake and to protect Swainson's hawk habitat and nesting areas. The HCP states that "to the maximum extent practicable, the [Natomas Basin] HCP will ensure that habitat acquisition will be provided *in advance* of habitat conversion resulting from urban development in the Natomas Basin." [ ] (emphasis added). Funding for land acquisition, however, is derived from the collection of mitigation fees for development. Thus, with regard to the phasing of land acquisition, the HCP actually requires only that, after an initial acquisition of 400 acres, which is to be made "as soon as possible," [ ], "no more than one year shall elapse between receipt of a fee and expenditure of that fee in the purchase or other acquisition of mitigation land." [ ]

The Plan is based on certain key principles and assumptions. First, the Plan assumes that only 17,500 acres of Basin land will be developed over the 50 year life of the permit, and that a substantial proportion of the undeveloped land will remain in agriculture, particularly rice, which is believed to have unique value as habitat for the GGS. The Plan's conclusion that a ratio of .5 acres of reserve lands for each 1 acre of developed land will ensure the biological needs of the protected species is based on the assumption that a considerable portion of the undeveloped and agricultural lands in the Basin will remain undeveloped, thereby augmenting the habitat value of the reserve lands.

Second, the Plan pursues a regional approach to conservation. Whereas without the Plan, individual landowners could pursue separate permit applications, or develop their land without securing an ITP,[6] the HCP is intended to provide a consolidated approach under which resources may be pooled and conservation lands may be purchased throughout the Basin. Third, the HCP treats all Basin lands as fungible, as equally valuable habitat. Thus, the HCP requires developers to "mitigate" for the anticipated take of individuals or habitat by payment of a fee for each acre developed. Rather than differentiating among lands according to their value as habitat for protected species, the HCP requires all landowners within the Permit area to pay a mitigation fee for developing their land, regardless of whether any particular parcel has or lacks habitat value. Depending on one's point of view, this uniform treatment is either a strength or a weakness of the Plan. It is a strength because mitigation fees are to be collected on all acreage and are used "to set aside 0.5 acres of habitat land for each 1.0 acres of gross development that occurs in the Basin." [ ] It is a potential weakness because the Plan does not attempt to identify, prior to intensified development under the ITP, particular parcels for acquisition as

---

6. An ITP is not a prerequisite for development, but simply insulates its holder from a § 9 suit in the event that incidental take results from development activities. *See* Part II.A, *infra.* The HCP provides local governments and water districts with umbrella permits such that these jurisdictions may in turn authorize particular development projects on Basin lands within their boundaries under the overall protection of the ITP.

reserves, based upon the importance of those parcels as habitat, but simply specifies acquisition criteria, and leaves specific reserve acquisition to the future decisionmaking of the NBC.

Finally, the Plan is based upon what it calls "adaptive management." The Plan recognizes that the current state of knowledge as to the conservation needs of protected species is imperfect, and that its assumptions as to the amount, location, and pace of development in the Basin and as to the adequacy of the mitigation fee to accommodate increased expenses may prove inaccurate. The Plan addresses these uncertainties through its "adaptive management" provisions, which permit the Plan's conservation strategy to be adjusted based on new information. [ ] The HCP's conservation program can be modified under the adaptive management provisions if: (1) new information results from ongoing research on the GGS or other covered species; (2) recovery strategies under Fish and Wildlife Service recovery plans for the GGS or the Swainson's hawk differ from the measures contemplated by the HCP; (3) certain of the HCP's mitigation measures are shown through monitoring to require modification; or (4) the HCP's required minimum block sizes for reserve lands are shown to require revision. [ ] The Plan anticipates that the NBC will make discretionary decisions in future years based upon new information. The NBC will decide, for example, which lands to purchase, depending on a variety of future considerations difficult now to predict, and whether to change the mix of in and out of Basin reserve lands and agricultural as opposed to marsh reserve lands.

The Plan provides for two distinct types of monitoring to assess its continuing effectiveness at meeting its conservation goals. First, periodic multi-species inventories across the Plan's entire system of reserve lands "shall be conducted throughout the [Natomas Basin] HCP plan area a minimum of once every five years." [ ] Second, "when necessary, as determined by the NBC and its Technical Advisory Committee (TAC), focused monitoring efforts [will be conducted] to assess the effectiveness of specific management and enhancement programs." [ ] The results of these monitoring efforts will "form an important component of the Adaptive Management" program. [ ]

Apart from the ongoing monitoring and adaptive management programs, the Plan addresses the "variety of uncertainties [that] exist in the Plan," including, among other things, the actual level of development that will occur in the basin, and the "extent, location and effectiveness of the habitat reserve system as it is developed under the Plan," by providing for "a comprehensive program review designed to evaluate the performance and effectiveness of the Plan." [ ] The program review is to be conducted at roughly the halfway point of the Plan, "when and if urban development [of currently undeveloped land] within the basin reaches a total of 9,000 acres." [ ] This program review is to be conducted by the NBC, the permittees, the Fish and Wildlife Service, and the California Department of Fish and Game ("CDFG"), and is to address whether the HCP is meeting its original goals with respect to four principal issues: (1) the status of the covered species; (2) the status and effectiveness of the reserve system; (3) the status and effectiveness of the Plan's funding mechanism; and, (4) the distribution of developed and reserve lands within the Basin. During the program review, no more than an additional 3,000 acres may be developed, so that, assuming that all Basin development proceeds under the auspices of the HCP, no more than 12,000 acres in total will have been developed in the Basin before the program review is completed.

C.   The 1997 Biological Opinion

As required by § 7(a)(2) of the ESA, the Service issued a Biological Opinion, ("1997 Biological Opinion"), [ ], in which it concludes that the issuance of the ITP is not likely to jeopardize the continued existence of any species covered by the Permit. In the 1997 Biological Opinion, the Service provides an account of the then current state of knowledge with respect to the "status and environmental baseline" of each covered species, including distribution and population....

. . .

The 1997 Biological Opinion briefly addresses the tension between the regional nature of the Plan and the local nature of the ITP. The Service acknowledges that, although the HCP is a regional plan that assumes permit applications from each of the three land use agencies and the two irrigation districts with interests in the Basin, complete participation is not assured, and "a lack of participation by Sacramento or Sutter County, could compromise the NBC's ability to assemble the required contiguous 400–acre and 2500–acre habitat blocks for the mitigation reserve system." [ ] The 1997 Biological Opinion ultimately brushes off these concerns, stating that mitigation "will keep pace with, and contribute to an overall balance between, habitat converted and habitat protected," [ ], and concluding that "the Plan would be self-sufficient within each permit area, to the extent that each permittee must mitigate for impacts to covered species that occur as a result of development within its respective jurisdiction * * * and the mitigation must meet the Plan's basic biological standards." [ ]

D.   The 1997 Findings and Recommendations

On December 31, 1997, the Service's Regional Director signed the "Findings and Recommendations Regarding Issuance of an Incidental Take Permit to the City of Sacramento" ("F & Rs"), which summarizes the provisions of the HCP, and discusses the 1997 Biological Opinion's analysis of the likely effect on covered species of the issuance of the permit. [ ] The F & Rs make each of the findings required under 16 U.S.C. § 1539(a)(2)(B), namely that: (1) the permitted taking will be incidental to otherwise lawful activity; (2) under the HCP, the City will, to the maximum extent practicable, minimize and mitigate the impacts of the taking; (3) the City will ensure that adequate funding for the HCP and procedures to deal with unforeseen circumstances would be provided; (4) the taking will not appreciably reduce the likelihood of the survival and recovery of the covered species in the wild; (5) any and all other measures required by the Service have been met; and (6) the Service has received the necessary assurances that the Plan will be implemented. [ ] Finally, the F & Rs summarize the HCP's analysis of the three alternatives considered by the City. [ ]

. . .

II.   Legal Background

Plaintiffs challenge the HCP and the Secretary's issuance of the ITP as in violation of the Endangered Species Act ("ESA"). The court reviews the Secretary's compliance with the ESA under the Administrative Procedure Act ("APA"), 5 U.S.C. § 701 *et seq. See, e.g., Bennett v. Spear,* 520 U.S. 154, 176–77 (1997).

A.   *The Endangered Species Act*

The ESA requires the Secretary to determine whether a given species qualifies for protection as endangered or threatened, and confers significant protection on species so listed. Section 9 of the ESA makes it unlawful for any person subject to the jurisdiction of the United States to "take" any member of any endangered or threatened species.[9] *See* 16 U.S.C. § 1538(a)(1). The ESA defines "take" as "to harass, harm, pursue, hunt, wound, kill, trap, capture, or collect." 16 U.S.C. § 1532(19). "Harm" is further defined by regulation to include killing or injuring a protected species through "significant habitat modification or degradation" that impairs "essential behavioral patterns, including breeding, feeding, or sheltering." 50 C.F.R. § 17.3.

Section 9's broad prohibition on take is limited by several exceptions identified in § 10. Most importantly for present purposes, § 10 allows the Secretary to issue an incidental take permit ("ITP"), which authorizes its holder to take some members of protected species when the taking is incidental to carrying out an otherwise lawful activity. *See* 16 U.S.C. § 1539(a). The permittee under an ITP is not liable for any taking that falls within the scope of the permit.

To obtain an ITP, an applicant must develop and submit a habitat conservation plan ("HCP"), which specifies (1) the likely impact from the proposed takings; (2) the steps the applicant will take to minimize and mitigate such impacts and the funding available for such mitigation; (3) alternative actions considered, and the reasons for not selecting them; and (4) such other measures as the Secretary may require as necessary or appropriate for the purposes of the plan. *See* 16 U.S.C. § 1539(a)(2)(A). Upon submission of a permit application and related conservation plan, "the Secretary shall issue the permit," if he finds, after opportunity for public comment, that

---

9. Of the species covered by the ITP, ten are currently listed under the ESA: the Aleutian Canada goose, giant garter snake, valley elderberry longhorn beetle, Conservancy fairy shrimp, vernal pool fairy shrimp, vernal pool tadpole shrimp, longhorn fairy shrimp, Colusa grass, slender Orcutt grass and Sacramento Orcutt grass. [ ] The Swainson's hawk is listed under the California ESA, and is covered by an ITP issued under the Plan by the California Department of Fish and Game, as well as by the federal ITP. [ ] The Permit also covers—that is, provides incidental take authority with respect to—a number of species not currently listed under either federal or state law on the theory that they could be listed at some point during the fifty year life of the Permit. [ ]

(i) the taking will be incidental;

(ii) the applicant will, to the maximum extent practicable, minimize and mitigate the impacts of such taking;

(iii) the applicant will ensure that adequate funding for the plan will be provided;

(iv) the taking will not appreciably reduce the likelihood of the survival and recovery of the species in the wild; and

(v) other measures required by the Secretary will be met.

16 U.S.C. § 1539(a)(2)(B). The permit "shall contain such terms and conditions as the Secretary deems necessary or appropriate to carry out the purposes of this paragraph, including ... such reporting requirements as the Secretary deems necessary for determining whether such terms and conditions are being complied with." *Id.* If the Secretary finds that a permittee is not complying with the terms and conditions of the permit, he "shall revoke" the permit. 16 U.S.C. § 1539(a)(2)(C).

In addition to his responsibility to review the permit application for compliance with the dictates of ESA § 10, the Secretary must insure that issuance of the permit is consistent with ESA § 7(a)(2). *See* 16 U.S.C. § 1536(a)(2). Section 7 requires each federal agency to "insure that any action authorized, funded, or carried out by such agency is not likely to jeopardize the continued existence of any endangered species or threatened species or result in the destruction or adverse modification of [critical habitat]." *Id.* To comply with § 7(a)(2), an agency considering action that may affect a protected species is required to engage in a consultation process with the Service. When the action agency is the Service itself, as when the Service is considering whether to issue an ITP, it must engage in internal consultation under § 7, and may issue the permit only upon a finding that it "is not likely to jeopardize the continued existence of" a protected species, or result in the destruction or adverse modification of critical habitat. *Id.;* 50 C.F.R. § 402.01(b). During the consultation process, the agency must consider direct, indirect,[10] and cumulative[11] effects. Any action that "may affect" listed species or critical habitat triggers the action agency's obligation to formally consult with the Service. *See* 50 C.F.R. 402.14; 51 Fed. Reg. 19926, 19949–50. Formal consultation typically culminates in the issuance of a biological opinion by the Service, which addresses whether jeopardy is likely to occur for any protected species, and if so, whether "reasonable and prudent alternatives" exist to avoid jeopardy. The Service must use "the best scientific and commercial data available" in making the required "no jeopardy" finding. 16 U.S.C. § 1536(a)(2). In every respect except for this "best scientific and commercial data" requirement, the no jeopardy finding required by ESA § 7(a)(2) is identical to the survival finding required under § 10(a)(2)(B)(iv). Where the "available data" is imperfect, the Service is not obligated to supplement it or to defer

---

10. "Indirect effects" are those that are reasonably certain to occur later in time, as a result of the proposed action. *See* 50 C.F.R. 402.02.

11. "Cumulative effects" are the effects of actions of third parties, whether state or private entities, "that are reasonably certain to occur within the action area." 50 C.F.R. § 402.02.

issuance of its biological opinion until better information is available. Rather, "the Service must develop its biological opinion based upon the best scientific and commercial data available regardless of the 'sufficiency' of that data." *See* 51 Fed.Reg. 19926, 19951 (final rulemaking with respect to 50 C.F.R. 402).

Under ESA regulations, certain conditions may trigger an agency's obligation to consult again on the same project. "Reinitiation of consultation" is required "where discretionary Federal involvement or control over the action has been retained or is authorized by law," and one of the following conditions occurs: (a) the extent of taking specified in the ITP is exceeded; (b) new information reveals that the action may affect the species or critical habitat in a manner or to an extent not previously considered; (c) the action is subsequently modified in a manner that causes an effect to the species or critical habitat that was not considered in the original biological opinion; or (d) a new species is listed or critical habitat designated that may be affected. *See* 50 C.F.R. § 402.16.

. . .

IV.   Endangered Species Act Claims

The nub of plaintiffs' challenge to the HCP concerns its strategy of adaptive management. Plaintiffs object that in the face of incomplete information as to a number of important issues—including the conservation needs of the covered species, the likely location and pace of development in the Basin, and the preferred location and availability of reserves—the Plan does not undertake studies to develop better information, but simply creates a structure and describes a process for reaching and adjusting decisions in the future based on developing information. Plaintiffs contend that many of the Service's findings are arbitrary because of the uncertainty inherent in the HCP's deferred decisionmaking scheme. As will be discussed below in greater detail, however, inconclusive data alone does not render the Service's findings arbitrary. *See* Part IV.D, *infra*.

With miscellaneous exceptions, plaintiffs' ESA claims fall into two categories. First, plaintiffs challenge as arbitrary the Service's findings as to the adequacy of the Plan's provisions, particularly those related to funding and mitigation; second, plaintiffs contend that the Service's findings regarding the biological effects of the Plan on covered species are arbitrary and capricious. As explained below, under the APA's deferential standard of review, the Service's findings largely pass muster with respect to the Plan as a whole; however, with respect to the City's Permit, the Service's findings do not. Many of the provisions of the HCP are based on the assumption that all of the land-use agencies with jurisdiction over parts of the Basin will become permittees. Similarly, the Service's findings are plainly geared toward the regional nature of the HCP, and do not adequately reckon with the local nature of the Permit or analyze what would happen if the City's lands were developed under the HCP, while the lands outside the City limits were developed piecemeal, by individual landowners, outside the HCP and the protections provided by the HCP. The importance of this point is most obvious with respect to the funding mechanism, which relies on future fee increases to fund current increases in land acquisition costs.

Because reserve land acquisition lags behind the development that funds it, the funding mechanism must play catch up, passing increased costs on to the next developer. The Plan can cope with increased expenses for mitigation, monitoring, and the like, only so long as there exists a ready supply of land to be developed under the HCP. The biological findings, too, are based on inadequate consideration of the tension between the regional Plan and the local Permit. The record contains no particularized analysis of the importance of the City's lands as habitat, and no consideration of how the species will fare if the City's lands are developed under the Plan and the some or all of the remainder of the Basin is fully developed outside the HCP. Similarly, although the 1997 Biological Opinion concedes that large blocks of reserve lands may not be possible if only the City is a permittee, there is no analysis of the consequences—particularly for the GGS—of abandoning the goal of large connected blocks of reserve lands.

A. *ESA § 10(a)(2)(A)—minimum criteria for a habitat conservation plan*

Plaintiffs argue that the Service's approval of the HCP is improper because the HCP does not adequately disclose its impacts on covered species and their habitat.... According to plaintiffs, the HCP must estimate the number of individual members of a species within the Permit area and must then estimate the number of members of the species that will be taken. Plaintiffs cite no authority for this interpretation of the ESA. The Secretary's contrary interpretation of the statute is entitled to deference. *See Chevron, U.S.A. Inc. v. Natural Resources Defense Council,* 467 U.S. 837, 844 (1984). The court finds that the HCP meets the minimum requirements for a habitat conservation plan.

B. *ESA § 10(a)(2)(B)(ii)—minimize and mitigate the impact of permitted takings "to the maximum extent practicable"*

Plaintiffs argue that the Service's (B)(ii) finding, that the Plan will minimize and mitigate takings to the maximum extent practicable, is arbitrary and capricious because the Service failed to consider any alternatives involving greater mitigation measures....

[T]he most reasonable reading of the statutory phrase "maximum extent practicable" nonetheless requires the Service to consider an alternative involving greater mitigation. *See Sierra Club v. Babbitt,* 15 F. Supp. 2d 1274, 1279–81 (S.D.Ala.1998). "The Administrative Record must contain some analysis of why the level or amount selected is appropriate for the particular project at issue." *Id.* at 1282. The linchpin of the HCP is the .5 to 1 preserved to developed acre ratio and the mitigation fee that is based on this ratio. Thus, to consider an alternative providing greater mitigation, in the context of this HCP, the record should provide some basis for concluding, not just that the chosen mitigation fee and land preservation ratio are practicable, but that a higher fee and ratio would be impracticable.

[The Secretary relied upon] conclusory statements ... to the effect that "the common and local wisdom is that a fee in the range from $2000 to $2500 per acre is practicable," [ ], but the record is devoid of evidence that the Service subjected this assumption to any examination or attempted to determine if a higher base fee would also be practicable. There is no economic analysis, discussion of mitigation fees in similar plans and circumstances, or even representations from particular landowners. . . . The plain language of the statutory provision requiring that the Plan minimize and mitigate its effects "to the maximum extent practicable" is not satisfied by a fee set, as here, at the minimum amount necessary to meet the minimum biological necessities of the covered species. The record lacks adequate evidence and analysis of whether a fee higher than that initially proposed by the working group would be economically practicable.

. . . . In short, the Secretary's conclusion that $2240 per acre is the maximum practicable initial base mitigation fee is unsupported by substantial evidence in the record, and therefore is arbitrary and capricious.

. . .

C. ESA § 10(a)(2)(B)(iii)—adequate funding

. . .

[P]laintiffs argue that the (B)(iii) finding was arbitrary and capricious with respect to the City's permit, in light of the City's explicit refusal to "ensure" funding in the event of a shortfall. This argument has merit. Plaintiffs argue that nothing in the record supports the HCP's assertion, endorsed in the F & Rs, that:

> The [Natomas Basin] HCP can be implemented independently by some individual permittees, but not by others, without adversely affecting the conservation program as a whole. This is because each land use agency is responsible under the Plan for mitigating the effects of urban development occurring within its respective permit area, regardless of the actions of other agencies.

[ ] Indeed, the record suggests a much more complicated picture than the Plan depicts concerning the consequences of nonparticipation by the other land-use agencies with jurisdiction over parts of the Basin. Given that the Plan does not permit retroactive fee increases, increases in the mitigation fee will be applied only to land developed after the need for a greater fee becomes apparent and the fee increase is approved. Thus, the Plan's funding mechanism depends on continual infusions of new developable land to provide funding for mitigation necessitated by previous development. Regardless of the City's incentives, if most or all of the City's land has been developed by the time the need for additional mitigation funding becomes apparent—a likelihood if the City lands are rapidly developed under the current fee—there may simply be no land left to which an increased fee could be applied. Given the Plan's acknowledgment that it is uncertain whether land-use agencies other than the City will submit applications, the statement that "each land use agency is *responsible* under the Plan for mitigating the effects of urban development occurring within its respective permit area," [ ], is not accurate with respect to the City, which refused to "ensure" funding for the mitigation necessitated by development under its permit.

The ESA requires that, before issuing an ITP, the Secretary must find, among other things, "that the applicant will ensure that adequate funding for the plan will be provided." 16 U.S.C. § 1539(a)(2)(B)(iii). The record reflects that the Service initially sought to require the City to ensure that funding would be available for necessary mitigation, rather than creating a funding scheme that was *projected* to be adequate. [ ] The City rejected the Service's proposed change, "because it broadly imposes liability on the City to 'ensure' the plan." [ ][20] The Service relented on the point and issued the permit, despite the possibility that, should funding under the City's Permit prove inadequate, no entity will be responsible for making up the funding shortfall, and there may not be any future permittee to whom increased costs may be shifted. This seems to frustrate the statutory requirement that funding for mitigation be ensured.

It is not clear that a funding mechanism that is not backed by the applicant's guarantee could ever satisfy the requirement of § 1539(a)(2)(B)(iii) that the applicant "ensure" funding for the Plan. Assuming, however, that a cost shifting mechanism "ensures" funding within the meaning of § 1539(a)(2)(B)(iii), in these circumstances, where the adequacy of funding depends on whether third parties decide to participate in the Plan, the statute requires the applicant's guarantee. *Cf. Sierra Club v. Babbitt,* 15 F. Supp. 2d 1274, 1282 (reliance on speculation as to funding from third parties is arbitrary and capricious); *Sierra Club v. Marsh,* 816 F.2d 1376 (9th Cir.1987) (action agency cannot "insure" project will not jeopardize species based on promise of future mitigation measures).

The City contends that the threat of permit revocation provides "the strongest protection possible," and thus satisfies the ESA's requirement that the applicant "ensure" funding. [ ] The Service's discretion to revoke a permit for violation of a condition, however, does not seem to satisfy the statute's requirement that the *applicant* ensure the adequacy of funding. *See* 16 U.S.C. § 1539(a)(2)(B)(iii).

In the face of the City's refusal to "ensure" funding, the Secretary's (B)(iii) finding with respect to the City's ITP is either at odds with the evidence in the record or is based on the City's untenable reading of the statute. In either case, while the Service's (B)(iii) finding is not arbitrary with respect to the Plan as a whole, it is arbitrary and capricious with respect to the City's Permit.

D.   ESA § 10(a)(2)(B)(iv)—Survival and Recovery, and § 7(a)(2)—No Jeopardy

Plaintiffs argue that in making the findings required by ESA §§ 10(a)(2)(B)(iv) and 7(a)(2) (collectively, the "no jeopardy" findings), the Service failed adequately to explain how habitat loss authorized by the HCP would avoid jeopardizing the continued survival of the Giant Garter Snake, Swainson's hawk, and other covered species.[23] Failure by the

---

20. The question whether the City's stated reason was valid is not before the court. Even assuming that the City's explanation—that it was without authority under the California Constitution to "ensure" funding—is meritorious, and that the City could not purchase private insurance with funds from a higher mitigation fee, § 10(a)(2)(B)(iii) makes no exception for applicants who are legally incapacitated from fulfilling the requirements of the ESA.

23. In most respects, as plaintiff concedes, the finding required by § 7(a)(2) is identical to that required by § 10(a)(2)(B)(iv).

Service to articulate a "rational connection" between the no jeopardy findings and the available facts may render the findings arbitrary and capricious. *See Friends of Endangered Species v. Jantzen*, 760 F.2d at 982. The no jeopardy findings, like the (B)(ii) and (B)(iii) findings, are undermined by the administrative record's focus on the regional HCP. Although the no jeopardy findings are adequately supported by the record if the Service's assumption that Sacramento and Sutter Counties will seek ITPs under the Plan is valid, the Service failed adequately to consider whether the findings could be made with respect to the issuance of an ITP to the City alone. In short, while the no jeopardy findings are not arbitrary with respect to the Plan, they are arbitrary with respect to the Permit.

(1) The Plan

Plaintiffs argue that the Service's no jeopardy findings are arbitrary and capricious for five reasons: (1) The Service "failed to articulate a rational connection between [the findings] and the fact that tens of thousands of acres of habitat will be destroyed and degraded under the HCP"; (2) the Service failed to explain its change in policy position on the habitat protections needed by covered species; (3) the Service "improperly ignored, and failed to explain its departure from, uncontradicted expert evidence regarding the survival and recovery needs of the imperiled species"; (4) the Service's no jeopardy findings are based on improper speculation; and (5) the Service failed to articulate a rational connection between the no jeopardy findings and the "admitted fact that the HCP's initial conservation strategy is highly uncertain to succeed." [ ]

As to plaintiffs' first argument, plaintiffs' principal contention is that the Service's reliance on the HCP's forecast of 17,500 acres of development over the 50 year term of the ITP is arbitrary. Plaintiffs argue that "up to 32,000 acres of habitat in the Natomas Basin" will be destroyed under the HCP. [ ] Plaintiffs have not established, however, that the Service's reliance on the 17,500 acre figure is unreasonable, and the Service adequately articulated its basis for the estimate.[24] Moreover, there are two important safeguards that justify reliance on the 17,500 acre figure. First, the HCP calls for a review at 9,000 acres, with a moratorium on development past 12,000 acres pending completion of the review. If the pace of development at that point exceeds expectations, various modifications may be requested or required, including a revocation of the permit. And second, because the 17,500 acre assumption is so central to the HCP, any significant departure from that figure would require reinitiation of consultation, again possibly leading to revocation or substantial modification of the permit. Based on the forecast of 17,500 acres, and using the 1:.5 development to preservation ratio, the Service concurred with the HCP's estimate that 8750 acres of reserve land would be protected under the Plan, and that

Section 7(a)(2) contains one additional requirement, however. In preparing a finding under that section, the agency must use the "best scientific and commercial data available." 16 U.S.C. § 1536(a)(2). *See* Part IV. D.3, *infra*.

24. The 1997 Biological Opinion explains that the 17,500 acre figure is a prediction based on the City's and Counties' General Plans, which the Service deemed to provide "a reasonable basis for predicting the extent and location of future urban development." [ ]

most of the remainder of the Basin would be in agricultural lands, which frequently provide excellent habitat. The Service concluded that the reserve lands, together with undeveloped land kept in agriculture, would suffice to maintain, and in some cases increase, the Basin's populations of covered species. [ ]

. . .

Plaintiffs' second major contention is that the Service retreated from earlier policy positions without providing a "reasoned analysis." The "earlier policy positions" identified by plaintiffs, however, involved mitigation proposals for a different, and larger, project. . . . [26]

Third, plaintiffs contend that the Service improperly ignored, and failed to explain its disregard of, "uncontradicted expert evidence" regarding the inadequacies of the Plan. . . . [M]any of the comments considered by the Service—indeed, many of the comments relied upon by plaintiffs—are inconsistent with one another. [ ] "When specialists express conflicting views, an agency must have discretion to rely on the reasonable opinions of its own qualified experts." *Marsh v. Oregon Natural Resources Council,* 490 U.S. at 378.

Plaintiffs' fourth contention is that the Service improperly speculated as to the likely success of the Plan's conservation measures. The subjects of "speculation" that plaintiffs identify include: (1) that habitat areas will be available for acquisition; (2) that local governments and landowners will cooperate in the NBC's efforts to acquire reserve lands; (3) that development under the plan will not exceed 17,500 acres; (4) that waterways and rice farms outside the reserves will be managed for the benefit of covered species; and (5) that reserve lands will have an adequate water supply.

The uncertainties to which plaintiffs object do not undermine the "rational connection" between the no jeopardy findings and the evidence in the record. Plaintiffs' first, second, and fifth charges of "speculation" are concerned with the uncertainties inherent in the market-based mitigation mechanism employed by the HCP. The NBC is given funds and acquisition criteria, and permitted to compete in the marketplace for land and for water rights. In the absence of any identified "critical habitat" in the Basin, or substantial evidence in the record that the market for land and water rights will not function—that is, that land and water rights will be unavailable to the NBC even if the Plan provides adequate funding—the adoption of such a market-based mitigation structure is not an arbitrary or otherwise impermissible exercise of the Secretary's discretion. As to the 17,500 acre estimate, as noted above, the Secretary's adoption of this forecast is not arbitrary or capricious. Plaintiffs' fourth charge of specula-

---

26. Plaintiffs' argue that there is evidence in the record suggesting that the Service may have been influenced by political pressure. Even were this the case, it would not require invalidation of the ITP. First, the evidence cited does not establish that the Service's motivations were other than scientific. Second, under the ESA, so long as the Secretary's decision is scientifically valid, he is not required "to justify his decision based solely on apolitical factors." *Southwest Center for Biological Diversity v. U.S. Bureau of Reclamation,* 143 F.3d 515, 523 & n. 5 (9th Cir.1998). It would be odd if in a democratic system of government those most affected by the Secretary's decisions were unable to contact their representatives to enlist their assistance.

tion concerning management of waterways and rice farms is equally merit-less. Plaintiffs offer no evidence that any such "assumption" is necessary for the Secretary's conclusion that the Plan will achieve its conservation goals. Moreover, the Secretary is powerless to control activities on private land other than by a § 9 suit. The Secretary is entitled to assume that under the Plan, as before it, the prospect of a § 9 suit will deter unpermit-ted take and that citizens generally obey the law.

As to plaintiffs' final challenge to the no jeopardy findings, which concerns the allegedly uncertain success of the HCP's initial conservation strategy, plaintiffs appear to contend that, in the face of incomplete data as to species' recovery needs and uncertainty as to the efficacy of the HCP, the Service's issuance of the ITP is arbitrary and capricious. Plaintiffs provide no authority for the duty they seek to impose on the Secretary, the resolution of all uncertainties before proceeding with a Plan, nor is any such duty apparent from the text of the ESA or case law. A certain degree of what plaintiffs label "speculation" and "uncertainty" is inevitable in any decisionmaking process, particularly one as complicated as that which led to the issuance of the ITP. The law does not require that the Secretary achieve certainty before acting. *See Greenpeace Action v. Franklin,* 14 F.3d 1324, 1336 (9th Cir.1992).

(2) *The Permit*

Although the Service's no jeopardy findings are not arbitrary and capricious with respect to the Plan as a whole—that is, assuming that Sacramento and Sutter Counties will seek permits under the Plan—the record is startlingly devoid of support for the findings with respect to the possibility that only the City would participate in the Plan. This is understandable, perhaps, given the regional approach of the HCP which is its greatest strength. But the court does not have before it what the drafters of the Plan apparently envisioned, a permit or permits for all of the jurisdictions within the Basin; rather, the court has for review only a permit for the City, and may not assume that other jurisdictions will also join in the HCP.

The Service's expert analysis of the likely impacts of the Plan assumes that all Basin development occurs under the HCP subject to the mitigation fee. As discussed above, the record provides insufficient consideration by the Service of whether funding for mitigation would be adequate if only the City's lands were developed under the Plan. Moreover, the record contains little or no analysis of the effect on the species of the City's permit considered on its own. Thus, there is no analysis of the importance of the City's lands as habitat for covered species. At oral argument, counsel for the Secretary asserted that the court could assume that the City's lands were less valuable habitat than other Basin lands, but the court cannot so assume; it must rely on the considered judgment of the Service and the record. Here, the Service did not assess the importance of the City's lands and made no analysis of the effects of the development of the City's lands were the protective features of the HCP not in place in the rest of the Basin. It cannot be assumed that if valuable habitat lands in the City are developed, equally valuable habitat lands may be protected elsewhere in the

Basin because those lands may be developed outside of the HCP and may not be protected.

Furthermore, there is little discussion of the effect on the GGS if the Plan's goal of large connected blocks of reserve lands cannot be met because only the City participates in the Plan. Such a fundamental change in the Plan's conservation strategy requires discussion. Yet the Service merely acknowledges the problem without explaining how the reserves set aside by the City's development will be adequate to protect the GGS and the other affected species.

The problem of the reserve lands is just an example of a larger problem when the Plan is applied only to the City's Basin lands. The Secretary concedes that the ITP will result in take of threatened species, including between 14 and 37% of the Basin population of the GGS, but relies on certain features of the Plan, including the monitoring, adaptive management, and 9,000 acre review provisions, to adequately mitigate the impact of the take. The Secretary's emphasis on these provisions, however, only underscores the tension between the HCP's regional nature and the local focus of the ITP and the Service's biological findings. Based on the projected development in City's area of the Basin, the midcourse review will come too late to result in any change with respect to the City's permit. The record shows that the portion of the Basin with approved development plans, most of which is in the City, is expected to be developed quickly, [ ], while the pace of development in the Counties is largely unknown. [ ] Thus, the halfway point moratorium and opportunity for mid-course correction, so important to the HCP, are irrelevant to the City's permit, which contains no analogous features for correction and reconsideration. Similarly, the record does not suggest that the Service considered whether the monitoring and adaptive management provisions of the regional Plan could be effective if the City is the sole permittee. Given the evidence that the City's lands will be developed quite quickly, the Service's failure to consider whether the survival of the species will be put at risk by the City's permit, if the regional mitigation approach of the HCP is not available, is arbitrary and capricious.

(3) Best Scientific Data Requirement

As noted above, the Service's § 7(a)(2) finding is subject to one additional statutory requirement to applicable to a finding under § 10(a)(2)(B)(iv). Under § 7(a)(2), the agency must use the "best scientific and commercial data available." 16 U.S.C. § 1536(a)(2). Plaintiffs argue that the "best scientific and commercial data" requirement should be interpreted to require the Service to refuse to issue a permit where the available data is incomplete. Plaintiffs' statutory interpretation is unpersuasive. On its face, § 7(a)(2)'s requirement that the Service use the "best available" data does not require perfect data. The most reasonable reading of the statute permits the Service to take action based on imperfect data, so long as the data is the best available. *See Greenpeace Action v. Franklin*, 982 F.2d at 1355 ("When an agency relies on the analysis and opinion of experts and employs the best evidence available, the fact that the evidence is * * * not dispositive, does not render the agency's determination 'arbitrary and capricious' "); *see also Greenpeace v. National Marine Fisheries*

Service, 55 F. Supp. 2d 1248, 1262 (W.D.Wash.1999) (Section 1536(a)(2) "requires 'far less' than conclusive proof"). The best scientific evidence requirement does not alter the general rule that "an agency must have discretion to rely on the reasonable opinions of its own qualified experts even if, as an original matter, a court might find contrary views more persuasive." *Aluminum Company of America v. Administrator, Bonneville Power Administration,* 175 F.3d 1156, 1162 (9th Cir.1999). The Service's § 7(a)(2) finding is not rendered arbitrary and capricious by the data gaps identified by plaintiffs.

. . .

VI. Conclusion

The record does not support the Service's finding under 16 U.S.C. § 1539(a)(2)(B)(ii), and it does not support the Service's findings under 16 U.S.C. §§ 1536(a)(2), and 1539(a)(2)(B)(iii) and (iv), as applied to the City's Permit. Plaintiffs' motion for summary judgment on their second, third, fourth, fifth, and ninth causes of action is GRANTED. Defendants' motion for summary judgment on those causes of action is DENIED. Defendants' motion for summary judgment is GRANTED as to Plaintiffs' first cause of action, and DENIED, without prejudice, as to plaintiffs' seventh and eighth causes of action. Defendants' motion to dismiss the sixth cause of action as unripe is GRANTED.

NOTES

(1) John Kostyack, lead counsel for the successful plaintiff's has extracted the following lessons from the district court ruling:

> Several important principles about conservation planning emerge from the court's extensive analysis of the facts and law. As discussed below, as a result of the court's ruling, in reviewing HCPs in the future, the FWS will need to take greater care to ensure that someone is legally and financially accountable for the success of the HCP's mitigation program, and it will need to do a more comprehensive analysis of the adequacy of the HCP's conservation measures. At a minimum, the following steps will need to be taken.

> *Ensure Success of Off–Site Mitigation Through Regional Planning*

> From the perspective of a smart growth advocate, one of the most important principles that emerges from *NWF v. Babbitt* is the notion that an HCP proposing to conserve habitats away from the site of the habitat destruction, *i.e.,* to implement off-site mitigation, would more likely satisfy ESA standards if it were to reflect planning at the regional scale. Throughout its opinion, the court strongly criticized the FWS for failing to address the nonparticipation of Natomas Basin jurisdictions outside the city, especially considering the fact that the HCP relied upon those jurisdictions both for conservation lands and for developable lands to generate mitigation fees.

> The court also went to great lengths to encourage multi-jurisdictional regional planning. After noting the FWS' failure to analyze the

problems created by the nonparticipation of other Natomas Basin jurisdictions, the court offered dicta concerning how well the Natomas Basin HCP would fare if such participation had been achieved.

Analyze the Relative Importance of Habitats to Be Destroyed and Conserved

NWF v. Babbitt makes clear that the FWS is obligated under ESA §§ 10(a)(2)(B)(iv) and 7(a)(2) to analyze the quality of the habitats to be sacrificed to development in the city and to weigh this carefully against the quality of the habitats that would be conserved outside the city. According to the court, "it cannot be assumed that if valuable habitat lands in the City are developed, equally valuable habitat lands may be protected elsewhere."[28]

The court criticized the FWS because the record had "no particularized analysis of the City's lands as habitat" and "no consideration of how species will fare if the City's lands are developed and some or all of the remainder of the Basin is developed." It also criticized the FWS for failing to address the impact on covered species if the HCP's goal of large, connected reserves cannot be achieved due to nonparticipation in the HCP by Natomas Basin jurisdictions outside the city. In essence, the ruling provides the FWS with a road map for a regional cumulative effects analysis, one that measures the habitat-altering impacts of both permitted development and anticipated future development in the region against the conservation value of offsetting mitigation measures. . . .

Analyze the Economic Practicalities of Securing Greater Mitigation

The court held that the FWS' ESA § 10(a)(2)(B)(ii) finding was arbitrary because the record failed to show how the harmful impacts of the amount of take contemplated in the plan would be minimized and mitigated "to the maximum extent practicable." According to the court, when examining alternatives to a proposed HCP, the FWS must "consider an alternative involving greater mitigation." The FWS wrongly accepted without analysis the developer-led Working Group's assertion that the proposed mitigation fee was "practicable," without even inquiring into what fee would be the "*maximum extent* practicable." . . .

Ensure a Reliable Funding Source

NWF v. Babbitt makes clear that the primary funding source for an HCP needs to be carefully spelled out. The court strongly criticized the HCP's reliance on future mitigation fee increases to pay for present-day increases in land acquisition costs, noting that such fee

---

28. 128 F. Supp. 2d at 1299. *See also id.* at 1291. The court did not address plaintiffs' contentions that the substantial net loss of habitats allowed by the HCP, and the HCP's failure to identify the location of the future reserves, violated the ESA's requirement that HCPs not "appreciably reduce the likelihood of survival and recovery" of a covered species. Instead, it accepted without analysis the FWS' contention in its biological opinion that "habitat enhancements [will] increase the amount and quality of [the covered species'] habitat." *Id.* at 1283.

increases could not be covered without a "ready supply of land to be developed under the HCP." . . .

Provide a Guaranteed Backup Funding Mechanism

In this author's view, the court's concern about the absence of a "ready supply of land to be developed under the HCP" does not necessarily point to a solution to the problem of the funding gap. That is, the funding gap identified by the court will not always be solved simply by identifying a larger "ready supply" of developable lands for inclusion in the HCP so that greater amounts of mitigation fees will be available. If the owners of the lands due to be developed in the later portion of the HCP's 50–year time frame are forced to pay substantially higher mitigation fees than previous developers, and if the reason for this higher fee is to remedy massive problems caused by the previous developers, the HCP might rightfully be rejected as an inequitable "Ponzi scheme." To avoid this scenario, planners crafting HCPs need a more reliable backup funding mechanism.

Fortunately, the court in *NWF v. Babbitt* anticipated this problem by requiring a financial guarantee of the HCP's performance. . . .

Avoid Severe Limits on Adaptive Management

NWF v. Babbitt raises serious questions about the legality of placing severe limits on adaptive management. In its analyses of each of the four ESA violations, the court questioned the logic of the HCP's adaptive management scheme, which placed a cap on fee increases for many types of expenditures, prohibited retroactive application of fee increases, called for a "mid-course review" that was too late to accomplish anything, and insulated the city from the cost of any funding shortfalls. The court suggested that this scheme could conceivably be valid if the HCP were to contain a mechanism to identify problems with HCP performance and to pay for necessary measures to correct these problems over the course of the plan. However, the restrictive adaptive management scheme in the Natomas Basin HCP did not pass muster because the review of the plan's performance would be too late to accomplish anything, and because no one had committed to remedy any problems with plan performance that might be identified.

The court's analysis of the Natomas Basin HCP's adaptive management strategy places into question many of the "no surprises" HCPs that have been negotiated in recent years. "No surprises" HCPs are HCPs in which the permittee takes advantage of the limits on responsibility set forth in the 1998 "no surprises"[43] rule or the nearly identical policy issued in 1994.[44] The rule states that once an ITP is issued, the FWS "will not require the commitment of additional land, water, or financial compensation or additional restrictions on the use of land, water, or other natural resources beyond the level otherwise

43. *See* Habitat Conservation Plan Assurances ("No Surprises") Rule, 63 Fed. Reg. 8859 (Feb. 23, 1998).

44. NMFS, U.S. FWS, No Surprises: Assuring Certainty for Private Landowners in Endangered Species Act Habitat Conservation Planning (1994) (available from the ELR Document Service, ELR Order No. AD–319).

agreed upon for the species covered by the conservation plan without the consent of the permittee." Permittees who avail themselves of this regulatory shield and refuse to consent to adaptive management in their HCPs effectively shift the risk of poor HCP performance to imperiled species. *NWF v. Babbitt* suggests that, to satisfy the ESA, permittees must agree to broad adaptive management provisions in which the permittee (or some other entity) takes financial responsibility for ensuring that the HCP achieves its stated objectives.

> *Do Not Rely on the FWS' Oversight and Permit Revocation Authority to Provide Accountability*

As noted earlier, the court in *Loggerhead Turtle*, held that an HCP requiring a permittee county to submit its annual appropriation to the FWS for review and providing the FWS with permit revocation authority to address any funding inadequacies satisfies ESA § 10(a)(2)(B)(iii)'s requirement that the permittee "ensure" adequate funding. The court in *NWF v. Babbitt* likewise considered an HCP with extensive FWS oversight and permit revocation authority. However, the court held that similar provisions did not satisfy § 10(a)(2)(B)(iii)'s requirement that the permittee "ensure" adequate funding because they did nothing more than give the FWS the discretion to address permit violations.

NWF v. Babbitt is the better reasoned of the two opinions. The mere fact that the FWS has discretion to revoke the permit does not mean that such discretion will in fact be exercised. In cases where the political ramifications of revoking a permit are severe, the FWS would likely avoid resorting to this tool at all costs. Moreover, even if the threat of permit revocation were credible, it is difficult to see how this threat would ensure adequate funding of an HCP's conservation program.

John Kostyack, NWF v. Babbitt: *Victory for Smart Growth and Imperiled Wildlife,* 31 Envtl. L. Rep. (Envtl. L. Inst.) 10712 (2001).

(2) Section 7 "incidental take statements" and section 10 "incidental take permits"—*Ramsey v. Kantor*: Although the two methods for authorizing incidental take share similarities, the requirements for incidental take permits under § 10 are more demanding than the requirements for incidental take statements under § 7.

(a) Protective standard: Under § 7, the Secretary may issue an incidental take statement only if the consultation process concludes that the proposed agency action "is not likely to jeopardize the continued existence of any [listed] species or result in the destruction or adverse modification of [critical] habitat of such species." 16 U.S.C. §§ 1536(b)(4)(A), 1536(a)(2). Under § 10, an incidental take permit may be issued only "the taking will not appreciably reduce the likelihood of the survival and recovery of the species in the wild." *Id.* § 1539(a)(2)(B)(iv). Congress appears to have thought that these two standards were "the same." H.R. CONF. REP. No. 835, 97th Cong., 2d Sess. at 29, *reprinted in* 1982 U.S.C.C.A.N. at 2870.

(b) Procedural requirements: The consultation procedures under § 7 are specified in some detail, require discussions between the action agency and the fish and wildlife agency, and are subject to time limits. *See* 16 U.S.C. § 1536(b)-(c). On the other hand, § 10 contains only a skeletal process for issuing incidental take permits. The statute shifts the responsibility and the cost to the permit applicant which must collect the necessary information and develop the requisite HCP; this is made more complex by the fact that the negotiations may involve a wide range of public and private entities. Furthermore, the incidental take permit application is subject to public comment requirements whereas § 7 consultation can occur behind closed doors, without public knowledge or participation. Finally, there are no time limits on the Secretary's consideration of a HCP. *See id.* § 1539(a)(1)(B)-(2).

(c) *Ramsey v. Kantor*: In December of 1991 and May of 1992, the National Marine Fisheries Service listed the Snake River fall chinook salmon, and the Snake River spring/summer chinook salmon as threatened under the ESA. The listing created a significant problem because, under current fishing methods, it is nearly impossible to catch hatchery chinook salmon in the Columbia River without also catching and killing wild chinook salmon. Such catching, however, is illegal under § 9. As a result, chinook salmon fishing violates the ESA unless it falls within one of the two exceptions to § 9's prohibition on the taking of a protected species:

> Under both the statutory exceptions to § 9, the incidental taking of an endangered species is permitted if it is determined that such action does not jeopardize the survival of the species. One exception is embodied in § 7 of the ESA, the other in § 10. The § 7 exception provides a procedure whereby federal agencies and certain statutorily-defined "applicants" may obtain determinations in the form of incidental take statements through a comparatively informal consultation process. By contrast, § 10 prescribes a more rigorous and time-consuming procedure whereby private parties may apply for and obtain permits authorizing incidental taking.[7]

Ramsey v. Kantor, 96 F.3d 434 (9th Cir.1996). In May 1993, NMFS issued a biological opinion under § 7 that included an incidental take statement that purported to include the salmon fisheries, fisheries that are regulated under state law—hence the question: does "the issuance of the § 7 statement enabl[e] Oregon and Washington to promulgate those regulations without first obtaining a § 10 permit"? Petitioners argued that the incidental take statement covered only the actions of the federal agencies whose actions affected the listed species and that the states were required to obtain a § 10 incidental take permit. The federal defendant argued that

---

7. Under Section 10, for example, it is the applicant's duty to submit an acceptable conservation plan, however long it takes to do so. Under Section 7, by contrast, this burden is shifted to the authorizing agency and the National Marine Fisheries Service (or the U.S. Fish and Wildlife Service), and they must normally conclude formal consultations within 90 days. Section 10 requires public participation, Section 7 does not. *See generally* David Farrier, *Conserving Biodiversity on Private Land: Incentives for Management or Compensation for Lost Expectations?,* 19 HARV. ENVTL. L. REV. 303, 378–79 (1995).

"any taking that is in compliance with the terms and conditions of the permit is permissible without more." The court agreed with the agency:

> The statutory language that was added to § 7 in 1982 to permit the incidental taking of listed species does not limit the protection afforded by an incidental take statement to federal agencies or applicants. That language reads in pertinent part:
>
> > [A]ny taking that is in compliance with the terms and conditions specified in a written statement provided under subsection (b)(4)(iii) of this section shall not be considered to be a taking of the species concerned.
>
> 16 U.S.C. § 1536(*o*)(2). The provision indicates that any taking— whether by a federal agency, private applicant, or other party—that complies with the conditions set forth in the incidental take statement is permitted. Moreover, the implementing regulations expressly provide that a taking that is in compliance with a § 7 incidental take statement need not be authorized by a § 10 permit or any other permit in order to be exempt from § 9's prohibition.

Id.

Are there reasons to demand more of non-federal actors than of federal agencies?

PERSPECTIVES

(1) Hoping for the best: A *New York Times'* headline about another California HCP captures the central issue: "California Environmentalists Cut a Deal, Hope for the Best." N.Y. Times, Mar. 28, 1993, at 4E. To what extent is "hoping for the best" a permissible agency strategy? Recall the listing decisions such as *Biodiversity Legal Foundation v. Babbitt,* 943 F.Supp. 23 (D.D.C.1996), in which the court reversed the FWS decision that listing the Alexander Archipelago wolf was not warranted because "we believe that the Forest Service's TLMP [Tongass Land Management Plan] revision process together with subsequent implementation of the revised TLMP will provide sufficient opportunity to reverse the declining population trend which we believe would occur under continued implementation of the current TLMP." The court held that "the Secretary . . . cannot use promises of proposed future actions as an excuse for not making a determination." Do HCPs face the same obstacle? How does the Natomas Basin HCP seek to overcome this obstacle? Why did the Natomas Basin HCP fail to meet the statute's requirements? Does this issue differ from the general question of decisionmaking in the face of uncertainty? How realistic is it to create a plan to manage multiple species over the next fifty years?

William H. Rodgers, Jr., *The Myth of the Win–Win: Misdiagnosis in the Business of Reassembling Nature*
42 Ariz. L. Rev. 297 (2000).

[T]he most serious obstacle to the ambitious campaign of environmental restoration . . . is the human brain. [H]uman cognitive processes are marvelous designers of serviceable self-deceptions. In the war on nature that we witnessed in the twentieth century the most functional of these is the firm belief in a non-zero sum world. This is the conviction that gains from economic development could be enjoyed without sacrifice of the natural world. This is a convenient, powerful, and serviceable myth although it happens to be faulty at its foundations.

. . .

Self-deception, by definition, is misdiagnosis. And misdiagnosis, by definition, is not where we should start in our campaigns to restore nature. The principal institutions we rely upon to resist misdiagnosis are law and science. . . .

Neither law nor science has done well in these environmental restoration circles. Law's problem . . . is that it is dependent on other entities for the development of facts. Courts have responded by inventing a "deference" doctrine that allows them to withdraw from the fray at the first hint of conflicting scientific opinion. The problem of science . . . is that it is confined to attempts to answer questions put forth by somebody else—frequently the wrong questions. Scientists have responded to law's encroachments the same way courts have responded to the encroachments of science: adopting a policy of complete deference. No question is too absurd to attempt to answer if it has been asked by a responsible political entity.

. . .

The Brain's Problem: Self–Deception

[S]elf-deception can thrive in environments of high uncertainty, complex interaction, low empirical feedback, and obscure second and third level adaptive responses. These characteristics are familiar domain to students of environmental degradation who stress cumulative effects, constant change, and sudden surprise.[4] And these characteristics are the essence of all strategies of environmental restoration that presume that interventions A and B will yield process changes C and D along with adaptive responses E and F that allow us to aspire to different endpoints G and H that are conceded to be temporary in any event. This sort of ecological theory, like a social theory, Trivers warns, "inevitably embraces a complex array of facts and these may be very partially remembered and very poorly organized.* * * Contradictions may be far afield and difficult to detect."[5] In other words, in these arenas of deep mystery, self-deception may be expected to thrive.

. . . . [M]isapprehension of reality serves [the] positive function of optimism. [I]n the last twenty years an important literature has grown up that "appears to demonstrate that there are intrinsic benefits to having a higher perceived ability to affect an outcome, a higher self-perception, and

---

4. *See generally, e.g.,* BARRIERS & BRIDGES TO THE RENEWAL OF ECOSYSTEMS AND INSTITUTIONS (Lance H. Gunderson *et al.* eds., 1995); NANCY LORD, DARKENED WATERS: A REVIEW OF THE HISTORY, SCIENCE AND TECHNOLOGY ASSOCIATED WITH THE EXXON VALDEZ OIL SPILL AND CLEANUP (1992).

5. Robert Trivers, *The Elements of a Scientific Theory of Self–Deception,* 907 ANNALS N.Y. ACAD. SCIENCES (forthcoming April 2000).

a more optimistic view of the future than facts would seem to justify."[7] This mild form of self-inflation produces benefits for those who practice it. Trivers explains, "[l]ife is intrinsically future-oriented and mental operations which keep a positive future orientation at the forefront result in better future outcomes [though perhaps not as good as those projected]."[8] Environmental lawyers would rush to confirm this speculation. Unwarranted optimism has triumphed in many corridors where careful calculators fear to tread. Environmental scientists would second the notion. The Corps of Engineers did not secure its reputation by calling itself a "Cannot Do" organization.

. . . . [In] the modern bureaucratic state . . . truth can become the first casualty in the multiple individual moves that add up to organizational behavior. Trivers' example is drawn from Richard Feynman's analysis of NASA's Challenger disaster where the muting of safety concerns developed from the agency's broader aims to promote the space shuttle.[9] . . .

The suggestion that organizational collectives can slip into gross patterns of self-deception strikes a convincing note. There is a large selection of literature on the topic that includes my personal favorite entitled *Extraordinary Popular Delusions and the Madness of Crowds*.[12] Today, few environmental lawyers pass up an opportunity to elaborate upon the folly, foolishness, or self-deception that befall bureaucracies known to them. They do not deny the phenomenon. They embrace it, extend it, and embellish it.

The grand self-deception that contributed mightily to the steady demise of the Columbia River salmon was the serviceable belief that the hydropower dams could be made compatible with the salmon's survival needs. The Bonneville Dam was constructed in the lower river (River Mile 146) between 1934 and 1937. It was designed with adult fish ladders that proved serviceable beyond expectations.[13] That some adult salmon made successful use of the fish ladders was taken as a harbinger of salmon-hydro coexistence. This "proof" that dams were compatible with fish buoyed later decisions to construct more dams. . . .

Of course, it is impossible to say definitively how widely disseminated the win-win myth of dams and salmon was. It was most popular among the construction and power agencies that were promoters of the projects. It was quite serviceable among political supporters. The win-win certainty was not embraced by the fisheries agencies. . . .

Some would say "we chose dams over salmon" in the political decisions approving the lower Snake dams. Others would say "we chose dams and

7. *Id.*

8. *Id.*

9. *See id. See also* Richard P. Feynman, "What Do You Care What Other People Think?" Further Adventures of a Curious Character 113–237 (1988).

12. Charles Mackay, Extraordinary Popular Delusions and the Madness of Crowds (Harmony Books 1980) (1st ed. 1841).

13. *See* Lisa Mighetto & Wesley J. Ebel, Saving the Salmon: A History of the U.S. Army Corps of Engineers' Efforts to Protect Anadromous Fish on the Columbia and Snake Rivers 53–54 (1994). *See also generally* Jim Lichatowich, Salmon Without Rivers: A History of the Pacific Salmon Crisis (1999).

salmon in the decisions, but subsequent events proved us wrong." But with self-deception there are always two voices. The facts were that the dams would come at the price of salmon. But political decisionmakers preferred to believe that they could have dams and salmon.

. . .

What can we do about these obstacles of institutional self-deception and pockets of cultural resistance to scientific findings? The only saviors nominated are the legal and scientific institutions or some combination of the two. Let us start with the law.

The Courts' Problem: Ignorance

[C]ourts are confined to a "highly restricted form of knowing.* * * "[23]

The enduring challenge of the courts in contributing to better decisions on environmental restoration is that they must take their facts from somebody else. Courts must decide what knowledge is legitimate and they must adhere to processes for obtaining it. To evaluate the performance of the courts, I will start with the question[:] "How well does the law integrate scientific findings into legal principles?" To elaborate further, I will borrow from consensus descriptions of the role of courts in scientific disputes[24] to ask whether courts have delivered on expectations that they resolve disputes, serve the function of public education, pursue justice, and encourage vigorous and effective adversary processes.

To test these postulations, I have explored a case sample of thirty-nine decisions addressing fisheries conflicts on the Columbia River. Have the courts met these high expectations that we have for them? Have they worked to overcome their ignorance? With rare exceptions, no. They have made ignorance a virtue and have disclaimed responsibility by deferring to the administrative agencies. Do these courts "integrate" scientific findings into law? Rarely. Their tolerance is so broad that if there is a hint of scientific "conflict" before the agencies,[26] the courts readily surrender their decisionmaking powers.

Do courts resolve disputes? No. They extend them. Do they fulfill the function of public education? They try. But how much educating can be done when these judicial explanations are nine parts arcane technicalities? Do these courts pursue justice? This goal figures so rarely in judicial decisionmaking that courts are more likely to disclaim it than embrace it.[27] Do they encourage vigorous and effective adversary processes? No. My

23. SHEILA JASANOFF, SCIENCE AT THE BAR: LAW, SCIENCE, AND TECHNOLOGY IN AMERICA 9 (1995). *See generally* D.H. Kaye, *Proof in Law and Science*, 32 JURIMETRICS J. 313 (1992).

24. *See generally* STEVEN GOLDBERG, CULTURE CLASH: LAW AND SCIENCE IN AMERICA (1994); JASANOFF, *supra* note 23.

26. SEE, E.G., WILLIAM H. RODGERS, ENVIRONMENTAL LAW § 9.3, at 851 (2d ed. 1994).

27. *See American Rivers v. National Marine Fisheries Serv.*, 109 F.3d 1484, 1492–93 (9th Cir.1997), *amended by* 126 F.3d 1118 (9th Cir.1997). The court applied mootness and the 60–day notice requirement to agencies that had been on notice for 20 years and said "we lack authority to consider the equities." *Id.* This language does not appear in the amended decision.

survey of the cases convinces me that a cathartic and decisive trial on the merits is the exception not the rule.

On the Columbia, help for the salmon in the courts is thus thrice stunted. Litigators try to push balky agencies into marginal change by asking rigid formalists to pull procedural strings. All works by indirection. The fish can be helped only through the crude tool of an agency. It is like trying to paddle with a broom. The agency can be moved only with the fine threads of procedure. It is like trying to pull a barge with a rope. The procedures will issue only if the judge is so disposed. It is like trying to tempt a mule with a stone.

I have no solutions to this state of affairs. A generation of federal judges has been selected for their docility. Advancement and honors are reserved for those who show the greatest deference. Fortunately, there is a skeleton crew still on the job.[28] Their work shows familiarity with the aggressive hard-look doctrine of judicial review that is at the foundation of modern environmental law. There are still some judges to be found who take seriously their duty to make science a part of their mandate. They have not forgotten that courts are supposed to resolve disputes, advance public understanding, and pursue justice.

The Scientists' Problem: Constraint and Direction

"[The turbines] are absolutely incapable of hurting the fish. If you could put a mule through there, and keep him from drowning he would go through without being hurt."[29]

This somewhat quaint example is offered to illustrate that the questions put to science are invariably constrained by legal and political choice. So far as I know, the mule experiment proposed by Colonel Robins for the Columbia was never conducted. Scientists used fish as the experimental animal rather than mules. The fish did not fare nearly as well as the mules in the mind of Colonel Robins. Though never answered by a decisive experiment, the issue of mule passage through the turbines somehow has lost its urgency.

The problem of being assigned the wrong question has haunted scientists who labor on the multiple fronts of environmental restoration. A number of years ago Alvin Weinberg invented the term "trans-scientific" to describe questions that could be asked of science but not answered.[30] In Weinberg's schema, "trans-scientific" questions were an oddity and a fluke. In today's world, "trans-scientific" questions are a common product of the political process. Pursuing unanswerable questions with a prolonged cam-

---

28. For example, recent commendable decisions include *Oregon Natural Desert Ass'n v. Singleton,* 75 F. Supp. 2d 1139 (D.Or.1999) (Redden, J.), *Pacific Coast Fed. of Fishermen's Ass'n v. National Marine Fisheries Serv.,* 71 F. Supp. 2d 1063 (W.D.Wash.1999) (Rothstein, J.), *Oregon Natural Resources Council Action v. United States Forest Service,* 59 F. Supp. 2d 1085 (W.D.Wash.1999) (Dwyer, J.).

29. MIGHETTO & EBEL, *supra* note 13, at 71 (quoting a 1941 statement by Thomas Robins, Assistant Chief of Engineers).

30. Alvin M. Weinberg, *Science and Trans–Science,* 10 MINERVA 209, 209 (1972).

paign of more study is a satisfactory outcome for many defenders of the status quo.[31]

Some lawyers are strongly interested in constraining scientific processes that show promise of asking the embarrassing questions. They much prefer inquiry into the safe questions....

As we did with law, I will borrow from consensus descriptions of the scientific process to evaluate the state of restoration science on the Columbia. Expectations of this science are progress orientation, falsifiable/testable conclusions, validation by normal processes, and conclusions subject to perpetual revision.

Does the science of the river meet these expectations? Erratically, at best. Progress on the most basic questions is grudging. After years of study, there is no consensus on flow-survival relationships for salmonids. There is no consensus on the efficacy of flow augmentation. There is no consensus on the use of artificially propagated fish to augment wild populations.[36]

There is little incremental progress dictated by the use of falsifiable and testable conclusions. Fads change—for example, the use of hatcheries for production has fallen out of favor and woody debris is now left in streams rather than removed from them. But classical hypothesis testing is not easily done in the context of ecological modification. While "adaptive management" is part of the gospel of environmental restoration,[37] actual experimentation (where methodologies are put in competition) is only getting started.

Scientific approaches on the Columbia River are certainly subject to validation by many different processes—ordinary and extraordinary. But the classical ideas of the gradual overthrow of paradigms are not telling and instructive.

. . .

Conclusion

The myth of the win-win has done much to justify damage to nature, and it has put the despoilers in the enviable position of the holders of the status quo. The facility of the courts and the insights of science are indispensable allies to the recovery of these lost opportunities. Courts must overcome their informational limitations and scientists must resist their directional constraints. The strategies of the hard look and the open book can help achieve these welcome independencies.

31. *See* K. Norman Johnson, *Science-Based Assessments of the Forests of the Pacific Northwest, in* CREATING A FORESTRY FOR THE 21ST CENTURY: THE SCIENCE OF ECOSYSTEM MANAGEMENT 397 (Kathryn A. Kohm & Jerry F. Franklin eds., 1997).

36. INDEPENDENT SCIENCE ADVISORY BOARD, LOOKING FOR COMMON GROUND: COMPARISON OF RECENT REPORTS PERTAINING TO SALMON RECOVERY IN THE COLUMBIA RIVER BASIN (Feb. 1, 1999) (ISAB 99–3) (ISAB Work-in-Progress Report).

37. *See, e.g.,* KAI N. LEE, COMPASS AND GYROSCOPE: INTEGRATING SCIENCE AND POLITICS FOR THE ENVIRONMENT 51–86 (1993); Kai N. Lee & Jody Lawrence, *Adaptive Management: Learning from the Columbia River Basin Fish and Wildlife Program*, 16 ENVTL. L. 431, 441–60 (1986).

NOTES

Is the 50–year duration of the Natomas Basin HCP an example of the self-deceptive win-win mentality that Rodgers examines? Do the Plan's monitoring provisions rise to the level of "science" in Rodgers's analysis?

(iii) 4(D) RULES

NOTES

(1) Generic vs. specific: As noted above, § 9 of the Act itself prohibits conduct that harms *endangered species* of *fish or wildlife* or that involves commercial transactions in such species. 16 U.S.C. § 1538(1)(A)-(F). *Threatened species* of *fish or wildlife*, on the other hand, are protected through regulations adopted by the Secretary. The two "Secretaries"—of the Interior and Commerce—have exercised this authority differently. The Secretary of the Interior has promulgated a generally applicable regulation that extends the statutory prohibitions applicable to endangered species to threatened species unless the rule listing an individual species provides otherwise. *See* 50 C.F.R. § 17.31(a). Thus, unless a regulation listing a species as threatened establishes less restrictive prohibitions, the statutory prohibitions are applicable. The Secretary's authority to promulgate generic—rather than species-specific—regulations was challenged in *Sweet Home Chapter of Communities for a Great Oregon v. Babbitt.* Although the panel was badly split on the question of whether "take" could include habitat destruction, all three judges concurred in holding that "[t]he statute does not unambiguously compel the agency to expand regulatory protection for threatened species only by promulgating regulations that are specific to individual species." 1 F.3d 1, 6 (D.C.Cir.), *rev'd on other grounds,* 17 F.3d 1463, 1464 (D.C.Cir.1994), *rev'd,* 515 U.S. 687, n. 5 (1995).

The Secretary of Commerce, on the other hand, extends § 9's prohibitions to threatened species on a case-by-case basis. *See* 50 C.F.R. pt. 223.

(2) Challenges to species-specific regulations have also been unsuccessful. In *Cayman Turtle Farm, Ltd. v. Andrus,* 478 F.Supp. 125 (D.D.C. 1979), [excerpted in Chapter 1] the petitioner challenged the regulations prohibiting the importation of green turtles that had been raised in captivity. Its argument that the regulation lacked a sufficient factual basis was rejected by the court which deferred to the Secretary's expert judgment. A similar result was reached in *Louisiana ex rel. Guste v. Verity,* 853 F.2d 322 (5th Cir.1988), in a challenge to both the evidentiary basis for regulations requiring shrimp nets to be equipped with "turtle excluder devices" as well as to the "necessity" of the devices to halt the decline of listed sea turtles.

(3) "Conservation" as a limit on 4(d) regulations: Section 4(d) directs the Secretary, "[w]henever any species is listed as threatened," to "issue such regulations as he deems necessary and advisable for the conservation of such species." 16 U.S.C. § 1533(d). Does the "conservation" requirement limit the Secretary's discretion in promulgating § 4(d) regulations?

In 1982, Secretary of the Interior James Watt published proposed regulation to permit a sport trapping season on gray wolves in Minnesota. The Sierra Club promptly challenged the proposal. Noting that the Secretary's authority to issue regulations was conditioned by the requirement that they be "necessary and advisable for the conservation of such species," the district court turned to the definition of conservation and focused on the final clause in the definition:

> "conservation" mean[s] ... the use of all methods and procedures which are necessary to bring any [listed] species to the point at which the measures provided pursuant to this Act are no longer necessary. Such methods and procedures ... , *in the extraordinary case where population pressures within a given ecosystem cannot be otherwise relieved, may include regulated taking.*

"The plain language of the Act," the court noted, "requires that before the taking of a threatened animal can occur, a determination must be made that population pressures within the animal's ecosystem cannot otherwise be relieved. In the present case, the government does not even attempt to argue that such an 'extraordinary case' exists." *Sierra Club v. Clark,* 577 F.Supp. 783, 787 (D.Minn.1984). The Eighth Circuit agreed: "the plain language of the statute ... compels us to agree with the district court.... Otherwise, such taking would not constitute an act of conservation under the Act and would fall without the scope of authority granted to the Secretary." *Sierra Club v. Clark,* 755 F.2d 608, 613 (8th Cir.1985).

The relationship between § 4(d) and the incidental-take-statement provisions of § 7 were briefly discussed in a subsequent decision involving the incidental harvest of listed species of salmon as a result of fishing for non-listed species. The court distinguished activities "directed at" a listed species from those that incidentally take a listed species, based upon the 1982 amendment of § 9 that permitted the Secretary to authorize incidental takes following consultation. *Pacific Northwest Generating Co–op. v. Brown,* 822 F.Supp. 1479, 1509 (D.Or.1993), *aff'd,* 25 F.3d 1443, 1452 (9th Cir.1994).

c. A MISCELLANY OF EXCEPTIONS

Section 10 also contains several narrowly drawn exceptions:

(1) the Secretary may permit otherwise prohibited activities "for scientific purposes or to enhance the propagation or survival of the affected species." 16 U.S.C. § 1539(a)(1)(A).

(2) the Secretary may grant an exception in a very narrowly defined class of cases involving "undue economic hardship." The exception only is available when a person enters into a contract before the date of publication of notice of a proposal to list a species and the subsequent listing of the species causes "substantial economic loss." *Id.* § 1539(b) (1988). The exception, however, can last only one year from the date of publication of the proposal to list. *Id.*

(3) Alaskan natives and non-native permanent residents of native villages may engage in subsistence hunting and sell the non-edible byproducts of species taken "primarily for subsistence purposes" when "made into authentic native articles of handicrafts and clothing" unless the Secretary determines that the taking "materially and negatively affects" the listed species. *Id.* § 1539(e).

(4) sperm whale oil and scrimshaw products held within the United States on the effective date of the 1973 Act are excepted from certain commercial prohibitions. *Id.* § 1539(f).

(5) antique products not less than 100 years old that contain listed species are excepted from the Act's prohibitions if their owner satisfy the documentation requirements established by the Secretary of the Treasury. *Id.* § 1539(h).

CHAPTER 14

BIODIVERSITY AND LAND HEALTH

This chapter brings our study of wildlife law to a close with an examination of the legal tools available to conserve wildlife populations at the landscape scale. As the materials—particularly Section 2 of Chapter 12—have revealed, the challenges of wildlife conservation are many—ranging from toxic contamination, overharvesting, and habitat degradation through the underlying cultural, economic, and political structure.

For centuries, a relatively few wild species have possessed direct value for humans, so that individual self-interest has provided motive to conserve them. Today, it is widely understood that vastly more species are valuable to humans in indirect ways, ways the market cannot value. The sense that wildlife ought to be protected without regard for any discernible, immediate benefits to humans is also far more widespread. Many observers, impressed by the vastness of human ignorance about nature's functioning, see wisdom in "saving all the parts," as Aldo Leopold so famously phrased it a half century ago. Many sense an obligation to maintain biodiversity for the enjoyment of future generations of humans. Also strong is the sense that other life forms have intrinsic value that deserves moral and legal recognition. Linked to these lines of thought is the perception that humans are thoroughly embedded into an intricate web of life—they are parts of the overall biotic community with their long-term health inextricably bound to the health of the larger whole. As farmer-writer Wendell Berry has forcefully argued, "the community—in the fullest sense: a place and all its creatures—is the smallest unit of health and to speak of the health of an isolated individual is a contradiction in terms." WENDELL BERRY, ANOTHER TURN OF THE CRANK 90 (1995).

Section 1 of this chapter sets the stage by drawing together materials from previous chapters to provide a brief overview of wildlife conservation. The first section also looks at the grave challenge to conservation posed by the fact that control over landscapes—and, hence, over interconnected wildlife habitats—is fragmented among many owners, who typically manage the lands for their own idiosyncratic needs while ignoring the needs of wildlife in the larger landscape. The consequences of these small decision by divided land managers can be tragic—the "tragedy of fragmentation." This tragedy is far more prevalent and damaging to wildlife than the related "tragedy of the commons."

As we have seen in Chapter 11, the traditional approach to these problems has been to establish preserves, whether as state game management areas (often funded under federal programs such as Pittman–Robertson Act) or as national wildlife refuges. Although the organic statute for the National Wildlife Refuge System now directs the FWS to expand the System so that it contributes to "the conservation of the ecosystems of the

United States," 16 U.S.C. § 668dd(4)(C), the System cannot achieve the objective by itself. Similarly, the National Parks, Wilderness Areas, and other federal conservation lands as we saw are too few, too small, and too fragmented to accomplish the necessary conservation of biological integrity. In Section 2, we examine the federal multiple-use lands—most notably the National Forest System. These "working" lands are the setting in which wildlife conservation been most prevalent.

At bottom, living with wildlife means accommodating wildlife in land-scapes that are occupied, used, and owned by individuals. While this includes the federal multiple-use lands, it cannot be limited to such lands. The fundamental building block of wildlife conservation must be the individual parcel of privately owned land. Since the beginning of the book, we have examined this issue—most particularly in Chapters 2 and 3—noting the inevitable tension between public rights in wildlife and the shifting mix of rights and responsibilities that the law vests in private landowners. Section 3 returns to this story, putting current developments into context and seeking to look ahead, to see how wildlife concerns might lead to yet another realignment of what it means to own land.

Sections 4 and 5 expand the spatial scale of analysis to consider wildlife planning over entire landscapes—landscapes that include intensive human activities. Section 4 returns to rivers and other bodies of water, not just because of the wildlife that inhabit them but also because so many human activities that are harmful to wildlife—even activities on dry land—end up degrading waterways. Measures to bring health to waterways often aid terrestrial ecosystems as well. From a legal perspective, the best way to assess land-use activities is often to begin with their effects on the waters they envelop.

The final section takes what is, by necessity, a quick glance at regional land planning efforts, some undertaken with wildlife needs in mind, some that benefit wildlife only unintentionally. If the "tragedy of fragmentation" is going to be addressed in ways that respect the landscape-scale needs of wildlife, it will be through the successful refinement of such efforts. As the materials here illustrate, however, landscape-level planning remains in its early stages, with its legal tools mostly experimental. Moreover, it has been met by stiff resistance, primarily by those espousing a cultural perspective that opposes planning as an infringement on personal autonomy. To understand humans as parts of a larger community of life, interwoven with it and dependent on its health, is to challenge directly the autonomy and liberty of the individual human. Wildlife law, then, rests at the heart of the conflict between individualistic and communitarian understandings of the human predicament.

SECTION 1.   THE GOALS AND CHALLENGES OF CONSERVATION

No American has been more responsible for turning wildlife manage-ment into a scientifically and economically grounded discipline than Aldo Leopold. In the 1920s, Leopold left the Southwest with its public lands and took up residence in Wisconsin, where he focused on the challenge of promoting conservation in the privately owned, farm-dominated landscapes around his new home. His writing from this period often was drafted with farmers in mind. Not surprisingly, he paid particular attention when addressing such audiences to the category of wildlife that he termed "farm game"—game that could live in farm landscapes and that farmers could enhance without significantly altering their land-use practices. Farm game was not the only wildlife that occupied his thoughts; he also addressed forest and rangeland game; migratory game; and wilderness game.

In the following essay, Leopold touches upon both the goals of wildlife management in human-occupied landscapes and also upon some of the challenges of achieving those goals:

ALDO LEOPOLD, *Planning for Wildlife, in* FOR THE HEALTH OF THE LAND

(J.B. Callicott & E.T. Freyfogle, eds., 1999).
(originally written in 1942).

Motives. No one can write a plan for accomplishing something until the reasons for desiring to accomplish it are defined. The reasons for restoring wildlife are two:

1. It adds to the satisfactions of living.

2. Wild plants and animals are parts of the land-mechanism, and cannot safely be dispensed with.

The land-mechanism, like any other mechanism, gets out of order. Abnormal erosion, loss of soil fertility, excessive floods and droughts, the spread of plant and animal pests, the replacement of useful by useless vegetation, and the dying out of protected species are all disorders of the land-mechanism.

Science understands these disorders superficially, but it seldom understands why they occur. Science, in short, has subjugated land, but it does not yet understand why some lands get out of order, others not. Stable (*i.e.,* healthy) land is essential to human welfare. Therefore it is unwise to discard any part of the land-mechanism which can be kept in existence by care and forethought. These parts might later be found to contribute to the stability of land. Most lands were stable before they were subjugated.

Many other motives have been asserted: economic profit, services to agriculture, stimulation of tourist business, etc. These hold good for some kinds of wildlife in some spots, but they break down in others. There is no economic profit in a ladyslipper. A peregrine falcon is detrimental to agriculture in every direct sense, but nevertheless worth conserving. A pheasant attracts more tourists than a prairie chicken, but has a far lesser value; he is not part of the native land-mechanism.

Man and Wildlife. The impact of civilization destroys many species of wildlife, some unavoidably (buffalo), many without any real reason (woods wildflowers). It greatly increases others, but a high proportion of these become pests, either native (rodents) or imported (carp, starling). It evicts species from one habitat and encourages then in others (shift of deer from the prairie border to the north woods).

The net result of these changes is a wild fauna and flora constantly decreasing in variety of species, in stability of populations, and in the ratio of benefits to damages. Another net result is a constantly increasing dependence on artificial replenishment from hatcheries and propagating plants, and on artificial control of "undesirable" species. Artificial replenishment and control are always costly and often ineffective.

The plan-wise adjustment of the impact of civilization can mitigate the losses and enlarge the gains in wildlife, and reduce the need for artificial interference.

Essentials of a Plan. The plan-wise adjustment is not primarily a matter of laws, appropriations, or administrative devices, but rather of modifying land-use so as to provide the habitat needed by each species. Hence the execution of a plan rests with farmers and landowners, rather than with government. The function of government is to teach, lead, and encourage.

The average farm has, or could have, a hundred resident bird species, a score of mammals, and several hundred plants. Of this total, perhaps a quarter will persist or disappear according to whether they are ignored or encouraged. These threatened species are usually the most interesting, useful, or beautiful ones. Each species has its own habitat requirements. Hence the retention of a rich fauna and flora is a rather complex job of habitat-engineering.

It does not suffice for the farmer to be interested in only one group of species. Exclusive interest in shootable game, for example, often means the deliberate extermination of the equally valuable predators. Exclusive interest in non-shootable wildlife means the needless elimination of wholesome sport. Exclusive interest in forests has, in parts of Europe, eliminated most other wildlife and ultimately damaged the forests themselves.

.   .   .

The farmer must also be willing to suffer losses, within reason, rather than eliminate a species from his community. The most useful hawks and owls, for example, occasionally take poultry; the finest songbirds take fruit; game birds eat grain.

Above all, the farmer must retain the fertility of his soil, for a rich fauna and flora, like a bountiful crop, is the direct expression of a rich and vigorous soil.

It is apparent that to accomplish these complex adjustments (which we may call collectively "wildlife management") the farmer must be moved by something more than a vague liking for wild things. He must be moved by a positive affection for the fauna and flora as a whole, and he must take pride in the skill and knowledge exercised in their management. In short, each farmer must build up, and cherish, his social "rating" as a producer of wild as well as tame animals and plants.

It is apparent, likewise, that the harvesting of game, fish, and fur crops must be the prerogative of the landowner, rather than the prerogative of the self-invited public. "Free shooting" in the end means nothing to shoot.

Wild Lands. Wildlife restoration on forests and ranges, as distinguished from farms, is likewise a matter of adjustments in land-use. These lands, being cheap, will have a higher proportion of public ownership, and hence a greater chance for quick governmental action as distinguished from slow landowner education. . . .

Completely wild lands have one function which is important, but as yet ill-understood. Every region should retain representative samples of its original or wilderness condition, to serve science as a sample of normality. Just as doctors must study healthy people to understand disease, so must the land sciences study the wilderness to understand disorders of the land-mechanism.

Education. A wildlife restoration plan is thus a plan for educating landowners, private and public, to want wildlife, and to understand how their wants may be fulfilled. This may sound like propaganda, but the shoe is on the other foot. We must *undo* the propaganda, brought to bear on landowners for the last century, which teaches that the land is a factory to be operated solely for profit. The land is a factory, but it is also a place to live, and wildlife helps make it a good place.

What took a century to do cannot be undone in a decade. Education must begin at the bottom and work upward. The land-philosophy of agricultural schools and extension agencies must be turned inside out. Wildlife education is no separate thing; it is part and parcel of land-education, and of social philosophy.

. . .

This face-about in land philosophy cannot, in a democracy, be imposed on landowners from without, either by authority or by pressure-groups. It can develop only from within, by self-persuasion, and by disillusionment with previous concepts. Short cuts like conservation text books, and conservation programs in youth organizations, help if they are sound and honest, but they are microscopic fractions of a deep and slow process. A wildlife plan is a constantly shifting array of small moves, infinitely repeated, to give wildlife due representation in shaping of the future minds and future landscapes of America.

NOTES

(1) Leopold, aesthetics and land health: In his condensed, plain-English style, Aldo Leopold was able to take complex ideas and translate them into terms that ordinary readers could understand. Behind the simple language, however, lay a great deal of serious thought and the best science that could be mustered.

Leopold's second reason for preserving wildlife had to do with its role in maintaining ecosystem processes that were essential to the maintenance of the land's health. Leopold's concept of land health was introduced in

Section 1 of Chapter 12. In his own mind, Leopold likely viewed that second purpose as the more important—yet he recognized that some readers might not agree; they might not understand the basic ecological realities underlying this valuation, and might be inattentive to the complex ways in which seemingly expendable species played key supporting roles. Leopold, therefore, listed the broad category of benefits that he often summed up with the term "aesthetics" as the first reason for promoting wildlife. Wildlife made the human predicament more enjoyable in many ways—ways that he would illustrate and explore in his now-classic collection, A SAND COUNTY ALMANAC AND SKETCHES HERE AND THERE (1949). Leopold on occasion would also refer to what he termed the "biotic right" of other species and rare communities to exist; perhaps these too were included within his broad claim that wildlife made the human predicament more satisfying.

(2) The Wildlands Project: Chapter 12 included excerpts by two leading conservation biologists, Reed Noss and Allen Cooperrider, who propose the restoration in North America of all native species in something close to their native ranges and historic populations. That vision underlies an important conservation effort—The Wildlands Project. According to its proponents, the Project is "a bold plan to halt and reverse" the on-going destruction of biodiversity and evolutionary processes:

> The mission of The Wildlands Project is to protect and restore the natural heritage of North America through the establishment of a connected system of wildlands. The idea is simple. To stem the disappearance of wildlife and wilderness we must allow the recovery of whole ecosystems and landscapes in every region of North America. Recovery on this scale will take time—100 years or more in some places. This vision for continental renewal rests on the spirit of social responsibility that has built so many great institutions in the past and acknowledges that the health of our society and its institutions depends on wildness. The land has given much to us; now it is time to give something back—to allow nature to thrive once more and to restore the links that will sustain both wilderness and the foundations of human communities.

The Wildlands Project: Mission, Vision, and Purpose, WILD EARTH 4 (Spring 2000). *See* <www.twp.org>.

(3) Compositionalist perspectives: The Wildlands Project is perhaps the most prominent and concrete example of what has come to be termed the "compositionalist approach" to natural areas conservation—an approach that focuses on maintaining in a given landscape those forms of life that inhabited the landscape at some point in the past or that would inhabit the landscape today but for major human disruptions. According to a prominent recent survey, this perspective is "an essentially entity-oriented, biological approach to ecology that begins with organisms aggregated into populations" which form and interact in "biotic communities." J. Baird Callicott, *et al., Current Normative Concepts in Conservation,* 13 CONSERVATION BIOLOGY 22, 23 (1999). Adherents of this approach commonly focus on the maintenance of biological diversity or the maintenance of a landscape's "biological integrity" (defined in this survey as "native species populations in their historic variety and numbers naturally interacting in naturally structured biotic communities"). Biological integrity differs from biological diversity by excluding exotic species, which could enhance local diversity even while eliminating native life forms. Biological integrity is also viewed as including ecological processes as well as the full range of biological components; as such, it is "the most comprehensive as well as the most rigorous of current norms in conservation." *Id.* at 24.

(4) Functionalist perspectives: In not-so-sharp contrast with compositionalist perspectives are the functionalist perspectives, which focus less on nature's parts than on its modes of functioning; they "perceive the world through the lens of ecosystem ecology," which is "an essentially process-oriented thermodynamical approach to ecology that begins with solar energy coursing through a physical system that includes but is not limited to the biota." *Id.* at 24. Functionalist goal statements are often phrased in terms of ecosystem health, ecological services, and ecological sustainability—or, as in the case of Aldo Leopold, land health. Compare the second paragraph from Leopold's essay above with a contemporary version of the same line of reasoning, phrased in more scientific terms:

> Ecosystem health, like organismic health, can alternatively be defined as the absence of its opposite, ecosystem disease (or "ecosystem distress syndrome"), which is indicated by, among other things, leaching of nutrients in terrestrial ecosystems and loading of nutrients in aquatic ecosystems, reduction in primary productivity in terrestrial ecosystems and increase in primary productivity in aquatic ecosystems, increased amplitude of oscillations in the species populations in the organic sector of ecosystems, and reduction in the size and longevity of organisms at the apex of the trophic pyramids of ecosystems.

Id. at 27. Functionalist perspectives and compositionalist perspectives differ in their willingness to allow exotic species to replace native ones in performing key ecological functions. Functionalists also show less concern over the decline and disappearance of species (and genetic variation within species) that are redundant—in the sense that their ecological roles could be performed by other life forms.

* * *

In addition to the issue of the goals of wildlife conservation, there are questions about how such goals might be talked about, given the generally limited ecological understanding of most Americans and their tendency to pay greatest attention to how policy questions affect them directly. The following excerpt takes up this issue of rhetoric, with particular reference to wildlife and wildlife habitat:

Holly Doremus, *The Special Importance of Ordinary Places,*
23:2 ENVIRONS ENVTL. L. & POL'Y J. 3 (Spring 2000).

For at least the past generation, and probably the past hundred years, it is fair to say that the environmental movement in the United States has concentrated on protecting special places and special things. Notwithstanding the understandable attraction, and perhaps even the inevitability, of that focus, advocates for nature protection should be cautious about placing too much emphasis on it. Only by remembering, and communicating to others, the special importance of ordinary places and ordinary things can we hope to save much nature.

. . .

The political power of the special places strategy is easy to understand. It gets people's attention and motivates them to action, two essential prerequisites to success in political battles. Merely by showing people Yellowstone, the Grand Canyon, or the Yosemite valley, in person or through the writings of John Muir or the photographs of Ansel Adams, we can convince many of them to support leaving the scenery in those places intact. A substantial number will even be inspired to take up the cause of those places themselves.

But the power of this strategy conceals serious shortcomings. The rhetoric of specialness sets up a dichotomy between special places, which are worth saving, and non-special ones, which by definition are not. If we truly want to protect nature, that distinction is ultimately untenable.

There are three problems with a strategy that calls for protection of nature because it is special, at least if that strategy swallows all others, as it has tended to do. Quantitatively, it assures that we cannot save as much nature as we should want, limiting us to a small number of special natural places. Qualitatively, it makes it difficult to save the things we have said we want, and impossible to save what we should want. Finally, a strategy focused exclusively on special places cannot build the support we will need from future generations to protect nature over the long term.

Past experience provides concrete examples of each of these drawbacks. First, take the quantitative problem. Special is a description that, by definition, can only fit a small percentage of the places and things in the world. Special things must be at least unusual, if not unique. Just as all the children in Lake Woebegon can't really be above average, all the places in the world can't really be special. By framing the argument for protection in terms of specialness, we invite the conclusion that, while some places or things are special enough to be worth protecting, many more are not.

We should not be surprised, then, that when we rely on specialness as the foundation for nature protection we are immediately hit with demands that we demonstrate that the resources we would like to save exceed some threshold level of specialness in order to justify their protection....

The specialness strategy also requires that we articulate precisely what makes the places or things we want to save special. In the search for a quick political victory, nature advocates have frequently fallen back on the most distinctive features of the most distinctive places, emphasizing them in a way that unintentionally, but quite effectively, devalues other places lacking those unique features....

There is an even more insidious danger in the strategic necessity of identifying special qualities that merit protection. Unwilling to trust the power of the "fuzzy" esthetic or moral arguments they themselves find most persuasive, nature advocates have frequently fallen back on claims of economic specialness as the justification for saving nature. The temptation to adopt this strategy is understandable. . . . Moral arguments face similar difficulties: it is hard to explain to those who do not already share the moral intuition that nature deserves protection why that view should determine public policy. Economic arguments appear to be grounded on a more solid, objective foundation. They appear to hold greater power to persuade an audience not already convinced of nature's beauty or moral considerability.

. . .

Arguments founded on economic value can sharply limit the extent to which we protect nature in many other contexts as well. Vast areas of nature have little apparent economic value. People will pay to see the spectacular Yosemite valley, for example, but not to see the far less striking Central Valley of California, just a few miles away. Of course, there are other kinds of economic value, but they do not get us much further along the protection spectrum. The discovery that the Pacific yew, once considered a junk tree of the northwest forests, contains taxol, a compound effective against some human cancers, made that tree suddenly seem valuable. But that value may be short lived; scientists quickly learned to synthesize taxol from sources other than yew bark. Moreover, there are many rarer plants with no such medicinal, or other material, bounty. . . .

Nature advocates who have recognized the shortcomings of the economic argument for nature have responded not by dropping that argument but by moving it to the most general level, denying that we know enough to evaluate it more closely. Some parts of nature, this refined claim runs, are surely essential to the material well-being, and even the survival, of humanity. Since we aren't sure exactly which parts those are, we had best keep all of nature around. The famous rivet popper story told by Paul and Anne Ehrlich provides a vivid example of this argument. The Ehrlichs put the reader in the position of a passenger about to board an airplane, watching with horror as someone pops rivets out of the plane's wings. Just as that passenger would be insane to board the plane, they argue, we as a society are insane if we allow rivets to be popped willy-nilly out of the planet on which we are all involuntary passengers.

Again the power of this argument is apparent. It is in no small way responsible for our current Endangered Species Act, and a variety of other environmental laws at the federal and state level.

But despite its power, the Ehrlichs argument is pernicious. By presenting species as simply rivets (the most ordinary, fungible piece of hardware we could imagine), it allows us to pop them without regret if we can be confident that they are not essential to the continued ecological functioning of the planet. And, contrary to one of the basic premises of this argument, it is increasingly apparent that there are many non-critical rivets. Ecological redundancy is common. . . .

. . .

Even many of the creatures fortunate enough to fall in the favored category of charismatic megafauna are undoubtedly ecologically redundant. The California condor provides an example. The condor's nine to ten foot wingspan makes it one of the largest North American birds. Undoubtedly it is physically special. But its ecological value is questionable at best. The condor subsists on carrion, scavenging the carcasses of large animals. That makes it a part of nature's crucial recycling system, freeing up nutrients from the last generation of creatures to make them available for the next. But there are plenty of other scavengers available to do that job, many of them far more abundant than the condor. The common turkey vulture is just as effective a recycler as the rare condor.

. . .

The second problem with the special places approach is that it cannot effectively save either what nature advocates have openly said they seek to protect, or what they ought to be trying to preserve. Actually, nature advocates have frequently ducked the question of what aspects of nature merit protection and why, perhaps because they have been so focused on individual battles for special places and things. When they have faced up to the issue, they have talked about species, about biodiversity, and even about natural processes such as evolution. Unfortunately, a strategy limited to special places is not likely to protect any of those.

To understand that, we have only to examine the word "special." Special carries several meanings, among them exceptional and particularly valued. Those are powerful concepts, lending strength to the argument that we should commit resources to protecting the places or things we label "special." But special also means un-usual or extra-ordinary. When we commit to a special places strategy, therefore, we treat nature as the exception rather than the rule. We concede that it is properly distinguished from what is ordinary, customary, or usual. Once we make that concession, we are almost forced to agree that although nature is important in a few special places it can be forbidden in many others. That, in turn, sends us down the path of dividing the world into natural zones and unnatural, or nature-free, zones.

. . .

The demand that we divide the world into natural zones and nature-free ones is problematic because we cannot protect species, ecosystems, or natural processes through a system of rigid nature zoning. For one thing, nature requires large areas. Demanding that the zones dedicated to nature be entirely free of human impacts reduces the likelihood that we will muster the political will to designate sufficiently large areas. For another, the strategy of designating a few places for nature encourages us to believe that no more is required of us than leaving those special places inviolate. . . .

Beyond these practical problems, when we change our protective focus slightly we see that nature zoning is not even theoretically compatible with the type of nature protection we should desire. Although nature advocates have not often gone beyond arguing for species or for evolution, those are not the only things that warrant protection. It is important that we also work to keep nature wild. Wild nature, functioning without our direction and outside our control, moving to its own rhythm rather than to a cadence we impose, provides an important counterpoint to humanity. . . . [W]e are so good at controlling the world that we are in danger of forgetting that anything lies outside our control. Wild nature checks that arrogance by reminding us that there is a world beyond us. It can provide a humility of which we are deeply in need.

. . .

Long term protection of wild nature can only come through learning to live with nature's impacts.... We cannot avoid that problem through nature zoning, because doing so sounds the death knell for wild nature. We must, therefore, offer people a reason to put up with the problems wild nature inevitably brings. Economics offers a reason, but only a weak one. It can justify protection of only a small slice of nature. What can perhaps move us the next step along the protective path is affection. Affection for nature, with the accompanying sense that nature brings something positive to our lives, can motivate us to make the sacrifices, economic and other, that long-term nature protection will require.

Unfortunately, the special places approach does not sufficiently nurture an affectionate human relationship with nature.... Our most special natural places are necessarily distant from the places most people live. Moreover, under the wilderness model, nature advocates often seek to maximize the physical challenge of accessing such places. Almost by definition, and certainly by design, few people can visit rugged, isolated wildernesses.

As a result, for all their value, those places cannot not help large numbers of people develop emotional ties to nature. They preach to the converted; only people who already care deeply about nature will make the effort to seek such places out....

The rhetoric of specialness on which we have so long relied cannot get us to the future we should seek, one in which wild nature co-exists with humanity. We should turn instead to the rhetoric of the ordinary. The message we should seek to communicate is that nature belongs in the world, including in the parts of the world we so thoroughly dominate. Nature is very special, something we should prize. But it is not, and should not be, un-usual. Nature is customary and ordinary. We should direct our efforts to keeping it so.

One small step we can take in that direction is simply to broaden the language we use to describe what is special about the places and things we seek to save. We should place less emphasis on their unique qualities, and more on their connection to the ordinary. When we want to have some land set aside, as a park, a wilderness, a wetland area, or a reserve for the spotted owl, red-cockaded woodpecker or some other species, we should not talk just about how spectacular, unique or rare it is. We should also make the effort to point out how ordinary it is. We can emphasize the similarities in soils, climate, and hydrology to surrounding, more developed, areas, and point out the extent to which those areas used to harbor the same flora and fauna, and perhaps someday could again. We should try to draw connections between our special places and the backyards of nearby settlements, using those connections to teach people to look differently at what they see at home....

We also need to emphasize what is special in the most ordinary nature. That means, for example, explaining that the vernal pools of California's central valley, with their endemic fairy shrimp and wildflowers, are wonderful because they belong there. We should treasure them, and encourage others to treasure them, as ordinary elements of their place, even if they are neither spectacular nor economically valuable.

NOTES

(1) What rhetorical justifications does Doremus present for the protection of wildlife? How does her reasoning differ from that of Leopold? Is it adequately grounded in ecology and economics? Does it need to be in order to succeed with the general public? To be taken seriously in courtroom and legislative chamber? To guide sound legal action? Might different arguments be needed for different audiences and settings?

(2) Leopold and the limiting factor: In his classic work, GAME MANAGEMENT (1933), Leopold proposed that readers view wildlife (especially game) as a "crop," which, like other crops, could often be increased through careful management. He explored the factors that affected particular populations, dividing them loosely into "decimating factors" (those that killed animals, such as predation and disease) and "welfare factors" (such as food, cover, and good breeding grounds) which, when inadequately supplied, weakened populations so as to make them more vulnerable to decimating factors. Leopold placed weather and certain disturbances into a separate category because game managers could not control them. Leopold's strong message to managers was that a game population was likely to be kept in check at a given time by one particular factor—whether lack of food at a key time of year, lack of cover, or excessive predation. This particular factor was, in Leopold's terminology, the "limiting factor," the one that, more than others, kept a population's natural reproductive powers from increasing its numbers. Game management was most effective when a manager could identify and then release that limiting factor, thereby allowing the population to rise. Once that factor was relieved, another factor typically became the limiting factor, and it, in turn, could then be addressed through management.[1] As Leopold emphasized, it made little sense to spend resources addressing a factor that was not the limiting factor—providing extra food, for instance, for a population that was kept in check by lack of cover or nesting spots, or eliminating predators when a game population would in any event die off over the winter for lack of food.

Wildlife managers have learned much since Leopold's day, but his basic focus on limiting factors remains useful. As the materials in Chapter 12 explored, wildlife species today are limited by a variety of factors—particularly the loss of habitat and the impacts of exotic species. Well-grounded management goes beyond such general lists to identify the particular limiting factor or factors affecting a given species in a given setting. Such management, however, can be extraordinarily complex, requiring vast

---

1. Leopold was well aware—and, indeed, was one of the first to study carefully—the tendency of some species to level off in population once a certain density was reached, without regard for external control factors.

amounts of unavailable data, particularly when management aims to protect a wide array of life forms, not just a few game species.

One recent study of wildlife in the United States argues that wildlife ecologists have been remiss in failing to identify economic growth (defined chiefly in terms of geographic expansion and resource consumption) as the key limiting factor affecting wildlife as a whole. Brian Czech, *Economic Growth as the Limiting Factor for Wildlife Conservation*, 28 WILDLIFE SOC'Y BULL. 415 (2000).

(3) The difficulties of calculating overall costs: Wildlife conservation is, of course, only one of many public goals, and resources devoted to it are unavailable to help achieve other goals. Many critics, particularly of the federal ESA, argue that more attention should be paid to questions of cost, to set conservation goals more sensibly and to apply available resources effectively. *E.g.*, CHARLES C. MANN & MARK L. PLUMMER, NOAH'S CHOICE: THE FUTURE OF ENDANGERED SPECIES (1995).[2] The assumption underlying such arguments is that conserving all species would be extremely expensive—far more than Americans are prepared to bear—and that a more realistic assessment of costs and benefits would lead society to embrace more modest, achievable aspirations.

One limitation of such analyses is that little is known about the costs of wildlife conservation. Indeed, no settled methodology is available to make such a calculation. Consider as an extreme case the Tellico Dam, at issue in the celebrated case of *TVA v. Hill* [Chapter 13]. So wasteful was the project, according to the calculation of the "God Squad," that it made economic sense to halt the project, even though it was more than 90 percent complete. When species conservation comes from halting wasteful projects, it generates savings, not costs. Consider, alternatively, the preservation of wetlands along waterways and of such important watersheds as New York's Catskill Mountains. The development of such lands can cause external harms—such as flooding and water quality degradation—that far exceed the land's development value; in such instances, preserving habitat can yield overall benefits rather than costs, even when the benefit to wildlife is ignored.

Even when less sensitive habitat is at issue—for instance, a large tract of open land at the edge of a metropolitan area—cost calculations can be difficult. Although land that is purchased as habitat costs money, from an overall, social perspective, no true expense is involved: money has merely changed hands in the form of a trade in assets. To the extent that a social cost is involved, the cost lies elsewhere. When a particular tract of land is conserved, its market value may, of course, fall precipitously. But the preservation of one tract often raises the value of surrounding land—both because the supply of developable land has been diminished and because adjacent land is made more desirable due to the protected habitat. Aside from issues of land valuation, much habitat protection yields a wide range of non-wildlife benefits, including public recreation, watershed protection,

---

2. For a comprehensive and generally devastating review of the book, see Jeffrey J. Rachlinski, Book Review, *Noah by the Num-* *bers: An Empirical Evaluation of the Endangered Species Act*, 82 CORNELL L. REV. 356 (1997).

flood reduction, maintenance of soil fertility, and the like. How should these benefits be taken into account? Is it fair to begin with overall costs and then reduce them by such non-wildlife benefits to determine the net cost, if any, for protecting wildlife? Alternatively, should the full costs of habitat protection be attributed to wildlife, with the various collateral benefits all viewed as free?

(4) Fairness to landowners: Without substantial research, it is hard to estimate the net costs of protecting wildlife in general and endangered species in particular: They could be substantial or they could be—save in a few situations—insignificant or even negative. What is far clearer, however, is that habitat protections, when imposed on private land, can significantly disrupt the economic hopes of individual landowners. Severely restricted land can be worth far less than land that an owner can alter at will without regard for spillover effects on other landowners and the community at large. It is this visible disruption of economic desires that draws attention, and that is often—though erroneously—cited as the "cost" of protecting wildlife. Without regard to cost, such disruptions raise serious questions of fairness, both to individual landowners, to neighboring landowners, and to the surrounding community as a whole. To what extent can a landowner be expected to make room for wildlife without compensation? When might compensation (or some other economic incentive) be appropriate? When might a burden be one that, in fairness, landowners should bear, given that wildlife populations are so often jeopardized by landowner activities?

Before-and-after comparisons of a parcel's market value would seem to provide a good measure of the economic disruption. Once again, however, the task of calculation is deceptively difficult. To estimate the pre-restriction value of property, numerous assumptions need to be made about the landowner's rights and about the presumed rights of surrounding landowners, including those whose property might compete for value in the same market. Given the longstanding *sic utere* limit on landowner rights—and given, also, the public's ownership of wildlife and its acknowledged power (akin to an easement, see Chapter 3) to protect that wildlife—what assumptions should be made about a landowner's development rights? Inevitably, valuation efforts are wrapped up in larger questions about what it means to own land in an era when society is placing higher value on wildlife conservation than it has in the past. Ownership norms have evolved significantly over the centuries. Should they continue to evolve in ways that reflect shifting social values, or should other tools (chiefly compensation) be used to achieve conservation aims? These questions are addressed in section 3 of this chapter.

Ultimately, the burdens of protecting wildlife need to be allocated fairly, either among all citizens or, in the case of wildlife harmed by habitat loss, by those responsible for causing that loss. Even if the overall costs of wildlife protection are low (or negative), fairness issues may remain. Until they are resolved, conservation measures are likely to be delayed.

PERSPECTIVE

(1) The Tragedy of Fragmentation: Many wildlife species range over large areas. Even in the case of species that are relatively sedentary, a given population can be at risk when it is isolated genetically from other populations of the same species. For these reasons and others, much wildlife conservation needs to be planned on large spatial scales. As Aldo Leopold recognized as soon as he arrived in Wisconsin, the fragmentation of natural landscapes poses grave threats to wildlife. Landscapes divided into private parcels, or divided among various governmental entities, fall under separate management regimes. The more division that occurs, the more legal boundaries there are. And the more boundaries there are, the greater the problem of "externalities"—that is, the consequences of land-use decisions by one owner that have positive or negative effects that spill across boundaries to neighboring lands. As externalities increase, land-use decisions commonly deviate further and further from efficient resource allocations. Of course, an undivided landscape can be rapidly degraded if no mechanism exists to control its use—as Garrett Hardin so famously explained in his essay, *The Tragedy of the Commons.* And as Hardin also pointed out, the division of a landscape into private parcels can help reduce such degradation. What Hardin did not note directly—and what is often overlooked—is that the "privatization" of a landscape can yield severe problems of its own, particularly when compared—not with unregulated use—but with a well-managed commons.

When a landscape is divided into private ownership, it is not the land but the management power over the land that is actually divided. At least initially, the landscape remains an integrated, natural whole and the wildlife ranges over it as before. The tragedy of fragmentation arises when individual landowners or land-managers are given full powers to make decisions concerning their lands, with no power reserved at the level of the commons to protect wandering wildlife—or hydrological processes and other ecosystem elements that sustain the health of the whole. No person or entity retains authority to set rules governing the use of individual parcels so as to avoid harm to shared interests. Individual owners, of course, could jointly arrange to impose limits on themselves—the "mutual coercion mutually agreed upon" that Hardin considered. But transactions costs to negotiate such agreement can be high and free-rider problems (and cultural resistance) can be insurmountable. The greater the fragmentation of a landscape, the less likely it is that joint action will occur—and the greater the likelihood of tragic consequences.

At the root of this tragedy is the fact that legal power to control the landscape has been fragmented to the point where no single person or entity (or even a small group) has either the power or the economic interest to protect wildlife. In the case of a well-run commons (as opposed to the uncontrolled, open-access commons that Hardin rightfully criticized) the community as a whole retains both the power to control and the economic incentive to act. It is the fragmentation of the landscape, without the retention of such power at the community level, that gives rise to the tragedy of fragmentation.

In important ways, the tragedy of fragmentation is much reduced in the wildlife setting because legal power over wildlife has been retained at the commons level: Under the state ownership doctrine, lawmakers can protect wildlife from direct harms. Thus, it is wildlife habitat rather than wildlife that has been fragmented. What needs reassembly, in some fair manner, is the power to control habitat to the extent necessary to achieve desired conservation goals. To a large extent, efforts to promote wildlife management above the individual parcel level entail attempts to respond to the tragedy of fragmentation by reassembling at the community level managerial power over wildlife habitat. We shall look briefly at such efforts, particularly in section 5.

(2) The tyranny of small decisions: Fragmentation is a significant problem in part because decisionmaking is increasingly likely to fall prey to the tyranny of small decisions:

> Ideally, society's problems are resolved through a system of nested levels of public decisions....

> Unfortunately, important decisions are often reached in an entirely different manner. A series of small, apparently independent decisions are made, often by individuals or small groups of individuals. The end result is that a big decision occurs (post hoc) as an accretion of these small decisions; the central question is never addressed directly at the higher decision-making levels. Usually, this process does not produce an optimal, desired, or preferred solution for society.

> This process of post hoc decision-making has been termed "the tyranny of small decisions" by the economist Alfred E. Kahn.[1] ...

> Clearly, "the tyranny of small decisions," or what might be called "small decisions effects," applies to much more than market economics. Much of the current confusion and distress surrounding environmental issues can be traced to decisions that were never consciously made, but simply resulted from a series of small decisions. Consider, for example, the loss of coastal wetlands on the east coast of the United States between 1950 and 1970. No one purposely planned to destroy almost 50% of the existing marshland along the coasts of Connecticut and Massachusetts. In fact, if the public had been asked whether coastal wetlands should be preserved or converted to some other use, preservation probably would have been supported. However, through hundred of little decisions and the conversion of hundreds of small tracts of marshland, a major decision was made without ever addressing the issue directly.

William E. Odum, *Environmental Degradation and the Tyranny of Small Decisions,* 32 BIOSCI. 728 (1982). "One key to avoiding the problem of cumulative effects of small environmental decisions," Odum writes, "lies in a holistic view of the world around us." He was not optimistic, however: "Few politicians, planners, or scientists have been trained with, or have developed a truly holistic perspective. Considering all of the pressures and short-term rewards that guide society toward simple solutions, it seems safe to assume that 'the tyranny of small decisions' will be an integral part of environmental policy for a long time to come."

* * *

---

1. Alfred E. Kahn, *The Tyranny of Small Decisions: Market Failures, Imperfec-* tions, and the Limits if Economics, 19 KYKLOS 23 (1966).

Although most efforts to promote landscape-level conservation take place either on publicly owned lands or by means of regulating private lands, there is increasing interest in physically re-uniting fragmented landscapes under shared ownership to reduce externality problems and to provide greater land-management flexibility. A provocative study of efforts to create and protect common lands in a New England town—Weston, Massachusetts—is recounted in the book from which the following excerpt is taken:

BRIAN DONAHUE, RECLAIMING THE COMMONS: COMMUNITY FARMS AND FORESTS IN A NEW ENGLAND TOWN
(1999).

In the medieval world of resource scarcity, traditional systems brought together common and private control over different kinds of land in useful ways. Commons systems were designed not to maximize production but to optimize ecological security. This was a conservative approach to landownership, and I think we will need something like it again as we approach a new set of ecological limits in the world. Lop off the overlords, insist on protecting ecological values on common forestland, acquire a measure of common protection for private farmland, and we will have a very effective and appropriate mix of landownership for the new millennium.

But aren't commons by their very nature hopelessly inefficient, if not prone to tragic abuse? I need to say a word here about the widely held but mistaken belief that commons are invariably wrecked by the commoners themselves, whereas private owners tend to take good care of their land— the so-called tragedy of the commons, in Garrett Hardin's unfortunate and misleading phrase. Hardin coined the term as a metaphor for the unlimited right to bear children in a crowded world, but it has been heartily endorsed in its literal sense by the property rights movement. The theory holds that because an individual has a strong personal incentive to cheat on the commons and a much weaker incentive to care for it, any commonly owned property is bound to be overexploited and thus degraded. This profoundly underestimates human nature—not private virtue, but collective jealousy. In actual historical fact, virtually all commons were closely guarded against individuals' cheating by the watchful eyes of their neighbors, backed up, when necessary, by law. Commons were vigorously defended against outside intruders. The term *commons* includes not only a common resource, but a mechanism for community control. There is no such thing as a free commons: if it's free, then it's not a commons. Commons have bounds and rules that limit access. Commons, like democracy, must always be defended. Given that, the system worked remarkably well for long periods of time in many parts of the world.

The corollary of the tragedy of the commons argument holds that private ownership ensures better treatment of land because the owner has a strong incentive to care for it. This assertion is so childishly simplistic as to be disingenuous. At best, it profoundly overestimates private virtue and resistance to the temptations of the market. A powerful incentive to care for the homestead might exist where a family hopes to live in one place for generations, and that is why I favor private ownership of farmland—once the urge to liquidate the ancestral land for profit has been eased. But in most cases in our culture, private ownership is brief. It is simply a license to exploit the land for all it is worth and then to cast it aside while reinvesting the profits elsewhere. The owner is not legally obligated to live on the property after finishing with it and often never lives there at all. To understand that private ownership is no panacea, one need look only at the cut-and-run practices of nineteenth-century timber barons (or at the similar behavior of some corporate forest owners today, for that manner), who let the land become a public charge after they had stripped it. Private ownership certainly does have a productive role to play if limitations can be placed on the rights of ownership and if the market system in which it is embedded can be modified to give the owner ecologically responsible signals.

Ideological quarrels that pit common against private property as ideal types are pointless. Each has its place. Common ownership cannot guarantee good management, but it is a sensible choice for that part of the landscape where the highest priority is restraint, rather than productivity. Private ownership is generally more productive but ecologically more risky. Even in long-settled New England, with its strong heritage of devotion to place, privatization of common forest and grazing land led in time to devastated woodlands and rundown pastures. Once the market system was firmly in the saddle by the nineteenth century, private farmers (some of whom represented the proverbial seventh generation) often chose to cash in their ancestral legacy by "skinning the land" rather than husband it any longer. Common ownership may not often lead to the most efficient production of wealth, but it is an appropriate means to safeguard long-term ecological health. The tragedy of the commons seldom lies in common ownership itself. The tragedy usually lies in the expropriation of common resources for unrestricted private gain. Privatization is seldom the solution to the tragedy of the commons—more often privatization *is* the tragedy of the commons. The solution is to reclaim and strengthen the commons.

The commons is not a utopian ideal of ownership of everything and everybody. There are things like the Earth's ozone layer than can be considered a global commons and need to be protected by international agreements. Our national and state forests are sometimes called commons, but, being so large, they must be controlled by bureaucracies; they become battlegrounds of competing interests. The kind of commons I am discussing here are small, and the bounds are not far from home. They can be perambulated in a day. One of the crucial ideas in a commons systems is that the land be controlled by the *local* community, by people who know it well and must live with the consequences of their actions upon it and with each other. This requires a community whose residents know how to speak with each other—which is perhaps why commons have reappeared in New England, with its town meeting form of direct democracy.

A commons also requires commoners who are productively engaged with the land, beyond weekend birding or mountain biking (I speak as an avid birder and biker, of course). For this reason a commons system and a revived local economy must go hand in hand. Such an economy will require broad participation, if that part of the community's land which is common is to be governed by residents who fully appreciate its value.

NOTES

(1) Is Donahue excessively optimistic in thinking that a tradition of careful commons management can arise in people who have long forgotten the entire institution? On the other hand, might a locally governed commons of the type Donahue proposes help bring about the kind of respect for ordinary places that Doremus views as essential? For a sympathetic but ultimately dubious assessment of locally-managed commons outside New England, see WENDELL BERRY, *Property and the Common Wealth, in* ANOTHER TURN OF THE CRANK (1995).

(2) However feasible Donahue's argument for the common ownership of community gardens and small forests, does it apply to wildlife habitat? Would it help wildlife species that need to live apart from humans? Is he perhaps focusing excessively on the harms to wildlife that come from timber harvesting and not enough on the harms that come from recreational users?

Glisson v. City of Marion

Supreme Court of Illinois.
720 N.E.2d 1034 (1999).

■ BILANDIC, J.:—Plaintiff, Joseph M. Glisson, filed a complaint for declaratory and injunctive relief in the circuit court of Williamson County against defendants, the City of Marion, Illinois, and its mayor, Robert Butler. Plaintiff's complaint sought a declaration that defendants' construction of a dam and reservoir on Sugar Creek, located in Williamson and Johnson Counties of Illinois, violates the Illinois Endangered Species Protection Act (520 ILCS 10/1 *et seq.* (1998)). The complaint alleged, *inter alia,* that the project will destroy the habitat for two species that Illinois lists as threatened and endangered, resulting in the elimination of those species from the area in violation of the Act. Plaintiff also sought to enjoin defendants from constructing such a project on Sugar Creek.... For the reasons that follow, we conclude that plaintiff lacks standing to bring this action against defendants.

BACKGROUND

The City of Marion has a water supply problem. In the past, the City has drawn most of its water from Marion City Lake. The City's requirement of 1.7 million gallons per day of water far exceeds Marion City Lake's capacity of 1.1 million gallons per day. Furthermore, the raw water from Marion City Lake is of poor quality, requiring substantial chemical treatment to render it suitable for human consumption. The City proposed to solve its shortage of water by constructing a dam and reservoir on Sugar Creek, located approximately seven miles southeast of Marion. The result would be a lake that is approximately 2,500 feet wide and 20,000 feet long, and a reservoir that is capable of supplying 8.9 million gallons of water per day.

. . .

[P]laintiff in this case filed a complaint for declaratory and injunctive relief. Plaintiff claimed that construction of the dam and reservoir violates sections 3 and 11(b) of the Illinois Endangered Species Protection Act (520 ILCS 10/3, 11(b) (1998)) because it will destroy the essential habitat of two species listed as threatened and endangered by Illinois, namely the least brook lamprey and the Indiana crayfish, and thereby will eliminate the species from the area. Plaintiff further claimed that he would suffer "intense harm" as a result of the dam and reservoir project because he is a naturalist who enjoys and uses Sugar Creek for "food gathering, recreation, spiritual, and educational activities," and because his lifestyle is "intertwined with and dependent on the natural world in general and Sugar Creek." Plaintiff requested that the circuit court (1) enter an order declaring that the dam and reservoir project violates the Illinois Endangered Species Protection Act, and (2) enjoin defendants from constructing the dam and reservoir.

Defendants filed a motion to dismiss plaintiff's complaint . . ., arguing, *inter alia,* that plaintiff lacks standing to sue under the Illinois Endangered Species Protection Act. . . .

During a hearing on both the City's motion to dismiss and plaintiff's motion for a preliminary injunction, plaintiff responded to defendants' claim of lack of standing by contending that article XI, section 2, of the Illinois Constitution of 1970 provides plaintiff with standing to pursue an action against the City.

. . .

ANALYSIS

The issue before this court is whether plaintiff has standing to maintain an action against defendants for an alleged violation of the Illinois Endangered Species Protection Act (520 ILCS 10/1 *et seq.* (1998)).

. . .

The basis of plaintiff's complaint is the Illinois Endangered Species Protection Act (Act). The Act is designed "to prohibit the possession, taking, disposal, or transport of specimens or products of animals or plants of species in danger of extinction and statewide extirpation, to provide penalties for violation thereof, and to create a Board to perform certain duties relative to the protection of such species and their habitats." 520 ILCS 10/1 (1998). The Act provides that it is unlawful for any person to take or otherwise dispose of any species on the Illinois list of endangered or threatened species without a permit issued by the Department of Natural Resources. 520 ILCS 10/3 (1998). The Act, among other things, limits the basis for the issuance of a permit; requires a consultation process between state and local agencies and the Department of Natural Resources regarding any project that may impact Illinois endangered or threatened species; and establishes that anyone who violates a provision of the Act is guilty of a

Class A misdemeanor. 520 ILCS 10/4, 9, 11 (1998). The Act also imposes an obligation on the Department of Natural Resources to implement a program for the conservation of endangered and threatened species and to adopt rules to implement the Act. 520 ILCS 10/11(a), (c) (1998).

The Act, however, does not expressly confer standing on plaintiff to bring this private cause of action. The Act does not contain any language that expressly grants a private cause of action for a violation of the Act, with the exception of allowing the enforcement of the consultation process by a writ of mandamus. 520 ILCS 10/11(b) (1998).

Defendants argue that plaintiff lacks standing because plaintiff's alleged injury is not an injury in fact to a legally cognizable interest. Plaintiff responds that he has standing pursuant to article XI, section 2, of the Illinois Constitution of 1970. Plaintiff argues that this provision grants him a constitutional right to a "healthful environment," and that the construction of the dam and reservoir on Sugar Creek would infringe on that right because the protection of endangered and threatened species is necessary to the maintenance of a "healthful environment." Plaintiff therefore contends that the Sugar Creek project results in injury to his legally cognizable interest in a "healthful environment," which includes the protection of endangered and threatened species.

. . .

We now address whether article XI, section 2, of the Illinois Constitution accords plaintiff standing. Article XI of the Illinois Constitution of 1970 is known as the environment article and consists of two sections. Section 1 provides that the "public policy of the State and the duty of each person is to provide and maintain a healthful environment for the benefit of this and future generations. The General Assembly shall provide by law for the implementation and enforcement of this public policy." ILL. CONST. 1970, art. XI, § 1. Section 2 provides that "[e]ach person has the right to a healthful environment. Each person may enforce this right against any party, governmental or private, through appropriate legal proceedings subject to reasonable limitation and regulation as the General Assembly may provide by law." ILL. CONST. 1970, art. XI, § 2.

In determining whether plaintiff has standing, we must interpret the provisions of article XI. It is well established that interpretation of a constitutional provision begins with the language of the provision. [ ] Where the language is not ambiguous, it will be given effect without resort to other aids for construction. [ ] Where, however, the meaning of a provision is not clear from its language, a court may consult the drafting history to ascertain the meaning of the provision. [ ]

The dispute in this appeal concerns whether article XI accords plaintiff standing to maintain an action against defendants to protect the least brook lamprey and the Indiana crayfish on the basis that their destruction violates plaintiff's right to a healthful environment. At the center of this dispute is the meaning of the term "healthful environment" and the scope of standing afforded to individuals pursuant to article XI, section 2. Plaintiff contends that "healthful environment" includes the health of the least brook lamprey and the Indiana crayfish. In contrast, defendants argue that the term "healthful environment" is limited to an environment conducive to human health.

What article XI means by the term "healthful environment" is not clear from the language itself. It is therefore appropriate to consult the drafting history of article XI to discern the meaning of "healthful environment." Our analysis of this history leads us to conclude that "healthful environment" was intended to refer to the relationship between the environment and human health. The primary concern of the drafters of article XI was the effect of pollution on the environment and human health. The right to a "healthful environment" was therefore not intended to include the protection of endangered and threatened species. We also conclude that the drafting history of article XI indicates that plaintiff's standing is limited to providing him with an opportunity to enforce his right to a "healthful environment."

Sections 1 and 2 of article XI were proposed to the constitutional convention by the General Government Committee as part of that Committee's Proposal No. 16, which proposed an environment article for the 1970 Constitution. 6 RECORD OF PROCEEDINGS, SIXTH ILLINOIS CONSTITUTIONAL CONVENTION 693, 695 (hereinafter cited as PROCEEDINGS). The Committee's explanatory report stated that the proposed environment article was designed to address the problem of environmental pollution. 6 PROCEEDINGS 696. The Committee sought to resolve the problem of environmental pollution by creating constitutional rights and duties concerning the environment. Particularly significant is the Committee report's explanation for its use of the term "healthful environment." The Committee stated:

> The Committee selects the word "healthful" as best describing the kind of environment which ought to obtain. "Healthful" is chosen rather than "clean," "free of dirt, noise, noxious and toxic materials" and other suggested adjectives because "healthful" describes the environment in terms of its *direct effect on human life* while the other suggestions describe the environment more in terms of its physical characteristics. A description in terms of physical characteristics may not be flexible enough to apply to new kinds of pollutants which may be discovered in the future.

(Emphasis added.) 6 PROCEEDINGS 697–98.

The Committee's proposal also outlined the right of each person to a "healthful environment" and each person's ability to enforce that right. This proposal ultimately became section 2 of article XI. The Committee determined that the right to a "healthful environment" is a "fundamental right" and that expression of this right "provides the vehicle for the individual to prosecute a violator." 6 PROCEEDINGS 700. The Committee explained that the standing provision set forth in section 2 was intended to "add practical significance" to the constitutional expression of the individual's right to a "healthful environment." (Emphasis omitted.) 6 PROCEEDINGS 702. The Committee further explained that, in drafting section 2, it recognized that individuals should "not be denied the opportunity to seek relief when so fundamental a right as that to a healthful environment is involved." 6 PROCEEDINGS 702. The Committee nevertheless limited the scope of section 2 as follows:

The Committee emphasizes that this Section [2] affords individuals the opportunity to seek relief. It wants to be very clear that it does *not*, by this Section (or by any Section in this Article for that matter) create or establish a new remedy. Nor does this Section assume the individual's ability to prove a violation of his right. It merely declares that individuals have "standing" to assert violations of his right.

. . .

Because the wrong here has reached crisis proportions and because it affects individuals in so fundamental a way, the Committee is of the view that the "special injury" requirement for standing is particularly inappropriate and ought to be waived. Section [2], therefore, allows the individual the opportunity to prove a violation of his right even though that violation may be a public wrong, or one common to the public generally.

. . .

This report evinces the intent of the General Government Committee in drafting what became article XI of the 1970 Constitution. The Committee intended to address environmental pollution and to encourage an environment conducive to human health. The Committee also intended to provide individuals with the opportunity to combat environmental pollution. The Committee sought to achieve this result by giving each person standing to bring suit to enforce the right to a healthful environment and restricted such standing by making it subject to limitations and regulations imposed by the General Assembly. It was the intent of the committee to broaden the law of standing by eliminating the traditional special injury prerequisite for standing to bring an environmental action. As such, § 2 gives standing to an individual for a grievance common to members of the public. The committee comments also indicate that § 2 is limited to granting standing and does not create any new causes of action. *See also City of Elgin v. County of Cook,* 169 Ill. 2d 53, 85, 660 N.E.2d 875 (1995) (holding that § 2 does not create any new causes of action).

. . .

Plaintiff nonetheless contends that another comment made in the Committee report reveals that the term "healthful environment" was intended to include the preservation of endangered and threatened species. Plaintiff refers to an instance where the Committee stated: "The word 'healthful' is meant to describe that quality of physical environment which a reasonable man would select for himself were a free choice available * * *. The word 'environment' means the aggregate of all conditions affecting the existence, growth and welfare of organisms." 6 Proceedings 701. Plaintiff takes these comments out of context. The Committee explained just prior to the aforementioned language that, in providing for a right to a "healthful environment," it gives "recognition to the problem of environmental pollution as one of fundamental significance." 6 Proceedings 700. The Committee also explained that it selected the word "healthful" as best describing the kind of environment that ought to be the objective. 6 Proceedings 697. Thus, the comments referred to by plaintiff do not support plaintiff's position that "healthful environment" includes conditions affecting threatened and endangered species.

We also reject the argument raised by *amici curiae* that the protection of endangered and threatened species is necessary for a "healthful environment." *Amici* contend that endangered and threatened species serve an important role in human health in the areas of medicine and economics, and as a food supply. Although this may be true, *amici* fail to recognize that "healthful environment," as that term is used in article XI, § 2, arose in the context of addressing the problem of environmental pollution. In view of the intention of the drafters of article XI, § 2, there is no basis for expanding the scope of "healthful environment" to include the preservation of endangered and threatened species.

We therefore conclude that plaintiff does not have standing under article XI, § 2, of the Illinois Constitution. . . .

■ HARRISON, dissenting:—Contrary to my colleagues, I believe that § 2 of Article XI of the Illinois Constitution of 1970 (ILL. CONST. 1970, art. XI, § 2) does authorize Dr. Glisson to bring this action to enforce the provisions of the Illinois Endangered Species Protection Act (520 ILCS 10/1 *et seq.* (1998)).

A proper analysis of § 2 should begin with the long-recognized principle that the meaning of any given constitutional provision depends on the common understanding of the citizens who, by ratifying the Constitution, "gave it life." [ ] To assess that understanding, we must give effect to the plain language of the Constitution, for it is the language itself which provides the best evidence of what the drafters intended to convey to the citizens for ratification. [ ]

The plain language of § 2 states that "[e]ach person has the right to a healthful environment" and that "[e]ach person may enforce this right against any party, governmental or private, through appropriate legal proceedings." ILL. CONST. 1970, art. XI, § 2. Nothing in this language suggests in any way that the right to bring an action to enforce the right to a healthful environment is restricted to cases of environmental pollution. That being so, we have no authority to create such a limitation ourselves. Our construction of § 2 is guided by the same principles applicable to the construction of statutes, [ ], and those principles dictate that where the language used is clear and unambiguous, we must give it effect as written, without reading into it exceptions, limitations, or conditions that the legislature did not express. [ ] (1996).

My colleagues' resort to legislative history is inappropriate. Justice Miller explained the principle clearly some years ago. He wrote that where the language of a constitutional provision is clear,

> we should have no occasion to consult the convention debates of th[at] provision[ ]. The same rules of construction applicable to statutes apply as well to the constitution [citations], and a basic rule of statutory construction forbids a court to canvass legislative history for evidence of legislative intent if the meaning of a provision can be determined from its text.

[ ]

Altering a watercourse in a way that will eradicate species of threatened or endangered wildlife clearly has obvious and important implications for the healthfulness of the environment. . . .

We protect threatened and endangered species because, in so doing, we protect ourselves and the welfare of the Illinoisans who will inherit this land when we are gone. It is our obligation and it is an obligation I believe that most Illinoisans believed they were assuming when they ratified § 2 of article XI of our Constitution. Under any fair reading, that provision cannot be confined to industrial pollution. To suggest, as my colleagues do, that the only environmental threats implicated by our Constitution are those that emanate from a smoke stack, drain pipe or car exhaust ignores wisdom, science and the plain language of the law.

. . .

For the foregoing reasons, I would hold that § 2 of article XI authorizes private citizens to bring suit to enforce the requirements of the Illinois Endangered Species Protection Act and that Dr. Glisson has standing to initiate such a proceeding. I therefore dissent.

NOTES

(1) Illinois is one of several states with endangered species statutes. The Illinois statute protects both federally listed species and species separately listed by the state. At the time *Glisson* was decided, the statute did not contain a provision under which a person could obtain an incidental take permit authorizing actions that would otherwise violate the take prohibition. Thus, the reservoir proposed by the City of Marion plainly violated the statute—and in a way that carried criminal sanctions. Given the clear violation, why did the state not take action? Would Glisson have fared better in his suit if he had brought it as a public nuisance action? Would he have satisfied the "special injury" standing rule applicable to such actions (as would have been necessary given that the more relaxed standing rules authorized by the state constitution did not apply)?

An overview of state endangered species statutes is set forth in Dale D. Goble *et al.*, *Local and National Protection of Endangered Species: An Assessment*, 2 ENVTL. SCI. & POL'Y 43 (1999).

(2) "Healthful," "healthy," and international human rights law: In light of this ruling, what protections do Illinois citizens enjoy as a result of their constitutional right to a "healthful" environment? Does it make sense—ecologically—to think that the human environment can be healthful when other species are disappearing? Although *Glisson* involved only two species, the state statute provides protection for any and all species that become imperilled. Is it sensible to argue that human health is unrelated to the plight of other species? What does the cited "legislative" history reveal about environmental understandings in the late 1960s (when the provision was drafted)? To what extent has public understanding and sentiment shifted since then?

Recall the discussion on Chapter 8 on the growing body of soft international law that a "healthy environment" is a basic human right.

Some commenters distinguish between documents calling for a "healthful environment" and those calling for a "healthy environment," arguing that the first is homocentric and the second biocentric. *E.g.*, Neil A.F. Popovic, *Pursuing Environmental Justice with International Human Rights and State Constitutions*, 15 STAN. ENVTL. L.J. 338, 344–47 (1996).

(3) Interpreting constitutions: Putting aside questions about whether an environment can be healthful if other species are disappearing, what protection does the Illinois constitution offer against direct invasions of human health? If the answer is none (or virtually none), has the court done its proper job interpreting the provision? Is it proper to interpret an entire article of a state constitution in such a way that it is meaningless—and arguably deceptive to citizens—even when the underlying "legislative" history is clear? Keep in mind that constitutions become effective only when approved by voters. How many Illinois voters likely read the convention record? What if a contemporary opinion poll of such voters revealed that most of them interpreted the provision in far different ways?

(4) Wildlife and the constitution: The Illinois court interpreted the state's constitution to empty it of any content (except, apparently, for broadening standing rules in a narrow range of public nuisance actions). Would a court—even one sympathetic to wildlife conservation—have trouble making sense out of an environmental protection provision phrased as an individual right?

Recall Aldo Leopold's vision of the land community and his claim that conservation ought to seek, above all, to promote the health of that *community*. How would such a communal goal mesh with an individual constitutional right to a healthful environment? As noted above, Leopold's vision falls within conservation approaches termed functionalist rather than compositionalist. Would an adherent of a functionalist perspective have deemed the least brook lamprey and the Indiana crayfish vital to the health of the larger ecosystem that included Dr. Glisson? Would the answer depend on whether other species performed essentially identical ecosystem roles? Is it conceivable that a constitutional provision such as Illinois' might be interpreted to embrace instead a compositionalist perspective, protective of all species?

Without regard for these issues, can one proceed from a general statement of individual right to meaningful legal restraints on land-use practices covering entire landscape? Most individual rights protected by constitutions are rights against government rather than rights that can be asserted to challenge the behavior of other citizens. In the case of wildlife, however, it is private conduct that creates the risk. To put the matter simply: Does the individual rights approach seem to offer much promise in protecting wildlife? For an argument that it does, see Rodger Schlickeisen, *Epilogue: The Argument for a Constitutional Amendment to Protect Living Nature, in* BIODIVERSITY AND THE LAW 221 (William J. Snape, ed. 1996). *See also* Carole L. Gallagher, *The Movement to Create an Environmental Bill of Rights: From Earth Day, 1970 to the Present*, 9 FORDHAM ENVTL. L.J. 107 (1997); J.B. Ruhl, *The Metrics of Constitutional Amendments: And Why Proposed Environmental Quality Amendments Don't Measure Up*, 74 NOTRE DAME L. REV. 245 (1999); Barton H. Thompson, Jr., *Environmental Policy and State Constitutions: The Potential Role of Substantive Guidance*, 27 RUTGERS L.J. 863 (1996).

SECTION 2.   MANAGING FEDERAL LANDSCAPES

In no setting has biodiversity played a more controversial role than on federal lands managed to promote multiple land uses. In Chapter 11, we considered wildlife issues as they arose on federal lands guided by "conservation" mandates—wildlife refuges, national parks, and wilderness areas. In the case of the National Forests and lands administered by the Bureau of Land Management, agency officials are obligated to balance a variety of conflicting land uses—grazing, timber harvesting, mining, recreation—and to protect watersheds and wildlife. The vast lands controlled by these agencies have provided vital testing grounds for protecting wildlife in and around extractive land uses. Over time, lessons learned about landscape management on these lands are likely to inform management efforts elsewhere. The materials here focus on the setting where conflict—and progress—has been greatest, the lands managed by the Forest Service.

Bradley C. Karkkainen, *Biodiversity and Land,*

83 CORNELL L. REV. 1 (1997).

The U.S. Department of Agriculture Forest Service is the nation's second-largest land management agency, responsible for 191 million acres of land. Although most Forest Service lands are in the West, the Forest Service also has a major presence in several important eastern ecoregions, including the upper Great Lakes, northern New England, the southern Appalachians, and the Ozarks....

Forest Service lands not subject to ... special designations are managed under a "multiple use-sustained yield" mandate.[148] In principle, this mandate gives the Forest Service broad discretionary authority to determine appropriate land uses and levels of commodity outputs. In practice, however, this mandate has historically resulted in an emphasis on commodity (especially timber) production and, secondarily, on recreational use.

In recent years, however, timber production from the national forests has declined dramatically under the constraints of the ESA and other environmental laws....

The National Forest Management Act of 1976 ("NFMA")[156] establishes an elaborate land-use and commodity production planning process. This process produces legally binding, long-term forest plans for each national

---

148. The Multiple Use–Sustained Yield Act of 1960, 16 U.S.C. §§ 528–531 (1994), provides that national forests "shall be administered for outdoor recreation, range, timber, watershed, and wildlife and fish purposes," *id.* § 528, and "utilized in the combi-

nation that will best meet the needs of the American people," including a "high-level annual or regular periodic output of the various renewable resources." *Id.* § 531(a)-(b).

156. 16 U.S.C. §§ 1601–1617 (1994).

forest, thus limiting the agency's management discretion once the forest plan has been adopted.

The Forest Service is the only federal land management agency with an explicit biodiversity conservation mandate in its organic statute. The NFMA directs the agency to "provide for diversity of plant and animal communities based on the suitability and capability of the specific land area in order to meet overall multiple-use objectives."[158] Implementing regulations require forests to be managed, "where appropriate and to the extent practicable," to "preserve and enhance the diversity of plant and animal communities * * * so that it is at least as great as that which would be expected in a natural forest"[159] and to provide sufficient habitat to "maintain viable populations of existing native and desired non-native vertebrate species."[160] The Forest Service carries out these directives primarily by identifying and monitoring "management indicator species"[161] for each national forest, "selected because their population changes are believed to indicate the effects of management activities,"[162] and by incorporating goals for the "maintenance and improvement of habitat for [these] species" in each forest management plan "to the degree consistent with overall multiple use objectives."[163]

Some of the northern spotted owl's most significant legal victories came from judicial rulings based on the threat of timber harvesting to the species, which had been identified as a management indicator species for forests in the Pacific Northwest even prior to its listing under the ESA. However, the Forest Service's biodiversity mandate is ultimately a weak one. The statutory language itself suggests that the goal of "providing for diversity" is subsidiary to the agency's broader mission of "meet[ing] overall multiple use objectives." The implementing regulations underscore this important qualification, instructing the Forest Service to manage forests to protect indicator species "to the degree consistent with overall multiple-use objectives," and pursue diversity objectives "where appropriate and to the extent practicable," with reductions in diversity allowable "where needed to meet overall multiple-use objectives." By thus subordinating biodiversity conservation to multiple-use management, the statute places less emphasis on biodiversity considerations, and appears to leave the Forest Service a free hand to continue its traditional emphasis on timber output. In practice, the Forest Service has often interpreted its biodiversity requirements in ways that many environmentalists and conservation biologists have found to be antithetical to biodiversity conservation goals. For example, the Forest Service has made questionable selections of indicator species, failed to adequately monitor populations of indicator species, and relied on single-species and site-specific mitigation rather than broader, ecosystem-protective conservation measures. Despite the dramatic

158. 16 U.S.C. § 1604(g)(3)(B).

159. 36 C.F.R. § 219.27(g) (1996).

160. *Id.* § 219.19.

161. *Id.* § 219.19(a).

162. *Id.* § 219.19(a)(1). Management indicator species may include listed endangered and threatened species, other species with special habitat needs, game species, nongame species of "special interest," or species whose population changes are believed to indicate the status and health of other species within the community. *See id.*

163. *Id.* § 219.19.

results in the spotted owl cases, courts have generally deferred to the Forest Service's "expert" determinations, holding the statutory and regulatory diversity mandates to be broadly discretionary.

Sierra Club v. Marita

Court of Appeals for the Seventh Circuit.
46 F.3d 606 (1995).

■ FLAUM, J.:—Plaintiffs Sierra Club, Wisconsin Forest Conservation Task Force, and Wisconsin Audubon Council, Inc. (collectively, "Sierra Club") brought suit against defendant United States Forest Service ("Service") seeking to enjoin timber harvesting, road construction or reconstruction, and the creation of wildlife openings at two national forests in northern Wisconsin. The Sierra Club claimed that the Service violated a number of environmental statutes and regulations in developing forest management plans for the two national forests by failing to consider properly certain ecological principles of biological diversity. . . .

I

The National Forest Management Act ("NFMA") requires the Secretary of Agriculture, who is responsible for the Forest Service, to develop "land and resource management plans" to guide the maintenance and use of resources within national forests. 16 U.S.C. §§ 1601–1604. In developing these plans the Secretary must determine the environmental impact these plans will have and discuss alternative plans, pursuant to the National Environmental Policy Act ("NEPA"), 42 U.S.C. § 4321 *et seq.* The Secretary must also consider the "multiple use and sustained yield of the several products and services obtained" from the forests, pursuant to the Multiple–Use Sustained Yield Act ("MUSYA"), 16 U.S.C. §§ 528–531.

The process for developing plans is quite elaborate. The Service must develop its management plans in conjunction with coordinated planning by a specially-designated interdisciplinary team, extensive public participation and comment, and related efforts of other federal agencies, state and local governments, and Indian tribes. 36 C.F.R. §§ 219.4–219.7. Directors at all levels of the Service participate in the planning process for a given national forest. The Forest Supervisor, who is responsible for one particular forest, initially appoints and then supervises the interdisciplinary team in order to help develop a plan and coordinate public participation. The Supervisor and team then develop a draft plan and draft environmental impact statement ("EIS"), which is presented to the public for comment. 36 C.F.R. §§ 219.10(a), 219.10(b). After a period of comment and revision, a final plan and final EIS are sent to the Regional Forester, who directs one of four national forest regions, for review. If the Regional Forester approves them, she issues both along with a Record of Decision ("ROD") explaining her reasoning. 36 C.F.R. § 219.10(c). An approved plan and final EIS may be appealed to the Forest Service Chief ("Chief") as a final administrative decision. 36 C.F.R. §§ 219.10(d), 211.18.

The final plan is a large document, complete with glossary and appendices, dividing a forest into "management areas" and stipulating how resources in each of these areas will be administered. The plans are ordinarily to be revised on a ten-year cycle, or at least once every fifteen years. 36 C.F.R. § 219.10(g).

The present case concerns management plans developed for two forests: Nicolet National Forest ("Nicolet") and Chequamegon (She–WA-megon) National Forest ("Chequamegon"). Nicolet spreads over 973,000 acres, of which 655,000 acres are National Forest Land, in northeastern Wisconsin, while Chequamegon encompasses 845,000 publicly-owned acres in northwestern and north-central Wisconsin. Collectively, the Nicolet and the Chequamegon contain hundreds of lakes and streams, thousands of miles of roads and trails, and serve a wide variety of uses, including hiking, skiing, snowmobiling, logging, fishing, hunting, sightseeing, and scientific research. The forests are important for both the tourism and the forest product industries in northern Wisconsin.

. . .

The Sierra Club brought an action against the Service in the district court on April 2, 1990, over the Nicolet plan and on October 10, 1990, over the Chequamegon plan. Suing under the Administrative Procedure Act ("APA"), 5 U.S.C. § 701–06, the Sierra Club argued in both cases that the Service had acted arbitrarily or capriciously in developing these forest management plans and FEISs. The Sierra Club requested both declaratory and injunctive relief.

The Sierra Club's primary contention concerned the Service's failure to employ the science of conservation biology, which failure led it to violate a number of statutes and regulations regarding diversity in national forests. Conservation biology, the Sierra Club asserted, predicts that biological diversity can only be maintained if a given habitat is sufficiently large so that populations within that habitat will remain viable in the event of disturbances. Accordingly, dividing up large tracts of forest into a patchwork of different habitats, as the Nicolet and Chequamegon plans did, would not sustain the diversity within these patches unless each patch were sufficiently large so as to extend across an entire landscape or regional ecosystem. *See generally* Reed F. Noss, *Some Principles of Conservation Biology, As They Apply to Environmental Law,* 69 CHI.-KENT L. REV. 893 (1994). Hence, the Sierra Club reasoned, the Service did not fulfil its mandates under the NFMA, NEPA and MUYSA to consider and promote biological diversity within the Nicolet and the Chequamegon.

. . .

III

The Sierra Club claims that the Service violated the NFMA and NEPA by using scientifically unsupported techniques to address diversity concerns in its management plans and by arbitrarily disregarding certain principles of conservation biology in developing those plans. The Sierra Club asserts that the Service abdicated its duty to take a "hard look" at the environmental impact of its decisions on biological diversity in the forests on the erroneous contentions that the Sierra Club's proposed theories and predictions were "uncertain" in application and that the Service's own methodology was more than adequate to meet all statutory requirements. According to the Sierra Club, the Service, rather than address the important ecological issues the plaintiffs raised, stuck its head in the sand. The result, the Sierra Club argues, was a plan with "predictions about diversity directly at odds with the prevailing scientific literature."

A

Several statutes and regulations mandate consideration of diversity in preparing forest management plans. Section 6(g) of the NFMA, the primary statute at issue, directs the Secretary of Agriculture in preparing a forest management plan to, among other things,

> provide for diversity of plant and animal communities based on the suitability and capability of the specific land area in order to meet overall multiple-use objectives, and within the multiple-use objectives of a land management plan adopted pursuant to this section, provide, where appropriate, to the degree practicable, for steps to be taken to preserve the diversity of tree species similar to that existing in the region controlled by the plan[.]

16 U.S.C. § 1604(g)(3)(B).

A number of regulations guide the application of this statute. The most general one stipulates that:

> Forest planning shall provide for diversity of plant and animal communities and tree species consistent with the overall multiple-use objectives of the planning area. Such diversity shall be considered throughout the planning process. Inventories shall include quantitative data making possible the evaluation of diversity in terms of its prior and present condition. For each planning alternative, the interdisciplinary team shall consider how diversity will be affected by various mixes of resource outputs and uses, including proposed management practices.

36 C.F.R. § 219.26. Another regulation addresses the substantive goals of the plan:

> Management prescriptions, where appropriate and to the extent practicable, shall preserve and enhance the diversity of plant and animal communities, including endemic and desirable naturalized plant and animal species, so that it is at least as great as that which would be expected in a natural forest and the diversity of tree species similar to that existing in the planning area. Reductions in diversity of plant and animal communities and tree species from that which would be expected in a natural forest, or from that similar to the existing diversity in the planning area, may be prescribed only where needed to meet overall multiple-use objectives.* * *

36 C.F.R. § 219.27(g); *see also* 36 C.F.R. § 219.27(a)(5) (requiring that all management prescriptions "provide for and maintain diversity of plant and animal communities to meet overall multiple-use objectives"). Diversity is defined for the purposes of these regulations as "[t]he distribution and abundance of different plant and animal communities and species within the area covered by a land and resource management plan." 36 C.F.R. § 219.3.

Regulations implementing the NFMA with regard to the management of fish and wildlife resources are more specific still. First,

> [f]ish and wildlife habitat shall be managed to maintain viable populations of existing native and desired non-native vertebrate species in the planning area.* * * In order to ensure that viable populations will be maintained, habitat must be provided to support, at least, a minimum number of reproductive individuals and that habitat must be well distributed so that those individuals can interact with others in the planning area.

36 C.F.R. § 219.19. In order to perceive the effects of management on these species, the Service must monitor the populations of specially selected "management indicator species" ("MIS"). 36 C.F.R. § 219.19(a)(1). The selection of MIS must include, where appropriate, "endangered and threatened plant and animal species" identified on state and federal lists for the area; species with "special habitat needs that may be influenced significantly by planned management programs; species commonly hunted, fished or trapped, non-game species of special interest; and additional * * * species selected because their population changes are believed to indicate the effects of management activities on other species * * * or on water quality." *Id.*

The NFMA diversity statute does not provide much guidance as to its execution; "it is difficult to discern any concrete legal standards on the face of the provision." Charles F. Wilkinson & H. Michael Anderson, [*Land and Resource Planning in the National Forests,* 64 Or. L. Rev. 1, 296 (1985)]. However, "when the section is read in light of the historical context and overall purposes of the NFMA, as well as the legislative history of the section, it is evident that section 6(g)(3)(B) requires Forest Service planners to treat the wildlife resource as a controlling, co-equal factor in forest management and, in particular, as a substantive limitation on timber production." *Id.*

In addition to the NFMA statute and regulations that specifically address diversity, NEPA also applies to the issue at hand.[6] *See* 16 U.S.C. § 1604(g)(1) (requiring that forest plans be developed in accordance with NEPA and its EIS provisions). Section 102(2)(C) of NEPA requires that when the Service, as a federal agency, undertakes a "major federal action," it must prepare an EIS containing a detailed statement of

> the environmental impact of the proposed action, * * * any adverse effects which cannot be avoided should the program be implemented, * * * alternatives to the proposed action, * * * the relationship between local short-term uses of man's environment and the maintenance and enhancement of long-term productivity, and * * * any irreversible and irretrievable commitments of resources which would be involved in the proposed action should it be implemented.

---

6. The district court considered the implications of MUSYA for diversity and determined that MUSYA added nothing to the NFMA requirements. *See Sierra Club v. Marita ("Nicolet"),* 843 F. Supp. 1526, 1540 (E.D.Wis.1994); *Sierra Club v. Marita ("Chequamegon"),* 845 F. Supp. 1317, 1328 (E.D.Wis.1994). The Sierra Club does not challenge that holding in this appeal.

42 U.S.C. § 4332(2)(C). Additionally, the Service is required to "utilize a systematic, interdisciplinary approach which will insure the integrated use of the natural and social sciences.* * *" 42 U.S.C. § 4332(2)(A). In the language of the case law, NEPA thus broadly requires that the Service take a "hard look" at the environmental consequences of its actions. *Robertson v. Methow Valley Citizens Council,* 490 U.S. 332, 350 (1989)....

B

The Service addressed diversity concerns in the Nicolet and Chequamegon in largely similar ways, both of which are extensively detailed in the district court opinions issued below. *See Nicolet,* 843 F. Supp. at 1533–40; *Chequamegon,* 845 F. Supp. at 1322–28. The Service defined diversity as "[t]he distribution and abundance of different plant and animal communities and species within the area covered by the Land and Resource Management Plan." The Service assumed that "an increase in the diversity of habitats increases the potential livelihood of diverse kinds of organisms."

The Service focused its attention first on vegetative diversity. Diversity of vegetation was measured within tree stands as well as throughout the forest, noting that such diversity is "desirable for diverse wildlife habitat, visual variety, and as an aid to protecting the area from wildfire, insects, and disease." The Service assessed vegetative diversity based on vegetative types, age class structure of timber types, within-stand diversity of tree species, and the spacial distribution pattern of all these elements across the particular forest. The Service also factored in other considerations, including the desirability of "large areas of low human disturbance" and amount of "old-growth" forest, into its evaluations. Using these guidelines, the Service gathered and analyzed data on the current and historical composition of the forests to project an optimal vegetative diversity.

The Service assessed animal diversity primarily on the basis of vegetative diversity. Pursuant to the regulations, the Service identified all rare and uncommon vertebrate wildlife species as well as those species identified with a particular habitat and subject to significant change through planning alternatives. The Service grouped these species with a particular habitat type, identifying 14 categories in the Nicolet and 25 (reduced to 10 similar types) in the Chequamegon. For each of these habitat types, the Service selected MIS (33 in the Nicolet and 18 in the Chequamegon) to determine the impact of management practices on these species in particular and, by proxy, on other species in general.[7] For each MIS, the Service calculated the minimum viable population necessary in order to ensure the continued reproductive vitality of the species. Factors involved in this calculation included a determination of population size, the spatial distribution across the forest needed to ensure fitness and resilience, and the kinds, amounts and pattern of habitats needed to support the population.

Taking its diversity analysis into consideration, along with the its numerous other mandates, the Service developed a number of plan alternatives for each of the forests (eight in the Nicolet and nine in the Chequame-

---

7. A number of the MIS selected were also chosen because their endangered status required the Service to monitor them directly.

gon). Each alternative emphasized a different aspect of forest management, including cost efficiency, wildlife habitat, recreation, and hunting, although all were considered to be "environmentally, technically, and legally feasible." In the Nicolet, the Service selected the alternative emphasizing resource outputs associated with large diameter hardwood and softwood vegetation; in the Chequamegon an alternative emphasizing recreational opportunities, quality saw-timber, and aspen management was chosen.

C

The Sierra Club argues that the diversity statute and regulations, as well as NEPA, required the Service to consider and apply certain principles of conservation biology in developing the forest plan. These principles, the Sierra Club asserts, dictate that diversity is not comprehensible solely through analysis of the numbers of plants and animals and the variety of species in a given area. Rather, diversity also requires an understanding of the relationships between differing landscape patterns and among various habitats. That understanding, the Sierra Club says, has led to the prediction that the size of a habitat—the "patch size"—tends to affect directly the survival of the habitat and the diversity of plant and animal species within that habitat.

A basic generalization of conservation biology is that smaller patches of habitat will not support life as well as one larger patch of that habitat, even if the total area of the smaller patches equals the total area of the large patch. This generalization derives from a number of observations and predictions. First, whereas a large-scale disturbance will wipe out many populations in a smaller patch, those in a larger patch have a better chance of survival. Second, smaller patches are subject to destruction through "edge effects." Edge effects occur when one habitat's environment suffers because it is surrounded by different type of habitat. Given basic geometry, among other factors, the smaller the patch size of the surrounded habitat, the greater the chance that a surrounding habitat will invade and devastate the surrounded habitat. Third, the more isolated similar habitats are from one another, the less chance organisms can migrate from one habitat to another in the event of a local disturbance. Consequently, fewer organisms will survive such a disturbance and diversity will decline. This third factor is known as the theory of "island biogeography." Thus, the mere fact that a given area contains diverse habitats does not ensure diversity at all; a "fragmented forest" is a recipe for ecological trouble. On the basis of these submissions, the Sierra Club desires us to rule that

> [t]o perform a legally adequate hard look at the environmental consequences of landscape manipulation across the hundreds of thousands of hectares of a National Forest, a federal agency must apply in some reasonable fashion the ecological principles identified by well accepted conservation biology. Species-by-species techniques are simply no longer enough. Ecology must be applied in the analysis, and it will be used as a criterion for the substantive results.

[ ]

As a way of putting conservation biology into practice, the Sierra Club suggested that large blocks of land (at least 30,000 to 50,000 acres per block), so-called "Diversity Maintenance Areas" ("DMAs"), be set aside in each of the forests. The Sierra Club proposed and mapped three DMAs for the Nicolet and two for the Chequamegon. In these areas, which would have included about 25% of each forest, habitats were to be undisturbed by new roads, timber sales, or wildlife openings. Neither forest plan, however, ultimately contained a DMA; the Chequamegon Forest Supervisor initially did include two DMAs, but the Regional Forester removed them from the final Chequamegon plan.

The Sierra Club contends that the Service ignored its submissions, noting that the FEISs and RODs for both the Nicolet and the Chequamegon are devoid of reference to population dynamics, species turnover, patch size, recolonization problems, fragmentation problems, edge effects, and island biogeography. According to the Sierra Club, the Service simply disregarded extensive documentary and expert testimony, including over 100 articles and 13 affidavits, supporting the Sierra Club's assertions and thereby shirked its legal duties.

The Service replies that it correctly considered the implications of conservation biology for both the Nicolet and Chequamegon and appropriately declined to apply the science. The Service asserts that it duly noted the "concern [of the Sierra Club and others] that fragmentation of the * * * forest canopy through timber harvesting and road building is detrimental to certain plant and animal species." The Service decided that the theory had "not been applied to forest management in the Lake States" and that the subject was worthy of further study. However, the Service found in both cases that while the theories of conservation biology in general and of island biogeography in particular were "of interest, * * * there is not sufficient justification at this time to make research of the theory a Forest Service priority." Given its otherwise extensive analysis of diversity, as well as the deference owed its interpretation of applicable statutory and regulatory requirements, the Service contends that it clearly met all the "diversity" obligations imposed on it.

IV

The case now turns to whether the Service was required to apply conservation biology in its analysis and whether the Service otherwise complied with its statutory mandates and regulatory prescriptions regarding diversity in national forests. We hold that the Service met all legal requirements in addressing the concerns the Sierra Club raises.

A

We note at the outset that the Sierra Club faces a high standard in challenging the Service's planning decisions. The APA, under which the Sierra Club has brought this suit, requires a court to set aside an agency action determined to be "arbitrary, capricious, an abuse of discretion, or otherwise not in accordance with law," or "without observance of procedure required by law." 5 U.S.C. §§ 706(2)(A), 706(2)(D). In so doing, "the court must consider whether the decision was based on a consideration of the relevant factors and whether there has been a clear error of judgment."

Citizens to Preserve Overton Park, Inc. v. Volpe, 401 U.S. 402, 416 (1971)....

B

The Sierra Club's arguments regarding the inadequacy of the Service's plans and FEISs can be distilled into five basic allegations, each of which we address in turn. First, the Sierra Club asserts that the law "treats ecosystems and ecological relationships as a separately cognizable issue from the species by species concepts driving game and timber issues." The Sierra Club relies on the NFMA's diversity language to argue that the NFMA treats diversity in two distinct respects: diversity of plant and animal communities and diversity of tree species. *See* 16 U.S.C. § 1604(g)(3)(B). The Sierra Club also points to NEPA's stipulations that environmental policy should focus on the "interrelations of all components of the natural environment," 42 U.S.C. § 4331, and regulations which require an EIS to include an analysis of "ecological" effects. *See* 40 C.F.R. § 1508.8. The Sierra Club concludes from these statutes and regulations that the Service was obligated to apply an ecological approach to forest management and failed to do so. In the Sierra Club's view, MISs and population viability analyses present only half the picture, a picture that the addition of conservation biology would make complete.

The Sierra Club errs in these assertions because it sees requirements in the NFMA and NEPA that simply do not exist. The drafters of the NFMA diversity regulations themselves recognized that diversity was a complex term and declined to adopt any particular means or methodology of providing for diversity. Report of the Committee of Scientists to the Secretary of Agriculture Regarding Regulations Proposed by the United States Forest Service to Implement Section 6 of the National Forest Management Act of 1976, 44 Fed. Reg. 26,599, 26,609 (1979). We agree with the district court that "[i]n view of the committee's decision not to prescribe a particular methodology and its failure to mention the principles that plaintiffs claim were by then well established, the court cannot fairly read those principles into the NFMA.* * *" *Nicolet,* 843 F. Supp. at 1542; *Chequamegon,* 845 F. Supp. at 1330. Thus, conservation biology is not a necessary element of diversity analysis insofar as the regulations do not dictate that the service analyze diversity in any specific way.

Furthermore, the Sierra Club has overstated its case by claiming that MIS and population viability analyses do not gauge the diversity of ecological communities as required by the regulations. Except for those species to be monitored because they themselves are in danger, species are chosen to be on an MIS list precisely because they will indicate the effects management practices are having on a broader ecological community. Indeed, even if all that the Sierra Club has asserted about forest fragmentation and patch size and edge effects is true, an MIS should to some degree indicate their impact on diversity. *See* Report of the Committee of Scientists, 44 Fed. Reg. at 26,627 (noting that MIS are chosen "because they indicate the consequences of management on other species whose populations fluctuate in some measurable manner with the indicator species"); Judy L. Meyer, *The Dance of Nature: New Concepts in Ecology,* 69 Chi.-Kent L. Rev. 875,

885 (1994) (noting that the most sensitive indicator of environmental stress is the population level). While the NFMA would not permit the Service to limit its choices to either enhancing diversity or protecting a particular species, *see Seattle Audubon Society v. Evans,* 952 F.2d 297, 301–02 (9th Cir.1991), such is not the case here. The Sierra Club may have wished the Service to analyze diversity in a different way, but we cannot conclude on the basis of the records before us that the Service's methodology arbitrarily or capriciously neglected the diversity of ecological communities in the two forests.

In a second and related argument, the Sierra Club submits that the substantive law of diversity necessitated the set-aside of large, unfragmented habitats to protect at least some old-growth forest communities. The Sierra Club points out that 36 C.F.R. § 219.27(g) requires that "where appropriate and to the extent practicable" the Service "shall preserve and enhance the diversity of plant and animal communities * * * so that it is at least as great as that which would be expected in a natural forest.* * * *" Furthermore, "[r]eductions in diversity of plant and animal communities and tree species from that which would be expected in a natural forest or from that similar to the existing diversity in the planning area[ ] may be prescribed only where needed to meet overall multiple-use objectives." *Id.* Diversity, the Sierra Club asserts, requires the Service to maintain a range of different, ecologically viable communities. Because it is simply not possible to ensure the survival of any old-growth forest communities without these large, undisturbed patches of land, the Service has therefore reduced diversity. The Service was thus bound to protect and enhance the natural forest or explain why other forest uses prevented the Service from doing so. The Sierra Club believes the Service did neither.

The Sierra Club asserts that the diversity regulations require a certain procedure and that because the substantive result of the Service's choices will produce, in the Sierra Club's view, results adverse to "natural forest diversity, the Service has violated its mandate. However, as the Service points out, the regulations do not actually require the promotion of "natural forest" diversity but rather the promotion of diversity at least as great as that found in a natural forest. The Service maintains that it did provide for such diversity in the ways discussed above. Additionally, the Service did consider the maintenance of some old-growth forest, even though the Sierra Club disputes that the Service's efforts will have any positive effects. . . .

Third, the Sierra Club asserts that the Service failed in its responsibility under NEPA to utilize "high quality" science in preparing EISs and evaluating diversity in them. 40 C.F.R. § 1500.1. The Sierra Club believes that it more than adequately demonstrated that conservation biology is (and was at the time the Service prepared its FEISs) an essential element of any proper scientific evaluation of diversity in the Nicolet and Chequamegon. . . .

Again, we disagree. The Service is entitled to use its own methodology, unless it is irrational. *See California v. Watt,* 712 F.2d 584, 597 (D.C.Cir. 1983); *Sierra Club v. Robertson,* 810 F. Supp. 1021, 1028 (W.D.Ark.1992), *aff'd in relevant part, vacated in part,* 28 F.3d 753 (8th Cir.1994). The

Service, as discussed at length in Section III, developed an appropriate method of analyzing diversity. The Sierra Club is correct that the Service did not employ conservation biology in its final analysis. However, the Service appropriately considered conservation biology and ultimately determined that science to be uncertain in application. . . .

Fourth, the Sierra Club contends that the rejection of its "high quality" science argument on the basis of "uncertainty" in the application of conservation biology was unscrupulous. The Sierra Club asserts that conservation biology represented well-accepted and well-respected science even at the time the Service developed its management plans in the mid–1980s and that this evidence was before the Service when it drafted the forest plans. Thus, if the Service's only argument against applying the "high quality" science of conservation biology was its uncertainty, the Service has utterly failed to respond to the challenge of conservation biology.

A brief look at available evidence suggests that the district court's understanding of uncertainty was correct and the Service's explanation principled. The Service, in looking at island biogeography, noted that it had been developed as a result of research on actual islands or in the predominantly old-growth forests of the Pacific Northwest and therefore did not necessarily lend itself to application in the forests of Wisconsin. . . .

V

The creation of a forest plan requires the Forest Service to make trade-offs among competing interests. *See Sierra Club v. Espy,* 38 F.3d at 802. The NFMA's diversity provisions do substantively limit the Forest Service's ability to sacrifice diversity in those trades, and NEPA does require that decisions regarding diversity comply with certain procedural requirements. However, the Service neither ignored nor abused those limits in the present case. Thus, while the Sierra Club did have standing to challenge the choices made by the Service, the Service made those choices within the boundaries of the applicable statutes and regulations.

NOTES

(1) Mandating conservation biology: The conservation groups that brought *Marita* sought, in essence, to hit a grand-slam home run: to force the Forest Service, not just to conserve biodiversity, but to use the principles of conservation biology as the fundamental building block for all land-use decisions. Note the precise language of the agency regulations at issue. Do they embrace—as conservation biology does—a compositionalist rather than a functionalist approach to conservation? Do they, in conjunction with the Endangered Species Act, mandate the preservation of all species that reside in a forest? If so, do they require maintenance of populations that are similar in number to those that would prevail in an unmanaged forest? Can the agency, consistent with the regulations, allow biodiversity gains in the form of exotic species to offset losses in native species? Is diversity properly measured by looking at a single National

Forest or by considering the overall diversity of the larger area that includes the Forest?

Is there any justification for the agency's argument that, "in looking at island biogeography, [it] noted that it had been developed as a result of research on actual islands or in the predominantly old-growth forests of the Pacific Northwest and therefore did not necessarily lend itself to application in the forests of Wisconsin"?

(2) Statutes versus regulations: *Marita* is typical of the decisions concerning biodiversity in the National Forests in that it focuses on the Forest Service regulations, which are far more demanding and inflexible than the statutory provision—16 U.S.C. § 1604(g)(3)(B)—on which they are based. The agency's duties under the statute are highly qualified by the phrases "where appropriate," "to the degree practicable," and "in order to meet multiple-use objectives." The legislative history behind the statute, however, suggests that Congress did intend the biodiversity requirement to have teeth. Oliver A. Houck, *On the Law of Biodiversity and Ecosystem Management,* 81 MINN. L. REV. 869, 886–89 (1997).

Courts routinely defer to agency judgments on the optimal mix of competing uses under the management standards of the Multiple–Use, Sustained Yield Act (MUSYA)—so much so that the statute rarely if ever constrains agency decision-making. *See* Michael Blumm, *Public Choice Theory and the Public Lands: Why "Multiple Use" Failed,* 18 HARV. ENVTL. L. REV. 405 (1994). George Coggins has pithily labeled the MUSYA a "vacuous platitude." George C. Coggins, *Of Succotash Syndromes and Vacuous Platitudes: The Meaning of "Multiple Use, Sustained Yield" for Public Land Management,* 53 U. COLO. L. REV. 229 (1982).

(3) Indicator species: Note the importance of the particular species selected as Management Indicator Species. By selecting species that thrive in and around timber harvest areas the Forest Service can more easily justify continued harvests; by selecting species that are disturbed by harvesting (or other intensive human activities), it can accomplish the opposite result. The selection of indicator species is a matter left to the sound discretion of the Forest Service, reviewable by courts only to determine whether the selection was arbitrary and capricious. *Oregon Natural Resources Council v. Lowe,* 109 F.3d 521 (9th Cir.1997) (upholding agency's refusal to designate the whiteheaded woodpecker as MIS).

Sierra Club v. Martin

Court of Appeals for the Eleventh Circuit.
168 F.3d 1 (1999).

■ BARKETT, J.:—The Sierra Club appeals the district court's grant of summary judgment to the United States Forest Service ("Forest Service") and intervenor timber companies in connection with the Forest Service's decision to allow seven timber sales in Georgia's Chattahoochee National Forest, which will enable logging (including clearcutting), road building and related activities. On appeal, Sierra Club asserts that the decision to permit the timber sales, which it contends will damage the forest environment, was arbitrary and capricious and thus violated the National Forest Management Act ("NFMA"), 16 U.S.C. § 1600, *et seq.*, and the substantive regulations promulgated under NFMA. *See* 36 C.F.R. §§ 219.1 *et seq.* We reverse.

Background

The Chattahoochee and Oconee National Forests ("Forest") encompass 741,000 acres in the Appalachian Mountains of northern Georgia. In 1991, the Forest Service proposed to sell the timber rights to seven tracts within the Forest, totaling approximately 2,000 acres. In addition to the logging itself, the timber projects would require the construction of eighteen miles of roads into wilderness areas of the Forest, leading to a discharge of 155.1 tons of sediment into surrounding rivers and streams.

The Forest Service adopted the Land and Resource Management Plan ("Forest Plan") for the Forest in 1985 and amended it in 1989. Before any sales of timber can occur within the Forest, the Plan requires the Forest Service to conduct a site-specific study to determine whether the proposed timber sale would harm the area or its resident species. After conducting a study of the projected impact of the sales in question, the Forest Service determined that there would be no adverse impact and approved the sales.

Sierra Club subsequently filed suit under the Administrative Procedure Act ("APA"), 5 U.S.C. § 706, contending that these timber cutting projects would harm plant and animal species in the Forest. Sierra Club argued that, in conducting its study, the Forest Service did not obtain, and therefore did not consider, population inventory and population trend data for proposed, endangered, threatened, or sensitive species of plants and animals (collectively, "PETS species"), as required by the Forest Plan and the Forest Service's own regulations. Without such data, Sierra Club claimed that the study of the affected area was inadequate, making the decision to sell the timber parcels arbitrary and capricious. Sierra Club also argued that the decision to approve the sales violated 36 C.F.R. §§ 219.12, 219.19 & 219.26 because the Forest Service lacked the population data required by those regulations as well. Finally, Sierra Club challenged the Forest Plan itself, contending that it does not conform with NFMA because the proposed clearcutting will not adequately protect the Forest's soil, watershed, fish, and wildlife as required by the statute. *See* 16 U.S.C. § 1604(g)(3)(F)(v)....

Discussion

1. *NFMA*

Sierra Club first argues that the Forest Service violated NFMA by failing to comply with the Forest Plan's requirement that population inventory information be gathered and considered before implementing any decision affecting areas within the Forest. For each proposed project within the Forest, the Plan requires that the Forest Service perform a site-specific Environmental Assessment (EA), including a Biological Evaluation (BE) of how the area will be affected by the project. Specifically, the Forest Plan states in relevant part:

A biological evaluation of how a project may affect any species federally listed as threatened, endangered, or proposed, or identified by the Forest Service as sensitive, is done as part of the site-specific environmental analysis. This evaluation considers all available inventories of threatened, endangered, proposed and sensitive species populations and their habitat for the proposed treatment area. When adequate population inventory information is unavailable, it must be collected when the site has high potential for occupancy by a [PETS] species.

Pursuant to the Forest Plan, a BE was done as part of the EA for each of the seven timber projects at issue. Thereafter, the Forest Service determined that no further evaluations were necessary and issued Findings of No Significant Impact (FONSIs) for each tract. The locus of this dispute is whether the Forest Service, in conducting its BEs and EAs, adequately researched the potential impact of the proposed timber sales before issuing FONSIs.

There is no disagreement between the parties that numerous plants and animals identified by the Forest Service as sensitive as well as several that are endangered inhabit the proposed timber project areas. In addition, the parties agree that the habitat in sections of the project areas are suitable for other sensitive and endangered species. However, the Forest Service had no population inventory information and little in the way of population data for thirty-two of the thirty-seven vertebrate PETS species that inhabit the Forest. Sierra Club contends that, in light of the acknowledged presence of many PETS species in the areas at issue, the Forest Service was required by the Forest Plan to gather population data before permitting the timber sales to proceed. By failing to collect these data, Sierra Club argues, the Forest Service violated the Forest Plan and the provision of NFMA mandating compliance with the Plan.

The Forest Service, on the other hand, argues that its data are adequate and that population studies are required only if the site has a high potential for occupancy by PETS species. It maintains that its field visits and consultation of compartment maps, CISC[5] data and Georgia Natural Heritage Program ("GNHP") maps indicate that the sites of the timber sales either do not have high potential for occupancy by PETS species, or suffice to demonstrate the continued viability of those PETS species that do occupy the areas. This habitat information, it asserts, is adequate to satisfy the requirements of the Forest Plan. Moreover, in its view, the Forest Service has the discretion to make determinations of potential impact based on information other than population inventory information, strictly defined. . . .

The Forest Service admits in numerous places in the record that sensitive species do occur within the project sites and acknowledges that those individuals would be destroyed by the proposed timber sales. It then notes in each case that because the species also exist elsewhere within the Forest, the timber projects would not significantly impact the species'

---

5. CISC stands for "Continuous Inventory of Stand Conditions;" it is a monitoring   system for the health of the forest's trees.

diversity or viability. Yet, the Forest Service reached this conclusion without gathering any inventory or population data on many of the PETS species. Though these species are, by definition, at risk, nothing in the record indicates that the Forest Service possessed baseline population data from which to measure the impact that their destruction in the project areas would have on the overall forest population. We are nevertheless asked to defer to the Forest Service's conclusion that there will be no significant impact upon these species from the proposed timber projects. Absent record support for the Forest Service's assertions, this we cannot do. Agency actions must be reversed as arbitrary and capricious when the agency fails to "examine the relevant data and articulate a satisfactory explanation for its action including a 'rational connection between the facts found and the choice made.' " *Motor Vehicle Mfrs. Ass'n v. State Farm Mut. Auto. Ins. Co.,* 463 U.S. 29, 43 (1983) (quoting *Burlington Truck Lines, Inc. v. United States,* 371 U.S. 156, 168 (1962)).

More basically, however, the Forest Service argues that nothing in the regulations requires it to keep data on sensitive species and that it is therefore not necessary for it to do so. While it is true that the regulations make no such demand, the Forest Plan explicitly does so. The Forest Plan states that when adequate population inventory information is unavailable and the site has a high potential for occupancy by PETS species, then the Forest Service must gather that information. Here, the Forest Service admits that the project areas actually contain PETS species. It nonetheless maintains that its data, though devoid of any inventory information as to some PETS species, remain adequate to assess potential impact upon the species, forest-wide. The information which the Forest Service deems "adequate" is in reality no information at all in terms of many of the PETS species. . . .

2. *36 C.F.R. § 219*

Sierra Club next claims that the Forest Service's decision to proceed with the timber sales violated 36 C.F.R. §§ 219.19 & 219.26 because it failed to collect population data specifically for Management Indicator Species (MIS) (as required by § 219.19), and for all affected species (as required by § 219.26).

Section 219.26 creates a general obligation that the Forest Service gather and keep data to ensure species diversity in the planning area. It states in relevant part:

> Forest Planning shall provide for the diversity of plant and animal communities and tree species consistent with the overall multiple use objectives of the planning area. Such diversity shall be considered throughout the planning process. Inventories shall include quantitative data making possible the evaluation of diversity in terms of its prior and present condition.

Section 219.19 specifically requires that the Forest Service monitor the population of Management Indicator Species, stating:

> Fish and wildlife habitat shall be managed to maintain viable populations of existing native and desired non-native vertebrate species in the planning area.* * * (1) In order to estimate the effects of each alterna-

tive on fish and wildlife populations, certain vertebrate and/or invertebrate species present in the area shall be identified and selected as
management indicator species.* * * (6) *Population trends of the management indicator species will be monitored and relationships to habitat
changes determined.*

[emphasis added]

Sierra Club contends that, taken together, these two regulations obli-
gate the Forest Service to maintain population data on all affected species
in the planning area. . . .

The Forest Service responds first that neither § 219.19 nor § 219.26
apply at the site-specific level. Rather, they are relevant only during the
formation of the Forest Plan and, because the Forest Plan is not a final
agency action, the Sierra Club cannot challenge the Forest Plan. Second,
the Forest Service contends that even if Sierra Club could bring its § 219
challenge at the site-specific level, it would still not be entitled to relief on
the merits of its claims. The Forest Service notes that § 219.19 does not
explicitly require the Forest Service to gather data on MIS. The regulation
simply states that population trends of the MIS must be monitored and
relationships to habitat changes determined. Furthermore, the Forest Service contends that to interpret § 219.26 to require that data be kept on *all*
species makes nonsense out of § 219.19's concept of management indicator
species. If the Forest Service must keep data on all species, it argues, then
no purpose is served by the MIS.

We agree that the regulations refer to the formulation of Forest Plans
rather than to specific projects proposed under already enacted Forest
Plans. Section 219 begins by explicitly stating that "[t]he regulations in
this subpart set forth a process for developing, adopting, and revising land
and resource management plans for the National Forest System," 36 C.F.R.
§ 219.1, and the regulations make repeated reference to the forest planning
process. However, the planning process does not end with the Forest Plan's
approval. The obligations of the Forest Service with regard to the Forest
Plan continue throughout the Plan's existence. The regulations require
that the Forest Service monitor the plan's impact and, when necessary,
revise the plan. Section 219.10(g) requires that forest plans be revised
every ten years and also whenever the Forest Supervisor "determines that
conditions or demands in the area covered by the plan have changed
significantly or when changes in * * * policies, goals, or objectives would
have a significant effect on forest level programs." 36 C.F.R. § 219.10(g).
One of the purposes of this constant oversight is to establish benchmarks in
order to better assess the impact of specific actions upon the forest
environment. Sierra Club is therefore entitled to challenge the Forest
Service's compliance with the Plan as part of its site-specific challenge to
the timber sales. *See Wilderness Society v. Alcock,* 83 F.3d 386, 390 (11th
Cir.1996) (court will not hear challenge to Forest Plan until site-specific
action is proposed). A contrary result would effectively make it impossible
for a plaintiff to ever seek review of the Forest Service's compliance with a
Forest Plan.

Furthermore, the Forest Service and intervenors' substantive argument—that 36 C.F.R. §§ 219.19 & 219.26 do not require the Forest Service

to collect any population data—is inconsistent with the language of the regulations. Section 219.19(a)(6) states that "[p]opulation trends of the management indicator species will be monitored and relationships to habitat changes determined." It is implicit that population data must be collected before it can be monitored and its relationships determined. Likewise, § 219.26 requires that inventories of quantitative data be used when evaluating the effect of management alternatives on forest diversity. Before inventories can be evaluated, they have to be collected. Thus we find no merit to the Forest Service's contention that they have no obligation under § 219 to collect population data.

We do agree with the Forest Service that the combination of §§ 219.26 and 219.19 require it only to collect inventory data on MIS rather than on all species in the Forest. To read § 219.26 to require inventory data on *all* species obviates the need for MIS and reduces § 219.19 to nonsense....

Turning now to the instant case, it becomes clear that the Forest Service's approval of the timber sales without gathering and considering data on the MIS is arbitrary and capricious. The regulations require that MIS be monitored to determine the effects of habitat changes. The timber projects proposed for the Chattahoochee and Oconee National Forests amount to 2,000 acres of habitat change. Yet, despite this extensive habitat change and the fact that the some MIS populations in the Forest are actually declining, the Forest Service has no population data for half of the MIS in the Forest and thus cannot reliably gauge the impact of the timber projects on these species.

NOTES

(1) Timber harvesting and the MBTA: Recall (Chapter 10) that the Migratory Bird Treaty Act's ban on the taking of migratory birds applies to "any person, association, partnership, or corporation." 16 U.S.C. § 707(a). In an earlier ruling in *Martin*, the appellate court set aside a district court injunction banning the challenged timber sales because of their expected harm to migratory birds; the MBTA, the court ruled, did not apply to activities of federal agencies. *Sierra Club v. Martin*, 110 F.3d 1551, 1555 (11th Cir.1997). The same conclusion was tentatively reached in *Newton County Wildlife Ass'n v. United States Forest Service*, 113 F.3d 110, 115 (8th Cir.1997). Recall, however, the ruling in *Humane Society v. Glickman*, 217 F.3d 882 (D.C.Cir.2000)—the resident Canada goose case excerpted in Chapter 10—where the District of Columbia Circuit Court expressly disagreed. *See also Robertson v. Seattle Audubon Society*, 503 U.S. 429, 438 (1992) (under the Northwest Timber Compromise, "the agencies could satisfy their MBTA obligations in either of two ways: by managing their lands so as neither to 'kill' nor 'take' any northern spotted owls ... or by managing their lands so as not to violate [other] prohibitions").

(2) Substance and process: Together, *Marita* and *Martin* offer important clues on the willingness of courts to second-guess agency decisions. In *Martin*, the agency's alleged error was procedural—it failed to gather data that it needed before it could proceed with timber sales. In *Marita*, the plaintiffs' request was more substantive: to compel the agency to alter its land-use plans in ways that dictated future on-the-ground decisions about how the land would be used. Courts are often willing to send agencies back to engage in more study or to conduct further hearings; they are more reluctant to overturn agency decisions absent a clear error of law.

(3) Diversity at larger scales: Particularly in the Midwest and East, National Forests are often composed of fragmented tracts of public land interspersed among private and state-owned lands. When managing such lands, should the Forest Service emphasize the conservation of species that lack suitable habitat on private lands or that are otherwise rare or under-represented in the larger region? The issue has arisen in particular with respect to interior forest nesting songbirds (chiefly neotropical migrants) that require large tracts of unbroken forest to nest. In *Sierra Club v. U.S. Dept. of Agriculture*, plaintiffs challenged the management of the Shawnee National Forest on this ground, attacking the Service's plan to maintain forest openings (chiefly through timber harvesting) so as to promote openland and edge species, species that were regionally abundant. Plaintiffs argued that, in determining populations of openland species, the Service should have included populations on private lands; had they done so, there would have been no need to promote them on public lands:

> The plaintiffs' argument presents a novel issue without an obvious resolution. As set forth above, section 219.19 of the Forest Service regulations require that "[f]ish and wildlife habitat shall be managed to maintain viable populations of existing native and desired non-native vertebrate species *in the planning area.*" 36 C.F.R. § 219.19 (1992) (emphasis added). The regulations define the term "planning area" as "[t]he area of the National Forest System covered by a regional guide or forest plan." 36 C.F.R. § 219.3 (1992). The most logical interpretation of this definition is that the planning area refers to lands within the formal boundaries of a designated national forest.

> . . . . When discussing the viability projections for certain openland species, the Forest Service based its population projections only upon Forest Service land acreage and did not consider the private lands in the calculations. [ ] But the FSEIS acknowledged that adjacent private lands contain openland habitat that might have increased the population levels for openland species. [ ] The Forest Service thus concluded that while forest lands alone were not projected to maintain viable populations of two openland species, the prairie warbler and the great crested flycatcher, careful monitoring of the two species would help determine the actual population trends to ensure that viable populations are maintained.

> In short, the Forest Service itself appears willing to consider, at least to a limited extent, the availability of suitable habitat on surrounding private lands. The Court need not determine, however, whether the Forest Service should have evaluated these lands to the extent that the plaintiffs would desire, *i.e.,* to determine whether openland species would remain viable if no artificial openings were created within the forest itself, because the Regional Forester's decision was not based solely on the issue of maintaining viability of openland species. Rather, as pointed out in an extended discussion

above, the regional forester's decision was also based upon a desire to maintain sufficient numbers of openland species on public lands for recreational purposes, such as hunting and wildlife watching, and to ensure appropriate habitat for the continuation of a program to reintroduce ruffed grouse in the Plank Hill area. Moreover, the Forest Service considered the openland habitat on surrounding lands to be inferior to that which could be maintained on the forest itself.

Thus, the Forest Service would be justified in seeking to maintain viable populations of openland species within the actual forest boundaries even if the forest regulations could be interpreted as allowing the Forest Service to consider whether surrounding private lands would provide habitat to ensure viability of openland species.

Sierra Club v. U.S. Dept. of Agriculture, 116 F.3d 1482 (7th Cir.1997) (adopting district court opinion as opinion of court). A similar argument, based chiefly on NEPA, was presented by plaintiffs in *Inland Empire Public Lands Council v. U.S. Forest Service* (distinguished in a footnote in *Martin*). Plaintiffs challenged the agency's EIS as inadequate because it did not study species populations on adjacent nonfederal lands. The court disagreed:

> [A]dopting Plaintiffs' position as a rule of law would be impractical. Under such a rule, an agency would have to analyze separately each species to determine the area covered by its particular ecosystem and then analyze its population viability in that area; this task could become particularly burdensome if there are a number of different species to examine, each with a different population ecosystem area to analyze. *See Seattle Audubon Soc'y v. Lyons,* 871 F.Supp. 1291, 1312 (W.D.Wash.1994) ("[T]o plan based on different geographic boundaries for every species in the same ecosystem would be impractical."). NEPA does not require the government to do the impractical. *Kleppe,* 427 U.S. at 414 (noting that "practical considerations of feasibility might well necessitate restricting the scope of comprehensive statements"); *Krichbaum v. Kelley,* 844 F.Supp. 1107, 1118 (W.D.Va.1994) ("This claim * * * would require a level of analysis sufficient to stop all action in the Forest while every conceivable effect is catalogued.* * * [P]laintiff's insistence [on this action] * * * is unavailing on an arbitrary and capricious standard."), *aff'd,* 61 F.3d 900 (4th Cir.1995). We therefore hold that the Forest Service did all it was obligated to do.

Inland Empire Public Lands Council v. U.S. Forest Service, 88 F.3d 754, 764 (9th Cir.1996). The conflict between *Martin* and *Inland Empire* on the obligation of the Forest Service to conduct detailed populations surveys is considered in Andrew Orlemann, Note, *Do the Forest Service Regulations Protect Biodiversity? An Analysis of the Continuing Viability of "Habitat Viability Analysis,"* 20 J. LAND RESOURCES & ENVTL. L. 357 (2000).

(4) Wildlife and soils: Recall again Aldo Leopold's particular focus, when writing about land health, on the maintenance of soil, both quantitatively and qualitatively. Though most wildlife-related litigation has focused directly on wildlife and actions immediately harmful to wildlife, the fate of wild species (including aquatic species) is linked to the way soil is treated. A useful exploration of this overlooked issue, focused on multiple-use federal lands, is Peter M. Lacy, Comment, *Our Sedimentation Boxes Runneth Over: Public Lands Soil Law as the Missing Link in Holistic Natural Resource Protection*, 31 ENVTL. L. 433 (2001).

* * *

Controversy over the management of the National Forests stimulated leaders of the Forest Service in the 1990s to establish an advisory committee to reconsider the agency's management methods. That effort led a report that strongly urged the agency to manage its lands so as to promote "sustainability." Although sustainability in the committee's view had several components, the foundational element—and hence an essential limit on all forest management—was what the authors termed ecological sustainability:

COMMITTEE OF SCIENTISTS, U.S. DEPARTMENT OF AGRICULTURE, SUSTAINING THE PEOPLE'S LANDS. RECOMMENDATIONS FOR STEWARDSHIP OF THE NATIONAL FORESTS AND GRASSLANDS INTO THE NEXT CENTURY

(March 15, 1999).

SUSTAINABILITY: THE OVERARCHING OBJECTIVE OF NATIONAL FOREST STEWARDSHIP

The national forests and grasslands constitute an extraordinary national legacy created by people of vision and preserved for future generations by diligent and far-sighted public servants and citizens. They are "the people's lands," emblems of our democratic traditions. These lands provide many and diverse benefits to the American people. Such benefits include: clean air and water, productive soils, biological diversity, goods and services, employment opportunities, community benefits, recreation, and naturalness. They also provide intangible qualities such as beauty, inspiration, and wonder.

Yet, these benefits depend upon the longterm sustainability of the watersheds, forests, and rangelands if the public is to enjoy the ecological, economic, and social values that these lands can provide. Accordingly, based on the statutory framework for the national forests and grasslands, the first priority for management is to retain and restore the ecological sustainability of these watersheds, forests, and rangelands for present and future generations.

The Committee believes that the policy of sustainability should be the guiding star for stewardship of the national forests and grasslands to assure the continuation of this array of benefits. Like other over-arching national objectives, sustainability is broadly aspirational and can be difficult to define in concrete terms. Yet, especially considering the increased human pressures on the national forests and grasslands, it becomes ever more essential that planning and management begin with this central tenet. Sustainability is broadly recognized to be composed of interdependent elements, ecological, economic, and social. . . .

ECOLOGICAL SUSTAINABILITY: A NECESSARY FOUNDATION FOR STEWARDSHIP

Ecological sustainability entails maintaining the composition, structure, and processes of a system. The National Forest Management Act (NFMA) establishes the goals of maintaining species' diversity and ecological productivity; these goals are consistent with the concept of ecological sustainability.

The Committee recommends that ecological sustainability provide a foundation upon which the management for national forests and grasslands can contribute to economic and social sustainability. This finding does not mean that the Forest Service is expected to maximize the protection of plant and animal species and environmental protection to the exclusion of other human values and uses. Rather, it means that planning for the multiple use and sustained yield of the resources of national forests and grasslands should operate within a baseline level of ensuring the sustainability of ecological systems and native species. Without ecologically sustainable systems, other uses of the land and its resources could be impaired.

. . .

Implementation of sustainability into plans for national forests and grasslands is not a precise process; there are many unknowns and potential pitfalls that are not under the control of resource managers. Therefore, planning must acknowledge the following features of ecological systems.

Acknowledge the Dynamic Nature of Ecological Systems

The dominant paradigm for ecological systems is that they are not in equilibrium; inherent dynamics are natural features of these systems. For example, ecological systems are regularly subjected to episodic, natural disturbances that shape their states. A part of this paradigm is the concept that ecological systems are hierarchical structures, best evaluated at a variety of spatial scales. Sustaining ecological processes within the expected bounds of variation is the only way to sustain ecological diversity and productivity for future generations.

Acknowledge the Significance of Natural Processes

National forests and grasslands contain a variety of natural resources that change overtime and space. These changes include succession, disturbance, changes in climate, loss of site productivity related to land-use activities, the establishment and spread of nonnative species, and the loss of native species diversity. However, some of these processes are natural, occurring independently of human activity. Anthropogenic disturbances need to be considered against the background of natural dynamics....

Acknowledge the Uncertainty and Inherent Variability of Ecological Systems

Uncertainty arises from an incomplete understanding of how ecological systems work and from insufficient information. However, even if these sources of uncertainty could be removed through more research and better theory, ecological systems are inherently variable. Thus, variability must be factored into expressions of desired future conditions as well as into expectations related to management actions and strategies....

Preserve Options

. . .

A core element of the concept of ecological sustainability is that it is future-oriented. The reason to ensure the long-term sustainability of ecological systems is to ensure that future generations live in a productive environment and have a broad range of choices. In assessing the ecological sustainability of complex and dynamic systems, the best single metric of sustainable use of the land is the persistence of the plant and animal species over time. The productivity of an ecosystem can be sustained over the long term only if species that provide the appropriate structure and function for the system are maintained.

Clearly, the concept of ecological sustainability means that national-forest planning and management must consider the larger landscape context and include lands and communities beyond the boundaries of the national forests and grasslands....

Conserve Habitat for Native Species and Productivity of Ecological Systems

The Committee believes that conserving habitat for native species and the productivity of ecological systems remains the surest path to maintaining ecological sustainability. We suggest the use of two general approaches in tandem to conserve these key elements of sustainability. First, we suggest a scientific assessment of the characteristic composition, structure, and processes of the ecosystems. This assessment should provide an understanding of the "ecological integrity" of the planning area. Ecosystems with integrity maintain their characteristic species diversity and ecological processes, such as productivity, soil fertility, and rates of biogeochemical cycling. Because ecosystems are dynamic and variable, the concept of the "historic range of variability" is used to characterize the variation and distribution of ecological conditions occurring in the past. This concept allows one to compare the ecological conditions that will be created under proposed management scenarios to past conditions. The more the prospective conditions differ from the conditions during recent millennia, the greater the expected risk to native species, their habitats, and their long-term ecological productivity.

Second, we suggest focusing on the viability of native species themselves. However, monitoring the status of all species and assessing their viability is impossible from a practical standpoint. Thus it is necessary to focus on a subset of species called "focal species." The key characteristic of a focal species is that its abundance, distribution, health, and activity over time and space are indicative of the functioning of the larger ecological system. In monitoring, the habitat needs of the focal species are analyzed, and projections are made of the habitat that will be needed for the species to be considered "viable," having self-sustaining populations well distributed throughout the species range. Self-sustaining populations, in turn, can be defined as those that have sufficient abundance and diversity to display the array of life-history strategies and forms that will provide for their persistence and adaptability in the planning area over time. The habitat that will be created under any management scenario is compared to the habitat needed for the viability of each selected focal species. The less adequate the habitat for each species, the greater the risk to native species and ecological productivity. Therefore, the Committee suggests a three-pronged strategy: (1) focusing on a set of selected "focal" species and their habitat needs; (2) maintaining conditions necessary for ecological integrity; and (3) monitoring the effectiveness of this approach in conserving native species and ecological productivity....

Reduce Uncertainty Through Adaptive Management and Continuous Learning

Adaptive management views management actions as experiments and accumulates knowledge to achieve continual learning. There are three ways to do adaptive management: (1) trial-and-error learning, in which initial management choices are made based on current understanding, and successful prescriptions are made routine; (2) passive-adaptive management, in which existing data are reviewed and used to inform decisions within a given management approach; and (3) active-adaptive management, in which different management approaches are tested in similar circumstances and the results are evaluated and used to select approaches and decisions. Of these alternative ways to learn, passive and active adaptive management accelerate the rate of learning how to best manage ecological systems.

All these modes of adaptive management require monitoring the results of the management action. That is, the only way in which learning is possible is to observe if the system responds as envisioned....

CONSIDERING THE LARGER LANDSCAPE

Sustainability as a vision and goal applies to all lands and resources on this planet, not just the lands and resources in public ownership. Thus, the global implications of decisions made in the management of public lands in the United States must be considered in developing policies and management strategies for the future. Moreover, because public lands often rest within a mosaic of land ownerships and administrative entities, public-land management must be integrated into a broader regional landscape....

Sustainability of watersheds and other areas in which national forests and grasslands are located may inevitably depend upon activities on nearby federal lands, tribal and state lands, and private lands as well as on the actions and attitudes of a wide variety of agencies, governments, and citizens. These neighboring landowners will vary in their abilities as well as their interest in providing the mix of uses, products, values, and services that people seek from forests and rangelands. Planning, therefore, must be outward-looking and done within the context of how individuals, communities, businesses, and governments conserve, regulate, and use the lands within and around the national forests and grasslands.

* * *

The Forest Service responded to this report on September 28, 1999, by proposing new agency regulations to replace the regulations at issue in *Marita* and *Martin*. The lengthy regulations included the following provisions:

§ 219.20   *Ecological sustainability.*

To achieve ecological sustainability, it is necessary to maintain and restore ecosystem integrity. Sustaining the integrity of ecological systems increases their resilience to natural disturbance events, allows renewal following use or degradation, and helps to preserve options for future generations.

(a) *Ecological information and analysis.* To maintain and restore ecological sustainability, the collection and analysis of information on ecosystem composition, structure, and processes at a variety of spatial and temporal scales is necessary. These include geographic scales such as bioregions and watersheds, scales of biological organization such as communities and species, and temporal scales ranging from months to centuries. Some ecological measures, such as landscape diversity, are meaningful only when information is collected and analyzed at large spatial scales. For other measures, such as species diversity, it may be appropriate to collect and analyze information at more than one scale, with analysis at each scale influencing and/or incorporating the analysis done at other scales.... As appropriate to the scale of the analysis, information and analyses, must include the following:

(1) The current biological and physical characteristics of ecosystems, such as plant and animal species, the composition, structural stages, and landscape distribution of major vegetation types, soil condition, air and water quality, stream channel morphology, and instream flows.

(2) The principal ecological processes that influence the characteristic structure and composition of an area. This includes the intensity, frequency, and magnitude of natural disturbance regimes, occurring at the multiple geographic and temporal scales.

(3) The effects of human activities, distinguishing activities prior to European settlement, which had an integral role in the landscape for a long period of time, from activities after European settlement, many of which are of a type, size, and rate that were not typical of disturbances under which native plant and animal species and ecosystems developed.

(4) Estimates of the historical range of variability of ecological conditions, which should include an analysis of the differences over time in the occurrence of key attributes of ecological systems,....

(5) A comprehensive status of ecosystem components and the contribution of National Forest System lands to ecosystem integrity, including species viability, based on consideration of all lands within the area under analysis.

. . .

(7) Identification of indicators of ecosystem integrity, which must include focal species and species at risk, and also may include other

physical and biological indicators. In general, the indicators should be consistent across different scales of analysis.

(i) Focal species. Focal species are used as surrogate measures in the evaluation of ecological integrity, including the diversity of native and desired non-native species. The key characteristic of a focal species is that its status and trend provide insights to the integrity of the larger ecological system to which it belongs. . . .

(ii) Species at risk. Species at risk include endangered, threatened, candidate, proposed, and sensitive species, and species for which significant local reductions in distribution or density are concerns.

(iii) Other physical and biological indicators. The status and trend of other physical or biological indicators, such as measures of air or water quality, soil conditions, fire and water flow regimes, the prevalence of invasive or noxious species, and the variety, distribution, and productivity of forest and grassland ecosystems, may be used to evaluate ecological integrity.

(8) An evaluation of ecosystem integrity, using measures of species viability and the condition of other indicators including analysis at appropriate spatial and temporal scales and the cumulative effects of human and natural disturbances. . . .

(b) *Decisions.* The responsible official must make decisions that provide for ecosystem integrity at the appropriate planning level. Decisions made at subsequent levels must be consistent with higher-level decisions. Subject to valid existing rights and other statutory requirements, land and resource management plan and site-specific decisions must maintain or restore ecosystem integrity, including species viability, and must:

(1) Be based on the application of the best available scientific information and analysis, including the information and analysis described in paragraph (a). . . .

(2) Provide for maintenance or restoration of the ecosystem composition, structure, and processes which are characteristic of an area over time and space.

(3) Provide for maintenance of the biological and physical components of ecosystems within the historical range of variability, except as provided in paragraph (b)(3)(iv). . . .

(4) Preserve options so that a range of future stewardship choices will be available.

(5) Designate appropriate reference landscapes to serve as benchmarks and to evaluate the effects of actions.

(6) Provide for the protection and/or restoration of soil and water resources, including, but not limited to, coastal waters, estuaries, groundwater, streams, stream banks, shorelines, lakes, wetlands, riparian areas, floodplains, and unstable soils, and comply with applicable Clean Water Act requirements. Identify current and foreseeable future Forest Service consumptive and non-consumptive water uses and quantities, and the water rights needed to maintain or restore watershed integrity, including instream flow needs.

§ 219.36   *Definitions.*

Definitions of the special terms used in this subpart are set out in alphabetical order in this section as follows:

Ecological composition: The biological components of an ecological system, which are the foundation of diversity at the genetic, species, and landscape scales. Genetic diversity is the variation in inheritable characteristics within and among individual organisms and populations. Species diversity is the number and different kinds of species present in a given area. Landscape diversity is the variety of plant communities (including their identity, distribution, juxtaposition, and seral stage) and habitats evaluated at the landscape scale.

Ecological sustainability: The maintenance or restoration of ecological system composition, structure, and function which are characteristic of a plan area over time and space, including but not limited to ecological processes, biological diversity, and the productive capacity of ecological systems.

Ecosystem integrity: The completeness of an ecosystem that, at multiple geographic and temporal scales, maintains its characteristic diversity of biological and physical components, spatial patterns, structure, and functional processes within its approximate range of historic variability. These processes include disturbance regimes, nutrient cycling; hydrologic functions, vegetation succession, and species adaptation and evolution....

Watershed integrity: A watershed that maintains its characteristic diversity of biological and physical components, structure, and functional processes within its approximate range of natural variability. Watersheds with integrity display processes that manifest their characteristic structure, function, and composition. These processes include natural disturbance regimes, nutrient cycling, hydrologic functions, vegetation succession, and species adaptation and evolution. Watersheds with integrity are resilient and capable of self-renewal within the cumulative effects of human and natural disturbances.

NOTES

(1) Is the conservation approach proposed in these regulations best understood as a compositionalist approach, a functionalist approach, or both? Do the regulations call for the restoration of wilderness-like conditions on National Forest lands, or could landscapes be devoted—at least in part—to intensive use? Consider the objections raised in *Inland Empire*, noted above, to the claim that the Forest Service should study the impacts of timber harvesting on wildlife populations on adjacent lands. If the court is correct in viewing such study as "impractical," how much more impractical are the data-collection demands set forth in the new regulations? Given the amount of data called for, might the Forest Service be immobilized by the study requirements? If followed, would the regulations reverse the outcome of *Marita* and mandate the embrace of conservation biology principles? What effect are such study requirements likely to have on the morale and sense of professionalism of forest managers?

(2) The Bureau of Land Management: The Bureau of Land Management (BLM) manages more land than any other organization in the United States: more than 264 million acres or 11.4% of the nation's lands. BUREAU OF LAND MANAGEMENT, DEPARTMENT OF THE INTERIOR, PUBLIC LAND STATISTICS 2000 table 1-4 (2001). Of these lands, the agency manages approximately 45 million acres (less than 20% of the land it manages) for conservation purposes: 5.2 millions acres are designated wilderness; an additional 18 million acres are in wilderness study areas; 14 million acres have been designated Areas of Critical Environmental Concern (ACEC); nearly 12 million acres are within National Conservation Areas. *Id.* tables 5–3,–4,–5,–15.

Often derided as the Bureau of Livestock and Mining, BLM has traditionally focused on commodity production, particularly forage and minerals. It is often cited as the paradigm of "agency capture": as George Coggins noted, BLM is "the very model of the agency capture phenomenon, the Rodney Dangerfield of agencies." George C. Coggins, *Some Directions for Reform of Public National Resource Law,* 3 ENVTL. L. 67, 72–73 (1988). The agency's organic act—the Federal Land Policy and Management Act, 43 U.S.C. §§ 1701–1784 (FLPMA)—has done relatively little to restrict the agency's broad management discretion. FLPMA enunciates a clear and consistent policy of something for everyone: "the public lands [shall] be managed in a manner that will protect the quality of scientific, scenic, historical, ecological, environmental, air and atmospheric, water resource, and archeological values; that, where appropriate, will preserve and protect certain public lands in their natural condition; that will provide food and habitat for fish and wildlife and domestic animals; and that will provide for outdoor recreation and human occupancy and use." 43 U.S.C. § 1701(8). And, were this list thought to have missed something: "the public lands [shall] be managed in a manner which recognizes the Nation's need for domestic sources of minerals, food, timber, and fiber from the public lands." *Id.* § (12). Finally, FLPMA does not contain a biodiversity maintenance requirement similar to that found in the NFMA that guides Forest Service planning.

(3) Grassland management: Among the most endangered ecosystems in North America are native grasslands. Because the legislative charter of the BLM does not contain an express biodiversity provision—and because agency regulations contain no counterparts to the Forest Service regulations—little wildlife-related litigation has arisen challenging the BLM's management of its massive grazing lands. A thoughtful look at the subject, with proposals for enhancing grassland habitats, is Joseph M. Feller & David E. Brown, *From Old–Growth Forests to Old–Growth Grasslands: Managing Rangelands for Structure and Function,* 42 ARIZ. L. REV. 319 (2000).

* * *

The proposed Forest Service regulations call for a highly refined form of ecosystem management, guided by a particular goal and fueled at every step along the way by massive infusions of scientific data. Ecosystem management of that type is less diffuse than similar management efforts that lack goals and that seek merely to ascertain and implement the policy choices of the parties participating in the process (recall the critique of the 1995 Federal Interagency Memorandum in Chapter 12). Still, "ecosystem" is a problematic and contested concept, not the least because it is offered as a means to reconcile interests that are often sharply divergent and that, in the end, perhaps cannot all be satisfied. Tough choices sometimes must be made; not every goal can be achieved on every tract of land.

The following study proposes that economic efficiency play a larger role in federal land management. The authors contend that multiple-use management is, in most settings, unachievable. They propose instead—as others have done before—that lands be assigned to dominant-use categories. They also assert that commodity production has become a less important activity on multiple-use lands. Finally, they argue that the chief conflict today is not between commodity production and preservation (including biodiversity preservation) but between recreation and preservation.

In the following excerpt, the authors question whether scientifically driven ecosystem management can adequately guide land-management on multiple-use lands, particularly in landscapes occupied by several federal agencies:

Jan G. Laitos & Thomas A. Carr, *The Transformation on Public Lands,*
26 ECOL. L.Q. 140 (1999).

The chief multiple-use statutes, MUSY, NFMA, and FLPMA, do not expressly mandate that the Forest Service or BLM consider, or manage, their lands in accordance with ecosystem management principles. Nevertheless, one can argue that ecosystem management is not inconsistent with multiple use and indeed may already be encompassed within relevant statutory law. Ecosystem management does not necessarily alter federal land management agencies' legislative mandates because coordinating human activities across large geographic areas to maintain or restore ecosystems could ensure the long-term use of natural resources, including the production of commodity resources. Also, to the extent that FLPMA and NFMA emphasize resource relationships, ecosystem management would support the multiple-use concept since it assumes interagency coordination and collaboration among federal and nonfederal parties within most ecosystems.

As a result of scientific and academic support for ecosystem management, as well as its seemingly close linkage to existing multiple-use concepts, virtually all federal land agencies are exploring how to integrate it into their management decisions. Each major land and natural resource management agency—the BLM, Forest Service, Park Service, and Fish and Wildlife Service—has begun to implement an ecosystem approach to managing its lands. In the case of the BLM and the Forest Service, however, the still-applicable statutory multiple-use mandates found in MUSY and FLPMA continue to encourage production of commodity resources, such as timber, grass, and minerals. Absent explicit congressional adoption of ecosystem management, it is unlikely that multiple-use agencies traditionally tied to the extraction and development of natural resources will pursue, with any vigor, current ecosystem initiatives.

One component of ecosystem management, biodiversity, has yet to be formally adopted and implemented by multiple-use agencies as a planning and management standard. This failure is not surprising because multiple-use laws were not designed to protect biological diversity. While other federal statutes, such as the Endangered Species Act, Clean Water Act, and the Wilderness Act, can be construed as mandating protection of species, habitats, and ecosystems, they do not form a coherent comprehensive framework for managing biodiversity on public lands.

A. *Reality: It May Be Quite Difficult (or Impossible) for Ecosystem Management, Alone, to Become a Viable Public Lands Policy*

Although many agencies are considering the adoption of ecosystem management, or have already drafted guidance regarding its adoption, the promise of ecosystem management as a long-term public land management strategy is problematic. Ecosystem management suffers from inherent difficulties that limit its effectiveness, especially if it is to become the sole management philosophy for public lands. These difficulties have caused the record of ecosystem management to be a mixed one in the courts, in Congress, and on the public lands.

* *Definitional Ambiguity*: "Ecosystem management" suffers from the absence of a generally accepted definition. As a result, the nature of ecosystems, as well as their management, often become whatever policymakers want them to be. It is common for federal agencies to use many different definitions of ecosystem management.

* *The Biocentric–Anthropocentric Dilemma*: Ecosystem management seeks to integrate the needs of humans and ecosystems. Unfortunately, those charged with implementing this management philosophy too often must choose between protecting the integrity of native ecosystems from humans and ensuring that humans and their needs get first priority. The former, which advocates a natural approach, is the biocentric model. The latter, which assumes that human activity is inevitable and must be an essential part of management decisions about resources, is the anthropocentric approach. Advocates of ecosystem management profess that humans and nature are interconnected and that a choice does not have to be made between one or the other. In truth, not all species are equal in an ecosystem. Indeed, the human species, particularly when it engages in commodity development or recreation, often dominates the land.

* *Delineating Ecosystem Boundaries:* Biodiversity and ecosystem planning require large, preferably undisturbed, tracts of land. In determining the appropriate geographic scale, decisions must be made regarding the relevant boundary for the ecosystem. Is a watershed the best ecosystem unit, or a biome? Ecosystems are interlinked and overlapping and are defined by nature, which means they are not easily segregated into tracts of land like those historically managed by federal multiple-use agencies.

* *Insufficient Data:* Federal agencies do not have adequate data to support full-scale ecosystem management. To understand the dynamics and characteristics of an ecosystem, one must collect and analyze large volumes of scientific data from several different disciplines. Socioeconomic data must also be gathered in order to identify relationships between humans and ecological conditions. Such collection and evaluation efforts are expensive and time-consuming. Moreover, even with adequate data, uncertainty regarding how ecosystems function, creates strong differences of opinion in the interpretation of scientific and socioeconomic evidence.

* *Coordination Problems:* In order for classic ecosystem management to occur, the relevant ecosystem must be defined by nature, not by artificial jurisdictional boundaries set by management agencies and private parties. This means that there must be coordination among all interested parties—federal, state, and private. Coordination between federal agencies within an ecosystem is made more difficult by their disparate missions and separate planning requirements. Collaboration and consensus-building with state and local governments, as well as with private landholders, is likely to be equally demanding.

[The problems associated with ecosystem management have prevented this management philosophy from succeeding in many individual cases.] Moreover, neither ecosystem management nor one of its primary components, biodiversity, have fared particularly well in court, especially when proponents have argued that these management standards must be employed by multiple-use agencies. Additionally, Congress has not been receptive to ecosystem management.

B. *A New Land Management Philosophy Is Needed*

Recently, federal lands agencies seem to have employed a land management strategy that is an uneasy hybrid of multiple use and ecosystem management. Despite this practice, dominant use, not multiple use, is the reality. Nor has ecosystem health resulted, particularly where mechanized recreation assaults deserts and forests. To compound matters, statutorily-recognized extractive uses are in decline, even though commodity resources from public lands should play an important role in this nation's economy. Because the country's current public land management template seems to be yielding unfortunate and unplanned side effects, a new public-lands philosophy is needed.

A next-generation public lands management philosophy must reflect certain realities. Primitive outdoor recreation and preservation of large segments of the public land base as wilderness, undisturbed ecosystems, or wildlife habitat, will likely continue to be the most popular uses of public lands, including those of the BLM and Forest Service. It must be understood, however, that recreation, even nonmotorized recreation, is often inconsistent with preservationist values. Recreation and preservation also foreclose commodity development of public lands, even though there are advantages to securing essential commodity resources from federal lands. A new management philosophy must therefore reckon with the inevitability of some human interaction with public lands. This human intervention will surely entail both noncommodity recreational use, some level of commodity development, and some incursions by recreationalists in preservation areas. Any proposed management strategy must accommodate these tensions. While multiple use and ecosystem management have certain attributes that should be retained by a new philosophy, their many internal limitations preclude a correct mix of uses.

SECTION 3.   WILDLIFE AND THE PRIVATE LANDOWNER

Although the federal lands have been the primary battleground over emerging approaches to landscape-level conservation of biodiversity, ultimately the federally owned lands are insufficient. Although the federal government owns some 630.3 million acres—27.7% of the total area of the United States—its lands are far from evenly distributed among the states: the federal government owns less than 1% of the land in Connecticut (0.5%), Maine (0.8%), New York (0.3%), and Rhode Island (0.6%) and more than 50% of the land in Alaska (62.4%), Idaho (62.5%), Nevada (82.9%), Oregon (52.5%), and Utah (64.5%). BUREAU OF LAND MANAGEMENT, DEPARTMENT OF THE INTERIOR, PUBLIC LAND STATISTICS 2000 table 1–3 (2001). Furthermore, the lands owned by the federal government are largely those that were left over—and thus are generally the least productive soils. As a result—particularly east of the Rocky Mountains—federal land managers will necessarily play only a limited role in the conservation of biological integrity. Of necessity, land in private ownership is central to the protection of wildlife at a landscape level.

Our exploration of wildlife law has returned repeatedly to the issue of how the public's rights in wildlife fit with the institution of private property in land—an institution that vests strong rights in individuals yet does so because of the ways that private property supports the common good. Recall *Barrett v. State* [Chapter 3], the 1917 New York decision in which the landowner was obliged to suffer beaver damage without compensation; the state law at issue barred, not just hunting or trapping beaver, but molesting the animal, disturbing it, or interfering with its dams or lodges. Two centuries earlier, the Queen's Bench in England had ruled in *Keeble v. Hickeringill* [Chapter 3] that a landowner had a right to attract wildlife onto his land and could complain of actions by a neighbor that unreasonably interfered with this activity. In *Cross v. State* [Chapter 3], the Wyoming court held that a landowner had a valid defense to the crime of killing a moose when he had tried every reasonable measure to keep the animals from damaging his land. Underlying such rulings is the general principle of *sic utere*—the principle that landowners have no vested right to use what they own in ways that cause harm to other landowners or to the public interest. Property law is the setting in which important and conflicting interests interact and are resolved. At times, public and private interests clash. Even more often, however, conflict arises between landowners whose land-use patterns are inconsistent. In both types of conflicts, property law is called upon to resolve the disputes.

Over the centuries, the meaning of land ownership has changed—often dramatically—in response to shifting circumstances and values. Change has always been contested. Some interests have been favored; others disfavored—as with all legal change. Looking ahead, what changes might we expect in the context of wildlife on private land? Can wildlife conservation be pursued by tinkering with the definition of landownership in ways that either (i) diminish the powers of landowners to harm wildlife, directly or indirectly, as in *Barrett*, or (ii) increase the powers of landowners to complain when neighbors disrupt wildlife that would otherwise reach their lands? Would such changes—if substantial—be fair to landowners? Would they unduly interfere with the ability of property law to fulfill its other important aims—stimulating economic enterprise, protecting privacy, and providing ballast for civil states?

As for the possibility of change, consider the following discussion by the Wisconsin Supreme Court in *Prah v. Maretti* (1982), a dispute involving a novel allegation that a newly built residence amounted to a common law nuisance because it unreasonably blocked the solar panels on an adjacent home:

> [T]he policy of favoring unhindered private development in an expanding economy is no longer in harmony with the realities of our society. *State v. Deetz*, 66 Wis.2d 1, 224 N.W.2d 407 (1974). The need for easy and rapid development is not as great today as it once was, while our perception of the value of sunlight as a source of energy has increased significantly.
>
> Courts should not implement obsolete policies that have lost their vigor over the course of the years. The law of private nuisance is better suited to resolve landowners' disputes about property development in the 1980's than is a rigid rule which does not recognize a landowner's interest in access to sunlight. As we said in *Ballstadt v. Pagel*, 202 Wis. 484, 489, 232 N.W. 862 (1930), "What is regarded in law as constituting a nuisance in modern times would no doubt have been tolerated without question in former times." We read *State v. Deetz*, 66 Wis.2d 1, 224 N.W.2d 407 (1974), as an endorsement of the application of common law nuisance to situations involving the conflicting interests of landowners and as rejecting *per se* exclusions to the nuisance law reasonable use doctrine.
>
> In *Deetz* the court abandoned the rigid common law common enemy rule with respect to surface water and adopted the private nuisance reasonable use rule, namely that the landowner is subject to liability if his or her interference with the flow of surface waters unreasonably invades a neighbor's interest in the use and enjoyment of land. *Restatement (Second) of Torts*, §§ 822, 826, 829 (1977) This court concluded that the common enemy rule which served society "well in the days of burgeoning national expansion of the mid-nineteenth and early-twentieth centuries" should be abandoned because it was no longer "in harmony with the realities of our society." *Deetz*, 66 Wis. 2d at 14–15, 224 N.W.2d 407. We recognized in *Deetz* that common law rules adapt to changing social values and conditions.[12]

12. This court has recognized "that the common law is susceptible of growth and adaptation to new circumstances and situations, and that courts have power to declare

Yet the defendant would have us ignore the flexible private nuisance law as a means of resolving the dispute between the landowners in this case and would have us adopt an approach, already abandoned in *Deetz*, of favoring the unrestricted development of land and of applying a rigid and inflexible rule protecting his right to build on his land and disregarding any interest of the plaintiff in the use and enjoyment of his land. This we refuse to do.

Prah v. Maretti, 108 Wis.2d 223, 321 N.W.2d 182 (1982). Not all courts are as willing as the Wisconsin Supreme Court to keep the law up to date. Still, the common law of property remains what it has always been—a judicial creation, with courts empowered to refine norms to keep them in line with current needs. Moreover, legislative bodies possess broad powers themselves to modernize ownership norms—the dissent in *Prah* believed that the court should have left the matter to the legislature. In either case, ownership norms shift, in ways that might either help or hinder the conservation of wildlife.

State v. Sour Mountain Realty, Inc.

New York Supreme Court, Appellate Division.
714 N.Y.S.2d 78 (2000).

■ PER CURIAM: On appeal we must construe a portion of Environmental Conservation Law § 11–0535 (hereinafter the New York State Endangered Species Act) to determine whether a "taking" of a threatened species includes the modification of its habitat. We hold that a prohibited taking of a protected species may occur upon the modification of its habitat. Moreover, under the particular circumstances before us, we conclude that the Supreme Court properly found that the defendant had committed a taking of a threatened species under the New York State Endangered Species Act and therefore affirm the order granting the preliminary injunction.

I

This appeal involves a timber rattlesnake den that was discovered approximately 260 feet from the property line of a parcel of real property owned by the defendant, Sour Mountain Realty, Inc. (hereinafter Sour Mountain) (*see State of New York v. Sour Mtn. Realty,* 183 Misc. 2d 313, 703 N.Y.S.2d 854). The timber rattlesnake (*Crotalus horridus*) has been designated a threatened species in the State of New York (*see* ECL 11–0535; 6 NYCRR 182.6[b][5]). The defendant's parcel is rugged, rocky, and undeveloped, and lies adjacent to land that is being used as part of Hudson Highlands State Park (*see Matter of Scenic Hudson v. Town of Fishkill Town Bd.,* 258 A.D.2d 654, 685 N.Y.S.2d 777). The defendant seeks to conduct mining operations on its 213 acre site and is in the process of applying for a mining permit from the New York State Department of

and effectuate what is the present rule in respect of a given subject without regard to the old rule.... The common law is not immutable, but flexible, and upon its own principles adapts itself to varying condi-

tions." *Dimick v. Schiedt,* 293 U.S. 474, 487 (1935), quoted with approval in *Schwanke v. Garlt,* 219 Wis. 367, 371, 263 N.W. 176 (1935).

Environmental Conservation (hereinafter the DEC) as required by the Mined Land Reclamation Law (*see generally* ECL article 23, title 27; *see also Matter of Sour Mtn. Realty v. New York State Dept. of Envtl. Conservation*, 260 A.D.2d 920, 688 N.Y.S.2d 842).

Upon learning of the existence of the rattlesnake den, the defendant informed the DEC that it intended to construct a four-foot-high snake-proof fence, running approximately 3500 feet along its property line. The obvious and acknowledged purpose of the fence was to keep timber rattle-snakes off of the defendant's property. The DEC responded to the defendant's plans by advising it that "should the placement and nature of the fencing or other activity unilaterally undertaken by [you] harass or harm or significantly modify, degrade, or limit the habitat of the identified [snakes], the Department would consider such activity to be violative of ECL § 11–0535 and 6 NYCRR part 182." The defendant nevertheless erected the fence.

After being informed of the erection of the fence, the State of New York and the Commissioner of the DEC commenced the instant action to permanently enjoin the defendant from continuing to use the fence.

II

The plaintiffs moved to preliminarily enjoin the defendant from continuing to use the fence and a hearing was held. At the hearing, Theodore Kerpez, a DEC biologist, described, in detail, the behavior of the timber rattlesnake and the significance of the snake's den to its survival. Kerpez observed that snake dens have very specific characteristics and generally face south so as to benefit from optimum sunlight. The dens, used by the snakes to hibernate during the winter months, are actually crevices or fissures in the earth. These formations extend deep enough to provide a stable, above-freezing temperature during periods of hibernation. There are only a limited number of such dens in New York State, and it appears that each such den has been used for generations by the same population of snakes.

Kerpez testified that once the spring arrives, the snakes disperse in all directions from the den, foraging for food. Studies have established that, during this time, the snakes will travel between two and one-half and three miles. Nevertheless, the snakes have "extremely high fidelity" to their den, habitually returning to it each winter.

Kerpez observed that the snakes were not really dangerous to people and that an individual has more of a chance of "being struck by lightning than being bitten by a rattlesnake."

Using various surveying techniques, including the satellite-based global positioning system, Kerpez located the den in question as being approximately 260 feet from Sour Mountain's property line.

Kerpez testified that the snake-proof fence erected by the defendant will have a negative impact upon the well-being of the snakes inhabiting the den because it will interfere, disrupt, and prevent the normal migratory patterns of the snakes. In addition, it will deprive the rattlesnakes inhabiting the den of a significant portion of their habitat, with attendant negative consequences.

A second biologist, William Brown, also testified for the plaintiffs. According to Brown, the timber rattlesnakes are "an ecologically important species" because "they form * * * part of the food web in the deciduous forest in which they are an important predatory animal" and "contribute to the energy transfer in the food web."

Brown believed that the installation of the fence along the boundary to Sour Mountain's property would have three basic negative impacts upon the snakes inhabiting the den in question. First, the fence would interfere with the snake's normal migratory movements. Second, the fence would deprive the snakes of summer habitats that are currently used for foraging. Third, the fence would divert or shunt the snakes in either direction along the length of the fence until they come to its terminus "at a great distance away from the den." This would potentially put the snakes "in harm's way" and increase "the potential for mortality on the snakes."

. . .

IV

The defendant does not contest the fact that the fence will interfere with the habitat and migratory patterns of the timber rattlesnake. Rather, the defendant asserts that the DEC does not have the statutory authority under the New York State Endangered Species Act to protect the habitat of a threatened or endangered species. According to the defendant, the DEC only has the authority to prevent the intentional harming or killing of such species. In the defendant's view, the DEC cannot prevent so tenuous a harm as habitat destruction. We disagree.

Under the New York State Endangered Species Act, "the taking * * * of any endangered or threatened species * * * is prohibited" (ECL 11–0535 [2]). "Taking" is defined as follows:

> "Taking" and "take" include pursuing, shooting, hunting, killing, capturing, trapping, snaring and netting fish, wildlife, game, shellfish, crustacea and protected insects, and all lesser acts such as disturbing, harrying, or worrying, or placing, setting, drawing or using any net or other device commonly used to take any such animal. Whenever any provision of the Fish and Wildlife Law permits "taking," the taking permitted is a taking by lawful means and in a lawful manner."

(ECL 11–0103[13]).

In light of the broad language of this statute, including the prohibition against "all lesser acts such as disturbing, harrying or worrying" an endangered or threatened species, we conclude that the DEC has the statutory authority to protect the habitats of such species (*see* ECL 11–0103[13]). We agree with the Supreme Court that the proscribed "lesser acts" logically include habitat modification. . . .

It should be observed that the definition of a "taking" included in the Federal Act is somewhat narrower than the definition under review. Nevertheless, as set forth above, the Federal courts have consistently held that habitat interference may constitute a "taking" of a threatened species. We find the reasoning of these cases persuasive. Upon the foregoing, we conclude that habitat interference may constitute a taking under ECL 11–0535.

V

Turning again to the facts of the instant case, we initially note the well-settled principle that a party seeking preliminary injunctive relief must demonstrate (1) a likelihood of success on the merits, (2) irreparable injury absent the granting of a preliminary injunction, and (3) that the balancing of the equities favors the movant's position. [ ]

We agree with the Supreme Court that the plaintiffs have established the likelihood of success on the merits. Contrary to the defendant's contention, the sole purpose of the fence on the perimeter of its property was to interfere with the normal migratory patterns of a threatened species. Moreover, the parcel in question is rural and undeveloped. While the propriety of the DEC's exercise of its regulatory power must be decided on a case-by-case basis, we conclude that under the particular facts of this case, the DEC's determination that the placement of the fence constituted a taking of a threatened species was neither arbitrary nor capricious (*see Babbitt v. Sweet Home Chapter,* 515 U.S. 687, 708 (1995); *see also Matter of Seymour v. New York State Dept. of Envtl. Conservation,* 184 A.D.2d 101, 104–105, 591 N.Y.S.2d 593; *New York State Thruway Auth. v. Dufel,* 129 A.D.2d 44, 516 N.Y.S.2d 981).

. . .

VI

Finally, we reject the defendant's assertion that the actions of the DEC can be equated with a taking of the defendant's property without just compensation. In this regard, we note that the removal of the fence cannot be deemed a regulatory taking of the defendant's parcel since any economic impact on the parcel would be tenuous at best (*cf. Lucas v. South Carolina Coastal Council,* 505 U.S. 1003; *Nollan v. California Coastal Commn.,* 483 U.S. 825). In addition, the State has not physically occupied or appropriated any portion of the parcel (*cf. Loretto v. Teleprompter Manhattan CATV Corp.,* 458 U.S. 419, 426; *Andrus v. Allard,* 444 U.S. 51, 65; *Penn Cent. Transp. v. New York City,* 438 U.S. 104). Rather, the State, through the exercise of its police power, is safeguarding the welfare of an indigenous species that has been found to be threatened with extinction (*see Barrett v. State of New York,* 220 N.Y. 423, 428, 116 N.E. 99; *In re Delaware River at Stilesville,* 131 App. Div. 403, 411–412, 115 N.Y.S. 745). The State's interest in protecting its wild animals is a venerable principle that can properly serve as a legitimate basis for the exercise of its police power (*see* ECL 11–0535; ECL 11–0105; *Barrett v. State of New York, supra; see also People v. Bootman,* 180 N.Y. 1, 8–9, 72 N.E. 505).

NOTES

(1) How different is the ruling in *Sour Mountain Realty* from the decision in *State v. Barrett* [Chapter 3]? Would the case have been decided differently if the snake had posed a greater danger to human health? If the planned land-use activity had been a day care center rather than a mine? Does the decision provide evidence of a shifting understanding of what constitutes harm in the land-use context, along the lines laid out in *Prah v. Maretti* or is it merely a straightforward application of the state ownership doctrine?

(2) ***Department of Community Affairs v. Moorman*****:** The county allowed landowner to construct a six-foot-high, 400–foot long fence on his property on the Florida Keys. The fence was designed to prevent the movement across the land of an endangered species, the miniature Florida Key deer. According to the court, "[h]uman development on the Key has put the deer perilously close to extinction, and their numbers are estimated to be only 350 to 400 animals." Because the land was located in a state-designated area of critical state concern, the fencing decision was subject to review by the Florida Land & Water Adjudicatory Commission, which rescinded the permit. Landowner challenged the action on various constitutional theories, including denial of equal protection, denial of due process, and violation of state right of privacy. The court rejected the arguments, holding that land-use restrictions are valid "unless they bear no substantial relationship to legitimate societal policies." Here, the record amply supported both the importance of the state's interest and the harm caused by the fence. The fencing law therefore was valid both on its face and as applied. *Department of Community Affairs v. Moorman*, 664 So.2d 930 (Fla.1995).

In re Southview Associates

Supreme Court of Vermont.
569 A.2d 501 (1989).

■ MORSE, J.:—Southview Associates appeals from a ruling of the Environmental Board denying its application for a permit to build a residential development in Stratton and Jamaica, Vermont. The Board based its decision on the finding that the proposed project failed to meet the requirements of Act 250 criterion 8 pertaining to "necessary wildlife habitat." 10 V.S.A. § 6086(a)(8)(A). We affirm.

Southview proposed to build a 33 lot subdivision for vacation homes on 88 acres of land, situated in a "deeryard" comprising some 280–320 acres. The Board found that, although Stratton once contained 600 acres of deeryard, the 280–320 acre area is the only "active deeryard" in a 10.7–square mile region. It supports approximately 20 deer over the winter.

The deeryard contains two significant areas of mature softwood cover, which is critical deer wintering habitat. One of these areas covers approximately half of the Southview property. The Board found that the softwood stand on the Southview property is necessary to the deer population. The development, it found, would destroy ten acres of this critical habitat, with likely secondary effects in a larger area.

Southview submitted a Wildlife Management Plan to mitigate the loss of the ten acres by increasing available deer food and encouraging the growth of immature softwood to replace the cover lost to the development.

The Board found, however, that increased food supply would only partially mitigate the adverse effect of the development on the deer, as availability of browse is less important to the deer's survival than good softwood cover, which provides shelter from winter elements and reduces heat loss by radiation. Also, it is critical to the deer population's survival during winter that the deer do not exhaust their fat reserves. Increased physical activity due to the presence of humans, pets, and vehicles would consume these reserves more rapidly.

The Board concluded:

As a result of the development, it is likely that there will be a loss of deer in this habitat. It is likely that the deer will abandon the remaining cover altogether and those that remain will be less likely to survive due to the high potential of stress created by wintertime noise and activity from people, vehicles, and pets.

The Board concluded further "that the environmental and recreational loss to the public from the destruction and imperilment of the habitat is not outweighed by the economic, social, cultural, recreational or other benefit to the public from the project." Nor did Southview, in the Board's opinion, employ "all feasible and reasonable means of preventing or lessening the destruction and imperilment of the deer habitat." Finally, the Board could not exclude "the possibility of less intensive development in other areas of the site." The Act 250 permit was accordingly denied.

Southview challenges the Board's construction of the relevant statute and argues that the record does not support several of the Board's findings and conclusions.

I

Under 10 V.S.A. § 6086(a)(8), a permit will be granted only if the subdivision or development "[w]ill not have an undue adverse effect on the scenic or natural beauty of the area, aesthetics, historic sites or rare and irreplaceable natural areas." The subsection further provides:

(A) Necessary wildlife habitat and endangered species. A permit will not be granted if it is demonstrated by any party opposing the applicant that a development or subdivision will destroy or significantly imperil necessary wildlife habitat or any endangered species, and

(i) the economic, social, cultural, recreational, or other benefit to the public from the development or subdivision will not outweigh the economic, environmental, or recreational loss to the public from the destruction or imperilment of the habitat or species, or

(ii) all feasible and reasonable means of preventing or lessening the destruction, diminution, or imperilment of the habitat or species have not been or will not continue to be applied, or

(iii) a reasonably acceptable alternative site is owned or controlled by the applicant which would allow the development or subdivision to fulfill its intended purpose.

The permit's opponents—here, the Agency of Natural Resources and the Vermont Natural Resources Council—thus have a dual burden: first, to show that the project "will destroy or significantly imperil necessary wildlife habitat or any endangered species" (only the former is involved in this case); and second, to prove one of the three statements prefaced by small roman numerals.

Southview's first claim on appeal pertains to the meaning of "necessary wildlife habitat." That term is defined at 10 V.S.A. § 6001(12) as a "concentrated habitat which is identifiable and is demonstrated as being decisive to the survival of a species of wildlife at any period in its life including breeding and migratory periods." Southview contends that the term refers to a habitat that is decisive to the survival of an entire species, rather than to the population of the species that resides in the habitat.

In reviewing a statute, we must construe its language so as to give effect to the legislative intent. We will avoid a construction that would render the legislation ineffective or irrational. [ ]

With this rule of construction in mind, we turn to the question stated succinctly by the Board as follows:

> The threshold issue that must be decided is whether the language "necessary wildlife habitat" in 10 V.S.A. § 6086(a) and defined in § 6001(12), as it applies to the white-tailed deer in Vermont, means habitat that is decisive to the survival of the entire population of deer in Vermont or decisive to the survival of the deer that are dependent upon the habitat.

If the former definition controlled, only the last landowner in the state to develop a deeryard would be subject to the provisions of criterion 8. All other developers would escape a criterion 8 challenge because, no matter how devastating to particular habitats, their projects would not decimate the entire deer herd in Vermont so long as one deeryard remained. This interpretation would render the statute largely ineffective to accomplish its purpose of regulating development throughout the state with an eye to the preservation of the natural environment. *See* 1969, No. 250 (Adj. Sess.), § 1. As the Board noted, "[t]he statute would be rendered meaningless if it were interpreted to mean that only the last deeryard in the state would be subject to review ... so that the state deer herd would have to be on the verge of extinction before Criterion 8(A) would apply." The Board must be afforded deference in its interpretation of its own enabling legislation. *In re Eastland, Inc.,* 151 Vt. 497, 499, 562 A.2d 1043, 1044 (1989). We affirm the Board's conclusion that a "necessary wildlife habitat" under Act 250 is one that is decisive to the survival of the population of a particular species that depends upon the habitat. The definition in § 6001(12) uses the words "a species" only to make clear that for habitat to be "necessary" under criterion 8 it need not be decisive to the survival of *all* species of wildlife that flourish there.

Southview vigorously argues that this construction of the statute produces its own absurdity: "For under the Board's definition, no matter how numerous and robust the deer herd in Vermont may be or become, and no matter how many acres of deeryard there may be in the State, if evidence indicates that a deeryard supports a few deer, and that part of it will be destroyed or significantly imperiled by development, that part is necessary wildlife habitat and may not be disturbed." [ ] Southview's concern is overstated. First, the habitat must be "concentrated" and "identifiable." If it is not of a certain quality, it will not be deemed "necessary" under the Act. Second, Southview ignores subparagraphs (i), (ii) and (iii) of criterion 8. The development's opponent must show not only that the development will destroy or imperil necessary wildlife habitat, but must *also* show that the benefits of the development to the public will not outweigh the loss, or that reasonable means of mitigating the loss have not been attempted, or that the developer owns or controls a reasonably acceptable alternative site for the project. In other words, contrary to Southview's dire predictions, the statute will not foreclose all useful and beneficial development projects whose negative impact on the natural environment is slight.

II

Southview next argues that there is inadequate support in the record for the Board's findings and conclusions that the property contains habitat that is decisive to the survival of the deer that use it. In support of this argument, Southview points to testimony by witnesses for both sides of the dispute expressing reservations about the severity of destruction to the deeryard that Southview's proposed development would cause. These doubts and reservations do not, however, undermine the Board's initial determination that the Southview property contains necessary wildlife habitat. There was ample evidence on that question, pertaining to the critical need of the deer population for softwood cover during the winter. . . .

III

The third claim on appeal challenges the Board's conclusions pertaining to the three considerations labeled by small roman numerals under criterion 8. The Board ruled in the opponents' favor on all three considerations. We reach only the first and hold that the Board's conclusion was adequately supported.

The Board stated:

> The Board concludes that the environmental and recreational loss to the public from the destruction and imperilment of the habitat is not outweighed by the economic, social, cultural, recreational, or other benefit to the public from the project. While the second homes will add to the tax base of the town, there is no evidence that the town needs the additional revenue. The Board is also not persuaded that the loss of the habitat will be outweighed by the social, cultural, or recreational benefit to the public from the additional 33 units in an area which is already predominated by second homes.

> On the other hand, the loss to the public from the destruction and imperilment of the deer habitat is significant. The deeryard on the Southview property is part of the last remaining deeryard in a 10.7 square mile watershed. There is only one other area in the entire 280–320 acre deeryard that provides as high quality softwood cover as the 44–acre shelter on the Southview property. This proposed project

would destroy ten acres of critical habitat and, through the secondary impacts of people living in the homes, imperil the remaining 34 acres. The existence of the deer in this area provides an opportunity to the public to hunt and to observe deer and provides the more intangible benefit of knowing that the deer exist. The loss of the deer in this area would be significant to the public who benefit from their existence.

Southview complains that the Board ignored evidence showing that second homes throughout the state contribute more to the economy of the state than does deer hunting. But this evidence simply was not relevant. The subcriterion requires only a comparison of the relative benefits and losses of the particular project. And that comparison must not be restricted to economic data only; the statute requires that the Board assess the less tangible effects, which are not reducible to mathematical formulae. The Board properly undertook this task.

NOTES

(1) *Southview Associates, Ltd. v. Bongartz*: Southview Associates continued its challenge to the Vermont law in federal court, adding the claim that the development restriction amounted to a taking of property without the payment of just compensation. The court determined that the takings and due process claims were not ripe for adjudication, given that it was unclear if development could still be undertaken on the land. The court did treat as ripe—and resolve—Southview's assertion that the restriction was a physical invasion of the property that constituted a *per se* taking by mandating deer be allowed to use the property.

> [N]o absolute, exclusive physical occupation exists. [ ] To the extent the Board has allowed the deer to "invade" Southview's land, this "invasion" is relatively minor, consisting of an occasional, seasonal, and limited habitation by no more than 20 deer. Minor physical intrusions are not physical takings. [ ] Indeed, the deer activity displaces only a few sticks in the bundle of rights that constitute ownership. *See* Oakes, *"Property Rights" in Constitutional Analysis Today,* 56 WASH. L. REV. 583, 589 (1981). In any event, no absolute dispossession of Southview's property rights has occurred. *See Loretto,* 458 U.S. at 435 n.12. Under *Loretto,* there has been no physical taking.
>
> Application of the government compulsion requirement—central to the results in *Florida Power Corp.* and *Yee*—yields a similar result. In *Yee,* there was no government compulsion because the mobile home park owners voluntarily rented their land to mobile home owners, and they were not compelled to continue to do so. [ ] The Court considered the park owners' submission to the rent control ordinance, as well as their submission to the resultant alleged physical invasion, to have been voluntary even though the owners were apparently engaged in this business before the ordinance was enacted.
>
> Here, even if the Board's action were a permanent physical occupation, there was no government compulsion. Just as the mobile home park owners voluntarily rented their land in *Yee* and, in so doing, engaged in activity that subjected them to the effects of the rent

control ordinance, *id.,* Southview voluntarily proposed to construct a residential subdivision development project, and, in so doing, engaged in activity that subjected it to the Act 250 review process. Moreover, at the time Southview purchased the land it knew that the project would be subjected to Act 250 scrutiny. Denial of the Act 250 permit—foreclosing one configuration of a development plan—represents a regulation of the use of Southview's property, rather than a *per se* physical taking.

Southview Associates, Ltd. v. Bongartz, 980 F.2d 84 (2d Cir.1992).

Although the Second Circuit determined that the state law did not authorize a physical invasion, it did not begin its analysis, as it might have (and arguably should have), by considering what rights the landowner had under state law to exclude wildlife. Given the state's preexisting power over wildlife, was the statute anything more than an expression of a pre-existing limit on landowner rights? Did existing law, even before Act 250, put the landowner on notice that rights to exclude wildlife were subject to legislative restriction at any time? Alternatively, is it more apt to say that the landowner had the right to exclude wildlife unless and until the government acted, and that the government's action then curtailed that right? Recall the decision in *Sierra Club v. Department of Forestry & Fire Protection* [Chapter 6] which discussed wildlife protection as a "background principle" of property law.

(2) The precautionary principle: The court notes that the burden of proving that the activity will significantly impact wildlife habitat is placed on the opponents of a permit; thus, a landowner seeking the permit enjoys the advantage of doubt on the issue. Should the burden instead be placed on the permit applicant to prove that the proposal will not harm habitat?

(3) Review processes for large projects: Vermont's Act 250 illustrates one legal approach to the protection of wildlife habitat: a state or regional review process under which developments of a certain minimum size are allowed to proceed only if a permit is obtained. Permits are available only after the proposed development is studied to determine whether its environmental effects comply with specific substantive standards. Frequently, permits are granted only after development proposals are scaled down and reconfigured to reduce adverse environmental effects.

Statutes of this type aid wildlife by reducing habitat degradation on lands where development takes place. On the other side, review processes are only triggered by permit applications, which are made on a parcel-by-parcel basis. Under such schemes, landscape-scale planning is difficult to undertake. In addition, review processes that are triggered only when projects reach a certain minimum size tend to encourage development slightly smaller projects that are specifically designed to avoid review. Cumulatively, such projects can be as damaging to wildlife habitat; indeed, standing alone they can promote increased dispersion of development across the landscape in ways that actually make the situation worse.

(4) Forestry practices statutes: A growing number of states have regulatory schemes governing forestry operations on private lands. These statutes typically operate similarly to Vermont's Act 250: private operations above a certain size require permits, which in turn are available only if the private actions are undertaken in such a way as to comply with specified environmental standards, including standards relating to the protection of wildlife habitat. California's forestry statute was at issue in *Sierra Club v. Department of Forestry & Fire Protection* [Chapter 6]; *see also Sierra Club v. State Board of Forestry*, 7 Cal.4th 1215 (1994) (Board of Forestry had power to withhold granting approval of timber harvesting plan covering old-growth forest until applicant obtained and submitted information about species present in old-growth forests, even though information was not required by forest practice rules; its approval of a timber harvesting plan without obtaining such information was an abuse of discretion). For a critical review of the application of the California regulation regime by state administrators, see Thomas N. Lippe & Kathy Bailey, *Regulation of Logging on Private Land in California Under Governor Gray Davis*, 31 GOLDEN GATE L. REV. 351 (2001).

(5) *Lee County v. Kiesel***:** Riparian landowners complained when the county constructed a bridge that blocked their views of the Caloosahatchee River. On appeal, the court held that riparian landowners possess a property right, appurtenant to their land, to view the river without substantial obstruction; the bridge amounted to a physical taking of that property right for which compensation was due. *Lee County v. Kiesel*, 705 So.2d 1013 (Fla.App.1998).

One commentator sees in this ruling a possible tool for allowing landowners, like the owner in the classic *Keeble v. Hickeringill* (Chapter 3), to expand their rights to complain when activities on neighboring lands disrupt wildlife:

> [T]he holding of *Kiesel* could expand to give landowners the right to see and enjoy the wildlife on their property. Environmentalists should press to expand the holding of *Kiesel*, which recognized the right to an unobstructed view of a river, to include the right to an unobstructed view of wildlife. Both rights can be important factors when a landowner purchases property, and may have an impact on the value of the property. Government infringement of the right to view wildlife would, under *Kiesel*, constitute a taking through physical invasion of the landowner's property. For example, a landowner may enjoy observing a bird population on his property. If the government drains a wetland on neighboring property that provides critical habitat for that bird population, the property owner could then sue the government for compensation. By destroying the wildlife that the property owner viewed on his property, the government has physically invaded a part of his property, and owes compensation.
>
> Using *Kiesel* to expand property rights could have consequences beyond the confines of takings jurisprudence. Landowners should enforce their property right to view wildlife against neighbors who destroy wildlife resources that the claimants view and enjoy on their own property.[17] For example, the neighbor might drain wetlands essen-

---

17. Several cases have held that damages to wildlife resources due to landowner actions can result in an actionable nuisance. *See, e.g., Colorado Div. of Wildlife v. Cox*, 843

tial to the survival of birds that roost on the plaintiff's property. Under the principle of *Kiesel*, the plaintiff landowner would sue his neighbor for trespass. The court in *Kiesel* held that construction of the bridge constituted a physical invasion that required compensation by the government; the analogous cause of action when a private actor physically invades another private party's property is trespass. The landowner could seek either an injunction or compensation.

Eric Biber, Note, *A House with a View*, 109 YALE L.J. 849, 851–52 (2000).

Other cases have reached similar results. In *Collens v. New Canaan Water Co.*, for example, the water company dewatered a stream by pumping from wells, killing fish and reducing the value of plaintiff's land. The court held that this was a nuisance to riparian landowners. *Collens v. New Canaan Water Co.*, 234 A.2d 825 (Conn.1967). *See also City of Los Angeles v. Aitken*, 52 P.2d 585 (Cal.App.1935); *Taylor v. Tampa Coal Co.*, 46 So.2d 392 (Fla.1950).

(6) Protecting sensitive land uses: As with *Prah v. Maretti*, *Kiesel* provides evidence of a rising inclination by courts to protect passive, sensitive land uses from unreasonable disruption by activities on neighboring lands. This reflects a fundamental fact: private property entails more than just the right to use land—it also includes a right to be protected when activities on adjoining land unreasonably disrupt a landowner's use of the land. One landowner's alleged right to drain can disrupt another landowner's alleged right to be free of flooding; one landowner's right to disrupt wandering wildlife must be set against her neighbor's right to have wildlife enter his land without interference. When law resolve such disputes, it inevitably favors one type of land use over another. No resolution of such disputes is inherently more favorable to property rights than any other. Rather, they are better understood as being either favorable to intensive land uses or favorable instead to more sensitive land uses.

A stark illustration of this interconnection of property rights arose in *Bormann v. Board of Supervisors of Kossuth County*, 584 N.W.2d 309 (Iowa 1998), in which the court held that a county unlawfully took property without compensation when it authorized a landowner to construct a large-scale animal confinement facility; the taking was of rights possessed by neighbors, whose quiet enjoyment of their rural land was being disrupted by the intensive livestock operation.

Perhaps the classic example is *Miller v. Schoene*, 276 U.S. 272 (1928), which involved the conflicting claims of red cedar and apple orchard owners. The Supreme Court held that "the state was under the necessity of making a choice between the preservation of one class of property and that of the other": "When forced to such a choice the state does not exceed its

---

P.2d 662, 664 (Colo.Ct.App.1992) (holding that the introduction of non-native wildlife may constitute a public nuisance because of the threat to native wildlife); *Wood v. Picillo*, 443 A.2d 1244, 1248 (R.I.1982) (holding that a toxic waste spill is a nuisance because of the threat to wildlife and humans). *Picillo* held that the plaintiffs had established both a public and a private nuisance for damage to wildlife resources. *See Picillo*, 443 A.2d at 1247–48. In finding a private nuisance, the court thus established that property owners have a property right to wildlife, which has been infringed by the party committing the nuisance.

constitutional powers by deciding upon the destruction of one class of property in order to save another which, in the judgment of the legislature, is of greater value to the public." *Id.* at 280.

(7) A new image of landownership and wildlife? One criticism of the federal Endangered Species Act has been that it imposes sometimes severe restrictions on a small number of landowners, while imposing no responsibilities on all others. The same fairness issues arise under other laws and at other levels of governance: some landowners are restricted, while many are unaffected.

Is it an answer to such fairness concerns to say simply that lands differ in their natural conditions, and that the laws at issue merely—and properly—reflect those natural differences? Wetlands are not the same as dry lands; sloping lands are not the same as flat ones; rare habitat is not the same as land with common vegetation and animal communities. Could property law essentially announce: Landowners can initiate new land-use activities only on lands that are naturally suited for such activities. Recall on this issue the much-debated language of *Just v. Marinette County* [Chapter 1]: "An owner of land has no absolute and unlimited right to change the essential natural character of his land so as to use it for a purpose for which it was unsuited in its natural state and which injures the rights of others.... This is not a case where an owner is prevented from using his land for natural and indigenous uses. The uses consistent with the nature of the land are allowed...." According to *Just,* ownership rights should be shaped by the land's natural features and be limited to those uses consistent with the maintenance of those features. Is this a plausible way to reform landed property rights? Would such a scheme lead to too much vagueness and unpredictability in terms of what landowners could or could not do? Or has this idea essentially been incorporated into statutes such as Vermont's Act 250 and the California Forestry Practice Act?

On the other hand, might the burdens of supporting wildlife be more bearable—and politically supported—if landowner duties were spread more broadly. Is it sensible to talk about a general duty, imposed on all landowners, to make reasonable accommodations for wildlife? Could such a fair-share approach provide the baseline for determining whether a particular landowner in a particular instance was shouldering an unfair burden so that compensation would be appropriate?

A vast literature exists on where property law ought to head and how it is being—and needs to be—reformulated to take into account ecological concerns. *See* Lynda L. Butler, *The Pathology of Property Norms: Living Within Nature's Boundaries,* 73 S. CAL. L. REV. 927 (2000); Myrl Duncan, *Property as a Public Conversation, Not a Lockean Soliloquy: A Role for Intellectual and Legal History in Takings Analysis,* 26 ENVTL. L. 1095 (1996); Terry W. Frazier, *Protecting Ecological Integrity Within the Balancing Function of Property Law,* 28 ENVTL. L. 53 (1998); Terry W. Frazier, *The Green Alternative to Classical Liberal Property Theory,* 20 VT. L. REV. 299 (1995) (a highly useful survey of literature); Eric T. Freyfogle, *Eight Principles for Property Rights in the Anti–Sprawl Age,* 23 WM. & MARY ENVTL. L. & POL'Y REV. 777 (1999); Eric T. Freyfogle, *The Owning and Taking of Sensitive Lands,* 43 U.C.L.A.L. REV. 77 (1995); Oliver A. Houck,

Why Do We Protect Endangered Species, and What Does That Say About Whether Restrictions on Private Property to Protect Them Constitute "Takings?," 80 IOWA L. REV. 297 (1995); John A Humbach, *Evolving Thresholds of Nuisance and the Takings Clause,* 18 COLUM. J. ENVTL. L. REV. 1 (1993); James M. McElfish Jr., *Property Rights, Property Roots: Rediscovering the Basis for Legal Protection of the Environment,* 24 Envtl. L. Rptr. (Envtl. L. Inst.) 10231 (1994); Marc R. Poirer, *Property, Environment, Community,* 12 J. ENVTL. L. & LITIG. 43 (1997); Joseph L. Sax, *Property Rights and the Economy of Nature: Understanding* Lucas v. South Carolina Coastal Council, 45 STAN. L. REV. 1433 (1993).

SECTION 4. BEGINNING WITH WATERS

Wildlife law has long paid considerable attention to waterways, chiefly because water bodies provide home and sustenance to so many species. In more recent decades, waterways have gained attention because their degraded conditions can provide clear evidence of unwise practices conducted on surrounding lands. The ill-effects of poorly conducted timber harvesting, for example, often show up most clearly in the form of polluted waterways and aggravated fluctuations in water flows—that is, worsened floods and droughts. Even landowners little aware of ecological interconnections generally can see how water flows unite all land parcels within a particular watershed. In many settings, ecological land planning is best undertaken by dividing the landscape along watershed lines.

A recurrent theme in these materials are issues relating to aquatic wildlife and to its dependence on water flows that are both uninterrupted and clean. Riparian landowners, we saw in Chapter 3, possess rights to complain about disruptions of water quantity and quality. In *Columbia River Fishermen's Protective Union* [Chapter 3], fishers in navigable waterways successfully challenged the pollution of a waterway by municipal sewage. Decisions in Chapter 5 explored the scope of governmental power to require dam owners to alter their structures to accommodate fish migrations. *Just v. Marinette County* in Chapter 1 and the Supreme Court's decision in *Solid Waste Agency of Northern Cook County* [Chapter 6] gave glimpses of some of the many laws and regulations protecting wetlands and coastal areas. Materials in Chapter 7 considered how Indian tribes have begun protecting their fishing rights by challenging land-use practices and waterway obstructions that disrupt them. As the Florida court's decision in *Kiesel* (noted above) demonstrates, waterway issues have been at the forefront of reconsidering what it means to own land.

The materials in this section focus on the ways that contemporary wildlife law has increasingly challenged activities that disrupt and pollute water flows. The first part explores legal tools being used to restore water flows to more natural conditions; it considers waterway obstructions as well as activities that alter flows in quantity and/or timing. The second part turns to questions of water quality, with particular reference to land-use activities. The concluding materials consider the prospects of using watersheds as the focal point for landscape-scale efforts to conserve wildlife.

a.   RESTORING FLOWS

A wide variety of human activities alter the quantity and timing of water flows. Physical obstructions—such as dams—and water diversions in which the water is consumed, used in ways that delay its return, or transferred entirely out of watershed all affect the quantity and timing of flows. Drainage activities can speed the passage of rainfall into nearby streams—and, in doing so, can exacerbate flooding after rains and worsen droughts during dry periods. Alterations in natural land cover—removing trees, for instance, or plowing grasslands—can also materially change natural hydrologic cycles.

Earlier materials examined laws restricting the drainage or filling of wetlands. Prominent among these is section 404 of the Clean Water Act, at issue in *Solid Waste Agency of Northern Cook County* [Chapter 6]. Federal laws relating to agriculture also contain provisions that protect wetlands, largely through limitations imposed on farmers who accept crop subsidy payments.[1]

Conservation Law Foundation v. Federal Energy Regulatory Commission

Court of Appeals for the District of Columbia Circuit.
216 F.3d 41 (2000).

■ RANDOLPH, J.:—The Department of the Interior and the Environmental Protection Agency, conservation groups, and the Penobscot Indian Nation petition for review of the Federal Energy Regulatory Commission's relicensing of a hydroelectric project in north-central Maine. The issues presented go mainly to the adequacy of the Commission's consideration of the various factors governing license renewals. Because the Commission gave sufficient attention to these factors and carefully explained its conclusions, the petitions are denied.

I

Located on the West Branch of the Penobscot River, the Ripogenus and Penobscot Mills Hydroelectric Projects produce approximately 108 megawatts of power for Great Northern Paper mills in Millinocket and East Millinocket, Maine. The projects consist of a series of reservoirs, dams, and powerhouses. This case focuses on one of the dams—the 1262 foot long Stone Dam, which is part of the Penobscot Mills Project. Constructed in 1899, Stone Dam diverts water through a canal to a 37 megawatt powerhouse. This diversion blocks the main channel of the Penobscot's West Branch for a 4.5 mile stretch known as the "Back Channel." Because of Stone Dam, the Back Channel receives only leakage flows of 2 to 5 cfs (cubic feet per second), except for occasional "spillage" when flows exceed power requirements.

---

1. An overview of these federal laws, focused on wildlife, is in Bradley C. Kark- kainen, *Biodiversity and Land*, 83 CORNELL L. REV. 1, 62–70 (1997).

The Penobscot Mills Project, like any project used for the "development, transmission, and utilization of power across, along, from, or in any of the streams or other bodies of water over which Congress has jurisdiction," requires a license from the Federal Energy Regulatory Commission. 16 U.S.C. § 797(e). When the original license for Penobscot Mills expired at the end of 1993, Great Northern applied for a new one. The Commission issued a Final Environmental Impact Statement analyzing three different proposals regarding the new license: the "Applicant's Proposal," in which Great Northern would "operate the project[ ] nearly as it has over the past 50 years" with some new environmental and recreational enhancements but no increased flows in the Back Channel; "Alternative 1," which reflected the Interior Department's recommendations for enhancements including minimum flows of 350 to 500 cfs in the Back Channel; and "Alternative 2," recommending "enhancement measures intermediate between those proposed by GNP and those in Alternative 1." [ ] As a baseline for comparison, the Commission adopted the terms and conditions of the existing license as the "no action" option. The impact statement recommended a modified version of Alternative 2 that did not include flow requirements for the Back Channel. [ ]

Shortly after issuance of the final impact statement, the Commission granted a new license for Penobscot Mills. *See* 77 F.E.R.C. ¶ 61,068 (1996). The order conditioned the license on Great Northern's commitment to wetland enhancements, project boundary expansion, and increased flows into Millinocket Stream. *See id.* at 61,275–79. As to the Back Channel, the Commission decided not to order minimum flows "given the modest fisheries benefit likely to occur and the significant adverse impact on the project's energy benefits," *id.* at 61,276, a decision it affirmed on rehearing, *see* 85 F.E.R.C. ¶ 61,316 (1998), and reconsideration, *see* 86 F.E.R.C. ¶ 61,184 (1999).

II

"In deciding whether to issue any license [for hydroelectric projects,] the Commission, in addition to the power and development purposes for which licenses are issued, shall give equal consideration to the purposes of energy conservation, the protection, mitigation of damage to, and enhancement of, fish and wildlife (including related spawning grounds and habitat), the protection of recreational opportunities, and the preservation of other aspects of environmental quality." 16 U.S.C. § 797(e). The Federal Power Act also requires the Commission to include conditions for the "protection, mitigation and enhancement" of fish and wildlife affected by the project, such conditions to be "based on recommendations received pursuant to the Fish and Wildlife Coordination Act (16 U.S.C. 661 *et seq.*) from the National Marine Fisheries Service, the United States Fish and Wildlife Service, and State fish and wildlife agencies." 16 U.S.C. § 803(j)(1). The Commission retains authority to decide that recommended conditions are "inconsistent with the purposes" of the FPA or other laws, in which event it shall of course reject them. 16 U.S.C. § 803(j)(2); *see United States Dep't of the Interior v. FERC,* 952 F.2d 538, 544 (D.C.Cir.1992). While the Commission must give "equal consideration" to environmental factors, those factors do not have "preemptive force." *Id.,* 952 F.2d at 545. The

Commission "still is charged with determining the 'public interest,' *i.e.,* balancing power and non-power values." *Id.*

The petitioners contend that the Commission's rejection of minimum flow requirements in the Back Channel violates these Federal Power Act provisions and the National Environmental Policy Act, *see* 42 U.S.C. § 4321 *et seq.* Their arguments can be grouped into two categories: that the Commission did not fully recognize the recreational and environmental (*i.e.,* nonpower) benefits that would have resulted if it had imposed minimum flow requirements; and that the Commission inflated the economic costs Great Northern would incur from increased Back Channel flows.

A. Nonpower Issues

The main argument of the federal petitioners is that the Commission should not have treated existing conditions at Stone Dam as the baseline "no action" option because this caused "the Commission to ignore ongoing impacts directly attributable to the new license.* * * " [ ] We think there is nothing to this objection. The statute—16 U.S.C. § 803(j)—invites a comparative inquiry. It charges the Commission with the duty of protecting, mitigating the damage to, and enhancing "fish and wildlife (including related spawning grounds and habitat) affected by the development, operation and management of the project." To do this properly the Commission must compare what might occur to fish and wildlife if the license does not include protection for nonpower resources against what will occur with conditions imposed. The statutory words "fish and wildlife * * * affected" by the project seems to refer to the fish and wildlife currently existing in the vicinity of the project, which supports the Commission's choice of existing conditions as a baseline. The quoted language surely cannot refer to the animals inhabiting the area in 1899, when the project came into being. They are long gone and so cannot be "affected" by a Commission licensing decision in the 1990s. Granted, it is possible to treat the words "fish and wildlife" generically, so that it is not just the animals currently residing in the region that get protected or enhanced, but different species that might be introduced or reintroduced. But this view of § 803(j) does not help petitioners because it says nothing about whether the baseline for the Commission's comparative inquiry should be today or sometime other than today. In other words, even if the statute refers generally to all "fish and wildlife" it hardly follows that the Commission must imagine the Back Channel as it existed before 1899 and assess the effect of relicensing by pretending that Stone Dam does not exist—at least when no one advocates decommissioning the Penobscot Mills Project and tearing down the dam.

Given the language of § 803(j), the Commission certainly had the leeway to conduct its comparative assessments using existing conditions as a baseline. To the reasons just mentioned, we incorporate by reference those given in *American Rivers v. FERC,* 201 F.3d 1186, 1195–99 (9th Cir.1999), which sustained the Commission's use of an existing conditions baseline as a reasonable construction of § 803(j).

In any event, the baseline business has the whiff of a red herring. Baseline or no baseline, the question is whether the Commission has fully examined options calling for greater or lesser environmental protection.

Here the Commission spoke of environmental "benefits" and the economic "costs" to Great Northern of options calling for stronger environmental protection. It could just as easily have spoken of economic "benefits" to Great Northern from licensing the project and environmental "costs." So long as the Commission adequately examines both the power and nonpower impacts of recommended licensing conditions, we do not see why it matters on which side of the equation environmental concerns are placed....

Petitioners also argue that the Commission did not give "equal consideration" to nonpower values because it refused to assess in economic terms the nonpower benefits that would result from restoring significant flows to the Back Channel. Restored flows, petitioners believe, would attract anglers and whitewater rafting enthusiasts to this 4.5 mile stretch of river. In the rehearing order, the Commission explained its refusal to quantify these nonpower benefits: "[T]he public-interest balancing of environmental and economic impacts cannot be done with mathematical precision, nor do we think our statutory obligation to weigh and balance all public interest considerations is served by trying to reduce it to a mere mathematical exercise.* * * [F]or non-power resources such as aquatic habitat, fish and wildlife, recreations, and cultural and aesthetic values, to name just a few, the public interest cannot be evaluated adequately only by dollars and cents." 85 F.E.R.C. at 62,244–45. Certainly nothing in the statute requires the Commission to place a dollar value on nonpower benefits. Nor does the fact that the Commission assigned dollar figures to Great Northern's economic costs require that the Commission do the same for nonpower benefits: " 'Equal consideration' is not the same as 'equal treatment.' " *State of California v. FERC,* 966 F.2d 1541, 1550 (9th Cir.1992). The refusal to quantify nonpower benefits did not "stack the deck" against those concerns. The Commission approved "a variety of enhancements related to instream flows for fisheries and recreation, stabilization of impoundment levels, wetlands, recreational facilities, shoreline protection, and cultural resources." 85 F.E.R.C. at 62,245; *see also id.* at 62,245 n.31. A critical factor in the Commission's refusal to impose minimum flows was the increased power expenses that would result, not the Commission's failure to appreciate nonpower values. Minimum flows of 350 cfs in the Back Channel would, the Commission concluded, increase annual power expenses by $916,300; the *total* increase in annual power costs of the enhancements the Commission approved for Penobscot Mills was $262,600. [ ]

. . .

B.   Power Issues

The Commission stated that the "reduction in the project's * * * annual energy benefits for the Back Channel flows outweighs the enhancement in aquatic resources that the flows would produce." 77 F.E.R.C. at 61,276. The Commission calculated this annual reduction as $916,000 (6% of the project's total benefits), *see id.*, based on the price of purchasing replacement power from the least-cost alternative source—Bangor Hydro & Electric Company, [ ].

Petitioners complain that the Commission failed to consider the alternative of Great Northern conserving energy, something the statute requires the Commission to consider. *See* 16 U.S.C. §§ 797(e), 808(a)(2)(C); *see also* 42 U.S.C. § 4332(2)(E); 40 C.F.R. § 1502.14. They put it this way: "By considering conserved power as the least cost alternative to hydropower, rather than the more expensive purchased power used by the Commission, the cost of environmental enhancements, such as Back Channel flows, are much lower." Final Brief for Petitioners Conservation Law Foundation, et al. and Trout Unlimited at 12. But the Commission did consider the alternative of energy conservation. After examining Great Northern's plant data, the Commission concluded that the mills had recently increased energy efficiency as the result of plant modernization efforts and the use of steam generation and that no reliable evidence supported petitioners' view that "enormous conserved power potential" still existed at the mills. *See* 77 F.E.R.C. at 61,269 n. 16; [ ]. The final impact statement also noted that Great Northern, "operating as a private for-profit enterprise, would have a strong economic incentive to maximize savings from conservation and not waste electric power, particularly as it manufactures an energy-intensive product." 85 F.E.R.C. at 62,243 n.14. Any conservation that did occur would be "used to displace higher cost fossil fuel power * * * [s]ince the entire output from the two projects supplies only a portion of GNP's total annual power needs.* * * " 85 F.E.R.C. at 62,243 n.14. We see no ground for disagreeing with this reasoning.

Petitioners' other cost-side argument is that the Commission relied on unsupported claims that the increased cost of Back Channel flows would result in job losses at the Great Northern mills. This misinterprets the Commission decision. In the original order, the Commission recognized "Great Northern's need for inexpensive power to remain competitive in its paper making operations." 77 F.E.R.C. at 61,275. Then, in a footnote, the Commission stated that it could not verify the company's claim that flows in the Back Channel "would result in the loss of approximately 238 jobs," so the Commission was just relying on what it did know—that "Great Northern's operating costs are high compared to other paper manufacturers, and cost increases *could* reduce the company's competitiveness." *Id.* at 61,275 n.31 (italics added). On rehearing, the Commission once again indicated that it was only relying on the *risk* of economic harm: "A 350–cfs minimum flow would reduce the annual energy benefit of Penobscot Mills substantially, with the *possibility* of causing Great Northern to further curtail operations at, or close, its paper mills.* * * " 85 F.E.R.C. at 62,242 (italics added). There is ample evidence in the record to support the Commission's findings. Papermaking is a highly competitive industry, [ ]; Great Northern is a high cost producer compared to other paper manufacturers, [ ], and Great Northern recently closed some Millinocket facilities, resulting in the elimination of about 350 jobs, [ ].

NOTES

(1) License renewals and dam removal: Because dams regulated by FERC are allowed to operate only as long as the operator has a valid license, a decision to refuse a new license means the dam must be removed.

According to many observers, the Tellico dam at issue in *TVA v. Hill* was hardly the only dam built in which the costs far exceeded benefits. *See* MARC REISNER, CADILLAC DESERT: THE AMERICAN WEST AND ITS DISAPPEARING WATER (1986). Waterway advocates are increasingly calling for the review of all existing dams, and for the removal of dams when the gains in terms of waterway health (including fisheries and recreational opportunities) exceed the benefits of dam continuance. *See* Christine A. Klein, *Dam Policy: The Emerging Paradigm of Restoration*, 31 Envtl. L. Rptr. (Envtl. L. Inst.) 10486 (2001).

FERC has been reluctant, critics say, to consider seriously the possibility of denying a license. One avenue of legal attack on such reluctance has been the EIS process under NEPA, which requires an agency to consider, not just a reasonable range of alternatives to a proposed action, but also the option of doing nothing—the "no action" alternative. In license renewal settings, FERC has viewed license *renewal* without change as tantamount to "no action," and dismisses with little study the alternative of denying a license. Note how the court in *Conservation Law Foundation* responds to this issue. Its ruling draws upon the Ninth Circuits opinion in *American Rivers v. FERC*, 187 F.3d 1007 (9th Cir.1999), in which the court agreed that renewal without change was properly viewed as the "no action" alternative. Even if this is true, has FERC considered a proper range of alternatives in its EIS if it fails to consider license denial? By choosing not to study license denial has the agency not, in effect, decided that the dam will remain—precisely the kind of major federal decision that should be made only after studying its environmental impacts? In *American Rivers*, FERC brushed aside the claim that it should consider license denial by asserting that "license denial and dam removal [would] in most proceedings not be considered a reasonable alternative by anyone." 187 F.3d at 1021.

(2) Equal consideration and conservation: In *Conservation Law Foundation*, the court decided that FERC did not need to quantify the benefits of imposing greater limits on the operating permit. Yet, how can it ensure "equal consideration" to nonpower values—including fish and wildlife—in the absence of quantification? Is "equal consideration" anything more than just a requirement that the agency take a hard look at the various options? If, as the court says, equal consideration is not the same as equal treatment, then what is it? Did the court deal fairly with the energy conservation option? In the court's view, the sole issue was whether the power company itself might conserve energy in its operations. But what of conservation measures by *customers* of the power company? What if conservation by customers could be undertaken more cheaply and with less ecological impact than continued operation of the hydropower facility? Would not this issue be relevant to public policy? Should FERC consider the option—or did it rightly ignore it on the ground that the power company had no way to force customers to conserve? Note that, under NEPA, an agency cannot exclude a reasonable alternative simply because it requires action by other agencies or even changes in law.

Recall also the discussion in Chapter 13 on the evolution of "consideration" requirements in congressional attempts to force single-use agencies such as FERC to value uses such as wildlife.

(3) Wildlife mitigation and fishways: As the court explains in *Conservation Law Foundation*, under section 10(j) of the Federal Power Act, 16 U.S.C. § 803(j), FERC is *empowered* to impose conditions on operating licenses for the "protection, mitigation, and enhancement" of fish and wildlife affected by the project. The conditions are to be based on recommendations received under the Fish and Wildlife Coordination Act from state fish and wildlife agencies, from the Fish and Wildlife Service, and from the National Marine Fisheries Service. In addition, under section 18 of the Act, 16 U.S.C. § 811, FERC is *obligated* to include in a license any "fishway" prescriptions recommended by the Secretary of Commerce or the Secretary of the Interior. In *American Rivers,* discussed in note (2), the court held that FERC had the power to refuse to accept recommendations under § 10(j) if it decided that the recommendations were inconsistent with the purposes of the Federal Power Act or other laws. FERC could not, however, refuse to accept a fishway proposal, nor could it even review a fishway proposal to determine whether it fit within the definition of "fishway" implicit in the statute. According to the court, FERC was obligated to adhere to any and all requests submitted to it "under color of section 18." 187 F.3d at 1030. On the facts of the case, FERC had accepted requests that it require fish ladders and fish screens, but it had resisted requests relating to (i) fish mortality standards at the fish screens, (ii) the construction of tailrace barriers, (iii) delays in raising lake levels, (iv) delays in constructing certain diversion structures, (v) fish salvage requirements, and (vi) inspection, monitoring, and enforcement duties. *Id.* at 1013 n.11. All such requests, the court held, had to be honored.

(4) *Alameda Water & Sanitation District v. Reilly***:** The Denver Water Board, acting for the city of Denver and for various other municipal entities, sought a permit from the Army Corps of Engineers under § 404 of the Clean Water Act to construct a water-storage reservoir on the South Platte River at a site known as Two Forks. The proposed reservoir would flood more than 30 miles of the river. The Corps of Engineers filed notice of its intent to issue the permit. Exercising its authority under § 404(c), the EPA vetoed the permit, citing its adverse effects on a "diverse riverine and wetland/upland complex with extremely high fisheries, wildlife and recreational values" along with the existence of less damaging alternatives to the project. Project proponents proposed modifications to mitigate the damage, but the EPA deemed the modifications insufficient. Various proponents then challenged the veto on the ground that the EPA based its veto, not on any water-quality considerations, but solely on wildlife and recreational effects. The court held that EPA has sufficient authority to consider all environmental effects of project and can veto a permit based chiefly on wildlife and recreational impacts. *Alameda Water & Sanitation Dist. v. Reilly,* 930 F.Supp. 486 (D.Colo.1996).

(5) Section 401 certifications: A tool just as potent as EPA's veto power is § 401 of the Clean Water Act, 33 U.S.C. § 1341(a), which allows states to veto the issuance of any federal license or permit (including hydropower dam licenses and § 404 permits) if the action being authorized is inconsistent with state water-quality standards. State power under the section was broadly construed in *PUD No. 1 v. Washington Dept. of Ecology,* 511 U.S. 700 (1994). A thoughtful consideration of the issue is Debra L. Donahue,

The Untapped Power of Clean Water Act Section 401, 23 ECOLOGY L.Q. 201 (1996).

(6) Water flows and water rights: Many waterway disruptions are caused by diversions by holders of private water rights. Wildlife law, therefore, is intertwined with the complex body of law on private rights in water flows. Although—as noted at the end of Chapter 3—water rights in some settings are held by state agencies expressly to promote "instream" uses, such as protecting aquatic life, and permits to make new appropriations are typically available only upon a showing that an appropriation is in the public interest—a review that also considers the effects of a proposed diversion on aquatic life—what about existing water diversions which either threaten existing life or stand in the way of restoring wildlife populations? This issue has been raised most forcefully in settings involving threatened and endangered species.

While diversion problems arise in all states that have adopted permit systems to allocate the use of water, they are most pressing in those states that have adopted the doctrine of prior appropriation. Water rights in such jurisdiction are, however, held under the continuing requirement that use of the water be "beneficial." Can a water use meet this requirement if the economic benefits to its holder are overshadowed by ecological harms caused by the diversion? In what sense would such a diversion be "beneficial"? In some Western states water uses must also be reasonable (as they must also be in riparian-rights jurisdictions). Defenders of existing water rights repeatedly assert that a water right that is beneficial when begun remains beneficial forever thereafter—that is, beneficial use does not evolve over time as does the *sic utere* doctrine and nuisance law. For a counter-argument criticizing courts for failing to keep the requirement up to date, see Eric T. Freyfogle, *Water Rights and the Common Wealth,* 26 ENVTL. L. 27 (1996). *See also* Reed D. Benson, *Maintaining the Status Quo: Protecting Established Water Uses in the Pacific Northwest, Despite the Rules of Prior Appropriation,* 28 ENVTL. L. 881 (1998). Recall also the decisions in *Shokal v. Dunn* [Chapter 3] and *National Audubon Society v. Superior Court* [Chapter 5] which involved restrictions on appropriative rights based upon public interest and public trust considerations. *See also Tulare Irrigation District v. Lindsay–Strathmore Irrigation District,* 45 P.2d 972, 1007 (Cal. 1935) ("What is a beneficial use at one time may, because of changed conditions, become a waste of water at a later time."); *State of Idaho, Department of Parks v. Idaho Department of Water Administration,* 530 P.2d 924, 931 (Idaho 1974) ("the concept of what is or is not a beneficial use must necessarily change with changing conditions").

Two useful considerations of these issues are Holly Doremus, *Water, Population Growth, and Endangered Species in the West,* 72 U. COLO. L. REV. 361 (2001), and Joseph L. Sax, *Environmental Law at the Turn of the Century: A Reportorial Fragment of Contemporary History,* 88 CALIF. L. REV. 2375 (2000). On the on-going transformation of western water policy, largely driven by environmental considerations, see David H. Getches, *The Metamorphosis of Western Water Policy: Have Federal Laws and Local Decisions Eclipsed the State's Role?,* 20 STAN. ENVTL. L.J. 3 (2001).

(7) The challenge of drainage: Drainage projects alter water flows by changing their timing: They speed up flows after rains, leading to diminished flows during dry times. Since a river's capacity to sustain aquatic life is often determined by the quality and quantity of its water at its lowest flow—that flow, in Leopold's term, is the ecosystem's limiting factor— drainage that diminishes low flows can severely harm wildlife. Aside from laws directly protecting wetlands, few legal limits are imposed on drainage activities on private lands. Indeed, even the most significant federal wetlands law—§ 404 of the Clean Water Act—does not protect wetlands altered solely by draining since it is triggered only when dredge or fill material is "deposited" into a waterway. Early in the nineteenth century, many jurisdictions adhered to the "civil law" approach to drainage, under which landowners cannot alter natural drainage in ways that harmed other landowners. Because that rule inhibited intensive land uses and thus economic development, it gradually gave way as landowners increasingly gained the right to undertake "reasonable" drainage—even when it caused harm to other landowners.

In many watersheds, excessive drainage offers a classic illustration of the tragedy of fragmentation and the tyranny of small decisions. Drainage by a few landowners poses no problems; drainage by most or all landowners can seriously damage a waterway. Efforts to reduce drainage, of course, encounter passionate arguments that such restrictions would interfere with private property rights. But is this true, given how substantially drainage rights have varied over time? Should a landowner's right to drain depend on the overall impact of all activities within a watershed? One effort to address excessive drainage in an Illinois watershed, led by The Nature Conservancy, is described in ERIC T. FREYFOGLE, BOUNDED PEOPLE, BOUNDLESS LANDS: ENVISIONING A NEW LAND ETHIC 151–170 (1998).

(8) Back to natural flow? Recall from Chapter 3 that water law in the United States began with a natural flow, riparian-rights doctrine, under which a landowner had no right to alter the quality or quantity of an adjacent waterway if it caused harm to others. Had that property rule remained in effect, America's waterways would be ecologically far healthier. The shift from natural flow to reasonable use—and, in western states, to prior appropriation—allowed landowners to use rivers in ways that led to significant ecological degradation and harm to downstream users and to the myriad species that depend directly and indirectly on the waterway. Can the environmental measures of the late twentieth century be viewed as a partial effort to shift back toward the natural flow rule? If the shift from natural flow to reasonable use was a legitimate shift in ownership norms, would a shift in the reverse direction not be equally legitimate? Note that the "takings" doctrine applicable to federal actions (*e.g.*, permit denials under § 404) dates from the Bill of Rights, adopted in 1791 when the natural flow rule was supreme. Should this history be relevant in deciding regulatory takings cases? Note also that those states adopting the prior appropriation doctrine "took" the previously existing riparian rights—and did so without payment of compensation. *See, e.g., Coffin v. Left Hand Ditch Co.*, 6 Colo. 443 (1882) (riparian rights never existed within state); *Albuquerque Land & Irrigation Co. v. Gutierrez*, 61 P. 357 (N.M. 1900), *aff'd* 188 U.S. 545 (1903) (same); *In re Hood River*, 227 P. 1065 (Or.1924) (statute adopting appropriation doctrine that saved "vested rights" and defined that term as including only those riparian rights actually beneficially used upheld); *Baumann v. Smrha,* 145 F.Supp. 617 (D.Kan.1956), *aff'd mem.,* 352 U.S. 863 (1956) (same). *See generally* Dale D. Goble, *Prior Appropriation and the Property Clause: A Dialogue of Accommodation,* 71 OR. L. REV. 381 (1992).

b.   RESTORING QUALITY

The most important legal protection of water quality is the federal Clean Water Act. The Act has substantially improved water quality in most parts of the country—largely as a result of the Act's requirement that polluters who discharge through "point sources" (such as pipes and ditches) reduce the discharges. Point-source polluters are required to obtain permits, which set limits on how much they can discharge. Violations of permit conditions can be remedied by suits brought by injured citizens. *E.g., Friends of the Earth, Inc. v. Gaston Copper Recycling Corp.,* 204 F.3d 149 (4th Cir.2000) (en banc).

Far less successful have been efforts to reduce waterway pollution that comes, not from discrete point sources, but from "nonpoint sources": that is, from the rainfall that runs off land, carrying pollutants with it. Urban run-off carries oil residues from parking lots and chemicals that homeowners spread on lawns. Run-off in industrial settings carries substances stored outside or washed from buildings and equipment. Construction sites can produce heavily polluted run-off unless measures are taken to cover disturbed land. In many states, the leading source of water pollution is agriculture, which produces eroded soil and a wide array of farm chemicals. Similarly, forestry activities can be major sources of pollution.

Land-use activities can degrade water quality not only by the pollutants they directly add to streams, but also by their indirect effects on waterways. The loss of wetlands, for example, diminishes the land's capacity to cleanse water before it enters rivers; the removal of vegetation along waterways exposes water flows to sunlight, increasing water temperatures and harming cold-water fisheries; accelerated water flows can significantly increase stream-bank erosion, further increasing sediment loads.

The case excerpted below traces efforts to restrict such nonpoint-source pollution. Federal law does not directly restrict polluting land-use activities. Instead, it requires states to establish water-quality standards—the maximum allowed concentrations of particular pollutants—for all water bodies. Once standards are set, the states must identify waterway segments that are in excess of the standards. The states are then to develop plans to reduce pollution loads to bring waterway segments into compliance with the standards. One way to do so is to further tighten discharge limits imposed on point-source polluters. In many settings, however, this option is not possible: pollution from nonpoint sources is so great that waterways would violate the standards even if point sources cut their discharges to zero. In addition, further reductions by point-source polluters may be far more expensive than pollution reduction steps available to nonpoint polluters.

For decades, states have faced obligations under the Clean Water Act to develop plans to reduce nonpoint-source pollution. Progress, however, has been slow, particularly in states where pollution comes from agricultural sources whose leaders ardently resist any regulatory restrictions. States have funded demonstration projects to show landowners how they might reduce run-off pollution, and have developed land-use guidelines—commonly termed "best management practices" or "BMPs"—to encourage reductions. But BMPs are almost entirely voluntary and many landowners ignore them.

Conservation advocates have long searched for Clean Water Act provisions that would enable them to push states (and the EPA) to become tougher on nonpoint polluters. Attention in recent years has focused on § 303(d) of the Act, which (as the following case explains) requires states to identify waterway segments that violate water quality standards and to submit a list of such segments to the EPA. The state is then required to calculate the total amount of each pollutant that each segment can accept *without* violating water quality standards. The quantity of allowable pollution—for a given waterway segment and a given pollutant—is the "total maximum daily load" or "TMDL." Once the TMDL is calculated for a waterway segment, then the even harder work begins: the state must identify the sources of the pollutant and decide which polluters will be required to cut back, and by how much. States have complete freedom in making such decisions; federal law only requires that they make the TMDL calculations, and then develop a workable plan to bring each segment into compliance with water-quality standards. In the case of waterways polluted by nonpoint sources, a state has no choice but to take action against them—largely by specifying mandatory land-use restrictions. If a state fails to make a TMDL calculation, the EPA is authorized to step in and make the calculation itself.

The following case describes this process. It also addresses—for the first time—a critical issue: must a state undertake a TMDL calculation for a waterway segment that is polluted entirely from nonpoint sources and, if it fails to do so, can the EPA do so on its behalf?

Pronsolino v. Marcus

District Court for the Northern District of California.
91 F. Supp. 2d 1337 (2000).

■ ALSUP, J.:—In this case of first impression, the issue is whether Section 303(d) of the Federal Water Pollution Control Act Amendments of 1972, later renamed the Clean Water Act, authorized the Environmental Protection Agency to determine "total maximum daily loads" for rivers and waters polluted only by logging and agricultural runoff and/or other nonpoint sources rather than by any municipal sewer and/or industrial point sources. 33 U.S.C. § 1313(d). The issue gathers importance from the fact that "nonpoint source pollution has become the dominant water quality problem in the United States, dwarfing all other sources * * *."

STATEMENT

Plaintiffs Guido and Betty Pronsolino own forested land along the Garcia River in the North Coast of California. When they obtained a permit to harvest timber, the California Department of Forestry ("CDF") imposed restrictions designed to reduce soil erosion into the Garcia River. The restrictions include measures such as leaving certain large conifers standing. Plaintiffs contend that the conditions are onerous and costly. They argue that CDF imposed these restrictions in order to implement a criterion known as a "total maximum daily load" ("TMDL") set by EPA for the Garcia River. Seeking to strike at the root of their problem, the Pronsolinos brought this action under the Administrative Procedure Act, 5 U.S.C. § 701 *et seq.*, to challenge EPA's authority to impose TMDLs on rivers polluted only by timber-harvesting and agricultural runoff and/or other nonpoint sources, as is concededly the case for the Garcia River. Joining them as plaintiffs are the Mendocino County Farm Bureau, the California Farm Bureau and the American Farm Bureau Federation, all of whom dispute EPA's authority to set TMDLs for such rivers.

The Garcia River runs through southwestern Mendocino County into the Pacific Ocean. The river was once flourished as a spawning ground for cold-water fish such as coho salmon and steelhead trout. Excess sediment from logging operations over many years in the region hurt, perhaps severely, the spawning and reproduction of these fish in the Garcia River (and other North Coast rivers). In 1966, one journal reported that one-half of "potential coho salmon's habitat in the Garcia River * * * was reported as moderately to severely damaged by ongoing logging practices" (quoted in Brown, *et al., Historical Decline & Current Status of Coho Salmon in California,* 14 No. AM. J. OF FISHERIES MANAGEMENT 237, 251 (May 1994)). By 1998, a staff report on the Garcia River by the California Regional Water Control Board stated that "[t]he Garcia River and its tributaries have experienced a reduction in the quality and amount of instream habitat that is capable of fully supporting the beneficial use of cold-water fishery, due to increased sedimentation." . . .

Although Section 303(d) of the Clean Water Act required the states and EPA to identify certain substandard waters and to set TMDLs for them a generation ago, the Garcia River and other North Coast rivers escaped their gaze until recently. In 1992, EPA required California to add the Garcia River and sixteen other North Coast waters to its list of substandard waters. Thereafter, California retained the same waters on its list in 1994, 1996 and 1998. Meanwhile, a group of fishermen and environmental groups sued EPA, alleging that the then-recent addition of the Garcia River and sixteen other water segments to California's list of substandard waters meant that California and/or the EPA had to prepare TMDLs for the rivers. That case ended in a consent decree in March 1997 requiring TMDLs for all the rivers. Consent Decree, *Pacific Coast Federation of Fishermen's Association v. Marcus, et al.,* No. 95–4474 MHP (Mar. 6, 1997).

Pursuant to the consent decree, EPA set March 16, 1998, as the deadline for the establishment of a TMDL for the Garcia River. California's North Coast Regional Water Quality Control Board initiated public comment on a draft TMDL but missed the deadline. EPA immediately released its own TMDL for the Garcia River (which was only slightly different from the state draft). The EPA TMDL was sensitive to the fish-habitat problem, [ ]:

> Brown *et al.* (1994) reports that coho salmon previously occurred in as many as 582 California streams from the Smith River near the Oregon border to the San Lorenzo River on the central coast. There are now probably less than 5,000 native coho salmon spawning in California each year, many in populations of less than 100 individuals. Coho populations today are probably less than 6% of what they were in the 1940s and there has been at least 70% decline since the 1960s. Brown *et al.* (1994) conclude that the reasons for the decline of coho salmon in California include: stream alterations brought about by poor land-use practices and by the effects of periodic floods and drought, the breakdown of genetic integrity of native stocks, introduced diseases, over harvest, and climatic change.

. . .

The Garcia River watershed has experienced a reduction in the quality and quantity of instream habitat which is capable of supporting the cold water fishery, particularly that of coho salmon and steelhead. Controllable factors contributing to this habitat loss include the acceleration of sediment production and delivery due to land management activities and the loss of instream channel structure necessary to maintain the system's capacity to efficiently store, sort and transport delivered sediment.

Overall, the TMDL for the Garcia River called for a sixty percent reduction of sediment. [ ][4] The TMDL set the total maximum amount of sediment loading at an average of 552 tons per square mile per year and allocated portions of this total load to various categories of nonpoint sources in the Garcia River watershed. [ ] The various categories of nonpoint sources were: (a) mass wasting associated with roads; (b) mass wasting associated with timber-harvesting activities; (c) erosion related to road surfaces; and (d) erosion related to road and skid trail crossings and gullies from diversions on roads and skid trails. [ ] In order to achieve these load allocations, the TMDL called for percentage reductions in sediment loading from these nonpoint sources. [ ] There were only "slight differ-

---

4. EPA's regulations on TMDLs were issued in 1985. 40 C.F.R. § 130.7. The record herein contains a summary of the TMDL process [ ]:

The TMDL process, in essence, is the following: States identify specific waters where problems exist or are expected; States set priorities; States allocate pollutant loadings among point and nonpoint sources; and EPA approves State actions or acts in lieu of the State if necessary. Point and nonpoint sources then reduce pollutants to achieve the pollutant loadings established by the TMDL through a wide variety of Federal, State, Tribal, and local authorities, programs, and initiatives.

States have primary responsibility for developing lists and TMDLs under section 303(d). Section 303(d)(1)(A) and the implementing regulations (at 40 C.F.R. § 130.7(b)) provide States with latitude to determine their own priorities for developing and implementing TMDLs. In particular, the flexibility to States offered by the priority ranking process of section 303(d)(1)(A) is a good opportunity for incorporating rotating basin or other watershed approaches into the TMDL process.

ences" between the regional board's pending TMDL and the EPA's TMDL as issued. [ ]

The regional board concluded that if it did not implement EPA's TMDL, then EPA could withdraw federal funding to the state agency. CDF, the state agency charged with approving timber-harvesting plans, such as those required of plaintiffs under state law, also believed that failure to implement the TMDL would imperil federal funding. In this connection, the Clean Water Act calls upon the states to incorporate whatever TMDLs are authorized for listed rivers and waters—the question here being whether a TMDL was authorized at all.

Plaintiffs' forester estimated that TMDL compliance would cost the Pronsolinos upwards of $750,000. Larry Mailliard and Bill Barr, members of plaintiff Mendocino County Farm Bureau, are similarly situated. They estimated their compliance would cost $10,602,000 and $962,000 respectively. This suit was filed on April 12, 1999, seeking a determination whether a TMDL for the Garcia River was authorized by the Clean Water Act.

ANALYSIS

The general issue presented is the extent to which logging and agricultural runoff and other nonpoint sources of pollution are relevant in the listing-and-TMDL process of section 303(d) of the Clean Water Act of 1972. 33 U.S.C. § 1313(d). Put more narrowly, the issue is whether listing and TMDLs are required for rivers and waters polluted only by logging and agricultural runoff and/or other nonpoint sources, such as the Garcia River.

[The court reviewed the history of the Act and concluded:]

The 1972 Act represented a major shift in enforcement policy—away from primary reliance on water-quality standards and toward primary reliance on specific effluent limits on all point sources, the latter being any discernible, confined and discrete conveyance such as a pipe or ditch. 33 U.S.C. § 1362(14). The Act established the National Pollution Discharge Elimination System ("NPDES") and required an NPDES permit for any discharge by any point source into any navigable water of the United States, interstate or intrastate. The new strategy sought to force the best technology practicable or achievable on dischargers. By 1977, industry was required to meet effluent limitations achievable through "best practicable control technology currently available." By 1983, it was to achieve control levels based on the "best available technology economically available." 33 U.S.C. § 1311. Instead of solely working backwards from the water-quality standards to develop acceptable levels of effluent from point sources, the new lead strategy was to require point sources to employ state-of-the-art treatment, even if it led, as a happy circumstance, to even cleaner water than called for by the standards. EPA was to issue NPDES permits except to the extent states adopted EPA-approved NPDES programs.

The Structure of the 1972 Act

Although the technology-based strategy of effluent limitations on all point sources (the NPDES permit program) was its capstone, the 1972 Act nonetheless carried forward the pre-existing regime of water-quality standards and even extended that regime to all navigable waters of the United States, interstate or intrastate. The Act explicitly recognized the separate problems of point versus nonpoint pollution and established different approaches to mitigate them. Point sources were subjected to NPDES regulation (under Sections 301–02 and 402). Nonpoint sources were left subject to state regulation. How TMDLs were supposed to fit into both branches of the solution is the problem presented by this case.

In analyzing this issue, it is important to bear in mind the comprehensive way in which *all* sources of pollution were addressed by the 1972 Act, albeit in different ways. It is important also to focus on the language actually adopted in 1972 (rather than in later amendments) because the issue here turns on the meaning of the 1972 language. The NPDES program has already been described. The following review of the structure of the 1972 Act focuses on those provisions arguably relevant to TMDLs and/or nonpoint-source pollution.

Under Section 102(a) of the 1972 Act, EPA was to cooperate with other state and federal agencies, municipalities and industry to "prepare or develop comprehensive programs for preventing, reducing or eliminating the pollution of the navigable waters," giving "due regard" to "the protection and propagation of fish and aquatic life and wildlife," among other purposes. [ ] Under Section 104(n) and (p), EPA was to promote "continuing comprehensive studies of the effects of pollution, including sedimentation in the estuaries and estuarine zones of the United States on fish and wildlife, on sport and commercial fishing * * *" [ ] and to "carry out a comprehensive study and research program to determine new and improved methods and the better application of existing methods of preventing, reducing, and eliminating pollution from agriculture * * *." [ ] In sum, while these provisions did not reference TMDLs, they called for "comprehensive" programs and studies, including protection of fish and wildlife.

Section 201 authorized grants for "waste treatment management" on an "areawide" basis to "provide control or treatment of all point and nonpoint sources of pollution * * *." § 201(c). In turn, Section 208 called for "areawide waste treatment management" planning by the states, expressly including plans for "nonpoint source" pollution. To that end, EPA was required to publish regulations guiding the identification of areas with "substantial water quality control problems." § 208(a)(1). The states were then to identify such areas. § 208(a)(2). Within one year thereof, responsible state organizations were called upon to "have in operation a continuing areawide waste treatment management planning process" with initial plans certified to EPA within two years. § 208(b)(1). Such plans were to include a number of components, the most germane of which was explicitly directed at "nonpoint source" pollution. Under Section 208(b)(2)(F), for example, the plans had to include:

a process to (i) identify, if appropriate, *agriculturally and silviculturally related nonpoint sources of pollution,* including runoff from manure disposal areas, and from land used for livestock and crop production,

and (ii) set forth procedures and methods (including land use requirements) to control to the extent feasible such sources [emphasis added];

. . .

Turning to Section 303, at the core of this controversy, its title was
"Water Quality Standards and Implementation Plans." Subsection (a)
required the states to adopt water-quality standards promptly, to the
extent not previously done, and to carry forward those already adopted
(subject to further EPA approval). Standards were to be set, as stated, for
both interstate and intrastate waters. Subsection (c) imposed periodic
updating of the standards and submission to EPA for review and approval.
Standards were to take into account the unique needs of each waterway,
including "propagation of fish and wildlife" as well as "agricultural * * *
and other purposes." 86 Stat. 848. Subsection (b) instructed EPA to impose
its own standards on any state failing to set standards. [ ] These standards,
the Supreme Court has said (once again), were meant by Congress to be
"comprehensive." *PUD No. 1 of Jefferson County v. Washington Dep't of
Ecology,* 511 U.S. 700, 704 (1994).

Significantly, in the process of setting standards, Section 303 did not
exempt any rivers or waters—all were covered to the full extent of federal
authority over navigable waters. Nor was any distinction drawn between
point sources and nonpoint sources. The goal was to set standards for all
navigable waterways in America, balanced and tailored to accommodate the
various needs of each, including, explicitly, the need for the protection of
fish and wildlife. The standards-setting process of Section 303 plainly
applied to waters polluted by point sources as well as nonpoint sources,
either alone or in combination. All parties agree on this conclusion.

It was onto this comprehensive standards regime that Congress imposed the requirement at issue, a requirement subdivided into a listing and
a TMDL. As to the first, Section 303(d)(1)(A) provided:

> Each state shall identify those waters within its boundaries for which
> the effluent limitations required by Section 301(b)(1)(A) and
> 301(b)(1)(B) are not stringent enough to implement any water quality
> standard applicable to such waters. The State shall establish a priority
> ranking for such waters, taking into account the severity of the
> pollution and the uses to be made of such waters.

Section 303(d) thus became an intersection between the old and new
strategies. It called for an assessment of the expected beneficial impact of
the main innovation of the Act—imposition of the best effluent reduction
technology could supply. If those reductions alone would bring a waterway
into compliance with standards, well and good. If not, then Section
303(d)(1) required the waterway to join a list of unfinished business. That
list, once completed, then had to be prioritized by the states. For each listed
river and water, Section 303(d)(1)(D) of the Act next required the states to
establish TMDLs:

> Each State shall establish for the waters identified in paragraph (1)(A)
> of this subsection, and in accordance with the priority ranking, the
> total daily maximum load, for those pollutants which the Administra-
> tor identifies under Section 304(a)(2) as suitable for such calculation.

Such load shall be established at a level necessary to implement the applicable water quality standards with seasonal variations and a margin of safety which takes into account any lack of knowledge concerning the relationship between effluent limitations and water quality.

TMDLs were thus required for all listed rivers and waters, at least as to pollutants identified by EPA as suitable for such calculation (and EPA long ago stated that "all" pollutants were suitable for such calculation). The controversy herein is whether the Garcia River should have been listed at all. Plaintiffs say no, it should not have been and, therefore, EPA should never have issued its TMDL. Before addressing this argument, it is instructive to complete the remainder of the structural review.

The next step—under Section 303(d)(2)—was for the State to submit the prioritized list and TMDLs for EPA review and for EPA to either approve or disapprove them. To repeat, EPA was statutorily required to approve or disapprove the lists and the TMDLs. . . .

As to nonlisted rivers and waters, Section 303(d)(3) imposed an "informational" TMDL requirement regarding fish and wildlife:

For the specific purpose of developing information, each State shall identify all waters within its boundaries which it has not identified under paragraph (1)(A) and (1)(B) of this subsection and estimate for such waters the total maximum daily load with seasonal variations and margins of safety, for those pollutants which the Administrator identifies under Section 304(a)(2) as suitable for such calculation and for thermal discharges, at a level that would assure protection and propagation of a balanced indigenous population of fish, shellfish and wildlife.

As stated, this provision applied only to nonlisted waters. The informational TMDLs were not subject to EPA review. EPA was not authorized to review or to issue the "informational" TMDLs. . . .

Section 303(e) imposed on the states "a continuing planning process" reviewable by EPA for consistency with the Act. EPA was to approve "any continuing planning process" that would result in "plans for *all* navigable waters within such state * * * which were to include, among other things, *total maximum daily loads for pollutants* in accordance with subsection (d)." (emphasis added). Subsection (d), in turn, covered both the TMDLs for listed waters and "informational" TMDLs. The plans also were required to include the "area-wide waste management plans" under Section 208. . . .

Section 304 was entitled "Information and Guidance." Section 304(a) generally called for EPA-set "criteria for water quality accurately reflecting the latest scientific knowledge" including impacts on fish and wildlife. EPA was to develop "information"

(A) on the factors necessary to restore and maintain the chemical, physical, and biological integrity of all navigable waters, ground waters, waters of the contiguous zone, and the oceans; (B) on the factors necessary for the protection and propagation of shellfish, fish, and wildlife for classes and categories of receiving waters and to allow recreational activities in and on the water; and (C) on the measurement and classification of water quality; and (D) *for the purposes of section 303, on and the identification of pollutants suitable for maximum daily load measurement correlated with the achievement of water quality objectives.*

§ 304(a)(2) (emphasis added). In requiring "identification of pollutants suitable" for the TMDL measurements of Section 303, no distinction was drawn between point and nonpoint sources in Section 304(a). That provision was comprehensive....

In summary, the 1972 Act addressed all sources of pollution, although each type in different ways. It sought comprehensively to protect and to restore all navigable waters in America....

Construction of Section 303(d)

The issue on which the parties divide is the extent to which nonpoint sources of pollution were to count in assembling the substandard-waters list required by Section 303(d) and in preparing the corresponding TMDLs. In their opening brief, plaintiffs contended that the listing and TMDL requirements of Section 303(d) were "exclusively reserved for point sources" [ ] and that "Section 303(d) focuses solely on point sources" [ ]. In their reply, plaintiffs stated: "A water body that is impaired by both point and nonpoint sources should be listed under both Section 303(d) and Section 319(a)(1)(A) and the point and nonpoint sources be addressed pursuant to those respective listings." A water polluted *only* by logging runoff or other nonpoint sources of pollution, like the Garcia River, plaintiffs argue, should not be listed and no TMDL should be prepared. Plaintiffs base their arguments on the fact that effluent limitations—which apply only to point sources—are referenced in the listing requirement of Section 303(d) whereas no reference is made to nonpoint sources:

> Each state shall identify those waters within its boundaries for which the effluent limitations required by Section 301(b)(1)(A) and 301(b)(1)(B) are not stringent enough to implement any water quality standard applicable to such waters. The State shall establish a priority ranking for such waters, taking into account the severity of the pollution and the uses to be made of such waters.

All versions of plaintiffs' arguments must be rejected....

First, the sole import of placing a river or water on a Section 303(d) list was that it would trigger the TMDL requirement. What use, then, did the statute contemplate for the TMDL? If the TMDL, for example, were to be used only to adjust NPDES effluent limitations for point sources, then plaintiffs' argument might have force. Such a narrower use, although a legitimate one, was not set forth in the statute as the sole use.... [T]he TMDLs had to be set at levels that would "implement" the applicable water-quality standards. It would have been impossible to do so without taking any nonpoint sources into account as well as any point sources....

Second, plaintiff's argument is inconsistent with the logic expressed in Section 303(d). Section 303 was entitled "Water Quality Standards And Implementation Plans." Water-quality standards were required for *all* navigable waters, intrastate or interstate. The first sentence of Section 303(d) required each state to "identify those waters within its boundaries" for which the new effluent limits would not be stringent enough to meet the standards. The starting point was, therefore, each and every substandard navigable water within the boundaries of the state. . . .

Third, while it is true that nonpoint-source pollution was not mentioned in Section 303(d), the reason seems obvious. The 1972 Act superimposed the technology-driven mandate of point-source effluent limitations. To assess the impact of the new strategy on the monumental clean-up task facing the nation, Congress called for a list of the unfinished business expected to remain even after application of the new cleanup strategy. In calling for such a list, it was unnecessary to reference nonpoint pollution. Any polluted waterway—whether its sources were point, nonpoint or a combination—had to be listed if it would not be cleansed by the new approach. To have excluded the large number of rivers and waters polluted solely by agricultural and logging runoff would have left a chasm in the otherwise "comprehensive" statutory scheme. . . .

. . .

The 1987 Amendment and Section 319

In 1987, Congress amended Section 319 to the Clean Water Act. It was specifically directed to nonpoint-source management programs. 33 U.S.C. § 1329; [ ]. This enactment, plaintiffs urge, would have been unnecessary and superfluous if Section 303(d) already comprehended nonpoint sources. In brief, Section 319(a)(1) required each governor to submit to EPA a report that identifies:

> Those navigable waters within the State which, without additional action to control nonpoint sources of pollution, cannot reasonably be expected to attain or maintain applicable water quality standards * * **

The report was to identify categories and subcategories of nonpoint sources, the state's process for identifying best management practices, the state's measures to control each such category and subcategory, and the state and local programs for controlling pollution from nonpoint sources. Section 319(b) also required each state to submit a "management program" for controlling nonpoint-source pollution, including an identification of the best management practices which will be undertaken to reduce "pollutant loadings" resulting from each category and subcategory. Plaintiffs are correct that the 1987 amendment covered some of the same general ground that EPA contends was already enacted. Nonetheless, plaintiffs' argument is rejected for three reasons:

First, while Section 319 addressed nonpoint pollution, it did not conflict with or duplicate the Listing/TMDL provisions at issue. The Section 303(d) list called for all unfinished business after application of technology-driven effluent limitations. Section 319, however, sought instead to list those rivers and waters which could not achieve standards "without additional action to control nonpoint sources of pollution." The two lists would partially overlap, to be sure, but were not the same. . . .

Second, while the 1987 enactment adopted newer and stronger measures to address the problem of nonpoint pollution, the 1972 enactment plainly spelled out—expressly so—medicine of its own. The phrase "nonpoint sources of pollution" was prominent in the 1972 Act (*see* §§ 201(c), 208(b)(2)(F), 304(e), 305(b)(1)(E)), as set forth above. It is inaccurate to argue, as do plaintiffs, that nonpoint-source pollution escaped attention under the 1972 Act.

Third, the Ninth Circuit has rejected a similar attempt to infer congressional intent for the 1972 Act from a later Clean Water Act amendment. . . .

Grants Versus Regulation

The word "regulate" pervades plaintiffs' argument. Congress did not, they say, authorize EPA to regulate state land-use practices. The Court agrees. EPA agrees. Unlike EPA's authority to revise individual NPDES permits issued by states for individual point sources, EPA received no authority to review land-use restrictions placed (or not placed) on timber-harvesting permits by CDF or any other practice permitted for agriculture or silviculture. The 1972 Act was clear that states should finally decide whether, and to what extent, land-management practices should be adopted to mitigate runoff. . . .

Under the Act, California must "incorporate" the TMDL in its planning. Nothing, however, requires that the TMDL be uncritically and mechanically passed through to every relevant parcel of land. California is free to select whatever, if any, land-management practices it feels will achieve the load reductions called for by the TMDL. California is also free to moderate or to modify the TMDL reductions, or even refuse to implement them, in light of countervailing state interests. Although such steps might provoke EPA to withhold federal environmental grant money, California is free to run the risk.

A practical reality, of course, is that once federal environmental grant money begins to flow, state regulatory agencies become dependent on it. They become sensitive to threats to terminate it—terminations that would entail job and programmatic cuts. This influences behavior. A state may knuckle under to coercive threats by EPA. A state may uncritically apply TMDL-loading reductions, like the ones at issue, without regard to other legitimate state interests or to the unique circumstances of an applicant. Even so, this is not direct federal regulation. The regulation is by California—though influenced by incentives established by Congress and the agency charged with protecting the environment. *Cf., North Carolina Dept. of Transportation v. Crest Street Community Council,* 479 U.S. 6, 8 (1986).

. . .

NOTES

(1) *Pronsolino* is noted in Debbie Schosteck, Note, Pronsolino v. Marcus, 28 ECOLOGY L.Q. 327 (2001).

(2) The challenge of controlling nonpoint-source pollution: As *Pronsolino* relates, Congress has tried repeatedly to push states to deal effectively with nonpoint sources—through § 208 planning processes, then with § 319, along with the longstanding requirement that they develop and seek to achieve water quality standards. Political realities are such that states lack the will to address the problem. The "polluter pays" principle, firmly established in all other areas of environmental law, has met stiff challenge.

It is hardly surprising that the same interests that resist nonpoint pollution controls also resist limits on the degradation or destruction of critical wildlife habitat, where the harm involved is even less clear than in the case of polluted runoff. In the early 1970s, Congress seriously considered the idea of federal land-use controls, but the political reaction against the idea was too strong. A perceptive survey of the problem is Robert W. Adler, *Controlling Nonpoint Source Water Pollution: Is Help on the Way (from the Courts or EPA)?*, 31 Envtl. L. Rptr. (Envtl. L. Inst.) 10270 (2001). *See also* Robin Kundis Craig, *Local or National? The Increasing Federalization on Nonpoint Source Pollution Regulation*, 15 J. ENVTL. L. & LITIG. 179 (2000). The particular challenges of dealing with agricultural pollution are taken up in John H. Davison, *Conservation Plans in Agriculture*, 31 Envtl. L. Rptr. (Envtl. L. Inst.) 10501 (2001); J.B. Ruhl, *The Environmental Law of Farms: 30 Years of Making a Mole Hill Out of a Mountain*, 31 Envtl. L. Rptr. (Envtl. L. Inst.) 10203 (2001). An earlier important study of the problem is Daniel R. Mandelker, *Controlling Nonpoint Source Water Pollution: Can It Be Done?*, 65 CHI.-KENT L. REV. 479 (1989). Suggestions for improving water-pollution control generally are set forth in Robert W. Adler, *Integrated Approaches to Water Pollution: Lessons from the Clean Air Act*, 23 HARV. ENVTL. L. REV. 203 (1999).

(3) TMDLs—the prognosis: Many conservation groups have focused energy on forcing states to prepare TMDLs for water-quality impaired stream segments. At least in some settings—as illustrated by *Pronsolino*—their efforts seem to be stimulating change. Note, however, that conservation plaintiffs cannot do more than get states (or, in their stead, the EPA) to make such calculations—which, of course, may or may not be accurate. Once the calculations are made, states still must take the lead in forcing polluters to change their ways. As the court notes, states can lose funding if they do not act, but the funding at issue is relatively modest—surely not enough to give most states adequate incentive to confront entrenched resistance. In addition, a decision to cut off funding is politically difficult for the federal government. A federal administration favorable to states and to extractive industries can remove any risk that states would lose funding, thus rendering the TMDL process of no greater effect than §§ 208 and 303. A detailed overview of the TMDL process—the beginning point for all research—is OLIVER A. HOUCK, THE CLEAN WATER ACT TMDL PROGRAM: LAW, POLICY, AND IMPLEMENTATION (1999). Recent commentary includes Sarah Birkeland, *EPA's TMDL Program*, 28 ECOLOGY L.Q. 297 (2001); Mary E. Christopher, Note, *Time to Bite the Bullet: A Look at State Implementation of Total Maximum Daily Loads (TMDLs) under Section 303(d) of the Clean Water Act*, 40 WASHBURN L.J. 480 (2001).

(4) Riparian vegetation: One setting in which states have commonly taken protective measures involves stream-side vegetation. Many states limit the ability of landowners to remove trees or to plow close to streambanks. Vegetation helps stabilize streambanks; can slow the entry of polluted runoff into waterways, and provides shade to keep summer water temperatures down. In waterways that support cold-water fisheries, water-quality standards include standards for maximum temperatures since heat added by human activities qualifies as a pollutant under the Clean Water Act. Such standards are among the most commonly violated. Violations of thermal standards can often be remedied only by major changes in surrounding land uses—not just maintaining and restoring riparian vegetation, but altering practices throughout the watershed to reduce the speed of run-off because rainwater that runs off land quickly is often warmer than water that percolates through soil. Measures to reduce run-off typically involve the retention of land cover that provides valuable wildlife habitat; thus, measures to protect cold-water fisheries often provide substantial benefits for terrestrial species as well.

(5) Other pollution statutes: Although the Clean Water Act provides the most potent tool for protecting wildlife, other federal pollution and toxics statutes are also important. The Safe Drinking Water Act, 42 U.S.C. §§ 300f to 300j–26, provides incentives for communities to protect drinking water supplies, including incentives to protect watersheds and aquifers. Steps taken to keep water supplies clean will often yield improvements in wildlife habitat. In the case of many water bodies (including the Great Lakes), the most damaging pollution arrives by air, including heavy metals and other dangerous elements and compounds. Acid rain caused by polluting activities can kill sensitive aquatic species in regions with thin soils that are low in buffering capabilities. In extreme cases, acid rain can render small lakes lifeless—with ripple effects that disrupt interdependent terrestrial life forms. Wildlife in such settings can be protected only by measures that halt the air pollution.

PERSPECTIVE

The Challenges of Watershed Management: Waterways have gained the attention of wildlife conservation interests in part because they provide a natural feature around which governance can take place. The area that drains into a particular river—its catchment basin, or more commonly today, its watershed—provides a logical, naturally-defined unit of land suitable for coordinated land-and water-management activities. The literature on the subject is vast. Much of it envisions a substantially greater role in land-use decisionmaking by people who live within the watershed— such management would be more a bottom-up process than a top-down approach. The challenges of such management are many, not the least, as Dan Tarlock has explained, is "the persistence of entitlements to use land and water without regard to the adverse environmental watershed impacts." A. Dan Tarlock, *Putting Rivers Back in the Landscape: A Revival of Watershed Management in the United States*, 6 HASTING W.-N.W.J. ENVTL. L. & POL'Y 167, 170 (2000). Many watersheds are inhabited by residents who embrace visions of land-and resource-ownership that are relics of an era when ecological degradation was ignored. Their cultural leanings can pose serious impediments to bottom-up processes. As J.B. Ruhl has noted, effective management typically requires an element of coercion from above. J.B. Ruhl, *The (Political) Science of Watershed Management in the Ecosystem Age*, 35 J. AM. WATER RESOURCES ASSN. 519 (1999). John Davison has urged that lessons be borrowed from the many special water districts—irrigation and drainage districts, for example—that have undertaken specialized tasks at the watershed level. John H. Davidson, *Commentary: Using Special Water Districts to Control Nonpoint Sources of Water Pollution*, 65 CHI.-KENT L. REV. 503 (1989).

One danger of watershed management is that it can be structured so as to give disproportionate influence to "stakeholders" who benefit economically from continued watershed degradation. That influence, together with processes that consume large amounts of time and resources (which tend to favor extractive industry groups), can undercut the ability of citizens concerned with conservation to play a meaningful role. A somber assessment of one such effort—centered on promoting protection for endangered species—is recounted in John D. Echeverria, *No Success Like Failure: The Platte River Collaborative Watershed Planning Process*, 25 WM. & MARY ENVTL. L. & POL'Y REV. 559 (2001). An even more-strongly worded critique, following similar lines attentive to allocations of power, is Rena I. Steinzor, *The Corruption of Civic Environmentalism*, 30 Envtl. L. Rptr. (Envtl. L. Inst.) 10909 (2000) ("Unless civic environmentalists grapple with the difficult problem of making their theories operational, they should be held responsible for the inevitable corruption of those ideals.")

Consider, finally, the following comments by Wendy Wagner:

> [W]atershed management and the associated requirements for clean waters have been misframed as technical issues, when in fact public discourse is required for significant progress to be made in restoring degraded waters. While experience suggests that the threat of rigorous federal standards is essential to improve water quality, experience also reveals that some of the greatest strides in environmental protection are made when these requirements form only the default rules for ensuring environmental quality, providing ample room for creative approaches that go above and beyond minimal federal guidelines. In the area of watershed-based water quality protection, however, the default requirements—the Total Maximum Daily Load (TMDL) program—impose a mandatory process that seems to have the effect of preempting more creative or public-spirited approaches to protecting water quality. The unrealistic technical demands imposed by the TMDL requirements not only consume agency resources that could be used to involve the public in enhancing water quality, but they may also alienate all but the most dedicated citizens and local communities from participating in water quality decisions. Yet without the support or involvement of the public, particularly at the state level where much of the regulatory authority rests, water protection programs are bound to drift aimlessly and ultimately fail.

Wendy E. Wagner, *Restoring Polluted Waters with Public Values*, 25 WM. & MARY ENVTL. L. & POL'Y REV. 429, 432 (2000).

SECTION 5.   THE CHALLENGES OF LANDSCAPE PLANNING

Biodiversity protection can succeed only if conservation work is undertaken at landscape levels. As we have seen, this necessarily includes landscapes that people occupy, use, and own. The challenges are many. Wildlife habitat and food sources require need protection. Disturbance regimes must be either restored or mimicked. Steps are needed to address the threats posed by exotics, both imports from distant places and the new exotics flowing from biotechnology laboratories. Basic ecosystem processes require protection and restoration, particularly soil-fertility cycles and hydrologic systems. And looming on the horizon are the threats posed by global climate change. Making such work harder is the fact that so many life forms are poorly equipped to live with humans, particularly the many K-selection species that evolved with low tolerances for habitat disruption.

In Chapter 12 we considered the prospects of ecosystem management as an organizing tool for biodiversity conservation. We also considered the fact that imperilled species are found disproportionately in biodiversity "hotspots"—places that, properly protected (with disturbance regimes intact), could provide home for many species now on the brink. Yet we ended our survey of biodiversity with two sobering reports—the story of the heath hen, which highlighted the dangers and practical problems that arise when a species reaches the brink, and David Wilcove's somber appraisal of our conservation record to date.

In this final section, we look briefly at tools available to promote wildlife at the landscape or ecosystem level. The initial excerpt, by two Australian authors, surveys the full range of such conservation tools, showing how property law and regulatory measures might fit together with voluntary measures, market-based tools, and public education. Attention then shifts to the legal context of regulatory measures, particularly the ways that law might promote more sensitive land-use practices without unfairly burdening private owners. For land planners, biodiversity protection presents a particularly knotty problem; in an excerpt below, a prominent planning scholar offers an appraisal of the challenge.

* * *

In the following excerpt, the authors set out what they view as the full range of tools available to protect and restore biodiversity in landscapes controlled by private owners. They place those tools in four categories: voluntary instruments, property-rights instruments, price-based instruments, and regulatory measures. Undergirding the four categories are mechanisms to inform citizens and motivate them to act. In the excerpt here, the authors assess the relative merits of these tools and comment on how they might best be used in concert.

Neil Gunningham & Michael D. Young, *Toward Optimal Environmental Policy: The Case of Biodiversity Conservation,*
24 ECOLOGY L.Q. 243 (1997).

A. *Motivational and Informational Mechanisms and Instruments*

Instruments falling within this general category are a part of almost all programs for the protection of biodiversity. It is useful to differentiate between: (a) motivational instruments that shift individual and community preference functions; and (b) mechanisms that inform people about relationships between resource management practice and the environment. In making this distinction, however, we observe that these two means of encouraging biodiversity conservation are frequently mixed with one another. We perceive that the personal preference functions of those who provide information about biodiversity typically are "greener" than those who receive and use the information; consequently, the processes used often involve conscious efforts to change individual biodiversity conservation attitudes and preferences.

1. Motivational Instruments

Motivational instruments include advertising and education campaigns, shaming, and the provision of awards to those who adopt best management practices. If people are positively motivated and persuaded that biodiversity conservation is worthwhile, then they are more likely to respond positively to the other types of instruments. For instance, those who understand and identify with the reasons for government regulation will similarly be more accepting of it. If school children, for example, can explain why mechanisms are needed to protect native vegetation, then their farming parents may be more likely to accept these regulations because of the pressure they exert on their parents to comply with emerging social norms. . . .

2. Informational Instruments

Informational instruments focus on information supply, including the dissemination of the results. There is considerable evidence to indicate that such instruments frequently repay substantial dividends in terms of improving management practice. Appropriately designed information programs may produce substantial benefits where informed resource users have a self interest in protecting biodiversity. If, for example, eutrophication of a lake is due to unnecessary over fertilization by farmers, merely bringing this to their attention may solve the problem. Thus, enlightened self interest may be sufficient to solve, or at least reduce, the problem. Provision of information can improve management of common property resources such as fisheries. . . .

Generally, informational instruments are considered to be equitable if the information is widely disseminated in a noninterventionist manner. Where such instruments provide information that harnesses self interest (as in the examples above), they prove financially attractive and self-enforcing, with continuing incentives for biodiversity conservation and sustainable use. Those who have been informed of the advantages of biodiversity conservation in certain contexts, such as ecotourism, will be more inclined to develop self-regulatory mechanisms that seek to maintain biodiversity values—agreements that restrict anchoring on coral reefs and restrict maneuvering to designated tracks, for example.

Motivational and educational instruments are sometimes combined. Victoria's Land for Wildlife Program rewards participants by publicizing the idea that participants are socially responsible citizens. The program also provides free advice to participants on ways to protect diversity.

We believe that motivational and informational instruments are so fundamental to a successful biodiversity conservation package that they should be invoked in almost all circumstances, and be incorporated in almost all policy mixes. They form a necessary foundation upon which all other instruments must rely if they are to achieve their optimal impact. . . .

We do not, however, suggest that this category of instruments is dependable. Nor do we suggest that they can be relied upon in isolation, particularly where there is a substantial tension between the public and private interests. . . .

B.   *Voluntary Instruments*

A variety of instruments and mechanisms can be classified under this heading but their main characteristic is that the principal resource manager has discretion in deciding whether or not to participate. They rely on voluntarism and self-regulation rather than coercion or continuing financial instruments. These mechanisms include self-regulation within an industry; support for projects undertaken by nongovernment organizations, community groups, or landholders (where the financial support is partial and there is heavy reliance on voluntary effort for successful completion); and personal land management agreements. Grants to facilitate specific projects also fall into this category. . . .

Voluntary assistance mechanisms may reinforce motivational instruments by encouraging positive community attitudes. Thus, motivational instruments are reinforced. The main problem of voluntary assistance mechanisms is that they can be difficult to target and monitor without incurring high administrative costs. For this reason, voluntarism is particularly appropriate in circumstances where there is a collective of people willing to protect biodiversity and areas of value, and where the self interest of individuals in obtaining a financial concession for themselves is therefore limited.

Voluntarism is noninterventionist, has high community acceptability, and raises minimal equity concerns. It also promotes an ethic of land custodianship. But in many cases, land owners will only voluntarily enter into an agreement or program when it is more profitable to do so than to follow market forces. Consequently, when the gap between the public and private interest is large, use of voluntary instruments becomes infeasible. In such circumstances, other instruments can be used to reduce the total cost of achieving biodiversity conservation.

. . .

Unfortunately, in most circumstances, there is a considerable gap between the public interest in biodiversity conservation and the private interests of individual land users.[79] Although many land users identify with

---

79. The basic problem derives from the fact that private landholders (or indeed other private users of resources) commonly lack any economic incentive to take account of the social costs of their actions. That is, we encounter a classic externalities problem where the direct benefits of biodiversity loss (for example, increased agricultural production

objectives of voluntary land protection schemes, their self interest in protecting biodiversity is not readily apparent in the short term. More commonly, there is a perceived tension between maximizing the use of productive land and protecting remnant vegetation. Despite providing long-term benefits (acting as a windbreak, reducing dryland salinity, etc.), the benefits of remnant vegetation are less tangible and less immediate than an increase in short-term productivity which remnant removal promises. For land users who are economically marginal, economic theory suggests that short-term production payoffs often outweigh longer-term conservation benefits.

History suggests that in these circumstances, unless backed by payments that make biodiversity conservation the most profitable strategy, voluntarism cannot be relied upon as an exclusive instrument to deliver biodiversity conservation.

Financial incentives are a powerful class of voluntary mechanism, but are not always necessary or wise. Once payments for biodiversity conservation become the norm, withdrawal of these payments threatens the loss of any realized conservation benefits unless measures, like a conservation covenant, are established to protect these benefits. Moreover, removal of the financial support may corrupt a carefully cultivated custodial ethic. Making clear that any payments are transitional reduces this risk. Transitional payments are characterized by statements that they will only be available for a period of time and that their purpose is to bring about a change in social expectations....

C.   *Property Rights and Price–Based Instruments*

In the case of biodiversity conservation, market failure is pervasive and results, inter alia, from externalities, the absence of markets for some aspects of biodiversity, and inadequately or incompletely defined property rights. Property right mechanisms have the potential to compensate for, or reverse, such market failure through mechanisms that make resource use opportunities consistent with social values. As with other instruments that modify prices directly, the aim "is to alter private costs and benefits so that any unaccounted social costs (and benefits) of environmental degradation can be 'internalized' to ensure the desired environmental improvement." Most property rights begin by defining what may be done and then restrict action through covenants and conditions. For example, easements and other legislative arrangements may grant rights to those other than landowners, a conservation covenant may prohibit clearing, or an individually transferable fishing right might confine fishing activity to a management plan.

A variety of techniques use a property rights approach. These are: exclusive use rights (of which bioprospecting contracts are a form); individually transferable property right mechanisms; covenants and easements; offset arrangements; and leasing and licensing. All property right instruments attempt to constrain legal entitlements so that there is a coincidence

from clearing land) go to individual property owners, whereas the costs (in terms of loss of species, ecosystems, genetic resources, and other potential uses) fall on society at large....

between social expectations and private self interest. For example, trade-able fishing quotas, identify the maximum quantity of fish that may be taken, and then use market mechanisms to prevent more than that quota from being taken.

The case for property rights instruments is usually presented in terms of the efficiency gains attainable within formal ecological targets. However, the strength of tradeable permits and licenses is that they offer a dependa-ble means to achieve a biodiversity target at minimum cost to individuals. As a mechanism, however, they are limited to resources that are relatively homogeneous. Hence, they are well suited to the control of threats associat-ed with water use, air pollution, fishing, and timber harvesting, but less so to issues involving irreversible losses like wetland drainage.

In contrast to property right instruments, which indirectly influence prices by changing the cost of certain activities and altogether preventing others, prices can be influenced directly via mechanisms such as charges, levies, use fees, and tax instruments. Conceptually, such price-based instru-ments could control most threats to biodiversity; but this is rarely done in practice. For pricing instruments to produce efficient solutions, it is neces-sary for transactions to be reversible in that any item consumed can be replaced. In the case of biodiversity, however, many habitats can never be recreated. Moreover, efficient markets need to be able to revise prices continuously through time and across space. In the case of biodiversity, a system must enable government institutions to constantly monitor and, when appropriate, change the prices they set.

Nevertheless, in selected circumstances, pricing mechanisms do have a significant role in revealing the cost of preventing and controlling adverse impacts on biodiversity. In particular, there is a strong case for removing perverse incentives that significantly raise the cost of biodiversity conserva-tion. At the global level, Panayotou has estimated that ninety cents in every dollar invested in biodiversity conservation is spent undoing the unintended effects of government subsidies, such as protecting people from competition, etc. There is also a strong case for charging people for the cost of gaining access to or adversely affecting biodiversity....

In theory, the virtues of property rights and price-based instruments lie in their ability to influence behavior through price signals without requiring direct intervention in the affairs of individuals. These instru-ments encourage individuals to seek out the most cost effective (and often innovative) solution to a problem....

It is less clear whether these mechanisms necessarily demonstrate these virtues in practice, due to a lack of empirical evidence. Since relative-ly few financial instruments have been implemented in the biodiversity policy area, and most of these only recently, we have very little knowledge of how they actually work....

Price-based and property right instruments have a particular advan-tage over command-and-control mechanisms that tend to be "targeted" on specific outcomes. As the OECD has pointed out:

[B]iodiversity is arguably different as an environmental and economic resource because the causes of species and ecosystem losses are extremely diffuse in nature and involve many difficult sectors. That is, it is pervasive to the economic system, being affected by land and water use decisions, by pollution and by economic activity generally.

As such, biodiversity conservation policies must themselves be pervasive; they must be capable of filtering through the entire economic system. All other things being equal, price-based approaches are less intrusive, more cooperative, and financially attractive. However, contrary to some claims, they are not self-enforcing and may involve considerable control costs. Indeed, one commentator recently concluded that "there is no reason to expect that the administrative costs of economic instruments are generally lower than those of regulatory instruments."[114] It must also be acknowledged that price-based and property right instruments are not generally well understood, and perhaps for this reason, do not rate highly in terms of community acceptance.

Price-based approaches may also be less appropriate than regulation in addressing two key characteristics of biodiversity. These characteristics are that biodiversity loss is often irreversible, and that ecosystems have limits and, if stressed beyond those limits, will collapse. . . .

D. *Regulatory Instruments*

In contrast to price-based instruments, regulation directly controls or restricts environmentally damaging activities by mandating the reduction or restriction of harmful activities. As such it is much more prescriptive than motivational, voluntary, and price-based instruments. The main regulatory instruments are well known and include zoning, land use restrictions, standards and bans, as well as some licenses and quotas.

Although regulation often lacks the flexibility and efficiencies associated with direct market-based approaches, it is perceived as being more certain (when adequate monitoring and enforcement exists). At a general level, regulation also provides an efficient means of discouraging the recalcitrant, the incompetent, or the intransigent, who may prove unresponsive to motivational, educational, voluntary, property right, and price-based instruments. Regulation in these circumstances may also be necessary to preserve the viability of other mechanisms. If all but one ecotourism operator are complying with a voluntary code of practice, then regulation to stop the recalcitrant offender might offer the most efficient way of protecting biodiversity at least administrative cost. . . .

[R]egulations have a particular role to play when biodiversity loss has proceeded so far that any further net loss is deemed unacceptable. In principle, regulation's strength is the greater certainty it provides, particularly where it takes the form of direct bans on destructive activity coupled with sanctions. In practice, the most common form of regulation has been to ban an activity while providing for exceptions (for example, for those who obtain a license). But past experience shows that the exemptions are

114. Kerry Turner & Hans Opschoor, *Environmental Economics and Environmental Policy Instruments: Introduction and Overview, in* ECONOMIC INCENTIVES AND ENVIRON- MENTAL POLICIES: PRINCIPLES AND PRACTICE 1, 22 (Hans Opschoor & Kerry Turner eds., 1994) (discussing the views of Lex De Savornin Lohman).

so routinely granted that the ban's conservation objectives often are undermined.

Even without the licensing exception, there will remain a temptation to cheat, particularly where breaches are not obvious. The strength of this temptation and the likelihood of people to succumb to it depends, in part, on the perceived legitimacy of the regulation (reinforcing the need for education and motivation) and, in part, on the likelihood of detection and the severity of any sanctions.

In spite of these constraints, regulation coupled with the moral force of law will, in some circumstances, provide greater assurance of compliance (certainty) than price-based instruments. . . .

As with other instruments, the effectiveness of regulation is likely to be context specific. For example, regulation reinforced by sanctions cannot serve to achieve biodiversity maintenance on privately managed semi-natural systems. As Bowers demonstrates, "where maintaining biodiversity requires people to perform actions that are not economic, sanctions will not in general work since primary operators (farmers or foresters who work the land) are likely to respond by abandoning management altogether."[131]

In contrast, when attempting to preserve a natural system by preventing use, a regulatory sanction is more effective than any other single instrument because it prevents certain types of land use change. Because land use change usually "cannot be brought about by doing nothing, the land-holder . . . cannot frustrate the intentions of the controlling authority by passive resistance,"[134] and defiance can be both identified and punished by law. Notably, however, some positive management will be necessary to protect biodiversity from feral animals and other threats, and management agreements can often achieve such protection in a way that regulation alone cannot.

. . .

F. *Mixing Voluntary, Property Right, Price-Based, and Regulatory Approaches*

In this Part, we explore the overall role of property right, price-based, and regulatory instruments in the broader policy mix, and the optimal relationship between these instruments. Before entering the details of this debate, it is important to recognize that the distinction between regulation on the one hand, and economic instruments on the other, is commonly overstated. In practice, there is no strict dichotomy between these two categories of instruments because economic instruments commonly rely on a substantial underpinning of government regulation for effective implementation. . . .

We begin with property rights. As indicated above, property right mechanisms encourage people to conserve biodiversity and limit its use to that which is sustainable. They do this by either constraining or expanding

---

131. John Bowers, Incentives and Mechanisms for Biodiversity: Observations and Issues 13 (Apr. 1994) (working document, on file with authors).

134. *Id.* at 14.

the opportunities available to resource users. Where markets for these rights can be created, change can often be achieved with less cost to society and with greater equity than is achievable under other mechanisms. . . .

There are also strong arguments favoring the use of price-based instruments. Mechanisms such as user charges and levies can change the economic signals given to those whose actions threaten biodiversity values. Furthermore, they embody the user-pays and polluter-pays principles. But should property right and price-based instruments be combined solely with voluntary and/or motivational instruments, or do they also require underpinning by regulation?

This last question is central, because price-based instruments have considerable virtues yet lack dependability. For example, a key characteristic of some price-based approaches is that a price is set and the market then decides how much biodiversity conservation to deliver. This encourages people to find efficient ways to profit from this trade-off and seek ways to do more or less damage depending upon the instrument's operation. However, setting prices at the optimal level to influence behavior is a "hit and miss" approach, with the result that if the price is set too low (which may only be apparent with hindsight) it will not have the anticipated effect on behavior.

Another problem with relying on prices rather than regulatory compulsion is that prices are not well suited to dealing with the wide range of responses people make to the same price signal. It may be that only those "at the margin" respond in the preferred direction. But for a variety of reasons, ranging from incompetence or ignorance to intransigence, there is likely to be a minority who, in the absence of more directive or even coercive policies, will continue to behave in a manner which threatens biodiversity conservation.[145] While probably relatively small, this minority cannot be ignored. If left unchecked, it will have a substantial impact on biodiversity, not just directly through its own behavior, but also through its impact in demotivating other target group members—particularly with respect to voluntary mechanisms. For example, there is evidence that land users and others who contribute to voluntary programs such as the Australian Landcare program may become dispirited if others are free to continue to degrade adjoining land. In many circumstances, the creation of a level playing field may be an essential prerequisite to the success of the sort of positive, less interventionist approach that we envisage for the large majority of circumstances.

In contrast, regulatory approaches mitigate both the uncertainty and irrationality problems. They decide how much conservation is required and then let the market reveal the action's economic consequences. The regulatory approach is often preferred over pricing policies because changes in physical processes and quantities, not prices, affect ecosystems most directly. Arguably, there is more dependability when ecological constraints are

---

145. The existence of such a minority has been acknowledged by a wide diversity of   stakeholders in Australia. [ ]

set and then price, demand and technological forces are allowed to work themselves out.

Voluntary management agreements, property right mechanisms, and regulations all do this. Voluntary management agreements can have the disadvantage, however, of creating an atmosphere where people are only prepared to conserve biodiversity when paid and implying that people are entitled to destroy biodiversity irrespective of social expectations. Moreover, because such agreements may create the impression that people have a right to destroy biodiversity, voluntary approaches can be expensive. . . .

In summary, where persuasion and education fail, where enterprises are unwilling to improve their environmental performances voluntarily, and where economic instruments or voluntarism lack dependability, then regulation may be the only technique capable of exerting pressure and compelling resource users and others to protect biodiversity. . . .

. . .

To summarize the discussion, we have moved through a series of arguments that began by pointing out the need for instrument mixes. We pointed out how the strengths of each instrument can be harnessed to build a framework that is as dependable as possible in terms of preventing irreversible losses yet trades off criteria like efficiency, equity, precaution, dynamism, administrative costs, and community acceptability. We have argued first for dependability, which implies the need for precautionary regulations and precautionary standards underpinned by a firm regulatory safety net that prohibits irreversible actions. However, we have also emphasized the importance of mechanisms that build community support.

Finally, we have emphasized the importance of using property rights and price-based and regulatory instruments in a complementary manner. In particular, the mere fact that a government makes clear its willingness to resort to regulation if other mechanisms fail, means that the latter are likely to work more effectively since resource users' decisions concerning the utilization of voluntary and property right instruments will be colored by their aversion to regulation. Thus, the threat of regulation is likely to render positive instruments more attractive to industry, and thus more effective.

. . .

Conclusion

The challenge for regulatory strategy in the late 1990s is to move beyond the market-government dichotomy to devise better ways of achieving environmental protection at an acceptable economic and social cost. . . .

In the case of biodiversity protection, we have argued that a variety of mechanisms exist that have only been used in a limited fashion but hold the potential to make a substantial contribution. In broad terms, these can be categorized as motivational, voluntary, property-based, price-based, and regulatory instruments.

In most circumstances, the multiple objectives of biodiversity conservation will be achieved most effectively through a mix of these instruments, targeted to the suite of threats extant at any location. An optimal strategy will harness the strengths of individual mechanisms while compensating for their weaknesses by using additional and complementary policy instruments....

NOTES

(1) Price-based mechanisms: Under price-based mechanisms, the authors lump together a wide variety of economic incentives. Although one such tool is the payment of money to landowners who use their lands consistently with biodiversity objectives, the authors see dangers in such payments other than to deal with transitional times when new land-use norms are taking effect. Aside from the sheer cost, payments undercut efforts to establish good land use as a requirement of citizenship, as well as efforts to convince the public that land degradation is a public harm. They also undercut voluntary conservation efforts by rewarding those who fail to do their part. The authors advocate instead that jurisdictions embrace the polluter-pays and user-pays principle, so that those who adversely affect biodiversity bear the costs of their behavior while those who peculiarly benefit from conservation (those who visit game preserves, for example) pay for the special benefits. One way to implement this idea is for those who harm valuable habitat to pay "biodiversity impact fees," tailored along the lines of other impact fees that local jurisdictions have charged for development that adversely affects urban infrastructures.

(2) Property-rights approaches and conservation easements: The various tools that the authors gather together under the "property rights" label also vary widely. The category would include, for example, steps to redefine habitat degradation as a land-use harm, akin to a private or public nuisance. Such a move would deny landowners the right to engage in degrading land uses—they would impose on owners the "ecological constraints" that the authors view as important.

Also included in the property rights category are arrangements whereby landowners restrict their land-use options by granting conservation easements to private or public conservation entities. At common law, only a few types of "negative easements"—easements that restricted how the owner could use property—were legally permitted. The list has been expanded by statutes which expressly authorize conservation easements. Because easements can be drafted in wide variety of ways, they are highly flexible tools in protecting wildlife while still allowing owners of burdened or servient estates to use their lands in ways not harmful to wildlife. In some settings, easements impose affirmative duties on landowners to manage lands to sustain desirable landscape features or processes. One useful survey is Melissa Waller Baldwin, *Conservation Easements: A Viable Tool for Land Preservation* 32 LAND & WATER L. REV. 89 (1997). The various settings in which the federal government obtains conservation easements are considered in Edward J. Heisel, Comment, *Biodiversity and Federal Land Ownership: Mapping a Strategy for the Future*, 25 ECOL. L.Q. 229, 292–300 (1998).

Useful as conservation easements are, the tool is not without its limitations and challenges. Owners of burdened estates may over time chafe at the restrictions imposed, particularly when the land passes into the hands of owners less supportive of conservation. Although easements are nominally permanent (unless otherwise created), some courts have shown a willingness to refuse to enforce limitations under significantly changed circumstances. Like other land-use restrictions, easements require monitoring and enforcement, which can pose additional problems, for public as well as private conservation entities. These problems and others are considered in Federico Cheever, *Public Good and Private Magic in the Law of Land Trusts and Conservation Easements: A Happy Present and a Troubled Future,* 73 DENV. U.L. REV. 1077 (1996). A useful overview of many easement-related problems and how they might be solved is James Boyd, Kathryn Caballero & R. David Simpson, *The Law and Economics of Habitat Conservation: Lessons from an Analysis of Easement Acquisitions,* 19 STAN. ENVTL. L.J. 209 (2000). The possible benefits of such transactions in aiding endangered species are explored in Federico Cheever, *Property Rights and the Maintenance of Wildlife Habitat: The Case for Conservation Land Transactions,* ___ Idaho L. Rev. ___ (2002).

The authors of the excerpt worry about the side effects of cash incentive payments to landowners unless such payments are clearly transitional. But are there not similar reasons to worry about easement-acquisition programs? Do they not also signal to landowners that conservation is optional and that they deserve payment when they undertake it? Consider: Is it fair for one landowner to receive compensation for a conservation easement when a neighbor is conserving ecologically similar land without compensation? What if one landowner sells a conservation easement, and then a government unit similarly restricts adjacent land by means of uncompensated regulation? Should payment for easements be limited to settings in which landowners clearly go beyond the conservation norm established for similarly situated landowners?

A special California easement acquisition program aimed at forest protection is considered in Stacy E. Gillespie, *The California Forest Legacy Program Act of 2000: A Long–Term Conservation Easement Program for Private Land,* 32 McGEORGE L. REV. 632 (2001).

(3) Regulatory approaches: As Gunningham and Young assess matters, regulatory measures are useful, not just in containing bad land uses, but in establishing norms for acceptable and unacceptable landowner conduct. Properly designed regulatory measures, they argue, can build upon and accentuate educational measures. Regulation can also level the playing field so that those who conserve do not feel that their efforts are being undercut by those who do not.

But note the limits on regulatory measures that the authors identify—limits that observers have commented upon since the days of Aldo Leopold: Regulation works best when compliance is easily monitored. When compliance is hard to determine, violations are far more likely. Moreover, it is most effective when it compels landowners to refrain from engaging in undesirable actions; regulations are less able to motivate landowners to manage their lands affirmatively in ways beneficial to wildlife—such as

mimicking disturbance regimes and affirmatively promoting habitat restoration and maintenance. They are ill-suited, also, to address the challenges
posed by exotics.

Although the authors distinguish between property-based and regulatory approaches, how different are they? Both entail imposing by law
"ecological constraints" on how owners can use their lands. At one time,
courts kept property law up to date by altering the common law of property
ownership. More recently, courts have deferred more to other lawmaking
bodies to fulfill this function. Today, statutes and regulations are just as
important as the common law in defining what it means to own.

(4) Mutual coercion and covenants: New residential developments
commonly involve land-use restrictions imposed by the developer/owner
during the development process; they are often termed real covenants
(enforceable generally), equitable servitudes (enforceable only in equity), or
simply servitudes. Some restrictions are fixed and inflexible. Many restrictions, however, envision the creation of a homeowners' association that
possesses power to alter restrictive terms and to levy fees to implement and
enforce them. "Private governance" measures of this type have been an
important part of the land-planning scene for nearly a century; the story of
their rise is told in Gerald Korngold, *The Emergence of Private Land Use
Controls in Large–Scale Subdivisions: The Companion Story to* Village of
Euclid v. Ambler Realty Co., 51 CASE-WESTERN L. REV. 617 (2001). Although
land-use restrictions are most commonly imposed during a development
process when a large tract of land is divided for sale, they can be imposed
thereafter if all affected landowners agree to them.

Like the conservation easement, the land-use covenant can be a useful
wildlife conservation tool when used to limit land-uses in ways that aid
wildlife. Unlike the typical easement, in which the beneficiary is a private
land trust or a government entity, the beneficiaries of covenants generally
are other landowners who are also bound by them; that is, landowners who
share a landscape are both burdened and benefited by the restrictions.
Could landowners within a given landscape band together to impose
restraints on one another for the common good—along the lines of the
"mutual coercion mutually agreed upon" that Garrett Hardin proposed?
Could such a method be used to address the tragedy of fragmentation? One
severe limitation on this approach is the rule that a landowner cannot be
bound against his or her will, despite the desires of surrounding landowners. Thus, an entire landscape can be protected only if the landowners in it
unanimously agree to the protections. Is the requirement of unanimity
necessary as a policy matter? Should not a supermajority of landowners,
acting to protect their shared interests, be able to constrain the recalcitrant
minority that would otherwise undercut the common good? For instance,
might a supermajority of landowners adjacent to a nonnavigable lake be
granted the power to set rules governing lake use (*e.g,* to protect waterfowl
habitat) that would bind all landowners? Could such a tool similarly help a
supermajority of landowners desirous of jointly managing their shared
landscape to restore disrupted disturbance regimes? *See* Robert C. Ellick-
son, *New Institutions for Old Neighborhoods*, 48 DUKE L.J. 75 (1998)
(urging a relaxation of the unanimity rule so that a supermajority could

impose land-use restrictions and levy fees for landscape maintenance). One precedent for such a legal shift are pooling and unitization laws applicable to oil and gas, under which a supermajority of landowners can obtain the power to manage jointly a fragmented oil field despite the objections of individual landowners.

(5) Selecting the right tools: In light of the comments in the excerpt, what conservation tool or tools might serve best to deal with the following problems:

(a) Airborne contaminants depositing heavy metals in a lake.

(b) Excessive drainage causes flooding and drought in a waterway.

(c) The spread of an exotic woodland plant (*e.g,* garlic mustard) that displaces native plants.

(d) Genetically engineered farm crops that pose threats to the genetic integrity of native plants.

Gardner v. New Jersey Pinelands Commission

New Jersey Supreme Court.
593 A.2d 251 (1991).

■ HANDLER, J.—The central issue in this case is whether the application of state regulations that limit the use of land in an environmentally-sensitive area constitutes an unconstitutional taking of private property. The regulations strictly limit residential development on such land and require that all remaining undeveloped acreage be subject to a recorded deed restriction limiting it to agriculture and related uses. A farmer contends that the application of this regulatory scheme to his farm effects a partial taking of his property without compensation.

Hobart Gardner lived and worked for almost seventy years on a 217–acre farm that had been owned by his family since 1902. The farm is located in Shamong Township, Burlington County, a part of the pinelands region subject to the regulations. Gardner, now deceased, and his son, who lives on the farm today, cultivated sod and grain. The farm includes a two-family house, barns, and out-buildings.

When confronted with the regulations, Gardner sought compensation, claiming that the land-use restrictions resulted in an unlawful taking of his property. After the State refused payment, Gardner, on February 7, 1988, initiated this action for inverse condemnation against the Commissioner of the Department of Environmental Protection and the New Jersey Pinelands Commission (Commission), which had promulgated the regulations. Gardner also contended that the regulations constituted an unlawful exaction and a denial of equal protection....

I

The value of the unique ecological, economic, and cultural features of the New Jersey Pine Barrens, or Pinelands, has been recognized for decades. [ ] Protection of the area, however, did not begin in earnest until Congress enacted the National Parks and Recreation Act of 1978, [ ] (codified at 16 U.S.C. § 471i), establishing over one-million acres as the Pinelands National Reserve. The Pinelands were the first natural resource to be protected by the innovative "national reserve" program. Designed to conserve areas of ecological sensitivity, natural beauty, and cultural importance, the national reserve concept combines limited public acquisition of property with land-use controls in a cooperative framework involving federal, state, and local governments, as well as concerned private groups and persons. . . .

Congress chose the Pinelands as the first protected site with good reason. New Jersey is the most densely populated state in the nation and lies at the midpoint of the emerging megalopolis that extends from Boston to Richmond. *Statistical Abstracts of the United States, 1990* at 21; JOHN MCPHEE, THE PINE BARRENS 4–5 (1981). The central corridor of the state between New York and Philadelphia has been described as "one great compression of industrial shapes, industrial sounds, industrial air, and thousands and thousands of houses webbing over the spaces between the factories." JOHN MCPHEE, *supra,* at 4. Astride that corridor in central and southern New Jersey is the Pinelands.

The pristine nature of the Pinelands sharply contrasts with its contiguous, dense urban and industrial surroundings. A "wilderness" of pine-oak forests and wild and scenic rivers, the Pinelands harbors a "wide variety of rare, threatened and endangered plant and animal species," and encompasses "many other significant and unique ecological, historical, recreational, and other resources." *Senate Committee Statement, supra;* JOHN MCPHEE, *supra,* at 4–5. The region overlies the vast, seventeen-trillion gallon Cohansey aquifer, "one of the largest virtually untapped sources of pure water in the world." *Senate Committee Statement, supra; see* JOHN MCPHEE, *supra,* at 13–16. There has been very little development within the Pinelands; there are no major retail centers, and developed property comprises only one to two percent of the land in most areas. New Jersey Pinelands Commission, *New Jersey Pinelands: Comprehensive Management Plan* 128–29 (1980) (*Comprehensive Management Plan*). Agriculture in the Pinelands, especially the cultivation of cranberries and blueberries, is particularly important both nationally and locally. New Jersey Department of Agriculture, *Annual Report—Ag Statistics* 38, 72–73 (1990).

In recent years, anxiety over the loss of farming and the fragile ecology of the Pinelands has produced increasingly stringent federal and state regulation. Both the federal and the implementing state legislation make clear that conservation, preservation, and protection are the principal ends of governmental regulation of land use in the Pinelands. The federal statute states its purpose is "to protect, preserve and enhance the significant values of the land and water resources of the Pinelands area." 16 U.S.C. § 471i(b)(1). Similarly, the New Jersey Pinelands Protection Act (Act), [ ], declares that its goals are, among others, to protect, preserve, continue, and expand agriculture and horticulture and to discourage piecemeal and scattered development within the Pinelands. [ ] The Act stresses preservation of the region:

> [T]he continued viability of [the Pinelands] area and resources is
> threatened by pressures for residential, commercial and industrial

development * * * [T]he protection of such area and resources is in the interests of the people of this State and of the Nation * * *.

. . .

The Legislature further finds and declares that the current pace of random and uncoordinated development and construction in the pinelands area poses an immediate threat to the resources thereof, especially to the survival of rare, threatened, and endangered plant and animal species and the habitat thereof, and to the maintenance of the existing high quality of surface and ground waters; that such development and construction increase the risk and extent of destruction of life and property which could be caused by the natural cycle of forest fires in this unique area * * *.

N.J.S.A. 13:18A–2.

The Act authorizes the designation of "protection areas" for promotion of agriculture, horticulture, and "appropriate patterns of compatible residential, commercial and industrial development in or adjacent to areas already utilized for such purposes." N.J.S.A. 13:18A–9b. It also calls for the establishment of an extensive "preservation area" to protect especially sensitive land in its natural state and to promote compatible agricultural, horticultural, and recreational uses. N.J.S.A. 13:18A–9c.

In keeping with the paramount objective of both federal and state governments, *i.e.,* protecting the Pinelands from overdevelopment and consequent ecological degradation, the plan for the Pinelands National Reserve calls for the full participation of federal, state, county, and municipal authorities. 16 U.S.C. § 471i(b), (d), (f)(4), (g), (h). To ensure that pressures for development do not overwhelm the need for preservation, actions of the lower levels of government that do not conform to that objective can be pre-empted by a higher authority.

The federal statute directs the Governor of New Jersey to create a planning commission. 16 U.S.C. § 471i(d). The New Jersey Pinelands Commission (the "Commission") is the instrumentality envisaged by federal and state law as having primary responsibility for planning in the Pinelands. N.J.S.A. 13:18A–4. Its charge is to develop a "comprehensive management plan" (CMP) to serve as the land-use blueprint for the region, subject to the approval of the federal Secretary of the Interior. 16 U.S.C. § 471i(d), (f), and (g); N.J.S.A. 13:18A–4,–5,–8,–9. To assist the State's efforts, the federal government provides funds for planning and land acquisition, which are subject to repayment if the State does not properly implement a preservation program. 16 U.S.C. § 471i(g)(5), (g)(6), (k).

A similar system of incentives to cooperate, reinforced by the power to pre-empt, characterizes the relations between the State and local governments under the Act. Initially, the Commission assumed all power to exercise traditional zoning functions within the Pinelands, promulgating minimum land-use standards under the CMP. N.J.S.A. 13:18A–8,–10. Thereafter, counties and municipalities were required to conform their master plans and zoning ordinances to the CMP and to have such plans and ordinances approved by the Commission. N.J.S.A. 13:18A–12(a), (b). If a county or municipality fails to conform to the CMP, the Commission will continue to exercise direct control over local land use. N.J.S.A. 13:18–12(c).

In developing the CMP, the Commission has been directed to "[r]ecognize existing economic activities within the area and provide for protection and enhancement of such activities as farming, forestry, proprietary recreational facilities, and those indigenous industries and commercial and residential developments which are consistent with such purposes and provisions." N.J.S.A. 13:18A–8(d)(3). To those ends, the Commission has been given broad authority to invoke

> a variety of land and water protection and management techniques, including but not limited to, zoning and regulation derived from State and local police powers, development and use standards, permit systems, acquisition of conservation easements and other interest [sic] in land, * * * transfer of development rights, dedication of private lands for recreation or conservation purposes and any other appropriate method of land and water protection and management which will help meet the goals and carry out the policies of the management plan.

N.J.S.A. 13:18A–8(d)(1).

Reflecting the aims of the federal and state statutes, the goals of the CMP include the "continuation and expansion of agricultural and horticultural uses." N.J.S.A. 13:18A–9(b)(3). The original CMP, adopted by the Commission in November 1980, stressed that agriculture contributes both to the unique characteristics of the Pinelands and to the environment "by creating open space, terrestrial and aquatic habitats, and wildlife feeding areas." *Comprehensive Management Plan, supra*, at 242. It also stated that suburban development contributes to "an unfavorable economic environment for farmers through escalating taxes, enactment of inhibiting local ordinances, and increased trespassing and vandalism." *Id.* Consequently, the original CMP called for several programs to accomplish the objective of agricultural preservation. It identified eight "Pinelands Management Areas" of varying ecological sensitivity, including a Preservation Area District, Forest Areas, Agricultural Production Areas, and Regional Growth Areas. N.J.A.C. 7:50–5.12(a).

The original CMP restricted residential development in Agricultural Production Areas, reserving them primarily for farm and farm-related purposes. Section 5–304 of the plan allowed residential units on lots with 3.2 acres as long as the applicant met certain stringent conditions. The original CMP also permitted ten-acre residential zoning, that is, one residential unit per ten acres, "provided that the dwelling unit is accessory to an active agricultural operation, and is intended for the use of the owners or employees of the agricultural operation."

The Commission further created a development-rights transfer program, under which it would award Pinelands Development Credits (PDCs) to landowners for recording permanent deed restrictions on their property limiting the land to specific uses set forth in the CMP. *See Comprehensive Management Plan, supra*, at 210–12 and sections 5–401 to–407; N.J.A.C. 7:50–5.41 to—5.47 (current version). The PDC program seeks to channel development by permitting holders of PDCs to transfer them to owners who wish to increase densities in specially-designated Regional Growth Areas. N.J.S.A. 13:18A-31; N.J.A.C. 7:50–5.41,–5.45. PDCs may be sold privately at market prices; according to the Assistant Director for Development Review at the Commission, Burlington County has a PDC bank that routinely pays $10,000 per credit. A landowner in an Uplands Agricultural Production Area—the designation that apparently includes the Gardner farm—receives two PDCs per thirty-nine acres. N.J.A.C. 7:50–5.43(b)(2)(i).

In the fall of 1987, Gardner explored the possibility of subdividing his property into fourteen to seventeen ten-acre "farmettes" in accordance with the CMP option allowing one farm-related residential unit per ten acres of land. Before the application was submitted, the Commission completed a periodic revision and amendment of the CMP, as required by the Act. N.J.S.A. 13:18A-8. The Commission determined, according to an affidavit submitted by its Assistant Director for Development Review, that the ten-acre farm option had deteriorated into a ten-acre subdivision requirement with no guarantee that the land actually would be used for farming, and had led in some situations "to the cessation of agricultural operations," "effectively eliminating existing agricultural uses, and threatening significant agricultural use of adjoining areas."

The revised CMP permits only three options for residential development of farmland in Agricultural Production Areas: (1) second-generation Pinelands residents or persons whose livelihood depends on traditional Pinelands economic activities may build homes on 3.2–acre lots, N.J.A.C. 7:50–5.24(a)(1),—5.32; (2) a home may be constructed on a ten-acre lot for an operator or employee of the farm, but that option may be exercised only once every five years, N.J.A.C. 7:50–5.24(a)(2); or (3) homes may be constructed at a density of one unit per forty acres, but only if the residences are clustered on one-acre lots and the remaining thirty-nine acres allocated to each residence are permanently dedicated to agricultural use by a recorded deed restriction, N.J.A.C. 7:50–5.24(a)(3),–5.24(c). The restriction of residential development to forty-acre tracts prompted the filing of Gardner's complaint.

II

Land use regulations span a wide spectrum, from conventional zoning, *e.g., Village of Euclid v. Ambler Realty,* 272 U.S. 365 (1926); *Cobble Close Farm v. Board of Adjustment,* 92 A.2d 4 (N.J.1952), to particularized restrictions on property with special characteristics, *e.g., Penn Cent. Transp. Co. v. City of New York,* 438 U.S. 104 (1978) (*Penn Central*). The Pinelands Protection Act virtually fills the entire spectrum. It imposes comprehensive and complex regulatory land-use controls over an extensive geographic region with distinctive natural, economic, cultural, and historic characteristics.

Because the Pinelands scheme is fundamentally a regime of zoning, takings doctrine dealing with zoning is particularly relevant. In its most general formulation, takings analysis makes two fundamental demands of any zoning scheme: it must substantially advance legitimate state interests, and it cannot deny an owner all economically viable use of the land....

A

There is not the slightest quarrel that the Act substantially advances several interrelated legitimate and important public purposes. We need refer only to the Legislature's declaration of the Act's objective: to protect the Pinelands, an area providing "a unique habitat for a wide variety of rare, threatened and endangered plant and animal species" and containing "significant and unique * * * resources." Protection of the Pinelands "is in the interests of the people of this State and of the Nation." N.J.S.A. 13:18A–2....

The preservation of agriculture and farmland constitutes a valid governmental goal. N.J. Const. art. VIII, § 1, para. 1(b) (lands used for agriculture or horticulture entitled to favorable tax treatment);....

The Act further advances a valid public purpose by preventing or reducing harm to the public. That is exemplified most dramatically by its measures to safeguard the environment and protect the water supply by severely limiting development....

That land itself is a diminishing resource cannot be overemphasized. *See Holmdel Builders v. Township of Holmdel,* 583 A.2d 277 (N.J.1990). Environmentally-sensitive land is all the more precious. Hence, a proposed development that may constitute only a small insult to the environment does not lessen the need to avoid such an offense. The cumulative detrimental impact of many small projects can be devastating....

We are satisfied that the Act and the regulations implementing it substantially advance legitimate and important governmental objectives.

B

The critical remaining question is whether the regulations impair to an impermissible degree valuable property rights and interests....

Plaintiff acknowledges that preserving agriculture is a legitimate governmental objective that can be achieved through land-use regulation. He contends, nonetheless, that the land-use regulations, including the required deed restrictions of the revised CMP, interfere to an intolerable degree with his right and freedom to use and enjoy his farmland property. The response to that contention is found in *Penn Central,* 438 U.S. 104, which amplified the takings principles applicable to specialized regulations seeking to preserve the status of distinctive property.

In *Penn Central,* New York City had enacted a landmarks preservation ordinance, requiring approval from the Landmarks Preservation Commission for exterior alterations. *Id.* at 109–12. Owners of affected buildings could transfer development rights from a landmark parcel to proximate lots. *Id.* at 113–14. Penn Central sued when that Commission refused to approve construction of a multi-story building atop Grand Central Terminal, a designated landmark. *Id.* at 116–19. It contended that New York had "taken" its air space and that the law had both significantly diminished the value of the site as a whole and unfairly singled out people who owned landmark properties to bear the public burden. *Id.* at 130–35. The Supreme Court rejected those arguments. It explained that takings jurisprudence focused on the nature and extent of interference with rights in the whole parcel, not discrete segments; that when laws are reasonably related to the general welfare even severe diminution in value will not effect a taking if viable uses remain; and that, far from being discriminatory, the law embodied a comprehensive plan to preserve structures of historic and aesthetic interest throughout the city. *Id.* at 129–35. Moreover, Penn Central could continue to use the parcel in a gainful fashion and could offset its loss by transferring valuable development rights to other parcels, even though such transfers did not fully compensate it. *Id.* at 137.

Plaintiff's claim fails under the *Penn Central* analysis. The CMP does not change or prohibit an existing use of the land when applied to plaintiff's farm. *See id.* at 129. Like Penn Central, plaintiff may continue the existing, admittedly beneficial use of the property. Further, although whether Penn Central could again make use of all of its property, particularly the airspace over its terminal, was unclear, plaintiff may gainfully use all of his property, including the right to build five homes clustered together on the restricted land. There also is no showing that the economic impact of the regulations interferes with distinct investment-backed expectations. In addition, Penn Central could offset its loss by transferring valuable property rights to other properties, even if such transfers did not fully compensate it. Plaintiff possesses the similar right to offsetting benefits; it may receive Pinelands Development Credits in return for recording the deed restrictions. Finally, there is no invidious or arbitrary unfairness in the application of the regulatory scheme. Gardner's neighbors in Uplands Agricultural Areas are burdened by exactly the same restrictions, and other landowners in the Pinelands must abide by comparable regulations as part of an integrated comprehensive plan designed to benefit both the region and the public.

III

Plaintiff contends that the regulations constitute a form of illegal "exaction," in effect requiring Pinelands farmers to pay the costs of zoning benefits for the public at large. He relies on a line of cases addressing the imposition of subdivision exactions, particularly *Longridge Builders v. Planning Board,* 245 A.2d 336 (N.J.1968). That case held that a municipality could not require, as a condition of subdivision approval, a developer to pave a dedicated off-site right-of-way from the proposed subdivision to an existing road. The Court explained that a developer "could be compelled to bear [only] that portion of the cost bearing a rational nexus to, and benefits conferred upon, the subdivision. It would be impermissible to saddle the developer with the full cost where other property owners receive a special benefit from the improvement." *Id.*; *see also Holmdel Builders Ass'n,* 583 A.2d 277 (traditionally strong, causal nexus between off-site public facilities and private development required to justify exactions).

Plaintiff's reliance on *Longridge Builders* is misplaced. On a conceptual level, applying the nexus requirement that governs responsibility for off-site improvements in connection with a single private development to a comprehensive environmental protection scheme that limits the use of land is difficult, if not impossible. [ ] Moreover, in the exactions cases, the development constitutes a lawful, permitted use; in that situation, the critical issue is the validity of imposing on the permissible development the costs for off-site improvements or for overcoming burdens occasioned by the development. In contrast, regulations that lawfully impose land-use constraints on an ecologically-sensitive area can validly disallow the development itself. If, in that context, the developer could not claim that the regulation effects an unlawful taking, it cannot claim that it constitutes an unlawful exaction.

Furthermore, unlike exactions for off-site improvements that unfairly or disproportionately penalize a developer and benefit the general public, the uniform land-use restrictions in the CMP are part of a comprehensive scheme. The CMP creates eight areas within the vast Pinelands region, prescribing different land uses according to the environmental, ecological, economic, and cultural characteristics of the respective areas. The CMP distributes and allocates the economic burdens among all property owners in order to promote the public good. . . .

NOTES

(1) Blending conservation tools: The Pinelands conservation approach is obviously a regulatory response to a large-scale challenge. But does it employ other tools described by Gunningham and Young? Note that land-owner property rights have been redefined, that conservation easements and land purchases are also featured prominently. The comprehensive management plan also has educational components and makes use of transferable development rights that give market forces a role. Some of the restrictions are involuntary, but in other cases landowners have options, with permanent conservation restrictions often triggered by voluntary landowner decisions to undertake particular types of development. Note the broad powers vested in the Commission, which it is authorized to employ so as to achieve overall management aims. Note too that the Commission did not displace all lower levels of local government; local bodies retain certain powers, including land-use regulatory powers, though they are obligated to make their master plans and land-use ordinances consistent with the larger-scale regional plan.

(2) The problem of large, minimum lot-size requirements: Note that the Commission originally allowed farmland owners to construct farm-related structures on their lands at a rate of one-building per 10 acres. The effect was that farmers wanting to develop commonly divided their lands into 10–acre "farmettes." Purchasers nominally built farmhouses on their farmettes, but many purchasers had no plans to continue agricultural operations. The result was a dispersal of new housing and an effective end to much farming. Plaintiff Gardner explored this development option before the law changed. The unanticipated ill effects of the rule led to the revised plan requirements that Gardner challenged in the case. Similar minimum-lot size zoning schemes have also had ill effects—and have been replaced by rules requiring the clustering of new dwellings to allow for larger, unbroken tracts of land for agricultural or conservation ends.

(3) Transforming the right to develop: In light of the Commission's comprehensive plan, what rights did Gardner have to develop his land? In effect, he could build one home per 40 acres, as long as the dwellings were clustered on one-acre lots and the remaining land was restricted to farming purposes. In addition, by agreeing to deed restrictions on his property Gardner gained certain transferable development rights (Pineland Development Credits) for use on other lands where more intensive development was permitted.

The approach employed by the Pinelands Commission has become increasingly common and is today widely viewed as a way to interject fairness into a regional scheme while protecting ecologically sensitive lands. Under the Pinelands comprehensive plan, certain lands were designated for more intensive development. The owners of such lands, however, did not obtain full rights to develop them. To undertake full development, they needed to acquire additional development rights from other landowners who, under the plan, received such rights but could not use them on their own, restricted lands. The economic effect of such a scheme, once rights are traded, is that development is concentrated in desired areas while all landowners in the region share in the economic benefits of development. Were the transferable rights not used, owners of land designated for intensive develop would benefit greatly, while those who owned restricted land would suffer.

Although transferable rights schemes are widely applauded by land planners and community groups of all types, the Supreme Court has viewed them with suspicion. Under the just compensation clause, the taking of property must be accompanied by the payment of the full fair-market value of the property taken. Although transferable development rights often have value, they typically are not valuable enough alone to qualify as just compensation. They are, instead, offered as a replacement for development rights that have been diminished—that is, they represent a legal reformulation of landowner rights. An unresolved issue in Supreme Court jurisprudence is whether the value of such rights should be taken into account, in a takings case, when assessing the economic impact of a regulatory scheme. If they are taken into account at that stage, they are likely, because of their value, to undercut a landowner's ability to demonstrate a regulatory taking. If instead they are viewed as partial compensation for rights, they would be ignored at the stage of determining whether a taking has occurred—thus making a taking more likely. *See Suitum v. Tahoe Regional Planning Agency,* 520 U.S. 725 (1997) (raising issue but disposing of case on unrelated ground); Julian Conrad Juergensmeyer, *et al., Transferable Development Rights and Alternatives After* Suitum, 30 URB. LAW. 441 (1998).

(4) ***Bonnie Briar Syndicate v. Town of Mamaroneck:*** Owner of land used for decades as a golf course brought suit challenging zoning ordinance that shifted the property from residential zoning category to one in which only recreational land uses were permitted. Development was restricted because the extensive regional development that had already occurred created a need for open space and recreational opportunities; the development had also altered hydrologic systems so that further development would exacerbate flooding. The court held that the zoning restriction substantially advanced legitimate state interests and, because it permitted continuance of existing land use, did not amount to a regulatory taking without payment of just compensation. *Bonnie Briar Syndicate, Inc. v. Town of Mamaroneck,* 721 N.E.2d 971 (N.Y.1999).

(5) Growth control ordinances: Biodiversity issues have sometimes played roles in community decisions to constrain urban sprawl, typically by means of plans that concentrate development within existing developed areas while protecting open spaces on the fringe. Courts generally have been receptive to well-planned growth-control programs, even when they severely constrain development possibilities. *E.g., Schenck v. City of Hudson,* 114 F.3d 590 (6th Cir.1997) (upholding growth control measure that severely limited development, even by landowners who already had received final plat approvals for development). The issue is discussed in Daniel Mandelker, *Managing Space to Manage Growth,* 23 WM. & MARY ENVTL. L. & POL'Y REV. 801 (1999). A thoughtful inquiry, presenting growth control as a means for community residents to wrest control of their shared landscape from developers and extractive industries, is offered in A. Dan Tarlock, *Contested Landscapes and Local Voice,* 3 WASH. U. J.L. & POL'Y 513 (2000).

* * *

Biodiversity issues have not gone unnoticed by professionals in the land-use planning field. The following overview of the subject, intended for planners, offers a sober assessment of the magnitude of the challenge:

Timothy Beatley, *Preserving Biodiversity: Challenges for Planners*

66 AM. PLANNING ASSOC. J. 5, 7–13 (2000).

For the most part, biodiversity conservation in the U.S. has been driven by the requirements of the federal Endangered Species Act (ESA). The ESA has accomplished much, and still represents one of the most important pieces of environmental legislation ever enacted....

But the approach of the ESA has many limitations and is in many ways not up to the present and future challenges we face. It has been largely a reactive law, an example of what some have called "emergency-room conservation": by the time species have gone through the federal listing process and receive protection, their ecological condition is often dire....

Also alarming is that many of the conservation actions and solutions undertaken are fragmented and piecemeal. Small-scale mitigation projects typically required under federal and state environmental mandates often produce only minor improvements. Project-by-project environmental analysis and mitigation will not solve our environmental problems and will not ensure that we will be able to maintain healthy ecosystems or biodiversity in the long run.

As the new millennium approaches, we must fundamentally rethink our conservation strategies. We need a new conservation vision and a redefined role for planners. As habitat loss continues and the number of species in jeopardy continues to rise, we must explore new alternatives. To be truly effective in the long run, our efforts must be intentionally multi-species in emphasis and must seek to protect the integrity and health of the broader habitats and ecosystems that support biodiversity—those of species that are endangered and threatened and of ones that are not. We need more integrated, comprehensive biodiversity conservation strategies that are long-range, proactive, and preventive in nature. We need to get ahead of the curve of decline and preserve species before their numbers and habitats are so reduced that emergency-room conservation is our only option.

Land Use Planning is the Key

Long-range land use planning must be the linchpin of our new biodiversity conservation strategies. Increasingly, this challenge must be faced by planners, as it will be a necessary part of any successful conservation strategy in the future. Those states and regions experiencing the greatest population and development growth pressures, moreover, also tend to be home to extensive numbers of species and diverse ecosystems. These clashes will continue and indeed become more intense in the future, and consequently finding ways to preserve biodiversity in the face of these pressures will become an even greater challenge.

Many of the current clashes between urban development and biobiodiversity—what Secretary of the Interior Babbitt has aptly called "train wrecks"—could have been avoided through careful, effective land use planning and growth guidance. In Austin, Texas, for instance, a forward-looking plan called Austin Tomorrow used an impressive series of ecological analyses to chart a growth corridor that would have minimized the ecological damage there. For a variety of political and other reasons, the plan was not implemented, and the booming growth that followed happened in some of the most ecologically sensitive areas of the region....

The story is much the same in many other parts of the country where ecological "train wrecks" have occurred. The threats to biodiversity in the Pacific Northwest and the tremendous protection and restoration costs to be incurred from salmon and steelhead listings might have been substantially avoided if more stringent and demanding land use controls had been in place earlier on. It is, of course, not too late in such places....

Comprehensive land use policies which protect essential habitat corridors and linkages must be at the core of these strategies. Land use and growth guidance techniques may steer development away from inappropriate and damaging locations, and prevent land use patterns and practices that fragment and isolate habitat....

A land use planning approach to biodiversity conservation will require more than simply redirecting future growth away from a few ecological hot spots or saving a small amount of habitat. Indeed, what will also be required is a fundamental rethinking of types and forms of urban growth. One of the most troubling aspects of many of our recent habitat conservation initiatives has been the acceptance of prevailing low-density, scattered development patterns and the belief that all that is needed to preserve biodiversity is to set aside a few areas of protected habitat. Biodiversity preservation will also require that we reevaluate the ways in which our communities and regions grow and develop. Containing urban growth in a compact urban form will be essential in protecting biodiversity.

Part of the agenda must also be how such comprehensive strategies are characterized in the regions in which they are envisioned. New land use planning restrictions and initiatives must be viewed as contributing substantially to the quality of life of residents (and thus to the economy). Perhaps at the deepest levels, biodiversity preservation must be redefined as self-preservation, an idea we have not yet been willing to accept. In an op-ed article in the Seattle Times, Alex Steffen puts it well:

> We know that what's bad for wild salmon is bad for us. Polluted waters, eroding land, wetlands which protect our communities from flooding being dredged and filled, lakes and bays whose bottoms are coated with toxic sludge, raw sewage churning out of open pipes, farmland being eaten up by runaway sprawl and the last nearby woods being clear cut and paved over for a strip mall—this is not what we want for our children, and we know, both in our guts and from the work of scientists, that it's hurting not only the salmon but the health of our whole region.

In many situations, the loss of habitat results in other substantial and significant societal costs. Clear cutting and developing in sensitive, steep-slope areas of the Northwest—major causes of the present plight of endangered salmon there—have also been instrumental in the extremely costly flooding and flood damage that have occurred in recent years. The connections between biodiversity conservation and other important local goals, such as economic development and enhancement of quality of life, will increasingly need to be made if comprehensive networks of habitat are to be preserved.

. . .

New Tools for Conservation

New biodiversity conservation tools are available to communities that will protect habitat and species, and greatly aid in effective land use planning. Several are worthy of special mention. One of these tools is the habitat conservation plan (HCP), a balancing tool that dates from the early 1980s. This tool has been used with much greater frequency in the last 5 years and has become a major plank in the conservation platform of the Clinton administration. . . .

While the early HCPs tended to focus on one or a few species and covered fairly limited geographical areas, many of the more recent ones have taken broader, multispecies-and ecosystem-oriented approaches. These are certainly positive trends, though the biological adequacy of these plans remains in question. They do allow for the potential to rise above the project-by-project conservation standards and the more fragmented mitigation and conservation measures that typically result. Regional HCPs have the potential to generate significant financial and political support for securing and managing substantial blocks of habitat and protected land, often in close proximity to metropolitan areas.

One of the most ambitious regional and multispecies HCP efforts to date is underway in southern California, one of the most significant biodiversity hot spots in the country. California's Natural Community

Conservation Planning (NCCP) program began in 1991 with its pilot application in the coastal sage scrub ecosystem. Stimulated largely by the impending federal listing of the California gnatcatcher, the NCCP was intended to support a scientifically-based, ecosystem-oriented habitat protection strategy. Under the program, a five-member scientific review panel was convened to prepare conservation guidelines. Choosing to focus on three target species (including the gnatcatcher), the panel delineated a series of "subregional focus areas," around which more detailed protection schemes have been focused. Multispecies plans have now been prepared (and approved locally) for two sub-areas: the Orange County Central/Coastal Plan and the San Diego Multiple Species Conservation Program Plan. The San Diego Plan is ambitious in scope, covering some 582,000 acres, 172,000 of which are included in a preserve network in the southwestern portion of the county.

There are many admirable attributes about the NCCP, including its collaborative, regional, multi-jurisdictional approach and its attempts to look at the habitat needs of a number of species (the San Diego plan includes 85 species, many of which appear on both federal and state endangered species lists). But the results to date also point out the difficulties in doing such regional habitat conservation and the challenges ahead for planners. Many environmental groups have been understandably critical of the adequacy of the results—plans that have not been subjected to scientific peer review, have not stopped continued habitat destruction, and, despite the obviously impressive land area involved, do not at all appear to provide sufficient habitat or adequate levels of funding. The southern California example, furthermore, while arguably setting aside important pieces, does not create or even envision an integrated ecosystem and habitat protection framework.

A recent comprehensive study of HCPs cosponsored by the American institute of Biological Sciences and the National Center for Ecological Analysis has raised a number of concerns about them. In particular, there are serious questions about the lack of information about the biology of the species covered by the plans, the failure of plans to estimate the numbers of species to be affected by take permits, and the lack of clear monitoring provisions....

For such plans to be truly effective, they will need to cover larger geographical areas and protect broader ecosystem functions. These plans need to be much more cautious in content, more ambitious in their habitat protection goals, and guided considerably less by political and legal expedience than they currently are. Moreover, while the best HCPs may lead to the setting aside of significant amounts of habitat, they also result in opening up for new development much larger areas of habitat. And the form and density of this new development—typically very-low-density residential—is rarely questioned as to the habitat it destroys.

. . .

Other tools help in analyzing and organizing information about species and ecosystems in need of protection. One of the more powerful tools is Gap Analysis. Historically, the absence of accurate biological data and inadequacy of mapping techniques that permit the identification of key areas in need of protection and management has substantially limited effective land use planning. Gap Analysis is an important technique for identifying these areas. By overlaying maps of land cover, vegetation, and vertebrate distribution onto maps of existing parks and protected areas (and with the heavy use of GIS), "gaps" in the existing protective system can be identified. Since the late 1980s, the U.S. Gap Analysis Program has been spearheaded by the Biological Resources Division of the U.S. Geological Service (Formerly the National Biological Resources Service). Gap analyses have been completed in eight states and are underway in a number of others.[1] While the technique has its limitations, it does represent a powerful tool for planners and land managers in designing biodiversity conservation strategies.

· · ·

Preserving Larger Ecosystems and Landscapes

There is considerable biological virtue to rediscovering Daniel Burnham's exhortation to make no little plans.[2] Indeed, while biodiversity conservation can and must happen at every scale, long-run effectiveness will require thinking on increasingly larger ecological scales. Too much effort in the past has been directed at preserving isolated patches of habitat, postage stamps that will eventually be surrounded by development, with questionable long-term ecological viability. What is ultimately needed are integrated, large-scale systems of protected natural green space and habitats, nested approaches in which regional systems connect with larger statewide and continental systems.

The vision of large-scale ecosystem protection and restoration is certainly not new. The Wildlands Project, a nonprofit grassroots organization of conservation biologists and environmentalists, has pushed for such a vision for years. Working to develop holistic visions of preserve systems in different parts of the country, their explicit goal is to set aside 50% of the nation's land base as "wildlands," organized into core areas (from 100,000 to 25 million acres in size), buffer zones, and corridors connecting habitat blocks. This is similar to the concept of biosphere reserves, which have been established around the world (including in the U.S.) under the UNESCO Man and the Biosphere Program. While in practice biosphere reserve status has tended not to result in the land use planning and management envisioned, there are now a number of them around the world, including the 47 in the U.S.

· · ·

An Emphasis on Integrated Ecological Networks

We must begin to think in terms of comprehensive, multiscale ecological networks. What is especially needed are integrated strategies, in which local habitats connect with and are meshed into regional systems, which

1. J.M. Scott & M.J. Jennings, *Large Area Mapping of Biodiversity*, 85 ANNALS MO. NOTANICAL GARDEN 34 (1998).

2. T. HINES, BURNHAM AND CHICAGO: ARCHITECT AND PLANNER (1979).

are in turn woven into larger continental-scale systems. And here, as well, there are inspiring examples.

At national and continental levels, Europe provides some important examples of efforts to visualize and create broader ecological networks. The most developed of these initiatives can be seen in the Netherlands' Nature Policy Plan. As a densely populated nation, the Netherlands has experienced tremendous stresses on its natural environment and indigenous biodiversity. As a result it has devised and adopted a national ecological network based on preserving and connecting large blocks of the remaining natural lands and representative sets of ecosystem types, which are of regional, national, and international significance. Based on extensive background studies, a map ... was prepared delineating a "coherent and robust" ecological network. This map serves as the framework for national, regional, and local conservation actions.

In the Dutch scheme, several categories of designation are included on the map. Core areas generally are existing natural areas of at least 500 hectares that are considered biological "hot spots, capable of recolonizing surrounding smaller ecosystems." Nature development areas are areas suitable for ecological regeneration or restoration, often farmlands that can be converted back to wetlands or woodlands. About 10% of the network will be made up of land currently in agricultural use. Ecological corridors are intended to provide connections and migration opportunities between core areas. In practice, these corridors are likely to be such things as "hedgerows, dikes, banks of waterways and roads." Buffer zones are also viewed as an important part of the network, but are not delineated on the map.

For each category, the map delineates more land or area than the final network will include, as its creators understood that not every parcel will actually be secured and protected. This allows flexibility in acquiring or redeveloping lands, and anticipates the working out of greater detail at the provincial and local levels. For nature development areas, about three times the actual target is contained on the map; for core areas, about twice as much land is indicated.

Under this Nature Policy Plan, most development or alteration of lands within core areas or development areas is prohibited. Implementation of the plan and realization of the national ecological network will require a variety of public actions and projects, including acquisition of lands and agreements with farmers willing to support nature values. The national ecological network places clear spatial parameters on planning and development at lower jurisdictional levels. In the Dutch system, decisions about which lands will actually be secured and restored and about specific boundaries are made at the provincial level. Each provincial government must work out the more precise details in its own Nature Policy Plan, and local municipal planning must build upon these regionally-specified networks.

. . .

The United States generally lacks and desperately needs such organizing ecological frameworks to guide planning and policy, and to ensure that the conservation investments we make (at a number of levels) will in the end protect biodiversity. Perhaps the most direct transfer of the Dutch experience in the U.S. could occur at the state level. Developing (and officially adopting) statewide ecological networks or integrated, connected systems of habitat would do much to provide such an important ecological planning framework.

NOTES

(1) Environmental land-use regulation: Though environmental law has long focused on pollution problems and toxic contaminants, its future— indeed, its present—has far more to do with land-use issues, which increasingly will require the kind of "organizing ecological frameworks" (as Beatley puts it) that are present in the laws of other countries but generally absent in the United States. An important survey of the subject in the United States is LINDA MALONE, ENVIRONMENTAL REGULATION OF LAND USE (1990). The most frequent call among conservationists has been for planning at the ecosystem level. *E.g.,* Richard Haeuber, *Setting the Environmental Policy Agenda: The Case for Ecosystem Management,* 36 NAT. RESOURCES J. 1 (1996). Efforts in the United States to date to undertake such management are explored in Oliver A. Houck, *On the Law of Biodiversity and Ecosystem Management,* 81 MINN. L. REV. 869 (1997). A useful wide-ranging study of U.S. efforts to conserve biodiversity—by an Australian scholar—is David Farrier, *Conserving Biodiversity on Private Land: Incentives for Management or Compensation for Lost Expectations?,* 19 HARV. ENVTL. L. REV. 303 (1995). J.B Ruhl has thoughtfully explored federal programs and various models for more coordinated federal land-related conservation efforts in *Biodiversity Conservation and the Ever–Expanding Web of Federal Laws Regulating Nonfederal Lands: Time for Something Completely Different?,* 66 U. COLO. L. REV. 555 (1995). The particular challenges of such management on private lands are set forth in Lee P. Breckenridge, *Reweaving the Landscape: The Institutional Challenges of Ecosystem Management for Lands In Private Ownership,* 19 VT. L. REV. 363 (1995). Also useful, in terms of state-based regulation, is Jeffrey L. Amestoy & Mark J. DiStefano, *Wildlife Habitat Protection Through State–Wide Land Use Regulation,* 14 HARV. ENVTL. L. REV. 45 (1990).

(2) California's NCCP Act: California's regional planning statute, described briefly by Beatley, is considered in DeAnne Parker, *Natural Community Conservation Planning: California's Emerging Ecosystem Management Alternative,* 6 U. BALT. J. ENVTL. L. 107 (1997); Marc J. Ebbin, *Is the Southern California Approach to Conservation Succeeding?,* 24 ECOL. L.Q. 695 (1997); John M. Gaffin, *Can We Conserve California's Threatened Fisheries Through Natural Community Conservation Planning?,* 27 ENVTL. L. 791 (1997).

(3) Citizen participation: Although Beatley does not highlight the issue, planning of the type he envisions is hard to undertake successfully without drawing ordinary citizens—particularly rural landowners—into the study and planning process. The idea is not without its dangers, however, particularly when, as often is the case, representatives of extractive industries and pro-development interests assume disproportionate roles. Perspectives on the subject are offered in Rena I. Steinzor, *The Corruption of Civic Environmentalism*, 30 Envtl. L. Rptr. (Envt. L. Inst.) 10909 (2000); Holly Doremus, *Preserving Citizen Participation in the Era of Reinvention: The Endangered Species Act Example*, 25 ECOL. L.Q. 707 (1999); Timothy P. Duane, *Community Participation in Ecosystem Management*, 24 ECOL. L.Q. 771 (1997); Matthew Schuckman, Note, *Making the Hard Choices: A Collaborative Governance Model for the Biodiversity Context*, 79 WASH. U.L.Q. 343 (2001).

Bolsa Chica Land Trust v. Superior Court

California Court of Appeal.
83 Cal.Rptr.2d 850 (1999).

■ BENKE, J.—This case concerns development plans for a large tract of land in southern Orange County known as Bolsa Chica. Although California Coastal Commission (Commission) approved a Local Coastal Program (LCP) for Bolsa Chica, the trial court found defects in the program and remanded it to Commission for further proceedings. In this court both the opponents and proponents of the LCP contend that the trial court erred.

The opponents of the LCP contend the trial court erred in finding a planned relocation of a bird habitat was permissible under the Coastal Act. The proponents of the LCP contend the trial court erred in preventing residential development of a wetlands area and in requiring preservation of a pond that would have been eliminated under the LCP in order to make room for a street widening. . . .

We find the trial court erred with respect to relocation of the bird habitat. The Coastal Act does not permit destruction of an environmentally sensitive habitat area [ESHA] simply because the destruction is mitigated offsite. At the very least, there must be some showing the destruction is needed to serve some other environmental or economic interest recognized by the act.

We agree with the trial court's rulings [that] on the record developed by Commission, neither residential development in the wetlands nor destruction of the pond are permissible.

FACTUAL BACKGROUND

Bolsa Chica is a 1,588–acre area of undeveloped wetlands and coastal mesas. Urban development surrounds Bolsa Chica on three sides. On the fourth side is the Pacific Ocean, separated from Bolsa Chica by a narrow strip of beach, coastal dunes and coastal bluffs.

Approximately 1,300 acres of Bolsa Chica consist of lowlands ranging from fully submerged saltwater in Bolsa Bay to areas of freshwater and saltwater wetlands and islands of slightly raised dry lands used by local wildlife for nesting and foraging. However, a large part of the lowlands is devoted to an active oil field and at one time the area was farmed.

The lowlands are flanked by two mesas, the Bolsa Chica Mesa on the north and the Huntington Mesa on the south. The Bolsa Chica Mesa consists of 215 acres of uplands hosting a variety of habitat areas. Although much of Huntington Mesa is developed, a long narrow undeveloped strip of the mesa abutting the lowlands is the planned site of a public park.

In 1973 the State of California acquired 310 contiguous acres of the Bolsa Chica lowlands in settlement of a dispute over its ownership of several separate lowland parcels and the existence of a public trust easement over other lowland areas.

In 1985 the County of Orange and Commission approved a land use plan for Bolsa Chica which contemplated fairly intense development. The 1985 plan allowed development of 5,700 residential units, a 75–acre marina and a 600–foot-wide navigable ocean channel and breakwater.

By 1988 substantial concerns had been raised with respect to the environmental impacts of the proposed marina and navigable ocean channel. Accordingly, a developer which owned a large portion of Bolsa Chica, a group of concerned citizens, the State Lands Commission, the County of Orange and the City of Huntington Beach formed the Bolsa Chica Planning Coalition (coalition). The coalition in turn developed an LCP for Bolsa Chica which substantially reduced the intensity of development. The coalition's LCP was eventually adopted by the Orange County Board of Supervisors. Commission approved the LCP with suggested modifications which were adopted by the board of supervisors.

As approved by Commission, the LCP eliminated the planned marina and navigable ocean channel, eliminated 3 major roads, reduced residential development from a total of 5,700 homes to 2,500 homes on Bolsa Chica Mesa and 900 homes in the lowlands and expanded planned open space and wetlands restoration to 1,300 acres.

The material features of the LCP which are in dispute here are: the replacement of a degraded eucalyptus grove on Bolsa Chica Mesa with a new raptor habitat consisting of nesting poles, native trees and other native vegetation on Huntington Mesa at the sight of the planned public park; the residential development in the lowland area which the LCP permits as a means of financing restoration of substantially degraded wetlands; and the elimination of Warner Pond on Bolsa Chica Mesa in order to accommodate the widening of Warner Avenue.

Throughout the approval process several interested parties and public interest groups, including the Bolsa Chica Land Trust, Huntington Beach Tomorrow, Shoshone–Gabrieleno Nation, Sierra Club and Surfrider Foundation (collectively the trust) objected to these and other portions of the LCP.

IV

Eucalyptus Grove

A.   History and Condition of the Grove

The LCP would permit residential development over five acres of a six and one-half-acre eucalyptus grove on Bolsa Chica Mesa. The five acres where development would be permitted is owned by Koll; the remainder of the grove is owned by the state.

The eucalyptus grove is not native to the area and was planted almost 100 years ago by a hunting club which owned large portions of Bolsa Chica. Since the time of its planting, the original 20–acre grove has diminished considerably because of development in the area and the lack of any effort to preserve it. Indeed, although the eucalyptus grove was nine and two-tenths acres large as recently as 1989, it had shrunk to no more than six and one-half acres by 1994 and portions of it were under severe stress. According to expert testimony submitted to Commission, the grove is probably shrinking because of increased salinity in the soil.

Notwithstanding its current diminished and deteriorating condition, Commission identified the grove as an ESHA within the meaning of Public Resources Code section 30107.5. The ESHA identification was based on the fact the grove provided the only significant locally available roosting and nesting habitat for birds of prey (raptors) in the Bolsa Chica area. At least 11 species of raptors have been identified as utilizing the site, including the white-tailed kite, marsh hawk, sharp skinned hawk, Cooper's hawk and osprey. According to Commission, a number of the raptors are dependent upon the adjacent lowland wetlands for food and the eucalyptus grove provides an ideal nearby lookout location as well as a refuge and nesting site.

B.   Section 30240

Under the Coastal Act, Commission is required to protect the coastal zone's delicately balanced ecosystem. § 30001, subds.(a)-(c); § 30001.5, subd. (a); *City of San Diego v. California Coastal Com.* 174 Cal. Rptr. 5 (1981); *Sierra Club v. California Coastal Com.*, 15 Cal. Rptr. 2d 779 (1993) (*Pygmy Forest*). Thus in reviewing all programs and projects governed by the Coastal Act, Commission must consider the effect of proposed development on the environment of the coast. *See City of San Diego v. California Coastal Com.*, 174 Cal. Rptr. 5.

. . .

In addition to the protection afforded by the requirement that Commission consider the environmental impact of all its decisions, the Coastal Act provides heightened protection to ESHA's. *Pgymy Forest,* 15 Cal. Rptr. 2d 779. Section 30107.5 identifies an ESHA as "any area in which plant or animal life or their habitats are either rare or especially valuable because of their special nature or role in an ecosystem and which could be easily disturbed or degraded by human activities and developments." "The consequences of ESHA status are delineated in section 30240: '(a) Environmentally sensitive habitat areas shall be protected against any significant disruption of habitat values, and only uses dependent on those resources shall be allowed within those areas. [¶] (b) Development in areas adjacent to environmentally sensitive habitat areas and parks and recreation areas shall be sited and designed to prevent impacts which would significantly degrade those areas, and shall be compatible with continuance of those habitat and recreation areas.' Thus development in ESHA areas themselves is limited to uses dependent on those resources, and development in adjacent areas must carefully safeguard their preservation." *Pygmy Forest,* 15 Cal. Rptr. 2d 779.

Commission found that residential development in the eucalyptus grove was permissible under section 30240 because the LCP required that an alternate raptor habitat be developed on Huntington Mesa. Commission reasoned that section 30240 only requires that "habitat values" be protected and that given the deteriorating condition of the grove, creation of a new raptor habitat on Huntington Mesa was the best way to promote the "habitat values" of the eucalyptus grove.

The reasoning Commission employed is seductive but, in the end, unpersuasive....

[T]he language of section 30240 does not permit a process by which the habitat values of an ESHA can be isolated and then recreated in another location. Rather, a literal reading of the statute protects *the area* of an ESHA from uses which threaten the habitat values which exist in the ESHA. Importantly, while the obvious goal of section 30240 is to protect habitat values, the express terms of the statute do not provide that protection by treating those values as intangibles which can be moved from place to place to suit the needs of development. Rather, the terms of the statute protect habitat values by placing strict limits on the uses which may occur in an ESHA and by carefully controlling the manner uses in the area around the ESHA are developed. *Pygmy Forest,* 15 Cal. Rptr. 2d 779.

[C]ontrary to Commission's reasoning, section 30240 does not permit its restrictions to be ignored based on the threatened or deteriorating condition of a particular ESHA. We do not doubt that in deciding whether a particular area is an ESHA within the meaning of section 30107.5, Commission may consider, among other matters, its viability. *See Pygmy Forest,* 15 Cal. Rptr. 2d 779. However, where, as is the case here, Commission has decided that an area is an ESHA, section 30240 does not itself provide Commission power to alter its strict limitations. *Id.* There is simply no reference in section 30240 which can be interpreted as diminishing the level of protection an ESHA receives based on its viability. Rather, under the statutory scheme, ESHA's, whether they are pristine and growing or fouled and threatened, receive uniform treatment and protection. *See Pygmy Forest,* 15 Cal. Rptr. 2d 779.

In this regard we agree with the trust that Commission's interpretation of section 30240 would pose a threat to ESHA's. As the trust points out, if, even though an ESHA meets the requirements of section 30107.5, application of section 30240's otherwise strict limitations also depends on the relative viability of an ESHA, developers will be encouraged to find threats and hazards to all ESHAs located in economically inconvenient locations. The pursuit of such hazards would in turn only promote the isolation and transfer of ESHA habitat values to more economically convenient locations. Such a system of isolation and transfer based on economic convenience would of course be completely contrary to the goal of the Coastal Act, which is to protect *all* coastal zone resources and provide heightened protection to ESHA's. §§ 30001, subds. (a)-(c), 30001.5, subd. (a); *Pygmy Forest,* 15 Cal. Rptr. 2d 779.

In short, while compromise and balancing in light of existing conditions is appropriate and indeed encouraged under *other* applicable portions of the Coastal Act, the power to balance and compromise conflicting interests cannot be found in section 30240.

V

Lowland Wetlands

The Coastal Act provides a separate protection regime for wetlands. Under section 30121: " 'Wetland' means lands within the coastal zone which may be covered periodically or permanently with shallow water and include saltwater marshes, freshwater marshes, open or closed brackish water marshes, swamps, mudflats, and fens."

Section 30233, subdivision (a), protects wetlands by providing: "The diking, filling, or dredging of * * * wetlands * * * shall be permitted in accordance with other applicable provisions of this division, where there is no feasible less environmentally damaging alternative, and where feasible mitigation measures have been provided to minimize adverse environmental effects, and shall be limited to the following:

(1) New or expanded port, energy, and coastal-dependent industrial facilities, including commercial fishing facilities.

(2) Maintaining existing, or restoring previously dredged, depths in existing navigational channels, turning basins, vessel berthing and mooring areas, and boat launching ramps.

(3) In wetland areas only, entrance channels for new or expanded boating facilities; and in a degraded wetland, identified by the Department of Fish and Game pursuant to subdivision (b) of Section 30411, for boating facilities if, in conjunction with such boating facilities, a substantial portion of the degraded wetland is restored and maintained as a biologically productive wetland. The size of the wetland area used for boating facilities, including berthing space, turning basins, necessary navigation channels, and any necessary support service facilities shall not exceed 25 percent of the degraded wetland.

(4) In open coastal waters, other than wetlands, including streams, estuaries, and lakes, new or expanded boating facilities and the placement of structural pilings for public recreational piers that provide public access and recreational opportunities.

(5) Incidental public service purposes, including, but not limited to, burying cables and pipes or inspection of pier and maintenance of existing and outfall lines.

(6) Mineral extraction, including sand for restoring beaches, except in environmentally sensitive areas.

(7) Restoration purposes.

(8) Nature study, aquaculture, or similar resource-dependent activities.

Although section 30233, subdivision (a), permits development of wetland areas when needed as a means of accommodating a whole host of varied uses, residential development is not a use permitted in wetlands. . . .

[The court held that, under the statute, the Commission lacked the flexibility to authorize any residential development in wetlands, even as part of a scheme to fund off-site restoration efforts.]

VI

Warner Avenue Pond

The parties agree Warner Avenue Pond, which is located on Bolsa Chica Mesa, is both an ESHA within the meaning of section 30107.5 and a wetland within the meaning of section 30121. As we have noted under section 30240, the habitat values in an ESHA may not be significantly disrupted and no use of an ESHA may occur which is not dependent on resources which exist in the ESHA. As we have also noted under section 30233, subdivision (a), wetlands are protected by specific limitations with respect to uses which may occur in a wetland and by the requirement that there be no feasible less environmentally damaging alternative to diking, filling or dredging of a wetland.

In approving the LCP, Commission found Warner Avenue Pond could be filled to permit the widening of Warner Avenue and that the filling could be mitigated by offsite restoration of other wetlands on a ratio of four to one. Commission found that widening of the road was an "incidental public service" within the meaning of section 30233, subdivision (a)(5), and therefore a permissible use of the wetland. Commission's findings do not discuss the pond's status as an ESHA.

[The court rejected the claim that the Commission had power under the provisions of the Act to authorize development in wetlands in contravention of section 30233.]

Practicality, as well as the need to maintain a consistent level of wetland protection, suggest that development of wetland ESHA's are governed by the very specific and uniform limitations set forth in section 30233, subdivision (a), rather than by way of the essentially ad hoc balancing process permitted by section 30007.5. . . .

Although we accept Commission's interpretation of sections 30233 and 30240, we do not accept Commission's application of that interpretation to Warner Avenue Pond. In particular we note that under Commission's interpretation, incidental public services are limited to temporary disruptions and do not usually include permanent roadway expansions. Roadway expansions are permitted only when no other alternative exists and the expansion is necessary to maintain existing traffic capacity. As the trust points out, Commission found that the widening of Warner Avenue was needed to accommodate future traffic created by local and regional development in the area. Contrary to Koll's argument, this limited exception cannot be extended by finding that a roadway expansion is permissible when, although it increases the vehicle capacity of a roadway, it is designed to maintain an existing level of traffic service. Such an interpretation of the exception would entirely consume the limitation Commission has put on the incidental public services otherwise permitted by section 30233, subdivision (a)(2).

In sum then, like the trial court we find that the LCP is defective insofar as it approves the filling of Warner Avenue Pond.

NOTES

(1) Coastal zone protection: California's Coastal Commission is similar to commissions created in many coastal states following passage of the federal Coastal Zone Management Act. The commissions are charged with the duty to protect, to one degree or another, ecologically sensitive coastal zones. The national program with its many state variants is discussed in LINDA MALONE, ENVIRONMENTAL REGULATION OF LAND USE (1990). Coastal zones are often rich in biological diversity, and they are under intense development pressure, particularly from sprawling urban areas and vacation-resort development. Of particular interest under the guiding federal statute are the provisions dealing with nonpoint-source water pollution, aimed at addressing such important, threatened ecological communities as Chesapeake Bay. Observers have long viewed these provisions as a model that might be used to give more force to the provisions of the Clean Water Act. Although coastal protection plans often focus on maintaining water quality and aquatic habitats, measures taken to achieve these goals commonly aid terrestrial wildlife as well.

(2) Mitigation measures and banking: As the court interpreted the California statute and the Local Coastal Plan, local planners had little authority to allow development to proceed in a sensitive area even when the harm was offset by mitigation measures taken elsewhere. This idea—allowing development subject to mitigation requirements—has been widely used in various settings and is often touted as a way both to add flexibility and to lower costs under resource-protection schemes. Under NEPA, federal agencies planning major federal activities must consider options to mitigate environmental harms—but they are not required to undertake such actions unless failure to do so would be arbitrary and capricious. *See, e.g., Robertson v. Methow Valley Citizens Council,* 490 U.S. 332 (1989). More rigorous are mitigation requirements included in wetland protection schemes. Under § 404 of the Clean Water Action, applicants for permits to deposit dredge or fill material into wetlands are often obligated in exchange to take steps to conserve or construct wetlands elsewhere. A perceptive overview of mitigation requirements as a conservation tool is offered in Michael J. Bean & Lynn E. Dwyer, *Mitigation Banking as an Endangered Species Conservation Tool,* 30 Envtl. L. Rptr. (Envtl. L. Inst.) 10537 (2000). As the authors note, wetland mitigation efforts often fail, either because they are more difficult to construct than first realized or because their continued success requires extensive on-going maintenance. The causes of such failure need to be identified and taken into account in designing mitigation programs aimed directly at wildlife conservation. A useful exploration, linking mitigation duties to the maintenance of ecosystem processes, is J.B. Ruhl & R. Juge Gregg, *Integrating Ecosystem Services into Environmental Law: A Case Study of Wetlands Mitigation Banking,* 20 STAN. ENVTL. L.J. 365 (2001).

(3) Ecologically sensitive places: Like the Pinelands Comprehensive Management Plan, California's coastal zone management program includes special protections for identified, ecologically sensitive places. Such places, in effect, are put off limits for intensive land use. The technique holds obvious promise for biodiversity conservation, given the number of biodiversity "hotspots" which provide habitat for large numbers of imperilled species. Recall the comments by Beatley on the technique known as "Gap Analysis," which is used to identify such species-rich places and to flag those that lack adequate protections. The term "gap analysis" has been defined by its developer as "the process by which species and natural communities not adequately represented in conservation lands are identified. These are the 'gaps' in our present-day efforts to maintain biological diversity, and it is these that are most likely to become endangered with extinction in the future." J Michael Scott and Michael D. Jennings, *Large-Area Mapping of Biodiversity*, 85 ANNALS MO. BOTANICAL GARDEN 34, 37 (1998). The gaps are identified by an iterative mapping process:

> The purpose of gap analysis is twofold. The first is to provide regional conservation assessments of native vertebrate species and natural land-cover types. The second is to facilitate the application of this information to land-management activities. These goals are accomplished by (a) mapping the vegetation alliances [ ] of the United States; (b) mapping predicted distributions of each native vertebrate species; (c) mapping the existing conservation lands and ranking them by their management status; (d) determining the degree of representation that vertebrate species and land-cover types have in conservation lands; (e) providing this information to the public and those entities charged with land-use research, policy, planning, and management; and (f) building institutional cooperation in the application of this information to state and regional management activities. This, then, provides an objective database of biogeographic information that allows researchers, planner, and managers to stratify the land surface for work at higher resolutions [ ] and to understand the regional and continental context of higher-resolution information from smaller areas.

Id. at 36. *See also* J. Michael Scott *et al.*, *Species Richness: A Geographic Approach to Protecting Future Biological Diversity*, 37 BIOSCI. 782 (1987); J. Michael Scott *et al.*, *Gap Analysis: A Geographic Approach to Protection of Biological Diversity*, 123 WILDLIFE MONOGRAPH 1 (1993); J. Michael Scott *et al.*, *Landscape Approaches to Mapping Biodiversity*, 46 BIOSCI. 74 (1996).

Many commentators have urged lawmakers to enact new programs—aimed specifically at protecting at such hotspots—to supplement single-species protection efforts. A particularly detailed exploration, linked to failings of the Endangered Species Act, is John Charles Kunich, *Preserving the Womb of the Unknown Species with Hotspots Legislation*, 52 HASTINGS L.J. 1149 (2001) (proposing a "Vital Ecosystems Preservation Act").

Sensitive-area designation programs are common in European nations. In England, for example, the governmental entity English Nature has broad powers to identify important natural features on private lands, including wildlife habitat. For years the agency could protect such features only by urging voluntary action by landowners and by helping landowners gain assistance from other agencies or not-for-profit groups. More recently, it has acquired powers to impose legal constraints, on agricultural and silvicultural practices as well as on more intensive development (which was already severely limited under the Town and Country Planning Act).

Sensitive-area designation programs raise obvious concerns about fairness to landowners. Those concerns are reduced when, as in *Gardner* (the Pinelands case) and *Bonnie Briar Syndicate* (the golf course case), an existing land use is allowed to continue. They are also reduced when landowners subject to severe limitations are given transferable development rights, which they can use elsewhere or sell. In the longer term, however, programs of this type raise fundamental questions about what it means to own land, and about the extent to which landowner rights should be defined abstractly, without regard for the natural features of the land that is owned. Recall the two questions raised in section 3 of this chapter (and even earlier, in Chapter 1): Should the degradation of ecologically sensitive natural features be viewed as a type of land-use harm that the community can constrain as a matter of self-preservation? Should the entitlements of ownership—particularly the owner's right to use land intensively—arise out of and be limited by the natural features of the land itself in the sense of being limited to those uses consistent with the achievement of ecological goals?

In considering this issue, keep in mind that many lands become ecologically sensitive only after similar lands have been altered in damaging ways: As the stock of that type of land (*e.g.,* a particular habitat type) dwindles, remaining unaltered lands become all the more vital. Is it fair to allow some landowners to develop and then, when the landscape reaches its ecological carrying capacity, to impose a ban on further development? Is this simply a type of first-in-time allocation system—long used in the law generally and accepted as legitimate, despite its elements of unfairness? Or does the unfairness here run deeper? Consider the following note.

(4) Carrying-capacity harms: Many land-use practices, such as drainage and the alteration of wildlife habitat, become damaging when and as they transform large portions of a landscape. Practices that cause little disruption when widely separated can degrade a landscape severely when undertaken by substantial numbers of landowners. Recall *Bonnie Briar Syndicate*, the golf-course case noted above: Because of residential development on similar, surrounding lands, the region lacked open space, suffered from declining recreational opportunities, and that excessive hydrologic modification had led to flooding. In the assessment of local officials and the New York Court of Appeals, the harmfulness of further residential development was properly determined by accepting all present development as given; if further development would be harmful in light of existing land uses it could be banned, even if the proposed development duplicated existing development. Other courts have embraced a similar view, although typically without raising the issue directly. *E.g., Christianson v. Gasvoda,* 789 P.2d 1234 (Mont.1990) (county can ban upland residential subdivision when existing development is sufficiently extensive to cause flooding to lower elevations); *Grant's Farm Associates, Inc. v. Town of Kittery,* 554 A.2d 799 (Me.1989) (town can ban residential subdivision, even when over 90 percent of land would be devoted to open space, because of threatened status of nearby shoreline due to prior development). On the role of carrying capacity analysis in land-use planning, see Jonathan Douglas Witten, *Carrying Capacity and the Comprehensive Plan: Establishing and Defending Limits to Growth*, 28 B.C. ENVTL. AFF. L. REV. 583 (2001).

(5) The local role: Conservation work by governments typically occurs at several levels, from the national—or even international—down to the most local. Recall how, under the Pinelands protection scheme, the regional Commission oversaw but did not displace further land-use regulation by local units of government. The same arrangement was employed in the California coastal protection plan in *Bolsa Chica*: the Local Coastal Program was prepared and approved by Orange County, and then reviewed for adequacy under state standards by the state Coastal Commission. A good discussion of the complex, state-local regulatory scheme developed in Maryland to protect the Chesapeake Bay is set forth in *Bucktail, LLC v. County Council of Talbot County*, 723 A.2d 440 (Md.1999). The prospects of local action generally are discussed in A. Dan Tarlock, *Local Government Protection of Biodiversity: What is Its Niche?*, 60 U. CHI. L. REV. 555 (1993).

* * *

In the end, no single tool, legal or otherwise, is likely to succeed in protecting the public's interest in the continent's biological riches. Aldo Leopold, it appears, had it right in the essay that began this chapter: A sound wildlife plan will likely comprise "a constantly shifting array of small moves, infinitely repeated, to give wildlife due representation in shaping of the future minds and future landscapes of America."

*

CHRONOLOGY OF FEDERAL WILDLIFE STATUTES

1900

Lacey Act, ch. 553, 31 Stat. 187 (May 25, 1900) [repealed in part] (currently codified at 16 U.S.C. § 701)

1906

Antiquities Act, 16 U.S.C. §§ 431–433

1913

Weeks–McLean Migratory Bird Act, ch. 145, 37 Stat. 828, 847 (Mar. 3, 1913)

1916

National Park Service Organic Act, 16 U.S.C. §§ 1, 2–4

1918

Migratory Bird Treaty Act, 16 U.S.C. §§ 703–711

1926

Black Bass Act, ch. 346, 44 Stat. 576 (May 20, 1926) [repealed]

1929

Migratory Bird Conservation Act, 16 U.S.C. §§ 715–715k

1930

Tariff Act of 1930, 19 U.S.C. § 1527

1931

Animal Damage Control, 7 U.S.C. § 426

1934

Fish & Wildlife Coordination Act, 16 U.S.C. §§ 661–666c

Migratory Bird Stamp Act [Duck Stamp Act], 16 U.S.C. §§ 718–718j

1935

Refuge Revenue Sharing Act, ch. 261, § 401, 49 Stat. 383 (June 15, 1935) [repealed]

1937

Federal Aid in Wildlife Restoration Act [The Pittman–Robertson Act], 16 U.S.C. §§ 669–669i; 26 U.S.C. §§ 4161(b), 4181

1940

Bald Eagle Protection Act, 16 U.S.C. §§ 668–668d

1946

Fish & Wildlife Coordination Act Amendments

1949

Migratory Bird Stamp Act Amendments [Duck Stamp Act], ch. 421, 63 Stat. 599 (Aug. 12, 1949)

1950

Federal Aid in Fish Restoration Act, [Dingell–Johnson Act], 16 U.S.C. §§ 777–777l; 26 U.S.C. § 9504(a)

1958

Fish & Wildlife Coordination Act Amendments

Migratory Bird Stamp Act Amendments [Duck Stamp Act], Pub. L. No. 85–585, 72 Stat. 486 (Aug. 1, 1958)

1959

Act Prohibiting the Use of Aircraft & Motor Vehicles to Hunt Feral Horse & Burros, 18 U.S.C. § 47

1960

Multiple–Use Sustained–Yield Act, 16 U.S.C. §§ 528–531

1961

Wetlands Loan Act, 16 U.S.C. §§ 715k–3 to 715k–5

1962

Refuge Recreation Act, 16 U.S.C. §§ 460k to 460k–4

Bald and Golden Eagle Protection Act Amendments, Pub. L. No. 87–884, 76 Stat. 1246 (Oct. 24, 1962)

1963

Land and Water Conservation Fund Act, 16 U.S.C. §§ 460l to 460l–11

1964

Wilderness Act, 16 U.S.C. §§ 1131–1136

Refuge Revenue Sharing Act, 16 U.S.C. § 715s

1965

The Anadromous Fish Act, 16 U.S.C. §§ 757a–757b

1966

Refuge Administration Act, 16 U.S.C. 16 U.S.C. §§ 668dd–668ee

Endangered Species Preservation Act, Pub. L. No. 89–669, 80 Stat. 926 [repealed]

Migratory Bird Conservation Act Amendments, 16 U.S.C. § 715i(a)

1968

Wild and Scenic River Act, 16 U.S.C. §§ 1271–1287

1969

National Environmental Policy Act of 1969, 42 U.S.C. §§ 4321, 4331–4335

Endangered Species Conservation Act, Pub. L. No. 91–135, 83 Stat. 275 [repealed]

1970

General Authorities Act [Park Service], 16 U.S.C. §§ 1a–1, 1c

Federal Aid in Wildlife Restoration Act Amendments [The Pittman–Robertson Act], Pub. L. No. 91–503, §§ 101–102, 84 Stat. 1097 (Oct. 23, 1970)

1971

Wild Free–Roaming Horses and Burros Act, 16 U.S.C. §§ 1331–1340

1972

Marine Mammal Protection Act, 16 U.S.C. §§ 1361–1407

Bald and Golden Eagle Protection Act Amendments, 16 U.S.C. § 668(a)

1973

Endangered Species Act, 16 U.S.C. §§ 1531–1544

1974

Sikes Act Extension, 16 U.S.C. §§ 670g–670o

1976

Magnuson Fisheries Conservation and Management Act of 1976, 16 U.S.C. §§ 1801–1883

National Forest Management Act, 16 U.S.C. §§ 1600–1614

Federal Land Policy and Management Act, 43 U.S.C. §§ 1701–1784

1980

Fish and Wildlife Conservation Act of 1980 [Non–Game Act], 16 U.S.C. §§ 2901–2911

The Pacific Northwest Electric Power Planning & Conservation Act, 16 U.S.C. §§ 839–839h

1981

Lacey Act Amendments, 16 U.S.C. §§ 3371–3378

1990

Nonindigenous Aquatic Nuisance Prevention and Control Act, 16 U.S.C. §§ 4701–4751

1992

Wild Bird Conservation Act, 16 U.S.C. §§ 4901–4916

1996

Magnuson Fishery Conservation and Management Act Amendments

1997

National Wildlife Refuge System Improvement Act, 16 U.S.C. §§ 668dd–668ee

1999

Neotropical Bird Conservation Act, 16 U.S.C. § 6101–6109

APPENDIX II

CHRONOLOGY OF INTERNATIONAL WILDLIFE AGREEMENTS

Interim Convention on the Conservation of North Pacific Fur Seals

37 Stat. 1542 (July 7, 1911) (no longer in force)

Convention for the Protection of Migratory Birds

39 Stat. 1702 (August 16, 1916)

Convention on Nature and Wildlife Preservation in the Western Hemisphere

56 Stat. 1354, 161 U.N.T.S. 193 (October 12, 1940) (entered into force May 1, 1942)

International Convention for the Regulation of Whaling

T.I.A.S. No. 1849, 161 U.N.T.S. 72 (December 2, 1946) (entered into force November 10, 1948)

General Agreements on Tariffs and Trade

T.I.A.S. No. 1700, 55 U.N.T.S. 187 (October 30, 1947) (provisionally entered into force January 1, 1948)

International Convention for the High Seas Fisheries of the North Pacific Ocean

4 U.S.T. 380, 205 U.N.T.S. 65 (May 9, 1952) (entered into force January 12, 1953)

Interim Convention of the Conservation of North Pacific Fur Seals

314 U.N.T.S. 105 (February 9, 1957) (entered into force October 1957)

Convention on Fishing and Conservation of the Living Resources of the High Seas

17 U.S.T. 138, 559 U.N.T.S. 285 (April 29, 1958) (entered into force March 20, 1966)

International Convention for the Conservation of Atlantic Tunas (ICCAT)

20 U.S.T. 2887, 673 U.N.T.S. 63 (May 14, 1966) (entered into force March 21, 1969)

Convention on Wetlands of International Importance especially as Waterfowl Habitat (Ramsar Convention)

T.I.A.S. No. 11984, 996 U.N.T.S. 245 (February 2, 1971) (entered into force December 21, 1975)

Convention on International Trade in the Endangered Species of Wild Fauna and Flora (CITES)

27 U.S.T. 1087, 993 U.N.T.S. 243 (March 3, 1973) (entered into force July 1, 1975)

Convention on the Conservation of Migratory Species of Wild Animals

19 I.L.M. 11 (1980) (June 23, 1979) (entered into force November 1, 1983)

Convention for the Conservation of Salmon in the North Atlantic Ocean

T.I.A.S. No. 10789, 1338 U.N.T.S. 33 (March 2, 1982) (entered into force October 10, 1986)

World Charter for Nature

G.A. Res.37/7 (Annex), U.N. Doc A/RES/37/51, 22 I.L.M. 455 (October 28, 1982)

Convention on Biological Diversity

31 I.L.M. 818 (1992) (June 5, 1992) (entered into force December 29, 1993)

Agreement for the Implementation of the Provisions of the United Nations Convention of the Law of the Sea of 10 December 1982, Relating to the Conservation and Management of Straddling Fish Stocks and Highly Migratory Fish Stocks

6th Sess., U.N. Doc. A/CONF. 164/37 (December 4, 1995), 34 I.L.M. 1542 (1995)

ACRONYMS

ADC	Animal Damage Control (now the more politically correct "Wildlife Services") [USDA/APHIS]
AEC	Atomic Energy Commission (now NRC)
ALJ	Administrative Law Judge
ANILCA	Alaska National Interest Lands Conservation Act, scattered sections of 16 & 43 U.S.C.
APA	Administrative Procedures Act, 5 U.S.C. §§ 551–559, 701–706
APHIS	Animal & Plant Health Inspection Service [USDA]
BA	Biological Assessment (ESA) [see 16 U.S.C. § 1536(c)]
BAT	Best Available Technology or, Best Available Technology Economically Achievable (CWA)
BCT	Best Conventional Control Technology (CWA)
BGEPA	Bald & Golden Eagle Protection Act, 16 U.S.C. §§ 668–668d
BIA	Bureau of Indian Affairs [DoI]
Bi Op	Biological Opinion (ESA) (BO) [see 16 U.S.C. § 1536(b)]
BLM	Bureau of Land Management [DoI]
BMP	Best Management Practices
BO	Biological Opinion (ESA) (Bi Op) [see 16 U.S.C. § 1536(b)]
BPA	Bonneville Power Administration [Department of Energy]
BRec	Bureau of Reclamation [DoI]
CBD	Convention on Biological Diversity
CEC	Commission on Environmental Cooperation [NAFTA]
CEQ	Council on Environmental Quality [executive office of the President]
CERCLA	Comprehensive Environmental Response, Compensation, and Liability Act, 42 U.S.C. §§ 9601–9675
CFR	Code of Federal Regulations
CITES	Convention on International Trade in Endangered Species
Corps	United States Army Corps of Engineers
CWA	Clean Water Act, 33 U.S.C. §§ 1251–1387 (FWPCA)
CZMA	Coastal Zone Management Act, 16 U.S.C. §§ 1451–1464
DEIS	Draft Environmental Impact Statement (NEPA)
DoE	United States Department of Energy
DoI	United States Department of Interior
DoJ	United States Department of Justice
DoT	United States Department of Transportation
EA	Environmental Assessment (NEPA)

EC	European Community
EEZ	Exclusive Economic Zone (FCMA and UNCLOS)
EIS	Environmental Impact Statement (NEPA)
EO	Executive Order
EPA	United States Environmental Agency
ESA	Endangered Species Act, 16 U.S.C. §§ 1531–1544
ESPA	Endangered Species Protection Act of 1966
ESCA	Endangered Species Conservation Act of 1969
EU	European Union
FAO	Food and Agriculture Organization [UN]
FEIS	Final Environmental Impact Statement (NEPA)
FEMA	Federal Emergency Management Agency
FERC	Federal Energy Regulatory Commission [Department of Energy]
FCMA	Magnuson Fisheries Conservation & Management Act, 16 U.S.C. §§ 1801–1882
FLPMA	Federal Land Policy and Management Act, 43 U.S.C. §§ 1701–1784
FMC	[regional] Fishery Management Council (FCMA)
FMP	fishery management plan (FCMA)
FOIA	Freedom of Information Act, 5 U.S.C. § 552
FONSI	Finding of No Significant Impact (NEPA)
FR	Federal Register
FWCA	Fish & Wildlife Coordination Act, 16 U.S.C. §§ 661–667e
FWPCA	Federal Water Pollution Control Act, 33 U.S.C. §§ 1251–1387 (CWA)
FWS	Fish and Wildlife Service [DoI]
GAO	General Accounting Office [Congress]
GATT	General Agreement on Tariffs and Trade
HCP	Habitat Conservation Plan (ESA)
ICJ	International Court of Justice [The World Court in the Hague]
IGO	InterGovernmental Organization or International Governmental Organization
IJC	International Joint Commission [US–Canada]
ILO	International Labor Organization
ISC	Interagency Scientific Committee (ESA)
IUCN	World Conservation Union [*formerly*, International Union for the Conservation of Nature]
IWC	International Whaling Commission
JPAC	Joint Public Advisory Committee [NAFTA]
MBTA	Migratory Bird Treaty Act, 16 U.S.C. §§ 703–711
MLA/MLLA	Mineral [Lands] Leasing Act, 30 U.S.C. §§ 181–287
MMPA	Marine Mammal Protection Act, 16 U.S.C. §§ 1361–1421h
MoA	Memorandum of Agreement
MoU	Memorandum of Understanding
MSY	Maximu Sustained Yield
MUSY	Multiple Use–Sustained Yield Act, 16 U.S.C. §§ 528–531

NAAEC	North American Agreement on Environmental Cooperation [NAFTA]
NACEC	North American Commission on Environmental Cooperation [NAFTA]
NAFTA	North American Free Trade Agreement [Canada–Mexico–United States]
NEPA	National Environmental Policy Act, 42 U.S.C. §§ 4321–4347
NFMA	National Forest Management Act, 16 U.S.C. §§ 1601–1614
NGO	Non–Governmental Organization
NMFS	National Marine Fisheries Service [Department of Commerce]
NOAA	National Oceanic and Atmospheric Administration [Department of Commerce]
NPDES	National Pollutant Discharge Elimination System (CWA)
NPS	National Park Service [DoI]
NRC	Nuclear Regulatory Commission [DoE]
NWR	National Wildlife Refuge
OAS	Organization of American States
OCS	Outer Continental Shelf
OCSLA	Outer Continental Shelf Lands Act, 43 U.S.C. §§ 1331–1343
OMB	Office of Management and Budget [executive office of the President]
OSY	Optimum Sustained Yield
PNEPPCA	Pacific Northwest Power Planning & Conservation Act, 16 U.S.C. §§ 839–839h
PPM	Processes or Production Methods (GATT/WTO)
PRIA	Public Rangelands Improvement Act, 43 U.S.C. §§ 1739, 1751–1753, 1901–1908
ROD	Record of Decision (NEPA)
SEIS	Supplemental Environmental Impact Statement (NEPA)
TIAS	Treaties and Other International Acts Series
TRO	Temporary Restraining Order
TVA	Tennessee Valley Authority
UN	United Nations
UNDP	United Nations Development Programme
UNCED	United Nations Conference on Environment and Development
UNCHE	United Nations Conference on the Human Environment
UNCLOS	United Nations Convention on the Law of the Sea (1982)
UNEP	United Nations Environmental Programme
UNTS	United Nations Treaty Series
USDA	United States Department of Agriculture
USFS	United States Forest Service [USDA]
USGS	United States Geological Survey [DoI]
UST	United States Treaties and Other International Agreements
WF–RHBA	Wild Free–Roaming Horses & Burros Act, 16 U.S.C. §§ 1331–1340
WHO	World Health Organization (UN)

WTO   World Trade Organization
WWF   World Wildlife Fund

INDEX

References are to pages.

†

1–58778–168–9

9 781587 781681

OHIO NORTHERN
UNIVERSITY

JUL 1 7 2002

TAGGART LAW LIBRARY